FINANCIAL INSTITUTIONS AND MARKETS

FINANCIAL INSTITUTIONS AND MARKETS

SECOND EDITION

BEN HUNT CHRIS TERRY

Nelson

an International Thomson Publishing company I(T)P®

Melbourne • Albany, NY • Belmont, CA • Bonn • Boston • Cincinnati
Detroit • Johannesburg • London • Madrid • Mexico City • New York
Paris • Singapore • Tokyo • Toronto • Washington

Nelson ITP®
102 Dodds Street
South Melbourne 3205

Nelson ITP® ***an International Thomson Publishing company***

First published as *Financial Instruments and Markets* by Ben Hunt and Chris Terry in 1991
This second edition first published 1997
10 9 8 7 6 5 4 3 2
05 04 03 02 01 00 99 98 97

National Library of Australia
Cataloguing-in-Publication data

Hunt, Ben.
Financial institutions and markets.

2nd ed.
Includes index.
ISBN 0 17 0092240 0.
1. Finance — Australia. 2. Financial institutions — Australia.
I. Terry, Chris, 1944 – . II. Title.

332.0994

Edited by Deidre Missingham
Designed by Mary Kerr
Cover designed by The Modern Art Production Group
Typeset in Perpetua and Univers
Printed in Australia by Australian Print Group

Nelson Australia Pty Limited ACN 004 603 454 (incorporated in Victoria) trading as Nelson ITP.

Contents

Acknowledgements

The authors and publisher would like to gratefully credit or acknowledge permission to reproduce text and diagrams.

ABS, pp. 207, 209–10, 218–19, 339. Cat. No. 5655.0, *Managed Funds*. Copyright in ABS data resides with the Commonwealth of Australia. Used with permission; ASSIRT, pp. 210–11, *Market Share Report*, June quarter, 1995; Austraclear, pp. 62, 273; AFIC, pp. 256–7, *Australian Financial Institutions Commission and the Financial Institutions Scheme, 1995*; pp. 494, 505, 530, 563, *Australian Financial Review*, 8 August 1995, 6 May 1996, 9 January 1996, 6 May 1996; Australian Government Publishing Service, pp. © Commonwealth of Australia 1997. All legislation herein is reproduced by permission but does not purport to be the official or authorised version. It is subject to Commonwealth of Australia copyright. The Copyright Act 1968 permits certain reproduction and publication of Commonwealth legislation. In particular, s.182A of the Act enables a complete copy to be made by or on behalf of a particular person. For reproduction or publication beyond that permitted by the Act, permission should be sought in writing from the Government Publishing Service. Requests in the first instance should be addressed to the Manager, Commonwealth Information Services, AGPS, GPO Box 84, Canberra, ACT 2601; ASX, pp. 336, 338, 339, 350–2, *Monthly Index Analyses*; Basle Committee on Banking Supervision, p. 253; C. Beelaerts and K. Forde, p. 219, *Understanding Unit Trusts*, Wrightbooks, Melbourne, 1994; E. Carew, pp. 282, 295, 299, *Derivatives Decoded*, Allen and Unwin, Sydney; E. Carew and W. Slayter, p. 372, Forex: The Techniques of Foreign Exchange, Heinemann, Melbourne, 1994; The Commercial Paper Review, p. 276, No. 5, June, 1995; P. J. Drake and D. W. Stammers, p. 336, in *The Australian Financial System*, eds. M. Lewis and R. Wallace, Longman Cheshire, Melbourne 1993, p. 286; G. Dufey and I. Giddy, p. 57, *The International Money Market*, 2nd edn, Prentice Hall, NJ, 1994, p. 9; M. Edey and B. Gray, pp. 75, 599, 602, *The Future of the Financial System*, Reserve Bank of Australia, Sydney, 1996; Ernst and Young, pp. 396–9, *Australian Capital Markets Survey*, Sydney, 1994; KPMG Peat Marwick, pp. 142–3, 184, 198, *1995 Financial Institutions Performance Survey*; J. Linklater, pp. 229–30, 365, 438, *Inside the Bank*, Allen and Unwin, Sydney, 1992; Macquarie Bank Limited, pp. 196–7, *1995 Annual Report*; M. McGrath, p. 343, Financial Institutions, Instruments and Markets in Australia, McGraw Hill, Sydney, 1994; Reserve Bank of Australia, pp. 40–1, 44–6, 48, 142, 144–5, 148, 152–3, 156–8, 165–6, 169, 172, 183, 185, 187, 190–3, 199–200, 236, 238–9, 242, 249–50, 270–1, 277, 281, 294, 296–8, 362, 364, 371, 391–2, *Bulletins*; R. H. Wallace, p. 182, *The Australian Financial System*, Longman Cheshire, Melbourne, 1993, pp. 214–8; Westpac, p. 150, 1994 Annual Report.

Every effort has been made to trace and acknowledge copyright holders. Where the attempt has been unsuccessful, the publisher welcomes information that would redress the situation.

Preface

We used the following words in the preface to the first edition of this book:

During the 1980s the financial system emerged as an exciting and vibrant sector of the economy. Its range of financial products and services greatly increased to better serve financial needs. In the process the system has become complex and plays a vital role in most business and personal decisions.

The aim of this book is to help you, the reader, to achieve an understanding of the operations of the new deregulated financial system.

These ideas also explain our primary motive in preparing the second edition. However, we have decided to substantially widen the coverage of our discussion of the role and operations of financial institutions and markets. This has resulted in ten new chapters that replace three in the first edition — increasing the total number of chapters from 13 to 20.

The second edition is divided into five parts. The first presents foundation material on the functions of the financial system and the operations of financial institutions and markets. In this discussion we distinguish between the payments, financing and risk-management functions of the financial system. We also provide an explanation of those aspects of financial mathematics that are applied in subsequent chapters.

Part two explains the operations of Australia's financial institutions, using concepts introduced in Chapter 2. The discussion is organised around the processes of retail banking, wholesale banking and funds management and applies the principles explained in Chapter 2. An attempt is made to distinguish clearly between the roles of financial institutions in intermediated and direct financing and explain the implications of these activities for financial institution management. This latter theme is reinforced by an explanation of the prudential supervision regime of the Reserve Bank.

Part three describes the operations of the four main physical markets: the short-term money market, the debt-capital market, the share market and the foreign exchange market. This discussion emphasises the operational principles presented in Chapter 3 and shows how financial markets replicate the basic financial services (e.g. maturity transformation) provided through intermediation.

Part four explains three aspects of interest-rate theory. We review the movements in interest and exchange rates over the past 25 years and introduce the major theories that explain movements in these variables. We examine yield curves to distinguish between spot and forward interest rates and show how forward rates can be revealed by multi-period spot rates. We also show how duration can be used to identify and manage the price risk associated with fixed-interest securities.

Part five is concerned with explaining the basic characteristics of derivatives and their use in hedging interest-rate and market risk. Our treatment is introductory. We explain the financial characteristics of the basic forms of futures contracts (particularly, the bill-futures contract), FRAs, interest-rate and currency swaps and exchange-traded options.

The book concludes with a brief discussion of financial innovation, and some emerging trends that might greatly influence the system's future development. This discussion was prepared during the deliberations of the Wallis Committee and thus may not accord with subsequent events and policy changes.

Potential adopters of this book should note that it gives you several levels of flexibility. The large number of chapters and their groupings provide inter-chapter choice, and the organisation of the discussion within chapters should provide considerable intra-chapter choice, without jeopardising the book's continuity.

The intra-chapter choice of material arises from the extensive provision of introductory material, including diagrams and models that show the general features of important financial arrangements and products. These are usually generalised representations which we trust will remain indicative even when changes occur in the depicted financial practice.

We have benefited from the writings and comments of many colleagues, practitioners and students. Our citations and lists of references represent a form of acknowledgment. We wish, though, to acknowledge other sources as assistance in this preface. Of our colleagues, Tiffany Hutcheson has been especially generous in reading and commenting upon earlier drafts of the manuscript. Tiffany has also prepared the answers to the book's discussion questions and exercises, which are available from the publisher.

Many leading practitioners have assisted us in various ways. We wish to acknowledge the help of Dr John Veal and Colleen Anderson (RBA), Peter McCray (Commonwealth Treasury), Dr David Morgan, Dr John Jarratt, Jane Grainger and Andrew Williamson (Westpac), Natalie O'Delle (AAP Reuters), Rebecca Wellwood (AFIC), Emma McPherson (Moody's), Susan Shore (Standard & Poor's), Paul Khoury (IFA), Kenton Farrow (AFMA), Mark Brennan (PUMA), Wayne Jordon (Austraclear) and Caroline Saunders (ASSIRT).

Through the use of a pre-publication draft of this edition we received useful feedback from a number of our students. Two graduate students in particular, Stephen Fisher and Colin Cunningham, provided helpful comment.

However, receiving good advice is no guarantee that our book is free of errors. Naturally, the authors accept responsibility for the errors that remain.

Ben Hunt
Chris Terry

Part ONE

Introduction to the financial system

The chapters in the opening part of the book serve to introduce the reader to the main functions performed by the financial system and to the basic principles that explain its operations.

Part One comprises five chapters. The first three introduce the roles and functions of the financial system and its constituent institutions and markets. Chapter 4 explains the various ways of calculating interest rates and market yields, while Chapter 5 introduces annuities and how they are used in the book to calculate bond prices, investment yields and the cash flows involved in reducible loans.

The key points explained in Chapter 1 are that the financial system performs three functions: arranging payments, financing and risk management, both domestically and internationally. Chapter 2 explains the principles of intermediated financing, whereas Chapter 3 explains the operations of financial markets.

In Chapter 4 we show how to calculate the growth in a present amount to a future amount, using simple and compound interest, whereas Chapter 5 shows how to use annuities in calculating reducible loans payments and bond prices.

Naturally, the role of these chapters is to provide a conceptual foundation for the material that is presented in the remainder of the book. But this does not mean that the introductory part is easy reading. A quick scan of the material is unlikely to result in the reader developing the conceptual foundation assumed by the book's remaining chapters.

1

The purposes of financial transactions

The aim of this chapter is to give readers an overview of the role of the financial system. Its approach is to describe the general types of transactions — payments, financing and financial risk management — performed through the financial system. The chapter also highlights some of the basic financial-market principles that are developed throughout the book.

Study objectives

From your study of this chapter you should be able to:

- describe the main components of the payments systems;
- describe the broad features of the financing system and the major categories of capital funds that are used for financing future payments;
- describe the processes of direct financing and financial intermediation;
- identify the four main physical financial markets;
- identify the main types of derivative and forward instruments;
- identify the risk-management purpose of derivative and forward instruments; and
- list ten important principles of finance.

INTRODUCTORY COMMENTS

Welcome to the study of the financial system! We, the authors, assume that you have embarked on this study because you want to understand this aspect of human endeavour, not simply because it is a requirement of the degree course you are undertaking.

It is easy to overlook the relevance of the financial system when it functions smoothly. However, its importance is evident in times of financial crisis, such as during periods of hyperinflation and when financial institutions collapse, inflicting losses on their shareholders and depositors.

At all times the financial system plays an important role within a country in determining the living standards of its citizens. The system does not create value directly through the production of goods (as does the manufacturing sector). Rather, it creates value through the provision of exchange services. These services are required in the production of goods and commodities and in their distribution to consumers.

The influence of the financial system on living standards (i.e. employment, output and income levels) arises mainly through the provision of funding. This is a major prerequisite for most production and many consumption decisions. As a consequence, the suppliers of funds have to be convinced that borrowers can repay with interest. In the case of businesses, the suppliers of funds may evaluate the viability of the intended use of the funds before making the funds available. Thus the suppliers of funds play an important role in the allocation of resources.

During the 1980s many governments around the world removed restrictions on their financial system. An important reason for this shift in policy was to allow financial markets to discipline economic decisions (by government, business and consumers) more effectively. These governments accepted the view that financial institutions and markets can attract funds efficiently and allocate them between competing uses.

Parties who wish to supply or gain access to funds need to be aware of the operations of financial institutions and markets, though these operations are not 'set in stone'. The removal of the regulations changed the way the financial system operates and accelerated the pace of financial innovation. As a consequence, the financial system has become more dynamic and complex and we can expect this process to continue indefinitely.

However, the movement to a deregulated financial system changed the way the value of financial variables, such as interest rates and exchange rates, is determined. Their value is determined by trading in financial markets. This has had two important consequences:

1 The influence of financial markets on economic activity has increased, by comparison with the previous era when governments directly set these variables. Governments do still attempt to influence these variables (mainly through monetary policy), but in the deregulated environment they implement such policies by themselves trading in financial markets.
2 Market-determined financial variables (such as interest rates) tend to vary moment-by-moment and this can be a source of risk for market participants. For instance, a company that plans to borrow, say, $10 million in three months' time is exposed to the risk that interest rates may rise unexpectedly over this period. The financial system expanded its operations through the development of instruments that can be used to manage exposure to the risk

of adverse movements in market-determined variables. This development is an important part of financial innovation and has served to improve the system's efficiency.

The determination of movements in interest rates and exchange rates (including the influence of monetary policy) is discussed in Chapter 14.

This book aims to help you to understand how Australia's financial markets, institutions and instruments — recognising that they are part of the global financial system — perform three basic tasks:

- making payments,
- arranging finance (i.e. the supply and use of funds), and
- managing the risks arising from the former two functions.

Although we focus on 'how' the system operates, we also refer to issues related to 'how well' it operates. The main criteria for judging performance of the financial system are:

- **Allocative efficiency**, which depends on the system's ability to arrange financing that is mutually beneficial to potential suppliers and users of capital. An allocationally-efficient system will ensure that finance will be extended when there are users prepared to pay the suppliers' required return (for the amount and term sought).
- **Operational efficiency**, which depends on the cost-effectiveness and reliability of the system.
- **Dynamic efficiency**, which depends on the innovativeness of the system and on the resulting benefits to the system's users.

It may be comforting to know that many readers of the first edition of this book indicated in surveys that they were satisfied with the understanding they gained from their reading. But this understanding was not achieved from a casual or hurried reading.

The authors have assumed that readers have not previously studied the operations of the financial system. Consequently, all of the terms used (which are shown initially in bold print) are defined. A glossary of these terms is provided at the end of the book.

It is important to recognise, at the outset, the practical nature of our study. Financial transactions are the basic activity of the financial system, and everyone undertakes financial transactions of one sort or another. In this chapter we describe the three main functions performed by the financial system. However, most of the following chapters deal with the second and third of the system's tasks.

THE PAYMENTS SYSTEM

One of the most common of people's activities is to exchange goods and services for money. It is so commonplace that we take for granted the system that allows us to transact with one another. These transactions are made through the **payments system** that comprises the various methods of making payments.

The role of the payments system is to provide the economy with a convenient and efficient means of payment. Payment services can be divided between **retail** and **wholesale** transactions. The former are payment services (based on cheque and card transactions) provided to individuals to facilitate (mainly) low-value transactions. The latter generally involve large-value payments by financial institutions, businesses and governments, by cheque and electronic means. Financial-market transactions are an important component of wholesale payments.

The main instruments of the payments system are cash (notes and coins), cheques, electronic transfers and plastic-card authorisations.

Cash transactions involve little supporting infrastructure, other than a note-issue process of high integrity. This is achieved through the issue of **legal tender**. Notes and coins issued by the government must be accepted when tendered to settle an account due. Cash transactions implicitly involve **real-time settlement**. This means that the payment is settled instantly. When payments are made through financial institutions, arrangements must be made to complete these transactions. These arrangements form the infrastructure of the payments system.

The introduction of **prepaid cards** (i.e. cards that store an amount of funds for particular expenses, such as for telephone calls and bus travel) and **smart cards** (i.e. cards that store cash, that can be used to make small-value purchases) provide an alternative to cash, and as such, do not require substantial additions to the payments system's infrastructure.

Legal tender is used to settle most transactions, although usually these are of a low value. The other forms of payment — cheques, plastic cards and electronic transfers — involve substantial support services. These include **clearing** and **settlement** arrangements.

A clearing process is a necessary step to allow the parties involved in the payments system (mainly banks) to exchange payment requests by their customers. Settlement is the actual exchange of funds. These arrangements have been in place for many years to support the cheque-payment system and have been extended to support card-based and electronic-payment systems. The relationship between these processes is shown in figure 1.1 and described further below.

The principal elements of the payments system are:

- the participants — the payer, the recipient and (where applicable) the financial institutions which implement the payment instruction;
- the payment instrument — such as a cheque or a plastic-card payment authorisation;
- the clearing process — the exchange of transfer instructions between financial institutions (mainly banks) and the calculation of each institution's net position (i.e. payments to an institution's accounts minus payments from its accounts);
- the settlement of payments — the payment by institutions that have a net debit position to the institutions that have a credit position; and
- the honouring process — the steps involved in establishing the validity of each cheque and that funds are available in the drawer's account.

The clearing and settlement processes are currently administered overnight (i.e. involving payment orders presented during that day), whereas the honouring process currently takes five days. Two features of this process should be noted:

1 Settlement is conducted on a **netting** basis. This means that institutions settle only their net position, not all individual transactions. This reduces the amount of each institution's exposure to counterparty risk.
2 Funds are credited to the individual depositor's account and debited to each drawer's account the day after the cheque is presented. This means that the calculation of interest due to each party is based on the settlement date and not the subsequent date when payments are formally honoured. Should a cheque be dishonoured both the original settlement and interest payments are reversed.

The honouring process involves the return of each cheque to the drawer's branch to confirm its validity. This involves an extensive paper distribution system. We can expect that new computer technology (such as signature recognition) will result in a shortening of the period of the honouring process.

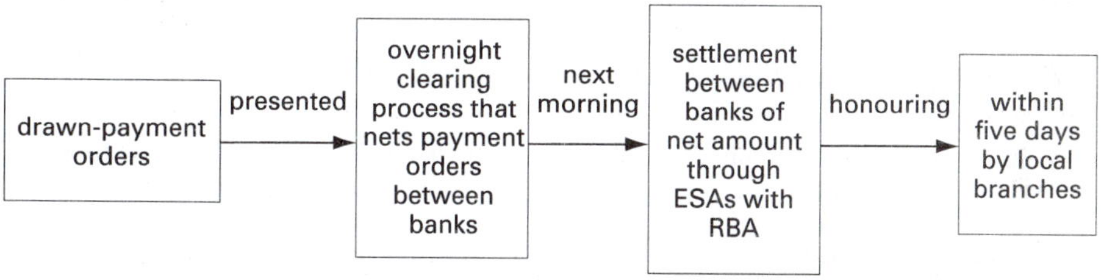

Figure 1.1 The clearing and settlement processes for payment orders

There is a very slight **counterparty risk** (i.e. the risk that the counterparty defaults) associated with the operation of the payments system. Banks that have a net credit position (i.e. are owed money as a result of the overnight clearing and settlement processes) are exposed to the risk that banks with a net debit position will not make the required payment. The risk that an individual payment will not be made is referred to as **settlement risk** (a specific form of default risk), whereas the risk that this could spread throughout the financial system is referred to as **contagion risk**. Contagion results when the default by one bank causes such severe liquidity problems for other banks that they default on their own payments.

The settlement of net positions is arranged through accounts held with the Reserve Bank, known as **Exchange Settlement Accounts** (ESAs). As at mid 1996, these payments must be made before 9.00 a.m. to comply with the bank's requirement that these accounts not be in debit.

In 1995 the Reserve Bank announced plans to introduce a system of real-time settlement, based on an existing electronic transfer system, for large-value (i.e. wholesale) payments by the end of 1997. One advantage of real-time settlement is that it eliminates inter-bank settlement risk (and hence reduces contagion risk). The present system works by an end-of-day settlement, which is a form of deferred settlement. Banks can make payments during the day even though settlement does not occur until the day's end. Should a bank default, it would cause liquidity problems for its bank counterparties. Under a real-time system, settlement occurs instantly. (RBA, 1995a)

While cheques have proven to be very convenient, electronic forms of payment, particularly for large-value transactions, have become, in value terms, the more important form of payment. The main forms of electronic payment are:

- **electronic funds transfer at point of sale** (EFTPOS), which is a retail payments service provided as a means of payment for consumer purchases,
- **Electronic Data Interchange** (EDI), which is a wholesale payment service based on computer-to-computer exchange of information, and
- **direct entry transactions**, which allow the payer to transfer funds to the accounts of a large number of recipients, such as in the payment of salaries by a large employer.

There are three types of plastic cards:

1. credit cards, which allow the user time to pay the card's provider and decide whether to pay the amount due in full or to pay off the amount due over time,
2. debit cards, which allow charges to be debited to the cardholder's account, and
3. automatic teller machine (ATM) cards, which give the user access to funds held in an account.

Debit and ATM cards can be used by EFTPOS machines. EFTPOS transactions have become very popular, partly because they also provide the user with access to cash from funds held in an account.

While cheques are a paper-based payment system (and this is a reason for its more cumbersome administration), electronic processes can be used to make the system more efficient. Do not assume therefore that this system is on the verge of becoming obsolete.

Approximately a billion cheques are drawn annually in Australia with a value (in 1993) of around $13 000 billion. This compares with 400 million transactions by credit and debit cards with a value of $25 billion, and 500 million electronic payments with an aggregate value of over $15 400 billion. (BIS, 1994, p. 1)

Providers of payment services

Banks (and in particular the major banks) have been the main providers of both retail and wholesale payment services. Their retail payment services include cheque and savings facilities, credit and debit cards, and ATM networks as well as EFTPOS systems. These services are provided through an extensive branch network — at the end of 1995 there were 6655 branches throughout Australia.

Prior to the deregulation of the financial system in the early 1980s, banks met the cost of their payment services mainly by way of a **cross-subsidy** from the income they generated through their **interest-rate spread**: the difference between the average interest rate they pay for funds and the average rate they receive on their loans and advances. In other words, banks did not charge for each of the payment services they provided but met the cost involved by (mainly) paying a low (often zero) rate of interest on deposit account balances. For many years **current** or

demand deposits (i.e. accounts that can be drawn upon by cheques) were interest free, and this allowed banks to cover the costs of administering payment orders.

The dominant position of the banks in the retail payments system gave them a competitive advantage over other financial institutions in raising funds from the public. Banks enjoyed a special relationship with the central bank because of their role in the payments system, which allowed them to attract funds at lower rates than non-banks. (In fact, the Reserve Bank is concerned primarily with the safety of depositors' funds and the integrity of the payments system, rather than with the viability of individual banks.)

Since deregulation, banks have gradually introduced charges for payment (and other) retail banking services. Given that the suppliers of funds to banks have become more sensitive to the return they earn on their funds from financial institutions generally, banks have found that their deposit rates were not competitive, despite the provision of subsidised payment services. The development of alternative payment processes, such as credit cards, which were issued by other institutions, further weakened the advantage banks had enjoyed due to their dominant position in the payment system.

Consequently, banks have been forced by their competitors to pay interest on demand deposits and are under pressure to pay competitive rates on their various other deposit accounts. However, the introduction of fees for payment services has met with resistance from the public, resulting in an inquiry into bank charges by the Prices Surveillance Authority (PSA).

In its report, the PSA accepted that:

- the imposition of charges for payment services should result in a more efficient payment system, particularly when service providers offer participants a choice between a range of different services and prices; and
- banks need to recover their costs when providing payment services, otherwise the provision of these services will place them at a competitive disadvantage. (PSA, 1995)

The PSA also advocated the development of a low-cost ('no frills') account which would be popular with low-income customers, such as the recipients of welfare benefits (e.g. age pensions), who must maintain a bank account to receive their benefit payments.

Building societies and credit unions are banks' main competitors in the provision of retail payment services (and retail banking services generally). Because they were not able to provide cheque-payment services directly, they provided equivalent services through payment orders and the issue of cheques as required by customers through agency agreements with banks. They also provide payment cards, ATM networks and EFTPOS services. However, in 1995 the Commonwealth Government finally decided to allow these institutions direct access to the cheque-payment system. (RBA, 1995b, p. 48) Even though these non-banks are small relative to the banks that offer retail-level payment services, the PSA considered that their capacity to compete with banks should not be impaired. In its report, the PSA argued that there should be competitive pressure on banks in the provision of payment services.

Other providers of payment services include American Express, Diners Club, major retailers, and several providers of consumer services (e.g. Telstra), which offer payment cards, as well as Australia Post which in 1995 introduced Giropost, a form of branch banking from post offices.

Official participants

The Reserve Bank is involved in the payments system in a number of ways. It prints and issues currency notes, provides settlement facilities (ESAs), conducts transactions as the banker for the Commonwealth Government (and certain other governments), operates an irrevocable electronic cash transfer facility and generally oversees the payments system.

The bank's electronic cash transfer system (RITS), is used as the registry in the market for Commonwealth Government securities (arranging delivery of the securities for cash settlement) as well as a real-time cash transfer system.

The bank has a statutory responsibility to protect depositors' funds, a large proportion of which forms part of the payments system, and to prudentially supervise banks.

The Reserve Bank is also an active participant in a number of industry organisations that oversee the payments system, including:

- the Australian Payments System Council (APSC), which was established in 1984 by the Federal Treasurer to monitor the payment system and oversee its development. Institutions involved in the provision of payment services are represented on the APSC as well as representatives of the users of the payment system (APSC, 1994); and
- the Australian Payments Clearing Association Limited (APCA), which was established in 1992 to oversee and manage on a day-to-day basis the development and operation of the payments system. The RBA is a shareholder, along with the other providers of payment services.

The activities of the Reserve Bank in the financial system are discussed further in Chapters 9, 13 and 14.

Payments in foreign currencies

It is important to realise that payment systems are essentially domestic in scope. Each country has its legal tender, thus cross-border payments require the conversion of one currency to another. Such payments involve **foreign exchange** markets.

For instance, when Australians need to make payments overseas it is usual to convert Australian dollars into the domestic currency of the other country. Australia's foreign exchange market is conducted by licensed dealers who buy and sell foreign currencies. Buying a foreign currency (for example, to pay for imports) is equivalent to selling the domestic currency; and selling a foreign currency (derived, say, from exports) is equivalent to buying the domestic currency.

Since the floating of the Australian dollar in December 1983 its value has been determined by trading in the foreign exchange market. Prior to that date, the value of the currency was set by the Reserve Bank.

The removal of foreign controls at the same time resulted in the integration of the Australian financial system within the global system. Australians can borrow and invest overseas and foreigners can borrow and invest in Australia. Individuals can also make payments overseas on various credit cards and can hold bank accounts in other countries. The operations of the foreign exchange market are discussed further in Chapter 13.

Even though the payments system is of great importance to the efficient operation of the economy, our attention in this book will be concentrated mainly on those transactions that are involved in the financing of payments. While we can distinguish between the purposes of the payment and financing systems, the two systems overlap. For example, bank deposits are used to make payments and to finance loans.

THE FINANCING SYSTEM

In formal terms, the financing system allocates funds from **surplus units** to **deficit units**. A surplus unit is any party whose income over a period exceeds its outlays. A deficit unit is any party whose income over a period is less than its outlays. For the Australian economy as a whole, the foreign sector has been the main source of surplus units, followed by the household sector, whereas the corporate and government sectors have generally been in deficit.

Put less formally, the financing system comprises suppliers and users of funds. The suppliers are investors who seek a return from supplying funds. However, these future returns involve some degree of risk. Hence suppliers of funds consider both the level of the promised return and the risk that the user of the funds will default and not pay the promised return.

The allocation of funds between suppliers and users creates financial assets and liabilities. The supplier exchanges cash for a financial asset — this being the promised future payments. These financial assets may take the form of bank deposits or a **financial security**. Typically, the former type of asset cannot be traded in financial markets, but most allow the holder to gain access to the funds when required. Most securities can be traded in financial markets, which allows their holder to exchange them for cash when required. Financial assets are described as being **liquid** when they can be exchanged for cash, as occurs when funds are withdrawn from a deposit account or when a security is sold.

Debt and equity capital

The various forms of financing are defined according to the terms of the arrangement. In broad terms, funds can be either lent on the basis of a promise to repay with **interest** at a future date, or contributed to the funds of a business on the basis of a promise to share in the distribution of its profits. The former arrangement (i.e. borrowing and lending) is referred to as **debt** financing, whereas the latter is **equity** financing. Equity funds are supplied by the owners of a business (such as a company's shareholders), whereas debt capital is lent to a business. Usually equity funds are provided for the life of a business, whereas debt funds are raised for a given **term** (i.e. the period of the loan).

The main instruments of debt capital are loans and advances by financial institutions (which operate in the domestic or overseas financial systems), and financial securities (known also as **financial instruments** or **paper**) that are issued in either domestic or overseas **capital** markets.

The term 'capital' is generally used instead of 'funds' when the financing arrangement extends beyond a year. This period, by convention, divides short-term from long-term financing. Hence there is both debt (i.e. long-term) and equity capital. Funds that are borrowed for a short term are, by convention, referred to as 'money'. Note that these words (i.e. short-term, long-term and capital) have different meanings in other fields, such as economics.

Borrowers have a legally enforceable commitment to meet their debt charges (i.e. interest together with the repayment of the amount lent). Interest payments are tax deductible (when the borrowing is for an income-earning purpose), though repayments of **principal** (i.e. the amount borrowed) are not.

The interest rate that a borrower is required to pay for debt capital depends on a number of variables. Two of the most important are:

- the current level of interest rates, as indicated by **benchmark** rates, and
- the borrower's **credit risk**.

The general level of interest rates is indicated by benchmark (or **marker**) rates, the most important of which are market-determined rates (i.e. are set by the rate in a particular financial market), such as the 90-day bank bill rate (BBR). They reflect the rate at a standard time each day in a particular market, such as the **yield** for 90-day bills in the short-term money market. A benchmark rate, as the name implies, serves as a base rate for the interest rates paid by borrowers.

The interest rate (or yield) in a market determines the basic cost of funds (or **credit**). This rate, r, is shown in figure 1.2 to depend on the demand and supply of loanable funds. This topic is examined in some detail in Chapter 14.

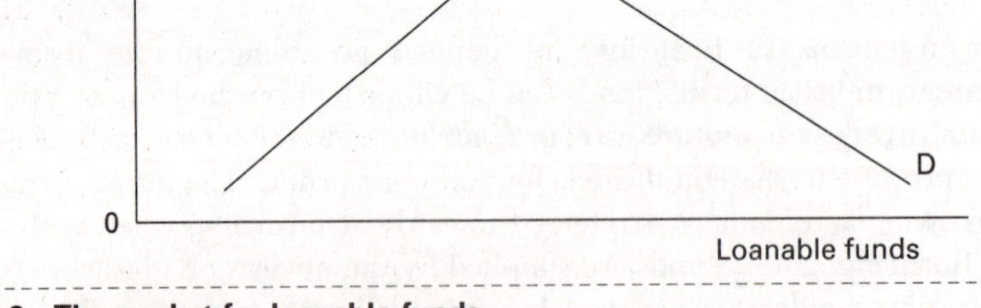

Figure 1.2 The market for loanable funds

In general, a **market yield** is a rate of interest. It is a measure of the return, expressed as an annual rate, that a security's future payments represent over its price. For instance, suppose a security that promises to pay $100 000 in three months is trading at a yield of 10% p.a. This means that at the current price, the security's face value, $100 000, generates a return of 10% p.a., over the next three months.

Frequent reference is made to market yields in the short-term and debt-capital markets, because they are the yield at which the securities are bought and sold. Generally they vary during the trading day and over time in response to changes in the demand for and supply of the security.

Credit (or default) risk refers to the probability that the borrower will not meet his or her loan payments when they are due. Borrowers who have a high **credit standing** (i.e. capacity to make loan payments) will have a small **credit risk premium** included in the interest rate they have to pay. For instance, such borrowers face an interest rate that is only a few **basis points** above the specified benchmark rate. Note that as interest rates are usually quoted to two decimal places, a basis point is one-hundredth of a percentage point (e.g. the last point in 10.01%). Usually it is the smallest interest rate movement that can occur. Whereas the general level of interest rates affects all borrowers, the size of the credit-risk premium varies between borrowers according to their credit standing.

Borrowers that have a very high credit standing, such as government enterprises, are able to borrow without providing **security** (such as a specified asset that reverts to the lender in the event of default), because of the strength of their credit standing. These are referred to as **unsecured** loans (or securities). Examples of the latter are bonds and promissory notes. (We describe these financial instruments in Chapter 3.) These borrowers also can borrow at rates that are close to the market's benchmark rate. In the case of Commonwealth Government bonds, they trade at **risk-free** rates, being free of credit risk, and their yield (i.e. the interest rate in the bond market) also serves as a benchmark rate.

Less creditworthy borrowers can reduce the credit risk they pose for lenders by providing security as **collateral** for the debt, which should reduce the interest rate payable on their debt. For example, a house buyer will be required to **mortgage** his or her house to the supplier of loan funds. Should the borrower default, the lender can take possession of the house for the purpose of selling it in order to obtain the amounts owing on the loan.

When providing security, borrowers are, in effect, sharing the exposure to their credit risk with the lender. As a result, they are risking the secured assets. Hence, security should be provided only when the interest reduction is worth more to the borrower than the risk being accepted.

The interest rate on debt may be a particular rate for the period of the loan, as in the case of a **fixed-rate** loan. Alternatively, the basis of the rate may be set to allow the interest rate to vary over the period of the loan in line with the general movements in interest rates (as in the case of a **variable** or **floating-rate** loan). The relationship between fixed and floating interest rates is discussed in Chapter 15 and Chapters 17–20.

The use of debt (in association with equity) is referred to as **financial leverage**. The higher the debt-to-equity ratio, the greater the degree of leverage. Most businesses will use debt funds to leverage their **capital structure** (i.e. their debt-to-equity ratio) when they expect to earn a higher rate of return than the cost of the debt funds. When this occurs leverage has the effect of improving the rate of return on equity capital.

However, leverage involves **financial risk** — the risk that the borrower's earnings will not cover its interest and loan repayment obligations when due. In general, lenders consider the level of a borrower's equity capital because this provides the borrower with a capacity to make debt payments when they exceed the borrower's earnings. Consequently, borrowers will have equity as well as debt funds.

Equity funds are raised either through the issue of **shares** or by a business retaining some or all of its earnings. The return to the suppliers of equity funds to a company is mainly in the form of **dividends**. These are a distribution of the company's profits that are payable only when profits (current or accumulated) are available for distribution. For this reason they may be referred to as **residual claims**. Because they are a distribution of after-tax profits their payment does not result in a tax deduction for the company. However, under Australia's system of **dividend imputation**, income tax paid by a company is in effect a pre-payment of the personal income tax liability of domestic shareholders on their dividend income.

Given that the payment of interest ranks ahead of the payment of dividends, equity capital may be referred to also as **risk capital**. The suppliers of equity funds face a greater risk of not receiving a return than the suppliers of debt capital.

Note that interest payments, being prescribed obligations (either fixed or floating), are both 'minimum' and 'maximum' amounts. Should the borrower make unexpectedly large profits from the use of borrowed funds, only the prescribed amount of interest is payable. Dividends payable to **ordinary** shareholders (i.e. the holders of the company's ordinary shares), in contrast, have both 'upside' potential and 'downside' risk. The amount of dividend payments can be more or less than the amount suggested by the company when the equity funds were raised.

The payment of dividends on **preference shares** is, though, related to the amount promised when the shares are issued and these payments rank ahead of dividend payments to ordinary shareholders (hence the term 'preference' shares).

Direct and intermediated financing

There are two methods of arranging finance: by **direct financing** and through **intermediation**. Direct financing occurs mainly in **capital markets.** In general, borrowers (deficit units) issue securities that are purchased by investors (surplus units). The process of direct financing is shown in figure 1.3, which indicates that a number of 'intermediaries' are often involved in arranging direct finance. However, these participants do not **intermediate** the finance because the funds are not supplied to and by the intermediary.

Refer to figure 1.4, which depicts intermediated financing. Under this process, surplus units lend to a financial intermediary which on-lends the funds to deficit units. In this process, the funds are intermediated because they are on-lent in the name of the intermediary. Should a borrower not repay, for instance, the immediate loss would be borne by the intermediary, who remains obligated to repay the funds borrowed from surplus units. In the case of direct financing, default by the borrower inflicts a loss on the supplier of the funds, not on the intermediaries who helped to arrange the financing.

Direct financing

Raising funds from financial markets involves the issue of securities. The issuer is the borrower and the buyer/investor is the supplier of the funds. Not all borrowers are able to issue securities. Well-established borrowers, such as large creditworthy companies, government enterprises and financial institutions, can issue unsecured instruments. Other enterprises can issue securities if their credit risk is accepted by a financial institution, such as a bank. However, most borrowers (such as individuals) have to approach a financial institution to raise funds.

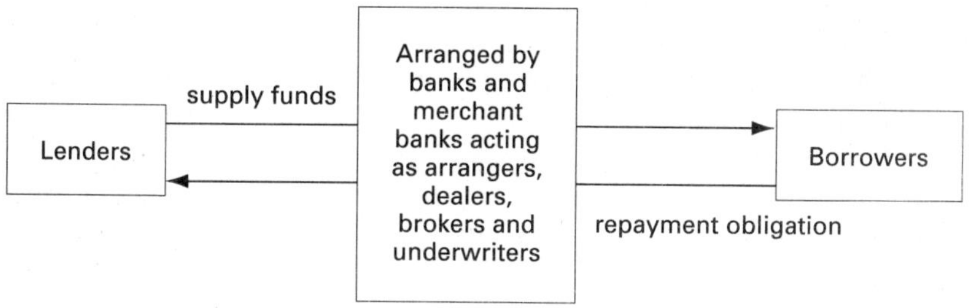

Figure 1.3 Direct financing

Funds are raised in an instrument's **primary market**. This term refers to arrangements for the issue (i.e. sale) of new securities to investors, the proceeds from which represent the funds raised.

When securities are issued in a financial market, usually they can be traded in what is referred to as the security's **secondary market**. Such trading is of considerable importance, in part because it determines the movement in market yields (i.e. interest rates). The role of secondary markets is explained in more detail in Chapter 3.

The main suppliers of funds to financial markets (i.e. holders of the securities issued in these markets) are financial institutions. Typically they hold large portfolios of securities and some on-sell newly-issued securities to their retail customers. Financial institutions usually apply **risk-averse** strategies in their acquisition of securities and the management of their portfolios. That is, they manage their affairs to minimise the risk of loss, even though this may remove the chance to make windfall profits.

The main incentive to engage in direct financing is that it offers a lower cost of funds to borrowers and better returns to investors compared with intermediation. The issue of new securities is generally arranged (and can be **underwritten**) by financial institutions. Usually the terms of an issue of new securities are based on the advice of a **lead manager**, who may also prepare the necessary documentation. A panel of institutions may be engaged to sell the securities and some may act as underwriters, who undertake to sell the securities and are obligated to buy those that remain unsold.

The process of issuing new securities is expensive, but when large amounts are raised, the cost can be spread very thinly per dollar raised. Moreover, the interest rate on funds provided by the market can be less than that required by intermediaries. This is reflected in the narrow **spread** between borrowing and lending rates in capital markets, compared with the spread between the lending and borrowing rates of financial institutions.

Intermediation

The alternative process to direct financing is intermediation. This occurs when a financial institution acts as the borrower to surplus units and the lender to deficit units. The process creates two sets of assets and liabilities. The intermediary's deposits are both its liabilities and the assets of the lenders. When these funds are lent to borrowers, they are the intermediary's assets as well as being liabilities for its borrowers.

As a consequence, intermediation involves a transformation of funds. Deposits with intermediaries (such as banks) are assets of depositors, but when the funds are lent by the intermediary they create assets for the intermediary. The transformation may also involve a change in the term of the funds. Typically, intermediated deposits are for shorter periods than for intermediated loans.

Intermediated funds are generally recorded on the balance sheets of the financial institutions that engage in this form of financing. Sources of intermediated funds (these typically are deposits) are shown as liabilities, whereas uses are shown as assets (these typically are the loans and securities held by the intermediary).

Note that not all 'intermediaries' engage in intermediation, and those that do may also arrange direct finance. Hence, intermediation is not the exclusive activity of a specific group of financial institutions.

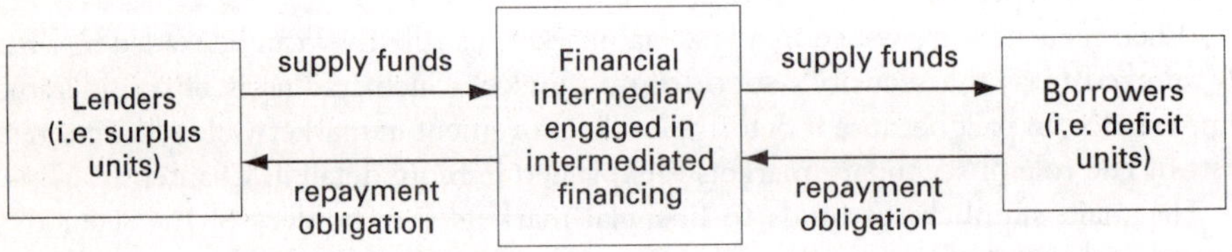

Figure 1.4 Intermediated financing

Because intermediation and direct financing are alternative processes, participants in the financing system may be in a position to choose between them. In general, borrowers and lenders who undertake large-value financing transactions are more likely to be able to engage in direct financing, whereas small-value transactions are usually handled by intermediaries. However, the development of the funds management sector has widened opportunities for those who invest relatively small amounts to participate collectively in direct financing and capital markets generally.

It is important to keep in mind that direct and intermediated financing perform the same basic function, despite the difference in their methods. Consider, for example, the supply of funds to a borrower for a period of five years:

- This can occur in the capital market through the sale of five-year securities that raise the amount borrowed, with the issuer undertaking to make regular interest payments to the holders of the securities and repaying the amount borrowed in five years by **redeeming** (i.e. retiring) the securities. The issue of the securities may be arranged by a specialist financial institution or a syndicate of such institutions (depending on the amount sought). Issuing securities involves their sale to investors, the proceeds from which (after issuing expenses have been deducted) represent the funds raised.

- Alternatively, the funds could be provided through a five-year bank loan, with the borrower undertaking to make regular interest payments and to repay the loan in five years. Given that the bank will not be repaid for five years, it must ensure that it can repay depositors who withdraw funds during this period.

The credit standing of the borrower will be assessed before finance is arranged by either process, and the cost of both intermediated and direct funds will reflect this assessment. In general, though, direct financing is confined (in the Australian financial markets) to borrowers with a very high credit standing, whereas intermediated funds can be provided to less well-established and secure borrowers.

As will be explained in later chapters, a number of securities have been modelled on forms of bank loans:

- There are short-term loans and short-term securities. These have a term of less than a year, but they can be **rolled over**, meaning that further loans (and securities) can be arranged, to extend the period of the finance.
- There are long-term loans and long-term securities. These have a term of a number of years, typically five to ten, and both can be arranged on either a fixed- or floating-rate basis.

The relative importance of direct and intermediated financing changes over time. This reflects cost considerations as well as improvements in financial products. One advantage of direct financing is that it produces marketable securities. They are liquid securities because they can be sold in the secondary market. Intermediated financing usually produces non-marketable assets that are not liquid. However, these assets can be transformed into securities through the process of **securitisation**.

This involves the conversion of loans (i.e. the future payments due on the loans) into marketable securities. The interest payments on the loans are the source of the interest payments on the issued securities. The securitiser issues the securities at a yield slightly below the yields on the original loans: the difference provides the securitiser's income.

Securitisation is well established in the USA but only began to develop in Australia from the late 1980s. It has the potential to provide intermediaries with greater flexibility in managing their assets because it allows them to sell the loans rather than being committed to maintaining sufficient deposits to fund them. Assets that are securitised include housing loans, credit card and other accounts receivable and the payments due on leases.

Securitisation has influenced the development of financial institutions because it separates the process of originating securitised assets (i.e. arranging the loans that are to be securitised) from their funding. The funds are raised when the securities are sold in the market. We discuss securities that are backed by the cash flows generated by securitised assets in Chapter 11.

Most financial institutions do not confine their activities to intermediation. In fact some (especially merchant banks) concentrate on the provision of direct financing services, such as arranging the issue of new securities, dealing in security markets and managing security portfolios. Others offer clients access to both their intermediated products and to financial market instruments (such as the major banks).

RISKS

Financial transactions can involve a wide range of risks, such as those already introduced in this chapter. The most basic arise because financing involves expected future payments. In our discussion of the financial system we are concerned mostly, but not exclusively, with three forms of risk:

1. Credit risk (known also as default or, more generally, counterparty risk), arises in the case of debt securities from the possibility that future payments will not be made. It forms part of the cost of finance, given that the suppliers of funds will seek to be compensated for accepting this risk. In the case of equity securities, risk arises from the possibility that future dividends and share prices will be lower than expected.
2. Market risk (known also as price risk) arises from volatile market prices. Often this term is defined by the particular market, such as foreign-exchange risk, where it refers to the risk of an adverse movement in the exchange rate. In debt markets it arises from adverse movements in interest rates because of the see-saw relationship between security prices and interest rates; increases in market yields cause security prices to fall. This see-saw relationship is explained in Chapter 4. When interest rates increase security prices fall, and vice versa.
3. Interest-rate risk is faced by both borrowers and lenders. This term can be used to cover a variety of interest-rate risks, but in this book it is used mainly to refer to the risks posed by unexpected future movement in interest rates. For instance, a company that plans to borrow in three months' time faces the risk that rates will increase unexpectedly over the next three months. It is faced also by financial institutions when they borrow, say, on a floating-rate basis and lend at a fixed rate. Should rates rise during the term of this financing, the institution will suffer a loss of income (i.e. interest-rate spread).

Risk management

Since the mid 1980s a third group of financial transactions has developed into a major area of the financial system. These transactions involve the purchase and sale of instruments that can be used to manage the **market risks** faced by participants in financial markets.

The main forms of market risk arise from actual or planned transactions in debt and foreign exchange markets. When interest and exchange rates vary continuously as a result of market trading (this movement is known as **volatility**), participants are exposed to the risk that the movements will adversely affect their financial position.

The movement in interest rates exposes participants in financial markets to a range of **interest-rate risks**, one of which is known also as **price risk**. In

Chapters 4, 10 and 11 we demonstrate that the price (or value) of most securities varies inversely with movements in interest rates. Holders of such securities are exposed to the risk of a rise in interest rates because this reduces the value of the securities.

Prospective borrowers also face the risk of a rise in interest rates. In their case it directly increases the interest payments that they will make on their loans, whereas prospective investors face the risk of a fall in interest rates. Movements in exchange rates are another source of market risk. For example, a fall in the value of the Australian dollar increases the domestic price of imported goods and services, and thus can have adverse effects on importers.

Given that adverse movements in interest and exchange rates can inflict substantial losses, there is a strong demand for instruments that can be used to manage market risks. In our discussion of risk management we refer to financial markets as **physical** markets because these are the markets in which finance (in one form or another) can be raised/lent. This term highlights the difference between the markets in which risk arises and the markets for instruments that can be used to manage these risks.

Managing market risks usually involves **hedging** the physical market position. This usually involves the use of another position to hedge the exposure in the physical market. It can be achieved in one of two ways:

1 creation of a position that counterbalances the risk associated with the participant's position in a physical market, or
2 acquisition of a forward contract that locks in the terms of a transaction before it will be undertaken.

The first approach can involve the use of a **derivative** instrument whose value matches that of the physical instrument. The market participant will acquire the position in the derivative market that moves in the opposite direction to the position in the **underlying** physical market. In such cases, the hedge position **covers** the position in the physical market.

For example, an investor can hedge an exposure to a fall in interest rates (which would otherwise lower the investor's return) by acquiring an instrument that increases in value when interest rates fall. Provided the two positions are of equal value, the effect of a fall in interest on the underlying position will be precisely offset by the rise in value in the derivative instrument. This approach is depicted by the see-saw in figure 1.5.

In concept, the second approach is less complex. It simply involves making a forward transaction, in much the same way as making an advance purchase of an airline ticket.

Market risks increased following the **deregulation** of financial systems around the world in the early 1980s. One purpose of financial deregulation is to allow interest rates and exchange rates to be determined by market forces. However, market-determined rates change almost moment-by-moment in ways that cannot be predicted easily. The volatility of values in financial markets has been an important reason why instruments that can be used to manage the risks arising from participation in capital and foreign exchange markets are needed.

Speculators are attracted by market volatility. They are participants who take a position in a market (i.e. either a buy or a sell position) which they expect will

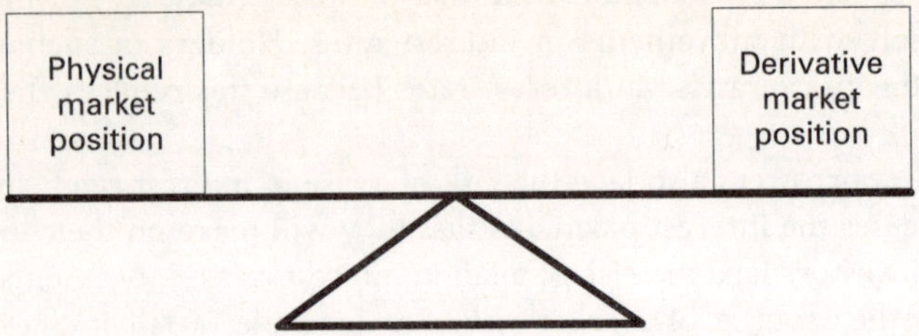

Figure 1.5 Using a derivative to hedge the risk of a financial-market position

increase in value from the movement in the market price. In effect, they seek to accept the risks arising from movements in market values because they aim to make a profit by correctly predicting such movements.

Speculators tend to trade in the markets for risk-management instruments because of the low cost of holding such positions compared with the cost of a similar position in the related physical market. Usually the outlay for a derivative instrument is a small fraction of its nominal value. Consequently, returns on the amount outlaid tend to be much higher in these instruments (than for an investment in the underlying physical instrument) when the speculator correctly predicts the market movement.

Trading in risk-management instruments can occur between **hedgers** (who acquire a position in a derivative market to cover an underlying position in a physical market) and speculators. Hedgers may trade with one another when one is exposed to the risk of a fall in, say, interest rates, and the other is exposed to the risk of an increase in interest rates.

The risk faced by a prospective borrower is the exact opposite of the risk faced by a prospective lender. A rise in rates increases the cost of funds whereas a fall in rates reduces the return that will be achieved by the lender. Borrowers and lenders are natural trading partners in instruments that hedge against movements in interest rates.

Similarly, speculators may trade with one another when one expects a fall and the other expects a rise in the market variable, such as security prices and foreign exchange.

Risk-management instruments

There are four main categories of risk-management instruments:

- forwards
- futures
- swaps and
- options.

A **forward** is simply a contract that establishes the 'price' prior to the exchange of the item for cash. For example, the per unit price of an amount of foreign currency can be agreed several months before the parties exchange their currencies. This contract, by establishing price in advance, removes the risk of an adverse movement in the exchange rate prior to the actual exchange. Typically, forward contracts cannot be sold during their life.

Futures are forward contracts that are traded on an exchange. In Australia this is the Sydney Futures Exchange. These contracts specify an amount of a specific physical item (or the value of an index) that takes effect at a future date. They can be traded prior to their contract date and their market value varies in response to changes in the expected value of the specified physical item on the contract date.

A **swap** is an exchange of financial payments. It must specify the basis of the payments. For example, the interest payments due on a fixed-rate loan of $10 million could be swapped for the interest payments on a $10 million floating-rate loan.

An **option** is simply the right to buy or sell a set amount of a specified asset at a set price (known as the **strike** or **exercise** price). Options are derivatives because their value depends on that of the specified (i.e. underlying) asset. For instance, an option to buy BHP shares at $20.00 will have value when these shares are trading at $30.00. Options have a term (i.e. life) at the end of which they expire. Options that can be traded on an exchange are known as **exchange-traded options**.

Transactions involving these derivative and forward instruments 'exploded' during the 1980s and by the mid 1990s their value, judged in terms of the nominal value of the contracts traded, greatly exceeded the value of physical financial assets. To illustrate, the value of these contracts held by Australian banks in June 1995 exceeded $2 trillion (i.e. $2416 billion) whereas the total value of banks' assets in June 1995 was $438 billion.

However, it is difficult to provide a basis for comparing their importance in the financial system with that of the payment and financing systems. The cost of acquiring, for instance, futures and options, is only a fraction of the contract's value. This is part of the reason for their popularity.

Risk-management instruments transfer the market risks faced by the issuers and holders of securities. In doing so they can help to facilitate the underlying financing transaction. As a consequence they play an important role in the performance by the financial system of its primary functions. These instruments are discussed further in Chapter 3 and are the subject of the chapters in Part Five, Derivative instruments.

In summary, the main functions of the financial system are to:

- facilitate payments (in both domestic and foreign currencies),
- arrange the allocation of finance (both debt and equity), and
- manage the risks associated with participation in financial markets.

These functions are performed by financial institutions and markets. An introduction to the role and functions of financial institutions and markets is provided in the next two chapters and we consider them in detail in Parts two and three of the book.

FINANCE-MARKET PRINCIPLES

To complete this opening chapter we introduce ten finance-market principles (or ideas) that are developed and applied throughout the book. Each represents an important part of financial market theory and is of practical importance to readers in guiding the financial decisions they make throughout their lifetime. Consequently an understanding of the principles highlighted here (as well as the other matters explained in the book) will be important for your exams and for the conduct of your financial affairs thereafter.

I Risk and return

Future returns are rarely (if ever) absolutely certain. Hence they are subject to the risk of not being fulfilled. There is a simple and direct relationship between the level of the return required by the suppliers of funds and the risk that the returns will be achieved. The greater the risk the higher the required return. This direct relationship is depicted in figure 1.6 by the upward-sloping line.

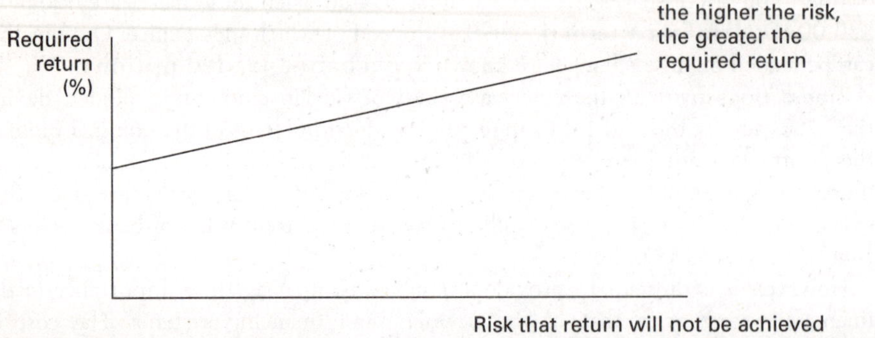

Figure 1.6 Risk-return trade-off

The direct relationship between risk and return holds for the various forms of risk. Consider, for example, default risk. In most financing transactions there is a risk that the borrower will not make the promised future payments. Lenders need to assess the risk of default when deciding whether to lend, and if so, what rate of return to require. Given that funds can be supplied to alternative borrowers, lenders will require a higher promised return from those borrowers who pose a higher risk of default.

Occasionally prospective borrowers will seek funds by promising a 'high and guaranteed safe return'. Your study of finance should instil in you a suspicion of such claims. You should wonder why the borrower has to offer high returns in order to attract funds for a 'safe' investment. The need to offer a high return will be due in part to the risk that prospective lenders face should they provide funds to the borrower. It is also possible that the prospective borrower is understating the default risk lenders would face.

It is logical to expect that when all the relevant information is available to prospective lenders, the level of default risk will be reflected in the rate of return that they require to supply funds. The greater the risk the greater the required return.

II Time value of money

In financial markets funds accrue interest over time, thus future amounts exceed present amounts. This implies that the value of a payment depends on the moment in time that it is made. **Present values** have no interest component because they represent payments that are made today, whereas **future values**, representing payments that are made at a future date, include interest.

One of the functions of financial markets is to establish the relationship between present and future values. They do this through determining the yield represented by the future payments of securities. The yield is a measure of the annual rate at which future values exceed present values.

The basic cause of the time value of money — interest — is the objective of the suppliers of funds to enhance their future purchasing power. This can be achieved through the payment of interest or through the appreciation of the eventual repayment amount (where the increase in the security's value represents interest).

Future values, because they include interest, can be converted into present values by removing their interest component. This is performed by **discounting** the future value using the interest rate that measures the time value of money. Any transaction that involves a delayed payment or future repayment should allow for the time value of money. The relationship between present and future values is shown in figure 1.7.

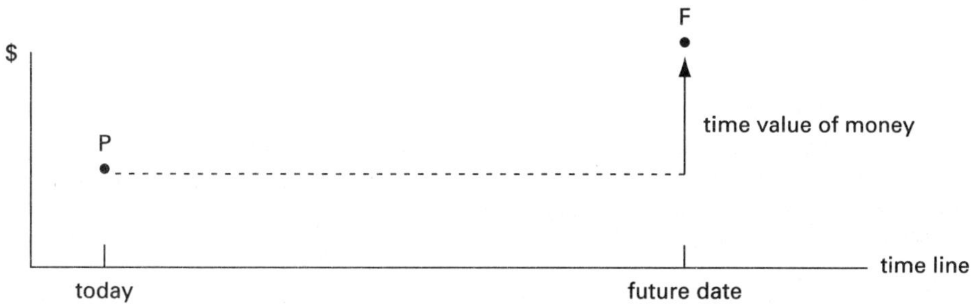

Figure 1.7 Present and future values

III Interest rates as market yields

A market yield is the annual rate of return represented by a security's future payment(s). These yields are set by the trading of securities in financial markets. The major benchmark yields are the 90-day bill rate and the 10-year bond rate. These yields are often referred to as interest rates and their movements are the underlying driving force behind movements in the interest rates set by financial institutions.

Yields measure the rate at which P increases to F (as in figure 1.7) over the 'term' of F (i.e. the period from the present day to the future date when F is paid).

IV Security prices and yields

Debt securities trade in financial markets on the basis of their yield. For those securities that provide fixed future payments, their price moves **inversely** to a change in their yield. This is an important relationship given that most of the debt securities traded in Australia's financial markets are of this kind.

The relationship between yields and prices, as depicted in figure 1.8, can be viewed either way:

- a decrease, say, in the yield causes the security's price to rise; or
- an increase, say, in the demand for a security will cause its yield to fall (and hence its price to rise).

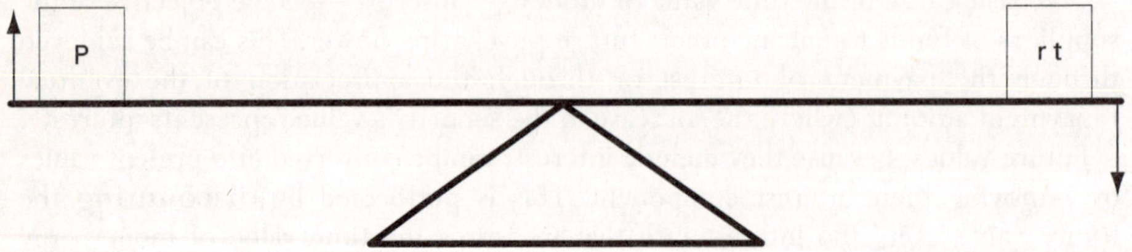

Figure 1.8 The relationship between a security's yield and its price

V Spreads in financial markets

The golden rule of trading is **buy low and sell high.** Consequently, 'bids' (buying orders) tend to be less than 'offers' (sell orders), resulting in a spread.

In Australia's markets for debt securities (mainly bills and bonds), bids and offers are expressed in yields rather than prices. Because yields and prices vary inversely to each other, bid yields are higher than offer yields in these markets.

Spreads exist also for dealings with financial institutions. They borrow at a low rate and lend at a high rate. Thus they have an interest-rate spread. The size of this spread is much greater than the spreads in financial markets, because intermediation involves the provision of more services than arranging a transaction.

VI Market volatility

Financial markets allow continuous trading during their business day. Even though the trading volume is usually very great, prices bounce about during a trading day and over the medium to long term. These movements in prices are referred to as the market's volatility.

Volatility is a source of risk for traders who enter financial markets. It can be an inhibiting force for risk-averse parties and so may depress economic activity. However, volatility can be a source of profit for speculators who trade on the expectation of buying low and selling high. Consequently, volatility is an important dimension of a market's behaviour.

VII Market risks

When interest rates rise, security prices fall (as implied in figure 1.8). Therefore holders of securities are exposed to the risk of a loss of value. Price risk is one form of market risk, the risk that market values (such as the value of shares, foreign exchange and securities) will move adversely for individual market participants.

Market risk can be substantial in markets that are not subject to price control. Consequently, the management of exposure to this risk is an important issue for financial-market participants.

VIII Risk management

The fundamental need for risk management is because financial variables, such as interest and exchange rates, vary continuously (i.e. are volatile), and the movements can impose serious losses on market participants. Risk management involves the identification of exposures, setting risk-management objectives and following risk-management strategies that achieve the objectives in a cost-effective way.

Given a risk-averse objective, one strategy is to establish an opposite position in the market for an equivalent derivative instrument. To illustrate, an investor in the money market can buy financial futures contracts that have the same face value as the money market investments, so that a profit is made in the futures market when interest rates fall. Such a fall reduces the yield on the investment in the money market but this is offset by the profit on the hedge position in the futures market.

Another strategy is to establish a **natural hedge** through offsetting positions in physical markets, such as offsetting the foreign exchange exposure arising from export income by borrowing in the foreign currency such that the payments match the foreign currency receipts.

The logic underpinning hedging was depicted in figure 1.5, where the hedge position is shown as counter-balancing the exposure arising from a position in a financial market (such as that of a borrower or lender).

IX Arbitrage and pricing parity

The term '**arbitrage**' refers to the practice of buying a product at a lower price in one market and selling it (or an exact equivalent product) immediately at a higher price in another market. This practice places upward pressure on the lower price and downward pressure on the higher price and so should result in **pricing parity** (i.e. the product selling at the same price in each market).

Provided the various markets for financial securities are open and competitive, equivalent securities that are traded in different markets should have the same price. Consequently, the price of a security in one market can be used to indicate the price of it or an equivalent security in another market.

Given that many securities (or their equivalent) are traded in different markets, both around the globe and within a country's financial system, arbitrage and the resulting parity pricing are important features of finance theory and practice.

X Information and expectations

Because of the huge value of turnover in financial markets, traders are under great pressure to use information about market conditions as efficiently as possible. When new information becomes available traders very quickly assess its impact on values and adjust their buying and selling positions accordingly. The faster prices adjust, the more efficient is the use of information.

This is not to imply that traders simply await the release of information and then react. They will form expectations, where possible, about the information that is to be released and adjust their bids and offers accordingly. Should the expectations of most traders prove correct, the subsequent release of the information will have no impact on market values, as these will have been adjusted in anticipation of the news. Market values will react to new information only when it takes the market by surprise, for example, when it differs from the expectations of most traders. It is difficult to exaggerate the importance of information and expectations in determining values set by financial markets.

Summary

The main points of this chapter are as follows:

- The financial system provides a variety of means for making payments.
- Future payments can be funded by either debt or equity capital.
- Lending and borrowing can be arranged through either direct financing or intermediation.
- Market transactions involve risks, the main ones being credit risk and market risks.
- Risk-management instruments (forwards, futures, swaps and options) are widely used for trading and risk-management purposes.
- A number of basic principles help explain the operations of the financial system.

DISCUSSION QUESTIONS AND EXERCISES

1 Discuss the financial system's contributions to the well-being of members of the community.
2 Discuss the three functions or tasks performed by the financial system.
3 Discuss four ways of making payments and whether we are headed toward a cashless society.
4 Describe the processes involved in the cheque-payment system, referring to the role of the Reserve Bank of Australia, and indicate whether depositors earn interest on deposited cheques prior to the release of the funds to the depositor.
5 What are net settlement positions within the payments system? What is real-time settlement and how does it reduce risk compared with delayed settlement?
6 Distinguish between the basic features of debt and equity capital and suggest several forms of each.
7 Discuss the advantages and risks of a borrower providing security for a loan.
8 Carefully distinguish between direct and intermediated financing, referring to the different roles of financial institutions.
9 Describe three forms of risk that arise through participation in the financial system.
10 Explain five principles of finance.

REFERENCES AND FURTHER READING

Australian Payments System Council 1994, *Report, 1993–94*, Sydney.
Bank for International Settlements 1994, *Payment Systems in Australia*, BIS, Basle.
Carew, Edna 1995, *Derivatives Decoded*, Allen & Unwin, Sydney.
Fabozzi, Frank J., Modigliani, Franco, & Ferri, Michael G. 1994, *Foundations of Financial Markets and Institutions*, Prentice-Hall, New Jersey, Chapter 1.
PSA 1995, *Inquiry into Fees and Charges imposed on Retail Accounts by Banks and other Financial Institutions and by Retailers on EFTPOS Transactions*, Melbourne, Chapter 2 and Appendix D.
RBA April 1995 (a), *The Case for Real Time Gross Settlement*, RBA, Sydney
RBA 1995 (b), *Annual Report, 1994–95*, RBA, Sydney.

2

Introduction to financial institutions

The purposes of this chapter are to explain the rationale for financial intermediation and to provide an introduction to the three main categories of financial institutions within the financial system. The chapter discusses the role of interest-rate spreads as the source of income for intermediation, as well as the fee income of institutions for their other activities. A more detailed discussion of the operations of financial institutions is presented in Part two of the book.

Study objectives

From your study of this chapter you should be able to:

- explain the main forms of financial services provided by financial institutions;
- explain the role and rationale of interest-rate spreads;
- explain the benefits of intermediation;
- describe the three main categories of financial institutions; and
- outline the role of the Reserve Bank of Australia within the financial system.

INTRODUCTION

A financial institution is a business that provides intermediated products and/or financial services. These institutions are distinguished from non-financial businesses that are engaged in the production of goods and/or non-financial services. This does not mean that financial institutions have exclusive rights to the provision of each and every financial service. Individuals and businesses undertake their own financing to some extent. For example, large retailers provide their own credit facilities, such as credit cards.

There is a wide range of financial institutions, reflecting, in the main, a 40-year period (early 1940s to early 1980s) of bank regulations that had the unintended effect of promoting the development of non-bank financial institutions. The regulations (e.g. controls on interest rates) had been applied to banks because when they were introduced in the early 1940s, banks dominated the financial system. There was little point in imposing controls on the interest rates set by, say, building societies, because they handled only a tiny proportion of the financial system's borrowing and lending.

Following the removal of these regulations in the early 1980s, there has been a rationalisation of the operations of financial institutions, leading to the reemergence of banks as the principal form of institution. However, banks are not homogeneous, and certain categories of non-banks compete with banks in the market for specific financial services.

You will recall from Chapter 1 that financing can be intermediated or raised directly from financial markets. In this chapter we will concentrate initially on the intermediation role of financial institutions. Their role in the operations of markets and in direct financing is referred to later in the chapter.

Remember that intermediation involves borrowing funds and lending them as the institution's funds, earning income through the interest-rate spread. The institutions engaged in intermediation offer a range of:

- investment and transaction products and services to depositors (and other suppliers of funds), and
- financing products and services to borrowers, through which they lend funds.

They also hold securities, mainly for liquidity (but also for investment) purposes and provide other related financial services, such as arranging payments.

As noted above, there is a range of financial institutions and wide variation in the activities of the institutions in each group. In large part this reflects their involvement in either intermediated or direct financing (or both). Officially, financial institutions are divided into several categories:

1. banks, which are licensed by the Reserve Bank,
2. non-bank financial institutions (NBFIs) that are classified under the *Financial Corporations Act*, 1974,
3. insurance offices and fund managers.

Following the removal, in the early 1980s, of the controls on banks, it has become increasingly difficult to distinguish between the operations of institutions in terms of the above categories. Under the current low-regulation regime, the distinctions between the operations of financial institutions (i.e. categories 1 and 2 above) are determined mainly by the business plans of each organisation and the segments of the markets for financial services in which they compete.

Not all banks are alike, nor do they all compete against one another. Likewise, not all NBFIs are alike. Their activities can be grouped, loosely, into **retail banking** and

wholesale banking in the same way that we group the activities of banks. Retail banking, which is discussed in Chapter 6, is the provision of financial services to small-value clients, and wholesale banking, which is discussed in Chapter 7, is the provision of financial services to large-value clients (mainly large companies and government enterprises).

The third general category also comprises institutions that provide different types of financial services, such as insurance products and investment-management services. The demarcation between banking and insurance, which applies in Australia (as at mid 1995), is one of the few remaining restrictions on the activities of banks. It has been removed in some countries, whereas in Australia it is being circumvented by a number of banks that have formed strategic alliances with insurance offices so that they can market a full range of financial services to their customers (even though the insurance products they sell are not 'produced' by them).

Although the official categories of financial institutions remain, the operations of most institutions are focused toward either the retail or wholesale segments (or both) of the market for financial products and services.

The retail segment is made up of the transactions of individuals, households and small business. These typically are small-value payment or financing transactions, whereas large businesses and enterprises are the customers in the wholesale (or corporate) segment. They typically undertake large-value payment and financing transactions and demand **treasury** products (i.e. capital, foreign exchange and risk-management instruments).

Financial innovation (that is, the development of new financial products, services, institutions and processes) accelerated following deregulation. But the application of new technology by the providers of financial services has been a more enduring cause of financial innovation. Consequently, we need to emphasise that the institutional structure in the financial sector is subject to perpetual change. And yet, despite this moving target, we need to start somewhere in our explanation of the general operations of financial institutions.

An indicative model

An indication of the organisational structure of a financial institution that provides traditional banking products and services is presented in figure 2.1. This model is an adaptation of the one presented by Burrows and Davis for the Prices Surveillance Authority inquiry into charges on retail accounts. (PSA, Appendix J, 1995) For the purposes of this section, we will use a bank to represent the operations of financial institutions. As shown by the data in table 2.2 (on p. 40), banks are the principal form of financial institution.

The model bank services the retail market through its branch and ATM networks. It provides deposit accounts for transaction and investment purposes, loans and other retail banking services. The wholesale/business market is serviced through its business banking and treasury departments.

A further indication of the operations of financial institutions is provided by the balance sheet of a hypothetical bank, SafeAsa Bank, presented in table 2.1, which shows assets and liabilities that are commonly held by banks. Data on the bank's **off-balance sheet** financial contracts accompany the balance sheet data. These are

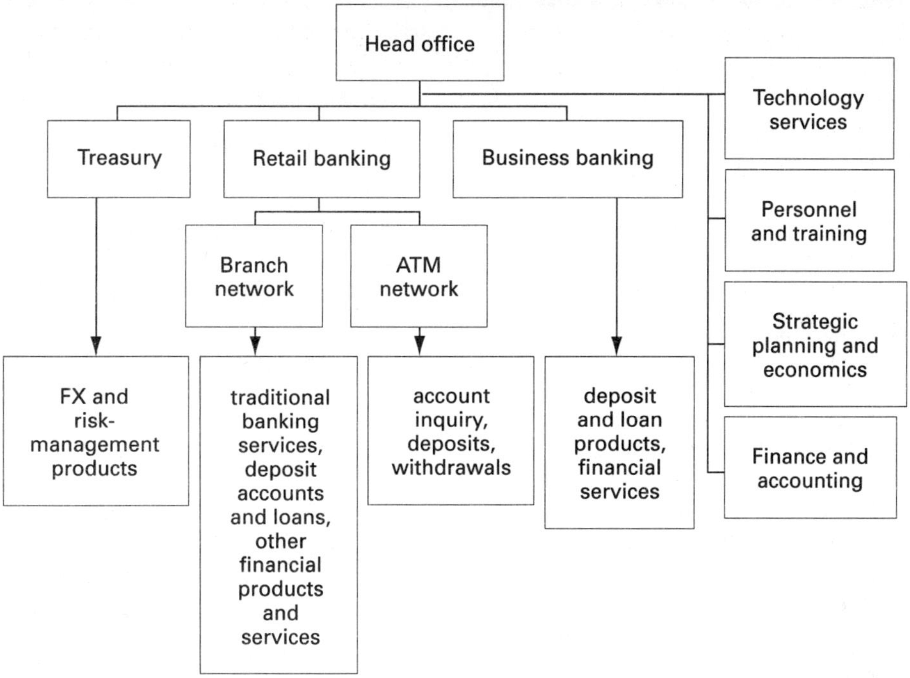

Figure 2.1 A model bank structure

mainly derivatives (held by the bank), the value of which is contingent in nature. Typically, their value depends on the future value of a financial variable.

Deposits are the bank's main source of funds (which are referred to as liabilities because the bank is obliged to repay them, usually with interest). Funds are mainly used as loans and advances and securities (which are referred to as assets because the bank earns interest on them and has a legal right to enforce their repayment).

The first three of the listed deposits are drawn mainly from the retail market. Individuals and businesses place funds in **current deposits** (these funds can be transferred by cheque) for transaction purposes. Individuals are the main suppliers of the funds held in **fixed-term deposit** and the 'other' accounts. The 'other retail' deposits are in investment savings and passbook accounts held by retail customers. The various types of bank accounts are explained more fully in Chapter 6.

Certificates of deposit (CDs) are drawn from business customers. These are large-value deposits (typically for amounts of $5 million and above) that have a short term (typically less than three months) and can be sold in the short-term money market should the depositor wish to exchange the repayment amount for cash prior to its maturity date.

Foreign currency liabilities are an alternative source of funds for the bank and may be used to finance its foreign currency assets.

All banks must hold an adequate amount of equity capital (mainly shareholders' funds). This requirement is discussed in Chapter 9.

Table 2.1 SafeAsa Bank — balance sheet

Assets	*$'000*	*Liabilities*	*$'000*
Cash	1 000	Current deposits	8 000
NCDs with RBA	300	Fixed-term deposits	12 000
Securities	5 200	Other retail deposits	5 000
Loans and advances	25 000	Certificates of deposit	4 000
Premises	1 000	Foreign-currency liabilities	3 500
Foreign-currency assets	2 500	Shareholders' funds	2 500
Totals	35 000		35 000

Off-balance sheet contracts:

Foreign-exchange contracts	$80 000 000
Interest-rate swap agreements	$40 000 000
Forward rate agreements (FRAs)	$20 000 000
Interest-rate futures contracts	$20 000 000

On the asset side, observe that the bank holds some cash even though it is a non-interest-earning asset, because it must meet its depositors' withdrawals. Securities are its other liquid asset. Its short-term securities can be sold for **next-day funds**, and thus are very liquid. Next-day funds are explained in Chapter 3. The bank's securities include Commonwealth Government securities (CGS), because they are a **prime asset**. The RBA requires (as at mid 1995) at least 6 per cent of a bank's assets to be in the form of prime assets (mainly cash, deposits with the RBA and CGSs).

NCDs are **non-callable deposits** with the Reserve Bank. Banks are required to hold at least 1 per cent of their Australian-dollar assets with the RBA.

The bank's loans and advances are made to both retail customers (e.g. housing loans) and business customers (e.g. term loans). Its foreign-currency assets include loans to an overseas affiliate bank.

You will observe that the bank relies principally on borrowed funds and thus its debt-to-equity ratio (13:1) is very high. Non-financial businesses tend to have a much lower ratio of debt-to-equity funds (typically the debt-to-equity ratio is less than 2:1).

The off-balance sheet data show the value of various contracts held by the bank, the value of which is contingent in nature. It can be seen that the total value of these items greatly exceeds the balance sheet total. The bank has entered many of these contracts to provide clients with risk-management instruments. For example, many of the foreign-exchange contracts serve to set future exchange rates for bank clients. Some of the contracts are held by the bank for its own risk-management purposes (arising from the bank's foreign exchange and borrowing/lending activities). These items are discussed more fully in later chapters.

The bank's shareholders expect that it will operate profitably and pay regular dividends. Historically, Australian banks have been very profitable, although during the last few years of the 1980s and the first few years of the 1990s their profitability declined, mainly as a result of large losses on certain of their loans. Bank profitability returned to its traditional high level by the mid-1990s.

INTEREST-RATE SPREAD

Deposit-taking institutions earn income from intermediation through their interest-rate spread. This is the difference between the average interest rate on their loans and the average interest rate paid on deposits.

There are several established methods of calculating interest rate spreads (or margins). One approach is:

$$\text{Net interest spread} = \frac{\text{interest received}}{\text{interest-earning assets}} - \frac{\text{interest paid}}{\text{total deposits}}$$

This approach shows a bank's spread from the viewpoint of its customers. The net spread is, in effect, the average return on the use of funds (paid by the customers who have borrowed from the institution) minus the average cost of the funds (paid to the customers who have placed funds with the institution). (RBA, 1992, p. 195)

While customers might object to a wide spread, because this is taken from them collectively by the institution, spreads depend on a range of factors that should be considered before an informed judgment can be made about the size of a spread.

Fundamentally, the cost of providing intermediation services and their value to the intermediary's customers should be reflected in the size of an institution's spread. One way of viewing intermediation services is to examine the assets and liabilities of intermediaries.

Loans and advances are relatively expensive to administer and thus institutions tend to seek a high rate of return from them compared with the return from simply holding securities. Moreover, small-value loans tend to be more expensive to administer, per loan dollar, than large-value loans. Thus, in general, institutions that hold most of their assets as low-value loans would have a higher interest-rate spread than institutions that mainly hold securities.

Allowance should be made also for the different characteristics of assets, such as their degree of risk, their liquidity and term. Generally, returns are higher for riskier assets and increase with the term of the asset (although this latter relationship does not always hold); whereas lower returns are usually expected on liquid (rather than illiquid) assets.

An institution could widen its interest-rate spread by investing more of its funds in risky, illiquid, long-term loans. But in the process it would be accepting a higher level of credit risk, for which it should be compensated, and it would have to manage with a less liquid portfolio of assets.

Nevertheless, investing in risky loans can result in an unplanned narrow interest-rate spread. This occurs when an unexpected proportion of them become bad loans. Loans are **non-performing** (or non-accrual) when the customers fail to make required interest and loan repayments. They do not contribute to interest earnings and so reduce the return on assets and the institution's interest-rate spread. This outcome is explained in example 2.1.

example 2.1

Suppose a bank made a $10 million loan to a property developer on the basis of quarterly interest payments with the principal to be repaid in two years, using the property as security. Suppose further that after six months the developer goes into liquidation and the bank resumes the partially-developed property from the developer. For the period until the bank can sell the property, during which it earns no interest income on the loan, it has to pay interest on the $10 million to its depositors. Thus, this non-performing loan reduces both its return on assets and its interest rate spread.

The average cost of funds also reflects many factors. Institutions pay a range of interest rates to their suppliers of funds, depending on such factors as:

- the services provided 'free' to the account holder, such as administration and payment services (when their cost is not fully recovered from bank charges on account holders),
- the balance in each account (the larger the balance the higher the interest rate),
- liquidity (i.e. the degree of access depositors have to the funds in the account), and
- the term of the placement (often the rate of interest increases with the term of deposits).

In general, rates vary inversely with the amount of services and liquidity provided to depositors, and vary directly with the balance in the account and the term of the deposit.

Institutions meet their operating costs from their interest-rate spread and from their non-interest income, such as fees and charges.

Because interest-rate spreads are influenced by many factors, care should be taken in their interpretation. A narrow spread can result from excessive bad loans, and this would indicate poor earnings for the bank. A narrow spread could result also when an institution invests mainly in securities and makes large, very secure loans. This would result in unspectacular but appropriate earnings, given the low level of credit risk involved.

Traditionally, most of a bank's net income is derived from its interest-rate spread. Since deregulation, though, the proportion of net income derived from fees for service has tended to rise, reflecting changes in the way banks conduct their business. Recovering the cost of payment services is one area where fees have been introduced. Another area where fee income has been increased is in the provision of financial services for large business customers and fund-management services for retail customers.

The interest-rate spread is much wider for retail than for wholesale transactions. Retail transactions are typically small and their processing cost represents a larger proportion of the amounts involved than for the typical wholesale transaction. Wholesale customers may be able to arrange direct finance and this places pressure on the rates institutions can charge. Also, the entry of new banks over the last decade has resulted in competition increasing most for wholesale business.

In 1994, for example, the overall spread for all banks averaged 4 per cent whereas the spreads for housing loans exceeded 5 per cent and for small business loans they exceeded 7.5 per cent. (PSA, 1995, p. 98) The lower overall spread reflects the lower spreads on large business loans.

The interest-rate spread charged by institutions represents a cost imposed on their customers. The wider the spread, the greater the cost; depositors receive a lower rate and borrowers pay a higher rate. Why then do lenders and borrowers transact through financial intermediaries? Presumably the cost is offset by the benefits provided by intermediaries.

Benefits of intermediation

Borrowing rates are less than lending rates because of the value of the financial services provided by financial institutions to depositors and to borrowers. Not all intermediaries provide the same set of services, but deposit-taking institutions generally provide the following:

- maturity intermediation,
- funds management,
- credit risk reduction,
- reduced transaction costs,
- payment services.

Maturity intermediation

Maturity intermediation occurs when funds are placed with intermediaries for a shorter term than the loans made by the institution. In general, surplus units prefer to lend for short periods whereas deficit units prefer to borrow for long periods. Observe in the SafeAsa Bank illustration in table 2.1 above that it holds substantial amounts of demand deposits, which have a short term, whereas most of its housing and business loans would have a much longer term — up to 30 years in the case of the housing loans.

The acceptance of short-term deposits to fund longer-term loans provides depositors with a much higher degree of liquidity than they would enjoy if they lent their funds direct to borrowers. From their viewpoint, maturity intermediation creates liquidity. However, the intermediary has to manage its short-term liabilities and longer-term assets.

Maturity intermediation also serves to better match the demand and supply of funds for both short-term and long-term transactions. This enhances the investment opportunities for surplus units and the borrowing opportunities for deficit units. It also reduces the rate of interest that longer-term borrowers would pay because it transforms short-term funds into longer-term funds. It also increases the rate of return received by short-term lenders because of its demand for such funds.

By providing the service of maturity intermediation, financial institutions greatly increase the efficiency of the financial system. That is, the difference between the maturity preferences of lenders and borrowers would otherwise be a major impediment to the borrowing and lending process. But providing this service poses a problem for a financial institution — that of managing its maturity mismatch.

Maturity intermediation exposes intermediaries to two forms of risk:

1 **Funding risk** This arises because the institution has to ensure that it can continuously maintain the level of deposits needed to finance (i.e. fund) its longer-term assets. Should its depositors withdraw their funds the institution would have a problem because it has agreed to lend funds for a specified period.

   To diminish funding risk, institutions attempt to attract funds from a variety of sources and from a large pool of depositors. This pooling strategy should ensure that the institution can always attract new deposits to replace those withdrawn — provided its depositors need cash at different times.

   Intermediaries are also exposed to **liquidity risk**, which is related to funding risk. This is the risk of a temporary lack of funds. This risk is managed through the holding of liquid assets, such as government securities, that can be sold in financial markets or sold to the Reserve Bank if funds need to be raised quickly.

2 **Interest-rate risk** This refers to losses that occur through adverse movements in interest rates. It arises when the interest-rate basis on an institution's loan differs from that on its deposits. Suppose an institution's loans are at a fixed rate of interest (say, 10 per cent p.a.) and it pays the current market interest rate on its deposits (say this is 5 per cent p.a.). Should the general level of interest rates rise (to say, 7 per cent p.a.), the institution's cost of funds would increase even though the rate it receives (10 per cent p.a.) is fixed. This would reduce its interest-rate spread and could even result in a negative spread should, for instance, short-term rates increase to 12 per cent p.a.

Suppose, though, that the rate of interest on the institution's long-term loans and on its short-term liabilities are both based on current rates (i.e. both have a floating rate). Usually the short-term rate of interest is less than the long-term rate. This helps institutions in their maturity intermediation. But there have been occasions when short-term rates have exceeded long-term rates. (We examine the relationship between short-term and long-term rates in Chapter 15.) This event could result also in a negative interest spread.

The ability to manage the risks that arise from maturity intermediation is an important part of the expertise of financial institutions which justifies their interest-rate spread. SafeAsa Bank's holdings of interest-rate swaps and futures contracts and FRAs play an important part in managing the risks arising from maturity intermediation.

Funds management

When institutions accept funds from surplus units they take on the responsibility for investing these funds. Institutions may lend the funds or invest them in financial assets, such as stocks and bonds. Being relieved of the need to make lending and investment decisions is an important benefit for the suppliers of intermediated funds.

Making loans and investments requires considerable expertise, which institutions need to possess. An important element of investment decisions is the risk that the user of the funds will fail to make loan payments as required. This matter is discussed below. Another element is the assessment of the likely return.

Generally, institutions that accept funds from the public (i.e. operate at the retail level) adopt a risk-averse investment strategy. They lend funds only where they believe the risk of default is low. This also means that they forgo investment opportunities that have high possible returns, because such opportunities tend to be too risky. By following a risk-averse lending strategy, these institutions can provide the public with low-risk avenues for investing their funds. However, institutions need to maximise their returns (given the risk level that they accept) to be able to offer competitive interest rates on their deposits. They must balance their pursuit of returns with their need to provide a safe haven for depositors' funds.

The management of funds is therefore a major part of the services provided by financial institutions.

Credit risk reduction

You will recall that credit risk refers to the risk that the borrower will default on loan repayments. It is referred to also as default risk or as a form of counterparty risk. An individual lender usually faces a lower level of credit risk when lending to a financial institution than when lending directly to a deficit unit.

Credit risk can be reduced through the diversification of loans. Institutions will make loans to a wide variety of industries and to a number of firms in each industry. Through diversification institutions reduce their exposure (i.e. risk of loss) to any one borrower or group of borrowers. Even though some lenders will default, the institutions that have diversified their loans are unlikely to suffer widespread defaults and so can continue to pay interest to their depositors.

Usually an individual lender is not able to lend to a diversified set of borrowers. This requires a substantial amount of funds because many investments require a sizeable minimum amount. Suppose, in the extreme case, that a lender is able to make only a single loan. If the borrower defaults, the lender may lose all of the amount lent. Consequently, individual lenders face a much lower level of credit risk by placing funds with an institution that has a diversified pattern of lending, rather than by lending directly to deficit units.

Credit risk can be reduced also by adopting prudent lending practices. This involves:

- analysis of the predicted cash flows the borrower expects to generate from the use of the borrowed funds, in order to identify the degree of riskiness,
- monitoring of the client's financial position over the period of the loan and the provision of financial advice to the borrower when required,
- establishing appropriate security over the assets acquired by the loan (or over the borrower's assets generally),

- imposition of a default-risk premium (i.e. a component of the interest rate charged on a loan that depends on the riskiness of each loan) to generate funds to cover losses from non-performing loans, and (as discussed above)
- the diversification of lending between borrowers and industries in order to reduce the institution's exposure to losses.

Institutions usually have greater lending expertise and, through economies of scale in lending, can undertake these activities at a lower unit cost than individual lenders can.

The losses incurred by financial institutions in the late 1980s and early 1990s can be attributed to their failure to apply these sound lending practices. Institutions corrected these mistakes in the early 1990s and, as a result, have become more financially secure themselves.

Reduced transaction costs

Financial institutions can reduce the transaction costs that customers would otherwise face when they plan their investments. We can divide the transaction costs of investors into three categories:

- information-processing costs that are involved in searching for potential borrowers and analysing the credit risks involved with each,
- contracting costs involved in negotiating and documenting the terms of each loan and investment, and
- access to (through branch and ATM networks) and choice among financial services and products.

Even though the interest-rate spreads set by institutions result in their depositors receiving a lower rate than that charged on loans, institutions attract customers because they absorb the transaction costs that customers would incur if they engaged in direct financing. These costs are reduced by institutions for the two basic reasons stated above:

1. institutions possess financial expertise in the lending and investment processes and in the management of loans and investments, and
2. institutions operate on a large scale that allows them to spread their transaction costs over many customers, lowering the per customer cost.

Retail banking institutions have traditionally reduced their customers' transaction costs by establishing a network of branches that are conveniently located and offer a range of financial products. The development of electronic delivery services tends to diminish the role of branches by providing better access to financial products.

Payment services

Most (but not all) financial institutions offer payment services to their customers. Traditionally, cheque accounts were the foundation instrument of the payment system. As noted in Chapter 1, plastic cards and electronic payment systems are important innovations. They allow customers to gain access to funds in other accounts for payment purposes.

A precondition for the provision of payment services is that customers have access to the funds they have deposited (i.e. liquidity). As noted above, this is achieved through the effective management of maturity intermediation. The main strategies adopted to provide customers with liquidity are:

- attract a large pool of depositors, because this tends to counterbalance the deposits and withdrawals of individual customers,
- invest in liquid assets that can be sold to raise cash whenever there is an overall decline in the amount of funds on deposit, and
- accept funds from different sectors of the community and from different parts of the global financial system.

In addition to liquidity, the provision of payment services also involves the transfer of funds as required by account holders. This involves the provision of the various payment systems described in Chapter 1, such as ATM machines, EFTPOS facilities and electronic banking.

DEREGULATION: IMPACT ON INSTITUTIONS

An extensive range of controls over the operations of banks was introduced in the early 1940s. The controls applied to banks (only) because at the time, they dominated the financial system. The regulations are described in Chapter 6. They had the (unintended) effect of impeding banks from attracting deposits (through the limits on the interest rates banks could pay on deposits) and thus restricted their capacity to lend.

During the 1960s and 1970s the financial system underwent a substantial development phase to provide the financial services and products sought by the developing real sector of the economy. Because of the restrictions on intermediation by banks, their effect was to provide non-bank institutions with the opportunity to develop by serving the growing financial needs of the community.

In 1974 a classification system of non-banks was set out in legislation. While no regulations over the operations of non-banks were introduced, the types of institutions classified by the *Financial Corporations Act* tended to operate in distinct ways. Thus, prior to financial deregulation in the early 1980s, it was possible to distinguish between the operations of many different types of financial institutions.

The regulations were kept in place after World War II as part of the then Government's low-interest-rate policy. There were various restrictions on banks (as well as on the foreign-exchange market). For instance, a ceiling was imposed on the level of interest rates that banks could charge. This was intended to prevent banks from profiting from the scarcity of funds during the war. The ceiling on the rate of interest banks could pay on deposits restricted their capacity to compete for funds, thus limiting their lending capacity.

The removal of these restrictions in the early 1980s (i.e. deregulation) allowed banks to expand their operations, attracting a greater proportion of funds and increasing their share of the market for loans. Moreover, a number of non-banks decided to become banks, either through amalgamation with an existing bank or by obtaining a bank licence.

Table 2.2 Financial institutions — assets, June 1984 to 1995

	1984	*1986*	*1988*	*1990*	*1992*	*1994*	*1995*
Banks $b	102.8	154.3	228.5	325.9	361.9	412.8	437.9
NBFIs $b	71.4	100.1	130.2	145.2	124.2	114.5	131.0
Managed funds $b	59.4	84.7	155.6	207.3	236.4	278.8	291.6
Total $b	233.5	347.5	514.2	678.3	722.5	806.0	860.5
% of total							
Banks	44.0	44.5	44.4	48.0	50.1	51.2	50.9
NBFIs	30.6	28.8	25.3	21.4	17.2	14.2	15.2
Managed funds	25.4	26.8	30.3	30.6	32.7	34.6	33.9
Total	100.0	100.0	100.0	100.0	100.0	100.0	100.0

Source: RBA, *Bulletin*, Table D.5

New technology and changing market conditions also have a major impact on the way institutions conduct their business and on the capacity of institutions to widen their range of services. Given that these are on-going processes, it follows that the institutional structure of the financial system is not stable; it evolves over time. In this chapter we discuss institutions according to the three official categories:

- banks
- non-bank financial institutions (such as merchant banks and credit unions) and
- fund managers (such as superannuation funds).

The share of financial assets held by banks, NBFIs and fund managers is shown by the data in table 2.2. Observe the relative growth in assets of banks and managed funds over the period, and the relative decline in the assets held by NBFIs.

BANKS

Banks are the principal form of financial institution. As noted earlier in this chapter, a wide range of activities are performed by banks, although the core business of banking involves:

- the provision of intermediated products (deposits and loans),
- providing payment services, and
- risk-management (of the bank and its customers). (Joss, 1996, p. 185)

Nevertheless, banks do not have an exclusive right to the provision of these core banking services. As previously noted, certain NBFIs offer these services. The distinction between banks and these NBFIs arises purely from their official status. Banks hold a banking licence (granted by the Commonwealth Treasurer on the advice of the RBA and the Treasury) and are subject to Reserve Bank requirements. However, the criteria for a banking licence do not help to distinguish banks from other financial institutions. In general they are concerned with establishing an applicant's capacity to operate effectively as a bank in accordance with the operating requirements of the RBA. As at mid 1996, there is no restriction on the number of bank licences that can be issued.

Table 2.3 Banks — assets, June 1981 to June 1995 ($m)

June	*Cash*	*Public sector securities*	*Loans, advances and bills*	*Other $A assets*	*Foreign currency assets*	***Total assets***
1981	755	15 368	38 011	10 809		64 943
1983	743	17 652	49 326	19 751		87 472
1985	875	21 761	68 684	28 848		120 169
1987	1 009	25 222	98 749	49 271	8 450	182 703
1989	1 280	26 573	167 322	75 548	12 950	283 672
1991	1 244	23 437	226 757	85 236	17 062	353 733
1992	1 283	24 975	238 604	82 685	14 362	361 908
1993	1 356	25 484	255 384	83 088	17 538	382 849
1994	1 452	28 179	277 136	85 891	20 185	412 844
1995	1 643	28 545	297 521	88 241	23 394	439 344

Source: RBA, *Bulletin*, Table B.1

As at the end of 1995 only banks can hold current deposits; but the RBA indicated in its 1994/95 *Annual Report* that this privilege will be extended to building societies and credit unions. Banks also hold a licence to trade in the foreign exchange market, but so can any other licensed foreign exchange dealer. Because of their involvement in the payment system, each bank has an exchange settlement account (ESA) with the Reserve Bank. Building societies and credit unions will also be given access to ESAs.

At one time the Reserve Bank provided banks with a lender-of-last-resort facility. This meant that they would lend funds to banks for short periods when banks were otherwise unable to raise the funds from the market. Currently, any holder of Treasury notes can rediscount them (i.e. sell them back) to the Reserve Bank. This facility serves to provide all such parties with access to liquidity if required. However, the rediscount rate is set so that the price is slightly below market value for the notes.

Banks, as a group, are the major financial intermediaries within the financial system. A summary of their holdings of assets over the period June 1981 to June 1995 is shown in table 2.3.

As at July 1995 there were 33 authorised banking groups in Australia and 16 authorised branches of foreign banks. (RBA, *Bulletin*, July 1995, pp 50–1) Nevertheless, the number of banks does change from time to time.

In its recent Financial Institutions Performance Surveys, KPMG Peat Marwick divides banks into three categories: major banks, regional banks and other banks.

The 'big four'

The major banks are known as the big four:

- Australia and New Zealand Bank (ANZ)
- Commonwealth Bank of Australia (CBA or 'which' bank)
- National Australia Bank (NAB) and
- Westpac Banking Corporation (WBC).

Referred to as the big four because of their size, each of these is a substantially larger bank than any of the remaining banks. Their respective size is indicated in table 2.4 by the data on total assets and number of branches/agencies. Collectively they held 65 per cent of bank assets and had 75 per cent of all bank branches (as at the end of 1995).

The big four are 'department store' (or 'one-stop-shop') banks, because of the wide range of financial products and services they provide. Their range of financial services spans all three of the above categories of financial institutions. The appointment of the Wallis Inquiry into Banking (in early 1996) was associated with speculation that mergers may be permitted between banks and insurance offices. This would allow the majors to provide insurance and fund-management services directly.

Table 2.4 The big four — Assets and number of branches (end 1995)

	Total assets ($ m)	*No. of branches*
ANZ Banking Group	64 382	1 186
Commonwealth Bank	77 240	1 474
National Australia Bank	83 596	1 214
Westpac Banking Corp.	68 120	1 092
Total: big four	293 338	4 966
Total: all banks	456 711	6 655

Source: RBA, *Bulletin*, Tables B.10 and B.20

Regional banks are mainly banks that are (or were) owned by a State government or were building societies that subsequently became banks. They are referred to as regional banks because their operations are concentrated within (usually) one state. These banks operate mainly as retail banks.

In 1995 there were clear indications that this group of 'second-tier' banks would undergo some form of rationalisation. For example, Advance Bank took over the Bank of South Australia, and a take-over battle emerged between St George Bank and several Queensland financial institutions for Metway (a Queensland-based bank).

The third group comprises all other banks, almost all of which are owned by large overseas banking groups (such as Citibank and Mitsubishi Bank), which we refer to as **investment banks**. These banks mainly operate in the wholesale sector of the financial system. They compete with the major banks and so-called merchant banks. Some of the regional banks also operate in this segment of the financial system.

Retail banking

The main distinguishing feature of retail banking as shown on a bank's balance sheet is the large volume of deposits and loans and advances (particularly housing loans). (See example 2.2.) Retail banking mainly involves the provision of intermediation services, particularly payment services.

The big four and the regional banks compete with each other through their branch networks for deposit funds from, and for loan business to, the general public. The nature of the business is characterised by many small-value transactions.

Traditionally, retail services have been provided through branches, and prior to deregulation, banks tended to compete on the basis of service, rather than price. (Arndt, 1960, p. 8) One way of improving service was to expand branch networks. But the provision of all retail-banking services through labour-intensive branches has become uneconomic, compared with the delivery of payment and other services by electronic means.

As mentioned in Chapter 1, banks had traditionally met the cost of providing many retail services from their interest-rate spread. That is, the cost was met through a cross-subsidy. In the 1980s, banks extended their fees to cover payment services. In theory this should result in customers buying only those services that provide them with value for their money. One consequence of this process should be the provision by banks of a more efficient set of products (especially deposit accounts). Another consequence should be a reduction in the overall amount of retail services consumed.

The 1995 PSA inquiry into charges for payment services accepted that bank charges should improve efficiency, but questioned whether banks had developed the right mix of retail products. It seems that the resistance of the public to the introduction of transaction fees was judged by the inquiry to be essentially a resistance to paying for services that previously were provided without an explicit charge.

However, the application of new communications technology at the retail level, for instance, in the development of home-based banking, will have major effects on this area of banking. The move toward electronic transactions will reduce the cost of providing retail services, but it will also diminish the value of branch banking. Banks have already begun to rationalise their branch networks (the number of branches declined in 1994 and again in 1995), and it appears that further rationalisation will occur through the latter half of the 1990s.

example 2.2

The Advance Bank is an example of a bank that operates mainly in the retail sector of banking. It had been a successful building society that operated in New South Wales prior to its acquisition of the Bank of South Australia. As at the end of June 1995 the combined institution had 400 branches, including 187 in New South Wales and 155 in South Australia. It raises most of its funds from Australian residents in the form of various $A deposit accounts and it lends mainly for housing purposes. It operates principally as a financial intermediary to the public, including small to medium businesses, and hence earns its income mainly from its balance sheet assets. A condensed version of its combined balance sheet follows.

Advance Bank — Selected balance sheet items ($m) (October 1995)

Assets		*Liabilities*	
Notes & coins	83	Current deposits	1 551
Non-callable deposits	185	Term deposits	8 036
Government securities	1 428	Certificates of deposit	3 006
Other S-T assets	1 137	Other deposits	3 602
Housing loans	8 061	Other liabilities	2 205
Other loans	9 864	Foreign currency liabilities	1 129
Foreign currency assets	480		
Total assets	21 238	**Total liabilities**[1]	19 529

[1] Shareholders' funds finance the difference between total assets and total liabilities.

Source: RBA, *Bulletin*, Tables B.9 and B.10

Advance Bank's successful bid for the Bank of South Australia reduced its exposure to the New South Wales economy.

Wholesale banking

Wholesale banking involves the provision of financial services to large businesses. This includes some intermediation, as large businesses require payment services, seek to earn a return on their liquid funds and borrow funds (usually in the form of term loans). Many also are large users of foreign exchange. Generally transactions involve large amounts and thus the cost per dollar is much lower than for retail transactions.

However, wholesale customers have the capacity to gain access to capital markets, both locally and overseas. Consequently, banks may assist these customers in their market dealings, say, through the issue of securities. They may also organise a **syndicated loan** (i.e. a large loan organised by a lead bank with a number of banks participating in the supply of the funds).

Large, financially-secure borrowers can generally borrow at a lower cost in financial markets than from financial institutions. These borrowers usually require capital market services from banks, including assistance in the marketing of new securities, underwriting and the management of interest-rate risk.

Because direct financing is more general at the wholesale level, many of the banks that operate in this segment of the market earn substantial fee income, in addition to the spreads from borrowing and lending. This is reflected in the balance sheet of Bankers Trust Australia Limited (see example 2.3), which concentrates on the wholesale segment of the financial system (as well as on funds management).

example 2.3

Bankers Trust Australia has been ranked among Australia's most successful banks by KPMG Peat Marwick in its annual surveys of financial institutions. Unlike Advance Bank, which is principally a financial intermediator, Bankers Trust concentrates on the provision of financial services to companies and other large organisations and is a leading funds manager, in association with its merchant bank subsidiary, BT Australia. In June 1995 it had only seven branches (at least one in each of the five largest mainland states) and has a relatively small balance sheet in relation to its income. Its 1994 after-tax profit was $260 million, representing a return on total assets of 4.6 per cent, compared with Advance Bank's return on assets of 1%. A condensed version of its balance sheet follows.

Bankers Trust Australia Limited — Selected balance sheet items ($m) (October 1995)

Assets		*Liabilities*	
Non-callable deposits	41	Current deposits	417
Public-sector securities	1 444	Term and other deposits	2 056
Other short-term assets	1 397	Certificates of deposit	32
Housing loans	nil	Other borrowing	156
Other loans	2 042	Other liabilities	867
Other assets	481	Foreign currency liabilities	1 205
Foreign currency assets	253		
Total assets	5 658	**Total liabilities**[1]	4 734

[1] Excludes shareholders' funds

Source: RBA, *Bulletin*, Tables B.9 and B.10

Non-bank financial institutions

The *Financial Corporations Act* categorises non-bank financial institutions (NBFIs). The main ones are building societies, credit unions, money market corporations (most of which are more commonly called **merchant banks**, even though they are not officially 'banks'), authorised money market dealers and finance companies. Some NBFIs compete with banks in the retail market, such as building societies, credit unions and certain finance companies, whereas others compete with banks in the wholesale market, such as merchant banks and the larger finance companies.

These institutions grew relative to banks during the 1960s and 1970s, prior to the deregulation of banks. They served the growing market for financial services that resulted from the development of the Australian economy during the post-war era. During this period building societies placed competitive pressure on banks in the retail market and merchant banks were responsible for important innovations in the wholesale segment of the financial system. Since deregulation most categories of NBFIs have lost market share, measured in terms of financial assets. Some of these institutions became banks, such as the Bank of Melbourne and St George.

The asset holdings of the main categories of NBFIs are shown in table 2.5. When interpreting the data it is important to keep in mind that the assets held are an indication of size of intermediation, and are not a good measure of the amount of financial services provided. Even though money market corporations are a major NBFI category by asset share, such data tend to understate the importance of merchant banks within the financial system.

Table 2.5 NBFIs: Financial assets — June 1981 to 1995 ($m)

30 June	*Building societies*	*Credit unions*	*Official dealers*	*Money market corps*	*Finance companies*	**Total**
1981	12 154	2 341	1 811	8 660	25 439	50 405
1983	15 201	3 548	2 007	13 774	30 621	65 150
1985	18 488	5 416	1 914	23 039	34 961	83 817
1987	18 301	7 328	2 172	39 572	44 031	111 404
1989	24 173	7 660	2 655	54 163	53 248	141 899
1991	21 905	9 019	4 093	48 367	49 531	132 916
1993	12 089	11 214	5 887	42 738	41 577	113 505
1994	12 011	12 514	6 771	43 048	40 142	114 488
1995	13 470	14 010	7 805	51 251	44 472	131 008

Source: RBA, *Bulletin*, Tables C.1 to C.8

FUND MANAGERS

Traditionally, fund managers invest funds in financial assets and property. They include institutions such as superannuation funds, insurance offices, unit trusts and friendly societies. A fund manager provides investment services on the basis of fee income. The funds usually remain the property of the investor who accepts the risk that the accumulated amount may be less than expected.

A fund manager does not engage in intermediation (and hence does not earn an interest-rate spread), but competes with banks and NBFIs in the retail segment of the financial system through the provision of investment services.

Superannuation funds play a major role in the financing system by organising the flow of savings into real and financial assets. Generally their source of funds involves a long-term savings commitment and these funds are not accessible for transaction purposes. In other words, superannuation funds do not form part of the payment system.

Life insurance offices raise funds through premiums that are related to the risk of future payments (such as on the death or injury of the contributor), but in the process they generate large balances that are invested to help meet payouts on insurance claims. In their case, the management of funds is a by-product of their main business.

Public unit trusts, including Cash Management Funds (CMFs), principally operate at the retail level where they compete for funds that are pooled for investment purposes. They offer retail investors access to the higher returns provided by wholesale market assets.

Funds in unit trusts are invested in a range of securities, whereas CMFs invest in short-term securities. Prior to deregulation the balance sheets of CMFs grew steadily because of their (then) unique position in the financial system. But when banks were permitted to offer similar (i.e. 'money market') accounts their growth slowed.

The assets of unit trusts are held by a trustee and are managed by a funds manager (such as a bank or a merchant bank). There are many unit trusts that can be distinguished by the area of their investments, such as imputation trusts that invest in the shares of companies that pay fully-franked dividends (i.e. dividends that allow the Australian shareholder to deduct the company tax paid from his or her personal income tax liability), property trusts that invest in real estate and balanced trusts that invest in a balanced portfolio of assets.

In the United States some of these institutions are referred to as **mutual funds** because they pool funds subscribed by retail sector customers for investment in wholesale market assets. They provide access to a 'balanced' or 'diversified' portfolio, which usually delivers a better level of return for a given level of risk, for small-value investors.

Trusts may be **listed** or **unlisted** on the stock exchange. Listed units can be traded on the basis of their current value. Unlisted trusts allow holders to convert their units for cash on the basis of their assessed value, provided notice is given. However, the illiquid nature of the assets of property trusts means that unlisted property trusts are not able to provide unitholders with easy access to their funds, unless they also hold some liquid assets. Of the various fund managers, only CMFs provide the liquidity required to allow depositors to use their funds for transaction purposes.

The market share of managed funds has risen in the 1990s and this trend can be expected to continue because of the Commonwealth Government's policy to require employers to contribute to the superannuation schemes of their employees. Even though such schemes usually allow benefits to be taken in a lump sum, these payouts tend to remain with institutions that manage funds.

The holdings of financial assets by the major categories of funds managers, over the period 1988 to 1995, are shown in table 2.6.

Table 2.6 Managed funds — assets, 1988 to 1995 ($m)

30 June	*Insurance offices*	*Super. funds*	*Cash mgt funds*	*Unit trusts*	*Other*	**Total**
1988	58 444	61 487	3 690	21 170	10 693	155 484
1989	71 620	66 555	3 749	25 733	13 026	180 683
1990	85 285	74 505	4 679	27 730	15 052	207 251
1991	92 700	78 183	5 755	25 778	15 016	217 432
1992	102 161	88 901	5 344	25 599	13 361	236 329
1993	107 918	97 332	5 316	28 406	13 755	252 727
1994	114 674	106 174	5 915	37 982	13 893	278 638
1995	118 880	113 282	5 625	40 265	13 554	291 606

Source: RBA, *Bulletin*, Table C.15

THE RESERVE BANK OF AUSTRALIA

The RBA is Australia's central bank. It was originally established in 1911 as part of the Commonwealth Bank. In 1960 it was established as a separate institution, pursuant to the *Reserve Bank Act*, 1959. Its mission is to adopt banking and monetary policies that best contribute to:

> *the stability of the currency of Australia; the maintenance of full employment in Australia; and the economic prosperity and welfare of the people of Australia. (Reserve Bank Act,* 1959*)*

In 1989 the *Reserve Bank Act* was amended to bestow on the RBA formal powers for the prudential supervision of banks. The objective of prudential supervision is to ensure that banks operate prudently so as to minimise contagion risk within the banking system. The key element of prudential supervision is the requirement that banks (and other financial institutions) maintain a minimum amount of equity capital (i.e. shareholder funds, or their equivalent). The minimum amount of equity is defined as a ratio of the risk-adjusted value of their balance sheet assets and off-balance sheet business. (These arrangements, known as capital adequacy requirements, are explained in Chapter 9.)

The RBA performs a range of functions. These include:

1 the determination and conduct of monetary policy. During the 1990s, monetary policy has been focused on the level of short-term interest rates. The RBA determines this policy in consultation with the Treasury and the Federal Treasurer. The bank's monetary policy goal has been to promote economic growth that maximises employment without causing inflation to exceed 2–3%. The RBA's low inflation target indicates that, of the three ultimate policy objectives listed in its Act, the RBA places greatest emphasis on the 'stability of the currency';
2 the provision of banking services to the Australian Government, several State Governments and certain other government instrumentalities and overseas official institutions. These services include maintaining their bank accounts and handling their account transactions, including foreign exchange transactions;
3 the provision of services covering the issue, registration, settlement and redemption of the debt securities of the Commonwealth Government and (currently) three State Government borrowing authorities, as well as certain other official organisations;
4 the recent move to provide many of the RBA's banking services by electronic means, replacing less efficient paper-based systems;
5 the management of the financial system's liquidity and stability. This function arises, in part, because transactions by the bank have an effect on the liquidity of the financial system. When the bank makes payments it increases liquidity and when it receives payments liquidity diminishes. The bank buys or sells Commonwealth securities in order to offset the effect of its banking transactions on the financial system's liquidity;
6 the overseeing of the payment system and provision of settlement facilities for the participants in the payments system;
7 the prudential supervision of banks, and liaison with the other members of the Council of Supervisors;
8 the overseeing of the financial markets and NBFIs, and issuing of licences for banks and participants in the foreign exchange market;
9 printing and distribution of currency notes.

The RBA's central banking role makes it the most influential and watched institution within the financial system. Consequently we examine its operations in a number of later chapters.

Summary

The main points of this chapter are as follows:

- Financial intermediaries derive their income from their interest-rate spread; that is, from the difference between the average rate of interest charged on loans and the average rate paid for funds.

- Interest-rate spreads tend to be wider for retail clients than for wholesale clients.
- The process of intermediation provides benefits to borrowers and lenders that can be categorised as (a) maturity intermediation, (b) management of funds, (c) credit risk reduction, (d) reduced transaction costs for clients, and (e) payment services.
- Financial institutions are categorised as banks, non-bank financial institutions, or fund managers.
- Australia's banks can be categorised as the majors (which currently are the big four), regional banks or investment banks.
- The clients of financial institutions may be categorised as either retail (small-value transactions) or wholesale (large-value transactions).
- The Reserve Bank is Australia's central bank.

DISCUSSION QUESTIONS AND EXERCISES

1 Briefly describe SafeAsa Bank's sources and uses of funds and suggest how it could calculate its average interest-rate spread.
2 Discuss the factors that influence an institution's interest-rate spread.
3 Describe the process of maturity intermediation and discuss its implications for institutions engaged in intermediated financing.
4 Briefly explain how intermediaries reduce the credit risks faced by the suppliers of deposit funds and discuss how intermediaries manage this risk.
5 Discuss how intermediaries can reduce the transaction costs of borrowers and lenders.
6 Briefly explain why the provision of payments services has traditionally reduced the interest cost of deposit funds.
7 Discuss the role played by the three official categories of financial institutions (banks, NBFIs and fund managers) since 1984.
8 Distinguish between retail and wholesale banking services and discuss the role of the major banks in these areas.
9 Compare the activities of Advance Bank with those of Bankers Trust Australia Limited.
10 Outline the functions of the Reserve Bank of Australia in the financial system.

REFERENCES AND FURTHER READING

Arndt, H. W. 1960, *The Australian Trading Banks*, Cheshire, Melbourne.

Burrows, Geoff, & Davis, Kevin 1995, 'Costs and the pricing of retail transactions accounts', in PSA 1995, Appendix J.

Fabozzi, Frank J., Modigliani, Franco, & Ferri, Michael G. 1994, *Foundations of Financial Markets and Institutions*, Prentice-Hall, New Jersey, Chapters 2 and 3.

House of Representatives Standing Committee on Finance and Public Administration, Martin, Stephen (Chair) 1991, *A Pocket Full of Change*, AGPS, Canberra.

Joss, Robert 1996, 'Developments in the business of banking', in Malcolm Edey (ed.) *The Future of the Financial System*, RBA, Sydney.
KPMG Peat Marwick 1995, *1995 Financial Institutions Performance Survey*, Sydney.
McGrath, Michael 1994, *Financial Institutions, Instruments and Markets in Australia*, McGraw-Hill, Sydney, Chapter 1.
PSA 1995, *Inquiry into Fees and Charges imposed on Retail Accounts by Banks and other Financial Institutions and by Retailers on EFTPOS Transactions*, Melbourne.
RBA December 1994 and July 1995, *Bulletin.*
RBA 1995, *Annual Report, 1994–95*, RBA, Sydney.

3

Introduction to financial markets

The purposes of this chapter are to introduce the general features of financial markets and to describe Australia's financial markets and instruments. The discussion in this chapter sets the scene for the chapters in Part three which examine financial markets in some detail.

Study objectives

From your study of this chapter you should be able to:

- describe the main features of Australia's financial markets;
- describe the trading conventions and practices used in financial markets;
- describe the functions of primary and secondary markets;
- describe the main instruments traded in physical financial markets;
- explain the role of risk-management instruments and describe the basic form of the four main derivative instruments;
- explain the efficient market hypothesis and its implications for security prices, market volatility and market risk.

INTRODUCTION

A financial market is an arrangement that organises trading in a related group of financial instruments. In a broad sense, a financial market performs the same functions as other markets. Items are 'produced' and initially sold (these are new securities). But unlike most other products, securities do not deteriorate in a physical sense, and can be traded until they mature. Consequently, financial markets serve two related purposes:

- to facilitate direct financing through the issue of new securities, and
- to organise trading in issued securities.

The first of these purposes is performed in the instrument's primary market, whereas the second is performed in the instrument's secondary market. The primary function of capital markets is to raise new funds through the issue of new securities. This function achieves comparable outcomes to borrowing from an institution. The borrower raises funds when the new securities are sold and repays these funds by redeeming the securities when they mature.

The arrangements for issuing new securities involve a number of specialised activities, such as preparing the documentation, deciding the terms of the offer and selling the new securities. Generally, the issue of new securities is undertaken only when large amounts of funds are raised. Borrowers seeking small amounts would approach an intermediary for the funds.

The trading activities of a financial market can be divided into two parts:

- the deal-making arrangements, and
- the back-room functions that result in the traded securities being exchanged for cash.

The details of these arrangements differ in the primary and secondary markets. The former is concerned only with the issue of the securities, whereas the latter is concerned with the transfer of the securities as a result of trading.

In secondary markets, trading is either confined to **dealers** who trade in wholesale amounts, or is conducted by the members of an **exchange** (i.e. an organisation that conducts a market at a particular place). In the former markets, trading is conducted by dealers over the telephone, because they operate from separate dealing rooms (e.g. the dealing room of a large bank). Whereas dealer markets are geographically dispersed, exchange markets, at least traditionally, operate in a central trading room, such as the floor of the Sydney Futures Exchange. Trading in an exchange-based market is undertaken by trading staff of **brokers** (i.e. members of the exchange), who relay (by **open outcry**, i.e. yelling, supported by hand signals) buying and selling prices to the market.

Note that the title 'dealer' is commonly used to refer to the individuals who trade in a market. Officially, the title applies to the organisations that deal in these markets. Dealer-organisations engage traders or 'dealers' to undertake their dealing operations. When referring to the individuals who deal we use either title.

Dealers and brokers perform different roles. The former actually buy and sell from one another, whereas brokers assist buyers and sellers by placing their bids and offers in the market. Should you purchase futures contracts by telephoning your futures exchange broker, the seller was the previous owner of the futures contracts, not your broker.

FINANCIAL MARKETS

In common with countries that have a well-developed financial system, Australia has three markets in which funds can be raised — the markets for short-term money, debt-capital and equity-capital — as well as a market for the exchange of foreign currencies. We refer to these as 'physical' financial markets to distinguish them from the markets for derivative instruments (forwards, futures, swaps and options) that can be used to hedge market risks when participating in the physical markets.

Physical markets

The main physical financial markets in Australia and the main instruments traded within them are set out in table 3.1.

Table 3.1 Domestic physical financial markets

Market	*Instrument*
Short-term money market	commercial bills (most being 'backed' by banks and referred to as bank bills), promissory notes, certificates of deposit, and Treasury notes
Debt-capital market	bonds and floating-rate notes/bonds
Equity-capital market	ordinary and preference shares
Foreign exchange market	foreign currencies

The short-term money market (or simply, the money market) is conducted by dealers who buy and sell securities that have a term of less than one year. Dealers also hold securities, funding them by accepting deposits, usually for short periods.

Funds placed with money-market dealers are either:

- **11 a.m. funds**, meaning that by 11 a.m. the next day either party can initiate the return of the funds, otherwise the funds roll over for a further day, or
- **24-hour-call funds**, which are placed at a fixed interest rate for a term of seven days, when the funds may be withdrawn or repaid, placed for a further term, or become 11 a.m. funds. (AFMA, 1994(a), p. 63)

Most of the dealer-organisations that operate in the money market are banks and money-market corporations. The five top dealers (based on the amount of new borrowing programs undertaken) in 1994 were:

1. Commonwealth Bank of Australia ($3450 million),
2. Westpac Banking Corporation ($3100 million),
3. Bankers Trust Australia Limited ($2950 million),
4. National Australia Bank ($2250 million),
5. ANZ Banking Group ($1725 million) (Ernst & Young, 1995, p. 9)

In 1959 the Reserve Bank established an official group of dealers within the short-term money market. These dealers were granted a licence on the condition that they trade with the RBA. They also were given an ESA through which their transactions with the bank were settled. As at June 1995 there were eight authorised money market dealers. In 1996 the RBA terminated the status of these **authorised**

dealers as part of its planned changes to the payment system's settlement process. Since July 1996 the RBA trades in the market with any dealer that is a member of RITS, its information and transfer system.

Instruments in the money market raise funds when they are first issued. The purchaser of the new securities is the lender and the issuer is the borrower. These securities usually have a term of 90 or 180 days when issued. They can be traded until they mature (in 90 or 180 days) when their redemption (i.e. the payment of their face value by their issuer) extinguishes the debt.

Most of the instruments that are traded in the money market are **discount instruments**, meaning that they are issued at a price that is less than their face value. The securities do not make an explicit interest payment. Interest is earned because they are purchased for less than their face value and are **redeemed** at maturity by the payment of their face value to their holder. Interest is the difference between the security's price and face value. (The instruments traded in financial markets are described in a later section of this chapter and are discussed further in Part three of the book.)

Turnover in the money market (i.e. the total value of securities sold) was reported by the Australian Financial Markets Association (AFMA) to have been $1024 billion in the year ending June 1994. (AFMA, 1994(b), p. 17) In round terms this turnover is $4 billion per trading day.

The short-term money market can be used to raise funds for longer periods through the **facility** process. A facility is an agreement, usually by a bank or merchant bank, to arrange the issue of a sequence of securities such that when the first parcel matures it is replaced (**rolled over**) by a second and so on. A two-year facility, for example, could involve the successive issue of eight parcels of 90-day securities.

The debt-capital market mainly involves trading in public sector securities, principally bonds. Some Australian companies issue bonds in this market, although they make greater use of overseas debt-capital markets. These are long-term securities, meaning that they are issued with a life of one year or longer.

The bonds issued by the Commonwealth Government (known also as **Treasury bonds**) are the principal instrument in this market. They are issued by the Reserve Bank on behalf of the government. Trading is undertaken by bond dealers. The main investors in bonds are fund managers, who tend to be risk averse (i.e. they will only hold bonds that are issued by very secure borrowers).

Most Treasury bonds pay a fixed amount of interest at specified dates during the bond's life and are redeemed at maturity by the payment of their face value. Interest payments on Treasury bonds are made each six months on the anniversary of their maturity date.

Turnover in the bond market during the year ended June 1994 was reported to be $1963 billion. (AFMA, 1994(b), p. 11) This represents a daily turnover of around $7.8 billion.

The equities market is conducted by the Australian Stock Exchange (ASX), which is an amalgamation of the stock exchanges that operate in the State capital cities. The ASX facilitates trading in the shares of listed companies. The ASX also arranges trading in options on shares through its subsidiary, the Australian Stock Exchange Derivatives (ASXD).

Shares can be treated as perpetual securities that provide an expected stream of future dividend payments. As noted in Chapter 1, dividends are not a financial obligation; they are disbursement of profits. Only preference shares offer a promised dividend payment.

Turnover in the equities market during the year ended June 1994 was reported by the ASX to be $128 billion. This represents a daily turnover of around $0.5 billion.

The foreign-exchange (FX) market is conducted by FX dealers who are licensed by the Reserve Bank. The big four banks are the major dealers, along with certain investment and merchant banks. Trade is mainly in the US dollar (known as **the dollar**), although dealers also trade third currencies (i.e. trade one overseas currency, say Japanese yen, for another, say, US dollars) because the Australian FX market operates when the main overseas markets (London and New York) are closed.

Average daily turnover in the FX market, as at April 1995, was $39.5 billion, measured in US dollars. Hence it is the most active of Australia's financial markets.

Eurocurrency markets

Following the removal of exchange controls and the floating of the currency in late 1983, Australia's capital markets became part of the global financial system. Not only could Australians borrow and lend in foreign currencies, they could invest and borrow in the markets of other countries and in the **eurocurrency market**.

The domestic capital markets of other developed countries are similar to those in Australia. Each has money, debt-capital and equity markets and similar instruments are traded in domestic markets.

Eurocurrency markets began to function in the 1960s, starting with USD transactions (i.e. bank loans and deposits and securities denominated in USD). Their principal function is to act as financing markets (they are not involved in the payments system) outside the jurisdiction of the various domestic capital markets. Consequently, borrowers and lenders can transact in AUD in countries such as Switzerland, Belgium and Hong Kong.

The eurocurrency market is the system of international markets that replicate domestic markets. It is conducted by banks (by accepting deposits and making loans) and through the issue of securities in overseas countries. The (US) **eurodollar** market is the largest segment, followed by the euroyen market.

There is an Aussie-eurodollar market in which Australian dollar capital can be raised overseas. Consequently an Australian borrower can raise an Aussie-dollar loan in either the domestic or the eurocurrency markets.

The forms of bank financing match those offered by the domestic banking system. Likewise, the securities issued in the eurodollar market are similar to those issued in the domestic capital market. The main short-term security is **euro-commercial paper** (these are promissory notes) and the main long-term securities are **euro-floating rate notes** and **eurobonds**. Borrowing in eurocurrency markets is usually undertaken in large amounts (often much larger than can be achieved in the Australian domestic markets) arranged by bank syndicates, whether the funds are provided through bank loans or the sale of securities.

Transactions between participants in the various eurocurrency markets are likely to involve an exchange of currencies. These transactions are undertaken in the various domestic FX markets; the eurocurrency market is not part of these FX markets.

Australian borrowers and lenders can also gain access to overseas domestic markets, such as those in the USA. Securities issued by foreigners in overseas domestic markets are referred to as **foreign** securities.

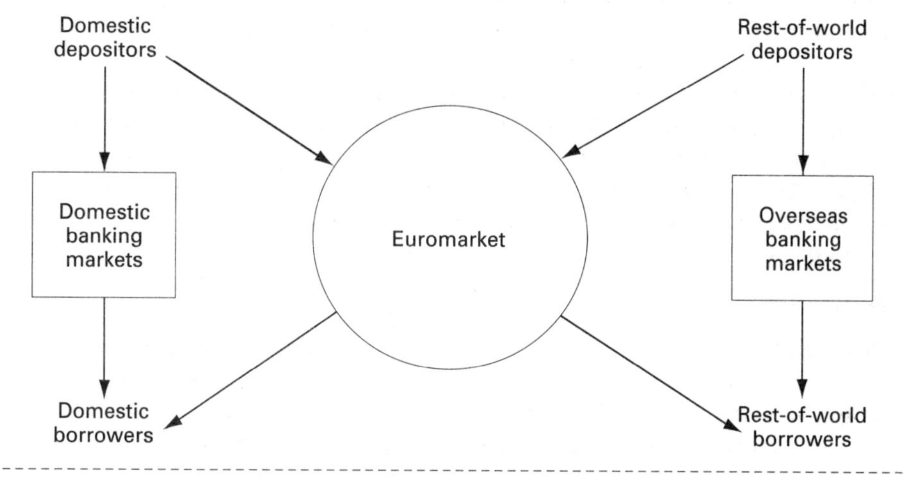

Figure 3.1 Domestic and international intermediation
Source: Adapted from Dufey and Giddy, 1994, p. 9

The relationships between domestic institutions and those involved in eurocurrency markets are depicted in figure 3.1 by the arrows from depositors to borrowers. The diagram shows that depositors can place funds with domestic or international banks that intermediate the funds to either domestic or overseas borrowers. Note that the proposed establishment of European Monetary Union involves the issue of a new currency, the **euro**, which should not be confused with the system of eurocurrency markets described above.

Derivative markets

As noted above, futures are traded in Australia through the Sydney Futures Exchange (SFE) and options are traded on the ASXD market, which is a subsidiary of the ASX. The SFE conducts trading in a variety of financial (and other) futures contracts. The 90-day bill futures contract generated the largest value of turnover in 1993–94. Its turnover was $3995 billion, representing approximately $16 billion a day. (AFMA, 1994, p. 34)

In terms of the number of contracts traded, the three-year Treasury bond futures contract generated the greatest turnover. In fiscal year 1994, 8647 three-year bond futures contracts were traded, compared with 6187 ten-year bond futures contracts and 7991 bill futures contracts. In value terms, the daily turnover in three-year bond futures is around $3.5 billion and around $2.5 billion for ten-year bond futures. (AFMA, 1994, p. 34)

The SFE conducts trading in a variety of futures contracts for equities including a contract that is based on the share price index (SPI). In fiscal year 1994, 2.2 million SPI futures contracts were traded. (AFMA, 1994, p. 25). As well as trading futures contracts the SFE also allows trading in options over the majority of its futures contracts.

The ASXD conducts trading in options on the shares of major companies. Turnover in this market was 11.6 million contracts in fiscal year 1994. (AFMA, 1994, p. 25) To some extent the SFE and the ASXD compete as markets for derivatives on equities.

Options are arranged on other financial instruments, such as foreign exchange and precious metals instruments, but these are not exchange-traded options. The value of currency option contracts written in fiscal year 1994 was $116 billion (AFMA, 1994, p. 62) The value of interest-rate options written in fiscal year 1994 was $67 billion. (AFMA, 1994, p. 52)

Prior to their maturity, options have some value, which in the case of exchange-traded options is revealed by their bids and offers in the option market. The value of any option can be estimated using complex formulae. We discuss options and their pricing in Chapter 19.

Swaps, as the name implies, entails an exchange of cash flows. The most active is the interest-rate swap market where fixed interest-rate payments are swapped for floating rate payments. The major banks and certain investment and merchant banks are the main participants in the swap market. Most swaps are between banks. Total turnover in swaps in fiscal year 1994 was reported to be $274 billion. (AFMA, 1994, p. 43) The major component of this turnover was for interest-rate swaps: $177 billion.

Forward markets exist for many financial assets. There are strong forward markets for FX, gold and for interest rates. The forward FX market organises the purchase and sale of **outright forward contracts**. These are agreements to exchange an amount of one currency for an amount of another, the ratio being determined by the forward exchange rate. The daily value of new forward FX agreements during fiscal year 1995 averaged around $2 billion.

The market also organises dealing in **FX swaps**. These involve the simultaneous purchase and sale of one currency against another currency, but for different delivery dates. An FX swap, for example, may consist of a forward contract to buy AUD, against USD, in September and a contract to sell AUD, against USD, in December. FX swaps are regularly used to facilitate offshore borrowing, with each leg of the FX swap used as part of the loan drawdown and repayment. Daily turnover in FX swaps during fiscal year 1995 averaged around $25 billion.

Forward contracts for short-term interest rates are called **forward rate agreements**, or **FRAs**. The market for FRAs allows borrowers and lenders to enter contracts that serve to establish a rate of interest that will apply for a specified period from a specified date. In fiscal year 1994, 14 681 FRA agreements were reported to AFMA. The nominal value of these contracts was $690 billion.

Recap

Financial markets and institutions comprise a country's domestic financial system. Institutions are the principal providers of payment services, whereas both markets and institutions offer competing financing and risk-management products. However, note that institutions are the principal players (e.g. dealers and arrangers) in the operation of financial markets.

The relationships between the four domestic physical markets and their related markets for risk-management instruments are shown in table 3.2.

Table 3.2 Physical and related risk-management markets

Domestic physical markets	*Risk-management instruments*
Short-term money market	bill futures, FRAs, interest-rate swaps and options
Fixed-interest market	bond futures, interest-rate swaps and options
Equity market	ASXD options, equity futures
Foreign exchange market	forward foreign exchange, FX swaps and options

MARKET PRINCIPLES

The purpose of this and the next section is to provide the reader with an understanding of the principles that explain the role and operations of Australia's financial markets.

As noted earlier, trading in financial markets is either dealer- or broker-based. In the former case, the markets are referred to as being **over the counter** (OTC), whereas the latter are called **auction** markets.

Exchange-organised and OTC markets

An auction market organises the bidding process between the buyers and sellers of a particular security or group of related securities. For many years the market for shares in Australia was conducted by an auction process within the exchange's trading room. This practice was initially replaced by an open-outcry system which involved continuous trading in all shares. Open outcry involves traders calling out bid and offer prices during the market's trading hours. In October 1987 the ASX introduced an electronic form of trading that allows bids and offers to be placed from each broker's office.

The term 'auction market' is still commonly used, even though auction trading has become obsolete within Australia's financial markets. Use of the term serves to distinguish between exchange-organised trading where the market is supervised by the exchange and arranged through its clearing house, and OTC trading, which generally is not subject to direct supervision.

In OTC markets, trades are conducted by telephone between geographically-dispersed dealers. In most cases standardised instruments are traded, although trades are struck according to the specific requirements of each customer.

Even though Australia's OTC markets are not officially supervised, the Australian Financial Markets Association promotes 'self regulation through the establishment of efficient and ethical practices and conventions.' (AFMA, 1995(a), p. 3)

To promote trading efficiency, AFMA encourages the use of standard trading terminology, market practices and documentation. Its concept of ethical trading is set out in its code of conduct. It uses an extensive committee system to review and monitor market practices. All dealers in Australia's financial markets are AFMA members. The Australian Tax Office, the Commonwealth Treasury and the RBA are associate members.

Market making

Dealers act as **market makers** when trading. They set buying (**bid**) and selling (**offer**) prices and are prepared to buy and sell instantly at these prices. The role of market making is performed by dealers when they:

- quote bid and offer prices to other dealers, and
- honour these quotes should they be accepted by another dealer.

Naturally, a dealer's bid is less than the offer; dealers earn income from their **dealing spread** (i.e. buying low and selling high). The **market spread** at any time is the difference between the best (i.e. highest) bid and the best (i.e. lowest) offer. In the debt markets, trading is in terms of **yields** (i.e. interest rates), rather than security prices. Thus a bid is a buying yield and an offer is a selling yield. We explain the relationship between security yields and prices (for short-dated securities) in the next chapter.

When reporting the movement of prices within financial markets, the media often reports a single price. This is usually the price of the last transaction or the **mid-point price** (i.e. the price mid-way between the market's bid and offer prices). Generally throughout the book we refer to mid-point prices (and yields). Given the narrowness of market (or trading) spreads, the mid-point value is a good indicator of market value.

A trade occurs when a bid matches an offer for an agreed parcel. Given the market spread, trades will be conducted at either the bid or the offer level. This results in a **bid-offer-bounce** price movement. To illustrate, a dealer who wants to sell must trade at another dealer's bid. This means that the price will be based on the bid level. This deal may be followed by one where a dealer seeks to buy, and thus accepts another dealer's offer. Hence the prices bounce from one side of the spread to the other.

Observe that the bid-offer-bounce occurs because initiating dealers trade on the 'wrong side' of the market spread. This practice is referred to as the 'screw rule'. However, the initiating dealer receives exchange services from the counter-party dealer. Moreover, the spreads in professional markets tend to be very small. Consequently, the cost of the transaction is not very great. The point is that spreads are necessary to ensure the supply of transaction services by dealers, but they should be as low as possible. (See example 3.1.)

The principal benefit of dealer-based markets is **immediacy**. This benefit is created by dealers being prepared to trade whenever another dealer accepts their bid or offer. To illustrate this point, suppose a dealer who is seeking to buy US dollars has telephoned a dealer whose offer is acceptable. The buying dealer simply indicates an acceptance of the selling price and confirms the details, and both dealers complete a simple **chit** that informs their back offices of the deal. The main dealer-based markets are for foreign exchange and debt securities.

example 3.1

Should dealers in the foreign exchange market quote the Australian dollar (AUD) at USD0.7750 and USD0.7754, the lower is the bid price and the higher is the offer price. The value of the Australian dollar would be quoted in the mass media as the mid-point price of USD0.7752. The spread is the difference between the bid and offer, being four points in this illustration.

A client who wants to sell Australian dollars (this could be a US exporter who has been paid in Australian dollars) could do so at the lower rate of USD0.7750. This means that the dollars would be purchased by a dealer at that bid. On the other hand, a client who wants to buy Australian dollars (such as a US importer who requires Australian dollars to pay for the Australian goods that will be imported into the USA) could do so at the higher price of USD0.7754. That is, the dealer would sell Australian dollars at the offer rate.

Should these trades occur, the dealer will earn the four-point spread; that is, the difference in the prices at which the deals were made with the two US clients. Of course, the dealer has provided an exchange service by agreeing to buy and sell and is entitled to be paid for these transactions.

In exchange-based markets, a prospective buyer's bid will be conveyed to the market and a deal will result only when it is matched by an offer (and other relevant terms). Brokers do not 'make a market', they help buyers and sellers to gain access to the market.

Australia has two exchange-organised markets, the stock exchange and the futures exchange. They promote the development of their markets by creating an environment that is conducive to efficient trading. This involves trading and other rules as well as the design of contracts that promote market **turnover** (i.e. the volume of trading).

Whereas OTC markets operate at the wholesale level, with transactions typically involving millions of dollars, the exchange-organised markets undertake both small-value trades on behalf of retail clients (subject to a minimum-sized transaction) and large-value trades on behalf of wholesale clients.

Execution of deals

Deals are executed through the market's clearing and settlement arrangements. The clearing process for a market involves checking that both traders agree on the terms of the transaction. You will recall that settlement is the actual exchange of the traded item for cash. Where a registry is kept of the traded securities, the new owner will replace the seller on the registry.

The back-room functions (i.e. trade confirmation, clearing, settlement and the transfer of title) resulting from each deal in an exchange-based market are organised by the exchange's clearing house (in the case of the futures market, its clearing house also guarantees the performance of each deal); whereas in the debt-security markets they are performed by either Austraclear (for non-Commonwealth securities) or the RBA (for Commonwealth securities) through RITS (which was described in Chapter 1).

AUSTRACLEAR

Austraclear is a company owned by the banks and other institutions that are professional dealers in Australia's debt-securities markets. It began operations in September 1984.

> *The Company performs the role of a national central securities depository for securities traded in the Australian money market. In addition, a real-time transaction confirmation recording and clearance facility, integrated with an electronic securities transfer and settlement system (the FINTRAC™ System) is provided to an approved Membership for money market securities and their derivatives.*
>
> *(Its) Regulations formalise a contractual relationship between Austraclear and its Members (wholesale market participants) and promote the efficient settlement and electronic transfer of the underlying securities . . . on a delivery versus payment basis..* (Austraclear, Mission Statement, *p. 2)*

The back-room functions performed by Austraclear are shown in figure 3.2. Following the market transaction, both the buyer and the seller advise Austraclear of the deal. Provided there is no discrepancy between this advice, Austraclear arranges settlement (cash for the securities) and the bank and security accounts of the parties are adjusted accordingly.

Figure 3.2 Austraclear's clearing and settlement arrangements
Source: Austraclear, p. 7

Primary and secondary markets

As emphasised above, financial markets have two related purposes. One is to facilitate direct financing (i.e. borrowing and lending), and the other is to organise trading in financial instruments. New securities are issued in the primary market. The sale of a new security results in the seller raising funds and the buyer supplying the funds. Existing securities are traded in the secondary market.

Primary market

The issue of new securities involves a number of specialist functions, such as the preparation of legal documents, the registration of the securities, their sale to the wholesale and/or retail markets, and the arrangements for making interest and the redemption payment.

Arrangements for the sale (i.e. issue) of new securities vary. The Reserve Bank issues Commonwealth Government securities to the wholesale market through a tender process. The tenders are held frequently, weekly in the case of Treasury notes. A specified amount of the securities is made available at each tender, with the securities being issued to the lowest bids (i.e. lowest yields). Under a previous arrangement, securities were issued 'on tap'. Under this arrangement the government set the yield and the market decided the amount issued through its purchases. The Reserve Bank issues the new securities and provides the registry, clearing and settlement services for the markets in Commonwealth securities.

In general, private sector and State government issuers seek the assistance of experienced market participants, such as banks and merchant banks. A panel of institutions may be used, one of which acts as the lead manager while others assist with the selling of securities to particular market segments. The panel may also be required by the issuer to help make the (secondary) market for the securities. (The relationship of the secondary market to the primary market is explained below.)

The process of arranging the sale of new securities on behalf of the issuer is generally referred to as underwriting. This may be arranged in a number of ways. One is a **bought deal** where one underwriter undertakes to sell the new securities at a price agreed with the issuer. The underwriter is paid a fee and a margin on the selling price. The underwriter accepts the risk that not all of the new securities will be sold. This risk depends in part on the way the issue is priced. Where a minimum price is specified, the underwriter will be required to acquire the unsold securities (if any), whereas an agreement to underwrite on a best endeavours basis eliminates the underwriter's risk because the price will fall until all securities are issued. (Juttner, 1994, pp. 299–302).

An underwriter may engage sub-underwriters to assist in the selling process, to reduce the risk of not being able to sell the issue. Usually an underwriter is a bank or merchant bank that has access to potential subscribers to the new issue (i.e. a client base) and is able to fund the purchase of unsold securities. In effect, an underwriter accepts the funding risk involved when raising new capital.

When securities are issued at tender, the issuer need not engage an underwriter because the tender process will usually establish a market-clearing price for the securities. However, institutions may be engaged to manage the issue process.

Generally the primary market is subject to stricter regulation than secondary markets, particularly when the public is invited to subscribe to the new issue. For instance, the issue of new securities to the public (such as share floats) is subject to strict prospectus requirements, whereas there are no requirements for sellers to provide information to the purchasers of existing securities. (See example 3.2.)

example 3.2

The Qantas float conducted in mid 1995 illustrates the distinction between the primary and secondary equity markets. The float involved the issue of new shares, for which the public was invited to apply via the prospectus. Once the shares were issued they were subsequently traded on the stock exchange. Applications closed on 21 July 1995 and trading in the shares commenced on 31 July 1995.

The Qantas prospectus (which was a 112-page document) presented relevant financial and business information about the affairs and prospects of Qantas, on a fair basis, for the purpose of providing potential subscribers with the necessary groundwork for deciding whether to apply for shares.

The Qantas float was not underwritten. The Commonwealth engaged a number of leading domestic and overseas financial institutions to manage the issue and assist in the sale of the 750 million shares being offered. The price of the new shares was based on the successful bids in the institutional offer. This determined the price paid by the public. In effect, the price was set through a constrained tender process because 'The Institutional Final Price will be in a range from $1.80 to $2.10'. (Qantas, *Public Share Offer Prospectus*, p. 70)

Ratings agencies

Ratings agencies play an important role in financial markets by publishing an informed opinion about the future ability of an issuer of debt securities to generate sufficient cash to meet its interest and principal repayment obligations. (Moody's, 1995, p. 4) (See example 3.3.) A credit rating is concerned with the probability of default over the life of a security, which could range from a few days to many years.

example 3.3

Moody's rating scales

Moody's began rating bonds issued by US railroad companies in 1909. Along with Standard & Poor's, it has developed into an international rating agency that applies a globally consistent rating system.

The main focus of a credit rating is the capacity of the issuer to meet its obligations under a specific debt issue. Moody's divides long-term debt issues into investment and speculative grades. Its investment grades range from Aaa (known as 'triple A') descending through three levels of Aa and A, to the third level of Baa (i.e. Baa3). Its speculative grades range from Ba1, through B to Caa, Ca and C. It has a simpler scale for short-term securities: Prime 1 that is aligned with the Aaa and Aa long-term ratings, Prime 2 that is aligned with the A long-term rating and Prime 3 that is aligned with the Baa and Ba long-term ratings.

The triple A rating indicates an extremely low probability of default. Such securities are often referred to as being 'gilt-edged'. Because of their premier rating, these securities can be issued at the lowest yield in the market. Securities that have been assigned a lower rating have a higher degree of uncertainty about their payments. As a result, they are usually issued (and trade) at a higher yield.

The rating assigned to a newly-issued security influences the issuer's cost of funds (i.e. the interest rate paid on the funds); the better the rating, the lower the cost. The rating may change over the security's life (depending on the issuer's financial circumstances) and this will influence the security's market value.

Two major ratings agencies — Moody's and Standard & Poor's — apply their international ratings scale when rating Australian securities.

Role of secondary market in assisting fund raising

Even though funds are not raised in a secondary market, it assists in the raising of new funds in four important ways.

First, a secondary market for an instrument enhances its value because the market can endow the instrument with liquidity (i.e. convertibility into cash). Investors are more likely to buy new securities that can be subsequently sold in a well-established secondary market. (See example 3.4.) This preference:

- will be reflected in a higher price for the security (than if there was no secondary market), and
- makes it easier for the instrument to be issued.

example 3.4

In late 1994 the Board of Macquarie Bank decided to seek listing of its shares on the Australian Stock Exchange in order to give its shareholders more liquidity. Satisfying the exchange's listing requirements posed certain problems for the bank and its largest shareholder, Hill Samuel, but these disadvantages were judged to be less important than the liquidity benefit gained by all of its shareholders.

Second, when a market endows a security with liquidity it is performing a maturity intermediation function. Lenders/investors who buy securities can have their preference for short terms satisfied when they are able to sell a long-term security for cash at any time. Secondary markets establish pools of investors who can buy and sell in accordance with their preferences. The borrower's preference for longer terms is satisfied by the market continuing to fund the security. This is achieved in the secondary market when one investor sells it to another.

Third, a secondary market performs a **price discovery** function. The prices of securities in the secondary market reveal to interested parties, such as the issuer of new securities and holders of existing securities, the market's assessment of their value.

Financial assets, unlike physical ones, do not depreciate. The value of an existing security will be the same as for a new security that has the same characteristics (such as, the issuer, term and cash flows). Hence, the price of a 180-day bank bill that was issued 90 days ago will serve to identify the price of a new issue of a 90-day bill that is identical in all other respects. Similarly, a new BHP share will have the same value as an existing BHP share.

Values in secondary markets are useful also in valuing portfolios of financial assets. The values of the securities in a portfolio are set by the continuous trading during the market's trading hours. Portfolio holders can value them at any time on the basis of the market price of each security. The process of revaluation of securities on the basis of their current market value is known as **marking-to-market**.

The price discovery function is best performed in a 'deep', well-informed market. A market's depth depends on its volume of turnover. A deep market can absorb a new bid or offer with little or no reaction in price, whereas in markets with little turnover an attempt to buy or sell could influence price. Hence, price in a deep market will provide prospective buyers and sellers with a reliable indication of the price at which they can trade.

Because of continuous trading during a market's trading hours, a large number of buyers and sellers is required to ensure that a random bunching of sell (or buy) orders will not cause the price to fluctuate. Should this result, prices will be excessively volatile and the market will not be effectively performing the price discovery function.

The movement of security prices is referred to as volatility. These movements can be classified to reflect, in general, their cause. Movements within a day result from the bid-offer-bounce, the placement of large or bunched orders and speculation by dealers. Longer-term volatility reflects changing economic conditions, which is inevitable in well-informed financial markets (Daugaard and Valentine, 1995, p. 3). But excessive short-term volatility can harm a market. It:

- is likely to discourage risk-averse traders because it increases the uncertainty about values, and
- can result in dealers widening the spread between their bids and offers.

However, the development of derivative markets provides a remedy for these potential problems because they allow participants with market exposures to remove the uncertainty arising from volatile market variables (such as interest and exchange rates).

Risk takers, though, are attracted by volatility. They expect to make a profit from price movements. Their trading may be beneficial for a market. When speculators successfully buy low and sell high they dampen volatility, capping both the potential falls and rises.

Note that ratings agencies play an important role in the price discovery function. The yields at which securities trade are related to their credit risk, which is indicated by their rating. The higher the rating, the lower the yield. From the issuer's viewpoint, a lower yield in the secondary market means it can issue new securities (i.e. raise funds in the primary market) at a lower interest cost of funds.

Yields in the secondary market serve to 'price' loans (i.e. new issues) in an equivalent way to the pricing of loans by intermediaries. That is, they contain two basic elements: the general level of interest rates, reflected in a market's benchmark yield, and a security's credit-risk premium. Further, movements in the yield of a security because of a change in its rating represent the market's monitoring of loans — a function also performed by institutions when managing the credit risk of their loans.

Fourth, a secondary market assists its primary market through its identification of potential buyers of new securities. This reduces the search costs of the issuers of new securities. When a market attracts many traders it may also reduce transaction costs (i.e. broker commissions and dealer spreads).

Through their identification and pooling of investors, deep markets can raise large amounts of new funds. They can therefore offer issuers scale economies when borrowing, which reduces the per dollar cost of funds. By adopting standardised documentation they further reduce transaction costs.

Because markets and institutions arrange financing in different ways they tend to serve different borrowers and different borrowing needs. In general terms, markets are better at providing funds for large, well-established borrowers and borrowing programs. By contrast, institutions can better serve the needs of smaller and less well-established borrowers.

Standardisation and liquidity

It was emphasised above that liquid markets generate more reliable and stable prices. One strategy followed by financial markets to achieve depth is to trade standardised products. Demand tends to be much greater for standardised rather than for individualised products.

Standardisation is achieved through:

- the size of financial instruments (e.g. commercial bills are usually issued with a face value of $100 000, $500 000 or $1 million),
- the term of the instrument (e.g. forward foreign exchange contracts usually are for monthly periods, such one, two and three months),
- specifying other features of financial instruments (e.g. futures contracts have only four settlement dates per year), and
- limiting the number of securities supplied to the market (e.g. concentrating the issue of bonds to a few series promotes turnover by increasing the availability of bonds in each series).

Not all potential purchasers will be suited by a standardised instrument. Their needs may be satisfied by alternative instruments or by customised products provided by specialist banks and merchant banks. However, there is little doubt that product standardisation promotes market turnover, and that this is sought by markets.

Market information

Market prices generally reflect the expectations of traders about the future value of securities. These expectations are formed on the basis of relevant information. Consequently, professional markets are major users of information, most of which is provided by electronic news services such as AAP, Telerate and Reuters. Electronic information (i.e. information that can be displayed on computer screens) is accessed through market reports that are displayed on specific 'pages' of a news service. Specialised trading software is provided by these news services and by software companies to assist in the interpretation and use of the data.

Mainly because of their retail customers, exchanges need to ensure that traders are given prompt and equal access to new information. Failure to provide market information is usually a breach of the listing rules of the exchange. The use of privileged information by traders is outlawed as **insider-trading**.

Participants

As noted earlier, trading in dealer-organised markets is confined to professional traders employed by dealer-organisations, such as the major banks. Through their trading they set prices (bids and offers) and hold inventories and create a market that can be accessed by wholesale clients, such as large companies and government-owned enterprises.

Dealers earn an income from their trading spreads (i.e. the spread between their bid and offer rates), which may be viewed as being equivalent to a broker's commission, and from trading profits, through arbitrage (buying and selling simultaneously at different prices) and speculation (buying at perceived low prices and selling when prices rise, or vice versa).

In exchange-organised markets, brokers assist buyers to locate sellers and vice versa. They buy and sell on behalf of clients, and thus are 'agents'. They earn an income by charging a commission on each trade. This varies according to the size of the transaction, and in the case of large transactions is subject to negotiation. (See example 3.5.)

Dealer spreads depend on the volume of trading, the size of transactions and the risks faced. The value of typical transactions in the markets for debt securities and foreign exchange is substantial ($5 or $10 million) and, as noted earlier in this chapter, daily turnover in these markets is also substantial. These factors contribute toward narrow trading spreads.

Because dealers hold securities they face the risk of an adverse movement in the price of the securities they are holding. Brokers do not face this risk because they merely communicate the orders of their clients to the market. The implicit commission element of a dealer's spread is therefore likely to be only a component of the spread.

Dealers set their own bids and offers. Generally they will fall within a narrow range and thus there will be a typical spread within the market. This is the difference between the highest bid and the lowest offer within the market.

When trading, dealers will adjust their bids and offers according to their trading strategy. When seeking to buy they will set their bids at the high end of the market's range of bids. When seeking to sell they will set their offers at the low end of the market's range of offers. In general, an aggressive trader will set a narrower-than-average spread.

Banks and merchant banks are the main dealer-organisations in the money and foreign exchange markets. They may also be brokers in the stock market and the SFE. At one time stockbroking was the domain of small independent firms. But following deregulation of financial markets, the ASX removed most of its restrictions on membership, and this allowed banks and merchant banks to become members.

example 3.5

Consider briefly the operating rules of the ASX, which controls the market for the ordinary shares of companies listed on the exchange. Trading is conducted by members of the exchange (brokers), during trading hours, through a computer-based trading system, the Stock Exchange Automated Trading System (SEATS). Originally trading was conducted on an auction basis. Bids and offers for the shares in each listed company were communicated by open outcry by traders on the floor of the sharemarket (i.e. traders shouted these to the auctioneer). Under SEATS, the computer matches bid and offer rates according to a clear set of impartial rules.

The ASX has developed detailed listing and business rules that determine which shares are traded and the trading practices of brokers. The exchange places great emphasis on ensuring that all relevant information about listed shares and their values is made available to the traders in the market.

In 1994 the exchange began to introduce a new computer-based system (the Clearing House Subregister System, or CHESS) to ensure that settlement occurs within three working days of each trade. Settlement is made through an electronic transfer system (replacing the previous cheque payment system), and changes in share ownership are automatically transferred to the share registries of each listed company.

Wholesale and retail clients

Financial institutions, governments, government business enterprises and large companies are the participants in wholesale markets, whereas individuals and small businesses are the main retail participants. The former engage in large-value transactions, whereas the latter undertake small-value transactions.

Most financial markets have large minimum-sized trading parcels which allow them to establish very low transaction costs. This usually means that they cannot serve the needs of retail clients. In such cases, institutions serve their needs. For example, the foreign exchange market is a wholesale market. The small-value foreign exchange needs of retail clients are served by banks through their branches. However, the spread at the retail level is much wider than in the foreign exchange market because of the small value of the transactions and their greater administrative costs.

However, the ASX and the SFE encourage the participation of both retail and wholesale clients. They have relatively small minimum-sized transactions. Trading in the other financial markets is the province of wholesale clients and is conducted by professional dealers.

In the markets for risk-management instruments, two groups of participants are commonly identified: hedgers who are taking a position to hedge (or **cover**) their position in a physical market, and speculators, who have an open (i.e. uncovered) position in the derivative market. The distinction between hedgers and speculators is not always obvious. Any party that has an uncovered position in any market is, in effect, speculating.

FINANCIAL INSTRUMENTS

Earlier in this chapter we listed four physical markets and the main instruments that are traded in these markets. We also referred to the markets for derivative instruments. This section provides a more detailed picture of the main forms of these instruments. We will start with the securities traded in the short-term money market.

Short-term securities

Each of the instruments traded in the short-term money market are single-payment securities. When they are originally issued, the borrower receives funds through their sale in the primary market. Borrowers repay (i.e. redeem) the securities by paying their face value at maturity. Because the original selling price is less than their face value, the payment of this amount includes an implicit interest payment. The general structure of short-dated securities is shown in figure 3.3.

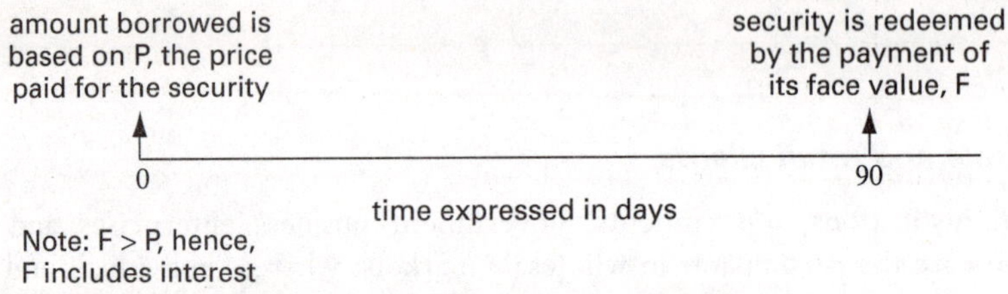

Figure 3.3 The payment structure of short-term securities

Short-dated securities include commercial bills, promissory notes (or commercial paper), Treasury notes and certificates of deposit. In fiscal year 1994, trading in bills represented approximately three-quarters of the turnover in this market.

Commercial bills

Commercial bills are a source of funds for business. Historically they were used to finance overseas trade; they allowed an exporter, for example, to be paid before the goods were received and sold by the importer. In such a case, the importer would draw a bill in favour of the exporter (the payee in this example) facilitating payment for the imports. In order to raise the funds for the payment, the importer would seek the bill's acceptance by a bank or some other financially secure party. The **acceptor**

agrees to redeem the bill when it matures on the condition that the importer provides the funds (when presumably the goods have been received and sold). Once a bill had been accepted it was sold in the market and the proceeds used to pay the exporter.

The unusual feature of bills is that the acceptor is responsible for its redemption at maturity (this being a liability for the acceptor), and not the bill's drawer. Hence the credit standing of the bill depends on this acceptor's financial credentials. The acceptor makes a separate **bill receivable** arrangement with the bill's **drawer** (this being an asset for the acceptor) to pay the acceptor the bill's face value at maturity, and these funds are used by the acceptor to redeem the bill.

A representation of the parties involved in the issue of bills accepted by a major bank (which is now the usual arrangement) is presented in figure 3.4. It shows the acceptor being liable for the bill's redemption ($F, being the face value) at maturity. The investor's purchase price ($P) is shown as being paid through the acceptor, who withholds an acceptance fee, to the drawer, who is responsible to pay $F at maturity through the acceptor to the holder (satisfying the acceptor's bill receivable).

Bills have become an important instrument for raising funds on a short-term basis. The drawer (i.e. the borrower) may be seeking funds simply to meet general operating expenses for a short period. In such cases the drawer is also the payee. Most bills are accepted by banks, and are known as **bank bills**. They are issued, typically, by selling them in the primary market, and they subsequently trade in the secondary market.

A bank will view bill acceptance as an alternative to a short-term advance because of the credit risk it accepts. The bill receivable agreement between the bank and the bill's drawer (under which the drawer provides the bank with the bill's face value at maturity) is comparable to a loan agreement between the bank and a borrower. If the bank is satisfied with the drawer's financial capacity to make this payment it will accept the bill for a fee. Upon signing as the acceptor, the bank usually sells the bill in the market. It will deduct its acceptance fee (which in practice may be a set of fees) from the proceeds of the bill's sale. The balance will be paid as required by the bill: either to the payee, if there is one, or to the drawer.

At a bill's maturity date, the drawer is liable to pay the bank the bill's face value, and this will be paid to the bill's holder, extinguishing the debt.

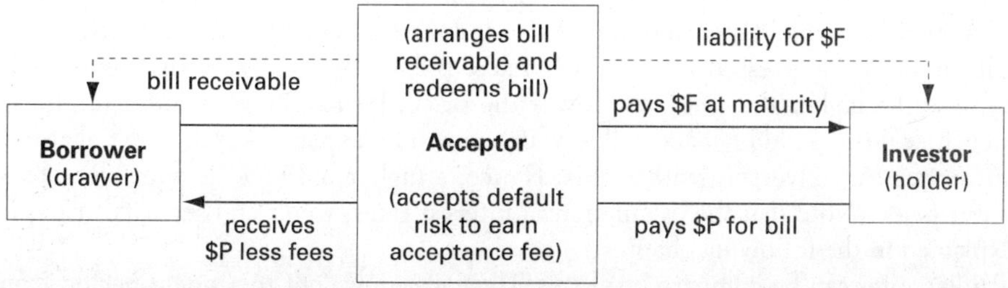

Figure 3.4 Parties to the issue of commercial bills

Treasury notes

Treasury notes are issued by the Reserve Bank on behalf of the Commonwealth Treasury. They are an important instrument, in part because they are a prime asset that banks are required to hold. Their credit standing is absolute given that the Commonwealth Government is responsible for the issue of legal tender. There is only limited turnover in Treasury notes within the short-term money market, mainly because trading is by banks to satisfy the RBA's prime asset ratio.

Promissory notes and CDs

Promissory notes (also referred to as **commercial paper**) are issued by very secure borrowers, such as large government enterprises and 'blue-chip' companies. They are redeemed by their issuer at maturity. Notes are 'one-name' paper because only the issuer is responsible for their redemption at maturity. By contrast, bills are 'two-name' paper because of the role of the acceptor.

In the previous chapter we noted that certificates of deposit (CDs) are similar to promissory notes issued by banks. However, many are issued for terms less than 90 days and their face value is usually $500 000 or $1 000 000, which is larger than is usual for bills and notes. CDs, because of their bank origin, have the characteristics of bank-accepted bills and trade as such.

Bills and notes are issued for short-term periods, usually for 90 or 180 days in the case of bills and promissory notes and 5, 13 and 26 weeks in the case of Treasury notes. As previously indicated, these instruments (as well as CDs) do not pay interest explicitly: interest is earned because they are issued at a discount to their face value. Investors in bills earn interest through the increase in the bill's price over time. A bill with a face value of $100 000 and maturing in 180 days may be issued for, say, $96 000. The difference between the face value and the issue price of $4000 represents the implicit interest paid by the borrower to the lender. Of course as time proceeds the price of the bill will steadily rise as the interest component decreases until eventually, at maturity, the price of the bill will be equal to its face (or redemption) value.

The interest cost a borrower incurs when bills/notes are issued is the difference between the funds received and the amount paid to redeem the bill on maturity (its face value). In the case of bills, as outlined above, the acceptance fee is deducted from the funds raised when the bills are issued. If the bank charges an acceptance fee of $750, the borrower will receive only $95 250, and the implicit interest charged is $4750.

Interest is not normally quoted in terms of dollar amounts. Rather, interest is expressed as a yield per annum. As noted above, dealer bids and offers for bills/notes are expressed in terms of yields. Bid yields are higher than sell yields because the higher the yield, the lower the price. Hence, in the market for these securities dealers bid high and sell low. But as will be explained in the next chapter, bill prices vary inversely with yields. Hence, a higher bid yield is equivalent to a lower price.(Note that the calculation of interest rates, yields and security prices is explained in the following chapter.)

Bills/notes can be compared to loans. They are equivalent to a single-period loan of an amount equal to the proceeds of the issue. The bill's redemption at maturity is equal to the repayment of the principal plus interest.

Debt-capital securities

There are two general forms of debt-capital securities: **bonds** and **floating rate notes** (FRNs). The latter are also referred to as **medium-term notes** (MTNs). Unlike the short-dated instruments, the distinction between these instruments is rather blurred.

Bonds

A bond is a long-term instrument that usually pays interest at regular intervals over its life. It is redeemed on its maturity date, usually by the payment of its face value. It is equivalent to a conventional interest-only loan because it makes interest payments during its life, and the redemption payment at maturity is equivalent to the repayment of the principal amount of the loan. The payment structure of a fixed-interest bond is depicted in figure 3.5.

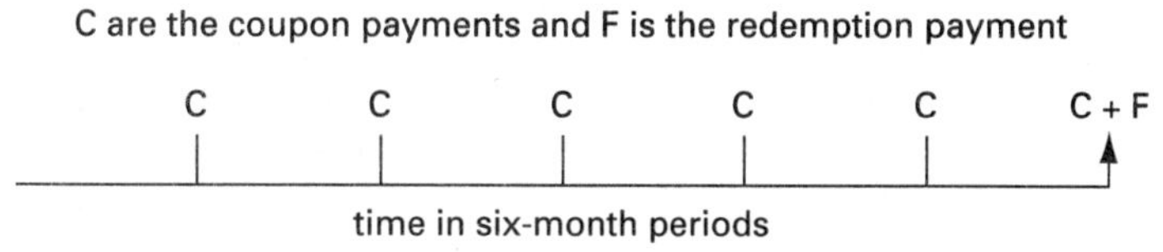

Figure 3.5 Payment structure of a three-year fixed-interest bond

In the Australian market, most bonds are fixed-interest securities. A bond's issuer promises to make the regular (usually six-monthly) interest (known also as **coupon**) payments until the bond matures. The amount and the timing of these (and the bond's redemption) payments are fixed when the bond is issued. Hence their description as **fixed-interest securities**.

In the mid 1980s, the Commonwealth first issued **indexed bonds**. Two types were issued: capital-indexed and interest-indexed bonds. In the former case, the face value of the bond is adjusted for inflation, and in the latter the rate of interest paid on the bonds increased with inflation. Issues of indexed bonds (TIBs) ceased in 1988, but in 1993 the Treasury recommenced issuing capital-indexed bonds.

In 1994 the Treasury introduced **adjustable rate bonds** (TABs) which make regular interest payments, based on the 90-day market rate of interest. They are referred to as adjustable-rate bonds because the rate of interest paid each quarter adjusts with movements in the 90-day rate over time. While the Treasury refers to these securities as bonds, they might well be referred to as FRNs (or MTNs) because the initial TABs had a term of only three years.

FRNs and MTNs

Whereas bonds are long-term securities, FRNs are medium-term (i.e. three- to five-year) securities. As noted above, there is not a clear distinction between these securities, especially as MTNs can be issued on either a fixed- or floating-rate basis and not all bonds have an issue term in excess of five years.

Each interest payment under an FRN is based on the level of a marker rate. This is the market's indicator rate that shows the movement of the market's yield over time. In the Australian market, the 90-day bank bill rate (referred to as BBSW or BBR), is used as the marker rate for FRNs.

An FRN must specify the dates each year when interest is paid (e.g. quarterly) and the relationship between the issuer's rate and the marker rate. For example, the Australian Postal Corporation issued five-year FRNs (in 1994) at BBSW plus 15 basis points (bps). Remember, a basis point is 0.01%. In this case, each time the corporation pays interest to the holders of its notes, it pays an amount based on the BBSW rate at the commencement of the interest period plus 15 bps. For instance, if the BBSW was 8.10% at the commencement of an interest period, the corporation would pay 8.25% p.a. for that interest period.

Commonwealth Treasury and semi-government bonds dominate the domestic market. In fiscal year 1994 the turnover in Treasury bonds was $995 billion and turnover in semi-government bonds was $921 billion. Total turnover in the bond market was $1963 billion. (AFMA, 1994(b), p. 12)

In the US fixed-interest market, bonds are extensively issued by corporations. A number of Australian companies have issued bonds in both the US domestic market and the eurocurrency markets. They have chosen to issue overseas rather than in the domestic bond market.

Foreign exchange

Foreign exchange (FX) is a physical instrument because the foreign currency is supplied in exchange for cash in terms of the domestic currency. We discuss forward foreign exchange in Chapter 13.

The Australian market is large relative to Australia's role in international trade. Trade in currencies against the Australian dollar is less than the trade in 'third-currencies'. The Australian market participates in third-currency (e.g. US dollars for German marks) trading because it operates after the New York market has closed and before the London market has opened.

Equity instruments

When issued, shares raise equity capital; that is, funds supplied by the owners of a company. Even though shares are usually issued by companies that intend to pay dividends, this intention does not constitute a legally-binding obligation on the company to make such payments.

Note that shares do not have a maturity date and thus may be thought of as perpetuities (i.e. instruments that make future payments in perpetuity). The value of a share depends largely upon expectations of future dividend payments.

As noted above, there are ordinary and preference shares. Given that the dividend paid on preference shares is usually a set amount, these securities make payments that are similar to the coupon payments paid by bonds (as shown in figure 3.5).

Hybrid instruments

Debt and equity can be classified on the basis of term and the nature of dividend payments. Debt has a limited life and makes a series of fixed dividend payments. On the other hand, equity has unlimited life and has variable dividend payments. There are some instruments whose classification lies somewhere between debt and equity. These hybrid instruments share some characteristics of both debt and equity.

A **convertible note** is debt that has some equity characteristics. Convertible notes have a fixed term and interest payments but may, at the behest of the holder, be converted to equity. A preference share represents equity with some debt characteristics. Preference shares, like ordinary shares, have an unlimited life, but unlike ordinary shares, preference shares generally pay a fixed dividend.

DERIVATIVE INSTRUMENTS

The purpose of this brief section is to give the reader a basic understanding of the main features of derivative instruments. Some of these are more complex than the physical instruments described above. Moreover, some may take a variety of forms, but we will concentrate on their basic form. Because reference will be made to these instruments prior to the chapters where each is discussed in detail, it is important that the reader have at least a basic knowledge of them.

A derivative is an instrument whose value depends on the value of an underlying asset, reference rate or index. As shown by the data presented in table 3.3, their use has greatly expanded since the mid 1980s because they allow financial institutions and other market participants to manage the market risks arising from their positions in financial markets (which increased when the markets were deregulated). As noted in Chapter 2, holdings of derivatives are shown off-balance sheet because of the contingent nature of their value.

Table 3.3 Average daily turnover in financial markets, 1980 to 1995 ($ billion)

Year to	*Treasury bonds*		*Bank bills*		*Equities*	
June	*physical*	*futures*	*physical*[1]	*futures*	*physical*	*futures*
1980	0.1	nil	—	nil	0.03	—
1985	0.3	nil	0.3	0.5	0.07	0.07
1990	1.2	1.7	1.7	11.4	0.23	0.19
1995	6.0	6.0	1.0	19.0	0.47	0.44

[1] Other short-term securities, such as commercial paper and CDs, are traded in a comparable way to bank bills
Source: Edey and Gray, 1996, p. 29

Forwards

Forward contracts establish prices and/or interest rates prior to the date of the transaction. As noted above, a forward FX contract simply provides for a delayed settlement at the agreed exchange rate. Whereas future and exchange-traded options are traded throughout their life, forward contracts are not traded. (See example 3.6.)

example 3.6

Two FX dealers could agree in March to exchange an amount of Australian dollars for an amount of US dollars in June. The forward contract establishes in March the rate of exchange that will be applied in June.

A forward rate agreement (FRA) is an agreement between a bank and either an investor or a borrower to make a settlement payment that will have the effect of fixing the rate of interest for an agreed amount that will be invested or borrowed at a future date. The agreement relates only to the interest rate; it is not an agreement to invest or borrow. FRAs are of value to investors and borrowers because they remove the risk of an adverse movement in interest rates prior to the intended transaction in the money market.

Futures

A futures contract is an obligation to buy (in the case of its holder) or sell (in the case of the seller) a defined item (such as a bank bill with a specified face value) at a specified future date (known as the settlement date). Futures contracts are traded on futures exchanges, such as the Sydney Futures Exchange. The main financial futures contracts are for 90-day bank bills, three-year and ten-year bonds and the share price index (SPI) contract.

A bank bill futures contract specifies 90-day bank-accepted bills with a face value of $1 million and the settlement date. They have the same appearance as a forward contract for bills. It is important to understand that the bills in the futures contract commence their term on the settlement date of the futures contract. The contracts can be traded prior to their settlement date.

example 3.7

At the end of 1994, the current yield on 90-day bank bills was 8.15%, whereas the value of March 1995 bank bill futures reflected a yield of 9.48% (which represents the expected 90-day yield in March 1995) and the June 1995 contract was trading at a yield of 10.45% (which represents the expected 90-day rate in June 1995).

Trading in bill futures contracts at the end of 1994 reflected the expectation that the 90-day interest rate would rise over the next six months. Consequently, the futures market provides a prediction of the movement in interest rates. It is worthwhile reflecting upon the outcome of the futures predicted rates. In fact, in March 1995 the physical bank bill rate was not 9.48% as predicted but rather was 8.20% and in June 1995 the bank bill rate was not 10.45% but was 7.50%. These are not insignificant errors and they underline the fallibility of market predictions.

The value of a bill futures contract depends on a 90-day interest rate, in the same way as for an actual bill. Bill futures differ from actual bills because futures contracts refer to bills that come into existence on the contract's settlement date (when the futures contract matures). Hence the 90-day interest rate relevant to a particular futures contract is the rate that is expected to occur on its settlement date. (See example 3.7.)

Bill futures contracts are widely traded because their value is related to future interest rates. They are typically used to create a position to hedge the risk of an adverse movement in interest rates arising from a position in the bill market. We explain how this is achieved in Chapter 17.

Swaps

Swaps are exchanges of financial payments. The most common form involves the exchange of interest payments by a fixed-rate borrower with those of a floating-rate borrower (e.g. a swap between the issuers of a bond and an FRN). For swaps covering a period of up to three years, interest is swapped on a quarterly basis, whereas for longer-term swaps interest is exchanged each six months.

Typically a bond issuer will swap with a party which has a floating-rate loan where the floating rate is set in relation to, say, the 90-day bank bill swap rate (BBSW). The floating-rate borrower pays a fixed rate (this is known as the **swap rate**) to the bond issuer, who in return pays a floating rate (based on the BBSW rate) to the floating-rate borrower. The swap transforms the bond issuer into a floating-rate payer and the floating-rate borrower into a fixed-rate payer.

In an interest-rate swap the level of the fixed-swap rate is usually set by swap dealers. Naturally, the fixed-rate payer would prefer to pay a lower rate while the fixed-rate receiver would prefer to receive a higher fixed rate. The swap rate agreed at the beginning of a swap is such that both parties are willing to exchange interest-rate payments without any supporting cash payment. This lack of valuable consideration defines any swap transaction.

The important feature of swaps is that they allow borrowers to de-couple their access to the capital market from the basis of their interest payments. This should be clear from the above illustration. The floating-rate borrower may not have been able to issue fixed interest bonds but was able to become a fixed-rate payer because of the swap. (See example 3.8.)

example 3.8

Suppose the issuer of a five-year bond who is obligated to make fixed six-monthly interest payments agreed to swap this set of payments for the interest payments on a five-year FRN. Under this arrangement the bond issuer's fixed-interest payments are met by the other party and the floating-rate borrower's interest payments are met by the fixed-rate borrower.

The effect of this swap is that the fixed-rate borrower makes the floating-rate payments and the floating-rate borrower makes the fixed-rate payments.

Options

Options are contractual rights to buy (or sell) a specified (i.e. underlying) item at a specified exercise price during (or at the end of) the option's term. For example, you could purchase an option to buy 1000 BHP shares at an exercise price of $20.00 at any time over the next three months.

The distinctive feature of an option is that it creates the right but not the obligation to proceed with the purchase (or sale) of the underlying asset. This feature is an important source of the value of options. (See example 3.9.)

Many options are arranged as specific deals between the buyer and seller. These are not traded in an options market. In Australia, ASX Derivatives, a subsidiary of the Australian Stock Exchange, conducts trading in a range of options on shares, such as options on BHP shares.

example 3.9

Suppose you purchased in March an option to buy 1000 BHP shares at an exercise price of $20.00 that expires in June. Should the share price rise to $25.00, the option allows you to buy them at the bargain price of $20.00, and this is part of the value of the option.

But should the share price fall to $18.00 you will not exercise the option, because now the $20.00 price under the option is not a bargain. In this event you let the option lapse. Its value, therefore, will be zero, and not minus $2.00.

Because options, prior to their expiry date, always have value, you must pay a price to acquire them. In the event that BHP shares fall in value below $20 by June, your option will expire worthless. Your loss is limited to the option purchase price.

In summary, an option has an unlimited upside potential (in this example, as the share price rises so does the value of the option) but has a downside risk limited to the purchase price.

INFORMATION AND EXPECTATIONS

Trading in financial markets is based on expectations about future movements in prices. Not all traders will have the same expectation. In most cases, the buyer in a trade expects the price will rise, whereas the seller expects the price will fall.

Expectations are formed on the basis of relevant information, previous experience and market sentiment (the optimistic or pessimistic bias imparted by traders when interpreting new information). Despite the role of sentiment, the immediate availability of new information about prices and the factors that influence prices is a vital ingredient for the successful operation of markets.

Fair-value prices can be generated by market trading only when traders possess relevant information about security values. Consequently relevant information (such as statements by the Reserve Bank and the release of economic data by the Australian Bureau of Statistics), is made available immediately to traders via their computer screens. Moreover, traders are advised by business economists and analysts who carefully review available data and make informed judgments about new figures before they are released.

Efficient-market hypothesis

We suggest that you carefully consider the implications of the **efficient-market hypothesis** (EMH) when attempting to understand and/or predict the movement in prices in financial markets. Its implications can serve as useful benchmarks when forming judgments about the movements in financial variables.

The EMH is based on the assumption that information is used efficiently by the traders in the market. In general, a market uses information efficiently when all relevant information is quickly taken into account in the bids and offers within a market.

A considerable amount of time and effort is applied within financial markets to the speedy provision of relevant information and to its interpretation by the business economists and security analysts who advise traders. This effort and the potential income that can be generated by market trading suggests that financial markets have the capacity and incentive to use information efficiently.

When bids and offers use information efficiently, it can be assumed that the market price represents a fair value for the item being traded. A fair price is one that best represents the item's value.

Many traders dispute the conclusions of the EMH, because of their experience of being able to make profits from spotting bargains. However, this experience is not inconsistent with the EMH. According to the hypothesis, when bargains arise, traders will quickly identify them and through their purchases the price will rise to the fair level. Hence traders in an efficient market are the means by which fair prices are quickly established.

Given the role of expectations in the formation of market prices, the EMH implies that today's price will be the best predictor of tomorrow's price. If this is not so — say we can consistently predict that tomorrow's price will be higher than today's price — we could profit by buying today and selling tomorrow. For this to occur, we have to make the implausible assumption that other traders in the market are not using information efficiently because they are failing to identify this pattern.

Another important conclusion of the EMH is that, because current security prices have been formed on the basis of existing knowledge and expectations about information to be released shortly, prices will change only when the new information arrives. New information must by definition arrive randomly — if it did not, it would not be new information. If information arrives randomly then prices will move randomly. This results in prices that follow a **random walk** over time.

The random walk pattern implies that prices do not trend. Should the market believe that prices will trend, say upwards, traders will buy immediately and sell later. But this will push up the current price and depress the future price — eliminating the expected trend. This view supports the proposition that today's price is the best predictor of tomorrow's price, and there is considerable evidence of this being the case.

The efficient use of information in forming expectations about the future movement in security prices does not imply that each trader will adopt the market's expectation, which is reflected in the current price. Not all traders are prepared to buy and sell at the current price. Moreover, we might assume that the buyer (at the current price) expects the price will rise, whereas the seller expects the price will fall.

If a market is efficient, with prices that are fair, a transaction will not provide a systematic advantage to either buyers or sellers. In zero-sum markets, such as those for futures, forwards and swaps, it means that 50% of the time the buyer will make a profit and 50% of the time the seller will make a profit. In non-zero-sum markets, such as those for bills, bonds and shares, an efficient market implies that any excess speculative returns over a normal rate of interest will be randomly shared between buyers and sellers.

Price volatility

It is important to understand that the EMH does not imply that market expectations about the level of future prices will be accurate. The October 1987 crash in share prices occurred in what was widely regarded as an efficient market. This event illustrates the implication of the EMH that future prices cannot be consistently predicted, and therefore risk-averse traders should hedge their exposure to future price movements (i.e. market risk). Hence the EMH provides an explanation for the growth in the use of risk-management instruments.

According to the EMH price movements result from new information. But experiences such as the October 1987 crash in share values suggest that price movements can 'over shoot'. This can occur on a less dramatic scale as a result of trading circumstances. For example, consider traders who have purchased securities in the expectation of a price rise. Suppose new information causes prices to fall. These traders will probably sell despite the price fall to 'cut their losses'. Their selling will place further downward pressure on prices, causing the market price to 'over react' (i.e. over shoot).

Generally, over shooting is kept in check by traders who take market positions (i.e. speculators). If they have some success (i.e. buy when prices are over shooting downwards and sell when they are over shooting upwards), their trading will reduce (but not eliminate) price volatility.

The EMH is an important explanation of both market prices and how they react to new information. It also provides a rationale for the practice of hedging exposures to market risk.

Summary

The main points of this chapter are as follows:

- Financial markets arrange the trading in securities and the settlement of deals.
- There are four physical financial markets in Australia: the markets for money (short-term securities such as bills and notes), for debt capital (bonds and FRNs), for equities and for foreign exchange.

- Primary markets perform the function of raising new capital, whereas secondary markets allow trading in existing securities, which assists the issue of new securities.
- Financial markets are either dealer-based or exchange-organised.
- Dealer-based markets are wholesale markets, whereas exchange-based markets serve both wholesale and retail markets.
- The forward, futures, options and swaps markets are the major derivative instruments markets.
- Financial markets operate within a framework of rules and trading conventions that generally promote their efficient operation.
- The efficient market hypothesis suggests that security prices reflect all relevant information and therefore are fair, and that their movement follows a random walk.
- When traders are not able to consistently predict future price movements, price volatility exposes their market positions to market risk, creating the need for risk-management instruments.

Discussion questions and exercises

1 Discuss the processes of deal making and settlement in financial markets.
2 Briefly describe the main physical and derivative financial markets.
3 Distinguish between the deal-making processes in exchange- and dealer-organised markets.
4 Describe the functions performed by primary markets. Refer to the role of ratings agencies in the issue of new securities.
5 Discuss the ways that a secondary market assists its corresponding primary market.
6 Discuss the ways that secondary markets (a) facilitate maturity intermediation and (b) assess credit risk.
7 Describe the four main discount instruments and specify their main issuers.
8 Distinguish between the payment structures of bills and bonds.
9 Explain how bank-accepted bills are issued and redeemed.
10 Briefly explain why prices in an efficient market might be regarded as being fair. Under what circumstances might security prices follow a random walk?

References and further reading

AFMA 1994(a), *Dealing Handbook*, AFMA, Sydney.

AFMA 1994(b), *1994 Australian Financial Markets Report*, AFMA, Sydney.

Austraclear (undated), *Mission Statement*.

Carew, Edna 1995, *Derivatives Decoded*, Allen & Unwin, Sydney, Chapter 1.

Daugaard, Dan, & Valentine, Tom 1995, *Financial Risk Management*, Harper Educational, Sydney, Chapter 1.

Dufey, Gunter, & Giddy, Ian H. 1994, *The International Money Market*, 2nd edn, Prentice-Hall, New Jersey, Chapters 1 and 2.

Edey, Malcolm, & Gray, Brian 1996, 'The evolving structure of the Australian financial system', in Malcolm Edey (ed.), *The Future of the Financial System*, RBA, Sydney.

Ernst & Young 1994, *Australian Capital Markets Survey*, Sydney.
Fabozzi, Frank, Modigliani, Franco, & Ferri, Michael G. 1994, *Foundations of Financial Markets and Institutions*, Prentice-Hall, New Jersey, Chapters 14 and 15.
Juttner, D. Johannes 1994, *Financial Markets, Interest Rates and Monetary Economics*, 3rd edn, Longman Cheshire, Melbourne, Chapters 8 and 18.
McGrath, Michael 1994, *Financial Institutions, Instruments and Markets in Australia*, McGraw-Hill, Sydney, Chapter 1.
Moody's Investors Service 1995(a), *Moody's Credit Ratings and Research*, New York.
Moody's Investors Service 1995(b), *Ratings Guide — Australasia*, Sydney.
RBA 1995, *A Proposal for Implementing Real Time Gross Settlement in Australia*, RBA, Sydney.

4

Introduction to interest rates and market yields

The main purpose of this chapter is to explain the conventional ways of measuring interest rates and yields. Emphasis is placed on the calculation of simple and semi-annual compound rates because of their use in Australia's financial markets. Interest rates are fundamental to the financial system and thus it is important to be able to calculate interest rates and yields and to understand what you have calculated.

Study objectives

From your study of this chapter you should be able to:

- explain the nature and measurement of interest;
- calculate the rate of accumulation of interest using simple and compound interest conventions;
- calculate the price of the instruments that are traded in the short-term money market;
- distinguish between market and holding-period yields;
- calculate effective rates of interest and understand their relationship to nominal rates;
- understand the relationship between present and future values.

INTRODUCTION

Interest is the cost of borrowed funds. It is paid to the lender by the borrower, for the use of the funds. Borrowers will pay interest when they judge that the immediate use of funds is worth the repayment of a larger amount (the amount borrowed plus interest) at a future date. In this sense, interest is the **time value** of money.

The payment of interest can be made in a variety of ways. In an interest-only loan, interest is paid periodically during the life of the loan and the amount borrowed is repaid at the end of the loan period. In a reducible loan, such as a housing loan, interest is paid through a regular payment that also reduces the amount outstanding.

For the moment it is convenient to concentrate on the simplest kind of loan, where funds are received immediately (at the **drawdown** of the loan), and a single payment is made at the end of the loan that both repays the borrowed amount and the interest due on this amount. This sort of loan may be arranged by the issue of a discount security that makes a single redemption payment at the end of its life.

At maturity, a discount security is redeemed by the payment of its face value, F. This payment includes the interest due, I, and the repayment of the borrowed amount, P. The interest paid on a discount security is implicit in the redemption payment, rather being a separate explicit payment.

The redemption payment of a discount security can be thought of as the **future value** of the loan. The proceeds raised when the security is issued are the **present value**. The difference between P and F is the amount of interest, I, paid by the borrower to the lender. That is:

$$F = P + I \qquad \textit{Equation (4.1)}$$

To illustrate, suppose a one-period loan of $100 is made on the condition that $110 is repaid at the end of the period. Thus:

$$110 = 100 + 10$$

In general, interest is discussed not as a dollar amount (i.e. $10, as in the above example), but as the rate at which P grows to F. Given that $10 was earned on a principal of $100 you might suggest that the rate of interest in the above example is 10%. Given further that interest rates are usually expressed as annual rates, this rate might be 10% per annum (p.a.). If the period over which $100 increased to $110 was a year, this would be the case.

There are, though, other equally correct answers, such as 9.53%, because there are various ways of calculating the rate of growth in an amount of money from P to F. That is, there are various measures of the rate of interest.

We encounter various things that have more than one measure, such as distance and temperature. Suppose Fangio left Milan at noon and reached Turin (500 km away) at 3 p.m. If Fangio was driving a Ferrari his speed would be measured as 167 km per hour. In these circumstances no confusion would arise if we simply stated that his speed was 167. But if Fangio was driving a Ford, his speed would have been calculated as 104 miles per hour. Both figures are correct; 167 km per hour is the same as 104 miles per hour, even though, in itself 104 is less than 167. Whether one expresses his speed as 167 or 104 depends entirely upon the basis of measuring distance. As long as everyone is aware of the basis used there should be no confusion.

Returning to our financial illustration, 9.53% p.a. is another correct measure of the rate at which $100 grows to $110 over a year. This may seem to be a lower rate of interest (than 10% p.a.) but we cannot make that judgment unless we know the basis on which it has been calculated. Is 167 a faster speed than 104? We need to know the basis on which distance is measured in each case to be able answer that question. Likewise, we need to know the basis on which the two interest rates are calculated to be able compare 10% with 9.53%.

There are two general ways of measuring the rate of interest:

1 on a simple interest basis or
2 a compound interest basis.

In the latter case the frequency of compounding must also be specified. The growth of $100 to $110 is 9.53% p.a. as a daily compounding basis; whereas it is 9.57% p.a. on a monthly compounding basis.

It is important to understand that each of the three rates (10.00, 9.57 and 9.53) is a correct measure of the growth of $100 to $110 over a year. They differ because they have been calculated on a different basis. Nevertheless, this will not cause confusion provided we know which one is being used.

Conventions have evolved in different financial markets that determine which method of calculating the rate of interest is used:

- rates in the short-term money market are calculated on the simple interest basis, whereas
- rates in the bond market are calculated on a semi-annual compound interest basis, and
- financial institutions, such as banks, generally calculate deposit rates on a daily compound basis and make loans on a monthly compound basis.

However, financial institutions do not uniformly use a particular basis for calculating interest. A comparison can be made of rates that have been calculated on different bases by converting them to an effective annual rate. An explanation of the calculation of effective rates is presented at the end of this chapter.

SIMPLE INTEREST

When the rate of interest is measured in simple interest terms, it accrues at a proportional rate over time in relation to the original amount of principal. Thus, the same amount of interest would accrue over, say, the first ten days of a simple interest investment as over the next ten days. This occurs because interest is not capitalised during the investment period.

The amount of interest is the principal amount times the (simple) rate of interest per annum times the period in years:

$$I = P * r * t \qquad \textit{Equation (4.2)}$$

where I is the amount of interest,
P is the principal amount,
r is rate of interest per annum,
t is time in years, and
* means multiply.

Recall that:

$$F = P + I \qquad (4.1)$$

Substituting equation (4.2) for I in equation (4.1) yields:

$$F = P + (Prt)$$

$$= P(1 + rt) \qquad \textit{Equation (4.3)}$$

This is an important formula that is referred to frequently, in one form or another, throughout this book. Note that the annual interest rate, r, is entered as a decimal and that t is in years, although when applied to the short-term market, it will be a fraction of a year, such as 90 over 365 days. The product, rt, is the interest rate over the period of the loan. A rate of 8% p.a. for a quarter of a year is:

$$rt = 0.08 * 0.25$$

$$= 0.02 \text{ per period (in this case a quarter of a year)}$$

When calculating (1 + rt) multiply r by t before the product is added to 1.

As an illustration we will calculate the value of $100 in 90 days given a rate of 12% p.a. Here:

$$F = 100\left(1 + 0.12\,\frac{90}{365}\right)$$

$$= \$102.96$$

Note that t is 90/365. In practice the number of days in the year depends on the convention in each country's financial markets. While there are 365 days in a year (except for a leap year), the financial markets in many countries adopt the convention that a year has 360 days. This convention has not been adopted in Australia, nor in many of the old British Commonwealth countries, where 365 days is the basis of their interest-rate year. Thus, in a country that uses a 360-day year, such as the United States, t would have been 0.25 and the future amount would be:

$$F = 100\left(1 + 0.12\,\frac{90}{360}\right)$$

$$= \$103.00$$

Observe in equation (4.3) that the amount of interest increases in proportion to the number of days. If 180 days was involved, F would amount to $106 (in the 360-day year case). The calculation of F using equation (4.3) is illustrated in the example 4.1.

example 4.1

Given an interest rate of 8.00% p.a., what is the future value of $98 066 in 90 days?

$$F = P(1 + rt)$$

$$= 98\,066\left(1 + 0.08\,\frac{90}{365}\right)$$

$$= \$100\,000$$

Calculating the present value

Observe that equation (4.3) has only four variables: F, P, r and t. The equation can be re-arranged to calculate any one of the four variables, assuming the value of the other three are known. The present value of a future amount can be found as:

$$P = \frac{F}{1 + rt} \qquad \textit{Equation (4.3a)}$$

Frequent reference will be made to equation (4.3a). Observe that P and rt (or r and t alone) vary in opposite directions to each other. An increase in the denominator term reduces the value of the right-hand term and so reduces P. Similarly, a reduction in r and/or t will increase the value of P.

The relationship between P and the denominator (this can be r or t individually) can be represented, in general terms, by a 'see saw', as shown in figure 4.1. For instance, when r falls, P increases, and vice versa.

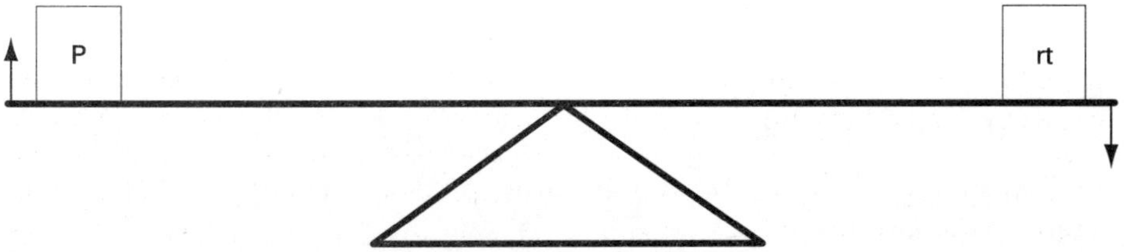

Figure 4.1 Inverse relationship between P and rt

In example 4.2 we illustrate how to calculate the present value of a future amount using simple interest. When the future value is the face value of a short-term (i.e. discount) security, equation (4.3a) serves to calculate the price of the security.

Hence, this equation can be used to price the securities traded in the short-term money market.

example 4.2

A short-term security promises to pay \$100 000 in 90 days. What is the present value of this amount given an interest rate of 8.00% p.a.? In order to answer this we solve the equation:

$$P = \frac{F}{1 + rt}$$

$$= \frac{100\,000}{1 + 0.08 * 90/365}$$

$$= \$98\,066$$

Calculating a simple-interest yield

Another important rearrangement of equation (4.3) is to calculate the rate of return, r, on an investment in a discount security:

$$r = \left(\frac{F}{P} - 1\right)\frac{1}{t} \qquad \textit{Equation (4.3b)}$$

When F represents the proceeds of the short-term investment, P represents the outlay, and t is the term of the investment, equation (4.3b) can be used to calculate the investment's yield as a percentage per annum. Given that t is a fraction of a year, it may be expressed as

d/diy

where d is the number of days in the period, and
diy is the number of days in the year.

In equation (4.3b), where the inverse (i.e. reciprocal) of t is shown, this term is diy/d. For example, if the term of the investment is 90 days in a 365-day year:

$$\frac{1}{t} = \frac{365}{90}$$

To illustrate, suppose F equals \$100, P equals \$98.00 and t is 91 days. The rate of return on this investment is:

$$r = \left(\frac{100.00}{98.00} - 1\right)\frac{365}{91}$$

$$= 8.19\% \text{ p.a.}$$

The use of equation (4.3b) is also illustrated in example 4.3.

example 4.3

Suppose you invest \$96 433 on the basis that in 180 days you will receive \$100 000. Your rate of return in simple interest can be calculated as follows by solving equation (4.3b):

$$r = \left(\frac{F}{P} - 1\right)\frac{1}{t}$$

$$= \left(\frac{100\,000}{96\,433} - 1\right)\frac{365}{180}$$

$$= 0.075 \text{ or } 7.50\% \text{ p.a.}$$

Calculating the term of an investment

The remaining rearrangement of the simple interest equation (4.3) shows the time taken for an investment to grow to a specific future amount:

$$t = \left(\frac{F}{P} - 1\right)\frac{1}{r} \qquad \textit{Equation (4.3c)}$$

Suppose an investor borrows \$96 433 and agrees to repay \$100 000. Calculate the investment period assuming the agreed interest rate is 7.50% p.a.

$$t = \left(\frac{F}{P} - 1\right)\frac{1}{r}$$

$$= \left(\frac{100\,000}{96\,433} - 1\right)\frac{1}{0.075}$$

$$= 0.4932 \text{ years (or } 0.4832 * 365 = 180 \text{ days)}$$

Pricing short-dated (discount) instruments

The main application of simple interest is in the pricing of instruments that are traded in the short-term money market. Reference was made to these instruments in the previous chapter. Recall that they are referred to as discount instruments, because they are sold at a discount to their face value. These are mainly Treasury notes, commercial bills, promissory notes (or commercial paper) and certificates of deposit. We describe these instruments in detail in Chapter 10.

The characteristic that discount securities have in common is that they do not provide their holder with an explicit interest payment. In order for the holder to receive the equivalent of an interest payment, the securities are sold at a price for less than their face value, which is the amount repaid by the borrower on the security's maturity date. Through this payment, the borrower redeems the debt represented by the bill as well as paying interest.

By convention the instruments traded in Australia's money market trade at a yield that is calculated as a nominal annual rate of simple interest. The price of a discount security is based on the simple interest equation (4.3a) in which F refers to the face value of the security, P refers to the security's price and r is the market yield:

$$P = \frac{F}{1 + rt}$$

To a lender (the security's initial purchaser), the market yield is an indication of the rate of return that will be received on the funds invested (i.e. the purchase price of the securities). To the borrower (i.e. the issuer of the securities), the yield indicates the cost of the borrowed funds (i.e. the proceeds from their sale). The market yield is an interest rate, because it measures the amount of interest that will be paid to the lender by the borrower.

As stated above, a discount security provides the holder with interest by virtue of its being priced at a discount to its face value. Thus:

$$P = F - I$$

To illustrate, suppose as a corporate treasurer you wish to borrow approximately \$500 000 for 90 days. Your company can do this by issuing a 90-day promissory note with a face value of \$500 000. The purchaser of the note becomes, in effect, the lender of these funds. However, as the note has a face value of \$500 000, the amount you will actually borrow will be less than this amount; it depends on the amount of interest that you will have to pay to the lender. Given that the current yield on your company's 90-day notes is 7.60% p.a., equation (4.3a) can be used to calculate the amount that will be raised when the note is sold in the market:

$$\begin{aligned} P &= \frac{F}{1 + rt} \\ &= \frac{500\,000}{1 + 0.076 * 90/365} \\ &= \$490\,802 \end{aligned}$$

Accordingly, you will borrow \$490 802 at an interest cost of \$9198 (\$500 000 − \$490 802) over the 90 days. The supplier of the funds will earn interest at the rate of 7.60% p.a. on a simple interest basis. This can be demonstrated as follows using equation (4.3b):

$$\begin{aligned} r &= \left(\frac{F}{P} - 1\right)\frac{1}{t} \\ &= \left(\frac{500\,000}{490\,802} - 1\right)\frac{365}{90} \\ &= 0.0760 \text{ or } 7.60\% \text{ p.a.} \end{aligned}$$

Note that it is often convenient to calculate the price of a security per $100 of face value. This simply means that F is set as $100 and once P is calculated this number is multiplied as required to arrive at the security's price. When following this practice, quote P correct to six decimal places to avoid a rounding error when establishing the security's actual price.

We will use the above $500 000 promissory note to illustrate:

$$P = \frac{100}{1 + 0.076 * 90/365}$$

$$= \$98.160499$$

The price ($490 802) is calculated by multiplying 98.160499 by 5000 (since there are this many hundreds in the note's face value).

Observe that $9198 will be earned (as interest) over the life of the promissory note. This accrues through the increase in the note's price, from $490 802 until it reaches $500 000 at maturity.

The accumulation of interest in a discount security's price is viewed by inspecting the movement in its price when only the time to maturity diminishes. Consider the price of a $1 000 000 bill when it is 90, 60, 30 and 0 days from maturity, assuming the market yield remains at 8.00% p.a.:

$$P_{90} = \frac{1\,000\,000}{1 + 0.08 * (90/365)} = \$980\,656$$

$$P_{60} = \frac{1\,000\,000}{1 + 0.08 * (60/365)} = \$987\,020$$

$$P_{30} = \frac{1\,000\,000}{1 + 0.08 * (30/365)} = \$993\,468$$

$$P_{0} = \frac{1\,000\,000}{1 + 0.08 * (0/365)} = \$1\,000\,000$$

Note that the increase in the price each 30 days is $6364 (from 90 to 60 days), $6448 (from 60 to 30 days) and $6532 (over the last 30 days). Even though simple interest on an amount accrues proportionally over time, the rise in the price of a discount security is not proportional to time. The rate of increase in price increases as time diminishes. This non-linear relationship between P and t is shown by the increase in the slope of the curve in figure 4.2. Note that the curve is not drawn to scale to emphasise the non-linear relationship.

Direct discounting: a comparison with market yield

In the previous section we showed how, in the Australian short-term money market, the price of a discount security is based on the market yield. An alternative method of pricing discount securities is used in many other countries.

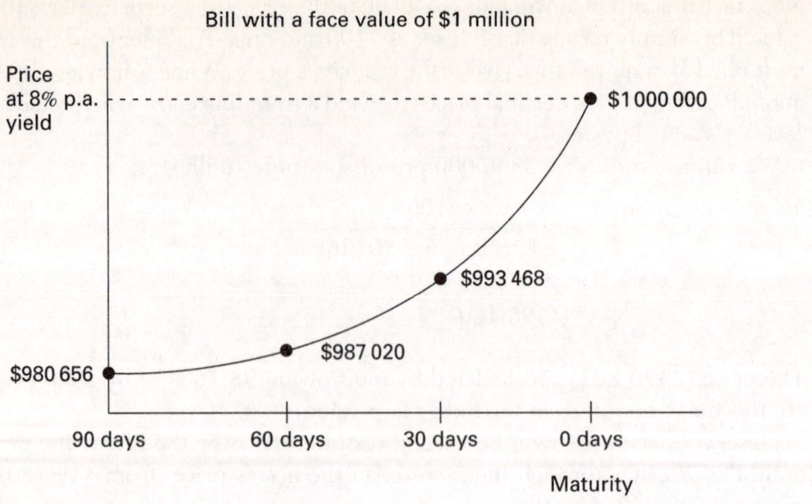

Figure 4.2 Bill price and time to maturity

This involves the use of a direct **discount rate**, d, which, like a market yield, r, is a rate per annum. Direct discounting is used to price short-term securities in the United States, Japan, Malaysia, South Africa and many other countries. The biggest market using direct discounting is that for US Treasury bills (T-bills).

The discount rate is used to find the amount that is deducted from the security's face value to derive the security's price. The amount subtracted is a proportion of the face value. This process can be expressed as:

$$P = F - D \qquad \textit{Equation (4.4)}$$

where D refers to the amount of the discount calculated with the discount rate as follows:

$$D = F * d * t \qquad \textit{Equation (4.4a)}$$

where d refers to the discount rate. Thus:

$$P = F(1 - dt) \qquad \textit{Equation (4.4b)}$$

In some ways direct discounting is simpler than the discount method embodied in equation (4.3a). With direct discounting a proportion is subtracted from the face value to produce the securities price. For example, the price of a one-year direct discount security, with a face value of $100, if the direct discount rate is 10% p.a., is simply the face value of $100 less 10% of the face value (i.e. $100 − 10 = $90). This is an application of equation (4.4b):

$$
\begin{aligned}
P &= F(1 - dt) \\
&= 100\,(1 - 0.10 * 1.0) \\
&= \$90
\end{aligned}
$$

The use of direct discounting is illustrated in example 4.4 concerning US T-bills.

example 4.4

Calculate the price of a \$1 million 90-day T-bill when the direct discount rate is 4.50% p.a. In the USA there are 360 days in a financial year, hence the term is 90/360 = 0.25 years. Thus:

$$
\begin{aligned}
P &= F(1 - dt) \\
&= 1\text{m}\,(1 - 0.045 * 0.25) \\
&= \$988\,750
\end{aligned}
$$

The price of a direct discount security increases linearly with time. This contrasts to the non-linear increase in the price of a security priced from its yield. While direct discounting makes for easier arithmetic, there is one severe disadvantage of using the direct discount rate. The direct discount rate is not an interest rate in that it does not reflect the return on invested funds. For example, consider the lender who purchases the one-year direct discount security, with a face value of \$100. If the direct discount rate is 10% p.a. its price is \$90. At the end of a year the lender will receive \$100. The rate of return on funds invested is 10/90 = 11.11% p.a., which is greater than 10% p.a. On the other hand, the discount yield to maturity does truly reflect the cost of funds. In this example \$100 discounted for a year at 11.11% p.a. would price the security at \$90.

A market yield is sometimes called the **add-on yield** to distinguish it from the direct discount yield. The yield represented by the future payment is added to the price to produce the future value:

$$F = P\,(1 + rt)$$

The relationship between a yield and a direct discount rate can be viewed by comparing a security's price given by equation (4.4b) to that given by equation (4.3a) that uses the market yield. If the two methods gave the same price these equations would be equal. Thus:

$$F(1 - dt) = \frac{F}{1 + rt}$$

Rearranging shows that:

$$d = \frac{r}{1 + rt} \qquad \textit{Equation (4.5)}$$

You can see from equation (4.5) that r must exceed d (given that r is divided by 1 + rt) to achieve the same price. This conclusion implies that for a given numerical rate (i.e. d = r), direct discounting will result in the lower security price.

Holding-period yields

The return from investing in a security can be split, conceptually, into an expected yield and an expected capital gain. A market yield provides an estimate of the cost of funds and the return to the investor. A bill purchased at 8% p.a., say, may be expected to generate a return of 8%. But this will result only when it is held to maturity and the investor receives the face value.

The **realised return** can vary from the yield when the bill is sold prior to its maturity. In this event, the return depends on the price at which the bill is sold and this, unlike F, is an uncertain amount until the sale is made. Should the bill be sold at a higher yield than the purchase yield, the return will incorporate a capital loss, whereas, if it is sold at a lower yield, the return will incorporate a capital gain.

Holding a discount security to maturity eliminates the possibility of a capital gain or loss. We know that at maturity a discount security is worth its face value. Thus if we purchase a discount security and hold it to maturity there can be no unanticipated capital gain or loss, so we must receive the yield at the time of purchase as the return on our investment.

Selling a security prior to maturity exposes the investor to the possibility of a capital gain or loss. The realised return on a security, held for part of its life, earns a yield, known as a **holding-period yield** (HPY).

Holding-period yields are calculated on the same interest rate basis as that for the underlying instrument. In other words, in the case of discount securities, the holding-period yield is calculated as an annual rate on a simple interest basis. Such yields can be calculated with equation (4.3b):

$$r = \left(\frac{F}{P} - 1\right)\frac{1}{t}$$

In the context of an investment in a discount security, F is replaced with the investment's proceeds (i.e. P_{sell}) and P by the investment outlay (i.e. P_{buy}). Suppose we purchased a $1 million, 91-day Treasury note at a yield of 7.50% p.a. Our investment outlay (the purchase price) is:

$$P = \frac{F}{1 + rt} = \frac{1\,000\,000}{1 + 0.075 * 91/365} = \$981\,645$$

If we hold our investment until maturity we receive proceeds of \$1 million when the note is redeemed. Our holding period yield, over 91 days is, as expected:

$$r = \left(\frac{F}{P} - 1\right)\frac{1}{t} = \left(\frac{1\ 000\ 000}{981\ 645} - 1\right)\frac{365}{91} = 7.50\%\text{ p.a.}$$

However, suppose we had sold the Treasury note after 30 days when yields were 7.00% p.a. The proceeds of our sale would be:

$$P = \frac{F}{1 + rt} = \frac{1\ 000\ 000}{1 + 0.070 * 61/365} = \$988\ 437$$

Our holding-period yield is:

$$r = \left(\frac{F}{P} - 1\right)\frac{1}{t} = \left(\frac{988\ 437}{981\ 645} - 1\right)\frac{365}{30} = 8.42\%\text{ p.a.}$$

Our holding-period yield incorporates a capital gain that adds some 92 basis points (i.e. 8.42% − 7.50%) in our realised return. (See figure 4.3.)

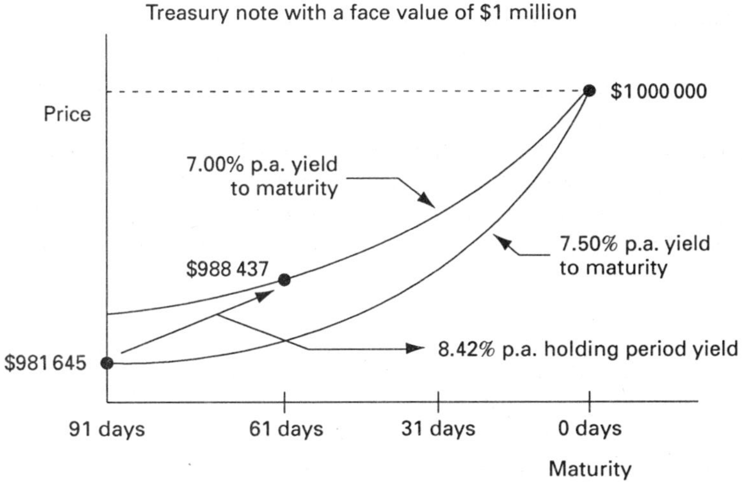

Figure 4.3 Capital gain and holding-period yield

In practice, yields differ over time. (You will recall the discussion in the previous chapter of the bid-offer bounce. We also discuss more general movements in market yields in later chapters.) Moreover, the 60-day rate is likely to differ from the 90-day rate that applied 30 days ago. As a consequence of volatility in market yields, capital gains and losses will influence actual yields on investments in short-term securities. (In Chapter 11 we show that capital gains and losses are more substantial in determining the actual yields on bonds.) Example 4.5 gives a further illustration of the influence of capital gains on investment yields.

example 4.5

Suppose after buying a 90-day bill with a face value of \$100 000 at 6% p.a., you sell it 45 days later when yields have risen to 7% p.a. Your investment outlay (the purchase price) is:

$$P_{buy} = \frac{F}{1 + rt} = \frac{1\,000\,000}{1 + 0.06 * 90/365} = \$98\,542$$

The proceeds of your sale after 45 days is:

$$P_{sell} = \frac{F}{1 + rt} = \frac{1\,000\,000}{1 + 0.070 * 45/365} = \$99\,144$$

Your holding-period yield is:

$$r_{HPY} = \left(\frac{F}{P} - 1\right)\frac{1}{t} = \left(\frac{99\,144}{98\,542} - 1\right)\frac{365}{45} = 4.96\% \text{ p.a.}$$

This holding-period yield incorporates a capital loss that results in the actual yield (4.96%) being less than the purchase yield of 6.00% p.a.

Compound interest

Compound interest entails the capitalisation of interest payments during the term of the loan so that, in effect, interest is earned on both the principal and on the capitalised interest. For example, suppose a person borrows \$100 for two periods at 10% per period on the basis that the interest is paid when the loan is repaid. The total amount of interest and principal to be paid, F, can be calculated, step-wise, as follows:

$$F_1 = 100\,(1 + 0.10)$$

$$= \$110$$

$$F_2 = 110\,(1 + 0.10)$$

$$= \$121$$

We can derive a general formula for compound interest as follows:

$$F_1 = P_0\,(1 + i),$$

$$F_2 = P_0\,(1 + i)^2,$$

and:

$$F_n = P_0\,(1 + i)^n \qquad \textit{Equation (4.6)}$$

Where i is the per compound period rate of interest.

DIGRESSION: USING A CALCULATOR — POWERS

If you do not use a financial calculator (which would allow you to make most calculations without following the formulae given in this book) you should use a scientific calculator that has the following exponential function key:

- Y^X and

Compound interest can be calculated with a scientific calculator as follows. Suppose, as in the future-value example on the next page:

$$1 + r/k = 1.075$$

$$kt = 10$$

Enter 1.075 in your calculator, then press the Y^X button and enter 10. Pressing the equals button gives 2.061032, which can then be multiplied by the amount of the principal to find the accumulated sum.

We will illustrate equation (4.6) with the above example:

$$F = 100\,(1 + 0.10)^2$$

$$= 100 * 1.21$$

$$= \$121$$

In the example above we used i to indicate the per period rate of interest. However, where the compound period is part of a year, such as a month, the annual interest rate is, by convention, divided by the number of compound periods per year, k, and n becomes k times the number of years, t. Hence the general equation for a future amount using a rate of compound interest is:

$$F = P\left(1 + \frac{r}{k}\right)^{kt} \qquad \textit{Equation (4.7)}$$

where r is the annual interest rate,
k is the number of compounds per year, and
t is time in years.

Interest rates and yields are calculated on a compound basis in the case of most loans and in the bond market. In the case of loans the frequency of compounding is relevant as this influences the amount of interest payable, given the quoted annual rate. In the case of the Australian bond market, yields are calculated on a semi-annual basis.

Future amount

We illustrate compound interest calculation with an elementary example. Suppose you arrange a loan of $10 000 at 15% p.a. over five years and you repay both the principal and interest at the end of the five years. If the compound period is six months, the sum that you will pay will be:

$$F = P\left(1 + \frac{r}{k}\right)^{kt}$$

$$= 10\,000\left(1 + \frac{0.15}{2}\right)^{5*2}$$

$$= 10\,000 * 1.075^{10}$$

$$= \$20\,610$$

Present amount

The present value, P, in the case of compound interest, can be found by simply rearranging equation (4.7) to show:

$$P = \frac{F}{(1 + r/k)^{kt}}$$ *Equation (4.7a)*

Thus, for example, we can calculate the principal amount that has to be invested at 15% p.a., compounded monthly, that will amount to $21 072 in five years, as follows:

$$P = \frac{21\,072}{(1 + 0.15/12)^{12*5}}$$

$$= \frac{21\,072}{2.107181}$$

$$= \$10\,000$$

In example 4.6, the price of single-payment bonds (known as **zero-coupon bonds**) is calculated on a semi-annual compound basis. (We discuss zero-coupon bonds in Chapter 15.)

example 4.6

Conventional bonds pay interest each six months, whereas no interest is paid on a zero-coupon bond. These bonds are priced as a pure discount security on a semi-annual compound interest basis. Hence, the price of a $100 000 zero-coupon bond that has five years to run when the market yield is 11% p.a., compounded semi-annually, can be calculated as:

$$P = \frac{F}{(1 + r/2)^{2t}}$$

$$= \frac{100\ 000}{(1 + 0.11/2)^{2*5}}$$

$$= \$58\ 543$$

Yields

We can also make the annual interest rate, r, the subject of the compound interest equation. Thus:

$$r = \left[\left(\frac{F}{P}\right)^{1/kt} - 1\right]k \qquad \textit{Equation (4.7b)}$$

Equation (4.7b) provides a basis for the calculation of compound interest rates of return and holding-period yield. For example, suppose we purchased Mount Isa Mining (MIM) shares for $1.80 and sold them three years later for $3.10, having received no dividends. What is our holding-period yield computed on a monthly compound basis? Here, P is the purchase price outlay of $1.80, F is the proceeds of the sale of $3.00, t is three years and k is 12. Thus:

$$r = \left[\left(\frac{3.10}{1.80}\right)^{1/12*3} - 1\right]12$$

$$= \left[1.7222^{\,1/36} - 1\right]12$$

$$= 18.26\%\ \text{p.a.}$$

Compounding frequency

An increase in the frequency of compounding, all else being equal, increases the future value. We show below, using equation (4.8), the future value of $1000 invested at 12% p.a. for two years on the basis of three compounding frequencies:

Semi-annual compounding:

$$F = 100 + \left(1 + \frac{0.12}{2}\right)^{2*2} = \$1262.48$$

Monthly compounding:

$$F = 1000\left(1 + \frac{0.12}{12}\right)^{12*2} = \$1269.73$$

Daily compounding:

$$F = 1000\left(1 + \frac{0.12}{365}\right)^{365*2} = \$1271.20$$

The results above illustrate the fact that the future value increases with the frequency of compounding. The upper limit to the frequency of compounding is **continuous compounding**.

Continuous compounding

This is a theoretical compounding concept deduced from the general compound-interest equation:

$$F = P\left(1 + \frac{r}{k}\right)^{kt} \qquad \textit{Equation (4.8)}$$

As k approaches infinity, F approaches a limit:

$$F = Pe^{r*t} \qquad \textit{Equation (4.9)}$$

where e is a constant (equal to 2.718218), and
r is a continuously compounded rate of interest expressed as a decimal.

In the above example the upper limit for F, the future value, is given by:

$$F = 1000\, e^{\,0.12(2)}$$

$$= \$1271.25$$

In practice no investment is compounded continuously, but the concept is important in providing tractable expressions in theoretical finance propositions. Simple interest and continuously compounded interest are at opposite ends of the compounding spectrum. In situations where there is no compounding convention it is sometimes convenient to use continuously compounded rates.

example 4.7

Express the growth of an investment over seven years from \$100 to \$250 as an annual rate of return on the basis of simple interest, semi-annual compounding and continuous compounding.

Simple interest:

$$r = \left(\frac{F}{P} - 1\right)\frac{1}{t} = \left(\frac{250}{100} - 1\right)\frac{1}{7} = 21.43\%\text{ p.a.}$$

Semi-annual compounds:

$$r = \left[\left(\frac{F}{P}\right)^{1/k*t} - 1\right]k = \left[\left(\frac{250}{100}\right)^{1/2*7} - 1\right]2 = 13.53\%\text{ p.a.}$$

Continuous compounding:

$$r = \ln\left(\frac{F}{P}\right)\frac{1}{t} = \ln\left(\frac{250}{100}\right)\frac{1}{7} = 13.09\% \text{ p.a.}$$

We illustrate the influence of compounding frequency on the rate that measures the growth in a sum from P to F over a given period in example 4.7. Observe that logarithms are required to calculate the continuously compounded yield. This approach is explained in the appendix at the end of this chapter. Note also that over seven years, the effect of compounding is considerable, such that on a simple-interest basis the growth in the sum occurs at a rate of over 21% p.a., whereas on a compound-interest basis it is at the rate of 13.53% p.a.

Interest-rate measurement: Summary

At the beginning of the chapter we observed that interest is the difference between the future value and the present amount:

$$I = F - P$$

Consequently, the present value of a future amount is arrived at by removing the amount of accumulated interest:

$$P = F - I$$

The way this is done depends on the interest-rate convention being used. We have discussed three general interest rate conventions:

- simple interest as a yield to maturity,
- simple interest on a direct discount basis, and
- compound interest including continuous compounding.

We have emphasised that the rate of growth between P and F can be measured in different ways. Even though each provides a different numerical rate of interest, each is a valid measure. The formula for each method of calculating the rate of interest is set out in table 4.1.

Table 4.1 Alternative interest-rate measures

Subject	*Simple interest*	*Direct discount*	*Compound interest*	*Continuous interest*
Future value, F	$P = \frac{F}{1 + rt}$	$P = F(1 - dt)$	$P = \frac{F}{(1 + r/k)^{kt}}$	$P = Fe^{-rt}$
Present value, P	$F = P(1 + rt)$	$F = \frac{P}{1 - rt}$	$F = P\left(1 + \frac{r}{k}\right)^{kt}$	$F = Pe^{rt}$
Interest rate, r	$r = \left(\frac{F}{P} - 1\right)\frac{1}{t}$	$d = \left(1 - \frac{P}{F}\right)\frac{1}{t}$	$r = \left[\left(\frac{F}{P}\right)^{1/kt} - 1\right]k$	$r = \ln\left(\frac{F}{P}\right)\frac{1}{t}$

NOMINAL VERSUS EFFECTIVE INTEREST RATES

As shown in table 4.1, the same annual rate of interest produces different future values for different compound frequencies. If an investment is compounded more than once a year the quoted annual rate is called the **nominal** rate. In order to properly compare investments with different compound frequencies it is helpful to transform the nominal rate of interest into an **effective annual rate of interest**. This is the simple interest rate that would produce the same future value as the compound nominal rate of interest. A limit of one year is usually placed upon the calculation of the effective rate.

Thus, as:

$$\text{simple sum} = \text{compound sum}$$

$$1 + r_e = \left(1 + \frac{r}{k}\right)^k$$

$$r_e = \left(1 + \frac{r}{k}\right)^k - 1 \qquad \textit{Equation (4.10)}$$

where r_e is the effective rate per annum,
r is the nominal rate per annum, and
k is the compound frequency.

For example, what is the effective rate on a one-year Bankcard debt if interest is calculated at 23% p.a. on the basis of monthly compounding? Hence:

$$r_e = \left(1 + \frac{0.23}{12}\right)^{12} - 1$$

$$= 0.2559 \text{ or } 25.59\% \text{ p.a.}$$

We will illustrate the importance of the distinction between nominal and effective rates with the following example. Can a bank earn an interest-rate spread by borrowing at 12% p.a. calculated annually and lending at 12% p.a. calculated daily? The answer to this question is **yes**! We can demonstrate this by comparing the effective annual rates on its deposits and its loans as follows:

$$r_e \text{ (loans)} = \left(1 + \frac{0.12}{365}\right)^{365} - 1$$

$$= 12.7475\% \text{ p.a.}$$

$$r_e \text{ (deposits)} = 12.0000\% \text{ p.a.}$$

$$\text{margin} = 0.7475\% \text{ p.a.}$$

Summary

The main points of this chapter are as follows:

- Interest is the difference between a present amount and an accumulated future value amount.
- The interest rate can be measured in different ways.
- Four variables are involved in interest-rate calculations: the principal (or present value or price), the future value, the yield and the term. When any three are known, the fourth can be calculated.
- Security prices (and yields) in the short-term money market are calculated on a simple interest basis. Direct discounting is used in many overseas money markets.
- Security prices vary inversely with changes in interest rates.
- An investment yield is the rate of return represented by the proceeds over the outlay. The holding-period yield from investing in discount securities is calculated on a simple interest basis.
- Compounding requires interest to be capitalised at the end of each compound period and so interest is earned on accumulated interest as well as the principal.
- The upper limit to the effect of compounding is achieved through continuous compounding.
- The more frequently interest is compounded the greater is the divergence between the effective and the nominal annual rate.

DISCUSSION QUESTIONS AND EXERCISES

1. Explain how the growth of $100 to $120 over a year can be correctly measured by more than one rate of interest.
2. What determines the time value of money?
3. What distinguishes a present from a future amount?
4. Calculate the future amount, on a simple interest basis, of $100 over six months at 6.00% p.a.
5. How much will $10 000 invested for 90 days amount to at 9% p.a. on a simple interest basis?
6. Calculate the price of a bill that has a face value of $500 000 and has 120 days to run when the interest rate is 7.80% p.a.
7. Explain the relationship between a bill's price and its yield.
8. Calculate the price of a 90-day bill with a face value of $100 000 at 7.40%, 7.80% and 8.20%.
9. How much would you have to pay for a Treasury note that has 90 days to run when the market interest rate is 8.10% p.a.? (Price the Treasury note per $100 of face value.)
10. Suggest the path taken by the price of a discount security as it moves to maturity.
11. Calculate the price of a $100 000 bill at a yield of 7.80% p.a. when it has 90, 60 and 30 days to maturity.

12 What is the price of a $100 000, 90-day US T-bill, given a direct discount rate of 8% p.a.?
13 Explain how an investment in a Treasury note can result in a different yield from its purchase yield.
14 Suppose you purchased a $100 000 bill with 120 days to run when the market yield was 7.60% and sold it 30 days later, assuming the yield had not changed. Calculate the rate of return on your 30-day investment.
15 Suppose in the previous question that the yield was 8.20% p.a. when you sold the bill. Calculate your return in this case. Explain the difference between this yield and that calculated in the previous question.
16 Suppose you purchased a $100 000 13-week Treasury note for $97 919.21 and held it to maturity. What was your rate of return on funds invested?
17 Suppose you expect that short-term yields are about to fall. Suggest an investment strategy that would profit if this does occur.
18 Calculate the future amount of $1000 in two years at 8.00%, compounded monthly and daily.
19 Calculate the present value of $100 that will be paid in three years, at 7.60% p.a. compounded semi-annually.
20 Calculate the price of a zero-coupon bond that pays $1000 in four years at a semi-annual yield of 8.20% p.a.
21 Why does more frequent compounding (other things being equal) increase the amount of interest payable on an investment?
22 Suppose you invest $12 000 in a fixed-deposit account with your local bank for one year. If the bank pays 5.80% p.a. compounded quarterly, how much will your investment amount to by the end of a year?
23 Suppose in the previous question that the bank compounded interest daily. What would be your accumulated sum?
24 How can you compare investments if the returns are quoted as nominal annual rates and the compounding periods differ?
25 Suppose Bank A offers a rate of 5.90% p.a. simple, Bank B offers 5.75% p.a. compounded monthly and Bank C offers 5.65% compounded daily. In which bank will you obtain the most interest from an investment of $8000 over two years?

FURTHER READING

Knox, D. M., *et. al.* 1990, *Mathematics of Finance*, McGraw-Hill, Sydney.

APPENDIX 4.1: LOGARITHMS

The emphasis of this chapter was on the use of simple interest rates. We showed how to calculate the present and future amounts and the interest rate when each was the only unknown variable. In this appendix we show how to calculate the time in years of an investment when it is the only unknown. To do so, we will use logarithms.

It is necessary to employ logarithms to solve equations with unknowns in the powers. In doing so we use the result that log $(Y^x) = x \log(Y)$. For example, solving:

$$Y^x = Z$$

for x, we take the **natural log**, ln, of this equation:

$$\ln (Y^x) = \ln Z$$

$$x (\ln Y) = \ln Z$$

or

$$x = \frac{\ln(Z)}{\ln(Y)}$$

Natural logs are logarithms to the base, e, which is a constant equal to 2.718218. A useful result is:

$$\ln (e^x) = x$$

Thus if, for example, $Y = e^x$ then taking logs of both sides of the equation produces $x = \ln Y$.

Suppose we wanted to know how much time it takes for a compound investment to reach a certain level. For example, how long does it take for an investment compounded monthly to double if interest rates are 10% p.a? To determine this the following equation must be solved for m:

$$F = P\left(1 + \frac{r}{k}\right)^m \qquad \textit{Equation (4A.1)}$$

where m is the number of months, and
k equals 12.

For simplicity we set P equal to one dollar, thus:

$$2 = 1 * \left(1 + \frac{0.12}{12}\right)^m$$

$$\ln z = m * \ln (1.01)$$

$$m = \frac{\ln(2)}{\ln (1.01)}$$

$$= 69.66 \text{ months or } 5.81 \text{ year.}$$

5

Annuities and their application

The main purposes of this chapter are to explain the mathematics of ordinary annuities and to demonstrate their application in valuing financial instruments and constructing loan repayment schedules.

Study objectives

From your study of this chapter you should be able to:

- understand and apply annuity factors;
- calculate the present and future values of ordinary annuities;
- calculate the price of a fixed-interest bond;
- calculate the present value of perpetuities;
- understand the structure of the repayment schedule for a reducible loan;
- calculate the mortgage constant and the remaining balance of a reducible loan;
- understand the basic elements of a pension scheme.

Introduction

A number of financial instruments and arrangements involve regular payments. In the previous chapter reference was made to the present and future values of a given amount. In this chapter we explain how to calculate and apply the present and future values of a series of regular payments.

A series of regular payments is called an **annuity**. The financial world abounds in instruments whose payments constitute an annuity. Commonly occurring examples are premiums on insurance policies, interest payments on bonds, lease and rental payments, and most loan repayment schemes.

Not all annuities have the same features. When an annuity's payments occur at the commencement of each period it is referred to as an **annuity due**. When its payments occur at the end of each period it is referred to as an **ordinary annuity**. The term of an annuity is the number of its payments, which is also the number of its periods for an ordinary annuity. For example, a three-year loan that requires monthly repayments is a 36-period annuity. When this number of payment periods is predetermined (as in the loan example) it is referred to as an **annuity certain**, whereas when the term is not pre-set (as in the case of a life insurance policy), it is referred to as a **contingent annuity**.

In this chapter we emphasise ordinary annuities that have a finite term. This is the form of annuity that we apply in subsequent chapters, particularly those that deal with bonds.

When referring to annuities we try to use accepted notation. In the previous chapter, P was used for present value and F for future value. In general we do not depart from this practice. However, the tradition within the annuity literature is that A, rather than P, stands for the present value (of an annuity) and S, rather than F, is used to represent the sum or future value of an annuity. Also, the rate of interest per annuity period will be referred to as i. This is the annual rate, r, divided by the number of annuity periods per year. Given that an annuity period need not be one year, we use n to refer to the number of annuity periods, rather than t, which refers to time in years.

Using specific notation for annuities has the practical benefit of distinguishing between the present and future values (P and F) of a given amount and the present and future values (A and S) of a series of payments.

The discussion in this chapter attempts to provide an understanding of the mathematics of annuities. Consequently the equations and formulae presented in this chapter (and elsewhere in the book) are designed to be solved by applying the rules of mathematics. This process is achieved most efficiently with a standard scientific calculator and thus we assume that the reader is competent in the use of one of these standard calculators.

We make this point because there are many financial calculators on the market that allow their user to make financial calculations by first selecting the type of calculation and then entering the data (such as the annual interest rate, the number of payments per annum and the amount of the regular payment). These calculators are popular because they generate answers very quickly. But they are effective only when the user is competent in their operation (and this involves a careful study of their operating manual and practice in their use) and understands the mathematics that has been programmed in the financial calculator.

ORDINARY ANNUITIES

An ordinary annuity is a series of regular periodic payments that are made at the end of each annuity period. An important example of an ordinary annuity is the interest (i.e. coupon) payments on a bond.

Future value

The future value of an annuity is the sum of the regular payments and the interest accrued on a compound basis. It is calculated as at the end of the term of the annuity and is sometimes referred to as the annuity's terminal value. To illustrate the calculation of an ordinary annuity's future value we will use a four-year annuity of $1 (i.e. the payments are made at the end of each of the four years). These payments are shown along a line, called a time line, in figure 5.1.

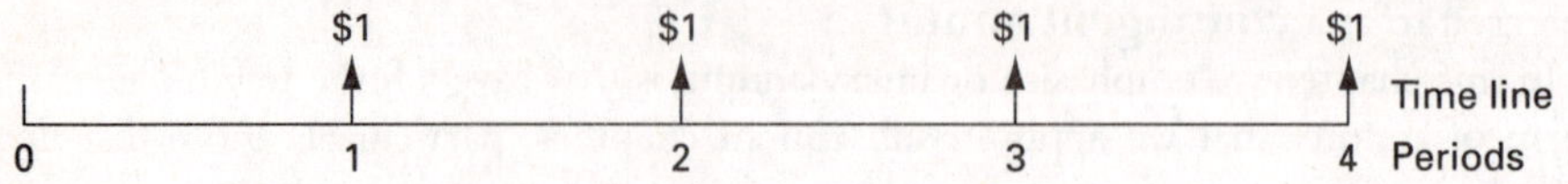

Figure 5.1 Ordinary annuity: time line

The future value of an annuity is the sum of the future value of each of an annuity's payments as at the end of the annuity. Its future value could be calculated by summing the future value for each of the annuity payments. Thus the future value of the $1 annuity depicted in figure 5.1 could be calculated as the sum of the following amounts:

$$\text{first dollar} = (1 + i)^3$$

$$\text{second dollar} = (1 + i)^2$$

$$\text{third dollar} = (1 + i)$$

$$\text{fourth dollar} = 1$$

Note that the first payment is compounded forward by three periods because, in the case of ordinary annuities, the payment is made at the end of each period (only three periods will elapse after the first payment is made). Similarly, the payment made at the end of the second period is compounded forward by only two periods, and as the third payment is made one period before the annuity period ends, no compounding is involved. Finally, in this example, the fourth payment is made when the annuity terminates and so it is also a future value.

Given the rate of interest that applies over the annuity period, this annuity's future value can be calculated as the sum of the four future values. To calculate the future value of an ordinary annuity in this way would be a very tiresome process, especially where the annuity comprises many payments. As shown below, a future-value annuity factor can be used to calculate the future value of an annuity irrespective of the number of payments.

The formula for the future-value annuity factor for an ordinary annuity (of $1, by definition), is derived in the boxed discussion opposite. In the formula, n refers to the number of annuity periods and i refers to the interest rate per annuity period.

DERIVATION OF THE FORMULA FOR THE FUTURE-VALUE FACTOR OF AN ORDINARY ANNUITY

The formula for the future-value factor is derived below from an annuity of $1 with an unspecified term. Note that n refers to the number of annuity periods (four in this case) and S represents the future value amount:

$$S = (1 + i)^{n-1} + (1 + i)^{n-2} + \ldots + (1 + i) + 1$$

Multiplying both sides by (1 + i):

$$S(1 + i) = (1 + i)^{n} + (1 + i)^{n-1} + \ldots + (1 + i)^{2} + (1 + i)$$

Subtracting the first equation from the second gives:

$$S(1 + i) - S = (1 + i)^{n} - 1$$

Hence:

$$iS = (1 + i)^{n} - 1$$

or

$$S = \frac{(1 + i)^{n} - 1}{i}$$

Given that the regular payment is $1, this equation is the formula for the future-value factor per one dollar of the regular payment. Hence, the general formula for the future amount is:

$$S = R\left[\frac{(1 + i)^{n} - 1}{i}\right]$$

In other words, the term inside the brackets is the formula for the future-value factor.

In the following formula for the future-value amount, S, the regular payment, is represented by R and $s_{\overline{n}|i}$ stands for the future-value factor for an ordinary annuity of one dollar per period:

$$S = Rs_{\overline{n}|i} \qquad \textit{Equation (5.1)}$$

where, $$s_{\overline{n}|i} = \frac{(1 + i)^{n} - 1}{i} \qquad \textit{Equation (5.2)}$$

(Note that the symbol ⌉ is used when designating an annuity factor. It is referred to as an angle.)

The sum of an ordinary annuity of a $1-per-period paid at the end of each of the next four periods, on the assumption that interest rates will remain at 12% per period, amounts to:

$$s_{\overline{n}|i} = s_{\overline{4}|0.12}$$

$$= \frac{(1 + 0.12)^4 - 1}{0.12}$$

$$= 4.7793$$

$$\approx \$4.78$$

Note that annuity factors should be calculated to six decimal places to avoid rounding errors. We show them correct to four decimal places for the sake of brevity.

We can confirm that the future-value annuity factor has correctly calculated the future value of the annuity, given an interest rate of 12% per period, as follows:

$$F_{\text{first dollar}} = (1.12)^3 = 1.4049$$

$$F_{\text{second dollar}} = (1.12)^2 = 1.2544$$

$$F_{\text{third dollar}} = 1.12 = 1.1200$$

$$F_{\text{fourth dollar}} = 1.00 = 1.0000$$

$$S = 4.7793$$

The value of $s_{\overline{n}|i}$ depends on the number of payments and the rate of interest. The future-value factor must exceed the number of payments because it incorporates interest on the payments (hence the factor exceeds four). Obviously, future-value factors increase in size as the number of payments increase, other things being equal. To illustrate, the future-value factor for a 10-period annuity that has the same interest rate is:

$$s_{\overline{10}|0.12} = \frac{(1 + 0.12)^{10} - 1}{0.12}$$

$$= 17.5487$$

Observe that the factor exceeds the number of payments by a greater amount than in the case of the four-period annuity, where the factor is not much more than the number of payments. This reflects the greater influence of compound interest as a component of the annuity factor, compared with its influence on the value of annuities with fewer periods.

Given that interest is part of the future-value factor, it follows that the factor's value will be larger when the rate of interest rate is higher (and vice versa), other things being equal. For example, if the interest rate was only 10%, the value of $s_{\overline{4}|i}$ would be less than \$4.78; that is:

$$s_{\overline{4}|0.1} = \frac{(1 + 0.10)^4 - 1}{0.10}$$

$$= \$4.64$$

Now consider an example where the annuity payment is not \$1. Suppose you are the recipient of a three-year scholarship which pays \$1000 per month. Its future value is, given an interest rate of 12% per annum or 1% per month:

$$S = Rs_{\overline{n}|i}$$

$$= 1000\ s_{\overline{36}|0.01}$$

$$= 1000\left[\frac{(1.01)^{36} - 1}{0.01}\right]$$

$$= 1000\ (43.0769)$$

$$= \$43\ 077$$

Observe that the annuity factor (43.0769) exceeds the number of payments (36), but not by much. The interest component is not particularly large because of the low rate (1% per period).

Present value

You will recall (from the previous chapter) that the present value of a future payment is arrived at by discounting it for its interest component. Hence, the present value of an ordinary annuity can be calculated by discounting each payment by the rate of interest and summing these present values. This long-hand approach is not time efficient, particularly when the annuity has many payments. The approach we follow is to use present-value annuity factors. These factors show the present value of an annuity of \$1 according to the number of payments and the rate of interest.

DERIVATION OF THE PRESENT-VALUE FACTOR OF AN ORDINARY ANNUITY

The present value of an annuity, A, can be calculated as the annuity's future value, S, discounted as a lump sum:

$$A = \frac{S}{(1 + i)^n}$$

Substituting equation (5.1) for S,

$$A = R\left[\frac{(1 + i)^n - 1}{i}\right]\left[\frac{1}{(1 + i)^n}\right]$$

the expression reduces to:

$$= R\left[\frac{1 - (1 + i)^{-n}}{i}\right]$$

The derivation of the present-value factor for an ordinary annuity of \$1 is explained in the boxed discussion on the previous page. It shows that the present-value amount can be calculated as:

$$A = R\left[\frac{1-(1+i)^{-n}}{i}\right] \qquad \textit{Equation (5.3)}$$

The term inside the large brackets is the present-value factor for an ordinary annuity. It is represented by $a_{\overline{n}|i}$. The term outside the brackets is the regular payment. Thus the present value, A, of an ordinary annuity is shown as:

$$A = Ra_{\overline{n}|i} \qquad \textit{Equation (5.3a)}$$

DIGRESSION ON POWERS OF THE INVERSE

Often we need to discount a future value back to a present value using a compound-interest discount factor.

$$P = \frac{F}{(1+i)^n}$$

The discount factor, $1/(1+i)^n$, may be expressed in a variety of ways. These are:

$$\frac{1}{(1+i)^n} = \left(\frac{1}{1+i}\right)^n = (1+i)^{-n}$$

The equality of these is shown using an example n = 10 and i = 0.12, Here:

$$\frac{1}{(1+i)^n} = \frac{1}{1.12^{10}} = 0.3220$$

$$\left(\frac{1}{1+i}\right)^n = \left(\frac{1}{1+0.12}\right)^{10} = 0.3220$$

$$(1+i)^{-n} = 1.12^{-10} = 0.3220$$

Some texts use $v = 1/(1+i)$ to express the discount factor as v^n. In this text we usually express the discount factor as $1/(1+i)^n$ or $(1+i)^{-n}$.

The Y^x button should be used to calculate the discount factor $(1+i)^{-n}$.

To calculate $(1+0.12)^{-10}$, enter 1.12, press Y^x, enter 10, press the equals button and then press the inverse button.

The size of present-value annuity factors depends on the number of payments. The larger the number, the larger is the present-value factor, other things being equal. For example, the present-value factor for a ten-period annuity, given an interest rate of 12% is:

$$a_{\overline{10}|0.12} = \frac{1-(1+0.12)^{-10}}{0.12} = 5.6502$$

whereas the present-value factor for a four-period annuity (at 12%) is 3.0373. This results because discounting of the future payments erodes the value of the future payments to a greater extent, the longer the annuity's term.

The size of the present-value factor depends also on the rate of interest. In contrast to the future-value factor, a higher interest rate results in a smaller present-value factor (and vice versa for a lower interest rate), because it is used to discount (rather than compound) the future payments. Consider, for example, the four-period annuity with the lower interest rate of 10%. Its present-value factor is:

$$a_{\overline{4}|0.10} = \frac{1 - (1.10)^{-4}}{0.10} = 3.1699$$

Notice that the present-value factor is larger with an interest rate of 10% (roundly 3.17) than with an interest rate of 12% (roundly 3.04).

We will refer again to the three-year scholarship to illustrate the use of a present-value annuity factor where the regular payment is more than \$1. The scholarship payment is \$1000 per month for 36 months and the interest rate is 1% per month. The present value of this annuity is:

$$\begin{aligned} A &= 1000\, a_{\overline{36}|0.01} \\ &= 1000\left(\frac{1 - (1.01)^{-36}}{0.01}\right) \\ &= 1000 * 30.1075 \\ &= \$30\ 108 \end{aligned}$$

We can check this answer by calculating the future value of \$30 108 as follows:

$$\begin{aligned} S &= 30\ 108 * (1.01)^{36} \\ &= \$43\ 077 \end{aligned}$$

Recall that we directly calculated the future value of this annuity (\$43 077) in the previous section.

The present value of a financial asset is most useful when it is marketable, because this represents its market value (i.e. price). You will remember our discussion of the present value of a bill in the previous chapter. Its price is the bill's present value. While you cannot sell your scholarship, you may be interested in calculating its present value. For instance, suppose the terms of your scholarship allowed you the choice of a lump sum of \$36 000, or \$1000 at the end of each month over the three years. The monthly scholarship, given an interest rate of 1% per month, was valued above at \$30 108. Thus, it is less valuable than the lump sum of \$36 000.

The use of annuity factors to calculate present and future amounts is illustrated in example 5.1.

example 5.1

Suppose you resolve to invest $1000 at the end of this and the next four years to provide yourself with some capital. Assuming that you can invest your funds at 15% p.a. compounded annually:

(a) how much capital will you have at the end of five years, and
(b) how much would you have to invest in one lump sum now to build up this capital in five years?

Solution:

(a) The future value can be calculated as:

$$S = Rs_{\overline{n}|i}$$
$$= 1000\, s_{\overline{5}|0.15}$$
$$= 1000\left[\frac{(1.15)^5 - 1}{0.15}\right]$$
$$= 1000 * 6.7424$$
$$= \$6742$$

(b) The present value may be calculated by a direct discount of the future value:

$$A = S\frac{1}{(1+i)^n}$$
$$= 6\,742.38 * \frac{1}{(1.15)^5}$$
$$= \$3352$$

or calculated directly from equation (5.3):

$$A = Ra_{\overline{n}|i}$$
$$= \frac{1000\ 1 - 1.15^{-5}}{0.15}$$
$$= 1000 * 3.3522$$
$$= \$3352$$

Finding the amount of the regular payment

The regular payment can be calculated by simply rearranging equation (5.1). For example, suppose you wish to accumulate $7500 in five years given an interest rate of 15% p.a., compounded annually. What you need to know is how much you should invest at the end of each year to reach this target sum. As,

$$S = Rs_{\overline{n}|i}$$

$$R = S/s_{\overline{n}|i}$$

$$= \frac{7500}{\dfrac{(1.15)^5 - 1}{0.25}}$$

$$= \frac{7500}{6.7424}$$

$$= \$1112.37$$

The calculation of the regular payment is further illustrated in example 5.2.

example 5.2

Suppose you worked for several years before commencing your studies in order to save $15 000 to meet your living costs whilst undertaking your three-year degree course. If you can invest your funds at 12% p.a., on a monthly compound basis (i.e. 1% per month), how much can you withdraw at the end of each month without exhausting your funds until you have finished your studies?

$$R = 15\,000/a_{\overline{36}|0.01}$$

$$= 15\,000 / \left[\frac{1 - (1 + 0.01)^{-36}}{0.01}\right]$$

$$= \frac{15\,000}{30.1075}$$

$$= \$498.21$$

Accordingly, you can spend almost $500 per month without prematurely exhausting your funds whilst undertaking your degree (provided the interest rate on your investment is fixed at 12% p.a.).

CALCULATING A BOND'S PRICE

In Chapter 3 we described a bond as a long-term instrument that makes regular interest (known as coupon) payments. In the case of a fixed-interest bond these regular payments are fixed for the life of the bond. In the Australian bond market, these coupon payments are made semi-annually at half the annual coupon rate.

It is usually convenient to calculate the price of bonds per $100 of face value. Using this approach, a three-year 12.00% bond makes six coupon payments of $6 at six-monthly intervals, aligned to the bond's maturity date and a redemption payment of $100 (i.e. its face value paid at maturity). These payments are shown in figure 5.2.

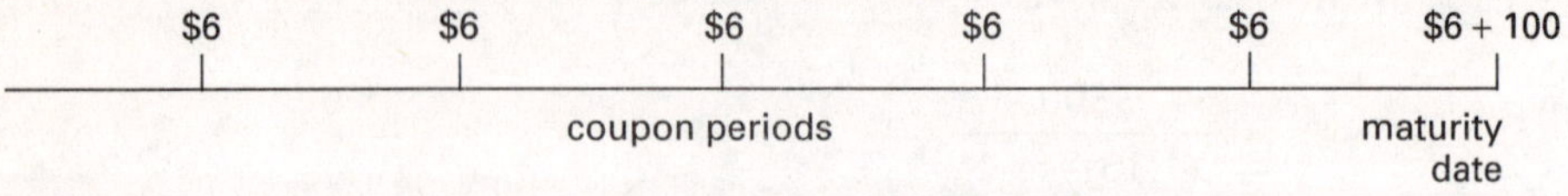

Figure 5.2 The remaining payments on a three-year 12% bond

A bond's price is the sum of the present value of its remaining payments. In the case of the three-year bond represented in figure 5.2, this amount could be calculated by discounting each of the remaining six payments and summing these amounts. Observe, though, in figure 5.2, that the bond's coupon payments take the form of an ordinary annuity. Hence, the present value of these payments can be calculated with the present value annuity factor. The bond's price is that amount plus the present value of the redemption payment ($100). Hence the bond's price can be calculated as the sum of two amounts:

$$P = C\,(a_{\overline{n}|r/2}) + F/(1 + r/2)^n \qquad \textit{Equation (5.4)}$$

$$= C\left[\frac{1 - (1 + r/2)^{-n}}{r/2}\right] + \frac{100}{(1 + r/2)^n}$$

where r is the annual yield at which the bond is purchased, and
n is the number of remaining complete coupon periods.

Observe that the coupon amount (C) and the redemption payment (F) are fixed. Hence the bond's price depends on the purchase yield (i.e. r/2) and the number of complete coupon periods. Suppose this three-year bond (i.e. n = 6) is purchased at a yield of 9.20%, its price would be, using equation (5.4):

$$P = 6\left(\frac{1 - (1.046)^{-6}}{0.046}\right) + \frac{100}{(1.046)^6}$$

$$= 6\,(5.141272) + 76.350150$$

$$= \$107.197782$$

Observe that time in equation (5.4) is in coupon periods, hence the annual yield, 9.20%, is divided by two and entered as a decimal (0.046). Bond pricing is examined in detail in Chapter 11. In this chapter we have shown how the annuity factor can be used to reduce the calculation to just two elements, irrespective of the number of remaining coupons. The calculation of bond prices is further illustrated in example 5.3.

example 5.3

Suppose you purchased a ten-year 8.00% bond at a yield of 9.50% p.a. and sold it two years later at a yield of 8.80%. Calculate the purchase and sale prices.

$$
\begin{aligned}
P_{buy} &= 4\left(\frac{1-(1.0475)^{-20}}{0.0475}\right) + \frac{100}{(1.0475)^{20}} \\
&= 50.922676 + 39.529322 \\
&= \$90.451998 \\
P_{sell} &= 4\left(\frac{1-(1.044)^{-16}}{0.044}\right) + \frac{100}{(1.044)^{16}} \\
&= 45.263447 + 50.210208 \\
&= \$95.473655
\end{aligned}
$$

Reducible loans

An interest-only loan requires the borrower to make interest payments over the term of the loan and to repay the amount borrowed (i.e. the principal) at the end of the loan's term. In the case of reducible loans, principal repayments are made concurrently with the payment of interest. They are referred to as 'reducible' loans because the repayments reduce the amount owing on the loan.

An intriguing feature of reducible loans is that they require the borrower to make a 'regular' payment, typically monthly. The regular payment satisfies both the interest due since the previous payment and a principal repayment that contributes to the loan's repayment by the end of its term.

Typically, at the start of the loan repayment the interest component is almost equal to the regular payment. This component gradually diminishes over time because the repayments of principal reduce the amount owing and this reduces the interest due each month. The principal repayments are initially small because most of the regular payment is required to cover the interest due, but as the interest component falls, a larger part of the regular payment becomes available for principal repayment.

Housing loans are typically structured as reducible loans. The payments are usually made monthly over a long term, such as 25 years, and if the interest rate does not change, the regular monthly payment will be unchanged over the term of the loan. Most housing loans are mortgages, because the loan is secured by the property that it finances. If the borrower defaults, the lender can sell the property to recover the amount due.

Even though innovations in housing finance have increased the variety of repayment conditions (such as fortnightly payments and capped interest rates), the principles explained below apply also to these types of loans.

An insight into the nature of a reducible loan can be gained from a consideration of the exchange between the borrower and the lender at the beginning of a loan. The borrower, by promising regular payments, is selling an annuity to the lender. The amount that a rational lender will pay for this annuity is the present value of the annuity. In other words, the present value of a loan's outstanding payments equals the principal amount due.

The task of determining the size of the periodic repayments comes down to solving equation (5.3a):

$$A = Ra_{\overline{n}|i}$$

where A is the principal of the loan.

The regular payment is found by simply rearranging this equation, as follows:

$$R = A/a_{\overline{n}|i}$$

Assuming the interest rate does not change, the borrower will repay the amount borrowed and meet the interest due by making the regular payment on the required dates over the term of the loan. We illustrate, step-by-step, the method of preparing a loan repayment schedule with a simple example. Suppose you borrowed $1000 on the basis of a reducible loan with monthly payments over a term of six months at a fixed interest rate of 18% p.a. or 1.5% per month.

Step 1: Calculate your monthly 'regular' payment:

$$R = 1000/a_{\overline{6}|0.015}$$

$$= 1000/\left[\frac{1 - (1 + 0.015)^{-6}}{0.015}\right]$$

$$= \frac{1000}{5.697187}$$

$$= \$175.53$$

Step 2: Calculate the amount of interest due at the end of the first month:

$$I = P * rt$$

$$I_1 = 1000 * 0.18/12$$

$$= \$15.00$$

Step 3: Calculate the loan repayment (LR) component (for the first month) of the regular payment:

$$LR_1 = R - I_1$$

$$= 175.53 - 15.00$$

$$= \$160.53$$

Step 4: Calculate the amount of loan outstanding at the end of the first month:

$$A = A - LR$$

$$= 1000 - 160.53$$

$$= \$839.47$$

This process is repeated for each of the six months of the loan. The resulting loan repayment schedule is presented in table 5.1.

Table 5.1 Loan repayment schedule — six-month loan

Period	*Balance at beginning of period*	*Regular payment*	*Interest component*	*Capital component*	*Balance at end of period*
1	1 000.00	175.53	15.00	160.53	839.47
2	839.47	175.53	12.59	162.93	676.54
3	676.54	175.53	10.15	165.38	511.16
4	511.16	175.53	7.67	167.86	343.31
5	343.31	175.53	5.15	170.38	172.93
6	172.93	175.53	2.59	172.93	0.00

A more typical loan repayment schedule is presented in table 5.2. It shows the first five and the last five monthly payments over the course of a $100 000 25-year loan that has an interest rate of 13.5% pa.

The amount of the regular payment is:

$$R = 100\,000/a_{\overline{300}|0.135/12}$$

$$= 100\,000 \;/ \left(\frac{1 - (1 + 0.135/12)^{-300}}{0.135/12}\right)$$

$$= \frac{100\,000}{85.789421}$$

$$= \$1165.64$$

The pay-out figure on a reducible loan

During the course of a loan the borrower may choose to pay out the amount due. Thus it is useful to be able to calculate the amount outstanding. You will recall that the amount of the loan is equivalent to the present value of the annuity represented by the series of regular payments. This implies that the amount outstanding is equal to the present value of the remaining payments at any time during the loan's term. For example, suppose two payments have been made on the loan shown in table 5.1. The outstanding balance is given by A_2 as there are four months remaining:

$$A_2 = Ra_{\overline{4|}0.15}$$

$$= 175.53 * 3.854385$$

$$= \$676.54$$

You can see from table 5.1 that this is the amount outstanding at the end of two years.

Table 5.2 Loan repayment schedule — initial five and last five payments

Period	*Balance at beginning of period*	*Regular payment*	*Interest component*	*Capital component*	*Balance at end of period*
1	100 000.00	1 165.64	1 125.00	40.64	99 959.36
2	99 959.36	1 165.64	1 124.54	41.10	99 918.25
3	99 918.25	1 165.64	1 124.08	41.56	99 876.69
4	99 876.69	1 165.64	1 123.61	42.03	99 834.66
5	99 834.66	1 165.64	1 123.14	42.50	99 792.15
6	99 792.15	1 165.64	1 122.66	42.98	99 749.17
—	—	—	—	—	—
295	6 726.54	1 165.64	75.67	1 089.97	5 636.57
296	5 636.57	1 165.64	63.41	1 102.23	4 534.34
297	4 534.34	1 165.64	51.01	1 114.63	3 419.70
298	3 419.70	1 165.64	38.47	1 127.17	2 292.53
299	2 292.53	1 165.64	25.79	1 139.85	1 152.68
300	1 152.68	1 165.64	12.97	1 152.68	0.00

Note that in the case of the six-month loan, the bulk of the regular payment goes to pay off the loan. However, the 25-year loan referred to in table 5.2 provides a more typical illustration of a reducible loan schedule. After five years of making the regular payment, the amount of the loan still outstanding is:

$$A_{20yrs} = R(a_{\overline{240|}0.135/12})$$

$$= 1165.64 * 82.824331$$

$$= \$96\ 543.35$$

In this case, after making 60 payments of \$1165.64 (which equals \$69 938.40 in total) the borrower still owes \$96 543.35. In other words, only \$3456.65 of the total amount paid over the first five years (\$69 938.40) went toward paying off the loan. The balance was interest paid. Another illustration of calculating the amount due during the repayment period is presented in example 5.4.

example 5.4

Suppose you work for a financial institution that specialises in home loans. A customer who took out a 20-year \$60 000 housing loan four years ago at a fixed rate of 12% p.a. compounded monthly wants to know the loan's outstanding balance.

The customer's monthly payment is:

$$R = 60\,000/a_{\overline{240}|0.01}$$

$$= 60\,000/\left[\frac{1-(1+0.01)^{-240}}{0.01}\right]$$

$$= \frac{60\,000}{90.819416}$$

$$= \$660.65$$

As 48 payments have been made by the customer, 192 further payments are required to fully repay the loan. Using equation (5.3) the amount outstanding is:

$$A_{192} = 660.65\,(a_{\overline{192}|0.01})$$

$$= 660.65 * 85.1988$$

$$= \$56\,287$$

Thus you advise the customer that \$56 287 is the amount outstanding; but you may need courage to advise your customer that of the \$31 711 paid so far (\$660.65 times 48) only \$3713 (\$60 000 less \$56 287) has gone towards repaying the loan. In other words, \$27 998 of the \$31 711 paid so far is interest income to the institution.

Changes in the interest rate

In Australia, most housing loans are made on the basis of a variable interest rate. That is, the loan is made at the lender's current interest rate. Usually lenders change their rate on housing loans periodically in line with the movements in interest rates generally. When a change occurs, the new rate will apply to the outstanding amount of the loan.

Each time the interest rate changes the loan repayment schedule has to be reset. If the term of the loan is not varied, the new interest rate will involve a new repayment amount. By contrast, if the amount of the repayment is not varied the term of the loan must change if the value of the annuity is to be preserved. However, when the interest rate increases it is possible that the regular payment is not sufficient to cover the interest due. In this event, the only way to avoid the amount outstanding from increasing is to increase the amount of the repayment.

We will consider first a change in the monthly payment. For example, suppose after five years of the 25-year $100 000 loan, the rate of interest increases from 13.50% to 14.50% p.a. The amount outstanding at that point was calculated above to be $96 543.35.

The new payments are derived by applying the new interest rate to this balance, as follows:

$$R_{new} = 96\,543.53/a_{\overline{240}|0.145/12}$$

$$= \frac{96\,543.53}{78.125136}$$

$$= \$1235.76$$

Thus the increase in the interest rate from 13.50% to 14.50% increased the regular payment by $70.12 (from $1165.64 to $1235.76).

Changes in the term of a loan

Increasing the term of a loan is an alternative to increasing the monthly repayment in response to an increase in the rate of interest. Providing that the existing regular payment will cover the new interest obligation, the borrower can continue with that payment by extending the loan's term. The new term can be found by first rearranging equation (5.1). Given that:

$$A = R\left[\frac{(1+i)^n - 1}{i}\right]$$

$$n = -\frac{\ln[1 - (Ai/R)]}{\ln(1+i)}$$

We will continue to use the 25-year loan as an illustration and assume that after ten years the interest rate increases from 13.50% to 14.50% p.a. Recall that the regular payment was $1165.64. Using the old interest rate, the outstanding balance after ten years is:

$$A_{15yrs} = 1165.64\,(a_{\overline{180}|0.135/12})$$

$$= \$89\,781$$

Continuing with the regular payment at the higher interest rate results in the remaining term being increased to:

$$n = \frac{\ln(1 - 89\,781 * (0.145/12)/1165.64}{\ln(1 + 0.145/12)}$$

$$= 222.23 \text{ months}$$

It is necessary to extend the term of the loan by some 42 periods, from 180 to 222 months (the last payment will be slightly bigger to adjust for the extra 0.23 months), if the existing repayments are to continue under the higher rate of interest.

PERPETUITIES

So far we have dealt with annuities that have a finite term. That is, at some point in time the payments stop. However, there are financial instruments with an infinite life. A perpetuity is such an instrument.

A **perpetuity** is an annuity that continues indefinitely. For instance, the British Government has in the past issued bonds called **consols** which have no maturity date and promise to make the regular interest payments forever. In general, equity instruments are perpetuities, assuming the company is not established with a finite life in mind.

While all forms of annuities could take the form of a perpetuity, we will consider only ordinary simple annuities. This means the regular payment commences at the end of the initial period and continues indefinitely, with interest being capitalised at the end of each period.

As a perpetuity is a never-ending series of payments it has no finite future (or terminal) value. It will, however, have a present value, which is the present value of an annuity when the number of periods is infinite.

From an inspection of equation (5.3) it can be seen that the term $(1+i)^{-n}$ tends to zero when n tends to infinity.

$$A = R\left[\frac{1 - (1 + i)^{-n}}{i}\right]$$

Thus for a perpetuity:

$$A = \frac{R}{i} \qquad \textit{Equation (5.5)}$$

We can use equation (5.5) to value perpetuities. For example, what is the value, per \$100 of face value, of a 2.50% p.a. consol if interest rates are 12.00% p.a.? Here the consol provides \$2.50 per year forever and thus, the value of this income stream is given by:

$$A = \frac{2.50}{0.12}$$

$$= \$20.83$$

An illustration of the calculation of the present value of a perpetuity is presented in example 5.5.

Annuities may be designed with constantly growing payment amounts. For example, an annuity may have payments that grow at, say, 2% per period. Obviously a growth annuity will always be worth more than an annuity with the payment remaining constant. Growth annuities are discussed as part of the general annuity material in Appendix 5.1.

example 5.5

Suppose BHP plans to issue preference shares on which it undertakes to pay a dividend of $0.50 per share in perpetuity. If the interest rate is 12% p.a., what will be the issue price of these shares?

$$A = \frac{0.50}{0.12}$$

$$= \$4.17$$

Suppose after several years the rate of interest falls to 10% p.a., will this alter the value of these shares? Yes, to:

$$A = \frac{0.50}{0.10}$$

$$= \$5.00$$

This also illustrates the inverse relationship that holds between the interest rate and the present value of any income stream including perpetuities.

A constantly increasing annuity also has a value as a perpetuity, provided that the rate of increase of the payments is less than the discount rate. Its present value can be calculated using equation (5.6), provided the interest rate, i, exceeds the growth rate, g:

$$A = \frac{R}{i - g} \qquad \textit{Equation (5.6)}$$

Example 5.6 shows the calculation of the present value of a constantly growing perpetuity.

OTHER ANNUITY FORMS

Because of the importance of ordinary annuities to the material covered in this book we have concentrated on this annuity form. A brief discussion of other annuity forms follows. We start with annuities due.

example 5.6

Suppose BHP has just paid its final dividend of $0.40 per share. Additionally, suppose it is expected that each dividend (the company pays two dividends a year, an interim and final) in the future is expected to be 3% higher than the previous one. If the interest rate is 13% p.a., (i.e. 6.5% per period) the price (being the present value) of BHP's shares should be approximately:

$$A = \frac{0.40}{0.065 - 0.03}$$

$$= \$11.43$$

If the dividend is expected to remain constant the price of BHP's shares ought to be:

$$A = \frac{0.40}{0.065}$$

$$= \$6.15$$

As one would expect, the price of a company's share would be higher when the dividend is expected to grow over time than if no growth was expected.

Annuities due

An annuity due is almost the same as an ordinary annuity. The only difference is that the regular payments occur at the commencement of each annuity period. The premiums due on insurance policies are an example of an annuity due; they are paid at the commencement of each period.

An annuity due extending over four periods is illustrated in figure 5.3. Observe that because the initial payment is made when the annuity period commences, it will earn compound interest for four periods. None of the payments in an equivalent ordinary annuity will have the future value of this payment. The second, third and fourth payments in an annuity due have the same future values as the first, second and third payments in an ordinary annuity. The fourth and final payment in the ordinary annuity earns no interest.

The future value of the annuity due will exceed that of the equivalent ordinary annuity (when each commences at the same moment in time) because each of its payments is compounded by an additional period. Consequently, the future value of an annuity due can be found by multiplying the future value of an equivalent ordinary annuity by 1 + i. Thus:

$$S_{due} = R\,(s_{\overline{n|}\,i})\,(1 + i) \qquad \textit{Equation (5.7)}$$

Refer again to figure 5.3 and you will see that when arriving at the present value of the annuity due, only three of the payments require discounting, because the first payment is a present value. As shown in figure 5.1, each of the four payments in the

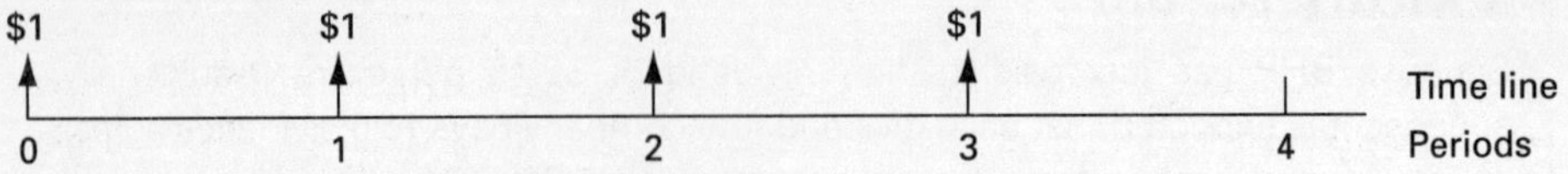

Figure 5.3 Annuity due — time line (a)

ordinary annuity must be discounted to arrive at its present value. This implies that the present value of an annuity due will exceed that of an equivalent ordinary annuity. If each of the payments in the ordinary annuity was multiplied by 1 + i, their combined present value would equal that of the equivalent annuity due that started at the same moment in time. Hence:

$$A_{due} = R\,(a_{\overline{n|}\,i})\,(1 + i) \qquad \textit{Equation (5.8)}$$

For example, suppose you decide to invest in a five-year endowment policy with a monthly premium of $100, the first being due now, on which the insurance company guarantees a net return of 1% per month. The terminal value of this 60-period policy (i.e. the amount you will receive after the five-year term) will equal:

$$S_{due} = 100\,(s_{5 * \overline{12|}\;0.01})\,(1 + 0.01)$$

$$= 100\left[\frac{(1.01)^{60} - 1}{0.01}\right] * 1.01$$

$$= 100 * 81.6697 * 1.01$$

$$= \$8249$$

The present value of this annuity due can be calculated with equation (5.8) and by discounting its sum, S, back n periods:

$$A_{due} = 100\left[\frac{1 - (1 + 0.01)^{60}}{0.01}\right] 1.01$$

$$= 100 * 44.955038 * 1.01$$

$$= \$4540$$

and:

$$A_{due} = \frac{S_{due}}{(1 + i)^n}$$

$$= \frac{8249}{(1.01)^{60}}$$

$$= \frac{8249}{1.816697}$$

$$= \$4540$$

Deferred annuities

The premiums paid into pension and superannuation schemes are examples of annuities due. Payments from pension and superannuation funds are examples of **deferred annuities** because these payments commence when the contributor reaches a specified age. A deferred annuity commences at a future date. The commencing date of an annuity is not necessarily the date of the first payment. It is for due annuities, but not for ordinary annuities because in their case the first payment occurs at the end of the annuity's first period.

A deferred ordinary annuity is illustrated in figure 5.4. It shows an annuity that commences after two periods have elapsed; that is, the regular payment commences at the end of the third period and has a term of four periods. We designate the number of deferred periods as k periods and, as usual, the term of the annuity is n periods. Thus, in figure 5.4, the deferred period, k, is two periods even though the first payment occurs at the end of the third period.

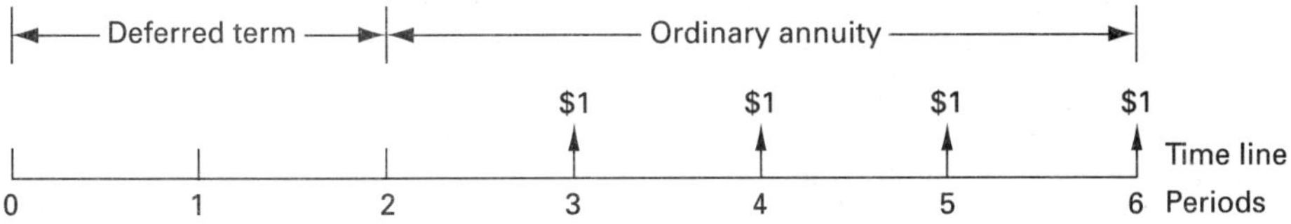

Figure 5.4 Annuity due — time line (b)

We can calculate the present value of a deferred annuity in several ways. Perhaps the simplest method is to calculate its value as though it was a conventional ordinary annuity and then discount this value over k periods. This produces

$$A = \frac{Ra_{\overline{n}|\,i}}{(1+i)^k} \qquad \textit{Equation (5.9)}$$

Pension and superannuation schemes

Suppose an insurance company is offering to assist parents with their children's future education expenses. The details are that a purchaser of this scheme will be provided with \$5000 on the nineteenth, twentieth and twenty-first birthdays of their child. If an insurance company offered the parents 10% p.a. on a single premium payment, how much will it cost the parents if their child is one year old? You should recognise that if the payments are treated as an ordinary annuity, the annuity commences on the child's eighteenth birthday. Thus the premium when the child is a year old is the present value of a three-year annuity deferred 17 years, thus:

$$A = 5000\left(\frac{a_{\overline{3}|\,0.10}}{(1.10)^{17}}\right)$$

$$= 5000\left(\frac{2.4869}{5.0545}\right)$$

$$= \$2460.05$$

Usually the benefits paid under a pension or superannuation scheme are for the whole of life; that is, the beneficiary receives a regular payment until he or she falls out of the tree of life. Our discussion does not extend to these policies nor to contingent annuities that terminate at death, which underpin them.

Summary

- An annuity is a series of regular periodic payments.
- In the case of an ordinary annuity, the regular payments occur at the end of each period.
- Future- and present-value annuity factors can be used to expedite the calculation of variables such as the future and present value of an annuity.
- An annuity's present value varies inversely with the level of interest rates, whereas its future value varies directly with the movement in interest rates.
- Arithmetically, an annuity comprises a regular payment, interest, its term and value (present and future). Knowing all but one of these amounts will enable the unknown one to be calculated.
- The price of a fixed-interest bond can be calculated as the sum of present-value amounts using the appropriate annuity factor for the coupons.
- The regular payments on a reducible loan, such as a mortgage, form an annuity, the present value of which equals the amount of the loan. The regular payment will gradually repay the principal while meeting the interest payments on the amount outstanding.
- A perpetuity is an annuity that continues indefinitely. It can be calculated by dividing the regular payment by the interest rate. The present value of a constantly growing perpetuity can be calculated by deducting the growth rate from the interest rate in the denominator.
- When the regular payment occurs at the commencement of each period, the series is called an annuity due. Its future and present values can be calculated in a similar fashion to the calculation of ordinary annuities.
- A deferred annuity is one in which the regular payments commence in a future period.

Discussion questions and exercises

1 Show on a time line the payments involved in a five-year ordinary annuity.

2 Explain the role of interest in determining the future value of an ordinary annuity.

3 Compare the future value of a three-period ordinary annuity with that of a ten-year annuity, when each has a regular payment of $100 and the interest rate is 8.00% per period.

4 Calculate the future value of an ordinary annuity of $1000 per year that has a term of ten years when the interest rate is 6.00% p.a. and 8.00% p.a. Explain the difference in the values.

5 Prepare a table of future-value annuity factors ($s_{\overline{n}|i}$) with the following interest rates listed as column headings, and the following number of periods shown as a column of line headings. Use your calculator to make these calculations. (You could also prepare a spreadsheet or consult financial tables to check your answers.) Briefly explain the pattern of your answers.

i	=	0.03	0.04	0.05	0.06	0.074
n	=	4	6	8	10	12

6 Prepare a table of present-value annuity factors with the data provided in the previous question. Briefly explain the pattern of your answers and compare them to those for the future-value factors.

7 Suppose you plan to invest $100 at the end of each month for the next five years at a fixed interest rate of 7.50% p.a., compounded monthly. What will be the future amount?

8 Calculate the present value of the sum arrived at in the previous question. Use two methods to check the correctness of your answer.

9 Suppose you wish to implement the plan referred to in the previous two questions, but not make the regular monthly investments over the first year. What sum must you invest at the end of the first year to reestablish the implementation of your plan?

10 Calculate the price (per $100 of face value) of a ten-year 9.00% bond at a purchase yield of 8.60%, and its price three years later when the yield is 9.40%.

11 Suppose you will receive $500 at the end of each of the next 12 months and you plan to invest these amounts at 8.00% p.a., compounded monthly. What will be your future sum, how much was the result of interest earnings and what is the present amount that is equivalent to the future sum?

12 Suppose you are a loans officer with a bank. Upon reviewing, you approve a loan application for $50 000 at 10% p.a., compounded half-yearly. Assuming the client is required to make ten equal payments at six-monthly intervals, prepare a loan repayment schedule for the client.

13 In your job as a loans officer you approve a housing loan application for $50 000, to be repaid in equal monthly instalments over 30 years. Given that the interest rate is currently 10.00% p.a., compounded monthly, what will be:

(a) the monthly payments,

(b) the total amount of interest that will be paid over the term of the loan, and

(c) the amount outstanding after five years?

14 Suppose, in the circumstances of the previous question, that the bank reduces the rate of interest to 9.00% p.a. after three years have elapsed because of a general easing of monetary policy. Calculate the new regular payment, assuming that the borrower decides to maintain the loan's term, and the total amount of interest that will be paid over the 30 years.

15 A client of your bank took out a loan of $30 000 at a fixed interest rate of 12.00% p.a., compounded monthly, over five years with monthly repayments. Having just made the twenty-sixth payment the client decides to pay off the outstanding balance of the loan. Advise the client of the amount to be paid. No interest penalty is involved.

16 Your company decides to issue preference shares that pay a dividend of $3 annually. If the interest rate is 12.00% p.a., estimate what will be the issue price of the shares.

17 Suppose your company's latest (six-monthly) dividend was $2.50 and the company expects its dividend pay-out to increase on average by 2% per year. Given an interest rate of 12.00% p.a., calculate a theoretical price for the company's shares.

18 Which of the following would you prefer to receive (i.e. which has the greatest present value), assuming an interest rate of 6.00% p.a., compounded monthly:
(a) $500 at the end of each month in perpetuity, or
(b) $10 000 immediately.

19 Show on a time line a four-year ordinary annuity that commences four years from now.

20 Suppose your parents decide to retire. They have a lump-sum insurance pay-out of $500 000 which they decide to invest in a 20-year annuity that provides a regular monthly payment. Calculate this payment if the interest rate is 9.00% p.a., compounded monthly.

FURTHER READING

Knox, D. M., *et. al.* 1990, *Mathematics of Finance*, McGraw-Hill, Sydney.

APPENDIX 5.1: A GENERAL DEFERRED-GROWTH ANNUITY

The most general annuity possible is one that can have an arbitrary:

1 number of periods,
2 interest rate,
3 payment growth per period, and
4 number of deferral periods.

The general formula for an n-period annuity of $1 that grows at a rate of g% per period, but deferred for k periods (for an annuity due k = −1), when the per period interest rate is i%, is:

$$a_{n,i,g,k} = \frac{1 - [(1 + g)/(1 + i)]^n}{(i - g)\,(1 + i)^k}$$

For example, what would it cost to purchase a pension of 20 annual payments of $1 million, indexed at 5% p.a., to begin in 35 years, if interest rates are 10% p.a? This is a growth annuity deferred 34 years.

$$a_{20,0.10,0.05,34} = 1\text{m} * \left[\frac{1 - [(1 + 0.05)/(1 + 0.10)]^{20}}{(0.10 - 0.05)\,(1 + 0.10)^{34}}\right]$$

$$= \$474\ 097$$

APPENDIX 5.2: CALCULATING THE INTEREST RATE USING LINEAR INTERPOLATION

If we know the regular payment, the term and either the present or future value, in principle we can find the interest rate. However, because of the non-linear nature of the relationship between changes in the rate of interest and a given annuity factor within the annuity formula, we have to adopt a trial-and-error process to find the rate of interest. That is, we cannot find the interest rate by merely rearranging equations (5.1) or (5.3).

The non-linear relationship between the value of an annuity (shown on the vertical axis) and the rate of interest (shown on the horizontal axis) is illustrated by the upward-sloping curve in figure 5A.1. This curve illustrates one method of locating the interest rate. It is called linear interpolation. The straight line drawn between i_2 and i_1 depicts a linear relationship between two rates of interest that is used to find the rate of interest. The horizontal gap between the curve and the straight line represents the error that arises when this method is used. However, as explained below, the error can be made to be very small.

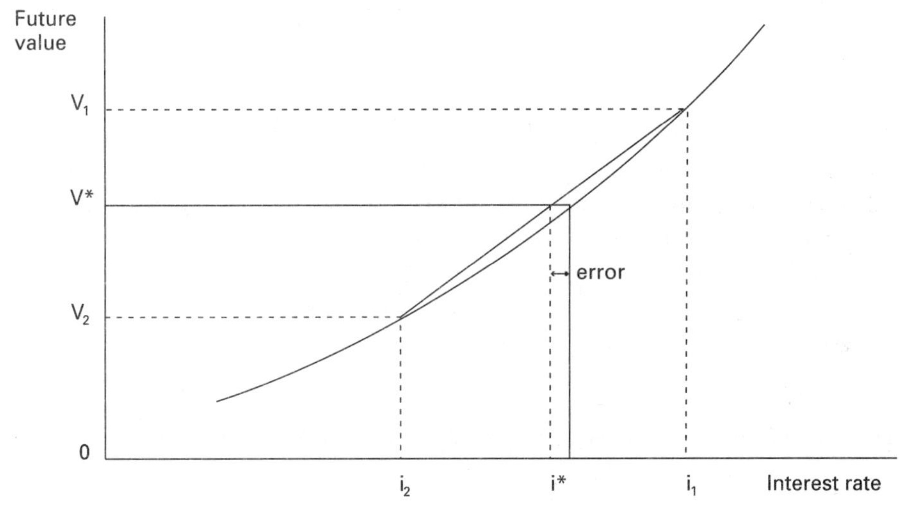

Figure 5A.1 Linear interpolation

The essence of all trial-and-error methods for finding the solution to an equation is to identify successively closer approximations to the true answer. The values for i_2 and i_1 are guesstimates that are intentionally above and below the expected rate of interest. In practice you can make many guesses until you have found two values that are only just above and below the answer, and this will minimise your error.

The value, either present or future, of an annuity can be expressed as a general function of the rate of interest, i:

$$V = f(i)$$

Our task is to find the interest rate, i*, that produces a required value, V*. We have made two guesses, V_1 (which has been calculated using i_1)and V_2 (which has been calculated using i_2). It can be seen from figure 5A.1 that:

$$\frac{V^* - V_1}{i^* - i_1} = \frac{V_2 - V_1}{i_2 - i_1}$$

or

$$i^* = i_1 + \frac{(i_2 - i_1)(V^* - V_1)}{(V_2 - V_1)} \qquad \textit{Equation (5A.1)}$$

Suppose you want to accumulate $200 000 over the next five years and you believe you can invest $2500 a month for this purpose. But as interest will form an important part of your future sum, you want to know the rate that must be earned for you to achieve your investment objective. Thus you wish to solve:

$$2500\ s_{\overline{60}|\,i} = 200\ 000$$

Suppose your first guess is:

$$i_1 = 1\% \rightarrow s_{\overline{60}|\,i} = 81.6697 \rightarrow S_1\ (= V_1) = 204\ 174$$

and your second guess is:

$$i_2 = 0.5\% \rightarrow s_{\overline{60}|\,i} = 69.7700 \rightarrow S_2\ (= V_2) = 174\ 425$$

Thus, the required interest rate is between 0.5% and 1.0% per month. You can use linear interpolation to find the rate.

$$i^* = 0.01 * \left[\frac{(0.005 - 0.01)\ (200\ 000 - 204\ 174)}{(174\ 425 - 204\ 174)}\right]$$

$$= 0.0092985 \text{ per month, or } 11.158\% \text{ p.a.}$$

The extent of the error involved in this approximation is indicated by:

$$\text{error} = 200\ 000 - 2500\ s_{\overline{60}|\,0.00929844}$$

$$= 200\ 000 - 2\ 500 * 79.8536$$

$$= 366$$

This means the rate of interest is larger than 0.00929844 per month; it is 0.009356. The size of the error could be reduced by choosing a larger value for i_2, one that generated a future value that is closer to but still less than 200 000.

Part TWO

Financial institutions

Financial institutions play a major role in the financial system, acting as intermediaries in the provision of payment services, the movement of funds from surplus to deficit units, and provision of risk-management services and products. They also are major participants in financial markets and in the provision of financial market services. The Reserve Bank, as Australia's central bank, plays a key role in the oversight of the managment of banks, which are the system's principal financial institutions.

Part Two comprises four chapters that describe the operations of retail and wholesale banking and fund management and their prudential supervision. Note that these are operational rather than institutional categories of financial institutions.

Chapter 6 explains the services provided by retail banking, which involve mainly payment services and intermediated financing, whereas Chapter 7 explains the activities of wholesale banking, which mainly involve the arrangement of direct financing through financial markets and the provision of risk-management services. Chapter 8 explains the activities of fund managers and their emergence as the main conduit for personal savings to the wholesale markets. Chapter 9 explains the RBA's system of prudential supervision and outlines the role of the other three supervisors. These chapters were written prior to the Wallis Committee's inquiry being finalised.

Chapters 6 to 9 also lay a foundation for the remaining chapters in the book. They provide an understanding of important aspects of the operations of financial markets and instruments and the risks posed by participation in the financial system.

6

Retail banking

The main purpose of this chapter is to describe the major features of retail banking as a sector of the financial system. We discuss the assets and liabilities of retail banking institutions. Most attention is given to banks, but reference is also made to building societies, credit unions and the retail activities of finance companies. The discussion applies the concepts and principles introduced in Chapter 2.

Study objectives

From your study of this chapter you should be able to:

- explain the development of financial institutions in Australia and, in particular, the impact of deregulation on this process;
- describe the main intermediation products provided by retail banking institutions;
- describe the main sources of bank funds and explain the characteristics of bank deposits;
- describe the use of funds by banks and explain the characteristics of bank lending; and
- explain the roles of building societies, credit unions and finance companies in the provision of retail banking products and services.

Even though we discuss retail and wholesale banking in separate chapters, and a number of banks have separate retail and wholesale banking divisions, there is no widely accepted way of dividing between retail and wholesale customers, especially for businesses. Also, a number of financial services and products are provided to both groups of customers.

This chapter presents a reasonably comprehensive picture of Australian banking though its primary focus is on retail banking activities. We therefore avoid some of the problems that arise when attempting to divide precisely between retail and wholesale banking.

Before commencing our discussion of retail banking products and services, we believe it is helpful to explain how Australia's financial institutions developed. The current set of institutions evolved in a round-about way and a knowledge of this history provides an understanding of their character and role in the financial system.

HISTORICAL INTRODUCTION

The history of financial institutions in Australia is related to the history of European settlement. The original British settlers did not bring currency with them and so the initial colony conducted its affairs without a monetary system. Governor Macquarie proposed that a government bank be established, but this was opposed by the British Colonial Office. (This brief historical introduction is based on *A Pocket Full of Change*, Chapter 2.)

The colony's first bank was established in 1817. It was called the Bank of New South Wales and it now operates as the Westpac Banking Corporation. Its focus was the provision of banking services for commerce (i.e. it functioned as a **trading bank**). Several years later the Savings Bank of New South Wales was established to attract small-value savings deposits from individuals. **Savings banks** (at this time) were established (often by a group of 'concerned citizens') to encourage 'frugality' among the 'lower classes'. (In 1989 the regulatory distinction between trading and savings banks was removed.) Other banks were subsequently established in the 1820s and 1830s as the colonies developed.

There was an economic slump in the 1840s and an inquiry was conducted into the role of banks and bank failures in this slump. In 1850 the New South Wales Government adopted Colonial Bank Regulations issued by the British Government. These were essentially prudential guidelines that dealt with the need for a minimum level of bank equity capital, limits on dividend payments, loans to directors, and the publication of half-yearly financial returns.

The development of pastoral lands and the gold discoveries in the 1850s led to the establishment of further banks. By 1888 there were an estimated 88 trading banks and ten savings banks in Australia. Some of these had established a branch network and the largest four banks held about one-third of banking funds.

The 1880s were a boom period when banks lent funds for highly speculative investments. During the subsequent crash in the early 1890s, all but nine banks either failed or closed for lengthy periods before reopening. The predecessors of three of the current major banks survived this crisis; the fourth current major, the Commonwealth Bank, was not established until 1911. These three majors achieved their current form in the early 1980s as a result of a series of bank mergers dating back to the 1890s. In 1991 the Commonwealth Bank was partially privatised and has since been fully privatised.

The 1893 crisis led to calls for the establishment of a central bank to issue notes and oversee the banking system. The Commonwealth Government eventually established the Commonwealth Bank (in 1911), but it was established as a savings bank (also performing trading-bank functions) rather than as a central bank. The government expected the bank to become Australia's principal savings bank. It was given access to post offices as agents and several years after its establishment it took over the Tasmanian and Queensland state savings banks. During the Depression it took over the New South Wales and Western Australian state savings banks.

At the commencement of this century, banks held 74% of financial assets. At the retail level they faced little competition. Building and friendly societies together only held about 3.5% of financial assets. Insurance offices and pension funds held about 12.5% of financial assets and pastoral finance companies held about 7.5% of financial assets, reflecting the agricultural base of the economy at that time. (Lewis and Wallace, 1993, p. 3)

Legislation was introduced in the 1920s to establish a central bank as part of the Commonwealth Bank. Its main functions were the issue of notes and provision of settlement services for the banking system.

The 1930s Depression affected the banking system, but did not result in widespread bank failures (as had occurred in the 1890s). The banks responded to the rise in bad loans by restricting credit. While this insulated them individually from losses, the practice represented a credit squeeze on the economy that probably intensified the recession.

A Royal Commission was held into the monetary and banking system, reporting in 1937. It recommended that the central bank division of the Commonwealth Bank be given wider powers over the conduct of monetary policy and the stability of the financial system. It also proposed that banks be licensed.

The outbreak of World War II overtook events. Many of the Royal Commission's recommendations were implemented, but as National Security Regulations. Banks were required to place funds with the Commonwealth Bank in Special Accounts, and were paid an interest rate that limited their profits to the pre-war level. The Commonwealth Bank was also given power to impose interest-rate ceilings on banks.

One of the country's most controversial pieces of legislation was introduced after the war (in 1945) to provide authority to continue to apply the controls on banks. When the banks successfully challenged part of this legislation in the courts, the then Labor government introduced legislation to nationalise the banks. The banks challenged the legislation in the courts and again won. Following the defeat of the Labor government at the next election, the issue of nationalisation was closed. The incoming government repealed the nationalisation provisions of the *Banking Act*, but not the provisions authorising the central banking powers. The banks accepted this outcome even though it involved the continued imposition of the controls that had been introduced during the war.

In summary, the controls on banks:

- placed a ceiling on the rates of interest they could offer to attract deposits and limited the maturities over which they could pay interest,
- placed a ceiling on the interest rates they could charge on loans,
- required banks to hold a minimum level of particular securities and allowed the central bank to influence their lending policies, and
- governed the number of banks. (De Lucia and Peters, 1993, p. 2)

Interest-rate ceilings restricted the capacity of banks to compete for funds, particularly during the 1970s when market interest rates rose to abnormally high levels. Non-bank financial institutions, such as building societies, were not subject to these controls and so they were able to expand their volume of deposits by offering higher interest rates.

Banks also were not permitted to pay interest on deposits with a term of less than 14 days. **Cash management funds** were established to attract such funds when short-term market rates rose in the late 1970s. Prior to the 1940s trading banks relied heavily on fixed-term deposits (with a term longer than three months). The interest-rate ceiling imposed on these accounts restricted the banks' capacity to attract fixed-term deposits, causing the banks to rely more heavily on current deposits.

The interest-rate ceilings on loans reduced the incentive for banks to lend and created the incentive for them to establish their own NBFIs. During this period banks rationed their loans by lending only to their most credit-worthy customers and by limiting the amount of such loans. The banks referred borrowers who required more funds to their associated NBFI (which was typically a finance company).

Banks were required to place funds in Special Accounts with the Reserve Bank of Australia. This requirement was later replaced by the statutory reserve deposits (SRD) ratio; and this, in turn, was replaced by non-callable deposits. The requirement to place funds with the RBA at uncommercial interest rates is a discriminatory tax that discourages the growth in bank deposits. Banks were also required to hold a minimum specified proportion of their assets in the form of cash and Commonwealth Government securities (CGSs), the 'liquids and government securities' — LGS — ratio.

Special regulations applied to savings banks. They could not accept current deposits (this was the exclusive domain of the trading banks until 1984) and were restricted in their provision of investment and fixed-term deposit accounts. They were also required to hold 70% of their assets in the form of liquid and government securities. The level of this requirement was progressively reduced to 40% by the end of the 1970s.

The central bank also influenced the volume and pattern of bank loans through its implementation of monetary policy (especially through changes in its SRD and LGS ratios) and its requests that banks vary their lending policies in accordance with the RBA's priorities.

The basic objective of the interest-rate ceilings and the requirements that banks hold CGSs was to maintain low interest rates. The low-interest-rate policy was intended to foster post-war economic development. Another factor was that increases in rates would have inflicted capital losses on the parties who held government securities. These had been issued to finance war-time expenditure.

Because banks were the main financial intermediators, their interest rates were of greatest importance. The requirements on banks (and the inducement for insurance offices) to hold government securities created a captive market for these securities and allowed the government to both set a low borrowing rate and control demand for the securities. Given that these were the main debt securities on issue, the government was able to implement effectively its low-interest policy for several decades after the war.

During this period, NBFIs were able to attract deposits away from banks, because they were not subject to bank regulations, and were able to lend these funds at rates above those charged by banks (because banks did not have sufficient deposits to satisfy the demand for finance). As a consequence, this group of institutions increased their share of intermediated assets within the financial system. This shift in market share did not totally disadvantage bank shareholders because they benefited from the growth and profitability of bank-owned NBFIs (particularly, bank-owned finance companies and money market corporations). However, it did weaken the effectiveness of the central bank because its influence was over banking business, not NBFIs.

In 1936 banks held 95% of intermediated financial assets (i.e. those held by banks and NBFIs combined); the balance of assets was held by pastoral financiers, building societies and finance companies. By the mid 1950s, the banks' share of assets had fallen below 90% and by 1980 it had fallen to less than 60% because of the relative growth in NBFIs.

A third group of institutions, collective-funds managers, also strengthened their position within the financial system. This group includes life offices and pension funds (which held 12.4% of financial assets in 1901), general insurers (which held 2.5% of financial assets in 1901), friendly societies, which have also operated throughout this century, and unit trusts, which commenced operations in the 1920s. By 1960 they held over 25% of financial assets.

The Reserve Bank commenced operations in 1960, having been separated from the Commonwealth Bank. During the 1960s the authorities recognised that they should either remove the controls on banks or extend them to cover all financial institutions. The *Financial Corporations Act* 1974 gave the authorities the opportunity to apply the controls to all institutions, but the relevant sections of this piece of legislation were not promulgated. Instead, the monetary authorities (i.e. the RBA and the Commonwealth Treasury) eventually decided to follow a free-market approach in their management of the financial system.

In 1979 the Commonwealth Government established a committee to inquire into the operations and efficiency of the financial system and the appropriateness of the regulatory system. This committee (known as the Campbell Committee) recommended in its report (1981) that, in relation to banking:

- the regulations should be replaced with 'market-oriented' forms of intervention that applied to financial institutions generally (i.e. not only banks),
- the restrictions on entry to the banking industry should be removed, and
- the government should introduce a system of prudential guidelines for financial institutions.

The committee also recommended the floating of the currency and the removal of exchange controls. In broad terms the committee formed the view that the system of controls was not very effective and that the controls impeded the efficiency of the operations of the financial system. The government began to implement these recommendations, but before much progress had been made in removing the regulations there was a change in government, in 1983.

The new (Labor) Government established a review group (the Martin Committee) to advise it on the appropriateness of the Campbell Committee's recommendations in terms of the government's 'economic and social objectives'.

This committee, in general terms, endorsed the Campbell Committee's recommendations. The Labor government promptly dismantled the regulations and the RBA developed and applied a market-oriented approach in its dealings with the financial system. However, a prudential supervision system was not introduced until 1988.

Since deregulation, banks have expanded their share of financial assets (refer back to table 2.2 in Chapter 2), for two main reasons:

- as a group they actively sought to expand their balance sheets (i.e. they have competed in the market for more deposits and loan business), and
- the number of banks has increased through the entry of foreign banks and conversion of some NBFIs to banks (such as the St George Bank, which previously was a building society).

The principal consequence of deregulation was that banks (including the newly admitted banks) became free to develop their business as they wished. Some banks, such as the big four, decided to offer a very wide range of financial services and products; whereas certain other banks decided to specialise in one or a few segments of the financial sector. Consequently, the role of banks in the financial system has gone full circle, from a position of dominance (until 1940) through a period of decline (to the early 1980s) back to a position of dominance.

During the immediate post-deregulation years (i.e. the latter half of the 1980s), most banks (and merchant banks) increased their lending too rapidly. They did this by lowering their **credit standards**. That is, they made loans that previously they would have regarded as being too risky and/or reduced their security requirements.

During the 1980s, corporate borrowers, in particular, sought to rely more heavily on debt (as opposed to equity) funds, creating a strong demand for loans. Banks that sought to strengthen their place in the market increased their borrowing to satisfy this increased demand for funds. The lending boom was severely halted by the end of the 1980s as a result of a series of events that included the October 1987 sharemarket crash, the subsequent collapse in the commercial property market and the 1990 recession. Many bank clients defaulted on their loans, leaving banks with excessive non-performing loans and heavy losses.

Banks have subsequently adopted more prudent lending practices and thus it cannot be validly argued that the excesses of the 1980s were a necessary result of deregulation. But this experience has led many people to question the value of deregulation.

In 1991 the Commonwealth Government conducted a parliamentary inquiry into post-deregulation banking. There was concern that competition had not improved operational efficiency. For instance, the inquiry considered whether interest-rate spreads had declined. The effectiveness of the new prudential supervision requirements was also questioned, given the high level of bad loans in the latter part of the 1980s. The inquiry also examined a number of retail banking concerns, such as the introduction of fees for credit cards and how customer disputes were handled by banks. Its report (released in November 1991) was entitled *A Pocket Full of Change*.

Concerns about bank charges for transaction accounts were the subject of a 1995 inquiry by the Prices Surveillance Authority. Its findings were discussed in Chapter 1.

Banks

Our discussion of retail banking activities centres on banks, but the retail banking activities of three NBFIs are discussed briefly at the end of the chapter. Two groups of banks, the majors and the regionals, are engaged in retail banking.

Recall the discussion in Chapter 2 that core banking business comprises borrowing/lending, payment services and risk management (of the bank and its customers). These activities are a related group (or 'bundle') of financial products and services that can be provided to different customer groups (such as retail and wholesale customers) or unbundled and provided as specific services and processes.

This bundling concept underpins the traditional practice of providing payment services to depositors rather than paying a competitive rate of interest on these funds. As noted in Chapter 1, the attempts by banks to unbundle and separately charge for these services have met with customer resistance; whereas banks have been more successful in their unbundling of the funding of a customer's borrowing requirement through the bill acceptance process. This process (of arranging but not providing a loan by accepting an investor's credit risk) is discussed further in Chapter 7.

As at mid 1995 there were 33 banking groups (some banks have bank subsidiaries) as well as 15 foreign banks with branches in Australia (some of which previously operated in Australia as local subsidiaries of the overseas bank). NBFIs operate under other legislation.

More than half of the 33 banks were admitted to the system in the mid 1980s, whereas the branch banks (all foreign owned) were admitted in the 1990s following a policy change announced in 1992. The major banks and most of the regionals were well-established institutions prior to deregulation, although some of the latter previously operated as building societies. These institutions are the main providers of financial intermediation services.

For the purposes of this and the next chapter banks are divided into four categories:

- the majors, which operate in the retail sector (as well as all other major sectors),
- regionals, which also operate in the retail sector (with some involvement in other sectors),
- investment banks (or the 'other' banks in the KPMG Peat Marwick surveys of financial institutions), which operate principally in the wholesale sector, and
- branch banks, which also operate in the wholesale sector.

The latter two groups are considered in the next chapter, together with the wholesale operations of the majors.

The major banks are the dominant players in the retail sector. Broad data on their operations are presented in table 6.1 Given that retail banking involves

Table 6.1 Major banks — operational indicators, 1994

	Assets ($m) [a]	*Number of employees*	*Number of branches*	*Net-II/ assets* [b] *(%)*	*Non-II/ assets* [c] *(%)*
ANZ	60 184	39 642	1 758	2.78	1.98
CBA	73 075	37 269	1 754	3.10	1.57
NAB	73 551	43 871	2 323	3.48	1.86
WBC	66 808	31 396	1 462	2.78	1.56
Totals	273 618	152 178	7 297	3.06	1.75

[a] Assets that form part of Australia's financial system (the majors operate in the domestic financial systems of other countries and therefore, as corporations, they hold more assets than shown by the RBA data on Australia's financial system)
[b] Net-interest income as a percentage of average total assets
[c] Non-interest income as a percentage of average total assets

Source: RBA, *Bulletin*, Table B.10 (for assets)
KPMG Peat Marwick, *1995 Financial Institutions Performance Survey*, pp. 36–7

Table 6.2 Regional banks — operational indicators, 1994

	Assets ($m)	*Number of employees*	*Number of branches*	*Net-II/ assets* [a] *(%)*	*Non-II/ assets* [b] *(%)*
Adelaide Bank	2 604	779	40	2.94	1.52
Advance Bank	11 641	2 409	246	3.37	0.37
Bank of Melbourne	7 755	1 537	123	3.42	0.49
Bank of Queensland	1 953	745	95	4.02	1.40
Bank of SA	7 790	n.a.	n.a.	1.51	0.53
Bank of WA	9 340	2 997	119	2.99	1.17
Challenge Bank	5 028	1 160	64	3.01	0.57
Metway Bank	5 952	1 476	107	3.65	0.82
St George Bank	14 127	3 732	299	3.48	0.64
State Bank of NSW	17 447	n.a.	n.a.	2.16	1.09
Trust Bank Tasmania	1 532	738	52	4.12	1.37
Totals	85 169	15 573	1145	2.94	0.93

[a] Net-interest income as a percentage of average total assets
[b] Non-interest income as a percentage of average total assets
n.a. Not provided in the source document

Source: RBA, *Bulletin*, Table B.10 (for bank assets)
KPMG Peat Marwick, *1995 Financial Institutions Performance Survey*, pp. 40–2

intermediation, the assets and liabilities of the financial institutions that operate in this sector provide a reasonable indication of their role in this sector. Observe that the indicators of size provide a clear picture of the dominance of the majors relative to the regional banks (shown in table 6.2) even though the majors are extensively involved in other areas of the financial system.

Most of the regional banks that existed in 1994 are listed in table 6.2. When interpreting this table, keep in mind that some of these banks were subject to takeover bids in 1995 (e.g. the bids by St George and Westpac for Challenge Bank) and Advance Bank had successfully bid for the Bank of South Australia. The overall picture provided by the data is that banks in this group are small compared to the majors. However, they are larger than the NBFIs that operate in this sector.

Apart from the difference of size between the major and the regional banks, observe that non-interest income as a percentage of assets is higher for the majors, reflecting their greater involvement in wholesale banking where fee-based services are of more importance than for retail banking.

The sources and uses of funds by all banks are discussed in this chapter to provide an overall view of the operations of banks. Retail sources and uses of funds are emphasised. An outline is provided in example 6.1 of the retail aspects of the operations of Westpac, the oldest of the big four.

example 6.1

The purpose of this illustration is to provide details of the retail operations of a major bank. The material (including the quoted passages) has been drawn from the 1994 *Annual Report* of the Westpac Banking Corporation.

The bank's extensive banking operations are provided by its:

- Retail Banking Group that, as at 30 September 1994, managed assets of $33 billion,
- Commercial Banking and Property Finance Group that managed assets of $15 billion,
- Institutional and International Banking Group that managed assets of $34 billion ($NZ12.5 billion of which are assets within New Zealand's financial system),
- Westpac Financial Services Group (the bank's funds manager), and
- Australian Guarantee Corporation, the bank's finance company that managed assets of $6 billion.

> *The Australian Retail Banking Group provides banking and financial products and services for the consumer and small-business markets via the branch and agency, ATM and EFTPOS networks, mobile bankers, Westpac Financial Consultants, the private banking network and the (bank's) . . . telephone banking service. The group also includes a product-management division, responsible for the development, pricing and marketing of deposit, loan and card products, and for the continued development of Westpac's distribution capabilities via channels other than branches. (p. 16)*

The bank is reengineering (through the mid 1990s) its branch operations by centralising administrative processes for the purpose of allowing branch staff to concentrate on customer service. The branches will service the banking needs of consumers and small businesses as well as the investment needs of individuals (in association with personnel from the bank's Financial Services Group). The reorganisation will assist the bank to develop its telephone banking service.

The operations of the Commercial Banking and Property Finance Group '. . . are targeted at medium-sized businesses with finance requirements generally in the range of $500 000 to $20 million and at all major finance transactions'. (pp. 16–17) The operations of this group straddle the retail- and wholesale-banking sectors. Consequently, part of the $15 billion of assets would be loans and advances to retail customers.

The operations of the Institutional and International Banking Group are directed toward Australia's wholesale banking sector and to overseas business (including what is the domestic business of other countries). We consider the operations of this group in the next chapter.

The operations of the bank's finance company (AGC) are directed mainly toward the retail sector. Its three main areas of business are financing vehicle sales by motor dealers, commercial and consumer finance. The financing of motor vehicles involves the provision of finance to dealers to acquire their stock of vehicles as well as the provision of finance to the car buyer.

> *The commercial unit provides finance for equipment and motor-vehicle leasing and asset purchases and is the market leader in factoring, a financial service that allows expanding businesses to turn their accounts receivable into cash. AGC's commercial customers include small- and medium-business and small corporate clients in industries ranging from construction and manufacturing to transport and storage to advertising. (p. 18)*

AGC provides finance to consumers, generally on a line-of-credit basis, for purchases of household consumer durables. It raises funds through the issue of fixed-rate, fixed-term retail debentures and by accepting call and short-term deposits.

> *Westpac Financial Services Group comprises the retail and wholesale funds-management operations which have between them $10 billion of funds under management, the general insurance broking unit, investment property operations and Westpac Custody Services with $51 billion in funds under administration . . . (p. 19)*

The group provides investment, retirement, superannuation and insurance products to retail customers. Its life and disability insurance products are manufactured by AMP.

LIABILITIES

In general, bank liabilities are sources of funds. There are four categories of bank liabilities, as shown by the data presented in table 6.3. They include domestic and foreign currency deposits, which together are the main sources of bank funds and bill-acceptance liabilities that are not a source of bank funds. Shareholders' funds are a source of funds, even though they are not bank liabilities. Given that we are discussing banks as financial intermediaries, this chapter emphasises their sources of borrowed funds.

Table 6.3 Bank liabilities — June 1981 to June 1995 ($ m)

June	*Deposits repayable ($A)*	*Other $A liabilities*	*Bill-acceptance liabilities*	*Foreign currency liabilities*	*Total liabilities*
1981	52 533	9 485[a]			62 018
1986	96 950	32 898[a]		9 552	139 400
1991	194 741	37 364	55 071	33 615	320 791
1994	238 477	39 852	49 421	47 947	375 697
1995	255 233	41 975	52 472	47 096	396 755

[a] Includes bill acceptance liabilities

Source: RBA, *Bulletin*, Table B.1

Deposits repayable in Australia

Table 6.4 provides data on Australian-dollar deposits for all banks. It should be noted that the deposit categories are those of the Reserve Bank. Individual banks can accept deposits on any basis they choose and there is a wider range of deposits than RBA categories.

Current accounts are cheque accounts. Cheques may be drawn against the balances in these accounts. Between 1981 and 1995 the proportion of these funds that earn interest increased from 10% to 76%. During this period the total amount of current deposits declined through the late 1980s and early 1990s, but returned to about 23% of total bank deposits by the mid 1990s.

Generally the rate of interest offered on balances in current accounts is low compared with balances in fixed-term deposits, for several reasons:

- the funds are highly liquid and this convenience has value to depositors and imposes costs on banks. The lower interest rate is the 'price' of this convenience,
- they provide customers with payment services that are being cross-subsidised through the low rate of interest paid on the funds.

Some banks allow customers a choice between current accounts that pay little or no interest but impose low or no transaction fees (a type of account that was advocated by the PSA) and accounts that pay close to retail-market interest rates but impose high transaction fees.

The increase in the proportion of interest-bearing current deposits is due to several factors. On the demand side, depositors have become more rational in their dealings with banks and seek the best deal, rather than simply remaining loyal to one bank.

On the supply side, banks, after a period of offering a diverse range of accounts as a means of attracting more deposits, have tended to promote 'all-in-one' accounts that provide depositors with payment services as well as giving a return for saving.

Table 6.4 Deposits repayable in Australia — all banks, June 1981 to June 1995

Type	*1981*	*1986*	*1991*	*1994*	*1995*
Dollar amounts ($m)					
Current					
— non-interest bearing	10 900	12 932	12 533	15 324	13 882
— interest bearing	1 218	4 803	18 636	42 873	44 040
Call	n.a.	n.a.	17 714	18 017	20 834
Fixed term	14 612*	39 619*	59 549	74 731	93 841
Certificates of deposit	2 576	6 616	32 773	31 085	31 228
Investment savings	9 752	16 355	24 898	29 630	25 745
Statement savings	n.a.	7 121	7 289	8 206	8 371
Passbook	n.a.	8 932	6 888	7 368	6 853
Other	13 475*	574	14 461	11 241	10 439
Totals	52 533	96 950	194 740	238 475	255 233
Percentages (%)					
Current					
— non-interest bearing	20.7	13.3	6.4	6.4	5.4
— interest bearing	2.3	5.0	9.6	18.0	17.2
Call			9.1	7.6	8.2
Fixed term	27.8	40.9	30.6	31.3	36.8
Certificates of deposit	4.9	6.8	16.8	13.0	12.2
Investment savings	18.6	16.9	12.8	12.4	10.1
Statement savings		7.3	3.8	3.5	3.3
Passbook		9.2	3.5	3.1	2.7
Other	25.7	0.6	7.4	4.7	4.1
Totals	100.0	100.0	100.0	100.0	100.0

* Includes the unavailable figure for the immediately above item(s)
n.a. Not provided in the source document

Source: RBA, *Bulletin*, Table B.2

Banks have also unbundled the pricing of the services provided to customers. They have introduced charges for services such as processing a customer's transaction, and this has allowed the banks to pay interest on the balances in these accounts.

The removal of the cross-subsidisation of banking services has been resisted by customers, who are accustomed to receiving these services free of charge. But as each customer has different needs it is more efficient (in an allocational sense) and equitable to charge for services according to their use by individual customers.

Call deposits are funds that require prior notice for withdrawals. They generally have a short term and are paid an interest rate that is marginally above the rate paid on interest-bearing current accounts (because they are marginally less liquid from the depositor's viewpoint). They represented about 7.5% of total bank deposits during the first half of the 1990s.

Fixed-term deposits are funds placed with banks for a fixed period. Banks usually accept fixed-term deposits for periods ranging from a month to five years. Their share of bank deposits increased from less than 28% in 1981 to 37% in 1995. Usually depositors can withdraw funds deposited in such accounts, but suffer an interest penalty when doing so. In other words, the interest rates on fixed-term deposits apply only when the deposits remain with the bank for their full term.

Fixed-term deposits generally offer a higher interest rate than for current deposits. They are less liquid and commonly rates are higher for longer-term deposits. (The reasons for this pattern are considered in Chapter 15.) These accounts offer retail customers interest rates that are closer to those available in money markets. However, the rates are usually lower than the yields in wholesale markets. For instance, in mid 1995, the rates on three-month CDs (and 90-day bank bills) was 7.55% p.a. whereas the three-month rate offered by banks on amounts over $100 000 averaged 6.10% p.a.

The general reasons for the difference between these rates were explained in Chapter 2 in the section dealing with the costs and benefits of intermediation. They include:

- that retail customers can invest smaller amounts in these accounts than the minimum values traded in the money market, although the rates for balances of less than $100 000 are lower than for the amount cited above, and
- that banks accept the market risks when investing funds in the short-term money market.

Typically (but not necessarily), interest rates on fixed-term deposits increase with the length of the term. For instance, in June 1995 rates on term deposits increased with the term. This pattern is illustrated by the fixed-term rates presented in table 6.5.

Banks (and other deposit-taking institutions) usually offer higher rates as the term increases for several reasons:

- These deposits reduce the institution's liquidity-management problems, compared with current and call deposits.
- Usually, the longer the period depositors forgo access to their funds, the higher the interest rate that has to be paid to compensate them for their loss of liquidity.

- Institutions are usually prepared to pay higher rates for longer terms because such deposits reduce their funding risks (on longer-term loans).
- Fixed-term deposits impose lower operating costs for banks because they cannot be used by customers for transaction purposes. Current (and other short-term) accounts in which customers have frequent transactions impose operating costs on banks.

Table 6.5 Indicative rates on fixed-term deposits — June 1995

Term	*Interest rate (% p.a.)*
One month	5.45
Three months	6.10
Six months	6.75
One year	7.15
Three years	7.50
Five years	7.80

Source: RBA, *Bulletin*, Table F.3

The data in table 6.4 show that banks have substantially increased their use of fixed-term deposits. In 1981, call and fixed-term deposits represented 27.8% of total bank deposits, whereas in 1995 the proportion was approximately 45%. (Fixed-term deposits are combined with call deposits in these calculations because in 1981 the RBA data did not distinguish between these accounts.) This shift in reliance on fixed-term deposits was quite deliberate.

Current deposits pose a liquidity-management problem for banks because they can be withdrawn at the discretion of the depositors. Banks hold marketable securities and other liquid assets, despite their lower yield, partly because of the need to be able to raise cash should the rate of withdrawals be greater than expected. Fixed-term deposits usually avoid this problem because depositors must leave their funds in these accounts for the full term in order to receive the quoted interest rate.

Fixed-term deposits are attractive to banks because they help them manage their risks when making fixed-term loans. When these loans are financed from current (or other short-term) deposits, banks are exposed to the liquidity risk arising from larger-than-expected withdrawals during the term of these loans. Fixed-term deposits are attractive when banks can lend these funds for an equivalent period, because this largely avoids funding risk (since the repayment of the deposit matches that of the loan).

When a bank lends for a fixed term and at a fixed rate and finances such loans from variable-rate deposits it is exposed to the risk of a rise in the general level of interest rates. This would increase the bank's cost of funds and reduce its interest spread on these loans. Funding such loans with fixed-rate deposits for a similar term removes this risk by locking-in a gross margin equal to the difference in the borrowing and lending rates.

Fixed-term deposits also reduce the exposure of banks to price risk, given that their assets have, on average, a longer term than their liabilities. Price risk arises from the mismatch in the maturities of bank tradeable assets and liabilities. (Changes in interest rates alter the value of fixed-interest securities according to their term; short-term securities are affected less than long-term securities. This outcome forms part of the risk of having a maturity mismatch between assets and liabilities. This problem is discussed further in Chapter 16.)

Certificates of deposit, known also as CDs (or negotiable CDs), are short-term securities issued by banks that have a face value payable at maturity. They are similar to promissory notes, in that they are discount instruments issued (and traded) in the short-term money market.

Generally, CDs are issued for large amounts (typically in denominations of $500 000 and $1 000 000) that are deposited with a bank for short periods at a yield set when issued. Provided CDs are held to maturity, the depositor receives the set (i.e. fixed) rate of interest that is implicit in the face value of the CD.

These are used to raise funds from wholesale customers and have become an important alternative source of funds to retail customers. Given the depth of the short-term money market, banks can raise large amounts of funds through the issue of CDs. It is more difficult to raise large amounts quickly from retail customers. As noted above, banks usually pay a higher interest rate on CDs, but being large-value transactions, they involve a lower transaction cost per dollar than when raising funds from the retail market. Hence the overall cost of these funds to banks need not exceed that of retail funds. The role of CDs as a source of wholesale funds is discussed further in the next chapter.

Investment savings accounts are those that have a minimum balance requirement, whereas **statement savings accounts** do not have a minimum balance. In both cases, interest is usually calculated daily and credited to the account on a periodic basis. The rate of interest usually depends on the size of the balance: the larger the balance the higher the rate.

Since deregulation, banks can set the rates they offer on investment savings accounts (along with fixed-term deposits and cash-management accounts) to compete against other banks and other deposit-taking institutions for funds.

Despite the growth in deposits in investment savings accounts (see the data in table 6.4) their share of total deposits declined between 1981 and 1995. One reason for this relative decline is the growth in cash-management accounts that pay interest rates that are closer to the rates in the short-term money market.

Passbook accounts traditionally pay a low rate of interest and have no minimum balance. Many pensioners maintain their savings in this form of account even though higher rates are available by placing the funds in other types of accounts. One reason for this behaviour is that many pensioners are not financially astute. Another reason is that their pension entitlements are income tested, and thus pensioners had little incentive to move their funds into higher interest-earning accounts. This practice benefited banks (by giving them cheap funds) at the expense of the pensioners involved and taxpayers. The Commonwealth Government took measures designed to ensure that banks paid pensioners a market-based rate of interest on their passbook-account balances. Even so, only 3% of deposits are derived from this source.

Other deposits include **cash management accounts** (CMAs) and pensioner deeming accounts. The interest rates on the cash management accounts depend on their balance. The rates shown in table 6.6 illustrate this practice.

Key points — bank deposits

1. Between June 1981 and June 1995, deposits repayable in Australia declined from 84.7% to 64.3% as a proportion of bank liabilities.
2. Even though banks increased their reliance on fixed-term deposits over the period (to 44.9% of total deposits), deposits in aggregate tend to have a short term.
3. Over the period the access of banks to 'cheap' funds (i.e. deposits on which they paid little or no interest) declined substantially.
4. Interest rates on retail accounts are lower than those for CDs, which attract funds from wholesale customers and are traded in the wholesale market.
5. Banks offer a range of retail deposit accounts that provide a mix of payment and investment services.

Table 6.6 Illustrative rates on cash management accounts — February 1995

Balance	*Interest rate % p.a.*
$250 000 and over	6.50
$100 000 and up to $249 999	6.30
$50 000 and up to $99 999	6.00
$20 000 and up to $49 999	5.85
$10 000 and up to $19 999	4.50
$5000 and up to $9999	4.25
up to $4999	1.00

Source: Westpac, 20 February 1995

Bill-acceptance liabilities

Recall from Chapter 3 that a bill is an instrument widely used by business to borrow funds for a short period (usually 90 or 180 days). It differs from other similar instruments because of its use of an acceptor. Bills are generally accepted on behalf of wholesale customers (although retail customers are able to draw bills). They are discussed in the next chapter.

Foreign-currency liabilities

As a consequence of the floating of the dollar and the effective removal of foreign-currency controls, banks have been able to raise funds from foreign sources. The Reserve Bank lists three categories of foreign-currency liabilities:

deposits (which include foreign-currency deposits by Australian residents); borrowing (e.g. by issuing securities in offshore capital markets); and loans from related corporations (e.g. loans to a foreign-owned bank by its foreign owner).

Borrowing is the largest source of foreign-currency liabilities, followed by deposits and balances due to related corporations. Reliance on offshore funds has increased considerably since the mid 1980s, as the figures in table 6.3 show. Reserve Bank data indicate that almost all banks have foreign-currency liabilities, not just the big four and foreign-owned banks. (See example 6.2.)

example 6.2

In the mid 1990s, Westpac issued euro-commercial paper and CDs in London and Hong Kong, commercial paper in New York, as well as subordinated debt in several overseas markets. It also accepted foreign-currency deposits from domestic clients.

Foreign liabilities are attractive to banks for several reasons:

- Since deregulation, interest rates have been much lower in the major offshore capital markets. Banks with a good credit rating have raised funds from these wholesale markets at much lower rates than they could from domestic money markets. When the funds are used to finance domestic business, banks usually swap the foreign-currency obligations into Australian-dollar obligations or buy foreign currency in the forward market to avoid being exposed to foreign-exchange risk. (The question of whether banks and other borrowers save by raising funds in foreign markets is examined in Chapters 13 and 14.)
- Raising offshore funds gives banks access to additional sources of funds (i.e. the savings of people in other countries) and this allows banks more flexibility in raising funds.
- Banks have acquired offshore assets and have funded them with offshore funds, since this creates a natural hedge against adverse movements in currency values. (Daugaard and Valentine, 1993, p. 77) (Note that this matter is discussed more fully in Chapter 13.)
- The trend toward global business creates a growing demand for financial services and products denominated in foreign currencies. Access to foreign-capital markets raises the global profile of a bank, which can enhance its capacity to provide such services.

Assets

The other side of intermediation is to on-lend the funds that have been raised. The use of funds by intermediaries is shown by the assets on their balance sheets. An overall picture of bank assets, over the period June 1981 to June 1995, is provided by the data in table 6.7 and figure 6.1.

Observe that loans and advances (and bills held) are the major use of funds. Most of these are in Australian dollars, but some are in foreign currencies. Bills receivable are equivalent to loans. Combining these with bank loans (excluding bills held) shows that nearly 78% of bank assets (as at June 1995) were held in these forms. The balance mainly comprises liquid assets.

The main liquid assets are cash and securities. Even though uncertainty about cash flows (due to maturity intermediation) means that banks will voluntarily hold liquid assets, the Reserve Bank imposes its prime asset ratio (PAR), which specifies a minimum level of prime assets as a ratio of Australian-dollar assets (less each bank's equity capital). Consequently, the mix of liquid assets is influenced by this requirement.

Table 6.7 Bank assets — June 1981 to 1995

Type	*1981*	*1986*	*1991*	*1994*	*1995*
Dollar amounts ($m)					
Cash	755	983	1 244	1 452	1 643
NCDs	1 853	3 301	2 541	3 256	3 535
Public-sector securities	15 368	22 637	23 437	28 179	28 545
Loans, advances & bills held	38 011	82 967	226 756	277 134	297 253
Bills receivable[a]			52 620	48 901	52 329
Premises	1 021	2 966	6 657	5 591	5 358
Other $A assets	7 935	32 268	22 465	28 144	26 986
Foreign-currency assets		6 128	17 062	20 185	22 236
Total assets	64 943	151 248	353 733	412 844	437 885
Percentages (%)					
Cash	1.2	0.6	0.4	0.4	0.4
NCDs	2.8	2.2	0.7	0.8	0.8
Public-sector securities	23.7	15.0	6.6	6.8	6.5
Loans, advances & bills held	58.5	54.9	64.3	67.1	67.9
Bills receivable[a]			14.9	11.8	11.9
Premises	1.6	2.0	1.9	1.4	1.2
Other $A assets	12.2	21.3	6.4	6.8	6.2
Foreign-currency assets		4.0	4.8	4.9	5.1
Total assets	100.0	100.0	100.0	100.0	100.0

[a] Included in other $A assets for 1981 and 1986

Source: RBA, *Bulletin*, Table B.1

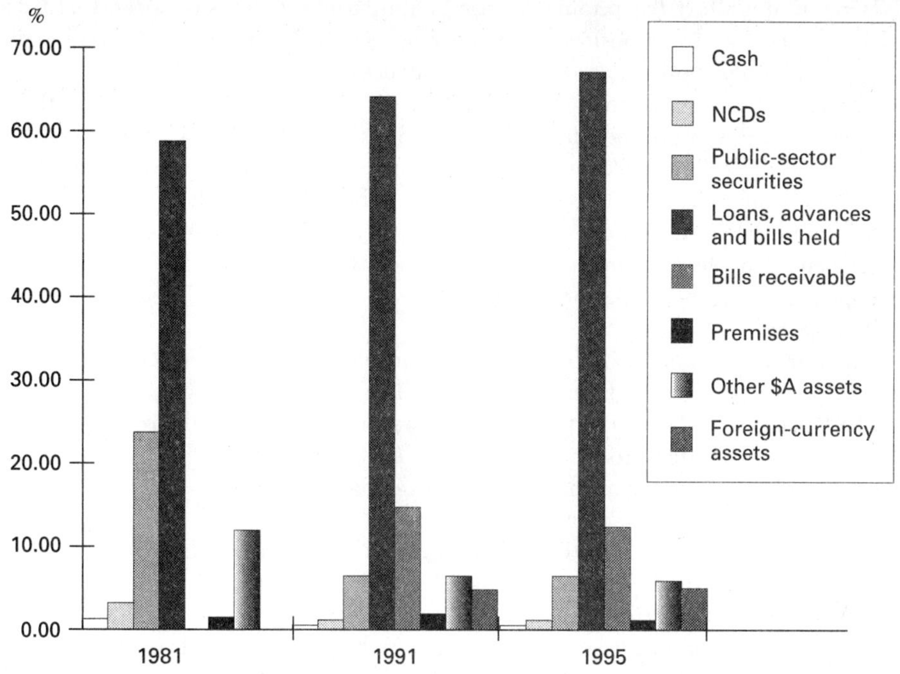

Figure 6.1 Assets as a percentage of total bank assets — June 1981 to June 1995, selected years
Source: RBA, *Bulletin*, Table B.1

Cash and liquid assets

The data in the first three rows of table 6.7 show bank holdings of liquid assets. A more detailed picture of these holdings over the decade June 1984 to June 1995, is presented by the data in table 6.8.

Liquid assets are required because of uncertainty about the timing and flow of deposits, withdrawals, loans and repayments. A large proportion of deposits are at call and so can be withdrawn at little or no notice. Even fixed-term deposits can be withdrawn before they mature. A proportion of loans allow customers to determine the timing of their use of these funds. These include overdrafts, 'revolving' loans and loans arranged on the basis that the funds can be 'drawn down' at the borrower's discretion. Also, loans can be repaid before they are due.

Even though liquid assets generally have a lower yield, they will be held by banks (and other financial institutions) because their liquidity has value. Institutions must be able to meet their obligations to customers, otherwise their viability will be undermined. Liquidity management is an important requirement for profitability, and liquid assets are the main instruments of liquidity management.

The historical pattern of liquid assets (as shown by the data in table 6.8) will be affected by the introduction of real-time gross settlement (RTGS) for the cheque system and for trading in CGS. (This proposal was discussed in Chapter 1.)

RTGS will not affect the amount of cash held by banks. Cash is required to satisfy cash withdrawals by depositors. The development of smart cards (discussed in Chapter 1) is also unlikely to make cash redundant over the next few years.

For many years prior to the introduction of RTGS, bank loans to the official dealers (AMMDs) were their next most-liquid asset. The RBA treated payments by the official dealers to banks as **same-day funds** when they were deposited in a bank's exchange settlement account (ESA) with the RBA, even though the cheques would not clear until the next day. Cheque payments are usually **next-day funds**. Inter-bank dealings also involve same-day funds when they pass through ESAs, as are dealings with the RBA, such as deposits with the bank. (De Lucia and Peters, 1993, pp. 84–9)

The introduction of RTGS by the RBA removed the need for banks to deal with the authorised dealers for liquidity purposes. The RBA commenced paying interest on ESA balances in July 1996 to allow these accounts to replace the role served by bank loans to (i.e. deposits with) AMMDs. Consequently, banks hold a substantial part of their liquid assets in the form of ESA deposits with the RBA. (This matter is discussed further in Chapter 10.).

As at June 1995 a total of $6783 million was deposited by banks with authorised dealers (most of which was secured by CGSs). Presumably bank deposits in their ESA will replace this prime asset once real-time settlement is implemented.

The RBA has for many years agreed to buy back (i.e. **rediscount**) Treasury notes at a stated rediscount rate. (See example 6.3.) In 1993 the bank announced that its rediscount rate would be set at a margin of 0.75 percentage points above the market yield for eligible Treasury notes (those with a residual maturity of between 8 and 90 days). Recall from Chapter 4 that the higher yield means that the bank will pay a lower price for rediscounted Treasury notes than would be available in the market. For banks, though, such proceeds are same-day funds, and when a bank is otherwise unable to prevent its ESA balance from becoming negative on a particular day, rediscounting Treasury notes with the RBA will allow it to overcome its lack of liquidity. In other words, by rediscounting Treasury notes the RBA is providing banks (and any other holder of Treasury notes) with a **lender-of-last-resort** facility.

In 1994 the RBA reduced the financial penalty involved on rediscounted notes by fixing the term of the margin at seven days. This provides banks with flexibility in deciding which notes to rediscount because the dollar amount of the penalty will not vary with the residual maturity (unless there is a very large variation in market yields for Treasury notes with a term between 8 and 90 days).

Apart from rediscounting Treasury notes with the RBA, which raises same-day funds, the proceeds from selling securities are generally next-day funds. Hence, holdings of government (and other public-sector) securities and commercial bills are the next most-liquid asset. They gain their liquidity from the deep secondary markets for these securities. The data in table 6.7 show a substantial fall in bank holdings of these securities in the 1980s. This is due mainly to the easing in the official requirements on banks (especially savings banks) over their holdings of such securities.

example 6.3

Suppose a bank needed to rediscount a $100 000 Treasury note to prevent the balance in its ESA falling below zero. It is holding Treasury notes with a residual maturity of 30 and 90 days. Given that the yield for 30-day bills is 7.50% p.a. and is 7.75% p.a. for 90-day bills, the penalty involved and the proceeds raised from rediscounting them is calculated below, using equation (4.3a) from Chapter 4.

Recall:

$$P = \frac{F}{1 + rt}$$

30-day notes:

$$\begin{aligned}
\text{Penalty} &= V_{mkt} - V_{RBA} \\
&= \frac{100\ 000}{1 + 0.075\ (7/365)} - \frac{100\ 000}{1 + 0.0825\ (7/365)} \\
&= 99\ 856.37 - 99\ 842.03 \\
&= \$14.3402
\end{aligned}$$

$$\begin{aligned}
\text{Proceeds} &= \frac{100\ 000}{1 + 0.075\ (30/365)} - \text{penalty} \\
&= 99\ 387.34 - 14.34 \\
&= \$99\ 373.00
\end{aligned}$$

90-day notes:

$$\begin{aligned}
\text{Penalty} &= \frac{100\ 000}{1 + 0.0775\ (7/365)} - \frac{100\ 000}{1 + 0.085\ (7/365)} \\
&= 99\ 851.59 - 99\ 837.25 \\
&= \$14.3388
\end{aligned}$$

$$\begin{aligned}
\text{Proceeds} &= \frac{100\ 000}{1 + 0.0775\ (90/365)} - \text{penalty} \\
&= 98\ 124.87 - 14.34 \\
&= \$98\ 110.53
\end{aligned}$$

Note that the amount of the penalty is just $14.34 (per $100 000 Treasury note) and that the variation in penalty between the two notes was insignificant, even though there was a difference, if only small, between their market yields.

The proceeds differ because the notes have different residual maturities.

The RBA's prime asset ratio (PAR) requires banks to hold a minimum amount of prime assets (i.e. those that have virtually no credit risk). As at July 1996, prime assets were:

- cash,
- CGSs, and
- ESA balances.

Note that these are highly liquid assets, which is the reason that the RBA requires them to be held. (The role of the PAR is discussed further in Chapter 9.) Data on prime assets are presented in table 6.8.

As at June 1995, prime assets of all banks represented 8.7% of their PAR base. This represents a margin of 2.7 percentage points over the required 6%. Given the amount of other liquid assets held by banks, it is evident that they assess their need to hold liquid assets to be well above the PAR. One reason for such a margin is that the requirement must be met, and hence it is only the extra prime assets that banks can immediately sell should they encounter an unexpected loss of liquidity.

Table 6.8 Liquid assets of banks — June 1991 to June 1995

Asset	*June 1991* ($m)	% of total	*June 1994* ($m)	% of total	*June 1995* ($m)	% of total
Prime						
—Cash	1 244		1 452		1 643	
—CGS	18 335		22 840		24 652	
—Loans to AMMD[a]	2 084		3 760		4 520	
Total: prime	21 663	36.7	28 052	41.1	30 815	47.1
Non-prime						
—NCDs	2 541		3 256		3 535	
—Loans to AMMD[b]	897		642		491	
—OPSS[c]	5 102		5 339		3 893	
—Bills	11 732		13 902		9 730	
—CDs	1 787		2 347		3 144	
—Loans to other banks	14 422		12 669		11 949	
—P-notes	909		2 009		1 860	
Total: non-prime	37 390	63.3	40 164	58.9	34 602	52.9
Totals	59 053	100.0	68 216	100.0	65 417	100.0

[a] Secured by CGSs from July 1996
[b] Not secured by CGSs
[c] Other public-sector securities

Source: RBA, *Bulletin*, Tables B.1, B.3, B.5 and B.8

Observe in table 6.7 that banks place non-callable deposits (NCDs) with the RBA. Since 1993, the RBA has paid a rate of interest on these funds that was based on the current yield for 13-week Treasury notes. But in 1995, the government decided to return to the previous arrangement of paying a rate that is five percentage points below the Treasury note rate. The monetary authorities suggested that they view this loss of revenue to the banks (estimated to be $185 million in 1995/96) as an indirect payment for their license and prudential supervision by the RBA. (RBA, June 1995, p. 1) This represents a change in official perception from that stated by the RBA in 1992. (RBA, October 1992, p. 25) Whether the banks get value for money from this implicit payment is another matter!

Given their below-market rate of return, banks will not place more than is required in their NCD accounts. Further, the funds that are placed in NCD accounts are not callable (i.e. cannot be withdrawn). The funds in these accounts therefore do not have the usual characteristics of liquid assets.

Liquid assets (as shown in table 6.8) represented 16.7% of total bank assets in June 1991, whereas in June 1994 they represented 16.5% and in June 1995 they represented 14.9%. These figures suggest that during the first half of the 1990s, banks have been able to operate with a lower proportion of liquid assets. Given that liquid assets usually provide a lower rate of return than non-liquid assets, the trend of reduced reliance on liquid assets should be associated with an increased return on bank assets.

A bank's need to hold liquid assets depends in part on the composition of its deposits and other assets. It was noted above that over recent years banks increased the proportion of their deposits held for a fixed term (and hence they reduced their reliance on deposits that can be withdrawn on demand or are at call). This trend reduces the need for banks to hold liquid assets.

Loans and advances

Banks make loans to individuals, businesses, governments and other financial institutions (including one another). This section will discuss 'loans and advances' as opposed to the loans that result when banks invest in securities issued by businesses and government agencies. There are four main forms of loans and advances:

- housing loans (mainly to individuals),
- personal loans (including credit-card advances),
- term loans to business, and
- overdrafts (mainly to businesses).

The data on loans and advances (and bills held) in table 6.7 (which are shown also in figure 6.1) indicate that reliance on loans declined in the 1980s, only to increase in the early years of the 1990s.

An important cause of the decline in loans and advances in the 1980s is not revealed by the data in table 6.7. During this period banks developed their role in the provision of bill financing. When accepting a bill the issuer agrees to pay the acceptor (i.e. the bank in this case) the bill's face value at maturity. These are shown as bills receivable. Their value grew during the 1980s but the amounts involved are included in 'other $A assets' for June 1981 and June 1986. Note the reduction in 'other $A assets' in June 1991 when bills receivable were shown separately.

Bill financing is, from a bank's viewpoint, an alternative to the provision of overdrafts and short-term loans. Overdrafts are a 'facility' because the customer determines the amount that is actually borrowed and the period of the financing is usually flexible. They are a notional form of short-term finance because they are subject to regular review and could be withdrawn if the customer's financial position deteriorated sufficiently.

Data on loans and advances (i.e. the amounts outstanding) for the period 1991 to 1995, are presented in table 6.9. Note that the value of bills held (i.e. bank holdings of bills as an investment) represents the difference between the total amount of loans and advances shown in table 6.9 and the amounts shown in the fourth row of table 6.7 for 1991 and 1995.

Housing loans

You will observe the absolute and relative increase in the provision of housing finance by banks during the first half of the 1990s. This reflects, in part, an upswing in housing expenditure. It was achieved despite the incursion into the housing finance market by other suppliers of funds. In addition, banks might have responded to the more favourable treatment of housing (compared with business) loans under the RBA's capital adequacy requirements, which were introduced in 1988.

Table 6.9 Bank loans and advances — June 1991, 1994 and 1995

	June 1991		*June 1994*		*June 1995*	
	($m)	% of total	($m)	% of total	($m)	% of total
To persons						
— housing	69 611	32.4	123 909	47.1	142 901	49.7
— other	27 693	12.9	27 359	10.4	28 905	10.0
To business						
— fixed	46 830	21.7	49 762	18.9	54 600	19.0
— overdrafts	20 406	9.5	11 326	4.3	12 723	4.4
— other	15 192	7.0	16 388	6.2	16 379	5.7
To institutions	31 991	14.9	28 699	10.9	28 388	9.9
To government	3 401	1.6	5 793	2.2	3 627	1.3
Total	215 025	100.0	263 235	100.0	287 523	100.0

Source: RBA, *Bulletin*, Tables B.3 to B.5

The traditional housing loan has a long term (typically 20–25 years), carries a floating rate of interest, is secured by a mortgage over the property, and the amount of the loan is usually less than the value of the property when the loan is taken out. Payments, which usually are made monthly, amortise the principal borrowed as well as meeting the interest due. In other words, they are reducible loans.

The mathematics of reducible loans was explained in Chapter 5. The regular payments over the term of the loan is an 'annuity' that covers the interest due and gradually amortises (i.e. repays) the loan. The amount outstanding over the course of the loan is equal to the present value of the remaining payments. Changes in the interest rate can result in either the regular payment or the term of the loan being adjusted.

Building societies were the main competitors of banks in this market, but in the 1990s new forms of competition emerged. Other institutions, such as credit unions, insurance offices and superannuation funds entered the market by offering funds at a lower rate than banks. The other source of competition came from **mortgage originators**, such as Aussie Home Loans. (See example 6.4.) They typically 'sell' housing loans direct to borrowers and are not otherwise engaged in the provision of retail banking services (particularly payment services). Originators do not continue to fund their loans. They sell them. The loan payments made by the borrowers are paid to a trustee under a securitisation arrangement, which involves the issue of mortgaged-backed securities. The payments made by borrowers are **passed through** to the holders of the **mortgage-backed securities** (less a narrow spread to pay for the services provided by the parties involved in the securitisation of these housing loans).

example 6.4

Aussie Home Loans (AHL) is a high-profile entrant in the housing-finance market as a mortgage originator. AHL uses finance raised by Puma Management, a subsidiary of Macquarie Bank. Puma is a fund manager that issues bonds backed by the mortgages written by AHL and other mortgage originators. In May 1995, Puma released an information memorandum prior to the issue of $650 million worth of fixed- and floating-rate bonds.

The most senior of these loans were rated triple A, allowing them to be issued at a low yield. A secondary market has been created for these securities, enhancing them with liquidity, which further contributed to their low issue yield.

Mortgage originators are well established in other countries, such as the United States, where they are the major providers of housing loans. As at 1995 they have a small share only in the Australian market, but their market share is rising and has been predicted to exceed 25% of the market by the year 2000.

Loan securitisation is a form of unbundling of bank lending products. Bank lending involves three phases:

- origination,
- funding, and
- servicing. (Joss, 1996, p. 185)

Origination is the selling of the loan and the development of loan originators shows that local branches are not essential to this process. Originators have pioneered low-cost methods of selling loan products, using 'mobile lenders' (loans officers who visit the home of potential borrowers) and direct marketing (telephone banking).

Traditionally, banks have funded loans from deposits, whereas loan originators have funded loans by issuing securities (which in some cases have been purchased by funds managers). Given that part of a bank's costs in providing payment services is met from its borrowing and lending products, banks are at a competitive disadvantage when funding housing loans.

Loan originators or the arrangers of their funding sources are responsible for the servicing of their loans. Banks have substantial experience in this process as well as in the process of assessing credit risk, and according to Joss (1996, p. 186) are likely to have a comparative advantage in these processes over loan originators. Time will tell whether loan originators will continue their erosion of banks' market share in the home-lending market.

The securitisation process is depicted in a generalised way in figure 6.2. It shows that investors are the source of the loan funds (which are channelled) through the loan originator, and that housing-loan repayments are the source of the interest payments to investors.

The originators are low-priced suppliers of housing funds, partly because their very low overheads allow them to be profitable when charging a narrow margin over their cost of funds. Their competitiveness depends also on the level of wholesale interest rates (domestically and overseas) relative to domestic retail rates. Their activities place competitive pressure on banks to contain the costs of the funds they raise through their retail operations.

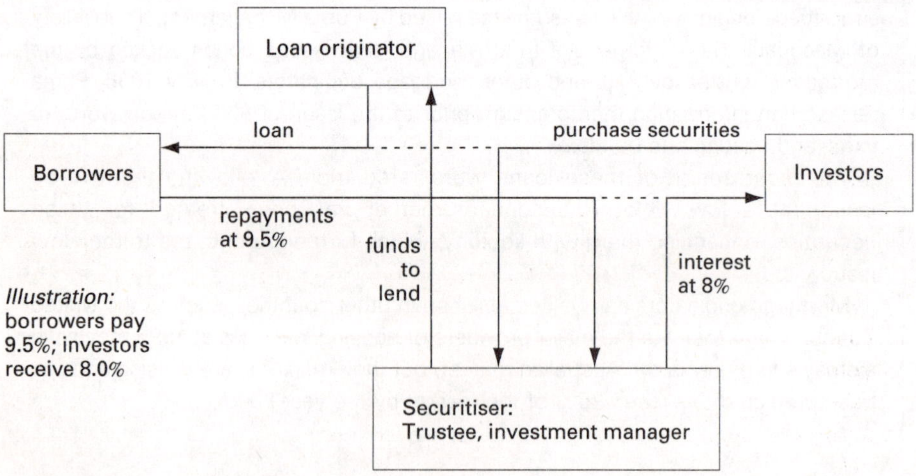

Figure 6.2 Loan originators and securitisation of housing loans

Banks responded by making loans that represent a higher than normal proportion of the assessed value of the residential property. This posed some concern for the RBA (which in 1994 increased its capital adequacy requirement for housing loans that exceeded 80% of the value of the property) because this practice resulted in an abnormal level of bad loans following the fall in real-estate values at the end of the 1980s.

The expectation that the value of real estate appreciates over time may imply that loans can be made for amounts that are similar to the value of the home or apartment being financed. But real-estate values do not increase steadily and when values are falling, the market tends to become illiquid, and during these periods the credit risk of these loans increases.

Given the amount of business involved, it is obvious that banks will respond to the new competition in the housing-finance market. Their attempts to impose fees that cover the cost of providing payment services to retail customers is part of this response. Banks are unlikely to be able to set competitive lending rates if the total cost of their funds (i.e. the interest rate plus cross-subsidies for services to retail customers) exceeds that of other suppliers of housing finance.

Personal loans

The data in table 6.9 show that personal loans are an important part of bank lending. Loans are made on either a secured or unsecured basis, with a higher rate generally applying on the unsecured loans. Some banks will allow borrowers to use the equity in their home (i.e. the value of the property minus the amount outstanding on the borrower's housing loan, if any) to secure their personal loans (especially for home-improvement loans). In the case of personal loans to purchase a motor vehicle, the vehicle is used to secure the loan.

Personal loans usually have a term of two to five years and are repaid by regular monthly payments that amortise the loan. Home-equity loans may take the form of a **revolving line of credit** that allows the borrower some discretion over the amount that is actually borrowed over time. A revolving line of credit means that the repayment of borrowed funds does not extinguish the line of credit.

Personal loans tend to be for small amounts. This poses a management problem for banks. Personal loans can involve a high level of credit risk but lenders are unlikely to be able to recoup their costs if they undertake a detailed assessment of every application for a personal loan. Banks (and other lenders) have responded to this problem by adopting standardised application forms and charging an interest-rate margin that is appropriate for classes of borrowers, rather than for individual borrowers.

Credit cards have become popular partly because they apply standardised and simple lending processes. However, the rates of interest on unpaid balances tend to be high because of the high credit risk on these loans. Despite the high rates charged on unpaid balances, and the charges imposed on retailers who allow credit-card purchases, banks claimed they lost money on their use. This claim, in part, led to the introduction of annual fees for bank credit cards.

The amount of funds lent through credit cards represents about 30% of approved borrowing limits. This poses a liquidity problem for banks because their customers determine how much is lent in this fashion. But the amount involved is not large ($5.7 billion in June 1995), relative to total bank assets.

The interest rates charged on the various types of personal loans are related to the risk faced by the lender. Usually all personal loans will involve a higher interest rate than housing loans. The most favourable rate applies to secured loans that are of a substantial amount. The rate on unsecured loans is usually higher, but is less than the rate on credit-card loans, especially where the issuer of the card does not impose an annual fee.

Business loans

The data in table 6.9 show that term loans are the largest category of business loans. While overdrafts are a traditional form of bank loan to business, the data in table 6.9 show the amount outstanding has declined throughout the 1990s. This decline is the continuation of a long-term trend away from the use of overdrafts in favour of term loans. (See example 6.5.)

Term loans Typically, a term loan extends for periods of two to five years and is repaid through regular monthly payments that amortise the loan. Term loans can be made on either a floating-rate or fixed-rate basis. In both cases, the rate is based on a marker (or reference) rate, such as a bank's **prime rate** (i.e. the rate for its prime customers) plus a margin that depends on the bank's assessment of the borrower's credit risk and how well the loan is secured. Interest is paid 'in arrears' (i.e. at the end of each reset period), on the rate set at the beginning of each period. Floating-rate loans are usually reset quarterly in line with movements (if any) in the level of the reference rate.

Term loans are typically used to finance major physical investments by businesses, such as the construction of a factory. They are made to businesses of all sizes and so are an example of a financing product that is provided to both retail and wholesale customers. Usually they are in the form of a reducible loan, which is amortised through the regular payments.

When evaluating applications for term loans, banks will pay special attention to the predicted cash flows that the acquired asset will generate. These cash flows provide the source of the borrower's capacity to meet the regular payments. Naturally, for longer-term loans, predicting cash flows many years ahead involves considerable uncertainty.

For this reason many term loans are secured and are subject to **loan covenants**. These are (usually) indicators of financial strength that the borrower must continue to maintain over the period of the loan, otherwise the bank can renegotiate the terms of the loan. Typical covenants are:

- the ratio of total liabilities to total net worth not to exceed 2:1,
- the ratio of earnings over interest obligations must exceed 1.5:1, and
- the maintenance of a positive amount of working capital. (Shanmugam *et. al.*, 1993, p. 338)

As noted in Chapter 2, a borrower can usually lower the margin over prime charged by a bank by providing good security. But in the process, the borrower is absorbing some of the credit risk of the loan. Where the borrower has a history of stable income that exceeds the regular payment on a loan by many times, a term loan may be unsecured.

Overdrafts As previously noted, overdrafts are a notional form of short-term financing that has been used in Australia for many years, usually to meet seasonal shortages of cash. An overdraft is a borrowing facility that, within the agreed limit, can be accessed through the borrower's cheque account.

Usually an overdraft is a revolving facility, with interest payable only on the amounts actually borrowed. The borrower is expected to access the overdraft for only part of a year. In other words, the borrower can 'reborrow' funds that have been repaid when experiencing the next seasonal shortfall of cash.

Overdrafts pose a liquidity problem for banks because once an overdraft limit has been set, the customer rather than the bank determines how much is borrowed and when. At one time banks charged a fee based on the unused amount of an overdraft limit to encourage customers to use their overdrafts. It is evident, though, from the data in table 6.9 that banks have switched to term loans. Because these are usually **fully drawn advances** and are repaid by regular payments, they permit banks to better calculate their cash requirements. (McGrath, 1994, pp. 33–4)

Banks usually charge establishment and line fees on overdrafts as well as transaction fees. These are in addition to the interest rate that is usually a margin above the bank's reference rate for overdrafts and is reset quarterly. The margin depends on the borrower's credit standing and on the quality of the security. Many overdrafts are unsecured, but those that are secured by residential real estate will usually incur a lower margin over the marker rate.

example 6.5

Following the slowdown in lending for housing in 1995, competition for business loans was reported to have intensified. The NAB launched a $1 billion small-business program, designed to attract better account customers from the other majors. Its competitors were reported to have cut margins in response.

It is difficult to compare the 'price' of business loans because banks tend to use their own marker (or reference) rate, rather than a market-wide rate, such as the 90-day bank-bill rate. Comparisons of the size of the margin charged to each customer need to be related to the bank's reference rate. Also, the charges imposed vary between banks, as does the quantity of services that are provided to the business customer.

In mid 1995 Citibank advertised extensively for new business-loan customers, on the basis that the loans and overdrafts are secured by residential property. Its advertisement stated that charges imposed by the majors for comparable overdrafts range from $990 p.a. to $1910 p.a. and that Citibank will not impose any charges on its business overdrafts. Whereas the margins imposed by the majors range from (up to) 1.75% p.a. to (up to) 4.5% p.a. (depending on the customer's credit standing), Citibank will not impose any margin over its reference rate, which was about only one percentage point above those set by the majors. (*Sydney Morning Herald*, 26 June 1995)

Overdrafts are extended to both retail and wholesale customers. The data presented in table 7.9 (p. 194) show that most floating-rate loans (which includes overdrafts) are made in the form of small- to medium-sized loans.

Bill financing Bill financing is an alternative to overdrafts. Bills are short-term instruments and can be used to raise funds as required, usually in amounts of $100 000. Should the drawer require funds for longer than their usual term of 90 or 180 days, a series of bills (this is known as a bill facility) can be drawn; each successive bill serves to roll over the previous maturing bill.

The cost of bill finance to the borrower is the sum of the yield in the bill market plus a margin (and fees) similar to those that would apply for overdraft financing. However, bill financing has one important advantage compared with overdrafts. Bills are liquid assets and can be sold either to raise the funds initially or during the bill's life. Because of this quality a bank will usually arrange bill financing at a slightly lower cost than overdraft finance.

The main advantage of overdrafts for borrowers is that, apart from some minor charges on unused limits, they pay interest only on the amount actually borrowed and they control the amount that is borrowed.

Banks also provide business finance for other purposes, such as for leasing, accounts receivable financing and bridging (or project) financing.

Leases There are two basic types of leases: financial and operating. An **operating lease** is similar to renting because the lessee (the user of the leased items, such as equipment) simply acquires the right to use the items by making regular lease payments to the lessor (their owner). On the other hand, a **financial lease** is a de facto hire-purchase agreement under which the lessee may acquire the leased items at the expiry of the lease. Usually financial leases can be for a short term, whereas operating leases usually have a term greater than a year.

Leased items are paid for by the lessor, who may borrow from banks (or finance companies, which were the traditional providers of lease finance) to finance their purchase. As at mid 1995, banks provided approximately $7 billion for lease finance. These funds are repaid from the regular lease payments of lessees to their lessors. Leasing is simply a tax-effective form of financing. Its popularity depends, therefore, on the provisions of the income-tax legislation.

Accounts receivable financing This is a form of collateralised lending, the payments on which flow from those received by the owner of the accounts receivable. These are amounts owing to a business that makes credit sales. Rather than wait until the payments are received, the business may borrow against these payments, raising funds to finance its future operations.

Factoring Factoring is an alternative form of finance that involves the sale of accounts receivable to a bank or finance company at a discount on their face value. The purchaser of the accounts becomes responsible for the collection of the amounts owing.

Bridging finance Also called project financing, this is a form of short-term finance that is used pending alternative financing. A property developer, for instance, might use bridging finance to acquire new property prior to the arrangement of long-term financing. Similarly, a bank may provide finance to another institution that is underwriting an issue of securities. The underwriter will repay the loan from the placement of the securities.

Term structure of lending

It was suggested in Chapter 2 that maturity intermediation is an important function performed by financial intermediaries. Unfortunately we cannot present precise data of the difference between the average term of bank assets and liabilities.

The data in table 6.8 indicate that in June 1995 banks held $24.6 billion of CGSs, more than half of these being Treasury bonds (the balance of which was $9.9 billion worth of Treasury notes). While bonds are long-term securities when issued, banks tend to hold (rather than trade) bonds with a residual maturity of less than a year. Consequently the majority of the CGSs held by banks are unlikely to be securities with long residual maturities.

The data in table 6.9 show that a large proportion of bank loans are for housing. These are mainly (very) long-term loans. A large proportion of these loans would be made on a variable-rate basis — the rate being reset at each bank's discretion in line with general movements in interest rates. Other housing loans would be fixed-rate and capped-rate loans that expose banks to the risk of an unexpected rise in interest rates (given that they would be funding the loans mainly with floating-rate deposits).

Business loans are the next largest form of bank lending. Data presented in table 7.7 in the next chapter (p. 191) indicate that (as at March 1995), 55% of business loans were made on a fixed-rate basis. The remaining business loans (including overdrafts) were made on a floating-rate basis. Usually these rates are reset quarterly in line with movements in market yields for 90-day bills.

Floating-rate loans reduce the exposure of Australian banks to the interest-rate risk that arises when lending for long terms and borrowing on a short-term basis. But they are not free of this risk, nor of the funding risk that arises from the difference in the length of the term of their assets and liabilities.

Pattern of lending

The data presented in tables 6.7 to 6.9 show the amounts outstanding; whereas the data presented in tables 6.10 and 6.11 show lending commitments on an average weekly basis according to the intended use of the funds. Total commitments indicate the amount of approved new lending, whereas net lending allows for repayments on existing loans.

Table 6.10 Average weekly lending commitments — 1991–92 to 1994–95 ($m)

	Personal loans			*Business loans*			*Total*	*Net*
	fixed	revolving	housing	lease	fixed	revolving		
1991–92	184	107	457	27	414	693	1881	1008
1992–93	229	118	654	32	441	780	2254	1381
1993–94	315	152	899	38	516	732	2653	1833
1994–95	360	169	798	38	559	763	2687	1789

Source: RBA, *Bulletin*, Table B.13

The data in table 6.10 show new lending for personal, housing and commercial purposes classified according to whether the approval is for a fixed amount (for a fixed term, repayable by regular payments that amortise the loan) or for a borrowing limit (i.e. revolving loan) that the borrower can draw down (i.e. draw upon) as required. Observe the strong growth in housing lending and the growth in the totals. This reflects the growth in the housing industry and the economy as a whole during the period.

The pattern of new commercial lending across the economy is indicated by the data in table 6.11. Individual banks should attempt to achieve a broad spread of lending across the economy because this reduces their exposure to a downturn in a particular industry or sector (agriculture is a sector whose prospects do not always vary with those of the rest of the economy).

Table 6.11 Percentage of new commercial lending commitments by industry sector — 1991–92 to 1995–96

	Agric.	*Mining*	*Manuf.*	*Constr.*	*Distrib.*	*Finance*	*Property*	*Other*
1991–92	9.5	4.6	14.5	6.1	16.4	17.0	14.0	17.9
1992–93	9.6	5.6	14.6	7.5	16.2	15.1	13.1	18.2
1993–94	9.1	3.6	13.9	7.9	15.4	14.4	15.8	19.9
1994–95	8.4	4.8	12.8	6.7	16.4	12.9	15.4	22.6
1995–96	8.5	5.3	13.4	6.7	18.4	13.7	15.7	18.3

Note that totals may not add to 100% due to rounding
Source: RBA, *Bulletin*, Table B.13

Bills receivable

We discussed bill financing earlier in this chapter and in Chapter 3. Bills receivable are the amounts owed to banks by the drawers of bank-accepted bills. The data in table 6.7 show that the amount outstanding for bills receivable has been of the order of $50 billion during the 1990s.

Banks earn an acceptance fee (together with a line fee) when they accept bills, rather than an interest-rate spread, which they would earn if they had made loans to these customers. Their profit from accepting bills depends on the level of their acceptance fee.

Foreign-currency assets

About half of the banks' foreign-currency assets are foreign-currency loans to residents. Banks also hold foreign-currency assets to assist their trading operations and make foreign-currency loans to subsidiaries and related companies.

Key points — bank lending

- About two-thirds of bank assets are in the form of loans and advances.
- Over half of the amount loaned by banks goes to persons.

- Just less than half of the funds loaned by banks is for housing.
- Commercial loans represent about 30% of the bank loans.
- Term loans are the main form of commercial lending.
- Overall, bank loans are for longer periods than bank deposits.
- The growth in fixed-rate deposits and floating-rate lending diminish the maturity-intermediation risks faced by banks.

NON-BANK FINANCIAL INSTITUTIONS

As noted in Chapter 2, there are a number of categories of non-bank financial institutions in Australia. Three operate in the retail banking sector:

- building societies,
- credit unions,
- finance companies and general financiers.

These institutions compete with banks in the provision of retail banking products. However, the activities of each category differ from one another. In broad terms, building societies and credit unions provide payment services and borrowing and lending products, whereas finance companies provide investment and borrowing opportunities for retail and business customers.

As at mid 1996, there were 25 building societies, 254 credit unions (or cooperatives), 92 finance companies and 95 general financiers classified by the RBA (under delegation from the Treasurer) under the *Financial Corporations Act*. (RBA July 1996)

Building societies generally operate in a region, or even a provincial city, whereas credit unions have generally been formed at work places and so their physical location depends on that of particular organisations and industries. Some finance companies are owned by banks and operate nationally, whereas others are small and have a localised clientele. The large number of companies might therefore give a false impression of the number of actual competitors in this institutional category.

Building societies and credit unions

Most building societies are cooperatives (i.e. most are 'owned' by their depositors, unlike banks, which usually are companies owned by shareholders) that have operated in Australia since the last century. They have traditionally competed with savings banks in the provision of housing loans, although only a few building societies became large institutions.

Building societies have experienced financial disasters, generally as a result of financing a building boom that collapsed leaving them with bad loans that forced some societies into bankruptcy. They have also, from time to time, come under financial pressure because of rumour. It is evident that the community has not always considered them as safe as banks.

Their period of strongest growth occurred prior to the deregulation of banks. In 1980 they held 8% of financial assets, whereas in June 1995 their share was only 1.6%. The major cause of this loss of market share was the conversion of the largest building societies to banks, moving about half of the assets of this category of institution to the banking sector. The following building societies became banks:

- NSW Building Society Ltd (with assets of $1.9 billion) and a smaller society merged to become Advance Bank on 1 June 1985;
- United Permanent Building Society Ltd (with assets of $1.7 billion) merged with the National Mutual to become the National Mutual Royal Savings Bank on 2 March 1987, which subsequently was taken over by ANZ);
- Perth Building Society (with assets of $1.3 billion) merged with a smaller Victorian-based building society to become the Challenge Bank on 21 April 1987;
- Metropolitan Permanent Building Society (with assets of $1.2 billion) became the Metway Bank Ltd on 1 July 1988;
- RESI-Statewide Building Society (with deposits of $3.0 billion) became the Bank of Melbourne on 1 July 1989;
- the Tasmanian Bank was formed on 1 September 1989 from the merger of a Tasmanian-based building society and savings bank (and has subsequently become part of Trust Bank Tasmania); and
- St George Building Society (the largest building society) became St George Bank on 1 July 1992. (O'Brien, 1993, pp. 94–5)

Credit unions emerged in the late 1940s. They usually operate as cooperatives under state legislation. This was a benefit prior to the deregulation of banks (which are regulated by the RBA) because these institutions were exempt from the RBA controls. But following deregulation, their operations remained subject to the controls and influence of State governments, which has not always been beneficial. Credit unions developed as providers of personal loans in competition with finance companies, when banks could not effectively enter this market.

The number of credit unions has declined steadily over the past 20 years or so, from 689 in 1978 to 259 by mid 1995. The decline in number is the result of mergers, which have increased the average size of credit unions.

Assets and liabilities

Both building societies and credit unions principally fund their assets through their deposits (although in the case of building societies these may be in the form of withdrawable shareholdings). Both accept deposits for transaction and investment purposes, including fixed deposits.

For a number of years both participated in the payments system through agency agreements with banks, prior to their direct participation in the cheque-payment system. Both offer a range of associated financial services, such as insurance products, cash-management type accounts and financial advice.

Data on the composition of the assets of building societies and credit unions are presented in table 6.12. When interpreting the percentage composition data in table 6.12, keep in mind that:

- the total value of building-society assets as at June 1991 was $21.9 billion, which represented 6.2% of bank assets;
- by comparison, in 1991 the value of credit-union assets was $8.8 billion, or 2.5% of bank assets;
- each held assets of between $13 and $14 billion in June 1995, which represents approximately 3% of bank assets;
- the fall in the value of building-society assets between June 1991 and June 1995 was due mostly to St George becoming a bank; and
- credit unions expanded their asset holdings during the first half of the 1990s.

Observe (in table 6.12) that more than half of the assets of building societies in 1995 were in the form of housing loans, whereas almost half of the assets of credit unions were in the form of personal loans. Further, housing loans by credit unions increased substantially.

Table 6.12 Assets of building societies and credit unions — percentage composition, June 1991 and June 1995

	Building societies		*Credit unions*	
Asset	1991	1995	1991	1995
Cash and bank deposits	5.1	7.5	3.3	3.0
Public-sector securities	4.3	0.8	0.3	0.1
Other deposits	1.5	0.2	9.5	12.0
Bills and P-notes	7.8	5.1	3.0	1.7
Housing loans	43.6	57.9	17.9	31.1
Personal loans	4.9	3.7	60.7	46.8
Other assets	32.8	24.7	5.3	5.2
Total	100.0	100.0	100.0	100.0

Source: RBA, *Bulletin*, Tables C.1 and C.2

Note their relative holdings of liquid assets. Building societies hold more cash, due no doubt to the less liquid nature of their assets. Maturity intermediation is a smaller problem for credit unions, given their greater reliance on personal loans that have a shorter term than housing loans.

You will notice the very low holdings of public-sector securities by both forms of institution, in comparison to banks which are subject to the PAR. Building societies hold bills instead, whereas credit unions have substantial funds placed with banks. Given that the PAR does not apply to these institutions, it might be inferred that banks might hold a smaller value of CGSs if they were not subject to the PAR.

Finance companies

There are three categories of finance company:

- pastoral,
- general financiers, and
- finance companies.

Pastoral finance companies were the third-largest institutional group in 1901, holding 7.4% of financial assets. (Lewis and Wallace, 1993, p. 3) This is not surprising, given the role of agriculture in Australia's early development. But their current role in the financial system is tiny. Their total assets in mid 1995 were just in excess of $2.6 billion, of which only $400 million was in the form of loans to rural producers.

Finance companies developed in the 1920s as providers of ('hire-purchase') funds for the purchase of motor vehicles, and developed in the 1950s and 1960s as providers of funds for the purchase of consumer durables more generally and as providers of finance for business, including lease finance. They developed **debentures** (a retail bond instrument) as a source of funds. These securities were popular with the public because, when they were developed, they provided access to interest rates that were close to wholesale market rates. When banks become owners of finance companies, the returns appeared even more attractive as bank ownership was interpreted as involving a lower level of risk.

General financiers and finance companies provide similar intermediation products; both lend to business and make personal loans, although general financiers (unlike finance companies) do not issue debentures as a source of funds. While they operate in the same market segments, they are categorised separately under the *Financial Corporations Act*.

Finance companies are specialised intermediaries. They do not provide payment services nor do they accept deposits from the public. However, finance companies (as opposed to the other two categories) issue securities to the retail sector as a source of funds. Their loans and sources of funds have a similar maturity structure and so they are not greatly involved in maturity intermediation. Their main business is lending funds, therefore managing credit risk is of importance. Their record in this regard has been blemished on occasions by reckless lending (mainly for property development) by a small number of finance companies, some of which paid the ultimate penalty.

The fact that there are close to 100 finance companies operating in Australia conceals the high degree of concentration that exists in this segment of the financial system. A large proportion of the assets ($44 billion) of the finance-company segment are held by a few finance companies. Examples of the largest finance companies (as shown in the 1995 Financial Institutions Performance Survey by KPMG Peat Marwick) include Esanda Finance Corporation (owned by ANZ), with assets of $7.9 billion; AGC (owned by Westpac), with assets of $6.4 billion; CBCF Limited (owned by CBC) with assets of $2.6 billion; Toyota Finance Australia Limited, with assets of $2 billion; and Ford Credit Australia Limited with assets of $1.7 billion.

A broad picture of the development of finance companies was presented earlier in this chapter in the discussion of the financial system prior to deregulation. Finance companies were one of the categories of NBFIs that sustained relative growth because they were not subject to bank controls. The banks circumvented these controls by establishing their own finance companies and redirected business to them.

Following deregulation, banks were able to incorporate some or all of their finance-company operations into their banking operations. Consequently, it was likely that the value of finance-company assets would decline, at least relative to the system as a whole.

It should be noted also that some of the business conducted by finance companies is risky — too risky for the banks to undertake. An example of such business is the financing of property development, an activity that is notoriously cyclical. Consequently, some finance companies have attempted to ride the boom and bust of property development and some incurred large losses in the process (resulting, for some, in liquidation or being absorbed by their owner). Several finance companies owned by State-owned banks incurred massive losses following the 1980s boom/bust cycle that eventually led to their demise, along with the demise of their owner. (See example 6.6.)

example 6.6

During the 1970s, FCA (owned by the Bank of Adelaide) grew rapidly and became much larger than its owner. Consequently, when it incurred large losses, the viability of the bank was undermined. At the instigation of the RBA the bank was purchased, through a tender process, by ANZ.

In the 1980s the State Bank of South Australia's finance company, Beneficial Finance, grew rapidly and invested heavily in property development, including developments in Adelaide that were supported by the State Government. When the property market collapsed, Beneficial incurred huge losses (of the order of $2 billion) as a result of which it was absorbed into the State Bank of South Australia. The disaster was the subject of a Royal Commission and led to the resignation of the then Premier. The Bank of South Australia was subsequently acquired by Advance Bank.

Assets and liabilities

Not all of the business of finance companies is based on property development. In fact, their main financing activity is the provision of funds for businesses (including leasing) and for consumers. An indication of their assets and liabilities is provided by the data in table 6.13.

While finance companies raise about half of their debt funds through the issue of debentures and unsecured notes to retail customers, these companies and general financiers rely heavily on other institutions (including their own related companies) for funds.

A debenture is a fixed-interest (retail-bond type) security that is issued in small denominations to retail investors. The issuing process is restrictive, requiring a prospectus and the imposition of covenants (on the financial position of the issuer) in a trust deed. Debentures are not readily marketable and thus are usually held to maturity by the original investors.

Observe in table 6.13 that holdings of liquid assets (cash plus marketable securities) are relatively small (compared to those of banks and building societies shown in tables 6.9 and 6.12). Presumably finance companies do not need a large holding of liquid assets. They do not accept deposits from the public: they raise funds from related companies and the maturity of their assets is similar to that of their liabilities. Most of their assets and liabilities have a term of less than five years.

Table 6.13 Finance companies — selected assets and liabilities, June 1991 and June 1995 ($m)

	Finance companies		*General financiers*	
	1991	1995	1991	1995
Liabilities				
— related corporations	1 125	2 601	1 992	1 099
— debentures and unsecured notes	16 462	13 279		
— banks	3 366	3 349	428	190
— other	4 504	4 187	6 069	4 415
— non-residents	4 719	2 986	1 833	2 367
Assets				
— cash	313	809	563	143
— marketable securities	332	319	1 635	399
— personal loans	6 678	7 429	2 043	2 298
— lease receivables	9 243	6 535	3 036	3 538
— other business loans	16 456	14 017	3 514	3 197
Total assets	35 809	31 563	11 788	10 166

Source: RBA, *Bulletin*, Tables C.6 and C.7

Their need for liquidity arises mainly from their revolving loans and they manage this by arranging lines of credit which they can draw upon as required. Finance companies make both fixed-term and revolving loans. They are usually repaid on a regular-payment basis that amortises the loan.

Lease receivables are an important asset. Their lending to the lease market ($10 billion in June 1995) exceeds that of banks ($7.1 billion). Finance companies are also a competitor of banks in both the personal-loan and business-loan markets. As at June 1995 their lending to individuals totalled $7.7 billion, whereas bank lending in this area was $28.9 billion. Their lending to business (other than for leasing) totalled $17.2 billion compared with $75.2 by banks.

Key points — NBFIs

- The participation of NBFIs in the provision of intermediation products has been undergoing rationalisation since deregulation and the process is still unfolding.
- The assets of some building societies and finance companies have been absorbed by banks.
- Credit unions, because of the common interests of their members, have been less affected by deregulation than the other institutions discussed here. But they have been undergoing a process of consolidation, resulting in larger, fewer credit unions.
- The asset composition of these institutions reflects their particular circumstances.

Summary

The main points of this chapter are as follows:

- Historically, banks have been the main providers of retail banking products and services.
- Payment services and borrowing/on-lending are basic activities of retail banks.
- The bulk of bank funds are as deposits in either current or fixed-term accounts (from retail customers) or as certificates of deposit (from wholesale customers).
- Banks have substantial foreign-currency liabilities.
- Loans and advances are the major uses of funds by banks.
- Banks are major providers of funds for housing, other personal loan requirements and business, through the provision of term loans.
- Banks hold liquid assets to satisfy the RBA's prime asset requirement and to meet their needs for same-day and next-day funds.
- Building societies and credit unions also provide basic intermediation services and products, but they operate on a smaller scale than most banks and almost all of the sizeable building societies have become banks.
- Finance companies and general financiers provide funds for business and individuals.

Discussion questions and exercises

1 Discuss the development of financial institutions in Australia up to the present. Refer, in particular, to the impact of regulations and deregulation on this development. Suggest what lessons should be learned from the historical development of financial institutions in Australia.

2 Briefly describe the activities of retail banking. Discuss the main sources and uses of funds, indicating their benefits to customers and the risks they pose for retail banks, and refer to recent trends in these items.

3 Prepare a schedule that lists current and fixed-term deposits and certificates of deposit and shows their characteristics and the relationship between their interest rates and liquidity.
4 Describe and assess the assets of banks (with reference to tables 6.7 and 6.8).
5 Describe the pattern of bank lending as at June 1995.
6 Describe the process of securitising housing loans through mortgage-backed securities and discuss the implications of loan origination for retail banking.
7 Discuss the process and forms of business loans by banks.
8 Explain the role of 'reference' interest rates and risk margins as determinants of the interest rate borrowers pay for funds.
9 Suggest several reasons for the growth in credit-card lending.
10 Discuss the past and future roles of NBFIs in retail banking.

REFERENCES AND FURTHER READING

Arndt, H.W. 1960, *The Australian Trading Banks*, Cheshire, Melbourne.

De Lucia, R. D., & Peters, J. 1993, *Commercial Bank Management: Functions and Objectives*, Serendip, Chapter 1.

Felmingham, Bruce, & Coleman, William 1995, *Money and Finance in the Australian Economy*, Irwin, Chapters 16 and 21.

House of Representatives Standing Committee on Finance and Public Administration, Martin, Stephen (Chair) 1991, *A Pocket Full of Change*, AGPS, Canberra.

Joss, Robert 1996, 'Developments in the business of banking' in Malcolm Edey (ed.), *The Future of the Financial System*, RBA, Sydney.

KPMG Peat Marwick, *1995 Financial Institutions Performance Survey*, Sydney.

Lewis, M. K., & Wallace, R. H. (eds) 1993, *The Australian Financial System*, Longman Cheshire, Melbourne: Chapter 1, 'Australia's evolving financial system' by M.K. Lewis and R. H. Wallace; Chapter 3, 'The banks' by D. Daugaard and T. J. Valentine; Chapter 4, 'The thrift institutions: building societies, credit unions and friendly societies' by K. P. O'Brien; and Chapter 6, 'The business financiers: merchant banks and finance companies' by R. H. Wallace.

McGrath, Michael 1994, *Financial Institutions, Instruments and Markets in Australia*, McGraw-Hill, Sydney, Chapter 2.

RBA October 1992, 'Foreign banks in Australia — policy issues and prospects', *Bulletin*, pp. 22–7.

RBA April 1995, *A Proposal for Implementing Real Time Gross Settlement in Australia*.

RBA June 1995, 'Non-callable deposits', *Bulletin*, p. 1.

RBA June 1996, 'The evolution of the housing loan market in Australia,' *Bulletin*, pp. 1–5.

RBA July 1996, *Bulletin*.

Shanmugam, Bala *et. al.* 1993, *Bank Management*, John Wiley & Sons, Chapters 10 and 11.

Westpac Banking Corporation, *1994 Annual Report*.

7

Wholesale banking

The main purpose of this chapter is to explain the operations of the institutions that are engaged in wholesale banking. The chapter discusses merchant banks (known officially as money market corporations), the major banks, international and investment banks, and branch banks. Reference is made to wholesale banking products and services, including the off-balance sheet holdings of banks.

Study objectives

From your study of this chapter you should be able to:

- describe the role of wholesale banking;
- recount the development of merchant banks in Australia;
- describe the assets and liabilities of wholesale banking institutions;
- compare the roles of merchant banks, major banks, investment banks and branch banks within the wholesale sector of Australia's financial system;
- describe the off-balance sheet holdings of banks.

INTRODUCTION

The previous chapter dealt with retail banking and the institutions that compete in that sector of the financial system. This chapter describes the institutions that provide products and services to wholesale customers. Whereas the previous chapter used banks as the basis for its discussion, this chapter commences with a discussion of merchant banks and their participation in the wholesale sector. The balance of the chapter discusses the role of banks in the wholesale sector and their off-balance sheet business.

In functional terms, wholesale banking is the preserve of investment banks. In Australia this group includes the majors, branches of foreign banks and certain merchant banks, along with the investment banks. According to Rob Ferguson (of Bankers Trust Australia Limited):

> *Investment banks aspire to be leading participants in all or nearly all of the following activities: corporate finance, both public and private; mergers and acquisitions; sales, trading and research of equities, foreign exchange, fixed-income securities and derivative products; and investment management and related operational services.* (1996, p. 205)

Most of the banks and non-bank institutions (i.e. merchant banks) that undertake the above activities (not including the majors) are members of the International Banks and Securities Association of Australia (IBSA), which formerly was known as the Australian Merchant Bankers' Association.

IBSA's *Annual Report 1994* (pp. 8–9) outlines the activities of its members. They include:

Corporate finance This covers corporate advisory and financing functions. In addition to providing advice to corporate clients on their financing needs in general, these functions include advice and assistance with, specifically:

- mergers and acquisitions and their financing,
- project finance (including financial planning for projects, as well as the provision of finance), and
- long-term debt and equity raising (undertaken with the lending departments of these institutions) from both domestic and overseas markets.

Corporate lending This covers various forms of lending, such as Australian- and foreign-currency loans, syndicated loans, letters of credit, bill facilities and leasing. Loans are provided on either a fixed- or floating-rate basis.

Money market This covers accepting short-term deposits from commercial clients, trading securities, such as bills, notes, CDs and bonds, underwriting security issues and making short-term advances. It also includes the provision of money-market advisory services and credit-enhancement facilities (such as letters of credit supporting security issues).

Swaps and options markets This covers the provision of risk-management instruments that assist clients in both the raising of capital and the management of the market risks that arise from having access to financial markets and holding financial assets.

Foreign exchange services As FX dealers, these institutions provide spot and forward foreign exchange as well as access to overseas financial markets. They also provide advice to clients on the management of exposures to FX risk.

Futures markets Most members, or their related organisation, are members of the Sydney (and/or overseas) Futures Market.

Investment management This covers the management of funds (raised through superannuation contributions and public unit trusts) and client portfolios.

Trade finance This involves drawing trade bills that are used to arrange short-term trade finance in domestic and foreign currencies.

Other activities These include stockbroking services, bullion trading and development-capital companies.

Four groups of institutions are engaged in wholesale activities. We discuss them in the following order:

- merchant banks,
- major banks,
- investment banks, and
- branch banks.

There is a wide disparity among the institutions engaged in the wholesale sector. Some, such as the major banks, are engaged in most of the activities listed above, and operate on a large scale; whereas many of the other institutions undertake only a few of these activities. Those institutions that concentrate on borrowing from and lending to large clients earn most of their income from their interest-rate spread; whereas those institutions that specialise in the provision of financial advice, market trading and the management of funds earn most of their income in non-interest forms. (See example 7.1.)

example 7.1

Banks and merchant banks act as arrangers of security issues for wholesale clients. According to the 1994 Capital Market Survey by Ernst & Young, the big four banks were the leading arrangers of new short-term debt programs in the domestic market and leading arrangers of such securities by domestic borrowers in offshore markets. Merchant and investment banks, such as Hambros Bank, Swiss Bank Corporation, Morgan Stanley and Nomura, were more prominent in arranging medium- to long-term debt securities, both in the domestic and off-shore markets.

The big four banks also dominated the provision of syndicated facilities in the domestic market in 1994, such as a $1 billion facility for Qantas (where the Commonwealth Bank was the lead arranger) and a similar amount for Nine Network Australia (where ANZ was the lead arranger).

More specific data are provided in the chapters in Part three that describe the operations of these security markets.

In the wholesale sector, markets have substantially displaced intermediated funding and thus bank balance sheets (that show bank loans and deposits) display only a small part of the activities of the banks engaged in this sector. According to William Ferguson (of Citibank Limited), '. . . markets are more efficient than institutions and the process of banks being disintermediated by capital markets and more efficient non-bank providers of financial services will not abate'. (1996, p. 195)

This view implies that traditional banking services to wholesale customers are being unbundled and that banks will remain as the main providers of financial services to wholesale customers only if they are competitive in the provision of each component service (such as loan arrangement, underwriting and investment management).

Merchant banks

Even though a study of the assets and liabilities of institutions engaged in wholesale banking provides an incomplete view of their activities, such a study is the best starting point for our discussion of these institutions.

Because the data on bank assets and liabilities are not divided into retail and wholesale segments, we commence this chapter with a study of merchant banks. As a group they are principally engaged in wholesale banking activities and they played the major role in the development of this sector of the financial system. Individually, though, they are neither large nor homogeneous.

At the outset it is important to clarify our reference to merchant banks as 'money market corporations' (MMCs) when discussing statistical data. The latter title arose from the need to classify non-bank institutions under the *Financial Corporations Act*. Even though the title 'merchant bank' was popularly used to refer to many of the institutions that raised funds from the short-term money market and made large-value loans, it was decided to call Category D institutions 'Money Market Corporations'. Presumably it was thought that 'merchant *bank*' was not appropriate, as it might give the false impression that these institutions were banks within the meaning of the *Banking Act*.

The classification of merchant banks as MMCs has significance only in the collection of statistics. The data provided by the RBA are for MMCs. Consequently, we use that title when discussing the data. In general discussion we use the title 'merchant bank', because we believe it is better known.

It is noted that in 1987 the government gave permission to registered MMCs to use the descriptive expression 'merchant bank', and that the RBA now refers to them as such in its *Bulletin*.

Historical introduction

The first institutions in Australia to undertake merchant bank activities were known as 'development finance institutions'. (Wallace, 1993, p. 220) They were formed in the 1950s by well-established stockbroking firms to undertake investment banking activities.

Initially they relied mainly on equity funds and for about a decade played only a minor role as a provider of corporate finance. However, in the early 1960s they were involved in the development of two important (and related) financial markets:

- the short-term money market, and
- the inter-company market.

Three of the original development finance institutions became official dealers in the short-term money market. They also developed the use of commercial bills as acceptors (in the primary market) and as market makers (in the secondary market).

As a result of tapping short-term funds themselves, their balance sheets grew and became highly geared. By the early 1970s they relied principally on short-term debt funds, only 8% of their funds being in the form of equity.

Two organisations were formed in the early 1970s:

- Accepting Houses of Australia (to promote the development of the bill market), and
- Issuing Houses Association of Australia (an association of companies engaged in investment-banking activities).

They merged in 1979 to form the Australian Merchant Bankers' Association. In January 1993 this organisation changed its name to the International Banks and Securities Association of Australia.

When the term 'money market corporation' was coined it applied to financial intermediaries that borrowed on a short-term basis from the corporate sector and on-lent the funds to official dealers and large-value borrowers such as companies. They used a proportion of their funds to hold government and commercial paper for liquidity purposes.

Banks could not be directly involved in the development of the short-term money market because of the regulation against them accepting large-value deposits (CDs) for terms of less than a month. Reserve Bank limits on their acceptance of bills and interest-rate ceilings also impeded their possible role in this area. They were indirectly involved through their part-ownership of merchant banks.

Several other regulations influenced the formation of merchant banks:

- foreign banks were not permitted to become Australian banks but they could become part-owners of Australian merchant banks and conduct their business through these companies,
- foreign-investment guidelines restricted the level of direct ownership by foreigners (i.e. overseas banks) of merchant banks, and
- limits were imposed on the extent to which domestic banks could hold shares in merchant banks.

As a result of these regulations most merchant banks in the 1970s were jointly owned by foreign and domestic institutions. The overseas institution usually possessed functional expertise. For example, several members of the London Accepting Houses Committee were part-owners of Australian merchant banks, as were a number of major US investment banks. The foreign banks also could provide access to substantial **standby facilities** (i.e. funds that could be drawn upon if required by the merchant bank). The domestic part-owners, being domestic banks or other financial institutions (such as insurance offices), were expected to provide the merchant bank with recognition in the Australian market as well as local knowledge to complement the expertise of the foreign co-owner(s).

Despite the ownership restrictions on merchant banks, there were 71 registered MMCs in 1983, which collectively held 5.5% of Australian financial assets.

> *There was a widespread view among financial writers that the deregulation would result in a substantial reduction in the merchant banking sector.* (Wallace, 1993, p. 230)

Large parts of the sector's activities relied on regulations that prevented intrusion by banks, both domestic and foreign. The removal of these regulations influenced merchant banks in various ways:

- The lifting of the restriction on ownership allowed each overseas and domestic bank to form its own wholly-owned merchant bank. Between 1985 and 1987, 59 new merchant banks were registered (RBA, 1992, p. 3), but it was thought that in time many of these institutions would either become banks or be incorporated into the operations of their owner.
- The entry of 15 new banks, most of which were subsidiaries of foreign banks, meant that these banks no longer needed to own a merchant bank to operate in Australia. Most of these banks (such as Citibank Limited, Bank America Australia Limited and Bank of Tokyo Australia Limited) became involved in merchant banking because they could not become an Australian bank. However, the decision whether to incorporate their 'non-bank' business into their new banking operations reflected other factors, such as the impact of the interest-withholding tax on foreign borrowings and the remaining regulations on banks that did not apply to non-banks. As at mid 1995, a number of foreign banks had maintained their merchant bank.
- It was expected that domestic banks would incorporate their merchant-bank activities within their operations, given that their participation in merchant banking arose only because they could not undertake the activities as a bank. Westpac, for example, after becoming the sole owner of Partnership Pacific Limited — the largest merchant bank in the mid 1980s — subsequently incorporated its activities into those of the bank.
- Banks became free to set competitive rates on CDs, allowing them to attract funds from wholesale customers (and they were able to compete with cash management funds, a number of which were operated by merchant banks, for retail funds). As they were able to compete for funds, banks could undertake merchant-banking activities as part of their banking operations.
- Banks were relieved of the constraint on their bill-acceptance activities and, given that their credit rating is generally higher than that of merchant banks, they became the dominant players in this market (displacing merchant banks).

Other aspects of deregulation opened new opportunities for merchant banks; for example:

- The floating of the currency and the removal of exchange control was accompanied by the licensing of approximately 50 merchant banks as FX dealers. This represented a new opportunity for merchant banks in the provision of spot and forward FX and in the provision of FX-risk-management services. It also allowed the foreign-owned merchant banks to gain readier access to overseas sources of funds.
- The market for CGSs developed following deregulation and a number of merchant banks became 'recognised dealers' in the bond market.
- The stock exchange reviewed its rules and decided to remove those that restricted competition. This allowed merchant banks (and any other institution) to become brokers and to increase their involvement in the equities market.

- The deregulation of the financial markets resulted in interest-rate (and FX) volatility and this created the need for risk-management instruments and advice. Merchant banks became members of the futures exchange and developed hedging instruments.
- A number of rapidly growing conglomerates (i.e. companies that are engaged in a range of industries) formed their own merchant banks.

Consequently, deregulation dislodged merchant banks from some market niches but created opportunities to develop others. Moreover, as noted previously, many foreign banks maintained their merchant-bank operations even though they were granted a banking licence. The domestic banks also maintained their merchant banks for some time through the 1980s, although by the 1990s they had incorporated their merchant-bank activities into their banking operations.

The aggregate balance sheet of MMCs continued to expand relative to the financial system until the late 1980s. This was the result of several specific features of this period, in addition to deregulation and the entry of new merchant banks:

- asset-price inflation,
- a general increase in the use of debt capital by companies, and
- the development of conglomerates by 'entrepreneurs'.

All these events were not unrelated and were not unique to Australia. They were features of a boom period in which merchant banks (particularly the newly established merchant banks that were attempting to secure a place in the Australian market) were aggressive participants. In other words, during the 1980s the amount of financial intermediation expanded strongly, partly because of the demand (from companies for debt capital) and partly because of the activities of suppliers (including merchant banks).

The October 1987 shareprice crash and their highly-geared capital structures caused the downfall of those companies that borrowed heavily to acquire assets (such as those represented by the shares of the companies being taken over) in the expectation that their value would rise. This simple business strategy had allowed the entrepreneurs to build massive conglomerates during the 1980s, but when asset prices fell they did not have sufficient cash flow to meet their debt obligations.

The institutions that provided funds to these conglomerates (which included, of course, the merchant banks that were owned by them) were left with bad debts. Those merchant banks that had sought business aggressively during the 1980s were most exposed to these bad debts and some became spectacular failures in the early 1990s. (See example 7.2.)

example 7.2

Following deregulation, a merchant bank (Tricontinental) that was co-owned by the State Bank of Victoria, the Rural and Industries Bank of Western Australia and five foreign banks, became wholly owned by the State Bank of Victoria. It was one of the largest merchant banks at the time, but following the change in its ownership it embarked on a massive expansion of its investment-banking business. However the assets it built up were loans to companies that subsequently collapsed, following the shareprice crash.

Tricontinental's bad debts resulted in losses of more than $1 billion, which greatly exceeded its equity and that of its owner, the State Bank of Victoria. The Government of Victoria was faced with having to use taxpayers' money to cover the losses and instead sold the bank to the Commonwealth Bank (allowing the Commonwealth Government to commence the process of privatising that bank).

Not all merchant banks went into bankruptcy (or even made losses) following the 1987 shareprice crash. Those that conducted business as usual (and this included merchant banks owned by Japanese banks) continued to grow and make good profits, as did those merchant banks that moved into new areas, such as funds management. BT Australia was a case in point. Its profits were substantial relative to its assets, partly because of its fee income from providing funds-management services.

An indication of the role of merchant banks within the financial system is provided by the data on total assets over the period June 1953 to June 1995 presented in table 7.1. Even though their asset share reached almost 10% in the late 1980s — and recognising that asset holdings understate their role within the financial system — it is clear that merchant banks have been specialists rather than major players in the financial system.

Observe the growth in market share between 1984 and 1989. As noted above, it had been widely expected that this group would lose market share following deregulation. The continued growth in market share after 1984 was due in part to the increase in the number of foreign-owned merchant banks and to the continued imposition of the statutory reserve deposit (SRD) requirements on banks. This requirement was replaced by the less-severe non-callable deposits ratio in September 1988. The SRD requirement impeded the growth of the new foreign banks because it tied up bank funds with the RBA at a non-commercial interest rate. (Hogan, 1991, p. 13)

Table 7.1 MMCs assets — Selected years, June 1953 to June 1995

June	*Total assets ($m)*	*% of all financial institutions*
1953	7	negligible
1966	70	0.5
1970	700	5.7
1980	7 000	2.0
1984	17 729	7.6
1989	54 163	8.9
1994	43 048	5.4
1995	51 251	6.0

Source: Wallace, 1993, p. 218; RBA, *Bulletin*, Tables C.4 and D.5

Despite some heavy losses and merchant-bank failures in the early 1990s, in the mid 1990s this group of NBFIs remains an important part of the wholesale banking sector, although no merchant bank is large when compared with their bank counterparts (the majors and the investment banks, which are discussed later in this chapter). The largest merchant banks (all foreign-owned) by assets held at the end of 1994 are:

- Société Générale Australia Limited, with assets of $3.1 billion,
- ABN AMRO Australia Limited, with assets of $2.4 billion,
- Toronto Dominion Australia Limited, with assets of $1.8 billion,
- BT Australia Limited, with assets of $1.65 billion, and
- Sumitomo International Finance Australia Limited, with assets of $1.6 billion.

Of the 40 or so MMCs included in the 1995 survey by KPMG Peat Marwick, only four had an Australian owner, one of which was J.B. Were Capital Markets Limited. The Melbourne-based stockbroking firm, J.B. Were, had established one of the original four development finance institutions, Capel Court Corporation.

Activities

A partial view of the activities of merchant banks is provided by the aggregate liabilities and assets of MMCs. Table 7.2 presents RBA data on selected liabilities of MMCs over the period June 1991 to June 1995. You will see that in most years shown in the table, the MMCs raised the majority of their liabilities from non-residents. The 'other' category includes short-term borrowing from domestic companies.

Domestic borrowing by merchant banks is usually on a short-term, unsecured basis. Accordingly, their cost of domestic funds is sensitive to movements in the overnight rate in the short-term money market. The rate paid by individual merchant banks depends on the credit standing of their parent. Skully (1987, p. 84) suggests that merchant-bank borrowing from non-residents is usually for medium terms.

Table 7.2 Liabilities of MMCs — June 1991 to June 1995 ($m)

June	*Related companies*	*Banks*	*Other*	*Non-residents*
1991	1 549	8 195	14 446	19 663
1992	2 053	7 181	13 818	19 896
1993	1 151	5 906	10 601	19 667
1994	2 374	5 359	10 391	17 333
1995	2 399	5 265	11 326	24 169

Source: RBA, *Bulletin*, Table C.4

Merchant banks use standby facilities to allow them to offer standby facilities to their customers. The unused amounts of their standby facilities are a source of liquidity for merchant banks.

Merchant banks lend funds at a base rate that applies a narrow margin (i.e. about one percentage point) over their cost of funds. (Wallace, 1993, pp. 224–25) Usually they lend large amounts to wholesale customers and provide no other banking services that could involve a cross-subsidy. The same practice is applied by the wholesale departments of banks.

The narrow spread reflects several factors:

- Wholesale operations are not labour intensive and usually involve large amounts. Data on operating income per employee for MMCs are provided in table 7.3. Observe that these amounts are much higher than for building societies and regional banks.
- The clients of merchant banks may be able to engage in direct financing and would do so if the spread set by merchant banks became too large.

Merchant banks use their funds mainly for lending purposes. Loans provide merchant banks with their highest yield, but, of course, involve more risk than their other assets. Data on the assets of MMCs are presented in table 7.4 for the period June 1991 to June 1995. Except for June 1995, loans and advances represent more than half of their assets.

Table 7.3 Operating income ($000) per employee — representative MMCs, building societies and regional banks, 1994

MMCs		*Building societies*		*Regional banks*	
	$		$		
BT Australia	854	Bendigo	113	Advance Bank	180
Société Générale	424	Newcastle Permanent	140	State Bank of NSW	107
Sumitomo International	518	Illawarra Mutual	142	Bank of Melbourne	180
Toronto Dominion	283	Heritage (Qld)	104	Challenge Bank	149
Average for group	493	**Average for group**	155	**Average for group**	170

Source: KPMG Peat Marwick, *1995 Financial Institutions Performance Survey*, pp. 43, 49, 51, 65 and 67

Merchant-bank lending parallels bank lending in a number of respects. While merchant banks cannot provide overdrafts, they provide short-term loans. These can be rolled over to provide a medium-term facility, on a floating-rate basis. When making large-value loans to business, they usually form a syndicate, given that merchant banks are not large financial intermediaries. They provide term loans, project finance and lease finance.

When providing finance for projects such as property and mining developments, merchant banks may accept some of the risks normally borne by the suppliers of equity funds, on the basis that they participate in the profits. For example, they provide funds on a **non-recourse** basis. This means that the finance payments come specifically from the project's income. Should this cash flow prove to be inadequate, the finance payments are not enforceable.

The average term of loans by merchant banks is longer than the average term of their liabilities. MMCs are classified as borrowers of short-term funds that are lent for short and medium terms. This requires them to undertake maturity intermediation. To the extent that their borrowings from non-residents involves medium-term funds, they reduce the extent of this problem.

It can be seen, though, that MMCs hold few overseas assets relative to their overseas liabilities. This exposes them to FX risk. Should the value of the Aussie dollar depreciate their net foreign-currency commitments would increase. No doubt MMCs hedge this exposure by either swapping their foreign-currency liabilities into Australian-dollar obligations, or by buying foreign currency in the forward market to meet their payments when due.

The asset composition of most merchant banks is influenced by the prudential supervision guidelines of the Bank for International Settlements (BIS) because the merchant banks are owned by banks and these requirements apply to the global operations of banks.

MMCs are not subject to the prime asset requirement (PAR) of the Reserve Bank. An indication of their holdings of liquid (although not necessarily, prime) assets is provided by the data in the first two rows of table 7.4. In total, these assets represented about 10% of their total assets over the past few years. However, CGSs (which are prime assets) represent only a tiny proportion of their assets (1.2% in June 1995 and 2.5% in June 1994). Given that they have a choice, it is evident that MMCs would hold more CGSs only if required to. In other words, not being subject to the PAR, they do not form part of the captive market for CGSs.

Observe also that they hold other liquid assets, such as cash and bank deposits, bills and P-notes. Even though there is a deep secondary market for bills and notes, their holdings of these securities may not be liquid. Merchant banks (in common with other institutions) accept deposits on the basis that they are secured by liquid securities. These securities, of course, must be held until the deposits have been repaid.

Table 7.4 MMCs — selected assets, June 1991 to June 1995, $m

	1991	*1992*	*1993*	*1994*	*1995*
Cash and bank deposits	3 065	2 597	1 519	1 739	3 584
Public-sector securities	1 907	3 005	2 883	2 220	1 627
Loans to related companies	1 382	1 799	1 296	1 573	2 345
Other placements and deposits	2 699	1 690	1 978	1 443	1 781
Balances with other NBFIs	3 126	2 436	2 256	2 125	3 459
Bills and P-notes	4 444	4 800	3 408	3 762	4 584
Loans and advances	27 236	24 502	23 324	23 061	24 430
Overseas assets	1 472	1 556	1 714	1 792	3 359
Total assets	48 367	46 657	42 738	43 048	51 251

Source: RBA, *Bulletin*, Table C.4

An indication of the activities of merchant banks that do not involve balance-sheet items is provided by their non-interest income, even though this may include abnormal sources of income. For the group of MMCs covered by the 1995 KPMG Peat Marwick survey, net-interest income as a ratio of the average total assets was 1.01%, whereas their non-interest income was 4.08% of their assets. The extent of non-interest income relative to their assets varied widely between MMCs because of the differences in their operations. For example, the non-interest income-to-assets ratio was 29.83% for McIntosh Securities Limited; 22.36% for BT Australia Limited; 15.37% for N. M. Rothchild & Sons; and 14.63% for SBC Australia Holdings Limited.

Key points — merchant banks

- Merchant banks remain as part of the wholesale sector despite (a) the removal of the regulations that served to protect their position; (b) the merchant banks owned by domestic banks being absorbed into the banking operations of their owner; and (c) some spectacular failures in the early 1990s.
- They are relatively small specialist companies, the most prominent of which are subsidiaries of foreign banks.
- Merchant banks raise funds domestically from the short-term money market and from overseas (this being their largest source of funds).
- They usually lend most of their funds to wholesale customers (generally on a floating-rate basis), transforming the maturity of the funds.
- Merchant banks that are subsidiaries of banks are subject to prudential guidelines, but are not subject to the PAR and NCD requirements of the RBA.

BANKS

Three groups of banks are active in the wholesale banking sector:

- the majors,
- investment banks (almost all of which are foreign-owned), and
- branches of foreign banks.

Some of the regional banks, such as the State Bank of New South Wales, have become active in the wholesale market, whereas others (such as Advance Bank) have remained focused on the retail banking sector. Some finance companies also compete in niches within the wholesale sector, such as the provision of lease finance and large-value business loans.

In this section we further consider three of the balance sheet items of banks that were discussed in the previous chapter, as well as the off-balance sheet business of banks.

Wholesale deposits

Banks raise funds from overseas and domestic wholesale markets. A number of banks have established short- and medium-term borrowing programs in Hong Kong,

London and New York. This allows them to raise funds as required by issuing more securities, such as euro-commercial paper. Data on the overall amount of foreign-currency liabilities (which include retail deposits of foreign currencies by domestic clients) was provided in table 6.1 (in the previous chapter, p. 142). Further discussion of offshore financing is presented in Chapter 13.

Certificates of deposit (CDs) are the main form of domestic wholesale deposits for banks. They are discount instruments similar to the promissory notes issued by non-financial organisations to raise funds.

Data were presented in table 6.2 (in Chapter 6, p. 142) on the role of CDs as a source of funds for banks. Generally, they are issued for large amounts (typically in denominations of $500 000 and $1 000 000) for short periods (see the data in table 7.5) at a yield set when issued. Provided CDs are held to maturity, the depositor receives the set (i.e. fixed) rate of interest that is implicit in the face value of the CD. Some variation can occur between the rates offered by different banks because not all banks have the same credit rating. Banks with a lower rating would have to offer a slightly higher rate.

As noted in the previous chapter, the issue yield on CDs usually is higher than the interest rate on retail deposits that have a similar term, but because large amounts are raised, the per dollar cost of the funds to banks need not exceed that of retail funds.

CDs give banks access to the money market as an alternative source of funds to retail customers. Given the liquidity of the short-term money market, banks can raise large amounts of funds through the issue of CDs. It is more difficult to raise large amounts quickly from retail customers. They can serve also as an alternative to selling securities to maintain a bank's liquidity.

Table 7.5 Certificates of deposit — all banks, amount issued ($m) according to term, January 1995

Week ending	*1 to <7 days*	*7 days to <3 months*	*3 to <6 months*	*6 months and over*
January 4	1 476	1 651	255	101
January 11	1 453	2 044	526	130
January 18	1 420	2 780	407	202
January 25	1 412	1 804	408	98

Source: RBA, *Bulletin*, Table B.11

The removal on the restriction that prevented banks from issuing CDs with a maturity of less than 14 days resulted in the banks relying more on this source of funds. In June 1981 only 4.9% of bank deposits came from CDs, whereas the proportion was 12.2% in June 1995.

Bill acceptances

As noted above, merchant banks pioneered the development of the commercial bill market. However, following deregulation, banks became the principal provider of acceptance facilities. The importance of bill-acceptance liabilities on the balance sheets of banks was shown by the data in table 6.1 (in Chapter 6, p. 142). A generalised representation of the parties involved in the issue of commercial bills was presented in figure 3.4 and is reproduced in this chapter, as figure 7.1, for ease of reference.

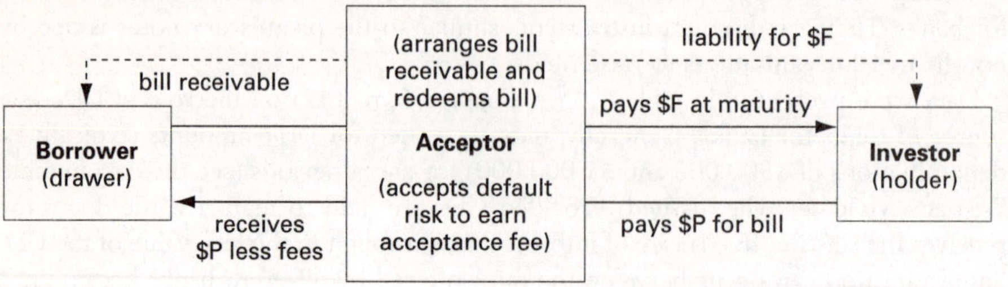

Figure 7.1 Parties to the issue of commercial bills

You will remember that the acceptor of a bill is responsible for its redemption at maturity (this is known as a **bill-acceptance liability**), but the acceptor will arrange for the bill's drawer to provide these funds (through a **bill-receivables** agreement). (Recall, the drawer is the borrower.) Thus, when a bill is issued, a parallel set of liabilities is created:

- the issuer's liability to pay the acceptor the bill's face value at maturity, and
- the acceptor's liability to make this payment to the bill's holder, known as **bill-acceptance liabilities**, and the amounts involved are shown on the acceptor's balance sheet. (RBA, 1988)

Bill acceptances also create a parallel set of assets:

- the promise of the drawer to pay the bill's face value to the acceptor (this being an asset for the acceptor), and
- the obligation of the acceptor to pay the bill's face value to its holder at maturity (this being an asset for the bill's holder).

As noted in the previous chapter, bill-acceptance liabilities are not a source of bank funds. Accepting this liability enhances the credit standing of the client's bill so that it can be sold in the short-term money market to raise funds for the client.

During the 1980s banks had an incentive to accept bills instead of providing their customers with overdrafts or advances, as a consequence of certain regulations on banks, and this resulted in a substantial growth in the acceptance of bills by banks.

Even though the regulations that resulted in the growth of bank-accepted bills have been repealed, the acceptance of bills has continued because it gives banks the option of funding or securitising assets. A bank can either make a short-term loan to a customer or agree to accept the customer's bill. The latter approach allows the bank to decide whether to fund (i.e. buy) the bill or discount it in the market.

Note that bill acceptance represents a form of unbundling of core banking business. Banks accept the investor's credit risk but do not (usually) fund the customer's borrowing. It represents a separation, therefore, of the credit assessment and funding components of loan products.

Bill facility

Because businesses often require funds for a longer term than the usual 90- or 120-day term of a bill, banks will provide a bill facility. This is an agreement to roll over bills on maturity by issuing a replacement set of bills. The bank redeems the first parcel of bills when they mature and arranges the issue of another parcel. The drawer is required to pay the difference between these amounts. This payment covers the bank's bill-facility charges and tops up the proceeds from the new issue to meet the redemption of the maturing bills.

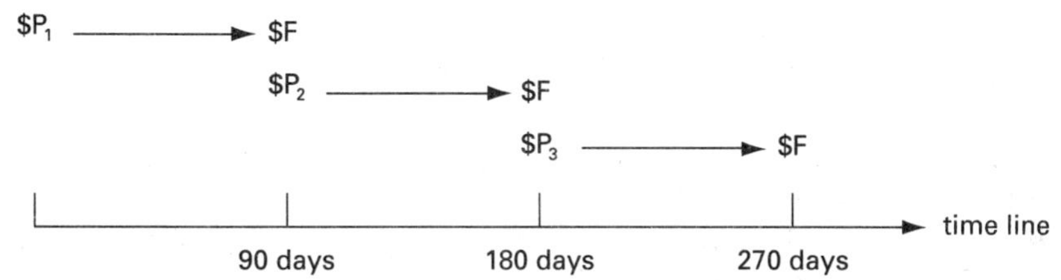

Figure 7.2 Notional cash flows on a 270-day bill facility

The cash flows involved in a 270-day bill facility are shown in figure 7.2. The proceeds of the issue of the first parcel of bills to the borrower is shown as $\$P_1$. New bills are issued under the facility when the initial bills mature. These raise $\$P_2$, which is used by the bank to redeem the initial parcel of bills, ($F), together with a payment from the borrower of $F - P_2$. The borrower will also be required to pay the bank's acceptance and facility fees each time the bills are rolled over.

The 270-day facility depicted in figure 7.2 is a floating-rate form of finance, because the amount paid by the borrower when the bills are rolled over $(F - P)$ depends on the proceeds from the sale of the replacement bills and this depends on the market yield each time the bills are issued. It therefore exposes the borrower to interest-rate risk. However, this exposure can be hedged through the use of derivatives, such as bill futures and FRAs, which are discussed in Chapter 17.

From a bank's viewpoint, a bill facility can substitute for the provision of an overdraft facility, which requires it to provide its funds. The advantage of the bill facility is that it does not involve the use of intermediated funds (i.e. the bank's funds). Both arrangements, though, require the bank to accept the credit risk on the repayment amount. This is covered in part by the bank imposing a higher margin on borrowers with a greater default risk. This pattern is reflected in the data presented in tables 7.6 and 7.7.

The big four banks dominate the bill-acceptance market and some banks do not accept bills. As at August 1995, the big four held 95% of the total amount of clients' commitments arising from bill acceptances.

The vast majority of bills outstanding are for amounts of $2 million and over (refer to the data in table 7.6.) Of the four categories provided in the RBA data, we treat

Table 7.6 Bills outstanding by size and interest rate, March 1995 ($m)

% p.a.	*<$100 000*	*$100 000 to >$0.5m*	*$0.5m to >$2m*	*$2m and over*	**Total**
Under 5	8	62	181	1 416	1 667
5 to <8	8	77	369	4 098	4 552
8 to <9	54	464	1 343	16 577	18 438
9 to <10	125	1 011	2 961	17 690	21 787
10 to <11	402	3 493	6 493	5 615	16 003
11 to <12	436	3 045	1 750	833	6 064
12 and over	409	1 341	991	924	3 584
Totals	1 442	9 493	14 008	47 153	72 095

Source: RBA, *Bulletin*, Table B.18

amounts of $2 million and over as representing loans to the wholesale sector. The smaller amounts are treated as loans to the retail sector. However, this distinction is purely arbitrary and each bank will distinguish between these sectors in its own way.

Observe also that the interest rate tends to be lower the larger the amount involved. This reflects differences in acceptance risk as a function of the amount of bill acceptance. Generally, larger borrowers have a lower credit risk. The interest rates do not incorporate the other charges imposed by banks when accepting bills (such as establishment, line and roll-over fees).

Term loans

The general features of term loans were explained in the previous chapter. As at June 1995, banks had term-loan outstandings of $54.6 billion, which represented 58% of their business loans. (Data on bank loans were presented in the previous chapter in table 6.9.) This amount does not distinguish between loans to retail customers (small- and medium-sized businesses) and the large-value loans (including syndicate loans) to wholesale customers.

As at March 1995, banks had almost $15 billion outstanding in the form of fixed-interest loans of amounts of $2 million or more. The majority of these were made at relatively low interest rates, compared with the rates that applied to small-value loans. (Refer to the data presented in table 7.7.) A further $9.9 billion was outstanding on loans of $2 million or more on a variable-rate basis.

Differences in credit risk and the amount of the loan are two reasons for the generally inverse relationship between loan size and the rate of interest. However, other factors are involved such as the age of the loan (in the case of fixed-rate loans, the rate depends on when the loan was granted); whether the credit risk of the customer has changed over the period of the loan; and what rate is reported on impaired loans (since 1994 they have been reported in the lowest interest-rate bands).

Treating loans of less than $2 million as retail, the data in table 7.7 indicate that variable-rate loans are made predominantly to retail customers (75%), and a slightly

Table 7.7 Loans to business by banks, classified by amount, interest-rate basis and the rate of interest, March 1996 ($m)

% p.a.	*<$100 000*	*$100 000 to <$0.5m*	*$500 000 to <$2m*	*$2m and over*	*Total*
Variable rate loans					
under 8	273	494	551	3 159	4 476
8 to <11	588	2 115	1 732	4 925	9 359
11 to <12	1 225	2 554	1 114	806	5 699
12 to <13	2 304	2 549	961	460	6 273
13 to <14	5 136	3 166	650	246	9 198
14 and over	1 104	629	180	311	2 224
Totals	10 629	11 507	5 187	9 907	37 229
Fixed-rate loans					
<6	27	110	146	1 757	2 039
6 to <8	38	99	239	3 625	4 000
8 to <9	371	910	941	2 822	5 045
9 to <10	1 777	3 191	2 738	3 495	11 201
10 to <11	2 324	4 579	2 455	1 841	11 198
11 to <12	1 540	2 646	1 051	790	6 027
12 to <13	574	1 102	575	541	2 793
13 and over	295	525	224	911	1 984
Totals	6 945	13 162	8 369	15 811	44 287

Source: RBA, *Bulletin*, Table B.17

lower proportion of fixed-rate loans (60%) are made to this sector. Overall, 67% of business lending is for amounts of less than $2 million.

Floating-rate lending and bill financing are alternative forms of financing. Recall (from the data in table 7.6) that bill financing is predominantly for amounts of $2 million or more. Aggregate data for loans and bill finance are presented in table 7.8, classified by amount and by economic sector.

Observe that, on an aggregate basis, the large-value loans (i.e. of $2 million or more) represent almost half of the credit extended directly or indirectly (through bill acceptances) by banks. The large-value loans were of greatest importance in the provision of credit to mining, manufacturing, construction, retail-trade (and related industries), finance and insurance and 'other' (the unspecified) sectors.

At the wholesale level, term loans compete with direct financing. Their main advantages over direct financing are as follows:

Table 7.8 Total bank credit outstanding by size and by sector, March 1996 ($m)

Sector	*<$100 000*	*$100 000 to <$0.5m*	*$0.5m to <$2m*	*$2m and over*	**Total**
Agriculture, etc.	3 419	6 303	2 854	2 491	15 068
Mining	103	204	290	2 514	3 110
Manufacturing	1 679	2 732	2 709	12 964	20 083
Construction	1 521	1 918	1 361	3 359	8 158
Retail-trade and related industries	5 086	6 944	4 185	8 615	24 829
Finance and insurance	871	2 766	3 818	21 924	29 379
Other	6 049	11 759	11 992	30 203	60 003
Total	18 728	32 625	27 208	82 070	160 631

Source: RBA, *Bulletin*, Table B.17

- Their usual maturity (two to five years) fills a gap between the short-term and long-term financial markets. Short-term securities can be issued so as to extend over several years (through a bill facility) and bonds can be issued for medium as well as long terms (such as medium-term notes). However, activity in the two financial markets is concentrated at either end of this term spectrum. (Shanmugam *et. al.*, p. 333)
- Raising funds in capital markets involves substantial costs that are only justified when the borrower has a large-scale borrowing program. The minimum amount of a term loan is much less than the minimum amount that can be raised through direct financing. Consequently, term loans are more cost effective for small- to medium-sized loans.
- The conditions of a term loan can be structured to suit the circumstances of the borrower while still satisfying the requirements of the lender. For example, a term loan that is used to finance extensions to a plant may be drawn down gradually to meet the payments to the builder and interest payments deferred until the plant becomes operational and able to generate cash flows.
- It is more convenient for a borrower to renegotiate a loan with a bank than with holders of securities, should the need arise.

In addition to term loans, banks provide overdraft finance to wholesale customers. Overdrafts are a 'facility' because the customer determines the amount that is actually borrowed. Overdrafts are a notional form of short-term finance because they are subject to regular review and could be withdrawn if the customer's financial position deteriorated sufficiently.

The data presented in tables 7.6 and 7.7 suggest that wholesale customers make much greater use of bill financing than overdrafts because bill financing generally involves a lower cost of funds. (This issue was discussed in the previous chapter.)

Banks also participate in large syndicate loans. This involves the provision of part of the loan funds. A syndicate loan requires a lead institution that organises the loan, the participating institutions and the loan documentation. Typically, the lead bank receives a margin for providing these services. The participating banks forgo this margin because they are relieved of the need to evaluate the borrower to the same degree as if they lent the money directly.

Syndicated loans usually are for large amounts and involve extensive documentation that specifies (among other things) the rights of the participating institutions against default by the borrower and the possible failure of any of the other participating banks.

Off-balance sheet business

Banks hold risk-management instruments to hedge their exposures to market risks and as counterparties to their customers (who may also be hedging their exposures). These instruments (forwards, futures, options and swaps) were described in Chapter 3. They are off-balance sheet items because of the contingent nature of their value.

These contracts are categorised in the RBA's data on off-balance sheet business as **market-related contracts**. There are three other categories:

- direct-credit substitutes, such as guarantees,
- trade- and performance-related items, such as letters of credit, and
- commitments, such as underwriting.

The amounts involved in the first two categories are tiny. Even though commitments amounted to \$132.6 billion in March 1995, that is a relatively small amount compared with the value of market-related contracts (\$2300 billion).

Market-related contracts have reference in the main to movements in:

- exchange rates, or
- interest rates.

The first three market-related contracts shown in table 7.9 serve to hedge exposure to movements in exchange rates, whereas the next four contracts are used to hedge exposure to movements in interest rates. The FX and currency contracts totalled \$1155.3 billion at the end of March 1995 and the interest-rate contracts totalled \$1110.7 billion.

The major categories of market-related contracts during the first half of the 1990s were:

- foreign-exchange contracts,
- interest-rate swap agreements,
- forward rate agreements, and
- interest-rate futures contracts.

Note that the data in table 7.9 is in billions of dollars, whereas the other tables are in millions of dollars, and note that the data cover the global operations of banks. This means that the data cover the global operations of Australian banks, as well as the operations of their bank and non-bank subsidiaries.

Table 7.9 Global off-balance sheet business of banks — March 1992 to March 1996 ($b)

	1992	*1993*	*1994*	*1995*	*1996*
Direct-credit substitutes	25.6	22.8	19.0	17.5	17.5
Trade- and performance-related items	15.1	16.4	15.2	16.0	16.2
Commitments	120.9	129.0	125.4	132.6	149.0
Market-related contracts					
— FX contracts	723.4	779.7	836.8	1 035.4	1 053.5
— currency swap contracts	82.2	88.2	92.6	80.0	83.4
— currency options purchased	29.0	35.1	39.1	39.8	32.3
— FRAs	302.4	304.2	296.9	267.6	180.0
— interest-rate swap agreements	382.7	493.3	532.8	538.0	568.3
— interest-rate futures contracts	169.2	211.8	265.7	243.0	288.3
— interest-rate options purchased	68.0	84.5	93.9	62.0	70.9
— other market-related contracts	12.3	18.6	48.9	34.3	32.9
Total market-related contracts	1 769.2	2 015.6	2 206.7	2 300.3	2 309.7
Total off-balance sheet business	1 930.8	2 183.8	2 366.3	2 466.4	2 492.4

Source: RBA, *Bulletin*, Table B.17

Observe in table 7.9 that off-balance sheet business involves substantial amounts that have increased steadily during the 1990s. Off-balance sheet items are products provided by banks to assist wholesale customers to manage their exposure to the risk of adverse movements in exchange and interest rates. When this exposes a bank to market risk, it will usually off-load this risk by entering further contracts with other banks. Moreover, banks are the principal dealers in the FX and domestic money markets. Consequently, one bank is often the counterparty to another in these derivative contracts.

Banks also enter risk-management contracts to hedge the risk arising from their balance-sheet business, such as the risk arising from their maturity intermediation.

The majors

In their previous existence as trading banks, the major banks provided funds to business. But prior to the 1960s the wholesale sector was both underdeveloped and supplied with few products and services. This was due in part to the financial system being highly regulated.

As outlined in the previous chapter, non-banks, especially merchant banks, were the main participants in the subsequent development of the wholesale sector. The major banks were involved in this process indirectly, through their co-ownership of merchant banks. Following deregulation they formed their own merchant banks, which were subsequently incorporated into their banking operations.

The big four banks are the main players in the wholesale sector. As noted above, they dominate the bill-acceptance market and are major lenders of funds to business. They are also leading providers of FX and risk-management instruments and have extensive overseas activities. They provide a comprehensive range of services and products to the wholesale market.

An indication of the wholesale business of a major bank (Westpac) is provided in the example that follows. Example 7.3 is an extension of the illustration presented in the previous chapter.

example 7.3

As stated in Chapter 6, Westpac had (in 1994) five operating groups:

- Retail Banking,
- Commercial Banking and Property Finance,
- Institutional and International Banking,
- Australian Guarantee Corporation,
- Westpac Financial Services.

A brief description of the bank's retail and commercial banking activities and those of AGC was presented in Chapter 6 (see p. 143).

The bank's wholesale activities are conducted mainly by its Institutional and International Banking Group, which also conducts the bank's overseas retail and wholesale operations. The bank's Financial Services Group, through its funds-management activities, is also a participant in the wholesale sector.

> *The* institutional banking division *has as its clientele large corporate, government and institutional customers for whom it provides domestic transaction banking and cash-management services, working-capital, term-lending and liquidity-enhancement facilities, and for whom it manages global banking arrangements . . . The division engages in international trade finance and funds transfer, provides project and structured finance and undertakes securitisation assignments on behalf of its clients.*
>
> *The* financial markets unit *. . . [provides] customers and the bank with foreign exchange services and currency and interest-rate risk-management products and services through its representation in the world's major financial centres.*
>
> *Customer-relationship management is integral to the division's operations in order to better bring together the various, often highly sophisticated, skills of the institutional bank's business units and ensure that all customers can potentially benefit from the products and services that are available within the bank.* (WBC, *1994 Annual Report, pp. 17–18)*

The bank's Institutional and International Banking Group held approximately $10 billion (of its $34 billion) in the form of (Australian) wholesale assets, which is over three times greater than the total assets of 1994's largest MMC (Société Générale Australia Limited, which had assets of just over $3 billion).

Investment banks

In the mid 1980s 15 new banking licences were issued to foreign banks as part of the process of deregulation. Sixteen offers were made but J. P. Morgan did not take up its offer. Most of these new banks were wholly-owned subsidiaries of foreign banks; the balance were co-owned with a domestic institution. Most of their efforts have been directed at the wholesale market.

A handful of new domestic banks also were created during the 1980s. Most of these were based on building societies and entered the retail banking sector. Macquarie Bank, in contrast, was based on a merchant bank (Hill Samuel Australia Limited) and directed most of its efforts toward the wholesale sector. The activities of this bank are summarised in example 7.4.

example 7.4

Macquarie Bank began operations in December 1969 as the merchant bank Hill Samuel Australia, with a staff of three. It was established by its British parent, Hill Samuel. In 1971 joint managing directors were appointed. One ran the money market and lending activities and the other was responsible for corporate advice. The former activities were transacted through the developing short-term money market.

In 1978 it established an international division that provided foreign-currency hedging advice and trading services in gold and commodity markets, including the contracts introduced by the Sydney Futures Exchange (of which it became a member).

In the early 1980s it established the first cash management trust. This took the merchant bank into the retail market, attracting larger deposits from individuals and small businesses. It also provided the basis for its subsequent entry to funds management.

At the time of the Campbell Committee's deliberations, the parent company decided to allow the Australian operation to pursue a banking licence as a locally-owned bank. It created a banking division in 1980 to consolidate its commercial-lending, money-market, Treasury and property-services activities. It also acquired part-ownership of a stockbroking firm, providing the basis for its Equities Group.

In 1984 the merchant bank was granted a licence to deal in foreign exchange. In February 1985 it was granted a banking licence. The bank's name (Macquarie Bank Limited) was chosen in recognition of the role played by Governor Macquarie (in the early 19th century) in the development of the then colony. Its mission was to develop a 'full service investment bank'.

Starting in 1983, the bank established a number of overseas offices, including its London office that traded Australian equities, foreign exchange and metals and arranged project and structured financing.

The bank avoided substantial exposure to the 'boom' firms and industries in the latter half of the 1980s and so did not suffer the profit reverses incurred by a number of its competitors.

In the early 1990s it developed its leading role in mortgage securitisation through its subsidiary, Puma.

As at March 1995, the bank had five major operating groups:

- the Corporate Banking Group, that has three divisions: Corporate Financing and Leasing, Property Investment Banking (which provides the bridging funds for Puma prior to the securitisation of the mortgage loans which it originates) and Banking Services.
- the Equities Group has five divisions: Macquarie Equities (which provides services to wholesale customers), Equity Structured Products, Macquarie Underwriting, Options and Private Clients Investments (which provides services to retail customers).
- the Macquarie Corporate Finance Group has two divisions, Corporate Advisory (providing advice on such matters as mergers and acquisitions, equity and debt raisings, and privatisations) and Project and Structured Finance (a global-oriented division that is a leader in infrastructure financing and cross-border leasing).
- the Treasury and Commodities Group has eight divisions: Bullion and Commodities, Capital Markets, Debt Markets (specialising in debt instruments other than CGSs and semi-government bonds), Energy and Agriculture, Foreign Exchange, Futures, Money Market (which manages the bank's liquidity position and trades in prime assets) and Risk Advisory Services.
- the Investment Services Group (with $11 billion under management, split equally between retail and institutional clients) has three divisions, Asset Management, Institutional Funds and Investment Products.

The bank has a number of smaller operating and support groups, such as Asia Resource Capital (a subsidiary that is engaged, for example, in metal projects in China), Quantitative Applications (in areas such as derivative pricing and risk analysis) and Economics and Fixed Interest Research. (Macquarie Bank Limited, *1995 Annual Report*)

We have given the title 'investment banks' to this category, principally to differentiate them from regional banks. It is a descriptive rather than an official title. As at mid 1995, all but one were owned or co-owned by an overseas bank. The domestic bank in this group, Macquarie Bank, referred to itself as an investment bank in its 1995 *Annual Report*. This group has been referred to as 'other banks' in the KPMG Peat Marwick surveys of financial institutions.

Each bank is principally (but not necessarily exclusively) involved in wholesale banking and does not have an extensive branch network, which is a feature of the operations of the big four and the regional banks. The 1995 KPMG Peat Marwick survey covers 13 of these banks. Some data on these banks for 1994 are presented in table 7.10.

These banks are equivalent institutions to merchant banks, although they are generally larger. The largest five banks each hold more assets than the largest MMC. The banks have to comply with the RBA's regulations, since they are part of Australia's banking system. They also obtain the benefits of being within the banking system. Merchant banks are NBFIs and are not subject to RBA regulation. You will recall that some of the foreign banks that have a bank subsidiary in Australia (such as Bankers Trust and the Industrial Bank of Japan) still operate their merchant bank.

Table 7.10 Selected data — investment banks, 1994

Bank Limited	*Assets ($m)*	*CAR[a] %*	*Op. Inc.[b] $000*	*Net II/A[c] %*	*Non II/A[d] %*
Arab Bank Australia	192	24.9	133.3	2.81	0.64
Bank of Singapore (Aust.)	681	14.5	392.1	2.05	1.94
Bank of Tokyo Australia	1 464	10.5	248.0	0.73	0.71
Bankers Trust Australia	5 695	37.2	483.9	2.92	9.65
Chase Manhattan Bank Aust.	1 418	19.0	216.2	2.27	4.04
Citibank	8 876	13.7	205.2	2.25	1.85
Hong Kong Bank of Australia	3 574	9.4	146.2	2.31	0.43
IBJ Australia Bank	1 950	15.2	1 127.0	2.42	1.09
Lloyds Bank NZA	817	14.8	176.3	1.39	1.39
Macquarie Bank	4 260	13.8	219.1	1.43	7.07
Mitsubishi Bank of Australia	1 406	11.0	295.8	1.05	0.28
Natwest Markets Australia	4 379	18.7	353.1	0.32	4.22
Standard Chartered Bank Aust.	607	14.1	207.0	1.68	2.65
Totals	43 487	18.7	289.0	1.65	3.75

[a] Capital adequacy ratio
[b] Operating income (in thousands) per employee
[c] Net-interest income as a ratio of average total assets
[d] Non-interest income as a ratio of average total assets

Source: KPMG Peat Marwick, *1995 Financial Institutions Performance Survey*, pp. 44–5

Coincidentally, as a group, the 13 banks held a similar amount of assets as MMCs did in December 1994 ($43.5 billion compared with $45.6 billion). Because of the similarity in their operations, they had similar ratios of net-interest income and non-interest income to assets in 1994 (1.65% compared with 1.01% for the net-interest income ratio and 3.75% compared with 4.08% for the non-interest income ratio), although the MMCs had a higher ratio of operating income to employees.

Observe the wide variation in the non-interest income ratio for the banks in table 7.10. Several are major funds managers (Bankers Trust Australia Limited and Macquarie Bank) and this earns them substantial amounts of fee income. You will recall that this applied also among MMCs.

Several of these banks, including Citibank and Deutsche Bank, undertake some retail business through their branches: 22 for Citibank and 18 for Deutsche Bank. These two banks plus Bankers Trust Australia and Macquarie Bank had, at the end of 1994, collectively, a staff of 5878 (equivalent full-time employees), which represented 70% of the total employment by this group of banks. The 40 MMCs covered by the KPMG 1995 survey had just over 3000 employees.

Branches of foreign banks

In 1992 the Commonwealth Government decided to:

- extend a licence to any foreign-bank applicant that meets the RBA's prudential and other regulatory requirements, and
- allow the new entrant to operate either as a subsidiary or as a branch of the foreign bank.

Newly admitted branches, including those that convert their bank subsidiary and/or their merchant bank to a branch of the foreign bank, will not be covered by the 'depositor protection' provisions of the *Banking Act*, and are not permitted to accept deposits from individuals of less than $250 000. In other words, branches will have to operate in the wholesale sector.

Branches are subject to the PAR and the NCD requirements of the Reserve Bank, but not to its prudential supervision requirements, such as its capital-adequacy requirement. The branches are subject to prudential supervision by their 'home' central bank. If applicants cannot demonstrate that they are subject to adequate prudential supervision by their home central bank, the government will refuse their application.

Approval will be granted for the establishment of a branch (subject to the above) where the applicant can show that its operations can be 'expected to make a worthwhile contribution to banking services in Australia . . . ' (RBA, 1992, p. 26) This contribution may be confined to certain banking services or to the more efficient functioning of a particular financial market. (RBA, 1994, p. 19)

By June 1995, 15 branches were in operation, the largest, Banque Nationale de Paris (BNP), having had a long involvement in Australia as a branch. (BNP, the Bank of China and the Bank of New Zealand established branches in Australia before the regulations that prohibited this practice were introduced.) However, as a group, branch banks are not large, although the larger branch banks are of a similar size to the larger MMCs. Data on the liabilities and assets of the larger branch banks and for the group overall are presented in tables 7.11 and 7.12.

The bulk of the Australian-dollar deposits of branch banks were in the form of term deposits and CDs. These are generally short-term deposits. About half of the branch banks also accept current deposits.

A few branch banks (Banque Nationale de Paris and the Bank of New Zealand, principally) accept bills, and thus have bill-acceptance liabilities. As a group, branch banks rely less on foreign-currency borrowing than MMCs, although the Bank of China can be seen to have relied almost totally on foreign-currency liabilities (which accounts for about a third of these liabilities for all branch banks in August 1995).

Observe in table 7.12 that branch banks hold very little cash because of their limited retail banking activities. They have, as a group, a very large proportion of their assets in the form of deposits and placements with, and loans to, other financial institutions (27%). While their Australian-dollar loans are their largest asset category, they represent only 35% of their assets. Their overseas assets ($4382m) are of a similar amount to their foreign-currency liabilities ($4585m).

Table 7.11 Branch banks — selected liabilities, August 1995 ($m)

Branch banks	*$A deposits*	*All $A liabilities*	*Foreign-currency liabilities*	**Total liabilities**
Bank of America NT and SA	278	590	857	1 447
Bank of China	109	378	1 618	1 996
Bank of New Zealand	1 173	1 523	476	2 008
Banque Nationale de Paris	3 413	3 826	624	4 450
Barclays Bank PLC	745	1 216	109	1 324
Dai-Ichi Kangyo Bank	796	813	424	1 237
Deutsche Bank AG	1 539	2 398	73	2 472
Midland Bank PLC	799	986	57	1 043
Other branch banks	1 764	1 965	347	2 313
Total	10 616	13 695	4 585	18 290

Source: RBA, *Bulletin*, Table B.9

Table 7.12 Branch banks — selected assets, August 1995 ($m)

Branch banks	*Cash*	*NCDs*	*CGSs*[a]	*Funds with other FIs*	*Loans*	*Total $A assets*	**Total assets**
Bank of America NT	9	6	57	590	75	763	1 439
Bank of China	1	8	40	133	577	821	2 373
Bank of New Zealand	1	13	—	377	839	1 437	1 844
Banque Nationale de Paris	—	36	208	1 260	1 824	3 721	4 783
Barclays Bank PLC	—	13	177	310	381	1 238	1 313
Dai-Ichi Kangyo Bank	1	9	76	331	667	1 088	1 215
Deutsche Bank	—	14	112	1 192	795	2 372	2 451
Midland Bank PLC	—	7	73	377	288	982	1 043
Other branch banks	—	18	182	585	1 243	2 053	2 396
Total	12	124	925	5 155	6 689	14 475	18 857

[a] Branch banks also held a total $432 million worth of other government securities ($326 million was held by two banks)

Source: RBA, *Bulletin*, Table B.10

Key points — banks

- Three categories of banks are engaged in wholesale banking.
- Individually, the big four banks are the biggest participants.
- The leading investment banks are also major players in the wholesale sector (or particular segments of it).
- Assets holdings are an incomplete measure of the wholesale activities of financial institutions.

Summary

The main points of this chapter are as follows:

- Wholesale banking is the provision of large-value financial products and services to companies and other large organisations.
- Four groups of institutions serve this sector of the financial system:
  - merchant banks,
  - major banks,
  - investment banks, and
  - branch banks.
- The main financial products provided to wholesale customers are:
  - certificates of deposit,
  - term loans,
  - bill financing, and
  - risk-management products.
- Banks' holdings of off-balance sheet contracts are very substantial, particularly holdings of market-risk management instruments.

Discussion questions and exercises

1 Discuss the development of merchant banks in Australia.
2 Describe the main financial products and services provided by wholesale banks. Distinguish between the intermediated and non-intermediated products and services.
3 Describe the wholesale banking activities of Macquarie Bank.
4 Discuss the activities of the institutions that operate in wholesale banking (the majors, merchant banks, investment banks and branch banks).
5 Describe the off-balance sheet holdings of banks.
6 Explain the relationship between bill acceptances and bank loans to business.
7 What are CDs and why have they become an important source of bank funds?
8 Explain the variation in interest rates on loans to business.

References and Further Reading

De Lucia, R. D., & Peters, J. 1993, *Commercial Bank Management: Functions and Objectives*, Serendip Publications.

Ferguson, Rob 1996, 'An investment banking perspective on the future of the financial system' in Malcolm Edey (ed.), *The Future of the Financial System*, RBA, Sydney.

Ferguson, William 1996, 'A banker's perspective on the future of the financial system' in Malcolm Edey (ed.), *The Future of the Financial System*, RBA, Sydney.

Hogan, Warren 1991, 'New banks: impact and response', *Economic Papers*, vol. 10, no. 1, pp. 11–33.

IBSA, *Annual Report 1994*.

Macquarie Bank Limited, *1995 Annual Report*, Sydney.

McGrath, Michael 1994, *Financial Institutions, Instruments and Markets in Australia*, McGraw-Hill, Sydney, Chapters 2 and 3.

KPMG Peat Marwick, *1995 Financial Institutions Performance Survey*, Sydney.

Peters, R.W. 1987, *The Commercial Bill Market in Australia*, CEDA

RBA August 1988, 'Bank bills', *Bulletin*, pp. 15–21.

RBA March 1992, 'Financial system: institutional and regulatory developments', *Bulletin*, pp. 1–9.

RBA October 1992, 'Foreign banks in Australia — policy issues and prospects', *Bulletin*, pp. 22–7.

RBA September 1994, 'Foreign banks in Australia', *Bulletin*, pp. 16–22.

Shanmugam, Bala, *et. al.* 1993, *Bank Management*, John Wiley & Sons, Chapter 10.

Skully, M. 1987, *Merchant Banking in Australia*, Oxford University Press, Melbourne.

Wallace, R. H. 1993, 'The business financiers: merchant banks and finance companies', in M. K. Lewis & R. H. Wallace (eds), *The Australian Financial System*, Longman Cheshire, Melbourne, pp. 214–48.

WBC, *1994 Annual Report*.

8

Managed funds

This chapter discusses the role and major forms of managed funds within the financial system and the activities of fund managers. This category includes insurance offices because they manage funds as a by-product of their primary business. Within this chapter, superannuation funds are emphasised because of their magnitude and their expected growth relative to intermediated funds.

Study objectives

From your study of this chapter you should be able to:

- define the main forms of managed funds;
- explain the functions performed by fund managers;
- describe the various forms of superannuation schemes;
- explain the rationale for the tax preferences given to superannuation schemes;
- describe the main types of portfolios used by funds managers;
- describe the main types of unit trusts;
- describe the other sources of managed funds.

INTRODUCTION

This chapter discusses the third sector of the financial system: managed funds. These are funds that are pooled for investment purposes. They are mainly invested by professional fund managers in financial assets and real property. Because most managed funds remain the property of the primary lender and are invested, rather than on-lent in the form of loans, they are not intermediated funds.

Most of these funds are long-term savings. They differ from bank deposits in character because they are invested mainly for income in retirement, whereas bank deposits tend to be used on a day-by-day basis. However, not all managed funds have a long-term savings horizon (e.g. unit trusts) and the character of some of these funds differs very little from bank deposits.

The title 'managed funds' is used because the funds are pooled for investment purposes, using the advice of professional fund managers. In terms of their origin (e.g. the superannuation contributions of an individual), these are retail funds, but once the funds are pooled (e.g. the total contributions to a superannuation scheme) they are invested as though they were wholesale funds. Not all of the institutions and parties that raise these funds have the expertise to invest them. Their funds are typically pooled (in, for example, a **pooled superannuation trust** that manages the funds for a number of superannuation schemes) and invested on the advice of professional funds managers.

There are three main forms of managed funds:

- those in superannuation schemes,
- those in public unit trusts, and
- the accumulated funds of insurance offices.

Superannuation forms the largest pool of funds.

Insurance offices play a role in both the superannuation and the insurance area. They have traditionally offered **endowment** policies that make a terminal payment which is similar to a lump-sum superannuation scheme. Their superannuation funds are held separately from their insurance funds.

Life, general and medical insurance policies also are a source of pooled funds. In these cases, the provider of the funds is receiving insurance services, but because of time lags between the premium payments and the payment of claims, the insurance provider has a pool of funds to invest. Particularly in the case of life insurance, these assets are sizeable and the investment income they earn is an important source of the payment of claims.

Institutions that receive managed funds provide different services from those of retail banks:

- Most fund managers provide investment services only; whereas most forms of bank deposits provide access to payment services as well as interest income and security.
- When the funds are supplied under a contractual savings arrangement, the funds manager does not face liquidity problems comparable with those faced by retail banks. In other words, funds managers do not have to engage in maturity transformation or provide the suppliers of funds with liquidity. (FitzGerald and Harper, 1992, p. 42)
- Banks cannot offer insurance services. These are provided by insurance offices under relevant legislation. Nevertheless, banks actively market insurance products to their customers.

Apart from insurance services, fund managers provide fewer services and as a consequence, their charges ought to represent a lower cost to the suppliers of funds than that represented by the interest-rate spread and charges (if any) imposed by retail banks. However, this proposition can be difficult to test because of the way fund managers charge for their services. They usually impose a mixture of up-front and exit fees and commissions. While an annual commission (provided it is disclosed) can be compared with a interest-rate spread, up-front and exit fees of say 4–5% (in total) cannot. These fees are once only and are not a set proportion of the amounts involved. Their effective annual cost, for instance, varies with the term of the advice.

Tax concessions are provided for long-term savings, especially those designed to generate income in retirement. Superannuation assets funded by contributions, for instance, earn an investment income (in the hands of the fund manager) and this is subject to a lower rate of tax than applies to the interest income earned on funds in, say, a bank account.

Tax concessions are provided because the community is judged to benefit from a higher level of long-term savings than would occur if no tax incentives were provided.

Arrangements for handling pooled funds tend to be more complex than for intermediated funds:

- There are the institutions that collect the funds. These include insurance offices, superannuation funds (including many small funds set up by self-employed individuals and small businesses), banks and financial advisers who 'sell' investments in managed funds.
- There are also professional fund managers (some of whom collect funds) who manage the investment of the funds. That is, they provide investment advice and are paid fees. Generally the assets remain the property of their trustee or their suppliers. Consequently, the assets acquired by funds do not usually appear on the balance sheet of the fund manager.
- Most schemes also involve a trustee, which could be a trust company (i.e. a professional trustee). The funds are placed in the hands of the trustee who invests them on the basis of the advice provided by a fund manager.
- The funds may be pooled for investment (with funds from other managed funds) according to explicit guidelines (e.g. in domestic equities) or managed as a separate portfolio.

Growth in funds under management

An indication of the relative growth of managed funds within the financial system was presented in table 2.2 (in Chapter 2, p. 40). Between June 1984 and June 1994, the main forms of managed funds, as a group, have increased their share of the assets of financial institutions from 25.4% to 34.2%.

When interpreting data of asset shares (by institutional category), keep in mind that they depend on:

- the rate of increase in the inflow of funds (to the institutions),
- the rate of increase in redemptions (or withdrawals), and
- the investment income on the pooled funds, which is retained for the benefit of the contributors.

Between the mid 1980s and 1990s, the flow of funds into superannuation increased for several reasons: first, the provision of employer contributions in awards; and second, the introduction, in 1992, of the **Superannuation Guarantee Charge** (SGC), which prescribed minimum contributions (mainly from employers). As at mid 1995, the minimum employer contribution was 6% of employee earnings, and the Labor Government's legislation provided for increases in the rate of contribution (including contributions from employees and the government) to 15% by 2002–03. (Willis, 1995)

However, these contributions were not the main cause of the increase in the relative share of assets held in managed funds since the mid 1980s. The third contributing factor was the main cause of the relative growth in the assets of fund managers. (Edey, Foster and Macfarlane, 1992, p. 22) During the 1980s, the returns achieved by fund managers were abnormally high, due in part to the very high real interest rates. Over the long run, though, there will be periods of low as well as high returns on superannuation and other managed funds.

Tax policy also influences the growth in contributions (and withdrawals). While tax provisions tend to support the objective of encouraging retirees to finance their retirement from an income stream, the tax concessions have become less generous, given that they tend to favour high-income over low-income individuals.

The ageing of the population is a further factor that explains the growth in funds under management. The post-war generation have reached their maximum earning capacity and, through their provision for retirement income, will boost the supply of funds to this sector.

The structure of managed funds

The value of the assets of the main forms of managed funds were presented in table 2.6 for the period June 1988 to June 1994. These amounts and their relative proportions as at March 1995 are shown in table 8.1.

In relation to the data in table 8.1, note that the insurance-office assets are 'Statutory superannuation funds' that are held separately from their other assets. These funds are held, in effect, as trust funds under Commonwealth legislation. **approved deposit funds** (ADFs) are established under Commonwealth legislation to receive **eligible termination payments**. They are superannuation funds because they preserve the superannuation benefits of workers when they change jobs prior to their retirement. Funds in ADFs receive the same tax preferences as funds in superannuation schemes.

One indicator of the importance of managed funds within the economy is that (in 1994–95) they represented over 60% of gross domestic product. They are also the principal domestic source of equity investment within the economy, providing about half of domestic investment and about a third overall (the balance being overseas investment). (Jones, 1992, p. 86)

Data on the main asset categories in which managed funds are invested are presented in table 8.2. Observe the relatively small amount of loans ($14 billion), compared with those made by banks ($287.5 billion, shown in table

6.9). Most of the managed funds (58.7% in March 1995) are held in the form of securities, including equities. This reflects the preferences of investors who can choose between funds according to their designated investments (as in the case of unit trusts) and industry practice (as in the case of superannuation funds).

An indication of the characteristics of the asset portfolios of fund managers is provided in example 8.1, which summarises the portfolios held by Westpac's Superannuation Division.

Table 8.1 Consolidated assets of managed funds, by type of fund, March 1995

Type of fund	*$m*	*% of total*
Statutory funds of life insurance offices	107 645	41.9
Superannuation and ADFs	95 872	37.4
Total of above	203 517	79.3
Public unit trusts	34 539	13.5
Friendly societies	8 524	3.3
Cash management trusts	5 329	2.1
Common funds	4 645	1.8
Totals	256 554	100.0

Source: ABS, *Managed funds*, Cat. No. 5655.0, Table 1

Table 8.2 Consolidated assets of managed funds by type of asset — June 1992 to March 1995 ($m)

	1992	*1993*	*1994*	*March 95*	*% of total*
Cash and bank deposits	14 278	12 155	15 010	12 453	4.9
Loans and placements	14 821	15 135	13 578	14 153	5.5
Short-term securities	27 218	28 257	28 660	27 724	10.8
Long-term securities	46 259	51 395	52 226	51 875	20.2
Equities and trust units	56 510	60 279	72 095	70 941	27.7
Land and buildings	30 140	26 776	29 352	32 088	12.5
Overseas assets	25 790	35 358	40 634	38 996	15.2
Other assets	7 927	8 299	7 899	8 325	3.2
Total	222 942	237 656	259 458	256 554	100.0

Source: ABS, *Managed funds*, Cat. No. 5655.0, Table 2

example 8.1

Reference was made in the previous two chapters to Westpac Financial Services, the group within Westpac that provides fund-management services. Its Superannuation Division is a major superannuation fund with a number of sub-plans. It markets its superannuation schemes to individuals (these are managed by its Personal Lifetime Superannuation Service) and to employers.

AMPAC Life Limited (a subsidiary of AMP) is the trustee of the Personal scheme. The Trust Deed defines the obligations and duties of the Trustee, the authorised investments that can be made by the manager and the rights and liabilities of investors.

The minimum contribution to a personal scheme is $120 per month, or a single contribution of $3000. The scheme offers five portfolios into which contributions can be paid, including ETPs that are being invested as ADFs. Contributors are permitted to switch between these portfolios. The portfolios and their fees are:

The Cash Portfolio This holds short-term securities only and is designed for single contributions, such as eligible termination payments. Its investment objective is to generate income with a high level of security. There are no entry or exit fees, but it has an investment management fee of 1.2% p.a. This fund suits older people who seek a low-risk income stream, rather than capital growth.

The Cash Plus Portfolio This is similar to the Cash Portfolio but with a longer investment horizon. It invests mainly in short-term securities and bonds, but includes small proportions of equities and property in the expectation of generating some capital gains. The diversified portfolio (in common with the following portfolios) should minimise the movement in the value of units. It imposes an entry fee of 3% on investments of up to $100 000 and 1.5% on the balance. The investment management fee is 1.5% p.a. These fees apply to each of the following portfolios.

The Diversified Stable Portfolio This portfolio comprises (in descending order of importance) short-term domestic securities, domestic and overseas long-term securities, domestic and overseas equities and property. It expects to provide a good income stream, together with potential for capital gain, while recognising a risk of capital depreciation. It suits investors with an investment horizon of five to ten years. The Diversified Stable Portfolio has a higher expected rate of return than the foregoing portfolios.

The Diversified Growth Portfolio This is similar to the previous portfolio except that a greater proportion of its funds are invested in domestic and overseas equities. This portfolio suits investors with an investment horizon of eight to ten years who are prepared to accept a higher capital-value risk in return for a higher expected rate of return, through the possibility of greater capital gains. The greater investment in domestic equities is expected to produce tax advantages for many investors, because of the receipt of franked dividends.

The Long-Term Growth Portfolio This portfolio has an even higher proportion of its funds invested in equities. The fund has a greater long-term growth potential but is subject to greater variation in unit values because of the cyclical movement in share values generally. It suits investors with an investment horizon of ten years or more.

Optional life insurance policies are offered by AMPAC Life Limited.

At the time of writing, commissions charged by financial consultants are met from the management fees and no margin is charged between the issue and redemption prices of units.

Westpac Financial Services participates, as a professional fund manager through Westpac Investment Management Pty Limited, in the market for employment-based schemes. These are referred to by Westpac as Corporate Superannuation Funds. They are pooled superannuation trusts that accept investments (of at least $50 000) from eligible investors (in terms of the *Superannuation Industry (Supervision) Act*, 1993). They have no entry or exit fees but they have a unit price spread of 0.5–1.0% between the purchase and redemption prices. The units are valued daily.

The fees charged on the pooled funds, as a percentage of assets (i.e. the 'management expense ratio' (MER)), are less than 1.0%, which is less than for the personal superannuation schemes. Their trustee is Westpac Securities Administration Limited, a Westpac subsidiary.

Contributions to these schemes can be invested in one or more of four portfolios, one being the Cash Plus Fund, described above, and the other three funds having progressively more equities in their portfolios (in a similar fashion to the portfolios described above). One of these portfolios, the Capital Growth Fund, is used in conjunction with the Cash Plus Fund to create a further portfolio.

Note that fund managers do not subscribe their own funds (i.e. equity capital) to their portfolios. These assets are acquired solely from the funds placed with them. This differs from the position of a bank, which holds equity funds as well as the depositors' funds. Should a bank make a loss, it forms a charge against shareholders' funds: whereas when a managed portfolio makes a loss, it forms a charge against contributors' funds.

The vast majority (86% as at March 1995) of managed funds are invested through professional fund managers. They are, in the main, insurance offices, banks, merchant banks and subsidiaries of these organisations that typically manage pooled funds (not to the exclusion of individual portfolios). The funds they manage remain the property of either the subscribers or the trustees of collective (or superannuation) funds. Professional fund managers earn fees for the investment services they provide. The role of professional fund managers within this sector is indicated by the data presented in table 8.3.

Industry leaders

Industry survey data are provided by ASSIRT, a fund management industry research company. The ten fund managers with the most assets under management are shown in table 8.4. Note that they are insurance offices and banks, including the two investment banks mentioned in the previous chapter as being leading funds managers, Bankers Trust Australia Limited and Macquarie Bank. Observe that the top ten, as a group, manage 60% of the funds under management.

Table 8.3 Professional fund managers, source of funds, June 1992 to March 1995 ($m)

Source	*June 1992*	*June 1993*	*June 1994*	*March 1995*
Managed funds				
— Life insurance offices	98 129	106 476	113 067	110 934
— Superannuation funds	45 409	51 935	60 015	61 424
— Approved deposit funds	9 183	9 607	9 180	8 340
— Public unit trusts	17 786	20 368	26 602	27 928
— Friendly societies	6 822	6 959	6 280	6 177
— Common funds	288	305	354	1 916
— Cash management funds	4 069	4 048	4 638	4 167
Total — managed funds	181 686	199 698	220 136	220 886
Percentage of managed funds	*81.5%*	*84.0%*	*84.8%*	*86.1%*
Other domestic sources	20 454	26 038	29 563	28 942
Overseas sources	1 858	2 439	4 443	5 206
Total — all sources	203 998	228 175	254 142	255 034

Source: ABS, *Managed funds*, Cat. No. 5655.0, Table 9

Table 8.4 Ten largest fund managers, June 1995

Rank	*Manager*	*$m*	*Market share %*
1	AMP	36 991.5	13.44
2	Bankers Trust Australia	26 532.5	9.64
3	Lend Lease	23 386.0	8.49
4	National Mutual	17 843.8	6.48
5	Commonwealth Bank	14 223.7	5.17
6	Macquarie Investment Management	11 829.0	4.29
7	Westpac	10 477.0	3.81
8	ANZ	8 350.0	3.03
9	Prudential	8 098.0	2.94
10	Commonwealth Funds Management	7 704.6	2.79
Total — top 10		165 436.1	60.08
Industry total		275 316.0	100.00

Source: ASSIRT, *Market Share Report*, June quarter 1995, Section 1, p. 5

Retail and wholesale funds

The funds within the fund-management industry can be divided into several categories. Most are **retail funds**. These include:

- unit trusts and cash management trusts,
- insurance, superannuation and friendly society bonds,
- superannuation and allocated pension/annuity retirement funds,
- roll overs (approved deposit funds and deferred annuities), and
- common funds.

Wholesale funds These are mainly pooled funds; that is, they are the proceeds of retail schemes that are pooled for investment by professional fund managers. For statistical purposes it is important that the retail proceeds that are invested in wholesale funds are shown only as wholesale assets, otherwise the funds are counted as both retail and wholesale assets.

Master funds These allow investors or fund managers to choose the underlying investment options (i.e. retail or wholesale funds). That is, they are a collection of funds that accept the proceeds of individual schemes (and hence are wholesale funds).

Discretely managed funds These are portfolios managed on behalf of private individuals, corporate and public-sector clients (and thus are retail funds).

In the following survey data published by ASSIRT, there is some double counting of assets because of funds being transferred between managers. Despite this shortcoming, the data in table 8.5 indicate the retail and wholesale assets of the ten largest fund managers.

Table 8.5 Ten largest fund managers, retail and wholesale assets ($m), June 1995

Fund manager	*Retail*	*Wholesale*	*Other*	*TAUM*[a]
AMP	25 541.8	11 787.0	(337.3)	36 991.5
Bankers Trust Australia	11 300.4	14 456.3	775.9	26 532.5
Lend Lease	13 707.0	6 369.0	3 310.0	23 386.0
National Mutual	12 592.0	5 251.8		17 843.8
Commonwealth Bank	7 524.2	6 679.5	20.0	14 223.7
Macquarie Investment Management	4 856.0	6 973.0		11 829.0
Westpac	3 265.0	6 743.0	119.0	10 477.0
ANZ	n.a.	n.a.		8 350.0
Prudential	5 307.9	2 790.1		8 089.0
Commonwealth Funds Management	256.0	7 448.6		7 704.6

[a] Total assets under management, which excludes Australian assets of overseas fund managers and internally managed corporate and public sector funds

Source: ASSIRT, *Market Share Report*, June quarter 1995, Sections 8 and 9

SUPERANNUATION FUNDS

As shown above, superannuation schemes are the principal source of managed funds. Assuming the SGC remains in place, it would seem that this source of savings is destined to grow, relative to other managed funds and to other forms of savings, such as bank deposits.

Even though there were approximately 100 000 superannuation schemes in the early 1990s (Robinson, p. 13), they can be divided into two categories — those that have a:

- **defined contribution**, or a
- **defined benefit**.

The former specifies the contributions to the scheme. The terminal value of the scheme to the beneficiary is undefined and depends on the accumulated value of the payments. This means that the beneficiary absorbs the investment risk of the scheme. Typically, these are employment-related schemes that define the contributions of both the employee and the employer, although in some schemes there is only the one contributor.

The latter category, defined benefit, specifies the value of the ultimate payout at retirement. Typically this amount is defined in terms of a multiple of the employee's salary prior to retirement. This means that the employer accepts the investment risk as well as the risk of a rapid escalation in salaries prior to retirement. Should earnings on the scheme's assets be less than expected, and the rate of increase in salaries be greater than expected, presumably the employer would have to meet substantial unfunded benefits.

In either case, where no adjustment is made for inflation, the retiree accepts the risk that greater than expected inflation will erode the real value of the retirement benefits. In Chapter 14 we discuss the relationship between inflation and interest rates. Should interest rates correctly adjust for future inflation, retirement benefits that are based on interest income need not be eroded by inflation. The outcome depends on how accurately interest rates allow for future inflation.

During the 1970s, defined-contribution schemes, including endowment insurance policies, did not adequately cope with inflation (from the beneficiary's point of view) and defined-benefit schemes became more popular in the 1980s. This caused a shift away from endowment policies (and their providers, insurance offices) toward defined-benefit schemes that were administered by subsidiaries of banks and merchant banks. Even though the Superannuation Guarantee Charge, which was announced in 1991, is a defined-contribution scheme, the new entrants to the industry have become important competitors to insurance offices in the management of the assets of superannuation funds.

Contribution schemes

Superannuation schemes are either marketed to the public (mainly to the self-employed and those individuals who have limited superannuation benefits) or are provided by employers as part of the remuneration package of employees. Most institutions market superannuation schemes, the main types of which are as follows:

- Regular-contribution schemes generate a lump-sum payment on maturity that reflects the contributions and the income earned on the investment of the contributions.
- Single-contribution schemes must have a life of at least ten years to attract the full tax benefits. **Superannuation** and **insurance bonds** are examples of single-payment schemes. Their terminal value also depends on the income earned by the assets in which the funds are invested.
- Roll-over schemes allow eligible termination payments (ETPs) to maintain their superannuation identity for tax deferment purposes until retirement. There are two types of roll-over schemes: approved deposit funds (ADFs) and deferred annuity funds (DAFs). They operate as trusts; the former generates an accumulated superannuation lump-sum payout, whereas the latter generates a stream of payments. Traditionally these have been offered only by insurance offices.

  Only ETPs can be deposited in ADFs and DAFs. Earnings on these funds are taxed as though they are superannuation funds. The funds in an ADF must be fully withdrawn at age 65 (e.g. used to purchase an annuity as retirement income) and can be withdrawn in part or full before that time, provided any tax liability is met. ADFs and DAFs are vehicles for creating superannuation portability for people who change jobs prior to retirement.
- **Annuities** that are paid to retirees. These are either 'whole of life' or have a fixed term. In the case of the former, the provider of the annuity is supplying an insurance service and accepts the risk that the annuitant lives longer than expected. Whereas the first three types of schemes listed above serve to accumulate funds for retirement, annuities provide retirement income. They are a form of dissaving, presumably from the proceeds of a lump-sum payout. The retiree invests the lump sum in an annuity and receives an income stream in return. The income payments are funded by the lump sum and the income from its diminishing amount of assets. Various forms of annuity that do not have a regular payment can be purchased. For example, the beneficiary might accept some of the investment risk by linking the payments to the income stream from a particular group of assets, or arrange to draw upon the funds as required, until they are exhausted.

Employment-related schemes can be 'contributory' (i.e. both the employee and employer make contributions), or 'non-contributory', where only the employer makes contributions. A trust deed prescribes how the funds are to be invested and the basis of payouts to employees at retirement. Private-sector funds are 'fully-funded', whereas for many years public-sector funds were 'unfunded'.

Governments that operated their superannuation schemes on an unfunded basis did not make their required contributions (as the employer) when due and therefore the funds available in the schemes could be less than the amount required to meet the defined benefits (i.e. payouts) as they became due. The governments met their share of the payouts, when required, from consolidated revenue. However, this practice created a substantial unfunded liability for these governments (given the ageing of their employees). For example, the Commonwealth Superannuation Scheme's unfunded liability was estimated to be $33 billion in 1990. (Edey, Foster and Macfarlane, 1992, p. 18) This practice was reformed to ensure that government budgets met superannuation costs on the basis of the annuity payment required (on an actuarial basis) to fund payouts at retirement.

Industry schemes were established following the inclusion of superannuation contribution payments within industrial awards in the late 1980s. These schemes were established by trade unions, and in some cases (through negotiated awards) they became the mandated repository of contributions made under the SGC.

Management functions

Superannuation schemes are managed under a trust deed. The main functions performed by a fund are the administration of cash flows (receipt of contributions and payment of entitlements), the investment of the balance in the fund and the provision of life insurance for beneficiaries (through a life-insurance office). (Covick and Lewis, 1993, p. 182)

The investment and administration of superannuation funds can be organised in various ways. Large schemes usually undertake these functions themselves, but some seek the advice of fund managers. Smaller schemes (of which there are many) often require the services of professional fund managers and administrators to ensure the effective conduct of their affairs. Some of the arrangements established are:

Master trusts These allow the funds of a number of schemes to be managed under one trust deed. This arrangement is attractive to smaller employer- or industry-based schemes (as well as personal schemes) for cost minimising purposes because there is only one trustee and all administrative activities are centralised. Master trusts are marketed by insurance offices and professional fund managers.

Pooled superannuation trusts These provide a centralised investment facility for the funds of schemes that comply with the *Superannuation Industry (Supervision) Act*, 1992 and other approved funds, such as ADFs (established under that Act).

Fund of fund arrangements These are superannuation funds placed with the statutory funds of life offices. (Australian Law Reform Commission, 1992, pp. 4 –13)

Various organisations rate the performance of fund managers. These ratings help investment advisers and fund managers within the industry to decide their recommendations and pooling decisions. An indication of the way these ratings are formed is provided in example 8.2 that discusses the ratings of ASSIRT.

example 8.2

The leading industry-research company, ASSIRT, rates funds and their management. This information is useful to investment advisers as well as fund managers, as it is an independent assessment of how well funds are likely to serve the needs of investors. These needs are deemed to be:

- security of original capital,
- wealth accumulation,
- income and tax efficiency,
- ease of withdrawal, and
- customer service in terms of simplicity, effective communication and comfort factor.

ASSIRT rates individual funds in terms of the likelihood that they will meet their investment objectives, and fund managers in terms of the ability of managers to ensure that their funds meet investor needs. The ASSIRT rating is the combination of the two ratings.

Funds are rated A through D. The top rating, A, is given to a 'fund which is *most likely* to achieve its investment objectives through the *high-quality* application of its investment strategy, risk management, quality controls and its value for money'.

Managers are rated a through c, with the top rating, a, given to a fund manager 'which is *most likely* to manage and service a quality managed fund. The manager has strong investment management, operating capability, propriety and customer service'. (p. 2)

The cost of preparing the rating is met by the fund being rated, which has to provide access and information to ASSIRT to allow it to reach an informed, balanced and independent opinion. The reporting of the rating is intended to be transparent, in order to provide financial advisers with a clear view of the strengths and perceived weaknesses of funds or their manager.

Ratings are not endorsements or investment advice: they are opinions based on information that is disclosed in the ratings report about various factors considered relevant to investor choice of funds and managers.

For example, in 1994 ASSIRT issued its ratings report on the IOOF Funds Management Group (a leading friendly society). It covered the fund manager, rated b, and 14 of its funds, 13 of which were given an investment grade, this being Bb and above.

The fund manager's rating of b means, 'In our [i.e. ASSIRT's] opinion, the fund manager is capable of managing and servicing a quality managed fund. Investment management, operating capability, propriety and customer service are adequate'. (ASSIRT, 1994(b), p. 2)

In 1995 ASSIRT issued a detailed non-rating report on BT Funds Management Limited (the subsidiary of Bankers Trust Australia Limited that conducts the bank's fund-management operations). The 43-page report provides extensive detail on the operating capability, investment management-approach and propriety and customer service of BT Funds Management. The report's research conclusion is that 'BT Funds Management is in a strong position to manage and service a quality managed fund'. (ASSIRT, 1995(a), p. 5)

Taxes and regulations

Superannuation and equivalent forms of savings are treated differently by the authorities from other forms of saving. As noted above, they are treated favourably under the tax laws to encourage people to provide their own income in retirement. (Knox, 1992, p. 65) The introduction of the SGC provides for the extension of superannuation coverage, given that in the late 1980s less than half of all workers were members of a superannuation scheme.

The tax provisions governing superannuation (and equivalent) schemes have undergone several changes over the past decade and they are unlikely to be 'set in stone' in the future. The main features are that a lower rate of tax applies to the income generated on savings within superannuation schemes (currently the tax rate is 15%) and dividend-imputation benefits are available on income generated from investments in equities. This latter feature is not unique to these income streams. It is important, though, to the decisions of fund managers. If the benefit was not available, the managers would be less likely to invest in equities. As shown in table 8.5, equities are an important asset of superannuation funds.

Superannuation is the subject of legislation because of the importance of retirement income to the community. In most developed countries, the central government operates a social-security system (that is distinct from its budget), which provides for retirement income in proportion to each person's compulsory contributions to the scheme. In Australia, the Commonwealth Government makes pension payments from consolidated revenue (i.e. from the government's budget).

The introduction of the SGC represents an alternative approach to social security. The aim of the charge is to encourage employers to make superannuation contributions for their employees. The charge does not apply when the employer's contribution satisfies the prescribed percentage of employee earnings. The contributions are paid to private funds, rather than a national fund (such as a social-security fund). Hence the SGC will contribute to the long-term development of the superannuation-funds industry.

The Labor Government claimed that the SGC will increase Australia's savings rate, which should help lower the current-account deficit within the balance of payments. It will lift the savings rate only if increased superannuation contributions do not replace other forms of savings. The impact of the SGC on the level of savings is a complex issue. (Morling and Subbaraman, 1995) Two of the main aspects to be considered are:

- the effect of increased savings through superannuation schemes on the level of deposits, and
- whether the SGC alters the behaviour of people when they approach their retirement. (Robinson, 1992)

Given that bank deposits (the other main form of personal savings) and superannuation contributions serve different purposes (bank deposits mainly serve transaction and short-term investment purposes and superannuation is a form of long-term contractual savings), it seems that increases in one should not cause the other to fall by the same amount.

The impact of the SGC on the pattern of life-time savings depends on the extent to which people, when approaching retirement, do not dissave for the purpose of becoming eligible for pension benefits. In the recent past there has been a clear pattern of people spending savings in order to achieve pension eligibility. This practice is referred to as 'double-dipping' because of the tax concessions provided for superannuation-based savings (a benefit received by many of the dissavers) and the tax-funded pension payments (and related benefits, particularly medical benefits) which they also received. Only those with substantial retirement income (and assets) remain self-reliant in their retirement.

If, over the next 40 years or so, superannuation contributions reach a sufficiently high level that most people are financially self-reliant in retirement (if in fact people retire!), enforced superannuation savings will probably lift the savings rate.

Assuming the assets of superannuation funds grow at the expense of intermediated funds, concern has been expressed (Jones, 1992, and Thom, 1992) about the consequences for small businesses that rely on banks for funds. As shown by the data in table 8.5, superannuation funds are invested mainly in high-quality securities and equities (which are mainly in 'blue-chip' companies or as equity participation in major development projects), whereas banks invest mainly in loans to individuals and small- to medium-sized businesses.

The main issue we face in our study of the financial system is the impact of the SGC on the level of assets of superannuation funds and fund managers generally. It seems highly likely that this sector of the financial system will continue to grow relative to the other sectors. There are several reasons for this view:

- the levy has greatly increased the number of people in superannuation schemes,
- the minimum rate of contributions is being increased, and
- the pool of assets will increase over the long run because of the accumulation of contributions and the earnings on this larger pool.

An important aspect of Australia's mandated superannuation arrangements is that it is a defined-contribution scheme (whereas most social-security schemes are defined-benefit schemes) and thus contributors accept the investment risk. (Kingston, Piggott and Bateman, 1992, p. 139)

Individuals' level of retirement income depends importantly on the rate of return achieved on the funds whilst they are being managed, and this depends partly on the prudential practices of fund managers. These points apply to all defined contribution schemes, but under the SGC an award can determine the fund into which payments are made. The individual contributor therefore cannot choose the fund manager. In these circumstances, the government ought to apply a regime of prudential guidelines as a form of contributor protection.

An extensive set of laws has applied to superannuation funds for some time, and it has been extended to cover the prudential supervision of institutions involved in the superannuation industry (Australian Law Reform Commission and Companies and Securities Advisory Committee, 1992). Major legislation is as follows:

- **The *Superannuation Industry (Supervision) Act*** This Act applies to superannuation schemes prescribing standards for scheme features (such as their vesting, preservation and portability benefits), the investment process, loans to the employer (i.e. limits on the amount that can be lent to the employer) and members, and audit and actuarial reports as well as regular reports to members on their entitlements.

- **The *Life Insurance Act*** This Act applies to the superannuation business of insurance offices, and is the legislative authority for the prudential requirements of the Insurance and Superannuation Commission (ISC) for such business. (Prudential supervision of banks by the Reserve Bank and the role of the Council of Supervisors are explained in the next chapter.)
- Corporations law covers a range of superannuation schemes and requires various approvals of the Australian Securities Commission (ASC), such as for the trust deeds and prospectuses. The ASC also prescribes and administers prudential supervision guidelines.

Use of funds

The asset shares of superannuation funds are broadly indicated by the data in table 8.2 for managed funds as a whole. The allocation of funds among assets is influenced by events, such as the 1987 sharemarket crash. However, the main theoretical issue is the appropriate proportion that should be held in the form of securities, equities and property.

Table 8.6 Assets of superannuation funds, March 1995, $m

Asset	*Statutory funds of life offices*	*Superannuation funds and ADFs*	*Total*	*% of total*
Cash and deposits	5 112	4 585	9 697	4.4
Loans and placements	5 603	6 430	12 033	5.4
Short-term securities				7.6
— bills	5 170	3 783	8 953	4.0
— other	4 546	3 381	7 927	3.6
Long-term securities				21.7
— Commonwealth	8 611	11 264	19 875	9.0
— semi-governmental	12 936	7 365	20 301	9.2
— other	5 516	2 188	7 704	3.5
Equities in				35.0
— non-financial co's	24 283	26 880	51 163	23.1
— financial companies	5 789	5 320	11 109	5.0
— units in trusts	6 963	8 203	15 166	6.9
Other financial assets	2 137	1 584	3 721	1.7
Non-financial assets	11 864	8 453	20 317	9.2
Overseas assets	16 333	16 941	33 274	15.0
Total assets	114 863	106 377	221 240	100.0

Source: ABS, *Managed funds*, Cat. No. 5655.0, Tables 3–4

The main forms of securities are cash, short-term and long-term securities. These assets have a very low default risk and, provided they are held to maturity, there is a low level of risk that the terminal value of the investment will not be realised. However, as noted above, these securities are exposed to the risk of a sudden and unexpected rise in the rate of inflation. While indexed and adjustable-rate bonds can provide a hedge against inflation risk, these securities have not been issued in large quantities.

Equities and real estate (i.e. property) usually increase in value over the long run in response to inflation and given the long-run nature of superannuation contributions, it is argued that these funds should be invested in such assets. Nevertheless, these assets also involve price risk. Consequently, superannuation funds are typically invested in all of these assets. A detailed listing of these assets, as at March 1995, is presented in table 8.6.

The main asset groups shown in table 8.6 are as follows:

- cash and short-term securities, 12.0%,
- long-term securities, 21.7%,
- equities, 35.0%,
- real estate, 8.0%, and
- overseas assets, 15.0%.

PUBLIC UNIT TRUSTS

Public unit trusts began operating in Australia in the 1930s but only began to play an important role in the financial system from the mid 1980s, following the development of cash management trusts (CMTs) in the early 1980s.

A unit trust is the classic form of collective investment. Members of the public can purchase units in these trusts because they have a small minimum investment, typically $2000. The funds of a unit trust (these being retail investments) are vested in a trustee, but they are invested collectively on the advice of a professional fund manager (as wholesale funds). The operation of each unit trust is governed by its trust deed.

> *The trust deed is the constitution of a unit trust. A trustee is appointed under the terms of the trust deed. The trustee's main responsibility is to represent unitholders and look after their interests. The trustee receives and holds all money, reviews the investment proposals of the manager, holds the investment in the name of the manager, distributes income, has the fund's accounts audited each year, and sends accounts and statements to unitholders. It is essential that the trustee be established, be independent, and be a reliable company approved by the ASC.* (Beelaerts and Forde, 1994, pp. 4 –5)

Unit trusts are identified according to the area in which their funds are invested. The assets of unit trusts and CMTs as at March 1995 are shown by the data in table 8.7. Observe that the main forms of unit trust assets are property, equities and securities. These assets can be held in various ways. Consequently there are more than three types of unit trusts. CMTs invest mainly in bills and other short-term securities.

Table 8.7 Assets of public unit trusts and CMTs, March 1995 ($m)

Asset	*Unit trusts*	*CMFs*	*Total*	*% of total*
Cash and deposits	1 304	606	2 000	4.7
Loans and placements	1 899	94	1 993	4.7
Short-term securities				
— bills	1 132	2 156	3 288	7.7
— other	381	2 299	2 680	6.3
Long-term securities	1 286	161	1 447	3.4
Equities	7 287		7 287	17.0
Units in trusts	2 923		2 923	6.8
Other assets	1 715	13	1 728	4.0
Land and buildings	13 927		13 297	31.0
Total Australian assets	31 853	5 329	37 182	86.6
Overseas assets	5 722		5 722	13.4
Total assets	37 575	5 329	42 904	100.0

Source: ABS, *Managed funds*, Cat. No. 5655.0, Tables 5 and 8

Types of trust

Trusts are identified by the area and nature of their assets. The following discussion is based on the description of trusts presented by Beelaerts and Forde (1994).

Equity trusts

Survey data collected by the Investment Funds Association of Australia (IFA), indicates that as at June 1995 there were 188 equity unit trusts with over 550 000 accounts (i.e. investors) which managed $11.3 billion worth of assets. These unit trusts invest their funds in shares and pay a return based on their dividend income and capital gains made from buying and selling shares.

The main attraction of equity trusts is that they provide access to share portfolios (i.e. part ownership) that would be beyond the savings of individual unitholders. They provide two further advantages. One is reduced transaction costs, because they trade in large parcels. The other is that their investments are made by professional fund managers who have access to expert information provided by security analysts.

Notwithstanding these advantages, equity trusts usually achieve returns that are in line with those generated by the market as a whole, and some do not match the market's performance. Equity trusts can be classified as follows:

- general equity trusts,
- growth equity trusts, and
- specialised equity trusts.

General equity trusts invest in a diversified (or 'balanced') portfolio of equities; that is, they hold shares in a wide range of companies. Growth equity trusts invest in the shares of companies that the investment manager believes will achieve a higher than average price rise. Theoretically, low dividend payout rates should result in a greater shareprice increase than high payout rates. But expected shareprice movements over a three- to five-year period depend on other factors, such as the prospects of particular industries, and fund managers generally hold different expectations about these factors. Consequently, the various growth equity trusts hold different share portfolios.

Examples of balanced equity trusts include Perpetual Industrial Share, with assets of $805 million in June 1995; Rothschild Australian Share, with assets of almost $420 million in June 1995; and J. B. Were Leaders Trust, with assets of $107 million in June 1995.

Specialised equity trusts have particular investment strategies, such as holding the shares of:

- companies in particular industries (such as Rothschild Natural Resources Trust, with assets of $86 million in June 1995),
- entrepreneurial companies,
- international (i.e. overseas) companies (such as BT Select Markets International, with assets of $1235 million in June 1995, and BT Select Markets Pacific Basin, with assets of $904 million in June 1995),
- small companies (such as the Rothschild Smaller Companies Trust, with assets of $180 million in June 1995), and
- companies that usually pay fully franked dividends (known as dividend-imputation funds).

Note that a fully franked dividend is one that is paid from company income that has been taxed at the company tax rate. It entitles the recipient to treat the company tax payment as a pre-payment of personal income tax. Should the recipient's income tax rate be less than the company rate, the pre-payment of tax may result in a refund of tax. Dividend-imputation schemes are therefore attractive to this group of investors.

Narrowly based share portfolios are usually subject to greater price risk than diversified portfolios because the prices of the shares in such portfolios tend to change in a similar way. (In the case of balanced portfolios, the price movements of individual stocks tend to offset each other, resulting in a lower variability in the portfolio's value over time.) In this circumstance, the specialised portfolios must have a higher expected rate of return (than for balanced portfolios) to attract subscriptions.

As noted above, imputation trusts have particular appeal to investors who face a low income-tax rate. Under the dividend-imputation arrangements, the company tax serves as a withholding tax against personal income liability. An investor with a personal tax rate that is less than the company rate will earn tax credits on fully franked shares (because the investor's tax rate is less than that paid by the company). The tax credits can be used to offset the income tax due on the investor's other income. Consequently investors might directly pay no personal income tax, because the tax liability on their income is fully met by the tax paid by companies whose shares form part of a dividend-imputation trust.

Examples of imputation trusts include BT Select Markets Equity Imputation, with assets of over $1 billion in June 1995; Advance Imputation Fund, with assets of $275 million in June 1995; and Westpac Imputation Trust, with assets of almost $200 million in June 1995.

Property trusts

IFA survey data indicates that there were 117 property trusts in June 1995, with over 535 000 accounts that managed $14.7 billion worth of assets. Examples of property trusts include AMP Property Securities, with assets of $107 million in June 1995; and National Mutual Australian Property, with assets of nearly $90 million in June 1995.

Property trusts purchase commercial, industrial and retail buildings with their pooled funds. Rental income is their source of returns to unitholders. Capital gain is also generated when property values are rising. However, the value of units in property trusts falls when property values decline. This poses problems for property trusts because unitholders are likely to attempt to redeem their units when property values are falling (or are expected to fall). At these times, property markets tend to become illiquid (i.e. it is difficult to sell even at depressed prices) and thus property trusts themselves become illiquid. This problem applies particularly to **unlisted** trusts. (We discuss this feature of trusts below.)

Nevertheless, property trusts provide investors with a much wider choice of property investments. For instance, an investor who has sufficient funds to purchase a small apartment could, as a unitholder in a property trust become a co-owner of a large piece of industrial property.

Mortgage trusts

A mortgage trust invests in mortgages, usually first mortgages that represent 65% of the value of the property being financed. They pay a return from the interest payments by the borrowers. Given the low default risk on first mortgages, the return of mortgage trusts is not as high as for most property trusts.

According to IFA data for June 1995, there were 15 mortgage trusts with nearly 95 000 accounts and assets worth $2.1 billion. Examples of mortgage funds include ANZ Mortgage Fund, with assets of $320 million in June 1995; and Perpetual Mortgage, with assets of $287 million in June 1995.

Fixed-interest trusts

Fixed-interest trusts invest in securities, such as CGSs, semi-government bonds and mortgage-backed securities. These assets have a low default risk but are exposed to price risk through increases in market yields. Should rates fall, the value of the securities will rise.

In June 1995, IFA data suggest there were 59 fixed-interest trusts with 75 000 accounts and assets worth $2.8 billion. There are both domestic and overseas fixed-interest trusts. Examples include Westpac Mortgage and Income Fund, with assets of $316 million in June 1995; ANZ Fixed Interest Trust, with assets of nearly $200 million in June 1995; and BT Select Bond Trust — Global, with assets of $103 million in June 1995.

Cash management trusts are similar to fixed-interest trusts, except that they invest principally in bills and other short-term securities, as shown by the data in table 8.7. Examples include Macquarie Cash Management, with assets of $1.8 billion in June 1995; and MLC Cash Management Trust, with assets of $540 million in June 1995.

Listed and unlisted trusts

Listed trusts have satisfied the listing requirements of the Australian Stock Exchange and therefore their units can be traded on the exchange. These are 'closed-end' trusts, meaning that unitholders can leave the trust only by selling on the exchange.

Most property trusts are listed (77% of the assets of property trusts were in listed trusts in June 1995) as this reduces their asset-valuation and liquidity-management problems. During the 1990 slump in property values a number of property trusts were unable to buy back units because they could not sell their assets to raise the cash. Moreover, if the assets were valued some months previously (their assets are usually valued annually), the assessed buy-back prices were too high, penalising the remaining unitholders. By being listed, unitholders can sell their units at a price that attracts a buyer. The value of the units, therefore, is set by the market. (See example 8.3.)

example 8.3

Westpac Financial Services offers a range of unit trusts that vary according to their investment strategy. These range from short-term securities only to portfolios that comprise mainly domestic and overseas shares. The characteristics of these funds are similar to those explained in the description of Westpac's superannuation funds (example 8.1). Their entry fees range from 3% to zero and their exit fees are zero (for the funds that impose an entry fee) or 2% for the funds with no entry fee.

Their minimum investment is either $1000 or $5000. Further investments or redemptions can be made at any time. The spread between unit-purchase and redemption values ranges between $1.15 and $1.01. The spread is based on the transaction costs of investing new subscriptions and selling assets to pay for redemptions. Units are valued daily, by dividing the portfolio's market value by the number of units held. Their MERs range from $2.25 to $1.37, depending on the portfolio.

However, most public unit trusts are unlisted. Unitholders can sell their units back to the trust. The price is set by the manager in accordance with the current market value of the trust's assets. The trust can either redeem these units (i.e. extinguish them) or re-sell them to new investors. Unlisted funds accept new subscriptions (on the basis of a prospectus) and so the size of these funds varies over time.

Other fund managers

The assets of the insurance business of insurance offices are the other major form of managed funds. Friendly societies, common funds and cash management funds are small players in this area of the financial system.

Insurance funds

Insurance policies generate substantial funds because of the lag in the timing of their receipt of premium income and payouts on insurance claims. The investment of these funds generates income that can be used to cover payouts.

The major insurance offices are mutuals (e.g. AMP, National Mutual and Colonial Mutual), although there are also insurance companies, such as those owned by banks.

The main insurance products are:

- life policies,
- superannuation schemes and similar products (discussed above),
- whole-of-life and term-endowment policies,
- employers' liability policies,
- motor-vehicle and compulsory third-party policies,
- medical and disability policies,
- fire, marine and household policies, and
- mortgage insurance.

Insurance is a risk-management industry. Insurance offices accept the risk of various events in return for policy premiums. The industry manages risk through **reinsurance**. This involves the sharing of risks and premiums by insurance offices with specialist reinsurers. Lloyds is an exception to this approach because, being a partnership, each partner accepts the risks arising from the policies written by Lloyds.

The insurance industry is subject to specific Commonwealth legislation and the supervision and surveillance of the ISC. The legislation prescribes a minimum amount of equity capital or reserves, minimum solvency requirements, and satisfactory arrangements for reinsurance. (Covick and Lewis, 1993, p. 201)

Friendly societies

Friendly societies are non-profit organisations that were formed in the early 1800s to provide health and welfare insurance products. The development of the welfare state in Australia reduced the need for such products, but these societies survived by entering the personal financial services field. They have received favourable tax treatment for their main source of funds, friendly society bonds (single premium insurance policies).

During the first half of the 1990s, friendly societies had aggregate assets of $8–9 billion, most of which was in the form of short-term securities ($3.3 billion in March 1995) and long-term securities ($2.4 billion). The largest friendly society (as at the end of 1995) had total assets of $3.2 billion, and two others had assets of more than $1 billion.

Cash management trusts

CMTs were established in the early 1980s. They accept deposits from retail investors which are invested in the short-term money market. They were the first institutions that gave retail investors the opportunity to earn a rate of return that was based on the rate in the short-term money market. By the mid 1990s, they were competing with banks and unit trusts in this market.

During the 1990s they managed assets of between $5 and $6 billion, most of which was invested in bills (over $2 billion) and other short-term securities (also over $2 billion). The average interest rate they paid to depositors during the mid 1990s was just over one percentage point below the yield on 90-day bills.

Common funds

Trustee companies pool their trust funds (and other funds deposited with them) for investment purposes. During the mid 1990s, common funds have been invested in assets of between $4 and 5 billion, most of which have been in the form of loans and advances (over $1 billion), bills (over $1 billion) and equities (just less than $1 billion).

Summary

The main points of this chapter are as follows:

- There are three main forms of managed funds: superannuation funds, public unit trusts and the accumulated funds of insurance offices.
- The largest fund managers are insurance offices, the major banks and several investment banks.
- Managed funds are invested mainly in debt and equity securities. The relative proportion in debt and equity securities varies according to the investment objectives of each fund.
- Managed funds differ from intermediated financing because they are mainly invested on behalf of the primary lenders.
- A substantial amount of managed funds is placed with professional fund managers.
- Superannuation schemes are taxed at a lower rate than other investments, partly to encourage people to provide for their retirement income.
- Public unit trusts pool retail subscriptions for investment purposes, which vary according to the specified investment objectives (such as equity and property trusts).

- Although insurance offices provide insurance services, in the process they accumulate substantial funds that are invested in debt and equity securities.

Discussion questions and exercises

1. Briefly describe the main components of the managed-funds industry. Compare the services provided by fund managers with those provided by retail banks.
2. Compare the use of funds by fund managers with the use of funds by retail banks. What are the variables that cause the assets of fund managers to vary over time? Which parties bear the investment risk faced by funds under management?
3. Discuss the superannuation component of the funds-management sector. Explain the pooling of retail funds into wholesale funds within this sector. Briefly describe the two main forms of superannuation schemes and the likely impact of the Superannuation Guarantee Charge on this sector of the managed-funds industry.
4. Briefly describe (a) roll-over funds, and suggest what will be their long-term importance within the managed-funds industry; and (b) the roles of deferred annuities and annuities within the managed-funds industry.
5. Describe five of the portfolios managed by Westpac. Suggest whether they are typical of the managed-funds industry. Explain the different preferences of investors between capital-stable (i.e. debt only) and growth funds.
6. Argue the case for the prediction that superannuation assets will increase relative to the assets of retail banks over the next 30 years. Suggest several reasons for the favourable tax treatment of superannuation schemes.
7. Describe the main types of unit trust, including cash management trusts. Distinguish between the role of the trust deed, the trustee and the fund manager in the administration of unit trusts.
8. Briefly explain how the provision of insurance products involves managed funds. Distinguish between the endowment and event-based (e.g. medical and life-insurance) schemes.
9. Briefly explain how the management of funds generates income for the fund manager without affecting the manager's balance sheet.

References and further reading

ASSIRT 1995(a), *Research, BT Funds Management Limited*.

ASSIRT 1995(b), *Market Share Report*, June 1995.

ASSIRT 1994(a), *Ratings, An Outline for Financial Advisers and Fund Managers*.

ASSIRT 1994(b), *Ratings, IOOF Funds Management Group*.

Australian Law Reform Commission and the Companies and Securities Advisory Committee 1992, *Collective Investment Schemes: Superannuation*, Discussion Paper 50.

Beelaerts, Charles, & Forde, Kevin 1994, *Understanding Unit Trusts*, Wrightbooks, Melbourne.

Cole, Tony 1996, 'An industry perspective on the future of the Australia financial system' in Malcolm Edey (ed.), *The Future of the Financial System*, RBA, Sydney.

Covick, O. E., & Lewis, M. K. 'Insurance, superannuation and collective investments', in Lewis & Wallace 1993.

Davis, E. Philip 1996, 'The role of institutional investors in the evolution of financial structure and behaviour', in Malcolm Edey (ed.), *The Future of the Financial System*, RBA, Sydney.

Davis, Kevin, & Harper, Ian (eds) 1992, *Superannuation and the Australian Financial System*, Allen & Unwin, Sydney.

Edey, Malcolm, Foster, Robin, & Macfarlane, Ian, 'The role of superannuation in the financial sector and in aggregate savings: a review of recent trends' in Davis & Harper 1992.

Ernst & Young 1994, *Australian Capital Markets Survey*, Sydney.

FitzGerald, Vince, & Harper, Ian, 'Banks, super funds and the future of financial intermediation', in Davis & Harper 1992.

Investment Funds Association, *Statistics*, June 1995.

Jones, Robert, 'Superannuation and the financing of risky investment', in Davis & Harper 1992.

Kingston, Geoffrey, Piggott, John, & Bateman, Hazel, 'Customised investment strategies for accumulations superannuation' in Davis & Harper 1992.

Knox, David M., 'The objectives and distribution of the taxation support provided to occupational superannuation', in Davis & Harper 1992.

Lewis, M. K., & Wallace, R. H. (eds) 1993, *The Australian Financial System*, Longman Cheshire, Melbourne.

Morling, Steven, & Subbaraman, Robert 1995, *Superannuation and Saving*, RBA Research Discussion Paper RDP 9511, RBA, Sydney.

Robinson, Ian, 'Superannuation — a policy perspective', in Davis & Harper 1992.

Saunders, Anthony, & Lange, Helen 1996, *Financial Institutions Management*, Irwin, Sydney, Chapter 2.

Thom, John, 'Capital formation friction', in Davis & Harper 1992.

Willis, The Hon. Ralph 1995, *Saving for our Future*, Commonwealth of Australia.

9

Supervision of financial institutions

This chapter explains the development of the system of prudential supervision of financial institutions. The focus is on the Reserve Bank of Australia and its prudential supervision of banks, the principal financial intermediators within the financial system. The supervision of other financial intermediators and fund managers is also considered.

Study objectives

From your study of this chapter you should be able to:

- explain the role of prudential supervision of banks;
- describe the evolution of central banks and the RBA in particular;
- describe the primary responsibilities of the RBA;
- list and explain the main functions performed by the RBA;
- explain the evolution of prudential supervision of banks;
- describe the RBA's supervisory approach;
- list and explain the role of the prudential statements issued by the RBA;
- explain the capital-adequacy requirement in relation to credit risk arising from on- and off-balance sheet assets;
- outline the treatment of market risks within the CAR; and
- outline the prudential supervision of other financial institutions.

INTRODUCTION

The principal purpose of this chapter is to explain the role (and dimensions) of the supervision of banks and other financial institutions. As shown in Chapter 2, banks are the principal intermediators, meaning that they accept deposit funds from the public (without issuing a prospectus) and on-lend the funds. The NBFIs that perform this function play only a small role in the financial system; and fund managers, who play a major and expanding role in the financial system, do not accept deposits (and are not participants in the payments system). Consequently, in this chapter we emphasise the RBA's prudential supervision of banks.

After presenting an overview of prudential supervision and the circumstances that led to its adoption (i.e. deregulation and the globalisation of banking), the chapter explains the development of the RBA. We discuss the RBA's evolution in order to provide an understanding of the bank's role in the financial system.

The regulations that were repealed by deregulation had served to protect banks (even though this was not generally their intention) from risks:

- normally associated with borrowing and lending activities, and
- arising from external competition and interest-rate and FX volatility.

The deregulation of banks allowed them to compete for business and the entry of foreign banks encouraged them to compete vigorously for market share (as a defensive business strategy). The major consequence of this pursuit of banking business was that banks exposed themselves (perhaps excessively in the 1980s) to risks they were not accustomed to managing.

The removal of exchange controls and the freeing of financial markets led to the globalisation of banking, with many foreign-owned banks entering the Australian banking industry, a number of Australian-owned banks undertaking banking activities overseas and most banks acquiring foreign-currency assets and liabilities. Australia's participation in the globalisation of banking followed similar trends in other countries and this created the need for a global approach to the supervision of banks that operate internationally. If countries adopted their own supervision standards (and they differed considerably), international banks would seek to be supervised where these requirements are the least severe. That is, banks would engage in **regulation arbitrage**.

The freeing of financial markets from price control (e.g. floating the exchange rate and removing interest-rate ceilings) also exposed banks (and other participants in the financial system) to market risks. This led to the development of the markets for derivatives (referred to in Chapter 3 and discussed in Part five of the book), but raised the question of the proficiency of banks in the management of their market risks.

The process of establishing a regime of prudential supervision began both within domestic banking systems and with the central banks of leading industrial countries and others concerned with the international banking community, such as the Bank for International Settlements (BIS), which sought to establish a 'level playing field' for international banks.

> *The Basle Committee on Banking Regulation and Supervisory Practice of the BIS, which reports to the governors of the group of ten central banks, began in 1975 to work toward assuring comprehensiveness of supervisory coverage of banks operating internationally. The 'Basle Concordat', which set the principles of allocation of responsibilities of host and parent supervisory authorities, was approved by the G10 governors at the end of 1975.*

In 1983, they adopted the Revised Basle Concordat, which was additionally addressed to assurance of appropriate standards of supervision. In 1988, a common framework of prudential requirements for banks addressing credit risk and capital adequacy was developed by the committee and adopted by the G10 governors. (Linklater, 1992, pp. 140–1)

The issue of the regulatory practices of 'host' and 'parent' supervisory authorities arises when banks operate overseas. A branch bank, for instance, may be admitted only if its host authority is satisfied that it (through its parent) is subject to an adequate level of supervision in its home country.

In order to assess the soundness of banks, prudential supervision should consider the range of risks to which they are exposed. The main ones are:

- credit risk, arising from the possibility of counterparty default, especially where the exposure is large (e.g. when a bank makes a particularly large loan to a client);
- market risks, arising from the possibility that movements in security prices and exchange rates will reduce earnings or the bank's net worth;
- interest-rate risk, arising from the possibility that a movement in interest rates will diminish earnings;
- funding and liquidity risks, which arise when bank loans are for longer periods than their deposits, exposing banks to the possibility of not being able to satisfy customers' requirements for cash (e.g. when making a withdrawal); and
- **operational risk**, arising from the possibility that the bank's management and operating procedures will fail and result in losses. (Example 9.1 discusses the collapse of Barings Bank because of fraud.)

The capacity of a bank to manage these risks depends on:

- the quality of its management and its management systems for monitoring and controlling its exposures,
- the quality and diversification of its assets,
- its pricing of the risks it incurs and its provisions for bad debts,
- the adequacy of its (equity-type) capital,
- its holding of secure liquefiable assets, and
- the spread of its shareholders and its relationship with its subsidiaries and associated companies. (Linklater, 1992, p. 141)

Banks (and other financial institutions that engage in intermediation), being exposed to so many risks, need to conduct their business affairs in a prudent (or cautious) way. That is, in their pursuit of profits they should pay special regard to the risks they are accepting. This involves thoroughly identifying and monitoring their exposures to risk and adopting effective risk-management strategies. Moreover, the roles of intermediaries as acceptors of deposits from the public on the basis of trust, and as participants in the payments system, place them in a position of responsibility to the public at large. A prudential supervision regime imposed by the authorities is an attempt to ensure that financial intermediaries accept these responsibilities by conducting their affairs prudently. (See example 9.1.)

example 9.1

In early 1995, a long-standing British bank, Baring Bros & Co., collapsed due to losses of nearly £1000 million. They arose from unreported trading losses within a subsidiary, Barings Futures Singapore (BFS). While these losses resulted from unauthorised trading on the Nikkei and Osaka futures exchanges, Baring's collapse was due more to 'the problems that arise when risk-management systems and practices and accounting procedures are ineffective. The experience also demonstrates the particular problems that can arise where there is deceptive activity and fraud on the part of senior bank staff.' (RBA, November 1995, p. 5)

The subsequent investigation by the Bank of England into the affair found that 'there was a lack of separation between the front and back offices within BFS'. (Nick Leeson, the general manager of BFS, controlled both sides of the trading operations, allowing him to conceal unauthorised deals.) 'The [bank's] matrix-based reporting system . . . made responsibility for oversight of his [i.e. Leeson's] activities ambiguous and ultimately ineffective'.

The bank's external auditors were also criticised for advising that BFS's internal controls were (in November 1994) satisfactory. (Dale, 1996, p. 239)

The collapse would have been prevented had the management of Barings Bros not provided funds to BFS to cover its losses on the futures positions taken by Nick Leeson. (In Chapter 17 we explain the requirement in the futures market for traders to make cash payments to cover the capital loss on futures positions.) Usually, a bank's risk-management system would require justification for large payments to a subsidiary, but in the case of Baring Bros, the bank's senior management simply made the payments sought by BFS (i.e. Nick Leeson).

The failure of the senior management of Baring Bros to adequately oversee the use of the bank's funds was explained (but not justified) by a misunderstanding about responsibility for BFS and a profit-sharing scheme that biased management decisions toward funding profitable ventures (and BFS had made large trading profits before making its catastrophic losses) without due regard to the risks involved.

The supervisory performance of the Bank of England, as the 'lead regulator' of Barings Bros, was also criticised. The failure of prudential supervision in this case was related to the need to supervise a bank (Barings Bros) that had a securities subsidiary (Barings Securities Ltd) that in turn had an overseas subsidiary (BFS). The supervisors failed to recognise that Baring Bros did not have in place an adequate risk-management system for reviewing the use of bank funds by a subsidiary (BFS). One solution in such cases is to establish 'funding firewalls' between bank deposits and funds raised by a subsidiary (such as a securities company in this case). (Dale, 1996, pp. 238–43)

In 1980 the RBA established a small supervision group to consider how to monitor the financial health of banks. (RBA, May 1991, p. 6) In 1985 the bank issued its first prudential statement. Most of the principles and intentions expounded in that statement have been followed by the bank, although the detailed arrangements have been extensively modified and extended in response to changing circumstances, especially those associated with the changes in the operations of banks.

The bank's prudential supervision regime is defined in a series of Prudential Statements. Some of these are described later in this chapter. Since issuing many of them, the bank has changed its numbering system, to distinguish the area of each statement. We use the new numbering system to cite these statements.

Prudential Statement PSA1

The need for prudential supervision was explained by the Reserve Bank in PSA1 in the following terms:

> *Banks provide the community with important payment services, both domestic and international, and are major depositories for small investors. Community confidence in banks is, therefore, a pre-requisite for a stable financial system.* (p. 1)

This is how the bank explained its approach to supervision:

> *The Bank's approach to supervision is predicated on the view that the prime responsibility for the prudential management of a bank's business lies with the bank itself. The Bank's system of supervision is directed toward satisfying itself that individual banks are following management practices which limit risks to prudent levels; and that banks' prudential standards are being observed and kept under review to take account of changing circumstances.*
>
> *The performance of each bank is continuously assessed, having regard to its global operations. Close attention is paid to capital and liquidity adequacy, earnings, loan loss experience, concentration of risks, the maturity structure of assets and liabilities, potential exposures through equity associations and international banking operations. To this end, the Bank looks for timely information from individual banks and regularly discusses with them both their domestic and international operations from a prudential viewpoint.* (p. 1)

The main features of prudential supervision set out in the statement are that each bank:

- must hold adequate amounts of 'capital' (i.e. equity-type capital, as defined by the RBA). It is a source of funds that can absorb losses. Banks, in common with all businesses, can suffer losses. Through holding an adequate amount of capital, each bank is providing for its long-term viability and contributing to the stability of the banking system over the long term;
- must hold adequate amounts of liquid assets so that it can meet the requirements of its customers for cash;
- should not undertake business such that potential losses from a customer or a group of related customers could threaten its (equity) capital base. In other words, each bank should manage its risk exposures, in part by applying operational limits (e.g. lending limits to individual customers) on its exposures to losses;
- should not undertake business through its subsidiaries such that it exposes the bank's capital base to excessive losses. The RBA emphasises that a bank's depositors have first call on a bank's equity and when a bank creates subsidiaries and associated companies, they must hold adequate amounts of capital to meet their potential losses;

- must comply with the RBA's exposure limits to movements in the exchange rate. These are net open positions in the foreign-exchange market.

The bank has since issued a number of Prudential Statements that either elaborate on its approach to these aspects of its prudential supervision or clarify the bank's approach to new developments in banking, from a prudential viewpoint. We explain the main features of the core aspects of its approach to prudential supervision, as they have been developed (by mid 1996), later in this chapter.

Once a formal system of bank supervision was established by the RBA, pressure emerged for similar supervision of other financial institutions. For instance, the House of Representatives' Standing Committee on Finance and Public Administration recommended in 1991 (*A Pocket Full of Change*, p. 231) that non-bank participants with assets of more than $1 billion be required to apply for a banking licence and so become subject to the RBA's prudential supervision. This recommendation was not adopted by the government.

The committee also recommended that other financial institutions be subject to prudential supervision (but not by the RBA) and that a Council of Supervisors be established to coordinate their supervisory approach. A Council of Supervisors was established in 1992 to coordinate and harmonise the supervision of the various financial institutions that operate in Australia. However, the approach of each of the four major supervisors, the RBA (for banks), the Australian Financial Institutions Commission (for building societies, credit unions and friendly societies), the Insurance and Superannuation Commission (for insurance offices and statutory superannuation funds) and the Australian Securities Commission (for unit trusts and other trustee-administered funds), is not identical because of the differences in the functions and operations of the institutions being supervised. (RBA, October 1995, pp. 34–8)

THE EVOLUTION OF THE RBA

According to the first governor of the RBA:

> *Central banking is a strange profession little understood by members of the public whose interests it exists to protect, by governments with which it shares responsibilities, or by financial institutions whose activities it to some degree controls.* (Coombs, 1981)

To help provide an understanding of the functions of the RBA we start this section with a discussion of the evolution of central banks.

The development of central banks

Central banks were first established in Europe in the 17th century. Their original function was to organise fund-raising for their governments. This activity evolved to the point where many central banks now act as their government's banker, which involves handling the government's financial transactions as well as marketing their securities.

The Bank of England, one of the first central banks, was established in 1694 as a joint-stock company (i.e. as a commercial bank). It initially acted as the government's banker. In the 1830s it became the sole issuer of notes; those issued by other banks were withdrawn. In 1844 its note issue was tied to its stock of gold bullion and this provided the basis for the **gold standard** (i.e. the amount of notes issued was based on the amount of gold held by the bank).

Over time, most central banks were granted the privilege of issuing notes, allowing them to reap the profits from this activity and to overcome the problems that arose from the unregulated issue of notes by individual banks. These notes were of different value, depending on the financial strength of their issuing bank, and were rendered worthless by bank failures. Unregulated note issue also meant that governments had no control over the amount of credit within their economy.

In the 1830s the Bank of England also began to issue (and buy back) consols (these are interest-paying securities that have no maturity date) and to rediscount secure commercial bills. This represented a rudimentary form of market operations that influenced credit conditions within the financial system. Selling consols had the effect of reducing liquidity whereas buying them back (and rediscounting bills) increased liquidity. It and other central banks also accepted deposits from commercial banks.

These activities led to central banks exercising control over the supply of money, a function which developed generally during the gold-standard period. They also became the first step toward central banks becoming responsible for the liquidity of the financial system generally.

In the 1860s the Bank of England developed its lender-of-last-resort facility, under which it lent (at a penalty rate) to banks that faced a liquidity crisis. (Jonson, 1993, pp. 23–6) In 1890 the Bank of England prevented the collapse of Barings Bank by arranging with other banks to guarantee its liabilities. (Linklater, 1992, p. 10) As noted above, in 1995 Barings Bank did collapse as a result of trading losses on the Singapore and Osaka futures markets by its subsidiary, Barings Futures (Singapore). (The transactions of one of the Barings traders was the immediate cause.) This collapse and its implications for prudential supervision were discussed earlier in this chapter.

The provision of reserve liquidity to banks led to the requirement that they supply information and financial data to their central bank. This further strengthened the position of central banks within the commercial banking system.

However, these developments did not crystallise a concept of the role of a central bank during the 19th century. One reason for the on-going debate about the role of central banks was that many operated as commercial banks as well as performing some of the above functions, which competitors regarded as privileges. Their competitors naturally resisted the development of these privileges. As a consequence, even today, not all central banks perform the same functions.

By the 1930s, though, the conceptual foundations were in place for the development of central banks as they are now generally known. According to a former governor of the central bank of South Africa, this was the result of:

- concern over the disruptive effects of the 1930s Depression,
- abandonment of the gold standard and a consequent need for government involvement in controlling the money supply,
- deliberate policies of cheap money — a reflationary tool during the Depression, and a financing measure during World War II and post-war reconstruction,

- an extension of war-time government control and intervention, and
- a trend toward socialism and development of welfare policies, and the use of monetary policy to support them. (quoted by Linklater, 1992, p. 11)

Regulatory powers were given to central banks to implement monetary policy, maintain low interest rates and fix the level of the exchange rate. In 1944, the Bretton Woods agreement (which we discuss in Chapter 13) required governments and central banks to apply monetary policies that maintained agreed exchange rates, further strengthening the role of central banks. Nevertheless, these developments did not result in all central banks being assigned the same set of responsibilities.

The development of Australia's central bank

In Australia, the debate over a central bank during the 19th and first half of the 20th century was no less confused. A major issue was resentment toward commercial banks, particularly among members of the Labor party, many of whom believed that they exploited the working class and should be nationalised. This view implied that the central bank should control commercial bank profits and direct their loans to designated areas (activities that now are clearly regarded as inappropriate for a central bank to perform). However, public resentment toward banks dates from the bank failures in the 1840s. (Linklater, 1992, Chapter 3)

As noted in Chapter 6, the Commonwealth Bank (CBA) began operating in 1912, following the passage of legislation by the Labor-controlled parliament in 1911. This legislation established what was primarily a savings bank that was to have limited central-banking functions. But the transformation of the CBA into a dual commercial and central bank still took some years to occur.

In 1920, the note-issue function was transferred from the Treasury to the CBA. In 1924 banks were required to conduct their settlements through the CBA, a practice that began during World War I. In 1929 the CBA was given control over gold, in response to the onset of the Depression. In 1931 it became responsible for the exchange rate, which it set weekly. In 1939 it was given exchange controls which were to be exercised for war-time purposes.

The CBA was given a range of powers to control the operations of the banking system in the early 1940s. Many of these regulations had been proposed by the 1937 Royal Commission into Money and Banking and were reformulated in the *Banking Act*, 1945. (These regulations were repealed by the process known as deregulation that was briefly described in Chapter 6.)

In 1953 the demarcation within the Commonwealth Bank between its commercial operations and its central bank (and other government-sponsored) operations was finally established. In 1959 the *Reserve Bank Act* formally established Australia's central bank as a separate organisation. (Linklater, 1992, pp. 24–6)

The RBA's responsibilities

The principal statutory responsibilities of the RBA, which were originally set out in the 1945 *Banking Act* for the CBA, are as follows:

It is the duty of the Board, within the limits of its powers, to ensure that the monetary and banking policy of the Bank is directed to the greatest advantage of the people of Australia and that the powers of the bank under this Act, the Banking Act *1959 and the regulations under that Act, are exercised in such a manner as, in the opinion of the Board, will best contribute to:*

(a) the stability of the currency of Australia;

(b) the maintenance of full employment in Australia; and

(c) the economic prosperity and welfare of the people of Australia.

It is remarkable that the principal responsibilities of the RBA have remained couched in these conflicting and vague terms. The first can be interpreted as an anti-inflationary goal which often requires measures that conflict with the achievement of the second responsibility. The third responsibility is so general (i.e. vague) that it could be interpreted to justify almost any measure.

The inherent conflict between the first two listed responsibilities is one faced by most central banks. Is it, or is the government of the day, responsible for inflation and unemployment? If it is responsible for unemployment and low inflation, which responsibility has the greater priority? Assuming that there is a degree of mutual exclusivity between these outcomes, when is the bank justified in taking measures that respond to one (e.g. reduce interest rates to help reduce unemployment) and aggravate the problems of the other (i.e. reduced interest rates are likely to add to inflationary pressures)?

A number of statements by the Governor of the RBA during the early 1990s (e.g. RBA, December 1991; RBA, September 1992; and RBA, December 1994) clarified his position toward these matters. The RBA gives priority to its anti-inflation responsibility (i.e. to protect the stability of the currency) with due concern for the rate of economic growth (which sustains employment). Part of this due concern is the expectation that monetary policy (this term refers to macroeconomic measures on the financial system that are designed to promote desired economic outcomes) is a less effective tool for promoting economic growth than it is for promoting price stability.

RBA independence

The issue of responsibility for economic outcomes is linked to the question of the independence of the bank. This matter has been debated since the development of central banks (as noted above). At one time it involved the role of a central bank as a provider of funds to allow governments to balance their budgets (i.e. they were used by the government as a money machine). Given the consequences of this practice (hyper inflation), most central banks in developed economies (including Australia) are no longer required to perform this function. That is, they are independent of the budgetary function of government.

In the 1990s, the main area in which central-bank independence arises is monetary policy. Here the concern is that the government of the day will adopt policies according to its electoral prospects, rather than according to the circumstances of the economy. In this context, growth will prevail over low inflation as an economic policy goal.

The then governor (of the RBA) contended in 1994 that an independent central bank is one that is given a charter that defines its goal(s) (e.g. the maintenance of price stability) and is free to implement it (or them).

> *. . . give central banks a charter which includes a strong commitment to price stability, and the freedom to pursue it. This does involve the government in setting the goals, but that is the way it should be: central banks cannot expect to determine the goals they should pursue, but they should have adequate scope to pursue the goals that have been set. In jargon, they should not have* goal independence *but they should have* instrument independence. (RBA, December 1994, p. 3)

Whether the RBA has instrument independence is not absolutely clear because the bank is required to consult with the Treasury and the treasurer. The governor stated that these consultations are desired by the bank because they enhance the bank's capacity to make correct decisions and do not diminish the bank's independence of action.

For the bank to be subject to the broad policy parameters (i.e. goals) of government seems appropriate in a democracy. It would be odd for a non-elected body (the board of the RBA) to determine goals in an area that is widely regarded as the government's responsibility, without reference to the treasurer and the Treasury (its principal policy department in this area).

The key issues in the debate about the independence of the RBA are whether it:

- would be able to better contain inflation if this was its sole objective, and
- should be required to gain the agreement of the treasurer of the day to its monetary-policy stance.

Should the bank and the government have irreconcilable differences of opinion over monetary policy, Section 11 of the Act specifies a dispute-resolution procedure that, in the end, allows the government's view to prevail. This provision has been interpreted by some commentators (but not the RBA) as implying that the bank's independence of government is excessively constrained.

Several central banks act in a very single-minded way in their conduct of monetary policy. The New Zealand Reserve Bank, for example, was given sole responsibility in 1990 for keeping inflation within 2% p.a. But the debate about independence is on-going because it is not clear which is the superior approach. The position of the RBA is similar to that of most central banks.

Depositor protection

Perhaps the most important responsibility of the RBA is to protect depositors' funds. This responsibility is set out in the Act. Under these provisions, the Reserve Bank may take over the assets of a bank that has placed its depositors' funds at risk, to ensure that these funds are repaid. Prior to the 1989 amendment of the Act, these depositor-protection provisions provided the authority for the bank's prudential supervision activities.

Given that bank deposits form the basis of the payments system, depositor protection is linked with the bank's responsibility to ensure the integrity of this system. The bank's goals for its prudential system can be traced to its responsibilities for:

- depositors' funds, and
- the stability of the payments system.

RBA functions

By the mid 1990s, the bank's main functions were to:

- determine and implement monetary policy settings,
- act as the government's banker, including issuing securities on behalf of the government,
- act to protect bank depositors' funds,
- recommend the issue of bank licences and supervise the banking system,
- oversee the payment system and facilitate its operation through provision of a data-handling system (RITS),
- issue CGSs on behalf of the Commonwealth Treasury and provide registration, clearing and settlement services that facilitate the operation of their secondary market,
- manage the financial system's liquidity and the government's holding of foreign exchange,
- oversee the operations of financial markets and NBFIs, and
- issue notes.

The operations of the RBA are reflected in its balance-sheet data. Table 9.1 presents a summary of the bank's balance sheet for selected years between June 1981 and June 1996.

In July 1996 the RBA began paying interest on balances in ESAs to accommodate the participation of banks in real-time settlement (discussed in Chapter 1). In August 1996, $6.8 billion was held in these accounts, increasing the RBA's liabilities (and hence its balance sheet). The funds were invested by the bank in foreign exchange and CGSs. The licences of the official dealers were withdrawn, closing this section of the short-term money market.

The bank's assets are mainly gold and foreign exchange (most of which is US dollars) and CGSs. Observe the increase in the bank's holding of gold through the 1980s. This reflects the appreciation in the $A value of its gold holdings during the period as well as the bank's net purchases of foreign currency. Note that this involved the net sale of Australian dollars (to acquire the foreign currency) by the bank over the period.

The fall in the bank's holdings of CGSs during the latter half of the 1980s resulted from the government's budget surplus. In particular, the surplus was used to redeem Treasury bonds and the bank sold down its holding of them to reduce the pressure on their supply in the bond market. (Jonson, 1993, pp. 32–4)

Table 9.1 RBA, balance sheet items, selected years, June 1981 to June 1996 ($m)

	1981	*1986*	*1991*	*1995*	*1996*
Assets					
— gold and FX	5 684	12 016	24 308	19 948	18 668
— CGSs	5 303	9 732	2 960	15 986	16 023
— other assets	1 103	1 256	861	690	805
Total assets	12 089	23 004	28 129	36 624	35 496
Liabilities					
— capital and reserves	75	182	248	633	634
— notes on issue	5 184	8 890	14 621	17 372	19 086
— SRDs/NCDs	1 853	3 301	2 541	3 256	3 918
— deposits of banks, governments	1 088	1 573	1 908	3 077	3 348
— other liabilities	3 496	8 709	8 573	7 934	8 510
Total liabilities	12 089	23 004	28 129	36 624	35 496

Source: RBA, *Bulletin*, Table A.1

Some of the bank's assets arise from their 'sale' of notes (i.e. the note-issue process) to the banking system. The RBA's assets can be viewed as backing for the notes on issue. However, these assets are used by the bank when conducting monetary policy, managing the financial system's liquidity and, as noted above, trading in the FX market.

The bank's main liability is notes on issue — these being promises to pay their face value. As noted above, the bank invests the proceeds it raises when issuing notes (financing the bank's assets). The interest earned on these investments is available to meet the bank's costs of issuing notes and the surplus is a source of profit for the bank.

The bank has four operating divisions (and a number of supporting departments) headed by an assistant governor:

- Economic, comprising Analysis and Research Departments,
- Financial Markets, comprising Domestic Markets and International Departments,
- Financial Institutions, comprising Supervision and Financial System Departments, and
- Business Services, with a Currency and Banking Department. (RBA, *1995 Report and Financial Statements,* pp. 84–5)

Refer back to the above list of functions. You will recall that we explained the role of the bank in the payments system in Chapter 1. In Chapter 14 we will discuss the bank's implementation of monetary policy, management of the system's liquidity and oversight of financial markets. In this chapter we explain the bank's approach to the prudential supervision of banks. This function is undertaken to protect the integrity of the payments system and depositors' funds.

Prudential supervision of banks: Part 1

We begin our discussion of the prudential supervision regime of the RBA by reviewing the domestic events that led (along with the BIS proposals) to the initial adoption of prudential supervision.

During the 1960s and 1970s, the RBA applied its various controls over banks and the financial system in performing its responsibilities. The controls on bank interest rates and their asset portfolios served to limit bank lending and to direct it to low-risk areas. It was said that banking followed the '3-6-3' rule — borrow at 3%, lend at 6% and close at 3 p.m. in time for a round of golf. As explained in Chapters 6 and 7, banks did not (i.e. could not) compete for funds on the basis of price and they lent only to the most creditworthy customers. Therefore they did not actively compete with one another (or with NBFIs) for funds or assets.

These regulations had been introduced mainly as war-time measures but they served to ensure that banks acted prudently.

> *As a former Reserve Bank deputy governor put it, during this period the authorities' attitude towards banks was 'if you did not let them do much, they would not get into much trouble'. (A Pocket Full of Change,* p. 181*)*

As noted in Chapter 6, it became apparent, even to the RBA, that its controls were becoming ineffective and were seriously distorting the operation of the financial system (i.e. were reducing the economic efficiency of the system).

At the beginning of the 1980s Australia's financial system was reviewed by the Campbell Committee. It recommended the dismantling of most of the regulations that restricted the operations of banks. Following the Martin Committee's review (1983) of the Campbell Committee's report, the new Labor Government completed the deregulation of the banking system, 'floated' the currency and, in 1985, admitted 16 new foreign banks.

It was recognised by the Campbell Committee that its recommendations to deregulate (for the purpose of improving the system's efficiency through greater competition) would greatly increase the exposure of banks to credit (and market) risks. The entry of foreign banks, in particular, posed a threat for the major banks. It was expected that the domestic banks would attempt to strengthen their market position by competing for funds and loan business. This led to the concern that banks might act imprudently when attempting to become more competitive.

> *On prudential matters, the Campbell Committee believed 'capital . . . should be seen as the cornerstone of prudential regulation' and capital requirements should be related to the nature of a bank's assets. They recommended 'the supervisory efforts of the Reserve Bank should continue to involve close liaison with bank management and place particular emphasis on periodic in-depth examinations'. They also recommended that 'a national framework for the prudential regulation of non-bank institutions which accept deposits primarily from households without issuing prospectuses should be developed'. (A Pocket Full of Change,* p. 29*)*

Since the mid 1980s the financial system has operated in a largely deregulated environment. This does not mean that banks were unregulated. Banks were still required, for example, to deposit funds with the RBA (non-callable funds) and hold at least 6% of their assets in the form of prime assets. They were also required to hold a licence and this meant satisfying various conditions. The introduction of prudential supervision in 1988 was considered by some commentators to be **reregulation**, although it can also be viewed (as described above) as a consequence (and 'complement') of deregulation.

The concerns about the consequences of deregulation of banking were not confined to Australia. There were a number of major bank failures in the US, UK and Europe and in the mid 1980s the Bank for International Settlements (BIS) proposed that central banks impose prudential supervision on their banking systems. The main instrument of supervision proposed by the BIS was the requirement that each bank hold a specified minimum amount of equity capital to ensure that it could sustain substantial losses without facing insolvency (i.e. without placing its depositors' funds at risk or posing a risk for the payments system).

The concern of central banks about the integrity of the payments system arises from the possibility that a bank failure could threaten the system because of the pressure it could place on the viability of other banks. This was referred to in Chapter 1 as contagion risk. When one bank fails, pressure on other banks can arise in several ways:

- depositors generally may lose confidence in banks that are in fact quite secure, causing a wave of withdrawals, and
- payment orders by its depositors are not honoured, which poses liquidity problems for the intended recipients who may also trigger a wave of withdrawals.

The main aims of the BIS proposals were to establish a regime of supervision that enhances the financial stability of banks throughout the global financial system, on the basis of an 'even playing field'.

The principal effect of deregulation on regulatory bodies (particularly the RBA) was to shift the focus from controlling the business of intermediaries to one of prudential supervision. The main aims of deregulation were to remove restrictions that impeded competition in the finance sector, to ensure that intermediaries take responsibility for their business decisions, and to protect the integrity of the payments system and depositors' funds, through a regime of prudential supervision.

The RBA began developing its supervisory policies in the early 1980s. Its first Prudential Statement, summarised above, set out the main features of its approach. While most of these remain of central concern, the bank's approach to prudential supervision has been somewhat evolutionary. This is to be expected because central banks will adjust their approach to supervision in the light of experience and because financial innovation by banks can require an extension of the scope of prudential supervision. Consequently the following description of the system will emphasise its principles rather than its details (which are likely to change over time).

Details of the RBA's prudential requirements are presented below. They relate to capital adequacy, the holding of liquid assets, lending and other risk-exposure limits which are monitored through the provision of statistical returns that external auditors verify. They also cover a bank's management system to control its operations within prudential guidelines on which external auditors provide advice to the RBA.

The RBA's system of prudential supervision is specified in a series of statements, the first of which, PSA1, was described earlier in this chapter. This statement is reviewed below, together with a statement describing the bank's involvement of external auditors in the supervision process, for the purpose of describing the bank's approach to (or philosophy of) prudential supervision. We describe each of these statements in this section of the chapter and discuss the most important and complex requirement, capital adequacy, in the following section.

The RBA approach

The RBA's approach to prudential supervision has not changed, in principle, from that described in the bank's first prudential statement. The RBA still maintains that each bank is primarily responsible for the prudent management of its affairs:

> *The central tenet of the Bank's supervisory philosophy is that the prime responsibility for effective management of banks, and for the introduction of systems which effectively control or limit risk, rests with the bank itself, its management and its board . . . It is the Bank's role to see that this process is on-going.* (RBA, May 1995, p. 7)

External auditors are called upon to report on '. . . (whether) prudential standards agreed with banks are being observed, that statutory and other banking requirements are being met and that banks' management systems limiting risks to prudent levels are operating effectively'. (PSH1, p. 1). Prudential statement PSH1, which defines the role of external auditors, was issued in April 1986.

The role of external auditors was subsequently widened in conjunction with the extension of prudential supervision to the use of derivatives by banks:

> *external auditors of banks are required . . . to give an opinion to the Reserve Bank on the adequacy of their internal management systems and controls; in particular, they advise on whether the bank's management systems to control and limit credit, liquidity and foreign-exchange risks are effective and are being observed. Consideration is currently being given to commissioning more detailed reports from auditors on particular aspects of banks' systems.* (RBA, May 1995, p. 4)

External auditors have been involved in the prudential-supervision process because this was judged to be the least intrusive and costly way of monitoring compliance. The RBA decided not to follow the inspection approach to monitoring compliance that has been adopted by certain other central banks (e.g. the US Federal Reserve Board) because of the expense and its philosophy of clearly identifying the primary responsibility of banks to manage the risks that arise from their business decisions.

However, the RBA has intensified its monitoring activities by adopting the practice of periodic on-site visits in addition to requiring banks to submit regular returns on features such as the quality of their assets.

> *Recognising the importance of sound management systems, in 1994 the Bank commenced a program of on-site visits to banks which have focused on how they identify, measure and manage market risks, including derivatives.* (RBA, May 1995, p. 3)

While on-site supervision should give staff in the RBA's supervisory division better insights into the management culture and practices of a bank, which may help it prevent problems from arising, tighter controls that require the RBA to review and/or approve the commercial judgments of banking staff pose other problems. For instance, this might undermine the sense of responsibility that directors and senior management should accept for a bank's lending and operating policies.

Ownership and control of banks

The ownership of a bank is regarded as relevant to prudential supervision because of the possibility that a bank which is controlled by one or a small group of shareholders might conduct its business in accordance with the interests of the controlling owner, without due regard to the interests of depositors. The bank's view on ownership is driven by its statutory obligation to protect depositors' funds and it believes that their interests are best served by a bank that has a wide range of shareholders and a board of directors that represents this broad range of shareholders.

As noted in Chapter 2, banks typically are highly geared through their use of deposits as a source of funds. Depositors cannot influence the operating decisions of banks, except in the marketplace for deposits. Shareholder interests are best served by a bank adopting policies that allow it to be successful in this marketplace. Such banks will conduct their business prudently and therefore will contribute to the stability of the banking and payments systems. These contentions are not universally endorsed, particularly by those who believe that competition and informed investors impose a discipline on banks, irrespective of their ownership position. (Hogan and Sharpe, 1990)

The bank's attitude toward ownership and control is set out in Prudential Statement B1 (PSB1). The main requirement is that any one shareholder (this could be a group of related shareholders) is limited to holding 15% of a bank's share capital (unless a larger shareholding is approved by the government) and this shareholder will be limited to proportional representation on the board (e.g. one member on a board that comprises six members or less). The authorisation (and therefore the ownership) of banks is determined by the government upon the advice of the RBA.

In PSB1, the RBA states that each bank's chair and a majority of its board members should be non-executive and not subject to a conflict of interests (e.g. through commercial dealings with the bank). The reason for this approach is that the RBA believes that a board which is independent of the bank's management is more likely to act in the interests of shareholders in general. In the case of foreign-owned banks, the RBA accepts that a non-executive director could be an executive of the parent bank.

Given that the government issues bank licences, the matter of ownership and control extends to proposed takeovers and other changes in the ownership of a bank. Such events require government approval.

In Chapter 7 we explained the 1992 policy change toward branch banks. Before then the RBA had opposed the admission of branch banks, mainly on prudential-supervision grounds. A branch of a foreign bank is part of that bank, whereas a subsidiary is a separate Australian legal entity. The RBA believed that it could meet its obligations to protect depositors' funds in respect of subsidiaries of foreign banks, but not branches. You will recall that one way the RBA could perform this obligation is to take over the Australian assets of a bank when its financial circumstances placed its depositors' funds at risk. The bank could perform this function in the case of a subsidiary of a foreign bank, because it could identify and gain access to the assets that were funded by Australian depositors; but it could not lay claim to the assets of a foreign bank when its Australian branch placed its depositors' funds at risk. (Linklater, 1992, pp. 145–7)

In 1992 the government decided to admit branch banks provided they do not operate in the retail-banking sector (therefore, they do not acquire retail deposit funds to place at risk); can demonstrate that their parent bank is adequately supervised by their central bank (in terms of the Basle concordat); and can demonstrate that they will contribute positively to the efficiency and competitiveness of the Australian banking system. (RBA, October 1992, pp. 22–7)

Liquidity requirements

The RBA's attitude toward bank liquidity is set out in PSD1:

> *The maintenance of an assured capacity to meet promptly all obligations as they fall due is fundamental to banking. It is the responsibility of a bank's management to ensure that its internal systems and controls are adequate to ensure resources are available to cover potential funds outflow. (PSD1, p.1)*

The bank has continued to impose its PAR (the history and form of which was discussed in Chapter 6), making it part of its liquidity requirements. Remember that prime assets are the most liquid and secure available to a bank (notes and coins, discretionary balances with the RBA and CGSs. The PAR is a ratio of prime assets to assets financed from Australian-dollar liabilities. In 1996 the required (i.e. minimum) ratio was 6%.

The RBA assumes that banks hold liquid assets in addition to those required to satisfy its PAR and, as shown in table 6.7 in Chapter 6 (p. 152), banks in fact do hold liquid assets in addition to those required to satisfy their PAR.

According to PSD1, a bank can sell down its holding of prime assets below the PAR, with RBA approval, 'in extreme circumstances'. It also states that banks that are 'in danger of breaching the PAR ratio — which should be a rare and exceptional situation — must advise the Bank immediately and, in consultation with the bank, take prompt action to correct the situation'.

As noted in Chapter 6, the strict operation of the PAR diminishes the liquidity of prime assets because they can be sold only in exceptional circumstances and with the approval of the RBA.

Large credit exposures

Banks are required to report 'large' credit exposures to the RBA. A large exposure is defined in terms of the amount of the bank's equity that is at risk should the borrower default. This requirement applies to the consolidated business of a bank (i.e. the bank and its banking and non-bank subsidiaries).

Under PSE1, which sets out the bank's prudential requirement regarding large credit exposures, each bank is required:

- to provide (and update as necessary) a statement of its policy in respect of large exposures to individual clients or groups of related clients;

- to report quarterly all exposures of the consolidated group to individual clients, or groups of related clients, above 10% of the capital base (i.e. its equity as defined by PSC1) of the consolidated group;
- to keep large exposures under review and to place a limit on their size relative to the capital base of the group;
- to give prior notification of its intention to enter an exceptionally large exposure to an individual client or group of related clients. In such cases, a bank should be able to show that the proposed exposure would not result in the consolidated group undertaking an excessive risk. (PSE1, p. 1)

Banks' association with non-banks

The RBA's approach to this matter is in terms of its depositor-protection obligations. These relationships between a bank and its associated businesses should not weaken the bank's capacity to service its depositors' requirements for access to their deposits. Chapter 6 presented illustrations of occasions when the losses of a bank's subsidiary exceeded the bank's capital. In each case, though, action was taken — the banks were sold — to avoid their possible failure.

The RBA also applies its 'separation policy' that requires banking conglomerates to limit and control their credit exposure to their subsidiaries and to clearly distinguish themselves from their subsidiaries within the marketplace. (RBA, April 1995, p. 32)

The RBA monitors the non-banking activities of bank conglomerates. It is also concerned to ensure that all of the operations of such conglomerates are appropriately supervised, and that information about conglomerates is shared by the various regulators.

PSG1 defines the bank's approach to the relationship between banks and their associated companies. According to this statement, these associations should not:

- weaken a bank's capital base; that is, a bank's equity investment in its associated companies should be financed by raising additional equity capital,
- involve an unlimited guarantee (explicit or implied) by a bank of the liabilities of its associated companies, or
- become excessively large relative to the bank.

The statement also requires banks to submit regular returns to the RBA disclosing its financial exposure (by way of equity, loans and standby guarantees) to its associated companies, and requires its subsidiaries to conduct their financial affairs in a prudent manner.

Asset quality

In 1993 the RBA required banks to report, by way of quarterly returns, data on their **impaired** assets. In PSL1, issued in January 1995, the bank added the following two further requirements relating to asset quality:

- regarding the principles to be adopted by banks when valuing security and determining the level of provisions, they require that security be valued on the basis of its net current market value where possible; and

- that banks should have in place appropriate credit-risk grading systems as an aid to assessing asset quality and credit exposures (and submit data on this basis along with their impaired asset returns). (RBA, Press release, 18 January 1995)

Impaired assets are those that are not generating their contractual cash flows. They comprise:

- non-accrual items — ones on which contractual payments to the bank cannot be relied upon,
- restructured items — ones where the bank has made financial concessions that render the business 'non-commercial' to itself, because of the customer's financial difficulties, and
- assets acquired through the enforcement of collateral or other security arrangements, which usually occurs when the bank cannot economically dispose of them.

Note that both balance sheet and off-balance sheet business can be impaired; it merely requires default, or likelihood of default, by the bank's counterparty.

According to PSL1:

> *The maintenance of sound asset quality is a fundamental aspect of banking. In its approach to the supervision of banks, the Reserve Bank takes the view that it is the prime responsibility of each bank's management to set policies and procedures to ensure that the bank maintains sound asset quality, strong portfolio management, prudent risk controls, effective credit review and classification procedures, and an appropriate methodology for dealing with problem exposures.*
>
> *To help improve prudential oversight of asset quality, the Reserve Bank is seeking to establish a set of minimum standards, and to apply a common language and methodology, for identifying impaired assets within banks. The guidelines on the measurement and reporting of impaired assets are designed to improve the quality and consistency of data received from banks.*
>
> *. . . The Reserve Bank also recommends that banks implement risk-grading systems which allow them to effectively monitor trends in asset quality.* (PSL1, p. 1)

Loan transfers and securitisation

Loan transfers and securitisation are addressed in Prudential Statement C1:

> *For the purpose of this Statement, securitisation is a process by which assets are sold by a bank and refinanced by the purchaser through the issue of securities backed by the cash flow from the assets; the cash flow is applied to meet the obligations attaching to the securities to pay interest and repay principal to investors. Assets such as bank loans, which are not always marketable in their original form are, in effect, converted into marketable securities.*
>
> *. . . a bank is relieved of the need to maintain capital in support of securitised assets only where their sale is clean and final, i.e. apart from any administrative function, the bank has no remaining obligation or interest in respect of the assets.* (PSC2, p. 1)

The Statement defines when capital will be required to support residual obligations — when, for instance, the bank provides a credit-enhancement facility (e.g. a guarantee) to the securities backed by the assets it has sold, and the notice that must be given by banks to the buyer of securitised assets to ensure that they will not have any recourse (legal or commercial) to the selling bank.

PRUDENTIAL SUPERVISION: PART 2 — CAR

The RBA's capital-adequacy requirement (CAR) is set out in PSC1. It defines the minimum amount of (equity) capital that banks must hold. It has been described:

> *. . . as the centrepiece of banking supervision and it is probably true that a bank's capital ratio, if measured accurately, is the single most useful indicator of its soundness and capacity to withstand adversity. (RBA, May 1991, p. 7)*

While the bank suggested in 1991 that its CAR is the centrepiece of its prudential supervision, the requirement represents a secondary form of protection against the risk of bank failures placing depositors' funds and the payments system at risk. The primary safeguard is effective management by banks of the risks they face. Only when circumstance or management shortcomings result in bank losses does the CAR perform an active role in protecting depositors' funds and the payment system.

When the requirement was introduced in August 1988, the RBA indicated that it 'will be watching closely the operation of the new guidelines to see if experience dictates the need for any changes'. (PSC1, p. 2) Experience over the past seven years has resulted in many changes being made to the requirement, so that it is now probably the most complex of the various elements of the bank's prudential requirements.

A brief inspection of a bank's notional balance sheet (shown in table 9.2) will allow you to focus on the main elements involved in the capital-adequacy requirement. Assets usually generate income for the bank, but are subject to credit (and other) risks, given that most are loans or securities. Liabilities involve interest payments (and/or services) that must be met from the bank's income. Should a bank's income be exceeded by its expenses, it incurs a loss, which must be met from shareholders' funds (i.e. the bank's equity capital) if the bank is to avoid bankruptcy: hence the role of 'capital' in respect of a bank's 'capacity to withstand adversity'.

Table 9.2 A bank's notional balance sheet

Assets	*Liabilities*
Loans, etc.	Deposits, etc.
Securities	Shareholders' funds
Off-balance sheet items	

In essence, the CAR specifies the minimum amount of shareholders' funds that must be held (8%) in relation to the bank's risk-adjusted balance-sheet assets and off-balance sheet credit exposures:

$$\text{CAR} = \frac{\text{capital}}{\text{risk-adjusted assets}}$$
$$= \text{at least } 8\%$$

General framework

Each bank is required to hold an amount of equity-type capital that is at least 8% of its **risk-adjusted assets**. The requirements define (as at mid 1996) two tiers of capital and the rules for determining how much has to be in the form of tier 1, the purest form of risk capital. These sources of bank funds form the numerator of the CAR ratio.

The requirements also define how to calculate the denominator term, which is the sum of the values of a bank's:

- risk-adjusted balance-sheet assets, and
- risk-adjusted off-balance sheet credit exposures.

The CAR applies 'to the consolidated global operations of a bank and its subsidiaries . . .' (PSC1, p. 3) However, the RBA requirements do not apply to the managed-funds activities of banks, which are subject to supervision by the ASC.

Observe that the CAR applies only to the credit exposures. In April 1995 the BIS released its revised proposal to incorporate market risks within the Basle Capital Accord. It expects to incorporate its supplement covering market risks (and a third tier of capital) by the end of 1997 and that member countries (i.e. the RBA in Australia's case) will apply the additional requirements by the end of 1997. Interest-rate risk will be considered after 1997. (BCBS, 1995, p. 7)

Given that, at the time of writing, incorporation for market risk was being developed, we will explain how the requirements allow for credit (or counterparty-default) risk first, and then explain the proposal for extending the requirements to cover market risks.

Credit risk

The amount of capital required for credit risk is based on the amount of a bank's global credit exposures adjusted by a set of prescribed **risk-adjustment factors**. A bank's credit exposures arise from its assets (i.e. its loans and holdings of securities). These have counterparties who are obliged to make payments to the bank. The risk-adjustment factors classify assets, in the main, according to their counterparty. Their effect is to reduce the value of a bank's assets (for CAR purposes) that have a very secure class of counterparty. As a consequence, less capital has to be held by a bank per dollar of such assets.

The amount of required capital is 8% of a bank's aggregate **risk-adjusted assets.**

Two classes of capital items were defined for the purpose of the CAR. **Tier 1** (or 'core') capital includes the purest forms of equity:

- paid-up ordinary shares,
- retained earnings, including general reserves and funds in non-repayable share-premium accounts,
- non-cumulative irredeemable preference shares, and
- minority interests in subsidiaries.

The sources of **tier 2** (or supplementary) capital, which are listed below, include forms of near-equity and funds that are available to meet unspecified losses. They also include perpetual and long-term subordinated debt, which is treated as capital because payments to the suppliers of such funds take priority only over shareholders. That is, the suppliers of these debt funds subordinate the usual payment priority of a debtholder:

- general provisions for doubtful debts (up to 1.25% of risk-adjusted assets),
- asset revaluation reserves,
- cumulative irredeemable preference shares,
- mandatory convertible notes and similar capital instruments,
- perpetual and (long-) term subordinated debt (the eligible amount of the term debt declines as its term to maturity diminishes),
- redeemable preference shares (subject to the special conditions that apply to long-term subordinated debt). (PSC1, as amended)

Equity and debt funds invested by banks in other banks and non-consolidated subsidiaries (for CAR purposes), goodwill and similar intangible assets must be deducted from the sum of tier 1 and tier 2 capital to calculate a bank's 'capital' for CAR purposes.

Banks are required to hold at least 4% of their risk-adjusted assets in the form of tier 1 capital; that is, tier 2 capital cannot exceed tier 1 for capital adequacy purposes. The data in table 9.3 show that during the 1990s, banks have held more tier 1 capital (than tier 2 sources) and during 1994 –95, tier 1 capital alone exceeded the 8% requirement.

Table 9.3 All banks — global consolidated group capital and risk-adjusted assets, June 1990 to March 1995 ($b)

	Tier 1	*Tier 2*	*Total*	*Risk-adjusted assets On-B S*	*Risk-adjusted assets Off-B S*	*Total risk-adjusted assets*	*Tier 1 ratio (%)*	*Tier 2 ratio (%)*
June 1990	26	14	40	362	64	425	6.1	9.3
June 1991	27	16	42	360	60	419	6.4	10.1
June 1992	29	14	42	354	58	412	7.0	10.2
June 1993	30	15	44	357	53	409	7.3	10.8
June 1994	34	14	47	355	43	398	8.5	11.9
March 1995	37	13	50	372	37	409	9.2	12.3

Note: totals may not add due to rounding.
Source: RBA, *Bulletin*, Table B.19

The key feature of the CAR is that banks must hold a minimum amount of capital to sustain losses, should they occur. In aggregate, the data in table 9.3 show that bank capital totalled $50 billion in March 1995. Banks were required to hold at least $32.72 billion, given their $409 billion worth of risk-adjusted assets ($409 billion times 0.08).

You will observe in table 9.3 that there are two groups of assets, those that appear on the balance sheet of banks and their off-balance sheet holdings. This distinction was explained in Chapter 2. Off-balance sheet items are contingent in nature; that is, their value depends on future events, such as the level of interest rates at a future date.

Table 9.4 Risk weighting for balance-sheet assets

Risk factor (i.e. risk weighting) (%)	*Selected assets in each category*
Nil	notes and coins, gold bullion, balances with the RBA, short-term Commonwealth securities
10	long-term claims on the Commonwealth and claims on State governments, central banks and governments of OECD countries
20	claims on local governments, Australian and OECD public-sector non-corporate entities (unless guaranteed by the government or a bank), Australian, OECD and other approved banks
50	loans secured by a mortgage on residential property which represent no more than 80% of the property's value
100	all other claims, such as those arising from commercial and personal loans, loans to NBFIs and long-term (or foreign-currency) loans to non-OECD central banks and governments

Source: RBA, Collection of press releases relating to prudential supervision, 1994; RBA, *Prudential statements*, 1990

The risk-adjusted value of balance-sheet assets is determined by grouping a bank's assets into the five risk categories, as shown in table 9.4. Observe that the main characteristic of each asset class is the bank's counterparty. The other relevant characteristics are the term of the asset (short-term assets in certain cases carry a lower risk weight), the currency of the asset (in certain cases, domestic-currency assets carry a lower risk weight) and the credit exposure's security (such as loans secured by a mortgage over residential property and loans guaranteed by banks or governments).

The calculation of the risk-adjusted value of balance-sheet assets is illustrated by the data in table 9.5. The sum of the value of the bank's assets in each risk-weighted category are shown in the first column. They are multiplied by the risk weight, shown in the second column and aggregated.

Observe that in the illustrative example presented in table 9.5, the risk-adjusted value of the bank's assets ($46.5 million) is considerably less than their monetary value because of the operation of the risk weights ($76.5 million). The risk weights can be interpreted in two ways. They can be viewed either as reducing (except for

Table 9.5 Calculation of the value of risk-adjusted balance-sheet assets

Asset values ($000)	*Risk weights*	*Risk-adjusted values $000*
1 500	zero	zero
5 000	0.1	500
5 000	0.2	1 000
40 000	0.5	20 000
25 000	1.0	25 000
76 500		**46 500**

the 100% weight) the value of the asset for risk-adjustment purposes, or as reducing the amount of capital required to finance the corresponding assets. For instance, the 50% weight on loans mortgaged by residential property can be viewed as reducing the value of these assets (as shown in table 9.5) or as reducing to 4% the amount of capital that has to be held against these loans.

The 50% weight assigned to loans secured by a mortgage over residential property, which is half of that assigned to other commercial and personal loans, is generally thought to bias the allocation of bank loans in favour of such loans. The data presented in table 6.8 (in Chapter 6, p. 156) are consistent with such an impression, although the CAR is not the only factor that has influenced the relative increase in bank lending to housing since the introduction of the requirements in 1988.

The calculation of the risk-adjusted value of a bank's off-balance sheet holdings is slightly more complicated than that for balance-sheet assets. The only additional calculation is to convert the nominal value of these holdings into values equivalent to balance-sheet assets. The key point is that most off-balance sheet holdings have a nominal value that is greatly in excess of the amount of a bank's exposure to loss due to counterparty default.

The amount of a loan by a bank is exposed to credit risk because the borrower may default and the bank might not be able to recover any of the loan funds. Therefore, the amount of the loan is the amount of the exposure to credit risk. The **credit equivalent** involved in many off-balance sheet holdings is not the nominal value of the contract, but the amount the bank could lose in the event of default by the counterparty to the contract.

The data on off-balance sheet holdings of banks presented in table 7.9 (in Chapter 7, p. 194) show that the vast majority of these holdings are contracts (futures, forwards, swaps and options) that serve to protect the counterparties from adverse movements in interest rates and exchange rates. The use of these instruments is explained in some detail in Part five of the book. Once you have studied these chapters (we trust) you will understand how the nominal value of these contracts greatly exceeds the amount a bank could lose from counterparty default. For the purposes of this chapter, simply accept this fact.

Banks can calculate the credit equivalent amount of their off-balance sheet contracts in one of two ways. One is the 'rule-of-thumb' approach defined by the

RBA in its CARs; and the other is that banks, with RBA approval, can directly calculate the amount they could lose (i.e. their 'current exposure') as a result of counterparty default on these contracts. Banks have developed information systems that compute their current exposure arising from off-balance sheet items and these have generally replaced the rule-of-thumb approach.

Once the value of off-balance sheet contracts is converted to equivalent balance-sheet values, they are categorised according to the same risk weights as for balance-sheet assets and the weights are applied in the same arithmetic way.

Even though the aggregate nominal value of banks' off-balance sheet contracts exceeded $2466 billion in March 1995 (shown in table 7.9, p. 194), their risk-adjusted value was $37 billion (shown in table 9.3). Consequently, for credit-risk adjustment purposes, balance-sheet assets ($372 billion in March 1995) were, in March 1995, approximately ten times more important than off-balance sheet contracts.

While the total balance-sheet assets of all banks increased from around $350 billion to $430 billion during the first half of the 1990s (shown in table 6.6, in Chapter 6, p. 150) and the nominal value of off-balance sheet contracts also increased (shown in table 7.9, in Chapter 7, p. 194), their risk-adjusted values have trended down (from around $426 billion to $409 billion, shown in table 9.3).

The relative growth in loans secured by mortgages largely explains the relatively slower growth in the risk-adjusted value of balance-sheet assets (relative to the growth in their monetary value); whereas the decline in the risk-adjusted value of off-balance sheet contracts is probably explained by the more extensive use of the current-exposure method of calculating their credit equivalent value.

Market risk

During the early 1990s, the Bank for International Settlement began developing a framework for extending the CARs to cover sources of potential bank losses in addition to defaults (that give rise to credit risk). In April 1995 the Basle Committee on Banking Supervision (BCBS) released a proposal for incorporating allowance for market risks with the capital requirements. It was expected that a general framework would be agreed upon by the end of 1995 and that central banks would implement their provisions by the end of 1997.

Incorporating allowance for market risks is a complex process. The following discussion aims only to provide an outline of the process proposed by the BCBS as amended by the RBA. In essence, it involves identifying another area of potential bank losses (i.e. losses on its marketable securities arising from adverse movements in market variables, such as interest and exchange rates) and requiring banks to hold further capital (at the minimum 8% level) as protection against the risk that such losses could cause banks to fail.

While the BCBS proposed the introduction of a third class (or tier) of capital as a source of funds to cover market losses, the RBA has indicated that it will not adopt this provision as part of its prudential supervision framework. (RBA, June 1996, p. 23) However, it will apply the requirement that each bank calculate its **market-risk capital charge**, which serves to determine the minimum amount of capital the bank must hold as protection against losses from market risk.

The proposal provides for a bank's 'market-risk capital charge' to be calculated directly from the value of its potential losses on its trading assets from the movement in market variables. The processes involved in making these calculations are complex and involve concepts that fall outside the scope of this book. Consequently, we do not attempt to explain how the capital charge can be calculated. Our purpose is merely to outline the proposed extension of the CAR to cover market risks.

Recall from the discussion in Chapter 1 that market risks arise from adverse movements in the value of marketable securities and other assets, such as debt and equity securities, foreign exchange, commodities and derivative contracts. Accordingly, market risks are confined to certain items on (and off) a bank's balance sheet. Specifically:

- the risks pertaining to *debt securities* and *equities* in (a bank's) trading book, and
- *foreign-exchange risk* and *commodities risk* throughout the bank. (BCBS, 1995, p. 1)

> *The trading book means the bank's proprietary positions in financial instruments (including derivative products and off-balance sheet instruments) which are intentionally held for short-term resale and/or which are taken on by the institution with the intention of benefiting in the short term from actual and/or expected differences between their buying and selling prices, or from other price or interest-rate variations, and positions in financial instruments arising from matched principal broking and market making, or positions taken in order to hedge other elements of the trading book.* (BCBS, 1995, p. 1)

When calculating a bank's 'value at risk', allowance is made for its holdings of those instruments that purely (and precisely) serve to hedge a bank's exposure to market risk. The net value of a bank's assets and other contractual positions that vary as a result of probable movements in market variables (e.g. interest and exchange rates) constitutes its value at risk against which it is proposed that banks hold further capital.

Within the proposed supervisory treatment of market risks, a distinction is drawn between a security's:

- **specific risk**, which arises from a change in the market's assessment of its issuer, and
- **general market risk**, which arises from general movements in market values.

The capital that is required to be held is calculated separately for these risks. The amount of capital required for specific risk varies with the issuer (nil for government, a low proportion for high-quality issuers and 8% for other issuers) and the term of the security (a larger proportion the longer the security's term).

Note that specific risk is not counterparty risk, which is covered by the credit-risk provisions of the CARs. Specific risk arises, for instance, when the rating of a security, particularly a long-term security, declines, causing its market value to fall. General market risk can arise, for instance, from an increase in the general level of interest rates in the case of securities held (known as a long position), and a fall in rates in the case of securities issued or sold (known as a short position).

The inclusion of market risks within the CAR means that each bank has to develop a valid and transparent way of identifying the securities and derivative instruments that form part of its trading book, as opposed to its banking book, so that their supervisor can be assured that it is complying with the requirements. It also implies that banks must mark these items to market (i.e. show them at their current market value).

Banks will be required to report their market risks on a global consolidated basis (consistent with the treatment of credit risks) and will generally be allowed to 'net' identical short and long positions in a specific security irrespective of their geographical location. However, international netting will not apply where there are obstacles to the movement of funds between the countries involved.

Banks have the option of valuing their market risks according to a standardised methodology, defined by the supervisor, or of using their own internal risk-management models, provided that the following conditions are satisfied:

- the bank's risk-management system can be shown to be adequate,
- the bank meets standards for internal oversight (by management) of the use of its models,
- the models apply an appropriate set of market-risk factors,
- the models satisfy quantitative standards for measuring risk, and
- the bank develops validation procedures for external oversight of the use of its models.

Rules also apply to banks that use a combination of their internal models and the standardised approach. In general, it is expected that banks and supervisors will 'learn by doing' in the application of internal models and that many refinements to the process will be made over time.

Banks will be expected to satisfy the capital requirements of market risk on a continuous basis (at least, at the end of each day), even though their reporting requirements may be at less frequent intervals, typically quarterly.

The standard method for calculating market risks for the instruments covered is too detailed and complex to be discussed in this chapter. Some of the issues involved will be explained in the chapters in Parts four and five, but in general, risk-management systems are beyond the scope of this book.

Key points — CAR

1. Banks are required to hold capital (defined as tier 1 or 2 capital, at least half of which must be from tier 1 sources) that at least covers 8% of its consolidated, risk-adjusted on- and off-balance sheet assets.
2. The required capital for credit risk is calculated by first computing the risk-adjusted value of a bank's balance-sheet assets and the credit equivalent amount of its off-balance sheet holdings and then multiplying this amount by 0.08 (the CAR requirement).
3. It is proposed that by the end of 1997, each bank will have to hold sufficient capital (i.e. tier 1 and tier 2) to cover its market-risk capital charge, as well as its 8% of its risk-adjusted assets.

CARs as a form of reregulation

The main impact of the CARs on banks arises from their need to hold equity to finance their banking and trading assets (either on- or off-balance sheet). It is argued that this represents a cost burden on the basis of two assumptions:

1 that a bank would not, as a matter of commercial judgment, maintain equity at 8% of its risk-adjusted assets. This assumption is questionable. If a bank judged this ratio to be commercially prudent, it follows that the CARs do not impose a burden on banks. The amount of capital a bank would hold in the absence of the CAR is presently a hypothetical question. On the one hand, holding substantial capital is beneficial because it is a source of a bank's financial strength and should result in it being able to raise funds at a lower cost;
2 on the other hand, that equity funds, being risk funds, should be more expensive than debt funds. (Recall the discussion in Chapter 1 of the difference between equity and debt capital. Equity does not involve an explicit cost, but shareholders' required return should exceed that of debtholders because of the greater risk involved in supplying equity.) If 8% is above the commercially preferred level of equity, the CAR represents a burden because equity is a more expensive source of funds to the bank than, say, further bank deposits. (Daaguard and Valentine, 1994)

If we accept that the CAR imposes a burden on banks but not on financial traders who are not subject to any prudential supervision (such as loan originators), it follows that the requirements place a competitive handicap on banks and so would distort the financial system. The global coverage of capital adequacy throughout the financial system (both internationally and across all the operations of financial institutions) means that 'level playing fields' have been established for most areas within the financial system.

In fact, experience since the requirements were introduced shows that banks have held a level of equity beyond the 8% requirement (recall the data presented in table 9.3). Over the first half of the 1990s, the total consolidated capital ratio has trended up from around 9.5% to over 12%, with the ratio of tier 1 capital rising from around 6% to around 9%. Also, certain banks hold capital well in excess of the CAR, such as Bankers Trust Australia Limited (37.2% as at the end of 1994); Chase Manhattan Bank Australia Limited (19.0%); and Westpac Banking Corporation (13.8%).

SUPERVISION OF OTHER INSTITUTIONS

There are four principal supervisors of financial institutions. Banks are supervised by the RBA, as described above. Building societies, credit unions and friendly societies are supervised by the Australian Financial Institutions Commission (AFIC). Fund managers are supervised either by the Insurance and Superannuation Commission (ISC) or the Australian Securities Commission (ASC).

The AFIC has generally adopted the RBA's approach to supervision, whereas the other bodies have adopted different techniques. This largely reflects the difference between the NBFIs that are engaged in intermediation (i.e. they accept deposits from the public and provide payment services) and fund managers who provide investment-management services.

AFIC

The AFIC was established in 1992 to develop a uniform code of supervision of building societies and credit unions throughout Australia. It is accountable to the Ministerial Council for Financial Institutions, comprising State and Territory ministers. Its prudential standards are enforced by State Supervisory Authorities (SSAs) under uniform State legislation. Consequently, AFIC is the central body for a program of national supervision over institutions that are subject to State and Territory laws.

> *To ensure compliance with the Prudential Standards and practices determined by AFIC, all building societies and credit unions regularly report to their SSAs on a range of matters involving the operation of the institution. In addition, SSAs regularly inspect these institutions and conduct meetings with their management and auditors. In support of their role and functions, SSAs have strong enforcement and intervention powers which include the power to place an institution under direction, suspend operations and appoint administrators as required.* (AFIC, 1995, p. 3)

In 1994 the Ministerial Council decided to extend the role of AFIC to cover friendly societies, which are also subject to State and Territory laws. However, the business of friendly societies differs from the retail-banking focus of the other two institutions. They mainly provide personal financial services and health insurance, raising funds through issuing friendly-society bonds that are similar to insurance bonds discussed in the previous chapter. You will recall that these are policies that often involve a single payment and have a term of at least ten years, during which the investment income is held by the fund and paid out as an accumulated lump sum.

Credit unions and building societies have formed Special Service Providers (SSPs) to undertake collective activities, such as to organise their participation in the payment system. Because these SSPs are entities that operate on behalf of these institutions, they are also subject to prudential supervision by AFIC.

AFIC's prudential supervision regime for building societies and credit unions follows the RBA (and BIS) approach. It comprises prudential standards in four areas:

1. Risk management — this covers five designated areas of risk. The foremost of these is liquidity risk, for which societies are required to hold prime assets and demonstrate a capacity to manage their operational liquidity needs. (However, AFIC has developed an emergency liquidity support scheme.) Societies are expected to employ risk-management techniques to identify and manage their market risks. They are also expected to be able to manage their credit risks through diversification of lending and applying sound credit-risk assessment and management techniques. Data and operational risks are also expected to be effectively managed.

2 Capital adequacy — the AFIC prudential standards follow closely the risk-adjusted approach of the RBA. The requirements for use of tier 1 and tier 2 capital varies, though, for credit unions and SSPs.
3 Accounting and disclosure requirements.
4 Other standards — these cover such matters as relationship with subsidiaries, diversification of ownership, guarantees, service contracts and the emergency liquidity support mechanism for 'well-managed societies facing a short-term loss of funds, but not to help insolvent or poorly managed societies'. (AFIC, 1995, p. 16)

Because some of these institutions are mutuals (i.e. they are 'owned' by the depositors as opposed to a company that is owned by shareholders), AFIC faces certain issues not faced by the RBA. For instance, equity can only take the form of retained earnings, as mutuals do not have shareholders and therefore cannot raise share capital. Also, certain building societies are fully owned (some by other financial institutions), whereas AFIC's prudential standard provides for a 10% ownership limit.

ASC and ISC

This section emphasises prudential supervision of superannuation funds. You will recall that these include, in addition to superannuation funds, approved deposit funds and pooled superannuation trusts.

The ISC is the Commonwealth's regulatory body for the insurance and superannuation sectors. The scope of its activities is reflected in the data in table 9.6.

Table 9.6 Coverage of ISC regulations

Sector	*Number*	*Assets ($b)*
Life insurance	52	116.0
General insurance	162	31.5
Superannuation entities	107 000	187.0

Source: ISC, *Annual Report 1994–95*, p. 1

The commission's stated objectives are to promote public confidence in the safety and integrity of the insurance and superannuation industries. The ISC's approach to supervision is expressed as follows:

> *The commission has adopted a market-oriented approach to the supervision of insurance companies and superannuation entities. This approach seeks to minimise interference in commercial activities except for prudential and other public-interest reasons.* (ISC, 1995, p. 2)

In relation to superannuation funds, the ISC's supervisory approach 'is based on the principle that trustees are primarily responsible for the viability and prudent operation of funds . . . ' (ISC, 1995, p. 2) Trustees, to gain ISC approval, must satisfy a minimum capital requirement (for public-offer funds) and demonstrate to the commission that they can reliably perform their responsibilities. By mid 1995, the commission had granted approvals for 167 trustees.

The commission audits funds to assess how well they are managed and to make recommendations to trustees where it believes improvements should be made. The ISC approach complies with the terms of the *Superannuation Industry (Supervision) Act* 1993, which aims 'to prevent imprudent and dishonest conduct in advance, rather than punish afterwards'. (ISC, 1995, p. 59)

In addition to its reliance on the fiduciary responsibilities of trustees, the commission imposes information-disclosure requirements on funds and has composition requirements (to ensure contributor representation) for the boards of superannuation funds. These requirements are judged necessary because of the Superannuation Guarantee Charge (discussed in the previous chapter).

The ISC responded to the Barings collapse (referred to earlier in this chapter) by requiring companies under its supervision to have in place a comprehensive risk-management strategy, including the necessary internal controls. The ISC has asked insurance and superannuation companies to produce a 'Risk Management Statement' that explicitly deals with the role, use and limits of derivative instruments in risk management.

The ISC is able to enforce compliance by fund managers because eligibility for tax concessions (which we discussed in the previous chapter) is determined by the commission.

The need for supervision of superannuation funds, according to the Senate Select Committee on Superannuation (SSCS), is based on five points:

1. the government has legislated for compulsory superannuation contributions to generate retirement income without accepting responsibility for the eventual benefits;
2. superannuation premiums are a major source of long-term savings within the economy;
3. for many people superannuation is their largest asset, after their family home;
4. superannuation is an illiquid asset and many contributors have no choice over who will manage the funds and little influence over or knowledge of their fund manager; and
5. substantial tax concessions are extended to superannuation funds. (SSCS, 1992, p. 31)

In its report the SSCS recounted an example of the misuse of superannuation funds by the director of a company who was also a trustee of the employees' superannuation fund. The director embezzled funds from both the company and the superannuation fund before committing suicide. Eventually the company dismissed its workers, who lost all of their superannuation funds. The case illustrates the need for the supervision of superannuation funds, especially when the government mandates superannuation contributions.

The main role of the Australian Securities Commission (ASC) is to regulate corporate business. In its own words:

> *The ASC aims to protect the interests of companies and investors by providing information about companies, helping business to interpret the law, and by taking action against offenders.* (ASC, *Annual Report 1994–95*)

The ASC is an independent government body established by the *Australian Securities Commission Act* 1989. The ASC is accountable to the Commonwealth Government via the Attorney-General, who may in certain circumstances give directions to the ASC.

> *The ASC sets and enforces standards for investment advice, fundraising and takeover documents, and financial reporting. It also provides public access to corporate information on more than 930 000 Australian companies.* (ASC, *Annual Report 1994–95*)

One of the requirements for a healthy financial sector is the free and unfettered flow of investment information. The ASC is the central investment information institution in Australia. The ASC, in the discharge of its obligations:

- requires companies to regularly lodge income and balance-sheet information and to disclose any other material investment information,
- examines and reviews all prospectuses concerning new capital raisings by Australian companies to ensure that the information contained within them is fair and will not mislead unsophisticated investors, and
- receives and examines all company takeover documents.

The ASC operates in cooperation with the Australian Stock Exchange. This relationship is discussed in Chapter 12.

Council of Supervisors

The council was established in 1992 'to improve communication and coordination among the main agencies responsible for regulation and prudential supervision in the financial system'. (RBA, October 1995, p. 34)

One of the main needs for coordination was the development of financial conglomerates, parts of which are subject to different supervisors. Given that the financial strength of a conglomerate depends on the health of each of its component parts, regulators of each part need to be aware of the financial standing of the rest of the conglomerate.

A further need for coordination is to avoid supervisory overlaps or gaps. These can arise because of financial innovation involving changes in products and how they are provided. Coordination can also help establish level playing fields.

A related function of the council is to develop a capacity to identify and respond to crises that spread across the financial system. The council is an ideal forum for multilateral discussions of systemic issues. (RBA, October 1995, p. 25)

The council comprises the RBA, AFIC, ASC and ISC. These supervisors cover the principal institutions within the financial system. A summary of their activities is presented in table 9.6.

In May 1996 the newly elected Federal Government announced the establishment of a Committee of Inquiry (the 'Wallis Inquiry') to recommend, among other matters, regulatory arrangements that will 'establish a consistent regulatory framework for similar financial functions, products or services which are offered by differing types of institutions'. (Press Release from the Office of the Treasurer) The RBA indicated in its submission to the Inquiry that it considers the prevailing arrangements to be generally appropriate. (RBA, July 1996, pp. 31–8, September 1996, pp. 4–8 and 35–42) Given that the Wallis Inquiry's final report will be submitted after this book has been published (by 31 March 1997), we have to await the outcome.

Table 9.6 Summary of the supervision of financial institutions

Financial institution	*Supervisor*	*Main aspects of supervision*
Banks	Reserve Bank	capital, liquidity, loan and FX exposure limits, associations with subsidiaries, risk-management systems
Merchant banks, finance companies (not bank owned)	ASC	capital, liquidity, dealing practices
Building societies, unions, friendly societies and SSPs	AFIC	capital, liquidity, risk management, credit disclosure, ownership
Insurance offices, superannuation funds	ISC	superannuation funds: fiduciary responsibilities of trustees, audits of management practices, information disclosure, composition of boards, minimum capital requirements for trustees of public-offer funds insurance offices: entry, solvency of statutory funds, investments in related companies, trusts, types of policies written, management structure, and information disclosure
Unit trusts/trustee companies	ASC	prospectus and trust deeds, role of funds manager and trustee, redemption procedures, liquidity (unit trusts), borrowing and capital/reserves.

SUMMARY

The main points of this chapter are as follows:

- The removal of controls on banks led to the need to introduce a system of prudential supervision.
- The globalisation of banking led to the need for an internationally uniform system of prudential supervision.
- The main aims of the prudential supervision of banks are to protect depositors' funds and the integrity of the payments system.
- Central banks evolved over several centuries as institutions with a variety of responsibilities. Most are responsible for the stability of their domestic currency and financial system and act as banker to their banking system and to their national government.

- The RBA was established as a separate central bank in 1960 after being part of the Commonwealth Bank.
- The RBA's system of prudential supervision is defined in a series of prudential statements, the most complex of which specifies its capital-adequacy requirements.
- The RBA's supervision philosophy is that banks should conduct their business in a prudent way and establish and apply effective risk-management systems that identify and manage their risk exposures.
- Banks (and other financial institutions) are required to hold a minimum amount of capital determined in relation to their credit-risk exposures and, by 1997, their market-risk exposures.
- There are four main bodies responsible for prudential supervision of financial institutions (RBA, AFIC, ASC and ISC) which come together to discuss and coordinate their activities as a Council of Supervisors.

Discussion questions and exercises

1 Discuss the factors (both domestic and overseas) that led to the RBA's introduction of a regime of prudential supervision.
2 List and briefly explain (a) five risks that should be addressed by a system of prudential supervision, and (b) six ways in which banks can manage the risks they face.
3 Discuss (a) the RBA's approach to prudential supervision, and (b) the main features of its regime of prudential supervision.
4 Discuss the evolution of central banks in general and the RBA in particular. Review the RBA's main goals and discuss the importance of its independence as a factor influencing its capacity to pursue these goals.
5 Briefly describe the RBA's responsibility for depositor protection. Explain its relevance to the purpose of its prudential-supervision regime.
6 Explain and critically review each of the main aspects of the RBA's prudential-supervision regime.
7 Present an overview of the RBA's capital requirements. Explain how the CAR deals with the credit-risk exposures arising from banks' balance-sheet assets and off-balance sheet items.
8 Briefly describe the 1995 proposal for supplementary capital to be held to cover market risks.
9 Discuss the contention that prudential supervision is a form of reregulation.
10 Briefly explain the role of the Council of Supervisors and the prudential-supervision approach of AFIC.

References and further reading

AFIC, *1993–94 Annual Report*.

AFIC (March 1995), *Introducing the Australian Financial Institutions Commission and the Financial Institutions Scheme*.

ASC, *Annual Report*, 1994–95.

Basle Committee on Banking Supervision April 1995, *Proposal to issue a Supplement to the Basle Capital Accord to cover Market Risks*, BIS, Basle.
Coombs, H. C. 1981, *Trial Balance*, Macmillan, Melbourne.
Dale, Richard 1996, 'Regulating the new financial markets', in Malcolm Edey (ed.), *The Future of the Financial System*, RBA, Sydney.
Daugaard, Dan, & Valentine, Tom 1994, 'The reregulation of banking: its implications for the industry and derivatives markets', *Economic Papers*, vol. 13, no. 1, pp. 17–40.
Hogan, W. P., & Sharpe, I. G. June 1990, 'Prudential supervision of Australian banks', *Economic Record*, pp. 127–45.
House of Representatives Standing Committee on Finance and Public Administration, Martin, Stephen (chair) 1991, *A Pocket Full of Change*, AGPS, Canberra.
ISC, *Annual Report, 1994–95*.
Jonson, P. D. 1993, 'The Reserve Bank', in M. K. Lewis & R. H. Wallace (eds), *The Australian Financial System*, Longman Cheshire, Melbourne, pp. 19–38.
Linklater, Joan 1992, *Inside the Bank*, Allen & Unwin, Sydney.
RBA June 1990, *Prudential Supervision of Banks, Prudential Statements*, RBA, Sydney.
RBA May 1991, 'Directions for prudential supervision in the 1990s', *Bulletin*, pp. 6 –13.
RBA December 1991, 'Some observations on the role of the Reserve Bank', *Bulletin*, pp. 8–13.
RBA September 1992, 'Two perspectives on monetary policy', *Bulletin*, pp. 1–8.
RBA October 1992, 'Foreign banks in Australia — policy issues and prospects' *Bulletin*, pp. 22–7.
RBA November 1994, Collection of Press Releases Related to Prudential Supervision.
RBA December 1994, 'Central bank independence: what does it mean? *Bulletin*, pp. 1–8.
RBA January 1995, *Asset Quality, PSL1*, RBA, Sydney.
RBA April 1995, 'Supervisory developments: the Reserve Bank's perspective', *Bulletin*, pp. 28–33.
RBA May 1995, 'Derivatives — bank activities and supervisory responses', *Bulletin*, pp. 1–7.
RBA, *1995 Report and Financial Statements*, RBA, Sydney.
RBA October 1995, 'The role of the Council of Financial Supervisors', *Bulletin*, pp. 34–8.
RBA November 1995, 'Implications of the Barings collapse for bank supervisors', *Bulletin*, pp. 1–5.
RBA June 1996, 'Supervision of market risk: the state of play', *Bulletin*, pp. 22–7.
RBA July 1996, 'Financial regulation and the financial system inquiry', *Bulletin*, pp. 31–8.
RBA September 1996, 'Submission to the financial system inquiry', *Bulletin*, pp. 4 –8.
RBA September 1996, 'The Wallis Inquiry: perspectives from the Reserve Bank', *Bulletin*, pp. 35– 42.
Senate Select Committee on Superannuation June 1992, *Safeguarding Super, The Regulation of Superannuation*, Parliament of the Commonwealth of Australia, AGPS, Canberra.
Thompson, Graeme 1996, 'Regulatory policy issues in Australia', in Malcolm Edey (ed.), *The Future of the Financial System*, RBA, Sydney.

Part THREE

Financial markets

In Part Three we turn to the operations of the system's physical financial markets. These chapters draw on the principles described in Chapter 2 and the measurement of yields and security prices presented in Chapters 4 and 5. Financial markets have emerged over the past decade or so as the main forum for wholesale financial transactions.

This part comprises four chapters that describe the operations of the three domestic physical markets for funds, together with the foreign-exchange and overseas-capital markets. These are referred to as physical financial markets because they arrange either finance or payments, and this term distinguishes them from the derivative markets that are discussed in Part Five.

Chapter 10 explains the operations of the short-term money market. It distinguishes between its primary and secondary markets and the instruments issued in this market, whereas Chapter 11 provides a similar coverage of the domestic debt-capital (i.e. bond) market. Chapter 12 explains the operations of the Australian Stock Exchange and the raising of equity funds generally, whereas Chapter 13 explains the operations of the foreign-exchange and overseas-capital markets. Chapter 13 also explains how forward foreign-exchange rates can be used to remove the uncertainty implicit in future foreign-exchange transactions.

These chapters, together with those in Part Two, show how participants in the physical financial markets can be exposed to market risk, the management of which is considered in the chapters in Part Five.

10

Short-term money market

This is the first of four chapters that explain the operation of Australia's financial markets and the instruments traded in them. The chapter deals with the short-term money market, commonly referred to as the money market. All of the instruments traded in this market have short terms when issued, but rolling them over allows them to be used to provide a medium-term supply of funds.

Study objectives

From your study of this chapter you should be able to:

- describe the main forms of short-dated instruments that are traded in the money market;
- describe the main features of the primary markets for short-dated instruments;
- explain the role of the principal participants in the market, such as the dealers, investors, issuers, the RBA, Austraclear and the ratings agencies;
- describe the two main ways of issuing new securities;
- explain how issuers determine their net proceeds and the cost of funds from a new issue of securities;
- explain the choice of instruments by the issuers in the money market;
- explain the main factors that determine the value of a short-dated security.

INTRODUCTION

This is the first of four chapters that describe the operations and functions of Australia's (physical) financial markets. These are the markets for short-dated securities, debt-capital securities, equities and foreign exchange (FX). The chapter commences by recapping the material presented in Chapter 3.

You will recall that debt and FX markets are self-regulated, over-the-counter (OTC) markets in which trading is conducted between professional dealers who trade in wholesale amounts. Because trading is conducted over the telephone, conversations between dealers are taped for verification purposes. A protocol exists for stating the terms of a deal and for handling cases where a genuine mistake occurs. (AFMA, 1994(a), pp. 136–9)

The three main screen information services for the financial markets are Telerate, Reuters and Bloomberg. They provide current information and news that influence market values, real-time and historical data, listings of indicative bid and offer rates, and trading software.

The main reason that these markets operate largely unregulated (apart from dealer licensing and supervision of exposure levels by the RBA, in the case of the FX market) is that trading occurs between professional dealers who have access to the most relevant information. When funds are being raised from the public, such as by unit trusts (discussed in Chapter 8) and through the issue of new shares to the public, the Companies Code requires that this be done only on the basis of a prospectus that has been approved by the ASC.

Information is an important ingredient of financial transactions and when an **information asymmetry** occurs (i.e. where one party knows more about the risk and potential return of a financial proposition than another), one party, usually the one seeking funds, is in a position to benefit at the expense of the other. The main reason for prospectuses is to require the release of information by the informationally-dominant party so that the other party is able to make an informed judgment.

In an efficient market (recall the discussion of the EMH in Chapter 3), prospectuses are unnecessary. Markets conducted by professional dealers are generally efficient, in the sense that dealers are well informed, and are able to make informed trading decisions. As noted in Chapter 3, considered in hindsight, not all decisions will have been correct. Trading decisions are based on expected future outcomes. Information merely allows dealers to form expectations on an informed basis. It does not allow dealers to accurately forecast the future.

Financial markets perform two important functions. They:

- facilitate the raising of funds (in the primary market), and
- organise trading in securities (in the secondary market) that create investment opportunities.

They facilitate the raising of funds by bringing together parties that wish to raise funds through the issue of new securities and parties that wish to invest surplus funds. That is, they achieve transaction cost economies. The secondary market also plays a part, by enhancing the value of new securities with liquidity. A deep secondary market allows the investors in new securities to sell them before they mature. It also performs a price-discovery function that assists the issuers of new securities to accurately set their price or, if they are issued at tender, it assists new issuers to estimate their market price (and hence the proceeds of the issue).

Underwriters may be used by the issuer of new securities to ensure that the funds are raised. Underwriters will use standby funds to hedge their risk of having to acquire unsold securities. However, they are not widely engaged by issuers in the money market.

Professional dealers are market makers. They quote both buy (bid) and sell (offer) rates. This exposes them to **trading risks** and, because they hold inventory, market risks. Trading risks arise because dealers stand ready to trade and, subject to the right of dealers to set their bid and offer rate, must satisfy a counterparty's requirement. For example, in the case of a money-market dealer who quotes a yield for funds that is accepted by a depositor, the dealer must accept the funds. Should yields then suddenly fall, the dealer will earn a lower-than-expected return on these funds.

Even though professional traders are very well informed, there are occasions when they have less information than their counterparty. Such information asymmetry forms part of a dealer's trading risks. (Fabozzi, Modigliani and Ferri, 1994, p. 314)

Dealers set their bids and offers to manage their trading intentions. For example, an FX dealer who is holding more US dollars than desired will shade his or her offer rate so that it is at the lower end of the market's range of offers. The dealer may also lower his or her bid by a point or two to reduce the possibility of actually acquiring more US dollars.

A dealer faces market risk because interest and exchange rates move almost continuously. Remember the discussion in Chapter 3 of continuous trading during a market's trading hours. For example, the dealer holding US dollars will suffer a loss of value should the currency's value suddenly fall.

In relation to the money market, you will recall from Chapter 3 that dealers accept wholesale deposits for short-term periods and trade short-term securities. The main securities are commercial bills (most of which are bank-accepted bills), promissory notes (known also as commercial paper), CDs and Treasury notes. Each is a discount instrument, meaning that the only payment their issuer is required to make is their face value on their maturity date. The securities trade at a price that is less than their face value (hence the term 'discount' instrument).

The money market developed from an inter-company market that was formed in the 1950s. This was an informal market which, by the 1970s, comprised at least several hundred companies that borrowed or lent surplus funds on a short-term basis. (Hill, 1993, pp. 379–80) During the 1970s when bank interest rates were subject to ceilings, companies were able to invest the (otherwise) unused portion of their overdraft in the inter-company market at a profit, because the inter-company rates exceeded the overdraft rate. (McGrath, 1994, pp. 175–6)

An inter-bank market also formed for broadly similar reasons. Banks necessarily will hold liquid funds, but due to daily variations in the transfer of funds between their customers' accounts, especially their cheque accounts, some banks will be short of liquid funds and others will have funds to invest. The development of the official short-term market (referred to below) provided banks with access to same-day-funds. The RBA's move to real-time settlement displaced the official dealers in July 1996 and the bank provides a market for these funds by paying interest on the balance in each bank's exchange settlement accounts.

An official segment of the money market was established in 1959 when seven dealers were granted special licences (the 'authorised' or official dealers). This group of dealers was granted lender-of-last-resort liquidity privileges and exchange settlement accounts with the central bank on the condition that the dealers made a market for CGSs and acted as counterparties for the RBA's market operations (i.e. buying and selling of short-dated CGSs, often through repurchase agreements). (RBA, 1991, pp. 19–25)

Their primary business function was to accept wholesale funds on a short-term basis (11 a.m. funds, described in Chapter 3) principally from banks. Because the dealers gave banks access to 'same-day funds' (i.e. exchange settlement account funds) they became the repository for an important part of the banks' liquid reserves. This meant that the dealers served to link the RBA's transactions with banks and the financial system generally.

In mid 1996 the RBA began the formal move to real-time gross settlement (discussed in Chapter 1) by terminating the licences of the authorised dealers. The bank commenced paying interest on ESA funds, at a comparable rate to the 'cash rate' (the rate the official dealers paid for funds deposited with them by the banks). The rate is set at 10 basis points below the overnight rate.

The RBA now trades in the short-term market with any market participant who is a RITS member. The bank's main trading counterparties are now the major banks.

In volume terms, the RBA principally trades in the form of repurchase agreements (repos). This involves the sale of securities (in the case of the RBA these are CGSs) on the basis of their agreed repurchase at a set date and price. Usually, the repurchase is made in a few days. In the case of the RBA, it is either selling repos or reverse repos (this is an agreement to buy a parcel of securities on the basis of a set resale date and price) for the purpose of injecting or withdrawing funds from the financial system when fulfilling its responsibility to stabilise liquidity in the financial system. We discuss this function of the RBA in Chapter 14.

Within the short-term money market, the official dealers were not ever an important quantitative force. Their significance related to the market for short-dated CGSs and their relationship with the RBA, rather than to the amount of assets on their balance sheets. Dealers in the unofficial money market dealt in 24-hour funds (which, as described in Chapter 3, means that the funds are deposited for seven days and can then be withdrawn with 24-hours' notice), bills, notes and CDs and so served the needs of financial institutions, companies and government enterprises for short-term funds and as a short-term repository for surplus wholesale funds.

As noted above, the RBA has displaced the official market by providing a secure place for the cash reserve funds of banks by paying a comparable yield on their ESA balances. Recall that up to mid 1996, no interest was paid on balances in ESAs. The payment of interest on these funds means that the RBA has become a de facto part of the short-term money market. It is likely that the commercial banks (particularly the majors) will question this role because it could be performed by market dealers.

The money market is a professional market in which the standard trading parcel of a particular issue (e.g. the promissory notes of a particular issuer that have the same maturity date) comprises securities with a face value of $1 million. Typically, short-term securities have a face value of $100 000, $500 000 or $1 million. (AFMA, 1994(a), pp. 57–8). According to survey data collected by AFMA, 63% of transaction parcels during 1993–94 had a value of less than $5 million, 34% had a value of between $5 million and less than $50 million, and the remaining 3% had a value of $50 million or more. (AFMA, 1994(b), p. 19)

The market's dealer-organisations are banks and merchant banks (i.e. money-market corporations) who trade over the counter. Traders quote indicative bid and offer yields. Remember that in Australia, debt securities are traded on the basis of their yield, quoted as a percentage per annum, to two decimal places. A security's price is calculated on the basis of the agreed yield. Payment is made on the same day for trades made in the morning, and the next day for trades made in the afternoon. (AFMA, 1994(a), p. 58)

Bids in the money market exceed offers, because yields vary inversely with security prices. A high bid yield is equivalent to a low bid price, and vice versa for offers. Hence, 'bid high and offer low' is the money market's version of the trading rule of 'buy low and sell high'.

The four main short-dated instruments are bills, commercial paper, CDs and Treasury notes. The primary market for short-dated securities tends to be more active than for long-dated securities, if only because their short terms require more frequent issuing to maintain a line of finance. When short-dated securities mature they are often rolled over by the issue of replacement securities, ensuring a continued line of finance.

Banks, particularly the major banks, dominate the primary bill market. Banks, of course, issue CDs, and they also play an important part in managing the issue of commercial paper (i.e. promissory notes). The RBA issues Treasury notes on behalf of the Commonwealth Treasury. The RBA is also the main user of repos.

Bills

Commercial bills are a major source of floating-rate funds for business. These instruments raise funds at a fixed rate of interest for short terms, typically 90 days. They are referred to as a floating-rate form of finance when they are issued through a bill facility that allows the issuer to issue new bills to replace maturing bills. Under this arrangement, the cost of the funds is reset each 90 days when the new bills are issued on the basis of the current 90-day bank-bill rate.

The process of issuing bills is more complex than for other short-dated securities. This process, which was explained in Chapter 3, requires the bill to be accepted in order to be issued. The borrower draws the bill in favour of a payee and once it has been accepted, the bill can be sold in the market. When a bill is sold, the market has regard to its acceptor, rather than its drawer. The acceptor is the party responsible for the payment of the bill's face value (i.e. redemption) at maturity, although the acceptor will require the drawer to furnish the funds (i.e. repay the amount borrowed plus interest).

Bills developed from trade bills which had been used for several hundred years to allow a producer/exporter to draw a bill for the value of the traded produce. Its acceptance by the customer/importer meant that payment would be made by the stated date. If the producer/exporter wanted the funds before that date, the bill would be sold at a discount (to its face value), typically to a bank. The amount of the discount depended on the credit standing of the acceptor. The drawer of the bill could pay a bank to **endorse** the bill (i.e. in effect, to guarantee the payment of its face value on the due date), which enhanced its value (and thereby increased the proceeds when discounting the bill).

The commercial bill has played an important part in Australia's commercial and financial history and development. There is an old Dad and Dave film in which Dad lets fly with a hail of shot-gun pellets at the departing rear end of Mabel's suitor, Bill. With a chuckle he says to Mabel 'There I've endorsed yer Bill for yer'. The humour was lost on Bill, but not on Australian audiences at the time, especially those in country areas. (Hill, 1993, p. 382)

The major banks have become the principal acceptors of bills and **bank-accepted bills** (BABs) have become the dominant instrument. The clients' commitments arising from bill acceptances of individual banks serve to indicate their respective role in accepting bills. Of the $59 billion worth of **bank bills** outstanding in August 1995 (these are bills accepted or endorsed by banks but almost all are accepted), most clients' commitments are to the major banks, as shown by the data in table 10.1.

Table 10.1 Bank bills, clients' commitments arising from bill acceptances, August 1995 ($m)

Bank	*$m*
ANZ Banking Group	11 818
Commonwealth Bank	10 627
National Australia Bank	15 273
Westpac Banking Corporation	11 998
Other banks	2 629
Total	52 345

Source: RBA, *Bulletin*, Tables B.10 and B.12

The primary market

Given that bills have a term of less than a year when issued, and that total bill outstandings (including bills accepted by merchant banks) during the first half of the 1990s ranged between $60 and $70 billion, the amount of new bills issued each year would have been about $200 billion.

The main investors in bills are financial institutions, which, as shown by the data in table 10.2, collectively hold about half of the bills on issue. Companies and other investors hold the remaining bills.

The issuer of bills receives cash proceeds when they are issued and is obliged to repay their face value at maturity (either to the acceptor, or direct to the holder, to extinguish the debt). The proceeds depend on the market yield for bills when they are issued and the fees charged by the acceptor. These can be divided into two categories: the 'acceptance fee' that is based on the drawer's credit risk, and establishment and line fees (similar to those that banks impose for overdrafts). Typically, when a bank accepts a bill, it combines its fees and quotes the drawer an

Table 10.2 Bank bills classified by holder, June 1994 and 1995, $m.

Holder	*June 1994*	*June 1995*
Banks	13 865	9 717
Money market corporations	2 169	3 100
Other NBFIs	1 798	1 390
Cash management trusts	1 814	2 891
Life offices	5 615	4 501
Superannuation funds	3 827	4 198
Other managed funds	3 914	4 328
Other holders	26 941	29 011
Total	59 943	59 136

Source: RBA, *Bulletin*, Table B.12

all-up yield to accept the bill that is based on the market rate for the bills when they are issued.

The cost of funds can be determined as a yield, by using equation (4.3b) explained in Chapter 4 (see p. 88). This equation applies the basic principle that the cost of funds as a yield depends on the initial proceeds and the subsequent repayment amount, expressed as an annual yield using simple interest:

$$r = \left(\frac{F}{P} - 1\right)\frac{1}{t}$$

Suppose a company issued 90-day bills with a face value of $5 million and its net proceeds, after meeting all bank charges, were $4 879 679. The cost of these funds was $120 321, or, as a yield:

$$r = \left(\frac{5\,000\,000}{4\,879\,679} - 1\right)\frac{365}{90}$$
$$= 10.00\%\text{ p.a.}$$

When bills are issued under a bill facility, the proceeds usually vary each time new bills are issued, in response to changes in the market rate since the bills were previously issued. The cost of the funds can be viewed as the difference between the repayment of the face value of the maturing bills and the proceeds of the new bills, as shown in example 10.1.

The illustrative 270-day bill facility depicted in Chapter 7 (as figure 7.2) is reproduced here in figure 10.1, where the initial parcel of bills raises $\$P_1$. This could be a parcel of ten bills each with a face value of $1 million (which would represent a $10m facility). The second and third parcels serve to roll over the initial bills, providing the issuer with funds for 270 days. The bank redeems the first two parcels with the proceeds of the replacement bills plus the interest payment ($F − $P) from the issuer. The facility ends with the redemption of the third parcel of bills.

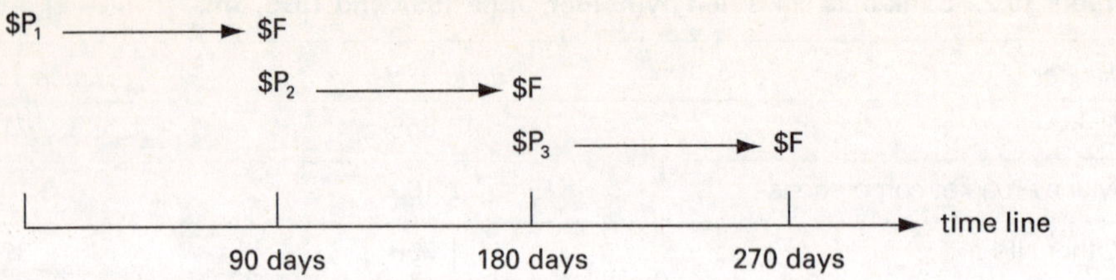

Figure 10.1 A 270-day bill facility

The net proceeds to the issuer when bills are rolled over (under a bill facility) are not known when the facility commences. They depend on the yield in the bill market when the replacement bills are issued and the fees charged by the bank for providing the bill facility. For instance, should the yield in the 90-day bill market increase before the initial bills are rolled over, $\$P_2$ will be less than $\$P_1$. The issuer under a bill facility therefore is exposed to interest-rate risk (i.e. the risk that rates will increase). In Chapters 17 and 18 we show how derivatives can be used by the bill issuer to manage this risk by locking in the interest rate when successive parcels of bills are issued.

example 10.1

Suppose a medium-sized company requires an estimated $2 million for a one-year period as a source of working capital. After studying the company's business plan and financial accounts, its bank suggests that it arrange a one-year bill facility with a face value of $2 million (e.g. a parcel of four $500 000 bills) at a cost of the issue yield in the bank-bill market plus 350 basis points (the percentage equivalent of the bank's fees for accepting the borrower's credit risk and arranging the facility).

Assume further that 90-day bills are issued and the bank-bill rate is 7.75%, 7.85%, 7.95% and 8.25% on the day each series of bills is issued. The amount raised and the company's cost of funds can be calculated as follows, using equation (4.3a), where F is $2m, r, for the first group of bills, is 0.1125 (0.0775 plus 0.035) and t is 90 over 365 days:

Initial proceeds, P_1:

$$P_1 = \frac{2\,000\,000}{1 + 0.1125 * 90/365}$$

$$= \$1\,946\,018$$

The company notionally pays the bank $2 million after 90 days (representing the repayment of $1 946 018 and interest of $53 982, which represents 11.25% p.a. for 90 days on the proceeds) and receives the proceeds from the issue of the second set of bills ($1 945 551). This amount is calculated below, with r equal to 0.1135, reflecting the ten basis point rise in the bill rate. Only the net amount (i.e. $54 449) would change hands (because the bank would redeem the maturing bills with the proceeds from the issue of the replacement bills). Note that the net amount is the interest cost of the new bills:

$$P_2 = \frac{2\,000\,000}{1 + 0.1135 * 90/365}$$

$$= \$1\,945\,551$$

Again, the company pays the net amount ($54 915 on this occasion) between $2 million and the proceeds of the new bill issue ($1 945 085), calculated below at the new rate of 11.45% p.a., reflecting the rise in the bank-bill rate over the past 90 days:

$$P_3 = \frac{2\,000\,000}{1 + 0.1145 * 90/365}$$

$$= \$1\,945\,085$$

The proceeds of the final series of bills, when r is 11.75%, is $1 943 686. At the end of the fourth 90-day period, the company pays $2 million to the bank. The cost of its funds for the 360-day period (paid, in effect, when each set of bills matured) was:

First set of bills:	$53 982
Second set:	$54 449
Third set:	$54 915
Final set:	$56 314

Note that the company's cost of funds rose over the year and that its overall cost of funds was not known when the company decided to use bill financing. Of course, had interest rates fallen, its cost of funds would also have fallen. The example illustrates the risk involved in arranging floating-rate funds. In Part five of this book we explain how the company could hedge its exposure to a rise in interest rates (one approach involves the use of bill-futures contracts and this activity links the physical and futures bill markets).

The example also illustrates other aspects of bill financing. By entering a bill facility, the company was able to borrow for longer periods than the term of the instrument. Given that the yield in the bank-bill market is common to all acceptors, competition between acceptors is reflected in the level of their fees.

The secondary market

Bills are the most actively traded short-dated securities. AFMA's survey data for 1993–94 indicates that of the total turnover of short-dated securities ($1024 billion), $766 billion was in bills and CDs (and bill turnover exceeded that for CDs). Because of the market's liquidity and the size of the transactions, dealer bid and offer spreads are very narrow. This means that the effective commission on each transaction is small. In our numerical examples we ignore these spreads and use mid-point values.

Two-way bank-bill rates as provided by financial intermediaries in, say, Reuters bank-bill swap-rate page (BBSW), usually show spreads of between 5 and 10 points (0.05% p.a.– 0.10% p.a.). These differences in fact overstate that market spread. On most days a professional dealer can obtain two-way bill yields with a spread of one to two points.

The credit standing of bills is determined by that of their acceptor. As at August 1995, Standard & Poor's counterparty rating for two of the major banks (NAB and the Commonwealth Bank) was A-1+, the top rating for short-term debt and the other two banks were rated A-1, the next highest rating. The difference in their ratings implies that the bills accepted by the first two banks should trade at yields that are several basis points below those for the other two banks.

The rating scale for short-term securities is broader (i.e. has fewer steps in the rating scale) than for long-term securities. Refer to the Moody's rating scales for short-term and long-term debt securities presented in Chapter 3 and to those of Standard & Poor's that are presented in the next chapter. One reason for the wider short-term scale is that there is less credit risk (as well as other forms of risk) involved in the shorter-term securities for any given issuer. This point is reflected in the CARs discussed in the previous chapter.

The registry, clearing and settlement functions for the bill market are performed by Austraclear Limited, a company formed (in 1981) by financial institutions that trade in Australia's professional markets for debt instruments.

> *The Company performs the role of a national central securities depository for securities traded in the Australian money market. In addition, real-time transaction confirmation recording and clearance facility, integrated with an electronic securities transfer and settlement system . . . is provided to an approved Membership for money market securities and their derivatives.*
>
> *The regulatory infrastructure is prescribed by in-house Regulations. These Regulations formalise a contractual relationship between Austraclear and its members (wholesale market participants) and promote the efficient settlement and electronic transfer of the underlying securities and their derivatives on a delivery versus payment basis.* (Austraclear, *Mission Statement)*

The seller of bills in the secondary market is responsible for recording the transaction. The transaction details are then confirmed by the buyer. Austraclear's cash-settlement arrangements mean that ownership of a traded security does not change hands until the payment is cleared. This, in 1995, was the same-day settlement system (i.e. T+0) that was adapted to real-time settlement when it was implemented by the RBA. The RBA's central securities depository operation for Treasury notes and bonds, known as the Reserve Bank Information and Transfer System (RITS), was developed by Austraclear and introduced in 1991.

Investors in bills typically hold them for part of their term. This may be the result of investors desiring liquidity because they have spare funds for only a few weeks and they prefer to invest in bills directly, rather than placing the funds with a money-market dealer at a fixed rate. The return for such investments depends on the (uncertain) holding-period yield, rather than the fixed rate quoted by the dealer. A classic investment strategy is to buy bills prior to an expected fall in bill yields. If this occurs the investor will make a capital gain as part of the holding-period yield.

Observe in example 10.2 that the capital gain was relatively small. This is due to the security's short period to maturity. The 15-basis-point fall in the yield applied to a security that had a term of only 60 days (i.e. about one-fifth of a year). When we discuss long-term securities in the next chapter we will show that a similar movement in the market yield for, say, a ten-year bond (with a $5 million face value), will have a much greater effect on that security's price.

example 10.2

Suppose a company has approximately $5 million in spare cash that it expects to use in 30 days. It could place these funds in a 30-day CD, buy bills with 30 days to mature or buy 90-day bills and sell them when it requires the cash. Suppose further that its bank quotes a 30-day CD rate of 7.60% p.a. and the market yields for 30-day and 90-day bank bills are 7.55% p.a. (These rates applied in June 1995.) If the company expects bill rates to fall over the next 30 days it may decide to buy 90-day bills (with a face value of $5 million) at 7.55% p.a. Suppose finally that the market yield for 60-day bills is 7.40% p.a. when the company sells the bills. Its holding period yield thus can be calculated as follows:

$$P_{buy} = \frac{5\ 000\ 000}{1 + 0.0755 * 90/365}$$

$$= \$4\ 908\ 619$$

Its proceeds from selling the bills 30 days later are:

$$P_{sell} = \frac{5\ 000\ 000}{1 + 0.074 * 60/365}$$

$$= \$4\ 939\ 909$$

Its holding-period yield is (using equation (4.3b) explained in Chapter 4, p. 88):

$$r_{HPY} = \left(\frac{4\ 939\ 909}{4\ 908\ 619} - 1\right)\frac{365}{30}$$

$$= 7.76\%\ \text{p.a.}$$

While this strategy achieved the highest yield, this outcome was the result of bill rates falling, which incorporated a capital gain in the selling price. This capital gain is the difference between the actual selling price and what it would have been ($4 938 706) had the yield remained at 7.55% p.a. (i.e. $1203).

Had the market yield increased, the selling price would have incorporated a capital loss, and resulted in a lower holding-period yield.

The yields in the bank-accepted bill market, especially the 90-day rate, are important indicator interest rates. Because of the volume of trading in the bill market (and the relationship between the yields in it and the bill futures market, which we discuss in Chapter 17), its yields tend to determine the interest rates set elsewhere in the financial system (with the exception of the cash rate, which is the object of the RBA's monetary-policy setting).

COMMERCIAL PAPER AND CDs

Commercial paper (or promissory notes) is short-term securities that are, in effect I-O-Us issued by a borrower who has a strong credit rating. The securities are referred to as 'one-name paper', because the issuer has the obligation to pay their face value at maturity. Certificates of deposit are similar instruments that are issued by banks. (Remember the discussion of CDs in Chapter 7.)

Both are discount securities that are issued to the wholesale market, mainly for very short terms. The majority of commercial paper is issued for periods of 45 days or less, and most CDs are issued for terms of less than three months. These are shorter terms than for bills, most of which are issued for 90 or 180 days.

The credit standing of the issuer is an important factor in the commercial-paper market, whereas in the bill market, the credit standing of the acceptor is important (rather than that of the issuer). Most commercial paper (65.6%) was rated A-1+ (the highest rating for short-term securities) by Standard & Poor's in August 1995, 24.1% was rated A-1 and 10.3% was rated A-2.

Because of the need to have a high credit ratings, many companies are not able to issue commercial paper in the Australian market. Issuers are classified in table 10.3 as State Central Borrowing Authorities (SCBA), such as the NSW Treasury Corporation, other government authorities (OGA), major companies (CORP), finance companies (FINC) and borrowers engaged in the creation of securitisation of assets (SECD). Survey data of the value of commercial paper outstandings as at June 1995 and for the amount issued in the quarter ending June 1995, collected from market participants, are presented in table 10.3.

Table 10.3 Activity in the commercial-paper market, June 1995

Segment	*Outstandings at June 1995 ($b)*	*Programs at June 1995 ($b)*	*Issues, June quarter ($b)*	*Average tenor in days*
SCBA	5.825	12.450	4.27	86.94
OGA	1.389	5.505	3.61	41.39
SECD	1.306	3.425	2.49	52.42
FINC	3.075	4.600	3.42	64.91
CORP	4.209	10.850	7.48	44.37
Total	15.493	36.830	21.27	56.65

Source: *The Commercial Paper Review*, no. 5, June 1995, Tables 1–3

Commercial paper is the only short-dated paper that is directly rated. As a consequence, ratings agencies play a smaller role in the money market than in the debt-capital market that is discussed in the next chapter.

During the first half of the 1990s, the value of CDs outstanding was relatively stable at about $30 billion. Austraclear data for April 1995 show that it held $21.2 billion worth of promissory notes. This suggests that the survey data in table 10.3 understate the size of the commercial-paper market. Comparing the RBA data for CDs with the Austraclear data for promissory notes suggests that as at mid 1995 the former market is a little larger than the commercial-paper market.

Primary market

CDs are issued by banks. They are usually negotiable, meaning that they can be traded by the depositor in the short-term money market (alongside bills and commercial paper), and so are liquid securities. As noted in Chapter 7, they are mostly issued at a discount to their face value. This means that if they are held to maturity, the depositor earns a fixed rate of return.

Data on the issue tenor and yield of CDs for September 1995 are presented in table 10.4; similar data, for January 1995, were presented in table 7.5 in Chapter 7.

Table 10.4 Weekly issues of CDs, September 1995, classified by tenor and yield

Week ending	*<7 days*	*7 days to <3 months*	*3<6 months*	*6 and over months*	**Total**	*<7 days*	*7 days to <3 months*	*3<6 months*	*6 and over months*
	($m)	($m)	($m)	($m)	($m)	% p.a.	% p.a.	% p.a.	% p.a.
September									
6	1 575	1 891	241	359	4 066	6.58	7.55	7.58	7.61
13	1 530	2 767	586	30	4 914	6.55	7.54	7.59	7.69
20	1 457	3 168	503	164	5 292	6.50	7.52	7.56	7.57
27	1 480	2 252	255	176	4 163	6.50	7.50	7.52	7.53

Source: RBA, *Bulletin*, Table B.11

The issue yield of the very short-term CDs is closely linked to the RBA's cash rate, which in September 1995 was 7.50% p.a. The rates for the longer terms reflect expectations about the future movement in the cash rate. This matter is examined in Chapter 15.

The issuing of commercial paper is usually undertaken as part of a program. A program is a borrowing limit, and because commercial paper has a short term, it involves the issue of new paper as existing paper matures. As at June 1995 the overall program utilisation rate was 41%. Issuers to this market need to maintain a program of issuing in order to help sustain the secondary market for their securities.

As at June 1995 there were approximately 100 issuers of commercial paper in the Australian market. Observe, in table 10.3, the importance of governmental borrowers. These include Australian Postal Corporation, Australian Wheat Board, Federal Airports Corporation and Telstra. Corporate issuers include Alcoa of Australia, Boral, BTR Nylex, Coles Myer, Email, Esso Australia Resources, James Hardie Industries, News Corporation, McDonald's Australia, Nestle Australia, and Shell Australia.

Commercial paper is issued mainly through dealer-tender panels that usually have up to five members. The role of these dealers is to bid for and place the commercial paper being issued and subsequently act as market makers for the paper. The dealers work closely with issuers and provide issuing advice about the amounts and terms of the paper being issued. The other process is **direct issuance** by the issuer, which is the way CDs are issued by banks and Treasury notes are issued by the RBA.

The administration of a program of commercial paper issuance usually involves four parties in addition to the issuer:

- the **lead manager**, which, because of its expertise in the market, arranges the program, its documentation and launch,
- **dealers**, who undertake to market and distribute the paper to their investor base,
- an **issuing** and **paying agent** that administers the exchange of paper for cash and eventual redemption of the paper at maturity, and
- **Austraclear**, as the central depository for these securities. It may also act as the issuing and paying agent. (*The Commercial Paper Review*, June 1995, p. 11)

The principal lead managers in the commercial-paper market are the major banks and Bankers Trust Australia Limited. Other important dealers in the market are investment banks (such as Citibank Limited and Macquarie Bank Limited), some regional banks (Advance Bank Australia Limited and State Bank of NSW Limited), some merchant banks (ABN Amro Australia Limited, Société Générale Australia Limited and Toronto Dominion Australia Limited), as well the Australian Mutual Provident Society.

Among the A-1+ issuers, government borrowers are able to issue at a yield very close to the bank-bill rate (BBR) and in some cases below that rate. But issue yields are generally lower for A-1+ issuers than for the issuers who have a lower rating (A-1 and then A-2), and there is a range of issue yields within each rating. Each of the three short-term ratings covers a wide range of issuers and therefore the market will not equally value all issues with the same rating. Further factors also influence issue yields, such as the size of the program and the market's experience with the issuer.

According to the Review, the securitisation and company issuers were able to issue, on average, at yields around five basis points above BBR, the margin varying with the term of the paper; it widens slightly for longer-term issues. Finance companies exhibit the widest range of issue margins against BBR (ranging from below BBR to 25 basis points above). (*The Commercial Paper Review*, June 1995, p. 8)

The issuers of commercial paper do so because they can achieve a lower cost of funds than if they issued bills. Commercial paper issuers generally have a sufficiently good rating and borrow on a sufficient scale to not require the support of bank acceptance. For them, the cost of this service is not worth its credit-enhancement value.

The reverse is the case for the less substantial and secure borrowers who issue bills. In their case, the credit enhancement of bank acceptance lowers their cost of funds from the market by more than the amount of the acceptance fee. Therefore, in their case, bill acceptance is cost effective. (Recall the discussion of this matter in Chapter 7.)

The costs of issuing commercial paper are based on their issue yields which, as noted, are similar to the BBR, and their direct issuing costs. These include the fees of the participants in the issue process, such as the lead manager, participating dealers and the issuing and paying agent. The issuer's proceeds are the amount raised (based on the issue yield) less fees paid. The cost of funds as an annual yield, r, is calculated, using equation (4.3b), as follows:

$$r = \left(\frac{F}{P_{net}} - 1\right)\frac{1}{t}$$

(See example 10.3.)

example 10.3

Suppose a company that has a rating of A-1+ for its short-dated securities issues 30-day commercial paper with a face value of $200 million at a yield of 7.60% p.a. and incurs issuance fees of $65 000. Its cost of funds can be calculated as follows:

$$P = \frac{200\ 000\ 000}{1 + 0.076 * 30/365}$$

$$= \$198\ 758\ 440$$

Hence its net proceeds are $198 693 440 (i.e. $198 758 440 − $65 000) and its cost of funds as an annual rate is:

$$r = \left(\frac{200\ 000\ 000}{198\ 693\ 440} - 1\right)\frac{365}{30}$$

$$= 8.00\%\ \text{p.a.}$$

The secondary market

Certificates of deposit and commercial paper are traded by money-market dealers in the same way as bills. There is, however, a much wider range of issuers of these securities and the market for each issue is not as deep as for bills (which largely have only four acceptors). (See example 10.4.)

Turnover in commercial paper in 1993–94 was $175 billion, which represented about 17% of the turnover in short-dated securities. (AFMA, 1994, p. 18) These securities are held by wholesale investors, such as financial institutions and large companies.

As noted above, non-government commercial paper is issued at a yield to maturity that ranges from a few basis points below BBR to as much as 25 basis points above.

Consequently, investors have the opportunity to earn a higher yield on commercial paper (by accepting greater risks) than on bills and CDs. For instance, in September 1995, when 30-day bills were trading at a yield of 7.50% p.a. and 30-day CDs were yielding 7.53% p.a., some 30-day commercial paper was trading at 7.60% pa. There were wider margins on 180-day commercial paper.

example 10.4

In the United States, commercial paper (CP) is the major form of short-dated paper. Generally, issues of CP are supported by forms of credit enhancement by banks and other security dealers which allow a much wider range of companies (in terms of their credit risk) to issue such paper. Typically, dealers contact potential investors to help ensure that the terms of the issue have market appeal and are able to place most (if not all) of a new issue the day it is released. If required, dealers will hold a small proportion of unsold paper as inventory for subsequent market-making purposes. Such purchases are typically financed with standby funds, which are repaid when the securities are sold.

CP is issued through a program administered by a group of banks. A program establishes the master documentation for successive issues. Sometimes CP will be issued when investors have funds to place, although the issuer ultimately decides whether new paper can be issued. (Dufey and Giddy, 1994, p. 57)

Treasury notes

Treasury notes (T-notes) are issued by the Treasury. Most are issued for terms of 13 or 26 weeks. Smaller quantities of five-week Treasury notes are also issued. All are issued at a discount to their face value.

Their main financing purpose is to provide funds for the Commonwealth during the financial year, needed because of differences in the timing of expenditures and receipts. Even though data on the amount of outstanding T-notes during the first half of the 1990s reflect a seasonal pattern (see the graph in figure 10.2), the outstanding amount rarely fell below $13 billion. This implies that these securities, by rolling over maturing notes, represented a form of long-term, floating-rate borrowing. (Treasury bonds, which we discuss in the next chapter, are the main source of funding for the Commonwealth Government's debt.)

T-notes are issued at weekly tenders, conducted by the RBA. The tender arrangements, as at September 1996, are as follows. At 4 p.m. each Tuesday the Treasury announces the securities that will be offered (i.e. the amount for each term). By 12.45 p.m. on the following day, bids are submitted by RITS members in terms of the amount and yield, and the bank announces the results of the tender at 2.00 p.m. that day. The bids are handled electronically, with the lowest bids (i.e. highest prices for the notes) being accepted. Successful bidders must settle the next day (Thursday). This is referred to as T+1 settlement, meaning that the notes are exchanged for cash (for many dealers this will be exchange-settlement funds) the day after the tender results are announced.

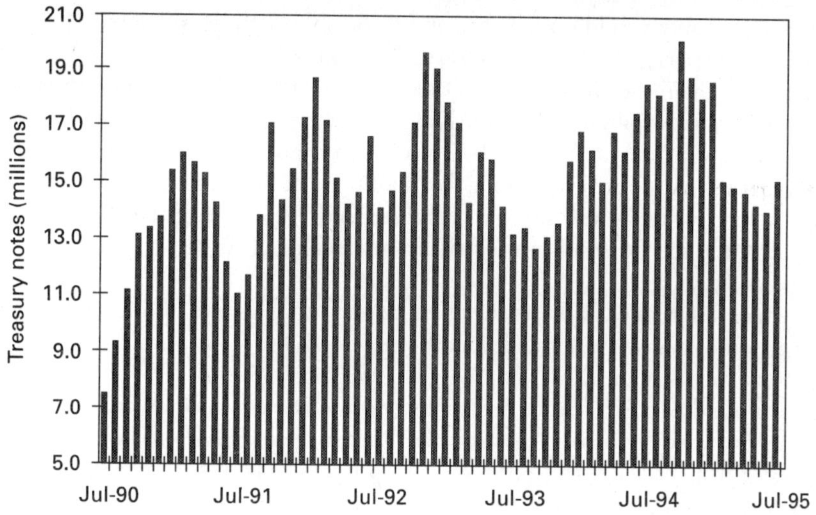

Figure 10.2 Treasury note outstandings, July 1990 to August 1995 ($m)
Source: Commonwealth Treasury

Table 10.5 Treasury note tender amounts and yields, September 1995

Date	*5-week ($m)*	*Average issue yield % p.a.*	*13-week ($m)*	*Average issue yield % p.a.*	*26-week ($m)*	*Average issue yield % p.a.*
September						
6	nil	n.a.	800	7.472	500	7.484
13	400	7.424	599	7.466	500	7.482
20	400	7.428	498	7.441	400	7.421
27	501	7.438	601	7.476	500	7.479

Source: RBA, *10*, Table E.4

The amounts offered at tender in September 1995 are shown in table 10.5. These are larger amounts than were offered earlier in the 1995–96 financial year because of the seasonal pattern of the government's requirement for funds (see figure 10.1).

As T-notes are sold by direct issuance, the proceeds of the tenders are simply the discounted value of the securities issued, using the issue yields. Of course, the Treasury incurs the expense of the RBA conducting the tenders, but this amount should not be great, given its established role as an issuer and that it also issues Treasury bonds.

The tenderers decide their bids after considering their prediction of future interest rates. If they quote a low rate (and are successful in the tender) and market yields rise shortly thereafter, they will have acquired T-notes at what turned out to be a high price only to experience a capital loss when rates rose. If they quoted a high yield they probably would not acquire any T-notes through the tender.

Given the experience of the tenderers, their knowledge of the current yields for T-notes and their extensive knowledge of the factors influencing short-term interest rates, we would expect their bids to be very similar. The range of accepted bids at a T-note tender in August 1995 was, for instance, three basis points for the 13-week notes and four basis points for the 26-week notes. Thirty per cent of the accepted bids were at the highest accepted bid (7.50% for the 13-week note and 7.58% for the 26-week note.) (Commonwealth of Australia, *Results of tender number 124*)

The small differences in the tender bids reflect some degree of uncertainty about the direction of market yields and the differing needs for T-notes among tenderers at the time of each tender. (Davis and Lewis, 1993, pp. 338–40)

The main bidders for T-notes are banks because these securities are prime assets (i.e. they are used by banks to satisfy the Reserve Bank's PAR). They are also the instrument that the RBA will rediscount to provide a last-resort source of cash. As at June 1995, banks held $10.3 billion of the $14.1 billion outstanding. The balance was held by the RBA itself ($1 billion), official dealers ($0.5 billion), public authorities ($0.7 billion), and $1.6 billion was held by other parties.

The secondary market is not very active: that is, their turnover as a proportion of their outstanding amount is low compared with the other short-dated securities discussed in this chapter. Turnover in 1993–94 was $84 billion compared with the turnover of $766 billion in bills and CDs.

Commonwealth bonds that have six months or less to maturity are traded as if they are T-notes. During the last six months of the term of a bond the security has only one payment to make — its face value and its final coupon — and the combined payment is made on the bond's maturity date. The security trades at a discount during this period in the same way as a T-note. Generally, though, such securities are held by banks to satisfy their PAR.

REPOS

Not all repurchase transactions are a form of finance, and so may not initially be thought of as a form of short-term security. Moreover, most of these transactions are conducted by the RBA for purposes other than to raise funds. But such transactions can and do serve a short-term financing purpose.

> *A repurchase agreement (repo or RP) is a series of transactions involving the sale of a security and the simultaneous agreement to buy it back, on an agreed date and at an agreed price. A repo gives the holder title to the security; it is not a secured loan.* (Carew, 1994, p. 9)

Most repos are for short periods, often for less than a week, even though they typically involve securities (such as Treasury bonds and semis) that have a much longer term to maturity. The repo's interest rate, which is an 'add-on' rate to the initial sale price of the securities, is based therefore on the term of the repo rather than on bond yields.

Repos were first transacted in the 1950s as a result of stockbrokers agreeing to buy back bonds. These deals served two purposes. They allowed investors access to bonds for short periods at a time when the supply of short-dated bonds did not match their demand. They also allowed sharebrokers to raise funds through the initial sale of the bonds. Investors were, in effect, lending funds to the sharebrokers, with the bonds serving as security. (Carew, 1994, pp. 9–10)

The RBA began transacting repos in 1957 and greatly increased its use of this arrangement as its main instrument for managing the financial system's liquidity (a function that is discussed in more detail in Chapter 14).

Repos are widely used by security dealers in the United States as a source of short-term funds. The funding role of a repurchase agreement is to generate funds for the seller of the repo. The seller raises funds by selling a parcel of securities and repays the funds when the securities are repurchased. (Dufey and Giddy, 1994, p. 56)

Repos may be used by funds managers who have large portfolios of bonds as a way of earning additional returns. A fund manager would sell repos when a higher return can be earned on the proceeds than the interest paid when repurchasing the securities. They would be demanded by traders who have taken a short position in bonds and require bonds temporarily to cover this short position. In this situation, a purchased repo is equivalent to borrowing bonds for an agreed period. (This practice is discussed in the next chapter.)

According to Carew (1994, p. 11), turnover in repos by the early 1990s could be of the order of $1.5 trillion, which is greater than the aggregate turnover of the short-dated securities discussed above. This is an estimate because precise data are not collected on the turnover in repos.

To summarise, repos are sold for official and commercial purposes. The RBA's use of repos is to move funds to and from the financial system. The three main commercial purposes of selling/buying repos are as follows:

- they are sold by fund managers to allow them to supplement their earnings from holding bonds;
- they are purchased for the purpose of acquiring bonds for a set period, because the bonds are otherwise difficult to obtain, or they are required for other purposes, such as to cover a short position in bonds; and
- they allow dealers to raise funds for short periods and give investors a return that is secured by bonds.

As noted above, the interest rate involved in a repo is an add-on, simple-interest rate that is based on the market yield for the term of the repo, regardless of the term of the securities involved. The repo rate determines the amount of interest that is added to the original sell price to arrive at the repurchase price. It is calculated as an amount of simple interest.

In the next chapter we explain how to calculate the price of bonds. But in the case of bonds with less than six months to maturity, they are priced as though they are Treasury notes. Thus we can illustrate the calculation of the sell and repurchase prices (including interest) of such securities through a repo. (See also example 10.5.)

Suppose the repo involves a sale, on Monday 16 December 1996, of a parcel of 12.50% p.a. coupon Treasury bonds that mature on 15 March 1997, and their repurchase seven days later. This bond will make a final payment of $106.25 on 15 March 1997 as bonds are redeemed by the payment of their face value and their final coupon. (These matters are explained in the next chapter.) Further, suppose that this bond is trading at a yield of 7.50% on Monday 16 December 1996. As the final payment is 89 days away, its sale price per $100 of face value under the repo will be:

$$P_{sold} = \frac{106.25}{1 + 0.075 * 89/365}$$

$$= \$104.3418$$

Suppose further that the agreed interest rate under the repo is 7.30% p.a. for seven days. This amounts to:

$$I = 104.3418\left(0.073\frac{7}{365}\right)$$

$$= \$0.1461$$

Thus the seller of the repo agrees to pay $104.4879 (104.3418 + 0.1461) for each of these bonds on 23 December 1996 to the buyer of the repo who, as a result, earns 7.30% p.a. for seven days on the amount paid for each bond. If the repo involved bonds with a face value of $1 million the amounts involved are:

Initial sale/buy:	$1 043 418
Interest:	$1 461
Repurchase/sale:	$1 044 879

Counterparty risk is involved in repos because market yields can vary between the sell and repurchase dates. The buyer faces the risk that market yields will rise during the repo period, reducing the value of the securities. Should the seller default, the buyer will be left with securities valued at less than the repo price. According to Carew (1994, p. 14), the parties may agree to an interim transaction in such an event which, in effect, terminates the repo and replaces it with another for the balance of the original term. The original repo rate will not be altered, but the value of the securities in the replacement repo will be reset according to the new higher yield.

Repos involving CGSs are settled through the RBA's RITS, and those involving semis are settled through Austraclear.

example 10.5

Suppose you enter into a repurchase agreement over 60-day Treasury notes, the effect of which is to provide you with a 14-day return of 6.05% p.a. You agree to purchase the Treasury notes at a price consistent with the prevailing 60-day yield of 6.00%:

$$P_{buy} = \frac{100}{1 + 0.06 * 60/365}$$

$$= 99.023332$$

and to sell back the Treasury notes 14 days later for:

$$P_{sell} = 99.023332\left(1 + 0.0605\frac{14}{365}\right)$$

$$= 99.253120$$

The increase in price is the interest earned at 6.05% p.a. over the 14 days.

Suppose the repurchaser defaults on the agreement after interest rates rise by 0.5% to 6.50% p.a. You are left with Treasury notes with 46 days to maturity, worth:

$$P = \frac{100}{1 + 0.065\frac{46}{365}}$$

$$= 99.187478$$

Thus, instead of realising a return of 6.05% p.a. for 14 days through the repo, i.e.:

$$r = \left(\frac{99.253120}{99.023332} - 1\right)\frac{365}{14}$$

you actually realise 4.32% p.a., i.e.:

$$r = \left(\frac{99.187478}{99.023332} - 1\right)\frac{365}{14}$$

when you sell the Treasury notes in the open market.

VALUATION PRINCIPLES

In Chapter 3 we explained how discount-security prices vary inversely with their market yield. This can be observed directly from equation (4.3a) where r is in the denominator of the value term:

$$P = \frac{F}{1 + rt}$$

The instant the market yield changes (meaning, other factors have not changed), the price of discount securities moves in the opposite direction. This is the source of the 'general market risk', referred to in the previous chapter, that arises from holding these securities.

Observe that t is also a denominator term. Therefore, the longer the security's term (other things being equal) the lower will be its price. This relationship reflects the 'time value of money' principle introduced in Chapter 1. The greater the period until the payment is made (F in the case of a discount security) the lower is its present value. The difference between F and P also reflects the accumulation of interest over time: the longer the period, the greater the amount of interest.

As noted above, the sensitivity of the price of these securities relative to a change in their market yield is not great, compared with that for long-term securities, because of the shorter period over which the rate applies. This is shown by the product of rt in the denominator. This difference in price sensitivity is explained in Chapter 16.

Recall the emphasis placed in this chapter on the credit rating of securities. A better rating for a particular security results in a higher price (and a lower market yield for that security). Movements in the price of particular securities because of changes in the credit standing of their issuers (or acceptors) are the source of 'specific risk' referred to in the CARs of banks (discussed in the previous chapter).

The general risk-return relationship introduced in Chapter 1 also implies that securities with a better rating will generally trade at a lower yield (command higher prices) than lower-rated securities. Thus, for example, T-notes will trade at a lower yield than commercial paper rated A-1, when all other features of these securities are the same.

In Chapter 3 it was emphasised that turnover in the secondary market can enhance the value of a security because its holders can easily sell them without disturbing the market price. Securities with deep secondary markets are endowed with liquidity and therefore will command a higher price (i.e. trade at a lower yield) than securities that have less liquidity.

In Chapter 14 we discuss the influence of inflation on yields, and thus on security prices. The expected inflation rate is a major determinant of the price of long-term securities, but has less influence on the price of short-dated securities (unless the rate of inflation is particularly severe). Short-term rates, though, are highly sensitive to the RBA's target for the 'cash rate', which is the bank's main instrument of monetary policy. A high inflation rate will be reflected in high long-term rates, and a tight monetary-policy setting will be reflected in high short-term rates.

To summarise, the value of short-dated securities:

- varies inversely with changes in the general level of their market yields,
- is lower, the longer their term,
- is higher, the better their credit rating,
- is higher, the greater their liquidity, and
- varies inversely with the tightening (i.e. their value falls) and easing (i.e. their value rises) of monetary policy.

Summary

The main points of this chapter are as follows:

- The market for short-dated securities is an unregulated, OTC professional market that deals in wholesale amounts.
- Four securities are traded in the market — bills, CDs, commercial paper and T-notes, together with repos.
- Bills, which are credit-enhanced securities (through bank acceptance), are the most widely used short-dated security.

- Banks issue CDs as a source of wholesale funds.
- Commercial paper is issued by very secure borrowers.
- T-notes are issued by the RBA on behalf of the Treasury.
- There is a deep secondary market for bills and CDs although there is less turnover in T-notes because a large proportion of them are held by banks to satisfy their PAR.
- Financial institutions are the principal participants in the money market, both on the issuing and investing sides.
- Non-financial wholesale borrowers and investors (e.g. large companies) are the other major participants in this market.
- The value of short-dated securities depends on the general level of interest rates, their term to maturity, their credit rating, their liquidity (which depends on the depth of their secondary market), and monetary policy.

DISCUSSION QUESTIONS AND EXERCISES

1 Discuss the primary and secondary markets for bills and commercial paper. Compare the differences between these instruments and the way they are issued. Comment also on the role of ratings agencies in the market for these securities.
2 Explain the operation of a one-year bill facility and identify the interest-rate risk it poses for the borrower. Refer to the discussion on this topic in Chapter 7.
3 Calculate the cost of funds, as a percentage per annum, when a company issues 90-day bank bills with a face value of $1 million at a market yield of 7.50% p.a., and is charged an acceptance fee of 200 basis points and other fees of $1000.
4 Prepare a statement showing a company's cost of funds, on the dates that the payments are made, when its bank provides a bill facility (using 90-day bills) with a face value of $2 million for 270 days, when the BBR is: 7.75% p.a. on the day the first set of bills are issued; 7.50% p.a. when the second set is issued; and 7.40% p.a. when the final set is issued, and imposes an overall charge of 300 basis points.
5 A well-established and financially secure company requires additional funds of roundly $1.5 million for approximately six months. Set out the factors that influence its choice between issuing bank-accepted bills and commercial paper and seeking a bank overdraft.
6 Compare the risks faced by two investors who purchased a $100 000 bill when one intends to hold the security to maturity and the other intends to hold it for a few weeks, assuming yields vary on average by ten basis points per week.
7 Compare the probable (and actual if you wish) yields on T-notes, bank-accepted bills, CDs and commercial paper that have the same term and explain any differences.
8 Describe the role of T-notes in the financial system. Suppose you work in the money-market section of a major bank which is submitting a tender for T-notes. Suppose the current yield on 13-week T-notes is 7.55% p.a. and the RBA has announced that $600 million of these notes will be available on Wednesday. Propose the bid(s) that your bank will submit to the RBA and explain your rationale for them.
9 Explain the operation of a repo and how interest is calculated.
10 Briefly explain the factors that influence the value of short-dated securities.

References and Further Reading

AFMA 1994(a), *Dealing Handbook*, AFMA, Sydney, pp. 53–60.

AFMA 1994(b), *1994 Australian Financial Markets Report*, AFMA, Sydney, pp. 17–20.

Austraclear, *Mission Statement*.

Carew, Edna 1994, *How Australia's Cash and Repo Markets Operate*, AFMA, Sydney.

The Commercial Paper Review, no. 5, June 1995.

Davis, K. T., & Lewis, M. K. 1993, 'Public sector securities market' in M. K. Lewis & R. H. Wallace (eds), *The Australian Financial System*, Longman Cheshire, Melbourne, pp. 318–57.

Dufey, Gunter & Giddy, Ian H. 1994, *The International Money Market*, 2nd edn, Prentice-Hall, New Jersey, Chapter 2.

Fabozzi, Frank J., Modigliani, Franco, & Ferri, Michael G. 1994, *Foundations of Financial Markets and Institutions*, Prentice-Hall, New Jersey, Chapters 14 and 15.

Hill, M. R. 1993, 'Short-term money markets,' in M. K. Lewis & R. H. Wallace (eds), *The Australian Financial System*, Longman Cheshire, Melbourne, pp. 358–90.

McGrath, Michael 1994, *Financial Institutions, Instruments and Markets in Australia*, McGraw-Hill, Sydney, Chapter 9.

RBA June 1991, 'Authorised short-term money market dealers', *Bulletin*, pp. 19–25.

RBA April 1995, *The Case for Real Time Gross Settlement*, RBA, Sydney.

Standard & Poor's August 1995, *Monthly Bulletin, Australia and New Zealand*.

11

Debt-capital market

This chapter explains the operations of Australia's debt-capital market and the features and financial characteristics of the main forms of long-term debt instruments. Emphasis is placed on the Commonwealth Treasury fixed-interest bond, which is the market's principal instrument. However, we also refer to other securities that have established a place within the market.

Study objectives

From your study of this chapter you should be able to:

- define the features of bonds;
- distinguish between the fixed- and floating-rate segments of the market;
- describe the role of Treasury bonds as a source of Commonwealth funds;
- explain the pattern of Treasury bonds on issue and the role of 'hot' or 'benchmark' series;
- describe the primary and secondary markets for Treasury bonds and for semis;
- calculate the price of Treasury bonds, using the market's trading conventions, on coupon dates and on the trading days between coupon dates;
- explain the behaviour of a bond's price in response to time and movements in their market yields;
- calculate holding-period yields for investments in bonds and distinguish their behaviour from that of yields to maturity;
- describe the floating-rate bonds issued by the Commonwealth; and
- describe mortgage-backed bonds, convertible notes, zero-coupon bonds and retail bonds.

INTRODUCTION

A general description of long-term debt instruments was presented in Chapter 3. Recall that they are generally known as bonds, are issued with a term longer than a year, and most make regular interest payments (known as 'coupons') of a fixed amount. Because of the dominance of the fixed-interest bond in this market, it has been traditionally referred to as the **fixed-interest market**. We refer to it as the debt-capital market because of the emergence, in the 1990s, of floating-rate securities from a diverse range of borrowers.

The Australian debt-capital market has been dominated by the Commonwealth Treasury (fixed-interest) bond, which we refer to as Treasury bonds. The other important bond issuers are the central borrowing authorities of the State governments, whose bonds are referred to as semi-governmental securities, or **semis**. Other potential issuers (such as major companies) have either issued long-term debt instruments in overseas bond markets or arranged term loans with domestic or overseas banks. As a consequence, Australia does not have a developed corporate bond market and its debt-capital market is dominated by public-sector securities. (Davis, 1993, p. 277)

A small number of companies and banks issue bonds in the wholesale market and some banks and finance companies issue into the retail market. But this scale of operations is not very significant compared with the activities of the Commonwealth and the States. This position contrasts with that in the USA where corporations are active in the debt-capital market, aided by investment banks. Major Australian companies have issued bonds in the US market (in either US or Australian dollars) and thus it and other overseas markets form part of the capital market from the perspective of major Australian borrowers. These markets are discussed in Chapter 13.

Bonds can be specified in terms of their:

- issuer,
- maturity date,
- coupon rate,
- frequency of coupon payments, and
- face value.

For each issuer, the maturity date of each bond is a key feature. It identifies each bond series for the issuer and determines the date of each bond's payments. Refer, for example, to the series of Treasury bonds listed in table 11.1, that were on issue in August 1995.

Typically, Treasury bonds are issued to ensure that there are one or two maturity dates each year up to a maximum term (currently) of 12 years (see the list of 'stocks' in table 11.1).

Each bond series specifies its coupon rate, as a percentage per annum, as well as its maturity date. These features are fixed when the bond is issued. In the fixed-interest segment of the Australian market, coupons are paid semi-annually (at half the annual rate) and bonds are redeemed at their face value.

Observe in table 11.1 that each bond series is identified by the month and year only. Each issuer will usually adopt a standard day in the month for payment purposes, and therefore this day need not be specified to identify each bond series.

In recent years, Treasury bonds have been issued with a minimum face value of $1000, but there are $100 face-value bonds still in the market. Thus, when calculating bond prices, we use the per $100 of face value practice. To arrive at the price of bonds with a face value of more than $100, you simply move the decimal point as required.

A bond's maturity date determines the timing of each of its redemption and coupon payments. For Treasury bonds, these payments are made on the 15th of the relevant month. The 9.00% September 2004 bond, for example, is redeemed on 15 September 2004 and its coupons are paid on 15 March and 15 September of each year until the bond matures.

Fixed-interest semis have similar features, although they generally do not follow the Treasury practice of always using the 15th of the month for payment purposes. The NSW Treasury Corporation (NSW T-Corp) bonds, for instance, currently use the first of the month for payment purposes and the South Australian Government Financing Authority (SAFA) uses the 15th for some bonds and the 16th for others.

Both Treasury bonds and semis are issued in the wholesale market and the subsequent trading of these bonds is undertaken by professional dealers in wholesale amounts (individual transactions are usually for parcels with a face value of $5 million). However, other long-term securities, such as the debentures issued by finance companies (referred to in Chapter 6) and retail bonds issued by banks, are issued to the retail sector. In some cases the issuer will repurchase them at prices based on the current market yield in the wholesale market (but this does not constitute a secondary market).

Since the late 1980s, mortgage-backed securities have been issued in increasing quantities. These are generally held by institutional investors and have not been extensively traded in the wholesale secondary markets.

In the early 1990s, a small number of overseas banks have issued $A bonds by private placement. These are known as **Matildas** (or 'global bonds'). As at May 1995, Austraclear provided settlement services for five issuers of 'Matildas'.

The fall and rise of semis

State governments, during the 19th and the early decades of the 20th century, competed vigorously with each other for funds (forcing up their borrowing rates); did not rigorously maintain sinking funds (these are provisions for the repayment of loans); and on occasions borrowed excessively to undertake development projects, not all of which proved successful.

In 1927 the Commonwealth and the States formed the Australian Loan Council to centralise borrowing under the terms of the *Financial Agreement*. Under this agreement, the Commonwealth took over responsibility for the States' debts and it issued bonds on behalf of itself and the State governments. Accordingly, only Commonwealth bonds were issued after 1927 (and this position remained in place for over 50 years).

The Loan Council (which has representatives from each State and the Commonwealth, but for various reasons was effectively under the Commonwealth's control) allocated the borrowed funds to State governments (funded from the issue of Commonwealth securities) and approved the overall amount of borrowing by each State's semi-governmental and local authorities (under the *Gentlemen's Agreement* of 1936).

During the 1980s, in association with the deregulation of the financial system, the Commonwealth began to return the borrowing independence of the States. In the early 1990s the Commonwealth decided to unwind its control through the Loan Council over State borrowing and to revert to the original position where State governments were responsible for their own debt and borrowing programs. This involves transferring to each State the portion of Commonwealth debt that was raised on its behalf. (Davis and Lewis, p. 323)

The States responded to their enlarged borrowing responsibilities by forming central borrowing authorities (CBAs) that served to raise and manage debt funds for all state organisations. Centralising each State's borrowing allows them to apply sound debt management principles and increase the scale of their borrowing programs.

Not all State CBAs, though, have been able to replicate the Commonwealth's AAA rating (in 1995 this rating applied to the securities of only the NSW T-Corp and the Queensland Treasury Corporation). As a consequence, some States pay higher issue yields than would have applied if the Commonwealth had continued to raised their debt funds.

Semi-governmentals firmly established their place in the debt-capital market during the late 1980s when the Commonwealth was redeeming some of its bonds and the States were expanding their bond issues. By the mid 1990s, semis (in aggregate) were of similar importance, quantitatively, as Treasury bonds in both the primary and secondary markets. Semi-governmental yields, though, tend to be five to ten basis points higher than for Treasury bonds (see figure 11.1).

PARTICIPANTS

The main participants in the debt-capital market are the issuers of securities, banks and fund managers as investors and service providers, such as the ratings agencies, information providers, dealers, banks and merchant banks that assist in the issuing of new securities.

The main instruments are the fixed-interest bonds issued on behalf of the Commonwealth and State governments. These securities dominate both the primary and secondary markets. Issues of floating-rate securities have emerged in the early 1990s, such as the Treasury's capital-indexed bonds (TIBs) and adjustable-rate bonds (TABs), and floating-rate notes (FRNs) issued by private sector borrowers. The TIBs were first issued in the mid 1980s, but issues were suspended until February 1993 and the TABs were introduced in November 1994. Many of the FRN issues are mortgage-backed securities.

Treasury bonds

The main focus of this chapter is on fixed-interest Treasury bonds. This is the largest security on issue and the most actively traded bond in the secondary market.

Moreover, an understanding of its financial characteristics applies to the other fixed-interest bonds issued in the Australian market.

Our discussion of Treasury bonds focuses on those issued in the Australian market rather than the bonds issued overseas. As at June 1994, the face value of outstanding Treasury bonds was $67 billion. In 1989, the government's issues of bonds in foreign currencies reached a peak at an Australian-dollar value of $9.5 billion. By June 1994, the amount outstanding had fallen to $4.4 billion. Most of these bonds were issued in US dollars and Japanese yen.

The Treasury bond also has the superior credit standing. Because of the Commonwealth's financial power (i.e. its extensive taxing authority and, perhaps, its monopoly on issuing legal tender), its securities are regarded as being free of credit risk. As a consequence, its securities (bonds and notes) trade at the lowest yields within the market (as shown in figure 11.1).

Moreover, the Treasury bond program has dominated the market for many years and has achieved a high degree of market liquidity by applying professional debt-management principles (such as issuing a limited number of series). This liquidity further enhances the value of these securities and contributes to their low yield.

Primary market

Treasury bonds are issued by the RBA (for the Treasury) through a tender process. The funds raised are used to fund the government's budget deficit. When the government's budget was in surplus in the late 1980s, it conducted a reverse tender to redeem some of its debt. (Davis and Lewis, 1993, p. 338)

The government's overall borrowing program is usually outlined as part of its budgetary statements. It considers the securities that are maturing during the year. Maturing bonds add to the government's financing needs; it has to raise the funds to meet their redemption payments. In 1995–96, as a result of the inclusion of indexed and adjustable-rate bonds, the program also specified the mix of the new issues during the year.

Even though the Commonwealth budgetary position is expected to move into surplus during the latter half of the 1990s, the Treasury expects to maintain an issuing program of about $5 billion a year because of the need to refinance a larger volume of maturing bonds. The expected surpluses therefore will not mean a cessation of new issues.

The amount of adjustable-rate bonds to be issued will depend on the market's acceptance of this form of security. This applies also for the capital-indexed bond that had been issued in the 1980s. Assuming that adjustable-rate bonds are accepted, their issue will reduce the amount of T-notes on issue, because both represent an exposure to floating rates. It was noted in the previous chapter that a core of T-notes have been maintained, providing the government with a floating-rate exposure. (Hinton, August 1995, p. 5)

As at 30 June 1994 there were 58 domestic bond series on issue. Each is defined by its maturity date and coupon rate. The current policy is to concentrate the issue of new bonds within a smaller number of series. The aim is to promote market turnover and by this means improve the liquidity of these bonds. As at August 1995, there were 20 series that had a substantial amount of outstanding securities (i.e. about $2 billion or more) and each had a weekly turnover (in the secondary market) of at least $0.5 billion. These are referred to as 'hot' or 'benchmark' bonds. They are listed in table 11.1 (except for the September 1995 series).

When issuing new securities, an attempt is made to ensure that there are three-year and ten-year benchmark bonds available to the market. As is evident from an inspection of the dates presented in table 11.1, these bonds need not have a term to maturity of precisely three and ten years and over time different bonds serve as the three-year and ten-year benchmark bonds.

Table 11.1 Treasury benchmark bonds, 10 –16 August 1995

Series	*Turnover ($m)*	*Total on issue ($m)*
13.00% July 1996	1 013	3 801
12.50% March 1997	1 894	2 497
12.50% September 1997	759	3 197
12.50% January 1998	2 050	4 125
7.00% August 1998	5 042	4 989
6.25% March 1999	1 676	4 393
12.00% July 1999	751	3 702
7.00% April 2000	1 557	4 896
13.00% July 2000	1 199	2 596
8.75% January 2001	1 567	3 698
12.00% November 2001	489	2 716
9.75% March 2002	1 743	1 997
10.00% October 2002	916	4 298
9.50% August 2003	2 509	5 290
9.00% September 2004	2 817	5 712
7.50% July 2005	4 042	5 502
10.00% February 2006	1 352	2 400
6.75% November 2006	2 544	4 599
10.00% October 2007	1 559	3 001

Source: RBA, Press release, 17 August 1995

Bonds with these terms are important because their market yield establishes the three-year and ten-year interest rates. These terms are also attractive to the market because their market risk can be hedged by taking a position in the three-year and ten-year bond futures contracts. Observe the turnover of the 7.00% August 1998 and 7.50% July 2005 bonds in table 11.1, which in August 1995 were the benchmark three-year and ten-year bonds.

Each bond's coupon rate is chosen so as to be similar to the bond's issue yield. This is indicated by the current market yield for bonds of that maturity (in the secondary market). The movement in the level of market yields over time explains the variation in coupon rates that is evident in table 11.1.

While the coupon rate and a bond's face value determine the amount of each coupon payment, the cost of funds raised is determined by the issue yield, which is set by a tender process described below. The issuer (i.e. the government) cannot achieve a low cost of funds by simply setting a low coupon rate. This point is explained in a following section.

Of the new bonds issued in 1994–95, 45% were in existing series, to increase their market supply, and 55% were new series bonds. Several of these (February 2006 and October 2007) served to extend the range of benchmark series with long terms and the other two (January 2001 and March 2002) widened the range of securities with medium terms. (Hinton, August 1995, p. 4)

During 1994–95 the RBA conducted 24 tenders, roughly two per month. In 1995–96 fewer tenders will be conducted because of the government's smaller borrowing program. The tender process is similar in principle to that for T-notes, described in the previous chapter. In the case of the fixed-rate bonds, each tender is announced (giving details of the amounts and the series being offered) at noon on Monday with a closing date of 12.45 p.m. the next day. The results of the tender are announced on the Tuesday at 2.00 p.m. Settlement is on a T+2 basis (i.e. successful tenderers have to exchange cash for securities through the RITS system by Thursday of that week). The T+2 settlement process was established in August 1995; previously it was T+3.

Bids, which can be submitted only by RITS members, are in the form of yields, to two decimal places, with the lowest yields being accepted. As in the case of T-notes, there is usually a very narrow range of issue yields, given the experience and knowledge of market yields possessed by bidding bond dealers. But at the June 1995 tender, there was no range for two of the three series on offer, and there was only a two-basis-point spread among the successful bids for the other bonds. Usually there is a small number of successful bidders; these are mainly banks and about 12 active bond-market participants.

> *Those bidding in the tenders are seeking stock either for their own purposes (such as fulfilling their PAR requirements or otherwise wanting to invest in bonds), or for clients. In the latter context, there may be an element of speculation as to how much will be demanded. Long gone are the days when bond buyers bought and held. Portfolio management has become paramount for most participants.* (Carew, 1993, p. 11)

The minimum bid at a tender is for a parcel of $100 000 worth of bonds (in face value), with increments being at least $1000. A standard process is followed when the bids at the highest accepted yield exceed the amount of bonds available. This serves to divide the remaining bonds between these bidders.

The RBA sells bonds in retail quantities (i.e. small parcels, with $1000 being the minimum-sized bond) and will buy them back at the current market yield, but this activity is of little overall importance. The Commonwealth has a history of issuing retail bonds, such as Australian Savings Bonds, which were first issued in 1976. But in the late 1980s when the government was scaling back its borrowing (because of its budget surpluses) it ceased issuing these bonds.

Treasury bonds are **inscribed stock** (rather than bearer bonds) and this allows the RBA to act as the clearing house, by maintaining the register of bond owners and making the required coupon and redemption payments (through RITS).

Data on the first two Treasury bond tenders conducted in 1995–96 are presented in table 11.2. The amounts issued are generally typical of bond tenders. Part of the government's debt-management activities is to judge the capacity of the market to absorb new bonds (allowing for redemptions of existing bonds, when this occurs). The RBA's take-up of $200 million worth of the 8.75% August 2008 bonds was at the weighted average yield. This acquisition of bonds is undertaken either to replace maturing bonds held by the RBA or to sterilise RBA sales of foreign currency. Since the mid 1980s, the government has fully funded its budget deficit through sales of securities. (RBA, 1993, pp. 1–5)

Table 11.2 Treasury bond tenders, August and September 1995

	Weighted average yield (%)	*Amount allotted ($m)*	*RBA take-up ($m)*
Tender 125 (22/8/95)			
12.00% Jul. 1999	8.327	302	nil
9.75% Mar. 2002	8.826	301	nil
10.00% Feb. 2006	9.103	402	nil
Total allotted		1 005	
Tender 126 (12/9/95)			
9.75% Mar. 2002	8.593	401	nil
8.75% Aug. 2008	8.994	596	200
Totals		997	200

Source: RBA, *Bulletin*, Table E.5

Secondary market

There is an active secondary market for Treasury bonds. The average daily turnover for all Treasury bonds throughout 1994–95 was $7.1 billion, excluding RBA trading and $5.9 billion when identifiable repo transactions (described in the previous chapter) are excluded. Data on total turnover for the years 1990–91 to 1994–95 are presented in table 11.3.

A more specific view of the depth of the bond market is provided by the data on turnover for each of the 'hot' bond series, which were presented in table 11.1. The most actively traded bonds are the benchmark three-year and ten-year bonds. The average daily turnover (for the week of 10–16 August 1995) for the three-year bond was roundly $1 billion and $0.8 billion for the ten-year bond.

Another indicator of the market's depth is the relationship between the turnover of bonds and the value on issue (i.e. the value of bonds in the market). Observe in table 11.3 that the net turnover of Treasury bonds during 1994–95 was $1477 billion and there were $67 billion worth of Treasury bonds on issue as at 30 June 1994. Hence, on average, each bond was traded over 20 times during the year. This represents a very deep market.

Table 11.3 Treasury bonds, total market turnover, 1990–91 to 1994–95, ($b)[a]

Year	*Gross turnover*		*Net of RBA[b]*		*Net of RBA & repos*	
1990–91	364	1.4	264	1.0	253	1.0
1991–92	671	2.6	529	2.1	469	1.8
1992–93	984	3.9	868	3.4	777	3.0
1993–94	1 436	5.6	1 299	5.1	1 049	4.1
1994–95	1 965	7.8	1 781	7.1	1 477	5.9

[a] The larger numbers are annual turnover and the smaller numbers are daily averages
[b] Gross turnover less trades involving the RBA
Source: RBA, Domestic Markets Department

The data in table 11.3 show the rapid growth in the secondary bond market during the 1990s and illustrate the point made by Carew, quoted above, about the shift (by market participants) from holding bonds to trading them within portfolios. Other reasons for the growth in turnover are:

- the shift from the previous practice in the secondary market of (sharemarket) brokers attempting to match equal and opposite parties;
- the movement of banks into bond trading, which also developed their knowledge of and ability to access the fixed-interest market. By developing their relationships with an investor base, banks became bidders for new issues for the purpose of making a profit from the distribution of newly-issued bonds to investors;
- the Commonwealth's decision to concentrate new issues in hot series;
- the development of the bond-futures contracts by the Sydney Futures Exchange, which gave the managers of bond portfolios hedging opportunities (for three- and ten-year bonds). (Carew, 1993, pp. 12–13)

Look at the data in table 11.3 relating to repos. These arrangements were explained in the previous chapter. Repurchase agreements are recorded as sales because formally they involve a change in bond ownership, even though this could be for a very short period. Notice also that the turnover volume (around $0.3 billion) is considerably less than the $1.5 billion estimate referred to in the last chapter. Part of the explanation for the discrepancy is that not all repo trades are reported to the RBA.

The main holders of Treasury bonds are financial institutions. Banks and money-market corporations are the main traders in bonds. The data in table 11.3 show that the RBA was a counterparty to bond trades in 1994 –95 of $184 billion (9.3% of total market turnover), and the data in table 11.4 show that it is an important holder of these bonds. Recall from Chapter 9 (table 9.1, p. 239) that the RBA greatly increased its holdings of bonds during the 1990s.

Table 11.4 Holders of Commonwealth bonds[a], March 1995 ($m)

	$m
Reserve Bank	11 069
Banks	16 769
Official dealers	4 021
Life insurance companies	9 098
Superannuation funds	11 264
Non-financial public authorities	2 979
Other	30 509
Total	85 709

[a] All types of Commonwealth bonds
Source: RBA, *Bulletin*, Tables C.12, C.13, E.3

Trading in bonds is mainly undertaken by professional dealers who quote buy and sell yields (i.e. act as market makers). Dealing is undertaken over the telephone on the basis of a standard trading protocol, under which dealers identify themselves and state the particular bond series and the amount for which they are seeking prices. The responding dealer will quote both a buy and sell price to another dealer.

Most deals are in parcels of $5–10 million, although trades involving larger parcels, up to $50 million, are not uncommon. The trading spreads are narrow, two to three basis points for a standard parcel. This represents a price spread of $694.50 for a $1 million parcel of ten-year bonds.

Trading with clients (rather than between dealers) is very competitive and dealers will provide good clients with prices without requiring them to trade and may quote them a better price than a fellow dealer. Dealers do not have to offer two-way quotes (i.e. bid and offer) to a client.

The major dealers are banks (particularly the big four and the leading investment banks, such as Bankers Trust Australia Limited and Macquarie Bank); merchant banks, such as Bain and Company, SBC Warburg and CS First Boston; and the AMP Society and other leading insurance offices.

Bond investors include the list of domestic bond holders presented in table 11.4, plus overseas investors. Approximately 25% of Treasury bonds are held by foreign investors. Likewise, bond portfolio managers hold both domestic and foreign-currency bonds.

Brokers are still active in the market, but rather than being stockmarket brokers, they provide specialised services to the professional dealers. They provide real-time price information, firm prices that allow anonymous trading, as well as information on potential counterparties. (Carew, 1993, p. 17)

As noted above, Treasury bond trades are mostly cleared and settled through RITS, operated by the RBA. When deals are made, the trader completes a deal chit that the back office implements. Once the deal has been confirmed by both parties to the RBA it will be irrevocably settled through RITS. Settlement is usually on the T+3 basis, but a non-standard settlement date can be negotiated. (AFMA, 1994, p. 77)

Ratings agencies do not play an important role in the Treasury bond market because of the financial strength of the Commonwealth. These agencies are more important to the issuers and investors in securities that have a degree of credit risk, such as the bonds issued by State government central borrowing authorities, public enterprises and corporations.

Semi-governmental bonds

In broad terms semis are an equivalent security to Treasury bonds, even though they trade at different yields (reflecting a lower credit standing) and the secondary market for certain individual semis is not as liquid as for Treasury bonds. The margins that two semis, T-Corp and SAFA, pay over the Treasury yield are illustrated in figure 11.1.

Semis are issued to dealer panels, whereas Treasury bonds are issued directly by the RBA through competitive tenders. Each borrower will select a panel of dealers who are required to both place new issues and make a market for them. Making a market means that they continuously quote bid and offer prices to other dealers.

> *From the point of view of an issuer, establishing a dealer panel has the advantage of cutting down the number of operators an issuer has to talk to, so there is better use of resources; it is also likely to improve marketability of the paper on offer and ensures the issuer has a group of traders who have an incentive to promote its securities.* (Carew, 1993, p. 12)

Issues to a dealer panel can be on a competitive basis among the panel dealers (i.e. a closed auction), or each may agree to buy a certain quantity at a set price. This is known as a 'bought deal'. Dealer panels may comprise as many as 15 dealers. The closed auction is more widely used than bought deals.

The NSW T-Corp and SAFA were the initial central borrowing authorities to issue through dealer panels. In 1988 the NSW T-Corp formed dealer panels to make markets for its hot stocks. As noted in the above discussion of Treasury bonds, the practice of concentrating issues in hot stocks improves the liquidity of these securities and this lowers their issue yields.

The NSW T-Corp also established a bond-lending facility which allows its dealers to sell bonds 'short'; that is, the facility allows dealers to sell bonds they do not possess. The seller borrows bonds for a short period so as to be able to exchange bonds for cash on the settlement date. A primary reason for short selling is a belief that bond prices will fall. A speculator who sells short a bond prior to a fall in bond prices can later buy back the bond for a profit.

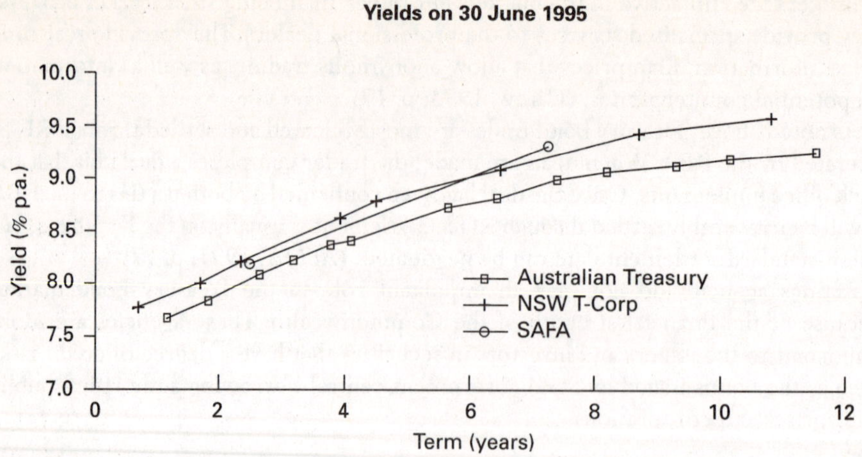

Figure 11.1 Treasury and semi-government yields

Short selling of bonds prior to new issues assists the issuer. It diffuses the impact of new securities on the market and it also improves the market's turnover. The T+3 settlement period also facilitates short selling. The short seller can cover these sales by buying bonds before the settlement date when bonds must be exchanged for cash.

The dealer spreads are wider for semis (their bid-offer spreads are up to five basis points) than for Treasury bonds. The standard trading parcel has a face value of $5 million. (Carew, 1993, p. 16)

Semis are cleared through Austraclear. It offers registry, safe custody and delivery (for cash) services for issuers and handles the settlement processes for both primary- and secondary-market transactions. As at April 1995, Austraclear held $68.5 billion worth of coupon-paying semis, most of which pay fixed-rate coupons.

Total turnover of semis for the year ending June 1994 was $921 billion, just a little less than for Treasury bonds. These trades are either on a straight buy/sell or a repurchase (repo) basis. Most of these trades are between banks, which are important dealers in the semi-governmental market. There are, of course, more securities in the semi market because each State government is an issuer.

Ratings agencies

As noted in the previous section, ratings agencies play an important role in security markets through the rating of securities that have some degree of credit risk. There are several ratings agencies and each decides what type of securities and institutions it rates. The main ratings agencies that operate in the debt-capital market are Moody's and Standard & Poor's. They express an informed opinion about the continued financial capacity of an issuer to meet the obligations associated with particular securities.

In general terms, debt-capital markets require the facilities of ratings agencies because the credit risk involved with long-term securities is much greater than for short-dated securities. Issuers may have considerable financial strength at the time they issue long-term debt, but may face predictable problems in servicing this debt over its full term.

The cost of preparing a rating is met by the issuer. Ratings provide a simple indication to the market of the credit standing of a security, and certain investors (such as trustee investments) are confined to only the highest rated securities. Therefore ratings provide useful information to the market.

A rating is an informed opinion about an issuer's capacity to meet its obligations under particular securities; it is not a trading recommendation. A rating reflects a view of an issuer's future financial capacity, and should events alter this view, the rating may be changed. Ratings agencies usually signal such events before determining whether a change in rating is required.

Moody's indicate that they form their ratings on the basis of an analytical hierarchy of variables, the most important of which is a qualitative analysis of the strategic direction and financial flexibility of the management of the issuer. The rationale for this as the most important factor is that an issuer's ability to meet financial obligations over a long period depends on its ability to cope with unexpected adverse events. This point applies particularly to corporate issuers.

The next most important piece of evidence is a quantitative analysis of an issuer's financial statements, including financial projections. This includes a study of the issuer's income flows available to meet interest obligations under particular securities.

Ratings agencies also consider:

- the competitive position of an issuer within its market and the prospects of the industry as a whole, and
- the issuer's regulatory environment, both domestic and overseas.

Even though the fees of ratings agencies are met by issuers, the views of the agencies are independent. They would be worthless if they were biased in favour of the issuer. They are formed only after an intensive study is made of each issuer's past, present and future financial capacity.

Standard & Poor's rating scale for long-term debt instruments is similar to Moody's scale shown in Chapter 3. It is divided into investment grades (AAA, AA, A and BBB) and speculative grades (BB, B and CCC). Lower ratings are CC, C and D. It also uses pluses and minuses for the ratings AA to CCC to further differentiate the credit standing of issues. The definitions of Standard & Poor's investment and speculative grades are presented in table 11.5.

Differences in rating are reflected in the market yields of rated securities. The lower the scale the higher the market yield. This means that new issues (in the primary market) are more expensive for the lower-rated issues and, in the secondary market, lower-rated securities have a lower value i.e. trade at higher yields.

Standard & Poor's calculate the difference between yields in the Australian bond market for AAA and AA bonds. The spread during June and July 1995 ranged from one to three basis points. Its assessment of the effect of rating on yields in the USA corporate bond market indicates much wider spreads, averaging 25 basis points between AAA and AA (for mid 1995), 45 basis points between AA and A, and 23 basis points between A and BBB. The margins are wider among the speculative grades. (Standard & Poor's, 1995, p. 16) Data supplied by Moody's to the authors on the US bond market are similar to that of Standard & Poor's.

Table 11.5 Standard & Poor's ratings definitions, AAA to CCC

Rating	*Definition*
AAA	**Extremely strong** capacity to meet financial commitments. Highest rating.
AA	**Very strong** capacity to meet financial commitments.
A	**Strong** capacity to meet financial commitments, but somewhat more susceptible to adverse economic conditions and changes in circumstances.
BBB	**Adequate** capacity to meet financial commitments, but more subject to adverse economic conditions. Lowest investment-grade rating.
BB	**Less vulnerable** in the near term but faces major ongoing uncertainties and exposures to adverse business, financial and economic conditions.
B	**More vulnerable** to adverse business, financial and economic conditions but currently has the capacity to meet financial commitments.
CCC	**Currently vulnerable** and dependent on favourable business, financial and economic conditions to meet financial commitments.
CC, C, D	**Highly speculative** with D referring to default.

Source: Standard & Poor's, 1995, p. 10

Information providers

The ratings agencies in the debt-capital market are an important source of market information, but they are not the only source of informed market opinion or of information generally. In an efficient market, prices will allow for the sorts of information available to ratings agencies and so ratings will serve merely to confirm the assessments of credit risk made by market traders. According to the EMH, a change in a security's rating would not alter its value; the market would have already changed its market value in line with the change in rating. However, ratings clearly play an important role in actual markets, otherwise issuers would not fund the reports of these agencies.

Chapter 3 explained that the main providers of information to the financial markets are news organisations such as AAP, Reuters, Dow Jones Telerate, Bloomberg Financial Services and Knight Ridder. They provide information electronically which allows traders to gain access to relevant information quickly on their computer screens. They also provide various trading support systems.

Each information provider has its own information products. For instance, AAP Corporate provides:

> *real-time price feeds for bonds, semis, bank bills and cash . . . This data (is) displayed in user-defined pages or pre-formatted displays. AAP Corporate also maintains a . . . historical database which covers all these instruments and displays them in graphical or tabular form. Data can also be manipulated in real time in spreadsheets and . . . analytical packages. AAP Corporate also gives access to futures markets, news and overseas money-market data to . . . complete the picture.'* (AAP Information Services)

Dow Jones Telerate organises its screen information numerically. For instance, its Australian Markets Report service provides a news headline on p. 22750, an events diary on pp. 22786–7, economic analysis on pp. 42905–22, and overnight market data on page 42929. Telerate also provides an overview of the bond market on pp. 2675 and 8122.

Information providers play an important role in allowing the professional traders in the bond market to use information efficiently in their trading decisions.

BOND PRICING

This section of the chapter presents an analysis of the pricing of fixed-interest bonds. It deals with Treasury bonds but the analysis applies to fixed-interest bonds generally. The section starts with an explanation of the basic pricing formula (i.e. equation (5.2) presented in Chapter 5, p. 109) for fixed-coupon bonds.

This section is mathematical and draws upon the explanation in Chapter 5 of annuity factors and equation (5.2) in particular. Some readers may find that a review of that chapter will assist their understanding of the bond-pricing formula used in this chapter. While we use a bond-pricing formula that includes an annuity factor, this is not the only way of pricing bonds.

However, competence in the use of a standard scientific calculator is necessary to be able to undertake the calculations illustrated in this section. In particular, the formula requires the use of a calculator's power and inverse functions.

While financial calculators and spreadsheets can calculate bond prices without directly following the pricing formula, we present and explain the application of the formula for two reasons. One is that the pricing formula can be applied with standard calculators and the other is that formula-based calculations help you to understand the elements and characteristics of a bond's price.

You will recall that the Treasury (fixed-interest) bond is a promise to pay a series of regular, fixed payments. These are its six-monthly coupons and its face value. Refer to the cash flows shown in figure 11.2 for the 7.00% August 1998 bond as at 15 August 1996. (Recall that Treasury bond payments are made on the 15th of the month.) Observe that coupon payments, C, are at half the coupon rate, c, times the bond's face value. As previously noted, we calculate bond prices per $100 of face value. Hence:

$$C = \frac{c}{2}(F)$$

$$= \frac{0.07}{2}(100)$$

$$= \$3.50$$

The value of a fixed-interest bond is simply the sum of the present value of each of its remaining payments. In Chapters 1 and 4 we explained that the present value of a future payment is found by removing its interest component. For bonds, this involves:

- the use of the current yield in the bond market, which is expressed as an annual rate, r, and
- semi-annual compounding, because the coupon payments are made semi-annually.

Therefore, the bond's price can be found by summing the present value of each of these payments as follows:

$$P = \frac{C_1}{1 + r/2} + \frac{C_2}{(1 + r/2)^2} + \frac{C_3}{(1 + r/3)^3} + \frac{C_4 + F}{(1 + r/2)^4}$$

Equation (11.1)

Assuming the bond is purchased at a market yield of 8%, its price is found as follows:

$$= \frac{3.50}{1.04} + \frac{3.50}{(1.04)^2} + \frac{3.50}{(1.04)^3} + \frac{103.50}{(1.04)^4}$$

$$= 3.3654 + 3.2359 + 3.1115 + 88.4722$$

$$= \$98.1850$$

In general, we will use four decimal places when pricing bonds, because this will accurately price bonds with a $1000 face value.

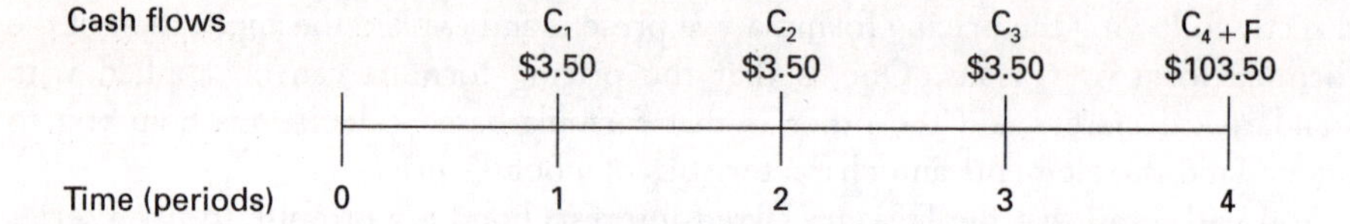

Figure 11.2 Cash flows for the 7% August 1998 Treasury bond on 15 August 1996

Had this been a longer bond (involving more coupon payments), this approach to calculating its value would have been rather tedious. One way of reducing the number of calculations is to treat the coupons as an ordinary annuity and value the stream of coupon payments separately from the payment of the bond's face value. According to this approach the price of a bond is calculated as the sum of:

- the present value of the coupon annuity, and
- the present value of the redemption payment.

In Chapter 5 we showed that the present value of an ordinary annuity can be calculated using the appropriate present-value annuity factor. In the above example, there are four coupon payments, each made at the end of successive six-month periods. Recall from the discussion in Chapter 5 that this series of payments constitutes an ordinary annuity and its present-value is the amount of the regular payment (C) times the present-value annuity factor. Further, the present value of the bond's face value is calculated as in equation (11.1).

The general formula we use for pricing bonds that pay semi-annual coupons, equation (5.2), is reproduced here as equation (11.2):

$$P = Ca_{\overline{n|}r/2} + F(1 + r/2)^{-n} \qquad \textit{Equation (11.2)}$$

where the power, $-n$, means that F is multiplied by the reciprocal of $(1 + r/2)^n$,
$a_{\overline{n|}r/2}$ is the present-value annuity factor for an annuity of n payments of \$1 given a market yield of r% p.a., and
C is the amount of the fixed-coupon payment.

Recall that the present-value annuity factor is calculated with equation (5.3):

$$a_{\overline{n|}r/2} = \frac{1 - (1 + r/2)^{-n}}{r/2}$$

When applying equation (11.2) it is important to understand several practices in the bond market.

First, trading is in terms of yields, thus r is determined by the market. Second, (as at 1996) settlement in the bond market occurs three business days after a deal is struck (this being in terms of the bond's yield). The amount paid for the bond (i.e. its price) is calculated using the purchase yield and the period from the settlement date. For instance, in the case of the 7.00% August 1998 bond purchased on 15 August 1996, the deal was made on 12 August 1996 at a yield of 8.00%.

We can use equation (11.2) to check the price paid for this bond calculated above using equation (11.1). Observe that as the yield was determined by the trade, the only unknown element in equation (11.2) is the number of coupon periods. In this case it is four. Thus:

$$P = 3.50\left(\frac{1 - (1.04)^{-4}}{0.04}\right) + \frac{100}{(1.04)^4}$$

$$= 12.7046 + 85.4804$$

$$= \$98.1850$$

As noted above, the use of the annuity factor is clearly more convenient when the bond has many remaining coupon payments. For instance, suppose a bond dealer sold a parcel of 9.50% August 2003 Treasury bonds on Monday 12 February 1996, at a market yield of 9.00%. The amount paid for these bonds is also based on their term from 15 February 1996 — this being three working days after the deal date — to their 15 August 2003 maturity date.

Observe that there are 15 coupon periods from 15 February 1996 to 15 August 2003, therefore the price of the bonds, per \$100 of face value, in this parcel, is:

$$P = 4.75\left(\frac{1-(1.045)^{-15}}{0.045}\right) + \frac{100}{(1.045)^{15}}$$

$$= 51.0128 + 51.6720$$

$$= \$102.6849$$

Note that a small rounding error can arise when the present values of the coupons and the bond's face value are expressed correct to four decimal places. Given the price of $102.6849 per $100 of face value, the value of a parcel of 10 000 of these bonds is $1 026 849. (See example 11.1.)

example 11.1

As a fixed-interest manager in a large superannuation fund you have agreed to purchase at a yield of 8.80% a $10 million (face value) parcel of 10% October 2007 Treasury bonds, with settlement being on 15 April 1997. Calculate the price of this parcel of bonds, per $100 of face value.

There are 21 interest periods between 15 April 1997 and maturity on 15 October 2007. The price per $100 of face value is:

$$P = 5\left(\frac{1-(1.044)^{-21}}{0.044}\right) + \frac{100}{(1.044)^{21}}$$

$$= 67.631171 + 40.484570$$

$$= \$108.115741$$

The price for bonds with a face value of $10m is 100 000 (108.115741) = $10 811 574.

Premium and discount prices

Notice that we calculated the price of the 9.50% August 2003 bond on its coupon date and that its price was $2.6849 above its par value of $100. It is customary to describe bonds that (on their coupon date) have a price above their face value as trading at (i.e. being priced at) a **premium** (to their face value). In this case the yield was 9.00%, whereas the bond's coupon rate was 9.50%.

As noted above, bond yields are set by market trading and tend to vary both throughout each trading day and over the business cycle. (We discuss interest rates and their movements in Chapter 14.) When a bond's yield falls below its coupon rate its price must rise above its face value, because the yield is the return represented by the bond's fixed cash flows to its price. In the above case, coupons paid at the rate of 9.50% of the bond's face value can only represent a yield of less than 9.50% if the bond's price is more than its face value.

Similarly, should a bond's yield exceed its coupon rate on a coupon date, this implies that its price is less than its face value. To illustrate, suppose the 9.50% August 2003 bond was trading at 10.00% on 12 February 1996. Its settlement price will be less than \$100 because this allows coupons that represent 9.50% of \$100 to yield more than that rate:

$$P = 4.75\left(\frac{1-(1.05)^{-15}}{0.05}\right)+\frac{100}{(1.05)^{15}}$$

$$= 49.3034 + 48.1017$$

$$= \$97.4051$$

Cum and ex-interest pricing

You will notice that the above price calculations assumed the bond was purchased (i.e. settled) on a coupon date. Since there are only two of these a year for each bond, we should understand how bonds are priced on other trading days. We continue to use equation (11.2) but we need to modify its application.

This equation has two terms and the first assumes that the bond's coupon payments are an ordinary annuity. When settlement is on a coupon date, all of the bond's remaining coupons form an ordinary annuity. But when settlement is on another date, the first of the remaining coupons will not be paid exactly six months from that date. Therefore, this coupon payment cannot be included in the annuity factor within the equation's first term. Annuity factors correctly value payment streams only when each occurs after a full payment period has elapsed.

However, we can use the annuity factor for all of the subsequent coupons (other than the one that is received during the current coupon period). The initial coupon will be allowed for in the modified form of equation (11.2) by simply adding it to the present value of the remaining coupons, as at the next coupon date (when appropriate).

Before explaining how to apply equation (11.2) to pricing bonds on non-coupon dates, we need to understand the role of **cum-interest** and **ex-interest** trading days. During the seven days prior to each coupon date, bonds are settled on an ex-interest basis, meaning that the buyer of the bond does not receive the coupon being paid on that coupon date (hence the expression 'ex-interest'). The **ex-interest date** (i.e. 8th of the coupon month) allows the RBA a week to process the payment of the coupon. On all other trading days, bonds are priced on a cum-interest basis, meaning that the buyer receives the next coupon.

The ex-interest period (i.e. from the 8th to the 15th of the coupon month) is liable to change over time as the processing time for paying coupons is reduced. In the early 1990s it was 14 days.

Pricing bonds on non-coupon dates adds two small complexities to the basic pricing formula (equation (11.2)):

- this equation assumes that *all* coupon payments form part of an ordinary annuity. This assumption holds when bonds are paid for on coupon dates, but not on other dates. On cum-interest dates, the period to the next coupon is less than the coupon period. Therefore this payment cannot be included in the annuity factor, and so is treated as a separate payment; and

- the annuity factor can be used for the remaining coupons by calculating the bond's price as at the next coupon date. This value must then be adjusted (i.e. discounted) to allow for the accumulation of interest during the coupon period.

Settlement price between coupon dates

In Australia, the conventional way of calculating the price of a bond on a settlement date other than its coupon dates, is to:

- first calculate the present value of its payments (on an ex-interest basis) at the next coupon date,
- second, add the coupon paid on that date if the settlement is in the cum-interest period (do not add the coupon if the settlement date is in the ex-interest period), and
- third, discount this sum back to the settlement date.

Refer to the time line in figure 11.3. The first step covers n periods (from the next coupon date); the second depends on whether settlement occurs during the ex-interest period; and the third step covers the period (w) between the ex-interest and the settlement dates.

The discount factor used in the third step is as follows:

$$(1 + r/2)^{-f/d} \qquad \textit{Equation (11.3)}$$

where f is the number of days between the settlement and the next coupon dates, and
d is the number of days in the current coupon period (i.e. the period in which settlement occurs).

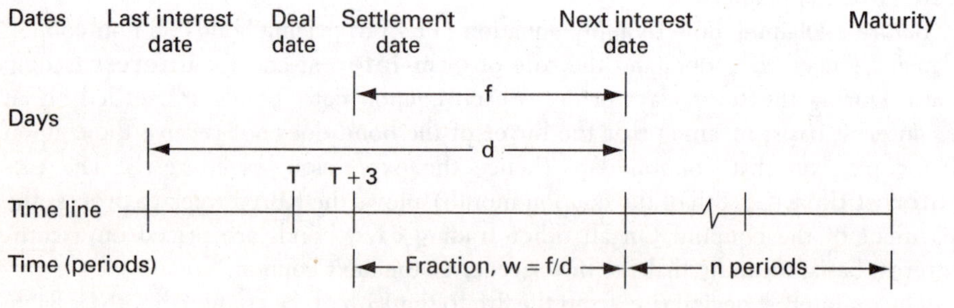

Figure 11.3 Time line for cum and ex-interest settlement

Suppose the 9.50% August 2003 bond (priced above on 15 February 1996 as $102.6849) was traded on Monday 6 May 1996 when its yield was 9.00%. Given T+3 settlement, its purchase price is based on the bond's term from Thursday 9 May 1996. This is a cum-interest date because the August 1996 coupon is more than seven days away, and in fact will be paid in precisely 98 days. The precise number of days in the current coupon period (i.e. the period ending 15 August 1996) is 182 days, as shown in figure 11.4.

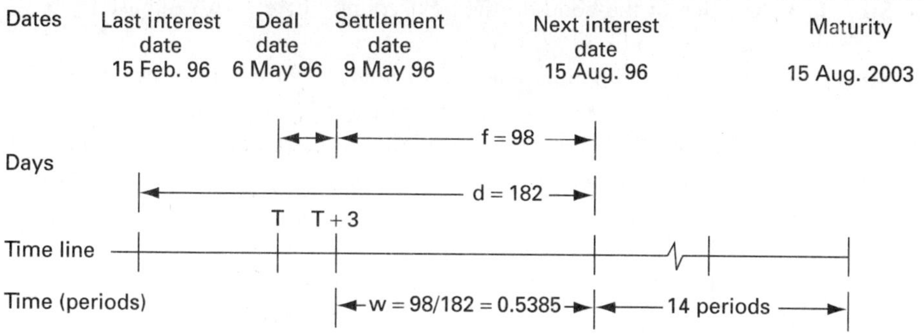

Figure 11.4 Time line for 9.50% August 2003 bond purchased (i.e. settled) on 9 May 1996

We follow three steps to apply equation (11.4) on cum-interest dates:

- **Step 1** We directly apply the bond-price equation (11.2) as though the purchase date was the next coupon date, 15 August 1996. Note, on this date the bond has 14 remaining coupons. In step 1 we set aside the next coupon (the one that will be paid on 15 August 1996):

$$
\begin{aligned}
P^{\text{ex-int}} &= 4.75\left(\frac{1-(1.045)^{-14}}{0.045}\right)+\frac{100}{(1.045)^{14}} \\
&= 48.5584 + 53.9973 \\
&= \$102.5557
\end{aligned}
$$

- **Step 2** We add in the next coupon (paid on 15 August 1996) because the bond is purchased cum-interest. This fully accounts for the bond's remaining 15 coupons:

$$
\begin{aligned}
P_{15/8/96} &= 102.5557 + 4.75 \\
&= \$107.3057
\end{aligned}
$$

- **Step 3** We discount the bond's value, on the next coupon date, back to the settlement date:

$$
\begin{aligned}
P_{9/5/96} &= \left(\frac{1}{(1.045)^{98/182}}\right)107.3057 \\
&= 0.9766(107.3057) \\
&= \$104.7923
\end{aligned}
$$

The same method is followed when calculating the price of a bond on ex-interest dates, except in such cases the imminent coupon is not included. Suppose the 9.50% August 2003 bond was traded on Tuesday 6 August 1996 at a yield of 9.00%. Settlement on Friday 9 August falls within an ex-interest period — 8 to 15 August 1996.

- **Step 1** The price of the bond on the next coupon date — 15 August 1996 — was calculated above to be $102.5557.
- **Step 2** Because the coupon payable on 15 August 1996 will not be paid to the bond's purchaser, we skip step 2 in the case of ex-interest pricing.
- **Step 3** We discount the bond's value at the next coupon date to its present value on the settlement date. There are six days between settlement on 9 August 1996 and 15 August 1996.

$$P_{9/8/96} = \left(\frac{01}{(1.045)^{6/182}}\right) 102.5557$$

$$= 0.9985(102.5557)$$

$$= \$102.4019$$

SUMMARY FORMULA

The above three-step approach is contained in equation (11.4). It applies equation (11.2) as at the next coupon date and multiplies this value by the discount factor shown as equation (11.3):

$$P = (1 + r/2)^{f/d} \left(C \left[\frac{1 - (1 + r/2)^{-n}}{r/2} \right] + \frac{F}{(1 + r/2)^n} + C_0 \right)$$

Equation (11.4)

where n is the number of complete coupon periods, and
C_0 is added only when the bond is purchased cum-interest.

Movement in a bond's price over time

Refer back to the calculation of the settlement price on 9 May 1996 of the August 2003 bond and its value on 15 August 1996. Observe that the price of the bond rose between these dates from $104.7923 to $107.3057. This increase in value, $2.5134 (per $100 of face value), represents the accumulation of interest over approximately half a coupon period. It forms part of the general increase in a bond's price between its ex-interest dates.

Should a bond's market yield (and credit rating) remain unchanged throughout its term, its market price will follow a saw-tooth pattern until it is finally redeemed on its maturity date. This pattern comprises an upward price trend from one ex-interest date to the next (because interest accumulates, as in the above example), followed by a fall in its price on each ex-interest date because the imminent coupon no longer forms part of the bond. This saw-tooth pattern is shown by the price line in figure 11.5.

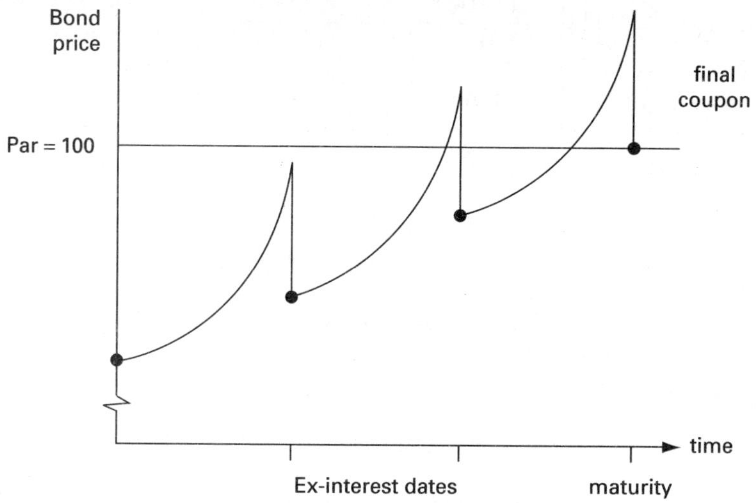

Figure 11.5 **A bond's price as a function of time**

The saw-tooth pattern in figure 11.5 applies to a bond that is trading at a discount. The pattern applies also to the price of bonds that are trading at a premium to their face value, except that the ex-interest prices are above \$100.

Observe the trend of the bond's price in figure 11.5 at each ex-interest date (ignoring the intra-coupon-period upward slope of the saw-tooth curve) until it matures. These values trend towards the bond's face value at maturity. For bonds trading at a discount the trend is upwards, whereas for a bond trading at a premium, its ex-interest-date prices trend downward to its face value.

Effect of changes in a bond's yield

Recall that in equation (11.1) the bond's yield appears in the denominator term for each of its payments. Consider, for example, the next coupon payment. Its value is given by:

$$PV(C) = \frac{C}{1 + r/2}$$

This implies that the bond's price (being the sum of the present value of its future payments) varies inversely with the direction of the change in its market yield. The yield, r, forms part of the denominator of the value term. Hence, the value of r forms a 'see-saw' relationship with bond prices. When r rises, P falls, and vice versa.

The price of the 9.50% August 2003 bond on 15 February 1996, given a yield of 10.00%, was calculated above to be \$97.4051 (per \$100 of face value). Suppose its yield fell to 9.00%. The see-saw relationship implies its price would rise, and this is confirmed by the following calculation:

$$P_{9.00\%} = 4.75\left[\frac{1-(1.045)^{-15}}{0.045}\right] + \frac{100}{(1.045)^{15}}$$

$$= 51.0128 + 51.6720$$

$$= \$102.6849$$

Note that the saw-tooth pattern of the movement of a bond's price over time assumes there is no change in its yield. When this occurs, the bond's price moves to another saw-tooth-shaped curve. A fall in the yield moves the price to a higher saw-tooth curve and an increase in its yield moves the price to a lower saw-tooth curve. (See example 11.2.)

example 11.2

In the USA, bonds are traded on the basis of their price. Bids and offers are expressed in terms of prices, not yields. US bond yields are calculated from market prices, as the **internal rate of return** represented by a bond's future payments in relation to its price. An internal rate of return is the rate, calculated on a compound-interest basis, that equates a bond's future payments with its current market price.

As US bonds are traded in terms of their price, we can use demand and supply curves directly to illustrate the cause of a change in bond yields. In the following diagram we have bond prices on the vertical axis. Given that D_0 and S_0 represent the current demand and supply curves for a particular bond, its price is P_0. Suppose there is an increase in demand for the bond. This is shown by the movement of the demand curve to D_1 which causes the bond's price to rise to P_1. The increase in demand could be caused by a fall in inflation expectations. (The causes of changes in the demand and supply of bonds are discussed in Chapter 14.) The rise in price implies that the bond's yield (i.e. the yield represented by its remaining payments in relation to the bond's price) has fallen.

DEMAND AND SUPPLY FOR BONDS

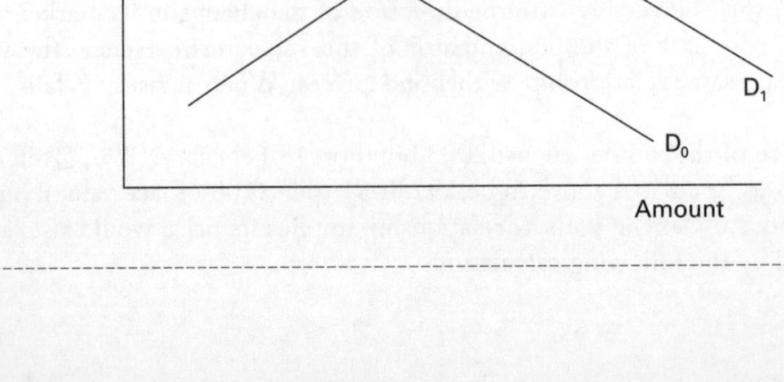

COST OF FUNDS

We have emphasised that while coupon rates determine the amount of the coupon paid to holders of Treasury bonds on each coupon date, this payment does not determine the cost of the funds to the Treasury. If it did, the Treasury would simply issue low-coupon-rate bonds.

Intuitively, the cost of funds can be represented by the relationships between a bond's payment and its proceeds when issued:

$$\text{cost of funds} = \frac{\text{future payments}}{\text{proceeds}} \qquad \textit{Equation (11.5)}$$

Given the market yield, issuing low-coupon-rate bonds will reduce the amount raised and thus not alter the cost of the borrowed funds. To illustrate, 12.00% July 1999 bonds issued in January 1995 at a yield of 8.40% would have raised (per \$100 of face value):

$$P = 6.00\left[\frac{1-(1.042)^{-9}}{0.042}\right] + \frac{100}{(1.042)^9}$$

$$= \$113.2625$$

Had this bond been issued with a coupon rate of only 2.00%, the proceeds would have been (only):

$$P = 1.00\left[\frac{1-(1.042)^{-9}}{0.042}\right] + \frac{100}{(1.042)^9}$$

$$= \$76.4223$$

Observe that the lower coupon payments raised less funds. In both cases the cost of the funds was determined by the market yield. This fact also can be viewed by nominating the amount to be raised. Given the amount of the denominator in equation (11.5), the cost of the funds depends on the numerator and this depends on the issue yield.

Suppose the Treasury was seeking to raise \$113.2625 million on 15 January 1995. The issue of \$100 million worth (in face-value terms) of 12% July 1999 bonds would raise this amount at a market yield of 8.40%. Had the yield been, say, 10.60%, the tender would have raised only \$104.9097 million and thus a higher coupon rate would be required.

Usually Treasury bonds are issued at or close to par. This is achieved by selecting the coupon rate for a new bond that is similar to the market yield when the bond is issued. Observe from table 11.1 that Treasury bonds have a wide range of coupon rates, reflecting the movement in market yields over the past 12 years.

Note that the actual issuing costs are in addition to the issue yield. These should be deducted from the proceeds of the bond issue (i.e. P in equation (11.5)) to arrive at the cost of funds as a percentage.

INVESTMENT YIELDS

Investors in bonds can earn a return from their future payments, coupons and the bond's face value. They are also assumed to earn interest on the reinvestment of the coupons received before the bond matures. Hence, the return to bond holders can be divided into three elements:

- the coupon payments,
- the interest on the reinvestment of the coupons, and
- the bond's face value.

Note that the coupon payments and the face value are fixed on issue, whereas the amount of interest earned on the coupons depends on the yield available when the coupons are received.

When bonds are be held to maturity they generate an actual yield to maturity whereas the market yield is a theoretical yield to maturity. We commence this section by explaining the difference between these concepts.

Market yield

The market yield is a rate of return based on a bond's future payments and its purchase price. It can be represented by a more formal form of equation (11.5) that separately shows the elements of a bond's future payments, as follows:

$$r = \left[\left(\frac{S_{coupons} + F}{P}\right)^{1/n} - 1\right]2 \qquad \textit{Equation (11.5a)}$$

where $S_{coupons}$ refers to the accumulated value of the coupons at maturity,
F refers to the redemption payment at maturity, and
n refers to the number of coupon periods between settlement and maturity.

Being a basic formula, equation (11.5a) assumes the bond is purchased on a coupon date. The expression is multiplied by two because the power (1/n) establishes a per coupon-period return.

Recall from Chapter 5 that $S_{coupons}$ is the accumulated value of the coupon stream. This includes the sum of their absolute value and the interest earned from their reinvestment, on a semi-annual compound basis. The formula for $S_{coupons}$ is:

$$S_{coupons} = C\left[\frac{(1 + r/2)^n - 1}{r/2}\right] \qquad \textit{Equation (5.1)}$$

We can display the elements of the market yield as a theoretical yield to maturity with the example used above in the discussion of the cost of funds. This involves the 12% July 1999 Treasury bond that was purchased on 15 January 1995 at a market yield of 8.40%. The accumulated value of the coupons is based on the market yield:

$$S_{coupons} = 6.00\left[\frac{(1.042)^9 - 1}{0.042}\right]$$

$$= \$64.0195$$

Hence the value of the bond's future payments is shown in the numerator of equation (11.5a), as follows, along with the cost of the investment, shown in the denominator:

$$r = \left[\left(\frac{100.000 + 64.0195}{113.2625}\right)^{1/9} - 1\right]2$$

$$= 8.40\%$$

Actual yield to maturity

Market yields are theoretical yields to maturity because they value the interest on the coupon stream at the current yield, rather than on the yields at which these future payments are invested. An actual yield to maturity uses the yields at which the coupons are reinvested.

The market yield might be used as a benchmark to assess the actual yield to maturity. Should future yields be less than a bond's purchase yield, and the bond is held to maturity, its actual yield to maturity will be less than the purchase yield, and vice versa when actual yields are higher.

Because future yields are unknown at the time a bond is purchased, the interest on the coupons, and thus, the yield to maturity on bonds, are uncertain and subject to **reinvestment risk**. This term refers to the risk that the actual yield to maturity will vary from the purchase yield. The level of this risk depends on the term of the bond (given the variability of market yields).

Bonds with few remaining coupons are not greatly exposed to reinvestment risk. In their case, purchase yields are likely to be similar to actual yields to maturity. Bonds with many remaining coupon payments are more exposed to this risk, and their actual yield to maturity can vary significantly from their purchase yield.

To illustrate the effect of coupons being invested at a yield different from the bond's purchase yield, consider a ten-year 12.00% bond that was purchased at a yield of 8.00%. Rates fell to 6.00% for the balance of its term. The purchase price of the bond was:

$$P = 6.00\left[\frac{1 - (1.04)^{-20}}{1.04}\right] + \frac{100}{(1.04)^{20}}$$

$$= 81.5420 + 45.6387$$

$$= \$127.1807$$

The accumulated value of the coupons is:

$$S_{coupons} = 6.00\left[\frac{(1.03)^{20} - 0}{0.03}\right]$$

$$= \$161.2222$$

At maturity, the coupons and the face value ($100) are worth $261.2222 and the bond's purchase price was $127.1807. Therefore the semi-annual return over the ten years is:

$$r = \left[\left(\frac{161.2222 + 100.00}{127.1807}\right)^{1/20} - 1\right]2$$

$$= 0.0733 \text{ or } 7.33\% \text{ p.a.}$$

Had this been a two-year bond, its actual yield to maturity, all other things being equal, would have been:

$$r = \left[\left(\frac{25.1018 + 100.00}{107.2598}\right)^{1/4} - 1\right]2$$

$$= 0.0784 \text{ or } 7.84\% \text{ p.a.}$$

Example 11.3 shows the three elements of the returns from holding to maturity for a two-year and a ten-year bond using two interest-rate scenarios. It demonstrates how a subsequent fall in market yields reduces the yield to maturity for bonds (compared with their purchase yield).

The relationship between yields and the length of a security's term is discussed further in Chapter 15.

example 11.3

The elements of the yield to maturity for a two-year and a ten-year 10.00% bond, when the purchase yield is 10.00% p.a. and the subsequent market yield is, first, 10.00%, and second, 9.00%, are:

Coupons invested at 10.00% p.a.

	2-year bond	10-year bond
Purchase price[1]	100.0000	100.0000
Coupons received[2]	20.0000	100.0000
Interest on coupons[3]	1.5506	65.3298
Accumulated value of coupons[4]	21.5506	165.3298
Redemption value of bond	100.0000	100.0000
Total income at maturity[5]	121.5506	265.3298
Yield to maturity[6]	10.00%	10.00%

Coupons invested at 9.00% p.a.

	2-year bond	10-year bond
Purchase price	100.0000	100.0000
Coupons received	20.0000	100.0000
Interest on coupons	1.3910	56.8571
Total value of coupons	21.3910	156.8571
Redemption value	100.0000	100.0000
Total income at maturity	121.3910	256.8571
Yield to maturity	9.93%	9.66%

Reinvestment of the coupons at 9% p.a. rather than 10% p.a. reduces the future value of the coupons of the two-year bond by only $0.16; whereas, it reduces the future value of the coupons of the ten-year bond by $8.47. As a result, the actual yield to maturity (on a semi-annual compound basis) for both bonds is less than their purchase yields. However, this reduction is greater for 10-year bond (9.66% p.a.) than for the two-year bond (9.93% p.a.).

1 Per $100 of face value
2 Two-year bond = 4*5 = $20; 10-year bond = 20*5 = $100
3 The difference between the accumulated value of the coupons and their absolute value
4 Calculated using equation (5.1)
5 Sum of the previous two amounts
6 Calculated using equation (11.5a)

Holding-period yield

A holding-period yield is a special case of the actual yield to maturity. Both are calculated, in the case of bonds, on a semi-annual compound basis. The only point of difference between them is that the bond's redemption payment forms part of the yield to maturity, whereas the bond's sale price forms part of a holding-period yield. Consequently, the elements of a holding-period yield are:

- the coupons received,
- the interest earned on these coupons, and
- the sale price of the bond.

Note that the sale price of the bond is unknown when the bond is purchased, whereas its redemption payment is known. It follows that holding-period yields are more uncertain than actual yields to maturity.

The general formula for calculating a holding-period yield is presented as equation (11.5b):

$$r_{HPY} = \left[\left(\frac{S_{coupons} + P_{sale}}{P_{buy}}\right)^{1/n} - 1\right]2 \qquad \textit{Equation (11.5b)}$$

We illustrate the application of the basic holding-period yield formula, equation (11.5b), for an investment in 9.50% August 2003 Treasury bonds, purchased on 15 February 1998 and sold exactly eighteen months later. These dates are shown in figure 11.6, along with the relevant number of coupon periods to form the bond and the holding period.

We further assume that the bond was purchased at a yield of 9.20% p.a., and that the market yield fell to 8.00% p.a. several months thereafter and remained at that rate until the bond was sold. Consequently, we can calculate its purchase price, the future value of the coupons received during the holding period and the proceeds when selling the bond, as follows.

The bond purchase price was:

$$P_{buy} = 4.75\left[\frac{1-(1.046)^{-11}}{0.046}\right] + \frac{100}{(1.046)^{11}}$$

$$= \$101.2726$$

The bond sale price is:

$$P_{sell} = 4.75\left[\frac{1-(1.04)^{-8}}{0.04}\right] + \frac{100}{(1.04)^{8}}$$

$$= \$105.0496$$

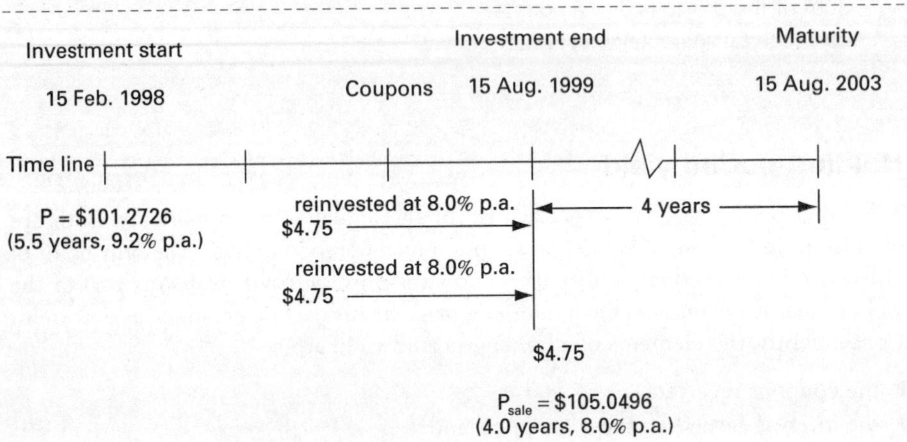

Figure 11.6 **Time line for holding-period yield calculation**

The value of the reinvested coupons is:

$$S_{coupons} = 4.75\left[\frac{(1.04)^3 - 1}{0.04}\right]$$

$$= \$14.8276$$

Consequently, the holding-period yield is:

$$r_{HPY} = \left[\left(\frac{14.8276 + 105.0496}{101.2726}\right)^{1/3} - 1\right]2$$

$$= 11.57\%\ \text{p.a.}$$

The holding-period yield was neither the purchase yield (9.20% p.a.), nor the yield (8.00% p.a.) at which the coupons were invested and the bond sold. In this case, the holding-period yield exceeded the purchase yield as a result of several partially offsetting factors. The investment:

- achieved a capital gain because of the effect on the bond's price of purchasing it at 9.20% p.a. and selling it at 8.00% p.a., and
- generated a lower-than-expected return on investment of the coupons, as they were reinvested at 8.00% p.a. rather than 9.20% p.a. Given the small number of coupons received during the holding period, this effect was not great and was outweighed by the capital gain.

As noted in the previous chapter, attempting to buy bonds before an expected fall in their yield is a traditional holding-period strategy. In general, bond traders, who hold bonds for short periods, suffer losses when bond yields are rising and make profits when yields are falling. This also applies to managed funds that are mainly invested in bonds. Their market value rises when bond yields fall, and vice versa.

When investors hold bonds for a long period, the coupon reinvestment effect is more important in determining the actual yield. These investors will achieve better earnings if reinvestment yields increase during the holding period. Of course, long-term investors will make lower earnings when the opposite occurs.

It is worth noting that a bond held to maturity cannot produce an unexpected capital gain or loss because the bond is redeemed at its known face value. Thus, for a bond held to maturity, increases in yields (above the purchase yield) will increase reinvestment return without any offsetting capital loss.

We discuss factors that influence the movement in yields/interest rates in Chapter 14. The differences in market risks and returns, for securities with different terms, are explored in Chapters 15 and 16.

Other bonds

In this chapter we emphasise Treasury fixed-rate bonds because of their dominance in the primary and secondary markets. We now briefly consider floating-rate instruments, which currently appear to be developing a larger role in the debt-capital market. Some States have developed programs of floating-rate securities and the Commonwealth introduced its adjustable-rate bonds in 1994. The private sector, especially through the development of mortgage-backed bonds, has also become a more important issuer of floating-rate securities.

Floating-rate bonds provide their issuer and holders with a different exposure to movements in interest rates. From the issuer's viewpoint, the cost of funds moves in conjunction with movements in market yields. The cost of funds raised by a fixed-rate security is set by the issue yield. Whilst floating-rate payers benefit when yields fall, they face higher rates when yields rise.

In the secondary market, the prices of floating-rate bonds are less sensitive to movements in yields than those of fixed-rate bonds. Typically, floating-rate securities pay quarterly coupons based on the prevailing marker yield (such as BBR). The value of a floating-rate note returns to par as the floating rate is reset to the prevailing rate on each coupon date. As its value will be at par on each coupon date, the value of a floating-rate security will not vary much from par.

The relative price stability of a floating-rate security contrasts to that of a fixed-interest bond. A bond's value is on the other side on the see-saw with its market yield. Should its yield be volatile, so too will be its value. This represents a much greater exposure to 'price' risk than for floating-rate securities.

Borrowers may prefer exposure to floating rates when, for instance, their income rises and falls with the level of interest rates, allowing them to cope with an increase in their cost of funds. Other borrowers may prefer fixed-rate obligations. Borrowers are likely to have a preference over the form of securities they issue. Similarly, investors/lenders will have a preference between fixed- and floating-rate securities. We discuss these preferences and the strategies available for managing the various interest-rate risks in Parts four and five.

In the section to follow, we describe (in some cases rather briefly) these floating-rate securities, along with zeros (which are an odd form of a fixed-rate security) and retail bonds (which also are issued on a fixed-rate basis).

The Commonwealth issues (as at mid 1995) two other types of bonds in the domestic bond market: adjustable-rate bonds (TABs) and capital-indexed bonds (TIBs). The former were first issued in November 1994, whereas the latter were issued in the 1980s before being reintroduced in February 1993.

Treasury adjustable-rate bonds

Treasury adjustable-rate bonds are medium-term, floating-rate notes. Their initial issue had a term of approximately three years and consideration is being given to the issue of five-year TABs. These are medium terms within this market. The coupons on the initial three-year TABs are paid quarterly, at a rate that is related to the bank-bill rate less 15 basis points.

The purpose of TABs is 'to meet the Commonwealth's portfolio management objectives for floating-rate exposure and this will reduce the Commonwealth's need to issue Treasury notes'. (Hinton, 1995, p. 5) As indicated in the previous chapter, the outstanding amount of Treasury notes during the first half of the 1990s rarely fell below $13 billion.

The Commonwealth's reliance on TABs depends on the level of their market demand. A TAB is equivalent to a rolled-over investment in Treasury notes. To a degree, TABs will compete with Treasury notes. The market for Treasury notes is relatively limited, depending primarily on the demand from banks for prime assets. Given the development of other floating-rate notes/bonds in the Australian market, it is likely that there will be broader demand for TABs.

The initial issues of TABs were made to a management group but the Commonwealth expects to make future issues through its tender process. Under the tender-issue process, the authorities will provide details of:

- each series of TABs for which bids will be invited,
- the amount to be offered of each series,
- the date and amount of the first interest payment and the date of subsequent interest payments and coupon resets,
- the coupon expressed as a margin to the interest-setting index;
- the closing time and date for bids, and
- the settlement arrangements. (Commonwealth of Australia, *Prospectus, Treasury bonds*, p. 2)

The minimum parcel size of the competitive bids at tender for TABs is five $100 000 (face-value) TABs.

Treasury indexed bonds

The return on a financial instrument, while quoted as a **nominal rate**, should be assessed in real terms (i.e. at the after-inflation rate of return). This indicates the increase in purchasing power provided by an investment. For example, a nominal yield of 10.00% p.a., when the inflation rate is 4.0% p.a., provides a real return of 6.00% p.a.

Logically, investors make their decisions on the basis of expected real, rather than expected nominal rates. In the early 1980s, the Cambell Committee recommended that the Australian Government issue securities that, by their nature, protect the investor from unanticipated changes in inflation. The response of the government was to issue two new **indexed securities**, Commonwealth interest-indexed and capital-indexed bonds.

Both of these bonds pay quarterly coupons that are linked to the quarterly release of the Consumer Price Index (CPI). The rate of inflation is defined as an average of the rate of increase of the CPI over two previous quarters for the purpose of the indexed bond.

Capital- and interest-indexed bonds were first issued in 1985. However the investor response to their release was unspectacular and gradually the Commonwealth phased out their issue. Interest in indexed bonds reemerged in the early 1990s and the Commonwealth is again issuing capital-indexed bonds.

Both the interest-indexed and capital-indexed bonds protect the holder against the effect of inflation. However, the method of protection differs between the two bonds. The interest-indexed bond pays a nominal coupon each quarter that is defined as a fixed real coupon rate plus the inflation rate prevailing at the time. The capital-indexed bond pays a fixed, real coupon rate on a face value that is indexed to the rate of inflation. The data in table 11.6 show the cash flows emanating from two-year bonds, both offering a real coupon rate of 4% p.a., for inflation rates of 8.00 and 12.00%.

The coupons of the interest-indexed bonds are one quarter of the real coupon rate of 4% p.a. plus a quarter of the annual inflation rate prevailing during the coupon period. For example, the first quarter coupon is $1 (being a quarter of the real coupon rate per annum) plus $2 (being a quarter of the annual inflation rate).

The capital-indexed bond pays each quarter a coupon based on the real coupon rate of 4% p.a. on a capital value that grows with inflation. For example, the capital value increased by 2% for the first quarter (being a quarter of the annual inflation rate) and the coupon rate was one quarter of 4% of $102.00.

At redemption the interest-indexed bond pays a face value of $100, whereas the capital-indexed bond pays the holder the inflation-adjusted capital value of $121.83.

Both bonds in table 11.6 provide the holder with a fixed real return of 4% p.a., ignoring coupon reinvestment. However, the method of compensating the holder for inflation differs. The interest-indexed bond compensates the holder for inflation during the life of the security with increases in the value of coupons received. In contrast, the capital-indexed bond, while providing an increased coupon stream, mainly compensates the holder for inflation with an increase in the bond's redemption value.

Table 11.6 4.00% p.a. real-rate indexed bonds — cash flows

Inflation rate (% p.a.)		Interest-indexed bond		Capital-indexed bonds	
		Face value	Coupons	Face value	Coupons
1	8.00	100.00	3.0000	102.00	1.0200
2	8.00	100.00	3.0000	104.04	1.0404
3	8.00	100.00	3.0000	106.12	1.0612
4	8.00	100.00	3.0000	108.24	1.0824
5	12.00	100.00	4.0000	111.49	1.1149
6	12.00	100.00	4.0000	114.84	1.1484
7	12.00	100.00	4.0000	118.28	1.1828
8	12.00	100.00	4.0000	121.83	1.2183

Corporate bonds

As noted in this chapter's introduction, corporate bonds, those issued by companies, have not established an important role within the Australian debt-capital market. Most potential issuers tend to issue in overseas markets. The only important development in the corporate bond market relates to securitised assets, which are the subject of the following section.

Austraclear and Standard & Poor's data for 1995 indicate that a number of banks, NBFIs, and a small number of companies, including publicly owned ones, constitute the corporate bond market in Australia. They have issued mainly floating-rate notes that have medium terms.

AFMA survey data (Financial Products Research Group, 1994, p. 12) indicate that turnover of corporate bonds (including those issued under asset securitisation programs) in the secondary market was only $29 billion during the year ending June 1994. This represented only 1.5% of the total market turnover of $1963 billion in the bond market.

Asset-backed securities

Asset-backed securities are issued in order to securitise assets that would otherwise be held on the balance sheets of financial institutions and other businesses. In Australia, most of the asset-backed securities that have been issued securitise home mortgages and are known as **mortgage-backed securities**. Other securitised assets include commercial mortgages, accounts receivable and lease receivables.

As explained in Chapter 6, assets, such as housing loans, are conventionally created when a bank (or other financial institution) approves (i.e. originates) these loans. The institution manages the asset (i.e. accepts the credit risk and collects the loan payments) and finances it through intermediation (i.e. from its deposits and other forms of borrowing). The institution also accepts the interest-rate and other risks associated with holding such assets.

The process of securitisation has to ensure that all of the above functions are performed, even though it merely represents an alternative way of financing assets. Essentially, it uses the capital market (i.e. direct financing) to finance assets rather than intermediated funds.

The development of securitisation has created an additional asset/liability management tool for retail banks (and other 'loan originators') which allows them to decide whether or not to hold (and fund) assets such as housing loans or hold asset-backed securities. Because financial institutions could sell such assets to one another, securitisation is an arrangement that extends beyond the simple sale of an asset.

In broad terms, securitisation converts (i.e. 'passes through') the cash flows from loans (we will use housing loans as our standard example) into the payments made by securities. It involves the creation of securities that ultimately serve to finance the loans. The securities themselves serve to develop the debt-capital market by giving investors wider investment choices.

The process of securitising housing loans was shown in figure 6.2 in Chapter 6 and is reproduced here as figure 11.7. A pool of 'approved' housing loans (i.e. loans that were made on an approved basis, the main condition being that the loans are for amounts that are less than a specified proportion of the value of the property) is established, which produces a flow of regular payments, from the 'borrowers' box in figure 11.7. These payments are at an interest rate that is greater than that paid out to security holders (shown in the right-hand box). The proceeds of the issue of the securities are used to fund the housing loans (i.e. they flow in the reverse direction to the loan payments). The interest-rate spread is used to meet the fees of the parties involved in the securitisation process. These parties are depicted by the central box in figure 11.7.

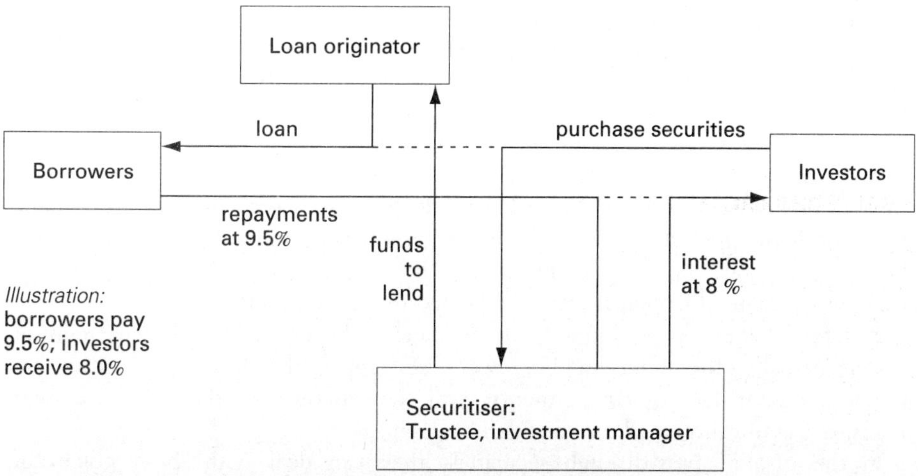

Figure 11.7 Loan originators and securitisation of housing loans

In broad terms, the securitisation of housing loans involves the following functions:

- the creation of a pool of approved mortgage loans. This function is performed by 'loan originators'. They could be financial institutions, such as retail banks, other financial institutions (such as insurance offices) or loan-originator specialists, such as Aussie Home Loans. They may also be engaged to service the loans, in the same way that a bank services its housing-loan customers;
- the issue of the mortgage-backed securities and the management of the cash flows associated with the securitised loans. This dual function is the responsibility of a trustee who typically engages a fund manager, such as an investment bank, to actually perform them. The trustee merely ensures that the functions are performed. A number of other participants are usually engaged to carry out the various aspects of the management of the securitisation process, such as credit enhancement, the sale of the securities and the establishment of a secondary market for them.

The management of the cash flows is a major function, partly because the timing of the payments by borrowers does not usually correspond with the payments to security holders, and partly because the payments by borrowers include both an interest and a principal repayment component and usually borrowers have the option to make unscheduled principal repayments.

The precise arrangements for each securitisation program are more complex than outlined above and vary according to the type of security issued. Provision must be made for servicing the housing loans and the management of their underlying default risk. Forms of credit enhancement are usually arranged, such as mortgage insurance, and access to standby funds (i.e. cash) is arranged to cover any shortfall in the cash flows resulting from defaults.

The fund manager may engage other parties to participate in the sale of the securities and in the management of the interest-rate risk involved in the securitisation process.

These securities are rated prior to their sale. Because of the low credit risk associated with home mortgages and the credit enhancement of the cash flows, mortgage-backed securities can receive very high credit ratings, including AAA. This serves to reduce the interest rate they pay when issued.

In Australia, mortgage-backed securities tend to be floating-rate bonds because most of the underlying loans are made on a floating-rate basis. This serves to reduce the underlying interest-rate risk of such securities. They generally have a very long term (e.g. 25 years), again reflecting the cash flows of the underlying assets, although early repayments of principal can be expected to shorten their life.

As inferred above, provision needs to be made for handling the early repayment of loan principal by the underlying borrowers. One approach is to issue securities that undertake to make regular payments until they mature. In this case, the fund manager has to reinvest all unscheduled payments.

In the case of pass-through securities, they can deal with the problem of unscheduled payments by being issued in **tranches** (separate classes of securities) that segregate the treatment of unscheduled payments, as well as establishing a priority order for payments generally. The payment rules for each tranche influence the level of their issue yield because they help to increase 'the certainty of the pattern of the cash flows the investor would receive'. (Midanek and Midanek, 1994, p. 29)

Mortgage-backed securities play an important role in the USA and this experience is often cited as the basis for the expected growth of such securities in Australia. However, there are important differences between the mortgage markets in the USA and in Australia which led to the earlier development of mortgage-backed securities in the USA. One of these differences is that the US Government supports the mortgage-backed securities market. This is provided through government-supported agencies, which have become popularly known as Fannie Mae (The Federal National Mortgage Association), Ginnie Mae (Government National Mortgage Association) and Freddie Mac (Federal Home Loan Mortgage Corporation). (Fabozzi, Modigliani and Ferri, 1994, pp. 480–2)

Asset-backed securities in Australia will become a sustainable component of the capital market only if:

- their risk/return profile is competitive with other securities, given their uncertain payment flows, and
- they provide finance at competitive rates for the assets they seek to securitise.

According to a survey of participants in this market, conducted by O'Connell (1994), the cost of securitisation arrangements is regarded as a major impediment to their development. However, the survey suggested that investor demand for these securities was strong and investors have developed an understanding of the characteristics of these securities.

As noted in Chapter 6, an analysis by Harding (1994) concluded that non-retail-bank mortgage originators will substantially increase their market share, to possibly 50%, by the year 2000. Given that many of these mortgage originators will be financed through securitisation, this prediction implies that over $100 billion worth of mortgage-backed securities will then be on issue. Should an active secondary market develop for these securities, they would accordingly play an important role in both the primary and secondary debt-capital markets.

As at mid 1995, the major two issuers of mortgage-backed securities are PUMA Sub-Funds and FANMAC Ltd, the former being an independently operating subsidiary of Macquarie Bank and the latter being part-owned and guaranteed by the NSW Government. (See example 11.4.) The major banks have begun to develop securitisation units and it appears that concerns about the RBA's prudential requirements in relation to securitisation have eased. As a consequence, this segment of the capital market appears set to grow significantly. (Standard & Poor's, 1995, pp. 5–7)

example 11.4

In June 1995 PUMA Management Limited issued $650 million worth of mortgage-backed bonds in four tranches:

- 1F, which pays fixed-rate coupons for three years and thereafter pays floating-rate quarterly coupons, and
- 2, 3 and 4, which pay floating-rate quarterly coupons.

Tranche 4 bonds are subordinated in relation to the other three tranches. This means that no payments are made to holders of the fourth tranche while ever payments are due to holders of the first three tranches. Whereas the first three are rated AAA, tranche 4 is rated AA-. The coupons are paid in arrears (i.e. at the end of the coupon periods) at rates based on the BBR. For example, the floating-rate for tranche 1F bonds is 35 basis points above BBR. The margin over BBR is greater for the fourth tranche than for the other three.

Each bond has a face value of $10 000, but they were issued in minimum parcels of $1 million. They mature in April 2020, but are likely to be redeemed early because of principal-reduction payments by borrowers. Each is a pass-through bond, although for the first three years only interest payments will be passed through. Thereafter, the coupons amortise the bonds. Provision has been made for the pass through of unscheduled principal repayments on a sequential basis, starting with tranche 1F.

Most of the bonds (90%) are in tranche 1F and 2. They were issued by a lead manager (Bain Capital Markets Limited) with assistance from a co-manager (Macquarie Bank Limited). Both are required to assist in the development of a secondary market for the securities.

Zero-coupon bonds

A zero-coupon bond, known also as a **zero**, is a bond that pays no coupons. These play an important role in the debt-capital market in the United States but are not widely issued in the Australian market. However, the concept of a zero has importance in all debt-capital markets and we will explain this role in Chapter 15.

The price of a zero is given by setting the coupon amount in equation (11.1) to zero.

$$P = \frac{F}{(1 + r/2)^n}$$

where r is the per annum yield, on a semi-annual compound basis, and
n is the number of coupon periods to maturity (or part thereof).

Even though a zero is, in effect, a discount security, its long term means that it is priced as a bond, using the interest-rate measure that is appropriate to the bond market — semi-annual compounding. (See example 11.5.)

example 11.5

Calculate the price of a zero-coupon bond that is five years and two months (i.e. 10.3333 semi-annual periods) from maturity if the yield on this bond is 8% p.a. The price per $100 of face value is:

$$P = \frac{100}{(1.04)^{10.3333}}$$

$$= \$66.6790$$

In the United States, zeros have either an impeccable credit standing or are unrated because of their inferior credit standing. The former arise from the stripping of coupons from large parcels of US Treasury bonds. The cash proceeds of the coupons are passed through a trust as the face value of a sequence of zeros, the terms being based on the payment date of the coupons. The redemption payment on the Treasury bond also forms a zero that has a term based on the bond's maturity date. These securities are actively traded in the US market, partly for risk-management purposes. We discuss this role of zeros in Chapter 16.

The zeros with an inferior credit standing form part of the **junk bond** market. Because of their higher default rate, their yields are higher than for investment-grade bonds. The other types of bonds in this market include **deferred-coupon bonds**, **step-up bonds** (i.e. the coupon rate increases during their term) and **payment-in-kind bonds** (which is a reinvestment-type bond). (Fabozzi, Modigliani and Ferri, p. 429)

These bonds either begin life in the junk-bond market (where they provide finance that would otherwise be borrowed from a financial institution) or fall into it because of a deterioration in the financial position of the issuer. These are known as 'fallen angels'. In the late 1980s, they experienced a higher than expected default rate and investor demand consequently fell. However, subsequent experience with these bonds has restored their place in the US market.

Convertible notes

Generally a clear distinction can be made between debt and equity securities. However, there are a number of hybrid securities that combine features of both debt and equity. Some hybrids begin life as debt instruments and can be converted to equity capital, such as **convertible unsecured notes**; whereas others are equity instruments but have features normally associated with debt instruments, such as redeemable preference shares (which are discussed in the next chapter).

Convertible unsecured notes are issued as debt-capital instruments that can be converted to shares at the discretion of their holder during specified periods (and on specified terms) before they mature. An unsecured note is a low-priority debt instrument that would normally be issued at a higher yield (for a given issuer and term) than a secured instrument; but when it is issued as a convertible note, the issuer is providing the subscribers with an option to convert and this enhances the value of the security. Hence the convertibility feature serves to lower the issue yield. But this feature is not without cost to the issuer. Such notes reduce the issuer's control over its capital structure. If the debtholders convert, the issuer's debt-to-equity ratio falls, but the issuer cannot ensure that this will occur, given that convertibility is at the option of the holders of the notes.

Convertible unsecured notes can be issued by way of private placements to parties who are either associated with their issuer or are regarded as being good potential shareholders. They are attractive to investors who are potential shareholders of the issuer because of the convertibility feature. However, should the issuer's financial position deteriorate unexpectedly, their holders are not required to convert the notes to shares.

The determination of their issue yield is based on the credit risk of the notes (given that they may not be converted to equity capital) and the value of the convertible option. We discuss the principles of option pricing in Chapter 19. In essence, the value of this option depends on the probability that the terms for conversion (such as the effective price of the shares) will become profitable to the holder of the notes.

Retail bonds

As noted previously, banks issue bonds to retail customers, usually on a fixed-coupon-rate basis for medium terms, and undertake to buy them back before they mature at the prevailing market yield. The RBA also sells Treasury bonds in retail amounts and will repurchase them at the prevailing yield.

Finance companies have been the major issuer of retail fixed-interest securities. They are more generally known as debentures. Whereas banks are able to issue retail bonds without a prospectus and are not required to issue under the restrictive terms of a trust deed, when they issue debentures finance companies must meet these requirements.

The rationale for the restrictions on the issue of debentures is that retail subscribers are not in a position to evaluate the credit standing of the issuer without the benefit of an approved prospectus and they are not in a position to enforce the conditions of a loan without the assistance of a trustee and a trust deed.

Despite the greater issuing cost represented by a prospectus and the security (e.g. a charge over assets), and restrictions imposed on the borrower by a trust deed (such as covenants that limit the issuer's overall level of borrowing), finance companies have continued to raise substantial amounts through debenture issues.

Summary

The main points of this chapter are as follows:

- Bonds are long-term securities that, except for zeros, make payments during their life.
- The Treasury fixed-rate bond is the dominant instrument in the Australian debt-capital market.
- Collectively, the States are the next most important issuer of bonds.
- Treasury bonds on issue have a range of maturity dates, which are being concentrated into hot or benchmark series.
- Treasury bonds are issued through a competitive tender system by the RBA, which also administers the secondary market (through RITS).
- Fixed-rate bonds trade at yields, which are used to calculate their price on settlement dates.
- Bond prices vary inversely with their market yield, and the price variation is greater, for a given change in yield, for long-term than for short-dated securities.

- Fixed-rate bond values reflect the accumulation of interest during ex-interest dates.
- Actual yields to maturity are subject to reinvestment risk.
- Holding-period yields are subject to general market risk.
- Floating-rate bonds are issued by governments and companies to provide an alternative interest-rate exposure to fixed-rate bonds.
- Mortgage-backed (i.e. flow-through) securities appear to be emerging as an important security in Australia's debt-capital market.

Discussion questions and exercises

1 Discuss the features of Treasury bonds and the structure of the bond series (i.e. their maturity dates and coupon rates) on issue. Briefly explain the reason for concentrating Treasury bonds into 'hot' series and the factors that determine the amount of new issues of Treasury bonds during a year.

2 Briefly describe the fall and rise of semis.

3 Discuss the operation of the primary market for Treasury bonds and present some evidence on the depth of the secondary market.

4 Compare the trading and settlement practices in the primary markets for Treasury and semi-governmental bonds. Refer to the role of ratings agencies in these markets.

5 Discuss the major factors that determine a bond's rating and the consequences of a security's rating.

6 'A bond's price is equal to the present value of its remaining payments.' Explain with reference to equation (11.1). Also show how equations (11.1) and (11.2) are equivalent.

7 What is meant by the T+3 settlement convention and how does it influence the pricing of Treasury bonds?

8 Assuming it is 15 January 1998, calculate:
   (a) the number of coupons remaining for the (i) 12.00% July 1999, (ii) 8.75% January 2001; and (iii) 7.50% July 2005 Treasury bonds,
   (b) the present-value annuity factor for the bonds listed in the previous question, assuming that on 15 January 1998 the market yield for each bond was 8.80% p.a.,
   (c) the present value of the remaining coupons for the bonds listed in (a),
   (d) the present value of the redemption payment for each of the bonds referred to above, and
   (e) the price of these bonds.

9 Calculate the settlement price (per $100 of face value) of the 10.00% October 2007 Treasury bond on 15 October 1997, assuming it was purchased at a yield of (a) 9.50% p.a.; (b) 10.00% p.a.; and (c) 10.60% p.a.

10 Explain what is meant by bonds trading at a premium, at par or at a discount. Refer to the prices in the previous question to illustrate your answer.

11 What is meant by cum-interest and ex-interest pricing? Explain the movement in a bond's price between ex-interest dates, assuming other variables remain unchanged.

12 (a) Describe the three-step process for pricing bonds on cum-interest dates and calculate:

(b) the present-value annuity factor that would be used in step 1 when pricing the 10.00% February 2006 Treasury bond on 20 March 1996 and 20 September 1998, assuming a purchased yield of 9.40% p.a. on both dates,
(c) the value of the bond as at the first coupon date following the two purchase dates,
(d) the discount factor that is used (in step 3) to determine the two cum-interest settlement prices, and
(e) the prices, per $100 of face value, for the bond at the two settlement dates.

13 Calculate the price of the 10.00% February 2006 Treasury bond on 12 February 1996, assuming it was purchased at a yield of 8.60% p.a.

14 Calculate the price of the 10.00% February 2006 Treasury bond on (a) 15 February 1996; (b) 15 February 1999; and (c) 15 February 2003, assuming on each occasion that the purchase yield was 9.60% p.a.

15 How and why is a holder of a Treasury bond exposed to price risk? Compare the price risk for two-year and ten-year Treasury bonds.

16 Suppose the RBA issued some 9.00% September 2004 bonds with a settlement date of 15 September 1997. What determines the cost of the funds raised and how much will be raised per bond if the market yield is 9.40% p.a?

17 What are the elements of an actual yield to maturity? Calculate:
(a) the future value of the coupons that an investor in the 7.50% July 2005 Treasury bond will receive, having purchased the bond on 15 January 1996 at a yield of 8.20%, and held it to maturity, assuming the market yield remains stable at 8.20% p.a.
(b) the sum of the coupons and the sum of the interest earned on their reinvestment, and
(c) the actual yield to maturity for the investment described in (a).

18 Compare the elements of a holding-period yield and a yield to maturity in the case of bonds. Explain why an investor who buys a bond and holds it to maturity is exposed to reinvestment risk, whereas the yield when the bonds are sold prior to maturity is subject also to price risk.

19 Suppose an investor purchased the 9.00% September 2004 bond on 15 March 1995 and held the bond till 15 September 1998, and that the market yield remained unchanged during the holding period at 8.60% p.a. Calculate the length of the holding period in terms of coupon periods, and the future value of the coupons received during the holding period.

20 Discuss the various floating-rate bonds that are issued in the Australian market.

REFERENCES AND FURTHER READING

AFMA 1994, *Dealing Handbook*, AFMA, Sydney.

Carew, Edna 1993, *How Australia's Fixed Interest Markets Operate*, AFMA, Sydney.

Commonwealth of Australia, *Prospectus, Treasury bonds*, p. 2.

Davis, K.T. 1993, 'Corporate debt markets', in M. K. Lewis & R. H. Wallace (eds), *The Australian Financial System*, Longman Cheshire, Melbourne, pp. 249–81.

Davis, K.T. & Lewis, M. K. 1993, 'Public sector securities markets' in M. K.Lewis & R. H.Wallace (eds), *The Australian Financial System*, Longman Cheshire, Melbourne, pp. 318–57.

Fabozzi, Frank J., Modigliani, Franco, & Ferri, Michael G. 1994, *Foundations of Financial Markets and Institutions*, Prentice-Hall, New Jersey, Chapters 21 and 24.
Financial Products Research Group Pty Ltd, *1994 Australian Financial Markets Report*, AFMA, Sydney, Chapter 2.
Harding, Ian 1994, 'Mortgage originators — the new kids on the block', *Company news % reports*, Bain Securities Research.
Harper, Ian 1995, 'Getting into bonds', in *Agenda*, vol. 2, no. 1, pp 81–92.
Hinton, Tony August 1995, 'Commonwealth Government's 1995–96 Financing Task and Debt Management Strategy, Paper presented to AFMA, Sydney, 1995.
McGrath, Michael 1994, *Financial Institutions, Instruments and Markets in Australia*, McGraw-Hill, Sydney, Chapters 8, 10 and 12.
Midanek, Deborah Hicks, & Midanek, James I. 1995, 'The development of the mortgage-backed securities market: a short history', *Derivatives Quarterly*, Fall, pp. 25–34.
O'Connell, Brendan 1994, 'Securitisation helps and hindrances', *JASSA*, September, pp. 26–9.
RBA November 1993, 'The separation of debt management and monetary policy', *Bulletin*, pp. 1–5.
Standard & Poor's August 1995, 'Securitisation market poised for growth', *Monthly Bulletin Australia & New Zealand*, pp. 5–7.

12

The equities market

Having considered the domestic markets for short-dated and debt-capital instruments in the previous two chapters, we now turn our attention to the market for equity instruments. At their polar extremes, equity instruments differ in nature to debt instruments, as do their markets. The market for equity instruments is organised by an exchange that, through its broker members, serves both wholesale and retail clients; whereas debt instruments are traded by professional dealers in over-the-counter wholesale markets.

Study objectives

From your study of this chapter you should be able to:

- explain the character and purpose of the listing rules of the ASX;
- explain the role of SEATS and CHESS within the operations of the ASX;
- describe the main indicators of the performance of a sharemarket;
- describe the process of, and the reasons for, floating a company;
- describe the process of, and the reasons for, a rights issue;
- calculate the theoretical value of rights from the terms of the issue;
- calculate the theoretical ex-rights price and explain its relationship to the value of the rights;
- explain the theoretical impact of a rights issue on the wealth and asset portfolio of shareholders;
- explain the process of and the reasons for the private placement of shares;
- describe the features of ordinary and the various preference shares;
- explain the role of a company's expected future earnings and dividends in determining its shareprice.

Introduction

In Chapter 1 we briefly described the nature of equity capital and distinguished it from debt capital. The most important point is that equity instruments represent ownership of a company, even when it is a minute share of its ownership.

The holders of equity instruments are entitled to a share in the company's earnings after tax and interest, which is paid in the form of dividends, and to a share in its net worth (should the company be liquidated). Despite the possibility of liquidation, most companies aim to operate indefinitely. Shares are therefore generally viewed as perpetual securities, whereas most debt instruments have a set term, when they must be redeemed.

Whereas the suppliers of debt capital are external to the business, shareholders, being owners, are entitled to vote at shareholders' meetings (on the basis of one vote per share owned) and participate in the election of the company's board of directors. Voting rights therefore form part of the entitlements of a shareholder that are not shared by debtholders.

A company's board of directors has the responsibility of ensuring that its management serves the objective of maximising shareholder wealth. A fundamental feature of the company form of business is the separation of management from ownership. The board of directors does not conduct the company's business: this is entrusted to professional managers who are hired by the board. Consequently, the suppliers of a company's equity capital normally have no say in its operating policies. Should they be dissatisfied with the performance of the company's managers, they can either sell their shares or encourage the board to change the management or their policies.

You will recall that the basic equity instrument is called an 'ordinary share', or 'common stock'. The latter term is derived from the initial corporate form: joint-stock companies that were formed in London in the 16th century. The first such company, the Russia Company, was formed in 1553 and raised £6000 (by selling 1200 shares at £5 each) to fund an expedition to find the north-east passage to the Orient. Following the establishment of further joint-stock companies, such as the Hudson Bay Company and the more descriptively named, 'Expedition in Search of Gold and Associated Treasures into East India', trading in common stock was conducted in a number of London coffee houses and in 1773, one of these establishments, New Jonathon's, near Change Alley, became known as the London Stock Exchange. (Bennetts, 1995, pp. 3–4)

Australian Stock Exchange

Australia's first stock exchange was established in Sydney in 1838 and turnover increased dramatically as a result of the 1850s gold boom. Moreover, other exchanges were established in provincial cities, near the sites of mineral discoveries and other centres of rapid economic development.

Over time, trading activity declined at the regional exchanges and an increasing proportion of trading was conducted by the Sydney and Melbourne exchanges, with smaller levels of turnover at the exchanges in the other State capitals. In 1937 the exchanges located in the then six State capitals formed an association as a national policy-making body. The Australian Stock Exchange (ASX) was formed on 1 April 1987 by the amalgamation of the exchanges in the State capital cities. The ASX continues to operate its exchanges in the State capital cities, despite the dominance of the Sydney and Melbourne exchanges.

The amalgamation of the exchanges 'came about primarily because of the recognition that the stockmarket is a national market, requiring a single national body to ensure that the industry developed in a cohesive and efficient manner which would compete effectively on an international basis.' (Drake and Stammer, 1993, p. 283)

Its principal function is to organise the efficient and fair trading in company securities. While it functions as a secondary market, the ASX facilitates the issue of new securities and its listing (and other) rules influence the operation of the primary market. Whereas Australia's exchanges historically organised trading in all securities (both debt and equity), almost all trading in debt instruments is now undertaken in the wholesale markets described in the previous two chapters. The ASX is principally concerned with the trading of equity securities (i.e. shares and equity derivatives).

The ASX is a non-profit organisation of broker members. Prior to 1984, the number of members was restricted and confined to non-incorporated businesses. However, the restriction on membership was judged to be anti-competitive and was thus removed.

By the early 1990s, almost all members had become companies, many of which were owned by banks and other financial institutions. Following the 1987 sharemarket crash, the number of members fell from 114 to less than 100. Part of this rationalisation process was the closure by NAB of its broking subsidiary, A.C. Goode, which had been a major broking firm before the deregulation of membership. Despite the large number of members, most trading is conducted by the ten largest brokers. (Drake and Stammer, 1993, pp. 288–91)

Even though the ASX is a member-based organisation, it is also a self-regulatory body that operates under the terms of Commonwealth legislation in association with the Australian Securities Commission (ASC). It has developed rules and regulations governing trading, the listing of companies, the disclosure of information by listed companies and the business conduct of its members. The exchange can censure, fine or dismiss a member who has been found to breach one or more of its rules. It may suspend or delist a company that has failed to comply with its rules.

The ASX has established a market-surveillance program to monitor its members' trading activities. Apparent breaches of trading rules, such as insider trading and market rigging, are referred to the ASC for further investigation and possible prosecution.

The rules of the exchange are overseen by the ASC and are enforceable by the courts. While the rules are backed by Commonwealth legislation, the ASX regards itself as being engaged in self regulation. That is, it establishes and enforces 'rules' rather than 'laws', and while it refers more serious breaches to the ASC, it has certain discretion in the application of its various rules.

Listing rules

The ASX is responsible for the conduct of the market for equity securities. Its listing rules, which are set out in its *Listing Manual*, limit access to the market to substantial public companies. In the early 1990s this was defined as companies that:

- have at least $1 million of issued capital, and
- have at least 500 shareholders, each with, at least, a minimum value of shares. (Drake and Stammers, 1993, pp. 293–4)

Similar rules apply to mining companies, which are listed separately from industrial companies. Mining companies include exploration companies provided they are actually engaged in commercial exploration. As mentioned in Chapter 8, many property trusts are listed on the exchange. They have met the listing rules for such organisations.

The ASX also imposes requirements for the continued listing of companies. These include:

- the provision of six-monthly accounts (within a specified period) that detail the company's financial position (including off-balance sheet items) and provide other information about its activities,
- the provision of immediate notice to the ASX of any change that could materially affect its financial position,
- the immediate reporting of transactions with its directors or associates,
- notifying the exchange of announcements to shareholders concerning matters such as the declaration of a dividend, the acquisition of another company and the issue of new shares. (McGrath, 1994, p. 106)

Again, separate (and more stringent) requirements are imposed on mining companies to keep the exchange informed about matters that are material to their financial position.

The purpose of these rules is to ensure that there is an efficient and fair market for listed shares. This requires a minimum turnover in a company's shares (i.e. a minimum market depth) and the immediate release of information that influences shareprices. The ASX has developed a comprehensive information service that uses the data supplied by listed companies to enhance the information available to the market. This service contributes to the market's efficiency.

Data on the number of companies listed on the exchange over the period 1984 to 1995 are presented in table 12.1. Observe the fall in the number of new listings following the 1987 sharemarket crash and the increase in delistings.

Electronic trading and settlement

The ASX introduced electronic trading and settlement processes in the latter half of the 1980s. These systems replaced the 'open outcry' trading system within the trading floor and largely replaced the previous 'paper-based' system for the transfer of shares. The move to electronic trading matched the trend overseas, such as the Toronto Stock Exchange's Computer Assisted Trading System (CATS), which has

Table 12.1 Companies listed on the ASX, 1984 to 1995

Financial year	*New listings*	*Delistings*	*Total listings*
1984	61	54	1 000
1985	92	36	1 056
1986	145	60	1 141
1987	271	26	1 386
1988	201	77	1 510
1989	53	180	1 302
1990	23	189	1 136
1991	23	154	1 005
1992	176	108	1 073
1993	104	70	1 107
1994	120	41	1 186
1995	45	53	1 178

Source: (to 1988) Drake and Stammer (1993), p. 286; (from 1989) ASX, *1996 Fact Book*

provided a model for electronic trading in a number of European countries. (Fabozzi, Modigliani and Ferri, 1994, pp. 390–2)

Trading on the ASX is conducted through SEATS, the Stock Exchange Automated Trading System. It was introduced in October 1987 (coincidentally, the day before the 1987 sharemarket crash) and extended to cover all trading three years later.

SEATS applies the principle of priority trading, where orders are ranked in priority of price and then in time within price. That is, the highest-priced buy orders and lowest-priced sell orders are matched first. Bids and offers are immediately entered into the system and, if no matching orders exist, are displayed on brokers' screens. If the computer matches bids and offers these transactions are also entered in the system for the information of brokers. (ASX, 1995, p. 3)

The system provides brokers with the sort of market information (i.e. details of the bids and offers for each stock and the volume of orders at each price, as well as details of actual trades) that was provided on the floor of the exchange when the open outcry system was used. Its main advantages are that trading can be instantaneous and brokers can operate from their offices.

The practice of trading hours still applies, so SEATS has a system for handling orders that were submitted prior to the opening of the market. In fact, most orders are handled during the opening of the market, rather than during the trading day.

The exchange's system for the transfer and settlement processes involved in trading is called CHESS: Clearing House Electronic Subregister System. Prior to the introduction of CHESS, the ASX introduced the system of uncertificated shareholdings. Most companies allow shareholders the choice of being uncertificated or being issued with share certificates.

In order to facilitate the operation of an uncertificated title system, the ASX established a subregister for the registration of shares. Changes in share ownership, through market trading, are recorded electronically and where the parties are CHESS participants (or are sponsored, say, by their stockbroker), settlement is arranged electronically to occur in T+5 days.

CHESS provides, periodically, each listed company with a current record of its shareholders and each shareholder is sent a statement (similar to a bank statement) showing their transactions and holdings.

Prior to the introduction of CHESS, companies maintained their own share registries and trading involved the transfer of share certificates. This paper-based system involved lengthy transfer and settlement delays and was much more costly to operate than the electronic system. Therefore, CHESS represents an important innovation that reduces the transaction costs within the Australian sharemarket.

Trading arrangements

As noted earlier, trading is conducted by brokers (who are members of the ASX) on behalf of clients. The broker is paid a commission for completing transactions. Clients either indicate a specific bid (when buying shares) or offer (when selling) or request their broker to trade 'at market' or 'at best'.

Where bids and offers specify a limit price, it is possible that they will not immediately result in a transaction. Therefore, for a given share, SEATS will hold data showing the volume of buying and selling orders at prices that are below and above the last sale price. Such bids and offers are likely to be placed for a period only. This practice serves to protect a trader from sudden changes in share values, which make the bid or offer inappropriate.

Generally, trading is in marketable parcels. These are very small compared with the trading parcels in the wholesale debt markets discussed in the previous two chapters. The number of shares in a marketable parcel decreases with the shareprice, such that its value is roundly \$500. For instance, it is 1000 shares when the shareprice is \$0.26 to \$0.50 and 50 shares when the shareprice is more than \$10 and up to \$50.

Commission rates are themselves open to negotiation. Prior to the deregulation of commission rates by the Trade Practices Commission, brokers charged according to a scale set by the Association of Australian Stock Exchanges. They comprised a flat fee of \$5 per transaction plus a percentage, on a sliding scale, according to the value of the parcel traded. This scale tended to be excessive for large parcels such as those transacted by fund managers and protected small-parcel transactions.

Following deregulation of commissions, the rates charged for large parcels fell. The concern that rates for retail-sized transactions would rise was eased by the entry of discount brokers, who offer low commissions by offering merely to make a transaction and not to provide advice on what shares to buy.

Brokers act on behalf of their clients, but they are liable for each transaction they conduct. Should a client default (i.e. not pay for shares purchased or not supply script for shares sold) the broker must honour the transaction. This means that when a client defaults in a selling transaction, the broker must buy shares to satisfy the sell transaction. The broker then charges the client for these shares, whatever their price. Should a broker default, the transaction is guaranteed through the provisions of the National Guarantee Fund.

In the United States stockmarkets, such as the New York Stock Exchange, large block trades, which usually are on behalf of institutions, are handled separately from the trading in usual parcel sizes. Such trading is conducted in the **upstairs market**, where the deals are negotiated and the identity of the clients is not disclosed. This market is used by non-US institutions for similar reasons. The upstairs market developed domestically as an alternative to the use of specialist dealers, who act as market makers for particular stocks. (Fabozzi, Modigliani and Ferri, 1994, pp. 364 –5) As noted above, only brokers deal on the ASX.

Indicators of activity

The main indicators of the exchange's activity are turnover, liquidity and market capitalisation. Data on the turnover of shares are presented in table 12.2 for the period 1984 to 1995. Observe that the value of turnover (not adjusted for inflation) has increased considerably but declined following the crash of 1987. This period is typical in that sharemarket activity, as well as the general level of shareprices, has displayed a cyclical pattern over time.

Table 12.2 ASX — average daily turnover, 1984 to 1995 ($m)

Financial year	*Value*
1984	48.8
1985	61.3
1986	124.2
1987	238.2
1988	269.5
1989	195.6
1990	225.3
1991	217.3
1992	247.3
1993	285.1
1994	507.6
1995	466.8

Source: ASX, *Monthly Index Analysis*

Market capitalisation is the total value of the shares available for trading. It is found by summing the market value of each listed company, and their value is the product of each company's share price and amount of issued share capital. This statistic increases with the growth in the number of issued shares and varies with the general movement in shareprices.

The movements in the general level of shareprices are measured by indices. These usually are weighted averages of the prices of a basket of shares. The main index prepared by the ASX is the **All Ordinaries Index** (AOI). The ASX also prepares two constituent indices of the AOI: the **All Resources** and **All Industrial** indices. Each has a value of 500 as at 1 June 1980. Index numbers show the movement in the weighted average level of the shares' prices within the index over time. Hence, an increase in an index from 500 to 2000 represents a fourfold increase over the period.

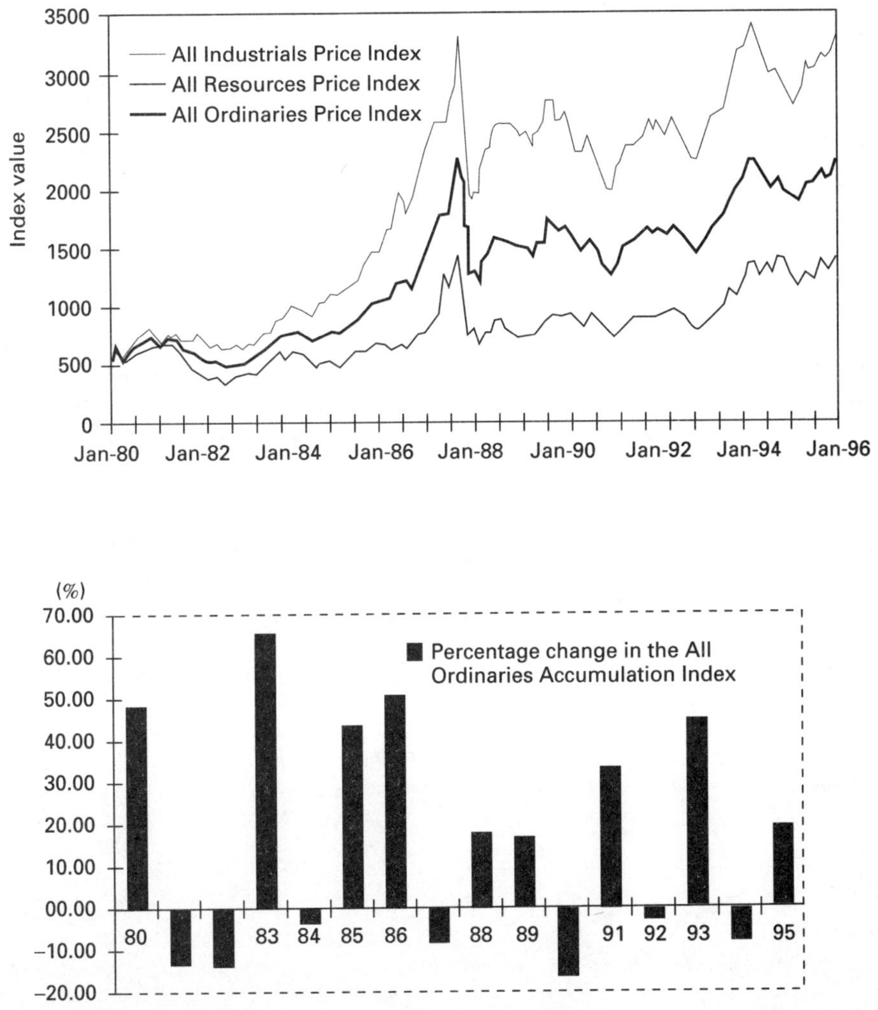

Figure 12.1 All Ordinaries, All Resources and All Industrial Indices, 1980 to 1996

Source: ABS

Each index comprises the shares of the larger companies within its category, weighted according to their market capitalisation. Because the future earnings of resource companies tend to vary according to different factors than the earnings of industrial companies, these indices do not follow the same path. The All Ordinaries Index comprises the shares of both resource and industrial companies. It is the indicator of the market as a whole.

The movements in this index and its constituent indices between 1980 and 1996, are shown in figure 12.1. Note the October 1987 crash in the general level of shareprices.

The data also show that the 1987 crash was preceded by a strong **bull** market (i.e. a period of strong growth in shareprices). When prices fall over a long period, it is referred to as a **bear** market. Sharemarket activity (such as turnover and the issue of new shares) tends to strengthen during bull markets and decline during bear markets.

The ASX also prepares the **All Ordinaries Accumulated Index** which includes the value of dividends and other benefits paid. This is a useful index for showing the overall returns from the market.

The ASX prepares other influential indices, including the Gold, 20 Leaders and 50 Leaders indices. Each of the ASX indices provides a potential benchmark for assessing the movement in a company's share price. Also, movement in the All Ordinaries Index is the major influence on the market's capitalisation.

The liquidity of sharemarkets is indicated by the ratio of turnover to market capitalisation. In the previous chapter data were presented on the liquidity of the bond market. By comparison, the data on turnover in the sharemarket, presented in table 12.3, indicate a much lower level of liquidity. Observe that the value of annual turnover is generally less than half of the value of market capitalisation, whereas in the debt-capital market, the value of turnover in 1994 was 15 times the value of Treasury bonds on issue. Note also that the average daily turnover for all shares was less than $0.5 billion in 1994 –95, a much smaller amount than the turnover in the debt-capital market which, as stated in the previous chapter, was around $6 billion per day for Treasury bonds alone.

Table 12.3 ASX — Turnover, market capitalisation and liquidity, 1989–90 to 1994–5

Financial year	*Average daily turnover ($m)*	*Average market capitalisation ($b)*	*Liquidity (% p.a.)*
1989–90	225.1	172.6	32.9
1990–91	217.2	156.3	34.9
1991–92	247.3	186.0	33.9
1992–93	285.1	201.8	36.0
1993–94	507.6	282.3	45.5
1994–95	466.8	291.1	40.6

Source: ASX, *Monthly Index Analysis*

As previously noted, deep markets allow traders to buy and sell without influencing prices. In the case of the sharemarket, there is usually insufficient depth to allow a large trade in a particular share to occur without disturbing its price. For instance, a buyer who seeks to acquire a large parcel of the shares in a company would have to bid up its price to extract the script from the market (i.e. from holders who are prepared to sell).

A buyer of a large parcel of the shares in a company (say 5% of its issued shares) might attempt to make a purchase off-market from one or more large shareholders. To be able to make such a deal, the buyer would usually make a bid that is above the current share price, recognising that if the shares were purchased from the market, many smaller parcels would have to be purchased at progressively higher prices.

However, market depth varies among the 1178 listed shares (as at June 1995). Some are actively traded without much immediate price movement, allowing trades to occur without disturbing price. But there are many shares that have a low turnover.

The growth in market capitalisation on the ASX has been modest over the past decade compared with that of most of South-east Asian markets. As at the end of 1990, market capitalisation as a proportion of GNP was less than 40% in Australia, whereas it exceeded 120% in Hong Kong, and exceeded 80% in Japan, Singapore and Malaysia. (George, 1991, p. 19)

MARKET PARTICIPANTS

As emphasised above, there are no dealers in the Australian sharemarket. Brokers act on the request of clients. There are two broad categories of market participants: companies whose shares are listed on the exchange and the holders of these shares.

Issuers

Companies seek listing on the exchange principally to gain better access to funds. The ASX, being a secondary market for shares, creates liquidity for the holders of shares. This makes it easier for the shares to be issued and thus assists companies to issue them. Listing also helps to establish a company's identity when raising funds from any source.

While shares can be issued on a **no liability** basis (these typically are the shares of exploration companies), most issuers of shares are **limited liability** companies. This means that shareholders are required to contribute only the issue price of their shares. Consequently, when shares are issued on the basis that part of their issue price is paid initially (these are known as partly-paid shares), the shareholders' liability is limited to the balance due on these shares. The company cannot require the shareholder to make further contributions, although it can invite shareholders to subscribe for additional shares through a **rights** issue, when the shareholder has the right (but not the obligation) to acquire these extra shares.

From a company's viewpoint, it can issue new equity or raise additional debt-capital when it requires additional funds. This question (i.e. the company's capital structure) was briefly discussed in Chapter 1. Each company has to assess what capital structure (i.e. the ratio of debt to equity capital) is in the shareholder's best interests. But this important (and essentially unresolved) question is not within the scope of this book, because it is a matter for each company to decide; it is not answered by an understanding of financial markets and institutions.

In Chapter 9 we considered this matter from the viewpoint of institutions in terms of the amount of equity that suits their business. Remember the discussion of the capital-adequacy requirements for financial institutions. The same basic principles about the role of equity capital apply to all companies.

- Equity is the riskier form of finance from the supplier's viewpoint and therefore tends to be more expensive (i.e. has a higher required rate of return) than debt capital. (We discuss the costs of issuing equity below.) Because the issuer of shares is not required to pay dividends, equity is sometimes viewed as being 'free' to the company. But this view ignores the fact that the suppliers of equity can liquidate their capital by selling their shares if the expected returns are below their required rate. Therefore, the required return is implicit in the shareprice. A fall in the shareprice is equivalent to a rise in the required rate of return, and vice versa.
- Equity capital reduces a company's exposure to financial risk (the risk that it cannot meet its interest obligations) and so is a source of financial strength. As such it serves to minimise its costs of borrowed funds.

The reason that most companies raise debt-capital is that it can improve a company's **earnings per share** (EPS). To illustrate, suppose a company has identified a project that has an expected return of 18% p.a. over five years and it can borrow for this period at a cost of funds of 12% p.a. If it raises the extra funds by issuing debt, the company can add a net return of 6% p.a. over five years to the earnings available to shareholders. That is, the project, when funded by debt capital, adds to the company's EPS over five years.

Floating a company

A company's initial issue of shares is referred to as a **float**, or an **initial public offering** (IPO). This occurs in the primary market. Nevertheless, the ASX is involved in the listing of these shares. The issuing of new shares is a similar process to the issue of new debt-capital. The shares may be issued through a tender, with the issue price being determined by the tender. This process should ensure all the shares are sold. Alternatively, the issue price may be set by the company, in which case not all of the shares may be sold.

Underwriters may be used to reduce the risk that the shares will not be sold. This involves an underwriting fee, because of the risk accepted by the underwriters that the shares (at the issue price) are not purchased by the market. This would occur when the subscription price has become unattractive, and so the underwriter could expect that it will have to on-sell these shares at a loss.

example 12.1

In July 1995, the Commonwealth 'floated' Qantas. It had previously sold 25% of Qantas shares to British Airways to establish a strategic alliance with a carrier that provides services within Europe and to the United States and other countries not served by Qantas. The float involved the sale of the balance of the shares (750 million) of Qantas (except for shares retained to meet certain obligations).

The offer was slightly unusual in that the government imposed some non-commercial limitations on the process. For example, new foreign investors were limited to 24% of the issue and some shares were retained to satisfy 'loyalty share entitlements', an arrangement that was designed to encourage members of the public to retain their shares for at least a year.

The offer was in two parts: one to the Australian public and the other to institutions and members of the ASX. The minimum number of shares that could be applied for in the public offer was 1000, whereas the minimum parcel for institutions was 50 000.

The price of the shares was set by parameters defined in the prospectus, within the range of $1.80 to $2.10. Subject to these parameters, the price of all shares was related to the outcome of the institutional tender process. If the institutional price was set at the low end of the set price range, the price to the public would be discounted to match this price. If the sale of shares to institutions was at the upper end of the price range, discounts would not be offered to the public. Therefore, the final price was set after the results of the institutional tender were known.

The offer was not underwritten. However, the Commonwealth engaged the services of a financial adviser (Bain Capital Markets Limited), Joint Lead Managers (McIntosh Corporate Limited in Melbourne and Potter Warburg Capital Markets in Sydney) and four domestic company lead managers and three international company lead managers.

As a result of the institutional tender, stock was offered to the public at the lower end of the possible range, for $1.90 per share.

The timing of a float is also an important factor. In bull markets there is a much greater capacity to acquire shares than in a bear market. Consequently, a company intending to float will probably seek advice, typically from a bank or merchant bank (recall our discussion of the activities of these institutions in Chapter 7), on both its terms and conditions and its timing. Data on the funds raised by newly listed companies are presented in table 12.6. (See also example 12.1.)

Partly because of the need to issue a prospectus when making a public float, the costs of the process are substantial:

> *The costs directly associated with the floatation process include: the fees charged by the adviser for the structuring, valuation and preparation of the documentation for the floatation; legal accounting and printing costs; and the stock exchange listing fees. The costs range between about 3 and 10% of the amount raised. The underwriting fee usually includes, as part of the fee, brokerage that is receivable on the sale of the shares. Thus, of a 3% underwriting fee, 1% may be payable as brokerage on allotted shares.* (McGrath, 1994, p. 100)

When a listed company seeks additional equity through the issue of new shares (of course, it can raise additional equity capital through retaining earnings rather than paying them as dividends) it conducts a rights issue.

Rights issue

A rights issue is a new share issue to a company's existing shareholders and certain other parties (as explained below). Generally rights issues involve less expense than a public issue. Their purpose is to raise additional equity, while allowing shareholders to maintain their proportionate holding in the company. The right to subscribe to the new shares is usually a given ratio to each shareholder's holding of existing shares and usually can be sold on the ASX prior to the issue's subscription date. Therefore the rights may become a short-term instrument.

Suppose a company seeks $6 million in additional equity by issuing two million new shares at a subscription price of $3.00. It presently has four million ordinary shares and no other parties (such as preference shareholders) participate in the issue. The terms of the rights issue are therefore one-for-two at a subscription price of $3.00. Should the current price for the company's shares be $6.00, the rights issue allows its shareholders to buy one new share at only $3.00 for each two they currently hold.

If for some reason not all of the rights are exercised (i.e. some are allowed to lapse), the company will raise less than the $6 million sought and fewer than one million new shares will be created. A company may decide to pay for its rights issue to be underwritten to avoid the risk of it not raising the amount sought.

The terms of a rights issue specify the purchase (i.e. subscription) price of the new shares, the maturity date for the offer and whether the rights are renounceable (i.e. can be sold in the marketplace). In this event the purchaser of the rights takes possession of the right to subscribe for the new shares. Usually rights are listed in ASX trading reports next to the company's ordinary shares and this shows the market value of the rights as a separate entity.

The process of a rights issue is shown by the time line in figure 12.2. Once a company has decided to make a rights issue it will advise the ASX and its shareholders. Following this announcement the company's shares will trade on a **cum-rights** basis.

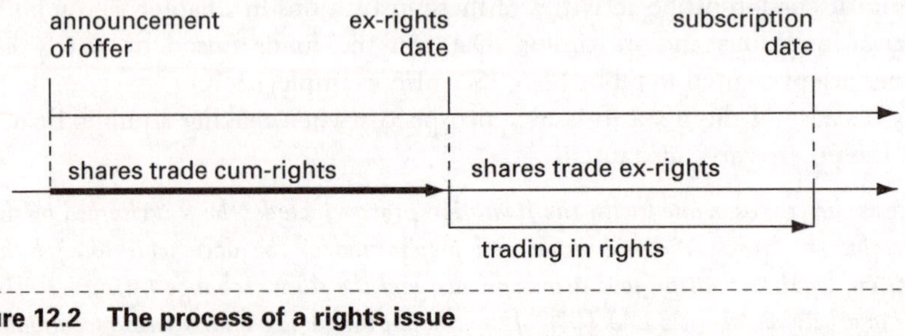

Figure 12.2 The process of a rights issue

The announcement of a rights issue will indicate the issue terms as well as the date the shares go **ex-rights** together with the subscription date for the issue. The ex-rights date serves to identify who owns the shares when the rights are allocated and indicates when the rights separate as a component of the benefits of the company's existing shares. The shareholders on the company's share register on the ex-rights date will be entitled to the right to subscribe to the new shares. (In practice a lead time of five days may be set to allow all trades just prior to the cut-off date to be recorded in the share register.) From the ex-rights date the rights usually are traded as a separate security, until they expire on the subscription date.

On the subscription date, the holder of the rights either exercises them by paying for the new shares or allows them to lapse.

Valuing rights

A right will have value if it allows its holder to purchase the new share at a lower price than that for the company's existing shares. Given that the process of issuing rights extends over a few months, as shown in figure 12.3, we will show how to calculate its theoretical value when the existing shares are trading on a cum-rights and then an ex-rights basis.

Almost certainly, the subscription price of a right will be less than the share price when the issue is announced. During the initial period when the shares are trading on a cum-rights basis, the value of the right is determined by the difference between the cum-rights price and the subscription price as well as by the number of shares that earn a right. Intuitively:

- the amount of the discount represented by the subscription price against the cum-rights price is an important source of the value of a right, and
- the number of existing shares required to earn a right determines the scarcity and therefore the value of the rights.

The formula that determines the theoretical value of a right is:

$$R = \frac{n(P - S)}{n + 1} \qquad \textit{Equation (12.1)}$$

where R stands for the value of the right to subscribe to one new share,
n stands for the number of existing shares that attract the right to subscribe to a new share,
P stands for the cum-rights price of existing shares, and
S stands for the subscription price for the new shares.

In our example, the theoretical value of the right to subscribe \$3.00 for a new share when two existing shares are held and trade at a cum-rights price of \$6.00, is:

$$R = \frac{2(6 - 3)}{2+1}$$

$$= \$2.00$$

Once the shares begin trading on an ex-rights basis, we would expect that the share price will fall. On the ex-rights date, ownership of the rights has been separated from that of the existing shares and thus the ex-rights price of the shares will be less than the cum-rights price. The extent of the fall is determined by the value of the rights on a per-share basis.

In our example, once the shares begin trading ex-rights, their price will fall to $5.00 which, as shown below, can be calculated as follows:

$$P_{\text{ex-rights}} = P - R/n \qquad \textit{Equation (12.2)}$$

Given that the rights will trade for a theoretical price of $2.00, and the cum-rights price was $6.00, the ex-rights price on the ex-rights date will be:

$$P_{\text{ex-rights}} = 6.00 - 2.00/2$$

$$= \$5.00$$

Alternatively, the theoretical ex-rights price can be calculated directly. This is the value of the shares assuming the rights have been exercised. Given that the rights issue is on a pro-rata basis, we can represent the ex-rights price by valuing the parcel of shares required to earn a right including the funds raised by the exercise of the right. Expressing this value on a per share basis (including the new shares created by the rights being exercised) gives the theoretical ex-rights price. Thus,

$$P_{\text{ex-rights}} = \frac{nP + S}{n + 1} \qquad \textit{Equation (12.3)}$$

In our above example of a one-for-two issue, equation (12.3) also shows the ex-rights price to be:

$$P_{\text{ex-rights}} = \frac{(2 * 6) + 3}{2 + 1}$$

$$= \$5.00$$

Remember that the market value of the company is the number of shares times their market price. Prior to the new issue, the company's value is $24 million (four million shares times $6.00). After the rights issue it will have a value of $30 million ($24 million plus the $6 million in new equity capital). In the above calculation we have subdivided the company into parcels of two cum-rights shares to which one new share has been added at $3.00 each.

The three shares are worth, on the ex-rights date, $5.00 each (i.e. $15.00 divided by three) and therefore the right to subscribe $3.00 for one of them is worth $2.00.

OBSERVATIONS

Notice that in equation (12.3) the ex-rights price increases with both S and n. A larger S injects more funds into the company and this increases its (and so its share's) ex-rights value. To illustrate, suppose the subscription price was $4.50 (rather than $3.00). The ex-rights price would be $5.50 rather than $5.00:

$$P_{ex\text{-}rights} = \frac{(2 * 6) + 4.50}{2 + 1}$$

$$= \$5.50$$

A larger n occurs when more existing shares have to be held to be entitled to the right to purchase a new share. In a one-for-five issue, for example, n would be five. A larger n means a smaller increase in the number of issued shares (i.e. less dilution in the value of the existing shares) and this results in a higher ex-rights price (i.e. a smaller fall from the cum-rights to the ex-rights price). Suppose the company sought less funds (say $1 million). The rights issue would be, therefore, one-for-four (i.e. n equals four rather than two). Given the $3.00 subscription price, the ex-rights value of the shares would be $5.40 rather than $5.00:

$$P_{ex\text{-}rights} = \frac{(4 * 6) + 3}{4 + 1}$$

$$= \$5.40$$

When valuing the rights we have assumed that the issue is fully subscribed and that only the company's ordinary shareholders are entitled to them. Should other parties be entitled to the rights (such as senior executives through their share options) the precise number of new shares will exceed the ratio of one for each parcel of two ordinary shares held. This would further reduce the ex-rights price and so reduce the value of the rights. (See example 12.2.)

We also assumed, for simplicity, that the subscription price is paid in full at the subscription date. On occasions the subscription process may involve an initial part-payment followed, at a later date, by further payments until the subscription price is fully paid. When this process is involved we need to allow for the reduced present value of the amount of the new equity raisings.

example 12.2

In May 1992, Westpac announced its intention to raise $1.2 billion through a three-for-ten rights issue. A prospectus was prepared to provide shareholders with relevant financial data. Initially, the bank did not plan to have the issue underwritten, because its shares were then trading at about $3.90 and the subscription price for the new shares was set at $3.00. But following the bank's announcement of a loss of $1.7 billion (for the half year ending March 1992), Westpac's shareprice fell to $3.50. This fall appears to have caused Westpac to appoint an underwriter (CS First Boston). The movement in Westpac's shareprice over the period of the rights issue is shown in figure 12.3.

The underwriter's role is to assist in promoting the issue and to purchase those shares not taken up through the rights offer. Other financial institutions (such as AMP, which held 15% of the bank's issued shares) are the major holders of Westpac shares and it would seem that Westpac believed an underwriter would be influential in encouraging these institutions (other than AMP, which was committed to the new issue) to take up the new shares. The underwriter's fee was set at $1.5 million plus 1.25% of the amount underwritten. This amounted to $16.5 million. Given that AMP had indicated it would support the new issue, it seems that Westpac wanted to hedge against a possible further reduction in its shareprice prior to the issue. The closing date for the issue was 23 September 1992.

During the period of the rights issue the All Ordinaries Index fell, which is not the ideal environment in which to raise additional capital. Whatever the reason, Westpac's rights issue failed in its attempt to raise funds from its shareholders because by September its shareprice had fallen below the subscription price for the new shares. Approximately 25% of the new shares (111 million of the 405 million offered) were taken up, a large proportion of which went to AMP because of its commitment to the rights issue. However, its move to underwrite the issue ensured that Westpac raised the additional funds sought.

The bank's $1.7 billion loss was the main reason for the new issue. This loss directly reduced the bank's equity and the new issue was required to replace the bank's capital for CAR purposes.

When Westpac shares were trading at $3.50 prior to the issue, the theoretical price for the rights was:

$$R = \frac{n(P - S)}{(n + 1)}$$

$$= \frac{10/3\ (3.50 - 3.00)}{10/3 + 1}$$

$$= \$0.38$$

As Westpac's shareprice fell prior to the subscription date, the value of the rights also fell and by September 1992, the shareprice was below the subscription price and so the rights had no value. For this reason, most were allowed by their holders to lapse.

Setting the terms of a rights issue

It is important to understand the role of the subscription price in the actual process of raising new share capital. The success of a rights issue depends on the level of the subscription price relative to the ex-rights price on the subscription date. Should S be set too close to P (the cum-rights price) there is a greater chance that the rights will not be exercised.

A company may attempt to reduce the risk of not actually raising the required extra share capital by negotiating an underwriter for the issue, on the basis that the underwriter will purchase any unsubscribed shares. But this arrangement will add to the costs of the issue, as the Westpac example indicated.

Notice in figure 12.3 that the date is shown in reverse order, with the year shown first, followed by the month and then the day.

Alternatively, a rights issue may be underpriced by setting a subscription price that is too low. In this event the rights issue will raise less new equity capital than was possible. It may appear to be successful when 100% of the new shares are purchased, but given the objective of raising new equity capital without unduly reducing the company's shareprice, the issue will be less than successful.

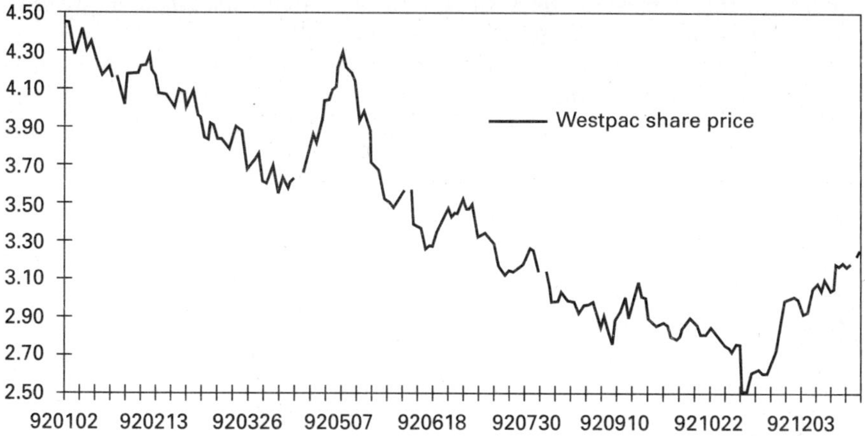

Figure 12.3 Westpac share price, 1992

Does a rights issue create wealth for shareholders?

At first thought, a rights issue might be viewed as a 'bonus' for shareholders. That is, because the subscription price for a new share is lower than the cum-rights price of a share, it may be assumed that the bargain price for the new shares serves to increase the wealth of shareholders.

Logic, however, indicates that a rights issue simply induces shareholders to exchange cash for new shares. It cannot, in normal circumstances, add to the wealth of a shareholder. If it could, all that companies would do is make rights issues.

The outcome of a rights issue on the wealth of the company's shareholders is illustrated by the following hypothetical example. Suppose a shareholder owns ten shares with a cum-rights price of \$9.00 and has \$10.00 cash. This represents \$100 in wealth. Further, suppose that the company has a one-for-five rights issue, with a subscription price of \$5.00, and the shareholder takes up the rights to two shares and so converts the \$10.00 cash into two more shares. The shareholder's wealth position is now based solely on the ex-rights value of the 12 shares. As shown below, their value is \$8.33 each, and so the shareholder's wealth remains at \$100.00:

$$P_{\text{ex-rights}} = \frac{(5 * 9) + 5}{5 + 1}$$

$$= \$8.33$$

Suppose the shareholder sold rather than exercised the rights. In this event, the shareholder would still have \$10.00 in cash, plus the proceeds from the sale of two rights (\$3.33 each), together with ten shares worth \$8.33 each, which totals roundly \$100. The value of each of the rights is:

$$R = \frac{5(9 - 5)}{5 + 1}$$

$$= \$3.33$$

In practice, the apparent effect of a rights issue on shareholder wealth is complicated by the fact that the price of a company's shares may increase in the wake of a rights announcement. However, this phenomenon is not the effect of the rights issue *per se* but is due to the implicit 'information' that the market reads into rights issue announcements. Often a rights issue signals that the management is about to undertake significant new investment which will add to the company's, and therefore the shareholders', wealth. The increase in the price of a share after a rights announcement ought to be interpreted as a reassessment of the company's value. It ought not to be interpreted as a creation of wealth through a rights issue.

In some cases, the market interprets a rights issue as a signal that the company is in need of funds, and assumes that its future earnings will be less than had been forecast. In this event, the shareprice will fall at the time of the announcement, but again, this is not due directly to the rights issue. It is a reaction to it.

While a rights issue does not of itself create wealth for a company's shareholders, it can transfer wealth among its participants. Depending upon the terms, others besides ordinary shareholders may participate in a rights issue. If the effective price of entry into the rights issue for another group is less than that for the ordinary shareholders, there will be a transfer of wealth from the ordinary shareholders to the other group. For instance, partially paid shares or company-issued options provide a cheaper entry into a rights issue than that afforded by ordinary shares.

The compensation package of senior management often includes low-priced options and partially paid shares. When these instruments give them access to a rights issue, their wealth can be increased at the expense of the ordinary shareholders.

Some recent examples of rights issues are listed in summary form in table 12.4.

Table 12.4 Examples of rights issues, 1995

Company	*Ratio*	*Amount raised ($m)*	*Underwriter*
Coca Cola Amatil	1:4	672.4	Potter Warburg Capital Markets
Advance Bank Corporate	7:10	563.2	J. B. Were & Son; McIntosh
Schroders Property Fund	1:4	157.9	ANZ McCaughan
Crown Ltd	2:7	130.0	E. L. & C. Baillieu
Australian Consolidated Investments	1:1	151.7	not underwritten

Source: ASX (Statex)

Private placements of new shares

While private placements can be made to either financial institutions (such as insurance companies) or to clients of sharebrokers, most are made to institutions. The raising of new equity capital by this means has three main advantages:

1 The placement can be made much more quickly than through a rights issue. (Private placements can be achieved in a few days whereas rights issues usually take at least two months.)
2 The price the company receives for the new shares is generally higher than through a rights issue (i.e. the subscription price representing a smaller discount on the market price is lower than the probable subscription price if the funds were raised through a rights issue).
3 The shares can be placed with 'friendly' institutions to reduce the risk of a takeover.

Table 12.5 Examples of private placements, 1993 and 1994

Year	*Company*	*Amount ($m)*	*Type of securities*
1993	TNT	210.3	preference shares
	News Corporation	500.0	preference shares
	Westpac	300.0	preference shares
	Lion Nathan	300.0	ordinary shares
1994	MIM	416.8	ordinary shares
	Amcor	150.5	convertible notes

Source: ASX, *Monthly Index Analysis*

The main disadvantage of private placements is that they dilute the proportionate claims of existing shareholders to the company's future profits. Because of the rules of the Australian Stock Exchange, private placements usually represent less than 10% of the number of shares (and equivalent securities) of a company.

While private placements could be viewed by the market as an attempt by a company to overcome financial difficulties, this is not usually the case. A summary of a few such placements made in 1993 and 1994 is presented in table 12.5.

Data on the amount of equity raisings are presented in table 12.6. Notice the cyclical nature of the amounts raised and the relative smallness of the primary market compared with the debt markets discussed in the previous two chapters.

Shareholders

Traditionally, individuals have been the main holders of shares. However, from the 1960s, insurance offices began to substantially increase their holdings of equities to improve their investment returns. Other institutions, such as superannuation funds, followed the lead of insurance offices. The subsequent development of unit trusts and their investments in equities continued the trend away from individuals as holders of shares to institutions. Recall that data on equity holdings by institutions were presented in Chapter 8.

Table 12.6 Equity raisings, 1987 to 1995 ($m)

Year	*Floats*	*Rights issues*	*Placements*	*Dividend reinvestment*	*Other*	*Total*
1987	5 272.0	8 005.8	4 220.1	482.1	1 105.9	19 085.9
1988	1 170.0	6 702.1	1 694.4	568.9	716.1	10 851.5
1989	1 704.2	2 314.2	1 698.6	2 418.0	1 082.1	9 217.1
1990	463.1	2 347.1	1 059.6	2 514.0	1 043.0	7 426.8
1991	1 937.3	2 724.5	1 780.2	2 017.1	615.5	9 074.6
1992	3 694.4	4 415.5	2 620.9	2 645.3	903.8	14 279.9
1993	5 347.7	978.7	5 450.3	2 738.1	1 330.5	15 845.3
1994	4 710.1	3 678.9	3 344.6	3 651.4	1 642.9	17 027.9
1995	4 111.8	2 867.0	2 103.8	3 264.0	1 632.8	13 979.4

Source: ASX, *Monthly Index Analysis*

> *In broad terms, from about 1950 to 1980 the proportion of shareholdings in individual hands seems to have fallen from 80% to 40%; by 1990 it was estimated at 10%. Only about 12% of the Australian adult population own shares directly — a figure about one third the level of the USA or Japan.* (Drake and Stammer, 1993, pp. 297–8)

Given the decline in individuals as holders of shares, the focus of many brokers is mainly toward the institutional client or the issuer. The extent of a broker's services, such as security analysis, depends on the firm's target clients. Institutions and issuers require more service, whereas discount broking is aimed at the retail client and generally provides no service other than the processing of buy and sell orders in the market.

Investment in shares does not involve credit risk because of the nature of shares as ownership instruments. Therefore shares are not rated by a credit ratings agency. However, they involve the more substantial risk of not receiving returns, because of the residual nature of their returns.

The risk involved in owning shares is a form of market risk; should expected returns decline, so will the shareprice. Therefore this risk can be measured by the variability in the movements of a share's price (particularly when the price is adjusted for dividends and bonus issues).

The risk of holding shares can be divided into two categories: **systematic risk**, which arises from the cyclical nature of the movement in shareprices generally; and **unsystematic risk**, which arises from the movements of the price of a particular share. This element of risk can be removed by investing in a balanced portfolio of shares, whose overall price movement is similar to that of the market as a whole.

Recall our discussion in Chapter 8 of unit trusts. They offer small investors ownership in a balanced portfolio, something that could not be achieved directly because of the cost of minimum parcels. When an investment's risk is reduced, without changing the expected rate of return, its value to the investor is increased.

This principle explains the trend in the market toward managed funds from the viewpoint of small investors.

Equity instruments

Equity instruments are issued by a company to raise equity funds. The principal instrument is the ordinary share (or common stock).

Ordinary shares

As explained above, the primary equity instrument is called (in Australia) an ordinary share. An ordinary share has a par value which is relevant for only a few purposes. When shares are issued at par, it determines how much has to be paid by the shareholder. But when shares have a different issue price (to par), the issue price determines the amount due. Unlike a debt security that is redeemed at par, shares are not usually refunded and if they are, it is not necessarily at par.

A share's par value has relevance also to a share split. This occurs rarely in Australia, but the process is adopted when the company judges its shareprice is too high and believes that, say, a halving of its value through doubling the number issued will improve market access to the share. The share split involves, in this case, a halving of the par value, although the aim is to halve the shareprice.

The closest instrument to the ordinary share is the preference share, which can be issued in a variety of forms, such as an irredeemable or a convertible preference share. These may be regarded as 'senior' instruments because in all cases, they are entitled to distributions of profits (and company assets) ahead of the company's ordinary shareholders. Of course, the suppliers of credit and debt capital to a company stand ahead of both groups of shareholders in the matter of payments by a company.

As discussed above, equity capital is the most risky because its returns depend on all other claims on the company being met. Moreover, should a company's gross earnings not be sufficient to meet its expenses, the loss must be funded from shareholders' funds, otherwise the unpaid creditors can liquidate the company's assets in order to be paid.

On the other hand, the returns to ordinary shareholders are not capped (as is the case with the interest payments on debt capital). Should the company's earnings per share (EPS) be substantial, the return to shareholders will be great, either through the dividend that distributes some or all of the earnings, or through an appreciation in the shareprice that results when earnings are retained.

A company's EPS is calculated by dividing the company's earnings after interest and taxes, less payments to preference shareholders, by the number of ordinary shares.

The value of an ordinary share is the price that will be paid for it in the market. Analysts commonly compare a share's price to its EPS. This is known as the **price–earnings ratio**. Should, for example, a company's shares trade at $20 and its EPS for the current year be $2, its price–earnings ratio is 10. This serves to indicate the market's confidence in the company's future earnings potential.

In Australia dividends are usually paid six-monthly (quarterly in the United States). Typically, companies prefer to sustain a particular dividend payment per share and make a special dividend payment when they make abnormally high profits. It is thought that lifting the dividend rate implies to the market that the company can sustain the new higher payment.

The rate of return represented by a dividend payment depends on the shareprice. A higher price means a lower rate of return for a given divided payment. But a higher price represents a higher price–earnings ratio and may precede a rise in the dividend rate.

Preference shares

The title 'preference share' arises from the fact that these are a form of shareholders' funds which rank ahead of ordinary shares in the payment of a dividend. Generally, preference shares are paid a promised dividend rate that, depending on their form, does not increase when the company achieves abnormally high profits. They are known as **non-participating preference shares**, and most take this form.

When the company promises to subsequently make up any missed dividend payments (should subsequent profits permit), they are known as **cumulative preference shares**. Should the preference shares also be **redeemable**, they become very similar to subordinated debt in that they receive a flow of regular payments that are made after most other obligations have been met from earnings.

Preference shares that have a redemption date are, in effect, a hybrid instrument, having both equity and debt features. This applies in particular to those shares that are redeemed by a fixed date at a set price, or when the company has the option to redeem them within a set range of dates and prices. Redeemable preference shares will specify whether the right to call for redemption is in the hands of the company or the shareholder.

The features of a preference-share issue can be designed creatively to achieve a wide range of outcomes. For example, they can be issued at a premium against a low par value. The dividend rate would appear to be high (given the low par value) and the premium could be retained as a reserve, to meet the eventual redemption payment.

Often preference shares are issued by private placement to a friendly or associated shareholder, and these tend to be the more creatively designed shares. They may also be issued to the company's shareholders through a rights issue. Preference shares that are similar to subordinated debt tend to be issued as a substitute for debt. Presumably, when a company has as much debt as it prefers, but requires additional funding, it will consider issuing preference shares.

The introduction of dividend imputation in the mid 1980s removed a tax impediment to the issue of preference shares. Dividend imputation allows for the taxes paid on the income stream that financed the dividend payment (by the issuer of the preference shares) to be credited against the income tax due by the shareholder.

Convertible preference shares are closest in nature to ordinary shares. They allow the shareholder to convert their preference shares, within a set period and at a set conversion rate, to ordinary shares. Usually, the holders of such shares participate in any share offers the company makes (e.g. a rights issue of ordinary shares or the granting of options to buy more shares) prior to the close of the conversion period.

Bonus shares

These are similar to rights issues except that no subscription price is imposed. They can be issued against the firm's reserves to move funds from reserves into the company's paid-up share capital. Despite their name, they do not provide a bonus to shareholders. They increase the number of shares on issue without adding to the company's value. Therefore they reduce the value of each share, such that, in theory, each shareholder's parcel of shares is larger but of no greater value.

The impact of a bonus issue on a company's shareprice is given by replacing S in equation (12.3) by zero, thus:

$$P_{\text{ex-bonus}} = \frac{nP}{n + 1}$$ *Equation (12.5)*

where n is the ratio of existing shares to bonus shares, and
P is the shareprice prior to the bonus issue.

For example, in a three-for-one bonus share issue, when P is $2.00, the ex-bonus price will be:

$$P_{\text{ex-bonus}} = \frac{(1/3) * 2.00}{(1/3) + 1}$$

$$= \$0.50$$

In this case there are four times as many shares in circulation, each with one quarter of their previous value. This confirms the general statement above that a bonus issue reduces the shareprice proportionally and it has no impact on shareholder wealth (unless it is used as a 'signalling' device by the company's management).

Share options

Share options give the holder the right to take up shares in a company at a pre-set price over a specified period. The holder is not obliged to subsequently purchase the shares, since these are options only. Presumably they will be purchased only if the shareprice exceeds that specified in the option.

New equity capital can be raised through the subscription price for the option and through the options being exercised. As rights and bonus issues affect the company's shareprice, the holders of options are usually allowed to participate in these issues. However, this practice can be very generous to the option holder who, for example, received shares through a rights issue, as this person would be able to sell the rights without first exercising his or her share options. In this way, options (as well as partly paid shares) can dilute the holdings of ordinary shareholders within the company.

Share options are given to employees, especially the most senior executives, as a motivational form of remuneration and to participants in new capital raisings (either equity or debt) to assist in this process.

Exchange-traded options and warrants

A number of instruments are referred to as options. In this chapter we have used the term to refer to instruments that raise funds on the basis that their holder has the right but not the obligation to subscribe to the new capital. In Chapter 19 we discuss options in the form of derivative instruments. Their general features were explained in Chapter 3.

Exchange-traded options (ETOs) are secondary market instruments that can be used to hedge an exposure in physical markets. Equity **warrants** are similar to ETOs in their purpose and operation (these matters are explained in Chapter 19). Their differences are that they are issued by an institution, approved by the ASX, over the shares of another company (usually one whose shares are actively traded), they have a longer term than ETOs, and responsibility for settlement rests with their issuer. (Carew, 1995, pp. 131–2)

Macquarie Bank issued the first equity warrants traded on the ASX in 1991; these were 15 million call warrants over Boral shares. Bankers Trust Australia Limited issued the first index warrants in the same year.

Given the various uses of the term 'option', it is important to understand which instrument you are dealing with. In this chapter we have referred to share options, rights issues and convertible securities. The former two give their holder the option to subscribe equity capital, and the latter creates the right to convert an instrument into another.

SHARE VALUES

The valuation of shares is a specialised endeavour that is beyond the scope of this book to handle in anything but the most superficial manner. Security analysts assess share values. In essence, they assess the earnings and dividend prospects of companies, considering their management, their place in their markets and the prospects for the industry and economy as a whole. (McGrath, 1994, pp. 135–41)

Security analysts usually apply **fundamental analysis** (as outlined in the previous paragraph) when valuing shares. An alternative approach adopted by some analysts is called **technical analysis**. In general, this approach involves a close inspection of past prices in the expectation of being able to identify a future trend. This approach is commonly referred to as 'charting' because price data are depicted as charts.

The collective effect of trading in shares on the basis of professional advice is that the market will use information efficiently, resulting in fair prices that follow a random walk. This is the efficient market hypothesis (EMH), which implies that informed predictions have about an even-money chance of correctly identifying a price trend. In other words, it implies that tossing a coin is as good as any other method for predicting price movements.

In theory, a share's value depends on its expected future income stream. Viewed this way, the current shareprice represents the market's best estimate of the present value of the company's future dividend stream per share. The present value should be based on the rate of return investors require on equity capital invested in the company's line of business. This dividend stream valuation method treats the share as a perpetuity, the formula for which was explained in Chapter 5.

Should the dividend stream (D) be expected to be constant over time and investors believe the required return for holding the shares of a particular company is k%, the share's price (P) should be:

$$P = \frac{D}{k} \qquad \textit{Equation (12.6)}$$

To illustrate, suppose the steady-state dividend is $0.50 and the required return of shareholders is 15.00%, the shareprice should be:

$$P = \frac{0.50}{0.15}$$

$$= \$3.33$$

Should the company's dividend stream be expected to grow at an average annual rate of 5.00%, this variable (g) is incorporated as a negative value in the denominator to produce a higher shareprice, to reflect the growth in dividend, as follows:

$$P_0 = \frac{D_1}{k - g} \qquad \textit{Equation (12.7)}$$

where P_0 refers to the current shareprice, and
D_1 refers to the next dividend payment, this being $D_0(1 + g)$.

To illustrate, using the above data:

$$P_0 = \frac{0.50\,(1.05)}{0.15 - 0.05}$$

$$= \$5.25$$

The required rate of return, k, will be influenced by the general level of interest rates (negatively) and shareprices in major overseas markets. (Valentine, 1995) Data presented by Valentine show that the All Ordinaries Index tends to move in line with profits and the Dow Jones Industrial Index (the New York based index) and in the opposite direction to interest rates.

Summary

The main points of this chapter are as follows:

- The ASX was established to facilitate trading in stocks and bonds and has developed rules that promote informed trading and efficient pricing.
- Trading is conducted electronically, with orders being handled by brokers.
- Turnover and the size of the primary market for equities is modest compared with that for debt securities.

- The ASX facilitates the raising of new equity, both through the floating of companies and the issue of additional shares by listed companies.
- While rights issues (and bonus issues) appear to create value for shareholders, in fact the former serves to raise extra share capital and the latter simply increases the number of shares.
- Preference shares can be designed with many different features, and some forms appear more like subordinated debt than equity.
- A company's shareprice reflects its expected future earnings and dividend stream, discounted by the required return of its shareholders.

DISCUSSION QUESTIONS AND EXERCISES

1 Discuss the development and functions of stock exchanges in general, and the ASX in particular.
2 Briefly describe the main requirements for listing on the ASX and to maintain listing and explain the purposes of these rules.
3 Briefly describe the role and trading protocol of SEATS and the settlement features of CHESS.
4 Briefly describe the All Ordinaries Index and indicate when movements in the index are described as 'bull' and 'bear' markets. What are the implications of such movements in the index for the issuers of shares?
5 Describe the process and the purpose of a rights issue. What are the main terms of a rights issue? Explain the reason for the subscription price being set below a share's current price when designing a rights issue.
6 (a) Calculate the theoretical value of the rights following the announcement of the issue, given the following terms:

Ratio	*Cum-right price*	*Subscription price*
2:5	$8.40	$6.00
1:3	$4.50	$3.00
1:4	$12.60	$10.00

(b) Calculate the theoretical ex-rights price for the shares in each of the above cases, using first equation (12.2) and then equation (12.3).
7 Discuss the Westpac 1992 rights issue. With the benefit of hindsight, was Westpac's decision to appoint an underwriter worth the expense?
8 Discuss the effect of a rights issue on shareholder wealth.
9 Discuss the various ways of raising new equity capital. Consider preference shares and describe the form that is most like subordinated debt.
10 Calculate the theoretical shareprice when the previous dividend was $0.50, the required cost of equity funds is 15% and the expected dividend growth is 3% p.a.

REFERENCES AND FURTHER READING

ASX May 1995, *SEATS, Overview*.
Bennetts, Ron 1995, *The Stockmarket*, ABC, Sydney.

Carew, Edna 1995, *Derivatives Decoded*, Allen & Unwin, Sydney.
Drake, P. J., & Stammers, D. W. 1993, 'The stock exchange' in M. K. Lewis & R. H. Wallace (eds), *The Australian Financial System*, Longman Cheshire, Melbourne, pp. 282–317.
Fabozzi, Frank J., Modigliani, Franco, & Ferri, Michael G. 1994, *Foundations of Financial Markets and Institutions*, Prentice-Hall, New Jersey, Chapters 18 and 19.
George, Robert Lloyd 1991, *Asian Stock Markets*, 2nd edn, Longman Cheshire, Melbourne.
McGrath, Michael 1994, *Financial Institutions, Instruments and Markets in Australia*, McGraw-Hill, Sydney, Chapters 4–7.
Valentine, Tom 1995, 'Fundmental influences on Australian share prices', *ASX Perspective*, pp. 38–40.

13

Foreign-exchange and overseas-capital markets

This chapter explains the operations of Australia's foreign-exchange (FX) market and overseas-capital markets. Trading in FX markets establishes the value of currencies as well as arranging the exchange of each country's legal tender, creating a global payments network. Overseas-capital markets offer borrowers and investors potential financing opportunities (in addition to those provided by the domestic markets).

Study objectives

From your study of this chapter you should be able to:

- identify from an exchange-rate quotation the currency being traded and its price;
- recognise an appreciation and a depreciation in a currency's value;
- describe the evolution of exchange rates from fixed- to floating-rate regime;
- describe the mechanics of spot and forward FX transactions;
- describe the trading practices in the FX market;
- distinguish between a two-way quote and a mid-point price for a currency;
- identify the source of exposures to the risk of an adverse movement in exchange rates;
- calculate cross-rates using either mid-point prices or two-way quotes;
- calculate forward rates (and points) using either mid-point exchange and interest rates or two-way quotes;
- explain the structure and cashflows of an FX swap;

- describe the main forms of bank lending in the eurocurrency bank credit market;
- describe the main instruments that are issued in eurocurrency markets; and
- explain several reasons for Australian entities borrowing from offshore capital markets.

INTRODUCTION

The foreign-exchange (FX or forex) market differs from those for securities because it is not a capital market. Selling a new security (in the primary market) serves to raise capital, whereas the sale of a currency serves to exchange it for another currency. The role of the FX market is to link each country's payment system, creating the international payments network.

The basic need for FX markets arises from each country's desire to issue its own currency as legal tender. Recall the discussion in Chapter 1 of the payment services available for transactions within Australia's financial system. To make a transaction in, say, Australian dollars, with a counterparty that requires payment in, say, Japanese yen, it is necessary to convert the Australian dollars into yen. This exchange of the two currencies occurs in the FX market.

The world's FX markets serve as linkages between each country's payment system, and thus they tend to be subject to official supervision, and in some cases, intervention. They are instrumental in the conduct of world trade and, as outlined below, have been the subject of international agreements.

When capital (and funds generally) is raised in another currency it will be exchanged in the FX market into the currency of use. Therefore, as shown in figure 3.1 (in Chapter 3, p. 57), the FX market performs a function (one of converting currencies) that is instrumental to the operations of the global capital market.

The FX market is Australia's largest and most dynamic financial market. The most actively-traded currencies, such as the US dollar and the Japanese yen, are traded in their domestic FX markets and in the FX market of other countries. Therefore trading in these currencies is conducted around the globe 24 hours a day.

The largest markets for foreign exchange are in London, Tokyo and New York. These markets operate in separate time zones, so that each mainly operates when the other is closed. Between them, these markets are responsible for more than half of the world's turnover in foreign exchange.

The Australian market, in terms of turnover, has been among the largest ten since the mid 1980s. This is a high ranking considering Australia's smaller share of world trade. Its prominence as an FX market is related to its time zone; to the strong economic growth of the countries in the Asia-Pacific region; and to the strong overseas demand for the Australian dollar as a hedging and speculative currency.

In April 1995, its daily turnover was $39.5 billion, measured in US dollars. This level of turnover is many times that (in value terms) of the security markets discussed in the previous three chapters. As a consequence, trading in FX is much more hectic, stressful, lucrative and noisy than security trading.

Foreign-currency transactions arise from international trade in goods and services and the capital flows involved in cross-border trading in real and financial assets.

> *Foreign-exchange markets developed to cater for the supply and demand for different currencies by governments, companies and individuals, including currency speculators. They exist to service international trade and the international movement of money and capital.* (Carew, 1995, p. 48)

The current account of a country's balance of payments shows the amount of currency exchange arising from trade in goods and services (including interest payments on overseas borrowing and transfers between citizens), whereas the capital account shows borrowing and direct investment by foreigners (net of these transactions by Australians).

Summary statistics of Australia's balance of payments for the years 1992–93 to 1994 –95, are presented in table 13.1. The current- and capital-account balances ought to exactly offset one another (i.e. one 'pays' for the other), but do not, due to statistical discrepancies.

Table 13.1 Balance of payments — summary statistics, 1992–93 to 1994–95 ($m)

Item	*1992–93*	*1993–94*	*1994–95*
Exports	60 022	63 852	66 514
Imports	59 427	64 400	74 696
Net services	−2 008	−809	−898
Net income and transfers	−13 252	−15 484	−17 902
Current-account balance	−14 664	−16 841	−26 982
Net official capital transactions	15 374	6 767	15 620
Net non-official capital transactions	557	9 556	5 678
Capital-account balance	15 930	16 323	21 297

Source: RBA, *Bulletin*, Tables H.1 and H.2

Exports and other foreign-currency payments generate a demand for the Australian dollar because they have to be exchanged for Australian dollars for the funds to be used within Australia's payment system. Imports and other foreign-currency payments generate a supply of Australian dollars in the FX market (i.e. a demand for foreign currency) because they have to be exchanged for foreign currencies to be used in the payment systems of other countries.

The exchange of currencies arising from current-account transactions accounts for a fraction (only) of the dealings in the FX market. Cross-border capital transfers are the main source of FX transactions, but their volume is not reflected by the balance on the capital account shown in table 13.1. 'Third-currency' transactions (those involving currencies other than the Australian dollar) are also important in the Australian market (and in others in the same time zone, such as Hong Kong), particularly when the London and New York markets are closed. Dealers also trade in foreign exchange to hedge their risks of an exposure to an adverse movement in exchange rates and to take advantage of arbitrage opportunities.

In April 1995, 77% of the average daily trading in the FX market involved three sets of currencies:

- 42.0% was for the Australian dollar in terms of the US dollar (i.e. AUD/USD),
- 21.7% was for the US dollar in terms of the German mark (i.e. USD/DEM), and
- 13.3% was for the US dollar in terms of the Japanese yen (i.e. USD/JPY). (RBA, 1995, Table 3)

The prices established in FX markets are the exchange rates between the various currencies. An exchange rate is the rate at which one currency is exchanged for another. Given the large number of currencies being traded, there are various ways of measuring a currency's value, but typically it is measured by its exchange rate with the US dollar. For example:

AUD1 = USD0.7515

This exchange rate prices one Australian dollar (AUD) in terms of US dollars (USD). In other words, the price of one Australian dollar (AUD1) is quoted in US dollars.

Every exchange rate treats one currency as the item (or commodity) being priced. In the above example, the Australian dollar is the commodity and its price tag is expressed in US dollars. In theory the choice of the **commodity** currency is entirely arbitrary. The above rate of exchange may also be expressed as:

USD1 = AUD1.3307

where the USD is the commodity currency and the AUD is the **terms** currency. Note that these exchange rates are the reciprocal of the other.

With the rise to prominence of the USD and its adoption as a *de facto* world currency, it is usually quoted as the commodity currency. The currencies of former British Empire countries are the main exceptions. They are also quoted as commodity currencies. The practice of using the local currency of a country as the terms currency (i.e. the foreign currency is the commodity currency) is called **direct quoting**. **Indirect quotes** use the local currency as the commodity currency.

However, the concept of the commodity/terms currency is more useful than the direct/indirect quotation classification. The first-listed currency (e.g. USD1) in any quote is the commodity currency being traded and its price is expressed in terms of the second currency. Increases in the price of a commodity currency mean that its value has **appreciated**, whereas a decrease in its price is a **depreciation** in its value.

Quoting the domestic currency as the commodity currency (indirect method), though, provides a more convenient expression for the local community. To illustrate, suppose the AUD (quoted on a direct basis, placing the USD as the commodity currency) moves as follows:

Day 1: USD = AUD1.3307

Day 2: USD1 = AUD1.3327

This means the USD has increased in value and thus the AUD has depreciated. In other words, the rise in this exchange rate implies a depreciation of the domestic currency. Had the rates been quoted with the AUD as the commodity, their movement would be shown as:

$$\text{Day 1: AUD1} = \text{USD0.7515}$$

$$\text{Day 2: AUD1} = \text{USD0.7504}$$

These quotations are easier for Australians to interpret, given that a fall in the rate indicates a decline in the value of the AUD. Similarly, from a trading viewpoint, it is clear from the latter quotations that, if you bought AUD at USD0.7515 and sold it at USD0.7504, you have made a loss.

The illustrative exchange rates presented in table 13.2 are the 12 most important from Australia's trade viewpoint, as shown by the percentages in the third column. Observe that each currency is given a three-letter code derived from the Reuters classification.

Table 13.2 Selected exchange rates, end September 1995

AUD1 in terms of	*Form of quotation*	*Trade-weight percentage*
Japanese yen	JPY74.22	22.6423
United States dollar	USD0.7550	16.1110
New Zealand dollar	NZD1.1488	6.4830
South Korean won	KRW580.03	5.6853
UK pound sterling	GBP0.4611	5.2241
Chinese renminbi	CNY6.2805	5.1486
German mark	DEM1.0726	4.6313
Singapore dollar	SGD1.0726	4.5931
New Taiwan dollar	TWD20.46	4.4155
Hong Kong dollar	HKD5.8384	2.7655
Malaysian ringgit	MYR1.8932	2.6962
Indonesian rupiah	IDR1717.6	2.5677

Source: RBA, *Bulletin*, October 1995, p. 16 and Table F.9

HISTORICAL DEVELOPMENT OF FX MARKETS

In Australia, foreign exchange is traded in an over-the-counter wholesale market. This is true also for the major FX markets around the world. Consequently, the value of most currencies (i.e. exchange rates) is set by continuous trading in the 24-hour global FX market. Currencies that are freely traded in FX markets are said to have **floating** exchange rates. These arrangements have evolved from a lengthy period in which exchange rates were **fixed**, meaning that the value of currencies was set in relation to a major currency or to gold.

Under the **gold standard**, which was introduced in 1881, the value of currencies was fixed at their rate of convertibility into gold. Therefore, exchange rates were fixed by the relative rates at which currencies were convertible into gold.

Countries held reserves of gold (and reserve currencies such as sterling) to maintain their fixed exchange rate. When, for example, a country encountered a balance-of-trade deficit, the consequent net outflow of reserves reduced its domestic money supply and required the government to deflate the economy to reverse the trade deficit.

Therefore, as trade-deficit problems were 'solved' through deflation of the economy, they did not require the devaluation of the exchange rate. In this way, the gold standard provided a stable exchange-rate environment. However, this was achieved through economies inflating or deflating.

World War I led to the suspension of the gold standard. Because the war had different and major impacts on the various national economies, the post-war values of currencies were no longer related to their pre-war gold parities. The changes in relative value of many countries' currencies frustrated attempts to return to a gold standard in the period between the world wars.

During the 1930s many currencies were devalued and countries imposed exchange controls to help contain their current-account deficits that arose because of an overvalued currency. Exchange controls are a direct control as they have the effect of limiting imports by rationing the supply of foreign currency to importers.

In order to promote international trade in the wake of World War II, a conference of representatives of 44 countries was held in July 1944 at Bretton Woods (a village in New Hampshire, USA) to plan post-war international financial arrangements. The Bretton Woods Agreement established a system of fixed exchange rates that would be managed by the newly created International Monetary Fund (IMF) in association with member countries.

The objectives of the Bretton Woods Agreement were to:

- establish stable exchange rates,
- eliminate exchange controls, and
- facilitate convertibility between all currencies.

Each member country of the IMF undertook to fix its currency in relation to either gold or the USD, and to maintain this parity within 1% above or below the official rate, by central-bank market operations. Periodic changes in official exchange rates were permitted in consultation with the IMF.

The USD became the key currency partly because its government agreed to fix its value in terms of gold (at the rate of USD35 per one ounce of gold) and partly because it became the medium for the settlement of international transactions.

The Bretton Woods system came under great pressure in the late 1950s and in the 1960s. In essence, it was a form of market regulation that was not flexible enough to cope with changing patterns of trade and economic growth. The need for flexibility arose mainly in relation to the USD, in terms of the **strong** currencies, such as the JPY and DEM.

While the USD had been a strong currency in the 1940s and 1950s, massive current-account deficits in the late 1960s and again in the early 1970s undermined the value of the USD, such that it became a **weak** currency (in terms of the new strong ones). However, the Bretton Woods Agreement did not provide for changes in its value and the United States government was reluctant to change its value in terms of gold. Moreover, no amount of central-bank trading could avoid this eventual outcome:

> *the US dollar was left 'unanchored'. That is, the agreement did not recognise external pressures on the US dollar — the key currency — and the possible need for the US dollar to devalue relative to other currencies.* (Linklater, 1992, p. 105)

Within Europe, the UK and France suffered a similar problem in the 1960s whereas Switzerland, Germany and Holland had the reverse problem. Despite this history of movements in exchange rates among European countries, the European Community (EC) decided to align currency values en route toward a single currency. Progress toward this goal is briefly outlined in example 13.1.

In August 1971 the United States government decided to abandon the convertibility of the USD into gold. In December 1971, under the terms of the Smithsonian Agreement, new exchange rates were adopted, with the USD being devalued (i.e. the price of an ounce of gold was increased to USD38), and wider tolerances (2.5% above or below) were set around the official exchange rates. The central banks of member countries and the IMF were to continue to act as exchange rate 'enforcers' whenever rates moved outside the upper or lower limits.

However, this arrangement lasted only to March 1973 when the USD (and several other currencies, such as the UK Pound Sterling and the Italian Lira) came under further selling pressure, sufficient to cause the system to be abandoned and replaced by floating exchange rates.

A floating-exchange-rate regime appears to be necessary within a global economy that displays national variations in productivity, inflation and prosperity. The attempts to sustain officially set exchange rates forced central banks to buy currencies that the market judged to be 'weak' and sell currencies the market judged to be 'strong'. This interfered with the monetary policies of the major central banks and inflicted losses on them.

example 13.1

Despite the lessons of the Bretton Woods period, several European Community countries attempted to establish a tight link between the value of their currencies. This was known as the 'snake in the tunnel'. It permitted limited fluctuations in exchange rates (the 'tunnel') in accordance with the Smithsonian agreement. However, by the late 1970s market pressures undermined the effectiveness of the snake.

In 1979, the European Monetary System (EMS) replaced the snake. It had wider limits, set in terms of the European Currency Unit (ECU), a weighted average of the eight currencies that comprised the EMS, plus Sterling. When a member's exchange rate with another member's currency reached the 'divergence indicator', new economic policies were called for to keep this exchange rate within the parity limit.

Experience with the EMS, though, was similar to that with the snake. Currency values changed over time, causing realignments and eventual withdrawal by a number of countries. In the next chapter we explain that differences in national inflation and growth rates (among other factors) cause exchange-rate movements, and this makes fixed rates unsustainable.

A new approach to monetary integration was proposed by the Delors Committee in 1989. This committee proposed a three-stage approach to achieve European Monetary Union (EMU) by 1999. It is based on the requirement that member countries pursue economic policies that bring about 'economic convergence' (of their economies) prior to the establishment of a single currency (the **euro**) and monetary system.

In December 1991, in the town of Maastricht (in the Netherlands) the *Treaty of European Union* was signed by the representatives of 15 European countries. It provided for the establishment of EMU on the basis of a three-stage time table. Stage one began in July 1990 with the aim of achieving a greater convergence in their economic performance, including the maintenance of stable exchange rates (under EMS). Stage two began on 1 January 1994 with the aim of establishing the basis for a single currency and monetary policy. However, as at the end of 1994 (Pollard, 1995, p. 6) only two countries would be eligible to join the EMU (based on their progress toward economic convergence). All five criteria of convergence (these are listed below) need to be satisfied to be eligible for membership of the EMU. The third stage must start by 1 January 1999.

A decision was made at the end of 1996 to proceed with the introduction of the EMU. Some further key dates in the plan for EMU are shown below:

1997	*1998*	*1999*	*2001*	*30 June 2002*
Decision on which countries can join the EMU, based on the five economic convergence criteria	Stage three: introduction of single currency (the 'euro'), the European Central Bank, a common monetary policy and real-time settlement		Completion of EMU, withdrawal of old currencies, etc.	

The five economic performance criteria for membership are:

- exchange-rate stability (judged by the currency's performance in the EMS),
- low inflation rate,
- low long-term interest rates,
- budget deficit not to exceed 3% of GDP, and
- the government's debt not to exceed 60% of GDP.

Should EMU occur, the euro will replace national currencies (such as the German mark), intra-European exchange rates will disappear and financial securities will be expressed in euros. This represents a major change to the financial landscape.

In 1996, the forward interest-rate markets in those countries most likely to join the EMU in 1999 reveal the financial market's expectation that this event will occur, given that entry will result in the adoption of a single interest rate (for any given class and term of security).

The degree of convergence between these rates has varied in response to political and economic events that have affected the likelihood of the euro's introduction. For instance, in 1995, the spreads in forward rates reflected uncertainty about the single currency's adoption, but by mid 1996,forward interest rates suggested that four countries are likely to adopt the single currency in 1999. These are Germany, the Netherlands, Belgium and France.

Floating the AUD

Prior to 1931 the then Australian pound was at parity with the GBP, but in that year it was devalued because of Australia's overseas debt and the adverse affect of the Depression on Australia's exports. From 1931 to 1967 the exchange rate was fixed at one Australian pound equals GBP0.8. Following the adoption of the dollar as the unit of currency in 1966 this rate became GBP1 = AUD2.5050.

From November 1967 (when the Australian government decided not to devalue in accord with the 14.3% devaluation of the GBP) until 1971, the exchange rate became GBP1 = AUD2.14715. In 1971 the AUD was fixed in relation to the USD at the rate AUD1 = USD1.2160. This shift in the reference rate was related to the declining importance of the UK as a trading partner and the dominant role of the USD in foreign-trade contracts. However, the Smithsonian Accord provided the opportunity for the change.

In the post-Smithsonian Accord period, the AUD was revalued upwards on three occasions, reaching USD1.4875 in September 1973. These rate adjustments reflected, in part, domestic economic conditions (e.g. a large balance-of-trade surplus in 1972–73) and, in part, a weakening USD.

The Australian government responded (on 25 September 1974) to the increasingly volatile international monetary conditions by modifying its fixed-rate regime, basing the exchange rate on the trade-weighted index. The AUD was devalued by 12% against the USD at the same time.

In November 1976, the fixed link with the TWI was replaced by a flexible peg mechanism, mainly because the exchange rate did not reflect the **bi-lateral** exchange rates in the global FX market. Under this mechanism the government frequently altered the value of the AUD against a basket of currencies. It amounted to a managed exchange rate. This regime remained in place until the AUD was floated on 8 December 1983.

The floating of the AUD meant the RBA was relieved of its obligation to support the official exchange rate. Exchange controls were substantially eased to facilitate the operations of the foreign-exchange market. In addition, banks were no longer required to settle their foreign-exchange positions with the RBA.

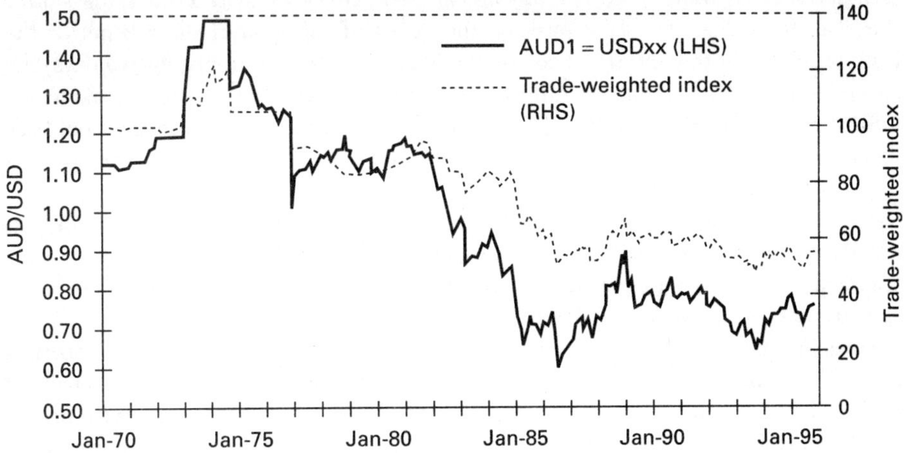

Figure 13.1 The value of the Australian dollar in terms of the USD and TWI, 1970 to 1995

Figure 13.1 charts the value of the AUD between 1970 and 1995. It shows the value of the AUD in terms of the USD and the trade-weighted index. Observe the volatility of the currency since 1983 and that even during the periods when the value of the currency was managed by the authorities, its value was volatile.

FX 'INSTRUMENTS'

Essentially, there is only one FX instrument: contracts to exchange one currency for another. Given that there are many currencies, there is a matrix of bilateral exchange rates, the values of which correspond to each other.

One basis for distinguishing between types of FX transactions is the timing of settlement (i.e. the exchange of the two currencies). The basic transaction (**spot**) involves settlement in two business days. Other transactions involve a later or earlier settlement, as shown in figure 13.2.

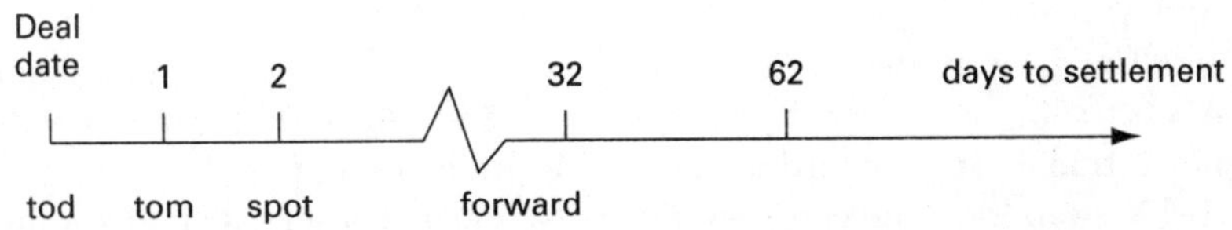

Figure 13.2 FX instruments according to settlement dates

Spot transactions

The day an FX transaction is made is referred to as the **deal date**. The settlement date of each transaction is referred to as the **value date**. In the case of spot transactions, the value date is T+2 (i.e. the deal is settled two business days after the deal date). The two days between the deal and value dates allow time for the back offices of both parties to process the deal. Each has to supply, in two days, the agreed amount of currency. To illustrate, assume a spot deal is made to exchange USD5 million for AUD6 802 721. The seller of the USD has to arrange its delivery in two business days and the seller of the AUD also has two days to arrange its delivery.

Spot transactions are an important part of the Australian market, making up 44.6% of the average daily transactions in April 1995. About 32% of these spot transactions involved the Australian dollar. A larger proportion (56%) were USD spot transactions. (RBA, 1995, Tables 1 and 2)

Foreign-currency deals can be arranged on a more immediate basis. **Tom** is market shorthand for a transaction that specifies tomorrow (i.e. the next business day) as the value date. The settlement amounts in such a transaction are based on the spot exchange rate discounted by one day's interest in the two currencies (i.e. discounted at the interest rate in their respective money markets). Settlement can also be arranged on the same day. This is referred to as the **tod** rate.

Forward transactions

All transactions that involve a settlement date after spot are at 'forward rates'. These deals can be arranged for any forward value date, but most are arranged on a monthly basis, such as the one-month and two-month forward rates. Settlement occurs on the monthly anniversary of the spot settlement date, provided it is a business day. To illustrate, suppose a one-month forward deal was made on Wednesday 9 October 1996. The spot date was Friday 11 October and therefore the settlement date was Monday 11 November 1996.

There are two forms of forward transactions: **outright forward** and **swaps**. The former is a one-way exchange of currencies at a forward date. The latter is a round-trip exchange of currencies. For instance, an exchange of AUD for USD at the spot rate followed by the exchange of USD for AUD at the agreed forward date. These should not be confused with capital-market swaps which will be discussed in Chapter 18.

Forward rates are usually expressed as a margin against the current spot rate. The amount of the margin (or points) is specific to each forward period. Typically, the **forward points** are greater for a two-month contract than for a one-month contract. The forward points are added to the spot rate when the commodity currency is trading at a forward premium and deducted from the spot rate when the currency is trading at a forward discount. (McGrath, 1994, p. 341)

In an FX swap 'one currency, say \$A, is swapped (converted) into another, say \$US, for a specified period. This is carried out by selling \$A today at the spot rate and buying \$A back for a future value date.' (Carew and Slayter, 1994, p. 138) It is an exchange of two cash flows; the first leg involves a spot transaction, say for AUD10m against USD, and the second is a forward transaction that reverses the spot transaction. For example, if the spot transaction sold AUD10m, the forward transaction would buy AUD10m. (Nguyen, 1993, p. 443) This is known as a sell/buy FX swap. (Allan *et. al.*, 1990, p. 11)

Notice that a sell/buy FX swap (i.e. sell the commodity currency spot and buy it forward) means that the party acquires the terms currency (USD in the case of an AUD/USD transaction) for the period of the swap, which is set by the term of the forward contract. The reverse applies in a buy/sell FX swap.

The forward rate, as explained above, is the sum of the spot rate and the forward points. In the case of an FX swap, the forward points are referred to as **swap points**, but the forward rate is set in the same way, as for an outright forward.

The use of FX swaps has increased considerably, representing 52% of the average daily transactions on the Australian FX market in April 1995, compared with 33% in April 1989. Just under half of the FX swap transactions were in terms of the AUD, the balance being against the USD.

Outright forward transactions represented only 3.3% of the average daily turnover in the Australian market in April 1995, compared with 5.2% in April 1989. While the outright forwards represent a small proportion of FX transactions, they comprise part of the FX swap transactions. And so the calculation of forward rates, explained below, is of considerable importance.

> *Most transactions in the forward and swap markets were for maturities of up to a year. In the forward market, around 29% of gross turnover had a term-to-maturity of up to one week and 69% had a term-to-maturity of between one week and one year; only 2% had a term-to-maturity of more than a year. In the swap market, 61% of gross turnover had a term-to-maturity of up to one week and 37% had a term-to-maturity between one week and one year, only 2% had a term-to-maturity of more than one year.* (RBA, 1995, p. 46)

Note that the turnover data presented above were collected by the RBA as part of the three-yearly surveys conducted for the Bank for International Settlements. These surveys have covered the month of April in the years 1989, 1992 and 1995.

MARKET PARTICIPANTS

The five main groups of market participants are dealers, overseas banks, clients, brokers and the RBA. Dealers are licensed by the RBA. They are mainly banks and merchant banks that serve the FX needs of their clients. However, these institutions also trade between one another and with overseas banks.

Dealers

Prior to the floating of the currency, only banks could deal in FX and, as outlined above, the exchange rate was set, one way or another, by the RBA. The float meant that the exchange rate was set through trading in the FX market. This trading is conducted by professional dealers who are licensed by the RBA. It was decided that licences would be granted to any company that:

- has shareholders' funds of at least $10 million,
- has a competent dealing team,
- maintains prudent internal controls and standards,

- complies with its end-of-day open position limit (which is based on the equity funds it commits to its trading activities),
- provides the statistical data (and other market information) sought by the RBA, and
- maintains appropriate operating standards. (Linklater, 1992, p. 119)

Subject to the RBA's licensing requirements, dealers aim to make a profit from trading FX. In essence, this boils down to buying low and selling high.

As explained below, not all trades are made with 'clients' (parties who have foreign currency to sell or who wish to buy foreign currency). Moreover, trading by dealers involves risks, such as the price (or market) risk that arises from adverse movements in exchange rates. The management of this risk might involve trading foreign currency and these deals aim to hedge potential losses rather than to make a profit.

Even though many other institutions (mainly merchant banks and foreign-owned banks) were issued with licences following the floating of the currency, the largest FX dealers are the major banks and the investment banks that specialise in foreign-exchange dealing. The ten largest FX dealers handled, in April 1995, 70% of the average daily turnover. This represents a high degree of market concentration, by world standards.

Trading foreign currencies is a specialised activity but, as explained below, the value of currencies, particularly on a forward basis, is related to the interest rates in domestic short-term money markets.

> *The dealing area is the hub of a bank or merchant bank's trading operations and encompasses activities in the short-term money market, futures and bond markets as well as foreign exchange. The . . . larger trading banks employ a wide range of dealers, each assigned to specialist areas such as spot, forward, $A, deutschmark and so on. In a major bank one trader might handle spot trading in yen exclusively; for show, he or she might have a small Japanese flag on the desk.* (Carew and Slayter, 1994, p. 99)

The larger FX dealer organisations, such as the major banks, have to coordinate the positions of their various traders, a role performed by a chief or senior trader. In general, professional dealers are risk-averse, and will make trades during the day to 'square' an excessive exposure to a currency. As previously noted, the RBA sets exposure limits on licensed dealers.

In a large dealing room, some traders may specialise in client work, whereas others trade in the inter-bank market. The former develop an understanding of the client's FX needs, whereas the latter concentrate on the market and make deals according to their instinct.

> *A good dealer* feels *where the market is going; he or she senses a move or reaction 20 or 30 seconds ahead of the pack and acts on that insight. It is an intangible quality but is one that clearly marks out the top dealers from the herd.* (Carew and Slayter, 1994, p. 104)

The main counterparties of the dealers in Australia's FX market are overseas banks. In April 1995, 57% of the average daily turnover was with overseas banks.

This reflects the role of the Australian market within the global FX market. In the same month about 20% of the market's turnover was between the domestic dealers.

In addition to their role as dealers, banks serve the FX needs of retail customers. These include the exchange of notes, the sale (and cashing) of traveller's cheques, and the transfers of funds overseas by various methods. The difference between the buying and selling rates (i.e. the spreads) in the retail market are much wider than in the wholesale market, partly because of the smaller value of each transaction and the greater amount of time required to complete the transaction.

Clients

The 'client market' includes companies that are engaged in foreign trade and/or conduct financing arrangements overseas (or in foreign currencies), financial institutions that borrow and lend/invest overseas or in foreign currencies. As noted in Chapters 6, 7 and 8, banks, non-banks and fund managers hold foreign-currency assets and, in some cases, have incurred foreign-currency liabilities.

The main purpose of the clients' FX transactions is to hedge their exposure to price risk. They usually have fewer dealings in the FX market than dealers, but some undertake large transactions (such as a large purchase of overseas equities by a fund manager or a large sale of USD by an exporter) and therefore can influence the market at the time of these transactions.

Large companies, government enterprises and non-dealer financial institutions that have substantial FX requirements employ their own traders within their Treasury departments. Mining companies, such as BHP, that generate substantial export earnings, monitor movements in exchange rates and trade in FX in much the same way as a bank. Their trading expertise would match that of most banks.

While companies tend to hedge their perennial FX exposure, they may 'speculate' through their trading strategies. This might involve leaving an exposure unhedged or over-hedged. While these terms are explained below, it should be noted that the dividing line between speculation and trading strategies is a fine one in the context of the FX market.

Transactions with clients represented 23% of the average daily turnover in the FX market in April 1995.

Brokers

Despite the dissemination of information to the market by the Reuters and Telerate services, currency **brokers** have a role to play. They comprehensively monitor exchange rates and provide dealers with information on the lowest (if buying) and highest (if selling) rates available in the market. Whereas dealers identify themselves when requesting bid/offer rates from other dealers, brokers can obtain this information without disclosing the identity of the buyer or seller.

The role of the broker is to bring together a buyer and a seller. Brokers do not deal in foreign exchange. They receive a commission for the deals that they help to broker. In April 1995, 25% of the average daily turnover was arranged by brokers. This represents a lower proportion than in April 1992.

Reserve Bank of Australia

In theory, floating exchange rates are regarded as 'clean' only when the central bank does not trade in the FX market, or take any other action that influences exchange rates. But in Australia, the RBA is an active participant in the FX market through:

- trading in the FX market for 'smoothing and testing' purposes,
- meeting the foreign-exchange requirements of its 'client': the Commonwealth Government,
- its influence on short-term interest rates for monetary-policy purposes, and
- its licensing and prudential supervision of FX dealers.

Trading in the market to reduce variability in the exchange rate ('testing') is intended to moderate what appear to be sharp changes in the exchange rate. Nevertheless, such intervention is not a form of 'managed float'. These activities are related the bank's responsibility to maintain the stability of the financial system.

In essence, the RBA attempts to influence the spot exchange rate when the bank believes it is either temporarily too low or too high. Its aim is to encourage 'the market' (i.e. dealers) to reassess current values; hence the term 'testing' the market. The objective is to eliminate excessive movements in exchange rates (i.e. 'smoothing' of exchange rates). The underlying assumption of these activities is that the FX market will, on occasions, cause the value of the currency to 'overshoot', and trade outside of the range implied by its 'fundamentals' (i.e. the conditions in the economy that are most relevant to the currency's value, such as economic growth, the inflation rate and interest rates).

> *The golden thread running through a central bank's activities is its abiding interest in stability. This also motivates its intervention in the foreign-exchange market, where we prefer to see orderliness rather than volatility. The objective of intervention is not to prevent an adjustment of the exchange rate to a new equilibrium but to ensure an orderly move to any new level that might be appropriate.* (Campbell, 1995, p. 50)

As noted in Chapter 2, the RBA is the Commonwealth Government's banker. Therefore it trades in the FX market to satisfy its client's needs. Whenever the bank buys or sells foreign exchange it **sterilises** the transaction as it would otherwise result in a change in the financial system's liquidity. To illustrate, suppose the bank purchased USD from a dealer in the FX market. Payment by the bank for this currency increases the financial system's liquidity (unintentionally) and so the bank would sell securities to dealers in the money market in order to offset the inflow of cash to the financial system.

When formulating monetary policy, the RBA takes into account the exchange rate, although this does not mean that it adopts a monetary-policy setting that is intended to support a particular exchange rate. Similarly, changing short-term rates for monetary policy purposes will have an effect on spot exchange rates, but this is not the only factor that affects the rate. In the next chapter we consider the relationship between interest rates and exchange rates. In general, for instance, the prospect of an increase in interest rates will cause the exchange rate to appreciate; but holding the exchange rate at the new level is another matter.

Despite the influence the RBA is able to exert on short-term interest rates, especially through the impact of its intervention on market expectations, it is widely accepted that central banks are not capable, given the depth of FX markets, of supporting an exchange rate over the longer term which the market regards as being too high or too low.

According to data presented in Campbell (1995, p. 51), the frequency and nature of the RBA's intervention in the FX market has changed considerably since the currency was floated. Initially after the float (December 1983 to June 1986) the bank intervened frequently but traded in small amounts. Over the next five years, when the exchange rate experienced sharp movements, the bank intervened more aggressively (i.e. by trading in larger amounts and in a more public way) to stem both falls (e.g. in July 1986 following the 'banana republic' episode) and increases (e.g. in February 1989 when the rate approached USD90 cents). During the 1990s the frequency of intervention has declined and, from December 1993 to mid 1995, the bank did not intervene at all because of the market's stability.

TRADING PRACTICES

Australia's FX market is a wholesale over-the-counter market that forms part of the global trading in FX. The core of the Australian market is formed by inter-bank dealing by professional dealers who act as market makers in various currencies.

Dealers operate from dealing rooms that are fitted out with the most up-to-date communication equipment and have access to the financial information (including data on bids and offers in the market) provided by Reuters and Telerate. Deals are made by telephone with the details confirmed in writing. Should a mistake occur, the deal agreed to on the telephone is honoured.

According to Carew and Slayter (1994, p. 51), deals between dealers in the inter-bank market are also made through the Reuters dealing system.

An FX deal must specify four matters:

1. the amount of the currency being bought or sold,
2. the agreed rate of exchange,
3. the agreed settlement date, and
4. settlement instructions.

Typical trading parcels are for amounts of $5–10 million, and should a deal be sought in an abnormally large parcel, this fact would be made known by the inquiring dealer.

Because of the pace of the market, trading is expressed in standard abbreviations. Currencies are given shortened names. Because of the prominence of the US dollar, it is referred to as 'the dollar'. Other dollar currencies are referred to in other ways. For example, the New Zealand dollar is referred to as the 'kiwi' and the Canadian dollar as 'Can'. Examples of written and spoken quotes are presented in table 13.3.

The agreed exchange rate is established when the calling dealer accepts either the bid or offer of the quoting dealer. The quoting dealer's bid will be the lower of the two prices, which will be expressed first, as shown by the illustrative quotes in

Table 13.3 Examples of FX quotes

Written quote	*Spoken quote*
USD/DEM1.3630-38	Dollar/Mark or Marks
USD/JPY115.25-30	Dollar/Yen or Yen
GBP/USD1.8325-30	Cable or Sterling or Pound
USD/CHF1.0920-25	Swiss franc or Swissy
AUD/USD0.7515-20	Australian dollar or Aussie
USD/HKD7.7510-15	Hong Kong dollar or Dollar/Honkie

table 13.3. The calling dealer always takes the opposite position to the quoting dealer. If the caller wishes to buy the commodity currency, it accepts the quoting bank's offer rate. If it wishes to sell the commodity currency, it accepts the quoting bank's bid rate.

As noted above, the quoting dealer will provide a two-way quotation regardless of the dealer's desire to buy or sell a currency. If the dealer has a preference regarding the transaction, this will be revealed in the level of the two-way price the trader quotes. Should the quoting dealer prefer to sell rather than buy, the first price will be below the general level of bids in the market and the second price will be at the low end of the market's range of offers. The low offer will attract those traders wishing to buy. This practice is referred to as **shading**. (Allan *et. al*, 1990, p. 67)

Look back to the illustrative quote in table 13.3 for the Aussie:

AUD/USD0.7515-20

Observe that the quotes are to four decimal places, whereas the yen is quoted to two decimal places. This practice is a market convention that determines the number of decimals on the basis of the level of the price for the commodity currency. In the case of the quotes for the Aussie, the last two decimals are referred to as 'points'. The second decimal place represents the **figure** (in this example the figure is five) and the first decimal place is called the **big figure**. When making a two-way quotation over the telephone it is assumed that both parties are aware of the figure and so only the points are stated.

In the above example, the quote would be 'Aussie is 15-20'. The 75 US cents is assumed to be understood.

A calling party has three responses to a two-way quote. An intention to purchase AUD is indicated by the phrase, 'mine at 20', an intention to sell AUD is indicated by 'yours at 15'. A call of 'no interest' is self evident.

In the event of a deal, the calling dealer will confirm the amount of the currency purchased/sold, the price, the settlement date and the settlement arrangements. This conversation will be taped to resolve any dispute that might arise.

The difference between the bid and the offer prices is the dealer's spread. It represents the basis of the profit (or trading commission) a dealer will make if he or she is fortunate enough to have two calling dealers simultaneously take opposite sides of a currency deal.

In 1995, the spreads in the inter-bank market for standard-sized trades (five to ten million) were only two to three points. So, if a dealer bought AUD10 million at USD0.7420 and sold this parcel for USD0.7423, the commission would amount to USD3000. It is a very rare occurrence for a dealer to be 'hit' on both sides of its quote. Consequently, over time and on average, dealers will buy currency at a price that is slightly lower than the price at which they will sell the currency.

The spread within the FX market reflects the market's depth, competitiveness and price volatility. Increases in turnover and competitiveness tend to reduce spreads, whereas increases in volatility intensify the price risk faced by market makers and so tend to widen the spread.

FX dealers trade for four general purposes. The first is to satisfy the needs of primary clients: companies that import and/or export or borrow or lend in foreign currencies. The dealer makes a profit on these transactions because of the spread between the dealer's bid and offer rates. In such a trade, the client 'hits' the dealer by accepting either the dealer's bid or offer. The dealer's bid for a foreign currency is accepted (typically) by an exporter who is selling that currency. The dealer's offer for a foreign currency would typically be accepted by an importer who requires the currency to complete a purchase.

The second purpose is to arbitrage between the various segments of the FX market. For example, a dealer might observe that the exchange rate for a currency in one centre differs from that quoted in another and so can profit by simultaneously buying (at the lower price) and selling (at the higher price).

The FX dealer's third purpose is to speculate in a currency. This involves 'taking a position' in a currency (either a **long** position by buying a currency or a **short** position by selling a currency) in the expectation that the exchange rate will move in a favourable direction. If the dealer is long in a currency, profits will result if the currency appreciates, because the dealer can sell at the higher price. If the dealer is short in a currency, profits will result if the currency depreciates, because the dealer can subsequently buy at a lower price. Usually dealers do not maintain open positions for very long, given their need to manage price risk.

Note that trading and speculating are very similar processes. A dealer who, for instance, buys foreign currency from an exporter as part of its normal trading activities, acquires a long position in that currency (unless by chance the dealer had a pre-existing short position). This is exactly the same position as would occur if the dealer set out to acquire the foreign currency because of an expectation that it would appreciate in value.

Fourth, a dealer trades to hedge his or her FX exposure. When dealers have made large transactions they may decide to offset their position rather than remain exposed to an adverse movement in the exchange rate. Suppose Bank A is hit by Bank B, which is selling a large parcel of USD. The senior dealer with Bank A may decide to sell some of this USD to reduce the bank's exposure arising from its long position in USD. Such trades do not add to the dealer's profits; they reduce the dealer's risk of losses.

The appendix to this chapter provides an explanation of how dealers keep track of their position when trading in the market.

FX EXPOSURES AND RISK

An FX exposure exists when a company's profits are affected by changes in exchange rates. The basic form of an FX exposure is price, or market, risk. It can arise when a company has future foreign-currency obligations or receipts. In the former case, the exposure arises because an appreciation of the foreign currency will increase the AUD cost of the obligations. In the latter case, the exposure is to a depreciation of the foreign currency, because this reduces the AUD value of the receipts.

Movements in exchange rates, because they alter the value of assets and liabilities valued in terms of the domestic currency, also involve **translation risk**, even if the party has no intention of making an FX transaction (that gives rise to the price risk). Dealers in the FX market (including 'clients' who manage their FX position) are also exposed to 'operational' risks, such as the risk that unauthorised transactions will be undertaken, resulting in an exposure that cannot be managed (because of its covert nature). In this section we confine our attention to the FX risk arising from a future FX transaction.

Most businesses have an FX exposure of some degree. An exposure constitutes a price risk because businesses cannot predict the future movements in exchange rates reliably. (We discuss the determinants of FX movements in the next chapter. Our conclusion is that in an efficient market, not even professional forecasters can consistently predict the movement in exchange rates.) Given that most businesses are risk-averse, they will manage their exposure.

Since price risk arises from uncertain future exchange rates, one way of managing this risk is to use forward rates to fix a particular exchange rate. If, for instance, an exporter will receive USD10 million in three months; the AUD value of this payment can be set by the exporter selling these US dollars at the three-month forward rate. If this action is taken, it does not matter what happens to the spot AUD/USD rate over the next three months, the exporter knows how much AUD will be generated by this payment.

If the USD depreciates (i.e. the AUD appreciates), the forward rate will in fact deliver a larger AUD receipt than if the dealer left this position unhedged and simply converted the USD into AUD at the spot rate in three months' time. But if the USD appreciates over this period, the forward rate will deliver a smaller amount of AUD than if the exporter exchanged the USD into AUD in three months.

Consequently, hedging the FX exposure does not imply a profitable outcome, compared with the future spot rate. The forward rate removes the uncertainty. It is a risk-management instrument. We explain how the value of forward rates is determined in the next section.

CALCULATING EXCHANGE RATES

Spot exchange rates are determined in the FX market. But certain other exchange rates, which we explain below, have to be calculated by traders from spot rates. For these purposes it is instructive if we show that an exchange rate can be derived from the amounts exchanged, as follows:

$$e = \frac{Q_{terms}}{Q_{commodity}}$$ *Equation (13.1)*

where Q_{terms} is the amount of the terms currency,
$Q_{commodity}$ is the amount of the commodity currency, and
e is the bilateral exchange rate.

Suppose you are supplying 1000 units of the commodity currency, say it is AUD, and your counterparty is supplying 750 units of the terms currency, say it is USD. The exchange rate is:

$$e_{AUD/USD} = 750/1000$$
$$= 0.7500$$

We can rearrange equation (13.1) to find the amount of the terms currency required to complete a transaction given the exchange rate and the quantity of the commodity currency, as follows:

$$Q_{terms} = e\,(Q_{commodity})$$ *Equation (13.1a)*

To illustrate, suppose you want to exchange AUD1000 for USD when the exchange rate, e, is AUD1 = USD0.7500. The amount of USD is:

$$USD? = 0.7500(1000)$$
$$= 750$$

Cross rates

We have mentioned that there is a matrix of exchange rates; each currency may be purchased/sold in terms of each other. But, in practice, the major currency that is traded in the FX market is the USD. In order to determine the exchange rate between two currencies that are not actively traded it is necessary to cross the currencies against a traded currency. These are referred to as **cross rates**.

Given the prominence of the USD in FX markets, it serves as the traded currency. Therefore, the rate of exchange between two non-USD currencies is calculated as a cross rate. For example, AUD/CHF is a cross rate. It is found by converting CHF into USD (i.e. buying USD with CHF) and using these funds to purchase AUD. Suppose USD1 = CHF1.3200 and AUD1 = USD0.7250, the CHF price of AUD1 is found as the product of these rates, as follows:

$$AUD1/CHF? = 1.3200(0.7250)$$
$$= 0.9570$$

Chain rule

However, the calculation of cross rates can be confusing, especially when direct and indirect quotes are involved.

> *A popular method for calculating cross rates is the chain, devised by Heinz Riehl, a Citibank Treasurer. The chain is particularly helpful in calculating the cross rate of two unfamiliar 'exotic' currencies.* (Carew and Slayter, 1994, p. 77)

The chain involves four steps. We will illustrate its use with the case of an Australian exporter who is due CHF10 million and requests its value in AUD, given the above exchange rates:

$$\text{AUD1} = \text{USD0.7250}$$

$$\text{USD1} = \text{CHF1.3200}$$

Step 1 State the rate that is sought (in this case, how much CHF is equivalent to AUD1):

$$\text{CHF?} = \text{AUD1}$$

Step 2 State the USD value of the currency that ended the first step:

$$\text{AUD1} = \text{USD0.7250}$$

Step 3 State the value of the USD in terms of the other currency:

$$\text{USD1} = \text{CHF1.3200}$$

Step 4 Divide the product of the right-hand-side numbers by the product of the left-hand-side numbers (in steps 2 and 3) to answer the question posed in step 1:

$$\text{CHF?} = \frac{0.7250 * 1.3200}{1 * 1}$$

$$= 0.9570$$

Therefore the exporter's receipt of CHF10 million is worth, using equation (13.1a):

$$\text{CHF10m} = 0.9570 * \text{AUD?}$$

$$\text{AUD} = \frac{10\,000\,000}{0.957}$$

$$= 10\,449\,321$$

example 13.2

Construct a cross rate for DEM/YEN on the basis that the USD/DEM rate is 1.5600 and the USD/YEN rate is 170.

Using the chain rule we have:

$$\text{YEN}_{xx} = \text{DEM1}$$

$$\text{DEM1.5600} = \text{USD1}$$

$$\text{USD1} = \text{YEN170.00}$$

Thus: $$\text{DEM/YEN} = \frac{1 * 170}{1 * 1.56}$$

$$= 108.97$$

Note in example 13.2 that we have used mid-point rates. In practice, there are bid and offer rates and the mid-point rates are averages of these two rates. So cross rates are calculated using the relevant bid and offer rates. Suppose the actual exchange rates in the above illustration are:

$$\text{AUD1} = \text{USD0.7245-55}$$

$$\text{USD1} = \text{CHF1.3195-05}$$

We need to calculate the dealer's bid rate as this is the rate at which the exporter will sell the CHF10 million:

Step 1 As stated above:

$$\text{CHF?} = \text{AUD1}$$

Step 2 This refers to the offer (i.e. sell) rate for the AUD:

$$\text{AUD1} = \text{USD0.7255}$$

Step 3 This refers to the offer (i.e. sell) rate for the USD:

$$\text{USD1} = \text{CHF1.3205}$$

Step 4 As stated above, to find the bank's bid rate for the CHF:

$$\text{AUD1} = \frac{0.7255 * 1.3205}{1 * 1}$$

$$= \text{CHF0.9580}$$

The exporter will actually receive less AUD for the CHF10 million, because of the dealer's spread:

$$\text{AUD} = \frac{10\,000\,000}{0.9580}$$

$$= 10\,438\,413$$

The dealer's offer rate for CHF, given the above two-way quotes is:

$$\text{AUD1} = \frac{0.7245 * 1.3195}{1 * 1}$$

$$= \text{CHF}0.9560$$

This is the rate at which the bank would sell CHF to, for example, an Australian importer of Swiss chocolate to meet the cost of a shipment.

Observe that the spread is wider for the cross rate (i.e. 20 points) than for the individual rates (i.e. 10 points). This results because the client is on the 'wrong' side of both rates when the cross rate is calculated.

Given that the above example focused on the AUD value of CHF, the reciprocal of the rates would provide a clearer view of the dealer's bid and offer rates. In the conventional quotation form, the bank sells AUD (i.e. buys CHF) at the offer rate (CHF0.9580) and buys AUD (sells CHF) at the bid rate (CHF0.9560), as follows:

AUD1 = CHF0.9560-80

From the Swiss viewpoint, the bank's bid (i.e. the reciprocal of CHF0.9580) and offer (i.e. the reciprocal of CHF0.9560) rates are:

CHF1 = AUD1.0438-60

This quotation clearly shows that the bank buys CHF at the lower rate and sells at the higher rate.

Forward rates

We explained in an earlier section that there are two ways of arranging forward rates: outright forwards and FX swaps. However, from a calculation viewpoint both rely on forward rates, which are explained in this section.

Before we present the formula for a forward rate, consider the elements of a forward FX transaction. It is simply an exchange of currencies at the agreed (forward) settlement date. The forward-rate formula determines how much of one currency will be exchanged for a given amount of the other.

For simplicity, assume that two parties each have funds that they plan to exchange in the FX market for use in three months. They could exchange at the spot rate and invest their respective proceeds in a three-month risk-free security (such as a Treasury note), yielding a future amount in the desired currency. Alternatively, they could invest in a three-month risk-free security in their domestic money market and exchange the proceeds for use in the other currency. Either way, they acquire the future amount of the other currency.

Recall from Chapter 4 that the future amount (in each currency, say AUD and USD) arising from an investment in a short-term money market is calculated as follows:

$$F_{AUD} = P_{AUD}\,(1 + rt_{AUD})$$

$$F_{USD} = P_{USD}\,(1 + rt_{USD})$$

The equivalent present-value amounts of each currency are determined by the spot rate. Assuming this is AUD/USD0.7400 and the AUD amount is $10 million, the equivalent USD amount is:

$$\begin{aligned} USD? &= 0.7400\,(AUD10m) \\ &= USD7.4m \end{aligned}$$

The ratio of the future amounts (in three months) will produce the forward rate. That is,

$$f_{AUD/USD} = F_{USD}\,/F_{AUD}$$

We can apply this simple logic to arrive at the formula for calculating a forward rate. It must start with the spot rate and be adjusted according to the ratio of the future value of the amount in the terms currency over the future value of the amount in the commodity currency, as follows:

$$f_{com/terms} = s_{com/terms}\left[\frac{1 + rt_{terms}}{1 + rt_{com}}\right] \qquad \textit{Equation (13.2)}$$

where s refers to the spot exchange rate,
r_{terms} is the interest rate in the terms country,
r_{com} is the interest rate in the commodity country, and
t is time in years.

To illustrate, suppose r_{USD} is 5.50% p.a., r_{AUD} is 7.50% p.a. and t is three months (roundly 3/12), the forward rate, using equation (13.2) will be:

$$\begin{aligned} f_{AUD/USD} &= 0.7400\left[\frac{1 + 0.055 * (3/12)}{1 + 0.075 * (3/12)}\right] \\ &= 0.7400*0.995092 \\ &= 0.7364 \end{aligned}$$

Notice that in this example, the forward rate for the AUD is less than the spot rate. In other words, the forward rate is at a discount to the spot rate and so the forward points, in this case, 36 (0.7400 − 0.7364), are deducted from the spot rate.

A simple inspection of equation (13.2) shows that the forward rate will trade at a discount to the spot rate when the expression in the large brackets is less than one, and this occurs when the interest rate in the terms currency (shown in the numerator) is less than the rate in the commodity currency (shown in the denominator); and vice versa. This is an important (and, perhaps, a counter-intuitive) principle. The currency of the country with the higher interest rate will trade at a forward discount (and vice versa).

Observe that the forward rate is calculated from the spot rate and the two interest rates. It is not a quote that dealers base on their expectation of the future exchange rate. But this does not mean that expectations about the movement in exchange rates are not relevant to either forward or spot rates. Dealers trade in both spot and forward rates, therefore if they thought one was too high they would sell at that rate and buy at the other.

Moreover, as will be explained in the next chapter, expectations play a part in determining interest rates (and interest differentials). Given that interest rates link spot and forward exchange rates, it follows that both are shaped by expectations.

The linkage between forward and spot exchange rates based on interest rates is enforced through arbitrage. Should the forward rate vary from that implied by the two interest rates, FX dealers can engage in arbitrage by manufacturing a forward rate by:

1 borrowing funds in one currency (say, P_{AUD} at r_{AUD}),
2 converting them at the spot rate (into, say, USD),
3 investing the proceeds in the short-term money market (at r_{USD}) for the term of the intended forward contract,
4 converting the future amount (F_{USD}) back at the agreed forward rate to the original currency (AUD), to
5 repay the original loan (F_{AUD}) and bank the profit.

This is an arbitrage deal because all of the variables ($s_{AUD/USD}$, $f_{AUD/USD}$, r_{AUD} and r_{USD}) are known (and have virtually no credit risk) when the deal is made. Note, though, that transaction costs allow a degree of variance between the forward rate and a manufactured forward. The potential for arbitrage is illustrated in example 13.3.

Observe that the difference between the amount of funds that would be exchanged through the spot (i.e. AUD9 815 951 for USD7 263 804) and the forward (i.e. AUD10 000 000 for USD7 363 681) rates arises from the difference in the interest rates. If the interest rate in each country's short-term money market was the same, the forward rate would be the same as the spot exchange rate.

example 13.3

Suppose a bank plans to convert AUD10 million into USD in three months. It could approach this transaction in two ways:

1 invest the present value of AUD10m in the AUD money market for three months, at say, 7.50% p.a., so that it will have AUD10m available for settlement at the agreed forward rate, or

2 it could convert the present value of the AUD funds at the spot exchange rate and invest the USD proceeds in the US money market at, say 5.50% p.a. for three months, so that it will have its USD in three months.

The present value in Australia of AUD10m (in three months) is, using equation (4.3a):

$$P_{AUD} = \frac{10\ 000\ 000}{1 + 0.075 * (3/12)}$$

$$= \text{AUD9 815 951}$$

Given that the AUD/USD spot rate is 0.7400, this converts the AUD9 815 951 into USD7 263 804. Investing this amount in the US money market generates the following amount in three months:

$$F_{USD} = 7\ 263\ 804 \left(1 + 0.055 \frac{3}{12}\right)$$

$$= \text{USD7 363 681}$$

This implies, using equation (13.1), a three-month forward rate, $f_{AUD/USD}$, that matches the rate found using equation (13.2):

$$f_{AUD/USD} = \frac{7\ 363\ 681}{10\ 000\ 000}$$

$$= 0.7364$$

The cashflows that occur through a forward contract and through a manufactured forward, by converting at the spot and investing in the foreign money market, are shown in figure 13.3.

If the forward rate is below that implied by the interest differential (e.g. $f_{AUD/USD} = 0.7250$), dealers will borrow AUD, convert to USD at the spot rate, invest the proceeds in the US money market and convert the future value of USD back to AUD at the forward rate to repay their borrowing and generate a riskless profit as follows. For the transaction described above, F_{AUD} (i.e. AUD10m) would convert (at $f_{AUD/USD} = 0.7250$) to USD7 250 000, yielding a risk-free profit of USD7 363 681 − 7 250 000 each time the transaction is made!

Likewise, if it is too high (e.g. $f_{AUD/USD} = 0.7550$) dealers will borrow USD, convert it to AUD at the spot rate, invest the proceeds in the Australian money market and convert the future value of the AUD to USD at the agreed forward rate to repay their borrowing and make a risk-free profit as follows. Given that F_{USD} is USD7 363 681, the above scenario implies that the dealer will generate USD 7 550 000 (by converting AUD10 m at $f_{AUD/USD} = 0.7550$), and so make a risk-free profit of USD186 319 (USD7 550 000 − 7 363 681) each time the deal is made. Note that in both cases the profit made is proportional to the degree of mispricing. In the last example a profit of $186 319 represents a gain of USD0.0186 per AUD1 traded forward, which is the difference between the high forward rate of AUD/USD0.7550 and the correct forward rate of AUD/USD0.7364.

So far in this chapter we have ignored the 360-day year used in the US money market and the 365-day year in the Australian market. If, for example, we calculated the

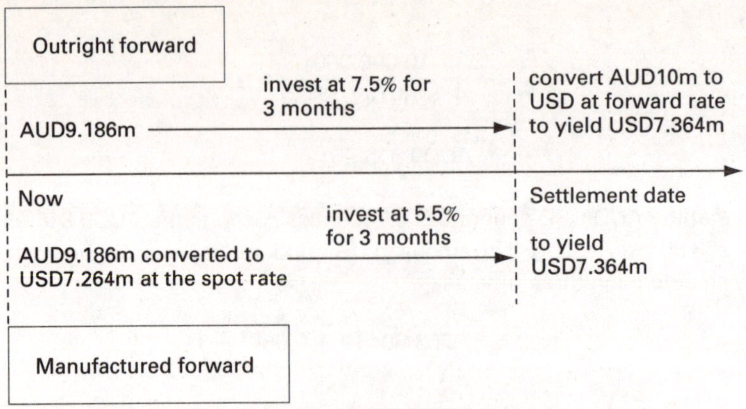

Figure 13.5 Cashflows associated with a forward and a simulated forward

90-day forward rate, t would be 90/360 in the USA and 90/365 in Australia. We have also used mid-point prices to further simplify the illustration. In practice, the appropriate bid and offer rates would be used. Note in example 13.4 the use of the 360-day interest-rate convention in Switzerland when calculating the 30-day forward rate.

example 13.4

Calculate the 30-day forward rate, $f_{AUD/CHF}$, given $s_{AUD/CHF}$ = 1.0250, the 30-day interest rate is 3.50% p.a. in Switzerland and 7.00% p.a. in Australia:

$$f_{AUD/CHF} = 1.0250\left(\frac{1 + 0.035 * (30/360)}{1 + 0.07 * (30/365)}\right)$$

$$= 1.0221$$

This example also shows the AUD trading at a forward discount (29 points) because the interest rate is higher in Australia (the commodity currency) than in Switzerland (the terms currency).

You will recall that a forward rate applies to any settlement that occurs more than two days from the deal date. The number of days involved in a forward-rate calculation starts after the spot settlement date. Typically, forward contracts are for monthly periods, with the number of days depending on the month. Consider the following examples of a one-month forward contract:

- a deal made on 4 April will be settled on 6 May (assuming it is a business day). This is a 30-day contract because there are 30 days between 6 April and 6 May, and
- a deal made on 4 May will be settled on 6 June. This is a 31-day contract because there are 31 days between 6 May and 6 June.

The general relationship between spot and forward exchange rates based on interest-rate differentials is shown by the diagram in figure 13.4.

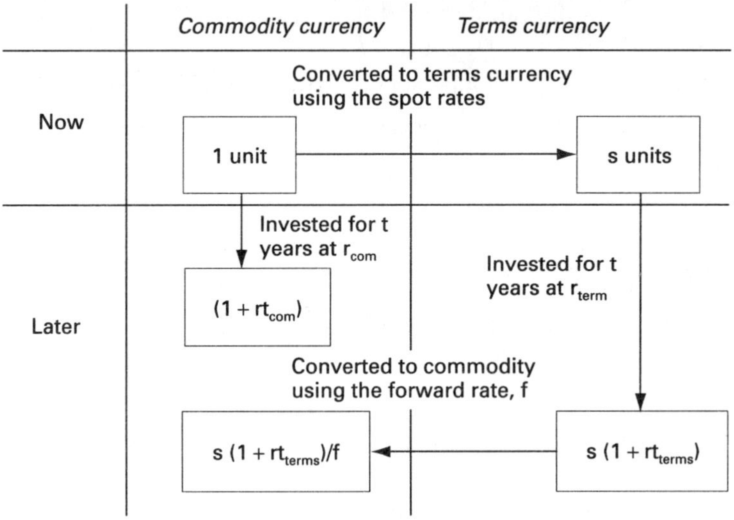

There are two ways to produce an amount of a commodity currency in the later period; by

1. direct investment at the commodity currency interest rate and
2. changing from the commodity currency to the terms currency, investing at the terms-currency interest rate and finally reconverting to the commodity currency at the forward rate, f. If there is to be no arbitrage then f must be such as to make the two sums equal. That is:

$$f = s\left(\frac{1 + rt_{terms}}{1 + rt_{com}}\right)$$

Figure 13.4 Relationship between spot and forward exchange rates

Two-way forward rates

Because currencies are bought and sold at forward rates, there are bid and offer rates. The spreads in the forward markets, as in the spot markets, are determined by the market, but must be limited by the ability of traders and clients to manufacture their forward rate in the fashion described above. That is, for example, a very creditworthy buyer of USD forward, in terms of JPY, could:

1. borrow the present value of the amount of JPY that will be exchanged on the settlement date (at the offer/lending interest rate in that country),
2. convert this amount at the (offer) spot rate for USD, and
3. invest this amount for the forward period in the US money market.

The proceeds of these transactions must set a lower limit on the USD funds that will be offered by the rates in the forward market.

Applying the above steps, the offer rate in the forward market can be determined as follows:

$$f_{offer} = s_{offer}\left(\frac{1 + rt_{terms/lend}}{1 + rt_{com/borrow}}\right) \qquad \textit{Equation (13.2a)}$$

By reverse logic, the market's bid rate in the forward market can be manufactured as:

$$f_{bid} = s_{offer}\left(\frac{1 + rt_{terms/borrow}}{1 + rt_{com/lend}}\right) \qquad \textit{Equation (13.2b)}$$

The use of these equations is illustrated by example 13.5.

example 13.5

Consider a three-month forward AUD/NZD rate. Assume:

	Bid	*Offer*
spot AUD/NZD	1.2800	1.2850
3-month money (%p.a.)	Borrow	Lend
AUD	14.25	14.50
NZD	17.25	17.50

$$\text{The bid rate} = 1.2800\left(\frac{1 + 0.1725 * (3/12)}{1 + 0.1450 * (3/12)}\right)$$

$$= 1.2885$$

$$\text{The offer rate} = 1.2850\left(\frac{1 + 0.1750 * (3/12)}{1 + 0.1425 * (3/12)}\right)$$

$$= 1.2951$$

The two-way price of 1.2885 − 1.2951 represents a spread of 66 points compared with the spot spread of 50 points. The forward prices calculated this way will always have a larger spread as they incorporate not only the spot spread but also the money-market spreads.

Market practice is to quote the forward points, these being the difference between the spot and forward rates for successively longer periods. When the forward rate is at a premium, the forward points are added to the spot rate. Also, in this case, the bid points will be less than the offer points. To illustrate, suppose $s_{AUD/USD} = 0.7400$ and the following forward points are quoted:

one month 12–17
two month 17–23
three month 20–27

These quotes imply the forward one-month bid and offer rates are USD0.7412–17, the two-month rates are USD0.7417–23, and the three-month rate is

USD0.7420–27. In this case, dealers who quote the highest bid points will attract business from dealers who wish to sell, and vice versa for offer rates.

When the bid is less than the offer, the currency is trading at a forward premium. When the bid is greater than the offer, the points are deducted from the spot rate because the currency is trading at a forward discount. To illustrate, suppose $s_{AUD/USD} = 0.7400$ and the following forward points are quoted:

one month	15–10
two month	18–12
three month	22–15

These quotes imply the forward one-month bid and offer rates are USD0.7385–90, the two-month forward rates are USD0.7382–88, and the three-month rate is USD0.7378–85.

FX swaps

As described in a previous section, an FX swap is the main way in which forward rates are used. FX swaps differ from an outright forward because they incorporate a spot transaction that is reversed by the forward. (The following illustrations are based on those presented in Allan *et. al.*, 1990, p. 22.)

In the case of a sell/buy swap, the dealer sells an amount of the commodity currency at the spot bid rate and buys it at the forward offer rate. To illustrate, suppose the swap is for AUD10 million in terms of USD, the spot rate is USD0.7400–05 and the three-month swap points are 37–27 (i.e. the forward offer rate is USD0.7378). The cash flows are:

Period	*AUD*	*USD*
Now	−10 000 000	+7 400 000
Three months	+10 000 000	7 378 000
Net flows	nil	22 000

In this transaction, the dealer acquired USD for three months and because that currency was trading at a forward premium (the AUD was trading at the forward discount) a small surplus arose in USD (because of the interest differential that underpinned the swap points).

In the case of a buy/sell swap, the commodity currency is bought at the spot offer rate and sold at the forward bid rate. The cash flows arising from this transaction are (using the same data as above):

Period	*AUD*	*USD*
Now	+10 000 000	−7 400 500
Three months	−10 000 000	+7 363 000
Net flows	nil	−37 500

Observe that the dealer acquires AUD10 million for three months and because of the higher interest rate in the AUD money market, the swap points result in a small loss in USD.

Notice also that the amount of the surplus/loss on the transaction depends solely on the forward (or swap) points which in turn are based on the interest differential as explained in the previous section.

A buy/sell FX swap as described above could be used by an Australian company to arrange a short-term USD loan which it repays at the forward rate. Similarly, the buy/sell FX swap could provide a vehicle for, say, a US company to lend AUD funds for three months to its Australian subsidiary, which repays the loan at the forward rate.

FX swaps could be used also by importers and exporters on a rolling basis to arrange forward cover for their FX exposures. An Australian importer could use a series of buy/sell FX swaps to continuously hedge an exposure to ongoing purchases of USD. The spot transaction of buying AUD/selling USD serves to close out the previous sell AUD/buy USD forward contract and the forward component of the current FX swap, sell AUD/buy USD, serves to hedge the AUD cost of the next purchase of imports.

Similarly, an Australian exporter could use a series of sell/buy FX swaps to hedge a continuous exposure to a fall in the value of the USD which would reduce the AUD value of the export income. The spot leg (sell AUD/buy USD) serves to close out the forward leg of the previous swap and the final leg of the current swap (buy AUD/sell USD) serves to hedge the value of the next export receipt. An example of the use of a series of swaps to hedge future USD receipts is shown in figure 13.5.

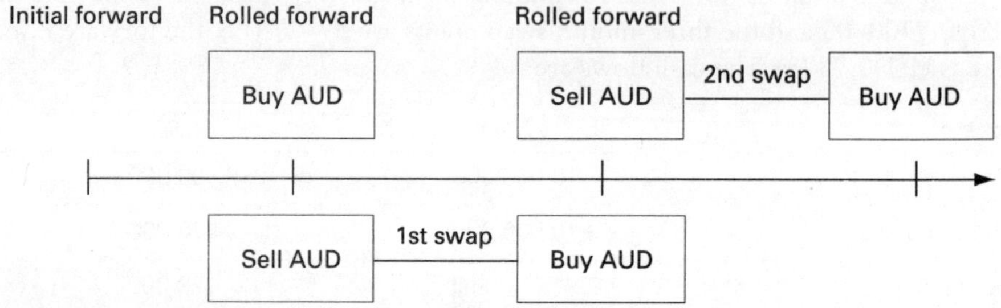

Figure 13.5 An FX swap

OVERSEAS CAPITAL MARKETS

Remember the brief discussion of overseas capital markets presented in Chapter 3. The diagram in figure 3.1 (p. 57) shows two types of overseas capital markets: eurocurrency and (other) domestic markets. Collectively, they comprise the global capital market.

A global capital market means that financing can be arranged in:

- the domestic capital market, with either local or overseas investors,
- another country's domestic capital market, with either their local or overseas investors, or
- eurocurrency markets, with investors from around the world.

Overseas capital markets are alternative sources of funds for borrowers and alternative investment opportunities for lenders. Overall, the former role of these markets traditionally has been more important for Australian entities than the latter. In other words, Australian entities have raised much more funds from these markets than they have placed in them. Data on investment in Australia and Australia's net foreign liabilities are presented in tables 13.4 and 13.5 for the period June 1976 to June 1995.

The scale of overseas borrowing by Australian entities is substantial compared with the level of borrowing from within the Australian financial system. Bank assets (which represent lending in one form or another), as at June 1994, were shown in table 2.2 (presented in Chapter 2, p. 40) to be just over twice the amount of overseas borrowing. Assets of NBFIs were shown in that table to be about half as large as overseas borrowing.

Table 13.4 Foreign investment in Australia, June 1976 to June 1995 ($m)

As at 30 June	*Borrowing*	*Equity*
1976	5 978	3 931
1980	13 498	21 298
1985	67 473	33 313
1990	162 770	85 545
1991	179 250	91 168
1992	191 268	96 539
1993	208 420	105 474
1994	205 927	137 328
1995	223 289	150 054

Source: RBA, *Bulletin*, Table H.5

Over the past two decades or so, the level of borrowing has exceeded equity investment in Australia, except in the early 1980s. Note also that in 1994, equity investment increased substantially, whereas borrowing declined. The shift between the supply of debt and equity capital reflects the preferences of both the suppliers and recipients of the funds.

During the 1990s, equity investment abroad increased more substantially than lending, so the data presented in table 13.5 show a much higher level of net borrowing than net equity investment. Observe also in table 13.5 that net non-official debt (issued by private businesses, financial institutions and public enterprises) is much greater than net official debt (issued by Commonwealth and State Governments for general governmental purposes only) but it has declined during the early years of the 1990s (along with the gap between it and official debt).

In macroeconomic terms, the level of net overseas funding (borrowing and equity raisings) is a function of the current-account deficit. Overseas funds have to be raised to finance the current-account deficit. This can be viewed in terms of the **twin deficits**, as follows:

$$\text{capital inflow} = \text{current-account deficit}$$
$$= \text{investment} + \text{PSBR} - \text{savings}$$

where PSBR stands for the public-sector borrowing requirement.

Table 13.5 Net foreign liabilities, June 1976 to 1994 ($m)

30 June	*Official borrowing*	*Non-official borrowing*	*Total borrowing*	*Equity*	*Other*	*Total*
1976	−1 717	4 116	2 399	4 517	n.a.	n.a.
1980	−25	6 889	6 863	19 426	43	26 334
1985	1 260	49 948	51 208	25 875	774	78 858
1990	16 802	114 952	131 754	40 558	−1 441	170 871
1991	17 366	125 417	142 782	50 439	−1 239	191 982
1992	22 858	130 707	153 565	47 020	238	200 824
1993	38 469	128 851	167 320	51 770	−608	218 481
1994	41 151	122 086	163 237	76 763	79	240 079
1995	56 159	125 068	181 228	77 267	325	258 820

Source: RBA, *Bulletin*, Table H.6

The twin deficits are PSBR and investment minus savings. (Allan *et. al.*, 1990, p. 45) However, participation in overseas capital markets does not depend on a current-account deficit; this determines the net involvement (whether the use of funds exceeds the supply of funds). Countries such as Japan have run current-account surpluses for many years and in their case, the net involvement is as a supplier of funds.

Funding arrangements

As noted above, overseas capital markets comprise eurocurrency markets and the principal overseas domestic markets. 'Euro' markets are the collection of markets and financial institutions that arrange financing in a currency outside the country of that currency. The institutions involved in these markets are mainly located in London and certain cities in Europe, the Middle East (such as Bahrain) and South-east Asia (such as Singapore).

Offshore banking units are engaged in the eurocurrency market. They generally are located in prominent financial centres, provide conventional banking services, but deal only with non-resident clients. Given the role of tax havens in the eurocurrency markets, most offshore banking units are subject to concessional tax rates. For instance, authorised offshore banking units in Australia are subject to tax at the rate of only 10%. (Linklater, 1992, pp. 149–50)

The major domestic markets, especially the US markets, form part of the international capital market because non-residents can issue securities in these markets, provided the issuer satisfies the requirements of the market regulator (the Securities and Exchange Commission, in the case of the US market). Such securities are referred as 'foreign' (e.g. foreign bonds).

Both euro and foreign markets involve direct and intermediated financing. The former involve the issue of securities with a range of maturities, interest-payment bases and various other features (such as the option of making payments in different currencies). The short-term securities are known generally as commercial paper; the medium-term securities are generally known as medium-term notes; and the longer-term securities are known as bonds (euro and foreign bonds). The latter involve the acceptance of deposits by institutions (principally international banks) in a eurocurrency (the principal one being the US dollar) and on-lending the funds to borrowers.

These international markets developed from the 1950s when UK banks began borrowing and lending in USD. The general removal of exchange controls during the 1970s and the generation of substantial USD export income by the Middle-Eastern oil-producing countries provided further impetus to the development of these markets. But their continued development results from their ability to perform their financing role compared with the individual domestic markets.

According to data presented in the 1995 *Annual Report* of the Bank for International Settlements, intermediated financing was the main form of cross-border financing, with bonds the principal instrument of direct financing. Euronote issues increased substantially during the first half of the 1990s; the amount outstanding in 1994 was close to that for bonds. (BIS, 1995, p. 167)

Intermediated financing

The principal source of offshore funds is the eurocurrency bank credit market, which in the case of the Australian dollar operates in Europe and Asia. The banks that operate in this market accept deposits and make loans (in AUD) in a similar fashion to domestically operating banks (without offering payment services) at interest rates that are competitive with those in the domestic financial system.

Whereas the interest rates charged on domestic loans are usually set in relation to domestic 'marker' rates (such as a bank's prime rate), interest rates in offshore markets are usually set in relation to an internationally recognised marker rate, such as one of the following:

- London Inter-bank Offered Rate (LIBOR)
- Singapore Inter-bank Offered Rate (SIBOR).

These rates are quoted for a wide range of maturities.

Because these marker rates assume a 360-day year, they must be multiplied by 365/360 for direct comparison with Australian interest rates. For example, a LIBOR rate of 8.50% p.a. is equivalent to an Australian domestic rate of 8.62% p.a.

The main forms of eurocurrency bank credit are:

- short-term advances,
- standby facilities,
- term loans, and
- syndicated facilities.

Short-term advances are repaid by a lump-sum payment at a specified time, although their period may be extended, creating a type of revolving loan, like a domestic overdraft facility. They can be arranged according to the requirements of the borrower, even allowing the repayment to be in a mixture of currencies.

A standby facility is a line of short-term credit that the borrower can draw upon, when needed, during the period of the facility. It can be arranged more easily offshore because the eurocurrency markets are much larger and therefore can be relied upon to provide the funds when they are needed. Usually a standby facility has a maturity of about two years and it will require the borrower to use the funds for only part of this period. The interest rate on the facility will be higher than for a term loan (other things being equal) because the facility serves as a fall-back for a borrower who is temporarily short of funds.

Term loans are usually arranged by a bank for amounts between five and 100 million USD, and for periods between five and 15 years. When the borrower arranges a gradual drawdown of the loan, a commitment fee is charged on the undrawn amount.

The rate of interest charged is set in relation to one of the marker rates listed above, depending on the credit standing of the borrower. The period of the interest rate is subject to agreement. If it was set for six months, at the end of each six-month period the rate is adjusted in relation to the movement in the marker rate. For example, assuming a loan was arranged at LIBOR plus 50 basis points, the loan rate would be 12.5% p.a. for the first six months if LIBOR was 12% at the commencement of the loan; and it would be 12% for the next six months if, at the end of the initial six-month period, LIBOR was at 11.5% p.a.

A term loan can be in any of the major currencies and the borrower can arrange to switch between currencies at the end of each interest period. The loans are typically based on security, such as a charge over assets owned by the borrower, and will usually impose financial covenants on the borrower, such as a limit on the borrower's debt/equity ratio.

Term loans can be written with a provision for the loan to be converted into **transferable loan certificates** (TLCs). These are issued at the discretion of the lender and have a term based on the underlying loan. They are, accordingly, a form of asset securitisation, which allows lenders to move assets from their balance sheet. They may also be exempt from Australia's interest-withholding tax, provided they satisfy the 'widely distributed' test. (McGrath, 1994, p. 227)

TLCs usually pay a floating rate of interest and so are similar to floating-rate notes which are discussed below briefly. In 1994, a number of regional banks and resource companies issued TLCs in USD, with interest payments between 33 and 85 basis points above LIBOR, reflecting their credit rating. The amount issued ranged between USD100 million and USD335 million. (Ernst and Young, 1994, Table 6.5)

A syndicated eurocurrency facility is usually arranged for amounts exceeding USD50 million. The facility is arranged by a lead bank, which may also underwrite the loan. The lead bank will attempt to organise sufficient participating banks to fund the loan. Syndicated loans involve complex documentation for which management fees are paid to the lead bank. When these loans are arranged it is common practice for the lead bank to then advertise the loan. Because this is undertaken after the loan has been fully subscribed, the advertisements are referred to as 'tombstones'.

Direct financing

One of the features of the evolving global financial system has been the ability of borrowers to raise capital by issuing securities in offshore markets. The two main types of debt instruments are short-term discount securities such as notes, commercial paper and certificates of deposit, and bonds, such as eurobonds and foreign bonds.

Short-term securities are typically issued under a facility (or 'program') that allows maturing securities to be rolled over through the issue of new securities providing medium-term financing. The securities have, more or less, the same features as those issued in domestic markets (as discussed in Chapter 10), being short-dated discount instruments that have a face value of between USD100 000 and USD500 000.

Notes are issued by tender to dealer panels (of around 20 dealers) in much the same way as promissory notes are issued in the Australian market (described in Chapter 10). Usually they are issued under a note-issuance facility (NIF), which is an arrangement to ensure continuity of finance over a period of years, even though the notes themselves have a term of between 30 and 180 days. NIFs are substantial programs, with a usual minimum size of USD50 million. (McGrath, 1994, p. 233)

The mechanics of the note market (i.e. registration of the paper, clearing and settlement processes) are similar to those used by Austraclear in the domestic short-term money market.

NIFs are underwritten, typically by a syndicate of banks. Even though notes are sold through dealer panels, there is a risk that issues will not be fully sold. Underwriting serves to hedge this risk, as the underwriters purchase any unsold notes at the agreed issue yield. However, the provision of underwriting services involves credit risk, against which banks (under the BIS prudential guidelines) need to commit equity capital, which forms part of the underwriting costs. According to McGrath (1994, p. 233), underwriting costs add about 0.5% p.a. to the cost of the funds raised.

Euro-commercial paper (ECP) developed an alternative to notes, especially for those issuers who did not require underwriting services. Their issue is arranged by a leading bank, and the risk that an issue is not fully subscribed is usually hedged by a standby arrangement. Paper is issued to (or through) small dealer panels who act as market makers in the secondary market.

According to the survey by Ernst and Young (1994), new commercial paper programs (by Australian issuers) with an aggregate value of AUD16 billion were established in 1994. This was three times greater than the value of new domestic commercial programs. Issuers were state central borrowing authorities, financial institutions and companies that have high credit ratings (e.g. Moody's P-1), which is representative of Australian issuers generally. The new programs are in USD, although some have multi-currency issue options. The five largest new programs in 1994 are listed in table 13.6.

Note that a 'program' defines the expected aggregate amount of a security that will be issued. The rate at which programs are issued depends on the market's acceptance of them and the issuer's need for funds. For instance, only about a quarter of the USD16 billion worth of new CP programs listed by Ernst & Young were issued in 1994.

Notes and ECP that are denominated in AUD have been sold mainly in Hong Kong and, to a lesser extent, in Singapore. The market for these securities developed in the mid 1980s because of the wide interest-rate differential between Australia and the United States and Hong Kong. The securities use an Australian marker interest rate (bank-bill rate), however in most other respects AUD issues are similar to USD issues.

Table 13.6 New offshore commercial paper programs, 1994

Borrower	*Program amount (m)*	*Maturity*	*Arranger*
NAB	USD2500[1]	Open	NAB
NAB	USD1500[2]	Open	NAB
Asset Collateralised Entity	USD1000[3]	Open	Société Générale
Bankers Trust Australia	USD1000	Open	Goldman Sachs
NSW Treasury Corp.	USD1000[4]	Open	Citibank

[1] Increase in existing USD program
[2] Global Commercial Paper program
[3] Funding for asset securitisation program
[4] Increase in existing program
Source: Ernst and Young, 1994, Table 2.2

The commercial paper market in the United States is another source of offshore funds, even though it originally provided working capital for United States corporations. Because there is no underwriting, issuers usually arrange standby lines of credit to guard against the possibility that the market will not roll over maturing paper.

Long-term securities

You will recall that a long-term security has a term to maturity of more than a year when issued. There are many forms of such securities. Reference is often made to 'medium-term notes' (MTNs) and to 'bonds' as though they are distinct types of securities, whereas they can have the same features.

MTNs are not a specific security — the term refers to those securities that usually have a term to maturity of between one and five years. (Skully, 1990, p. 23) They are usually issued on an unsecured basis at a fixed coupon rate, and can be issued in any currency in the eurocurrency market or in USD in the US market. On a global basis, most are issued in USD, although in 1994 issues by Australian borrowers were mainly in JPY and AUD.

They may be issued in small-denomination securities for subsequent sale to retail investors, particularly in Europe and Japan, or in large denominations for the wholesale market. They are issued by dealer panels under the direction of a lead manager, either periodically or continuously.

Some examples of MTNs issued in 1994 by Australian borrowers are listed in table 13.7.

Floating-rate notes (FRNs) are medium-term bearer securities whose interest payments are based on a marker rate, principally LIBOR. (Skully, 1990, p. 21) They commonly make quarterly interest payments at a set margin above or below LIBOR, according to the credit standing of the issuer.

Table 13.7 Examples of MTNs issued offshore by Australian borrowers in 1994

Borrower	*Amount (m [a])*	*Coupon rate*	*Maturity date*	*Lead manager*
AIDC	JPY15 000	2.9–4.1[1]	July 1997	Credit Suisse/ CS First Boston
Qld Treasury Corp.	AUD100	8.2	Nov. 1996	Nikko Securities
State Bank of NSW	JPY10 000[2]	3–3.8[3]	July 1997	Merrill Lynch
TNT	USD100	11.5	April 2004	Morgan Stanley
Treasury Corp. of Victoria	JPY10 000[4]	3.2	June 1997	Nomura
Treasury Corp. of Victoria	AUD110	6.75	Sept. 1999	SG Warburg

[a] In millions in the specified currency
[1] 2.9% in year 1, 3.5% in year 2, then 4.1%
[2] One of a number of new programs that total over JPY50 billion
[3] 3.0% in year 1, 3.4% in year 2, 3.8% in year 3
[4] One of a number of new programs that total over JPY30 billion
Source: Ernst and Young, 1994, Table 6.4

FRNs are issued in a similar manner to MTNs. Note that their exposure to interest-rate risk is similar to that of NIFs and CP programs. Examples of FRNs issued in 1994 by Australian borrowers are listed in table 13.8.

Bonds are the principal long-term instrument issued offshore by Australian borrowers. They also are the major security in the eurocurrency market generally. Recall that there are two main types of international bonds: eurobonds, which are issued in the borrower's currency (such as AUD bonds issued in London or Singapore), and foreign bonds, which are issued by non-residents in the host country's currency (such as USD bonds issued in the United States by an Australian company).

> *A Eurobond is essentially a medium- to long-term, fixed-rate bearer debt instrument sold outside of the country in whose currency the security is denominated.* (Skully, 1990, p. 20)

Note that eurobonds are generally 'bearer' bonds. You will recall that in Australia, Treasury bonds are inscribed stock and therefore their owner is registered with the

Table 13.8 New offshore FRN issues, 1994

Borrower	*Amount (m [a])*	*Interest margin [b]*	*Maturity date*	*Lead manager*
Advance Bank	USD250	L+35bp	June 1999	JP Morgan
ANZ Bank	GBP200	L+12.5bp	July 1997	Union Bank of Switzerland
Dai-Ichi Kangyo Australia	USD60	L+75bp[1]	May 2004	Dai-Ichi Kangyo
SAFA	DEM350	L	June 1996	Swiss Bank Corp.
St George Bank	USD250	L+30bp	Jan. 2000	Union Bank of Switzerland
Tasmanian Public Finance Corp.	JPY3000	L+20bp	Oct. 1997	Nikko Securities

[a] Amount in millions in the stated currency
[b] The margin is specified in basis points against three-month LIBOR
[1] Hybrid FRN. First three years floating against six-month LIBOR, then 8%
Source: Ernst and Young, 1994, Table 6.3

RBA. The owner of a bearer bond is not registered by the issuer and this gives investors anonymity and, if widely distributed, exemption from Australia's 10% withholding tax. This, together with the high coupon rate, has made AUD eurobonds popular in those countries with a strong 'retail' investor sector (such as Germany, Japan, Switzerland and Belgium).

Bonds are fixed-interest securities with periodic coupons attached to the bonds (being bearer bonds). Eurobonds are mainly sold to retail investors (i.e. not to financial institutions), who usually hold them to maturity, although there is a secondary bond market. Because investors usually do not undertake their own credit analysis of issuers, they have a strong preference for well-known and very credit-worthy issuers.

Eurobond issues are usually undertaken only for large amounts (USD50 million minimum). They are arranged by an international bank as the lead manager of a syndicate of banks that manage the issue by advising on the bond's features and choosing the underwriters, selling institutions, trustee and paying agents in major financial centres (who help disperse coupon payments and the eventual redemption payment).

There are three broad types of eurobonds:

- 'straight' or fixed-interest bonds, which is the principal form,
- floating-rate bonds (the FRNs discussed above), and
- 'exotics', some of which give the holder the option to convert the bond into another security (either shares, known as 'equity-linked securities', or another debt instrument) or the right (known as a 'warrant') to acquire other securities issued by the borrower.

The provision of options as part of a bond enhances its value and allows the issuer to raise funds at a lower issue yield. But the provision of options imposes other costs on the issuer (there are no free lunches).

In the mid 1990s, the amount of **dual-currency** bonds issued increased substantially. A dual-currency bond raises funds in one currency and makes coupon and/or the redemption payments in another currency. For example, a bond might raise funds in JPY and make its coupon and/or redemption payments in AUD. This exposes the investor to the risk of a depreciation in the AUD, but given the higher interest rates in Australia, the investor receives a higher coupon rate than on a JPY bond. This risk is reduced when the coupon payments are in JPY, but in such cases, the coupon rate would be lower, given the FX risk faced by the issuer.

Representative examples of new offshore issues by Australian borrowers are listed in table 13.9. Semi-governmentals have been the main issuers of dual bonds, followed by financial institutions. (RBA, 1996, p. 3) The main investors are wealthy Japanese (the so-called Japanese housewife, as opposed to the Belgian dentists who represented the basis of the retail demand for AUD securities in Europe).

A number of well-known European banks issued AUD bonds in 1994 in the eurobond market for the purpose of swapping the payments with another borrower. These banks can reduce their interest costs because of their comparative advantage in issuing these securities. (Cross-currency swaps are discussed in Chapter 18.)

Table 13.9 Selected offshore bond issues, 1994

Borrower	*Currency*	*Amount (m [a])*	*Coupon rate (%)*	*Maturity date*	*Lead manager*
Australian Wheat Board	JPY	5 000	zero	Nov. 1996	Yamaichi
Coca-Cola Amatil	AUD	75	10.75	Dec. 1997	Hambros Bank
Commonwealth Bank of Australia	AUD	100	8.625	Oct. 1997	CBA
FAI Insurance	USD	100	9.625	Jul. 1999	Merrill Lynch
Ford Credit Australia	AUD	75	9.625	Sept. 1999	Macquarie Bank
Mobil Australia Finance	AUD	100	6.625	March 2001	Morgan Stanley
SAFA	JPY	10 000	4.45	Feb. 2004	Nomura
Toyota Finance Australia	AUD	100	9.75	Dec. 1997	Nomura
Treasury Corp. of Victoria	JPY	50 000	2.0[1]	July 1998	Nomura

[a] Amount in millions in stated currency
[1] 2% for two years then six-month LIBOR plus 45 basis points
Source: Ernst and Young, 1994, Table 6.2

Foreign bonds issued in the US market are known as 'yankee' bonds whereas those issued in the Japanese market are known as 'Samurai' bonds. Issuers have to satisfy the requirements of the domestic authorities (the Ministry of Finance in Japan and the Securities and Exchange Commission in the USA). Periodically, Australian companies (such as News Corporation, BHP and CRA) have made large (and in some cases, very long-term) bond issues in the US market.

In addition to debt finance, offshore markets trade equity and hybrid securities. A number of large Australian companies have arranged for their shares to be listed on foreign stock exchanges. Also, Australian companies can participate in the **American Depository Receipts** (ADRs) program which allows US investors to purchase their shares. This is an alternative to listing on a US stock exchange.

Reasons for raising funds overseas

It was emphasised in Chapter 3 that international markets out-perform domestic markets (in arranging the supply of funds), because they are free of the regulatory and tax regimes imposed on domestic participants in domestic markets. (Dufey and Giddy, 1994, p. 35) The use of bearer securities, as opposed to inscribed ones, illustrates this point.

Given that Australia is a net user of overseas funds, we will concentrate our discussion on the borrowing side. There are three main reasons for raising funds overseas: lower interest rates, availability of funds, and risk management.

Lower interest rates

The main element of the cost of funds is the rate of interest. For many years interest rates in Australia have been higher than those in many overseas countries. Many borrowers of overseas funds have expected to take advantage of these lower rates. However, the cost of foreign-currency funds (as will be explained in more detail in the next chapter) depends on both the interest rate due and the movement in the exchange rate between the time the funds are raised and repaid.

The low interest rates quoted in tables 13.7–13.9 for securities denominated in JPY cannot be regarded simply as a source of cheap funds. Allowance should be made for the forward margin in the FX market for the term of each loan. The interest differential results in the AUD trading at a forward discount against the JYP (as explained above). Should the AUD depreciate by this margin, the effective interest rate for JPY funds will match that for AUD loans. Consequently, the expected cost of foreign-currency funds depends, at least in part, on the interest rate overseas and the expected movement in the AUD:

$$r_{fc} = r_{US} + \delta e \qquad \textit{Equation (13.3)}$$

where r_{fc} refers to the net cost of foreign-currency funds,

r_{US} refers to the interest rate paid on foreign-currency funds (US being the example), and

δe refers to the expected change in the exchange rate (AUD/USD).

Borrowers who expect that r_{fc} will be less than the interest rate in Australia will borrow offshore because of their belief that they will get the funds more cheaply.

This judgment is based on the belief that the currency will not depreciate as much as assumed by the money markets (in which the interest differential between r_{AUD} and r_{USD} is set).

During the mid 1980s, many foreign-currency loans were issued to such borrowers. In many of these cases the AUD depreciated much more than these borrowers expected and movement more than offset the interest differential. As a consequence, the effective interest rate was greater than the 'high' Australian rate.

This episode illustrates the point that lower interest rates overseas need not result in a lower effective borrowing rate; the outcome depends on the movement in the exchange rate over the term of the loan. Of course, as explained above, the risk of an unexpectedly large depreciation in the AUD can be hedged in the forward FX market. However, if this strategy is followed, the cost of funds is fixed by the forward rate at the level of rates in Australia (because the forward points are determined by the interest differential). Forward rates give effect to 'interest-rate parity', a theory that is explained in the next chapter.

Other hedging strategies may be used (such as a currency swap, that is described in Chapter 18) to attempt to lock in a lower effective borrowing rate: 'The banks made their overseas borrowings in conjunction with swaps to produce medium-term funds at costs below those which could be obtained domestically.' (Daugaard and Valentine, 1993, p. 77)

Even if it is assumed that equation (13.3) applies to borrowers (i.e. they borrow, on average, at rates similar to those prevailing in Australia), international markets can generally operate at lower costs (than domestic banks) because:

- the eurocurrency markets are not subject to domestic regulation,
- suppliers of funds may face lower tax rates than apply to domestic interest income, and
- the international markets operate only at the wholesale level (they do not provide payment services). (McGrath, 1994, p. 220)

These factors can be expected to be reflected in narrower spreads, slightly higher rates on deposits and marginally lower lending rates.

Availability of funds

The cost of funds is also related to availability. The eurocurrency and certain overseas domestic markets are very large compared to the Australian market. Their much greater depth gives borrowers access to funds on conditions (such as large standby facilities) not so readily available domestically, and permit the raising of funds on a large scale.

By accommodating large-scale fund raising, offshore markets can provide funds at a lower cost per dollar raised than small-scale domestic programs. This reflects the benefits arising from liquidity (i.e. the liquidity of the securities that are issued in substantial quantities) and lower overheads (per dollar raised) achieved by large-scale borrowing.

Overseas markets also provide borrowers with alternative sources of funds. Being able to borrow from both domestic and offshore markets provides borrowers with greater flexibility, such as the ability to borrow where market conditions are favourable.

Risk management

Borrowing in a foreign currency can be a source of exposure to FX and **sovereign** risk (the risk that governments will impose FX controls that restrict the cross-border movement of funds) but it can also be arranged as a natural hedge. A borrower who already has an FX exposure, such as an exporter, can hedge this risk by creating an offsetting exposure through a foreign-currency loan.

An exporter is exposed to the risk of a depreciation of the foreign currency (this reduces the AUD value of the export receipts) and could hedge this risk by arranging a loan in that foreign currency that makes payments of about the same size as the export receipts. In the event of a depreciation of the foreign currency, the AUD value of the loan payments will also be reduced, thus counter-balancing the adverse effect of the currency's depreciation on the borrower's profits.

Borrowers may also issue securities in different currencies for the purpose of hedging their exposure to the movements in the value of any one.

Summary

The main points of this chapter are as follows:

- FX markets serve to link domestic payment systems into a global payments network.
- Offshore capital markets provide alternative borrowing and lending opportunities to those available in the domestic financial system.
- An exchange rate is the value of one currency (the 'commodity') in terms of another.
- During this century most countries have converted from a fixed to a floating exchange-rate regime.
- The main two forms of FX transactions are on a spot- and forward-rate basis.
- The FX market is the most active financial market, with trading being conducted by professional dealers in wholesale amounts.
- Dealers buy low (at their bid quote) and sell high (at their offer quote) which means the party who trades with a dealer buys at the dealer's offer quote and/or sells at the dealer's bid quote.
- Most businesses have an exposure to adverse movements in an exchange rate and might manage this exposure by hedging the position.
- Forward exchange rates are determined by interest-rate differentials, given that both exchange and interest rates are influenced by expectations.
- Forward rates (and FX swaps) are commonly used to hedge an exposure to a movement in exchange rates.
- Borrowers in offshore markets can use banks to provide loans/funds or issue securities (in much the same way as occurs in the domestic financial system).
- A low interest rate in another currency does not necessarily result in a lower effective interest rate for a borrower.

Discussion questions and exercises

1 Discuss the role and scale of Australia's FX market. Suggest reasons for its importance among the world's FX markets.
2 Discuss the practices of quoting exchange rates. Explain the commodity currency and show, with an actual example, when it is appreciating. Explain the difference between actual bid and offer rates and mid-point rates. Cite yesterday's USD value of the AUD and explain what are the 'points', the 'figure' and the 'big figure'.
3 What lessons do you draw (in relation to exchange-rate harmonisation) from the experience with the Bretton Woods Agreement?
4 Explain the mechanics of spot and forward FX rates and an FX swap arranged by an Australian borrower of USD funds for three months.
5 Discuss the role of dealers and brokers in the Australian FX market. Suggest how dealers earn income from their trading and briefly describe the risks faced by an FX dealer.
6 Describe several sources of an FX exposure. Explain how a forward FX rate can serve as a hedging instrument for an Australian company that has decided to purchase equipment at a contract price of USD20 million.
7 Indicate whether DEM1 = USD0.6750 is a cross rate. Explain. Calculate the GBP/CHF rate when:
(a) USD1 = GBP0.7350 and USD1 = CHF1.3250, and
(b) USD1 = GBP0.6750 and USD1 = CHF1.2450
8 Calculate two-way rates for GBP/CHF when the spot spreads are ten points (i.e. five points above and below the mid-point prices given in the previous question).
9 Calculate the 30-day forward rate for AUD/USD (recall that the US adopts a 360-day year) when:
(a) the spot rate is 0.7850, r_{AUD} is 7.60% p.a. and r_{USD} is 5.40% p.a.;
(b) the spot rate is 0.7640, r_{AUD} is 6.50% p.a. and r_{USD} is 5.20% p.a.
10 What are 'swap points'? Calculate the forward rate in a buy/sell FX swap, given that the spot rate is AUD/USD0.7850 and the one-month swap points are 15-10.
11 Discuss the role of eurocurrency markets. Briefly describe how the interest payments on a USD10 million three-year term loan are determined when they are based on three-month LIBOR plus 40 basis points. Briefly describe NIFs, ECP, MTNs, FRNs, 'straight' bonds and equity-linked bonds.
12 If the NSW T-Corp. can issue ten-year JPY eurobonds at par with a fixed coupon rate of 3.50% p.a., suggest several reasons that could explain why it also issues bonds in the Australian market at a yield in excess of 8.00% p.a?

References and further reading

Allan, Richard, Elstone, Rob, Lock, Geoff, & Valentine, Tom 1990, *Foreign Exchange Management*, Allen & Unwin, Sydney.
Bank for International Settlements 1995, *Annual Report*, BIS, Basle.
Campbell, Frank 1995, 'The exchange rate and the Reserve Bank's role in the foreign exchange market' in *Seminar for Teachers*, RBA, pp. 39–54.
Carew, Edna, & Slayter, Will 1994, *Forex: The Techniques of Foreign Exchange*, Heinemann, Melbourne.

Davis, K. T. 1993, 'Corporate debt markets', in M. K. Lewis & R. H. Wallace (eds), *The Australian Financial System*, Longman Cheshire, Melbourne, pp. 249–81.
Dufey, Gunter, & Giddy, Ian 1994, *The International Money Market*, 2nd edn, Prentice-Hall, New Jersey.
Ernst & Young 1994, *Australian Capital Markets Survey*, Sydney.
Juttner, D. Johannes 1989, *International Finance and Global Financial Markets*, Longman Cheshire, Melbourne.
Linklater, Joan 1992, *Inside the Bank*, Allen & Unwin, Sydney, Chapters 9 and 10.
McGrath, Michael 1994, *Financial Institutions, Instruments and Markets in Australia*, McGraw-Hill, Sydney.
Nguyen, D. T. 1993, 'The foreign exchange market', in M. K. Lewis & R. H. Wallace (eds), *The Australian Financial System*, Longman Cheshire, Melbourne, pp. 435–84.
RBA October 1995, 'Survey of foreign exchange market activity in Australia', *Bulletin*, pp. 45–7.
RBA March 1996, 'Recent developments in the Australian dollar offshore bond market', *Bulletin*, pp. 1–4.
Skully, Michael T. (ed.) 1990, *International Corporate Finance*, Butterworths, Sydney.

Appendix 13.1: Position taking

This appendix presents a brief discussion of the trading activities of a dealer.

A dealer has an **open position** in a currency when the dealer stands to make a profit or loss consequent upon a movement in its price. If an FX dealer has bought more of a currency than the dealer has sold, the dealer is said to be 'long' in the currency and will be favoured by an increase in its value. On the other hand, a net seller of a currency is said to have a 'short' position and will be advantaged by a decrease in its value. In a two-currency situation, if a dealer is long in one currency, the dealer is necessarily short in the other currency.

A dealer's exposure to unfavourable fluctuations in exchange rates is directly related to the extent of the dealer's open FX position. Dealers keep account of their FX position, and hence their exposure, by recording the cumulative amount of commodity currency traded on a 'dealer's blotter'. Table 13A.1 presents a stylised AUD/USD dealer's blotter.

Dealers take positions in FX in an attempt to make speculative profits. For example, suppose a dealer expects the AUD/USD rate will decline. The dealer would sell AUD with the aim of buying AUD following the expected decline in its value (i.e. sell high and buy low). The dealer could achieve a short AUD by quoting a low two-way price (compared with the other prices in the market). To illustrate, suppose the market is currently at AUD/USD0.8130-35; the dealer, if called, might quote AUD/USD0.8129-34 to attract buyers of Aussie at USD0.8134.

A more immediate method of shorting the Aussie (but at a less attractive sell price) is to 'hit' another bank (i.e. another dealer) at the market bid rate of USD0.8130. In this case the dealer is selling on the wrong side of the spread and so would require a larger fall in the AUD/USD rate to earn a profit when buying back the currency to reestablish a 'square' position.

Table 13A.1 Record of AUD/USD transactions

Transaction	*Position*	*Description of position*
Buy 20	+20	long AUD (will benefit if AUD/USD appreciates)
Buy 10	+30	as above (but increased risk of depreciation in AUD)
Sell 20	+10	bought USD, reduced exposure to risk of AUD depreciating
Sell 20	−10	short AUD (or long USD)
Sell 10	−20	as above (will benefit if AUD depreciates against USD)
Sell 5	−25	as above (greater exposure to risk of depreciation of USD)
Buy 25	0	square AUD against USD

Cash-flows and T accounts

A dealer's position can be conveniently shown in **T accounts**, which are a set of stylised cash-flow diagrams. In a T account, positive cash-flows are set down on the left of the 'T' and negative flows are set down on the right. In currency transactions, cash-flows arise from buying (or borrowing) or selling (or lending) a currency.

To illustrate, consider a round transaction of AUD1m purchased at AUD/DEM1.1500 and sold at AUD/DEM1.1300. It is obvious that there has been a loss of 200 points on the transaction. The loss in DEM is given by:

$$\text{Profit}_{\text{DEM}} = 1\,000\,000\ (1.1300 - 1.1500)$$

$$= -20\,000$$

This transaction is shown in T-account form in table 13A.2.

Table 13A.2 Dealer's T account

Cash-flows			
AUD		DEM	
1 000 000			−1 150 000
	−1 000 000	1 130 000	
0			−20 000

The use of T accounts is further illustrated by example 13A.1.

example 13a.1

What is the position and the unrealised profit associated with the following series of transactions, given a subsequent spot rate of AUD/DEM 1.5605–15?

1 buy 2m AUD at AUD/DEM1.5620
2 sell 5m AUD at AUD/DEM1.5625
3 sell 3m AUD at AUD/DEM1.5630

The transactions are recorded in T-account form as follows:

AUD		DEM	
2 000 000			−3 124 000
	−5 000 000	7 812 500	
	−3 000 000	4 689 000	
	−6,000 000	9 377 500	

To value position, buy AUD6m at 1.5615 with DEM9.369m.

AUD		DEM	
6 000 000			−9 369 000
0		8 500	

After three transactions the dealer is short AUD6m. To compute the unrealised profit the position is 'squared off'. To accomplish this we must calculate the cost of buying AUD6m at the current market selling price of AUD/DEM1.5615. The net result is an unrealised profit of DEM8500.

Part FOUR

Analysis of interest rates

Interest rates can be viewed as the cost of (or return on) funds. Hence they are the main financial variable within the financial system. Following the deregulation of financial institutions and markets the general level of interest rates is free to vary according to the demand and supply of funds, both immediately and over the foreseeable future.

Because interest rates are market variables, their future movement cannot be known and this creates risk for the suppliers and users of funds whose transactions extend into the future. In Part Four of the book we turn our attention to both the causes of the movements in interest and exchange rates, to the formation of implied forward rates in the markets for funds, and to the price risk arising from interest-rate movements in the bond market.

This part comprises three chapters that analyse different aspects of interest rates. Chapter 14 reviews the factors and theories that attempt to explain the movements in market rates. It covers both interest and exchange rates because of the close relationship between these variables. Chapter 15 explains the difference between forward and spot rates and how forward rates influence the level of multi-period spot rates. Chapter 16 introduces the concept of duration and shows how it provides a simple measure of the price sensitivity of fixed-interest bonds and thus their price risk.

These chapters serve to provide a conceptual basis for the discussion of hedge instruments in Part Five. These instruments provide the opportunity for parties that have a risk exposure in the physical financial markets to remove uncertainty by locking in forward rates. Through the use of these instruments, financing can be conducted at pre-set rates, despite the volatility of market variables.

14

Determinants of the movements in interest and exchange rates

The main two financial-market variables are interest and exchange rates, and their movement is a source both of possible profit and risk of loss. Therefore participants in the financial system have a keen interest in predicting their movements. It is hardly surprising that many theories have been developed to explain, or help to explain, their level and movement. This chapter presents a basic explanation of those theories commonly considered by market participants when forming a view about future movements in these variables.

Study objectives

From your study of this chapter you should be able to:

- explain the general relationship between interest and exchange rates and economic activity;
- explain the interest-rate cycle arising from the business cycle, using loanable-funds theory;
- explain the formation of the Fisher effect and suggest how it explains the level (and movement) of interest rates;
- indicate how dominant overseas interest rates influence domestic rates;
- explain the influence of monetary policy on interest rates;
- distinguish between the influences on short-term and long-term interest rates;
- describe market operations by the RBA and their purposes;

- explain purchasing-power parity and its influence on exchange rates;
- explain interest-rate parity and the expected movement in exchange rates;
- suggest the relationship between commodity prices generally and the value of the Australian dollar;
- suggest the relationship between the balance of payments and exchange rates;
- describe the inter-relationship between actual and expected interest and exchange rates.

INTRODUCTION

The two most important financial-market variables are interest and exchange rates. Following deregulation, their values are determined by market forces. In the case of interest rates, a number of influential rates had been controlled by the government — bank deposit and loan rates and those set by the Commonwealth government on its securities — but these are now set in the markets for intermediated funds and for Commonwealth Government securities. As noted in the previous chapter, the exchange rate was floated in 1983, following a gradual move from a fixed-rate regime.

As at the mid 1990s, the pre-eminent interest rates were those set in the short-term and debt-capital markets. The major short-term rates were the cash (or overnight) rate and the 90-day bank-bill rate. The main long-term rates were the two-year, three-year and ten-year bond rates. Financial institutions set their rates on intermediated funds on a competitive basis, with reference to market yields.

In this chapter we focus on the perceived causes of the movements in interest rates generally, as well as the causes of the movements in exchange rates. Consequently we ignore differences that occur between the movements in market and institutional rates, although we distinguish between the movements in short-term and long-term rates.

Even though we discuss the determinants of the movements in interest rates separately from those that influence exchange rates, we emphasise that these rates are inter-related and each is, to some extent, a cause of movements in the other. Also, both rates influence economic conditions and are themselves influenced by economic conditions. Hence we encounter some problems of the 'chicken and egg' type.

Consider briefly the second of these 'chicken and egg' relationships. In general terms, interest and exchange rates respond to changes in economic conditions (such as the rate of **real** output and inflation) as well as being themselves important determinants of the level and pattern of economic activity. This interaction is shown in figure 14.1. Note that real output refers to the quantity of output of goods and services, and inflation refers to the increase in the general level of prices.

In broad terms, strong economic growth places upward pressure on interest rates because of the resulting demand for funds, whereas slow growth results in a weaker demand for funds and lower interest rates. But, as shown in figure 14.1, interest rates, in particular real rates, are themselves a determinant of economic conditions. We can distinguish three aspects of their influence on economic activity:

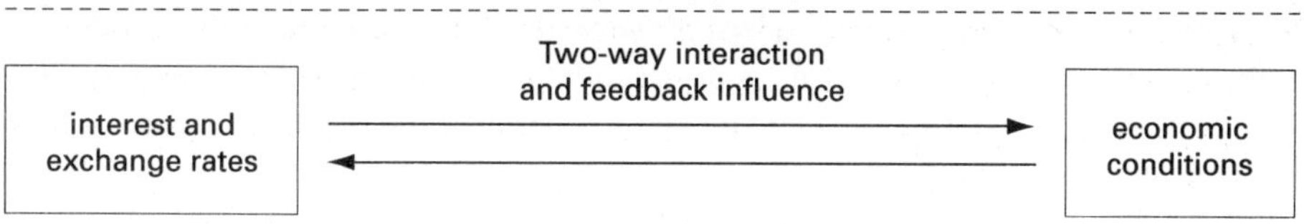

Figure 14.1 Interaction between interest and exchange rates and economic activity

- the level of real interest rates inversely affects the value of economic activity; that is, high rates slow economic activity whereas low rates encourage activity,
- changes in interest rates cause the value of economic activity to respond after a period of about 12 months, and
- interest rates have a greater influence on inflation than the growth in real economic output.

The third of these points partly explains the use of interest rates by the Reserve Bank as an instrument of monetary policy, given its primary focus on containing inflation. However, the bank's instrument is the cash rate in the short-term money market. Therefore we can refine the picture presented in figure 14.1 by suggesting that economic conditions (especially inflation) have a direct influence on long-term rates, whereas they indirectly influence short-term rates, given that they are considered by the RBA when it determines its monetary-policy setting (i.e. its desired level for the cash rate).

Turning to exchange rates, the value of the Australian dollar is influenced by economic conditions. Strong growth in the global economy, for instance, will tend to increase commodity prices, and as these are an important determinant of the value of Australia's exports, this will result in an appreciation of the Australian dollar (and vice versa).

Exchange rates, in turn, directly influence the traded-goods sector (i.e. importing and exporting industries) of the economy:

- An appreciation of the Australian dollar reduces the value of imports and exports in Australian-dollar terms. Imports become cheaper in comparison to domestic output, whereas exports either generate a lower return in Australian dollars (when sales contracts are expressed in the foreign currency), or become more expensive in foreign markets (when sales contracts are expressed in Australian dollars). Therefore, an appreciation of the currency tends to adversely affect the traded-goods sector.
- A depreciation of the currency increases the Australian-dollar value of imports and exports, which improves the price competitiveness of import-competing and exporting industries.
- Exchange rates also determine effective interest rates in a global setting. For instance, borrowing in a foreign currency involves two repayment transactions: interest payments (which are made in the foreign currency) and the purchase of the foreign currency. A depreciation of the Australian dollar increases the effective overseas interest rate because the foreign currency required to make the interest payments become more expensive in Australian-dollar terms, whereas an appreciation of the currency reduces the Australian cost of the interest payments.

Because interest and exchange rates influence the level and pattern of economic activity, governments use them as instruments of macroeconomic policy. For instance, the Reserve Bank can be expected to place upward pressure on short-term interest rates when it believes that inflationary pressures within the economy need to be subdued. When deciding the timing and extent of the upward pressure, the bank will focus on expected economic conditions in 12 months or so.

The Reserve Bank very publicly influences short-term interest rates. Its main instrument of monetary policy, its desired level for the cash rate, is clearly articulated to the market (and the community at large), along with its inflation-control objective, which in the mid 1990s is an 'underlying' rate of 2–3%, (Debelle and Stevens, 1995, p. 3). Nevertheless, the bank does not set (at least not publicly) a target exchange rate. The bank's influence on the exchange rate is related to 'micro' market management (for the purpose of subduing excessive volatility in the rate), rather than the pursuit of a particular rate for macroeconomic purposes.

While the main focus of this chapter is on the factors that influence the movement in interest and exchange rates, including the influence of the Reserve Bank, we also explain the bank's **smoothing** and **testing** practices in the money and foreign-exchange markets. These activities are designed to minimise the day-to-day volatility of these rates, without impeding their general movements.

INTEREST RATES

In this section we use the **loanable funds** framework to show how economic variables, including action by the Reserve Bank, influence the movement in interest rates. While a basic knowledge of the causes of interest-rate movements provides a general understanding of them, it cannot be relied upon to provide a basis for consistently predicting tomorrow's movement in interest rates. Indeed, there would be something amiss if it could, given that these relationships are well known to participants in the financial market.

Recall the discussion of the efficient-market hypothesis, which suggests that market values reflect available information and therefore their movements are the result of 'new' information. Often this takes the form of data (such as the release of balance-of-payments figures) that differs from the market's expectations. The basic propositions explained in this chapter can be used to project changes in market variables implied by new data, but they cannot predict future information.

A further precautionary note: variables such as interest and exchange rates depend on many factors and on the inter-relationships between them. We attempt in this chapter to merely explain the main relationships that influence the movement in these variables. We do not attempt to present a general explanation (or theory) of the behaviour of these variables (which is the province of macroeconomics).

Loanable-funds theory

Loanable-funds theory provides a simple framework for showing how variables influence interest rates. The theory assumes that interest rates are set by market forces, and so predicts their level by the intersection of the demand and supply curves for loanable funds, such as those presented in figure 14.2. The supply curve (S) represents the aggregate supply of funds at different interest rates and the demand curve (D) represents the aggregate demand for funds at different interest rates. The market clearing rate is r, where Q funds are lent and borrowed.

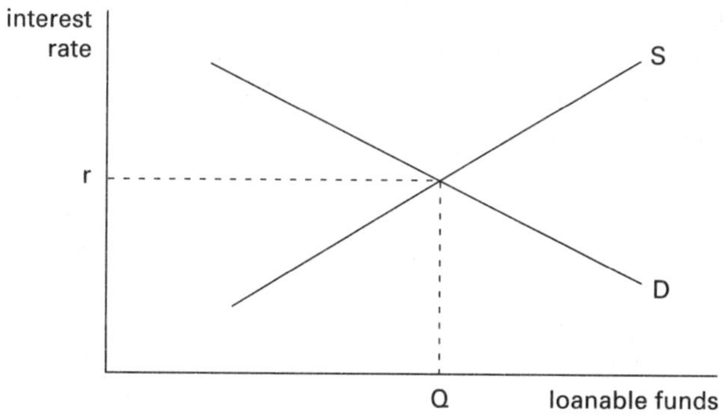

Figure 14.2 The demand and supply of loanable funds

According to loanable-funds theory, an increase in interest rates comes from either an increase in the demand for funds or a decrease in the supply of funds. Interest-rate falls are the consequence of either a decrease in the demand for funds or an increase in the supply of funds. This approach focuses on the effect of a change in one variable, by assuming other factors remain unchanged. Consequently it does not display the inter-relationships between the factors and so does not fully explain the movements in interest rates.

In broad terms, funds are supplied by surplus units for the purpose of earning interest, whereas funds are demanded by deficit units having regard to the interest cost of the funds. The upward-sloping supply curve and the downward-sloping demand curve reflect assumptions about the relationship between the amount of funds that will be supplied and demanded at different interest-rate levels.

Supply of funds

The actual relationship between funds supplied and interest rates is complex, because funds are supplied by different sectors of the economy (as well as by overseas suppliers) and each may respond in various ways to changes in interest rates.

In general, households might respond to higher interest rates (and vice versa for lower rates) for several offsetting reasons. Higher interest rates make the supply of funds more rewarding (and spending them more expensive), which might cause more to be supplied. However, higher rates allow savers to achieve a target return (in absolute terms) by saving less. They also reduce the value of securities (as emphasised in Chapters 10 and 11), which might diminish the wealth of investors and, in turn, diminish their rate of savings.

The business sector is an important source of loanable funds, even though, as a whole, it supplies less than the amount it demands. Each company's internal funds can be invested within the company or supplied to the financial market. The standard argument is that, given an expected rate of return on a company's assets, higher interest rates will induce a company to supply more funds to the market than at lower rates. Accordingly, the corporate sector's supply-of-funds curve will have an upward slope.

The government sector will to some degree behave like the business sector. But the Commonwealth Government can directly alter the overall supply of loanable funds. While this topic will be examined later in this chapter, we can observe that when the government, through the RBA, makes more payments to the private sector than it receives, bank deposits will expand and so will the supply of loanable funds. Of course, a contraction occurs when the government is a net recipient of funds from the private sector. Therefore, in loanable funds theory, governments can shift the supply curve.

Factors other than the rate of interest influence the supply and demand for loanable funds within a domestic market. These factors include the level of economic activity and investment opportunities overseas. If any of these change (and the rate of interest remains the same), the supply and/or demand curves may shift. For instance, should companies in general expect their future earnings to decline, they would be less inclined to reinvest within their operations and more likely to supply surplus funds to the market, shifting the supply curve to the right (and, perhaps, the demand curve to the left). Such a movement is illustrated in figure 14.3 by the supply curve moving from S_0 to S_1, resulting in a fall in the general level of interest rates (to r_1).

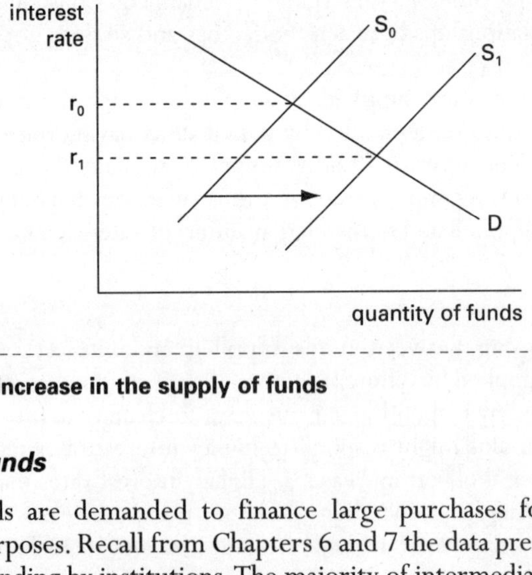

Figure 14.3 An increase in the supply of funds

Demand for funds

In general, funds are demanded to finance large purchases for investment and consumption purposes. Recall from Chapters 6 and 7 the data presenting the volume and pattern of lending by institutions. The majority of intermediated funds is lent to people (for housing in particular), whereas direct financing arranged through financial markets is used by companies and governments (mainly to finance capital expenditure).

As noted above, business planners compare the rate of interest with the expected rate of return on an envisaged investment project. An investment project is given the go-ahead if the project's expected return exceeds the rate of interest on funds to be employed in the project. This is another way of saying that rational investors undertake any project that has a positive net present value.

It follows that businesses' demand for funds, at a given rate of interest, is governed by the number of projects with a positive net present value. Clearly the higher the interest rate, the smaller are the number of projects with a positive net present value and thus the smaller is the demand for funds. Accordingly, the demand for funds by the corporate sector tends to be negatively related to the level of interest rates, which partly shapes the downward-sloping demand curve.

The demand for funds for consumption expenditure (particularly for large-value items such as housing) tends also to vary inversely with the level of interest rates. A higher rate makes the ultimate outlay more expensive.

The use of funds by government reflects several diverse factors, such as 'community needs' and the impact of economic conditions on government expenditure programs and tax collections. The government's influence on interest rates depends mainly on its use of short-term rates as an instrument of monetary policy, but its budgetary position also forms part of the overall demand and supply of funds (depending on whether the government's budget is in deficit or surplus).

The business-cycle effect

A business cycle covers a period during which the rate of economic activity accelerates, reaches a peak, declines and may become negative (when an economy is said to be in **recession**) prior to a return to the growth phase of the cycle. The business cycle is usually shown by the percentage change in an economy's real gross domestic product (GDP) over successive quarters, as depicted by the stylised chart in figure 14.4.

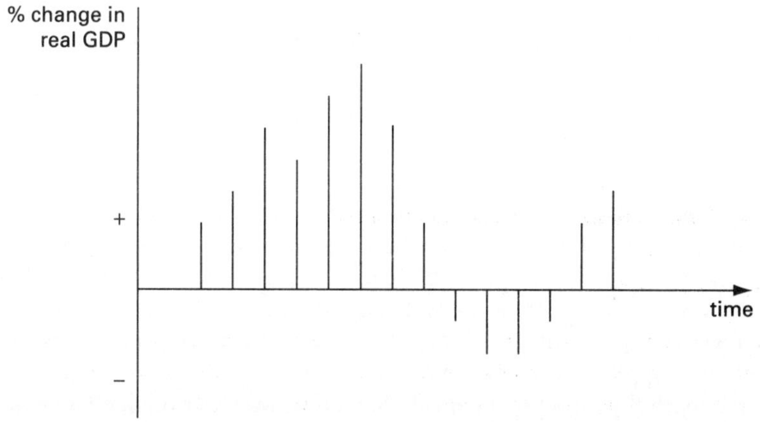

Figure 14.4 A stylised business cycle

Business cycles do not follow a uniform pattern and therefore their turning points are not easy to predict. Look at the variation in the rate of annual growth in real GDP over the period, 1970 to 1995, shown in figure 14.5. The most distinct cycles involved the recessions in the early 1980s and 1990s.

The influence of the business cycle on interest rates is shown by loanable-funds theory through movements in the demand and supply of funds, as depicted in figure 14.6. Because income is generated through economic activity (i.e. output of goods and services), the business cycle causes an income cycle as well as employment and unemployment cycles, because jobs are created by growth and destroyed by recessions. Given that income (both personal and corporate) is the source of savings, the business cycle can be expected to influence the supply of funds. It will also influence the demand for funds, because business will tend to invest and consumers will tend to spend more strongly when they expect the economy to grow strongly (and vice versa when they expect the growth in activity will decline).

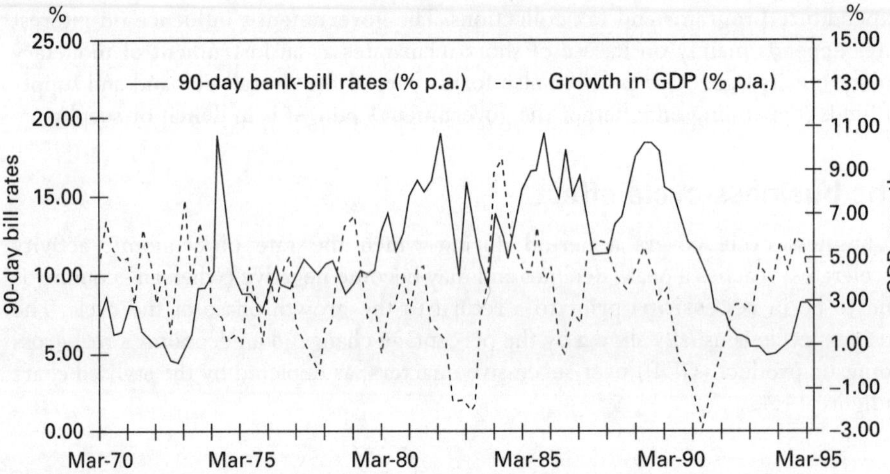

Figure 14.5 Rate of annual growth in real GDP and 90-day bank bills, 1970 to 1995

In recession, both the demand and supply of funds are low. An acceleration in the rate of economic activity will increase the demand for funds. This increase is due to greater business investment and to an increased demand by the household sector for consumer finance. At the same time an increase in economic activity will cause an increase in the supply of funds. Increased economic activity means increased income and therefore increased saving for both the business and the household sector. Provided the supply effect does not outweigh the demand effect, the net result of increased economic activity will be an increase in interest rates. The reverse argument also applies. A movement into recession will be accompanied by a reduction in both the supply and demand for funds, with an overall effect of a lower level of interest rates.

The conclusion from this brief discussion is that the business cycle will influence interest rates in a cyclical fashion. This view is supported by Stevens (1995, p. 25) who stated, after a more detailed discussion, that 'cycles in interest rates are associated, at the broadest level, with a cycle in economic activity'. The interest-rate cycle referred to by Stevens (the movement in the 90-day bank-bill rate over the period, 1970 to 1995) is presented in figure 14.5. Note especially the similarity of the interest-rate and business cycles since the early 1980s. Even though interest rates have displayed a cyclical pattern, the business cycle is not the sole cause of their movements.

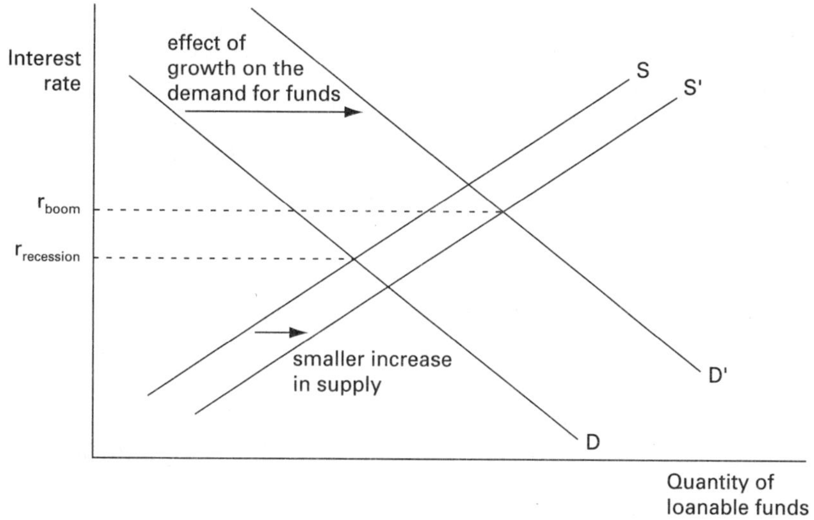

Figure 14.6 The business cycle and interest rates

Inflation

The effect of inflation on market interest rates depends on whether participants draw a distinction between market (i.e. nominal) interest rates and real interest rates. Rational suppliers and users of funds will focus upon the real or inflation-adjusted cost of funds because this attempts to relate future and present values in terms of differences in purchasing power. Suppliers of funds expect to be able to purchase a larger quantity of goods and services in the future than they could if they spent all their funds presently.

In order to allow for the effects of inflation, suppliers and users of finance must form some expectation of the rate of inflation over the period of their financing transaction. This is neither an easy nor a certain process. Predicted inflation rates do not always match the actual outcome. But this does not imply that inflation will be ignored.

The effect of inflation on nominal interest rates can be illustrated in a loanable-funds diagram (which shows market rates on the vertical axis) by basing the supply and demand curves on a particular expected inflation rate. Changes in this expectation will then be shown by a new demand and/or supply curve.

We start by assuming there is no inflation (and none is expected). The no-inflation supply and demand curves are shown in figure 14.7, resulting in a market rate of r, which is both the nominal and real rate, given the absence of inflation. Suppose conditions change and most participants in the market expect inflation will be 2%. This discourages the supply of funds, shown by the shift of the supply curve to $S_{inflation}$, and encourages the demand for funds, represented by the shift of the demand curve to $D_{inflation}$, resulting in the market rate increasing to r plus an inflation premium.

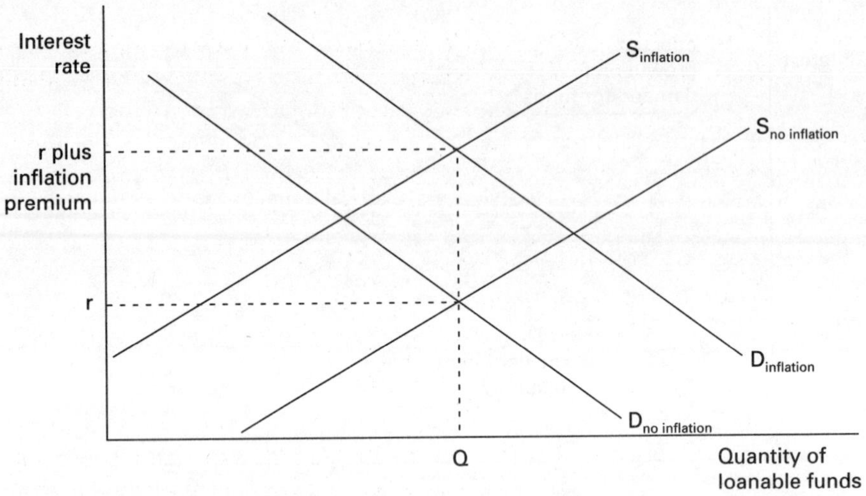

Figure 14.7 Allowing for inflation

Borrowers will seek to increase their demand for funds, at the current interest rate, when there is an upward adjustment in expected inflation, because this will ease the real value of their future repayments. For the reverse reason, suppliers will be discouraged from making funds available (because the real value of the repayments they receive will be eroded should higher inflation occur).

Assuming there is a constant rate of inflation, the implication of figure 14.7 is that the market rate of interest can be derived from:

$$1 + r = (1 + r_r)(1 + p) \qquad \textit{Equation (14.1)}$$

where r_r stands for the real interest rate, and
p stands for the inflation rate.

Multiplying through and taking one from both sides of equation (14.1) gives:

$$r = r_r + p + (r_r * p) \qquad \textit{Equation (14.1a)}$$

Equation (14.1a) shows the various contributions to nominal interest rate. It is made up of the real rate, r_r, a premium that compensates for the effect of inflation on the loan principal, p, and a further premium (r_r * p) that compensates for the decline in the worth of the interest received. Provided r_r and p are relatively small, their product can be ignored because of its small size. Hence, equation (14.1a) can be approximated by:

$$r = r_r + p \qquad \textit{Equation (14.1b)}$$

Fisher effect

Equation (14.1b) is traditionally known as the **Fisher equation**, in recognition of Fisher's 1896 article on interest rates. When the inflation rate is unstable, p should be treated as the expected inflation rate over the period of the transaction.

Given the real interest rate, the market rate can be predicted by the Fisher equation in terms of the expected inflation rate. To illustrate, suppose the real rate is 4.00% p.a. and the inflation rate for the next year is expected to be 3%. The Fisher equation implies that the one-year market interest rate will be:

$$r = 0.04 + 0.03$$

$$= 0.07 \text{ (or 7\%)}$$

The Fisher equation can be used also to predict movements in market rates on the basis of changes in expected inflation. If, for example, the expected inflation rate were to increase to 5%, the equation predicts that market rates will increase to:

$$r = 0.04 + 0.05$$

$$= 0.09 \text{ (or 9\%)}$$

In practice, a movement in the expected inflation rate will change the market rate by a wider margin because of the operation of the income-tax system. Assuming suppliers of funds are seeking an after-tax real rate of return, the market rate will adjust by more than the increase in the inflation rate because part of the increased interest income will be paid in taxes.

The after-tax nominal interest rate, r_{AT} is given by:

$$r_{AT} = r(1 - t)$$

where t is the marginal rate of income taxation.

Equation (14.1b) can be modified to calculate the after-tax nominal interest rate as follows:

$$r(1 - t) = r_r + p \qquad \textit{Equation (14.1c)}$$

Rearranging this equation provides the before-tax market rate as:

$$r = \frac{r_r}{(1 - t)} + \frac{p}{(1 - t)} \qquad \textit{Equation (14.1d)}$$

Equation (14.1d) is referred to as the tax-adjusted Fisher effect. It is particularly relevant during periods of high inflation. To illustrate, suppose the tax rate is 20 cents in the dollar, the real interest rate is 4% p.a. and inflation is 3% p.a. The market interest rate (this is the before-tax rate) is predicted to be:

$$r = \frac{0.04}{1 - 0.2} + \frac{0.03}{1 - 0.2}$$

$$= 0.0875 \text{ or } 8.75\% \text{ p.a.}$$

Observe that this is a higher rate than that predicted by the simple Fisher equation (i.e. 7%). The tax-adjusted Fisher effect also implies that a given percentage change in the inflation rate will cause a larger percentage increase in the market rate. For instance, a one percentage point increase in the inflation rate (from 3 to 4%) is predicted to increase the market rate by 1.25% (from 8.75 to 10.0%), given the assumed 20% tax rate:

$$r = \frac{0.04}{1 - 0.2} + \frac{0.04}{1 - 0.2}$$

$$= 0.1 \text{ or } 10\% \text{ p.a.}$$

POINT OF INTEREST

Is it always the case that borrowers win and lenders lose as a result of inflation?

Contrary to popular opinion, the answer is no! Provided both borrowers and lenders make their financing decisions on the basis of the same expected inflation rate and the actual inflation rate matches this expectation, both parties will be satisfied with the outcome of any loan. Should future inflation turn out to be less than expected the lender wins, whereas the borrower wins when actual inflation is greater than the expected rate.

Accordingly, it is unexpected inflation that produces winners and losers.

Does the Fisher effect hold?

The simple Fisher effect assumes that interest rates are set by supply and demand and that the real interest rate is observable and stable. It implies that market rates will vary above the real rate in relation to movements in expected inflation. While we do not scientifically test the applicability of the Fisher effect, we examine the movements in the inflation rate and interest rates.

The interest rates that are more likely to behave in accordance with the Fisher equation are long-term rates. In the next section we explain that the Reserve Bank uses short-term rates as an instrument of monetary policy, therefore these rates are not free to respond to changes in expected inflation. Moreover, given their longer terms, long-term rates are more exposed (and so more sensitive) to expected changes in the inflation rate than short-term rates.

A general indication of the accuracy of the Fisher effect is provided by a simple comparison of the movements in the five-year bond yield and the inflation rate, shown in figure 14.8, over the period 1960 to 1995, and the real five-year interest rate shown in figure 14.9. Before we interpret the data, note that observing *ex poste* real interest rates (i.e. the actual interest rate minus actual inflation) is not observing expected (or *ex ante*) real rates. Therefore, the data do not provide a precise measure of the influence of inflation expectations on the two-year interest rate.

Note that:

- market interest rates provided a negative real rate of return between 1971 and 1977, and
- the actual real rate was far from being stable over the period 1960 to 1995.

The first of these observations seems to imply that suppliers of funds acted irrationally because they lost purchasing power by saving. This experience can be explained in several ways. It is possible that the market's expectation of inflation over the period 1971 to 1977 was consistently below the actual rate, and that investors expected real rates would be positive, but this did not eventuate. Inflation expectations may have been consistently too low over this period because the sustained high rates of inflation that occurred were unprecedented and so market expectations were very slow to adjust.

An alternative explanation is that an inflation premium did not emerge during the 1970s because of the government's low-interest-rate policy and so rates were not free to adjust with inflation expectations. (Juttner, 1994, p. 415)

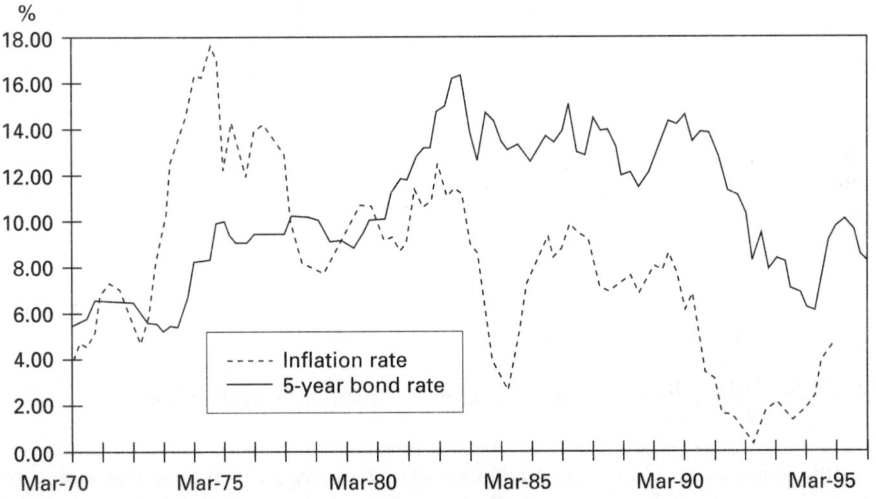

Figure 14.8 The five-year bond rate and the inflation rate, 1960 to 1995

While the actual real rates were negative during the 1970s, they were abnormally high during the 1980s when bond yields were determined by the market. It is possible that given the experience of the 1970s, investors became particularly cautious in formulating inflation expectations and demanded an inflation-risk

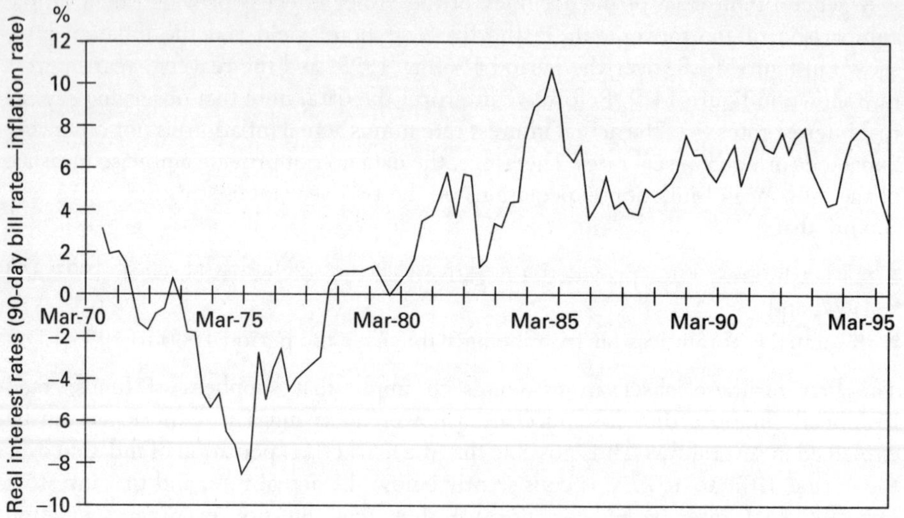

Figure 14.9 The real interest on five-year bonds

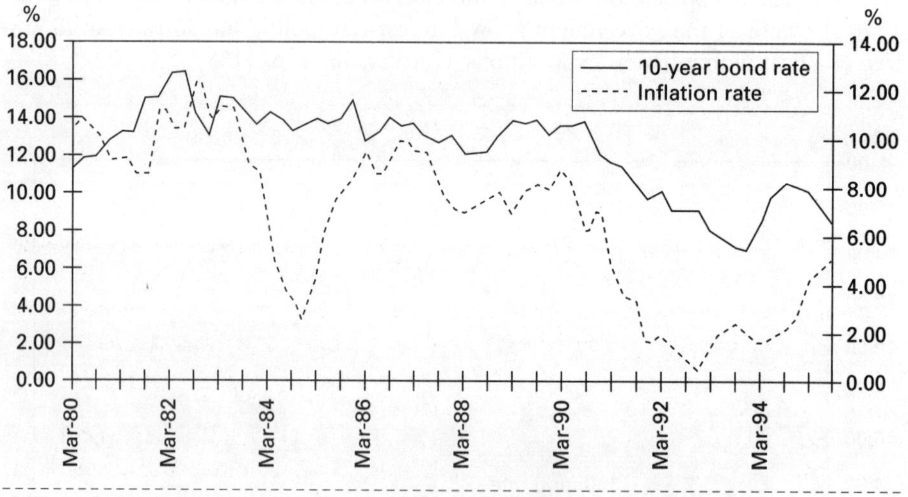

Figure 14.10 The ten-year bond rate and the inflation rate, 1985 to 1995

premium. That is, in addition to their expected real rate, a premium was added to compensate for the risk that actual inflation will exceed expected inflation. Also, the tax effect would partly explain their higher level.

Given that long-term interest rates were determined by the market over the past decade, we also compare the movements in the ten-year bond rate with the movement in the inflation rate over the period 1985 to 1995, shown in figure 14.10, and plot the implied real rate in figure 14.11. This experience is consistent with the Fisher effect, because the movements in the ten-year rate matched the movement in the inflation rate (and the implied real rate was comparatively stable).

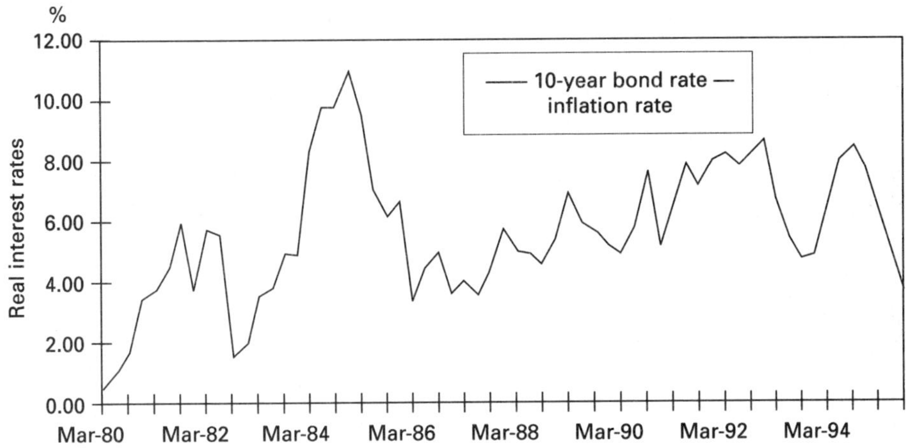

Figure 14.11 The implied real ten-year bond rate, 1985 to 1995

In summary, the Australian experience since the 1960s provides only limited support for the Fisher effect, although the more recent experience (since the mid 1980s) provides stronger support. A more technically precise study of the Fisher effect in Australia (Mishkin and Simon, 1994) confirms this conclusion.

Overseas interest rates

In a global financial system, overseas rates exert considerable influence on domestic interest rates because funds are free to flow between domestic markets. The dominant interest rates are likely to be the US and Japanese rates because of the size of their capital markets and the demand for funds in these currencies. The relationship between the ten-year bond rate in Australia with that in the USA over the period 1980 to 1995 is shown by the data in figure 14.12.

The influence of interest rates in dominant markets (such as in the USA) on rates in other countries depends on the freedom and volume of movement of funds between the markets and the expected movement in the exchange rate between the currencies. It was suggested in the previous chapter that borrowers and lenders in a country who are free and able to transact in different currencies will choose on the basis of their expectations of effective interests. This relationship was presented in Chapter 13 as equation (13.3) and is reproduced below as equation (14.2) which shows that the Australian interest rate equals the US rate plus the expected percentage movement in the AUD/USD exchange rate, $\dot{e}$:

$$r_{AUS} = r_{US} + \dot{e} \qquad \textit{Equation (14.2)}$$

To illustrate, suppose the 90-day bank-bill rates are 7.60% in Australia and 5.60% in the USA. An Australian borrower, for instance, who expected the Australian dollar would depreciate against the US dollar by more than two percentage points over the next 90 days would choose to borrow AUD funds. If the borrower expected the Australian dollar to depreciate over the next 90 days by only one percentage point, USD funds would be borrowed.

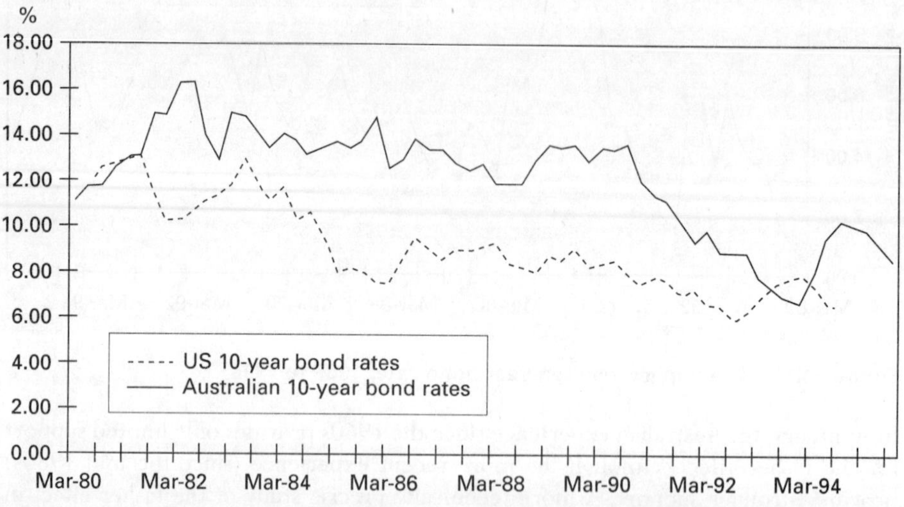

Figure 14.12 Australian and USA ten-year bond rates, 1980 to 1995

In an active global capital market, transactions between borrowers and lenders will establish an expected parity between interest rates in different countries, as specified by equation (14.2). This equation may be interpreted in either of two ways (or some of both):

- r_{AUS} changes in response to changes in r_{US}, given the exchange rate, or
- r_{AUS} responds to changes in the AUD/USD exchange rate, given r_{US}.

We specify below that forward exchange rates (such as the AUD/USD rate in 90 days) depend on the ratio of interest rates in the two countries, which may imply that the exchange rate responds to interest rates. But if the bulk of potential capital-market transactions are made on the basis of an expected movement in the exchange rate that differs from the forward rate, the interest rate in Australia would be expected to change to reestablish parity (given the dominance of r_{US}). Therefore, the relationship depicted in equation (14.2) is another example of an inter-relationship as characterised in figure 14.13.

Monetary policy

Perhaps the greatest influence on short-term interest rates is exercised by monetary policy. As noted in the introduction to this chapter, the main objective of monetary policy is to promote low inflation. This currently is defined as an underlying annual rate of 2–3%, having regard to the inflation experience of Australia's trading partners. Policy also attempts to promote growth consistent with the inflation objective, for the purposes of minimising unemployment and maximising economic well-being.

The mechanics of monetary policy and its implementation have changed since deregulation. During the 1990s, the bank has used the cash rate as its monetary policy instrument. This was the rate paid by the official dealers in the short-term money market on deposits (mainly from banks) that are secured by investments in Commonwealth Government securities. The official dealer status was established by the bank to provide a market for its trading in securities. In 1995, the RBA announced proposed changes to its settlement procedures that remove the need for official dealers.

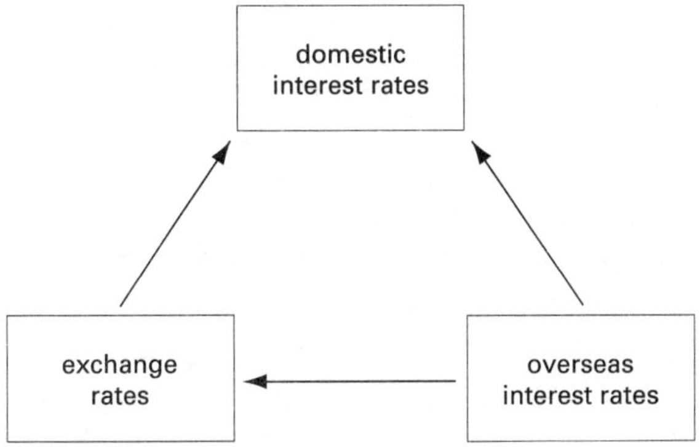

Figure 14.13 The inter-relationship between interest and exchange rates

Under real-time settlement, the bank implements monetary policy (and conducts its trading in the money market generally) by trading with any dealer that is a member of RITS (the bank's electronic system for settling transactions). The major banks, being the principal dealers in the short-term money market, are now the RBA's main counterparties to its market operations. These transactions are settled in real time through their ESAs. Recall that from mid July 1996 the bank paid a market-based rate on balances in ESAs. As at the end of July 1996, $6.8 billion was held in these accounts.

Given the movement of bank reserves from the authorised dealers to ESAs, the RBA will implement changes in monetary policy by trading with members of RITS to change the cash rate in the short-term money market to that desired by the bank. Changes in this rate will flow through to the other short-term money-market rates, especially, the 90-day bank-bill rate (Lowe, 1995, p. 9).

In general, the bank can be expected to raise short-term rates (in both real and nominal terms) when it is concerned about the level of inflation expectations (i.e. when they exceed 2–3%), and will lower them when it believes growth has fallen below the non-inflationary rate.

In practice, the determinants of monetary policy settings are more complicated because other factors might be involved (such as the exchange rate, in the context of a severe current-account deficit) and because of the lag in the effect of policy changes on the economy. In this chapter, though, our focus is on the influence of monetary policy on interest rates, rather than the formulation of monetary-policy settings (which is the concern of macroeconomics).

As stated above, the bank's monetary-policy setting most directly affects short-term rates. But because its aim is to contain inflation, its actions eventually will have an impact on long-term rates, should monetary policy prove to be effective. To illustrate, suppose inflation expectations appear to be rising above the tolerated level. The bank will trade in the money market (i.e. sell securities) to increase short-term rates in the belief that this will eventually subdue the economy, and in particular, inflation. Given the Fisher effect, this will lead, eventually, to a fall in long-term rates. Therefore, an intended consequence of an induced increase in short-term rates is a subsequent reduction in long-term rates.

Given the use of the cash rate as the instrument of monetary policy, it will tend to vary more widely through the interest-rate cycle than long-term rates. This pattern is evident from the short-term and long-term interest-rate data presented in figure 14.14. Observe that the cyclical movement in the cash rate exceeds that of the ten-year bond rate, over the decade or so since deregulation.

In terms of the Fisher equation, monetary policy will increase the real cash rate when the bank is attempting to subdue inflation expectations and will allow the real rate to fall when the economy's growth rate has fallen below the non-inflationary growth rate; whereas long-term rates can be expected to respond mainly to changes in inflation expectations.

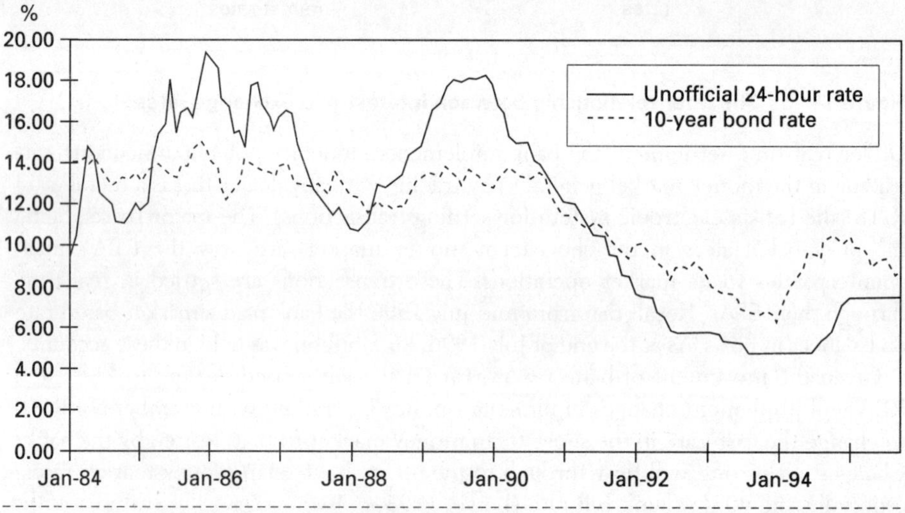

Figure 14.14 Movements in the cash rate and the ten-year bond rate, 1984 to 1995

Dealers in the money market will carefully monitor the economy to form an expectation of both the need for a change in policy and the likelihood of the bank changing its monetary-policy setting. On occasions, the cash rate (and other short-term market rates) have moved in anticipation of action by the bank. Recall that profit can be made by holding securities when their yield falls and losses can be made when rates rise. Therefore, changes in monetary policy are not made in a vacuum and on occasions very little effort is required by the bank to change short-term rates in accordance with the new policy setting.

Implementing monetary policy

Prior to the payment of interest on ESA balances, banks invested their surplus funds with the authorised dealers in the short-term money market, where they were paid the 'cash rate'. During this period, the RBA specified its monetary setting in terms of a desired level for the cash rate and it changed its monetary-policy setting by announcing a new desired cash rate. It implemented this change of policy by trading with the authorised dealers. This trading, which was known as **market operations**, involved selling short-dated Commonwealth Government securities (CGSs) when it sought to establish a higher rate, and buying CGSs when it sought to lower the rate. Note that market operations by the bank are conducted for the purpose of liquidity management as well as monetary policy. We discuss liquidity management in the next section.

The effect of market operations with RITS members (rather than the authorised dealers) is shown in figure 14.15. The effect of selling (for instance) CGSs is to reduce the market's holding of cash, because of the payments by dealers for the securities. Naturally, a reduction in cash will increase the cost of these funds; that is, the interest rate on the funds will rise. Note that selling of securities by the bank simultaneously causes their price to fall and their yield to rise. The reverse occurs when the bank buys CGSs.

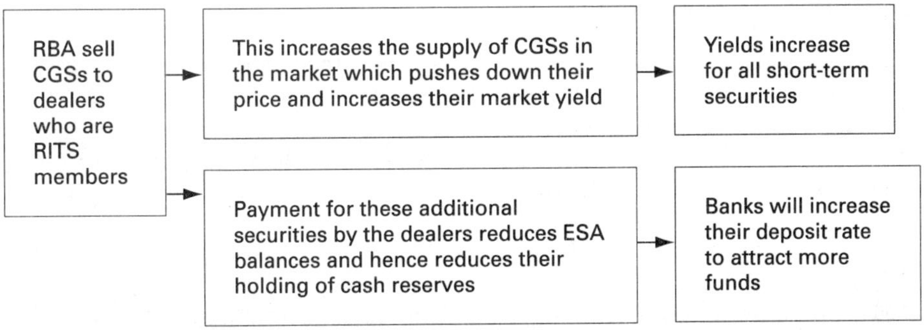

Figure 14.15 Transmission effects of RBA selling CGSs

While market operations have generally allowed the bank to keep the cash rate at the desired level, there have been occasions when the rate has varied from this level. This reflects the fact that it is a market rate, even though the bank is able to manipulate exchange-settlement funds to achieve its desired rate. (Rankin, 1992, pp. 1–6).

Market operations are conducted in CGSs because of their liquidity and freedom from credit risk. In the late 1980s when the government was able to redeem debt because of its budget surpluses, some thought was given to the instruments that could be used should their supply be severely reduced. This discussion underlined the point that any security could serve as the instrument of market operations. The increased issue of CGSs to fund the government's deficits during the 1990s has removed the need (at least temporarily) for the bank to consider the use of other instruments.

The transmission of the bank's market operations through the financial system to the real sector of the economy is represented by the flow chart presented in figure 14.16. It is based on the chart presented in Rankin. (1995, p. 35) Note that the process applies with or without the official dealers.

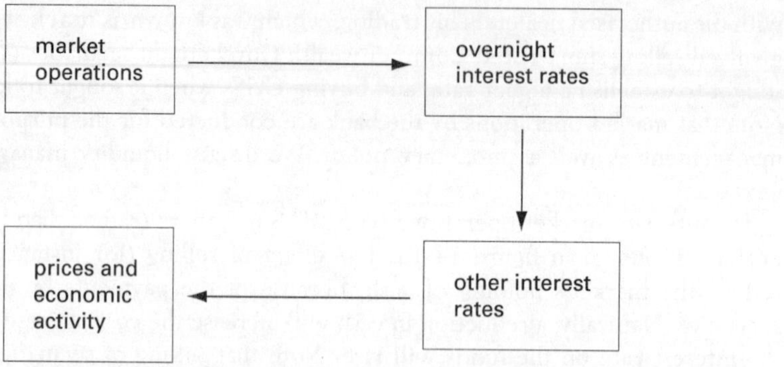

Figure 14.16 Transmission of monetary policy through market operations

Liquidity management

Market operations are much more frequently conducted by the bank to prevent the cash rate from changing unintentionally. The need for these operations arises from the bank's role as the government's banker. On any day when its payments on behalf of the government exceed its receipts, the bank is increasing the supply of cash. Unless the bank simultaneously withdraws an equivalent amount of cash (by selling CGSs to the market), rates will fall. Likewise, should the bank's receipts exceed its payments on that day, the supply of cash will fall, causing rates to rise, unless the bank sterilises the cashflows.

Liquidity management by the bank is the process of moving funds into and from the market to counterbalance the net flow of funds from and to the bank resulting from transactions on behalf of the government. This process has been referred to as 'smoothing' because of the intended effect of eliminating unintended movements in interest rates.

Examples of payments on behalf of the government include welfare benefits, interest and redemption payments on Treasury bonds and payments to State governments. Examples of receipts include tax payments by companies and settlement payments following the issue of Treasury notes at weekly tenders.

Market operations for liquidity management purposes mainly involve repos (i.e. repurchase agreements, discussed in Chapter 11) because some days the net cashflow on behalf of the government is to the financial system and on other days it is in the reverse direction. To illustrate, suppose the bank estimates that on Thursday net payments to the financial system will be $500 million and that on the following Tuesday the net inflow to the government will also be $500 million. The RBA will sell repos worth $500 million on Tuesday that it will repurchase the following Tuesday.

The objective of liquidity management is to reduce the day-to-day movements in the cash rate (and short-term rates generally) that would occur simply because of the movement of funds to and from the government's accounts with the bank. Market operations for liquidity-management purposes are presented in example 14.1.

example 14.1

At 9.30 a.m. on 16 June 1995 the bank announced to the market its estimate that the financial system would be in surplus to the extent of $400 million on that day. It also announced its intention to sell CGSs and repos, presumably to remove the surplus funds, and sought bids from dealers by 10.00 a.m. for the securities.

EXCHANGE RATES

The forces that affect the level of exchange rates are both real and imaginary. Unfounded rumour is just as likely to move the price of foreign exchange as is news founded in fact. Usually it is not possible to attribute a particular exchange-rate movement to the influence of a change in any one variable. Many exchange-rate movements appear to be counter-intuitive and contrary to accepted wisdom. The foreign-exchange market has consistently defied attempts by experts to predict future movements in the rate of exchange. Notwithstanding this, there is agreement of sorts as to a number of theories of the principal influences on the level of exchange rates. We will look briefly at the influence that the following may have on the AUD:

- inflation rates,
- interest rates,
- commodity prices,
- the current-account balance, and
- the Reserve Bank.

Purchasing-power parity

Purchasing-power parity (PPP) is a long-run theory of exchange rates that rests on the assumption that arbitrage will eventually force adjustments to exchange rates so that comparable goods will cost the same in any number of countries. (Arbitrage is the process of buying or selling a product at the most favourable price and its effect is to reduce, or even eliminate, price differentiation for the same product.)

On an economy-wide basis, purchasing power is diminished by inflation. Therefore the relative purchasing power of two currencies depends on the difference in their inflation rates. The country with the higher inflation rate is predicted by the theory to experience a depreciation of its currency in terms of the other. The effect of the resulting movement in exchange rates is to equate each currency's purchasing power.

The *Economist* magazine termed PPP the 'McDonald's Hamburger' theory of exchange rates. That is, according to this theory, exchange rates will adjust so that the effective price of a Big Mac will be the same around the globe (presumably with Hindu India being an exception). However, it is unlikely that arbitrage will force exact pricing parity. Few people will travel to the country where a Big Mac is cheapest, simply to enjoy the price advantage.

The theory relies upon equilibrating trade flows. The country with the higher inflation rate will suffer a fall in demand for its exports (because of their higher prices) and will increase its demand for imports (because of their relative cheapness compared with domestic output) and these trade flows will cause the currency to depreciate. But such forces occur only over many years. Consequently, PPP considerations have virtually no influence over day-to-day movements in exchange rates.

Table 14.1 Inflation rate differentials and the depreciation of AUD, 1970 to 1995

Country	*Inflation (% p.a.)*	*Inflation differential (%)*	*Depreciation of AUD (%)*
Australia	12.24		
Canada[1]	6.49	−2.75	−1.34
France[1]	7.88	−1.36	−1.48
Germany	5.73	−6.50	−7.11
Italy	16.95	4.72	3.56
Japan	6.95	−5.29	−9.10
Switzerland	6.32	−5.91	−9.13
UK	13.19	0.96	0.67
USA	8.74	−3.50	−2.35
NZ	15.09	2.85	0.86

[1] The data for Canada and France cover the period 1970 to 1990

The data presented in table 14.1 provide evidence that gives weight to the importance of PPP. Where Australia's inflation rate has exceeded that of another country, the AUD has depreciated against its currency. Average annual inflation rates in various countries (over the period 1970 to 1995) are shown in the first column of the table. The difference between each rate and the Australian rate (negative values indicate that the Australian inflation rate was higher than the other country) is shown in the second column (as percentage points). The third column shows the rate of appreciation of the AUD against each currency (a negative value indicates a depreciation of the AUD) as average per annum percentage points. If the PPP held perfectly over the period, the numbers in the second and the third columns would be identical. While this is not so, there is clearly a very strong positive relationship between the inflation differentials and the extent of depreciation of the bilateral exchange rates.

The numbers in the body of table 14.1 have been estimated from ABS and OECD data over the period January 1970 to July 1995. All rates of change were computed on the basis of annual compounding.

The data in table 14.1 supports the view that over the long run, the PPP theory has predictive power. This conclusion is further supported by the downward-sloping curve in figure 14.17 which predicts the AUD/DEM exchange rate in terms of PPP from 1970 to 1995. While it should be remembered that the results are somewhat sensitive to the starting point, it is nevertheless clear that the theory of purchasing-power parity provides a good explanation of most of the fall in value of the AUD against the DEM over that period.

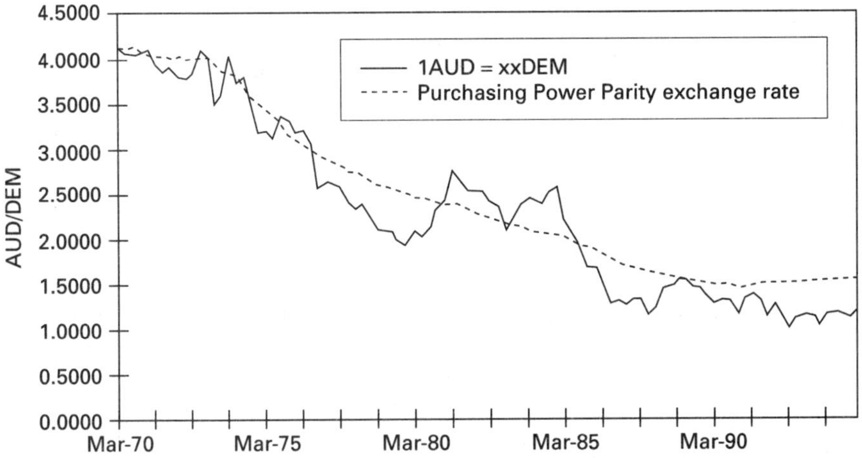

Figure 14.17 The AUD/DEM exchange rate and the implied PPP rate, 1970 to 1994

Nevertheless, observe in figure 14.17 that PPP does not hold at all points in time; indeed, over some periods there is prolonged and extensive deviation of AUD/DEM away from that predicted by PPP. This pattern is consistent with the proposition (stated above) that PPP is unlikely to apply over the short run.

The uncertainty surrounding exchange rate movements due to purchasing power differences may be likened to that surrounding the occurrence of an earthquake. While participants in the market may recognise the build-up of pressure for a substantial change in the value of a particular currency, no one can be certain of the timing of the currency realignment or of the extent of the realignment. The earthquake analogy can be continued in that the longer a currency continues a stable relationship against another currency in the face of building pressure from differential inflation rates, the more likely it is that the exchange rate will change sharply. In other words, the foreign-exchange risk is greatest when there has been a period of relative exchange-rate stability despite a substantial difference in inflation rates.

Interest-rate parity

Recall our discussion of the relationship between interest rates in different countries. The effective rate for a domestic transaction is the market rate, whereas the effective rate for a cross-currency transaction is the rate in the other country adjusted for the movement (if any) in the exchange rate between the borrowing and repayment of the funds. Interest-rate-parity theory (IRP) states that the expected movement in a bilateral exchange rate should equalise the effective interest rates between the two countries.

For example, if comparable one-year interest rates in Australia and the USA are 9.50% and 7.50% p.a. respectively, it follows under IRP theory that the AUD is expected to depreciate by two percentage points against the USD over the year. The expectation of a depreciation of the AUD (because of the interest-rate differential) serves to equate the expected returns in each financial market. If expectations are fulfilled, the effective cost of US funds for an Australian borrower, for example, would be the interest rate of 7.50% and the increase in the AUD cost of the USD (2% p.a.) required to repay the loan.

The theory of IRP provides a guide to expected short-run exchange-rate changes. The difference between interest rates in Australia and other countries represents the market's expectation (i.e. the equilibrium expectation of financial-market participants) of the movement in exchange rates over the period of a financing transaction. Data presented in table 14.2 generally support the proposition, known as **uncovered interest-rate parity**, that exchange-rate movements adjust for interest-rate differences; or, in other words, that the actual change in exchange rates generally follows the expected movement.

Table 14.2 Interest-rate differences and the actual movement in exchange rates, 1975 to 1995

Country	*Market interest rate (%)*	*Effective interest rate (%)*	*Depreciation of AUD (%)*
Australia	10.59		
US	7.15	9.62	3.33
Japan	5.85	12.65	8.92
UK	10.19	10.16	1.58
Germany	6.41	10.60	6.33
Switzerland[1]	3.83	10.10	6.94
NZ[1]	12.78	10.82	−1.86

[1] The data for Switzerland and New Zealand are for the period 1975 to 1990

The data in table 14.2 consist of quarterly interest-rate observations over the period March 1975 to March 1995 for Australia and some of its trading partners. The market interest rate, the effective interest rate and the depreciation of the AUD against the currency of the other countries was computed on a quarterly compound basis. The market interest rate is the average three-month rate in each country. This is the rate that, on average, would be paid by a domestic borrower in each country. The effective rate allows for the depreciation of the AUD on the cost of an offshore loan taken by an Australian. The rate of depreciation measures the decline in the value of the AUD on a quarterly compound basis. (A negative figure indicates an appreciation of the AUD.)

The data in table 14.2 show that the variation between each country's domestic interest rate, shown in the first column, is greater than for the effective rates shown in the second column. What has happened is that the currencies of the low-interest-rate countries, relative to Australia, have tended to appreciate against the AUD, but the movement in the exchange rates has not precisely achieved uncovered interest-rate parity. Accordingly, offshore borrowing can be advantageous, or more expensive, than domestic borrowing.

The exchange-rate risk inherent in offshore borrowing can be eliminated by taking **forward cover** by entering into a forward foreign-exchange contract to purchase sufficient currency to cover the repayment of principal and interest. However, the forward exchange rate (as explained in the previous chapter) is based on the interest-rate differential and thus a covered offshore loan has the same effective cost as a domestic loan.

It is important to understand that interest-rate parity implies that the exchange rate of a high-interest-rate currency is expected to depreciate against the currency of a low-interest-rate country. This principle may appear to be counter-intuitive because high interest rates, assuming other factors are constant, tend to attract foreign capital, and the inflow of funds would support the exchange rate.

However, usually all other things are not equal. High interest rates occur in countries with a high inflation rate or some other structural weakness (such as a current-account deficit). Structural weaknesses place downward pressure on the exchange rate and the high interest rates are normally there to compensate overseas investors for the likely depreciation of the currency during the time of their investment.

Consider the case of countries with high inflation rates. Their interest rates will tend to be relatively high, given the **international Fisher effect**. In such cases, the higher interest rate serves to compensate for the expected weakness in the exchange rate that can be explained by PPP.

Note that PPP and IRP are compatible when countries have the same real interest rate. For example, suppose country A has an interest rate of 8.00% p.a. and an inflation rate of 5%; and country B has an interest rate of 4.00% p.a. and an inflation rate of 1%. Both A and B have a real interest rate of 3% p.a. Under PPP we would expect A's exchange rate to depreciate in terms of B's currency at a rate of 4% (i.e. 5 − 1 percentage points). Likewise, under IRP we would expect A's exchange rate to depreciate relative to B's currency at a rate of 4% (i.e. 8 − 4 percentage points).

There are sound reasons for believing that the real interest rate will equate across countries (if we ignore **sovereign risk**, which is the risk that foreign-currency transactions will not be honoured). In a global capital market investors seek the highest real return. Their actions will force down high real rates and force up low-real-rates countries until a common real rate is established. The consequence is a tendency for real rates to be the same across the global market. This tendency removes the potential inconsistency between the IRP and the PPP.

Differences exist between real rates around the globe mainly because of differences in sovereign risk. Such differences can be ignored for the purpose of our discussion because they serve to compensate investors for accepting different degrees of risk. The interest rates referred to in our discussion have the same low risk class.

The tendency for the exchange rates of high-interest countries to depreciate, rather than appreciate, can be best understood by distinguishing between differences in the relative level of interest rates and changes in interest rates. An increase in interest rates, for instance, is likely to increase the inflow of funds and therefore result in an appreciation in the exchange rate, provided the FX market had not adjusted the rate in anticipation of the interest-rate rise. Whereas interest-rate differentials (following the change) reflect the subsequent expected movements in exchange rates.

We can illustrate the inter-relationship between interest and exchange rates with several general cases. Suppose there is an unexpected increase in interest rates in a country. It is likely to be associated with an immediate appreciation of the exchange rate and a subsequent further appreciation, when the increase leaves the country's interest rate below that of its trading partners. In a high-interest-rate country, a similar unexpected increase in the interest rate is likely to cause an immediate appreciation of the exchange rate, followed by a subsequent depreciation, when its interest rates are higher than those of other countries.

The data in table 14.2 support the principle that the currencies of high-interest-rate countries have a propensity to depreciate rather than appreciate against low-interest-rate countries.

Commodity prices

Over many years commodities have been Australia's dominant exports, although their share has trended down since the 85% in the 1950s and fell more sharply during the 1990s (from 71% in the 1980s to 62% for the first half of the 1990s). (RBA, 1996, p. 25) Consequently, movements in the general level of commodity prices influence the value of the AUD.

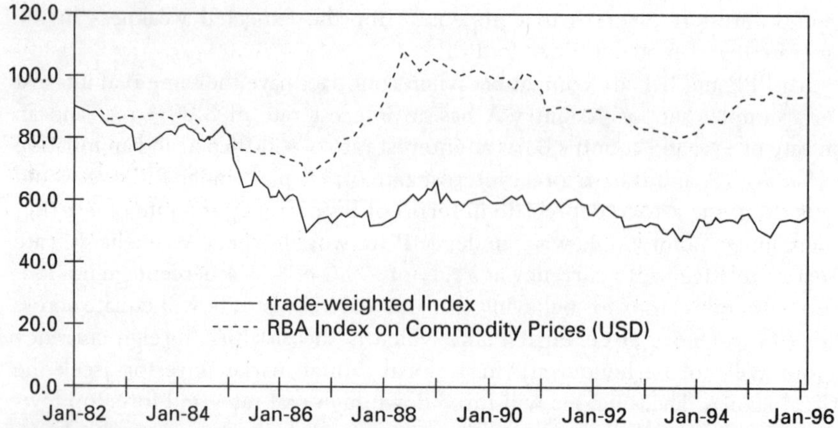

Figure 14.18 Movements in TWI value of AUD and the RBA's Commodity Price Index, 1982 to 1996

The movements in the value of the AUD (as reflected by the TWI) and the RBA's commodity price index between 1982 and 1995 are shown in figure 14.18. Clearly there is some correlation between the value of the AUD and the prices received for commodities, shown by the similarity of the directional changes in the two indices. Given that many other factors influenced the movement in the TWI, it is unlikely that the two graphs would move in a precise parallel fashion.

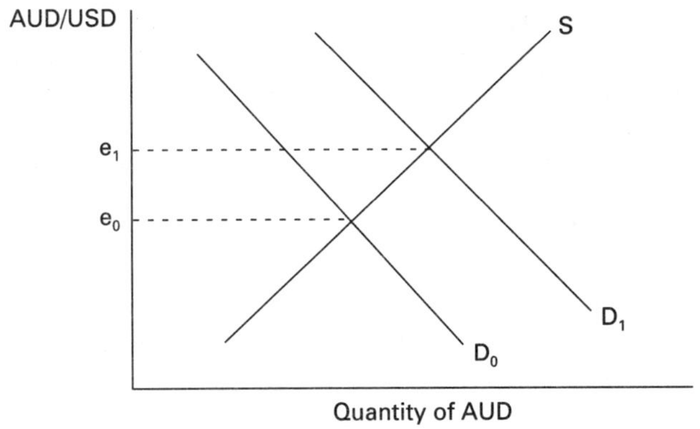

Figure 14.19 Demand and supply of foreign exchange

The relationship between the value of the AUD and commodity prices is explained with reference to the demand and supply curves presented in figure 14.19. These curves relate to the AUD in the FX market in terms of a major foreign currency, such as the USD.

Suppose world commodity prices increase. This will generally result in greater foreign-currency earnings. Exporters will accordingly increase their demand for Australian dollars when converting them to AUD, and this will increase the value of the AUD. This is shown in figure 14.19 by the demand curve shifting to the right (to D_1) and the exchange rate increasing to e_1. Similarly, when commodity prices fall, the amount of FX earned by Australian exporters will decline. This will reduce the demand for Australian dollars by exporters (shown by the demand curve shifting to the left to D_0, causing the AUD to depreciate (to e_0).

The influence of commodity price movements on the AUD is a specific application of the relationship between exchange rates and a country's **terms of trade**, which is an index of the general level of its export prices over its import prices. Increases in world commodity prices usually result in an improvement in Australia's terms of trade and this is positively related to the value of the AUD. Similarly, a fall in the terms of trade is associated with a depreciation in the AUD.

Balance of payments

A country's balance-of-payments position is typically judged on the basis of the current account, even though transactions on the capital account must counterbalance this position. The level of a country's net external debt is also an important factor.

Typically, countries with an accumulated current-account deficit have 'weak' exchange rates, whereas countries with an accumulated current-account surplus (i.e. which are a net external supplier of funds) tend to have a 'strong' currency. Weak currencies have depreciated over the long term, whereas strong currencies have appreciated. This pattern is illustrated by the Australian and Japanese experience over the 25 years to 1995, as shown by the data in figures 14.20(a) and 14.20(b).

The main reason for this long-term relationship is that an accumulated current deficit must be funded, resulting in an increased demand for foreign currency to meet the interest and repayments on these funds. The 'banana republic' comment by the then Commonwealth Treasurer (Paul Keating) in 1986 brought into sharp focus Australia's accumulated foreign debt, which caused the exchange rate to depreciate sharply.

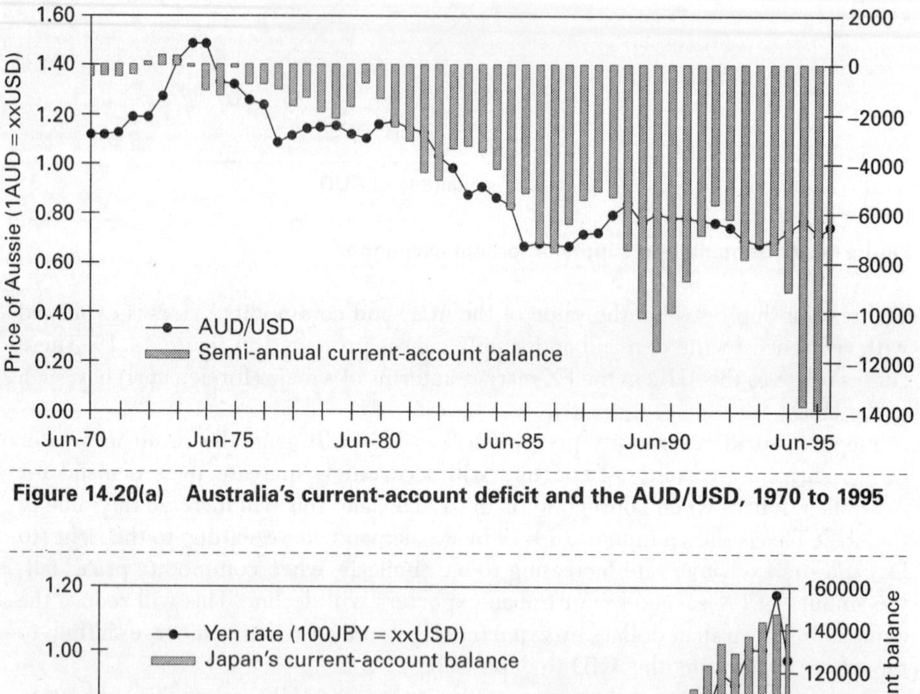

Figure 14.20(a) Australia's current-account deficit and the AUD/USD, 1970 to 1995

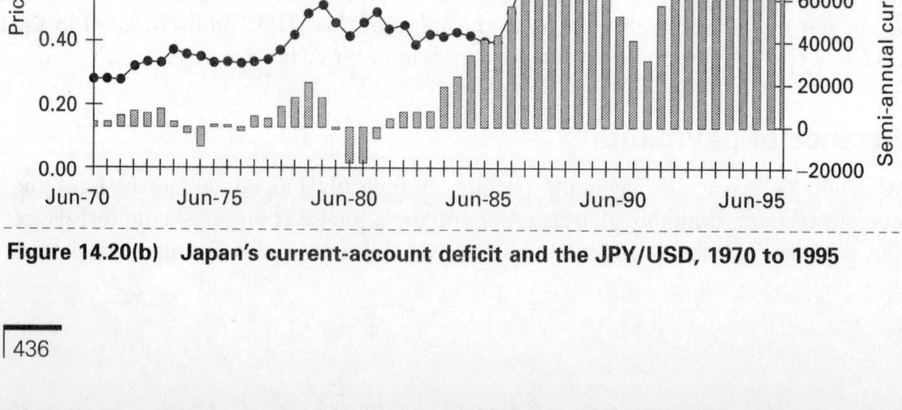

Figure 14.20(b) Japan's current-account deficit and the JPY/USD, 1970 to 1995

Over the very long run, a country may experience alternating periods of sustained current-account surpluses and deficits. In such cases, movements in the exchange rate may follow a cyclical pattern without seriously impeding the movement from deficit to surplus. But when a country has a severe current-account deficit, it can be trapped in deficit. This can occur because a depreciation in the exchange rate increases the amount of foreign exchange required to meet the country's existing foreign debt-servicing requirement. Should the debt-servicing requirement exceed the country's potential export income it will be trapped into a deficit position. This possibility for Australia prompted the 'banana republic' comment. According to the then governor of the RBA (Fraser, 1995) Australia's overseas indebtedness does not pose this problem, although it does require an increase in the national savings rate.

In common with inflation, a country's balance-of-payments position influences its exchange rate over the long run. Usually, it does not provide a basis for predicting short-term movements in the exchange rate.

Official influence

Recall from the discussion in the previous chapter that the Reserve Bank trades in the foreign-exchange market for two main purposes: to make foreign-currency transactions on behalf of the Commonwealth Government and to test the market's sentiment whenever the exchange-rate changes appear (to the bank) to be too high or too low. It was noted earlier in this chapter that such trading in the domestic money market is referred to as 'smoothing and testing'.

Two questions arise about the bank's intervention to reduce the variability in the exchange rate:

1 Is the variability in exchange rates excessive? The efficient-market hypothesis implies that markets do not over shoot and so there is no need for the bank to intervene. However, the bank contends (Campbell, p. 50) that over shooting occurs.
2 Is intervention effective? One test is whether the bank makes a profit from intervening to reduce variability. A profit indicates that intervention is effective because the bank buys to prevent the exchange rate from falling too far and sells to prevent it from appreciating too much. If the intervention is not effective (i.e. does not smooth movements in exchange rates) the bank would make a loss. Over the period since the floating of the exchange rate to June 1994, the bank made an overall profit of $3.4 billion from such intervention. (Andrew and Broadbent, 1994)

Accepting that, in general, the bank intervenes in the market to promote stability rather than to maintain the exchange rate at a desired level (Campbell, p. 50), there is some evidence that the bank has, on occasions, attempted to keep the exchange rate within certain bounds.

In recent years, the Bank has intervened heavily in the market for the purposes of stabilisation, of preventing a fall in the Australian-dollar rate in the context of a loss of confidence, and of preventing a rise in the Australian-dollar rate when it felt it was being pushed unrealistically high. Examples of the former were in September 1986, October

1987 and January/February 1992, of the latter in February 1987 and October 1990.
(Linklater, 1992, p. 111)

During the 1990s, the RBA's holding of foreign exchange has been relatively stable at around $20 billion (although the bank increased its holding of foreign exchange and gold by $3 billion following the receipt of $7 billion in ESA funds in July 1996), which gives the bank a capacity to influence the value of the currency through trading in the market, even though the daily turnover in the foreign-exchange market was much greater (USD40 billion). However, the bank's potential influence on the exchange rate depends more on other factors, such as announcement effects, monetary-policy settings and coordinated action with a number of central banks.

Monetary-policy settings also affect the exchange rate because, as discussed above, interest rates and their expected movements will influence the demand and supply of the AUD. A tightening of monetary policy (i.e. an increase in short-term interest rates) may increase demand for AUD securities because of the higher yield, and this may increase the value of the currency, and vice versa for an easing of monetary policy.

Nevertheless, it is not clear that maintaining high short-term rates will support the value of the currency at an artificially high level. Where the interest rate exceeds that in other countries, interest-rate parity theory implies that the value of the currency is expected to fall.

Also, because monetary policy responds to developments within the economy, market sentiment may ignore an economic event, such as a lift in the rate of inflation (which in terms of fundamentals would cause the exchange rate to fall), deciding instead to mark up the currency in anticipation of a tightening of monetary policy (i.e. an increase in short-term interest rates).

Unfortunately we cannot conclude this discussion of the determinants of the movements in exchange rates with a formula for predicting their future movements. It would involve accurately forecasting movements in the fundamental factors that influence the exchange rate as well as consistently predicting the market's response to expected future events. We have an understanding of the relationship between many variables and the exchange rate, but so do the market's participants.

Efficient-market implications

Day-to-day changes in the exchange rate are indistinguishable from that of a random series. Such exchange-rate behaviour is consistent with the efficient-market hypothesis. You will recall that this theory implies that recognisable trends in exchange rates do not arise because they represent exploitable profit opportunities. It is assumed that arbitrage will almost instantly remove any such unexploited opportunities for profit, and therefore the only force for change in exchange rates is the random arrival of new information. The numerous components of market information which impinge upon the value of the AUD range from news on fundamental factors of currency supply and demand to unsubstantiated rumour and hearsay about these factors.

In an efficient market all relevant information is incorporated in the ruling market price. It follows that the weight of money and expectations about all future movements (whether short-term or long-term) in the exchange rate are centred around this price. This must be so or the price would have moved.

Recall two important implications of the efficient-market/random-walk theory. These are that:

1 price changes are random and so future prices cannot be predicted with any degree of precision, and
2 the best predictor of future price is today's price.

Table 14.3 Weekly forecasts of the movement in the exchange rate

Bank	*Forecast error* average % (1)	standard deviation % (2)	*Correct direction* % (3)
BT	0.08	2.11	49.13
ANZ	−0.28	2.29	38.79
Aust. Bank	−0.14	2.05	48.27
BA	−0.26	2.00	50.00
Barclays	−0.13	2.29	44.82
Citibank	0.07	2.25	48.27
CBA	−0.05	2.26	42.24
Elders	0.08	2.08	39.65
Macquarie Bank	−0.16	2.19	50.00
Lloyds	0.19	2.28	58.62
NAB	−0.33	2.17	56.03
R. & I.	−0.16	2.16	49.13
Schroders	0.10	2.38	46.55
Westpac	−0.08	2.14	46.55
BNP	0.08	2.05	45.68
Average forecast	−0.04	1.89	49.13
Random walk	−0.08	1.83	n.a.

Table 14.3 displays the results of a comparison of FX forecasting by 16 banks and merchant banks with actual movements. The figures in the body of the table are based on weekly surveys conducted over the period February 1985 to September 1987. Respondents were asked in a telephone poll to forecast next week's AUD/USD exchange rate. The data tend to be consistent with the random-walk (efficient-market) conclusions.

Column (1) in table 14.3 presents the average error of 116 weekly predictions and column (2) presents the standard deviation of the prediction errors. The higher the figures in these two columns, the worse is the prediction record. The data in column (3) show the percentage of occasions that the direction of the weekly movement in the exchange rate was forecast correctly. When this result is compared with a coin-toss forecast method that would score 50%, the scores of (3) appear in perspective.

A random walk of foreign-exchange prices, as is expected in an efficient market, is to some counter-intuitive. The naive gambler might, mistakenly, conclude that the occurrence of three reds in a row makes the probability of a black in the next spin more likely than a red. In an efficient market, like that for FX, a fall in exchange rates is equally as likely to be followed by a further fall as it is to be followed by a rise.

The description of exchange-rate movements as a random process highlights the fact that while one cannot be certain of either the direction or extent of future rate changes, one can be sure that there is a considerable degree of risk associated with foreign-currency ventures. This general conclusion is supported by leading practitioners. According to White (1994), forecasting is a worthwhile activity even though it does not generate the predictions that are consistently profitable.

Summary

The main points of this chapter are as follows:

- Loanable-funds theory can show the impact of economic conditions on market interest rates.
- The business cycle induces an interest-rate cycle.
- The market's expected inflation rate forms part of market interest rates (in addition to the real rate). This is known as the Fisher effect.
- The Fisher effect is more evident in long-term than short-term rates.
- The Fisher effect did not hold during the 1970s, mainly because of interest-rate ceilings during a period of high inflation.
- Domestic interest rates are influenced by dominant overseas interest rates, subject to expected movements in the exchange rate.
- Changes in monetary policy influence short-term rates immediately and long-term rates eventually.
- Monetary policy and liquidity management are implemented by market operations by the RBA.
- Over the long run, exchange rates tend to establish purchasing power parity.
- The expected movement in exchange rates aligns with interest-rate differentials.
- The AUD is sensitive to movements in commodity prices.
- Over the long run, exchange rates are influenced by a country's current-account position.
- A change in monetary policy can immediately change the exchange rate, and the exchange rate influences monetary policy.
- The efficient-market hypothesis suggests that exchange rates follow a random walk, and there is evidence that supports this claim.

Discussion questions and exercises

1 Discuss the relationship between interest and exchange rates and economic activity. Refer to the main effects of interest rates on economic activity and the main effects of the exchange rate on the economy.
2 Discuss the volatility of the 90-day bank-bill rate and the five-year bond rate between 1970 and 1995 and the level of *ex poste* real rates over this period.
3 Discuss the movement in interest rates using loanable-funds theory. Refer to figure 14.5 when explaining the link between the business cycle and the level of interest rates. Consider also the effect of inflation on interest rates.
4 Discuss the Fisher effect and assess its relevance to Australian interest rates between 1970 and 1995. Distinguish between the inflation rate and inflationary expectations, and between short- and long-run interest rates. Use the Fisher equation to predict the movement in interest rates when the inflation rate is expected to increase from 2% to 5%, given a real rate of 4% p.a.
5 Describe the implementation process for changes in monetary policy and discuss the influence of monetary policy on Australia's interest rates. Explain how an increase in the cash rate can serve to reduce long-term rates.
6 Explain and discuss liquidity management by the RBA.
7 Explain purchasing-power parity and its implications for movements in the exchange rate. Present evidence of the effect of PPP on the movements in the exchange rate.
8 Explain interest-rate parity. Distinguish between the expected movement in exchange rates and the subsequent movement in spot rates (i.e. uncovered interest-rate parity).
9 Discuss the relationship between IRP and PPP.
10 Explain the influence of commodity prices on the value of the Australian dollar. Is this factor linked to the influence of the balance of payments on the exchange rate?
11 Discuss the RBA's involvement in the FX market and its influence over exchange rates.
12 Suggest an explanation for the observed inability of professional economists to correctly predict movements in the Australian dollar.

References and further reading

Andrew, Robert, & Broadbent, John 1994, *Reserve Bank Operations in the Foreign Exchange Market: Effectiveness and Profitability*, RDP 9406, RBA.

Campbell, Frank 1995, 'The exchange rate and the Reserve Bank's role in the foreign exchange market', in *Seminar for Teachers*, RBA, pp. 39–54.

Felmington, Bruce, & Coleman, William 1995, *Money and Finance in the Australian Economy*, Irwin, Chapters 8 and 25.

Fraser, B.W. 1995, 'Australia in hock?', *Bulletin*, RBA, Sydney, pp. 1–8.

Juttner, D. Johannes 1994, *Financial Markets, Interest Rates and Monetary Economics*, 3rd edn, Longman Cheshire, Melbourne, Chapters 21–23.

Linklater, Joan 1992, *Inside the Bank*, Allen & Unwin, Sydney.

Lowe, Philip 1995, *The Link between the Cash Rate and Market Interest Rates*, RDP 9504, RBA, Sydney.

Mishkin, Frederick, & Simon, John 1994, *An Empirical Examination of the Fisher Effect in Australia*, RDP 9410, RBA.

Paul-Choudhury, Sumit 1996, 'Union blues', *Risk*, vol. 9, no. 3, March 1996.

Pollard, Patricia S. 1995, 'EMU: will it fly?', *Review*, Federal Reserve Bank of St Louis, vol. 77, no. 4, July 1995.

Rankin, R.W. 1992, *The Cash Market in Australia*, RDP 9214, RBA.

Rankin, Bob 1995, 'The Reserve Bank's domestic market operations', in *Seminar for Teachers*, RBA.

RBA January 1996, 'Diversity of exports and Australia's terms of trade', in *Bulletin*.

Stevens, Glenn 1995, 'Monetary policy in Australia', in *Seminar for Teachers*, RBA, Sydney.

White, Garry 1994, 'Forecasting: a mug's game or a productive role for economists?', *Agenda*, vol. 1, no. 1, pp. 63–70.

15

The term structure of interest rates

This chapter examines the relationship between interest rates and the term over which they apply. This is an important topic because it introduces forward interest rates — that is, rates that apply from future dates. Multi-period market rates implicitly provide financial-market participants with choices between rates with different terms. When making these choices, participants are revealing their expectation about the future movement in interest rates, because multi-period rates (i.e. yield curves) implicitly incorporate forward rates.

Study objectives

From your study of this chapter you should be able to:

- identify generalised yield-curve shapes;
- calculate implicit forward interest rates from yields in the short-term money market;
- explain how expectations about future rates determine the shape of yield curves;
- explain the formation of liquidity premiums and discuss their role in determining the slope of yield curves;
- explain the possible influence of market segmentation and preferred habitats on the shape of the yield curve;
- explain how bond-market yields can be converted into zero-coupon spot rates;
- calculate implied forward rates from zero-coupon spot rates; and
- show how forward rates can be set through trading in financial markets.

Introduction

The **term structure** of interest rates refers to the relationship between interest rates and the period over which they apply. We can view it through the **yield curve**, which traces the yields on a particular instrument (or risk-class of instruments) according to maturities that are traded in the market. For example, bills with various terms to maturity (up to 180 days) are traded each day in the money market. A yield curve is formed by tracing their market yields according to the term to maturity.

A security's term is simply the length of time to the security's maturity (or redemption) date. Ideally, a yield curve will trace yields on securities that make a single payment on their maturity date. In these cases, the yield applies to the term of the payment. For instance, the yield on a 90-day bill is precisely the yield on a payment that has a 90-day term. We return to this point in the next section.

There is virtually no limit to the variety of shapes that may be embodied in a yield curve. Figure 15.1 presents three generalised yield-curve shapes. The upward-sloping curve is referred to as the **normal yield curve**, implying, perhaps, that it normally occurs. The downward-sloping curve is referred to as an **inverse yield curve**.

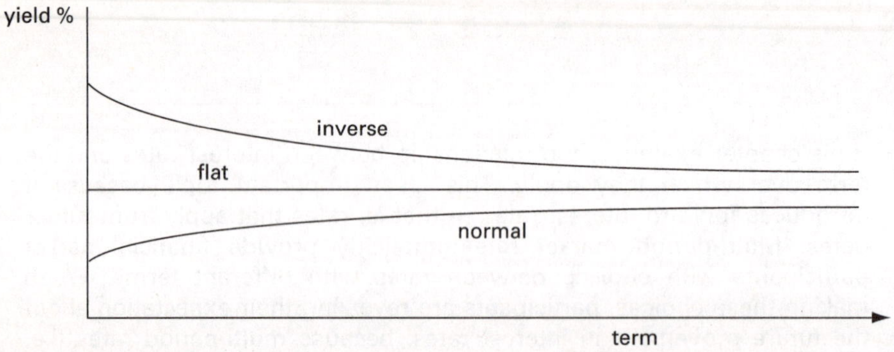

Figure 15.1 Generalised yield-curve shapes

In practice, yield-curve shapes are not rigid, changing whenever short-term rates vary by a different margin to long-term rates. Several yield curves for Treasury bonds, based on market yields, are presented in figure 15.2. Note that the yields are identified by the maturity dates for particular bonds.

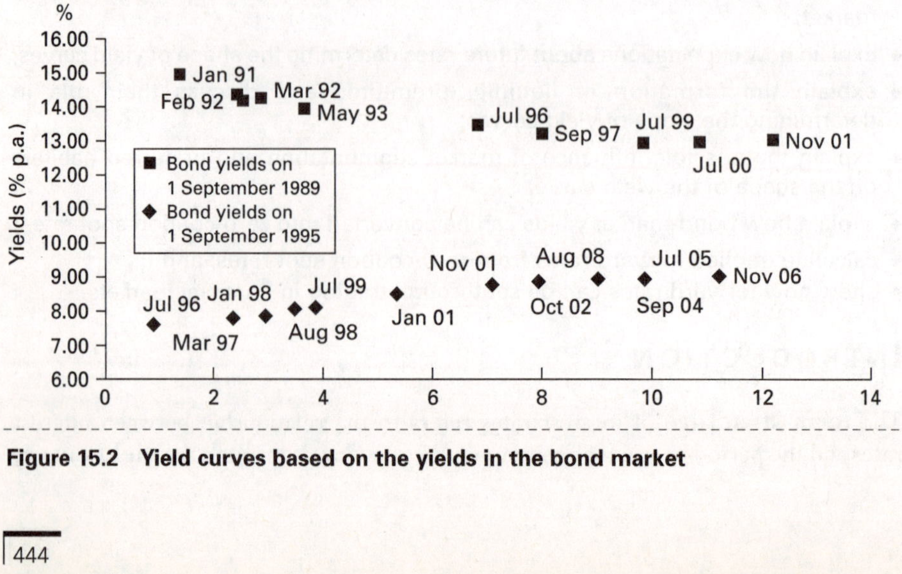

Figure 15.2 Yield curves based on the yields in the bond market

Note that the rates in figure 15.2 are market yields, rather than interest rates set by institutions. We analyse yields (rather than deposit rates) for two main reasons. They reflect trading in liquid securities and so provide a better view of yields as a function of term. The rates set by institutions, such as for fixed-term deposits, apply to the retail market, which is subservient to the wholesale markets, and reflect the illiquid nature of these accounts, as well as their term.

As noted above, a term structure is based on the yields for securities that have the same risk-class. It serves to identify the sole influence of 'term' on yields. Other factors that influence yields, such as default risk and liquidity, have to be held constant when constructing a yield curve. For example, recall the separate yield curves for Treasury and semi-government bonds presented in figure 11.1 (p. 300). The differences in yields (or spread) between these two security classes, for the same term (or tenor), are due to differences in credit rating and liquidity.

Australia's yield-curve experience

In general terms, the shape of the yield curve is reflected in the relative level of short-term to long-term yields. When the short-term yields are higher, the yield curve will have an inverse shape, and vice versa for the normal yield-curve shape.

The data in figures 15.3 and 15.4 provide some insight into the changing Australian term structure between 1970 and 1995. Figure 15.3 plots the yield to maturity on two instruments, 13-week Treasury notes and ten-year Treasury bonds, over this period. Given that the yields on Treasury securities have the same credit standing, it follows that in the periods when the short-term yields were lower than the long-term yields, a normal yield curve resulted. These periods are shown in figure 15.4 by the curve being above the horizontal. When short-term yields exceeded long-term yields (indicating an inverse yield curve), the curve in figure 15.4 is below the horizontal.

Observe (in figure 15.4) that during the 1970s, short-term yields were generally less than long-term yields, and so the normal yield curve was generally prevalent. But in the 1980s, the reverse generally applied. During these two decades, the yield curve twisted from normal to inverse when the economy 'over-heated' (in say, 1975 and 1985) and the monetary authorities tightened monetary policy. This was particularly evident during the 1980s, when the government's anti-inflation policy imposed very high short-term rates.

It is also evident that the yield curve twisted from being inverse to being normal when the economy fell into recession, when the authorities eased short-term rates to promote a recovery in the economy. This is evident, for example, in 1990–91. You will see that during the first half of the 1990s, the yield curve had a normal shape. This reflected the low level of expected inflation, which meant that the authorities did not have to place severe upward pressure on short-term yields.

Australia's experience in the 1980s was consistent with that of other countries that experienced relatively high inflation (such as Italy, Great Britain and New Zealand), whereas the normal yield-curve shape was more evident in the low-inflation countries (such as Japan, Germany and Switzerland).

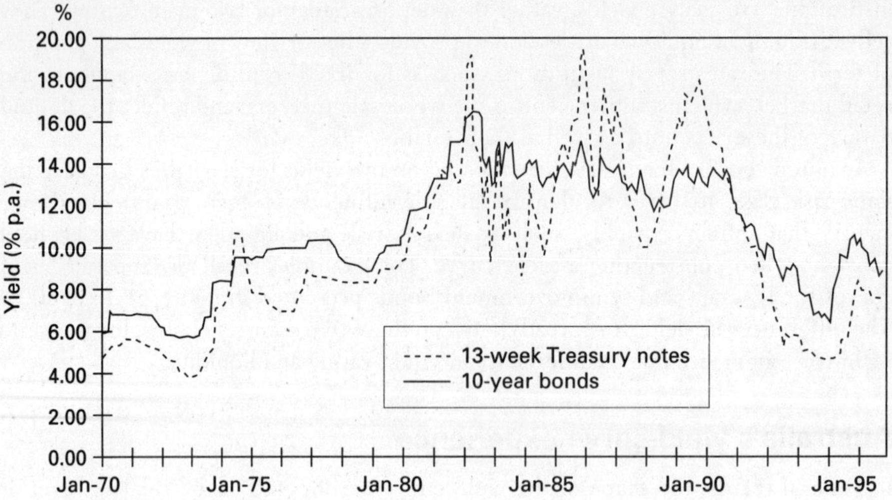

Figure 15.3 Yields on Treasury bonds and notes, 1970 to 1995

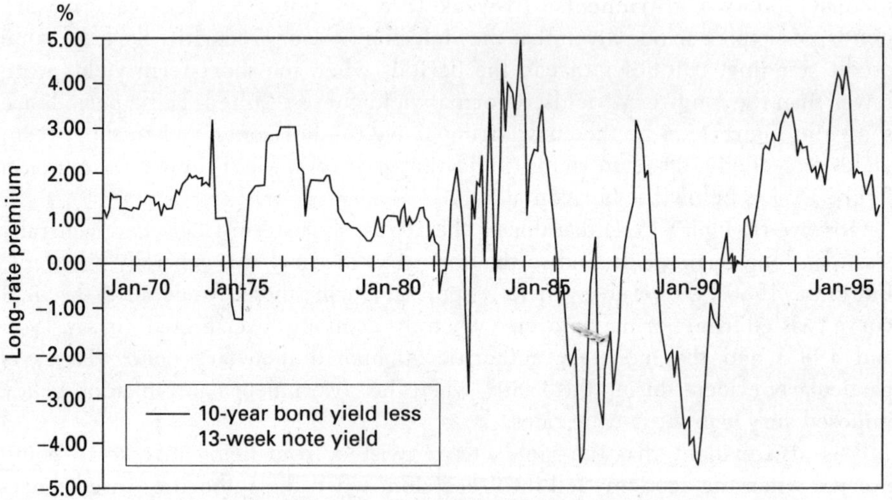

Figure 15.4 Treasury bond yield minus Treasury note yield, 1970 to 1995

In general, interest rates are **mean-reverting**. That is, interest rates tend to return to some long-run average rate, after periods of high and low rates. This behaviour is reflected in the shape of yield curves. An inverse yield curve is more likely to occur when interest rates are historically high, whereas a normal yield curve is more frequently associated with low interest-rate levels.

Forward rates in the short-term market

The main learning objective of this chapter is that you understand the role of forward interest rates (i.e. rates that start in the future) in shaping the yield curve. Forward rates can be identified from a yield curve when the yields apply to single-payment securities. Such yields provide a precise measure of yield according to term.

In our discussion in Chapters 10 and 11 of short- and long-term securities we emphasised that the former make one payment only — on their maturity date — whereas bonds make a series of payments, including a large payment (the last coupon plus the bond's face value) on their maturity date. For the purposes of this chapter we can use the yields in the short-term market directly because they provide a precise measure of yield according to the term of the payment.

In our discussion of forward rates we refer to current market yields for single-payment securities as **spot rates**. They provide the precise measure of yields as a function of term that is a prerequisite for identifying implicit forward rates. Note that spot rates can apply for single or multiple periods, whereas we will treat forward rates as single-period rates that start at a future date. This treatment of spot and forward rates is designed to simplify the discussion of forward rates.

We further assume that a month constitutes a period in the short-term money market. Therefore the basic spot rate is the yield for 30-day bills, the 60-day rate is the two-period rate and the 90-day rate is the three-period yield. These rates are quoted in daily newspapers. They are spot rates because they measure the growth in P to a single payment, F, over the term of the security.

Our basic proposition is that a two-period spot rate comprises the one-period spot rate and an implicit one-period forward rate. Using subscripts to identify when rates commence and finish, this proposition can be stated as:

$$ {}_0r_2 = \frac{{}_0r_1 + {}_1r_2}{2} \qquad \textit{Equation (15.1)} $$

To illustrate, suppose the two-period spot rate is 8.00% and the one-period spot rate is 7.50%, the forward rate that is embedded in the two-period rate is 8.50%. This rate serves to equate the two-period rate with the two successive one-period rates. It also shows that the two-period rate is the average of the constituent one-period rates. This principle can be extended to all multi-period rates.

NOTATION OF SPOT AND FORWARD RATES

The notation used in the balance of this chapter serves to distinguish spot from forward rates and identify their terms. The general form of the notation is, ${}_{t1}r_{t2}$, where t_1 refers to the time when the rate commences (e.g. t_1 equals zero for a spot rate) and t_2 refers to the time when the rate matures. We treat six months as a single period in the discussion of bond yields. Hence, a spot rate that applies for one period is shown as ${}_0r_1$ and a forward rate that commences in six months' time and matures in a year (i.e. at the end of two periods) is shown as ${}_1r_2$. The term of this rate is t_2 minus t_1 (i.e. one period).

This notation system is consistent with that used in the market for forward rates (i.e. FRAs), which we discuss in Chapter 17. FRAs are one of the arrangements that are used to lock in a forward interest rate. For example, a 1:4 FRA commences in one month and extends for a term of three months (i.e. matures at the end of four months).

It is usual to refer to single-period forward rates. Examples of such rates, in terms of the notation used in this book, are ${}_1r_2$ and ${}_2r_3$.

It is shown below that, say, a three-period spot rate, ${}_0r_3$, covers three single-period rates, ${}_0r_1$, ${}_1r_2$ and ${}_2r_3$ (i.e. the three-period rate is the average of its constituent single-period spot and forward rates).

Note that in using yields in the short-term market, being simple-interest yields, we need not be concerned with compounding effects, whereas they must be taken into account when we consider multi-period yields in the bond market.

The rationale for equation (15.1) is that traders in the market would view two successive single-period rates as an alternative to a two-period rate. Therefore, trading in the market would establish a relationship between the single- and two-period spot rates based on the expected forward rate (i.e. ${}_1r_2$). The implicit forward rate serves to ensure that the two-period rate is the average of its constituent single-period rates (the observable single-period spot rate and the implicit forward rate).

In practice, short-term forward rates are not derived from multi-period market yields. They are determined by trading in the bill-futures market. We show in Chapter 17 that three-month forward rates are revealed by the prices of bill-futures contracts in the futures market. In this market, we treat three months as the basic period. Hence, identifying short-term forward rates is simply a matter of observing the prices that are quoted in the daily newspapers.

However, long-term forward rates (i.e. six-month rates) have to be derived from the multi-period spot rates in the bond market and as bonds are not single-payment securities, their market yields must be adjusted before they can be used to calculate implicit forward rates. The following section explains this adjustment process. Nevertheless, it is important to keep in mind that the process is undertaken solely to provide yields that can be used to derive six-monthly implicit forward rates.

THE DERIVATION OF SPOT RATES FROM BOND YIELDS

The actual yield curves presented in figure 15.2 are based on the market yields for Treasury bonds on 1 September 1989 and 1995. The yield curves display an approximate relationship (only) between yield and term, because the yields are for bonds that make a series of payments over their term. These yields have to be converted to spot i.e. single-payment yields to show their precise relationship with the term of the bond's final payment. This involves **stripping** the bond of its coupon payments prior to its final payment, converting it into a theoretical single-payment instrument.

The payments on a two-and-a-half-year bond and the payment on a discount instrument are shown in figure 15.5. The bond makes four coupon payments and a final payment at maturity that comprises the last coupon and the bond's face value (this being the 'redemption' payment), whereas the short-dated security makes only one payment (on its maturity date).

A precise relationship between yield and term could be shown for bonds if they made no payments prior to their maturity date. Such bonds are traded in other bond markets where they are known as zero-coupon bonds (or zeros) because they make only one payment at maturity and their yield is calculated on a semi-annual compound basis. However, such bonds do not trade in Australia's bond market.

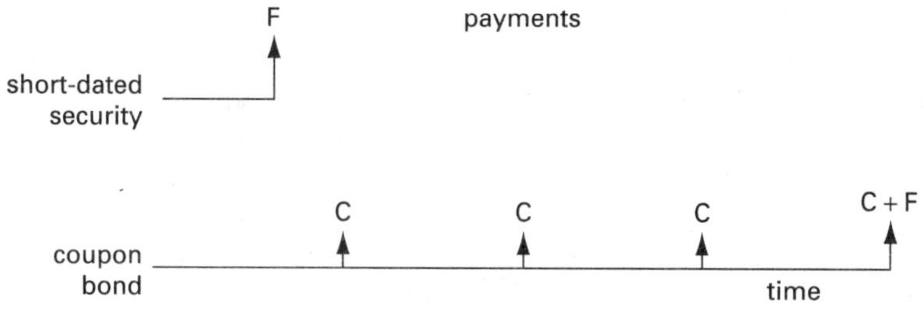

Figure 15.5 The timing of security payments

In the United States, zeros are created by selling securities whose one and only payment is based on the coupon payments of US Treasury bonds. This is arranged by a financial institution that buys a large parcel of Treasury bonds that are designed for this purpose. The parcel provides a series of coupon payments, as well as a final redemption payment that the institution can pass through to the holders of the zeros it has issued. Each zero has the term that matches each payment from the Treasury bond. Hence the institution converts (or strips) the Treasury bonds into a series of zero-coupon bonds.

Trading in zeros establishes yields in the same way as trading in coupon-paying bonds. These are referred to as **zero-coupon yields** and are simply the yields on zero-coupon (i.e. single-payment) bonds. We refer to them also as spot yields, as explained above. When zeros are issued with a range of maturities, their yields can be plotted as a spot-yield curve. However, the market for zeros in the United States is not sufficiently liquid or deep to ensure that the observed yields provide a pure measure of yields as a function of term. (Fabozzi, Modigliani and Ferri, 1994, p. 236)

Consequently, even in the USA, zero-coupon yields are derived theoretically from market yields for Treasury coupon-paying bonds. This simply involves the simulated sale of a bond's coupons, stripping it down to its final single payment (its face value plus its last coupon). The sale of the coupons on a two-and-a-half-year bond is shown in example 15.1.

The problem posed by coupons when representing long-term yields as a function of their term is evident when the yield curve is not flat. Suppose, for instance, there is a normal yield curve. This means that the yield appropriate for the first coupon, for instance, will be less than the yield appropriate for the bond's final payment. If there is an inverse yield curve, the reverse would be true. Only by stripping the coupons at the yield that is appropriate to their individual terms can we determine the yield that corresponds to the term of the bond's final payment.

The calculation of zero-coupon yields from the market yields for coupon bonds, to construct the spot-yield curve, is performed by sequentially deriving zero-coupon rates, starting with a one-year (i.e. two payment) bond, and moving to successively longer coupon-paying bonds. A simple example will illustrate the technique. Note that we adopt six months as the basic period for bond yields, because interest is calculated on a semi-annual compound basis.

example 15.1

A two-and-a-half-year 10.00% Treasury bond can be stripped of its coupon payments that are made prior to its maturity as follows:

2.5-year coupon bond

- sell first coupon as six-month zero for $C/(1 + {}_0r_1/2)$
- sell second coupon as 12-month zero for $C/(1 + {}_0r_2/2)^2$
- sell third coupon as 1.5-year zero for $C/(1 + {}_0r_3/2)^3$
- sell fourth coupon as two-year zero for $C/(1 + {}_0r_4/2)^4$
- convert security to a 2.5-year single-payment bond, worth $(C + F)/(1 + {}_0r_5/2)^5$

where ${}_0r_n$ = the spot rate (% p.a.) appropriate to a term of n coupon periods.

Consider three 10.00% coupon bonds. The first matures in six months. Because this bond has only one payment to make ($C + F in six months), it is in effect a zero-coupon bond and its market yield is already a zero-coupon rate. We ignore that the bond's final payment includes its last coupon when we describe its market yield as being a 'zero-coupon' yield. The important feature is that the yield is for a single payment. For the purpose of the illustration we assume that this yield, which is a spot yield, is 8.00% p.a.

The second bond matures in a year's time, and its market yield is 9.00%. This bond has two payments to make. The first is its second-last coupon, worth $5.00 (calculated as half of 10.00% times $100, which represents its face value) and the final payment is $105 (the last coupon plus F, i.e. $100). Before we strip this bond of the coupon that will be paid in six months, we first calculate the bond's price by discounting all cash-flows at its yield of 9% p.a.:

$$P_{1\,yr} = \frac{5}{1.045} + \frac{105}{1.045^2}$$

$$= \$100.936334$$

Observe that this two-payment bond is worth just over $100. In other words, the remaining two payments form a yield of 9.00% p.a. when the bond is purchased at this price. To convert the bond to a (notional) single-payment instrument we strip this bond of the coupon due in six months by selling it (at least, notionally) and deducting the proceeds from the above price (which includes the value of the coupon). The coupon's value is found, as follows, using the six-month spot yield of 8.00% p.a.:

$$PV_{1st\ cpn} = \frac{5}{1.04}$$

$$= \$4.807692$$

Deducting this amount from the bond's price provides the present value of the bond's final (and only remaining) payment:

$$100.936334 - 4.807692 = \$96.128642$$

Accordingly, we have established that the bond's remaining payment (in a year) of $105 is worth $96.128642 and represents a one-year spot (i.e. two-period spot) yield of:

$${}_0r_2 = \left[\left(\frac{105.00}{96.128642}\right)^{1/2} - 1\right]2$$

$$= 9.025\%$$

Now we turn to the third bond. Suppose that it has a term of 1.5 years and is trading at a yield of 9.80%. Its price is:

$$P = \frac{5}{1.049} + \frac{105}{1.049^2} + \frac{105}{1.049^3}$$

$$= \$100.272836$$

Next we strip it of its initial two coupon payments. The one due in six months' time has a present value of $4.807692 (as calculated above). The second one is worth $5 discounted at the one-year spot rate:

$$PV_{2nd\ cpn} = \frac{5}{(1 + 0.09025/2)^2}$$

$$= \$4.577555$$

Deducting the proceeds from selling these coupons from the price of the coupon bond provides a present value of:

$$P_{zero} = 100.272836 - (4.577555 + 4.807692)$$

$$= \$90.887589$$

The theoretical three-period spot yield represented by the bond's final payment of $105 is:

$${}_0r_3 = \left[\left(\frac{105}{90.887589}\right)^{1/3} - 1\right]2$$

$$= 0.0986 \text{ (or } 9.86\%)$$

To summarise, we have calculated three spot yields from the corresponding market yields for coupon bonds, and could continue the process to fully strip a ten-year bond, if desired. These rates are:

	6 months	*12 months*	*18 months*
Market rates	8.000	9.000	9.800
Spot (or zero-coupon) rates	8.000	9.025	9.860

Observe that the spot yields differ only slightly from the market yields for the coupon bonds. This occurs because we have used bonds with only a few coupons. For longer-term bonds, the differences are wider. Consider the one-year spot yield. It removes the influence of only one $5 coupon, for which the appropriate yield is 8.00% p.a., rather than the bond's yield of 9.00%.

Note also that the spot yield is greater than the market yield for the coupon bond. This occurs because the market yield (9.00%) is a weighted average of the yield on the first coupon (8.00%) and the yield on the final payment (9.025%). This relationship between coupon bond and the derived spot yields is shown more generally by the curves in figure 15.6. (See also example 15.2.)

Having shown how spot yields can be calculated from bond-market yields, we are able to identify the six-month forward rates that are embedded in multi-period spot rates for bonds. But before we explain how the forward rates can be derived we will examine the main theories that attempt to explain yield-curve shapes. In this discussion we refer to spot and forward rates and so it should help your understanding of these concepts.

example 15.2

The term structure of interest rates can be depicted as a plot of coupon-bond yields against term without any reference to the actual coupons rate, as shown in Monday's edition of the *Australian* newspaper. These are the yields on par bonds (i.e. bonds whose yield is equal to their coupons). It is relatively easy to derive a zero-coupon-yield curve from a par-yield curve. A method of so doing is set out in the Appendix to this chapter.

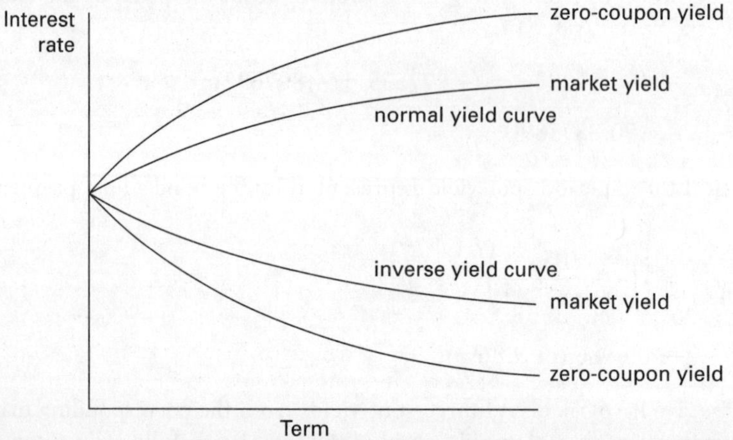

Figure 15.6 Market yields for coupon bonds and derived zero-coupon yields

EXPLANATIONS OF YIELD-CURVE SHAPES

In this section we introduce four basic theories that attempt to explain the shape of yield curves. The first two of these theories receive greater emphasis. We begin with the unbiased-expectations hypothesis.

Unbiased-expectations hypothesis

In essence, the **unbiased-expectations hypothesis** attributes the shape of the yield curve to the market's expectation about the level of future interest rates. For instance, if the market expects interest rates to be higher in the future than presently, the theory implies that the yield curve will be upward sloping; whereas the theory implies that a downward-sloping curve is established by expectations of reductions in interest rates some time in the future.

The theory does not prescribe the basis of market expectations. Any of the variables that influence interest rates (such as those discussed at the beginning of this chapter and in the previous chapter) would play a role in shaping market expectations. The crux of the theory is that once expectations have been formed they will set in place market forces that will determine the shape of the yield curve.

The hypothesis assumes that traders are not biased on the basis of term in their choice of securities. For instance, an investor with a one-year investment plan has no preference about holding:

- a one-year security to maturity, or
- a six-month security and reinvesting its proceeds at maturity in another six-month security which is held to maturity.

If investors view the one-year and two successive six-month securities as perfect substitutes, their trading will establish the same yield for the one-year security as the expected yield on the two successive six-month securities. This does not mean that all investors have the same expectation about the future six-month yield. Some investors will decide to invest in the two-period (i.e. one-year) security and hold it to maturity, whereas others will invest in two successive one-period (i.e. six-month) securities, depending on which approach they expect will achieve the higher return.

The choice between the above two investment strategies is based on the following relationship, where the yields are percentage per annum and the term of the rates is in coupon periods (i.e. six months):

$$\left(1 + \frac{{}_0r_2}{2}\right)^2 = \left(1 + \frac{{}_0r_1}{2}\right)\left(1 + \frac{E_1r_2}{2}\right) \qquad \textit{Equation (15.2)}$$

The relationship shows that the yield on the one-year (zero) security (${}_0r_2$) is expected to match the return from a six-month (zero) security reinvested in another six-month security. Note that the one-year rate (${}_0r_2$) and the six-month rate (${}_0r_1$) are spot yields and the six-month rate that applies in six months (shown as ${}_1r_2$) is an expected future yield.

The unbiased-expectations hypothesis claims that the expected yield (E_1r_2) determines the relationship between the one-period and two-period spot rates:

- When the market expects six-month rates will be higher in six months' time (i.e. the expected six-month rate exceeds the spot six-month rate), the two-period spot rate will exceed the one-period spot rate. In terms of equation (15.2), the expected increase in rates will result in the product of the two six-month rates being higher than the spot six-month rate and so the one-year rate will exceed the six-month spot rate. Accordingly, the spot yields will start to trace a normal yield curve when the market expects interest rates to increase.
- When the market expects six-month rates to be lower in six months' time, the one-year spot rate will be less than the six-month spot rate, indicating an inverse yield curve.
- Finally, when the market expects six-month rates to remain unchanged into the future, the yield curve will be flat.

The unbiased-expectations hypothesis relies on the proposition that when the market treats securities of differing maturities as being perfect substitutes, the shape of the yield curve must reflect expected future rates. If it did not, one would have to conclude that traders were ignoring expected arbitrage opportunities.

You should note that the unbiased-expectations hypothesis ignores transaction costs. For instance, the choice between the investment strategies discussed above assumed that it is no more expensive to roll over two short securities than it is to purchase one longer security. (Juttner, 1994, p. 463)

BASIC PRINCIPLE

If we ignore the compound effect when comparing a one-year spot yield and two successive six-month yields, the two-period yield is the average of its constituent one-period yields.

To repeat the example presented earlier in the chapter, if the one-period spot rate is 7.50% p.a. and the expected one-period forward rate is 8.50% p.a., the two-period spot rate will be 8.00% p.a.:

$$8.00 = 0.5*(7.50 + 8.50)$$

Should the expected forward rate be 6.50% p.a., the two-period rate will be 7.00% p.a. (approximately):

$$7.00 = 0.5*(7.50 + 6.50)$$

Strictly, longer-term spot yields are the geometric average of their constituent yields, because this allows for compounding.

Liquidity-premium theory

This explanation of the normal yield curve does not share the assumption of the expectations hypothesis that securities with different terms (but otherwise identical) are perfect substitutes. It is built on the reverse assumption: that risk factors influence the choice of securities according to their term.

Before explaining this theory we should clarify that the theory does not assume that short-term bonds are more liquid than their long-term counterparts. The market for government bonds in Australia, as elsewhere, is both active and efficient. It is no more difficult to realise quickly the value of a ten-year bond than it is to realise the value of a one-year bond. So a ten-year bond is no less liquid than a one-year bond.

Funds placed on fixed-term deposits with financial institutions involve a loss of liquidity the longer the term and so deposit rates usually increase with the term. But, as emphasised above, both short- and long-term bonds are highly liquid because of the substantial turnover in these markets. In their case, the liquidity issue derives from the price risk involved when selling longer-term securities.

Consider again a one-year investment. This can be achieved by investing in a one-year security and holding it to maturity. It can also be arranged with a ten-year bond that is sold after one year. In this case, the return is calculated as a holding-period yield (HPY).

Examine the following formulae for a semi-annual yield to maturity and an HPY, which were discussed in Chapter 11:

$$r_{\text{to maturity}} = \left[\left(\frac{S_{\text{coupons}} + F}{P_{\text{buy}}}\right)^{1/2*t} - 1\right]2$$

$$r_{\text{HPY}} = \left[\left(\frac{S_{\text{coupons}} + P_{\text{sell}}}{P_{\text{buy}}}\right)^{1/2*t} - 1\right]2$$

Observe that the yield-to-maturity formula includes two variables that are known when the investment was made (i.e. P_{buy} and F), and one ($S_{coupons}$) that is exposed to reinvestment risk. By contrast, the HPY formula shows that these yields are exposed to both reinvestment risk through $S_{coupons}$ and price risk arising from P_{sell} (whereas F is not subject to price risk).

The price risk of selling a ten-year bond after one year arises because of the chance that bond yields will rise after the bond has been purchased. The risk also reflects the greater price sensitivity of long-term bonds to a given change in yields. To illustrate, suppose the yield on two-year and nine-year bonds (both paying coupons at 8.00% p.a.) rose by two percentage points, from 8.00% to 10.00% following their purchase. The percentage change in their prices is as follows.

Given that both bonds traded at par (i.e. their yield equalled their coupon rate), their purchase price was \$100. The selling prices of the bonds are:

$$P_{\text{2-years}} = 4\left(\frac{1 - 1.05^{-4}}{0.05}\right) + \frac{100}{1.05^4}$$

$$= \$96.454049$$

$$P_{\text{9-year}} = 4\left(\frac{1 - 1.05^{-18}}{0.05}\right) + \frac{100}{1.05^{18}}$$

$$= \$88.310413$$

The two-year bond's price reduction represents 3.55% of its purchase price, whereas the price reduction of the nine-year bond represents 11.69% of its purchase price.

The greater exposure of longer-term bonds to price risk than shorter-term bonds is shown in table 15.1 by the greater volatility of holding-period yields for longer bonds than for shorter-term securities. If the holders of bonds are risk-averse, they will require compensation in the form of increased yields in order that they hold the riskier long-term bonds. This compensation can be termed a **liquidity premium**.

Notionally, the premium is the result of lower prices for longer-term bonds because of the preference by investors for shorter-term bonds. Remember that lower prices represent higher yields. Consequently, should the market expect that rates will remain unchanged, and the yield curve has a normal shape, the higher yields for longer bonds could be explained by liquidity premiums.

Table 15.1 Yield volatility, July 1972 to February 1996

Part (a) Yield to maturity

Instrument	*Average (%)*	*Volatility (%)*
180-day T-note	10.31	14.53
5-year bond	10.79	9.72
10-year bond	10.98	9.09

Part (b) 6-month holding-period yields

Instrument	*Average (%)*	*Volatility (%)*
180-day T-note	10.31	14.53
5-year bond	10.75	15.78
10-year bond	10.91	19.28

The sample period was from July 1972 to February 1996. Rates were obtained from RBA data and are expressed on a semi-annual compound basis. Volatility is calculated as the annual standard deviation of holding-period yields.

The evidence in figure 15.3, that the shorter-term interest rates are more volatile than the longer-term interest rates, is supported by the summary statistics in table 15.1 for 180-day Treasury-note rates, five-year bond rates and ten-year bond rates. The volatility statistics in part (a) of the table show that the standard deviation of the changes in rates diminished with the length of the term to maturity. You will recall, however, that the market yield on a bond is only achieved if it is held until maturity and all coupons are reinvested at the purchase yield.

The more relevant measure of volatility for yield-curve analysis is the volatility of holding-period yields. Part (b) of table 15.1 shows the volatility of six-month holding-period yields for each of the instruments over the period July 1972 to February 1996. The statistics show that holding-period-yield volatility increases with term to maturity. This indicates that the effect of lower volatility on longer-run yields was outweighed by the greater price sensitivity of longer-run instruments. The recent

Australian experience is that holding long-term securities, at least for reasonably short investment terms, entails greater risk than holding short-term securities.

The data in table 15.2 show that there is only a low correlation between the holding-period yields for instruments of different terms, except between five- and ten-year bonds.

The existence of liquidity premiums, by themselves, implies an upward-sloping yield curve. This is the strength of the liquidity-preference theory. No other theory of the yield curve provides an explanation for this 'normal' (perhaps) state of affairs.

Table 15.2 Correlation between holding-period yields

Instrument	*180-day T-note*	*5-year bond*	*10-year bond*
180-day T-note	1.0000		
5-year bond	0.5276	1.0000	
10-year bond	0.3885	0.9335	1.0000

Note: The sample period was from July 1972 to February 1996. Rates were obtained from RBA data. Holding-period yields were computed over six-month intervals and expressed on a semi-annual compound basis.

However, there are a number of weaknesses in the liquidity-premium theory. First, it provides no explanation for shapes other than the upward-sloping yield curve. Second, it ignores the risk preference of the suppliers of bonds. Issuers of bonds are exposed to holding-period risk when they decide to redeem bonds before they mature. If they are also risk-averse, they would prefer to borrow short and so would require a liquidity discount to supply long-term bonds. Consequently, for the liquidity-premium theory to hold, lenders must be more exposed to holding-period-yield risk than borrowers.

The effect of liquidity premiums on the yield curve is illustrated in example 15.3. Notice that the unobservable liquidity premium for each period is added to the unobservable expected yield. The required return for each period forms the basis of the market (i.e. spot) yields, which are, in effect, the geometric average of the constituent zero-coupon rates.

example 15.3

Suppose the bond market expects future one-period rates to be the same as the current one-period rate, and that the potential holders of longer bonds demand a liquidity premium, as indicated in the table below. Estimate the yield curve that incorporates the relevant liquidity premium in each of the nominated spot yields. Note that the yields are percentage per annum on a semi-annual compound basis.

Forward yield	*Expected yield*	*Liquidity premium*	*Required yield*
${}_0r_1$	9.00	0.00	9.00
E_1r_2	9.00	1.00	10.00
E_2r_3	9.00	1.00	10.00
E_3r_4	9.00	2.00	11.00

The six-month spot yield is 9.00% p.a. The one-year spot yield is found as the geometric average of the required return for its constituent spot and forward rate:

$$_0r_2 = \left[\left(\left(1+\frac{0.09}{2}\right)\left(1+\frac{0.10}{2}\right)\right)^{1/2} - 1\right]2$$

$$= 9.50\%\text{ p.a.}$$

$$_0r_3 = \left[\left(\left(1+\frac{0.09}{2}\right)\left(1+\frac{0.10}{2}\right)\left(1+\frac{0.10}{2}\right)\right)^{1/3} - 1\right]2$$

$$= 9.67\%\text{ p.a.}$$

$$_0r_4 = \left[\left(\left(1+\frac{0.09}{2}\right)\left(1+\frac{0.10}{2}\right)\left(1+\frac{0.10}{2}\right)\right)^{1/4} - 1\right]2$$

$$= 10.00\%\text{ p.a.}$$

The effect of liquidity premiums is to generate a normal yield curve. This outcome is illustrated in figure 15.7.

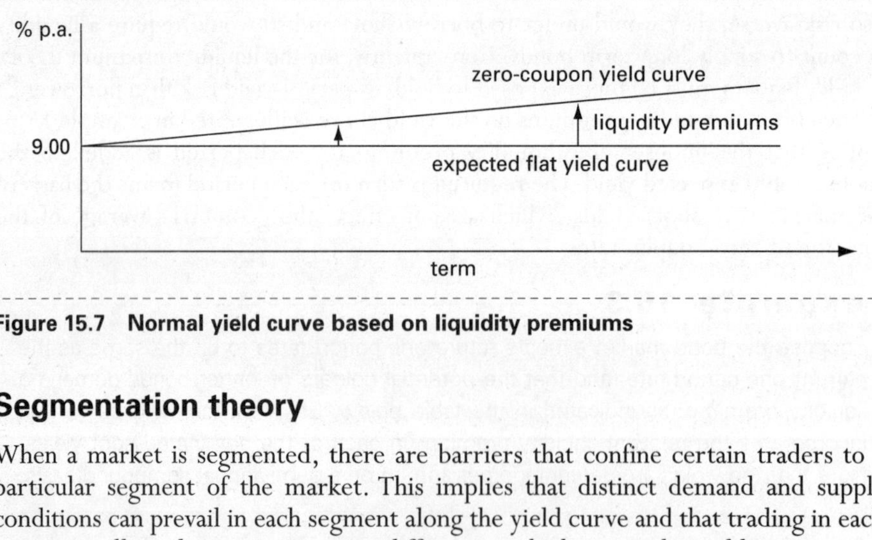

Figure 15.7 Normal yield curve based on liquidity premiums

Segmentation theory

When a market is segmented, there are barriers that confine certain traders to a particular segment of the market. This implies that distinct demand and supply conditions can prevail in each segment along the yield curve and that trading in each segment will produce security-price differences which create the yield curve.

To illustrate, suppose that the supply of funds, relative to demand, is much greater for short-term investments than for long-term investments. Given the segmentation of the market between the short and long term, the market yield in the short-term segment will be lower than in the long-term segment, creating a normal yield curve.

Figure 15.8 schematically depicts the two market segments of this example and their influence on the term structure.

The segmentation theory assumes that traders in the market do not arbitrage this yield differential; otherwise, funds would rush to the long-term segment to take advantage of the higher yield. If funds were mobile, the segmentation theory would collapse as the movement in funds would eliminate the interest-rate differential. Such an investment strategy is known as 'riding the yield curve'. Investors would borrow at short-term rates and lend at long-term rates to generate a constant supply of income. But as noted above, the shape of the yield curve is not predictable. If it was, a normal yield curve, for instance, would allow all investors to make easy money by borrowing short and lending long.

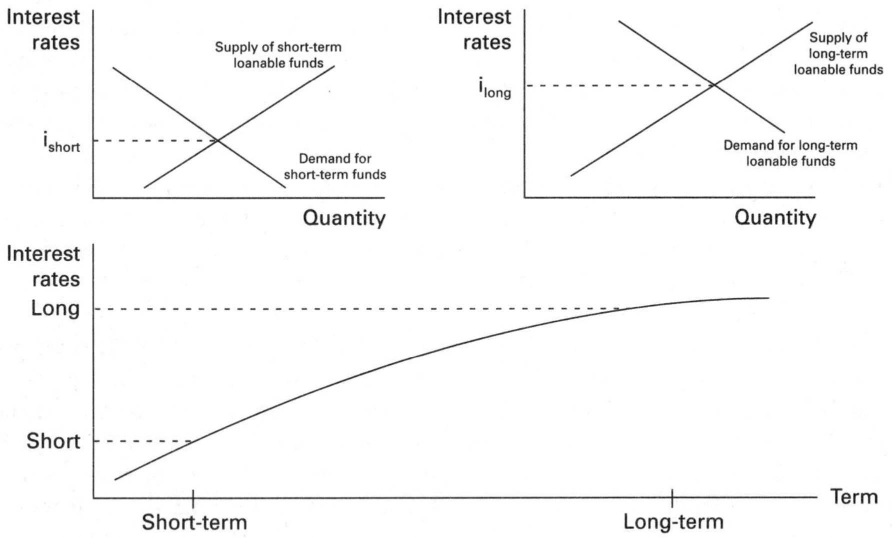

Figure 15.8 Segmented financial markets

The plausibility of the theory rests largely on there being a basis for the existence of market segments. Prior to the deregulation of the financial system a number of regulations had the effect of segmenting the market according to term. But with their repeal, the main basis for segmentation is provided by the hedging strategies of certain traders. (Juttner, 1994, pp. 474–5)

We will discuss hedging in some detail in subsequent chapters. It is a trading strategy designed to reduce risk. Such a trading strategy may create segments within financial markets because it ignores yield differentials. To illustrate: financial institutions with mainly short-term liabilities (such as cash management trusts) will try to hedge their risks by displaying a preference for short-term assets. This strategy could lead to a normal yield curve, as these financial institutions will ignore (when they are hedging in this manner) the higher yields available on long-term investments.

The relative shift in the supply of funds from short-term deposits with intermediaries to long-term savings schemes associated with superannuation and other forms of fund managers (discussed in Chapters 6 to 8) may have implications for the shape of the yield curve. But market segmentation will have a role in this process only if these institutions are locked into particular market segments in their use of funds, and following deregulation, this is not the case.

Preferred-habitat theory

The final explanation of yield curves is a combination of the segmentation and the liquidity-premium theories. It is known as the **preferred-habitat theory**. Its basic assumption is that investors have preferred maturities but they are prepared to modify the maturity of their investments provided they are compensated for doing so.

Recall that the expectations theory assumes that investments with different maturities are perfect substitutes, whereas the segmentation theory assumes they are not substitutable by investors. The preferred-habitat theory lies somewhere in between these two opposite assumptions. The preferred-habitat theory, like the segmented-market theory, acknowledges that investors do not view bonds of different maturities as perfect substitutes. The preferred-habitat theory assumes that investors have definite maturity preferences. But, unlike the segmented-markets theory, the preferred-habitat theory assumes that investors can be persuaded by higher interest rates to purchase bonds whose maturities are adjacent to their preferred maturity.

The liquidity-premium theory is consistent with the preferred-habitat theory. Under the liquidity-premium theory, investors are assumed to prefer shorter maturities to longer maturities. The liquidity-premium theory assumes that investors are only persuaded to purchase longer maturities by the incorporation of a liquidity premium into the yield of longer-term bonds. The theory rests on the assumption that longer bonds are more risky. The preferred-habitat theory is more general than the liquidity-premium theory in that it allows for the possibility that short bonds could be more risky than long bonds. It is quite plausible that shorter-maturity bonds are more risky to some investor groups than longer-maturity bonds.

In truth, the riskiness of a bond depends upon the investment horizon of the investor. If an investor has a one-year horizon, it follows that a one-year bond is less risky than a ten-year bond. On the other hand, for an investor with a ten-year horizon, the one-year bond is a riskier investment than a ten-year bond. To complete this longer investment, a one-year bond has to be rolled over nine times. The investor faces, at each roll over, the possibility of an unfavourable rate of interest. In contrast, investment in a ten-year bond is a less risky alternative as investment in this instrument locks in a rate over the entire investment horizon and is subject only to reinvestment risk. It is evident that the ten-year investor may require an interest-rate premium in order to invest at the short end of the maturity spectrum.

The preferred-habitat theory allows for the possibility of the incorporation of a liquidity premium at the short end of the term structure. Consequently, the preferred-habitat theory is consistent with any yield-curve shape. For example, a hill-shaped curve results if there are two distinct investor groups, one whose preferred habitats lie at the very short end and the other whose lie at the very long end of the interest-rate spectrum.

Yield-curve determinants: concluding comments

A considerable amount of investigation has been conducted overseas (together with some Australian studies) to test the foregoing theories. According to Juttner (1994, pp. 468–9), researchers have generally found little evidence to support the expectations hypothesis. It appears that future spot rates do not systematically behave in accordance with the implications of the yield curve. However, researchers have found considerable support for the existence of risk premiums in long-term yields. (Juttner, 1994, pp. 470–4)

Nevertheless these findings do not explain the inverse yield curves that were most prevalent in Australia during the 1980s. Economic conditions and monetary policy appear to have been important influences on the shape of the yield curve and on the movement of the yield curve over time (twists) between the inverse and normal shapes.

Yield-curve movements, though, are predominantly up and down rather than twists. That is, movements in rates more often occur uniformly along the yield curve. An increase, for instance, in the expected inflation rate will usually cause all rates along the term structure to rise (and vice versa). The inverse yield curve presented in figure 15.2 occurred in 1989 when the RBA was applying a tight monetary policy (i.e. a high real cash rate), whereas the normal curve in 1995 reflected an easier monetary policy stance (i.e. a lower real cash rate).

FORWARD INTEREST RATES

The major purpose of this chapter is to identify forward rates from the yield curve. Forward rates play a major role in financial decisions because most transactions either commence at a future date or extend over a number of periods. Accordingly, it is very important to be able to distinguish between spot and forward rates. You will recall that spot rates are current yields on single-payment securities (or stripped coupon bonds), whereas we have defined forward rates as single-period yields that begin life at some time in the future.

Spot and forward interest rates are intimately related one to the other. A multi-period spot rate comprises a single-period spot rate plus successive single-period forward rates. We use this principle in this section to show how to calculate these embedded forward rates from spot yields (derived from bond-market yields). We can also show that the reverse applies. That is, a spot rate can be found from its constituent single-period forward rates and the one-period spot rate.

Both spot and forward interest rates are determined simultaneously by the shape of the yield curve.

Calculating forward rates from spot rates

The ability to subdivide any investment into shorter sub-period investments provides a method of deducing forward interest rates. This is illustrated in figure 15.9 by the return on a two-period spot rate (${}_0i_2$) being equal to the return on the single-period spot rate (${}_0i_1$) times the return on the forward single-period rate (${}_1i_2$). Note that $i = r/2$.

Consider two alternative routes to making a two-period investment. One can either:

- make a single investment for two periods, or
- make an investment for one period that is rolled into another one-period investment so that the combined investment is for two periods.

Obviously, if there is to be no arbitrage opportunity, the sum generated from either of these investments must be the same regardless of the route taken. That is:

$$(1 + {}_0i_2)^2 = (1 + {}_0i_1)(1 + {}_1i_2) \qquad \textit{Equation (15.1a)}$$

Rearranging, we can find the forward rate from the two spot rates, as follows:

$${}_1i_2 = \frac{(1 + {}_0i_2)^2}{(1 + {}_0i_1)} - 1 \qquad \textit{Equation (15.1b)}$$

To illustrate, given a two-period rate of 8.00% and a one-period rate of 7.50%, the one-period forward rate is:

$${}_1i_2 = \frac{(1.08)^2}{1.075} - 1$$

$$= 8.50\%$$

As noted earlier in this chapter, the two-period rate is approximately the average of its constituent single-period rates.

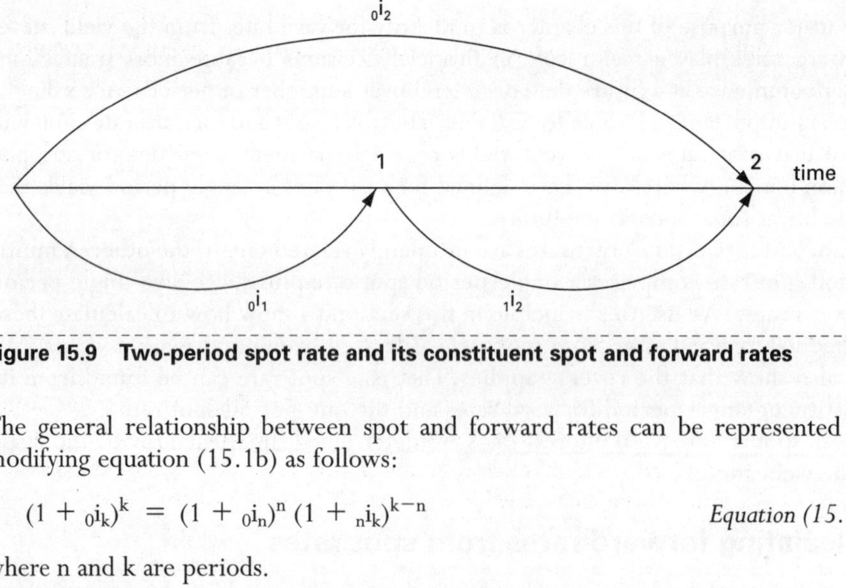

Figure 15.9 Two-period spot rate and its constituent spot and forward rates

The general relationship between spot and forward rates can be represented by modifying equation (15.1b) as follows:

$$(1 + {}_0i_k)^k = (1 + {}_0i_n)^n (1 + {}_ni_k)^{k-n} \qquad \textit{Equation (15.1c)}$$

where n and k are periods.

This equation can be rearranged to show the forward rate, ${}_ni_k$, as follows:

$${}_ni_k = \left(\frac{(1 + {}_0i_k)^k}{(1 + {}_0i_n)^n}\right)^{1/k-n} - 1 \qquad \textit{Equation (15.1d)}$$

or, as follows, when using annual rates:

$$ {}_{n}r_{k} = \left[\left(\frac{(1 + {}_{0}r_{k}/2)^{k}}{(1 + {}_{0}r_{n}/2)^{n}}\right)^{1/k-n} - 1\right]2 \qquad \textit{Equation (15.1e)} $$

where n and k refer to coupon periods as defined above, and
r is percent per annum.

This equation is the general form of equation (15.1b). To illustrate, using the same rates as assumed above, (i.e. a one-year spot rate of 8.00% and a six-month spot rate of 7.50%), the six-month forward rate (which applies for six months) is:

$$ {}_{1}r_{2} = \left[\left(\frac{(1 + 0.08/2)^{2}}{(1 + 0.075/2)}\right)^{1/2-1} - 1\right]2 $$

$$ = \left[\left(\frac{(1.04)^{2}}{1.0375}\right)^{1} - 1\right]2 $$

$$ = 0.085 $$

The more general use of equation (15.1e) is illustrated in example 15.4.

example 15.4

Given a one-year spot rate of 6.00% p.a. and a three-year spot rate of 8.00% p.a., calculate the implied forward two-year rate one year from now (${}_{2}r_{6}$). Using equation (15.1e):

$$ {}_{2}r_{6} = \left[\left(\frac{(1 + 0.08/2)^{6}}{(1 + 0.06/2)^{2}}\right)^{1/4} - 1\right]2 $$

$$ = 9.01\% \text{ p.a.} $$

Deriving forward rates with future amounts

Forward rates can be calculated using future amounts also. This approach uses future amounts (referred to also as a **capital sum**) as an intermediate variable. The capital sum is the future sum of $1 invested at the appropriate rate. Using the data in example 15.3, the capital sums involved are shown in the following chart:

Term in coupon periods	*Spot rates*	*Capital sum*
0		1.0000
2	6.00%	1.0609
6	8.00%	1.2653

The capital column, cs, is computed using spot yields and coupon periods, as follows:

$$cs_n = \left(1 + \frac{{}_0r_n}{2}\right)^n \qquad \textit{Equation (15.3)}$$

For example, the capital sum at the end of the sixth period, given the spot yield of 8.00%, is calculated as:

$$cs_6 = \left(1 + \frac{0.08}{2}\right)^6$$

$$= 1.2653$$

The two-year forward rate in one year is implied from the growth of the capital sum from \$1.0609 to \$1.2653. That is:

$${}_2r_6 = \left[\left(\frac{1.2653}{1.0609}\right)^{1/4} - 1\right]2$$

$$= 9.01\% \text{ p.a.}$$

A more detailed illustration of the use of capital sums to calculate forward rates is presented in table 15.3. The spot yields in the first column have been used to calculate the capital sums shown in the second column from which the forward rates have been calculated. For instance, the one-period forward rate that applies from the commencement of the fourth period can be calculated as:

$${}_3r_4 = \left(\frac{1.2063}{1.1412} - 1\right)2$$

$$= 11.41\% \text{ p.a.}$$

Table 15.3 Alternative calculation of forward yields

Coupon period	*Spot yield ${}_0r_n$ (%)*	*Capital sum*	*Forward rate ${}_nr_{n+1}$ (%)*
0		1.0000	
1	6.00	1.0300	6.00
2	8.00	1.0816	10.02
3	9.00	1.1412	11.01
4	9.60	1.2063	11.41
5	10.00	1.2763	11.61
6	10.29	1.3512	11.75
7	10.50	1.4307	11.76
8	10.67	1.5156	11.86
9	10.80	1.6053	11.84
10	10.91	1.7009	11.90

The forward-rate curve

The shape of the spot-yield curve is related to the embedded forward rates because, as explained above, multi-period spot rates are the average of their constituent single-period spot and forward rates. Hence, when the forward rates trace an upward-sloping curve they imply a normal spot-yield curve (and vice versa for an inverse spot-yield curve).

It is well recognised that most finance phenomena may be explained with reference to the most noble game of all — cricket. The relationship between the forward and the spot rates is no exception to this rule. If Mark Taylor's batting average is increasing with each innings, his most recent score must have exceeded his average score. So it is with an upward-sloping yield curve. The forward rate must lie above the 'average' spot-rate equivalent. Similarly, like Mike Atherton's falling average, the forward rate for an inverse yield curve must lie below the spot-rate curve. These relationships are illustrated in figure 15.10 for normal and inverse yield curves.

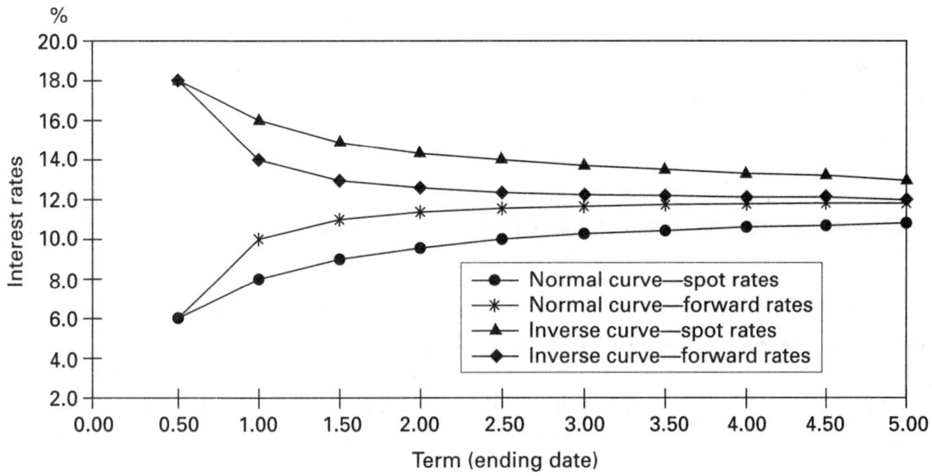

Figure 15.10 Spot and forward yield curves

Locking in forward rates through financial market transactions

Forward rates can also be derived from the market yields (assuming they are spot rates) by undertaking offsetting transactions that have different terms. For example, a bank could establish a forward lending rate simultaneously:

- borrowing funds (that will be repaid on the date when the investment will be made), and
- investing these funds (with a maturity date that corresponds with that of the intended investment).

This process is illustrated in figure 15.11, where the funds are borrowed for a year and simultaneously invested for three years. These simultaneous transactions involve no net cash flows initially, but serve to establish the two-year rate that commences in one year (${}_2r_6$).

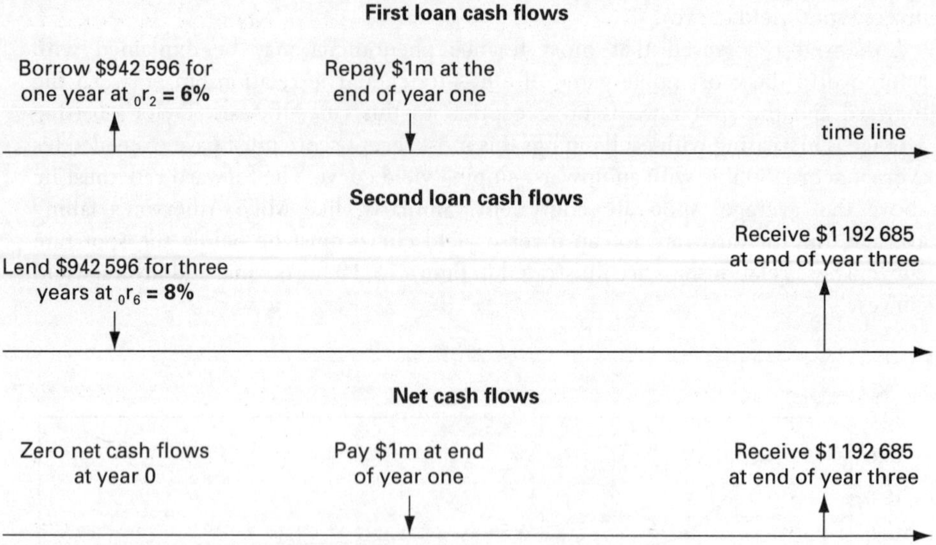

Figure 15.11 Forward rate established in the capital market

The illustration in figure 15.11 ignores transaction costs. It represents the possible case of a bank that will have $1 million at its disposal in one year to lend for a period of two years. It locks in the forward (lending) rate implied by the above spot yields by selling a one-year zero-coupon security, yielding 6% p.a., with a face value of $1 million. The proceeds will be:

$$\frac{1\ 000\ 000}{(1 + 0.06/2)^2} = \$942\ 596$$

This amount is lent for three years by buying a three-year zero-coupon security, yielding 8% p.a., with a face value of $942 596. The redemption proceeds of this security after three years will be:

$$942\ 596 * (1 + 0.08/2)^6 = \$1\ 192\ 685$$

The net effect of these transactions in cash-flow terms is:

- a $1 million cash outflow (i.e. investment) in one year's time (to repay the borrowed funds), and
- a cash inflow in three years' time of $1 192 685 (i.e. the proceeds from the investment).

The semi-annual compound rate implied by these two flows is:

$$\left[\left(\frac{1\,192\,685}{1\,000\,000}\right)^{1/4} - 1\right]2 = 9.01\%$$

A borrowing rate can be locked in by using the reverse transactions: that is, by buying a one-year security and selling a three-year security. Naturally the locked-in borrowing rate will also be 9.01% p.a.

Typically, forward rates are established by the use of derivative instruments, such as bill-futures contracts, FRAs and interest-rate swaps. These instruments, which we discuss in Chapters 17 and 18, are used mainly because of their small transaction costs.

Summary

The main points of this chapter are as follows:

- A yield curve can be viewed, approximately, by tracing market yields for securities according to their term to maturity.
- A normal yield curve has an upward slope, as opposed to a flat or an inverse yield curve.
- During the 1980s, inverse yield curves were common in Australia, but during the first half of the 1990s, normal yield curves have predominated.
- A yield curve is most clearly revealed by the yields on a series of single-payment securities with a range of terms.
- The yields for short-dated securities can be directly plotted as a yield curve and can be used to calculate implicit forward rates.
- Zero-coupon (or spot) yields can be derived from bond-market yields by notionally selling the coupons that are to be paid prior to each bond's maturity.
- The unbiased-expectations hypothesis states that expected future rates determine the slope of the yield curve.
- Monetary policy is an important variable in relation to the yield curve and to expectations of future interest rates.
- Investors in longer-term securities are exposed to price risk and this can create liquidity premiums that could result in the formation of a normal yield curve.
- The segmentation theory states that interest rates will differ according to maturity because supply and demand conditions vary with maturity.
- The preferred-habitat theory states that investors are prepared to trade outside their preferred term to maturity provided the market offers a premium.
- Implicit forward interest rates can be calculated from the spot yields with different terms, either directly or through the calculation of capital sums.
- Forward interest rates can be locked in by trading in securities with different maturities.

DISCUSSION QUESTIONS AND EXERCISES

1 Discuss the data traced by a yield curve based on market yields. Construct a yield curve based on the market yields published in a recent newspaper, such as the *Financial Review,* and describe its general shape (even though you may have only a few observations).

2 Discuss the existence of implicit forward rates in multi-period short-term money market yields. Explain the virtue of using the yields on single-payment securities when displaying the term structure of interest rates.

3 Describe how the market yield on a coupon bond could be converted into a theoretical spot yield on a single payment through the stripping process. Distinguish between market and spot yields in your discussion.

4 Calculate spot yields for a 10.00% Treasury bond, given the following yields to maturity:

Term (coupon periods)	*Yield to maturity*
1	7.00% p.a.
2	7.50% p.a.
3	8.00% p.a.

5 Calculate the spot yields for an 11.00% Treasury bond, given the following yields:

Term (coupon periods)	*Yield to maturity*
1	9.50% p.a.
2	9.00% p.a.
3	8.50% p.a.

6 Discuss the assumptions of the unbiased-expectations hypothesis and how it can explain an upward-sloping yield curve.

7 Discuss the liquidity-premium theory. Explain the difference in the volatility of yields to maturity and holding-period yields and the risk involved in treating securities with different terms to maturity as perfect substitutes. Explain the formation of liquidity premiums when the market expects no change in spot yields.

8 Construct the yield curve when the expected future rates and liquidity premiums are as follows and the current one-period rate ($_0r_1$) is 8.50% p.a.:

$E(_1r_2)$	8.75%	$_1L_2 = 0.25\%$
$E(_2r_3)$	9.00%	$_2L_3 = 0.50\%$
$E(_3r_4)$	9.25%	$_3L_4 = 0.75\%$

9 Discuss the segmentation theory and preferred-habitat explanations of the yield curve. State their assumptions and conclusions.

10 Discuss multi-period spot and single-period forward rates. How many single-period forward rates are there in a three-period spot rate? Calculate the following forward rates from the given spot rates.

Spot rates	*Forward rates*
$_0r_1 = 8.00\%$ p.a.	
$_0r_2 = 8.50\%$ p.a.	$_1r_2$
$_0r_3 = 9.00\%$ p.a.	$_2r_3$

11 Calculate the forward rates listed in the previous question using the capital-sum method.

12 Show how a financial institution, by trading in the following securities, can lock in the rate on a two-year borrowing to commence in one year, given:

Zero-coupon bond term	*Yield (%)*
0	
2	6.00
6	8.00

REFERENCES

Fabozzi, Frank J., Modigliani, Franco, & Ferri, Michael G. 1994, *Foundations of Financial Markets and Institutions*, Prentice-Hall, New Jersey, Chapter 12.

Juttner, D. Johannes 1994, *Financial Markets, Interest Rates and Monetary Economics,* 3rd edn, Longman Cheshire, Melbourne, Chapter 24.

APPENDIX 15.1 ZERO-COUPON YIELDS CALCULATED FROM PAR-BOND YIELDS

If one has access to a par yield curve, one can easily derive the associated zero-coupon yield curve. A par bond's coupon rate is equal to the yield ensuring that its price is equal to its face value. For the purpose of the analysis below we will consider par bonds with a face value of $1.

The price of any bond can be expressed in terms of its cash-flows and a set of discount factors. A discount factor, d_t, is a number that when multiplied with a cash-flow in period t converts that cash-flow to its present value.

The value of a bond is simply the sum of its cash-flows multiplied by their appropriate discount factors. A $1-face-value bond pays a coupon of $c per period, where c is the per period coupon rate. Thus:

$$P = cd_1 + cd_2 + \ldots + (c + F)\, d_n$$

Where P is the bond price,
c is the coupon payment, and
F is the face value.

For a $1-face-value par bond paying $c per period the following equation holds:

$$1 = cd_1 + cd_2 + \ldots + (c + 1)\, d_n \qquad \textit{Equation (15A.1)}$$

The left-hand side of equation (15A.1) is the price of a $1 par bond, while the right-hand side is the discounted value of the bond's cash-flows. This equation provides us with a simple method for sequentially computing discount factors as:

$$\begin{aligned} d_n &= 1 - (cd_1 + cd_2 + \ldots + cd_{n-1}) \\ &= 1 - c(d_1 + d_2 + \ldots + d_{n-1}) \\ &= \frac{1 - c * cumd_{n-1}}{1 + c} \end{aligned}$$

Where c is the coupon rate per period, and
$cumd_{n-1}$ is the sum of the previous n − 1 discount factors.

We can easily compute a zero-coupon rate for time, t, once we have the discount factor, d_t. The capital sum of an investment of $1 made for t periods is simply the inverse of the discount factor (i.e. $1/d_t$). Thus, the semi-annual zero-coupon rate for t years is computed as:

$$r_t^{zero} = \left[\left(\frac{1}{d_t}\right)^{\frac{1}{2t}} - 1\right]2$$

Table 15A.1 Worksheet for calculating zero-coupon rates

Term (in years)	*Par yield (%)*	*Discount factor*	*Cumulative discount factor*	*Capital sum*	*Zero coupon rate (%)*
0.00			0.0000		
0.50	5.00	0.9756	0.9756	1.0250	5.00
1.00	5.80	0.9443	1.9199	1.0590	5.81
1.50	6.33	0.9104	2.8304	1.0984	6.36
2.00	6.71	0.8757	3.7060	1.1420	6.75
2.50	7.00	0.8409	4.5469	1.1893	7.05
3.00	7.22	0.8067	5.3536	1.2396	7.29
3.50	7.40	0.7733	6.1269	1.2932	7.48
4.00	7.55	0.7407	6.8677	1.3500	7.64
4.50	7.67	0.7094	7.5771	1.4096	7.78
5.00	7.77	0.6792	8.2563	1.4722	7.89
5.50	7.86	0.6500	8.9063	1.5385	7.99
6.00	7.93	0.6222	9.5285	1.6072	8.07
6.50	8.00	0.5951	10.1236	1.6805	8.15
7.00	8.06	0.5691	10.6926	1.7572	8.22
7.50	8.11	0.5443	11.2370	1.8371	8.28
8.00	8.16	0.5203	11.7573	1.9220	8.34
8.50	8.20	0.4976	12.2548	2.0098	8.38
9.00	8.24	0.4755	12.7303	2.1030	8.43
9.50	8.27	0.4548	13.1851	2.1988	8.47
10.00	8.30	0.4348	13.6199	2.3000	8.51

Table 15A.1 presents a worksheet for deriving a set of zero-coupon rates from a set of par yield curves.

As the first bond (term = 0.50) is already a zero, the first discount factor is computed as:

$$d_{0.5} = \frac{1}{1 + 0.05/2} = 0.9756$$

The second discount factor is computed as:

$$d_{1.0} = \frac{1 - (0.058/2) * 0.9756}{1 + 0.058/2} = 0.9443$$

The third discount factor is computed as:

$$d_{1.5} = \frac{1 - (0.0633/2)\,(1.9199)}{1 + 0.0633/2} = 0.9104$$

The third capital sum is calculated as:

$$cs_{1.5} = \frac{1}{0.9104} = 1.0948$$

The third zero coupon rate is computed as:

$$r_{1.5}^{zero} = [(1.0948)_{\frac{1}{3}} - 1] * 2 = 6.36\%$$

The par yield and zero-coupon yield curves are graphed in figure 15A.1.

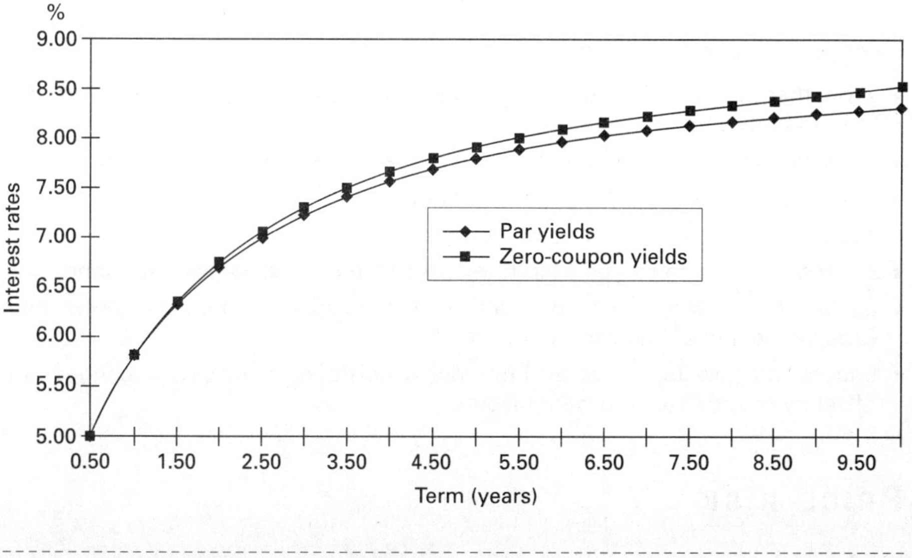

Figure 15A.1 Par and zero-coupon yields

16

Price risk and duration

It is commonly believed that the fixed-interest market (such as the market for Treasury bonds) is a safe place to invest funds, where the return is certain although at a relatively low rate. The purposes of this chapter are to explain the risks of trading in the fixed-interest market and to explain how duration can be used in the management of interest-rate risk. While we consider fixed-interest securities, the discussion is relevant to asset-liability management generally.

Study objectives

From your study of this chapter you should be able to:

- show that the price sensitivity of a bond varies directly with the length of the term to maturity;
- show that the price sensitivity of bonds increases, the lower the coupon rates;
- explain the concept of Macaulay's duration;
- calculate the modified duration of a bond;
- show how duration can be used to measure the price sensitivity of bonds;
- explain how duration can be used as the basis for managing assets and liabilities to hedge interest-rate risk; and
- understand how to design an immunised portfolio where price changes are offset by coupon-reinvestment income.

PRICE RISK

The basis of price risk is unexpected increases in interest rates. The relevance of this risk to market traders depends on the volatility of interest rates and on the ability of traders to forecast interest-rate changes. In Chapter 14 we presented evidence of interest-rate volatility, which appears to have increased since deregulation. While the Reserve Bank has been successful in smoothing movements in the volume of funds in financial markets, it has not eliminated interest-rate volatility and cannot do so.

Interest-rate volatility would not pose a risk to traders and financial managers if they could accurately forecast these movements. But neither the market as a whole nor individual traders are able to forecast interest-rate movements consistently. Consequently market participants generally seek to manage their exposure to market risks.

It was noted in Chapter 11 that changes in yields impinge on fixed-interest returns in two ways. First, increases in interest rates reduce the value of bonds (i.e. $\uparrow r \Rightarrow \downarrow P$), which exposes bond holders to price risk; and second, a fall in interest rates reduces the value of reinvested coupons (i.e. $\downarrow r \Rightarrow \downarrow S_{coupons}$ over the holding period), which exposes bond holders to reinvestment risk.

Unexpected increases in bond yields reduce the market value of the securities, which is reflected in the value of portfolios that are marked-to-market. However, a capital loss will be realised only when the securities are sold. Price risk may not be important to bond holders who actually hold them until they mature, but is important to portfolio managers who are regularly trading them.

Price sensitivity

In general, bond values vary inversely with changes in yields (remember the see-saw analogy). But the movement is not uniform for all bonds. Consider the reaction of the three bonds listed in table 16.1 when yields increase from 10% to 12% p.a.

Table 16.1 Price sensitivity

Term in years	*Coupon rate (% p.a.)*	*Price when yield is: 10%*	*12%*	*Change in price (%)*
2	10	100.00	96.53	−3.47
10	10	100.00	88.53	−11.47
10	6	75.08	65.59	−14.47

Observe that the ten-year bond is more price sensitive than the two-year bond and that the 6% bond is more price sensitive than the 10% coupon bond. The data in table 16.1 (as well as the data presented in figures 16.1 and 16.2) illustrate the following general relationship between bond values and a given change in yields:

1 the prices of low-coupon bonds are, all else being equal, more sensitive to a given change in market yields than the prices of high coupon bonds; and
2 the price of longer-tenor bonds are, all else being equal, more sensitive to changes in yields than the prices of shorter maturity bonds.

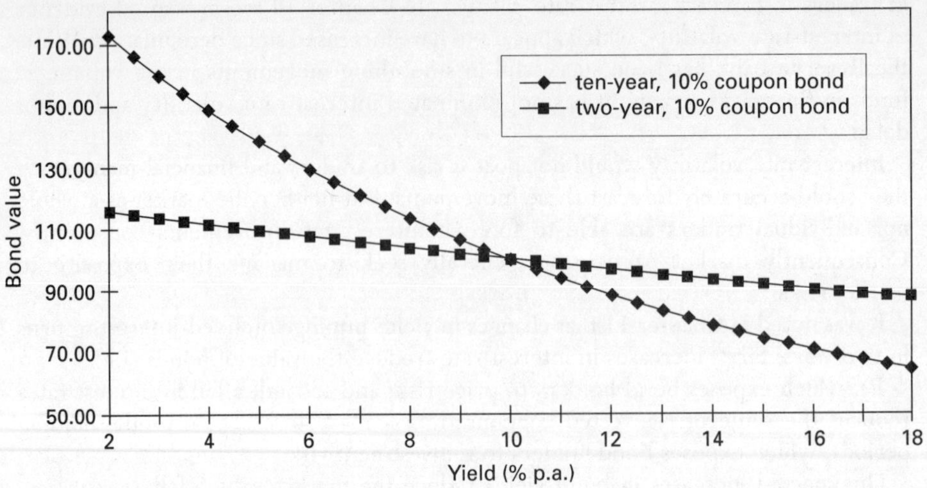

Figure 16.1 Price sensitivity and maturity

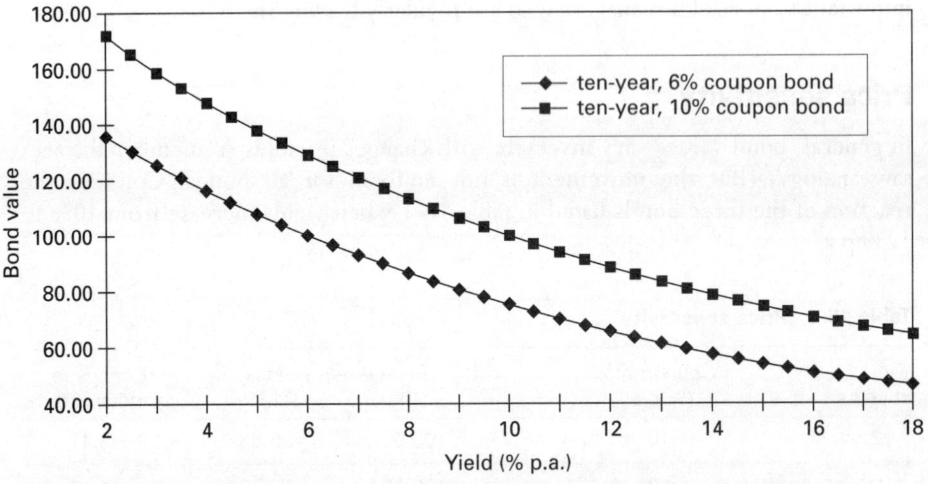

Figure 16.2 Price sensitivity and the coupon rate

DURATION

Duration is a measure of the average time in which an instrument's payments are made. While duration is commonly applied to bonds, the concept is applicable to any series of future cashflow. A two-year 10% bond, for instance, makes four payments over two years. However, only the final coupon and the redemption payment have a term of two years. The initial three coupon payments have a shorter term. Therefore, on average, the bond's payments have a term of less than two years.

The duration of a multi-payment security is a measure of its equivalent zero-coupon security. Recall that a zero makes one payment at maturity. Duration calculates the term of a single-payment security that is equivalent to a multi-payment instrument, such as a coupon-paying bond.

The duration of a coupon-paying bond, being a measure of the average time of payment, represents the 'effective' term or tenor of an equivalent hypothetical zero (or, 'pure security'). Many of the risk properties of a multi-payment security are a reflection of the properties of its equivalent pure security.

For example, suppose we are to receive \$100 in one month and \$100 in three months' time. It could be said that on average we are to receive \$200 in two months' time. The duration of this cashflow would be about two months, which is the average time of payment.

However, duration is measured not as a simple average of the time of payments, but as a weighted average, based on the present value of those payments. The traditional formula for calculating a bond's duration, shown below, was developed by Macaulay and therefore is known as Macaulay's duration:

$$D = \frac{\sum_{i=1}^{n} t_i \, Pv_i}{\sum_{i=1}^{n} Pv_i}$$

$$= \frac{\sum_{i=1}^{n} t_i \, Pv_i}{P} \qquad \textit{Equation (16.1)}$$

where D is Macaulay's duration (average time) in t units,
P is the price of the bond (or instrument),
t_i is the time of the ith payment, and
Pv_i is the present value of the payment made at t_i.

The calculation of duration is straightforward, although somewhat repetitive. It is illustrated in table 16.2, for a three-year 8% bond with a face value of \$100, given the market yield is 9%.

Note that we have designated t in years so that D is also in years.

$$D = \text{weighted time/price}$$

$$= 272.5911/100.00$$

$$= 2.7259 \text{ years or } 5.4518 \text{ coupon periods}$$

The duration of 2.7259 years is less than the bond's tenor of three years. That duration in this case is less than maturity is a consequence of the coupon payments made prior to maturity. Although the payment of the bond's face value plus interest

Table 16.2 Calculation of Macaulay's duration

Term t_i	Cashflow C_i	Discounted PV_i	$t_i{*}Pv_i$
0.5	4	$4/1.04 = 3.8462$	1.9231
1.0	4	$4/1.04^2 = 3.6982$	3.6982
1.5	4	$4/1.04^3 = 3.5560$	5.3340
2.0	4	$4/1.04^4 = 3.4192$	6.8384
2.5	4	$4/1.04^5 = 3.2877$	8.2193
3.0	104	$104/1.04^6 = 82.1927$	246.5781
Totals		100.0000	272.5911

in three years' time is the single largest bond payment, there are five other payments at times prior to this which reduce the length of time of the average payment.

It is worth noting that the only bond with a duration equal to its tenor is a zero-coupon bond whose only payment occurs at maturity.

Measurement of price sensitivity

Duration as a measure of the average time of payment can serve as a measure of the effective length of a security. While this interpretation of duration is of some interest it is not the principal reason for its use in finance. Duration is mostly used as a measure of a security's price sensitivity to changes in interest rates. This use of duration is best served when it is expressed as **modified duration**, (D′), which is duration discounted one period:

$$D' = \frac{D}{1 + i} \qquad \textit{Equation (16.2)}$$

The relationship between the sensitivity of a bond's price to changes in interest rates and the bond's duration is given by the approximation:

$$\frac{\Delta P}{P} \cong -D'\Delta r \qquad \textit{Equation (16.3)}$$

where Δ indicates a small change,
P is the price of a bond,
D is duration expressed as a number of years, and
r is the market yield.

The left-hand side of the above equation is the percentage change in the price of a bond which indicates that the percentage change in the price of an asset is approximately equal to −D′ for a change of one percentage point in the market yield.

The modified duration of the three-year 8% bond (used in table 16.2) is:

$$D' = \frac{D}{1+i} = \frac{27\,259}{1+0.04}$$

$$= 2.6211 \text{ years}$$

We would expect that when interest rates go down one percentage point the value of the bond would rise by approximately 2.62%.

We can test the accuracy of the duration-based prediction of bond-price change by computing the price of the three-year, 8% bond at a yield to maturity of 7% p.a.

$$P_{7\%} = 4 * a_{\overline{6}|0.035} + \frac{100}{1.035^6}$$

$$= 102.6643$$

You will recall that the price of the bond when the yield was 8%, $P_{8\%}$, was $100.00. The actual percentage change in the price of the bond is 2.66%. This figure differs from the modified-duration predicted value of 2.62% because of the curvilinear nature of the relationship between price and yield. Modified-duration predicted price changes will be accurate only for small and parallel changes in the yield curve.

The above equation shows that the sensitivity of a bond's price, as indicated by the percentage change in its price, to a small change in the yield is indirectly proportional to the bond's duration.

Approximation

For coupon bonds the modified duration is approximately equal to the annuity factor.

$$D' \approx a_{n|i} \qquad \textit{Equation (16.4)}$$

This relationship is exact for par bonds (where coupon equals yield). Consider the three-year 8% coupon bond when yields are 8% p.a.

$$D' = a_{\overline{6}|0.04} = \frac{1 - 1.04^{-6}}{0.04}$$

$$= 5.24 \text{ periods or } 2.62 \text{ years}$$

Duration properties

Duration can serve as a measure of price sensitivity because, all other things being equal, a bond's duration will be larger:

1 the smaller the coupon payments relative to the redemption value,
2 the lower its yield, and
3 the longer the time to redemption.

Each of the above factors drag the average time of payment, and therefore the duration, upwards.

First, bonds with a higher coupon rate, that are identical in all other respects, will have a shorter duration than bonds with a lower coupon rate. Higher coupon rates cause a larger proportion of a bond's payments to be made over the life of the bond, rather than at maturity. Therefore higher coupon rates result in shorter durations.

Second, duration varies inversely with the market yield. At higher discount rates the relative importance of the payments toward the end of the bond's maturity diminishes and this shortens the bond's duration. This has an important implication as it shows that each time the market yield changes, the duration of bonds varies in the reverse direction.

Third, bonds that have a long term to maturity will tend to have a lower duration relative to their maturity than short-term bonds. This relationship arises because the discount factor reduces the present value of the redemption payment as a proportion of a bond's present value, the longer the term to maturity. The relationship is shown in figure 16.3 for coupon bonds, depending on whether they are trading at par, at a discount or at a premium.

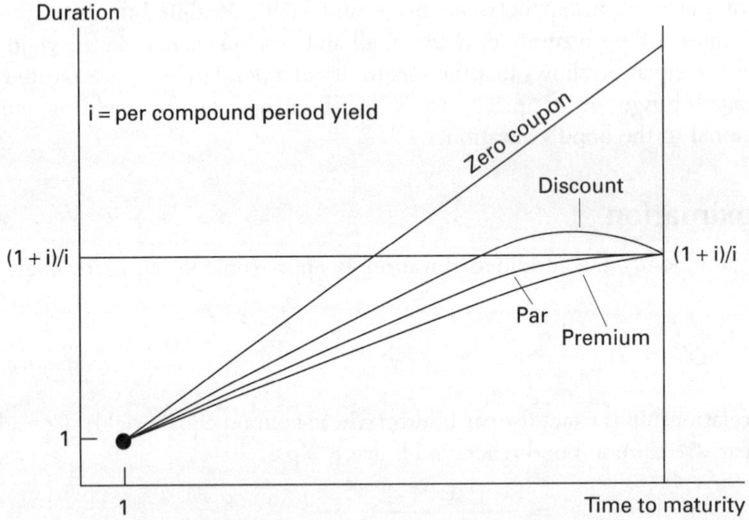

Figure 16.3 Duration and maturity

Figure 16.3 also shows that as coupon-paying bonds become very long (i.e. approach a consol) the duration approaches a limit:

$$D_{consol} = \frac{(1 + i)}{i} \qquad \textit{Equation (16.5)}$$

where D_{consol} is the Macaulay duration of a consol (this is a perpetual bond), and

i is the per coupon rate of interest (i.e. r/2).

(See example 16.1.)

example 16.1

Compute the modified duration of three 7% p.a. semi-annual coupon bonds when yields are also 7% p.a. The first is a five-year bond, the second a ten-year bond and the third a consol.

As all are par bonds, the modified duration is given by the annuity factor $a_{\overline{n}|i}$.

$$D'_{5\text{-years}} = a_{\overline{10}|0.035} = \frac{1 - 1.035^{-10}}{0.035} = 8.32 \text{ periods} = 4.16 \text{ years}$$

$$D'_{10\text{-years}} = a_{\overline{20}|0.035} = \frac{1 - 1.035^{-20}}{0.035} = 14.21 \text{ periods} = 7.11 \text{ years}$$

$$D'_{\text{consol}} = a_{\overline{\infty}|0.035} = \frac{1 - 1.035^{-\infty}}{0.035} = 28.57 \text{ periods} = 14.29 \text{ years}$$

Note that in the case of consols, the amount of the coupon payments is irrelevant.

ASSET/LIABILITY MANAGEMENT

Interest-rate movements affect the value of both assets and liabilities. If an interest-rate change induces a different change in the value of liabilities to that of assets then the balance sheet is exposed to interest-rate risk.

One obvious way for an institution to avoid interest-rate risk is to match cash flows. Interest-rate risk is avoided if assets and liabilities with single payments mature at the same time. For most institutions that have a great variety of assets and liabilities, many of which have multiple cashflows, exact cash-flow matching is not feasible. Indeed, many traditional financial institutions exist because of their willingness to borrow short and lend long — a policy of cash-flow mismatching.

One way in which a firm can measure its exposure to interest-rate risk is to estimate the difference between the modified duration of its assets and liabilities.

D-gap analysis

The duration of the assets and liabilities of a financial institution can be calculated as a weighted average of the duration of each asset and liability. A comparison of these average durations reveals whether the institution has a D-gap. Suppose the assets of an institution have an average modified duration of five years and its liabilities have an average modified duration of two years. It therefore has a D-gap, such that its assets are more price sensitive than its liabilities.

The value of both assets and liabilities will fall when interest rates rise, but liabilities will fall by 2% while assets will fall by 5% for each one-percentage-point rise in market yields, causing a 3% deterioration in the institution's net worth (when marked-to-market).

Duration becomes a management tool when action is taken to close the gap between the duration of a portfolio's assets and liabilities. Managing a portfolio by closing its D-gap reduces its exposure to price risk. For example, when the modified duration, D'_{asset}, is 11 and $D'_{liabilities}$ is 2, the portfolio's net worth will fall much more (by 9%), should yields rise, than it would if the portfolio manager was able to close the D-gap, to say, $D'_{asset} = 7$ and $D'_{liabilities} = 5$. This would limit the fall in the overall portfolio's net worth to 2% whenever yields rise by one percentage point.

Asset/liability management could involve changing the term structure of the assets and liabilities. An institution could also use financial futures (or other derivative instruments) to create artificial assets and liabilities that alter the portfolio's average duration. These instruments can reduce the portfolio's exposure to price risk without changing its existing physical asset/liability structure.

HOLDING-PERIOD IMMUNISATION

There are two factors that influence the return received from an investment in coupon-paying bonds:

1. the coupons received and the associated income from reinvesting the coupons, and
2. the capital gains/losses that arise from changes in the value of the bond over the holding period.

Shifts in the term structure influence both factors, but in offsetting directions. A general rise in interest rates will increase reinvestment income but induce a capital loss; whereas a fall in rates will decrease reinvestment income and produce a capital gain.

It ought to be noted that:

- a zero-coupon bond, because it makes a single payment only, does not have any reinvestment risk, and
- any bond that matures at the end of the holding period has no price risk (i.e. no unexpected capital gain or loss) as it must have a par value at the end of the period.

Therefore a portfolio manager having an investment horizon of t years can completely avoid interest-rate risk by investing in zero-coupon bonds of length t.

If an investment in zero-coupon bonds is not feasible, an investment in coupon bonds with duration t will remove almost all interest-rate risk for an investor with an investment horizon of t years. This is because the risk characteristics of a coupon bond, with duration D, are, to a degree, a reflection of the risk characteristics of a zero-coupon bond of length D.

A bond investment may be tracked by plotting the future value of the investment over time. The value at any point in time is the sum of the capital value of the bond plus the accumulated value of the coupons received.

The effect of a 'once and for all time' change in interest rates is illustrated in figure 16.4, which shows the future (i.e. accumulated) value of a 10% ten-year coupon bond. The flatter curve assumes the market yield starts and remains at 10% p.a., whereas the steeper curves assume the market yield of 10% p.a. has jumped to 15% p.a. immediately after the bond is purchased. Notice that the jump in yields causes a substantial fall in the bond's price but also increases the rate of interest accumulation associated with the reinvestment of the bond's coupons, which is shown by the steeper slope.

The duration of the bond when the market yield is 10% p.a. is approximately 6.5 years. Note that the two lines cross at about 6.5 years. That is, the future value of the bond investment is the same regardless of whether yields are 10% or 15%. This means that the return from investment in the bond six and a half years from now is immune from changes in market yields, even a jump from 10% p.a. to 15% p.a.

This property of duration can be used by a bond trader to immunise a bond portfolio's future value at a particular date from interest-rate changes, provided the period to this date equals the portfolio's duration. This property of duration is relevant when the trader has a particular investment horizon.

An alternative approach to hedging the terminal value of a portfolio is to use zero-coupon bonds that mature on the terminal date. Zero-coupon bonds are not exposed to reinvestment risk (as there are no coupon payments to invest) and if they are held to maturity they will realise the portfolio's intended terminal value. Zero-coupon bonds are not common in Australia, but they are in the United States where there is an active corporate bond market and housing loans are more generally made on a fixed-interest basis.

Fund managers will generally consider duration when they are hedging their portfolio of fixed-interest securities. However, for hedging purposes they can choose strategies other than asset/liability management, such as financial futures, swaps and forward-rate agreements. These instruments are explained in the following two chapters.

From figure 16.4 and table 16.3 it can be seen that if duration is less than the investment horizon, the reinvestment effect dominates the price effect and a fund is advantaged (disadvantaged) by an increase (decrease) in yields. If duration is greater than the investment horizon, the reinvestment effect is less than the price effect and a fund is advantaged (disadvantaged) by a decrease (increase) in yields.

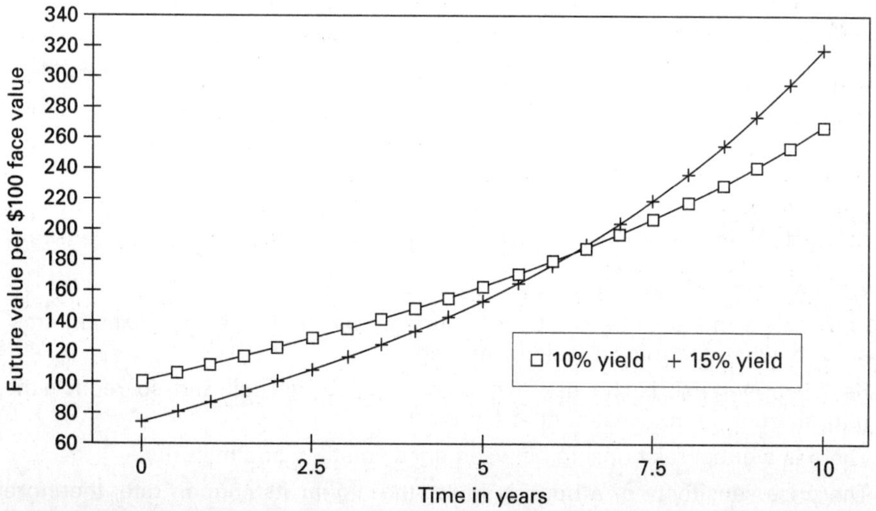

Figure 16.4 Portfolio future value

The trade off between capital gain/loss and reinvestment income is shown in table 16.3. Here we examine the holding-period yield associated with a seven-year investment in three alternative 8.25% p.a. semi-annual coupon bonds. These three bonds have maturities of seven, ten and 15 years. They have durations of 5.45, 7.00 and 8.86 years respectively. Each bond has a price of $100 at the commencement of the investment because the yield of 8.25% p.a. is equal to the coupon rate. We examine the effect of an immediate 'once and for all time' change in the yield to either 7.00% p.a. or 9.50% p.a.

The interest accumulated at the end of the investment is either $72.92 ($57.75 interest and $15.17 interest on interest) if the yield falls to 7.0% or $79.46 if yields rise to 9.5%.

The data in table 16.3 show that the return on a seven-year investment in the ten-year bond with a duration of seven years is approximately 8.25% p.a. regardless of whether yields rise or fall. This immunisation is the result of reinvestment income offsetting the capital gain/loss.

Table 16.3 Duration and holding-period yields for three 8.25% bonds

Bonds according to term		*After seven years*			
Initial yield = 8.25%		Yield = 7.00% p.a.		Yield = 9.50% p.a.	
Term	7 years	Price	$100.00	Price	$100.00
Price	$100.00	$S_{coupons}$	$72.92[a]	$S_{coupons}$	$79.46[b]
Duration	5.45 years	Total	$172.92	Total	$179.46
		HPY	7.98%	HPY	8.53%
Term	10 years	Price	$103.33	Price	$96.80
Price	$100.00	$S_{coupons}$	$72.92	$S_{coupons}$	$79.46
Duration	7.00 years	Total	$176.25	Total	$176.26
		HPY	$8.26%	HPY	8.26%
Term	15 years	Price	$107.56	Price	$93.10
Price	$100.00	$S_{coupons}$	$72.92	$S_{coupons}$	$79.46
Duration	8.86 years	Total	$180.48	Total	$172.56
		HPY	8.62%	HPY	$7.95%

[a] $S_{coupons}$ = $57.75 worth of coupons + $15.17 accumulated interest at 7.00% p.a.
[b] $S_{coupons}$ = $57.75 worth of coupons + $21.71 accumulated interest at 9.50% p.a.

Summary

The main points of this chapter are as follows:

- Price risk is the risk of a capital loss suffered by the holder of a fixed-interest security when the market yield increases.
- Reinvestment risk is the risk that market yields will fall and so reduce the returns from the reinvestment of funds.
- There is a direct relationship between price volatility and maturity.
- The price sensitivity of a bond is lower the higher its coupon rate, therefore traders with fixed-interest assets and liabilities may be exposed to price risk if the coupon rates on the assets differ from the rates on the liabilities.

- The price risk faced by a portfolio of assets and liabilities can be hedged such that its net worth is unaffected by interest-rate movements.
- Duration is a measure of the average maturity of a bond's cash payments.
- Duration varies inversely with the coupon rate; that is, bonds with a higher coupon rate will have a shorter duration, other things being equal.
- Duration varies inversely with the market yield; that is, the higher the yield, the shorter the duration, other things being equal.
- The relationship between duration and maturity widens as maturity increases, provided the bond makes coupon payments.
- Macaulay's duration provides a linear measure of the relationship between interest rates and price sensitivity, whereas in truth the relationship is curvilinear. Therefore Macaulay's measure is more accurate when changes in interest rates are small.
- Matching the duration of fixed-interest assets and liabilities hedges the overall portfolio's net worth against interest-rate risk.
- Duration provides the basis for hedging a bond portfolio's accumulated value at a given date against interest-rate risk.
- Zero-coupon bonds can provide a simple solution to the hedging of a portfolio's terminal value.

Discussion questions and exercises

1 Discuss price risk. Illustrate your answer with reference to the price sensitivity of (a) a two-year and a ten-year 10% Treasury bond, and (b) the following four-year bonds, when the market yield falls from 11.00% to 10.00%:

Bond	*Coupon rate (% p.a.)*
A	14
B	10
C	6

2 If you were a bond trader and you were convinced interest rates would rise (even though there is a flat yield curve), how would you structure the composition (according to term) of your assets and liabilities?

3 Calculate Macaulay's duration of the 7.00% April 2000 Treasury bond in April 1997, assuming the market yield was 8.00%. Compare your answer with the duration of a three-year zero-coupon bond. Which of these bonds has the greater price risk? Explain.

4 Explain the general relationship between maturity and duration of a bond as time rolls along.

5 Calculate the modified duration of the 7.00% April 2000 bond in April 1997 when its yield was 8.00% and indicate its price sensitivity.

6 Suppose you manage a bond portfolio that has a D-gap of four years (i.e. D'_{assets} is six years and $D'_{liabilities}$ is two years). What is the extent of the portfolio's price risk?

7 Explain how a trader could maintain the terminal value of a portfolio of bonds.

8 How could zero-coupon bonds be of use in hedging against interest-rate risk when the trader has a definite investment horizon?

REFERENCES AND FURTHER READING

Fabozzi, F. J. 1993, *Fixed Income Mathematics*, Probus, Chapter 9.
Van Horne, James C. 1993, *Financial Markets, Rates and Floors*, 4th edn, Prentice-Hall, New Jersey.

Part FIVE

Derivative instruments

Following the deregulation of financial institutions and markets, financial variables became more volatile, increasing the uncertainty for participants in the system. This created the need for risk-management products and services and resulted in rapid growth in the markets for derivatives. The professional use of these instruments allows financial-market participants to conduct their underlying transactions with a high degree of certainty.

The chapters in Part Five describe the main forms of derivative instruments and their markets and show how they can be used as risk-management instruments.

Chapter 17 explains financial futures and forward-rate agreements (FRAs) and shows how they can be used to pre-set future interest rates as a result of their settlement payment counter-balancing unexpected movements in interest rates. Chapter 18 explains the operations of interest-rate and currency swaps and shows how they can be used to hedge exposures in domestic and foreign-currency financial markets. Chapter 19 explains the characteristics of options and shows how they can be used as hedging (and speculative) instruments.

The treatment of derivatives is introductory and should allow all readers to understand their role and operation. Whereas derivatives are commonly viewed with some suspicion in the community as risky instruments, we emphasise their role as risk-management instruments.

Chapter 20 completes the book, summarising the major innovations that have followed the deregulation of the financial system in the early 1980s, and reviewing the emerging changes to the system. It is suggested that new technology will radically alter the practices of retail banking in particular.

17

Financial futures and FRAs

In the previous two chapters we analysed multi-period interest rates and securities and considered several sources of interest-rate risk. Futures markets organise the trading in contracts which can be used to hedge interest-rate risk, even though they first evolved to permit trading in commodity price futures. Forward-rate agreements are an alternative arrangement for hedging interest-rate risk. In this and the next two chapters we discuss derivative instruments that can be used to hedge risk exposures in financial markets.

Study objectives

From your study of this chapter you should be able to:

- explain the role of derivatives as risk-management instruments;
- describe the operations of the Sydney Futures Exchange;
- explain the functions of the clearing house;
- describe the SPI futures contract and show how it can be used to hedge a share portfolio from price risk;
- describe the bank-accepted bill-futures contract and show how it can be used to hedge the interest-rate risks faced by borrowers and lenders;
- describe the bond-futures contracts and show how they can be used to hedge bond portfolios against interest-rate risk;
- describe FRAs and show how they can lock in a forward borrowing and/or lending rate.

DERIVATIVES AS HEDGING INSTRUMENTS

In this and the next two chapters we consider four derivative instruments and show how they can be used to hedge interest-rate and price risk arising from positions in physical financial markets. We briefly described these instruments — futures, forwards, swaps and options — in Chapter 3. Recall also that in Chapter 13 we showed how forward FX contracts can be used to hedge exposures to FX risk.

In this chapter we will consider financial futures and FRAs. We will show how they can be used to hedge an exposure to interest-rate risk. In the next chapter we will show how swaps can also serve this purpose. These instruments can be used for other hedging (and speculative) purposes, but for the purposes of this book, we concentrate on their role as interest-rate hedge instruments.

Derivatives are extensively used by financial institutions and business corporations generally to hedge their exposures to interest-rate and foreign-exchange risk. The off-balance sheet data for banks presented in Chapter 9 shows their extensive use of these instruments. Similarly, the results of a survey of major corporations revealed their extensive use of these instruments. (Price Waterhouse, 1994)

The purpose of hedging instruments is to remove the risks arising from the uncertainty of future movements in the rates in the underlying physical market, which for our purposes are the short-term money and debt-capital markets (as well as the FX and equity markets). In simplistic terms, a hedge may be represented by a see-saw, as in figure 17.1, in which the value of the position in the underlying physical market is at one end and the value of the hedging instrument is at the other end. The aim of the hedge is to 'lock in' a forward rate as an effective future spot rate. It was noted in Chapter 15 that forward interest rates are revealed through futures market trading. Consequently, positions can be taken in the futures market by parties that are exposed to the risk of an adverse movement in interest rates, which serve to establish, in effect, the prevailing forward rate as their future spot rate.

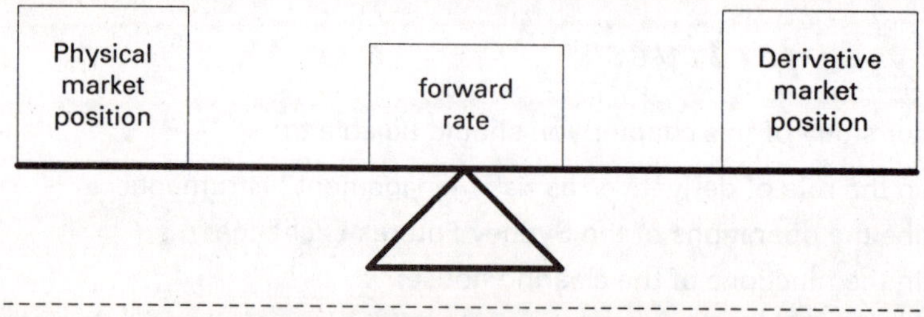

Figure 17.1 The counterbalancing role of hedging instruments

The process by which the hedge position establishes the forward rate involves, in the case of a number of hedge instruments, a profit or loss from the hedge position that counterbalances the change in the value of the underlying position in the associated physical market (relative to the established hedge position). Hence the see-saw analogy.

To be effective, the value of the hedge instrument must be able to vary up or down because underlying market positions are exposed to either an upward or downward movement. This requires hedge instruments that can be either bought or sold. The bought position profits when prices subsequently rise, whereas the sold position profits when prices subsequently fall. In this respect derivatives usually differ from physical instruments, which can be sold only when they are possessed. In derivative markets, either the long (i.e. bought) or short (i.e. sold) position can be acquired. Given that performance under the contract occurs at a future time, the holder of the short position can simply **close out** this position (by acquiring an offsetting long position) making a profit or loss and avoiding the obligation of actually supplying the underlying physical instrument.

In practice, hedging instruments do not always provide an exact counterbalance to the movement in the underlying position. That is, they do not always achieve a perfect hedge. In this chapter, our main aim is to explain how futures and FRAs can serve to hedge an interest-rate-risk exposure, and this is best approached by using simplified examples that ensure a perfect hedge. Thus we defer our comments on imperfect hedges until the end of the chapter.

Elementary futures-hedging theory

Before we discuss futures, we provide a brief explanation of the theory and practice of hedging, using a forward, given that you should be familiar with forwards from our discussion of FX forwards in Chapter 13. But in this section we use gold as the underlying physical.

Suppose a gold miner will have 1000 ounces mined, refined and ready to sell in six months' time and a manufacturing jeweller will require 1000 ounces in six months. Both parties are subject to the risk that the price of gold will change over this period. The miner is exposed to the risk that gold prices will fall, whereas the jeweller is exposed to the risk that gold prices will rise. Both can hedge their price risk by entering a forward contract with one another. The forward contract sets the price (now) and commits both parties to the exchange of gold in six months.

Suppose that the gold prices shown in table 17.1 apply in spot and forward markets for gold. You will notice that the September forward price exceeds the March spot price. This relationship is typical of forward markets. Observe also that in September a forward contract (with September delivery) will be a spot contract and thus have the then spot price.

Table 17.1 Gold prices

		Time
	Now (March)	6 months later (September)
Spot price	$380	$420
Forward price (for September delivery)	$385	$420

If the gold miner and the gold manufacturer enter into a forward contract now, they both pre-set a price of $385 per ounce. In six months, the producer delivers the gold and receives $385 per ounce and the jeweller accepts the gold and pays $385 per ounce. They trade at this price even though the September spot price is $420 per ounce at the time of delivery.

A futures market provides the same hedging services as a forward market (i.e. allows parties to pre-set future prices) but works in a slightly different way. The central tenet of a successful hedge (as shown in figure 17.1) is to take a position in the hedge market (in this case the futures market) that is opposite to that in the physical market. This ensures that any changes in the value of the underlying physical position will be offset by changes in the value of the hedge contract. Let us examine how the gold miner and the jeweller would use a futures market to lock in the price of gold.

The gold miner has a long position in gold. To hedge this position, the miner takes the opposite position in the futures market. That is, the miner takes a short position in the futures market by selling futures contracts that mature when the gold is to be sold. The jeweller has a short position in gold and so takes a long futures position (i.e. buys futures contracts that mature when the gold is to be purchased).

Note that the positions taken by the miner and the jeweller in the futures market are identical to those taken in the forward market (as discussed above). That is, the miner sells a forward/futures contract and the jeweller buys a forward/futures contract. The difference between a futures and a forward hedge emerges at the time of exchange.

Futures contracts do not normally provide for delivery of the underlying asset when they mature. The day the futures contracts mature, the two hedgers:

- sell and buy the underlying asset in the spot market at the going price, and
- close out their futures position by making the reverse trade and receive (or make) a cash settlement depending on the change in the value of their futures position.

Using the spot/forward prices in table 17.1, the miner delivers its gold to the spot market and receives \$420 per ounce. The miner simultaneously closes out the futures position by buying September contracts at the going rate of \$420 per ounce. The effective price received by the miner is the sum of the revenue received from delivering the gold to the spot market and the cash settlement from the futures market. In the example, the miner sold September futures contracts at \$385 and bought at \$420, making a loss of \$35. Thus the miner's effective price is \$420 less \$35, which equals the pre-set (i.e. forward) price of \$385.

The jeweller's actions and results are the opposite of those of the miner. The jeweller buys gold in the physical market at \$420 per ounce and closes out its long futures position by selling futures contracts at \$420 per ounce. The jeweller makes a profit on its futures transactions of \$35 per ounce (i.e. \$420 − \$385 = \$35) which offsets the gold purchased at \$420 to give a net effective price of \$385 per ounce.

Observe that the miner took a short position in the futures market to establish the hedge, and subsequently offset it by purchasing the September contracts. As noted above, a hedge position may require taking a short position. The question often asked is — how can a short futures position be taken in the futures market? One needs to examine the nature of the contract to understand the legitimacy of **short selling** (i.e. selling without owning the underlying physical) in the futures market.

A short futures position commits the holder to deliver a quantity of the underlying asset, at a time in the future, at an agreed selling price. This obligation can be extinguished by acquiring a subsequent long position prior to the maturity (i.e. contract date) of the sold futures contracts. The long position means the party sold first and bought second, removing the party from the futures market with a potential profit/loss, depending on the relative value of the long and short positions.

The role played by a hedging instrument can also be shown with a simple equation, where V_t refers to the overall value of a market participant's position at time t, $A_{t,T}$ refers to the future value, at time, t, of the participants' underlying asset position, for delivery at time, T, and $H_{t,T}$ refers to the value of the hedge instrument at time, t, for delivery at time T, as follows:

$$V_t = A_{t,T} + H_{t,T} \qquad \textit{Equation (17.1)}$$

In general, $A_{t,T}$ is unknown for future time periods. In the above example, $A_{t,T}$ is the spot price of gold in September. If no hedge is established, V_t, the value of the overall position, fluctuates with movement in the gold price.

The theory of hedging requires that a hedge position is established such that any fluctuations in the value of the underlying asset position, $A_{t,T}$, is offset by changes in the value of the hedge position, $H_{t,T}$, so that the overall position value, V_t, remains constant. This is achieved in the gold example.

Table 17.2 Hedged values

Time		*Underlying asset value*	*Hedge position*	*Overall position*
		Miner		
t=0	March	385	0	385
t= 6 months	September	420	(35)	385
		Jeweller		
t=0	March	(385)	0	(385)
t= 6 months	September	(420)	35	(385)

The above gold example illustrates the principles of hedging that apply equally to hedging the risks that arise from movements in interest rates. In financial markets the underlying physical can be the securities that are issued by a borrower and held by an investor. We explain this process after we introduce the operations of futures markets in the next section.

To summarise, the key features of the use of derivatives to hedge interest-rate risk, as discussed in this and the next two chapters, are that they:

- use forward rates to pre-set future spot rates, and
- operate through a cash settlement that serves to counterbalance the difference between the actual spot and the forward interest rates.

INTRODUCTION TO FUTURES

Futures markets had their origins in the United States in the mid 1800s. Since that time they have been established in cities around the world. Australia's largest futures market, the Sydney Futures Exchange (SFE), began its life in 1960 as a market for wool futures.

Since then the range of contracts offered for trade has been increased, particularly in the area of financial futures, which include contracts for 90-day bank-accepted bills, three-year Treasury bonds, ten-year Treasury bonds and the Share Price Index (SPI).

Forward contracts are similar to futures in that they specify a future (as opposed to spot) settlement date. There is evidence that futures, rather than forward contracts, were being traded on the Chicago Board of Exchange by the 1860s. Since that time the basic structure, settled on in Chicago, has been adopted around the world. It is important to understand both the similarities and differences between forward and futures contracts.

Because none of the current SFE financial futures contracts are based on a simple deliverable 'commodity' we use the (now obsolete) gold futures contract to illustrate the basic features of futures trading. The gold contract was traded on the SFE during the late 1970s and although it has since been removed from the SFE, it remains a popular contract on the New York Commodity Exchange (COMEX). Briefly, the SFE gold futures contract was an agreement to deliver, or accept delivery of, 50 ounces of gold.

Trading in futures contracts involves five principal arrangements:

1. the organised exchange,
2. the standardised contract specifications,
3. the clearing house,
4. the daily 'marking-to-market', and
5. the ability to enact reversing transactions.

The Sydney Futures Exchange

Futures contracts are always traded on an organised exchange. The SFE is a voluntary, non-profit association of members. It is also a self-regulatory body that enforces trading and business rules. These rules 'ensure that the futures market is fair and orderly and that the interests of all participants are safeguarded.' (SFE).

The SFE has three types of members:

- Full members (called **floor members**) have access to the facilities offered by the clearing house. They are brokers who are entitled to trade on behalf of their clients. They are required to have a minimum net asset backing of $1 000 000. As at 1995, there were 29 floor members. Clients' orders are announced in the market by the method of open outcry and deals are struck when another trader on the floor agrees to deal at the price for a particular number of contracts (or lots).
- **Associate members** (of which there are three classes) can either trade on behalf of clients or through floor members. Full associate members must be licensed and have a minimum net asset backing of $250 000. Both floor members and full associate members are permitted to handle clients' monies. The other categories of associate members are introducing brokers and market associates. In 1995 there were 116 associate members.
- **Local members** are permitted to undertake business for floor members. As at 1995 there were 137 local members. (SFE)

Generally, trading takes place during official hours (morning and afternoon sessions that vary slightly for the different contracts) and in the designated trading areas, called 'pits'. A small but increasing proportion of the SFE's total business is conducted after the floor has closed using the SYCOM system, which enables SFE contracts to be quoted and traded off a computer screen.

A pit consists of a depressed area of the trading floor and is presided over by a pit-boss who supervises trading and adjudicates over any disputed transactions. Futures contracts are traded by a system of open outcry. In this system, any offer to buy or sell must be made to all the traders present in the pit. An esoteric, highly developed system of hand signals is also used by traders to express their wish to buy or sell. However, the official means of communication remains the technique of open outcry. The pit staff ensure that bid and offer prices are communicated to the exchange's computer system.

The best bid (highest) and offer (lowest) are continually displayed on monitors on the floor. An example of the floor screen and the sort of information printed in daily papers is set out in tables 17.3 and 17.4.

Observe the large number of outstanding positions for the next three or four contract dates. As noted in Chapter 3, approximately eight million contracts were traded in fiscal year 1994, with a market value of $3995 million. This high level of turnover means the bill-futures market is of considerable influence within the short-term money market generally.

The organised structure for the trading of futures contracts differs from the organisation of forward markets. Forward markets are loosely organised and have no physical location devoted to their trading. In other words, they are over-the-counter markets. Perhaps the best-developed forward market is for foreign exchange. As noted in Chapter 13, this is a worldwide network of participants, largely banks and brokers, who communicate with each other electronically. There is no organised exchange and no central trading point.

Table 17.3 Reporting of bill-futures trading

Contract month		*Jun.*	*Sep.*	*Dec.*
First price today	OPN	91.11	91.53	91.47
Highest price today	HI	91.17	91.56	91.50
Lowest price today	LO	91.11	91.47	91.44
Yesterday's final settlement price	SET	91.10	91.51	91.46
Change from previous day	CHG	+0.04	−0.01	0.00
Number of trades done	VOL	32 564	17 256	8 659
Fourth last trade	4TH	91.11	91.50	91.44
Third last trade	3RD	91.13	91.49	91.44
Second last trade	2ND	91.14	91.50	91.45
Latest trade	LST	91.14	91.50	91.45
Seller's price (offer)	ASK	91.14	91.50	91.45
Buyer's price	BID	91.13	91.49	91.44

Table 17.4 Reporting of futures trading in the *Financial Review*

SYDNEY FUTURES EXCHANGE MARKETS: *FINANCIAL REVIEW*, Tuesday 8 August 1995

	Prev. Price	*First Trade*	*High*	*Low*	*Settlement Price*	*Change*	*$ Value of Chg*	*Volume*	*Prev O/P*
All Ordinaries Share Price Index (A$25 x All Ordinaries Index)									
Sep 95	2184.0	2190.0	2199.0	2180.0	2181.0	−3.0	−75.00	2662	100685
Dec 95	2197.0	2203.0	2210.0	2196.0	2193.0	−4.0	−100.00	11	4113
Mar 96	2215.0	—	—	—	2212.0	−3.0	−75.00	0	1289
Jun 96	2236.0	—	—	—	2233.0	−3.0	−75.00	0	81
TOTALS: SYCOM Vol. 41 2 Trading Floor Vol. 2673 Prev O/P. 1 06168									
ANZ Share Futures (based on 1000 shares)									
Oct 95	5.31	—	—	—	5.25	−0.06	−60.00	0	11
TOTALS: SYCOM Vol. 0 Trading Floor Vol. 0 Prev O/P. 11									
BHP Share Futures (based on 1100 shares)									
Sep 95	20.19	20.12	20.24	20.12	20.21	+0.02	22.00	7	1486
TOTALS: SYCOM Vol. 0 Trading Floor Vol. 7 Prev O/P. 1490									
90-Day Bank Bills (100.00 minus yield % p.a.)									
Sep 95	92.34	92.36	92.37	92.36	92.37	+0.03	71.26	300	48241
Dec 95	92.20	92.25	92.27	92.24	92.27	+0.07	166.18	817	39706
Mar 96	92.03	92.08	92.13	92.08	92.14	+0.11	260.94	167	20842
Jun 96	91.93	—	92.02	92.00	92.02	+0.09	213.39	59	12144
Sep 96	91.80	91.88	91.88	91.88	91.88	+0.08	189.56	16	5892
Dec 96	91.70	—	—	—	91.75	+0.05	118.41	0	6010
Mar 97	91.58	—	—	—	91.64	+0.06	142.01	0	4130
Jun 97	91.44	—	—	—	91.52	+0.08	189.23	0	3231
Sep 97	91.30	—	—	—	91.40	+0.10	236.39	0	1999
Dec 97	91.14	—	—	—	91.24	+0.10	236.21	0	1760
TOTALS: SYCOM Vol. 2221 Trading Floor Vol. 1359 Prev O/P. 14531									
3-year Treasury Bonds (100.00 minus yield % p.a.)									
Sep 95	91.59	91.69	91.69	91.66	91.69	+0.10	275.97	1528	157375
Dec 95	91.38	—	—	—	91.48	+0.10	274.12	0	255
TOTALS: SYCOM Vol. 5154 Trading Floor Vol. 1528 Prev O/P. 157630									
10-year Treasury Bonds (100.00 minus yield % p.a.)									
Sep 95	90.575	90.680	90.700	90.665	90.700	+0.125	891.13	899	94491
Dec 95	90.495	—	—	—	90.665	+0.170	1206.11	0	96
TOTALS: SYCOM Vol. 5380 Trading Floor Vol. 899 Prev O/P. 94587									

Standardised contracts

A futures exchange will only allow trading of very specific contracts. Futures contracts are standardised with respect to:

1 **The contract unit** This specifies the size of the contract. For example, the contract unit of the SFE Bank Accepted Bill contract is bank bills with a face value of $1 000 000.
2 **Delivery months** This varies with the traded contract. However, in the case of the SFE-traded contracts there are commonly four equally spaced delivery months per calender year; these are shown in table 17.4.
3 **Quotation** This specifies the method of quotation and the minimum unit of price quotation. Therefore it also represents the smallest possible change in the last traded price. In the case of the interest-rate futures, the method of quotation is 100 minus the interest rate, quoted as a whole number correct to two decimal places for bills and three-year bonds and three decimal places for ten-year bonds. For example, if the market yield for bills is 7.55% p.a., the quoted price of the futures contract will be 92.45 (100 minus 7.55).
4 **Settlement details** The contract will specify whether contracts remaining open at the close of trading on the settlement day will be settled by delivery of the item specified in the contract (this is known as a **deliverable contract**), or whether they will be settled by the payment of cash (known as **cash settlement**). Because they evolved from forward markets, early futures markets invariably provided for delivery of the specified commodity. Deliverable contracts specify delivery sites and acceptable quality requirements. Cash settlement has since become the more popular method of settling outstanding positions at the maturity of a contract. There are three reasons for this. First, in some contracts, the 'commodity' does not exist, such as the SPI. Second, cash settlement gets around some of the problems of guaranteeing the quality of the delivered commodity. Lastly, cash settlement is often more convenient and less costly than physical delivery.

Throughout our discussion of futures markets reference will be made to delivery (or settlement). Even though some contracts will specify cash settlement, meaning that the cash difference between the contract's value at delivery and the contract amount when it was traded is paid by the losing party to the other party, we will refer to delivery as though it involves the whole contract amount. This, of course, is the way a deliverable contract is settled when the product is exchanged.

The clearing house

To ensure the smooth functioning of trading, each futures exchange operates a clearing house which plays a crucial role in the functioning of the futures market. The essential purpose of the clearing house is to guarantee performance to all the participants in the market. It serves this role by adopting the position of buyer to every seller and seller to every buyer. This means that every trader in the futures market has obligations only to the clearing house and has expectations that the clearing house will maintain its side of the bargain. The clearing house takes no active position in the market, but interposes itself between the parties to every transaction. This process is known as **novation**.

Two positions are opened when a contract is agreed upon. The buyer of a contract has the long position, whereas the seller has the short position. Because of the two-sided nature of any position, the number of bought contracts will always equal the number sold. So, for every party expecting to receive delivery of a commodity, the opposite trading partner must be prepared to make delivery. If we were to add up all of the outstanding long and short futures market positions, the total would always equal zero.

A representative trading situation is shown in table 17.5. On 1 September, the Union Bank of Switzerland (Party A, in table 17.5) buys one gold-futures contract for delivery in December. In order for the Swiss bank to be able to buy the contract, some other participant must sell to it. Let us suppose that Gold Corp. (a subsidiary of the Perth mint) is the party agreeing to a sell a contract. In panel (a) of the table it is apparent that the two parties to the gold-futures transaction have exactly complementary positions in the futures market. Notice that the time of delivery, the amount of gold to be delivered and the price all match. Otherwise, there could have been no transaction.

Table 17.5 Hypothetical gold futures trade

Panel (a)	*Panel (b)*
1 September	
Party A	**Clearing house**
Buys 1 December 50 oz gold-futures contract at AUD465/oz	Agrees to deliver to Party A a December gold contract
Party B	**Clearing house**
Sells 1 December 50 oz gold-futures gold contract at AUD465/oz	Agrees to accept from Party B a December contract

Invariably the two trading parties will be unknown to one another. Each party is concerned with the position they have taken, rather than with the identity of the other party. They have traded with one another for their own mutual benefit through the agency of the futures brokers, the market and the clearing house. Performance of both sides to each contract is guaranteed by the clearing house. This is shown in panel (b) of table 17.5.

After the initial sale is made, the clearing house steps in and acts as the seller to the buyer and as the buyer to the seller. The buyer of the futures contract is guaranteed by the clearing house that it will make delivery at the initially agreed time and price. To the seller, the clearing house agrees that it will receive delivery at the agreed time and price.

In order to be able to guarantee the performance of each contract the clearing house must protect itself against the failure of individual transactors. The chief safeguard the clearing house has against the possibility that a counterparty to a transaction may default, is its administration of a system of **deposits (initial margin)** and **margins**.

Prior to being permitted to trade, an individual must post a specified amount of money. Thereafter, the system of initial deposits and **daily resettlement** ensures that the clearing house has funds to make good any defaulted contract. Initial deposits are not the price of a futures contract, they are a down-payment and thus are held by the clearing house on behalf of the trader.

Table 17.6 Initial margins and values of selected financial futures contracts

Contract	*Face value*	*Initial margin*	*Minimum price movement*	*Value of minimum move*
SPI	AOI[1] times 25	$1 600	1.0 point of AOI	$25.00
90-day BABs	$1 000 000	$1 000	1 basis point	$24.00[2]
3-year bonds	$100 000	$1 200	1 basis point	$27.00[2]
10-year bonds	$100 000	$2 800	0.5 basis point	$36.00[2]

[1] All Ordinaries Index
[2] These amounts depend on the level of the market yield, especially for ten-year bonds
Source: Sydney Futures Exchange

Initial deposits for various futures contracts as at November 1995 are set out in the final column of table 17.6. Deposits are approximately equal in value to the estimated maximum possible daily price fluctuation for the contract in question. This is the first of possibly many payments that a futures trader may have to make while holding an open futures position.

Daily resettlement

The SFE clearing house monitors the market value of each position. This process is known as **mark-to-market**. The clearing house undertakes this process because of its responsibility to ensure the performance of each position. Each day the clearing house posts changes in the value of a trader's position to their margin accounts. This may require further payments to a trader's margin account, depending on the extent of the fall in the value of the trader's position. These payments must be made, or the clearing house will close out the trader's position. In practice the clearing house holds brokers responsible for their clients' margin payments.

Observe (in table 17.6) that initial margins are less than five per cent of the contract's value. This is practical because of the system of daily resettlement, described in the previous paragraph. Using the example of the gold-futures contract, let us examine the consequence of the price of the December gold contract falling from AUD465/oz to AUD450/oz. Consider the unrealised profit/loss associated with each side of the deal.

The buyer (Union Bank of Switzerland):

Unrealised loss = (market price − purchase price) * 50
= (450 − 465) * 50
= $750

The seller (Gold Corp.):

Unrealised profit = (selling price − market price) * 50
= (465 − 450) * 50
= $750

The Union Bank of Switzerland, which bought one contract for $465 per ounce on 1 September, has sustained a loss of $15 per ounce. Since there are 50 ounces in the contract, this represents a loss of $750. This amount is deducted from the bank's margin deposited with its broker. When the value of the funds on deposit with the broker reaches a certain level, called the **maintenance** or **variation margin**, the trader is required to replenish the margin, bringing it back to its initial level. The maintenance margin is generally about 75% of the amount of the initial margin. When the initial margin is $1000, the maintenance threshold would be $800. Hence, once the loss exceeds $200 a further margin payment would be required. As the bank has sustained a loss of $750, the broker will require the Swiss bank to top up its margin account, to bring it back up to the $1000 initial margin. This additional payment must be paid in immediately and in cash.

When the bank sells its gold-futures contracts, assuming the sale price is less than the purchase price, the funds it had contributed (i.e. its initial margin and daily resettlement amounts) are used to meet its obligation on settlement.

In the above circumstance, the value of the position of the other party, Gold Corp., has increased by $750. Apart from the initial deposit, the surplus represented by the current value of its futures position minus the original value of its short position, 'belongs' to this party and can be withdrawn from its account with the clearing house; or, if the funds are left in the account, the company is paid interest on them by the clearing house.

Closing out a futures position

In the case of non-deliverable futures contracts, holders of positions must, on the settlement date, take an opposite position to close out the position. So, for instance, the holder of 100 short positions must buy 100 of these contracts. This party settles by paying or receiving the balance between the value of the long position (taken that day) and the value of the short position when it was acquired. In the case of deliverable contracts, traders may elect to close out or implement the delivery requirements.

Consider again the situation shown in table 17.5. The buyer of the contract, Union Bank of Switzerland, has an obligation to the clearing house to accept 50 ounces of gold in December and to pay $465 per ounce at that time. Perhaps the Union Bank of Switzerland does not wish to actually receive the gold or it decides to withdraw from the market on, say, 10 September.

The bank will fulfil its futures-market commitment by entering the futures market and selling its contracts as shown in table 17.7. The first line of this table merely repeats the initial trade that was made on 1 September. On 10 September, the Union Bank of Switzerland, wishing to cut its losses, takes exactly the opposite position by selling a December gold contract for a futures price of $450 per ounce. This time the bank transacts with a new entrant to the market, say Macquarie Bank. After this trade, the Swiss bank's net position is zero.

Table 17.7 The effect of a closing-out transaction

1 September	
Party A:	Union Bank of Switzerland
Buys 1 December gold-futures contract at $465/oz	
Party B:	Gold Corp.
Sells 1 December gold-futures contract at $465/oz	
10 September	
Party A:	Union Bank of Switzerland
Sells 1 December gold-futures contract at $450/oz	
Party C:	Macquarie Bank
Buys 1 December gold-futures contract at $450/oz	

The price of December gold-futures contracts fell $15 per ounce during this period, inflicting a loss of $750 on the bank. Gold Corp., the original seller, is not affected by the Union Bank of Switzerland's reversing trade. Gold Corp. still has the same commitment, since the clearing house continues to stand ready to complete this transaction.

From 10 September the clearing house assumes a complementary obligation to the new market entrant, Macquarie Bank. Note that the position of the clearing house has not really changed due to the transactions that took place on 10 September. Also, Gold Corp. and Macquarie Bank have complementary obligations after the new trades, just as the Union Bank of Switzerland and Gold Corp. had complementary obligations after the initial transactions on 1 September.

A further illustration of position taking in the futures market is provided in example 17.1. Even though this example also applies to gold futures, it illustrates position taking in any futures contract.

example 17.1

Suppose A sells five 50-ounce March gold-futures contracts for $410/oz. Subsequently, A buys four contracts from B at $430/oz and one from C at $435. What are the positions and profits of A, B and C if the current futures price is $420?

Party A has no position, having offset the original short five contracts through the subsequent purchase of five contracts. A's profit is computed as:

$$\text{Sales} = 5*410*50$$
$$= \$102\,500$$
$$\text{Purchases} = (4*430 + 435)*50$$
$$= \$107\,750$$

hence
$$\text{Profit} = -\$5\,250$$

Party B, having sold to A, has an open short position of four contracts. B also has an unrealised profit on this open position:

$$\text{Profit} = 4*(430 - 420)*50$$
$$= \$2000$$

Party C, having sold to A, has an open short position of one contract. C has an unrealised profit on this open position:

$$\text{Profit} = (435 - 420)*50$$
$$= \$750$$

When entering the reversing trade, it is crucial that Party A (in table 17.7) sell exactly the same contracts that were originally bought. Note, in table 17.7, the close-out trade matches the original trade in all respects. If it does not, the trader takes a new obligation instead of cancelling the old. For instance, if Party A had sold a June contract on 10 September instead of the December contract, A would be obligated to receive gold in December and to deliver gold in June. Such a transaction would result in a 'spread': a position in two or more related contracts, instead of a reversing trade.

FUTURES-MARKET PARTICIPANTS

Participants in the future markets can be somewhat arbitrarily divided into three groups: hedgers, arbitragers and speculators. A hedger has a position in another market, whereas a speculative futures position is not covering an underlying position. Arbitragers seek to exploit occasions when prices of equivalent instruments differ: buying at the lower price and simultaneously selling at the higher price.

Hedge positions

To hedge is to reduce risk by removing uncertainty. A hedger is a party with commitments, usually in the physical market that underlies the futures contract, who enters the futures market in order to reduce risk arising out of those commitments. A hedger might make a short or a long hedge.

In the gold example discussed above, the gold miner with gold in the ground hedged its exposure to a fall in prices by selling sufficient future contracts to cover the anticipated mine production, and the manufacturing jeweller took the opposite position (buying futures contracts) to hedge its exposure to a rise in gold prices.

Hedge positions can be shown by the pay-off lines in figure 17.2. The pay-off line for a long future is a positive-sloping 45-degree line that intersects the horizontal axis at the entry price, shown as X. This is the delivery price agreed to in the futures contract. Observe that the price is multiplied by 50 because a gold-futures contract comprises 50 ounces of gold, and the price is expressed in ounces. The negatively sloped pay-off line illustrates the profit applying to the seller of the futures contract. Note that potential profit or loss on any futures position is effectively unbounded. The unlimited upside/downside to a futures position is to be contrasted with that of options positions, which we will discuss in Chapter 19.

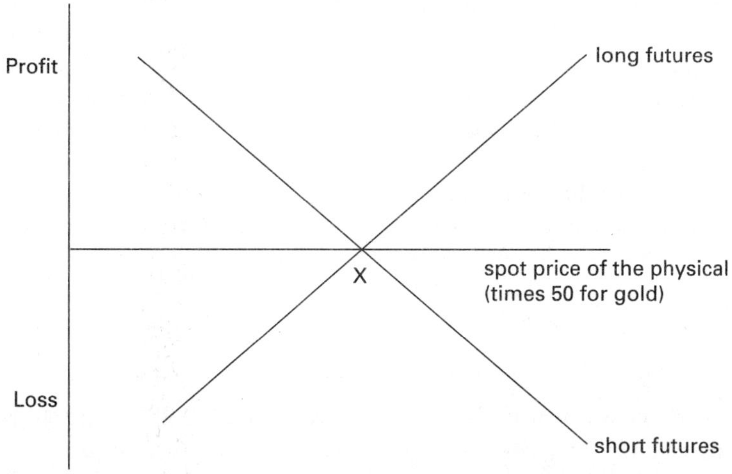

Figure 17.2 Pay-off lines for a long and short futures position

The miner has a long position that is exposed to the future movement in its market price. This exposure is represented in figure 17.2 by the upward-sloping line. Should the price of gold increase above X, the value of the mine increases, and vice versa. (Note that the exposure from holding 50 ounces of gold is the same as the exposure of holding a long gold-futures position.)

The miner can hedge the risk of a fall in the price of gold by taking the opposite position in the gold-futures market. The trader would sell gold-futures contracts at X because a fall in price below X will allow the trader to earn a profit by buying back the gold-futures contracts at the lower price and this profit would offset the fall in value of the trader's holding of gold. Hence the short futures position (shown by the downward-sloping line in figure 17.2) can hedge the exposure of a gold miner to a fall in the value of its gold holdings.

Likewise, the jeweller's exposure to the risk of a rise in the price prior to the jeweller's purchase of gold is represented by the downward-sloping curve and this risk can be hedged by taking a long futures position, the value of which is shown by the upward-sloping curve in figure 17.2.

It is clear that hedging involves a fundamental trade off. The hedger is giving up the potential profit from a favourable price movement in order to avoid an unfavourable movement. In the case of the gold miner, the short futures position yields a counteracting profit when the price falls below X, but inflicts a counteracting loss when the price of gold exceeds X. The hedger's objective is to lock in a future price and the hedger is prepared to forego possible profits from a favourable price movement to gain the certainty of a future price. Given the difficulty of predicting future movements in interest rates, exchange rates and stock prices, financial institutions and companies tend to hedge their financial exposures and use the futures market as one of the means for reducing uncertainty.

A completely successful hedge is one that, in the face of volatile prices, maintains without variation the value of a trader's underlying position (i.e. guarantees the value of A in equation (17.1)). As noted above, the process of hedging often involves the problem of basis risk. This is the risk that the futures price is not perfectly correlated with the price of the underlying security. It arises when the changes in the position being hedged are not exactly matched by changes in the value of the futures contract.

To illustrate, suppose a fund manager takes a position in SPI futures in order to hedge a particular portfolio. Should the composition of the portfolio being hedged differ from that of the All Ordinaries Index, the reaction of the portfolio to changing market conditions might not be matched by changes in the value of the SPI futures contract. As a consequence, the hedge will be imperfect. Another example is the case of a borrower who uses a position in the BAB futures market to hedge an exposure to an unexpected increase in the overdraft rate. In both of these cases, the movement of the value of the position being hedged (the left-hand side of the see-saw in figure 17.1), will not necessarily match that of the futures position (the right-hand side of the see-saw).

A further problem is that the value of futures contracts will not match the value of the hedger's underlying position. For example, because the bill-futures contract has a value of $1 000 000 it cannot precisely hedge a borrower's interest-rate risk on a planned loan of $800 000.

Arbitragers

Arbitragers take a position in both the physical (or the spot) and futures markets simultaneously, to profit from price differences. For example, if the futures price exceeds the spot price by more than the cost of carrying the commodity (as in the case of gold futures), a riskless profit can be made by buying spot, selling futures and later making delivery of the commodity to complete the futures contract. Similarly, if the spot price is greater than the futures price it is possible for a manufacturer who needs the commodity at a later date to sell the commodity, buy futures and take delivery later.

Speculators

Speculators take a position in the market and so accept the risk of an adverse price movement. They take a speculative (or open) position in the market in the hope that future market movements are consistent with their views. Because trading by speculators and arbitragers adds to the market's liquidity, they assist in the operation of the futures market.

The unrealised profit attached to an open futures position is the difference between the price of the contract and the current market price in the futures market. An open long position gains from an increase in the futures market price, while an open short position gains from a fall in the futures market price. The unrealised profit on an open position can be expressed as:

$$\text{Profit} = \text{Position} * \text{Quantity} * (P_{\text{Market}} - P_{\text{Entry}}) \qquad \textit{Equation (17.2)}$$

where, Position = 1 long position,
= − 1 short position,
Quantity = number of contracts,
P_{Market} = current futures price,
P_{Entry} = entry or contract price.

The relationship between the profit on a futures position and the current price is set out in equation (17.2) and is illustrated in example 17.2. This relation can be expressed graphically in a plot called a pay-off or profit diagram, such as the pay-off lines in figure 17.2 for a single long position and a single short position.

example 17.2

Suppose a trader sells ten 50-ounce gold futures contracts for \$400/oz. What is the unrealised profit on this open short position if the current market price is \$375?

$$\begin{aligned}\text{Profit} &= \text{Position} * \text{Quantity} * (P_{\text{Market}} - P_{\text{Entry}})\\ &= -1 * 10 * 50 * (375 - 400)\\ &= \$12\,500\end{aligned}$$

FINANCIAL FUTURES

Of the four financial-futures contracts, the SPI and the three interest-rate futures, bank bills, three-year and ten-year Treasury bonds that we consider, more attention will be given to bank-bill futures. We commence this section with a discussion of the bank-bill futures contracts and their use for hedging underlying transactions in the short-term money market.

BAB futures

Bank-accepted bill (BAB) futures began trading on the SFE in 1979, and are currently the most active market on the exchange, trading contracts with a nominal value of more than $4 billion each day.

The features of the BAB futures contract are summarised in table 17.8. Note in particular that its face value is $1 million, its price is quoted as 100 minus the yield, and that there are four contract dates (i.e. the dates when each futures contract matures) per year for the next three years.

Table 17.8 Summary of the BAB futures contract, as at November 1995

Contract unit	$A1 000 000 face value of 90-day bank-accepted bills of exchange.
Standard delivery	Ten bank-accepted bills or bank-negotiable certificates of deposit (NCDs), each of face value $A100 000; or two BABs or NCDs of face value $A500 000; or one $A1 000 000 BAB or NCD, maturing 85–95 days from settlement day.
Quotations	One hundred minus annual percentage yield to two decimal places. (The minimum fluctuation of 0.01% equals approximately $11 per contract, varying with the level of interest rates.)
Contract months	March, June, September and December up to five years ahead.
Termination of trading	12.00 noon on the business day immediately prior to settlement day.
Settlement day	The second Friday of the delivery month.
Trading hours	8.30 a.m. to 12.30 p.m.; 2.00 p.m. to 4.30 p.m. SYCOM: 4.40 p.m. to 6.00 a.m.

A BAB futures contract is effectively an agreement to borrow or lend the present value of $1 000 000 for 90 days from a given future date at an interest rate agreed on today, because it is a contract to deliver 90-day BABs with a face value of $1 000 000. The price of a BAB futures contract is a specific application of the general bill-pricing formula, explained in Chapter 4:

$$P_{futures} = \frac{F}{1 + r_{fwd}t} \qquad \textit{Equation (17.3)}$$

where F is $1 million,

r_{fwd} is the forward yield embedded in the price of a futures contract (i.e. $= 100 - P_{futures}$),

$P_{futures}$ is the price of a BAB futures contract,

t is 90 over 365.

To illustrate, suppose the December BAB futures are trading at 92.40, representing a (forward) yield of 7.60%. The price of this contract will be:

$$P_{Dec} = \frac{1\ 000\ 000}{1 + 0.076 * 90/365}$$

$$= \$981\ 605$$

Trading in each contract can be represented by the demand and supply at the yield in the futures market. For instance, suppose in June the December BAB futures contract is trading at 92.40. Traders who believe that price is too low (i.e. the implied forward yield is too high) will buy and traders who believe the price is too high (i.e. the implied forward yield is too low), will sell. Of course, other trades will serve a hedging purpose. When the market clearing price is 92.40, it indicates that the market currently expects the 90-day yield in December (i.e. the December forward rate) will be 7.60%.

It is important to understand that the yield implied by trading in each futures contract is a forward rate that commences when the contract matures. These contracts, as stated above, specify 90-day BABs that commence their term when the futures contract matures — on its contract date. Consequently, BAB futures contract dates specify when the 90-day forward rates apply.

To illustrate, examine the BAB futures prices on 3 March 1996, shown in table 17.9 and figure 17.3. The embedded yields are the 90-day forward rates over this period. They provide a measure of the expected future rates, as discussed in Chapter 15. For instance, the December 1996 yield of 8.17% resulted from trading in the December 1996 contract and so represented the market's expectation (on 3 March 1996) about the 90-day spot rate in December 1996.

Table 17.9 BAB futures prices and yields, 3 March 1996

Contract month	*Price*	*Yield (% p.a.)*
June 1996	92.41	7.59
Sept. 1996	92.16	7.84
Dec. 1996	91.83	8.17
March 1997	91.52	8.48
June 1997	91.28	8.72
Sept. 1997	91.13	8.87
Dec. 1997	91.03	8.97
March 1998	90.27	9.73
June 1998	90.92	9.08

Source: *Australian Financial Review*, 6 May 1996

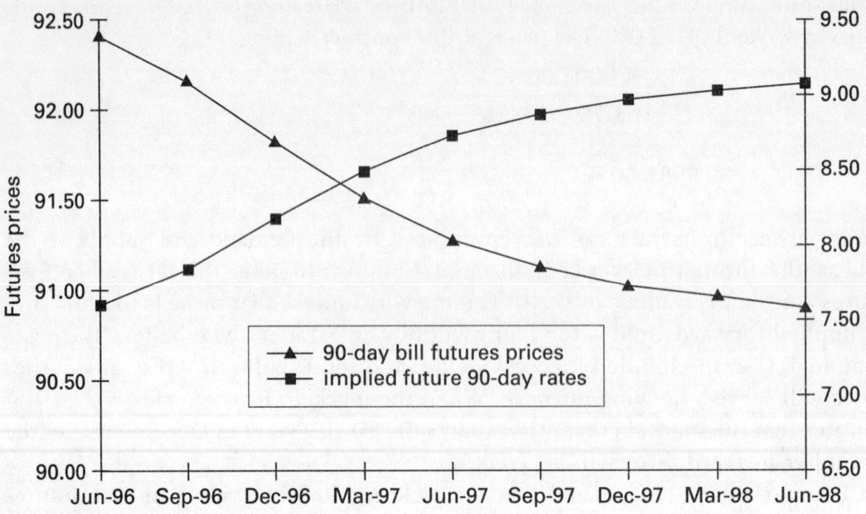

Figure 17.3 BAB futures and yields

Bill futures and the term structure

The yields embedded in futures prices are forward rates that apply when the contracts mature. They are not spot rates. But using the theory explained in Chapter 15, a yield curve can be constructed by incorporating the forward rates in multi-period spot rates.

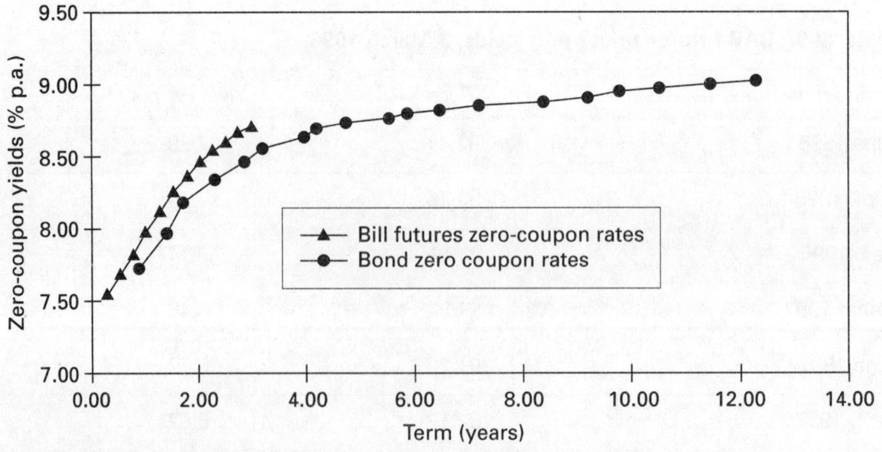

Figure 17.4 Zero-coupon rate on bill futures and Treasury bonds

Term structures of interest rates are based on the yields for dominant short-term and long-term financial instruments. For longer terms, the dominant market is for Treasury bonds (discussed in Chapter 11), whereas the main market for short-term rates is the bill-futures market. Figure 17.4 presents spot (or zero-coupon) rates derived from the BAB market with those obtained in the Commonwealth Treasury bond market. The zero-coupon bill rates exceed their bond equivalents because BABs have a higher credit risk than Treasury bonds which, you will remember, are free of default risk. Note that the bill-futures data in figure 17.4 are for three years. On 29 July 1996, the futures market added two further years of contract dates.

BAB futures as a hedge instrument

Future borrowers and lenders of funds face interest-rate uncertainty. A borrower is concerned that interest rates will rise prior to a future loan, while naturally a lender is concerned about a possible fall in interest rates. This exposure arises from intended or actual dealings in the physical market, which is usually the short-term money market when it is being hedged by transactions in the BAB futures market.

For example, a company expecting to issue BABs in the future is exposed to the risk that interest rates will rise before the bills are issued. Given that they are discount securities, the company will raise less funds (i.e. pay a higher yield for the funds sought) in the event that the issue yield is higher than expected. Such a company could use a position in the BAB futures market to pre-set its effective borrowing rate — removing uncertainty about the interest cost of the future borrowing.

We will illustrate how bill futures can hedge this risk. Suppose the company plans to issue a parcel of ten promissory notes, each with a face value of $1 million in June, on which it will pay the bank-bill rate. Because its plans are being made in February, it seeks to pre-set its effective issue yield. This can be achieved if the company sells ten June bill-futures contracts in February. In other words, the company will acquire a short position — holding ten 'sold' contracts — in the market for June bill futures.

With reference to equation (17.1), in this illustration, $A_{t,T}$ refers to the actual proceeds of the issue of the ten notes in June, $H_{t,T}$ refers to the profit or loss that arises from the company's short position in June bill futures, and V_t refers to the company's net proceeds — from the actual issue of the notes adjusted for the profit/loss on its futures position ($A_{t,T} + H_{t,T}$).

The company takes a short position in the June bill-futures market because it will generate profits should interest rates rise. Recall the see-saw diagram. The role of the hedge is to appreciate in value in response to the variable that causes the physical position to depreciate. If the company acquired the long position in ten contracts and interest rates rose, its futures position would depreciate in value and so would not perform as a hedge.

Observe that the value of the short position increases should the actual issue yield exceed that embedded in the purchase price of the short position. Assuming the contracts were sold at 91.65 (i.e. a yield of 8.35%), the value of this sold position is:

$$V_{sold} = 10\left(\frac{1\ 000\ 000}{1 + 0.0835 * 90/365}\right)$$

$$= \$9\ 798\ 263$$

Further, assume that in June the futures position is reversed (i.e. ten June contracts are purchased) at a BBR of 8.75%, this being the yield at which the notes are issued. The value of the bought position is:

$$V_{bought} = 10\left(\frac{1\ 000\ 000}{1 + 0.0875 * 90/365}\right)$$

$$= \$9\ 788\ 803$$

Because the yield in the money market in June exceeded the forward rate that was embedded in the June futures contracts, the hedge (ten short June contracts at 8.35%) when closed out in June at 8.75%, created a profit of $9460 which supplements the proceeds the company receives when issuing its notes at 8.75%. In terms of equation (17.1), where V is the company's net proceeds from issuing the notes and completing its hedge:

$$= 9\ 788\ 800 + 9460$$

$$= \$9\ 798\ 260$$

The net proceeds is equal to an issue yield of 8.35%, the forward rate which the company pre-set by taking the short position in bill futures:

$$r = \left(\frac{F}{P - 1}\right)/t$$

$$= \left(\frac{10\ 000\ 000}{9\ 798\ 260} - 1\right)/\left(\frac{90}{365}\right)$$

$$= 8.35\%\ \text{p.a.}$$

As noted above, the yields in the futures market are forward rates, whereas the yields in the money market are spot rates. But on contract dates, when the bills in the futures contract are about to be (notionally) issued, the yields for that contract and in the money market will be the same. Traders would arbitrage between these markets on that day if the yields differed. Hence, in the foregoing illustration we assumed that the short futures position would be closed out at the same rate as the notes were issued (i.e. the BBR in the money market).

The role of the hedge is to pre-set the forward rate. Note that had the company been able to issue its notes at 8.00%, because rates had fallen unexpectedly, the hedge would negate this benefit. The short position will fall in value, being reversed at 8.00% — shown as follows:

$$V_{bought} = 10\left(\frac{1\ 000\ 000}{1 + 0.08 * 90/365}\right)$$

$$= \$9\ 806\ 556$$

The loss on the short futures position is, $V_{bought} - V_{sold}$

$$9\,806\,556 - 9\,798\,263 = \$8293$$

In this event the company will raise $9 806 560 when it issues the notes at 8.00%, but lose $8300 on its hedge position. Hence, its effective proceeds will be $9 798 260 which, as calculated above, represents a yield of 8.35%.

In either situation, the futures position fulfils its objective of allowing the company to set its borrowing cost in advance. Using the see-saw metaphor, it counterbalances the unexpected movements in yields (i.e. actual yields being different from the forward yield), and establishes the forward yield.

Purposes of bank-accepted bill-futures contracts

BAB futures have a wide range of uses, but are principally employed to manage interest-rate risk for borrowers and lenders. Although not an exhaustive list, the following is a summary of the principal uses of bank-bill futures:

- to hedge a borrowing cost. A company intending to borrow short-term funds in the future can sell bank-bill futures to set the borrowing rate;
- to hedge an investment yield. A company intending to lend short-term funds in the future can buy bank-bill futures to set the lending rate, to insure against rates dropping below the forward rate;
- to hedge over a longer period. By using a series of futures contracts for delivery in consecutive financial quarter months (March, June, September and December), a borrower or lender can set an interest rate for a period of up to five years. This is known as **strip hedging** and effectively creates a synthetic long-term security. We demonstrate this process below;
- for arbitrage. At times, when futures prices are out of line with the physical bank-bill market, it is possible to undertake what is known as **cash and carry**. This involves buying physical bank bills with a term longer than 90 days and later delivering them as 90-day bills against sold futures contracts. **Reverse cash and carry** involves buying a short-term bill and then taking delivery of bills under a bought futures contract to lengthen the term of the investment.

The terms **tic**, **pip**, or **point** are used in many markets, including the futures market. Each of these words is a synonym for the smallest possible movement in value of a contract. The tic value is important in interest-rate contracts as it provides an easy approximation of trading profit or loss. Given the curvilinear relationship between the value of a bank-bill futures contract and changes in the market yield (this relationship was shown in Chapter 4 for bills) it is difficult to compute changes in the value of a bank-bill futures contract consequent upon a basis-point change in the forward yield. However, if we know the tic value, changes in the value of a contract may be approximated by multiplying changes in the number of points by the tic value. Observe the tic values presented in the final column of table 17.6.

Strip hedge

A **strip hedge** is a sequence of single-period instruments with successive contract (or expiry) dates that are simultaneously acquired to hedge an exposure to a series of movements in a market variable. In the case of a **futures strip**, a sequence of futures contracts is acquired to hedge interest-rate risk over a number of 90-day periods. Suppose the following futures contracts are traded at the prices shown below. The simultaneous sale (or purchase) of the contracts would establish a strip hedge in relation to the spot rates on each of the future dates.

September	92.50	(i.e. a forward yield of 7.50%)
December	92.20	(i.e. a forward yield of 7.80%)
March	92.00	(i.e. a forward yield of 8.00%)

A strip hedge converts a single-period hedge instrument, such as the September bill-futures contract, into a component of a multi-period hedge arrangement, when it is acquired along with futures contracts with subsequent contract dates. One source of demand for a futures strip arises from the interest-rate risk implicit in a bill-facility arrangement.

Suppose a bank approves (in June) a 270-day bill facility for a company with a face value of $5 million, with the first parcel of bills being issued in mid September. This company is exposed to the risk that the spot rates for 90-day bills in September, December and next March will be higher than the prevailing forward rates in the bill-futures market. The company could hedge this risk by immediately selling five bill-futures contracts for the corresponding contract dates.

The above contract prices indicate the forward rates that the company could lock in as their future effective spot rates when the bills are rolled over. The company could leave its interest-rate risk exposure unhedged. It might decide to follow that path if its management believed that interest rates will be lower than the forward rates. Alternatively, it could decide to lock in these rates if the company was satisfied with the cost of funds they imply.

The effect of this strip hedge in locking in the forward rates can be demonstrated with the following worksheet that assumes the bill-market spot rates are 8.00% in September, 8.00% December and 7.50% March:

Contract date	*V_{sell} five bill futures*	*V_{buy} five (close-out)*	*Profit*	*Issue proceeds*	*Net proceeds*	*Effective yield (%)*
September	4 909 213	4 903 278	5 935	4 903 278	4 909 213	7.50
December	4 905 650	4 903 278	2 372	4 903 278	4 905 650	7.80
March	4 903 278	4 909 213	(5 935)	4 909 213	4 903 278	8.00

Note that the futures strip established the forward rate as the effective yield by offsetting the difference between that rate and the actual spot rate when the bills were issued. This outcome is summarised in table 17.10.

Table 17.10 Strip hedging with bill futures

Contract date	*Contracts sold at*	*Actual market rate on contract dates*	*Effective interest rate on roll-over dates (% p.a.)*
September	92.50	${}_0r_1 = 8.00\%$	${}_0r_1 + (7.50 - {}_0r_1) = 7.50$
December	92.20	${}_0r_1 = 8.00\%$	${}_0r_1 + (7.80 - {}_0r_1) = 7.80$
March	92.00	${}_0r_1 = 7.50\%$	${}_0r_1 + (8.00 - {}_0r_1) = 8.00$

Note that in the foregoing illustration the acceptance and bill-facility fees were ignored for simplicity. They can be allowed for in the issue proceeds and effective yield columns. To illustrate, suppose these fees amounted to 150 basis points. The net proceeds in September would be, given the assumed spot rate of 8.00%, as follows:

$$P = \frac{5\ 000\ 000}{1 + (0.08 + 0.015)\ 90/365}$$

$$= \$4\ 885\ 557$$

The effective yield for the initial issue of bills would be:

$$r = \left(\frac{5\ 000\ 000}{4\ 885\ 557 + 5935} - 1\right)\frac{365}{90}$$

$$= 9.00\%\ (\text{i.e. } 7.50 + 1.50)$$

Basis risk

Before completing this discussion of bill futures, we will briefly discuss the assumptions that underpinned the perfect hedge that was demonstrated above. As noted earlier in this chapter, hedging often involves basis risk because of imperfect hedges. This can arise when:

- the yield in the money market is not the BBR. For instance, many borrowers pay a floating rate that differs from BBR and so the settlement payment when the futures position is closed-out might not precisely adjust the issue yield so as to match the forward rate;
- the amount borrowed is not some multiple of $1 million, the face value of the bill-futures contract, and the securities are not issued in contract months;
- the dates when the securities are issued do not match the contract dates in the futures market. This can arise with a bill facility that sustains funding over a multiple of 90-day periods, whereas the four contract dates in the futures market are neither exactly 90 days apart nor do they match the 360-day year covered by a four-period 90-day bill facility.

Despite these practical imperfections, futures contracts are very efficient hedging instruments, considering their low cost and absence of credit risk. Evidence of this is provided by the very heavy use of futures by parties exposed to interest-rate and price risk.

Bond-futures contracts

Ten-year Commonwealth Treasury bond futures are among the most active of the Sydney Futures Exchange's markets. The contracts provide the means for holders of Treasury bond portfolios and potential investors in Treasury bonds to protect themselves from the adverse effects of changing interest rates. A summary of the ten-year bond futures contract is presented in table 17.11 and of the three-year contract in table 17.12.

Table 17.11 Summary of the ten-year bond-futures contract

Contract unit	Commonwealth Government Treasury bonds with a face value of $100 000, a coupon rate of 12% per annum and a term to maturity of ten years, no tax rebate allowed.
Cash settlement price	The arithmetic mean of quotations provided at 9.45 a.m., 10.30 a.m. and 11.15 a.m. on the last day of trading provided by 12 dealers, randomly selected for each time, at which they would buy and sell bonds in a basket of maturities set down in advance by the exchange, excluding the two highest and two lowest buying quotations and the two highest and two lowest selling quotations.
Cash settlement process	All bought and sold contracts in existence as at the close of trading in the contract months shall be settled by the clearing house at the cash settlement price.
Quotations	Prices shall be quoted in yield per annum per 100 dollars face value in multiples of 0.005%. For quotation purposes the yield shall be deducted from 100.00. (The minimum fluctuation of 0.005% equals approximately $44 per contract, varying with the levels of interest rates.)
Contract months	March, June, September and December up to two quarterly months ahead.
Termination of trading	The fifteenth day of the cash settlement month (or the next succeeding business day where the fifteenth day is not a business day). Trading ceases at 12.00 noon.
Settlement day	The business day following the last permitted day for trading.

A ten-year bond futures contract is effectively an agreement to buy or sell ten-year Treasury bonds with a face value of $100 000 on a specified date in the future. A three-year bond futures contract is effectively an agreement to buy or sell three-year bonds with a face value of $100 000, on a specified date in the future. In practice, the contracts can be used either as a temporary substitute for holding bonds, or as a means of protection against a downturn in the value of a bond portfolio. Because no delivery can take place under the contract as it is now constituted, the effect of the agreement is that one party will either pay to or receive from another party a sum of money, according to whether the value of the contract has increased or decreased after the contract was made.

A bond dealer expecting to invest in Treasury bonds in the future is at risk because, if interest rates fall, the bonds will be more expensive and the dealer will be investing at a lower interest rate. The dealer could hedge this risk by purchasing bond-futures contracts in the meantime to fix the rate at which the money will be invested.

On the other side of the coin, a portfolio manager responsible for the management of a large holding of Treasury bonds is at risk if interest rates rise, since this would reduce the value of the portfolio's assets. To hedge this price risk the portfolio manager would sell the required number of bond-futures contracts because this will generate a profit on the futures contracts should rates rise, to offset the fall in the value of the actual bonds. If interest rates fall, there will be a loss on the futures position, offsetting the increase in the value of the physical bonds.

Table 17.12 Summary of the three-year bond-futures contract

Contract unit	Commonwealth Government Treasury bonds with a face value of $100 000, a coupon rate of 12% per annum and a term to maturity of three years, no tax rebate allowed.
Cash settlement price	The arithmetic mean of quotations provided at 9.45 a.m., 10.30 a.m. and 11.15 a.m. on the last day of trading provided by 12 dealers, randomly selected for each time, at which they would buy and sell bonds in a basket of maturities set down in advance by the exchange, excluding the two highest and two lowest buying quotations and the two highest and two lowest selling quotations.
Mandatory cash settlement	All bought and sold contracts in existence as at the close of trading in the contract month shall be settled by the clearing house at the cash settlement price.
Price quotations	Prices shall be quoted in yield per annum per 100 dollars face value in multiples of 0.01%. For quotation purposes the yield shall be deducted from 100.00. (The minimum fluctuation of 0.01% equals approximately $28 per contract, varying with the level of interest rates.)
Contract months	March, June, September and December up to two quarterly months ahead.
Termination of trading	The fifteenth day of the cash settlement month (or the next succeeding business day where the fifteenth day is not a business day). Trading ceases at 12.00 noon.
Settlement day	The business day following the last permitted day of trading.

To illustrate, suppose you manage a bond portfolio with a face value of $10 million and by June half of the bonds have a ten-year term and the other half a three-year term. You believe that between March and June the ten-year bond rate is likely to rise by one percentage point and the three-year rate is likely to rise by 50 basis points. How could you use bond futures to hedge your perceived interest-rate risk?

You would sell 50 ten-year and 50 three-year bond-futures contracts (recall that each has a face value of $100 000) to establish your hedge. Given that you hold 12% coupon bonds, your hedge would protect the present value of your portfolio as follows, assuming the following movements in interest rates:

	March	*June*
three-year	8.5% p.a.	10.0% p.a.
ten-year	9.0% p.a.	10.0% p.a.

Change in the portfolio's value in June:
three-year 12% bonds with a face value of $5 000 000:

$P_{8.5\%}$ = $5 454 977

$P_{10.0\%}$ = $5 253 785

fall in value = $201 192

ten-year 12% bonds with a face value of $5 000 000:

$P_{9\%}$ = $5 975 595

$P_{10.0\%}$ = $5 623 110

fall in value = $352 485

fall in value
of portfolio = $553 677

Futures position:
three-year futures:

sell at 91.50 (= 8.5%): value = 109 100 * 50 = $5 454 977

buy at 90.00 (= 10%): value = 105 075.70 * 50 = $5 253 785

profit = $201 192

ten-year bond futures:

sell at 91.00 (= 9%): value = 119 512 * 50 = $5 623 110

buy at 90.00 (= 10%): value = 112 462 * 50 = $5 975 595

profit = $352 485

Total profit in futures market = $553 677

(See example 17.3.)

example 17.3

Suppose you purchase five ten-year bond futures at $89.50 and sell a number of three-year bond futures at $90.50. Roughly how many three-year bond futures must be sold in order that your overall position would remain unaffected by a 1% across-the-board increase in interest rates?

$$P_{(10\text{ year: }90.50)} = 6000 * a_{\overline{20}|\,0.095/2} + \frac{100\,000}{(1 + 0.095/2)^{20}} = \$115\,913$$

$$P_{(10\text{ year: }89.50)} = 6000 * a_{\overline{20}|\,0.105/2} + \frac{100\,000}{(1 + 0.105/2)^{20}} = \$109\,152$$

Change of value on five contracts = 5 * (115 913 − 109 152) = $33 805

$$P_{(3\text{ year: }90.50)} = 6000 * a_{\overline{6}|\,0.095/2} + \frac{100\,000}{(1 + 0.095/2)^{6}} = \$106\,396$$

$$P_{(3\text{ year: }89.50)} = 6000 * a_{\overline{6}|\,0.105/2} + \frac{100\,000}{(1 + 0.105/2)^{6}} = \$103\,777$$

Change of value on 1 contract = 106 396 − 103 777 = $2619

Thus the number of three-year bond-futures contracts needed for the hedge is:

$$\frac{33\,805}{2619} = 12.9$$

A wide range of risk-management strategies is available using bond futures. Although not exhaustive, the following is a summary of the principal uses of bond futures.

- to hedge a portfolio of bonds. An institution holding physical bonds could sell ten-year bond futures to protect itself against a decline in their value caused by rising interest rates;
- to price a future investment in bonds. A life office with maturing investments that it plans to reinvest could buy bond futures to reduce the risk of a fall in interest rates in the interim;
- as a substitute for holding physical bonds. A bond dealer unable to obtain physical bonds could buy futures as a temporary substitute until actual bonds became available. Also, dealers can use a futures position to change a portfolio's duration;
- to hedge portfolios of similar instruments. An institution holding long-term semi-government bonds could sell bond futures as a hedge, provided the difference in yields was taken into account and volatilities were correctly matched;
- for arbitrage and spreads. When futures prices are not aligned with yields in the bond market, arbitrage opportunities are created. Futures can be used to exploit these opportunities as well as those that arise from yield-curve changes. For example, when the yield curve shifts from inverse to flat, traders would profit if they were long short-term bond futures because the fall in short-term yields would increase the value of their futures position.

Share Price Index

Trading in SPI futures began on the Sydney Futures Exchange in 1983, about a year after their introduction in the United States. SPI futures have had considerable success in Australia, although futures trading volume has fluctuated in line with the volumes traded in the actual stockmarket. A summary of the features of SPI futures contracts is presented in table 17.13.

SPI futures are, in effect, agreements to buy or sell a broadly based parcel of shares on a future contract date. The futures contract is based on the Australian Stock Exchange (ASX) All Ordinaries Share Price Index, which, in turn, is based on the prices of about 300 listed shares, representing over 80% of the value of shares traded on the ASX.

In practice, no delivery of actual shares takes place. Instead, the effect of the agreement is that one party will either pay to or receive from another party, a sum of money, according to whether the value of the contract on the futures market has increased or decreased after the contract was made.

Table 17.13 Summary, SPI futures contract

Contract unit	A sum of money equal to 25 times the Australian Stock Exchange's All Ordinaries Share Price Index expressed in Australian dollars.
Cash settlement price	The closing quotation for the Australian Stock Exchange's All Ordinaries Share Price Index on the last day of trading calculated to one decimal place, as adjusted and provided by Australian Stock Exchange (Sydney) Limited to the clearing house at 12.00 noon on the business day following the last day of trading.
Cash settlement process	All bought and sold contracts in existence as at the close of trading in the contract month shall be settled by the clearing house at the cash settlement price.
Price quotations	Prices shall be quoted in the same form as the Australian Stock Exchange's All Ordinaries Share Price Index expressed to one full index point. On the final trading day only, provision exists for the minimum fluctuation to be in 0.1 index points.
Contract months	March, June, September and December up to six quarters ahead.
Termination of trading	The last business day of the contract month. On this day, trading terminates at 4.10 p.m. or such other time as determined by the board.
Settlement day	The second business day following the last permitted day of trading.

Source: Sydney Futures Exchange

The value of the contract at its maturity is the actual All Ordinaries Index on the last day of trading, multiplied by 25 and expressed in Australian dollars. So, if the index is 2250, the value of the contract is $A56 250. A participant who had previously entered into a futures contract to buy at 2125 would have an unrealised profit of \$3125 (\$56 250 − \$53 125). A further illustration of trading in SPI futures contracts is presented in example 17.4.

example 17.4

What is the profit attached to a round transaction of a bearish speculator who sold two SPI contracts at 2455, in anticipation of a sharemarket decline, only to be forced to buy them back, after the market rallied, at 2490?

Profit = 100 * Quantity * (Sale price − Purchase price)

= 100 * 2 * (2455 − 2490)

= −\$7000

The SPI is a convenient medium for speculation on the future direction of the share market. A speculator, convinced that the market is about to rise, may buy SPI contracts. On the other hand, a speculator who believes the market will fall will sell SPI futures. The SPI contract, as well as facilitating speculative transactions, also provides services to hedgers.

The SPI futures contract can be used as either a temporary substitute for holding shares, or as a means of protection against a fall in the value of a share portfolio. The holder of a share portfolio would agree to sell in the futures market to manage the risk of a downturn in share prices. This is a short hedge. At any time before the contract matures, the trader may close out the position to remove any obligation under the contract. If, in the meantime, the All Ordinaries Index has fallen, there will be a futures profit to offset the decline in the value of the actual shares. If the sharemarket rises, there will be a loss on the futures market, but this will be offset by the increase in the value of the shares.

If a contract is still open on the last trading day, the clearing house requires traders to close out their positions at the current contract value, based on the price of the actual All Ordinaries Index on that day.

Similarly, traders can create a long hedge by purchasing future contracts. This enables investors who intend to invest in a broad range of shares in the future to pre-set their entry price to the sharemarket.

example 17.5

How would you protect a fund, with a total portfolio value of \$337 500, from a general decline in share prices if the value of the portfolio generally correlates with movements in the value of the All Ordinaries Index? Assume the AOI is currently 2230 and the December futures price is 2250.

The value of a December contract is currently:

25 * 2250 = \$56 250

The portfolio can thus be hedged by selling:

$$337\,500/56\,250 = 6 \text{ contracts}$$

The hope with this strategy is that any decline in the value of the portfolio will be offset by a profit on the six futures contracts.

Suppose after selling six SPI contracts at 2250 the index subsequently fell by 8% and the December contract fell to 2070. The portfolio's position would be:

$$\text{Value of the portfolio} = 337\,500 * (1 - 0.08) = \$310\,500$$

$$\text{Futures profit} = 25 * 6 * (2250 - 2070) = \$27\,000$$

$$\text{Total value} = \$337\,500$$

The loss on the value of the portfolio was compensated for by the profit on the futures contract.

In example 17.5, the value of the portfolio varied precisely with the change in the AOI. Often the value of a portfolio of shares will not be perfectly correlated with the movements in the AOI and so the hedge will not be perfect. This problem might be overcome by using the number of contracts that best correlates with the movement in the index. If the portfolio's value is more volatile than the index, for instance, a larger number of futures contracts may provide a close hedge.

Another way of adjusting for differences between the index and a particular share portfolio is to use the **beta** of the portfolio. This shows the relationship between movements in the value of the portfolio and the value of the index. Suppose, in the above example, that the portfolio had a beta of 1.25, which indicates that on average the value of the portfolio will fluctuate 12.5% for every 10% movement in the index. The number of futures contracts needed is given by:

$$\text{Contracts} = \frac{(\text{value of portfolio} * \text{beta})}{(25 * \text{value of index})} \qquad \textit{Equation (17.4)}$$

Relationship between the price of SPI futures contracts and the current AOI

It is worth taking a moment to consider the nature of the relationship between the value of the All Ordinaries Index and the theoretical value of the SPI futures price. We show below that the future price should be related to the rate of interest (which determines the relationship between future and present values generally) adjusted for the average dividend yield.

Consider two portfolios:

Portfolio A: A long futures contract negotiated at a price, F, and an amount of cash equal to the discounted value of F.

Portfolio B: An amount of the All Ordinaries 'commodity' equal to $1/(1 + d * t)$, where d is the average dividend rate and t is the time to maturity, with all dividends being reinvested, so that at maturity there will be a unit of the All Ordinaries commodity.

At the maturity of the contract, both portfolios will consist of one unit of the All Ordinaries 'commodity'. (The cash in Portfolio A is used to purchase the contract on the futures contract's maturity date.) Thus the portfolios must have the same value now. That is:

$$\frac{F}{(1 + rt)} = \frac{S}{(1 + dt)}$$

or

$$F = S(1 + (r - d)t) \qquad \textit{Equation (17.5)}$$

where S is the value of the All Ordinaries Index,
r is the risk-free rate of interest,
t is time in years, and
d is the average dividend yield.

To illustrate, the June SPI contract will have the following theoretical value in March when the current index is 2280, the risk-free interest rate is 8.00% and the average dividend yield over the next three months is 4% p.a.:

$$F = 2280\,(1 + ((0.08 - 0.04) * 3/12))$$

$$= 2280\,(1.1)$$

$$= \$2302$$

Forward-rate agreements

A forward-rate agreement, known also as an FRA, is an arrangement between two parties that determines an interest rate for a period that commences at a pre-set future date. An FRA is not an agreement to provide funds; rather, it determines a future borrowing or lending rate. The forward interest rate would be set having in mind the forward rates in the bill-futures market.

> *The FRA market began in London in 1983 and quickly spread to Australia where it is a large sector of the OTC derivatives markets.* (Carew, 1994, p. 4)

During the period 1991 to 1994, 64% of FRAs covered in the AFMA annual surveys were for periods of three months or less, the majority of which were between financial institutions. A very small proportion were for periods beyond a year. As at June 1994, the reported value of outstanding FRAs was $260 billion. (AFMA, 1994, pp. 37–42)

The essential features of an FRA are illustrated in figure 17.5. These are the settlement date, when the agreed forward rate commences and the maturity date.

The period of the FRA (three months in figure 17.5) determines the amount of the settlement payment along with the difference between the rate in the money market and the agreed rate and the amount of funding involved. This is either the face value of short-dated securities or the amount borrowed from an institution.

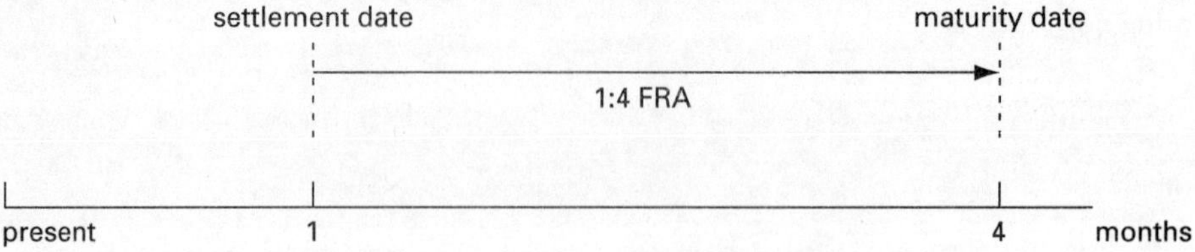

Figure 17.5 Forward-rate agreement

The purpose of FRAs is to facilitate borrowing or lending forward. They are, in effect, a non-deliverable discount bill contract. In this and other senses they are very similar to the bank-bill futures contracts that are traded on the SFE. However, FRAs are dealt party to party (usually by a bank or a merchant bank) and, to some extent, contract specifications are customised to meet the needs of the borrower and lender. The SFE futures contracts are based on 90-day paper, whereas FRAs can establish forward rates that exceed 90 days.

FRAs are distinguished by their:

- starting and ending dates. For example, the 1:4 FRA shown in figure 17.5 covers a three-month period that starts in a month;
- their agreed rate. This could be 8.55% p.a. for three months;
- the amount of the funding at risk such as $5 million face value of a planned bill issue; and
- the settlement payment. This is structured to be to the lender (a negative amount is paid by the lender to the borrower), and is paid at the commencement of the funding period.

The settlement procedure involves a cash payment by or to the lender. The settlement amount provided by the lender is based on the difference between the value of a discounted bill at the agreed FRA rate and the value of the bill at the market rate at the time the loan is notionally to commence. The settlement amount, when hedging a short-dated security, is:

$$\begin{aligned} \text{Settlement}_{\text{(to lender)}} &= \text{Value}_{\text{market}} - \text{Value}_{\text{agreed}} \\ &= \frac{F}{1 + rt_{mkt}} - \frac{F}{1 + rt_{agd}} \end{aligned}$$

Equation (17.6)

where, F is the face value of the bill being discounted,
r_{agd} is FRA agreed rate,
r_{mkt} is market rate at settlement date, and
t is term of the security in years.

To illustrate, suppose a company requires additional funds and decides to issue bills with a face value of $2 million in July. Its bank agrees to accept these bills and offers the company an FRA rate of 8.45%, which the company accepts. If this deal occurred in April it would be referred to as a 3:6 FRA that is settled in July when the bills are issued. Suppose further that when the bills are issued, the market yield is 8.25%. The settlement payment will be, treating t as a quarter of the year:

$$\text{Settlement} = \frac{2\ 000\ 000}{1 + 0.0825 * 0.25} - \frac{2\ 000\ 000}{1 + 0.0845 * 0.25}$$

$$= 1\ 959\ 584 - 1\ 958\ 624$$

$$= \$960$$

The company is required to pay the bank $960 when the bills are issued because the payment is to the lender by the borrower. The settlement payment by the borrower is plausible given that the bills were issued at 8.25%; the borrower benefited from the market yield being less than the agreed rate. Recall again equation (17.1). V refers to the net proceeds, A is the proceeds at 8.25% and H is the hedge which, in this example, is a negative amount that has the effect of locking in the agreed rate, 8.45%. This outcome is demonstrated as follows:

$$r = \left(\frac{2\ 000\ 000}{1\ 959\ 584 - 960} - 1\right) / \left(\frac{3}{12}\right)$$

$$= 8.45\%$$

In the case of a bank loan, the principal amount can be converted to the future amount at the agreed rate to calculate the settlement payment with equation (17.6).

To illustrate, suppose a bank agrees in February to lend $1.5 million to a company in May for three months, with interest paid at the end of the quarter at the May BBR. The company is exposed to the risk that the BBR will increase between February and May. It decides to enter a 3:6 FRA with the bank at an agreed rate of 8.35% (having in mind the forward rate in the futures market for June is 8.40%). The future amount of the loan in May (at the agreed rate) is:

$$F = 1\ 500\ 000\ (1 + 0.0835 * 0.25)$$

$$= \$1\ 531\ 312.50$$

Suppose the BBR in May is 8.55%. The FRA's settlement payment will be:

$$\text{Settlement} = \frac{1\ 531\ 312.50}{1 + 0.0855 * 0.25} - \frac{1\ 531\ 312.50}{1 + 0.0835 * 0.25}$$

$$= 1\ 499\ 265.70 - 1\ 500\ 000$$

$$= -\$734$$

Being a negative payment to the lender, this amount is received by the borrower to counterbalance the effect of the higher interest rate on the loan. That is, the borrower receives $1 500 734 in May and repays:

$$F_{8.55\%} = 1\ 500\ 000 * (1 + 0.0855 * 0.25)$$
$$= 1\ 532\ 062.50$$

Hence the effective cost of the funds is:

$$r = \left(\frac{1\ 532\ 062.50}{1\ 500\ 734} - 1\right)\frac{12}{3}$$
$$= 8.35\%$$

An illustration of the use of FRAs to hedge the return to an investor is presented in example 17.6.

example 17.6

As the company treasurer you are aware that in three months' time your company will be able to invest $5 million for six months. You are satisfied with the forward rate of 9% p.a. (available in the futures market), but you are worried by the possibility that rates will fall over the next three months. You decide to hedge your future borrowings by 'buying' a 3:9 FRA at 9% p.a. (Note that the lender buys and the borrower sells the FRA.)

It transpires that in three months, consistent with your fears, interest rates have fallen to 8% p.a. What will be the settlement payment, assuming there are 182 days in the six-month period covered by the FRA?

The future value of the company's investment in 182 days will be:

$$F = 5\ 000\ 000\ (1 + 0.09 * 182/365)$$
$$= 5\ 224\ 384$$

$$\text{Settlement} = \frac{5\ 224\ 384}{1 + 0.08\ (182/365)} - \frac{5\ 224\ 384}{1 + 0.09\ (182/365)}$$
$$= 5\ 023\ 976 - 5\ 000\ 000$$
$$= \$23\ 976$$

Hence, $23 976 is paid to your company (as the lender) to compensate for the lower actual investment rate. When the company invests, it will have to pay $5 023 976 for securities with a face value of $5 224 384 because of the 8.00% market yield. But it will receive $23 976 from its FRA, and thus the company only outlays $5 million. Its effective investment yield will be:

$$r = \left(\frac{5\ 224\ 384}{5\ 023\ 976 - 23\ 976} - 1\right)\frac{365}{182} = 9.00\%$$

PRICING FORWARD-RATE AGREEMENTS

FRAs are priced off the bill-futures strip. Bill futures dominate the market for short-term funds. FRA rates are set with reference to the forward rates set in the futures market. The FRA market, being an OTC market, caters to a wide range of clients, ranging from very small to very large (e.g. $1 billion) transactions. As a consequence, there is a range of spreads in the FRA market, although generally they are wider than those in the bill-futures market. This phenomenon is illustrated in figure 17.6.

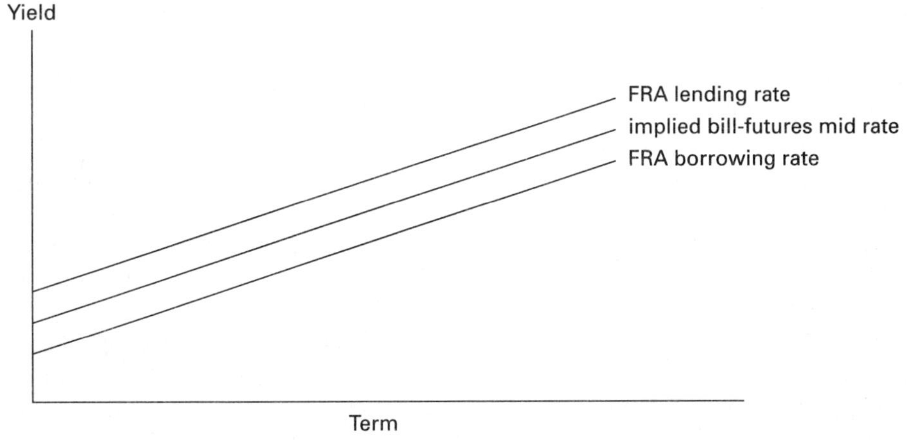

Figure 17.6 Bid and offer FRA rates and bill-futures forward rates

Forward-rate agreements versus bill futures

The main alternative instrument to an FRA is interest-rate futures. The main differences between them are as follows:

- FRAs are arranged in relation to the party's actual interest-rate risk; that is, in relation to the rate, amount and timing of the intended borrowing or lending. Bill futures may involve basis risk unless the features of the physical transactions align with the timing of the futures settlement dates and are at BBR.
- The credit risk of FRAs is limited to the settlement amount, whereas in the futures market, the clearing house carries the credit risk.
- There is no secondary market in FRAs, whereas there is for futures. However, an FRA counterparty may be able to close-out the position, if an opposite deal can be made.
- FRAs are sold by banks to both borrowers and lenders and earn a spread between these rates. The spread is usually only one or two basis points, but this can represent a greater transaction cost than for futures.
- FRAs involve no associated daily resettlement payments as can (but need not) occur with bill futures.

In the case of hedging a floating-rate facility, a futures strip can be established (up to five years ahead). The same can be arranged through a strip of FRAs, although the bulk of FRAs are for periods of less than a year.

Summary

The main points of this chapter are as follows:

- Futures markets facilitate risk management as well as speculation.
- A futures position is a contractual arrangement with upside and downside risk.
- Futures are traded through an exchange, such as the Sydney Futures Exchange.
- The clearing house absorbs the counterparty risk of futures contracts and facilitates trading with minimal margins.
- There are four settlement dates each year and trading is conducted, in the case of the bank-bill contract, up to five years ahead.
- The prices of bill-futures contracts reveal 90-day forward rates.
- Bill and bond futures can be used to hedge a future borrowing cost and a future investment yield.
- SPI futures can be used to hedge a share portfolio from adverse movements in share prices, but in the process the upside potential is traded to eliminate the downside risk.
- An FRA is an agreement between two parties to establish a forward interest rate.
- The FRA involves a settlement amount which is paid at the commencement of the term of the FRA by the party that is favoured by the difference between the contract rate and the actual interest rate on settlement day.
- The payment of the settlement amount results in both parties achieving the agreed forward rate.
- FRAs are an alternative hedging device to interest-rate futures. They have the advantage of being an over-the-counter instrument, but they have no secondary market.

Discussion questions and exercises

1 Briefly explain the theory of hedging using derivative instruments and suggest why it is important that the value of a hedge should vary with the variable that causes risk in the underlying physical market.

2 Discuss the trading and settlement operations of the Sydney Futures Exchange (and its clearing house). Refer in your answer to the role and features of the system of deposits and daily margins.

3 Explain how long and short positions can be acquired in the futures market and the role of the close-out transaction generally, and for non-deliverable futures contracts in particular.

4 Discuss the bill-futures contract. Use a current example to show how the value of a contract differs from its price. Also, demonstrate that the movement in prices matches the direction of the change in the value of the contracts.

5 Explain (a) how the prices for bill-futures contracts reveal forward 90-day interest rates, and (b) why the yield embedded in a bill-futures contract equals the spot rate in the bill market on its contract date.

6 Explain how a long futures position can hedge an investor who in June will be reinvesting $1 000 000 in the 90-day bill market. Illustrate your answer with reference to the following circumstance. Suppose the June bill-futures contract is trading (in April) at 92.75 and that in June the actual market yield on a 90-day bank bill is 6.75% p.a. Calculate the investor's profit/loss position in the futures market. Repeat your calculations, assuming the spot rate in June is 6.00% p.a.

7 What is a futures strip? How is it established and how does it convert a single-period hedging instrument into a multi-period hedging instrument?

8 Explain how a borrower can use the bill-futures market to lock in the forward rates to remove the uncertainty arising from a one-year bill facility with a face value of $10 million. Refer to the futures prices published in the daily newspaper in your answer and demonstrate how positions in the futures market pre-set the market cost of funds during the one-year facility.

9 What is basis risk? Suggest how it can arise in the case of a strip of bill futures that has been acquired to hedge the interest-rate risk arising from a one-year bill facility.

10 Suppose you hold ten 12.00% July 1999 Treasury bonds with a face value of $100 000 each, which you plan to sell in September 1996. You notice that September 1996 three-year bond futures are trading at 91.15 and you believe that by September the three-yield bond yield will be above 9.00% p.a. Explain how you can use bond futures to hedge your interest-rate risk. Demonstrate your explanation, assuming the three-year bond yield is:
(a) 9.50% p.a.
(b) 8.50% p.a.

11 Explain how SPI futures contracts are traded. Suppose your share portfolio is currently (i.e. in June) worth $1 200 000 and you expect share prices to fall over the next three months. Given that the beta of your portfolio is 1.1, the All Ordinaries Index is currently 2150 and September SPI futures are trading at 2160, how can you trade in the futures market (using whole contracts only) to hedge your perceived risk? Support your answer with relevant calculations.

12 What are the basic features of an FRA? Compare its operation as a hedging instrument with that of a bill-futures position. Suggest the relationship between the yields in the bill-futures market and the mid-point of the bid and offer FRA rates for three-month FRAs that commence in bill-futures contract months.

13 Suppose a three-month FRA is arranged between a bank and a company in March with a settlement date of 1 May, with an agreed rate of 8.00% p.a., to hedge the interest-rate risk on 90-day bills with a face value of $4 million. If the 90-day rate on 1 May is 7.00% p.a., what is the settlement amount and which party makes this payment?

14 Suppose a bank accepts a $20 million deposit at 6.50% p.a. for six months and invests this amount in a parcel of 90-day bank bills yielding 7.50% p.a. Explain whether the bank might be interested in entering an FRA and what position it would take.

15 Calculate the settlement amount and explain how it ensures that each party locks in a three-month rate of 8.00% p.a. when the settlement date is 1 May, and one party is issuing bills with a face value of $4 000 000 and the other is investing in these bills, given that market yield is 7.50% p.a. on 1 May.

References and Further Reading

AFMA 1994, *1994 Australian Financial Markets Report*, AFMA, Sydney, Chapters 6 and 7.

Carew, Edna 1995, *Derivatives Decoded*, Allen & Unwin, Sydney.

Carew, Edna 1994, *How Australia's Forward-rate Agreement Markets Operate*, AFMA, Sydney.

Daugaard, Dan, & Valentine, Tom 1995, *Financial Risk Management*, Harper Educational, Sydney, Chapters 4 and 5.

Juttner, D. Johannes 1994, *Financial Markets, Interest Rates and Monetary Economics*, 3rd edn, Longman Cheshire, Chapters 26 and 27.

Lewis, M. K. 1993, 'Derivative markets', in M. K. Lewis & R. H. Wallace (eds), *The Australian Financial System*, Longman Cheshire, Melbourne, pp. 391–434 .

Price Waterhouse 1994, *Corporate Derivatives Survey*, Australian Society of Corporate Treasurers.

Sydney Futures Exchange, *Corporate Profile and Contract Specifications*.

18

Swaps

The purposes of this chapter are to explain the operation of fixed-for-floating interest-rate and currency swaps and their use as instruments of interest (and FX) risk management. Interest-rate swaps link the fixed-rate and floating-rate domestic capital markets, whereas currency swaps link domestic capital markets within the global system.

Study objectives

From your study of this chapter you should be able to:

- describe the main forms of interest-rate and currency swaps;
- show how a fixed-for-floating interest-rate swap operates;
- calculate the settlement payments under a fixed-for-floating swap, given the swap rate;
- explain the role and formation of the swap rate in an interest-rate swap;
- explain the principles of swap valuation;
- explain the main purposes of interest-rate swaps;
- describe the main conventions of the Australian swap market; and
- explain the purposes of currency swaps.

INTRODUCTION

Swaps emerged as financial-market instruments in the early 1980s, mainly to allow borrowers to raise funds under the most favoured terms, and convert the proceeds and obligations into their preferred funds. Their development has been an important part of the globalisation of financial markets.

Swaps are used by participants in a domestic capital market to convert interest obligations from one basis to another, such as from a floating-rate to a fixed-rate. Such swaps could change the obligations from a bill facility or a floating-rate note to those of a fixed-rate bond.

You will recall from the discussion in Chapters 10 and 11 that fixed-interest bonds are issued mainly by governmental borrowers, whereas companies are the main issuers of floating-rate paper, such as bills and commercial paper. Most companies that have fixed-interest debt have either issued securities in overseas capital markets or have arranged a term loan from a bank or a syndicate of banks.

Given the predominance of governmental issuers of fixed-rate bonds, companies that would prefer to raise fixed-rate funds from the debt market can achieve this effect by issuing floating-rate paper and arranging a swap with, say, a semi-governmental that has issued bonds and is seeking a floating-rate exposure. (Daugaard and Valentine, 1995, pp. 152–3)

Swaps are made also between parties in different domestic markets, to exchange currency obligations. To illustrate, a company that can readily borrow in the AUD debt market but prefers to raise USD can achieve that outcome indirectly, by swapping its payments on its AUD loan with a company that can readily borrow in the USD debt market but prefers to make payments on an AUD loan.

In the foregoing instances, the swap forms part of a capital market transaction. It would be arranged along with the capital raising itself. In fact, without the swap, a different capital-market transaction would be undertaken.

Almost any set of cash flows that have the same present value can be swapped, including, for example, proceeds from the sale of two commodities. In financial markets, the cash flows that are swapped are generally interest payments and foreign exchange. Given the variety of interest rates, many different cash flows can be swapped. However, the discussion in this chapter is confined to the two most basic (and common) forms of swaps:

- fixed-for-floating interest-rate swaps, and
- currency swaps.

The first is a form of **interest-rate swap**. These are the most widely used interest-rate swap, involving the exchange of fixed-interest obligations for floating-rate obligations. They are known as a **fixed-for-floating** swap, or as a **plain vanilla** swap. Note that the parties do not also swap the principal amounts of their loans.

The second category, **currency swaps**, involves an exchange of all currency payments; that is, both interest and principal amounts are swapped on an agreed-exchange-rate basis. Note that currency swaps are not FX swaps, which, as discussed in Chapter 13, are typically a combined spot and forward FX transaction.

Swaps serve to uncouple the source of financial obligations, such as a loan raised in the bill market, from the interest (and, in the case of currency swaps, foreign-exchange) payments. The benefits of this uncoupling are that borrowers can:

- use swaps to change their interest/FX obligations, typically for risk-management purposes, and
- raise funds under the best terms available, and swap the obligations as desired.

The swap market has developed considerably, even though financial markets have become more widely accessible to borrowers. The main participants in the swap market are financial institutions, although large business enterprises are also important users of swaps.

Table 18.1 Respondents to AFMA's 1994–95 swaps survey

Advance Bank Australia Limited
Australian and New Zealand Banking Group Ltd
Bank of America
Bank of Melbourne
BT Australia Limited
Challenge Bank Limited
Chase AMP Bank Limited
CIBC Australia Limited
Citibank Limited
Commonwealth Bank of Australia
Deutsche Bank Australia Ltd
First Chicago
J. P. Morgan Australia Ltd
Lloyds
National Australia Bank Limited
Nat West
SBC
Schroeders
Société Générale
St George
State Bank of NSW
UBS Australia Ltd
Westpac Banking Corporation

Since the late 1980s, the Swap Dealers Committee of the Australian Financial Markets Association has published the results of annual surveys of the Australian-dollar swap market. The 1994–95 survey (the respondents to which are shown in table 18.1) revealed that $317 billion worth of swaps were dealt in that year (by the survey's respondents) — an increase of 16% on the previous year. Of this overall amount, fixed-to-floating interest-rate swaps totalled $246 billion (up 36% on the previous year) and currency swaps totalled $68 billion (valued in AUD).

The survey indicated the volume of swaps according to the following counterparty categories:

In-house transactions: (transactions with other divisions or subsidiaries of the respondent bank)	AUD152 billion
Respondents: (known participant banks and merchant banks)	AUD40 billion
Other banks: (offshore interbank market dealings)	AUD56 billion
Government and semi-government:	AUD32 billion
Corporate:	AUD36 billion

This pattern of swap users is similar to that in the United States market. (Fabozzi, Modigliani and Ferri, 1994, p. 609)

Table 18.2 Australian interest rates, 9 January 1996

	Dec. 18 %	Jan. 8 %
Official call, average 11 a.m. rate	7.40	7.50
Unofficial overnight, average 11 a.m. rate	7.45	7.45
Domestic Rates:		
90-day dealers-bill rate	7.43	7.47
180-day dealers-bill rate	7.40	7.40
5-year bond yield	7.85	7.72
10-year bond yield	8.41	8.13
Bank-bill swap reference rate (Source: Bloomberg):		
30 days	7.498	7.50
60 days	7.467	7.446
90 days	7.424	7.429
180 days	7.392	7.338
AUD forward-rate agreements (Source: Macquarie Bank):		
1/4	7.36	7.36
3/6	7.25	7.24
6/9	7.17	7.17
Swap rates. Quarterly in arrears versus mean bank bill (Source: CBA):		
1 year	7.33	7.29
3 years	7.66	7.47
5 years	7.98	7.75

Source: *Australian Financial Review*, 9 January 1996

Swaps are traded over the counter by a number of Australian financial intermediaries. Interest-rate swaps are one of the growing number of interest-rate derivative products. Indicative swap rates, along with other important Australian interest rates, are published on a daily basis, as shown in table 18.2. Note that swap rates are quoted by swap dealers in the same way that borrowing and lending rates are quoted by money-market dealers.

Interest-rate swaps

Interest-rate swaps include fixed-for-floating, fixed-for-fixed and floating-for-floating arrangements. In the latter two cases, the counterparties have rates that are set on a different basis. For instance, one borrower could be paying the BBR whereas the other is paying a bank reference rate on an overdraft. By far the most common arrangement is the fixed-for-floating and we will confine our discussion to this type.

The fixed rate in a swap is known as the **swap rate**. Its term defines the term (i.e. length) of the swap. Therefore it can be compared with the yield in the bond market. The floating rate in a swap is based on the market's 'marker' rate. In the Australian market this is the **bank-bill swap rate** (BBSW). It is equivalent to BBR, which is the marker rate in the short-term money market.

In an individual swap, depending on the credit rating of the two parties, the swap payments could be at rates that are above or below the market's swap rate and the BBSW rate. A floating-rate payer could, for instance, pay BBSW less 20 basis points (i.e. 0.002%). Thus, if BBSW was 7.60%, that particular floating-rate swap payment would be at the rate of 7.40% p.a.

We illustrate a fixed-for-floating swap with the following hypothetical example. Suppose Party A enters a swap as the fixed-rate payer, at a rate of 8% p.a. of a notional capital amount of $1 million, for a period of one year. These payments will be made to the other swap party, B, in exchange for floating-rate payments, which are at the rate of BBSW. Naturally, Party B assumes the opposite obligations to Party A by agreeing to receive the fixed-rate interest payments (from A) and to pay BBSW on $1 million for a year. Hence, in the swap, A pays fixed/receives floating and B pays floating/receives fixed. An indication of the cash flows associated with this swap is presented in figure 18.1 and table 18.3.

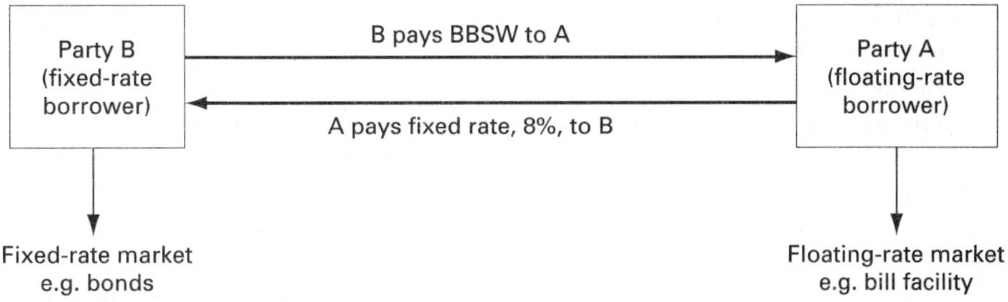

Figure 18.1 Model of a fixed-for-floating interest-rate swap

Observe, in figure 18.1, that as a result of the swap, Party A transforms its floating-rate obligations to the bill market by making fixed-rate payments to B (shown by the heavy arrows), and Party B has transformed its interest obligations to the bond market by making floating-rate payments to A. However, the swap does not change each party's responsibility for the interest obligations under their loans. That is, A remains liable for the payments on its bill facility and B remains responsible for making the payments on the bonds it has issued.

The exact amount of each party's obligations under the swap depends on the interest rates involved and the number of interest periods per year. In Australia, short-term swaps, covering periods up to three years, have four payment periods per year, whereas longer-term swaps have two payment periods per year. Hence, four interest payments are involved in the swap illustration.

Swap payments are made 'in arrears' (i.e. at the end of each payment period), based on the floating rate at the commencement of each payment period. They are calculated as the fixed payment minus the floating-rate payment. Negative amounts represent payments by the floating-rate payer.

Interest-rate swaps are 'priced' by their fixed rate, which is 8.00% p.a. in this illustration. So swap payments made by one party to the other depend upon the BBSW at the commencement of each of the four payment periods. Assuming the BBSW is 7.00% p.a. when the swap is agreed, the initial net payment made by A (the fixed-rate payer under the swap) at the end of the first interest period is calculated as:

$$\$1\,000\,000\ (0.08/4 - 0.07/4) = \$2500$$

The full set of actual net payments made by A to B are shown in table 18.3, given the assumed BBSW rates at the commencement of the four payment periods.

Observe that A makes the net payment at the end of the first quarter because the fixed rate (8.00%) exceeded the floating rate (7.00%) for this quarter. Hence, at the end of the first quarter, A makes two interest payments:

- the interest payment to its bill holders, at the rate of 7.00% p.a., plus
- the payment in the swap.

The combined value of these payments represents an interest rate of 8.00% p.a. Therefore, the effect of the swap has been to change A's effective interest rate to the fixed rate (8.00% in this example). Given that B has received the swap payment, its effective interest rate is reduced from the 8.00% it pays its bond holders, to 7.00% p.a. for the quarter.

No payment is made at the end of the second quarter because both the fixed and floating rates are 8.00%. Finally, B makes the net payments at the end of the third and fourth quarters because the floating rate exceeded the fixed rate. The effect of these payments is to maintain A's effective interest rate at 8.00% and B's at the BBSW rates, which is the function of the swap.

Observe also that the net payments are small relative to the principal amount. This occurs whenever the floating rate is similar to the fixed rate.

Table 18.3 Net payments under an interest-rate swap

Period	*Notional principal ($)*	*Fixed rate (%)*	*BBSW (%)*	*Net payment (A to B) ($)*
First quarter	1 000 000	8.00	7.00	2 500
Second quarter	1 000 000	8.00	8.00	$0
Third quarter	1 000 000	8.00	8.50	-1 250
Fourth quarter	1 000 000	8.00	9.00	-2 500

Even though this swap example is a simplification of an actual swap, we will refer to it throughout this chapter to illustrate a number of swap principals.

The value of a swap

The value of a swap depends on the present value of the two payment streams that are being exchanged. In Chapter 11 we showed how to value a fixed-interest bond. This approach can be used to value the fixed-rate payments in a swap. The value of the floating-rate payments depends, when the swap is established, on the expected future BBSW rates. You will recall from the discussion in the previous chapter that the prices of bill-futures contracts reveal the market's forward rates. Hence these rates can be used to determine the present value of the expected floating-rate payments.

Given that the swap rate is a market-determined rate (i.e. parties are free to enter either side of a swap), the value of the fixed-rate payments can be expected to equal the present value of the expected floating-rate payments. Otherwise, market participants will attempt to pay the lower-valued payment stream and receive the higher-valued payments. Accordingly:

- the payment streams will have the same expected present value at the commencement of a swap, and
- the swap will have a zero value when it is established.

In a later section we explain that the swap rate is set so as to establish a zero value. In the appendix to this chapter, we show how to calculate the swap rate.

When the last swap payment has been made, the swap will also have a zero net value. Thus, at its commencement, and its finish, a swap has zero value. However, depending on the movement in short-term interest rates (i.e. the BBSW), a swap will have either a positive or a negative value during its term. This occurs when the actual floating rates vary from the forward rates that existed when the swap was established.

Given that the swap rate is based on the forward rates when it is established, an unexpected fall in interest rates will cause the present value of the new expected floating-rate payments to fall relative to the present value of the fixed payments. Hence the position of the floating-rate payer/fixed-rate receiver (i.e. Party B in figure 18.1) will have a positive net present value; whereas the position of the fixed-rate payer/floating-rate receiver (i.e. Party A in figure 18.1) develops a negative net present value.

Should interest rates increase during the swap, the position of the fixed-rate payer/floating-rate receiver (i.e. Party A in figure 18.1) will develop a positive net present value, because of the fall in the forward rates (relative to the fixed payments), and the position of the other side (i.e. Party B in figure 18.1) develops a negative net present value.

Swap participants

Swap transactions can, like futures trades, be categorised into either speculative or hedging transactions. A speculative position is not matched by an underlying position in the capital market, which is the case for a hedge transaction. Such a position is represented by that of Party B in figure 18.2. Observe that Party B has no obligations to the fixed-interest market.

Speculative positions

A speculator enters a swap in the expectation that interest-rate movements will enhance the value of the position taken. For example, a speculator who believes interest rates will fall will enter a swap to pay floating/receive fixed. A speculator who believes interest rates are about to rise will enter a swap to pay fixed/receive floating.

To illustrate, suppose interest rates fall after the swap (in figure 18.2) has been established. Party B's position develops positive net present value. B could realise this value by either selling the position in the secondary market to make a cash profit, or entering an offsetting swap as the fixed-rate payer/floating-rate receiver. The new swap will have a lower fixed rate because of the fall in interest rates. (Remember that the fixed rate at the time a swap is established is based on the prevailing forward rates.)

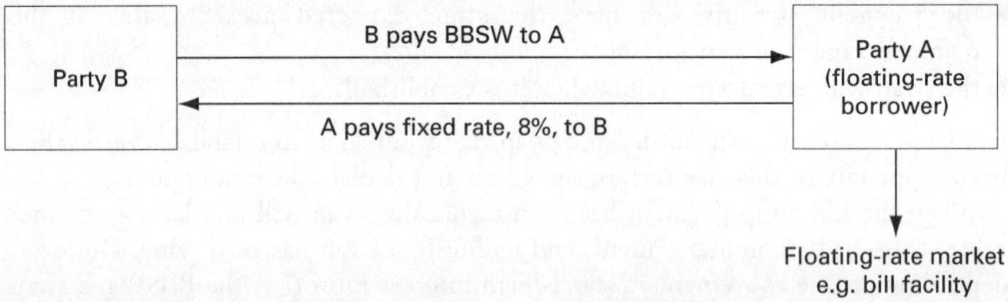

Figure 18.2 Speculative swap position

Taking on the offsetting swap position removes B's obligations under the original swap, while generating a cash flow during the balance of the swap's term. This dual outcome occurs because:

- the BBSW obligation in the original swap is offset by the receive BBSW position in the offsetting swap, and
- the fixed-rate paid under the new swap position will be lower than the fixed-rate being received under the initial swap.

Hedge positions

Hedgers enter swaps as a way of hedging the interest-rate exposure of their underlying interest commitments to the capital market. The swap shown in figure 18.1 illustrates the position of two hedgers. Party A has floating-rate and B has fixed-rate obligations and each has entered the swap to manage the interest-rate risk exposure posed by these obligations.

Party A's interest-rate exposure could arise because it is earning a fixed rate on the funds that it has borrowed on a floating-rate basis in the bill market. In this situation, a rise in interest rates will reduce the spread between A's borrowing and lending rates and, if rates rose sufficiently, A's floating rate could even exceed the fixed rate that it earns. By swapping its floating-rate obligations to a fixed rate, Party A removes its exposure to an increase in interest rates and locks in a spread between its lending rate and its cost of funds.

Party B's exposure could arise because it has made a floating-rate loan (at, say, BBR plus 200 basis points) which it is funding with a bond issue. Should rates fall, so will its income stream on the loan. It enters the swap to establish floating-rate interest payments (BBR and BBSW are equivalent rates) to lock in a spread between its lending and borrowing rates and remove its exposure to a fall in interest rates.

The overall positions of both A and B are shown in table 18.4, given their underlying interest obligations and their swap obligations, assuming the BBSW rate at the commencement of each quarter is as shown in the second column. Given A's fixed-rate income stream the swap has fixed its quarterly interest payments at the rate of 8.00% p.a. (i.e. $20 000 per quarter). Given B's floating-rate income stream, the swap has locked in its interest payments at BBSW, and so fixes a spread between the floating-rate income and BBSW.

Table 18.4 Swap and underlying cash flows

Period (quarter)	*BBSW (%)*	*Party A*			*Party B*		
		Payments to market	*Swap payments*	*Effective payments*	*Payments to market*	*Swap payments*	*Effective payments*
First	7.00	17 500	2 500	20 000	20 000	−2 500	17 500
Second	8.00	20 000	nil	20 000	20 000	nil	20 000
Third	8.50	21 250	−1 250	20 000	20 000	1 250	21 250
Fourth	9.00	22 500	−2 500	20 000	20 000	2 500	22 500

The rationale for swaps

Interest-rate (as well as currency) swaps are financial-market instruments because they add value to a hedger's capital-market dealings for two reasons:

- they provide interest-rate hedging services, and
- they allow the borrower to exploit its comparative advantage in the market for funds.

Hedging services

As described above, borrowers in the fixed- and floating-rate markets are exposed to interest-rate risk when the return on the use of the funds is related to the opposite interest-rate basis. We also showed how a one-year swap can serve to hedge these risks. Two other instruments that could hedge these risks, bill futures and FRAs, were discussed in the previous chapter. These instruments are not only substitutes, their interest rates are linked because the forward rates on which the swap rate is based are those revealed in the futures market.

In this section we explain in more detail how interest-rate swaps perform as hedging instruments and compare their approach to that of bill futures and FRAs. In this discussion we will refer to the following illustration. Suppose a company plans (prior to December 1996) to issue 90-day bank-accepted bills under a one-year bill facility in December, 1996 and observes that the current prices of bank-bill futures contracts in the futures market are:

Contracts	*Futures price*	*Implied rate (% p.a.)*
December 1996	94.00	6.00
March 1997	93.00	7.00
June 1997	92.50	7.50
September 1997	92.00	8.00

The planned initial issue of bills in December 1996 is exposed to interest-rate risk, because 90-day rates could increase by December. This risk can be eliminated by selling December 1996 bill futures contracts or by entering a 3:6 FRA (as explained in the previous chapter).

Given the price of the December futures contracts, the company can lock in an effective rate of 6.00% for the December issue of bills by immediately selling December 1996 contracts in the futures market. If the December issue of bills was left unhedged, they would be issued at the then prevailing yield for 90-day bank-accepted bills (i.e. they would be issued on a 'floating-rate' basis). Using December futures, this floating rate has been swapped for a forward rate. The same outcome could be arranged through a 3:6 FRA. In both cases, a cash payment would be made in December 1996 that fixes the effective interest rate for these bills. These arrangements are equivalent to those that would occur under a one-period interest-rate swap (assuming the initial bills are issued at 6.00%), except that the cash payment is made at the commencement of the interest period and the payment under the swap is made in arrears (i.e. at the end of the period).

While swaps are a multi-period instrument and bill futures and FRAs are single-period instruments the latter can be extended by taking a sequence of contracts. For example, the company could also lock in the forward rates for March, June and September 1997 by selling March, June and September futures contracts (i.e. selling a strip of futures contracts). Using an overall strip of futures locks in 90-day rates of 6.00% p.a. for December, 7.00% p.a. for March, 7.50% p.a. for June and 8.00% p.a. for September. The same outcome can be arranged through a strip of FRAs.

Observe that the strip of futures/FRAs locks in the forward rates for a multi-period loan. In this example, the forward rates imply a normal yield curve. Only when the yield curve is flat will the strip approach lock in the same 90-day rate for each quarter. In contrast, an interest-rate swap locks in a fixed rate for a multi-period loan. Figure 18.3 contrasts the interest rates associated with a futures strip and the swap rate on an equivalent swap.

In this example the swap rate is 7.11% p.a. It is, approximately, an average of the spot and forward rates (6.00%, 7.00%, 7.50% and 8.00%) for each 90-day period in this example. However, it is not a simple average of these 90-day rates (which is 7.125% p.a.), but rather it is that rate which equates the swap's discounted fixed- and floating-interest-rate cash flows.

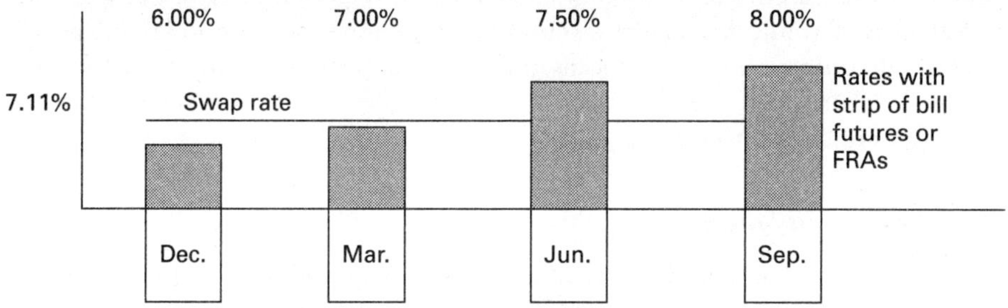

Figure 18.3 One-year hedge with a futures strip or a swap

While strips (futures and FRAs) and swaps can be used to hedge multi-period loans, only the swap establishes a fixed rate for a loan.

We demonstrate the hedging services of a swap between a borrower who agrees to pay fixed/receive floating in order to hedge a multi-period loan and a lender who agrees to receive fixed/pay floating in example 18.1.

example 18.1

Suppose a finance company has a substantial portion of its assets in five-year commercial loans paying an average rate of 10% p.a. on a semi-annual basis. Further, suppose it has financed these loans by issuing 180-day bank bills at an issuance cost of 25 basis points (i.e. the cost of funds is 180-day BBR plus 25 basis points).

The finance company is exposed to the risk that the 180-day rate will rise over the five years. If, for example, the rate rises above 9.75% p.a., the finance company begins to earn a negative spread.

The finance company can remove its interest-rate risk by swapping floating for fixed rates. Should it receive the 180-day rate in exchange for paying 8.00% p.a. fixed, it locks in a spread of 1.75% p.a.

Consider a life assurance company that has issued a five-year guaranteed-return product paying 6.00% p.a. It is using the funds raised by this product to make short-term investments. Suppose it receives the 180-day bank-bill rate minus 50 basis points from these investments. The life assurance company is exposed to the risk of a fall in short-term rates. If the 180-day rate falls beneath 6.50% p.a. the company faces a negative spread on its product.

The life assurance company can remove its interest-rate risk by exchanging fixed for floating rates. Should it pay the 180-day bank-bill rate in exchange for receiving 8.00% p.a. fixed, it locks in a spread of 1.50% p.a.

In this example both parties can avoid interest-rate risk by agreeing to an interest-rate swap at a swap rate of 8.00% p.a. The finance company agrees to pay the swap rate (and receive 180-day BBR) while the life assurance company agrees to receive 8.00% p.a. fixed (and pay 180-day BBR).

Before we discuss the second reason for swaps, it should be emphasised that swaps, when used as a hedge (in common with the other risk-management instruments), are a counterbalance to a position in a capital market. Hence, should a movement in interest rates result in a party making a loss under a swap, that party's position in the capital market would have been favoured by the interest-rate movement. In this context, the loss on the swap means the party successfully achieved the hedged outcome, even though the party would have been better off if the hedge (i.e. the swap) had not been established.

Comparative advantage

There is another school of thought that explains the existence of the swap market by the comparative advantage that exists between two borrowers of different credit standing. A central proposition of this explanation is that a borrower of a lesser credit standing will receive a greater interest-rate penalty in the market for fixed-rate funds than it will receive in the market for floating-rate funds. This difference creates a comparative advantage for each borrower (the borrower with the lower credit standing will borrow in the floating-rate market) that uses a swap to establish its desired fixed/floating position.

According to this view, the fixed-rate payer in the swap enjoys a lower rate than would apply if it borrows in the fixed-rate market and shares part of the benefit with the floating-rate payer. Because of this benefit, the floating-rate payer issues fixed-rate securities even though it prefers floating-rate obligations.

To illustrate, suppose that A and B have been offered the following rates:

Market	*Company A*	*Bank B*
Fixed	10.00%	9.00%
Floating	BBR+50 bps	BBR

Observe that A cannot borrow as favourably as B in either market, but it has a comparative advantage in the floating-rate market, because its borrowing rate is only 50 bps (basis points) more than A's borrowing rate; whereas B's comparative advantage lies in the fixed-rate market, where it can borrow at a rate 100 basis points below A. This creates an opportunity for both parties to lower their effective borrowing rates through a swap:

$$\text{gain} = \text{Absolute value of } (\alpha - \beta) \qquad \textit{Equation (18.1)}$$

where α is the difference between each borrower's rate in the fixed-rate market (100 bps) and,

β is the difference between each borrower's rate in the floating-rate market (50 bps).

Hence:

$$\text{gain} = 100 - 50$$

$$= 50 \text{ bps}$$

You can check this analysis by comparing the combined interest rates the two parties will pay if B issues in the fixed-rate market and A in the floating-rate market (9.00% + BBR+50 bps = 9.50% + BBR) with A issuing in the fixed-rate market and B in the floating-rate market (10.00% + BBR). The difference is 50 basis points.

Given their comparative advantages:

- the bank borrows in the fixed-rate market at 9.00%, and
- the company borrows in the floating-rate market at BBR+50bps.

Under a swap, they share the 50-bps gain. To illustrate, suppose the swap rate is 9.25% (which the company pays to the bank) and the bank pays BBR to the company. The reduction in interest cost is 25 basis points each:

- the company pays 9.25% plus 50 bps (BBR + 50 bps − BBR), a saving of 25 bps on its quoted rate (10.00%) in the fixed-rate market, and
- the bank pays BBR less the 25 basis points between the 9.25% received in the swap and the 9.00% it pays to the fixed-rate market.

This arrangement is shown in figure 18.4.

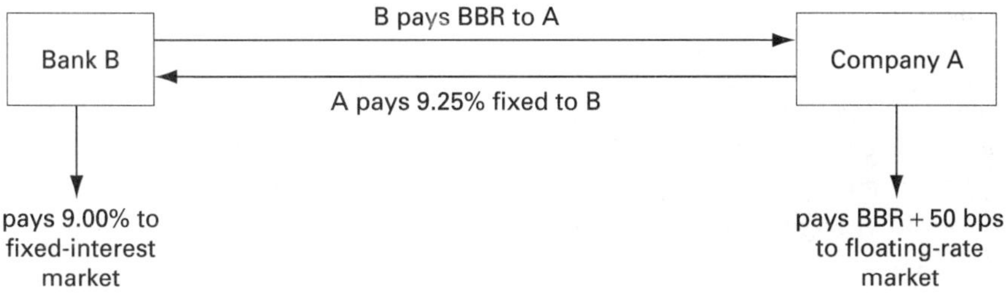

Figure 18.4 Swap terms that are based on comparative advantage

How can comparative advantages arise in financial markets? The basic reason is market segmentation. This can arise in at least three ways.

First, fixed-rate investors tend to be more sensitive to credit risk than floating-rate lenders and thus impose higher-risk premiums on borrowers with a lower credit standing. This characteristic is related to the type of investor in the fixed- and floating-rate markets. 'Trustee' investors, such as pension funds and insurance companies, as well as individual investors, are more important in the fixed-rate market, whereas banks are more important in the floating-rate market. Banks are the main suppliers of floating-rate funds (through the acceptance of bills), and as a consequence of their superior risk analysis and loan-management skills, they impose lower risk premiums on less creditworthy borrowers.

Whether comparative advantage arises in this way is debatable. (Allan, 1990, pp. 118–19) It begs the question of why the fixed-rate receiver in the swap would accept a rate from the less creditworthy party that is lower than that set in the capital market for that borrower. In the above example, why would Party B accept 9.25% from Party A when the market requires 10.00%? One possible answer is that this does not occur.

When swaps first developed, both domestic markets and the global system of markets were segmented and so particular borrowers experienced a 'home-ground advantage' in their borrowing. But as markets become more efficient, differences in the rates charged for a borrower will narrow and this reduces the scope for comparative advantage: 'The exploitation of borrowing-cost differentials through arbitrage should eventually lead to their disappearance.' (Juttner, 1994, p. 556)

However, this logical implication of the argument may not apply in practice. That is, comparative advantages may narrow but not be removed in all cases, at all times. (Fabozzi, Modigliani and Ferri, 1994, p. 608)

Second, a borrower will enjoy a comparative advantage in the domestic market where it is a well-established and respected borrower. For example, many Australian companies can borrow more favourably domestically because they are well known to that market, but unknown to foreign markets. In this situation the Australian company would borrow domestically and swap its interest obligations with a company that is well known (and so can borrow on more favourable terms) in the foreign market.

A third reason is the existence of taxes and regulations that affect groups of borrowers differently. Australia's interest-withholding tax is an example of an asymmetrical tax, as it applies only to certain borrowers. Those to whom it does not apply will enjoy a comparative advantage. Also, the severe requirements for the issuing of debentures encourages companies to borrow in the floating-rate market and to swap these obligations with a fixed-rate borrower.

> *Consequently, we can say that the swap market originally developed around the purpose of exploiting real or perceived imperfections in the capital market, but eventually evolved into a transactionally efficient market for accomplishing asset/liability objectives.* (Fabozzi, Modigliani and Ferri, 1994, p. 609)

Australian specifications

Swaps are traded over the counter, and as such do not have standard specifications. Interest-rate swap specifications are negotiated and agreed to by each party to a swap. However, as in all liquid over-the-counter markets, there are a number of conventions to which most interest-rate swaps adhere. The components necessary to specify an interest-rate swap are listed below.

Principal

All interest-rate swaps have a notional principal from which both floating- and fixed-rate interest-rate payments are based. The principal amount is called a notional amount because there is no actual exchange of principal. This is an important legal consideration as it limits each party's obligation to the net difference between interest payments. The principal is never at risk in the event of a default on an interest-rate swap.

Swap amounts

Swap principals are large. The conventional minimum amount is $10 million, although much larger parcels, such as $30 and $50 million, are frequently traded.

Start date

Most interest-rate swaps commence almost immediately after an agreement between the two parties has been determined. However, it is possible to obtain delayed-start swaps. This is a forward swap in that the fixed rate, agreed upon now, takes effect at a time in the future.

Term

Parties to a swap must agree upon the term of the swap. This is usually based on the term of the underlying interest-rate obligation. Data on the term of outstanding fixed-to-floating interest-rate swaps, as at 30 June 1995, are presented in figure 18.5. The average term for these swaps was a comparatively short 2.35 years.

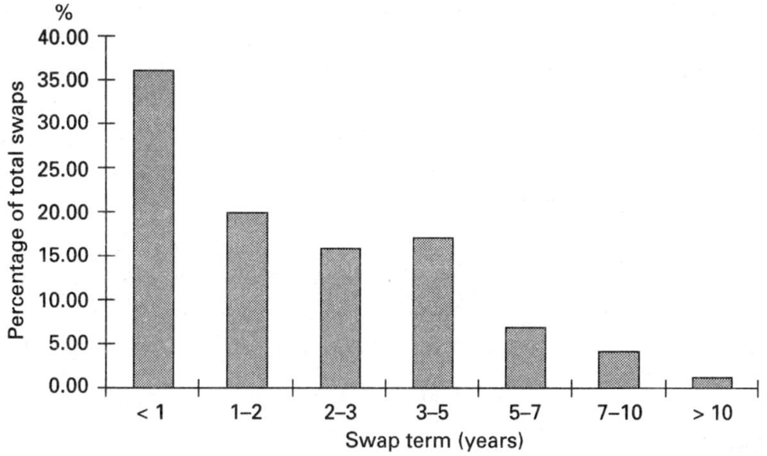

Figure 18.5 Fixed-to-floating-rate swaps according to their term, June 1995

Reset frequency

At the end of each interest period, one counterparty pays to the other counterparty an amount sufficient to cover the difference between the fixed and the floating payments on the notional principal of the swap. The times these payments fall due are called reset dates. On each reset date the floating rate that applies to the next interest period is determined. Note that in an ordinary interest-rate swap, the payment due at the end of an interest period is known at the beginning of the period when the floating rate is determined (i.e. BBSW).

In Australia, most short-term swaps (less than three years) are specified with quarterly reset dates. On the other hand, most longer-term swaps (greater than three years) have semi-annual reset dates. That short swaps have quarterly resets and long swaps have semi-annual resets is due to the nature of the instruments that dealers use to hedge swap agreements.

Short-term swaps are hedged using bank bills, and more importantly bank-bill futures. These instruments provide quarterly cash flows. It makes sense to design swaps with quarterly resets to match the hedging instruments. Longer-term swaps are hedged using bonds and bond futures. Again, it makes sense to design longer swaps with semi-annual resets to match the bond's coupon-payment frequency.

Floating rate

A floating interest rate must be employed to compute a swap's floating-rate payment. Clearly, in order to initially specify a swap and to quantify subsequent payments associated with the swap, it is necessary to have a standard reference floating rate. This floating rate is set at the beginning of the swap and is reset at the beginning of each interest period as it arises.

In Australia, the BBSW is used as the reference floating rate. The BBSW is displayed in a 'page' as part of the Reuters financial data service. This particular page consists of bank-bill bid and offer rates provided by eight leading Australian banks. The two highest and the two lowest mid-rate quotations are discarded, and the remaining mid rates are then averaged and this becomes the BBSW for that day. It forms the basis of the setting and the resetting of floating-rate legs of plain vanilla interest-rate swaps. Table 18.5 sets out data obtained from a Reuters BBSW page.

Table 18.5 Calculation of BBSW[1]

Contributor	*Three-month rates*	*Six-month rates*
	Bid[2] Offer[2]	Bid Offer
1	7.60–7.50	7.53–7.43
2	7.60–7.50	7.51–7.41
3	7.60–7.50	7.50–7.40
4	7.60–7.50	7.50–7.40
5	7.59–7.49	7.50–7.40
6	7.56–7.51	7.50–7.40
7	7.58–7.48	7.47–7.40
8	7.55–7.50	7.46–7.41[1]
Average	7.5425	7.4492

[1] Note that the bid rate is greater than the offer rate. This ordering is necessary to ensure that the implied bill bid price is less than the implied bill offer price.

[2] The rates in the body of the table were taken from the Reuters data service on 1 April 1992.

Swap rate

As previously noted, the swap rate is a market-determined variable. A receiver of the swap fixed rate would naturally want this rate to be as high as possible. On the other hand, the payer of the fixed rate would want the rate to be as low as possible. The rate will balance the demand and supply of both swap sides (subject to any negotiation for particular swaps) and is thus a fair rate.

A fair swap rate is one that does not, in any systematic way, advantage either the fixed-rate payer or the fixed-rate receiver. This means that the present value of the fixed-rate payments or receipts must equal the present value of the expected floating-rate receipts or payments. The calculation of a swap rate is discussed in the appendix to this chapter.

The swap rate (for swaps up to three years) is approximately the average of the forward rates revealed in the futures market. It is a fixed spot rate and so (as explained in Chapter 15) is based on the average of its constituent spot and forward rates.

However, the swap rate is set to equate the present value of two payment streams in a swap. When there is a normal yield curve, the fixed rate will exceed the forward rates during the first half of the swap and be less than the forward rates for the balance of the swap. Hence the fixed-rate payer can expect to make the initial swap payments and the floating-rate payer can expect to make the later payments, as shown by the example in tables 18.3 and 18.4.

Should the respective payments have the same absolute values in total, the present value of the fixed-rate payments will exceed those of the floating-rate payer. Hence the swap rate will be less than the average. This will reduce the absolute value of the expected swap payments by the fixed-rate payer but equalise their present value with that of the floating-rate payer. This relationship is illustrated by the swap rate shown in figure 18.3, where the average of the forward rates is 7.125% and the swap rate is 7.11%.

In the event of an inverse yield curve, the reverse relationships would hold. The floating-rate payer would make the initial payments and so the swap rate would be marginally above the average of the constituent spot and forward rates.

Swap rates are not set in isolation, but are closely related to the rates on other financial instruments with similar tenors. Given that there is no clearing house that accepts the credit risk associated with the swap payments, as in the case of the futures market, the swap rate reflects the default risk of the market's participants. Given that these are mainly banks, swap payments have a risk akin to that of commercial paper and semi-governmental securities.

In Australia, swap rates are usually quoted as a margin over the yields on NSW T-Corp bonds. However, the relationship between the swap rate and semi-governmental yields is not fixed. The yield-curve data in figure 18.6 depict the relationship between the swap rate and the yields on Commonwealth Treasury and the NSW T-Corp bonds on 8 January 1996.

The amount of credit-risk exposure arising from swaps is small relative to the notional principal involved. Default by one party in a swap exposes the other to a loss whenever the present value of the receiving party's remaining payments is positive. As shown above in table 18.3, net swap payments often are a tiny fraction of the notional principal.

The potential loss from counterparty default in a swap increases when there is a steeply sloping yield curve, because this gives rise (whether it has a normal or inverse shape) to larger payments. Given a normal yield curve, the fixed-rate payer is more exposed to credit risk because this party makes the net payments during the

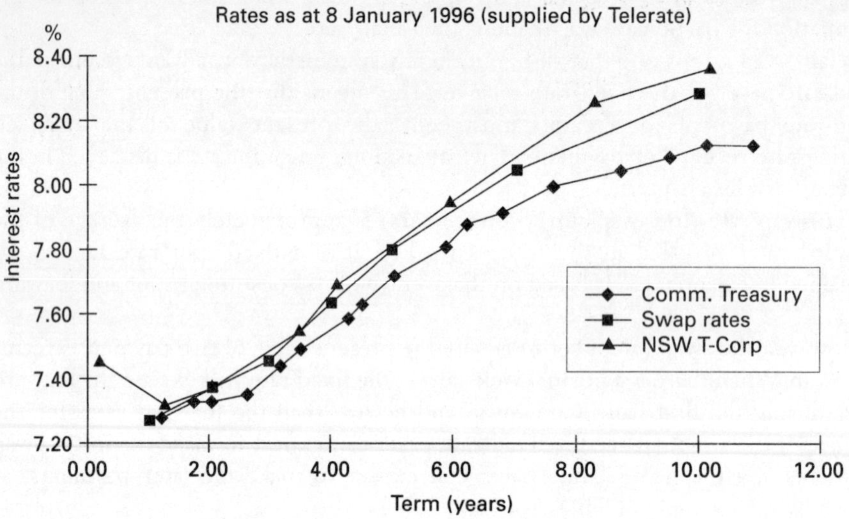

Figure 18.6 Yield curves — swap rate, Treasury and T-Corp bonds

first half of the swap, whereas the floating-rate payer is more exposed when the yield curve has an inverse shape.

Changes in yields also increase credit risk because they create present value for one side of a swap during its term. For example, when yields fall unexpectedly, the floating-rate payer's position will increase in value but expose this party to credit risk, because this value is dependent on the fixed-rate payer continuing to make payments.

In contrast, a series of FRAs has no value, and therefore no credit risk, if interest rates evolve as anticipated and reflected in the FRA rates. For this reason, a series of FRAs has less credit risk than a similar swap.

Pricing schedules

Swap dealers usually quote two-way swap prices based on a **pricing schedule**. This lists swap rates not as absolute rates, but as a margin over the rate on a reference security. In Australia, swap rates are usually referenced to T-Corp yields. A pricing schedule assumes that swap margins are more stable than swap rates. If swap margins are stable, a swap dealer can continue to quickly quote swap rates as a margin above or below the reference rate, even in situations where interest rates are volatile.

A pricing schedule listing swap rates relative to T-Corp bond yields is presented in table 18.6. Observe the difference between the fixed rate that a dealer will pay, and that which a dealer will receive. This is the dealers' spread.

Settlement

In Australia, settlement of the fixed- and floating-interest obligations is invariably conducted on a net basis. That is, one party, instead of paying (receiving) the full amount of the fixed interest and receiving (paying) the full amount of the floating interest, simply pays or receives the difference between the two amounts.

Table 18.6 Indicative pricing schedule, 8 January 1996

Term	*Interpolated NSW T-Corp yields (%)*	*Swap-point margins (in basis points) over NSW T-Corp yields*	
		Pay fixed, receive BBSW	*Receive fixed, pay BBSW*
1.00	7.33	−5	−2
2.00	7.38	0	3
3.00	7.50	−3	0
4.00	7.70	−5	−2
5.00	7.86	−5	−2
7.00	8.12	−6	−3
10.00	8.36	−6	−3

Periodic settlements are made by comparing the floating and the fixed rates and multiplying by the notional principal. The amount paid by the fixed-rate payer is:

$$S = Q\,(r_{\text{fixed}} - r_{\text{floating}})\,\frac{d}{DIY} \qquad \textit{Equation (18.2)}$$

where S is each net settlement amount (fixed minus floating payment),
Q is the notional swap principal,
r_{fixed} is the swap fixed rate,
r_{float} is the swap floating rate,
d is the number of days in the interest period, and
DIY is the days in a year.

We illustrate the calculation of net settlement amounts in example 18.2.

Swap intermediaries

Many Australian banks and merchant banks act as intermediaries in the swap market, as shown in table 18.1. They perform their intermediary role by bringing together swap parties with offsetting swap requirements. Intermediaries in the swap market provide the same general benefits that are provided by intermediaries in any financial market. Most importantly, they reduce the search cost of parties requiring swap transactions. Clearly, the end users of swaps must reward the intermediary for the provision of its services. This reward can either be in the form of an up-front fee, as is paid to swap brokers, or as a spread, in the case of swap dealers. Spreads are shown in table 18.6 and in the swap presented in figure 18.7.

When the swap market originally developed, financial intermediaries acted as brokers. That is, they helped parties to arrange direct swaps. The market has developed to become mainly dealer-based, where dealers take one side of a swap transaction. An intermediated swap is illustrated in figure 18.7, where the dealer's spread arises on both the floating- and fixed-rate sides of the swap.

example 18.2

Suppose your firm undertakes an 18-month interest-rate swap on 20 January 1996 as the fixed-rate payer, receiving BBSW (with quarterly resets) on a notional principal of $1 million. Compute the six settlement payments on the basis of the following data.

On 20 January 1996 the swap rate was 7.00% and the three-month bank-bill swap rate (BBSW) was 6.50% p.a. Over the term of the swap, the BBSW rates were:

Date	*BBSW (%)*	*d (in each three-month period)*
20 Jan. 1996	6.50	
20 Apr. 1996	6.50	91
20 Jul. 1996	7.00	91
20 Oct. 1996	7.25	92
20 Jan. 1997	8.00	92
20 Apr. 1997	8.25	90
20 Jul. 1997		91

Your firm's net payments can be expressed as:

$$S = Q\,(r_{fixed} - r_{float}) * d/365$$

Hence, the settlement amounts are:

$$20.04.96,\ S = 1\,000\,000 * (0.07 - 0.0650) * 91/365 = \$1247$$

$$20.07.96,\ S = 1\,000\,000 * (0.07 - 0.0650) * 91/365 = \$1247$$

$$20.10.96,\ S = 1\,000\,000 * (0.07 - 0.0700) * 92/365 = \$0$$

$$20.01.97,\ S = 1\,000\,000 * (0.07 - 0.0725) * 92/365 = -\$630$$

$$20.04.97,\ S = 1\,000\,000 * (0.07 - 0.0800) * 90/365 = -\$2466$$

$$20.07.97,\ S = 1\,000\,000 * (0.07 - 0.0825) * 91/365 = -\$3116$$

Should a dealer have an imbalance between its swap counterparties, this creates an open swap position that requires careful management. The position can be (a) closed out, by taking an opposite swap position, (b) hedged in another market, with, for example, a position in interest-rate futures, or (c) kept open and let run, with the prospect that future financial movements will increase the value of the open swap.

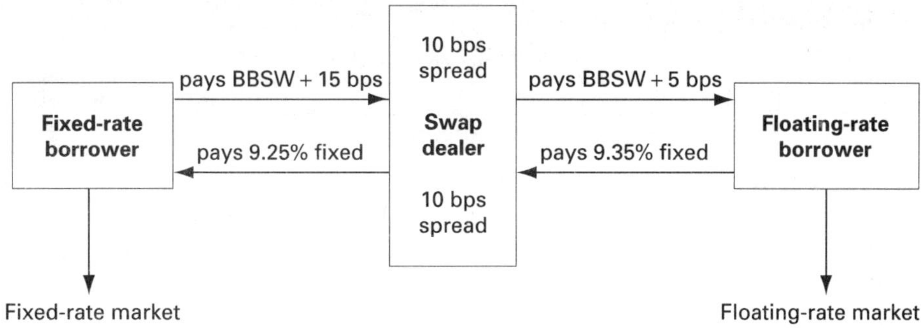

Figure 18.7 Intermediated interest-rate swap

CURRENCY SWAPS

Currency swaps, in their simplest form, involve the exchange of loan payments in one currency for the payments on a loan in another currency. Hence, in a fixed-for-fixed currency swap, both the loan principal and fixed-interest payments in one currency are exchanged for the principal and fixed-interest payments in another currency. For example, an Australian company that has borrowed in AUD, but prefers a loan in USD, may swap principal and interest payments with another company that has borrowed USD. The flow of the payments in such a swap is shown in figure 18.8.

Observe in figure 18.8 that company AUS borrows in the AUD market but exchanges these cash flows for USD in the swap with corporation NKY, which borrows in USD and exchanges USD cash flows for AUD. Observe also that the payments can be divided into three stages:

- the exchange of the amounts borrowed at the commencement of the swap,
- the exchange of interest payments on each settlement date during the swap, and
- the repayment of the loans at the swap's maturity date.

In contrast to interest-rate swaps, the payments between the swap counterparties are not netted. Both parties make their required payments in the currency involved. In the swap example depicted in figure 18.8, for instance, the principal amount borrowed in AUD by company AUS is paid to company NKY in exchange for the USD raised by NKY at the commencement of the swap. Interest payments are swapped throughout the swap's term, and NKY repays the AUD principal received from AUS, in exchange for the USD principal amount, at the end of the swap.

Using a currency swap to change the currency of a loan

The effect of such currency swaps is to convert a loan raised in one currency to a ('synthetic') loan in another currency. AUS, for example, having raised funds in AUD, has exchanged them for the USD funds raised by NKY. It makes interest payments to NKY in USD and repays the USD funds when the swap ends. While such swaps do not raise funds directly, they are undertaken as part of a borrower's capital-raising program.

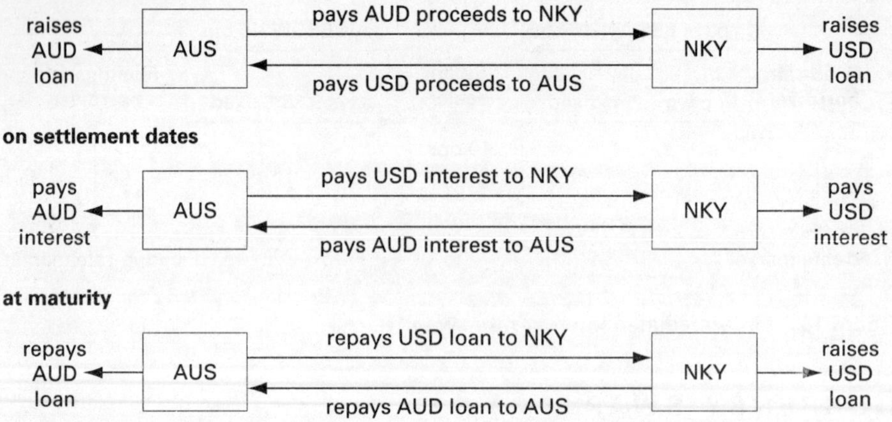

Figure 18.8 Cash flows in a currency swap

As illustrated by the above example, the Australian company is using the swap to convert its AUD obligations to USD, rather than borrowing in the market for USD. It is exploiting its comparative advantage in the Australian capital market as a vehicle for raising USD. The same reason applies for the USD borrower when it has an established place in the USD market but not in the AUD market, yet prefers to raise AUD funds.

Suppose that an Australian company, AUS, and an American company, NKY, are offered fixed rates of interest in both AUD and USD.

	USD	AUD
Company AUS	6.00%	9.00%
Company NKY	4.00%	8.50%

These figures indicate that NKY has a better credit rating than AUS in both capital markets, but AUS has a comparative advantage in the AUD market, because its relative disadvantage is smaller in this market (50 basis points compared with 200 basis points in the USD market). Suppose that NKY requires AUD to purchase a factory for its Australian subsidiary, while AUS requires USD to purchase a number of United States newspapers. A currency swap allows each company to borrow in the currency where its enjoys a comparative advantage, and receive the currency it requires.

The extent of the savings from the currency swap, to be shared by the two companies, is 150 basis points, which is the difference between the 200-point difference in the USD market compared with the 50-basis-point difference in the AUD market (recall equation (18.1)). There are many possible permutations, though, of the way in which this 150-basis-point gain may be shared. Figure 18.9 sets out one way that the currency swap might be organised.

As shown in figure 18.9, the swap converts the payments under NKY's borrowings to an AUD loan at 8.25%. This rate is 50 basis points less than NKY would have achieved had it gone directly to the AUD market for funds. Similarly, AUS has, by means of the swap, achieved a 50 bps reduction compared with its quoted USD borrowing rates. The financial intermediary has also gained from the swap. The intermediary has achieved a net borrowing/lending spread of 150 bps in USD and −75 bps in AUD. Ignoring the different exchange rates, it can be seen that the financial intermediary has a net margin of 75 bps p.a.

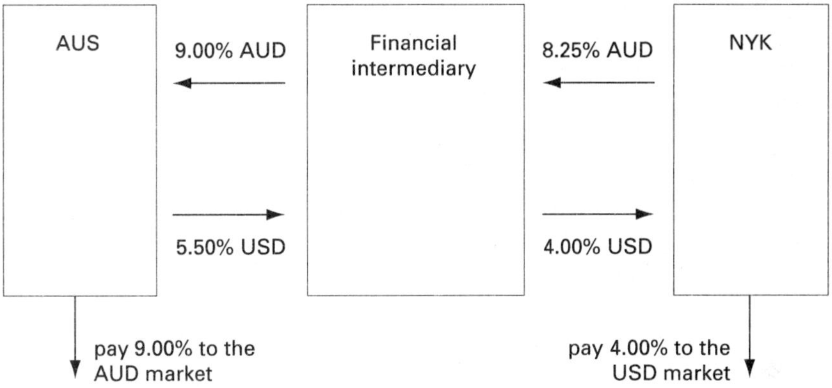

Gains	AUS	Financial intermediary	NYK
AUD	0.00%	–0.75%	+0.25%
USD	+0.50%	+1.50%	0.00%
Net	+0.50%	+0.75%	+0.25%

Figure 18.9 Currency swap

Unless the swap also specifies the rate of exchange for the swap payments, foreign-exchange risk is involved. In this example, the financial institution has contracted to receive net 1.50% USD and to pay net 0.75% AUD. The actual net margin received by the financial intermediary during the swap depends on the AUD/USD exchange rate remaining unchanged. Given that the intermediary is making AUD interest payments and receiving USD interest payments, it will be disadvantaged by any increase in future AUD/USD rates. This foreign-exchange exposure could be removed by the intermediary entering into a series of forward FX contracts, corresponding to the swap payment dates, that lock in its margin in the currency of its choice. But generally other arrangements are made. (Allan, 1990, p. 121)

Typically, a currency swap will either specify the exchange rate for the future payments, or, in the case of swaps where each party makes swap payments in its domestic currency, use the spot rate when the swap is established to repay the swapped principal. (Nguyen, 1993, p. 456)

Valuation of currency swaps

The value of a currency swap, like an interest-rate swap, is computed as the discounted value of all cash flows attached to the swap. The cash flows associated with a currency swap can be conceptually broken down into two bonds that are denominated in different currencies. In the example above, AUS has simultaneously sold a USD-denominated bond and purchased an AUD denominated bond. The net value of the swap to AUS is given by the value of the sold bond less the value of the purchased bond, provided that the value of each bond is expressed in a common currency.

The value of a currency swap is determined by three factors:

- the term structure of interest rates in the country of the commodity currency,
- the term structure of interest rates in the country of the terms currency and,
- the spot exchange rates.

At the time the swap is made, the present value of the future payments has the same value, but during the swap the above listed factors may change, and create value on one side of the swap at the expense of the other side. (See also example 18.3.)

example 18.3

A financial institution has on its books a currency swap with 15 months of its life to run. Under the terms of this swap the institution will pay a floating rate of interest, twice a year, on a principal of NZD15 million. In return the institution receives 12.00% p.a. fixed on AUD10 million. On the last interest date the NZ interest rate was 6.00% p.a. The current zero-coupon semi-annual interest rates are:

Tenor	*Zero-coupon swap rates*	
	New Zealand	Australian
3 months	4.50	8.00
9 months	5.00	9.00
15 months	5.00	10.00

Compute a fair price, in AUD, for the swap if the spot exchange rate is AUD/NZD1.2500.

The interest due on the NZ bond at the next interest payment in three months' time is NZD0.450 million (= 15 000 000*0.06/2). The value of the bond is the value of this payment plus the face value of the bond discounted back three months:

$$B_{terms} = \frac{15\,000\,000 + 450\,000}{(1 + 0.045/2)^{3/6}}$$

$$= \text{NZD15 279 067}$$

The interest payments associated with the AUD fixed-interest bond are AUD0.6 million (=10 000 000*0.12/2). The value of this bond is:

$$B_{com} = \frac{600\,000}{(1 + 0.08/2)^{2*3/12}} + \frac{600\,000}{(1 + 0.09/2)^{2*9/12}} + \frac{10\,600\,000}{(1 + 0.10/2)^{2*15/12}}$$

$$= \text{AUD10 532 816}$$

The value of the bond is thus:

$$V_{com} = (10\ 532\ 816 - 15\ 279\ 067)/1.2500$$

$$= -AUD1\ 690\ 437$$

Types of currency swaps

In general, a cross-currency interest-rate swap can be on any basis, fixed rate to fixed rate, floating to floating, or fixed to floating. The example 18.3 illustrates the method of valuation of currency swaps from a fixed rate in one currency to a floating rate in another currency.

Hedging purposes of currency swaps

Currency swaps can hedge foreign-exchange as well as interest-rate exposures. As noted in Chapter 13, exporters are exposed to the risk of a depreciation in the foreign currency (i.e. the currency in which it is paid). Exporters could use a swap to convert a series of debt payments into that currency to create a natural hedge. Should that currency depreciate, the fall in the AUD value of the export income is offset by the fall in the AUD value of debt payments under the swap.

To illustrate, Qantas earns JPY income, and so is exposed to the risk of a depreciation of JPY. It also has substantial USD outlays as lease payments for aircraft. Qantas could establish a natural hedge by borrowing in USD, where it is an established borrower, and entering a swap with a JPY borrower who wants to convert JPY payments to USD payments. Such a swap would create a stream of JPY outlays as a natural hedge for its stream of JPY receipts.

Summary

The main points of this chapter are as follows:

- Swaps are an exchange of cash flows over an agreed period.
- The two most common swap forms are interest-rate and currency swaps.
- The Australian swap market was established in 1983 and has grown substantially. In 1994–95 AUD246 billion worth (i.e. notional principals) of swaps were written.
- Swaps may be arranged directly between two counterparties or intermediated by a dealer (which usually is a bank or merchant bank).
- Interest-rate swaps are an exchange of interest payments on set dates during their term. The principal amounts are not exchanged. Typically, the net amount only is paid at each settlement date by the counterparty with the larger payment obligation.
- Swaps are often used in conjunction with capital-market dealings, either to manage interest-rate risk or to exploit a borrower's comparative advantage to lower the effective cost of funds.
- The Australian interest-rate swap market has a number of conventions. For example, swaps that have a term of less than three years have quarterly

settlement and reset dates, whereas longer-term swaps have six-monthly settlement and reset dates.

- The fixed rate on Australian interest-rate swaps, while being determined by swap-market forces, is often closely aligned to the rate on the best semi-government paper.
- Brokers who charge a fixed fee for their services play an important role in the market for Australian swaps.
- Interest-rate swaps begin and end with a value of zero. At other times a swap probably will have either a negative or a positive value.
- The swap rate is set such that a swap has zero value at its inception, given the forward rates at the time the swap is established.
- Interest-rate swaps can be used to profit from term structure shifts, but are used more generally by borrowers to hedge their exposure to interest-rate and/or foreign-currency risks.
- Currency swaps involve an exchange of both interest and principal payments of a loan denominated in one currency for a loan in another currency.
- Currency swaps, depending on each party's FX risk, specify the exchange rate for swap payments.
- Currency swaps, like interest-rate swaps, are valued as the net of two bonds. However, unlike interest-rate swaps, currency swaps bonds must be brought to a common currency for valuation.

DISCUSSION QUESTIONS AND EXERCISES

1. Discuss the form, operation and hedging role of a one-year plain vanilla swap. Refer to the derivation and level of the swap rate.
2. Briefly explain the concept of a zero value for a swap at the time it is established. How can a swap position gain value during the course of a swap?
3. Suppose the spot BBR is 8.00% and the forward rates embedded in bill-futures contracts that mature over the next nine months are 7.90%, 7.70% and 7.60%. Suggest the approximate swap rate in a one-year fixed-for-floating swap.
4. Suppose that the spot 180-day BBR is 7.80% at the commencement of an interest period in a five-year fixed-for-floating swap that has a swap rate of 8.00% and a notional principal of $10 million. Calculate the interest payment that will be made in 182 days at the next settlement date.
5. Set out the payments that will be made during the final year of a two-year fixed-for-floating swap with a notional principal of $10 million, assuming remaining BBRs are (in succession) 7.50%, 7.60%, 7.70% and 7.80%, the quarterly periods are 92 days and the swap rate is 7.62% p.a.
6. In an interest-rate swap, which party loses when interest-rates rise? Consider, separately, the cases of a speculative and hedged position when answering this question.
7. Compare the way a one-year fixed-for-floating swap serves to hedge the interest-rate exposure on a one-year bill facility with the hedge provided by a strip of bill futures, assuming the spot and forward 90-day rates are 7.60%, 7.80%, 7.90% and 8.00%.

8 Suppose Bank A has borrowed at BBR plus 25 basis points and lent at 10% p.a. fixed for three years, whereas Bank B has borrowed at 9.00% p.a. and lent at BBR less 25 basis points. Specify the interest-rate risk each bank faces and calculate the overall position of each after they enter into a swap where A pays a swap rate of 9.50% p.a. (to B) and receives BBR.

9 Suppose company A can borrow at 12.00% p.a. fixed for three years or at BBR, whereas company B can borrow at 14.00% p.a. fixed or at BBR plus 1% and the swap rate is 12.00%. Explain whether these companies could benefit from being swap counterparties.

10 Describe the main features of a currency swap and suggest two purposes that are served by currency swaps. Use a flow chart to show the cash flows involved.

References and further reading

Allan, Richard, *et. al* 1990, *Foreign Exchange Management*, Allen & Unwin, Sydney, Chapter 10.

Carew, Edna 1995, *Derivatives Decoded*, Allen & Unwin, Sydney, Chapter 4.

Das, S. 1994, *Swap Financing and Derivatives*, 2nd edn, The Law Book Company, Sydney.

Daugaard, Dan 1991, *The Swaps Handbook*, Financial Training & Analysis Services.

Daugaard, Dan, & Valentine, Tom 1995, *Financial Risk Management*, Harper Educational, Sydney, Chapters 6 and 7.

Fabozzi, Frank J, Modigliani, Franco, & Ferri, Michael G. 1994, *Foundations of Financial Markets and Institutions*, Prentice-Hall, New Jersey, Chapter 29.

Juttner, D. Johannes 1994, *Financial Markets, Interest Rates and Monetary Economics*, 3rd edn, Longman Cheshire, Melbourne, Chapter 28.

Lewis, M. K. 1993, 'Derivative markets', in M. K. Lewis & R. H. Wallace (eds), *The Australian Financial System*, Longman Cheshire, Melbourne, Chapter 11.

Nguyen, D. T. 1993, 'The foreign exchange market', in M. K. Lewis & R. H. Wallace (eds), *The Australian Financial System*, Longman Cheshire, Melbourne, Chapter 12.

Appendix 18.1 Determining the swap rate

The swap fixed rate is an approximate average of the forward rates over the life of the swap. This average is neither a simple nor a geometric average. Rather, it is computed as the rate that equates the value of a swap's floating-rate payments with the fixed-rate payments.

For short-term swaps, the rates used in computing the expected floating rates and the discount factors are, in practice, taken from the bill-futures market. For longer swaps, the rates are taken from an appropriate zero-coupon yield curve.

In the simple example given in table 18A.1, we employ futures prices as the basis for expected floating rates and discount factors. In order to simplify the calculations we have assumed that each futures contract covers a quarter of a year (i.e. 91.25 days). The computation of the fair swap rate is set out in table 18A.1.

Table 18A.1 The swap rate given bill-futures prices

Fixed rate => 7.11%

Contract	*Futures price*	*Implied rate (%)*	*Days*	*Cum. sum*	*Floating payments*	*Discounted*	*Fixed payments*	*Discounted*	*Net*
	(1)	(2)	(3)	(4)	(5)	(6)	(7)	(8)	(9)
December	94.00	6.00	91.25	1.0000					
March	93.00	7.00	91.25	1.0150	15 000	14 778	17 775	17 512	−2 734
June	92.50	7.50	91.25	1.0328	17 500	16 945	17 775	17 211	− 266
September	92.00	8.00	91.25	1.0521	18 750	17 821	17 775	16 894	927
				1.0732	20 000	18 636	17 775	16 563	2 073
Totals						68 181		68 181	0

Column (1) of the table contains the futures prices. Column (2) consists of the futures' implied future interest rates. Column (4) contains the cumulative sum of $1.00 invested in December, and rolled over each 91.25 days. That is, $(4)_{t+1} = (4)_t*(1 + (2)_t * 91.25/365)$. These cumulative-sum figures are used to discount future cash flows back to the start of the swap. The interest payments, on $1 million, under the expected floating rates, are set out in column (5). That is, $(5)_{t+1} = 1\,000\,000 * (2)_t * 91.25/365$. The discounted values of column (5) are set out in column (6); that is, (6) = (5)/(4). Columns (7) and (8) contain the fixed-rate flows and discounted flows respectively. That is, (7) = 1 000 000 * 0.0711 * 91.25/365 and (8) = (7)/(4). Column (9) is the discounted value of the difference between the fixed and the floating flows. That is, (9) = (6) − (8).

Table 18A.1 shows that a fixed rate of 7.11% p.a. ensures that the discounted value of the fixed-rate cash flows equals the floating rate, hence, the swap has a zero net value.

The analysis so far has avoided the question of how we find the rate that guarantees this equality. One method is by trial and error. Any increase in the value of the fixed rate increases the swap value and any decrease lowers the swap value. So, it is a relatively simple process to find the fixed rate that gives the swap a zero value. However, there is another way.

In assessing swap cash flows we have ignored the notional capital value of a swap on the grounds that the fixed-rate notional capital value is offset by the floating-rate notional capital value. But it is important to recognise that the cash flows associated with a pay fixed (receive floating) swap are identical to those arising from a two-asset portfolio consisting of:

- short (long) a coupon bond, and
- long (short) a floating-rate note (FRN).

For example, a $1 million 8.00% pay fixed/receive BBSW swap, can be replicated by issuing a $1 million 8% p.a. bond and simultaneously buying a $1 million floating-rate note paying coupons equal to the bank-bill rate. Table 18A.2 summarises each side of an interest-rate swap and the bond portfolio that replicates the swap's cash flow.

Table 18A.2 Swap and its equivalent bond portfolio

Swap	*Equivalent bond portfolio*
pay fixed	sell a coupon bond
receive floating	buy an FRN
receive fixed	buy a coupon bond
pay floating	sell an FRN

The interpretation of a swap as a combination of a floating- and a fixed-rate bond is useful in valuing a swap at any time during its life. Further, the fact that a swap has zero value at its inception can be used to determine the 'fair' fixed rate of a swap.

The value of the underlying fixed-coupon bond must equal the value of the underlying floating-rate bond if a swap is to have a value of zero. The value of a floating-rate bond, just prior to its issue, is always equal to its face value. This means that the value of the fixed-rate bond must also equal its face value. That is, the fixed-rate bond is a par bond with its coupon equal to its yield to maturity.

It follows that the swap rate is the same as the coupon rate on a par bond. This equivalence can be employed as the basis of a method for determining the swap fixed rate. Consider a \$1-face-value par-coupon bond. The bond's value of \$1 can be expressed as the sum of its discounted cash flows:

$$P = cd_1 + cd_2 + \ldots + cd_n + Fd_n$$

if P and F are both 1

$$1 = cd_1 + cd_2 + \ldots + cd_n + d_n$$

where P is the price of the bond,
F is the face value,
c is the coupon rate per period, and
d_i is the discount factor applicable to the ith period cash flow.

Equation (18A.1) can be rearranged to focus on c:

$$c = \frac{1 - d_n}{\sum_{i=1}^{n} d_i}$$

As the coupon rate c is equal to the yield per period for a year bond the per annum swap fixed rate can be calculated as:

$$r_{fixed} = k\left(\frac{1 - d_n}{\sum_{i=1}^{n} d_i}\right) \qquad \textit{Equation 18A.2}$$

where k is the number of compounds per annum.

Table 18A.3 Calculation of the swap rate

Contract	Futures price	Implied rate (%)	Days	Cumulative sum	Discount factor
	(1)	(2)	(3)	(4)	(5)
December	94.00	6.00	91.25	1.0000	
March	93.00	7.00	91.25	1.0150	0.9852
June	92.50	7.50	91.25	1.0328	0.9683
September	92.00	8.00	91.25	1.0521	0.9505
				1.0732	0.9318
Total					3.8358

example 18.A1

The first step in calculating the fair swap rate on a three-year $1 million swap, using a semi-annual zero-coupon yield curve, is to compute the cumulative sum column in the table below. This shows the accumulated sum of $1 invested at the zero-coupon rate for t periods. Column (3) = $(1 + \text{column }(2)/2)^{2*(1)}$. The discount factors are the inverse of the cumulative sums. Column (5) = 1/(4). The fixed rate is computed as the coupon rate on a par bond.

Notional Principal =>1 000 000 Fixed Rate=>9.59%

Periods	*Zero coupon rate (%)*	*Cumulative sum*	*Discount factors*	*Floating rate (%)*	*Floating payments*	*Discounted*	*Fixed payments*	*Discounted*	*Net*
(1)	(2)	(3)	(4)	(5)	(6)	(7)	(8)	(9)	(10)
0.00	12.00	1.0000		12.00					
0.50	11.00	1.0600	0.9434	10.00	60 000	56 604	47 960	45 246	11 358
1.00	10.50	1.1130	0.8985	9.50	50 024	44 944	47 960	43 090	1 854
1.50	10.00	1.1659	0.8577	8.51	47 518	40 756	47 960	41 135	−380
2.00	9.75	1.2155	0.8227	8.75	42 536	34 994	47 960	39 457	−4 463
2.50	9.50	1.2687	0.7882	8.25	43 765	34 496	47 960	37 803	−3 307
3.00		1.3211	0.7570		41 272	31 242	47 960	36 304	−5 063
Totals			5.0674			243 035		243 035	0

We can check that the swap fixed rate is indeed 9.59% p.a., confirming that under this rate the swap has a zero net value. The floating rates are implied in the growth of the cumulative sums from one period to the next, $(5)_t = [(3)_{t+1}/(3)_t]*2$. The figures in columns (6) and (8) are the cash flows associated with the floating- and fixed-interest-rate payments on $1 million. Column $(6)_{t+1}$ = $1 000 000*$(5)_t$/2 and Column (8) = $1 000 000*0.0959/2. Columns (7) and (9) are the discounted values of (6) and (8); (7) = (8)/(3), (9) = (8)/(3), and (1) = (7) − (9).

The data presented in table 18A.3 relate to the simple one-year swap presented at the beginning of the chapter. The discount-factor column is obtained as the inverse of the cumulative sum column, (5) = 1/(4). The swap fixed rate is computed as:

$$r_{fixed} = K\left(\frac{1 - d_n}{\sum_{i=1}^{n} d_i}\right)$$

$$= 4\left(\frac{1 - 0.9381}{3.8358}\right)$$

$$= 7.11\% \text{ p.a.}$$

The simple swap used thus far has employed the forward rates embedded in futures contracts as a base for computing floating rates and discount factors. In Australia, bill futures are only traded out for five years. Longer swaps must employ an appropriate zero-coupon yield curve in order to compute the fair fixed rate. The swap rate for a three-year swap using a zero-coupon yield curve is calculated in example 18A.1.

Appendix 18.1 exercises

1 Compute a fair 18-month swap rate on the basis of the following futures prices:

March	92.0
June	93.0
September	94.0
December	95.0
March	95.0
June	95.5

Assume that the swap rate is calculated on the contract date for March futures and the implied forward rates apply for a quarter of a year. Show that the net value of the swap is zero at commencement.

2 Compute a fair 18-month swap rate on the basis of the following futures prices:

March	95.0
June	95.0
September	94.0
December	94.0
March	93.0
June	93.0

Assume that the swap rate is calculated on the contract date for March futures and that the implied forward rates apply to a quarter of a year. Show that the net value of the swap is zero at commencement.

3 Compute a fair three-year swap rate and show that the net value of the swap is zero at its commencement, on the basis of the following zero-coupon swap rates:

Term (years)	*Zero-coupon rates* (% p.a.)
0.5	5
1.0	6
1.5	7
2.0	7
2.5	8
3.0	8

19

Options

Following the deregulation of the financial system, greater attention has been given by traders to the risks created by volatile interest rates, exchange rates and stock prices. As a result, hedgers have turned to risk-management instruments such as futures and forward rates. In this chapter we consider a further instrument, options, that can be used to hedge exposure to price risk, and to open speculative positions.

Study objectives

From your study of this chapter you should be able to:

- describe the features of options and distinguish between a call and a put;
- define and calculate an option's intrinsic value;
- define an option's time value;
- explain the pattern of an option's time value;
- explain the shape and position of an option's price line;
- explain the five factors that can be used to price options;
- distinguish between historic and implied volatility;
- construct profit diagrams for call and put options and the physical asset;
- show how combinations, or option strategies, can be devised to suit particular hedge or speculative requirements.

OPTION MARKETS AND CONTRACTS

Options are widely used in financial risk management. The use of options is entirely due to the unique attributes of an option contract. While options retain some aspects of forward contracts, in that settlement is generally at a future date, they differ from forward or futures contracts in a fundamental respect.

In a forward contract the participating parties are locked in (i.e. committed) to a future transaction. In contrast, the holder of an option contract has the right but not the obligation to complete that transaction. It is this flexibility that makes options such an attractive financial instrument.

There are some who say, rather unkindly, that the discipline of finance consists of 10% mathematics, 10% economics and 80% jargon. If this is the case it results from the contribution of inventive American writers to finance jargon generally and to option jargon in particular. As a consequence of this inventive expression there are many synonyms to describe a particular aspect of an option. We will attempt to highlight and define the more esoteric of these as we progress.

Before we explain the formal features of option contracts and markets we will briefly explain the general nature of options. They exist in many forms. A 14-day cooling-off period that is a feature of certain sales contracts is an option because the intending buyer has, in effect, 14 days in which to decide whether to proceed with the purchase. In options jargon, the buyer has a 14-day option to purchase the product at the contract (or 'exercise') price. Consider another example. When a company borrows funds it is creating an option for the lenders who, in the event of default, have the right to sell the company's assets. In this case, the creditors are not given an exercise price for the assets, so the right to foreclose has only certain features of a 'put' option. We explain put options (the right to sell) below.

In Chapter 12 we discussed rights issues and convertible notes. Both of these instruments have option features. Rights issues provide shareholders with the right, but not the obligation, to subscribe for new shares. In this case, the subscription price represents, in options terminology, an exercise price. Convertible notes allow their holders to convert the notes into shares at a pre-set price. This arrangement creates the right, but not the obligation, to acquire shares at a pre-set price and over a set period.

In this chapter we use formal option contracts to illustrate the features and capabilities of options. Hence, in our discussion we treat options as financial instruments that are traded in an options market. Such options have a market price which is likely to vary from day to day. These options create the right to buy or sell the specified underlying asset (or the underlying 'physical').

Options are a derivative product because, in common with futures and swaps, their value is based on the yield or price (or index) in the market for the underlying asset. Moreover, buying an option is not the same as buying the asset; the option is merely the right to buy (sell) an underlying asset on pre-set terms. In options markets the terms are set out in standard contracts, whereas for untraded options the terms are arranged by the parties to the transaction.

Option trading

Options are traded in both over-the-counter and exchange-organised markets. In the former case, specific option contracts are designed and the price is negotiated between the buyer and the seller, whereas exchange-traded options are standardised options that are traded in the marketplace — usually by open outcry. Australia has two main option exchanges. These are the ASX Derivatives (ASXD) and the Sydney

Futures Exchange (SFE). The former trades options on Australian equities while the latter trades options written on futures contracts.

An option contract is defined by its specifications. Let us examine the sorts of specifications that are necessary to define an option contract.

Option specifications

Type of option

An option contract is either a **put** or a **call**:

- a call option gives the holder the right (but not the obligation) to buy an underlying asset by a certain date at a certain price, and
- a put option gives the holder the right (but not the obligation) to sell an asset by a certain date at a certain price.

The buyer of an option holds the long position, whereas the seller (or **writer**) holds the short position. It is the holder who does not have to proceed with the transaction. It is the ability to not exercise an option contract that distinguishes it from other types of contracts. The seller of an option has no choice in the matter. If the holder decides to exercise the right to complete the transaction, the writer is obliged to comply. On the other hand, if the holder decides not to complete, again, the writer must acquiesce with the holder's wishes.

Underlying asset

An option contract must specify the underlying asset. For example, ordinary shares in NAB are one of the underlying assets of contracts traded in the ASXD. It also specifies the quantity of the underlying asset. In the ASXD the quantity or lot size is 1000 shares.

Options are also traded in the SFE, such as the options on bill and bond futures. In such cases, futures contracts are the assets that underlie option contracts. If the holder of a call option on March 1998 bank bills exercises the right to buy, the holder acquires a March 1998 bank-bill futures contract. In the SFE the quantity is one futures contract.

In this chapter we focus on the ASXD options on shares.

Exercise price

The **strike** or **exercise price** in an option is the price at which the underlying asset can be purchased (in the case of a call option) or sold (in the case of a put option). For example, a $13 put option on NAB gives the holder the right to sell NAB shares at $13 per share. Note that an option's strike price is not the price of the option itself (this is its premium, which is discussed below).

It is usual for an option exchange to determine a range of strike prices at the commencement of trading of a particular contract. Further, the exchange ensures that there is always at least one strike price above and below the current price of the underlying asset. Should the price of the underlying asset rise above the highest current strike price (or fall below the lowest), the exchange adds a new higher (lower) strike contract to the list of contracts being traded.

Expiration date

A holder has until the expiration date (which determines when an option matures) to exercise the right to complete. After this date the option lapses. Exchanges have regular expiration dates that vary with the particular option contract. ASXD contracts expire on the last Thursday of the maturity month, unless this day happens to be the last day in the month, in which case the contract expires on the previous Thursday. Originally the ASXD traded three maturity months for each stock, each three months apart. However, for some of the most active stocks, the ASXD ensures that there is always a contract (the spot contract) that is less than one month from expiration. In addition, the ASXD have recently added long-dated contracts expiring in two and three years for several stocks.

The range of expiry dates for options on News Corp shares is set out in table 19.1, starting with the current month, May. Observe the data on trading volumes and open positions. Many of the contracts were not traded at all on 6 May 1996 and some have been traded only lightly. This pattern of liquid and illiquid contracts is indicative of the option market in general.

American or european-form option

An **american** option can be exercised at any time up to the expiry date, whereas a **european** option can be exercised only on the expiry date. Both the SFE and the ASXD trade american options; whereas a number of over-the-counter options, notably FX and gold options, are written as european options.

An american option has all of the properties of its european counterpart plus the extra degree of freedom of being able to be exercised prior to expiration. It follows that the value of an american option must be equal to or greater than the value of a similar european option.

The valuation of american options is more complex than for european options. But as an american option can have the same value as a european option, this relationship is helpful when valuing american options. In this chapter we confine our attention to european-form options.

Option premium

An option's price (or premium) is established by trading in the market. In common with other traded instruments, the price of an option is liable to vary during its term. Various models have been developed to predict the price of options. They have helped the development of option markets because they assist traders to place a value on options. Later in this chapter we explain the relationship between an option's price and the five factors included in the Black and Scholes option-pricing model.

Market liquidity

Option markets are intrinsically illiquid. This derives from the multiplicity of options attached to a single underlying asset. It was explained above that there are:

- call and put options on each underlying asset (e.g. News Corp shares),

- a number of expiry dates, and
- for each expiry date, a range of strike prices.

Table 19.1 ASXD, options on News Corp shares, 3 May 1996

DERIVATIVES — SHARE OPTIONS
(*Australian Financial Review* 6 May 1996)

CALL OPTIONS

Stock	*Strike price*	*Buyer*	*Seller*	*Last sale*	*Vol. (000s)*	*Open int.*	*Implied volatility Buyer*	*Implied volatility Seller*	*Delta*	*Annual return (%)*
NCP Last Sale Price $7.20:										
1996:										
May	6.00	1.20	1.26	1.39	3	24	—	45.4	+.94	5.63
May	6.50	.71	.77	.92	2	829	—	33.5	+.89	7.51
May	7.00	.28	.32	.29	1335	6851	15.9	22.5	+.75	18.77
May	7.50	.06	.07	.07	3313	22279	20.0	21.7	+.28	13.77
May	8.00	.01	.02	.02	1617	8114	22.8	26.7	+.07	3.25
May	8.50	—	.01	.02	—	1741	—	31.1	+.03	1.87
May	9.00	—	.01	.01	—	118	—	40.0	+.03	1.87
May	9.50	—	.01	.01	—	300	—	49.3	+.03	1.87
Jun.	7.00	.40	.42	.58	5	5	21.3	23.2	+.69	19.35
Jun.	7.50	.17	.20	.25	20	296	23.2	25.9	+.40	17.51
Jun.	8.00	.05	.07	.10	15	33	22.5	25.2	+.17	5.50
Jul.	7.50	.20	.24	—	1150	1150	20.0	23.0	+.43	13.43
Aug.	6.00	1.33	−1.39	1.55	−146	—		28.2	+.92	6.87
Aug.	6.50	.91	.97	1.01	—	52	20.0	26.1	+.85	10.31
Aug.	7.00	.56	.62	.60	—	302	21.6	25.5	+.68	16.75
Aug.	7.50	.31	.35	.46	1802	5646	22.3	24.7	+.48	14.17
Aug.	8.00	.15	.17	.18	595	7125	21.9	23.6	+.29	6.87
Aug.	8.50	.07	.08	.11	2	3275	22.4	23.4	+.15	3.43
Nov.	7.00	.73	.79	.64	—	27	20.8	23.8	+.69	13.58
Nov.	7.50	.48	.54	.68	—	38	21.7	24.6	+.54	12.37
Nov.	8.00	.31	.36	.29	—	108	22.6	24.9	+.40	8.24
Nov.	8.50	.18	.22	.35	—	5494	22.5	24.6	+.27	4.85
1997:										
Feb.	7.00	.90	.97	—	—	—	21.3	24.3	+.71	12.50
Feb.	7.50	.65	.71	—	—	—	22.2	24.6	+.58	11.45
Feb.	8.50	.30	.35	.53	—	6	22.3	24.5	+.35	5.57

PUT OPTIONS

Stock	Strike price	Buyer	Seller	Last sale	Vol. (000s)	Open int.	Implied volatility Buyer	Implied volatility Seller	Delta	Annual return (%)
NCP Last Sale Price $7.20:										
1996:										
May	6.00	—	.01	.02½	—	992	—	40.0	−.04	1.87
May	6.50	.02	.04	.02	200	3964	29.2	35.0	−.10	5.63
May	7.00	.07	.07	.07½	821	7609	20.8	21.5	−.27	13.14
May	7.50	.32	.36	.32	4128	10562	18.5	24.8	−.74	7.51
May	8.00	.77	.83	.90	—	85	22.7	37.0	−.93	1.76
Jun.	6.50	.03	.05	.03	40	50	22.3	26.8	−.11	3.68
Jun.	7.00	.13	.16	.15	23	158	21.9	24.7	−.32	13.82
Jun.	7.50	.37	.38	.27	5	35	20.0	21.3	−.67	7.37
Jul.	7.00	.16	.19	—	1150	1150	21.2	23.5	−.33	10.99
Aug.	5.50	—	.01	.02½	—	185	—	24.6	−.02	.42
Aug.	6.00	.02	.04	.03	20	135	21.5	26.8	−.06	1.28
Aug.	6.50	.08	.10	.07	10	1235	22.5	24.4	−.16	3.86
Aug.	7.00	.21	.25	.19	2173	7027	22.1	24.7	−.34	9.88
Aug.	7.50	.45	.50	.44	585	1204	21.7	24.8	−.57	7.73
Aug.	8.00	.82	.88	.51	—	455	21.4	27.5	−.78	2.14
Nov.	6.00	.05	.09	.06	—	334	21.8	26.5	−.10	1.69
Nov.	6.50	.14	.18	.18	—	102	22.7	25.4	−.20	3.88
Nov.	7.00	.29	.34	.34	—	275	22.6	25.1	−.34	7.76
Nov.	7.50	.54	.60	.50	—	102	23.1	25.0	−.51	6.54
1997:										
Feb.	7.00	.36	.41	.44	—	20	23.4	25.6	−.34	6.59

Even if there is considerable interest in the market for the underlying asset, this interest per option contract will be considerably diminished by the time it is diluted down to a particular option. In other words, each option instrument is defined by its type, maturity and strike price.

The degree of dilution that exists in the option market can be observed from the list of News Corp options in table 19.1. This underlying asset supports some 20 option instruments. Observe, from the turnover column, that a number of the News Corp options had an insignificant volume of transactions. The multiplicity of option instruments ensures that some of these instruments will be illiquid.

The more liquid options are:

- calls rather than puts,
- those that are near their expiry date (rather than options with a long term), and

- those that are 'at the money' rather than those that are either 'in' or 'out of the money'. (These terms are defined below.)

There is no convincing theoretical reason to explain the liquidity structure of option series — it is simply an observable market phenomenon.

ELEMENTS OF AN OPTION'S VALUE

The total value of an option comprises its **intrinsic** and **time values**.

Intrinsic value

The **intrinsic value** of an option is its value if it is exercised immediately. This depends on the level of the price of the underlying asset and the option's strike price. It also reflects the fact that an option does not have to be exercised. Should the price of the underlying asset be less than the option's strike price, the option's holder will not exercise the option (i.e. will not buy the shares through the option). This implies that an option's intrinsic value cannot be less than zero. And this is the distinguishing feature of options.

Consequently, the value of a call option may be expressed as:

$$C = \max(0, S - X) \qquad \textit{Equation (19.1)}$$

where C is the value of the call option
S is the price of the asset, and
X is the exercise price.

For example, when S = \$14.00 and X = \$13.00, C = \$1.00. This results from the call option holder having the right to buy the stock at \$13.00 and then to sell it at the market price of \$14.00, thus yielding the holder a profit of \$1.00. On the other hand, if the current stock price, S, was equal to \$12.00, the intrinsic value of the option is zero (i.e. maximum (0, 12.00 − 13.00) = 0). This value reflects the fact that one would not exercise the right to buy at \$13.00 if one could instead buy in the market at \$12.00.

Table 19.2 Intrinsic value of a call and a put option with a \$13.00 strike

Shareprice (\$)	*Intrinsic value of call (\$)*	*Intrinsic value of put (\$)*
10.00	0.00	3.00
11.00	0.00	2.00
12.00	0.00	1.00
13.00	0.00	0.00
14.00	1.00	0.00
15.00	2.00	0.00
16.00	3.00	0.00

It is easy to calculate the intrinsic value of an option for a range of prices of the underlying asset, S. The intrinsic value of a call option is zero whenever the asset price is less than the strike price. Once the asset price reaches the exercise price, the intrinsic value of the option rises dollar for dollar with the price of the underlying asset. This relationship for a call option is illustrated by the data in figure 19.1 and table 19.2.

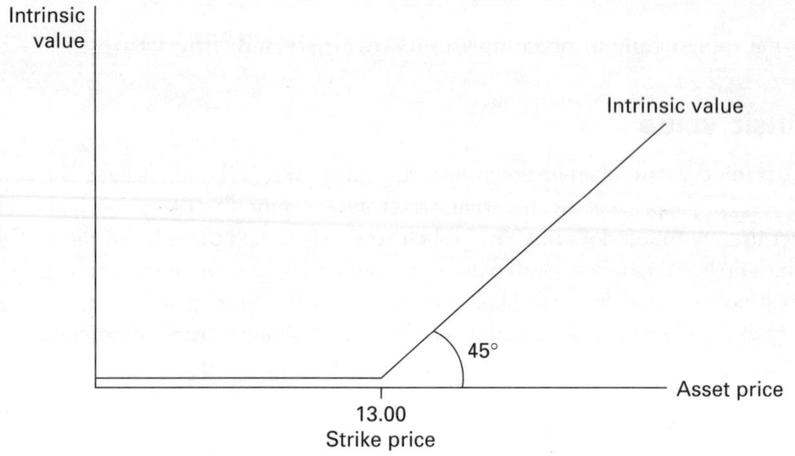

Figure 19.1 Intrinsic value of a \$13.00 call

The intrinsic value of a call option is defined as being:

- in the money, when $S > X$,
- at the money, when $S = X$, or
- out of the money, when $S < X$.

Observe in figure 19.1 that the in-the-money position is shown by the upward-sloping part of the curve, the at-the-money position is at the share price where the curve bends, and the out-of-the-money position is where the curve is flat.

The fact that an option is a right, but not an obligation, to purchase an underlying asset is reflected in its intrinsic value diagram by the asymmetrical response to changes in the value of the underlying asset. When the price of the underlying asset rises above the exercise price, the option fully participates in any change in the value of the underlying asset. However, if the price of the underlying asset falls below the exercise price, then the intrinsic value of the option is unaffected by further falls in the price of the underlying asset. We shall see later that it is this pay-off asymmetry that generates much of an option's value.

The intrinsic value of a put option is given by:

$$P = \text{maximum}\ (0, X - S) \qquad \textit{Equation (19.2)}$$

where P is the value of the put option.

For example, when the exercise price, X, equals \$13.00 and the asset price, S, equals \$11.00, the option's intrinsic value equals \$2.00. This value arises because the holder of a put option can buy the asset at \$11.00 and, by exercising the option, sell it at \$13.00, thus making a profit of \$2.00. See table 19.2 and figure 19.2 for an illustration of a put option's intrinsic value.

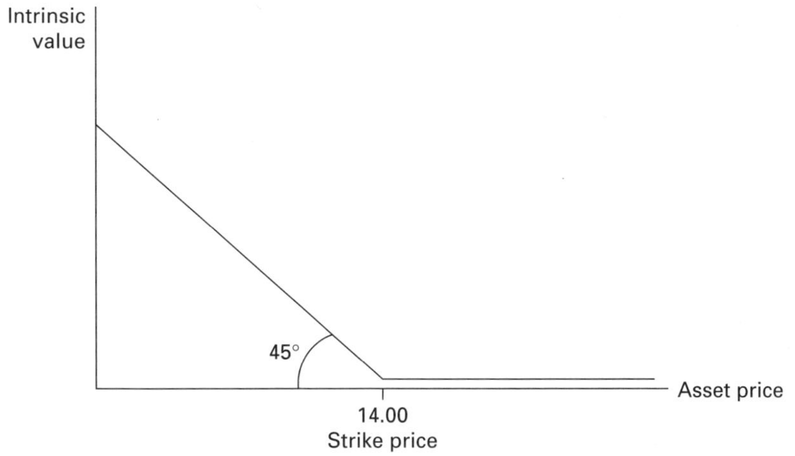

Figure 19.2 Put option, intrinsic value diagram

A put option's intrinsic value diagram can be constructed, in a similar manner to that of the call option, by plotting the intrinsic value of a particular put option against a range of prices of the underlying asset. A put option is in the money when $S < X$, at the money when $S = X$, and out of the money when $S > X$.

Time value

So far, we have concentrated on the intrinsic value of an option (its value if exercised now). This amount is calculated very easily, as explained above. (See example 19.1.) By its very nature, an option has an uncertain value component, which arises from the chance that at expiry it will be in the money. This is referred to as an option's **time value**.

example 19.1

What would be the price of BHP shares if both a \$20.00 call and a \$20.50 put have the same intrinsic value?

$$\text{Call value} = \text{Put value}$$

$$(S - X) = (X - S)$$

$$(S - 20.00) = (20.50 - S)$$

or:

$$S = \frac{20.00 + 20.50}{2}$$

$$= \$20.25$$

An option's value is determined by its market price. Conceptually, this can be divided into two parts: its intrinsic value and its time value. That is:

$$\text{Option value} = \text{Intrinsic value} + \text{Time value}$$

Given that we can calculate an option's intrinsic value from its strike price and the price of the underlying asset and that we can observe an option's market price, we can calculate an option's time value as:

$$\text{Time value} = \text{Option price} - \text{Intrinsic value}$$

To illustrate, the time value of some of the News Corp options listed in table 19.1 is shown in table 19.3. The data illustrate two general features of time value. First, time value is positively related to time to maturity. For each strike, the time value of the April series exceeds that of the January series. Second, the time value of the at-the-money series (the $7.00 strike options are close to the at-the-money position) is greater than that of either the in-the-money ($6.00 strike) or the out-of-the-money ($8.00 strike) series.

Table 19.3 Time value, News Corp. shares (price is $7.20)

Series	*Strike price ($)*	*Option's price[1] ($)*	*Intrinsic value ($)*	*Time value ($)*
May 1996	6.00	1.23	1.20	0.03
	7.00	0.30	0.20	0.10
	8.00	0.02	0.00	0.02
August 1996	6.00	1.36	1.20	0.16
	7.00	0.59	0.20	0.39
	8.00	0.16	0.00	0.16

[1] mid-point price, from Table 19.1

An understanding of the value patterns revealed by the data in table 19.3 rests on an option's asymmetric intrinsic value pattern, given the uncertain future movements in the value of the underlying asset.

Asymmetric value pattern

An option's asymmetric intrinsic value line serves to create value because it shows that an option participates in the benefit of price increases above the strike (i.e. has 'upside potential'), but does not participate in the loss should the price of the underlying asset fall below the strike. The upside potential and 'capped' downside value lines for a call and a put are shown in figures 19.1 and 19.2. A symmetric value line (such as that for a futures position, illustrated in Chapter 17) intersects the horizontal axis (i.e. has upside and downside potential), whereas an option has no negative zone.

The pattern of possible future price movements is shown by the frequency distributions in figures 19.3 and 19.4. According to the efficient-market hypothesis, prices follow a random walk and thus are equally as likely to rise as to fall. Therefore the frequency distributions of possible future prices (for the option's underlying asset) have a normal distribution shape.

These factors imply that an option fully participates in a favourable movement in the price of the underlying asset but does not fully participate in an unfavourable movement. The way unfavourable price movements influence an option's value depends on whether the option is at an in-the-money position. This point is explained further in example 19.2.

example 19.2

A loose parallel can be drawn between the asymmetry of an option's return and gambling. Suppose you played a game of two-up even though you are risk-averse. The value of this game is zero, given that over a long period the wins will be balanced by the losses. In other words, you cannot expect that the game will increase your wealth; you should depart the game with the same amount of money you had before it commenced.

But suppose the rules of the game were modified, so that they became 'heads you win, tails you do not lose'. This game has value because of its 'unlimited upside potential and capped downside'. Hence, playing this game should result in your wealth being increased. As a consequence, you would be prepared to pay to participate in the game.

An option participates in favourable price movements but escapes unfavourable ones when they would result in a loss. And so, a price has to be paid to acquire an option. (We explain below that this claim applies especially to at-the-money options.)

When possible future movements in the price of the underlying asset (i.e. its volatility):

- can increase an option's value (when they are in a favourable direction),
- without reducing its value by an equivalent amount (when the price movement is unfavourable),

they become the source of the time value of options.

In figure 19.3 a distribution of future values for the underlying asset is superimposed on a value diagram for a call option at maturity. (Note that at maturity, by definition, an option's intrinsic value is also its total value — as it has no time value.) We have constructed the diagram such that the distribution of future asset prices is centred around the exercise price of the option. That is, it is equally likely that asset prices in the future will end up such that the option is in or out of the money.

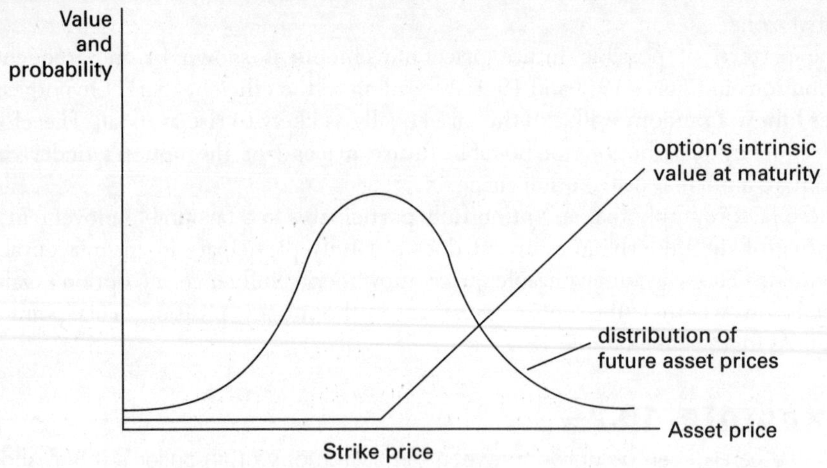

Figure 19.3 Possible future values of share price and a call's intrinsic value

While the distribution of future asset prices is symmetrical, the pay-off to the holder of the option is not, when the option is at the money. If at maturity the price of the asset exceeds the strike price, the holder of the option wins, whereas if at maturity the asset's price is less than the exercise price, the zero intrinsic value floor protects the holder against loss. An option has a positive time value because if the asset price increases the option holder benefits, while if the asset price falls the holder does not lose. The disparity between the option's upside gain and downside loss gives the option time value.

It follows that the greater the disparity between the upside gain and the downside loss, the greater the time value. This upside/downside disparity is greatest when the distribution of future prices is spread around the exercise price. As illustrated in figure 19.4, this occurs when the exercise price is at today's asset price. The disparity between upside gain and downside loss for an at-the-money option means that, of all options, the time value is greatest for an at-the-money option.

When the option is out-of-the-money, there can be only a limited degree of upside/downside disparity. In figure 19.4, refer to the frequency distribution of future possible shareprices that is situated over the out-of-the-money position. Here, upward price movements (in common with downward movements) will not affect the option's value and therefore do not contribute time value.

When the option is in-the-money, movements in future prices (shown by the frequency distribution in figure 19.4 situated over the in-the-money position) follow a symmetric pattern because price rises add value and price falls reduce value. Given the reduced asymmetry, the option has less time value when it is in the money than when it is at the money.

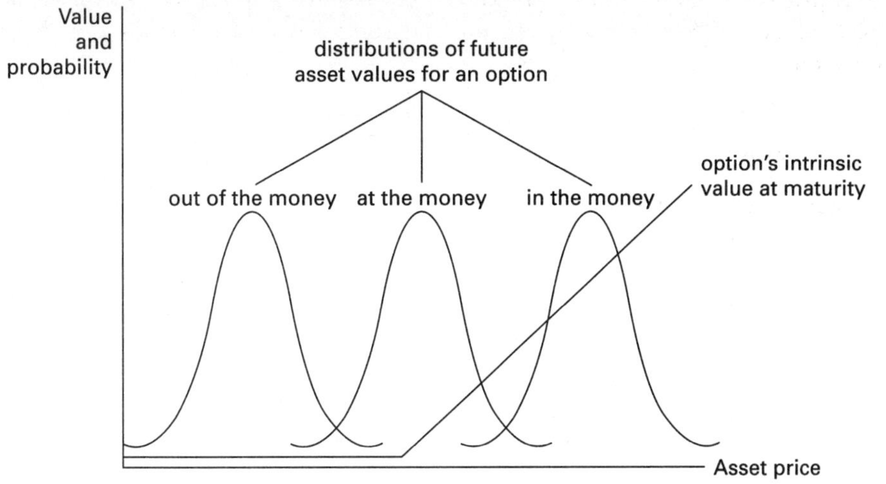

Figure 19.4 Possible future shareprices at various option values

The time value of a call option is represented in part (a) of figure 19.5 by the pyramid-shaped curve. Its maximum height occurs when the option is at-the-money. The addition of an option's time value to its intrinsic value is shown in part (b) of figure 19.5 by the option's **price line** which shows its price as a function of the price of the underlying asset, given the other factors that determine the option's value. Observe that:

- an out-of-the-money option has only time value, and
- an in-the-money option has both intrinsic and time values, although as the intrinsic value increases, the time value diminishes.

Whereas an option's intrinsic value line shows its value at maturity, its price line traces its possible prices during its term. Points on a price line show an option's price at a moment in time in relation to the price of the underlying asset. Changes in other factors cause the price line to shift. These other factors are discussed below.

Degree of volatility

All other things being equal, the greater the distribution of future asset prices the greater the time value, because of the greater possibility of a profitable pay-off.

The distribution of future asset prices depends on:

1. the price volatility of the underlying asset, and
2. the time to the expiration of the option.

Some assets, simply by their nature, have greater price volatility than other assets. A bank like ANZ, because of the nature of its business, has or ought to have a relatively stable shareprice. On the other hand, WMC, a company whose profit depends on volatile metal prices, will naturally have a volatile stock price. As a consequence, the time value of the more volatile stock, WMC, will be greater than the time value of the less volatile stock, ANZ. The wider of the bell-shaped curves in figure 19.6 depicts a shareprice with greater volatility.

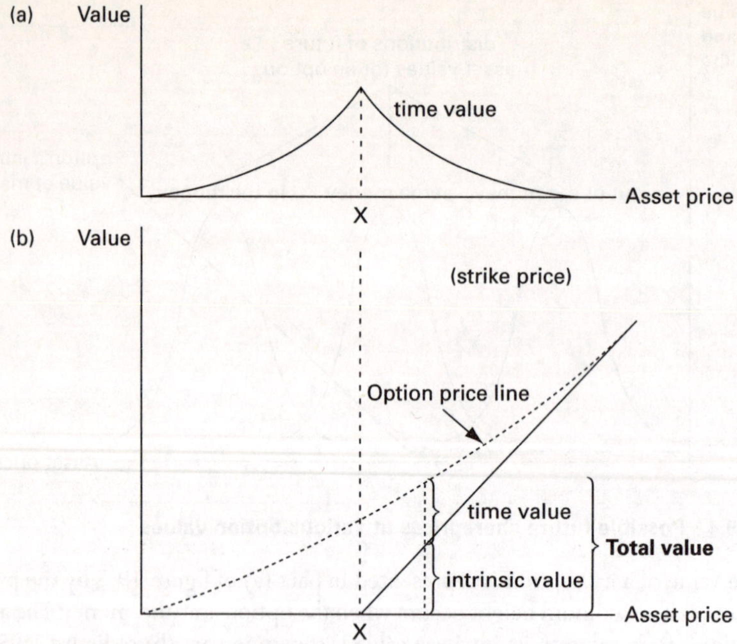

Figure 19.5 A call option's price line — intrinsic plus time value

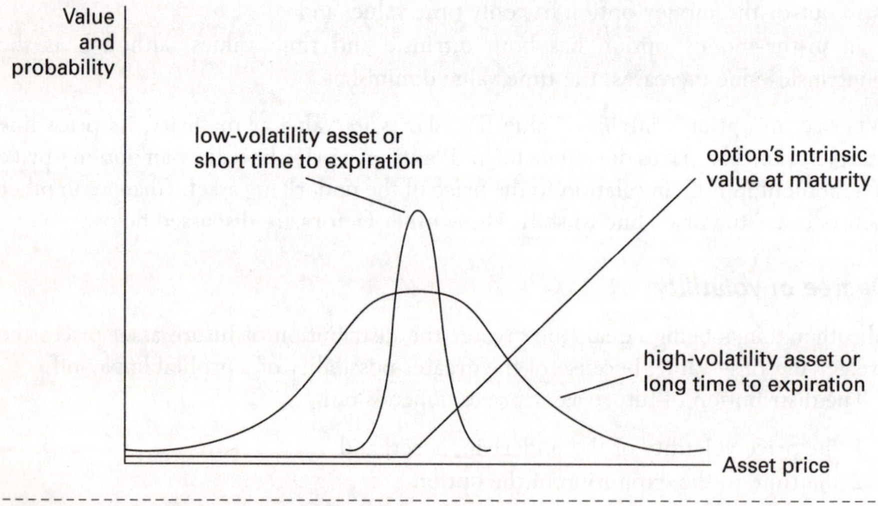

Figure 19.6 Volatility of an asset's future prices

The degree of price volatility is reflected in the option's price line. The greater the volatility, the greater the time value. Therefore, the price line for an option on a share with greater volatility will be further from the intrinsic value line than for an option on a share that has less volatility. This relationship is represented in figure 19.7 by the price line further from the intrinsic value line.

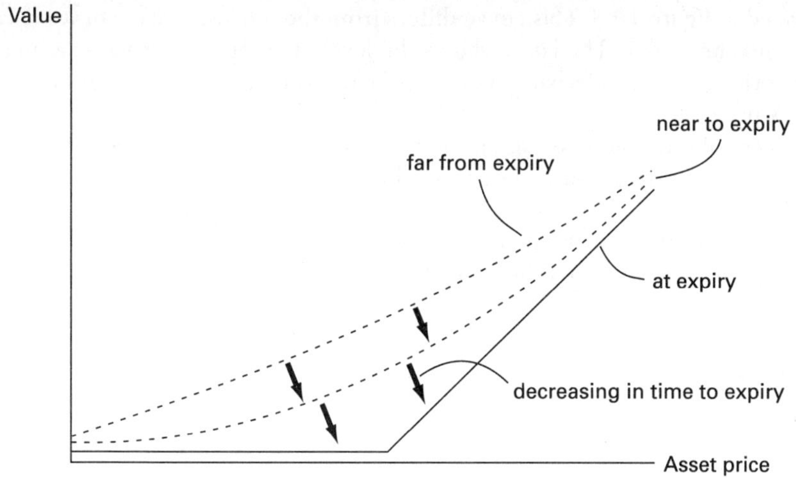

Figure 19.7 Volatility and the passage of time and an option's price line

The position of the price line for an option depends also on the option's time to run. An option's time value diminishes with the passage of time because the spread of future prices depends directly on the length of time within which they can occur. For example, for any stock, the spread of possible prices for next week must be narrower than the spread of possible prices for next month. As an option's time to maturity diminishes, so will its volatility and this will be reflected in a fall in its time value. This is depicted in figure 19.7 by the inward movement of the price line.

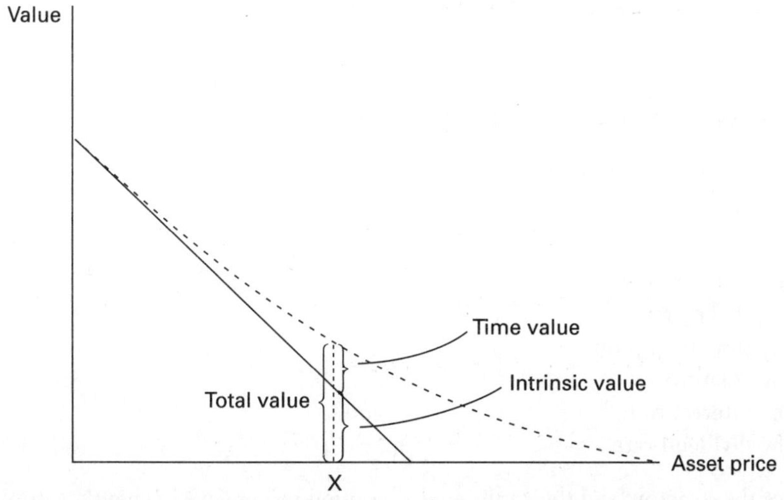

Figure 19.8 Time and intrinsic value for a put, shown by the price line

The total value of a put option (the time value and the intrinsic value) is illustrated in figure 19.8. This curve differs from the intrinsic value curves because it includes time value. The curve shows the level of an option's price as a function of the price of the underlying asset, given the other factors that influence the option's price.

The lapse of time decreases an option's time value and this is shown by the inward movement of the option price line toward the angle of the option's intrinsic value. This effect is illustrated in figure 19.8. A decrease in volatility works in the same way. However, volatility can increase, forcing the option price line away from the intrinsic value angle. This is illustrated in figure 19.9.

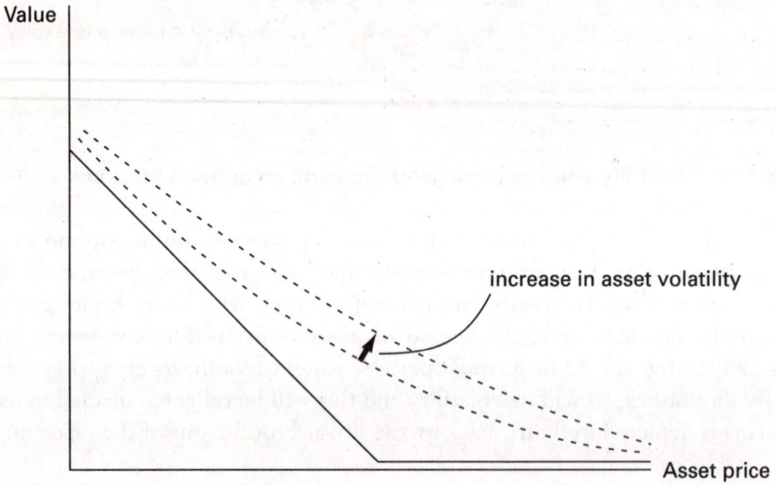

Figure 19.9 Volatility and a put option's time line

FACTORS THAT DETERMINE AN OPTION'S PRICES

There are six factors that affect the price of an option on a dividend-paying asset:

1 the asset price, S,
2 the strike price, X,
3 the time to expiration, t,
4 the volatility, σ,
5 the interest rate, r, and
6 the dividend rate, q.

Most of these factors and their influence on option prices have been either implicitly or explicitly discussed. The direction of the influence of each of these factors on the value of a call and a put option is summarised in table 19.4.

Table 19.4 Determinants of option prices

Factor	*Direction of effect on prices of:* Call	Put
asset price, S	+	–
strike price, X	–	+
time to expiry, t	+	+
volatility, δ	+	+
interest rate, r	+	–
dividend interest rate, q	–	+

Asset and strike prices

The value of both put and call options, if exercised, depends on the relationship between the asset price and the strike price. In the case of the call option, provided the asset price exceeds the exercise price, the option is worth the asset price less the exercise price. Thus, the higher the asset price or the lower the strike price the greater the value of the call option.

Put options embody a right to sell an asset. The future pay-off depends on the exercise price less the asset price. The higher the strike price or the lower the asset price, the greater the value of the put option.

Volatility

The distribution of possible future asset prices (coupled with an option's asymmetrical pay-off and an option's time to expiration) is a primary source of an option's time value. The greater the volatility of the asset's price, the more diffuse the distribution of possible future asset prices. Therefore the greater the price volatility of the underlying asset, the greater the price of both put and call options.

Of the six variables listed above, only the price volatility of the underlying asset over the term of the option cannot be directly observed. It indicates the range of possible price movements in the underlying security that can occur prior to the maturity of an option and as such is clearly an important variable in the pricing of an option.

The most obvious indicator of an asset's current volatility is its **historic volatility** represented by its actual volatility over the recent past. However, in option pricing there is another important concept of volatility: the **implied volatility**. This is implied by an option's current market price. For example if, given all other variables, using a volatility of 25% produces a theoretical option price of $2.00 and the market price for the option is also $2.00, the implied volatility is 25%.

Table 19.5 Asset-price volatility

Month	*Price*	*Continuously compounded returns (%)*
December 1989	10.00	
January 1990	9.73	−2.74
February 1990	9.58	−1.55
March 1990	9.51	−0.73
April 1990	9.47	−0.42
May 1990	9.70	2.40
June 1990	9.95	2.54
July 1990	9.97	0.20
August 1990	10.30	3.26
September 1990	10.42	1.16
October 1990	9.90	−5.12
November 1990	9.77	−1.32
December 1990	9.75	−0.20
Calculated data		
Monthly average return		−0.21
Monthly standard deviation		2.28
Yearly standard deviation		2.28% * $12^{0.5}$ = 7.90

Ideally the volatility that ought to be used in pricing options is the future volatility of the price of the underlying asset, between now and the expiry of the option. This volatility is, by the immutable law of time, unobtainable. As a consequence, option practitioners must obtain and employ a reasonable proxy for the unobservable future volatility. Historical volatility is one such proxy.

Estimating historical volatility

An asset's price volatility is the standard deviation of its annual returns. In practice the returns are estimated from regular observations of the price of the underlying asset. An example of the calculation of historical volatility using monthly asset prices is presented below using the data in table 19.5.

Note that the first step in calculating volatility requires that prices (shown in table 19.5) be converted to per period returns, as shown in the table. This is accomplished by taking the natural logs of the ratio of this period's price to last period's price. Next, the standard deviation of the per period returns is calculated. This can be accomplished either through the command @STD in Lotus (or similar commands in other spreadsheet programs), or by using a standard statistical formula for the standard deviation. Finally, the per period standard deviation is annualised by multiplying it by the square root of the number of periods in a year. Thus, in the example above:

$$\sigma_{\text{annual}} = \sigma_{\text{monthly}} * 12^{0.5}$$

$$= 0.0228 * 3.4641$$

$$= 7.90\%$$

The problems of correctly specifying volatility estimators have led most practitioners to consider another approach to the estimation of volatility. This approach uses as a measure of volatility an option's market price. This measure is called an option's **implied volatility**. Note that implied volatility for News Corp options is recorded in table 19.1 for the buyer and seller. These are the implied volatility numbers associated with each bid and offer price.

Volatility is always positively related to the price of an option. A typical relationship between volatility and price is set out in figure 19.10. This relationship makes it easy to 'reverse' the usual relationship and go from option price to volatility, rather than from volatility to option price.

Interest rates

An increase in the rate of interest affects options in two ways. First, it increases the average of the distribution of future asset prices. This results because future (or accumulated) values vary directly with the rate of interest (i.e. F values are increased by higher interest rates). Second, an increase in interest rates decreases the present value of the strike price that must be paid should the holder exercise an option. For example, an increase in interest rates decreases the present value of the strike and thus increases the value of a call option and decreases the value of a put option.

For put options, these two effects work in the same direction to decrease the value of a put option. For call options, these effects of an increase in interest rates oppose one another. However, it can be shown that on balance, an increase in interest rates increases the value of a call option.

Dividend rates

When an asset pays a dividend, its price will drop by the amount of the dividend. It follows that the greater the dividend, or the higher the dividend rate, the lower will be the price of the underlying asset. Therefore a high dividend rate will reduce the value of any call option written over an asset because it decreases the value of an underlying asset.

A put option is advantaged by a high dividend rate. A high dividend rate reduces the value of an asset and so increases the value of any put option written on that asset.

The Black and Scholes option-pricing model

The estimation of the 'fair' value of an option requires complex mathematical models. The most common of these models, the Black-Scholes, is named after its

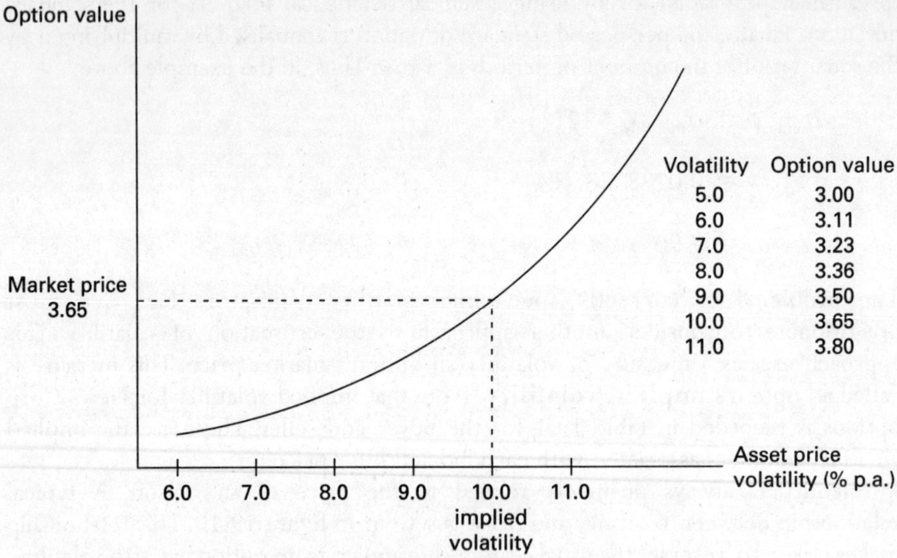

Figure 19.10 Relationship between option price and volatility

originators. An exploration of the nature of this model is outside the scope of this text. However the Black-Scholes formulae and an example of their use is presented in the appendix at the end of this chapter.

PROFIT DIAGRAMS

The single most important determinant of option value is the price of the underlying asset. Profit diagrams show how the profit on an option, or a combination of options, varies with the price of the underlying asset. Observe in the diagrams that the price of the underlying asset (a particular share in our applications), is shown along the horizontal axis, whereas profit, which is the option's value minus its price, is shown along the vertical axis.

The pay-off lines in these diagrams show the profit/loss that would arise given the price of the underlying asset at the option's expiration. Profit/loss is calculated as an option's intrinsic value minus its (entry) price. Even though these diagrams ignore an option's time value, they remain a useful tool in the design and analysis of option strategies.

Call options

For the holder of a call option at expiration, profit is given by:

$$\text{Profit}_{\text{call}} = \max(0, S - X) - E \qquad \textit{Equation (19.3)}$$

where $Profit_{call}$ is the net value of the call option,
S is the price of the asset,
X is the exercise price, and
E is the entry cost (i.e. price of the option).

For example, suppose we bought an April call option on BHP, strike price $19.00, for $1.50. Further, suppose at the expiration of the option the price of BHP is $18.00.

$$\text{Profit} = \max(0, 18.00 - 19.00) - 1.50$$
$$= -\$1.50$$

We can see in this case that the holder of the call option loses $1.50 per share, this being the purchase price of the option. Alternatively, if at expiration BHP was $21.50, the holder makes $1.00 per share.

$$\text{Profit} = \max(0, 21.50 - 19.00) - 1.50$$
$$= \$1.00$$

We have made similar calculations over a range of possible asset prices for this call option, the results of which are set out in table 19.6.

Table 19.6 Pay-off line for a $19.00 strike call option

Asset price ($)	*Profit ($)*
18.00	−1.50
19.00	−1.50
20.00	−0.50
21.00	0.50
22.00	1.50
23.00	2.50

A plot of profit against asset price is called a pay-off diagram. Figure 19.11 shows the pay-off diagram for the table 19.6 call option.

You will see that in figure 19.11 the graph consists of two distinct sections:

- a flat section reflecting the fact that the intrinsic value of an option is never less than zero, and
- an upward-sloping line, starting at the exercise price, reflecting the fact that once an option is in the money, its value at maturity increases, dollar for dollar, with the value of the underlying asset.

What about the returns to the seller (i.e. writer) of a call option? The writer's return is the mirror image of that accruing to the call option holder. The writer is paid the

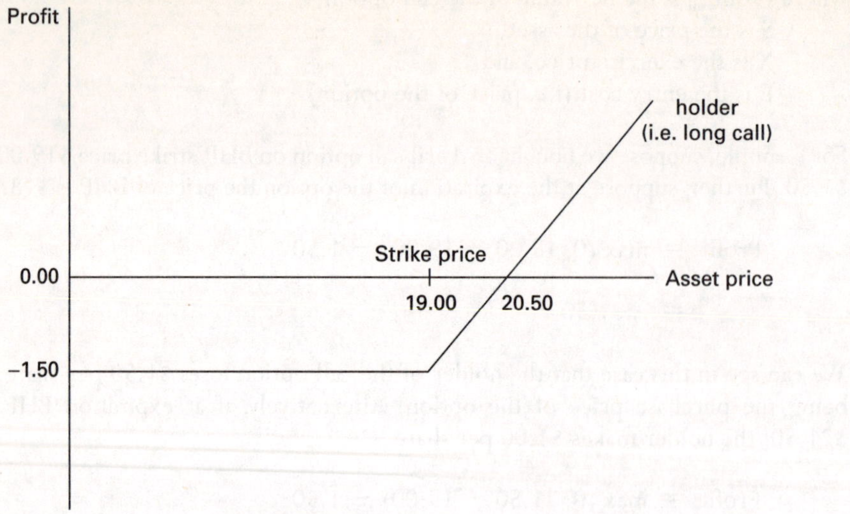

Figure 19.11 Call option pay-off diagram

option premium, by the holder, at the commencement of the transaction. The writer's profit is given by the difference between the premium and the intrinsic value. Using the above example, suppose BHP shares are at $19.50, when the option expires, then:

$$\text{Profit} = [1.50 - \max(0, 19.50 - 19.00)]$$

$$= \$1.00$$

In this case the holder of the option will exercise the right to buy at $19.00 because the 50-cent price advantage will partly meet the cost of the option. This reduces the holder's loss from $1.50 to $1.00 and consequently the profit to the writer will be $1.00. Figure 19.12 shows the profit diagram for the writer of a call option.

The break-even point, where both the holder and writer of the call option realise zero profit, is equal to the strike price plus the premium paid.

Put options

The profit accruing to the holder of a put option is given by:

$$\text{Profit}_{put} = \max(0, X - S) - E \qquad \textit{Equation (19.4)}$$

Observe that the return to the purchaser of a put option at maturity is given by the intrinsic value less the premium received. To illustrate, suppose a $20.00 strike BHP put option was sold at $1.50, and the shares were selling for $19.00 at its expiry date. The holder of the option would exercise the option (i.e. sell the shares at $20.00) and buy the shares in the market at $19.00, yielding a gross return of

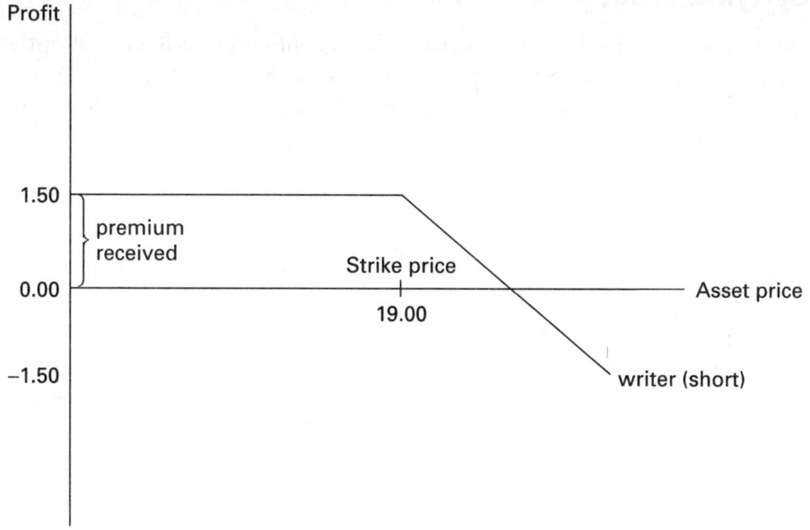

Figure 19.12 Pay-off diagram for a short call

\$1.00. Given the purchase price of \$1.50, the holder would lose \$0.50 per option.

The pay-off diagram for the long and short put-option positions is shown in figure 19.13, where the short put position is shown by the broken line.

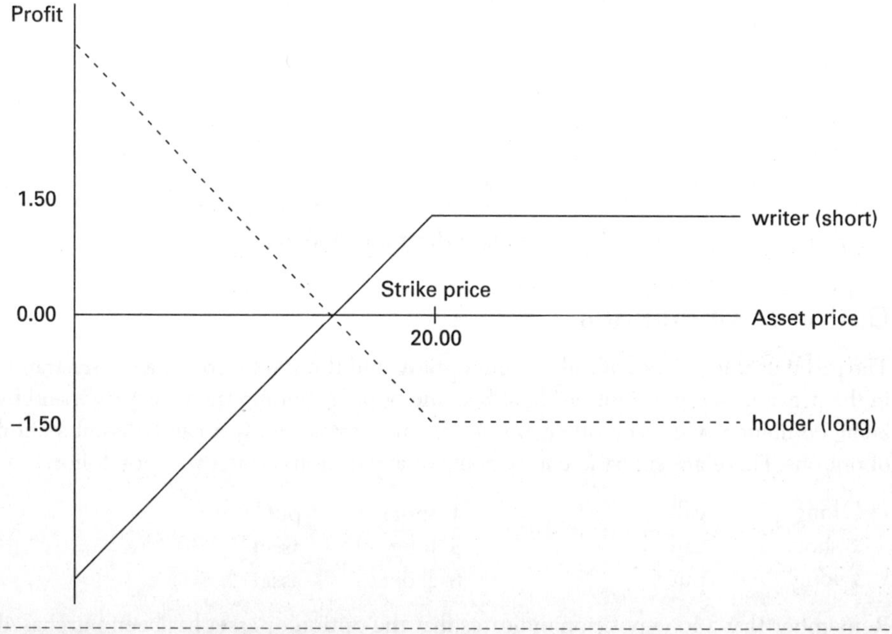

Figure 19.13 Pay-off lines for a put option

Underlying asset

The discussion of profit diagrams has so far been confined to call and put options. It is a simple matter to extend the profit analysis to the underlying asset. If a long position in the underlying asset is taken, the buyer will profit by the amount that the price of the asset rises above the entry price. That is:

$$\text{Profit}_{\text{asset}} = S - E \qquad \textit{Equation (19.5)}$$

where $\text{Profit}_{\text{asset}}$ is the value of the position,
S is the price of the asset,
E is the entry cost.

Of course the profit attached to a short position in the asset is the negative of any long-position profit. These pay-off lines are illustrated in figure 19.14, where the short position is shown by the broken line.

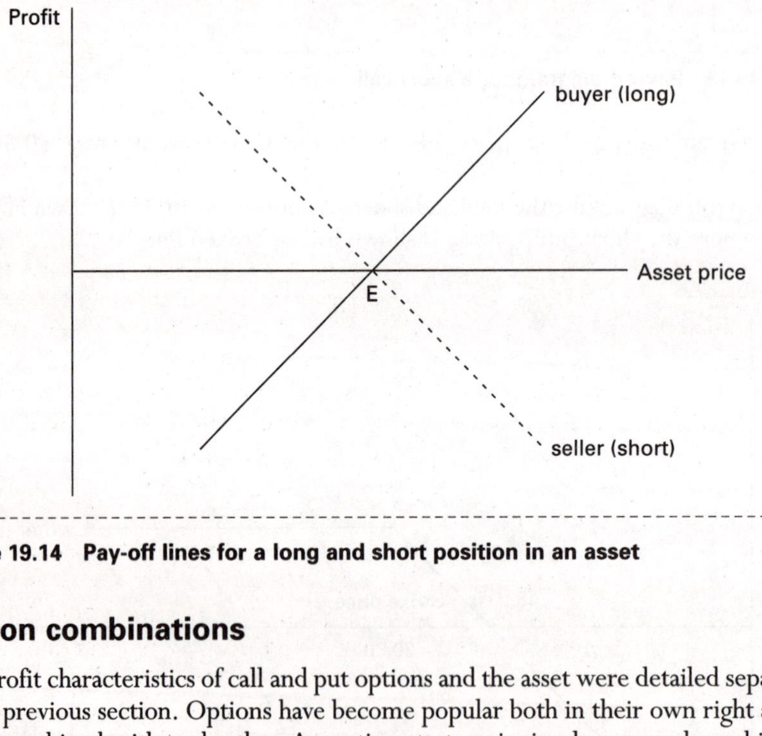

Figure 19.14 Pay-off lines for a long and short position in an asset

Option combinations

The profit characteristics of call and put options and the asset were detailed separately in the previous section. Options have become popular both in their own right and by being combined with each other. An option strategy is simply a named combination of options. There are six basic components of any options strategy or portfolio:

1 long	call	4 short	put
2 short	call	5 long	asset
3 long	put	6 short	asset

Remember that a long position indicates that the option or asset has been purchased and a short position indicates that the option or asset has been sold. It is a relatively simple task to evaluate the profit diagram of a combination of basic option positions. The profit attached to a portfolio is the sum of each of the profits attached to its individual components. So the pay-off diagram for a combination is the vertical sum of the underlying option positions.

The number of option combinations, and hence option strategies, is unlimited. We will examine a few of the simpler strategies in order to illustrate their general properties. Each strategy is designed to take advantage of an expected set of future asset prices. Hedge and speculation strategies may be formed so as to protect against untoward movements in the price of the underlying asset or to profit from such price movements.

In general, a combination alters the pay-off line for a single position, but in doing so, its effect on the upside is reflected also in the downside. A combination that reduces the upside potential, for example, can be expected to reduce its downside. Combinations may also change the pattern of the upside and this can be expected also to reduce the pattern of the downside.

Buy and write

A buy and write strategy is the combination of the long asset and the short call (over the asset) positions. The short call position is taken at a strike price that is less than the purchase price of the shares. This combination uses the price received for the short call to substantially offset the downside of the long asset position. However, the short call caps the upside of the long asset position. Therefore it has a conservative pay-off line compared with the unlimited upside and downside of the long asset position.

This combination is illustrated with a short August call on News Corp shares, with a $6.00 strike (sold at $1.55) and the purchase of the shares at $7.20. The value of the constituent positions, together with that for the combined position, over the range of possible shareprices at expiry, is shown by the data in table 19.7. Observe that the pay-off values of the combined position are simply the sum of the pay-offs of the constituent positions at each possible shareprice. For example, should News Corp shares be at $4.50 in August 1996, the long asset position would have a negative pay-off of $2.70, the short call would have a positive value of $1.55, and thus the pay-off on the combined position would be negative $1.15.

Figure 19.15 plots the pay-off diagram for the individual components of the buy/write strategy as for the position as a whole. The conservative pay-off line for the buy/write strategy provides a fund manager, for example, with downside protection (against a possible fall in the value of News Corp shares) and some upside potential ($0.35).

The buy/write pay-off diagram illustrates two general points. First, strategies do not create wealth. There are no free lunches! Adding a second position (creating a combination) that alters the downside, also alters the upside. The buy and write strategy reduces the downside (shown by the thick line in figure 19.15 being above the downside of the long asset position), but also caps the upside, shown by the horizontal section of the combination's pay-off line. However, it also improves the profit of the long stock position should the shareprice, at expiry, be less than $7.55. On the other hand, if the stock ends up above $7.55, the long stock position would outperform the buy and write strategy.

Table 19.7 Pay-off data for a buy/write combination on News Corp

Shareprice at expiry ($)	*Pay-off on long asset ($)*	*Pay-off on short call ($)*	*Pay-off on buy/write ($)*
4.50	−2.70	+1.55	−1.15
5.00	−2.20	+1.55	−0.65
5.50	−1.70	+1.55	−0.15
6.00	−1.20	+1.55	+0.35
6.50	−0.70	+1.05	+0.35
7.00	−0.20	+0.55	+0.35
7.50	+0.30	+0.05	+0.35
8.00	+0.80	−0.45	+0.35
8.50	+1.30	−0.95	+0.35
9.00	+1.80	−1.45	+0.35

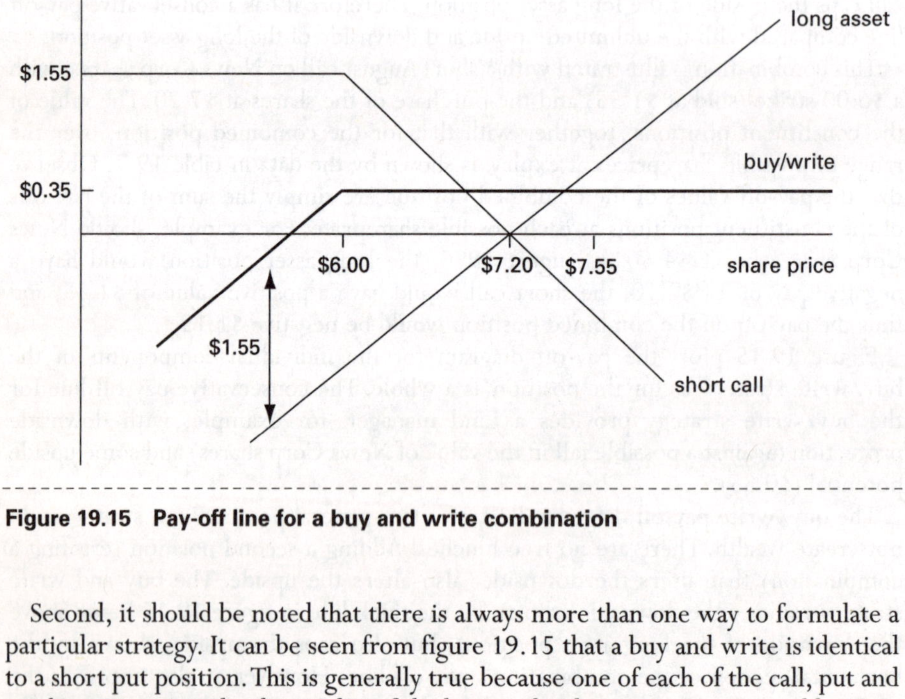

Figure 19.15 Pay-off line for a buy and write combination

Second, it should be noted that there is always more than one way to formulate a particular strategy. It can be seen from figure 19.15 that a buy and write is identical to a short put position. This is generally true because one of each of the call, put and stock positions is redundant. A list of the basic redundancies is set out in table 19.8. The equalities shown in the left-hand side of the table are redundant when the right-hand side portfolios are created.

Table 19.8 Option-position redundancies

Long call	=	long asset	+	long put
Short call	=	short asset	+	short put
Long put	=	short asset	+	long call
Short put	=	long asset	+	short call
Long asset	=	long call	+	short put
Short asset	=	short call	+	long put

Bull/bear spreads

A **bull spread** comprises a low strike option (X = \$13.50 in figure 19.16) and a high strike option (X = \$15.00). A **call-bull spread** combines a long call and a short call (with a higher strike price) as illustrated in figure 19.16. The net pay-off values can be calculated as in table 19.9. The price of the \$13.50 strike call option is assumed to be \$1.15 and the price of the \$15.00 strike call is assumed to be \$0.40.

Table 19.9 Pay-off pattern for a call-bull spread

Shareprice at expiry (\$)	*\$13.50 long call (\$)*	*\$15.00 long call (\$)*	*Combined pay-off (\$)*
12.50	−1.15	+0.40	−0.75
13.00	−1.15	+0.40	−0.75
13.50	−1.15	+0.40	−0.75
14.00	−0.65	+0.40	−0.25
14.50	−0.15	+0.40	+0.25
15.00	+0.35	+0.40	+0.75
15.50	+0.85	−0.10	+0.75
16.00	+1.35	−0.60	+0.75

The pay-off line for the call-bull spread is not dissimilar to that for the long call. The effect of the strategy is to give up some upside potential (the pay-off line being capped) in return for reduced downside potential.

On the other hand, the pay-off line for a **bear spread** is not dissimilar to that of a long put, except again, its upside potential is capped in order to reduce its price. A bear spread is constructed by taking the opposite position to that taken to construct the bull spread. That is, a bear spread is a short bull spread. Its pay-off line is illustrated in figure 19.18.

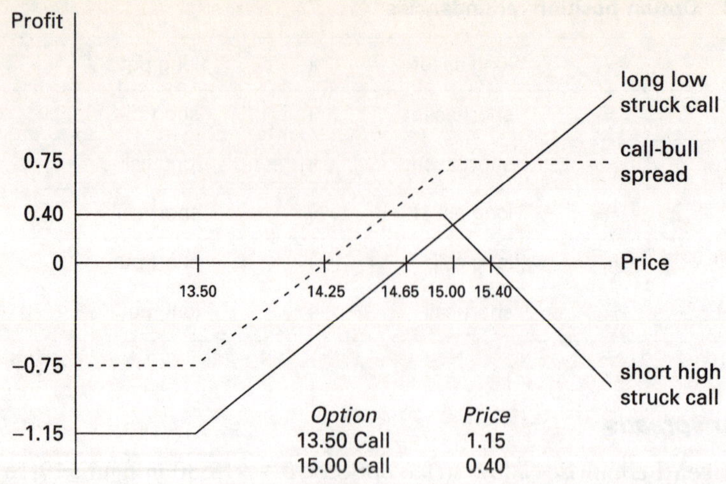

Figure 19.16 Call-bull spread

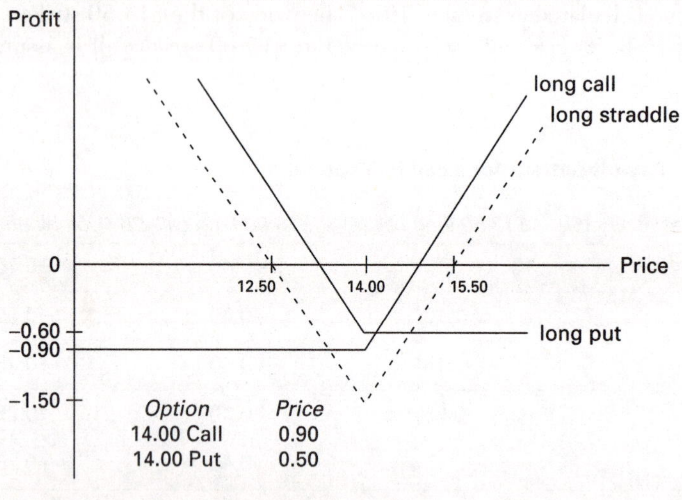

Figure 19.17 Pay-off diagram for a long straddle

Straddles, strangles and butterflies

A **straddle** entails the simultaneous purchase (or sale) of a put and a call option with identical strike prices. The profit diagram for a long straddle is given in figure 19.17. It can be seen from this figure that the holder of the long straddle will profit if the price of the asset fluctuates well away from its initial position. On the other hand, the short straddle benefits from the underlying asset price remaining relatively constant over the option's terms. Long straddles are favoured by traders expecting an increase in the price volatility of the underlying stock, while short straddles are an appropriate strategy for those expecting a decrease in stock volatility.

Strangles and **butterflies** are straightforward elaborations of the basic straddle position. A strangle, like a straddle, is constructed from two options. However, whereas a straddle uses two options with a single strike, a strangle uses two options with different strikes. A butterfly is a straddle with the addition of an upside ceiling and a downside floor. Figure 19.18 presents illustrative profit profiles for a bear spread, a long butterfly, a long strangle and a long condor.

INTEREST-RATE OPTIONS

In the previous chapter we showed how borrowers and lenders can use the futures/FRA contracts to remove the uncertainty surrounding future interest rates. A borrower can establish a forward interest rate by selling bank-bill futures or equivalent FRA contracts. On the other hand, a lender can establish a forward lending rate by buying bank-bill futures or equivalent FRA contracts. Using futures/FRA contracts to hedge interest-rate risk does have one significant drawback.

A futures/FRA contract locks borrowers and lenders into a specific interest rate. Whilst this removes interest-rate risk, and insulates borrowers and lenders from the effects of an unfavourable movement in rates, it also prevents borrowers and lenders from participating in the benefits of a favourable movement in rates. That is, hedging with futures/FRA contracts prevents a borrower from enjoying a drop in rates and a lender from benefiting from an increase in rates.

We have emphasised that options are different from futures/forward contracts in that they provide protection against untoward movements in rates/prices, while still allowing the upside of favourable movements. In this regard, interest-rate options are no different from equity or any other option.

Interest-rate options provide a guaranteed interest rate without locking in the holder. For example, a borrower facing an uncertain future interest rate can use an interest-rate option to place an upper limit on the cost of funds borrowed, if interest rates rise, without necessarily forgoing the benefits of lower rates should interest rates fall. On the other hand, a lender facing an uncertain future lending rate can use an interest-rate option to secure a floor on the lending rate without forgoing the benefit of a rise in future lending rates.

Interest-rate options are regularly traded in many Australian financial markets. The market for bank-bill futures is central to the determination of Australian interest rates within a term of three years. Bank-bill futures options are traded on the SFE and provide Australia's most liquid market for exchange-traded interest-rate options. The SFE also trades options on three and ten-year bond futures. Australia has a healthy over-the-counter market for options on bonds for a variety of maturities.

Taking an option over a bank-bill future provides a hedger with protection for a single interest payment. Naturally, there is demand for an interest-rate option product that provides a hedge against multiple interest payments. Interest-rate **caps** and **floors** provide a hedge for multiple interest payments. A number of financial institutions offer interest-rate caps to protect borrowers from future interest increases, and interest-rate floors, to protect lenders from interest-rate falls.

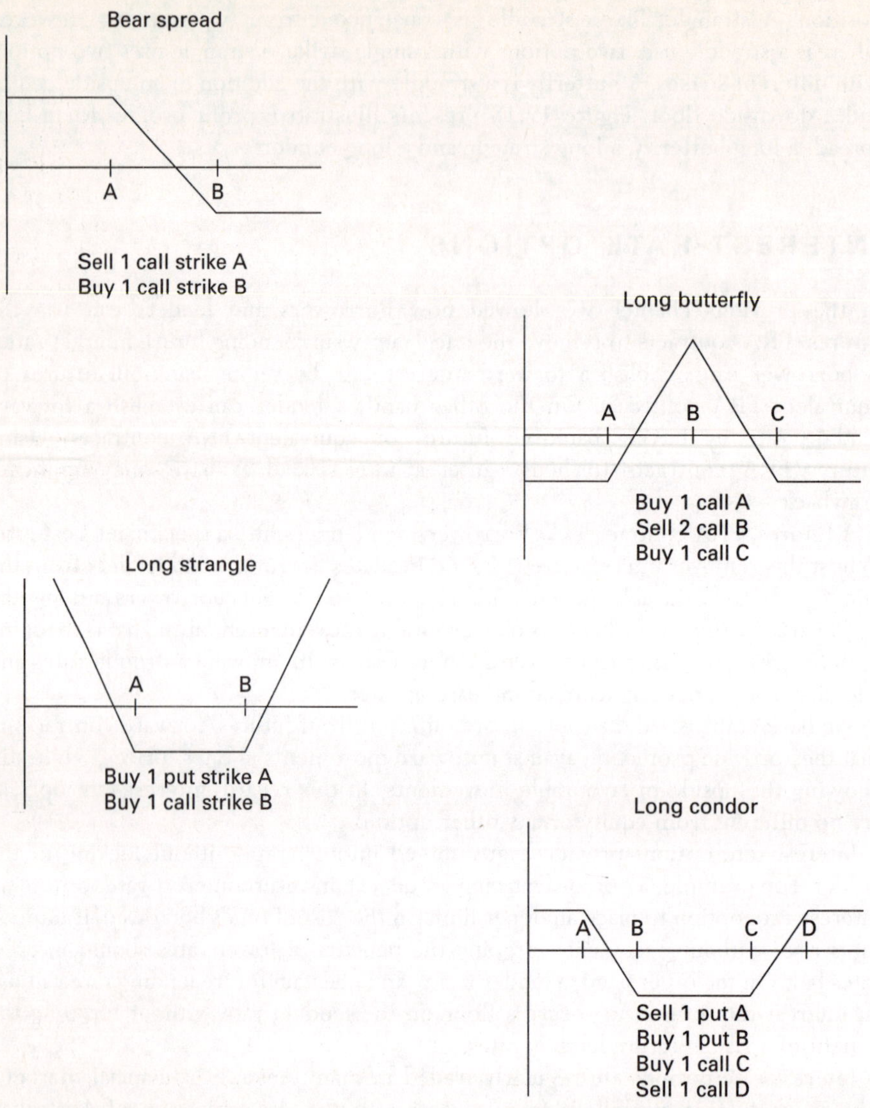

Figure 19.18 Pay-off lines for a bear spread, a long butterfly, a long strangle and a long condor

The mechanics of an interest-rate option

Interest rates are largely determined in the market for funds as the yields on traded financial instruments. As previously discussed, yields and prices are simply opposite sides of a single coin. A particular yield will imply a specific instrument price and a particular price will imply a specific instrument yield. For example, a yield of 7.00% p.a. on a $1 million 90-day bank bill implies a yield of:

$$P = \frac{1\,000\,000}{1 + 0.07 * 90/365}$$

and a bill price of $983 033 for a 90-day bill represents a market yield of 7.00% p.a.

Suppose a borrower wished to establish the interest rate on a future 90-day loan at a maximum rate of 7.00% p.a. Securing a put option, which provides the right but not the obligation, to sell a $1 million 90-day bill for $983 033, will do the trick. Alternatively, suppose a lender wished to enter into an arrangement whereby the lending rate was guaranteed to equal or exceed 7% p.a. In this case a call, which provides the right but not the obligation, to buy a $1 million, 90-day bill for $983 033, is an instrument that achieves this outcome.

example 19.3

Suppose you plan to invest in a two-year 10.00% bond in six months' time and you wish to place a floor on your expected investment return of 8.00% p.a. What kind of a contract would you use to support your investment aims?

Assuming that you plan to hold the bond until it matures, you can establish an expected yield (subject to the re-investment risk on the coupons) of 8.00% by acquiring a call option on two-year bonds that mature in six months at a strike price that represents a yield of 8.00%. The option's strike price would be:

$$P = 5.0\left[\frac{1 - (1.04)^{-4}}{0.04}\right] + \frac{100}{(1.04)^4}$$

$$= \$103.629895$$

Thus, if you can buy the bond in six months for $103.629895 per $100 of face value, you will have secured an expected return of 8.00% p.a.

You could consider the purchase of a forward contract to buy the bond at this price, as this would lock in the expected yield. But a forward contract would prevent you from benefiting should the two-year bond yield exceed 8.00% in six months.

However, a call option with a strike price of $103.629895 will give you the right to acquire the bond (without the obligation). You would exercise the option in the event that two-year bonds are trading at a yield lower than 8.00% in six months. In this event their price will exceed $103.629895, but your option allows you to buy the bond at the price consistent with an expected return of 8.00%.

Should the market yield exceed 8.00%, you will allow the option to lapse and purchase the bond in the market at the lower price, consistent with the higher yield.

Because of the inverse relationship between bill prices and yields, a call option on prices is equivalent to a put option on rates. A put option contract to sell a $1 million 90-day bill at a strike price of $983 000 is equivalent to a call option contract to 'buy' an interest rate of 7% p.a.

Australian interest-rate futures are traded using a pseudo price of 100 minus the interest rate. This futures price convention dictates that a borrower requires a futures put option while a lender requires a futures call option to hedge interest-rate risk.

The option requirements of borrowers and lenders are set out in the chart below.

Hedger	*Option specified in* interest rates	instrument price	futures price
Borrower	Call	Put	Put
Lender	Put	Call	Call

The use of an interest-rate option is illustrated in example 19.3.

Options on bank-bill futures contracts

The SFE organises trading in 90-day bill-futures contracts and put and call options on these futures contracts. The options on bank-bill futures contracts are american-form options with maturities that correspond with the maturity of the underlying futures contracts.

Bank-bill futures options are priced in the same terms as the underlying contract: that is, as 100 minus the yield. Suppose that the settlement price for the March bill-futures contract is \$92.72 (implying an expected interest rate of 7.28%) and the March \$92.50 strike call option has a settlement price of \$0.27. How is this price to be interpreted?

The price of a bank-bill futures option has two interpretations. First, it can be interpreted as an interest rate of 0.27%. A call option with a strike of \$92.50 provides a lender with the right to lend at 7.50% p.a. A call option price of \$0.27, interpreted as 0.27% p.a, means that a lender has the right to establish a net lending rate of 7.50% p.a. less 0.27% — that is, 7.23% p.a.

The second interpretation of a call option price of \$0.27 is as an indicator of the value of the option. The option value is the amount that is paid by the buyer of the option to the seller of the option. A price of \$0.27 represents 27 tics evaluated at the strike price. The tic value at a strike of \$92.50 is:

$$\text{Tic}_{92.50(7.5\%)} = \frac{1\,000\,000}{1 + 0.0750 * 90/365} - \frac{1\,000\,000}{1 + 0.0751 * 90/365} = 23.7697$$

The cost of the option for a purchaser is 27 * 23.7697 = \$641.78. Because this is more expensive than a futures/forward hedge, the extra benefit provided by an option (to participate in the upside) comes at a price. Recall the no-free-lunch principle!

Buying a bank-bill futures contract locks in a 90-day lending rate. Buying a call option over a bank-bill futures contract provides the holder with the right to purchase a bank-bill futures contract. Exercising a call option effectively locks in an interest rate for a lender at the option strike price.

Selling a bank-bill futures contract locks in a 90-day borrowing rate. Buying a put option on a bank-bill futures contract gives the holder the right to sell a bank-bill futures contract. Exercising a bank-bill put option effectively locks in a borrower's interest rate at the strike price.

In example 19.4 we show how a bank-bill put option serves to hedge a future borrowing and how it compares with alternative hedging strategies.

example 19.4

Suppose a company that is to commence a 90-day borrowing facility beginning in June 1998 is considering (in January) how to manage its interest-rate risk. It observes the current prices in the futures and options markets for June contracts. The company can pursue three alternative strategies:

- do nothing and leave the borrowing unhedged,
- sell a bill-futures contract (the settlement price of the June contract is $92.84) and lock in a borrowing rate of 7.16%, or
- purchase a put option, say, with a strike of $92.75.

Obviously the first strategy requires no cash payment. Whether this turns out to be the best decision depends on whether interest rates rise or fall in the period between now and June 1998. If interest rates fall it will be the best strategy because the second locks in a higher rate and the third requires a cash payment (the option's purchase price).

Apart from the payment of futures margins, the second strategy also requires no cash payment. Margins payments are not fees but, rather, are security lodgments. A futures contract at initiation has zero value. Selling a June futures contract locks the company into an interest rate of 7.16% p.a. (assuming the company can sell the contract at the settlement price of $92.84). The second strategy is preferable to the first if, in June, interest rates are greater than 7.16%.

A bank-bill put option places a ceiling on the borrowing rate without forgoing the potential of participating in any fall in rates that may occur before June 1998. The June $92.75 strike bank-bill put option has a settlement price of $0.25. That is, the price is 25 tics or 0.25% p.a. This option gives the company the right to sell a bill at $92.75 (i.e. at 7.25% p.a.).

If rates in June exceed 7.25%, the company will exercise its right to sell the bill and obtain funds at 7.25% p.a. This does not, of course, represent the true cost of funds, as we have not factored in the purchase price of the option. The net price we receive for the bill is the strike price of $92.75 less the put option price of $0.25: that is, $92.50. Using the put option guarantees a ceiling rate of 7.50% p.a. This is greater than the futures fixed rate of 7.16%. However, if interest rates fall below 7.16% less the option price of 0.25% (i.e. 6.91%) by June, the option is a better alternative than the futures contract. For example, should the yield in the bill market be 6.75% in June, the company would let the put option lapse and borrow funds at this rate. The company's net cost of funds would be 6.75% + 0.25% = 7.00% p.a., which is lower than the rate established by the futures contracts (7.16%).

Summary

The main points of this chapter are as follows:

- An option is a contractual right (but not the obligation) to buy or sell an underlying asset.
- A european option can be exercised only on its maturity date, whereas an american option can be exercised at any time during its life.
- Options may have an intrinsic and a time value.
- Time value of an option depends mainly on the price volatility of the underlying asset and the length of time to maturity.
- Six variables determine option prices in the Black-Scholes model. Their relationship to a call option's price is as follows:

Current price of underlying physical	positive
Exercise price of option	negative
Price variability of underlying physical	positive
Time to maturity	positive
Risk-free interest rate	positive
Dividend yield	negative

- The underlying asset's price volatility can be measured by observing past price movements or by deriving it from prices in option markets.
- The basic option structures are calls and puts; the long position is held by the buyer and the short position is held by the option's seller. The long call has upside profit potential but a capped downside potential. The long put has limited upside potential and a capped downside potential.
- Pay-off lines show the value of an option (allowing for its premium) in relation to its exercise price and the price of the underlying physical.
- The profit position in relation to an option must have an equivalent loss position for the other party.
- Option strategies, using perhaps different exercise prices and/or basic structures, provide a high degree of flexibility in relation to the needs of traders.
- Options on financial futures contracts provide an alternative strategy for managing interest-rate risk.

DISCUSSION QUESTIONS AND EXERCISES

1 Describe the main features of european form calls and puts. Show and explain their asymmetric intrinsic value lines, assuming a strike price of $10.00.

2 Briefly explain how options are traded on the ASXD.

3 When are options out of the money, in the money and at the money?

4 Describe in your own words the characteristics of an option's time value. How can an option's time value be deduced from an option's market value? Illustrate your answer with an actual example taken from the prices quoted by the *Financial Review*.

5 What is meant by the price volatility of an underlying asset and how can it be displayed on a graph? Why should an option's price depend on the volatility of the price of the underlying asset?
6 What is shown by an option's price line? What factors cause an option's price line to vary its position?
7 Draw pay-off lines for:
(a) a short call,
(b) a long call,
(c) a short put,
(d) a long put,
(e) long the asset,
(f) short the asset.
8 How can put and call options serve as a hedging instrument? Compare them to futures positions as hedge instruments.
9 What are option combinations? Explain the structure of a buy and write combination and how its pay-off pattern differs from its constituent parts.
10 Explain how options on bill futures can be used to manage the interest-rate risk faced by a prospective issuer of 90-day bills.

References and Further Reading

Carew, Edna 1995, *Derivatives Decoded*, Allen & Unwin, Sydney, Chapter 5.
Das, S. 1994, *Swap Financing and Derivatives*, 2nd edn, The Law Book Company, Sydney.
Daugaard, Dan, & Valentine, Tom 1995, *Financial Risk Management*, Harper Educational, Chapter 9.
Fabozzi, Frank J, Modigliani, Franco, & Ferri, Michael G. 1994, *Foundations of Financial Markets and Institutions*, Prentice-Hall, New Jersey, Chapters 26–8.
Juttner, D. Johannes 1994, *Financial Markets, Interest Rates and Monetary Economics*, 3rd edn, Longman Cheshire, Melbourne, Chapter 29.
Lewis, M. K. 1993, 'Derivative markets', in M. K. Lewis & R. H. Wallace (eds), *The Australian Financial System*, Longman Cheshire, Melbourne, Chapter 11.

Appendix 19.1: Black-Scholes Model

In a ground-breaking piece of work, Black and Scholes were able to obtain exact formulae for the prices of european call and put options on a non-dividend-paying security. Their formulae were extended by Merton to allow for dividends. The Black-Scholes equations are:

$$C = Se^{-qt}N(d_1) - Xe^{-rt}N(d_2)$$

$$P = -Se^{-qt}(1 - N(d_1)) + Xe^{-rt}(1 - N(d_2))$$

$$d_1 = \frac{\ln(S/X) + (r - q + \sigma^2/2)t}{\sigma\sqrt{t}}$$

$$d_2 = d_1 - \sigma\sqrt{t}$$

where C = call price
P = put price
S = stock price
X = exercise price
r = interest rate
q = dividend rate
t = time to maturity
N() = cumulative normal distribution
σ = volatility

In example 19A.1 we illustrate the use of the Black-Scholes/Merton formula to price a european put option dividend paying stock.

example 19A.1

Compute the value of a two-year $10.00 strike, european put option on a stock paying dividends at a rate of 4% p.a. when the stock price is $11.00. The volatility of the stock is estimated to be 20% p.a. and the interest rate is 7% p.a.

In this case:

$$S = 11.00$$
$$X = 10.00$$
$$t = 2$$
$$\sigma = 0.20$$
$$r = 0.08$$
$$q = 0.04$$

Thus:
$$d_1 = \frac{1n(11/10) + (0.08 - 0.04 + 0.20^2/2) * 2}{0.20 * \sqrt{2}}$$
$$= 0.76$$
$$d_2 = 0.76 - 0.20 * \sqrt{2}$$
$$= 0.48$$

From a set of normal tables we find:

$$N(d_1) = 0.78 \text{ and } N(d_2) = 0.68$$

Thus:
$$P = -11.00 * e^{-0.04*2} * (1 - 0.78) + 10.00 * e^{-0.08*2} * (1-0.68)$$
$$= 0.49$$

20

Financial innovation

The purposes of this brief final chapter are to review the major features of the financial system and, in the process, to highlight the role of financial innovation in shaping its form and practices. Even though the financial system changed more over the past decade than during any previous decade (due to deregulation), the experience of 1996 suggests that the pace of change is unlikely to slacken over the next decade.

Study objectives

From your study of this chapter you should be able to:

- identify the main forms and sources of financial innovation, and
- integrate your understanding of the operations of the financial system.

FORMS AND SOURCES OF INNOVATION

Financial innovation refers to the changes that occur within the financial system. These changes can be classified in terms of the system's institutional structure and the products and services provided. For instance, before deregulation, the institutional structure of the system developed through the growth of NBFIs and the relative decline in banks. NBFIs were also responsible for the introduction of new financing arrangements and markets, such as bill financing and the development of the short-term money market.

These changes can be classified in terms of the system's institutional structure and the type and range of products provided. The banking regulations introduced in the 1940s greatly influenced the institutional structure of Australia's financial system, impeding innovation by banks, while encouraging innovation by (and development of) non banks. Deregulation reversed this pattern, allowing banks to regain their dominance and, through the release of competitive pressures, stimulating their dynamic efficiency.

Deregulation also stimulated the development of new products and markets, given the concurrent development of electronic information and trading systems. The physical markets began to replace intermediated funding, both domestically and offshore, particularly for large-scale borrowers, even though the removal of controls on interest and exchange rates initially resulted in greater volatility in these market variables.

A flow-on effect of this environment was the growth in demand for derivative instruments to allow participants to hedge their market exposures. Hence, even though the removal of controls over interest and exchange rates exposed participants to greater market risk, the system developed products (i.e. derivatives) that allow participants to manage the risks arising from the greater volatility in these market variables.

New technology was also an important source of innovation in the post-deregulation decade as it allowed institutions to offer new products and services and adopt more efficient ways of handling data. As time progresses, technological change will become the principal source of innovation. It will alter the way the system operates, resulting in further change to the institutional structure of the system, as well as providing the basis for new products and services.

The pattern of demand for financial products and services also changed, reflecting most importantly, a growth in demand for retail investment products (for post-retirement income) compared with the stable demand for deposit account facilities for transaction purposes. (Edey and Gray, 1996)

A summary of the main forms and sources of financial innovation is presented in table 20.1 as a matrix. Illustrative examples are shown in the table, although readers can extend the table as a review exercise, having regard to the list of important economic events that is presented in the appendix to this chapter.

Table 20.1 Forms and sources of financial innovation

Sources/forms	*New products/services*	*Institutional structure*
Regulation/deregulation	imputation trusts	rise and fall of NBFIs
Globalisation	eurocurrency loans	entry of foreign-owned banks
New technology	EFTPOS	downsizing of retail banks
Changes in demand	approved deposit funds	growth in funds under management

Innovation and efficiency

It was suggested in Chapter 1, that when judging the financial system's economic performance, consideration should be given to its:

- allocative efficiency,
- technical efficiency, and
- dynamic efficiency.

Allocative efficiency is concerned with the fit of the pattern of the financial products and services provided by the system in relation to the wants and needs of consumers. Technical (or operational) efficiency is concerned with the amount of scarce resources used to produce these products and services. Dynamic efficiency is concerned with the rate at which the sector improves the quality and range of its products and services. (Valentine, 1991, pp. 37–8)

The efficiency of the system can be assessed in terms of:

- the stability of the payments system,
- the cost and convenience of payment and other financial services,
- the interest-rate margin involved in intermediated financing,
- the spreads (between bid and offer rates) involved in financial and foreign-exchange markets and the cost of associated services provided to participants in these markets,
- the depth of trading (i.e. turnover) in financial markets, as this underpins the liquidity of financial instruments,
- the allocation of funds between potential borrowers according to their economic value, which is indicated by their risk and expected return dimensions,
- the extent to which the range of financial needs within the economy is satisfied by financial institutions, instruments and markets, and
- the speed with which new technology is applied within the financial sector.

Other goals are pursued through the financial system, such as those associated with monetary policy and equal opportunity (whether all members of the community are treated equally by financial institutions and markets).

Review of innovation

Financial innovation in Australia began with the establishment of the Bank of New South Wales in 1817 and the further establishment of banks through the last century. However, the pace of change was slow until the NBFIs began to respond to the demand for finance from a growing post-war economy, during the 1960s and 1970s. During this period, the system of financial regulations, applying to banks and not NBFIs, placed a bias on the development of the system's institutional structure.

Following deregulation, the institutional structure began to unwind, as banks became the dominant intermediaries and NBFIs declined as institutional groups. High inflation, from the mid 1970s to the late 1980s, had weakened the role of insurance as a form of savings, but through the growth in superannuation-type savings schemes (including those developed by insurance offices), along with unit trusts, fund managers emerged in the 1990s as the other dominant institutional form.

Institutional structure

In this book most of the discussion focused on explaining the operations of the financing system. Two main ways of arranging finance were considered: through intermediation or through markets. Whereas the former is mainly arranged through retail banking institutions, the latter is mainly organised by wholesale banking institutions and fund managers.

Prior to deregulation, the institutional arrangements developed mainly in response to the regulations that restricted the activities of banks (but not the activities of NBFIs). In this era, NBFIs were the innovators — especially building societies and finance companies in the retail sector and merchant banks in the wholesale sector.

Following deregulation, the domestic banks (particularly the majors) reorganised their activities and by the mid 1990s had become the dominant institutions and the leaders in financial innovation. Foreign-owned banks have become important providers of financial services in the wholesale sector.

During the 1980s, deregulation was a major cause of change in the financial system. It not only allowed the institutional structure of the system to become more flexible, it created the competitive environment in which service providers are required to be innovative and efficient.

In the immediate post-deregulation period, the extent of intermediation increased substantially, to finance a swing by the corporate sector toward more highly leveraged capital structures. (Phelps, 1991, p. 89) This expansion of the provision of debt finance was possible, in part, because of a general decline in credit standards set by institutions, and a sustained period of asset appreciation. This period ended ignominiously with the share market 'crash' in October 1987 and the collapse of the property market, especially the commercial market, several years later. These events resulted in major losses for a number of financial institutions which, in some cases, were too large for the institution to survive.

These events led to the parliamentary inquiry into banking and deregulation (*A Pocket Full of Change*), which examined several aspects of the performance of the banking sector, including the response of interest-rate spreads since deregulation, and the need for changes in the supervision of financial institutions.

Product and market innovation

Deregulation had important consequences for Australia's financial markets. They became part of the global system of markets, and interest and exchange rates were set through market trading. Consequently, it is important to understand the forces that cause these rates to change and that their volatility is a source of risk for market participants.

In response to these forces, the financial system developed instruments and services that are used for managing risk exposures. These are known mainly as derivative instruments. In the main, they are designed to replicate financing instruments for the purpose of becoming counterbalances to adverse movements in interest and exchange rates. Of course, these instruments can generally be used for both hedging and speculative purposes.

> *Financial deregulation was expected to bring a variety of efficiency gains, and a convincing argument can be made that many of these have been delivered — for example, increased diversity of choice for buyers of financial services, increased product innovation including a*

wide range of new retail banking services, higher returns to depositors and removal of non-price credit rationing induced by regulatory constraints. (Edey and Gray, 1996, p. 33)

The growth in derivatives

In the previous three chapters we described four types of derivative instruments and, in the case of three (forwards, futures and swaps) we showed how they can be used to manage interest-rate risk. Low transaction costs and credit risk were mentioned as factors that have contributed to the rise of derivatives as hedging instruments that allow financial-market participants to cope with the volatility of market determined variables.

Following several catastrophic losses from the use of derivatives to open speculative positions (e.g. the collapse of Barings Bank), and the capacity of derivatives to inter-relate markets, concern has arisen about the possible destabilising effect of derivatives on the financial system. (Valentine, 1995, p. 321)

According to Valentine:

> *(T)here is little evidence to show that derivatives have made financial markets more volatile or that they have created a potential for systematic instability . . . A good argument can be made, however, that bank supervisors should pay some attention to the risks that can arise from the derivative activities of banks. Such supervision should ensure that banks measure these risks accurately and control them effectively.* (1995, pp. 321–2)

EMERGING DEVELOPMENTS

It would be wrong to view the major changes that have occurred in the operations of the financial system since deregulation as defining a new and stable system. The factors that influence the efficient provision of financial products and services, such as technology, are themselves continuously changing and so the financial system should be viewed as an evolving set of arrangements.

In May 1996, following the federal elections, the treasurer in the new government, Peter Costello, announced the formation of a new inquiry (i.e. the 'Wallis Inquiry', reflecting the name of the inquiry's chairman) into the financial system. The inquiry's mission was defined by the treasurer as follows:

> *The Inquiry is charged with providing a stocktake of the results arising from the financial deregulation of the Australian financial system since the early 1980s. The forces driving further change will be analysed, in particular, technological development. Recommendations will be made on the nature of the regulatory arrangements that will best ensure an efficient, responsive, competitive and flexible financial system to underpin stronger economic performance consistent with financial stability, prudence, integrity and fairness.* (Press release from the Office of the Treasurer)

The inquiry was given a deadline of 31 March 1997 for the submission of its final report. Given that this chapter was written in 1996, the authors are not able to evaluate the role of the Wallis Inquiry on the financial system's development. It seems likely, from its very limited scope for making recommendations and its short deliberation period, that the inquiry will not have a comparable impact to that of the Campbell Committee. (Recommendations were sought from the inquiry only in relation to regulatory arrangements and related matters affecting the operation of the financial system, such as mergers between financial institutions.)

However, the inquiry has triggered considerable debate about the future of the financial system. It was required to review the factors that drive further change, of which four were listed in the inquiry's terms of reference:

- technological and marketing advances,
- international competition and integration of financial markets,
- domestic competition in all its forms, and
- consumer needs and demand.

Some of these factors are related (only) to the area in which the inquiry will make recommendations and thus this list does not address the factors that are shaping the system's future comprehensively. The following (brief) discussion is organised around a slightly different set of headings.

Technological change and retail banking

During the 1990s, the financial sector has been moving toward a paperless, cashless and locationless banking system. (Murray, 1995) Reference was made to these developments in Chapter 1 when discussing the payment system and in the chapters that dealt with the clearing and settlement processes in financial markets. A further indication of the trend toward cashless transactions during the first half of the 1990s is provided by the data presented in table 20.2.

Table 20.2 Non-cash payments, 1991 and 1995 (%)

	Volume		*Value*	
	1991	*1995*	*1991*	*1995*
Paper	60	50	59	35
Electronic				
— retail	40	50	2	1
— wholesale	<0.1	<0.1	39	64
Total	100	100	100	100

Source: Thompson, 1996, p. 3

The development of electronic banking systems allows customers to use banking services without actually ever visiting their bank. These systems allow the financial system to become more efficient in each of the three ways identified above, through:

- the development of new products and services, such as phone banking,
- the development of cheaper and more effective management information systems, and
- the development of Internet banking to support (global) home shopping.

However, these developments pose consumer protection and privacy problems as well as changing the focus and capacity of supervisors. The former problem is being addressed through codes of bank behaviour and a banking-industry ombudsman. Supervisors have focused on the way institutions manage their exposure to operational risks and to the security of computing systems used in the payments system.

The use of new technology will change the economics of branches as the vehicle of retail banking, as well as optimum size of a retail bank. It has been an important factor behind the takeovers and mergers among the former regional banks during the 1990s. It also provides large non-financial corporations with the capacity to provide financial services to their customers in competition with financial institutions.

Unbundling of financial services

The economics of the provision of intermediated products (deposits, loans and transaction services) versus direct financing products depends in part on the relative advantages of providing a bundle of services compared with providing services and products individually. To illustrate, recall the discussion in Chapter 1 of the cross-subsidy banks have traditionally provided for payment services from their earnings generated through the provision of financing services, and the discussion in Chapter 6 of the securitisation of lending products. The capacity of intermediaries to cross-subsidise payment services is eroded when competitors, who do not have to cross-subsidise payment services, enter the market for the financing products.

The initial growth in the market share of home-loan originators in the mid 1990s is based in part on their focus on one product compared with the multi-products provided by retail banks. This experience suggests that in some areas, at least, narrowly based providers of financial products might be competitive with multi-product providers and this has implications for competition policy as it applies to financial institutions. For instance, it suggests that the 'six pillars' policy (the Keating Government opposed mergers between the four major banks and the two largest insurance offices) might be excessively restrictive.

It seems that the unbundling of financial services has a different effect on the way financial services and products are marketed from its effect on the size of the financial institutions that provide them. It is widely expected that mergers will occur among the big institutions (and the regional banks) and result in fewer larger banks/financial institutions. Hence, while unbundling may foster the development of more specialised providers, this development seems unlikely to eliminate the role of large financial institutions.

Changes in the pattern of savings

The growth of superannuation during the past ten years or so has been associated with a decline in the use of retail banks as a vehicle for personal savings. This trend is likely to continue, placing pressure on banks to both develop savings products that compete with superannuation products and to enter the superannuation market.

In each decade since the 1960s the proportion of household savings going into deposit-type accounts with retail banks has declined. During the 1990s, less than 40 per cent of households' net acquisition of financial assets has been with retail banks, compared with

> *around 45 per cent in the 1980s and 55 per cent in the 1970s. Correspondingly, the proportion of household savings going to funds managers (including superannuation) and life offices has been on the rise.* (Thompson, 1996, p. 1)

As indicated in Chapter 8, banks have become important fund managers, although this has been through subsidiaries, rather than as part of their general operations.

> *The banks clearly believe there are advantages to be gained from combining their intermediation role with funds-management activities, and have pushed for allowance of more direct involvement in retirement-savings products, as well as having introduced a range of over-the-counter investment products in recent years. These developments, and the changing nature of the funds-management sector itself, point to increasing areas of overlap between the products offered by banks and funds managers.* (Edey and Gray, 1996, p. 41)

Likewise, some fund managers believe they can successfully provide bank-type products and are seeking to be allowed to enter these markets. Hence, there is an expectation that functional distinctions between the providers of financial services will become harder to sustain.

Markets versus intermediation

During the 1980s, the development of the bank-accepted bill market allowed banks to arrange short-term finance without having to lend their own funds. As a result, bills play a much greater role in the provision of finance than bank overdrafts.

In the 1990s, the securitisation of housing and other loans has further shifted the balance toward markets as a provider of funds. Securitisation has grown in part as a result of the success (during the first half of the 1990s, at least) of the loan arrangers in the housing-finance industry, and as an investment vehicle for fund managers. Assuming the trend for savings to be placed with fund managers (as opposed to retail banks) continues, the market for securitised loans will expand to support the further growth of securitisation: 'The point is that markets are more efficient than institutions and the process of banks being disintermediated by capital markets . . . will not abate.' (William Ferguson, 1996, p. 195)

This view applies most to wholesale banking and complements the expectation that the development of global financial markets will result in a small number of (globally) dominant investment banks. (Rob Ferguson, 1996)

The emerging technological and institutional developments briefly reviewed above suggest that retail banking will undergo fundamental change over the balance of the 1990s and may become a technologically based global market. While it and wholesale banking will change over time, banks will continue to be the main players in the financial system. (Joss, 1996, p. 193)

THE FINANCIAL SYSTEM IN SUMMARY

The financial system was described in Chapter 1 as comprising:

- the payment system. This is essentially a domestic system comprising the banks that provide the main payment systems. However, it is linked to the systems in

other countries through the foreign-exchange market. It is supervised by the RBA and operated through the bank's RITS and exchange-settlement funds system.
- the financing system. This comprises intermediated and direct financing, the former being the mainstream activity of banks, especially retail banking, whereas the latter is the mainstream activity of three financial markets. However, these markets are largely conducted by financial institutions that operate at the wholesale level.
- the risk-management system. This comprises the markets for derivative instruments and the services provided by wholesale banking institutions.

Whereas the payment system involves the immediate transfer of funds, the financing system moves funds through time. Because of the time value of money, future amounts accumulate interest, the rate of which depends on the risks involved.

Intermediated and direct financing involve broadly the same functions, but they are performed in different ways. Intermediated financing can be viewed as internal markets that are managed by institutions, whereas financial markets are more transparent in the functions performed when borrowing and investing.

Market volatility (given the efficient-market hypothesis) is a source of risk. It is important to understand both the causes of the movements in market variables, and the instruments that can be used to manage the risk and uncertainty arising from volatility.

Given that much of the uncertainty relates to planned future financing, it is important to understand the distinction (and relationship) between spot and forward rates and how the markets for forward rates can be used when managing interest-rate and market risks.

The basic principle of hedging is to establish a second position (preferably at a small cost) the value of which varies inversely with that of the underlying position in the physical market. The hedge instrument should be established such that its value counteracts any adverse movement in the underlying physical market.

Discussion questions and exercises

1. Briefly describe the goals of the financial system.
2. Explain the development of banking regulations.
3. Describe the forces that led to financial deregulation.
4. Explain the impact of deregulation on prudential supervision.
5. Explain the growth in intermediation during the 1980s.
6. Discuss the impact of deregulation on credit-risk management by banks.
7. Assess the credit-risk management skills displayed by banks during the latter half of the 1980s.
8. Assess the efficiency gains achieved through deregulation.
9. Compare the importance of new technology and volatility in financial markets as causes of financial innovation.
10. Review the development of financial products in the 1980s and explain the purpose they serve.

References and further reading

Edey, Malcolm (ed.) 1996, *The Future of the Financial System*, RBA, Sydney.
Edey, Malcolm, & Gray, Brian 1996, 'The evolving structure of the Australian financial system', in Malcolm Edey (ed.) 1996.
Ferguson, Rob 1996, 'An investment banking perspective on the future of the financial system', in Malcolm Edey (ed.) 1996.
Ferguson, William 1996, 'A banker's perspective on the future of the financial system', in Malcolm Edey (ed.) 1996.
House of Representatives Standing Committee on Finance and Public Administration, Martin, Stephen (Chair) 1991, *A Pocket Full of Change*, AGPS, Canberra.
Joss, Robert 1996, 'Developments in the business of banking', in Malcolm Edey (ed.) 1996.
Murray, David 1995, *Creating the Future,* Commonwealth Bank.
Phelps, Les 1991, 'Competition: profitability and margins', in Ian Macfarlane (ed.), *The Deregulation of Financial Intermediaries*, RBA, pp. 87–110.
Thompson, G. J. 1996, *Retail Banking, Technology and Prudential Supervision*, RBA, Sydney.
Valentine, Tom 1991, 'What the Campbell Committee expected', in Ian Macfarlane (ed.), *The Deregulation of Financial Intermediaries*, pp. 36–60.
Valentine, Tom 1995, 'Derivatives in their proper place', *Agenda*, vol. 2, no. 3, pp. 321–32.

Appendix 20.1: Monetary milestones

August 1937 The Royal Commission into Banking reported. The commission's recommendations provided a framework for the regulation of the banking system, some aspects of which are still in existence. A major part of the recommendations concerned the development of the Commonwealth Bank as the central bank. One specific recommendation was that the central bank publish a monthly statistical bulletin.

September 1939 The outbreak of World War II led to certain wartime banking regulations. Exchange controls were introduced at the outbreak of war, replacing the 1930s Exchange Mobilisation Agreement. Controls were extended in 1941–42 to cover interest rates and bank lending/profitability.

August 1945 The *Commonwealth Bank Act* 1945 and the *Banking Act* 1945 came into operation. The Acts, extending the 1937 Royal Commission's recommendations, provided the framework for much of the post-war regulation of the banking system. The Commonwealth Bank, as the central bank, retained control over interest rates, banks' lending policies and various other aspects of banking.

April 1953 The *Commonwealth Bank Act* 1953 came into operation. The General Banking Division of the Commonwealth Bank was reconstituted as the Commonwealth Trading Bank.

February 1959 The first Authorised Short-Term Money Market dealers commenced operations. This marked the establishment of what has since been known as the official short-term money market.

November 1959 **Seasonal securities** were issued for the first time. These securities helped in the management of the seasonal liquidity flows arising mainly from the pattern of Commonwealth Government payments and receipts.

January 1960 The *Reserve Bank Act* 1959 and the *Banking Act* 1959 came into operation. This legislation established a separate Commonwealth Banking Corporation, and vested the central banking functions in the Reserve Bank of Australia. The predecessor of the Sydney Futures Exchange began trading wool futures.

July 1962 **Treasury notes** were first issued to replace seasonal securities.

January 1965 The authorised money-market dealers were permitted to trade in commercial bills.

November 1965 The Reserve Bank suspended the practice of issuing qualitative guidelines on bank lending.

March 1967 Controls over the granting of personal loans by banks were lifted.

July 1967 Trading banks were permitted to extend short-term mortgages and bridging loans.

November 1967 **Sterling depreciated against the USD but the AUD did not follow.** This was the first change in the exchange rate of the AUD against Sterling since the 1930s. The 26-week Treasury note was introduced.

May 1968 Trading banks were permitted to provide lease finance.

May 1969 Trading banks were allowed to issue certificates of deposits.

August 1971 The US **suspended convertibility of the USD** into gold. Foreign-exchange markets abroad closed temporarily. The Reserve Bank withdrew temporarily the banks' authorities to deal in foreign exchange. Disturbances to international markets continued, with trading interrupted on several occasions during 1971 and 1972. Trading banks were allowed to deal as principals with the Reserve Bank in foreign exchange and set their own charges on forward cover.

December 1971 The **Australian dollar** was fixed to the USD. This broke the long-standing link to Sterling, which later floated against the USD, as did a number of major currencies.

September 1973 The interest-rate ceiling on certificates of deposit was abolished.

August 1974 The *Financial Corporations Act* became operative. The Act governs some aspects of non-bank financial corporations and provides for the collection of statistics from these corporations. Part IV of the Act, which provides for the Reserve Bank to exercise direct control over various aspects of the operations of these intermediaries, has not been proclaimed.

September 1974 The fixed link of the **Australian dollar to the USD** was discontinued. The dollar was thereafter maintained at a constant value against a trade-weighted basket of currencies.

October 1974 Bankcard was launched.

February 1976 The fixed link of the **Australian dollar to the trade-weighted basket of currencies** was discontinued. Following a devaluation of 17%, a flexible link was introduced. The exchange rate was kept under constant review and adjusted frequently. The Australian options market commenced trading.

January 1979 The **Committee of Inquiry into the Australian Financial System** was established. The 'Campbell Committee' issued its Interim Report in May 1980, and its Final Report in September 1981. The committee's findings provided a major impetus to the deregulation of the financial system which occurred in the 1980s.

December 1979 **Treasury notes offered at tender** for the first time.

December 1980 Ceilings on **interest rates paid on bank deposits** were removed. While movement in the direction of freer markets had been under way for a number of years, this was one of the first big steps in the deregulatory process which took place in the first half of the 1980s.

June 1981 The Bank of New South Wales (now Westpac) merged with the Commercial Bank of Australia and the National Bank of Australasia (now National Australia Bank) merged with the Commercial Banking Company of Sydney Ltd.

June 1982 The Loan Council agreed to the introduction of a **tender system for Treasury bonds**. The first tender was announced in July 1982. This, together with the tender arrangements for Treasury notes, improved the processes of debt and liquidity management.

May 1983 The **Review Group on the Australian Financial System** was commissioned by the treasurer. The 'Martin Review Group' reported on the recommendations of the Committee of Inquiry into the Australian Financial System, the government's economic and social objectives, and the need to improve the efficiency of the financial system. The report was published in December 1983.

December 1983 The **Australian dollar floated**. Most **exchange controls** were abolished. These were major steps in the process of deregulation of the financial system. The float of the dollar improved control over domestic liquidity. The removal of exchange controls allowed much freer flows of capital into and out of Australia.

February 1984 The Martin Review Group's report was released, recommending that the Labor Government continue the process of deregulation.

April 1984 Macquarie Bank Ltd was established.

June 1984 Forty NBFIs were granted a licence to trade in foreign exchange.

August 1984 The Reserve Bank established a separate **Supervision Unit.** This provided a focal point for discussions with banks on prudential matters. The broad principles of prudential supervision policy were subsequently set out in a series of papers published by the bank. **Maturity restrictions on bank deposits** were removed. This enabled banks to offer interest on call deposits and short-term fixed deposits. The Reserve Bank introduced repurchase agreements (involving CGSs) as an instrument for trading with AMMDs.

February 1985 The treasurer announced that sixteen **foreign banks** would be invited to establish operations in Australia. Discussions between the potential new banks, the Reserve Bank, and the Treasury followed, and the first bank with significant foreign ownership commenced business later that year. Approval was granted for 16 new banks.

April 1985 Further deregulation of banks. The remaining ceilings on lending rates (other than for loans for owner-occupied housing of amounts less than $100 000) were removed. The ceiling on new loans for housing was removed in April 1986.

May 1985 The prime asset requirement (PAR) was introduced, replacing the LGS convention.

June 1985 The NSW Building Society became the Advance Bank Australia.

April 1986 The interest-rate ceiling for new housing loans was removed.

November 1986 The *Cheques and Payment Orders Act* was passed by parliament. This Act extended to non-bank financial institutions and customers certain legal protections regarding cheques. It also provided for new cheque-like instruments called payment orders.

May 1987 Announcement of **proposed amendments to the *Banking Act* 1959**. The government foreshadowed amendments to the *Banking Act* that would make more explicit the Reserve Bank's supervisory powers.

August 1988 The RBA issued guidelines for its risk-adjusted, capital-adequacy requirements.

September 1988 The SRD ratio was replaced by NCDs.

December 1989 The *Banking Act* was changed to remove the distinction between trading and savings banks.

February 1990 PAR was reduced to 6%.

October 1990 The House of Representatives Standing Committee on Finance and Public Administration was requested to inquire into various aspects of the banking system. The report was published in November 1991.

Sources: 1 RBA, *Bulletin*, November, 1987, pp. 2–4
2 Edna Carew 1991, *Fast Money 3*, Allen & Unwin, Sydney, pp. 1–30

Glossary

acceptance liability The liability to redeem commercial bills that arises when the bills are accepted.

accounts receivable financing The use of accounts receivable as collateral for a loan. The amount raised is usually the discounted value of the accounts receivable.

add-on yield An alternative term to describe the theoretical yield to maturity used to price securities in the Australian short-term money market.

ADRs Certificates held by US banks that represent shares in a foreign company owned by American citizens. They have the same financial characteristics as the underlying shares, and allow the company to have their shares issued and traded in the USA without meeting the listing requirements of the Securities and Exchange Commission.

allocational efficiency The financial system's ability to provide borrowers and lenders with products and services that best fit their needs.

american option The right, but not the obligation, to buy (or sell) at any time before an option's expiry date.

annuity A sequence of regular payments valued on a compound-interest basis. Its accumulated (or terminal) value is the sum of the payments with interest at its maturity date, and its present value is this accumulated value discounted to the present.

annuity certain An annuity for a specified number of annuity periods.

annuity due An annuity in which the regular payments are made at the commencement of each period.

approved deposit funds Funds that extend the period of superannuation tax benefits. They provide portability of superannuation benefits.

arbitrage The simultaneous buying and selling of a product to take advantage of price differences. It serves to eliminate the price difference — buying increases the lower price and selling increases the higher price until the price difference is eliminated.

asset-liability management The practice of adjusting the composition of a fund's (or a financial institution's) assets and liabilities to achieve the preferred risk-return combination.

at-the-money option When the price of the asset equals the option's exercise price.

ATM An automated teller machine that can be operated 24 hours a day.

auction market Markets conducted at a particular place (i.e. at an exchange) that traditionally used the auction process for trading.

Authorised Money Market Dealers A small number of money-market dealers who were licensed by the Reserve Bank for the purpose of providing trading opportunities for the bank. Their licences were withdrawn by the RBA upon the introduction of real-time settlement.

bank-accepted bills (BAB) Commercial bills that have been accepted by a bank.

bank bill A commercial bill that has been either accepted or endorsed by a bank.

bank-bill rate The average rate for BABs with a particular maturity, calculated at 10 a.m. on each trading day.

bank-bill swap rate (BBSW) This is the bank-bill rate used in swaps.

banking regulations Laws and regulations that directly control aspects of the business of lending and borrowing by banks.

basis point The smallest movement possible in market yields that are quoted to two decimal points (i.e. 0.01%). It is also known as a 'point'.

basis risk This arises when the value of the hedge instrument does not precisely correlate with the movement in the value of the underlying asset.

bear market A pattern of falling prices in a market, caused by pessimistic market sentiment.

bearer bond A bond that makes coupon payments to the holder (or bearer) of the bond.

benchmark rates Interest rates that indicate the rate for a particular term or for particular (e.g. very creditworthy) borrowers.

beta The relationship between the volatility of a security's value and that for the market as a whole.

bilateral exchange rate The value of one currency in terms of another.

bid-offer bounce The price movement in markets that results when deals are made alternatively between bid and offer prices.

bids Financial market jargon for buying quotes.

bill facility An arrangement by a lender to renew (i.e. reissue, or roll over) a series of bills. It creates a medium-term source of finance with interest determined each time the bills are rolled over.

bill receivable The contractual obligation of the drawer of a bill to pay the acceptor the bill's face value at maturity.

BITS A method of transferring large sums of money between the banks that are members of the Reserve Bank's Bank Interchange and Transfer System.

Black and Scholes option-pricing model A widely used option-pricing model.

bond A long-term financial instrument that makes regular (usually six-monthly) coupon payments and a redemption payment (usually its face value).

bond stripping The process of removing the coupons from a bond, leaving it as a single-payment instrument. The aim is to measure the yield represented by the net present value and the bond's single payment at maturity.

bond tender The process of issuing bonds to the highest bidders (i.e. those who are prepared to lend to the issuer at the lowest interest rate).
bonds Long-term securities that usually make regular interest payments.
bonus shares Shares issued free to existing shareholders.
bought deal The practice of an underwriter agreeing to arrange the sale of a complete parcel of securities at an agreed price.
bridging finance Short-term finance commonly used to fund property development prior to its sale.
brokers Agents who arrange financial dealings, such as the sale or purchase of shares, on behalf of a client.
bull market A pattern of rising market prices, resulting from optimistic market sentiment.
buy and write An option strategy that combines a long asset (i.e. holding the asset) and a short call (i.e. a sold call option on the asset).
call An option to buy an asset at a set price within a set period.
call-bull spread An option strategy that combines a long call with a low exercise price and a short call with a high exercise price.
call deposit Funds that are placed in an account on the basis that prior notice must be given for withdrawals.
capital markets This term may refer to those financial markets in which funds can be raised, such as the money and debt-capital markets.
capital structure The ratio of an enterprise's debt capital to its equity capital.
capital sum The future value of $1.
capital-indexed bonds The face value of these bonds is indexed to the Consumer Price Index, to adjust for the capital-eroding effect of inflation.
cash and carry The combination of a spot transaction (i.e. for cash) and a forward position.
cash management accounts Bank accounts that compete with cash management funds.
cash management fund A fund manager that invests mainly in short-term money market instruments.
cash rate The rate of interest the Reserve Bank targets when implementing monetary policy. Before July 1996 it was the rate of interest paid by authorised dealers for deposits at call.
certificates of deposit (CDs) Wholesale deposits that are placed with banks for short periods at a set interest rate. They can be traded in the short-term money market, and thus are very liquid.
chain rule A method of calculating cross rates.
cheque An instruction (or payment order) to a bank to transfer funds from the drawer's account to the bearer or to the payee's account.
clearing The process of checking transaction details prior to settlement.
clearing house A body established to organise the exchange of financial transactions, such as the exchange of cheques and futures contracts.
commercial bill A short-term discount instrument issued to raise working capital. The bill's drawer raises funds equal to the bill's face value discounted at the issue yield. The bill's acceptor guarantees (for an acceptance fee) the bill's redemption at maturity.

commercial paper An alternative name for promissory notes.
commodity currency FX market jargon for the currency that is priced in terms of another currency.
Commonwealth Treasury bonds Bonds issued by the Commonwealth Treasury. This term is used commonly to refer to the Commonwealth's fixed-interest bonds.
compound interest The capitalisation of interest during the term of the loan.
compound period The period over which interest is capitalised.
consol A perpetual bond that pays coupons in perpetuity.
contagion risk The chance that the failure of a bank to settle its payment-system obligations will result in the failure of other banks to settle.
contingent annuity An annuity for an unspecified number of annuity periods.
continuous compounding The continuous addition of interest to the principal amount (plus accumulated interest).
convertible note A coupon-paying debt security that may be converted into the issuer's ordinary shares.
corporate bonds Bonds issued by non-government borrowers.
counterparty risk The chance that a counterparty to a transaction (or contract) will fail to perform (i.e. default).
coupons The interest payments under a bond or medium-term note.
covered position An exposure that is counterbalanced by a second position, usually in a derivative market.
credit Funds that have been loaned.
credit risk The possibility that a borrower will fail to meet the financial obligations under the loan. It is a form of 'default risk'.
credit-risk premium A margin incorporated in the interest rate charged on a loan to cover the credit risk faced by the lender.
credit standard The degree of risk that a lender will accept.
credit standing A borrower's assessed capacity to make future payments.
cross rates The exchange rate between two currencies, neither of which is the USD.
cross-subsidy The practice of meeting some or all of the costs of a product or service from the revenue generated from the provision of other goods and services.
cum-interest dates Trading days on which a bond's purchaser will receive its next coupon.
cum-rights price The price of shares that provide the buyer with the right to a new share issue.
currency swap An agreement between two parties to exchange the interest and principal payments associated with a loan in one currency with the interest and principal payments associated with a loan in another currency. These arrangements are usually intermediated by a swap dealer.
current deposits Funds in the accounts that can be accessed for cheque-payment purposes. Known also as demand deposits.
D-gap The difference between the duration of a fund's assets and its liabilities. A D-gap is managed by changing the maturity composition of the fund's assets and liabilities to close the gap.

daily resettlement The procedure adopted by the futures-market clearing house of requiring the holder of a position that fell in value the previous day to make a margin payment to cover the unrealised loss on the contract up to the level of the original deposit.
deal date The day a deal is made, as opposed to the day a deal is settled.
dealers Market makers for securities. In Australia they are the organisations that buy and sell debt securities and foreign exchange. The individuals who conduct the trading are known as professional dealers.
dealing spread The difference between a dealer's bid and offer quotes.
debenture A medium-term fixed-interest security that is usually issued in small denominations to the public. Debentures are a form of retail bond mainly issued by finance companies. They are not traded in the wholesale market, but may be redeemed by the issuer prior to their maturity.
debt finance Funds that are borrowed and the repayment of which is a contractual obligation.
deep market A market with a substantial turnover.
default risk The possibility that a borrower (or, more generally, a counterparty to a transaction) will fail to meet its financial obligations.
deferred annuity A sequence of regular payments that commence at a future date.
deficit units Those members of the financial system whose outlays exceed their income, and who either incur new debts or dispose of assets.
demand deposits Funds in accounts that can be accessed for cheque-payment purposes.
deregulation The process of lifting the regulations that control dealings in the financial system. It occurred over the period from the late 1970s to the mid 1980s.
derivative Any instrument whose value depends principally on the value of another financial product, interest rate or index.
direct financing The process of borrowing from surplus units. It is usually arranged by financial institutions acting as dealers, underwriters and market makers for the issued paper.
direct issuance The sale of securities by their issuer.
direct quote The value of a foreign currency (typically the US dollar) in terms of the domestic currency.
discount bond When the market yield for a bond exceeds its coupon rate, its price is less than its face value and it is thus referred to as a discount bond.
discount instruments Single-payment securities that are sold at a discount to their face value.
discount rate The rate used when pricing securities on a direct discount basis (as in the USA), rather than on the basis of a theoretical yield to maturity (as in Australia).
discounting The practice of selling short-dated securities at a price less than their face (or redemption) value.
dividend imputation The practice of treating company income tax as a prepayment of personal income tax due on dividend income.
dividends Payments to the owners of shares. They are known as residual claims because they can be made only after the company has met its financial obligations.

the dollar The US dollar when traded in foreign exchange markets.
drawdown The actual take-up of borrowed funds.
due annuity A sequence of regular payments made at the beginning of each period.
duration A measure of the average time at which payments are made.
dynamic efficiency The innovativeness of the financial system.
earnings per share A company's earnings (after meeting all expenses) divided by the number of issued shares.
effective annual rate of interest The simple interest rate that would produce the same future value as the compound nominal rate of interest.
efficient-market hypothesis The contention that financial markets use information efficiently and thus prices are fair in the sense that they reflect all relevant information about the value of the assets being traded.
EFTPOS A method of accessing accounts with banks and NBFIs to pay for purchases. It refers to electronic funds transfer at point of sale.
electronic trading The use of either telephones or computers to conduct trading. For example, the Australian Stock Exchange uses SEATS to match buy and sell quotes.
eligible termination payments Payments that carry tax benefits, being treated as superannuation payouts.
endorse The practice of verifying ownership of an instrument (such as a cheque or a bill) and confirming the valid transfer of the funds stated on the instrument. In the case of a bill, endorsement is a form of guarantee that it will be redeemed.
endowment policies These are insurance products that are similar to an investment, because they make a payment to the policyholder on maturity.
equilibrium rate of interest The interest rate that balances the demand for and the supply of loanable funds.
equity Funds contributed by the owner(s) of a business. It usually takes the form of paid-up share capital and retained profits.
the euro The proposed single currency of the members of the European Monetary Union.
eurobonds Long-term securities issued to foreign investors.
euro-commercial paper Short-term securities issued in a foreign currency, typically USD, to overseas investors.
Eurocommercial paper (ECP) An alternative to the notes covered by an NIF, that are issued by well-established foreign borrowers in the European or Asian markets.
eurocurrency This refers to the raising of funds in the domestic currency outside the country. For example, the raising of a US-dollar loan in London.
eurocurrency markets The external markets for funds.
Euronote Issuance Facility (NIF) An arrangement involving a series of short-term securities issued on the eurodollar market.
European Monetary System The arrangement that fixed the exchange rates (under the 'exchange rate mechanism') between the European Union countries.
european option The right, but not the obligation, to buy (or sell) at an option's expiry date.

ex-interest date Trading days on which a bond's purchaser will not receive the next coupon.
ex-rights price The price of shares that do not provide the buyer with the rights to a rights issue.
exchange-rate risk The risk that arises from unexpected adverse movement in the exchange rate.
exchange settlement account (ESA) The account each bank has with the Reserve Bank for purposes of settling their financial dealings with the bank.
exchange traded option An option contract that is traded on an exchange, such as the SFE and the ASX.
exercise price The price at which an option is to be exercised, also known as the 'strike price'.
expected real rate of interest The market rate minus the expected rate of inflation.
face value The value of a security that is usually payable on maturity.
factoring The sale of accounts receivable, usually at a discounted value.
financial futures Futures contracts that are based on financial securities or indices, such as the SPI and bank-bill contracts.
financial innovation The on-going process of change in the financial sector that improves the quality of financial services and the productivity of this sector.
financial institution An enterprise that specialises in the provision of financial services and products.
financial instruments Securities (or contracts) that are traded in financial markets.
financial lease A financial arrangement that might allow the user of equipment to subsequently acquire the asset. Usually they have a term of a few years.
financial leverage The use of debt funds (as full or partial substitute for equity funds) to finance the acquisition of assets.
financial risk The chance that an enterprise will be unable to meet its financing obligations.
financial securities Contractual arrangements that specify future financial obligations or benefits that typically are traded in financial markets.
financing facility The method of providing finance for a term longer than that of the security (or loan arrangement) that raises the funds.
Fisher effect The contention that interest rates adjust for the expected rate of inflation so that the market rate is the sum of the real rate and the (expected) inflation rate.
fixed exchange rate The practice of a government setting the value of its currency in FX markets.
fixed rate The rate of interest on a loan or security that is fixed for the term of the loan (or security).
fixed-interest market That segment of the capital market in which bonds and other fixed-interest securities are traded.
fixed-term deposits Retail funds that are placed with financial institutions for a specified term at a set interest rate.
flat yield curve A horizontal yield curve, indicating that the same yield applies irrespective of term.

float The issue of ordinary shares to form a company. The aim is to raise the equity capital required to establish the business. Also referred to as 'initial public offering' (IPO).
floating exchange rate The exchange rate for a currency set by trading in FX markets.
floating rate The rate of interest on a loan or security that might vary (i.e. be reset) during the term of the loan.
floating rate notes (FRNs) Long-term securities that have a floating rate of interest.
foreign bonds Long-term securities issued by a foreign borrower in a domestic market (e.g. US dollar bonds issued in the US by an Australian borrower).
foreign exchange (FX) The currency of another country.
foreign-exchange market The market in which foreign exchange is traded.
forward This term generally refers to a delayed-settlement transaction.
forward cover The use of the forward FX market to cover a future spot exposure to the FX market.
forward foreign exchange The purchase of foreign exchange on a delayed settlement basis.
forward interest rates Interest rates that apply at a future date (as opposed to spot rates).
forward margin The difference between the forward and spot exchange rates for a currency. A forward discount means that the forward rate is lower than the spot rate. A forward premium means the forward rate is higher than the spot rate.
forward market The market for contracts that provide for delayed settlement.
forward points The difference between the forward and spot rates for a currency.
forward rate agreement (FRA) An agreement between a borrower and lender for the purpose of fixing the rate of interest at which both parties will borrow and lend at a future date. The agreement requires the party who benefits from the difference between the actual interest rate and the agreed rate to make a payment to the other party and this payment ensures that each transacts at the agreed interest rate.
forwards Instruments that arrange a transaction on the basis of a delayed settlement.
friendly society bonds These are similar to superannuation bonds.
fully drawn advances Loans that must be drawndown fully at the outset.
funding risk The risks arising from financing assets when the maturity of the borrowed funds is shorter than the maturity of the assets.
funds management The practice of managing a portfolio of financial assets and liabilities. The term refers also to the sector of the financial system that manages pooled retail funds by investing them in wholesale markets.
future value The accumulated value of a sum of money at a future time.
futures contracts The (forward) contracts traded in a futures market.
futures market The place where futures contracts are traded.
FX swap A round trip transaction in the foreign-exchange market, such as buying a currency in the spot market and simultaneously selling it in the forward market.
gold standard A fixed-exchange-rate regime that sets the value of a currency in relation to an ounce of gold.

gross interest margin The difference between the average rate of interest paid by an intermediary for funds and the average rate received on the funds lent by the intermediary. It represents the intermediary's income on its intermediated business.
hedger A trader who enters a market for the purpose of establishing a pay-off potential that counterbalances the exposure of the trader's existing commitment. For example, a borrower who sells bill futures to hedge an exposure as a borrower in the money market.
hedging The process of establishing a second position to counterbalance an exposed position. Typically, but not necessarily, the exposure arises from a position in a physical market.
historic volatility The previous variability (standard deviation) in an asset's returns.
holding-period yield The return from holding a security for part of its term. It is calculated as a simple interest rate for discount securities and as a semi-annual compound rate for bonds.
impaired assets In banking circles this refers to bank loans on which payments are incomplete.
implied volatility The level of volatility implied by the market price of an option.
in-the-money option When the price of the asset exceeds the exercise price for a call option; and the reverse for a put option.
indexed bonds Long-term securities that make payments that are adjusted for the inflation rate.
indirect quoting The practice, followed mostly in the FX markets of cricket-playing nations, of quoting the domestic currency in terms of a foreign currency.
inflation-risk premium The idea that savers/investors require a risk premium to compensate for the risk that inflation will be higher than they expect.
information asymmetry The circumstance of one party to a transaction having more relevant information than the counterparty.
initial public offering The initial issue of shares in a company.
inscribed stock Securities that are registered so that ownership is based on the registry rather than on the possession of certificates.
insider trading Trading in a market by a party that possesses knowledge that is the property of the market.
interest The increase in a future amount over the present amount.
interest-rate parity The hypothesis that the difference in the rate of interest between two countries is offset by the expected movement in their exchange rate. Hence, the effective interest rate is expected to be the same whether funds are borrowed domestically or overseas.
interest-rate risk The chance that interest-rate movements have an adverse effect on a position, such as that faced by a fixed-rate borrower who has lent the funds on a floating-rate basis.
interest-rate spread The difference between an institution's average interest rate on its assets and its average interest rate paid for funds.
interest-rate swap An agreement between two borrowers to swap their interest payments, usually, but not necessarily, when one party has fixed-interest payments and the other has floating-rate obligations.

interest-indexed bonds The coupon rate of these bonds adjusts over time to keep pace with inflation.
intermediated swap The involvement of a financial institution as the counterparty to both primary swap counterparties. Swap dealers usually operate a swap book, with many counterparties on both sides.
intermediation The process of raising funds from surplus units for the purpose of on-lending them to deficit units in the name of the intermediary. It is an expensive form of financing because of the benefits provided to borrowers and lenders and risks accepted by the intermediary.
international Fisher effect The claim that differences in domestic interest rates result from inflation differences between the countries.
International Monetary Fund (IMF) The body established under the Bretton Woods Agreement (July 1944) to help manage the international financial system following World War II.
intrinsic value An option's value if exercised immediately. Only in-the-money options have intrinsic value.
inverse yield curve A downward-sloping yield curve, indicating that yields are lower for securities that have longer terms to maturity.
investment banks Financial institutions that operate mainly in the wholesale segment of the financial system.
investment savings accounts Bank accounts that provide retail customers with a higher interest rate than current deposits. The rate of interest paid usually increases with the size of the balance in the account.
investment yields Actual yields to maturity and holding-period yields.
junk bond A bond that has a rating of BB or below. These are also known as high-yield bonds.
lead manager The institution that arranges the sale of a parcel of securities (or a loan) on behalf of a syndicate of institutions.
legal tender The notes and coins issued on behalf of the government that must be accepted for payment purposes.
lender of last resort facility The preparedness of the RBA to buy securities from banks at a penalty rate to provide same-day funds. It is intended to solve a temporary liquidity problem and does not protect banks from losses.
life insurance bonds These are similar to superannuation bonds.
limited liability The concept that shareholders are required only to make payments that result in their shares being fully paid. They are not required to subscribe further funds to the company. This concept is one of the foundations of the corporate form of business ownership.
linear interpolation The procedure of estimating the value of a variable with two values that are either side of the true value.
liquidity This term has several meanings, each of which is based on the notion of the convertibility of an asset for cash.
liquidity management The practice of the Reserve Bank to sterilise its daily net transactions as the government's banker for the purpose of maintaining the liquidity of the financial system.
liquidity preference theory The contention that investors have a preference to lend for short periods and that a liquidity premium must be offered on long-term

securities to make them attractive to investors. The premium is required because of the greater volatility in the value of long-term (compared with short-term) securities.

liquidity premium Compensation for holding securities that have long terms to maturity. As both short- and long-term securities can be traded for cash in financial markets, the basis for the premium is the contention that holding-period yields are more volatile than short-term interest rates.

liquidity risk The risk of not being able to make contractual payments when required. Financial intermediaries face this risk mainly because of maturity intermediation.

loan covenants Restrictions imposed by a lender on the financial position of a borrower.

loanable funds theory The contention that the rate of interest is set by the demand for and supply of loanable funds.

London Interbank Offered Rate (LIBOR) A widely used marker rate of interest.

long Financial market jargon that represents the buyer's position.

Macaulay's duration One way of measuring duration.

margins Payments by a trader to a clearing house to cover the discrepancy between the value of the trader's position and its market value.

marker rate The rate that defines the market yield on a particular day.

market makers The dealers in wholesale markets who make bids and offers and will trade immediately.

market operations The practice of the Reserve Bank to trade short-dated Commonwealth securities in the money market. The bank undertakes these operations for the purpose of both monetary policy and liquidity management.

market risk The chance that changes in a market variable (such as exchange rates) will adversely affect the value of a market position (such as holding an amount of foreign exchange).

market spread The spread between the bid and offer rates in a financial market.

market yield Trading in Australia's debt-security markets is in terms of the yield represented by the security's remaining payment(s). These are theoretical yields to maturity which are quoted as annual interest rates.

market-related contracts These are mainly derivatives. The term is used by the Reserve Bank in its presentation of data on the off-balance sheet business of banks.

marking-to-market The practice of valuing securities on a regular (say daily) basis according to their market value.

Matildas Australian-dollar bonds issued by overseas borrowers (usually banks).

maturity intermediation The transformation of short-term funds into long-term loans.

maturity matching The strategy of balancing the maturities of a fund's assets and liabilities to reduce exposure to interest-rate risk.

maturity mismatch This arises when a trader's assets and liabilities have different terms to maturity; for example, when an intermediary borrows on a short-term basis and lends on a long-term basis.

mean reverting The idea that certain variables vary around their average value.

medium-term notes Interest-paying securities that usually have a term of between three and five years.
merchant banks These are known officially as money-market corporations in Australia. They are equivalent to investment banks, except they do not hold a banking licence.
mid-point price The average of a market's bid and offer quotes.
modified duration An adaptation of duration that provides a more convenient way of using duration to indicate the price sensitivity of a bond.
monetary policy The use of short-term interest rates as an instrument of macroeconomic policy. Its main purpose is to contain inflation, having regard to the economy's overall economic performance.
money The economy's medium of exchange.
mortgage constant The reciprocal of the annuity factor based on the term and interest rate of a mortgage. When multiplied by the amount of the loan it determines the amount of the regular payment.
mortgage loans Loans that are secured by a charge over an asset, such as a house. Reducible loans are often referred to as mortgages.
mortgage originators Parties that arrange housing loans. They might (but need not) subsequently service the loan.
mortgage-backed security A long-term security that transforms an asset's cash flows into coupon and redemption payments.
mutual funds US financial institutions that are engaged in funds management.
natural hedge The use of a position in a physical market to counterbalance the exposure arising from a position in another market.
net worth The value of a portfolio's assets minus the value of its liabilities.
netting The process of offsetting amounts due by each counterparty to the other prior to settlement.
next-day funds The proceeds raised by financial institutions when they sell securities in the short-term money market are referred to as next-day funds because payment occurs the following day.
no liability shares These are usually issued as partly paid shares and the holder is not required to make the further payments. They are not commonly issued.
non-bank financial institution A financial intermediary, such as a building society or a merchant bank, that is not licensed (as a bank) by the Reserve Bank.
non-callable deposit Funds that banks must place with the RBA.
non-performing loans Loans on which the borrower is not meeting the financing requirement, such as the payment of interest.
normal yield curve An upward-sloping yield curve indicating that yields increase with the length of their term.
novation The practice of a clearing house offsetting individual obligations.
off-balance sheet business Financial contracts that are recorded off the balance sheet because of accounting conventions.
official short-term money market A group of dealers that provided a market for trading by the RBA prior to the bank's decision in July 1996 to trade with any dealer who is a member of RITS.
offshore banking units Banking facilities that are confined to non-domestic currency transactions. They usually enjoy a preferential level of taxation.

open outcry A method of trading on the floor of an exchange that involves communicating through yelling and a system of hand signals.
operating lease A financing arrangement that is an alternative to renting an asset. These usually have a short term.
operational efficiency The cost-effectiveness and reliability of the financial system.
operational risk The risk of loss that arises from the failure of a financial institution's operational systems.
option The right, but not the obligation, to undertake a specified transaction within a set period.
option premium The price of an option.
option strategies These are combinations of the four basic option positions together with positions in the asset, such as strangles, butterflies and condors.
ordinary annuity A sequence of regular payments that are made at the end of each period.
ordinary shares The class of shares that provide the right to vote and to receive dividends.
out-of-the-money option An option that has no intrinsic value. In the case of a call option, its strike price is greater than the price of the underlying asset; with the reverse for a put option.
outright forward contract A contract to buy or sell a currency in the forward foreign-exchange market.
over-the-counter markets Dealer- (rather than exchange-) organised markets. In Australia, their operations are overseen by various committees of the Australian Financial Markets Association (AFMA).
overdraft A borrowing facility that is accessed through a borrower's cheque account.
paper A generic term for financial instruments.
par bonds Bonds that are trading at a yield equal to their coupon rate.
pass-through securities Asset-backed securities that convert all of an asset's cash flows (i.e. interest and principal reduction) into payments to their holders. Hence, these securities can be redeemed prior to their maturity date.
pay-off diagram Shows the movement in the value of an asset in relation to the movement in price of the underlying asset.
payments system The methods by which payments can be effected, such as the use of notes and coins, cheques and credit cards.
pension A form of post-retirement income.
per annum standardisation The expression of the rate of interest as an annual rate. In Australia, this involves a 365-day year, whereas in the USA and in Europe it involves a 360-day year.
perpetuity A series of regular payments that continue indefinitely.
physical markets Those financial markets that arrange the exchange of funds on a spot basis. The term is used to distinguish them from derivative markets.
plain vanilla swap A fixed-for-floating interest-rate swap.
point The smallest change in the value of a market variable, such as a market yield. It is also referred to as a 'tic'.

pooled superannuation trust An arrangement that allows small superannuation schemes to pool their funds for investment purposes.
position taking The strategy of buying in the expectation of a future price increase, or selling in the expectation of a future price fall, for the purpose of making a trading profit. The practice is, in effect, speculation.
preference shares The class of shares that has a prior right to dividends (over that of ordinary shareholders).
preferred habitat theory The contention that investors prefer to place funds in securities with particular maturities. The theory implies that investors will place funds at less preferred maturities if offered a premium and that these premiums determine the shape of the yield curve.
premium bond Bonds that are trading at a yield that is less than their coupon rate.
prepaid cards Cards that store value for use when settling specific transactions.
present value The current value of a sum of money that is typically a future payment.
price risk A specific form of market risk, arising from movements in security prices. It is related to interest-rate risk, because the price of debt securities is set by their market yield.
price sensitivity of a bond The percentage change in a bond's price in response to a small change in interest rates.
price-earnings ratio A share price divided by the company's earnings per share.
primary market The arrangements for the sale of new securities for the purpose of raising funds.
prime asset As a generic term, prime refers to the lowest level of credit risk. Prime assets are those that the RBA accepts as being eligible under its prime asset requirement.
private placement The issue of new securities to particular investors such as life offices and superannuation funds.
promissory notes Short-term discount securities that are issued by very creditworthy borrowers in their own name. They are referred to also as 'commercial paper'.
purchasing power parity The theory that implies that exchange rates adjust for inflation differences, so that the effective price of goods and services is the same whether they are purchased locally or overseas. It implies that a country's currency will depreciate when its inflation rate exceeds that of its trading partners.
put An option to sell an asset at a set price within a set period.
random walk The consequence of an efficient market is that prices follow a random walk. This occurs when current prices reflect all available information relevant to an asset's value and thus price changes in response to the random flow of new information.
rate of interest The rate of increase between the present and future value of an amount of money over time, usually a year.
real This term refers to actual (or nominal) values that have been adjusted for inflation. For instance, the real interest rate is the actual rate less the inflation rate.

real-time settlement Arrangements that result in the immediate exchange of cash to settle transactions.
recession A fall in the real value of an economy's output (i.e. real GDP) over two successive quarters.
redemption value The amount payable to the holder of a security on its maturity. In Australia, it is usually the security's face value.
rediscounting The repurchase of a discount security, illustrated by the Reserve Bank's repurchase of Treasury notes.
reducible loan A loan that has a regular payment that meets the interest due each period and contributes to the loan's repayment.
regional banks An informal category of banks that operate mainly in one or a few states. They usually provide retail services and products.
regulation arbitrage The practice of businesses (including financial institutions) to locate in an area that offers the lowest level of regulation.
reinvestment risk The chance that the return on an interest-paying investment is reduced because of a fall in the yield at which the payments are invested.
repurchase agreements Contracts for the sale and subsequent repurchase (or vice versa) of securities, such as Commonwealth Treasury bonds. They are used extensively by the Reserve Bank when it is adjusting the liquidity of the financial system.
reregulation The idea that changes in the regulatory environment following deregulation represent a return to the regulatory environment.
Reserve Bank bond formula A formula that calculates the price of a bond whether it is traded on an ex-interest or cum-interest date.
Reserve Bank of Australia Australia's central bank. It operates under Commonwealth legislation that defines its responsibilities.
retail banking The operations of deposit-taking institutions that involve small-value transactions. It usually covers the transactions of individuals and small to medium-sized businesses.
retail bonds Long-term securities, such as debentures and bank bonds, that are sold in small parcels to retail customers.
retail transactions Small-value financial transactions, typically made by individuals.
reversing transaction The practice in futures markets of traders closing out their position. For example, a trader who holds ten gold futures contracts would sell ten contracts to reverse (or close out) the original position.
revolving line of credit A borrowing limit, such that repayments can be subsequently reborrowed.
rights A financial security that creates the right to subscribe to new shares at a set price within a given period.
rights issue The issue of new shares to existing shareholders with the aim of raising additional share capital.
risk The possibility that financial transactions will not achieve their desired outcome.
risk capital Equity funds.
risk management The practice of assessing exposures to undesirable outcomes and deciding what measures are to be taken to cover these exposures. For example,

a borrower who is exposed to the risk of future interest-rate increases may decide to enter forward rate agreements (FRAs) to pre-set an agreed forward rate.
risk-adjusted assets The value of bank assets for capital-adequacy purposes. It is calculated by multiplying the value of each asset by the appropriate risk-adjustment factor and aggregating these values.
risk-adjustment factors The five risk factors used in calculating the risk-adjusted value of assets for capital adequacy purposes.
risk-free rate of interest The rate of interest on securities that have no default risk. Treasury bonds are generally regarded as (credit) risk-free securities.
risk-return trade-off The proposition that risk increases the return required by the suppliers of funds.
roll over The issue of new securities to finance the redemption of maturing securities. It has the effect of extending the period of the financing arrangement.
same-day funds Funds that pass through the exchange settlement accounts with the RBA are treated as cash, and hence are known as same-day funds, even though cheques normally are not cleared until the next day.
savings banks Refer to trading banks.
secondary market The arrangements for trading existing securities (and the settlement of these transactions). It provides liquidity for investors in new securities and thus enhances the value of tradeable securities.
securitisation The process of funding loans with securities, as opposed to intermediated funds. It can have the effect of converting assets into traded securities.
securitised asset The creation of securities based on an asset's expected future payments.
security Either, a financial instrument, or the collateral for a loan.
segmentation theory The contention that the shape of the yield curve is determined by yields in different maturity segments of security markets.
semi-government bonds Bonds issued by Australia's semi-government and State government borrowing authorities, such as the New South Wales Treasury Corporation.
sentiment Financial-market jargon for the general mood of the traders in the market.
settlement The exchange of cash to complete a transaction, such as the exchange of cash for a security, following a market transaction.
settlement risk A specific form of counterparty risk. It is the chance that a transaction will not be settled.
shading The practice of dealers to improve their quoted prices (usually by a point) to attract business.
share float The initial issue of shares in a company. Usually it is undertaken to allow the company's shares to be listed on the stock exchange.
share options Securities that allow their holder to subscribe to new shares at a set price within a given period.
shares Financial instruments (known also as common stock) that represent equity funds invested in a company.
short Financial market jargon that represents the seller's position.
short selling The practice of selling without owning the asset. It is accommodated in the futures market because the contracts are either non-

deliverable or the delivery date is a future date and the seller can close out the position before the delivery date.
short-term money market The market in which short-term securities are issued and traded.
short-term securities These have been issued with a term to maturity of less than one year.
simple interest A method of measuring the growth in a present to a future amount when interest is calculated at the end of the period. Yields in the money market are calculated in simple-interest terms.
Singapore Interbank Offered (SIBOR) A widely used marker rate of interest in the South-east Asian market.
smart cards Cards that store value for use in settling transactions generally.
smoothing and testing Jargon used by the Reserve Bank, particularly prior to 1995, to represent its objectives when conducting market operations for the purpose of liquidity management in the domestic money and FX markets. Testing occurred mainly in the foreign-exchange market when the bank believed the market sentiment was out of line with the fundamental factors that determine the value of the currency.
sovereign risk The risk that FX exchange transactions will be adversely affected by the domestic government, for example, through the imposition of exchange controls.
speculator A trader who takes a position in a market in the hope of making a profit from the future price movement.
spot This term is generally used in financial markets to refer to transactions for non-delayed delivery. The practices in each market determine the period between the deal and settlement dates. In the short-term money market it is usually the same day, in the FX market it is two days and in the bond market it is three.
spot interest rates The rates (i.e. yields) that currently apply for single-payment securities.
spread The difference between buying and selling quotations. A foreign-exchange dealer, for instance, makes a profit when currency is bought at the dealer's bid rate and sold at the dealer's offer rate. This means the counterparties to these two transactions dealt at different prices (on the wrong side of the spread).
standby facility The agreement to provide funds should this be required by the borrower. Usually, it is for a very large amount.
step-up bond A bond that has a coupon rate that increases over its term.
sterilise This refers to a transaction that offsets the effect of another.
stock exchange The organisation that arranges trading in shares and share options.
straddle The combination of a long put and a long call with the same exercise price.
strip hedging The practice of taking a sequence of single-period hedge contracts to create a sequence of hedge positions. A strip hedge would be used, for instance, by a borrower under a bill facility, to hedge the interest-rate risk on the bill roll-over dates.
strong currency A currency that has been increasing in FX markets.
superannuation A form of post-retirement income that can be taken as a lump sum or as an annuity that has a term (usually) of the beneficiary's life.

superannuation bonds Single-payment superannuation policies that can be redeemed with tax benefits if held for a specified period (ten years).
Superannuation Guarantee Charge A scheme introduced in the late 1980s by the then federal government to require employers to contribute to their employees' superannuation scheme. The charge was not imposed if the required contributions were made.
surplus units Participants in the financial system that receive more income during a period than the sum of their outlays, and therefore they either reduce their financial liabilities or increase their financial assets.
swap points These are the forward points in an FX swap transaction.
swap rate The fixed rate in an interest-rate swap.
swaps An instrument that arranges an exchange of cash flows between two parties.
Sydney Futures Exchange (SFE) Australia's futures market. With its clearing house, it organises trading in futures contracts. The clearing house acts as the counterparty to each trader and accepts the risk of default by each trader.
Sydney Stock Exchange Automated Trading System (SEATS) The computer-based trading system that matches buy and sell orders in the stockmarket.
syndicated loan A large loan that is provided by a syndicate of lenders, usually arranged by a lead banker.
tax-adjusted Fisher effect The contention that interest rates adjust to inflation and to the effect of the income tax on the after-tax return to lenders.
technical analysis A method of predicting the movement in shareprices based on the patterns formed by past price movements.
term (or **tenor**) The length of period prior to a payment(s). It may refer also to the length of the period to a security's maturity date.
term loans Medium- to long-term loans by financial institutions. They can be on a reducible or interest-only basis.
term structure The relationship between spot (interest) rates and their term.
terminal value The accumulated value of an investment or portfolio of investments at a particular date.
terms currency FX-market jargon for the currency in which another currency is priced.
theoretical zero-coupon yields The zero-coupon rates deduced from coupon bond yields.
time value The value of the chance that an option will have value when exercised.
time value of money Interest indicates the time value of money because it is the difference between the present and future value of an amount.
tombstone An advertisement that announces the successful completion of the raising of a syndicated loan.
trade weighted index An index that expresses the value of the Australian dollar in terms of a weighted average of the currencies of our trading partners.
trading banks Until 1989, banks in Australia were classified as being either a trading or a savings bank. The former provided cheque-account facilities and made loans to business, whereas the latter mainly borrowed from and lent to individuals.
tranche Portions, or classes, of securities.

transaction costs The cost of making (in the context of this book) financial deals, such as the lending of funds and the costs of issuing new securities.
translation risk The risk of changes in the value of assets and liabilities due to changes in market values. It arises in particular when the assets and liabilities are in other currencies.
Treasury bonds Commonwealth Government bonds. The term is used mainly to refer to Treasury fixed-interest bonds.
Treasury note A short-term security issued by the Commonwealth Treasury at a discount on its face value.
treasury products These include financial capital, foreign exchange and derivatives. They are the products used by an enterprise's treasury department.
turnover The volume of trading in a market.
twin deficits The relationship between a country's current-account deficit and its budget deficit. It is a national accounting identity that may reflect causation.
two-way cross rates The bid and offer rates for a non-USD exchange rate, such as JPY/DEM.
unbiased-expectations hypothesis The proposition that the market's expectations about the level of future spot rates relative to the current spot rate determine the shape of the yield curve.
uncovered interest-rate parity The outcome should interest-rate parity actually occur.
underwriting The practice of selling securities on the basis that the seller will acquire the script that has not been sold.
value date The settlement date for a market transaction.
vanilla swap A fixed-for-floating interest-rate swap.
volatility The movements in a market variable.
warrants These are traded options, such as a warrant over shares, that have a term longer than those for exchange-traded options, that are issued by a party (typically an investment bank) other than the issuer of the underlying instrument.
weak currency A currency that has been falling in FX markets.
wholesale banking The operations of financial institutions that involve large-value (e.g. $2m and above) transactions.
wholesale transactions Large-value financial transactions, typically made by large enterprises and by the dealers in financial markets.
yield The rate of growth, usually expressed as a percentage per annum, in an amount of funds.
yield curve A curve showing spot yields according to their term.
yield to maturity The return from holding a security until it matures. It is equal to the purchase yield for discount (and zero-coupon) securities. For coupon-paying securities it depends on the interest rate when the securities are purchased and the rate at which coupon payments are invested.
zero-coupon bond A bond that pays no coupons.
zero-coupon yield curve A yield curve based on spot (or zero-coupon) yields according to their term.

Index

THE NEW JERUSALEM BIBLE

The New Jerusalem Bible

POCKET EDITION

DARTON · LONGMAN + TODD

Darton, Longman & Todd Ltd
1 Spencer Court
140–142 Wandsworth High Street
London SW18 4JJ

Pocket Edition published 1990

Nihil obstat Anton Cowan
Imprimatur Rt Rev John Crowley V.G.
Bishop in Central London
Westminster 4th September 1989

The Nihil obstat *and* Imprimatur *are a declaration that a book or pamphlet is considered to be free from doctrinal or moral error. It is not implied that those who have granted the* Nihil obstat *and* Imprimatur *agree with the contents, opinions or statements expressed.*

2/13

ISBN 10 0 232 51890 4
ISBN 13 978 0 232 51890 0 (Printed cased edition)
ISBN 10 0 232 51891 2
ISBN 13 978 0 232 51891 7 (Leather zipped edition: black)
ISBN 10 0 232 51892 0
ISBN 13 978 0 232 51892 4 (Leather zipped edition: red)
ISBN 10 0 232 52312 6
ISBN 13 978 0 232 52312 6 (White Leather Presentation Bible)
ISBN 10 0 232 52705 9
ISBN 13 978 0 232 52705 6 (White Leather Confirmation Bible)
ISBN 10 0 232 52706 7
ISBN 13 978 0 232 52706 3 (White Leather First Communion Bible)

Phototypeset by Input Typesetting Ltd, London
Printed in China
FT4936-22M

CONTENTS

THE OLD TESTAMENT

THE PENTATEUCH

THE DEUTERONOMIC HISTORY

THE WISDOM BOOKS

THE PROPHETS

THE NEW TESTAMENT

SUPPLEMENTS

EDITOR'S FOREWORD

The Bible is not a book but a library, joining together dozens of writings, history, stories, poetry and letters. Almost the only common factor is that they all speak to us of God, revealing his nature, his awesome sovereignty and his tender love.

The Old Testament is normally divided into three sections. The histories (including the Pentateuch, the basic first five books, the great Law of Israel) show God's loving guidance and correction of Israel from nomad beginnings through all the trials and infidelities of the settled civilisation in Palestine. The Wisdom books (including the Psalms, the prayerbook of Israel) express the wisdom of Israel drawn from God for the practical art of living. The prophetic writings gather the warnings and promises of God expressed through those special messengers who strove to keep Israel faithful for the centuries before Christ. By all these means God was forming his people, preparing them for the fulfilment of his purposes in Christ.

The New Testament is best divided into two sections. First come the four gospels, the record of the message of Good News brought by Jesus. Then the letters written by Paul and other apostolic figures to the nascent churches of Mediterranean Christianity, to give them instruction and help to solve their problems, but also to be a source of understanding and guidance for every generation of Christians. The last book of the Bible, the Revelation to John, sums all up in the vision of deliverance from persecution and a glorious establishment of the reign of God in the New Jerusalem.

This Pocket Edition of *The New Jerusalem Bible* is based on the much larger Standard Edition first published in 1985. While the biblical text remains unchanged, the notes and introductory material have been pared to make the volume more accessible and manageable. There will be questions left unanswered here for which the answer can be found in the Standard Edition. The Index of Persons and the Chronological Table at the end have been simplified. A new help has, however, been added, in the form of a Theological Glossary; this gives succinct notes on nearly 200 key words and concepts of the Bible; each note ends with half a dozen references to the key passages in the Bible for the concept, thus providing also a sort of mini-concordance.

The translation follows the original Hebrew, Aramaic and Greek texts. For the Old Testament (OT) the 'Massoretic Text' (MT), established in the 8–9th centuries AD by Jewish scholars, is used. Only when this presents insuperable difficulties have emendations or other versions, such as the ancient Greek translation begun in 200 BC at Alexandria, the 'Septuagint' (abbreviated 'LXX'), been used. In certain OT books passages exist only in the LXX version; these passages have been printed in italics. Italics are used also, and in the New Testament (NT) exclusively, to indicate quotations from other books of the Bible. Occasionally the verse-numbering shows a disturbed order; the verse-numbers always follow the MT, but versions or logic may show that another order of printing the verses is preferable. On occasion also a gap may be left (. . .); this indicates an unintelligible word or an incomplete sentence in the original, which scholars have not been able to fill out satisfactorily. Brackets in the OT text indicate that the passage is considered a gloss, an addition or explanation later than the original text. = This sign indicates a parallel passage within the same book. It also can signify simply 'equals'. || indicates a parallel passage within another book.

The work of many devoted scholars has contributed to this Bible: those who produced the parent *Bible de Jérusalem* in 1956, the collaborators on the first English *Jerusalem Bible* (1966), the revisers of the *Bible de Jérusalem* (1973), and those who combined to produce the Standard Edition of *The New Jerusalem Bible* in 1985. The grateful reader might spare a prayer of thanks and blessing on them.

'So now let us begin our narrative, without adding any more to what has been said above; there would be no sense in expanding the preface to the history and curtailing the history itself' (2 Mc 2:32).

Feast of the Assumption, 1989
Ampleforth Abbey HENRY WANSBROUGH

THE OLD TESTAMENT

INTRODUCTION TO THE PENTATEUCH

Genesis and the next four books of the Bible (the 'Pentateuch' or fivefold scroll) form the basic *torah* or Law of Israel. They are the memorial of the beginnings of God's people. They record God's call to the patriarchs who followed him in trusting faith, the choice and formation of the people whom he called in the desert to be his own, and the way of life laid down for them to make them a people able to associate with the holiness of God. He is a God who saves his people, and by a series of covenants leading up to the great covenant on Sinai, commits himself to being their protector for always. Israel in its turn commits itself to fidelity as the holy people of God, who reveals himself to them in love and tenderness.

Yahweh, the God of Israel did not pluck his people out of their surroundings, but educated them gradually, 'leading them with human ties, with the leading-strings of love' (Ho 11:3). These books draw on the folklore and traditions of Israel over many centuries, reflecting all the phases of the development of the life of the nation and its devotion to Yahweh. The memories of its origins are preserved in a variety of ways. There are personal stories of the great ancestors of the people, their attachment to Yahweh or their astuteness. Some stories are centred on particular localities, while others explain usages or provide legislation in the form of anecdotes.

Two collections of these ancient memories were recorded, one about the time of King Solomon (*c.* 980 BC) and the other two centuries later after the fall of the northern kingdom of Israel (*c.* 720 BC). At the time of the Babylonian exile (587–538 BC) these were joined by a third body of tradition concerned mostly with worship and its origins and with genealogical and cultic matters. A fourth stream of tradition, the deuteronomic tradition, is associated with the religious reform of 620 BC and reflects the concerns seen both in Deuteronomy and also in the accounts of the later history. But it was not until after the Babylonian exile, *c.* 450 BC, that the Pentateuch reached its definitive and final form.

Firmly rooted in the nomadic culture of the ancient Near East, Israel was a primitive people, whose customs and morality may seem barbaric by some modern standards. Secure in the championship of Yahweh, they learnt gradually his nature and his purpose for the people he had chosen as his own.

THE BOOK OF GENESIS

Genesis, the story of origins, sets the scene for the whole Bible. The very first episode shows that God is the all-powerful creator of the universe, and that he chose Adam to administer it. The second episode already shows human failure and God's forgiveness, themes woven together especially in Gn 1–11, through stories couched in the remote past, but relevant to every phase of human history. Much of the imagery is similar to that of other ancient religions, but the conception of God and the world is wholly different. Instead of the fantastic world of quarrelling deities who use human beings as mere pawns, God is a loving creator who repeatedly acts to save the human race even when it fails him.

The stories of the ancestors which follow represent the oldest traditions of Israel. Their world is that of the Hebrews, pastoral nomads on the fringes of civilisation. Abraham stands out as the friend of God at the origin of faith, reckless in his trust in Yahweh, and a partner in the first of the series of covenants which lead up to the great covenant on Sinai. Isaac receives a confirmation of this covenant, and so does Jacob, that figure of cunning and intrigue. Finally, the extended story of Joseph shows that God is able to save his people in Egypt through the very man they had rejected and sold into slavery.

The origin of these traditions is diverse. Many of the stories explain customs such as circumcision or abstention from eating blood; some comment on features of the landscape or the existence of shrines; others explain the origin of names. Although identification of persons is not always certain, details of legal observances often show a striking correspondence with ancient codes of Law, e.g. on ownership of land or on marital customs. Through it all shines the faith of these ancestors and their certainty that they are chosen and protected by their God.

PLAN OF THE BOOK

Sons of God and women

6 When people began being numerous on earth, and daughters had been born to them, 2the sons of God, looking at the women, saw how beautiful they were and married as many of them as they chose. 3Yahweh said, 'My spirit cannot be indefinitely responsible for human beings, who are only flesh; let the time allowed each be a hundred and twenty years.' 4The Nephilim were on earth in those days (and even afterwards) when the sons of God resorted to the women, and had children by them. These were the heroes of days gone by, men of renown.

B: THE FLOOD

The corruption of humanity

5Yahweh saw that human wickedness was great on earth and that human hearts contrived nothing but wicked schemes all day long. 6Yahweh regretted having made human beings on earth and was grieved at heart. 7And Yahweh said, 'I shall rid the surface of the earth of the human beings whom I created—human and animal, the creeping things and the birds of heaven—for I regret having made them.' 8But Noah won Yahweh's favour.

9This is the story of Noah:

Noah was a good man, an upright man among his contemporaries, and he walked with God. 10Noah fathered three sons, Shem, Ham and Japheth. 11God saw that the earth was corrupt and full of lawlessness. 12God looked at the earth: it was corrupt, for corrupt were the ways of all living things on earth.

Preparations for the flood

13God said to Noah, 'I have decided that the end has come for all living things, for the earth is full of lawlessness because of human beings. So I am now about to destroy them and the earth. 14Make yourself an ark out of resinous wood. Make it of reeds and caulk it with pitch inside and out. 15This is how to make it: the length of the ark is to be three hundred cubits, its breadth fifty cubits, and its height thirty cubits. 16Make a roof to the ark, building it up to a cubit higher. Put the entrance in the side of the ark, which is to be made with lower, second and third decks.

17'For my part I am going to send the flood, the waters, on earth, to destroy all living things having the breath of life under heaven; everything on earth is to perish. 18But with you I shall establish my covenant and you will go aboard the ark, yourself, your sons, your wife, and your sons' wives along with you. 19From all living creatures, from all living things, you must take two of each kind aboard the ark, to save their lives with yours; they must be a male and a female. 20Of every species of bird, of every kind of animal and of every kind of creature that creeps along the ground, two must go with you so that their lives may be saved. 21For your part, provide yourself with eatables of all kinds, and lay in a store of them, to serve as food for yourself and them.' 22Noah did this; exactly as God commanded him, he did.

7 Yahweh said to Noah, 'Go aboard the ark, you and all your household, for you alone of your contemporaries do I see before me as an upright man. 2Of every clean animal you must take seven pairs, a male and its female; of the unclean animals you must take one pair, a male and its female 3(and of the birds of heaven, seven pairs, a male and its female), to preserve their species throughout the earth. 4For in seven days' time I shall make it rain on earth for forty days and forty nights, and I shall wipe every creature I have made off the face of the earth.' 5Noah did exactly as Yahweh commanded him.

6Noah was six hundred years old when the flood came, the waters over the earth.

7Noah with his sons, his wife, and his sons' wives boarded the ark to escape the waters of the flood. 8(Of the clean animals and the animals that are not clean, of the birds and all that creeps along the ground, 9one pair boarded the ark with Noah, one male and one female, as God had commanded Noah.) 10Seven days later the waters of the flood appeared on earth.

11In the six hundredth year of Noah's life, in the second month, and on the seventeenth day of the month, that very day all the springs of the great deep burst through, and the sluices of heaven opened. 12And heavy rain fell on earth for forty days and forty nights.

13That very day Noah and his sons Shem, Ham and Japheth boarded the ark, with Noah's wife and the three wives of his sons, 14and with them every species of wild animal, every species of cattle, every species of creeping things that creep along the ground, every species of bird, everything that flies, everything with wings. 15One pair of all that was alive and had the breath of life boarded the ark with Noah, 16and those that went aboard were a male and female of all that was alive, as God had commanded him.

Then Yahweh shut him in.

The flood

17The flood lasted forty days on earth. The waters swelled, lifting the ark until it floated off the ground. 18The waters rose, swelling higher above the ground, and the ark drifted away over the waters. 19The waters rose higher and higher above the ground until all the highest mountains under the whole of heaven were submerged. 20The waters reached their peak fifteen cubits above the submerged mountains. 21And all living things that stirred on earth perished; birds, cattle, wild animals, all the creatures swarming over the earth, and all human beings. 22Everything with the least breath of life in its nostrils, everything on dry land, died. 23Every living thing on the face of the earth was wiped out, people, animals, creeping things and birds; they were wiped off the earth and only Noah was left, and those with him in the ark. 24The waters maintained their level on earth for a hundred and fifty days.

The flood subsides

8 But God had Noah in mind, and all the wild animals and all the cattle that were with him in the ark. God sent a wind across the earth and the waters began to subside. 2The springs of the deep and the sluices of heaven were stopped up and the heavy rain from heaven was held back. 3Little by little, the waters ebbed from the earth. After a hundred and fifty days the waters fell, 4and in the seventh month, on the seventeenth day of the month, the ark came to rest on the mountains of Ararat. 5The waters gradually fell until the tenth month when, on the first day of the tenth month, the mountain tops appeared.

6At the end of forty days Noah opened the window he had made in the ark 7and released a raven, which flew back and forth as it waited for the waters to dry up on earth. 8He then released a dove, to see whether the waters were receding from the surface of the earth. 9But the dove, finding nowhere to perch, returned to him in the ark, for there was water over the whole surface of the earth; putting out his hand he took hold of it and brought it back into the ark with him. 10After waiting seven more days, he again released the dove from the ark. 11In the evening, the dove came back to him and there in its beak was a freshly-picked olive leaf! So Noah realised that the waters were receding from the earth. 12After waiting seven more days, he released the dove, and now it returned to him no more.

13It was in the six hundred and first year of Noah's life, in the first month and on the first of the month, that the waters began drying out on earth. Noah lifted back the hatch of the ark and looked out. The surface of the ground was dry!

14In the second month, on the twenty-seventh day of the month, the earth was dry.

They disembark

15Then God said to Noah, 16'Come out of the ark, you, your wife, your sons, and your sons' wives with you. 17Bring out all the animals with you, all living things, the birds, the cattle and all the creeping things that creep along the ground, for them to swarm on earth, for them to breed and multiply on earth.' 18So Noah came out with his sons, his wife, and his sons' wives. 19And all the wild animals, all the cattle, all the birds and all the creeping things that creep along the ground, came out of the ark, one species after another.

20Then Noah built an altar to Yahweh and, choosing from all the clean animals and all the clean birds he presented burnt offerings on the altar. 21Yahweh smelt the pleasing smell and said to himself, 'Never again will I curse the earth because of human beings, because their heart contrives evil from their infancy. Never again will I strike down every living thing as I have done.

22As long as earth endures:
seed-time and harvest,
  cold and heat,
summer and winter,
  day and night
  will never cease.'

The new world order

9 God blessed Noah and his sons and said
to them, 'Breed, multiply and fill the
earth. [2]Be the terror and the dread of all the
animals on land and all the birds of heaven,
of everything that moves on land and all the
fish of the sea; they are placed in your hands.
[3]Every living thing that moves will be yours
to eat, no less than the foliage of the plants.
I give you everything, [4]with this exception:
you must not eat flesh with life, that is to say
blood, in it. [5]And I shall demand account of
your life-blood, too. I shall demand it of
every animal, and of man. Of man as regards
his fellow-man, I shall demand account for
human life.

[6]He who sheds the blood of man,
by man shall his blood be shed,
for in the image of God
was man created.
[7]Be fruitful then and multiply,
teem over the earth and subdue it!'

[8]God spoke as follows to Noah and his
sons, [9]'I am now establishing my covenant
with you and with your descendants to come,
[10]and with every living creature that was with
you: birds, cattle and every wild animal with
you; everything that came out of the ark,
every living thing on earth. [11]And I shall
maintain my covenant with you: that never
again shall all living things be destroyed by
the waters of a flood, nor shall there ever
again be a flood to devastate the earth.'

[12]'And this', God said, 'is the sign of the
covenant which I now make between myself
and you and every living creature with you
for all ages to come: [13]I now set my bow in
the clouds and it will be the sign of the
covenant between me and the earth. [14]When
I gather the clouds over the earth and the
bow appears in the clouds, [15]I shall recall the
covenant between myself and you and every
living creature, in a word all living things,
and never again will the waters become a
flood to destroy all living things. [16]When the
bow is in the clouds I shall see it and call to
mind the eternal covenant between God and
every living creature on earth, that is, all
living things.'

[17]'That', God told Noah, 'is the sign of the
covenant I have established between my-
self and all living things on earth.'

C: FROM THE FLOOD TO ABRAHAM

Noah and his sons

[18]The sons of Noah who came out of the ark
were Shem, Ham and Japheth—Ham being
the father of Canaan. [19]These three were
Noah's sons, and from these the whole earth
was peopled.

[20]Noah, a tiller of the soil, was the first to
plant the vine. [21]He drank some of the wine,
and while he was drunk, he lay uncovered in
his tent. [22]Ham, father of Canaan, saw his
father naked and told his two brothers
outside. [23]Shem and Japheth took a cloak and
they both put it over their shoulders, and
walking backwards, covered their father's
nakedness; they kept their faces turned away,
and they did not look at their father naked.
[24]When Noah awoke from his stupor he
learned what his youngest son had done to
him, [25]and said:

Accursed be Canaan,
he shall be
his brothers' meanest slave.

[26]He added:

Blessed be Yahweh, God of Shem,
let Canaan be his slave!
[27]May God make space for Japheth,
may he live in the tents of Shem,
and let Canaan be his slave!

[28]After the flood Noah lived three hun-
dred and fifty years. [29]In all, Noah's life
lasted nine hundred and fifty years; then he
died.

The peopling of the earth

10 These are the descendants of Noah's
sons, Shem, Ham and Japheth, to
whom sons were born after the flood:

[2]Japheth's sons: Gomer, Magog, the
Medes, Javan, Tubal, Meshech, Tiras.
[3]Gomer's sons: Ashkenaz, Riphath,
Togarmah. [4]Javan's sons: Elishah, Tarshish,
the Kittim, the Dananites. [5]From these came
the dispersal to the islands of the nations.

These were Japheth's sons, in their
respective countries, each with its own
language, by clan and nation.

[6]Ham's sons: Cush, Mizraim, Put,
Canaan. [7]Cush's sons: Seba, Havilah,

Sabtah, Raamah, Sabteca. Raamah's sons: Sheba, Dedan.

[8]Cush fathered Nimrod who was the first potentate on earth. [9]He was a mighty hunter in the eyes of Yahweh, hence the saying, 'Like Nimrod, a mighty hunter in the eyes of Yahweh'. [10]The mainstays of his empire were Babel, Erech and Accad, all of them in the land of Shinar. [11]From this country came Asshur, and he built Nineveh, Rehoboth-Ir, Calah, [12]and Resen between Nineveh and Calah (this being the capital).

[13]Mizraim fathered the people of Lud, of Anam, Lehab, Naphtuh, [14]Pathros, Casluh and Caphtor, from which the Philistines came.

[15]Canaan fathered Sidon, his first-born, then Heth, [16]and the Jebusites, the Amorites, Girgashites, [17]Hivites, Arkites, Sinites, [18]Arvadites, Zemarites and Hamathites. Later, the Canaanite clans spread out. [19]The Canaanite frontier stretched from Sidon all the way to Gerar near Gaza, and all the way to Sodom, Gomorrah, Admah and Zeboiim near Lesha.

[20]These were Ham's sons, by clans and languages, by countries and nations.

[21]Shem too fathered sons, being ancestor of all the sons of Eber and Japheth's elder brother.

[22]Shem's sons: Elam, Asshur, Arpachshad, Lud, Aram. [23]Aram's sons: Uz, Hul, Gether and Mash.

[24]Arpachshad fathered Shelah, and Shelah fathered Eber. [25]To Eber were born two sons: the first was called Peleg, because it was in his time that the earth was divided, and his brother was called Joktan. [26]Joktan fathered Almodad, Sheleph, Hazarmaveth, Jerah, [27]Hadoram, Uzal, Diklah, [28]Obal, Abima-El, Sheba, [29]Ophir, Havilah, Jobab; all these were sons of Joktan. [30]They occupied a stretch of country from Mesha all the way to Sephar, the eastern mountain range.

[31]These were Shem's sons, by clans and languages, by countries and nations.

[32]Such were the clans of Noah's descendants, listed by descent and nation. From them, other nations branched out on earth after the flood.

The tower of Babel

11 The whole world spoke the same language, with the same vocabulary. [2]Now, as people moved eastwards they found a valley in the land of Shinar where they settled. [3]They said to one another, 'Come, let us make bricks and bake them in the fire.' For stone they used bricks, and for mortar they used bitumen. [4]'Come,' they said, 'let us build ourselves a city and a tower with its top reaching heaven. Let us make a name for ourselves, so that we do not get scattered all over the world.'

[5]Now Yahweh came down to see the city and the tower that the people had built. [6]'So they are all a single people with a single language!' said Yahweh. 'This is only the start of their undertakings! Now nothing they plan to do will be beyond them. [7]Come, let us go down and confuse their language there, so that they cannot understand one another.' [8]Yahweh scattered them thence all over the world, and they stopped building the city. [9]That is why it was called Babel, since there Yahweh confused the language of the whole world, and from there Yahweh scattered them all over the world.

The patriarchs after the flood

[10]These are Shem's descendants:

When Shem was a hundred years old he fathered Arpachshad, two years after the flood. [11]After the birth of Arpachshad, Shem lived five hundred years and fathered sons and daughters.

[12]When Arpachshad was thirty-five years old he fathered Shelah. [13]After the birth of Shelah, Arpachshad lived four hundred and three years and fathered sons and daughters.

[14]When Shelah was thirty years old he fathered Eber. [15]After the birth of Eber, Shelah lived four hundred and three years and fathered sons and daughters.

[16]When Eber was thirty-four years old he fathered Peleg. [17]After the birth of Peleg, Eber lived four hundred and thirty years and fathered sons and daughters.

[18]When Peleg was thirty years old he fathered Reu. [19]After the birth of Reu, Peleg lived two hundred and nine years and fathered sons and daughters.

[20]When Reu was thirty-two years old he fathered Serug. [21]After the birth of Serug, Reu lived two hundred and seven years and fathered sons and daughters.

[22]When Serug was thirty years old he fathered Nahor. [23]After the birth of Nahor, Serug

lived two hundred years and fathered sons
and daughters.
24When Nahor was twenty-nine years old
he fathered Terah. 25After the birth of Terah,
Nahor lived a hundred and nineteen years
and fathered sons and daughters.
26When Terah was seventy years old he
fathered Abram, Nahor and Haran.

The descendants of Terah

27These are Terah's descendants:
Terah fathered Abram, Nahor and Haran.
Haran fathered Lot. 28Haran died in the
presence of his father Terah in his native
land, Ur of the Chaldaeans. 29Abram and
Nahor both married: Abram's wife was called
Sarai, Nahor's wife was called Milcah
daughter of Haran, father of Milcah and
Iscah. 30Sarai was barren, having no child.
31Terah took his son Abram, his grand-
son Lot son of Haran, and his daughter-in-
law the wife of Abram, and made them
leave Ur of the Chaldaeans to go to the land
of Canaan. But on arrival in Haran they
settled there.
32Terah's life lasted two hundred and five
years; then he died at Haran.

II: THE STORY OF ABRAHAM

The call of Abram

12 Yahweh said to Abram, 'Leave your
country, your kindred and your
father's house for a country which I shall
show you; 2and I shall make you a great
nation, I shall bless you and make your name
famous; you are to be a blessing!

3I shall bless those who bless you,
and shall curse those who curse you,
and all clans on earth
will bless themselves by you.'

4So Abram went as Yahweh told him, and
Lot went with him. Abram was seventy-five
years old when he left Haran. 5Abram took
his wife Sarai, his nephew Lot, all the
possessions they had amassed and the people
they had acquired in Haran. They set off for
the land of Canaan, and arrived there.
6Abram passed through the country as far
as the holy place at Shechem, the Oak of
Moreh. The Canaanites were in the country
at the time. 7Yahweh appeared to Abram
and said, 'I shall give this country to your
progeny.' And there, Abram built an altar to
Yahweh who had appeared to him. 8From
there he moved on to the mountainous
district east of Bethel, where he pitched his
tent, with Bethel to the west and Ai to the
east. There he built an altar to Yahweh
and invoked the name of Yahweh. 9Then
Abram made his way stage by stage to the
Negeb.

Abram in Egypt[a]

10There was a famine in the country, and
Abram went down to Egypt to stay there for
a time, since the famine in the country was
severe. 11When he was about to enter
Egypt, he said to his wife Sarai, 'Look, I
know you are a beautiful woman. 12When the
Egyptians see you they will say, "That is his
wife," and they will kill me but leave you
alive. 13Therefore please tell them you are my
sister, so that they may treat me well because
of you and spare my life out of regard for
you.' 14When Abram arrived in Egypt
the Egyptians did indeed see that the woman
was very beautiful. 15When Pharaoh's
officials saw her they sang her praises to
Pharaoh and the woman was taken into
Pharaoh's household. 16And Abram was very
well treated because of her and received
flocks, oxen, donkeys, men and women
slaves, she-donkeys and camels. 17But
Yahweh inflicted severe plagues on Pharaoh
and his household because of Abram's wife
Sarai. 18So Pharaoh summoned Abram and
said, 'What is this you have done to me? Why
did you not tell me she was your wife?
19Why did you say, "She is my sister," so
that I took her to be my wife? Now, here is
your wife. Take her and go!' 20And Pharaoh
gave his people orders about him; they sent
him on his way with his wife and all his
possessions.

12a =20; =26:1–11.

Abram and Lot separate

13 From Egypt Abram returned to the
Negeb with his wife and all he
possessed, and Lot with him. 2 Abram was
very rich in livestock, silver and gold. 3 By
stages he went from the Negeb to Bethel,
where he had first pitched his tent, between
Bethel and Ai, 4 at the place where he had
formerly erected the altar. There Abram
invoked the name of Yahweh.

5 Lot, who was travelling with Abram, had
flocks and cattle of his own, and tents too.
6 The land was not sufficient to accommodate
them both at once, for they had too many
possessions to be able to live together.
7 Dispute broke out between the herdsmen of
Abram's livestock and those of Lot. (The
Canaanites and Perizzites were living in the
country at the time.) 8 Accordingly Abram
said to Lot, 'We do not want discord between
us or between my herdsmen and yours, for
we are kinsmen. 9 Is not the whole land open
before you? Go in the opposite direction to
me: if you take the left, I shall go right; if you
take the right, I shall go left.'

10 Looking round, Lot saw all the Jordan
plain, irrigated everywhere—this was before
Yahweh destroyed Sodom and Gomorrah—
like the garden of Yahweh or the land of
Egypt, as far as Zoar. 11 So Lot chose all
the Jordan plain for himself and moved off
eastwards. Thus they parted company:
12 Abram settled in the land of Canaan; Lot
settled among the cities of the plain, pitching
his tents on the outskirts of Sodom. 13 Now
the people of Sodom were vicious and great
sinners against Yahweh.

14 Yahweh said to Abram after Lot had
parted company from him, 'Look all round
from where you are, to north and south, to
east and west, 15 for all the land within sight
I shall give to you and your descendants for
ever. 16 I shall make your descendants like the
dust on the ground; when people succeed in
counting the specks of dust on the ground,
then they will be able to count your descend-
ants too! 17 On your feet! Travel the length
and breadth of the country, for I mean to
give it to you.'

18 So Abram moved his tent and went to
settle at the Oak of Mamre, at Hebron, and
there he built an altar to Yahweh.

The campaign of the four great kings

14 When Amraphel king of Shinar,
Arioch king of Ellasar, Chedor-
Laomer king of Elam, and Tidal king of the
Goiim, 2 made war on Bera king of Sodom,
Birsha king of Gomorrah, Shinab king of
Admah, Shemeber king of Zeboiim, and the
king of Bela (that is, Zoar), 3 all the latter
joined forces in the Valley of Siddim (now
the Salt Sea). 4 For twelve years they had been
under the yoke of Chedor-Laomer, but in
the thirteenth year they revolted. 5 In the
fourteenth year Chedor-Laomer arrived and
the kings who had allied themselves with
him. They defeated the Rephaim at
Ashteroth-Carnaim, the Zuzim at Ham, the
Emim in the Plain of Kiriathaim, 6 the Horites
in the mountainous district of Seir near El-
Paran, which is on the edge of the desert.
7 Wheeling round, they came to the Spring of
Judgement (that is, Kadesh); they conquered
all the territory of the Amalekites and also
the Amorites who lived in Hazazon-Tamar.
8 Then the kings of Sodom, Gomorrah,
Admah, Zeboiim and Bela (that is, Zoar)
marched out and engaged them in the Valley
of Siddim: 9 Chedor-Laomer king of Elam,
Tidal king of the Goiim, Amraphel king of
Shinar and Arioch king of Ellasar: four kings
against five. 10 Now there were many bitumen
wells in the Valley of Siddim, and in their
flight the kings of Sodom and Gomorrah fell
into them, while the rest fled into the hills.
11 The conquerors seized all the possessions
of Sodom and Gomorrah, and all their
provisions, and made off. 12 They also took
Lot (the nephew of Abram) and his
possessions and made off; he had been living
at Sodom.

13 A survivor came to tell Abram, and Aner
the Hebrew, who was living at the Oak of the
Amorite Mamre, the brother of Eshcol; these
were allies of Abram. 14 When Abram heard
that his kinsman had been taken captive,
he mustered his retainers born in his own
household, numbering three hundred and
eighteen, and gave chase as far as Dan.
15 He and his retainers deployed against them
under cover of dark, defeated them and
pursued them as far as Hobah, north of
Damascus. 16 He recaptured all the goods as
well as his kinsman Lot and his possessions,
together with the women and people.

Melchizedek

17 When Abram returned from defeating
Chedor-Laomer and the kings who had been
on his side, the king of Sodom came to meet
him in the Valley of Shaveh (that is, the
Valley of the King). 18 Melchizedek king of
Salem brought bread and wine; he was a
priest of God Most High. 19 He pronounced
this blessing:

Blessed be Abram by God Most High,
Creator of heaven and earth.
And blessed be God Most High
for putting your enemies
into your clutches.

20 And Abram gave him a tenth of every-
thing.
21 The king of Sodom said to Abram,
'Give me the people and take the possessions
for yourself.' 22 But Abram replied to the
king of Sodom, 'I swear by God Most High,
Creator of heaven and earth: 23 not one thread,
not one sandal strap, will I take of what is
yours, for you to be able to say, "I made
Abram rich." 24 For myself, nothing—except
what the troops have used up, and the share
due to the men who came with me, Eshcol,
Aner and Mamre; let them take their share.'

The divine promises and covenant[a]

15 Some time later, the word of Yahweh
came to Abram in a vision:

Do not be afraid, Abram!
I am your shield
and shall give you a very great reward.

2 'Lord Yahweh,' Abram replied, 'what use
are your gifts, as I am going on my way
childless? . . .[b] 3 Since you have given me
no offspring,' Abram continued, 'a member
of my household will be my heir.' 4 Then
Yahweh's word came to him in reply, 'Such
a one will not be your heir; no, your heir will
be the issue of your own body.' 5 Then taking
him outside, he said, 'Look up at the sky and
count the stars if you can. Just so will your
descendants be,' he told him. 6 Abram put
his faith in Yahweh and this was reckoned to
him as uprightness.
7 He then said to him, 'I am Yahweh who
brought you out of Ur of the Chaldaeans to
give you this country as your possession.'
8 'Lord Yahweh,' Abram replied, 'how can I
know that I shall possess it?' 9 He said to him,
'Bring me a three-year-old heifer, a three-
year-old she-goat, a three-year-old ram, a
turtledove and a young pigeon.' 10 He brought
him all these, split the animals down the
middle and placed each half opposite the
other; but the birds he did not divide. 11 And
whenever birds of prey swooped down on the
carcases, Abram drove them off.
12 Now, as the sun was on the point of
setting, a trance fell on Abram, and a deep
dark dread descended on him. 13 Then
Yahweh said to Abram, 'Know this for
certain, that your descendants will be exiles
in a land not their own, and be enslaved and
oppressed for four hundred years. 14 But I
shall bring judgement on the nation that
enslaves them and after this they will leave,
with many possessions. 15 For your part, you
will join your ancestors in peace; you will be
buried at a happy old age. 16 In the fourth
generation they will come back here, for until
then the iniquity of the Amorites will not
have reached its full extent.'
17 When the sun had set and it was dark,
there appeared a smoking firepot and a
flaming torch passing between the animals'
pieces. 18 That day Yahweh made a covenant
with Abram in these terms:

'To your descendants I give this country,
from the River of Egypt
to the Great River,

the River Euphrates, 19 the Kenites, the
Kenizzites, the Kadmonites, 20 the Hittites,
the Perizzites, the Rephaim, 21 the Amorites,
the Canaanites, the Girgashites, and the
Jebusites.'

The birth of Ishmael[a]

16 Abram's wife Sarai had borne him no
child, but she had an Egyptian slave-
girl called Hagar. 2 So Sarai said to Abram,
'Listen, now! Since Yahweh has kept me
from having children, go to my slave-girl.
Perhaps I shall get children through her.'
And Abram took Sarai's advice.
3 Thus, after Abram had lived in the land
of Canaan for ten years, Sarai took Hagar her
Egyptian slave-girl and gave her to Abram

15a =17; 12:2–7.
15b The remainder of the v. is unintelligible.
16a =21:8–19.

as his wife. [4]He went to Hagar and she conceived. And once she knew she had conceived, her mistress counted for nothing in her eyes. [5]Then Sarai said to Abram, 'This outrage done to me is your fault! It was I who put my slave-girl into your arms but, now she knows that she has conceived, I count for nothing in her eyes. Yahweh judge between me and you!' [6]'Very well,' Abram said to Sarai, 'your slave-girl is at your disposal. Treat her as you think fit.' Sarai accordingly treated her so badly that she ran away from her.

[7]The angel of Yahweh found her by a spring in the desert, the spring on the road to Shur. [8]He said, 'Hagar, slave-girl of Sarai, where have you come from, and where are you going?' 'I am running away from my mistress Sarai,' she replied. [9]The angel of Yahweh said to her, 'Go back to your mistress and submit to her.' [10]The angel of Yahweh further said to her, 'I shall make your descendants too numerous to be counted.' [11]Then the angel of Yahweh said to her:

Now, you have conceived
and will bear a son,
and you shall name him Ishmael,
for Yahweh has heard
your cries of distress.
[12]A wild donkey of a man he will be,
his hand against every man,
and every man's hand against him,
living his life in defiance
of all his kinsmen.

[13]Hagar gave a name to Yahweh who had spoken to her, 'You are El Roi,' by which she meant, 'Did I not go on seeing here, after him who sees me?' [14]This is why the well is called the well of Lahai Roi; it is between Kadesh and Bered.

[15]Hagar bore Abram a son, and Abram gave his son borne by Hagar the name Ishmael. [16]Abram was eighty-six years old when Hagar bore him Ishmael.

The covenant and circumcision[a]

17 When Abram was ninety-nine years old Yahweh appeared to him and said, 'I am El Shaddai. Live in my presence, be perfect, [2]and I shall grant a covenant between myself and you, and make you very numerous.' [3]And Abram bowed to the ground.

God spoke to him as follows, [4]'For my part, this is my covenant with you: you will become the father of many nations. [5]And you are no longer to be called Abram; your name is to be Abraham, for I am making you father of many nations. [6]I shall make you exceedingly fertile. I shall make you into nations, and your issue will be kings. [7]And I shall maintain my covenant between myself and you, and your descendants after you, generation after generation, as a covenant in perpetuity, to be your God and the God of your descendants after you. [8]And to you and to your descendants after you, I shall give the country where you are now immigrants, the entire land of Canaan, to own in perpetuity. And I shall be their God.'

[9]God further said to Abraham, 'You for your part must keep my covenant, you and your descendants after you, generation after generation. [10]This is my covenant which you must keep between myself and you, and your descendants after you: every one of your males must be circumcised. [11]You must circumcise the flesh of your foreskin, and that will be the sign of the covenant between myself and you. [12]As soon as he is eight days old, every one of your males, generation after generation, must be circumcised, including slaves born within the household or bought from a foreigner not of your descent. [13]Whether born within the household or bought, they must be circumcised. My covenant must be marked in your flesh as a covenant in perpetuity. [14]The uncircumcised male, whose foreskin has not been circumcised—that person must be cut off from his people: he has broken my covenant.'

[15]Furthermore God said to Abraham, 'As regards your wife Sarai, you must not call her Sarai, but Sarah. [16]I shall bless her and moreover give you a son by her. I shall bless her and she will become nations: kings of peoples will issue from her.' [17]Abraham bowed to the ground, and he laughed,[b] thinking to himself, 'Is a child to be born to a man one hundred years old, and will Sarah have a child at the age of ninety?' [18]Abraham said to God, 'May Ishmael live in your presence! That will be enough!' [19]But God

17a =15.
17b Play on the Hebr. root 'laugh' in the name Isaac, which in fact means 'God will smile'.

replied, 'Yes, your wife Sarah will bear you a son whom you must name Isaac. And I shall maintain my covenant with him, a covenant in perpetuity, to be his God and the God of his descendants after him. [20]For Ishmael too I grant you your request. I hereby bless him and will make him fruitful and exceedingly numerous. He will be the father of twelve princes, and I shall make him into a great nation. [21]But my covenant I shall maintain with Isaac, whom Sarah will bear you at this time next year.' [22]When he had finished speaking to Abraham, God went up from him.

[23]Then Abraham took his son Ishmael, all the slaves born in his household or whom he had bought, in short all the males among the people of Abraham's household, and circumcised their foreskins that same day, as God had said to him. [24]Abraham was ninety-nine years old when his foreskin was circumcised. [25]Ishmael his son was thirteen years old when his foreskin was circumcised. [26]Abraham and his son Ishmael were circumcised on the very same day, [27]and all the men of his household, those born in the household and those bought from foreigners, were circumcised with him.

The apparition at Mamre

18 Yahweh appeared to him at the Oak of Mamre while he was sitting by the entrance of the tent during the hottest part of the day. [2]He looked up, and there he saw three men standing near him. As soon as he saw them he ran from the entrance of the tent to greet them, and bowed to the ground. [3]'My lord,' he said, 'if I find favour with you, please do not pass your servant by. [4]Let me have a little water brought, and you can wash your feet and have a rest under the tree. [5]Let me fetch a little bread and you can refresh yourselves before going further, now that you have come in your servant's direction.' They replied, 'Do as you say.'

[6]Abraham hurried to the tent and said to Sarah, 'Quick, knead three measures of best flour and make loaves.' [7]Then, running to the herd, Abraham took a fine and tender calf and gave it to the servant, who hurried to prepare it. [8]Then taking curds, milk and the calf which had been prepared, he laid all before them, and they ate while he remained standing near them under the tree.

[9]'Where is your wife Sarah?' they asked him. 'She is in the tent,' he replied. [10]Then his guest said, 'I shall come back to you next year, and then your wife Sarah will have a son.' Sarah was listening at the entrance of the tent behind him. [11]Now Abraham and Sarah were old, well on in years, and Sarah had ceased to have her monthly periods. [12]So Sarah laughed to herself, thinking, 'Now that I am past the age of childbearing, and my husband is an old man, is pleasure to come my way again?' [13]But Yahweh asked Abraham, 'Why did Sarah laugh and say, "Am I really going to have a child now that I am old?" [14]Nothing is impossible for Yahweh. I shall come back to you at the same time next year and Sarah will have a son.' [15]Sarah said, 'I did not laugh,' lying because she was afraid. But he replied, 'Oh yes, you did laugh.'

Abraham intercedes for Sodom

[16]From there the men set out and arrived within sight of Sodom, with Abraham accompanying them to speed them on their way. [17]Now Yahweh had wondered, 'Shall I conceal from Abraham what I am going to do, [18]as Abraham will become a great and powerful nation and all nations on earth will bless themselves by him? [19]For I have singled him out to command his sons and his family after him to keep the way of Yahweh by doing what is upright and just, so that Yahweh can carry out for Abraham what he has promised him.' [20]Then Yahweh said, 'The outcry against Sodom and Gomorrah is so great and their sin is so grave, [21]that I shall go down and see whether or not their actions are at all as the outcry reaching me would suggest. Then I shall know.'

[22]While the men left there and went to Sodom, Yahweh remained in Abraham's presence. [23]Abraham stepped forward and said, 'Will you really destroy the upright with the guilty? [24]Suppose there are fifty upright people in the city. Will you really destroy it? Will you not spare the place for the sake of the fifty upright in it? [25]Do not think of doing such a thing: to put the upright to death with the guilty, so that upright and guilty fare alike! Is the judge of the whole world not to act justly?' [26]Yahweh replied, 'If I find fifty upright people in the city of Sodom, I shall spare the whole place because of them.'

[27]Abraham spoke up and said, 'It is

presumptuous of me to speak to the Lord, I who am dust and ashes: [28]Suppose the fifty upright were five short? Would you destroy the whole city because of five?' 'No,' he replied, 'I shall not destroy it if I find forty-five there.' [29]Abraham persisted and said, 'Suppose there are forty to be found there?' 'I shall not do it,' he replied, 'for the sake of the forty.'

[30]Abraham said, 'I hope the Lord will not be angry if I go on: Suppose there are only thirty to be found there?' 'I shall not do it,' he replied, 'if I find thirty there.' [31]He said, 'It is presumptuous of me to speak to the Lord: Suppose there are only twenty there?' 'I shall not destroy it,' he replied, 'for the sake of the twenty.' [32]He said, 'I trust my Lord will not be angry if I speak once more: perhaps there will only be ten.' 'I shall not destroy it,' he replied, 'for the sake of the ten.'

[33]When he had finished talking to Abraham Yahweh went away, and Abraham returned home.

The destruction of Sodom

19 When the two angels reached Sodom in the evening, Lot was sitting at the gate of Sodom. As soon as Lot saw them, he stood up to greet them, and bowed to the ground. [2]'My lords,' he said, 'please come down to your servant's house to stay the night and wash your feet. Then you can make an early start on your journey.' 'No,' they said, 'we shall spend the night in the square.' [3]But he pressed them so much that they went home with him and entered his house. He prepared a meal for them, baking unleavened bread, and they had supper.

[4]They had not gone to bed when the house was surrounded by the townspeople, the men of Sodom both young and old, all the people without exception. [5]Calling out to Lot they said, 'Where are the men who came to you tonight? Send them out to us so that we can have intercourse with them.'

[6]Lot came out to them at the door and, having shut the door behind him, [7]said, 'Please, brothers, do not be wicked. [8]Look, I have two daughters who are virgins. I am ready to send them out to you, for you to treat as you please, but do nothing to these men since they are now under the protection of my roof.' [9]But they retorted, 'Stand back! This fellow came here as a foreigner, and now he wants to play the judge. Now we shall treat you worse than them.' Then they forced Lot back and moved forward to break down the door. [10]But the men reached out, pulled Lot back into the house with them, and shut the door. [11]And they dazzled those who were at the door of the house, one and all, with a blinding light, so that they could not find the doorway.

[12]The men said to Lot, 'Have you anyone else here? Your sons, your daughters and all your people in the city, take them away, [13]for we are about to destroy this place, since the outcry to Yahweh against those in it has grown so loud that Yahweh has sent us to destroy it.' [14]So Lot went off and spoke to his future sons-in-law who were to marry his daughters. 'On your feet!' he said, 'Leave this place, for Yahweh is about to destroy the city.' But his sons-in-law thought he was joking.

[15]When dawn broke the angels urged Lot on, 'To your feet! Take your wife and your two daughters who are here, or you will be swept away in the punishment of the city.' [16]And as he hesitated, the men seized his hand and the hands of his wife and his two daughters—Yahweh being merciful to him—and led him out and left him outside the city.

[17]When they had brought him outside, he was told, 'Flee for your life. Do not look behind you or stop anywhere on the plain. Flee to the hills or you will be swept away.' [18]'Oh no, my lord!' Lot said to them, [19]'You have already been very good to your servant and shown me even greater love by saving my life, but I cannot flee to the hills, or disaster will overtake me and I shall die. [20]That town over there is near enough to flee to, and is small. Let me flee there—after all it is only a small place—and so survive.' [21]He replied, 'I grant you this favour too, and will not overthrow the town you speak of. [22]Hurry, flee to that one, for I cannot do anything until you reach it.' That is why the town is named Zoar.

[23]The sun rose over the horizon just as Lot was entering Zoar. [24]Then Yahweh rained down on Sodom and Gomorrah brimstone and fire of his own sending. [25]He overthrew those cities and the whole plain, with all the people living in the cities and everything that grew there. [26]But Lot's wife looked back, and was turned into a pillar of salt.

[27]Next morning, Abraham hurried to the

place where he had stood before Yahweh,
[28]and looking towards Sodom and Gomorrah
and the whole area of the plain, he saw the
smoke rising from the ground like smoke
from a furnace.
[29]Thus it was that, when God destroyed
the cities of the plain, he did not forget
Abraham and he rescued Lot from the midst
of the overthrow, when he overthrew the
cities where Lot was living.

The origin of the Moabites and the Ammonites[a]

[30]After leaving Zoar Lot settled in the hill
country with his two daughters, for he dared
not stay at Zoar. He lived in a cave, he and
his two daughters.
[31]The elder said to the younger, 'Our
father is an old man, and there is no one here
to marry us in the normal way of the world.
[32]Come on, let us ply our father with wine
and sleep with him. In this way we can
preserve the race by our father.' [33]That
night they made their father drunk, and the
elder slept with her father though he was
unaware of her coming to bed or of her
leaving. [34]The next day the elder said to the
younger, 'Last night, I was the one who slept
with our father. Let us make him drunk again
tonight, and you go and sleep with him. In
this way we can preserve the race by our
father.' [35]They made their father drunk
that night too, and the younger went and
slept with him, though he was unaware of
her coming to bed or of her leaving. [36]Both
Lot's daughters thus became pregnant by
their father. [37]The elder gave birth to a son
whom she named Moab; and he is the
ancestor of the Moabites of our own times.
[38]The younger also gave birth to a son
whom she named Ben-Ammi; and he is the
ancestor of the Bene-Ammon of our own
times.

Abraham at Gerar[a]

20 Abraham left there for the region of the
Negeb, and settled between Kadesh
and Shur. While staying in Gerar,
[2]Abraham said of his wife Sarah, 'She is
my sister,' and Abimelech the king of Gerar
had Sarah brought to him. [3]But God visited
Abimelech in a dream one night. 'You are to
die,' he told him, 'because of the woman you
have taken, for she is a married woman.'
[4]Abimelech, however, had not gone near her;
so he said, 'Lord, would you kill someone
even if he is upright? [5]Did he not tell me
himself, "She is my sister"? And she herself
said, "He is my brother." I did this with a
clear conscience and clean hands.' [6]'Yes, I
know,' God replied in the dream, 'that you
did this with a clear conscience and I myself
prevented you from sinning against me. That
was why I did not let you touch her. [7]Now
send the man's wife back; for he is a prophet
and can intercede on your behalf for your
life. But understand that if you do not send
her back, this means death for you and all
yours.'
[8]Early next morning, Abimelech
summoned his full court and told them the
whole story, at which the people were very
much afraid. [9]Then summoning Abraham,
Abimelech said to him, 'What have you done
to us? What wrong have I done you, for
you to bring such guilt on me and on my
kingdom? You had no right to treat me like
this.' [10]Abimelech then said to Abraham,
'What possessed you to do such a thing?'
[11]'Because', Abraham replied, 'I thought
there would be no fear of God here and that
I should be killed for the sake of my wife.
[12]Anyway, she really is my sister, my father's
daughter though not my mother's, besides
being my wife. [13]So when God made me
wander far from my father's home I said to
her, "There is an act of love you can do me:
everywhere we go, say of me that I am your
brother." '
[14]Abimelech took sheep, cattle, men and
women slaves, and presented them to
Abraham, and gave him back his wife Sarah.
[15]And Abimelech said, 'Look, my land is
open to you. Settle wherever you please.'
[16]To Sarah he said, 'Look, I am giving your
brother a thousand pieces of silver. This will
allay suspicions about you, as far as all the
people round you are concerned; you have
been completely vindicated.' [17]Abraham
then interceded with God, and God healed
Abimelech, his wife and his slave-girls, so
that they could have children, [18]for Yahweh
had made all the women of Abimelech's

19a Popular explanations of the name Moab as 'from my father' and of Ben Ammon as 'son of my kinsman'.
20a =12:10–20; =26:1–11.

household barren on account of Sarah, Abraham's wife.

The birth of Isaac

21 Yahweh treated Sarah as he had said, and did what he had promised her. 2 Sarah conceived and bore Abraham a son in his old age, at the time God had promised. 3 Abraham named the son born to him Isaac, the son to whom Sarah had given birth. 4 Abraham circumcised his son Isaac when he was eight days old, as God had commanded him. 5 Abraham was a hundred years old when his son Isaac was born to him. 6 Sarah said:

> God has given me cause to laugh!
> All who hear about this
> will laugh with me!

7 She added:

> Whoever would have told Abraham
> that Sarah would nurse children!
> Yet I have borne a son in his old age.

The dismissal of Hagar and Ishmael[a]

8 The child grew and was weaned, and Abraham gave a great banquet on the day Isaac was weaned. 9 Now Sarah watched the son that Hagar the Egyptian had borne to Abraham, playing with her son Isaac. 10 'Drive away that slave-girl and her son,' she said to Abraham, 'this slave-girl's son is not to share the inheritance with my son Isaac.' 11 This greatly distressed Abraham, because the slave-girl's child too was his son, 12 but God said to him, 'Do not distress yourself on account of the boy and your slave-girl. Do whatever Sarah says, for Isaac is the one through whom your name will be carried on. 13 But the slave-girl's son I shall also make into a great nation, for he too is your child.' 14 Early next morning, Abraham took some bread and a skin of water and, giving them to Hagar, put the child on her shoulder and sent her away.

She wandered off into the desert of Beersheba. 15 When the skin of water was finished she abandoned the child under a bush. 16 Then she went and sat down at a distance, about a bowshot away, thinking, 'I cannot bear to see the child die.' Sitting at a distance, she began to sob.

17 God heard the boy crying, and the angel of God called to Hagar from heaven. 'What is wrong, Hagar?' he asked. 'Do not be afraid, for God has heard the boy's cry in his plight. 18 Go and pick the boy up and hold him safe, for I shall make him into a great nation.' 19 Then God opened Hagar's eyes and she saw a well, so she went and filled the skin with water and gave the boy a drink.

20 God was with the boy. He grew up and made his home in the desert, and he became an archer. 21 He made his home in the desert of Paran, and his mother got him a wife from Egypt.

Abraham and Abimelech at Beersheba[b]

22 About then, Abimelech and Phicol, the commander of his army, said to Abraham, 'Since God is with you in everything you do, 23 swear to me by God, here and now, that you will not act treacherously towards me or my kith and kin, but behave with the same faithful love to me and the land of which you are a guest as I have behaved to you.' 24 'Yes,' Abraham replied, 'I swear it.'

25 Abraham then reproached Abimelech about a well that Abimelech's servants had seized. 26 'I do not know who has done this,' Abimelech said. 'You yourself have never mentioned it to me and, for myself, I heard nothing of it till today.' 27 Abraham then took sheep and cattle and presented them to Abimelech, and the two of them made a covenant. 28 Abraham put seven lambs of the flock on one side. 29 'Why have you put these seven lambs on one side?' Abimelech asked Abraham. 30 He replied, 'You must accept these seven lambs from me as evidence that I have dug this well.' 31 This was why the place was called Beersheba: because there the two of them swore an oath.

32 After they had made a covenant at Beersheba, Abimelech and Phicol, the commander of his army, left and went back to Philistine territory. 33 And Abraham planted a tamarisk at Beersheba and there he invoked the name of Yahweh. 34 Abraham stayed for a long while in Philistine territory.

21a =16.
21b Fragments using two explanations of the name as 'Well of the Seven' and 'Well of the Oath'. The story is parallel with 26:15–33.

Abraham's sacrifice

22 It happened some time later that God put Abraham to the test. 'Abraham, Abraham!' he called. 'Here I am,' he replied. 2 God said, 'Take your son, your only son, your beloved Isaac, and go to the land of Moriah, where you are to offer him as a burnt offering on one of the mountains which I shall point out to you.'

3 Early next morning Abraham saddled his donkey and took with him two of his servants and his son Isaac. He chopped wood for the burnt offering and started on his journey to the place which God had indicated to him. 4 On the third day Abraham looked up and saw the place in the distance. 5 Then Abraham said to his servants, 'Stay here with the donkey. The boy and I are going over there; we shall worship and then come back to you.'

6 Abraham took the wood for the burnt offering, loaded it on Isaac, and carried in his own hands the fire and the knife. Then the two of them set out together. 7 Isaac spoke to his father Abraham. 'Father?' he said. 'Yes, my son,' he replied. 'Look,' he said, 'here are the fire and the wood, but where is the lamb for the burnt offering?' 8 Abraham replied, 'My son, God himself will provide the lamb for the burnt offering.' And the two of them went on together.

9 When they arrived at the place which God had indicated to him, Abraham built an altar there, and arranged the wood. Then he bound his son and put him on the altar on top of the wood. 10 Abraham stretched out his hand and took the knife to kill his son.

11 But the angel of Yahweh called to him from heaven. 'Abraham, Abraham!' he said. 'Here I am,' he replied. 12 'Do not raise your hand against the boy,' the angel said. 'Do not harm him, for now I know you fear God. You have not refused me your own beloved son.' 13 Then looking up, Abraham saw a ram caught by its horns in a bush. Abraham took the ram and offered it as a burnt offering in place of his son. 14 Abraham called this place 'Yahweh provides', and hence the saying today: 'On the mountain Yahweh provides.'

15 The angel of Yahweh called Abraham a second time from heaven. 16 'I swear by my own self, Yahweh declares, that because you have done this, because you have not refused me your own beloved son, 17 I will shower blessings on you and make your descendants as numerous as the stars of heaven and the grains of sand on the seashore. Your descendants will gain possession of the gates of their enemies. 18 All nations on earth will bless themselves by your descendants, because you have obeyed my command.'

19 Abraham went back to his servants, and together they set out for Beersheba, and Abraham settled in Beersheba.

The descendants of Nahor

20 It happened some time later that Abraham received word that Milcah, too, had now borne sons to his brother Nahor: 21 Uz his first-born, Buz his brother, Kemuel father of Aram, 22 Chesed, Hazo, Pildash, Jidlaph, Bethuel 23 (and Bethuel was the father of Rebekah). These were the eight children Milcah gave Nahor, Abraham's brother. 24 He had a concubine named Reumah, and she too had children: Tebah, Gaham, Tahash and Maacah.

The tomb of the patriarchs

23 The length of Sarah's life was a hundred and twenty-seven years. 2 She died at Kiriath-Arba—now Hebron—in the land of Canaan, and Abraham proceeded to mourn and bewail her.

3 Then rising from beside his dead, Abraham spoke to the Hittites, 4 'I am a stranger resident here,' he said. 'Let me have a burial site of my own here, so that I can remove my dead for burial.' 5 The Hittites replied to Abraham, 6 'Please listen to us, my lord, we regard you as a prince of God; bury your dead in the best of our tombs; not one of us would refuse you his tomb for you to bury your dead.'

7 At this, Abraham rose and bowed low to the local people, the Hittites, 8 and pleaded with them as follows, 'If you consent to my removing my dead for burial, you must agree to intercede for me with Ephron son of Zohar, 9 for him to let me have the cave he owns at Machpelah, which is on the edge of his field. Let him sell it to me in your presence at its full price, for a burial site of my own.' 10 Now Ephron was sitting among the Hittites, and Ephron the Hittite answered Abraham in the hearing of the Hittites, of all the inhabitants of his town. 11 'No, my lord, listen to me,' he said. 'I give you the field and the cave in it; I

make this gift in the presence of my kinsmen.
Bury your dead.'
12 Abraham bowed low to the local people
13 and, in the hearing of the local people,
replied to Ephron as follows, 'Be good
enough to listen to me. I shall pay the price
of the field; accept it from me and I shall
bury my dead there.' 14 Ephron replied to
Abraham, 15 'Please listen to me, my lord.
What is a plot of land for four hundred
shekels of silver between me and you? Bury
your dead.' 16 Abraham agreed to Ephron's
terms, and Abraham weighed out for Ephron
the silver he had stipulated in the hearing of
the Hittites, namely four hundred shekels of
silver, according to the current commercial
rate.
17 Thus Ephron's field at Machpelah,
facing Mamre—the field and the cave in
it and all the trees anywhere within the
boundaries of the field—passed 18 into Abra-
ham's possession in the sight of the Hittites,
of all the inhabitants of his town. 19 And after
this, Abraham buried his wife Sarah in the
cave of the field of Machpelah, facing
Mamre—now Hebron—in the land of
Canaan. 20 And so the field and the cave in
it passed from the Hittites into Abraham's
possession as a burial site of his own.

The marriage of Isaac

24 By now Abraham was an old man, well
on in years, and Yahweh had blessed
Abraham in every way. 2 Abraham said to the
senior servant in his household, the steward
of all his property, 'Place your hand under
my thigh: 3 I am going to make you swear by
Yahweh, God of heaven and God of earth,
that you will not choose a wife for my son
from the daughters of the Canaanites among
whom I live 4 but will go to my native land
and my own kinsfolk to choose a wife for my
son Isaac.' 5 The servant asked him, 'What if
the girl does not want to follow me to this
country? Should I then take your son back
to the country from which you come?'
6 Abraham replied, 'On no account are you to
take my son back there. 7 Yahweh, God of
heaven and God of earth, who took me from
my father's home, and from the land of my
kinsfolk, and who promised me on oath, "I
shall give this country to your descend-
ants"—he will now send his angel ahead of
you, so that you can get a wife for my son
from there. 8 If then the girl refuses to follow
you, you will be quit of this oath to me. Only
do not take my son back there.' 9 And the
servant placed his hand under the thigh of
his master Abraham, and swore to him that
he would do it.
10 The servant took ten of his master's
camels and, carrying all kinds of gifts from
his master, set out for the city of Nahor in
Aram Naharaim. 11 In the evening, at the time
when women come out to draw water, he
made the camels kneel outside the town near
the well. 12 And he said, 'Yahweh, God of my
master Abraham, give me success today and
show faithful love to my master Abraham.
13 While I stand by the spring as the young
women from the town come out to draw
water, 14 I shall say to one of the girls, "Please
lower your pitcher and let me drink." And if
she answers, "Drink, and I shall water your
camels too," let her be the one you have
decreed for your servant Isaac; by this I shall
know you have shown faithful love to my
master.'
15 He had not finished speaking when out
came Rebekah—who was the daughter of
Bethuel son of Milcah, the wife of Abraham's
brother Nahor—with a pitcher on her
shoulder. 16 The girl was very beautiful, and
a virgin; no man had touched her. She went
down to the spring, filled her pitcher and
came up again. 17 Running towards her, the
servant said, 'Please give me a sip of water
from your pitcher.' 18 She replied, 'Drink,
my lord,' and quickly lowered her pitcher on
her arm and gave him a drink. 19 When she
had finished letting him drink, she said, 'I
shall draw water for your camels, too, until
they have had enough.' 20 She quickly
emptied her pitcher into the trough, and ran
to the well again to draw, and drew for all
the camels. 21 All the while, the man stood
watching her, not daring to speak, wondering
whether Yahweh had made his journey
successful or not.
22 When the camels had finished drink-
ing, the man took a gold ring weighing
half a shekel, and put it through her nose,
and put two bracelets weighing ten gold
shekels on her arms, 23 and said, 'Whose
daughter are you? Please tell me. Is there
room at your father's house for us to spend
the night?' 24 She replied, 'I am the daughter
of Bethuel, the son whom Milcah bore to
Nahor.' 25 And she went on, 'We have plenty
of straw and fodder, and room to spend the
night.' 26 Then the man bowed down and

worshipped Yahweh 27saying, 'Blessed be
Yahweh, God of my master Abraham, for
not withholding his faithful love from my
master. Yahweh has led me straight to the
house of my master's brother.'
28The girl ran to her mother's house to
tell what had happened. 29Now Rebekah
had a brother called Laban, and Laban ran
out to the man at the spring. 30As soon as
he had seen the ring and the bracelets his
sister was wearing, and had heard his sister
Rebekah saying, 'This is what the man said
to me,' he went to the man and found him
still standing by his camels at the spring. 31He
said to him, 'Come in, blessed of
Yahweh, why stay out here when I have
cleared the house and made room for the
camels?' 32The man went to the house, and
Laban unloaded the camels. He provided
straw and fodder for the camels and water
for him and his companions to wash their
feet.
33They offered him food, but he said, 'I
will eat nothing before I have said what I have
to say.' Laban said, 'Speak.' 34He said, 'I am
Abraham's servant. 35Yahweh has loaded my
master with blessings, and Abraham is now
very rich. He has given him flocks and herds,
silver and gold, men and women slaves,
camels and donkeys. 36Sarah, my master's
wife, bore my master a son in his old age, and
he has made over all his property to him.
37My master made me take this oath, "You
are not to choose a wife for my son from the
daughters of the Canaanites in whose country
I live. 38Instead, you are to go to my father's
home and to my own kinsfolk to choose a
wife for my son." 39I said to my master,
"Suppose the girl will not agree to come with
me?" 40and his reply was, "Yahweh, in whose
presence I have walked, will send his angel
with you and make your journey successful,
for you to choose a wife for my son from
my own kinsfolk, from my father's house.
41Then you will be quit of my curse: if you
go to my family and they refuse you, you will
be quit of my curse." 42Arriving today at the
spring I said, "Yahweh, God of my master
Abraham, please grant a successful outcome
to the course I propose to take. 43While I
stand by the spring, if a girl comes out to
draw water and I say to her, 'Please give me
a little water to drink from your pitcher,' 44if
she replies, 'Drink by all means, and I shall
draw water for your camels too,' let her be
the girl whom Yahweh has decreed for my
master's son." 45I was still saying this in my
mind when Rebekah came out, her pitcher
on her shoulder. She came down to the spring
and drew water. I said to her, "Please give
me a drink." 46Quickly she lowered her
pitcher saying, "Drink, and I shall water
your camels too." 47I asked her, "Whose
daughter are you?" She replied, "I am the
daughter of Bethuel, whom Milcah bore to
Nahor." Then I put this ring through her
nose and these bracelets on her arms. 48I
bowed down and worshipped Yahweh, and
I blessed Yahweh, God of my master
Abraham, who had led me by a direct path
to choose the daughter of my master's brother
for his son. 49Now tell me whether you are
prepared to show constant and faithful love
to my master; if not, say so, and I shall know
what to do.'
50Laban and Bethuel replied, 'This is
from Yahweh; it is not for us to say yes or
no to you. 51Rebekah is there before you.
Take her and go; and let her become the
wife of your master's son, as Yahweh has
decreed.' 52On hearing this, Abraham's
servant bowed to the ground before Yahweh.
53He brought out silver and gold ornaments
and clothes which he gave to Rebekah; he
also gave rich presents to her brother and to
her mother.
54They ate and drank, he and his com-
panions, and spent the night there. Next
morning when they were up, he said, 'Let
me go back to my master.' 55Rebekah's
brother and mother replied, 'Let the girl stay
with us for ten days or so; then she can go.'
56But he replied, 'Do not delay me, since
Yahweh has made my journey successful;
let me leave and go back to my master.'
57They replied, 'Let us call the girl and
find out what she has to say.' 58They called
Rebekah and asked her, 'Will you go with
this man?' She replied, 'I will.' 59Accordingly
they let their sister Rebekah go, with her
nurse, and Abraham's servant and his men.
60They blessed Rebekah and said to
her:

Sister of ours, from you may there spring
thousands and tens of thousands!
May your descendants gain possession
of the gates of their enemies!

61And forthwith, Rebekah and her maids

mounted the camels, and followed the man. The servant took Rebekah and departed.

62 Isaac meanwhile had come back from the well of Lahai Roi and was living in the Negeb. 63 While Isaac was out walking towards evening in the fields, he looked up and saw camels approaching. 64 And Rebekah looked up and saw Isaac. She jumped down from her camel, 65 and asked the servant, 'Who is that man walking through the fields towards us?' The servant replied, 'That is my master.' So she took her veil and covered herself up. 66 The servant told Isaac the whole story. 67 Then Isaac took her into his tent. He married Rebekah and made her his wife. And in his love for her, Isaac was consoled for the loss of his mother.

The descendants of Keturah

25 Abraham married another wife whose name was Keturah; 2 and she bore him Zimram, Jokshan, Medan, Midian, Ishbak and Shuah. 3 Jokshan was the father of Sheba and Dedan, and the descendants of Dedan were the Asshurites, the Letushim and the Leummim. 4 The descendants of Midian were Ephah, Epher, Hanoch, Abida and Eldaah. All these were sons of Keturah.

5 Abraham left all his possessions to Isaac. 6 To the sons of his concubines Abraham made grants during his lifetime, sending them away from his son Isaac eastward, to the Land of the East.

The death of Abraham

7 The number of years Abraham lived was a hundred and seventy-five. 8 When Abraham had breathed his last, dying at a happy ripe age, old and full of years, he was gathered to his people. 9 His sons Isaac and Ishmael buried him in the cave of Machpelah facing Mamre, in the field of Ephron the Hittite son of Zohar. 10 This was the field that Abraham had bought from the Hittites, and Abraham and his wife Sarah were buried there. 11 After Abraham's death, God blessed his son Isaac. Isaac settled near the well of Lahai Roi.

The descendants of Ishmael

12 These are the descendants of Ishmael son of Abraham by Hagar, Sarah's Egyptian slave-girl. 13 These are the names of the sons of Ishmael by name and line: Ishmael's first-born was Nebaioth; then Kedar, Adbeel, Mibsam, 14 Mishma, Dumah, Massa, 15 Hadad, Tema, Jetur, Naphish and Kedemah. 16 These are the sons of Ishmael, and these are their names, according to their settlements and encampments, twelve chiefs of as many tribes.

17 The number of years Ishmael lived was one hundred and thirty-seven. When he breathed his last and died, he was gathered to his people.

18 He lived in the territory stretching from Havilah-by-Shur just outside Egypt on the way to Assyria, and he held his own against all his kinsmen.

III: THE STORY OF ISAAC AND JACOB

The birth of Esau and Jacob

19 This is the story of Isaac son of Abraham.

Abraham fathered Isaac. 20 Isaac was forty years old when he married Rebekah the daughter of Bethuel the Aramaean of Paddan-Aram, and sister of Laban the Aramaean. 21 Isaac prayed to Yahweh on behalf of his wife, for she was barren. Yahweh heard his prayer, and his wife Rebekah conceived. 22 But the children inside her struggled so much that she said, 'If this is the way of it, why go on living?' So she went to consult Yahweh, 23 and Yahweh said to her:

There are two nations in your womb,
your issue will be two rival peoples.
One nation will have the mastery
of the other,
and the elder will serve the younger.

24 When the time came for her confinement, there were indeed twins in her womb. 25 The first to be born was red, altogether like a hairy cloak; so they named him Esau. 26 Then his brother was born, with his hand

give you my special blessing.' He served it to
him and he ate; he offered him wine, and he
drank. 26 His father Isaac said to him, 'Come
closer, and kiss me, son.' 27 He went closer
and kissed his father, who sniffed the smell
of his clothes. Then he blessed him, saying:

Ah, the smell of my son
is like the smell of a fertile field
which Yahweh has blessed.
28 May God give you
dew from heaven,
and the richness of the earth,
abundance of grain and wine!
29 Let peoples serve you
and nations bow low before you!
Be master of your brothers;
let your mother's other sons
bow low before you!
Accursed be whoever curses you
and blessed be whoever blesses you!

30 As soon as Isaac had finished blessing
Jacob, and just as Jacob was leaving his
father Isaac, his brother Esau returned from
hunting. 31 He too made an appetising dish
and brought it to his father, 'Father, please
eat some of your son's game and then give
me your special blessing.' 32 His father Isaac
asked, 'Who are you?' 'I am your first-born
son, Esau,' he replied. 33 At this Isaac was
seized with a violent trembling and said,
'Who was it, then, that went hunting and
brought me the game? I finished eating it just
before you came; I blessed him, and now
blessed he will remain!' 34 On hearing his
father's words, Esau cried out loudly and
bitterly and said to his father, 'Father, bless
me too!' 35 But he replied, 'Your brother came
by fraud and took your blessing.' 36 Esau said,
'His name should be Jacob right enough, for
he has now supplanted me twice. First he
took my birthright, and look, now he has
gone and taken my blessing! But', he added,
'have you not kept a blessing for me?' 37 Isaac
replied to Esau, 'I have already made him
your master; I have given him all his brothers
as servants, I have given him grain and wine
to sustain him. So what can I *do* for you,
son?' 38 Esau said to his father, 'Can you bless
only once, father? Father, bless me too.'
Isaac remained silent, and Esau began to
weep aloud. 39 Then his father Isaac spoke
again and said:

'Far from the richness of the earth
and the dew of heaven above,
your home will be.
40 By your sword you will live,
and your brother will you serve.

But when you win your freedom, you will
shake his yoke off your neck.'

41 Esau hated Jacob because of the blessing
his father had given him, and Esau said to
himself, 'The time to mourn for my father
will soon be here. Then I shall kill my brother
Jacob.' 42 When the words of Esau, her elder
son, were repeated to Rebekah, she sent for
her younger son Jacob and said to him,
'Look, your brother Esau means to take
revenge and kill you. 43 Now, son, listen to
me; go at once and take refuge with my
brother Laban in Haran. 44 Stay with him a
while, until your brother's fury cools, 45 until
your brother's anger is diverted from you and
he forgets what you have done to him.
Then I shall send someone to bring you
back. I do not want to lose you both on
one day!'

Isaac sends Jacob to Laban

46 Rebekah said to Isaac, 'The Hittite women
sicken me to death. If Jacob were to marry a
Hittite woman like these, one of the local
women, what would there be left in life for
me?'

28 So Isaac summoned Jacob and blessed
him; and he gave him this order: 'You
are not to marry any of the Canaanite women.
2 Go off to Paddan-Aram, the home of Bethuel
your mother's father, and there choose a wife
for yourself from the daughters of Laban
your mother's brother. 3 May El Shaddai
bless you; may he make you fruitful and
make you multiply so that you become a
group of nations. 4 May he grant you the
blessing of Abraham, you and your descend-
ants after you, so that one day you may own
the country where you are now living as
a stranger—which God gave to Abraham.'
5 Then Isaac sent Jacob away, and Jacob went
to Paddan-Aram, to Laban son of Bethuel
the Aramaean and brother of Rebekah the
mother of Jacob and Esau.

Another marriage of Esau

6 When Esau saw that Isaac had blessed Jacob
and sent him to Paddan-Aram to choose a
wife there, and that in blessing him he had

given him this order: 'You are not to choose a wife from the Canaanite women,' 7and that, in obedience to his father and mother, Jacob had gone to Paddan-Aram, 8Esau then realised how much his father Isaac disapproved of the Canaanite women. 9So Esau went to Ishmael and chose for a wife, in addition to the wives he had, Mahalath daughter of Abraham's son Ishmael and sister of Nebaioth.

Jacob's dream

10Jacob left Beersheba and set out for Haran. 11When he had reached a certain place, he stopped there for the night, since the sun had set. Taking one of the stones of that place, he made it his pillow and lay down where he was. 12He had a dream: there was a ladder, planted on the ground with its top reaching to heaven; and God's angels were going up and down on it. 13And there was Yahweh, standing beside him and saying, 'I, Yahweh, am the God of Abraham your father, and the God of Isaac. The ground on which you are lying I shall give to you and your descendants. 14Your descendants will be as plentiful as the dust on the ground; you will spread out to west and east, to north and south, and all clans on earth will bless themselves by you and your descendants. 15Be sure, I am with you; I shall keep you safe wherever you go, and bring you back to this country, for I shall never desert you until I have done what I have promised you.' 16Then Jacob awoke from his sleep and said, 'Truly, Yahweh is in this place and I did not know!' 17He was afraid and said, 'How awe-inspiring this place is! This is nothing less than the abode of God, and this is the gate of heaven!' 18Early next morning, Jacob took the stone he had used for his pillow, and set it up as a pillar, pouring oil over the top of it. 19He named the place Bethel, but before that the town had been called Luz.

20Jacob then made this vow, 'If God remains with me and keeps me safe on this journey I am making, if he gives me food to eat and clothes to wear, 21and if I come home safe to my father's home, then Yahweh shall be my God. 22This stone I have set up as a pillar is to be a house of God, and I shall faithfully pay you a tenth part of everything you give me.'

Jacob arrives at Laban's home

29 Continuing his journey, Jacob reached the Land of the Easterners. 2And there, out in the open, he saw a well with three flocks of sheep lying beside it; this well was used for watering the flocks. Now the stone on the mouth of the well was a large one, 3and only when all the flocks had collected there, did they roll the stone off the mouth of the well and water the sheep; then they would replace the stone over the mouth of the well. 4Jacob said to the shepherds, 'Friends, where are you from?' They replied, 'We are from Haran.' 5He asked them, 'Do you know Laban son of Nahor?' They replied, 'We do.' 6Then he asked them, 'Is he well?' 'He is,' they replied, 'and here comes his daughter Rachel with the flock.' 7Then he said, 'But it is still broad daylight, not the time to round up the animals. Why don't you water the sheep and take them back to graze?' 8To which, they replied, 'We can't, until all the shepherds have assembled to roll the stone off the mouth of the well; then we can water the sheep.'

9He was still talking to them, when Rachel arrived with her father's flock, for she was a shepherdess. 10As soon as Jacob saw Rachel, his uncle Laban's daughter, with his uncle Laban's flock, he went up and, rolling the stone off the mouth of the well, watered his uncle Laban's sheep. 11Jacob then kissed Rachel and burst into tears. 12He told Rachel he was her father's kinsman and Rebekah's son, and she ran to tell her father. 13As soon as he heard her speak of his sister's son Jacob, Laban ran to greet him, embraced him, kissed him and took him to his house. Jacob told Laban everything that had happened, 14and Laban said to him, 'You are indeed my bone and flesh!'

Jacob's two marriages

After Jacob had been staying with him for a month, 15Laban said to Jacob, 'Just because you are my kinsman, why should you work for me for nothing? Tell me what wages you want.' 16Now Laban had two daughters, the elder named Leah, and the younger Rachel. 17Leah had lovely eyes, but Rachel was shapely and beautiful, 18and Jacob had fallen in love with Rachel. So his answer was, 'I shall work for you for seven years in exchange for your younger daughter Rachel.' 19Laban

replied, 'It is better for me to give her to you
than to a stranger; stay with me.'
[20]So Jacob worked for seven years for
Rachel, and they seemed to him like a few
days because he loved her so much. [21]Then
Jacob said to Laban, 'Give me my wife, for
my time is up and I should like to go to her.'
[22]Laban gathered all the people of the place
together, and gave a banquet. [23]But when
night came, he took his daughter Leah and
brought her to Jacob, and he slept with her.
[24](Laban gave his slave-girl Zilpah to his
daughter Leah as her slave.) [25]When morning
came, it was Leah! So Jacob said to Laban,
'What have you done to me? Did I not work
for you for Rachel? Why then have you
tricked me?' [26]Laban replied, 'It is not the
custom in our place to marry off the younger
before the elder. [27]Finish this marriage week
and I shall give you the other one too in return
for your working for me for another seven
years.' [28]Jacob agreed and, when he had
finished the week, Laban gave him his
daughter Rachel as his wife. [29](Laban gave
his slave-girl Bilhah to his daughter Rachel
as her slave.) [30]So Jacob slept with Rachel
too, and he loved Rachel more than Leah.
He worked for Laban for another seven
years.

Jacob's children

[31]When Yahweh saw that Leah was unloved,
he opened her womb, while Rachel remained
barren. [32]Leah conceived and gave birth to
a son whom she named Reuben, meaning
'Yahweh has seen my misery'; and she said,
'Now my husband will love me.' [33]Con-
ceiving again, she gave birth to a son and
said, 'Yahweh heard that I was unloved, and
so he has given me this one too'; and she
named him Simeon. [34]Again she conceived
and gave birth to a son, and said, 'This time
my husband will become attached to me,
because I have borne him three sons.'
Accordingly, she named him Levi. [35]Again
she conceived and gave birth to a son, and
said, 'Now I shall praise Yahweh!' Accord-
ingly, she named him Judah. Then she had
no more children.
30 Rachel, seeing that she herself gave
Jacob no children, became jealous of
her sister. And she said to Jacob, 'Give me
children, or I shall die!' [2]This made Jacob
angry with Rachel, and he retorted, 'Am I in
the position of God, who has denied you
motherhood?' [3]So she said, 'Here is my slave-
girl, Bilhah. Sleep with her and let her give
birth on my knees; through her, then, I too
shall have children!' [4]So she gave him her
slave-girl Bilhah as concubine. Jacob slept
with her, [5]and Bilhah conceived and gave
birth to a son by Jacob. [6]Then Rachel said,
'God has done me justice; yes, he has heard
my prayer and given me a son.' Accordingly
she named him Dan. [7]Again Rachel's slave-
girl Bilhah conceived and gave birth to a
second son by Jacob. [8]Then Rachel said,
'I have fought a fateful battle with my
sister, and I have won!' So she named him
Naphtali.
[9]Now Leah, seeing that she had ceased to
bear children, took her slave-girl Zilpah and
gave her to Jacob as concubine. [10]So Leah's
slave-girl Zilpah gave birth to a son by Jacob.
[11]Then Leah exclaimed, 'What good
fortune!' So she named him Gad. [12]Leah's
slave-girl Zilpah gave birth to a second son by
Jacob. [13]Then Leah said, 'What blessedness!
Women will call me blessed!' So she named
him Asher.
[14]One day, at the time of the wheat harvest,
Reuben found some mandrakes[a] in the field
and brought them to his mother Leah. Rachel
said to Leah, 'Please give me some of your
son's mandrakes.' [15]Leah replied, 'Is it not
enough to have taken my husband, without
your taking my son's mandrakes as well?' So
Rachel said, 'Very well, he can sleep with you
tonight in return for your son's mandrakes.'
[16]When Jacob came back from the fields that
night, Leah went out to meet him and said,
'You must come to me, for I have hired you
at the price of my son's mandrakes.' So he
slept with her that night. [17]God heard Leah,
and she conceived and gave birth to a fifth
son by Jacob. [18]Then Leah said, 'God has
given me my reward for giving my slave-girl
to my husband.' So she named him Issachar.
[19]Again Leah conceived and gave birth to a
sixth son by Jacob, [20]and said, 'God has given
me a fine gift; now my husband will bring me
presents, for I have borne him six sons.' So
she named him Zebulun. [21]Later she gave
birth to a daughter and named her Dinah.
[22]Then God remembered Rachel; he heard
her and opened her womb. [23]She conceived
and gave birth to a son, and said, 'God has

30a The Hebr. name is similar to 'love'; and it was considered an aphrodisiac by the ancients.

taken away my disgrace!' [24]She named him
Joseph, saying, 'May Yahweh add another
son for me!'

How Jacob became rich

[25]When Rachel had given birth to Joseph,
Jacob said to Laban, 'Release me and let me
go home to my own country. [26]Give me my
wives for whom I have worked for you, and
my children, and let me go. You are well
aware how long I have worked for you.'
[27]Laban replied, 'If I have done what pleases
you . . . I have learnt by divination that
Yahweh has blessed me because of you. [28]So
name your wages,' he added, 'and I will pay.'
[29]He replied, 'You know how hard I have
worked for you, and how your stock has fared
in my charge. [30]The little you had before I
came has increased enormously, and Yahweh
has blessed you wherever I have been. When
am I to provide for my own household too?'
[31]Laban said, 'How much am I to pay you?'
Jacob replied, 'You need not pay me
anything. I shall change my mind and go on
tending your flock, if you do this one thing
for me.

[32]'Go through your entire flock today and
remove every black animal among the sheep,
and every speckled or spotted one among the
goats. These will be my wages, [33]and my
uprightness will answer for me later: when
you come to check my wages, every goat I
have that is not speckled or spotted, and
every sheep that is not black will count as
stolen by me.' [34]Laban replied, 'Good, just
as you say.' [35]That same day he removed the
striped and speckled he-goats and all the
spotted and speckled she-goats, every one
that had white on it, and all the black sheep,
and entrusted these to his sons. [36]Then he
put a three days' journey between himself
and Jacob, while Jacob grazed the rest of
Laban's flock.

[37]Jacob then got fresh shoots from poplar,
almond and plane trees, and peeled them in
white strips, laying bare the white part of the
shoots. [38]He set up the shoots he had peeled
in front of the animals, in the troughs, in the
water-holes where the animals came to drink.
Since they mated when they came to drink,
[39]the goats thus mated in front of the shoots
and so the goats produced striped, spotted
and speckled young. [40]The ewes, on the
other hand, Jacob kept apart and made these
face whatever was striped or black in Laban's
flock. Thus he built up droves of his own
which he did not put with Laban's flocks.
[41]Furthermore, whenever the sturdier
animals were mating, Jacob put the shoots
where the animals could see them, in the
troughs, so that they would mate in front of
the shoots. [42]But when the animals were
feeble, he did not put them there; so Laban
got the feeble, and Jacob the sturdy. [43]Thus
the man grew extremely rich, and came to
own large flocks, men and women slaves,
camels and donkeys.

Jacob's flight

31 Jacob learned that Laban's sons were
saying, 'Jacob has taken everything
that belonged to our father; it is at our father's
expense that he has acquired all this wealth,'
[2]and Jacob also saw that Laban's manner
towards him was not as it had been in the
past. [3]Yahweh said to Jacob, 'Go back to the
land of your ancestors, where you were born,
and I shall be with you.' [4]So Jacob had Rachel
and Leah called to the fields where his flocks
were, [5]and he said to them, 'I can see that
your father's manner towards me is not as it
was in the past, but the God of my father has
been with me. [6]You yourselves know that I
have worked for your father with all my
might, [7]and that your father has tricked me,
changing my wages ten times over, and yet
God has not allowed him to harm me.
[8]Whenever he said, "The spotted ones will
be your wages," all the animals produced
spotted young; whenever he said, "The
striped ones will be your wages," all the
animals produced striped young. [9]Thus God
has reclaimed your father's livestock and
given it to me. [10]Once, when the animals
were on heat, I suddenly saw in a dream
that the he-goats covering the females were
striped or spotted or piebald. [11]In the dream
the angel of God called to me, "Jacob!" I
said, "Here I am." [12]He said, "Now take
note: all the he-goats covering the females
are striped or spotted or piebald—for I too
have noted all the things that Laban has been
doing to you, [13]I am the God who appeared
to you at Bethel, where you poured oil on a
pillar and made a vow to me. On your feet,
then, leave this country and return to the
land of your birth." '

[14]In answer Rachel and Leah said to him,
'Are we still likely to inherit anything from

our father's estate? 15 Does he not think of us
as outsiders now? For not only has he sold
us, but he has completely swallowed up the
money he got for us. 16 All the wealth that
God has reclaimed from our father belonged
to us and our children in any case. So do
whatever God has told you.'

17 Forthwith, Jacob put his children and
his wives on camels, 18 and drove off all his
livestock—with all the possessions he had
acquired, the livestock belonging to him
which he had acquired in Paddan-Aram—to
go to his father Isaac in Canaan. 19 Laban
was away, shearing his sheep; Rachel in the
meanwhile had appropriated the household
idols belonging to her father, 20 and Jacob had
outwitted Laban the Aramaean so that he
would not be forewarned of his flight. 21 Thus
he got away with all he had. He was soon
across the River and heading for Mount
Gilead.

Laban pursues Jacob

22 Three days later Laban was told that Jacob
had fled. 23 Taking his brothers with him, he
pursued him for seven days and overtook
him at Mount Gilead. 24 But God appeared to
Laban the Aramaean in a dream that night
and said to him, 'On no account say any-
thing whatever to Jacob.' 25 Laban caught
up with Jacob, who had pitched his tent
in the hills; and Laban pitched camp on
Mount Gilead.

26 Laban said to Jacob, 'What do you mean
by outwitting me and then carrying off my
daughters like prisoners of war? 27 Why did
you flee in secret, stealing away without
letting me know, so that I could send you on
your way rejoicing, with songs and the music
of tambourines and harps? 28 You did not
even let me kiss my sons and daughters. You
have behaved like a fool. 29 It is in my power
to harm you, but the God of your father said
to me last night, "On no account say anything
whatever to Jacob." 30 Now it may be you
really went because you had such a longing
for your father's house, but why did you steal
my gods?'

31 Jacob answered Laban, 'I was afraid,
thinking you were going to snatch your
daughters from me. 32 But whoever is found
in possession of your gods shall not remain
alive. In the presence of our brothers,
examine for yourself what I have, and take
what is yours.' Now Jacob did not know that
Rachel had appropriated them. 33 Laban went
into Jacob's tent, and then into Leah's tent
and the tent of the two slave-girls, but he
found nothing. He came out of Leah's tent
and went into Rachel's. 34 Now Rachel had
taken the household idols and put them inside
a camel cushion, and was sitting on them.
Laban went through everything in the tent
but found nothing. 35 Then Rachel said to her
father, 'Do not look angry, my lord, because
I cannot rise in your presence, for I am
as women are from time to time.' Laban
searched but did not find the idols.

36 Then Jacob lost his temper and took
Laban to task. And Jacob said to Laban,
'What is my offence, what is my crime, for
you to have hounded me like this? 37 You have
gone through all my belongings; have you
found anything belonging to your house-
hold? Produce it here in the presence of my
brothers and yours, and let them decide
between the two of us. 38 In all the twenty
years I was under you, your ewes and your
she-goats never miscarried, and I never ate
rams from your flock. 39 Those mauled I
never brought back to you, but bore the loss
myself. You demanded compensation from
me, whether the animal was stolen in daylight
or at night. 40 In the daytime the heat
devoured me, and frost at night; I never had
a good night's sleep. 41 It was like this for the
twenty years I spent in your household.
Fourteen years I slaved for you for your two
daughters, and six years for your flock, since
you changed my wages ten times over. 42 If
the God of my father, the God of Abraham,
the Kinsman of Isaac, had not been with me,
you would have sent me away empty-handed.
But God saw my plight and my labours, and
last night he delivered judgement.'

A treaty between Jacob and Laban

43 Laban replied to Jacob, 'These daughters
are my daughters and these children are
my children, this livestock is my livestock:
everything you see belongs to me. But what
can I do today about my daughters here or
about the children they have borne? 44 So
come, let us make a pact, you and me . . . ,[a]
and let that serve as a witness between us.'

45 Jacob then took a stone and set it up as
a memorial. 46 Jacob said to his kinsmen,
'Collect some stones,' and gathering some

31a Some words have probably fallen out of the text at this point.

stones they made a cairn. They had a meal
there, on the cairn, and [47]Laban called it
Jegar-Sahadutha while Jacob called it
Galeed. [48]Laban said, 'May this cairn be a
witness between us today.' That is why
he named it Galeed, [49]and also Mizpah,
because he said, 'Let Yahweh act as
watchman between us when we are no
longer in sight of each other. [50]If you ill-treat
my daughters or marry other women besides
my daughters, even though no one be with
us, remember: God is witness between us.'
[51]Then Laban said to Jacob, 'Here is this
cairn I have thrown up between us, and here
the pillar. [52]This cairn is a witness, and the
pillar is a witness, that I am not to cross to
your side of this cairn and you are not to cross
to my side of this cairn and pillar, with hostile
intent. [53]May the God of Abraham and the
god of Nahor judge between us.' Then Jacob
swore by the Kinsman of his father Isaac.
[54]He offered a sacrifice on the mountain
and invited his kinsmen to the meal. They
ate the meal, and passed the night on the
mountain.

32 Early next morning, Laban kissed his
grandchildren and daughters and
blessed them. Then Laban left to return
home. [2]While Jacob was going on his way,
angels of God encountered him, [3]and on
seeing them he said, 'This is God's camp,'
and he named the place Mahanaim.

Jacob prepares for his meeting with Esau

[4]Jacob sent messengers ahead of him to his
brother Esau in Seir, the open country of
Edom, [5]with these instructions, 'Say this to
my lord Esau, "Here is the message of your
servant Jacob: I have been staying with
Laban and have been delayed there until
now, [6]and I own oxen, beasts of burden and
flocks, and men and women slaves. I send
news of this to my lord in the hope of winning
your favour." ' [7]The messengers returned
to Jacob and told him, 'We went to your
brother Esau, and he is already on his way
to meet you; there are four hundred men
with him.'

[8]Jacob was greatly afraid and distressed.
He divided the people with him, and the
flocks and cattle, into two camps, [9]think-
ing, 'If Esau comes to one of the camps
and attacks it, the remaining camp may
be able to escape.' [10]Jacob said, 'God of
my father Abraham, and God of my father
Isaac, Yahweh who told me, "Go back to
your native land and I will be good to you,"
[11]I am unworthy of all the faithful love and
constancy you have shown your servant. I
had only my staff when I crossed this Jordan,
and now I have grown into two camps.
[12]I implore you, save me from my brother
Esau's clutches, for I am afraid that he may
come and attack me, mothers and children
alike. [13]Yet it was you who said, "I shall be
very good to you, and make your descendants
like the sand of the sea, which is too numerous
to count." ' [14]Then Jacob passed that night
there.

From what he had with him he chose a gift
for his brother Esau: [15]two hundred she-
goats and twenty he-goats, two hundred ewes
and twenty rams, [16]thirty camels in milk with
their calves, forty cows and ten bulls, twenty
female donkeys and ten male. [17]He put them
in the charge of his servants, in separate
droves, and told his servants, 'Go ahead of
me, leaving a space between each drove and
the next.' [18]He gave the leading man this
order: 'When my brother Esau meets you
and asks, "Whose man are you? Where are
you going? Whose are those animals that
you are driving?" [19]you will answer, "Your
servant Jacob's. They are a gift sent to my
lord Esau. And Jacob himself is just behind
us." ' [20]He gave the same order to the second
and the third, and to all who were following
the droves. 'That is what you must say to
Esau when you find him. [21]And you must
add, "Your servant Jacob himself is just
behind us." ' For he thought, 'If I conciliate
him by sending a gift in advance, perhaps he
will be well inclined towards me when I face
him.' [22]The gift went ahead of him, but he
himself spent that night in the camp.

Jacob wrestles with God

[23]That same night he got up and, taking his
two wives, his two slave-girls and his eleven
children, crossed the ford of the Jabbok.
[24]After he had taken them across the stream,
he sent all his possessions over too. [25]And
Jacob was left alone.

Then someone wrestled with him until
daybreak [26]who, seeing that he could not
master him, struck him on the hip socket,
and Jacob's hip was dislocated as he wrestled
with him. [27]He said, 'Let me go, for day is
breaking.' Jacob replied, 'I will not let you
go unless you bless me.' [28]The other said,

'What is your name?' 'Jacob,' he replied.
29He said, 'No longer are you to be called
Jacob,[a] but Israel since you have shown
your strength against God and men and have
prevailed.' 30Then Jacob asked, 'Please tell
me your name.' He replied, 'Why do you ask
my name?' With that, he blessed him there.
31Jacob named the place Peniel, 'Because
I have seen God face to face,' he said, 'and
have survived.' 32The sun rose as he passed
Peniel, limping from his hip. 33That is why
to this day the Israelites do not eat the thigh
sinew which is at the hip socket: because he
had struck Jacob at the hip socket on the
thigh sinew.

The meeting with Esau

33 Looking up, Jacob saw Esau coming
and with him four hundred men. He
then divided the children between Leah,
Rachel and the two slave-girls. 2He put the
slave-girls and their children in front, with
Leah and her children following, and Rachel
and Joseph behind. 3He himself went ahead
of them and bowed to the ground seven
times, until he reached his brother. 4But
Esau ran to meet him, took him in his arms,
threw himself on his neck and wept as he
kissed him. 5Then looking up he saw the
women and children. 'Who are these with
you?' he asked. Jacob answered, 'The chil-
dren whom God has bestowed on your
servant.' 6The slave-girls then came up with
their children, and they all bowed low. 7Then
Leah too came up with her children, and they
all bowed low. Finally Rachel and Joseph
came up and bowed low.
8Esau asked, 'What was the purpose of
that whole camp I just met?' 'To win my
lord's favour,' he replied. 9'Brother, I have
plenty,' Esau answered, 'keep what is yours.'
10Jacob protested, 'No, if I have won your
favour, please accept the gift I offer, for in
fact I have come into your presence as into
the presence of God, since you have received
me kindly. 11So accept the gift I have brought
for you, since God has been generous to me
and I have all I need.' And he urged him, and
Esau accepted.

Jacob parts company with Esau

12Esau said, 'Let us break camp and move
off; I shall go beside you.' 13But Jacob replied,
'As my lord knows, the children are weak,
and the sheep and cows which have
calved make it hard for me. If they are driven
too hard, even for one day, the whole drove
will die. 14May it please my lord to go on
ahead of his servant. For my part, I shall
move at a slower pace, to suit the flock I am
driving and the children, until I join my lord
in Seir.' 15Esau then said, 'At least let me
leave you some of the people who are with
me.' 'What for?' Jacob asked. 'Please indulge
me, my lord!' 16So that day Esau turned
back towards Seir, 17but Jacob made his
way to Succoth, where he built himself a
house and made shelters for his livestock;
that is why the place was given the name of
Succoth.

Jacob arrives at Shechem

18Jacob arrived safely at the town of Shechem
in Canaanite territory, on his return from
Paddan-Aram. He encamped opposite the
town 19and for one hundred pieces of silver
he bought from the sons of Hamor father of
Shechem the piece of land on which he had
pitched his tent. 20There he erected an altar
which he called 'El, God of Israel'.

The rape of Dinah

34 Dinah, who was Jacob's daughter by
Leah, went out to visit some of the
women of that region. 2Shechem son of
Hamor the Hivite, headman of the region,
saw her, seized her and forced her to sleep
with him. 3He was captivated by Dinah
daughter of Jacob; he fell in love with the girl
and tried to win her heart. 4Accordingly
Shechem said to his father Hamor, 'Get me
this girl; I want to marry her.' 5Mean-
while, Jacob had heard how his daughter
Dinah had been dishonoured, but since his
sons were out in the countryside with his
livestock, Jacob said nothing until they
came back.

A matrimonial alliance with the Shechemites

6Hamor father of Shechem was visiting
Jacob to discuss the matter with him, 7when
Jacob's sons returned from the countryside

32a =35:10.

and heard the news; the men were outraged
and infuriated that Shechem had insulted
Israel by sleeping with Jacob's daughter—
a thing totally unacceptable. 8 Hamor
reasoned with them as follows, 'My son
Shechem's heart is set on your daughter.
Please allow her to marry him. 9 Intermarry
with us; give us your daughters and take our
daughters for yourselves. 10 We can live
together, and the country will be open to
you, for you to live in, and move about in,
and acquire holdings.' 11 Then Shechem
addressed the girl's father and brothers,
'Grant me this favour, and I will give you
whatever you ask. 12 Demand as high a
bride-price from me as you please, and I will
pay as much as you ask. Only let me marry
the girl.'

13 Jacob's sons gave Shechem and his father
Hamor a crafty answer, speaking as they
did because he had dishonoured their sister
Dinah. 14 'We cannot do this,' they said to
them. 'To give our sister to an uncircumcised
man would be a disgrace for us. 15 We can
agree only on one condition: that you become
like us by circumcising all your males. 16 Then
we will give you our daughters, taking yours
for ourselves; and we will stay with you to
make one nation. 17 But if you will not agree
to our terms about being circumcised, we
shall take our daughter and go.' 18 Hamor and
Shechem son of Hamor were pleased with
what they heard. 19 The young man did not
hesitate about doing this, for he was deeply
in love with Jacob's daughter. Moreover he
was the most respected member of his entire
family.

20 Hamor and his son Shechem went to the
gate of their town and spoke to their fellow-
townsmen as follows, 21 'These men are
friendly; let them settle in the region and
move about freely in it; there is plenty of
room here for them; we shall marry their
daughters and give our daughters to them.
22 But these men will agree to settle with us
and become a single nation only on this
condition: that all our males be circumcised
like them. 23 Will not the livestock they own,
all their animals, become ours? Then let us
give our assent to this, so that they can settle
with us.' 24 All the citizens of the town agreed
to the proposal made by Hamor and his son
Shechem, and all the males were cir-
cumcised.

The treacherous revenge of Simeon and Levi

25 Now on the third day, when the men were
still in pain, Jacob's two sons Simeon and
Levi, Dinah's brothers, each took his sword
and advanced unopposed against the town
and slaughtered all the males. 26 They killed
Hamor and his son Shechem with the sword,
removed Dinah from Shechem's house and
came away. 27 When Jacob's other sons
came on the slain, they pillaged the town in
reprisal for the dishonouring of their sister.
28 They seized their flocks, cattle, donkeys,
everything else in the town and in the
countryside, 29 and all their possessions. They
took all their children and wives captive
and looted everything to be found in the
houses.

30 Jacob said to Simeon and Levi, 'You
have done me an ill turn by bringing me into
bad odour with the people of the region, the
Canaanites and the Perizzites. I have few
men, whereas they will unite against me to
defeat me and destroy me and my family.'
31 They retorted, 'Should our sister be treated
like a whore?'

Jacob at Bethel

35 God said to Jacob, 'Move on, go to
Bethel and settle there. Make an altar
there for the God who appeared to you when
you were fleeing from your brother Esau.'

2 Jacob said to his family and to all who
were with him, 'Get rid of the foreign gods
you have with you; cleanse yourselves, and
change your clothes. 3 We must move on and
go to Bethel. There I shall make an altar for
the God who heard me when I was in distress,
and gave me his help on the journey I made.'
4 They gave Jacob all the foreign gods in their
possession, and the earrings that they were
wearing. Jacob buried them under the oak
tree near Shechem. 5 They broke camp; a
divine terror struck the towns round about,
and no one pursued the sons of Jacob.

6 When Jacob arrived at Luz in Canaan—
that is, Bethel—and all the people with him,
7 he built an altar there and named the place
El-Bethel, since it was there that God had
appeared to him when he was fleeing from his
brother. 8 Deborah, who had been Rebekah's
nurse, died and was buried below Bethel,
under the oak tree; so they named it the Oak
of Tears.

9 God again appeared to Jacob on his return
from Paddan-Aram, and blessed him. 10 God
said to him, 'Your name is Jacob,[a] but from
now on you will be called not Jacob but
Israel.' Thus he came by the name Israel.
11 God said to him, 'I am El Shaddai. Be
fruitful and multiply. A nation, indeed an
assembly of nations, will descend from you,
and kings will issue from your loins. 12 The
country which I gave to Abraham and Isaac,
I now give to you; and this country I shall
give to your descendants after you.' 13 Then
God went up from him.
14 Jacob raised a monument at the spot
where he had spoken to him, a standing-
stone, on which he made a libation and
poured oil. 15 Jacob named the place Bethel
where God had spoken to him.

The birth of Benjamin and the death of Rachel

16 They left Bethel, and while they were still
some distance from Ephrath, Rachel went
into labour, and her pains were severe.
17 When her labour was at its hardest, the
midwife said to her, 'Do not worry, this is
going to be another boy.' 18 At the moment
when she breathed her last, for she was
dying, she named him Ben-Oni. His father,
however, named him Benjamin. 19 So Rachel
died and was buried on the road to Ephrath,
now Bethlehem. 20 Jacob raised a monument
on her grave, that same monument of
Rachel's Tomb which is there today.

Reuben's incest

21 Israel left and pitched his tent beyond
Migdal-Eder. 22 While Israel was living in
that district, Reuben went and slept with
Bilhah his father's concubine, and Israel
found out.

The twelve sons of Jacob

The sons of Jacob were now twelve. 23 The
sons of Leah: Jacob's eldest son Reuben,
then Simeon, Levi, Judah, Issachar and
Zebulun. 24 The sons of Rachel: Joseph
and Benjamin. 25 The sons of Bilhah, Rachel's
slave-girl: Dan and Naphtali. 26 The sons of
Zilpah, Leah's slave-girl: Gad and Asher.
These were the sons born to Jacob in Paddan-Aram.

The death of Isaac

27 Jacob came home to his father Isaac at
Mamre, at Kiriath-Arba—now Hebron—
where Abraham and Isaac had stayed. 28 Isaac
was one hundred and eighty years old 29 when
he breathed his last. He died and was gathered to his people, an old man who had
enjoyed his full span of life. His sons Esau
and Jacob buried him.

Esau's wives and children in Canaan

36 These are the descendants of Esau, that
is, Edom. 2 Esau chose his wives from
the women of Canaan: Adah daughter of Elon
the Hittite, Oholibamah daughter of Anah,
son of Zibeon the Horite, 3 Basemath
daughter of Ishmael and sister of Nebaioth.
4 Adah bore Eliphaz to Esau, Basemath bore
Reuel, 5 Oholibamah bore Jeush, Jalam and
Korah. These were the sons of Esau born to
him in Canaan.

Esau's migration

6 Esau took his wives, his sons and daughters,
all the members of his household, his livestock, all his cattle and all the goods he had
acquired in Canaan and left for Seir, away
from his brother Jacob. 7 For they had
acquired too much to live together. The land
in which they were at that time could not
support them both because of their livestock.
8 That is why Edom settled in the mountainous region of Seir. Esau is Edom.

Esau's descendants in Seir

9 These are the descendants of Esau, ancestor of Edom, in the mountainous region
of Seir.
10 These are the names of Esau's sons:
Eliphaz son of Esau's wife Adah, and Reuel
son of Esau's wife Basemath.
11 The sons of Eliphaz were: Teman, Omar,
Zepho, Gatam and Kenaz. 12 Eliphaz son of
Esau had Timna for concubine and she bore
him Amalek. These were the sons of Esau's
wife Adah.
13 These were the sons of Reuel: Nahath,

35a =32:29.

Zerah, Shammah and Mizzah. These were
the sons of Esau's wife Basemath.
14 And these were the sons of Esau's wife
Oholibamah daughter of Anah, son of
Zibeon: she bore him Jeush, Jalam and
Korah.

The chieftains of Edom

15 These are the chieftains of Esau.
The descendants of Eliphaz, Esau's eldest
son: the chieftains of Teman, Omar, Zepho,
Kenaz, 16 Gatam and Amalek. These are the
chieftains of Eliphaz in Edom and are
descended from Adah.
17 The descendants of Esau's son Reuel: the
chieftains of Nahath, Zerah, Shammah and
Mizzah. These are the chieftains of Reuel in
Edom and are descended from Esau's wife
Basemath.
18 The descendants of Esau's wife Oholi-
bamah: the chieftains of Jeush, Jalam and
Korah. These are the chieftains of Esau's
wife Oholibamah daughter of Anah.
19 These were the sons of Esau—that is,
Edom—and these are their chieftains.

The descendants of Seir the Horite

20 These are the sons of Seir the Horite, natives
of the country: Lotan, Shobal, Zibeon,
Anah, 21 Dishon, Ezer and Dishan; these
were the Horite chieftains descended from
Seir, in Edom. 22 The sons of Lotan were Hori
and Hemam, and Lotan's sister was Timna.
23 These are the sons of Shobal: Alvan,
Manahath, Ebal, Shepho and Onam. 24 These
are the sons of Zibeon: Aiah, Anah—the
Anah who found the hot springs in the desert
while pasturing his father Zibeon's donkeys.
25 These are the children of Anah: Dishon,
and Oholibamah daughter of Anah. 26 These
are the sons of Dishon: Hemdan, Eshban,
Ithran and Cheran. 27 These are the sons of
Ezer: Bilhan, Zaavan and Akan. 28 These are
the sons of Dishan: Uz and Aran.
29 These are the Horite chieftains: the chief-
tains of Lotan, Shobal, Zibeon, Anah,
30 Dishon, Ezer and Dishan. These are the
chieftains of the Horites, by their clans, in
Seir.

The kings of Edom

31 These are the kings who reigned in Edom
before an Israelite king. 32 In Edom reigned
Bela son of Beor; his city was called
Dinhabah. 33 Bela died and Jobab son of
Zerah, from Bozrah, succeeded. 34 Jobab died
and Husham from the land of the Temanites
succeeded. 35 Husham died and Hadad son of
Bedad succeeded; he defeated the Midianites
in Moab, and his city was called Avith.
36 Hadad died and Samlah of Masrekah
succeeded. 37 Samlah died and Shaul of
Rehoboth-ha-Nahar succeeded. 38 Shaul died
and Baal-Hanan son of Achbor succeeded.
39 Baal-Hanan died and Hadad succeeded; his
city was called Pau and his wife's name
was Mehetabel daughter of Matred, from
Mezahab.

More chieftains of Edom

40 These are the names of the chieftains of
Esau—according to their clans and localities:
the chieftains of Timna, Alvah, Jetheth,
41 Oholibamah, Elah, Pinon, 42 Kenaz,
Teman, Mibzar, 43 Magdiel and Iram. These
are the chieftains of Edom, as settled in the
territory which they own. Esau was Edom's
ancestor.
37 But Jacob settled in the land where his
father had stayed, the land of Canaan.

IV: THE STORY OF JOSEPH

Joseph and his brothers

2 This is the story of Joseph.
Joseph was seventeen years old. As he was
young, he was shepherding the flock with his
brothers, with the sons of his father's wives,
Bilhah and Zilpah; and Joseph brought his
father bad reports about them.
3 Jacob loved Joseph more than all his other
sons, for he was the son of his old age, and
he had a decorated tunic made for him. 4 But
his brothers, seeing how much more his
father loved him than all his other sons, came
to hate him so much that they could not say
a civil word to him.
5 Now Joseph had a dream, and he repeated
it to his brothers, who then hated him more
than ever. 6 'Listen', he said, 'to the dream I

had. [7]We were binding sheaves in the field, when my sheaf suddenly rose and stood upright, and then your sheaves gathered round and bowed to my sheaf.' [8]'So you want to be king over us,' his brothers retorted, 'you want to lord it over us?' And they hated him even more, on account of his dreams and of what he said. [9]He had another dream which he recounted to his brothers. 'Look, I have had another dream,' he said. 'There were the sun, the moon and eleven stars, bowing down to me.' [10]He told his father and brothers, and his father scolded him. 'A fine dream to have!' he said to him. 'Are all of us then, myself, your mother and your brothers, to come and bow to the ground before you?' [11]His brothers held it against him, but his father pondered the matter.

Joseph sold by his brothers

[12]His brothers went to pasture their father's flock at Shechem. [13]Then Israel said to Joseph, 'Your brothers are with the flock at Shechem, aren't they? Come, I am going to send you to them.' 'I am ready,' he replied. [14]He said to him, 'Go and see how your brothers and the flock are doing, and bring me word.' He sent him from the valley of Hebron, and Joseph arrived at Shechem.

[15]A man found him wandering in the countryside and asked him, 'What are you looking for?' [16]'I am looking for my brothers,' he replied. 'Please tell me where they are pasturing their flock.' [17]The man answered, 'They have moved on from here; indeed I heard them say, "Let us go to Dothan." ' So Joseph went after his brothers and found them at Dothan.

[18]They saw him in the distance, and before he reached them they made a plot to kill him. [19]'Here comes that dreamer,' they said to one another. [20]'Come on, let us kill him now and throw him down one of the storage-wells; we can say that some wild animal has devoured him. Then we shall see what becomes of his dreams.'

[21]But Reuben heard, and he saved him from their clutches. 'We must not take his life,' he said. [22]'Shed no blood,' said Reuben to them, 'throw him down that well out in the desert, but do not kill him yourselves'—intending to save him from them and to restore him to his father. [23]So, when Joseph reached his brothers, they pulled off his tunic, the decorated tunic which he was wearing, [24]and catching hold of him, threw him into the well. The well was empty, with no water in it. [25]They then sat down to eat.

Looking up, they saw a group of Ishmaelites who were coming from Gilead, their camels laden with gum tragacanth, balsam and resin, which they were taking to Egypt. [26]Then Judah said to his brothers, 'What do we gain by killing our brother and covering up his blood? [27]Come, let us sell him to the Ishmaelites, then we shall not have laid hands on him ourselves. After all, he is our brother, and our own flesh.' His brothers agreed.

[28]Now some Midianite merchants were passing, and they pulled Joseph out of the well. They sold Joseph to the Ishmaelites for twenty shekels of silver, and these men took Joseph to Egypt. [29]When Reuben went back to the well, there was no sign of Joseph. Tearing his clothes, [30]he went back to his brothers. 'The boy has gone,' he said. 'What am I going to do?'

[31]They took Joseph's tunic and, slaughtering a goat, dipped the tunic in the blood. [32]Then they sent off the decorated tunic and had it taken to their father, with the message, 'This is what we have found. Do you recognise it as your son's tunic or not?' [33]He recognised it and cried, 'My son's tunic! A wild animal has devoured him! Joseph has been torn to pieces!' [34]Tearing his clothes and putting sackcloth round his waist, Jacob mourned his son for many days. [35]All his sons and daughters tried to comfort him, but he refused to be comforted. 'No,' he said, 'I will go down to Sheol in mourning and join my son.' Thus his father wept for him.

[36]Meanwhile the Midianites had sold him in Egypt to Potiphar, one of Pharaoh's officials and commander of the guard.

The story of Judah and Tamar

38 It happened at about that time that Judah left his brothers, to go down and settle with a certain Adullamite called Hirah. [2]There Judah saw the daughter of a Canaanite called Shua. He made her his wife and slept with her. [3]She conceived and gave birth to a son whom she named Er. [4]She conceived again and gave birth to a son whom she named Onan. [5]Yet again she gave birth to a son whom she named Shelah. She was at Chezib when she gave birth to him.

6 Judah took a wife for his first-born Er, and her name was Tamar. 7 But Er, Judah's first-born, offended Yahweh, and Yahweh killed him. 8 Then Judah said to Onan, 'Take your brother's wife, and do your duty as her brother-in-law, to maintain your brother's line.' 9 But Onan, knowing that the line would not count as his, spilt his seed on the ground every time he slept with his brother's wife, to avoid providing offspring for his brother. 10 What he did was offensive to Yahweh, who killed him too. 11 Then Judah said to his daughter-in-law Tamar, 'Go home as a widow to your father, until my son Shelah grows up,' for he was thinking, 'He must not die like his brothers.' So Tamar went home to her father.

12 A long time passed, and then Shua's daughter, the wife of Judah, died. After Judah had been comforted he went up to Timnah for the shearing of his sheep, he and his friend Hirah the Adullamite. 13 When Tamar was told, 'Look, your father-in-law is going up to Timnah for the shearing of his sheep,' 14 she changed out of her widow's clothes, wrapped a veil around her to disguise herself, and sat down at the entrance to Enaim, which is on the way to Timnah; for she saw that, although Shelah was grown up, she had not been given to him as his wife.

15 Judah, seeing her, took her for a prostitute, since her face was veiled. 16 Going up to her on the road, he said, 'Here, let me sleep with you.' He did not know that she was his daughter-in-law. 'What will you give me for sleeping with you?' she asked. 17 'I will send you a kid from the flock,' he said. 'Agreed, if you give me a pledge until you send it,' she replied. 18 'What pledge shall I give you?' he asked. 'Your seal and cord and the staff you are holding,' she replied. He gave them to her and slept with her, and she conceived by him. 19 Then she got up and left him and, taking off her veil, resumed her widow's weeds.

20 Judah sent the kid by his friend the Adullamite, to recover the pledge from the woman. But he did not find her. 21 He enquired from the men of the place, 'Where is the prostitute who was by the roadside at Enaim?' 'There has been no prostitute there,' they answered. 22 So returning to Judah he said, 'I did not find her. What is more, the men of the place told me there had been no prostitute there.' 23 'Let her keep the things,' Judah said, 'or we shall become a laughing-stock. At least I sent her this kid, even though you did not find her.'

24 About three months later, Judah was told, 'Your daughter-in-law has played the harlot; furthermore, she is pregnant, as a result of her misconduct.' 'Bring her out,' Judah ordered, 'and let her be burnt alive!' 25 But as she was being led off, she sent word to her father-in-law, 'It was the owner of these who made me pregnant. Please verify', she said, 'whose seal and cord and staff these are.' 26 Judah recognised them and said, 'She was right and I was wrong, since I did not give her to my son Shelah.' He had no further intercourse with her.

27 When the time for her confinement came, there were twins in her womb! 28 During the delivery, one of them put out a hand, and the midwife caught it and tied a scarlet thread to it, indicating that this was the first to arrive. 29 Whereupon, he drew back his hand, and out came his brother. Then she said, 'What a breach you have opened for yourself!' So he was named Perez. 30 Then his brother came out with the scarlet thread on his hand, so he was named Zerah.

Joseph's early days in Egypt

39 Now Joseph had been taken down into Egypt. Potiphar the Egyptian, one of Pharaoh's officials and commander of the guard, bought him from the Ishmaelites who had taken him down there. 2 Yahweh was with Joseph, and everything he undertook was successful. He lodged in the house of his Egyptian master, 3 and when his master saw how Yahweh was with him and how Yahweh made everything he undertook successful, 4 he was pleased with Joseph and made him his personal attendant; and his master put him in charge of his household, entrusting him with all his possessions. 5 And from the time he put him in charge of his household and all his possessions, Yahweh blessed the Egyptian's household out of consideration for Joseph; Yahweh's blessing extended to all his possessions, both household and estate. 6 So he left Joseph to handle all his possessions, and with him there, concerned himself with nothing beyond the food he ate.

The attempt to seduce Joseph

Now Joseph was well built and handsome, 7 and it happened some time later that his master's wife cast her eyes on Joseph and said, 'Sleep with me.' 8 But he refused. 'Look,' he said to his master's wife, 'with me here, my master does not concern himself with what happens in the house, having entrusted all his possessions to me. 9 He himself wields no more authority in this house than I do. He has exempted nothing from me except yourself, because you are his wife. How could I do anything so wicked, and sin against God?' 10 Although she spoke to Joseph day after day, he would not agree to sleep with her or be with her.

11 But one day when Joseph came into the house to do his work, and none of the men of the household happened to be indoors, 12 she caught hold of him by his tunic and said, 'Sleep with me.' But he left the tunic in her hand, took to his heels and got out. 13 When she saw that he had left the tunic in her hands as he ran out, 14 she called her servants and said to them, 'Look at this! My husband brought in a Hebrew to make a fool of me! He burst in on me, but I screamed, 15 and when he heard me scream, he left his tunic beside me and ran out of the house.'

16 She kept his tunic by her until his master came home. 17 Then she told him the same tale, 'The Hebrew slave you brought to us burst in on me to make a fool of me. 18 But when I screamed, he left his tunic beside me and ran away.' 19 When his master heard his wife say, 'This was how your slave treated me,' he became furious. 20 Joseph's master had him arrested and committed to the gaol where the king's prisoners were kept.

Joseph in gaol

And there in gaol he stayed. 21 But Yahweh was with Joseph. He showed him faithful love and made him popular with the chief gaoler. 22 The chief gaoler put Joseph in charge of all the prisoners in the gaol, making him responsible for everything done there. 23 The chief gaoler did not bother about anything put in his charge, since Yahweh was with him, and Yahweh made everything he undertook successful.

Joseph interprets the dreams of Pharaoh's officials

40 It happened some time later that the king of Egypt's cup-bearer and his baker offended their master the king of Egypt. 2 Pharaoh was angry with his two officials, the chief cup-bearer and the chief baker, 3 and put them in custody in the house of the commander of the guard, in the gaol where Joseph was a prisoner. 4 The commander of the guard assigned Joseph to them to attend to their wants, and they remained in custody for some time.

5 Now both of them had dreams on the same night, each with its own meaning for the cup-bearer and the baker of the king of Egypt, who were prisoners in the gaol. 6 When Joseph came to them in the morning, he saw that they looked gloomy, 7 and he asked the two officials who were in custody with him in his master's house, 'Why these sad looks today?' 8 They replied, 'We have each had a dream, but there is no one to interpret it.' 'Are not interpretations God's business?' Joseph asked them. 'Tell me about them.'

9 So the chief cup-bearer described his dream to Joseph, telling him, 'In my dream there was a vine in front of me. 10 On the vine were three branches; no sooner had it budded than it blossomed, and its clusters became ripe grapes. 11 I had Pharaoh's cup in my hand; I picked the grapes and squeezed them into Pharaoh's cup, and put the cup into Pharaoh's hand.' 12 'This is what it means,' Joseph told him. 'The three branches are three days. 13 In another three days Pharaoh will lift up your head by restoring you to your position. Then you will hand Pharaoh his cup, as you did before, when you were his cup-bearer. 14 But be sure to remember me when things go well with you, and keep faith with me by kindly reminding Pharaoh about me, to get me out of this house. 15 I was kidnapped from the land of the Hebrews in the first place, and even here I have done nothing to warrant being put in the dungeon.'

16 The chief baker, seeing that the interpretation had been favourable, said to Joseph, 'I too had a dream; there were three wicker trays on my head. 17 In the top tray there were all kinds of pastries for Pharaoh, such as a baker might make, and the birds were eating them off the tray on my head.' 18 Joseph replied as follows, 'This is what it means: the three trays are three days. 19 In another three days Pharaoh will lift up your head by hanging you on a gallows, and the birds will eat the flesh off your bones.'

20 And so it happened; the third day was

Pharaoh's birthday and he gave a banquet for
all his officials. Of his officials he lifted up
the head of the chief cup-bearer and the chief
baker, [21]the chief cup-bearer by restoring
him to his cup-bearing, so that he again
handed Pharaoh his cup; [22]and by hanging
the chief baker, as Joseph had explained to
them. [23]But the chief cup-bearer did not
remember Joseph; he had forgotten him.

Pharaoh's dreams

41 Two years later it happened that
Pharaoh had a dream: there he was,
standing by the Nile, [2]and there, coming up
from the Nile, were seven cows, sleek and
fat, and they began to feed among the rushes.
[3]And then seven other cows, wretched and
lean, came up from the Nile, behind them;
and these went over and stood beside the
other cows on the bank of the Nile. [4]The
wretched and lean cows ate the seven sleek
and fat cows. Then Pharaoh woke up.
[5]He fell asleep and dreamed a second time:
there, growing on one stalk, were seven ears
of grain, full and ripe. [6]And then sprouting
up, behind them, came seven ears of grain,
meagre and scorched by the east wind. [7]The
scanty ears of grain swallowed the seven full
and ripe ears of grain. Then Pharaoh woke
up; it had been a dream.
[8]In the morning Pharaoh, feeling
disturbed, had all the magicians and wise
men of Egypt summoned to him. Pharaoh
told them his dream, but there was no one to
interpret it for Pharaoh. [9]Then the chief cup-
bearer addressed Pharaoh, 'Today, I recall
having been at fault. [10]When Pharaoh was
angry with his servants, he put myself and
the chief baker in custody in the house of the
commander of the guard. [11]We had a dream
on the same night, he and I, and each man's
dream had a meaning for himself. [12]There
was a young Hebrew with us, one of the
slaves belonging to the commander of the
guard. We told our dreams to him and he
interpreted them for us, telling each of us
what his dream meant. [13]It turned out exactly
according to his interpretation: I was restored
to my position, but the other man was
hanged.'
[14]Then Pharaoh had Joseph summoned,
and they hurried him from the dungeon.
He shaved and changed his clothes, and
presented himself before Pharaoh. [15]Pharaoh
said to Joseph, 'I have had a dream, and there
is no one to interpret it. But I have heard it
said of you that you can interpret a dream the
instant you hear it.' [16]'Not I,' Joseph replied
to Pharaoh, 'God will give Pharaoh a favour-
able answer.'
[17]So Pharaoh told Joseph, 'In my dream
there I was, standing on the bank of the Nile.
[18]And there were seven cows, fat and sleek,
coming up out of the Nile, and they began to
feed among the rushes. [19]And then seven
other cows came up, behind them, starved,
very wretched and lean; I have never seen
such poor cows in all Egypt. [20]The lean and
wretched cows ate up the first seven fat cows.
[21]But when they had eaten them up, it was
impossible to tell they had eaten them, for
they looked as wretched as ever. Then I woke
up. [22]And then again in my dream, there,
growing on one stalk, were seven ears of
grain, beautifully ripe; [23]but then sprouting
up behind them came seven ears of grain,
withered, meagre and scorched by the east
wind. [24]Then the shrivelled ears of grain
swallowed the seven ripe ears of grain. I have
told the magicians, but no one has given me
the answer.'
[25]Joseph said to Pharaoh, 'Pharaoh's
dreams are one and the same: God has
revealed to Pharaoh what he is going to do.
[26]The seven fine cows are seven years and the
seven ripe ears of grain are seven years; it is
one and the same dream. [27]The seven gaunt
and lean cows coming up behind them are
seven years, as are the seven shrivelled ears
of grain scorched by the east wind: there will
be seven years of famine. [28]It is as I have told
Pharaoh: God has revealed to Pharaoh what
he is going to do. [29]Seven years are coming,
bringing great plenty to the whole of Egypt,
[30]but seven years of famine will follow them,
when all the plenty in Egypt will be forgotten,
and famine will exhaust the land. [31]The
famine that is to follow will be so very severe
that no one will remember what plenty the
country used to enjoy. [32]The reason why
Pharaoh had the same dream twice is that the
event is already determined by God, and God
will shortly bring it about.
[33]'Pharaoh should now find someone intel-
ligent and wise to govern Egypt. [34]Pharaoh
should take action and appoint supervisors
for the country, and impose a tax of one-fifth
on Egypt during the seven years of plenty.
[35]They will collect all the food produced
during these good years that are coming, and
store the grain under Pharaoh's authority,

putting it in the towns and keeping it. 36 This food will form a reserve for the country against the seven years of famine which are coming on Egypt, so that the country will not be destroyed by the famine.'

Joseph's promotion

37 Pharaoh and all his ministers approved of what he had said. 38 Then Pharaoh asked his ministers, 'Can we find anyone else endowed with the spirit of God, like him?' 39 So Pharaoh said to Joseph, 'Since God has given you knowledge of all this, there can be no one as intelligent and wise as you. 40 You shall be my chancellor, and all my people shall respect your orders; only this throne shall set me above you.' 41 Pharaoh said to Joseph, 'I hereby make you governor of the whole of Egypt.' 42 Pharaoh took the ring from his hand and put it on Joseph's. He dressed him in robes of fine linen and put a gold chain round his neck. 43 He made him ride in the best chariot he had after his own, and they shouted *'Abrek!'* ahead of him. Thus he became governor of the whole of Egypt.

44 Pharaoh said to Joseph, 'Although I am Pharaoh, no one is to move hand or foot without your permission throughout Egypt.' 45 Pharaoh named Joseph Zaphenath-Paneah, and gave him Asenath daughter of Potiphera, priest of On, to be his wife. And Joseph began to journey all over Egypt.

46 Joseph was thirty years old when he entered the service of Pharaoh king of Egypt. After leaving Pharaoh's presence, Joseph travelled throughout the length and breadth of Egypt. 47 During the seven years of plenty, the soil yielded generously. 48 He collected all the food of the seven years while there was an abundance in Egypt, and stored the food in the towns, placing in each the food from the surrounding countryside. 49 Joseph gathered in grain like the sand of the sea, in such quantity that he gave up keeping count, since it was past accounting.

Joseph's sons

50 Before the year of famine came, two sons were born to Joseph: Asenath daughter of Potiphera, priest of On, bore him these. 51 Joseph named the first-born Manasseh, 'Because', he said, 'God has made me completely forget my hardships and my father's House.' 52 He named the second Ephraim, 'Because', he said, 'God has made me fruitful in the country of my misfortune.'

53 Then the seven years of plenty that there had been in Egypt came to an end, 54 and the seven years of famine set in, as Joseph had predicted. There was famine in every country, but throughout Egypt there was food. 55 But when all Egypt too began to feel the famine and the people appealed to Pharaoh for food, Pharaoh told all the Egyptians, 'Go to Joseph and do whatever he tells you.' 56 There was famine all over the world. Then Joseph opened all the granaries and rationed out grain to the Egyptians, as the famine grew even worse in Egypt. 57 People came to Egypt from all over the world to get supplies from Joseph, for the famine had grown severe throughout the world.

The first meeting between Joseph and his brothers

42 Jacob, seeing that there were supplies to be had in Egypt, said to his sons, 'Why do you keep staring at one another? 2 I hear', he said, 'that there are supplies in Egypt. Go down and procure some for us there, so that we may survive and not die.' 3 So ten of Joseph's brothers went down to procure grain in Egypt. 4 But Jacob did not send Joseph's brother Benjamin with his brothers. 'Nothing must happen to him,' he thought.

5 Thus the sons of Israel were among the other people who came to get supplies, there being famine in Canaan. 6 It was Joseph, as the man in authority over the country, who allocated the rations to the entire population. So Joseph's brothers went and bowed down before him, their faces touching the ground. 7 As soon as Joseph saw his brothers he recognised them. But he did not make himself known to them, and he spoke harshly to them. 'Where have you come from?' he asked. 'From Canaan to get food,' they replied.

8 Now when Joseph recognised his brothers, but they did not recognise him, 9 Joseph remembered the dreams he had had about them, and said to them, 'You are spies. You have come to discover the country's weak points.' 10 'No, my lord,' they said, 'your servants have come to get food. 11 We

are all sons of the same man. We are honest
men, your servants are not spies.' [12]'Oh no,'
he replied, 'you have come to discover the
country's weak points.' [13]'Your servants were
twelve brothers,' they said, 'sons of the same
man in Canaan, but the youngest is at present
with our father, and the other one is no more.'
[14]To which Joseph retorted, 'It is as I said,
you are spies. [15]This is the test you are to
undergo: as sure as Pharaoh lives you shall
not leave unless your youngest brother comes
here. [16]Send one of your number to fetch
your brother; you others will remain under
arrest, so that your statements can be tested
to see whether or not you are honest. If not,
then as sure as Pharaoh lives you are spies.'
[17]Whereupon, he put them all into custody
for three days.

[18]On the third day Joseph said to them,
'Do this and you will live, for I am a man
who fears God. [19]If you are honest men, let
one of your brothers be detained where you
are imprisoned; the rest of you, go and take
supplies home for your starving families.
[20]But you must bring your youngest brother
back to me; in this way, what you have said
will be verified, and you will not have to die!'
And this is what they did. [21]And they said to
one another, 'Clearly, we are being punished
for what we did to our brother. We saw his
deep misery when he pleaded with us, but
we would not listen, and now this misery has
come home to us.' [22]Reuben retorted to them,
'Did I not tell you not to wrong the boy?
But you would not listen. Now comes the
accounting.' [23]They did not know that Joseph
understood, because there was an interpreter
between them. [24]He turned away from them
and wept. When he was able to speak to them
again, he chose Simeon out of their number
and had him bound while they looked on.

Jacob's sons return to Canaan

[25]Joseph gave the order to fill their panniers
with grain, to put back each man's money in
his sack, and to give them provisions for the
journey. This was done for them. [26]Then
they loaded their supplies on their donkeys
and went away. [27]But when they camped for
the night, one of them opened his sack to
give his donkey some fodder and saw his
money—there it was in the mouth of his sack.
[28]He said to his brothers, 'My money has
been put back; here it is, in my sack!' Their
hearts sank, and they looked at one another
in panic, saying, 'What is this that God has
done to us?'

[29]Returning to their father Jacob in
Canaan, they gave him a full report of what
had happened to them, [30]'The man who is
lord of the country spoke harshly to us,
accusing us of spying on the country. [31]We
told him, "We are honest men, we are not
spies. [32]We were twelve brothers, sons of the
same father. One of us is no more, and the
youngest is at present with our father in
Canaan." [33]But the man who is lord of the
country said to us, "This is how I shall know
whether you are honest: leave one of your
brothers with me. Take supplies for your
starving families and be gone, [34]but bring me
back your youngest brother and then I shall
know that you are not spies but honest men.
Then I shall give your brother back to you
and you will be free to move about the
country." '

[35]As they emptied their sacks, each disco-
vered his bag of money in his sack. On seeing
their bags of money they were afraid, and so
was their father. [36]Then their father Jacob
said to them, 'You are robbing me of my
children; Joseph is no more; Simeon is no
more; and now you want to take Benjamin.
I bear the brunt of all this!'

[37]Then Reuben said to his father, 'You
may put my two sons to death if I do not
bring him back to you. Put him in my care
and I will bring him back to you.' [38]But he
replied, 'My son is not going down with you,
for now his brother is dead he is the only one
left. If any harm came to him on the journey
you are undertaking, you would send my
white head down to Sheol with grief!'

Jacob's sons leave again with Benjamin

43 But the famine in the country grew
worse, [2]and when they had finished
eating the supplies which they had brought
from Egypt their father said to them, 'Go
back and get us a little food.' [3]'But', Judah
replied, 'the man expressly warned us, "You
will not be admitted to my presence unless
your brother is with you." [4]If you are ready
to send our brother with us, we will go down
and get food for you. [5]But if you are not ready
to send him, we will not go down, in view of
the man's warning, "You will not be admitted
to my presence unless your brother is with

you." '[6]Then Israel said, 'Why did you bring
this misery on me by telling the man you had
another brother?' [7]They replied, 'He kept
questioning us about ourselves and our
family, asking, "Is your father still alive?"
and, "Have you another brother?" That is
why we told him. How could we know he
was going to say, "Bring your brother down
here"?' [8]Judah then said to his father Israel,
'Send the boy with me, and let us be off and
go, if we are to survive and not die, we, you,
and our dependants. [9]I will go surety for him,
and you can hold me responsible for him. If
I do not bring him back to you and produce
him before you, let me bear the blame all my
life. [10]Indeed, if we had not wasted so much
time we should have been there and back
twice by now!'

[11]Then their father Israel said to them, 'If
it must be so, then do this: take some of the
country's best products in your baggage and
take them to the man as a gift: some balsam,
some honey, gum tragacanth, resin, pistachio
nuts and almonds. [12]Take double the amount
of money with you and return the money put
back in the mouths of your sacks; it may have
been a mistake. [13]Take your brother, and go
back to the man. [14]May El Shaddai move the
man to be kind to you, and allow you to bring
back your other brother and Benjamin. As
for me, if I must be bereaved, bereaved I
must be.'

The meeting with Joseph

[15]The men took this gift; they took double the
amount of money with them, and Benjamin.
They set off, went down to Egypt and
presented themselves before Joseph. [16]When
Joseph saw Benjamin with them he said to
his chamberlain, 'Take these men into the
house. Slaughter a beast and prepare it, for
these men are to eat with me at midday.'
[17]The man did as Joseph had ordered, and
took the men to Joseph's house.

[18]The men were afraid at being taken to
Joseph's house and said, 'We are being taken
there because of the money replaced in our
sacks the first time. They will set on us; they
will fall on us and make slaves of us, and
take our donkeys too.' [19]So they went up to
Joseph's chamberlain and spoke to him at
the entrance to the house. [20]'By your leave,
sir,' they said, 'we came down once before to
get supplies, [21]and when we reached camp
and opened our sacks, there was each man's
money in the mouth of his sack, to the full.
But we have brought it back with us, [22]and
we have brought more money with us for the
supplies. We do not know who put our money
in our sacks.' [23]'Set your minds at ease,' he
replied, 'do not be afraid. Your God and the
God of your father put treasure in your sacks
for you. I received your money.' And he
brought Simeon out to them.

[24]The man then took the men into Joseph's
house. He offered them water to wash their
feet, and gave their donkeys fodder. [25]They
arranged their gift while they waited for
Joseph to come at midday, for they had heard
they were to dine there.

[26]When Joseph arrived at the house they
offered him the gift they had with them,
bowing low before him. [27]He greeted them
pleasantly, asking, 'Is your father well, the
old man you told me of? Is he still alive?'
[28]'Your servant our father is well,' they
replied, 'he is still alive,' and they bowed
respectfully. [29]Looking about, he saw his
brother Benjamin, his mother's son. 'Is this
your youngest brother', he asked, 'of whom
you told me?' And he added, 'God be good
to you, my son.' [30]Joseph hurried out; so
strong was the affection he felt for his brother
that he wanted to cry. He went into his room
and there he wept. [31]After washing his face
he returned and, controlling himself, gave
the order: 'Serve the meal.' [32]He was served
separately; so were they, and so were
the Egyptians who ate in his household,
for the Egyptians could not take food with
Hebrews; Egyptians have a horror of doing
so. [33]They were placed facing him in order
of seniority, from the eldest to the youngest,
and the men looked at one another in amaze-
ment. [34]He had portions carried to them
from his own dish, the portion for
Benjamin being five times larger than
any of the others. And they feasted with
him and drank freely

Joseph's cup in Benjamin's sack

44 Then Joseph instructed his chamber-
lain as follows: 'Fill these men's sacks
with as much food as they can carry, and put
each man's money in the mouth of his sack.
[2]And put my cup, the silver one, in the mouth
of the youngest one's sack as well as the
money for his rations.' He did as Joseph had
instructed.

[3]At daybreak, the men were sent off with

their donkeys. 4They had gone only a little
way from the city, when Joseph said to his
chamberlain, 'Away now and follow those
men. When you catch up with them, say to
them, "Why have you repaid good with evil?
5Is this not what my lord uses for drinking
and also for reading omens? What you have
done is wrong." '

6So when he caught up with them he
repeated these words. 7They asked him,
'What does my lord mean? Your servants
would never think of doing such a thing.
8Look, we brought you back the money we
found in the mouths of our sacks, all the way
from Canaan. Are we likely to have stolen
silver or gold from your master's house?
9Whichever of your servants is found to have
it shall die, and the rest of us shall be slaves
of my lord.' 10'Very well, then, it shall be as
you say,' he replied, 'the one on whom it is
found shall become my slave, but the rest of
you can go free.' 11Each of them quickly
lowered his sack to the ground, and each
opened his own. 12He searched, beginning
with the eldest and ending with the youngest,
and found the cup in Benjamin's sack. 13Then
they tore their clothes, and when each man
had reloaded his donkey they returned to the
city.

14When Judah and his brothers arrived
at Joseph's house he was still there, so they
fell on the ground in front of him. 15'What
do you mean by doing this?' Joseph asked
them. 'Did you not know that a man such as
I am is a reader of omens?' 16'What can we
answer my lord?' Judah replied. 'What can
we say? How can we clear ourselves? God
himself has uncovered your servants' guilt.
Here we are then, my lord's slaves, we no
less than the one in whose possession the cup
was found.' 17'I could not think of doing
such a thing,' he replied. 'The man in whose
possession the cup was found shall be my
slave, but you can go back unhindered to
your father.'

Judah intervenes

18At this, Judah went up to him and said,
'May it please my lord, let your servant have
a word privately with my lord. Do not be
angry with your servant, for you are like
Pharaoh himself. 19My lord questioned his
servants, "Have you father or brother?"
20And we said to my lord, "We have an old
father, and a younger brother born of his old
age. His brother is dead, so he is the only one
by that mother now left, and his father loves
him." 21Then you said to your servants,
"Bring him down to me, so that I can set eyes
on him." 22We replied to my lord, "The boy
cannot leave his father. If he leaves him,
his father will die." 23But you said to your
servants, "If your youngest brother does
not come down with you, you will not be
admitted to my presence again." 24When we
went back to your servant my father, we
repeated to him what my lord had said. 25So
when our father said, "Go back and get us a
little food," 26we said, "We cannot go down.
We shall go only if our youngest brother is
with us for, unless our youngest brother is
with us, we shall not be admitted to the man's
presence." 27So your servant our father said
to us, "You know that my wife bore me two
children. 28When one of them left me, I
supposed that he must have been torn to
pieces, and I have never seen him since. 29If
you take this one from me too and any harm
comes to him, you will send my white head
down to Sheol with grief." 30If I go to your
servant my father now, and we do not have
the boy with us, he will die as soon as he sees
that the boy is not with us, for his heart is
bound up with him; 31and your servants will
have sent your servant our father's white
head down to Sheol with grief. 32Now your
servant went surety to my father for the boy.
I said: "If I do not bring him back to you, let
me bear the blame before my father all my
life." 33Let your servant stay, then, as my
lord's slave in place of the boy, I implore you,
and let the boy go back with his brothers.
34How indeed could I go back to my father
and not have the boy with me? I could not
bear to see the misery that would overwhelm
my father.'

Joseph makes himself known

45 Then Joseph could not control his
feelings in front of all his retainers,
and he exclaimed, 'Let everyone leave me.'
No one therefore was present with him
while Joseph made himself known to his
brothers, 2but he wept so loudly that all
the Egyptians heard, and the news reached
Pharaoh's palace.

3Joseph said to his brothers, 'I am
Joseph. Is my father really still alive?' His
brothers could not answer him, they were so

dumbfounded at seeing him. 4Then Joseph
said to his brothers, 'Come closer to me.'
When they had come closer to him he said,
'I am your brother Joseph whom you sold
into Egypt. 5But now, do not grieve, do not
reproach yourselves for having sold me here,
since God sent me before you to preserve
your lives. 6For this is the second year there
has been famine in the country, and there are
still five years to come without ploughing or
harvest. 7God sent me before you to assure
the survival of your race on earth and to save
your lives by a great deliverance. 8So it was
not you who sent me here but God, and he
has set me up as a father to Pharaoh, as lord
of all his household and governor of the whole
of Egypt.
9'Return quickly to your father and tell
him, "Your son Joseph says this: 'God has
made me lord of all Egypt. Come down to me
without delay. 10You will live in the region
of Goshen where you will be near me, you,
your children and your grandchildren, your
flocks, your cattle and all your possessions.
11There I shall provide for you—for there are
five years of famine still to come—so that
you, your household and all yours are not
reduced to penury.' " 12You can see with
your own eyes, and my brother Benjamin can
see too, that I am who I say I am. 13Give my
father a full report of all the honour I enjoy
in Egypt, and of all you have seen; and
quickly bring my father down here.'
14Then throwing his arms round the neck
of his brother Benjamin he wept;
and Benjamin wept on his shoulder. 15He
kissed all his brothers, weeping on each
one. Only then were his brothers able to talk
to him.

Pharaoh's invitation

16News reached Pharaoh's palace that
Joseph's brothers had come, and Pharaoh
was pleased to hear it, as were his servants.
17Pharaoh told Joseph, 'Say to your brothers,
"Do this: load your beasts and hurry away
to Canaan. 18Fetch your father and your
families, and come back to me. I will give
you the best territory in Egypt, where you
will live off the fat of the land." 19And you,
for your part, give them this order: "Do this:
take waggons from Egypt, for your little ones
and your wives. Get your father and come.
20Never mind about your property, for the
best of all Egypt will be yours." '

The return to Canaan

21Israel's sons did as they were told. Joseph
gave them waggons as Pharaoh had ordered,
and he gave them provisions for the journey.
22To each and every one he gave new clothes,
and to Benjamin three hundred shekels
of silver and five changes of clothes. 23And
to his father he sent ten donkeys laden
with the best that Egypt offered, and ten
she-donkeys laden with grain, bread and
food for his father's journey. 24And so he
sent his brothers on their way. His final words
to them were, 'And let there be no upsets on
the way!'
25And so they left Egypt. When they
reached their father Jacob in Canaan, 26they
gave him this report, 'Joseph is still alive. He
is at this moment governor of all Egypt!' But
he was as one stunned, for he did not believe
them. 27However, when they told him all
Joseph had said to them, and when he saw
the waggons that Joseph had sent to fetch
him, the spirit of their father Jacob revived,
28and Israel said, 'That is enough! My son
Joseph is still alive. I must go and see him
before I die.'

Jacob leaves for Egypt

46 So Israel set out with all his possessions.
Arriving at Beersheba, he offered sacri-
fices to the God of his father Isaac. 2God
spoke to Israel in a vision at night, 'Jacob,
Jacob,' he said. 'Here I am,' he replied. 3'I
am El, God of your father,' he said. 'Do not
be afraid of going down to Egypt, for I will
make you into a great nation there. 4I shall
go down to Egypt with you and I myself shall
bring you back again, and Joseph's hand will
close your eyes.' 5So Jacob left Beersheba.
Israel's sons conveyed their father Jacob,
their little children and their wives in the
waggons Pharaoh had sent to fetch him.
6Taking their livestock and all that they
had acquired in Canaan, they arrived in
Egypt—Jacob and all his offspring. 7With
him to Egypt, he brought his sons and grand-
sons, his daughters and granddaughters—all
his offspring.

Jacob's family[a]

8 These were the names of the Israelites, Jacob and his descendants, who arrived in Egypt:

Reuben, Jacob's first-born, 9 and the sons of Reuben: Hanoch, Pallu, Hezron and Carmi. 10 The sons of Simeon: Jemuel, Jamin, Ohad, Jachin, Zohar, and Shaul the son of the Canaanite woman. 11 The sons of Levi: Gershon, Kohath and Merari. 12 The sons of Judah: Er, Onan, Shelah, Perez, and Zerah (Er and Onan had died in Canaan), and Hezron and Hamul sons of Perez. 13 The sons of Issachar: Tola, Puvah, Jashub and Shimron. 14 The sons of Zebulun: Sered, Elon and Jahleel. 15 These were the sons that Leah had borne to Jacob in Paddan-Aram, besides his daughter Dinah; in all, his sons and daughters numbered thirty-three.

16 The sons of Gad: Ziphion, Haggi, Shuni, Ezbon, Eri, Arodi and Areli. 17 The sons of Asher: Jimnah, Jishvah, Jishvi, Beriah, with their sister Serah; the sons of Beriah: Heber and Malchiel. 18 These were the sons of Zilpah whom Laban gave to his daughter Leah; she bore these to Jacob—sixteen persons.

19 The sons of Rachel wife of Jacob: Joseph and Benjamin. 20 Born to Joseph in Egypt were: Manasseh and Ephraim sons of Asenath, daughter of Potiphera priest of On. 21 The sons of Benjamin: Bela, Becher, Ashbel, Gera, Naaman, Ehi, Rosh, Muppim, Huppim and Ard. 22 These were the sons that Rachel bore to Jacob—fourteen persons in all.

23 The sons of Dan: Hushim. 24 The sons of Naphtali: Jahzeel, Guni, Jezer and Shillem. 25 These were the sons of Bilhah whom Laban gave to his daughter Rachel; she bore these to Jacob—seven persons in all.

26 Altogether, the members of Jacob's family who arrived with him in Egypt—his own issue, not counting the wives of Jacob's sons—numbered sixty-six all told. 27 With Joseph's sons born to him in Egypt—two persons—the members of Jacob's family who went to Egypt totalled seventy.

Joseph welcomes them

28 Israel sent Judah ahead to Joseph, so that Judah might present himself to Joseph in Goshen. When they arrived in Goshen, 29 Joseph had his chariot made ready and went up to Goshen to meet his father Israel. As soon as he appeared he threw his arms round his neck and for a long time wept on his shoulder. 30 Israel said to Joseph, 'Now I can die, now that I have seen you in person and seen you still alive.'

31 Then Joseph said to his brothers and his father's family, 'I shall go back and break the news to Pharaoh. I shall tell him, "My brothers and my father's family who were in Canaan have come to me. 32 The men are shepherds and look after livestock, and they have brought their flocks and cattle and all their possessions." 33 Thus, when Pharaoh summons you and asks, "What is your occupation?", 34 you are to say, "Ever since our boyhood your servants have looked after livestock, we and our fathers before us," so that you can stay in the Goshen region—for the Egyptians have a horror of all shepherds.'

Pharaoh grants an audience

47 So Joseph went and told Pharaoh, 'My father and brothers have arrived from Canaan with their flocks and cattle and all their possessions. Here they are, in the region of Goshen.' 2 He had taken five of his brothers, and he now presented them to Pharaoh. 3 Pharaoh asked his brothers, 'What is your occupation?' and they gave Pharaoh the answer, 'Your servants are shepherds, like our fathers before us.' 4 They went on to tell Pharaoh, 'We have come to stay in this country for the time being, since there is no pasturage for your servants' flocks, Canaan being stricken with famine. So now please allow your servants to settle in the region of Goshen.' 5a Then Pharaoh said to Joseph, 6b 'They may stay in the region of Goshen, and if you know of any capable men among them, put them in charge of my own livestock.'

Another version

5b Jacob and his sons went to Egypt where Joseph was. Pharaoh king of Egypt heard

---

46a || Nb 26:5seq.

about this and said to Joseph, 'Your father
and brothers have come to you.6a The country
of Egypt is open to you: settle your father
and brothers in the best region.' 7Joseph
brought his father and presented him to
Pharaoh. Jacob paid his respects to Pharaoh.
8Pharaoh asked Jacob, 'How many years
have you lived?' 9Jacob said to Pharaoh, 'The
years of my stay on earth add up to one
hundred and thirty years. Few and unhappy
my years have been, falling short of my
ancestors' years in their stay on earth.'
10Jacob then took leave of Pharaoh and with-
drew from his presence. 11Joseph then settled
his father and brothers, giving them land
holdings in Egypt, in the best part of the
country, the region of Rameses, as Pharaoh
had ordered.
12Joseph provided his father, brothers and
all his father's family with food, down to the
least of them.

Joseph's agrarian policy

13And on all the earth around there was now
no food anywhere, for the famine had grown
very severe, and Egypt and Canaan were both
weak with hunger. 14Joseph accumulated all
the money to be found in Egypt and Canaan,
in exchange for the supplies being handed
out, and put the money in Pharaoh's
palace.
15When all the money in Egypt and
Canaan was exhausted, all the Egyptians
came to Joseph, pleading, 'Give us food,
unless you want us to die before your eyes!
For our money has come to an end.'
16Joseph replied, 'Hand over your livestock
and I shall issue you food in exchange for
your livestock, if your money has come to an
end.' 17So they brought their livestock to
Joseph, and Joseph gave them food in exch-
ange for horses and livestock, whether sheep
or cattle, and for donkeys. Thus he saw them
through that year with food in exchange for
all their livestock.
18When that year was over, they came to
him the next year, and said to him, 'We
cannot hide it from my lord: the truth is, our
money has run out and the livestock is in my
lord's possession. There is nothing left for
my lord except our bodies and our land. 19If
we and our land are not to perish, take us and
our land in exchange for food, and we with
our land will become Pharaoh's serfs; only
give us seed, so that we can survive and not
die and the land not revert to desert!'
20Thus Joseph acquired all the land in
Egypt for Pharaoh, since one by one the
Egyptians sold their fields, so hard pressed
were they by the famine; and the whole
country passed into Pharaoh's possession,
21while the people he reduced to serfdom
from one end of Egypt to the other. 22The
only land he did not acquire belonged to the
priests, for the priests received an allowance
from Pharaoh and lived on the allowance that
Pharaoh gave them. Hence they had no need
to sell their land.
23Then Joseph said to the people, 'This is
how we stand: I have bought you out, with
your land, on Pharaoh's behalf. Here is seed
for you to sow the land. 24But of the harvest
you must give a fifth to Pharaoh. The other
four-fifths you can have for sowing your
fields, to provide food for yourselves and
your households, and food for your children.'
25'You have saved our lives!' they replied. 'If
it please my lord, we will become serfs to
Pharaoh.' 26So Joseph made a law, still in
force today, as regards the soil of Egypt, that
one-fifth should go to Pharaoh. Only the land
of the priests did not go to Pharaoh.

Jacob's last wishes

27Thus Israel settled in Egypt, in the region
of Goshen. They acquired property there;
they were fruitful and grew very numerous.
28Jacob lived seventeen years in Egypt; thus
Jacob's total age came to a hundred and forty-
seven years. 29When Israel's time to die drew
near he sent for his son Joseph and said to
him,[a] 'If you really love me, place your hand
under my thigh as pledge that you will act
with faithful love towards me: do not bury
me in Egypt! 30When I lie down with my
ancestors, carry me out of Egypt and bury
me in their tomb.' 'I shall do as you say,' he
replied. 31'Swear to me,' he insisted. So he
swore to him, and Israel sank back on the
pillow.

Jacob adopts Joseph's two sons and blesses them

48 Some time later, Joseph was informed,
'Your father has been taken ill.' So he

47a =49:29–32; =50:6.

took with him his two sons Manasseh and
Ephraim. 2When Jacob was told, 'Look,
your son Joseph has come to you,' Israel,
summoning his strength, sat up in bed. 3'El
Shaddai appeared to me at Luz in Canaan,'
Jacob told Joseph, 'and he blessed me,
4saying to me, "I shall make you fruitful
and numerous, and shall make you into an
assembly of peoples and give this country
to your descendants after you, to own in
perpetuity." 5Now your two sons, born to
you in Egypt before I came to you in Egypt,
shall be mine; Ephraim and Manasseh shall
be as much mine as Reuben and Simeon.
6But with regard to the children you have
had since them, they shall be yours, and they
shall be known by their brothers' names for
the purpose of their inheritance.

7'When I was on my way from Paddan, to
my sorrow death took your mother Rachel
from me in Canaan, on the journey while
only a short distance from Ephrath. I buried
her there on the road to Ephrath—now
Bethlehem.'

8When Israel saw Joseph's two sons, he
asked, 'Who are these?' 9'They are my sons,
whom God has given me here,' Joseph
told his father. 'Then bring them to me',
he said, 'so that I may bless them.' 10Now,
Israel's eyes were dim with age, and he could
not see. So Joseph made them come closer to
him and he kissed and embraced them.
11Then Israel said to Joseph, 'I did not
think I should ever see you again, and now
God has let me see your children as well!'
12Then Joseph took them from his lap and
bowed to the ground.

13Then Joseph took the two of them,
Ephraim with his right hand so that he should
be on Israel's left, and Manasseh with his left
hand, so that he should be on Israel's right,
and brought them close to him. 14But Israel
held out his right hand and laid it on the head
of Ephraim, the younger, and his left on
the head of Manasseh, crossing his hands—
Manasseh was, in fact, the elder. 15Then he
blessed Joseph saying:

May the God in whose presence
  my fathers Abraham and Isaac walked,
the God who has been my shepherd
  from my birth until this day,
16the Angel who has saved me
  from all harm, bless these boys,
so that my name may live on in them,
  and the names of my ancestors
    Abraham and Isaac,
and they grow into teeming multitudes
  on earth!

17Joseph saw that his father was laying
his right hand on the head of Ephraim, and
this he thought was wrong, so he took his
father's hand and tried to shift it from the
head of Ephraim to the head of Manasseh.
18Joseph protested to his father, 'Not like
that, father! This one is the elder; put your
right hand on his head.' 19But his father
refused. 'I know, my son, I know,' he said.
'He too shall become a people; he too will be
great. But his younger brother will be greater,
his offspring will be sufficient to constitute
nations.'
20So he blessed them that day, saying:

By you shall Israel bless itself, saying,
'God make you like Ephraim
  and Manasseh!'

putting Ephraim before Manasseh.
21Then Israel said to Joseph, 'Now I am
about to die. But God will be with you and
take you back to the land of your ancestors.
22As for me, I give you a Shechem[a] more
than your brothers, the one I took from the
Amorites with my sword and bow.'

Jacob's testament

49 Jacob called his sons and said, 'Gather
round, so that I can tell you what is in
store for you in the final days.

2Gather round, sons of Jacob, and listen;
listen to Israel your father.

3Reuben, you are my first-born,
my vigour, and the first-fruit
  of my manhood,
foremost in pride, foremost in strength,
4uncontrolled as water:
  you will not be foremost,
for you climbed into your father's bed,
and so defiled my couch, to my sorrow.

5Simeon and Levi are brothers
in carrying out their malicious plans.
6May my soul not enter their council
nor my heart join their company,
for in their rage they have killed men
and hamstrung oxen at their whim.

48a *Shekem* = shoulder, but it is also the name of Joseph's burial-town.

7Accursed be their rage for its ruthlessness,
their wrath for its ferocity.
I shall disperse them in Jacob,
I shall scatter them through Israel.

8Judah, your brothers will praise you:
you grip your enemies by the neck,
your father's sons will do you homage.
9Judah is a lion's whelp;
You stand over your prey, my son.
Like a lion he crouches and lies down,
a mighty lion: who dare rouse him?
10The sceptre shall not pass from Judah,
nor the ruler's staff from between his feet,
until tribute be brought him
and the peoples render him obedience.
11He tethers his donkey to the vine,
to its stock the foal of his she-donkey.
He washes his clothes in wine,
his robes in the blood of the grape.
12His eyes are darkened with wine
and his teeth are white with milk.

13Zebulun will live by the seashore
and be a sailor on board the ships,
with Sidon on his flank.

14Issachar is a strong donkey
lying down among sheepfolds.
15When he saw how good the resting-place
and how pleasant the country,
he bowed his shoulder to the load
and became a slave to forced labour.

16Dan will govern his people
like any other of the tribes of Israel.
17May Dan be a snake on the road,
a viper on the path,
who bites the horse on the hock
so that its rider falls off backwards!

18I long for your deliverance, Yahweh!

19Gad will be raided by raiders,
and he will raid at their heels.

20Rich the food produced by Asher:
he will furnish food fit for kings.

21Naphtali is a swift hind
bearing lovely fawns.

22Joseph is a fruitful plant near a spring
whose tendrils reach over the wall.
23Archers in their hostility
drew their bows and attacked him.
24But their bows were broken
by a mighty One,
the sinews of their arms were snapped
by the power of the Mighty One of Jacob,
by the Name of the Stone of Israel,
25the God of your father who assists you,
El Shaddai who blesses you:
blessings of heaven above,
blessings of the deep lying below,
blessings of the breasts and womb,
26blessings of the grain and flowers,
blessings of the eternal mountains,
bounty of the everlasting hills—
may they descend on Joseph's head,
on the crown of the one dedicated
from among his brothers!

27Benjamin is a ravening wolf,
in the morning he devours the prey,
in the evening
he is still sharing out the spoil.'

28All these make up the tribes of Israel, twelve in number, and this is what their father said to them as he bade them farewell, giving each an appropriate blessing.

Jacob's last moments and death[a]

29Then he gave them these instructions, 'I
am about to be gathered to my people. Bury
me with my ancestors, in the cave that is in
the field of Ephron the Hittite, 30in the cave
in the field at Machpelah, facing Mamre,
in Canaan, which Abraham bought from
Ephron the Hittite as a burial site of his own.
31There Abraham and his wife Sarah were
buried. There Isaac and his wife Rebekah
were buried; and there I buried Leah—32the
field and the cave in it which were bought
from the Hittites.'
33When Jacob had finished giving his instructions to his sons, he drew his feet up into the bed, and breathing his last was gathered to his people.

Jacob's funeral

50 At this Joseph threw himself on his
father's face, covering it with tears and
kisses. 2Then Joseph ordered the doctors in
his service to embalm his father. The doctors
embalmed Israel, 3and it took them forty
days, for embalming takes forty days to
complete.
The Egyptians mourned him for seventy
days. 4When the period of mourning for him
was over, Joseph said to Pharaoh's house-

49a =47:29–31; =50:6.

hold, 'If you have any affection for me, see
that this message reaches Pharaoh's ears,
5"My father put me under oath, saying: I am
about to die. In the tomb which I dug for
myself in Canaan, that is where you are to
bury me. So may I have leave to go up and
bury my father, and then come back?" '
6Pharaoh replied, 'Go up and bury your
father, as he made you swear to do.'[a]

7Joseph went up to bury his father, and
with him went all Pharaoh's officials, the
dignitaries of his palace and all the dignitaries
of Egypt, 8as well as all Joseph's family, his
brothers and his father's family. The only
people they left behind in Goshen were those
unfit to travel, and their flocks and cattle.
9Chariots and horsemen went up with him
too; it was a very large retinue.

10On arriving at Goren-ha-Atad, which is
across the Jordan, they there held a long and
solemn lamentation, and Joseph observed
seven days' mourning for his father. 11When
the Canaanites, the local inhabitants,
witnessed the mourning at Goren-ha-Atad,
they said, 'This is a solemn act of mourning
by the Egyptians,' which is why the place
was given the name Abel-Mizraim—it is
across the Jordan.

12His sons did what he had ordered them
to do for him. 13His sons carried him to
Canaan and buried him in the cave in the
field at Machpelah, facing Mamre, which
Abraham had bought from Ephron the
Hittite as a burial site of his own.

14Then Joseph returned to Egypt with his
brothers and all those who had come up with
him to bury his father.

From the death of Jacob to the death of Joseph

15Seeing that their father was dead, Joseph's
brothers said, 'What if Joseph intends
to treat us as enemies and pay us back for all
the wrong we did him?' 16So they sent this
message to Joseph: 'Before your father died,
he gave us this order: 17"You are to say to
Joseph: Now please forgive the crime and
faults of your brothers and all the wrong they
did you." So now please forgive the crime of
the servants of your father's God.' Joseph
wept at the message they sent to him.

18Then his brothers went to him them-
selves and, throwing themselves at his feet,
said, 'Take us as your slaves!' 19But Joseph
replied, 'Do not be afraid; is it for me to put
myself in God's place? 20The evil you planned
to do me has by God's design been turned to
good, to bring about the present result: the
survival of a numerous people. 21So there is
no need to be afraid; I shall provide for
you and your dependants.' In this way he
reassured them by speaking affectionately to
them.

22So Joseph stayed in Egypt with his
father's family; and Joseph lived a hundred
and ten years. 23Joseph saw the third gener-
ation of Ephraim's line, as also the children
of Machir son of Manasseh, who were born
on Joseph's lap. 24At length Joseph said to
his brothers, 'I am about to die; but God will
be sure to remember you kindly and take you
out of this country to the country which he
promised on oath to Abraham, Isaac and
Jacob.' 25And Joseph put Israel's sons on
oath, saying, 'When God remembers you
with kindness, be sure to take my bones away
from here.'

26Joseph died at the age of a hundred and
ten; he was embalmed and laid in a coffin in
Egypt.

50a =47:29–31; =49:29–32.

THE BOOK OF
EXODUS

Israel always looked back on the deliverance from Egypt as the supreme act of God's power and love, leading on to the great meeting with God on Sinai. It gave them the overwhelming experience of God's majesty and power, and was also the decisive moment when God chose Israel to be his own people. The covenant with God on Sinai was the basis of the whole way of life of Israel. Though there is an infinite gulf between the holy God and humanity, the holiness of God's people must correspond to his own. This awareness determines the whole body of Israel's Law.

For its details the Law draws on the case-law of other Near Eastern peoples, and much of it reflects later practice, when Israel had a large, settled, agricultural population. Particularly the instructions of chh. 25–31 (fulfilled in chh. 35–39) mix elements of Moses' time with more recent ones, though as it is the foundation of Israel's life it is still presented as dictated by Yahweh.

Similarly, the story of the exodus from Egypt itself is simplified and schematised. There were probably two groups of Hebrews involved: one was expelled and the other escaped, only one being led by Moses; this would account for a certain overlap in the telling. At the crossing of the sea two accounts are interwoven: the earlier mentions only the destruction of the Egyptians in the water, but the wonder of God's protection of his people is later expressed by the introduction of 'walls of water'. In later books of the Bible (e.g. Wisdom) this tendency is carried still further.

PLAN OF THE BOOK

EXODUS

I: THE LIBERATION FROM EGYPT

A: ISRAEL IN EGYPT

The prosperity of the Hebrews in Egypt

1 These are the names of the Israelites who
went with Jacob to Egypt, each of them
went with his family: 2Reuben, Simeon, Levi
and Judah, 3Issachar, Zebulun and
Benjamin, 4Dan and Naphtali, Gad and
Asher. 5In all, the descendants of Jacob
numbered seventy persons. Joseph was in
Egypt already. 6Then Joseph died, and his
brothers, and all that generation. 7But the
Israelites were fruitful and prolific; they
became so numerous and powerful that
eventually the whole land was full of
them.

The Hebrews oppressed

8Then there came to power in Egypt a new
king who had never heard of Joseph. 9'Look,'
he said to his people, 'the Israelites are now
more numerous and stronger than we are.
10We must take precautions to stop them
from increasing any further, or if war should
break out, they might join the ranks of our
enemies. They might take arms against us
and then escape from the country.'
11Accordingly they put taskmasters over the
Israelites to wear them down by forced
labour. In this way they built the store-cities
of Pithom and Rameses for Pharaoh. 12But
the harder their lives were made, the more
they increased and spread, until people came
to fear the Israelites. 13So the Egyptians gave
them no mercy in the demands they made,
14making their lives miserable with hard
labour: with digging clay, making bricks,
doing various kinds of field-work—all sorts
of labour that they imposed on them without
mercy.

15The king of Egypt then spoke to the
Hebrew midwives, one of whom was called
Shiphrah, and the other Puah. 16'When you
attend Hebrew women in childbirth,' he
said, 'look at the two stones. If it is a boy,
kill him; if a girl, let her live.' 17But the
midwives were God-fearing women and did
not obey the orders of the king of Egypt, but
allowed the boys to live. 18So the king of
Egypt summoned the midwives and said to
them, 'What do you mean by allowing the
boys to live?' 19The midwives said to
Pharaoh, 'Hebrew women are not like Egyp-
tian women, they are hardy and give birth
before the midwife can get to them.' 20For
this, God was good to the midwives, and the
people went on increasing and growing
more powerful; 21and since the midwives
feared God, he gave them families of their
own.

22Pharaoh then gave all his people this
command: 'Throw every new-born boy into
the river, but let all the girls live.'

B: EARLY LIFE OF MOSES

The birth of Moses[a]

2 There was a man descended from Levi
who had taken a woman of Levi as his
wife. 2She conceived and gave birth to a
son and, seeing what a fine child he was, she
kept him hidden for three months. 3When
she could hide him no longer, she got a
papyrus basket for him; coating it with
bitumen and pitch, she put the child inside
and laid it among the reeds at the River's
edge. 4His sister took up position some
distance away to see what would happen to
him.

5Now Pharaoh's daughter went down to
bathe in the river, while her maids walked
along the riverside. Among the reeds she
noticed the basket, and she sent her maid to
fetch it. 6She opened it and saw the child: the
baby was crying. Feeling sorry for it, she
said, 'This is one of the little Hebrews.'
7The child's sister then said to Pharaoh's
daughter, 'Shall I go and find you a nurse

2a Popular Hebr. explanation of an Egyptian name.

among the Hebrew women to nurse the child for you?' 8'Yes,' said Pharaoh's daughter, and the girl went and called the child's own mother. 9Pharaoh's daughter said to her, 'Take this child away and nurse it for me. I shall pay you myself for doing so.' So the woman took the child away and nursed it. 10When the child grew up, she brought him to Pharaoh's daughter who treated him like a son; she named him Moses 'because', she said, 'I drew him out of the water.'

Moses escapes to Midian

11It happened one day, when Moses was grown up, that he went to see his kinsmen. While he was watching their forced labour he also saw an Egyptian striking a Hebrew, one of his kinsmen. 12Looking this way and that and seeing no one in sight, he killed the Egyptian and hid him in the sand. 13On the following day he came back, and there were two Hebrews, fighting. He said to the man who was in the wrong, 'What do you mean by hitting your kinsman?' 14'And who appointed you', the man retorted, 'to be prince over us and judge? Do you intend to kill me as you killed the Egyptian?' Moses was frightened. 'Clearly that business has come to light,' he thought. 15When Pharaoh heard of the matter, he tried to put Moses to death, but Moses fled from Pharaoh. He went into Midianite territory and sat down beside a well.

16Now there was a priest of Midian with seven daughters. They used to come to draw water and fill the troughs to water their father's flock. 17Some shepherds came and drove them away, but Moses sprang to their help and watered their flock. 18When they returned to their father Reuel, he said to them, 'Why are you back so early today?' 19'An Egyptian protected us from the shepherds,' they said, 'and he even drew water for us and watered the flock.' 20'And where is he?' he asked his daughters. 'Why did you leave the man there? Ask him to eat with us.' 21Moses agreed to stay on there with the man, who gave him his daughter Zipporah in marriage. 22She gave birth to a son, whom he named Gershom 'because', he said, 'I am an alien in a foreign land.'

C: THE CALL OF MOSES

God remembers Israel

23During this long period the king of Egypt died. The Israelites, groaning in their slavery, cried out for help and from the depths of their slavery their cry came up to God. 24God heard their groaning; God remembered his covenant with Abraham, Isaac and Jacob. 25God saw the Israelites and took note.

The burning bush[a]

3 Moses was looking after the flock of his father-in-law Jethro, the priest of Midian; he led it to the far side of the desert and came to Horeb, the mountain of God. 2The angel of Yahweh appeared to him in a flame blazing from the middle of a bush. Moses looked; there was the bush blazing, but the bush was not being burnt up. 3Moses said, 'I must go across and see this strange sight, and why the bush is not being burnt up.' 4When Yahweh saw him going across to look, God called to him from the middle of the bush. 'Moses, Moses!' he said. 'Here I am,' he answered. 5'Come no nearer,' he said. 'Take off your sandals, for the place where you are standing is holy ground. 6I am the God of your ancestors,' he said, 'the God of Abraham, the God of Isaac and the God of Jacob.' At this Moses covered his face, for he was afraid to look at God.

The mission of Moses

7Yahweh then said, 'I have indeed seen the misery of my people in Egypt. I have heard them crying for help on account of their taskmasters. Yes, I am well aware of their sufferings. 8And I have come down to rescue them from the clutches of the Egyptians and bring them up out of that country, to a country rich and broad, to a country flowing with milk and honey, to the home of the Canaanites, the Hittites, the Amorites, the Perizzites, the Hivites and the Jebusites. 9Yes indeed, the Israelites' cry for help has reached me, and I have also seen the cruel way in which the Egyptians are oppressing them. 10So now I am sending you to Pharaoh,

---

3a =6:2–13.

for you to bring my people the Israelites out
of Egypt.'
11Moses said to God, 'Who am I to go
to Pharaoh and bring the Israelites out of
Egypt?' 12'I shall be with you,' God said, 'and
this is the sign by which you will know that
I was the one who sent you. After you have
led the people out of Egypt, you will worship
God on this mountain.'

The divine name[b] revealed

13Moses then said to God, 'Look, if I go to
the Israelites and say to them, "The God of
your ancestors has sent me to you," and they
say to me, "What is his name?" what am I to
tell them?' 14God said to Moses, 'I am he
who is.' And he said, 'This is what you are
to say to the Israelites, "I am has sent me to
you." ' 15God further said to Moses, 'You
are to tell the Israelites, "Yahweh, the God
of your ancestors, the God of Abraham, the
God of Isaac and the God of Jacob, has sent
me to you." This is my name for all time,
and thus I am to be invoked for all generations
to come.

Moses instructed for his mission

16'Go, gather the elders of Israel together
and tell them, "Yahweh, the God of your
ancestors, has appeared to me—the God of
Abraham, of Isaac and of Jacob—and has
indeed visited you and seen what is being
done to you in Egypt, 17and has said: I shall
bring you out of the misery of Egypt to the
country of the Canaanites, the Hittites, the
Amorites, the Perizzites, the Hivites and
the Jebusites, to a country flowing with milk
and honey." 18They will listen to your words,
and you and the elders of Israel are to go to
the king of Egypt and say to him, "Yahweh,
the God of the Hebrews, has encountered us.
So now please allow us to make a three-
days' journey into the desert and sacrifice to
Yahweh our God." 19I am well aware that the
king of Egypt will not let you go unless he is
compelled by a mighty hand; 20he will not let
you go until I have stretched out my arm and
struck Egypt with all the wonders I intend to
work there.

The Egyptians to be plundered

21'I shall ensure that the Egyptians are so
much impressed with this people that when
you go, you will not go empty-handed.
22Every woman will ask her neighbour and
the woman staying in her house for silver and
golden jewellery, and clothing. In these you
will dress your own sons and daughters,
despoiling the Egyptians of them.'

Moses granted miraculous powers

4 Moses replied as follows, 'But suppose
they will not believe me or listen to my
words, and say to me, "Yahweh has not
appeared to you"?' 2Yahweh then said,
'What is that in your hand?' 'A staff,' he said.
3'Throw it on the ground,' said Yahweh.
Moses threw it on the ground; the staff turned
into a snake and Moses recoiled from it.
4Yahweh then said to Moses, 'Reach out your
hand and catch it by the tail.' He reached out
his hand, caught it, and in his hand it turned
back into a staff. 5'Thus they may believe
that Yahweh, the God of their ancestors, the
God of Abraham, the God of Isaac and the
God of Jacob, has appeared to you.'
6Next, Yahweh said to him, 'Put your
hand inside your tunic.' He put his hand
inside his tunic, then drew it out again:
and his hand was diseased, white as snow.
7Yahweh then said, 'Put your hand back
inside your tunic.' He put his hand back
inside his tunic and when he drew it out,
there it was restored, just like the rest of his
flesh. 8'Even so: should they not believe you
nor be convinced by the first sign, the second
sign will convince them; 9but should they not
be convinced by either of these two signs and
refuse to listen to what you say, you are to
take some water from the River and pour it
on the ground, and the water you have taken
from the River will turn to blood on the dry
land.'

Aaron, the mouthpiece of Moses

10Moses said to Yahweh, 'Please, my Lord,
I have never been eloquent, even since you
have spoken to your servant, for I am slow
and hesitant of speech.' 11'Who gave a
person a mouth?' Yahweh said to him. 'Who

3b 'Yahweh' may be some form of the verb 'to be'. God either refuses to give a name or reveals that he is the key to existence. The Gk understands it as a statement that God is Being itself.

makes a person dumb or deaf, gives sight or makes blind? Is it not I, Yahweh? [12]Now go, I shall help you speak and instruct you what to say.'

[13]'Please, my Lord,' Moses replied, 'send anyone you decide to send!' [14]At this, Yahweh's anger kindled against Moses, and he said to him, 'There is your brother Aaron the Levite, is there not? I know that he is a good speaker. Here he comes to meet you. When he sees you, his heart will be full of joy. [15]You will speak to him and tell him what message to give. I shall help you speak, and him too, and instruct you what to do. [16]He will speak to the people in your place; he will be your mouthpiece, and you will be as the god inspiring him. [17]And take this staff in your hand; with this you will perform the signs.'

Moses leaves Midian and returns to Egypt

[18]Moses went back to his father-in-law Jethro and said to him, 'Give me leave to return to my kinsmen in Egypt and see if they are still alive.' And Jethro said to Moses, 'Go in peace.'

[19]Yahweh said to Moses in Midian, 'Go, return to Egypt, for all those who wanted to kill you are dead.' [20]So Moses took his wife and his son and, putting them on a donkey, started back for Egypt; and Moses took the staff of God in his hand. [21]Yahweh said to Moses, 'Think of the wonders I have given you power to perform, once you are back in Egypt! You are to perform them before Pharaoh, but I myself shall make him obstinate, and he will not let the people go. [22]You will then say to Pharaoh, "This is what Yahweh says: Israel is my first-born son. [23]I told you: Let my son go and worship me; but since you refuse to let him go, well then! I shall put your first-born son to death." '

The son of Moses circumcised

[24]On the journey, when he had halted for the night, Yahweh encountered him and tried to kill him. [25]Then Zipporah, taking up a flint, cut off her son's foreskin and with it touched his feet and said, 'You are my blood-bridegroom!' [26]So he let him go. She said, 'Blood-bridegroom' then, with reference to the circumcision.

Moses meets Aaron

[27]Yahweh said to Aaron, 'Go into the desert to meet Moses.' So he went, and met him at the mountain of God and kissed him. [28]Moses then told Aaron all that Yahweh had said when sending him and all the signs he had ordered him to perform. [29]Moses and Aaron then went and gathered all the elders of the Israelites together, [30]and Aaron repeated everything that Yahweh had said to Moses, and in the sight of the people performed the signs. [31]The people were convinced, and they rejoiced that Yahweh had visited the Israelites and seen their misery, and they bowed to the ground in worship.

The first audience with Pharaoh

5 After this, Moses and Aaron went to Pharaoh and said to him, 'This is what Yahweh, God of Israel, says, "Let my people go, so that they can hold a feast in my honour in the desert." ' [2]'Who is Yahweh,' Pharaoh replied, 'for me to obey what he says and let Israel go? I know nothing of Yahweh, and I will not let Israel go.' [3]'The God of the Hebrews has encountered us,' they replied. 'Give us leave to make a three-days' journey into the desert and sacrifice to Yahweh our God, or he will strike us with a plague or with the sword.' [4]The king of Egypt said to them, 'Moses and Aaron, what do you mean by distracting the people from their work? Get back to your forced labour.' [5]And Pharaoh said, 'Now that the people have grown to such numbers in the country, what do you mean by interrupting their forced labour?'

Instructions to the taskmasters

[6]That very day, Pharaoh gave the order to the people's taskmasters and their scribes, [7]'Do not go on providing the people with straw for brickmaking as before; let them go and gather straw for themselves. [8]But you will exact the same quantity of bricks from them as before, not reducing it at all, since they are lazy, and that is why their cry is, "Let us go and sacrifice to our God." [9]Give these people more work to do, and see they do it instead of listening to lying speeches.'

[10]The people's taskmasters and scribes

went out to speak to the people and said,
'Pharaoh says this, "I shall not provide you
with any more straw. [11]Go and collect straw
for yourselves where you can find it. But your
output is not to be any less." ' [12]So the people
scattered all over Egypt to gather stubble
for their straw. [13]The taskmasters harassed
them. 'You must complete your daily quota,'
they said, 'just as when the straw was there.'
[14]And the Israelites' foremen whom
Pharaoh's taskmasters had put in charge of
them, were flogged and asked, 'Why have
you not fulfilled your quota of bricks made
today as before?'

The Hebrew scribes complain

[15]The Israelites' foremen went and appealed
to Pharaoh. 'Why do you treat your servants
like this?' they said. [16]'No straw is provided
for your servants, yet still the cry is, "Make
bricks!" And now your servants are being
flogged!. . .' [17]'You are lazy, lazy,' he
retorted. 'That is why you say, "Let us go
and sacrifice to Yahweh." [18]Get back to your
work at once. You will not be provided with
straw; all the same, you will deliver the quota
of bricks.'

Recriminations of the people
Prayer of Moses

[19]The Israelites' foremen saw they were in a
difficult position on being told, 'You will not
reduce your daily production of bricks.' [20]As
they left Pharaoh's presence, they met Moses
and Aaron who were standing in their way.
[21]'May Yahweh look down at you and judge!'
they said to them. 'You have brought us into
bad odour with Pharaoh and his officials; you
have put a sword into their hand to kill us.'
[22]Moses went back to Yahweh and said,
'Lord, why do you treat this people so
harshly? Why did you send me? [23]Ever since
I came to Pharaoh and spoke to him in your
name, he has ill-treated this people, and you
have done nothing at all about rescuing your
people.'

6 Yahweh then said to Moses, 'Now you
will see what I am going to do to Pharaoh.
A mighty hand will force him to let them go,
a mighty hand will force him to expel them
from his country.'

Another account of the call of Moses[a]

[2]God spoke to Moses and said to him, 'I am
Yahweh. [3]To Abraham, Isaac and Jacob I
appeared as El Shaddai, but I did not make
my name Yahweh known to them. [4]I also
made my covenant with them to give them
the land of Canaan, the country in which they
were living as aliens. [5]Furthermore, I have
heard the groaning of the Israelites, enslaved
by the Egyptians, and have remembered my
covenant. [6]So say to the Israelites, "I am
Yahweh. I shall free you from the forced
labour of the Egyptians; I shall rescue you
from their slavery and I shall redeem you
with outstretched arm and mighty acts of
judgement. [7]I shall take you as my people
and I shall be your God. And you will know
that I am Yahweh your God, who have freed
you from the forced labour of the Egyptians.
[8]Then I shall lead you into the country which
I swore I would give to Abraham, Isaac and
Jacob, and shall give it to you as your heritage,
I, Yahweh." ' [9]And Moses repeated this to
the Israelites, but they would not listen to
Moses, so crushed was their spirit and so
cruel their slavery.

[10]Yahweh then said to Moses, [11]'Go to
Pharaoh, king of Egypt, and tell him to
let the Israelites leave his country.' [12]But
Moses spoke out in Yahweh's presence and
said, 'The Israelites have not listened to me,
so why should Pharaoh take any notice of a
poor speaker like me?' [13]Yahweh spoke to
Moses and Aaron and sent them to Pharaoh
king of Egypt, to lead the Israelites out of
Egypt.

The genealogy of Moses and Aaron

[14]These were their heads of families:

The sons of Reuben, Israel's first-born:
Hanoch, Pallu, Hezron and Carmi: these are
the clans of Reuben.

[15]The sons of Simeon: Jemuel, Jamin,
Ohad, Jachin, Zohar, and Shaul son of the
Canaanite woman: these are the clans of
Simeon.

[16]These were the names of the sons of Levi
with their descendants: Gershon, Kohath
and Merari. Levi lived for a hundred and
thirty-seven years.

[17]The sons of Gershon: Libni and Shimei,
with their clans.

6a =3:1—4:23.

18 The sons of Kohath: Amram, Izhar,
Hebron and Uzziel. Kohath lived for a
hundred and thirty-three years.
19 The sons of Merari: Mahli and Mushi.
These are the clans of Levi with their
descendants.
20 Amram married Jochebed, his aunt, who
bore him Aaron and Moses. Amram lived for
a hundred and thirty-seven years.
21 The sons of Izhar were: Korah, Nepheg
and Zichri.
22 And the sons of Uzziel: Mishael, Elza-
phan and Sithri.
23 Aaron married Elisheba daughter of
Amminadab and sister of Nahshon, and she
bore him Nadab, Abihu, Eleazar and
Ithamar.
24 The sons of Korah: Assir, Elkanah and
Abiasaph. These are the clans of the
Korahites.
25 Eleazar, son of Aaron, married one of
Putiel's daughters who bore him Phinehas.
These were the Levitical heads of families,
according to clan.
26 It was to this Aaron and Moses that
Yahweh said, 'Lead the Israelites out of
Egypt in their armies.' 27 It was they who
spoke to Pharaoh, king of Egypt, to lead the
Israelites out of Egypt—namely Moses and
Aaron.

The narrative of Moses' call, continued

28 Now the day when Yahweh spoke to Moses
in Egypt, 29 Yahweh said to Moses, 'Tell
Pharaoh king of Egypt everything that I am
going to say to you.' 30 But Moses said to
Yahweh's face, 'I am a poor speaker, so why
should Pharaoh take any notice of me?'

7 Yahweh then said to Moses, 'Look, I have
made you as a god for Pharaoh, and your
brother Aaron is to be your prophet. 2 You
must say whatever I command you, and your
brother Aaron will repeat to Pharaoh that he
is to let the Israelites leave his country. 3 But
I myself shall make Pharaoh stubborn and
shall perform many a sign and wonder in
Egypt. 4 Since Pharaoh will not listen to
you, I shall lay my hand on Egypt and with
great acts of judgement lead my armies, my
people, the Israelites, out of Egypt. 5 And
the Egyptians will know that I am Yahweh
when I stretch out my hand against the
Egyptians and lead the Israelites out of their
country.'
6 Moses and Aaron did exactly as Yahweh
had ordered. 7 Moses was eighty years old
and Aaron eighty-three, when they spoke to
Pharaoh.

D: THE PLAGUES OF EGYPT

The staff turned into a snake

8 Yahweh said to Moses and Aaron, 9 'If
Pharaoh says to you, "Display some marvel,"
you must say to Aaron, "Take your staff and
throw it down in front of Pharaoh, and let it
turn into a serpent!" ' 10 Moses and Aaron
went to Pharaoh and did as Yahweh had
ordered. Aaron threw down his staff in front
of Pharaoh and his officials, and it turned
into a serpent. 11 Then Pharaoh in his turn
called for the sages and sorcerers, and by
their spells the magicians of Egypt did the
same. 12 Each threw his staff down and these
turned into serpents. But Aaron's staff swal-
lowed up theirs. 13 Pharaoh, however,
remained obstinate and, as Yahweh had fore-
told, refused to listen to Moses and Aaron.

The first plague: the water turns to blood

14 Yahweh then said to Moses, 'Pharaoh is
adamant. He refuses to let the people go.
15 Go to Pharaoh tomorrow morning as he
makes his way to the water, confront him on
the river bank and in your hand take the
staff that turned into a snake. 16 Say to him,
"Yahweh, God of the Hebrews, sent me to
say: Let my people go and worship in the
desert. Up till now, you have refused to
listen. 17 This is what Yahweh says: You
will know that I am Yahweh by this: with the
staff that is in my hand I shall strike the
waters of the River and they will turn to
blood. 18 The fish in the river will die, and
the River will stink, and the Egyptians will
not be able to drink the river water." '
19 Yahweh said to Moses, 'Say to Aaron,
"Take your staff and stretch out your hand
over the waters of Egypt—over their rivers
and canals, their marshland, and all their
reservoirs—and they will turn to blood.
There will be blood throughout the whole of
Egypt, even in sticks and stones." '
20 Moses and Aaron did as Yahweh ordered.
He raised his staff and struck the waters of
the River, with Pharaoh and his officials
looking on, and all the water in the River
turned to blood. 21 The fish in the River

died, and the River stank; and the Egyptians
could no longer drink the River water.
Throughout the whole of Egypt there was
blood. 22But by their spells the magicians
of Egypt did the same; Pharaoh remained
obstinate and, as Yahweh had foretold,
refused to listen to Moses and Aaron.
23Pharaoh turned away and went back into
his palace, taking no notice even of this.
24And the Egyptians all dug holes along the
river-bank in search of drinking water, since
they could not drink the River water. 25After
Yahweh struck the River, seven days went
by.

The second plague: the frogs

26Then Yahweh said to Moses, 'Go to
Pharaoh and say to him, "Yahweh says this:
Let my people go and worship me. 27If you
refuse to let them go, I shall strike your whole
territory with frogs. 28The River will swarm
with frogs; they will make their way into your
palace, into your bedroom, onto your bed,
into the houses of your officials and subjects,
into your ovens, into your kneading bowls.
29The frogs will actually clamber onto you,
onto your subjects and onto all your
officials." '
8 Yahweh then said to Moses, 'Say to Aaron,
"Stretch out your hand with your staff,
over the rivers, the canals and the marshland,
and bring the frogs up over the land of
Egypt." ' 2So Aaron stretched out his hand
over the waters of Egypt, and the frogs came
up and covered the land of Egypt. 3But
by their spells the magicians did the same,
bringing frogs over the land of Egypt.
4Pharaoh then summoned Moses and
Aaron and said, 'Entreat Yahweh to take the
frogs away from me and my subjects, and I
promise to let the people go and sacrifice to
Yahweh.' 5Moses said to Pharaoh, 'You are
the one to gain by it: when would you like
me to pray for you, your officials and your
subjects, so as to rid you and your houses of
the frogs so that they will be left only in the
River?' 6'Tomorrow,' he said. Moses said,
'It shall be as you say, so that you will know
that there is no one like Yahweh our God.
7The frogs will leave you, your houses, your
officials and your subjects and will be left
only in the River.' 8Moses and Aaron left
Pharaoh's presence, and Moses pleaded with
Yahweh about the frogs which he had
inflicted on Pharaoh. 9Yahweh did as Moses
asked, and in house and courtyard and field
the frogs died. 10They piled them up in heaps
and the country stank. 11But once Pharaoh
saw that there had been a respite, he became
obstinate and, as Yahweh had foretold,
refused to listen to them.

The third plague: the mosquitoes

12Yahweh then said to Moses, 'Say to Aaron,
" Stretch out your staff and strike the dust of
the earth, and it will turn into mosquitoes
throughout the whole of Egypt." ' 13Aaron
stretched out his hand, with his staff, and
struck the dust of the earth, and there were
mosquitoes on man and beast; all the dust of
the earth turned into mosquitoes throughout
the whole of Egypt. 14By their spells the
magicians tried to produce mosquitoes in
the same way but failed, and there were
mosquitoes on man and beast. 15So the
magicians said to Pharaoh, 'This is the finger
of God.' But Pharaoh was obstinate and, as
Yahweh had foretold, refused to listen to
them.

The fourth plague: the horseflies

16Yahweh then said to Moses, 'Get up early
in the morning and confront Pharaoh as he
makes his way to the water. Say to him,
"Yahweh says this: Let my people go and
worship me. 17But if you will not let my
people go, I shall send horseflies on you, on
your officials, your subjects and your houses.
The Egyptians' houses will swarm with
horseflies, and so will the very ground they
stand on. 18But I shall exempt the region of
Goshen, where my people are living, that
day; there will be no horseflies there, so that
you will know that I am Yahweh, here in this
country. 19I shall make a distinction between
my people and your people. This sign will
take place tomorrow." ' 20Yahweh did this,
and great swarms of horseflies found their
way into Pharaoh's palace, into his officials'
houses and all over Egypt; the country was
ruined by the horseflies.
21Pharaoh then summoned Moses and
Aaron and said, 'Go and sacrifice to your
God, inside the country.' 22'That would never
do,' Moses said, 'since what we sacrifice
to Yahweh our God is outrageous to the
Egyptians. If the Egyptians see us offering
sacrifices which outrage them, won't they
stone us? 23We shall make a three-days'

journey into the desert to sacrifice to Yahweh
our God, as he has ordered us.' 24Pharaoh
said, 'I will let you go and sacrifice to Yahweh
your God in the desert, provided you do not
go very far. Pray for me.' 25'The moment
I leave you,' Moses said, 'I shall pray to
Yahweh. Tomorrow morning the horseflies
will leave Pharaoh, his officials and his
subjects. But Pharaoh must stop trifling with
us by not allowing the people to go and
sacrifice to Yahweh.' 26Moses then left
Pharaoh's presence and prayed to Yahweh,
27and Yahweh did as Moses asked; the horse-
flies left Pharaoh, his officials and his
subjects: not one remained. 28But Pharaoh
became obstinate this time too and did not
let the people go.

The fifth plague: death of the Egyptians' livestock

9Yahweh then said to Moses, 'Go to
Pharaoh and say to him, "Yahweh, God
of the Hebrews, says this: Let my people go
and worship me. 2If you refuse to let them
go and detain them any longer, 3look, the
hand of Yahweh will strike your livestock in
the fields, horses, donkeys, camels, oxen and
flocks with a deadly plague. 4Yahweh will
discriminate between the livestock of Israel
and the livestock of Egypt: nothing of what
belongs to the Israelites will die. 5Yahweh
has fixed the time. Tomorrow, he has said,
Yahweh will do this in the country." ' 6Next
day Yahweh did this: all the Egyptians' live-
stock died, but nothing of the livestock
owned by the Israelites died. 7Pharaoh had
enquiries made, and found that of the live-
stock owned by the Israelites not a single
beast had died. But Pharaoh was obstinate
and did not let the people go.

The sixth plague: the boils

8Yahweh then said to Moses and Aaron,
'Take handfuls of soot from the kiln, and
before Pharaoh's eyes let Moses throw it in
the air. 9It will turn into fine dust over the
whole of Egypt and produce boils breaking
into sores on man and beast throughout the
whole of Egypt.' 10So they took soot from the
kiln and stood in front of Pharaoh, and Moses
threw it in the air, and on man and beast it
brought out boils breaking into sores. 11And
the magicians could not compete with Moses
in the matter of the boils, for the magicians
were covered with boils like all the other
Egyptians. 12But Yahweh made Pharaoh
stubborn and, as Yahweh had foretold to
Moses, he did not listen to them.

The seventh plague: the hail

13Yahweh then said to Moses, 'Get up early
in the morning and confront Pharaoh. Say to
him, "Yahweh, God of the Hebrews, says
this: Let my people go and worship me. 14For
this time I am going to inflict all my plagues
on you, on your officials and on your subjects,
so that you will know that there is no one like
me in the whole world. 15Had I stretched out
my hand to strike you and your subjects with
pestilence, you would have been swept from
the earth. 16But I have let you survive for this
reason: to display my power to you and
to have my name talked of throughout the
world. 17Since you take a high hand with my
people, refusing to let them go, 18very well,
at about this time tomorrow, I shall cause so
severe a hail to fall as was never known in
Egypt from the day of its foundation until
now. 19So now send word to have your live-
stock and everything else you own in the
fields put under cover. On man or beast, all
that happen to be in the fields and are not
brought indoors, the hail will fall and they
will die." '

20Those of Pharaoh's officials who
respected what Yahweh said, brought their
slaves and livestock indoors, 21but those who
did not take to heart what Yahweh said left
their slaves and livestock in the fields.

22Yahweh then said to Moses, 'Stretch out
your hand towards heaven so that it hails
throughout the whole of Egypt, on man and
beast and on everything growing anywhere
in Egypt.' 23Moses stretched out his staff
towards heaven, and Yahweh thundered and
rained down hail. Lightning struck the earth
and Yahweh rained down hail on Egypt.
24And so there was hail, and lightning
accompanied the hail, very severe, such as
had never been known anywhere in Egypt
since it first became a nation. 25All over Egypt
the hail struck down everything in the fields,
man and beast, and the hail beat down every-
thing growing in the fields and shattered all
the trees in the fields. 26The only place where
there was no hail was in the Goshen region,
where the Israelites lived.

27Pharaoh then sent for Moses and Aaron
and said, 'This time, I have sinned. Yahweh

is in the right; I and my subjects are in the
wrong. 28Pray to Yahweh, for we cannot bear
any more of this thunder and hail. I promise
to let you go. You need stay no longer.'
29Moses said to him, 'The moment I leave
the city I shall stretch out my hands to
Yahweh. The thunder will stop, and there
will be no more hail, so that you may know
that the earth belongs to Yahweh. 30But as
for you and your officials, I know very well
that you still have no respect for Yahweh
God.' 31The flax and the barley were ruined,
since the barley was in the ear and the flax in
bud, 32but the wheat and spelt were not
destroyed, being late crops.

33Moses left Pharaoh and went out of the
city. He stretched out his hands to Yahweh
and the thunder and hail ceased and the rain
stopped pouring down on the earth. 34When
Pharaoh saw that rain and hail and thunder
had stopped, he relapsed into sin, 35and
he and his officials became obstinate again.
Pharaoh was stubborn and, as Yahweh had
foretold through Moses, refused to let the
Israelites go.

The eighth plague: the locusts

10 Yahweh then said to Moses, 'Go to
Pharaoh, for I have made him and his
officials stubborn, to display these signs of
mine among them; 2so that you can tell
your sons and your grandsons how I made
fools of the Egyptians and what signs I
performed among them, so that you would
know that I am Yahweh.' 3Moses and
Aaron then went to Pharaoh and said to him,
'Yahweh, God of the Hebrews, says this,
"How much longer will you refuse to submit
to me? Let my people go and worship me.
4Or, if you refuse to let my people go,
tomorrow I shall send locusts into your
country. 5They will cover the surface of the
soil so that the soil cannot be seen. They will
devour the remainder of what has escaped,
of what you have been left after the hail; they
will devour all your trees growing in the
fields; 6they will fill your houses, all your
officials' houses and all the Egyptians'
houses—something your ancestors and your
ancestors' ancestors have never seen from the
day they first appeared on earth until now." '
Then he turned on his heel and left Pharaoh's
presence. 7At which, Pharaoh's officials said
to him, 'How much longer are we to be
tricked by this fellow? Let the people go and
worship Yahweh their God. Do you not
finally realise that Egypt is on the brink of
ruin?'

8So Moses and Aaron were brought back
to Pharaoh who said to them, 'Go and worship
Yahweh your God. But who are to go?'
9Moses replied, 'We shall take our young
men and our old men, we shall take our sons
and daughters, our flocks and our herds,
since we are going to hold a feast in Yahweh's
honour.' 10Pharaoh said, 'So I must let you go
with your wives and children! May Yahweh
preserve you! Plainly, you are up to no good!
11Oh no! You men may go and worship
Yahweh, since that was your original
request.' With that, they were driven from
Pharaoh's presence.

12Yahweh then said to Moses, 'Stretch out
your hand over Egypt for the locusts. Let
them invade Egypt and devour whatever is
growing in the country, whatever the hail has
left!' 13Moses stretched his staff over Egypt,
and over the country Yahweh sent an east
wind which blew all that day and night. By
morning, the east wind had brought the
locusts.

14The locusts invaded the whole of Egypt
and settled all over Egypt, in great swarms;
never had there been so many locusts before,
nor would there be again. 15They covered
the surface of the ground till the land was
devastated. They devoured whatever was
growing in the fields and all the fruit on the
trees that the hail had left. No green was left
on tree or plant in the fields anywhere in
Egypt.

16Pharaoh sent urgently for Moses and
Aaron and said, 'I have sinned against
Yahweh your God and against you. 17Now
forgive my sin, I implore you, just this once,
and entreat Yahweh your God to turn this
deadly thing away from me.' 18When Moses
left Pharaoh's presence he prayed to Yahweh,
19and Yahweh changed the wind into a west
wind, very strong, which carried the locusts
away and swept them into the Sea of Reeds.
There was not one locust left in the whole of
Egypt. 20But Yahweh made Pharaoh stub-
born, and he did not let the Israelites go.

The ninth plague: the darkness

21Yahweh then said to Moses, 'Stretch out
your hand towards heaven, and let darkness,
darkness so thick that it can be felt, cover
Egypt.' 22So Moses stretched out his hand

towards heaven, and for three days there was thick darkness over the whole of Egypt. [23]No one could see anyone else or move about for three days, but all the Israelites did have light where they were living.

[24]Pharaoh summoned Moses and said, 'Go and worship Yahweh, but your flocks and herds are to stay here. Your wives and children can go with you too.' [25]Moses said, 'But now you must give us sacrifices and burnt offerings to offer to Yahweh our God. [26]And our livestock will go with us too; not a hoof will be left behind; for we may need animals from these to worship Yahweh our God; for until we get there we ourselves cannot tell how we are to worship Yahweh.'

[27]But Yahweh made Pharaoh stubborn, and he refused to let them go. [28]Pharaoh said to Moses, 'Out of my sight! Be sure you never see my face again, for the next time you see my face you die!' [29]Moses then said, 'You yourself have said it. I shall never see your face again.'

Announcement of the death of the first-born

11 Yahweh then said to Moses, 'I shall inflict one more plague on Pharaoh and Egypt, after which he will let you go away. When he lets you go, he will actually drive you out! [2]Now instruct the people that every man is to ask his neighbour, and every woman hers, for silver and golden jewellery.' [3]And Yahweh made the Egyptians impressed with the people, while Moses himself was a man of great importance in Egypt in the opinion of Pharaoh's officials and the people.

[4]Moses then said, 'Yahweh says this, "At midnight I shall pass through Egypt, [5]and all the first-born in Egypt will die, from the first-born of Pharaoh, heir to his throne, to the first-born of the slave-girl at the mill, and all the first-born of the livestock. [6]And throughout Egypt there will be great wailing, such as never was before, nor will be again. [7]But against the Israelites, whether man or beast, never a dog shall bark, so that you may know that Yahweh discriminates between Egypt and Israel. [8]Then all these officials of yours will come down to me and, bowing low before me, say: Go away, you and all the people who follow you! After which, I shall go." ' And, hot with anger, he left Pharaoh's presence.

[9]Yahweh then said to Moses, 'Pharaoh will not listen to you, so that more of my wonders may be displayed in Egypt.' [10]Moses and Aaron worked all these wonders in Pharaoh's presence, but Yahweh made Pharaoh stubborn, and he did not let the Israelites leave his country.

E: THE PASSOVER[a]

12 Yahweh said to Moses and Aaron in Egypt, [2]'This month must be the first of all the months for you, the first month of your year. [3]Speak to the whole community of Israel and say, "On the tenth day of this month each man must take an animal from the flock for his family: one animal for each household. [4]If the household is too small for the animal, he must join with his neighbour nearest to his house, depending on the number of persons. When you choose the animal, you will take into account what each can eat. [5]It must be an animal without blemish, a male one year old; you may choose it either from the sheep or from the goats. [6]You must keep it till the fourteenth day of the month when the whole assembly of the community of Israel will slaughter it at twilight. [7]Some of the blood must then be taken and put on both door-posts and the lintel of the houses where it is eaten. [8]That night, the flesh must be eaten, roasted over the fire; it must be eaten with unleavened bread and bitter herbs. [9]Do not eat any of it raw or boiled in water, but roasted over the fire, with the head, feet and entrails. [10]You must not leave any of it over till the morning: whatever is left till morning you must burn. [11]This is how you must eat it: with a belt round your waist, your sandals on your feet and your staff in your hand. You must eat it hurriedly: it is a Passover in Yahweh's honour. [12]That night, I shall go through Egypt and strike down all the first-born in Egypt, man and beast alike, and shall execute justice on all the gods of Egypt, I, Yahweh! [13]The blood will be a sign for you on the houses where you are. When I see the blood I shall pass over you, and you will escape

---

12a Once a herdsmen's new year festival, it receives a new meaning as the memorial of the exodus. The Feast of Unleavened Bread, an agricultural feast, is of separate origin.

the destructive plague when I strike Egypt. [14]This day must be commemorated by you, and you must keep it as a feast in Yahweh's honour. You must keep it as a feast-day for all generations; this is a decree for all time.

The feast of Unleavened Bread

[15]"For seven days you must eat unleavened bread. On the first day you must clean the leaven out of your houses, for anyone who eats leavened bread from the first to the seventh day must be outlawed from Israel. [16]On the first day you must hold a sacred assembly, and on the seventh day a sacred assembly. On those days no work may be done; you will prepare only what each requires to eat. [17]You must keep the feast of Unleavened Bread because it was on that same day that I brought your armies out of Egypt. You will keep that day, generation after generation; this is a decree for all time. [18]In the first month, from the evening of the fourteenth day until the evening of the twenty-first day, you must eat unleavened bread. [19]For seven days there may be no leaven in your houses, since anyone, either stranger or citizen of the country, who eats leavened bread will be outlawed from the community of Israel. [20]You will eat nothing with leaven in it; wherever you live, you will eat unleavened bread." '

Injunctions relating to the Passover

[21]Moses summoned all the elders of Israel and said to them, 'Go and choose a lamb or kid for your families, and kill the Passover victim. [22]Then take a bunch of hyssop, dip it in the blood that is in the basin, and with the blood from the basin touch the lintel and both door-posts; then let none of you venture out of the house till morning. [23]Then, when Yahweh goes through Egypt to strike it, and sees the blood on the lintel and on both door-posts, he will pass over the door and not allow the Destroyer to enter your homes and strike. [24]You will observe this as a decree binding you and your children for all time, [25]and when you have entered the country which Yahweh will give you, as he has promised, you will observe this ritual. [26]And when your children ask you, "What does this ritual mean?" [27]you will tell them, "It is the Passover sacrifice in honour of Yahweh who passed over the houses of the Israelites in Egypt, and struck Egypt but spared our houses." ' And the people bowed in worship. [28]The Israelites then went away and did as Yahweh had ordered Moses and Aaron.

The tenth plague: death of the first-born

[29]And at midnight Yahweh struck down all the first-born in Egypt from the first-born of Pharaoh, heir to his throne, to the first-born of the prisoner in the dungeon, and the first-born of all the livestock. [30]Pharaoh and all his officials and all the Egyptians got up in the night, and there was great wailing in Egypt, for there was not a house without its dead. [31]It was still dark when Pharaoh summoned Moses and Aaron and said, 'Up, leave my subjects, you and the Israelites! Go and worship Yahweh as you have asked! [32]And take your flocks and herds as you have asked, and go! And bless me too!' [33]The Egyptians urged the people on and hurried them out of the country because, they said, 'Otherwise we shall all be dead.' [34]So the people carried off their dough still unleavened, their bowls wrapped in their cloaks, on their shoulders.

The Egyptians plundered

[35]The Israelites did as Moses had told them and asked the Egyptians for silver and golden jewellery, and clothing. [36]Yahweh made the Egyptians so much impressed with the people that they gave them what they asked. So they despoiled the Egyptians.

Israel's departure

[37]The Israelites left Rameses for Succoth, about six hundred thousand on the march—men, that is, not counting their families. [38]A mixed crowd of people went with them, and flocks and herds, quantities of livestock. [39]And with the dough which they had brought from Egypt they baked unleavened cakes, because the dough had not risen, since they had been driven out of Egypt without time to linger or to prepare food for themselves. [40]The time that the Israelites spent in Egypt was four hundred and thirty years. [41]And on the very day the four hundred and thirty years ended, all Yahweh's armies left Egypt. [42]The night when Yahweh kept vigil to bring them out of Egypt must be kept as

a vigil in honour of Yahweh by all Israelites,
for all generations.

Ordinances for the Passover

43 Yahweh said to Moses and Aaron, 'This is
the ritual for the Passover: no alien may eat
it, 44 but any slave bought for money may eat
it, once you have circumcised him. 45 No
stranger and no hired servant may eat it. 46 It
must be eaten in one house alone; you will
not take any of the meat out of the house; nor
may you break any of its bones.

47 'The whole community of Israel must
keep it. 48 Should a stranger residing with
you wish to keep the Passover in honour of
Yahweh, all the males of his household must
be circumcised: he will then be allowed to
keep it and will count as a citizen of the
country. But no uncircumcised person may
eat it. 49 The same law will apply to the citizen
and the stranger resident among you.' 50 The
Israelites all did as Yahweh had ordered
Moses and Aaron, 51 and that same day
Yahweh brought the Israelites out of Egypt
in their armies.

The first-born

13 Yahweh spoke to Moses and said,
2 'Consecrate all the first-born to me,
the first birth from every womb, among the
Israelites. Whether man or beast, it is mine.'

The feast of Unleavened Bread

3 Moses said to the people, 'Remember this
day, on which you came out of Egypt, from
the place of slave-labour, for by the strength
of his hand Yahweh brought you out of it; no
leavened bread may be eaten. 4 On this day,
in the month of Abib, you are leaving, 5 and
when Yahweh has brought you into the
country of the Canaanites, the Hittites, the
Amorites, the Hivites and the Jebusites,
flowing with milk and honey, which he swore
to your ancestors that he would give you,
then you must observe this rite in the same
month. 6 For seven days you will eat
unleavened bread, and on the seventh day
there must be a feast in Yahweh's honour.
7 During these seven days unleavened bread
may be eaten; no leavened bread may be seen
among you, no leaven among you throughout
your territory. 8 And on that day you will
explain to your son, "This is because of what
Yahweh did for me when I came out of
Egypt." 9 This will serve as a sign on your
hand would serve, or a reminder on your
forehead, and in that way the law of Yahweh
will be ever on your lips: for with a mighty
hand Yahweh brought you out of Egypt.
10 You shall observe this law at its appointed
time, year by year.

The first-born

11 'When Yahweh has brought you into the
Canaanites' country, as he swore to you and
your ancestors that he would, and given it
to you, 12 to Yahweh you must make over
whatever first issues from the womb, and
every first-born cast by animals belonging to
you: these males belong to Yahweh. 13 But
every first-born donkey you will redeem with
a lamb or kid; if you do not redeem it, you
must break its neck. All the human first-
born, however, among your sons, you will
redeem. 14 And when your son asks you in
days to come, "What does this mean?" you
will tell him, "By the strength of his hand
Yahweh brought us out of Egypt, out of
the place of slave-labour. 15 When Pharaoh
stubbornly refused to let us go, Yahweh
killed all the first-born in Egypt, of man and
beast alike. This is why I sacrifice every male
first issuing from the womb to Yahweh and
redeem every first-born of my sons." 16 This
will serve as a sign on your hand would serve,
or a headband on your forehead, for by the
strength of his hand Yahweh brought us out
of Egypt.'

F: THE DEPARTURE FROM EGYPT

The departure of the Israelites

17 When Pharaoh had let the people go, God
did not let them take the road to the Phili-
stines' territory, although that was the
shortest, 'in case', God thought, 'the prospect
of fighting makes the people change their
minds and turn back to Egypt.' 18 Instead,
God led the people a roundabout way through
the desert of the Sea of Reeds. The Israelites
left Egypt fully armed. 19 Moses took with
him the bones of Joseph, since Joseph had
put the Israelites on solemn oath with the
words, 'It is sure that God will visit you,' he
had said, 'and when that day comes you must
take my bones away from here with you.'

[20]They set out from Succoth and
encamped at Etham, on the edge of the
desert.
[21]Yahweh preceded them, by day in a pillar
of cloud to show them the way, and by night
in a pillar of fire to give them light, so that
they could march by day and by night. [22]The
pillar of cloud never left its place ahead of the
people during the day, nor the pillar of fire
during the night.

From Etham to the Sea of Reeds

14 Yahweh spoke to Moses and said, [2]'Tell
the Israelites to turn back and pitch
camp in front of Pi-Hahiroth, between
Migdol and the sea, facing Baal-Zephon. You
must pitch your camp opposite this place,
beside the sea, [3]and then Pharaoh will think,
"The Israelites are wandering to and fro in
the countryside; the desert has closed in on
them." [4]I shall then make Pharaoh stubborn
and he will set out in pursuit of them; and I
shall win glory for myself at the expense of
Pharaoh and his whole army, and then the
Egyptians will know that I am Yahweh.' And
the Israelites did this.

The Egyptians pursue the Israelites

[5]When Pharaoh king of Egypt was told that
the people had fled, he and his officials
changed their attitude towards the people.
'What have we done,' they said, 'allowing
Israel to leave our service?' [6]So Pharaoh had
his chariot harnessed and set out with his
troops, [7]taking six hundred of the best char-
iots and all the other chariots in Egypt, with
officers in each. [8]Yahweh made Pharaoh king
of Egypt stubborn, and he gave chase to the
Israelites. The Israelites marched confidently
away, [9]but the Egyptians, all Pharaoh's
horses, his chariots, his horsemen and his
army, gave chase and caught up with them
where they lay encamped beside the sea
near Pi-Hahiroth, facing Baal-Zephon. [10]As
Pharaoh approached, the Israelites looked
up—and there were the Egyptians in pursuit
of them! The Israelites were terrified and
cried out to Yahweh for help. [11]To Moses
they said, 'Was it for lack of graves in Egypt,
that you had to lead us out to die in the desert?
What was the point of bringing us out of
Egypt? [12]Did we not tell you as much in
Egypt? Leave us alone, we said, we would
rather work for the Egyptians! We prefer to
work for the Egyptians than to die in the
desert!' [13]Moses said to the people, 'Do not
be afraid! Stand firm, and you will see what
Yahweh will do to rescue you today: the
Egyptians you see today you will never see
again. [14]Yahweh will do the fighting for you;
all you need to do is to keep calm.'

The miracle of the sea

[15]Yahweh then said to Moses, 'Why cry out
to me? Tell the Israelites to march on. [16]Your
part is to raise your staff and stretch out your
hand over the sea and divide it, so that the
Israelites can walk through the sea on dry
ground, [17]while I, for my part, shall make
the Egyptians so stubborn that they will
follow them, and I shall win glory for myself
at the expense of Pharaoh and all his army,
chariots and horsemen. [18]And when I have
won glory for myself at the expense of
Pharaoh and his chariots and horsemen, the
Egyptians will know that I am Yahweh.'
[19]Then the angel of God, who preceded
the army of Israel, changed station and
followed behind them. The pillar of cloud
moved from their front and took position
behind them. [20]It came between the army
of the Egyptians and the army of Israel. The
cloud was dark, and the night passed without
the one drawing any closer to the other the
whole night long. [21]Then Moses stretched
out his hand over the sea, and Yahweh drove
the sea back with a strong easterly wind all
night and made the sea into dry land. The
waters were divided [22]and the Israelites
went on dry ground right through the sea,
with walls of water to right and left of them.
[23]The Egyptians gave chase, and all
Pharaoh's horses, chariots and horsemen
went into the sea after them. [24]In the
morning watch, Yahweh looked down on the
army of the Egyptians from the pillar of fire
and cloud and threw the Egyptian army into
confusion. [25]He so clogged their chariot
wheels that they drove on only with difficulty,
which made the Egyptians say, 'Let us flee
from Israel, for Yahweh is fighting on their
side against the Egyptians!' [26]Then
Yahweh said to Moses, 'Stretch out your
hand over the sea and let the waters flow back
on the Egyptians and on their chariots and
their horsemen.' [27]Moses stretched out his
hand over the sea and, as day broke, the sea
returned to its bed. The fleeing Egyptians
ran straight into it, and Yahweh overthrew

the Egyptians in the middle of the sea.
28The returning waters washed right over
the chariots and horsemen of Pharaoh's
entire army, which had followed the Israel-
ites into the sea; not a single one of them
was left. 29The Israelites, however, had
marched through the sea on dry ground,
with walls of water to right and left of them.
30That day, Yahweh rescued Israel from
the clutches of the Egyptians, and Israel saw
the Egyptians lying dead on the sea-shore.
31When Israel saw the mighty deed that
Yahweh had performed against the Egyp-
tians, the people revered Yahweh and put
their faith in Yahweh and in Moses,
his servant.

Song of victory

15 It was then that Moses and the Israelites sang this song in Yahweh's honour:

I shall sing to Yahweh,
for he has covered himself in glory,
horse and rider
he has thrown into the sea.
2Yah is my strength and my song,
to him I owe my deliverance.
He is my God and I shall praise him,
my father's God and I shall extol him.
3Yahweh is a warrior;
Yahweh is his name.

4Pharaoh's chariots and army
he has hurled into the sea
the pick of his officers
have been drowned in the Sea of Reeds.
5The ocean has closed over them;
they have sunk to the bottom like a stone.
6Your right hand, Yahweh,
wins glory by its strength,
your right hand, Yahweh,
shatters your foes,
7and by your great majesty
you fell your assailants;
you unleash your fury,
it consumes them like chaff.
8A blast from your nostrils
and the waters piled high;
the waves stood firm as a dyke;
the bed of the sea became firm ground.

9The enemy said,
'I shall give chase and overtake,
'I shall share out the spoil
and glut myself on them,
'I shall draw my sword,
my hand will destroy them.'
10You blew with your breath,
the sea closed over them;
they sank like lead in the terrible waters.
11Yahweh, who is like you,
majestic in sanctity,
who like you among the holy ones,
fearsome of deed, worker of wonders?
12You stretched your right hand out,
the earth swallowed them!
13In your faithful love you led out
the people you had redeemed,
in your strength you have guided them
to your holy dwelling.

14Hearing of this, the peoples tremble;
pangs seize on the people of Philistia;
15the chieftains of Edom are dismayed,
Moab's princes—panic has seized them,
all the inhabitants of Canaan
have melted away.
16On them fall terror and dread;
through the power of your arm
they are still as stone
while your people are passing, Yahweh,
while the people you have purchased
are passing.
17You will bring them in and plant them
on the mountain which is your heritage,
the place which you, Yahweh,
have made your dwelling,
the sanctuary, Yahweh,
prepared by your own hands.
18 Yahweh will be king
for ever and ever.

19For when Pharaoh's cavalry, with his
chariots and horsemen, had gone into the
sea, Yahweh brought the waters of the sea
back over them, though the Israelites went
on dry ground right through the sea.
20The prophetess Miriam, Aaron's sister,
took up a tambourine, and all the women
followed her with tambourines, dancing,
21while Miriam took up from them the
refrain:

Sing to Yahweh,
for he has covered himself in glory,
horse and rider
he has thrown into the sea.

II: THE JOURNEY THROUGH THE DESERT

Marah

22Moses led Israel away from the Sea of
Reeds, and they entered the desert of Shur.
They then travelled through the desert for
three days without finding water. 23When
they reached Marah, they could not drink
the Marah water because it was bitter; this is
why the place was named Marah. 24The
people complained to Moses saying, 'What
are we to drink?' 25Moses appealed to Yahweh
for help, and Yahweh showed him a piece of
wood. When Moses threw it into the water,
the water became sweet.

There he laid down a statute
and law for them
and there he put them to the test.

Then he said, 26'If you listen carefully to
the voice of Yahweh your God and do what
he regards as right, if you pay attention to his
commandments and keep all his laws, I shall
never inflict on you any of the diseases that I
inflicted on the Egyptians, for I am Yahweh
your Healer.'

27So they came to Elim where there were
twelve springs and seventy palm trees;
and there they pitched camp beside the
water.

The manna and the quails[a]

16 Setting out from Elim, the whole
community of Israelites entered the
desert of Sin, lying between Elim and Sinai—
on the fifteenth day of the second month
after they had left Egypt. 2And the whole
community of Israelites began complaining
about Moses and Aaron in the desert 3and
said to them, 'Why did we not die at Yahweh's
hand in Egypt, where we used to sit round
the flesh pots and could eat to our heart's
content! As it is, you have led us into this
desert to starve this entire assembly to death!'

4Yahweh then said to Moses, 'Look, I shall
rain down bread for you from the heavens.
Each day the people must go out and collect
their ration for the day; I propose to test them
in this way to see whether they will follow
my law or not. 5On the sixth day, however,
when they prepare what they have brought
in, this must be twice as much as they collect
on ordinary days.'

6Moses and Aaron then said to the whole
community of Israelites, 'This evening you
will know that it was Yahweh who brought
you out of Egypt, 7and tomorrow morning
you will see the glory of Yahweh, for Yahweh
has heard your complaints about him. What
are we, that your complaint should be against
us?' 8Moses then said, 'This evening Yahweh
will give you meat to eat, and tomorrow
morning bread to your heart's content, for
Yahweh has heard your complaints about
him. What do we count for? Your complaints
are not against us, but against Yahweh.'

9Moses then said to Aaron, 'Say to the
whole community of Israelites, "Approach
Yahweh's presence, for he has heard your
complaints." ' 10As Aaron was speaking
to the whole community of Israelites, they
turned towards the desert, and there the
glory of Yahweh appeared in the cloud.
11Yahweh then spoke to Moses and said,
12'I have heard the Israelites' complaints.
Speak to them as follows, "At twilight you
will eat meat, and in the morning you will
have bread to your heart's content, and
then you will know that I am Yahweh your
God." '

13That evening, quails flew in and
covered the camp, and next morning there
was a layer of dew all round the camp.
14When the layer of dew lifted, there on the
surface of the desert was something fine and
granular, as fine as hoarfrost on the ground.
15As soon as the Israelites saw this, they
said to one another, 'What is that[b]?' not
knowing what it was. 'That', Moses told
them, 'is the food which Yahweh has given
you to eat. 16These are Yahweh's orders:
Each of you must collect as much as he needs
to eat—a *homer* per head for each person in
his tent.'

17The Israelites did this. They collected it,
some more, some less. 18When they measured
out what they had collected by the *homer*, no
one who had collected more had too much,
no one who had collected less had too little.

16a ‖ Nb 11.
16b Hebr. *Man hu*. Popular explanation of the name. Manna is an insect secretion found on tamarisks.

Each had collected as much as he needed to
eat.
19 Moses then said, 'No one may keep any
of it for tomorrow.' 20 But some of them took
no notice of Moses and kept part of it for the
following day, and it bred maggots and smelt
foul; and Moses was angry with them.
21 Morning by morning they collected it, each
man as much as he needed to eat, and once
the sun grew hot, it melted away.
22 Now, on the sixth day they collected
twice the amount of food: two *homer* per
person, and all the leaders of the community
came and told Moses this. 23 Moses replied,
'This is what Yahweh said, "Tomorrow is a
day of complete rest, a Sabbath sacred to
Yahweh. Bake what you want to bake, boil
what you want to boil; put aside what is left
over, to be kept for tomorrow." 24 So, as
Moses ordered, they put it aside for the
following day, and its smell was not foul nor
were there maggots in it. 25 'Eat it today,'
Moses said, 'for today is a Sabbath for
Yahweh; you will find none in the fields
today. 26 For six days you will collect it, but
on the seventh day, the Sabbath, there will
be none.' 27 On the seventh day some of the
people went out to collect it, but they found
none. 28 Yahweh then said to Moses, 'How
much longer will you refuse to obey my
commandments and laws? 29 Look,
Yahweh has given you the Sabbath; this is
why he gives you two days' food on the sixth
day; each of you must stay in his place;
on the seventh day no one may leave his
home.' 30 So on the seventh day the people
rested.
31 The House of Israel named it 'manna'.
It was like coriander seed; it was white and
its taste was like that of wafers made with
honey.
32 Moses then said, 'These are Yahweh's
orders: Fill a *homer* with it and preserve it for
your descendants, so that they can see the
bread on which I fed you in the desert when
I brought you out of Egypt.' 33 Moses then
said to Aaron, 'Take a jar and in it put a full
homer of manna and store it in Yahweh's
presence, to be kept for your descendants.'
34 Accordingly, Aaron stored it in front of the
Testimony, to be preserved, as Yahweh had
ordered Moses.
35 The Israelites ate manna for forty years,
up to the time they reached inhabited
country: they ate manna up to the time they
reached the frontiers of Canaan. 36 A *homer* is
one-tenth of an *ephah*.

The water from the rock[a]

17 The whole community of Israelites left
the desert of Sin, travelling by stages
as Yahweh ordered. They pitched camp at
Rephidim where there was no water for the
people to drink. 2 The people took issue with
Moses for this and said, 'Give us water to
drink.' Moses replied, 'Why take issue with
me? Why do you put Yahweh to the test?'
3 But, tormented by thirst, the people com-
plained to Moses. 'Why did you bring us
out of Egypt,' they said, 'only to make us,
our children and our livestock, die of thirst?'
4 Moses appealed to Yahweh for help. 'How
am I to deal with this people?' he said. 'Any
moment now they will stone me!' 5 Yahweh
then said to Moses, 'Go on ahead of the
people, taking some of the elders of Israel
with you; in your hand take the staff with
which you struck the River, and go. 6 I shall
be waiting for you there on the rock (at
Horeb). Strike the rock, and water will come
out for the people to drink.' This was what
Moses did, with the elders of Israel looking
on. 7 He gave the place the names Massah and
Meribah because of the Israelites' conten-
tiousness and because they put Yahweh to
the test by saying, 'Is Yahweh with us, or
not?'

A battle against the Amalekites

8 The Amalekites then came and attacked
Israel at Rephidim. 9 Moses said to Joshua,
'Pick some men and tomorrow morning go
out and engage Amalek. I, for my part, shall
take my stand on the hilltop with the staff of
God in my hand.' 10 Joshua did as Moses had
told him and went out to engage Amalek,
while Moses, Aaron and Hur went up to the
top of the hill. 11 As long as Moses kept his
arms raised, Israel had the advantage; when
he let his arms fall, the advantage went to
Amalek. 12 But Moses' arms grew heavy, so
they took a stone and put it under him and
on this he sat, with Aaron and Hur supporting
his arms on each side.
Thus his arms remained unwavering till

17a || Nb 20:1–13.

sunset, 13and Joshua defeated Amalek,
putting their people to the sword. 14Yahweh
then said to Moses, 'Write this down in a
book to commemorate it, and repeat it over
to Joshua, for I shall blot out all memory of
Amalek under heaven.' 15Moses then built an
altar and named it Yahweh-Nissi 16meaning,
'Lay hold of Yahweh's banner! Yahweh will
be at war with Amalek generation after
generation.'

The meeting of Jethro and Moses

18 Jethro, priest of Midian, Moses' father-
in-law, had heard all about what God
had done for Moses and for Israel his people:
how Yahweh had brought Israel out of Egypt.
2Jethro, Moses' father-in-law, then took back
Zipporah, Moses' wife, whom Moses had
sent home, 3with her two sons; one of them
was called Gershom because, he had said, 'I
am an alien in a foreign land,' 4and the other
called Eliezer because 'My father's God is my
help and has delivered me from Pharaoh's
sword.'

5Then Jethro, Moses' father-in-law,
with Moses' sons and wife, came to Moses in
the desert where he was encamped, at the
mountain of God. 6'Here is your father-in-
law Jethro approaching', Moses was told,
'with your wife and her two sons.' 7So
Moses went out to greet his father-in-law,
bowed low to him and kissed him; and when
each had asked how the other was they went
into the tent. 8Moses then told his father-
in-law all about what Yahweh had done to
Pharaoh and the Egyptians for Israel's sake,
and about all the hardships that they had
encountered on the way, and how Yahweh
had rescued them. 9And Jethro was
delighted at all Yahweh's goodness to Israel
in having rescued them from the clutches of
the Egyptians. 10'Blessed be Yahweh', Jethro
exclaimed, 'for having rescued you from the
clutches of the Egyptians and the clutches of
Pharaoh, for having rescued the people from
the grasp of the Egyptians! 11Now I know that
Yahweh is greater than all other gods. . .'

12Jethro, Moses' father-in-law, then
offered a burnt offering and other sacrifices
to God; and Aaron and all the elders of
Israel came and ate with Moses' father-in-
law in the presence of God.

The appointment of judges[a]

13On the following day, Moses took his seat
to administer justice for the people, and
the people were standing round him from
morning till evening. 14Seeing all he did for
the people, Moses' father-in-law said to him,
'Why do you do this for the people, why sit
here alone with the people standing round
you from morning till evening?' 15Moses
replied to his father-in-law, 'Because the
people come to me to consult God. 16When
they have a problem they come to me, and I
give a ruling between the one and the other
and make God's statutes and laws known to
them.' 17Moses' father-in-law then said to
him, 'What you are doing is not right. 18You
will only tire yourself out, and the people
with you too, for the work is too heavy for
you. You cannot do it all yourself. 19Now
listen to the advice I am going to give you,
and God be with you! Your task is to represent
the people to God, to lay their cases before
God, 20and to teach them the statutes and
laws, and show them the way they ought to
follow and how they ought to behave. 21At
the same time, from the people at large choose
capable and God-fearing men, men who are
trustworthy and incorruptible, and put them
in charge of them as heads of thousands,
hundreds, fifties and tens, 22and make them
the people's permanent judges. They will
refer all important matters to you, but all
minor matters they will decide themselves,
so making things easier for you by sharing
the burden with you. 23If you do this—and
may God so command you—you will be able
to stand the strain, and all these people will
go home satisfied.'

24Moses took his father-in-law's advice and
did just as he said. 25Moses chose capable
men from all Israel and put them in charge of
the people as heads of thousands, hundreds,
fifties and tens. 26These acted as the people's
permanent judges. They referred hard cases
to Moses but decided minor matters
themselves.

27Moses then set his father-in-law on his
way, and he travelled back to his own
country.

18a || Dt 1:9–18.

III: THE COVENANT AT SINAI

A: THE COVENANT AND THE DECALOGUE

The Israelites reach Sinai

19 Three months to the day after leaving Egypt, the Israelites reached the desert of Sinai. 2 Setting out from Rephidim, they reached the desert of Sinai and pitched camp in the desert; there, facing the mountain, Israel pitched camp.

Yahweh promises the covenant

3 Moses then went up to God, and Yahweh called to him from the mountain, saying, 'Say this to the House of Jacob! Tell the Israelites, 4 "You have seen for yourselves what I did to the Egyptians and how I carried you away on eagle's wings and brought you to me. 5 So now, if you are really prepared to obey me and keep my covenant, you, out of all peoples, shall be my personal possession, for the whole world is mine. 6 For me you shall be a kingdom of priests, a holy nation." Those are the words you are to say to the Israelites.' 7 So Moses went and summoned the people's elders and acquainted them with everything that Yahweh had bidden him, 8 and the people all replied with one accord, 'Whatever Yahweh has said, we will do.' Moses then reported to Yahweh what the people had said.

Preparing for the covenant

9 Yahweh then said to Moses, 'Look, I shall come to you in a dense cloud so that the people will hear when I speak to you and believe you ever after.' Moses then told Yahweh what the people had said.

10 Yahweh then said to Moses, 'Go to the people and tell them to sanctify themselves today and tomorrow. They must wash their clothes 11 and be ready for the day after tomorrow; for the day after tomorrow, in the sight of all the people, Yahweh will descend on Mount Sinai. 12 You will mark out the limits of the mountain and say, "Take care not to go up the mountain or to touch the edge of it. Anyone who touches the mountain will be put to death. 13 No one may lay a hand on him: he must be stoned or shot by arrow; whether man or beast, he shall not live." When the ram's horn sounds a long blast, they must go up the mountain.'

14 So Moses came down from the mountain to the people; he made the people sanctify themselves and they washed their clothes. 15 He then said to the people, 'Be ready for the day after tomorrow; do not touch a woman.'

The theophany on Sinai

16 Now at daybreak two days later, there were peals of thunder and flashes of lightning, dense cloud on the mountain and a very loud trumpet blast; and, in the camp, all the people trembled. 17 Then Moses led the people out of the camp to meet God; and they took their stand at the bottom of the mountain. 18 Mount Sinai was entirely wrapped in smoke, because Yahweh had descended on it in the form of fire. The smoke rose like smoke from a furnace and the whole mountain shook violently. 19 Louder and louder grew the trumpeting. Moses spoke, and God answered him in the thunder. 20 Yahweh descended on Mount Sinai, on the top of the mountain, and Yahweh called Moses to the top of the mountain; and Moses went up. 21 Yahweh then said to Moses, 'Go down and warn the people not to break through to look at Yahweh, or many of them will perish. 22 Even the priests, who do have access to Yahweh, must sanctify themselves, or Yahweh may burst out against them.' 23 Moses said to Yahweh, 'The people cannot come up Mount Sinai, since you yourself warned us to mark out the limits of the mountain and declare it sacred.' 24 Yahweh said, 'Away with you! Go down! Then come back bringing Aaron with you. But do not allow the priests and people to break through to come up to Yahweh, or he may burst out against them.' 25 So Moses went down to the people and spoke to them.

The Decalogue[a]

20 Then God spoke all these words. He said, 2 'I am Yahweh your God who

20a || Dt 5:6–22.

brought you out of Egypt, where you lived
as slaves.
3 'You shall have no other gods to rival
me.
4 'You shall not make yourself a carved
image or any likeness of anything in heaven
above or on earth beneath or in the waters
under the earth.
5 'You shall not bow down to them or serve
them. For I, Yahweh your God, am a jealous
God and I punish a parent's fault in the
children, the grandchildren, and the great-
grandchildren among those who hate me;
6 but I act with faithful love towards thou-
sands of those who love me and keep my
commandments.
7 'You shall not misuse the name of Yahweh
your God, for Yahweh will not leave unpun-
ished anyone who misuses his name.
8 'Remember the Sabbath day and keep it
holy. 9 For six days you shall labour and do
all your work, 10 but the seventh day is a
Sabbath for Yahweh your God. You shall do
no work that day, neither you nor your son
nor your daughter nor your servants, men or
women, nor your animals nor the alien living
with you. 11 For in six days Yahweh made the
heavens, earth and sea and all that these
contain, but on the seventh day he rested;
that is why Yahweh has blessed the Sabbath
day and made it sacred.
12 'Honour your father and your mother so
that you may live long in the land that Yahweh
your God is giving you.
13 'You shall not kill.
14 'You shall not commit adultery.
15 'You shall not steal.
16 'You shall not give false evidence against
your neighbour.
17 'You shall not set your heart on your
neighbour's house. You shall not set your
heart on your neighbour's spouse, or servant,
man or woman, or ox, or donkey, or any of
your neighbour's possessions.'
18 Seeing the thunder pealing, the lightning
flashing, the trumpet blasting and the moun-
tain smoking, the people were all terrified and
kept their distance. 19 'Speak to us yourself,'
they said to Moses, 'and we will obey; but do
not let God speak to us, or we shall die.'
20 Moses said to the people, 'Do not be afraid;
God has come to test you, so that your fear
of him, being always in your mind, may keep
you from sinning.' 21 So the people kept their
distance while Moses approached the dark
cloud where God was.

B: THE BOOK OF THE COVENANT

Law concerning the altar

22 Yahweh said to Moses, 'Tell the Israelites
this, "You have seen for yourselves how I
have spoken to you from heaven. 23 You must
not make gods of silver to rival me, nor must
you make yourselves gods of gold.
24 "You must make me an altar of earth on
which to sacrifice your burnt offerings and
communion sacrifices, your sheep and cattle.
Wherever I choose to have my name remem-
bered, I shall come to you and bless you. 25 If
you make me an altar of stone, do not build
it of dressed stones; for if you use a chisel on
it, you will profane it. 26 You must not go up
to my altar by steps, in case you expose your
nakedness on them." '

Laws concerning slaves

21 1 'These are the laws you must give them:
2 'When you buy a Hebrew slave, his
service will last for six years. In the seventh
year he will leave a free man without paying
compensation. 3 If he came single, he will
depart single; if he came married, his wife
will depart with him. 4 If his master gives him
a wife and she bears him sons or daughters,
the wife and her children will belong to her
master, and he will depart alone. 5 But if the
slave says, "I love my master and my wife
and children; I do not wish to be freed,"
6 then his master will bring him before God
and then, leading him to the door or the
doorpost, his master will pierce his ear with
an awl, and the slave will be permanently his.
7 If a man sells his daughter as a slave, she
will not leave as male slaves do. 8 If she does
not please her master who intended her for
himself, he must let her be bought back: he
has not the right to sell her to foreigners, for
this would be a breach of faith with her. 9 If
he intends her for his son, he must treat her
as custom requires daughters to be treated.
10 If he takes another wife, he must not reduce
the food, clothing or conjugal rights of the
first one. 11 Should he deprive her of these
three things she will leave a free woman,
without paying compensation.

Homicide

12 'Anyone who by violence causes a death
must be put to death. 13 If, however, he has

not planned to do it but it comes from God
by his hand, he can take refuge in a place
which I shall appoint for you. 14 But should
any person dare to kill another with deliberate
planning, you will take that person even from
my altar to be put to death.
15 'Anyone who strikes father or mother
will be put to death. 16 Anyone who abducts
a person—whether that person has since been
sold or is still held—will be put to death.
17 Anyone who curses father or mother will
be put to death.

Blows and wounds

18 'If people quarrel and one strikes the other
a blow with stone or fist so that the injured
party, though not dead, is confined to bed,
19 but later recovers and can go about, even
with a stick, the one who struck the blow will
have no liability, other than to compensate
the injured party for the enforced inactivity
and to take care of the injured party until the
cure is complete.
20 'If someone beats his slave, male or
female, and the slave dies at his hands, he
must pay the penalty. 21 But should the slave
survive for one or two days, he will pay no
penalty because the slave is his by right of
purchase.
22 'If people, when brawling, hurt a preg-
nant woman and she suffers a miscarriage
but no further harm is done, the person
responsible will pay compensation as fixed
by the woman's master, paying as much as
the judges decide. 23 If further harm is done,
however, you will award life for life, 24 eye for
eye, tooth for tooth, hand for hand, foot for
foot, 25 burn for burn, wound for wound,
stroke for stroke.
26 'If anyone strikes the eye of his slave,
male or female, and destroys the use of it, he
will give the slave his freedom to compensate
for the eye. 27 If he knocks out the tooth of
his slave, male or female, he will give the
slave his freedom to compensate for the tooth.
28 'If an ox gores a man or woman to
death, the ox will be stoned and its meat will
not be eaten, but the owner of the ox will not
be liable. 29 But if the ox has been in the habit
of goring before, and if its owner has been
warned but has not kept it under control,
then should this ox kill a man or woman, it
will be stoned and its owner put to death. 30 If
a ransom is imposed on the owner, he will
pay whatever is imposed, to redeem his life.
31 If the ox gores a boy or a girl, it will be
treated in accordance with this same rule. 32 If
the ox gores a slave, male or female, its owner
will pay the price—thirty shekels—to their
master, and the ox will be stoned.
33 'If anyone leaves a pit uncovered, or digs
a pit and does not cover it, and an ox, or
donkey falls into it, 34 then the owner of the
pit will make good the loss by compensating
its owner, and the dead animal will be his.
35 If anyone's ox injures anyone else's ox
causing its death, the owners will sell and
share the money for it; they will also share the
dead animal. 36 But if it is common knowledge
that the ox has been in the habit of goring
before, and its owner has not kept it under
control, the owner will repay ox for ox, and
will keep the dead animal.

Theft of animals

37 'If anyone steals an ox or a sheep and
slaughters or sells it, he will pay back five
beasts from the herd for the ox, and four
animals from the flock for the sheep.'

22 'If a thief is caught breaking in and is
struck a mortal blow, his blood may
not be avenged, 2 but if it happens after
sunrise, his blood may be avenged. He will
make full restitution; if he has not the means,
he will be sold to pay for what he has stolen.
3 If the stolen animal is found alive in his
possession, be it ox, donkey or animal from
the flock, he will pay back double.

Offences requiring compensation

4 'If anyone puts his animals out to graze in a
field or vineyard and lets them graze in
someone else's field, he will make restitution
for the part of the field that has been grazed
on the basis of its yield. But if he has let the
whole field be grazed, he will make restitution
in proportion to the best crop of the field or
vineyard.
5 'If a fire breaks out, setting light to thorn
bushes and burning stacks, standing corn or
the field as a result, the person who started
the fire will make full restitution.
6 'If anyone entrusts money or goods to
someone else's keeping and these are stolen
from that person's house, the thief, if he can
be discovered, will repay double. 7 Should
the thief not be discovered, the owner of the
house will come into the presence of God, to

declare that he has not laid hands on the other
person's property.
8'In every case of law-breaking involving
an ox, donkey, animal from the flock,
clothing or lost property of any sort, the
ownership of which is disputed, both parties
will lay their case before God. The party
whom God pronounces guilty will pay back
double to the other.
9'If anyone entrusts a donkey, ox, animal
from the flock or any other animal to someone
else's keeping, and it dies or breaks a limb or
is carried off without anyone seeing,
10an oath
by Yahweh will decide between the two
parties whether the keeper has laid hands on
the other's property or not. The owner will
take what remains, the keeper will not have
to make good the loss.
11Only if the animal
has been stolen from him, will he make
restitution to the owner.
12If it has been
savaged by a wild animal, he must bring the
savaged remains of the animal as evidence,
and will then not have to make restitution.
13'If anyone borrows an animal from
someone else, and it breaks a limb or dies
in the owner's absence, he will make full
restitution.
14But if the animal's owner has
been present, he will not have to make good
the loss. If the owner has hired it out, he will
get the cost of its hire.

Violation of a virgin

15'If a man seduces a virgin who is not
engaged to be married, he will pay her bride-price and make her his wife.
16If her father
absolutely refuses to let him have her, he will
pay a sum equivalent to the bride-price of a
virgin.

Moral and religious laws

17'You will not allow a sorceress to live.
18'Anyone who has intercourse with an
animal will be put to death.
19'Anyone who sacrifices to other gods will
be put under the curse of destruction.
20'You will not molest or oppress aliens,
for you yourselves were once aliens in Egypt.
21You will not ill-treat widows or orphans;
22if you ill-treat them in any way and they
make an appeal to me for help, I shall
certainly hear their appeal,
23my anger will
be roused and I shall put you to the sword;
then your own wives will be widows and your
own children orphans.
24'If you lend money to any of my people,
to anyone poor among you, you will not play
the usurer with him: you will not demand
interest from him.
25'If you take someone's cloak in pledge,
you will return it to him at sunset.
26It is all
the covering he has; it is the cloak he wraps
his body in; what else will he sleep in? If he
appeals to me, I shall listen. At least with me
he will find compassion!
27'You will not revile God, nor curse your
people's leader.

First-fruits and first-born

28'Do not be slow about making offerings
from your abundance and your surplus. You
will give me the first-born of your children;
29you will do the same with your flocks and
herds. For the first seven days the first-born
will stay with its mother; on the eighth day
you will give it to me.
30'You must be people consecrated to me.
You will not eat the meat of anything in the
countryside savaged by wild animals; you
will throw it to the dogs.'

Justice. Duties towards enemies

23 'You will not spread false rumours.
You will not lend support to the wicked
by giving untrue evidence.
2You will not be
led into wrong-doing by the majority nor,
when giving evidence in a lawsuit, side with
the majority to pervert the course of justice;
3nor will you show partiality to the poor in a
lawsuit.
4'If you come on your enemy's ox or
donkey straying, you will take it back to him.
5If you see the donkey of someone who hates
you fallen under its load, do not stand back;
you must go and help him with it.
6'You will not cheat the poor among you
of their rights at law.
7Keep clear of fraud.
Do not cause the death of the innocent or
upright, and do not acquit the guilty.
8You
will accept no bribes, for a bribe blinds the
clear-sighted and is the ruin of the cause of
the upright.
9'You will not oppress the alien; you know
how an alien feels, for you yourselves were
once aliens in Egypt.

The sabbatical year and the Sabbath

10'For six years you will sow your land and
gather its produce,
11but in the seventh year

you will let it lie fallow and forgo all produce from it, so that those of your people who are poor can take food from it and the wild animals eat what they have left. You will do the same with your vineyard and your olive grove.

[12]'For six days you will do your work, and on the seventh you will rest, so that your ox and your donkey may rest and the child of your slave-girl have a breathing space, and the alien too.

[13]'Take notice of everything I have told you and do not mention the name of any other god: let none ever be heard from your lips.

The great feasts

[14]'Three times a year you will hold a festival in my honour. [15]You will observe the feast of Unleavened Bread. For seven days you will eat unleavened bread, as I have commanded you, at the appointed time in the month of Abib, for in that month you came out of Egypt. No one will appear before me empty-handed. [16]You will also observe the feast of Harvest, of the first-fruits of your labours in sowing the fields, and the feast of Ingathering, at the end of the year, once you have brought the fruits of your labours in from the fields. [17]Three times a year all your menfolk will appear before Lord Yahweh.

[18]'You will not offer the blood of my victim with leavened bread, nor will the fat of my feast be kept till the following day.

[19]'You will bring the best of the first-fruits of your soil to the house of Yahweh your God.

'You will not boil a kid in its mother's milk.

Promises and instructions for the entry into Canaan

[20]'Look, I am sending an angel to precede you, to guard you as you go and bring you to the place that I have prepared. [21]Revere him and obey what he says. Do not defy him: he will not forgive any wrong-doing on your part, for my name is in him. [22]If, however, you obey what he says and do whatever I order, I shall be an enemy to your enemies and a foe to your foes. [23]My angel will precede you and lead you to the home of the Amorites, the Hittites, the Perizzites, the Canaanites, the Hivites and the Jebusites, whom I shall exterminate. [24]You will not bow down to their gods or worship them or observe their rites, but throw them down and smash their cultic stones. [25]You will worship Yahweh your God, and then I shall bless your food and water, and keep you free of sickness. [26]In your country no woman will miscarry, none be sterile, and I shall give you your full term of life.

[27]'I shall send terror of myself ahead of you; I shall throw all the peoples you encounter into confusion, and make all your enemies take to their heels. [28]I shall send hornets ahead of you to drive Hivite, Canaanite and Hittite out before you. [29]I shall not drive them out ahead of you in a single year, or the land might become a desert where wild animals would multiply to your cost. [30]I shall drive them out little by little before you, until your numbers grow sufficient for you to take possession of the land. [31]And your frontiers I shall fix from the Sea of Reeds to the Sea of the Philistines, and from the desert to the River, for I shall put the inhabitants of the territory at your mercy, and you will drive them out before you. [32]You will make no pact with them or with their gods. [33]They may not stay in your country or they might make you sin against me, for you would serve their gods, and that would be a snare for you!'

C: THE RATIFICATION OF THE COVENANT

24 He then said to Moses, Come up to Yahweh, you and Aaron, Nadab and Abihu, and seventy of the elders of Israel and bow down at a distance. [2]Moses alone will approach Yahweh; the others will not approach, nor will the people come up with him.'

[3]Moses went and told the people all Yahweh's words and all the laws, and all the people answered with one voice, 'All the words Yahweh has spoken we will carry out!' [4]Moses put all Yahweh's words into writing, and early next morning he built an altar at the foot of the mountain, with twelve standing-stones for the twelve tribes of Israel. [5]Then he sent certain young Israelites to offer burnt offerings and sacrifice bullocks to Yahweh as communion sacrifices. [6]Moses then took half the blood and put it into basins, and the other half he sprinkled on the altar. [7]Then, taking the Book of the Covenant, he

read it to the listening people, who then said, 'We shall do everything that Yahweh has said; we shall obey.' [8]Moses then took the blood and sprinkled it over the people, saying, 'This is the blood of the covenant which Yahweh has made with you, entailing all these stipulations.'

[9]Moses, Aaron, Nadab, Abihu and seventy elders of Israel then went up, [10]and they saw the God of Israel beneath whose feet there was what looked like a sapphire pavement pure as the heavens themselves, [11]but he did no harm to the Israelite notables; they actually gazed on God and then ate and drank.

Moses on the mountain

[12]Yahweh said to Moses, 'Come up to me on the mountain. Stay there, and I will give you the stone tablets—the law and the commandment—which I have written for their instruction.' [13]Moses made ready, with Joshua his assistant, and they went up the mountain of God. [14]He said to the elders, 'Wait here for us until we come back to you. You have Aaron and Hur with you; if anyone has any matter to settle, let him go to them.' [15]Moses then went up the mountain.

Cloud covered the mountain. [16]The glory of Yahweh rested on Mount Sinai and the cloud covered it for six days. On the seventh day Yahweh called to Moses from inside the cloud. [17]To the watching Israelites, the glory of Yahweh looked like a devouring fire on the mountain top. [18]Moses went right into the cloud and went on up the mountain. Moses stayed on the mountain for forty days and forty nights.

IV: INSTRUCTIONS ON THE BUILDING OF THE SANCTUARY AND ON ITS MINISTERS[a]

Contributions for the sanctuary

25 Yahweh spoke to Moses and said, [2]'Tell the Israelites to set aside a contribution for me; you will accept a contribution from everyone whose heart prompts him to give it. [3]And this is what you will accept from them: gold, silver and bronze; [4]materials dyed violet-purple, red-purple and crimson, fine linen, goats' hair; [5]rams' skins dyed red, fine leather, acacia wood; [6]oil for the light, spices for the anointing oil and fragrant incense; [7]cornelian and other stones to be set in the *ephod* and breastplate. [8]Make me a sanctuary so that I can reside among them. [9]You will make it all according to the design for the Dwelling and the design for its furnishings which I shall now show you.

The Dwelling and its furnishings
The ark[b]

[10]'You must make me an ark of acacia wood, two and a half cubits long, one and a half cubits wide and one and a half cubits high. [11]You will overlay it, inside and out, with pure gold and make a gold moulding all round it. [12]You will cast four gold rings for it and fix them to its four supports: two rings on one side and two rings on the other. [13]You will also make shafts of acacia wood and overlay them with gold [14]and pass the shafts through the rings on the sides of the ark, by which to carry it. [15]The shafts will stay in the rings of the ark and not be withdrawn. [16]Inside the ark you will put the Testimony which I am about to give you.

[17]'You will also make a mercy-seat[c] of pure gold, two and a half cubits long and one and a half cubits wide, [18]and you will model two great winged creatures of beaten gold, you will make them at the two ends of the mercy-seat. [19]Model one of the winged creatures at one end and the other winged creature at the other end; you will model the winged creatures of a piece with the mercy-seat at either end. [20]The winged creatures must have

---

25a =35–40.
25b A wooden chest, symbol of God's presence, finally housed in the Temple. It disappeared in the destruction of 586 BC.
25c This covering of the ark is the place of God's appearing to Moses. The winged creatures correspond to Babylonian *karibu*, half-animal, half-human guards of the temples.

their wings spread upwards, protecting the mercy-seat with their wings and facing each other, their faces being towards the mercy-seat. 21 You will put the mercy-seat on the top of the ark, and inside the ark you will put the Testimony which I am about to give you. 22 There I shall come to meet you; from above the mercy-seat, from between the two winged creatures which are on the ark of the Testimony, I shall give you all my orders for the Israelites.

The table for the loaves of permanent offering

23 'You must also make a table of acacia wood, two cubits long, one cubit wide and one and a half cubits high. 24 You will overlay it with pure gold, and make a gold moulding all round it. 25 You will fit it with struts of a hand's breadth and make a gold moulding round the struts. 26 You will make four gold rings for it and fix the four rings at the four corners where the four legs are. 27 The rings must lie close to the struts to hold the shafts for carrying the table. 28 You must make the shafts of acacia wood and overlay them with gold. The table must be carried by these. 29 You must make dishes, cups, jars and libation bowls for it; you must make these of pure gold, 30 and on the table, in my presence, you will always put the loaves of permanent offering.

The lamp-stand

31 'You will also make a lamp-stand of pure gold; the lamp-stand must be of beaten gold, base and stem. Its cups, calyxes and petals, must be of a piece with it. 32 Six branches must spring from its sides: three of the lamp-stand's branches from one side, three of the lamp-stand's branches from the other. 33 The first branch must carry three cups shaped like almond blossoms, each with its calyx and petals; the second branch, too, must carry three cups shaped like almond blossoms, each with its calyx and bud, and similarly for all six branches springing from the lamp-stand. 34 The lamp-stand itself must carry four cups shaped like almond blossoms, each with its calyx and bud: 35 one calyx under the first two branches springing from the lamp-stand, one calyx under the next pair of branches and one calyx under the last pair of branches—thus for all six branches springing from the lamp-stand. 36 The calyxes and the branches will be of a piece with the lamp-stand, and the whole made from a single piece of pure gold, beaten out. 37 You will also make seven lamps for it and mount the lamps in such a way that they light up the space in front of it. 38 The snuffers and trays must be of pure gold. 39 You will use a talent of pure gold for the lamp-stand and all its accessories; 40 and see that you work to the design which was shown you on the mountain.'

The Dwelling. Fabrics and hangings

26 'The Dwelling itself you will make with ten sheets of finely woven linen dyed violet-purple, red-purple and crimson. You will have them embroidered with great winged creatures. 2 The length of a single sheet is to be twenty-eight cubits, its width four cubits, all the sheets to be of the same size. 3 Five of the sheets are to be joined to one another, and the other five sheets are to be joined to one another. 4 You will make violet loops along the edge of the first sheet, at the end of the set, and do the same along the edge of the last sheet in the other set. 5 You will make fifty loops on the first sheet and fifty loops along the outer edge of the sheet of the second set, the loops corresponding to one another. 6 You will also make fifty gold clasps, and join the sheets together with the clasps. In this way the Dwelling will be a unified whole.

7 'You will make sheets of goats' hair to form a tent over the Dwelling; you will make eleven of these. 8 The length of a single sheet must be thirty cubits and its width four cubits, the eleven sheets to be all of the same size. 9 You will join five sheets together into one set, and six sheets into another; the sixth you will fold double over the front of the tent. 10 You will make fifty loops along the edge of the first sheet, at the end of the first set, and fifty loops along the edge of the sheet of the second set. 11 You will make fifty bronze clasps and insert the clasps into the loops, to draw the tent together and to make it a unified whole.

12 'Of the extra part of the sheets that overlap, half is to hang down the back of the Dwelling. 13 The extra cubit on either side along the length of the tent sheets must hang down the sides of the Dwelling on either side to cover it.

14‘And for the tent you will make a cover
of rams’ skins dyed red and a cover of fine
leather over that.

The framework

15‘For the Dwelling you will make vertical
frames of acacia wood. 16Each frame must
be ten cubits long and one and a half cubits
wide. 17Each frame must have twin tenons;
that is how all the frames for the Dwelling
must be made. 18You will make frames for
the Dwelling: twenty frames for the south
side, to the south, 19and make forty silver
sockets under the twenty frames, two sockets
under one frame for its two tenons, two
sockets under the next frame for its two
tenons; 20and for the other side of the
Dwelling, the north side, twenty frames
21and forty silver sockets, two sockets
under one frame, two sockets under the next
frame. 22For the back of the Dwelling, on the
west, you will make six frames, 23and
make two frames for the corners at the back
of the Dwelling; 24these must be coupled
together at the bottom, and right up to the
top, to the level of the first ring; this for the
two frames that must form the two corners.
25Thus there will be eight frames with their
silver sockets: sixteen sockets; two sockets
under one frame and two sockets under the
next frame.

26‘You will make crossbars of acacia wood:
five for the frames of the first side of the
Dwelling, 27five crossbars for the frames of
the opposite side of the Dwelling, and five
crossbars for the frames which form the back
of the Dwelling, to the west. 28The middle
bar must join the frames from one end to the
other, halfway up. 29You will overlay the
frames with gold, make gold rings for them,
through which to place the crossbars, and
overlay the crossbars with gold. 30This is how
you must erect the Dwelling, following the
design shown you on the mountain.

The curtain

31‘You will make a curtain of finely woven
linen, dyed violet-purple, red-purple and
crimson, and embroidered with great winged
creatures, 32and put it on four poles of acacia
wood overlaid with gold, with golden hooks
for them, set in four sockets of silver. 33You
will put the curtain below the clasps, so that
inside behind the curtain, you can place the
ark of the Testimony, and the curtain will
mark the division for you between the Holy
Place and the Holy of Holies. 34You will put
the mercy-seat on the ark of the Testimony
in the Holy of Holies. 35You will place the
table outside the curtain, and the lamp-stand
on the south side of the Dwelling, opposite
the table; you will put the table on the north
side. 36For the entrance to the tent you will
make a screen of finely woven linen embroid-
ered with violet-purple, red-purple and
crimson, 37and for the screen you
will make five poles of acacia wood and
overlay them with gold, with golden
hooks, and for them you will cast five sockets
of bronze.’

The altar of burnt offerings

27 ‘You will make the altar of acacia wood,
five cubits long and five cubits wide;
the altar will be square and three cubits high.
2At its four corners you will make horns, the
horns must be of a piece with it, and you will
overlay it with bronze. 3And for it you will
make pans for taking away the fatty ashes,
and shovels, sprinkling basins, hooks and fire
pans; you will make all the altar accessories of
bronze. 4You will also make a grating for it
of bronze network, and on the four corners
of the grating you will make four bronze
rings. 5You will put it below the ledge of the
altar, underneath, so that it comes halfway
up the altar. 6You will make shafts for the
altar, shafts of acacia wood and overlay them
with bronze. 7The shafts will be passed
through the rings in such a way that the shafts
are on either side of the altar, for carrying it.
8You will make the altar hollow, out of
boards; you will make it as you were shown
on the mountain.

The court

9‘Then you will make the court of the
Dwelling. On the south side, the curtaining
of the court must be of finely woven linen,
one hundred cubits long (for the first side),
10its twenty poles and their twenty sockets
being of bronze, and the poles’ hooks and
rods of silver. 11So too for the north side,
there must be a hundred cubits of curtaining,
its twenty poles and their twenty sockets
being of bronze, and the poles’ hooks and
rods of silver. 12Across the width of the court,
on the west side, there must be fifty cubits of

curtaining, with its ten poles and their ten
sockets. [13]The width of the court on the east
side, facing the sunrise, must be fifty cubits,
[14]with fifteen cubits of curtaining on one side
of the entrance, with its three poles and their
three sockets, [15]and on the other side of the
entrance, fifteen cubits of curtaining, with
its three poles and their three sockets; [16]and
for the gateway to the court there must be a
twenty-cubit screen of finely woven linen
embroidered with violet-purple, red-purple
and crimson, with its four poles and their
four sockets. [17]All the poles round the court
must be connected by silver rods; their hooks
must be of silver and their sockets of bronze.
[18]The length of the court must be one
hundred cubits, its width fifty cubits and its
height five cubits. All the curtaining must be
made of finely woven linen, and their sockets
of bronze. [19]All the accessories for general
use in the Dwelling, all its pegs and all the
pegs of the court, must be of bronze.

The oil for the lamps

[20]'You will order the Israelites to bring you
pure pounded olive oil for the light, and to
keep a lamp burning all the time. [21]Aaron
and his sons will tend it in the Tent of
Meeting, outside the curtain hanging in front
of the Testimony, from dusk to dawn, before
Yahweh. This is a perpetual decree for all
generations of Israelites.'

The priestly vestments

28 'From among the Israelites, summon
your brother Aaron and his sons to be
priests in my service: Aaron and Aaron's sons
Nadab, Abihu, Eleazar and Ithamar. [2]For
your brother Aaron you will make sacred
vestments to give dignity and magnificence.
[3]You will instruct all the skilled men, whom
I have endowed with skill, to make Aaron's
vestments for his consecration to my priest-
hood. [4]These are the vestments which they
must make: a pectoral, an *ephod*, a robe, an
embroidered tunic, a turban and a belt. They
must make sacred vestments for your brother
Aaron and his sons, for them to be priests in
my service. [5]They will use gold and violet
material, red-purple and crimson, and finely
woven linen.

The *ephod*[a]

[6]'They will make the *ephod* of finely woven
linen embroidered with gold, violet-purple,
red-purple and crimson. [7]It will have two
shoulder-straps joined to it; it will be joined
to them by its two edges. [8]The waistband on
the *ephod* to hold it in position must be of the
same workmanship and be of a piece with
it: of gold, violet-purple, red-purple and
crimson materials and finely woven linen.
[9]You will then take two cornelians and
engrave them with the names of the sons of
Israel, [10]six of their names on one stone, the
remaining six names on the other, in the
order of their birth. [11]By the stone-carver's
art—seal engraving—you will engrave the
two stones with the names of the sons of
Israel. You will have them mounted in gold
settings [12]and will put the two stones on the
shoulder-straps of the *ephod*, to commem-
orate the sons of Israel. In this way Aaron
will bear their names on his two shoulders,
before Yahweh, as a reminder. [13]You will
also make golden rosettes, [14]and two chains
of pure gold twisted like cord, and will attach
the cord-like chains to the rosettes.

The breastplate of judgement

[15]'You will make the breastplate of judge-
ment of the same embroidered work as the
ephod; you will make it of gold, violet-purple,
red-purple and crimson materials and finely
woven linen. [16]It must be square and doubled
over, a span in length and a span in width.
[17]In it you will set four rows of stones: a sard,
topaz and emerald for the first row; [18]for the
second row, a garnet, sapphire and diamond;
[19]for the third row, a hyacinth, a ruby and an
amethyst; [20]and for the fourth row, a beryl,
a cornelian and a jasper. These must be
mounted in gold settings. [21]The stones will
correspond to the names of the sons of Israel,
twelve like their names, engraved like seals,
each with the name of one of the twelve
tribes. [22]For the breastplate you will make
chains of pure gold twisted like cords, [23]and
on the breastplate you will make two gold
rings, putting the two rings on the two outside
edges of the breastplate [24]and fastening the
two gold cords to the two rings on the outside
edges of the breastplate. [25]The other two ends
of the cords you will fasten to the two rosettes,

28a This can mean 1 a sort of pouch, 2 a priest's loin-cloth, 3 the high priest's breastplate.

putting these on the shoulder-straps of the *ephod*, on the front. 26You will also make two gold rings and put them on the two edges of the breastplate, on the inner side, against the *ephod*; 27and you will make two gold rings and put them low down on the front of the two shoulder-pieces of the *ephod*, close to the join, above the waistband of the *ephod*. 28The breastplate will be secured by a violet-purple cord passed through its rings and those of the *ephod*, so that the breastplate will sit above the waistband and not come apart from the *ephod*. 29Thus Aaron will bear the names of the sons of Israel on the breastplate of judgement, on his heart, when he enters the sanctuary, as a reminder, before Yahweh, always. 30To the breastplate of judgement you will add the *urim* and the *thummim*, and these will be on Aaron's heart when he goes into Yahweh's presence, and Aaron will bear the Israelites' judgement on his heart, in Yahweh's presence, always.

The robe

31'You will make the robe of the *ephod* entirely of violet-purple. 32In the centre it will have an opening for the head, the opening to have round it a border woven like the neck of a coat of mail, so that it will not get torn. 33On its lower hem, you will make pomegranates of violet-purple, red-purple and crimson, and finely woven linen all round the hem, with golden bells between them all round: 34a golden bell and then a pomegranate, alternately, all round the lower hem of the robe. 35Aaron must wear it when he officiates, and the tinkling will be heard when he goes into the sanctuary into Yahweh's presence, or leaves it, and so he will not incur death.

The symbol of consecration

36'You will make a flower of pure gold and on it, as you would engrave a seal, you will engrave, "Consecrated to Yahweh". 37You will put it on a violet-purple cord; it will go on the turban; the front of the turban is the place where it must go. 38This will go on Aaron's brow, and Aaron will thus take on himself the short-comings in the holy things consecrated by the Israelites, in all their holy offerings. It will be on his brow permanently, to make them acceptable to Yahweh. 39The tunic you will weave of fine linen, and make a turban of fine linen, and an embroidered waistband.

The vestments of the priests

40'For the sons of Aaron you will make tunics and waistbands. You will also make them head-dresses to give dignity and magnificence. 41You will dress your brother Aaron and his sons in these; you will then anoint them, invest them and consecrate them to serve me in the priesthood. 42You will also make them linen breeches reaching from waist to thigh, to cover their bare flesh. 43Aaron and his sons will wear these when they go into the Tent of Meeting and when they approach the altar to serve in the sanctuary, as a precaution against incurring mortal guilt. This is a perpetual decree for Aaron and for his descendants after him.'

The consecration of Aaron and his sons
Preparations

29 'This is what you will do to them, to consecrate them to my priesthood. Take one young bull and two rams without blemish; 2also unleavened bread, unleavened cakes mixed with oil, and unleavened wafers spread with oil, made from fine wheat flour, 3and put these into a basket and present them in the basket, at the same time as the bull and the two rams.

Their purification, clothing and anointing

4'You will bring Aaron and his sons to the entrance of the Tent of Meeting and bathe them. 5You will then take the vestments and dress Aaron in the tunic, the robe of the *ephod*, the *ephod*, and the breastplate, and tie the waistband of the *ephod* round his waist. 6Then you will place the turban on his head, and on it put the symbol of holy consecration. 7You will then take the anointing oil and pour it on his head and so anoint him.

8'Next, you will bring his sons and dress them in tunics, 9and fasten waistbands round their waists and put the head-dresses on their heads. By perpetual decree the priesthood will be theirs. Then you will invest Aaron and his sons.

The offerings

10 'You will bring the bull in front of the Tent
of Meeting, and Aaron and his sons will lay
their hands on the bull's head. 11 You will
then slaughter the bull before Yahweh at the
entrance to the Tent of Meeting. 12 You will
then take some of the bull's blood and with
your finger put it on the horns of the altar.
Next, pour out the rest of the blood at the
foot of the altar. 13 And then take all the fat
covering the entrails, the fatty mass over the
liver, the two kidneys with their covering fat,
and burn them on the altar. 14 But the young
bull's flesh, its skin and its offal, you will
burn outside the camp, for this is a sin
offering.

15 'Next, you will take one of the rams,
and Aaron and his sons will lay their hands
on the ram's head. 16 You will then slaughter
the ram, take its blood and pour it against
the altar, all round. 17 Next, cut the ram into
quarters, wash the entrails and legs and put
them on the quarters and head. 18 Then burn
the whole ram on the altar. This will be a
burnt offering for Yahweh, a pleasing smell,
a food offering burnt for Yahweh.

19 'Next, you will take the other ram, and
Aaron and his sons will lay their hands on
the ram's head. 20 You will then slaughter the
ram, take some of its blood and put it on
the lobe of Aaron's right ear, on the lobes of
his sons' right ears, the thumbs of their right
hands, and the big toes of their right feet,
and pour the rest of the blood against the
altar, all round. 21 You will then take some
of the blood on the altar and some of the
anointing oil, and sprinkle it on Aaron and
his vestments and on his sons and on his sons'
vestments: so that he and his vestments will
be consecrated and his sons too, and his sons'
vestments.

The investiture of the priests

22 'You will then take the fatty parts of the
ram: the tail, the fat covering the entrails,
the fatty mass over the liver, the two kidneys
with their covering fat and also the right
thigh—for this is a ram of investiture— 23 and
a loaf of bread, a cake of bread made with oil,
and a wafer, from the basket of unleavened
bread before Yahweh, 24 and put it all on the
palms of Aaron and his sons, and make the
gesture of offering before Yahweh. 25 Then
you will take them back and burn them on
the altar, on top of the burnt offering, as a
smell pleasing before Yahweh, a food offering
burnt for Yahweh.

26 'You will then take the forequarters of
the ram of Aaron's investiture and with it
make the gesture of offering before Yahweh;
this will be your portion. 27 You will conse-
crate the forequarters that have been thus
offered, as also the thigh that is set aside—
what has been offered and what has been set
aside from the ram of investiture of Aaron
and his sons. 28 This, by perpetual decree,
will be the portion that Aaron and his sons
will receive from the Israelites, since it is the
portion set aside, the portion set aside for
Yahweh by the Israelites from their
communion sacrifices: a portion set aside for
Yahweh.

29 'Aaron's sacred vestments must pass to
his sons after him, and they will wear them for
their anointing and investiture. 30 Whichever
of the sons of Aaron succeeds him in the
priesthood and enters the Tent of Meeting to
serve in the sanctuary, will wear them for
seven days.

The sacred meal

31 'You will take the ram of investiture and
cook its meat in a holy place. 32 Aaron and his
sons will eat the meat of the ram and the
bread which is in the basket, at the entrance
to the Tent of Meeting. 33 They will eat what
was used in making expiation for them at
their investiture and consecration. No
unauthorised person may eat these; they are
holy things. 34 If any of the meat from the
investiture sacrifice, or the bread, should be
left till morning, you will burn what is left.
It may not be eaten; it is a holy thing. 35 This
is what you will do for Aaron and his sons,
implementing all the orders I have given
you. You will take seven days over their
investiture.

The consecration of the altar of burnt offerings

36 'On each of the days you will also offer a
young bull as a sacrifice for sin, in expiation.
You will offer a sin sacrifice for the altar when
you make expiation for it; then you will
consecrate it by anointing it. 37 For seven days
you will make expiation for the altar, then
you will consecrate it; it will then be especially

holy, and whatever touches the altar will
become holy.

The daily burnt offering

38 'This is what you must offer on the altar: two
yearling male lambs each day in perpetuity.
39 The first lamb you will offer at dawn, and
the second at twilight, 40 and with the first
lamb, one-tenth of a measure of fine flour
mixed with one-quarter of a *hin* of pounded
olive oil and, for a libation, one-quarter of a
hin of wine. 41 The second lamb you will offer
at twilight, and do it with a similar cereal
offering and libation as at dawn, as a pleasing
smell, as an offering burnt for Yahweh, 42 a
perpetual burnt offering for all your gener-
ations to come, at the entrance to the Tent of
Meeting before Yahweh, where I shall meet
you and speak to you.
43 'There I shall meet the Israelites in the
place consecrated by my glory. 44 I shall conse-
crate the Tent of Meeting and the altar; I
shall also consecrate Aaron and his sons, to
be priests in my service. 45 And I shall live
with the Israelites and be their God, 46 and
they will know that I am Yahweh their God,
who brought them out of Egypt to live among
them: I, Yahweh their God.'

The altar of incense

30 'You will make an altar on which to
burn incense; you will make it of acacia
wood, 2 one cubit long, and one cubit wide—
it must be square—and two cubits high; its
horns must be of a piece with it. 3 You will
overlay its top, its sides all round and its horns
with pure gold and make a gold moulding to
go all round. 4 You will make two gold rings
for it below the moulding on its two opposite
sides, to take the shafts used for carrying it.
5 You will make the shafts of acacia wood and
overlay them with gold.
6 'You will put it in front of the curtain by
the ark of Testimony, in front of the mercy-
seat which is on the Testimony, where I shall
meet you. 7 On it Aaron will burn fragrant
incense each morning; when he trims the
lamps, he will burn incense on it; 8 and when
Aaron puts back the lamps at twilight, he will
burn incense on it, incense perpetually before
Yahweh for all your generations to come.
9 You will not offer unauthorised incense, or
burnt offering, or cereal offering on it, and
you will not pour any libation over it. 10 Once
a year, Aaron will perform the rite of
expiation on the horns of the altar; once a
year, on the Day of Expiation, with the
blood of the sacrifice for sin, he will make
expiation for himself, for all your genera-
tions to come. It is especially holy for
Yahweh.'

The poll tax

11 Yahweh then spoke to Moses and said,
12 'When you count the Israelites by census,
each one of them must pay Yahweh a ransom
for his life, to avoid any incidence of plague
among them while you are holding the
census. 13 Everyone subject to the census will
pay half a shekel, reckoning by the sanctuary
shekel: twenty *gerah* to the shekel. This
half-shekel will be set aside for Yahweh.
14 Everyone subject to the census, that is to
say of twenty years and over, will pay the
sum set aside for Yahweh. 15 The rich man
must not give more, nor the poor man less,
than half a shekel when he pays the sum set
aside for Yahweh in ransom for your lives.
16 You will take the ransom money of the
Israelites and apply it to the service of the
Tent of Meeting, for it to be a reminder of
the Israelites before Yahweh, as the ransom
for your lives.'

The bronze basin

17 Yahweh then spoke to Moses and said,
18 'You will also make a bronze basin on its
bronze stand, for washing. You will put it
between the Tent of Meeting and the altar
and put water in it, 19 in which Aaron and
his sons will wash their hands and feet.
20 Whenever they are to enter the Tent of
Meeting, they will wash, to avoid incurring
death; and whenever they approach the altar
for their service, to burn an offering for
Yahweh, 21 they will wash their hands and
feet, to avoid incurring death. This is a
perpetual decree for him and his descendants
for all their generations to come.'

The anointing oil

22 Yahweh spoke further to Moses and said,
23 'Take the finest spices: five hundred shekels
of fresh myrrh, half as much (two hundred
and fifty shekels) of fragrant cinnamon, two
hundred and fifty shekels of scented reed,
24 five hundred shekels (reckoning by the

sanctuary shekel) of cassia, and one *hin* of olive oil. 25You will make this into a holy anointing oil, such a blend as the perfumer might make; this will be a holy anointing oil. 26With it you will anoint the Tent of Meeting and the ark of the Testimony, 27the table and all its accessories, the lamp-stand and its accessories, the altar of incense, 28the altar of burnt offerings and all its accessories, and the basin with its stand, 29consecrating them, so that they will be especially holy and whatever touches them will become holy. 30You will also anoint Aaron and his sons and consecrate them to be priests in my service. 31You will then speak to the Israelites and say, "This anointing oil will be holy for you for all your generations to come. 32It must not be used for anointing the human body, nor may you make any of the same mixture. It is a holy thing; you will regard it as holy. 33Anyone who makes up the same oil or uses it on an unauthorised person will be outlawed from his people." '

The incense

34Yahweh then said to Moses, 'Take sweet spices: storax, onycha, galbanum, sweet spices and pure frankincense in equal parts, 35and compound an incense, such a blend as the perfumer might make, salted, pure, and holy. 36You will grind some of this up very fine and put it in front of the Testimony in the Tent of Meeting, where I shall meet you. You will regard it as especially holy. 37You may not make any incense of similar composition for your own use. You will regard it as holy, reserved for Yahweh. Anyone who makes up the same thing to use as perfume will be outlawed from his people.'

The craftsmen for the sanctuary

31 Yahweh then spoke to Moses and said, 2'Look, I have singled out Bezalel son of Uri, son of Hur, of the tribe of Judah, 3and have filled him with the spirit of God in wisdom, knowledge and skill in every kind of craft: 4in designing and carrying out work in gold and silver and bronze, 5in cutting stones to be set, in wood carving and in executing every kind of work. 6And to help him I have given him Oholiab son of Ahisamach, of the tribe of Dan, and have endowed the hearts of all the skilled men with the skill to make everything I have ordered you: 7the Tent of Meeting; the ark of the Testimony; the mercy-seat above it; and all the furniture of the tent; 8the table and all its accessories; the pure lamp-stand and all its equipment; the altar of incense; 9the altar of burnt offerings and all its accessories; the basin and its stand; 10the liturgical vestments, the sacred vestments for Aaron the priest, and the vestments for his sons, for their priestly functions; 11the anointing oil and the fragrant incense for the sanctuary. They will do everything as I have ordered you.'

The Sabbath rest

12Yahweh then said to Moses, 13'Speak to the Israelites and say, "You will keep my Sabbaths properly, for this is a sign between myself and you for all your generations to come, so that you will know that it is I, Yahweh, who sanctify you. 14You will keep the Sabbath, then; you will regard it as holy. Anyone who profanes it will be put to death; anyone who does any work on that day will be outlawed from his people. 15Work must be done for six days, but the seventh day will be a day of complete rest, consecrated to Yahweh. Anyone who works on the Sabbath day will be put to death. 16The Israelites will keep the Sabbath, observing the Sabbath for all their generations to come: this is an eternal covenant. 17Between myself and the Israelites, this is a sign for ever, for in six days Yahweh made heaven and earth, but on the seventh day he rested and drew breath." '

The tablets of the Law committed to Moses

18When he had finished speaking to Moses on Mount Sinai, he gave him the two tablets of the Testimony, tablets of stone inscribed by the finger of God.

V: THE GOLDEN CALF AND THE RENEWAL OF THE COVENANT[a]

The golden calf

32 When the people saw that Moses was
a long time before coming down the
mountain, they gathered round Aaron and
said to him, 'Get to work, make us a god to
go at our head; for that Moses, the man who
brought us here from Egypt—we do not
know what has become of him.' [2]Aaron
replied, 'Strip off the gold rings in the ears
of your wives and your sons and daughters,
and bring them to me.' [3]The people all
stripped off the gold rings from their ears and
brought them to Aaron. [4]He received what
they gave him, melted it down in a mould
and with it made the statue of a calf. 'Israel,'
the people shouted, 'here is your God who
brought you here from Egypt!' [5]Observing
this, Aaron built an altar before the statue
and made this proclamation, 'Tomorrow will
be a feast in Yahweh's honour.'
[6]Early next morning they sacrificed
burnt offerings and brought communion
sacrifices. The people then sat down to eat
and drink, and afterwards got up to amuse
themselves.

Moses forewarned by Yahweh

[7]Yahweh then said to Moses, 'Go down at
once, for your people whom you brought
here from Egypt have become corrupt. [8]They
have quickly left the way which I ordered
them to follow. They have cast themselves a
metal calf, worshipped it and offered sacrifice
to it, shouting, "Israel, here is your God who
brought you here from Egypt!" ' [9]Yahweh
then said to Moses, 'I know these people; I
know how obstinate they are! [10]So leave me
now, so that my anger can blaze at them and
I can put an end to them! I shall make a great
nation out of you instead.'

The prayer of Moses

[11]Moses tried to pacify Yahweh his God.
'Yahweh,' he said, 'why should your anger
blaze at your people, whom you have brought
out of Egypt by your great power and mighty
hand? [12]Why should the Egyptians say, "He
brought them out with evil intention, to
slaughter them in the mountains and wipe
them off the face of the earth?" Give up
your burning wrath; relent over this disaster
intended for your people. [13]Remember your
servants Abraham, Isaac and Jacob, to whom
you swore by your very self and made this
promise: "I shall make your offspring as
numerous as the stars of heaven, and this
whole country of which I have spoken, I shall
give to your descendants, and it will be their
heritage for ever." ' [14]Yahweh then relented
over the disaster which he had intended to
inflict on his people.

Moses breaks the tablets of the Law

[15]Moses turned and came down the mountain
with the two tablets of the Testimony in
his hands, tablets inscribed on both sides,
inscribed on the front and on the back. [16]The
tablets were the work of God, and the writing
on them was God's writing, engraved on the
tablets.
[17]When Joshua heard the noise of the
people shouting, he said to Moses, 'There is
the sound of battle in the camp!' [18]But he
replied:

> No song of victory is this sound,
> no lament for defeat this sound;
> but answering choruses I hear!

[19]And there, as he approached the camp,
he saw the calf and the groups dancing. Moses
blazed with anger. He threw down the tablets
he was holding, shattering them at the foot
of the mountain. [20]He seized the calf they
had made and burned it, grinding it into
powder which he scattered on the water, and
made the Israelites drink it. [21]Moses then
said to Aaron, 'What have these people done
to you for you to have brought so great a sin
on them?' [22]Aaron replied, 'My lord should
not be so angry. You yourself know what a
bad state these people are in! [23]They said to
me, "Make us a god to go at our head; for
that Moses, the man who brought us here
from Egypt—we do not know what has
become of him." [24]I then said to them,

32a ‖ Dt 9:7seq.

"Anyone with gold, strip it off!" They gave
it to me. I threw it into the fire and out came
this calf!'

The zeal of the Levites

25When Moses saw that the people were out
of hand—for Aaron had let them get out of
hand to the derision of their enemies all round
them—26Moses then stood at the gate of the
camp and shouted, 'Who is for Yahweh? To
me!' And all the Levites rallied round him.
27He said to them, 'Yahweh, God of Israel,
says this, "Buckle on your sword, each of
you, and go up and down the camp from
gate to gate, every man of you slaughtering
brother, friend and neighbour." ' 28The
Levites did as Moses said, and of the people
about three thousand men perished that day.
29'Today', Moses said, 'you have consecrated
yourselves to Yahweh, one at the cost of his
son, another of his brother; and so he bestows
a blessing on you today.'

Moses prays again

30On the following day Moses said to the
people, 'You have committed a great sin. But
now I shall go up to Yahweh: perhaps I can
secure expiation for your sin.' 31Moses then
went back to Yahweh and said, 'Oh, this
people has committed a great sin by making
themselves a god of gold. 32And yet, if it
pleased you to forgive their sin. . . ! If not,
please blot me out of the book you have
written!' 33Yahweh said to Moses, 'Those
who have sinned against me are the ones I
shall blot out of my book. 34So now go and
lead the people to the place I promised to
you. My angel will indeed go at your head
but, on the day of punishment, I shall punish
them for their sin.' 35And Yahweh punished
the people for having made the calf, the one
Aaron had made.

The Israelites ordered to depart

33 Yahweh then said to Moses, 'Leave,
move on from here, you and the people
whom you have brought here from Egypt, to
the country that I swore to Abraham, Isaac
and Jacob that I would give to their descend-
ants. 2I shall send an angel in front of you
and drive out the Canaanites, the Amorites,
the Hittites, the Perizzites, the Hivites and
the Jebusites. 3Move on towards a country
flowing with milk and honey, but I myself
shall not be going with you or I might
annihilate you on the way, for you are an
obstinate people.' 4On hearing these stern
words the people went into mourning and no
one wore his ornaments.
5Yahweh then said to Moses, 'Say to the
Israelites, "You are an obstinate people. If I
were to go with you even for a moment, I
should annihilate you. So now take off your
ornaments, and then I shall decide how to
deal with you!" ' 6So, from Mount Horeb
onwards, the Israelites stripped themselves
of their ornaments.

The Tent

7Moses used to take the Tent and pitch it
outside the camp, far away from the camp.
He called it the Tent of Meeting. Anyone
who wanted to consult Yahweh would go out
to the Tent of Meeting, outside the camp.
8Whenever Moses went out to the Tent, the
people would all stand up and every man
would stand at the door of his tent and watch
Moses until he went into the Tent. 9And
whenever Moses went into the Tent, the
pillar of cloud would come down and station
itself at the entrance to the Tent, while
Yahweh spoke with Moses. 10The people
could all see the pillar of cloud stationed at
the entrance to the Tent and the people would
all stand up and bow low, each at the door of
his tent. 11Yahweh would talk to Moses face
to face, as a man talks to his friend, and
afterwards he would come back to the camp,
but the young man who was his servant,
Joshua son of Nun, never left the inside of
the Tent.

Moses prays

12Moses said to Yahweh, 'Look, you say to
me, "Make the people move on," but you
have not told me whom you are going to send
with me, although you have said, "I know
you by name and you enjoy my favour." 13If
indeed I enjoy your favour, please show me
your ways, so that I understand you and
continue to enjoy your favour; consider too
that this nation is your people.' 14Yahweh
then said, 'I myself shall go with you and I
shall give you rest.' 15To which he said, 'If
you do not come yourself, do not make us
move on from here, 16for how can it be
known that I and my people enjoy your

favour, if not by your coming with us? By this we shall be marked out, I and your people, from all the peoples on the face of the earth.' 17 Yahweh then said to Moses, 'Again I shall do what you have asked, because you enjoy my favour and because I know you by name.'

Moses on the mountain

18 He then said, 'Please show me your glory.' 19 Yahweh said, 'I shall make all my goodness pass before you, and before you I shall pronounce the name Yahweh; and I am gracious to those to whom I am gracious and I take pity on those on whom I take pity. 20 But my face', he said, 'you cannot see, for no human being can see me and survive.' 21 Then Yahweh said, 'Here is a place near me. You will stand on the rock, 22 and when my glory passes by, I shall put you in a cleft of the rock and shield you with my hand until I have gone past. 23 Then I shall take my hand away and you will see my back; but my face will not be seen.'

The covenant renewed
The tablets of the Law

34 Yahweh said to Moses, 'Cut two tablets of stone like the first ones and come up to me on the mountain, and I will write on the tablets the words that were on the first tablets, which you broke. 2 Be ready at dawn; at dawn come up Mount Sinai and wait for me there at the top of the mountain. 3 No one may come up with you, no one may be seen anywhere on the mountain; the flocks and herds may not even graze in front of this mountain.' 4 So he cut two tablets of stone like the first and, with the two tablets of stone in his hands, Moses went up Mount Sinai in the early morning as Yahweh had ordered. 5 And Yahweh descended in a cloud and stood with him there and pronounced the name Yahweh.

God appears

6 Then Yahweh passed before him and called out, 'Yahweh, Yahweh, God of tenderness and compassion, slow to anger, rich in faithful love and constancy, 7 maintaining his faithful love to thousands, forgiving fault, crime and sin, yet letting nothing go unchecked, and punishing the parent's fault in the children and in the grandchildren to the third and fourth generation!' 8 Moses immediately bowed to the ground in worship, 9 then he said, 'If indeed I do enjoy your favour, please, my Lord, come with us, although they are an obstinate people; and forgive our faults and sins, and adopt us as your heritage.'

The covenant

10 He then said, 'Look, I am now making a covenant: I shall work such wonders at the head of your whole people as have never been worked in any other country or nation, and all the people round you will see what Yahweh can do, for what I shall do through you will be awe-inspiring. 11 Mark, then, what I command you today. I am going to drive out the Amorites, the Canaanites, the Hittites, the Perizzites, the Hivites and the Jebusites before you. 12 Take care you make no pact with the inhabitants of the country which you are about to enter, or they will prove a snare in your community. 13 You will tear down their altars, smash their cultic stones and cut down their sacred poles, 14 for you will worship no other god, since Yahweh's name is the Jealous One; he is a jealous God. 15 Make no pact with the inhabitants of the country or, when they prostitute themselves to their own gods and sacrifice to them, they will invite you and you will partake of their sacrifice, 16 and then you will choose wives for your sons from among their daughters, and their daughters, prostituting themselves to their own gods, will induce your sons to prostitute themselves to their gods.

17 'You will not cast metal gods for yourself.

18 'You will observe the feast of Unleavened Bread. For seven days you will eat unleavened bread, as I have commanded you, at the appointed time in the month of Abib, for in the month of Abib you came out of Egypt.

19 'All that first issues from the womb belongs to me: every male, every first-born of flock or herd. 20 But the first-born donkey you will redeem with an animal from the flock; if you do not redeem it, you must break its neck. All the first-born of your sons you will redeem, and no one will appear before me empty-handed.

21 'For six days you will labour, but on the

seventh day you will rest; you will stop work even during ploughing and harvesting.
[22]'You will observe the feast of Weeks, of the first-fruits of the wheat harvest, and the feast of Ingathering at the close of the year.
[23]'Three times a year all your menfolk will appear before Lord Yahweh, God of Israel,
[24]for I shall dispossess the nations before you and extend your frontiers, and no one will set his heart on your territory when you go away to appear before Yahweh your God three times a year.
[25]'You will not offer the blood of my sacrificial victim with leavened bread, nor is the victim offered at the feast of Passover to be left until the following day.
[26]'You will bring the best of the first-fruits of your soil to the house of Yahweh your God.

'You will not boil a kid in its mother's milk.'

[27]Yahweh then said to Moses, 'Put these words in writing, for they are the terms of the covenant which I have made with you and with Israel.'
[28]He stayed there with Yahweh for forty days and forty nights, eating and drinking nothing, and on the tablets he wrote the words of the covenant—the Ten Words.

Moses comes down from the mountain

[29]When Moses came down from Mount Sinai with the two tablets of the Testimony in his hands, as he was coming down the mountain, Moses did not know that the skin of his face was radiant because he had been talking to him. [30]And when Aaron and all the Israelites saw Moses, the skin on his face was so radiant that they were afraid to go near him. [31]But Moses called to them, and Aaron and all the leaders of the community rejoined him, and Moses talked to them, [32]after which all the Israelites came closer, and he passed on to them all the orders that Yahweh had given to him on Mount Sinai. [33]Once Moses had finished speaking to them, he put a veil over his face. [34]Whenever Moses went into Yahweh's presence to speak with him, he took the veil off until he came out. And when he came out, he would tell the Israelites what orders he had been given, [35]and the Israelites would see Moses' face radiant. Then Moses would put the veil back over his face until he went in to speak to him next time.

VI: THE FURNISHING AND BUILDING OF THE SANCTUARY

The Sabbath rest

35 Moses assembled the whole community of Israelites and said, 'These are the things Yahweh has ordered to be done: [2]Work must be done for six days, but the seventh must be a holy day for you, a day of complete rest, in honour of Yahweh. Anyone who does any work on that day will be put to death. [3]You will not light a fire on the Sabbath day in any of your homes.'

The materials are collected

[4]Moses spoke to the whole community of Israelites. 'This', he said, 'is what Yahweh has ordered: [5]Set aside a contribution for Yahweh out of your possessions. Everyone whose heart prompts him to do so should bring a contribution for Yahweh: gold, silver and bronze; [6]materials dyed violet-purple, red-purple and crimson, finely woven linen, goats' hair, [7]rams' skins dyed red, fine leather, acacia wood, [8]oil for the light, spices for the anointing oil and for the fragrant incense; [9]cornelian and other stones to be set in the *ephod* and breastplate. [10]And all those of you who have the skill must come and make everything that Yahweh has ordered: [11]the Dwelling, its tent and its covering, its clasps and its frames, its crossbars, its pillars and its sockets; [12]the ark, its shafts and all its accessories, the mercy-seat and the screening curtain; [13]the table, its shafts and all its accessories, and the loaves of permanent offering; [14]the lamp-stand for the light, its accessories, its lamps, and the oil for the light; [15]the altar of incense and its shafts, the anointing oil, the fragrant incense, and the screen for the entrance, for the entrance of the tent; [16]the altar of burnt offerings and its bronze grating, its shafts, and all its accessories; the basin and its stand; [17]the curtaining

for the court, its poles, its sockets, and the
screen for the entrance to the court; [18]the
pegs for the Dwelling and the pegs for the
court, and their cords; [19]the liturgical vest-
ments for service in the sanctuary—the
sacred vestments for Aaron the priest, and
the vestments for his sons, for their priestly
functions.'

[20]The whole community of Israelites then
withdrew from Moses' presence. [21]And all
those whose heart stirred them and all those
whose spirit prompted them brought a
contribution for Yahweh, for the work on
the Tent of Meeting, for its general service
and for the sacred vestments. [22]Men and
women, they came, all those whose heart
prompted them, bringing brooches, rings,
bracelets, necklaces, golden objects of every
kind—all those who had vowed gold to
Yahweh, [23]while all those who happened to
own violet-purple, red-purple or crimson
materials, finely woven linen, goats' hair,
rams' skins dyed red, or fine leather, brought
that. [24]All those offering a contribution of
silver or bronze brought their contribution
for Yahweh and all who happened to own
acacia wood, suitable for any of the work
to be done, brought that. [25]All the skilled
women set their hands to spinning, and
brought what they had spun: violet-purple,
red-purple or crimson materials, and fine
linen, [26]while all those women whose heart
stirred them by virtue of their skill, spun
goats' hair. [27]The leaders brought cornelians
and other stones to be set in the *ephod* and
breastplate, [28]and the spices and oil for the
light, for the anointing oil and for the fragrant
incense. [29]All those Israelites, men and
women, whose heart prompted them to
contribute to the entire work that Yahweh
had ordered through Moses to be done,
brought a contribution to Yahweh.

The craftsmen for the sanctuary

[30]Moses then said to the Israelites, 'Look,
Yahweh has singled out Bezalel son of Uri,
son of Hur, of the tribe of Judah, [31]and has
filled him with the spirit of God in wisdom,
knowledge and skill in every kind of craft:
[32]in designing and carrying out work in gold
and silver and bronze, [33]in cutting stones to
be set, in wood carving and in executing
every kind of work. [34]And on him and on
Oholiab son of Ahisamach, of the tribe of
Dan, he has bestowed the gift of teaching,
[35]and filled them with the skill to carry out
every kind of work, that of the engraver, that
of the embroiderer, that of the needleworker
in violet-purple, red-purple and crimson
materials and fine linen, that of the weaver,
and indeed that of every kind of craftsman
and designer.'

36 'Bezalel, Oholiab and all the men whom
Yahweh has endowed with the skill and
knowledge to know how to carry out all the
work to be done on the sanctuary, will do
exactly as Yahweh has ordered.'

A halt is called to the collection

[2]Moses then summoned Bezalel, Oholiab and
all the skilled men whose hearts Yahweh had
endowed with skill, all whose heart stirred
them to come forward and do the work.
[3]From Moses they received everything that
the Israelites had brought as contributions
for carrying out the work of building the
sanctuary, and, as they went on bringing
their offerings every morning, [4]the skilled
men who were doing all the work for the
sanctuary, all left their particular work [5]and
said to Moses, 'The people are bringing more
than is needed for the work Yahweh has
ordered to be done.' [6]Moses then gave the
order and proclamation was made
throughout the camp, 'No one, whether man
or woman, must do anything more towards
contributing for the sanctuary.' So the people
were prevented from bringing any more, [7]for
the material to hand was enough, and more
than enough, to complete all the work.

The Dwelling

[8]All the most skilled of the men doing the
work made the Dwelling. Moses made it with
ten sheets of finely woven linen, dyed violet-
purple, red-purple and crimson and
embroidered with great winged creatures.
[9]The length of a single sheet was twenty-
eight cubits, its width four cubits, all the
sheets being of the same size. [10]He joined five
of the sheets to one another, and the other
five sheets to one another. [11]He made violet
loops along the edge of the first sheet, at the
end of the set, and did the same along the
edge of the last sheet in the other set. [12]He
made fifty loops on the first sheet and fifty
loops along the outer edge of the sheet of the
second set, the loops corresponding to one
another. [13]He made fifty gold clasps and

joined the sheets together with the clasps. In
this way the Dwelling was a unified whole.
14 Next he made sheets of goats' hair for the
tent over the Dwelling; he made eleven of
these. 15 The length of a single sheet was thirty
cubits and its width four cubits; the eleven
sheets were all of the same size. 16 He joined
five sheets together into one set and six sheets
into another. 17 He made fifty loops along the
edge of the last sheet of the first set, and fifty
loops along the edge of the sheet of the second
set. 18 He made fifty bronze clasps, to draw
the tent together and make it a unified whole.
19 And for the tent he made a cover of rams'
skins dyed red, and a cover of fine leather
over that.

The framework

20 For the Dwelling he made vertical frames
of acacia wood. 21 Each frame was ten cubits
long and one and a half cubits wide. 22 Each
frame had twin tenons; this was how he made
all the frames for the Dwelling. 23 He made
frames for the Dwelling: twenty frames for
the south side, to the south, 24 and made
forty silver sockets under the twenty frames,
two sockets under one frame for its two
tenons, two sockets under the next frame for
its two tenons; 25 and for the other side of
the Dwelling, the north side, twenty frames
26 and forty silver sockets, two sockets under
one frame, two sockets under the next frame.
27 For the back of the Dwelling, on the west,
he made six frames. 28 He also made two
frames for the corners at the back of the
Dwelling; 29 these were coupled together at
the bottom, staying so up to the top, to the
level of the first ring; this he did with the two
frames forming the two corners. 30 Thus there
were eight frames with their sixteen silver
sockets; two sockets under each frame. 31 He
made crossbars of acacia wood: five for the
frames of the first side of the Dwelling, 32 five
crossbars for the frames of the other side of
the Dwelling and five crossbars for the frames
which formed the back of the Dwelling, to
the west. 33 He made the middle bar, to join
the frames from one end to the other, halfway
up. 34 He overlaid the frames with gold, made
gold rings for them, through which to place
the crossbars, and overlaid the crossbars with
gold.

The curtain

35 He made a curtain of finely woven linen,
dyed violet-purple, red-purple and crimson
and embroidered with great winged crea-
tures, 36 and for it he made four poles of
acacia wood, overlaying them with gold, with
golden hooks for them, for which he cast four
sockets of silver. 37 For the entrance to the
tent he made a screen of finely woven linen
embroidered with violet-purple, red-purple
and crimson, 38 as also the five columns for it
and their hooks; he overlaid their capitals
and rods with gold, but their five sockets
were of bronze.

The ark

37 Bezalel made the ark of acacia wood,
two and a half cubits long, one and a
half cubits wide and one and a half cubits
high. 2 He overlaid it, inside and out, with
pure gold, and made a gold moulding all
round it. 3 He cast four gold rings for it at its
four supports: two rings on one side and two
rings on the other. 4 He also made shafts of
acacia wood and overlaid them with gold,
5 and passed the shafts through the rings on
the sides of the ark, by which to carry it.
6 He also made a mercy-seat of pure gold, two
and a half cubits long and one and a half cu-
bits wide, 7 and modelled two great winged
creatures of beaten gold, putting them at
the two ends of the mercy-seat, 8 one winged
creature at one end and the other winged crea-
ture at the other end, making the winged
creatures of a piece with the mercy-seat at
either end. 9 The winged creatures had their
wings spread upwards, protecting the ark
with their wings and facing each other, their
faces being towards the mercy-seat.

The table for the loaves of permanent offering

10 He made the table of acacia wood, two
cubits long, one cubit wide and one and a
half cubits high, 11 and made a gold moulding
all round it. 12 He fitted it with struts a hand's
breadth wide and made a gold moulding
round the struts. 13 He cast four gold rings
for it and fixed the rings at the four corners
where the four legs were. 14 The rings lay
close to the struts to hold the shafts for
carrying the table. 15 He made the shafts of
acacia wood and overlaid them with gold;

these were for carrying the table. 16He made
the accessories which were to go on the table:
its dishes, cups, jars and libation bowls, of
pure gold.

The lamp-stand

17He also made the lamp-stand of pure gold,
making the lamp-stand, base and stem, of
beaten gold, its cups, calyxes and bud being
of a piece with it. 18Six branches sprang from
its sides: three of the lamp-stand's branches
from one side, three of the lamp-stand's
branches from the other. 19The first branch
carried three cups shaped like almond blos-
soms, each with its calyx and bud; the second
branch, too, carried three cups shaped like
almond blossoms, each with its calyx and
bud, and similarly all six branches springing
from the lamp-stand. 20The lamp-stand itself
carried four cups shaped like almond blos-
soms, each with its calyx and bud: 21one calyx
under the first two branches springing from
the lamp-stand, one calyx under the next pair
of branches and one calyx under the last
pair of branches—thus for all six branches
springing from the lamp-stand. 22The calyxes
and the branches were of a piece with the
lamp-stand, and the whole was made from a
single piece of pure gold, beaten out. 23He
also made its seven lamps, its snuffers and
trays of pure gold. 24He made the lamp-stand
and all its accessories from a talent of pure
gold.

The altar of incense
The anointing oil and incense

25He made the altar of incense of acacia wood,
one cubit long, and one cubit wide—it was
square—and two cubits high, its horns were
of a piece with it. 26He overlaid its top, its
sides all round and its horns with pure gold
and made a moulding to go all round. 27He
made two gold rings for it below the moulding
on its two opposite sides, to take the shafts
used for carrying it. 28He made the shafts of
acacia wood and overlaid them with gold.
29He also made the holy anointing oil and the
fragrant incense, blending it as a perfumer
would.

The altar of burnt offerings

38 He made the altar of burnt offerings of
acacia wood, five cubits long and five
cubits wide; it was square and three cubits
high. 2At its four corners he made horns,
the horns being of a piece with it, and overlaid
it with bronze. 3He made all the altar
accessories: the ash pans, shovels, sprinkling
basins, hooks and fire pans; he made all the
altar accessories of bronze. 4He also made
a grating for the altar of bronze network,
below its ledge, underneath, coming halfway
up. 5He cast four rings for the four corners
of the bronze grating to take the shafts. 6He
made the shafts of acacia wood and overlaid
them with bronze. 7He passed the shafts
through the rings on the sides of the altar for
carrying it. He made the altar hollow, out of
boards.

The bronze basin

8He made the bronze basin and its bronze
stand from the mirrors of the women who
served at the entrance to the Tent of Meeting.

The court

9He made the court. On the south side, on
the south, the curtaining of the court was of
finely woven linen a hundred cubits long.
10Its twenty poles and their sockets being of
bronze, and their hooks and rods of silver;
11and on the north side, a hundred cubits of
curtaining, its twenty poles and their twenty
sockets being of bronze, and their hooks and
rods of silver. 12On the west side there were
fifty cubits of curtaining, with its ten poles
and their ten sockets, the poles' hooks and
rods being of silver; 13and on the east side on
the east, there were fifty cubits. 14On the one
side there were fifteen cubits of curtaining,
with its three poles and their three sockets,
15and on the other side—either side of the
gateway to the court—there were fifteen
cubits of curtaining with its three poles and
their three sockets. 16All the curtaining round
the court was of finely woven linen, 17the
sockets for the poles were of bronze, the
poles' hooks and rods of silver, their capitals
were overlaid with silver and all the poles of
the court had silver rods. 18The screen for
the gateway to the court was of finely woven
linen embroidered with violet-purple, red-
purple and crimson, twenty cubits long and
five cubits high (all the way along) like the
curtaining of the court, 19its four poles and
their four sockets being of bronze, their
hooks of silver, their capitals overlaid with

silver, and their rods of silver. [20]All the pegs
round the Dwelling and the court were of
bronze.

The amount of metal used

[21]These are the accounts for the Dwelling—
the Dwelling of the Testimony—drawn up
by order of Moses, the work of Levites,
produced by Ithamar son of Aaron, the
priest.
[22]Bezalel son of Uri, son of Hur, of the
tribe of Judah, made everything that Yahweh
ordered Moses to make, [23]his assistant being
Oholiab son of Ahisamach, of the tribe of
Dan, an engraver, embroiderer and needle-
worker in violet-purple, red-purple and
crimson materials and fine linen.
[24]The amount of gold used for the work,
for the entire work for the sanctuary (the gold
consecrated for the purpose) was twenty-nine
talents and seven hundred and thirty shekels,
reckoned by the sanctuary shekel. [25]The
silver from the census of the community was
one hundred talents and one thousand seven
hundred and seventy-five shekels, reckoned
by the sanctuary shekel, [26]one *beqa* per head,
half a shekel reckoned by the sanctuary
shekel, for everyone of twenty years and over
included in the census, for six hundred and
three thousand five hundred and fifty
persons. [27]A hundred talents of silver were
used for casting the sockets for the sanctuary
and the sockets for the curtain: a hundred
sockets from a hundred talents, one talent
per socket. [28]From the one thousand seven
hundred and seventy-five shekels he made
the hooks for the poles, overlaid their capitals
and made the rods for them. [29]The bronze
consecrated for the purpose amounted to
seventy talents and two thousand four
hundred shekels, [30]and from it he made
the sockets for the entrance of the Tent of
Meeting, the bronze altar, its bronze grating
and all the altar accessories, [31]the sockets all
round the court, the sockets for the gateway
to the court, all the pegs for the Dwelling and
all the pegs round the court.

The vestments of the high priest

39 From the violet-purple, red-purple and
crimson materials, they made the
liturgical vestments for service in the sanc-
tuary. They made the sacred vestments for
Aaron, as Yahweh had ordered Moses.

The *ephod*

[2]They made the *ephod* of gold, of violet-
purple, red-purple and crimson materials
and finely woven linen. [3]They beat gold into
thin plates and cut these into threads to
work into the violet-purple, red-purple and
crimson materials and the fine linen by
needlework. [4]For the *ephod* they made shoul-
der-straps which were joined to it at its two
edges. [5]The waistband on the *ephod* to hold
it in position, was of a piece with it and of the
same workmanship: of gold, violet-purple,
red-purple and finely woven linen, as
Yahweh had ordered Moses. [6]They worked
the cornelians, mounted in gold setting, and
engraved, like an engraved seal, with the
names of the sons of Israel, [7]and put the
stones on the shoulder-straps of the *ephod*, to
commemorate the sons of Israel, as Yahweh
had ordered Moses.

The breastplate of judgement

[8]They made the breastplate of the same
embroidered work as the *ephod*: of gold,
violet-purple, red-purple and crimson
materials and finely woven linen. [9]It was
square and doubled over, a span in length
and a span in width. [10]In it they set four rows
of stones: a sard, a topaz and an emerald, for
the first row; [11]for the second row, a garnet,
a sapphire and a diamond; [12]for the third
row, a hyacinth, a ruby and an amethyst;
[13]and for the fourth row, a beryl, a cornelian
and a jasper: mounted in gold settings, [14]the
stones corresponding to the names of the sons
of Israel, twelve like their names, engraved
like seals, each with the name of one of the
twelve tribes. [15]For the breastplate they made
chains of pure gold twisted like cords, [16]and
they made two gold rosettes and two gold
rings, putting the two rings on the two outside
edges of the breastplate [17]and fastening the
two gold cords to the two rings on the outside
edges of the breastplate. [18]The other two ends
of the cords they fastened to the two rosettes,
putting these on the shoulder-straps of the
ephod, on the front. [19]They also made two
gold rings and put them on the two outside
edges of the breastplate, on the inner side,
against the *ephod*; [20]and they made two more
gold rings and put them low down on the
front of the two shoulder-straps of the *ephod*,
close to the join, above the waistband of the
ephod. [21]They secured the pectoral by a violet-

purple cord passed through its rings and those of the *ephod*, so that the pectoral would sit above the waistband and not come apart from the *ephod*, as Yahweh had ordered Moses.

The robe

[22]They made the robe of the *ephod* woven entirely of violet-purple. [23]The opening in the centre of the robe was like the neck of a coat of mail; round the opening was a border, so that it would not get torn. [24]On the lower hem of the robe, they made pomegranates of violet-purple, red-purple and crimson and finely woven linen, [25]and made bells of pure gold, putting the bells between the pomegranates all round the lower hem of the robe: [26]alternately, a bell and then a pomegranate, all round the lower hem of the robe of office, as Yahweh had ordered Moses.

The vestments of the priests

[27]They made the tunics of finely woven linen for Aaron and his sons, [28]the turban of fine linen, the head-dresses of fine linen, the breeches of finely woven linen, [29]the waistbands of finely woven linen embroidered with violet-purple, red-purple and crimson, as Yahweh had ordered Moses.

[30]They also made the flower—the symbol of holy consecration—of pure gold and on it, like an engraved seal, they engraved, 'Consecrated to Yahweh'. [31]They put it on a violet-purple cord, to fasten it high up on the turban, as Yahweh had ordered Moses.

[32]So all the work for the Dwelling, for the Tent of Meeting, was completed. They had done everything exactly as Yahweh had ordered Moses.

The finished work presented to Moses

[33]They then brought Moses the Dwelling, the Tent and all its accessories: its clasps, frames, crossbars, poles and sockets; [34]the cover of rams' skins dyed red, the cover of fine leather and the screening curtain; [35]the ark of the Testimony and its shafts, and the mercy-seat; [36]the table, all its accessories and the loaves of permanent offering; [37]the lamp-stand of pure gold, its lamps—the array of lamps—and all its accessories, and the oil for the light; [38]the golden altar, the anointing oil, the fragrant incense and the screen for the entrance to the tent; [39]the bronze altar and its bronze grating, its shafts and all its accessories; the basin and its stand; [40]the curtaining for the court, its poles, its sockets, and the screen for the gateway to the court, its cords, its pegs and all the accessories for the service of the Dwelling, for the Tent of Meeting; [41]the liturgical vestments for officiating in the sanctuary—the sacred vestments for Aaron the priest, and the vestments for his sons—for the priestly functions. [42]The Israelites had done all the work exactly as Yahweh had ordered Moses.

[43]Moses inspected all the work: they had indeed done it as Yahweh had ordered; and Moses blessed them.

The sanctuary erected and consecrated

40 Yahweh then spoke to Moses and said, [2]'On the first day of the first month, you will erect the Dwelling, the Tent of Meeting, [3]and place the ark of the Testimony in it and screen the ark with the curtain. [4]You will then bring in the table and arrange what has to be arranged on it. You will then bring in the lamp-stand and set up its lamps. [5]You will place the golden altar of incense in front of the ark of the Testimony, and place the screen at the entrance to the Dwelling. [6]You will place the altar of burnt offerings in front of the entrance to the Dwelling, the Tent of Meeting, [7]and you will place the basin between the Tent of Meeting and the altar, and fill it with water. [8]You will then set up the surrounding court and hang the screen at the gateway of the court. [9]Then, taking the anointing oil, you will anoint the Dwelling and everything inside, consecrating it and all its accessories; it will then be holy. [10]You will then anoint the altar of burnt offerings and all its accessories, consecrating the altar; the altar will then be especially holy. [11]You will then anoint the basin and its stand, and consecrate it. [12]You will then bring Aaron and his sons to the entrance of the Tent of Meeting, bathe them thoroughly [13]and then dress Aaron in the sacred vestments, and anoint and consecrate him, to serve me in the priesthood. [14]You will then bring his sons, dress them in tunics [15]and anoint them as you anointed their father, to serve me in the priesthood. Their anointing will confer an everlasting priesthood on them for all their generations to come.'

The divine commands are carried out

16 Moses did this; he did exactly as Yahweh
had ordered him. 17 On the first day of the
first month in the second year the Dwelling
was erected. 18 Moses erected the Dwelling.
He fixed its sockets, set up its frames, put its
crossbars in position and set up its poles.
19 He spread the tent over the Dwelling and
the covering for the tent over that, as Yahweh
had ordered Moses. 20 He took the Testimony
and put it in the ark, positioned the shafts on
the ark and put the mercy-seat on top of the
ark. 21 He brought the ark into the Dwelling
and put the screening curtain in place,
screening the ark of the Testimony, as
Yahweh had ordered Moses. 22 He put the
table inside the Tent of Meeting, against the
side of the Dwelling, on the north, outside
the curtain, 23 and on it arranged the loaves
before Yahweh, as Yahweh had ordered
Moses. 24 He put the lamp-stand inside the
Tent of Meeting, opposite the table, on the
south side of the Dwelling, 25 and set up
the lamps before Yahweh, as Yahweh had
ordered Moses. 26 He put the golden altar
inside the Tent of Meeting, in front of the
curtain, 27 and on it burnt fragrant incense,
as Yahweh had ordered Moses. 28 He then put
the screen at the entrance to the Dwelling.
29 He put the altar of burnt offerings at the
entrance to the Dwelling, to the Tent of
Meeting, and on it offered the burnt offering
and cereal offering, as Yahweh had ordered
Moses. 30 He put the basin between the Tent
of Meeting and the altar and put water in it
for the ablutions, 31 where Moses, Aaron and
his sons washed their hands and feet,
32 whenever they entered the Tent of Meeting
or approached the altar they washed, as
Yahweh had ordered Moses. 33 He then set
up the court round the Dwelling and the altar
and set up the screen at the gate-way to the
court. Thus Moses completed the work.

Yahweh takes possession of the sanctuary

34 The cloud then covered the Tent of Meeting
and the glory of Yahweh filled the Dwelling.
35 Moses could not enter the Tent of Meeting,
since the cloud stayed over it and the glory
of Yahweh filled the Dwelling.

The cloud guides the Israelites

36 At every stage of their journey, whenever
the cloud rose from the Dwelling, the Israel-
ites would resume their march. 37 If the cloud
did not rise, they would not resume their
march until the day it did rise. 38 For
Yahweh's cloud stayed over the Dwelling
during the daytime and there was fire in-
side the cloud at night, for the whole
House of Israel to see, at every stage of their
journey.

THE BOOK OF LEVITICUS

The book draws together various bodies of law and ritual, starting with laws concerning Levites. The keynote is the holiness of God, to which his people must correspond. For this especially, certain classes of people, certain objects and certain actions are set apart from common usage. Israel must remain fully aware that its God is totally other than the common world of human experience.

In fact this system of holiness developed over several centuries. Burnt offerings and cereal offerings stem only from Canaan; the law of the single sanctuary at Jerusalem (to combat the contamination of the local shrines) dates from King Josiah; the

Law of Holiness (chh. 17—26) with its emphasis on the awesome transcendence of God, dates from the Babylonian exile; the full rite of consecration of priests may be even later than this.

Many of the regulations are drawn from the body of law widespread in the Near East, some based on hygiene appropriate to hot and desert lands. But two principles are paramount, setting this legislation apart from the laws of Israel's neighbours: **1** all life, both human and animal, and its processes are sacred to Yahweh, and **2** Israelites must be free to serve Yahweh, neither subject to, nor humiliated by, any human being.

PLAN OF THE BOOK

LEVITICUS

I: THE RITUAL OF SACRIFICE

The burnt offering

1 Yahweh summoned Moses and, speaking
to him from the Tent of Meeting, said,
[2]"Speak to the Israelites; say to them, "When
any of you brings an offering to Yahweh, he
can offer an animal either from the herd or
from the flock.
[3]"If his offering is to be a burnt offering
from the herd, he must offer an unblemished
male; he will offer it at the entrance to the
Tent of Meeting, to make it acceptable to
Yahweh. [4]He must lay his hand on the
victim's head, and it will be accepted as
effectual for his expiation. [5]He will then
slaughter the bull before Yahweh, and the
priests descended from Aaron will offer the
blood. They will pour it all around the altar
which stands at the entrance to the Tent of
Meeting. [6]He will then skin the victim and
quarter it. [7]The priests descended from
Aaron will put a fire on the altar and arrange
wood on the fire. [8]The priests descended
from Aaron will then arrange the quarters,
the head and the fat on the wood on the fire
on the altar. [9]He will wash the entrails and
shins in water, and the priest will burn it all
on the altar as a burnt offering, food burnt as
a smell pleasing to Yahweh.
[10]"If his offering is to be of an animal from
the flock, of a lamb or a goat to be offered as a
burnt offering, he must offer an unblemished
male. [11]He will slaughter it on the north side
of the altar, before Yahweh, and the priests
descended from Aaron will pour the blood
all around the altar. [12]He will then quarter it,
and the priest will arrange the quarters, the
head and the fat on the wood on the fire on
the altar. [13]He will wash the entrails and shins
in water, and the priest will burn it all on the
altar as a burnt offering, food burnt as a smell
pleasing to Yahweh.
[14]"If his offering to Yahweh is to be a burnt
offering of a bird, he must offer a turtledove
or a young pigeon. [15]The priest will offer it
at the altar and wring off its head, which he
will burn on the altar; its blood must then be
squeezed out on the side of the altar. [16]He
will then remove the crop and the feathers
and throw them on the eastern side of the
altar, where the fatty ashes are put. [17]He will
then split it in half with a wing on each side,
but without separating the two parts. The

priest will then burn it on the altar, on the
wood which is on the fire, as a burnt offering,
food burnt as a smell pleasing to Yahweh." '

The cereal offering

2' "If anyone offers Yahweh a cereal
offering, his offering must consist of
wheaten flour on which he must pour wine
and put incense. 2He will bring it to the
priests descended from Aaron; he will take a
handful of the wheaten flour, some of the oil
and all the incense, and this the priest will
burn on the altar as a memorial, as food
burnt as a smell pleasing to Yahweh. 3The
remainder of the cereal offering will revert to
Aaron and his sons, an especially holy portion
of the food burnt for Yahweh.
4"When you offer a cereal offering of
dough baked in the oven, the wheaten flour
must be prepared either in the form of
unleavened cakes mixed with oil, or in the
form of unleavened wafers spread with oil.
5"If your offering is a cereal offering
cooked on the griddle, the wheaten flour
mixed with oil must contain no leaven. 6You
will break it in pieces and pour oil over it. It
is a cereal offering.
7"If your offering is a cereal offering
cooked in the pan, the wheaten flour must be
prepared with oil.
8"You will bring Yahweh the cereal
offering thus prepared and present it to the
priest; he will take it to the altar. 9And from
the cereal offering the priest will take the
memorial and burn it on the altar, food
burnt as a smell pleasing to Yahweh. 10The
remainder of the cereal offering will revert to
Aaron and his descendants: it is especially
holy since it is taken from the food burnt for
Yahweh.
11"None of the cereal offerings which you
offer to Yahweh must be prepared with
leaven, for you must never include leaven or
honey in food burnt for Yahweh. 12You may
offer them to Yahweh as an offering of first-
fruits, but they will not make a pleasing smell
if they are burnt on the altar. 13You will put
salt in every cereal offering that you offer,
and you will not fail to put the salt of the
covenant of your God on your cereal offering;
to every offering you will add an offering of
salt to your God. 14If you offer Yahweh a
cereal offering of first-fruits, you will offer it
in the form of roasted ears of wheat or of
bread made from ground wheat. 15You will
add oil to it and put incense on it; it is a cereal
offering; 16and from it the priest will burn
the memorial with some bread and oil (and
all the incense) as food burnt for Yahweh." '

The communion sacrifice

3' "If his sacrifice is a communion sacrifice,
and if he offers an animal from the herd,
be it male or female, whatever he offers before
Yahweh must be unblemished. 2He will lay
his hand on the victim's head and slaughter
it at the entrance to the Tent of Meeting. The
priests descended from Aaron will then pour
the blood all around the altar. 3He will offer
part of the communion sacrifice as food burnt
for Yahweh: the fat covering the entrails, all
the fat on the entrails, 4both kidneys, the fat
on them and on the loins, the mass of fat
which he will remove from the liver and
kidneys. 5The priests descended from Aaron
will then burn this on the altar, in addition
to the burnt offering, on the wood of the fire,
food burnt as a smell pleasing to Yahweh.
6"If it is an animal from the flock which he
offers as a communion sacrifice to Yahweh,
be the animal that he offers male or female,
it must be unblemished.
7"If he offers a sheep, he will offer it before
Yahweh, 8he will lay his hand on the victim's
head and slaughter it in front of the Tent of
Meeting; the priests descended from Aaron
will then pour its blood all around the altar.
9Of the communion sacrifice he will offer the
following as food burnt for Yahweh: the fat,
all the tail taken off near the base of the spine,
the fat covering the entrails, all the fat on the
entrails, 10both kidneys, the fat on them and
on the loins, the mass of fat which he will
remove from the liver and kidneys. 11The
priest will then burn this on the altar as food,
as food burnt for Yahweh.
12"If his offering is a goat, he will offer it
before Yahweh, 13he will lay his hand on the
victim's head and slaughter it in front of the
Tent of Meeting, and the descendants of
Aaron will then pour its blood all around the
altar. 14This is what he will then offer of it as
food burnt for Yahweh: the fat covering the
entrails, all the fat on the entrails, 15both
kidneys, the fat on them and on the loins, the
mass of fat which he will remove from the
liver and kidneys. 16The priest will then burn
these pieces on the altar as food burnt as a
smell pleasing to Yahweh.
"All the fat belongs to Yahweh. 17This is

a perpetual law for all your descendants, wherever you may live: that you will not eat either fat or blood." '

The sacrifice for sin:

a: of the high priest

4 Yahweh spoke to Moses and said: 2'Speak to the Israelites and say:

"If anyone sins inadvertently against any of Yahweh's commandments and does anything prohibited by them, 3if the one who sins is the anointed priest, thus making the people guilty, then for the sin which he has committed he must offer Yahweh a young bull, an unblemished animal from the herd, as a sacrifice for sin. 4He will bring the bull before Yahweh at the entrance to the Tent of Meeting, will lay his hand on its head and slaughter it before Yahweh. 5The anointed priest will then take some of the bull's blood and carry it into the Tent of Meeting. 6He will then dip his finger in the blood and sprinkle it seven times in front of the sanctuary curtain, before Yahweh. 7The priest will then put some of the blood on the horns of the altar of incense smoking before Yahweh in the Tent of Meeting, and will pour all the rest of the bull's blood at the foot of the altar of burnt offerings at the entrance to the Tent of Meeting.

8"Of the bull offered as a sacrifice for sin, he will set aside all the fat: the fat covering the entrails, all the fat on the entrails, 9both kidneys, the fat on them and on the loins, the mass of fat which he will remove from the liver and kidneys—10exactly as was done with the portion set aside in the communion sacrifice—and the priest will burn these pieces on the altar of burnt offerings.

11"The bull's skin and all its meat, its head, its shins, its entrails and its offal, 12the whole bull he will then have carried out of the camp to a clean place, the place where the fatty ashes are thrown, and will burn it on a wood fire; it must be burnt where the ashes are thrown.

b: of the community of Israel

13"If the whole community of Israel has sinned inadvertently and, without being aware of it has incurred guilt by doing something forbidden by Yahweh's commandments, 14once the sin of which it is guilty has been discovered, the community must offer a young bull, an unblemished animal from the herd, as a sacrifice for sin, and bring it in front of the Tent of Meeting. 15The elders of the community will then lay their hands on the bull's head before Yahweh, and the bull will be slaughtered before Yahweh.

16"The anointed priest will then take some of the bull's blood into the Tent of Meeting. 17He will then dip his finger in the blood and sprinkle it seven times in front of the curtain, before Yahweh. 18He will then put some of the blood on the horns of the altar standing before Yahweh inside the Tent of Meeting, and then pour all the rest of the blood at the foot of the altar of burnt offerings at the entrance to the Tent of Meeting.

19"He will then set aside all the fat from the animal and burn it on the altar. 20He will then deal with the bull as he did with the bull in the sacrifice for sin. It will be dealt with in the same way; and once the priest has performed the rite of expiation for the people, they will be forgiven.

21"He will then have the bull carried out of the camp and will burn it as he burned the first one. This is the sacrifice for the sin of the community.

c: of a leader of the community

22"When a leader has sinned and inadvertently incurred guilt by doing something forbidden by the commandments of Yahweh his God 23(or if the sin which he has committed is drawn to his attention), he must bring a he-goat as his offering, an unblemished male. 24He will then lay his hand on the goat's head and slaughter it on the spot where the burnt offerings are slaughtered before Yahweh. This is a sacrifice for sin; 25the priest will take some of the victim's blood on his finger and put it on the horns of the altar of burnt offerings. He will then pour the rest of its blood at the foot of the altar of burnt offerings 26and burn all the fat on the altar, as with the fat in the communion sacrifice. This is how the priest must perform the rite of expiation for him to free him from his sin, and he will be forgiven.

d: of a private individual

27"If one of the country people sins inadvertently and incurs guilt by doing something forbidden by Yahweh's commandments 28(or

if the sin which he has committed is drawn to his attention), he must bring a she-goat as his offering for the sin which he has committed, an unblemished female. 29 He will then lay his hand on the victim's head and slaughter it on the spot where the burnt offerings are slaughtered. 30 The priest will take some of its blood on his finger and put it on the horns of the altar of burnt offerings. He will then pour all the rest of the blood at the foot of the altar. 31 He will then remove all the fat, as the fat was removed for the communion sacrifice, and the priest will burn it on the altar as a smell pleasing to Yahweh. This is how the priest must perform the rite of expiation for him, and he will be forgiven.

32 "If he wishes to bring a lamb as an offering for this kind of sacrifice, he must bring an unblemished female. 33 He will then lay his hand on the victim's head and slaughter it as a sacrifice for sin on the spot where the burnt offerings are slaughtered. 34 The priest will take some of the victim's blood on his finger and put it on the horns of the altar of burnt offerings. He will then pour all the rest of the blood at the foot of the altar. 35 He will then remove all the fat, as was done for the sheep in the communion sacrifice, and the priest will burn it as food burnt for Yahweh. This is how the priest must perform for him the rite of expiation for the sin which he has committed, and he will be forgiven." '

Some cases of sacrifice for sin

5 1 ' "If someone sins in any of these following cases:

"He should have come forward to give evidence when he heard the formal adjuration, having seen the incident or known the facts; but he has not spoken out, and so bears the consequences of his guilt;

2 "or someone touches something unclean, whatever it may be—the dead body of an unclean animal, wild or tame, or of one of the unclean reptiles—and without realising it becomes unclean, he becomes answerable for it;

3 "or he touches some human uncleanness, whatever it may be, contact with which makes him unclean; he does not notice it, then, realising it later, he becomes answerable for it;

4 "or someone lets slip an oath to do something either evil or good, in any of those matters on which someone may let slip an oath; he does not notice it, then, realising it later, he becomes answerable for it;

5 "if he is answerable in any of those cases, he will have to confess the sin committed. 6 As a sacrifice of reparation for the sin committed, he will bring Yahweh a female from the flock (sheep or goat) as a sacrifice for sin; and the priest will perform the rite of expiation for him to free him from his sin.

Sins of private individuals (continued)

7 "If he cannot afford an animal from the flock as a sacrifice of reparation for the sin he has committed, he will bring Yahweh two turtledoves or two young pigeons—one as a sacrifice for sin and the other as a burnt offering. 8 He will bring them to the priest who will first offer the one intended for the sacrifice for sin. The priest will wring its neck but not remove the head. 9 He will sprinkle the side of the altar with the victim's blood, and then squeeze out the rest of the blood at the foot of the altar. This is a sacrifice for sin. 10 He will then offer the other bird as a burnt offering according to the ritual. This is how the priest must perform the rite of expiation for the person for the sin he has committed, and he will be forgiven.

11 "If he cannot afford two turtledoves or two young pigeons, he will bring a tenth of an *ephah* of wheaten flour as an offering for the sin committed; he must not mix oil with it or put incense on it, since this is a sacrifice for sin. 12 He will bring it to the priest, who will take a handful of it as a memorial, and burn this on the altar in addition to the offerings of food burnt for Yahweh. This is a sacrifice for sin. 13 This is how the priest must perform the rite of expiation for the person for the sin he has committed in any of those cases, and he will be forgiven. In this case, the priest has the same rights as in the case of a cereal offering." '

The sacrifice of reparation

14 Yahweh spoke to Moses and said:

15 'If someone is unfaithful and sins inadvertently by infringing Yahweh's sacred rights, as a sacrifice of reparation he must bring Yahweh an unblemished ram from his flock, the value of which will be decided by you in silver shekels according to the rate of the sanctuary-shekel. 16 He will make amends for what his sin subtracted from the sacred

rights, adding one-fifth to the value, and give
it to the priest. The priest will then perform
the rite of expiation for him with the ram for
the sacrifice of reparation and he will be
forgiven.
[17]'If someone sins and without realising it
does one of the things forbidden by Yahweh's
commandments, he will answer for it and
bear the consequences of his guilt. [18]As a
sacrifice of reparation he must bring the
priest an unblemished ram from his flock to
the value which you decide, and the priest
will perform the rite of expiation for him for
the oversight unwittingly committed, and
he will be forgiven. [19]This is a sacrifice of
reparation; the man was certainly answerable
to Yahweh.'
[20]Yahweh spoke to Moses and said:
[21]'If someone sins and is unfaithful against
Yahweh by deceiving his fellow-countryman
over a deposit or a security, or by withholding
something due to him or by exploiting him;
[22]'or if he finds lost property and denies it;
'or if he perjures himself about anything
that a human being may do criminally in such
matters;
[23]'if he sins and so becomes answerable, he
must restore what he has taken or demanded
in excess: the deposit confided to him, the
lost property that he has found, [24]or any
object about which he has perjured himself.
He will add one-fifth to the principal and pay
the whole to the person who held the property
rights on the day when he incurred the guilt.
[25]He will then bring Yahweh an unblemished
ram from his flock to the value which you
decide, to the priest as a sacrifice of repar-
ation, [26]and the priest will perform the rite
of expiation for him before Yahweh and he
will be forgiven, whatever the act by which
he incurred guilt.'

Priesthood and sacrifice

a: The burnt offering

6 Yahweh spoke to Moses and said:
[2]'Give these orders to Aaron and his sons:
"This is the ritual for the burnt offering
(that is, the burnt offering that stays on the
altar brazier all night until morning and is
consumed by the altar fire).
[3]"The priest will put on his linen tunic and
put his linen drawers on to cover himself. He
will then remove the fatty ashes of the burnt
offering consumed by the altar fire and put
them at the side of the altar. [4]He will then
take off his clothes, put on others and carry
the ashes to a clean place outside the camp.
[5]"The fire on the altar that consumes the
burnt offering must not be allowed to go out.
Every morning the priest will make it up with
wood, arranging the burnt offering on it
and burning the fat from the communion
sacrifices. [6]The fire must always be burning
on the altar; it must never go out.

b: The cereal offering

[7]'This is the ritual for the cereal offering:
"One of the descendants of Aaron will
bring it into Yahweh's presence in front of
the altar, [8]will take a handful of the wheaten
flour (with the oil and all the incense which
have been added to it) and burn the memorial
on the altar as a smell pleasing to Yahweh;
[9]and Aaron and his sons will eat the
remainder in the form of unleavened loaves.
They will eat it inside the holy place, in the
court of the Tent of Meeting. [10]The portion
I give them of the food burnt for me must
not be baked with leaven; it is especially holy,
like the sacrifice for sin and the sacrifice of
reparation. [11]All male descendants of Aaron
are entitled to eat this portion of the food
burnt for Yahweh (this is a perpetual law
for all your descendants) and anyone who
touches it will become holy." '
[12]Yahweh spoke to Moses and said:
[13]'This is the offering that Aaron and his
sons must make to Yahweh on the day they
are anointed: one-tenth of an *ephah* of
wheaten flour as a perpetual cereal offering,
half in the morning and half in the evening.
[14]It will be prepared on the griddle and mixed
with oil; you will bring the paste as a cereal
offering in several pieces, offering them as a
smell pleasing to Yahweh. [15]When one of his
sons is anointed priest to succeed him, he will
do the same. This is a perpetual law.
'The entire cereal offering will be burnt
for Yahweh. [16]Every cereal offering made by
a priest will be a total sacrifice; none of it will
be eaten.'

c: The sacrifice for sin

[17]Yahweh spoke to Moses and said, [18]'Speak
to Aaron and his sons and say:
"This is the ritual for the sacrifice for sin:
"The victim must be slaughtered before
Yahweh on the spot where the burnt offerings

are slaughtered. It is especially holy. [19]The
priest who offers this sacrifice will eat it. It
will be eaten inside the holy place, in the
court of the Tent of Meeting. [20]Everything
touching the victim's meat will become holy,
and if any of the blood splashes on clothing,
the stain will be washed off inside the holy
place. [21]The earthenware vessel in which the
meat is cooked must be broken; if a bronze
vessel has been used for the cooking, it
must be scrubbed and thoroughly rinsed with
water. [22]Any male who is a priest may eat the
sacrifice. It is especially holy. [23]But no one
may eat any of the victims offered for sin, the
blood of which has been taken into the Tent
of Meeting to make expiation inside the
sanctuary. These must be burnt." '

d: The sacrifice of reparation

7 ' "This is the ritual for the sacrifice of
reparation:
"It is especially holy. [2]The victim must be
slaughtered where the burnt offerings are
slaughtered, and the priest will pour the
blood all around the altar. [3]He will then offer
all the fat: the tail, the fat covering the
entrails, [4]both kidneys, the fat on them and
on the loins, the mass of fat which he will
remove from the liver and kidneys. [5]The
priest will burn these pieces on the altar as
food burnt for Yahweh. This is a sacrifice of
reparation. [6]Every male who is a priest may
eat it. It will be eaten inside the holy place;
it is especially holy.

The rights of the priests

[7]"As with the sacrifice for sin, so with the
sacrifice of reparation—the ritual is the same
for both. The offering with which the priest
performs the rite of expiation will revert to
the priest. [8]The hide of the victim presented
by someone to the priest to be offered as a
burnt offering will revert to the priest. [9]Every
cereal offering baked in the oven, every cereal
offering cooked in the pan or on the griddle
will revert to the priest who offers it. [10]Every
cereal offering, mixed with oil or dry, will
revert to all the descendants of Aaron without
distinction.

e: The communion sacrifice

(i) Sacrifice with praise
[11]"This is the ritual for the communion sacrifice to be offered to Yahweh:

[12]"If this is offered as a sacrifice with
praise, to the latter must be added an offering
of unleavened cakes mixed with oil,
unleavened wafers spread with oil, and
wheaten flour in the form of cakes mixed
with oil. [13]This offering, then, must be added
to the cakes of leavened bread and to the
communion sacrifice with praise. [14]One of
the cakes of this offering must be presented
as an offering to Yahweh; it will revert to
the priest who pours out the blood of the
communion sacrifice. [15]The meat of the
victim will be eaten on the day the offering
is made; nothing may be left until next
morning.

(ii) Votive or voluntary sacrifices
[16]"If the victim is offered as a votive or a
voluntary sacrifice, it must be eaten on the
day it is offered, and the remainder may be
eaten on the following day; [17]but on the third
day whatever is left of the meat of the victim
must be burnt.

General rules

[18]"If any of the meat of a victim offered as a
communion sacrifice is eaten on the third
day, the person who has offered it will not be
acceptable and will receive no credit for it. It
will count as rotten meat, and the person who
eats it will bear the consequences of the guilt.
[19]"Meat that has touched anything unclean
cannot be eaten; it must be burnt.
"Anyone clean may eat the meat, [20]but
anyone unclean who eats the meat of a
communion sacrifice offered to Yahweh will
be outlawed from his people. [21]Furthermore,
if anyone touches anything unclean, human
or animal, or any foul thing, and then eats
the meat of a communion sacrifice offered to
Yahweh, that individual will be outlawed
from his people." '
[22]Yahweh spoke to Moses and said,
[23]'Speak to the Israelites and say:
"You may not eat the fat of ox, sheep or
goat. [24]The fat of an animal that has died a
natural death or been savaged by beasts may
be used for any other purpose, but you are
not to eat it. [25]Anyone who eats the fat of an
animal offered as food burnt for Yahweh will
be outlawed from his people.
[26]"Wherever you live, you will never eat
blood, whether it be of bird or of beast.
[27]Anyone who eats any blood will be outlawed
from his people." '

The priest's portion

[28]Yahweh spoke to Moses and said, [29]'Speak to the Israelites and say:

"Anyone who offers Yahweh a communion sacrifice must bring him part of his sacrifice as an offering. [30]He must bring the food to be burnt for Yahweh, that is to say, the fat adhering to the forequarters, with his own hands. He will bring it, and also the forequarters, with which he will make the gesture of offering before Yahweh. [31]The priest will then burn the fat on the altar, and the forequarters will revert to Aaron and his descendants. [32]You will set aside the right thigh from your communion sacrifice and give it to the priest. [33]The right thigh will be the portion of the descendant of Aaron who offers the blood and fat of the communion sacrifice. [34]For I have deprived the Israelites of the forequarter offered and the thigh presented in their communion sacrifices, and given them to the priest Aaron and his descendants; this is a perpetual law for the Israelites." '

Conclusion

[35]Such was the portion of Aaron and his descendants in the food burnt for Yahweh, the day he presented them to Yahweh for them to become his priests. [36]This was what Yahweh ordered the Israelites to give them on the day they were anointed: a perpetual law for all their descendants.

[37]Such was the ritual for burnt offering, cereal offering, sacrifice for sin, sacrifice of reparation, investiture sacrifice and communion sacrifice, [38]which Yahweh laid down for Moses on Mount Sinai, the day he ordered the Israelites to make their offerings to Yahweh in the desert of Sinai.

II: THE INVESTITURE OF THE PRIESTS

Consecration rites[a]

8 Yahweh spoke to Moses and said:

[2]'Take Aaron and with him his sons, the vestments, the anointing oil, the bull for the sacrifice for sin, the two rams and the basket of unleavened bread. [3]Then call the whole community together at the entrance to the Tent of Meeting.'

[4]Moses did as Yahweh ordered; the community gathered at the entrance to the Tent of Meeting, [5]and Moses said to them, 'This is what Yahweh has ordered to be done.'

[6]He made Aaron and his sons come forward and washed them with water.

[7]He then dressed him in the tunic, passed the waistband round his waist, vested him in the robe and put the *ephod* on him. He then put the waistband of the *ephod* round his waist, fastening it to him. [8]He put the breastplate on him, and placed the *urim* and *thummim* in it. [9]He put the turban on his head, and on the front of the turban, the golden flower; this was the symbol of holy consecration, which Yahweh had prescribed to Moses.

[10]Moses then took the anointing oil and anointed the Dwelling and everything inside it, to consecrate them. [11]He sprinkled the altar seven times and anointed the altar and its accessories, the basin and its stand, to consecrate them. [12]He then poured some of the anointing oil on Aaron's head and anointed him to consecrate him.

[13]Moses then made Aaron's sons come forward; he dressed them in tunics, passed the waistbands round their waists and put on their head-dresses, as Yahweh had ordered him.

[14]He then had the bull for the sacrifice for sin brought forward. Aaron and his sons laid their hands on the victim's head [15]and Moses slaughtered it. He then took the blood and with his finger put some of it on the horns on the corners of the altar to purify the altar. He then poured the rest of the blood at the foot of the altar, which he consecrated by performing the rite of expiation over it. [16]He then took all the fat covering the entrails, the mass of fat over the liver, both kidneys and their fat; and he burnt this on the altar, [17]but the bull's skin, its meat and its offal he burnt outside the camp, as Yahweh had ordered Moses.

[18]He then had the ram for the burnt

8a || Ex 28:1—29:35.

offering brought forward. Aaron and his sons laid their hands on the ram's head [19]and Moses slaughtered it. He poured its blood all around the altar. [20]He then quartered the ram and burned the head, the quarters and the fat. [21]He then washed the entrails and shins, and burnt the whole ram on the altar, as a burnt offering, offered to be a pleasing smell, as food burnt for Yahweh, as Yahweh had ordered Moses.

[22]He then had the other ram brought forward, the ram for the investiture sacrifice. Aaron and his sons laid their hands on its head [23]and Moses slaughtered it. He took some of its blood and put it on the lobe of Aaron's right ear, on the thumb of his right hand, and on the big toe of his right foot. [24]He then made Aaron's sons come forward and he put some of the blood on the lobes of their right ears, on the thumbs of their right hands and on the big toes of their right feet. Next, Moses poured the rest of the blood all around the altar. [25]He then took the fat: the tail, all the fat covering the entrails, the mass of fat over the liver, both kidneys and their fat, and the right thigh. [26]From the basket of unleavened bread placed before Yahweh, he took an unleavened cake, a cake of bread made with oil, and a wafer; he placed these on the fat and the right thigh, [27]and put it all into Aaron's hands and those of his sons, and made the gesture of offering before Yahweh. [28]Moses then took them away from them and burned them on the altar, with the burnt offering. This was the investiture sacrifice, offered to be a pleasing smell, as food burnt for Yahweh. [29]Moses then took the fore-quarter and made the gesture of offering before Yahweh. This was the portion of the ram of investiture that reverted to Moses, as Yahweh had ordered Moses.

[30]Moses then took some of the anointing oil and some of the blood that was on the altar and sprinkled Aaron and his vestments, and his sons and their vestments, with it. In this way he consecrated Aaron and his vestments and his sons and their vestments.

[31]Moses then said to Aaron and his sons, 'Cook the meat at the entrance to the Tent of Meeting, and eat it there, as also the bread of the investiture sacrifice still in the basket of the investiture offerings, as I ordered, when I said, "Aaron and his sons must eat it." [32]What remains of the meat and bread you will burn. [33]For seven days you will not leave the entrance to the Tent of Meeting, until the time of your investiture is complete; for your investiture will require seven days. [34]Yahweh has ordered us to do as we have done today to perform the rite of expiation for you; [35]hence, for seven days, day and night, you will remain at the entrance to the Tent of Meeting observing Yahweh's ritual; do this, and you will not incur death. For this was the order I received.' [36]So Aaron and his sons did everything that Yahweh had ordered through Moses.

The priests assume their functions

9 On the eighth day Moses summoned Aaron and his sons and the elders of Israel; [2]he said to Aaron, 'Take a calf to offer a sacrifice for sin, and a ram for a burnt offering, both without blemish, and bring them before Yahweh. [3]Then say to the Israelites, "Take a goat to be offered as a sacrifice for sin, a calf and a lamb one year old (both without blemish) for a burnt offering, [4]a bull and a ram for communion sacrifices to be slaughtered before Yahweh, and a cereal offering mixed with oil. For Yahweh will appear to you today." '

[5]They brought what Moses had ordered in front of the Tent of Meeting; then the whole community approached and stood before Yahweh. [6]Moses then said, 'This is what Yahweh has ordered you to do, so that his glory may be visible to you.' [7]Moses then addressed Aaron, 'Go to the altar and offer your sacrifice for sin and your burnt offering, and so perform the rite of expiation for yourself and your family. Then present the people's offering and perform the rite of expiation for them, as Yahweh has ordered.'

[8]Aaron went to the altar and slaughtered the calf as a sacrifice for his own sin. [9]Aaron's sons then presented the blood to him; he dipped his finger in it and put some on the horns of the altar, and then poured the rest of the blood at the foot of the altar. [10]The fat of the sacrifice for sin and the kidneys and the mass of fat over the liver he burned on the altar, as Yahweh had ordered Moses, [11]and the meat and the skin he burned outside the camp.

[12]He then slaughtered the burnt offering; Aaron's sons then handed him the blood, which he poured all around the altar. [13]They then handed him the quartered victim and the head, and he burned these on the altar. [14]He then washed the entrails and shins and

burned them with the burnt offering on the
altar.
15He then presented the people's offering.
He took the goat for the people's sacrifice for
sin, slaughtered it, and made a sacrifice for
sin with it in the same way as with the first.
16He then had the burnt offering brought
forward and proceeded according to the
ritual. 17He then had the cereal offering
brought forward, took a handful of it and
burned it on the altar in addition to the
morning burnt offering.
18Then he slaughtered the bull and the ram
as a communion sacrifice for the people.
Aaron's sons handed him the blood and he
poured it all around the altar. 19The fat of the
bull and the ram, the tail, the covering fat,
the kidneys, the mass of fat over the liver,
20he placed on the ribs and then burned on
the altar. 21With the ribs and the right thigh
Aaron made the gesture of offering as
Yahweh had ordered Moses.
22Aaron then raised his hands towards
the people and blessed them. Having thus
performed the sacrifice for sin, the burnt
offering and the communion sacrifice, he
came down 23and entered the Tent of Meeting
with Moses. Then they came out together to
bless the people and the glory of Yahweh
appeared to the entire people: 24a flame leapt
out from Yahweh's presence and consumed
the burnt offering and fat on the altar. At this
sight the entire people shouted for joy and
fell on their faces.

Complementary legislation

a: A lesson in exact observance

10 Aaron's sons Nadab and Abihu each
took his censer, put fire in it and incense
on the fire, and presented unauthorised fire
before Yahweh, which was not in accordance
with his orders. 2At this a flame leapt out
from Yahweh's presence and swallowed them
up, and they perished before Yahweh.
3Moses then said to Aaron, 'That is what
Yahweh meant when he said:

In those who are close to me
I show my holiness,
and before all the people I show my glory.'

Aaron remained silent.

b: Removal of bodies

4Moses summoned Mishael and Elzaphan,
sons of Aaron's uncle Uzziel, and said to
them, 'Come here and take your brothers
away from the sanctuary, out of the camp.'
5They came and carried them away, still in
their tunics, out of the camp, as Moses had
said.

c: Rules for priestly mourning

6Moses said to Aaron and his sons Eleazar
and Ithamar, 'Do not disorder your hair or
tear your clothes; or you may incur death
and his retribution may overtake the whole
community. No, it is for the entire House of
Israel to lament your brothers who have
been the victims of Yahweh's fire. 7To avoid
incurring death, do not leave the entrance to
the Tent of Meeting, for Yahweh's anointing
oil is on you.' And they did as Moses said.

d: Wine forbidden

8Yahweh spoke to Aaron and said:
9'When you come to the Tent of Meeting,
you and your sons with you, to avoid incur-
ring death you may not drink wine or any
other fermented liquor. This is a perpetual
law for all your descendants. 10And so shall
it be also when you separate the sacred from
the profane, the unclean from the clean, 11and
when you teach the Israelites any of the
decrees that Yahweh has pronounced for
them through Moses.'

e: The priests' portion in offerings

12Moses said to Aaron and his surviving
sons, Eleazar and Ithamar, 'Take the cereal
offering left over from the food burnt for
Yahweh. Eat the unleavened part of it beside
the altar, since it is especially holy. 13Eat it in
the holy place, since it is the portion of the
food burnt for Yahweh that is prescribed for
you and your sons; this is the order I have
received.
14'You, your sons and daughters with you,
will eat in a clean place the forequarter offered
and the thigh presented, for these have been
given to you and your children as your due
from the Israelites' communion sacrifices.
15The thigh presented and the forequarter
offered, once the fat has been burnt, revert
to you and your sons with you, after they

have been presented before Yahweh with the gesture of offering, in virtue of a perpetual law as Yahweh has ordered.'

f: A special regulation concerning sacrifice for sin

[16]Moses then enquired carefully about the goat offered as a sacrifice for sin, and found that they had burnt it. He was angry with Eleazar and Ithamar, Aaron's surviving sons, and said, [17]'Why did you not eat this victim for sin in the holy place, since it is especially holy and was given to you to take away the community's guilt, by performing the rite of expiation for them before Yahweh? [18]Since its blood was not taken inside the sanctuary, you should have eaten its meat there, as I ordered you.' [19]Aaron said to Moses, 'Look, today they offered their sacrifice for sin and their burnt offering before Yahweh, and these disasters have befallen me. If I had eaten the sin offering today, would this have met with Yahweh's approval?' [20]And when Moses heard this, he was satisfied.

III: RULES CONCERNING THE CLEAN AND UNCLEAN

Clean and unclean animals[a]

a: On land

11 Yahweh spoke to Moses and Aaron and said to them, [2]'Speak to the Israelites and say:

"Of all animals living on land these are the creatures you may eat:

[3]"You may eat any animal that has a cloven hoof, divided into two parts, and that is a ruminant. [4]The following, which either chew the cud or have a cloven hoof, are the ones that you may not eat: you will regard the camel as unclean, because though it is ruminant, it does not have a cloven hoof; [5]you will regard the coney as unclean, because though it is ruminant, it does not have a cloven hoof; [6]you will regard the hare as unclean, because though it is ruminant, it does not have a cloven hoof; [7]you will regard the pig as unclean, because though it has a cloven hoof, divided into two parts, it is not a ruminant. [8]You will not eat the meat of these or touch their dead bodies; you will regard them as unclean.

b: In water

[9]"Of all that lives in water, these you may eat:

"Anything that has fins and scales, and lives in the water, whether in sea or river, you may eat. [10]But anything in sea or river that does not have fins and scales, of all the small water-creatures and all the living things found there, you will regard as detestable. [11]You will regard them as detestable; you must not eat their meat and you will regard their carcases as detestable. [12]Anything that lives in water, but not having fins and scales, you will regard as detestable.

c: Birds

[13]"Of the birds these are the ones that you will regard as detestable; they may not be eaten, they are detestable for eating:

"The tawny vulture, the griffon, the osprey, [14]the kite, the various kinds of buzzard, [15]all kinds of raven, [16]the ostrich, the screech owl, the seagull, the various kinds of hawk, [17]horned owl, night owl, cormorant, barn owl, [18]ibis, pelican, white vulture, [19]stork, the various kinds of heron, the hoopoe and the bat.

d: Winged insects

[20]"All winged insects moving on four feet you will regard as detestable for eating. [21]Of all these winged insects you may eat only the following: those with the sort of legs above their feet which enable them to leap over the ground. [22]These are the ones you may eat: the various kinds of migratory locust, the various kinds of *solham* locust, *hargol* locust and *hagab* locust. [23]But all other winged insects on four feet you will regard as detestable for eating.

11a || Dt 14:3–21.

Contact with unclean animals

24"By the following you will be made unclean. Anyone who touches the carcase of one will be unclean until evening. 25Anyone who picks up their carcases must wash his clothing and will be unclean until evening. 26Animals that have hoofs, but not cloven, and that are not ruminant, you will regard as unclean; anyone who touches them will be unclean. 27Those four-footed animals which walk on the flat of their paws you will regard as unclean; anyone who touches their carcases will be unclean until evening, 28and anyone who picks up their carcases must wash his clothing and will be unclean until evening. You will regard them as unclean.

e: Small ground animals

29"Of the small creatures which crawl along the ground, these are the ones which you will regard as unclean: the mole, the rat, the various kinds of lizard: 30gecko, *koah*, *letaah*, chameleon and *tinshamet*.

Further rules on contact with things unclean

31"Of all the small creatures, these are the animals which you must regard as disgusting. Anyone who touches them when they are dead will be unclean until evening.

32"Any object on which one of these creatures falls when it is dead becomes unclean: wooden utensil, clothing, skin, sacking, any utensil whatever. It must be immersed in water and will remain unclean until evening: then it will be clean. 33If the creature falls into an earthenware vessel, the vessel must be broken; whatever the vessel contains is unclean. 34Any edible food will be unclean if the water touches it; any drinkable liquid will be unclean, no matter what its container. 35Anything on which the carcase of such a creature may fall will be unclean: be it oven or stove, it must be destroyed; for they are unclean and you will regard them as unclean 36(although springs, wells and stretches of water will remain clean); anyone who touches one of their carcases will be unclean. 37If one of their carcases falls on any kind of seed, the seed will remain clean; 38but if the seed has been moistened and one of their carcases falls on it, you will regard it as unclean.

39"If one of the animals that you use as food dies, anyone who touches the carcase will be unclean until evening; 40anyone who eats any of the carcase must wash his clothing and will remain unclean until evening; anyone who picks up the carcase must wash his clothing and will remain unclean until evening.

The religious aspect

41"Any creature that swarms on the ground is detestable for eating; it must not be eaten. 42Anything that moves on its belly, anything that moves on four legs or more—in short all the creatures that swarm on the ground—you will not eat, since they are detestable. 43Do not make yourselves detestable with all these swarming creatures; do not defile yourselves with them, do not be defiled by them. 44For it is I, Yahweh, who am your God. You have been sanctified and have become holy because I am holy: do not defile yourselves with all these creatures that swarm on the ground. 45Yes, it is I, Yahweh, who brought you out of Egypt to be your God: you must therefore be holy because I am holy." '

Conclusion

46Such is the law concerning animals, birds, all living creatures that move in water and all creatures that swarm on the ground. 47Its purpose is to distinguish the clean from the unclean, the creatures that may be eaten from those that may not be eaten.

Purification of a woman after childbirth

12 Yahweh spoke to Moses and said, 2"Speak to the Israelites and say: "If a woman becomes pregnant and gives birth to a boy, she will be unclean for seven days as when in a state of pollution due to menstruation. 3On the eighth day the child's foreskin must be circumcised, 4and she will wait another thirty-three days for her blood to be purified. She will not touch anything consecrated nor go to the sanctuary until the time of her purification is over.

5"If she gives birth to a girl, she will be unclean for two weeks, as during her monthly periods; and will wait another sixty-six days for her blood to be purified.

6"When the period of her purification is

over, for either boy or girl, she will bring the
priest at the entrance to the Tent of Meeting
a lamb one year old for a burnt offering, and
a young pigeon or turtledove as a sacrifice
for sin. 7The priest must offer this before
Yahweh, perform the rite of expiation for her,
and she will be purified from her discharge of
blood.

"Such is the law concerning a woman who
gives birth to either a boy or a girl. 8If she
cannot afford a lamb, she must take two
turtledoves or two young pigeons, one for
the burnt offering and the other for the
sacrifice for sin. The priest will perform the
rite of expiation for her and she will be
purified." '

Human skin-diseases

a: Swellings, scabs, discolorations

13 Yahweh said to Moses and Aaron, 2'If
a swelling or scab or spot appears on
someone's skin, which could develop into a
contagious skin-disease, that person must
then be taken to the priest, either Aaron or
one of his sons. 3The priest will examine the
disease on the skin. If the hair on the diseased
part has turned white, or if the disease bites
into the skin, the skin-disease is contagious,
and after examination the priest will declare
the person unclean. 4But if there is a white
spot on the skin without any visible
depression of the skin or whitening of the
hair, the priest will isolate the sick person for
seven days. 5On the seventh day he will
examine the person, and if he observes that
the disease persists though without spreading
over the skin, he will isolate the person for a
further seven days 6and examine him again
on the seventh. If he finds that the disease
has faded and has not spread over the skin,
the priest will declare the person clean. This
was merely a scab. Once he has washed his
clothing he will be clean.

7'But if the scab spreads over the skin after
the sick person has been examined by the
priest and declared clean, then he will let
himself be examined again by the priest.
8After examining him and certifying the
spread of the scab over the skin, the priest
will declare him unclean: it is a contagious
skin-disease.

b: Cases of dormant skin-disease

9'Someone who has a contagious skin-disease
must be taken to the priest. 10The priest will
examine the sick person, and if he finds a
whitish swelling with whitening of the hair
and an ulcer forming on the skin, 11this is a
dormant skin-disease, and the priest will
declare the person unclean. He will not isolate
him; he is obviously unclean.

12'But if the disease spreads all through the
skin, if it covers the person entirely from
head to foot so far as the priest can see, 13the
priest will then examine the sick person and,
if he finds that the skin-disease covers his
whole body, declare the sick person clean.
Since it has all become white, he is clean.
14But as soon as an ulcer appears on him, he
will be unclean. 15After examining the ulcer,
the priest will declare him unclean: the ulcer
is unclean, it is contagious. 16But if the ulcer
becomes white again, the sick person will go
to the priest; 17the priest will examine him
and if he finds that the disease has turned
white, he will declare the sick person clean:
he is clean.

c: Ulcers

18'When an ulcer appears on someone's skin,
and then gets better, 19and if then a white
swelling or a reddish-white spot forms on the
same place, the sick person will show himself
to the priest. 20The priest will examine him,
and if he finds a visible depression in the skin
and a whitening of the hair, he will declare
the person unclean: this is a case of contagious
skin-disease breaking out in an ulcer. 21But
if on examination the priest finds neither
white hair nor depression of the skin, but a
fading of the affected part, he will isolate the
sick person for seven days. 22If the disease
has then spread over the skin, he will declare
the person unclean: this is a case of contagious
skin-disease. 23But if the spot has stayed
where it was and has not spread, it is the scar
of the ulcer and the priest will declare the
person clean.

d: Burns

24'If someone has a burn on the skin and an
abscess, a reddish-white or white spot, forms
on the burn, 25the priest will then examine
it. If he finds a whitening of the hair or a

visible depression of the mark on the skin, a contagious disease has broken out in the burn. The priest will declare the sick person unclean: this is a contagious skin-disease. [26]If on the other hand the priest on examination does not find white hair on the mark or depression of the skin, but a fading of the mark, the priest will isolate the person for seven days. [27]He will examine the person on the seventh day and, if the disease has spread over the skin, he will declare the sick person unclean: this is a case of contagious skin-disease. [28]If the mark has stayed where it was and has not spread over the skin, but has faded instead, it was only a swelling due to the burn. The priest will declare the person clean: it is merely a burn scar.

e: Diseases of the scalp and chin

[29]'If a man or a woman has a sore on the head or chin, [30]the priest will examine the sore; and if he finds a depression visible in the skin, with the hair on it yellow and thin, he will declare the sick person unclean: this is tinea, that is to say, a contagious skin-disease of the head or chin. [31]If on examining this case of tinea the priest finds no visible depression in the skin and no yellow hair, he will isolate the person so affected for seven days. [32]He will examine the infected part on the seventh day, and if he finds that the tinea has not spread, that the hair on it is not yellow, and that there is no visible depression in the skin, [33]the sick person will shave his hair off, all except the part affected with tinea, and the priest will again isolate him for seven days. [34]He will examine the infected part on the seventh day, and if he finds that it has not spread over the skin, and that there is no visible depression of the skin, the priest will declare the sick person clean. After washing his clothes the person will be clean. [35]But if after this purification the tinea does spread over the skin, [36]the priest will examine the person; if he finds that the tinea has indeed spread over the skin, the sick person is unclean, and there is no need to verify whether the hair is yellow. [37]Whereas if, so far as he can see, the tinea is arrested and dark hair is beginning to grow on it, the sick person is cured. He is clean, and the priest will declare him clean.

f: Rash

[38]'If spots break out on the skin of a man or woman, and if these spots are white, [39]the priest will examine them. If he finds that the spots are of a dull white, this is a rash that has broken out on the skin: the sick person is clean.

g: Loss of hair

[40]'If someone loses the hair of the scalp, this is baldness of the scalp but the person is clean. [41]If he loses hair off the front of the head, this is baldness of the forehead but the person is clean. [42]If, however, a reddish-white sore appears on scalp or forehead, a contagious skin-disease has broken out on the scalp or forehead. [43]The priest will examine it, and if he finds a reddish-white swelling on scalp or forehead, looking like a contagious skin-disease, [44]the person has such a disease: he is unclean. The priest will declare him unclean; he has a contagious skin-disease of the head.

The law governing cases of contagious skin-diseases

[45]'Anyone with a contagious skin-disease will wear torn clothing and disordered hair; and will cover the upper lip and shout, "Unclean, unclean." [46]As long as the disease lasts, such a person will be unclean and, being unclean, will live alone and live outside the camp.

Infections of clothing

[47]'When a piece of clothing is infected with mould, be it woollen or linen clothing, [48]linen or woollen fabric or covering, or leather or anything made of leather, [49]if the spot on the clothing, leather, fabric, covering or object made of leather is a greenish or reddish colour, it is a disease to be shown to the priest. [50]The priest will examine the infection and isolate the object for seven days. [51]If on the seventh day he observes that the infection has spread on the clothing, fabric, covering, leather or object made of leather, whatever it may be, this is a contagious disease and the object is unclean. [52]He will burn this clothing, fabric, linen or woollen covering or leather object whatever it may be, on which the infection has appeared; for this is a

contagious disease which must be destroyed
by fire.
53'But if on examination the priest finds
that the infection has not spread on the
clothing, fabric, covering, or leather object
whatever it may be, 54he will order the
infected object to be washed and will isolate
it again for a period of seven days. 55After the
washing, he will examine the infection and
if he finds that there is no change in its
appearance, even though it has not spread,
the article is unclean. You will burn it; it is
infected through and through.
56'But if on examination the priest finds
that the infection has diminished after
washing, he will tear it out of the clothing,
leather, fabric or covering. 57But if the infec-
tion reappears on the same clothing, fabric,
covering or leather object whatever it may
be, this means that the infection is active;
you will burn whatever is infected. 58The
clothing, fabric, covering or leather object
whatever it may be, from which the infection
disappears after being washed, will be clean
after it has been washed a second time.
59'Such is the law governing disease in a
linen or woollen garment, a fabric or covering
or leather object whatever it may be, when it
is a question of declaring them clean or
unclean.'

Purification from contagious skin-diseases

14 Yahweh spoke to Moses and said:
2'This is the law to be applied on the
day of the purification of someone who has
suffered from a contagious skin-disease.
Such a person will be taken to the priest, 3and
the priest will go outside the camp. If he finds
on examination that the person has recovered
from the disease, 4he will order the following
to be brought for his purification: two live
birds that are clean, some cedar wood, scarlet
material and hyssop. 5He will then order
one of the birds to be slaughtered in an
earthenware pot over running water. 6He will
then take the live bird, the cedar wood, the
scarlet material and the hyssop and dip all
this (including the live bird) into the blood
of the bird slaughtered over running water.
7He will then sprinkle the person to be
purified of the skin-disease seven times, and
having declared the person clean, will set the
live bird free to fly off into the countryside.
8The person who is being purified will then
wash all clothing, shave off all hair, and wash,
and will then be clean. After this he will
return to the camp, although he will remain
outside his tent for seven days. 9On the
seventh day he will shave off all his hair—
head, beard and eyebrows; he will shave off
all his hair. After washing his clothing and
his body he will be clean.
10'On the eighth day he will take two
unblemished lambs, an unblemished ewe one
year old, three-tenths of wheaten flour mixed
with oil for the cereal offering, and one *log*
of oil. 11The priest who is performing the
purification will place the person who is being
purified, with all his offerings, at the entrance
to the Tent of Meeting, before Yahweh. 12He
will then take one of the lambs and offer it as
a sacrifice of reparation, as also the *log* of
oil. With these he will make the gesture
of offering before Yahweh. 13He will then
slaughter the lamb on that spot inside the
holy place where the victims for the sacrifice
for sin and for the burnt offering are slaugh-
tered. This reparatory offering, like the sacri-
fice for sin, will revert to the priest: it is
especially holy. 14The priest will then take
some blood of this sacrifice and put it on the
lobe of the right ear, the thumb of the right
hand, and the big toe of the right foot of the
person who is being purified. 15He will then
take the *log* of oil and pour a little into the
hollow of his left hand. 16He will dip a finger
of his right hand into the oil in the hollow of
his left hand, and sprinkle the oil with his
finger seven times before Yahweh. 17He will
then take some of the oil left in the hollow of
his hand and put it on the lobe of the right
ear, the thumb of the right hand, and the big
toe of the right foot of the person being
purified, in addition to the blood of the
sacrifice of reparation. 18The rest of the oil in
the hollow of his hand he will put on the head
of the person who is being purified. This
is how the priest will perform the rite of
expiation for such a person before Yahweh.
19'The priest will then offer the sacrifice
for sin, and perform the rite of expiation for
uncleanness for the person who is being
purified. After this, he will slaughter the
burnt offering 20and offer this and the cereal
offering on the altar. So, when the priest has
performed the rite of expiation for him the
person will be clean.
21'If he is poor and cannot afford all this,
he need take only one lamb, the one for
the sacrifice of reparation, and this will be

presented with the gesture of offering to perform the rite of expiation for him. And for the cereal offering he will only take one-tenth of wheaten flour mixed with oil, and the *log* of oil, 22 and two turtledoves or two young pigeons, whichever he can afford, one for a sacrifice for sin and the other for the burnt offering. 23 He will bring these on the eighth day to the priest at the entrance to the Tent of Meeting before Yahweh, for his purification. 24 The priest will take the lamb for the sacrifice of reparation and the *log* of oil, and present them before Yahweh with the gesture of offering. 25 He will then slaughter the lamb for the sacrifice of reparation, take some of its blood and put it on the lobe of the right ear, the thumb of the right hand and the big toe of the right foot of the person who is being purified. 26 He will pour the oil into the hollow of his left hand, 27 and with his finger sprinkle the oil in the hollow of his left hand seven times before Yahweh. 28 He will then put some of the oil on the lobe of the right ear, the thumb of the right hand and the big toe of the right foot of the person who is being purified, as he did with the blood of the sacrifice of reparation. 29 The remainder of the oil in the hollow of his hand he will put on the head of the person who is being purified, thus performing the rite of expiation for him before Yahweh. 30 Of the two turtledoves or two young pigeons—whatever he has been able to afford—he will offer 31 a sacrifice for sin with one, and with the other a burnt offering with a cereal offering—whatever he has been able to afford. This is how the priest will perform before Yahweh the rite of expiation for the person who is being purified.

32 'Such is the law concerning someone with a contagious skin-disease who cannot afford the means of purification.'

Similar infections of houses

33 Yahweh spoke to Moses and Aaron and said:

34 'When you reach Canaan, which I am giving you as your possession, if I infect a house with a disease in the country which you are to possess, 35 the owner will come and inform the priest and say, "I have seen something like a skin-disease in the house." 36 The priest will order the house to be emptied before he goes to examine the infection, or everything in the house will become unclean; after which, the priest will go inside and examine the house; 37 and if on examination he finds the walls of the house pitted with reddish or greenish depressions which appear to be eating away the wall, 38 the priest will then go out of the house, to the door, and shut it up for seven days. 39 On the seventh day, the priest will come back and if on examination he finds that the infection has spread over the walls of the house, 40 he will order the infected stones to be removed and thrown into some unclean place outside the town. 41 He will then have all the inside of the house scraped, and the plaster that comes off will be emptied in an unclean place outside the town. 42 The stones will then be replaced with new ones and the house given a new coat of plaster.

43 'If the infection spreads again after the stones have been removed and the house scraped and replastered, 44 the priest will come and examine it. If he finds that the infection has spread, this means that there is a contagious disease in the house: it is unclean. 45 It must be pulled down and the stones, woodwork and all the plaster be taken to an unclean place outside the town.

46 'Anyone who enters the house while it is closed will be unclean until evening. 47 Anyone who sleeps there will wash his clothes. Anyone who eats there will wash his clothes. 48 But if the priest finds, when he comes to examine the infection, that it has not spread in the house since it was plastered, he will declare the house clean, for the infection is cured.

49 'As a sacrifice for the defilement of the house, he will take two birds, some cedar wood, scarlet material and hyssop. 50 He will slaughter one of the birds in an earthenware pot over running water. 51 He will then take the cedar wood, the hyssop, the scarlet material and the live bird, dip them into the blood of the slaughtered bird and into the running water and sprinkle the house seven times; 52 and after offering the sacrifice for the defilement of the house with the blood of the bird, the running water, the live bird, the cedar wood, the hyssop and the scarlet material, 53 he will set the live bird free to fly out of the town into the countryside. Once the rite of expiation has been performed for the house in this way it will be clean.

54 'Such is the law governing all kinds of skin-disease and tinea, 55 diseases of clothing and houses, 56 swellings, scabs and spots. It

defines the occasions when things are unclean and when clean. 57 Such is the law on skin-diseases.'

Sexual impurities

a: Of men

15 Yahweh spoke to Moses and Aaron and said:

2 'Speak to the Israelites and say to them:

"When a man has a discharge from his body, that discharge is unclean. 3 While the discharge continues, the nature of his uncleanness is as follows.

"Whether his body allows the discharge to flow or whether it retains it, he is unclean.

4 "Any bed the man lies on and anything he sits on will be unclean.

5 "Anyone who touches his bed must wash clothing and body and will be unclean until evening.

6 "Anyone who sits where the man has sat must wash clothing and body and will be unclean until evening.

7 "Anyone who touches the body of the man with the discharge must wash clothing and body and will be unclean until evening.

8 "If the man with the discharge spits on someone who is clean, that person must wash clothing and body and will be unclean until evening.

9 "Any saddle the man has ridden on will be unclean.

10 "All those who touch any object that has been under him will be unclean until evening.

"Anyone who picks up such an object must wash clothing and body and will be unclean until evening.

11 "All those whom the man with the discharge touches without having washed his hands must wash clothing and body and will be unclean until evening.

12 "The earthenware vessel he touches must be broken and any wooden utensil must be rinsed.

13 "Once the man with the discharge is cured, he will allow seven days for his purification. He will wash his clothes and wash his body in running water and he will be clean. 14 On the eighth day he will take two turtledoves or two young pigeons and come before Yahweh at the entrance to the Tent of Meeting and give them to the priest. 15 The priest will offer one of them as a sacrifice for sin and the other as a burnt offering. And in this way the priest will perform the rite of expiation for him before Yahweh for his discharge.

16 "When a man has a seminal discharge, he must wash his whole body with water and will be unclean until evening. 17 Any clothing or leather touched by the seminal discharge must be washed and will be unclean until evening. 18 When a woman has had intercourse with a man, both of them must wash and will be unclean until evening.

b: Of women

19 "Whenever a woman has a discharge and the discharge from her body is of blood, she will remain in a state of menstrual pollution for seven days.

"Anyone who touches her will be unclean until evening.

20 "Anything she lies on in this polluted state will be unclean; anything she sits on will be unclean.

21 "Anyone who touches her bed must wash clothing and body and will be unclean until evening.

22 "Anyone who touches anything she has sat on must wash clothing and body and will be unclean until evening. 23 If there is anything on the bed or where she is sitting, anyone who touches it will be unclean until evening.

24 "If a man goes so far as to sleep with her, he will contract her menstrual pollution and will be unclean for seven days. Any bed he lies on will be unclean.

25 "If a woman has a prolonged discharge of blood outside the period, or if the period is prolonged, during the time this discharge lasts she will be in the same state of uncleanness as during her monthly periods. 26 Any bed she lies on during the time this discharge lasts will be polluted in the same way as the bed she lies on during her monthly periods. Anything she sits on will be unclean as during her monthly periods. 27 Anyone who touches it will be unclean and must wash clothing and body and will be unclean until evening.

28 "Once she is cured of her discharge, she will allow seven days to go by; after that she will be clean. 29 On the eighth day she will take two turtledoves or two young pigeons and bring them to the priest at the entrance to the Tent of Meeting. 30 The priest will offer one of them as a sacrifice for sin and the other as a burnt offering. And in this way the priest

will perform the rite of expiation for her before Yahweh for the discharge which made her unclean.

Conclusion

[31]"Hence you will warn the Israelites against contracting a state of uncleanness, rather than incurring death by defiling my Dwelling which is among them.

[32]"Such is the law governing a man with a discharge or who is made unclean by a seminal discharge, [33]a woman in a state of pollution due to menstruation, a man or a woman with a discharge, or a man who sleeps with a woman when she is unclean." '

The great Day of Expiation[a]

16 Yahweh spoke to Moses after the death of the two sons of Aaron who died when offering unauthorised fire. [2]Yahweh spoke to Moses and said:

'Tell Aaron your brother that he may not enter the sanctuary inside the curtain in front of the mercy-seat on the ark whenever he chooses, in case he incurs death, for I appear in a cloud on the mercy-seat.

[3]'This is how he must enter the sanctuary: with a young bull for a sacrifice for sin and a ram for a burnt offering. [4]He will put on a tunic of consecrated linen, wear linen drawers on his body, a linen waistband round his waist, and a linen turban on his head. These are the sacred vestments he will put on after washing himself.

[5]'From the community of Israelites he will receive two he-goats for a sacrifice for sin and a ram for a burnt offering. [6]After offering the bull as a sacrifice for his own sin and performing the rite of expiation for himself and his family, [7]he will take the two he-goats and place them before Yahweh at the entrance to the Tent of Meeting. [8]Aaron will then draw lots over the two goats, one lot to be for Yahweh and the other lot for Azazel. [9]Aaron will then take the goat on which the lot "For Yahweh" has fallen, and offer it as a sacrifice for sin. [10]But the goat on which the lot "For Azazel" has fallen, will be placed alive before Yahweh, for the rite of expiation to be performed with it, and for it then to be sent to Azazel in the desert.

[11]'Having offered the bull as a sacrifice for his own sin and performed the rite of expiation for himself and for his family, and slaughtered the bull as a sacrifice for sin, [12]Aaron will then fill a censer with live coals from the altar before Yahweh, take two handfuls of finely ground aromatic incense and bring this inside the curtain. [13]He will then put the incense on the fire before Yahweh, so that the cloud of incense hides the mercy-seat which is on the Testimony and he does not incur death. [14]He will then take some of the bull's blood and sprinkle it with his finger on the eastern side of the mercy-seat. He will sprinkle some of the blood seven times with his finger in front of the mercy-seat.

[15]'He will then slaughter the goat for the sacrifice for the sin of the people, and take its blood inside the curtain, and with this blood do as he did with the blood of the bull, sprinkling it on the mercy-seat and in front of it. [16]This is how he must perform the rite of expiation for the sanctuary for the uncleanness of the Israelites, for their acts of rebellion and all their sins.

'And this is what he must do for the Tent of Meeting which remains with them, surrounded by their uncleanness. [17]No one must be inside the Tent of Meeting, from the moment he enters to make expiation in the sanctuary until the time he comes out.

'When he has made expiation for himself, for his family, and for the whole community of Israel, [18]he must come outside, go to the altar before Yahweh and perform the rite of expiation for it. He will take some of the bull's blood and some of the goat's blood and put it on the horns at the corners of the altar all around it, [19]and sprinkle some of the blood on it seven times with his finger, thus purifying it and setting it apart from the uncleanness of the Israelites.

[20]'Once expiation for the sanctuary, the Tent of Meeting and the altar is complete, he will bring the goat which is still alive. [21]Aaron will then lay both his hands on its head and over it confess all the guilt of the Israelites, all their acts of rebellion and all their sins. Having thus laid them on the goat's head, he will send it out into the desert under the charge of a man waiting ready, [22]and the goat will bear all their guilt away into some desolate place.

16a An important annual festival combining **1** a sacrifice of expiation by blood and **2** a primitive ritual of driving the bearer of sin away from the community.

'When he has sent the goat into the desert, 23 Aaron will go back into the Tent of Meeting and take off the linen vestments which he wore to enter the sanctuary and leave them there. 24 He will then wash his body inside the holy place, put on his vestments and come outside to offer his own and the people's burnt offering. He will perform the rite of expiation for himself and for the people, 25 and burn the fat of the sacrifice for sin on the altar.

26 'The man who led the goat away to Azazel will wash his clothes and body before entering the camp. 27 The bull and the goat offered as a sacrifice for sin, the blood of which was taken into the sanctuary for the rite of expiation, must be taken outside the camp, where their skin, meat and offal are to be burnt. 28 The man who burns them will wash his clothes and body before entering the camp.

29 'This will be a perpetual law for you.

'On the tenth day of the seventh month you will fast and refrain from work, both citizen and resident alien; 30 for this is the day on which the rite of expiation will be performed for you to purify you, to purify you before Yahweh from all your sins. 31 It will be a sabbatical rest for you and you will fast. This is a perpetual law.

32 'The rite of expiation will be performed by the priest who has been anointed and installed to officiate in succession to his father. He will put on the linen vestments, the sacred vestments, 33 and perform the rite of expiation for the holy sanctuary, the Tent of Meeting and the altar, and will then perform the rite of expiation for the priests and all the people of the community. 34 This will be a perpetual law for you; once a year the rite of expiation will be made for the Israelites for all their sins.'

And as Yahweh ordered Moses, so it was done.

IV: THE LAW OF HOLINESS

Slaughtering and sacrifice

17 Yahweh spoke to Moses and said: 2 'Speak to Aaron and his sons and all the Israelites and say:

"This is the order that Yahweh has given:

3 "Any man of the House of Israel who slaughters a bull, lamb or goat, whether inside the camp or outside it, 4 without bringing it to the entrance to the Tent of Meeting to make an offering of it to Yahweh in front of his Dwelling, that man will be answerable for bloodshed; he has shed blood, and that man will be outlawed from his people. 5 The purpose of this is that the Israelites should instead bring their sacrifices, which they would otherwise offer in the countryside, to Yahweh at the entrance to the Tent of Meeting, to the priest, and offer them as communion sacrifices to Yahweh; 6 and the priest will sprinkle the blood on Yahweh's altar at the entrance to the Tent of Meeting and will burn the fat as a smell pleasing to Yahweh. 7 No longer may they offer their sacrifices to the satyrs in whose service they used to prostitute themselves. This is a perpetual law for them and for their descendants."

8 'You will also say to them, "Any member of the House of Israel or any resident alien who offers a burnt offering or sacrifice 9 without bringing it to the entrance to the Tent of Meeting to offer it to Yahweh, will be outlawed from his people.

10 "If any member of the House of Israel or any resident alien consumes blood of any kind, I shall set my face against that individual who consumes blood and shall outlaw him from his people. 11 For the life of the creature is in the blood, and I have given it to you for performing the rite of expiation on the altar for your lives, for blood is what expiates for a life. 12 That is why I told the Israelites: None of you will consume blood, nor will any resident alien consume blood.

13 "Anyone, whether Israelite or resident alien, who hunts and catches game, whether animal or bird, which it is lawful to eat, must pour out its blood and cover it with earth. 14 For the life of every creature is its blood, and I have told the Israelites: You will not consume the blood of any creature, for the life of every creature is its blood, and anyone who consumes it will be outlawed.

15 "Anyone, citizen or alien, who eats an animal that has died a natural death or been

savaged, must wash clothing and body, and will be unclean until evening, but will then be clean. [16]But anyone who does not wash clothing and body will bear the consequences of his guilt." '

Sexual prohibitions

18 Yahweh spoke to Moses and said: [2]'Speak to the Israelites and say:

"I am Yahweh your God: [3]You must not behave as they do in Egypt where you used to live; you must not behave as they do in Canaan where I am taking you, nor must you follow their laws. [4]You must observe my customs and keep my laws, following them.

"I, Yahweh, am your God: [5]hence you will keep my laws and my customs. Whoever complies with them will find life in them.

"I am Yahweh.

[6]"None of you will approach a woman who is closely related to him, to have intercourse with her. I am Yahweh.

[7]"You will not have intercourse with your father or your mother. She is your mother—you will not have intercourse with her.

[8]"You will not have intercourse with your father's wife; it is your father's sexual prerogative.

[9]"You will not have intercourse with your sister, whether she is your father's or your mother's daughter. Whether she was born in the same house or elsewhere, you will not have intercourse with her.

[10]"You will not have intercourse with your son's or your daughter's daughter; for their sexual privacy is your own.

[11]"You will not have intercourse with the daughter of your father's wife, born to your father. She is your sister; you will not have intercourse with her.

[12]"You will not have intercourse with your father's sister; for she is your father's own flesh and blood.

[13]"You will not have intercourse with your mother's sister; for she is your mother's own flesh and blood.

[14]"You will not have intercourse with your father's brother; you will not approach his wife. She is your aunt.

[15]"You will not have intercourse with your daughter-in-law. She is your son's wife; you will not have intercourse with her.

[16]"You will not have intercourse with your brother's wife; it is your brother's sexual prerogative.

[17]"You will not have intercourse with a woman and her daughter; nor will you take her son's or her daughter's daughter, to have intercourse with them. They are your own flesh and blood; it would be incest.

[18]"You will not take a woman and her sister into your harem at the same time, to have intercourse with the latter while the former is still alive.

[19]"You will not approach and have intercourse with a woman who is in a state of menstrual pollution.

[20]"Furthermore, you will not have intercourse with your fellow-citizen's wife; you would become unclean by doing so.

[21]"You will not allow any of your children to be sacrificed to Molech,[a] thus profaning the name of your God. I am Yahweh.

[22]"You will not have intercourse with a man as you would with a woman. This is a hateful thing.

[23]"You will not have intercourse with any kind of animal; you would become unclean by doing so. Nor will a woman offer herself to an animal, to have intercourse with it. This would be a violation of nature.

[24]"Do not make yourselves unclean by any of these practices, for it was by such things that the nations that I am driving out before you made themselves unclean. [25]The country has become unclean; hence I am about to punish it for its guilt, and the country itself will vomit out its inhabitants.

[26]"You, however, must keep my laws and customs and not do any of these hateful things: none of your citizens, none of your resident aliens. [27]For all these hateful things were done by the people who lived in the country before you, and the country became unclean. [28]If you make it unclean, will it not vomit you out as it vomited out the nations there before you? [29]Yes, anyone who does any of these hateful things, whatever it may be, any person doing so, will be outlawed from his people; [30]so keep my rules and do not observe any of the hateful laws which were in force before you came; then you will not be made unclean by them. I am Yahweh your God." '

18a A sacrifice by fire, Phoenician in origin, practised in Jerusalem right up to the Exile.

Moral and religious regulations

19 Yahweh spoke to Moses and said:
2 'Speak to the whole community of
Israelites and say:
"Be holy, for I, Yahweh your God, am
holy.
3 "Each of you will respect father and
mother.
"And you will keep my Sabbaths; I am
Yahweh your God.
4 "Do not turn to idols and do not cast
metal gods for yourselves. I am Yahweh your
God.
5 "If you offer a communion sacrifice to
Yahweh, make it in such a way as to be
acceptable. 6 It must be eaten the same day or
the day after; whatever is left on the third
day must be burnt. 7 If eaten on the third day
it would be rotten food and not be acceptable.
8 Anyone who eats it must bear the conse-
quences of this guilt, having profaned
Yahweh's holiness; that person will be
outlawed from his people.
9 "When you reap the harvest of your land,
you will not reap to the very edges of the
field, nor will you gather the gleanings of the
harvest; 10 nor will you strip your vineyard
bare, nor pick up the fallen grapes. You will
leave them for the poor and the stranger. I
am Yahweh your God.
11 "You will not steal, nor deal deceitfully
or fraudulently with your fellow-citizen.
12 You will not swear by my name with intent
to deceive and thus profane the name of your
God. I am Yahweh. 13 You will not exploit or
rob your fellow. You will not keep back the
labourer's wage until next morning. 14 You
will not curse the dumb or put an obstacle in
the way of the blind, but will fear your God.
I am Yahweh.
15 "You will not be unjust in administering
justice. You will neither be partial to the
poor nor overawed by the great, but will
administer justice to your fellow-citizen
justly. 16 You will not go about slandering
your own family, nor will you put your
neighbour's life in jeopardy. I am Yahweh.
17 You will not harbour hatred for your
brother. You will reprove your fellow-
countryman firmly and thus avoid burdening
yourself with a sin. 18 You will not exact
vengeance on, or bear any sort of grudge
against, the members of your race, but will
love your neighbour as yourself. I am
Yahweh.

19 "You will keep my laws.
"You will not mate your cattle with those
of another kind; you will not sow two kinds
of grain in your field; you will not wear a
garment made from two kinds of fabric.
20 "If someone has intercourse with a
woman who is the concubine slave of a man
from whom she has not been redeemed and
she has not been given her freedom, he will
be liable for a fine, but they will not incur
death, since she was not a free woman. 21 He
will bring a sacrifice of reparation for Yahweh
to the entrance of the Tent of Meeting. This
will be a ram of reparation, 22 and with the
ram of reparation the priest will perform the
rite of expiation for him before Yahweh
for the sin committed; and the sin he has
committed will be forgiven.
23 "Once you have entered the country and
planted any kind of fruit tree, you will regard
its fruit as uncircumcised. For three years
you will count it as uncircumcised and it will
not be eaten; 24 in the fourth year, all its fruit
will be consecrated to Yahweh in a feast of
praise; 25 and in the fifth year you may eat its
fruit, so that it may yield you even more. I
am Yahweh your God.
26 "You will eat nothing with blood in it.
You will not practise divination or magic.
27 "You will not round off your hair at the
edges or trim the edges of your beard. 28 You
will not gash your bodies when someone dies,
and you will not tattoo yourselves. I am
Yahweh.
29 "Do not profane your daughter by
making her a prostitute, or the country itself
will become prostituted and filled with incest.
30 "You will keep my Sabbaths and revere
my sanctuary. I am Yahweh.
31 "Do not have recourse to the spirits of
the dead or to magicians; they will defile you.
I, Yahweh, am your God.
32 "You will stand up in the presence of
grey hair, you will honour the person of the
aged and fear your God. I am Yahweh.
33 "If you have resident aliens in your
country, you will not molest them. 34 You will
treat resident aliens as though they were
native-born and love them as yourself—for
you yourselves were once aliens in Egypt. I
am Yahweh your God.
35 "You will not be unjust in administering
justice as regards measures of length, weight
or capacity. 36 You will have just scales, just
weights, a just *ephah* and a just *hin*. I am
Yahweh your God who brought you out of

Egypt; 37 hence you are to keep all my laws and
all my customs and put them into practice. I
am Yahweh." '

Penalties

a: Religious offences

20 Yahweh spoke to Moses and said:
2 'Say to the Israelites:
"Anyone, be he Israelite or alien resident
in Israel, who gives any of his children to
Molech, will be put to death. The people of
the country must stone him, 3 and I shall set
my face against that man and outlaw him
from his people; for by giving a child of his
to Molech he has defiled my sanctuary and
profaned my holy name. 4 If the people of the
country choose to close their eyes to the man's
action when he gives a child of his to Molech,
and do not put him to death, 5 I myself shall
turn my face against that man and his clan. I
shall outlaw them from their people, both
him and all those after him who prostitute
themselves by following Molech.
6 "If anyone has recourse to the spirits of
the dead or to magicians, to prostitute himself
by following them, I shall set my face against
him and outlaw him from his people.
7 "Sanctify yourselves and be holy, for I
am Yahweh your God.

b: Offences against the family

8 "You will keep my laws and put them into
practice, for it is I, Yahweh, who make you
holy. 9 Hence:
"Anyone who curses father or mother will
be put to death. Having cursed father or
mother, the blood will be on that person's
own head.
10 "The man who commits adultery with
his neighbour's wife will be put to death, he
and the woman.
11 "The man who has intercourse with his
father's wife has infringed his father's sexual
prerogative. Both of them will be put to
death; their blood will be on their own
heads.
12 "The man who has intercourse with his
daughter-in-law: both of them will be put to
death; they have violated nature, their blood
will be on their own heads.
13 "The man who has intercourse with a
man in the same way as with a woman: they
have done a hateful thing together; they will
be put to death; their blood will be on their
own heads.
14 "The man who marries a woman and her
mother: this is incest. They will be burnt
alive, he and they; you will not tolerate incest.
15 "The man who has intercourse with an
animal will be put to death; you will kill the
animal too.
16 "The woman who approaches any animal
to have intercourse with it: you will kill the
woman and the animal. They will be put to
death; their blood will be on their own heads.
17 "The man who marries his father's or his
mother's daughter: if they have intercourse
together, this is an outrage. They will be
executed in public, for the man has had
intercourse with his sister; he will bear the
consequences of his guilt.
18 "The man who has intercourse with a
woman during her monthly periods and
exposes her nakedness: he has laid bare the
source of her blood, and she has exposed the
source of her blood, and both of them will be
outlawed from their people.
19 "You will not have intercourse with your
mother's sister or your father's sister.
Whoever does so, has had intercourse with a
close relation; they will bear the consequences of their guilt.
20 "The man who has intercourse with the
wife of his paternal uncle has infringed his
uncle's sexual prerogative; they will bear the
consequences of their guilt and die childless.
21 "The man who marries his brother's
wife: this is pollution; he has infringed his
brother's sexual prerogative; they will die
childless.

Concluding exhortation

22 "You will keep all my laws, all my decisions,
and put them into practice, so that the
country where I am taking you to live will
not vomit you out. 23 You will not follow the
laws of the nations whom I am driving out
before you; they practised all these things,
which is why I detested them. 24 As I have
already told you, you will take possession of
their soil, I myself shall give you possession
of it, a country flowing with milk and honey.
"Since I, Yahweh your God, have set you
apart from these peoples, 25 you for your part
will make a distinction between clean
animals and unclean ones and between
unclean birds and clean ones, and will not
make yourselves detestable with any animal

or bird or reptile, which I have set apart from you as unclean.

26"Be consecrated to me, for I, Yahweh, am holy, and I shall set you apart from all these peoples, for you to be mine.

27"Any man or woman of yours who is a necromancer or magician will be put to death; they will be stoned to death; their blood will be on their own heads." '

The holiness of the priesthood

a: The priests

21 Yahweh said to Moses: 'Speak to the priests descended from Aaron and say:

"None of them must make himself unclean by touching the corpse of one of his people, 2unless it be of one of his closest relations—father, mother, son, daughter, brother, 3or virgin sister, since she being unmarried is still his close relation: he can make himself unclean for her; 4but for a close female relation who is married he will not make himself unclean; he would profane himself.

5"They will not make tonsures on their heads, shave the edges of their beards, or gash their bodies. 6They will be consecrated to their God and will not profane the name of their God. For their function is to offer the food burnt for Yahweh, the food of their God, and so they must be holy.

7"They will not marry a woman profaned by prostitution, or one divorced by her husband, for the priest is consecrated to his God.

8"You will treat him as holy, for he offers the food of your God. For you, he will be a holy person, for I, Yahweh, who sanctify you, am holy.

9"If a priest's daughter profanes herself by prostitution, she profanes her father and will be burnt alive.

b: The high priest

10"The priest who is pre-eminent over his brothers, on whose head the anointing oil has been poured, and who, robed in the sacred vestments, has received investiture, will not disorder his hair or tear his clothes; 11he will not go near any corpse or make himself unclean even for his father or mother. 12He will not leave the holy place in such a way as to profane the sanctuary of his God; for he bears the consecration of the anointing oil of his God. I am Yahweh.

13"He will marry a woman who is still a virgin. 14He will not marry a woman who has been widowed or divorced or profaned by prostitution, but will marry a virgin from his own people: 15he must not make his own children profane, for I, Yahweh, have sanctified him." '

c: Impediments to the priesthood

16Yahweh spoke to Moses and said:

17'Speak to Aaron and say:

"None of your descendants, for all time, may come forward to offer the food of his God if he has any infirmity, 18for none may come forward if he has an infirmity, be he blind or lame, disfigured or deformed, 19or with an injured foot or arm, 20a hunchback, someone with rickets or ophthalmia or the scab or running sores, or a eunuch. 21No descendant of the priest Aaron may come forward to offer the food burnt for Yahweh if he has any infirmity; if he has an infirmity, he will not come forward to offer the food of his God.

22"He may eat the food of his God, things especially holy and things holy, 23but he will not go near the curtain or approach the altar, since he has an infirmity and must not profane my holy things; for I, Yahweh, have sanctified them." '

24And Moses promulgated this to Aaron, to his sons, and to all the Israelites.

Holiness in consuming sacred food

a: The priests

22 Yahweh spoke to Moses and said: 2'Speak to Aaron and his sons. They must be consecrated by the holy offerings of the Israelites and must not profane my holy name; for my sake they must sanctify it; I am Yahweh. 3Say to them:

"Any one of your descendants, for all time, who in a state of uncleanness approaches the holy offerings consecrated to Yahweh by the Israelites, will be outlawed from my presence. I am Yahweh.

4"Anyone of Aaron's line who is afflicted with a contagious skin-disease or a discharge will not eat holy things until he is clean. Anyone who touches anything made unclean by a dead body, or who has a seminal

discharge, 5or who is made unclean by
touching any kind of reptile or any one
who has contaminated him with his own
uncleanness, be it what it may, 6in short,
anyone who has had any such contact will be
unclean until evening, and must not eat holy
things until he has washed his body. 7At
sunset he will be clean and may then eat holy
things, for these are his food.

8"He must not eat an animal that has died
a natural death or been savaged; he would
contract uncleanness from it. I am Yahweh.

9"They must keep my rules and not burden
themselves with sin. If they profane them,
they will incur death; I, Yahweh, have sancti-
fied them.

b: Lay people

10"No lay person may eat anything holy; no
guest or employee of a priest may eat anything
holy. 11But if the priest has acquired a slave
by purchase, the slave may eat it like anyone
born in his household; they will share his
food.

12"If a priest's daughter marries a layman,
she will have no share in the holy things set
aside, 13but if she is widowed or divorced
and, being childless, has had to return to her
father's house as when she was young, she
may share her father's food. No lay person
may share it; 14 anyone who does eat a holy
thing by inadvertence, will restore it to the
priest with one-fifth added.

15"They may not profane the holy offerings
which the Israelites have set aside for
Yahweh. 16By eating these, they would
burden them with guilt requiring a sacrifice
of reparation; for I, Yahweh, have sanctified
these offerings." '

c: Sacrificial animals

17Yahweh spoke to Moses and said:

18'Speak to Aaron, to his sons, and to all
the Israelites and say:

"Any member of the House of Israel or
any alien resident in Israel who brings an
offering either in payment of a vow or as a
voluntary gift, and offers it as a burnt offering
to Yahweh, 19must, if he is to be acceptable,
offer an unblemished male, be it bull or sheep
or goat. 20You will not offer anything with a
blemish, for it would not make you
acceptable.

21"If anyone offers Yahweh a communion
sacrifice, either to fulfil a vow or as a voluntary
offering, the animal, be it from the herd
or flock, must be perfect, if he is to be
acceptable; it must be unblemished. 22You
will not offer Yahweh any animal which is
blind, lame, mutilated, ulcerous, scabby or
covered in sores. No part of such an animal
will be offered on the altar as food burnt for
Yahweh. 23As a voluntary offering, you may
offer a bull or a lamb that is underdeveloped
or deformed; but such will not be acceptable
in payment of a vow. 24You will not offer
Yahweh an animal if its testicles have been
bruised, crushed, torn or cut off. You may
not do that in your country, 25and you may
not accept any such from the hands of a
stranger, to be offered as food for your God.
Their deformity is a blemish, and they would
not make you acceptable." '

26Yahweh spoke to Moses and said:

27'A calf, lamb, or kid will stay with its
dam for seven days after being born. From
the eighth day onwards, it will be acceptable
as food burnt for Yahweh. 28But no animal,
whether cow or ewe, will be slaughtered on
the same day as its young.

29'If you offer Yahweh a sacrifice with
praise, do it in the acceptable manner; 30it
must be eaten the same day; you will leave
nothing over till next morning. I am Yahweh.

d: Concluding exhortation

31'You will keep my commands and put them
into practice. I am Yahweh. 32You will not
profane my holy name—so that I may be
honoured as holy among the Israelites, I,
Yahweh, who make you holy, 33I who
brought you out of Egypt, to be your God, I,
Yahweh.'

The ritual for the annual feasts

23 Yahweh spoke to Moses and said:
2'Speak to the Israelites and say:

(The solemn festivals of Yahweh to which
you will summon them are my sacred
assemblies.)

"These are my solemn festivals:

a: The Sabbath

3"You will work for six days, but the seventh
will be a day of complete rest, a day for the
sacred assembly on which you do no work at

all. Wherever you live, this is a Sabbath for Yahweh.

4"'These are Yahweh's solemn festivals, the sacred assemblies to which you will summon the Israelites on the appointed day:

b: The Passover and the feast of Unleavened Bread

5"'The fourteenth day of the first month, at twilight, is the Passover of Yahweh; 6and the fifteenth day of the same month is the feast of Unleavened Bread for Yahweh. For seven days you will eat unleavened bread. 7On the first day you will hold a sacred assembly; you will do no heavy work. 8For seven days you will offer food burnt for Yahweh. On the seventh day there will be a sacred assembly; you will do no heavy work." '

c: The first sheaf

9Yahweh spoke to Moses and said:

10'Speak to the Israelites and say:

"When you enter the country which I am giving you and reap the harvest there, you will bring the priest the first sheaf of your harvest, 11and he will present it to Yahweh with the gesture of offering, for you to be acceptable. The priest will make this offering on the day after the Sabbath, 12and on the same day as you make this offering, you will offer Yahweh an unblemished lamb one year old as a burnt offering. 13The cereal offering for that day will be two-tenths of wheaten flour mixed with oil, as food burnt as a smell pleasing to Yahweh. The libation will be a quarter of a *hin* of wine. 14You will eat no bread, roasted ears of wheat or fresh produce before this day, before making the offering to your God. This is a perpetual law for all your descendants, wherever you live.

d: The feast of Weeks

15"'From the day after the Sabbath, the day on which you bring the sheaf of offering, you will count seven full weeks. 16You will count fifty days, to the day after the seventh Sabbath, and then you will offer Yahweh a new cereal offering. 17You will bring bread from your homes to present with the gesture of offering—two loaves, made of two-tenths of wheaten flour baked with leaven; these are first-fruits for Yahweh. 18In addition to the bread, you will offer seven unblemished lambs a year old, a young bull and two rams, as a burnt offering to Yahweh with a cereal offering and a libation, as food burnt as a smell pleasing to Yahweh. 19You will also offer a goat as a sacrifice for sin, and two lambs a year old as communion sacrifice. 20The priest will present them before Yahweh with the gesture of offering, in addition to the bread of the first-fruits. These, and the two lambs, are holy things for Yahweh, and will revert to the priest.

21"On the same day, you will hold an assembly; for you this will be a sacred assembly; you will do no heavy work. This is a perpetual law for your descendants, wherever you live.

22"When you reap the harvest in your country, you will not reap to the very edges of your field, nor will you gather the gleanings of the harvest. You will leave them for the poor and the stranger. I am Yahweh your God." '

e: The first day of the seventh month

23Yahweh spoke to Moses and said:

24'Speak to the Israelites and say:

"The first day of the seventh month[a] will be a day of rest for you, of remembrance and acclamation, a sacred assembly. 25You will do no heavy work and you will offer food burnt for Yahweh." '

f: The Day of Expiation

26Yahweh spoke to Moses and said:

27'But the tenth day of this seventh month will be the Day of Expiation. You will hold a sacred assembly. You will fast and offer food burnt for Yahweh. 28You will do no work that day, for it is the Day of Expiation, on which the rite of expiation will be performed for you before Yahweh your God. 29Anyone who fails to fast that day will be outlawed from his people; 30anyone who works that day I shall eliminate from his people. 31No work will be done—this is a perpetual law for your descendants wherever you live. 32It must be a day of complete rest for you. You will fast; on the evening of the ninth day of the month, from this evening

23a A Canaanite new-moon festival, but held now in one month only, the first of autumn.

till the following evening, you will rest
completely.'

g: The feast of Shelters

33Yahweh spoke to Moses and said:
34'Speak to the Israelites and say:
"On the fifteenth day of this seventh month
there will be the feast of Shelters for Yahweh,
lasting for seven days. 35The first day will be
a day of sacred assembly; you will do no
heavy work. 36For seven days you will offer
food burnt for Yahweh. On the eighth day
you will hold a sacred assembly and you will
offer food burnt for Yahweh. It is a day of
solemn meeting; you will do no heavy
work.

Conclusion

37"These are Yahweh's solemn festivals to
which you will summon the Israelites, the
sacred assemblies for the purpose of offering
food burnt for Yahweh, consisting of burnt
offerings, cereal offerings, sacrifices and
libations, each on its appropriate day,
38besides Yahweh's Sabbaths, and your
presents and all your votive and voluntary
gifts that you make to Yahweh.

Recapitulation on the feast of Shelters

39"But on the fifteenth day of the seventh
month, when you have gathered in the
produce of the land, you will celebrate the
feast of Yahweh for seven days. The first and
eighth days will be days of rest. 40On the first
day you will take choice fruit, palm branches,
boughs of leafy trees and flowering shrubs
from the river bank, and for seven days enjoy
yourselves before Yahweh your God. 41You
will celebrate a feast for Yahweh in this way
for seven days every year. This is a perpetual
law for your descendants.
"You will keep this feast in the seventh
month. 42For seven days you will live in
shelters: all the citizens of Israel will live
in shelters, 43so that your descendants may
know that I made the Israelites live in
shelters when I brought them out of Egypt,
I, Yahweh your God." '
44Moses then promulgated Yahweh's
solemn festivals to the Israelites.

Complementary ritual prescriptions

a: The perpetual flame

24 Yahweh spoke to Moses and said:
2'Order the Israelites to bring you
crushed-olive oil for the lamp-stand, and
keep a flame burning there continually.
3Aaron will keep it permanently in trim from
evening to morning, outside the curtain of
the Testimony in the Tent of Meeting, before
Yahweh. This is a perpetual decree for your
descendants: 4Aaron will keep the lamps
permanently trimmed on the pure lamp-
stand before Yahweh.

b: The loaves of permanent offering on the golden table

5'You will take wheaten flour and with it bake
twelve loaves, each of two-tenths of an *ephah*.
6You will then place them in two rows of six
on the pure table before Yahweh 7and put
pure incense on each row, to make it food
offered as a memorial, food burnt for
Yahweh. 8Every Sabbath they will be
arranged before Yahweh. The Israelites will
provide them as a permanent covenant.
9They will belong to Aaron and his sons, who
will eat them inside the holy place since, for
him, they are an especially holy part of the
food burnt for Yahweh. This is a permanent
law.'

A case of blasphemy
The law of retaliation

10There was a man whose mother was an
Israelite woman and whose father was an
Egyptian. He came out of his house and, in
the camp, surrounded by the Israelites, he
began to quarrel with a man who was an
Israelite. 11Now the son of the Israelite
woman blasphemed the Name and cursed it.
He was then taken to Moses (his mother's
name was Shelomith daughter of Dibri, of
the tribe of Dan). 12He was then put under
guard until Yahweh's will should be made
clear to them.
13Yahweh spoke to Moses and said:
14'Take the man who pronounced the curse
outside the camp. All those who heard him
must then lay their hands on his head, and
the whole community must then stone him.
15Then say to the Israelites:
"Anyone who curses his God will bear the

consequences of his sin, 16 and anyone who
blasphemes the name of Yahweh will be put
to death; the whole community will stone
him; be he alien or native-born, if he blas-
phemes the Name, he will be put to death.
17 "Anyone who strikes down any other
human being will be put to death.
18 "Anyone who strikes down an animal
will make restitution for it: a life for a life.
19 "Anyone who injures a neighbour shall
receive the same in return, 20 broken limb for
broken limb, eye for eye, tooth for tooth. As
the injury inflicted, so will be the injury
suffered. 21 Whoever strikes down an animal
will make restitution for it, and whoever
strikes down a human being will be put to
death. 22 The sentence you pass will be the
same, whether on native-born or on alien; for
I am Yahweh your God." '
23 Moses having told the Israelites this, they
took the man who had pronounced the curse
out of the camp and stoned him. And so
the Israelites carried out Yahweh's order to
Moses.

The holy years

a: The sabbatical year

25 Yahweh spoke to Moses on Mount
Sinai and said:
2 'Speak to the Israelites and say to them:
"When you enter the country which I am
giving you, the land must keep a Sabbath's
rest for Yahweh. 3 For six years you will sow
your field, for six years you will prune your
vineyard and gather its produce. 4 But in the
seventh year the land will have a sabbatical
rest, a Sabbath for Yahweh. You will neither
sow your field, nor prune your vineyard, 5 nor
reap any grain which has grown of its own
accord, nor gather the grapes from your
untrimmed vine. It will be a year of rest for
the land. 6 But what the land produces in its
Sabbath will serve to feed you, your slave,
male or female, your employee and your
guest residing with you; 7 for your cattle
too, and the wild animals of your country,
whatever it produces will serve as food.

b: The year of jubilee

8 "You will count seven weeks of years—
seven times seven years, that is to say a period
of seven weeks of years, forty-nine years.
9 And on the tenth day of the seventh month
you will sound the trumpet; on the Day
of Expiation you will sound the trumpet
throughout the land. 10 You will declare this
fiftieth year to be sacred and proclaim the
liberation of all the country's inhabitants.
You will keep this as a jubilee: each of you
will return to his ancestral property, each to
his own clan. 11 This fiftieth year will be a
jubilee year for you; in it you will not sow,
you will not harvest the grain that has come
up on its own or in it gather grapes from your
untrimmed vine. 12 The jubilee will be a holy
thing for you; during it you will eat whatever
the fields produce.
13 "In this year of jubilee, each of you will
return to his ancestral property. 14 If you
buy land from, or sell land to, your fellow-
countryman, neither of you may exploit the
other. 15 In buying from your fellow-
countryman, you will take account of the
number of years since the jubilee; the sale-
price he fixes for you will depend on the
number of productive years still to run. 16 The
greater the number of years, the higher the
price you will ask for it; the fewer the number
of years, the greater the reduction; for what
he is selling you is a certain number of
harvests. 17 So you will not exploit one
another, but fear your God, for I am Yahweh
your God.

Divine guarantee for the sabbatical year

18 "Hence, you will put my laws and customs
into practice; you will keep them and put
them into practice, and you will live securely
in the country. 19 The land will give its fruit,
and you will eat your fill and live in security.
20 "In case you should ask: What shall we
eat in this seventh year if we do not sow
or harvest our produce? 21 I shall order my
blessing to be on you in the sixth year, which
will yield you enough produce for three years.
22 You will have the old produce to eat while
you are sowing in the eighth year, and even
in the ninth year, you will be eating the old
produce, while waiting for the harvest of that
year.

Redemption of land

23 "Land will not be sold absolutely, for the
land belongs to me, and you are only strangers
and guests of mine. 24 You will allow a right
of redemption over any ancestral property.
25 If your brother becomes impoverished and

sells off part of his ancestral property, his nearest male relative will come and exercise his family rights over what his brother has sold. 26 The man who has no one to exercise this right may, once he has found the means to effect the redemption, 27 calculate the number of years that the alienation would have lasted, repay to the purchaser the sum due for the time still to run, and so recover his ancestral property. 28 If he cannot find the sum in compensation, the property sold will remain in the possession of the purchaser until the jubilee year. In the jubilee year, the latter will vacate it and return to his own ancestral property.

29 "If anyone sells a dwelling house inside a walled town, he will have the right of redemption until the expiry of the year following the sale. His right of redemption is limited to the year; 30 and if the redemption has not been effected by the end of the year, the house in the walled town will become the property of the purchaser and his descendants in perpetuity; he need not vacate it at the jubilee. 31 But houses in villages not enclosed by walls will be considered as situated in the open country; they carry the right of redemption, and the purchaser will vacate them at the jubilee.

32 "As regards the towns of the Levites, town houses forming part of their ancestral property will carry a perpetual right of redemption in their favour. 33 If a Levite is the one to be affected by the right of redemption, at the jubilee he will vacate the purchased property and return to his own home, to the town in which he has a title to property. The houses in the Levites' towns represent their ancestral property in Israel, 34 and the arable land depending on these towns cannot be sold, being their ancestral property for ever.

Redemption of persons

35 "If your brother becomes impoverished and cannot support himself in the community, you will assist him as you would a stranger or guest, so that he can go on living with you. 36 Do not charge him interest on a loan, but fear your God, and let your brother live with you. 37 You will not lend him money on interest or give him food to make a profit out of it. 38 I am Yahweh your God who brought you out of Egypt to give you the land of Canaan and be your God.

39 "If your brother becomes impoverished while with you and sells himself to you, you will not make him do the work of a slave; 40 you will treat him like an employee or guest, and he will work for you until the jubilee year. 41 He will then leave you, both he and his children, and return to his clan and regain possession of his ancestral property. 42 For they are my servants whom I have brought out of Egypt, and they may not be bought and sold as slaves. 43 You will not oppress your brother-Israelites harshly but will fear your God.

44 "The male and female slaves you have will come from the nations round you; from these you may purchase male and female slaves. 45 As slaves, you may also purchase the children of aliens resident among you, and also members of their families living with you who have been born on your soil; and they will become your property, 46 and you may leave them as a legacy to your sons after you as their perpetual possession. These you may have for slaves; but you will not oppress your brother-Israelites.

47 "If a stranger or guest living with you gets rich and your brother, in the course of dealings with him, becomes impoverished and sells himself to this stranger or guest, or to the descendant of a stranger's family, 48 he will enjoy the right of redemption after being sold, and one of his brothers may redeem him. 49 His paternal uncle, his uncle's son, or a member of his own family may redeem him; if he has the means, he may redeem himself. 50 By agreement with his purchaser, he will count the number of years between the year of sale and the jubilee year; his sale-price will be proportionate to the number of years, his time being valued as that of an employee. 51 If there are still many years to run, in proportion to their number he will refund part of his sale-price as payment for his redemption. 52 And if there are only a few years still to run before the jubilee year, he will calculate with him what should be refunded for his redemption, in proportion to their number, 53 as though he were hired by the year. You will see to it that he is not harshly oppressed.

54 "If he has not been redeemed in any of these ways, he will go free in the jubilee year, both he and his children; 55 for the Israelites are my servants; they are my servants whom I brought out of Egypt. I am Yahweh your God." '

Summary: conclusion

26 1"You will not make idols for your-
selves; you will not erect statues or
cultic stones, or erect carved stones in your
country, for you to worship: for I, Yahweh,
am your God. 2You will keep my Sabbaths
and revere my sanctuary. I am Yahweh.

Blessings

3"If you live according to my laws, if you
keep my commandments and put them into
practice, 4I shall give you the rain you need
at the right time; the soil will yield its produce
and the trees of the countryside their fruit;
5you will thresh until vintage time and gather
grapes until sowing time. You will eat your
fill of bread and live secure in your land.
6"I shall give peace in the land, and you
will go to sleep with no one to frighten you.
I shall rid the land of beasts of prey. The
sword will not pass through your land. 7You
will pursue your enemies and they will fall
before your sword; 8five of you pursuing a
hundred of them, one hundred pursuing ten
thousand; and your enemies will fall before
your sword.
9"I shall turn towards you, I shall make
you fertile and make your numbers grow,
and I shall uphold my covenant with you.
10"Having eaten all you need of last year's
harvest, you will throw out the old to make
room for the new.
11"I shall fix my home among you and
never reject you. 12I shall live among you; I
shall be your God and you will be my people,
13I, Yahweh your God, who brought you out
of Egypt so that you should be their slaves
no longer, and who broke the bonds of your
yoke and made you walk with head held high.

Curses

14"But if you will not listen to me and do not
put all these commandments into practice,
15if you reject my laws and detest my customs,
and you break my covenant by not putting
all my commandments into practice, 16this is
how I shall treat you:
"I shall subject you to terror, consumption
and fever, making you dim of sight and short
of breath. You will sow your seed in vain, for
your enemies will eat it. 17I shall turn against
you and you will be defeated by your enemies.
Your foes will have the mastery over you,
and you will flee when no one is pursuing
you.
18"And if, in spite of this, you will not
listen to me, I shall punish you seven times
over for your sins. 19I shall break your proud
strength. I shall make the sky like iron for
you, and your soil like bronze. 20You will
wear out your strength in vain, your land will
not yield its produce, nor the trees of the
country their fruit.
21"And if you go against me and will not
listen to me, I shall heap seven times more
plagues on you for your sins. 22I shall send
wild animals to attack you and rob you of
your children, destroy your cattle and reduce
your numbers until your roads are deserted.
23"And if that does not reform you, and
you still go against me, 24then I shall go
against you and punish you another seven
times over for your sins. 25I shall bring the
sword on you, which will avenge the
covenant, and when you huddle inside your
towns, I shall send pestilence among you,
and you will fall into the enemy's clutches.
26When I take away the bread which supports
you, ten women will be able to bake your
bread in one oven and will then dole your
bread out by weight; you will eat but not be
satisfied.
27"And if, in spite of this, you will not
listen to me but go against me, 28I shall go
against you in fury and punish you seven
times over for your sins. 29You will eat the
flesh of your own sons, you will eat the flesh
of your own daughters. 30I shall destroy your
high places and smash your incense-altars; I
shall pile your corpses on the corpses of your
foul idols and shall reject you. 31I shall reduce
your cities to ruins; I shall lay waste your
sanctuary and refuse to inhale from you
smells intended to please. 32I shall make such
a desolation of the country that your enemies
who come to live there will be appalled by it.
33And I shall scatter you among the nations.
I shall unsheathe the sword against you,
reducing your country to desert and your
towns to ruins. 34Then the country will
indeed observe its Sabbaths, all the while it
lies deserted, while you are in the country of
your enemies. Then indeed the country will
rest and observe its Sabbaths. 35And as it lies
deserted it will rest, as it never did on your
Sabbaths when you were living there. 36I
shall strike such fear into the hearts of those
of you who survive in the countries of their
enemies that the sound of a falling leaf will

set them fleeing; they will flee as though
fleeing from the sword, and fall when no one
is pursuing. 37They will stumble over one
another as though fleeing before the sword,
when no one is pursuing. You will be power-
less to stand up to your enemies; 38you will
perish among the nations, and the land of
your enemies will swallow you up. 39Those
of you who survive will pine away in their
guilt in the countries of their enemies and,
bearing the guilt of their ancestors too, will
pine away like them.
40"Then they shall admit their guilt and
that of their ancestors and their infidelities
against me, and further, their setting them-
selves against me.
41"I in my turn will go against them and
bring them into the land of their enemies.
Then their uncircumcised hearts will grow
humble and then they will accept the punish-
ment for their guilt. 42I shall remember my
covenant with Jacob, I shall remember my
covenant with Isaac and my covenant with
Abraham; and I shall remember the country
too.
43"Abandoned, the country will keep its
Sabbaths, as it lies deserted in their absence,
and they will have to accept the punishment
for their guilt, since they detested my
customs and rejected my laws.
44"Yet, in spite of all this, when they are
in the land of their enemies, I shall not so
utterly reject or detest them as to destroy
them completely and break my covenant with
them; for I am Yahweh their God. 45For their
sake I shall remember the covenant I made
with those first generations that I brought
out of Egypt while other nations watched,
so that I should be their God, I,
Yahweh." '
46Such were the decrees, customs and laws
which Yahweh established between himself
and the Israelites on Mount Sinai through
Moses.

APPENDIX
TARIFFS AND VALUATIONS

a: Persons

27 Yahweh spoke to Moses and said:
2'Speak to the Israelites and say:
"If anyone vows the value of a person to
Yahweh and wishes to discharge the vow:
3"a man between twenty and sixty years of
age will be valued at fifty silver shekels—the
sanctuary shekel; 4a woman will be valued at
thirty shekels;
5"between five and twenty years, a boy will
be valued at twenty shekels, a girl at ten
shekels;
6"between one month and five years, a boy
will be valued at five silver shekels, a girl at
three silver shekels;
7"at sixty years and over, a man will be
valued at fifteen shekels and a woman at ten
shekels.
8"If the person who made the vow cannot
meet this valuation, he will present the person
concerned to the priest, and the priest will
set a value proportionate to the resources of
the person who made the vow.

b: Animals

9"In the case of an animal suitable for offering
to Yahweh, any such animal given to Yahweh
will be holy. 10It cannot be exchanged or
replaced, a good one instead of a bad one, or
a bad one instead of a good one. If one animal
is substituted for another, both of them will
become holy. 11In the case of an unclean
animal unsuitable for offering to Yahweh,
whatever it may be, it will be presented to
the priest 12and he will set a value on it, in
relation to its worth. His valuation will be
decisive; 13but if the person wishes to redeem
it, he will add one-fifth to the valuation.

c: Houses

14"If a man consecrates his house to Yahweh,
the priest will set a value on it, in relation to
its worth. His valuation will be decisive. 15If
the man who has vowed his house wishes
to redeem it, he will add one-fifth to the
valuation, and it will revert to him.

d: Fields

16"If a man consecrates one of the fields of his ancestral property to Yahweh, its value will be calculated in terms of its yield, at the rate of fifty silver shekels to one *homer* of barley.

17"If he consecrates the field during the jubilee year, he will abide by this valuation. 18But if he consecrates it after the jubilee, the priest will calculate the price in terms of the number of years still to run until the next jubilee and the valuation will be reduced accordingly.

19"If he wishes to redeem the field, he will add one-fifth to the valuation, and the field will revert to him. 20If he does not redeem it but sells it to someone else, the right of redemption ceases; 21when the purchaser has to vacate it at the jubilee year, it becomes consecrated to Yahweh, like a field vowed unconditionally; ownership of it passes to the priest.

22"If he consecrates to Yahweh a field which he has bought, but which is not part of his ancestral property, 23the priest will calculate the valuation in terms of the number of years still to run before the jubilee year; and the man will pay this sum the same day since it is consecrated to Yahweh. 24In the jubilee year the field will revert to the vendor, the man to whose ancestral property the land belongs. 25All your valuations will be made in sanctuary shekels, at the rate of twenty *gerah* to the shekel.

Particular rules for the redemption

a: of the first-born

26"The first-born of livestock is born to Yahweh; no one may consecrate it, whether it be cattle or sheep, for it belongs to Yahweh anyway. 27But if it is an unclean animal, it may be redeemed at the valuation price with one-fifth added; if the animal is not redeemed, it will be sold at the valuation price.

b: of things vowed unconditionally

28"Nothing, however, that someone vows unconditionally to Yahweh may be redeemed, nothing he possesses, be it a human being or animal or field of his ancestral property. What is vowed unconditionally is especially holy and belongs to Yahweh. 29A human being vowed unconditionally cannot be redeemed but will be put to death.

c: of tithes

30"All tithes on land, levied on the produce of the soil or on the fruit of trees, belong to Yahweh; they are consecrated to Yahweh. 31If anyone wishes to redeem part of his tithe, he will add one-fifth to its value.

32"In all tithes on herds or flocks, the tenth animal of all that pass under the herdsman's staff will be consecrated to Yahweh; 33there will be no examining whether it is good or bad, and no substitution. If substitution takes place, the animal and its substitute will both become holy without possibility of redemption." '

34Such were the orders which Yahweh gave Moses on Mount Sinai for the Israelites.

THE BOOK OF NUMBERS

A collection of varied material, the book concludes Israel's wanderings, including the abortive attempt to enter Canaan from the south. Much of the legislation, chiefly on ritual and priestly matters, comes in the form of incidents, the natural source of case-law. Several of these highlight the punishment for infidelity, and so point to the absolute demands of God's holiness, which brooks no rivalry or opposition. There is some overlap with other books, but sources vary from very ancient poetic fragments to post-exilic material. There are traces of some primitive magical practices, some echoes of David's majesty and conquests, and the provisions of the late, priestly legislation (never fully observed) on the holy war.

PLAN OF THE BOOK

NUMBERS

I: THE CENSUS[a]

1 Yahweh spoke to Moses, in the desert of Sinai, in the Tent of Meeting, on the first day of the second month, in the second year after the exodus from Egypt, and said:
2 "Take a census of the whole community of Israelites by clans and families, taking a count of the names of all the males, head by head. 3 You and Aaron will register all those in Israel, twenty years of age and over, fit to bear arms, company by company; 4 you will have one man from each tribe, the head of his family, to help you.

The census officials

5 "These are the names of those who must help you:
For Reuben, Elizur son of Shedeur.
6 For Simeon, Shelumiel son of Zurishaddai.
7 For Judah, Nahshon son of Amminadab.

1a Israel is shown as a settled community, centred on the Levites. The numbers fit that period.

8 For Issachar, Nethanel son of Zuar.
9 For Zebulun, Eliab son of Helon.
10 Of the sons of Joseph: for Ephraim,
Elishama son of Ammihud; for Manasseh,
Gamaliel son of Pedahzur.
11 For Benjamin, Abidan son of Gideoni.
12 For Dan, Ahiezer son of Ammishaddai.
13 For Asher, Pagiel son of Ochran.
14 For Gad, Eliasaph son of Reuel.
15 For Naphtali, Ahira son of Enan.'
16 These were men of repute in the
community; they were the leaders of their
ancestral tribes, the heads of Israel's
thousands.
17 Moses and Aaron took these men who
had been named 18 and on the first day of
the second month they mustered the whole
community. The Israelites established their
pedigrees by clans and families, and one by
one the names of all men of twenty years
and over were recorded. 19 As Yahweh had
ordered, Moses registered them in the desert
of Sinai.

The census

20 Once the pedigrees of the descendants of
Reuben, Israel's first-born, had been estab-
lished by clans and families, the names of all
the males of twenty years and over, fit to bear
arms, were recorded one by one. 21 The total
of these for the tribe of Reuben was forty-six
thousand five hundred.
22 Once the pedigrees of Simeon's descend-
ants had been established by clans and
families, the names of all the males of twenty
years and over, fit to bear arms, were recorded
one by one. 23 The total of these for the
tribe of Simeon was fifty-nine thousand three
hundred.
24 Once the pedigrees of Gad's descendants
had been established by clans and families,
the names of all the males of twenty years
and over, fit to bear arms, were recorded one
by one. 25 The total of these for the tribe of
Gad was forty-five thousand six hundred and
fifty.
26 Once the pedigrees of Judah's descend-
ants had been established by clans and
families, the names of all the males of twenty
years and over, fit to bear arms, were recorded
one by one. 27 The total of these for the
tribe of Judah was seventy-four thousand six
hundred.
28 Once the pedigrees of Issachar's descend-
ants had been established by clans and
families, the names of all the males of twenty
years and over, fit to bear arms, were recorded
one by one. 29 The total of these for the
tribe of Issachar was fifty-four thousand four
hundred.
30 Once the pedigrees of Zebulun's
descendants had been established by clans
and families, the names of all the males of
twenty years and over, fit to bear arms, were
recorded one by one. 31 The total of these for
the tribe of Zebulun was fifty-seven thousand
four hundred.
32 As regards the descendants of Joseph:
once the pedigrees of Ephraim's descendants
had been established by clans and families,
the names of all the males of twenty years
and over, fit to bear arms, were recorded one
by one. 33 The total of these for the tribe of
Ephraim was forty thousand five hundred.
34 Once the pedigrees of Manasseh's
descendants had been established by clans
and families, the names of all the males of
twenty years and over, fit to bear arms, were
recorded one by one. 35 The total of these
for the tribe of Manasseh was thirty-two
thousand two hundred.
36 Once the pedigrees of Benjamin's
descendants had been established by clans
and families, the names of all the males of
twenty years and over, fit to bear arms, were
recorded one by one. 37 The total of these
for the tribe of Benjamin was thirty-five
thousand four hundred.
38 Once the pedigrees of Dan's descendants
had been established by clans and families,
the names of all the males of twenty years
and over, fit to bear arms, were recorded one
by one. 39 The total of these for the tribe of
Dan was sixty-two thousand seven hundred.
40 Once the pedigrees of Asher's descend-
ants had been established by clans and
families, the names of all the males of twenty
years and over, fit to bear arms, were recorded
one by one. 41 The total of these for the
tribe of Asher was forty-one thousand five
hundred.
42 Once the pedigrees of Naphtali's
descendants had been established by clans
and families, the names of all the males of
twenty years and over, fit to bear arms, were
recorded one by one. 43 The total of these for
the tribe of Naphtali was fifty-three thousand
four hundred.
44 Such were the men registered by Moses,
Aaron and the leaders of Israel, of whom
there were twelve, each representing his

family. 45All the Israelites of twenty years
and over, fit to bear arms, were counted by
families. 46Altogether, the total came to six
hundred and three thousand five hundred
and fifty.
47But the Levites and their tribes were not
included in the count.

Statute for the Levites

48Yahweh spoke to Moses and said:
49'Do not, however, take a census of the
Levites, or register them with the other
Israelites, 50but enrol the Levites to take
charge of the Dwelling where the Testimony
is and of all its furnishings and belongings.
They must carry the Dwelling and all its
furnishings; they must look after the
Dwelling and pitch their camp round it.
51Whenever the Dwelling is moved, the
Levites will dismantle it; whenever the
Dwelling stops for the night, the Levites will
erect it. Any unauthorised person coming
near it will be put to death. 52The Israelites
will pitch their tents, each in their own
encampment and by their own standard,
company by company, 53but the Levites will
pitch their tents round the Dwelling where
the Testimony is. In this way Retribution
will be kept from falling on the whole
community of Israelites, and the Levites will
keep charge of the Dwelling of the
Testimony.'
54The Israelites did exactly as Yahweh had
ordered Moses. They did as he said.

Order of the tribes

2 Yahweh spoke to Moses and to Aaron and
said:
2'The Israelites must pitch their tents, each
man by his own standard, under their family
emblems. They must pitch their tents round
the Dwelling where the Testimony is, some
distance away.
3'Encamped on the east side:
'Furthest towards the east, the standard of
the camp of Judah, unit by unit. Leader of
the Judahites: Nahshon son of Amminadab.
4His company: seventy-four thousand six
hundred men.
5'Next to him:
'The tribe of Issachar. Leader of the Issa-
charites: Nethanel son of Zuar. 6His
company: fifty-four thousand four hundred
men.
7'The tribe of Zebulun. Leader of the
Zebulunites: Eliab son of Helon. 8His com-
pany: fifty-seven thousand four hundred
men.
9'The tribal forces in the camp of Judah
number in all a hundred and eighty-six thou-
sand four hundred. These will be the first to
break camp.
10'On the south side, the standard of the
camp of Reuben, unit by unit. Leader of the
Reubenites: Elizur son of Shedeur. 11His
company: forty-six thousand five hundred
men.
12'Next to him:
'The tribe of Simeon. Leader of the
Simeonites: Shelumiel son of Zurishaddai.
13His company: fifty-nine thousand three
hundred men.
14'The tribe of Gad. Leader of the Gadites:
Eliasaph son of Reuel. 15His company: forty-
five thousand six hundred and fifty men.
16'The tribal forces in the camp of Reuben
number in all a hundred and fifty-one thou-
sand four hundred and fifty. They will be
second to break camp.
17'Next, the Tent of Meeting will move,
since the camp of the Levites is situated in
the middle of the other camps. The order of
movement will be the order of encampment,
each man under his own standard.
18'On the west side, the standard of the
camp of Ephraim, unit by unit. Leader of
the Ephraimites: Elishama son of Ammihud.
19His company: forty thousand five hundred
men.
20'Next to him:
'The tribe of Manasseh. Leader of the
Manassehites: Gamaliel son of Pedahzur.
21His company: thirty-two thousand two
hundred men.
22'The tribe of Benjamin. Leader of the
Benjaminites: Abidan son of Gideoni. 23His
company: thirty-five thousand four hundred
men.
24'The tribal forces in the camp of Ephraim
number in all a hundred and eight thousand
one hundred. They will be third to break
camp.
25'On the north side, the standard of the
camp of Dan, unit by unit. Leader of the
Danites: Ahiezer son of Ammishaddai. 26His
company: sixty-two thousand seven hundred
men.
27'Next to him:
'The tribe of Asher. Leader of the Asher-

ites: Pagiel son of Ochran. 28His company: forty-one thousand five hundred men.

29'The tribe of Naphtali. Leader of the Naphtalites: Ahira son of Enan. 30His company: fifty-three thousand four hundred men.

31'The tribal forces in the camp of Dan number in all a hundred and fifty-seven thousand six hundred. They will be the last to break camp.

'All under their appropriate standards.'

32Such was the tally of the Israelites when the census was taken by families. The full count of the entire camp, unit by unit, came to six hundred and three thousand five hundred and fifty. 33But, as Yahweh had ordered Moses, the Levites were not included in the census of the Israelites.

34The Israelites did exactly as Yahweh had ordered Moses. This was how they pitched camp, grouped by standards. This was how they broke camp, each man in his own clan, each man with his own family.

The tribe of Levi

a: The priests

3 These were the descendants of Aaron and Moses, at the time when Yahweh spoke to Moses on Mount Sinai.

2These were the names of Aaron's sons: Nadab the eldest, then Abihu, Eleazar and Ithamar.

3Such were the names of Aaron's sons, priests anointed and invested with the powers of the priesthood. 4Nadab and Abihu died in Yahweh's presence, in the desert of Sinai, when they offered unauthorised fire before Yahweh. They left no children and so it fell to Eleazar and Ithamar to exercise the priesthood under their father Aaron.

b: The Levites: their duties

5Yahweh spoke to Moses and said:

6'Muster the tribe of Levi and put it at the disposal of the priest Aaron: they must be at his service. 7They will undertake the duties incumbent on him and the whole community before the Tent of Meeting, in serving the Dwelling, 8and they will be in charge of all the furnishings of the Tent of Meeting and undertake the duties incumbent on the Israelites in serving the Dwelling. 9You will present the Levites to Aaron and his sons as men dedicated; they will be given to him by the Israelites.

10'You will register Aaron and his sons, who will carry out their priestly duty. But any unauthorised person who comes near must be put to death.'

c: Their privileged status

11Yahweh spoke to Moses and said:

12'Look, I myself have chosen the Levites from the Israelites instead of all the first-born, those who emerge first from the womb in Israel; the Levites therefore belong to me. 13For every first-born belongs to me. On the day when I struck down all the first-born in Egypt, I consecrated all the first-born in Israel, human and animal, to be my own. They are mine, Yahweh's.'

d: Census of the Levites

14Yahweh spoke to Moses in the desert of Sinai and said:

15'You must take a census of Levi's descendants by families and clans; all the males of the age of one month and over will be counted.'

16At Yahweh's word Moses took a census of them, as Yahweh had ordered. 17These were the names of Levi's sons: Gershon, Kohath and Merari.

18These were the names of Gershon's sons by their clans: Libni and Shimei; 19Kohath's sons by their clans: Amram, Izhar, Hebron and Uzziel; 20Merari's sons by their clans: Mahli and Mushi. These were the clans of Levi, grouped by families.

21From Gershon were descended the Libnite and Shimeite clans; these were the Gershonite clans. 22Their full number, counting the males of one month and over, came to seven thousand five hundred. 23The Gershonite clans pitched their camp behind the Dwelling, on the west side. 24The leader of the House of Gershon was Eliasaph son of Lael. 25As regards the Tent of Meeting, the Gershonites had charge of the Dwelling, the Tent and its covering, the screen for the entrance to the Tent of Meeting, 26the curtaining of the court, the screen for the entrance to the court surrounding the Dwelling and the altar, and the cords required in dealing with all this.

27From Kohath were descended the Amramite, Izharite, Hebronite and Uzzielite

clans; these were the Kohathite clans. [28]Their
full number, counting the males of one month
and over, came to eight thousand three
hundred. They were in charge of the sanc-
tuary. [29]The Kohathite clans pitched their
camp on the south side of the Dwelling. [30]The
leader of the house of the Kohathite clans
was Elizaphan son of Uzziel. [31]They were in
charge of the ark, the table, the lamp-stand,
the altars, the sacred vessels used in the
liturgy, and the curtain with all its fittings.
[32]The chief of the Levite leaders was
Eleazar, son of Aaron the priest. He super-
vised the people responsible for the
sanctuary.
[33]From Merari were descended the
Mahlite and Mushite clans; these were the
Merarite clans. [34]Their full number, count-
ing the males of one month and over, came
to six thousand two hundred. [35]The leader of
the House of the Merarite clans was Zuriel,
son of Abihail. They pitched their camp
on the north side of the Dwelling. [36]The
Merarites were in charge of the framework
of the Dwelling, with its crossbars, poles,
sockets and all its accessories and fittings,
[37]and also the poles round the court, with
their sockets, pegs and cords.
[38]Finally, on the east side, in front of the
Dwelling, in front of the Tent of Meeting,
towards the east, was the camp of Moses and
Aaron and his sons, who had charge of the
sanctuary on behalf of the Israelites. Any
unauthorised person coming near was to be
put to death.
[39]The total number of male Levites of the
age of one month and over, whom Moses
counted by clans as Yahweh had ordered,
came to twenty-two thousand.

e: The Levites and the ransoming of the first-born

[40]Yahweh said to Moses:
'Take a census of all the first-born of the
Israelites, all the males from the age of one
month and over; take a census of them by
name. [41]You will then present the Levites to
me, Yahweh, instead of Israel, and similarly
the Levites' cattle instead of the first-born
cattle of the Israelites.'
[42]As Yahweh ordered, Moses took a census
of all the first-born of the Israelites. [43]The
total count, by name, of the first-born from
the age of one month and over came to
twenty-two thousand two hundred and
seventy-three.
[44]Yahweh then spoke to Moses and said:
[45]'Take the Levites instead of all the first-
born of the Israelites, and the Levites' cattle
instead of their cattle; the Levites will be
mine, Yahweh's. [46]For the ransom of the two
hundred and seventy-three first-born of the
Israelites in excess of the number of Levites,
[47]you will take five shekels for each, by
the sanctuary shekel, at twenty *gerah* to the
shekel; [48]you will then give this money to
Aaron and his sons as the ransom for the
extra number.'
[49]Moses took the ransom money for the
extra ones unransomed by the Levites; [50]he
took the money for the first-born of the
Israelites: one thousand three hundred and
sixty-five shekels, by the sanctuary shekel;
[51]and Moses then handed over their ransom
money to Aaron and his sons, at Yahweh's
bidding, as Yahweh had ordered Moses.

The Levite clans

a: The Kohathites

4 Yahweh spoke to Moses and said:
[2]'Take a census by clans and families of
the Levites descended from Kohath: [3]all the
men between thirty and fifty years of age and
eligible for military service, who will have
their duties in the Tent of Meeting.
[4]'These are the duties of the Kohathites:
looking after those things that are especially
holy.
[5]'When camp is broken, Aaron and his
sons must come and take down the screening
curtain, and cover the ark of the Testimony
with it. [6]Over this, they will put a covering
of fine leather, over which they will spread a
cloth entirely of violet-purple. They will then
fix the poles to the ark.
[7]'Over the offertory table they will spread
a violet cloth, and on it put the dishes,
cups, bowls and libation jars; the bread of
permanent offering will also be on it. [8]Over
these they will spread a scarlet cloth and
cover the whole with a covering of fine
leather. They will then fix the poles to the
table.
[9]'They will then take a violet cloth and
cover the lamp-stand, its lamps, snuffers,
trays and all the oil jars used for it, [10]and will
lay it and all its accessories in a covering of
fine leather and put it on the litter.

[11]'Over the golden altar they will spread a violet cloth, and cover that with a covering of fine leather. They will then fix the poles to it.

[12]'They will then take all the other objects used in the service of the sanctuary, put them in a violet cloth, with a covering of fine leather, and put it all on the litter.

[13]'When they have removed the ashes from the altar, they will spread a scarlet cloth over it, [14]and on this place all the objects used in the liturgy, the fire pans, hooks, scoops, sprinkling basins and all the altar accessories. Over this they will spread a covering of fine leather. They will then fix the poles to it.

[15]'Once Aaron and his sons have finished covering the holy things and all their accessories at the breaking of camp, the Kohathites will come and carry them, but without touching any of the holy things on pain of death. Such is the load for the Kohathites in the Tent of Meeting. [16]But Eleazar, son of Aaron the priest, is responsible for looking after the oil for the light, the fragrant incense, the daily cereal offering and the anointing oil, and for supervising the entire Dwelling and everything in it, the holy things and their accessories.'

[17]Yahweh spoke to Moses and said:

[18]'You must not let the group of Kohathite clans be lost to the rest of the Levites. [19]But deal with them in this way, so that they may survive and not incur death by approaching those things that are especially holy. Aaron and his sons will go in and assign to each of them his task and load, [20]in such a way that they have no need to incur the death penalty by going in and setting eyes on the holy things, even for an instant.'

b: The Gershonites

[21]Yahweh spoke to Moses and said:

[22]'Take a census of the Gershonites by families and clans, too: [23]all the men between thirty and fifty years of age, eligible for military service, who will have their duties in the Tent of Meeting.

[24]'These are the duties of the Gershonite clans, their functions and their loads. [25]They will carry the curtaining of the Dwelling, the Tent of Meeting with its covering and the covering of fine leather that goes over it, the screen for the entrance to the Tent of Meeting, [26]the curtaining of the court, the screen for the entrance to the court surrounding the Dwelling and the altar, the cords, all the accessories for worship, and all the necessary equipment.

'They will be responsible for these things. [27]All the duties of the Gershonites, their functions and their loads, will be carried out under the direction of Aaron and his sons: you will see that they fulfil their charge. [28]Such are the duties of the Gershonite clans in the Tent of Meeting. Their work will be supervised by Ithamar, son of Aaron the priest.

c: The Merarites

[29]'You will take a census of the Merarites by clans and families. [30]You will take a census of all the men between thirty and fifty years of age, eligible for military service, who will have their duties in the Tent of Meeting.

[31]'The load they carry and the duties incumbent on them in the Tent of Meeting will be as follows: the framework of the Dwelling, its cross-bars, poles and sockets, [32]the poles round the court with their sockets, pegs, cords and all their tackle. You will draw up a list of their names with the loads for which each is responsible.

[33]'Such are the duties of the Merarite clans. All their duties in the Tent of Meeting will be supervised by Ithamar, son of Aaron the priest.'

Census of the Levites

[34]Moses, Aaron and the leaders of the community took a census of the Kohathites by clans and families: [35]all the men between thirty and fifty years of age, eligible for military service, for duties in the Tent of Meeting. [36]The number of men counted in their clans came to two thousand seven hundred and fifty. [37]Such was the total number of men in the Kohathite clans who were eligible for duties in the Tent of Meeting and whom Moses and Aaron counted at Yahweh's bidding through Moses.

[38]A census was taken of the Gershonites by clans and families: [39]all the men between thirty and fifty years of age, eligible for military service, for duties in the Tent of Meeting. [40]The number of men counted in their clans and families came to two thousand six hundred and thirty. [41]Such was the total number of men in the Gershonite clans who were eligible for duties in the Tent of

Meeting, and whom Moses and Aaron
counted at Yahweh's bidding.
42A census was taken of the Merarite clans
by clans and families: 43all the men between
thirty and fifty years of age, eligible for
military service, for duties in the Tent of
Meeting. 44The number of men counted in
their clans came to three thousand two
hundred. 45Such was the total number of
men in the Merarite clans, whom Moses and
Aaron counted at Yahweh's bidding through
Moses.

46The total number of Levites whom
Moses, Aaron and the leaders of Israel
counted in their clans and families, 47all the
men between thirty and fifty years of age,
eligible for religious duties and for those of
transporting the Tent of Meeting 48came to
eight thousand five hundred and eighty. 49At
Yahweh's bidding through Moses, a census
was taken of them and each man was assigned
his duty and load. And so the census was
conducted by Moses as Yahweh had ordered
him.

II: VARIOUS LAWS

Expulsion of the unclean

5 Yahweh spoke to Moses and said:
2'Order the Israelites to expel from the
camp all those suffering from a contagious
skin-disease or from a discharge, or who
have become unclean by touching a corpse.
3Whether man or woman, you will expel
them; you will expel them from the camp, so
that they do not pollute their encampments,
in the heart of which I dwell.'
4The Israelites did so: they expelled them
from the camp. The Israelites did as Yahweh
had told Moses.

Restitution

5Yahweh spoke to Moses and said, 6'Speak
to the Israelites:
"If a man or woman commits any of the
sins by which people break faith with
Yahweh, that person incurs guilt.
7"The person must confess the sin
committed and restore in full the amount
owed, with one-fifth added. Payment is to be
made to the person wronged.
8"If, however, the latter has no relation
to whom restitution can be made, the
restitution due to Yahweh reverts to the
priest, apart from the ram of expiation with
which the priest makes expiation for the
guilty party. 9For of everything the Israel-
ites consecrate and bring to the priest he
has a right to the portion set aside.
10Whatever anyone consecrates is his own;
whatever is given to the priest belongs to
the priest." '

Cereal offering in cases of suspicion

11Yahweh spoke to Moses and said, 12'Speak
to the Israelites and say:
"If anyone has a wife who goes astray and
is unfaithful to him, 13if some other man
sleeps with the woman without the husband's
knowledge, and she secretly makes herself
unclean, without any witness against her,
and without anyone catching her in the act;
14if, then, a spirit of suspicion comes over the
husband and makes him suspicious of the
wife who has disgraced herself, or again if
this spirit of suspicion comes over him and
makes him suspicious of his wife even when
she is innocent, 15the man will bring his wife
before the priest, and on her behalf make an
offering of one-tenth of an *ephah* of barley
meal. He will not pour oil over it or put
incense on it, because this is a cereal offering
for a case of suspicion, a memorial offering
to recall guilt to mind.
16"The priest will then bring the woman
forward and place her before Yahweh. 17The
priest will then take fresh water in an earthen
jar, and on the water throw dust that he has
taken from the floor of the Dwelling. 18After
he has placed the woman before Yahweh, he
will unbind her hair and put the commemor-
ative cereal offering (that is, the cereal
offering for a case of suspicion) into her
hands. In his own hands the priest will hold
the water of bitterness and cursing.
19"The priest will then put the woman on
oath. He will say to her: If it is not true that
a man has slept with you, that you have gone
astray and made yourself unclean while under

your husband's authority, may this water of bitterness and cursing do you no harm. [20]But if it is true that you have gone astray while under your husband's authority, that you have made yourself unclean and that a man other than your husband has slept with you . . . [21]Here the priest will impose an imprecatory oath on the woman. He will say to her: . . . May Yahweh make you the object of your people's execration and curses, by making your sexual organs shrivel and your belly swell! [22]May this water of cursing entering your bowels, make your belly swell and your sexual organs shrivel! To which the woman will reply: Amen! Amen!

[23]"Having written these curses on a scroll and washed them off in the water of bitterness, [24]the priest will make the woman drink the water of bitterness and cursing; when the water of cursing enters into her, it will become bitter.

[25]"The priest will then take the cereal offering for a case of suspicion from the woman's hands, and hold it up before Yahweh with a gesture of offering, and so carry it up to the altar. [26]He will take a handful of it as a memorial and burn it on the altar.

"After this, he will make the woman drink the water. [27]After he has made her drink it, if it is true that she has made herself unclean and been unfaithful to her husband, the water of cursing then entering into her will indeed be bitter: her belly will swell and her sexual organs shrivel, and she will be an object of execration to her people. [28]But if she has not made herself unclean, but is clean, then she will go unscathed and will bear children.

[29]"Such is the ritual in cases of suspicion, when a woman has gone astray and made herself unclean while under her husband's authority, [30]or when a spirit of suspicion has come over a man and made him suspicious of his wife. When a husband brings such a woman before Yahweh, the priest will apply this ritual to her in full. [31]The husband will be guiltless, but the woman will bear the consequences of her guilt." '

The nazirite

6 Yahweh spoke to Moses and said, [2]"Speak to the Israelites and say:
"If a man or a woman wishes to make a vow, the nazirite vow, to vow himself to Yahweh, [3]he will abstain from wine and fermented liquor, he will not drink vinegar derived from one or the other, he will not drink grape-juice or eat grapes, be they fresh or dried. [4]For the duration of his vow he will eat nothing that comes from the vine, not even juice of unripe grapes or skins of grapes. [5]As long as he is bound by his vow, no razor will touch his head; until the time for which he has vowed himself to Yahweh is completed, he remains consecrated and will let his hair grow freely. [6]For the entire period of his vow to Yahweh, he will not go near a corpse, [7]he will not make himself unclean for his father or his mother, or his brother or his sister, should they die, since on his head he carries his vow to his God. [8]Throughout the whole of his vow he is a person consecrated to Yahweh.

[9]"If anyone suddenly dies near him, making his vowed hair unclean, he will shave his head on the day he is purified, he will shave his head on the seventh day. [10]On the eighth day, he will bring two turtledoves or two young pigeons to the priest, at the entrance to the Tent of Meeting. [11]The priest will offer one as a sacrifice for sin, and the other as a burnt offering and will then perform for the person the rite of expiation for the pollution which he has contracted from the corpse. He will consecrate his head that same day; [12]he will vow himself to Yahweh for the period of his nazirate, and will bring a male yearling lamb as a sacrifice of reparation. The time already spent will not count, since his hair had become unclean.

[13]"This is the ritual for the nazirite on the day when the period of his vow is completed. He will be led to the entrance of the Tent of Meeting, [14]bringing his offering to Yahweh: an unblemished male yearling lamb as a burnt offering, an unblemished yearling ewe lamb as a sacrifice for sin, an unblemished ram as a peace offering, [15]and a basket of unleavened loaves made of fine flour mixed with oil, and of unleavened wafers spread with oil, with the cereal offerings and libations appropriate to them. [16]The priest, having brought all this before Yahweh, will offer the nazirite's sin sacrifice and burnt offering. [17]The latter will then offer the ram as a communion sacrifice with the basket of unleavened bread, and the priest will offer the accompanying cereal offering and libation. [18]The nazirite will then shave off his vowed hair at the entrance to the Tent of Meeting and, taking the locks of his vowed head, he will put them in the fire of the communion sacrifice. [19]The priest will

take the shoulder of the ram, as soon as it is cooked, with an unleavened cake from the basket, and an unleavened wafer, and put them into the hands of the nazirite once he has shaved off his hair. 20With these he will make the gesture of offering before Yahweh; as it is a holy thing, it reverts to the priest, in addition to the forequarter that has been presented and the thigh that has been set aside. After this, the nazirite may drink wine.

21"Such is the ritual for the nazirite. If, besides his hair, he has also vowed a personal offering to Yahweh, he will (apart from anything else that his means allow) fulfil the vow that he has made, in addition to what the ritual prescribes for his hair." '

The form of blessing

22Yahweh spoke to Moses and said, 23'Speak to Aaron and his sons and say:

"This is how you must bless the Israelites. You will say:

24May Yahweh bless you and keep you.
25May Yahweh let his face shine on you
and be gracious to you.
26May Yahweh show you his face
and bring you peace."

27This is how they must call down my name on the Israelites, and then I shall bless them.'

III: OFFERINGS OF THE LEADERS AND CONSECRATION OF THE LEVITES

Offering of wagons

7On the day Moses finished erecting the Dwelling, he anointed and consecrated it and all its furniture, as well as the altar and all its equipment. When he had anointed and consecrated it all, 2the leaders of Israel made an offering; they were the heads of their families, the tribal leaders who had presided over the census. 3They brought their offering before Yahweh: six covered wagons and twelve oxen, one wagon for every two leaders and one ox each. They brought them in front of the Dwelling. 4Yahweh spoke to Moses and said, 5'Accept these from them, and let them be set apart for the service of the Tent of Meeting. You will give them to the Levites, to each as his duties require.' 6Moses took the wagons and oxen, and gave them to the Levites. 7To the Gershonites he gave two wagons and four oxen for the duties they had to perform. 8To the Merarites he gave four wagons and eight oxen for the duties they had to perform under the direction of Ithamar, son of Aaron the priest. 9But to the Kohathites he gave none at all, because the sacred charge entrusted to them had to be carried on their shoulders.

Dedication offering

10The leaders then made an offering for the dedication of the altar, on the day it was anointed. They brought their offering before the altar, 11and Yahweh said to Moses, 'Each day one of the leaders must bring his offering for the dedication of the altar.'

12On the first day an offering was brought by Nahshon son of Amminadab, of the tribe of Judah. 13His offering consisted of: one silver bowl weighing a hundred and thirty shekels, one silver sprinkling bowl weighing seventy shekels (sanctuary shekels), both of them full of fine flour mixed with oil as a cereal offering, 14one golden bowl weighing ten shekels, full of incense, 15one young bull, one ram and one male yearling lamb as a burnt offering, 16one he-goat as a sacrifice for sin, 17and two bulls, five rams, five he-goats and five male yearling lambs as a communion sacrifice. Such was the offering of Nahshon son of Amminadab.

18On the second day an offering was brought by Nethanel son of Zuar, leader of Issachar. 19His offering consisted of: one silver bowl weighing a hundred and thirty shekels, one silver sprinkling bowl weighing seventy shekels (sanctuary shekels), both of them full of fine flour mixed with oil as a cereal offering, 20one golden bowl weighing ten shekels, full of incense, 21one young bull, one ram and one male yearling lamb as a burnt offering, 22one he-goat as a sacrifice for sin, 23and two bulls, five rams, five he-goats and five male yearling lambs as a communion

sacrifice. Such was the offering of Nethanel son of Zuar.

24On the third day an offering was brought by Eliab son of Helon, leader of the Zebulunites. 25His offering consisted of: one silver bowl weighing a hundred and thirty shekels, one silver sprinkling bowl weighing seventy shekels (sanctuary shekels), both of them full of fine flour mixed with oil as a cereal offering, 26one golden bowl weighing ten shekels, full of incense, 27one young bull, one ram and one male yearling lamb as a burnt offering, 28one he-goat as a sacrifice for sin, 29and two bulls, five rams, five he-goats and five male yearling lambs as a communion sacrifice. Such was the offering of Eliab son of Helon.

30On the fourth day an offering was brought by Elizur son of Shedeur, leader of the Reubenites. 31His offering consisted of: one silver bowl weighing a hundred and thirty shekels, one silver sprinkling bowl weighing seventy shekels (sanctuary shekels), both of them full of fine flour mixed with oil as a cereal offering, 32one golden bowl weighing ten shekels, full of incense, 33one young bull, one ram and one male yearling lamb as a burnt offering, 34one he-goat as a sacrifice for sin, 35and two bulls, five rams, five he-goats and five male yearling lambs as a communion sacrifice. Such was the offering of Elizur son of Shedeur.

36On the fifth day an offering was brought by Shelumiel son of Zurishaddai, leader of the Simeonites. 37His offering consisted of: one silver bowl weighing a hundred and thirty shekels, one silver sprinkling bowl weighing seventy shekels (sanctuary shekels), both of them full of fine flour mixed with oil as a cereal offering, 38one golden bowl weighing ten shekels, full of incense, 39one young bull, one ram and one male yearling lamb as a burnt offering, 40one he-goat as a sacrifice for sin, 41and two bulls, five rams, five he-goats and five male yearling lambs as a communion sacrifice. Such was the offering of Shelumiel son of Zurishaddai.

42On the sixth day an offering was brought by Eliasaph son of Reuel, leader of the Gadites. 43His offering consisted of: one silver bowl weighing a hundred and thirty shekels, one silver sprinkling bowl weighing seventy shekels (sanctuary shekels), both of them full of fine flour mixed with oil as a cereal offering, 44one golden bowl weighing ten shekels, full of incense, 45one young bull, one ram and one male yearling lamb as a burnt offering, 46one he-goat as a sacrifice for sin, 47and two bulls, five rams, five he-goats and five male yearling lambs as a communion sacrifice. Such was the offering of Eliasaph son of Reuel.

48On the seventh day an offering was brought by Elishama son of Ammihud, leader of the Ephraimites. 49His offering consisted of: one silver bowl weighing a hundred and thirty shekels, one silver sprinkling bowl weighing seventy shekels (sanctuary shekels), both of them full of fine flour mixed with oil as a cereal offering, 50one golden bowl weighing ten shekels, full of incense,51 one young bull, one ram and one male yearling lamb as a burnt offering, 52one he-goat as a sacrifice for sin, 53and two bulls, five rams, five he-goats and five male yearling lambs as a communion sacrifice. Such was the offering of Elishama son of Ammihud.

54On the eighth day an offering was brought by Gamaliel son of Pedahzur, leader of the Manassehites. 55His offering consisted of: one silver bowl weighing a hundred and thirty shekels, one silver sprinkling bowl weighing seventy shekels (sanctuary shekels), both of them full of fine flour mixed with oil as a cereal offering, 56one golden bowl weighing ten shekels, full of incense, 57one young bull, one ram and one male yearling lamb as a burnt offering, 58one he-goat as a sacrifice for sin, 59and two bulls, five rams, five he-goats and five male yearling lambs as a communion sacrifice. Such was the offering of Gamaliel son of Pedahzur.

60On the ninth day an offering was brought by Abidan son of Gideoni, leader of the Benjaminites. 61His offering consisted of: one silver bowl weighing a hundred and thirty shekels, one sprinkling bowl weighing seventy shekels (sanctuary shekels), both of them full of fine flour mixed with oil as a cereal offering, 62one golden bowl weighing ten shekels, full of incense, 63one young bull, one ram and one male yearling lamb as a burnt offering, 64one he-goat as a sacrifice for sin, 65and two bulls, five rams, five he-goats and five male yearling lambs as a communion sacrifice. Such was the offering of Abidan son of Gideoni.

66On the tenth day an offering was brought by Ahiezer son of Ammishaddai, leader of the Danites. 67His offering consisted of: one silver bowl weighing a hundred and thirty shekels, one silver sprinkling bowl weighing seventy shekels (sanctuary shekels), both of

them full of fine flour mixed with oil as a cereal offering, 68one golden bowl weighing ten shekels, full of incense, 69one young bull, one ram and one male yearling lamb as a burnt offering, 70one he-goat as a sacrifice for sin, 71and two bulls, five rams, five he-goats and five male yearling lambs as a communion sacrifice. Such was the offering of Ahiezer son of Ammishaddai.

72On the eleventh day an offering was brought by Pagiel son of Ochran, leader of the Asherites. 73His offering consisted of: one silver bowl weighing a hundred and thirty shekels, one silver sprinkling bowl weighing seventy shekels (sanctuary shekels), both of them full of fine flour mixed with oil as a cereal offering, 74one golden bowl weighing ten shekels, full of incense, 75one young bull, one ram and one male yearling lamb as a burnt offering, 76one he-goat as a sacrifice for sin, 77and two bulls, five rams, five he-goats and five male yearling lambs as a communion sacrifice. Such was the offering of Pagiel son of Ochran.

78On the twelfth day an offering was brought by Ahira son of Enan, leader of the Naphtalites. 79His offering consisted of: one silver bowl weighing a hundred and thirty shekels, one silver sprinkling bowl weighing seventy shekels (sanctuary shekels), both of them full of fine flour mixed with oil as a cereal offering, 80one golden bowl weighing ten shekels, full of incense, 81one young bull, one ram and one male yearling lamb as a burnt offering, 82one he-goat as a sacrifice for sin, 83and two bulls, five rams, five he-goats and five male yearling lambs as a communion sacrifice. Such was the offering of Ahira son of Enan.

84Such were the offerings made by the leaders of Israel for the dedication of the altar on the day it was anointed: twelve silver bowls, twelve silver sprinkling bowls, and twelve golden bowls. 85Each silver bowl weighed a hundred and thirty shekels, and each sprinkling bowl seventy, the silver of these objects weighing in all two thousand four hundred sanctuary shekels. 86The twelve golden bowls full of incense each weighed ten shekels (sanctuary shekels), the gold of these bowls weighing in all a hundred and twenty shekels.

87The sum total of animals for the burnt offering: twelve bulls, twelve rams, twelve male yearling lambs, with their cereal offerings. For the sacrifice for sin, twelve he-goats. 88The sum total of animals for the communion sacrifice: twenty-four bulls, sixty rams, sixty he-goats and sixty male yearling lambs.

Such were the offerings for the dedication of the altar, after it had been anointed.

89When Moses went into the Tent of Meeting to speak with him, he heard the voice speaking to him from above the mercy-seat on the ark of the Testimony, from between the two great winged creatures. He then spoke to him.

The lamps for the lamp-stand

8 Yahweh spoke to Moses and said: 2'Speak to Aaron and say, "When you set up the lamps, the seven lamps must throw their light towards the front of the lamp-stand." '

3Aaron did this. He set up the lamps to the front of the lamp-stand, as Yahweh had ordered Moses. 4This lamp-stand was worked in beaten gold, including its stem and its petals, which were also of beaten gold. This lamp-stand had been made according to the pattern Yahweh had shown to Moses.

The Levites are offered to Yahweh

5Yahweh spoke to Moses and said, 6'Separate the Levites from the Israelites and purify them. 7This is how you must purify them: you will sprinkle them with purifying water, and they will shave their bodies all over and wash their clothes. They will then be clean. 8They will then take a young bull, with the accompanying cereal offering of fine flour mixed with oil, and you will take a second young bull for a sacrifice for sin. 9You will then bring the Levites in front of the Tent of Meeting, and assemble the whole community of Israelites. 10Once you have brought the Levites before Yahweh, the Israelites will lay their hands on them. 11Aaron will then offer the Levites, making the gesture of offering before Yahweh on behalf of the Israelites, admitting them to Yahweh's service.

12'The Levites will then lay their hands on the heads of the bulls, one of which you will offer as a sacrifice for sin, and the other as a burnt offering to Yahweh, to perform the rite of expiation for the Levites. 13Having brought the Levites before Aaron and his sons, you will present them to Yahweh with the gesture of offering. 14That is how you will

set the Levites apart from the Israelites, for them to be mine. 15The Levites will then begin their ministry in the Tent of Meeting.

'You will purify them and offer them with the gesture of offering 16because, of the Israelites, they have been dedicated to me in place of all those who first emerge from the womb, instead of the first-born; of all the Israelites, I have taken them for my own. 17For all the first-born of the Israelites, whether human or animal, do indeed belong to me: the day I struck down all the first-born in Egypt, I consecrated them to myself, 18and now, in place of all the first-born of the Israelites, I have taken the Levites. 19Of the Israelites, I give the Levites to Aaron and his sons, as dedicated men, to minister in the Tent of Meeting on behalf of the Israelites and perform the rite of expiation for them, so that no disaster befalls the Israelites when the Israelites come close to the sanctuary.'

20Moses, Aaron and the whole community of Israelites dealt with the Levites exactly as Yahweh had ordered Moses concerning them; this is what the Israelites did with them. 21The Levites purified themselves and washed their clothes, and Aaron presented them with the gesture of offering before Yahweh. He then performed the rite of expiation for them to purify them. 22The Levites were then allowed to perform their ministry in the Tent of Meeting in the presence of Aaron and his sons. As Yahweh had ordered Moses concerning the Levites, so it was done with them.

The duration of their ministry

23Yahweh spoke to Moses and said:

24'This concerns the Levites. From the age of twenty-five onwards, the Levite will exercise his ministry and do duty in the Tent of Meeting. 25After the age of fifty, he is no longer bound to the ministry; he will have no further duties; 26but he will still help his brothers to assure the services in the Tent of Meeting, though he himself will no longer have any ministry. That is how you will act as regards the ministry of the Levites.'

IV: THE PASSOVER AND THE DEPARTURE

Date of the Passover

9 Yahweh spoke to Moses, in the desert of Sinai, in the second year after the exodus from Egypt, in the first month, and said:

2'The Israelites must keep the Passover at its appointed time. 3The fourteenth day of this month, at twilight, is the time appointed for you to keep it. You will keep it with all the laws and customs proper to it.'

4Moses told the Israelites to keep the Passover. 5They kept it, in the desert of Sinai, in the first month, on the fourteenth day of the month, at twilight. The Israelites did everything as Yahweh had ordered Moses.

Individual cases

6It happened that some men had become unclean by touching a dead body; they could not keep the Passover that day. They came the same day to Moses and Aaron, 7and said, 'We have become unclean by touching a dead body. Why should we be excluded from bringing an offering to Yahweh at the proper time with the rest of the Israelites?' 8Moses replied, 'Wait here until I hear what order Yahweh gives about you.'

9Yahweh spoke to Moses and said, 10'Speak to the Israelites and say:

"Any of you or your descendants who becomes unclean by touching a dead body, or is away on a long journey, can still keep a Passover for Yahweh. 11Such persons will keep it in the second month, on the fourteenth day, at twilight. They will eat it with unleavened bread and bitter herbs; 12nothing of it must be left over until morning, nor will they break any of its bones. They will keep it, following the entire Passover ritual. 13But anyone who is clean, or who is not on a journey, but fails to keep the Passover, such a person will be outlawed from his people. For not having brought the offering to Yahweh at its appointed time, the person will bear the consequences of the sin.

14"A resident alien who keeps a Passover for Yahweh, will keep it in accordance with the ritual and customs of the Passover. You will have one law for alien and citizen alike." '

The cloud

15On the day the Dwelling was erected, the cloud covered the Dwelling, the Tent of the Testimony. From nightfall until morning it remained over the Dwelling looking like fire. 16So the cloud covered it all the time, and at night it looked like fire.

17Whenever the cloud rose from the Tent, the Israelites broke camp, and wherever the cloud halted, there the Israelites pitched camp. 18At Yahweh's order, the Israelites set out and, at Yahweh's order, the Israelites pitched camp. They remained in camp for as long as the cloud rested on the Dwelling. 19If the cloud stayed for many days on the Dwelling, the Israelites performed their duty to Yahweh and did not set out. 20But if the cloud happened to stay for only a few days on the Dwelling, just as they had pitched camp at Yahweh's order, at Yahweh's order they set out. 21If the cloud happened to remain only from evening to morning, they set out when it lifted the next morning. Or, if it stayed for a whole day and night, they set out only when it lifted. 22Sometimes it stayed there for two days, a month, or a longer time; however long the cloud rested on the Dwelling, the Israelites remained in camp, and when it lifted they set out. 23At Yahweh's order they pitched camp, and at Yahweh's order they set out. They performed their duty to Yahweh, as Yahweh had ordered through Moses.

The trumpets

10 Yahweh spoke to Moses and said: 2'Make yourself two trumpets; make them of beaten silver, so that you can use them for summoning the community, and for sounding the order to break camp. 3Whenever they are sounded, the whole community must gather round you, at the entrance to the Tent of Meeting. 4But if only one trumpet is sounded, then only the leaders, the heads of Israel's thousands, must gather round you.

5'When the trumpet blast is accompanied by a battle cry,[a] the encampments pitched to the east will set out. 6At the second blast accompanied by a battle cry, the encampments pitched to the south will set out. For breaking camp, the trumpet blast will be accompanied by a battle cry, 7but for assembling the community the trumpets will be sounded without battle cry. 8The Aaronite priests will sound the trumpets; this is a perpetual decree for you and your descendants.

9'When in your country you go to war against an enemy who is oppressing you, you will sound trumpets with a battle cry, and Yahweh your God will remember you, and you will be delivered from your enemies. 10At your festivals, solemnities and new-moon feasts, you will sound the trumpets over your burnt offerings and communion sacrifices, so that they recall you to the remembrance of your God. I am Yahweh your God.'

The order of march

11In the second year, in the second month, on the twentieth day of the month, the cloud rose from where the Dwelling of the Testimony was, 12and the Israelites set out, in marching order, from the desert of Sinai. The cloud came to rest in the desert of Paran.

13These were the men who set out in the vanguard, at Yahweh's order through Moses: 14first went the standard of the camp of the Judahites and their units, with Nahshon son of Amminadab commanding that contingent; 15Nethanel son of Zuar commanding the tribal contingent of the Issacharites; 16and Eliab son of Helon commanding the tribal contingent of the Zebulunites.

17The Dwelling was then dismantled and the Gershonites and Merarites set out, carrying the Dwelling.

18Then came the standard of the camp of the Reubenites and their units, with Elizur son of Shedeur commanding that contingent; 19Shelumiel son of Zurishaddai commanding the tribal contingent of the Simeonites; 20and Eliasaph son of Reuel commanding the tribal contingent of the Gadites.

21Then came the Kohathites carrying the sanctuary (the Dwelling was erected before they arrived).

22Then came the standard of the camp of the Ephraimites and their units, with Elishama son of Ammihud commanding that contingent; 23Gamaliel son of Pedahzur commanding the tribal contingent of the Manassehites; 24and Abidan son of Gideoni

10a Battle cry or cry of acclamation used also on royal occasions and in worship.

commanding the tribal contingent of the Benjaminites.

25 Last of all, the rearguard of all the camps, came the standard of the camp of the Danites and their units, with Ahiezer son of Ammishaddai commanding that contingent; 26 Pagiel son of Ochran commanding the tribal contingent of the Asherites; 27 and Ahira son of Enan commanding the tribal contingent of the Naphtalites.

28 Such was the order of march for the Israelites, unit by unit. So they set out.

Moses' proposal to Hobab

29 Moses said to Hobab son of Reuel the Midianite, his father-in-law, 'We are setting out for the country of which Yahweh has said: I shall give it to you. Come with us, and we will treat you well, for Yahweh has promised good things for Israel.' 30 'I will not come with you,' he replied, 'but shall go to my own country and kin.' 31 'Do not leave us,' Moses said, 'for you know where we can camp in the desert, and so you will be our eyes. 32 If you come with us, we shall share with you whatever blessings Yahweh gives us.'

The departure

33 They set out from Yahweh's mountain and travelled for three days, while the ark of the covenant of Yahweh preceded them on the three-day journey, searching out a place for them to halt.

34 In the daytime, Yahweh's cloud was over them, once they had broken camp. 35 Whenever the ark set out, Moses would say:

Rise, Yahweh,
may your enemies be scattered
and those who hate you
flee at your approach!

36 And when it halted, he would say:

Come back, Yahweh,
to the countless thousands of Israel!

V: THE HALTS IN THE DESERT

Taberah

11 Now the people began to complain, which was offensive to Yahweh's ears. When Yahweh heard, his anger was aroused and the fire of Yahweh broke out among them; it devoured one end of the camp. 2 The people appealed to Moses who interceded with Yahweh and the fire died down. 3 So the place was called Taberah, because the fire of Yahweh had broken out among them.

Kibroth-ha-Taavah
The people complain[a]

4 The rabble who had joined the people were feeling the pangs of hunger, and the Israelites began to weep again. 'Who will give us meat to eat?' they said. 5 'Think of the fish we used to eat free in Egypt, the cucumbers, melons, leeks, onions and garlic! 6 But now we are withering away; there is nothing wherever we look except this manna!'

7 The manna was like coriander seed and had the appearance of bdellium. 8 The people went round gathering it, and ground it in a mill or crushed it with a pestle; it was then cooked in a pot and made into pancakes. It tasted like cake made with oil. 9 When the dew fell on the camp at night-time, the manna fell with it.

The prayer of Moses

10 Moses heard the people weeping, each family at the door of its tent. Yahweh's anger was greatly aroused; Moses too found it disgraceful, 11 and he said to Yahweh:

'Why do you treat your servant so badly? In what respect have I failed to win your favour, for you to lay the burden of all these people on me? 12 Was it I who conceived all these people, was I their father, for you to say to me, "Carry them in your arms, like a foster-father carrying an unweaned child, to the country which I swore to give their fathers"? 13 Where am I to find meat to give all these people, pestering me with their tears and saying, "Give us meat to eat"? 14 I cannot

11a || Ex 16.

carry all these people on my own; the weight
is too much for me. 15If this is how you mean
to treat me, please kill me outright! If only I
could win your favour and be spared the sight
of my misery!'

Yahweh replies

16Yahweh said to Moses, 'Collect me seventy
of the elders of Israel, men you know to be
the people's elders and scribes. Bring them
to the Tent of Meeting, and let them stand
beside you there. 17I shall come down and
talk to you there and shall take some of the
spirit which is on you and put it on them.
Then they will bear the burden of the people
with you, and you will no longer have to bear
it on your own.

18'And say to the people, "Purify yourselves for tomorrow and you will have meat
to eat, since you have wept in Yahweh's
hearing, saying: Who will give us meat to
eat? How happy we were in Egypt! Very well,
Yahweh will give you meat to eat. 19You will
eat it not for one day, or two, or five, or ten
or twenty, 20but for a whole month, until it
comes out of your nostrils and sickens you,
since you have rejected Yahweh who is among
you, and have wept before him saying: Why
did we ever leave Egypt?" '

21Moses said, 'The people round me
number six hundred thousand foot soldiers,
and you say, "I shall give them meat to eat
for a whole month"! 22If all the flocks and
herds were slaughtered, would that be
enough for them? If all the fish in the seas
were collected, would that be enough for
them?' 23Yahweh said to Moses, 'Is the arm
of Yahweh so short? You shall see whether
the promise I have made to you comes true
or not.'

The spirit given to the elders

24Moses went out and told the people what
Yahweh had said. Then he collected seventy
of the people's elders and stationed them
round the Tent. 25Yahweh descended in the
cloud. He spoke to him and took some of the
spirit that was on him and put it on
the seventy elders. When the spirit came on
them they prophesied—but only once.

26Two men had stayed back in the camp;
one was called Eldad and the other Medad.
The spirit came down on them; though they
had not gone to the Tent, their names were
enrolled among the rest. These began to
prophesy in the camp. 27A young man ran to
tell Moses this. 'Look,' he said, 'Eldad and
Medad are prophesying in the camp.'
28Joshua son of Nun, who had served Moses
since he was a boy, spoke up and said, 'My
lord Moses, stop them!' 29Moses replied,
'Are you jealous on my account? If only all
Yahweh's people were prophets, and
Yahweh had given them his spirit!' 30Moses
then went back to the camp with the elders
of Israel.

The quails

31A wind, sent by Yahweh, started blowing
from the sea bringing quails which it
deposited on the camp. They lay for a
distance of a day's march either side of the
camp, two cubits thick on the ground. 32The
people were up all that day and night and
all the next day collecting quails: the least
gathered by anyone was ten *homer*; then they
spread them out round the camp. 33The
meat was still between their teeth, not even
chewed, when Yahweh's anger was aroused
by the people. Yahweh struck them with a
very great plague.

34The name given to this place was
Kibroth-ha-Taavah, because it was there that
they buried the people who had indulged
their greed.

35From Kibroth-ha-Taavah the people set
out for Hazeroth, and at Hazeroth they
pitched camp.

Miriam and Aaron criticise Moses

12 Miriam, and Aaron too, criticised
Moses over the Cushite woman he had
married. He had indeed married a Cushite
woman. 2They said, 'Is Moses the only one
through whom Yahweh has spoken? Has he
not spoken through us too?' Yahweh heard
this. 3Now Moses was extremely humble, the
humblest man on earth.

God's answer

4Suddenly Yahweh said to Moses, Aaron and
Miriam, 'Come out, all three of you, to the
Tent of Meeting.' They went, all three of
them, 5and Yahweh descended in a pillar of
cloud and stood at the entrance of the Tent.
He called Aaron and Miriam and they both
came forward. 6Yahweh said:

Listen to my words!
if there is a prophet among you,
I reveal myself to him in a vision,
I speak to him in a dream.
7Not so with my servant Moses;
to him my whole household
is entrusted;
8to him I speak face to face,
plainly and not in riddles,
and he sees Yahweh's form.
How, then, could you dare
to criticise my servant Moses?

9Yahweh's anger was aroused by them. He went away, 10and as soon as the cloud left the Tent, there was Miriam covered with a virulent skin-disease, white as snow! Aaron turned to look at her and saw that she had contracted a virulent skin-disease.

The prayer of Aaron and Moses

11Aaron said to Moses:

'Oh, my Lord, please do not punish us for the sin we have been foolish enough to commit. 12Do not let her be like some monster with its flesh half eaten away when it leaves its mother's womb!'

13Moses pleaded with Yahweh. 'O God,' he said, 'I beg you, please heal her!'

14Yahweh then said to Moses, 'If her father had done no more than spit in her face, would she not be unclean for seven days? Have her shut out of the camp for seven days, and then have her brought in again.'

15Miriam was shut out of the camp for seven days. The people did not set out until she returned. 16Then the people moved on from Hazeroth and pitched camp in the desert of Paran.

The reconnaissance in Canaan[a]

13 1Yahweh spoke to Moses and said, 2'Send out men, one from each tribe, to reconnoitre the land of Canaan which I am giving the Israelites. Each of them is to be a leading man of the tribe.'

3At Yahweh's order, Moses sent them from the desert of Paran. All of them were leading men of Israel. 4These were their names:

For the tribe of Reuben, Shammua son of Zaccur;

5for the tribe of Simeon, Shaphat son of Hori;

6for the tribe of Judah, Caleb son of Jephunneh;

7for the tribe of of Issachar, Igal son of Joseph;

8for the tribe of Ephraim, Hoshea son of Nun;

9for the tribe of Benjamin, Palti son of Raphu;

10for the tribe of Zebulun, Gaddiel son of Sodi;

11for the tribe of Joseph, for the tribe of Manasseh, Gaddi son of Susi;

12for the tribe of Dan, Ammiel son of Gemalli;

13for the tribe of Asher, Sethur son of Michael;

14for the tribe of Naphtali, Nahbi son of Vophsi;

15for the tribe of Gad, Geuel son of Machi.

16Such were the names of the men whom Moses sent to reconnoitre the country. Moses then gave Hoshea son of Nun the name Joshua.

17Moses sent them to reconnoitre the land of Canaan, 'Go up into the Negeb,' he said, 'then go up into the highlands. 18See what sort of country it is, and what sort of people the inhabitants are, whether they are strong or weak, few or many, 19what sort of land they live on, whether it is good or poor; what sort of towns they live in, whether they are open or fortified; 20what sort of land it is, fertile or barren, wooded or open. Be bold, and bring back some of the country's produce.'

It was the season for early grapes. 21They went up and reconnoitred the country from the desert of Zin to Rehob, the Pass of Hamath. 22They went up by way of the Negeb as far as Hebron, where Ahiman, Sheshai and Talmai, the Anakim, lived. (Hebron was founded seven years before Tanis in Egypt.) 23Reaching the Vale of Eshcol, there they lopped off a vine branch with a cluster of grapes, which two of them carried away on a pole, as well as pomegranates and figs. 24This place was called the Vale of Eshcol after the cluster which the Israelites cut there.

The expedition's report

25After forty days they returned from reconnoitring the country. 26Making their way to Moses, Aaron and the whole community of

13a || Dt 1:20–29.

Israel, in the desert of Paran, at Kadesh, they
made their report to them and the whole
community, and displayed the country's
produce.
27This was the report they gave: 'We made
our way into the country where you sent us.
It does indeed flow with milk and honey;
here is what it produces. 28At the same time,
its inhabitants are a powerful people; the
towns are fortified and very big; yes, and we
saw the Anakim there. 29The Amalekites
occupy the Negeb area, the Hittites, Jebu-
sites and Amorites the highlands, and the
Canaanites the sea coast and the banks of the
Jordan.'
30Caleb called the people round Moses to
silence and then said, 'We must march in
immediately and take it; we are certainly able
to conquer it.' 31But the men who had been
with him said, 'We cannot attack these
people; they are stronger than we are.' 32And
they began disparaging to the Israelites the
country they had reconnoitred, saying, 'The
country we have been to reconnoitre is a
country that devours its inhabitants. All the
people we saw there were of enormous size.
33We saw giants there too (the Anakim,
descended from the Giants). We felt like
grasshoppers, and so we seemed to them.'

The rebellion of Israel[a]

14 The whole community then cried out
in dismay, and the people wept all that
night. 2All the Israelites muttered at Moses
and Aaron, and the whole community said
to them, 'Would to God we had died in
Egypt, or even that we had died in this desert!
3Why has Yahweh brought us to this country,
for us to perish by the sword and our wives
and children to be seized as booty? Should
we not do better to go back to Egypt?' 4And
they said to one another, 'Let us appoint a
leader and go back to Egypt.'
5At this, Moses and Aaron threw them-
selves on their faces in front of the whole
assembled community of Israelites, 6while
Joshua son of Nun and Caleb son of
Jephunneh, two of the men who had
reconnoitred the country, tore their clothes
7and addressed the whole community of
Israelites as follows, 'The country we went
to reconnoitre is a good country, an excellent
country. 8If Yahweh is pleased with us, he
will lead us into this country and give it to
us. It is a country flowing with milk and
honey. 9But do not rebel against Yahweh or
be afraid of the people of the country, for we
shall gobble them up. Their protecting shade
has deserted them, while we have Yahweh
on our side. Do not be afraid of them.'

Yahweh's anger. Moses intercedes[b]

10The whole community was talking of
stoning them, when the glory of Yahweh
appeared to all the Israelites, inside the Tent
of Meeting, 11and Yahweh said to Moses:
'How much longer will these people treat
me with contempt? How much longer will
they refuse to trust me, in spite of all the
signs I have displayed among them? 12I shall
strike them with pestilence and disown them.
And of you I shall make a new nation, greater
and mightier than they are.'
13Moses said to Yahweh:
'Suppose the Egyptians hear about this—
for by your power you brought these people
out of their country—14and tell the people
living in this country. They have heard that
you, Yahweh, are with this people, and that
you, Yahweh, show yourself to them face to
face; that your cloud stands over them and
that you go before them in a pillar of cloud
by day and a pillar of fire by night. 15If you
kill this people now as though it were one
man, then the nations who have heard about
you will say, 16"Yahweh was not able to bring
this people into the country which he had
sworn to give them, and so he has slaughtered
them in the desert." 17No, my Lord! Now is
the time to assert your power as you promised
when you said, earlier, 18"Yahweh, slow to
anger and rich in faithful love, forgiving
faults and transgression, and yet letting
nothing go unchecked, punishing the
parents' guilt in the children to the third and
fourth generation." 19In your most faithful
love, please forgive this people's guilt, as you
have done from Egypt until now.'

Pardon and punishment[c]

20Yahweh said, 'I forgive them as you ask.
21But—as I live, and as the glory of Yahweh

14a ‖ Dt 1:26–32.
14b ‖ Ex 32:7–14; 34:6–7.
14c ‖ Dt 1:34–40.

fills the whole world—22of all these people who have seen my glory and the signs that I worked in Egypt and in the desert, who have put me to the test ten times already and not obeyed my voice, 23not one shall see the country which I promised to give their ancestors. Not one of those who have treated me contemptuously will see it. 24However, since my servant Caleb is of another spirit and since he has obeyed me completely, I shall bring him into the country where he has been, and his descendants will own it 25(the Amalekites and Canaanites occupy the plain). Tomorrow you will turn about and go back into the desert, in the direction of the Sea of Suph.'

26Yahweh then spoke to Moses and Aaron and said:

27'How much longer am I to endure this perverse community muttering against me? I have heard what the Israelites mutter against me. 28Say to them, "As I live, Yahweh declares, I shall do to you what I have heard you saying. 29In this desert your dead bodies will fall, all you who were counted in the census, from the age of twenty years and over who have muttered against me. 30I swear none of you will enter the country where I swore most solemnly to settle you, except Caleb son of Jephunneh, and Joshua son of Nun. 31Your children, who you said would be seized as booty, will be the ones whom I shall bring in so that they get to know the country you disdained, 32but, as for you, your dead bodies will fall in this desert 33and your children will be nomads in the desert for forty years, bearing the consequences of your faithlessness, until the last one of you lies dead in the desert. 34For forty days you reconnoitred the country. Each day will count as a year: for forty years you will bear the consequences of your guilt and learn what it means to reject me." 35I, Yahweh, have spoken: this is how I swear to treat this entire perverse community united against me. In this desert, to the last man, they shall die.'

36The men whom Moses had sent to reconnoitre the country and who on their return had incited the whole community of Israel to mutter about him by disparaging it, 37these men who had disparaged the country were all struck dead before Yahweh. 38Of the men who had gone to reconnoitre the country, only Joshua son of Nun and Caleb son of Jephunneh were left alive.

An abortive attempt by the Israelites

39When Moses told all the Israelites what had been said, the people set up a great outcry. 40Early next morning they set out for the heights of the hill country saying, 'Look, we will set out for the place about which Yahweh said that we have sinned.' 41To which, Moses said, 'Why disobey Yahweh's order? No success will come of doing so. 42Do not go, for Yahweh is not among you, and you will be defeated by your enemies. 43For the Amalekites and the Canaanites are ahead of you, and you will be put to the sword, since you have turned away from Yahweh, and Yahweh is not with you.' 44All the same, they presumptuously set off for the heights of the hill country. Neither the ark of the covenant of Yahweh nor Moses left the camp. 45The Amalekites and Canaanites living in those highlands then came down, defeated them and harried them all the way to Hormah.

VI: LAWS GOVERNING SACRIFICES. POWERS OF PRIESTS AND LEVITES

Cereal offerings to accompany sacrifices

15 Yahweh spoke to Moses and said, 2'Speak to the Israelites and say:

"When you have arrived in the country where you are to live and which I am giving to you, 3and you burn food as an offering to Yahweh either as a burnt offering or as a sacrifice, whether in payment of a vow, or as a voluntary gift, or on the occasion of one of your solemn feasts, from your herds and flocks as a smell pleasing to Yahweh: 4the offerer will, as his personal gift to Yahweh, bring a cereal offering of one-tenth of an *ephah* of fine flour mixed with one-quarter of a *hin* of oil. 5You will also make a libation of wine, one-quarter of a *hin* to each lamb, in addition to the burnt offering or sacrifice.

[6]For a ram, you will make a cereal offering
of two-tenths of an *ephah* of fine flour mixed
with one-third of a *hin* of oil, [7]and a libation
of one-third of a *hin* of wine as a smell pleasing
to Yahweh. [8]If you offer a bull as a burnt
offering or sacrifice, in payment of a vow or
as a communion sacrifice for Yahweh, [9]in
addition to the animal you will offer a cereal
offering of three-tenths of an *ephah* of fine
flour mixed with half a *hin* of oil, [10]and you
will offer a libation of half a *hin* of wine, as
food burnt as a smell pleasing to Yahweh.
[11]This will be done for every bull, every ram,
every lamb or kid. [12]Whatever the number
of victims you intend to offer, you will do the
same for each of them, however many there
are.

[13]"Every citizen of the country will act in
this way whenever he offers food burnt as a
smell pleasing to Yahweh; [14]and if an alien
residing with you or with your descendants
intends to offer food burnt as a smell pleasing
to Yahweh, he will do as you do. [15]There
will be one law for you, members of the
community, and the resident alien alike, a
law binding your descendants for ever: before
Yahweh you and the resident alien are no
different.' [16]One law, one statute, will apply
for you and the resident alien." '

The first-fruits of bread

[17]Yahweh spoke to Moses and said, [18]'Speak
to the Israelites and say:

"When you have entered the country to
which I am bringing you, [19]you will set a
portion aside for Yahweh when you eat that
country's bread. [20]You will set one cake aside
as the first-fruits of your dough; you will set
this offering aside like the one set aside from
your threshing. [21]For all future generations
you will set a portion of your dough aside for
Yahweh.

Expiation for faults of inadvertence

[22]"If through inadvertence you fail in any of
these orders which Yahweh has given to
Moses [23](whatever orders Yahweh has given
you or your descendants through Moses,
from the day when Yahweh gave his orders),
[24]this is what must be done:

"If it is an inadvertence on the part of the
community, the community as a whole will
offer a young bull as a burnt offering, as a
smell pleasing to Yahweh, with the
prescribed accompanying cereal offering and
libation, and a he-goat as a sacrifice for sin.
[25]The priest will perform the rite of expiation
for the entire community of Israelites, and
they will be forgiven, since it was an inadver-
tence. Once they have brought their offering
as food burnt for Yahweh, and have
presented their sacrifice for sin before
Yahweh to make amends for their inadver-
tence, [26]the whole community of Israelites
will be forgiven, as also the alien residing
with them, since the entire people acted by
inadvertence.

[27]"If it is an individual who has sinned by
inadvertence, he will offer a yearling kid as a
sacrifice for sin. [28]The priest will perform the
rite of expiation before Yahweh for the person
who has gone astray owing to this sin of
inadvertence and, expiation having been
made for him, he will be forgiven; [29]whether
he is an Israelite citizen or a resident alien,
you will have one law for anyone who sins by
inadvertence.

[30]"But the individual who acts deliber-
ately, be he citizen or alien, commits an
outrage against Yahweh, and such a man will
be outlawed from his people. [31]Since he has
treated Yahweh's word with contempt and
has disobeyed his order, such a man will
be outlawed absolutely and will bear the
consequences of his guilt." '

Sabbath-breaking

[32]While the Israelites were in the desert,
a man was caught gathering wood on the
Sabbath day. [33]Those who caught him gath-
ering wood brought him before Moses, Aaron
and the whole community. [34]He was kept
in custody, because the penalty he should
undergo had not yet been fixed. [35]Yahweh
said to Moses, 'This man must be put to
death. The whole community will stone him
outside the camp.' [36]The whole community
took him outside the camp and stoned him
till he was dead, as Yahweh had ordered
Moses.

Tassels on clothes

[37]Yahweh spoke to Moses and said, [38]'Speak
to the Israelites and tell them, for all gener-
ations to come, to put tassels on the hems of
their clothes and work a violet thread into
the tassel at the hem. [39]You will thus have a
tassel, and the sight of it will remind you of

all Yahweh's orders and how you are to put
them into practice, and not follow the dictates
of your own heart and eyes, which have led
you to be unfaithful.
[40]'This will remind you of all my orders;
put them into practice, and you will be
consecrated to your God. [41]I, Yahweh your
God, have brought you out of Egypt, to be
your God, I, Yahweh your God.'

The rebellion of Korah, Dathan and Abiram

16 Now Korah son of Izhar, son of Kohath
the Levite, and the Reubenites Dathan
and Abiram sons of Eliab, and On son of
Peleth were proud [2]and rebelled against
Moses with two hundred and fifty Israelites
who were leaders of the community, promi-
nent at the solemn feasts, men of repute.
[3]These banded together against Moses and
Aaron and said to them, 'You take too much
on yourselves! The whole community, all its
members, are consecrated, and Yahweh lives
among them. Why set yourselves higher than
Yahweh's community?'
[4]On hearing this, Moses threw himself on
his face. [5]Then he said to Korah and all in
his party, 'Tomorrow morning Yahweh will
reveal who is his, who the consecrated man
whom he will allow to approach him. The
one he allows to approach is the one whom
he has chosen. [6]This is what you must do:
take the censers of Korah and all in his party,
[7]put fire in them and put incense in them
before Yahweh tomorrow, and the one whom
Yahweh chooses will be the consecrated man.
Levites, you take too much on yourselves!'
[8]Moses then said to Korah, 'Now listen,
you Levites! [9]Is it not enough for you that
the God of Israel has singled you out of the
community of Israel, and called you to be
near him, to serve in Yahweh's Dwelling and
to represent the community by officiating on
its behalf? [10]He has called you to be near him,
you and all your brother Levites with you,
and now you want to be priests as well! [11]For
which reason, you and all in your party have
banded together against Yahweh himself: for
what is Aaron, that you should mutter against
him?'
[12]Moses then summoned Dathan and
Abiram sons of Eliab. They replied, 'We will
not come. [13]Is it not enough for you to have
brought us away from a country flowing with
milk and honey to kill us in the desert,
without your making yourself our absolute
ruler? [14]What is more, you have not brought
us to a country flowing with milk and honey
and you have not given us fields and vineyards
for our heritage. Do you think you can hood-
wink these people? We will not come.'
[15]Moses flew into a rage and said to Yahweh,
'Disregard their cereal offering! I have not
taken so much as a donkey from them, nor
have I wronged any of them.'

The punishment

[16]Moses said to Korah, 'You and all your
party, come before Yahweh tomorrow, you
and they, and Aaron too. [17]Each will take his
censer, put incense in it, and bring his censer
before Yahweh—two hundred and fifty
censers. You and Aaron too will each bring
his censer.' [18]Each of them took his censer,
put fire in it and placed incense on it, and
stood at the entrance to the Tent of Meeting
with Moses and Aaron. [19]Then, Korah
having assembled the whole community to
confront them at the entrance to the Tent of
Meeting, the glory of Yahweh appeared to
the whole community.
[20]Yahweh then spoke to Moses and Aaron.
He said, [21]'Get away from this community. I
am going to destroy them here and now.'
[22]They threw themselves on their faces and
cried out, 'O God, God of the spirits that give
life to every living thing, will you be angry
with the whole community because one man
has sinned?' [23]Yahweh then said to Moses,
[24]'Speak to the community and say, "Stand
well clear of Korah's tent." '
[25]Moses stood up and went to Dathan and
Abiram; the elders of Israel followed him.
[26]He spoke to the community and said, 'Stand
away, I tell you, from the tents of these
sinners, and touch nothing that belongs to
them, for fear that with all their sins you too
will be swept away.' [27]So they moved away
from Korah's tent.
Dathan and Abiram had come out and
were standing at their tent doors, with their
wives, their sons and their little ones. [28]Moses
said, 'This is how you will know that Yahweh
himself has sent me to perform all these tasks
and that I am not doing them of my own
accord. [29]If these people die a natural death
such as people commonly die, then Yahweh
has not sent me. [30]But if Yahweh does some-
thing utterly new, if the earth should open
its mouth and swallow them and all their

belongings, so that they go down alive to Sheol, then you will know that they held Yahweh in contempt.'

31 The moment he finished saying all this, the ground split apart under their feet, 32 the earth opened its mouth and swallowed them, their families, all Korah's people and all their property.

33 They went down alive to Sheol with all their belongings. The earth closed over them and they disappeared in the middle of the community. 34 At their cries, all the Israelites round them took to their heels, saying, 'We do not want the earth to swallow us too!'

35 Fire then shot out from Yahweh and consumed the two hundred and fifty men offering incense.

The censers

17 Yahweh then spoke to Moses and said, 2 'Tell Eleazar son of Aaron the priest to pick the censers out of the smouldering remains and scatter the fire from them away from here, 3 for these sinful censers have become sanctified at the price of human lives. Since they were brought before Yahweh and thus became consecrated, they must be hammered into sheets to cover the altar. They will be an object-lesson to the Israelites.'

4 The priest Eleazar took the bronze censers which had been carried by the men destroyed by the fire. They were hammered into sheets to cover the altar. 5 They are a reminder to the Israelites that no unauthorised person, no one not of Aaron's line, may approach and offer incense before Yahweh, on pain of suffering the fate of Korah and his party, as Yahweh had said through Moses.

Aaron intercedes

6 On the following day, the whole community of Israelites were muttering against Moses and Aaron and saying, 'You are responsible for killing Yahweh's people!' 7 Now, as the community was banding together against Moses and Aaron, they turned towards the Tent of Meeting, and there was the cloud covering it, and the glory of Yahweh appeared. 8 Moses and Aaron then went to the front of the Tent of Meeting.

9 Yahweh spoke to Moses and said, 10 'Get away from this community. I am going to destroy them here and now.' They threw themselves on their faces. 11 Moses then said to Aaron, 'Take a censer, put fire in it from the altar, place incense on it and hurry to the community to perform the rite of expiation for them: for retribution has come from Yahweh, plague has broken out.' 12 Aaron took it as Moses said and ran into the middle of the community, but plague had already broken out among the people. He put in the incense and performed the rite of expiation for the people. 13 Then he stood between the living and the dead, and the plague stopped. 14 There were fourteen thousand seven hundred victims of the plague, apart from those who died because of Korah. 15 Aaron then went back to Moses at the entrance to the Tent of Meeting; the plague had been halted.

Aaron's branch

16 Yahweh spoke to Moses and said, 17 'Tell the Israelites to give you a branch for each of their families, one for each leader of each family: twelve branches. Write the name of each on his branch; 18 and on the branch of Levi write Aaron's name, since the head of the Levite families must have a branch too. 19 You will then put them inside the Tent of Meeting in front of the Testimony, where I make myself known to you. 20 The man whose branch sprouts will be the one I have chosen; this is how I shall put an end to the mutterings of the Israelites about you.'

21 Moses spoke to the Israelites, and all their leaders gave him one branch each, twelve branches in all for their families; Aaron's branch was among them. 22 Moses placed them before Yahweh in the Tent of the Testimony. 23 On the following day Moses went to the Tent of the Testimony and there, already sprouting, was Aaron's branch, representing the House of Levi; buds had formed, flowers had bloomed and almonds had already ripened. 24 Moses then brought out all the branches from before Yahweh to all the Israelites; they examined them and each one took back his own branch.

25 Yahweh then said to Moses, 'Put Aaron's branch back in front of the Testimony, where it will have its ritual place as a warning to the rebellious; thus you will rid me of their muttering for good, without their incurring death.' 26 Moses did as Yahweh had ordered. That is what he did.

Expiation: the function of the priesthood

27The Israelites then said to Moses, 'We are
lost! We are dead men! We are all dead
men! 28Anyone who approaches Yahweh's
Dwelling with an offering will die. Are we to
be doomed to the last man?'

18 Yahweh then said to Aaron:
'You, your sons and your ancestor's
line with you will be answerable for offences
against the sanctuary. You and your sons
with you will be answerable for the offences
of your priesthood. 2You will admit your
brothers of the branch of Levi, your ances-
tor's tribe, to join you and serve you, yourself
and your sons, before the Tent of the Testi-
mony. 3They must be at your service and the
service of the whole Tent. Provided they do
not come near the sacred vessels or the altar,
they will be in no more danger of death than
you. 4They must join you, they must take
charge of the Tent of Meeting for the entire
ministry of the Tent, and no unauthorised
person will come near you. 5You will take
charge of the sanctuary and charge of the
altar, and retribution will never again befall
the Israelites. 6Of the Israelites, I myself have
chosen your brothers the Levites as a gift to
you. As men dedicated, they will belong to
Yahweh, to serve at the Tent of Meeting.
7You and your sons will undertake the
priestly duties in all that concerns the altar
and all that lies behind the curtain. You will
perform the liturgy, the duties of which I
entrust to your priesthood. But an unauth-
orised person approaching will incur death.'

The priests' portion

8Yahweh said to Aaron:
'I myself have put you in charge of every-
thing set aside for me. Everything conse-
crated by the Israelites I give to you and your
sons as your portion by perpetual decree. 9Of
the things especially holy, of the food offered,
this is what will revert to you: every offering
that the Israelites give back to me, whether
it be a cereal offering, a sacrifice for sin or a
sacrifice of reparation, is a thing especially
holy and will revert to you and your sons.
10You will eat the things especially holy.
Every male may eat them. You will regard
them as sacred.
11'To you will revert also whatever is set
aside from the offerings of the Israelites,
whatever is held out with the gesture of
offering; this I give to you and your sons and
daughters, by perpetual decree. All members
of your household may eat it unless they are
unclean. 12All the best of the oil, all the best
of the new wine and wheat, these first-fruits
offered by them to Yahweh I give to you.
13All the first produce of the country brought
by them to Yahweh will revert to you. All
members of your household may eat it unless
they are unclean. 14Everything in Israel put
under the curse of destruction will revert
to you. 15Every first-born of all creatures
brought to Yahweh, human or animal, will
revert to you, but you will have to redeem
the first-born of man; you will also redeem
the first-born of an unclean animal. 16You
will redeem it in the month in which it
is born, valuing it at five shekels, at the
sanctuary shekel, which is twenty *gerah*.
17But you will not redeem the first-born of
cow, sheep and goat. They are holy: you will
sprinkle their blood on the altar and burn the
fat as food burnt to be a smell pleasing to
Yahweh; 18the meat will revert to you, as will
the forequarter that has been presented with
the gesture of offering, and the right thigh.
19Everything the Israelites set aside for
Yahweh from the holy things, I give to you
and your sons and daughters, by perpetual
decree. This is a covenant of salt for ever
before Yahweh, for you and your descend-
ants too.'

The Levites' portion

20Yahweh said to Aaron:
'You will have no heritage in their country,
you will not have a portion like them; I shall
be your portion and your heritage among the
Israelites.
21'Look, as heritage I give the Levites all
the tithes collected in Israel, in return for
their services, for the ministry they render in
the Tent of Meeting. 22The Israelites will no
longer approach the Tent of Meeting, on
pain of committing a deadly sin. 23Levi will
discharge the duties of the Tent of Meeting,
and the Levites will bear the consequences
of their own guilt. This is a perpetual decree
binding all your descendants: the Levites will
have no heritage among the Israelites, 24for
the tithe which the Israelites set aside for
Yahweh is the heritage I have given the
Levites. This is why I have told them that
they will have no heritage among the
Israelites.'

Tithes

25 Yahweh spoke to Moses and said, 26 'Speak
to the Levites and say:
"When from the Israelites you receive the
tithe which I have given you from them as
your heritage, you will set a portion of this
aside for Yahweh: a tithe of the tithe. 27 It will
take the place of the portion set aside that
is due from you, like the wheat from the
threshing-floor and new wine from the press.
28 Thus you too will set a portion aside for
Yahweh out of all the tithes you receive from
the Israelites. You will give what you have
set aside for Yahweh to the priest Aaron.
29 Out of all the gifts you receive, you will set
a portion aside for Yahweh. Out of all these
things, you will set aside the best, the sacred
portion."
30 'You will say to them, "After you have
set the best aside, the remainder will take the
place, in the Levites' case, of the produce of
the threshing-floor and wine-press. 31 You
may consume this anywhere, you and the
members of your households; this is your
recompense for serving in the Tent of
Meeting, 32 and you will not incur sin by doing
so, once you have set aside the best; you will
not be profaning the things consecrated by
the Israelites and will not incur death." '

The ashes of the red heifer

19 Yahweh spoke to Moses and Aaron and
said:
2 'This is a decree of the Law which Yahweh
has prescribed. Tell the Israelites, they are
to bring you a red heifer without fault or
blemish that has never borne the yoke. 3 You
will give it to the priest Eleazar. It will then
be taken outside the camp and slaughtered
in his presence. 4 The priest Eleazar will then
take some of the victim's blood on his finger,
and sprinkle this blood seven times towards
the entrance to the Tent of Meeting. 5 The
heifer will then be burnt while he looks on;
its hide, flesh, blood and offal will be burnt.
6 The priest will then take some cedar wood,
hyssop and scarlet material and throw them
on the fire where the heifer is burning. 7 He
will then wash his clothes and bathe himself;
after which he will go back to the camp,
though he will remain unclean until evening.
8 The man who has burnt the heifer will wash
his clothes and bathe himself and will remain
unclean until evening. 9 The man who gathers
up the ashes of the heifer must be ritually
clean; he will deposit them outside the camp,
in a clean place. They will be kept for the
ritual use of the Israelite community for
making water for purification; it is a sacrifice
for sin. 10 The man who has gathered up the
ashes of the heifer will wash his clothes
and remain unclean until evening. For the
Israelites as for the resident alien, this will be
a perpetual decree.

Cases of uncleanness

11 'Anyone who touches the corpse of anyone
whatever will be unclean for seven days.
12 Such a person must be purified with these
waters on the third and seventh day and will
then be clean; otherwise he will not be clean.
13 Anyone who touches the corpse of anyone
who has died and is not purified, defiles
Yahweh's Dwelling; such a person will be
outlawed from Israel, since the water for
purification has not been sprinkled over him;
he is unclean, and his uncleanness remains
in him.
14 "This is the law when someone dies in a
tent. Anyone who goes into the tent, or
anyone who is already in it, will be unclean
for seven days, 15 and every open vessel with
no cover tied over it will also be unclean.
16 'Anyone in the open country who touches
a murder victim, a corpse, human bones or
a grave will be unclean for seven days.

The ritual of water for purification

17 'For someone thus unclean, some of the
ashes of the victim burnt as a sacrifice for sin
will be taken and spring water must be poured
over them, in a vessel. 18 Someone who is
ritually clean will then take some hyssop and
dip it in the water. This person will then
sprinkle the tent, all the vessels and people
who were there, and similarly anyone who
has touched human bones, a murder victim,
a corpse or a grave. 19 On the third and the
seventh day the clean one will sprinkle the
unclean, who on the seventh day will be
clean. The latter will then wash his clothes
and bathe in water, and in the evening he will
be clean. 20 Anyone who fails to be purified in
this way will be outlawed from the
community, and would defile Yahweh's sanc-
tuary. Such a person is unclean, not having
been sprinkled with the water for puri-
fication.

[21]‘This will be a perpetual decree for them.
The person who sprinkles the water for puri-
fication will wash his clothes, and anyone
who touches the water for purification will
be unclean until evening. [22]Anything that an
unclean person touches will be unclean, and
anyone who touches it will be unclean until
evening.’

VII: FROM KADESH TO MOAB

The Waters of Meribah[a]

20 The Israelites, the whole community,
arrived in the first month at the desert
of Zin. The people settled at Kadesh. There
Miriam died and was buried.
[2]There was no water for the community,
so they banded together against Moses and
Aaron. [3]The people laid the blame on Moses.
‘We would rather have died’, they said, ‘as
our brothers died before Yahweh! [4]Why have
you brought Yahweh’s community into this
desert, for us and our livestock to die here?
[5]Why did you lead us out of Egypt, only to
bring us to this wretched place? It is a place
unfit for sowing, it has no figs, no vines, no
pomegranates, and there is not even water to
drink!’
[6]Leaving the assembly, Moses and Aaron
went to the entrance of the Tent of Meeting.
They threw themselves on their faces, and the
glory of Yahweh appeared to them. [7]Yahweh
then spoke to Moses and said, [8]‘Take the
branch and call the community together, you
and your brother Aaron. Then, in full view
of them, order this rock to release its water.
You will release water from the rock for them
and provide drink for the community and
their livestock.’
[9]Moses took up the branch from before
Yahweh, as he had directed him. [10]Moses
and Aaron then called the assembly together
in front of the rock. He then said to them,
‘Listen now, you rebels. Shall we make water
gush from this rock for you?’ [11]Moses then
raised his hand and struck the rock twice with
the branch; water gushed out in abundance,
and the community and their livestock
drank.

The punishment of Moses and Aaron

[12]Yahweh then said to Moses and Aaron,
‘Because you did not believe that I could
assert my holiness before the Israelites’ eyes,
you will not lead this assembly into the
country which I am giving them.’
[13]These were the Waters of Meribah,
where the Israelites laid the blame on Yahweh
and where, by their means, he asserted his
holiness.

Edom refuses right of way

[14]Moses sent messengers from Kadesh: ‘To
the king of Edom. Your brother Israel says
this: You are aware of the great hardships
we have encountered. [15]Our ancestors went
down to Egypt and there we stayed for a long
time. But the Egyptians treated us badly, as
they had our ancestors. [16]When we appealed
to Yahweh, he heard our cry and, sending an
angel, brought us out of Egypt, and here we
are, now, at Kadesh, a town on the borders
of your territory. [17]We ask permission to
pass through your country. We shall not go
through the fields or vineyards; we shall not
drink the water from the wells; we shall keep
to the king’s highway without turning to
right or left until we have passed through
your territory.’ [18]To which, Edom replied,
‘You will not pass through my country; if
you do, I shall oppose you by force of arms.’
[19]To which the Israelites replied, ‘We shall
keep to the high road; if I and my flocks drink
any of your water, I am willing to pay for it.
All I am asking is to pass through on foot.’
[20]Edom replied: ‘You shall not pass,’ and
Edom opposed them in great numbers and
great force. [21]At Edom’s refusal to grant
Israel passage through his territory, Israel
turned away.

The death of Aaron

[22]They set out from Kadesh, and the Israel-
ites, the whole community, came to Mount
Hor. [23]Yahweh spoke to Moses and Aaron at
Mount Hor, on the frontier of Edom, and
said, [24]‘Aaron is to be gathered to his people;

20a || Ex 17:1–7.

he will not enter the country which I have
given to the Israelites, since you both
disobeyed my order at the Waters of
Meribah. 25Take Aaron and his son Eleazar
and bring them up Mount Hor. 26Then take
Aaron's robes off him and dress his son
Eleazar in them. Aaron will then be gathered
to his people; that is where he will die.'
27Moses did as Yahweh ordered. With the
whole community watching, they went up
Mount Hor. 28Moses took Aaron's robes off
him and dressed his son Eleazar in them,
and there Aaron died, on the mountain-top.
Moses and Eleazar then came back down the
mountain. 29The whole community saw that
Aaron had died, and for thirty days the whole
House of Israel mourned for Aaron.

The capture of Hormah

21 The king of Arad, the Canaanite living
in the Negeb, learned that Israel was
coming by way of Atharim. He attacked
Israel and took some prisoners. 2Israel then
made this vow to Yahweh, 'If you deliver this
people into my power, I shall curse their
towns with destruction.' 3Yahweh heard
Israel's words and delivered the Canaanites
into their power, and they destroyed them in
accordance with their curse. Hence the place
was given the name Hormah.

The bronze serpent

4They left Mount Hor by the road to the Sea
of Suph, to skirt round Edom. On the way
the people lost patience. 5They spoke against
God and against Moses, 'Why did you bring
us out of Egypt to die in the desert? For there
is neither food nor water here; we are sick of
this meagre diet.'
6At this, God sent fiery serpents among the
people; their bite brought death to many in
Israel. 7The people came and said to Moses,
'We have sinned by speaking against Yahweh
and against you. Intercede for us with
Yahweh to save us from these serpents.'
Moses interceded for the people, 8and
Yahweh replied, 'Make a fiery serpent and
raise it as a standard. Anyone who is bitten
and looks at it will survive.' 9Moses then
made a serpent out of bronze and raised it as
a standard, and anyone who was bitten by a
serpent and looked at the bronze serpent
survived.

By stages to Transjordan

10The Israelites set out and camped at Oboth.
11Then they left Oboth and camped at Iye-
Abarim, in the desert on the eastern border
of Moab. 12They set out from there and
camped in the gorge of the Zered. 13They set
out from there and camped on the other side
of the Arnon.
This gorge in the desert begins in the
territory of the Amorites. For the Arnon is
the frontier of Moab, between the Moabites
and the Amorites. 14That is why it says in the
Book of the Wars of Yahweh:
'. . .Waheb near Suphah and the gorges
of the Arnon 15and the slope of the ravine
running down to the site of Ar and over
against the frontier of Moab.'
16And from there they went to Beer, that
being the well in connection with which
Yahweh had said to Moses, 'Call the people
together and I will give them water.' 17Then
it was that Israel sang this song:

Spring up, well!
Sing out for the well,
18sunk by the princes,
dug by the people's leaders
with the sceptre, with their staves!

—and from the desert to Mattanah, 19and
from Mattanah to Nahaliel, and from
Nahaliel to Bamoth, 20and from Bamoth to
the valley that opens into the country of
Moab, towards the heights of Pisgah over-
looking the desert.

The conquest of Transjordan[a]

21Israel sent messengers to say to Sihon
king of the Amorites, 22'I wish to pass through
your country. We shall not stray into the
fields or vineyards; we shall not drink the
water from the wells; we shall keep to the
king's highway until we have passed through
your territory.'
23But Sihon would not give Israel leave to
pass through his country. He assembled all
his people, marched into the desert to meet
Israel, and reached Jahaz, where he gave
battle to Israel. 24Israel defeated him by force
of arms and conquered his country from the

21a || Dt 2:26–36.

Arnon to the Jabbok, as far as the Ammon-
ites, for Jazer marked the Ammonite frontier.
25 Israel took all these towns. Israel occu-
pied all the Amorite towns, Heshbon and
all its dependencies, 26 Heshbon being the
capital of Sihon king of the Amorites, who
had made war on the first king of Moab and
captured all his territory as far as the Arnon.
27 Hence the poets say:

Come to Heshbon!
Let the city of Sihon
be rebuilt on firm foundations!

28 For fire has burst from Heshbon,[b]
a flame from the city of Sihon,
devouring Ar of Moab,
engulfing the heights of the Arnon.
29 Oh, unhappy Moab!
People of Chemosh, you are lost!
He has resigned his sons as fugitives,
and his daughters as prisoners
to Sihon king of the Amorites.
30 Their posterity has been destroyed
from Heshbon all the way to Dibon,
and we have lit a fire
all the way from Nophah to Medeba.

31 Thus Israel occupied the Amorites' terri-
tory. 32 Moses then sent men to reconnoitre
Jazer, and Israel took it and its dependencies,
evicting the Amorites who lived there.
33 They then turned and marched on
Bashan. Og king of Bashan and all his people
marched to meet them and give battle at
Edrei. 34 Yahweh said to Moses, 'Do not be
afraid of him, for I have put him, all his
people and his country at your mercy. Treat
him as you treated Sihon king of the
Amorites, who lived in Heshbon.' 35 So they
pressed their attack against him, his sons and
all his people until there was no one left alive.
And they took possession of his country.

22 The Israelites then set out and pitched
their camp in the Plains of Moab,
beyond the Jordan opposite Jericho.

The king of Moab appeals to Balaam

2 Balak son of Zippor saw all that Israel had
done to the Amorites, 3 and Moab was terri-
fied of the people, because there were so
many of them.
Moab was afraid of the Israelites; 4 he said
to the elders of Midian, 'This horde will soon
have cropped everything round us as closely
as an ox crops grass in the countryside.'
Now Balak son of Zippor was king of Moab
at the time. 5 He sent messengers to summon
Balaam son of Beor, at Pethor on the River,
in the territory of the Amawites, saying,
'Look, a people coming from Egypt has
overrun the whole countryside; they have
halted at my very door. 6 I beg you come and
curse this people for me, for they are stronger
than I am. We may then be able to defeat
them and drive them out of the country. For
this I know: anyone you bless is blessed,
anyone you curse is accursed.'
7 The elders of Moab and the elders of
Midian set out, taking the fee for the divi-
nation with them. They found Balaam and
gave him Balak's message. 8 He said to them,
'Stay the night here, and I will answer as
Yahweh directs me.' So the chiefs of Moab
stayed with Balaam. 9 God came to Balaam
and said, 'Who are these men staying with
you?' 10 Balaam said to God, 'Balak son of
Zippor, king of Moab, has sent me this
message, 11 "Look, a people coming from
Egypt has overrun the whole countryside.
Come now and curse them for me; I may then
be able to defeat them and drive them out." '
12 God said to Balaam, 'You are not to go with
them. You are not to curse the people, for
they are blessed.' 13 In the morning Balaam
got up and said to the chiefs sent by Balak,
'Go back to your country, for Yahweh will
not let me go with you.' 14 So the chiefs of
Moab got up, went back to Balak and said,
'Balaam refuses to come with us.'
15 And again Balak sent chiefs, more
numerous and more renowned than the first.
16 They came to Balaam and said, 'A message
from Balak son of Zippor, "Now do not
refuse to come to me. 17 I will load you with
honours and do whatever you say. I beg you
come and curse this people for me." ' 18 In
reply, Balaam said to Balak's envoys, 'Even
if Balak gave me his house full of silver and
gold, I could not go against the order of
Yahweh my God in anything, great or small.
19 Now please stay the night here yourselves,
and I will learn what else Yahweh has to tell
me.' 20 God came to Balaam during the night
and said to him, 'Have not these men come
to summon you? Get up, go with them, but
do only what I tell you to do.' 21 Balaam got

21b || Jr 48:45–46.

up and saddled his donkey and set out with
the chiefs of Moab.

Balaam's donkey

22 His going kindled Yahweh's anger, and the
angel of Yahweh took his stand on the road
to bar his way. Balaam was riding his donkey
and his two servants were with him. 23 Now
the donkey saw the angel of Yahweh standing
in the road with a drawn sword in his hand,
and she turned off the road into the open
country. Balaam then struck the donkey to
turn her back onto the road.
24 The angel of Yahweh then went and
stood on a narrow path among the vineyards,
with a wall to the right and a wall to the left.
25 The donkey saw the angel of Yahweh and
scraped against the wall, scraping Balaam's
foot against it, so he struck her again.
26 The angel of Yahweh then moved and
stood in a place so narrow that there was no
room to pass either to right or left. 27 When
the donkey saw the angel of Yahweh, she lay
down under Balaam. Balaam flew into a rage
and struck the donkey with his stick.
28 Yahweh then gave the donkey the power
to talk, and she said to Balaam, 'What harm
have I done you, for you to strike me three
times like this?' 29 Balaam answered the
donkey, 'Because you have been making a
fool of me! If I had been carrying a sword, I
should have killed you by now.' 30 The donkey
said to Balaam, 'Am I not your donkey, and
have I not been your mount all your life?
Have I ever behaved like this with you
before?' 'No,' he replied.
31 Yahweh then opened Balaam's eyes and
he saw the angel of Yahweh standing in the
road with a drawn sword in his hand; and he
bowed his head and threw himself on his
face. 32 And the angel of Yahweh said to him,
'Why did you strike your donkey three times
like that? I myself had come to bar your way;
while I am here your road is blocked. 33 The
donkey saw me and turned aside because of
me three times. You are lucky she did turn
aside, or I should have killed you by now,
though I would have spared her.' 34 Balaam
said to the angel of Yahweh, 'I have sinned.
I did not know you were standing in the road
to stop me. But if what I am doing displeases
you, I will go home again.' 35 The angel of
Yahweh said to Balaam, 'Go with these men,
but say only what I tell you to say.' So Balaam
went on with the chiefs sent by Balak.

Balaam and Balak

36 Balak learned that Balaam was coming and
went out to meet him, in the direction of
Ar in Moab, at the Arnon frontier on the
country's furthest boundary. 37 Balak said
to Balaam, 'Did I not send messengers to
summon you? Why did you not come to me?
Did you think, perhaps, I could confer no
honours on you?' 38 Balaam said to Balak, 'I
have come to you after all. I suppose you
know I cannot say anything on my own? The
words God puts into my mouth are what I
shall say.'
39 Balaam set out with Balak. They came to
Kiriath-Huzoth. 40 Balak sacrificed oxen and
sheep, and offered portions to Balaam and the
chiefs who were with him. 41 Next morning
Balak took Balaam and brought him up to
Bamoth-Baal, from where he could see the
edge of the camp.

23 Balaam said to Balak, 'Build me seven
altars here and prepare me seven bulls
and seven rams.' 2 Balak did as Balaam said
and offered a burnt offering of one bull and
one ram on each altar. 3 Balaam then said to
Balak, 'Stand beside your burnt offerings
while I go away. Perhaps Yahweh will come
and meet me. If he does, I shall tell you
whatever he reveals to me.' And he withdrew
to a bare hill.

Balaam's prophecies

4 God came to meet Balaam, who said to him,
'I have prepared the seven altars and offered
a burnt offering of one bull and one ram on
each altar.' 5 Yahweh then put a prophecy
into his mouth and said to him, 'Go back to
Balak, and that is what you must say to him.'
6 So Balaam went back to him, and found him
still standing beside his burnt offering, with
all the chiefs of Moab. 7 He then declaimed
his poem as follows:

Balak has brought me from Aram,
the king of Moab from the hills
of Kedem:
'Come and curse Jacob for me,
come and denounce Israel!'
8 How shall I curse someone
whom God has not cursed,
how denounce someone
God has not denounced?
9 Yes, from the top of the crags I see him,
from the hills I descry him:
a people that dwells on its own,

to your people, as Aaron your brother was. [14]For you both rebelled in the desert of Zin when the community disputed with me and when I ordered you to assert my holiness before their eyes by means of the water.' (These were the Waters of Meribah of Kadesh, in the desert of Zin.)

[15]Moses then said to Yahweh, [16]'May it please Yahweh, God of the spirits that give life to all living creatures, to appoint a leader for this community, [17]to be at their head in all their undertakings, a man who will lead them out and bring them in, so that Yahweh's community will not be like sheep without a shepherd.' [18]Yahweh then said to Moses, 'Take Joshua son of Nun, a man in whom the spirit dwells, and lay your hand on him. [19]Bring him before the priest Eleazar and the whole community and give him your orders in their presence, [20]conferring some of your own authority on him, so that the whole community of Israelites will obey him. [21]He will present himself to the priest Eleazar who will consult Yahweh on his behalf by means of the rite of the *urim*; at his command, they will go out and, at his command, they will come in, he and all the Israelites with him, the whole community.'

[22]Moses did as Yahweh had ordered. He took Joshua, brought him before the priest Eleazar and the whole community, [23]laid his hands on him and gave him his orders, as Yahweh had directed through Moses.

Regulations for sacrifices

28 Yahweh spoke to Moses and said, [2]'Give the Israelites this order:

"Take care to bring me my offering, my sustenance in the form of food burnt as a smell pleasing to me, at the proper time."

[3]'You will then say to them: "This is the food which you will burn in offering to Yahweh:

a: Daily sacrifices

"Every day, two unblemished yearling lambs as a perpetual burnt offering. [4]You will offer the first lamb in the morning and the second lamb at twilight, [5]with a cereal offering of one-tenth of an *ephah* of fine flour mixed with one-quarter of a *hin* of crushed-olive oil. [6]Such was the perpetual burnt offering made on Mount Sinai as a pleasing smell, as food burnt for Yahweh. [7]The accompanying libation will be of one-quarter of a *hin* for each lamb; the libation of fermented liquor for Yahweh will be poured inside the sanctuary. [8]The second lamb you will offer at twilight, offering it with the same cereal offering and the same libation as in the morning, as food burnt as a smell pleasing to Yahweh.

b: The Sabbath

[9]"On the Sabbath day, you will offer two unblemished yearling lambs and two-tenths of an *ephah* of fine flour as a cereal offering, mixed with oil, as well as the accompanying libation. [10]The Sabbath burnt offering will be offered every Sabbath in addition to the perpetual burnt offering, and the accompanying libation similarly.

c: The feast of New Moon

[11]"At the beginning of each of your months you will offer a burnt offering to Yahweh: two young bulls, one ram and seven yearling lambs, without blemish; [12]for each bull a cereal offering of three-tenths of an *ephah* of fine flour mixed with oil; for each ram, a cereal offering of two-tenths of fine flour mixed with oil; [13]for each lamb, a cereal offering of one-tenth of fine flour mixed with oil: as a burnt offering, as a pleasing smell, as food burnt for Yahweh. [14]The accompanying libations will be of half a *hin* of wine for a bull, one-third of a *hin* for a ram and one-quarter of a *hin* for a lamb. This will be the monthly burnt offering, month after month, every month of the year. [15]In addition to the perpetual burnt offering, a goat will be offered to Yahweh, as a sacrifice for sin, with its accompanying libation.

d: The feast of Unleavened Bread

[16]"The fourteenth day of the first month is the Passover of Yahweh, [17]and the fifteenth day of this month is a feast day. For seven days unleavened bread will be eaten. [18]On the first day there will be a sacred assembly; you will do no heavy work. [19]As food burnt as a burnt offering you will offer Yahweh two young bulls, a ram and seven yearling lambs, without blemish. [20]The accompanying cereal offering of fine flour mixed with oil will be three-tenths of an *ephah* for a bull, two-tenths for a ram, [21]and one-tenth for each of the

seven lambs. 22There will also be a goat as a sacrifice for sin, for performing the rite of expiation for you. 23You will offer these in addition to the morning burnt offering, which is a perpetual burnt offering. 24You will do this every day for seven days. It is sustenance, food burnt as a smell pleasing to Yahweh, to be offered in addition to the perpetual burnt offering and its accompanying libation. 25On the seventh day you will hold a sacred assembly; you will do no heavy work.

e: The feast of Weeks

26"On the day of the first-fruits, when you make your offering of new fruits to Yahweh at your feast of Weeks, you will hold a sacred assembly; you will do no heavy work. 27As a burnt offering as a smell pleasing to Yahweh, you will offer two young bulls, one ram and seven yearling lambs. 28The accompanying cereal offering of fine flour mixed with oil will be three-tenths of an *ephah* for each bull, two-tenths for the ram, 29and one-tenth for each of the seven lambs. 30There will also be a goat as a sacrifice for sin, for performing the rite of expiation for you. 31You will offer these in addition to the perpetual burnt offering and its accompanying cereal offering and libations." '

f: The feast of Acclamations

29 ' "In the seventh month, on the first day of the month, you will hold a sacred assembly; you will do no heavy work. For you this will be a day of Acclamations. 2As a burnt offering, as a smell pleasing to Yahweh, you will offer one young bull, one ram and seven yearling lambs, without blemish. 3The accompanying cereal offering of fine flour mixed with oil will be three-tenths of an *ephah* for the bull, two-tenths for the ram, 4and one-tenth for each of the seven lambs. 5There will also be a goat as a sacrifice for sin, for performing the rite of expiation for you. 6This is in addition to the monthly burnt offering and its cereal offering, the perpetual burnt offering and its cereal offering, and the accompanying libations enjoined by law, as a pleasing smell, as food burnt for Yahweh.

g: The Day of Expiation

7"On the tenth day of this seventh month, you will hold a sacred assembly; you will fast and do no work. 8As a burnt offering for Yahweh, as a pleasing smell, you will offer one young bull, one ram and seven yearling lambs, which you will choose as being without blemish. 9The accompanying cereal offering of fine flour mixed with oil will be three-tenths of an *ephah* for the bull, two-tenths for the ram, 10and one-tenth for each of the seven lambs. 11And a goat will be offered as a sacrifice for sin. This is in addition to the victim for sin at the feast of Expiation, to the perpetual burnt offering and its cereal offering, and their accompanying libations.

h: The feast of Shelters

12"On the fifteenth day of the seventh month you will hold a sacred assembly; you will do no heavy work, and for seven days you will celebrate a feast for Yahweh. 13As a burnt offering, as food burnt as a smell pleasing to Yahweh, you will offer thirteen young bulls, two rams and fourteen yearling lambs, without blemish. 14The accompanying cereal offering of fine flour mixed with oil will be three-tenths of an *ephah* for each of the thirteen bulls, two-tenths for each of the two rams, 15and one-tenth for each of the fourteen lambs; 16also one goat as a sacrifice for sin. This is in addition to the perpetual burnt offering and its cereal offering and libation.

17"On the second day: twelve young bulls, two rams and fourteen yearling lambs, without blemish; 18the accompanying cereal offering and libations, as prescribed, in proportion to the number of bulls, rams and lambs; 19also one goat as a sacrifice for sin. This is in addition to the perpetual burnt offering and its cereal offering and libations.

20"On the third day: eleven bulls, two rams and fourteen yearling lambs, without blemish; 21the accompanying cereal offering and libations, as prescribed, in proportion to the number of bulls, rams and lambs; 22also one goat as a sacrifice for sin. This is in addition to the perpetual burnt offering and its cereal offering and libations.

23"On the fourth day: ten bulls, two rams and fourteen yearling lambs, without blemish; 24the accompanying cereal offering and libations, as prescribed, in proportion to the number of bulls, rams and lambs; 25also one goat as a sacrifice for sin. This is in addition to the perpetual burnt offering and its cereal offering and libation.

26"On the fifth day: nine bulls, two rams

and fourteen yearling lambs, without blemish; 27the accompanying cereal offering and libations, as prescribed, in proportion to the number of bulls, rams and lambs; 28also one goat as a sacrifice for sin. This is in addition to the perpetual burnt offering and its cereal offering and libation.

29"On the sixth day: eight bulls, two rams and fourteen yearling lambs, without blemish; 30the accompanying cereal offering and libations, as prescribed, in proportion to the number of bulls, rams and lambs; 31also one goat as a sacrifice for sin. This is in addition to the perpetual burnt offering and its cereal offering and libations.

32"On the seventh day: seven bulls, two rams and fourteen yearling lambs, without blemish; 33the accompanying cereal offering and libations, as prescribed, in proportion to the number of bulls, rams and lambs; 34also one goat as a sacrifice for sin. This is in addition to the perpetual burnt offering and its cereal offering and libation.

35"On the eighth day you will hold an assembly; you will do no heavy work. 36As a burnt offering, as food burnt as a smell pleasing to Yahweh, you will offer one bull, one ram and seven yearling lambs, without blemish; 37the accompanying cereal offering and libations, as prescribed, in proportion to the number of bulls, rams and lambs; 38also one goat as a sacrifice for sin. This is in addition to the perpetual burnt offering and its cereal offering and libation.

39"This is what you are to do for Yahweh at your solemn feasts, over and above your votive offerings and your voluntary offerings, your burnt offerings, cereal offerings and libations, and your peace offerings." '

30 Moses told the Israelites exactly what Yahweh had ordered him.

Laws concerning vows

2Moses spoke to the tribal leaders of the Israelites and said, 'This is what Yahweh has ordered:

3"If a man makes a vow to Yahweh or a formal pledge under oath, he must not break his word: whatever he promises by word of mouth he must do.

4"If a woman makes a vow to Yahweh or a formal pledge during her youth, while she is still in her father's house, 5and if her father hears about this vow or pledge made by her and says nothing to her, her vow, whatever it may be, will be binding, and the pledge she has taken, whatever it may be, will be binding. 6But if her father on the day he learns of it expresses his disapproval of it, then none of the vows or pledges she has taken will be binding. Yahweh will not hold her to it, since her father has expressed his disapproval.

7"If, being bound by vows or by a pledge voiced without due reflection, she then marries, 8and if her husband hears of it but says nothing on the day he learns of it, her vows will be binding and the pledges she has taken will be binding. 9But if on the day he learns of it he expresses his disapproval to her, this will annul the vow that she has made or the pledge that binds her, voiced without due reflection. Yahweh will not hold her to it.

10"The vow of a widow or a divorced woman and all pledges taken by her are binding on her.

11"If she has made a vow or taken a pledge under oath while in her husband's house, 12and if when the husband learns of it he says nothing to her and does not express disapproval to her, then the vow, whatever it is, will be binding, and the pledge, whatever it is, will be binding. 13But if the husband when he hears of it annuls it on the day he learns of it, no undertaking of hers, be it vow or pledge, will be binding. Since the husband has annulled it, Yahweh will not hold her to it.

14"Every vow or oath that is binding on the wife may be endorsed or annulled by the husband.

15"If by the following day the husband has said nothing to her, it means that he endorses her vow, whatever it may be, or her pledge, whatever it may be. He endorses them if he says nothing on the day he learns of them. 16But if, having learnt of them, he annuls them later, he will bear the consequences for his wife's guilt." '

17Such were the laws which Yahweh prescribed to Moses, concerning the relationship between a man and his wife, and between a father and his daughter while still young and living in her father's home.

IX: BOOTY AND ITS ALLOCATION

The holy war against Midian

31 Yahweh spoke to Moses and said, 2'Exact the full vengeance for the Israelites on the Midianites. Afterwards you will be gathered to your people.'

3Moses said to the people, 'Some of you are to take up arms for Yahweh's campaign against Midian, to carry out the vengeance of Yahweh on Midian. 4You will put a thousand men in the field from each of the tribes of Israel.'

5In this way Israel's thousands provided twelve thousand men equipped for war, one thousand from each tribe: 6Moses put them in the field, one thousand from each tribe, with Phinehas, son of the priest Eleazar, to go with them carrying the sacred objects and the trumpets for the battle cry.

7They made war on Midian, as Yahweh had ordered Moses, and put every male to death. 8What is more, they killed the kings of Midian, Evi, Rekem, Zur, Hur and Reba, the five Midianite kings; they also put Balaam son of Beor to the sword. 9The Israelites took the Midianite women and their little ones captive and carried off all their cattle, all their flocks and all their goods as booty. 10They set fire to the towns where they lived and to all their encampments. 11Then, taking all their booty, everything they had captured, human and animal, 12they brought the captives, spoil and booty to Moses, the priest Eleazar and the whole community of Israelites at the camp on the Plains of Moab, near the Jordan by Jericho.

The slaughter of the women and purification of the booty

13Moses, the priest Eleazar and all the leaders of the community went out of the camp to meet them. 14Moses was enraged with the officers of the army, the commanders of the thousands and commanders of the hundreds, who had come back from this military expedition. 15He said, 'Why have you spared the life of all the women? 16They were the very ones who, on Balaam's advice, caused the Israelites to be unfaithful to Yahweh in the affair at Peor: hence the plague which struck Yahweh's community. 17So kill all the male children and kill all the women who have ever slept with a man; 18but spare the lives of the young girls who have never slept with a man, and keep them for yourselves. 19As for you, bivouac outside the camp for seven days, everyone who has killed anyone or touched a corpse. Purify yourselves and your prisoners on the third and seventh days, 20and purify all clothing, everything made of skin, everything woven of goat's hair and everything made of wood.'

21The priest Eleazar said to the soldiers who had come back from the campaign, 'This is an article of the Law which Yahweh prescribed to Moses: 22although gold, silver, bronze, iron, tin and lead, 23everything that can withstand fire can be cleaned by being passed through fire, it must still be purified with water for purification. Whatever cannot resist fire you must pass through water.

24'Wash your clothes on the seventh day and you will then be clean. You may then re-enter the camp.'

The allocation of the booty

25Yahweh spoke to Moses and said:

26'With the priest Eleazar and the heads of families in the community, take a count of the spoils and captives, human and animal. 27You will then share out the spoil, half and half, between those who fought the campaign and the rest of the community. 28From the share of the combatants who took part in the campaign, you will set aside one out of every five hundred persons, oxen, donkeys and sheep as Yahweh's portion. 29You will take this from the half share coming to them and give it to the priest Eleazar as the portion set aside for Yahweh. 30From the half coming to the Israelites, you will take one out of every fifty persons, oxen, donkeys, sheep, and all other animals, and give them to the Levites who are responsible for Yahweh's Dwelling.'

31Moses and the priest Eleazar did as Yahweh had ordered Moses. 32The spoils, the remainder of the booty captured by the soldiers, came to six hundred and seventy-five thousand sheep and goats, 33seventy-two thousand head of cattle, 34sixty-one thousand donkeys, 35and in persons, women who had never slept with a man, thirty-two thousand in all. 36Half was assigned to those who had taken part in the war, namely three hundred

and thirty-seven thousand five hundred
sheep and goats, 37 of which Yahweh's portion
was six hundred and seventy-five, 38 thirty-six
thousand head of cattle, of which Yahweh's
portion was seventy-two, 39 thirty thousand
five hundred donkeys, of which Yahweh's
portion was sixty-one, 40 and sixteen thousand
persons, of which Yahweh's portion was
thirty-two. 41 Moses gave the priest Eleazar
the portion set aside for Yahweh, as Yahweh
had ordered Moses.

42 As for the half coming to the Israelites
which Moses had separated from that of
the combatants, 43 this half, the community's
share, came to three hundred and thirty-
seven thousand five hundred sheep and goats,
44 thirty-six thousand head of cattle, 45 thirty
thousand five hundred donkeys 46 and sixteen
thousand persons. 47 From this half, the
Israelites' share, Moses took one out of every
fifty, human and animal, and gave them to the
Levites who were responsible for Yahweh's
Dwelling, as Yahweh had ordered Moses.

The offerings

48 The officers of the thousands who had
fought the campaign, the commanders of the
thousands and commanders of the hundreds,
came to Moses 49 and said, 'Your servants
have numbered the soldiers under their
command: none of our men is missing. 50 So,
as an offering for Yahweh, we have brought
what each of us has found in the way of
gold ornaments, armlets and bracelets, rings,
earrings and breastplates, to make expiation
for ourselves before Yahweh.' 51 Moses and
the priest Eleazar accepted this gold from
them, all this jewellery. 52 This portion of
gold given to Yahweh by the commanders
of the thousands and commanders of the
hundreds amounted to sixteen thousand
seven hundred and fifty shekels.

53 Each of the soldiers took his own booty.
54 But Moses and the priest Eleazar, having
accepted the gold from the commanders of
the thousands and commanders of the
hundreds, brought it into the Tent of
Meeting, to be a reminder of the Israelites
before Yahweh.

The allocation of Transjordan[a]

32 Now, the Reubenites and Gadites
owned very large herds of cattle.
Having seen that the territories of Jazer and
Gilead formed an ideal region for raising
stock, 2 the Gadites and Reubenites went to
Moses, the priest Eleazar and the leaders of
the community, and said to them, 3 'The
territory of Ataroth, Dibon, Jazer, Nimrah,
Heshbon, Elealeh, Sebam, Nebo and Beon,
4 which Yahweh has conquered before the
advancing community of Israel, is ideal land
for raising stock, and your servants are cattle
breeders. 5 So', they said, 'if you approve,
give your servants this land for us to own; do
not make us cross the Jordan.'

6 Moses said to the Gadites and Reubenites,
'Do you intend your brothers to go into
battle while you stay here? 7 Why are you
discouraging the Israelites from crossing to
the country which Yahweh has given them?
8 Your fathers behaved in the same way when
I sent them from Kadesh-Barnea to see the
country, 9 for, having gone as far as the Valley
of Eshcol and seen the country, they discour-
aged the Israelites from entering the country
which Yahweh had given them. 10 Hence
Yahweh's anger was aroused that day and he
swore this oath, 11 "No man of twenty years
and over, who left Egypt, shall set eyes on
the country which I promised on oath to
Abraham, Isaac and Jacob . . . , for they
have not followed me absolutely, 12 except for
Caleb son of Jephunneh the Kenizzite, and
Joshua son of Nun: these indeed have
followed Yahweh absolutely." 13 Yahweh's
anger being aroused by Israel, he made them
wander in the desert for forty years, until the
generation that offended Yahweh had all
disappeared. 14 And now you rise up in your
father's place, offshoot of sinful stock, to
increase Yahweh's burning anger with Israel
even more! 15 If you turn away from him, he
will prolong the time spent in the desert, and
you will bring about this entire people's ruin.'

16 They came to Moses and said, 'We should
like to build sheepfolds here for our flocks
and towns for our little ones. 17 We ourselves
will take up arms and lead the Israelites until
we have brought them to the place appointed
for them, while our little ones stay in the
fortified towns to be safe from the local
inhabitants. 18 We will not return to our
homes until every one of the Israelites has
taken possession of his heritage. 19 For we
shall have no heritage with them on the other
bank of the Jordan or beyond, since our

32a ‖ Dt 3:12–20.

heritage has fallen to us here, east of the
Jordan.'
[20]Moses said to them, 'If you do as you
have said, if you are prepared to fight before
Yahweh, [21]and if all those of you who bear
arms cross the Jordan before Yahweh, until
he has driven all his enemies out before him,
[22]then, once the country has become subject
to Yahweh, you may go back, and will have
discharged your obligation to Yahweh and
Israel, and Yahweh will consider this terri-
tory yours. [23]But if you do not, you will sin
against Yahweh, and be sure your sin will
find you out. [24]Build towns, then, for your
little ones and folds for your flocks; but do
what you have promised.'
[25]The Gadites and Reubenites said to
Moses, 'Your servants will do as my lord
directs. [26]Our little ones, our wives, our
flocks and all our livestock will stay in the
towns of Gilead, [27]but your servants, each
armed for war, will cross in Yahweh's name
and fight, as my lord says.'
[28]So Moses gave orders about them to the
priest Eleazar, Joshua son of Nun, and the
heads of families in the Israelite tribes.
[29]Moses said to them, 'If the Gadites and
Reubenites, all those under arms, cross the
Jordan with you to fight in Yahweh's name,
then, once the country has become subject
to you, you will give them the territory of
Gilead as theirs. [30]But if they will not cross
with you under arms, they will receive their
domains in Canaan with the rest of you.'
[31]To this, the Gadites and Reubenites
replied, 'What Yahweh has said to your
servants, we shall do. [32]Under arms, we shall
cross in Yahweh's name into Canaan, so that
ownership of our heritage on this side of
the Jordan will be ours.' [33]Moses then gave
them—the Gadites, the Reubenites and the
half-tribe of Manasseh son of Joseph—the
kingdom of Sihon king of the Amorites and
the kingdom of Og king of Bashan, the
country and the towns within its territory,
and the country's frontier-towns.
[34]The Gadites rebuilt Dibon, Ataroth,
Aroer, [35]Atroth-Shophan, Jazer, Jogbehah,
[36]Beth-Nimrah and Beth-Haran as fortified
towns with folds for the flocks.
[37]The Reubenites rebuilt Heshbon,
Elealeh, Kiriathaim, [38]Nebo and Baal-Meon
(the names of which were altered), and
Sibmah, giving new names to the towns
which they rebuilt.
[39]The descendants of Machir son of
Manasseh went to Gilead. They conquered
it and drove out the Amorites who were
there. [40]Moses gave Gilead to Machir son of
Manasseh, and he settled there. [41]Jair son of
Manasseh went and seized their encamp-
ments, renaming them the Encampments of
Jair. [42]Nobah went and seized Kenat with its
dependent townships, and called it Nobah
after himself.

The stages of the Exodus

33 These were the stages of the journey
made by the Israelites when they left
Egypt in their companies under the leader-
ship of Moses and Aaron. [2]Moses recorded
their starting-points in writing whenever
they moved on at Yahweh's order. The
stages, from one starting-point to another,
were as follows:
[3]They left Rameses in the first month. It
was the fifteenth day of the first month,
the day following the Passover, when the
Israelites confidently set out, under the eyes
of all Egypt. [4]The Egyptians were burying
those of their own people whom Yahweh had
struck down, all the first-born; Yahweh had
carried out his judgement on their gods.
[5]The Israelites left Rameses and camped
at Succoth. [6]Then they left Succoth and
encamped at Etham which is on the edge of
the desert. [7]They left Etham, turned back
to Pi-Hahiroth, opposite Baal-Zephon, and
encamped before Migdol. [8]They left Pi-
Hahiroth, crossed the sea into the desert, and
after marching for three days in the desert of
Etham they encamped at Marah. [9]They left
Marah and reached Elim. At Elim there were
twelve springs of water and seventy palm
trees; they encamped there. [10]They left Elim
and encamped by the Sea of Reeds. [11]They
left the Sea of Reeds and encamped in the
desert of Sin. [12]They left the desert of Sin and
encamped at Dophkah. [13]They left Dophkah
and encamped at Alush. [14]They left Alush
and encamped at Rephidim; the people found
no drinking water there. [15]They left
Rephidim and encamped in the desert of
Sinai. [16]They left the desert of Sinai and
encamped at Kibroth-ha-Taavah. [17]They left
Kibroth-ha-Taavah and encamped at
Hazeroth. [18]They left Hazeroth and
encamped at Rithmah. [19]They left Rithmah
and encamped at Rimmon-Perez. [20]They left
Rimmon-Perez and encamped at Libnah.
[21]They left Libnah and encamped at Rissah.

22They left Rissah and encamped at Kehel-
athah. 23They left Kehelathah and encamped
at Mount Shepher. 24They left Mount
Shepher and encamped at Haradah. 25They
left Haradah and encamped at Makheloth.
26They left Makheloth and encamped at
Tahath. 27They left Tahath and encamped
at Terah. 28They left Terah and encamped at
Mithkah. 29They left Mithkah and encamped
at Hashmonah. 30They left Hashmonah and
encamped at Moseroth. 31They left Moseroth
and encamped at Bene-Jaakan. 32They left
Bene-Jaakan and encamped at Hor-Gidgad.
33They left Hor-Gidgad and encamped at
Jotbathah. 34They left Jotbathah and
encamped at Abronah. 35They left Abronah
and encamped at Ezion-Geber. 36They left
Ezion-Geber and encamped in the desert of
Zin, that is, at Kadesh. 37They left Kadesh
and encamped at Mount Hor, on the borders
of the land of Edom. 38The priest Aaron went
up Mount Hor on Yahweh's orders and died
there in the fortieth year of the exodus of the
Israelites from Egypt, in the fifth month, on
the first day of the month. 39Aaron was a
hundred and twenty-three years old when he
died on Mount Hor. 40The king of Arad, the
Canaanite who lived in the Negeb of Canaan,
heard of the Israelites' arrival. 41They left
Mount Hor and encamped at Zalmonah.
42They left Zalmonah and encamped at
Punon. 43They left Punon and encamped at
Oboth. 44They left Oboth and encamped in
Moabite territory at Iye-Abarim. 45They left
Iyim and encamped at Dibon-Gad. 46They
left Dibon-Gad and encamped at Almon-
Diblathaim. 47They left Almon-Diblathaim
and encamped in the Abarim mountains
facing Nebo. 48They left the Abarim moun-
tains and encamped on the Plains of Moab,
near the Jordan opposite Jericho. 49They
encamped near the Jordan between Beth-
ha-Jeshimoth and Abel-ha-Shittim, on the
Plains of Moab.

The allocation of Canaan. God's order

50Yahweh spoke to Moses on the Plains of
Moab, near the Jordan by Jericho, and said:
51'Speak to the Israelites and say:
"When you have crossed the Jordan into
Canaan, 52you will drive out all the local
inhabitants before you. You will destroy
all their painted images, you will destroy all
their metal statues and you will demolish all
their high places. 53You will take possession
of the country and settle in it, for I have given
you the country as your property. 54You will
share it out by lot among your clans. To a
large clan you will give a larger heritage, and
to a smaller clan you will give a smaller
heritage. Where the lot falls for each, that
will be his. Your heritage will depend on the
size of your tribe. 55If, however, you do not
drive out the local inhabitants before you,
the ones you allow to remain will be thorns
in your eyes and thistles in your sides and
will harass you in the country where you are
living, 56and I shall treat you as I intended to
treat them." '

The boundaries of Canaan

34 Yahweh spoke to Moses and said,
2'Give the Israelites this order. Say:
"When you enter the country (Canaan), this
will be the country which forms your heri-
tage. This is Canaan as defined by its
boundaries:

3"The southern part of your country will
start from the desert of Zin, on the borders
of Edom. Your southern boundary will start
on the east at the end of the Salt Sea. 4It will
then turn south towards the Ascent of the
Scorpions and go by Zin to end in the south
at Kadesh-Barnea. It will then run towards
Hazar-Addar and pass through Azmon.
5From Azmon the boundary will turn
towards the Torrent of Egypt and end at the
Sea.

6"Your seaboard will be on the Great Sea;
this will be your western boundary.

7"Your northern boundary will be as
follows: you will draw a line from the Great
Sea to Mount Hor, 8then from Mount Hor
you will draw a line to the Pass of Hamath,
and the boundary will end at Zedad. 9From
there it will run on to Ziphron and end
at Hazar-Enan. This will be your northern
boundary.

10"You will then draw your eastern
boundary from Hazar-Enan to Shepham.
11The boundary will run down from
Shepham towards Riblah on the east side of
Ain. Further down it will keep to the eastern
shore of the Sea of Chinnereth. 12The frontier
will then follow the Jordan and end at the
Salt Sea.

"Such will be your country with the
boundaries surrounding it." '

13Moses then gave the Israelites this order:
'This is the country, where your heritages

will be assigned by lot, and which Yahweh has ordered to be given to the nine tribes and the half-tribe, 14for the tribe of the Reubenites with their families and the tribe of the Gadites with their families have already received their heritage; the half-tribe of Manasseh has also received its heritage. 15These two tribes and the half-tribe have received their heritage on the other side of the Jordan by Jericho, to the east, towards the sunrise.'

The leaders in charge of the allocation

16Yahweh spoke to Moses and said:

17'Here are the names of the men who will divide the country up for you: the priest Eleazar and Joshua son of Nun, 18and you will take one leader from each tribe to divide the country up into heritages. 19Here are the names of these men:

'For the tribe of Judah, Caleb son of Jephunneh;

20'for the tribe of the Simeonites, Shemuel son of Ammihud;

21'for the tribe of Benjamin, Elidad son of Chislon;

22'for the tribe of the Danites, the leader Bukki son of Jogli;

23'for the sons of Joseph: for the tribe of Manasseh, the leader Hanniel son of Ephod;

24'for the tribe of the Ephraimites, the leader Kemuel son of Shiphtan;

25'for the tribe of the Zebulunites, the leader Elizaphan son of Parnach;

26'for the tribe of the Issacharites, the leader Paltiel son of Azzan;

27'for the tribe of the Asherites, the leader Ahihud son of Shelomi;

28'for the tribe of the Naphtalites, the leader Pedahel son of Ammihud.'

29These were the men whom Yahweh ordered to divide Canaan into heritages for the Israelites.

The portion of the Levites

35 Yahweh spoke to Moses on the Plains of Moab, near the Jordan by Jericho, and said:

2'Order the Israelites, from the heritage they possess, to give the Levites towns in which to live and pasture land round the towns. You will give these to the Levites. 3The towns must be their homes and the surrounding pasture land must be for their cattle, their possessions and all their animals. 4The pasture land surrounding the towns which you give to the Levites will extend, from the walls of the towns, for a thousand cubits all round.

5'Outside the town, measure two thousand cubits to the east, two thousand cubits to the south, two thousand cubits to the west and two thousand cubits to the north, the town lying in the centre; such will be the pasture lands of these towns. 6The towns you give to the Levites will be six cities of refuge, ceded by you as sanctuary for those who commit manslaughter; and you will give forty-two towns in addition. 7Altogether you will give the Levites forty-eight towns, with their pasture lands. 8Of the towns which you give from the Israelites' possessions, you will give more from those who have more, and less from those who have less. Each will give some of his towns to the Levites, in proportion to the heritage he himself has received.'

Cities of refuge

9Yahweh spoke to Moses and said:

10'Speak to the Israelites and say:

"Once you have crossed the Jordan into Canaan, 11you will find towns, some of which you will make into cities of refuge where those who have accidentally committed manslaughter can take sanctuary. 12These towns will afford you refuge from the avenger of blood, so that the killer will not be put to death before standing trial before the community. 13Of the towns you give, six will serve you as cities of refuge: 14as cities of refuge, you will give three towns on the other side of the Jordan and will give three towns in Canaan. 15These six towns will serve as refuge for the Israelites, for the foreigner and for the resident alien, where anyone who has accidentally killed someone can take sanctuary.

16"But if he has struck the person with an iron object so as to cause death, he is a murderer. The murderer will be put to death. 17If he has struck him with a stone meant for killing, and has killed him, he is a murderer. The murderer will be put to death. 18Or if he has struck him with a wooden instrument meant for killing, and has killed him, he is a murderer. The murderer will be put to death. 19The avenger of blood will put the murderer to death. Whenever he finds him, he will put him to death.

20"If the killer has maliciously manhandled
his victim, or thrown some lethal missile to
strike him down, 21or out of enmity dealt him
the death-blow with his fist, then he who
struck the blow will be put to death; he is a
murderer; the avenger of blood will put
him to death whenever he finds him. 22If,
however, he has manhandled his victim by
chance, without malice, or thrown some
missile at him not meaning to hit him 23or,
without seeing him, dropped on him a stone
meant for killing and so killed him, so long
as he bore him no malice and wished him no
harm, 24then the community will decide in
accordance with these rules between the one
who struck the blow and the avenger of
blood, 25and will save the killer from the
clutches of the avenger of blood. They will
send him back to the city of refuge where he
had taken sanctuary, and there he will stay
until the death of the high priest who has
been anointed with the holy oil. 26Should the
killer leave the bounds of the city of refuge
in which he has taken sanctuary 27and the
avenger of blood encounter him outside the
bounds of his city of refuge, the avenger of
blood may kill him without fear of reprisal;
28since the killer should stay in his city of
refuge until the death of the high priest; only
after the death of the high priest is he free to
go back to his own piece of property. 29Such
will be the legal rule for you and your
descendants, wherever you may live.

30"In any case of homicide, the evidence
of witnesses will determine whether the killer
must be put to death; but a single witness is
not enough to sustain a capital charge. 31You
will not accept a ransom for the life of a
murderer condemned to death; he must die.
32Nor will you accept a ransom for anyone
who, having taken sanctuary in his city or
refuge, wishes to come back and live at home
before the death of the high priest. 33Do
not profane the country you live in. Blood
profanes the country and, for the country,
the only expiation for the blood shed in it is
the blood of the man who shed it. 34So do not
defile the country which you live in and
where I live; for I, Yahweh, live among the
Israelites." '

A wife's inheritance

36 Then the heads of families of the clan
descended from Gilead, son of Machir,
son of Manasseh, one of the clans descended
from Joseph, came forward and, addressing
Moses and the leaders, the Israelite heads of
families, 2they said:

'Yahweh has ordered my lord to apportion
the Israelites' heritages in the country by lot
and my lord has been ordered by Yahweh to
give the heritage of our brother Zelophehad
to his daughters. 3Now, if they marry
someone from another Israelite tribe, their
heritage will be alienated from our ancestral
heritage. The heritage of the tribe to which
they will then belong will be increased, and
the heritage allotted to us will be diminished.
4And when the jubilee for the Israelites comes
round, these women's heritage will become
part of the heritage of the tribe to which
they then belong, and be alienated from the
heritage of our ancestral tribe.'

5At Yahweh's bidding, Moses gave the
Israelites this order. He said:

'What the Josephite tribe says is true.
6This is Yahweh's ruling for Zelophehad's
daughters: "They may marry whom they
please, providing they marry into a clan of
their father's tribe. 7But the heritages of
Israelites are not to be transferred from tribe
to tribe; each Israelite will stick to the heritage
of his own tribe. 8Any daughter who owns a
heritage in an Israelite tribe will marry into
a clan of her own paternal tribe, so that the
Israelites may each preserve the heritage of
his father. 9No heritage may be transferred
from one tribe to another; each Israelite tribe
will stick to its own heritage." '

10Zelophehad's daughters did as Yahweh
had ordered Moses. 11Mahlah, Tirzah,
Hoglah, Milcah and Noah, daughters of
Zelophehad, married the sons of their
father's brothers. 12Since they married into
clans descended from Manasseh son of
Joseph, their heritage reverted to the tribe of
their father's clan.

Conclusion

13Such were the commandments and laws
that Yahweh prescribed for the Israelites
through Moses on the Plains of Moab near
the Jordan by Jericho.

THE BOOK OF DEUTERONOMY

The Book of Deuteronomy is, as its name implies, a second version or copy of the Law. It may well be the book of the Law discovered in the Temple at the time of the reform of King Josiah (622 BC). Although it clearly incorporates a great deal of earlier material, it contains many religious emphases characteristic of the prophets and must have received its definitive moulding at that time. After an introductory summary on Israel's history and the need for fidelity, it is structured on three great discourses of Moses, the second of which sandwiches the Deuteronomic Code of Law (12:1—26:15).

It is dominated by the twin ideas of love and law: God's passionate and exclusive love for Israel, his chosen nation, and his affectionate intimacy with Israel, and Israel's response in whole-hearted love and filial obedience to the Law. This response is expressed in the tribute of tithes, first-born and first-fruits, a recognition that Yahweh is master of the land and its produce. But the Israelites must also imitate God's generosity to themselves through a code of law which excludes exploitation or humiliation of one Israelite by another.

PLAN OF THE BOOK

DEUTERONOMY

I: INTRODUCTORY DISCOURSES

A: THE FIRST DISCOURSE OF MOSES

Time and place

1 These are the words which Moses addressed to all Israel beyond the Jordan, in the desert, in the Arabah facing Suph, between Paran and Tophel, Laban, Hazeroth and Dizahab. 2 It is eleven days' journey from Horeb by way of Mount Seir to Kadesh-Barnea. 3 It was in the fortieth year, on the first day of the eleventh month, that Moses told the Israelites everything that Yahweh had ordered him to tell them.

4 ‘He had defeated Sihon king of the Amorites, who lived at Heshbon, and Og king of Bashan, who lived at Ashtaroth and Edrei. 5 There, in Moab beyond the Jordan, Moses resolved to expound this Law. He said:

The final instructions at Horeb

6 ‘Yahweh our God said to us at Horeb, “You have stayed long enough at this mountain. 7 Move on, continue your journey, go to the highlands of the Amorites, to all those who live in the Arabah, in the highlands, in the lowlands, in the Negeb and in the coastland; go into Canaan and to Lebanon as far as the great River Euphrates. 8 Look, that is the country I have given you; go and take possession of the country that Yahweh promised on oath to give to your ancestors, Abraham, Isaac and Jacob, and to their descendants after them.”

9 ‘At the same time, I told you,[a] “I cannot be responsible for you by myself. 10 Yahweh your God has increased your numbers, until you are now as numerous as the stars of heaven. 11 And Yahweh your God is going to increase you a thousand times more, and bless you as he has promised you. 12 So how can I cope by myself with the bitter burden that you are, and with your bickering? 13 From each of your tribes pick wise, shrewd and experienced men for me to make your leaders.” 14 You replied, “Your plan is good.” 15 So I took your tribal leaders, wise, experienced men, and appointed them to lead you, as captains of thousands, hundreds, fifties, tens, and as scribes for your tribes. 16 At that same time I told your judges, “You must give your brothers a fair hearing and see justice done between one person and his brother or the foreigner living with him. 17 You must be impartial in judgement and give an equal hearing to small and great alike. Do not be afraid of any human person, for the verdict is God’s. Should a case be too difficult, bring it for me to hear. 18 And on that occasion I gave you instructions about everything you were to do.”

Kadesh: the Israelites lose faith[b]

19 ‘So, as Yahweh our God had ordered, we left Horeb and made our way through that vast and terrible desert, which you saw on the way to the Amorite highlands, and arrived at Kadesh-Barnea. 20 I then said, “You have now reached the Amorite highlands, which Yahweh our God has given us. 21 Look, Yahweh your God has given you this country. March in, take possession of it as Yahweh, the God of your ancestors, has said; do not be afraid or discouraged.” 22 Then you all came to me and said, “Let us send men ahead of us to explore the country; they shall report to us which way we ought to take and what towns we shall come to.” 23 This seemed good advice to me and I selected twelve men from among you, one from each tribe. 24 These men made towards the highlands and went up into them; they reached the Valley of Eshcol and reconnoitred it. 25 They collected some of the produce of the country and brought it down to us; and they made us this report, “Yahweh our God has given us a fine country.” 26 You, however, refused to go up there and rebelled against the voice of Yahweh your God. 27 You muttered in your tents, saying, “Yahweh hates us, and that is why he has brought us out of Egypt, to put us into the Amorites’ power and so destroy us. 28 What kind of place are we making for? Our brothers have discouraged us by saying that the people are stronger and taller than we are, the cities immense, with walls reaching to the sky. And we have seen Anakim[c] there too.”

29 ‘And I said to you, “Do not take fright, do not be afraid of them. 30 Yahweh your God goes ahead of you and will be fighting on your side, just as you saw him act in Egypt. 31 You have seen him in the desert too: Yahweh your God continued to support you, as a man supports his son, all along the road you followed until you arrived here.” 32 But for all this, you put no faith in Yahweh your God, 33 going ahead of you on the journey to find you a camping ground, by night in the fire to light your path, and in the cloud by day.

1a ‖ Ex 18:13–26.
1b ‖ Nb 13:1–14:9.
1c According to legend, the Anakim and Rephaim are the original dwellers in Palestine, pictured as giants.

Yahweh's instructions at Kadesh[d]

34'Yahweh heard what you were saying and in his anger swore this oath, 35"Not one of these people, this perverse generation, will see the fine country I swore to give your ancestors, 36except Caleb son of Jephunneh. He will see it. To him and to his children I shall give the land he has set foot on, for he has been perfectly obedient to Yahweh." 37Yahweh was angry with me too, because of you. "You will not go in either," he said. 38"Your assistant, Joshua son of Nun, will be the one to enter. Encourage him, since he is to bring Israel into possession of the country. 39And your little ones too, who, you said, would be seized as booty, these children of yours who do not yet know good from evil, they will go in; I shall give it to them and they will own it. 40But, as regards yourselves, turn round, go back into the desert, towards the Sea of Suph."

41"In reply, you then said to me, "We have sinned against Yahweh our God. We shall go up and fight just as Yahweh our God has ordered us." And each one of you buckled on his arms and equipped himself to march up into the highlands. 42But Yahweh said to me, "Tell them this: Do not go up and fight. I am not with you. Do not let yourselves be defeated by your enemies." 43So I told you, but you would not listen, and you rebelled against the voice of Yahweh; presumptuously you marched into the highlands. 44The Amorites, who live in that country of hills, came swarming out against you like bees, pursued you and beat you from Seir to Hormah. 45On your return, you wept in Yahweh's presence, but he would not listen to your cries or pay attention. 46That was why you had to stay at Kadesh as long as you did.'

From Kadesh to the Arnon

2 'We then turned round and made for the desert, in the direction of the Sea of Suph, as Yahweh had ordered me. For many days we skirted Mount Seir. 2Yahweh then said to me, 3"You have gone far enough round this mountain; now turn north. 4And give the people this order: You are about to pass through the territory of your kinsmen, the sons of Esau who live in Seir. They are afraid of you, and you will be well protected. 5Do not provoke them, for I shall give you none of their land, no, not so much as a foot's length of it. I have given the highlands of Seir to Esau as his domain. 6Pay them in money for what food you eat; and pay them in money for the water you drink. 7Yahweh your God has blessed you in all you do; he has watched over your journeying through this vast desert. Yahweh your God has been with you these forty years and you have never been in want."

8'So we passed beyond those relatives of ours, the children of Esau who live in Seir, by the road through the Arabah, Elath and Ezion-Geber; then, changing direction, we took the road towards the Plains of Moab. 9Yahweh then said to me, "Do not attack Moab, do not provoke him to fight, for I shall give you none of his land, since I have given Ar to the children of Lot as their domain." 10(At one time the Emim lived there, a great and numerous people, tall as the Anakim; 11and, like the Anakim, they were considered to be Rephaim, though the Moabites call them Emim. 12The Horites, too, lived in Seir at one time; these, however, were dispossessed and exterminated by the children of Esau who settled there in place of them, just as Israel has done in the country given to it by Yahweh as a heritage.) 13"On your way, then! Cross the Wadi Zered!"

'And so we crossed the Wadi Zered. 14From Kadesh-Barnea to the crossing of the Wadi Zered our wanderings had taken thirty-eight years; as a result of which, the entire generation of those of age to bear arms had been eliminated, as Yahweh had sworn to them. 15Yahweh's hand had been against them, to eliminate them completely from the camp.

16'When death had carried off from the people those of age to bear arms, to the last man, 17Yahweh said this to me, 18"You are now crossing Ar, the country of Moab, 19and soon you will encounter the children of Ammon. Do not attack them, do not provoke them, for I shall give you none of the land belonging to the children of Ammon as your domain. I have given it to the children of Lot as theirs." 20(This used also to be considered as Rephaim territory; at one time the Rephaim lived there, though the Ammonites call them Zamzummim, 21a great and numerous people, and tall like the Anakim.

1d || Nb 14:21–35.

Yahweh exterminated them for the Ammon-
ites who dispossessed them and settled there
in place of them, 22 just as he had done for the
children of Esau who live in Seir, so that they
dispossessed the Horites and settled there
instead of them and are still there now. 23 It
was the same with the Avvites who occupied
encampments as far as Gaza: the Caphtorim,
coming from Caphtor, exterminated them
and settled there instead.) 24 "On your way!
Break camp and cross the Wadi Arnon. See,
I am putting Sihon the Amorite, king of
Heshbon, at your mercy, and his country
too. Set about the conquest; engage him in
battle. 25 Today and henceforth, I shall fill the
peoples under all heaven with fear and terror
of you; whoever hears word of your approach
will tremble and writhe in anguish because
of you."

Conquest of the kingdom of Sihon[a]

26 'So, from the desert of Kedemoth I sent
envoys to Sihon king of Heshbon with this
peaceful message, 27 "I intend to cross your
country. I shall go my way, straying neither
to right nor to left. 28 I shall eat and pay for
the food you choose to sell me, and I shall
drink and pay for the water you let me have.
I only want to march through, 29 just as the
children of Esau who live in Seir permitted,
as well as the Moabites who live in Ar, until
I cross the Jordan into the country that
Yahweh our God is giving us."

30 'But Sihon king of Heshbon would not
give us leave to pass through his territory;
Yahweh our God had made his spirit obsti-
nate and his heart stubborn, to put him at
your mercy, as he still is. 31 Yahweh said to
me, "You see, I am starting to give you
Sihon and his country. Begin the conquest by
seizing his country." 32 Sihon marched out
against us, he and all his people, to give battle
at Jahaz. 33 And Yahweh our God handed him
over to us: we defeated him and his sons and
all his people. 34 We captured all his towns
and laid all these towns under the curse of
destruction: men, women and children, we
left no survivors 35 except the livestock which
we took as our booty, and the spoils of the
captured towns. 36 From Aroer on the edge
of the Arnon valley and from the town down
in the valley, as far as Gilead, not one town
was beyond our reach; Yahweh our God
delivered them all to us. 37 You did not,
however, go near the country of the Ammon-
ites, or the region of the River Jabbok, or
the towns in the highlands, or anywhere
forbidden us by Yahweh our God.'

Conquest of the kingdom of Og[a]

3 'We then turned on Bashan and invaded
that. And Og king of Bashan marched out
against us, he and all his people, to give battle
at Edrei. 2 Yahweh said to me, "Do not be
afraid of him, for I have put him at your
mercy, him, all his people and his country.
You will treat him as you treated Sihon king
of the Amorites who lived in Heshbon." 3 So,
Yahweh our God put Og king of Bashan at
our mercy too, with all his people. We beat
him so thoroughly that nobody was left.
4 That was when we captured all his towns;
there was not a town of theirs we did not
take: sixty towns, the whole confederation of
Argob, Og's kingdom in Bashan, 5 all of
them fortresses defended by high walls and
fortified with gates and bars, not to mention
the Perizzite towns, which were very
numerous. 6 We laid them under the curse of
destruction as we had done Sihon king of
Heshbon, laying all these towns under the
curse of destruction: men, women and chil-
dren—7 but we seized the livestock and spoils
of the towns as booty for ourselves.

8 'Thus, by then we had taken the country
of the two Amorite kings beyond the Jordan,
stretching from the Wadi Arnon to Mount
Hermon 9 (the Sidonians call Hermon 'Sirion'
and the Amorites call it 'Senir'): 10 all the
towns of the tableland, all Gilead, and all
Bashan as far as Salecah and Edrei, the capital
cities of Og in Bashan. 11 (Og king of Bashan
was the last survivor of the Rephaim; his bed
was the iron bed that can be seen at Rabbah-
of-the-Ammonites, nine cubits long and four
wide, according to the human cubit.)

The partitioning of Transjordan[b]

12 'Then we took possession of this country,
from Aroer on the Wadi Arnon. To the
Reubenites and Gadites I gave half the high-
lands of Gilead with its towns. 13 To the half-

2a ‖ Nb 21:21–25.
3a ‖ Nb 21:33–35.
3b ‖ Nb 32.

tribe of Manasseh I gave the rest of Gilead and the whole of Bashan, Og's kingdom. (The whole confederation of Argob and the whole of Bashan is called the country of the Rephaim. [14]Since Jair son of Manasseh occupied the whole confederation of Argob as far as the frontiers of the Geshurites and Maacathites, after him Bashan is called the Encampments of Jair even today.) [15]To Machir I gave Gilead. [16]To the Reubenites and the Gadites I gave the region from Gilead to the Wadi Arnon, the middle of the ravine marking the boundary, and up as far as the Jabbok, the ravine marking the frontier of the Ammonites. [17]The Arabah and the Jordan serve as frontiers from Chinnereth down to the Sea of the Arabah (the Salt Sea), at the foot of the slopes of Pisgah on the east.

Further instructions from Moses

[18]'I then gave you this order: "Yahweh your God has given you this country to be yours. Armed, every one of you fit to fight must go ahead of your brothers the Israelites. [19]Only your wives, your children and your flocks (you have many flocks, I know) must stay behind in the towns which I have given you, [20]until Yahweh has brought your brothers to rest as he has already brought you, and they too possess the territory which Yahweh your God is giving them on the other side of the Jordan; after that, you can go home, each to the domain I have given you." [21]I then gave Joshua this order, "You can see for yourself everything that Yahweh our God has done to these two kings; Yahweh will do the same to all the kingdoms through which you pass. [22]Do not be afraid of them: Yahweh your God himself is fighting for you."

[23]'I then pleaded with Yahweh. [24]"My Lord Yahweh," I said, "now that you have begun to reveal your greatness and your power to your servant with works and mighty deeds no God in heaven or on earth can rival, [25]may I not go across and see this fine country on the other side of the Jordan, that fine upland country and the Lebanon?" [26]But, because of you, Yahweh was angry with me and would not listen. "Enough!" he said, "Do not mention this subject again! [27]Climb to the top of Pisgah; turn your eyes to the west, the north, the south, the east. Look well, for across this Jordan you shall not go. [28]Give Joshua your instructions; encourage him, strengthen him; for he will be the one to cross at the head of this people; he will be the one to bring them into possession of the country which you will see."

[29]'We then stayed in the valley, close to Beth-Peor.'

The apostasy at Beth-Peor contrasted with true wisdom

4 'And now, Israel, listen to the laws and customs which I am teaching you today, so that, by observing them, you may survive to enter and take possession of the country which Yahweh, God of your ancestors, is giving you. [2]You must add nothing to what I command you, and take nothing from it, but keep the commandments of Yahweh your God just as I lay them down for you. [3]You can see for yourselves what Yahweh has done about the Baal of Peor; Yahweh your God has destroyed all those of you who followed the Baal of Peor; [4]but those of you who stayed faithful to Yahweh your God are all alive today. [5]Look: as Yahweh my God commanded me, I have taught you laws and customs, for you to observe in the country of which you are going to take possession. [6]Keep them, put them into practice, and other peoples will admire your wisdom and prudence. Once they know what all these laws are, they will exclaim, "No other people is as wise and prudent as this great nation!" [7]And indeed, what great nation has its gods as near as Yahweh our God is to us whenever we call to him? [8]And what great nation has laws and customs as upright as the entirety of this Law which I am laying down for you today?

The revelation at Horeb; its demands

[9]'But take care, as you value your lives! Do not forget the things which you yourselves have seen, or let them slip from your heart as long as you live; teach them, rather, to your children and to your children's children. [10]The day you stood at Horeb in the presence of Yahweh your God, Yahweh said to me, "Summon the people to me; I want them to hear me speaking, so that they will learn to fear me all the days they live on earth, and teach this to their children." [11]So you came and stood at the foot of the mountain, and the mountain flamed to the very sky, a sky darkened by cloud, murky and thunderous. [12]Yahweh then spoke to you from the heart

of the fire; you heard the sound of words but saw no shape; there was only a voice. [13]He revealed his covenant to you and commanded you to observe it, the Ten Words which he inscribed on two tablets of stone. [14]Yahweh then ordered me to teach you the laws and customs that you were to observe in the country into which you are about to cross, to take possession of it.

[15]'Hence, be very careful what you do. Since you saw no shape that day at Horeb when Yahweh spoke to you from the heart of the fire, [16]see that you do not corrupt yourselves by making an image in the shape of anything whatever: be it statue of man or of woman, [17]or of any animal on the earth, or of any bird that flies in the heavens, [18]or of any reptile that crawls on the ground, or of any fish in the waters under the earth. [19]When you raise your eyes to heaven, when you see the sun, the moon, the stars—the entire array of heaven—do not be tempted to worship them and serve them. Yahweh your God has allotted these to all the other peoples under heaven, [20]but Yahweh has chosen you, bringing you out of the iron-foundry, Egypt, to be his own people, his own people as you still are today.

Of punishment to come, and of conversion

[21]'Yahweh is angry with me because of you; he has sworn that I shall not cross the Jordan or enter the fine country which Yahweh your God is giving you as your heritage. [22]Yes, I am to die in this country; I shall not cross this Jordan; you will go over and take possession of that rich land. [23]Be careful not to forget the covenant which Yahweh your God has made with you, by sculpting an image or making a statue of anything, since Yahweh your God has forbidden this; [24]for Yahweh your God is a consuming fire, a jealous God.

[25]'When you have fathered children and grandchildren and have grown old in the country, when you have grown corrupt and made some image, doing what Yahweh regards as wrong and so provoking his anger—[26]today I call heaven and earth to witness against you—you will quickly vanish from the country which you are crossing the Jordan to possess. Your days will not be prolonged there, for you will be utterly destroyed. [27]Yahweh will scatter you among the peoples, and only a small number of you will remain among the nations where Yahweh will have driven you. [28]There you will serve gods made by human hand, of wood and of stone, that cannot see or hear, eat or smell.

[29]'If, however, from there you start searching once more for Yahweh your God, and if you search for him honestly and sincerely, you will find him. [30]You will suffer; everything I have said will befall you, but in the final days you will return to Yahweh your God and listen to his voice. [31]For Yahweh your God is a merciful God and will not desert or destroy you or forget the covenant which he made on oath with your ancestors.

The glory of having been chosen by God

[32]'Put this question, then, to the ages that are past, that have gone before you, from when God created the human race on earth: Was there ever a word so majestic, from one end of heaven to the other? Was anything like it ever heard? [33]Did ever a people hear the voice of the living God speaking from the heart of the fire, as you have heard it, and remain alive? [34]Has it ever been known before that any god took action himself to bring one nation out of another one, by ordeals, signs, wonders, war with mighty hand and outstretched arm, by fearsome terrors—all of which things Yahweh your God has done for you before your eyes in Egypt?

[35]'This he showed you, so that you might know that Yahweh is the true God and that there is no other. [36]To instruct you, he made you hear his voice from heaven, and on earth he let you see his great fire, and from the heart of the fire you heard his words. [37]Because he loved your ancestors and, after them, chose their descendants, he has brought you out of Egypt, displaying his presence and mighty power, [38]dispossessing for you nations who were larger and stronger than you, to make way for you and to give you their country as your heritage, as it still is today.

[39]'Hence, grasp this today and meditate on it carefully: Yahweh is the true God, in heaven above as on earth beneath, he and no other. [40]Keep his laws and commandments as I give them to you today, so that you and your children after you may prosper and live long in the country that Yahweh your God is giving you for ever.'

The cities of refuge

41 Moses then set aside three towns in the east,
beyond the Jordan, 42 to which any killer
might flee who had accidentally, without any
previous feud, killed his fellow; by taking
refuge in one of these towns he could save his
life. 43 These were, for the Reubenites, Bezer
in the desert on the tableland; for the Gadites,
Ramoth in Gilead; for the Manassehites,
Golan in Bashan.

B: THE SECOND DISCOURSE OF MOSES

Time and place

44 This is the Law which Moses presented to
the Israelites. 45 These are the stipulations,
the laws and the customs which Moses
gave the Israelites after they had left Egypt,
46 beyond the Jordan in the valley near Beth-
Peor, in the country of Sihon the Amorite
king who had lived at Heshbon. Moses and
the Israelites had defeated him when they left
Egypt, 47 and had taken possession of his
country, as well as that of Og king of
Bashan—two Amorite kings to the east
beyond the Jordan, 48 from Aroer on the edge
of the Arnon Valley, all the way to Mount
Sion (that is, Hermon) — 49 and of the whole
Arabah east of the Jordan as far as the Sea of
the Arabah, at the foot of the slopes of Pisgah.

The Ten Commandments

5 Moses called all Israel together and said
to them, 'Listen, Israel, to the laws and
customs that I proclaim to you today. Learn
them and take care to observe them.
2 'Yahweh our God made a covenant with
us at Horeb. 3 Yahweh made this covenant
not with our ancestors, but with us, with all
of us alive here today. 4 On the mountain,
from the heart of the fire, Yahweh spoke to
you face to face, 5 while I stood between you
and Yahweh to let you know what Yahweh
was saying, since you were afraid of the fire
and had not gone up the mountain. He said:
6 ' "I am Yahweh your God who brought
you out of Egypt, out of the place of slave-
labour.[a]
7 ' "You will have no gods other than me.
8 ' "You must not make yourselves any
image or any likeness of anything in heaven
above or on earth beneath or in the waters
under the earth; 9 you must not bow down to
these gods or serve them. For I, Yahweh your
God, am a jealous God and I punish the
parents' fault in the children, the grand-
children and the great-grandchildren, among
those who hate me; 10 but I show faithful love
to thousands, to those who love me and keep
my commandments.
11 ' "You must not misuse the name of
Yahweh your God, for Yahweh will not leave
unpunished anyone who uses his name for
what is false.
12 ' "Observe the Sabbath day and keep it
holy, as Yahweh your God has commanded
you. 13 Labour for six days, doing all your
work, 14 but the seventh day is a Sabbath for
Yahweh your God. You must not do any
work that day, neither you, nor your son, nor
your daughter, nor your servants—male or
female—nor your ox, nor your donkey, nor
any of your animals, nor the foreigner who
has made his home with you; 15 so that your
servants, male and female, may rest, as you
do. Remember that you were once a slave in
Egypt, and that Yahweh your God brought
you out of there with mighty hand and
outstretched arm; this is why Yahweh your
God has commanded you to keep the Sabbath
day.
16 ' "Honour your father and your mother,
as Yahweh your God has commanded you,
so that you may have long life and may
prosper in the country which Yahweh your
God is giving you.
17 ' "You must not kill.
18 ' "You must not commit adultery.
19 ' "You must not steal.
20 ' "You must not give false evidence
against your fellow.
21 ' "You must not set your heart on your
neighbour's spouse, you must not set your
heart on your neighbour's house, or field, or
servant—man or woman—or ox, or donkey
or any of your neighbour's possessions."
22 'These were the words Yahweh spoke to
you when you were all assembled on the
mountain. Thunderously, he spoke to you
from the heart of the fire, in cloud and thick
darkness. He added nothing, but wrote them
on two tablets of stone which he gave to me.

5a || Ex 20:1–17.

Moses the mediator

23'Now, having heard this voice coming out of the darkness, while the mountain was all on fire, you came to me, all of you, heads of tribes and elders, 24and said, "Yahweh our God has shown us his glory and his greatness, and we have heard his voice from the heart of the fire. Today we have seen that God can speak with a human being and that person still live. 25So why should we expose ourselves to death again? For this great fire might devour us if we go on listening to the voice of Yahweh our God, and then we should die. 26For what creature of flesh could possibly live after hearing, as we have heard, the voice of the living God speaking from the heart of the fire? 27Go nearer yourself and listen to everything that Yahweh our God may say, and then tell us everything that Yahweh our God has told you; we shall listen and put it into practice!"

28'Yahweh heard what you were saying to me, and he then said to me, "I have heard what these people are saying. Everything they have said is well said. 29If only their heart were always so, set on fearing me and on keeping my commandments, so that they and their children might prosper for ever! 30Go and tell them to go back to their tents. 31But you yourself stay here with me, and I shall tell you all the commandments, the laws and the customs which you are to teach them and which they are to observe in the country which I am giving them as their possession."

To love Yahweh is the essence of the Law

32'Keep them and put them into practice: such is Yahweh's command to you. Stray neither to right nor to left. 33Follow the whole way that Yahweh has marked for you, and you will survive to prosper and live long in the country which you are going to possess.'

6 'Such, then, are the commandments, the laws and the customs which Yahweh your God has instructed me to teach you, for you to observe in the country which you are on your way to possess. 2And hence, if, throughout your lives, you fear Yahweh your God and keep all his laws and commandments, which I am laying down for you today, you will live long, you and your child and your grandchild. 3Listen then, Israel, keep and observe what will make you prosperous and numerous, as Yahweh, God of your ancestors, has promised you, in giving you a country flowing with milk and honey.

4'Listen, Israel: Yahweh our God is the one, the only Yahweh. 5You must love Yahweh your God with all your heart, with all your soul, with all your strength. 6Let the words I enjoin on you today stay in your heart. 7You shall tell them to your children, and keep on telling them, when you are sitting at home, when you are out and about, when you are lying down and when you are standing up; 8you must fasten them on your hand as a sign and on your forehead as a headband; 9you must write them on the doorposts of your house and on your gates.

10'When Yahweh has brought you into the country which he swore to your ancestors Abraham, Isaac and Jacob that he would give you, with great and prosperous cities you have not built, 11with houses full of good things you have not provided, with wells you have not dug, with vineyards and olive trees you have not planted, and then, when you have eaten as much as you want, 12be careful you do not forget Yahweh who has brought you out of Egypt, out of the place of slave-labour. 13Yahweh your God is the one you must fear, him alone you must serve, his is the name by which you must swear.

An appeal for loyalty

14'Do not follow other gods, gods of the peoples round you, 15for Yahweh your God among you is a jealous God; the wrath of Yahweh your God would blaze out against you, and he would wipe you off the face of the earth. 16Do not put Yahweh your God to the test as you tested him at Massah. 17Keep the commandments of Yahweh your God, and his instructions and laws which he has laid down for you, 18and do what Yahweh regards as right and good, so that you may prosper and take possession of the fine country which Yahweh swore to give your ancestors, 19driving out your enemies before you; such was Yahweh's promise.

20'In times to come, when your child asks you, "What is the meaning of these instructions, laws and customs which Yahweh our God has laid down for you?" 21you are to tell your child, "Once we were Pharaoh's slaves in Egypt, and Yahweh brought us out of Egypt by his mighty hand. 22Before our eyes, Yahweh worked great and terrible signs and wonders against Egypt, against Pharaoh and

his entire household. [23]And he brought us
out of there, to lead us into the country which
he had sworn to our ancestors that he would
give us. [24]And Yahweh has commanded us
to observe all these laws and to fear Yahweh
our God, so as to be happy for ever and to
survive, as we do to this day. [25]For us, right
living will mean this: to keep and observe
all these commandments in obedience to
Yahweh our God, as he has commanded
us." '

Israel a people apart

7 'When Yahweh your God has brought you
into the country which you are going to
make your own, many nations will fall before
you: Hittites, Girgashites, Amorites,
Canaanites, Perizzites, Hivites and Jebu-
sites, seven nations greater and stronger than
yourselves. [2]Yahweh your God will put them
at your mercy and you will conquer them.
You must put them under the curse of
destruction. You must not make any treaty
with them or show them any pity. [3]You must
not intermarry with them; you must not give
a daughter of yours to a son of theirs, or take
a daughter of theirs for a son of yours, [4]for
your son would be seduced from following
me into serving other gods; the wrath of
Yahweh would blaze out against you and he
would instantly destroy you. [5]Instead, treat
them like this: tear down their altars, smash
their standing-stones, cut down their sacred
poles and burn their idols. [6]For you are a
people consecrated to Yahweh your God; of
all the peoples on earth, you have been chosen
by Yahweh your God to be his own people.

God's election and his favour

[7]'Yahweh set his heart on you and chose you
not because you were the most numerous of
all peoples—for indeed you were the smallest
of all—[8]but because he loved you and meant
to keep the oath which he swore to your
ancestors: that was why Yahweh brought you
out with his mighty hand and redeemed
you from the place of slave-labour, from the
power of Pharaoh king of Egypt. [9]From this
you can see that Yahweh your God is the true
God, the faithful God who, though he is true
to his covenant and his faithful love for a
thousand generations as regards those who
love him and keep his commandments,
[10]punishes in their own persons those that
hate him. He destroys anyone who hates him,
without delay; and it is in their own persons
that he punishes them. [11]Hence, you must
keep and observe the commandments, laws
and customs which I am laying down for you
today.

[12]'Listen to these ordinances, be true to
them and observe them, and in return
Yahweh your God will be true to the covenant
and love which he promised on oath to your
ancestors. [13]He will love you and bless you
and increase your numbers; he will bless the
fruit of your body and the produce of your
soil, your corn, your new wine, your oil, the
issue of your cattle, the young of your flock, in
the country which he swore to your ancestors
that he would give you. [14]You will be the
most blessed of all peoples. None of you,
man or woman, will be sterile, no male or
female of your beasts infertile. [15]Yahweh will
deflect all illness from you; he will not afflict
you with those evil plagues of Egypt which
you have known, but will inflict them on all
who hate you.

[16]'So, devour all the peoples whom
Yahweh your God puts at your mercy, show
them no pity, do not serve their gods: or you
will be ensnared.

The power of Yahweh

[17]'You may say in your heart, "These nations
outnumber me; how shall I be able to dispos-
sess them?" [18]Do not be afraid of them:
remember how Yahweh your God treated
Pharaoh and all Egypt, [19]the great ordeals
that you yourselves have seen, the signs and
wonders, the mighty hand and outstretched
arm with which Yahweh your God brought
you out. This is how Yahweh your God will
treat all the peoples whom you fear to face.
[20]And what is more, Yahweh your God will
send hornets to destroy those who are left
and who hide from you.

[21]'Do not be afraid of them, for Yahweh
your God is among you, a great and terrible
God. [22]Little by little, Yahweh your God will
clear away these nations before you; you
cannot destroy them all at once, or wild
animals will breed and be disastrous for you.
[23]But Yahweh your God will put them at
your mercy, and disaster after disaster will
overtake them until they are finally des-
troyed. [24]He will put their kings at your
mercy and you will blot out their names

under heaven; no one will be able to resist
you—until you have destroyed them all.
[25]'You must burn the statues of their gods,
not coveting the gold and silver that covers
them; take it and you will be caught in a
snare: it is detestable to Yahweh your God.
[26]You must not bring any detestable thing
into your house: or you, like it, will come
under the curse of destruction. You must
regard them as unclean and loathsome, for
they are under the curse of destruction.'

The ordeal in the desert

8 'You must keep and put into practice all
the commandments which I enjoin on you
today, so that you may survive and increase
in numbers and enter the country which
Yahweh promised on oath to your ancestors,
and make it your own. [2]Remember the long
road by which Yahweh your God led you for
forty years in the desert, to humble you,
to test you and know your inmost heart—
whether you would keep his commandments
or not. [3]He humbled you, he made you feel
hunger, he fed you with manna which neither
you nor your ancestors had ever known, to
make you understand that human beings live
not on bread alone but on every word that
comes from the mouth of Yahweh. [4]The
clothes on your back did not wear out and
your feet were not swollen, all those forty
years.
[5]'Learn from this that Yahweh your God
was training you as a man trains his child,
[6]and keep the commandments of Yahweh
your God, and so follow his ways and fear
him.

The Promised Land and its temptations

[7]'But Yahweh your God is bringing you into
a fine country, a land of streams and springs,
of waters that well up from the deep in valleys
and hills, [8]a land of wheat and barley, of
vines, of figs, of pomegranates, a land of
olives, of oil, of honey, [9]a land where you will
eat bread without stint, where you will want
nothing, a land where the stones are iron and
where the hills may be quarried for copper.
[10]You will eat and have all you want and
you will bless Yahweh your God in the fine
country which he has given you.
[11]'Be careful not to forget Yahweh your
God, by neglecting his commandments,
customs and laws which I am laying down
for you today. [12]When you have eaten all you
want, when you have built fine houses to live
in, [13]when you have seen your flocks and
herds increase, your silver and gold abound
and all your possessions grow great, [14]do not
become proud of heart. Do not then forget
Yahweh your God who brought you out of
Egypt, out of the place of slave-labour, [15]who
guided you through this vast and dreadful
desert, a land of fiery snakes, scorpions,
thirst; [16]who in this waterless place brought
you water out of the flinty rock; who in this
desert fed you with manna unknown to your
ancestors, to humble you and test you and so
make your future the happier.
[17]'Beware of thinking to yourself, "My
own strength and the might of my own hand
have given me the power to act like this."
[18]Remember Yahweh your God; he was the
one who gave you the strength to act effec-
tively like this, thus keeping then, as today,
the covenant which he swore to your ances-
tors. [19]Be sure: if you forget Yahweh your
God, if you follow other gods, if you serve
them and bow down to them—I testify to you
today—you will perish. [20]Like the nations
Yahweh is to destroy before you, so you
yourselves will perish, for not having listened
to the voice of Yahweh your God.'

Yahweh, not Israel, wins the victory

9 'Listen, Israel; today you are about to
cross the Jordan, to go and dispossess
nations greater and stronger than yourself,
and cities immense, with walls reaching to
the sky. [2]A people great and tall, these
Anakim, as you know; you have heard the
saying: Who can stand up to the sons of
Anak? [3]Know then today that Yahweh your
God himself will go ahead of you, destroying
them like a devouring fire, and that he himself
will subdue them before you so that you can
dispossess and quickly make an end of them,
as Yahweh has already said. [4]Do not think to
yourself, once Yahweh your God has driven
them before you, "Yahweh has brought me
into possession of this country because I
am upright," when Yahweh is dispossessing
these nations for you, because they do wrong.
[5]You are not going into their country to take
possession because of any right behaviour or
uprightness on your part; rather, it is because
of their wickedness that Yahweh is dispos-
sessing these nations for you, and also to keep
the pact which he swore to your ancestors,

Abraham, Isaac and Jacob. 6Be clear about this: Yahweh is not giving you possession of this fine country because of any right conduct on your part, for you are an obstinate people.

Israel's conduct at Horeb; Moses intercedes[a]

7'Remember; never forget how you provoked Yahweh your God in the desert. From the very day that you left Egypt until you arrived here, you have been rebels against Yahweh. 8At Horeb, you provoked Yahweh, and Yahweh was so angry with you that he was ready to destroy you. 9I had gone up the mountain to receive the stone tablets, the tablets of the covenant that Yahweh was making with you. I stayed forty days and forty nights on the mountain, with nothing to eat or drink. 10Yahweh gave me the two stone tablets inscribed by the finger of God, exactly corresponding to what Yahweh had said to you on the mountain, from the heart of the fire, on the day of the Assembly. 11After forty days and forty nights, having given me the two stone tablets, the tablets of the covenant, 12Yahweh said to me, "Get up, go down quickly, for your people, whom you have brought out of Egypt, are corrupting one another. They have been quick to leave the way I marked out for them; they have cast themselves a metal idol." 13Yahweh then said to me, "I have seen this people, and what an obstinate people they are! 14Leave me, I am going to destroy them and wipe out their name under heaven; and I shall make you into a mightier and more numerous nation than they are!"

15'I went back down the mountain, which was blazing with fire, and in my hands were the two tablets of the covenant. 16When I looked, I saw that you had been sinning against Yahweh your God. You had cast yourselves a metal calf; you had been quick to leave the way marked out for you by Yahweh. 17I seized the two tablets and with my two hands threw them down and broke them before your eyes. 18Then I fell prostrate before Yahweh; as before, I spent forty days and forty nights with nothing to eat or drink, on account of all the sins which you had committed, by doing what was displeasing to Yahweh and thus arousing his anger. 19For I was afraid of this anger, of the fury which so roused Yahweh against you that he was ready to destroy you. And, once again, Yahweh heard my prayer. 20Yahweh was enraged with Aaron and was ready to destroy him too; I also pleaded for Aaron on that occasion. 21That work of sin, the calf you had made, I took and burned and broke to pieces; having ground it to the finest dust, I threw its dust into the stream that comes down from the mountain.

Israel sins again. A prayer of Moses

22'At Taberah too and at Massah and Kibroth-ha-Taavah, you provoked Yahweh. 23And when Yahweh, meaning you to leave Kadesh-Barnea, said, "Go up and take possession of the country which I have given you," you rebelled against the command of Yahweh your God and would not believe him or listen to his voice. 24You have been rebels against Yahweh from the day he first knew you.

25'So I fell prostrate before Yahweh and lay there those forty days and forty nights, Yahweh having said that he was going to destroy you. 26And I pleaded with Yahweh. "My Lord Yahweh," I said, "do not destroy your people, your heritage whom in your greatness you have redeemed, whom you have brought out of Egypt with your mighty hand. 27Remember your servants, Abraham, Isaac, and Jacob; take no notice of this people's stubbornness, their wickedness, and their sin, 28so that, in the country from which you have brought us, it may not be said, 'Yahweh was not able to bring them to the country which he had promised them. He hated them; that was why he brought them out—to slaughter them in the desert.' 29But these are your people, your heritage, whom you yourself have brought out by your great power and your outstretched arm." '

The ark of the covenant; the choice of Levi

10 1'Yahweh then said to me, "Cut two stone tablets like the first ones, and come up to me on the mountain. Make an ark of wood; 2on the tablets I shall inscribe the words that were on the first tablets, which you broke; put them in the ark." 3So I made an ark of acacia wood, cut two stone tablets

9a || Ex 32.

like the first and went up the mountain with
the two tablets in my hand. 4And he inscribed
the tablets, as he had inscribed them before,
with the Ten Words which Yahweh had said
to you on the mountain, from the heart of the
fire, on the day of the Assembly. Yahweh
then gave them to me. 5I turned and came
down from the mountain and put the tablets
in the ark I had made, and there they stayed,
as Yahweh had commanded me.
6'The Israelites left the wells of the Bene-
Jaakan for Moserah, where Aaron died; he
was buried there, and his son Eleazar
succeeded him in the priesthood. 7From
there, they set out for Gudgodah, and from
Gudgodah for Jotbathah, an area rich in
streams. 8Yahweh then set apart the tribe of
Levi to carry the ark of Yahweh's covenant,
to stand in the presence of Yahweh, to serve
him and to bless in his name, as they still do
today. 9This is why Levi has no share or
heritage with his brothers: Yahweh is his
heritage, as Yahweh your God then told him.
10'And, as before, I stayed on the mountain
for forty days and forty nights. And again
Yahweh heard my prayer and agreed not to
destroy you. 11And Yahweh said to me, "Be
on your way at the head of this people, so
that they can go and take possession of the
country which I swore to their ancestors that
I would give them."

Circumcision of the heart

12'And now, Israel, what does Yahweh your
God ask of you? Only this: to fear Yahweh
your God, to follow all his ways, to love him,
to serve Yahweh your God with all your heart
and all your soul, 13to keep the command-
ments and laws of Yahweh, which I am laying
down for you today for your own good.
14'Look, to Yahweh your God belong
heaven and the heaven of heavens, the earth
and everything on it; 15yet it was on your
ancestors, for love of them, that Yahweh set
his heart to love them, and he chose their
descendants after them, you yourselves, out
of all nations, up to the present day.
16Circumcise your heart then and be obstinate
no longer; 17for Yahweh your God is God
of gods and Lord of lords, the great God,
triumphant and terrible, free of favouritism,
never to be bribed. 18He it is who sees justice
done for the orphan and the widow, who
loves the stranger and gives him food and
clothing. 19(Love the stranger then, for you
were once strangers in Egypt.) 20Yahweh
your God is the one whom you must fear and
serve; to him you must hold firm; in his name
take your oaths. 21Him you must praise, he
is your God: for you he has done these great
and terrible things which you have seen for
yourselves; 22and, although your ancestors
numbered only seventy persons when they
went down to Egypt, Yahweh your God has
now made you as many as the stars of heaven.'

Israel's past experiences

11 'You must love Yahweh your God and
always keep his observances, his laws,
his customs, his commandments. 2You are
the ones who have had the experience, not
your children. They have not had the experi-
ence, they have not witnessed the lessons of
Yahweh your God, his greatness, his mighty
hand and his outstretched arm, 3the signs
and the deeds which he performed in the
heart of Egypt, against Pharaoh king of Egypt
and his entire country, 4what he did to the
armies of Egypt, to their horses and their
chariots, by overwhelming them with the
waters of the Sea of Reeds when they were
pursuing you, and leaving no trace of them
to this day; 5what he did for you in the desert,
until you arrived here; 6what he did to Dathan
and Abiram the sons of Eliab the Reubenite,
when, with all Israel standing round, the
earth opened its mouth and swallowed them,
with their families, their tents and all their
supporters. 7All these great deeds of Yahweh
you have seen with your own eyes.

Promises and warnings

8'You must keep all the commandments
which I enjoin on you today, so that you may
have the strength to conquer the country
into which you are about to cross, to take
possession of it, 9and so that you may live
long in the country which Yahweh promised
on oath to bestow on your ancestors and their
descendants, a country flowing with milk and
honey.
10'For the country which you are about to
enter and make your own is not like the
country of Egypt from which you have come,
where, having done your sowing, you had
to water the seed by foot, as though in a
vegetable garden. 11No, the country which
you are about to enter and make your own,
is a country of hills and valleys watered by

the rain of heaven. [12]Yahweh your God looks after this country, the eyes of Yahweh your God are always on it, from the beginning of the year to the end. [13]Depend on it: if you faithfully obey the commandments I enjoin on you today, loving Yahweh your God and serving him with all your heart and all your soul, [14]I shall give your country rain at the right time, rain in autumn, rain in spring, so that you can harvest your wheat, your new wine and your oil. [15]I shall provide grass in the fields for your cattle, and you will eat to your heart's content. [16]Beware of letting your heart be seduced: if you go astray, serve other gods and bow down to them, [17]Yahweh's anger will be kindled against you, he will shut the heavens, there will be no more rain, the soil will not yield its produce and, in the fine country given you by Yahweh, you will quickly perish.

Conclusion

[18]'Let these words of mine remain in your heart and in your soul; fasten them on your hand as a sign and on your forehead as a headband. [19]Teach them to your children, and keep on telling them, when you are sitting at home, when you are out and about, when you are lying down and when you are standing up. [20]Write them on the doorposts of your house and on your gates, [21]so that you and your children may live long in the country which Yahweh swore to your ancestors that he would give them for as long as there is a sky above the earth.

[22]'For if you faithfully keep and observe all these commandments that I enjoin on you today, loving Yahweh your God, following all his ways and holding fast to him, [23]Yahweh will dispossess all these nations before you, and you will dispossess nations greater and more powerful than yourselves. [24]Wherever the sole of your foot treads will be yours; your territory will run from the desert all the way to the Lebanon; and from the River, from the River Euphrates, as far as the Western Sea, will be your territory. [25]No one will be able to resist you; Yahweh your God will make you feared and dreaded throughout the territory you tread, as he has promised you.

[26]'Today, look, I am offering you a blessing and a curse: [27]a blessing, if you obey the commandments of Yahweh your God which I enjoin on you today; [28]a curse, if you disobey the commandments of Yahweh your God and leave the way which today I have marked out for you, by following other gods hitherto unknown to you. [29]And when Yahweh your God has brought you into the country which you are about to enter and make your own, you must set the blessing on Mount Gerizim and the curse on Mount Ebal. [30](These mountains, as everyone knows, are on the other side of the Jordan on the westward road, in the territory of the Canaanites who live in the Arabah, opposite Gilgal, near the Oak of Moreh.) [31]For you are about to cross the Jordan, to enter and take possession of the country given you by Yahweh your God. You will possess it, you will live in it, [32]and you must keep and observe all the laws and customs promulgated by me to you today.'

II: THE DEUTERONOMIC CODE

12 'Now, these are the laws and customs which you must keep in the country which Yahweh, God of your ancestors, is giving you as yours, and which you must observe every day that you live in that country.

The place of worship

[2]'You must completely destroy all the places where the nations you dispossess have served their gods, on high mountains, on hills, under any spreading tree; [3]you must tear down their altars, smash their sacred stones, burn their sacred poles, hack to bits the statues of their gods and obliterate their name from that place.

[4]'Not so must you behave towards Yahweh your God. [5]You must seek Yahweh your God in the place which he will choose from all your tribes, there to set his name and give it a home: that is where you must go. [6]That is where you must bring your burnt offerings and your sacrifices, your tithes and offerings

held high, your votive offerings and your
voluntary offerings, and the first-born of
your herd and flock; 7and that is where you
must eat in the presence of Yahweh your
God, rejoicing over your labours, you and
your households, because Yahweh your God
has blessed you.
8'You must not behave as we are behaving
here today, each of you doing what he himself
sees fit, 9since you have not yet come to the
resting place and the heritage that Yahweh
your God is going to give you. 10You are
about to cross the Jordan and live in the
country given you by Yahweh your God as
your heritage; he will grant you peace from
all the enemies surrounding you, and you
will live in safety. 11To the place chosen by
Yahweh your God as a home for his name, to
that place you must bring all the things
that I am laying down for you: your burnt
offerings and your sacrifices, your tithes and
offerings held high, and all the best of your
possessions dedicated by you to Yahweh.
12That is where you will rejoice in the pres-
ence of Yahweh your God, you and your
sons and daughters, your serving men and
women, and the Levite living in your
community since he has no share or heritage
of his own among you.

Sacrificial regulations

13'Take care you do not offer your burnt
offerings in all the sacred places you see;
14only in the place that Yahweh chooses in
one of your tribes may you offer your burnt
offerings and do all the things which I have
commanded you.
15'This notwithstanding, and whenever
you wish, you may slaughter and eat meat
wherever you live—as much as the blessing
of Yahweh affords you. Clean or unclean may
eat it, as though it were gazelle or deer. 16You
will not, however, eat the blood, but will
pour that like water on the ground.
17'You must not eat the tithe of your wheat,
of your new wine or of your oil, or the first-
born of your herd or flock, or any of your
votive offerings or voluntary offerings, or
your offerings held high to Yahweh, at home.
18You must eat these in the presence of
Yahweh your God in the place Yahweh your
God chooses and there alone, you, your son
and your daughter, your serving man and
serving woman, and the Levite living in your
community, expressing your joy in all your
labours in the presence of Yahweh your God.
19As long as you live on your soil, be careful
not to neglect the Levite.
20'When Yahweh your God enlarges your
territory as he has promised you, and you
say, "I should like to eat meat," if you want
to eat meat you may eat as much as you like.
21If the place in which Yahweh your God
chooses to set his name is too far away, you
may slaughter any of your herd or flock that
Yahweh has given you, as I have prescribed
for you; you may eat as much of it as you
please at home. 22But you must eat it as you
would gazelle or deer; clean and unclean may
eat it together. 23Take care, however, not to
eat the blood, since blood is life, and you
must not eat the life with the meat.
24You must not eat it, but must pour it like
water on the ground. 25You must not eat it—
so that you, and your children after you, may
prosper, doing what is right in Yahweh's
eyes. 26But the holy things of yours and the
things which you have dedicated, you must
go and take to the place chosen by Yahweh.
27The burnt offerings of meat and blood must
be presented on the altar of Yahweh your
God; whereas, in your sacrifices, the blood
must be poured on the altar of Yahweh
your God; the meat you yourselves may eat.
28Faithfully keep and obey all these orders
which I am giving you, so that you and your
children after you may prosper for ever,
doing what is good and right in the eyes of
Yahweh your God.

Against Canaanite cults

29'When Yahweh your God has annihilated
the nations confronting you, whom you are
going to dispossess, and when you have
dispossessed them and made your home in
their country, 30beware of being entrapped
into copying them, after they have been
destroyed to make way for you, and do not
enquire about their gods, saying, "How did
these nations worship their gods? I am going
to do the same too." 31This is not the way to
treat Yahweh your God. For in honour of
their gods they have done everything detest-
able that Yahweh hates; yes, in honour of
their gods, they even burn their own sons
and daughters as sacrifices!'

13 'Whatever I am now commanding you,
you must keep and observe, adding
nothing to it, taking nothing away.

Against the enticements of idolatry

2'If a prophet or a dreamer of dreams arises
among you, offering you some sign or
wonder, 3and the sign or wonder comes
about; and if he then says to you, "Let us
follow other gods (hitherto unknown to you)
and serve them," 4you must not listen to that
prophet's words or to that dreamer's dreams.
Yahweh your God is testing you to know if
you love Yahweh your God with all your
heart and all your soul. 5Yahweh your God
is the one whom you must follow, him you
must fear, his commandments you must
keep, his voice you must obey, him you must
serve, to him you must hold fast. 6That
prophet or that dreamer of dreams must be
put to death, since he has preached apostasy
from Yahweh your God who brought you out
of Egypt and redeemed you from the place
of slave-labour; and he would have diverted
you from the way in which Yahweh your God
has commanded you to walk. You must
banish this evil from among you.
7'If your brother, the son of your father or
of your mother, or your son or daughter, or
the spouse whom you embrace, or your most
intimate friend, tries secretly to seduce you,
saying, "Let us go and serve other gods,"
unknown to you or your ancestors before
you, 8gods of the peoples surrounding you,
whether near you or far away, anywhere
throughout the world, 9you must not
consent, you must not listen to him; you
must show him no pity, you must not spare
him or conceal his guilt. 10No, you must kill
him, your hand must strike the first blow in
putting him to death and the hands of the
rest of the people following. 11You must stone
him to death, since he has tried to divert you
from Yahweh your God who brought you out
of Egypt, from the place of slave-labour. 12All
Israel, hearing of this, will be afraid, and
none of you will do such a wicked thing again.
13'If you hear that in one of the towns
which Yahweh your God has given you for a
home, 14there are men, scoundrels from your
own stock, who have led their fellow-citizens
astray, saying, "Let us go and serve other
gods," hitherto unknown to you, 15it is your
duty to look into the matter, examine it, and
enquire most carefully. If it is proved and
confirmed that such a hateful thing has taken
place among you, 16you must put the inhabi-
tants of that town to the sword; you must lay
it under the curse of destruction—the town
and everything in it. 17You must pile up all
its loot in the public square and burn the
town and all its loot, offering it all to Yahweh
your God. It is to be a ruin for all time, and
never rebuilt. 18From what is thus put under
the curse of destruction you must keep
nothing back, so that Yahweh may turn from
the ferocity of his anger and show you mercy,
and have pity on you and increase your
numbers, as he swore he would to your
ancestors, 19on condition that you listen to
the voice of Yahweh your God by keeping all
his commandments which I am enjoining on
you today, and by doing what is right in the
eyes of Yahweh your God.'

Against an idolatrous practice

14 'You are children of Yahweh your God.
You must not gash yourselves or shave
your foreheads for the dead. 2For you are a
people consecrated to Yahweh your God, and
Yahweh has chosen you to be his own people
from all the peoples on the earth.

Clean and unclean animals[a]

3'You must not eat anything disgusting.
4These are the animals you may eat: ox,
sheep, goat, 5deer, gazelle, roebuck, ibex,
antelope, oryx, mountain sheep. 6You may
eat any animal that has a divided and cloven
hoof and that is a ruminant. 7Of those,
however, that are ruminants and of those that
have a divided and cloven hoof you may not
eat the following: the camel, the hare and the
coney, which are ruminants but have no
cloven hoof; you must class them as unclean.
8So also the pig, which though it has a cloven
hoof is not a ruminant; you must class it as
unclean. You must neither eat the meat of
such animals nor touch their dead bodies.
9'Of whatever lives in water you may eat
the following: you may eat anything that
has fins and scales. 10But you must not eat
anything without fins and scales: you must
class it as unclean.
11'You may eat all clean birds, 12but the
following birds you must not eat: the tawny
vulture, the griffon, the osprey, 13the kite
and the several kinds of buzzard, 14all kinds
of raven, 15the ostrich, the screech owl, the

14a || *Lv 11:1.*

seagull, the several kinds of hawk, 16owl, barn owl, ibis, 17pelican, white vulture, cormorant, 18stork, the several kinds of heron, hoopoe and bat. 19You are to class all winged insects as unclean and must not eat them. 20You may eat any clean fowl.

21'You must not eat any animal that has died a natural death. You may give it to a resident foreigner to eat, or sell it to a foreigner. For you are a people consecrated to Yahweh your God.

'You must not boil a kid in its mother's milk.

The annual tithe

22'Every year, you must take a tithe of what your fields produce from what you have sown 23and, in the presence of Yahweh your God, in the place where he chooses to give his name a home, you must eat the tithe of your wheat, of your new wine and of your oil, and the first-born of your herd and flock; and by so doing, you will learn always to fear Yahweh your God.

24'If the road is too long for you, if you cannot bring your tithe because the place in which Yahweh chooses to make a home for his name is too far away, when Yahweh your God has blessed you, 25you must convert it into money and, with the money clasped in your hand, you must go to the place chosen by Yahweh your God; 26there you may spend the money on whatever you like, oxen, sheep, wine, fermented liquor, anything you please. There you must eat in the presence of Yahweh your God and rejoice, you and your household. 27Do not neglect the Levite living in your community, since he has no share or heritage of his own among you.

The third-year tithe

28'At the end of every three years, you must take all the tithes of your harvests for that year and collect them in your community. 29Then the Levite—since he has no share or heritage of his own among you—the foreigner, the orphan and the widow living in your community, will come and eat all they want. And so Yahweh your God will bless you in all the labours that you undertake.'

The sabbatical year

15 'At the end of every seven years, you must grant remission. 2The nature of the remission is as follows: any creditor holding a personal pledge obtained from his fellow must release him from it; he must not exploit his fellow or his brother once the latter has appealed to Yahweh for remission. 3A foreigner you may exploit, but you must remit whatever claim you have on your brother. 4There must, then, be no poor among you. For Yahweh will grant you his blessing in the country which Yahweh your God is giving you to possess as your heritage, 5only if you pay careful attention to the voice of Yahweh your God, by keeping and practising all these commandments which I am enjoining on you today. 6If Yahweh your God blesses you as he has promised, you will be creditors to many nations but debtors to none; you will rule over many nations, and be ruled by none.

7'Is there anyone poor among you, one of your brothers, in any town of yours in the country which Yahweh your God is giving you? Do not harden your heart or close your hand against that poor brother of yours, 8but be open handed with him and lend him enough for his needs. 9Do not allow this mean thought in your heart, "The seventh year, the year of remission, is near," and scowl at your poor brother and give him nothing; he could appeal against you to Yahweh, and you would incur guilt! 10When you give to him, you must give with an open heart; for this, Yahweh your God will bless you in all your actions and in all your undertakings. 11Of course, there will never cease to be poor people in the country, and that is why I am giving you this command: Always be open handed with your brother, and with anyone in your country who is in need and poor.

Slaves

12'If your fellow Hebrew, man or woman, sells himself to you, he can serve you for six years. In the seventh year you must set him free, 13and in setting him free you must not let him go empty handed. 14By way of present, you will load his shoulders with things from your flock, from your threshing-floor and from your winepress; as Yahweh your God has blessed you, so you must give to him. 15Remember that you were once a slave in Egypt and that Yahweh your God redeemed you; that is why I am giving you this order today.

16'But if he says to you, "I do not want to
leave you," because he loves you and your
household and is happy with you, 17you must
take an awl and drive it through his ear into
the door and he will be your servant for ever.
You must do the same to a female slave.
18'Do not think it hard on you to have to
give him his freedom; he is worth twice what
a paid servant would cost you, and has served
you for six years. And Yahweh your God will
bless you in everything you do.

The first-born

19'You must consecrate every first-born male
from your herd and flock to Yahweh your
God. You must not put the first-born of
your herd to work, or shear the first-born of
your flock. 20You must eat it, you and your
household, each year, in the presence of
Yahweh your God, in the place which
Yahweh chooses. 21If it has any defect, if it
is lame or blind—any serious defect—you
must not sacrifice it to Yahweh your God.
22You will eat it at home, unclean and clean
together, as you would gazelle or deer; 23only,
you will not eat its blood, but pour that like
water on the ground.'

The feasts: Passover and Unleavened Bread

16 'Observe the month of Abib and
celebrate the Passover for Yahweh your
God, because it was in the month of Abib
that Yahweh your God brought you out
of Egypt by night. 2You must sacrifice a
Passover from your flock or herd for Yahweh
your God in the place where Yahweh chooses
to give his name a home. 3You must not eat
leavened bread with this; for seven days you
must eat it with unleavened bread—the bread
of affliction—since you left Egypt in great
haste; this is so that, as long as you live, you
will remember the day you came out of
Egypt. 4For seven days no leaven must be
found in any house throughout your terri-
tory, nor must any of the meat that you
sacrifice in the evening of the first day be kept
overnight until the next day. 5You must
sacrifice the Passover not in any of the towns
given you by Yahweh your God, 6but in the
place where Yahweh your God chooses to
give his name a home; there you must sacrifice
the Passover, in the evening at sunset, at the
hour when you came out of Egypt. 7You will
cook it and eat it in the place chosen by
Yahweh your God, and in the morning you
must return and go to your tents. 8For six
days you will eat unleavened bread; on the
seventh day there will be an assembly for
Yahweh your God; and you must do no work.

Other feasts

9'You must count seven weeks, counting
these seven weeks from the time you begin
to put your sickle into the standing corn.
10You will then celebrate the feast of Weeks
for Yahweh your God with the gift of a
voluntary offering proportionate to the
degree in which Yahweh your God has
blessed you. 11You must rejoice in the pres-
ence of Yahweh your God, in the place where
Yahweh your God chooses to give his name
a home, you, your son and your daughter,
your serving men and women, the Levite
living in your community, the foreigner, the
orphan and the widow living among you.
12Remember that you were once a slave in
Egypt, and carefully observe these laws.
13'You must celebrate the feast of Shelters
for seven days, at the time when you gather
in the produce of your threshing-floor and
winepress. 14You must rejoice at your feast,
you, your son and your daughter, your
serving men and women, the Levite, the
foreigner, the orphan and the widow living
in your community. 15For seven days, you
must celebrate the feast for Yahweh your
God in the place chosen by Yahweh; for
Yahweh your God will bless you in all your
produce and in all your undertakings, so that
you will have good reason to rejoice.
16'Three times a year all your menfolk must
appear before Yahweh your God in the place
chosen by him: at the feast of Unleavened
Bread, at the feast of Weeks, at the feast of
Shelters. No one must appear empty-handed
before Yahweh, 17but each must give what
he can, in proportion to the blessing which
Yahweh your God has bestowed on you.

Judges

18'You must appoint judges and scribes in
each of the towns that Yahweh your God is
giving you, for all your tribes; these are to
mete out proper justice to the people. 19You
must not pervert the law; you must be impar-
tial; you will take no bribes, for a bribe blinds
the eyes of the wise and ruins the cause of the

upright. [20]Strict justice must be your ideal,
so that you may live long in possession of the
country given you by Yahweh your God.

Abuses in worship

[21]'You must not plant a sacred pole of any
wood whatsoever beside the altar which you
erect for Yahweh your God; [22]nor will
you set up a standing-stone, a thing Yahweh
your God would abhor.'

17 'To Yahweh your God you must sacri-
fice nothing from herd or flock that
has any blemish or defect whatsoever, for
Yahweh your God holds this detestable.
[2]'If there is anyone, man or woman, among
you in any of the towns given you by Yahweh
your God, who does what is wrong in the
eyes of Yahweh your God by violating his
covenant, [3]who goes and serves other gods
and worships them, or the sun or the moon
or any of heaven's array—a thing I have
forbidden—[4]and this person is denounced to
you: if after careful enquiry it is found true
and confirmed that this hateful thing has
been done in Israel, [5]you must take the man
or woman guilty of this evil deed outside your
city gates, and there you must stone that man
or woman to death. [6]A death sentence may
be passed only on the word of two witnesses
or three; and no one must be put to death
on the word of one witness alone. [7]The
witnesses' hands must strike the first blow in
putting the condemned to death, the rest of
the people following. You must banish this
evil from among you.

Levitical judges

[8]'If a case comes before you which is too
difficult for you, a case of murder, conflicting
claims, damage to property—any kind of
dispute—in your towns, you must make your
way to the place chosen by Yahweh your
God, [9]and approach the levitical priests and
the judge then in office. They will hold an
enquiry and let you know their sentence.
[10]You must abide by the verdict which they
give you in this place chosen by Yahweh, and
you will take care to carry out all their
instructions. [11]You will abide by the decision
which they give you and by the sentence
which they pronounce, not deviating to right
or to left from the verdict which they have
given you. [12]If anyone presumes to disobey
either the priest who is there in the service of
Yahweh your God, or the judge, that person
must die. You must banish this evil from
Israel. [13]And when the people hear of this
they will all be afraid and not act presumptu-
ously any more.

Kings

[14]'If, having reached the country given by
Yahweh your God and having taken
possession of it and, while living there, you
think, "I should like to appoint a king to rule
me—like all the surrounding nations," [15]the
king whom you appoint to rule you must be
chosen by Yahweh your God; the appoint-
ment of a king must be made from your own
brothers; on no account must you appoint as
king some foreigner who is not a brother of
yours.
[16]'He must not, however, acquire more
and more horses, or send the people back to
Egypt with a view to increasing his cavalry,
since Yahweh has told you, "You must never
go back that way again." [17]Nor must he keep
on acquiring more and more wives, for that
could lead his heart astray. Nor must he
acquire vast quantities of silver and gold.
[18]Once seated on his royal throne, and for his
own use, he must write a copy of this Law on
a scroll, at the dictation of the levitical priests.
[19]It must never leave him, and he must read
it every day of his life and learn to fear
Yahweh his God by keeping all the words of
this Law and observing these rules, [20]so that
he will not think himself superior to his
brothers, and not deviate from these
commandments either to right or to left. So
doing, long will he occupy his throne, he and
his sons, in Israel.'

The levitical priesthood

18 'The levitical priests, the whole tribe
of Levi will be without share or heritage
of their own in Israel; they will live on the
foods offered to Yahweh and on his heritage.
[2]Levi will have no heritage of his own among
his brothers; Yahweh will be his heritage, as
he has promised him.
[3]'This is what is due to the priests from the
people, from those who offer an ox or a sheep
in sacrifice: the priest must be given the
shoulder, the cheeks and the stomach. [4]You
must give him the first-fruits of your wheat,
of your new wine and of your oil, as well as
the first-fruits of your sheep-shearing. [5]For

Yahweh your God has chosen him from all your tribes to stand before Yahweh your God, to do the duties of the sacred ministry, and to bless in Yahweh's name—him and his sons for all time.

6'If a Levite living in one of your towns anywhere in Israel decides to move to the place chosen by Yahweh, 7he shall minister there in the name of Yahweh his God like all his fellow Levites who stand ministering there in the presence of Yahweh, 8eating equal shares with them—what he has from the sale of his patrimony notwithstanding.

Prophets

9'When you have entered the country given you by Yahweh your God, you must not learn to imitate the detestable practices of the nations there already. 10There must never be anyone among you who makes his son or daughter pass through the fire of sacrifice, who practises divination, who is soothsayer, augur or sorcerer, 11weaver of spells, consulter of ghosts or mediums, or necromancer. 12For anyone who does these things is detestable to Yahweh your God; it is because of these detestable practices that Yahweh your God is driving out these nations before you.

13'You must be faultless in your relationship with Yahweh your God. 14For these nations whom you are going to dispossess have listened to soothsayers and mediums, but Yahweh your God does not permit you to do this. From among yourselves, from among your own brothers, 15Yahweh your God will raise up a prophet like me; you will listen to him. 16This is exactly what you asked Yahweh your God to do—at Horeb, on the day of the Assembly, when you said, "Never let me hear the voice of Yahweh my God or see this great fire again, or I shall die." 17Then Yahweh said to me, 18"What they have said is well said. From their own brothers I shall raise up a prophet like yourself; 19I shall put my words into his mouth and he will tell them everything I command him. Anyone who refuses to listen to my words, spoken by him in my name, will have to render an account to me. 20But the prophet who presumes to say something in my name which I have not commanded him to say, or who speaks in the name of other gods, that prophet must die."

21'You may be privately wondering, "How are we to tell that a prophecy does not come from Yahweh?" 22When a prophet speaks in the name of Yahweh and the thing does not happen and the word is not fulfilled, then it has not been said by Yahweh. The prophet has spoken presumptuously. You have nothing to fear from him.'

Homicide and cities of refuge

19 'When Yahweh your God has annihilated the nations whose country Yahweh your God is going to give you, and you have dispossessed them and are living in their towns and in their houses, 2you must set aside three towns, centrally placed in the country which Yahweh your God is giving you for your own. 3You will keep the approaches to them in good order, dividing the area of the country which Yahweh your God is giving you as your heritage, into three parts, so that any killer can flee to these towns. 4Here is an example of how someone may save his life by fleeing to them.

'If anyone has struck his fellow accidentally, without any previous feud with him 5(for example, he goes with his fellow into the forest to cut wood; his arm swings the axe to fell a tree; the head slips off the handle and strikes his companion dead), that man may take refuge in one of these towns and save his life. 6It must not be allowed that the avenger of blood, in the heat of his anger, should pursue the killer and that the length of the road should help him to overtake and wound him fatally; for the man has not deserved to die, having had no previous feud with his victim.

7'Hence I am giving you this order: You must set aside three towns, 8and if Yahweh your God enlarges your territory, as he swore to your ancestors that he would, and gives you the whole country which he promised to give to your ancestors—9provided that you keep and observe all the commandments which I am enjoining on you today, loving Yahweh your God and always following his ways—then, to those three towns you will add three more. 10In this way, innocent blood will not be shed in the country which Yahweh your God is going to give you as your heritage; otherwise you would incur blood-guilt.

11'But if it happens that a man has a feud with his fellow and lies in wait for him and attacks him and fatally wounds him and he dies, and the man takes refuge in one of these towns, 12the elders of his own town must send

there and have him taken and handed over
to the avenger of blood, to be put to death.
[13]You must show him no pity. You must
banish the shedding of innocent blood from
Israel, and then you will prosper.

Boundaries

[14]'You must not displace your neighbour's
boundary mark, positioned by men of old in
the heritage soon to be yours, in the country
which Yahweh your God is about to give you.

Witnesses

[15]'A single witness will not suffice to convict
anyone of a crime or offence of any kind;
whatever the misdemeanour, the evidence of
two witnesses or three is required to sustain
the charge.
[16]'If someone gives false evidence against
anyone, laying a charge of apostasy, [17]both
parties to this dispute before Yahweh must
appear before the priests and judges then
in office. [18]The judges will make a careful
enquiry, and if it turns out that the witness
is a liar and has made a false accusation
against his brother, [19]you must treat the
witness as he would have treated his brother.
You must banish this evil from among you.
[20]The rest, hearing of this, will be afraid and
never again do such an evil thing among you.
[21]You must show no pity.

Limits of retaliation

'Life for life, eye for eye, tooth for tooth,
hand for hand, foot for foot.'

War and combatants

20 'When you go to war against your
enemies and see horses and chariots
and an army greater than your own, you must
not be afraid of them; Yahweh your God is
with you, he who brought you out of Egypt.
[2]When you are about to join battle, the priest
must come forward and address the people.
[3]He must say to them, "Listen, Israel: today
you are about to join battle with your
enemies. Do not be faint hearted. Let there
be no fear or trembling or alarm as you face
them. [4]Yahweh your God is marching with
you, to fight your enemies for you and make
you victorious."
[5]'The scribes will then address the people,
as follows:
"Has anyone built a new house and not yet
dedicated it? Let him go home, in case he
dies in battle and someone else performs the
dedication.
[6]"Has anyone planted a vineyard and not
yet enjoyed its fruit? Let him go home, in
case he dies in battle and someone else enjoys
its fruit.
[7]"Has anyone contracted to marry a girl
and not yet married her? Let him go home,
in case he dies in battle and someone else
marries her."
[8]'Finally, the scribes will say to the people:
"Is anyone frightened or faint hearted?
Let him go home, in case he makes his
brothers faint hearted too!"
[9]'Then, when the scribes have finished
speaking to the people, commanders will be
appointed to lead them.

Captured towns

[10]'When you advance on a town to attack it,
first offer it peace-terms. [11]If it accepts these
and opens its gates to you, all the people
inside will owe you forced labour and work
for you. [12]But if it refuses peace and gives
battle, you must besiege it. [13]Yahweh your
God having handed it over to you, you will
put the whole male population to the sword.
[14]But the women, children, livestock and
whatever the town contains by way of spoil,
you may take for yourselves as booty. You
will feed on the spoils of the enemies whom
Yahweh your God has handed over to you.
[15]'That is how you will treat towns far away
and not belonging to the nations near you.
[16]But as regards the towns of those peoples
whom Yahweh your God is giving you as
your heritage, you must not spare the life of
any living thing. [17]Instead, you must lay
them under the curse of destruction: Hittites,
Amorites, Canaanites, Perizzites, Hivites
and Jebusites, as Yahweh your God has
commanded, [18]so that they may not teach
you to do all the detestable things which they
do to honour their gods: in doing these, you
would sin against Yahweh your God.
[19]'If, when attacking a town, you have to
besiege it for a long time before you capture
it, you must not destroy its trees by taking
the axe to them: eat their fruit but do not cut
them down. Is the tree in the fields human,
that you should besiege it too? [20]Any trees,

however, which you know are not fruit trees, you may destroy and cut down and use to build siege-works against the hostile town until it falls.'

The unidentified murderer

21 'If, in the country which Yahweh your God gives you as your possession, a victim of murder is found lying in the open country and it is not known who has killed that person, 2your elders and scribes must measure the distance between the victim and the surrounding towns, 3and establish which town is the nearest to the victim. The elders of that town must then take a heifer that has not yet been put to work or used as a draught animal under the yoke. 4The elders of that town must bring the heifer down to a permanently flowing river, to a spot that has been neither ploughed nor sown, and there by the river they must break the heifer's neck. 5The priests, the sons of Levi, will then step forward, these being the men whom Yahweh your God has chosen to serve him and to bless in Yahweh's name, and it being their business to settle all cases of dispute or of violence. 6All the elders of the town nearest to the victim of murder must then wash their hands in the stream, over the slaughtered heifer. 7They must pronounce these words, "Our hands have not shed this blood and our eyes have seen nothing. 8O Yahweh, forgive your people Israel whom you have redeemed, and let no innocent blood be shed among your people Israel. May this bloodshed be forgiven them!" 9You must banish all shedding of innocent blood from among you, if you mean to do what is right in the eyes of Yahweh.

Women taken in war

10'When you go to war against your enemies and Yahweh your God delivers them into your power and you take prisoners, 11and among the prisoners you see a beautiful woman, and you fall in love with her, and you take her to be your wife 12and bring her home; she must shave her head and cut her nails, 13and take off her prisoner's garb; she must stay inside your house and mourn her father and mother for a full month. You may then go to her and be a husband to her, and she will be your wife. 14Should she cease to please you, you will let her go where she wishes, not selling her for money: you must not make any profit out of her, since you have exploited her.

Birthright

15'If a man has two wives, one loved and the other unloved, and the loved one and the unloved both bear him children, and if the first-born son is of the unloved wife, 16when the man comes to bequeath his goods to his sons, he may not treat the son of the wife whom he loves as the first-born, at the expense of the son of the wife whom he does not love, the true first-born. 17As his first-born he must acknowledge the son of the wife whom he does not love, giving him a double share of his estate; this son being the first-fruit of his vigour, the right of the first-born is his.

The rebellious son

18'If a man has a stubborn and rebellious son who will not listen to the voice either of his father or of his mother and, even when they punish him, still will not pay attention to them, 19his father and mother must take hold of him and bring him out to the elders of his town at the gate of that place. 20To the elders of his town, they will say, "This son of ours is stubborn and rebellious and will not listen to us; he is a wastrel and a drunkard." 21All his fellow-citizens must then stone him to death. You must banish this evil from among you. All Israel, hearing of this, will be afraid.

Various rulings

22'If a man guilty of a capital offence is to be put to death, and you hang him from a tree, 23his body must not remain on the tree overnight; you must bury him the same day, since anyone hanged is a curse of God, and you must not bring pollution on the soil which Yahweh your God is giving you as your heritage.'

22 'If you see your brother's ox or one of his sheep straying, you must not disregard it: you must take it back to your brother. 2And if he is not close at hand or you do not know who he is, you must take it home with you and keep it by you until your brother comes to look for it; you will then return it to him.

3'You must do the same with his donkey, the same with his cloak, the same with anything that your brother loses and that you find; you must not disregard it.

4 'If you see your brother's donkey or ox fall over on the road, you must not disregard it, but must help your brother get it on its feet again.

5 'A woman must not dress like a man, nor a man like a woman; anyone who does this is detestable to Yahweh your God.

6 'If, when out walking, you come across a bird's nest, in a tree or on the ground, with chicks or eggs and the mother bird sitting on the chicks or the eggs, you must not take the mother as well as the chicks. 7 Let the mother go; the young you may take for yourself. Thus will you have prosperity and long life.

8 'When you build a new house, you must give your roof a parapet; then your house will not incur blood-vengeance, should anyone fall off the top.

9 'You must not sow any other crop in your vineyard, or the whole yield may become forfeit, both the crop you have sown and the yield of your vines.

10 'You must not plough with ox and donkey together.

11 'You must not wear clothing woven part of wool, part of linen.

12 'You must make tassels for the four corners of the cloak in which you wrap yourself.

A young wife's reputation

13 'If a man marries a woman, has sexual intercourse with her and then, turning against her, 14 taxes her with misconduct and publicly defames her by saying, "I married this woman and when I had sexual intercourse with her I did not find evidence of her virginity," 15 the girl's father and mother must take the evidence of her virginity and produce it before the elders of the town, at the gate. 16 To the elders, the girl's father will say, "I gave this man my daughter for a wife and he has turned against her, 17 and now he taxes her with misconduct, saying, I have found no evidence of virginity in your daughter. Here is the evidence of my daughter's virginity!" 18 They must then display the cloth to the elders of the town. 19 The elders of the town in question will have the man arrested and flogged, and fine him a hundred silver shekels for publicly defaming a virgin of Israel, and give this money to the girl's father. She will remain his wife; as long as he lives, he may not divorce her.

20 'But if the accusation that the girl cannot show evidence of virginity is substantiated, 21 she must be taken out, and at the door of her father's house her fellow-citizens must stone her to death for having committed an infamy in Israel by bringing disgrace on her father's family. You must banish this evil from among you.

Adultery and fornication

22 'If a man is caught having sexual intercourse with another man's wife, both must be put to death: the man who has slept with her and the woman herself. You must banish this evil from Israel.

23 'If a virgin is engaged to a man, and another man encounters her in the town and has sexual intercourse with her, 24 you will take them both to the gate of the town in question and stone them to death: the girl, for not having called for help in the town; the man, for having exploited his fellow-citizen's wife. You must banish this evil from among you. 25 But if the man ran into the betrothed girl in the open country and slept with her, having taken her by force, her ravisher alone must die; 26 you must do nothing to the girl, she has not committed a capital offence. The case is like that of a man who attacks and kills his fellow: 27 since he came across her in the open country, the betrothed girl may have called out, without anyone's coming to her rescue.

28 'If a man meets a young virgin who is not betrothed and seizes her, sleeps with her and is caught in the act, 29 her ravisher must give the girl's father fifty silver shekels; since he has exploited her, she must be his wife and, as long as he lives, he may not divorce her.'

23 'A man must not take his father's wife; he must not withdraw the skirt of his father's cloak from her.

Participation in public worship

2 'A man whose testicles have been crushed or whose male member has been cut off must not be admitted to the assembly of Yahweh. 3 No half-breed may be admitted to the assembly of Yahweh; not even his descendants to the tenth generation may be admitted to the assembly of Yahweh. 4 No Ammonite or Moabite may be admitted to the assembly

of Yahweh; not even his descendants to the
tenth generation may be admitted to the
assembly of Yahweh, and this is for all time;
[5]since they did not come to meet you with
food and drink when you were on your way
out of Egypt, and even hired Balaam son of
Beor to oppose you by cursing you, from
Pethor in Aram Naharaim. [6]But Yahweh
your God refused to listen to Balaam, and
Yahweh your God turned the curse on you
into a blessing, because Yahweh your God
loved you. [7]Never, as long as you live, must
you seek their welfare or their prosperity.
[8]'You must not regard the Edomite as
detestable, for he is your brother; you must
not regard the Egyptian as detestable, since
you were once a foreigner in his country.
[9]The third generation of children born to
these may be admitted to the assembly of
Yahweh.

Hygiene in camp

[10]'When you are in camp, at war with your
enemies, you must avoid anything bad. [11]If
any one of you is unclean by reason of a
nocturnal emission, he must leave and not
come back into camp, [12]but towards
evening wash himself, and return to camp
at sunset.
[13]'You must have a latrine outside the
camp, and go out to this; [14]you must have a
trowel in your equipment and, when you
squat outside, you must scrape a hole with
it, then turn round and cover up your excre-
ment. [15]For Yahweh your God goes about
the inside of your camp to guard you and put
your enemies at your mercy. Your camp must
therefore be a holy place; Yahweh must not
see anything indecent there or he will desert
you.

Miscellaneous

[16]'You must not allow a master to imprison a
slave who has escaped from him and come to
you. [17]Let him make his home with you and
yours, wherever he pleases in whichever of
your towns he prefers; you must not molest
him.
[18]'There must be no sacred prostitute
among the women of Israel, and no sacred
prostitute among the men of Israel. [19]You
must not bring the wages of a prostitute or
the earnings of a 'dog'[a] to the house of
Yahweh your God, whatever vow you may
have made: both are detestable to Yahweh
your God.
[20]'You must not lend on interest to your
brother, whether the loan be of money, of
food, or of anything else that may earn
interest. [21]You may demand interest on a
loan to a foreigner, but you must not demand
interest from your brother; so that Yahweh
your God may bless you in all your labours,
in the country which you are about to enter
and make your own.
[22]'If you make a vow to Yahweh your God,
you must not be slack about fulfilling it:
Yahweh your God will certainly hold you
answerable for it and you will incur guilt.
[23]If, however, you make no vow, you do not
incur guilt. [24]Whatever passes your lips you
must keep to, and the vow that you have
made to Yahweh, your generous God, you
must fulfil.
[25]'If you go into your neighbour's vine-
yard, you may eat as many grapes as you
please, but you must not put any in your
basket. [26]If you go into your neighbour's
standing corn, you may pick ears by hand,
but you must not put a sickle into your
neighbour's corn.'

Divorce

24 'Suppose a man has taken a wife and
consummated the marriage; but she
has not pleased him and he has found some
impropriety of which to accuse her; he has
therefore made out a writ of divorce for her
and handed it to her and then dismissed her
from his house; [2]she leaves his home and goes
away to become the wife of another man.
[3]Then suppose this second man who has
married her takes a dislike to her and makes
out a writ of divorce for her and hands it to
her and dismisses her from his house or if
this other man who took her as his wife dies,
[4]her first husband, who has repudiated her,
may not take her back as his wife now that
she has been made unclean in this way. For
that is detestable in Yahweh's eyes and you
must not bring guilt on the country which
Yahweh your God is giving you as your
heritage.

23a Contemptuous term for a male prostitute.

Protection of the individual

5 ‘If a man is newly married, he must not join the army, nor must he be pestered at home; he must be left at home, free of all obligations for one year, to make his new wife happy.

6 ‘No one may take a mill or a millstone in pledge; that would be to take life itself in pledge.

7 ‘If anyone is caught, having kidnapped one of his brother-Israelites, whether he makes him his slave or sells him, that thief must die. You must banish this evil from among you.

8 ‘In a case of a virulent skin-disease, take care you faithfully observe and exactly carry out everything that the levitical priests direct you to do. You must keep and observe everything that I have commanded them. 9 Remember what Yahweh your God did to Miriam when you were on your way out of Egypt.

10 ‘If you are making your brother a loan on pledge, you must not go into his house and seize the pledge, whatever it may be. 11 You must stay outside, and the man to whom you are making the loan must bring the pledge out to you. 12 And if the man is poor, you must not go to bed with his pledge in your possession; 13 you must return it to him at sunset so that he can sleep in his cloak and bless you; and it will be an upright action on your part in God's view.

14 ‘You must not exploit a poor and needy wage-earner, be he one of your brothers or a foreigner resident in your community. 15 You must pay him his wages each day, not allowing the sun to set before you do, since he, being poor, needs them badly; otherwise he may appeal to Yahweh against you, and you would incur guilt.

16 ‘Parents may not be put to death for their children, nor children for parents, but each must be put to death for his own crime.

17 ‘You must not infringe the rights of the foreigner or the orphan; you must not take a widow's clothes in pledge. 18 Remember that you were once a slave in Egypt and that Yahweh your God redeemed you from that. That is why I am giving you this order.

19 ‘If, when reaping the harvest in your field, you overlook a sheaf in that field, do not go back for it. The foreigner, the orphan and the widow shall have it, so that Yahweh your God may bless you in all your undertakings.

20 ‘When you beat your olive tree, you must not go over the branches twice. The foreigner, the orphan and the widow shall have the rest.

21 ‘When you harvest your vineyard, you must not pick it over a second time. The foreigner, the orphan and the widow shall have the rest.

22 ‘Remember that you were once a slave in Egypt. That is why I am giving you this order.’

25 ‘If people fall out, they must go to court for judgement; the judges must declare the one who is right to be in the right, the one who is wrong to be in the wrong. 2 If the one who is in the wrong deserves a flogging, the judge must have him laid on the ground and flogged in his presence, the number of strokes proportionate to his offence. 3 He may impose forty strokes but no more; otherwise, by the infliction of more, serious injury may be caused and your brother be humiliated before you.

4 ‘You must not muzzle an ox when it is treading out the corn.

The levirate law

5 ‘If brothers live together and one of them dies childless, the dead man's wife may not marry a stranger outside the family. Her husband's brother must come to her and, exercising his duty as brother, make her his wife, 6 and the first son she bears must assume the dead brother's name; by this means his name will not be obliterated from Israel. 7 But if the man declines to take his brother's wife, she must go to the elders at the gate and say, “I have no brother-in-law willing to perpetuate his brother's name in Israel; he declines to exercise his duty as brother in my favour.” 8 The elders of the town must summon the man and talk to him. If, on appearing before them, he says, “I refuse to take her,” 9 then the woman to whom he owes duty as brother must go up to him in the presence of the elders, take the sandal off his foot, spit in his face, and pronounce the following words, “This is what is done to the man who refuses to restore his brother's house,” 10 and his family must henceforth be known in Israel as House of the Unshod.

Modesty in brawls

11 ‘If, when two men are fighting, the wife of one intervenes to protect her husband from the other’s blows by reaching out and seizing the other by his private parts, 12 you must cut off her hand and show no pity.

Appendices

13 ‘You must not keep two different weights in your bag, one heavy, one light. 14 You must not keep two different measures in your house, one large, one small. 15 You must keep one weight, full and accurate, so that you may have long life in the country given you by Yahweh your God. 16 For anyone who does things of this kind and acts dishonestly is detestable to Yahweh your God.

17 ‘Remember how Amalek treated you when you were on your way out of Egypt. 18 He met you on your way and, after you had gone by, he fell on you from the rear and cut off the stragglers; when you were faint and weary, he had no fear of God. 19 When Yahweh your God has granted you peace from all the enemies surrounding you, in the country given you by Yahweh your God to own as your heritage, you must blot out the memory of Amalek under heaven. Do not forget.’

First-fruits

26 ‘When you have entered the country which Yahweh your God is giving you as heritage, when you have taken possession of it and are living in it, 2 you must set aside the first-fruits of all the produce of the soil raised by you in your country, given you by Yahweh your God. You must put these in a basket and go to the place where Yahweh your God chooses to give his name a home. 3 You will go to the priest then in office and say to him, “Today I declare to Yahweh my God that I have reached the country which Yahweh swore to our ancestors that he would give us.”

4 ‘The priest will then take the basket from your hand and lay it before the altar of Yahweh your God. 5 In the presence of Yahweh your God, you will then pronounce these words:

“My father was a wandering Aramaean, who went down to Egypt with a small group of men, and stayed there, until he there became a great, powerful and numerous nation. 6 The Egyptians ill-treated us, they oppressed us and inflicted harsh slavery on us. 7 But we called on Yahweh, God of our ancestors. Yahweh heard our voice and saw our misery, our toil and our oppression, 8 and Yahweh brought us out of Egypt with mighty hand and outstretched arm, with great terror, and with signs and wonders. 9 He brought us here and has given us this country, a country flowing with milk and honey. 10 Hence, I now bring the first-fruits of the soil that you, Yahweh, have given me.”

‘You will then lay them before Yahweh your God, and prostrate yourself in the presence of Yahweh your God. 11 You must then rejoice in all the good things that Yahweh your God has bestowed on you and your family—you, the Levite and the foreigner living with you.

The third-year tithe

12 ‘In the third year, the tithing year, when you have finished taking the tithe of your whole income and have given it to the Levite, the foreigner, the orphan and the widow so that, in your towns, they may eat to their heart’s content, 13 in the presence of Yahweh your God, you must say:

“I have cleared my house of what was consecrated. Yes, I have given it to the Levite, the foreigner, the orphan and the widow, in accordance with all the commandments you have imposed on me, neither going beyond your commandments nor neglecting them. 14 When in mourning, I have not eaten any of it; when unclean, I have taken none of it away; I have given none of it for the dead. I have obeyed the voice of Yahweh my God and I have behaved in every way as you have commanded me. 15 Look down from your holy dwelling, from heaven, and bless your people Israel and the country which you have given us, as you swore to our ancestors, a country flowing with milk and honey.” ’

III: CONCLUDING DISCOURSE

A: END OF THE SECOND DISCOURSE

Israel, the people of Yahweh

16‘Yahweh your God commands you today to
observe these laws and customs; you must
keep and observe them with all your heart
and with all your soul.
17‘Today you have obtained this declar-
ation from Yahweh: that he will be your God,
but only if you follow his ways, keep his
statutes, his commandments, his customs,
and listen to his voice. 18And today Yahweh
has obtained this declaration from you: that
you will be his own people—as he has said—
but only if you keep all his commandments;
19then for praise and renown and honour, he
will raise you higher than every other nation
he has made, and you will be a people conse-
crated to Yahweh, as he has promised.’

The writing of the Law and religious ceremonies

27 Moses and the elders of Israel gave the
people this command: ‘Keep all the
commandments which I am laying down for
you today. 2After you have crossed the Jordan
into the country which Yahweh your God is
giving you, you must set up tall stones, coat
them with lime 3and on them write all the
words of this Law, when you have crossed
and entered the country which Yahweh your
God is giving you, a country flowing with
milk and honey, as Yahweh, God of your
ancestors, has promised you.
4‘When you have crossed the Jordan, you
must erect these stones on Mount Ebal, as I
command you today, and coat them with
lime. 5There, for Yahweh your God, you
must build an altar of stones, on which no
iron has been used. 6You must build the altar
of Yahweh your God of rough stones, and on
this altar you will present burnt offerings to
Yahweh your God, 7and immolate com-
munion sacrifices and eat them there,
rejoicing in the presence of Yahweh your
God. 8On these stones you must write all the
words of this Law; cut them carefully.’
9Moses and the levitical priests then said
to all Israel: ‘Be silent, Israel, and listen.
Today you have become a people for Yahweh
your God. 10You must listen to the voice of
Yahweh your God and observe the command-
ments and laws which I am laying down for
you today.’
11That day Moses gave the people this
order: 12‘When you have crossed the Jordan,
the following will stand on Mount Gerizim
to bless the people: Simeon and Levi, Judah
and Issachar, Joseph and Benjamin. 13And
the following will stand on Mount Ebal for
the curse: Reuben, Gad and Asher, Zebulun,
Dan and Naphtali. 14The Levites will then
speak, proclaiming loudly to all the
Israelites:
15“Accursed be anyone who makes a
carved or cast idol, a thing detestable to
Yahweh, a workman’s artefact, and sets it up
in secret.” And the people are all to respond
by saying, Amen.
16“Accursed be anyone who treats father
or mother dishonourably.” And the people
must all say, Amen.
17“Accursed be anyone who displaces a
neighbour’s boundary mark.” And the
people must all say, Amen.
18“Accursed be anyone who leads the blind
astray on the road.” And the people must all
say, Amen.
19“Accursed be anyone who violates the
rights of the foreigner, the orphan and the
widow.” And the people must all say,
Amen.
20“Accursed be anyone who has sexual
intercourse with his father’s wife and with-
draws the skirt of his father’s cloak from
her.” And the people must all say, Amen.
21“Accursed be anyone who has sexual
intercourse with any kind of animal.” And
the people must all say, Amen.
22“Accursed be anyone who has sexual
intercourse with his sister, the daughter of
his father or of his mother.” And the people
must all say, Amen.
23“Accursed be anyone who has sexual
intercourse with his mother-in-law.” And
the people must all say, Amen.
24“Accursed be anyone who secretly
strikes down his neighbour.” And the people
must all say, Amen.
25“Accursed be anyone who accepts a bribe
to take an innocent life.” And the people
must all say, Amen.

[26]"'Accursed be anyone who does not make the words of this Law effective by putting them into practice." And the people must all say, Amen.'

Promised blessings

28 [1]'But if you faithfully obey the voice of Yahweh your God, by keeping and observing all his commandments, which I am laying down for you today, Yahweh your God will raise you higher than every other nation in the world, [2]and all these blessings will befall and overtake you, for having obeyed the voice of Yahweh your God.

[3]'You will be blessed in the town and blessed in the countryside; [4]blessed, the offspring of your body, the yield of your soil, the yield of your livestock, the young of your cattle and the increase of your flocks; [5]blessed, your basket and your kneading trough. [6]You will be blessed in coming home, and blessed in going out. [7]The enemies who attack you, Yahweh will defeat before your eyes; they will advance on you from one direction and flee from you in seven. [8]Yahweh will command blessedness to be with you, on your barns and on all your undertakings, and he will bless you in the country given you by Yahweh your God.

[9]'From you Yahweh will make a people consecrated to himself, as he has sworn to you, if you keep the commandments of Yahweh your God and follow his ways. [10]The peoples of the world, seeing that you bear Yahweh's name, will all be afraid of you. [11]Yahweh will make you abound in possessions: in the offspring of your body, in the yield of your cattle and in the yield of your soil, in the country which he swore to your ancestors that he would give you. [12]For you Yahweh will open his treasury of rain, the heavens, to give your country its rain at the right time, and to bless all your labours. You will make many nations your subjects, yet you will be subject to none. [13]Yahweh will put you at the head, not at the tail; you will always be on top and never underneath, if you listen to the commandments of Yahweh your God, which I am laying down for you today, and then keep them and put them into practice, [14]not deviating to right or to left from any of the words which I am laying down for you today, by following other gods and serving them.

Curses

[15]'But if you do not obey the voice of Yahweh your God, and do not keep and observe all his commandments and laws which I am laying down for you today then all these curses will befall and overtake you.

[16]'You will be accursed in the town and accursed in the countryside; [17]accursed, your basket and your kneading trough; [18]accursed, the offspring of your body, the yield of your soil, the young of your cattle and the increase of your flock. [19]You will be accursed in coming home, and accursed in going out.

[20]'Yahweh will send a curse on you, a spell, an imprecation on all your labours until you have been destroyed and quickly perish, because of your perverse behaviour, for having deserted me. [21]Yahweh will fasten the plague on you, until it has exterminated you from the country which you are about to enter and make your own. [22]Yahweh will strike you down with consumption, fever, inflammation, burning fever, drought, wind-blast, mildew, and these will pursue you to your ruin. [23]The heavens above you will be brass, the earth beneath you iron. [24]Your country's rain Yahweh will turn into dust and sand; it will fall on you from the heavens until you perish. [25]Yahweh will have you defeated by your enemies; you will advance on them from one direction and flee from them in seven; and you will be a terrifying object-lesson to all the kingdoms of the world. [26]Your carcase will be carrion for all wild birds and all wild animals, with no one to scare them away.

[27]'Yahweh will strike you down with Egyptian ulcers, with swellings in the groin, with scurvy and the itch, for which you will find no cure. [28]Yahweh will strike you down with madness, blindness, distraction of mind, [29]until you grope your way at noon like a blind man groping in the dark, and your steps will lead you nowhere.

'You will never be anything but exploited and plundered, with no one to save you. [30]Get engaged to a woman, another man will have her; build a house, you will not live in it; plant a vineyard, you will not gather its first-fruits. [31]Your ox will be slaughtered before your eyes and you will eat none of it; your donkey will be carried off in front of you and not be returned to you; your sheep will be given to your enemies, and no one will come to your help. [32]Your sons and daughters will be handed over to another people, and every day you will wear your eyes out watching for them, while your hands are powerless. [33]A nation hitherto unknown to you will eat the yield of your soil and of all your hard work. You will never be anything but exploited and crushed. [34]You will be driven mad by the sights you will see. [35]Yahweh will strike you down with foul ulcers on knee and leg, for which you will find no cure—from the sole of your foot to the top of your head.

[36]'Yahweh will send away both you and the king whom you have appointed to rule you to a nation unknown either to you or to your ancestors, and there you will serve other gods, made of wood and stone. [37]And you will be the astonishment, the byword, the laughing-stock of all the peoples where Yahweh is taking you.

[38]'You will cast seed in plenty on the fields but harvest little, since the locust will devour it. [39]You will plant and till your vineyards but not drink the wine or gather the grapes, since the grub will eat them up. [40]You will grow olive trees throughout your territory but not anoint yourself with the oil, since your olive trees will be cut down. [41]You will father sons and daughters but they will not belong to you, since they will go into captivity. [42]All your trees and the whole yield of your soil will be the prey of insects.

[43]'The foreigners living with you will rise higher and higher at your expense, while you yourself sink lower and lower. [44]You will be subject to them, not they to you; they will be the ones at the head, and you the one at the tail.

[45]'All these curses will befall you, pursue you and overtake you until you have been destroyed, for not having obeyed the voice of Yahweh your God by keeping his commandments and laws which he has laid down for you. [46]They will be a sign and a wonder over you and your descendants for ever.

Of war and exile to come

[47]'For not having joyfully and with happy heart served Yahweh your God, despite the abundance of everything, [48]you will have to serve the enemy whom Yahweh will send against you, in hunger, thirst, lack of clothing and total privation. He will put an iron yoke on your neck, until he has destroyed you.

[49]'Against you Yahweh will raise a distant nation from the ends of the earth like an eagle taking wing: a nation whose language you do not understand, [50]a nation grim of face, with neither respect for the old, nor pity for the young. [51]He will eat the yield of your cattle and the yield of your soil until you have been destroyed; he will leave you neither wheat, nor wine, nor oil, nor the young of your cattle, nor increase of your flock, until he has made an end of you. [52]He will besiege you inside all your towns until your loftiest and most strongly fortified walls collapse, on which, throughout your country, you have relied. He will besiege you inside all the towns throughout your country, given you by Yahweh your God. [53]During the siege and in the distress to which your enemy will reduce you, you will eat the offspring of your own body, the flesh of the sons and daughters given you by Yahweh your God. [54]The gentlest and tenderest of your men will scowl at his brother, and at the wife whom he embraces, and at his remaining children, [55]not willing to give any of them any of his own children's flesh, which he is eating; because of the siege and the distress to which your enemy will reduce you in all your towns, he will have nothing left. [56]The most refined and fastidious of your women, so refined, so fastidious that she has never ventured to set the sole of her foot to the ground, will scowl at the husband whom she embraces, and at her son and daughter, and at the after-birth when it leaves her womb, and at the child to which she has given birth— [57]she will hide away and eat them, so complete will be the starvation resulting from the siege and the distress to which your enemy will reduce you in all your towns.

[58]'If you do not keep and observe all the words of this Law, which are written in this book, in the fear of this glorious and awe-inspiring name: Yahweh your God, [59]Yahweh will strike you down with monstrous plagues, you and your descendants: with plagues grievous and lasting, diseases pernicious and enduring. [60]He will afflict you with all the maladies of Egypt which you used to dread, and they will fasten on you. [61]What is more, Yahweh will afflict you with all the plagues and all the diseases not mentioned in the book of this Law, until you have been destroyed. [62]There will only be a small group of you left, you who were once as numerous as the stars of heaven.

'For not having obeyed the voice of

Yahweh your God, [63]just as Yahweh used to
delight in making you happy and in making
your numbers grow, so will he take delight
in ruining you and destroying you. You will
be torn from the country which you are about
to enter and make your own. [64]Yahweh will
scatter you throughout every people, from
one end of the earth to the other; there you
will serve other gods made of wood and stone,
hitherto unknown either to you or to your
ancestors. [65]Among these nations there will
be no repose for you, no rest for the sole of
your foot; there Yahweh will give you a
quaking heart, weary eyes, halting breath.
[66]Your life ahead of you will hang in doubt;
you will be afraid day and night, uncertain
of your life. [67]In the morning you will say,
"How I wish it were evening!", and in the
evening you will say, "How I wish it were
morning!", such terror will grip your heart
and such sights you will see! [68]Yahweh will
send you back to Egypt, either by ship or by
a road which I promised you would never
see again. And there you will want to offer
yourselves for sale to your enemies as
serving men and women, but no one will
buy you.'

B: THE THIRD DISCOURSE

[69]These are the words of the covenant which
Yahweh ordered Moses to make with the
Israelites in Moab, in addition to the covenant
which he had made with them at Horeb.

Historical introduction

29 Moses called all Israel together and said
to them:
'You have seen everything that Yahweh did
before your eyes in Egypt, to Pharaoh, to his
servants and to his whole country—[2]the great
ordeals which you yourselves witnessed,
those signs and the great wonders. [3]But until
today Yahweh has not given you a heart to
understand, eyes to see, or ears to hear.
[4]'I have been leading you for forty years in
the desert, yet the clothes which you have
been wearing have not worn out, nor have
the sandals on your feet. [5]You have had
no bread to eat, you have had no wine or
fermented liquor to drink, so that you would
learn that I, Yahweh, am your God.
[6]'When you reached this place, Sihon king
of Heshbon and Og king of Bashan came out
to do battle against us; we defeated them.
[7]We conquered their country and gave it as
heritage to Reuben, Gad and the half-tribe
of Manasseh.
[8]'Keep the words of this covenant, put
them into practice, and you will thrive in
everything you do.

The covenant in Moab

[9]'All of you are standing here today in the
presence of Yahweh your God: your tribal
leaders, your elders, your scribes, all the men
of Israel, [10]with your children and your wives
(and the foreigner too who is in your camp, be
he your wood-cutter or your water-carrier),
[11]and you are about to pass into the covenant
of Yahweh your God, sworn with impre-
cation, which he has made with you today,
[12]and by which, today, he makes you a nation
for himself and he himself becomes a God to
you, as he has promised you, and as he swore
to your ancestors Abraham, Isaac and Jacob.
[13]Not only on your behalf am I today making
this covenant and pronouncing this solemn
curse, [14]not only on behalf of those standing
here with us in the presence of Yahweh our
God today, but also on behalf of those not
here with us today.
[15]'Yes, you know the people with whom
we used to live in Egypt, and those through
whose countries we have travelled—the
nations through whom we have passed. [16]You
have seen their abominations and their idols
made of wood and stone, silver and gold,
which were there.
[17]'Let there be no man or woman of you,
no clan or tribe, whose heart turns away from
Yahweh your God today, to go and serve the
gods of these nations. Among you let there
be no root which bears poison or wormwood.
[18]If, after hearing this imprecation, anyone,
blessing himself, should say in his heart, "I
shall do well enough if I follow the dictates
of my heart; much water drives away thirst,"
[19]Yahweh will not pardon him. The wrath
and jealousy of Yahweh will blaze against
such a person; every curse written in this
book will fall on him, and Yahweh will blot
his name out under heaven. [20]Yahweh will
single him out of all the tribes of Israel for
misfortune, in accordance with all the curses
of the covenant written in the book of this
Law.

A threat of exile

21‘The future generation, that of your chil-
dren coming after you, and the foreigner
arriving from some far-away land, on seeing
the plagues and diseases inflicted on this
country by Yahweh, will exclaim,
22“Sulphur! Salt!—The whole country is
burning! No one will sow, nothing grow, no
vegetation spring ever again! Devastation
like that of Sodom and Gomorrah, Admah
and Zeboiim, devastated by Yahweh in his
furious wrath!” 23And all the nations will
exclaim, “Why has Yahweh treated this
country like this? Why this great blaze of
anger?”
24‘And people will say, “Because they
deserted the covenant of Yahweh, God of
their ancestors, the covenant which he made
with them when he brought them out of
Egypt; 25because they went and served other
gods and worshipped them, gods hitherto
unknown to them, gods that were no part
of their heritage from him: 26this is why
Yahweh’s anger has blazed against this
country, afflicting it with all the curses
written in this book. 27In anger, in fury, in
fierce wrath, Yahweh has torn them from
their own country and flung them into
another country, where they are today.”
28Things hidden belong to Yahweh our God,
but things revealed are ours and our chil-
dren’s for ever, so that we can put all the
words of this Law into practice.’

Return from exile and conversion

30 ‘And when all these words have come
true for you—the blessing and the
curse, which I have offered you—if you
meditate on them in your heart wherever
among the nations Yahweh your God has
driven you, 2if you return to Yahweh your
God, if with all your heart and with all
your soul you obey his voice, you and your
children, in everything that I am laying down
for you today, 3then Yahweh your God will
bring back your captives, he will have pity
on you and gather you back from all the
peoples among whom Yahweh your God
has scattered you. 4Should you have been
banished to the very sky’s end, Yahweh your
God will gather you again even from there,
will come there to reclaim you 5and bring you
back to the country which belonged to your
ancestors, so that you may possess it in your
turn, and be made prosperous there and more
numerous than your ancestors.
6‘Yahweh your God will circumcise your
heart and the heart of your descendants, so
that you will love Yahweh your God with all
your heart and soul, and so will live. 7Yahweh
your God will make all these curses recoil
on your foes and on your enemies who have
persecuted you. 8And once again you will
obey the voice of Yahweh your God and you
will put all his commandments into practice,
which I am laying down for you today.
9Yahweh your God will make you prosper in
all your labours, in the offspring of your
body, in the yield of your cattle and in the
yield of your soil. For once again Yahweh
will delight in your prosperity as he used
to take delight in the prosperity of your
ancestors, 10if you obey the voice of Yahweh
your God, by keeping his commandments
and decrees written in the book of this Law,
and if you return to Yahweh your God with
all your heart and soul.
11‘For this Law which I am laying down
for you today is neither obscure for you nor
beyond your reach. 12It is not in heaven, so
that you need to wonder, “Who will go up to
heaven for us and bring it down to us, so that
we can hear and practise it?” 13Nor is it
beyond the seas, so that you need to wonder,
“Who will cross the seas for us and bring it
back to us, so that we can hear and practise
it?” 14No, the word is very near to you, it is
in your mouth and in your heart for you to
put into practice.

The two ways

15‘Look, today I am offering you life and
prosperity, death and disaster. 16If you obey
the commandments of Yahweh your God,
which I am laying down for you today, if you
love Yahweh your God and follow his ways,
if you keep his commandments, his laws
and his customs, you will live and grow
numerous, and Yahweh your God will bless
you in the country which you are about to
enter and make your own. 17But if your heart
turns away, if you refuse to listen, if you let
yourself be drawn into worshipping other
gods and serving them, 18I tell you today, you
will most certainly perish; you will not live
for long in the country which you are crossing
the Jordan to enter and possess. 19Today, I
call heaven and earth to witness against you:
I am offering you life or death, blessing or

curse. Choose life, then, so that you and your
descendants may live, [20]in the love of Yahweh
your God, obeying his voice, holding fast to
him; for in this your life consists, and on this
depends the length of time that you stay in
the country which Yahweh swore to your
ancestors Abraham, Isaac and Jacob that he
would give them.'

IV: LAST ACTIONS AND DEATH OF MOSES

The commissioning of Joshua

31 Moses went and spoke to all Israel as
follows, [2]'Today, I am one hundred
and twenty years old, and can no longer act
as leader. Yahweh has told me, "You shall
not cross this Jordan." [3]Yahweh your God
himself will lead you across, he himself will
destroy and dispossess these nations
confronting you; Joshua too will lead you
across, as Yahweh has said. [4]Yahweh will
treat them as he has treated Sihon and Og
the Amorite kings and their country—he
destroyed them. [5]Yahweh will put them at
your mercy, and you will deal with them
exactly as prescribed by the commandments
which I have laid down for you. [6]Be strong,
stand firm, have no fear, do not be afraid of
them, for Yahweh your God is going with
you; he will not fail you or desert you.'
[7]Moses then summoned Joshua and, in the
presence of all Israel, said to him, 'Be strong,
stand firm; you will be the one to go with this
people into the country which Yahweh has
sworn to their ancestors that he would give
them; you are to be the one who puts them
into possession of it. [8]Yahweh himself will
lead you; he will be with you; he will not fail
you or desert you. Have no fear, do not be
alarmed.'

The ritual reading of the Law

[9]Moses committed this Law to writing and
gave it to the priests, the sons of Levi, who
carried the ark of Yahweh's covenant, and to
all the elders of Israel. [10]And Moses gave
them this command, 'At the end of every
seven years, at the time fixed for the year of
remission, at the feast of Shelters, [11]when all
Israel assembles in the presence of Yahweh
your God in the place chosen by him, you
must proclaim this Law in the hearing of
all Israel. [12]Call the people together, men,
women, children, and the foreigner residing
with you, so that, hearing it, they may learn
to fear Yahweh your God and keep and
observe all the words of this Law. [13]Their
children, who as yet do not know it, will hear
it and learn to fear Yahweh your God, all the
time you live in the country which you are
crossing the Jordan to possess.'

Yahweh's instructions

[14]Yahweh said to Moses, 'And now the time
is near when you must die. Summon Joshua
and take your places at the Tent of Meeting,
so that I can give him his orders.' Moses and
Joshua went and took their places at the Tent
of Meeting, [15]and Yahweh showed himself at
the Tent in a pillar of cloud; the pillar of
cloud stood at the door of the Tent.
[16]Yahweh said to Moses, 'You will soon be
sleeping with your ancestors, and this people
is about to play the harlot by following the
gods of the foreigners of the country, among
whom they are going to live. They will desert
me and break my covenant, which I have
made with them. [17]That very day, my anger
will blaze against them; I shall desert them
and hide my face from them. A host of
disasters and misfortunes will overtake them
to devour them, and when that day comes
they will say, "If such disasters overtake me,
surely Yahweh my God cannot be with me?"
[18]Yes indeed, I shall hide my face that day,
on account of all the evil which they will have
done by turning to other gods.

The song of witness

[19]'Now write down this song for you to use;
teach it to the Israelites, put it into their
mouths, for it to be a witness on my behalf
against the Israelites: [20]against Israel, whom
I am bringing into the country which I swore
to his ancestors that I would give him, a
country flowing with milk and honey: against
Israel, who will eat to his heart's content and
grow fat, and will then turn to other gods and
serve them, despising me and breaking my
covenant. [21]When a host of disasters and
misfortunes overtakes him, this song, like a

witness, will give evidence against him, since
his descendants will not have forgotten it.
Yes, even today, before I have brought him
to the country which I have promised him on
oath, I know what plans he has in mind.'
22 So, that day, Moses wrote out this song and
taught it to the Israelites.
23 To Joshua son of Nun, Yahweh gave this
order, 'Be strong and stand firm, for you are
to be the one to bring the Israelites into the
country which I have promised them on oath,
and I myself shall be with you.'

The Law placed beside the ark

24 When Moses had completely finished
writing the words of this Law in a book, 25 he
gave this command to the Levites who carried
the ark of Yahweh's covenant: 26 'Take the
book of this Law and put it beside the ark of
the covenant of Yahweh your God. Let it lie
there as evidence against you. 27 For I know
how rebellious and stiff-necked you are. If
today, while I am still alive and with you,
you rebel against Yahweh, how much more
will you rebel against him after my death!

Israel assembles to hear the song

28 'Gather all your tribal elders and scribes
round me, so that I may be sure that they
hear these words, as I call heaven and earth
to witness against them. 29 For I know that
after my death you are certain to grow
corrupt; you will leave the way which I have
marked out for you; in the final days disaster
will befall you for having done what is evil
in Yahweh's eyes, for having provoked his
anger by your behaviour.'
30 In the hearing of the whole assembly of
Israel, Moses then recited the words of this
song to the end:

32 Listen, heavens, while I speak;
hear, earth, the words that I shall say!
2 May my teaching fall like the rain,
may my word drop down like the dew,
like showers on the grass,
like light rain on the turf!
3 For I shall proclaim the name of Yahweh.
Oh, tell the greatness of our God!

4 He is the Rock, his work is perfect,
for all his ways are equitable.
A trustworthy God who does no wrong,
he is the Honest, the Upright One!
5 They have acted perversely,
those he fathered without blemish,
a deceitful and underhand brood.
6 Is this the return you make to Yahweh?
O people brainless and unwise!
Is this not your father, who gave you being,
who made you, by whom you subsist?
7 Think back on the days of old,
think over the years, down the ages.
Question your father,
let him explain to you,
your elders, and let them tell you!
8 When the Most High gave the nations
each their heritage,
when he partitioned out the human race,
he assigned the boundaries of nations
according to the number
of the children of God,
9 but Yahweh's portion was his people,
Jacob was to be the measure
of his inheritance.

10 In the desert he finds him,
in the howling expanses of the wastelands.
He protects him, rears him, guards him
as the pupil of his eye.
11 Like an eagle watching its nest,
hovering over its young,
he spreads out his wings to hold him,
he supports him on his pinions.

12 Yahweh alone is his guide;
no alien god for him!
13 He gives him the heights
of the land to ride,
he feeds him on the yield of the mountains,
he gives him honey from the rock to taste,
and oil from the flinty crag;
14 curds from the cattle, milk from the flock,
and the richness of the pasture,
rams of Bashan's breed, and goats,
the richness of the wheat kernel;
the fermented blood of the grape for drink.

15 Jacob has eaten to his heart's content,
Jeshurun,[a] grown fat, has now lashed out.
(You have grown fat, gross, bloated.)
He has disowned the God who made him,
and dishonoured the Rock, his salvation,
16 whose jealousy they aroused
with foreigners—
with things detestable they angered him.

32a A name for Israel (also in 33:5) of uncertain sense and origin.

17They sacrificed to demons
who are not God,
to gods hitherto unknown to them,
to newcomers of yesterday
whom their ancestors had never respected.
18(You forget the Rock who fathered you,
the God who made you,
you no longer remember.)
19Yahweh saw it and, in anger,
he spurned his sons and daughters.
20'I shall hide my face from them,' he said,
'and see what will become of them.
For they are a deceitful brood,
children with no loyalty in them.
21They have roused me to jealousy
with a non-god,
they have exasperated me with their idols.
In my turn I shall rouse them to jealousy
with a non-people,
I shall exasperate them
with a stupid nation.
22Yes, a fire has blazed from my anger,
it will burn right down
to the depths of Sheol;
it will devour the earth and all its produce,
it will set fire to the footings
of the mountains.
23I shall hurl disasters on them,
on them I shall use up all my arrows.
24They will be weakened by hunger,
eaten away by plague
and the bitter scourge.
Against them I shall send the fang
of wild animals
and the poison of snakes
that glide in the dust.
25Outside, the sword bereaves,
while inside terror will reign.
Young man and girl alike will perish,
suckling and greybeard both together.
26I should crush them to dust, I said,
I should wipe out all memory of them,
27did I not fear the boasting of the enemy.'
But do not let their foes be mistaken!
Do not let them say,
'We have got the upper hand
and Yahweh plays no part in this.'
28What a short-sighted nation this is,
how thoroughly imperceptive!
29Were they wise, they would succeed,
they would be able to read their destiny.
30How else could one man rout a thousand,
how could two put ten thousand to flight,
were it not that their Rock has sold them,
that Yahweh has delivered them up?
31But their rock is not like our Rock;
our enemies cannot pray for us!
32For their vine springs
from the stock of Sodom
and from the groves of Gomorrah:
their grapes are poisonous grapes,
their clusters are bitter;
33their wine is snakes' poison,
the vipers' cruel venom.
34But he, is he not safe with me,
sealed inside my treasury?
35Vengeance is mine, I will pay them back,
for the time when they make a false step.
For the day of their ruin is close,
doom is rushing towards them,
for he will see to it that their power fails,
that neither serf nor free man remains.
36(For Yahweh will see his people righted,
he will take pity on his servants.)
37'Where are their gods then?' he will ask,
'the rock where they sought refuge,
38who ate the fat of their sacrifices
and drank the wine of their libations?'
Let these arise and help you,
let these be the shelter above you!
39See now that I, I am he,
and beside me there is no other god.
It is I who deal death and life;
when I have struck, it is I who heal
(no one can rescue anyone from me).

40Yes, I raise my hand to heaven,
and I say, 'As surely as I live for ever,
41When I have whetted my flashing sword,
I shall enforce justice,
I shall return vengeance to my foes,
I shall take vengeance on my foes.
42I shall make my arrows drunk with blood,
and my sword will feed on flesh:
the blood of the wounded
and the prisoners,
the dishevelled heads of the enemy!'

43Heavens, rejoice with him,
let all the children of God pay him homage!
Nations, rejoice with his people,
let God's envoys tell of his power!
For he will avenge the blood of his servants,
he will return vengeance to my foes,
he will repay those who hate him
and purify his people's country.

44Moses came with Joshua son of Nun and recited all the words of this song in the people's hearing.

The Law, the source of life

[45]When Moses had finished reciting these words to all Israel, [46]he said to them, 'Take all these words to heart; I intend them today to be evidence against you. You must order your children to keep and observe all the words of this Law. [47]You must not think of this as empty words, for the Law is your life, and by its means you will live long in the country which you are crossing the Jordan to possess.'

Moses' death foretold

[48]Yahweh spoke to Moses that same day and said to him, [49]'Climb this mountain of the Abarim, Mount Nebo, in the country of Moab, opposite Jericho, and view the Canaan which I am giving to the Israelites as their domain. [50]Die on the mountain you have climbed, and be gathered to your people, as your brother Aaron died on Mount Hor and was gathered to his people. [51]Because, with the other Israelites, you broke faith with me at the Waters of Meribah-Kadesh in the desert of Zin, because you did not make my holiness clear to the Israelites; [52]you may only see the country from outside; you cannot enter it—the country which I am giving to the Israelites.'

Moses blesses the tribes

33 This is the blessing that Moses, man of God, pronounced over the Israelites before he died. [2]He said:

Yahweh came from Sinai,
from Seir he dawned on us,
from Mount Paran blazed forth,
For them he came,
after the mustering at Kadesh,
from his zenith as far as the foothills.

[3]You who love the ancestors!
Your holy ones are all at your command.
At your feet they fell,
under your guidance went swiftly on.

[4](Moses enjoined a law on us.)
The assembly of Jacob
comes into its inheritance;
[5]there was a king in Jeshurun
when the heads of the people foregathered
and the tribes of Israel were all assembled!

[6]May Reuben survive and not die out,
survive though his men be few!

[7]Of Judah he said this:
Listen, Yahweh, to the voice of Judah,
and bring him back to his people.
That his hands may defend his rights,
come to his help against his foes!

[8]Of Levi he said:
To Levi, give your *urim*,
to your faithful one, your *thummim*,
having tested him at Massah,
having striven with him
at the Waters of Meribah.
[9]Of his father and mother, he says,
'I have not seen them.'
He does not acknowledge his brothers,
nor does he know his own children.
Yes, they have kept your word,
they hold firmly to your covenant.
[10]They will teach your customs to Jacob,
and your Law to Israel.
They will put incense before you
and burnt offerings on your altar.
[11]Yahweh, bless his worthiness,
and accept the actions he performs.
Crush the loins
of those who rise against him
and of his foes,
so that they rise no more!

[12]Of Benjamin he said:
Beloved of Yahweh,
he rests trustfully near him.
The Most High protects him day after day
and dwells between his hillsides.

[13]Of Joseph he said:
His land is blessed by Yahweh.
For him the best of heaven's dew
and of the deep that lies below,
[14]the best of what the sun makes grow,
of what springs with every month,
[15]the first-fruits of the ancient mountains,
the best from the hills of old
[16]the best of the land and all it holds,
the favour of him who dwells in the Bush.
May the hair grow thick
on the head of Joseph,
on the brow of the consecrated one
among his brothers!
[17]First-born of the Bull, his the glory.
His horns are the wild ox's horns,
with which he gores the peoples
to the very ends of the earth.
Such are the myriads of Ephraim,
such are the thousands of Manasseh.

18 Of Zebulun he said:
Prosper, Zebulun, in your expeditions,
and you, Issachar, in your tents!
19 On the mountain
where the people come to pray
they offer upright sacrifices,
for they taste the riches of the seas
and the treasures hidden in the sands.

20 Of Gad he said:
Blessed be he
who gives Gad space enough!
He lies there like a lioness;
he has savaged arm and face and head.
21 Then he took the first portion for himself,
saw that there was stored up for him
a leader's share.
He has come at the head of the people,
has carried out
the saving justice of Yahweh
and his judgements on Israel.

22 Of Dan he said:
Dan is a lion cub
leaping from Bashan.

23 Of Naphtali he said:
Naphtali, sated with favours,
filled with the blessings of Yahweh:
the west and south are to be his domain.

24 Of Asher he said:
Most blessed of the sons let Asher be!
Let him be the most privileged
of his brothers
and let him bathe his feet in oil!
25 Be your bolts of iron and of bronze
and your security as lasting as your days!

26 No one is like the God of Jeshurun:
he rides the heavens to your rescue,
rides the clouds in his majesty!
27 The God of old is your refuge,
his the eternal arm which here below
drives the enemy before you;
he it is who says, 'Destroy!'
28 Israel rests trustfully.
The well-spring of Jacob is chosen out
for a land of corn and wine;
there heaven itself rains down dew.

29 Blessed are you, O Israel!
Who is like you, O victorious people?
Yahweh is the shield that protects you
and the sword that leads you to triumph.
Your enemies will try to corrupt you,
but you yourself
will trample on their backs.

The death of Moses

34 Then, leaving the Plains of Moab,
Moses went up Mount Nebo, the peak
of Pisgah opposite Jericho, and Yahweh
showed him the whole country: Gilead as far
as Dan, 2 the whole of Naphtali, the country
of Ephraim and Manasseh, the whole country
of Judah as far as the Western Sea, 3 the
Negeb, and the region of the Valley of
Jericho, city of palm trees, as far as Zoar.
4 Yahweh said to him, 'This is the country
which I promised on oath to give to Abraham,
Isaac and Jacob, saying: I shall give it to your
descendants. I have allowed you to see it for
yourself, but you will not cross into it.'
5 There in the country of Moab, Moses,
servant of Yahweh, died as Yahweh decreed;
6 he[a] buried him in the valley, in the country
of Moab, opposite Beth-Peor; but to this day
no one has ever found his grave. 7 Moses was
a hundred and twenty years old when he died,
his eye undimmed, his vigour unimpaired.
8 The Israelites wept for Moses on the Plains
of Moab for thirty days. The days of weeping
for the mourning rites of Moses came to an
end. 9 Joshua son of Nun was filled with the
spirit of wisdom, for Moses had laid his
hands on him, and him the Israelites obeyed,
carrying out the order which Yahweh had
given to Moses.
10 Since then, there has never been such a
prophet in Israel as Moses, the man whom
Yahweh knew face to face. 11 What signs and
wonders Yahweh caused him to perform in
Egypt against Pharaoh, all his servants and
his whole country! 12 How mighty the hand
and great the fear that Moses wielded in the
eyes of all Israel!

34a i.e. Yahweh, but Sam. and some Greek texts read 'they'.

THE DEUTERONOMIC HISTORY

The books of Joshua, Judges, Samuel and Kings form one great history, telling the story of Israel from the settlement in Palestine until the Babylonian exile. The materials on which the author draws vary enormously, from folk-tales, through cycles of stories about Elijah and Elisha, to court records of the kings. But the final editor is concerned above all with one viewpoint: fidelity to Yahweh brings prosperity, while desertion of him brings punishment.

Throughout these 600 years Israel again and again deserts the covenant and needs to be drawn back to its duty. This lesson of history is taught both by the selection and shaping of material and by the editorial comment which points the moral from time to time. The theological angle is typical of the religious reforms of 622 BC and of the Book of Deuteronomy which is associated with them, and for this reason modern scholars have given the group of books this name, though there must have been a final edition some fifty years later after the destruction of Jerusalem.

THE BOOK OF JOSHUA

This first book of the deuteronomic history begins by recounting the conquest of the Promised Land. It gives the impression of a sweeping and quick victory by Yahweh and his lieutenant Joshua—a way of stressing that Israel owes its land to Yahweh. In fact almost all the stories of conquest (chh. 2—9) concern the territories of the small tribe of Benjamin and contain folk traditions of the tribe. Many of them give historical reasons for notable features of the countryside, e.g. the two stories to explain a group of stones in the Jordan and at Gilgal (4:1–9, 19–24), or the explanation of the spectacular ruin at Ai. The story of the destruction of Jericho is presented as a religious, almost liturgical, act to emphasise that Yahweh alone is responsible for the victory, and to relate this fine empty site (in fact destroyed long before) to the conquest. Other biblical passages make clear that large tracts remained too strong for Israel until David's time. And even in the course of this conquering progress there are warnings, when victory is turned to defeat because of disobedience to Yahweh's commands.

The distribution of land by Joshua in the second part of the book is a formal justification of the later holdings of the tribes and the theoretical boundaries of the Holy Land. Since cities of refuge were not instituted before Solomon's time this list (ch. 20) must also be later. The title of all the tribes to their ancestral land was its grant by Yahweh through his servant Joshua.

In fact the land was acquired in many different ways: some elements in Israel never went down to Egypt, some infiltrated peacefully, some invaded from the south, only some (with Joshua) from the east. The great assembly at Shechem which forms the conclusion of the book seals the religious bonds of the various Semitic groups in Palestine which join Joshua and thus commit themselves to his victorious God.

PLAN OF THE BOOK

I The Conquest of the Promised Land 1—12
- **A** The Preparations 1—2
- **B** The Crossing of the Jordan 3—5:12
- **C** The Conquest of Jericho 5:13—7
- **D** The Capture of Ai 8:1–29
- **E** Sacrifice and Reading of the Law on Mount Ebal 8:30–35
- **F** The Treaty between Israel and the Gibeonites 9
- **G** Coalition of Five Amorite Kings— Conquest of Southern Palestine 10
- **H** The Conquest of the North 11
- **I** Recapitulation 12

II Distribution of the Country among the Tribes 13—21
- **A** Description of the Transjordanian Tribes 13:8–33
- **B** Description of the Three Large Tribes to the West of Jordan 14—17
- **C** Description of the Seven Other Tribes 18—19
- **D** Privileged Towns 20—21

III The Close of Joshua's Career 22—24
- **A** The Return of the Eastern Tribes— The Question of their Altar 22
- **B** Last Discourse of Joshua 23
- **C** The Great Assembly at Shechem 24:1–28
- **D** Two Additions 24:29–34

THE BOOK OF JOSHUA

I: THE CONQUEST OF THE PROMISED LAND

A: THE PREPARATIONS

The summons to enter the Promised Land

1 When Moses, servant of Yahweh, was
dead, Yahweh spoke to Joshua son of
Nun, Moses' adjutant. He said, 2 'Moses my
servant is dead; go now and cross this Jordan,
you and this whole people, into the country
which I am giving to them (the Israelites).
3 Every place you tread with the soles of your
feet I shall give you, as I declared to Moses
that I would. 4 From the desert and the
Lebanon, to the Great River, the Euphrates

(the entire country of the Hittites), and as far
as the Great Sea to westward, is to be your
territory. 5As long as you live, no one will be
able to resist you; I shall be with you as I was
with Moses; I shall not fail you or desert you.

God's help conditional on faithfulness to the Law

6'Be strong and stand firm, for you are the
man to give this people possession of the land
which I swore to their ancestors that I would
give them. 7Only be strong and stand very
firm and be careful to keep the whole Law
which my servant Moses laid down for you.
Do not swerve from this either to right or to
left, and then you will succeed wherever you
go. 8Have the book of this Law always on
your lips; meditate on it day and night, so
that you may carefully keep everything that
is written in it. Then your undertakings will
prosper, then you will have success. 9Have I
not told you: Be strong and stand firm? Be
fearless and undaunted, for go where you
may, Yahweh your God is with you.'

Support from the Transjordanian tribes

10Joshua then gave the people's officials this
instruction: 11'Go through the camp and give
the people this order, "Make provisions
ready, for in three days' time you will cross
this Jordan and go on to take possession of
the land which Yahweh your God is giving
you as your own." ' 12Joshua then said to the
Reubenites and Gadites and the half-tribe of
Manasseh, 13'Remember the order given you
by Moses, servant of Yahweh: Yahweh your
God, in bringing you to rest, has given
you the land where we are. 14Your wives,
your little ones and your cattle must stay in
the country given you by Moses beyond the
Jordan. But all you fighting men must cross in
battle formation at the head of your brothers
and help them, 15until Yahweh grants rest to
your brothers and you alike, when they too
have taken possession of the land which
Yahweh your God is giving to them. Then
you may go back and take possession of the
land which belongs to you and which Moses,
servant of Yahweh, has given you on the
eastern side of the Jordan.' 16They answered
Joshua, 'We will do whatever you order us,
and wherever you send us we will go. 17We
obeyed Moses in everything, and now we will
obey you. Only may Yahweh your God be
with you as he was with Moses! 18If anyone
rebels against your orders or will not listen
to your commands, let him be put to death.
Only be strong and stand firm.'

Joshua's spies at Jericho

2 From Shittim, Joshua son of Nun secretly
sent two men to reconnoitre. He said, 'Go
and explore the country and Jericho.' They
left; they went into the house of a prostitute
called Rahab, to spend the night there. 2The
king of Jericho was told, 'Some men have
come here tonight from the Israelites, to
reconnoitre the country.' 3The king of
Jericho then sent a message to Rahab, 'Send
out the men who came to you and are lodging
in your house, for they have come to
reconnoitre the whole country.' 4But the
woman took the two men and hid them. 'It
is true,' she said, 'the men did come to me,
but I did not know where they came from.
5When the city gate was about to be closed
at nightfall, the men went out and I cannot say
where they have gone. Follow them quickly
and you will overtake them.'

6She had taken them up to the roof and
hidden them under some stalks of flax which
she had laid out there. 7The men hurried in
pursuit of them towards the Jordan, as far as
the fords, and the gate was shut once the
pursuers had gone through.

The pact between Rahab and the spies

8The two men had not yet settled down for
the night when Rahab came up to them
on the roof. 9She said to them, 'I know that
Yahweh has given you this country, that we
are afraid of you and that everyone living in
this country has been seized with terror at
your approach; 10for we have heard how
Yahweh dried up the Sea of Reeds before you
when you came out of Egypt and what you
did to the two Amorite kings across the
Jordan, Sihon and Og, whom you put under
the curse of destruction. 11When we heard
this, our hearts failed us, and now no one has
any courage left to resist you, since Yahweh
your God is God both in heaven above and
on earth beneath. 12So, swear to me now by
Yahweh, since I have been kind to you, 13that
you in your turn will be kind to my father's
family; and give me a sure sign of this: that
you will spare the lives of my father and
mother, my brothers and sisters and all who

belong to them, and will preserve us from death.'

[14]The men replied, 'We pledge you our lives, provided that you say nothing about our mission. When Yahweh has given us the country, we shall treat you kindly and faithfully.' [15]She then let them down from the window on a rope, as her house was against the city wall and she actually lived in the wall. [16]'Make for the hills,' she said, 'or you may run into your pursuers. Hide there for three days, until your pursuers have come back, and then go on your way.' [17]The men said, 'This is how we shall fulfil the oath which you have made us swear: [18]when we invade the country, you must tie this scarlet cord to the window from which you let us down, and collect your father, mother, brothers and entire family inside your house. [19]If anyone goes out of the doors of your house into the street, his blood will be on his own head and we shall not be to blame; but the blood of all staying inside the house with you will be on our heads if a hand is laid on any of them. [20]But if you divulge our mission in the meanwhile, we shall be free of the oath which you have made us swear.' [21]She replied, 'Let it be as you say.' She let them go, and they left. She then tied the scarlet cord to the window.

The spies return

[22]They left and made for the hills. They stayed there for three days, until their pursuers had gone home, having scoured the countryside without finding them. [23]The two men then came down again from the hills, crossed over and, going to Joshua son of Nun, told him everything that had happened to them. [24]To Joshua they said, 'Yahweh has put the whole country at our mercy, and its inhabitants are all panic-stricken at our approach.'

B: THE CROSSING OF THE JORDAN

Before the crossing

3 Early in the morning, Joshua struck camp and set out from Shittim with all the Israelites. They went as far as the Jordan and there they camped before they crossed. [2]Three days later, the officials went through the camp [3]and gave the people these instructions, 'When you see the ark of the covenant of Yahweh your God being carried by the levitical priests, you will leave your position and follow it, [4b]so that you may know which way to take, since you have never gone this way before. [4a]Between you and the ark, however, keep a distance of about two thousand cubits: do not go near it.' [5]Joshua said to the people, 'Sanctify yourselves, since tomorrow Yahweh will work wonders among you.' [6]Joshua then said to the priests, 'Take up the ark of the covenant and cross at the head of the people.' They took up the ark of the covenant and moved to the head of the people.

Final instructions

[7]Yahweh said to Joshua, 'This very day, I shall begin to make you great in the eyes of all Israel so that they will know that, as I was with Moses, so I shall be with you. [8]Now, give this order to the priests carrying the ark of the covenant, "When you have reached the brink of the waters of the Jordan, you must halt in the Jordan itself." ' [9]To the Israelites, Joshua then said, 'Come closer and hear the words of Yahweh your God.' [10]Joshua said, 'By this, you are to know that the living God is with you and without a doubt will expel the Canaanites, the Hittites, the Hivites, Perizzites, Girgashites, Amorites and Jebusites before you. [11]Look, the ark of the covenant of the Lord of the whole earth is about to move into the Jordan at your head. [12]Now choose twelve men from the tribes of Israel, one man from each tribe. [13]As soon as the priests carrying the ark of Yahweh, Lord of the whole earth, have set the soles of their feet in the waters of the Jordan, the waters of the Jordan will be cut off; the upper waters flowing down will stop as a single mass.'

Crossing the Jordan

[14]Accordingly, when the people left their tents to cross the Jordan, the priests carried the ark of the covenant ahead of the people. [15]As soon as the bearers of the ark reached the Jordan and the feet of the priests carrying the ark touched the waters—the Jordan is in spate throughout the harvest season—[16]the upper waters stood still and formed a single mass over a great distance, at Adam, the town near Zarethan, while those flowing down to

the Sea of the Arabah, the Salt Sea, were completely separated. The people crossed opposite Jericho. 17The priests carrying the ark of the covenant of Yahweh stood firm on dry ground in mid-Jordan, while all Israel crossed on dry ground, until the whole nation had completed its crossing of the Jordan.

The twelve memorial stones

4 When the whole nation had finished crossing the Jordan, Yahweh spoke to Joshua and said, 2'Choose twelve men from the people, one man from each tribe, and give them this order, 3"Here, from mid-Jordan, from the place where the priests' feet were standing, take twelve stones; carry them with you and set them down in the camp where you pass the night." ' 4Joshua called the twelve men whom he had selected from the Israelites, one man from each tribe, 5and Joshua said to them, 'Go on ahead of the ark of Yahweh your God into mid-Jordan, and each of you take one stone on his shoulder, corresponding to the number of the tribes of Israel, 6to make this a sign among you; and when, in the future, your children ask you, "What do these stones mean for you?" 7you will then tell them, "The waters of the Jordan separated before the ark of the covenant of Yahweh; when it crossed the Jordan, the waters of the river separated. These stones are an everlasting reminder of this to the Israelites." ' 8The Israelites did as Joshua ordered; they took twelve stones from mid-Jordan corresponding to the number of the tribes of Israel, as Yahweh had told Joshua; they carried them over to the camp and set them down there. 9Joshua then erected twelve stones in mid-Jordan, on the spot where the feet of the priests carrying the ark of the covenant had stood; and they are still there today.

The crossing ends

10The priests carrying the ark stood still in mid-Jordan, until everything had been done that Yahweh had ordered Joshua to tell the people (in accordance with everything that Moses had ordered Joshua); and the people hurried across. 11When the people had finished crossing, the ark of Yahweh then crossed, with the priests, to the head of the people. 12The sons of Reuben, the sons of Gad and the half-tribe of Manasseh crossed in battle formation at the head of the Israelites, as Moses had told them. 13Some forty thousand warriors in arms, they crossed in Yahweh's presence, ready for battle, towards the plain of Jericho. 14That day, Yahweh made Joshua great in the eyes of all Israel, who respected him as they had respected Moses, as long as he lived. 15Yahweh said to Joshua, 16'Order the priests carrying the ark of the Testimony to come up out of the Jordan.' 17And Joshua gave the order to the priests, 'Come up, out of the Jordan!' 18Now, when the priests carrying the ark of the covenant of Yahweh came up out of mid-Jordan, no sooner had the soles of the priests' feet touched solid ground, than the waters of the Jordan returned to their bed and ran on, in spate as before.

Arrival at Gilgal

19It was the tenth day of the first month when the people came up from the Jordan and made their camp at Gilgal, on the eastern border of Jericho. 20As regards those twelve stones, which they had taken from the Jordan, Joshua set them up at Gilgal. 21He then said to the Israelites, 'When, in the future, your children ask their fathers, "What are these stones?" 22you will explain to your children, "Israel crossed this Jordan dry-shod. 23For Yahweh your God dried up the waters of the Jordan in front of you until you had crossed, just as Yahweh your God did to the Sea of Reeds, which he dried up before us until we had crossed it; 24so that all the peoples of the earth may know how mighty the hand of Yahweh is, and always stand in awe of Yahweh your God." '

Terror of the peoples west of the Jordan

5 When all the kings of the Amorites living to westward across the Jordan, and all the kings of the Canaanites living on the seaboard, heard that Yahweh had dried up the waters of the Jordan before the Israelites until they had crossed, their hearts failed and they lost all courage to resist the Israelites.

Circumcision of the Hebrews at Gilgal

2At this time Yahweh said to Joshua, 'Make flint knives and circumcise the Israelites again (a second time). 3Joshua made flint

knives and circumcised the Israelites on the
Hill of Foreskins.
4The reason why Joshua circumcised them
was this. All the males of the people who had
come out of Egypt of age to bear arms had
died in the desert on their journey after
leaving Egypt. 5Now, all the people who
came out had been circumcised; but none of
those born in the desert, during the journey,
after leaving Egypt, had been circumcised;
6for the Israelites walked the desert for forty
years, until the whole nation had died out,
that is, the men who had come out of Egypt
of age to bear arms; they had not obeyed the
voice of Yahweh, and Yahweh had sworn to
them never to let them see the land which he
had sworn to their ancestors that he would
give us, a land flowing with milk and honey.
7But in place of these he set their sons, and
these were the ones whom Joshua circum-
cised: they were uncircumcised because they
had not been circumcised during the journey.
8When the circumcising of the whole nation
was finished, they stayed resting in the camp
till they were well again. 9Yahweh then said
to Joshua, 'Today I have taken the shame of
Egypt away from you.' Hence, the place has
been called Gilgal[a] ever since.

Celebration of the Passover

10The Israelites pitched their camp at Gilgal
and kept the Passover there on the fourteenth
day of the month, at evening, in the plain of
Jericho. 11On the very next day after the
Passover, they ate what the land produced,
unleavened bread and roasted ears of corn.
12The manna stopped the day after they had
eaten the produce of the land. The Israelites
from that year onwards ate the produce of
Canaan and had no more manna.

C: THE CONQUEST OF JERICHO

Prelude: a theophany

13Now when Joshua was near Jericho, he
looked up and saw a man standing in front of
him, grasping a naked sword. Joshua walked
towards him and said to him, 'Are you on our
side or on that of our enemies?' 14He replied,
'On neither side. I have come now as the
captain of the army of Yahweh.' Joshua fell
on his face to the ground, worshipping him,
and said, 'What has my Lord to say to
his servant?' 15The captain of the army of
Yahweh answered Joshua, 'Take your
sandals off your feet, for the place where you
are standing is holy.' And Joshua did so.

Capture of Jericho[a]

6 Now, Jericho had shut and barricaded its
gates (against the Israelites): no one came
out and no one went in. 2Yahweh then said
to Joshua, 'Look, I am putting Jericho, its
picked troops and its king, at your mercy.
3All you warriors must march round the city
(go right round the city once, doing the same
on six successive days. 4Seven priests must
carry seven ram's-horn trumpets in front of
the ark. On the seventh day, you will go
seven times round the city and the priests
will blow their trumpets). 5When the ram's
horn sounds (when you hear the sound of the
trumpet), the entire people must utter a
mighty war cry and the city wall will collapse
then and there; the people will then go into
the assault, each man straight ahead.'
6Joshua son of Nun summoned the priests
and said to them, 'Take up the ark of the
covenant, and let seven priests carry seven
ram's-horn trumpets ahead of the ark of
Yahweh.' 7To the people he then said,
'Forward! March round the city, and let the
vanguard march ahead of the ark of Yahweh!'
8(Everything was done as Joshua had given
orders to the people.) Seven priests, carrying
seven ram's-horn trumpets ahead of Yahweh,
moved forward blowing their trumpets; the
ark of the covenant of Yahweh came behind
them, 9the vanguard marched ahead of the
priests, who blew their trumpets, the rear-
guard followed behind the ark; the men
marched, the trumpets sounded.
10Joshua had given the people the following
orders, 'Do not raise a war cry, do not let
your voice be heard (not a word must pass
your lips), until the day when I say, "Raise
the war cry." That is when you must raise
the war cry.'
11He made the ark go round the city (going
round it once), then they went back to camp,
where they spent the night. 12Joshua got up
early, and the priests took up the ark of

5a Word-play with *galloti* (=I have taken away). In fact Gilgal =circle, cf. 4:20.
6a The Hebr. text is longer than the Gk, which omits passages given here in brackets.

Yahweh. [13]Carrying the seven ram's-horn
trumpets, the seven priests walked ahead of
the ark of Yahweh, blowing their trumpets
as they went, while the vanguard marched
ahead of them and the rearguard behind the
ark of Yahweh, and the march went on to the
sound of the trumpet.
[14]They marched once round the city (on
the second day) and went back to camp; and
so on for six days. [15]On the seventh day, they
got up at dawn and marched (in the same
manner) round the city seven times. (This
was the only day when they marched round
the city seven times.) [16]At the seventh time,
the priests blew their trumpets and Joshua
said to the people, 'Raise the war cry, for
Yahweh has given you the city!

Jericho placed under the curse of destruction

[17]'The city and everyone in it must be devoted
to Yahweh under the curse of destruction;
the life of Rahab the prostitute alone must be
spared, with all those with her in her house,
since she hid the messengers we sent. [18]But
beware of the curse of destruction, your-
selves, for fear that, moved by greed, you
take something lying under the curse; that
would put the camp of Israel under the same
curse and bring disaster on it. [19]All the silver
and all the gold, everything made of bronze
or iron, will be consecrated to Yahweh and
put in his treasury.'
[20]The people raised the war cry, the trum-
pets sounded. When the people heard the
sound of the trumpet, they raised a mighty
war cry and the wall collapsed then and there.
At once the people stormed the city, each
man going straight forward; and they
captured the city. [21]They enforced the curse
of destruction on everyone in the city: men
and women, young and old, including the
oxen, the sheep and the donkeys, slaugh-
tering them all.

Rahab's house preserved

[22]Joshua said to the two men who had
reconnoitred the country, 'Go into the prosti-
tute's house, and bring the woman out with
all who belong to her, as you swore to her
that you would.' [23]The young men who had
been spies went and brought Rahab out, with
her father and mother and brothers and all
who belonged to her. They brought out all
her clansmen too, and put them in a place of
safety outside the camp of Israel.
[24]They burned the city and everything
inside it, except the silver, the gold and the
things of bronze and iron; these they put into
the treasury of Yahweh's house. [25]But Rahab
the prostitute, her father's family and all
who belonged to her, these Joshua spared.
She is still living in Israel even today, for
having hidden the messengers whom Joshua
sent to reconnoitre Jericho.

A curse on anyone who rebuilds Jericho

[26]At that time Joshua made them take this
oath before Yahweh:

Accursed before Yahweh
  be the man who rises up
and rebuilds this city (Jericho)!
On his first-born
  will he lay its foundations,
on his youngest son set up its gates!

[27]So Yahweh was with Joshua, whose fame
spread throughout the country.

Violation of the curse of destruction

7 But the Israelites were unfaithful to the
curse of destruction. Achan son of Carmi,
son of Zabdi, son of Zerah, of the tribe of
Judah, took something that fell under the
curse of destruction, and the anger of Yahweh
was aroused against the Israelites.

The sacrilege punished by a repulse at Ai

[2]Now Joshua sent men from Jericho to Ai[a]
(which is near Beth-Aven), to the east of
Bethel, having said to them, 'Go up and
reconnoitre the country.' They went up and
reconnoitred Ai. [3]Coming back to Joshua,
they said, 'There is no need for the whole
people to go up; let some two or three thou-
sand go and attack Ai. Spare the whole people
such an effort; there are only a few of them!'
[4]Of the people, some three thousand
marched up, but these broke before the
people of Ai, [5]who killed some thirty-six of
them and pursued them from the town gate
as far as Shebarim, and on the slope cut them

7a The word *ai* = ruin, and the site is a spectacular ruin.

to pieces. The hearts of the people melted
away and turned to water.

Joshua's prayer

6Joshua then tore his clothes and prostrated
himself before the ark of Yahweh till night-
fall; the elders of Israel did the same, and all
poured dust on their heads. 7And Joshua
said, 'Alas, Lord Yahweh, why did you
bother to bring this nation across the Jordan,
if it was only to put us at the mercy of the
Amorites and destroy us? If only we could
have settled down on the other side of the
Jordan! 8Forgive me, Lord, but what can I
say, now that Israel has turned tail on the
enemy? 9The Canaanites, all the inhabitants
of the land, will hear of it; they will unite
against us to wipe our name from the earth.
And what will you do about your great Name
then?'

Yahweh's answer

10Yahweh said to Joshua, 'Stand up! Why are
you lying prostrate like this? 11Israel has
sinned; they have violated the covenant
which I imposed on them. They have gone
so far as to take what was under the curse of
destruction, they have even stolen it; they
have actually hidden it; they have put it in
their baggage. 12That is why the Israelites
cannot stand up to their foes, why they have
turned tail on their enemies: because they
have come under the curse of destruction
themselves. Unless you get rid of the object
among you which has been put under the
curse of destruction, I shall be with you no
longer.'

13'Get up, sanctify the people and say,
"Sanctify yourselves for tomorrow, since
Yahweh, the God of Israel, declares: The
curse of destruction has now fallen on you,
Israel; you will not be able to stand up to
your enemies, until you have rid yourselves
of that object which has been put under the
curse of destruction. 14Tomorrow morning,
therefore, you will come forward tribe by
tribe, and then the tribe which Yahweh
selects by lot will come forward clan by clan,
and the clan which Yahweh selects by lot will
come forward family by family, and the
family which Yahweh selects by lot will come
forward man by man. 15And the man indi-
cated by lot as regards the object which has
been put under the curse of destruction will
be delivered to the flames, he and all his
possessions, for having violated the covenant
with Yahweh and for having committed an
infamy in Israel." '

The culprit discovered and punished

16Joshua got up early; he made Israel come
forward tribe by tribe, and the lot indicated
the tribe of Judah. 17He summoned the clans
of Judah, and the lot indicated the clan of
Zerah. He summoned the clan of Zerah,
family by family, and the lot indicated Zabdi.
18Joshua then summoned the family of Zabdi,
man by man, and the lot indicated Achan son
of Carmi, son of Zabdi, son of Zerah, of the
tribe of Judah.

19Joshua then said to Achan, 'My son, give
glory to Yahweh, God of Israel, and confess;
tell me what you have done and hide nothing
from me.' 20Achan replied to Joshua, 'Yes, I
am the man who has sinned against Yahweh,
God of Israel, and this is what I have done.
21In the loot, I saw a fine robe from Shinar
and two hundred shekels of silver and an
ingot of gold weighing fifty shekels, I set my
heart on them and I took them. They are
hidden in the ground inside my tent, with
the silver underneath.'

22Joshua sent messengers; they ran to the
tent, and the robe was indeed hidden in the
tent, with the silver underneath. 23They took
the things out of the tent and, bringing them
to Joshua and all the Israelites, laid them out
before Yahweh.

24Joshua then took Achan son of Zerah and
led him up to the Vale of Achor, with the
silver and the robe and the ingot of gold, his
sons, his daughters, his oxen, his donkeys,
his sheep, his goats, his tent and all his
belongings. All Israel went with him.

25Joshua said, 'Why have you brought
misfortune on us? Today may Yahweh bring
misfortune on you!' And all Israel stoned him
to death (and they burned them and threw
stones at them).

26Over him, they raised a great mound of
stones, which is still there today. Yahweh
then relented from his fierce anger. That was
why the place was called the Vale of Achor,[b]
as it still is today.

7b Word-play with *'akar* (=bring bad luck).

D: THE CAPTURE OF AI

The command given to Joshua

8 Yahweh then said to Joshua, 'Be fearless
and undaunted. Take all your fighting
men with you. Up! March against Ai. Look,
I have put the king of Ai, his people, his town
and his territory at your mercy. 2 You must
treat Ai and its king as you treated Jericho
and its king. The only booty you will take are
the spoils and the cattle. Take up a concealed
position by the town, to the rear of it.'

Joshua's stratagem

3 Joshua set out to march against Ai with
all the fighting men. Joshua chose thirty
thousand of the bravest and sent them out
under cover of dark, 4 having given them
these orders, 'Pay attention! You must take
up a concealed position by the town, at the
rear, not very far from the town, and be sure
you all keep alert! 5 I, and the whole people
with me, shall advance on the town, and
when the people of Ai come out to engage us
as they did the first time, we shall run away
from them. 6 They will then give chase, and
we shall draw them away from the town,
since they will think, "They are running
away from us as they did the first time." 7 You
will then burst out of your concealed position
and seize the town; Yahweh your God will
put it at your mercy. 8 When you have
captured the town, set fire to it, in obedience
to Yahweh's command. Well then, these are
my orders.'
9 Joshua sent them off, and they made their
way to the place of ambush and took up
position between Bethel and Ai, to the west
of Ai. Joshua spent the night with the people,
10 then, getting up early next morning,
reviewed the people and, with the elders of
Israel, marched on Ai at their head. 11 All the
warriors marching with him advanced on the
front of the town and pitched camp north of
Ai, with the valley between them and the
town. 12 Joshua took about five thousand men
and concealed these between Bethel and Ai,
to the west of the town. 13 The people pitched
the main camp to the north of the town and
set up its ambush to the west of the town.
Joshua went that night into the middle of the
plain.

The capture of Ai

14 The king of Ai had seen this; the people of
the town got up early and hurried out, so that
he and all his people could engage Israel in
battle on the slope facing the Arabah; but he
did not know that an ambush had been laid
for him to the rear of the town. 15 Joshua and
all Israel pretended to be beaten by them and
took to their heels along the road to the
desert. 16 All the people in the town joined in
the pursuit and, in pursuing Joshua, were
drawn away from the town. 17 Not a man was
left in Ai (nor in Bethel), who had not gone
in pursuit of Israel; and in pursuing Israel
they left the town undefended.
18 Yahweh then said to Joshua, 'Point the
sabre in your hand at Ai; for I am about to
put the town at your mercy.' Joshua pointed
the sabre in his hand towards the town. 19 No
sooner had he stretched out his hand than
the men in ambush burst from their position,
ran forward, entered the town, captured it
and quickly set it on fire.
20 When the men of Ai looked back, they
saw smoke rising from the town into the sky.
None of them had the courage to run in any
direction, for the people fleeing towards the
desert turned back on their pursuers. 21 For,
once Joshua and all Israel saw that the town
had been seized by the men in ambush, and
that smoke was rising from the town, they
turned about and attacked the men of Ai.
22 The others came out from the town to
engage them too, and the men of Ai were
thus surrounded by Israelites, some on this
side and some on that. The Israelites struck
them down until not one was left alive and
none to flee; 23 but the king of Ai was taken
alive, and brought to Joshua. 24 When Israel
had finished killing all the inhabitants of Ai
in the open ground, and in the desert where
they had pursued them, and when every
single one had fallen to the sword, all Israel
returned to Ai and slaughtered its remaining
population. 25 The number of those who fell
that day, men and women together, was
twelve thousand, all people of Ai.

The curse of destruction; the destruction of the town

26 Joshua did not draw back the hand with
which he had pointed the sabre until he had
subjected all the inhabitants of Ai to the
curse of destruction. 27 For booty, Israel took

only the cattle and the spoils of this town, in accordance with the order that Yahweh had given to Joshua. 28 Joshua then burned Ai, making it a ruin for evermore, a desolate place even today. 29 He hanged the king of Ai from a tree till evening; but at sunset Joshua ordered his body to be taken down from the tree. It was then thrown down at the entrance to the town gate and on top of it was raised a great mound of stones, which is still there today.

E: SACRIFICE AND READING OF THE LAW ON MOUNT EBAL

The altar of undressed stones

30 Joshua then built an altar to Yahweh, God of Israel, on Mount Ebal, 31 as Moses, servant of Yahweh, had ordered the Israelites, as is written in the law of Moses: an altar of undressed stones, on which no iron has been used. On this they presented burnt offerings to Yahweh and communion sacrifices as well.

The reading of the Law

32 There, Joshua wrote on the stones a copy of the Law of Moses, which Moses had written in the presence of the Israelites. 33 All Israel, with their elders, their officials and their judges, stood on either side of the ark, facing the levitical priests who were carrying the ark of the covenant of Yahweh, foreigners with the native-born, half of them on the upper slopes of Mount Gerizim, and half of them on the upper slopes of Mount Ebal, as Moses, servant of Yahweh, had originally ordered for the blessing of the people of Israel. 34 After this, Joshua read all the words of the Law—the blessing and the cursing—exactly as it stands written in the Book of the Law. 35 Of every word laid down by Moses, not one was left unread by Joshua in the presence of the whole assembly of Israel, including the women and children, and the foreigners living with them.

F: THE TREATY BETWEEN ISRAEL AND THE GIBEONITES

A coalition against Israel

9 Hearing these things, all the kings on this side of the Jordan, in the highlands and in the lowlands, all along the coast of the Great Sea towards the Lebanon, Hittites, Amorites, Canaanites, Perizzites, Hivites and Jebusites, with one consent 2 formed a fighting alliance against Joshua and Israel.

The ruse of the Gibeonites

3 When the inhabitants of Gibeon learned how Joshua had treated Jericho and Ai, for their part, 4 they had recourse to a ruse. They provided themselves with supplies, and loaded their donkeys with old sacks and with old wineskins which had burst and been sewn up again. 5 They put on patched old sandals and worn-out clothes. The only bread they took with them to eat was dried up and crumbling.

6 They came to Joshua in the camp at Gilgal, and to him and the men of Israel they said, 'We come from a distant country, so make a treaty with us.' 7 The Israelites answered these Hivites, 'For all we know, you may live right among us. How then could we make a treaty with you?' 8 They said to Joshua, 'We are your servants.' 'But who are you?' Joshua asked them, 'and where do you come from?' 9 They said, 'Your servants have come from a country very far away, because of the fame of Yahweh your God; for we have heard of him and of all that he did in Egypt, 10 and of all that he did to the two Amorite kings who used to live on the other side of the Jordan: Sihon king of Heshbon, and Og king of Bashan, who used to live at Ashtaroth. 11 Because of which, our elders and all the people of our country said to us, "Take provisions with you for the journey; go and meet them and say to them: We are your servants; so make a treaty with us." 12 Here is our bread; it was warm when we took it from home to provide for our journey the day we set out to come to you, and now, you can see, it is dried up and crumbling. 13 These wineskins were new when we filled them; you can see, they have burst; and these clothes and sandals of ours are worn out from travelling such a long way.'

14 The leaders sampled some of the food they offered, but they did not ask Yahweh's orders. 15 Joshua made peace with them, and struck a treaty with them guaranteeing their lives, and the leaders of the community ratified it by oath.

16 Now it so happened that three days after the treaty had been made, it became known

that they were a neighbouring people, living
in Israel's region. 17 The Israelites set out
from camp, arriving in their towns three days
later. Their towns were Gibeon, Chephirah,
Beeroth and Kiriath-Jearim. 18 The Israelites
did not attack them, since the leaders of the
community had sworn to them by Yahweh,
God of Israel, but the whole community
muttered against the leaders.

The Gibeonites' place in the community

19 The leaders, however, all said to the whole
community, 'Since we have sworn an oath to
them by Yahweh, God of Israel, we cannot
touch them now. 20 This is what we shall do
with them: let them live, rather than bring
retribution down on ourselves on account of
the oath which we have sworn to them.'
21 And the leaders went on, 'Let them live,
but let them be wood-cutters and water-
carriers for the whole community.' Thus
spoke the leaders. 22 Joshua sent for the
Gibeonites and asked them, 'Why did you
deceive us by saying, "We live very far
away," when in fact you live right among us?
23 From now on, you are accursed and will for
ever be serfs, as wood-cutters and water-
carriers in the house of my God.' 24 Their
answer to Joshua was, 'We did it because your
servants had been rightly told that Yahweh
your God had ordered his servant Moses to
give you the whole of this country and destroy
all its inhabitants before you; also because,
as you advanced on us, we feared very greatly
for our lives. That was why we did this.
25 Now, as you see, we are at your mercy; do
to us whatever you think good and right.'
26 What he did with them was this: he saved
them from the hand of the Israelites, who did
not kill them. 27 But that very day Joshua
made them wood-cutters and water-carriers
for the community and for the altar of
Yahweh, at the place which he would eventu-
ally choose; and so they are today.

G: COALITION OF FIVE AMORITE KINGS—CONQUEST OF SOUTHERN PALESTINE

Five kings make war on Gibeon

10 Now, it happened that Adoni-Zedek
king of Jerusalem, learned that Joshua
had conquered Ai and put the town under
the curse of destruction, treating Ai and its
king as he had already treated Jericho and
its king; and also that the inhabitants of
Gibeon had made peace with Israel and were
living with them. 2 There was consternation
at this, since Gibeon was as important a town
as any of the royal towns themselves (it was
larger than Ai), while all its citizens were
fighting men. 3 Consequently, Adoni-Zedek
king of Jerusalem sent word to Hoham king
of Hebron, Piram king of Jarmuth, Japhia
king of Lachish, and Debir king of Eglon,
4 'Join me up here and help me to conquer
Gibeon, since it has made peace with Joshua
and the Israelites.' 5 The five Amorite kings
joined forces and went up there, that is, the
king of Jerusalem, the king of Hebron, the
king of Jarmuth, the king of Lachish and the
king of Eglon, they and all their armies;
laying siege to Gibeon, they attacked it.

Joshua comes to the rescue of Gibeon

6 The men of Gibeon sent word to Joshua in
the camp at Gilgal, 'Do not desert your
servants; come up here quickly to save us and
help us, since all the Amorite kings living in
the highlands have allied themselves against
us.' 7 Joshua came up from Gilgal, he, all the
fighting men and all the bravest of his army.
8 Yahweh said to Joshua, 'Do not be afraid of
these people; I have put them at your mercy;
not one of them will put up any resistance.'
9 Having marched from Gilgal throughout the
night, Joshua caught them unawares.

Aid from on high

10 Yahweh threw them into disorder at the
sight of Israel, defeating them completely at
Gibeon; furthermore, he pursued them by
way of the Descent of Beth-Horon and
harassed them as far as Azekah (and as far as
Makkedah). 11 And as they fled from Israel
down the Descent of Beth-Horon, Yahweh
hurled huge hailstones from heaven on them
all the way to Azekah, and they died. More
of them died under the hailstones than under
the swords of the Israelites. 12 Joshua then
spoke to Yahweh, the day Yahweh delivered
the Amorites to the Israelites. In the presence
of Israel, Joshua said:

Sun, stand still over Gibeon,
and, moon, you too,
over the Vale of Aijalon!

13And the sun stood still, and the moon
halted, until the people had taken vengeance
on their enemies.

Is this not written in the Book of the Just?
The sun stood still in the middle of the sky
and delayed its setting for almost a whole
day. 14There was never a day like that before
or since, when Yahweh obeyed the voice of
a man—for Yahweh was fighting for Israel.
15Joshua, and all Israel with him, then went
back to the camp at Gilgal.

The five kings in the cave at Makkedah

16As regards the five kings, these had fled and
hidden in the cave of Makkedah, 17and news
of this was brought to Joshua. 'The five
kings have been found hiding in the cave at
Makkedah.' 18Joshua said, 'Roll great stones
over the mouth of the cave and post men
there to keep guard. 19You yourselves, do not
stay there doing nothing; pursue the enemy,
cut off their line of retreat and do not let them
enter their towns, for Yahweh your God has
put them at your mercy.'

20When Joshua and the Israelites had
finished inflicting a very great defeat on them,
to the point of destroying them, those who
had escaped alive took refuge in their
fortresses. 21The people came back to
Joshua's camp at Makkedah; they were all
safe and sound, and no one dared to attempt
anything against the Israelites.

22Joshua then said, 'Clear the mouth of the
cave and bring the five kings out to me.'
23They did so, and brought the five kings out
of the cave to take them to him: the king of
Jerusalem, the king of Hebron, the king of
Jarmuth, the king of Lachish and the king
of Eglon. 24When these kings had been
brought out, Joshua assembled all the men
of Israel and said to the chiefs of the warriors
who had fought with him, 'Come forward
and put your feet on the necks of these kings!'
They came forward and put their feet on their
necks. 25'Be fearless and undaunted,' Joshua
went on, 'be strong and stand firm, for this
is how Yahweh will deal with all the enemies
you fight.' 26With this, Joshua struck and
killed them and had them hanged on five
trees; they hung there till evening.

27At the hour of sunset, on Joshua's orders,
they were taken down from the trees and
thrown into the cave where they had been
hiding. Great stones were laid over the mouth
of the cave, and these are still there to this
very day.

The conquest of the southern towns of Canaan

28The same day Joshua captured Makkedah,
putting it and its king to the sword; he
delivered them over to the curse of destruc-
tion, with every living creature there, and
let no one escape, and he treated the king of
Makkedah as he had treated the king of
Jericho.

29Joshua, and all Israel with him, went on
from Makkedah to Libnah and attacked it
30and Yahweh put this, too, and its king at
Israel's mercy; and Israel put every living
creature there to the sword, and left none
alive, and treated its king like the king of
Jericho.

31Joshua, and all Israel with him, went on
from Libnah to Lachish and besieged it and
attacked it. 32Yahweh put Lachish at Israel's
mercy, and Israel took it on the second day
and put it and every living creature in it
to the sword, as they had treated Libnah.
33Horam king of Gezer then marched up to
help Lachish, but Joshua beat him and his
people until not one was left alive.

34Joshua, and all Israel with him, went on
from Lachish to Eglon. They besieged it and
attacked it. 35The same day they took it and
put it to the sword. That day he delivered
over to the curse of destruction every living
creature there, treating it as he had treated
Lachish.

36Joshua, and all Israel with him, went on
up from Eglon to Hebron. They attacked it,
37took it and put it to the sword, with its king,
its dependencies and every living creature in
it. As he had treated Eglon, so here, he left
no one alive. He delivered it over to the curse
of destruction, with every living creature in
it.

38Joshua, and all Israel with him, then
turned back on Debir and attacked it. 39He
took it and its king and all the places
belonging to it; they put them to the sword,
and every living creature there they delivered
over to the curse of destruction. He left no
one alive. As he had treated Hebron, as he
had treated Libnah and its king, so he treated
Debir and its king.

The southern conquests recapitulated

40 Thus Joshua subjugated the whole country: the highlands, the Negeb, the lowlands and watered foothills, and all their kings. He left not one survivor and put every living thing under the curse of destruction, as Yahweh, God of Israel, had commanded. 41 Joshua conquered them from Kadesh-Barnea to Gaza, and the whole region of Goshen as far as Gibeon. 42 All these kings and their territory Joshua captured in a single campaign, because Yahweh, God of Israel, fought for Israel. 43 And then Joshua, and all Israel with him, went back to the camp at Gilgal.

H: THE CONQUEST OF THE NORTH

11 When Jabin king of Hazor heard about this, he sent word to Jobab king of Merom, to the king of Shimron, to the king of Achshaph 2 and to the kings in the northern highlands, in the plain south of Chinneroth, and those in the lowlands and on the slopes of Dor to the west. 3 To eastward and to westward lived the Canaanites: in the highlands, the Amorites, Hittites, Perizzites and Jebusites; the Hivites, at the foot of Hermon in the area of Mizpah. 4 They set out with all their troops, a people as numerous as the sands of the sea, with a huge number of horses and chariots.

The victory at Merom

5 These kings, having all agreed on a meeting place, came and set up camp together at the Waters of Merom, to fight Israel. 6 Yahweh then said to Joshua, 'Do not be afraid of them, for by this time tomorrow I shall hand them all over, cut to pieces, to Israel; you will hamstring their horses and burn their chariots.' 7 With all his warriors Joshua caught them unawares near the Waters of Merom and fell on them. 8 Yahweh put them at Israel's mercy and they defeated them and pursued them as far as Sidon the Great, and as far as Misrephoth to the west, and as far as the Vale of Mizpah to the east; they harried them until not one of them was left alive. 9 Joshua treated them as Yahweh had told him; he hamstrung their horses and burned their chariots.

The capture of Hazor and of the other northern towns

10 Joshua then turned back and captured Hazor, putting its king to the sword. Hazor in olden days was the capital of all these kingdoms. 11 In compliance with the curse of destruction, they put every living creature there to the sword. Not a living soul was left, and Hazor was burnt to the ground.

12 All these royal cities and all their kings Joshua put to the sword in compliance with the curse of destruction, as Moses, servant of Yahweh, had ordered.

13 Yet of all these towns standing on their mounds, Israel burned none, apart from Hazor, burnt by Joshua. 14 All the spoils of these towns, including the livestock, the Israelites took as booty for themselves. But they put all the human beings to the sword till they had destroyed them completely; they did not leave a living soul.

The orders of Moses carried out by Joshua

15 What Yahweh had ordered his servant Moses, Moses in turn had ordered Joshua, and Joshua carried it out, leaving nothing undone of what Yahweh had ordered Moses. 16 In consequence, Joshua captured this entire country: the highlands, the whole Negeb and the whole of Goshen, the lowlands, the Arabah, the highlands and lowlands of Israel.

17 From Mount Halak, which rises towards Seir, to Baal-Gad in the Vale of Lebanon at the foot of Mount Hermon, he captured all their kings, struck them down and put them to death. 18 For many a day Joshua made war on all these kings; 19 no city had made peace with the Israelites except the Hivites who lived at Gibeon; all the rest had been captured in battle. 20 For Yahweh had decided to harden the hearts of these men, so that they would engage Israel in battle and thus come under the curse of destruction and so receive no quarter but be exterminated, as Yahweh had ordered Moses.

Extermination of the Anakim

21 Joshua then went and wiped out the Anakim of the highlands, of Hebron, of Debir, of Anab, of all the highlands of Judah and of all the highlands of Israel; he delivered them and their towns over to the curse of destruction. 22 No Anakim were left in the

territory of the Israelites, except at Gaza, Gath and Ashdod. [23]Joshua captured the entire country, just as Yahweh had told Moses, and he gave it as heritage to Israel, to be shared out between their tribes.

And the country had rest from warfare.

I: RECAPITULATION

The kings conquered east of the Jordan

12 The kings of the country, whom the Israelites conquered and whose territory they took, on the further, eastern side of the Jordan, from the Wadi Arnon to Mount Hermon, with the entire Arabah to the east, were as follows:

[2]Sihon king of the Amorites, who lived at Heshbon, ruled from Aroer which is on the edge of the Arnon Valley, including the bottom of the valley, half Gilead and as far as the Jabbok, the river forming the frontier
with the Ammonites; [3]the eastern Arabah up to the Sea of Chinneroth, and as far as the Sea of the Arabah, or Salt Sea, on the eastern side, in the direction of Beth-Jeshimoth, and, in the south, the watered foothills of Mount Pisgah.

[4]Og king of Bashan, one of the last of the Rephaim, who lived at Ashtaroth and Edrei,
[5]ruled over Mount Hermon and Salecah, the whole of Bashan to the frontier of the Geshurites and Maacathites, and half Gilead to the frontier of Sihon king of Heshbon.

[6]Moses, servant of Yahweh, and the Israelites conquered these, and Moses, servant of Yahweh, conferred their territory on the Reubenites, the Gadites and the half-tribe of Manasseh.

The kings conquered west of the Jordan

[7]The kings of the country whom Joshua and the Israelites conquered on the nearer, western side of the Jordan, from Baal-Gad in the Vale of Lebanon to Mount Halak rising towards Seir, and whose heritage Joshua distributed to the tribes of Israel, dividing it up between them, were as follows:

[8]In the highlands and the lowlands, in the Arabah and in the watered foothills, in the desert and in the Negeb, belonging to the Hittites, the Amorites, the Canaanites, the Perizzites, the Hivites and the Jebusites:

[9]the king of Jericho, one;
the king of Ai near Bethel, one;
[10]the king of Jerusalem, one;
the king of Hebron, one;
[11]the king of Jarmuth, one;
the king of Lachish, one;
[12]the king of Eglon, one;
the king of Gezer, one;
[13]the king of Debir, one;
the king of Geder, one;
[14]the king of Hormah, one;
the king of Arad, one;
[15]the king of Libnah, one;
the king of Adullam, one;
[16]the king of Makkedah, one;
the king of Bethel, one;
[17]the king of Tappuah, one;
the king of Hepher, one;
[18]the king of Aphek, one;
the king of Sharon, one;
[19]the king of Merom, one;
the king of Hazor, one;
[20]the king of Shimron Meron, one;
the king of Achshaph, one;
[21]the king of Taanach, one;
the king of Megiddo, one;
[22]the king of Kedesh, one;
the king of Jokneam in Carmel, one;
[23]the king of Dor,
on the Slopes of Dor, one;
the king of the nations in Galilee, one;
[24]the king of Tirzah, one;
Total number of all these kings: thirty-one.

II: DISTRIBUTION OF THE COUNTRY AMONG THE TRIBES

Lands remaining unconquered

13 Now Joshua had grown old and advanced in years. Yahweh said to him, 'You are now old and advanced in years, yet there is still a great deal of territory left to be taken possession of. [2]This is all the territory left:

'All the districts of the Philistines and the whole country of the Geshurites; [3]from the Shihor, facing Egypt, to the frontier of Ekron in the north, is reckoned as Canaanite terri-

tory. The five rulers of the Philistines have
their seats at Gaza, Ashdod, Ashkelon, Gath
and Ekron, respectively; the Avvites are in
4the south. The entire territory of the
Canaanites, and Mearah which belongs to the
Sidonians, as far as Aphekah and as far as
the frontier of the Amorites; 5and then the
country of the Gebalites with the entire
Lebanon eastwards from Baal-Gad at the foot
of Mount Hermon to the Pass of Hamath.
6'All who live in the highlands from the
Lebanon to Misrephoth in the west—all the
Sidonians—I myself shall dispossess before
the Israelites. All you have to do is to
distribute the territory as a heritage for the
Israelites as I have ordered you. 7The time
has come to divide this territory as a heritage
between the nine tribes and the half-tribe of
Manasseh: from the Jordan as far as the Great
Sea in the west, you must give it them; the
Great Sea will be their limit.'

A: DESCRIPTION OF THE TRANSJORDANIAN TRIBES

A general survey

8As regards the other half-tribe of Manasseh,
this and the Reubenites and Gadites had
already received their heritage, given them
by Moses on the further, eastern side of the
Jordan, the one which Moses, servant of
Yahweh, had already given them: 9The
country onwards from Aroer on the edge
of the Arnon Valley, with the town in the
bottom of the valley and the entire tableland
from Medeba to Dibon; 10all the towns of
Sihon king of the Amorites, who had reigned
in Heshbon, to the frontier of the Ammon-
ites; 11then Gilead and the territory of the
Geshurites and Maacathites with the whole
Hermon range and the whole of Bashan as
far as Salecah; 12and in Bashan, the whole
kingdom of Og, who had reigned in Ashta-
roth and Edrei, and was the last of the
survivors of the Rephaim. Moses had con-
quered and dispossessed these two kings.
13The Israelites did not, however, dispossess
either the Geshurites or the Maacathites,
hence Geshur and Maacah survive inside
Israel even today.
14To the tribe of Levi alone no heritage
was given; Yahweh, God of Israel, was his
heritage, as he had told him.

The tribe of Reuben

15Moses had given the tribe of the sons of
Reuben a share by clans. 16Thus, their terri-
tory was the entire tableland from Aroer on
the edge of the Arnon Valley, with the town
in the bottom of the valley, as far as Medeba,
17Heshbon with all the towns on the table-
land: Dibon, Bamoth-Baal, Beth-Baal-
Meon, 18Jahaz, Kedemoth, Mephaath,
19Kiriathaim, Sibmah and, in the highlands
of the Arabah, Zereth-Shahar; 20Beth-Peor,
the watered foothills of Mount Pisgah, Beth-
ha-Jeshimoth, 21all the towns on the tableland
and the entire kingdom of Sihon king of the
Amorites, who had reigned in Heshbon; he
had been defeated by Moses, and with him
the princes of Midian, Evi, Rekem, Zur, Hur
and Reba, vassals of Sihon, formerly living
in the country.
22As regards Balaam son of Beor, the sooth-
sayer, the Israelites had put him to the sword
with those whom they had killed.
23The boundary of the Reubenites was the
Jordan and its territory.
Such was the heritage of the sons of
Reuben, by clans, with the towns and villages
belonging to them.

The tribe of Gad

24Moses had given the tribe of Gad, the sons
of Gad, a share by clans. 25Their territory was
Jazer, all the towns of Gilead, half the country
of the Ammonites as far as Aroer facing
Rabbah, 26and from Heshbon to Ramath-
Mizpeh and Betonim; from Mahanaim as far
as the territory of Lo-Debar, 27and in the
valley: Beth-Haram, Beth-Nimrah, Succoth,
and Zaphon—the rest of the kingdom of
Sihon king of Heshbon—the Jordan and the
territory running to the tip of the Sea of
Chinneroth, on the further, eastern side of
the Jordan.
28Such was the heritage of the sons of
Gad, by clans, with their towns and villages
belonging to them.

The half-tribe of Manasseh

29Moses had given the half-tribe of Manasseh
a share by clans. 30Their territory, starting
from Mahanaim, was the whole of Bashan,
the entire kingdom of Og king of Bashan, all
the Encampments of Jair in Bashan: sixty
towns. 31Half of Gilead, with Ashtaroth, and

Edrei, the royal cities of Og in Bashan, were allotted to the sons of Machir son of Manasseh, to half of the sons of Machir, by clans.

32This was what Moses had conferred in heritage on the Plains of Moab on the further, eastern side of the Jordan opposite Jericho. 33To the tribe of Levi, however, Moses gave no heritage; Yahweh, God of Israel, was his heritage, as he had told him.

B: DESCRIPTION OF THE THREE LARGE TRIBES TO THE WEST OF THE JORDAN

Introduction

14 This was what the Israelites received as their heritage in Canaan, which was given them as their heritage by the priest, Eleazar, and by Joshua son of Nun, with the heads of families of the tribes of Israel. 2They received their heritage by lot, as Yahweh had ordered through Moses, as regards the nine tribes and the half-tribe. 3For Moses himself had given the two-and-a-half tribes their heritage on the further side of the Jordan, although to the Levites he had given no heritage with them. 4Since the sons of Joseph formed two tribes, Manasseh and Ephraim, no share in the country was given to the Levites, apart from some towns to live in, with their pasture lands for their livestock and their possessions. 5The Israelites did as Yahweh had ordered Moses, and shared out the country.

Caleb's share

6Some sons of Judah came to Joshua at Gilgal, and Caleb son of Jephunneh the Kenizzite said to him, 'You know what Yahweh said to Moses, man of God, at Kadesh-Barnea concerning you and me. 7I was forty years old when Moses, servant of Yahweh, sent me from Kadesh-Barnea to reconnoitre this country, and I made him a completely honest report. 8The brothers, however, who had gone up with me discouraged the people, whereas I myself scrupulously obeyed Yahweh my God. 9That day Moses swore this oath, "Be sure of this, that the country your foot has trodden will be a heritage for you and your children for ever, since you have scrupulously obeyed Yahweh my God." 10From then till now, Yahweh has kept me alive in observance of his promise. It is forty-five years since Yahweh said this to Moses—Israel was then going through the desert—and now I am eighty-five years old. 11Today I am still as strong as the day when Moses sent me out on that errand; for fighting, for going and coming, I am as strong now as then. 12It is time you gave me the highlands, of which Yahweh spoke to me that day. You heard that day that there were Anakim and large, fortified towns there; but if Yahweh is with me, I shall drive them out, as Yahweh has said.'

13Joshua blessed Caleb son of Jephunneh and gave him Hebron as heritage. 14And hence Hebron down to the present day has remained the heritage of Caleb son of Jephunneh the Kenizzite, since he had scrupulously obeyed Yahweh, God of Israel. 15Hebron in olden days was called Kiriath-Arba. Arba had been the greatest of the Anakim.

And the country had rest from warfare.

The tribe of Judah

15 The portion falling to the tribe of the sons of Judah, by clans, was near the frontier of Edom, from the desert of Zin southwards to Kadesh in the south. 2Their southern frontier began at the tip of the Salt Sea, at the southerly bay; 3it proceeded south of the Ascent of Scorpions, crossed Zin and came up to Kadesh-Barnea from the south; past Hezron, it went on to Addar and turned towards Karka; 4the frontier then went on to Azmon, came out at the Torrent of Egypt and reached as far as the sea. This is to be your southern frontier.

5The eastern frontier was the Salt Sea as far as the mouth of the Jordan.

6The northern boundary began at the bay at the mouth of the Jordan. The boundary went up to Beth-Hoglah, passed north of Beth-ha-Arabah and went on to the Stone of Bohan son of Reuben. 7The boundary then went on to Debir from the Vale of Achor and turned north towards the stone circle opposite the Ascent of Adummim, which is south of the Torrent; the boundary went on to the Waters of En-Shemesh and came out at En-Rogel. 8It then went back up the Valley of Hinnom, coming from the south to the flank of the Jebusite—that is, Jerusalem—and climbed to the crest of the mountain

barring the Valley of Hinnom to the west,
at the northern end of the Valley of the
Rephaim. 9From the mountain top, the
boundary curved round to the spring of
the Waters of Nephtoah, went on to the
towns of Mount Ephron and then turned
towards Baalah—that is, Kiriath-Jearim.
10From Baalah, the boundary curved west-
wards to the highlands of Seir, skirted the
northern slope of Mount Jearim—that is,
Chesalon—went down to Beth-Shemesh and
through Timnah, 11came out on the northern
flank of Ekron, turned towards Shikkeron
and, passing through the highlands of
Baalah, came out at Jabneel, and reached as
far as the sea.

12The western boundary was the Great Sea
itself. Such was the frontier surrounding the
sons of Judah, by clans.

The Calebites occupy the territory of Hebron

13Caleb son of Jephunneh was given a share
within that of the sons of Judah, in accord-
ance with Yahweh's order to Joshua: Kiriath-
Arba, the town of the father of Anak—that
is, Hebron. 14Caleb drove out the three sons
of Anak: Sheshai, Ahiman and Talmai,
descended from Anak. 15From there he
marched on the inhabitants of Debir; Debir
in olden days was called Kiriath-Sepher.
16Caleb then said, 'To the man who attacks
and takes Kiriath-Sepher, I shall give my
daughter Achsah as wife.' 17The man who
captured it was Othniel son of Kenaz, brother
of Caleb, who gave him his daughter Achsah
as wife. 18When she arrived, he urged her to
ask her father for arable land, but when she
alighted from the donkey and Caleb asked
her, 'What is the matter?' 19she said to him,
'Grant me a blessing! As the land you have
given me is the Negeb, give me springs
of water too!' So Caleb gave her what she
wanted, the upper springs and the lower
springs.

20Such was the heritage of the tribe of the
sons of Judah, by clans.

Names of places owned by Judah

21Towns at the extremity of the tribe of the
sons of Judah, near the frontier of Edom in
the Negeb:

Kabzeel, Arad, Jagur, 22Kinah, Dimon,
Aroer, 23Kedesh, Hazor-Ithnan, 24Ziph,
Telem, Bealoth, 25Hazor-Hadattah, Kiriath-
Hezron—that is, Hazor—26Amam, Shema,
Moladah, 27Hazar-Gaddah, Heshmon, Beth-
Pelet, 28Hazar-Shual, Beersheba and its
dependencies, 29Baalah, Iim, Ezem,
30Eltolad, Chesil, Hormah, 31Ziklag,
Madmannah, Sansannah, 32Lebaoth,
Shilhim, Ain and Rimmon: in all, twenty-
nine towns with their villages.

33In the lowlands:

Eshtaol, Zorah, Ashnah, 34Zanoah, En-
Gannim, Tappuah, Enam, 35Jarmuth,
Adullam, Socoh, Azekah, 36Shaaraim,
Aditaim, Ha-Gederah and Gederothaim:
fourteen towns with their villages.

37Zenan, Hadashah, Migdal-Gad,
38Dilean, Ha-Mizpeh, Jokteel, 39Lachish,
Bozkath, Eglon, 40Cabbon, Lahmas,
Chitlish, 41Gederoth, Beth-Dagon, Naamah
and Makkedah: sixteen towns with their
villages.

42Libna, Ether, Asham, 43Iphtah, Ashnah,
Nezib, 44Keilah, Achzib and Mareshah: nine
towns with their villages.

45Ekron with its dependencies and its
villages. 46From Ekron to the sea, everything
to the side of Ashdod, with its villages.
47Ashdod with its dependencies and its
villages; Gaza with its dependencies and its
villages as far as the Torrent of Egypt, the
Great Sea forming the boundary.

48In the highlands:

Shamir, Jattir, Socoh, 49Dannah, Kiriath-
Sepher, now Debir, 50Anab, Eshtemoh,
Anim, 51Goshen, Holon and Giloh: eleven
towns with their villages.

52Arab, Dumah, Eshan, 53Janum, Beth-
Tappuah, Aphekah, 54Humtah, Kiriath-
Arba, now Hebron, and Zior: nine towns
with their villages.

55Maon, Carmel, Ziph, Juttah, 56Jezreel,
Jokdeam, Zanoah, 57Ha-Kain, Gibeah and
Timnah: ten towns with their villages.

58Halhul, Beth-Zur, Gedor, 59Maarath,
Beth-Anoth and Eltekon: six towns with
their villages.

Tekoa, Ephrathah, now Bethlehem, Peor,
Etam, Kulon, Tatam, Sores, Carem, Gallim,
Bether and Manach: eleven towns with their
villages.

60Kiriath-Baal, that is Kiriath-Jearim, and
Rabbah: two towns with their villages.

61In the desert:

Beth-Arabah, Middin, Secacah,
62Nibshan, Salt Town and En-Gedi: six
towns with their villages.

63The Jebusites, however, who lived in
Jerusalem, the sons of Judah were unable to
dispossess, and the Jebusites still live in
Jerusalem today, side by side with the sons
of Judah.

The tribe of Ephraim

16 The portion of the sons of Joseph
started on the east at the Jordan
opposite Jericho (the Waters of Jericho)
through the desert rising from Jericho into
the highlands of Bethel; 2from Bethel it went
to Luz, and on towards the frontier of the
Archites at Ataroth; 3then passed downwards
and westwards to the frontier of the Japhle-
tites as far as the border of Lower Beth-
Horon and on to Gezer, and reached as far as
the sea.
4Such was the heritage of the sons of
Joseph, Manasseh and Ephraim.
5As regards the territory of the sons of
Ephraim, by clans, the frontier of their heri-
tage ran from Ataroth-Arach to Upper Beth-
Horon; 6the frontier then reached as far as
the sea . . . the Michmethath in the north,
and the frontier turned east to Tanaath-
Shiloh which it crossed in an easterly direc-
tion to Janoah; 7it ran down to Ataroth and
Naarah, touched Jericho and ended at the
Jordan. 8From Tappuah, the frontier ran
westwards to the Torrent of Kanah and
reached as far as the sea.
Such was the heritage of the tribe of the
sons of Ephraim, by clans, 9apart from the
towns reserved for the sons of Ephraim inside
the heritage of the sons of Manasseh, all these
towns and their villages. 10The Canaanites
living in Gezer were not driven out; they have
remained in Ephraim to the present day but
are obliged to do forced labour.

The tribe of Manasseh

17 The portion of the tribe of Manasseh,
who was in fact Joseph's first-born—
went to Machir, Manasseh's first-born,
father of Gilead, for he was a warrior; he
had Gilead and Bashan. 2The other sons of
Manasseh had theirs, by clans: for the sons
of Abiezer, for the sons of Helek, for the
sons of Asriel, for the sons of Shechem, for
the sons of Hepher, and for the sons of
Shemida: these were the male children of
Manasseh son of Joseph, by clans.
3Zelophehad son of Hepher, son of Gilead,
son of Machir, son of Manasseh, had no sons
but only daughters, whose names were these:
Mahlah, Noah, Hoglah, Milcah and Tirzah.
4These approached the priest Eleazar, Joshua
son of Nun and the leaders, and said,
'Yahweh ordered Moses to give us a heritage
among our brothers.' In compliance with
Yahweh's order, therefore, they were given
a heritage among their father's brothers. 5In
this way ten portions fell to Manasseh, apart
from Gilead and Bashan lying on the further
side of the Jordan, 6since Manasseh's daugh-
ters received a heritage as well as his sons.
Gilead itself belonged to Manasseh's other
sons.
7On the side of Asher, the frontier of
Manasseh was the Michmethath, which is
opposite Shechem, and thence continued to
the right to Jashib, which is at the spring of
Tappuah. 8The territory of Tappuah
belonged to Manasseh, but Tappuah on
Manasseh's border belonged to the sons of
Ephraim. 9The boundary went down to the
Torrent of Kanah; south of the Torrent
were the towns of Ephraim, excluding those
owned by Ephraim among the towns of
Manasseh; the boundary of Manasseh was
north of the Torrent and reached as far as the
sea. 10The south belonged to Ephraim and
the north to Manasseh and reached as far as
the sea; they touched Asher to the north and
Issachar to the east. 11With Issachar and
Asher, Manasseh shared Beth-Shean and its
dependent towns, Ibleam and its dependent
towns, the inhabitants of Dor and of its
dependent towns, the inhabitants of Taanach
and Megiddo and of their dependent towns:
the Three of the Slopes. 12But because the
sons of Manasseh could not take possession
of these towns, the Canaanites managed to
live on in that territory. 13When, however,
the Israelites became stronger, they
subjected the Canaanites to forced labour,
though they never dispossessed them.

Land reclamation by the sons of Joseph

14The sons of Joseph spoke as follows to
Joshua, 'Why have you given me only one
share, only one portion, as heritage, when I
am a numerous people, since Yahweh has so
blessed me?' 15Joshua replied, 'If your people
are so many, go up to the wooded area
and clear space for yourselves in the area
belonging to the Perizzites and Rephaim,
since the highlands of Ephraim are too small

for you.' 16The sons of Joseph replied, 'The highlands are not enough for us, and what is more, all the Canaanites living on the land of the plain have iron chariots, so do those in Beth-Shean and its dependent towns, and those in the plain of Jezreel.' 17Joshua said to the House of Joseph, to Ephraim and to Manasseh, 'You are a numerous people and your strength is great; you will not only have one share, 18but a mountain will be yours as well; even if it is a forest, you can clear it and its territories will be yours. And you will dispossess the Canaanites, although they have iron chariots and although they are strong.'

C: DESCRIPTION OF THE SEVEN OTHER TRIBES

The land survey for these seven tribes

18 The whole community of the Israelites assembled at Shiloh, and the Tent of Meeting was set up there; the whole country had been subdued for them. 2But among the Israelites there were still seven tribes left who had not received their heritage. 3Joshua then said to the Israelites, 'How much more time are you going to waste before you go and take possession of the country which Yahweh, God of your ancestors, has given to you? 4Choose three men from each tribe for me to send all over the country so that they can make a survey with a view to their inheritances and then come back to me. 5They will divide the country into seven portions. Judah will remain in his territory in the south, and those of the House of Joseph will remain in their territory in the north. 6You must survey the country in seven sections and bring your findings to me here, so that I can cast lots for you here, in the presence of Yahweh our God. 7The Levites, however, will have no portion with the rest of you; the priesthood of Yahweh will be their heritage. As regards Gad and Reuben and the half-tribe of Manasseh, they have received their heritage on the further, eastern side of the Jordan, the one given them by Moses, servant of Yahweh.'

8The men stood up and set off. To those who were to survey the country Joshua gave this order, 'Start out, then, go all over the country, survey it, and then come back to me; and I shall cast lots for you here, in the presence of Yahweh, at Shiloh.' 9The men left, went all over the country and surveyed it by towns, in seven sections, writing down their findings in a book, and then went back to Joshua in the camp at Shiloh.

10Joshua cast lots for them in Yahweh's presence at Shiloh, and there Joshua divided the country between the Israelites, share by share.

The tribe of Benjamin

11A portion fell first to the tribe of the sons of Benjamin, by clans: the territory of their portion lay between the sons of Judah and the sons of Joseph. 12Their northern frontier began at the Jordan, went up the flank of Jericho to the north, climbed westwards through the highlands and came out at the desert of Beth-Aven. 13Thence, the frontier went on to Luz, on the southern flank of Luz —now Bethel—and then down to Ataroth-Arach, on the mountain south of Lower Beth-Horon. 14At this westerly point, the frontier curved round and turned south, from the mountain facing Beth-Horon from the south and came out at Kiriath-Baal, now Kiriath-Jearim, a town of the sons of Judah. That was the western side.

15This was the south side: from the tip of Kiriath-Jearim, the frontier went to Gasin and came out near the spring of the Waters of Nephtoah, 16it then went down to the edge of the mountain facing the Valley of Hinnom, in the Valley of the Rephaim to the north; it then went down into the Valley of Hinnom, past the southerly flank of the Jebusite, and went down to En-Rogel. 17It then curved northwards, coming out at En-Shemesh, and came out at the stone circle opposite the Ascent of Adummim, then went down to the Stone of Bohan son of Reuben. 18It then went on to Cheteph on the flank of Beth-ha-Arabah northwards, and went down into the Arabah; 19the frontier then passed round the northern flank of Beth-Hoglah, and the frontier came out at the northern bay of the Salt Sea, at the southern end of the Jordan. Such was the southern frontier. 20The Jordan itself formed the frontier on the east.

Such was the heritage of the sons of Benjamin as defined by their frontier, by clans.

The towns of Benjamin

21The towns of the tribe of the sons of
Benjamin, by clans, were:
22Jericho, Beth-Hoglah, Emek-Keziz;
23Beth-Arabah, Zemaraim, Bethel; Avvim,
Parah, Ophrah; 24Chephar-Ammoni, Ophni,
Geba: twelve towns and their villages.
25Gibeon, Ramah, Beeroth; 26Mizpeh,
Chephirah, Mozah; 27Rekem, Irpeel,
Taralah; 28Zela-ha-Eleph, the Jebusite—that
is, Jerusalem—Gibeah and Kiriath: fourteen
towns with their villages.

Such was the heritage of the sons of Benjamin, by clans.

The tribe of Simeon

19 The second lot to come out was for
Simeon, for the tribe of the sons of
Simeon, by clans; their heritage was within
the heritage of the sons of Judah. 2As heri-
tage, they received:
3Beersheba, Shema, Moladah, 4Hazar-
Shual, Balah, Ezem, Eltolad, Bethul,
Hormah, 5Ziklag, Beth-ha-Marcaboth,
Hazar-Susa, 6Beth-Lebaoth and Sharuhen:
thirteen towns and their villages.
7Ain, Rimmon, Ether and Ashan: four
towns and their villages, 8with all the villages
situated near these towns as far as Baalath-
Beer and Ramah of the Negeb.
Such was the heritage of the tribe of the
sons of Simeon, by clans. 9The heritage of
the sons of Simeon was taken out of the
portion of the sons of Judah, because the
share of the sons of Judah was too large for
them; hence, the sons of Simeon received
their heritage within the heritage of the sons
of Judah.

The tribe of Zebulun

10The third lot fell to the sons of Zebulun, by
clans; the territory of their heritage stretched
as far as Sadud; 11their frontier climbed west-
wards to Maraalah, touching Dabbesheth
and the torrent facing Jokneam. 12From
Sadud, the frontier turned east, towards the
rising sun, as far as the frontier of Chisloth-
Tabor; it came out at Dobrath and went up
to Japhia. 13Thence, it went east, towards the
sunrise, to Gath-Hepher and Ittah-Kazin,
came out at Rimmon and turned towards
Neah. 14The northern frontier turned
towards Hannathon and came to an end
in the Valley of Iphtah-El; 15with Kattath,
Nahalal, Shimron, Iralah and Bethlehem:
twelve towns with their villages.
16Such was the heritage of the sons of
Zebulun, by clans: these towns with their
villages.

The tribe of Issachar

17The fourth lot came out for Issachar, for the
sons of Issachar, by clans. 18Their territory
stretched towards Jezreel and included
Chesulloth, Shunem, 19Hapharaim, Shion,
Anaharath, 20Dobrath, Kishion, Ebez,
21Remeth, En-Gannim, En-Haddah and
Beth-Pazzez. 22Their frontier touched
Tabor, Shahazimah and Beth-Shemesh, and
the frontier came to an end at the Jordan:
sixteen towns with their villages.
23Such was the heritage of the tribe of the
sons of Issachar, by clans: the towns and their
villages.

The tribe of Asher

24The fifth lot came out for the tribe of the
sons of Asher, by clans. 25Their territory
included Helkath, Hali, Beten, Achshaph,
26Alammelech, Amad and Mishal. 27On the
west, it touched Carmel and the course of the
Libnath. On the side of the rising sun, it
went as far as Beth-Dagon, touched Zebulun,
the Valley of Iphtah-El on the north side,
Beth-ha-Emek and Neiel, coming out with
Cabul on the left, 28with Abdon, Rehob,
Hammon and Kanah as far as Sidon the
Great. The frontier then turned towards
Ramah, as far as the fortress-town of Tyre;
29the frontier then went to Hosah and reached
as far as the sea at Mahalab and Achzib,
30with Acco, Aphek and Rehob: twenty-two
towns with their villages.
31Such was the heritage of the tribe of the
sons of Asher, by clans; these towns and their
villages.

The tribe of Naphtali

32To the sons of Naphtali fell the sixth
portion, to the sons of Naphtali, by clans.
33Their frontier went from Heleph and the
Oak of Zanaannim, with Adami-ha-Negeb
and Jabneel, as far as Lakkum, and ended at
the Jordan. 34The westward boundary ran
to Aznoth-Tabor and thence came out at
Hukkok, marching with Zebulun in the

south, Asher in the west and the Jordan in
the east. 35The fortified towns were Ziddim,
Zer, Hammath, Rakkath, Chinnereth,
36Adamah, Ramah, Hazor, 37Kedesh, Edrei,
En-Hazor, 38Jiron, Migdal-El, Horem, Beth-
Anath and Beth-Shemesh: nineteen towns
and their villages.
39Such was the heritage of the sons of
Naphtali, by clans: the towns and their
villages.

The tribe of Dan

40To the tribe of the sons of Dan, by clans,
fell the seventh portion. 41The territory of
their heritage comprised: Zorah, Eshtaol, Ir-
Shemesh, 42Shaalbim, Aijalon, Silatha,
43Elon, Timnah, Ekron, 44Eltekeh,
Gibbethon, 45Baalath, Azor, Bene-Berak and
Gath-Rimmon; 46and, by the sea, Jerakon
with the territory facing Jaffa.
47The territory of the sons of Dan eluded
them, however, and the sons of Dan conse-
quently went up and attacked Leshem,
captured it and put it to the sword. Having
gained possession of it, they settled there
and called Leshem, Dan, after Dan their
ancestor.
48Such was the heritage of the tribe of the
sons of Dan, by clans: these towns and their
villages.
49Having finished dividing the country,
frontier by frontier, the Israelites gave Joshua
son of Nun a heritage among themselves; 50at
Yahweh's command, they gave him the town
which he had asked for, Timnath-Serah in
the highlands of Ephraim; he rebuilt the
town and settled there.
51Such are the heritages which the priest
Eleazar, Joshua son of Nun, and the heads
of each family apportioned by lot between
the tribes of Israel at Shiloh, in Yahweh's
presence, at the door of the Tent of Meeting;
and thus the apportioning of the country was
completed.

D: PRIVILEGED TOWNS

The cities of refuge

20 Yahweh said to Joshua, 2'Speak to the
Israelites and say to them, "Choose
yourselves the cities of refuge of which I
spoke to you through Moses, 3to which
anyone who has accidentally (unintention-
ally) killed someone else may flee, and which
will serve you as refuge from the avenger of
blood. 4(The killer must flee to one of these
towns. He will stop at the entrance to the
town gate and explain his case to the town
elders. These will admit him to their town
and assign him a place to live among them.
5If the avenger of blood pursues him, they
must not hand the killer over to him, since
he has killed his fellow unintentionally and
was not motivated by long-standing hatred
for him. 6He must stay in this town) until he
is brought to trial before the community
(until the death of the high priest then in
office. Only then may the killer go back to
his own town and to his own house in the
town from which he has fled)." '
7For this purpose they designated Kedesh
in Galilee, in the highlands of Naphtali,
Shechem in the highlands of Ephraim, and
Kiriath-Arba—now Hebron—in the high-
lands of Judah. 8On the other, eastern, side
of the Jordan opposite Jericho, in the desert
of the tableland, they chose Bezer of the tribe
of Reuben, Ramoth in Gilead of the tribe of
Gad, and Golan in Bashan of the tribe of
Manasseh. 9Such were the towns designated
for all the Israelites and for foreigners living
among them, so that anyone who had acci-
dentally killed someone could flee there and
might escape the hand of the avenger of
blood, until brought to trial before the
community.

The levitical cities

21 The heads of families of the Levites
then came to the priest, Eleazar, Joshua
son of Nun and the heads of families of the
tribes of Israel—2they were then at Shiloh in
Canaan. They said to them, 'Through Moses,
Yahweh ordered us to be given towns to live
in, with their pasture lands for our livestock.'
3In compliance with Yahweh's order, the
Israelites consequently and from their own
heritage gave the Levites the following towns
with their pasture lands:
4Lots were cast for the clans of the
Kohathites: to those Levites who were sons
of Aaron the priest, fell thirteen towns from
the tribes of Judah, Simeon and Benjamin;
5to the other sons of Kohath, by clans, 6fell
ten towns from the tribes of Ephraim, Dan,
and the half-tribe of Manasseh. To the sons
of Gershon, by clans, fell thirteen towns from
the tribes of Issachar, Asher, Naphtali and

the half-tribe of Manasseh in Bashan. 7To
the sons of Merari, by clans, fell twelve towns
from the tribes of Reuben, Gad and Zebulun.
8The Israelites assigned these towns and
their pasture lands to the Levites by lot, as
Yahweh had ordered through Moses.

The portion of the Kohathites

9From the tribe of Judah and the tribe of
Simeon, they gave the towns named below.
10The first portion was for the sons of Aaron,
belonging to the clans of the Kohathites, to
the sons of Levi, since the first lot was theirs.
11They gave them Kiriath-Arba, Anak's
father's town—now Hebron—in the high-
lands of Judah, with its surrounding pasture
lands. 12The fields and villages of this town,
however, they gave to Caleb son of
Jephunneh as his property. 13To the sons
of Aaron the priest they gave Hebron, a city
of refuge for those who had killed, with its
pasture lands, as well as Libnah with its
pasture lands, 14Jattir with its pasture lands,
Eshtemoa with its pasture lands, 15Holon
with its pasture lands, Debir with its pasture
lands, 16Ashan with its pasture lands, Juttah
with its pasture lands, and Beth-Shemesh
with its pasture lands: nine towns taken from
these two tribes; 17and, from the tribe of
Benjamin, Gibeon with its pasture lands,
Geba with its pasture lands, 18Anathoth with
its pasture lands and Almon with its pasture
lands: four towns.
19Total number of towns for the priests,
the sons of Aaron: thirteen towns with their
pasture lands.
20As regards the clans of the sons of
Kohath, those Levites still left of the sons
of Kohath, the towns of their lot were taken
from the tribe of Ephraim. 21They were given
Shechem, a city of refuge for those who had
killed, with its pasture lands, in the highlands
of Ephraim, as well as Gezer with its pasture
lands, 22Kibzaim with its pasture lands, and
Beth-Horon with its pasture lands: four
towns; 23from the tribe of Dan, Elteke with
its pasture lands, Gibbethon with its pasture
lands, 24Aijalon with its pasture lands and
Gath-Rimmon with its pasture lands: four
towns; 25and, from the half-tribe of
Manasseh, Taanach with its pasture lands
and Jibleam with its pasture lands: two
towns.
26In all: ten towns with their pasture
lands for the remaining clans of the sons
of Kohath.

The portion of the sons of Gershon

27To the sons of Gershon, of the levitical
clans, were given: from the half-tribe of
Manasseh, Golan in Bashan, a city of refuge
for those who had killed, with its pasture
lands, and Ashtaroth with its pasture lands—
two towns; 28from the tribe of Issachar,
Kishion with its pasture lands, Dobrath with
its pasture lands, 29Jarmuth with its pasture
lands and En-Gannim with its pasture
lands—four towns; 30from the tribe of Asher,
Mishal with its pasture lands, Abdon with its
pasture lands, 31Helkath with its pasture
lands and Rehob with its pasture lands—four
towns; 32and, from the tribe of Naphtali,
Kedesh in Galilee, a city of refuge for those
who had killed, with its pasture lands,
Hammoth-Dor with its pasture lands and
Kartan with its pasture lands—three towns.
33Total number of towns of the Gershon-
ites, by clans: thirteen towns with their
pasture lands.

The portion of the sons of Merari

34To the clans of the sons of Merari, the
remainder of the Levites, fell: from the tribe
of Zebulun, Jokneam with its pasture lands,
Kartah with its pasture lands, 35Rimmon
with its pasture lands and Nahalal with its
pasture lands—four towns; 36on the other
side of the Jordan opposite Jericho, from the
tribe of Reuben, Bezer in the desert, on the
tableland, a city of refuge for those who had
killed, with its pasture lands, Jahaz with its
pasture lands, 37Kedemoth with its pasture
lands and Mephaath with its pasture lands—
four towns; 38and, from the tribe of Gad,
Ramoth in Gilead, a city of refuge for those
who had killed, with its pasture lands,
Mahanaim with its pasture lands, 39Heshbon
with its pasture lands and Jazer with its
pasture lands—four towns.
40Total number of towns forming the lot of
the sons of Merari by clans, of the remaining
levitical clans: twelve towns.
41The total number of towns for the Levites
in Israelite territory was forty-eight towns
with their pasture lands. 42These towns
consisted in each case of the town itself and
the pasture land round it. This was the case
with all the towns.

End of the distribution

[43]This was how Yahweh gave the Israelites the entire country which he had sworn to give to their ancestors. They took possession of it and settled in it. [44]Yahweh granted them tranquillity on all their frontiers just as he had sworn to their ancestors and, of all their enemies, not one succeeded in resisting them. Yahweh put all their enemies at their mercy. [45]Of all the promises that Yahweh had made to the House of Israel, not one failed; all were fulfilled.

III: THE CLOSE OF JOSHUA'S CAREER

A: THE RETURN OF THE EASTERN TRIBES— THE QUESTION OF THEIR ALTAR

The Transjordanian tribes are sent home

22 Joshua then summoned the Reubenites, the Gadites and the half-tribe of Manasseh [2]and said to them, 'You have observed everything that Moses, servant of Yahweh, ordered you, and whenever I have given you an order you have listened to me. [3]You have not deserted your brothers, from long ago until today, keeping the observance of the commandment of Yahweh your God. [4]Now that Yahweh your God has granted your brothers the rest that he promised them, go back to your tents, to the country belonging to you which Moses, servant of Yahweh, gave you on the other side of the Jordan. [5]But take great care to practise the commandments and the Law which Moses, servant of Yahweh, has given you: to love Yahweh your God, always to follow his paths, to keep his commandments, to be loyal to him and to serve him with all your heart and with all your soul.'

[6]Joshua blessed them and sent them away, and they went home to their tents.

[7]To one half of the tribe of Manasseh, Moses had given a territory in Bashan; to the other half, Joshua gave another among their brothers on the west bank of the Jordan. As Joshua sent them home to their tents, he blessed them [8]and said to them, 'You are going back to your tents with great wealth, with a great deal of livestock, with silver and gold, bronze and iron and great quantities of clothing; share the spoils of your enemies with your brothers.'

An altar is built beside the Jordan

[9]The Reubenites, the Gadites and the half-tribe of Manasseh returned home, leaving the Israelites at Shiloh in Canaan, and made for Gilead, the territory which belonged to them as a result of Yahweh's order given through Moses. [10]When they came to the stone circle by the Jordan, in Canaanite territory, the Reubenites, the Gadites and the half-tribe of Manasseh built an altar there beside the Jordan, a large, imposing altar.

[11]This came to the ears of the Israelites. 'Look,' the word went round, 'the Reubenites, the Gadites and the half-tribe of Manasseh have built this altar on the Canaanite side, near the stone circle by the Jordan, on the Israelites' bank.'

[12]At this news, the whole community of the Israelites mustered at Shiloh, to march against them and make war on them.

Reproaches addressed to the eastern tribes

[13]The Israelites sent the priest Phinehas son of Eleazar to the Reubenites, the Gadites and the half-tribe of Manasseh, in Gilead, [14]and with him ten leading men, one man from a leading family from each of the tribes of Israel, each of them being head of his family in the clans of Israel. [15]Having reached the Reubenites, the Gadites and the half-tribe of Manasseh in Gilead, they said this:

[16]'The whole community of Israel says as follows, "What do you mean by this infidelity, which you have committed against the God of Israel by now repudiating your allegiance to Yahweh, and by building yourselves an altar with the intention now of rebelling against Yahweh?

[17]"Was the crime which we committed at Peor so slight—although we have not

managed to purify ourselves from that even
now, in spite of the plague which has ravaged
the community of Yahweh — 18that you must
now repudiate your allegiance to Yahweh?
For since you are in rebellion against him
today, tomorrow his anger will be aroused
against the whole community of Israel.
19"Is the country in which you have settled
unclean? Then cross over into the country
where Yahweh has settled, there where
Yahweh's Dwelling now stands, and settle
among us. But do not rebel against Yahweh
or involve us in your rebellion by building a
rival altar to the altar of Yahweh our God.
20When Achan son of Zerah was unfaithful
to the curse of destruction, did not the retri-
bution come down on the whole community
of Israel, although he was only one man? Did
he not have to die for his crime?" '

The Transjordanian tribes justify their action

21The Reubenites, the Gadites and the half-
tribe of Manasseh spoke in their turn and
answered the heads of the clans of Israel:
22'The God of gods, Yahweh, the God of
gods, Yahweh well knows, and let Israel
know it too: if there has been rebellion or
infidelity to Yahweh on our part, may he
refuse to save us today! 23And if we have
built ourselves an altar with the intention of
repudiating our allegiance to Yahweh and of
presenting burnt offering and oblation or
of offering communion sacrifices on it, may
Yahweh himself call us to account for it!
24The truth is, we have done this as a
precaution: in the future, your descendants
might say to ours, "What connection do you
have with Yahweh, God of Israel? 25Has
not Yahweh set the frontier of the Jordan
between us and you, you Reubenites and
Gadites? You have no share in Yahweh."
Thus, your descendants would be the cause
of stopping ours from fearing Yahweh.
26'So we said to each other, "Let us build
this altar, not for burnt offerings or other
sacrifices 27but as a witness between us and
you and between our descendants after us,
attesting that we too have the right to worship
Yahweh, in his presence, with our burnt
offerings, our victims and our communion
sacrifices. And so, in the future your descend-
ants will not be able to say to ours: You have
no share in Yahweh." 28And we furthermore
said, "If ever it were to happen that they did
say this either to us or to our descendants in
the future, we should reply: Look at this
structure, Yahweh's altar, made by our
ancestors not for burnt offerings or other
sacrifices but as a witness between us and
you." 29Far be it from us to rebel against
Yahweh or now to repudiate our allegiance
to Yahweh by building an altar for burnt
offerings or oblations or sacrifices, in rivalry
with the altar of Yahweh our God that stands
before his Dwelling!'

Peace restored

30When the priest Phinehas, the leaders of
the community and the heads of the clans of
Israel who were with him, heard the words
spoken by the Gadites, the Reubenites and
the Manassehites, they approved of them.
31The priest Phinehas son of Eleazar then
said to the Reubenites, the Gadites and the
Manassehites, 'Today, we can see that
Yahweh is among us, since you have not been
unfaithful to Yahweh in this matter; this
means that you have spared the Israelites
from Yahweh's avenging hand.'
32The priest Phinehas son of Eleazar and
the leaders left the Reubenites and the
Gadites and went back from Gilead to Canaan
and the Israelites, to whom they reported the
answer. 33The Israelites were pleased to hear
this; the Israelites gave thanks to God and
spoke no more of marching against them to
make war on them and to ravage the country
inhabited by the Reubenites and the Gadites.
34The Reubenites and the Gadites called the
altar . . . , 'Because', they said, 'it will be a
witness between us that Yahweh is God.'

B: LAST DISCOURSE OF JOSHUA

Joshua sums up his work

23 Now long after Yahweh had given
Israel rest from all the enemies
surrounding them — Joshua was old now, far
advanced in years — 2Joshua summoned all
Israel, their elders, leaders, judges and
officials, and said to them, 'I myself am old,
far advanced in years; 3you for your part have
witnessed all that Yahweh your God has done
to all these nations for your sake; Yahweh
your God himself has fought for you. 4Look,
these nations still remaining, and all the
nations which I have exterminated from

the Jordan all the way to the Great Sea in the
west, I have allotted to you as the heritage for
your tribes. 5 Yahweh your God will himself
drive them out before you; he will dispossess
them before you and you will take possession
of their country, as Yahweh your God has
promised you.

Rules of conduct when living among foreigners

6 'So be very firm about keeping and doing
everything written in the Book of the Law of
Moses, not swerving from that either to right
or to left. 7 Never mix with the peoples who
are still left beside you. Do not utter the
names of their gods, do not swear by them,
do not serve them and do not bow down to
them. 8 On the contrary, you must be loyal to
Yahweh your God as you have been till
now. 9 Yahweh has dispossessed great and
powerful nations before you, and no one so
far has been able to resist you. 10 One man of
you was able to rout a thousand of them,
since Yahweh your God was himself fighting
for you, as he had promised you. 11 Be very
careful, as you value your life, to love Yahweh
your God.

12 'But should you in any way relapse, if
you make friends with the remnant of these
nations still living beside you, if you inter-
marry with them, if you mix with them and
they with you, 13 then know for certain that
Yahweh your God will stop dispossessing
these nations before you, and for you they
will be a snare, a pitfall, thorns in your sides
and thistles in your eyes, until you vanish
from this fine country given you by Yahweh
your God.

14 'Today, you see, I am going the way of
all the earth. Acknowledge with all your heart
and soul that of all the promises made to you
by Yahweh your God, not one has failed: all
have been fulfilled—not one has failed.

15 'As every promise made to you by
Yahweh your God has been fulfilled for you,
by the same token Yahweh will fulfil all his
threats against you, even to exterminating
you from this fine country given you by
Yahweh your God.

16 'For if you violate the covenant which
Yahweh your God has imposed on you, if you
go and serve other gods and bow down to
them, then Yahweh's anger will be roused
against you and you will quickly vanish from
the fine country which he has given you.'

C: THE GREAT ASSEMBLY AT SHECHEM

24 Joshua gathered all the tribes of Israel
together at Shechem; he then sum-
moned all the elders of Israel, its leaders,
judges and officials, and they presented
themselves in God's presence. 2 Joshua then
said to all the people:

'Yahweh, the God of Israel, says this,
"From time immemorial, your ancestors,
Terah, father of Abraham and Nahor, lived
beyond the River, and served other gods. 3 I
then brought your ancestor Abraham from
beyond the River and led him through the
length and breadth of Canaan. I increased his
descendants and I gave him Isaac. 4 To Isaac
I gave Jacob and Esau. To Esau I gave
possession of the mountainous country of
Seir. Jacob and his sons went down into
Egypt. 5 I then sent Moses and Aaron, and
plagued Egypt with the wonders that I
worked there; finally I brought you out. 6 I
brought your ancestors out of Egypt, and you
came to the Sea; the Egyptians pursued your
ancestors with chariots and horsemen, to the
Sea of Reeds. 7 They then called to Yahweh,
and he spread a thick fog between you and
the Egyptians, and made the sea go back on
them and cover them. You saw with your
own eyes what I did in Egypt. Then, for a
long while, you lived in the desert. 8 I then
brought you into the country of the Amorites,
who used to live on the further side of the
Jordan; they made war on you and I put
them at your mercy; after which, you took
possession of their country, since I destroyed
them before you. 9 Next, Balak son of Zippor,
king of Moab, rose to make war on Israel,
and sent for Balaam son of Beor to come and
curse you. 10 But I would not listen to Balaam;
instead, he had to bless you, and I saved you
from his power.

11 "You then crossed the Jordan and came
to Jericho, but the inhabitants of Jericho
made war on you: Amorites, Perizzites,
Canaanites, Hittites, Girgashites, Hivites
and Jebusites, and I put them all at your
mercy. 12 I sent hornets ahead of you, which
drove out the two Amorite kings before you;
this was not the work of your sword or of
your bow. 13 And now I have given you a
country for which you have not toiled, towns
you have not built, although you live in

them, vineyards and olive groves you have
not planted, although you eat their fruit." '

Israel chooses Yahweh

14 'So now, fear Yahweh and serve him truly
and sincerely; banish the gods whom your
ancestors served beyond the River and in
Egypt, and serve Yahweh. 15 But if serving
Yahweh seems a bad thing to you, today you
must make up your minds whom you do
mean to serve, whether the gods whom your
ancestors served beyond the River, or the
gods of the Amorites in whose country you
are now living. As regards my family and me,
we shall serve Yahweh.'
16 The people replied, 'Far be it from us
to desert Yahweh and to serve other gods!
17 Yahweh our God was the one who brought
us and our ancestors here from Egypt, from
the place of slave-labour, who worked those
great wonders before our eyes and who kept
us safe all along the way we travelled and
among all the peoples through whom we
passed. 18 And Yahweh has driven all the
nations out for us, including the Amorites
who used to live in the country. We too shall
serve Yahweh, for he is our God.'
19 Joshua then said to the people, 'You will
not be able to serve Yahweh, since he is a
holy God, he is a jealous God who will not
tolerate either your misdeeds or your sins. 20 If
you desert Yahweh and serve the foreigners'
gods, he will turn and maltreat you anew
and, in spite of having been good to you in
the past, will destroy you.' 21 The people
replied to Joshua, 'No! Yahweh is the one we
mean to serve.' 22 Joshua then said to the
people, 'You are witnesses to yourselves that
you have chosen Yahweh, to serve him.'
They replied, 'Witnesses we are!' 23 'Then
banish the foreign gods which you have with
you and give your allegiance to Yahweh, God
of Israel!' 24 The people replied to Joshua,
'Yahweh our God is the one whom we shall
serve; his voice we shall obey!'

The covenant at Shechem

25 That day Joshua made a covenant for the
people; he laid down a statute and ordinance
for them at Shechem. 26 Joshua wrote these
words in the Book of the Law of God. He
then took a large stone and set it up there,
under the oak tree in Yahweh's sanctuary.
27 Joshua then said to all the people, 'Look,
this stone will be a witness to us, since it has
heard all the words that Yahweh has spoken
to us: it will be a witness against you, in case
you should deny your God.' 28 Joshua then
dismissed the people, every one to his own
heritage.

D: TWO ADDITIONS

The death of Joshua

29 After this, Joshua son of Nun, servant of
Yahweh, died; he was a hundred and ten
years old. 30 He was buried on the estate which
he had received as his heritage, at Timnath-Serah
which lies in the highlands of Ephraim,
north of Mount Gaash. 31 Israel served
Yahweh throughout the lifetime of Joshua
and throughout the lifetime of those elders
who outlived Joshua and had known all the
deeds which Yahweh had done for the sake
of Israel.

The bones of Joseph
The death of Eleazar

32 As regards the bones of Joseph, which the
Israelites had brought from Egypt, these
were buried at Shechem in the plot of ground
which Jacob had bought for a hundred pieces
of silver from the sons of Hamor father of
Shechem, and which had become the heritage
of the sons of Joseph. 33 Eleazar son of Aaron
then died and was buried at Gibeah, the town
of his son Phinehas, which had been given to
him in the highlands of Ephraim.

THE BOOK OF
JUDGES

The book covers the two centuries of Israel's history between the settlement in Canaan and the beginning of monarchy. As the first chapter shows, Israel was not in a position of strength: the tribes were struggling to establish themselves against the settled powers in the land. They were fragmented and disunited, constantly under attack from outside. Later tradition represents Israel neatly as twelve federated and fraternal tribes descended from Jacob's twelve sons, but at this time even the names and identity of the groups seem still to be fluid; Deborah's call to arms certainly produces no concerted action.

The 'judges' themselves are charismatic figures, inspired by the Spirit of Yahweh either as leaders in war or as authorities to guide some section of the people in peace. They are very varied: some have wide influence, others are territorially very restricted; some appear only for a moment, others almost found a dynasty; one (Samson) seems to have been little more than a legendary strong man, drawing his strength from Yahweh and using it to taunt the Philistines. Towards the end of the period the growing power of the Philistines and the disunited anarchy within Israel show that the time is ripe for a more stable rule.

In this varied material the deuteronomic editor sees a repeated fourfold pattern: *infidelity* to Yahweh leads to *punishment* until Israel *repents* and turns to Yahweh, at which he *delivers* them through a charismatic leader. The religious lesson of the history is this constant failure and return, to which Yahweh equally constantly replies.

PLAN OF THE BOOK

THE BOOK OF JUDGES

I: FIRST INTRODUCTION

SUMMARY OF THE SETTLEMENT IN CANAAN

The settlement of Judah, Simeon, Caleb and the Kenites

1 Now after Joshua's death, the Israelites
consulted Yahweh, asking, 'Which of us
is to march on the Canaanites first, to make
war on them?' 2And Yahweh replied, 'Judah
is to march on them first; I am delivering the
country into his hands.' 3Judah then said to
his brother Simeon, 'March with me into the
territory allotted to me; we shall make war
on the Canaanites, and then I in my turn shall
march into your territory with you.' And
Simeon marched with him. 4So Judah
marched on them, and Yahweh delivered the
Canaanites and Perizzites into their hands,
and they defeated them at Bezek—ten thou-
sand of them! 5At Bezek they came upon
Adoni-Bezek; they joined battle with him
and defeated the Canaanites and Perizzites.
6Adoni-Bezek took to flight, but they chased
and captured him and cut off his thumbs and
big toes. 7Adoni-Bezek said, 'Seventy kings
with their thumbs and big toes cut off used
to pick up the crumbs under my table. As I
did, God does to me.' He was taken to
Jerusalem, and there he died. 8(The sons of
Judah attacked Jerusalem and took it: they
put its people to the sword and set fire to the
city.)

9After this the sons of Judah went down to
make war on the Canaanites who were living
in the highlands, the Negeb and the lowlands.
10Judah next marched on the Canaanites
living in Hebron—the name of Hebron in
olden days was Kiriath-Arba—and beat
Sheshai, Ahiman and Talmai. 11From there,
he marched on the inhabitants of Debir—the
name of Debir in olden days was Kiriath-
Sepher. 12Caleb said, 'To the man who
conquers and captures Kiriath-Sepher, I
shall give my daughter Achsah as wife.' 13The
man who captured it was Othniel son of
Kenaz, younger brother of Caleb, who gave
him his daughter Achsah as wife. 14When she
arrived, he urged her to ask her father for
arable land, but when she alighted from the
donkey and Caleb asked her, 'What is the
matter?' 15she said to him, 'Grant me a
blessing! As the land you have given me is
the Negeb, give me springs of water, too!' So
Caleb gave her what she wanted: the upper
springs and the lower springs.

16The sons of Hobab the Kenite, father-
in-law of Moses, marched up with the sons
of Judah from the City of Palm Trees into
the desert of Judah lying in the Negeb of
Arad, where they went and settled among
the people.

17Judah then set out with his brother
Simeon. They beat the Canaanites who lived
in Zephath and delivered it over to the curse
of destruction; hence the town was given the
name of Hormah. 18Judah then captured
Gaza and its territory, Ashkelon and its terri-
tory, Ekron and its territory. 19bAnd Yahweh
was with Judah, who made himself master
of the highlands; 19ahe could not, however,
dispossess the inhabitants of the plain, since
they had iron chariots.

20As Moses had directed, Hebron was
given to Caleb, and he drove the three sons
of Anak out of it. 21As regards the Jebusites
living in Jerusalem, the sons of Benjamin did
not dispossess them, and the Jebusites have
been living in Jerusalem with the sons of
Benjamin ever since.

The capture of Bethel

22Similarly, the House of Joseph marched on
Bethel, and Yahweh was with them. 23The
House of Joseph made a reconnaissance of
Bethel. (In olden days, the name of the town
was Luz.) 24The scouts saw a man coming
out of the town and said to him, 'Show us
how to get into the town and we shall show
you faithful love.' 25And when he had shown
them a way into the town, they put the town

to the sword but let the man and his whole clan go. 26The man went off to the country of the Hittites and built a town which he called Luz; and that has been its name ever since.

The northern tribes

27Manasseh did not dispossess Beth-Shean and its dependencies, nor Taanach and its dependencies, nor the inhabitants of Dor and its dependencies, nor the inhabitants of Ibleam and its dependencies, nor the inhabitants of Megiddo and its dependencies; in those parts the Canaanites held their ground. 28But when the Israelites became stronger, they subjected the Canaanites to forced labour, although they did not dispossess them. 29Nor did Ephraim dispossess the Canaanites living in Gezer; thus, the Canaanites went on living in Gezer with him. 30Zebulun did not dispossess the inhabitants of Kitron or of Nahalol. The Canaanites lived on with Zebulun but were subjected to forced labour. 31Asher did not dispossess the inhabitants of Acco, nor those of Sidon, of Mahalab, of Achzib, of Helbah, of Aphek or of Rehob. 32So the Asherites lived among the Canaanite inhabitants of the country, not having dispossessed them. 33Naphtali did not dispossess the inhabitants of Beth-Shemesh or of Beth-Anath; they settled among the Canaanite inhabitants of the country, but the inhabitants of Beth-Shemesh and of Beth-Anath were subjected to forced labour for them. 34The Amorites drove the Danites back into the highlands and would not let them come down into the plain. 35The Amorites held their ground at Har-Heres and Shaalbim, but when the hand of the House of Joseph grew heavier, they were subjected to forced labour.

(36The territory of the Edomites begins at the Ascent of Scorpions, runs to the Rock and continues on upwards.)

The Angel of Yahweh tells Israel of disasters to come

2 The Angel of Yahweh[a] went up from Gilgal to Bethel and said, 'I have brought you out of Egypt and led you into this country, which I promised on oath to your ancestors. I said, "I shall never break my covenant with you. 2You for your part must make no covenant with the inhabitants of this country; you will destroy their altars." But you have not listened to my voice. What is the reason for this? 3Very well, I now say this, "I am not going to drive these nations out before you. They will become your oppressors, and their gods will be a snare for you." ' 4When the angel of Yahweh had spoken these words to all the Israelites, the people began to wail at the top of their voices. 5And they called the place Bochim, and offered sacrifices to Yahweh there.

II: SECOND INTRODUCTION

GENERAL REFLECTIONS ON THE PERIOD OF THE JUDGES

6Joshua having dismissed the people, the Israelites then went away, each one to his own heritage, to occupy the country.[b] 7The people served Yahweh throughout the lifetime of Joshua and throughout the lifetime of those elders who outlived Joshua and had known all the great deeds which Yahweh had done for the sake of Israel. 8Joshua son of Nun, servant of Yahweh, was a hundred and ten years old when he died. 9He was buried on the estate which he had received as his heritage at Timnath-Heres in the highlands of Ephraim, north of Mount Gaash. 10And when that whole generation had been gathered to its ancestors, another generation followed it which knew neither Yahweh nor the deeds which he had done for the sake of Israel.

Religious interpretation of the period of the Judges

11The Israelites then did what is evil in Yahweh's eyes and served the Baals. 12They deserted Yahweh, God of their ancestors,

---

2a An expression for Yahweh himself in visible form.
2b || Jos 24:29–31.

who had brought them out of Egypt, and
they followed other gods, from those of the
surrounding peoples. They bowed down to
these; they provoked Yahweh; [13]they
deserted Yahweh to serve Baal and Astartes.[c]
[14]Then Yahweh's anger grew hot against
Israel. He handed them over to pillagers who
plundered them; he delivered them to the
enemies surrounding them, and they were
no longer able to resist their enemies.
[15]Whenever they mounted an expedition,
Yahweh's hand was there to foil them, as
Yahweh had told them and as Yahweh had
sworn to them, so that they were in dire
distress.

[16]Yahweh then appointed them judges,
who rescued them from the hands of their
plunderers. [17]But even to their judges they
refused to listen. They prostituted them-
selves to other gods and bowed down before
these. Very quickly they left the path which
their ancestors had trodden in obedience to
the orders of Yahweh; they did not follow
their example. [18]When Yahweh appointed
judges for them, Yahweh was with the judge
and rescued them from the hands of their
enemies as long as the judge lived, since
Yahweh relented at their groans under their
persecutors and oppressors. [19]But once the
judge was dead, they relapsed into even
worse corruption than their ancestors. They
followed other gods; they served them and
bowed before them and would not give up
the practices and stubborn ways of their
ancestors at all.

Why foreign nations survived in Canaan

[20]Yahweh's anger then blazed out against
Israel, and he said, 'Since this people has
broken the covenant which I laid down for
their ancestors, since they have not listened
to my voice, [21]in future I shall not drive
before them any one of those nations which
Joshua left when he died, [22]in order, by
means of them, to put Israel to the test, to
see whether or not they would tread the
paths of Yahweh as once their ancestors had
trodden them.' [23]Hence, Yahweh allowed
these nations to remain; he did not hurry to
drive them out, and did not deliver them into
the hands of Joshua.

3 These are the nations which Yahweh
allowed to remain, by their means to put
all those Israelites to the test who had not
experienced any of the Canaanite wars [2](this
was only to instruct the Israelites' descend-
ants, to teach them the art of war, those at
least who had not experienced it previously):
[3]the five chiefs of the Philistines, all the
Canaanites, the Sidonians, and the Hittites
who lived in the range of the Lebanon, from
the uplands of Baal-Hermon to the Pass of
Hamath. [4]They were used to put Israel to the
test and see if they would keep the orders
which Yahweh had given their ancestors
through Moses. [5]The Israelites lived among
the Canaanites, Hittites and Amorites, the
Perizzites, Hivites and Jebusites; [6]they mar-
ried their daughters, they gave their own sons
to their daughters and they served their gods.

III: HISTORY OF THE JUDGES

A: OTHNIEL

[7]The Israelites did what is evil in Yahweh's
eyes. They forgot Yahweh their God and
served Baals and Asherahs. [8]Then Yahweh's
anger blazed out against Israel: he handed
them over to Cushan-Rishathaim king of
Edom, and the Israelites were enslaved to
Cushan-Rishathaim for eight years.

[9]The Israelites then cried to Yahweh and
Yahweh raised for the Israelites a deliverer
who rescued them, Othniel son of Kenaz,
Caleb's younger brother. [10]The spirit of
Yahweh was on him; he became judge in
Israel and set out for war. Yahweh delivered
Cushan-Rishathaim king of Edom into his
hands, and he triumphed over Cushan-
Rishathaim. [11]The country then had peace
for forty years. Othniel son of Kenaz then
died.

2c Canaanite deities, the male and female fertility gods. Astarte is also called Asherah.

B: EHUD

12 Again the Israelites began doing what is evil
in Yahweh's eyes, and Yahweh strengthened
Eglon king of Moab against Israel, since they
were doing what is evil in Yahweh's eyes.
13 Eglon in conjunction with the sons of
Ammon and Amalek marched on Israel, beat
them and captured the City of Palm Trees.[a]
14 The Israelites were enslaved to Eglon king
of Moab for eighteen years.

15 The Israelites then cried to Yahweh, and
Yahweh raised a deliverer for them, Ehud
son of Gera, a Benjaminite; he was left-
handed. The Israelites appointed him to take
their tribute to Eglon king of Moab. 16 Ehud
made himself a dagger—it was double-edged
and a foot long—and strapped it under his
clothes on his right thigh. 17 He presented the
tribute to Eglon king of Moab. This Eglon
was a very fat man. 18 Having presented the
tribute, Ehud sent away the men who had
been carrying it; 19 but he himself, on reaching
the Idols which are near Gilgal, went back
and said, 'I have a secret message for you, O
king.' The king commanded silence, and all
his attendants withdrew. 20 Ehud went up
to him; he was sitting in his private room
upstairs, where it was cool. Ehud said to him,
'I have a message from God for you, O king.'
The latter immediately rose from his seat.
21 Then Ehud, reaching with his left hand,
drew the dagger he was carrying on his right
thigh and thrust it into the king's belly. 22 The
hilt too went in after the blade, and the fat
closed over the blade, since Ehud did not
pull the dagger out of his belly again. 23 Ehud
went out through the privies, having shut
and bolted the doors of the upstairs room
behind him.

24 When he had gone, the servants came
back and looked; the doors of the upstairs
room were bolted. They thought, 'He is
probably covering his feet in the inner part
of the cool room.' 25 They waited until they
became embarrassed, but still he did not open
the doors of the upstairs room. Eventually,
they took the key and opened the door; and
there lay their master, dead, on the ground.

26 Meanwhile, Ehud had got away, passed
the Idols and made good his escape to safety
in Seirah. 27 Once there, he sounded the horn
in the highlands of Ephraim, and the Israel-
ites came down from the hills with him at
their head. 28 And he said to them, 'Follow
me, because Yahweh has delivered your
enemy Moab into your hands.' So they
followed him, seized the fords of the Jordan
against Moab and allowed no one to cross.
29 On that occasion they beat the Moabites,
some ten thousand men, all tough and
seasoned fighters, and not one escaped.
30 That day Moab was humbled under the
hand of Israel, and the country had peace for
eighty years.

C: SHAMGAR

31 After him came Shamgar son of Anath. He
routed six hundred of the Philistines with an
ox-goad; he too was a deliverer of Israel.

D: DEBORAH AND BARAK

Israel oppressed by the Canaanites

4 Once Ehud was dead, the Israelites again
began doing what is evil in Yahweh's eyes,
2 and Yahweh handed them over to Jabin
king of Canaan, who reigned at Hazor. The
commander of his army was Sisera, who lived
in Haroshet-ha-Goiim.

3 The Israelites then cried to Yahweh; for
Jabin had nine hundred iron chariots and had
cruelly oppressed the Israelites for twenty
years.

Deborah

4 Deborah, a prophetess, wife of Lappidoth,
was judging Israel at the time. 5 She used to
sit under Deborah's Palm between Ramah
and Bethel in the highlands of Ephraim, and
the Israelites would come to her for justice.
6 She sent for Barak son of Abinoam from
Kedesh in Naphtali, and said to him, 'Has
not Yahweh, God of Israel, commanded,
"Go! March to Mount Tabor and with you
take ten thousand of the sons of Naphtali and
the sons of Zebulun. 7 I shall entice Sisera,
the commander of Jabin's army, to encounter
you at the Torrent of Kishon with his chariots
and troops; and I shall put him into your
power"? ' 8 Barak replied, 'If you come with
me, I shall go; if you will not come, I shall

3a Jericho, well within the territory of Benjamin.

not go, for I do not know how to choose the
day when the angel of Yahweh will grant me
success.' 9'I shall go with you then,' she said,
'but, the way you are going about it, the glory
will not be yours; for Yahweh will deliver
Sisera into the hands of a woman.' Deborah
then stood up and went with Barak to
Kedesh. 10Barak summoned Zebulun and
Naphtali. Ten thousand men marched
behind him, and Deborah went with him.

Heber the Kenite

11Heber the Kenite had parted company with
the tribe of Kain and with the sons of Hobab,
father-in-law of Moses; he had pitched his
tent near the Oak of Zaanannim, not far from
Kedesh.

Defeat of Sisera

12Sisera was informed that Barak son of
Abinoam had encamped on Mount Tabor.
13Sisera summoned all his chariots—nine
hundred iron chariots—and all the troops
he had, from Harosheth-ha-Goiim to the
Torrent of Kishon. 14Deborah said to Barak,
'Up! For today is the day when Yahweh has
put Sisera into your power. Is not Yahweh
marching at your head?' And Barak charged
down from Mount Tabor with ten thousand
men behind him. 15At Barak's advance,
Yahweh struck terror into Sisera, all his
chariots and his entire army. Sisera leapt
down from his chariot and fled on foot.
16Barak pursued the chariots and the army as
far as Harosheth-ha-Goiim. Sisera's whole
army fell by the edge of the sword; not one
man was spared.

Death of Sisera

17Sisera meanwhile fled on foot towards the
tent of Jael, the wife of Heber the Kenite.
For there was peace between Jabin king of
Hazor and the family of Heber the Kenite.
18Jael came out to meet Sisera and said to
him, 'Stay here, my lord, with me; do not be
afraid!' He stayed with her in her tent, and
she covered him with a rug. 19He said to her,
'Please give me a little water to drink, for I
am thirsty.' She opened the skin of milk,
gave him some to drink and covered him up
again. 20Then he said to her, 'Stand at the
tent door, and if anyone comes and questions
you—if he asks, "Is there a man here?" say,
"No." ' 21But Jael the wife of Heber took a
tent-peg and picked up a mallet; she crept up
softly to him and drove the peg into his
temple right through to the ground. He was
lying fast asleep, worn out; and so he died.
22And now Barak came up in pursuit of
Sisera. Jael went out to meet him and said,
'Come in, and I will show you the man you
are looking for.' He went into her tent; and
there was Sisera dead, with the tent-peg
through his temple.

Israel delivered

23Thus God that day humbled Jabin king
of Canaan before the Israelites. 24And the
Israelites bore down more and more heavily
on that king of Canaan, Jabin, until he was
utterly destroyed.

THE SONG OF DEBORAH AND BARAK

5 They sang a song that day, Deborah and
Barak son of Abinoam, and the words
were:

2That the warriors in Israel
unbound their hair,
that the people came forward with a will,
bless Yahweh!

3Listen, you kings! Give ear, you princes!
From me, from me
comes a song for Yahweh.
I shall glorify Yahweh, God of Israel.

4Yahweh, when you set out from Seir,
when you marched
from the field of Edom,
the earth shook,
the heavens pelted,
the clouds pelted down water.
5The mountains melted
before Yahweh of Sinai,
before Yahweh, God of Israel.

6In the days of Shamgar son of Anath,
in the days of Jael,
there were no more caravans;
those who went forth on their travels
took their way along by-paths.

7The villages in Israel were no more,
they were no more
until you arose, O Deborah,
until you arose, mother of Israel!

8 They were choosing new gods
when war was at the gates.
Was there one shield,
one spear to be found
among the forty thousand men in Israel?

9 My heart is with the leaders of Israel,
with the people who came forward
with a will!
Bless Yahweh!

10 You who ride white donkeys
and sit on saddle-blankets as you ride,
and you who go on foot,
11 sing—to the sound of the shepherds
at the watering places!
There they extol Yahweh's blessings,
his saving acts for his villages in Israel!
(Then Yahweh's people
marched down to the gates.)

12 Awake, awake, Deborah!
Awake, awake, declaim a song!
Take heart, to your feet, Barak,
capture your captors, son of Abinoam!

13 Then Israel marched down to the gates;
like champions, Yahweh's people
marched down to fight for him!

14 The princes of Ephraim are in the valley.
Behind you, Benjamin is in your ranks.

Captains have come down from Machir,
those who wield the commander's staff,
from Zebulun.
15 The princes of Issachar are with Deborah;
Naphtali, with Barak, in the valley
follows in hot pursuit.

In the clans of Reuben
there was much searching of heart.
16 Why did you stay among the sheepfolds,
listening for the whistle, with the flocks?
(In the clans of Reuben,
there was much searching of heart.)

17 Gilead stayed
on the other side of the Jordan,
and why should Dan have stayed
aboard ship?
Asher remained beside the sea,
peacefully living within his ports.

18 Zebulun is a people
who have braved death,
Naphtali too,
on the high ground of the country.

19 The kings came and they fought,
how they fought, those kings of Canaan,
at Taanach, near the Waters of Megiddo,
but no booty of silver did they take!

20 The stars fought from heaven,
from their orbits
they fought against Sisera.

21 The torrent of Kishon swept them away,
the torrent of old, the torrent of Kishon.
—March on, be strong my soul!

22 The horses' hooves
then hammer the ground:
galloping, galloping go his steeds.

23 'Curse Meroz,' said the Angel of Yahweh,
'curse, curse the people living there
for not having come to Yahweh's help,
to Yahweh's help as warriors!'

24 Most blessed of women be Jael
(the wife of Heber the Kenite);
of tent-dwelling women,
may she be most blessed!

25 He asked for water; she gave him milk;
she offered him curds in a lordly dish.
26 She reached her hand out to seize the peg,
her right hand
to seize the workman's mallet.

She hammered Sisera,
she crushed his head,
she pierced his temple and shattered it.
27 Between her feet, he crumpled,
he fell, he lay;
at her feet, he crumpled, he fell.
Where he crumpled,
there he fell, destroyed.

28 At the window, she leans and watches,
Sisera's mother, through the lattice,
'Why is his chariot so long coming?
Why so delayed
the hoof-beats from his chariot?'

29 The wisest of her ladies answers,
and she to herself repeats,
30 'Are they not collecting
and sharing out the spoil:
a girl, two girls for each warrior;
a booty of coloured and embroidered
stuff for Sisera,
one scarf, two embroidered scarves
for me!'

31 So perish all your enemies, Yahweh!
And let those who love you be like the sun
when he emerges in all his strength!

And the country had peace for forty years.

E: GIDEON AND ABIMELECH

1: THE CALL OF GIDEON

Israel oppressed by the Midianites

6 The Israelites did what is evil in Yahweh's eyes, and for seven years Yahweh handed them over to Midian; [2]and Midian bore down heavily on Israel. To escape from the Midianites[a] the Israelites used the mountain clefts and the caves and shelters. [3]Whenever Israel sowed seed the Midianites would march up with Amalek and the sons of the East. They would march on Israel. [4]They would pitch camp on their territory and destroy the produce of the country as far as Gaza. They left Israel nothing to live on, not a sheep or an ox or a donkey, [5]for they came up as thick as locusts with their cattle and their tents; they and their camels were innumerable, they invaded the country to pillage it. [6]Thus, Midian brought Israel to great distress, and the Israelites cried to Yahweh.

A message from a prophet

[7]When the Israelites cried to Yahweh because of Midian, [8]Yahweh sent a prophet to the Israelites. He said to them, 'This is what Yahweh, God of Israel, says, "It was I who brought you out of Egypt, and led you out of the place of slave-labour. [9]I rescued you from the power of the Egyptians and from the power of all who oppressed you. I drove them out before you and gave their country to you. [10]And I said to you: I am Yahweh your God. You are not to fear the gods of the Amorites in whose country you are now living. But you have not listened to my voice." '

The Angel of Yahweh appears to Gideon

[11]The Angel of Yahweh came and sat under the terebinth at Ophrah which belonged to Joash of Abiezer. Gideon his son was threshing wheat inside the wine-press, to keep it hidden from Midian, [12]and the Angel of Yahweh appeared to him and said, 'Yahweh is with you, valiant warrior!' [13]Gideon replied, 'Excuse me, my lord, but if Yahweh is with us, why is all this happening to us? And where are all his miracles which our ancestors used to tell us about when they said, "Did not Yahweh bring us out of Egypt?" But now Yahweh has deserted us; he has abandoned us to Midian.'

[14]At this, Yahweh turned to him and said, 'Go in this strength of yours, and you will rescue Israel from the power of Midian. Am I not sending you myself?' [15]Gideon replied, 'Forgive me, my lord, but how can I deliver Israel? My clan is the weakest in Manasseh and I am the least important of my father's family.' [16]Yahweh replied, 'I shall be with you and you will crush Midian as though it were one man.' [17]Gideon said, 'If I have found favour in your sight, give me a sign that you are speaking to me. [18]Please do not go away from here until I come back to you, bringing you my offering and laying it before you.' And he replied, 'I shall stay until you come back.'

[19]Gideon went away, he prepared a young goat and from an *ephah* of flour he made unleavened cakes. He put the meat into a basket and the broth into a pot, then brought it all to him under the terebinth. As he approached, [20]the Angel of Yahweh said to him, 'Take the meat and unleavened cakes, put them on this rock and pour the broth over them.' Gideon did so. [21]The Angel of Yahweh then stretched out the tip of the staff which he was carrying, and touched the meat and unleavened cakes. Fire sprang from the rock and consumed the meat and unleavened cakes, and the Angel of Yahweh vanished before his eyes. [22]Gideon then knew that this was the Angel of Yahweh, and he said, 'Alas, my Lord Yahweh! Now I have seen the Angel of Yahweh face to face!' [23]Yahweh answered, 'Peace be with you; have no fear; you will not die.' [24]Gideon built an altar there to Yahweh and called it Yahweh-Peace. This altar stands in our own day at Ophrah of Abiezer.

Gideon against Baal

[25]Now that night, Yahweh said to Gideon, 'Take your father's bull, the seven-year-old bull, and pull down the altar to Baal belonging to your father and cut down the sacred pole beside it. [26]Then, on top of this strong-point, build a proper altar to Yahweh your God. Then take the bull and burn it as a burnt offering on the wood of the sacred pole which you have cut down.' [27]Gideon

6a Nomads based in north-west Sinai, near the Amalekites.

then took ten of his servants and did as Yahweh had ordered him. But, being too frightened of his family and of the townspeople to do it in daylight, he did it at night. [28]Next morning, when the townspeople got up, they found that the altar to Baal had been destroyed, the sacred pole standing beside it had been cut down and the bull had been sacrificed as a burnt offering on the newly built altar. [29]'Who has done this?' they asked one another. They searched, made enquiries and declared, 'Gideon son of Joash has done it.' [30]The townspeople then said to Joash, 'Bring out your son; he must die for having destroyed Baal's altar and cut down the sacred pole which stood beside it.' [31]To the people all crowding round him, Joash replied, 'Is it your job to plead for Baal? Is it your job to champion his cause? (Anyone who pleads for Baal must be put to death before dawn.) If he is a god, let him plead for himself, now that Gideon has destroyed his altar.' [32]That day, Gideon was given the name Jerubbaal, because, they said, 'Baal must plead against him, because he has destroyed his altar!'

The call to arms

[33]All Midian and Amalek and the sons of the East joined forces and, having crossed the Jordan, pitched camp in the plain of Jezreel. [34]And the spirit of Yahweh clothed Gideon around; he sounded the horn and Abiezer rallied behind him. [35]He sent messengers throughout Manasseh, and Manasseh too rallied behind him; he sent messengers to Asher, Zebulun and Naphtali, and they marched out to meet him.

The sign of the fleece

[36]Gideon said to God, 'If it is really you delivering Israel by means of me, as you have said, [37]look, I am going to put a woollen fleece on the threshing-floor; if there is dew only on the fleece and all the ground stays dry, then I shall know that you will deliver Israel by means of me, as you have said.' [38]And so it happened. Early next morning, Gideon got up, squeezed the fleece and wrung enough dew out of the fleece to fill a cup. [39]Gideon then said to God, 'Do not be angry with me if I speak just once more. Allow me to make the fleece-test just once more: let the fleece alone be dry and there be dew all over the ground!' [40]And God did so that night. The fleece alone stayed dry, and there was dew all over the ground.

2: GIDEON'S CAMPAIGN TO THE WEST OF THE JORDAN

Yahweh reduces the numbers of Gideon's army

7 Jerubbaal (that is, Gideon) got up very early, as did all the people who were with him; he pitched camp at En-Harod; the camp of Midian was north of his, under the Hill of Moreh in the valley. [2]Yahweh then said to Gideon, 'There are too many people with you for me to put Midian into their power; Israel might claim the credit for themselves at my expense: they might say, "My own hand has rescued me." [3]So now make this proclamation to the people, "Anyone trembling with fear is to go back and watch from Mount Gilboa." ' Twenty-two thousand of the people went back, and ten thousand remained.

[4]Yahweh said to Gideon, 'There are still too many people. Take them down to the waterside and I shall sort them out for you there. If I say of someone, "He is to go with you," that man is to go with you. And if I say of anyone, "He is not to go with you," that man is not to go.' [5]So Gideon took the people down to the waterside, and Yahweh said to him, 'All those who lap the water with their tongues, as a dog laps, put these on one side. And all those who kneel down to drink, put these on the other side.' [6]The number of those who lapped with their hands to their mouth was three hundred; all the rest of the people had knelt to drink. [7]Yahweh then said to Gideon, 'With the three hundred who lapped the water, I shall rescue you and put Midian into your power. Let the people as a whole disperse to their homes.' [8]So they took the people's provisions and their horns, and then Gideon sent all the Israelites back to their tents, keeping only the three hundred. The camp of Midian was below his in the valley.

An omen of victory

[9]Now it happened, that same night, that Yahweh said to him, 'Get up and go down to the camp. I am putting it into your power. [10]If, however, you are nervous about going

down, go down to the camp with your servant
Purah; 11listen to what they are saying, and
that will encourage you to go down to the
camp.' So, with his servant Purah, he went
down to the edge of the outposts of the camp.
12Midian, Amalek and all the sons of the
East were deployed in the valley as thick as
locusts; their camels were as innumerable as
the sand on the seashore. 13Gideon got there
just as a man was telling his comrade a dream;
he was saying, 'This was the dream I had: a
cake made of barley bread came rolling into
the camp of Midian; it came to a tent, struck
against it and turned it upside down.' 14His
comrade replied, 'This can only be the sword
of Gideon son of Joash the Israelite. God has
put Midian and the whole camp into his
power.' 15When Gideon heard the dream thus
told and interpreted, he bowed in reverence;
he then went back to the camp of Israel and
said, 'On your feet, for Yahweh has put the
camp of Midian into your power!'

The surprise attack

16Gideon then divided his three hundred men
into three groups. To each he gave a horn
and an empty pitcher, with a torch inside
each pitcher. 17He said to them, 'Watch me,
and do as I do. When I reach the edge of the
camp, whatever I do, you must do also. 18I
shall blow my horn, and so will all those who
are with me; you too will then blow your
horns all round the camp and shout, "For
Yahweh and for Gideon!" '
19Gideon and his hundred companions
reached the edge of the camp at the beginning
of the middle watch, when the new sentries
had just been posted; they blew their horns
and smashed the pitchers in their hands.
20The three groups blew their horns and
smashed their pitchers; with their left hands
they grasped the torches, with their right
hands the horns for blowing them; and they
shouted, 'The sword for Yahweh and for
Gideon!' 21And they stood still, spaced out
round the camp. The whole camp was thrown
into confusion and the Midianites fled,
shouting. 22While the three hundred blew
their horns, Yahweh made each man turn his
sword against his comrade throughout the
entire camp. They all fled as far as Beth-ha-
Shittah in the direction of Zarethan, as far as
the bank of Abel-Meholah opposite Tabbath.

The pursuit

23The men of Israel mustered from Naphtali,
Asher and all Manasseh, and pursued
Midian. 24Gideon sent messengers
throughout the highlands of Ephraim to say,
'Come down to meet Midian, seize the water-
points ahead of them as far as Beth-Barah
and the Jordan.' All the men of Ephraim
mustered and seized the water-points as far as
Beth-Barah and the Jordan. 25They captured
the two Midianite chieftains, Oreb and Zeeb;
they killed Oreb at Oreb's Rock and Zeeb at
Zeeb's Winepress.[a] They pursued Midian;
and they brought the heads of Oreb and Zeeb
to Gideon on the other side of the Jordan.

The Ephraimites take offence

8 Now the men of Ephraim said to Gideon,
'What do you mean by treating us like
this, not summoning us when you went to
fight Midian?' And they reproached him
bitterly. 2He replied, 'What have I achieved,
compared with you? Is not the gleaning of
Ephraim's grapes better than the vintage of
Abiezer? 3God delivered Oreb and Zeeb, the
chieftains of Midian, into your power. What
was I able to do, in comparison with what
you have done?' At these words, their anger
with him died down.

3: GIDEON'S CAMPAIGN IN TRANSJORDAN HIS END

Gideon pursues the enemy beyond the Jordan

4Gideon reached the Jordan and crossed it,
but he and his three hundred companions
were exhausted with the pursuit. 5So he
said to the men of Succoth, 'Please give my
followers some loaves of bread, since they are
exhausted, and I am pursuing Zebah and
Zalmunna the kings of Midian.' 6The
headmen of Succoth replied, 'Are the hands
of Zebah and Zalmunna already in your
grasp, that we should give bread to your
army?' 7'Very well,' retorted Gideon, 'when
Yahweh has put Zebah and Zalmunna into
my power, I shall tear your flesh off with

7a Fragment explaining two place-names and independent of the main story.

desert-thorn and thistles.' 8From there he
went up to Penuel and asked the men of
Penuel the same thing; they replied as those
of Succoth had done. 9And to those of Penuel
he made a similar retort, 'When I return
victorious, I shall destroy this tower.'

The defeat of Zebah and Zalmunna

10Zebah and Zalmunna were in Karkor with
their army, about fifteen thousand men, all
that was left of the entire army of the sons of
the East. Of men bearing arms, a hundred
and twenty thousand had fallen. 11Gideon
approached them by the tent-dwellers' route,
east of Nobah and Jogbehah, and attacked
the army when it thought itself in safety.
12Zebah and Zalmunna fled. He pursued
them; he took the two kings of Midian pris-
oner—Zebah and Zalmunna—and the whole
army he routed in panic.

Gideon's acts of vengeance

13After the battle Gideon came back by the
Ascent of Heres. 14He caught a young man,
one of the people of Succoth, and questioned
him, and the latter wrote down the names of
the headmen and elders of Succoth for him—
seventy-seven men. 15Gideon son of Joash
then went to the people of Succoth and said,
'Here you see Zebah and Zalmunna, about
whom you taunted me and said, "Are the
hands of Zebah and Zalmunna already in
your grasp, that we should give bread to your
exhausted troops?"' 16He then seized the
elders of the town and, taking desert-thorn
and thistles, tore the men of Succoth to
pieces. 17He destroyed the tower of Penuel
and slaughtered the townsmen. 18He then
said to Zebah and Zalmunna, 'The men you
killed at Tabor—what were they like?' They
replied, 'They looked like you. Every one of
them carried himself like the son of a king.'
19Gideon replied, 'They were my brothers,
the sons of my own mother; as Yahweh lives,
if you had spared their lives I would not kill
you.' 20To Jether his eldest son he said, 'Stand
up and kill them!' But the boy did not draw
his sword; he dared not; he was still only a
lad. 21Zebah and Zalmunna then said, 'Stand
up yourself, and strike us down; for as a man
is, so is his strength.' Then Gideon stood up
and killed Zebah and Zalmunna; and he
took the crescents from round their camels'
necks.

Latter days of Gideon

22The men of Israel said to Gideon, 'Rule
over us, you, your son and your grandson,
since you have rescued us from the power of
Midian.' 23But Gideon replied, 'I will not
rule you, neither will my son. Yahweh
shall rule you.' 24Gideon went on, however,
'Let me make you one request. Each of you
give me one ring out of his booty'—for the
vanquished had had gold rings, being
Ishmaelites. 25'We shall give them gladly,'
they replied. So he spread out his cloak, and
on it each of them threw a ring from his
booty. 26The weight of the gold rings which
he had asked for amounted to seventeen
hundred shekels of gold, besides the cres-
cents and the earrings and purple garments
worn by the kings of Midian, and besides the
collars round their camels' necks. 27From
this Gideon made an *ephod*[a] and set it
up in his town, in Ophrah. All Israel, fol-
lowing his example, prostituted themselves
to it, and it was a snare for Gideon and
his family.

28Thus Midian was humbled before the
Israelites. He did not raise his head again,
and the country had peace for forty years, as
long as Gideon lived. 29So Jerubbaal son of
Joash went to live at home. 30Gideon had
seventy sons begotten by him, for he had
many wives. 31His concubine, who lived in
Shechem, also bore him a son, to whom he
gave the name Abimelech. 32Gideon son of
Joash died after a happy old age and was
buried in the tomb of Joash his father, at
Ophrah of Abiezer.

Israel relapses into idolatry

33After Gideon's death, the people of Israel
again began to prostitute themselves to the
Baals, taking Baal-Berith for their god. 34The
Israelites no longer remembered Yahweh
their God, who had rescued them from all
the enemies round them. 35And to the family
of Jerubbaal—Gideon—they showed no
faithful gratitude for all the good which it
had done for Israel.

8a Here a cult-object, cf. Ex 28:6.

4: THE REIGN OF ABIMELECH

9 Abimelech son of Jerubbaal confronted
his mother's brothers at Shechem and, to
them and to the whole clan of his maternal
grandfather's family, he said, 2 'Please put
this question to the leading men of Shechem:
Which is better for you: to be ruled by seventy
people—all Jerubbaal's sons—or to be ruled
by one? Remember too that I am your own
flesh and bone.' 3 His mother's brothers said
all this on his behalf to all the leading men of
Shechem, and their feelings swayed them to
follow Abimelech, since they argued, 'He is
our brother.' 4 So they gave him seventy
shekels of silver from the temple of Baal-
Berith, and with this Abimelech paid violent
adventurers to follow him. 5 He then went to
his father's house at Ophrah and put his
brothers, Jerubbaal's seventy sons, to death
on one and the same stone. Jotham, however,
Jerubbaal's youngest son, escaped by going
into hiding. 6 All the leading men of Shechem
and all Beth-Millo then met and proclaimed
Abimelech king at the oak of the cultic stone
at Shechem.

Jotham's diatribe

7 News of this was brought to Jotham. He
went and stood on the top of Mount Gerizim
and shouted at the top of his voice:

Hear me, leaders of Shechem,
so that God may also hear you!

8 One day the trees went out
to anoint a king to rule them.
They said to the olive tree, 'Be our king!'

9 The olive tree replied,
'Must I forgo my oil
which gives honour to gods and men,
to stand and sway over the trees?'

10 Then the trees said to the fig tree,
'You come and be our king!'

11 The fig tree replied,
'Must I forgo my sweetness,
forgo my excellent fruit,
to go and sway over the trees?'

12 Then the trees said to the vine,
'You come and be our king!'

13 The vine replied,
'Must I forgo my wine
which cheers gods and men,
to go and sway over the trees?'

14 Then the trees all said to the thorn bush,
'You come and be our king!'

15 And the thorn bush replied to the trees,
'If you are anointing me in good faith
to be your king,
come and shelter in my shade.
But, if not,
fire will come out of the thorn bush
and devour the cedars of Lebanon.'

16 'Now then, if you have acted in sincerity
and good faith in making Abimelech king, if
you have dealt honourably with Jerubbaal
and his family, and have treated him as his
actions deserved, 17 my father having fought
for you, risked his life and rescued you from
the power of Midian, 18 and you today having
risen up against my father's family, murdered
his sons—seventy of them on one and the
same stone—and appointed Abimelech, his
slave-girl's son, to rule the leading men of
Shechem, because he is your brother!— 19 if,
I say, you have acted in sincerity and good
faith towards Jerubbaal and his family, then
may Abimelech be your joy and may you be
his! 20 If not, may fire come out of Abimelech
and devour the leading men of Shechem and
Beth-Millo, and fire come out of the leading
men of Shechem and Beth-Millo to devour
Abimelech!'

21 Jotham then took to his heels; he fled and
made his way to Beer; and there he stayed,
to be out of his brother Abimelech's reach.

Shechem revolts against Abimelech

22 Abimelech ruled Israel for three years.
23 God then sent a spirit of discord between
Abimelech and the leaders of Shechem, and
the leaders of Shechem betrayed Abimelech.
24 And this was so that the crime committed
against Jerubbaal's seventy sons should be
avenged, and their blood recoil on their
brother Abimelech who had murdered them,
and on those leaders of Shechem who had
helped him to murder his brothers.

25 The leaders of Shechem put men to
ambush him on the mountain tops, and these
robbed anyone travelling their way. Abime-
lech was told of this. 26 Gaal son of Obed,
with his brothers, happened to pass through
Shechem and win the confidence of the
leaders of Shechem. 27 These went out into
the countryside to harvest their vineyards;

they trod the grapes and made merry and went into the temple of their god. They ate and drank there and cursed Abimelech. [28]Gaal son of Obed said, 'Who is Abimelech, and what is Shechem, for us to be his slaves? Should not Jerubbaal's son and his lieutenant, Zebul, be serving the men of Hamor, father of Shechem? Why should we be his slaves? [29]Who will put this people under my command, so that I can expel Abimelech? I should say to him, "Reinforce your army and come out!" ' [30]Zebul the governor of the town was told what Gaal son of Obed had said, and he was furious. [31]He sent messengers secretly to Abimelech to say, 'Look! Gaal son of Obed has come to Shechem with his brothers, and they are stirring up the town against you. [32]So, move under cover of dark, you and the men you have with you, and take up concealed positions in the countryside; [33]then in the morning at sunrise, break cover and rush on the town. When Gaal and his supporters come out to meet you, treat them as occasion offers.' [34]So Abimelech set off under cover of dark with all his own supporters and took up concealed positions over against Shechem, in four groups. [35]As Gaal son of Obed was coming out and pausing at the entrance of the town gate, Abimelech and his supporters rose from their ambush. [36]Gaal saw these men and said to Zebul, 'Look, there are men coming down from the tops of the mountains!' Zebul answered, 'You mistake the shadow of the mountains for men.' [37]But Gaal insisted, 'Look, there are men coming down from the Navel of the Earth and another group is coming from the direction of the Diviners' Oak.' [38]Zebul then said, 'Where are your mouthings now about "Who is Abimelech, for us to be his slaves?" Are not these the men you made light of? Sally out, then, and fight him.' [39]Gaal sallied out at the head of the leaders of Shechem and engaged Abimelech. [40]Abimelech drove Gaal off, who turned tail, many of his men falling dead before they could reach the gate. [41]Abimelech then stayed at Aruma, and Zebul expelled Gaal and his brothers and prevented them from living in Shechem.

Destruction of the town and citadel of Shechem

[42]Next day, when the people went out into the countryside, Abimelech was told of this. [43]He took his men, divided them into three groups and lay in wait in the fields. When he saw the people leaving the town, he bore down on them and slaughtered them. [44]While Abimelech and his group rushed forward and took position at the entrance to the town gate, the two other groups fell on everyone in the fields and slaughtered them. [45]All that day Abimelech attacked the town. He stormed it and slaughtered the people inside, razed the town and sowed it with salt. [46]On hearing this, all the leading men inside Migdal-Shechem took refuge in the crypt of the temple of El-Berith. [47]As soon as Abimelech heard that the leading men inside Migdal-Shechem had all gathered there, [48]he went up Mount Zalmon with all his men. Then taking an axe in his hands, he cut off the branch of a tree, picked it up and put it on his shoulder, and said to the men with him, 'Hurry and do what you have seen me do.' [49]Each of his men similarly cut off a branch; then, following Abimelech, they piled the branches over the crypt and set it on fire over those who were inside; so that all the people in Migdal-Shechem died too, about a thousand men and women.

Siege of Thebez and death of Abimelech

[50]Abimelech then marched on Thebez, besieged it and captured it. [51]In the middle of the town there was a fortified tower in which all the men and women and all the leading men of the town took refuge. They locked the door behind them and climbed up to the roof of the tower. [52]Abimelech reached the tower and attacked it. As he was approaching the door of the tower to set it on fire, [53]a woman threw down a millstone on his head and cracked his skull. [54]He instantly called his young armour-bearer and said, 'Draw your sword and kill me, so that it will not be said of me that "A woman killed him".' His armour-bearer ran him through, and he died. [55]When the men of Israel saw that Abimelech was dead, they dispersed to their homes.

[56]Thus God made to recoil on Abimelech the evil he had done his father by murdering his seventy brothers, [57]and all the evil that the men of Shechem had done God made recoil on their heads too. And so the curse of Jotham son of Jerubbaal came true for them.

JEPHTHAH AND THE 'MINOR' JUDGES

F: TOLA

10 After Abimelech, Tola son of Puah,
son of Dodo, rose to deliver Israel. He
belonged to Issachar and lived at Shamir in
the mountain country of Ephraim. 2He was
judge in Israel for twenty-three years; he then
died and was buried at Shamir.

G: JAIR

3After him rose Jair of Gilead, who judged
Israel for twenty-two years. 4He had thirty
sons who rode on thirty young donkeys and
who owned thirty towns, still known today
as the Encampments of Jair, in the territory
of Gilead. 5Jair then died and was buried at
Kamon.

H: JEPHTHAH

Oppression by the Ammonites

6The Israelites again began doing what is evil
in Yahweh's eyes. They served Baal and
Astarte, and the gods of Aram and Sidon, the
gods of Moab and those of the Ammonites
and Philistines. They deserted Yahweh and
served him no more. 7Yahweh's anger then
grew hot against Israel and he gave them over
into the power of the Philistines and the
power of the Ammonites, 8who from that
year onwards crushed and oppressed the
Israelites for eighteen years—all those Israel-
ites living on the other side of the Jordan in
Amorite territory, in Gilead. 9Furthermore,
the Ammonites would cross the Jordan and
also make war on Judah, Benjamin and the
House of Ephraim, so that Israel was in
distress. 10The Israelites then cried to
Yahweh and said, 'We have sinned against
you, because we have turned from Yahweh
our God to serve Baals.' 11And Yahweh said
to the Israelites, 'When Egyptians and
Amorites, Ammonites and Philistines,
12when the Sidonians, Amalek and Midian
oppressed you and you cried to me, did I not
rescue you from their power? 13But it is you
who have forsaken me and served other gods;
and so I shall rescue you no more. 14Go and
cry to the gods whom you have chosen. Let
them rescue you in your time of trouble.'
15The Israelites replied to Yahweh, 'We have
sinned. Treat us as you see fit, but please
rescue us today.' 16They got rid of their
foreign gods and served Yahweh, who could
bear Israel's suffering no longer.

17The Ammonites gathered and pitched
camp in Gilead. The Israelites rallied and
pitched camp at Mizpah. 18The people, the
chieftains of Gilead, then said to one another,
'Who will volunteer to attack the Ammon-
ites? He shall be chief of all who live in
Gilead!'

Jephthah lays down his terms

11 Jephthah the Gileadite was a valiant
warrior. He was a prostitute's son.
Gilead was Jephthah's father, 2but Gilead's
wife also bore him sons, and the sons of this
wife, when they grew up, drove Jephthah
away, saying, 'No share of the paternal heri-
tage for you, since you are a son of another
woman.' 3Jephthah fled far from his brothers
and settled in the territory of Tob. Jephthah
enlisted a group of adventurers who used to
go raiding with him.

4It was some time after this that the
Ammonites made war on Israel. 5And when
the Ammonites had attacked Israel, the
elders of Gilead went to fetch Jephthah from
the territory of Tob. 6'Come', they said, 'and
be our commander, so that we can fight the
Ammonites.' 7Jephthah replied to the elders
of Gilead, 'Didn't you hate me and drive me
out of my father's house? Why come to me
now, when you are in trouble?' 8The elders
of Gilead said to Jephthah, 'That is why we
are turning to you now. Come with us; fight
the Ammonites and be our chief, chief of all
the people living in Gilead.' 9Jephthah then
said to the elders of Gilead, 'If you bring me
home to fight the Ammonites and Yahweh
defeats them for me, I am to be your chief?'
10And the elders of Gilead then said to
Jephthah, 'Yahweh be witness between us,
if we do not do as you have said!' 11So
Jephthah set off with the elders of Gilead.
The people put him at their head as chief
and commander; and Jephthah repeated all
his conditions at Mizpah in Yahweh's
presence.

Jephthah negotiates with the Ammonites

12 Jephthah sent messengers to the king of the
Ammonites to say to him, 'What do you have
against us, for you to come and make war on
my country?' 13 The king of the Ammonites
replied to Jephthah's messengers, 'The
reason is that when Israel came up from
Egypt, they seized my country from the
Arnon to the Jabbok and to the Jordan; so
now restore it to me peacefully.' 14 Jephthah
sent messengers back to the king of the
Ammonites 15 with this answer, 'Jephthah
says this, "Israel seized neither the country
of Moab nor the country of the Ammonites.
16 When Israel came out of Egypt, they
marched through the desert as far as the
Sea of Reeds and, having reached Kadesh,
17 Israel then sent messengers to the king of
Edom to say: Please let me pass through your
country, but the king of Edom would not
listen. They sent similarly to the king of
Moab, but he refused, and Israel remained
at Kadesh; 18 later, moving on through the
desert and skirting the countries of Edom
and Moab until arriving to the east of Moabite
territory, the people camped on the other
side of the Arnon but did not enter Moabite
territory, the Arnon being the Moabite fron-
tier. 19 Israel then sent messengers to Sihon,
king of the Amorites, ruling in Heshbon.
Israel's message was: Please let me pass
through your country to my destination.
20 But Sihon would not let Israel pass through
his territory; he mustered his whole army;
they encamped at Jahaz, and he then joined
battle with Israel. 21 Yahweh, God of Israel,
delivered Sihon and his whole army into the
power of Israel, who defeated them; as the
result of which, Israel took possession of the
entire territory of the Amorites living in that
region. 22 Israel took possession of all the
Amorite territory from the Arnon to the
Jabbok and from the desert to the Jordan.
23 And now that Yahweh, God of Israel, has
dispossessed the Amorites before his people
Israel, do you think you can dispossess us?
24 Will you not keep as your possession what-
ever Chemosh, your god, has given you?
And, just the same, we shall keep as ours
whatever Yahweh our God has given us, to
inherit from those who were before us! 25 Are
you a better man than Balak son of Zippor,
king of Moab? Did he pick a quarrel with
Israel? Did he make war on them? 26 When
Israel settled in Heshbon and its depen-
dencies, and in Aroer and its dependencies,
or in any of the towns on the banks of the
Arnon (three hundred years ago), why did
you not recover them then? 27 I for my part
have done you no harm, but you are wronging
me by making war on me. Let Yahweh the
Judge give judgement today between the
Israelites and the king of the Ammonites." '
28 But the king of the Ammonites took no
notice of the message that Jephthah sent
him.

Jephthah's vow and his victory

29 The spirit of Yahweh was on Jephthah, who
crossed Gilead and Manasseh, crossed by
way of Mizpah in Gilead, and from Mizpah
in Gilead crossed into Ammonite territory.
30 And Jephthah made a vow to Yahweh, 'If
you deliver the Ammonites into my grasp,
31 the first thing to come out of the doors of
my house to meet me when I return in
triumph from fighting the Ammonites shall
belong to Yahweh, and I shall sacrifice it as
a burnt offering.' 32 Jephthah crossed into
Ammonite territory to attack them, and
Yahweh delivered them into his grasp. 33 He
beat them from Aroer to the border of
Minnith (twenty towns) and to Abel-
Keramim. It was a very severe defeat,
and the Ammonites were humbled by the
Israelites.

34 As Jephthah returned to his house at
Mizpah, his daughter came out to meet him,
dancing to the sound of tambourines. She
was his only child; apart from her, he had
neither son nor daughter. 35 When he saw her,
he tore his clothes and exclaimed, 'Oh my
daughter, what misery you have brought
upon me! You have joined those who bring
misery into my life! I have made a promise
before Yahweh which I cannot retract.' 36 She
replied, 'Father, you have made a promise to
Yahweh; treat me as the promise that you
have made requires, since Yahweh has
granted you vengeance on your enemies the
Ammonites.' 37 She then said to her father,
'Grant me this! Let me be free for two
months. I shall go and wander in the moun-
tains, and with my companions bewail my
virginity.' 38 He replied, 'Go,' and let her go
away for two months. So she went away with
her companions and bewailed her virginity
in the mountains. 39 When the two months
were over she went back to her father, and
he treated her as the vow that he had uttered

bound him. She had remained a virgin. And
hence, the custom in Israel 40for the
daughters of Israel to leave home year by
year and lament over the daughter of
Jephthah the Gileadite for four days every
year.

War between Ephraim and Gilead
The death of Jephthah

12 The men of Ephraim mobilised; they
crossed the Jordan near Zaphon and
said to Jephthah, 'Why did you go and make
war on the Ammonites without asking us to
go with you? We shall burn down your house
over your head!' 2Jephthah replied, 'My
people and I were in serious conflict with the
Ammonites. I summoned you, but you did
not come to rescue me from them. 3When I
saw that no one was coming to rescue me, I
took my life in my hands and marched against
the Ammonites, and Yahweh handed them
over to me. So why advance on me today to
make war on me?' 4Jephthah then mustered
all the men of Gilead and made war on
Ephraim, and the men of Gilead defeated
Ephraim—since the latter used to say, 'You
are only fugitives from Ephraim, you Gilead-
ites in the heart of Ephraim and Manasseh.'
5Gilead then cut Ephraim off from the fords
of the Jordan, and whenever Ephraimite
fugitives said, 'Let me cross,' the men of
Gilead would ask, 'Are you an Ephraimite?'
If he said, 'No,' 6they then said, 'Very
well, say Shibboleth.'[a] If anyone said,
"Sibboleth", because he could not pro-
nounce it, then they would seize him and kill
him by the fords of the Jordan.

Forty-two thousand Ephraimites fell on
this occasion.

7Jephthah judged Israel for six years.
Jephthah the Gileadite then died and was
buried in his town, in Gilead.

I: IBZAN

8After him, Ibzan of Bethlehem was judge
in Israel. 9He had thirty sons and thirty
daughters. He gave his daughters in marriage
outside his clan and brought in thirty brides
from outside for his sons. He was judge in
Israel for seven years. 10Ibzan then died and
was buried in Bethlehem.

J: ELON

11After him, Elon of Zebulun was judge in
Israel. He was judge in Israel for ten years.
12Elon of Zebulun then died and was buried
at Aijalon in the territory of Zebulun.

K: ABDON

13After him, Abdon son of Hillel of Pirathon
was judge in Israel. 14He had forty sons and
thirty grandsons who rode seventy young
donkeys. He was judge in Israel for eight
years. 15Abdon son of Hillel of Pirathon
then died and was buried at Pirathon in
the territory of Ephraim, in the Amalekite
highlands.

L: SAMSON

Samson's birth foretold

13 Again the Israelites began doing what
is evil in Yahweh's eyes, and Yahweh
delivered them into the power of the Phili-
stines for forty years.

2There was a man of Zorah of the tribe of
Dan, called Manoah. His wife was barren;
she had borne no children. 3The Angel of
Yahweh appeared to this woman and said to
her, 'You are barren and have had no child,
but you are going to conceive and give birth
to a son. 4From now on, take great care.
Drink no wine or fermented liquor, and
eat nothing unclean. 5For you are going to
conceive and give birth to a son. No razor is
to touch his head, for the boy is to be God's
nazirite from his mother's womb; and he will
start rescuing Israel from the power of the
Philistines.' 6The woman then went and told
her husband, 'A man of God has just come
to me, who looked like the Angel of God, so
majestic was he. I did not ask him where he
came from, and he did not tell me his name.
7But he said to me, "You are going to conceive
and will give birth to a son. From now on,
drink no wine or fermented liquor, and eat
nothing unclean. For the boy is to be God's
nazirite from his mother's womb to his dying
day." '

12a The word (= 'ear of corn') is chosen simply to show up local pronunciation.

The Angel appears a second time

8Manoah then pleaded with Yahweh and
said, 'I beg you, Lord, let the man of God
that you sent come to us again and instruct
us what to do about the child when he is
born.' 9Yahweh heard Manoah's prayer, and
the Angel of Yahweh visited the woman again
while she was sitting in a field and when her
husband Manoah was not with her. 10The
woman quickly ran and told her husband,
'Look,' she said, 'the man who came to me
the other day has appeared to me again.'
11Manoah got up, followed his wife, came to
the man and said to him, 'Are you the man
who spoke to this woman?' He replied, 'I
am.' 12Manoah then said, 'When your words
come true, what will be the boy's way of life?'
13The Angel of Yahweh replied to Manoah,
'From everything that I forbade this woman,
let her abstain. 14Let her swallow nothing
that comes from the vine, let her drink no
wine or fermented liquor, let her eat nothing
unclean and let her obey all the orders that I
have given her.' 15Manoah then said to the
Angel of Yahweh, 'Allow us to detain you
while we prepare a kid for you'—16bfor
Manoah did not know that this was the Angel
of Yahweh. 16aThe Angel of Yahweh said to
Manoah, 'Even if you did detain me, I should
not eat your food; but if you wish to prepare a
burnt offering, offer it to Yahweh.' 17Manoah
then said to the Angel of Yahweh, 'What is
your name, so that we may honour you
when your words come true?' 18The Angel of
Yahweh replied, 'Why ask my name? It is
a name of wonder.' 19Manoah then took
the kid and the oblation and offered it on the
rock as a burnt offering to Yahweh the
Wonderworker. Manoah and his wife looked
on. 20Now, as the flame rose heavenwards
from the altar, the Angel of Yahweh ascended
in this flame before the eyes of Manoah and
his wife, and they fell face downwards on the
ground. 21After this, the Angel of Yahweh
did not appear any more to Manoah and his
wife, but Manoah understood that this had
been the Angel of Yahweh. 22And Manoah
said to his wife, 'We are certain to die, because
we have seen God.' 23His wife replied, 'If
Yahweh had meant to kill us, he would not
have accepted a burnt offering and oblation
from us, he would not have let us see all this
and, at the same time, have told us such
things.' 24The woman gave birth to a son and
called him Samson. The child grew, and
Yahweh blessed him; 25and the spirit of
Yahweh began to stir him in the Camp of
Dan, between Zorah and Eshtaol.

Samson marries

14 Samson went down to Timnah, and at
Timnah he noticed a woman, a Phili-
stine girl. 2He went home again and told his
father and mother this. 'At Timnah', he said,
'I noticed a woman, a Philistine girl. So now
get her for me, to be my wife.' 3His father
and mother said to him, 'Is there no woman
among your brothers' daughters or in our
entire nation, for you to go and take a wife
among these uncircumcised Philistines?' But
Samson said to his father, 'Get that one for
me; she is the one I am fond of.' 4His father
and mother did not know that all this came
from Yahweh, who was seeking grounds for
a quarrel with the Philistines, since at this
time the Philistines dominated Israel.

5Samson went down to Timnah and, as he
reached the vineyards of Timnah, he saw a
young lion coming roaring towards him.
6The spirit of Yahweh seized on him and he
tore the lion to pieces with his bare hands as
though it were a kid; but he did not tell his
father or mother what he had done. 7He went
down and talked to the woman, and he
became fond of her. 8Not long after this,
Samson went back to marry her. He went out
of his way to look at the carcase of the lion,
and there was a swarm of bees in the lion's
body, and honey. 9He took up some honey
in his hand and ate it as he went along. On
returning to his father and mother, he gave
some to them, which they ate too, but he did
not tell them that he had taken it from the
lion's carcase. 10His father then went down
to the woman, and Samson made a feast
there, as is the custom for young men. 11And
when the Philistines saw him, they chose
thirty companions to stay with him.

Samson's riddle

12Samson then said to them, 'Let me ask you
a riddle. If you can give me the answer during
the seven days of feasting, I shall give you
thirty pieces of fine linen and thirty festal
robes. 13But if you cannot tell me the answer,
then you in your turn must give me thirty
pieces of fine linen and thirty festal robes.'
'Ask your riddle,' they replied, 'we are lis-
tening.' 14So he said to them:

Out of the eater came what is eaten,
and out of the strong came what is sweet.

But three days went by and they could not
solve the riddle.
15 On the fourth day they said to Samson's
wife, 'Cajole your husband into explaining
the riddle to us, or we shall burn you and
your father's family to death. Did you invite
us here to rob us?' 16 Samson's wife then went
to him in tears and said, 'You only hate me,
you do not love me. You have asked my
fellow countrymen a riddle and told not even
me the answer.' He said to her, 'I have not
told even my father or mother; why should I
tell you?' 17 She wept on his neck for the seven
days that their feasting lasted. She was so
persistent that on the seventh day he told
her the answer, and she told her fellow-
countrymen.
18 So on the seventh day, before he went
into the bedroom, the men of the town said
to him:

What is sweeter than honey,
and what stronger than a lion?

He retorted:

If you had not ploughed with my heifer,
you would never have solved my riddle.

19 Then the spirit of Yahweh seized on him.
He went down to Ashkelon, killed thirty men
there, took what they wore and gave the festal
robes to those who had answered the riddle,
then burning with rage returned to his
father's house. 20 Samson's wife was then
given to the companion who had acted as his
best man.

Samson burns the Philistines' harvest

15 Not long after this, at the time of the
wheat harvest, Samson visited his wife,
with a kid; he said, 'I wish to go to my wife
in her room.' But her father would not let
him enter. 2 'I felt sure', he said, 'that you
had taken a real dislike to her, so I gave
her to your companion. But would not her
younger sister suit you better? Have her
instead.' 3 But Samson answered them, 'I can
get my revenge on the Philistines now only
by doing them some damage.' 4 So Samson
went off and caught three hundred foxes,
then took torches and, turning the foxes tail
to tail, put a torch between each pair of tails.
5 He lit the torches and set the foxes free in
the Philistines' cornfields. In this way he
burned both sheaves and standing corn, and
the vines and olive trees as well.
6 The Philistines asked, 'Who has done
this?' and received the answer, 'Samson, who
married the Timnite's daughter; his father-
in-law took the wife back again and gave her
to his companion instead.' The Philistines
then went and burned the woman and her
father's family to death. 7 Samson said to
them, 'If that is how you behave, I swear I
will not rest till I have had my revenge on
you.' 8 And he fell on them systematically and
caused great havoc. Then he went down to
the cave in the Rock of Etham and lived
there.

The donkey's jawbone

9 The Philistines came up and encamped in
Judah and made a foray against Lehi.
10 The men of Judah said to them, 'Why
are you attacking us?' They replied, 'We
have come to seize Samson and to treat him
as he has treated us.' 11 Three thousand men
of Judah then went down to the cave of the
Rock of Etham and said to him, 'Don't you
know that the Philistines have us in their
power? Now what have you done to us?' He
replied, 'I have treated them only as they
treated me.' 12 They then said, 'We have come
down to take you, to hand you over to the
Philistines.' He said, 'Swear to me not to kill
me yourselves.' 13 They replied, 'No; we only
want to bind you and hand you over to them;
we certainly do not want to kill you.' They
then bound him with two new ropes and
brought him up from the Rock.
14 As he was approaching Lehi, and the
Philistines came running towards him with
triumphant shouts, the spirit of Yahweh was
on him; the ropes on his arms became like
burnt strands of flax and the cords round his
hands came untied. 15 Coming across the fresh
jawbone of a donkey, he reached out and
snatched it up; and with it he slaughtered a
thousand men. 16 And Samson said:

With the jawbone of a donkey
I have laid them in heaps,
with the jawbone of a donkey
I have felled a thousand men.

17 And with that he hurled the jawbone away;
and that is why the place was called Ramath-

Lehi.[a] [18]And as he was very thirsty, he called on Yahweh and said, 'You yourself have worked this great deliverance by the hand of your servant; and now must I die of thirst and fall into the hands of the uncircumcised?' [19]Then God opened a hollow in the ground, the hollow there is at Lehi, and water gushed out of it. Samson drank; his vigour returned and he revived. And therefore this spring was called En-ha-Kore;[b] it is still at Lehi today. [20]Samson was judge in Israel in the days of the Philistines for twenty years.

The gates of Gaza

16 Samson then went to Gaza and, seeing a prostitute there, went in to her. [2]The men of Gaza being told, 'Samson has arrived,' surrounded the place and kept watch for him the whole night at the town gate. All that night they were going to make no move, thinking, 'Let us wait until daybreak, and then kill him.' [3]Till midnight, however, Samson stayed in bed, and then at midnight he got up, seized the doors of the town gate and the two posts as well; he tore them up, bar and all, hoisted them on to his shoulders and carried them to the top of the hill overlooking Hebron.

Samson is betrayed by Delilah

[4]After this, he fell in love with a woman in the Vale of Sorek; she was called Delilah. [5]The Philistine chiefs visited her and said, 'Cajole him and find out where his great strength comes from, and how we can master him, so that we can bind him and subdue him. In return we shall each give you eleven hundred silver shekels.'

[6]Delilah said to Samson, 'Please tell me where your great strength comes from, and what would be needed to bind and subdue you.' [7]Samson replied, 'If I were bound with seven new bowstrings which had not yet been dried, I should lose my strength and become like any other man.' [8]The Philistine chiefs brought Delilah seven new bowstrings which had not yet been dried and she took them and bound him with them. [9]She had men concealed in her room, and she shouted, 'The Philistines are on you, Samson!' Then he snapped the bowstrings as a strand of tow snaps at a touch of the fire. So the secret of his strength remained unknown.

[10]Delilah then said to Samson, 'You have been laughing at me and telling me lies. But now please tell me what would be needed to bind you.' [11]He replied, 'If I were bound tightly with new ropes which have never been used, I should lose my strength and become like any other man.' [12]Delilah then took new ropes and bound him with them, and she shouted, 'The Philistines are on you, Samson!' She had men concealed in her room, but he snapped the ropes round his arms like thread.

[13]Delilah then said to Samson, 'Up to now you have been laughing at me and telling me lies. Tell me what would be needed to bind you.' He replied, 'If you wove the seven locks of my hair into the warp of a cloth and beat them together tight with the reed, I should lose my strength and become like any other man.' [14]She lulled him to sleep, then wove the seven locks of his hair into the warp, beat them together tight with the reed and shouted, 'The Philistines are on you, Samson!' He woke from his sleep and pulled out both reed and warp. So the secret of his strength remained unknown.

[15]Delilah said to him, 'How can you say that you love me, when your heart is not with me? Three times now you have laughed at me and have not told me where your great strength comes from.' [16]And day after day she pestered him with her talk, nagging him till he grew sick to death of it. [17]At last he confided everything to her; he said to her, 'A razor has never touched my head, because I have been God's nazirite from my mother's womb. If my head were shorn, then my power would leave me and I should lose my strength and become like any other man.' [18]Delilah then realized that he had really confided in her; she sent for the Philistine princes with the message, 'Come just once more: he has confided everything to me.' And the Philistine chiefs came to her with the money in their hands. [19]She lulled Samson to sleep in her lap, summoned a man and had him shear off the seven locks from his head. Thus for the first time she got control over him, and his strength left him. [20]She cried, 'The Philistines are on you, Samson!' He awoke from sleep, thinking, 'I shall break

---

15a Lit. 'hill of the jawbone'.
15b 'The Spring of the Caller', where Samson called on Yahweh.

free as I have done time after time and shake
myself clear.' But he did not know that
Yahweh had left him. 21 The Philistines seized
him, put out his eyes and took him down to
Gaza. They fettered him with a double chain
of bronze and he spent his time turning the
mill in the prison.
22 But his hair began to grow again when it
had been cut off.

Samson's revenge and death

23 The Philistine chiefs assembled to offer a
great sacrifice to Dagon their god. And amid
their festivities they said:

> Into our hands our god has delivered
> Samson our enemy.

24 And as soon as the people saw their god,
they acclaimed him, shouting his praises:

> Into our hands our god has delivered
> Samson our enemy,
> the man who laid our country waste
> and killed so many of us.

25 And as their hearts were full of joy, they
shouted, 'Summon Samson out to amuse us.'
So Samson was summoned from prison, and
he performed feats in front of them; then
he was put to stand between the pillars.
26 Samson then said to the boy who was
leading him by the hand, 'Lead me where I
can touch the pillars supporting the building,
so that I can lean against them.' 27 Now the
building was crowded with men and women.
All the Philistine chiefs were there, while
about three thousand men and women were
watching Samson's feats from the terrace.
28 Samson called on Yahweh and cried out,
'Lord Yahweh, I beg you, remember me;
give me strength again this once, O God, and
let me be revenged on the Philistines at one
blow for my two eyes.' 29 And Samson took
hold of the two central pillars supporting the
building, and braced himself with his right
arm round one and his left round the other;
30 and he shouted, 'Let me die with the Phili-
stines!' He then heaved with all his might,
and the building fell on the chiefs and on all
the people there. Those whom he brought to
their death by his death outnumbered those
whom he had done to death during his life.
31 His brothers and the whole of his father's
family came down and carried him away.
They took him back and buried him between
Zorah and Eshtaol in the tomb of Manoah
his father. He had judged Israel for twenty
years.

IV: APPENDICES

A: THE SANCTUARY OF MICAH AND THE SANCTUARY OF DAN

Micah's domestic shrine

17 In the highlands of Ephraim there was
a man called Micayehu. 2 He said to his
mother, 'The eleven hundred silver shekels
which were taken from you and concerning
which you uttered a curse, having said in my
hearing . . .[a] Look, I have got that silver. I
was the one who took it.' His mother said,
'May Yahweh bless my boy!' 3 He gave the
eleven hundred shekels back to his mother,
who said, 'I have indeed vowed to give this
silver to Yahweh for my son, to have a statue
carved and an idol cast in metal, but now I
should like to give it back to you.' He,
however, returned the money to his mother.
4 His mother then took two hundred silver
shekels and gave them to the metalworker.
With them, he carved a statue (and cast an
idol in metal) which was put in Micayehu's
house. 5 This man Micah owned a shrine; he
made an *ephod* and some domestic images,
and installed one of his sons to be his priest.
6 In those days there was no king in Israel,
and everyone did as he saw fit.
7 There was a young man of Bethlehem in
Judah, of the clan of Judah, who was a Levite
and resided there as a stranger. 8 This man
left the town of Bethlehem in Judah to settle
wherever he could find a home. On his travels
he came to the highlands of Ephraim and to
Micah's house. 9 Micah asked him, 'Where
do you come from?' The other replied, 'I am
a Levite from Bethlehem in Judah. I am
travelling, and am going to settle wherever I

17a The words of the curse are omitted lest even to quote them might have its effect.

can find a home.' 10Micah said to him, 'Stay here with me; be my father and priest and I shall give you ten silver shekels a year, and clothing and food.' 11The Levite agreed to remain in the man's house, and the young man became like one of his sons to him. 12Micah installed the Levite; the young man became Micah's priest and stayed in his house. 13And Micah said, 'Now I know that Yahweh will treat me well, since I have this Levite as priest.'

The Danites in search of a territory

18 In those days there was no king in Israel.

Now in those days the tribe of Dan was in search of a territory to live in, for until then no territory had fallen to them among the tribes of Israel. 2From their clan the Danites sent five brave men from Zorah and Eshtaol to reconnoitre the country and explore it. They said to them, 'Go and explore the country.' The five men came to the highlands of Ephraim, as far as Micah's house, and spent the night there. 3When they were near Micah's house, they recognised the voice of the young Levite and, going nearer, said to him, 'Who brought you here? What are you doing here? What is keeping you here?' 4He replied, 'Micah has made certain arrangements with me. He pays me a wage and I act as his priest.' 5They replied, 'Then consult God, so that we may know whether the journey we are on will lead to success.' 6The priest replied, 'Go in peace; Yahweh is watching over your journey.'

7The five men then left and, arriving at Laish, saw that the people living there had an untroubled existence, according to the customs of the Sidonians, peaceful and trusting, that there was no lack or shortage of any sort in the territory, that they were a long way away from the Sidonians and that they had no contact with the Aramaeans.

8They then went back to their brothers at Zorah and Eshtaol and, when the latter asked them, 'What have you to report?' 9they said, 'Up! we must go against them, since we have looked at the country and it is excellent, though you take no action! Waste no time in setting out and taking possession of the country. 10When you get there, you will find a trusting people. The country is wide, and God has put it at your mercy. It is a place where there is no lack of anything on earth.'

The migration of the Danites

11From these places, consequently, from the clan of Danites at Zorah and Eshtaol, six hundred men set out equipped for war. 12They went up and camped at Kiriath-Jearim in Judah; and for this reason the place is still called the Camp of Dan today. It lies to the west of Kiriath-Jearim. 13From there they entered the highlands of Ephraim and came to Micah's house.

14The five men who had been to reconnoitre the country then spoke to their brothers. 'Do you know', they said, 'that in these houses there is an *ephod*, some domestic images, a carved statue and an idol cast in metal? So now work out what you have got to do!'

15So, turning off the road, they went to the young Levite's dwelling, to Micah's house, and greeted him peacefully. 16While the six hundred men of the Danites, equipped for war, stood at the threshold of the gate, 17the five who had been to reconnoitre the country went on into the house and took the carved statue, the *ephod*, the domestic images and the idol cast in metal; meanwhile the priest remained at the threshold of the gate with the six hundred men equipped for war. 18These men, having entered Micah's house, took the carved statue, the *ephod*, the domestic images and the idol cast in metal. The priest, however, said, 'What are you doing?' 19'Be quiet,' they replied. 'Put your hand over your mouth and come with us, and become our father and priest. Are you better off as domestic priest to one man, or as priest to a tribe and clan in Israel?' 20The priest was delighted; he took the *ephod*, the domestic images and the carved statue, and went off among the people.

21Resuming their original line of march, they set off, having put the women, children, livestock and baggage out in front. 22They had gone some distance from Micah's house, when the people living in the houses near Micah's house raised the alarm and set off in pursuit of the Danites. 23As they shouted after the Danites, the latter, turning about, said to Micah, 'What is the matter with you, that you are shouting like this?' 24He replied, 'You have taken away my god, which I have had made, and the priest as well. You are going away, and what have I got left? And now you ask me, "What is the matter?" ' 25The Danites said, 'Let us hear no more from you, or quick-tempered men may set about you, and this might cost you your life and the lives of your family!' 26So the Danites went on their way; and Micah, seeing that they were the stronger, turned and went home.

Capture of Laish Foundation of Dan and the sanctuary there

27So, having taken the god made by Micah, and the priest who had been his, the Danites marched on Laish, on a peaceful and trusting people. They put it to the sword and they burned down the town. 28There was no one to come to the rescue, since it was a long way from Sidon and had no contact with the Aramaeans. It lay in the valley running towards Beth-Rehob. They rebuilt the town and settled in it 29and called it Dan, from the name of Dan their ancestor who had been born to Israel; originally, however, the town had been called Laish. 30The Danites erected the carved statue for themselves. Jonathan son of Gershom, son of Moses, and his sons after him were priests for the tribe of Dan till the day when the inhabitants of the country were carried away into exile. 31The carved statue made by Micah they installed for their own use, and there it stayed as long as the house of God remained at Shiloh.

B: THE CRIME AT GIBEAH AND THE WAR AGAINST BENJAMIN

The Levite of Ephraim and his concubine

19 In those days, when there was no king in Israel, there was a man, a Levite, whose home was deep in the highlands of Ephraim. He took as concubine a woman from Bethlehem in Judah. 2In a fit of anger his concubine left him and went back to her father's house at Bethlehem in Judah, and she stayed there for some time—four months. 3Her husband then set out after her, to appeal to her affections and fetch her back; he had his servant and two donkeys with him. As he was arriving at the house of the girl's father, the father saw him and came happily to meet him. 4His father-in-law, the girl's father, kept him there; and he stayed with him for three days; they ate and drank and spent the nights there. 5On the fourth day they got up early, and the Levite was preparing to leave when the girl's father said to his son-in-law, 'Have something to eat to gather strength; you can leave later.' 6So they sat down and began eating and drinking, the two of them together; then the girl's father said to the young man, 'Please agree to spend tonight here too and enjoy yourself.' 7And when the man got up to leave, the father-in-law pressed him again, and he spent another night there. 8On the fifth day, the Levite got up early to leave, but the girl's father said to him, 'Please gather strength first!' So they stayed on until the sun began to go down, and the two men had a meal together. 9The husband was getting up to leave with his concubine and his servant when his father-in-law, the girl's father, said, 'Look, day is fading into evening. Please spend the night here. Look, the day is nearly over. Spend the night here and enjoy yourself. Then, early tomorrow, you can leave on your journey and go back home.' 10But the man, refusing to stay the night, got up and went on his way, until he arrived within sight of Jebus—that is, Jerusalem. He had with him two donkeys saddled, his concubine and his servant.

The crime of the men of Gibeah

11By the time they were near Jebus, the light was going fast. The servant said to his master, 'Come on, please, let us turn off into this Jebusite town and spend the night there.' 12His master replied, 'We shall not turn off into a town of foreigners, of people who are not Israelites; we shall go on to Gibeah.' 13He then said to his servant, 'Come on, we shall try to reach one or other of those places, either Gibeah or Ramah, and spend the night there.' 14So they kept going and went on with their journey. As they approached Gibeah in Benjamin, the sun was setting. 15So they turned that way to spend the night in Gibeah. Once inside, the Levite sat down in the town square, but no one offered to take them in for the night.

16Eventually, an old man came along at nightfall from his work in the fields. He too was from the highlands of Ephraim, although he was living in Gibeah; the people of the place, however, were Benjaminites. 17Looking up, he saw the traveller in the town square. 'Where are you going?' said the old man, 'And where have you come from?' 18'We are on our way', the other replied,

'from Bethlehem in Judah to a place deep in
the highlands of Ephraim. That is where I
come from. I have been to Bethlehem in
Judah and now I am going home, but no
one has offered to take me into his house,
19although we have straw and provender for
our donkeys, and I also have bread and wine
for myself, and this maidservant and the
young man who is travelling with your
servant; we are short of nothing.'
20'Welcome,' said the old man. 'I shall see
that you have all you want. You cannot spend
the night in the square.' 21So he took him
into his house and gave the donkeys prov-
ender. The travellers washed their feet, then
ate and drank.

22While they were enjoying themselves,
some townsmen, scoundrels, came crowding
round the house; they battered on the door
and said to the old man, master of the house,
'Send out the man who went into your house,
we should like to have intercourse with him!'
23The master of the house went out to them
and said, 'No, brothers, please, do not be so
wicked. Since this man is now under my roof,
do not commit such an infamy. 24Here is my
daughter; she is a virgin; I shall bring her out
to you. Ill-treat her, do what you please with
her, but do not commit such an infamy
against this man.' 25But the men would not
listen to him. So the Levite took hold of his
concubine and brought her out to them. They
had intercourse with her and ill-treated her all
night till morning; when dawn was breaking
they let her go.

26At daybreak the girl came and fell on the
threshold of her husband's host, and she
stayed there until it was light. 27In the
morning her husband got up and, opening
the door of the house, was going out to
continue his journey when he saw the woman,
his concubine, lying at the door of the house
with her hands on the threshold. 28'Get up,'
he said, 'we must leave!' There was no
answer. He then loaded her on his donkey
and began the journey home. 29Having
reached his house, he took his knife, took
hold of his concubine and cut her, limb by
limb, into twelve pieces; he then sent her
throughout the territory of Israel. 30He gave
instructions to his messengers, 'This is what
you are to say to all the Israelites, "Has
anything like this been done since the day
when the Israelites came out of Egypt until
today? Take this to heart, discuss it; then
give your verdict." ' And all who saw it
declared, 'Never has such a thing been done
or been seen since the Israelites came out of
Egypt until today.'

The Israelites vow to avenge the crime at Gibeah

20 The Israelites then all turned out and,
as one man, the entire community from
Dan to Beersheba, including Gilead,
assembled in Yahweh's presence at Mizpah.
2The leaders of the entire people, of all the
tribes of Israel, were present at this assembly
of God's people, four hundred thousand
trained infantry. 3The Benjaminites heard
that the Israelites had gone up to Mizpah.
The Israelites then said, 'Tell us how this
crime was committed.' 4The Levite, husband
of the murdered woman, spoke in reply and
said, 5'The men of Gibeah ganged up against
me and, during the night, surrounded the
house where I was lodging. They intended
to murder me. They raped my concubine to
death. 6I then took my concubine, cut her up
and sent her throughout the entire territory
of the heritage of Israel, since these men had
committed a shameful act, an infamy, in
Israel. 7Now, all you Israelites, discuss the
matter and give your decision here and
now.'

8The whole people stood up as one man
and said, 'None of us will go home, none of
us will go back to his house! 9And this is what
we are now going to do to Gibeah. We shall
draw lots 10and, throughout the tribes of
Israel, select ten men out of a hundred, a
hundred out of a thousand and a thousand
out of ten thousand to collect food for the
people, so that, on their arrival, the latter
may treat Gibeah in Benjamin as this infamy
perpetrated in Israel deserves.' 11Thus, as
one man, all the men of Israel mustered
against the town.

Obduracy of the Benjaminites

12The tribes of Israel sent messengers
throughout the tribe of Benjamin to say,
'What is this crime which has been
committed in your territory? 13Now, give
up these men, these scoundrels, living in
Gibeah, so that we can put them to death
and wipe out this evil from Israel.' The
Benjaminites, however, would not listen to
their brother Israelites.

The first engagements

14 The Benjaminites left their towns and mustered at Gibeah to fight the Israelites. 15 At the time, a count was made of the Benjaminites from the various towns: there were twenty-six thousand swordsmen; and the count excluded the inhabitants of Gibeah. 16 In this great army there were seven hundred first-rate left-handers, every man of whom could sling a stone at a hair and not miss it.

17 A count was also held of the men of Israel, excluding Benjamin: there were four hundred thousand men, all experienced swordsmen. 18 They moved off, up to Bethel, to consult God. The Israelites put the question, 'Which of us is to go first into battle against the Benjaminites?' And Yahweh replied, 'Judah is to go first.'

19 In the morning, the Israelites moved off and pitched their camp over against Gibeah. 20 The men of Israel advanced to do battle with Benjamin; they drew up their battle line in front of Gibeah. 21 But the Benjaminites sallied out from Gibeah and that day massacred twenty-two thousand Israelites. 23 The Israelites went and wept before Yahweh until evening; they then consulted Yahweh; they asked, 'Shall we join battle again with the sons of our brother Benjamin?' Yahweh replied, 'March against him!' 22 The army of the men of Israel then took fresh heart and again drew up their battle line in the same place as the day before. 24 This second day, the Israelites advanced against the Benjaminites, 25 and, this second day, Benjamin sallied out from Gibeah to meet them and massacred another eighteen thousand Israelites, all experienced swordsmen.

26 Then all the Israelites and the whole people went off to Bethel; they wept and sat in Yahweh's presence; they fasted all day till the evening and presented burnt offerings and communion sacrifices before Yahweh. 27 The Israelites then consulted Yahweh. In those days, the ark of the covenant of God was there, 28 and Phinehas son of Eleazer, son of Aaron was its minister at the time. They said, 'Ought I to go into battle against the sons of my brother Benjamin again, or should I stop?' Yahweh replied, 'March! For tomorrow I shall deliver him into your hands.'

Defeat of Benjamin

29 Israel then positioned troops in ambush all round Gibeah. 30 On the third day the Israelites marched against the Benjaminites and, as before, drew up their line in front of Gibeah. 31 The Benjaminites sallied out to engage the people and let themselves be drawn away from the town. As before, they began by killing those of the people who were on the roads, one of which runs up to Bethel, and the other to Gibeah through open country: some thirty men of Israel. 32 The Benjaminites thought, 'We have beaten them, as we did the first time,' but the Israelites had decided, 'We shall run away and draw them away from the town along the roads.'

33 All the Israelites then retreated and re-formed at Baal-Tamar, while the Israelite troops in ambush surged from their positions to the west of Gibeah. 34 Ten thousand picked men, chosen from the whole of Israel, launched their attack on Gibeah. The battle was fierce; and the others knew nothing of the disaster impending. 35 Yahweh defeated Benjamin before Israel and that day the Israelites killed twenty-five thousand one hundred men of Benjamin, all of them trained swordsmen.

36 The Benjaminites saw that they were beaten. The Israelites had given ground to Benjamin, since they were relying on the ambush which they had positioned close to Gibeah. 37 The troops in ambush threw themselves against Gibeah at top speed; fanning out, they put the whole town to the sword. 38 Now it had been agreed between the Israelites and those of the ambush that the latter should raise a smoke signal from the town, 39 whereupon the Israelites in the thick of the battle would turn about. Benjamin began by killing some of the Israelites, about thirty men, and thought, 'We have certainly beaten them, as we did in the first battle.' 40 But the signal, a column of smoke, began to rise from the town, and the Benjaminites looking back saw the whole town going up in flames to the sky. 41 The Israelites then turned about, and the Benjaminites were seized with terror, for they saw that disaster had struck them.

42 They broke before the Israelite onslaught and made for the desert, but the fighters pressed them hard, while the others coming out of the town took and slaughtered them

from the rear. 43They hemmed in the Benjaminites, pursued them relentlessly, crushing them opposite Gibeah on the east. 44Of Benjamin, eighteen thousand men fell, all of them brave men. 45They then turned tail and fled into the desert, towards the Rock of Rimmon. Five thousand of them were picked off on the roads, and the rest were relentlessly pursued as far as Gideon, two thousand of them being killed. 46The total number of Benjaminites who fell that day was twenty-five thousand swordsmen, all of them brave men. 47Six hundred men, however, turned tail and escaped into the desert, to the Rock of Rimmon, and there they stayed for four months.

48The men of Israel then went back to the Benjaminites, and put them to the sword—people, livestock and everything else that came their way in the town. And they fired all the towns involved.

Remorse of the Israelites

21 The men of Israel had sworn this oath at Mizpah, 'None of us is to give his daughter in marriage to Benjamin.' 2The people went to Bethel and stayed there until evening, sitting before God and raising their voices, made a great lament, 3and exclaiming, 'Yahweh, God of Israel, why has this happened in Israel that a tribe should be missing from Israel today? 4The next day the people got up early and built an altar there; they presented burnt offerings and communion sacrifices. 5The Israelites then said, 'Out of all the tribes of Israel, who has not come to Yahweh, to the assembly?'—for they had sworn a solemn oath that anyone who did not come to Yahweh at Mizpah would certainly die.

6Now the Israelites felt sorry about Benjamin their brother. 'Today', they said, 'a tribe has been amputated from Israel. 7What shall we do to provide wives for those who are left, since we have sworn by Yahweh not to give them any of our own daughters in marriage?'

The girls of Jabesh given to the Benjaminites

8They then asked, 'Out of the tribes of Israel, who is it that has not come to Yahweh at Mizpah?' It was discovered that no one from Jabesh in Gilead had come to the camp for the assembly; 9for, a muster having been called of the people, none of the inhabitants of Jabesh in Gilead was present. 10The community then despatched twelve thousand of their bravest men there, with these orders: 'Go and slaughter all the inhabitants of Jabesh in Gilead, including the women and children. 11This is what you are to do. All males and all those women who have ever slept with a man, you will put under the curse of destruction, but the lives of the virgins you will spare.' And this they did. 12Among the inhabitants of Jabesh in Gilead they found four hundred young virgins who had never slept with a man, and brought them to the camp (to Shiloh in the territory of Canaan).

13The whole community then sent messengers to offer peace to the Benjaminites who were at the Rock of Rimmon. 14Benjamin then came home: they were given those of the women of Jabesh in Gilead whose lives had been spared, but there were not enough for all.

The rape of the daughters of Shiloh

15The people felt sorry about Benjamin, Yahweh having made a breach in the tribes of Israel. 16And the elders of the community said, 'What shall we do to provide wives for the survivors, since the women of Benjamin have been wiped out?' 17They went on, 'How can we preserve a remnant for Benjamin so that a tribe may not be lost to Israel? 18We cannot give them our own daughters in marriage'—for the Israelites had taken an oath, 'Accursed be the man who gives a wife to Benjamin!'

19'However,' they said, 'there is the feast of Yahweh, held every year at Shiloh.' (The town lies north of Bethel, east of the highway that runs from Bethel up to Shechem, and south of Lebonah.) 20So they told the Benjaminites to do as follows, 'Put yourselves in ambush in the vineyards. 21Keep watch: when the girls of Shiloh come out in groups to dance, you then come out of the vineyards, each of you seize a wife from the girls of Shiloh and make for Benjaminite territory. 22If their fathers or brothers come and complain to us, we shall say, "Let us have them, since we could not take wives for everyone in the battle; and you could not give them to them, or you would then have been guilty." '

23The Benjaminites did this and, from the

dancers whom they caught, took as many
wives as there were men and then, setting
off, went back to their heritage, rebuilt the
towns and settled down in them.
24The Israelites then dispersed, each man
to rejoin his tribe and clan, each leaving that
place for his own heritage.
25In those days there was no king in Israel,
and everyone did as he saw fit.

THE BOOK OF RUTH

Ruth is not part of the deuteronomic history, but is a tale of family loyalty, probably written *c.* 800 BC, though possibly some centuries later. It is inserted here because the loyalty of Ruth, the foreigner, enables her to become the ancestress of David.

PLAN OF THE BOOK

THE BOOK OF RUTH

I: RUTH AND NAOMI

1 In the days when the Judges were
governing, a famine occurred in the
country and a certain man from Bethlehem
of Judah went—he, his wife and his two
sons—to live in the Plains of Moab. 2The
man was called Elimelech, his wife Naomi
and his two sons Mahlon and Chilion;[a] they
were Ephrathites from Bethlehem of Judah.
Going to the Plains of Moab, they settled
there. 3Elimelech, Naomi's husband, died,
and she and her two sons were left. 4These
married Moabite women: one was called
Orpah and the other Ruth. They lived there
for about ten years. 5Mahlon and Chilion
then both died too, and Naomi was thus
bereft of her two sons and her husband. 6She
then decided to come back from the Plains
of Moab with her daughters-in-law, having
heard in the Plains of Moab that God had
visited his people and given them food. 7So,
with her daughters-in-law, she left the place
where she was living and they took the road
back to Judah.
8Naomi said to her two daughters-in-law,
'Go back, each of you to your mother's house.
9May Yahweh show you faithful love, as you
have done to those who have died and to
me. Yahweh grant that you may each find
happiness with a husband!' She then kissed
them, but they began weeping loudly, 10and
said, 'No, we shall go back with you to
your people.' 11'Go home, daughters,' Naomi

1a The names are chosen for their meanings: Mahlon = sickness, Chilion = passing away.

replied. 'Why come with me? Have I any
more sons in my womb to make husbands for
you?[b] 12Go home, daughters, go, for I am
now too old to marry again. Even if I said, "I
still have a hope: I shall take a husband this
very night and shall bear more sons," 13would
you be prepared to wait for them until they
were grown up? Would you refuse to marry
for their sake? No, daughters, I am bitterly
sorry for your sakes that the hand of Yahweh
should have been raised against me.' 14They
started weeping loudly all over again;
Orpah then kissed her mother-in-law and
went back to her people. But Ruth stayed
with her.

15Naomi then said, 'Look, your sister-in-
law has gone back to her people and to her
god. Go home, too; follow your sister-in-
law.'

16But Ruth said, 'Do not press me to leave
you and to stop going with you, for

wherever you go, I shall go,
wherever you live, I shall live.
Your people will be my people,
and your God will be my God.
17Where you die, I shall die
and there I shall be buried.
Let Yahweh bring unnameable ills[c] on me
and worse ills, too,
if anything but death
should part me from you!'

18Seeing that Ruth was determined to go
with her, Naomi said no more.

19The two of them went on until they came
to Bethlehem. Their arrival set the whole
town astir, and the women said, 'Can this be
Naomi?' 20To this she replied, 'Do not call
me Naomi, call me Mara,[d] for Shaddai has
made my lot bitter.

21I departed full,
and Yahweh has brought me home empty.
Why, then, call me Naomi,
since Yahweh has pronounced against me
and Shaddai has made me wretched?'

22This was how Naomi came home with
her daughter-in-law, Ruth the Moabitess, on
returning from the Plains of Moab. They
arrived in Bethlehem at the beginning of the
barley harvest.

II: RUTH IN THE FIELDS OF BOAZ

2 Naomi had a kinsman on her husband's
side, well-to-do and of Elimelech's clan.
His name was Boaz.

2Ruth the Moabitess said to Naomi, 'Let
me go into the fields and glean ears of corn
in the footsteps of some man who will look on
me with favour.' She replied, 'Go, daughter.'
3So she set out and went to glean in the fields
behind the reapers. Chance led her to a plot
of land belonging to Boaz of Elimelech's clan.
4Boaz, as it happened, had just come from
Bethlehem. 'Yahweh be with you!' he said to
the reapers. 'Yahweh bless you!' they replied.
5Boaz said to a servant of his who was in
charge of the reapers, 'To whom does this
young woman belong?' 6And the servant in
charge of the reapers replied, 'The girl is the
Moabitess, the one who came back with
Naomi from the Plains of Moab. 7She said,
"Please let me glean and pick up what falls
from the sheaves behind the reapers." Thus
she came, and here she stayed, with hardly a
rest from morning until now.'

8Boaz said to Ruth, 'Listen to me,
daughter. You must not go gleaning in any
other field. You must not go away from here.
Stay close to my work-women. 9Keep your
eyes on whatever part of the field they are
reaping and follow behind. I have forbidden
my men to molest you. And if you are thirsty,
go to the pitchers and drink what the servants
have drawn.' 10Ruth fell on her face, pros-
trated herself and said, 'How have I attracted
your favour, for you to notice me, who am
only a foreigner?' 11Boaz replied, 'I have been
told all about the way you have behaved to
your mother-in-law since your husband's
death, and how you left your own father and
mother and the land where you were born to
come to a people of whom you previously

1b A dead husband's nearest male relative must marry the childless widow and father heirs to his name.
1c The disasters are not named because mere mention might bring their effect.
1d Mara = the bitter one, Naomi = my sweetness.

knew nothing. [12]May Yahweh repay you for what you have done, and may you be richly rewarded by Yahweh, the God of Israel, under whose wings you have come for refuge!' [13]She said, 'My lord, I hope you will always look on me with favour! You have comforted and encouraged me, though I am not even the equal of one of your work-women.'

[14]When it was time to eat, Boaz said to her, 'Come and eat some of this bread and dip your piece in the vinegar.' Ruth sat down beside the reapers and Boaz made a heap of roasted grain for her; she ate till her hunger was satisfied, and she had some left over. [15]When she had got up to glean, Boaz gave orders to his work-people, 'Let her glean among the sheaves themselves. Do not molest her. [16]And be sure you pull a few ears of corn out of the bundles and drop them. Let her glean them, and do not scold her.' [17]So she gleaned in the field till evening. Then she beat out what she had gleaned and it came to about a bushel of barley.

[18]Taking it with her, she went back to the town. Her mother-in-law saw what she had gleaned. Ruth also took out what she had kept after eating all she wanted, and gave that to her. [19]Her mother-in-law said, 'Where have you been gleaning today? Where have you been working? Blessed be the man who took notice of you!' Ruth told her mother-in-law in whose field she had been working. 'The name of the man with whom I have been working today', she said, 'is Boaz.' [20]Naomi said to her daughter-in-law, 'May he be blessed by Yahweh who does not withhold his faithful love from living or dead! This man', Naomi added, 'is a close relation of ours. He is one of those who have the right of redemption over us.' [21]Ruth the Moabitess said to her mother-in-law, 'He also said, "Stay with my work-people until they have finished my whole harvest." ' [22]Naomi said to Ruth, her daughter-in-law, 'It is better for you, daughter, to go with his work-women than to go to some other field where you might be ill-treated.' [23]So she stayed with Boaz's work-women, and gleaned until the barley and wheat harvests were finished. And she went on living with her mother-in-law.

III: BOAZ SLEEPS

3 Her mother-in-law Naomi then said, 'Daughter, is it not my duty to see you happily settled? [2]And Boaz, the man with whose work-women you were, is he not our kinsman? Tonight he will be winnowing the barley on the threshing-floor. [3]So wash and perfume yourself, put on your cloak and go down to the threshing-floor. Don't let him recognise you while he is still eating and drinking. [4]But when he lies down, take note where he lies, then go and turn back the covering at his feet and lie down yourself. He will tell you what to do.' [5]Ruth said, 'I shall do everything you tell me.'

[6]So she went down to the threshing-floor and did everything her mother-in-law had told her. [7]When Boaz had finished eating and drinking, he went off happily and lay down beside the pile of barley. Ruth then quietly went, turned back the covering at his feet and lay down. [8]In the middle of the night, he woke up with a shock and looked about him; and there lying at his feet was a woman. [9]'Who are you?' he said; and she replied, 'I am your servant Ruth. Spread the skirt of your cloak over your servant for you have the right of redemption over me.' [10]'May Yahweh bless you, daughter,' he said, 'for this second act of faithful love of yours is greater than the first, since you have not run after young men, poor or rich. [11]Don't be afraid, daughter, I shall do everything you ask, since the people at the gate of my town all know that you are a woman of great worth. [12]But, though it is true that I have the right of redemption over you, you have a kinsman closer than myself. [13]Stay here for tonight and, in the morning, if he wishes to exercise his right over you, very well, let him redeem you. But if he does not wish to do so, then as Yahweh lives, I shall redeem you. Lie here till morning.' [14]So she lay at his feet till morning, but got up before the hour when one man can recognise another; and he thought, 'It must not be known that this woman came to the threshing-floor.' [15]He then said, 'Let me have the cloak you are wearing, hold it out!' She held it out while he put six measures of barley into

it and then loaded it on to her; and off she
went to the town.
16 When Ruth got home, her mother-in-
law asked her, 'How did things go with you,
daughter?' She then told her everything that
the man had done for her. 17 'He gave me
these six measures of barley and said, "You
must not go home empty-handed to your
mother-in-law." ' 18 Naomi said, 'Do
nothing, daughter, until you see how things
have gone; I am sure he will not rest until he
has settled the matter this very day.'

IV: BOAZ MARRIES RUTH

4 Boaz, meanwhile, had gone up to the gate
and sat down, and the relative of whom
he had spoken then came by. Boaz said to
him, 'Here, my friend, come and sit down';
the man came and sat down. 2 Boaz then
picked out ten of the town's elders and said,
'Sit down here'; they sat down. 3 Boaz then
said to the man who had the right of redemp-
tion, 'Naomi, who has come back from the
Plains of Moab, is selling the piece of land
that belonged to our brother, Elimelech. 4 I
thought I should tell you about this and say,
"Acquire it in the presence of the men who
are sitting here and in the presence of the
elders of my people. If you want to use your
right of redemption, redeem it; if you do not,
tell me so that I know, for I am the only
person to redeem it besides yourself, and I
myself come after you." ' The man said, 'I
am willing to redeem it.' 5 Boaz then said,
'The day you acquire the field from Naomi,
you also acquire Ruth the Moabitess, the wife
of the man who has died, to perpetuate the
dead man's name in his inheritance.' 6 The
man with the right of redemption then said,
'I cannot use my right of redemption without
jeopardising my own inheritance. Since I
cannot use my right of redemption, exercise
the right yourself.'
7 Now, in former times, it was the custom
in Israel to confirm a transaction in matters
of redemption or inheritance by one of the
parties taking off his sandal and giving it to
the other.[a] This was how agreements were
ratified in Israel. 8 So, when the man with the
right of redemption said to Boaz, 'Acquire it
for yourself,' he took off his sandal.
9 Boaz then said to the elders and all the
people there, 'Today you are witnesses that
from Naomi I acquire everything that used
to belong to Elimelech, and everything that
used to belong to Mahlon and Chilion 10 and
that I am also acquiring Ruth the Moabitess,
Mahlon's widow, to be my wife, to perpetuate
the dead man's name in his inheritance, so
that the dead man's name will not be lost
among his brothers and at the gate of his
town. Today you are witnesses to this.' 11 All
the people at the gate said, 'We are witnesses';
and the elders said, 'May Yahweh make the
woman about to enter your family like Rachel
and Leah who together built up the House
of Israel.

Grow mighty in Ephrathah,
be renowned in Bethlehem!

12 And through the children Yahweh will give
you by this young woman, may your family
be like the family of Perez, whom Tamar
bore to Judah.'
13 So Boaz took Ruth and she became his
wife. And when they came together, Yahweh
made her conceive and she bore a son. 14 And
the women said to Naomi, 'Blessed be
Yahweh who has not left you today without
anyone to redeem you. May his name be
praised in Israel! 15 The child will be a comfort
to you and the prop of your old age, for he
has been born to the daughter-in-law who
loves you and is more to you than seven sons.'
16 And Naomi, taking the child, held him to
her breast; and she it was who looked after
him.
17 And the women of the neighbourhood
gave him a name. 'A son', they said, 'has
been born to Naomi,' and they called him
Obed. This was the father of Jesse, the father
of David.

4a A distortion of the legislation given in Dt 25:9–10. To plant a sandal (or foot) on a field marks a claim to it. Here, taking off the sandal signifies renunciation of a claim.

THE GENEALOGY OF DAVID

18These are the descendants of Perez. Perez fathered Hezron, 19Hezron fathered Ram, Ram fathered Amminadab, 20Amminadab fathered Nahshon, Nahshon fathered Salmon, 21Salmon fathered Boaz, Boaz fathered Obed, 22Obed fathered Jesse, and Jesse fathered David.

THE BOOKS OF SAMUEL

The Books of Samuel, originally one book, form a continuation of the great deuteronomic history. The story is dominated at first by the figure of Samuel, the last of the judges, who struggles to keep Israel faithful to Yahweh under increasing pressure from the Philistines. Defeats and the loss of the Ark, symbol of God's protection, show that Israel needs a new kind of leadership, so Samuel anoints the first two kings, Saul and his successor, David. Saul constructs the beginnings of a stable monarchy but incurs the divine displeasure and ends his rule in fits of black despondency and murderous hatred of David.

David leads Israel in its most glorious period, when it was for a brief moment a major power in the Near East. More than this, he is the model for all kingship in Israel. The greater part of the story of his reign is from a near-contemporary source, whose vivid delineation makes David one of the first clear figures in any history. He is a forceful yet attractive character, very human in his failings but passionate and intimate in his devotion to Yahweh. To him and to his line is promised endless rule, the basis of all future hope for a Messiah.

FIRST SAMUEL: PLAN OF THE BOOK

- I Samuel 1–7
  - A The Childhood of Samuel 1:1–4:1
  - B The Ark in Philistine Hands 4:1–7:17
- II Samuel and Saul 8–15
  - A The Institution of the Monarchy 8–12
  - B The Beginning of Saul's Reign 13–15
- III Saul and David 16–31
  - A David at Court 16:1–19:7
  - B The Flight of David 19:8–21:16
  - C David the Outlaw 22–26
  - D David among the Philistines 27–31

SECOND SAMUEL: PLAN OF THE BOOK

I David 2–20
- **A** David King of Judah 2–4
- **B** David King of Judah and of Israel 5–8
- **C** David's Family and the Intrigues over the Succession 9–20 (+1 K 1–2)

II Supplements 21–24

THE BOOKS OF SAMUEL

THE FIRST BOOK OF SAMUEL

I: SAMUEL

A: THE CHILDHOOD OF SAMUEL

The pilgrimage to Shiloh

1 There was a man of Ramathaim, a Zuphite
from the highlands of Ephraim whose
name was Elkanah son of Jeroham, son of
Elihu, son of Tohu, son of Zuph, an
Ephraimite. 2He had two wives, one called
Hannah, the other Peninnah; Peninnah had
children but Hannah had none. 3Every year
this man used to go up from his town to
worship, and to sacrifice to Yahweh Sabaoth[a]
at Silo. (The two sons of Eli, Hophni and
Phinehas, were there as priests of Yahweh.)
4One day Elkanah offered a sacrifice. Now
he used to give portions to Peninnah and to
all her sons and daughters; 5to Hannah,
however, he would give only one portion:
for, although he loved Hannah more,
Yahweh had made her barren. 6Further-
more, her rival would taunt and provoke her,
because Yahweh had made her womb barren.
7And this went on year after year; every time
they went up to the temple of Yahweh she
used to taunt her. On that day she wept and
would not eat anything; 8so her husband
Elkanah said, 'Hannah, why are you crying?
Why are you not eating anything? Why are
you so sad? Am I not more to you than ten
sons?'

Prayer of Hannah

9When they had finished eating in the room,
Hannah got up and stood before Yahweh. Eli
the priest was sitting on his seat by the
doorpost of the temple of Yahweh. 10In the
bitterness of her soul she prayed to Yahweh
with many tears, 11and she made this vow,
'Yahweh Sabaoth! Should you condescend
to notice the humiliation of your servant and
keep her in mind instead of disregarding your
servant, and give her a boy, I will give him
to Yahweh for the whole of his life and no
razor shall ever touch his head.'
12While she went on praying to Yahweh,
Eli was watching her mouth, 13for Hannah
was speaking under her breath; her lips were
moving but her voice could not be heard, and
Eli thought that she was drunk. 14Eli said,

1a A mysterious title stemming from the shrine at Silo and interpreted as 'Lord of armies'.

'How much longer are you going to stay
drunk? Get rid of your wine.' 15'No, my
lord,' Hannah replied, 'I am a woman in
great trouble; I have not been drinking wine
or strong drink—I am pouring out my soul
before Yahweh. 16Do not take your servant
for a worthless woman; all this time I have
been speaking from the depth of my grief and
my resentment.' 17Eli then replied, 'Go in
peace, and may the God of Israel grant what
you have asked of him.' 18To which she said,
'May your servant find favour in your sight.'
With that, the woman went away; she began
eating and was dejected no longer.

Birth and consecration of Samuel

19They got up early in the morning and, after
worshipping Yahweh, set out and went home
to Ramah. Elkanah lay with his wife Hannah,
and Yahweh remembered her. 20Hannah
conceived and, in due course, gave birth to a
son, whom she named Samuel,[b] 'since', she
said, 'I asked Yahweh for him.' 21Elkanah,
the husband, went up with all his family to
offer the annual sacrifice to Yahweh and to
fulfil his vow. 22However, Hannah did not go
up, having said to her husband, 'Not before
the child has been weaned. Then I shall bring
him and present him before Yahweh and
he will stay there for ever.' 23Elkanah her
husband then said to her, 'Do what you think
fit; wait until you have weaned him. May
Yahweh bring about what he has said.' So
the woman stayed behind and nursed her
child until she weaned him.

24When she had weaned him, she took him
up with her, as well as a three-year-old bull,
an *ephah* of flour and a skin of wine, and took
him into the temple of Yahweh at Shiloh; the
child was very young. 25They sacrificed the
bull and led the child to Eli. 26She said, 'If
you please, my lord! As you live, my lord, I
am the woman who stood beside you here,
praying to Yahweh. 27This is the child for
which I was praying, and Yahweh has granted
me what I asked of him. 28Now I make him
over to Yahweh for the whole of his life.
He is made over to Yahweh.' They then
worshipped Yahweh there.

Song of Hannah

2 Hannah then prayed as follows:

My heart exults in Yahweh,
in my God is my strength lifted up,
my mouth derides my foes,
for I rejoice in your deliverance.

2There is no Holy One like Yahweh,
(indeed, there is none but you)
no Rock like our God.

3Do not keep talking so proudly,
let no arrogance come from your mouth,
for Yahweh is a wise God,
his to weigh up deeds.

4The bow of the mighty has been broken
but those who were tottering
are now braced with strength.
5The full fed
are hiring themselves out for bread
but the hungry need labour no more;
the barren woman bears sevenfold
but the mother of many is left desolate.

6Yahweh gives death and life,
brings down to Sheol and draws up;
7Yahweh makes poor and rich,
he humbles and also exalts.

8He raises the poor from the dust,
he lifts the needy from the dunghill
to give them a place with princes,
to assign them a seat of honour;
for to Yahweh belong the pillars
of the earth,
on these he has poised the world.

9He safeguards the steps of his faithful
but the wicked vanish in darkness
(for human strength can win no victories).
10Yahweh, his enemies are shattered,
the Most High thunders in the heavens.

Yahweh judges the ends of the earth,
he endows his king with power,
he raises up the strength of his Anointed.

11Elkanah then went home to Ramah, but
the child stayed in Yahweh's service, in the
presence of Eli the priest.

The sons of Eli

12Now the sons of Eli were scoundrels; they
cared nothing for Yahweh 13nor for what was
due to the priests from the people. Whenever
anyone offered a sacrifice, the priest's servant
would come with a three-pronged fork in his
hand while the meat was being cooked; 14he

1b Samuel is derived from *shem-'el* (=the Name of God), but is here related to *sha'al* (=ask).

would thrust this into cauldron or pan, or
dish or pot, and the priest claimed for his
own whatever the fork brought up. That was
how they behaved with all the Israelites who
came there to Shiloh. 15The priest's servant
would even come up before the fat had been
burnt and say to the person who was making
the sacrifice, 'Give the priest some meat for
him to roast. He will not accept boiled meat
from you, only raw.' 16Then, if the person
replied, 'Let the fat be burnt first, and then
take for yourself whatever you choose,' he
would retort, 'No! You must give it to me
now or I shall take it by force.' 17The young
men's sin was very great in Yahweh's eyes,
because they treated with contempt the
offering made to Yahweh.

Samuel at Shiloh

18Samuel was in Yahweh's service, a child
wearing a linen loincloth. 19His mother used
to make him a little coat which she brought
him each year when she came up with her
husband to offer the yearly sacrifice. 20Eli
would bless Elkanah and his wife and say,
'May Yahweh grant you an heir by this
woman in exchange for the one which she has
made over to Yahweh,' and they would go
home. 21Yahweh visited Hannah; she
conceived and gave birth to three sons and
two daughters. Meanwhile, the child Samuel
grew up in Yahweh's presence.

More about the sons of Eli

22Although very old, Eli heard about every-
thing that his sons were doing to all Israel,
23and said, 'Why are you behaving as all the
people say you are? 24No, my sons, what I
hear reported by the people of Yahweh is not
good. 25If one person sins against another,
God will be the arbiter, but if he sins against
Yahweh, who will intercede for him?' But
they did not listen to their father's words, for
Yahweh was bent on killing them.

26Meanwhile, the child Samuel went on
growing in stature and in favour both with
Yahweh and with people.

Punishment foretold

27A man of God came to Eli and said to him,
'This is what Yahweh says, "Did I not reveal
myself to your father's family when they were
in Egypt as slaves in Pharaoh's household?
28Did I not single him out of all the tribes of
Israel to be my priest, to go up to my altar,
to burn the offering, to carry the *ephod*[a] in
my presence; and did I not grant all the
burnt offerings made by the Israelites to your
father's family? 29Why do you trample on the
offering and on the sacrifice which I have
ordered for my Dwelling, and honour your
sons more than me, by growing fat on the
best of the offerings of Israel, my people?
30Whereas—this is what Yahweh, God of
Israel, declares—I had promised that your
family and your father's family would walk
in my presence for ever, now, however—this
is what Yahweh declares—nothing of the
sort! Those who honour me I honour in my
turn, and those who despise me will be an
object of contempt. 31Be sure, the days are
coming when I shall cut off your strength and
the strength of your father's family, so that
no one in your family will live to old age.
32Beside the Dwelling, you will see all the
benefits that I shall confer on Israel, but no
one in your family will ever live to old age.
33I shall keep one of you at my altar for his
eyes to go blind and his soul to wither, but
the bulk of your family will die by the sword.

34' "What happens to your two sons
Hophni and Phinehas will be a sign for you:
on the same day both will die. 35I shall raise
myself a faithful priest, who will do as I
intend and as I desire. I shall build him an
enduring House and he will walk in the
presence of my Anointed for ever. 36The
members of your House who survive will
come and beg him on their knees for a silver
coin and a loaf of bread and say: Please give
me some priestly work, so that I can have a
scrap of bread to eat." '

God calls Samuel

3 Now, the boy Samuel was serving Yahweh
in the presence of Eli; in those days it
was rare for Yahweh to speak; visions were
uncommon. 2One day, it happened that Eli
was lying down in his room. His eyes were
beginning to grow dim; he could no longer
see. 3The lamp of God had not yet gone out,
and Samuel was lying in Yahweh's sanctuary,
where the ark of God was, 4when Yahweh
called, 'Samuel! Samuel!' He answered,

2a Not a garment as elsewhere, but a holder for the sacred lots.

'Here I am,' 5and, running to Eli, he said,
'Here I am, as you called me.' Eli said, 'I did
not call. Go back and lie down.' So he went
and lay down. 6And again Yahweh called,
'Samuel! Samuel!' He got up and went to Eli
and said, 'Here I am, as you called me.' He
replied, 'I did not call, my son; go back and
lie down.' 7As yet, Samuel had no knowledge
of Yahweh and the word of Yahweh had not
yet been revealed to him. 8Again Yahweh
called, the third time. He got up and went to
Eli and said, 'Here I am, as you called me.'
Eli then understood that Yahweh was calling
the child, 9and he said to Samuel, 'Go and lie
down, and if someone calls say, "Speak,
Yahweh; for your servant is listening." ' So
Samuel went and lay down in his place.

10Yahweh then came and stood by, calling
as he had done before, 'Samuel! Samuel!'
Samuel answered, 'Speak, Yahweh; for your
servant is listening.' 11Yahweh then said to
Samuel, 'I am going to do something in Israel
which will make the ears of all who hear of it
ring. 12I shall carry out that day against Eli
everything that I have said about his family,
from beginning to end. 13You are to tell him
that I condemn his family for ever, since
he is aware that his sons have been cursing
God and yet has not corrected them.
14Therefore—I swear it to the family of Eli—
no sacrifice or offering shall ever expiate the
guilt of Eli's family.'

15Samuel lay where he was until morning
and then opened the doors of Yahweh's
temple. Samuel was afraid to tell Eli about
the vision, 16but Eli called Samuel and said,
'Samuel, my son.' 'Here I am,' he replied.
17Eli asked, 'What message did he give you?
Please do not hide it from me. May God bring
unnameable ills on you and worse ones, too,
if you hide from me anything of what he said
to you.' 18Samuel then told him everything,
hiding nothing from him. Eli said, 'He is
Yahweh; let him do what he thinks good.'

19Samuel grew up. Yahweh was with him
and did not let a single word fall to the ground
of all that he had told him. 20All Israel knew,
from Dan to Beersheba, that Samuel was
attested as a prophet of Yahweh. 21Yahweh
continued to manifest himself at Shiloh,
revealing himself to Samuel there,

4 and, for all Israel, the word of Samuel was
as the word of Yahweh; since Eli was very
old and his sons persisted in their wicked
behaviour towards Yahweh.

B: THE ARK IN PHILISTINE HANDS

Defeat of the Israelites and capture of the ark

It happened at that time that the Philistines
mustered to make war on Israel and Israel
went out to meet them in war, pitching camp
near Ebenezer while the Philistines pitched
camp at Aphek. 2The Philistines drew up
their battle-line against Israel, the fighting
was fierce, and Israel was beaten by the
Philistines: about four thousand men in their
ranks were killed on the field of battle. 3When
the troops returned to camp, the elders of
Israel said, 'Why has Yahweh caused us to
be beaten by the Philistines today? Let us
fetch the ark of our God from Shiloh so that,
when it goes with us, it may save us from the
clutches of our enemies.' 4So the troops
sent to Shiloh and brought away the ark of
Yahweh Sabaoth enthroned on the winged
creatures; the two sons of Eli, Hophni and
Phinehas, came with the ark. 5When the ark
of Yahweh arrived in the camp, all Israel
raised a great war cry so that the earth
resounded. 6When the Philistines heard the
noise of the war cry, they said, 'What can
this great war cry in the Hebrew camp mean?'
And they realised that the ark of Yahweh had
come into the camp. 7At this, the Philistines
were afraid; for they said, 'God has come into
the camp. Disaster!' they said. 'For nothing
like this has ever happened before. 8Disaster!
Who will rescue us from the clutches of this
mighty God? This was the God who struck
down Egypt with every kind of misfortune
in the desert. 9But take courage and be men,
Philistines, or you will become slaves to the
Hebrews as they have been slaves to you. Be
men and fight.' 10So the Philistines gave
battle and Israel was defeated, each man
fleeing to his tent. The slaughter was very
great: on the Israelite side, thirty thousand
foot soldiers fell. 11The ark of God was
captured too, and Hophni and Phinehas the
two sons of Eli died.

Death of Eli

12A Benjaminite ran from the battle-line and
reached Shiloh the same day, his clothes torn
and dust on his head. 13When he arrived,
Eli was sitting on his seat beside the gate
watching the road, for his heart was trem-
bling for the ark of God. The man came into

the town and told the news, whereupon cries of anguish filled the town. 14 Eli heard the sound and asked, 'What does this uproar mean?' The man hurried on and told Eli. 15 Eli was ninety-eight years old; his gaze was fixed; he was blind. 16 The man said to Eli, 'I have come from the camp. I escaped from the battle-line today.' 'My son,' said Eli, 'what happened?' 17 The messenger replied, 'Israel has fled before the Philistines; the army has been utterly routed. What is worse, your two sons are dead and the ark of God has been captured.' 18 When he mentioned the ark of God, Eli fell backwards off his seat by the gate and broke his neck and died, for he was old and heavy. He had been judge of Israel for forty years.

Death of the wife of Phinehas

19 Now his daughter-in-law, the wife of Phinehas, was with child and near her time. When she heard the news that the ark of God had been captured and that her father-in-law and husband were dead she crouched down and gave birth, for her labour pains had come on. 20 When she was at the point of death, the women at her side said, 'Do not be afraid; you have given birth to a son.' But she did not answer and took no notice. 21 She named the child Ichabod,[a] saying, 'The glory has gone from Israel,' alluding to the capture of the ark of God and to her father-in-law and husband. 22 She said, 'The glory has gone from Israel, because the ark of God has been captured.'

The ark brings disaster to the Philistines

5 When the Philistines had captured the ark of God, they took it from Ebenezer to Ashdod. 2 Taking the ark of God, the Philistines put it in the temple of Dagon, setting it down beside Dagon. 3 When the people of Ashdod got up the following morning and went to the temple of Dagon, there lay Dagon face down on the ground before the ark of Yahweh. They picked Dagon up and put him back in his place. 4 But when they got up on the following morning, there lay Dagon face down on the ground before the ark of Yahweh, and Dagon's head and two hands lay severed on the threshold; only the trunk of Dagon was left in its place. 5 This is why the priests of Dagon and the people frequenting Dagon's temple never step on Dagon's threshold in Ashdod, even today.

6 Yahweh oppressed the people of Ashdod; he ravaged them and afflicted them with tumours—Ashdod and its territory. When the people of Ashdod saw what was happening they said, 7 'The ark of the God of Israel must not stay here with us, for he is oppressing us and our god Dagon.' 8 So they summoned all the Philistine chiefs to them, and said, 'What shall we do with the ark of the God of Israel?' They decided, 'The ark of the God of Israel shall be taken away to Gath.' So they took the ark of the God of Israel to Gath. 9 But after they had taken it there, Yahweh oppressed that town and a great panic broke out; afflicting the people of the town from highest to lowest, he brought them out in tumours too. 10 They then sent the ark of God to Ekron, but when it came to Ekron the Ekronites shouted, 'They have brought me the ark of the God of Israel to kill me and my people!' 11 They summoned all the Philistine chiefs and said, 'Send the ark of the God of Israel away; let it go back to where it belongs and not kill me and my people'—for there was mortal panic throughout the town; God was oppressing them. 12 The people who did not die were afflicted with tumours, and the wailing from the town rose to the sky.

Return of the ark

6 The ark of Yahweh was in Philistine territory for seven months. 2 The Philistines then called for their priests and diviners and asked, 'What shall we do with the ark of Yahweh? Tell us how to send it back to where it belongs.' 3 They replied, 'If you send the ark of the God of Israel away, you must certainly not send it away without a gift; you must pay him a guilt offering. You will then recover and will realise why he continually oppressed you.' 4 They then asked, 'What guilt offering ought we to pay him?' They replied, 'Corresponding to the number of Philistine chiefs: five golden tumours and five golden rats, since the same plague afflicted your chiefs as the rest of you. 5 So make models of your tumours and models of your rats ravaging the territory, and pay honour to the God of Israel. Then perhaps

4a *Ei-kabod* = Where is the glory?

he will stop oppressing you, your gods and your country. 6Why should you be as stubborn as Egypt and Pharaoh were? After he had brought disasters on them, did they not let the people leave? 7Now, then, take and fit out a new cart, and two milch cows that have never borne the yoke. Then harness the cows to the cart and take their calves back to the byre. 8Then take the ark of Yahweh, place it on the cart, and put the golden objects which you are paying him as guilt offering in a box beside it; and then send it off on its own. 9Watch it; if it goes up the road to its own territory, towards Beth-Shemesh, then he was responsible for this great harm to us; but if not, we shall know that it was not his hand that struck us, and that this has happened to us by chance.'

10The people did this. They took two milch cows and harnessed them to the cart, shutting their calves in the byre. 11They then put the ark of Yahweh on the cart, with the box and the golden rats and the models of their tumours.

12The cows made straight for Beth-Shemesh, keeping to the one road, lowing as they went and turning neither to right nor to left. The Philistine chiefs followed them as far as the boundaries of Beth-Shemesh.

The ark at Beth-Shemesh

13The people of Beth-Shemesh were reaping the wheat harvest in the plain when they looked up and saw the ark and went joyfully to meet it. 14When the cart came to the field of Joshua of Beth-Shemesh, it stopped. There was a large stone there, and they cut up the wood of the cart and offered the cows as a burnt offering to Yahweh. 15The Levites had taken down the ark of Yahweh and the box with it containing the golden objects and put these on the large stone. That day the people of Beth-Shemesh presented burnt offerings and made sacrifices to Yahweh. 16The five chiefs of the Philistines, having witnessed this, went back to Ekron the same day.

17The golden tumours paid by the Philistines as a guilt offering to Yahweh were as follows: one for Ashdod, one for Gaza, one for Ashkelon, one for Gath, one for Ekron; 18and golden rats to the number of all the Philistine towns, those of the five chiefs, from fortified towns down to open villages: still to this day the large stone in the field of Joshua of Beth-Shemesh, on which they put the ark of Yahweh, is a witness. 19Of the people of Beth-Shemesh the sons of Jeconiah had not rejoiced when they saw the ark of Yahweh, and Yahweh struck down seventy of them. The people mourned because Yahweh had struck them so fiercely.

The ark at Kiriath-Jearim

20The people of Beth-Shemesh then said, 'Who can stand his ground before Yahweh, this holy God? To whom shall he go, so that we are rid of him?' 21So they sent messengers to the inhabitants of Kiriath-Jearim, to say, 'The Philistines have sent back the ark of Yahweh; come down and take it up to your town.'

7 The men of Kiriath-Jearim came and, taking up the ark of Yahweh, brought it to the house of Abinadab on the hill, and consecrated his son Eleazar to guard the ark of Yahweh.

Samuel, judge and liberator

2From the day when the ark was installed at Kiriath-Jearim, a long time went by—twenty years—and the whole House of Israel longed for Yahweh. 3Samuel then spoke as follows to the whole House of Israel, 'If you are returning to Yahweh with all your heart, banish the foreign gods and Astartes which you now have, and set your heart on Yahweh and serve him alone; and he will deliver you from the power of the Philistines.' 4And the Israelites banished the Baals and Astartes and served Yahweh alone.

5Samuel then said, 'Muster all Israel at Mizpah and I shall plead with Yahweh for you.' 6So they mustered at Mizpah and drew water and poured it out before Yahweh. They fasted that day and declared, 'We have sinned against Yahweh.' And Samuel was judge over the Israelites at Mizpah.

7When the Philistines heard that the Israelites had mustered at Mizpah, the Philistine chiefs marched on Israel; and when the Israelites heard this, they were afraid of the Philistines. 8They said to Samuel, 'Do not stop calling on Yahweh our God to rescue us from the power of the Philistines.' 9Samuel took a sucking lamb and presented it as a burnt offering to Yahweh, and he called on Yahweh on behalf of Israel and Yahweh heard him.

10While Samuel was in the act of presenting
burnt offering, the Philistines joined battle
with Israel, but that day Yahweh thundered
violently over the Philistines, threw them
into panic and Israel defeated them. 11The
men of Israel sallied out from Mizpah in
pursuit of the Philistines and beat them all
the way to below Beth-Car. 12Samuel then
took a stone and erected it between Mizpah
and the Tooth, and gave it the name
Ebenezer,[a] saying, 'Yahweh helped us as far
as this.'
13So the Philistines were humbled and no
longer came into Israelite territory; Yahweh
oppressed the Philistines throughout the life
of Samuel. 14The towns which the Philistines
had taken from Israel were given back to
Israel, from Ekron all the way to Gath, and
Israel freed their territory from the power
of the Philistines. There was peace, too,
between Israel and the Amorites.
15Samuel was judge over Israel throughout
his life. 16Each year he went on circuit
through Bethel and Gilgal and Mizpah and
judged Israel in all these places. 17He would
then return to Ramah, since his home was
there; there too he judged Israel. And there
he built an altar to Yahweh.

II: SAMUEL AND SAUL

A: THE INSTITUTION OF THE MONARCHY

The people ask for a king

8 When Samuel grew old, he appointed his
sons as judges of Israel. 2His eldest son
was called Joel and his second one, Abijah;
they were judges at Beersheba. 3His sons did
not follow his example but, seduced by the
love of money, took bribes and gave biased
verdicts. 4The elders of Israel all assembled,
went back to Samuel at Ramah, and said,
5'Look, you are old, and your sons are not
following your example. So give us a king to
judge us, like the other nations.' 6Samuel
thought that it was wrong of them to say,
'Let us have a king to judge us,' so he prayed
to Yahweh. 7But Yahweh said to Samuel,
'Obey the voice of the people in all that they
say to you: it is not you they have rejected
8but me, not wishing me to reign over them
any more. They are now doing to you exactly
what they have done to me since the day
I brought them out of Egypt until now,
deserting me and serving other gods. 9So, do
what they ask; only, you must give them a
solemn warning, and must tell them what the
king who is to reign over them will do.'

Disadvantages of a monarchy

10Everything that Yahweh had said, Samuel
then repeated to the people who were asking
him for a king. 11He said, 'This is what the
king who is to reign over you will do. He
will take your sons and direct them to his
chariotry and cavalry, and they will run in
front of his chariot. 12He will use them as
leaders of a thousand and leaders of fifty; he
will make them plough his fields and gather
in his harvest and make his weapons of war
and the gear for his chariots. 13He will take
your daughters as perfumers, cooks and
bakers. 14He will take the best of your fields,
your vineyards and your olive groves and
give them to his officials. 15He will tithe
your crops and vineyards to provide for his
courtiers and his officials. 16He will take the
best of your servants, men and women, of
your oxen and your donkeys, and make them
work for him. 17He will tithe your flocks,
and you yourselves will become his slaves.
18When that day comes, you will cry aloud
because of the king you have chosen for
yourselves, but on that day Yahweh will not
hear you.'
19The people, however, refused to listen to
Samuel. They said, 'No! We are determined
to have a king, 20so that we can be like the
other nations, with our own king to rule us
and lead us and fight our battles.' 21Samuel
listened to all that the people had to say
and repeated it in Yahweh's ear. 22Yahweh
then said to Samuel, 'Do as they ask and
give them a king.' Samuel then said to the
Israelites, 'Go home, each of you, to his
own town.'

7a *Eben-ezer* = Stone of help.

Saul and his father's donkeys

9 Among the men of Benjamin was a man
called Kish son of Abiel, son of Zeror, son
of Becorath, son of Aphiah; a Benjaminite
and a person of rank. 2He had a son called
Saul, a handsome man in the prime of life.
Of all the Israelites there was no one more
handsome than he; he stood head and shoul-
ders taller than anyone else.
3Now since the donkeys belonging to Kish,
Saul's father, had strayed, Kish said to his
son Saul, 'My son, take one of the servants
with you and be off; go and look for the
donkeys.' 4They went through the highlands
of Ephraim, they went through the territory
of Shalishah, and did not find them; they
went through the territory of Shaalim but
they were not there; they went through the
territory of Benjamin and did not find them.
5When they reached the territory of Zuph,
Saul said to the servant who was with him,
'Come on, let us go back or my father will
stop worrying over the donkeys and start
being anxious about us.' 6The servant,
however, replied, 'Look, there is a man of
God in this town, a man who is held in
honour; everything he says comes true. Let
us go there, then; perhaps he will be able to
show us the way that we should take.' 7Saul
said to his servant, 'But if we do go, what can
we take to the man? The food in our sacks is
finished, and we have no present to offer the
man of God. What else have we got?' 8The
servant spoke up again and said to Saul,
'Look, I happen to have a quarter of a silver
shekel; I shall give that to the man of God,
for him to tell us which way to go.' 10Saul
then said to his servant, 'Well said! Come on,
let us go.' And they went off to the town
where the man of God was.

Saul meets Samuel

11As they were going up the slope to the town
they came across some girls going out to draw
water, and said to them, 'Is the seer there?'
9In Israel, in olden days, when anyone used
to go to consult God, he would say, 'Come
on, let us go to the seer,' for a man who is
now called a 'prophet' used to be called a
'seer' in olden days. 12The girls replied, 'He
is. He arrived a moment or two ahead of you.
You had better hurry: he has just come to
town because the people are having a sacrifice
today on the high place. 13You can catch him
as soon as you go into the town, before he
goes up to the high place for the meal. The
people will not eat until he comes, since he
must bless the sacrifice; after that, the guests
will start eating. If you go up now, you will
find him straight away.'
14So they went up to the town and, as they
were going through the gate, Samuel came
out towards them on his way to the high
place. 15Now, Yahweh had given Samuel a
revelation the day before Saul came, saying,
16'About this time tomorrow, I shall send you
a man from the territory of Benjamin; you
are to anoint him as prince of my people
Israel, and he will save my people from the
power of the Philistines; for I have seen the
misery of my people and their cries of anguish
have come to me.' 17When Samuel saw Saul,
Yahweh told him, 'That is the man of whom
I said to you, "He is to govern my people." '
18Saul accosted Samuel in the gateway and
said, 'Tell me, please, where the seer's house
is.' 19Samuel replied to Saul, 'I am the seer.
Go up ahead of me to the high place. You
must eat with me today. Tomorrow, when I
let you go, I shall tell you whatever is on your
mind. 20As regards your donkeys, however,
which strayed three days ago, do not worry
about them; they have been found. And for
whom is the whole wealth of Israel destined,
if not for you and for all the members of your
father's family?' 21To this, Saul replied, 'Am
I not a Benjaminite, from the smallest of the
tribes of Israel? And is not my family the
least of all the families of the tribe of
Benjamin? Why are you saying a thing like
this to me?'
22Samuel then took Saul and his servant
and brought them into the hall and gave them
a place at the head of the guests, of whom
there were about thirty. 23Samuel then said
to the cook, 'Serve the portion which I gave
you and told you to put on one side.' 24The
cook then picked up the leg and the tail and
put it in front of Saul, saying, 'This is for
you. This is what was left. Make a good
meal . . .' That day, Saul ate with Samuel.
25They came down from the high place
into the town. A bed was made for Saul on
the roof and he lay down there.

Consecration of Saul

26At dawn, Samuel called to Saul on the roof,
'Get up, and I shall send you on your way.'
Saul got up, and Samuel and he went outside

together. [27]They had walked as far as the end of the town when Samuel said to Saul, 'Tell the servant to go on ahead of us, but you stand still for a moment, so that I can make known to you the word of God.'

10 Samuel took a phial of oil and poured it on Saul's head; he then kissed him and said, 'Has not Yahweh anointed you as leader of his people Israel? You are the man who is to govern Yahweh's people and save them from the power of the enemies surrounding them. The sign for you that Yahweh has anointed you as prince of his heritage is this: [2]after leaving me today, you will meet two men near the tomb of Rachel, on the frontier of Benjamin . . . and they will say to you, "The donkeys which you went looking for have been found, and your father has lost interest in the matter of the donkeys and is worrying about you and wondering, What am I to do about my son?" [3]Going on from there, you will come to the Oak of Tabor, where you will meet three men going up to God at Bethel; one will be carrying three kids, one three loaves of bread and the third a skin of wine. [4]They will greet you and give you two loaves of bread which you must accept from them. [5]After this, you will come to Gibeah of God (where the Philistine garrison is) and, when you are just outside the town, you will meet a group of prophets coming down from the high place, headed by lyre, tambourine, pipe and harp; they will be in a state of ecstasy. [6]The spirit of Yahweh will then seize on you, and you will go into ecstasy with them, and be changed into another man. [7]When these signs have occurred, act as occasion serves, for God is with you. [8]You will then go down, ahead of me, to Gilgal, and I shall join you there to make burnt offerings and to offer communion sacrifices. You must wait seven days for me to come to you, and I shall then reveal to you what you must do.'

Return of Saul

[9]As soon as he had turned his back to leave Samuel, God changed his heart. And all these signs occurred that very day . . . [10]From there, they came to Gibeah: and there was a group of prophets coming to meet him! The spirit of God seized on him and he fell into ecstasy with them. [11]Seeing him prophesying with the prophets, all the people who had known him previously said to one another, 'What has come over the son of Kish? Is Saul one of the prophets too?' [12]And one of the local people retorted, 'But who is their father?' Hence the origin of the proverb: Is Saul one of the prophets too?

[13]When he came out of his ecstasy, he went into Gibeah. [14]Saul's uncle asked him and his servant, 'Where have you been?' 'Looking for the donkeys,' he replied, 'and when we could not find them anywhere, we went to Samuel.' [15]Saul's uncle said, 'Tell me please what Samuel said to you.' [16]Saul said to his uncle, 'He merely told us that the donkeys were already found,' but did not mention anything that Samuel had said about the kingship.

Saul is designated king by lot

[17]Samuel summoned the people to Yahweh at Mizpah [18]and said to the Israelites, 'Yahweh, God of Israel, says this, "I brought Israel out of Egypt and delivered you from the power of the Egyptians and of all the kingdoms that were oppressing you." [19]But today you have rejected your God, him who saves you from all your difficulties and troubles; and you have said, "No, you must set a king over us." Very well, take your positions before Yahweh, tribe by tribe and clan by clan.'

[20]Samuel then made all the tribes of Israel come forward, and the lot indicated the tribe of Benjamin. [21]He then made the tribe of Benjamin come forward clan by clan, and the lot indicated the clan of Matri; he then made the clan of Matri come forward one by one, and the lot indicated Saul son of Kish, but when they looked for him, he was not to be found.

[22]Again they consulted Yahweh, 'Has the man come here?' Yahweh replied, 'There he is, hiding among the baggage.' [23]So they ran and fetched him out and, as he stood among the people, he was head and shoulders taller than any of them. [24]Samuel then said to all the people, 'You have seen the man whom Yahweh has chosen, and that among the whole people he has no equal.' And all the people acclaimed him, shouting, 'Long live the king!'

[25]Samuel then explained the king's constitutional position to the people and inscribed this in a book which he placed before Yahweh. Samuel then sent all the people away, everyone back to his home. [26]Saul too went home to Gibeah and with him went

those strong men whose hearts God had touched. 27But there were some scoundrels who said, 'How can this fellow save us?' These treated him with contempt and offered him no present.

Victory over the Ammonites

11 About a month later, Nahash the Ammonite marched up and laid siege to Jabesh in Gilead. All the men of Jabesh said to Nahash, 'Make a treaty with us and we will be your subjects.' 2Nahash the Ammonite replied, 'I shall make a treaty with you only on this condition, that I put out all your right eyes, and I will make it a taunt to the whole of Israel.' 3The elders of Jabesh said to him, 'Give us seven days' grace while we send messengers throughout the territory of Israel, and if no one comes to our help, we will come out to you.' 4The messengers came to Gibeah of Saul, and reported this to the people, and all the people wept aloud.

5Now Saul was just then coming in from the fields behind his oxen, and he said, 'What is wrong? Why are the people weeping?' They explained to him what the men of Jabesh had said. 6And the spirit of Yahweh seized on Saul when he heard these words, and he fell into a fury. 7He took a yoke of oxen, cut them into pieces and sent these by messengers throughout the territory of Israel with these words, 'Anyone who will not march with Saul will have the same done to his oxen!' At this, a panic from Yahweh swept on the people and they marched out as one man. 8Saul inspected them at Bezek; there were three hundred thousand of Israel and thirty thousand of Judah. 9Then he said to the messengers who had come, 'This is what you are to say to the people of Jabesh in Gilead, "Tomorrow, by the time that the sun is hot, help will reach you." ' The messengers went and reported this to the people of Jabesh who were overjoyed; 10they said to Nahash, 'Tomorrow we shall come out to you and you can do whatever you like to us.'

11The next day, Saul disposed the army in three contingents, which burst into the middle of the camp during the dawn watch and slaughtered the Ammonites until high noon. The survivors were so scattered that no two of them were left together.

Saul is proclaimed king

12The people then said to Samuel, 'Who said, "Must we have Saul reigning over us?" Hand the men over, for us to put them to death.' 13'No one must be put to death today,' Saul said, 'for today Yahweh has intervened to rescue Israel.' 14Samuel then said to the people, 'Let us now go to Gilgal and reaffirm the monarchy there.'

15The people then all went to Gilgal. And there, at Gilgal, they proclaimed Saul king before Yahweh; they offered communion sacrifices before Yahweh, and there Saul and all the people of Israel gave themselves over to great rejoicing.

Samuel gives way to Saul

12 Samuel said to all Israel, 'I have faithfully done all that you asked of me, and have appointed you a king. 2In future, the king will lead you. As for me, I am old and grey, and in any case you have my sons. I have been your leader ever since I was young until today. 3Here I am. Bear witness against me before Yahweh and before his anointed. Whose ox have I taken? Whose donkey have I taken? Have I wronged or oppressed anyone? Have I taken a consideration from anyone for looking the other way? If so, I will make amends.' 4They said, 'You have neither wronged nor oppressed us nor accepted anything from anyone.' 5He said to them, 'Yahweh is your witness and his anointed is witness today that you have found nothing in my hands?' They replied, 'He is witness.'

6Samuel then said to the people, 'Yahweh is witness, he who raised up Moses and Aaron and who brought your ancestors out of Egypt. 7So now, stay where you are, while I plead with you before Yahweh and remind you of all the saving acts which he has done for you and for your ancestors. 8After Jacob had arrived in Egypt, the Egyptians oppressed them, and your ancestors cried to Yahweh. Yahweh then sent Moses and Aaron, who brought your ancestors out of Egypt and gave them a settled home here. 9They then forgot Yahweh their God and he sold them into the power of Sisera, general of the army of Hazor, and also into the power of the Philistines and of the king of Moab, who made war on them. 10They cried to Yahweh, "We have sinned," they said, "for we have deserted Yahweh and served the Baals and the Astartes. Rescue us now from the power of our enemies, and we will serve you." 11 Yahweh then sent Jerubbaal, Barak, Jephthah, and Samuel. He rescued you from the power of the enemies surrounding you, and you lived in security.

12 'But when you saw Nahash, king of the Ammonites, marching on you, you said to me, "No, we must have a king to rule us"—although Yahweh your God is your king. 13 So, here is the king whom you have chosen; Yahweh has appointed you a king. 14 If you fear and serve Yahweh and obey his voice and do not rebel against his commands, and if both you and the king who rules you follow Yahweh your God, all will be well. 15 But if you do not obey Yahweh's voice but rebel against his commands, Yahweh's hand will be against you and against your king.

16 'Stay where you are and see the wonder which Yahweh will do before your eyes. 17 Is it not now the wheat harvest? I shall call on Yahweh and he will send thunder and rain, so that you may clearly understand what a very wicked thing you have done, in Yahweh's eyes, by asking for a king.' 18 Samuel then called on Yahweh, and Yahweh sent thunder and rain the same day, and all the people held Yahweh and Samuel in great awe. 19 They all said to Samuel, 'Pray for your servants to Yahweh your God, to save us from death; for to all our sins we have added this wrong of asking for a king.'

20 Samuel said to the people, 'Do not be afraid. Although you have done all these wicked things, do not withdraw your allegiance from Yahweh. Instead, serve Yahweh with all your heart. 21 Do not transfer your allegiance to useless idols which, being useless, are futile and cannot save anybody; 22 Yahweh, for the sake of his great name, will not desert his people, for it has pleased Yahweh to make you his people. 23 For my part, far be it from me to sin against Yahweh by ceasing to pray for you or to instruct you in the good and right way. 24 Fear none but Yahweh, and serve him faithfully with all your heart, bearing in mind the wonder which he has just performed. But, if you persist in wickedness, you and your king will perish.'

B: THE BEGINNING OF SAUL'S REIGN

Revolt against the Philistines

13 Saul was . . . years old when he became king, and reigned over Israel for . . . years. 2 Saul selected three thousand men of Israel; two thousand of them were with Saul at Michmash and in the highlands of Bethel, and one thousand with Jonathan at Geba of Benjamin; the rest of the people Saul sent home, everyone to his tent.

3 Jonathan killed the Philistine governor stationed at Gibeah and the Philistines were informed that the Hebrews had risen in revolt. Saul had the trumpet sounded throughout the country, 4 and all Israel heard the news, 'Saul has killed the Philistine governor, and now Israel has antagonised the Philistines.' So all the people rallied behind Saul at Gilgal. 5 The Philistines mustered to make war on Israel, three thousand chariots, six thousand horse and a force as numerous as the sand on the seashore. They came up and pitched camp at Michmash, to the east of Beth-Aven. 6 When the Israelites saw that their plight was desperate, being so hard pressed, the people hid in caves, in holes, in crevices, in vaults, in wells. 7 Some also crossed the Jordan fords into the territory of Gad and Gilead.

Samuel breaks with Saul

Saul was still at Gilgal and all the people who followed him were trembling. 8 He waited for seven days, the period fixed by Samuel, but Samuel did not come to Gilgal, and the army, deserting Saul, began dispersing. 9 Saul then said, 'Bring me the burnt offering and the communion sacrifices.' And he presented the burnt offering. 10 Just as he had finished presenting the burnt offering, Samuel arrived, and Saul went out to meet and greet him. 11 Samuel said, 'What have you been doing?' Saul replied, 'I saw the army deserting me and dispersing, and you had not come at the time fixed, while the Philistines were mustering at Michmash. 12 So I thought: Now the Philistines are going to fall on me at Gilgal and I have not implored the favour of Yahweh. So I felt obliged to make the burnt offering myself.' 13 Samuel said to Saul, 'You have acted like a fool. You have not obeyed the order which Yahweh your God gave you.

Otherwise, Yahweh would have confirmed your sovereignty over Israel for ever. 14But now your sovereignty will not last; Yahweh has discovered a man after his own heart and designated him as leader of his people, since you have not carried out what Yahweh ordered you.' 15Samuel then got up and left Gilgal to continue his journey.

Those people remaining followed Saul as he went to join the warriors, and went from Gilgal to Geba of Benjamin. Saul reviewed the force that was with him; there were about six hundred men.

Preparations for battle

16Saul, his son Jonathan, and the force that was with them took up their quarters in Geba of Benjamin while the Philistines camped at Michmash. 17The raiding company sallied out of the Philistine camp in three groups: one group made for Ophrah in the territory of Shual; 18one group made for Beth-Horon; and one group made for the high ground overlooking the Valley of the Hyenas, in the direction of the desert.

19There was not a single blacksmith throughout the territory of Israel, the Philistines' reasoning being, 'We do not want the Hebrews making swords or spears.' 20Hence, the Israelites were all in the habit of going down individually to the Philistines to sharpen their ploughshares, axes, mattocks and scythes. 21The price was two-thirds of a shekel for ploughshares and axes, and one-third for sharpening mattocks and straightening goads. 22So it was that on the day of the battle, no one in the army with Saul and Jonathan was equipped with either sword or spear; only Saul and his son Jonathan were so equipped.

23A Philistine unit set out for the Pass of Michmash.

Jonathan attacks the outpost

14 One day, Jonathan son of Saul said to his armour-bearer, 'Come on, let us go across to the Philistine outpost over on the other side.' But he did not inform his father. 2Saul was on the outskirts of Geba, sitting under the pomegranate tree that stands near the threshing-floor; the force with him numbered about six hundred men. 3Ahijah son of Ahitub, brother of Ichabod, son of Phinehas, son of Eli, the priest of Yahweh at Shiloh, was carrying the *ephod*.[a] The force did not know that Jonathan had left.

4In the pass that Jonathan was trying to cross to reach the Philistine outpost, there is a rocky spur on one side and a rocky spur on the other; one is called Bozez, the other Seneh. 5The first spur stands to the north facing Michmash, the other to the south facing Geba. 6Jonathan said to his armour-bearer, 'Come on, let us go across to these uncircumcised people's outpost; perhaps Yahweh will do something for us, for Yahweh is free to grant deliverance through a few men, just as much as through many.' 7His armour-bearer replied, 'Do exactly as you think. I am with you; our hearts are as one.' 8Jonathan then said, 'Look, we will go across to these people and let ourselves be seen. 9If they say, "Do not move until we come to you," we shall stay where we are and not go up to them. 10But if they say, "Come up to us," we shall go up, for that will be the sign for us that Yahweh has given them into our power.'

11When the two of them let themselves be seen by the Philistine outpost, the Philistines said, 'Look, the Hebrews are coming out of the holes where they have been hiding.' 12The men of the outpost then hailed Jonathan and his armour-bearer. 'Come up to us,' they said, 'we have something to tell you.' Jonathan then said to his armour-bearer, 'Follow me up; Yahweh has given them into the power of Israel.' 13Jonathan clambered up on hands and feet, with his armour-bearer behind him; the Philistines fell at Jonathan's onslaught, and his armour-bearer, coming behind, finished them off. 14This first killing made by Jonathan and his armour-bearer accounted for about twenty men . . .

Battle is engaged

15There was panic in the camp, in the field and throughout the army; outpost and raiding company too were panic-stricken; the earth quaked: it was a panic from Yahweh. 16Saul's look-out men in Geba of Benjamin could see the camp scattering in all directions. 17Saul then said to the force that was with him, 'Call the roll and see who has left us.' So they

14a *See* note to 2:28.

called the roll, and Jonathan and his armour-
bearer were missing.
18 Saul then said to Ahijah, 'Bring the
ephod,' since he was the man who carried the
ephod in Israel. 19 But while Saul was speaking
to the priest, the turmoil in the Philistine
camp grew worse and worse; and Saul said
to the priest, 'Withdraw your hand.' 20 Saul
and the whole force with him then formed
up and advanced to where the fighting was
going on: and there they all were, drawing
their swords on one another in wild
confusion. 21 Those Hebrews who had earlier
taken service with the Philistines and had
accompanied them into camp, now defected
to the Israelites who were with Saul and
Jonathan. 22 Similarly, all those Israelites
who had been hiding in the highlands of
Ephraim, hearing that the Philistines were
on the run, chased after them and joined in
the fight. 23 That day Yahweh gave Israel the
victory.

Jonathan violates Saul's prohibition

The fighting reached the other side of Beth-
Horon. 24 As the men of Israel were hard
pressed that day, Saul pronounced this
imprecation over the people, 'A curse on
anyone who eats food before evening,
before I have taken revenge on my enemies!'
So none of the people so much as tasted
food.
25 Now there was a honeycomb out in the
open. 26 The people came to the honeycomb,
the honey was dripping out, but no one put
a hand to his mouth, the people being in awe
of the oath. 27 Jonathan, however, not having
heard his father bind the people with the
oath, reached with the end of the stick which
he was carrying, thrust it into the honeycomb
and put it to his mouth; whereupon his eyes
grew brighter. 28 One of the people then spoke
up. 'Your father', he said, 'has bound the
people with this oath: "A curse on anyone
who eats anything today." ' 29 'My father has
brought trouble on the country,' Jonathan
replied. 'See how much brighter my eyes are
for having eaten this mouthful of honey.
30 By the same token, if the people had been
allowed to eat some of the booty which they
had captured from the enemy today, would
not the defeat of the Philistines have been all
the greater?'

The people commit a ritual fault

31 That day the Philistines were beaten from
Michmash all the way to Aijalon, until the
people were utterly exhausted. 32 The people
flung themselves on the booty and, taking
sheep, bullocks and calves, slaughtered them
there on the ground and ate them with the
blood. 33 Saul was informed, 'The people are
sinning against Yahweh by eating with the
blood!' He said, 'You have not kept faith!
Roll me a large stone here!' 34 Saul then
said, 'Scatter among the people and say,
"Everyone is to bring his bullock or his sheep
to me here." You will slaughter them here
and eat, and not sin against Yahweh by eating
with the blood.' Each individual brought
what he happened to have that night, and
they all slaughtered in the same place. 35 Saul
built an altar to Yahweh; it was the first altar
he had built to Yahweh.

Jonathan's guilt is discovered, but he is saved by the people

36 Saul said, 'Let us go down under cover of
dark and plunder the Philistines until dawn;
we shall not leave one of them alive.' 'Do
whatever you think right,' they replied. But
the priest said, 'Let us approach God here.'
37 Saul consulted God, 'Shall I go down and
pursue the Philistines? Will you hand them
over to Israel?' But he gave him no reply that
day. 38 Saul then said, 'Come forward, all
you leaders of the people; consider carefully
where today's sin may lie; 39 for as Yahweh
lives who gives victory to Israel, even if the
sin lies with Jonathan my son, he shall be put
to death.' But not one out of all the people
answered. 40 He then said to all Israel, 'Stand
on one side, and I and Jonathan my son will
stand on the other.' And the people replied
to Saul, 'Do as you think right.' 41 Saul then
said, 'Yahweh, God of Israel, why did you
not answer your servant today? Yahweh, God
of Israel, if the fault lies with me or with my
son Jonathan, give *urim*: if the fault lies with
your people Israel, give *thummim*.'[b] Jonathan
and Saul were indicated and the people went
free. 42 Saul said, 'Cast the lot between me
and my son Jonathan,' and Jonathan was
indicated.
43 'I only tasted a mouthful of honey off the
end of the stick which I was carrying. But I

14b A simple yes/no answer is obtained by drawing one of the lots out of the *ephod*.

am ready to die.' 44Saul said, 'May God bring
unnameable ills on me, and worse ones too,
if you do not die, Jonathan!' 45But the people
said to Saul, 'Must Jonathan die after winning
this great victory for Israel? We will never
allow that! As Yahweh lives, not one hair of
his head shall fall to the ground, for his deeds
today have been done with the help of God.'
And so the people ransomed Jonathan and
he was not put to death.
46Saul decided not to pursue the Philistines,
and the Philistines retired to their own
territory.

Summary of Saul's reign

47Saul consolidated his rule over Israel and
made war on all his enemies on all fronts: on
Moab, the Ammonites, Edom, the king of
Zobah and the Philistines; whichever way he
turned, he was victorious. 48He did great
deeds of valour; he defeated the Amalekites
and delivered Israel from those who used to
pillage him.
49Saul's sons were: Jonathan, Ishvi and
Malchishua. The names of his two daughters
were: the elder, Merab, and the younger,
Michal. 50The name of Saul's wife was
Ahinoam daughter of Ahimaaz. The name of
his army commander was Abner son of Ner,
Saul's uncle. 51Kish father of Saul, and Ner
father of Abner were the sons of Abiel.
52There was fierce warfare with the Philistines
throughout Saul's life. Any strong
or valiant man who caught Saul's eye, he
recruited into his service.

Holy war against the Amalekites

15 Samuel said to Saul, 'I am the man
whom Yahweh sent to anoint you as
king of his people Israel, so now listen to the
words of Yahweh. 2This is what Yahweh
Sabaoth says, "I intend to punish what
Amalek did to Israel—laying a trap for him
on the way as he was coming up from Egypt.
3Now, go and crush Amalek; put him under
the curse of destruction with all that he
possesses. Do not spare him, but kill man
and woman, babe and suckling, ox and sheep,
camel and donkey." '
4Saul summoned the people and reviewed
them at Telaim: two hundred thousand foot
soldiers (and ten thousand men of Judah).
5Saul advanced on the town of Amalek and
lay in ambush in the river bed. 6Saul said to
the Kenites, 'Go away, leave your homes
among the Amalekites, in case I destroy
you with them—you acted with faithful love
towards all the Israelites when they were
coming up from Egypt.' So the Kenites
moved away from the Amalekites.
7Saul then crushed the Amalekites, beginning
at Havilah in the direction of Shur,
which is to the east of Egypt. 8He took Agag
king of the Amalekites alive and, executing
the curse of destruction, put all the people to
the sword. 9But Saul and the army spared
Agag with the best of the sheep and cattle,
the fatlings and lambs and all that was good.
They did not want to consign these to the
curse of destruction; they consigned only
what was poor and worthless.

Saul is rejected by Yahweh

10The word of Yahweh came to Samuel, 11'I
regret having made Saul king, since he has
broken his allegiance to me and not carried
out my orders.' Samuel was appalled and
cried to Yahweh all night long.
12In the morning, Samuel set off to find
Saul. Samuel was told, 'Saul has been to
Carmel, to raise himself a monument there,
but now has turned about, moved on and
gone down to Gilgal.' 13When Samuel
reached Saul, Saul said, 'May you be blessed
by Yahweh! I have carried out Yahweh's
orders.' 14Samuel replied, 'Then what is this
bleating of sheep in my ears and the lowing
of cattle that I hear?' 15Saul said, 'They
have been brought from Amalek, the people
having spared the best of the sheep and cattle
to sacrifice them to Yahweh, your God; the
rest we have consigned to the curse of
destruction.'
16Samuel then said to Saul, 'Stop! Let me
tell you what Yahweh said to me last night.'
He said, 'Go on.' 17Samuel said, 'Small as
you may be in your own eyes, are you not the
leader of the tribes of Israel? Yahweh has
anointed you as king of Israel. 18When
Yahweh sent you on a mission he said to you,
"Go and put those sinners, the Amalekites,
under the curse of destruction and make war
on them until they are exterminated." 19Why
then did you not obey Yahweh's voice?
Why did you fall on the booty and do what
is wrong in Yahweh's eyes?' 20Saul replied to
Samuel, 'But I did obey Yahweh's voice. I
went on the mission which Yahweh gave me;
I brought back Agag king of the Amalekites;

I put Amalek under the curse of destruction; 21 and from the booty the people have taken the best sheep and cattle of what was under the curse of destruction only to sacrifice them to Yahweh your God in Gilgal.' 22 To which, Samuel said:

> Is Yahweh pleased by burnt offerings
> and sacrifices
> or by obedience to Yahweh's voice?
> Truly, obedience is better than sacrifice,
> submissiveness than the fat of rams.
> 23 Rebellion is a sin of sorcery,
> presumption a crime of idolatry!

'Since you have rejected Yahweh's word, he has rejected you as king.'

Saul asks in vain for pardon

24 Saul then said to Samuel, 'I have sinned, having broken Yahweh's order and your instructions because I was afraid of the people and yielded to their demands. 25 Now, please forgive my sin and come back with me, so that I can worship Yahweh.' 26 Samuel said to Saul, 'I will not come back with you, since you have rejected Yahweh's word and Yahweh has rejected you as king of Israel.' 27 As Samuel turned away to leave, Saul caught at the hem of his cloak and it tore, 28 and Samuel said to him, 'Today Yahweh has torn the kingdom of Israel from you and given it to a neighbour of yours who is better than you.' 29 (The Glory of Israel, however, does not lie or go back on his word, not being human and liable to go back on his word.) 30 'I have sinned,' Saul said, 'but please still show me respect in front of my people's elders and in front of Israel, and come back with me, so that I can worship Yahweh your God.' 31 Samuel followed Saul back and Saul worshipped Yahweh.

Death of Agag and departure of Samuel

32 Samuel then said, 'Bring me Agag king of the Amalekites!' Agag came towards him unsteadily saying, 'Truly death is bitter!' 33 Samuel said:

> As your sword has left women childless,
> so will your mother be left childless
> among women!

Samuel then butchered Agag before Yahweh at Gilgal.

34 Samuel left for Ramah, and Saul went up home to Gibeah of Saul. 35 Samuel did not see Saul again till his dying day. Samuel indeed mourned over Saul, but Yahweh regretted having made Saul king of Israel.

III: SAUL AND DAVID

A: DAVID AT COURT

David is anointed

16 Yahweh said to Samuel, 'How much longer do you mean to go on mourning over Saul, now that I myself have rejected him as ruler of Israel? Fill your horn with oil and go. I am sending you to Jesse of Bethlehem, for I have found myself a king from among his sons.' 2 Samuel replied, 'How can I go? When Saul hears of it he will kill me.' Yahweh then said, 'Take a heifer with you and say, "I have come to sacrifice to Yahweh." 3 Invite Jesse to the sacrifice, and I shall reveal to you what you must do; and you will anoint for me the one I indicate to you.'

4 Samuel did what Yahweh ordered and went to Bethlehem. The elders of the town came trembling to meet him and asked, 'Seer, is your coming favourable for us,' 5 'Yes,' he replied. 'I have come to sacrifice to Yahweh. Purify yourselves and come with me to the sacrifice.' He purified Jesse and his sons and invited them to the sacrifice.

6 When they arrived, he looked at Eliab and thought, 'This must be Yahweh's anointed now before him,' 7 but Yahweh said to Samuel, 'Take no notice of his appearance or his height, for I have rejected him; God does not see as human beings see; they look at appearances but Yahweh looks at the heart.' 8 Jesse then called Abinadab and presented him to Samuel, who said, 'Yahweh has not chosen this one either.' 9 Jesse then presented Shammah, but Samuel said, 'Yahweh has not chosen this one either.' 10 Jesse thus presented seven of his sons to Samuel, but Samuel said to Jesse, 'Yahweh has not chosen these.' 11 He

then asked Jesse, 'Are these all the sons you have?' Jesse replied, 'There is still one left, the youngest; he is looking after the sheep.' Samuel then said to Jesse, 'Send for him, for we shall not sit down to eat until he arrives.' 12 Jesse had him sent for; he had ruddy cheeks, with fine eyes and an attractive appearance. Yahweh said, 'Get up and anoint him: he is the one!' 13 At this, Samuel took the horn of oil and anointed him, surrounded by his brothers; and the spirit of Yahweh seized on David from that day onwards. Samuel, for his part, set off and went to Ramah.

David enters Saul's service[a]

14 Now the spirit of Yahweh had withdrawn from Saul, and an evil spirit from Yahweh afflicted him with terrors. 15 Saul's servants said to him, 'An evil spirit from God is undoubtedly the cause of your terrors. 16 Let our lord give the order, and your servants who wait on you will look for a skilled harpist; when the evil spirit from God comes over you, he will play and it will do you good.' 17 Saul said to his attendants, 'Find me, please, a man who plays well, and bring him to me.' 18 One of the servants then spoke up and said, 'I have seen one of the sons of Jesse the Bethlehemite: he is a skilled player, a brave man and a fighter, well spoken, good-looking and Yahweh is with him.' 19 So Saul sent messengers to Jesse with the order, 'Send me your son David (who is with the sheep).' 20 Jesse took five loaves, a skin of wine and a kid, and sent them to Saul by his son David. 21 David went to Saul and entered his service; Saul became very fond of him and David became his armour-bearer. 22 Saul then sent a message to Jesse, 'Let David stay in my service, since he has won my favour.' 23 And whenever the spirit from God came over Saul, David would take a harp and play; Saul would then be soothed; it would do him good, and the evil spirit would leave him.

Goliath challenges the Israelite army

17 The Philistines mustered their troops for war; they assembled at Socoh in Judah and pitched camp between Socoh and Azekah, in Ephes-Dammim. 2 Saul and the Israelites also mustered, pitching camp in the Valley of the Terebinth, and drew up their battle-line opposite the Philistines. 3 The Philistines occupied the high ground on one side and the Israelites occupied the high ground on the other side, with the valley between them.

4 A champion stepped out from the Philistine ranks; his name was Goliath, from Gath; he was six cubits and one span tall. 5 On his head was a bronze helmet and he wore a breastplate of scale-armour; the breastplate weighed five thousand shekels of bronze. 6 He had bronze greaves on his legs and a bronze scimitar slung across his shoulders. 7 The shaft of his spear was like a weaver's beam, and the head of his spear weighed six hundred shekels of iron. A shield-bearer walked in front of him.

8 Taking position in front of the Israelite lines, he shouted, 'Why have you come out to range yourselves for battle? Am I not a Philistine and are you not Saul's lackeys? Choose a man and let him come down to me. 9 If he can fight it out with me and kill me, we will be your servants; but if I can beat him and kill him, you become our servants and serve us.' 10 The Philistine then said, 'I challenge the ranks of Israel today. Give me a man and we will fight it out!' 11 When Saul and all Israel heard what the Philistine said, they were dismayed and terrified.

David arrives in the camp

12 David was the son of an Ephrathite from Bethlehem of Judah whose name was Jesse; Jesse had eight sons and, by Saul's time, he was old and well on in years. 13 Jesse's eldest three sons followed Saul to the war. The names of the three sons who went to the war were: the eldest Eliab, the second Abinadab and the third Shammah. 14 David was the youngest; the eldest three followed Saul. 15 David alternated between serving Saul and looking after his father's sheep at Bethlehem. 16 Morning and evening, the Philistine advanced, presenting himself thus for forty days. 17 Jesse said to his son David, 'Take your brothers this *ephah* of roasted grain and these ten loaves, and hurry to the camp, to your brothers. 18 And take these ten cheeses to their commanding officer; find out how

---

16a There are two separate versions: 1 David is a court musician; 2 He is a shepherd visiting his brothers. In this part of David's story there is a series of doublets: 18:11 = 19:8–10; 18:17–19 = 18:20–27; 19:1–7 = 20:1–42; 24 = 26; 21:11–16 = 27:1–12.

your brothers are and bring some token back
from them; 19they are with Saul and all the
men of Israel in the Valley of the Terebinth,
fighting the Philistines.'
20David got up early in the morning and,
leaving the sheep with someone to guard
them, took up his load and went off as Jesse
had ordered; he reached the encampment
just as the troops were leaving to take up
battle stations and shouting the war cry.
21Israel and the Philistines drew up their lines
facing one another. 22David left his bundle
in charge of the baggage guard and, running
to the battle-line, went and asked his brothers
how they were.
23While he was talking to them, the cham-
pion (Goliath, the Philistine from Gath) came
up from the Philistine ranks and made his
usual speech, which David heard. 24As soon
as the Israelites saw this man, they all ran
away from him and were terrified. 25The
Israelites said, 'You saw that man who just
came up? He comes to challenge Israel. The
king will lavish riches on the man who kills
him, he will give him his daughter in marriage
and exempt his father's family from all taxes
in Israel.'
26David asked the men who were standing
near him, 'What would be the reward for
killing this Philistine and saving Israel from
disgrace? Who is this uncircumcised Phili-
stine, to challenge the armies of the living
God?' 27The people told him what they had
been saying, 'That would be the reward for
killing him,' they said. 28His eldest brother
Eliab heard David talking to the men and
grew angry with him. 'Why have you come
down here?' he said. 'Whom have you left in
charge of those few sheep in the desert? I
know how impudent and artful you are;
you have come to watch the battle!' 29David
retorted, 'What have I done? May I not even
speak?' 30And he turned away from him to
someone else and asked the same question, to
which the people replied as before. 31David's
words were noted, however, and reported to
Saul, who sent for him.

David volunteers to accept the challenge

32David said to Saul, 'Let no one be discour-
aged on his account; your servant will go and
fight this Philistine.' 33Saul said to David,
'You cannot go and fight the Philistine; you
are only a boy and he has been a warrior since
his youth.'
34David said to Saul, 'Your servant used
to look after the sheep for his father and
whenever a lion or a bear came and took a
sheep from the flock, 35I used to follow it up,
lay into it and snatch the sheep out of its jaws.
If it turned on me, I would seize it by the
beard and batter it to death. 36Your servant
has killed both lion and bear, and this uncir-
cumcised Philistine will end up like one of
them for having challenged the armies of the
living God.' 37'Yahweh,' David went on,
'who delivered me from the claws of lion and
bear, will deliver me from the clutches of this
Philistine.' Then Saul said to David, 'Go,
and Yahweh be with you!'
38Saul dressed David in his own armour;
he put a bronze helmet on his head, dressed
him in a breastplate 39and buckled his own
sword over David's armour. David tried to
walk but, not being used to them, said to
Saul, 'I cannot walk in these; I am not used
to them.' So they took them off again.

David and Goliath

40He took his stick in his hand, selected five
smooth stones from the river bed and put
them in his shepherd's bag, in his pouch;
then, sling in hand, he walked towards the
Philistine. 41The Philistine, preceded by his
shield-bearer, came nearer and nearer to
David. 42When the Philistine looked David
up and down, what he saw filled him with
scorn, because David was only a lad, with
ruddy cheeks and an attractive appearance.
43The Philistine said to David, 'Am I a dog
for you to come after me with sticks?' And
the Philistine cursed David by his gods.
44The Philistine said to David, 'Come over
here and I will give your flesh to the birds of
the air and the wild beasts!' 45David retorted
to the Philistine, 'You come to me with
sword, spear and scimitar, but I come to you
in the name of Yahweh Sabaoth, God of the
armies of Israel, whom you have challenged.
46Today, Yahweh will deliver you into my
hand; I shall kill you, I shall cut off your
head; today, I shall give your corpse and the
corpses of the Philistine army to the birds of
the air and the wild beasts, so that the whole
world may know that there is a God in Israel,
47and this whole assembly know that Yahweh
does not give victory by means of sword and
spear—for Yahweh is lord of the battle and
he will deliver you into our power.'
48No sooner had the Philistine started

forward to confront David than David darted
out of the lines and ran to meet the Philistine.
49Putting his hand in his bag, he took out a
stone, slung it and struck the Philistine on the
forehead; the stone penetrated his forehead
and he fell face downwards on the ground.
50Thus David triumphed over the Philistine
with a sling and a stone; he hit the Philistine
and killed him, though he had no sword in
his hand. 51David ran and stood over the
Philistine, seized his sword, pulled it from
the scabbard, despatched him and cut off his
head.

When the Philistines saw that their cham-
pion was dead, they fled. 52The men of Israel
and of Judah started forward, shouting their
war cry, and pursued the Philistines as far as
the approaches of Gath and the gates of
Ekron. The Philistine dead lay all along the
road from Shaaraim as far as Gath and Ekron.
53Turning back from their ferocious pursuit
of the Philistines, the Israelites plundered
their camp. 54And David took the Philis-
tine's head and brought it to Jerusalem; his
weapons, however, he put in his own tent.

David the conqueror of Goliath is presented to Saul

55When Saul saw David going to engage
the Philistine he said to Abner, the army
commander, 'Abner, whose son is that boy?'
'On your life, O king,' Abner replied, 'I do
not know.' 56The king said, 'Find out whose
son the lad is.'

57When David came back after killing the
Philistine, Abner took him and brought him
before Saul with the Philistine's head in his
hand. 58Saul asked him, 'Whose son are you,
young man?' David replied, 'The son of your
servant Jesse of Bethlehem.'

18 When David had finished talking to
Saul, Jonathan felt an instant affection
for David; Jonathan loved him like his very
self; 2Saul engaged him that very day and
would not let him go home to his father.
3Jonathan made a pact with David, since he
loved him like his very self; 4Jonathan took
off the cloak which he was wearing and
gave it to David, and his armour too, even
including his sword, his bow and his belt.
5Wherever David was sent on a mission by
Saul, he was successful, and Saul put him in
command of the fighting men; all the people
respected him and so did Saul's staff.

Saul starts being jealous

6On their return, when David was coming
back from killing the Philistine, the women
came out of all the towns of Israel singing
and dancing to meet King Saul, with
tambourines, sistrums and cries of joy; 7and
as they danced the women sang:

Saul has killed his thousands,
and David his tens of thousands.

8Saul was very angry; the incident
displeased him. 'They have given David the
tens of thousands,' he said, 'but me only
the thousands; what more can he have, except
the throne?' 9And Saul watched David jeal-
ously from that day onwards.

10The following day, an evil spirit from
God seized on Saul and he fell into a frenzy
while he was indoors. David played the harp
as on other occasions; Saul had a spear in his
hand. 11Saul brandished the spear; he said,
'I will pin David to the wall!' David evaded
him twice.

12Saul feared David, since Yahweh was
with him and had withdrawn from Saul. 13So
Saul removed him from his presence and
appointed him commander of a thousand; he
led the people on campaign. 14In all his
expeditions, David was successful and
Yahweh was with him. 15And Saul, seeing
how very successful he was, was afraid of
him. 16All Israel and Judah loved David,
however, since he was their leader on
campaign.

David's marriage

17Saul said to David, 'This is my elder
daughter Merab; I shall give her to you in
marriage; but you must serve me bravely and
fight Yahweh's wars.' Saul thought, 'Better
than strike the blow myself, let the Philistines
do it!' 18David replied to Saul, 'Who am I
and what is my lineage—and my father's
family—in Israel, for me to become the king's
son-in-law?' 19When the time came for Merab
daughter of Saul to be given to David, she
was given to Adriel of Meholah instead.

20Now Michal daughter of Saul fell in love
with David. When Saul heard this he was
pleased. 21He thought, 'Yes, I shall give her
to him; she can be the snare for him, so
that the Philistines will get him.' (On two
occasions, Saul told David, 'Today, you shall
be my son-in-law.') 22Saul gave instructions

to his servants, 'Have a private word with David and say, "Look, the king is fond of you and all his servants love you—why not be the king's son-in-law?" ' 23Saul's servants repeated these words in David's ear, to which David replied, 'Do you think that becoming the king's son-in-law is a trivial matter; I have neither wealth nor position.' 24Saul's servants then reported back, 'This is what David said.' 25Saul replied, 'Tell David this, "The king desires no bride-price except one hundred Philistine foreskins, in vengeance on the king's enemies." ' Saul was counting on getting David killed by the Philistines.

26When his servants repeated this to David, David thought it would be a fine thing to be the king's son-in-law. And no time was lost 27before David got up to go, he and his men, and killed two hundred of the Philistines. David brought their foreskins back and counted them out before the king, so that he could be the king's son-in-law. Saul then gave him his daughter Michal in marriage.

28Saul could not but see that Yahweh was with David, and that the whole House of Israel loved him; 29Saul became more afraid of David than ever, and became his inveterate enemy. 30The Philistine chiefs kept mounting their campaigns but, whenever they did so, David proved more successful than any of Saul's staff; consequently he gained great renown.

Jonathan intercedes for David

19 Saul let his son Jonathan and all his servants know of his intention to kill David. But Jonathan, Saul's son, held David in great affection; 2and Jonathan warned David, 'My father Saul is looking for a way to kill you, so be on your guard tomorrow morning; go into hiding, stay out of sight. 3I shall go out and keep my father company in the countryside where you will be, and shall talk to my father about you; I shall see what the situation is and then tell you.'

4Jonathan spoke highly of David to Saul his father and said, 'The king should not harm his servant David; far from harming you, what he has done has been greatly to your advantage. 5He took his life in his hands, he killed the Philistine, and Yahweh brought about a great victory for all Israel. You saw for yourself. How pleased you were! Why then sin against innocent blood by killing David for no reason?' 6Saul was impressed by Jonathan's words. Saul swore, 'As Yahweh lives, I will not kill him.' 7Jonathan called David and told him all this. Jonathan then brought him to Saul, and David remained in attendance as before.

B: THE FLIGHT OF DAVID

Saul's attempt on David's life

8War broke out again and David sallied out to fight the Philistines; he inflicted a great defeat on them and they fled before him. 9An evil spirit from Yahweh came over Saul while he was sitting in his house with his spear in his hand; David was playing the harp. 10Saul tried to pin David to the wall with his spear, but he avoided Saul's thrust and the spear stuck in the wall. David fled and made good his escape.

David is saved by Michal

That same night 11Saul sent agents to watch David's house, intending to kill him in the morning. But Michal, David's wife, warned him, 'If you do not escape tonight, you will be a dead man tomorrow!' 12Michal then let David down through the window, and he made off, took to flight and so escaped.

13Michal then took a domestic image, laid it on the bed, put a tress of goats' hair at the head of the bed and put a cover over it. 14When Saul sent the agents to arrest David, she said, 'He is ill.' 15Saul sent the agents back to see David, with the words, 'Bring him to me on his bed, for me to kill him!' 16So in the agents went, and there in bed was the image, with the tress of goats' hair on its head! 17Saul then said to Michal, 'Why have you deceived me like this and let my enemy go, and so make his escape?' Michal replied to Saul, 'He said, "Let me go, or I shall kill you!" '

Saul and David at Ramah with Samuel

18David, having fled and made his escape, went to Samuel at Ramah and told him exactly how Saul had treated him; he and Samuel went and lived in the huts. 19Word was brought to Saul, 'David is in the huts at Ramah.' 20Saul accordingly sent agents to

capture David; when they saw the
community of prophets prophesying, and
Samuel there as their leader, the spirit of God
came over Saul's agents, and they too fell into
frenzy. [21]When Saul was told of this, he sent
other agents, and they too fell into frenzy;
Saul then sent a third group of agents, and
they fell into frenzy too.
[22]He then went to Ramah himself and,
arriving at the large storage-well at Seku,
asked, 'Where are Samuel and David?' And
someone said, 'Why, they are in the huts at
Ramah!' [23]Making his way from there to the
huts at Ramah, the spirit of God came over
him too, and he went along in a frenzy until
he arrived at the huts at Ramah. [24]He too
stripped off his clothes and he too fell into a
frenzy in Samuel's presence, then collapsed
naked on the ground for the rest of that day
and all night. Hence the saying: Is Saul one
of the prophets too?

Jonathan helps David to escape

20 Fleeing from the huts at Ramah, David
went and confronted Jonathan, 'What
have I done, what is my guilt, how have I
wronged your father, for him to want to take
my life?' [2]He replied, 'You must not think
that! You are not going to die. My father, you
see, does nothing, important or unimportant,
without confiding in me, so why should my
father hide this from me? It is not true.' [3]In
reply, David swore, 'Your father knows very
well that I enjoy your favour, and thinks,
"Jonathan must not know about this or he
will be upset." But, as Yahweh lives and as
you yourself live, there is only a step between
me and death.'
[4]At which, Jonathan said to David, 'What-
ever you think best, I will certainly do for
you.' [5]David replied, 'Look, tomorrow is
New Moon and I ought to sit at table with
the king, but you must let me go and hide in
the countryside until the evening. [6]If your
father notices my absence, you must say,
"David insistently asked me for permission
to hurry over to Bethlehem, his home town,
because they are holding the annual sacrifice
there for the whole clan." [7]If he says, "Very
well," your servant is safe, but if he flies into
a rage, you may be sure that he has some evil
plan. [8]Show your servant faithful love, since
you have bound your servant to you by a pact
in Yahweh's name. But if I am guilty, then kill
me yourself—why take me to your father?'
[9]Jonathan replied, 'Perish the thought! If I
knew for sure that my father was determined
to do you a mischief, would I not have told
you?' [10]David then said to Jonathan, 'Who
will let me know if your father gives you a
harsh answer?'
[11]Jonathan then said to David, 'Come on,
let us go out into the country,' and the pair
of them went out into the country. [12]Jonathan
then said to David, 'By Yahweh, God of
Israel! I shall sound my father this time
tomorrow; if all is well for David and I do
not then send and inform you, [13]may Yahweh
bring unnameable ills to Jonathan and worse
ones too! If my father intends to do you a
mischief, I shall tell you so and let you get
away, so that you can be safe. And may
Yahweh be with you as he used to be with
my father! [14]If I am still alive, show your
servant faithful love; if I die, [15]never with-
draw your faithful love from my family.
When Yahweh has exterminated every
enemy of David's from the face of the earth,
[16]do not let Jonathan's name be exterminated
with Saul's family, or may Yahweh call David
to account!' [17]Jonathan then renewed his oath
to David, since he loved him like his very
soul.
[18]Jonathan then said to David, 'Tomorrow
is New Moon; your absence will be noticed,
since your place will be empty. [19]The day
after tomorrow your absence will be very
marked, and you must go to the place where
you hid on the day of the deed, and stay
beside that mound. [20]For my part, the day
after tomorrow I shall shoot three arrows in
that direction, as though at a target. [21]I shall
then send a servant to go and find the arrows.
If I say to him, "The arrows are this side of
you, get them," come out, since all will be
well for you and nothing the matter, as sure
as Yahweh lives. [22]But if I say to him, "The
arrows are ahead of you," then be off, for
Yahweh himself will be sending you away.
[23]And as regards the agreement we made,
you and I, why, Yahweh is witness between
us for ever.'
[24]So David hid in the country; New Moon
came and the king sat down to his meal. [25]He
sat in his usual place with his back to the
wall, Jonathan sat facing him and Abner sat
next to Saul; but David's place was empty.
[26]Saul said nothing that day, thinking, 'It is
sheer chance; he is unclean.' [27]On the day
after New Moon, the second day, David's
place was still empty. [28]Saul said to his son

Jonathan, 'Why did not the son of Jesse come to the meal either yesterday or today?' 29 Jonathan answered Saul, 'David insistently asked me for permission to go to Bethlehem. "Please let me go," he said, "for we are holding the clan sacrifice in the town and my brothers have ordered me to attend. So now, if I enjoy your favour, let me get away and see my brothers." That is why he has not come to the king's table.'

30 Saul flew into a rage with Jonathan and said, 'Son of a rebellious slut! Don't I know that you side with the son of Jesse to your own shame and your mother's dishonour? 31 As long as the son of Jesse lives on earth, neither you nor your royal rights are secure. Now have him fetched and brought to me; he deserves to die.' 32 Jonathan retorted to his father Saul, 'Why should he die? What has he done?' 33 But Saul brandished his spear at him to strike him, and Jonathan realised that his father was determined that David should die. 34 Hot with anger, Jonathan got up from the table and ate nothing on the second day of the month, being upset about David—and because his father had insulted him.

35 Next morning, Jonathan went out into the country at the time agreed with David, taking a young servant with him. 36 He said to his servant, 'Run and find the arrows which I am going to shoot,' and the servant ran while Jonathan shot an arrow ahead of him. 37 When the servant reached the spot to which Jonathan had shot the arrow, Jonathan shouted after him, 'Is not the arrow ahead of you?' 38 Again Jonathan shouted after the servant, 'Quick! Hurry, do not stand around.' Jonathan's servant picked up the arrow and brought it back to his master. 39 The servant suspected nothing; only Jonathan and David knew what was meant.

40 Jonathan then gave his weapons to his servant and said, 'Go and carry them to the town.' 41 As soon as the servant had gone, David stood up beside the mound, threw himself to the ground, prostrating himself three times. They then embraced each other, both weeping copiously. 42 Jonathan then said to David, 'Go in peace. And as regards the oath that both of us have sworn by the name of Yahweh, may Yahweh be witness between you and me, between your descendants and mine for ever.'

21 David then got up and left, and Jonathan went back to the town.

David and the priest at Nob

2 David then went to Nob, to Ahimelech the priest. Ahimelech came out trembling to meet David and said, 'Why are you alone? Why is nobody with you?' 3 David replied to Ahimelech the priest, 'The king has given me an order and said to me, "Do not let anyone know anything about the mission on which I am sending you, or about the order which I have given you." I have arranged to meet the guards at such and such a place. 4 Meanwhile, if you have five loaves of bread to hand, give them to me, or whatever there is.' 5 The priest replied to David, 'I have no ordinary bread to hand; there are only consecrated loaves of permanent offering—provided that the men have kept themselves from women?'

6 David replied to the priest, 'Certainly, women have been forbidden to us, as always when I set off on a campaign. The men's things are clean. Though this is a profane journey, they are certainly clean today as far as their things are concerned.' 7 The priest then gave him what had been consecrated, for the only bread there was the loaves of permanent offering, which is taken out of Yahweh's presence, to be replaced by warm bread on the day when it is removed.

8 Now one of Saul's servants happened to be there that day, detained in Yahweh's presence; his name was Doeg the Edomite and he was the strongest of Saul's shepherds.

9 David then said to Ahimelech, 'Have you no spear or sword here to hand? I did not bring either my sword or my weapons with me, because the king's business was urgent.' 10 The priest replied, 'The sword of Goliath the Philistine whom you killed in the Valley of the Terebinth is here, wrapped in a piece of clothing behind the *ephod*;[a] if you care to take it, do so, for that is the only one here.' David said, 'There is nothing like that one; give it to me.'

David with the Philistines

11 David journeyed on and that day fled out of Saul's reach, going to Achish king of Gath. 12 Achish's servants said to him, 'Is not this

21a Here either the container of the sacred lots or some object used in worship.

David, the king of the country? Was it not of him that they sang as they danced:

Saul has killed his thousands,
and David his tens of thousands?'

[13]David pondered on these words and became very frightened of Achish king of Gath. [14]When their eyes were on him, he played the madman and, when they held him, he feigned lunacy. He drummed his feet on the doors of the gate and let his spittle run down his beard.

[15]Achish said to his servants, 'You can see that this man is mad. Why bring him to me? [16]Have I not enough madmen, without your bringing me this one to weary me with his antics? Is he to join my household?'

C: DAVID THE OUTLAW

22 David left there and took refuge in the Cave of Adullam; his brothers and his father's whole family heard this and joined him there. [2]All those in distress, all those in debt, all those who had a grievance, gathered round him and he became their leader. There were about four hundred men with him.

[3]From there David went to Mizpah in Moab and said to the king of Moab, 'Allow my father and mother to stay with you until I know what God intends to do for me.' [4]He left them with the king of Moab and there they stayed all the time that David was in the stronghold.

[5]The prophet Gad, however, said to David, 'Do not stay in the stronghold; leave and make your way into the territory of Judah.' David then left and went to the forest of Hereth.

Massacre of the priests of Nob

[6]When Saul heard that David and the men with him had been discovered, Saul was at Gibeah, seated under the tamarisk on the high place, spear in hand, with all his staff standing round him. [7]'Listen, Benjaminites!' said Saul to them, 'Is the son of Jesse going to give you all fields and vineyards and make all of you commanders of thousands and commanders of hundreds [8]that you all conspire against me? No one warned me when my son made a pact with the son of Jesse; none of you felt sorry for me or warned me when my son incited my servant to become my enemy, as he is now.'

[9]Then, up spoke Doeg the Edomite, who was in command of Saul's staff, 'I saw the son of Jesse coming to Nob, to Ahimelech son of Ahitub. [10]That man consulted Yahweh on his behalf, gave him provisions and also the sword of Goliath the Philistine.' [11]The king then sent for the priest Ahimelech son of Ahitub and his whole family, the priests of Nob; they all came to the king.

[12]Saul said, 'Now listen, son of Ahitub!' He replied, 'Here I am, my lord.' [13]'Why have you conspired against me,' said Saul, 'you and the son of Jesse, giving him bread and a sword and consulting God on his behalf, for him to rebel against me as is now the case?' [14]Ahimelech replied to the king, 'Of all those in your service, who is more loyal than David son-in-law to the king, captain of your bodyguard, honoured in your household? [15]Was today the first time I ever consulted God on his behalf? Indeed it was not! The king has no grounds for bringing any charge against his servant or against his whole family, for your servant knew nothing whatever about all this.' [16]The king retorted, 'You must die, Ahimelech, you and your whole family.'

[17]The king said to the scouts who were standing round him, 'Forward! and put the priests of Yahweh to death, for they too are on David's side, they knew that he was escaping, yet did not warn me of it.' The king's professional soldiers, however, would not lift a hand to strike the priests of Yahweh. [18]The king then said to Doeg, 'Forward, you! Fall on the priests!' Doeg the Edomite stepped forward and fell on the priests, himself that day killing eighty-five men who wore the linen *ephod*. [19]Nob, the town of the priests, Saul put to the sword: men and women, children and infants, cattle, donkeys and sheep.

[20]One son of Ahimelech son of Ahitub alone escaped. His name was Abiathar, and he fled away to join David. [21]When Abiathar told David that Saul had slaughtered the priests of Yahweh, [22]David said to Abiathar, 'I knew, that day when Doeg the Edomite was there, that he would be sure to inform Saul. I am responsible for the death of all your kinsmen. [23]Stay with me, do not be afraid, for he who seeks your life seeks mine; you will be safe with me.'

David at Keilah

23 News was then brought to David, 'The Philistines are besieging Keilah and plundering the threshing-floors'. 2 David consulted Yahweh, 'Shall I go and fight these Philistines?' Yahweh replied to David, 'Go and fight the Philistines and save Keilah.' 3 But David's men said to him, 'We are already afraid here in Judah; how much more, then, if we go to Keilah to fight the Philistine troops!' 4 So David consulted Yahweh again and Yahweh replied, 'Be on your way; go down to Keilah, since I shall give the Philistines into your power.' 5 So David and his men went to Keilah and fought the Philistines and carried off their cattle and inflicted a great defeat on them. Thus David saved the inhabitants of Keilah. 6 When Abiathar son of Ahimelech took refuge with David, he went down to Keilah with the *ephod* in his hand.

7 When word was brought to Saul that David had gone to Keilah he said, 'God has delivered him into my power: he has trapped himself by going into a town with gates and bars.' 8 Saul called all the people to arms, to go down to Keilah and besiege David and his men. 9 David, however, was aware that Saul was plotting evil against him, and said to Abiathar the priest, 'Bring the *ephod*.' 10 David said, 'Yahweh, God of Israel, your servant has heard that Saul is preparing to come to Keilah and destroy the town because of me. 11 Will Saul come down as your servant has heard? Yahweh, God of Israel, I beg you, let your servant know.' Yahweh replied, 'He will come down.' 12 David then went on to ask, 'Will the notables of Keilah hand me and my men over to Saul?' Yahweh replied, 'They will hand you over.' 13 At this, David made off with his men, about six hundred in number; they left Keilah and went where they could. When Saul was told that David had escaped from Keilah, he abandoned the expedition.

14 David stayed in the desert, in the strongholds; he stayed in the mountains, in the desert of Ziph; Saul kept looking for him day after day, but God did not deliver him into his power.

David at Horesh. Visit from Jonathan

15 David was aware that Saul had mounted an expedition to take his life. David was then at Horesh in the desert of Ziph. 16 Jonathan son of Saul set off and went to David at Horesh and encouraged him in the name of God. 17 'Do not be afraid,' he said, 'for my father Saul's hand will not reach you. You are to reign over Israel, and I shall be second to you. Saul my father is himself aware of this.' 18 And the two made a pact before Yahweh. David stayed at Horesh and Jonathan went home.

David has a narrow escape from Saul

19 Some men from Ziph then went up to Saul at Gibeah and said, 'Look, David is hiding among us in the strongholds at Horesh, on the Hill of Hachilah to the south of the wastelands. 20 Now whenever you wish to go down, my lord king, do so; we shall make it our task to hand him over to the king.' 21 Saul replied, 'May you be blessed by Yahweh for sympathising with me. 22 Go and make doubly sure, find out exactly what place he frequents, for I have been told that he is very cunning. 23 Take careful note of all the hiding places where he lurks, and come back to me when you are certain. I shall then come with you and, if he is in the country, I shall track him down through every clan in Judah!'

24 Setting off they went to Ziph ahead of Saul. Meanwhile, David and his men were in the desert of Maon, in the plain to the south of the wastelands. 25 When Saul and his men set out in search, David was told and went down to the gorge running through the desert of Maon. 26 Saul and his men proceeded along one side of the mountain, David and his men along the other. David was hurrying to escape from Saul, while Saul and his men were trying to cross over to David and his men's side, to capture them, 27 when a messenger came to Saul and said, 'Come at once, the Philistines have invaded the country.' 28 So Saul broke off his pursuit of David and went to oppose the Philistines. That is why the place is called the Gorge of Separations.

David spares Saul

24 From there David went up and installed himself in the strongholds of En-Gedi. 2 Once Saul was back from pursuing the Philistines, he was told, 'David is now in the desert of En-Gedi.' 3 Saul thereupon took three thousand men selected from all Israel and went in search of David and his men east

of the Rocks of the Mountain Goats. 4He
came to the sheepfolds along the route, where
there was a cave, and went in to cover his
feet. Now David and his men were sitting in
the recesses of the cave; 5David's men said
to him, 'Today is the day of which Yahweh
said to you, "I shall deliver your enemy into
your power; do what you like with him." '
David got up and, unobserved, cut off the
border of Saul's cloak. 6Afterwards David
reproached himself for having cut off the
border of Saul's cloak. 7He said to his men,
'Yahweh preserve me from doing such a thing
to my lord as to raise my hand against him,
since he is Yahweh's anointed.' 8By these
words David restrained his men and would
not let them attack Saul.
9Saul then left the cave and went on his
way. After this, David too left the cave and
called after Saul, 'My lord king!' Saul looked
behind him and David, bowing to the
ground, prostrated himself. 10David then
said to Saul, 'Why do you listen to people
who say, "David intends your ruin"? 11This
very day you have seen for yourself how
Yahweh put you in my power in the cave and
how, refusing to kill you, I spared you saying,
"I will not raise my hand against my lord,
since he is Yahweh's anointed." 12Look,
father, look at the border of your cloak in my
hand. Since, although I cut the border off
your cloak, I did not kill you, surely you
realise that I intend neither mischief nor
crime. I have not wronged you, and yet you
hunt me down to take my life. 13May Yahweh
be judge between me and you, and may
Yahweh avenge me on you; but I shall never
lay a hand on you! 14(As the old proverb says:
Wickedness comes out of wicked people, but
I shall never lay a hand on you!) 15On whose
trail is the king of Israel campaigning? Whom
are you pursuing? On the trail of a dead dog,
of a flea! 16May Yahweh be the judge and
decide between me and you; may he examine
and defend my cause and give judgement for
me by rescuing me from your clutches!'
17When David had finished saying this to
Saul, Saul said, 'Is that your voice, my son
David?' And Saul began to weep aloud.
18'You are upright and I am not,' he said to
David, 'since you have behaved well to me,
whereas I have behaved badly to you. 19And
today you have shown how well you have
behaved to me, since Yahweh had put me in
your power but you did not kill me. 20When
a man comes on his enemy, does he let him
go unmolested? May Yahweh reward you for
the good you have done me today! 21Now I
know that you will indeed reign and that
the sovereignty in Israel will pass into your
hands. 22Now swear to me by Yahweh that
you will not suppress my descendants once I
am gone, or blot my name out of my family.'
23This David swore to Saul, and Saul went
home while David and his men went back to
the stronghold.

Death of Samuel
Story of Nabal and Abigail

25 Samuel died and all Israel assembled
to mourn for him. They buried him at
his home in Ramah.
David then set off and went down to the
desert of Maon.
2Now, there was a man in Maon whose
business was at Carmel; the man was very
rich: he owned three thousand sheep and a
thousand goats. He was then at Carmel,
having his sheep shorn. 3The man's name
was Nabal and his wife's Abigail. She was a
woman of intelligence and beauty, but the
man was miserly and churlish. He was a
Calebite.
4When David heard in the desert that
Nabal was at his sheepshearing, 5he sent ten
men off, having said to them, 'Go up to
Carmel, visit Nabal and greet him from me.
6And this is what you are to say to my brother,
"Peace to you, peace to your family, peace to
all that is yours! 7I hear that you now have
the shearers; your shepherds were with us
recently: we did not molest them, nor did
they lose anything all the while they were at
Carmel. 8Ask your young men and they will
tell you. I hope that you will give the men a
welcome, coming as we do on a festival.
Whatever you have to hand please give to
your servants and to your son David." '
9David's men went and said all this to
Nabal for David, and waited. 10Nabal
retorted to the men in David's service, 'Who
is David? Who is the son of Jesse? 11There
are many servants nowadays who run away
from their masters. Am I to take my bread
and my wine and the meat that I have slaugh-
tered for my shearers and give it to men who
come from I know not where?' 12David's men
turned on their heels and went back, and on
their arrival told him exactly what had been
said. 13David then said to his men, 'Every
man buckle on his sword!' And they buckled

on their swords, and David buckled on his
too; about four hundred followed David
while two hundred stayed with the baggage.
14 Now one of the young men told Abigail,
Nabal's wife. He said, 'David sent messen-
gers from the desert to greet our master, but
he flared up at them. 15 Now, these men were
very good to us; they did not molest us and
we lost nothing all the time we had anything
to do with them while we were out in the
country. 16 Night and day, they were like a
rampart to us, all the time we were with
them, minding the sheep. 17 So now make up
your mind what you should do, for the ruin
of our master and his whole family is a
certainty, and he is such a brute that no one
can say a word to him.'
18 Abigail hastily took two hundred loaves,
two skins of wine, five sheep ready prepared,
five measures of roasted grain, a hundred
bunches of raisins and two hundred cakes of
figs and loaded them on donkeys. 19 She said
to her servants, 'Go on ahead, I shall follow
you'—but she did not tell her husband Nabal.
20 As she was riding her donkey down
behind a fold in the mountain, David and his
men happened to be coming down in her
direction; and she met them. 21 Now, David
had decided, 'It was a waste of time my
guarding all this man's property in the desert
so that he lost nothing at all! He has repaid
me bad for good. 22 May God bring unname-
able ills on David and worse ones, too, if by
morning I leave a single manjack alive of all
who belong to him!' 23 As soon as Abigail saw
David, she quickly dismounted from the
donkey and, falling on her face in front of
David, prostrated herself on the ground.
24 She fell at his feet and said, 'Let me take
the blame, my lord. Let your servant speak
in your ear; listen to what your servant has
to say! 25 My lord, please pay no attention to
this brute Nabal[a] for his nature is like his
name; "Brute" is his name and brutal he is.
But I, your servant, did not see the men
whom my lord sent. 26 And now, my lord, as
Yahweh lives and as your soul lives, by
Yahweh who kept you from the crime of
bloodshed and from taking vengeance with
your own hand, may your enemies and all
those ill-disposed towards you become like
Nabal. 27 As for the present which your
servant has brought my lord, I should like
this to be given to the men in your service.
28 Please forgive your servant for any offence
I have given you, for Yahweh will certainly
assure you of a lasting dynasty, since you are
fighting Yahweh's battles and no fault has
been found in you throughout your life.
29 Should anyone set out to hunt you down
and try to kill you, your life will be kept close
in the wallet of life with Yahweh your God,
while your enemies' lives he will fling out of
the pouch of the sling. 30 Once Yahweh has
done for you all the good things which he has
said he will do for you, and made you ruler
of Israel, 31 you must have no anxiety, my
lord, no remorse, over having wantonly shed
blood, over having taken a revenge. When
Yahweh has done well by you, then
remember your servant.'
32 David said to Abigail, 'Blessed be
Yahweh, God of Israel, who sent you to meet
me today! 33 Blessed be your wisdom and
blessed you yourself for today having
restrained me from the crime of bloodshed
and from exacting revenge! 34 But as Yahweh,
God of Israel, lives, who prevented me from
harming you, had you not hurried out to
meet me, I swear Nabal would not have
had a single manjack left alive by morning!'
35 David then accepted what she had brought
him and said, 'Go home in peace; yes, I have
listened to you and have pardoned you.'
36 Abigail returned to Nabal. He was
holding a feast, a princely feast, in his house;
Nabal was in high spirits, and as he was very
drunk she told him nothing at all till it was
daylight. 37 In the morning, when Nabal's
wine had left him and his wife told him
everything that had happened, his heart died
within him and he became like a stone.
38 About ten days later Yahweh struck Nabal,
and he died.
39 When David heard that Nabal was dead,
he said, 'Blessed be Yahweh for having
defended my cause over the insult which I
received from Nabal, and for having
restrained his servant from doing wrong!
Yahweh has made Nabal's wickedness
rebound on his own head!'
40 David then sent Abigail an offer of
marriage. When the men in David's service
came to Abigail at Carmel, they said, 'David
has sent us to take you to him, to be his wife.'
41 She stood up, then prostrated herself on the
ground. 'Consider your servant a slave', she
said, 'to wash the feet of my lord's servants.'

25a *Nabal* =fool.

42 Quickly Abigail stood up again and
mounted a donkey; followed by five of her
servant-girls, she followed David's messen-
gers and became his wife.
43 David had also married Ahinoam of
Jezreel and he kept them both as wives. 44 Saul
had given his daughter Michal, David's wife,
to Palti son of Laish, from Gallim.

David spares Saul

26 Some men from Ziph went to Saul
at Gibeah and said, 'Look, David is
hiding on the Hill of Hachilah on the edge of
the wastelands!' 2 So Saul set off and went
down to the desert of Ziph, accompanied
by three thousand picked men of Israel, to
search for David in the desert of Ziph. 3 Saul
pitched camp on the Hill of Hachilah, which
is on the edge of the wastelands near the road.
David was then living in the desert and saw
that Saul had come after him into the desert.
4 Accordingly, David sent out spies and
learned that Saul had indeed arrived. 5 Setting
off, David went to the place where Saul had
pitched camp. He saw the place where Saul
and Abner son of Ner, commander of his
army, had bedded down. Saul had bedded
down inside the camp with the troops bivou-
acking round him.
6 Speaking to Ahimelech the Hittite and
Abishai son of Zeruiah and brother of Joab,
David said, 'Who will come down with me
to the camp, to Saul?' Abishai answered, 'I
will go down with you.' 7 So in the dark David
and Abishai made their way towards the
force, where they found Saul lying asleep
inside the camp, his spear stuck in the ground
beside his head, with Abner and the troops
lying round him.
8 Abishai then said to David, 'Today God
has put your enemy in your power; so now
let me pin him to the ground with his own
spear. Just one stroke! I shall not need to
strike him twice.' 9 David said to Abishai,
'Do not kill him, for who could raise his hand
against Yahweh's anointed and go unpun-
ished? 10 As Yahweh lives,' David said,
'Yahweh himself will strike him down: either
the day will come for him to die, or he will
go into battle and perish then. 11 Yahweh
forbid that I should raise my hand against
Yahweh's anointed! But now let us take the
spear beside his head and the pitcher of water,
and let us go away.'
12 David took the spear and the pitcher of
water from beside Saul's head, and they made
off. No one saw, no one knew, no one woke
up; they were all asleep, because a torpor
from Yahweh had fallen on them.
13 David crossed to the other side and halted
on the top of the mountain a long way off;
there was a wide space between them.
14 David then called out to the troops and to
Abner son of Ner, 'Abner, why don't you
answer?' Abner replied, 'Who is that calling?'
15 David said to Abner, 'Are you not a man?
Who is your equal in Israel? Why, then, did
you not guard the king your lord? One of the
people came to kill the king your lord. 16 What
you did was not well done. As Yahweh lives,
you all deserve to die since you did not guard
your lord, Yahweh's anointed. Look where
the king's spear is now, and the pitcher of
water which was beside his head!'
17 Recognising David's voice, Saul said,
'Is that your voice, my son David?' David
replied, 'It is my voice, my lord king. 18 Why
is my lord pursuing his servant?' he said.
'What have I done? What crime have I
committed? 19 May my lord king now listen
to his servant's words: if Yahweh has incited
you against me, may he be appeased with an
offering; but if human beings have done it,
may they be accursed before Yahweh, since
they have as effectively banished me today
from sharing in Yahweh's heritage as if they
had said, "Go and serve other gods!" 20 So I
pray now that my blood shall not be shed on
soil remote from Yahweh's presence, when
the king of Israel has mounted an expedition
to take my life, as one might hunt a partridge
in the mountains!'
21 Saul replied, 'I have done wrong! Come
back, my son David; I shall never harm you
again, since today you have shown respect
for my life. Yes, I have behaved like a fool, I
have been profoundly in the wrong.' 22 In
reply, David said, 'Here is the king's spear.
Let one of the men come across and get it.
23 May Yahweh reward each as each has been
upright and loyal. Today Yahweh put you in
my power but I would not raise my hand
against Yahweh's anointed. 24 As today I set
great value by your life, so may Yahweh
set great value by my life and deliver me from
every tribulation!'
25 Saul then said, 'May you be blessed, my
son David! In what you undertake, you will
certainly succeed.' David then went on his
way and Saul returned home.

D: DAVID AMONG THE PHILISTINES

David takes refuge at Gath

27 'One of these days,' David thought, 'I
shall perish at the hand of Saul. The
best thing that I can do is to get away into the
country of the Philistines; then Saul will
give up tracking me through the length and
breadth of Israel and I shall be safe from
him.' [2]So David set off and went over, he and
his six hundred men, to Achish son of Maoch,
king of Gath. [3]He settled at Gath with Achish,
he and his men, each with his family and
David with his two wives, Ahinoam of
Jezreel and Abigail widow of Nabal of Car-
mel. [4]When news reached Saul that David
had fled to Gath, he stopped searching for
him.

David as vassal of the Philistines

[5]David said to Achish, 'If I have won your
favour, let me be given a place in one of the
outlying towns, where I can live. Why should
your servant live in the royal city with you?'
[6]That very day Achish gave him Ziklag; and
this is why Ziklag has been the property of
the kings of Judah to the present day. [7]The
time that David stayed in Philistine territory
amounted to a year and four months.

[8]David and his men went out on raids
against the Geshurites, Girzites and Amalek-
ites, for these are the tribes inhabiting the
region which, from Telam, goes in the direc-
tion of Shur, as far as Egypt. [9]David laid the
countryside waste and left neither man nor
woman alive; he carried off the sheep and
cattle, the donkeys, camels and clothing, and
then came back again to Achish. [10]Achish
would ask, 'Where did you go raiding today?'
David would reply, 'Against the Negeb of
Judah,' or 'the Negeb of Jerahmeel,' or 'the
Negeb of the Kenites.' [11]David spared
neither man nor woman to bring back alive
to Gath, 'in case', as he thought, 'they inform
on us and say, "David did such and such." '
This was the way David conducted his raids
all the time he stayed in Philistine territory.
[12]Achish trusted David. 'He has made
himself detested by his own people Israel,'
he thought, 'and so will be my servant for
ever.'

The Philistines go to war with Israel

28 It then happened that the Philistines
mustered their forces for war, to fight
Israel, and Achish said to David, 'It is under-
stood that you and your men go into battle
with me.' [2]David said to Achish, 'In that
case, you will soon see what your servant can
do.' Achish replied to David, 'Right, I shall
appoint you as my permanent bodyguard.'

Saul and the witch of En-Dor

[3]Now Samuel was dead, and all Israel had
mourned him and buried him at Ramah, his
own town. Saul had expelled the necroman-
cers and wizards from the country.

[4]Meanwhile the Philistines had mustered
and had come and pitched camp at Shunem.
Saul mustered all Israel and they encamped
at Gilboa. [5]When Saul saw the Philistine
camp, he was afraid and his heart trembled
violently. [6]Saul consulted Yahweh, but
Yahweh gave him no answer, either by
dream, divination or prophet. [7]Saul then said
to his servants, 'Find a necromancer for me,
so that I can go and consult her.' His servants
replied, 'There is a necromancer at En-Dor.'
[8]And so Saul, disguising himself and
changing his clothes, set out accompanied by
two men; their visit to the woman took place
at night. 'Disclose the future to me', he said,
'by means of a ghost. Conjure up the one I
shall name to you.' [9]The woman replied,
'Look, you know what Saul has done, how
he has outlawed necromancers and wizards
from the country; why are you setting a trap
for my life, then, to have me killed?' [10]But
Saul swore to her by Yahweh, 'As Yahweh
lives,' he said, 'no blame shall attach to
you for this business.' [11]The woman asked,
'Whom shall I conjure up for you?' He
replied, 'Conjure up Samuel.'

[12]The woman then saw Samuel and, giving
a great cry, she said to Saul, 'Why have you
deceived me? You are Saul!' [13]The king said,
'Do not be afraid! What do you see?' The
woman replied to Saul, 'I see a ghost rising
from the earth.' [14]'What is he like?' he asked.
She replied, 'It is an old man coming up; he
is wrapped in a cloak.' Saul then knew that
it was Samuel and, bowing to the ground,
prostrated himself.

[15]Samuel said to Saul, 'Why have you
disturbed my rest by conjuring me up?' Saul
replied, 'I am in great distress; the Philistines

are waging war on me, and God has aban-
doned me and no longer answers me either
by prophet or by dream; and so I have
summoned you to tell me what I ought to
do.' 16 Samuel said, 'Why consult me, when
Yahweh has abandoned you and has become
your enemy? 17 Yahweh has treated you as he
foretold through me; he has snatched the
sovereignty from your hand and given it
to your neighbour, David, 18 because you
disobeyed Yahweh's voice and did not
execute his fierce anger against Amalek. That
is why Yahweh is treating you like this today.
19 What is more, Yahweh will deliver Israel
and you too, into the power of the Philistines.
Tomorrow you and your sons will be with
me; and Yahweh will hand over the army of
Israel into the power of the Philistines.'

20 Immediately Saul fell full length on the
ground. He was terrified by what Samuel had
said and was also weak from having eaten
nothing all that day and night. 21 The woman
went to Saul and, seeing his terror, said,
'Look, your servant has obeyed your order;
I have taken my life in my hands and obeyed
the command which you gave me. 22 Now
please, you in your turn listen to what your
servant has to say. Let me offer you a piece
of bread. Eat something and get some
strength for your journey.' 23 But he refused.
'I will not eat,' he said. His servants however
pressed him, and so did the woman. Allowing
himself to be persuaded by them, he got up
from the ground and sat on the bed. 24 The
woman owned a fattened calf which she
quickly slaughtered, and she took some flour
and kneaded it and with it baked some
unleavened cakes 25 which she served to Saul
and his servants; they ate, and then set off
and left the same night.

David is sent away by the Philistine leaders

29 The Philistines mustered all their
forces at Aphek while the Israelites
pitched camp near the spring in Jezreel. 2 The
Philistine commanders marched past with
their hundreds and their thousands, and
David and his men brought up the rear with
Achish. 3 The Philistine chiefs asked, 'What
are these Hebrews doing?' Achish replied to
them, 'Why, this is David the servant of Saul,
king of Israel, who has been with me for the
last year or two. I have had no fault to find
with him from the day he gave himself up to
me until the present time.' 4 But the Philistine
chiefs were angry with him. 'Send the man
back,' they said, 'make him go back to the
place which you assigned to him. He cannot
go into battle with us, in case he turns on us
once battle is joined. Would there be a better
way for the man to regain his master's favour
than with the heads of these men here? 5 Is
not this the David of whom they sang as they
danced:

Saul has killed his thousands,
and David his tens of thousands'?

6 So Achish called David and said, 'As
Yahweh lives, you are loyal, and I am quite
content with all your doings in our
campaigning together, since I have found no
fault with you from the day you came to
me until the present time. But you are not
acceptable to the chiefs. 7 So go home, in
peace, rather than antagonise them.'

8 'But what have I done,' David asked
Achish, 'what fault have you had to find with
your servant from the day I entered your
service to the present time, for me not to be
allowed to go and fight the enemies of my
lord the king?' 9 In reply, Achish said to
David, 'In my opinion, it is true, you are as
good as an angel of God; but the Philistine
chiefs have said, "He must not go into battle
with us." 10 So get up early tomorrow
morning, with your master's servants who
came with you, and go to the place which I
assigned to you. Do not harbour resentment,
since personally I have no fault to find with
you. Get up early tomorrow morning and, as
soon as it is light, be off.'

11 So David and his men got up early to
leave at dawn and go back to Philistine terri-
tory. And the Philistines marched on Jezreel.

Reprisals against the Amalekites

30 Now by the time David and his men
reached Ziklag three days later, the
Amalekites had raided the Negeb and Ziklag;
they had sacked Ziklag and burnt it down.
2 They had taken the women prisoner, and
everyone who was there, both small and
great. They had not killed anyone, but had
carried them off and gone away. 3 When
David and his men arrived, they found the
town burnt down and their wives and sons
and daughters taken captive. 4 Then David
and the people with him wept aloud till they
were too weak to weep any more. 5 David's
two wives had been captured: Ahinoam of

Jezreel and Abigail widow of Nabal of
Carmel.
6 David was in great trouble, since the
people were talking of stoning him; the
people all felt very bitter, each man for his
own sons and daughters. But David took
courage from Yahweh his God. 7 To the priest
Abiathar son of Ahimelech, David said,
'Bring me the *ephod*.' Abiathar brought the
ephod to David. 8 David then consulted
Yahweh, 'Shall I go in pursuit of these
raiders? Will I overtake them?' The answer
was, 'Go in pursuit; you will certainly over-
take them and rescue the captives.' 9 David
accordingly set off with the six hundred men
who were with him and reached the torrent
of Besor. 10 David then continued the pursuit
with four hundred men, two hundred staying
behind who were too exhausted to cross the
torrent of Besor.
11 Out in the country they found an Egyp-
tian and brought him to David. They gave
him some bread to eat and some water to
drink; 12 they also gave him a piece of fig cake
and two bunches of raisins; he ate these and
his spirits revived—he had had nothing to
eat or drink for three days and three nights.
13 David then said to him, 'Whose man are you
and where do you come from?' He replied,
'I am a young Egyptian, the slave of an
Amalekite; my master abandoned me
because I fell sick three days ago. 14 We raided
the Negeb of the Cherethites, and the Negeb
of Judah, and the Negeb of Caleb too, and
we burnt Ziklag down.' 15 David said, 'Will
you guide me to these raiders?' He replied,
'Swear to me by God not to kill me or hand
me over to my master, and I will guide you
to these raiders.'
16 He guided him to them, and there they
were, scattered over the whole countryside,
eating, drinking and celebrating, on account
of the enormous booty which they had
brought back from the territory of the Phili-
stines and the territory of Judah. 17 David
slaughtered them from dawn until the
evening of the following day. No one escaped,
except four hundred young men who
mounted camels and fled. 18 He rescued
everything that the Amalekites had taken—
David also rescued his two wives. 19 Nothing
of theirs was lost, whether small or great,
from the booty or sons and daughters—
everything that had been taken from them;
David recovered everything. 20 They
captured the flocks and herds as well and
drove them in front of him. 'This is David's
booty,' they shouted.
21 When David reached the two hundred
men who had been too exhausted to follow
him and whom he had left at the torrent of
Besor, they came out to meet David and the
party accompanying him; David approached
with his party and greeted them. 22 But all the
rogues and scoundrels among the men who
had gone with David began saying, 'Since
they did not go with us, we shall not give
them any of the booty which we have rescued,
except that each of them can have his wife
and children. Let them take them away and
be off.' 23 But David said, 'Do not behave like
this, brothers, with what Yahweh has given
us; he has protected us and has handed over
to us the raiders who attacked us. 24 Who
would agree with you on this? No:

As the share of the man
who goes into battle,
so is the share of the man
who stays with the baggage.

They will share alike.' 25 And from that day
on, he made that a rule and custom for Israel,
which obtains to the present day.
26 When David reached Ziklag, he sent
parts of the booty to the elders of Judah,
town by town, with this message, 'Here is a
present for you, taken from the booty of
Yahweh's enemies':

27 to those in Bethel,
to those in Ramoth of the Negeb,
28 to those in Jattir,
to those in Aroer,
to those in Siphmoth,
to those in Eshtemoa,
29 to those in Carmel,
to those in the towns of Jerahmeel,
to those in the towns of the Kenites,
30 to those in Hormah,
to those in Borashan,
to those in Athach,
31 to those in Hebron

and to all the places which David and his men
had frequented.

Battle of Mount Gilboa and death of Saul

31 The Philistines gave battle to Israel,
and the Israelites, fleeing from the
Philistines, fell and were slaughtered on
Mount Gilboa. 2 The Philistines bore down on
Saul and his sons, and they killed Jonathan,

Abinadab and Malchishua, Saul's sons. [3]The fighting grew fiercer round Saul; the archers came upon him, and he was severely wounded [4]by the archers. Saul then said to his armour-bearer, 'Draw your sword and run me through with it; I do not want these uncircumcised men to come and make fun of me.' But his armour-bearer was very much afraid and would not do it. So Saul took his own sword and fell on it. [5]His armour-bearer, seeing that Saul was dead, fell on his sword too and died with him. [6]Thus died Saul, his three sons and his armour-bearer, together on the same day. [7]When the Israelites who were on the other side of the Jordan saw that the Israelites had been routed and that Saul and his sons were dead, they abandoned their towns and fled. The Philistines then came and occupied them.

[8]When the Philistines came on the following day to strip the dead, they found Saul and his three sons lying on Mount Gilboa. [9]They cut off his head and, stripping him of his armour, had these carried round the territory of the Philistines to proclaim the good news to their idols and their people. [10]They put his armour in the temple of Astarte; and his body they fastened to the walls of Beth-Shean.

[11]When the inhabitants of Jabesh in Gilead heard what the Philistines had done to Saul, [12]the warriors all set out and, having marched all night, took the bodies of Saul and his sons off the walls of Beth-Shean; they brought them to Jabesh and burned them there. [13]They then took their bones and buried them under the tamarisk of Jabesh, and fasted for seven days.

THE SECOND BOOK OF SAMUEL

David learns of Saul's death

1 Saul was dead and David, returning after his victory over the Amalekites, had been at Ziklag for two days. [2]On the third day, a man arrived from Saul's camp with his clothes torn and earth on his head. When he came to David, he fell to the ground and prostrated himself. [3]David asked him, 'Where have you come from?' 'I have escaped from the Israelite camp,' he said. [4]David said, 'What has happened? Tell me.' He replied, 'The people fled from the battle, and many of them have fallen and are dead. Saul and his son Jonathan are dead too.'

[5]Then David asked the young man who brought the news, 'How do you know that Saul and his son Jonathan are dead?' [6]The young man replied, 'I happened to be on Mount Gilboa, and there was Saul, leaning on his spear, with the chariots and the cavalry bearing down on him. [7]Glancing behind him and seeing me, he shouted to me. I replied, "Here I am!" [8]He said, "Who are you?" I replied, "I am an Amalekite." [9]He then said, "Come here and kill me. My head is swimming, although I still have all my strength." [10]So I went over to him and killed him, because I knew that once he fell he could not survive. I then took the crown which he had on his head and the bracelet on his arm, and have brought them here to my lord.'

[11]David then took hold of his clothes and tore them, and all the men with him did the same. [12]They mourned and wept and fasted until the evening for Saul and his son Jonathan, for the people of Yahweh and for the House of Israel, because they had fallen by the sword.

[13]David said to the young man who had brought the news, 'Where are you from?' He replied, 'I am the son of a resident foreigner, an Amalekite.' [14]David said, 'How was it that you were not afraid to lift your hand to destroy Yahweh's anointed?' [15]Then David called one of the young men. 'Come here,' he said, 'strike him down.' The man struck him and he died. [16]David said, 'Your blood be on your own head. You convicted yourself out of your own mouth by saying, "I killed Yahweh's anointed." '

David's elegy over Saul and Jonathan

[17]David sang the following lament over Saul and his son Jonathan [18](it is for teaching

archery to the children of Judah; it is written in the Book of the Just):[a]

[19]Does the splendour of Israel
lie dead on your heights?
How did the heroes fall?

[20]Do not speak of it in Gath,
nor broadcast it in the streets of Ashkelon,
for fear the daughters
of the Philistines rejoice,
for fear the daughters
of the uncircumcised gloat.

[21]You mountains of Gilboa,
no dew, no rain fall on you,
O treacherous fields
where the heroes' shield lies dishonoured!

Not greased with oil, the shield of Saul,
[22]but with the blood of wounded men,
the fat of warriors!
The bow of Jonathan never turned back,
the sword of Saul
never came home unsated!

[23]Saul and Jonathan,
beloved and handsome,
were divided neither in life, nor in death.
Swifter than eagles were they,
stronger than lions.

[24]O daughters of Israel, weep for Saul
who gave you scarlet
and fine linen to wear,
who pinned golden jewellery
on your dresses!

[25]How did the heroes fall
in the thick of the battle?

Jonathan, by your dying I too am stricken,
[26]I am desolate for you,
Jonathan my brother.
Very dear you were to me,
your love more wonderful to me
than the love of a woman.

[27]How did the heroes fall
and the weapons of war succumb!

I: DAVID

A: DAVID KING OF JUDAH

David consecrated king at Hebron

2 After this David consulted Yahweh, asking, 'Shall I go up to one of the towns of Judah?' Yahweh replied, 'Go up!' 'Which one shall I go to?' David asked. 'To Hebron,' was the reply. [2]So David went up, with his two wives Ahinoam of Jezreel and Abigail widow of Nabal of Carmel. [3]In addition David brought up the men who were with him, each with his family, and they settled in the towns of Hebron. [4]The men of Judah came, and there they anointed David as king of the House of Judah.

David's message to the people of Jabesh

They told David that the people of Jabesh in Gilead had given Saul burial, [5]so David sent messengers to the people of Jabesh in Gilead. 'May you be blessed by Yahweh,' he said, 'for showing this faithful love to Saul your lord, and for burying him. [6]And now may Yahweh show faithful love and constancy towards you! I too shall treat you well because you have done this. [7]And now take courage and be men of valour. Saul your lord is dead, but the House of Judah has anointed me to be their king.'

Abner imposes Ishbaal as king of Israel

[8]Abner son of Ner, Saul's army commander, had taken Ishbaal son of Saul and brought him over to Mahanaim. [9]He had made him king of Gilead, of the Asherites, of Jezreel, of Ephraim, of Benjamin and indeed of all Israel. [10]Ishbaal son of Saul was forty years old when he became king of Israel, and he reigned for two years. Only the House of Judah supported David. [11]The length of David's reign over Judah in Hebron was seven years and six months.

War between Israel and Judah
The battle of Gibeon

[12]Abner son of Ner, with the retainers of Ishbaal son of Saul, marched out from

1a Poetry from this book is quoted elsewhere too in the Bible.

Mahanaim to Gibeon. 13 Joab son of Zeruiah, with David's retainers, also took the field, encountering them at the pool of Gibeon. There they halted, one party on one side of the pool, and the other opposite.

14 Abner then said to Joab, 'Let the men come forward and fight it out between us!' Joab replied, 'Let them come forward.' 15 So they came forward and were numbered off, twelve from Benjamin for Ishbaal son of Saul, and twelve of David's retainers. 16 Each caught his opponent by the head and drove his sword into his side; and thus they all fell together. Hence the place was called the Field of Sides; it is at Gibeon.

17 That day a very fierce battle took place, and Abner and the men of Israel were beaten by David's retainers. 18 The three sons of Zeruiah were there, Joab, Abishai, and Asahel. Now Asahel could run like a wild gazelle. 19 Asahel chased Abner, not swerving to the right or left from pursuing him. 20 Abner turned and said, 'Asahel, is that you?' He replied, 'It is.' 21 Abner said, 'Turn to your right or your left, catch one of the men and take his spoil!' But Asahel would not break off the pursuit. 22 Again Abner spoke to Asahel, 'Stop following me, unless you want me to strike you to the ground; and then how could I look your brother Joab in the face?' 23 But he refused to be diverted, so Abner struck him in the belly with the butt of his spear so that the shaft came out through his back; and he fell at his feet and died on the spot. On coming to the place where Asahel had fallen and died, everyone halted.

24 Joab and Abishai took up the pursuit of Abner and at sunset reached the Hill of Ammah, which is to the east of Giah on the road through the desert of Gibeon. 25 The Benjaminites gathered in close formation behind Abner and halted on the top of a hill. 26 Abner called out to Joab, 'Is the sword to go on devouring for ever? Surely you see that this can only end in bitterness? How long will it be before you order those people to stop pursuing their brothers?' 27 Joab replied, 'As Yahweh lives, if you had not spoken, these men would not have given up the pursuit of their brothers until morning.' 28 Joab then sounded the trumpet and all the troops halted; they pursued Israel no further and fought no more.

29 All that night Abner and his men made their way through the Arabah; they crossed the Jordan and, marching throughout the morning, came to Mahanaim. 30 Joab, having stopped pursuing Abner, mustered the whole contingent; David's retainers had lost nineteen men in addition to Asahel, 31 but had killed three hundred and sixty of Benjamin, Abner's men. 32 They took up Asahel and buried him in his father's tomb, which is at Bethlehem. Joab and his men then marched throughout the night, reaching Hebron at daybreak.

3 So the war dragged on between the House of Saul and the House of David, but David grew steadily stronger and the House of Saul steadily weaker.

The sons born to David at Hebron

2 The sons born to David at Hebron were: his first-born Amnon, by Ahinoam of Jezreel; 3 his second Chileab, by Abigail widow of Nabal of Carmel; the third Absalom son of Maacah, daughter of Talmai king of Geshur; 4 the fourth Adonijah son of Haggith; the fifth Shephatiah son of Abital; 5 the sixth Ithream, by David's wife, Eglah. These were born to David at Hebron.

The rift between Abner and Ishbaal

6 This is what took place during the war between the House of Saul and the House of David. Abner took complete control in the House of Saul. 7 Now, there was a concubine of Saul's called Rizpah daughter of Aiah, and Abner took her. Ishbaal said to Abner, 'Why have you slept with my father's concubine?' 8 At these words of Ishbaal, Abner flew into a rage. 'Am I a dog's head?' he shouted. 'Here am I, full of faithful love towards the House of Saul your father, his brothers and his friends, not leaving you to the hands of David, and now you find fault with me over a woman! 9 May God bring unnameable ills on Abner, and worse ones, too, if I do not bring about what Yahweh has sworn to David: 10 to take the sovereignty from the House of Saul, and establish David's throne over Israel as well as Judah, from Dan to Beersheba!' 11 Ishbaal dared not say a single word to Abner in reply, as he was afraid of him.

Abner negotiates with David

12 Abner sent messengers on his own behalf
to say to David, '. . . and furthermore, come
to an agreement with me and I will give you
my support to win all Israel over to you.'
13 'Very well,' David said, 'I will come to an
agreement with you. I impose one condition
however; you will not be admitted to my
presence unless you bring me Michal, Saul's
daughter, when you come to see me.' 14 David
then sent messengers to say to Ishbaal son of
Saul, 'Give me back my wife Michal, whom
I acquired for a hundred foreskins of the
Philistines.' 15 So Ishbaal sent for her to be
taken from her husband Paltiel son of Laish.
16 Her husband set off with her and followed
her, weeping as he went, as far as Bahurim;
but Abner said to him, 'Go back!' and he
went.

17 Now Abner conferred with the elders of
Israel. 'For a long time now,' he said, 'you
have wanted David as your king. 18 Now you
must take action, since Yahweh has said of
David, "By the hand of my servant David
I shall deliver my people Israel from the
clutches of the Philistines and all their
enemies." ' 19 Abner also spoke to the men of
Benjamin and then went to Hebron to tell
David everything that had been agreed by
Israel and the House of Benjamin.

20 Abner, accompanied by twenty men,
came to David at Hebron, and David held a
feast for Abner and the men who were with
him. 21 Abner then said to David, 'I must get
up and go. I am going to rally all Israel to my
lord the king, so that they will make an
alliance with you, and you will reign over all
that you desire.' So David allowed Abner to
go, and he went unmolested.

The murder of Abner

22 David's retainers were just then coming
back with Joab from a raid, bringing a great
quantity of booty with them. Abner was no
longer with David at Hebron, since David
had allowed him to go, and he had gone
unmolested. 23 When Joab and the whole
company with him had arrived, Joab was
told, 'Abner son of Ner has been to the king,
and the king has allowed Abner to go away
unmolested.' 24 Joab then went to the king
and said, 'What have you done? Abner comes
to you and you let him go away and now he
has gone—why? 25 You know Abner son of
Ner! He came to trick you, to discover
your every move, to find out what you
are doing.'

26 Joab left David's presence and sent mess-
engers after Abner and these, unknown to
David, brought him back from the storage-
well at Sirah. 27 When Abner reached
Hebron, Joab took him aside in the town-
gate, as if to have a quiet word with him, and
there struck him a mortal blow in the belly
to avenge the blood of his brother Asahel.
28 Afterwards, when David heard of this, he
said, 'I and my kingdom are for ever innocent
before Yahweh of the blood of Abner son of
Ner; 29 may it fall on the head of Joab and on
all his family! May the House of Joab never
be free of men afflicted with haemorrhage or
a virulent skin-disease, whose strength is in
the distaff, who fall by the sword, who lack
food.' 30 (Joab and his brother Abishai had
murdered Abner because he killed their
brother Asahel at the battle of Gibeon.)
31 David then said to Joab and the whole
company with him, 'Tear your clothes, put
on sackcloth, and mourn over Abner,' and
King David walked behind the bier. 32 They
buried Abner at Hebron, and the king wept
aloud on his grave, and the people all wept
too. 33 The king made this lament over
Abner:

Should Abner have died as a brute dies?
34 Your hands were not tied,
    your feet not chained;
you fell as a man falls
    at the hands of criminals.

And all the people wept for him louder than
ever.

35 The people then all tried to persuade
David to have some food while it was still
daylight, but David swore this oath, 'May
God bring unnameable ills on me, and worse
ills, too, if I taste bread or anything whatever
until the sun is down!' 36 All the people took
note of this and it pleased them; indeed,
everything the king did pleased the people.
37 That day, all the people and all Israel under-
stood that the king had had no part in the
murder of Abner son of Ner.

38 The king said to his retainers, 'Do you
not realise that a prince, a great man, has
fallen in Israel today? 39 I, though anointed
king, am weak at present, and these men, the
sons of Zeruiah, are too strong for me. May
Yahweh repay the criminal as his crime
deserves!'

The murder of Ishbaal

4 When Saul's son heard that Abner had
died at Hebron, his heart failed him, and
all Israel was alarmed. 2Now, Saul's son had
two freebooting chieftains; one was called
Baanah, the other Rechab. They were the
sons of Rimmon of Beeroth, and Ben-
jaminites—for Beeroth is regarded as
belonging to Benjamin. 3The people of Beer-
oth had taken refuge in Gittaim, where they
have remained to this day as resident
foreigners.
4Jonathan son of Saul had a son with
crippled feet. He was five years old when the
news about Saul and Jonathan came from
Jezreel. His nurse picked him up and fled
but, as she hurried away, he fell and was
lamed. His name was Meribbaal.
5The sons of Rimmon of Beeroth, Rechab
and Baanah, set out; they came to Ishbaal's
house at the hottest part of the day when he
was taking his midday rest. 6The woman who
kept the door had been cleaning wheat and
had drowsed off to sleep. 7Rechab and his
brother Baanah stole past her and entered
the house, where he was lying on his bed in
his bedroom. They struck him and killed
him, then cut off his head and, taking the
head with them, travelled all night by way of
the Arabah. 8They brought Ishbaal's head to
David at Hebron. 'Here', they said to the
king, 'is the head of Ishbaal son of Saul, your
enemy, who meant to take your life. Yahweh
has avenged my lord the king today on Saul
and on his offspring.'
9But David answered Rechab and his
brother Baanah, the sons of Rimmon, by
saying, 'As Yahweh lives, who has rescued
me from every danger, 10when someone told
me, "Saul is dead!" supposing himself to be
bringing me good news, I seized and put
him to death at Ziklag, and that was how I
rewarded him for his news! 11How much
more when bandits have killed an upright
man in his house, and on his bed! Am I not
to demand an account of his blood from you,
and rid the earth of you?' 12David then gave
an order to the men, who put them to death,
cut off their hands and feet, and hung them
up beside the pool of Hebron. Ishbaal's head
they took and buried in Abner's grave at
Hebron.

B: DAVID KING OF JUDAH AND OF ISRAEL

David is anointed king of Israel

5 All the tribes of Israel then came to David
at Hebron and said, 'Look, we are your
own flesh and bone. 2In days past when Saul
was our king, it was you who led Israel on its
campaigns, and to you it was that Yahweh
promised, "You are to shepherd my people
Israel and be leader of Israel." ' 3So all the
elders of Israel came to the king at Hebron,
and King David made a pact with them
in Yahweh's presence at Hebron, and they
anointed David as king of Israel.
4David was thirty years old when he
became king, and he reigned for forty years.
5In Hebron he reigned over Judah for seven
years and six months; then he reigned in
Jerusalem over all Israel and Judah for thirty-
three years.

The capture of Jerusalem

6The king and his men then marched on
Jerusalem, on the Jebusites living in the
territory. These said to David, 'You will not
get in here. The blind and the lame will hold
you off.' (That is to say: David will never get
in here.) 7But David captured the citadel of
Zion, that is, the City of David. 8That day,
David said, 'Whoever gets up the tunnel and
kills a Jebusite . . .'[a] As for the blind and
the lame, David hated them with his whole
being. (Hence the saying: the blind and the
lame may not enter the Temple.) 9David
went to live in the citadel and called it the
City of David. David then built a wall round
it, from the Millo inwards. 10David grew
stronger and stronger, and Yahweh, God of
Sabaoth, was with him.
11Hiram king of Tyre sent envoys to
David, with cedar wood, carpenters and
stone-cutters, who built David a palace.
12David then knew that Yahweh had con-
firmed him as king of Israel and, for the
sake of his people Israel, had extended his
sovereignty.

The sons born to David in Jerusalem

13After coming from Hebron, David took
other concubines and wives in Jerusalem,
and sons and daughters were born to him.

5a The sentence breaks off. The tunnel, a secret passage from the spring to the interior of the city, still exists.

[14]These are the names of those born to him in Jerusalem: Shammua, Shobab, Nathan, Solomon, [15]Ibhar, Elishua, Nepheg, Japhia, [16]Elishama, Eliada, Eliphelet.

Victory over the Philistines

[17]When the Philistines heard that David had been anointed as king of Israel, they all went up to seek him out. On hearing this, David went down to the stronghold. [18]When the Philistines arrived, they deployed in the Valley of the Rephaim. [19]David consulted Yahweh and asked, 'Shall I attack the Philistines? Will you deliver them into my power?' Yahweh replied to David, 'Attack! I shall certainly deliver the Philistines into your power.' [20]Accordingly, David went to Baal-Perazim and there David defeated them. He said, 'Yahweh has made a breach in my enemies for me, as though they had been breached by a flood.' This is why the place was given the name Baal-Perazim. [21]They had left their gods behind them there, and David and his men carried them off.

[22]Again the Philistines invaded and deployed in the Valley of the Rephaim. [23]David consulted Yahweh, who replied, 'Do not attack them from the front; go round to their rear and engage them opposite the balsam trees. [24]When you hear the sound of footsteps in the tops of the balsam trees, advance, for that will be Yahweh going out ahead of you to defeat the Philistine army.' [25]David did as Yahweh had ordered and beat the Philistines from Gibeon to the Pass of Gezer.

The ark in Jerusalem

6 David again mustered all the picked troops of Israel, thirty thousand men. [2]Setting off with the whole force then with him, David went to Baalah of Judah, from there to bring up the ark of God, who bears the title 'Yahweh Sabaoth, enthroned on the winged creatures'. [3]They transported the ark of God on a new cart and brought it out of Abinadab's house which is on the hill. Uzzah and Ahio, the sons of Abinadab, drove the cart, [4]Uzzah walked alongside the ark of God and Ahio went in front. [5]David and the whole House of Israel danced before Yahweh with all their might, singing to the accompaniment of harps, lyres, tambourines, sistrums and cymbals. [6]When they came to Nacon's threshing-floor, Uzzah reached his hand out to the ark of God and steadied it, as the oxen were making it tilt. [7]This roused Yahweh's anger against Uzzah, and for this crime God struck him down on the spot, and there he died beside the ark of God. [8]David resented Yahweh's having broken out against Uzzah, and the place was given the name Perez-Uzzah,[a] which it still has today.

[9]That day David felt afraid of Yahweh. 'How can the ark of Yahweh come to be with me?' he said. [10]So David decided not to take the ark of Yahweh with him into the city of David but diverted it to the house of Obed-Edom of Gath. [11]The ark of Yahweh remained in the house of Obed-Edom of Gath for three months, and Yahweh blessed Obed-Edom and his whole family.

[12]King David was informed that Yahweh had blessed Obed-Edom's family and everything belonging to him on account of the ark of God. David accordingly went and, amid great rejoicing, brought the ark of God up from Obed-Edom's house to the City of David. [13]When the bearers of the ark of Yahweh had gone six paces, he sacrificed an ox and a fat sheep. [14]And David danced whirling round before Yahweh with all his might, wearing a linen loincloth. [15]Thus with war cries and blasts on the horn, David and the entire House of Israel brought up the ark of Yahweh. [16]Now as the ark of Yahweh entered the City of David, Michal daughter of Saul was watching from the window and when she saw King David leaping and whirling round before Yahweh, the sight of him filled her with contempt. [17]They brought the ark of Yahweh in and put it in position, inside the tent which David had erected for it; and David presented burnt offerings and communion sacrifices in Yahweh's presence. [18]And when David had finished presenting burnt offerings, he blessed the people in the name of Yahweh Sabaoth. [19]To all the people, to the whole multitude of Israelites, men and women, he then distributed to each a loaf of bread, a portion of dates and a raisin cake. Then the people all went back to their homes.

[20]As David was coming back to bless his household, Michal daughter of Saul came out to meet him. 'Much honour the king of Israel has won today,' she said, 'making an

6a 'Uzzah's Breach', a popular explanation of the name.

exhibition of himself under the eyes of his
servant-maids, making an exhibition of
himself like a buffoon!' 21 David replied to
Michal, 'I was dancing for Yahweh, not for
them. As Yahweh lives, who chose me in
preference to your father and his whole family
to make me leader of Israel, Yahweh's people,
I shall dance before Yahweh and 22 lower
myself even further than that. In your eyes I
may be base, but by the maids you speak of,
by them, I shall be held in honour!' 23 And to
the day of her death, Michal, daughter of
Saul, had no children.

Nathan's prophecy

7 Once the king had settled into his palace
and Yahweh had granted him rest from
all the enemies surrounding him, 2 the king
said to the prophet Nathan, 'Look, I am
living in a cedar-wood palace, while the ark
of God is under awnings.' 3 Nathan said to
the king, 'Go and do whatever you have in
mind, for Yahweh is with you.'
4 But that very night, the word of Yahweh
came to Nathan:
5 'Go and tell my servant David, "Yahweh
says this: Are you to build me a temple for
me to live in? 6 I have never lived in a house
from the day when I brought the Israelites
out of Egypt until today, but have kept
travelling with a tent for shelter. 7 In all my
travels with all the Israelites, did I say to
any of the judges of Israel, whom I had
commanded to shepherd my people Israel:
Why do you not build me a cedar-wood
temple?" 8 This is what you must say to my
servant David, "Yahweh Sabaoth says this:
I took you from the pasture, from following
the sheep, to be leader of my people Israel;
9 I have been with you wherever you went; I
have got rid of all your enemies for you. I am
going to make your fame as great as the fame
of the greatest on earth. 10 I am going to
provide a place for my people Israel; I shall
plant them there, and there they will live and
never be disturbed again; nor will they be
oppressed by the wicked any more, as they
were in former times 11 ever since the time
when I instituted judges to govern my people
Israel; and I shall grant you rest from all your
enemies. Yahweh furthermore tells you that
he will make you a dynasty. 12 And when your
days are over and you fall asleep with your
ancestors, I shall appoint your heir, your own
son to succeed you (and I shall make his
sovereignty secure. 13 He will build a temple
for my name)[a] and I shall make his royal
throne secure for ever. 14 I shall be a father to
him and he a son to me; if he does wrong, I
shall punish him with a rod such as men use,
with blows such as mankind gives. 15 But my
faithful love will never be withdrawn from
him as I withdrew it from Saul, whom I
removed from before you. 16 Your dynasty
and your sovereignty will ever stand firm
before me and your throne be for ever
secure." '
17 Nathan related all these words and this
whole revelation to David.

David's prayer

18 King David then went in, sat down in
Yahweh's presence and said:
'Who am I, Lord Yahweh, and what is my
lineage, for you to have led me as far as this?
19 Yet, to you, Lord Yahweh, this seemed too
little, and now you extend your promises for
your servant's family into the distant future.
Such is human destiny, Lord Yahweh.
20 What more can David say to you, since you,
Lord Yahweh, know all about your servant?
21 Because of your promise and since you were
so inclined, you have had the generosity to
reveal this to your servant. 22 That is why you
are great, Lord Yahweh; there is no one like
you, no God but you alone, as everything that
we have heard confirms. 23 Is there another
people on earth like your people, like Israel,
whom a god proceeded to redeem, to make
them his people and to make a name for
himself by performing great and terrible
things on their behalf, by driving out nations
and their gods before his people?—24 for you
constituted your people Israel your own
people for ever and you, Yahweh, became
their God.
25 'Now, Yahweh God, may the promise
which you have made for your servant and
for his family stand firm forever as you have
said, 26 so that your name will be exalted for
ever and people will say, "Israel's God is
Yahweh Sabaoth." Your servant David's
dynasty will be secure before you, 27 since
you, Yahweh Sabaoth, the God of Israel,
have disclosed to your servant, "I am going
to build you a dynasty." Hence, your servant

7a The words in brackets were probably added during Solomon's reign.

has ventured to offer this prayer to you.
28 Yes, Lord Yahweh, you are God indeed,
your words are true and you have made this
generous promise to your servant. 29 What
is more, you have deigned to bless your
servant's dynasty, so that it may remain for
ever before you; for you, Lord Yahweh, have
spoken; and may your servant's dynasty be
blessed with your blessing for ever.'

David's wars

8 After this, David defeated the Philistines
and subdued them. From the grip of the
Philistines he wrested . . . 2 He also defeated
the Moabites and, making them lie on the
ground, measured them off by the line; he
measured out two lines to be put to death and
one full line to have their lives spared. The
Moabites became David's subjects and paid
him tribute.

3 David defeated Hadadezer son of Rehob,
king of Zobah, when the latter mounted
an expedition to extend his power over the
River. 4 David captured one thousand seven
hundred charioteers and twenty thousand
foot soldiers from him; David hamstrung all
the chariot teams, keeping only a hundred of
them. 5 The Aramaeans of Damascus came to
the help of Hadadezer king of Zobah, but
David killed twenty-two thousand of the
Aramaeans. 6 David then imposed governors
on Aram of Damascus, and the Aramaeans
became David's subjects and paid him
tribute. Wherever David went, Yahweh gave
him victory. 7 David took the golden shields
carried by Hadadezer's guards and brought
them to Jerusalem. 8 From Betah and Bero-
thai, towns belonging to Hadadezer, King
David captured a great quantity of bronze.

9 When Tou king of Hamath heard that
David had defeated Hadadezer's entire army,
10 he sent his son Hadoram to King David to
greet him and to congratulate him on having
made war on Hadadezer and on having
defeated him, since Hadadezer was at war
with Tou. Hadoram brought with him
objects made of silver, gold and bronze,
11 which King David also consecrated to
Yahweh, as he had already consecrated the
silver and gold taken from all the nations
which he had subjugated— 12 from Aram,
Moab, the Ammonites, the Philistines and
Amalek; and from the spoil of Hadadezer son
of Rehob, king of Zobah.

13 David became famous when he came
home from defeating the Edomites in the
Valley of Salt—eighteen thousand of them.
14 He imposed governors on Edom and
all the Edomites became David's subjects.
Wherever David went, Yahweh gave him
victory.

The administration of the kingdom[a]

15 David ruled over all Israel, administering
law and justice to all his people. 16 Joab son
of Zeruiah was in command of the army;
Jehoshaphat son of Ahilud was herald;
17 Zadok and Abiathar son of Ahimelech,
son of Ahitub, were priests; Seraiah was
secretary; 18 Benaiah son of Jehoiada was in
command of the Cherethites and Pelethites;
David's sons were priests.

C: DAVID'S FAMILY AND THE INTRIGUES OVER THE SUCCESSION

1: MERIBBAAL

David's kindness to Jonathan's son

9 David asked, 'Is there anyone belonging
to Saul's family left, to whom I might
show faithful love for Jonathan's sake?' 2 Now
Saul's family had a servant whose name was
Ziba. When he had been summoned to
David, the king said, 'Are you Ziba?' 'At
your service,' he replied. 3 The king said, 'Is
there no one left, belonging to Saul's family,
for me to treat with God's own faithful love?'
Ziba said to the king, 'There is still one of
Jonathan's sons. He has crippled feet.' 4 The
king asked 'Where is he?' Ziba replied, 'He
is living in the household of Machir son of
Ammiel, at Lo-Debar.' 5 So King David sent
for him to be fetched from the house of
Machir son of Ammiel at Lo-Debar.

6 On entering David's presence, Meribbaal
son of Jonathan, son of Saul, fell on his face
and prostrated himself. David said, 'Merib-
baal!' He replied, 'Here I am, at your service.'
7 David then said, 'Do not be afraid; I will
indeed treat you with faithful love for your
father Jonathan's sake. I shall restore all your

8a =20:23–26.

grandfather Saul's estates to you, and you will always eat at my table.' 8Meribbaal prostrated himself and said, 'Who is your servant, for you to show favour to a dead dog like me?'

9The king then summoned Saul's servant Ziba and said, 'Everything belonging to Saul and his family, I give to your master's son. 10You must work the land for him, you and your sons and your slaves; you must harvest the produce to provide food for your master's family to eat. But Meribbaal, your master's son, will always take his own meals at my table.' Now, Ziba had fifteen sons and twenty slaves. 11Ziba said to the king, 'Your servant will do everything my lord the king has ordered his servant.'

So Meribbaal ate at David's table like one of the king's sons. 12Meribbaal had a young son whose name was Micha. All the people living in Ziba's household entered Meribbaal's service. 13Meribbaal lived in Jerusalem, since he always ate at the king's table. He was crippled in both feet.

2: THE AMMONITE WAR— BIRTH OF SOLOMON

David's ambassadors are insulted

10 After this, when the king of the Ammonites died and his son Hanun succeeded him, 2David thought, 'I shall show Hanun son of Nahash the same faithful love as his father showed me.' And David sent his representatives to offer him condolences over his father. But, when David's representatives reached the Ammonites' country, 3the Ammonite princes said to Hanun their master, 'Do you really think David means to honour your father when he sends you messengers with sympathy? On the contrary, the reason why David has sent his representatives to you is to explore the city, to reconnoitre and so overthrow it.' 4Whereupon Hanun seized David's representatives, shaved off half their beards, cut their clothes off halfway up, at their buttocks, and sent them away. 5When David was told, he sent someone to meet them, since the men were overcome with shame. 'Stay in Jericho', the king said, 'until your beards have grown again, and come back then.'

The first Ammonite campaign

6When the Ammonites realised that they had antagonised David, they sent agents to hire twenty thousand foot soldiers from the Aramaeans of Beth-Rehob and the Aramaeans of Zobah, one thousand men from the king of Maacah and twelve thousand men from the prince of Tob. 7When David heard this, he sent Joab with the whole army, the champions. 8The Ammonites marched out and drew up their line of battle at the city gate, while the Aramaeans of Zobah and of Rehob and the men of Tob and Maacah kept their distance in the open country. 9Joab, seeing that he had to fight on two fronts, to his front and to his rear, chose the best of Israel's picked men and drew them up in line facing the Aramaeans. 10He entrusted the rest of the army to his brother Abishai, and drew them up in line facing the Ammonites. 11'If the Aramaeans prove too strong for me,' he said, 'you must come to my help; if the Ammonites prove too strong for you, I shall come to yours. 12Be brave! Let us acquit ourselves like men for the sake of our people and for the cities of our God. And let Yahweh do as he thinks right!' 13Joab and the force with him joined battle with the Aramaeans, who fled at his onslaught. 14When the Ammonites saw that the Aramaeans had fled, they too fled from Abishai and withdrew into the city. Hence, Joab broke off his campaign against the Ammonites and returned to Jerusalem.

Victory over the Aramaeans

15The Aramaeans, realising that Israel had got the better of them, concentrated their forces. 16Hadadezer sent messengers and mobilised the Aramaeans living on the other side of the river; and these arrived at Helam, with Shobach the commander of Hadadezer's army, at their head. 17David, being informed of this, mustered all Israel, crossed the Jordan and arrived at Helam. The Aramaeans drew up in line facing David and engaged him. 18But the Aramaeans fled from Israel, and David killed seven hundred of their chariot teams and forty thousand men; he also cut down Shobach the commander of their army, who died there. 19When all Hadadezer's vassal kings saw that Israel had got the better of them, they made peace with the Israelites and became their subjects. The Aramaeans were afraid to give any more help to the Ammonites.

The second Ammonite campaign
David's sin

11 At the turn of the year, at the time when kings go campaigning, David sent Joab and with him his guards and all Israel. They massacred the Ammonites and laid siege to Rabbah-of-the-Ammonites. David, however, remained in Jerusalem.

2 It happened towards evening when David had got up from resting and was strolling on the palace roof, that from the roof he saw a woman bathing; the woman was very beautiful. 3 David made enquiries about this woman and was told, 'Why, that is Bathsheba daughter of Eliam and wife of Uriah the Hittite.' 4 David then sent messengers to fetch her. She came to him, and he lay with her, just after she had purified herself from her period. She then went home again. 5 The woman conceived and sent word to David, 'I am pregnant.'

6 David then sent word to Joab, 'Send me Uriah the Hittite,' whereupon Joab sent Uriah to David. 7 When Uriah reached him, David asked how Joab was and how the army was and how the war was going. 8 David then said to Uriah, 'Go down to your house and wash your feet.' Uriah left the palace and was followed by a present from the king's table. 9 Uriah, however, slept at the palace gate with all his master's bodyguard and did not go down to his house.

10 This was reported to David; 'Uriah', they said 'has not gone down to his house.' So David asked Uriah, 'Haven't you just arrived from the journey? Why didn't you go down to your house?' 11 To which Uriah replied, 'The ark, Israel and Judah are lodged in huts; my master Joab and my lord's guards are camping in the open. Am I to go to my house, then, and eat and drink and sleep with my wife? As Yahweh lives, and as you yourself live, I shall do no such thing!' 12 David then said to Uriah, 'Stay on here today; tomorrow I shall send you off.' So Uriah stayed that day in Jerusalem. 13 The next day, David invited him to eat and drink in his presence and made him drunk. In the evening, Uriah went out and bedded down with his master's bodyguard, but did not go down to his house.

14 Next morning David wrote a letter to Joab and sent it by Uriah. 15 In the letter he wrote, 'Put Uriah out in front where the fighting is fiercest and then fall back, so that he gets wounded and killed.' 16 Joab, then besieging the city, stationed Uriah at a point where he knew that there would be tough fighters. 17 The people of the city sallied out and engaged Joab; there were casualties in the army, among David's guards, and Uriah the Hittite was killed as well.

18 Joab sent David a full account of the battle. 19 To the messenger he gave this order: 'When you have finished telling the king all about the battle, 20 if the king's anger is aroused and he says, "Why did you go near the town to give battle? Didn't you know that they would shoot from the ramparts? 21 Who killed Abimelech son of Jerubbaal? Wasn't it a woman who dropped a millstone on him from the ramparts, causing his death at Thebez? Why did you go near the ramparts?" you are to say, "Your servant Uriah the Hittite is dead too." '

22 So the messenger set off and, on his arrival, told David everything that Joab had instructed him to say. David flew into a rage with Joab and said to the messenger, 'Why did you go near the ramparts? Who killed Abimelech son of Jerubbaal? Wasn't it a woman who dropped a millstone on him from the ramparts, causing his death at Thebez? Why did you go near the ramparts?' 23 The messenger replied to David, 'Their men had won an initial advantage and then came out to engage us in the open. We then drove them back into the gateway, 24 but the archers shot at your retainers from the ramparts; some of the king's retainers lost their lives, and your servant Uriah the Hittite is dead too.'

25 David then said to the messenger, 'Say this to Joab, "Do not take the matter to heart; the sword devours now one and now another. Attack the town in greater force and destroy it." That will encourage him.' 26 When Uriah's wife heard that her husband Uriah was dead, she mourned for her husband. 27 When the period of mourning was over, David sent to have her brought to his house; she became his wife and bore him a son. But what David had done displeased Yahweh.

David is rebuked by Nathan
His repentance

12 Yahweh sent the prophet Nathan to David. He came to him and said:

In the same town were two men,
one rich, the other poor.
2 The rich man had flocks and herds
in great abundance;
3 the poor man had nothing but a ewe lamb,
only a single little one
which he had bought.
He fostered it and it grew up with him
and his children,
eating his bread, drinking from his cup,
sleeping in his arms;
it was like a daughter to him.
4 When a traveller came to stay,
the rich man
would not take anything
from his own flock or herd
to provide for the wayfarer
who had come to him.
Instead, he stole the poor man's lamb
and prepared that for his guest.

5 David flew into a great rage with the man. 'As Yahweh lives,' he said to Nathan 'the man who did this deserves to die. 6 For doing such a thing and for having shown no pity, he shall make fourfold restitution for the lamb.'

7 Nathan then said to David, 'You are the man! Yahweh, God of Israel, says this, "I anointed you king of Israel, I saved you from Saul's clutches, 8 I gave you your master's household and your master's wives into your arms, I gave you the House of Israel and the House of Judah; and, if this is still too little, I shall give you other things as well. 9 Why did you show contempt for Yahweh, by doing what displeases him? You put Uriah the Hittite to the sword, you took his wife to be your wife, causing his death by the sword of the Ammonites. 10 For this, your household will never be free of the sword, since you showed contempt for me and took the wife of Uriah the Hittite, to make her your wife."

11 'Yahweh says this, "Out of your own household I shall raise misfortune for you. Before your very eyes I shall take your wives and give them to your neighbour, who will lie with your wives in broad daylight. 12 You have worked in secret, but I shall work this for all Israel to see, in broad daylight." '

13 David said to Nathan, 'I have sinned against Yahweh.' Nathan then said to David, 'Yahweh, for his part, forgives your sin; you are not to die. 14 But, since you have outraged Yahweh by doing this, the child born to you will die.' 15 And Nathan went home.

Death of Bathsheba's child Birth of Solomon

Yahweh struck the child which Uriah's wife had borne to David and it fell gravely ill. 16 David pleaded with Yahweh for the child; he kept a strict fast and went home and spent the night lying on the ground, covered with sacking. 17 The officials of his household stood round him, intending to get him off the ground, but he refused, nor would he take food with them. 18 On the seventh day the child died. David's retinue were afraid to tell him that the child was dead. 'Even when the child was alive', they thought, 'we reasoned with him and he would not listen to us. How can we tell him that the child is dead? He will do something desperate.' 19 David, however, noticed that his retinue were whispering among themselves, and realised that the child was dead. 'Is the child dead?' he asked the officers. They replied, 'He is dead.'

20 David got off the ground, bathed and anointed himself and put on fresh clothes. Then he went into Yahweh's sanctuary and prostrated himself. On returning to his house, he asked to be served with food and ate it. 21 His retinue said, 'Why are you acting like this? When the child was alive, you fasted and wept; now that the child is dead, you get up and take food!' 22 'When the child was alive', he replied, 'I fasted and wept because I kept thinking, "Who knows? Perhaps Yahweh will take pity on me and the child will live." 23 But now that he is dead, why should I fast? Can I bring him back again? I shall go to him but he cannot come back to me.'

24 David consoled his wife Bathsheba. He went to her and slept with her. She conceived and gave birth to a son, whom she called Solomon. Yahweh loved him 25 and made this known by means of the prophet Nathan, who named him Jedidiah, as Yahweh had instructed.

Capture of Rabbah

26 Joab assaulted Rabbah-of-the-Ammonites and captured the royal town. 27 He then sent messengers to tell David, 'I have assaulted Rabbah and captured the water supply. 28 So now muster the rest of the army, lay siege to the town and take it, or I will take it and the town will be called after me!' 29 So David mustered the whole army and marched on

Rabbah; he assaulted the town and captured it. [30]He took the crown off Milcom's head; it weighed one talent of gold, and in it was set a precious stone which went on David's head instead. He carried off great quantities of booty from the town.' [31]And he expelled its inhabitants, setting them to work with saws, iron picks and iron axes, employing them at brickmaking. He treated all the Ammonite towns in the same way. David and the whole army returned to Jerusalem.

3: ABSALOM

Amnon violates his sister Tamar

13 After this, the following events took place. Absalom son of David had a beautiful sister whose name was Tamar; Amnon son of David fell in love with her. [2]Amnon was so obsessed with his sister Tamar that it made him ill, since she was a virgin and Amnon thought it impossible to do anything to her. [3]But Amnon had a friend called Jonadab son of Shimeah, David's brother, and Jonadab was a very shrewd man. [4]'Son of the king,' he said, 'tell me why, morning after morning, you look so worn? Won't you tell me?' Amnon replied, 'I am in love with Tamar, my brother Absalom's sister.' [5]Then Jonadab said, 'Take to your bed, pretend to be ill and, when your father comes to visit you, say, "Please let my sister Tamar come and give me something to eat; let her prepare the food where I can see. What she gives me I shall eat." ' [6]So Amnon lay down and pretended to be ill. The king then came to visit him and Amnon said to the king, 'Please let my sister Tamar come and make a cake or two where I can watch. What she gives me, I shall eat.' [7]David then sent word to Tamar at the palace, 'Go to your brother Amnon's house and prepare some food for him.' [8]Tamar went to the house of her brother Amnon who was lying there in bed. She took dough and kneaded it, and she made some cakes while he watched, and baked the cakes. [9]She then took the pan and dished them up in front of him, but he refused to eat. Amnon said, 'Let everyone leave me!' So everyone withdrew. [10]Amnon then said to Tamar, 'Bring the food to the inner room, so that I can eat what you give me.' So Tamar took the cakes which she had made and brought them to her brother Amnon in the inner room. [11]And as she was offering the food to him, he caught hold of her and said, 'Come to bed with me, sister!' [12]She replied, 'No, brother! Do not force me! This is no way to behave in Israel. Do not do anything so disgraceful! [13]Wherever should I go? I should be marked with this shame, while you would become disgraced in Israel. Why not go and speak to the king? He will not refuse to give me to you.' [14]But he would not listen to her; he overpowered her and raped her.

[15]Amnon was then seized with extreme hatred for her; the hatred he now felt for her was greater than his earlier love. 'Get up and go!' he said. [16]She said, 'No, brother! To send me away would be worse than the other wrong you have done me!' But he would not listen to her. [17]He called his personal servant. 'Rid me of this woman!' he said. 'Throw her out and bolt the door behind her!' [18](She was wearing a magnificent dress, for this was what the king's unmarried daughters wore in days gone by.) So the servant put her out and bolted the door behind her.

[19]Tamar put dust on her head, tore the magnificent dress which she was wearing, laid her hand on her head, and went away, crying aloud as she went.

[20]Her brother Absalom said to her, 'Has Amnon your brother been with you? Sister, be quiet; he is your brother; do not take the matter to heart!' Tamar, however, went back to her brother Absalom's house inconsolable.

[21]When King David heard the whole story, he was very angry; but he had no wish to harm his son Amnon, whom he loved because he was his first-born. [22]Absalom, however, would not so much as speak to Amnon, since he hated Amnon for having raped his sister Tamar.

Absalom kills Amnon and flees

[23]Two years later, when Absalom had the sheep-shearers at Baal-Hazor, which is near Ephraim, he invited all the king's sons. [24]Absalom went to the king and said, 'Now sir, your servant has the sheep-shearers. Will the king and his retinue be pleased to come with your servant?' [25]'No, my son,' the king replied, 'we must not all come and be a burden to you.' And though Absalom was insistent, he would not go but dismissed him. [26]Absalom persisted, 'Then at least let my brother Amnon come with us.' The king said, 'Why should he go with you?' [27]On Absalom's insistence, however, he let

Amnon and all the king's sons to go with
him.
Absalom prepared a royal banquet 28and
then gave this order to the servants, 'Listen
carefully; when Amnon's heart is merry with
wine and I say, "Strike Amnon down", then
kill him. Don't be afraid. Have I not myself
given you the order? Use your strength and
show your mettle!' 29Absalom's servants
treated Amnon as Absalom had ordered. The
king's sons all leapt to their feet, mounted
their mules and fled.
30While they were on the road, word
reached David, 'Absalom has killed all the
king's sons; not one of them is left.' 31The
king stood up, tore his clothes and threw
himself on the ground. All his officers tore
their clothes too. 32Jonadab son of Shimeah,
David's brother, then spoke up and said, 'Do
not let my lord take to heart the report that
all the young men, the king's sons, have
been killed, since only Amnon is dead: for
Absalom has been promising himself to do
this since the day when Amnon raped his
sister Tamar. 33So my lord the king must not
imagine that all the king's sons are dead; only
Amnon is dead 34and Absalom has fled.'
The man on sentry duty looked up and saw
a large troop coming along the road from
Bahurim. The sentry came to tell the king,
'I have seen some people coming down the
Bahurim road on the mountainside.'
35Jonadab then said to the king, 'These are
the king's sons arriving: what your servant
said is exactly what happened.' 36He had
scarcely finished speaking when the king's
sons arrived and wept aloud; the king and all
his retinue wept aloud too. 37Absalom had
gone to Talmai son of Ammihud, king of
Geshur. The king mourned for his son every
day.

Joab negotiates Absalom's return

38When Absalom had gone to Geshur, he
stayed there for three years. 39Once the king
was consoled over Amnon's death, his anger
against Absalom subsided.

14 Now, Joab son of Zeruiah observed
that the king was favourably inclined
to Absalom. 2Joab therefore sent to Tekoa
for a wise woman. 'Pretend to be in
mourning,' he said. 'Dress yourself in
mourning, do not perfume yourself; act like
a woman who has long been mourning for
the dead. 3Then go to the king and say this
to him.' And Joab put the words into her
mouth which she was to say.
4So the woman of Tekoa went to the king
and, falling on her face to the ground, pros-
trated herself. 'Help, my lord king!' she said.
5The king said, 'What is the matter?'
'As you see,' she replied, 'I am a widow;
my husband is dead. 6Your servant had two
sons and out in the fields, where there was
no one to intervene, they had a quarrel. And
one of them struck the other one and killed
him. 7And now the whole clan has risen
against your servant. "Give up the man who
killed his brother," they say, "so that we can
put him to death, to atone for the life of the
brother whom he has murdered; and thus we
shall destroy the heir as well." By this means,
they will extinguish the ember still left to
me, leaving my husband neither name nor
survivor on the face of the earth.' 8Then the
king said to the woman, 'Go home; I myself
shall give orders about your case.' 9The
woman of Tekoa said to the king, 'My lord
king! May the guilt be on me and on my
family; the king and his throne are innocent
of it.' 10'Bring me the man who threatened
you,' the king replied, 'and he shall never
hurt you again.' 11She then said, 'Let the
king be pleased to pronounce the name of
Yahweh your God, so that the avenger of
blood may not do greater harm and destroy
my son.' 'As Yahweh lives,' he said, 'not one
of your son's hairs shall fall to the ground!'
12Then the woman said, 'Permit your
servant to say something else to my lord the
king.' 'Go on,' he said. 13The woman said,
'Why then has the king, who by giving this
verdict has condemned himself, conceived
the idea, against God's people's interests, of
not bringing home the son whom he has
banished? 14We are all mortal; we are like
water spilt on the ground, which cannot be
gathered up again, nor does God raise up a
corpse; let the king therefore make plans for
his banished son not to remain far away from
him in exile.
15'Now, the reason why I came to speak
about this to my lord the king is that I was
being intimidated, and your servant thought,
"I shall speak to the king; perhaps the king
will do what his servant asks. 16Surely the
king will consent to save his servant from the
clutches of the man who is trying to cut both
me and my son off from God's heritage. 17Let
a word from my lord the king, restore the
peace!" your servant thought, "for my lord

the king is like the Angel of God in under-
standing good and evil." May Yahweh your
God be with you!'
18 Replying to the woman, the king said,
'Now do not evade the question which I am
going to ask you.' The woman said, 'Let my
lord the king ask his question.' 19 'Is not Joab's
hand behind you in all this?' the king asked.
The woman replied, 'As you live, my lord
king, I cannot escape what my lord the king
says, either to right or to left. Yes, it was your
servant Joab who gave me my orders; he put
all these words into your servant's mouth.
20 Your servant Joab did this to approach the
matter indirectly, but my lord has the wisdom
of the Angel of God; he knows everything
that happens on earth!'
21 The king then said to Joab, 'Very well,
the suit is granted. Go and bring the young
man Absalom back.' 22 Joab fell on his face to
the ground, prostrated himself and blessed
the king. 'My lord king,' Joab said, 'today
your servant knows that he has won your
favour, since the king has done what his
servant asked.' 23 Joab then set off, went
to Geshur, and brought Absalom back to
Jerusalem. 24 The king, however, said, 'Let
him retire to his own house; he is not to
appear in my presence.' So Absalom retired
to his own house and was not received by the
king.

Some details about Absalom

25 In all Israel there was no one more praised
for his beauty than Absalom; from the sole
of his foot to the crown of his head, he could
not be faulted. 26 When he cut his hair—he
shaved it once a year because his hair got
too heavy—he would weigh the hair: two
hundred shekels, king's weight. 27 To
Absalom were born three sons and one
daughter called Tamar; she was a beautiful
woman.

Absalom obtains his pardon

28 Absalom lived in Jerusalem for two years
without being received by the king.
29 Absalom then summoned Joab, intending
to send him to the king, but Joab would not
come to him. He sent for him a second
time, but still he would not come. 30 At this,
Absalom said to his retainers, 'Look, Joab's
field is next to mine and he has barley in it;
go and set it on fire.' Absalom's retainers set
fire to the field. 31 Joab then stirred himself,
went to Absalom in his house and asked,
'Why have your retainers set my field on
fire?' 32 Absalom replied to Joab, 'Look, I
sent word to you: Come here, so that I can
send you to the king to say, "Why come back
from Geshur? Better for me to have been
there still!" Now I want to be received by the
king, and if I am guilty, let him put me to
death!' 33 Joab went to the king and told
him this. He then summoned Absalom, who
prostrated himself with his face to the ground
before the king. And the king kissed
Absalom.

Absalom's intrigues

15 After this, Absalom procured a chariot
and horses, with fifty men to run ahead
of him. 2 He would get up early and stand
beside the road leading to the city gate; and
whenever a man with some lawsuit had to
come before the king's tribunal, Absalom
would call out to him and ask, 'Which town
are you from?' If he answered, 'Your servant
is from one of the tribes of Israel,' 3 then
Absalom would say, 'Look, your case is
sound and just, but not one of the king's
deputies will listen to you.' 4 Absalom would
say, 'Oh, who will appoint me judge in the
land? Then anyone with a lawsuit or a plea
could come to me and I should see he had
justice!' 5 And whenever anyone came up to
him to prostrate himself, he would stretch
out his hand, draw him to him and kiss him.
6 Absalom acted like this with every Israelite
who appealed to the king's tribunal, and so
Absalom won the Israelites' hearts.

Absalom's rebellion

7 When four years had gone by, Absalom said
to the king, 'Allow me to go to Hebron and
fulfil the vow which I have made to Yahweh;
8 for, when I was in Geshur, in Aram, your
servant made this vow, "If Yahweh brings
me back to Jerusalem, I shall pay my devo-
tions to Yahweh in Hebron." ' 9 The king
said to him, 'Go in peace.' So he set off and
went to Hebron.
10 Absalom sent couriers throughout the
tribes of Israel to say, 'When you hear the
trumpet sound, you are to say, "Absalom is
king at Hebron!" ' 11 With Absalom went two
hundred men from Jerusalem; they had been
invited and had gone in all innocence,

unaware of what was going on. 12 Absalom sent for Ahithophel the Gilonite, David's counsellor, from Giloh his town, and had him with him while offering the sacrifices. The conspiracy grew in strength, since Absalom's supporters grew in number.

David's flight

13 A messenger came and told David, 'The men of Israel have shifted their allegiance to Absalom.' 14 David said to all his retinue then with him in Jerusalem, 'Up, let us flee, or we shall not escape from Absalom! Leave as quickly as you can, in case he mounts a sudden attack, overcomes us and puts the city to the sword.' 15 The king's retinue replied, 'Whatever my lord the king decides, we are at your service.' 16 The king set out on foot with his whole household, leaving ten concubines to look after the palace. 17 The king set out on foot with everyone following, and they halted at the last house. 18 All his officers stood at his side. All the Cherethites and all the Pelethites, with Ittai and all the six hundred Gittites who had come in his retinue from Gath, marched past the king. 19 The king said to Ittai the Gittite, 'You, why are you coming with us? Go back and stay with the king, for you are a foreigner, indeed an exile from your homeland. 20 You arrived only yesterday; should I take you wandering with us today, when I do not know myself where I am going? Go back, take your fellow countrymen with you, and may Yahweh show you mercy and faithful love!' 21 Ittai replied to the king, 'As Yahweh lives, and as my lord the king lives, wherever my lord the king may be, for death or life, your servant will be there too.' 22 David then said to Ittai, 'Go ahead, march past!' And Ittai of Gath marched past with all his men and with all his children too. 23 The entire population was weeping aloud as the king stood in the bed of the Kidron and everyone marched past him, making for the desert.

The ark is left in Jerusalem

24 Zadok was there too, and all the Levites with him, carrying the ark of God. They set the ark of God down beside Abiathar until everyone had finished marching out of the town. 25 The king then said to Zadok, 'Take the ark of God back into the city. Should I win Yahweh's favour, he will bring me back and allow me to see it and its tent once more. 26 But should he say, "You displease me," here I am: let him treat me as he sees fit.' 27 The king said to Zadok the priest, 'Look, you and Abiathar go back quietly into the city, with your two sons, your own son Ahimaaz and Jonathan son of Abiathar. 28 You see, I shall wait in the passes of the desert plain until word comes from you bringing me news.' 29 So Zadok and Abiathar took the ark of God back to Jerusalem and stayed there.

Hushai is briefed to work for David

30 David then made his way up the Mount of Olives, weeping as he went, his head covered and his feet bare. And all the people with him had their heads covered and made their way up, weeping as they went. 31 David was then informed that Ahithophel was among the conspirators with Absalom. David said, 'I beg you, Yahweh, turn Ahithophel's advice to folly.'

32 As David reached the summit, where God is worshipped, he saw Hushai the Archite, his friend, coming to meet him with his tunic torn and with earth on his head. 33 David said, 'If you go along with me, you will be a burden to me. 34 But if you go back to the city and say to Absalom, "I am at your service, my lord king; once I was in your father's service, but now I shall serve you," you will be able to thwart Ahithophel's advice for me. 35 Surely the priests Zadok and Abiathar will be with you? Anything you hear from the palace you must report to the priests Zadok and Abiathar. 36 You see, their two sons are there with them, Zadok's son Ahimaaz, and Abiathar's son Jonathan; through these, you will send me word of everything you hear.' 37 Hushai, David's friend, entered the city just as Absalom was reaching Jerusalem.

David and Ziba

16 When David had passed a little beyond the summit, Meribbaal's retainer, Ziba, met him with a pair of donkeys, saddled and laden with two hundred loaves of bread, a hundred bunches of raisins, a hundred of the season's fruits, and a skin of wine. 2 The king said to Ziba, 'What are you going to do with that?' 'The donkeys', Ziba replied, 'are

for the king's family to ride, the bread and the fruit for the soldiers to eat, the wine is for drinking by those who get exhausted in the desert.' [3]The king asked 'And where is your master's son?' Ziba replied to the king, 'Why, he has stayed in Jerusalem because, he says, "Today, the House of Israel will give me back my father's kingdom." ' [4]Then the king said to Ziba, 'Everything owned by Meribbaal is yours.' Ziba said, 'I prostrate myself! May I be worthy of your favour, my lord king!'

Shimei curses David

[5]As David was reaching Bahurim, out came a man of the same clan as Saul's family. His name was Shimei son of Gera and, as he came, he uttered curse after curse [6]and threw stones at David and at all King David's retinue, even though the whole army and all the champions formed an escort round the king on either side. [7]The words of his curse were these, 'Off with you, off with you, man of blood, scoundrel! [8]Yahweh has paid you back for all the spilt blood of the House of Saul whose sovereignty you have usurped; and Yahweh has transferred the sovereign power to Absalom your son. Now your wickedness has overtaken you, man of blood that you are.' [9]Abishai son of Zeruiah said to the king, 'Why should this dead dog curse my lord the king? Let me go over and cut his head off.' [10]But the king replied, 'What concern is my business to you, sons of Zeruiah? Let him curse! If Yahweh has said to him, "Curse David!" what right has anyone to say, "Why have you done so?" ' [11]David said to Abishai and all his retinue, 'Why, the son sprung from my own body is now seeking my life; all the more reason for this Benjaminite to do so! Let him curse on, if Yahweh has told him to! [12]Perhaps Yahweh will look on my wretchedness and will repay me with good for his curses today.' [13]So David and his men went on their way, and Shimei kept pace with him along the opposite mountainside, cursing as he went, throwing stones and flinging dust. [14]The king and all the people who were with him arrived exhausted at . . .[a] . . . and there they drew breath.

Hushai ingratiates himself with Absalom

[15]Absalom entered Jerusalem with all the men of Israel; with him was Ahithophel. [16]When Hushai the Archite, David's friend, reached Absalom, Hushai said to Absalom, 'Long live the king! Long live the king!' [17]Absalom said to Hushai, 'Is this your faithful love for your friend? Why didn't you go away with your friend?' [18]Hushai replied to Absalom, 'No, the man whom Yahweh and this people and all the men of Israel have chosen, he is the man for me, and with him will I stay! [19]Besides, whom should I serve, if not his son? As I served your father, so shall I serve you.'

Absalom and David's concubines

[20]Absalom said to Ahithophel, 'Think carefully. What shall we do?' [21]Ahithophel replied to Absalom, 'Go to your father's concubines whom he left to look after the palace; then all Israel will hear that you have thoroughly antagonised your father, and the resolution of all your supporters will be strengthened.' [22]So a tent was pitched for Absalom on the flat roof and, with all Israel watching, Absalom went to his father's concubines. [23]At the time, whatever advice Ahithophel gave was treated like a decision obtained from God; as by David, so by Absalom, was all Ahithophel's advice regarded.

Hushai thwarts Ahithophel's plans

17 Ahithophel said to Absalom, 'Let me choose twelve thousand men and set off this very night in pursuit of David. [2]I shall fall on him while he is tired and dispirited; I shall strike terror into him, and all the people who are with him will run away. I shall kill only the king, [3]and I shall then bring all the people back to you, like a bride returning to her husband. You seek the life of one individual only; the people as a whole will have peace.' [4]The suggestion seemed a good one to Absalom and all the elders of Israel.

[5]Then Absalom said, 'Now call Hushai the Archite, for us to hear what he too has to say.' [6]When Hushai had come to Absalom, Absalom said, 'This is what Ahithophel says. Are we to do as he suggests? If not, suggest

16a A place-name is missing.

something yourself.' [7]Hushai said to
Absalom, 'On this occasion the advice given
by Ahithophel is not good. [8]You know',
Hushai went on, 'that your father and his
men are great fighters and that they are now
as angry as a wild bear robbed of her cubs.
Your father is a man of war: he will not let
the army rest during the night. [9]At this
moment he is concealed in some hollow or
other place. If at the outset there are casualties
among our troops, word will go round that
the army supporting Absalom has met with
disaster. [10]And then even the valiant, the
truly lion-hearted, will be demoralised; for
all Israel knows that your father is a champion
and that the men with him are valiant. [11]For
my part, I offer this advice: Summon all
Israel, from Dan to Beersheba, to rally to
you, as numerous as the sand on the seashore,
and you take the field in person with them.
[12]We shall reach him wherever he is to be
found; we shall fall on him as the dew falls
on the ground, and not leave him or any one
of the men with him. [13]Should he retire into
a town, all Israel will bring ropes to that
town, and we shall drag it into the river-bed
until not a pebble of it is to be found.' [14]Then
Absalom and all the people of Israel said,
'Hushai the Arkite's advice is better than
Ahithophel's,' Yahweh having resolved to
thwart Ahithophel's shrewd advice and so
bring disaster on Absalom.

[15]Hushai then told the priests Zadok and
Abiathar, 'Ahithophel gave such and such
advice to Absalom and the elders of Israel,
but I advised so and so. [16]Send with all speed
to David and say, "Do not camp in the desert
passes tonight, but get through them as fast
as you can, or the king and his whole army
may be annihilated." '

David is warned and crosses the Jordan

[17]Jonathan and Ahimaaz were posted at the
Fuller's Spring; a servant-girl was to go and
warn them and they in turn were to warn King
David, since they could not give themselves
away by coming into the city themselves. [18]A
young man saw them nonetheless and told
Absalom. The pair of them, however, made
off quickly, reaching the house of a man in
Bahurim. In his courtyard was a storage-well
and they got down into it. [19]The woman took
a piece of canvas and, spreading it over the
mouth of the storage-well, scattered crushed
grain on it so that nothing showed.

[20]When Absalom's servants reached the
woman at the house, they said, 'Where are
Ahimaaz and Jonathan?' The woman said,
'They have gone further on, towards the
water.' They searched but, having found
nothing, went back to Jerusalem.

[21]When they had gone, the men climbed
out of the storage-well and went to warn King
David. 'Set out!' they told David. 'Cross the
water quickly, for Ahithophel has given such
and such advice against you!' [22]So David and
all the troops with him set off and crossed the
Jordan. By dawn no one was left, all had
crossed the Jordan.

[23]When Ahithophel saw that his advice had
not been followed, he saddled his donkey and
set off and went home to his own town. Then,
having set his house in order, he hanged
himself. He was buried in his father's tomb.

Absalom crosses the Jordan
David at Mahanaim

[24]David had reached Mahanaim by the time
that Absalom crossed the Jordan with all the
men of Israel. [25]Absalom had put Amasa in
command of the army in place of Joab. This
Amasa was the son of a man called Ithra
the Ishmaelite, who had married Abigail,
daughter of Jesse and sister of Zeruiah,
mother of Joab. [26]Israel and Absalom pitched
their camp in the territory of Gilead.

[27]When David reached Mahanaim, Shobi
son of Nahash from Rabbah-of-the-Ammon-
ites, Machir son of Ammiel from Lo-Debar,
and Barzillai the Gileadite from Rogelim
[28]brought bedding, rugs, bowls and
crockery; and wheat, barley, meal, roasted
grain, beans, lentils, [29]honey, curds and
cows' cheese and sheep's cheese, which they
presented to David and the people with him
for them to eat. 'The army', they said, 'must
have been hungry, tired and thirsty in the
desert.'

Defeat of Absalom's party

18 David reviewed the troops who were
with him and appointed commanders
of thousands and commanders of hundreds
to lead them. [2]David divided the army into
three groups, one under the command of
Joab, another under the command of Abishai
son of Zeruiah and brother of Joab, and the
third under the command of Ittai the Gittite.
David then said to the troops, 'I shall take

the field in person with you.' 3But the troops replied, 'You are not to take the field. No one will bother about us if we run away, they will not even bother about us if half of us are killed, but you are ten thousand times more valuable. So it is better if you stay inside the town, in case we need reinforcements.' 4David said, 'I will do what you think best.' And the king stood beside the gate as the troops marched out by their hundreds and their thousands. 5The king gave orders to Joab, Abishai and Ittai, 'For my sake, treat young Absalom gently!' And the troops all heard the king give all the commanders these orders about Absalom. 6So the troops marched out into the open to engage Israel, and the battle took place in the Forest of Ephraim. 7There, the army of Israel was beaten by David's retainers; it was a great defeat that day, with twenty thousand casualties. 8The fighting spread throughout the region and that day the forest claimed more victims than the sword.

Death of Absalom

9Absalom happened to run into some of David's guards. Absalom was riding his mule and the mule passed under the thick branches of a great oak. Absalom's head got caught in the oak and he was left hanging between heaven and earth, while the mule he was riding went on. 10Someone saw this and reported to Joab, 'I have just seen Absalom hanging from an oak.' 11Joab said to the man who had informed him, 'If you saw him, why did you not strike him to the ground then and there? I would have made it my business to give you ten silver shekels and a belt!' 12The man replied to Joab, 'Even if I could feel the weight of a thousand silver shekels in my hand, I would not lift my hand against the king's son. In our own hearing, the king gave you and Abishai and Ittai these orders, "For my sake, spare young Absalom." 13Even if I had deceived myself, nothing stays hidden from the king and you would have dissociated yourself from me.' 14Joab then said, 'I cannot waste time arguing with you!' And, taking three darts in his hand, he planted them in Absalom's heart, while he was still alive, deep in the oak-tree. 15Ten soldiers, Joab's armour-bearers, then came in close, struck Absalom and killed him.

16Joab then had the trumpet sounded, and the troops left off pursuing Israel, since Joab held the troops back. 17They took Absalom, flung him into a deep pit in the forest and raised a huge cairn over him. All the Israelites had fled, dispersing to their homes.

18Now, during his lifetime, Absalom had made and erected a pillar to himself, which is in the Valley of the King. 'I have no son', he said, 'to preserve the memory of my name.' He gave his own name to the pillar, and today it is still called Absalom's Monument.

The news is brought to David

19Ahimaaz son of Zadok said, 'Let me run and tell the king the good news that Yahweh has vindicated his cause by ridding him of his enemies.' 20But Joab said, 'Today you would be no bearer of good news, some other day you may be; but today you would not be bringing good news, since the king's son is dead.' 21Joab then said to the Cushite, 'Go and tell the king what you have seen.' The Cushite prostrated himself to Joab and ran off. 22But Ahimaaz son of Zadok persisted. 'Come what may,' he said to Joab, 'please let me run after the Cushite.' 'My son,' Joab said, 'why run? You will get no reward for your news.' 23But he replied, 'Come what may, let me run!' and Joab said 'Run, then!' So Ahimaaz ran off along the road through the Plain, outrunning the Cushite.

24David was sitting between the two gates. The sentry, having gone up to the roof of the gate, looked out from the ramparts and saw a man running alone. 25The sentry called down to the king and told him. The king said, 'If he is alone, he is bringing good news.' 26As the man drew steadily nearer, the lookout man saw another man running, and the sentry above the gate shouted, 'Here comes another man, running alone!' David said, 'He too is a bearer of good news.' 27The sentry said, 'I recognise the way the first man runs; Ahimaaz son of Zadok runs like that.' 'He is a good man', said the king, 'and comes with good news.'

28Ahimaaz went up to the king. 'All hail!' he said, prostrating himself on the ground before the king. 'Blessed be Yahweh your God', he said, 'who has handed over the men who rebelled against my lord the king!' 29'Is all well with young Absalom?' the king asked. Ahimaaz replied, 'I saw a great commotion when Joab, the king's servant, sent your servant off, but I do not know what it was.'

[30]The king said, 'Go and stand over there.'
He stood to one side and waited.
[31]Then the Cushite arrived. 'Good news
for my lord the king!' the Cushite shouted.
'Today Yahweh has vindicated your cause,
by ridding you of all who had risen up against
you.' [32]'Is all well with young Absalom?' the
king asked the Cushite. 'May the enemies of
my lord the king', the Cushite answered,
'and all who rise up to harm you, share the
fate of that young man!'

David mourns for Absalom

19 The king shuddered. He went up to
the room over the gate and burst into
tears; and, as he wept, he kept saying, 'Oh,
my son Absalom! My son! My son Absalom!
If only I had died instead of you! Oh, Absalom
my son, my son!' [2]Word was brought to
Joab, 'The king is weeping and mourning for
Absalom.' [3]And for the entire army that day,
victory was turned to mourning, the troops
having learnt that the king was grieving
for his son. [4]And that day the troops came
furtively back into town, like troops creeping
shamefacedly away when deserting in battle.
[5]The king had covered his face and kept
crying aloud, 'My son Absalom! Oh,
Absalom my son, my son!'
[6]Joab went inside to the king and said,
'Today you have made all your servants feel
ashamed—today, when they have saved your
life, the lives of your sons and daughters, the
lives of your wives and the lives of your
concubines!—because you love those who
hate you and hate those who love you. [7]Today
you have made it plain that commanders and
soldiers mean nothing to you—for today I
can see that you would be content if we were
all dead, provided that Absalom was alive!
[8]Now get up, come out and reassure your
soldiers; for if you do not come out, I swear
by Yahweh, not one man will stay with you
tonight; and this will be a worse misfortune
for you than anything that has happened to
you from your youth until now!' [9]The king
got up and took his seat at the gate. An
announcement was made to the whole army:
'The king is sitting at the gate.' And the
whole army assembled in front of the king.

Preparations for David's return

[10]Israel had fled, dispersing to their homes.
Throughout the tribes of Israel all was dissen-
sion and people began saying, 'The king,
having freed us from the clutches of our
enemies, having saved us from the clutches
of the Philistines, has himself had to flee the
country to escape from Absalom; [11]and now
Absalom, whom we had anointed to reign
over us, has died in battle. Why does no one
suggest that the king should be brought
back?'
[12b]What was being said throughout Israel
reached the king. [12a]King David then sent
word to the priests Zadok and Abiathar, 'Say
to the elders of Judah, "Why should you be
the last to bring the king home? [13]You are
my brothers, you are my own flesh and bone:
why should you be the last to bring the king
back?" [14]And say to Amasa, "Are you not
my own flesh and bone? May God bring
unnameable ills on me and worse ills, too, if
you do not become my permanent army
commander instead of Joab!" ' [15]Thus he
rallied the hearts of the men of Judah to a
man and, as a result, they sent word to the
king, 'Come back, you and all who serve
you.'

Episodes connected with David's return: Shimei

[16]So the king started home and reached the
Jordan. Judah, coming to meet the king to
escort him across the Jordan, had arrived at
Gilgal. [17]Shimei son of Gera, the Benjaminite
of Bahurim, hurried down with the men of
Judah to meet King David. [18]With him were
a thousand men from Benjamin. Ziba,
servant of the House of Saul, with his fifteen
sons and twenty servants, arrived at the
Jordan before the king [19]and worked
manfully ferrying the king's family across
and doing whatever he required.
While the king was crossing the Jordan,
Shimei son of Gera fell at the king's feet
[20]and said to the king, 'I hope my lord does
not regard me as guilty of a crime! Forget
about the wrong your servant did on the day
my lord the king left Jerusalem. Let my lord
not hold my guilt against me. [21]For your
servant is aware of having sinned, and that is
why I have come today—the first member of
the whole House of Joseph to come down to
meet my lord the king.'
[22]At this, Abishai son of Zeruiah spoke up
and said, 'Does Shimei not deserve death
for having cursed Yahweh's anointed?' [23]To
which David replied, 'What concern is my

business to you, sons of Zeruiah, that you
should oppose my wishes today? Could
anyone be put to death in Israel today? Today
I know for sure that I am king of Israel?'
24 'Your life is spared,' the king said. And the
king gave him his oath.

Meribbaal

25 Meribbaal son of Saul also went down to
meet the king. He had not cared for his feet
or hands, he had not trimmed his moustache
or washed his clothes from the day of the
king's departure till the day of his peaceful
return.
26 When he arrived from Jerusalem to greet
the king, the king asked him, 'Why did you
not come with me, Meribbaal?' 27 'My lord
king,' he replied, 'my retainer deceived
me. Your servant said to him, "Saddle the
donkey for me to ride, so that I can go with
the king," your servant being lame. 28 He has
slandered your servant to my lord the king.
My lord the king, however, is like the Angel
of God, so do as you think right. 29 My father's
entire family deserved no better than death
from my lord the king, and yet you admitted
your servant to the ranks of those who eat at
your table. What right have I to make any
further appeal to the king?' 30 The king said,
'You need say no more. I rule that you and
Ziba divide the property between you.' 31 'Let
him take it all,' Meribbaal said to the king,
'since my lord the king has come back home
in peace!'

Barzillai

32 Barzillai the Gileadite had come down from
Rogelim and accompanied the king towards
the Jordan, intending to take leave of him at
the Jordan. 33 Barzillai was a man of great age;
he was eighty years old. He had kept the king
in provisions during his stay at Mahanaim,
being a very wealthy man. 34 'Come with me',
the king said to Barzillai, 'and I will provide
for you at my side in Jerusalem.' 35 Barzillai
replied to the king, 'How many years have I
left to live, for me to go up to Jerusalem with
the king? 36 I am now eighty years old; can I
tell the good from the bad? Has your servant
any taste for his food and drink? Can I still
hear the voices of men and women singers?
Why should your servant be a further burden
to my lord the king? 37 Your servant will go a
little way across the Jordan with the king; but
why should the king reward me so generously
for that? 38 Please allow your servant to go
home again, so that I can die in my own town
near the grave of my father and mother. But
here is your servant Chimham; let him go
with my lord the king; treat him as you think
right.' 39 The king said, 'Let Chimham come
along with me then; I shall do whatever you
wish for him, and anything you request I
shall do for your sake.' 40 The people then
all crossed the Jordan, and the king, having
crossed, kissed Barzillai and blessed him,
and the latter went home.

Judah and Israel dispute over the king

41 The king went on to Gilgal and Chimham
went with him. All the people of Judah
accompanied the king, and also half the
people of Israel. 42 All the men of Israel then
came to the king. 'Why', they asked the king,
'have our brothers, the men of Judah, carried
you off and brought the king and his family
across the Jordan, and all David's men with
him?' 43 All the men of Judah retorted to the
men of Israel, 'Because the king is more
closely related to us. Why do you take offence
at this? Have we been eating at the king's
expense? Have we taken any position for
ourselves?' 44 The men of Israel replied to the
men of Judah, 'We have ten shares in the
king and, what is more, we are your elder
brothers, so why have you slighted us? Were
we not the first to suggest bringing back our
king?' The men of Judah's words were even
more intemperate than those of the men of
Israel.

Sheba's revolt

20 Now there happened to be a scoundrel
there called Sheba son of Bichri, a
Benjaminite, who sounded the trumpet and
shouted:

> We have no share in David,
> we have no heritage in the son of Jesse.
> Every man to his tents, O Israel!

2 At this all the men of Israel deserted David
and followed Sheba son of Bichri. But the
men of Judah stuck close to their king, from
the Jordan all the way to Jerusalem.
3 David returned to his palace in Jerusalem.
The king took the ten concubines, whom he
had left to look after the palace, and put them

under guard. He provided for their upkeep but never went near them again; they were shut away until the day they died, widows, as it were, of a living man.

Assassination of Amasa

[4]The king said to Amasa, 'Summon me the men of Judah and be here yourself within three days.' [5]Amasa went off to summon Judah, but he took longer than the time fixed by David. [6]David then said to Abishai, 'Sheba son of Bichri is now in a position to do us more damage even than Absalom. Take your master's retainers and be after him, before he can reach any fortified towns and elude us.' [7]Joab, the Cherethites, the Pelethites and all the champions took the field under Abishai, setting off from Jerusalem in pursuit of Sheba son of Bichri. [8]They were near the great stone at Gibeon when Amasa met them, coming the other way. Joab was wearing his uniform, over which he had buckled on a sword hanging from his waist in its scabbard; the sword came out and fell. [9]Joab said to Amasa, 'Are you well, brother?' and, with his right hand, took Amasa by the beard to kiss him. [10]Amasa paid no attention to the sword, which Joab had now picked up, and Joab struck him with it in the belly, spilling his entrails all over the ground. He did not need to strike a second blow; and Amasa died, while Joab and Abishai hurried on in pursuit of Sheba son of Bichri.

[11]One of Joab's men stood on guard beside Amasa, shouting, 'Whoever is on Joab's side, whoever is for David, follow Joab!' [12]Amasa meanwhile lay wallowing in his blood in the middle of the road. Seeing that everyone was stopping, the man dragged Amasa off the road into the field and threw a cloak over him, having realised that everyone passing would stop. [13]Once Amasa had been taken off the road, the men all carried on, following Joab in pursuit of Sheba son of Bichri.

End of the revolt

[14]Sheba crossed all the tribes of Israel as far as Abel Beth-Maacah, and the Bichrites all . . . They formed up and followed him. [15]Laying siege to him in Abel Beth-Maacah, they threw up a ramp against the outer wall of the town, [16]while the whole army accompanying Joab undermined the wall to bring it down. A quick-witted woman shouted from the town, 'Listen! [17]Listen! Say to Joab, "Come here, I want to speak to you." ' He came forward, and the woman said, 'Are you Joab?' 'I am', he replied. She said, 'Listen to what your servant says.' 'I am listening,' he replied. [18]She then spoke as follows, 'In olden days people used to say, "Abel and Dan are where you should enquire [19]whether a tradition established by the faithful of Israel has finally died out." And yet you are trying to destroy a town, a metropolis of Israel. Why do you want to devour Yahweh's heritage?' [20]'The last thing I want to do', said Joab, 'is either to devour or to destroy. [21]This is not the issue; a man from the highlands of Ephraim, called Sheba son of Bichri, has revolted against the king, against David. Hand that one man over and I will raise the siege of the town.' 'Very well,' the woman said to Joab, 'his head will be thrown over the wall to you.' [22]The woman went and spoke to all the people as her wisdom dictated. They cut off the head of Sheba son of Bichri and threw it down to Joab. He had the trumpet sounded and they withdrew from the town and all went home, while Joab himself went back to the king in Jerusalem.

David's principal officials[a]

[23]Joab commanded the whole army; Benaiah son of Jehoiada commanded the Cherethites and Pelethites; [24]Adoram was in charge of forced labour; Jehoshaphat son of Ahilud was herald; [25]Shiya was secretary; Zadok and Abiathar were priests; [26]also: Ira the Jairite was David's priest.

20a =8:16–18.

II: SUPPLEMENTS[a]

The great famine and the execution of Saul's descendants

21 In the days of David there was a famine which lasted for three years on end. David consulted Yahweh, and Yahweh said, 'Saul and his family have incurred bloodguilt, by putting the Gibeonites to death.' [2]Then the king summoned the Gibeonites and said—now, the Gibeonites were not Israelites, but were a remnant of the Amorites, to whom the Israelites had bound themselves by oath; Saul, however, in his zeal for the Israelites and for Judah, had done his best to exterminate them—hence David said to the Gibeonites, [3]'What can I do for you? How can I make amends, so that you will call a blessing down on Yahweh's heritage?' [4]The Gibeonites replied, 'Our quarrel with Saul and his family cannot be settled for silver or gold, nor by putting to death one man in Israel.' David said, 'Say what you want and I will do it for you.' [5]Then they replied to the king, 'The man who dismembered us and planned to annihilate us, so that we should not exist anywhere in Israelite territory—[6]we want seven of his descendants handed over to us; and we shall dismember them before Yahweh at Gibeon on Yahweh's hill.' 'I shall hand them over,' said the king. [7]The king, however, spared Meribbaal son of Jonathan, son of Saul, on account of the oath by Yahweh binding them together, binding David and Jonathan son of Saul. [8]The king took the two sons born to Saul by Rizpah daughter of Aiah: Armoni and Meribbaal; and the five sons borne by Merab daughter of Saul to Adriel son of Barzillai, of Meholah. [9]He handed these over to the Gibeonites who dismembered them before Yahweh on the hill. The seven of them perished together; they were put to death in the first days of the harvest, at the beginning of the barley harvest.

[10]Rizpah daughter of Aiah, wearing sacking and spreading some out for herself on the rock, from the beginning of the barley harvest until the rain fell on them from heaven, kept the birds of the sky away from them in the daytime, and the wild animals away at night. [11]David was told of what Saul's concubine, Rizpah daughter of Aiah, had done.

[12]David went and recovered the bones of Saul and his son Jonathan from the notables of Jabesh in Gilead. The latter had stolen them from the square in Beth-Shean, where the Philistines had hung them, when the Philistines had defeated Saul at Gilboa. [13]David fetched the bones of Saul and his son Jonathan. The bones of the men who had been dismembered were collected [14]and these, with the bones of Saul and his son Jonathan, were buried in the territory of Benjamin, at Zela, in the tomb of Saul's father, Kish. The king's orders were carried out to the letter and after that, God took pity on the country.

Various exploits against the Philistines

[15]Once again the Philistines made war on Israel. David went down with his retainers; they fought the Philistines and David began to tire. [16]There was a champion, one of the sons of Rapha. His spear weighed three hundred shekels of bronze; he was wearing a new sword and was confident of killing David. [17]Abishai son of Zeruiah came to his rescue, however, attacking the Philistine and killing him. Then it was that David's men swore the following oath to him, 'You are never to go into battle with us again, in case you should extinguish the lamp of Israel!'

[18]After this, war with the Philistines broke out again at Gob. This was when Sibbecai of Hushah killed Saph, one of the sons of Rapha.

[19]Again, war with the Philistines broke out at Gob, and Elhanan son of Jair, of Bethlehem, killed Goliath of Gath, the shaft of whose spear was like a weaver's beam.

[20]There was further warfare at Gath, where there was a man of huge stature with six fingers on each hand and six toes on each foot, twenty-four in all. He too was a son of Rapha. [21]When he defied Israel, Jonathan son of Shimea, brother of David cut him down.

[22]These four were sons of Rapha in Gath

21a Chh. 21—24 interrupt the succession narrative with 6 appendices in balancing pairs: famine and plague (21:1–14; 24), military exploits (21:15–22; 23:8–39), hymns of David (22; 23:1–7).

and fell at the hands of David and his retainers.

A hymn of victory [a]

22 David addressed the words of this song to Yahweh, when Yahweh had delivered him from the clutches of all his enemies and from the clutches of Saul. 2He said:

Yahweh is my rock and my fortress,
3my deliverer is my God.
I take refuge in him, my rock,
my shield, my saving strength,
my stronghold, my place of refuge.

My Saviour, you have saved me
from violence;
4I call to Yahweh, who is worthy of praise,
and I am saved from my foes.

5With Death's breakers closing in on me,
Belial's torrents ready to swallow me,
6Sheol's snares on every side of me,
Death's traps lying ahead of me,

7I called to Yahweh in my anguish,
I cried for help to my God,
from his Temple he heard my voice,
my cry came to his ears!

8Then the earth quaked and rocked,
the heavens' foundations shuddered,
they quaked at his blazing anger.
9Smoke rose from his nostrils,
from his mouth devouring fire
(coals were kindled at it).

10He parted the heavens and came down,
a storm-cloud underneath his feet;
11riding one of the winged creatures,
he flew,
soaring on the wings of the wind.

12He wrapped himself in darkness,
his pavilion dark waters and dense cloud.
13A brightness lit up before him,
hail and blazing fire.

14Yahweh thundered from the heavens,
the Most High made his voice heard.
15He shot his arrows and scattered them,
his lightning flashed and routed them.

16The very springs of ocean were exposed,
the world's foundations were laid bare,
at the roaring of Yahweh,
at the blast of breath from his nostrils!

17He reached down from on high,
snatched me up,
pulled me from the watery depths,
18rescued me from my mighty foe,
from my enemies
who were stronger than I.

19They assailed me on my day of disaster,
but Yahweh was there to support me,
20he freed me, set me at large,
he rescued me, because he loves me.

21Yahweh rewards me for my uprightness,
as my hands are pure so he repays me,
22since I have kept the ways of Yahweh,
and not fallen away from my God.

23His judgements are all before me,
his statutes I have not put away from me;
24I am blameless before him,
I keep myself clear of evil.

25Hence Yahweh repaid me
for acting uprightly
because he could see I was pure.
26Faithful you are to the faithful,
blameless with the blameless,

27sincere to the sincere
but cunning to the crafty,
28you save a people that is humble
and humiliate those with haughty looks.

29Yahweh, you yourself are my lamp,
my God lights up my darkness;
30with you I storm the rampart
with my God I can scale any wall.

31This God, his way is blameless;
the word of Yahweh
is refined in the furnace,
for he alone is the shield
of all who take refuge in him.

32For who is God but Yahweh,
who is a rock but our God:
33this God who girds me with strength,
who makes my way free from blame,

34who makes me as swift as a deer
and sets me firmly on the heights,
35who trains my hands for battle
my arms to bend a bow of bronze.

36You give me your invincible shield,
you never cease to listen to me,
37you give me the strides of a giant,
give me ankles that never weaken—

22a =Ps 18.

38I pursue my enemies
and exterminate them,
not turning back till they are annihilated;
39I strike them down, and they cannot rise,
they fall, they are under my feet.

40You have girded me with strength
for the fight,
bent down my assailants beneath me,
41made my enemies retreat before me;
and those who hate me I destroy.

42They cry out, there is no one to save,
to Yahweh, but no answer comes.
43I crumble them like the dust
of the squares,
trample them like the mud of the streets.

44You free me from the quarrels
of my people,
you place me at the head of the nations,
a people I did not know
are now my servants,

45foreigners come wooing my favour,
no sooner do they hear
than they obey me,
46foreigners grow faint of heart,
they come trembling
out of their fastnesses.

47Life to Yahweh! Blessed be my rock!
Exalted be the God of my salvation,
48the God who gives me vengeance
and crushes the peoples under me,

49who takes me away from my enemies.
You lift me high above those
who attack me,
you deliver me from the man of violence.

50For this I will praise you, Yahweh,
among the nations,
and sing praise to your name.
51He saves his king, time after time,
displays faithful love for his anointed,
for David and his heirs for ever.

Last words of David

23 These are the last words of David:

Thus speaks David son of Jesse,
thus speaks the man raised to eminence,
the anointed of the God of Jacob,
the singer of the songs of Israel:

2The spirit of Yahweh speaks through me,
his word is on my tongue;
3the God of Jacob has spoken,
the Rock of Israel has said to me:

He whose rule is upright on earth,
who rules in the fear of God,
4is like the morning light at sunrise
(on a cloudless morning)
making the grass of the earth
sparkle after rain.

5Yes, my House stands firm with God:
he has made an eternal covenant with me,
all in order, well assured;
does he not bring to fruition
my every victory and desire?

6But men of Belial he rejects like thorns,
for these are never taken up in the hand:
7no one touches them
except with a pitchfork or spear-shaft,
and then only to burn them to nothing!

David's champions

8These are the names of David's champions:
Ishbaal the Hachmonite leader of the Three;
it was he who brandished his spear over eight
hundred men whom he had killed at one
time. 9Next, there was Eleazar son of Dodo,
the Ahohite, one of the three champions. He
was with David at Pas-Dammim when the
Philistines mustered for battle there and the
men of Israel had disbanded. 10But he stood
his ground and cut down the Philistines until
his hand was so stiff that he could not let go
of the sword. Yahweh brought about a great
victory that day, and the people rallied
behind him, although only to plunder.
11Next, there was Shamma son of Elah, the
Hararite. The Philistines had mustered at
Lehi. There was a field full of lentils there;
the people fled from the Philistines, 12but he
took his stand in the middle of the field, held
it, and cut down the Philistines; and Yahweh
brought about a great victory.

13Three members of the Thirty went down
at the beginning of the harvest and came
to David at the Cave of Adullam while a
company of Philistines was encamped in the
Valley of the Rephaim. 14David was then in
the stronghold, and there was a Philistine
garrison in Bethlehem. 15Longingly David
said, 'If only someone would fetch me a drink
of water from the well that stands by the gate
at Bethlehem!' 16At this, the three cham-
pions, forcing their way through the Phili-
stine camp, drew water from the well that
stands by the gate of Bethlehem and, taking

it away, presented it to David. He, however,
would not drink any of it, but poured it out
as a libation to Yahweh. 17'Yahweh preserve
me', he said, 'from doing such a thing! This
is the blood of men who went at risk of their
lives.' That was why he would not drink.
Such were the deeds of these three
champions.
18Abishai, brother of Joab and son of
Zeruiah, was leader of the Thirty. It was he
who brandished his spear over three hundred
men whom he had killed, winning himself a
name among the Thirty. 19He was a most
illustrious member of the Thirty and became
their captain, but he was not equal to the
Three.
20Benaiah of Kabzeel was the son of Jeho-
iada and hero of many exploits. He it was
who slaughtered two formidable Moabites
and, one snowy day, climbed down and
slaughtered the lion in the storage-well. 21He
also slaughtered an Egyptian of great stature.
The Egyptian was armed with a spear, but
he took him on with a staff, tore the spear
from the Egyptian's hand and killed the man
with it. 22Such were the exploits of Benaiah
son of Jehoiada, winning him a name among
the thirty champions. 23He was a most illus-
trious member of the Thirty, but he was
not equal to the Three. David put him in
command of his bodyguard.

24Asahel brother of Joab was one
of the Thirty;
Elhanan son of Dodo, of Bethlehem;
25Shammah of Harod;
Elika of Harod;
26Helez of Beth-Pelet;
Ira son of Ikkesh, of Tekoa;
27Abiezer of Anathoth;
Sibbecai of Hushah;
28Zalmon of Ahoh;
Maharai of Netophah;
29Heled son of Baanah, of Netophah;
Ittai son of Ribai, of Gibeah in Benjamin;
30Benaiah of Pirathon;
Hiddai of the Torrents of Gaash;
31Abibaal of Beth-ha-Arabah;
Azmaveth of Bahurim;
32Eliahba of Shaalbon;
Jashen of Gimzo;
Jonathan 33son of Shammah, of Harar;
Ahiam son of Sharar, of Harar;
34Eliphelet son of Ahasbai, of Beth-Maacah;
Eliam son of Ahithophel, of Gilo;
35Hezro of Carmel;
Paarai of Arab;
36Igal son of Nathan, of Zobah;
Bani the Gadite;
37Zelek the Ammonite;
Naharai of Beeroth squire to Joab,
son of Zeruiah;
38Ira of Jattir;
Gareb of Jattir;
39Uriah the Hittite—

thirty-seven in all.

The census

24 Again, Yahweh's anger was aroused
against Israel, and he incited David
against them. 'Go,' he said, 'take a census of
Israel and Judah.' 2The king said to Joab and
the senior army officers who were with him,
'Now, go through all the tribes of Israel from
Dan to Beersheba, and take a census of
the people; I wish to know the size of the
population.' 3Joab said to the king, 'May
Yahweh your God multiply the people a
hundred times—however many there are—
while my lord the king still has eyes to see it,
but why should my lord the king be set on
this?' 4The king nonetheless enforced his
order on Joab and the senior officers, and
Joab and the senior officers left the king's
presence, to take a census of the people of
Israel.
5They crossed the Jordan and made a start
with Aroer and the town in the middle of the
valley, then moved on to the Gadites and to
Jazer. 6They then went to Gilead and the
territory of the Hittites, to Kadesh; they then
went to Dan and from Dan cut across to
Sidon. 7They then went to the fortress of
Tyre and to all the towns of the Hittites and
Canaanites ending up in the Negeb of Judah
at Beersheba. 8Having travelled throughout
the country, after nine months and twenty
days they returned to Jerusalem.
9Joab gave the king the census results
for the people; Israel had eight hundred
thousand fighting men who could wield a
sword, and Judah five hundred thousand.

The pestilence. God's forgiveness

10But afterwards David's heart misgave him
for having taken a census of the people. David
then said to Yahweh, 'I have committed a
grave sin by doing this. But now, Yahweh, I
beg you to forgive your servant for this fault,

for I have acted very foolishly.' 11When,
however, David got up next morning, the
following message had come from Yahweh
to the prophet Gad, David's seer, 12'Go and
say to David, "Yahweh says this: I offer you
three things; choose which one of them I am
to inflict on you." ' 13So Gad went to David
and said, 'Which do you prefer: to have three
years of famine befall your country; to flee
for three months before a pursuing army;
or to have three days of epidemic in your
country? Now think, and decide how I am to
answer him who sends me.' 14David said
to Gad, 'I am very apprehensive . . . Better
to fall into Yahweh's hands, since his mercies
are great, than to fall into the hands of men!'
15So David chose the epidemic.

It was the time of the wheat harvest. So
Yahweh unleashed an epidemic on Israel
from that morning until the time determined;
plague ravaged the people and, of the people
from Dan to Beersheba, seventy thousand
died. 16But when the angel stretched his hand
towards Jerusalem to destroy it, Yahweh felt
sorry about the calamity and said to the angel
who was destroying the people, 'Enough
now! Hold your hand!' The angel of Yahweh
was standing by the threshing-floor of
Araunah the Jebusite. 17When David saw the
angel who was ravaging the people, he said
to Yahweh, 'I was the one who sinned. I was
the one who acted wrongly. But these, the
flock, what have they done? Let your hand
lie heavy on me and on my family!'

The building of an altar

18Gad went to David that day and said, 'Go
up and raise an altar to Yahweh on the
threshing-floor of Araunah the Jebusite.'
19So, at Gad's bidding, David went up, as
Yahweh had ordered. 20When Araunah
looked up and saw the king and his retinue
advancing towards him—Araunah was
threshing the wheat—Araunah came for-
ward and prostrated himself on the ground
at the king's feet. 21'Why has my lord the
king come to his servant?' Araunah asked.
David replied, 'To buy the threshing-floor
from you, to build an altar to Yahweh, so
that the plague may be lifted from the people.'
22Araunah said to David, 'Let my lord the
king take it and make what offerings he
thinks fit. Here are the oxen for the burnt
offering, the threshing-sleds and the oxen's
yokes for the wood. 23My lord the king's
servant will give the king everything. And',
Araunah said to the king, 'may Yahweh your
God accept what you offer!'

24'No,' said the king to Araunah, 'I shall
give you a price for it; I will not offer Yahweh
my God burnt offerings which have cost me
nothing.' David bought the threshing-floor
and the oxen for fifty shekels of silver.
25David built an altar to Yahweh and offered
burnt offerings and communion sacrifices.
Yahweh then took pity on the country and
the plague was lifted from Israel.

THE BOOKS OF THE
KINGS

The two Books of Kings, originally forming one whole, make up the final part of the deuteronomic history. They trace the gradual decline of the monarchy from the splendour of Solomon until the final destruction. Solomon himself, though he lost some territory, developed a trade empire and was the centre of a glittering court where the arts and literature flourished; his greatest achievement was the building of the Temple. But the north and the south had never welded together and after his death they split into two kingdoms. The prophetic movement in the northern kingdom failed to prevent a slide into worship of false gods and materialism, until Samaria was sacked by Assyrian armies in 721 BC and the people were deported. The promises to David's line gave the southern kingdom more stability, but foreign influences and especially political alliances again corrupted the true worship of Yahweh. Despite short-lived reforms and the warnings of the great prophets, Judah could be purged only by deportations to Babylon starting in 597, and finally by the destruction of Jerusalem in 586.

The Books of Kings are essentially a religious history, and the deuteronomic editor traces his fourfold pattern of infidelity, punishment, repentance and deliverance through the material he brings together from a variety of sources. Every king is assessed on his fidelity to Yahweh, rather than on any material or political achievement, and more particularly on his resistance to, or encouragement of, false worship. The significance of this period lies in the failure of the institutions of Temple, priesthood and monarchy to ensure fidelity to Yahweh. The prophets called for a more personal and interior religion to replace them, a new heart and a new spirit.

PLAN OF THE BOOKS

THE BOOKS OF THE KINGS

THE FIRST BOOK OF THE KINGS

I: THE DAVIDIC SUCCESSION

Last days of David and activities of Adonijah

1 King David was now a very old man, and
though wrapped in bedclothes he could
not keep warm. 2So his servants said to him,
'Let us find a young girl for my lord the king,
to wait on the king and look after him; she
will lie close beside you and this will keep my
lord the king warm.' 3Having searched for a
beautiful girl throughout the territory of
Israel, they found Abishag of Shunem and
brought her to the king. 4The girl was very
beautiful. She looked after the king and
waited on him but the king did not have
intercourse with her. 5Now Adonijah son of

Haggith was growing pretentious and saying,
'I shall be king!' Accordingly, he procured a
chariot and team with fifty guards to run
ahead of him. 6Never once in his life had his
father crossed him by saying, 'Why are you
behaving like that?' He was very handsome
too; his mother had given birth to him after
Absalom. 7He conferred with Joab son of
Zeruiah and with the priest Abiathar, who
both rallied to Adonijah's cause; 8but neither
Zadok the priest, nor Benaiah son of
Jehoiada, nor the prophet Nathan, nor
Shimei and Rei, nor David's champions,
supported Adonijah.
9One day when Adonijah was sacrificing
sheep, oxen and fattened calves at the Sliding
Stone which is beside the Fuller's Spring, he
invited all his brothers, the royal princes, and
all the men of Judah in the king's service;
10but he did not invite the prophet Nathan,
or Benaiah, or the champions, or his brother
Solomon.

The intrigues of Nathan and Bathsheba

11Nathan then said to Bathsheba, Solomon's
mother, 'Have you not heard that, unknown
to our lord David, Adonijah son of Haggith
has become king? 12Well, this is my advice
to you if you want to save your own life and
the life of your son Solomon. 13Go straight in
to King David and say, "My lord king, did
you not make your servant this promise on
oath: Your son Solomon is to be king after
me; he is the one who is to sit on my throne?
How is it, then, that Adonijah is king?"
14And while you are still there talking to the
king, I shall come in after you and confirm
what you say.'
15So Bathsheba went to the king in his room
(he was very old and Abishag of Shunem was
in attendance on him). 16She knelt, pros-
trated herself before the king, and the king
said, 'What do you want?' 17'My lord,' she
replied, 'you swore to your servant by
Yahweh your God, "Your son Solomon is to
be king after me; he is the one who is to sit
on my throne." 18And now here is Adonijah
king, and you, my lord king, knowing
nothing about it! 19He has sacrificed quan-
tities of oxen, fattened calves and sheep,
and invited all the royal princes, the priest
Abiathar, and Joab the army commander;
but he has not invited your servant Solomon.
20Yet you are the man, my lord king, to whom
all Israel looks, to tell them who is to succeed
my lord the king. 21And when my lord the
king falls asleep with his ancestors, Solomon
and I shall be made to suffer for this.'
22She was still speaking to the king when
the prophet Nathan came in. 23The king was
told, 'The prophet Nathan is here'; and he
came into the king's presence and prostrated
himself on his face before the king. 24'My
lord king,' said Nathan, 'is this, then, your
decree, "Adonijah is to be king after me; he
is the one who is to sit on my throne"?
25For he has gone down today and sacrificed
quantities of oxen, fattened calves and sheep,
and invited all the royal princes, the army
commanders, and the priest Abiathar; and
they are there now, eating and drinking in
his presence and shouting, "Long live King
Adonijah!" 26He has not, however, invited
me your servant, Zadok the priest, Benaiah
son of Jehoiada, or your servant Solomon.
27Can it be that this is done with my lord the
king's approval and that you have not told
those loyal to you who is to succeed to the
throne of my lord the king?'

Solomon is consecrated king on David's nomination

28King David then spoke. 'Call Bathsheba to
me,' he said. And she came into the king's
presence and stood before him. 29Then the
king swore this oath, 'As Yahweh lives, who
has delivered me from all adversity, 30just as
I swore to you by Yahweh, God of Israel, that
your son Solomon should be king after me
and take my place on my throne, so I shall
bring it about this very day.' 31Bathsheba
knelt down, prostrated herself on her face
before the king and said, 'May my lord King
David live for ever!' 32Then King David
said, 'Summon Zadok the priest, the prophet
Nathan and Benaiah son of Jehoiada.' So
they came into the king's presence. 33'Take
the royal guard with you,' said the king,
'mount my son Solomon on my own mule and
escort him down to Gihon. 34There Zadok the
priest and the prophet Nathan are to anoint
him king of Israel; then sound the trumpet
and shout, "Long live King Solomon!"
35Then you are to escort him back, and he is
then to assume my throne and be king in
place of me, for he is the man whom I have
appointed as ruler of Israel and of Judah.'
36Benaiah son of Jehoiada answered the king.
'Amen!' he said. 'And may Yahweh, God of

my lord the king, confirm it! 37As Yahweh
has been with my lord the king, so may he
be with Solomon and make his throne even
greater than the throne of my lord King
David!'
38Zadok the priest, the prophet Nathan,
Benaiah son of Jehoiada, and the Cherethites
and Pelethites then went down; they
mounted Solomon on King David's mule and
escorted him to Gihon. 39Zadok the priest
took the horn of oil from the Tent and
anointed Solomon. They sounded the
trumpet and all the people shouted, 'Long
live King Solomon!' 40The people all escorted
him back, with pipes playing and loud
rejoicing and shouts to split the earth.

Adonijah is afraid

41Adonijah and his guests, who had by then
finished their meal, all heard the noise. Joab
too heard the sound of the trumpet and said,
'What is that noise of uproar in the city?'
42While he was still speaking, Jonathan son
of Abiathar the priest arrived. 'Come in,'
Adonijah said, 'you are an honest man, so
you must be bringing good news.' 43'The
truth is,' Jonathan answered, 'our lord King
David has made Solomon king. 44With him,
the king sent Zadok the priest, the prophet
Nathan, Benaiah son of Jehoiada and the
Cherethites and Pelethites; they mounted
him on the king's mule, 45and Zadok the
priest and the prophet Nathan have anointed
him king at Gihon; and they have gone back
again with shouts of joy and the city is now
in an uproar; that was the noise you heard.
46What is more, Solomon is seated on the
royal throne. 47And further, the king's offi-
cers have been to congratulate our lord King
David with the words, "May your God make
the name of Solomon more glorious than
yours, and his throne more exalted than your
own!" And the king bowed down on his bed,
48and then said, "Blessed be Yahweh, God
of Israel, for setting one of my own sons on
the throne while I am still alive to
see it!" '
49At this, all Adonijah's guests, taking
fright, got up and made off in their several
directions. 50Adonijah, in terror of Solomon,
got up and ran off to cling to the horns of the
altar. 51Solomon was told, 'You should know
that Adonijah is terrified of King Solomon
and is now clinging to the horns of the altar,
saying, "Let King Solomon first swear to me
that he will not have his servant executed." '
52'Should he bear himself honourably,'
Solomon answered, 'not one hair of his shall
fall to the ground; but if he proves difficult,
he shall die.' 53King Solomon then sent for
him to be brought down from the altar; he
came and threw himself prostrate before
King Solomon; Solomon said to him, 'Go to
your house.'

David's testament. His death

2 As David's life drew to its close he laid
this charge on his son Solomon, 2'I am
going the way of all the earth. Be strong and
show yourself a man. 3Observe the injunc-
tions of Yahweh your God, following his ways
and keeping his laws, his commandments, his
ordinances and his decrees, as stands written
in the Law of Moses, so that you may be
successful in everything you do and under-
take, 4and that Yahweh may fulfil the promise
which he made me, "If your sons are careful
how they behave, and walk loyally before me
with all their heart and soul, you will never
want for a man on the throne of Israel."
5'You know too what Joab son of Zeruiah
did to me, and what he did to the two
commanders of the army of Israel, Abner son
of Ner and Amasa son of Jether; how he
murdered them, shedding the blood of war
in time of peace and staining the belt round
my waist and the sandals on my feet with the
blood of war. 6You will be wise not to let his
grey head go down to Sheol in peace. 7As
regards the sons of Barzillai of Gilead, treat
them with faithful love, let them be among
those who eat at your table, for they were as
kind to me when I was fleeing from your
brother Absalom. 8You also have with you
Shimei son of Gera, the Benjaminite from
Bahurim. He called down a terrible curse on
me the day I left for Mahanaim, but he came
down to meet me at the Jordan and I swore
to him by Yahweh that I would not put him
to death. 9But you, you must not let him go
unpunished; you are a wise man and will
know how to deal with him, to bring his grey
head down to Sheol in blood.'
10So David fell asleep with his ancestors
and was buried in the City of David. 11David
was king of Israel for a period of forty years:
he reigned at Hebron for seven years, and in
Jerusalem for thirty-three.

The death of Adonijah

12 Solomon then sat on the throne of David,
and his sovereignty was securely established.
13 Adonijah son of Haggith went to
Bathsheba mother of Solomon. 'Do you bring
peace?' she asked. He replied, 'Yes, peace.'
14 Then he said, 'I have something to say to
you.' 'Say on,' she replied. 15 'You know', he
said, 'that the kingdom should have come to
me, and that all Israel expected me to be
king; but the crown eluded me and fell to my
brother, since it came to him from Yahweh.
16 Now I have one request to make you; do
not refuse me.' 'Go on,' she said. 17 He went
on, 'Please ask King Solomon—for he will
not refuse you—to give me Abishag of
Shunem in marriage.' 18 'Very well,'
Bathsheba replied, 'I shall speak to the king
about you.' 19 So Bathsheba went to King
Solomon to speak to him about Adonijah;
the king got up to meet her and bowed before
her; he then sat down on his throne; a seat
was brought for the king's mother, and she
sat down on his right. 20 She said, 'I have one
small request to make you; do not refuse
me.' 'Mother,' the king replied, 'make your
request, for I shall not refuse you.' 21 'Let
Abishag of Shunem', she said, 'be given in
marriage to your brother Adonijah.' 22 King
Solomon replied to his mother, 'And why do
you request Abishag of Shunem for Adon-
ijah? You might as well request the kingdom
for him, since he is my elder brother and
Abiathar the priest and Joab son of Zeruiah
are on his side.' 23 And King Solomon swore
by Yahweh: 'May God bring unnameable ills
on me, and worse ills, too,' he said, 'if
Adonijah does not pay for these words of his
with his life! 24 As Yahweh lives who has set
me securely on the throne of my father David,
and who, as he promised, has given him a
dynasty, Adonijah shall be put to death this
very day.' 25 And King Solomon com-
missioned Benaiah son of Jehoiada to strike
him down, and that was how he died.

The fate of Abiathar and Joab

26 As for Abiathar the priest, the king said to
him, 'Go to Anathoth to your estate. You
deserve to die, but I am not going to put you
to death now, since you carried the ark of
Yahweh in the presence of my father David
and shared all my father's hardships.'
27 Solomon deprived Abiathar of the priest-
hood of Yahweh, thus fulfilling the prophecy
which Yahweh had uttered against the House
of Eli at Shiloh.
28 When the news reached Joab—for Joab
had lent his support to Adonijah, though he
had not supported Absalom—he fled to the
Tent of Yahweh and clung to the horns of
the altar. 29 King Solomon was told, 'Joab has
fled to the Tent of Yahweh; he is there beside
the altar.' On this, Solomon sent word to
Joab, 'What reason did you have for fleeing
to the altar?' Joab replied, 'I was afraid of
you and fled to Yahweh.' Solomon then sent
Benaiah son of Jehoiada. 'Go', he said, 'and
strike him down.' 30 Accordingly Benaiah
went to the Tent of Yahweh. 'By order of the
king,' he said, 'come out!' 'No,' he said, 'I
will die here.' So Benaiah brought word back
to the king, 'This is what Joab said, and the
answer he gave me.' 31 'Do as he says,' the
king replied. 'Strike him down and bury him,
and so rid me and my family today of the
innocent blood which Joab has shed.
32 Yahweh will bring his blood down on his
own head, because he struck down two more
upright and better men than he, and, without
my father David's knowledge, put to the
sword Abner son of Ner, commander of the
army of Israel, and Amasa son of Jether,
commander of the army of Judah. 33 May
their blood come down on the head of Joab
and his descendants for ever, but may David,
his descendants, his dynasty, his throne, have
peace for ever from Yahweh.' 34 Whereupon
Benaiah son of Jehoiada went out, struck
Joab down and put him to death; he was
buried at his home in the desert. 35 In his place
as head of the army the king appointed
Benaiah son of Jehoiada and, in place of
Abiathar, the priest Zadok.

The disobedience and death of Shimei

36 The king had Shimei summoned to him.
'Build yourself a house in Jerusalem,' he told
him. 'You are to live there; do not leave it to
go anywhere at all. 37 The day you go out and
cross the ravine of the Kidron, be sure you
will certainly die. Your blood will be on your
own head.' 38 'That is a fair demand,' Shimei
replied to the king, 'your servant will do as
my lord the king orders.' And for a long time
Shimei lived in Jerusalem.
39 But when three years had gone by, it
happened that two of Shimei's slaves ran

away to Achish son of Maacah, king of Gath;
Shimei was told, 'Your slaves are in Gath.'
40On this, Shimei got up and saddled his
donkey and went to Akish at Gath to find his
slaves. He went off and brought his slaves
back from Gath. 41Solomon was informed
that Shimei had left Jerusalem for Gath and
come back again.

42The king had Shimei summoned to him.
'Did I not make you swear by Yahweh,' he
said, 'and did I not warn you, "The day you
leave to go anywhere at all, be sure you will
certainly die"? To which you replied, "That
is a fair demand." 43Why did you not keep
the oath to Yahweh and the order which I
imposed on you?' 44The king then said to
Shimei, 'You know well all the evil you did
to my father David. Yahweh is about to bring
your wickedness down on your own head.
45But may King Solomon be blessed, and
may the throne of David be kept secure
before Yahweh for ever!' 46The king gave
orders to Benaiah son of Jehoiada; he went
out and struck Shimei down; and that was
how he died. And now the kingdom was
securely in Solomon's hands.

II: SOLOMON IN ALL HIS GLORY

A: SOLOMON THE SAGE

Introduction

3 Solomon became the son-in-law of
Pharaoh king of Egypt; he married
Pharaoh's daughter, and took her to the City
of David until he could complete the building
of his palace, the Temple of Yahweh and
the ramparts of Jerusalem. 2The people,
however, were still sacrificing on the high
places, because at that time a dwelling-place
for the name of Yahweh had not yet been
built. 3Solomon loved Yahweh: he followed
the precepts of his father David, except that
he offered sacrifice and incense on the high
places.

Solomon's dream at Gibeon

4The king went to Gibeon to sacrifice there,
since that was the principal high place—
Solomon presented a thousand burnt offer-
ings on that altar. 5At Gibeon Yahweh
appeared to Solomon in a dream during the
night. God said, 'Ask what you would like
me to give you.' 6Solomon replied, 'You
showed most faithful love to your servant
David, my father, when he lived his life
before you in faithfulness and uprightness
and integrity of heart; you have continued
this most faithful love to him by allowing a
son of his to sit on his throne today. 7Now,
Yahweh my God, you have made your servant
king in succession to David my father. But I
am a very young man, unskilled in leader-
ship. 8And here is your servant, surrounded
with your people whom you have chosen, a
people so numerous that its number cannot
be counted or reckoned. 9So give your servant
a heart to understand how to govern your
people, how to discern between good and
evil, for how could one otherwise govern
such a great people as yours?' 10It pleased
Yahweh that Solomon should have asked for
this. 11'Since you have asked for this,' God
said, 'and not asked for long life for yourself
or riches or the lives of your enemies but
have asked for a discerning judgement for
yourself, 12here and now I do what you ask.
I give you a heart wise and shrewd as no one
has had before and no one will have after you.
13What you have not asked I shall give you
too: such riches and glory as no other king
can match. 14And I shall give you a long life,
if you follow my ways, keeping my laws
and commandments, as your father David
followed them.' 15Then Solomon woke up; it
had been a dream. He returned to Jerusalem
and stood before the ark of the covenant of
Yahweh; he presented burnt offerings and
communion sacrifices and held a banquet for
all those in his service.

The judgement of Solomon

16Later two prostitutes came to the king and
stood before him. 17'If it please you, my lord,'
one of the women said, 'this woman and I
live in the same house, and while she was in
the house I gave birth to a child. 18Now it
happened on the third day after my delivery
that this woman also gave birth to a child.
We were alone together; there was no one

else in the house with us; just the two of us
in the house. 19Now one night this woman's
son died; she overlaid him. 20And in the
middle of the night she got up and took my
son from beside me while your servant was
asleep; she took him in her arms and put her
own dead son in mine. 21When I got up to
suckle my child, there he was, dead. But in
the morning I looked at him carefully, and
he was not the child I had borne at all.' 22Then
the other woman spoke. 'That is not true!
My son is the live one, yours is the dead one';
and the first retorted, 'That is not true! Your
son is the dead one, mine is the live one.' And
so they wrangled before the king. 23'This one
says,' the king observed, ' "My son is the
one who is alive; your son is dead," while the
other says, "That is not true! Your son is the
dead one, mine is the live one." 24Bring me
a sword,' said the king; and a sword was
brought into the king's presence. 25'Cut the
living child in two,' the king said, 'and give
half to one, half to the other.' 26At this the
woman who was the mother of the living
child addressed the king, for she felt acutely
for her son. 'I beg you, my lord,' she said,
'let them give her the live child; on no account
let them kill him!' But the other said, 'He
shall belong to neither of us. Cut him in half!'
27Then the king gave his decision. 'Give the
live child to the first woman,' he said, 'and
do not kill him. She is his mother.' 28All Israel
came to hear of the judgement which the king
had pronounced and held the king in awe,
recognising that he possessed divine wisdom
for dispensing justice.

Solomon's high officials

4 King Solomon was king of all Israel, 2and
these were his high officials:

Azariah son of Zadok, priest;
3Elihaph and Ahijah sons of Shisha,
secretaries;
Jehoshaphat son of Ahilud, herald.
4(Benaiah son of Jehoiada,
commander of the army.
Zadok and Abiathar, priests);
5Azariah son of Nathan,
chief administrator;
Zabud son of Nathan, Friend of the King;
6Ahishar, master of the palace;
Eliab son of Joab, commander of the army;
Adoram son of Abda,
in charge of forced labour.

Solomon's administrators

7Solomon had twelve administrators for all
Israel who saw to the provisioning of the king
and his household; each had to provide for
one month in the year.
8These are their names:
Son of Hur, in the mountain country of
Ephraim.
9Son of Deker, in Makaz, Shaalbim, Beth-
Shemesh, Aijalon, Beth-Hanan.
10Son of Hesed, in Arubboth; his district
was Socoh and the whole territory of Hepher.
11Son of Abinadab, all the Slopes of Dor.
Tabaath Solomon's daughter was his wife.
12Baana son of Ahilud, in Taanach and
Megiddo as far as the other side of Jokmeam,
and all Beth-Shean below Jezreel, from Beth-
Shean as far as Abel-Meholah by Zarethan.
13Son of Geber, in Ramoth-Gilead: his
district was the Encampments of Jair son of
Manasseh, which are in Gilead; he had the
region of Argob, which is in Bashan: sixty
fortified towns, walled and with bolts of
bronze.
14Ahinadab son of Iddo, in Mahanaim.
15Ahimaaz in Naphtali; he too married a
daughter of Solomon, Basemath.
16Baana son of Hushai, in Asher and in the
highlands.
17Jehoshaphat son of Paruah, in Issachar.
18Shimei son of Ela, in Benjamin.
19Geber son of Uri, in the territory of Gad,
the territory of Sihon king of the Amorites
and of Og king of Bashan.
In addition, there was one administrator
in the country.
5 7These[b] administrators provided the food
for Solomon and for all those who were
admitted by him to the royal table, each for
the period of a month; they ensured that
nothing was wanting. 8They also provided
the barley and straw for the horses and
draught animals, where required, each
according to the quota demanded of him.
2The daily provisions for Solomon were:
thirty measures of fine flour and sixty meas-
ures of meal, 3ten fattened oxen, twenty free-
grazing oxen, one hundred sheep, besides
deer and gazelles, roebucks and fattened
poultry. 4For he was master of all Transeu-

5b This edition follows the order of the Gk, as more logical.

phrates—of all the kings of Transeuphrates
from Tiphsah to Gaza—and he enjoyed peace
on all his frontiers. 5 Judah and Israel lived in
security, everyone under his vine and his fig
tree, from Dan to Beersheba, throughout the
lifetime of Solomon.

4 20 Judah and Israel were numerous, as
numerous as the sand on the sea-shore;
they ate and drank and were happy.

5 1 Solomon was overlord of all the kingdoms
from the River[a] to the territory of the
Philistines and the Egyptian border. They
brought tribute and served him all his life
long. 6 And Solomon had four thousand stalls
of horses for his chariots and twelve thousand
cavalrymen.

Solomon's fame

9 God gave Solomon immense wisdom and
understanding, and a heart as vast as the sand
on the sea-shore. 10 The wisdom of Solomon
surpassed the wisdom of all the sons of the
East and all the wisdom of Egypt. 11 He was
wiser than anyone else, wiser than Ethan the
Ezrahite, than the sons of Mahol, Heman,
Calcol and Darda; his fame spread to all the
surrounding nations. 12 He composed three
thousand proverbs, and his songs numbered
a thousand and five. 13 He could discourse on
plants from the cedar in Lebanon to the
hyssop growing on the wall; and he could
discourse on animals and birds and reptiles
and fish. 14 Men from all nations came to hear
Solomon's wisdom, and he received gifts
from all the kings in the world, who had
heard of his wisdom.

B: SOLOMON THE BUILDER

Preparations for building the Temple

15 Hiram king of Tyre sent an embassy to
Solomon, having learnt that he had been
anointed king in succession to his father and
because Hiram had always been a friend of
David. 16 And Solomon sent this message to
Hiram, 17 'You are aware that my father David
was unable to build a temple for the name of
Yahweh his God, on account of the wars
waged on him from every side, until Yahweh
put his enemies under the soles of his feet.
18 But now Yahweh my God has given me
peace on every side: not one enemy, no
calamities. 19 I propose, then, to build a
temple for the name of Yahweh my God, in
accordance with what Yahweh told my father
David, "Your son whom I shall place on your
throne to succeed you will be the man to
build a temple for my name." 20 So now have
cedars of Lebanon cut down for me; my
servants will work with your servants, and I
shall pay for the hire of your servants at
whatever rate you fix. As you know, we
have no one as skilled in felling trees as
the Sidonians.' 21 When Hiram heard what
Solomon had said, he was delighted. 'Now
blessed be Yahweh,' he said, 'who has given
David a wise son to rule over this great
people!' 22 And Hiram sent word to Solomon,
'I have received your message. For my part,
I shall supply you with all you require in
the way of cedar wood and juniper. 23 Your
servants will bring these down from Lebanon
to the sea, and I shall have them towed by
sea to any place you name; I shall discharge
them there, and you will take them over. For
your part, you will see to the provisioning
of my household as I desire.' 24 So Hiram
provided Solomon with all the cedar wood
and juniper he wanted 25 while Solomon gave
Hiram twenty thousand *kor* of wheat to feed
his household, and twenty thousand *kor* of
pure oil. Solomon gave Hiram this every
year. 26 Yahweh gave Solomon wisdom as he
had promised him; good relations persisted
between Solomon and Hiram, and the two of
them concluded a treaty.

27 King Solomon raised a levy throughout
Israel for forced labour: the levy numbered
thirty thousand men. 28 He sent these to
Lebanon in relays, ten thousand a month;
they spent one month in Lebanon and two
months at home. Adoram was in charge of
the forced labour. 29 Solomon also had seventy
thousand porters and eighty thousand
quarrymen in the mountains, 30 as well as the
administrators, officials who supervised the
work, three thousand three hundred of them
in charge of the men employed in the
work. 31 At the king's orders they quarried
huge stones, special stones for the laying
of the temple foundations, dressed stones.
32 Solomon's workmen and Hiram's
workmen and the Giblites cut and assembled
the wood and stone for the building of the
Temple.

5a The Euphrates.

The Temple building

6 In the four hundred and eightieth year after the Israelites came out of Egypt, in the fourth year of Solomon's reign over Israel, in the month of Ziv, which is the second month, he began building the Temple of Yahweh. [2]The temple which King Solomon built for Yahweh was sixty cubits long, twenty cubits wide and twenty-five high. [3]The portico in front of the Hekal of the Temple was twenty cubits long across the width of the Temple and ten cubits wide along the length of the Temple. [4]He made windows for the Temple with frames and latticework. [5]He also built an annex against the Temple wall, right round the Hekal and Debir. He built lateral storeys all round; [6]the lowest lateral storey was five cubits wide, the middle one six cubits, and the third seven cubits, for he had made the outside of the Temple wall correspondingly stepped back all round, so that the annex was not attached to the Temple walls. [7](The building of the Temple was done with quarry-dressed stone; no sound of hammer or pick or any iron tool was to be heard in the Temple while it was being built.) [8]The entrance to the lowest storey was at the right-hand corner of the Temple; access to the middle storey was by a spiral staircase, and so from the middle storey to the third. [9]Having finished building the Temple, he roofed the Temple with a coffered ceiling of cedar wood. [10]Round the outside of the Temple he then built the annex which was five cubits high and was joined to the Temple by cedar-wood beams. [11]And the word of Yahweh came to Solomon, [12]'With regard to this temple which you are now building, if you follow my statutes and obey my ordinances and faithfully follow my commandments, I shall fulfil the promise which I made about you to your father David. [13]And I shall make my home among the Israelites and never forsake Israel my people.'

[14]Solomon finished building the Temple.

Interior furnishings. The Holy of Holies

[15]He lined the inside of the Temple walls with panels of cedar wood—panelling them on the inside from the floor of the Temple to the beams of the ceiling—and laid the floor of the Temple with juniper planks. [16]The twenty cubits measured from the end of the Temple he built of cedar planks from the floor to the beams, and this part was reserved as the Debir, the Holy of Holies. [17]The Temple measured forty cubits—the Hekal—in front of the Debir. [18]There was cedar wood round the inside of the Temple, ornamentally carved with gourds and rosettes; all was cedar wood, with no stone showing. [19]In the inner part of the Temple he designed a Debir, to contain the ark of the covenant of Yahweh. [20]The Debir was twenty cubits long, twenty cubits wide, and twenty high, and he overlaid it on the inside with pure gold. He made an altar of cedar wood [21]in front of the Debir and overlaid it with gold. [22]He overlaid the whole Temple with gold, the whole Temple entirely.

The great winged creatures

[23]In the Debir he made two great winged creatures of wild-olive wood. . .It was ten cubits high. [24]One winged creature's wing was five cubits long and the other wing five cubits: ten cubits from wing tip to wing tip. [25]The other winged creature also measured ten cubits; both had the same measurements and the same shape. [26]The height of one was the same as the other's. [27]He placed them in the middle of the inner chamber; their wings were spread out so that the wing of one touched one of the walls and the wing of the other touched the other wall, while their wings met in the middle of the chamber wing to wing. [28]And he overlaid them with gold. [29]All round the Temple walls he carved figures of winged creatures, palm trees and rosettes, both inside and outside. [30]He overlaid the floor of the Temple with gold, both inside and outside.

The doors. The court

[31]He made the door of the Debir with uprights of wild-olive wood, and door jambs with five indented sections, [32]and the two leaves of wild-olive wood. He carved figures of great winged creatures, palm trees and rosettes which he overlaid with gold, and he gilded winged creatures and palm trees. [33]Similarly, he made uprights of wild-olive wood for the door of the Hekal, and door jambs with four indented sections, [34]and the two leaves of juniper: one leaf had two ribs binding it, and the other had two ribs binding it. [35]He carved winged creatures, palm trees

and rosettes, which he overlaid with gold laid evenly over the carvings.

[36]He built the wall of the inner court in three courses of dressed stone and one course of cedar beams.

The date

[37]In the fourth year, in the month of Ziv, the foundations of the Temple were laid; [38]in the eleventh year, in the month of Bul—that is, the eighth month—the Temple was completed exactly as it had been planned and designed. Solomon took seven years to build it.

Solomon's palace

7 As regards his palace, Solomon spent thirteen years on it before the building was completed. [2]He built the House of the Forest of Lebanon, a hundred cubits long, fifty cubits wide, and thirty cubits high, on four rows of cedar-wood pillars, [3]with lengths of cedar wood laid horizontally on the pillars. The upper part was panelled with cedar right down to the tie-beams on forty-five pillars, fifteen in each row. [4]There were three rows of window-frames, with the windows corresponding to one another at three levels. [5]All the doorways and windows were rectangular, with the windows corresponding to one another at three levels. [6]He also made the Colonnade, fifty cubits long and thirty cubits broad, with a cornice in front. [7]He also made the Hall of the Throne where he used to dispense justice, that is, the Hall of Justice; it was panelled in cedar from floor to beams. [8]His own living quarters, in the other court and inwards from the Hall, were of the same construction. And there was a house similar to this Hall for Pharaoh's daughter whom he had taken in marriage.

[9]All these buildings were of special stones cut to measure, trimmed on the inner and outer sides with the saw, from the foundations to the coping—[10]the foundations were of special stones, huge stones, of ten and eight cubits, [11]and, above these, special stones, cut to measure, and cedar wood—[12]and, on the outside, the great court had three courses of dressed stone round it and one course of cedar beams; so also had the inner court of the Temple of Yahweh and the vestibule of the Temple.

Hiram, the bronzeworker

[13]King Solomon sent for Hiram of Tyre; [14]he was the son of a widow of the tribe of Naphtali, but his father had been a Tyrian, a bronzeworker. He was a highly intelligent craftsman, skilled in all types of bronzework. He came to King Solomon and did all this work for him.

The bronze pillars

[15]He cast the two bronze pillars; the height of one pillar was eighteen cubits, and a cord twelve cubits long gave the measurement of its girth; so also was the second pillar. [16]He made two capitals of cast bronze for the tops of the pillars; the height of one capital was five cubits, and the height of the other five cubits. [17]He made two sets of filigree to cover the moulding of the two capitals surmounting the pillars, one filigree for one capital and one filigree for the other. [18]He also made pomegranates: two rows of them round each filigree, [19b]four hundred in all, [20]applied on the raised moulding behind the filigree; there were two hundred pomegranates round one capital and the same round the other capital. [19a]The capitals surrounding the pillars were lily-shaped. [21]He erected the pillars in front of the portico of the Temple, he erected the right-hand pillar and named it Jachin; he erected the left-hand pillar and named it Boaz. [22]Thus, the work on the pillars was completed.

The bronze Sea

[23]He made the Sea of cast metal, ten cubits from rim to rim, circular in shape and five cubits high; a cord thirty cubits long gave the measurement of its girth. [24]Under its rim and completely encircling it were gourds surrounding the Sea; over a length of thirty cubits the gourds were in two rows, of one and the same casting with the rest. [25]It rested on twelve oxen, three facing north, three facing west, three facing south, three facing east; on these, their hindquarters all turned inwards, stood the Sea. [26]It was a hand's breadth in thickness, and its rim was shaped like the rim of a cup, lily-shaped. It could hold two thousand measures.

The wheeled stands and the bronze basins

27 He made the ten bronze stands; each stand
was four cubits long, four cubits wide, and
three high. 28 They were designed as follows;
they had an undercarriage and crosspieces
to the undercarriage. 29 On the crosspieces of
the undercarriage were lions and bulls and
winged creatures, and on top of the undercar-
riage was a support; under the lions and oxen
there were scrolls in the style of. . . 30 Each
stand had four bronze wheels with bronze
axles; its four feet had shoulderings under the
basin, and the shoulderings were cast. . . 31 Its
mouth measured one and a half cubits from
where the shoulderings met to the top; its
mouth was round like a stand for a vessel,
and on the mouth there were engravings too;
the crosspieces, however, were rectangular
and not round. 32 The four wheels were under
the crosspieces. The axles of the wheels were
inside the stands; the height of the wheels
was one and a half cubits. 33 The wheels were
designed like chariot wheels: their axles,
felloes, spokes and naves had all been cast.
34 There were four shoulderings at the four
corners of each stand: the stand and the
shoulderings were all of a piece. 35 At the top
of the stand there was a support, circular in
shape and half a cubit high; and on top of the
stand there were lugs. The crosspieces were
of a piece with the stand. 36 On the bands he
engraved winged creatures and lions and
palm leaves. . . and scrolls right round. 37 He
made the ten stands like this: the same casting
and the same measurements for all.

38 He made ten bronze basins; each basin
held forty measures and each basin measured
four cubits, one basin to each of the ten
stands. 39 He arranged the stands, five on the
right-hand side of the Temple, five on the
left-hand side of the Temple; the Sea he
placed on the right-hand side of the Temple,
to the south east.

The utensils. Summary

40 Hiram made the ash containers, the scoops
and the sprinkling bowls. He finished all
the work that he did for King Solomon on
the Temple of Yahweh:

41 Two pillars; the two mouldings of the
capitals surrounding the pillars; the two sets
of filigree to cover the two mouldings of the
capitals surmounting the pillars; 42 the four
hundred pomegranates for the two sets of
filigree—two rows of pomegranates for each
set of filigree;

43 the ten stands and the ten basins
on the stands;

44 the one Sea and the twelve oxen
beneath the Sea;

45 the ash containers, the scoops,
and sprinkling bowls.

All these objects made by Hiram for King
Solomon for the Temple of Yahweh were of
burnished bronze. 46 He made them by the
process of sand casting, in the plain of the
Jordan between Succoth and Zarethan.
47 There were so many of them, that the
weight of the bronze was never calculated.

48 Solomon made all the objects designed
for the Temple of Yahweh: the golden altar
and the gold table for the loaves of permanent
offering; 49 the lamp-stands, five on the right
and five on the left in front of the Debir, of
pure gold; the floral work, the lamps, the
tongs, of gold; 50 the basins, the snuffers, the
sprinkling bowls, the incense ladles and
the pans, of real gold; the door panels—
for the inner shrine—that is, the Holy of
Holies—and for the Hekal, of gold.

51 Thus all the work done by King Solomon
for the Temple of Yahweh was completed,
and Solomon brought in the gifts which
his father David had consecrated; and he
had the silver, the gold and the utensils put
into the treasuries of the Temple of
Yahweh.

The ark is brought into the Temple

8 Solomon then summoned the elders of
Israel to Jerusalem to bring the ark of the
covenant of Yahweh up from the City of
David, that is, Zion. 2 All the men of Israel
assembled round King Solomon in the month
of Ethanim, at the time of the feast (that is,
the seventh month). 3 When all the elders of
Israel had arrived, the priests took up the ark
4 and the Tent of Meeting and all the sacred
utensils which were in the Tent. 5 King
Solomon and all Israel, present with him
before the ark, sacrificed countless, innumer-
able sheep and oxen. 6 The priests brought
the ark of the covenant of Yahweh to its
place, in the Debir of the Temple, that is, in
the Holy of Holies, under the wings of the
winged creatures 7 for the winged creatures
spread their wings over the place where the
ark stood, forming a canopy over the ark and
its shafts. 8 These were so long, however, that

the ends of the shafts could be seen from the Holy Place in front of the Debir, though they could not be seen from outside. They are still there today. 9There was nothing in the ark except the two stone tablets which Moses had placed in it at Horeb, the tablets of the covenant which Yahweh made with the Israelites when they came out of Egypt.

Yahweh takes possession of his Temple

10Now when the priests came out of the Holy Place, the cloud filled the Temple of Yahweh, 11and because of the cloud the priests could not stay and perform their duties. For the glory of Yahweh filled the Temple of Yahweh.

12Then Solomon said:

Yahweh has chosen to dwell
in thick cloud.
13I have built you a princely dwelling,
a residence for you for ever.

Solomon addresses the people

14The king then turned round and blessed the whole assembly of Israel, while the whole assembly of Israel stood. 15He said, 'Blessed be Yahweh, God of Israel, who has carried out by his hand what he promised with his mouth to my father David, when he said, 16"From the day I brought my people Israel out of Egypt I chose no city, in any of the tribes of Israel, to have a temple built where my name should be; but I did choose David to rule my people Israel." 17My father David had set his heart on building a temple for the name of Yahweh, God of Israel, 18but Yahweh said to my father David, "You have set your heart on building a temple for my name, and in this you have done well; 19and yet, you are not the man to build the temple; but your son, yet to be born to you, will be the one to build the temple for my name." 20Yahweh has kept the promise which he made: I have succeeded my father David and am seated on the throne of Israel, as Yahweh promised; I have built the temple for the name of Yahweh, God of Israel, 21and in it I have made a place for the ark containing the covenant of Yahweh which he made with our ancestors when he brought them out of Egypt.'

Solomon's prayer for himself

22Then, in the presence of the whole assembly of Israel, Solomon stood facing the altar of Yahweh and, stretching out his hands towards heaven, 23said, 'Yahweh, God of Israel, there is no god like you in heaven above or on earth beneath, as loyal to the covenant and faithful in love to your servants as long as they walk wholeheartedly in your way. 24You have kept the promise you made to your servant, my father David, as you promised him you would. Today you have carried it out by your power. 25And now, Yahweh, God of Israel, keep the promise which you made to your servant David when you said, "You will never lack for a man to sit before me on the throne of Israel, provided that your sons are careful how they behave, walking before me as you yourself have done." 26So now, God of Israel, let the words come true which you spoke to your servant, my father David. 27Yet will God really live with human beings on earth? Why, the heavens, the highest of the heavens, cannot contain you. How much less this temple built by me! 28Even so, listen favourably to the prayer and entreaty of your servant, Yahweh my God; listen to the cry and to the prayer which your servant makes to you today: 29day and night may your eyes watch over this temple, over this place of which you have said, "My name will be there." Listen to the prayer which your servant offers in this place.

Solomon's prayer for the people

30'Listen to the entreaty of your servant and of your people Israel; whenever they pray in this place, listen from the place where you reside in heaven; and when you hear, forgive.

31'If someone has wronged his neighbour and a curse is laid on him to make him swear an oath here before your altar in this Temple, 32then listen from the place where you reside in heaven and do justice between your servants: condemning the guilty one by making him suffer for his conduct, and acquitting the upright by rewarding him as his uprightness deserves.

33'When your people Israel are defeated by the enemy because they have sinned against you, but then return to you and acknowledge your name, and pray and seek your favours in this Temple, 34then listen from the place where you reside in heaven; forgive the sin

of your people Israel, and bring them back to
the country which you gave to their ancestors.
35‘When the heavens are shut and there is
no rain because they have sinned against you,
if they pray in this place and praise your name
and, having been humbled by you, desist
from their sin, 36then listen from the place
where you reside in heaven and forgive the
sin of your servant and your people Israel—
for you are constantly showing them the good
way which they must follow—and send rain
on your country, which you have given to
your people as their heritage.
37‘Should there be famine in the country,
or pestilence, wind-blast or mildew, locust
or caterpillar; should their enemy lay siege
to one of their gates; should there be any
plague or any disease: 38whatever be the
prayer or entreaty of any individual aware
of a particular affliction: when that person
stretches out the hands towards this Temple,
39then listen from heaven where you reside;
forgive and, since you know what is in the
heart, deal with each as their conduct
deserves—for you alone know what is in
every human heart—40so that they may rever-
ence you throughout their lives in the country
which you gave to our ancestors.

Supplementary section

41‘Even the foreigner, not belonging to your
people Israel but coming from a distant
country, attracted by your name—42for they
too will hear of your name, of your mighty
hand and outstretched arm—if a foreigner
comes and prays in this Temple, 43listen from
heaven where you reside, and grant all that
the foreigner asks of you, so that all the
peoples of the earth may acknowledge your
name and, like your people Israel, revere you
and know that this Temple, which I have
built, bears your name.
44‘If your people go out to war against the
enemy, on whatever missions you send them,
and they pray to Yahweh, turning towards
the city which you have chosen and towards
the Temple which I have built for your name,
45then listen from heaven to their prayer and
their entreaty, and uphold their cause.
46‘When they sin against you—for there is
no one who does not sin—and you are angry
with them and abandon them to the enemy,
and their captors carry them off to a hostile
country, be it far away or near, 47if they come
to their senses in the country to which they
have been taken as captives and repent and
entreat you in the country of their captors,
saying, “We have sinned, we have acted
perversely and wickedly,” 48and turn back to
you with all their heart and soul in the country
of the enemies who have taken them captive,
and pray to you, turning towards
the country which you gave to their ances-
tors, towards the city which you have chosen
and towards the Temple which I have built
for your name, 49listen to their prayer and
their entreaty from the place where you reside
in heaven, uphold their case, 50forgive your
people for having sinned against you and for
all the crimes against you of which they have
been guilty, and allow them to arouse the
pity of their captors so that these may have
pity on them: 51for they are your people
and your heritage whom you brought out of
Egypt, that iron foundry!

Conclusion of the prayer and blessing of the people

52‘May your eyes be open to the entreaty of
your servant and the entreaty of your people
Israel, to listen to them, whatever they ask
of you. 53For you it was who set them apart
from all the peoples of the earth to be your
heritage, as you declared through your
servant Moses when you brought our ances-
tors out of Egypt, Lord Yahweh.’
54When Solomon had finished offering to
Yahweh this whole prayer and entreaty, he
rose from where he was kneeling with hands
stretched out towards heaven before the altar
of Yahweh, 55and stood upright. And in a
loud voice he blessed the whole assembly of
Israel. 56‘Blessed be Yahweh,’ he said, ‘who
has granted rest to his people Israel, keeping
all his promises. Of all the promises of good
that he made through his servant Moses, not
one has failed. 57May Yahweh our God be
with us, as he was with our ancestors; may
he never desert us or cast us off. 58May he
turn our hearts towards him so that we may
follow all his ways and keep the command-
ments and laws and ordinances which he gave
to our ancestors. 59May these words of mine,
of my entreaty before Yahweh, be present
with Yahweh our God day and night, that he
may uphold the cause of his servant and
the cause of Israel his people, as each day
requires, 60so that all the peoples of the earth
may come to know that Yahweh is God
indeed and that there is no other. 61May your

hearts be wholly with Yahweh our God, following his laws and keeping his commandments as at this present day.'

The sacrifices on the feast of Dedication

62 The king and all Israel with him offered sacrifice before Yahweh. 63 Solomon offered a communion sacrifice of twenty-two thousand oxen and a hundred and twenty thousand sheep to Yahweh; and thus the king and all the Israelites dedicated the Temple of Yahweh. 64 On the same day the king consecrated the middle part of the court in front of the Temple of Yahweh; for that was where he presented the burnt offerings, oblations and fatty parts of the communion sacrifices, since the bronze altar which stood before Yahweh was too small to hold the burnt offering, oblation and the fatty parts of the communion sacrifice. 65 And then Solomon and with him all Israel from the Pass of Hamath to the Torrent of Egypt—a great assembly—celebrated the feast before Yahweh our God for seven days. 66 On the eighth day he dismissed the people, who bade farewell to the king and went home joyful and happy of heart over all the goodness which Yahweh had shown to his servant and his people Israel.

Yahweh appears a second time

9 When Solomon had finished building the Temple of Yahweh, the royal palace and everything else which Solomon had wanted to do, 2 Yahweh appeared to Solomon a second time, as he had appeared to him at Gibeon. 3 Yahweh said to him, 'I have heard your prayer and the entreaty which you have before me. I consecrate this temple which you have built: I place my name there for ever; my eyes and my heart will be there always. 4 For your part, if you walk before me in innocence of heart and in honesty, like your father David, if you do everything that I command and keep my laws and my ordinances, 5 I shall make your royal throne secure over Israel for ever, as I promised your father David when I said, "You will never lack for a man on the throne of Israel." 6 But if you turn away from me, either you or your descendants, and instead of keeping my commandments and laws which I have laid down for you, you go and serve other gods and worship them, 7 then I shall banish Israel from the country which I have given them, and shall disown this Temple which I have consecrated for my name, and Israel will be a proverb and a byword among all peoples. 8 As for this once-exalted Temple, everyone who passes by will be appalled, and they will whistle and say, "Why has Yahweh treated this country and this Temple like this?" 9 And the answer will be, "Because they deserted Yahweh their God who brought their ancestors out of Egypt, and they adopted other gods and worshipped and served them; that is why Yahweh has brought all these disasters on them." '

The bargain with Hiram

10 At the end of the twenty years that it took Solomon to erect the two buildings, the Temple of Yahweh and the royal palace 11 (Hiram king of Tyre had provided Solomon with all the cedar wood, juniper wood and gold that he wanted), King Solomon gave Hiram twenty towns in the territory of Galilee. 12 But when Hiram came from Tyre to view the towns that Solomon had given him, he was not pleased with them. 13 He said, 'What kind of towns are these you have given me, brother?' And to this day they are known as 'cabul-land'. 14 Hiram sent the king one hundred and twenty talents of gold.

Forced labour for Solomon's building programme

15 This is an account of the forced labour levied by King Solomon for building the Temple of Yahweh, his own palace, the Millo and the fortifications of Jerusalem, Hazor, Megiddo, Gezer 16 (Pharaoh king of Egypt mounted an expedition, captured Gezer, burnt it down and massacred the Canaanites living there; he then gave the town as a dowry to his daughter, Solomon's wife, 17 and Solomon rebuilt Gezer), Lower Beth-Horon, 18 Baalath, Tamar in the desert, inside the country, 19 all Solomon's storage towns owned by Solomon, all the towns for his chariots and horses, and whatever Solomon was pleased to build in Jerusalem, in the Lebanon and in all the countries under his rule. 20 All those who survived of the Amorite, Hittite, Perizzite, Hivite and Jebusite peoples, who were not Israelites— 21 their descendants still remaining in the country on whom the Israelites had not been able to

enforce the curse of destruction—these
Solomon levied as forced labourers, as is still
the case today. 22Solomon did not, however,
impose forced labour on the Israelites; for
they were soldiers, his officials, his
administrators, his officers and his chariot
and cavalry commanders. 23There were five
hundred and fifty officials in charge of the
foremen over Solomon's work, who super-
vised the people employed on the work.
24After Pharaoh's daughter had moved
from the City of David up to the palace which
he had built for her, he then built the Millo.
25Three times a year Solomon presented
burnt offerings and communion sacrifices on
the altar which he had built for Yahweh
and set his burnt offerings smoking before
Yahweh.

Thus he completed the Temple.

C: SOLOMON THE TRADER

Solomon as ship-owner

26King Solomon equipped a fleet at Ezion-
Geber, which is near Elath on the shores of
the Red Sea, in Edom. 27For this fleet Hiram
sent men of his, experienced sailors, to serve
with those in Solomon's service. 28They went
to Ophir and took on four hundred and
twenty talents of gold, which they brought
back to Solomon.

The queen of Sheba visits Solomon

10 The queen of Sheba heard of Solomon's
fame and came to test him with difficult
questions. 2She arrived in Jerusalem with a
very large retinue, with camels laden with
spices and an immense quantity of gold and
precious stones. Having reached Solomon,
she discussed with him everything that she
had in mind, 3and Solomon had an answer
for all her questions; not one of them was too
obscure for the king to answer for her.
4When the queen of Sheba saw how very wise
Solomon was, the palace which he had built,
5the food at his table, the accommodation for
his officials, the organisation of his staff and
the way they were dressed, his cupbearers,
and the burnt offerings which he presented in
the Temple of Yahweh, it left her breathless,
6and she said to the king, 'The report I heard
in my own country about your wisdom in
handling your affairs was true then! 7Until I
came and saw for myself, I did not believe
the reports, but clearly I was told less than
half: for wisdom and prosperity, you surpass
what was reported to me. 8How fortunate
your wives are! How fortunate these courtiers
of yours, continually in attendance on you
and listening to your wisdom! 9Blessed be
Yahweh your God who has shown you his
favour by setting you on the throne of Israel!
Because of Yahweh's everlasting love for
Israel, he has made you king to administer
law and justice.' 10And she presented the
king with a hundred and twenty talents of
gold and great quantities of spices and
precious stones; no such wealth of spices ever
came again as those which the queen of
Sheba gave to King Solomon. 11Similarly,
Hiram's fleet, which brought the gold from
Ophir, also brought back great cargoes of
almug timber and precious stones. 12Of
the *almug* timber the king made supports
for the Temple of Yahweh and for the royal
palace, and harps and lyres for the musicians;
no more of this *almug* timber has since come
or been seen to this day. 13And King
Solomon, in his turn, presented the queen of
Sheba with everything that she expressed a
wish for, besides those presents which he
gave her with a munificence worthy of King
Solomon. After which, she went home to her
own country, she and her servants.

Solomon's wealth

14The weight of gold received annually by
Solomon amounted to six hundred and sixty-
six talents of gold, 15besides what tolls and
foreign trade, as well as everything the Arab
kings and the provincial governors brought
in. 16King Solomon made two hundred great
shields of beaten gold, six hundred shekels
of gold going into one shield; 17also three
hundred small shields of beaten gold, three
mina of gold going into one shield; and the
king put these into the House of the Forest
of Lebanon. 18The king also made a great
ivory throne which he overlaid with refined
gold. 19The throne had six steps, a back with
a rounded top, and arms on each side of the
seat; two lions stood beside the arms, 20and
twelve lions stood on each side of the six
steps. Nothing like it has ever been made in
any other kingdom.

21All King Solomon's drinking vessels
were of gold, and all the plate in the House
of the Forest of Lebanon was of pure gold;

silver was little thought of in Solomon's days,
[22]since the king had a fleet of Tarshish[a] at sea
with Hiram's fleet, and once every three years
the fleet of Tarshish would come back laden
with gold and silver, ivory, apes and baboons.
[23]For riches and for wisdom, King Solomon
surpassed all kings on earth, [24]and the whole
world consulted Solomon to hear the wisdom
which God had implanted in his heart; [25]and
everyone would bring a present with him:
things made of silver, things made of gold,
robes, armour, spices, horses and mules; and
this went on year after year.

Solomon's chariots and cavalry

[26]Solomon then built up a force of chariots
and cavalry; he had one thousand four
hundred chariots and twelve thousand
horses, these he stationed in the chariot towns
and near the king in Jerusalem. [27]In Jeru-
salem the king made silver as common as
stones, and cedar wood as plentiful as syca-
more in the lowlands. [28]Solomon's horses
were imported from Muzur and Cilicia. The
king's dealers acquired them from Cilicia at
the prevailing price. [29]A chariot was imported
from Egypt for six hundred silver shekels
and a horse from Cilicia for a hundred and
fifty. They also supplied the Hittite and
Aramaean kings, who all used them as
middlemen.

D: HIS DECLINE

Solomon's wives

11 King Solomon loved many foreign
women: not only Pharaoh's daughter
but Moabites, Edomites, Sidonians and
Hittites, [2]from those peoples of whom
Yahweh had said to the Israelites, 'You are
not to go among them nor they among you,
or they will be sure to sway your hearts to
their own gods.' But Solomon was deeply
attached to them. [3]He had seven hundred
wives of royal rank and three hundred concu-
bines. [4]When Solomon grew old his wives
swayed his heart to other gods; and his heart
was not wholly with Yahweh his God as his
father David's had been. [5]Solomon became
a follower of Astarte, the goddess of the
Sidonians, and of Milcom, the Ammonite
abomination. [6]He did what was displeasing
to Yahweh, and was not a wholehearted
follower of Yahweh, as his father David had
been. [7]Then it was that Solomon built a
high place for Chemosh, the abomination
of Moab, on the mountain to the east of
Jerusalem, and to Milcom, the abomination
of the Ammonites. [8]He did the same for all
his foreign wives, who offered incense and
sacrifice to their gods.

[9]Yahweh was angry with Solomon because
his heart had turned away from Yahweh, God
of Israel, who had twice appeared to him
[10]and had forbidden him to follow other gods;
but he did not carry out Yahweh's order.
[11]Yahweh therefore said to Solomon, 'Since
you have behaved like this and have not kept
my covenant or the laws which I laid down
for you, I shall tear the kingdom away from
you and give it to one of your servants. [12]For
your father David's sake, however, I shall
not do this during your lifetime, but shall
tear it out of your son's hands. [13]Even so, I
shall not tear the whole kingdom from him.
For the sake of my servant David, and for
the sake of Jerusalem which I have chosen, I
shall leave your son one tribe.'

Solomon's foreign enemies

[14]Yahweh raised an enemy against Solomon,
Hadad the Edomite, of the kingly stock of
Edom. [15]After David had crushed Edom,
Joab the army commander had gone to bury
the dead and had slaughtered the entire male
population of Edom [16](Joab stayed there
with all Israel for six months until he had
exterminated the entire male population of
Edom), [17]but Hadad with a number of
Edomites in his father's service had fled to
Egypt. Hadad had been only a boy at the
time. [18]They set out from Midian, and on
reaching Paran, took a number of men from
Paran with them and went on to Egypt, to
Pharaoh the king of Egypt, who provided
him with a house, undertook to maintain
him, and assigned him an estate. [19]Hadad
became a great favourite of Pharaoh who
gave him his own wife's sister in marriage,
the sister of the Great Lady Tahpenes. [20]The
sister of Tahpenes bore him his son Genubath
whom Tahpenes brought up in Pharaoh's
palace, Genubath living in Pharaoh's palace
with Pharaoh's own children. [21]But when
news reached Hadad in Egypt that David had

10a Meaning uncertain, perhaps a place-name. Or 'refinery ships', so ships for carrying metal.

fallen asleep with his ancestors and that Joab the army commander was dead, he said to Pharaoh, 'Give me leave to go that I may return to my own country.' 22'What do you lack here with me,' Pharaoh said, 'for you to want to go back to your country?' 'Nothing,' he replied, 'but please let me go.' 25bHence the harm which Hadad caused: he loathed Israel and ruled Edom.

23God raised a second enemy against Solomon, Rezon son of Eliada. He had fled from his master, Hadadezer king of Zobah. 24A number of men having rallied to him, he became leader of a marauding band (which was then massacred by David). Rezon captured Damascus and settled there and became king of Damascus. 25aHe was hostile to Israel as long as Solomon lived.

The revolt of Jeroboam

26Jeroboam was the son of Nebat, an Ephraimite from Zeredah; the name of his mother, a widow, was Zeruah; he was in Solomon's service but revolted against the king. 27This is the account of his revolt.

Solomon was building the Millo and closing the breach in the City of David his father. 28Now this Jeroboam was a man of great energy; Solomon, noticing how the young man set about his work, put him in charge of all the forced labour of the House of Joseph. 29One day when Jeroboam had gone out of Jerusalem, the prophet Ahijah of Shiloh accosted him on the road. Ahijah was wearing a new cloak; the two of them were in the open country by themselves. 30Ahijah took the new cloak which he was wearing and tore it into twelve strips, 31saying to Jeroboam: 'Take ten strips for yourself, for Yahweh, God of Israel, says this, "I am going to tear the kingdom from Solomon's hand and give ten tribes to you. 32He will keep one tribe for the sake of my servant David and for the sake of Jerusalem, the city which I have chosen out of all the tribes of Israel; 33for he has forsaken me to worship Astarte the goddess of the Sidonians, Chemosh the god of Moab, Milcom the god of the Ammonites; he has not followed my ways by doing what I regard as right, or by keeping my laws and ordinances as his father David did. 34But it is not from his hands that I will take the kingdom, since I have made him a prince for as long as he lives, for the sake of my servant David who kept my commandments and laws. 35I shall, however, take the kingdom from the hand of his son, and I shall give it to you, that is, the ten tribes. 36I shall give one tribe to his son, so that my servant David may always have a lamp in my presence in Jerusalem, the city which I have chosen as a dwelling-place for my name. 37You nonetheless I shall appoint to rule over as much as you wish, and you will be king of Israel. 38If you listen to all my orders and follow my ways, by doing what I regard as right and by keeping my laws and commandments as my servant David did, then I shall be with you and shall build you as enduring a dynasty as the one which I built for David. I shall give Israel to you, 39and I shall humble the descendants of David, but not for ever." '

40Solomon tried to kill Jeroboam but he made off and fled to Egypt, to Shishak king of Egypt, and he remained in Egypt until Solomon's death.

The end of the reign of Solomon

41The rest of the history of Solomon, his entire career, his wisdom, is this not recorded in the Book of the Annals of Solomon? 42Solomon's reign in Jerusalem over all Israel lasted forty years. 43When Solomon fell asleep with his ancestors, he was buried in the City of David his father; his son Rehoboam succeeded him.

III: THE POLITICAL AND RELIGIOUS SCHISM

The assembly at Shechem

12 Rehoboam then went to Shechem, all Israel having come to Shechem to proclaim him king. 2(As soon as Jeroboam son of Nebat heard the news—he was still in Egypt, where he had taken refuge from King Solomon—he returned from Egypt. 3They now sent for him, and Jeroboam and the whole assembly of Israel came.) And they spoke as follows to Rehoboam, 4'Your father laid a cruel yoke on us; if you will lighten your father's cruel slavery, that heavy yoke which he imposed on us, we are willing to

serve you.' 5He said to them, 'Go away for
three days and then come back to me.' And
the people went away.
6King Rehoboam then consulted the elders
who had been in attendance on his father
Solomon while he was alive, and said, 'How
do you advise me to answer this people?'
7They replied, 'If you become the servant of
this people today, and submit to them and
give them a fair reply, then they will remain
your servants for ever.' 8But he rejected the
advice given him by the elders and consulted
the young men in attendance on him, who
had grown up with him. 9He said, 'How do
you advise us to answer these people who
have been saying, "Lighten the yoke which
your father imposed on us!"? ' 10The young
men who had grown up with him replied,
'This is the way to answer these people who
have been saying, "Your father made our
yoke heavy, you must lighten it for us!" This
is the right thing to say to them, "My little
finger is thicker than my father's loins.
11Although my father laid a heavy yoke on
you, I shall make it heavier still. My father
controlled you with the whip, but I shall
apply a spiked lash!" '
12On the third day Jeroboam and all the
people came to Rehoboam in obedience to
the king's instruction: 'Come back to me in
three days' time.' 13And the king gave the
people a harsh answer, rejecting the advice
given him by the elders 14and speaking to
them as the young men had recommended,
'My father made your yoke heavy, I shall
make it heavier still! My father controlled
you with the whip, but I shall apply a spiked
lash!'
15Thus the king refused to listen to the
people, and this was brought about by
Yahweh to fulfil the promise which he had
made through Ahijah of Shiloh to Jeroboam
son of Nebat. 16When all Israel saw that the
king refused to listen to them, the people
answered the king thus:

What share have we in David?
—No heritage in the son of Jesse!
Away to your tents, Israel!
Now look after
your own House, David!

So Israel went home again. 17Rehoboam,
however, reigned over those Israelites who
lived in the towns of Judah. 18When King
Rehoboam sent Adoram, who was in charge
of forced labour, all Israel stoned him to
death, while King Rehoboam managed to
mount his chariot and escape to Jerusalem.
19And Israel has remained in rebellion against
the House of David from that day to this.

The political schism

20When all Israel heard that Jeroboam had
returned, they summoned him to the
assembly and made him king of all Israel; no
one remained loyal to the House of David,
except the tribe of Judah.
21When Rehoboam reached Jerusalem he
mustered the whole House of Judah and the
tribe of Benjamin, a hundred and eighty
thousand picked warriors, to fight the House
of Israel and win back the kingdom for
Rehoboam son of Solomon. 22But the word
of Yahweh came to Shemaiah, man of God,
23'Say this to Rehoboam son of Solomon,
king of Judah, to the whole House of Judah,
to Benjamin and to the rest of the people,
24"Yahweh says this: Do not go and make
war on your brothers, the Israelites; let
everyone go home, for this is my doing." '
They obeyed the command of Yahweh and
turned back in accordance with his word.
25Jeroboam fortified Shechem in the
mountain country of Ephraim and made
that his residence. Then, leaving there, he
fortified Penuel.

The religious schism

26Jeroboam thought to himself, 'As things
are, the kingdom will revert to the House of
David. 27If this people continues to go up to
the Temple of Yahweh in Jerusalem to offer
sacrifices, the people's heart will turn back
again to their lord, Rehoboam king of Judah,
and they will put me to death.' 28So the king
thought this over and then made two golden
calves; he said to the people, 'You have been
going up to Jerusalem long enough. Here is
your God, Israel, who brought you out of
Egypt!' 29He set one up at Bethel, 30and the
people went in procession in front of the
other one all the way to Dan. In Israel this
gave rise to sin, for the people went to Bethel
to worship the one, and all the way to Dan to
worship the other. 31He set up shrines on
the high places and appointed priests from
ordinary families, who were not of levitical
descent. 32Jeroboam also instituted a feast in
the eighth month, on the fifteenth of the
month, like the feast kept in Judah, when he

offered sacrifices on the altar. This he did at Bethel, offering sacrifices to the calves which he had made and, at Bethel, installing the priests of the high places which he had set up. 33On the fifteenth of the eighth month, the month which he had chosen deliberately, he offered sacrifices on the altar which he had made at Bethel; he instituted a feast for the Israelites and himself went up to the altar to burn the sacrifice.

The condemnation of the altar in Bethel

13 There came to Bethel at Yahweh's command a man of God from Judah, just as Jeroboam was standing by the altar to offer the sacrifice, 2and at Yahweh's command this man denounced the altar. 'Altar, altar,' he said, 'Yahweh says this, "A son is to be born to the House of David, Josiah by name, and on you he will slaughter the priests of the high places who have offered sacrifice on you, and on you he will burn human bones." ' 3At the same time he gave a sign. 'This is the sign', he said, 'that Yahweh has spoken, "This altar will burst apart and the ashes which are on it will be spilt." ' 4When the king heard how the man of God denounced the altar of Bethel, he stretched out his hand from the altar, saying, 'Seize him!' But the hand he stretched out against the man withered, and he could not draw it back, 5and the altar burst apart and the ashes from the altar were spilt, in accordance with the sign given by the man of God at Yahweh's command. 6The king said to the man of God, 'I beg you to placate Yahweh your God, and so restore me the use of my hand.' The man of God placated Yahweh; the king's hand was restored as it had been before. 7The king then said to the man of God, 'Come home with me and refresh yourself, and I shall give you a present,' 8but the man of God replied to the king, 'Were you to give me half your palace, I would not go with you. I will eat and drink nothing here, 9for I have had Yahweh's order, "You are to eat or drink nothing, nor to return by the way you came." ' 10And he left by another road and did not return by the way he had come to Bethel.

The man of God and the prophet

11Now there was an old prophet living in Bethel, and his sons came to tell him all that the man of God had done in Bethel that day; and the words which he had said to the king, they told these to their father too. 12'Which road did he take?' their father asked. His sons showed him the road which the man of God who came from Judah had taken. 13'Saddle the donkey for me,' he said to his sons; they saddled the donkey for him and he mounted. 14He followed the man of God and found him sitting under a terebinth. 'Are you the man of God', he said, 'who came from Judah?' 'I am,' he replied. 15'Come home with me,' he said, 'and take some food.' 16'I cannot go back with you,' he answered, 'or eat or drink anything here, 17for I have received Yahweh's order, "You are to eat or drink nothing there, nor to return by the way you came." ' 18'I too am a prophet like you,' the other replied, 'and an angel told me this by Yahweh's command, "Bring him back with you to your house to eat and drink." ' He was lying to him. 19The man of God went back with him; he ate and drank at his house.

20As they were sitting at table a word of Yahweh came to the prophet who had brought him back, 21and he addressed the man of God who came from Judah. 'Yahweh says this,' he said. ' "Since you have defied Yahweh's command and not obeyed the orders which Yahweh your God gave you, 22but have come back and eaten and drunk where he forbade you to eat and drink, your corpse will never reach the tomb of your ancestors." ' 23After he had eaten and drunk, the prophet saddled the donkey for him, and he turned about and went away. 24A lion met him on the road and killed him; his corpse lay stretched out on the road; the donkey stood there beside it; the lion stood by the corpse too. 25People going by saw the corpse lying on the road and the lion standing by the corpse, and went and spoke about it in the town where the old prophet lived. 26When the prophet who had made the man turn back heard about it, he said, 'That is the man of God who defied Yahweh's command! Yahweh has handed him over to the lion, which has mauled and killed him, just as Yahweh had foretold it would.' 27He said to his sons, 'Saddle the donkey for me,' and they saddled it. 28He set off and found the man's corpse lying on the road with the donkey and the lion standing beside the corpse; the lion had neither eaten the corpse nor mauled the donkey. 29The prophet lifted the corpse of the man of God and put it on

the donkey and brought it back to the town
where he lived to hold mourning for him and
bury him. 30 He laid the corpse in his own
tomb, and they raised the mourning cry for
him, 'Alas, my brother!' 31 After burying
him, the prophet said to his sons, 'When I
die, bury me in the same tomb as the man of
God, lay my bones beside his. 32 For the word
he uttered at Yahweh's command against the
altar of Bethel and against all the shrines of
the high places in the towns of Samaria will
certainly come true.'
33 Jeroboam did not give up his wicked ways
after this incident, but went on appointing
priests for the high places from the common
people. He consecrated as priests of the high
places any who wished to be. 34 Such conduct
made the House of Jeroboam a sinful House,
and caused its ruin and extinction from the
face of the earth.

IV: THE TWO KINGDOMS UNTIL ELIJAH

Continuation of the reign of Jeroboam I (931–910)

14 At that time Abijah, Jeroboam's son,
fell sick, 2 and Jeroboam said to his
wife, 'Come, please disguise yourself so that
no one will recognise you as Jeroboam's wife,
and go to Shiloh; the prophet Ahijah is there,
the man who said I was to be king of this
people. 3 Go to him, and take ten loaves and
some savoury food and a jar of honey; he
will tell you what will happen to the child.'
4 Jeroboam's wife did this: she set out, went
to Shiloh and came to Ahijah's house. 5 Now
Ahijah could not see, his eyes were fixed with
age, but Yahweh had told him, 'Jeroboam's
wife is now on her way to ask you for a
prophecy about her son, as he is sick. You
will tell her such and such. When she comes,
she will pretend to be some other woman.'
6 So when Ahijah heard her footsteps at the
door, he called, 'Come in, wife of Jeroboam;
why pretend to be someone else? I have
bad news for you. 7 Go and tell Jeroboam,
"Yahweh, God of Israel, says this: I raised
you from the people and made you leader of
my people Israel; 8 I tore the kingdom from
the House of David and gave it to you. But
you have not been like my servant David who
kept my commandments and followed me
with all his heart, doing only what I regard
as right; 9 you have done more evil than all
your predecessors, you have gone and made
yourself other gods, idols of cast metal,
provoking my anger, and you have turned
your back on me. 10 For this I shall bring
disaster on the House of Jeroboam, I shall
wipe out every manjack of the family of
Jeroboam, fettered or free in Israel, I shall
sweep away the House of Jeroboam as a man
sweeps dung away till none is left. 11 Those of
Jeroboam's family who die in the city, the
dogs will eat; and those who die in the open
country, the birds of the air will eat, for
Yahweh has spoken." 12 Now get up and go
home; at the moment your feet enter the
town, the child will die. 13 All Israel will
mourn for him, and bury him; and he alone
of Jeroboam's family will have a proper
burial, for in him alone of the House of
Jeroboam can Yahweh, God of Israel, find
anything good. 14 Yahweh will set a king over
Israel, who will put an end to the House of
Jeroboam. 15 Yahweh will make Israel shake,
till it quivers like a reed in the water; he
will uproot Israel from this prosperous land
which he gave to their ancestors and scatter
them beyond the River for provoking
Yahweh to anger by making their sacred
poles. 16 He will abandon Israel for the sins
which Jeroboam has committed and made
Israel commit.' 17 Jeroboam's wife rose and
left. She arrived at Tirzah, and when she
crossed the threshold of the palace, the child
was already dead. 18 They buried him, and all
Israel mourned for him, just as Yahweh
had foretold through his servant Ahijah the
prophet.
19 The rest of the history of Jeroboam, what
wars he waged, how he governed, this is
recorded in the Book of the Annals of the
Kings of Israel. 20 Jeroboam's reign lasted
twenty-two years. Then he fell asleep with
his ancestors; his son Nadab succeeded him.

The reign of Rehoboam (931–913)

21 In Judah, Rehoboam son of Solomon
became king; he was forty-one years old when
he came to the throne and he reigned for
seventeen years in Jerusalem, the city which

Yahweh had chosen out of all the tribes of Israel, to give his name a home there. His mother's name was Naamah, the Ammonite. [22]He did what is displeasing to Yahweh, arousing his resentment more than his ancestors by all the sins which they had committed; [23]they had built themselves high places, and had set up pillars and sacred poles on every high hill and under every spreading tree. [24]There were even male sacred prostitutes in the country. He copied all the shameful practices of the nations whom Yahweh had dispossessed for the Israelites.

[25]And so it happened that in the fifth year of King Rehoboam, Shishak king of Egypt advanced on Jerusalem [26]and carried off all the treasures of the Temple of Yahweh and the treasures of the royal palace; he took everything away, including all the golden shields which Solomon had made. [27]To replace those King Rehoboam made bronze shields, entrusting them to the commanders of the guard who guarded the king's palace gate. [28]Whenever the king went to the Temple of Yahweh, the guards would carry them, returning them to the guardroom afterwards.

[29]The rest of the history of Rehoboam, his entire career, is this not recorded in the Book of the Annals of the Kings of Judah? [30]Warfare between Rehoboam and Jeroboam went on throughout the period. [31]When Rehoboam fell asleep with his ancestors, he was buried in the City of David; his son Abijam succeeded him.

The reign of Abijam in Judah (913–911)

15 In the eighteenth year of King Jeroboam son of Nebat, Abijam became king of Judah [2]and reigned for three years in Jerusalem. His mother's name was Maacah descendant of Absalom. [3]In everything he followed the sinful example of his father before him; his heart was not wholly with Yahweh his God, as the heart of David his ancestor had been. [4]However, for David's sake, Yahweh his God gave him a lamp in Jerusalem, with a son to succeed him, so keeping Jerusalem secure; [5]for David had done what Yahweh regarded as right and had never in all his life disobeyed whatever he commanded him (except in the matter of Uriah the Hittite).[a]

[7]The rest of the history of Abijam, his entire career, is this not recorded in the Book of the Annals of the Kings of Judah? Abijam and Jeroboam made war on each other. [8]When Abijam fell asleep with his ancestors, he was buried in the City of David; his son Asa succeeded him.

The reign of Asa in Judah (911–870)

[9]In the twentieth year of Jeroboam king of Israel, Asa became king of Judah [10]and reigned for forty-one years in Jerusalem. His mother's name was Maacah descendant of Absalom. [11]Asa did what Yahweh regards as right, as his ancestor David had done. [12]He drove the male prostitutes out of the country and got rid of all the idols which his ancestors had made. [13]He even deprived his grandmother Maacah of the dignity of Great Lady for having made an obscenity for Asherah; Asa cut down her obscenity and burnt it in the ravine of the Kidron. [14]Though the high places were not abolished, Asa's heart was loyal to Yahweh throughout his life. [15]He deposited his father's and his own dedicated gifts of silver, gold and sacred vessels in the Temple of Yahweh.

[16]Asa and Baasha king of Israel were at war with each other throughout their reigns. [17]Baasha king of Israel marched on Judah and fortified Ramah to blockade Asa king of Judah. [18]Asa then took all the remaining silver and gold left in the treasuries of the Temple of Yahweh and the royal palace. Entrusting this to his servants, King Asa sent them with the following message to Ben-Hadad son of Tabrimmon, son of Hezion, the king of Aram who lived in Damascus, [19]'Let us make an alliance between myself and yourself, between my father and your father! Look, I have sent you a gift of silver and gold. Come, break off your alliance with Baasha king of Israel, which will make him withdraw from me.' [20]Ben-Hadad listened favourably to King Asa, and sent the generals of his armies to attack the towns of Israel; he ravaged Ijon, Dan, Abel-Beth-Maacah, all Chinneroth, and the whole territory of Naphtali. [21]When Baasha heard this he gave up fortifying Ramah and retired to Tirzah. [22]King Asa then summoned all Judah, no one was exempt; they took away the stones and timber with which Baasha had been fortifying

15a v. 6 is omitted as in some Gk texts; it doubles 14:30.

Ramah, and King Asa used them to fortify
Geba of Benjamin and Mizpah.
23 The rest of the history of Asa, all his
valour, his entire career, is this not recorded
in the Book of the Annals of the Kings of
Judah? In his old age, however, he contracted
a disease of his feet. 24 When Asa fell asleep
with his ancestors, he was buried with his
ancestors in the City of his ancestor David;
his son Jehoshaphat succeeded him.

The reign of Nadab in Israel (910–909)

25 Nadab son of Jeroboam became king of
Israel in the second year of Asa king of Judah,
and he reigned over Israel for two years. 26 He
did what is displeasing to Yahweh; he copied
his father's example and the sin into which
he had led Israel. 27 Baasha son of Ahijah, of
the House of Issachar, plotted against him
and murdered him at Gibbethon, a Philistine
town which Nadab and all Israel were
besieging. 28 Baasha killed Nadab and
succeeded him in the third year of Asa king
of Judah. 29 No sooner was he king than he
butchered the entire House of Jeroboam, not
sparing a soul, and put an end to it, just as
Yahweh had foretold through his servant
Ahijah of Shiloh, 30 because of the sins which
he had committed and into which he had led
Israel, and because he had provoked the
anger of Yahweh, God of Israel.
31 The rest of the history of Nadab, his
entire career, is this not recorded in 32 the
Book of the Annals of the Kings of Israel?

The reign of Baasha in Israel (909–886)

33 In the third year of Asa king of Judah,
Baasha son of Ahijah became king of Israel
at Tirzah for twenty-four years. 34 He did
what is displeasing to Yahweh; he copied the
example of Jeroboam and the sin into which
he had led Israel.

16 The word of Yahweh came to Jehu son
of Hanani against Baasha: 2 'I raised
you from the dust and made you leader of
my people Israel, but you have followed
Jeroboam's example and led my people Israel
into sins which provoke my anger. 3 Now I
shall sweep away Baasha and his House; I
shall make your House like the House of
Jeroboam son of Nebat. 4 Those of Baasha's
family who die in the city, the dogs will eat;
and those who die in the open country, the
birds of the air will eat.'

5 The rest of the history of Baasha, his
career, his valour, is this not recorded in the
Book of the Annals of the Kings of Israel?
6 When Baasha fell asleep with his ancestors,
he was buried in Tirzah; his son Elah
succeeded him.
7 Furthermore, the word of Yahweh was
delivered through the prophet Jehu son of
Hanani against Baasha and his House, first
because of the many ways in which he had
displeased Yahweh, provoking him to anger
by his actions and becoming like the House
of Jeroboam; secondly because he had
destroyed that House.

The reign of Elah in Israel (886–885)

8 In the twenty-sixth year of Asa king of
Judah, Elah son of Baasha became king
of Israel at Tirzah, for two years. 9 Zimri, one
of his officers, captain of half his chariotry,
plotted against him. While he was at Tirzah,
drinking himself senseless in the house of
Arza who was master of the palace in Tirzah,
10 Zimri came in, struck him down and killed
him in the twenty-seventh year of Asa king
of Judah, and succeeded him. 11 On his
accession, as soon as he was seated on the
throne, he butchered Baasha's entire family,
not leaving him one manjack of them alive,
neither relative nor friend. 12 Zimri destroyed
the whole House of Baasha, in accordance
with the word which Yahweh had spoken
against Baasha through the prophet Jehu,
13 because of all the sins of Baasha and his
son Elah into which they had led Israel,
provoking the anger of Yahweh, God of
Israel, with their worthless idols.
14 The history of Elah, his entire career, is
this not recorded in the Book of the Annals
of the Kings of Israel?

The reign of Zimri in Israel (885)

15 In the twenty-seventh year of Asa king of
Judah, Zimri became king for seven days, at
Tirzah. The people were then encamped
in front of Gibbethon, a Philistine town.
16 When news reached the camp of how Zimri
had not only plotted against but actually
killed the king, all Israel proclaimed the army
commander Omri as king of Israel in the
camp that very day. 17 Omri, and all Israel
with him, raised the siege of Gibbethon and
laid siege to Tirzah. 18 When Zimri saw that
the town had been captured, he went into the

keep of the royal palace, burned the palace
over his own head, and died. 19 This was
because of the sin which he had committed
in doing what is displeasing to Yahweh, by
copying the example of Jeroboam and the sin
into which he had led Israel.
20 The rest of the history of Zimri and of
his conspiracy, is this not recorded in the
Book of the Annals of the Kings of
Israel?
21 The people of Israel then split into two
factions: one half following Tibni son of
Ginath to make him king, the other half
following Omri. 22 But the faction of Omri
proved stronger than that of Tibni son of
Ginath; thus Tibni lost his life and Omri
became king.

The reign of Omri in Israel (885–874)

23 In the thirty-first year of Asa king of Judah,
Omri became king of Israel and reigned for
twelve years. He reigned for six years at
Tirzah. 24 Then for two talents of silver he
bought the hill of Samaria from Shemer and
on it built a town which he named Samaria
after Shemer who had owned the hill. 25 Omri
did what is displeasing to Yahweh, and was
worse than all his predecessors. 26 In every
way he copied the example of Jeroboam son
of Nebat and the sins into which he had led
Israel, provoking the anger of Yahweh, God
of Israel, with their worthless idols.
27 The rest of the history of Omri, his
career, his valour, is this not recorded in the
Book of the Annals of the Kings of Israel?
28 When Omri fell asleep with his ancestors,
he was buried in Samaria; his son Ahab
succeeded him.

Introduction to the reign of Ahab (874–853)

29 Ahab son of Omri became king of Israel in
the thirty-eighth year of Asa king of Judah,
and reigned over Israel for twenty-two years
in Samaria. 30 Ahab son of Omri did what is
displeasing to Yahweh, and was worse than
all his predecessors. 31 The least that he did
was to follow the sinful example of Jeroboam
son of Nebat: he married Jezebel daughter
of Ethbaal, king of the Sidonians, and then
proceeded to serve Baal and worship him.
32 He erected an altar to him in the temple of
Baal which he built in Samaria. 33 Ahab also
put up a sacred pole and committed other
crimes as well, provoking the anger of
Yahweh, God of Israel, more than all the
kings of Israel his predecessors. 34 It was in
his time that Hiel of Bethel rebuilt Jericho.
Laying its foundations cost him his eldest
son Abiram and erecting its gates cost him
his youngest son Segub, just as Yahweh had
foretold through Joshua son of Nun.[a]

V: THE ELIJAH CYCLE

A: THE GREAT DROUGHT

Elijah foretells the drought

17 Elijah the Tishbite, of Tishbe in
Gilead, said to Ahab, 'By the life of
Yahweh, God of Israel, whom I serve, there
will be neither dew nor rain these coming
years unless I give the word.'

In the ravine of the Cherith

2 The word of Yahweh came to him, 3 'Go
away from here, go east and hide by the
torrent of Cherith, east of the Jordan. 4 You
can drink from the stream, and I have ordered
the ravens to bring you food there.' 5 So he
set out and did as Yahweh had said; he went
and stayed by the torrent of Cherith, east of
the Jordan. 6 The ravens brought him bread
in the morning and meat in the evening, and
he quenched his thirst at the stream.

At Zarephath
The miracle of the flour and the oil[a]

7 But after a while the stream dried up, for
the country had had no rain. 8 And then the
word of Yahweh came to him, 9 'Up and go
to Zarephath in Sidonia, and stay there. I

16a Jos 6:26.
17a ‖ 2 K 4:1–7.

have ordered a widow there to give you food.' [10]So he went off to Sidon. And when he reached the city gate, there was a widow gathering sticks. Addressing her he said, 'Please bring a little water in a pitcher for me to drink.' [11]She was on her way to fetch it when he called after her. 'Please', he said, 'bring me a scrap of bread in your hand.' [12]'As Yahweh your God lives,' she replied, 'I have no baked bread, but only a handful of meal in a jar and a little oil in a jug; I am just gathering a stick or two to go and prepare this for myself and my son to eat, and then we shall die.' [13]But Elijah said to her, 'Do not be afraid, go and do as you have said; but first make a little scone of it for me and bring it to me, and then make some for yourself and for your son. [14]For Yahweh, God of Israel, says this:

Jar of meal shall not be spent,
jug of oil shall not be emptied,
before the day when Yahweh sends
rain on the face of the earth.'

[15]The woman went and did as Elijah told her and they ate the food, she, himself and her son. [16]The jar of meal was not spent nor the jug of oil emptied, just as Yahweh had foretold through Elijah.

The widow's son raised to life[b]

[17]It happened after this that the son of the mistress of the house fell sick; his illness was so severe that in the end he expired. [18]And the woman said to Elijah, 'What quarrel have you with me, man of God? Have you come here to bring my sins home to me and to kill my son?' [19]'Give me your son,' he said and, taking him from her lap, he carried him to the upper room where he was staying and laid him on his bed. [20]He cried out to Yahweh, 'Yahweh my God, by killing her son do you mean to bring grief even to the widow who is looking after me?' [21]He stretched himself on the child three times and cried out to Yahweh, 'Yahweh my God, may the soul of this child, I beg you, come into him again!' [22]Yahweh heard Elijah's prayer and the child's soul came back into his body and he revived. [23]Elijah took the child, brought him down from the upper room into the house, and gave him to his mother. 'Look,' Elijah said, 'your son is alive.' [24]And the woman replied, 'Now I know you are a man of God and the word of Yahweh in your mouth is truth itself.'

Elijah and Obadiah

18 A long time went by, and the word of Yahweh came to Elijah in the third year, 'Go, present yourself to Ahab, and I will send rain on the country.' [2]So Elijah set off to present himself to Ahab.

As the famine was particularly severe in Samaria, [3]Ahab summoned Obadiah, the master of the palace—Obadiah held Yahweh in great reverence: [4]when Jezebel was butchering the prophets of Yahweh, Obadiah took a hundred of them and hid them, fifty at a time, in a cave, and kept them provided with food and water—[5]and Ahab said to Obadiah, 'Come along, we must scour the country, all the springs and all the ravines in the hope of finding grass to keep horses and mules alive, or we shall have to slaughter some of our stock.' [6]They divided the country for the purpose of their survey; Ahab went one way by himself and Obadiah went another way by himself. [7]While Obadiah was on his way, whom should he meet but Elijah. Recognising him he fell on his face and said, 'So it is you, my lord Elijah!' [8]'Yes,' he replied, 'go and tell your master, "Elijah is here." ' [9]But Obadiah said, 'What sin I have committed, for you to put your servant into Ahab's power and cause my death? [10]As Yahweh your God lives, there is no nation or kingdom where my master has not sent in search of you; and when they said, "He is not there," he made the kingdom or nation swear an oath that they did not know where you were. [11]And now you say to me, "Go and tell your master: Elijah is here." [12]But as soon as I leave you, the spirit of Yahweh will carry you away and I shall not know where; I shall go and tell Ahab; he will not be able to find you, and then he will kill me. Yet from his youth your servant has revered Yahweh. [13]Has no one told my lord what I did when Jezebel butchered the prophets of Yahweh, how I hid a hundred of them in a cave, fifty at a time, and kept them provided with food and water? [14]And now you say to me, "Go and tell your master: Elijah is here." Why, he will kill me!' [15]Elijah replied, 'As Yahweh Sabaoth lives,

17b ‖ 2 K 4:18–37.

whom I serve, I shall present myself to him
today!'

Elijah and Ahab

16 Obadiah went to find Ahab and tell him the
news, and Ahab then went to find Elijah.
17 When he saw Elijah, Ahab said, 'So there
you are, you scourge of Israel!' 18 'Not I,' he
replied, 'I am not the scourge of Israel,
you and your family are; because you have
deserted Yahweh and followed Baal. 19 Now
give orders for all Israel to gather round me
on Mount Carmel, and also the four hundred
prophets of Baal who eat at Jezebel's table.'

The sacrifice on Carmel

20 Ahab called all Israel together and
assembled the prophets on Mount Carmel.
21 Elijah stepped out in front of all the people.
'How long', he said, 'do you mean to hobble
first on one leg then on the other? If Yahweh
is God, follow him; if Baal, follow him.' But
the people had nothing to say. 22 Elijah then
said to them, 'I, I alone, am left as a prophet
of Yahweh, while the prophets of Baal are
four hundred and fifty. 23 Let two bulls be
given us; let them choose one for themselves,
dismember it but not set fire to it. I in my
turn shall prepare the other bull, but not set
fire to it. 24 You must call on the name of your
god, and I shall call on the name of Yahweh;
the god who answers with fire, is God indeed.'
The people all answered, 'Agreed!' 25 Elijah
then said to the prophets of Baal, 'Choose
one bull and begin, for there are more of you.
Call on the name of your god but light no
fire.' 26 They took the bull and prepared it,
and from morning to midday they called on
the name of Baal. 'O Baal, answer us!' they
cried, but there was no voice, no answer, as
they performed their hobbling dance round
the altar which they had made. 27 Midday
came, and Elijah mocked them. 'Call louder,'
he said, 'for he is a god: he is preoccupied or
he is busy, or he has gone on a journey;
perhaps he is asleep and needs to be woken
up!' 28 So they shouted louder and gashed
themselves, as their custom was, with swords
and spears until the blood flowed down them.
29 Midday passed, and they ranted on until
the time when the offering is presented; but
there was no voice, no answer, no sign of
attention.
30 Then Elijah said to all the people, 'Come
over to me,' and all the people came over to
him. He repaired Yahweh's altar which had
been torn down. 31 Elijah took twelve stones,
corresponding to the number of tribes of the
sons of Jacob, to whom the word of Yahweh
had come, 'Israel is to be your name,' 32 and
built an altar in the name of Yahweh. Round
the altar he dug a trench of a size to hold two
measures of seed. 33 He then arranged the
wood, dismembered the bull, and laid it on
the wood. 34 Then he said, 'Fill four jars with
water and pour it on the burnt offering and
on the wood.' They did this. He said, 'Do it
a second time;' they did it a second time. He
said, 'Do it a third time;' they did it a third
time. 35 The water flowed round the altar until
even the trench itself was full of water. 36 At
the time when the offering is presented,
Elijah the prophet stepped forward.
'Yahweh, God of Abraham, Isaac and Israel,'
he said, 'let them know today that you are
God in Israel, and that I am your servant,
that I have done all these things at your
command. 37 Answer me, Yahweh, answer
me, so that this people may know that you,
Yahweh, are God and are winning back their
hearts.'
38 Then Yahweh's fire fell and consumed
the burnt offering and the wood and licked
up the water in the trench. 39 When all the
people saw this they fell on their faces.
'Yahweh is God,' they cried, 'Yahweh is
God!' 40 Elijah said, 'Seize the prophets of
Baal: do not let one of them escape.' They
seized them, and Elijah took them down to
the Kishon, and there he slaughtered them.

The drought ends

41 Elijah said to Ahab, 'Go back now, eat and
drink; for I hear the approaching sound of
rain.' 42 While Ahab went back to eat and
drink, Elijah climbed to the top of Carmel
and bowed down to the ground, putting his
face between his knees. 43 'Now go up', he
told his servant, 'and look out to sea.' He
went up and looked. 'There is nothing at all,'
he said. Seven times Elijah told him to go
back. 44 The seventh time, the servant said,
'Now there is a cloud, small as a man's hand,
rising from the sea.' Elijah said, 'Go and say
to Ahab, "Harness the chariot and go down
before the rain stops you." ' 45 And with that
the sky grew dark with cloud and storm,
and rain fell in torrents. Ahab mounted his
chariot and made for Jezreel. 46 But the hand

of Yahweh had come on Elijah and, hitching
up his clothes, he ran ahead of Ahab all the
way to Jezreel.

B: ELIJAH AT HOREB

The journey to Horeb

19 When Ahab told Jezebel everything
that Elijah had done, and how he had
put all the prophets to the sword, 2 Jezebel
sent a messenger to Elijah to say, 'May the
gods bring unnameable ills on me and worse
ills too, if by this time tomorrow I have not
made your life like one of theirs!' 3 He was
afraid and fled for his life. He came to Beer-
sheba, a town of Judah, where he left his
servant. 4 He himself went on into the desert,
a day's journey, and sitting under a furze
bush wished he were dead. 'Yahweh,' he
said, 'I have had enough. Take my life; I am
no better than my ancestors.' 5 Then he lay
down and went to sleep. Then all of a sudden
an angel touched him and said, 'Get up and
eat.' 6 He looked round, and there at his head
was a scone baked on hot stones, and a jar of
water. He ate and drank and then lay down
again. 7 But the angel of Yahweh came back
a second time and touched him and said, 'Get
up and eat, or the journey will be too long for
you.' 8 So he got up and ate and drank, and
strengthened by that food he walked for forty
days and forty nights until he reached Horeb,
God's mountain.

The encounter with God

9 There he went into a cave and spent the
night there. Then the word of Yahweh came
to him saying, 'What are you doing here,
Elijah?' 10 He replied, 'I am full of jealous zeal
for Yahweh Sabaoth, because the Israelites
have abandoned your covenant, have torn
down your altars and put your prophets to
the sword. I am the only one left, and now
they want to kill me.' 11 Then he was told,
'Go out and stand on the mountain before
Yahweh.' For at that moment Yahweh was
going by. A mighty hurricane split the moun-
tains and shattered the rocks before Yahweh.
But Yahweh was not in the hurricane. And
after the hurricane, an earthquake. But
Yahweh was not in the earthquake. 12 And
after the earthquake, fire. But Yahweh was
not in the fire. And after the fire, a light
murmuring sound. 13 And when Elijah heard
this, he covered his face with his cloak and
went out and stood at the entrance of the
cave. Then a voice came to him, which said,
'What are you doing here, Elijah?' 14 He
replied, 'I am full of jealous zeal for Yahweh,
God Sabaoth, because the Israelites have
abandoned your covenant, have torn down
your altars and put your prophets to the
sword. I am the only one left and now they
want to kill me.' 15 'Go,' Yahweh said, 'go
back by the same way to the desert of Dama-
scus. You must go and anoint Hazael as king
of Aram. 16 You must anoint Jehu son of
Nimshi as king of Israel, and anoint Elisha
son of Shaphat, of Abel-Meholah, as prophet
to succeed you. 17 Anyone who escapes the
sword of Hazael will be put to death by
Jehu; and anyone who escapes the sword of
Jehu will be put to death by Elisha. 18 But I
shall spare seven thousand in Israel; all the
knees that have not bent before Baal, all the
mouths that have not kissed him.'

The call of Elisha

19 Leaving there, he came on Elisha son of
Shaphat as he was ploughing behind twelve
yoke of oxen, he himself being with the
twelfth. Elijah passed near to him and threw
his cloak over him. 20 Elisha left his oxen and
ran after Elijah. 'Let me kiss my father and
mother, then I will follow you,' he said.
Elijah answered, 'Go, go back; for have I
done anything to you?' 21 Elisha turned away,
took a yoke of oxen and slaughtered them.
He used the oxen's tackle for cooking the
meat, which he gave the people to eat. He
then rose and, following Elijah, became his
servant.

C: THE ARAMAEAN WARS

The siege of Samaria

20 Ben-Hadad king of Aram mustered
his whole army—thirty-two kings were
with him, and horses and chariots—and
marched on Samaria, to besiege it and take
it by assault. 2 He sent messengers into the
city to Ahab king of Israel to tell him, 'Ben-
Hadad says this, 3 "Your silver and gold
are mine. Your wives and children remain
yours." ' 4 The king of Israel replied, 'As you

command, my lord king. Myself and all I
have are yours.'
5The messengers came again, this time
they said, 'Ben-Hadad says this, "I have
already sent you an order to hand over your
silver and your gold, your wives and your
children; 6but I swear, this time tomorrow,
I shall send my servants to ransack your
house and your servants' houses and lay
hands on everything that they value and take
it away." '
7The king of Israel summoned all the elders
of the country and said, 'You can see clearly
how this man intends to ruin us. He has
already demanded my wives and my chil-
dren, although I have not refused him my
silver and gold.' 8All the elders and all the
people said, 'Take no notice. Do not
consent.' 9So he gave this answer to Ben-
Hadad's messengers, 'Say to my lord the
king, "All you first required of your servant
I will do, but this I cannot do." ' And the
messengers went back with the answer.
10Ben-Hadad then sent him the following
message, 'May the gods bring unnameable
ills on me and worse ills too, if there is enough
dust in Samaria for each of my followers to
have a handful!' 11But the king of Israel
returned this answer, 'Say: the man who puts
on his armour is not the one to boast, but the
man who takes it off.' 12When Ben-Hadad
heard this message—he was under the
awnings drinking with the kings—he gave
orders to his servants, 'Take up position!'
And they took up their positions against the
city.

Victory for Israel

13A prophet then arrived, looking for Ahab
king of Israel. 'Yahweh says this,' he said.
' "You have seen this huge army? This very
day I shall deliver it into your hands, and you
will know that I am Yahweh." ' 14'By whose
means?' Ahab asked. The prophet replied,
'Yahweh says this, "By means of the guards
of the district governors." ' 'Who will co-
ordinate the attack?' Ahab asked. 'You will,'
the prophet replied.
15So Ahab inspected the guards of the
district governors: there were two hundred
and thirty-two. After these he reviewed the
army, all the Israelites: there were seven
thousand. 16They made a sortie at midday,
when Ben-Hadad was drinking himself
senseless under the awnings, he and the
thirty-two kings who were allies. 17The
guards of the district governors led the sortie.
A report was made to Ben-Hadad: 'Some
men have come out of Samaria.' 18He said,
'If they have come out for peace, take them
alive; if they have come out for war, take
them alive too.' 19So they made a sortie from
the city, the district governors' guards and
behind them the army, 20and each struck
down his man. Aram took to flight and Israel
pursued; Ben-Hadad king of Aram escaped
on horseback. 21The king of Israel then
advanced, capturing horses and chariots and
inflicting a great defeat on Aram.

Respite

22The prophet then went to the king of Israel
and said, 'Now is the time to be resolute and
think carefully about what you should do,
for at the turn of the year the king of Aram
will march against you.'
23The servants of the king of Aram said to
him, 'Their gods are gods of the mountains;
that is why they have proved stronger than
we are. But if we fight them on level ground,
we shall certainly beat them. 24This is what
you must do: remove all these kings from
their commands and appoint professional
soldiers in their place. 25You, for your part,
must recruit an army as large as the one which
deserted you, with as many horses and as
many chariots; then if we fight them on level
ground, we shall certainly beat them.' He
listened to their advice and acted accordingly.

The victory of Aphek

26At the turn of the year, Ben-Hadad
mustered the Aramaeans and marched on
Aphek to fight Israel. 27The Israelites were
already mobilised and provisioned, and
marched out to meet them. Encamped
opposite them, the Israelites looked like two
herds of goats, whereas the Aramaeans filled
the countryside.
28The man of God then went to the king of
Israel and said, 'Yahweh says this, "Since
Aram has said that Yahweh is a god of the
mountains and not a god of the plains, I shall
put the whole of this huge army into your
power, and you will know that I am
Yahweh." ' 29For seven days they were
encamped opposite each other. On the
seventh day battle was joined and the Israel-
ites slaughtered the Aramaeans, a hundred

thousand foot soldiers in one day. 30The rest fled to Aphek, into the citadel, but the city walls collapsed on twenty-seven thousand of the survivors.

Now Ben-Hadad had fled and taken refuge in an inner room inside the citadel. 31'Look,' his servants said to him, 'we have heard that the kings of Israel are faithful and kind kings. Let us put sackcloth round our waists and cords round our heads and go out to the king of Israel; perhaps he will spare your life.' 32So they wrapped sackcloth round their waists and put cords round their heads and went to the king of Israel, and said, 'Your servant Ben-Hadad says, "Spare my life." ' 33'So he is still alive?' he replied. 'He is my brother.' The men took this for a good omen and quickly seized on his words. 'Yes,' they said, 'Ben-Hadad is your brother.' Ahab said, 'Go and fetch him.' Then Ben-Hadad came out to him and Ahab made him get up into his chariot. 34Ben-Hadad said, 'I shall restore the towns which my father took from your father and you may set up a trading quarter for yourself in Damascus as my father did in Samaria.' 'With a treaty,' Ahab said, 'I shall set you free.' Granting him a treaty, Ahab let him go.

A prophet condemns Ahab's policy

35At Yahweh's command a member of the brotherhood of prophets said to a companion of his, 'Strike me,' but the man refused to strike him. 36So he said to him, 'Since you have disobeyed Yahweh's order, the very moment you leave me a lion will kill you.' And no sooner had he left him than he met a lion, which killed him. 37The prophet then went to find another man and said, 'Strike me,' and the man struck him and wounded him. 38The prophet then went and stood waiting for the king on the road, disguising himself with a bandage over his eyes. 39As the king passed, he called out to him, 'Your servant was making his way to where the fight was thickest when someone left the fighting to bring a man to me, and said, "Guard this man; if he is found missing, your life will pay for his, or else you will have to pay one talent of silver." 40But your servant was busy with one thing and another, the man disappeared.' The king of Israel said, 'That is your sentence then. You have pronounced it yourself.' 41At this the man quickly pulled off the bandage over his eyes, and the king of Israel recognised him as one of the prophets. 42He said to the king, 'Yahweh says this, "Since you have let the man escape who was under my curse of destruction, your life will pay for his, your people for his people." ' 43And the king of Israel went home, gloomy and out of temper, back to Samaria.

D: NABOTH'S VINEYARD

Naboth refuses to hand over his vineyard

21 This is what happened next: Naboth of Jezreel had a vineyard close by the palace of Ahab king of Samaria, 2and Ahab said to Naboth, 'Give me your vineyard to be my vegetable garden, since it adjoins my palace; I will give you a better vineyard for it or, if you prefer, I will give you its value in money.' 3Naboth, however, said to Ahab, 'Yahweh forbid that I should give you my ancestral heritage!'

Ahab and Jezebel

4Ahab went home gloomy and out of temper at the words of Naboth of Jezreel, 'I will not give you my heritage from my ancestors.' He lay down on his bed and turned his face away and refused to eat. 5His wife Jezebel came to him. 'Why are you so dispirited,' she said, 'that you refuse to eat?' 6He said, 'I have been talking to Naboth of Jezreel. I said, "Give me your vineyard either for money or, if you prefer, for another vineyard in exchange." But he said, "I will not give you my vineyard." ' 7Then his wife Jezebel said, 'Some king of Israel you make! Get up, eat and take heart; I myself shall get you the vineyard of Naboth the Jezreelite.'

Naboth is murdered

8So she wrote a letter in Ahab's name and sealed it with his seal, sending the letter to the elders and notables of the city where Naboth lived. 9In the letter, she wrote, 'Proclaim a fast, and put Naboth in a prominent place among the people. 10There confront him with a couple of scoundrels who will accuse him as follows, "You have cursed God and the king." Then take him outside and stone him to death.'

11 The men of Naboth's city, the elders and notables living in his city, did what Jezebel ordered, as was written in the letter which she had sent him. 12 They proclaimed a fast and put Naboth in a prominent place among the people. 13 The two scoundrels then came and confronted him, and the scoundrels then publicly accused Naboth as follows, 'Naboth has cursed God and the king.' He was then taken outside the city and stoned to death. 14 They then sent word to Jezebel, 'Naboth has been stoned to death.' 15 When Jezebel heard that Naboth had been stoned to death, she said to Ahab, 'Get up! Take possession of the vineyard which Naboth of Jezreel refused to sell you, for Naboth is no longer alive, he is dead.' 16 When Ahab heard that Naboth was dead, he got up to go down to the vineyard of Naboth of Jezreel and take possession of it.

Elijah pronounces God's sentence

17 Then the word of Yahweh came to Elijah the Tishbite, 18 'Up! Go down to meet Ahab king of Israel, in Samaria. You will find him in Naboth's vineyard; he has gone down to take possession of it. 19 You are to say this to him, "Yahweh says this: You have committed murder and now you usurp as well. For this—and Yahweh says this— in the place where the dogs licked the blood of Naboth, the dogs will lick your blood too." '[a] 20 Ahab said to Elijah, 'So you have caught me, O my enemy!' Elijah answered, 'I have caught you! For your double dealing, and since you have done what is displeasing to Yahweh, 21 I shall now bring disaster down on you; I shall sweep away your descendants and wipe out every manjack of the House of Ahab, fettered or free in Israel. 22 I shall treat your House as I treated the house of Jeroboam son of Nebat and of Baasha son of Ahijah, for provoking my anger and leading Israel into sin. 23 (Against Jezebel too Yahweh spoke these words, "The dogs will eat Jezebel in the Field of Jezreel.") 24 Those of Ahab's family who die in the city, the dogs will eat; and those who die in the open country, the birds of the air will eat.'

25 And indeed there never was anyone like Ahab for double dealing and for doing what is displeasing to Yahweh, urged on by Jezebel his wife. 26 He behaved in the most abominable way, adhering to idols, just as the Amorites had, whom Yahweh had dispossessed for the Israelites.

Ahab repents

27 When Ahab heard these words, he tore his garments and put sackcloth next to his skin and fasted; he slept in the sackcloth; he walked with slow steps. 28 Then the word of Yahweh came to Elijah the Tishbite, 29 'Have you seen how Ahab has humbled himself before me? Since he has humbled himself before me, I shall not bring the disaster in his days; I shall bring the disaster down on his House in his son's days.'[b]

E: ANOTHER WAR WITH ARAM

Ahab plans a campaign against Ramoth in Gilead

22 There was a lull of three years, with no fighting between Aram and Israel. 2 Then, in the third year, Jehoshaphat king of Judah paid a visit to the king of Israel. 3 The king of Israel said to his officers, 'You are aware that Ramoth in Gilead belongs to us? And yet we do nothing to wrest it away from the king of Aram.' 4 He said to Jehoshaphat, 'Will you come with me to attack Ramoth in Gilead?' Jehoshaphat replied to the king of Israel, 'I will be as you, my men as yours, my horses as yours.'

The spurious prophets predict success

5 Jehoshaphat, however, said to the king of Israel, 'First, please enquire what the word of Yahweh is.' 6 The king of Israel then called the prophets together, about four hundred of them. 'Should I go and attack Ramoth in Gilead,' he asked, 'or should I hold back?' 'Go ahead,' they replied, 'for Yahweh has already given it to the king.' 7 Jehoshaphat, however, said, 'Is there no other prophet of Yahweh here, so that we can enquire through him?' 8 The king of Israel said to Jehoshaphat, 'There is one more man through whom we can consult Yahweh, but I hate him because he never has a favourable prophecy for me,

---

21a ‖ 2 K 9:25–26.
21b *See* 2 K 9–10.

only unfavourable ones; he is Micaiah son of
Imlah.' 'I hope the king's words are unjusti-
fied,' said Jehoshaphat. 9The king of Israel
then summoned a court official and said,
'Bring Micaiah son of Imlah immediately.'

10The king of Israel and Jehoshaphat king
of Judah were sitting each on his throne,
wearing their robes, in an open space just
outside the gate of Samaria, with all the
prophets in a state of ecstasy before them.
11Zedekiah son of Kenaanah, who had made
himself some iron horns, said, 'Yahweh says,
"With horns like these you will gore the
Aramaeans till you make an end of them." '
12And all the prophets cried ecstatically in
the same vein, saying, 'March on Ramoth
in Gilead! Success is sure, for Yahweh has
already given it to the king!'

The prophet Micaiah predicts defeat

13The messenger who had gone to summon
Micaiah said to him, 'Look here, what the
prophets are saying is uniformly favourable
to the king. I hope you will say the same as
they do and speak favourably.' 14Micaiah
said, 'As Yahweh lives, I shall speak as
Yahweh tells me!' 15When he came to the
king, the king said, 'Micaiah, should we go
and attack Ramoth in Gilead, or should we
hold back?' He replied, 'Go ahead! Success
is sure, for Yahweh has already given it to
the king!' 16The king then said, 'How often
must I put you on oath to tell me nothing but
the truth in the name of Yahweh?' 17Then he
spoke out:

I saw all Israel
scattered on the mountains
like sheep without a shepherd.
And Yahweh said,
'These have no master,
let them all go safely home!'

18At this the king of Israel said to Jeho-
shaphat, 'Did I not tell you that he never
gives me favourable prophecies, but only
unfavourable ones?' 19Micaiah went on,
'Now listen to the word of Yahweh. I saw
Yahweh seated on his throne with the whole
array of heaven standing by him, on his right
and on his left. 20Yahweh said, "Who will
entice Ahab into marching to his death at
Ramoth in Gilead?" At which some answered
one way, and some another. 21A spirit then
came forward and stood before Yahweh and
said, "I will entice him." 22"How?" Yahweh
asked. He replied, "I shall go and be a
deceptive spirit in the mouths of all his
prophets." Yahweh said, "You will succeed
in enticing him. Go and do it." 23And now,
you see, Yahweh has put a deceptive spirit
into the mouths of all your prophets here, for
in fact Yahweh has pronounced disaster on
you.'

24Zedekiah son of Chenaanah then came
up, struck Micaiah on the cheek and said,
'Which way did Yahweh's spirit leave me, to
speak to you?' 25'That is what you will find
out,' Micaiah retorted, 'the day you go from
room to room, trying to hide.' 26The king of
Israel said, 'Seize Micaiah and hand him over
to Amon, governor of the city, and Joash,
the king's son, 27and say, "These are the
king's orders: Put this man in prison and feed
him on nothing but bread and water until I
am safely home." ' 28Micaiah said, 'If you
ever do get home safely, Yahweh has not
spoken through me.'

Ahab falls at Ramoth in Gilead

29The king of Israel and Jehoshaphat king of
Judah marched on Ramoth in Gilead. 30The
king of Israel said to Jehoshaphat, 'I shall
disguise myself to go into battle, but you put
on your robes.' So the king of Israel disguised
himself and went into battle. 31Now, the king
of Aram had given his chariot commanders
the following order, 'Do not attack anyone
of whatever rank, except the king of Israel.'
32So, when the chariot commanders saw
Jehoshaphat, they thought, 'That is obvi-
ously the king of Israel,' and surrounded him
to attack. But when Jehoshaphat shouted his
war cry 33the chariot commanders, realising
that he was not the king of Israel, broke off
their pursuit.

34Someone, however, drawing his bow
without any special aim, shot the king of
Israel between the joints of his armour. 'Turn
about!' said the king to his charioteer. 'Get
me out of the fighting; I am collapsing.' 35But
the battle grew fiercer as the day went on and
the king had to be held upright in his chariot
facing the Aramaeans, the blood from the
wound running into the bottom of the
chariot, until in the evening he died. 36At
sundown a shout ran through the ranks,
'Every man back to his town, every man back
to his country! 37The king is dead.' He was
taken to Samaria and in Samaria the king was
buried. 38They washed the chariot at the Pool

of Samaria; the dogs licked up the blood, and
the prostitutes washed in it, in accordance
with the word which Yahweh had spoken.

F: AFTER THE DEATH OF AHAB

The end of the reign of Ahab

39 The rest of the history of Ahab, his entire
career, the ivory house he erected, all the
towns he built, is this not recorded in the
Book of the Annals of the Kings of Israel?
40 When Ahab fell asleep with his ancestors,
his son Ahaziah succeeded him.

The reign of Jehoshaphat in Judah (870–848)

41 Jehoshaphat son of Asa became king of
Judah in the fourth year of Ahab king of Israel.
42 Jehoshaphat was thirty-five years old when
he came to the throne, and he reigned for
twenty-five years in Jerusalem. His mother's
name was Azubah daughter of Shilhi. 43 In
every way he followed the example of his
father Asa undeviatingly, doing what is
pleasing to Yahweh. 44 The high places,
however, were not abolished; the people still
offered sacrifice and incense on the high
places. 45 Jehoshaphat was at peace with the
king of Israel.

46 The rest of the history of Jehoshaphat,
the valour he showed, the wars he waged, is
this not recorded in the Book of the Annals
of the Kings of Judah? 47 The few male sacred
prostitutes left over from the days of his
father Asa, he expelled from the country.
48 At the time, Edom had no king, and King
49 Jehoshaphat built ships of Tarshish to go
to Ophir for gold, but they never made the
voyage since the ships were wrecked at Ezion-
Geber. 50 Ahaziah son of Ahab then proposed
to Jehoshaphat, 'Let my men go to sea with
yours.' But Jehoshaphat would not agree.
51 When Jehoshaphat fell asleep with his
ancestors he was buried in the City of his
ancestor, David; his son Jehoram succeeded
him.

King Ahaziah of Israel (853–852) and the prophet Elijah

52 Ahaziah son of Ahab became king of Israel
in Samaria in the seventeenth year of Jeho-
shaphat king of Judah, and reigned over
Israel for two years. 53 He did what is
displeasing to Yahweh, by following the
example of his father and mother, and of
Jeroboam son of Nebat who had led Israel
into sin. 54 He served Baal and worshipped
him, and provoked the anger of Yahweh God
of Israel just as his father had done.

THE SECOND BOOK OF THE KINGS

1 After Ahab's death Moab rebelled against
Israel.
2 Ahaziah had fallen from the balcony of
his upper room in Samaria, and was lying ill;
so he sent messengers, saying to them, 'Go
and consult Baal-Zebub[a] god of Ekron and
ask whether I shall recover from my illness.'
3 But the angel of Yahweh said to Elijah the
Tishbite, 'Up! Go and intercept the king of
Samaria's messengers. Say to them, "Is there
no God in Israel, for you to go and consult
Baal-Zebub god of Ekron? 4 Yahweh says
this: You will never leave the bed you have
got into; you are certainly going to die." '
And Elijah set out.

5 The messengers returned to the king, who
said, 'Why have you come back?' 6 'A man
came to meet us,' they answered. 'He said,
"Go back to the king who sent you and tell
him: Yahweh says this: Is there no God in
Israel, for you to go and consult Baal-Zebub
god of Ekron? For this, you will never leave
the bed you have got into; you are certainly
going to die." '
7 He said, 'This man who met you and said
all this, what was he like?' 8 'A man wearing
a hair cloak', they answered, 'and a leather
loincloth.' 'It was Elijah the Tishbite,' he
said.
9 He then sent a captain of fifty soldiers

1a A mocking pun (=Baal of Flies). The god's real name was Baal-Zebul (=Baal the Prince).

with his fifty men to Elijah, whom they found
sitting on top of a hill; the captain went up
to him and said, 'Man of God, the king
says, "Come down." ' [10]Elijah answered the
captain, 'If I am a man of God, may fire fall
from heaven and destroy both you and your
fifty men.' And fire fell from heaven and
destroyed him and his fifty men. [11]The king
sent a second captain of fifty to him, again
with fifty men, and he too went up and said,
'Man of God, this is the king's order, "Come
down at once." ' [12]Elijah answered them, 'If
I am a man of God, may fire fall from heaven
and destroy both you and your fifty men.'
And lightning fell from heaven and destroyed
him and his fifty men. [13]The king then sent
a third captain of fifty to him, with another
fifty men. The third captain of fifty came up
to Elijah, fell on his knees before him and
pleaded with him. 'Man of God,' he said,
'may my life and the lives of these fifty
servants of yours count for something in
your eyes. [14]Fire has fallen from heaven and
destroyed two captains of fifties and their
companies, but this time may my life count
for something in your eyes!' [15]The angel of
Yahweh said to Elijah, 'Go down with him;
do not be afraid of him.' He rose and
accompanied him down to the king, [16]and
said to him, 'Yahweh says this, "Since you
sent messengers to consult Baal-Zebub god
of Ekron, you will never leave the bed you
have got into; you are certainly going to
die." '

[17]And, in accordance with the word of
Yahweh which Elijah had uttered, he died.
Since he had no son, his brother Jehoram
succeeded him, in the second year of
Jehoram son of Jehoshaphat, king of Judah.
[18]The rest of the history of Ahaziah, and his
career, is this not recorded in the Book of the
Annals of the Kings of Israel?

VI: THE ELISHA CYCLE

A: ITS OPENING

Elijah is taken up to heaven and Elisha succeeds him

2 This is what happened when Yahweh
took Elijah up to heaven in the whirlwind:
Elijah and Elisha set out from Gilgal, [2]and
Elijah said to Elisha, 'You stay here, for
Yahweh is only sending me to Bethel.' But
Elisha replied, 'As Yahweh lives and as you
yourself live, I will not leave you!' and they
went down to Bethel. [3]The brotherhood of
prophets living at Bethel came out to meet
Elisha and said, 'Do you know that Yahweh
will carry your lord and master away today?'
'Yes, I know,' he said, 'be quiet.' [4]Elijah
said, 'Elisha, you stay here, Yahweh is only
sending me to Jericho.' But he replied, 'As
Yahweh lives and as you yourself live, I will
not leave you!' and they went on to Jericho.
[5]The brotherhood of prophets living at
Jericho went up to Elisha and said, 'Do you
know that Yahweh will carry your lord and
master away today?' 'Yes, I know,' he said,
'be quiet.' [6]Elijah said, 'Elisha, you stay here,
Yahweh is only sending me to the Jordan.'
But he replied, 'As Yahweh lives and as you
yourself live, I will not leave you!' And they
went on together.

[7]Fifty of the brotherhood of prophets
followed them, halting some distance away
as the two of them stood beside the Jordan.
[8]Elijah took his cloak, rolled it up and struck
the water; and the water divided to left and
right, and the two of them crossed over dry-
shod. [9]When they had crossed, Elijah said to
Elisha, 'Make your request. What can I do
for you before I am snatched away from you?'
Elisha answered, 'Let me inherit a double
share of your spirit.' [10]'Your request is diffi-
cult,' Elijah said. 'If you see me while I am
being snatched away from you, it will be as
you ask; if not, it will not be so.' [11]Now as
they walked on, talking as they went, a
chariot of fire appeared and horses of fire
coming between the two of them; and Elijah
went up to heaven in the whirlwind. [12]Elisha
saw it, and shouted, 'My father! My father!
Chariot of Israel and its chargers!' Then he
lost sight of him, and taking hold of his own
clothes he tore them in half. [13]He picked up
Elijah's cloak which had fallen, and went
back and stood on the bank of the Jordan.

[14]He took Elijah's cloak and struck the
water. 'Where is Yahweh, the God of Elijah?'
he cried. As he struck the water it divided to

right and left, and Elisha crossed over. 15The
brotherhood of prophets saw him in the
distance, and said, 'The spirit of Elijah has
come to rest on Elisha'; they went to meet
him and bowed to the ground before him.
16'Look,' they said, 'your servants have fifty
strong men with them, let them go and look
for your master; the Spirit of Yahweh may
have taken him up and thrown him down on
a mountain or into a valley.' 'Send no one,'
he replied. 17But they so shamed him with
their insistence that he consented. So they
sent fifty men who searched for three days
without finding him. 18They then came back
to Elisha who had stayed in Jericho; he said,
'Didn't I tell you not to go?'

Two miracles of Elisha

19The people of the city said to Elisha, 'The
city is pleasant to live in, as my lord indeed
can see, but the water is foul and the country
suffers from miscarriages.' 20'Bring me a new
bowl,' he said, 'and put some salt in it.' They
brought it to him. 21Then he went to the
source of the water, threw salt into it and
said, 'Yahweh says this, "I make this water
wholesome: neither death nor miscarriage
shall come from it any more." ' 22And the
water became wholesome, as it is today,
exactly as Elisha had said it would.

23From there he went up to Bethel, and
while he was on the road, some small boys
came out of the town and jeered at him.
'Hurry up, baldy!' they shouted. 'Come on
up, baldy!' 24He turned round and looked at
them; and he cursed them in the name of
Yahweh. And two bears came out of the
forest and savaged forty-two of the boys.
25From there he went on to Mount Carmel
and then returned to Samaria.

B: THE MOABITE WAR

Introduction to the reign of Jehoram in Israel (852–841)

3 Jehoram son of Ahab became king of
Israel in Samaria in the eighteenth year of
Jehoshaphat king of Judah, and reigned for
twelve years. 2He did what is displeasing
to Yahweh, though not like his father and
mother, for he did away with the pillar to Baal
which his father had made. 3Nonetheless, he
continued to practise the sins into which
Jeroboam son of Nebat had led Israel and did
not give them up.

The expedition of Israel and Judah against Moab

4Mesha king of Moab was a sheep-breeder
and used to pay the king of Israel in tribute
a hundred thousand lambs and a hundred
thousand rams with their wool. 5But when
Ahab died, the king of Moab rebelled against
the king of Israel.

6At once King Jehoram left Samaria and
mustered all Israel. 7After this he sent word
to the king of Judah, 'The king of Moab has
rebelled against me. Will you go to war with
me against Moab?' 'I will,' he replied. 'I will
be as you, my men as yours, my horses as
yours,' 8and added, 'Which way are we to
attack?' 'Through the desert of Edom,' the
other answered.

9So they set out, the king of Israel, the king
of Judah and the king of Edom. They carried
out a flanking movement for seven days, until
there was no water left for the troops or for
the beasts of their baggage train. 10'Alas!'
the king of Israel exclaimed, 'Yahweh has
summoned us three kings, only to put us into
the power of Moab.' 11But the king of Judah
said, 'Is there no prophet of Yahweh here for
us to consult Yahweh through him?' One of
the king of Israel's servants answered, 'Elisha
son of Shaphat is here, who used to pour
water on the hands of Elijah.' 12'The word of
Yahweh is with him,' the king of Judah said.
So the king of Israel, the king of Judah and
the king of Edom went to consult him. 13But
Elisha said to the king of Israel, 'What busi-
ness have you with me? Go to your father's
and your mother's prophets.' 'No,' the king
of Israel answered, 'Yahweh is the one who
has summoned us three kings, only to put us
into the power of Moab.' Elisha replied, 14'By
the life of Yahweh Sabaoth whom I serve, if
I did not respect the king of Judah, I would
take no notice of you, nor so much as look at
you. 15Now bring me someone who can play
the lyre.' And as the musician played, the
hand of Yahweh came on him 16and he said,
'Yahweh says this, "Dig in this valley ditch
after ditch," 17for Yahweh says, "You will
see no wind, you will see no rain, but this
valley will become full of water, and you and
your troops and your baggage animals will
drink." 18But this is only a trifle in Yahweh's
eyes, for he will put Moab itself into your

power. 19 You will storm every fortified town,
fell every productive tree, block every water-
hole, ruin all the best fields with stones.'
20 Next morning at the time when the oblation
was being offered, water came from the direc-
tion of Edom, and the whole terrain was
flooded.
21 When the Moabites learned that the
kings were advancing to fight them, all those
of an age to bear arms were mobilised; they
took up position on the frontier. 22 In the
morning when they got up, the sun was
shining on the water; and in the distance the
Moabites saw the water as red as blood.
23 'This is blood!' they said. 'The kings must
have fought among themselves and killed one
another. So now for the booty, Moab!' 24 But
when they reached the Israelite camp, the
Israelites launched their attack and the
Moabites fled before them, and as they
advanced they cut the Moabites to pieces.
25 They laid the towns in ruins, and each man
threw a stone into all the best fields to fill
them up, and they blocked every water-hole
and felled every productive tree. In the end,
there was only Kir-Hareseth left, which the
slingers surrounded and bombarded.
26 When the king of Moab saw that the battle
had turned against him, he mustered seven
hundred swordsmen in the hope of breaking
a way out and going to the king of Aram, but
he failed. 27 Then he took his eldest son who
was to succeed him and offered him as a
sacrifice on the city wall. Alarmed at this, the
Israelites withdrew and retired to their own
territory.

C: SOME MIRACLES OF ELISHA

The widow's oil[a]

4 The wife of a member of the prophetic
brotherhood appealed to Elisha. 'Your
servant my husband is dead,' she said, 'and
you know how your servant revered Yahweh.
A creditor has now come to take my two
children and make them his slaves.' 2 Elisha
said, 'What can I do for you? Tell me, what
have you got in the house?' 'Your servant has
nothing in the house,' she replied, 'except a
flask of oil.' 3 Then he said, 'Go outside and
borrow jars from all your neighbours, empty
jars and not too few. 4 When you come back,
shut the door on yourself and your sons, and
pour the oil into all these jars, putting each
aside when it is full.' 5 So she left him; and
she shut the door on herself and her sons;
they passed her the jars and she went on
pouring. 6 When the jars were full, she said
to her son, 'Pass me another jar.' 'There are
no more,' he replied. Then the oil stopped
flowing. 7 She went and told the man of God,
who said, 'Go and sell the oil and redeem
your pledge; you and your children can live
on the remainder.'

The woman of Shunem and her son

8 One day as Elisha was on his way to Shunem,
a woman of rank who lived there pressed him
to stay and eat there. After this he always
broke his journey for a meal when he passed
that way. 9 She said to her husband, 'Look, I
am sure the man who is constantly passing
our way must be a holy man of God. 10 Let us
build him a small walled room, and put him
a bed in it, and a table and chair and lamp;
whenever he comes to us he can rest there.'
11 One day when he came, he retired to the
upper room and lay down. 12 He said to his
servant Gehazi, 'Call our Shunammite.' He
called her and when she appeared, Elisha
said, 13 'Tell her this: "Look, you have gone
to all this trouble for us, what can we do for
you? Is there anything you would like said
for you to the king or to the commander of
the army?" ' But she replied, 'I live with my
own people about me.' 14 'What can I do for
you then?' he asked. Gehazi replied, 'Well,
she has no son and her husband is old.'
15 Elisha said, 'Call her.' The servant called
her and she stood at the door. 16 'This time
next year', he said, 'you will hold a son in
your arms.' But she said, 'No, my lord, do
not deceive your servant.' 17 But the woman
did conceive, and she gave birth to a son at
the time that Elisha had said she would.
18 The child grew up; one day he went to
his father who was with the reapers, 19 and
exclaimed to his father, 'Oh, my head! My
head!' The father told a servant to carry him
to his mother.[b] 20 He lifted him up and took
him to his mother, and the boy lay on her lap
until midday, when he died. 21 She went
upstairs, laid him on the bed of the man of

4a ‖ 1 K 17:8–15.
4b ‖ 1 K 17:17–24.

God, shut the door on him and went out.
22She called her husband and said, 'Send me
one of the servants with a donkey. I must
hurry to the man of God and back.' 23'Why
go to him today?' he asked. 'It is not New
Moon or Sabbath.' But she replied, 'Never
mind.' 24She had the donkey saddled and
said to her servant, 'Lead on, go! Do not
draw rein until I give the order.' 25She set off
and made her way to the man of God at
Mount Carmel. When the man of God saw
her in the distance, he said to his servant
Gehazi, 'Look, here comes our Shunammite!
26Now run and meet her and ask her, "Are
you well? Is your husband well? Your child
well?" ' 'Yes,' she replied. 27When she came
to the man of God there on the mountain,
she took hold of his feet. Gehazi stepped
forward to push her away, but the man of
God said, 'Leave her; there is bitterness in
her soul and Yahweh has hidden it from me,
he has not told me.' 28She said, 'Did I ask my
lord for a son? Did I not say: Don't deceive
me?'

29Elisha said to Gehazi, 'Hitch up your
clothes, take my staff in your hand and go.
If you meet anyone, do not greet him; if
anyone greets you, do not answer him. You
are to stretch out my staff over the child.'
30But the child's mother said, 'As Yahweh
lives and as you yourself live, I will not leave
you.' Then he stood up and followed her.
31Gehazi had gone ahead of them and had
stretched out the staff over the child, but
there was no sound or response. He went
back to meet Elisha and told him. 'The child
has not woken up,' he said. 32Elisha then
went to the house, and there on his bed lay
the child, dead. 33He went in and shut the
door on the two of them and prayed to
Yahweh. 34Then he climbed on to the bed
and stretched himself on top of the child,
putting his mouth on his mouth, his eyes to
his eyes, and his hands on his hands, and as
he lowered himself on to him, the child's
flesh grew warm. 35Then he got up and
walked to and fro inside the house, and then
climbed on to the bed again and lowered
himself on to the child seven times in all;
then the child sneezed and opened his eyes.
36He then summoned Gehazi. 'Call our
Shunammite,' he said. He called her. When
she came to him, he said, 'Pick up your
son.' 37She went in and, falling at his feet,
prostrated herself on the floor and then
picked up her son and went out.

The poisoned soup

38Elisha went back to Gilgal while there was
famine in the country. As the brotherhood
of prophets were sitting with him, he said to
his servant, 'Put the large pot on the fire and
cook some soup for the brotherhood.' 39One
of them went into the fields to gather herbs
and came on some wild vine, off which he
gathered enough gourds to fill his lap. On his
return, he cut them up into the pot of soup;
they did not know what they were. 40They
then poured the soup out for the men to eat,
but they had no sooner tasted the soup than
they cried, 'Man of God, there is death in the
pot!' And they could not eat it. 41'Bring some
meal then,' Elisha said. This he threw into
the pot, and said, 'Pour out, for the company
to eat!' And there was nothing harmful in the
pot.

The multiplication of loaves

42A man came from Baal-Shalishah, bringing
the man of God bread from the first-fruits,
twenty barley loaves and fresh grain still in
the husk. 'Give it to the company to eat,'
Elisha said. 43But his servant replied, 'How
can I serve this to a hundred men?' 'Give it
to the company to eat,' he insisted, 'for
Yahweh says this, "They will eat and have
some left over." ' 44He served them; they ate
and had some left over, as Yahweh had said.

Naaman is healed

5 Naaman, army commander to the king
of Aram, was a man who enjoyed his
master's respect and favour, since through
him Yahweh had granted victory to the
Aramaeans. 2But the man suffered from a
virulent skin-disease. Now, on one of their
raids into Israelite territory, the Aramaeans
had carried off a little girl, who became a
servant of Naaman's wife. 3She said to her
mistress, 'If only my master would approach
the prophet of Samaria! He would cure him
of his skin-disease.' 4Naaman went and told
his master. 'This and this', he reported, 'is
what the girl from Israel has said.' 5'Go by
all means,' said the king of Aram, 'I shall
send a letter to the king of Israel.' So Naaman
left, taking with him ten talents of silver, six
thousand shekels of gold and ten festal robes.
6He presented the letter to the king of Israel.
It read, 'With this letter, I am sending my

servant Naaman to you for you to cure him
of his skin-disease.' 7When the king of Israel
read the letter, he tore his clothes. 'Am I a
god to give death and life,' he said, 'for him
to send a man to me and ask me to cure him
of his skin-disease? Listen to this and take
note of it and see how he intends to pick a
quarrel with me.'
8When Elisha heard that the king of Israel
had torn his clothes, he sent word to the king,
'Why have you torn your clothes? Let him
come to me, and he will find there is a prophet
in Israel.' 9So Naaman came with his team
and chariot and drew up at the door of Elisha's
house. 10And Elisha sent him a messenger to
say, 'Go and bathe seven times in the Jordan,
and your flesh will become clean once more.'
11But Naaman was indignant and went off,
saying, 'Here was I, thinking he would be
sure to come out to me, and stand there, and
call on the name of Yahweh his God, and
wave his hand over the spot and cure the
part that was diseased. 12Surely, Abana and
Parpar, the rivers of Damascus, are better
than any water in Israel? Could I not bathe
in them and become clean?' And he turned
round and went off in a rage. 13But his
servants approached him and said, 'Father,
if the prophet had asked you to do something
difficult, would you not have done it? All the
more reason, then, when he says to you,
"Bathe, and you will become clean." ' 14So
he went down and immersed himself seven
times in the Jordan, as Elisha had told him
to do. And his flesh became clean once more
like the flesh of a little child.
15Returning to Elisha with his whole
escort, he went in and, presenting himself,
said, 'Now I know that there is no God
anywhere on earth except in Israel. Now,
please, accept a present from your servant.'
16But Elisha replied, 'As Yahweh lives, whom
I serve, I will accept nothing.' Naaman
pressed him to accept, but he refused. 17Then
Naaman said, 'Since your answer is "No,"
allow your servant to be given as much earth
as two mules may carry, since your servant
will no longer make burnt offerings or sacri-
fice to any god except Yahweh. 18Only—and
may Yahweh forgive your servant for this—
when my master goes to the temple of
Rimmon to worship there, he leans on my
arm, and I bow down in the temple of
Rimmon when he does; may Yahweh forgive
your servant for doing this!' 19'Go in peace,'
Elisha replied.
20Naaman had gone a small distance, when
Gehazi, Elisha's servant, said to himself, 'My
master has let this Aramaean Naaman off
lightly, by not accepting what he offered. As
Yahweh lives, I will run after him and get
something out of him.' 21So Gehazi set off in
pursuit of Naaman. When Naaman saw him
running after him, he jumped down from his
chariot to meet him. 'Is all well?' he asked.
22'All is well,' he said. 'My master has sent
me to say, "This very moment two young
men of the prophetic brotherhood have
arrived from the highlands of Ephraim. Be
kind enough to give them a talent of silver
and two festal robes." ' 23'Please accept two
talents,' Naaman replied, and pressed him,
tying up the two talents of silver in two bags
with the two festal robes and consigning them
to two of his servants who carried them ahead
of Gehazi. 24When he reached Ophel, he took
these from them and put them away in the
house. He then dismissed the men, who went
away.
25He, for his part, went and presented
himself to his master. Elisha said, 'Gehazi,
where have you been?' 'Your servant has not
been anywhere,' he replied. 26But Elisha said
to him, 'Was not my heart present there when
someone left his chariot to meet you? Now
you have taken the money, you can buy
gardens with it, and olive groves, sheep and
oxen, male and female slaves. 27But
Naaman's disease of the skin will cling to you
and your descendants for ever.' And Gehazi
left his presence white as snow from skin-
disease.

The axe lost and found

6 The brotherhood of prophets said to
Elisha, 'Look, the place where we are
living with you is too small for us. 2Let us go
to the Jordan, then, and each of us cut a beam
there, and we will make our living quarters
there.' He replied, 'Go.' 3'Be good enough to
go with your servants,' one of them said. 'I
will go,' he replied, 4and went with them. On
reaching the Jordan they began cutting down
timber. 5But, as one of them was felling his
beam, the iron axehead fell into the water.
'Alas, my lord,' he exclaimed, 'and it was a
borrowed one too!' 6'Where did it fall?' the
man of God asked; and he showed him the
spot. Then, cutting a stick, Elisha threw it
in at that point and made the iron axehead

float. 7'Lift it out,' he said; and the man
stretched out his hand and took it.

D: THE ARAMAEAN WARS

Elisha captures an armed band of Aramaeans

8The king of Aram was at war with Israel.
He conferred with his officers and said, 'You
must attack at such and such a place.' 9Elisha,
however, sent word to the king of Israel, 'Be
on your guard about such and such a place,
because the Aramaeans are going to attack
it.' 10The king of Israel accordingly sent men
to the place which Elisha had named. And
he kept warning the king, and the king stayed
on the alert; and this happened more than
once or twice.
11The king of Aram grew very much
disturbed over this. He summoned his offi-
cers, and said, 'Tell me which of you is
betraying us to the king of Israel.' 12'No one,
my lord king,' one of his officers replied. 'It
is Elisha, the prophet in Israel. The words
you utter in your bedchamber, he reveals to
the king of Israel.' 13'Go and find out where
he is,' the king said, 'so that I can send people
to capture him.' Word was brought to him,
'He is now in Dothan.' 14So he sent horses
and chariots there, and a large force; and
these, arriving during the night, surrounded
the town.
15Next day, Elisha got up early and went
out; and there surrounding the town was an
armed force with horses and chariots. 'Oh,
my lord,' his servant said, 'what are we to
do?' 16'Do not be afraid,' he replied, 'for
there are more on our side than on theirs.'
17And Elisha prayed. 'Yahweh,' he said,
'open his eyes and make him see.' Yahweh
opened the servant's eyes, and he saw the
mountain covered in fiery horses and chariots
surrounding Elisha.
18As the Aramaeans came down towards
him, Elisha prayed to Yahweh, 'I beg you
to strike these people sun-blind.' And, at
Elisha's word, he struck them sun-blind.
19Then Elisha said to them, 'This is not the
road, nor is this the town. Follow me; I shall
lead you to the man you are looking for.' But
he led them to Samaria. 20As they entered
Samaria, Elisha said, 'Yahweh, open these
people's eyes, and let them see.' Yahweh
opened their eyes and they saw; they were
inside Samaria.
21When the king of Israel saw them, he
said to Elisha, 'Shall I kill them, father?'
22'Do not kill them,' he replied. 'Do you kill
your own prisoners with sword and bow?
Offer them food and water, so that they can
eat and drink, and then let them go back to
their master.' 23So the king provided a great
feast for them; and when they had eaten and
drunk, he sent them off and they went back
to their master. Aramaean raiding parties
never invaded the territory of Israel again.

Samaria besieged; the famine

24It happened after this that Ben-Hadad king
of Aram, mustering his whole army, marched
on and laid siege to Samaria. 25In Samaria
there was great famine, and so strict was the
siege that the head of a donkey sold for eighty
shekels of silver, and one quarter-*kab* of wild
onions for five shekels of silver.
26Now as the king was passing along the
city wall, a woman shouted, 'Help, my lord
king!' 27'If Yahweh does not help you,' he
retorted, 'where can I find help for you? From
the threshing-floor? From the winepress?'
28Then the king asked, 'What is the matter?'
'This woman here', she answered, 'said to
me, "Give up your son; we will eat him today,
and eat my son tomorrow." 29So we cooked
my son and ate him. Next day, I said to her,
"Give up your son for us to eat." But she has
hidden her son.' 30On hearing the woman's
words, the king tore his clothes; the king was
walking on the wall, and the people saw that
underneath he was wearing sackcloth next
his body. 31'May God bring unnameable ills
on me, and worse ills, too,' he said, 'if the
head of Elisha son of Shaphat remains on
his shoulders today!'

Elisha foretells imminent relief

32Elisha was sitting in his house, and the
elders were sitting with him. The king sent a
messenger ahead but, before the man arrived,
Elisha had said to the elders, 'Do you see how
this son of a murderer has given orders to cut
off my head? Look, when the messenger
comes, shut the door; hold the door against
him. Isn't that the sound of his master's step
behind him?' 33He was still actually speaking,
when the king arrived and said, 'This misery

plainly comes from Yahweh. Why should I
still trust in Yahweh?'

7 'Listen to the word of Yahweh,' Elisha
said. 'Yahweh says this, "By this time
tomorrow a measure of finest flour will sell
for one shekel, and two measures of barley
for one shekel, at the gate of Samaria." ' 2The
equerry on whose arm the king was leaning
retorted to Elisha, 'Even if Yahweh made
windows in the sky, could this word come
true?' 'You will see it with your own eyes,'
Elisha replied, 'though you will eat none of
it.'

The Aramaean camp is found abandoned

3Now at the entrance to the gate—for they
were afflicted with virulent skin-disease—
there were four men and they debated among
themselves, 'Why sit here waiting for death?
4If we decide to go into the city, what with
the famine in it, we shall die there; if we stay
where we are, we shall die just the same.
Come on, let us go over to the Aramaean
camp; if they spare our lives, we live; if they
kill us, well, then we die.' 5So at dusk they
set out and made for the Aramaean camp,
but when they reached the confines of the
camp there was not a soul there. 6For Yahweh
had caused the Aramaeans in their camp to
hear a noise of chariots and horses, the noise
of a great army; and they had said to one
another, 'Listen! The king of Israel has hired
the Hittite and Egyptian kings against us, to
attack us.' 7So in the dusk they had made off
and fled, abandoning their tents, their horses
and their donkeys; leaving the camp just as
it was, they had fled for their lives. 8The men
with skin-disease, then, reached the confines
of the camp. They went into one of the tents
and ate and drank, and from it carried off
silver and gold and clothing; these they took
and hid. Then they came back and, entering
another tent, looted it too, and took and hid
their booty.

The siege at an end; the famine ceases

9Then they said to one another, 'We are doing
wrong. This is a day of good news, yet we are
holding our tongues! If we wait till morning,
we shall certainly be punished. Come on, let
us go and take the news to the palace.' 10Off
they went and shouted out to the guards on
the city gate, 'We have been to the Aramaean
camp. There was not a soul there, no sound
of anyone, only tethered horses and tethered
donkeys, and their tents just as they were.'
11The gatekeepers shouted the news, which
was reported inside the palace.

12The king got up while it was still dark
and said to his officers, 'I can tell you what
the Aramaeans have done to us. They know
we are starving, so they have left the camp to
hide in the open country. "They will come
out of the city," they think, "we shall catch
them alive and get into the city." ' 13One of
his officers replied, 'Five of the surviving
horses still left us had better be taken—they
would die in any case like all the rest. Let us
send them and see.' 14So they took two chariot
teams and the king sent them after the
Aramaean army, saying, 'Go and see.' 15They
followed them as far as the Jordan, finding
the whole way strewn with clothes and gear
which the Aramaeans had thrown away in
their panic. The scouts returned and
informed the king.

16Then the people went out and plundered
the Aramaean camp: a measure of finest flour
sold for one shekel, and two measures of
barley for one shekel, as Yahweh had prom-
ised they would. 17The king had detailed
the equerry, on whose arm he leaned, as
commander of the guard on the gate, but the
people trampled on him in the gateway and
he died, as the man of God had foretold when
the king had come down to him. 18(What
Elisha had said to the king came true, 'Two
measures of barley will sell for one shekel,
and a measure of finest flour for one shekel, by
this time tomorrow at the gate of Samaria.'
19And the equerry in question had replied to
the man of God, 'Even if Yahweh made
windows in the sky, could this word come
true?' 'You will see it with your own eyes,'
Elisha had answered, 'though you will eat
none of it.' 20And that was what happened to
him: for the people trampled on him in the
gateway and he died.)

**Epilogue to the story of
the woman of Shunem**

8 Elisha had said to the woman whose son
he had raised to life, 'Move away with
your family, and live where you can in some
foreign country, for Yahweh has called up a
famine—it is already coming on the
country—for seven years.' 2The woman
hurried to do what the man of God had told
her: she set out, she and her family, and for

seven years she lived in Philistine territory.
3When the seven years were over, the woman
returned from Philistine territory and went
to lodge a claim with the king for her house
and land.
4Now the king was talking to Gehazi, the
servant of the man of God. 'Tell me', he was
saying, 'all about the marvels which Elisha
did.' 5Gehazi was just telling the king how
Elisha had raised the dead child to life,
when the woman whose son Elisha had raised
lodged her claim with the king for her house
and land. 'My lord king,' Gehazi said, 'this
is the very woman, and that is her son whom
Elisha raised to life.' 6The king questioned
the woman, who told him the story. The king
then delegated one of the officials to her
with this order, 'See that all her property is
restored to her, and all the revenue from her
land from the day she left the country until
now.'

Elisha and Hazael of Damascus

7Elisha went to Damascus. Ben-Hadad king
of Aram was ill, and was told, 'The man of
God has come all the way to us.' 8Then the
king said to Hazael, 'Take a present with you
and go and meet the man of God; consult
Yahweh through him, and find out if I shall
recover from my illness.'
9So Hazael went to meet Elisha, taking
with him as a present the best that Damascus
could offer, a load for forty camels. He
arrived and, presenting himself, said, 'Your
son Ben-Hadad king of Aram has sent me to
ask you, "Shall I recover from my illness?" '
10Elisha replied, 'Go and tell him, "You
might recover," though Yahweh has shown
me that he will certainly die.' 11Then the face
of the man of God went rigid, and his look
grew strangely fixed, and he wept. 12'Why',
Hazael asked, 'does my lord weep?' 'Because
I know', Elisha replied, 'what harm you will
do to the Israelites: you will burn down their
fortresses, put their picked warriors to the
sword, dash their little children to pieces,
disembowel their pregnant women.' 13'But
what is your servant?' Hazael said. 'How
could this dog achieve anything so great?' 'In
a vision from Yahweh,' Elisha replied, 'I
have seen you king of Aram.'
14Leaving Elisha, Hazael went back to his
master who asked, 'What did Elisha say to
you?' He replied, 'He told me that you might
recover.' 15Next day he took a blanket,
soaked it in water, and spread it over his face.
So died Ben-Hadad, and Hazael succeeded
him.

The reign of Jehoram in Judah (848–841)

16In the fifth year of Jehoram son of Ahab,
king of Israel, Jehoram son of Jehoshaphat
became king of Judah. 17He was thirty-two
years old when he came to the throne, and he
reigned for eight years in Jerusalem. 18He
followed the example of the kings of Israel
as the House of Ahab were doing; he had
married one of Ahab's daughters; and he did
what is displeasing to Yahweh. 19But Yahweh
was unwilling to destroy Judah, because of
his servant David, and was faithful to the
promise which he had made him to leave him
a lamp for ever in his presence.
20In his time Edom threw off the domi-
nation of Judah and set up a king for itself.
21Jehoram crossed to Zair, and with him all
the chariots . . . Under cover of dark, he and
his chariot commanders broke through the
Edomites surrounding him; the people fled
to their tents. 22Even so, Edom threw off the
domination of Judah, remaining free to the
present day. Libnah also revolted at that
time.
23The rest of the history of Jehoram, his
entire career, is this not recorded in the Book
of the Annals of the Kings of Judah? 24Then
Jehoram fell asleep with his ancestors and
was buried with them in the City of David;
his son Ahaziah succeeded him.

The reign of Ahaziah in Judah (841)

25In the twelfth year of Jehoram son of Ahab,
king of Israel, Ahaziah son of Jehoram, king
of Judah, became king. 26Ahaziah was
twenty-two years old when he came to the
throne, and he reigned for one year in Jeru-
salem. His mother's name was Athaliah
granddaughter of Omri king of Israel. 27He
followed the example of the House of Ahab
and did what is displeasing to Yahweh, as the
House of Ahab were doing, to whom he was
related by marriage.
28He went with Jehoram son of Ahab to
make war on Hazael king of Aram at Ramoth
in Gilead, but the Aramaeans wounded
Jehoram. 29King Jehoram returned to Jezreel
to recover from the wounds which he had
received at Ramah, fighting against Hazael
king of Aram. Ahaziah son of Jehoram, king

of Judah, went down to Jezreel to visit
Jehoram son of Ahab because he was ailing.

E: THE HISTORY OF JEHU

A disciple of Elisha anoints Jehu king

9 The prophet Elisha summoned a member
of the prophetic brotherhood to him,
'Hitch up your clothes, take this flask of oil,
and go to Ramoth in Gilead. [2]When you
arrive there, look for Jehu son of Jeho-
shaphat, son of Nimshi. Then, when you
find him, tell him to get up and leave his
companions, and take him into an inner
room. [3]Take the flask of oil then and pour it
over his head, and say, "Yahweh says this: I
have anointed you king of Israel." Then open
the door and flee as fast as you can.'
[4]The young man left for Ramoth in Gilead
[5]and when he arrived, found the senior offi-
cers of the army sitting together. 'I have a
message for you, commander,' he said. 'For
which of us?' asked Jehu. 'For you,
commander,' he answered. [6]Jehu then got
up and went into the house. And the young
man poured the oil on his head, saying,
'Yahweh, God of Israel, says this, "I have
anointed you king of Yahweh's people, of
Israel. [7]You will strike down the family of
Ahab your master, and I shall avenge the
blood of my servants the prophets and all of
Yahweh's servants, on Jezebel [8]and on the
whole family of Ahab. I shall destroy every
manjack of Ahab's family, fettered or free in
Israel. [9]I shall make the House of Ahab like
the House of Jeroboam son of Nebat and of
Baasha son of Ahijah. [10]As for Jezebel, the
dogs will eat her in the field of Jezreel; no one
will bury her." ' With this, he opened the
door and made his escape.

Jehu proclaimed king

[11]Jehu came out to his master's officers. 'Is
all well?' they asked him. 'Why did this
madman come to you?' 'You know the fellow
and how he talks,' he answered. [12]'Evasion!'
they cried, 'Come on, tell us.' He replied,
'He said this and that to me. He said,
"Yahweh says this: I have anointed you king
of Israel." ' [13]Whereupon they all took their
cloaks and spread them under him on the
bare steps; they sounded the trumpet and
shouted, 'Jehu is king!'

Jehu prepares to usurp power

[14]Jehu son of Jehoshaphat, son of Nimshi
plotted against Jehoram. (At the time,
Jehoram, with all Israel, was holding Ramoth
in Gilead against an attack by Hazael king of
Aram, [15]but King Jehoram had gone back to
Jezreel to recover from the wounds which he
had received from the Aramaeans while he
was fighting against Hazael king of Aram.)
'If you agree,' Jehu said, 'let no one leave the
town to go and take the news to Jezreel.'
[16]Jehu then mounted his chariot and left for
Jezreel; Jehoram had taken to his bed there,
and Ahaziah king of Judah had gone down
to visit him.
[17]The lookout posted on the tower of
Jezreel saw Jehu's troop approaching. 'I can
see a body of men,' he shouted. Jehoram gave
the order: 'Have a horseman sent to meet
them and ask, "Is all well?" ' [18]The horseman
went to meet Jehu and said, 'The king says,
"Is all well?" ' 'What has it to do with you
whether all is well?' Jehu replied. 'Fall in
behind me.' The lookout reported, 'The
messenger has reached them and is not
coming back.' [19]The king sent a second
horseman who reached them and said, 'The
king says, "Is all well?" ' 'What has it to do
with you whether all is well?' Jehu replied.
'Fall in behind me.' [20]The lookout reported,
'He has reached them and is not coming
back. The manner of driving is like that
of Jehu son of Nimshi: he drives like a
madman.' [21]'Harness!' Jehoram cried; and
they harnessed his chariot. Then Jehoram
king of Israel and Ahaziah king of Judah,
each in his chariot, set out to meet Jehu.
They reached him in the field of Naboth of
Jezreel.

The assassination of Jehoram

[22]As soon as Jehoram saw Jehu he asked, 'Is
all well, Jehu?' 'What a question!' he replied,
'when all the while the prostitutions and
countless sorceries of your mother Jezebel go
on.' [23]At this, Jehoram wheeled and fled,
saying to Ahaziah, 'Treason, Ahaziah!' [24]But
Jehu had drawn his bow; he struck Jehoram
between the shoulder-blades, the arrow went
through the king's heart, and he sank down
in his chariot. [25]'Pick him up,' Jehu said to
Bidkar, his equerry, 'and throw him into the
field of Naboth of Jezreel. Remember how,
when you and I manned a chariot together

behind Ahab his father, Yahweh pronounced
this sentence against him,[a] 26"This I swear.
Yesterday I saw the blood of Naboth and the
blood of his sons—Yahweh says this. And in
this same field I shall requite you—Yahweh
says this." So pick him up, and throw him
into the field, as Yahweh declared should
happen!'

The assassination of Ahaziah

27When Ahaziah king of Judah saw this, he
fled along the Beth-ha-Gan road, but Jehu
went in pursuit of him. 'Strike him down
too,' he said. And they wounded him in his
chariot at the slope of Gur, which is near
Ibleam, and he took refuge in Megiddo,
where he died. 28His servants carried him in
a chariot to Jerusalem and buried him in his
tomb in the City of David. 29Ahaziah had
become king of Judah in the eleventh year of
Jehoram son of Ahab.

The assassination of Jezebel

30When Jehu went back to Jezreel, Jezebel
was told. She made up her eyes with mascara,
adorned her head and appeared at the
window. 31As Jehu came through the gateway
she said, 'How did Zimri get on after killing
his master?' 32Jehu looked up to the window
and said, 'Who is on my side? Who?' And
two or three officials looked down at him.
33'Throw her down,' he said. They threw her
down and her blood spattered the walls and
the horses; and Jehu rode over her. 34He went
in and ate and drank, then said, 'See to this
accursed woman, and give her burial; after
all, she was a king's daughter.' 35But when
they went to bury her, they found nothing
but her skull, feet and hands. 36They came
back and told Jehu, who said, 'This is the
word of Yahweh which he spoke through his
servant Elijah the Tishbite, "The dogs will
eat the flesh of Jezebel in the field of Jezreel;
37the corpse of Jezebel will be like dung
spread on the fields, so that no one will be
able to say: This was Jezebel." '

The massacre of the royal family of Israel

10 There were seventy of Ahab's sons in
Samaria. Jehu sent to Samaria, to the
authorities of the city, to the elders and to
the guardians of Ahab's children. He said,
2'Now, when this letter reaches you, you
have your master's sons with you; you also
have chariots and horses, a fortified city and
weapons. 3See which of your master's sons is
the best and worthiest, put him on his father's
throne and fight for your master's dynasty!'
4They were utterly terrified. 'We have seen
how the two kings could not stand up to him,'
they said, 'so how could we?' 5Consequently
the master of the palace, the governor of the
city, the elders and the guardians sent word
to Jehu, 'We are your servants. We shall do
whatever you order us. We shall not proclaim
a king; act as you think best.'

6Jehu then wrote them a second letter. He
said, 'If you are for me and if you are prepared
to accept orders from me, take the heads of
the men of your master's family and come to
me at Jezreel by this time tomorrow.' (There
were seventy of Ahab's sons being educated
there by the leading men of the city.) 7When
this letter reached them, they took the king's
sons and butchered all seventy of them, put
their heads in baskets and sent them to him
at Jezreel.

8The messenger came and told Jehu, 'They
have brought the heads of the king's sons.'
'Leave them in two heaps at the entrance to
the gate until morning,' he replied. 9When
morning came, he went out and, standing,
said to all the people, 'No guilt attaches to
you! I did indeed plot against my master and
have killed him; but what about all these?
Who struck them? 10Know, then, that
nothing will fail to be fulfilled of the proph-
ecy uttered by Yahweh against the House of
Ahab; Yahweh has done what he said through
his servant Elijah.' 11Jehu then killed every
member of the House of Ahab surviving in
Jezreel, all his leading men, his close friends,
his priests; he did not leave a single one alive.

The massacre of the princes of Judah

12Jehu then set out for Samaria. As he was on
his way, at Beth-Eked of the Shepherds, 13he
met the brothers of Ahaziah king of Judah.
'Who are you?' he asked. 'We are Ahaziah's
brothers,' they replied, 'and we are on our
way to pay our respects to the king's sons
and the queen mother's sons.' 14'Take them
alive,' he said. They took them alive, and he
slaughtered them at the storage-well of Beth-

9a || 1 K 21:19.

Eked, forty-two of them; he did not spare a
single one.

Jehu and Jehonadab

15 Leaving there, he came on Jehonadab son
of Rechab who was on his way to meet him.
He greeted him and said, 'Is your heart true
to mine, as my heart is to yours?' Jehonadab
replied, 'Yes.' 'If so,' Jehu said, 'give me
your hand.' Jehonadab gave him his hand,
and Jehu took him up beside him in his
chariot. 16 'Come with me,' he said, 'and
witness my zeal for Yahweh,' and took him
along in his chariot. 17 When he entered
Samaria, he killed all the survivors of Ahab's
family there; he destroyed it, as Yahweh had
told Elijah it would happen.

The destruction of Baal's adherents and temple

18 Then Jehu assembled all the people. 'Ahab
did Baal some small service,' he said, 'but
Jehu will do him a great one. 19 Now call me
all the prophets of Baal and all his priests.
Not one is to be absent: I have a great sacrifice
to offer to Baal. If anyone is absent, he will
forfeit his life.' This was a trick on Jehu's part
to destroy the devotees of Baal. 20 'Summon a
sacred assembly for Baal,' he commanded;
and they summoned it. 21 Jehu sent messen-
gers throughout Israel, and all the devotees
of Baal arrived, not a man was left who did
not attend. They crowded into the temple of
Baal until it was full from wall to wall. 22 Jehu
then said to the keeper of the wardrobe,
'Bring out vestments for all the devotees of
Baal'; he brought out the vestments for them.
23 Jehu then went into the temple of Baal with
Jehonadab son of Rechab and said to Baal's
devotees, 'Make quite sure that there are no
devotees of Yahweh in here with you, but
only devotees of Baal.' 24 He then proceeded
to present sacrifices and burnt offerings.

Now Jehu had stationed eighty of his men
outside, having said, 'Whoever lets one of
the people go whom I am now putting within
your clutches, will pay for it with his life.'
25 When he had finished making the burnt
offering, he gave the order to the guards and
equerries, 'Go in, strike them down! Let no
one out!' The guards and equerries went in,
putting everyone to the sword all the way to
the sanctuary of Baal's temple. 26 They took
the sacred pole out of Baal's temple and
burned it. 27 They demolished Baal's image
and demolished Baal's temple too, making it
into a latrine, which it still is today.

The reign of Jehu in Israel (841–814)

28 Thus Jehu rid Israel of Baal. 29 Even so,
Jehu did not give up the sins into which
Jeroboam son of Nebat had led Israel, the
golden calves of Bethel and Dan. 30 Yahweh
said to Jehu, 'Since you have done well in
carrying out what pleases me, and have done
everything I required to be done to the House
of Ahab, your sons will occupy the throne of
Israel down to the fourth generation.' 31 Jehu,
however, did not faithfully and whole-
heartedly follow the law of Yahweh, God of
Israel; he did not give up the sins into which
Jeroboam son of Nebat had led Israel.

32 At that time Yahweh began to whittle
Israel down, and Hazael defeated the Israel-
ites throughout the territory east of the
Jordan: 33 the whole territory of Gilead—of
the Gadites, the Reubenites and the Manas-
sehites—from Aroer on the River Arnon:
Gilead and Bashan.

34 The rest of the history of Jehu, his entire
career, all his prowess, is this not recorded
in the Book of the Annals of the Kings of
Israel? 35 Then he fell asleep with his ancestors
and was buried in Samaria; his son Jehoahaz
succeeded him. 36 Jehu's reign over Israel in
Samaria lasted twenty-eight years.

F: FROM THE REIGN OF ATHALIAH TO THE DEATH OF ELISHA

Athaliah (841–835)

11 When Athaliah mother of Ahaziah
learned that her son was dead, she
promptly murdered all those of royal stock.

2 But Jehosheba, daughter of King
Jehoram and sister of Ahaziah, surrep-
titiously rescued Jehoash son of Ahaziah from
among the princes who were to be murdered,
and put him with his nurse in the sleeping
quarters; in this way she hid him from
Athaliah, and he was not killed. 3 He stayed,
hidden with her in the Temple of Yahweh
for six years, while Athaliah governed the
country.

4 In the seventh year, Jehoiada sent for the
regimental commanders of the Carians and
the guards, and had them brought to him

in the Temple of Yahweh. He made a pact
with them, put them on oath, then showed
them the king's son. He gave them this order,
[5]'This is what you must do: a third of you
who come on duty on the Sabbath must
mount guard at the royal palace,[a] [7]and your
two other sections who come off duty on the
Sabbath and mount guard at the Temple of
Yahweh [8]must surround the king, each man
with his weapons in his hand; anyone forcing
his way through the ranks is to be killed. And
you will escort the king as he leaves and as
he comes in.'

[9]The regimental commanders did every-
thing as Jehoiada the priest had ordered, and
each one brought his men, those coming on
duty on the Sabbath and those going off duty
on the Sabbath, and reported to Jehoiada the
priest. [10]The priest then issued the regi-
mental commanders with King David's
spears and shields, which were kept in the
Temple of Yahweh. [11]The guards then took
position, each man with his weapons in his
hand, from the south corner of the Temple
to the north corner of the Temple, all round
the altar and the Temple. [12]Then Jehoiada
brought the king's son out—crowned him
and gave him a copy of the covenant; and
they made him king and anointed him, and
they clapped their hands and shouted, 'Long
live the king!'

[13]On hearing the people shouting, Athaliah
joined the people in the Temple of Yahweh.
[14]When she looked, there stood the king on
a dais, as the custom was, with the officers
and trumpeters at the king's side, and all the
people of the country rejoicing and blowing
the trumpets; then Athaliah tore her clothes
and shouted, 'Treason, treason!' [15]Jehoiada
the priest then gave the orders to the
commanders in charge of the troops, 'Take
her out under guard and put to death anyone
who follows her.' 'For', the priest had already
said, 'she must not be killed inside the
Temple of Yahweh.' [16]They seized her, and
when she reached the horses' entry to the
palace, she was killed there.

[17]Jehoiada made a covenant between
Yahweh, the king and the people that they
would remain Yahweh's people; and another
one between the king and the people. [18]All
the people of the country then went to the
temple of Baal and demolished it; they
smashed its altars and its images and killed
Mattan the priest of Baal in front of the
altars.

The priest made arrangements for the
security of the Temple of Yahweh. [19]He
then took the regimental commanders, the
Carians, the guards and all the people of the
country, and they escorted the king down
from the Temple of Yahweh, entering the
palace through the Gate of the Guards.
Jehoash took his seat on the throne of the
kings. [20]All the people of the country were
delighted; the city, however, made no move.
And Athaliah was put to death inside the
palace.

The reign of Jehoash in Judah (835–796)

12 Jehoash was seven years old when he
came to the throne. [2]Jehoash became
king in the seventh year of Jehu, and reigned
for forty years in Jerusalem. His mother's
name was Zibiah of Beersheba. [3]All his life
Jehoash did what Yahweh regards as right,
having been instructed by Jehoiada the
priest. [4]The high places, however, were not
abolished, and the people still offered sacri-
fices and incense on the high places.

[5]Jehoash said to the priests, 'All the money
from the sacred revenues brought to the
Temple of Yahweh, the money from personal
taxes, and all the money voluntarily offered
to the Temple—[6]the priests are to receive
this individually from people of their
acquaintance and will carry out all the repairs
to the Temple which need to be made.' [7]Now
in the twenty-third year of King Jehoash the
priests had done no repairs to the Temple;
[8]so King Jehoash summoned Jehoiada the
priest and the other priests. 'Why are you not
repairing the Temple?' he asked. 'You are no
longer to accept money from people of your
acquaintance but are to hand it over for
the Temple repairs.' [9]The priests agreed to
accept no money from the people and no
longer to be responsible for repairs to the
Temple.

[10]Jehoiada the priest took a chest, bored a
hole in the lid and placed it beside the pillar,
to the right of the entry to the Temple of
Yahweh; in it the priests who guarded the
threshold put all the money which was given
for the Temple of Yahweh. [11]Whenever they
saw that there was a great deal of money in
the chest, the king's secretary would come,

11a v. 6 is omitted as a confused gloss.

and they would empty it out and reckon the money then in the Temple of Yahweh. [12]Once checked, they paid this money over to the masters of works attached to the Temple of Yahweh, and these in turn spent it on carpenters and builders working on the Temple of Yahweh, [13]on masons and stone-cutters, and on buying timber and dressed stone to be used for repairs to the Temple of Yahweh; in short, for all the costs of the Temple repairs. [14]But no silver basins, knives, sprinkling bowls, trumpets or gold or silver objects were made for the Temple of Yahweh out of the money presented, [15]which was all given to the masters of works for repairing the Temple of Yahweh. [16]No accounts were kept with the men to whom the money was paid over to be spent on the workmen, since they were honest with their work. [17]Money offered in expiation of an offence or of a sin was not given to the Temple of Yahweh; that was for the priests.

[18]At that time Hazael king of Aram went to war against Gath, and captured it; he then prepared to attack Jerusalem. [19]Jehoash king of Judah took all the sacred offerings dedicated by his ancestors, the kings of Judah, Jehoshaphat, Jehoram and Ahaziah, with those which he himself had dedicated, and all the gold which was to be found in the treasuries of the Temple of Yahweh and of the palace; he sent it all to Hazael king of Aram, who retired from Jerusalem.

[20]The rest of the history of Joash, his entire career, is this not recorded in the Book of the Annals of the Kings of Judah? [21]His own retainers rebelled and hatched a plot; they murdered Joash in the palace of the Millo . . . [22]Jozacar son of Shimeath and Jehozabad son of Shomer were the retainers who struck the blows from which he died. He was buried with his ancestors in the City of David; his son Amaziah succeeded him.

The reign of Jehoahaz in Israel (814–798)

13 In the twenty-third year of Joash son of Ahaziah, king of Judah, Jehoahaz son of Jehu became king of Israel in Samaria. He reigned for seventeen years. [2]He did what is displeasing to Yahweh and copied the sin into which Jeroboam son of Nebat had led Israel; he did not give it up.

[3]This aroused Yahweh's anger against the Israelites, and he delivered them without respite into the power of Hazael king of Aram and of Ben-Hadad son of Hazael. [4]Jehoahaz, however, tried to placate Yahweh, and Yahweh heard him, for he had seen the oppression which the king of Aram was inflicting on Israel. [5]Yahweh gave Israel a saviour who freed them from the grip of Aram, and the Israelites lived in their tents as in the past. [6]But they did not give up the sin into which Jeroboam had led Israel; they persisted in it, and even the sacred pole stayed standing in Samaria. [7]Of Jehoahaz's army Yahweh left only fifty horsemen, ten chariots and ten thousand foot soldiers. The king of Aram had destroyed them, making them like dust trampled under foot.

[8]The rest of the history of Jehoahaz, his entire career, his prowess, is this not recorded in the Book of the Annals of the Kings of Israel? [9]Then Jehoahaz fell asleep with his ancestors, and was buried in Samaria; his son Joash succeeded him.

The reign of Jehoash in Israel (798–783)

[10]In the thirty-seventh year of Joash king of Judah, Jehoash son of Jehoahaz, became king of Israel in Samaria. He reigned for sixteen years. [11]He did what is displeasing to Yahweh, he did not give up the sin into which Jeroboam son of Nebat had led Israel; he persisted in it.

[12]The rest of the history of Joash, his entire career, his prowess, how he waged war on Amaziah king of Judah, is this not recorded in the Book of the Annals of the Kings of Israel? [13]Then Joash fell asleep with his ancestors, and Jeroboam ascended his throne. Joash was buried in Samaria with the kings of Israel.

The death of Elisha

[14]When Elisha had fallen ill of the illness of which he was to die, Joash king of Israel went down to him and shedding tears over him said, 'Father! Father! Chariot of Israel and its chargers!' [15]Elisha said to him, 'Bring bow and arrows,' and he sent for a bow and arrows. [16]Then Elisha said to the king, 'Draw the bow,' and he drew it. Elisha put his hands over the hands of the king, [17]then he said, 'Open the window towards the east,' and he opened it. Then Elisha said, 'Shoot!' And he shot. Elisha said, 'Arrow of victory over Aram! You will defeat Aram at Aphek—completely.'

[18]Elisha said, 'Take the arrows,' and he took them. Then he said to the king, 'Strike the ground,' and he struck it three times, then stopped. [19]At this the man of God grew angry with him. 'You should have struck half a dozen times,' he said, 'and you would have beaten Aram completely; now you will beat Aram only three times.'

[20]Elisha died and was buried. Bands of Moabites were making incursions into the country every year. [21]Some people happened to be carrying a man out for burial; at the sight of one of these bands, they flung the man into the tomb of Elisha and made off. The man had no sooner touched the bones of Elisha than he came to life and stood up on his feet.

Victory over the Aramaeans

[22]Hazael king of Aram had oppressed the Israelites throughout the lifetime of Jehoahaz, [23]but Yahweh was kind and took pity on them. Because of the covenant which he had made with Abraham, Isaac and Jacob, he relented towards them; he had no wish to destroy them, he did not cast them out of his presence. [24]Hazael king of Aram died, and his son Ben-Hadad succeeded him. [25]From Ben-Hadad son of Hazael, Jehoash son of Jehoahaz recaptured the towns which Hazael had seized from his father Jehoahaz by force of arms. Joash defeated him three times and recovered the Israelite towns.

VII: THE TWO KINGDOMS UNTIL THE FALL OF SAMARIA

The reign of Amaziah in Judah (796–781)

14 In the second year of Joash son of Jehoahaz, king of Israel, Amaziah son of Joash became king of Judah. [2]He was twenty-five years old when he came to the throne, and he reigned for twenty-nine years in Jerusalem. His mother's name was Jehoaddin of Jerusalem. [3]He did what Yahweh regards as right, though not like his ancestor David; he imitated his father Joash in all respects. [4]The high places, however, were not abolished, and the people still offered sacrifices and incense on the high places.

[5]Once the kingdom was firmly under his control, he killed those of his retainers who had murdered the king his father. [6]But he did not put the murderers' sons to death, in accordance with what is written in the Book of Moses, where Yahweh has commanded: '*Parents may not be put to death for their children, nor children for parents, but each must be put to death for his own crime.*'[a]

[7]It was he who slaughtered the Edomites in the Valley of Salt, ten thousand of them, and captured the Rock; he gave it the name Joktheel, which it bears to the present day.

[8]Amaziah then sent messengers to Jehoash son of Jehoahaz, king of Israel, saying, 'Come and make a trial of strength!' [9]Jehoash king of Israel sent back word to Amaziah king of Judah, 'The thistle of Lebanon sent a message to the cedar of Lebanon, saying, "Give my son your daughter in marriage"; but a wild animal of the Lebanon ran over the thistle and squashed it. [10]You have conquered Edom and now aspire to even greater glory. Stay where you belong! Why provoke disaster, to your own and Judah's ruin?'

[11]But Amaziah would not listen, so Jehoash king of Israel marched to the attack. And at Beth-Shemesh, which belongs to Judah, he and Amaziah king of Judah made their trial of strength. [12]Judah was defeated by Israel, and everyone fled to his tent. [13]The king of Judah, Amaziah son of Jehoash, son of Ahaziah, was taken prisoner at Beth-Shemesh by Jehoash king of Israel who led him off to Jerusalem, where he demolished four hundred cubits of the city wall between the Ephraim Gate and the Corner Gate; [14]all the gold and silver, and all the vessels to be found in the Temple of Yahweh and in the palace treasury, and hostages besides, he then took back with him to Samaria.

[15]The rest of the history of Jehoash, his entire career, his prowess, how he waged war on Amaziah king of Judah, is this not recorded in the Book of the Annals of the Kings of Israel? [16]Then Joash fell asleep with his ancestors, and was buried in Samaria

14a Dt 24:16.

with the kings of Israel; his son Jeroboam
succeeded him.
17Amaziah son of Joash, king of Judah,
lived for fifteen years after the death of
Jehoash son of Jehoahaz, king of Israel.
18The rest of the history of Amaziah, is this
not recorded in the Book of the Annals of the
Kings of Judah? 19A plot having been hatched
against him in Jerusalem, he fled to Lachish;
but he was followed to Lachish where he was
murdered. 20He was then transported by
horse and buried in Jerusalem with his ances-
tors in the City of David. 21All the people of
Judah then chose Uzziah, who was sixteen
years old, and made him king in succession
to his father Amaziah. 22It was he who rebuilt
Elath, recovering it for Judah, after the king
had fallen asleep with his ancestors.

The reign of Jeroboam II in Israel (783–743)

23In the fifteenth year of Amaziah son of
Joash, king of Judah, Jeroboam son of Joash
became king of Israel in Samaria. He reigned
for forty-one years. 24He did what is
displeasing to Yahweh and did not give up
any of the sins into which Jeroboam son of
Nebat had led Israel.
25It was he who recovered the territory of
Israel from the Pass of Hamath to the Sea
of the Arabah, in accordance with the word
which Yahweh, God of Israel, had spoken
through his servant Jonah son of Amittai, the
prophet from Gath-Hepher. 26For Yahweh
had seen how very bitter the affliction of
Israel was, with no one, either fettered or
free, to come to Israel's help. 27But Yahweh
had resolved not to blot out the name of Israel
under heaven; he rescued them by means of
Jeroboam son of Joash.
28The rest of the history of Jeroboam, his
entire career, his prowess, what wars he
waged, how he brought Damascus and
Hamath back to their allegiance to Judah and
Israel, is this not recorded in the Book of
the Annals of the Kings of Israel? 29Then
Jeroboam fell asleep with his ancestors and
was buried in Samaria with the kings of
Israel; his son Zechariah succeeded him.

The reign of Uzziah in Judah (781–740)

15 In the seventeenth year of Jeroboam
king of Israel, Uzziah son of Amaziah
became king of Judah. 2He was sixteen years
old when he came to the throne, and he
reigned for fifty-two years in Jerusalem. His
mother's name was Jecoliah of Jerusalem.
3He did what Yahweh regards as right, just
as his father Amaziah had done. 4The high
places, however, were not abolished, and the
people still offered sacrifices and incense on
the high places.
5But Yahweh struck the king, and he was
afflicted with a virulent skin-disease till his
dying day. He lived confined to his room,
while Jotham the king's son, who was master
of the palace, governed the country.
6The rest of the history of Uzziah, his
entire career, is this not recorded in the Book
of the Annals of the Kings of Judah? 7Then
Uzziah fell asleep with his ancestors and was
buried in the City of David; his son Jotham
then succeeded him.

The reign of Zechariah in Israel (743)

8In the thirty-eighth year of Uzziah king of
Judah, Zechariah son of Jeroboam became
king of Israel in Samaria for six months. 9He
did what is displeasing to Yahweh, as his
fathers had done; he did not give up the sins
into which Jeroboam son of Nebat had led
Israel.
Shallum son of Jabesh plotted against him,
murdered him at Ibleam, 10and succeeded
him.
11The rest of the history of Zechariah is
recorded in the Book of Annals of the Kings
of Israel. 12This was the word which Yahweh
had spoken to Jehu, 'Your sons will sit on
the throne of Israel to the fourth generation.'
And so it turned out.

The reign of Shallum in Israel (743)

13Shallum son of Jabesh became king in the
thirty-ninth year of Uzziah king of Judah and
reigned for one month in Samaria.
14Then Menahem son of Gadi marched
from Tirzah, entered Samaria, murdered
Shallum son of Jabesh there and succeeded
him.
15The rest of the history of Shallum, and
the plot he hatched, is recorded in the Book
of the Annals of the Kings of Israel.
16Menahem then sacked Tappuah—killing
all who were in it—and its territory from
Tirzah onwards, because it had not opened
its gates to him; he sacked the town and
disembowelled all the pregnant women.

The reign of Menahem in Israel (743–738)

17In the thirty-ninth year of Uzziah king of
Judah, Menahem son of Gadi became king
of Israel. He reigned for ten years in Samaria.
18He did what is displeasing to Yahweh, he
did not give up the sins into which Jeroboam
son of Nebat had led Israel.

In his days 19Pul[a] king of Assyria invaded
the country. Menahem gave Pul a thousand
talents of silver in return for his support in
strengthening his hold on the royal power.
20Menahem levied this sum from Israel, from
all the men of rank, at the rate of fifty shekels
a head, to be given to the king of Assyria,
who then withdrew and did not stay in the
country.

21The rest of the history of Menahem, his
entire career, is this not recorded in the Book
of the Annals of the Kings of Israel? 22Then
Menahem fell asleep with his ancestors; his
son Pekahiah succeeded him.

The reign of Pekahiah in Israel (738–737)

23In the fiftieth year of Uzziah king of Judah,
Pekahiah son of Menahem became king of
Israel in Samaria. He reigned for two years.
24He did what is displeasing to Yahweh; he
did not give up the sins into which Jeroboam
son of Nebat had led Israel.

25Pekah son of Remaliah, his equerry,
plotted against him and assassinated him in
the palace keep . . .[b] He had fifty Gileadites
with him. He killed the king and succeeded
him.

26The rest of the history of Pekahiah, his
entire career, is recorded in the Book of the
Annals of the Kings of Israel.

The reign of Pekah in Israel (737–732)

27In the fifty-second year of Uzziah king of
Judah, Pekah son of Remaliah became king
of Israel in Samaria. He reigned for twenty
years. 28He did what is displeasing to
Yahweh; he did not give up the sins into
which Jeroboam son of Nebat had led
Israel.

29In the days of Pekah king of Israel,
Tiglath-Pileser king of Assyria came and
captured Ijon, Abel-Beth-Maacah, Janoah,
Kedesh, Hazor, Gilead and Galilee—the
whole territory of Naphtali and deported the
population to Assyria. 30Hoshea son of Elah
hatched a plot against Pekah son of Remaliah;
he murdered the king and succeeded him.

31The rest of the history of Pekah, his
entire career, is recorded in the Book of the
Annals of the Kings of Israel.

The reign of Jotham in Judah (740–736)

32In the second year of Pekah son of Rema-
liah, king of Israel, Jotham son of Uzziah
became king of Judah. 33He was twenty-five
years old when he came to the throne, and he
reigned for sixteen years in Jerusalem. His
mother's name was Jerusha daughter of
Zadok. 34He did what Yahweh regards as
right, just as his father Uzziah had done.
35The high places, however, were not abol-
ished, and the people still offered sacrifices
and incense on the high places.

It was he who built the Upper Gate of the
Temple of Yahweh.

36The rest of the history of Jotham, his
entire career, is this not recorded in the Book
of the Annals of the Kings of Judah? 37At
that time Yahweh began sending Razon king
of Aram and Pekah son of Remaliah against
Judah. 38Then Jotham fell asleep with his
ancestors and was buried in the City of David,
his ancestor; his son Ahaz succeeded him.

The reign of Ahaz in Judah (736–716)

16 In the seventeenth year of Pekah son of
Remaliah, Ahaz son of Jotham became
king of Judah. 2Ahaz was twenty years old
when he came to the throne, and he reigned
for sixteen years in Jerusalem. He did not do
what Yahweh his God regards as right, as his
ancestor David had done. 3He followed the
example of the kings of Israel, even causing
his son to pass through the fire of sacrifice,
also copying the disgusting practices of the
nations whom Yahweh had dispossessed for
the Israelites. 4He offered sacrifices and
incense on the high places, on the hills and
under every luxuriant tree.

5Then it was that Razon king of Aram
and Pekah son of Remaliah, king of Israel,
launched their campaign against Jerusalem.
They besieged it but could not reduce it. 6(At
that time, the king of Edom recovered Elath
for Edom; he drove the Judaeans out of

15a Name taken by Tiglath-Pileser III of Assyria when he assumed power also in Babylon.
15b Hebr. adds 'Argob and Arieh', a gloss on 'Gileadites'.

Elath, and the Edomites occupied it and have been there ever since.) 7 Ahaz then sent messengers to Tiglath-Pileser king of Assyria to say, 'I am your servant and your son. Come and rescue me from the king of Aram and the king of Israel who are making war on me.' 8 And Ahaz took what silver and gold was to be found in the Temple of Yahweh and in the palace treasury, and sent this as a present to the king of Assyria. 9 The king of Assyria granted his request and, marching on Damascus, captured it; he deported its population to Kir and put Razon to death.

10 When King Ahaz went to Damascus to meet Tiglath-Pileser king of Assyria, he saw the altar which was in Damascus. King Ahaz then sent a picture and model of the altar, with details of its construction, to Uriah the priest. 11 Uriah the priest constructed the altar; all the instructions sent by King Ahaz from Damascus were carried out by Uriah the priest before King Ahaz returned from Damascus. 12 When the king arrived from Damascus, he inspected the altar, he approached it and ascended it. 13 And on the altar he made his burnt offering and his oblation; he poured out his libation and sprinkled the blood of his communion sacrifices. 14 The altar which used to stand before Yahweh he removed from the front of the Temple, where it had stood between the new altar and the Temple of Yahweh, and placed it at the north side of the new altar. 15 King Ahaz gave this order to Uriah the priest, 'In future you will present the morning burnt offering, the evening oblation, the king's burnt offering and oblation, the burnt offering, the oblation and the libations of all the people of the country on the large altar; on it you will pour out all the blood of the burnt offerings and sacrifices. As regards the bronze altar, I shall see to that.' 16 Uriah the priest did everything that King Ahaz had ordered.

17 King Ahaz broke up the wheeled stands; removed the crosspieces and the basins from them, and took the bronze Sea off the oxen supporting it, and rested it on the stone pavement. 18 And from the Temple of Yahweh, in deference to the king of Assyria, he removed the dais for the throne which had been built inside, and the royal entrance on the outside.

19 The rest of the history of Ahaz, his entire career, is this not recorded in the Book of the Annals of the Kings of Judah? 20 Then Ahaz fell asleep with his ancestors and was buried in the City of David; his son Hezekiah succeeded him.

The reign of Hoshea in Israel (732–724)

17 In the twelfth year of Ahaz king of Judah, Hoshea son of Elah became king of Israel in Samaria, and reigned for nine years. 2 He did what is displeasing to Yahweh, though not like the preceding kings of Israel.

3 Shalmaneser king of Assyria made war on Hoshea who submitted to him and paid him tribute. 4 But the king of Assyria discovered that Hoshea was playing a double game with him; he had sent messengers to Sais, to the king of Egypt, and had not, as in previous years, handed over the tribute to the king of Assyria. For this the king of Assyria imprisoned him in chains.

The fall of Samaria (721)

5 The king of Assyria invaded the whole country and, coming to Samaria, laid siege to it for three years. 6 In the ninth year of Hoshea the king of Assyria captured Samaria and deported the Israelites to Assyria. He settled them in Halah on the Habor, a river of Gozan, and in the cities of the Medes.

Observations on the fall of the Northern Kingdom

7 This happened because the Israelites had sinned against Yahweh their God who had brought them out of Egypt, out of the grip of Pharaoh king of Egypt. They worshipped other gods, 8 they followed the practices of the nations which Yahweh had dispossessed for them. 9 The Israelites spoke slightingly of Yahweh their God. They built themselves high places wherever they lived, from watchtower to fortified town. 10 They set up pillars and sacred poles for themselves on every high hill and under every luxuriant tree. 11 They sacrificed on all the high places like the nations which Yahweh had expelled for them, and did wicked things there, provoking Yahweh's anger. 12 They served idols, although Yahweh had told them, 'This you must not do.'

13 And yet through all the prophets and the seers, Yahweh had given Israel and Judah this warning, 'Turn from your wicked ways

and keep my commandments and my laws in accordance with the entire Law which I laid down for your fathers and delivered to them through my servants the prophets.' [14]But they would not listen, they were as stubborn as their ancestors, who had no faith in Yahweh their God. [15]They despised his laws and the covenant which he had made with their ancestors and the warnings which he had given them. Pursuing futility, they themselves became futile through copying the nations round them, although Yahweh had ordered them not to act as they did. [16]They rejected all the commandments of Yahweh their God and cast themselves metal idols, two calves; they made themselves sacred poles, they worshipped the whole array of heaven, and they served Baal. [17]They caused their sons and daughters to pass through the fire of sacrifice, also they practised divination and sorcery, they sold themselves to doing what displeases Yahweh, provoking his anger. [18]Because of which, Yahweh became enraged with Israel and thrust them away from him. The tribe of Judah was the only one left.

[19]Judah did not keep the commandments of Yahweh their God either but copied the practices which Israel had introduced. [20]Yahweh rejected the whole race of Israel; he brought them low, delivering them into the hands of marauders, until at length he thrust them away from him. [21]And indeed he had torn Israel away from the House of David, and they had made Jeroboam son of Nebat king; Jeroboam had drawn Israel away from Yahweh and led them into a great sin. [22]The Israelites copied the sin which Jeroboam had committed; they did not give it up, [23]until at length Yahweh thrust Israel away from him, as he had foretold through all his servants the prophets; he deported the Israelites from their own country to Assyria, where they have been ever since.

The origin of the Samaritans

[24]The king of Assyria brought people from Babylon, Cuthah, Avva, Hamath and Sepharvaim, and settled them in the towns of Samaria to replace the Israelites; these took possession of Samaria and lived in its towns.

[25]When they first came to live there, they did not worship Yahweh; hence, Yahweh set lions on them, which killed a number of them. [26]Consequently, the king of Assyria was informed as follows, 'The nations whom you deported and settled in the towns of Samaria do not know how to worship the local god, and he has set lions on them; and now these are killing them because they do not know how to worship the local god.' [27]So the king of Assyria gave this order, 'Send back one of the priests whom I deported from there; let him go and live there and teach them how to worship the local god.' [28]Accordingly, one of the priests who had been deported from Samaria came to live in Bethel; he taught them how to worship Yahweh.

[29]Each nationality made gods of its own and put them in the shrines on the high places built by the Samaritans; each nationality did this in the towns where it lived. [30]The people from Babylon had made a Succoth-Benoth, the people from Cuthah a Nergal, the people from Hamath an Ashima, [31]the Avvites a Nibhaz and a Tartak; while the Sepharvites caused their children to pass through the fire of sacrifice to Adrammelech and Anammelech, gods of Sepharvaim. [32]They worshipped Yahweh as well, and they appointed priests out of their own number for the high places, and these officiated in the shrines on the high places. [33]They worshipped Yahweh and served their own gods at the same time, with the rites of the countries from which they had been deported. [34]They still follow their old rites even now.

They did not worship Yahweh and did not conform to his statutes or ritual, or the law or the commandments, which Yahweh had laid down for the sons of Jacob to whom he gave the name Israel. [35]Yahweh had made a covenant with them and had given them this command, 'You are not to worship alien gods, you are not to bow down to them or serve them or offer them sacrifices. [36]You are to bow down and offer sacrifice only to Yahweh who brought you out of Egypt with great power and outstretched arm. [37]You are to observe the statutes and ritual, the law and the commandments which he has given you in writing and to which you are always to conform; you are not to worship alien gods. [38]Do not forget the covenant which I have made with you, and do not venerate alien gods. [39]But venerate Yahweh your God, and he will deliver you from the clutches of all your enemies.' [40]But they would not listen and still followed their old rites.

[41]These nationalities, then, worshipped

Yahweh and served their idols as well, as did their children; and their children's children still behave today as their ancestors behaved in the past.

VIII: THE LAST YEARS OF THE KINGDOM OF JUDAH

A: HEZEKIAH
THE PROPHET ISAIAH
ASSYRIA

Introduction to the reign of Hezekiah (716–687)

18 In the third year of Hoshea son of Elah, king of Israel, Hezekiah son of Ahaz became king of Judah. [2]He was twenty-five years old when he came to the throne, and he reigned for twenty-nine years in Jerusalem. His mother's name was Abijah daughter of Zechariah. [3]He did what Yahweh regards as right, just as his ancestor David had done. [4]He abolished the high places, broke the pillars, cut down the sacred poles and smashed the bronze serpent which Moses had made; for up to that time the Israelites had offered sacrifices to it; it was called Nehushtan.

[5]He put his trust in Yahweh, God of Israel. No king of Judah after him could be compared with him—nor any of those before him. [6]He was devoted to Yahweh, never turning from him, but keeping the commandments which Yahweh had laid down for Moses. [7]And so Yahweh was with him, and he was successful in all that he undertook. He rebelled against the king of Assyria and refused to serve him. [8]He beat the Philistines back to Gaza, laying their territory waste from watchtower to fortified town.

The fall of Samaria; recapitulation

[9]In the fourth year of Hezekiah, which was the seventh year of Hoshea son of Elah, king of Israel, Shalmaneser king of Assyria marched on Samaria and laid siege to it. [10]He captured it after three years. Samaria fell in the sixth year of Hezekiah, which was the ninth year of Hoshea king of Israel. [11]The king of Assyria deported the Israelites to Assyria and settled them in Halah on the Habor, a river of Gozan, and in the cities of the Medes. [12]This happened because they had not obeyed the voice of Yahweh their God and had broken his covenant, everything that Moses servant of Yahweh had laid down. They neither listened to it nor put it into practice.

Sennacherib's invasion[a]

[13]In the fourteenth year of King Hezekiah, Sennacherib king of Assyria advanced on all the fortified towns of Judah and captured them. [14]Then Hezekiah king of Judah sent this message to the king of Assyria at Lachish, 'I have been at fault. Call off the attack, and I will submit to whatever you impose on me.' The king of Assyria exacted three hundred talents of silver and thirty talents of gold from Hezekiah king of Judah, [15]and Hezekiah gave him all the silver in the Temple of Yahweh and in the palace treasury. [16]At which time, Hezekiah stripped the facing from the leaves and jambs of the doors of the Temple of Yahweh, which an earlier king of Judah had put on, and gave it to the king of Assyria.

The embassy of the cupbearer-in-chief

[17]From Lachish the king of Assyria sent the cupbearer-in-chief with a large force to King Hezekiah in Jerusalem. He marched on Jerusalem and, on his arrival, took up position near the conduit of the upper pool which is on the road to the Fuller's Field. [18]He summoned the king. The master of the palace, Eliakim son of Hilkiah, Shebnah the secretary and the herald Joah son of Asaph went out to him. [19]The cupbearer-in-chief said to them, 'Say to Hezekiah, "The great king, the king of Assyria, says this: What makes you so confident? [20]Do you think empty words are as good as strategy and military strength? Who are you relying on, to dare to rebel against me? [21]There you are,

18a The whole of 18:13—20:19 is repeated with minor variations in Is 36—39.

relying on that broken reed Egypt, which pricks and pierces the hand of whoever leans on it. That is what Pharaoh king of Egypt is like to all who rely on him. 22 You may say to me: We rely on Yahweh our God. But have his high places and altars not been suppressed by Hezekiah who told Judah and Jerusalem: Here, in Jerusalem, is the altar before which you must worship? 23 Very well, then, make a wager with my lord the king of Assyria: I will give you two thousand horses if you can find horsemen to ride them. 24 How could you repel a single one of the least of my master's soldiers? And yet you have relied on Egypt for chariots and horsemen. 25 And lastly, have I marched on this place to lay it waste without warrant from Yahweh? Yahweh himself said to me: March on this country and lay it waste." '

26 Eliakim, Shebnah and Joah said to the cupbearer-in-chief, 'Please speak to your servants in Aramaic, for we understand it; do not speak to us in the Judaean language within earshot of the people on the ramparts.' 27 But the cupbearer-in-chief said, 'Do you think my lord sent me here to say these things to your master or to you? On the contrary, it was to the people sitting on the ramparts who, like you, are doomed to eat their own dung and drink their own urine.'

28 The cupbearer-in-chief then drew himself up and shouted loudly in the Judaean language, 'Listen to the word of the great king, the king of Assyria. 29 The king says this, "Do not let Hezekiah delude you. He will be powerless to save you from my clutches. 30 Do not let Hezekiah persuade you to rely on Yahweh by saying: Yahweh is sure to save us; this city will not fall into the king of Assyria's clutches. 31 Do not listen to Hezekiah, for the king of Assyria says this: Make peace with me, surrender to me, and every one of you will be free to eat the fruit of his own vine and of his own fig tree and to drink the water of his own storage-well 32 until I come and take you away to a country like your own, a land of corn and good wine, a land of bread and vineyards, a land of oil and honey: and so you will survive and not die. Do not listen to Hezekiah; he is deluding you when he says: Yahweh will save us. 33 Has any god of any nation been able to save his country from the king of Assyria's clutches? 34 Where are the gods of Hamath and Arpad? Where are the gods of Sepharvaim and Hena and Ivvah? Where are the local gods of Samaria? Did they save Samaria from my clutches? 35 Of all the local gods, which ones have saved their countries from my clutches, for Yahweh to be able to save Jerusalem from my clutches?" '

36 The people, however, kept quiet and said nothing in reply, since the king had given the order, 'You are not to answer him.' 37 The master of the palace, Eliakim son of Hilkiah, Shebnah the secretary and the herald Joah son of Asaph, with their clothes torn, went to Hezekiah and reported what the cupbearer-in-chief had said.

The prophet Isaiah is consulted

19 On hearing this, King Hezekiah tore his clothes, put on sackcloth and went to the Temple of Yahweh. 2 He sent Eliakim master of the palace, Shebnah the secretary and the elders of the priests, wearing sackcloth, to the prophet Isaiah son of Amoz. 3 They said to him, 'This is what Hezekiah says, "Today is a day of suffering, of punishment, of disgrace. Children come to birth, and there is no strength to bring them forth. 4 May Yahweh your God hear the words of the cupbearer-in-chief whom his master, the king of Assyria, has sent to insult the living God, and may Yahweh your God punish the words he has heard. Offer your prayer for the remnant still remaining." '

5 King Hezekiah's ministers went to Isaiah, 6 and Isaiah said to them, 'Say to your master, "Yahweh says this: Do not be afraid of the words which you have heard or the blasphemies which the king of Assyria's minions have uttered against me. 7 Look, I am going to put a spirit in him and, on the strength of a rumour, he will go back to his own country, and in that country I shall make him fall by the sword." '

The cupbearer returns to his master

8 The cupbearer turned about and rejoined the king of Assyria, who was then attacking Libnah, as the cupbearer had learnt that the king had already left Lachish 9 on hearing that Tirhakah king of Cush was on his way to attack him.

Sennacherib's letter to Hezekiah

10 Sennacherib again sent messengers to Hezekiah, saying, 'Tell Hezekiah king of

Judah this, "Do not let your God on whom
you are relying deceive you with the promise:
Jerusalem will not fall into the king of Assy-
ria's clutches. 11 You have learnt by now what
the kings of Assyria have done to all the other
countries, devoting them to destruction. Are
you likely to be saved? 12 Did the gods of the
nations whom my ancestors devastated save
them—Gozan, Haran, Rezeph and the Eden-
ites who were in Tel Basar? 13 Where is the
king of Hamath, the king of Arpad, the king
of Lair, of Sepharvaim, of Hena, of Ivvah?" '

14 Hezekiah took the letter from the mess-
engers' hands and read it; he then went up to
the Temple of Yahweh and spread it out
before Yahweh. 15 Hezekiah said this prayer
in the presence of Yahweh, 'Yahweh
Sabaoth, God of Israel, enthroned on the
winged creatures, you alone are God of all
the kingdoms of the world, you made heaven
and earth. 16 Give ear, Yahweh, and listen;
open your eyes, Yahweh, and see! Hear the
words of Sennacherib, who has sent to insult
the living God. 17 It is true, Yahweh, that the
kings of Assyria have destroyed the nations,
18 they have thrown their gods on the fire, for
these were not gods but human artefacts—
wood and stone—and hence they have
destroyed them. 19 But now, Yahweh our
God, save us from his clutches, I beg you,
and let all the kingdoms of the world know
that you alone are God, Yahweh.'

Isaiah intervenes

20 Isaiah son of Amoz then sent the following
message to Hezekiah, 'Yahweh, God of
Israel, says this, "I have heard the prayer
which you have addressed to me about Sen-
nacherib king of Assyria." 21 Here is the
pronouncement which Yahweh has made
about him:

"She despises you, she scorns you,
the virgin daughter of Zion;
she tosses her head at you,
the daughter of Jerusalem!
22 Whom have you insulted,
whom have you blasphemed?
Against whom raised your voice
and lifted your haughty eyes?
Against the Holy One of Israel!
23 Through your envoys
you have insulted the Lord,
thinking: With my many chariots
I have climbed the mountain-tops,
the utmost peaks of Lebanon.
I have felled
its mighty cedars,
its finest cypresses,
have reached its furthest recesses,
its forest garden.
24 Yes, I have dug
and drunk of foreign waters;
under the soles of my feet
I have dried up all Egypt's rivers.

25 "Do you hear? Long ago
I prepared this,
from days of old I actually planned it,
now I carry it out.
You were to lay walled cities
in heaps of ruins;
26 that was why their inhabitants,
feeble of hand,
were dismayed and discomfited,
were weak as grass,
were frail as plants,
were like grass of housetop and meadow
under the east wind.
27 But whether you stand up
or you sit down,
whether you go out or you come in,
I know it.
28 Because you have raved against me,
and your arrogance has reached my ears,
I shall put a hook through your nostrils
and a muzzle on your lips,
and make you return by the road
by which you came.

A sign for Hezekiah

29 "And this will be the sign for you:

this year will be eaten the self-sown grain,
next year what sprouts in the fallow;
but in the third year sow and reap,
plant vineyards and eat their fruit.
30 The surviving remnant
of the House of Judah will bring forth
new roots below and fruits above;
31 for a remnant will issue from Jerusalem,
and survivors from Mount Zion.
Yahweh Sabaoth's jealous love
will accomplish this.

32 "This, then, is what Yahweh says about the
king of Assyria:

"He will not enter this city,
will shoot no arrow at it,
confront it with no shield,
throw up no earthwork against it.

33 By the road by which he came,
by that he will return;
he will not enter this city,
declares Yahweh.
34 I shall protect this city and save it
for my sake
and my servant David's sake." '

Sennacherib is punished

35 That same night the angel of Yahweh went
out and struck down a hundred and eighty-
five thousand men in the Assyrian camp. In
the early morning when it was time to get up,
there they lay, so many corpses.
36 Sennacherib struck camp and left; he
returned home and stayed in Nineveh. 37 One
day when he was worshipping in the temple
of his god Nisroch, his sons Adrammelech
and Sharezer struck him down with the sword
and escaped into the territory of Ararat. His
son Esarhaddon succeeded him.

The illness and cure of Hezekiah

20 About then Hezekiah fell ill and was at
the point of death. The prophet Isaiah
son of Amoz came and said to him, 'Yahweh
says this, "Put your affairs in order, for
you are going to die, you will not live." '
2 Hezekiah turned his face to the wall and
addressed this prayer to Yahweh, 3 'Ah,
Yahweh, remember, I beg you, that I have
behaved faithfully and with sincerity of heart
in your presence and done what you regard
as right.' And Hezekiah shed many tears.
4 Isaiah had not left the middle court,
before the word of Yahweh came to him,
5 'Go back and say to Hezekiah, prince of my
people, "Yahweh, the God of your ancestor
David, says this: I have heard your prayer
and seen your tears. I shall cure you: in three
days' time you will go up to the Temple of
Yahweh. 6 I shall add fifteen years to your
life. I shall save you and this city from the
king of Assyria's clutches and defend this
city for my sake and my servant David's
sake." '
7 'Bring a fig poultice,' Isaiah said; they
brought one, applied it to the ulcer, and the
king recovered.
8 Hezekiah said to Isaiah, 'What is the sign
to tell me that Yahweh will cure me and that
I shall be going up to the Temple of Yahweh
in three days' time?' 9 'Here', Isaiah replied,
'is the sign from Yahweh that he will do what
he has said; would you like the shadow to go
forward ten steps, or to go back ten steps?'
10 'It is easy for the shadow to lengthen ten
steps,' Hezekiah replied. 'No, I would rather
the shadow went back ten steps.' 11 The
prophet Isaiah then called on Yahweh, who
made the shadow cast by the declining sun on
the steps — the steps to Ahaz's roof-room — go
back ten steps.

The Babylonian embassy

12 At that time the king of Babylon, Merod-
ach-Baladan son of Baladan, sent letters and
a gift to Hezekiah, for he had heard of
his illness and his recovery. 13 Hezekiah was
delighted at this and showed the ambassadors
his entire treasury, the silver, gold, spices,
precious oil, his armoury too, and everything
to be seen in his storehouses. There was
nothing in his palace or in his whole domain
that Hezekiah did not show them.
14 The prophet Isaiah then came to King
Hezekiah and asked him, 'What have these
men said, and where have they come from?'
Hezekiah answered, 'They have come from
a distant country, from Babylon.' 15 Isaiah
said, 'What have they seen in your palace?'
'They have seen everything in my palace,'
Hezekiah answered. 'There is nothing in my
storehouses that I have not shown them.'
16 Then Isaiah said to Hezekiah, 'Listen to
the word of Yahweh, 17 "The days are coming
when everything in your palace, everything
that your ancestors have amassed until
now, will be carried off to Babylon. Not a
thing will be left," Yahweh says. 18 "Sons
sprung from you, sons fathered by you, will
be abducted to be eunuchs in the palace of
the king of Babylon." ' 19 Hezekiah said to
Isaiah, 'This word of Yahweh that you
announce is reassuring,' for he was thinking,
'And why not? So long as there is peace and
security during my lifetime.'

The end of the reign of Hezekiah

20 The rest of the history of Hezekiah, all his
prowess, how he constructed the pool and
the conduit to bring water into the city, is
this not recorded in the Book of the Annals
of the Kings of Judah? 21 Then Hezekiah fell
asleep with his ancestors; his son Manasseh
succeeded him.

B: TWO WICKED KINGS

The reign of Manasseh in Judah (687–642)

21 Manasseh was twelve years old when he came to the throne and he reigned for fifty-five years in Jerusalem. His mother's name was Hephzibah. 2He did what is displeasing to Yahweh, copying the disgusting practices of the nations whom Yahweh had dispossessed for the Israelites.

3He rebuilt the high places which his father Hezekiah had destroyed, he set up altars to Baal and made a sacred pole as Ahab king of Israel had done, he worshipped the whole array of heaven and served it. 4He built altars in the Temple of Yahweh of which Yahweh had said, 'Jerusalem is where I shall put my name.' 5He built altars to the whole array of heaven in the two courts of the Temple of Yahweh. 6He caused his son to pass through the fire of sacrifice, he also practised soothsaying and divination and set up mediums and spirit guides. He did very many more things displeasing to Yahweh, thus provoking his anger. 7He had an image of Asherah carved and placed it inside the Temple of which Yahweh had said to David and his son Solomon, 'In this Temple and in Jerusalem, the city which I have chosen out of all the tribes of Israel, I shall put my Name for ever. 8Nor shall I ever again set Israel's footsteps wandering outside the country which I gave to their ancestors, provided they are careful to observe all I have commanded them as laid down in the whole Law which my servant Moses prescribed for them.' 9But they would not listen, and Manasseh misled them into doing worse things than the nations whom Yahweh had destroyed for the Israelites.

10Then Yahweh spoke through his servants the prophets as follows, 11'Since Manasseh king of Judah has done these shameful deeds, doing more wicked deeds than anything which the Amorites did before him, and has led Judah too into sin with his idols, 12Yahweh, God of Israel, says this, "Look, I shall bring such disaster on Jerusalem and Judah as will make the ears of all who hear of it tingle. 13Over Jerusalem I shall stretch the same measuring line as over Samaria, the same plumb-rule as for the House of Ahab; I shall scour Jerusalem as someone scours a dish and, having scoured it, turns it upside down. 14I shall cast away the remnant of my heritage, delivering them into the clutches of their enemies and making them the prey and booty of all their enemies, 15because they have done what is displeasing to me and have provoked my anger from the day their ancestors came out of Egypt until now." '

16Manasseh shed innocent blood, too, in such great quantity that he flooded Jerusalem from one end to the other, besides the sins into which he led Judah by doing what is displeasing to Yahweh.

17The rest of the history of Manasseh, his entire career, the sins he committed, is this not recorded in the Book of the Annals of the Kings of Judah? 18Then Manasseh fell asleep with his ancestors and was buried in the garden of his palace, the Garden of Uzza; his son Amon succeeded him.

The reign of Amon in Judah (642–640)

19Amon was twenty-two years old when he came to the throne, and he reigned for two years in Jerusalem. His mother's name was Meshullemeth daughter of Haruz, of Jotbah. 20He did what is displeasing to Yahweh, as Manasseh his father had done. 21In every respect he followed the example of his father, serving the idols which his father had served, and worshipping them. 22He abandoned Yahweh, God of his ancestors; he did not follow the way of Yahweh.

23Amon's retinue plotted against the king and killed him in his own palace. 24The people of the country, however, slaughtered all those who had plotted against King Amon and proclaimed his son Josiah as his successor.

25The rest of the history of Amon, his entire career, is this not recorded in the Book of the Annals of the Kings of Judah? 26He was buried in his father's tomb in the Garden of Uzza; his son Josiah succeeded him.

C: JOSIAH AND THE RELIGIOUS REFORM

Introduction to the reign of Josiah (640–609)

22 Josiah was eight years old when he came to the throne, and he reigned for thirty-one years in Jerusalem. His mother's

name was Jedidah daughter of Adaiah, of
Bozkath. [2]He did what Yahweh regards as
right, and in every respect followed the
example of his ancestor David, not deviating
from it to right or left.

The Book of the Law discovered

[3]In the eighteenth year of King Josiah, the
king sent the secretary Shaphan son of
Azaliah, son of Meshullam to the Temple of
Yahweh. [4]'Go to Hilkiah the high priest,' he
told him, 'and tell him to melt down the silver
contributed to the Temple of Yahweh and
collected by the guardians of the threshold
from the people. [5]He is to hand it over to the
masters of works attached to the Temple of
Yahweh, for them to pay it over to men
working on the Temple of Yahweh, to repair
the damaged parts of the Temple: [6]to the
carpenters, builders and masons, and for
buying timber and dressed stone for the
Temple repairs.' [7]The latter were not
required to render account of the money
handed over to them, since they were
conscientious in their work.
[8]The high priest Hilkiah said to Shaphan
the secretary, 'I have found the Book of the
Law in the Temple of Yahweh.' And Hilkiah
gave the book to Shaphan, who read it.
[9]Shaphan the secretary went to the king,
reporting furthermore to him as follows,
'Your servants have melted down the silver
which was in the Temple and have handed it
over to the masters of works attached to the
Temple of Yahweh.' [10]Then Shaphan the
secretary informed the king, 'The priest
Hilkiah has given me a book'; and Shaphan
read it aloud in the king's presence.

The prophetess Huldah consulted

[11]On hearing the words of the Book of the
Law he tore his clothes. [12]Then the king gave
the following order to the priest Hilkiah,
Ahikam son of Shaphan, Achbor son of
Micaiah, Shaphan the secretary and Asaiah
the king's minister: [13]'Go and consult
Yahweh on behalf of me and the people
about the words of the book that has been
discovered; for Yahweh's furious wrath has
been kindled against us because our an-
cestors disobeyed the word of Yahweh by
not doing what this book says they ought to
have done.'
[14]The priest Hilkiah, Ahikam, Achbor,
Shaphan and Asaiah went to the prophetess
Huldah wife of Shallum son of Tikvah, son
of Harhas the keeper of the wardrobe; she
lived in Jerusalem in the new town. They put
the matter to her, [15]and she replied, 'Yahweh,
God of Israel, says this, "To the man who
sent you to me say this: [16]Yahweh says this:
I am going to bring disaster on this place and
the people who live in it—all the words of the
book read by the king of Judah. [17]Because
they have abandoned me and sacrificed to
other gods, so as to provoke my anger by their
every action, my wrath is kindled against this
place, and nothing can stop it. [18]As for the
king of Judah who sent you to consult
Yahweh, say this to him: As regards the
words you have heard . . . [19]But since your
heart has been touched and you have
humbled yourself before Yahweh on hearing
what I have decreed against this place and
the people who live in it, how they will
become an object of horror and cursing, and
have torn your clothes and wept before me,
I too have heard—Yahweh says this. [20]So
look, when I gather you to your ances-
tors, you will be gathered into your grave in
peace; you will not live to see the great
disaster that I am going to bring on this
place." ' They took this answer to the
king.

The solemn reading of the Law and renewal of the covenant

23 The king then had all the elders of
Judah and of Jerusalem summoned to
him, [2]and the king went up to the Temple of
Yahweh with all the people of Judah and all
the inhabitants of Jerusalem, priests,
prophets and the whole populace, high and
low. In their hearing he read out the entire
contents of the Book of the Covenant discov-
ered in the Temple of Yahweh. [3]The king
then, standing on the dais, bound himself
by the covenant before Yahweh, to follow
Yahweh, to keep his commandments,
decrees and laws with all his heart and soul,
and to carry out the terms of the covenant as
written in this book. All the people pledged
their allegiance to the covenant.

Religious reform in Judah

[4]The king ordered Hilkiah with the priest
next in rank and the guardians of the thresh-

old to remove all the cult objects which had
been made for Baal, Asherah and the whole
array of heaven; he burnt them outside Jeru-
salem in the fields of the Kidron and had the
ashes taken to Bethel. 5He exterminated the
spurious priests whom the kings of Judah
had appointed and who offered sacrifice on
the high places, in the towns of Judah and
the neighbourhood of Jerusalem; also those
who offered sacrifice to Baal, to the sun, the
moon, the constellations and the whole array
of heaven. 6And from the Temple of Yahweh
he took the sacred pole outside Jerusalem to
the Kidron valley and in the Kidron valley
he burnt it, reducing it to ashes and throwing
its ashes on the common burial-ground. 7He
pulled down the house of the sacred male
prostitutes which was in the Temple of
Yahweh and where the women wove veils for
Asherah.

8He brought all the priests in from the
towns of Judah, and from Geba to Beersheba
he rendered unsanctified the high places
where these priests had offered sacrifice. He
pulled down the High Place of the Gates,
which stood at the gate of Joshua, the
governor of the city, to the left of the entry
to the city. 9The priests of the high places,
however, did not officiate at the altar of
Yahweh in Jerusalem, although they did
share the unleavened bread of their brother-
priests. 10He rendered unsanctified Tophet
in the Valley of Ben-Hinnom, so that no one
could pass his son or daughter through the
fire of sacrifice to Molech. 11He destroyed
the horses which the kings of Judah had
dedicated to the sun at the entrance to the
Temple of Yahweh, near the apartment of
Nathan-Melech the official, in the precincts,
and he burned the solar chariot. 12The king
pulled down altars which the kings of Judah
had built on the roof and those which
Manasseh had built in the two courts of the
Temple of Yahweh, and broke them to pieces
on the spot, throwing their rubble into the
Kidron valley. 13The king rendered unsancti-
fied the high places facing Jerusalem, to
the south of the Mount of Olives, which
Solomon king of Israel had built for Astarte
the Sidonian abomination, for Chemosh the
Moabite abomination, and for Milcom the
Ammonite abomination. 14He also smashed
the sacred pillars, cut down the sacred poles,
and covered with human bones the places
where they had stood.

The reform is extended to the former Northern Kingdom

15As for the altar which was at Bethel, the
high place built by Jeroboam son of Nebat
who had led Israel into sin, he demolished
this altar and this high place as well, in
the same way, breaking up its stones and
reducing them to powder. The sacred pole
he burned.

16On looking round, Josiah saw the tombs
there on the hillside; he had the bones
fetched from the tombs and burned them on
the altar. This he rendered unsanctified, in
accordance with the word of Yahweh which
the man of God had proclaimed when Jero-
boam was standing by the altar at the time of
the feast. On looking round, Josiah caught
sight of the tomb of the man of God who
had foretold these things. 17'What is that
monument I see?' he asked. The townspeople
replied, 'It is the tomb of the man of God
who came from Judah and foretold what you
have done to the altar.' 18'Let him rest,' the
king said, 'and let no one disturb his bones.'
So they left his bones untouched, with the
bones of the prophet who came from Samaria.

19Josiah also destroyed all the shrines on
the high places which were in the towns of
Samaria and which the kings of Israel had
built to provoke Yahweh's anger; he treated
these places exactly as he had treated the one
at Bethel. 20All the priests of the high places
who were there he slaughtered on the altars,
and on those altars burned human bones.
Then he returned to Jerusalem.

The Passover

21The king gave this order to the whole
people: 'Celebrate a Passover to Yahweh
your God, as prescribed in this Book of the
Covenant.' 22No Passover like this had ever
been celebrated since the days when the
judges ruled Israel, nor throughout the entire
period of the kings of Israel and the kings of
Judah. 23The eighteenth year of King Josiah
was the only time when such a Passover was
celebrated in Yahweh's honour in Jerusalem.

Final comments on the religious reform

24What is more, the spirit-guides and
mediums, the household gods and idols, and
all the abominations to be seen in the country
of Judah and in Jerusalem, were swept away

by Josiah to give effect to the words of the
Law written in the book found by the priest
Hilkiah in the Temple of Yahweh. [25]No king
before him turned to Yahweh as he did, with
all his heart, all his soul, all his strength, in
perfect loyalty to the Law of Moses; nor did
any king like him arise again.
[26]Yet Yahweh did not renounce the heat
of his great anger which had been aroused
against Judah by all the provocations which
Manasseh had caused him. [27]Yahweh said, 'I
shall thrust Judah away from me too, as I
have already thrust Israel; I shall cast off
Jerusalem, this city which I have chosen, and
the Temple of which I have said: My Name
shall be there.'

The end of the reign of Josiah

[28]The rest of the history of Josiah, his entire
career, is this not recorded in the Book of the
Annals of the Kings of Judah?
[29]In his times, Pharaoh Necho king of
Egypt was advancing to meet the king of
Assyria at the River Euphrates, and King
Josiah went to intercept him; but Necho
killed him at Megiddo in the first encounter.
[30]His retainers carried his body from
Megiddo by chariot; they brought him to
Jerusalem and buried him in his own tomb.
The people of the country then took Jehoahaz
son of Josiah and anointed him, proclaiming
him king in succession to his father.

D: THE DESTRUCTION OF JERUSALEM

The reign of Jehoahaz in Judah (609)

[31]Jehoahaz was twenty-three years old when
he came to the throne, and he reigned for
three months in Jerusalem. His mother's
name was Hamutal daughter of Jeremiah,
of Libnah. [32]He did what is displeasing to
Yahweh, just as his ancestors had done.
[33]Pharaoh Necho put him in chains at
Riblah in Hamath, to prevent his reigning
any longer in Jerusalem, and imposed a levy
of a hundred talents of silver and ten talents
of gold on the country. [34]Pharaoh Necho then
made Eliakim son of Josiah king in succession
to Josiah his father, and changed his name to
Jehoiakim. Carrying off Jehoahaz, he took
him to Egypt, where he died.
[35]Jehoiakim paid over the silver and gold
to Pharaoh, but first had to tax the people of
the country before he could raise the sum
which Pharaoh demanded: he levied the
silver and gold to be paid over to Pharaoh
Necho from each according to his means.

The reign of Jehoiakim in Judah (609–598)

[36]Jehoiakim was twenty-five years old when
he came to the throne, and he reigned for
eleven years in Jerusalem. His mother's name
was Zebidah daughter of Pedaiah of Rumah.
[37]He did what is displeasing to Yahweh, just
as his ancestors had done.
24 In his times, Nebuchadnezzar king
of Babylon invaded, and Jehoiakim
became his vassal for three years, but then
rebelled against him a second time. [2]So he
sent armed bands of Chaldaeans, Aramaeans,
Moabites and Ammonites against him; he
sent these against Judah to destroy it, in
accordance with the word which Yahweh had
spoken through his servants the prophets. [3]It
was entirely due to Yahweh's anger that this
happened to Judah; he had resolved to thrust
them away from him because of Manasseh's
sins and all that he had done, [4]and also
because of the innocent blood which he had
shed, flooding Jerusalem with innocent
blood. Yahweh would not forgive.
[5]The rest of the history of Jehoiakim, his
entire career, is this not recorded in the Book
of the Annals of the Kings of Judah? [6]Then
Jehoiakim fell asleep with his ancestors; his
son Jehoiachin succeeded him.
[7]The king of Egypt did not leave his own
country again, because the king of Babylon
had conquered everywhere belonging to the
king of Egypt, from the Torrent of Egypt to
the River Euphrates.

Introduction to the reign of Jehoiachin (598–597)

[8]Jehoiachin was eighteen years old when he
came to the throne, and he reigned for three
months in Jerusalem. His mother's name was
Nehushta daughter of Elnathan of Jeru-
salem. [9]He did what is displeasing to
Yahweh, just as his father had done.

The first deportation

[10]At that time the troops of Nebuchadnezzar
king of Babylon advanced on Jerusalem,
and the city was besieged. [11]Nebuchadnezzar

king of Babylon advanced on the city and his generals laid siege to it. 12 Jehoiachin king of Judah—he, his mother, his retinue, his nobles and his officials—then surrendered to the king of Babylon, and the king of Babylon took them prisoner in the eighth year of his reign.

13 The latter carried off all the treasures of the Temple of Yahweh and the treasures of the palace and broke up all the golden furnishings which Solomon king of Israel had made for the sanctuary of Yahweh, as Yahweh had foretold. 14 He carried all Jerusalem off into exile, all the nobles and all the notables, ten thousand of these were exiled, with all the blacksmiths and metalworkers; only the poorest people in the country were left behind. 15 He deported Jehoiachin to Babylon, as also the king's mother, his officials and the nobility of the country; he made them all leave Jerusalem for exile in Babylon. 16 All the men of distinction, seven thousand of them, the blacksmiths and metalworkers, one thousand of them, all the men capable of bearing arms, were led off into exile in Babylon by the king of Babylon.

17 The king of Babylon deposed Jehoiachin in favour of his paternal uncle Mattaniah, whose name he changed to Zedekiah.

Introduction to the reign of Zedekiah in Judah (598–587)[a]

18 Zedekiah was twenty-one years old when he came to the throne, and he reigned for eleven years in Jerusalem. His mother's name was Hamital daughter of Jeremiah, of Libnah. 19 He did what is displeasing to Yahweh, just as Jehoiakim had done. 20 It was entirely due to Yahweh's anger that this happened to Jerusalem and Judah. It resulted in his casting them from his presence. Zedekiah rebelled against the king of Babylon.

The siege of Jerusalem

25 In the ninth year of his reign, in the tenth month, on the tenth day of the month, Nebuchadnezzar king of Babylon advanced on Jerusalem with his entire army; he pitched camp in front of the city and threw up earthworks round it. 2 The city lay under siege till the eleventh year of King Zedekiah. 3 In the fourth month, on the ninth day of the month, when famine was raging in the city and there was no food for the populace, 4 a breach was made in the city wall. The king then made his escape under cover of dark, with all the fighting men, by way of the gate between the two walls, which is near the king's garden—the Chaldaeans had surrounded the city—and made his way towards the Arabah. 5 The Chaldaean troops pursued the king and caught up with him in the Plains of Jericho, where all his troops deserted. 6 The Chaldaeans captured the king and took him to the king of Babylon at Riblah, who passed sentence on him. 7 He had Zedekiah's sons slaughtered before his eyes, then put out Zedekiah's eyes and, loading him with chains, carried him off to Babylon.

The sack of Jerusalem
The second deportation

8 In the fifth month, on the seventh day of the month—it was in the nineteenth year of Nebuchadnezzar king of Babylon—Nebuzaradan commander of the guard, a member of the king of Babylon's staff, entered Jerusalem. 9 He burned down the Temple of Yahweh, the royal palace and all the houses in Jerusalem. 10 The Chaldaean troops who accompanied the commander of the guard demolished the walls surrounding Jerusalem. 11 Nebuzaradan commander of the guard deported the remainder of the population left in the city, the deserters who had gone over to the king of Babylon, and the rest of the common people. 12 But the commander of the guard left some of the poor country people behind as vineyard workers and ploughmen.

13 The Chaldaeans broke up the bronze pillars from the Temple of Yahweh, the wheeled stands and the bronze Sea, which were in the Temple of Yahweh, and took the bronze away to Babylon. 14 They also took the ash containers, the scoops, the knives, the incense boats, and all the bronze furnishings used in worship. 15 The commander of the guard also took the censers and the sprinkling bowls, everything made of gold and everything made of silver. 16 As regards the two pillars, the one Sea and the wheeled stands, which Solomon had made for the Temple of Yahweh, there was no reckoning the weight

24a ‖ Jr 52.

of bronze in all these objects. [17]The height of
one pillar was eighteen cubits, and on it stood
a capital of bronze, the height of the capital
being five cubits; round the capital were
filigree and pomegranates, all in bronze. So
also for the second pillar.
[18]The commander of the guard took pris-
oner Seraiah the chief priest, Zephaniah the
priest next in rank, and the three guardians
of the threshold. [19]In the city he took prisoner
an official who was in command of the
fighting men, five of the king's personal
friends who were discovered in the city, the
secretary to the army commander, respon-
sible for military conscription, and sixty
men of distinction discovered in the city.
[20]Nebuzaradan commander of the guard took
these men and brought them to the king of
Babylon at Riblah, [21]and at Riblah in the
territory of Hamath the king of Babylon had
them put to death. Thus Judah was deported
from its country.

Gedaliah governor of Judah

[22]For the people remaining in the country
of Judah whom Nebuchadnezzar king of
Babylon had left behind, he appointed Geda-
liah son of Ahikam, son of Shaphan as
governor. [23]When the military leaders and
their men all heard that the king of Babylon
had appointed Gedaliah as governor, they
went to him at Mizpah: Ishmael son of
Nethaniah, Johanan son of Kareah, Seraiah
son of Tanhumeth the Netophathite,
Jaazaniah the Maacathite, they and their
men. [24]To them and to their men Gedaliah
swore an oath. 'Do not be afraid of the
Chaldaeans,' he said, 'stay in the country,
serve the king of Babylon, and all will go well
with you.'
[25]But in the seventh month, Ishmael son
of Nethaniah, son of Elishama, who was of
royal descent, and ten men with him, came
and murdered Gedaliah, as well as the
Judaeans and Chaldaeans who were with him
at Mizpah. [26]Then all the people, high and
low, with the military leaders, set off and
went to Egypt, being afraid of the
Chaldaeans.

King Jehoiachin pardoned

[27]In the thirty-seventh year of the exile of
Jehoiachin king of Judah, in the twelfth
month, on the twenty-seventh day of the
month, Evil-Merodach king of Babylon, in
the year he came to the throne, pardoned
Jehoiachin king of Judah and released him
from prison. [28]He treated him with kindness
and allotted him a seat above those of the
other kings who were with him in Babylon.
[29]So Jehoiachin laid aside his prisoner's garb,
and for the rest of his life always ate at the
king's table. [30]And his upkeep was perma-
nently ensured by the king, day after day, for
the rest of his life.

THE BOOKS OF CHRONICLES

These books present a reinterpretation of the period from David to the end of the monarchy. Everything is seen from the point of view of worship, and the Temple personnel are prominent at every stage. David, as founder of the Temple liturgy, is the central figure, comparable to Moses. He himself is beyond criticism and anything to his discredit (his adultery, the revolts and intrigues of his reign) is carefully suppressed. The initial genealogies are directed chiefly towards him and Judah his tribe, and the full Temple liturgy begins as soon as he brings the Ark up to Jerusalem.

Solomon is given similar treatment (his harem, an important source of contamination with foreign gods, is not mentioned). Subsequent kings also are assessed by their fidelity, not to the covenant as in the deuteronomic history, but to prayer and the Temple worship. Most marked is the optimistic conclusion: the work ends with King Cyrus' proclamation in 538 BC for the rebuilding of the Temple, after the exile in Babylon.

Long passages are adopted word for word from Samuel and Kings, so that the change of emphasis, where it occurs, is all the clearer. The details of design and worship in the Temple are clearly post-exilic. The work is best seen as a celebration of the restored worship in the Temple at a period when it was at the centre of Jewish life, *c.* 300 BC.

PLAN OF THE BOOKS

THE BOOKS OF CHRONICLES

THE FIRST BOOK OF CHRONICLES

I: THE GENEALOGIES

A: FROM ADAM TO ISRAEL

The origin of the three ethnic groups

1 Adam, Seth, Enosh, [2]Kenan, Mahalalel,
Jared, [3]Enoch, Methuselah, Lamech,
[4]Noah, Shem, Ham and Japheth.

The Japhethites

[5]Sons of Japheth: Gomer, Magog, the Medes,
Javan, Tubal, Meshech, Tiras.
[6]Sons of Gomer: Ashkenaz, Riphath,
Togarmah. [7]Sons of Javan: Elishah,
Tarshish, the Kittim, the Dananites.

The Hamites

[8]Sons of Ham: Cush, Mizraim, Put, Canaan.
[9]Sons of Cush: Seba, Havilah, Sabta,
Raama, Sabeteca. Sons of Raamah: Sheba,
Dedan. [10]Cush fathered Nimrod, the first
mighty warrior on earth.
[11]Mizraim fathered the people of Lud, of
Anam, of Lehab, of Naphtuh, [12]of Pathros,
Casluh and Caphtor, from which the Phili-
stines came. [13]Canaan fathered Sidon, his
first-born, then Heth, [14]and the Jebusites,
the Amorites, Girgashites, [15]Hivites,
Arkites, Sinites, [16]Arvadites, Zemarites,
Hamathites.

The Semites

17 Sons of Shem: Elam, Asshur, Arpachshad, Lud, Aram.

Sons of Aram: Uz, Hul, Gether and Meshech.

18 Arpachshad fathered Shelah, and Shelah fathered Eber. 19 To Eber were born two sons; the first was called Peleg, because it was in his time that the earth was divided into districts, and his brother was called Joktan.

20 Joktan fathered Almodad, Sheleph, Hazarmaveth, Jerah, 21 Hadoram, Uzal, Diklah, 22 Ebal, Abimael, Sheba, 23 Ophir, Havilah, Jobab; all these are sons of Joktan.

From Shem to Abraham

24 Arpachshad, Shelah, 25 Eber, Peleg, Reu, 26 Serug, Nahor, Terah, 27 Abram, that is, Abraham. 28 Sons of Abraham: Isaac and Ishmael. 29 These are their descendants:

The Ishmaelites

The first-born of Ishmael, Nebaioth; then Kedar, Adbeel, Mibsam, 30 Mishma, Dumah, Massa, Hada, Tema, 31 Jetur, Naphish and Kedemah. These are the sons of Ishmael.

32 Sons of Keturah, Abraham's concubine: she gave birth to Zimran, Jokshan, Medan, Midian, Ishbak, and Shuah. Sons of Jokshan: Sheba and Dedan. 33 Sons of Midian: Ephah, Epher, Hanoch, Abida, Eldaah. All these are sons of Keturah.

Isaac and Esau

34 Abraham fathered Isaac. Sons of Isaac: Esau and Israel.

35 Sons of Esau: Eliphaz, Reuel, Jeush, Jalam and Korah. 36 Sons of Eliphaz: Teman, Omar, Zephi, Gatam, Kenaz, Timna, Amalek. 37 Sons of Reuel: Nahath, Zerah, Shammah, Mizzah.

Seir

38 Sons of Seir: Lotan, Shobal, Zibeon, Anah, Dishon, Ezer, Dishan. 39 Sons of Lotan: Hori and Homam. Sister of Lotan: Timma. 40 Sons of Shobal: Alian, Manahath, Ebal, Shephi, Onam. Sons of Zibeon: Aiah and Anah. 41 Son of Anah: Dishon. Sons of Dishon: Hamran, Eshban, Ithran, Cheran. 42 Sons of Ezer: Bilhan, Zaavan, Jaakan. Sons of Dishan: Uz and Aran.

The kings of Edom

43 These are the kings who ruled in Edom before an Israelite king ruled: Bela son of Beor; his city was called Dinhabah. 44 Bela died and Jobab son of Zerah, from Bozrah, succeeded. 45 Jobab died and Husham from the territory of the Temanites succeeded. 46 Husham died and Hada son of Bedad succeeded; he defeated the Midianites in Moab, and his city was called Avith. 47 Hadad died and Samlah of Masrekah succeeded. 48 Samlah died and Shaul of Rehoboth-ha-Nahar succeeded. 49 Shaul died and Baal-Hanan son of Achbor succeeded. 50 Baal-Hanan died and Hadad succeeded. His city was called Pai; his wife's name was Mehetabel daughter of Matred, daughter of Mezahab.

The chiefs of Edom

51 Hadad died, and then there were chiefs in Edom: Chief Timna, Chief Aliah, Chief Jetheth, 52 Chief Oholibamah, Chief Elah, Chief Pinon, 53 Chief Kenaz, Chief Teman, Chief Mibzar, 54 Chief Magdiel, Chief Iram. These were the chiefs of Edom.

B: JUDAH

The sons of Israel

2 These are the sons of Israel: Reuben, Simeon, Levi, Judah, Issachar, and Zebulun. 2 Dan, Joseph, and Benjamin, Naphtali, Gad, and Asher.

The descendants of Judah

3 Sons of Judah: Er, Onan and Shelah. These three were born to him by Bath-shua the Canaanite woman. Er, Judah's first-born, displeased Yahweh who put him to death. 4 Tamar, Judah's daughter-in-law, bore him Perez and Zerah. Judah had five sons in all.

5 Sons of Perez: Hezron and Hamul.

6 Sons of Zerah: Zimri, Ethan, Heman, Calcol and Dara, five in all.

7 Sons of Carmi: Achar, who brought trouble on Israel by being unfaithful to the curse of destruction.

8 Sons of Ethan: Azariah.

The ancestors of David

9 Sons of Hezron: there were born to him
Jerahmeel, Ram, Chelubai.
10 Ram fathered Amminadab, Amminadab
fathered Nahshon chief of the sons of Judah,
11 Nahshon fathered Salma, Salma fathered
Boaz. 12 Boaz fathered Obed, Obed fathered
Jesse. 13 Jesse fathered Eliab, his first-born,
Abinadab second, Shimea third, 14 Nethanel
fourth, Raddai fifth, 15 Ozem sixth, David
seventh. 16 Their sisters were Zeruiah and
Abigail. Sons of Zeruiah: Abishai, Joab and
Asahel: three. 17 Abigail gave birth to
Amasa; father of Amasa was Jether the
Ishmaelite.

Caleb

18 Caleb son of Hezron fathered Jerioth by
Azubah his wife; these are her sons: Jesher,
Shobab and Ardon. 19 Azubah died, and
Caleb married Ephrath, who bore him Hur.
20 Hur fathered Uri, Uri fathered Bezalel.
21 Afterwards, Hezron married the
daughter of Machir, father of Gilead; he
married her when he was sixty years old and
she bore him Segub. 22 Segub fathered Jair
who held twenty-three towns in the territory
of Gilead. 23 From them, however, Geshur
and Aram took the Encampments of Jair and
Kenath with its dependencies: sixty towns.
All these used to belong to the sons of Machir
father of Gilead.
24 After Hezron's death, Caleb married
Ephrathah, wife of Hezron his father, who
bore him Ashhur father of Tekoa.

Jerahmeel

25 Jerahmeel, Hezron's eldest son, fathered
Hezron, his first-born, Ram, Bunah, Oren,
Ozem, Ahijah. 26 Jerahmeel had another wife
called Atarah; she was the mother of Onam.
27 Sons of Ram, Jerahmeel's first-born:
Maaz, Jamin and Eker.
28 Sons of Onam: Shammai and Jada. Sons
of Shammai: Nadab and Abishur.
29 Abishur's wife was called Abihail; she bore
him Ahban and Molid. 30 Sons of Nadab:
Seled and Ephraim. Seled died leaving no
son. 31 Son of Ephraim: Ishi; son of Ishi:
Sheshan; son of Sheshan: Ahlai. 32 Sons of
Jada, Shammai's brother: Jether and
Jonathan. Jether died leaving no sons. 33 Sons
of Jonathan: Peleth and Zaza.
These were the sons of Jerahmeel.
34 Sheshan had no sons, only daughters.
He had an Egyptian slave Jarha 35 to whom
Sheshan gave his daughter in marriage. She
bore him Attai. 36 Attai fathered Nathan,
Nathan fathered Zabad, 37 Zabad fathered
Ephlal, Ephlal fathered Obed, 38 Obed fath-
ered Jehu, Jehu fathered Azariah, 39 Azariah
fathered Helez, Helez fathered Eleasah,
40 Eleasah fathered Sismai, Sismai fathered
Shallum, 41 Shallum fathered Jekamiah,
Jekamiah fathered Elishama.

Caleb

42 Sons of Caleb, Jerahmeel's brother: Mesha,
his first-born, who fathered Ziph. His son
was Mareshah, father of Hebron. 43 Sons of
Hebron: Korah, Tappuah, Rekem and
Shema. 44 Shema fathered Raham, father of
Jorkeam. Rekem fathered Shammai.
45 Shammai's son was Maon, and Maon fath-
ered Beth-Zur.
46 Ephah, Caleb's concubine, gave birth to
Haran, Moza and Gazez. Haran fathered
Gazez.
47 Sons of Jahdai: Regem, Jotham, Geshan,
Pelet, Ephah and Shaaph.
48 Maacah, Caleb's concubine, gave birth
to Sheber and Tirhanah. 49 She gave birth to
Shaaph, who fathered Madmannah, and
Sheva, who fathered Machbenah and
Gibea.
The daughter of Caleb was Achsah.
50 These were the sons of Caleb.

Hur

Sons of Hur, the first-born of Ephrathah:
Shobal fathered Kiriath-Jearim; 51 Salma
fathered Bethlehem; Hareph fathered Beth-
Gader. 52 Shobal, father of Kiriath-Jearim,
had sons: Haroeh, that is, half of the Manah-
athites, 53 and the clans of Kiriath-Jearim: the
Ithrites, Puthites, Shumathites and
Mishraites. Their descendants are the people
of Zorah and Eshtaol.
54 Sons of Salma: Bethlehem, the Neto-
phathites, Atroth Beth-Joab, half of the
Manahathites, the Zorathites, 55 the Sophrite
clans living at Jabez, the Tirathites, the
Shimeathites, the Sucathites. They were the
Kenites descended from Hammath, father of
the House of Rechab.

C: THE HOUSE OF DAVID

The sons of David

3 These are the sons of David who were
born to him in Hebron: the first-born
Amnon, by Ahinoam of Jezreel; second,
Daniel, by Abigail of Carmel; [2]third,
Absalom son of Maacah, daughter of Talmai
king of Geshur; fourth, Adonijah son of
Haggith; [3]fifth, Shephatiah by Abital, sixth,
Ithream by his wife Eglah. [4]Six, therefore,
were born to him in Hebron, where he
reigned for three years and six months.
He reigned for thirty-three years in Jeru-
salem. [5]These are the sons who were born to
him in Jerusalem: Shimea, Shobab, Nathan,
Solomon, the four of them children of Bath-
Shua daughter of Ammiel; [6]Ibhar, Elishama,
Eliphelet, [7]Nogah, Nepheg, Japhia,
[8]Elishama, Eliada, Eliphelet: nine.
[9]All these were sons of David, not count-
ing the sons of the concubines. Tamar was
their sister.

The kings of Judah

[10]Sons of Solomon: Rehoboam; Abijah his
son, Asa his son, Jehoshaphat his son,
[11]Joram his son, Ahaziah his son, Joash his
son, [12]Amaziah his son, Azariah his son,
Jotham his son, [13]Ahaz his son, Hezekiah his
son, Manasseh his son, [14]Amon his son,
Josiah his son. [15]Sons of Josiah: Johanan,
the first-born, Jehoiakim second, Zedekiah
third, Shallum fourth. [16]The sons of Jeho-
iakim: Jeconiah his son, Zedekiah his son.

The royal line after the exile

[17]Sons of Jeconiah the captive: Shealtiel his
son, [18]then Malchiram, Pedaiah, Shenazzar,
Jechamiah, Hoshama, Nedabiah. [19]Sons of
Pedaiah: Zerubbabel and Shimei. Sons of
Zerubbabel: Meshullam and Hananiah;
Shelomith was their sister. [20]Sons of
Meshullam: Hashubah, Ohel, Berechiah,
Hasadiah, Jushab-Hesed: five. [21]Sons of
Hananiah: Pelatiah; Jeshaiah his son,
Rephaiah his son, Arnan his son, Obadiah his
son, Shecaniah his son. [22]Sons of Shecaniah:
Shemaiah, Hattush, Igal, Bariah, Neariah,
Shaphat: six. [23]Sons of Neariah: Elioenai,
Hizkiah, Azrikam: three. [24]Sons of Elioenai:
Hodaviah, Eliashib, Pelaiah, Akkub,
Johanan, Delaiah, Anani: seven.

D: THE SOUTHERN TRIBES

Judah. Shobal

4 Sons of Judah: Perez, Hezron, Carmi,
Hur, Shobal. [2]Reaiah son of Shobal fath-
ered Jahath, and Jahath fathered Ahumai
and Lahad. These are the Zoreathite clans.

Hur

[3]These are Abi-Etam, Jezreel, Ishma, and
Idbash, whose sister was called Hazzelelponi.
[4]Penuel fathered Gedor, and Ezer father-
ed Hushah.
These were the sons of Hur, first-born of
Ephrathah and father of Bethlehem.

Ashhur

[5]Ashhur, father of Tekoa, had two wives:
Helah and Naarah.
[6]Naarah bore him Ahuzzam, Hepher, the
Timnites, and the Ahashtarites—these were
the sons of Naarah.
[7]Sons of Helah: Zereth, Zohar, Ethnan.
[8]Koz fathered Anub, Hazzobebah and the
clans of Aharhel son of Harum. [9]Jabez was
better known than his brothers. His mother
gave him the name Jabez, 'because', she said,
'in distress I gave birth to him.' [10]Jabez called
on the God of Israel. 'If you truly bless me,'
he said, 'you will extend my lands, your hand
will be with me, you will keep harm away
and my distress will cease.' God granted him
what he had asked.

Caleb

[11]Chelub, Shuhah's brother, fathered Mehir,
who fathered Eshton. [12]Eshton fathered
Bethrapha, Paseah and Tehinnah father of
Irnahash. These were the men of Recab.
[13]Sons of Kenaz: Othniel and Seraiah.
Sons of Othniel: Hathath and Meonothai;
[14]Meonothai fathered Ophrah. Seraiah fath-
ered Joab, father of Geharashim—for they
were craftsmen.
[15]Sons of Caleb son of Jephunneh: Iru,
Elah and Naam. Sons of Elah: Kenaz.
[16]Sons of Jehallelel: Ziph, Ziphah, Tiria,
Asarel.
[17]Sons of Ezrah: Jether, Mered, Epher,
Jalon. She conceived Miriam, Shammai, and
Ishbah, the father of Eshtemoa, [18]whose
Judaean wife gave birth to Jered father of

Gedor, Heber father of Soco, and Jekuthiel, father of Zanoah. These were the sons of Bithiah the daughter of Pharaoh whom Mered had married.

[19]The sons of Hodiah's wife, sister of Naham father of Keilah the Garmite and of Eshtemoa the Maacathite . . .

[20]Sons of Shimon: Amnon, Rinnah, Ben-Hanan, Tilon.

Sons of Ishi: Zoheth and Ben-Zoheth.

Shelah

[21]Sons of Shelah son of Judah: Er father of Lecah, Laadah father of Mareshah, and the clans of linenworkers at Beth-Ashbea, [22]Jokim, the men of Cozeba, Joash and Saraph where Moab found wives and then returned to Bethlehem. (These are old traditions.) [23]These were potters and lived at Netaim and Gederah; they resided there, working for the king.

Simeon

[24]Sons of Simeon: Nemuel, Jamin, Jarib, Zerah, Saul; [25]Shallum was his son, Mibsam his son, Mishma his son. [26]The sons of Mishma: Hammuel his son, Zaccur his son, Shimei his son. [27]Shimei had sixteen sons and six daughters, but his brothers did not have many children, and the sum of their clans did not multiply as the sons of Judah did.

[28]They lived in Beersheba, Moladah and Hazar-Shual, [29]Bilhah, Ezem and Tolad, [30]Bethuel, Hormah and Ziklag, [31]Beth-Marcaboth, Hazar-Susim, Beth-Biri, Shaaraim. [32]These were their towns until the reign of David. Their settlements were: Etam, Ain, Rimmon, Tochen and Ashan, five towns, [33]and all the dependencies surrounding these towns as far as Baalath. That was where they lived and they had an official genealogy. [34]Meshobab, Jamlech, Joshah son of Amaziah, [35]Joel, Jehu son of Joshibiah, son of Seraiah, son of Asiel, [36]Elioenai, Jaakobah, Jeshohaiah, Asaiah, Adiel, Jesimiel, Benaiah, [37]Ziza, Ben-Shiphi, Ben-Allon, Ben-Jedaiah, Ben-Shimri, Ben-Shemaiah—[38]these above named were princes in their clans in their ancestral home. Their numbers increased enormously. [39]In search of pasture for their flocks, they spread from the Pass of Gerar to the eastern end of the valley, [40]where they found good, fat pasture; the land was broad, untroubled, peaceful. Hamites had been living there before them.

[41]These Simeonites, recorded by name, arrived there in the time of Hezekiah king of Judah; they overran their tents and the dwellings which they found there. They put them under a curse of destruction still in force today and settled in their place, since there was pasturage for their flocks.

[42]Five hundred of them, of the Simeonites, went to Mount Seir, their leaders being Pelatiah, Neariah, Rephaiah, and Uzziel, the sons of Ishi.

[43]They defeated the surviving fugitives of Amalek and still live there today.

E: THE TRANSJORDANIAN TRIBES

Reuben

5 Sons of Reuben, first-born of Israel. He was indeed the first-born but, when he defiled his father's bed, his birthright was given to the sons of Joseph son of Israel, and he was no longer reckoned as the eldest son.

[2]Although Judah grew greater than his brothers and a leader came from him, the birthright was Joseph's.

[3]Sons of Reuben, first-born of Israel: Henoch, Pallu, Hezron, Carmi.

Joel

[4]Sons of Joel: Shemaiah his son, Gog his son, Shimei his son, [5]Micah his son, Reaiah his son, Baal his son. [6]Beerah his son, whom Tiglath-Pileser king of Assyria carried off into exile, was the chief of the Reubenites.

[7]His brothers, by families, were grouped according to relationship. Jeiel was first, then Zechariah [8]and Bela son of Azaz, son of Shema, son of Joel.

Territory of Reuben

It was Reuben who lived in Aroer and his territory extended as far as Nebo and Baal-Meon. [9]To eastward, what he occupied extended to the edge of the desert and the River Euphrates, for they had many herds in Gilead.

[10]In the time of Saul, they made war on the Hagrites, whom they defeated and who were then living in their tents throughout the eastern front of Gilead.

Gad

[11]Next to them, in Bashan as far as Salecah,
lived the sons of Gad. [12]Joel was the first,
Shapham the second, then Janai and Shaphat
in Bashan.
[13]Their brothers, by families, were
Michael, Meshullam, Sheba, Jorai, Jacan,
Zia, Eber: seven. [14]These were the sons of
Abihail: Ben-Huri, Ben-Jaroah, Ben-Gilead,
Ben-Michael, Ben-Jeshishai, Ben-Jahdo,
Ben-Buz. [15]Ahi son of Abdiel, son of Guni,
was the head of their families. [16]They
inhabited Gilead, Bashan and its depen-
dencies, as well as all the pasture lands of
Sharon on their extremities. [17]In the time
of Jotham king of Judah and in the time of
Jeroboam king of Israel, all of them were
included in the official genealogy.
[18]The sons of Reuben, the Gadites and the
half-tribe of Manasseh had warriors, men
armed with shield and sword who could
handle the bow and were trained for war, to
the number of forty-four thousand seven
hundred and sixty fit for service. [19]They
made war on the Hagrites, on Jetur, Naphish
and Nodab. [20]God came to their help, and
the Hagrites and all their allies fell into their
hands, for they called on God as they fought,
and because they put their trust in him he
heard their prayer. [21]Of their livestock they
carried off fifty thousand camels, two
hundred and fifty thousand sheep, two thou-
sand donkeys and a hundred thousand
people. [22]Because the war was of God, the
slaughter was great. They continued to live
in their territory until the exile.

The half-tribe of Manasseh

[23]The sons of the half-tribe of Manasseh lived
in the territory between Bashan and Baal-
Hermon, Senir and Mount Hermon.
They were numerous. [24]These were the
heads of their families: Epher, Ishi, Eliel,
Azriel, Jeremiah, Hodaviah, Jahdiel—stout
fighting men, men of renown, heads of their
families.
[25]But since they were unfaithful to the God
of their ancestors and prostituted themselves
to the gods of the peoples of the country
whom God had destroyed before them, [26]the
God of Israel roused the hostility of Pul, king
of Assyria, that is the wrath of Tiglath-
Pileser, king of Assyria who deported them—
the Reubenites, the Gadites and the half-
tribe of Manasseh—taking them off to Halah,
Habor, Hara and the river of Gozan. They
are still there today.

F: LEVI

The lineage of the high priests

[27]Sons of Levi: Gershom, Kohath and
Merari. [28]Sons of Kohath: Amram, Izhar,
Hebron, Uzziel. [29]Children of Amram:
Aaron, Moses and Miriam. Sons of Aaron:
Nadab and Abihu, Eleazar and Ithamar.
[30]Eleazar fathered Phinehas, Phinehas
fathered Abishua, [31]Abishua fathered Bukki,
Bukki fathered Uzzi. [32]Uzzi fathered
Zerahiah, Zerahiah fathered Meraioth.
[33]Meraioth fathered Amariah, Amariah fath-
ered Ahitub, [34]Ahitub fathered Zadok,
Zadok fathered Ahimaaz. [35]Ahimaaz fath-
ered Azariah, Azariah fathered Johanan.
[36]Johanan fathered Azariah. He it was who
officiated as priest in the Temple which
Solomon built in Jerusalem. [37]Azariah fath-
ered Amariah, Amariah fathered Ahitub,
[38]Ahitub fathered Zadok, Zadok fathered
Shallum, [39]Shallum fathered Hilkiah,
Hilkiah fathered Azariah, [40]Azariah fathered
Seraiah, Seraiah fathered Jehozadak, [41]and
Jehozadak went into exile when, at the hands
of Nebuchadnezzar, Yahweh exiled Judah
and Jerusalem.

The line of Levi

6 Sons of Levi: Gershom, Kohath and
Merari. [2]These are the names of the sons
of Gershom: Libni and Shimei. [3]Sons of
Kohath: Amram, Izhar, Hebron, Uzziel.
[4]Sons of Merari: Mahli and Mushi.
These are the levitical clans according to
their father.
[5]Of Gershom: Libni his son, Jahath his
son, Zimmah his son, [6]Joah his son, Iddo his
son, Zerah his son, Jeatherai his son.
[7]Sons of Kohath: Amminadab his son,
Korah his son, Assir his son, [8]Elkanah his
son, Ebiasaph his son, Assir his son. [9]Tahath
his son, Uriel his son, Uzziah his son, Shaul
his son. [10]Sons of Elkanah: Amasai and
Ahimoth. [11]Elkanah his son, Zophai his son,
Nahath his son, [12]Eliab his son, Jeroham his
son, Elkanah his son. [13]Sons of Elkanah:
Samuel his first-born, the second Abijah.
[14]Sons of Merari: Mahli, Libni his son,

15Shimei his son, Haggiah his son, Asaiah his son.

The singers

16These are the men whom David nominated to lead the singing in the Temple of Yahweh after the ark had come to rest there. 17They were responsible for the singing before the Dwelling, the Tent of Meeting, until Solomon had built the Temple of Yahweh in Jerusalem and then continued their customary duties.

18These were the persons in office, with their sons:

Of the sons of Kohath: Heman the singer, son of Joel, son of Samuel, 19son of Elkanah, son of Jeroham, son of Eliel, son of Toah, 20son of Zuph, son of Elkanah, son of Mahath, son of Amasai, 21son of Elkanah, son of Joel, son of Azariah, son of Zephaniah, 22son of Tahath, son of Assir, son of Ebiasaph, son of Korah, 23son of Izhar, son of Kohath, son of Levi, son of Israel.

24His brother Asaph stood on his right: Asaph son of Berechiah, son of Shimea, 25son of Michael, son of Baaseiah, son of Malchijah, 26son of Ethni, son of Zerah, son of Adaiah, 27son of Ethan, son of Zimmah, son of Shimei, 28son of Jahath, son of Gershom, son of Levi.

29On the left, the sons of Merari: Ethan son of Kishi, son of Abdi, son of Malluch, 30son of Hashabiah, son of Amaziah, son of Hilkiah, 31son of Amzi, son of Bani, son of Shemer, 32son of Mahli, son of Mushi, son of Merari, son of Levi.

The other Levites

33Their brother Levites were dedicated for all the other duties of the Dwelling, the Temple of God, 34but Aaron and his sons burned the offerings on the altar of burnt offering and on the altar of incense; they were entirely responsible for the most holy things and for the ritual of expiation for Israel, in accordance with all that Moses, servant of God, had commanded.

35These were the sons of Aaron: Eleazar his son, Phinehas his son, Abishua his son, 36Bukki his son, Uzzi his son, Zerahiah his son, 37Meraioth his son, Amariah his son, Ahitub his son, 38Zadok his son, Ahimaaz his son.

Towns of the Aaronites

39These were their places of settlement within their prescribed territory:

The sons of Aaron of the Kohathite clan—for to these the first lot fell— 40were given Hebron in the territory of Judah with its surrounding pasture lands. 41But the open country of the town and its dependencies were given to Caleb son of Jephunneh. 42The sons of Aaron were also given the cities of refuge, Hebron, Libnah with its pasture lands, Jattir, Eshtemoa with its pasture lands. 43Hilen with its pasture lands, Debir with its pasture lands, 44Ashan with its pasture lands and Beth-Shemesh with its pasture lands; 45and, from the tribe of Benjamin, Geba with its pasture lands, Alemeth with its pasture lands and Anathoth with its pasture lands. In all, the towns distributed among their clans numbered thirteen.

Towns of the other Levites

46The remaining sons of Kohath were allotted ten towns from the clans of the tribe, that is, from the half-tribe of Manasseh. 47The sons of Gershom and their clans were allotted thirteen towns from the tribe of Issachar, from the tribe of Asher, from the tribe of Naphtali and from the tribe of Manasseh in Bashan. 48The sons of Merari and their clans were allotted twelve towns from the tribe of Reuben, from the tribe of Gad and from the tribe of Zebulun. 49The Israelites gave these towns with their pasture lands to the Levites. 50From the tribe of the sons of Judah, from the tribe of the sons of Simeon and from the tribe of the sons of Benjamin, they also allotted them those towns to which they gave their names.

51Towns from the tribe of Ephraim were also assigned to the territory of some clans of the sons of Kohath. 52They were given the cities of refuge: Shechem in the highlands of Ephraim with its pasture lands, Gezer and its pasture lands, 53Jokmeam with its pasture lands, Beth-Horon with its pasture lands, 54Aijalon with its pasture lands and Gath-Rimmon with its pasture lands 55and from the half-tribe of Manasseh, Aner with its pasture lands and Bileam with its pasture lands. So much was given to the remaining families of the sons of Kohath.

56From the half-tribe of Manasseh, the sons of Gershom according to family were

given Golan in Bashan with its pasture lands
and Ashtaroth with its pasture lands; 57 from
the tribe of Issachar, Kedesh with its pasture
lands, Daberath with its pasture lands,
58 Ramoth with its pasture lands and Anem
with its pasture lands; 59 from the tribe of
Asher: Mashal with its pasture lands, Abdon
with its pasture lands. 60 Hukok with its
pasture lands and Rehob with its pasture
lands; 61 from the tribe of Naphtali, Kedesh
in Galilee with its pasture lands, Hammon
with its pasture lands and Kiriataim with its
pasture lands.

62 To the remainder of the sons of Merari:
from the tribe of Zebulun, Rimmon with its
pasture lands and Tabor with its pasture
lands; 63 in Transjordan, near Jericho, east of
the Jordan, from the tribe of Reuben: Bezer
in the desert with its pasture lands, Jahzah
with its pasture lands, 64 Kedemoth with its
pasture lands and Mephaath with its pasture
lands; 65 from the tribe of Gad: Ramoth in
Gilead with its pasture lands, Mahanaim with
its pasture lands, 66 Heshbon with its pasture
lands and Jazer with its pasture lands.

G: THE NORTHERN TRIBES

Issachar

7 For the sons of Issachar: Tola, Puah,
Jashub, Shimron: four.

2 Sons of Tola: Uzzi, Rephaiah, Jeriel,
Jahmai, Ibsam, Shemuel, heads of their
families of Tola. In the time of David, these
numbered twenty-two thousand six hundred
stout fighting men, grouped according to
their kinship.

3 Sons of Uzzi: Izrahiah. Sons of Izrahiah:
Michael, Obadiah, Joel, Isshiah. In all five
chiefs, 4 responsible for fighting companies
amounting to thirty-six thousand troops,
according to relationship and family, for they
had many women and children. 5 They had
kinsmen belonging to all the clans of Issachar,
eighty-seven thousand stout fighting men, all
belonging to one related group.

Benjamin

6 Sons of Benjamin: Bela, Becher, Jediael:
three.

7 Sons of Bela: Ezbon, Uzzi, Uzziel,
Jerimoth and Iri: five, chiefs of families and
warriors. Their official genealogy included
twenty-two thousand and thirty-four
members.

8 Sons of Becher: Zemirah, Joash, Eliezar,
Elioenai, Omri, Jeremoth, Abijah,
Anathoth, Alemeth, all these were the sons
of Becher. 9 The official genealogy of the
descendants of the chiefs of their families
included twenty thousand two hundred
warriors.

10 Sons of Jediael: Bilhan. Sons of Bilhan:
Jeush, Benjamin, Ehud, Chenaanah,
Zethan, Tarshish, Ahishahar. 11 All these
sons of Jediael, became heads of families,
stout fighting men, numbering seventeen
thousand two hundred men fit for active
service.

Naphtali

12 Shuppim and Huppim. Son of Ir: Hushim;
his son: Aher.

13 Sons of Naphtali: Jahziel, Guni, Jezer,
Shallum.

These were the sons of Bilhah.

Manasseh

14 Sons of Manasseh: Asriel, born of his
Aramaean concubine. She gave birth to
Machir, father of Gilead. 15 Machir took a
wife for Huppim and Shuppim. His sister's
name was Maacah.

The name of the second son was
Zelophehad. Zelophehad had daughters.

16 Maacah the wife of Machir gave birth to
a son whom she called Peresh. His brother
was called Sheresh and his sons Ulam and
Rakem.

17 Sons of Ulam: Bedan. These were the
sons of Gilead son of Machir, son of
Manasseh.

18 His sister Hammoleketh gave birth to
Ishod, Abiezer and Mahlah.

19 Shemida had sons: Ahian, Shechem,
Likhi and Aniam.

Ephraim

20 Sons of Ephraim: Shuthelah, Bered his son,
Tahath his son, Eleadah his son, Tahath his
son, 21 Zabad his son, Shuthelah his son and
Ezer and Elead whom the men of Gath,
natives of the country, killed when they
came down to raid their cattle. 22 Their father
Ephraim mourned for a long time and his
brothers came to comfort him. 23 He had

intercourse with his wife, who conceived and
gave birth to a son whom he called Beriah
because his house was in misfortune. 24He
had a daughter, Sheerah, who built Upper
and Lower Beth-Horon and Uzzen-Sheerah.
25Rephah was his son, Shuthelah his son,
Tahan his son, 26Ladan his son, Ammihud
his son, Elishama his son, 27Nun his son,
Joshua his son.
28They had lands and settlements in Bethel
and its dependencies from Naaran on the east
to Gezer and its dependencies on the west, as
well as Shechem and its dependencies as far
as Ayyah and its dependencies. 29Beth-Shean
with its dependencies, Taanach and its
dependencies, Megiddo and its dependencies
and Dor with its dependencies were in the
hands of the sons of Manasseh. There lived
the sons of Joseph son of Israel.

Asher

30Sons of Asher: Imnah, Ishvah, Ishvi,
Beriah; their sister Serah.
31Sons of Beriah: Heber and Malchiel. He
fathered Birzaith. 32Heber fathered Japhlet,
Shomer, Hotham and their sister Shua.
33Sons of Japhlet: Pasach, Bimhal and
Ashvath. These were the sons of Japhlet.
34Sons of Shomer his brother: Rohgah,
Hubbah and Aram.
35Sons of Helem his brother: Zophah,
Imna, Shelesh and Amal. 36Sons of Zophah:
Suah, Harnepher, Shual, Beri and Imrah.
37Bezer, Hod, Shamma, Shilshah, Ithran and
Beerah. 38Sons of Ithran: Jephunneh, Pispa,
Ara.
39Sons of Ulla: Arah, Hanniel, Rizia.
40All these were the sons of Asher, heads
of families, picked men, warriors and senior
princes. They were registered in fighting
companies to the number of twenty-six thou-
sand men.

H: BENJAMIN AND JERUSALEM

The line of Benjamin

8 Benjamin was father of Bela, his first-
born, Ashbel second, Ahiram third,
2Nohah fourth, Rapha fifth. 3Bela had sons:
Addar, Gera father of Ehud, 4Abishua,
Naaman, Ahoah, 5Gera, Shephuphan and
Huram.

In Geba

6These are the sons of Ehud. They were
heads of families of the inhabitants of Geba
and led them into exile at Manahath:
7Naaman, Ahijah and Gera. It was he who
led them into exile; he became the father of
Uzza and Ahihud.

In Moab

8Shaharaim had children in the Plains of
Moab after he had dismissed his wives,
Hushim and Baara. 9By his new wife he had
sons: Jobab, Zibia, Mesha, Malcam, 10Jeuz,
Sachia, Mirmah. These were his sons, heads
of families.

In Ono and Lud

11By Hushim he had sons: Abitub and Elpaal.
12The sons of Elpaal were Eber, Misham and
Shemed, who built Ono and Lud and its
dependencies.

In Aijalon

13Beriah and Shema were the chiefs of the
families who lived at Aijalon; they routed the
inhabitants of Gath.
14His brother was Shashak.

In Jerusalem

Jeremoth, 15Zebadiah, Arad, Eder,
16Michael, Ishpah, Joha were the sons of
Beriah.
17Zebadiah, Meshullam, Hizki, Haber,
18Ishmerai, Izliah, Jobab were the sons of
Elpaal.
19Jakim, Zichri, Zabdi, 20Elienai, Zille-
thai, Eliel, 21Adaiah, Beraiah, Shimrath were
the sons of Shimei.
22Ishpan, Eber, Eliel, 23Abdon, Zichri,
Hanan, 24Hananiah, Elam, Anthothijah,
25Iphdeiah, Penuel were the sons of Shashak.
26Shamsherai, Shehariah, Athaliah,
27Jaareshaiah, Elijah, Zichri were the sons of
Jeroham.
28These were chiefs of families according to
their relationship. They lived in Jerusalem.

In Gibeon

29At Gibeon lived Jeiel the father of Gibeon,
whose wife was called Maacah. 30His first-

born son was Abdon, then Zur, Kish, Baal, Ner, Nadab, 31 Gedor, Ahio, Zecher 32 and Mikloth. Mikloth fathered Shimeah. But they, unlike their brothers, lived at Jerusalem with their brothers.

Saul and his family

33 Ner fathered Kish, Kish fathered Saul, Saul fathered Jonathan, Malchishua, Abinadab and Eshbaal. 34 Son of Jonathan: Meribbaal. Meribbaal fathered Micah. 35 Sons of Micah: Pithon, Melech, Tarea, Ahaz. 36 Ahaz fathered Jehoaddah, Jehoaddah fathered Alemeth, Azmaveth and Zimri. Zimri fathered Moza, 37 Moza fathered Binea, Raphah his son, Eleasah his son and Azel his son. 38 Azel had six sons, whose names were these: Azrikam, his first-born, then Ishmael, Sheariah, Obadiah, Hanan. All these were sons of Azel.

39 Sons of Eshek his brother: Ulam, his first-born, Jeush second, Eliphelet third.

40 The sons of Ulam were warriors—archers. They had as many as a hundred and fifty sons and grandsons.

All these belonged to the sons of Benjamin.

Jerusalem, the holy city of Israel

9 Thus, all Israel's official genealogies had been entered in the records of the kings of Israel and Judah before they were deported to Babylon for their infidelity.

2 Now the first citizens to return to their property in their cities were the Israelites, the priests, the Levites and the temple slaves. 3 In Jerusalem, there settled Judaeans, Benjaminites, Ephraimites and Manassehites.

4 Uthai son of Ammihud, son of Omri, son of Imri, son of Bani, one of the sons of Perez son of Judah. 5 Of the descendants of Shelah: Asaiah, the first-born, and his sons. 6 Of the sons of Zerah: Jeuel. And six hundred and ninety of their kinsmen.

7 And of the sons of Benjamin: Sallu son of Meshullam, son of Hodaviah, son of Hassenuah; 8 Ibneiah son of Jeroham; Elah son of Uzzi, son of Michri; and Meshullam son of Shephatiah, son of Reuel, son of Ibnijah. 9 Their kinsmen, according to their relationship, numbered nine hundred and fifty-six. All these men were chiefs of their families.

10 Of the priests there were Jedaiah, Jehoiarib, Jachin, 11 Azariah son of Hilkiah, son of Meshullam, son of Zadok, son of Meraioth, son of Ahitub, the chief of the Temple of God; 12 Adaiah son of Jeroham, son of Pashhur, son of Malchijah; and Maasai son of Adiel, son of Jahzerah, son of Meshullam, son of Meshillemith, son of Immer. 13 Their kinsmen, heads of families, numbered one thousand seven hundred and sixty—men expert in the ministerial service of the Temple of God.

14 Of the Levites there were Shemaiah son of Hasshub, son of Azrikam, son of Hashabiah of the sons of Merari, 15 Bakbakar, Heresh, Galai, Mattaniah son of Mica, son of Zichri, son of Asaph. 16 Obadiah son of Shemaiah, son of Galal, son of Jeduthun and Berechiah son of Asa, son of Elkanah, who lived in the dependencies of the Netophathites.

17 The gatekeepers were Shallum, Akkub, Talmon, Ahiman and their kinsmen. Shallum was the chief 18 and is still gatekeeper of the King's Gate to the east. They were the gatekeepers of the camps of the sons of Levi.

19 Shallum son of Kore, son of Ebiasaph, son of Korah, and his brothers belonging to his family, the Korahites, were also in charge of the ministerial service as doorkeepers of the Tent, as their ancestors had been keepers of the entrance to the camp of Yahweh. 20 Formerly, Phinehas son of Eleazar had been in charge of them—Yahweh be with him! 21 Zechariah son of Meshelemiah was gatekeeper at the door of the Tent of Meeting. 22 All the keepers of the gate at the thresholds were picked men; there were two hundred and twelve of them. They were grouped by relationship in their various villages. These were confirmed in office by David and Samuel the seer because of their dependability. 23 They and their sons continued in charge as guards of the gates of the Temple of Yahweh, the house of the Tent. 24 The gatekeepers were assigned to the four sides, east, west, north and south, 25 and their brothers in their villages were required to assist them from time to time for a week, 26 since the four head gatekeepers were permanently on duty.

They were Levites and were in charge of the accommodation and supplies of the Temple of God. 27 They spent the night in the precincts of the Temple of God, their duties

being to guard it and open it every morning.
28 Some of them were in charge of the
implements of worship, having to count
them when they took them out and when
they put them away. 29 Others of them were
put in charge of the implements, of all the
objects in the sanctuary and of the flour, the
wine, the oil, the incense and the perfume.
30 Members of the priestly caste, however,
mixed the ointment for the perfume.
31 One of the Levites, Mattithiah—he was
the first-born of Shallum the Korahite—had
regular charge of baking operations. 32 Some
of their kinsmen the Kohathites were respon-
sible for the loaves to be set out in rows
Sabbath by Sabbath.
33 In addition, there were the singers, the
heads of the levitical families, who were
accommodated in the Temple, free of other
responsibilities because they were on duty
day and night.
34 Such were the chiefs of the levitical
families, according to their relationship;
these lived in Jerusalem.

I: SAUL, DAVID'S PREDECESSOR

The ancestors of Saul

35 Jeiel father of Gibeon lived at Gibeon and
his wife was called Maacah. 36 His first-born
son was Abdon, then Zur, Kish, Baal, Ner,
Nadab, 37 Gedor, Ahio, Zechariah and
Mikloth. 38 Mikloth fathered Shimeam. But
they, unlike their brothers, lived at Jerusalem
with their brothers.
39 Ner fathered Kish, Kish fathered Saul,
Saul fathered Jonathan, Malchishua, Abin-
adab and Eshbaal. 40 Son of Jonathan: Merib-
baal. Meribbaal fathered Micah. 41 Sons of
Micah: Pithon, Melech, Tahrea. 42 Ahaz
fathered Jarah, Jarah fathered Alemeth,
Azmaveth and Zimri; Zimri fathered Moza,
43 Moza fathered Binea, Rephaiah his son,
Eleasah his son and Azel his son. 44 Azel had
six sons; their names were these: Azrikam
his first-born, Ishmael, Sheariah, Obadiah,
Hanan. These were the sons of Azel.

Death of Saul

10 The Philistines gave battle to Israel and
the Israelites, fleeing from the Phili-
stines, fell and were slaughtered on Mount
Gilboa. 2 The Philistines bore down on Saul
and his sons, and they killed Jonathan, Abi-
nadab and Malchishua, Saul's sons. 3 The
fighting grew fiercer round Saul; the archers
came upon him, and he was wounded by the
archers. 4 Saul then said to his armour-bearer,
'Draw your sword and run me through with
it. I do not want these uncircumcised men to
come and make fun of me.' But his armour-
bearer was very much afraid and would not
do it. So Saul took his own sword and fell on
it. 5 His armour-bearer, seeing that Saul was
dead, fell on his sword too and died with him.
6 Thus died Saul, his three sons and his entire
household together. 7 When all the Israelites
who were in the valley saw that the Israel-
ites had been routed and that Saul and his
sons were dead, they abandoned their towns
and fled. The Philistines then came and
occupied them.
8 When the Philistines came on the
following day to strip the dead, they found
Saul and his sons lying on Mount Gilboa.
9 They stripped him and, taking his head and
his armour, had these carried round the
territory of the Philistines to proclaim the
good news to their idols and their people.
10 They placed his armour in the temple of
their gods and nailed his head up in the
temple of Dagon.
11 When all the inhabitants of Jabesh in
Gilead heard everything that the Philistines
had done to Saul, 12 the warriors all set out
and took the bodies of Saul and his sons away;
they brought them to Jabesh and buried their
bones under the tamarisk of Jabesh and fasted
for seven days.
13 Thus died Saul in the infidelity of which
he had been guilty towards Yahweh, in that
he had not obeyed the word of Yahweh and
because he had consulted a necromancer for
guidance. 14 He had not consulted Yahweh,
who therefore caused his death and trans-
ferred the monarchy to David son of Jesse.

II: DAVID, FOUNDER OF THE TEMPLE LITURGY

A: DAVID THE KING

David is anointed as king of Israel

11 All Israel then rallied to David at Hebron and said, 'Look, we are your own flesh and bone. 2 In days past when Saul was king, it was you who led Israel on its campaigns, and Yahweh your God promised you, "You are to shepherd my people Israel and be leader of my people Israel." ' 3 So all the elders of Israel came to the king at Hebron, and David made a pact with them in Yahweh's presence at Hebron, and they anointed David as king of Israel, in accordance with the word of Yahweh through Samuel.

The capture of Jerusalem

4 David and all Israel then marched on Jerusalem (that is to say, Jebus); the inhabitants of the territory were the Jebusites. 5 The inhabitants of Jebus said to David, 'You will not get in here.' But David captured the citadel of Zion, that is, the City of David. 6 David said, 'The first man to kill a Jebusite will be made army commander and chief.' Joab son of Zeruiah was the first man to go up, and was made commander of the army. 7 David went to live in the citadel, and that is how it came to be called the City of David. 8 He then built a wall round the city, all round, beginning from the Millo, and Joab restored the rest of the city. 9 Thus David grew stronger and stronger, for Yahweh Sabaoth was with him.

David's champions

10 These are David's principal champions who joined forces with him in his kingdom, with all Israel, to make him king in accordance with the word of Yahweh concerning Israel. 11 This is the roll of David's champions: Jashobeam son of Hachmoni, head of the Three; he it was who brandished his spear over three hundred men whom he had killed at one time.

12 Next, there was Eleazar son of Dodo, the Ahohite, one of the three champions. 13 He was with David at Pas-Dammim when the Philistines mustered for battle there. There was a field full of barley there; and the people fled from the Philistines. 14 And they took their stand in the middle of the field, held it and cut down the Philistines; and Yahweh brought about a great victory.

15 Three members of the Thirty went down to David at the rock near the Cave of Adullam while a company of Philistines was encamped in the Valley of the Rephaim. 16 David was then in the stronghold and there was a Philistine garrison in Bethlehem. 17 Longingly, David said, 'If only someone would fetch me a drink of water from the well that stands by the gate at Bethlehem!' 18 At this the three champions, forcing their way through the Philistine camp, drew water from the well that stands by the gate of Bethlehem and, bringing it away, presented it to David. David, however, would not drink any of it, but poured it out as a libation to Yahweh. 19 'God preserve me', he said, 'from doing such a thing! Am I to drink these men's blood? For at the risk of their lives they brought it.' And so he would not drink. Such were the deeds of the three champions.

20 Abishai, brother of Joab, was leader of the Thirty. He it was who brandished his spear over three hundred men whom he had killed, winning himself a name among the Thirty. 21 He was a most illustrious member of the Thirty and became their captain, but he was not equal to the Three.

22 Benaiah son of Jehoiada from Kabzeel was the hero of many exploits; he it was who slaughtered two formidable Moabites and, one snowy day, climbed down and slaughtered the lion in the storage-well. 23 He also slaughtered an Egyptian, a man who was seven and a half feet tall. The Egyptian was armed with a spear in his hand like a weaver's beam, but he took him on with a staff, tore the spear from the Egyptian's hand and killed the man with it. 24 Such were the exploits of Benaiah son of Jehoiada, winning him a name among the thirty champions. 25 He was a most illustrious member of the Thirty, but he was not equal to the Three. David put him in command of his bodyguard.

26 The military champions were:

Asahel brother of Joab;

Elhanan son of Dodo, of Bethlehem;
27 Shammoth of Haror;
Helez the Pelonite;
28 Ira son of Ikkesh, of Tekoa;
Abiezer of Anathoth;
29 Sibbecai of Hushah;
Ilai of Ahoh;
30 Maharai of Netophah;
Heled son of Baanah, of Netophah.
31 Ithai son of Ribai, of Gibeah in Benjamin.
Benaiah of Pirathon;
32 Hurai of the Torrents of Gaash;
Abiel of Beth-ha-Arabah;
33 Azmaveth of Bahurim;
Eliahba of Shaalbon;
34 the sons of Hashem of Gizon;
Jonathan son of Shagee, of Harar;
35 Ahiam son of Sachar, of Harar;
Eliphelet son of Ur;
36 Hepher of Mecherah;
Ahijah the Pelonite;
37 Hezro of Carmel;
Naarai son of Ezbai;
38 Joel brother of Nathan;
Mibhar son of Hagri;
39 Zelek the Ammonite;
Naharai of Beeroth,
armour-bearer to Joab son of Zeruiah;
40 Ira of Jattir;
Gareb of Jattir;
41 Uriah the Hittite;
Zabad son of Ahlai;
42 Adina son of Shiza the Reubenite,
chief of the Reubenites and commander
of the Thirty;
43 Hanan son of Maacah;
Joshaphat the Mithnite;
44 Uzzia of Ashteroth;
Shama and Jeiel sons of Hotham of Aroer;
45 Jediael son of Shimri,
and Joha his brother, the Tizite;
46 Eliel the Mahavite;
Jeribai and Joshaviah sons of Elnaam;
Ithmah the Moabite;
47 Eliel, Obed, and Jaasiel of Zobah.

Early defections to David

12 These are the men who rallied to David
at Ziklag while he was still being kept
away from Saul son of Kish; they were among
the champions, the warriors.
2 They were
equipped with bows and could sling stones
or shoot arrows from the bow with either
right hand or left.
Of Saul's fellow-tribesmen from
Benjamin:
3 Ahiezer the leader, and Joash,
sons of Hassemar of Gibeah, Jeziel and
Peleth, sons of Azmaveth, Berachah and
Jehu of Anathoth,
4 Ishmaiah of Gibeon, one
of the champions in the Thirty and
commander of the Thirty,
5 Jeremiah,
Jahaziel, Johanan and Jozabed of Gederoth,
6 Eluzai, Jerimoth, Bealiah, Shemariah,
Shephatiah of Hariph,
7 Elkanah, Isshiah,
Azarel, Joezer and Jashobeam the Korahites,
8 Joelah, Zebadiah, sons of Jeroham of Gedor.
9 From the Gadites, some good, capable
fighting men defected and came to David at
the stronghold in the desert—all skilled with
shield and spear, fierce as lions and nimble
as mountain gazelles.
10 Ezer was the leader,
Obadiah second, Eliab third,
11 Mishmannah
fourth, Jeremiah fifth,
12 Attai sixth, Eliel
seventh,
13 Johanan eighth, Elzabad ninth,
14 Jeremiah tenth, Machbannai eleventh.
15 These Gadites were the leaders of the
troops, the least of them a match for a
hundred men and the greatest a match for a
thousand.
16 These were the men who once
crossed the Jordan in the first month, when
it had overflowed its banks and had driven
out all the lowlanders to east and west.
17 Some of the Benjaminites and Judahites
also joined David at the stronghold.
18 When
David came forward to meet them, he
responded to them by saying, 'If you have
come to me with peaceful intent to help me,
you will find me a good friend. But if it is to
betray me to my enemies, seeing that I have
done nothing wrong, may the God of our
ancestors take note and condemn you.'
19 Then the Spirit invested Amasai the
leader of the Thirty:

'We are your men, David;
with you, son of Jesse!
Peace be with you, peace be with you;
peace be with those who help you!
For your God has helped you!'

And David accepted them, including them
among his more senior officers.
20 Some Manassehites also defected to
David as he was setting out with the Phili-
stines to fight Saul. But he did not help the
Philistines because, after consultation, their
chiefs sent him away, saying, 'He will defect
to his master Saul and it will cost us our
heads!'
21 He was on his way to Ziklag when
these Manassehites deserted to him: Adnah,
Jozabad, Jediael, Michael, Jozabad, Elihu,
Zillethai, chiefs of thousands in Manasseh.

22They helped David and his band, since they were all men of standing and became officers in the army.

23Indeed reinforcements reached David day after day, so that his camp grew into a camp of prodigious size.

The warriors who assured David's kingship

24These are the numbers of fully armed men who joined David at Hebron to transfer Saul's kingdom to him in accordance with the order of Yahweh:

25Judahites carrying shield and spear: six thousand eight hundred fully armed warriors;

26Simeonites; seven thousand one hundred champions valiant in war;

27Levites: four thousand six hundred, 28in addition to Jehoiada, in command of the Aaronites, with three thousand seven hundred of these, 29Zadok, a young and valiant champion, and twenty-two commanders of his family;

30Benjaminites: three thousand kinsmen of Saul, most of them hitherto in the service of the House of Saul;

31Ephraimites: twenty thousand eight hundred valiant champions, men famous in their families;

32of the half-tribe of Manasseh: eighteen thousand men assigned by name to go and proclaim David king;

33Issacharites, sound judges of the times when Israel should take action, and the way to do it: two hundred chiefs and all their kinsmen under their command;

34Zebulunites: fifty thousand men fit for service, marshalled for battle, with warlike weapons of every kind, staunch-hearted auxiliaries;

35Naphtalites: a thousand commanders, and with them thirty-seven thousand men armed with shield and spear;

36Danites: twenty-eight thousand six hundred men marshalled for battle;

37Asherites: forty thousand men fit for service, marshalled for battle;

38from Transjordan: a hundred and twenty thousand men of Reuben, Gad and the half-tribe of Manasseh, with warlike weapons of every kind.

39All these warriors in battle array came to David at Hebron with the firm determination of making David king of all Israel; and the rest of Israel, too, was of one mind in wanting to make David king. 40For three days they stayed there with David, eating and drinking, their fellow-tribesmen having made preparations for them; 41their neighbours too, from as far away as Issachar and Zebulun and Naphtali, came bringing food on donkeys, camels, mules and oxen—supplies of flour, fig cakes, bunches of raisins, wine, oil, quantities of oxen and sheep—for there was joy in Israel.

The ark brought back from Kiriath-Jearim

13 David conferred with the commanders of the thousands and the hundreds, in fact with all the leaders. 2Then, to the whole assembly of Israel, David said, 'If this has your approval, and if Yahweh our God wills it so, we shall send messengers to the rest of our brothers throughout the territories of Israel, and also to the priests and Levites in their towns and pasture lands, bidding them join us. 3And then we will go and recover the ark of our God, for in the days of Saul we neglected to do it.'

4The whole assembly agreed to this, because all the people thought that this was the right thing to do. 5So David summoned all Israel from the Shihor of Egypt to the Pass of Hamath, to bring the ark of God from Kiriath-Jearim. 6David and all Israel then went up to Baalah, to Kiriath-Jearim in Judah, from there to bring up the ark of God, which bears the title 'Yahweh enthroned on the winged creatures'. 7They transported the ark of God out of Abinadab's house on a new cart. Uzzah and Ahio drove the cart. 8David and all Israel danced before God with all their might, singing to the accompaniment of harps, lyres, tambourines, cymbals and trumpets. 9When they came to the threshing-floor of the Javelin, Uzzah reached out his hand to steady the ark, as the oxen were making it tilt. 10This roused Yahweh's anger against Uzzah, and he struck him down because he had laid his hand on the Ark, and there he died before God. 11David resented Yahweh's having broken out against Uzzah, and the place was given the name Perez-Uzzah, which it still has today.

12That day David felt afraid of God. 'How can I bring the ark of God to be with me?' he said. 13So David did not take the ark with him into the City of David but had it put in the house of Obed-Edom of Gath. 14The ark of God remained with Obed-Edom, in his house, for three months, and Yahweh blessed Obed-Edom's family and everything that belonged to him.

David in Jerusalem, his palace, his children

14 Hiram king of Tyre sent envoys to David, with cedar wood, stone-cutters and carpenters, to build him a palace. 2 David then knew that Yahweh had confirmed him as king of Israel and, for the sake of his people, had extended his sovereignty.

3 David took more wives in Jerusalem and fathered more sons and daughters. 4 These are the names of the children born to him in Jerusalem: Shammua, Shobab, Nathan, Solomon, 5 Ibhar, Elishua, Elpelet, 6 Nogah, Nepheg, Japhia, 7 Elishama, Beeliada, Eliphelet.

Victories over the Philistines

8 When the Philistines heard that David had been anointed as king of all Israel, they all invaded to seek him out. On hearing this, David marched out towards them. 9 When the Philistines arrived, they deployed in the Valley of the Rephaim. 10 David consulted God and asked, 'Shall I attack the Philistines? Will you deliver them into my power?' Yahweh replied to him, 'Attack! I shall deliver them into your power.' 11 Accordingly, they went up to Baal-Perazim and there David defeated them. David said, 'Through me God has made a breach in my enemies, as though they had been breached by a flood.' This is why the place was given the name Baal-Perazim. 12 They had left their gods behind there, and David ordered them to be burnt.

13 Again the Philistines deployed in the valley. 14 David again consulted God, and God replied, 'Do not attack them from the front; go round and engage them opposite the balsam trees. 15 When you hear the sound of footsteps in the tops of the balsam trees, launch your attack, for that will be God going out ahead of you to defeat the Philistine army.' 16 David did as God had ordered, and they beat the Philistine army from Gibeon to Gezer.

17 David's fame then spread to every country, and Yahweh made him feared by every nation.

B: THE ARK IN THE CITADEL OF DAVID

Preparations for moving the ark

15 After he had put up buildings for himself in the City of David, he prepared a place for the ark of God and pitched a tent for it. 2 David then said, 'No one but the Levites should carry the ark of God, since Yahweh has chosen them to carry the ark of Yahweh and to minister to him for ever.'

3 David then summoned all Israel to Jerusalem, to move the ark of Yahweh to the place which he had prepared for it. 4 David also called the sons of Aaron and the Levites together: 5 of the sons of Kohath: Uriel the chief and his hundred and twenty kinsmen; 6 of the sons of Merari: Asaiah the chief and his two hundred and twenty kinsmen; 7 of the sons of Gershom: Joel the chief and his hundred and thirty kinsmen; 8 of the sons of Elizaphan: Shemaiah the chief and his two hundred kinsmen; 9 of the sons of Hebron: Eliel the chief and eighty kinsmen; 10 of the sons of Uzziel: Amminadab the chief and his hundred and twelve kinsmen.

11 David then sent for the priests Zadok and Abiathar, and the Levites Uriel, Asaiah, Joel, Shemaiah, Eliel and Amminadab. 12 To them he said, 'You are the heads of the levitical families. Sanctify yourselves, you and your kinsmen, so that you can move the ark of Yahweh, God of Israel, to the place which I have prepared for it. 13 Because you were not there the first time, Yahweh our God broke out at us because we did not handle it properly.' 14 So the priests and the Levites sanctified themselves, to move the ark of Yahweh, God of Israel, 15 and the Levites carried the ark of God with the shafts on their shoulders, as Moses had ordered in accordance with the word of Yahweh.

16 David also told the heads of the Levites to appoint their kinsmen as singers with the accompaniment of musical instruments, lyres, harps, and cymbals to play joyfully. 17 The Levites then appointed Heman son of Joel, Asaph son of Berechiah, one of his brothers, Ethan son of Kushaiah, one of their Merarite kinsmen; 18 and with them their kinsmen of the second rank: Zechariah, Uzziel, Shemiramoth, Jehiel, Unni, Eliab, Benaiah, Maaseiah, Mattithiah, Eliphelehu,

Mikneiah, and Obed-Edom and Jehiel the
gatekeepers. [19]The singers, Heman, Asaph
and Ethan, were to play the bronze cymbals.
[20]Zechariah, Uzziel, Shemiramoth, Jehiel,
Unni, Eliab, Maaseiah and Benaiah were
to play the lyre. [21]Mattithiah, Eliphelehu,
Mikneiah, Obed-Edom, Jehiel and Azaziah,
giving the beat, were to play the harp.
[22]Chenaniah, the levitical director of trans-
port was in charge of the transport, being
skilful at it. [23]Berechiah and Elkanah were
gatekeepers for the ark. [24]The priests Sheb-
aniah, Joshaphat, Nethanel, Amasai, Zech-
ariah, Benaiah and Eliezer blew trumpets
before the ark of God, while Obed-Edom and
Jehiah were also gatekeepers for the ark.

The ark is brought to Jerusalem

[25]David, the elders of Israel and the
commanders of the thousands accordingly
went, amid great rejoicing, to bring the ark
of the covenant of Yahweh up from Obed-
Edom's house, [26]and since God was helping
the Levites who carried the ark of the
covenant of Yahweh, they sacrificed seven
bulls and seven rams. [27]David, all the Levites
who carried the ark, the singers and Chen-
aniah, director of transport, wore cloaks of
fine linen. David also wore a linen *ephod*.
[28]Thus, with war-cries and the sounding of
the horn, the trumpets and the cymbals,
and the music of lyres and harps, all Israel
transported the ark of the covenant of
Yahweh. [29]Now, as the ark of the covenant
of Yahweh entered the City of David, Michal
daughter of Saul was watching from the
window and, when she saw King David
dancing and playing, the sight of him filled
her with contempt.

16 They brought the ark of God in and
put it inside the tent which David had
erected for it, and brought burnt offerings
and made communion sacrifices in God's
presence. [2]And when David had finished
making burnt offerings and communion
sacrifices, he blessed the people in the name
of Yahweh. [3]To all the Israelites, both men
and women, to each, he then distributed a
loaf of bread, a portion of meat and a raisin
cake.

The service of the Levites before the ark

[4]He appointed some of the Levites as minis-
ters before the ark of Yahweh, to extol,
glorify and praise Yahweh, God of Israel;
[5]first Asaph, second Zechariah, then Uzziel,
Shemiramoth, Jehiel, Mattithiah, Eliab,
Benaiah, Obed-Edom and Jeiel, who played
the lyre and harp, while Asaph played the
cymbals. [6]The priests Benaiah and Jahaziel
continually blew the trumpet before the ark
of the covenant of God. [7]On that day, David
was the first to assign to Asaph and his
kinsmen the giving of thanks to Yahweh:

[8]Give thanks to Yahweh,
call his name aloud,
proclaim his deeds to the peoples.
[9]Chant to him, play to him,
sing about all his wonders!

[10]Take pride in his holy name,
let your heart rejoice,
you seekers of Yahweh!
[11]Seek out Yahweh, seek his strength,
continually seek out his presence!

[12]Remember what wonders he has done,
what miracles, what rulings he has given,
[13]you offspring of Israel his servant,
you children of Jacob his chosen one!

[14]For he is Yahweh our God,
his authority extends
throughout the world.

[15]For ever remember his covenant,
the pact imposed
for a thousand generations,
[16]which he concluded with Abraham,
which was sworn by him to Isaac,

[17]since he confirmed it as a law for Jacob,
as an eternal covenant for Israel,
[18]saying, 'I will give you the country;
Canaan is the measure
of your inheritance,

[19]'though you are few in number,
only a few strangers there!'

[20]As they wandered from nation to nation,
from this kingdom to that people,
[21]he would not let anyone oppress them
and on their account
he admonished kings,
[22]'You are not to touch my anointed ones,
my prophets are not to be harmed!'

[23]Sing to Yahweh, all the earth,
day after day proclaim his salvation!
[24]Declare his glory among the nations,
his marvels to every people!

[25]Great is Yahweh, worthy of all praise,

more awesome than any of the gods.
26 Nothingness, all the gods of the nations.

Yahweh it was who made the heavens,
27 in his presence are splendour and majesty,
in his sanctuary strength and joy.
28 Give Yahweh his due, families of peoples,
give Yahweh his due of glory and power,
29 give Yahweh the glory due to his name!

Bring an offering and enter his courts,
bow down to Yahweh in his sacred court,
30 tremble before him, all the earth!

The world is firm, it cannot be moved,
31 let the heavens rejoice and earth be glad!
Say among the nations, 'Yahweh is king!'
32 Let the sea thunder and all it holds,
the countryside exult
and everything that is in it,
33 and all the trees of the forest
cry out for joy
at Yahweh's approach,
for he is coming to judge the earth.
34 Give thanks to Yahweh, for he is good,
for his faithful love lasts for ever!

35 Say, 'Save us, God of our salvation,
gather us together
and free us from the nations,
so that we may give thanks
to your holy name—
to be extolled whenever you are praised!'

36 Blessed be Yahweh, God of Israel,
from everlasting to everlasting!

To which all the people said,
'Amen, Alleluia!'

37 There before the ark of the covenant of
Yahweh David left Asaph and his kinsmen
to maintain a permanent ministry before the
ark as each day's ritual required, 38 and also
Obed-Edom with his sixty-eight kinsmen.
Obed-Edom son of Jeduthun, and Hosah
were gatekeepers.
39 Zadok the priest and the priests, his
kinsmen, he left before the dwelling of
Yahweh on the high place at Gibeon 40 to
bring burnt offerings to Yahweh unfailingly,
morning and evening, on the altar of burnt
offering, and to carry out all that is written
in the Law of Yahweh laid down for Israel.
41 With them were Heman and Jeduthun and
the rest of those who were chosen and
assigned by name to give thanks to Yahweh,
'for his faithful love lasts for ever'. 42 With
them were Heman and Jeduthun to play
trumpets and cymbals, as well as instruments
for accompanying sacred song. The sons of
Jeduthun were in charge of the gates.
43 Then all the people went back to their
homes, and David went back to bless his
household.

Nathan's prophecy

17 It happened, once David had settled
into his palace, that David said to the
prophet Nathan, 'Here am I living in a cedar-
wood palace, while the ark of the covenant
of Yahweh is under awnings.' 2 Nathan said
to David, 'Do whatever you have in mind,
for God is with you.'
3 But that very night the word of God came
to Nathan, as follows:
4 'Go and tell my servant David, "Yahweh
says this: You must not build a temple for
me to live in. 5 I have never lived in a house
from the day when I brought Israel out until
today, but have kept travelling from tent to
tent and from shelter to shelter. 6 In all my
travels with all Israel, did I say to any of the
judges of Israel, whom I had commanded to
shepherd my people: Why do you not build
me a cedar-wood temple? 7 This is what you
must say to my servant David: Yahweh
Sabaoth says this: I took you from the
pasture, from following the sheep, to be
leader of my people Israel. 8 I have been with
you wherever you went; I have got rid of all
your enemies for you. I am going to make
your fame like that of the greatest men on
earth. 9 I am going to provide a place for my
people Israel; I shall plant them there and
there they will live and never be disturbed
again; nor will they be oppressed by the
wicked as they were in former times 10 ever
since I instituted judges to govern my people
Israel; I shall subdue all your enemies.
Yahweh moreover tells you that he will build
you a dynasty. 11 And when your days are
over and you have gone to join your ancestors,
I shall appoint your heir—who will be one of
your sons—to succeed you, and I shall make
his sovereignty secure. 12 He will build a
temple for me and I shall make his throne
secure for ever. 13 I shall be his father and he
will be my son, and I shall not withdraw my
favour from him, as I withdrew it from your
predecessor. 14 I shall set him over my temple
and kingdom for ever and his throne will be
for ever secure." '

15 Nathan related all these words and this
whole revelation to David.

David's prayer

16 King David then went in, sat down in
Yahweh's presence and said:
'Who am I, Yahweh God, and what is my
lineage, that you have led me as far as this?
17 Yet, to you, O God, this seemed too little,
and now you extend your promises for your
servant's family into the distant future,
making me see as it were a whole succession
of men, and it is Yahweh God himself who
raises it up. 18 What more can David reply to
you for the honour you have given to your
servant? You yourself have singled out your
servant. 19 For your servant, and since you
were so inclined, you have had the generosity
to reveal all this greatness to come. 20 Yahweh,
there is no one like you, no God but you
alone, as everything that we have heard
confirms. 21 Is there another people on earth
like your people Israel, whom a god has
proceeded to redeem, to make them his
people and to make them famous and do for
them great and terrible deeds, by driving
out nations before your people, whom you
redeemed from Egypt?—22 for you made your
people Israel your own people for ever and
you, Yahweh, became their God.
23 'Now, Yahweh, may the promise which
you have made for your servant and as regards
his family hold good for ever, and do as you
have said. 24 May it hold good, so your name
will be exalted for ever and people will say,
"Israel's God is Yahweh Sabaoth; he is God
for Israel." Your servant David's dynasty
will be secure before you 25 since you, my
God, have disclosed to your servant that you
are going to build him a dynasty. Hence,
your servant has ventured to offer this prayer
to you. 26 Yes, Yahweh, you are God indeed,
and you have made this generous promise
to your servant. 27 What is more, you have
deigned to bless your servant's dynasty, so
that it may remain for ever before you; and
since you, Yahweh, have blessed it, blessed
will it be for ever.'

David's wars

18 After this David defeated the Phili-
stines and subdued them. From the
grip of the Philistines he wrested Gath and
its dependencies. 2 He also defeated the
Moabites; the Moabites became David's
subjects and paid him tribute.
3 David also defeated Hadadezer king of
Zobah, which lies in the direction of Hamath,
when the latter mounted an expedition to
assert his rule on the River Euphrates. 4 David
captured one thousand chariots, seven thou-
sand charioteers and twenty thousand foot
soldiers from him; David hamstrung all the
chariot teams, keeping only a hundred of
them. 5 The Aramaeans of Damascus came to
the help of Hadadezer king of Zobah, but
David killed twenty-two thousand of the
Aramaeans. 6 David then imposed governors
in Aram of Damascus, and the Aramaeans
became David's subjects and paid him
tribute. Wherever David went, Yahweh gave
him victory. 7 David took the golden shields
carried by Hadadezer's guards and brought
them to Jerusalem. 8 From Tibhath and from
Cun, towns belonging to Hadadezer, David
captured a great quantity of bronze, with
which Solomon made the bronze Sea, the
pillars and the bronze implements.
9 When Tou king of Hamath heard that
David had defeated the entire army of
Hadadezer king of Zobah, 10 he sent his son
Hadoram to King David to greet him and to
congratulate him on having made war on
Hadadezer and on having defeated him, since
Hadadezer was at war with Tou. He also sent
all sorts of objects made of gold, silver and
bronze, 11 which King David also consecrated
to Yahweh, as well as the silver and gold
which he had levied from all the nations,
from Edom, Moab, the Ammonites, the
Philistines and Amalek.
12 Abishai son of Zeruiah defeated the
Edomites in the Valley of Salt—eighteen
thousand of them. 13 He stationed garrisons in
Edom, and all the Edomites became David's
subjects. Wherever David went, Yahweh
gave him victory.

The administration of the kingdom

14 David ruled over all Israel, administering
law and justice to all his people. 15 Joab son
of Zeruiah was in command of the army;
Jehoshaphat son of Ahilud was herald;
16 Zadok son of Ahitub and Abiathar son of
Ahimelech were priests; Shusha was
secretary; 17 Benaiah son of Jehoiada was in
command of the Cherethites and Pelethites;
David's sons took first place after the king.

David's ambassadors are insulted

19 After this, when Nahash king of the Ammonites died and his son Hanun succeeded him, [2]David thought, 'I shall show Hanun son of Nahash the same faithful love as his father showed me.' And David sent representatives to offer him condolences over his father. But when David's representatives reached Hanun in the Ammonites' country to present these condolences, [3]the Ammonite leaders said to Hanun, 'Do you really think David means to honour your father when he sends you messengers with sympathy? On the contrary, the reason why his representatives have come to you is to explore, overthrow and reconnoitre the country.' [4]Whereupon Hanun seized David's representatives, shaved them, cut their clothes off half-way up, right by their buttocks, and sent them away. [5]As soon as David was told how the men had been treated, he sent someone to meet them, since the men were overcome with shame. 'Stay in Jericho,' the king said, 'until your beards have grown, and come back then.'

The first Ammonite campaign

[6]When the Ammonites realised that they had antagonised David, Hanun and the Ammonites sent a thousand talents of silver to hire chariots and cavalry from the Aramaeans of Upper Mesopotamia, of Maacah and of Zobah. [7]They hired thirty-two thousand chariots and the king of Maacah with his people, who came and encamped before Medeba, while the Ammonites, having left their towns and mustered, were advancing to the war. [8]When David heard this, he sent Joab with the whole army, the champions. [9]The Ammonites marched out and drew up their line of battle at the city gate, while the kings who had come kept their distance in the open country. [10]Joab, seeing that he had to fight on two fronts, to his front and to his rear, chose the best of Israel's picked men and drew them up in line facing the Aramaeans. [11]He entrusted the rest of the army to his brother Abishai, and drew them up in line facing the Ammonites. [12]'If the Aramaeans prove too strong for me,' he said, 'you must come to my help; if the Ammonites prove too strong for you, I shall come to yours. [13]Be brave and let us fight valiantly, for the sake of our people and for the cities of our God! And let Yahweh dispose as he thinks fit!' [14]Joab and the force with him joined battle with the Aramaeans, who fled at his onslaught. [15]When the Ammonites saw that the Aramaeans had fled, they too fled from his brother Abishai and withdrew into the city. Joab then returned to Jerusalem.

Victory over the Aramaeans

[16]The Aramaeans, realising that Israel had got the better of them, sent messengers and mobilised the Aramaeans living on the other side of the River, with Shophach, commander of Hadadezer's army, at their head. [17]David, being informed of this, mustered all Israel, crossed the Jordan, made contact with them and took up position near them. David drew up his line of battle facing the Aramaeans, who then engaged him. [18]But the Aramaeans fled from Israel, and David killed seven thousand of their chariot teams and forty thousand men; and also Shophach, the commander of the army. [19]When Hadadezer's vassals saw that Israel had got the better of them, they made peace with David and became his subjects. The Aramaeans were unwilling to give any more help to the Ammonites.

The second Ammonite campaign

20 At the turn of the year, at the time when kings go campaigning, Joab led out the troops and, having ravaged the Ammonites' territory, proceeded to lay siege to Rabbah. David, however, remained in Jerusalem. Joab reduced Rabbah and dismantled it. [2]David took the crown off Milcom's head and found that it weighed a talent of gold, and in it was set a precious stone which went on David's head instead. He carried off great quantities of booty from the city. [3]And he expelled its inhabitants, setting them to work with saws, iron picks and axes. David treated all the Ammonite towns in the same way. David and all the people then returned to Jerusalem.

Various exploits against the Philistines

[4]After this war broke out with the Philistines at Gezer. This was when Sibbecai of Hushah killed Sippai, one of the Rephaim, and the Philistines were subdued.

[5]Again, war with the Philistines broke out,

and Elhanan son of Jair killed Lahmi brother
of Goliath of Gath, the shaft of whose spear
was like a weaver's beam.
6There was further warfare at Gath, where
there was a man of huge stature with six
fingers on each hand and six toes on each
foot, twenty-four in all. He too was a son of
Rapha. 7When he defied Israel, Jonathan son
of Shimea, brother of David cut him down.
8These men were sons of Rapha in Gath
and fell at the hands of David and his guards.

C: PRELUDE TO THE BUILDING OF THE TEMPLE

The census

21 Satan took his stand against Israel and
incited David to take a census of Israel.
2David said to Joab and the people's princes,
'Go, and take a census of Israel, from Beer-
sheba to Dan, then bring it back to me and
let me know the total.' 3Joab replied, 'May
Yahweh multiply his people to a hundred
times what they are today! But my lord king,
are they not all my lord's servants in any case?
Why should my lord insist on this? Why
should he involve Israel in guilt?' 4But the
king enforced his order on Joab, and Joab set
out, travelled throughout all Israel, and then
returned to Jerusalem. 5Joab gave David the
census results for the people: all Israel had
eleven hundred thousand men who could
wield a sword; Judah had four hundred and
seventy thousand men who could wield a
sword. 6Joab had found the king's command
so distasteful that he did not include Levi
and Benjamin.

The pestilence. God's forgiveness

7God looked with displeasure on this and
punished Israel in consequence. 8David then
said to God, 'I have committed a grave sin by
doing this. But now I beg you to forgive your
servant for this fault, for I have acted very
foolishly.' 9Yahweh then spoke to Gad,
David's seer, 10'Go and say to David,
"Yahweh says this: I offer you three things;
choose which one of them I am to inflict on
you."' 11So Gad went to David and said,
'Yahweh says this, 12"Take your choice
between three years of famine; or three
months of disaster at the hands of your
enemies, with your enemies' sword over-
taking you; or three days of Yahweh's sword,
an epidemic in the country, while the angel
of Yahweh wreaks havoc throughout the
territory of Israel." Now decide how I am to
answer him who sends me.' 13David said to
Gad, 'I am very apprehensive. Better for me
to fall into Yahweh's hand, since his mercies
are very great, than for me to fall into the
hands of human enemies.'
14So Yahweh unleashed an epidemic on
Israel, and seventy thousand Israelites
succumbed. 15Next, God sent the angel to
Jerusalem to destroy it, but as he was about
to destroy it, Yahweh looked down and felt
sorry about the calamity; and he said to the
destroying angel, 'Enough now! Hold your
hand!' The angel of Yahweh was standing by
the threshing-floor of Ornan the Jebusite.
16David, raising his eyes, saw the angel of
Yahweh standing between earth and heaven,
a drawn sword in his hand stretched out
towards Jerusalem. David and the elders
then put on sackcloth and fell on their faces,
17and David said to God, 'Did I not order the
people to be counted? I was the one who
sinned and actually committed the wrong.
But these, the flock, what have they done?
Yahweh my God, let your hand lie heavy on
me and on my family; but spare your people
from the plague!'

The altar is built

18The angel of Yahweh then ordered Gad to
tell David that David should go up and erect
an altar to Yahweh on the threshing-floor of
Ornan the Jebusite. 19So, at Gad's bidding,
given in Yahweh's name, David went up.
20Ornan had turned round and seen the angel,
and he and his four sons with him had hidden.
21When David arrived Ornan was threshing
wheat. He looked up and saw David and
came off the threshing-floor and prostrated
himself on the ground at David's feet.
22David then said to Ornan, 'Let me have the
site of the threshing-floor, so that I can build
an altar to Yahweh on it; let me have it at the
full price—so that the plague may be lifted
from the people.' Ornan said to David,
23'Take it, and let my lord the king do what
he thinks fit. Look, I shall give you the oxen
for burnt offerings, the threshing-sleds for
the wood and the wheat for the oblation. I
shall give everything.'
24'No,' said King David to Ornan, 'I insist
on buying it at the full price. I will not offer

Yahweh what belongs to you or bring burnt
offerings which have cost me nothing.' 25So
David gave Ornan six hundred shekels of
gold by weight for the site.
26There David built an altar to Yahweh and
brought burnt offerings and peace offerings.
He called on Yahweh, and Yahweh answered
him with fire from heaven on the altar of
burnt offering. 27Then Yahweh ordered the
angel to sheathe his sword. 28Whereupon,
seeing that Yahweh had answered him on the
threshing-floor of Ornan the Jebusite, David
offered sacrifice there. 29The Dwelling which
Moses had made in the desert and the altar
of burnt offering were at that time on the
high place at Gibeon, 30but David could not
go there to consult God because he was
terrified of the angel's sword.
22 David then said, 'This is to be the
house of Yahweh God and this the altar
of burnt offering for Israel.'

Preparations for the building of the Temple

2David then gave orders for all foreigners
in Israel to be rounded up, and appointed
quarrymen to cut dressed stone for building
the house of God. 3David also prepared great
quantities of iron to make nails for the leaves
of the doors and for the clamps, and more
bronze than could be weighed, 4as well as
innumerable cedar-wood logs, as the Sidon-
ians and Tyrians had brought cedar logs to
David in great quantities.
5David then said, 'My son Solomon is
young and immature, and the house to be
built for Yahweh must be superlatively fine,
the most famous and splendid in any country.
I shall now make the preparations for it.'
And so, before he died, David made ample
preparations. 6He then summoned his son
Solomon and commanded him to build a
house for Yahweh, God of Israel. 7'My son,'
David said to Solomon, 'my heart was set on
building a house for the name of Yahweh my
God. 8But the word of Yahweh came to me,
"You have shed much blood and fought great
wars; it is not for you to build a house for my
name, since you have shed much blood in my
sight on earth. 9Look, a son will be born to
you. He will be a man of peace, and I shall
give him peace from his enemies on all sides;
for Solomon is to be his name,[a] and in his
days I shall give Israel peace and tranquillity.
10He must build a house for my name; he will
be my son and I shall be his father, and I shall
make the throne of his kingdom secure over
Israel for ever." 11Now, my son, may
Yahweh be with you and give you success in
building a house for Yahweh your God, as he
has promised about you. 12And especially,
may Yahweh give you discretion and discern-
ment, may he give you his orders for Israel,
so that you may observe the Law of Yahweh
your God. 13Success will be yours, only if you
observe the statutes and ordinances which
Yahweh gave Moses as regulations for Israel.
Be strong and stand fast, be fearless, be
dauntless. 14Now, poor as I am, I have set
aside for the house of Yahweh a hundred
thousand talents of gold, a million talents of
silver and more bronze and iron than can be
weighed, there being so much. I have also
provided timber and stone, to which you may
add more. 15Furthermore, you have a large
number of workmen, quarrymen, masons,
carpenters and all sorts of craftsmen for every
kind of work, 16while your gold and silver,
bronze and iron will be beyond reckoning.
Set to work, then, and may Yahweh be with
you!'
17David then commanded all the leaders of
Israel to help his son Solomon. 18'Has not
Yahweh your God been with you and given
you peace on all sides, having put the inhabi-
tants of the country into my power and
the country now having been subdued for
Yahweh and his people? 19So now devote
heart and soul to searching for Yahweh your
God. Set to and build the sanctuary of
Yahweh God, so that you can bring the ark
of the covenant of Yahweh and the holy
vessels of God into the house built for the
name of Yahweh.'

The orders and functions of the Levites

23 When David had become old and full
of days, he made his son Solomon
king of Israel, 2and then summoned all the
leaders of Israel, with the priests and Levites.
3A census was taken of those Levites thirty
years old and upwards. On a count of heads,
they numbered thirty-eight thousand men;
4twenty-four thousand were responsible for
the service of the House of Yahweh, six
thousand were officials and judges, 5four

22a The name is here derived from *shalom* = peace.

thousand were gatekeepers and four thousand praised Yahweh on the instruments which David had made for praising him.

6 David then divided the Levites into classes: Gershon, Kohath and Merari.

7 Of the Gershonites there were Ladan and Shimei. 8 Sons of Ladan: Jehiel first, Zetham, Joel; three in all. 9 Sons of Shimei: Shelomoth, Haziel, Haran; three in all. These are the heads of families of Ladan. 10 Sons of Shimei: Jahath, Zina, Jeush, Beriah; these were the sons of Shimei; four in all. 11 Jahath was the eldest, Zizah the second, then Jeush and Beriah, who had not many children and were reckoned as one family.

12 Sons of Kohath: Amram, Izhar, Hebron, Uzziel; four in all. 13 Sons of Amram: Aaron and Moses. Aaron was set apart to consecrate the things that were especially holy, he and his sons for ever, to burn incense in the presence of Yahweh, to serve him and to bless in his name for ever. 14 Moses, man of God, and his sons were reckoned with the tribe of Levi. 15 Sons of Moses: Gershom and Eliezer. 16 Sons of Gershom: Shebuel, the first. 17 Of the sons of Eliezer, Rehabiah was the first. Eliezer had no other sons, but the sons of Rehabiah were very numerous. 18 Sons of Izhar: Shelomith, the first. 19 Sons of Hebron: Jeriah first, Amariah second, Jahaziel third, Jekameam fourth. 20 Sons of Uzziel: Micah first, Isshiah second.

21 Sons of Merari: Mahli and Mushi. Sons of Mahli: Eleazar and Kish. 22 Eleazar died without sons, but he did have daughters, whom their cousins, the sons of Kish, married. 23 Sons of Mushi: Mahli, Eder, Jeremoth: three in all.

24 These were the sons of Levi by their families, the heads of families, and those registered by name, individually; whoever was twenty years old or upwards had his function in the service of the Temple of Yahweh.

25 For David said, 'Since Yahweh, God of Israel, has given rest to his people Israel and has taken up residence in Jerusalem for ever, 26 the Levites need no longer carry the Dwelling or any of the objects required for its service.' 27 For, according to the last words of David, the Levites who had been registered were of twenty years and upwards. 28 Their duty now is to help the sons of Aaron in the service of the House of Yahweh, in the care of the courts and rooms, the purification of all the holy things, the work for the service of the House of God, 29 the loaves of permanent offering, the flour for the oblation, the wafers of unleavened bread, the pan-baked materials, the unmixed materials and all measures of volume and length. 30 Furthermore, they have to be present every morning to give thanks and praise to Yahweh, and also in the evening, 31 and at the bringing of every burnt offering to Yahweh on Sabbath, New Moon or solemn feast, appearing regularly before Yahweh in accordance with the numbers required of them. 32 In serving the Temple of Yahweh they observe the ritual of the Tent of Meeting, the ritual of the sanctuary and the ritual of their kinsmen, the sons of Aaron.'

The classification of the priests

24 Orders of the sons of Aaron: Sons of Aaron: Nadab, Abihu, Eleazar, Ithamar. 2 Nadab and Abihu died in their father's lifetime leaving no children, so Eleazar and Ithamar filled the office of priest. 3 With Zadok of the sons of Eleazar, and Ahimelech of the sons of Ithamar, David allocated them according to the classification of their duties. 4 Since the sons of Eleazar were found to have more headmen than the sons of Ithamar, they allocated sixteen heads of families to the sons of Eleazar and eight heads of families to the sons of Ithamar. 5 They allocated them by lot, both alike, there being religious officials and officials of God among the sons of Eleazar, as among the sons of Ithamar. 6 The levitical scribe Shemaiah son of Nethanel, recorded them in the presence of the king, the leaders, Zadok the priest, Ahimelech son of Abiathar and the heads of the priestly and levitical families, so that two families were selected for Eleazar for each one selected for Ithamar.

7 The first lot fell to Jehoiarib, the second to Jedaiah, 8 the third to Harim, the fourth to Seorim, 9 the fifth to Malchijah, the sixth to Mijamin, 10 the seventh to Hakkoz, the eighth to Abijah, 11 the ninth to Jeshua, the tenth to Shecaniah, 12 the eleventh to Eliashib, the twelfth to Jakim, 13 the thirteenth to Huppah, the fourteenth to Ishbaal, 14 the fifteenth to Bilgah, the sixteenth to Immer, 15 the seventeenth to Hezir, the eighteenth to Happizzez, 16 the nineteenth to Pethahiah, the twentieth to Jehezkel, 17 the twenty-first to Jachin, the twenty-second to Gamul, 18 the twenty-

third to Delaiah and the twenty-fourth to
Maaziah.
19 These were their classifications for their
duties when they entered the House of
Yahweh in accordance with their prescrip-
tions laid down by Aaron their ancestor as
Yahweh, God of Israel, had commanded
him.
20 As regards the rest of the sons of Levi:
Of the sons of Amram: Shubael. Of the
sons of Shubael: Jehdeiah. 21 As regards
Rehabiah, of the sons of Rehabiah: Isshiah,
the first one. 22 Of the sons of Izhar: Shelo-
moth; of the sons of Shelomoth: Jahath. 23 Of
the sons of Hebron: Jeriah the first, Amariah
the second, Jahaziel the third, Jekameam the
fourth. 24 The son of Uzziel was Micah; of the
sons of Micah: Shamir. 25 The brother of
Micah was Isshiah; of the sons of Isshiah,
Zechariah. 26 The sons of Merari were Mahli
and Mushi; of his sons: Jaaziah his son.
27 The sons of Merari by his son Jaaziah were
Shoham, Zaccur and Ibri. 28 Of Mahli, there
was Eleazar who had no sons, 29 and Kish;
and of the sons of Kish: Jerahmeel. 30 The
sons of Mushi were Mahli, Eder and
Jerimoth.
These were the Levites according to
families. 31 Like their kinsmen, the sons of
Aaron, these heads of families, senior and
junior alike, also drew lots in the presence of
King David, Zadok, Ahimelech, and the
heads of the priestly and levitical families.

The cantors

25 For the liturgy, David and the religious
officials selected the sons of Asaph,
of Heman and of Jeduthun, who were to
prophesy to the accompaniment of harps,
lyres and cymbals. The list of ministrants for
this service was as follows:
2 Of the sons of Asaph: Zaccur, Joseph,
Nethaniah, Asharelah; the sons of Asaph
were under the direction of Asaph who
prophesied at the king's direction.
3 Of Jeduthun there were the sons of Jedu-
thun: Gedaliah, Zeri, Jeshaiah, Hashabiah
and Mattithiah, six, under the direction of
their father Jeduthun who, with the harp,
prophesied when thanks and praise were to
be given to Yahweh.
4 Of Heman there were the sons of Heman:
Bukkiah, Mattaniah, Uzziel, Shebuel,
Jerimoth, Hananiah, Hanani, Eliathah,
Giddalti, Romamti-Ezer, Joshbekashah,
Mallothi, Hothir, Mahazioth. 5 All these were
sons of Heman, the king's seer; at God's
word they blew the horn. God gave Heman
fourteen sons and three daughters. 6 Under
the king's direction all these had the duty of
singing to the accompaniment of cymbal,
lyre and harp for the liturgy of the house of
God under the direction of their fathers.
Asaph, Jeduthun and Heman, 7 trained in
the songs of Yahweh, with their brothers,
numbered two hundred and eighty-eight, all
expert. 8 Junior and senior, master and pupil
alike, they drew lots for their term of duty.
9 The first to whom the lot fell was the
Asaphite, Joseph. The second was Gedaliah,
who with his sons and brothers made twelve.
10 The third was Zaccur, who with his sons
and brothers made twelve. 11 The fourth was
Izri, who with his sons and brothers made
twelve. 12 The fifth was Nethaniah, who with
his sons and brothers made twelve. 13 The
sixth was Bukkiah, who with his sons and
brothers made twelve. 14 The seventh was
Jesharelah, who with his sons and brothers
made twelve. 15 The eighth was Jeshaiah, who
with his sons and brothers made twelve.
16 The ninth was Mattaniah, who with his
sons and brothers made twelve. 17 The tenth
was Shimei, who with his sons and brothers
made twelve. 18 The eleventh was Azarel, who
with his sons and brothers made twelve.
19 The twelfth was Hashabiah, who with his
sons and brothers made twelve. 20 The thir-
teenth was Shubael, who with his sons and
brothers made twelve. 21 The fourteenth was
Mattithiah, who with his sons and brothers
made twelve. 22 The fifteenth was Jeremoth,
who with his sons and brothers made twelve.
23 The sixteenth was Hananiah, who with
his sons and brothers made twelve. 24 The
seventeenth was Joshbekashah, who with
his sons and brothers made twelve. 25 The
eighteenth was Hanani, who with his sons
and brothers made twelve. 26 The nineteenth
was Mallothi, who with his sons and brothers
made twelve. 27 The twentieth was Eliathah,
who with his sons and brothers made twelve.
28 The twenty-first was Hothir, who with
his sons and brothers made twelve. 29 The
twenty-second was Giddalti, who with his
sons and brothers made twelve. 30 The
twenty-third was Mahazioth, who with his
sons and brothers made twelve. 31 The
twenty-fourth was Romamti-Ezer, who with
his sons and brothers made twelve.

The gatekeepers

26 As regards the orders of the gate-
keepers:
Of the Korahites there was Meshelemiah
son of Kore, one of the sons of Ebiasaph,
2and Meshelemiah's sons: Zechariah the
first-born, Jediael the second, Zebadiah the
third, Jathniel the fourth, 3Elam the fifth,
Jehohanan the sixth, Elioenai the seventh.
4Obed-Edom's sons were: Shemaiah the
first-born, Jehozabad the second, Joah the
third, Sacar the fourth, Nethanel the fifth,
5Ammiel the sixth, Issachar the seventh,
Peullethai the eighth; God had indeed blessed
him. 6His son Shemaiah also had sons who
wielded authority in their family, because
they were men of outstanding quality. 7The
sons of Shemaiah were: Othni, Rephael,
Obed and Elzabad, whose brothers Elihu and
Semachiah were outstanding men. 8All these
were sons of Obed-Edom, who with their
sons and brothers were men of standing, well
fitted for their task. Obed-Edom had sixty-
two.
9Meshelemiah had eighteen outstanding
sons and brothers.
10Hosah, one of the sons of Merari, had
sons: Shimri was the first, for although he
was not the first-born his father had made
him the chief. 11Hilkiah was the second,
Tebaliah the third, Zechariah the fourth:
Hosah had thirteen sons and brothers
in all.
12These orders of gatekeepers, allocated
according to their headmen, had duties, just
like their brothers, of serving in the house of
Yahweh. 13Similarly, they drew lots for each
gate, whether their families were large or
small. 14For the eastern one, the lot fell to
Shelemiah; and when they drew lots for
Zechariah his son, a shrewd counsellor, his
lot came out for the north. 15To Obed-Edom
went the south, and to his sons the store-
houses. 16To Shuppim and Hosah went the
west with the Gate of the Felled Tree-trunk
on the upper road. The corresponding guards
were as follows: 17for the east gate, six per
day; for the north gate, four per day; for the
south gate, four per day; for the storehouses,
two each; 18for the Parbar at the west gate,
four by the road and two for the Parbar.
19These were the orders of the gatekeepers
of the sons of Korah and the sons of
Merari.

Other levitical duties

20The Levites, their brothers, who were
responsible for the treasures of the house of
God and for the treasures of consecrated
gifts, 21were the sons of Ladan and belonged
to the Gershonites—the heads of the families
of Ladan were descended from Ladan the
Gershonite—that is to say, the Jehielites.
22The sons of the Jehielites, Zetham and
Joel his brother, were responsible for the
treasures of the house of Yahweh.
23Over the Amramites, Izharites, Hebron-
ites, and Uzzielites 24was Shebuel son of
Gershom, son of Moses, who was governor
of the treasures; 25and his brothers of the line
of Eliezer were Rehabiah his son, Jeshaiah
his son, Joram his son, Zichri his son and
Shelomoth his son. 26This Shelomoth and
his kinsmen were responsible for all the
consecrated treasures dedicated by King
David, by the heads of families, by the
commanders of the thousands and hundreds
and by the commanders of the army, 27who
had dedicated a part of the spoils of war to
the service of the house of Yahweh, 28and
also for all that Samuel the seer, Saul son of
Kish, Abner son of Ner and Joab son of
Zeruiah had dedicated. In fact, whatever was
dedicated was the responsibility of Shelo-
moth and his kinsmen.
29Of the Izharites, Chananiah and his sons
were assigned to secular duties for Israel as
officials and judges.
30Of the Hebronites, Hashabiah and his
kinsmen, one thousand seven hundred
outstanding men were in charge of Israel west
of Jordan in everything pertaining to Yahweh
and to the service of the king. 31Of the
Hebronites, Jerijah was the head. In the
fortieth year of David's reign research was
done on the lineage and relationships of the
Hebronites, and men of outstanding quality
from among them were found at Jazer in
Gilead. 32There were twenty-seven hundred
outstanding men, heads of families, whom
King David put in charge of the Reubenites,
the Gadites and the half-tribe of Manasseh in
all matters pertaining to God and the king.

Military and civil organisation

27 The Israelites listed according to heads
of families, commanders of thousands
and hundreds, with their officials in the
king's service who dealt with all matters

affecting the companies on monthly duty, month by month throughout the year, each company consisting of twenty-four thousand men:

2 The commander of the first company detailed for the first month was Jashobeam son of Zabdiel, whose company consisted of twenty-four thousand men. 3 He belonged to the family of Perez and was the senior military officer of all those detailed for the first month.

4 The commander of the company for the second month was Dodai the Ahohite, whose company consisted of twenty-four thousand men.

5 The officer commanding the third body of men for the third month was Benaiah son of Jehoiada, the chief priest, whose company consisted of twenty-four thousand men. 6 This was the Benaiah who was an important member of the Thirty and his company. His son was Ammizabad.

7 The fourth for the fourth month was Asahel brother of Joab, and his son Zebadiah after him, whose company consisted of twenty-four thousand men.

8 The fifth officer commanding for the fifth month was Shamhuth the Zerahite, whose company consisted of twenty-four thousand men.

9 The sixth for the sixth month was Ira son of Ikkesh of Tekoa, whose company consisted of twenty-four thousand men.

10 The seventh for the seventh month was Helez the Pelonite, one of the Ephraimites, whose company consisted of twenty-four thousand men.

11 The eighth for the eighth month was Sibbecai of Hushah, a Zerahite, whose company consisted of twenty-four thousand men.

12 The ninth for the ninth month was Abiezer of Anathoth, a Benjaminite, whose company consisted of twenty-four thousand men.

13 The tenth for the tenth month was Maharai of Netophah, a Zerahite, whose company consisted of twenty-four thousand men.

14 The eleventh for the eleventh month was Benaiah of Pirathon, an Ephraimite, whose company consisted of twenty-four thousand men.

15 The twelfth for the twelfth month was Heldai of Netophah, of Othniel, whose company consisted of twenty-four thousand men.

List of tribal chiefs

16 Responsible for the tribes of Israel were chief Eliezer son of Zichri for the Reubenites, Shephatiah son of Maacah for the Simeonites, 17 Hashabiah son of Kemuel for the Levites, Zadok for the Aaronites, 18 Elihu, one of David's brothers, for Judah, Omri son of Michael for Issachar, 19 Ishmaiah son of Obadiah for Zebulun, Jerimoth son of Azriel for Naphtali, 20 Hoshea son of Azaziah for the Ephraimites, Joel son of Pedaiah for the half-tribe of Manasseh, 21 Iddo son of Zechariah for the half-tribe of Manasseh in Gilead, Jaasiel son of Abner for Benjamin, 22 and Azarel son of Jeroham for Dan.

These were the tribal chiefs of Israel.

The uncompleted census

23 Now in the census David did not include those who were twenty years old and under, since Yahweh had promised to make Israel as numerous as the stars of heaven. 24 Joab son of Zeruiah began the count but never finished. This is why retribution came upon Israel, and the number did not come up to that recorded in the annals of King David.

25 Overseer of the king's supplies: Azmaveth son of Adiel. Overseer of supplies in the countryside, towns, villages and fortresses: Jonathan son of Uzziah. 26 Overseer of the farmers who tilled the land: Ezri son of Chelub. 27 Overseer of vineyards: Shimei of Ramah. Overseer of those in the vineyards who looked after the wine cellars: Zabdi of Shepham. 28 Overseer of olive and sycamore trees in the Shephelah: Baal-Hanan of Geder. Overseer of oil supplies: Joash. 29 Overseer of cattle at pasture in the plains of Sharon: Shitrai of Sharon. Overseer of cattle in the valleys: Shaphat son of Adlai. 30 Overseer of camels: Obil the Ishmaelite. 31 Overseer of donkeys: Jehdeiah of Meranoth. Overseer of flocks: Jaziz the Hagrite.

All the above supervised the property belonging to King David.

The king's personal advisers

32 Jonathan, David's uncle, a councillor, wise man and scribe, and Jehiel son of Hachmoni took care of the king's sons. 33 Ahitophel was the king's counsellor and Hushai, the Archite, was Friend of the King. 34 Jehoiada son of Benaiah and Abiathar succeeded

Ahitophel—Joab was commander of the
king's army.

David's instructions for the Temple

28 David then summoned to Jerusalem all
the officials of Israel—the tribal chiefs,
the senior officials in the royal service, the
commanders of the thousands, the
commanders of the hundreds and the over-
seers of all the property and livestock
belonging to the king and to his sons—
including the court officials, the champions
and all the men of standing. 2King David
then rose to his feet and said:
'My brothers and my people, listen to me.
I have set my heart on building a settled home
for the ark of the covenant of Yahweh, for
the footstool for our God, but when I was
ready to build it, 3God said to me, "You must
not build a house for my name, for you have
been a man of war and have shed blood."
4'Even so, out of my entire family, it was
I whom Yahweh, God of Israel, chose to reign
over Israel for ever. Having chosen Judah as
leader, and my family out of the House of
Judah, it pleased him out of all my father's
sons to make me king of all Israel. 5Out of all
my sons—for Yahweh has given me many—
he has chosen my son Solomon to sit on
Yahweh's sovereign throne over Israel.
6Furthermore, he has told me, "Solomon
your son is the man to build my house and
my courts, for I have chosen him to be my
son and I shall be his father. 7I shall make his
sovereignty secure for ever if he sturdily
carries out my commandments and ordi-
nances as he does now."
8'So now in the sight of all Israel, the
assembly of Yahweh, and in the hearing of
our God, I charge you to observe and adhere
strictly to all the commandments of Yahweh
your God, so that you may retain possession
of this fine country and leave it to your sons
after you as a heritage for ever.
9'And you, Solomon my son, know the
God of your father and serve him with an
undivided heart and willing mind; for
Yahweh scrutinises all hearts and under-
stands whatever plans they may devise. If
you seek him, he will let you find him; but
forsake him and he will cast you off for ever.
10So, since Yahweh has chosen you to build
a house for his sanctuary, go resolutely to
work!'
11David then gave his son Solomon the
plans for the portico, the plans for the build-
ings, its storehouses, its upper rooms, its
inner rooms and the room for the throne of
mercy 12as well as the plans for everything
that he had in mind: for the courts of the
house of Yahweh, for all the surrounding
rooms, for the treasuries of the house of God
and for the sacred treasuries, 13for the orders
of priests and Levites, for all the duties to be
carried out in the service of the house of
Yahweh, and for all the liturgical objects to
be used in the house of Yahweh; 14for the
gold bullion, for all the golden liturgical
objects of various uses; for the silver bullion,
for all the silver liturgical objects of various
uses; 15for the gold bullion for the golden
lamp-stands and for their lamps, and for the
silver bullion for the silver lamp-stands and
their lights, depending on the function of
each lamp-stand; 16for the gold bullion for
each of the tables for the loaves of permanent
offering and the silver for the silver tables;
17for the pure gold for the forks, the bowls
and the jars, for the gold bullion for each of
the golden basins and for the silver bullion
for each of the silver basins; 18and for the
refined gold bullion for the altar of incense;
also for the gold for the model of the chariot
and of the great winged creatures which cover
the ark of the covenant of Yahweh with wings
outspread—19all this was in the document
conveying Yahweh's instructions, by which
he revealed the pattern of what was to be
done.
20David then said to his son Solomon, 'Be
resolute and courageous in your work, do not
be afraid or disheartened, because Yahweh
God, my God, is with you. He will not fail
you or forsake you before you have finished
all the work to be done for the house of
Yahweh. 21And besides, there are the orders
of priests and Levites for whatever is needed
in connection with the house of God, and you
have at your disposal every kind of craftsman
for whatever has to be done, as well as the
officials and all the people entirely at your
command.'

The voluntary offerings

29 David then addressed the whole
assembly, 'Solomon my son, whom
Yahweh has specifically chosen, is young and
immature, and the work is great; this palace
is not for any human being but for Yahweh
God. 2With all the resources I can command,

for the house of my God I have provided gold
for what must be made of gold, silver for
what must be made of silver, bronze for what
must be made of bronze, iron for what must
be made of iron, wood for what must be made
of wood, as well as cornelian for inlay work,
slabs of multi-coloured mosaic, every kind of
precious stone and quantities of alabaster.
3Furthermore, because my affections are set
on the house of my God, I have also given
what gold and silver I personally own for
the house of my God, over and above every-
thing which I have already provided for the
holy Temple—4that is to say, three thou-
sand talents of gold of Ophir, and seven
thousand talents of refined silver for over-
laying the walls of the buildings, 5the gold
being for what must be made of gold, and the
silver for what must be made of silver: and
for whatever the craftsmen must make. Who,
then, is willing to devote himself to Yahweh's
service today?'

6At this, the heads of families, the tribal
chiefs of Israel, the commanders of the thou-
sands and the hundreds and those who
managed the king's affairs, 7volunteered a
gift of five thousand talents and ten thousand
darics of gold, ten thousand talents of silver,
eighteen thousand talents of bronze and a
hundred thousand talents of iron, 8while
those who owned precious stones presented
them to the treasury of the house of Yahweh
in the custody of Jehiel the Gershonite. 9The
people rejoiced at what these had given so
readily, since they had presented their free-
will offerings wholeheartedly to Yahweh.
King David too was filled with joy.

David's thanksgiving

10Hence, in the presence of the whole
assembly David blessed Yahweh. David said:

'May you be blessed, Yahweh, God of
Israel our ancestor, for ever and for ever!
11Yours, Yahweh, is the greatness, the
power, the splendour, length of days and
glory, everything in heaven and on earth is
yours. Yours is the sovereignty, Yahweh;
you are exalted, supreme over all. 12Wealth
and riches come from you, you are ruler of
all, in your hand lie strength and power, and
you bestow greatness and might on whomso-
ever you please. 13So now, our God, we give
thanks to you and praise your majestic name,
14for who am I and what is my people, for us
to be able to volunteer offerings like this?—
since everything has come from you and we
have given you only what you bestowed in
the first place, 15and we are guests before
you, and passing visitors as were all our
ancestors, our days on earth fleeting as a
shadow and without hope. 16Yahweh our
God, all this wealth, which we have provided
to build a house for your holy name, has come
from you and all belongs to you.

17'Knowing, my God, how you examine
our motives and how you delight in integrity,
with integrity of motive I have willingly given
all this and have been overjoyed to see your
people, now present here, willingly offering
their gifts to you. 18Yahweh, God of
Abraham, Isaac and Israel our ancestors,
watch over this for ever, shape the purpose
of your people's heart and direct their hearts
to you, 19and give an undivided heart to
Solomon my son to keep your command-
ments, your decrees and your statutes, to put
them all into effect and to build the palace
for which I have made provision.'

20David then addressed the whole
assembly: 'Now bless Yahweh your God!'
And the whole assembly blessed Yahweh,
God of their ancestors, bowing down in
homage to Yahweh, and to the king.

Accession of Solomon and the end of the reign of David

21On the day following this, they slaughtered
sacrifices and brought burnt offerings to
Yahweh on behalf of Israel—a thousand
bulls, a thousand rams, a thousand lambs
with their libations, as well as many other
sacrifices—22and they ate and drank that day
in Yahweh's presence with great joy. They
then made Solomon son of David king a
second time, anointing him as leader for
Yahweh, and Zadok as priest. 23Solomon
took his seat on Yahweh's throne, to reign in
succession to David his father. He prospered,
and all Israel obeyed him. 24All the chiefs, all
the leading citizens and all King David's
other sons pledged allegiance to King
Solomon. 25Yahweh made Solomon exceed-
ingly powerful, as all Israel could see, and
gave him a reign of such splendour as no
previous king of Israel ever had.

26David son of Jesse was king of all Israel.
27He was king of Israel for a period of forty
years; he reigned at Hebron for seven years,
and in Jerusalem for thirty-three. 28He died
at a good old age, full of days, riches and

honour. Then his son Solomon succeeded
him. 29The history of King David, from first
to last, is all written down in the records of
Samuel the seer, the records of Nathan the
prophet and the records of Gad the seer,
30with his entire reign, his mighty deeds and
the times which he, Israel and all the kings
of other countries, had experienced.

THE SECOND BOOK OF CHRONICLES

III: SOLOMON AND THE BUILDING OF THE TEMPLE

God confers wisdom on Solomon

1 Solomon son of David then made himself
secure over his kingdom. Yahweh his God
was with him, making him more and more
powerful. 2Solomon then spoke to all Israel,
to the commanders of thousands and of
hundreds, to the judges and to every leader
in all Israel, the heads of families. 3Solomon,
and the whole assembly with him, then went
to the high place at Gibeon, where God's
Tent of Meeting was, which Moses, servant
of God, had made in the desert. 4The ark of
the covenant, however, David had brought
from Kiriath-Jearim to the place which he
had prepared for it, having pitched a tent for
it in Jerusalem. 5The bronze altar which
Bezalel son of Uri, son of Hur, had made was
there, in front of Yahweh's Dwelling, where
Solomon and the assembly consulted him.
6There Solomon presented a burnt offering
before Yahweh on the bronze altar of the
Tent of Meeting, making on it one thousand
burnt offerings.
7That night God appeared to Solomon and
said, 'Ask what you would like me to give
you.' 8Solomon replied to God, 'You showed
most faithful love to David my father, and
you have made me king in succession to him.
9Yahweh God, the promise you made to
David my father has now been fulfilled, since
you have made me king over a people as
numerous as the dust of the earth.
10Therefore give me wisdom and knowledge
to act as leader of this people, for how other-
wise could such a great people as yours be
governed?'
11'Since that is what you want,' God said
to Solomon, 'since you have asked, not for
riches, treasure, honour, the lives of your
enemies, or even for a long life, but for
wisdom and knowledge to govern my people
of whom I have made you king, 12therefore
wisdom and knowledge are granted you. I
give you riches too, and treasure, and honour
such as no king had before you and none will
have after you.'
13So Solomon came away from the high
place at Gibeon, from the Tent of Meeting,
to Jerusalem and reigned over Israel.
14Solomon then built up a force of chariots
and cavalry; he had one thousand four
hundred chariots and twelve thousand
horses; these he kept in the chariot towns and
near the king at Jerusalem. 15In Jerusalem
the king made silver and gold as common
as stones, and cedar wood as plentiful as
sycamore in the lowlands. 16Solomon's horses
were imported from Muzur and Cilicia. The
king's dealers acquired them in Cilicia at the
prevailing price. 17A chariot was imported
from Egypt for six hundred silver shekels
and a horse from Cilicia for a hundred and
fifty. They also supplied the Hittite and
Aramaean kings, who all used them as
middlemen.

The final preparations. Huram of Tyre

18Solomon then gave the order to build a
house for the name of Yahweh and a palace
in which to reign.
2 And Solomon allocated seventy thousand
men to be porters and eighty thousand to
quarry in the hills and three thousand six
hundred overseers for them. 2And Solomon
sent this message to Huram king of Tyre,
'Do as you did for my father David when you
sent him cedars for him to build himself a
palace to live in. 3You see, I am building a
house for the name of Yahweh my God, to
acknowledge his holiness so that perfumed
incense may be burnt before him, the loaves
of permanent offering be perpetually laid out
and the burnt offerings be made morning and

evening, on the Sabbaths, New Moons and
solemn festivals of Yahweh our God, as
prescribed to Israel for ever; 4and the house
which I am building must be large, for our
God is greater than all gods; 5even so, who
would not find it an impossible task to build
a house for him, when the heavens and the
heavens of the heavens cannot contain him?
And who am I to build a house for him except
to burn incense before him? 6So now send
me a man skilled at working in gold, silver,
bronze, iron, scarlet, crimson and violet
materials, and who knows the art of
engraving too; he is to work with my skilled
men in Judah and Jerusalem, whom my
father David has provided. 7Also send me
cedar, juniper and *algum* trunks from the
Lebanon, for I know that your servants know
the art of felling timber in the Lebanon. And,
my servants will work with your servants 8in
preparing a vast quantity of timber for me,
since the house which I intend to build is to
be of a size to marvel at. 9Furthermore, for
the upkeep of the woodcutters whom you
employ to cut the timber, I shall provide
twenty thousand *kor* of wheat, twenty thou-
sand *kor* of barley, twenty thousand *bat* of
wine and twenty thousand *bat* of oil.'

10In a letter sent to King Solomon, Huram
king of Tyre replied, 'Because Yahweh loves
his people he has made you their king!'
11Huram went on to say, 'Praised be Yahweh,
God of Israel, who made heaven and earth
and has given King David a wise son,
endowed with discretion and discernment,
to build a house for Yahweh and a palace in
which to reign!—12I am now sending you a
skilled and intelligent man, Huram-Abi 13the
son of a Danite woman by a Tyrian father.
He knows the arts of working in gold, silver,
bronze, iron, stone, wood, scarlet, violet,
fine linen and crimson materials, and is
competent to carry out any kind of engraving
and to execute any design which may be
entrusted to him, in collaboration with your
skilled men and those of my lord David, your
father.

14'So now let my lord send his servants the
wheat, barley, oil and wine as promised 15and
we will fell all the wood you need from
Lebanon, and bring it you in rafts by sea to
Jaffa; and it will be your responsibility to
transport it to Jerusalem.'

16Solomon then took a census of all the
aliens resident in Israel similar to the census
which his father David had taken; it was
found that there were a hundred and fifty-
three thousand six hundred. 17He impressed
seventy thousand of them as porters, eighty
thousand as quarrymen in the hills and three
thousand six hundred as overseers to make
sure the people worked.

Solomon builds the Temple

3Solomon then began building the house
of Yahweh in Jerusalem on Mount Moriah
where David his father had had a vision—on
the site which David had prepared—on the
threshing-floor of Ornan the Jebusite. 2He
began building it on the second day of the
second month of the fourth year of his reign.
3These are the dimensions which Solomon
fixed for the structure of the house of God:
its length in cubits, according to the old
standard, was sixty cubits and its width
twenty cubits; 4and the portico in front of the
house was the full width of the house, that
is, twenty cubits, and its height was a
hundred and twenty cubits; on the inside he
overlaid it with pure gold. 5The Great Hall
he lined with juniper, which he overlaid with
fine gold and ornamented with palm trees
and festoons, 6and he decorated the hall
beautifully with precious stones and with
gold from Parvaim, 7overlaying the hall, its
beams and its thresholds, its walls and its
doors, with gold and engraving the walls with
great winged creatures.

8He also made the Holy of Holies, the
length of which corresponded to the width
of the Great Hall, being twenty cubits, with
a width of twenty cubits, and this he overlaid
with fine gold weighing six hundred talents,
9while the weight of the gold nails was fifty
shekels. He also overlaid the upper rooms
with gold. 10In the Holy of Holies he modelled
two winged creatures of wrought metal work
and overlaid them with gold. 11The total span
of their wings was twenty cubits; one wing,
being five cubits long, touched the wall of
the house and the other wing, being five
cubits long, touched the wing of the other
winged creature; 12while one wing of the
other, five cubits long, touched the other wall
of the house and the other wing, five cubits
long, touched the wing of the other winged
creature. 13The spread of these creatures'
wings was twenty cubits. They stood in an
upright position, with their faces towards the
Hall.

14He also made the Curtain of violet,

scarlet, crimson and fine linen, working a
design of winged creatures on it.
15 In front of the Hall he made two pillars
thirty-five cubits high, and on the top of each
a capital measuring five cubits. 16 He made
festoons, in the Debir, to go at the tops of the
pillars, and made a hundred pomegranates
to go on the festoons. 17 He erected the pillars
in front of the Temple, one on the right, the
other on the left; the one on the right he
called Jachin and the one on the left, Boaz.

4 He made a bronze altar, twenty cubits
long, twenty cubits wide and ten cubits
high. 2 He made the Sea of cast metal, ten
cubits from rim to rim, circular in shape and
five cubits high; a cord thirty cubits long gave
the measurement of its girth. 3 Under it and
completely encircling it were things like
oxen, ten to the cubit round the entire Sea;
the oxen were in two rows, of one and the
same casting with the rest. 4 It rested on
twelve oxen, three facing north, three facing
west, three facing south, three facing east; on
these, their hindquarters all turned inwards,
stood the Sea. 5 It was a hand's breadth in
thickness, and its rim was shaped like the
rim of a cup—lily-shaped. It could hold three
thousand *bat*.
6 He made ten basins, putting five on the
right and five on the left, for washing in; the
things to be offered as burnt offerings were
to be rinsed in these, but the Sea was for the
priests to wash in. 7 He made the ten golden
lamp-stands according to the pattern and
placed them in the Hekal, five on the right
and five on the left. 8 He made ten tables
which he set up in the Hekal, five on the right
and five on the left. He also made a hundred
golden sprinkling bowls.
9 He made the court of the priests and the
great court with its gates and plated the gates
with bronze. 10 The Sea he placed on the right-
hand side of the Temple, to the south-east.
11 Huram made the ash containers, the
scoops and the sprinkling bowls. Thus
Huram completed all the work done for King
Solomon for the Temple of God: 12 the two
pillars; the mouldings of the capitals
surmounting the two pillars; the two sets of
filigree to cover the two mouldings of the
capitals surmounting the pillars; 13 the four
hundred pomegranates for the two sets of
filigree—two rows of pomegranates for each
set of filigree; 14 the ten stands and the ten
basins on the stands; 15 the one Sea and the
twelve oxen beneath it; 16 the ash containers,
scoops and forks.
All these utensils made by Huram-Abi for
King Solomon for the Temple of Yahweh
were of burnished bronze. 17 The King made
them by the process of sand casting, in the
plain of the Jordan between Succoth and
Zeredah. 18 There was such an enormous
quantity of them that the weight of the bronze
could not be calculated.
19 Solomon made all the objects designed
for the Temple of God, as well as the golden
altar and the tables for the loaves of perma-
nent offering; 20 the lamp-stands with their
lamps to burn, as prescribed, in front of the
Debir, of pure gold; 21 the floral work, the
lamps, the tongs, of gold (and it was pure
gold); 22 the snuffers, the sprinkling bowls,
incense ladles and the pans, of real gold; and
the entrance to the Temple, the inner doors
(for the Holy of Holies) and the doors of the
Temple itself, that is of the Hekal, were also
made of gold.

5 Thus all the work done by Solomon for
the Temple of Yahweh was completed,
and Solomon brought in the gifts which his
father David had consecrated; and he had
the silver, the gold and all the utensils put
into the treasuries of the Temple of God.

The ark is brought to the Temple

2 Solomon then assembled the elders of Israel
to Jerusalem, all the tribal chiefs, the princes
of the families of Israel, to bring the ark of
the covenant of Yahweh up from the City of
David, that is, Zion. 3 All the men of Israel
assembled round the king at the time of the
feast, that is, in the seventh month. 4 When
all the elders of Israel had arrived, the Levites
took up the ark; 5 they brought up the ark
and the Tent of Meeting and all the sacred
utensils which were in the Tent; the levitical
priests brought them up.
6 King Solomon and the whole assembly
of Israel present with him before the ark
sacrificed countless, innumerable sheep and
oxen. 7 The priests brought the ark of the
covenant of Yahweh to its place, in the Debir
of the Temple, that is, in the Holy of Holies,
under the wings of the winged creatures; 8 for
they spread their wings over the place where
the ark stood, forming a canopy over the ark
and its shafts. 9 The shafts were so long,
however, that the ends of the shafts of the
ark could be seen in front of the Holy Place

in front of the Debir, though they could not be seen from outside. They are still there today. [10]There was nothing in the ark except the two tablets which Moses had placed in it at Horeb, when Yahweh made a covenant with the Israelites when they came out of Egypt.

The Lord takes possession of his Temple

[11]Now when the priests came out of the Holy Place—for all the priests present had sanctified themselves regardless of the orders to which they belonged, [12]and all the levitical singers, Asaph, Heman and Jeduthun with their sons and brothers, dressed in linen, were standing to the east of the altar with cymbals, lyres and harps and with them one hundred and twenty priests blowing the trumpets, [13]and the harmony between trumpeters and singers was such that only one melody could be heard as they praised and gave thanks to Yahweh—and the singing began, to the accompaniment of trumpets, cymbals and musical instruments, and they praised Yahweh 'for he is good, for his faithful love is everlasting'—then the Temple was filled with the cloud of the glory of Yahweh, [14]and because of the cloud the priests could not stay and perform their duties. For the glory of Yahweh filled the Temple of God.

6 Then Solomon said:

Yahweh has chosen
to dwell in thick cloud,
[2]and I have built you a princely dwelling,
a residence for you for ever.

Solomon addresses the people

[3]Then the king turned round and blessed the whole assembly of Israel, while the whole assembly of Israel stood. [4]He said, 'Blessed be Yahweh, God of Israel, who has carried out by his hand what he promised verbally to my father David, when he said, [5]"From the day I brought my people out of Egypt I chose no city, in any of the tribes of Israel, to have a temple built where my name should be, nor did I choose anyone to be prince of my people Israel; [6]but I did choose Jerusalem for my name to be there, and I did choose David to rule my people Israel." [7]My father David had set his heart on building a temple for the name of Yahweh, God of Israel, [8]but Yahweh said to my father David, "You have set your heart on building a temple for my name, and in this you have done well; [9]and yet, you are not the man to build the temple; but your son, yet to be born to you, will be the one to build the temple for my name." [10]Yahweh has kept the promise which he made: I have succeeded my father David and am seated on the throne of Israel, as Yahweh promised; I have built the temple for the name of Yahweh, God of Israel, [11]and I have placed in it the ark containing the covenant of Yahweh, which he made with the Israelites.'

Solomon's prayer for himself

[12]Then in the presence of the whole assembly of Israel, he stood facing the altar of Yahweh and stretched out his hands—[13]for Solomon had made a bronze platform, five cubits long, five cubits wide and five cubits high, which he had placed in the middle of the court and on which he was standing; he knelt down in front of the whole assembly of Israel, stretched out his hands to heaven—[14]and said, 'Yahweh, God of Israel, there is no god like you in heaven or on earth, you who are loyal to the covenant and show faithful love to your servants as long as they walk wholeheartedly in your way. [15]You have kept it with your servant, my father David, as you promised him you would. What you promised verbally today you have carried out by your hand. [16]And now, Yahweh, God of Israel, keep the promise which you made to your servant David when you said, "You will never lack for a man to sit in my presence before me on the throne of Israel, provided that your sons are careful how they behave, following my law as you yourself have done." [17]So now, God of Israel, let the words come true which you spoke to your servant, my father David. [18]Yet will God really live with the people on earth? Why, the heavens and the heavens of the heavens cannot contain you! How much less this temple built by me! [19]Even so, listen favourably to the prayer and entreaty of your servant, Yahweh my God; listen to the cry and to the prayer which your servant makes to you: [20]Day and night, may your eyes watch over this temple, over this place in which you have promised to put your name. Listen to the prayer which your servant offers in this place.

Solomon's prayer for the people

21'Listen to the entreaties of your servant and
of your people Israel; whenever they pray in
this place, listen from the place where you
reside in heaven; and when you hear, forgive.
22'If someone has wronged his neighbour
and a curse is laid on him to make him swear
here before your altar in this Temple, 23then
listen from heaven and do justice between
your servants, paying back the guilty one
by making him suffer for his conduct, and
acquitting the upright by rewarding him as
his uprightness deserves.
24'If your people Israel are defeated by the
enemy because they have sinned against you,
but then return to you and acknowledge your
name, and pray and seek your favour in this
temple, 25then listen from heaven; forgive
the sin of your people Israel, and bring them
back to the country which you gave to them
and their ancestors.
26'When the heavens are shut and there is
no rain because they have sinned against you,
if they pray in this place and praise your name
and, having been humbled by you, desist
from their sin, 27then listen from heaven and
forgive the sin of your servant and of your
people Israel—for you are constantly
showing them the good way which they must
follow—and send rain on your country,
which you have given to your people as their
heritage.
28'Should there be famine in the country,
or pestilence, wind-blast or mildew, locust
or caterpillar; should their enemy lay siege
to their territory; should there be any plague
or any disease; 29whatever be the prayer or
entreaty of any individual, or of all your
people Israel, each being aware of his own
affliction and pain; when he stretches out his
hands towards this Temple, 30then listen
from heaven where you reside; forgive and,
since you know what is in his heart, deal with
each as his conduct deserves—for you alone
know what is in the human heart—31so that
they may revere you by following your direc-
tions, which you gave to our ancestors,
throughout their lives on earth.
32'Even the foreigner, not belonging to
your people Israel but coming from a distant
country, attracted by your great name, your
mighty hand and outstretched arm, if he
comes and prays in this Temple, 33then listen
from heaven where you reside, and grant all
that the foreigner asks of you, so that all the
peoples of the earth may acknowledge your
name and, like your people Israel, revere
you, and know that this Temple, which I
have built, bears your name.
34'If your people go out to war against
their enemies, on whatever mission you send
them, and they pray to you, turning towards
this city which you have chosen and towards
the Temple which I have built for your name,
35then listen from heaven to their prayer and
their entreaty, and uphold their cause.
36'When they sin against you—for there is
no one who does not sin—and you are angry
with them and abandon them to the enemy,
and their captors carry them off to a country
be it far away or near, 37if they come to their
senses in the country to which they have been
taken as captives and pray to you once again
in the country of their captivity, saying, "We
have sinned, we have acted wrongly and
wickedly," 38and turn back to you with all
their heart and soul in the country of their
captivity to which they have been carried
away as captives, and pray, turning towards
the country which you gave to their ances-
tors, towards the city you have chosen, and
towards the Temple which I have built for
your name, 39then listen from heaven where
you reside, hear their prayer and entreaties,
uphold their cause and forgive your people
for having sinned against you.

Conclusion of the prayer

40'Now, O my God, may your eyes be open
and your ears attentive to prayer offered in
this place. 41And now

Yahweh God, go up to your resting-place,
you and your fortress, the Ark!
Let your priests, Yahweh God,
be robed in salvation,
let your faithful rejoice in what is good!
42Yahweh God,
do not rebuff your Anointed—
remember the faithful love
of your servant David!'

The dedication

7 When Solomon had finished his prayer,
fire came down from heaven and con-
sumed the burnt offering and the sacrifices;
and the glory of Yahweh filled the Temple.
2The priests could not enter the Temple of
Yahweh, because the glory of Yahweh filled

the Temple of Yahweh. 3When all the Israel-
ites saw the fire come down and the glory of
Yahweh resting on the Temple, they bowed
down on the pavement with their faces to
the earth, worshipping and praising Yahweh
with 'For he is good, for his faithful love lasts
for ever!'

4Then the king and all the people offered
sacrifices before Yahweh. 5King Solomon
offered a sacrifice of twenty-two thousand
oxen and a hundred and twenty thousand
sheep; and thus the king and all the people
dedicated the Temple of God. 6The priests
stood in their places, as did the Levites with
Yahweh's musical instruments which King
David had provided, to render 'Give thanks
to Yahweh, for his faithful love lasts for
ever!' whenever David offered praise to their
accompaniment. Opposite them, the priests
blew trumpets, while all Israel stood.

7Solomon also consecrated the middle part
of the court in front of the Temple of Yahweh;
for that was where he presented the burnt
offerings and the fatty parts of the com-
munion sacrifices, since the bronze altar
which Solomon had made could not hold the
burnt offering, the oblation and the fatty
parts. 8And then Solomon and with him all
Israel from the Pass of Hamath to the Torrent
of Egypt—a very great assembly—celebrated
the feast for seven days. 9On the eighth day
they held the assembly, for they had devoted
seven days to the dedication of the altar
and seven days to the feast. 10On the twenty-
third day of the seventh month Solomon
dismissed the people to their homes, rejoicing
and happy of heart over the goodness which
Yahweh had shown to David, to Solomon
and to his people Israel.

Yahweh appears and gives a warning

11Thus Solomon finished the Temple of
Yahweh and the royal palace, and he success-
fully concluded everything that he was of a
mind to do in the Temple of Yahweh and in
his own palace. 12Then Yahweh appeared to
Solomon in the night and said, 'I have heard
your prayer and have chosen this place for
myself as a house of sacrifice. 13If I shut the
heavens so that there is no rain, or if I
command the locusts to devour the country,
or if I send pestilence among my people,
14if my people who bear my name humble
themselves, and pray and seek my presence
and turn from their wicked ways, then I will
listen from heaven and forgive their sins and
restore their country. 15Now and for the
future my eyes are open and my ears attentive
to prayer offered in this place, 16for now I
have chosen and consecrated this Temple,
for my name to be there for ever; my eyes
and my heart will constantly be there. 17And
if, for your part, you walk before me as your
father David did, and do everything that I
have commanded you to do, and keep my
laws and my ordinances, 18I shall make your
royal throne secure, as I covenanted with
your father David when I said: You will never
lack for a male to rule in Israel. 19But if
you turn away and forsake my laws and
commandments which I have laid down for
you, and go and serve other gods and worship
them, 20then I shall uproot them from the
country which I have given them, and shall
disown this Temple which I have consecrated
for my name and make it a proverb and a
byword among all the peoples. 21And at this
once-exalted Temple, everyone who passes
by will be appalled, and will say, "Why has
Yahweh treated this country and this Temple
like this?" 22And the answer will be,
"Because they deserted Yahweh, the God of
their ancestors, who brought them out of
Egypt, and adopted other gods and wor-
shipped and served them; that is why he has
brought all these disasters on them." '

Conclusion: The completion of the building programme

8 At the end of the twenty years which it
took Solomon to build the Temple of
Yahweh and his own palace, 2and to rebuild
the towns which Huram had given him and
settle them with Israelites, 3Solomon
mounted an expedition against Hamath-
Zobah and captured it. 4He also fortified
Tadmor in the desert and all the storage
towns which he had built in Hamath. 5He
also built Upper Beth-Horon and Lower
Beth-Horon as fortified towns with walls
and gates and bars, 6also Baalath and all
Solomon's storage towns, all the towns for
his chariots and horses, and everything which
Solomon was pleased to build in Jerusalem,
in the Lebanon and throughout the territory
under his rule. 7All those who survived of
the Hittite, Amorite, Perizzite, Hivite and
Jebusite peoples, who did not belong to
Israel—8those of their descendants still
remaining in the country, whom the Israelites

had not exterminated, these Solomon levied
for forced labour, as is still the case today.
[9]Solomon did not, however, impose forced
labour on the Israelites for his work—for
they were soldiers, his senior officers and his
chariot and cavalry commanders. [10]There
were two hundred and fifty of King Solo-
mon's officials in charge of the foremen who
supervised the people.

[11]Solomon moved Pharaoh's daughter up
from the City of David to the palace which
he had built for her. 'I must not be respon-
sible', he said, 'for a woman living in the
palace of David king of Israel, for these
buildings to which the ark of Yahweh has
come are sacred.'

[12]Thereafter, Solomon made burnt offer-
ings to Yahweh on the altar of Yahweh which
he had built in front of the portico, [13]in
accordance with the regular prescriptions for
burnt sacrifice as commanded by Moses, on
the Sabbaths, New Moons and the three
annual feasts; the feast of Unleavened Bread,
the feast of Weeks and the feast of Shelters.
[14]Following the prescriptions of his father
David, he assigned the orders of priests to
their duties and the Levites to their tasks of
praise and of assisting the priests in accord-
ance with day-to-day requirements; as also
the gatekeepers in their various orders to
each gate—for such was the command of
David, man of God. [15]Nor was there devi-
ation on any point from the king's command
as regards the priests, the Levites or even the
storehouses.

[16]Thus, all the work was over which
Solomon had put in hand when the Temple
of Yahweh was founded until it was finished.
The Temple of Yahweh was complete in
every detail.

Solomon in his glory

[17]Solomon then mounted an expedition to
Ezion-Geber and Elath on the sea-coast of
Edom. [18]Huram sent him ships through his
agents, as well as experienced sailors, who
went to Ophir with men in Solomon's service,
where they took on four hundred and fifty
talents of gold, which they brought back to
King Solomon.

9 The queen of Sheba heard of Solomon's
fame and came to Jerusalem to test
Solomon with difficult questions, with a very
large retinue with camels laden with spices
and an immense quantity of gold and precious
stones. Having reached Solomon, she dis-
cussed everything that she had in mind with
him, [2]and Solomon had an answer for all her
questions; not one of them was too obscure
for Solomon to answer for her. [3]When the
queen of Sheba saw how wise Solomon was,
the palace which he had built, [4]the food at
his table, the accommodation for his officials,
the organisation of his staff and the way they
were dressed, his cupbearers and the way
they were dressed, and the burnt offerings,
which he made in the Temple of Yahweh, it
left her breathless, [5]and she said to the king,
'The report I heard in my own country about
you and about your wisdom in handling your
affairs was true, then! [6]Until I came and saw
for myself, I did not believe the reports, but
clearly I was told less than half about the true
extent of your wisdom. You surpass what
was reported to me. [7]How fortunate your
people are! How fortunate your courtiers,
continually in attendance on you and listen-
ing to your wisdom! [8]Blessed be Yahweh
your God. Because your God loved Israel and
meant to keep it secure for ever, he has made
you its king to administer law and justice.'
[9]And she presented the king with a hundred
and twenty talents of gold and great quan-
tities of spices and precious stones. There
never were such spices as those which the
queen of Sheba gave to King Solomon.
[10]Similarly, the men employed by Huram
and the men employed by Solomon, who
brought the gold from Ophir, also brought
back *algum* wood and precious stones. [11]Of
the *algum* wood the king made steps for the
Temple of Yahweh and for the royal palace,
and harps and lyres for the musicians, the
like of which had never before been seen in
Judah. [12]And King Solomon, in his turn,
presented the queen of Sheba with everything
that she expressed a wish for, besides what
he gave her in exchange for what she had
brought to the king. After which, she went
home to her own country, she and her
servants.

[13]The weight of the gold received annually
by Solomon amounted to six hundred and
sixty-six talents of gold, [14]besides what tolls
and foreign trade brought in; all the Arab
kings and the provincial governors also
brought gold and silver to Solomon. [15]King
Solomon made two hundred great shields of
beaten gold, six hundred shekels of beaten

gold going into one shield; [16]also three
hundred small shields of beaten gold, three
hundred shekels of gold going into one shield;
and the king put these into the House of the
Forest of Lebanon. [17]The king also made a
great ivory throne which he overlaid with
refined gold. [18]The throne had six steps with
a golden foot-rest attached to the throne, and
arms on each side of the seat and two lions
standing beside the arms, [19]and twelve lions
stood on either side of the six steps. Nothing
like it had ever been made in any other
kingdom.
[20]All King Solomon's drinking vessels
were of gold, and all the plate in the House
of the Forest of Lebanon was of pure gold;
silver was little thought of in Solomon's days,
[21]since the king's ships went to Tarshish with
Huram's employees, and once every three
years the merchantmen would come back
laden with gold and silver, ivory, apes and
baboons. [22]For riches and for wisdom, King
Solomon surpassed all kings on earth, [23]and
all the kings in the world consulted Solomon
to hear the wisdom which God had implanted
in his heart, [24]and everyone would bring a
present with him: objects of silver and of
gold, robes, armour, spices, horses and
mules; and this went on year after year.
[25]Solomon also had four thousand stalls for
horses and chariots, and twelve thousand
cavalrymen; these he stationed in the chariot
towns and near the king in Jerusalem. [26]He
was overlord of all the kings from the River
to the territory of the Philistines and the
Egyptian border. [27]In Jerusalem the king
made silver as common as stones, and cedar
wood as plentiful as sycamore in the
Lowlands. [28]Horses were imported for
Solomon from Muzur and all the other coun-
tries too.

The death of Solomon

[29]The rest of the history of Solomon, from
first to last, is this not all written down in
the records of Nathan the prophet, in the
Prophecy of Ahijah of Shiloh, and in the
Vision of Iddo the seer concerning Jeroboam
son of Nebat? [30]Solomon reigned in Jeru-
salem over all Israel for forty years. [31]When
Solomon fell asleep with his ancestors, he
was buried in the City of his father David;
Rehoboam his son succeeded him.

IV: FIRST REFORMS OF THE MONARCHICAL PERIOD

A: REHOBOAM AND THE REGROUPING OF THE LEVITES

The schism

10 Rehoboam then went to Shechem, all
Israel having come to Shechem to pro-
claim him king. [2]As soon as Jeroboam son of
Nebat heard the news—he was in Egypt,
where he had taken refuge from King
Solomon—he returned from Egypt. [3]They
now sent for him, so Jeroboam and all Israel
came and spoke as follows to Rehoboam,
[4]'Your father laid a cruel yoke on us; if you
will lighten your father's cruel slavery, that
heavy yoke which he imposed on us, we are
willing to serve you.' [5]He said to them, 'Come
back to me in three days' time.' And the
people went away.
[6]King Rehoboam then consulted the
elders, who had been in attendance on his
father Solomon while he was alive, and said,
'How do you advise me to answer this
people?' [7]They replied, 'If you are fair to
these people, pleasant to them and give them
a fair reply, they will remain your servants
for ever.' [8]But he rejected the advice given
him by the elders and consulted the young
men in attendance on him, who had grown
up with him. [9]He said, 'How do you advise
us to answer these people who have been
saying, "Lighten the yoke which your father
imposed on us"?' [10]The young men who had
grown up with him replied, 'This is the way
to answer the people who have been saying,
"Your father made our yoke heavy, you must
lighten it for us!" This is the right thing to
say to them, "My little finger is thicker than
my father's loins! [11]Although my father laid
a heavy yoke on you, I shall make it heavier
still! My father controlled you with the whip,
but I shall apply a spiked lash!" ' [12]On the
third day, Jeroboam and all the people came
to Rehoboam in obedience to the king's
instructions, 'Come back to me in three days'
time.' [13]And the king gave them a harsh

answer. King Rehoboam, rejecting the advice of the elders, [14]spoke to them as the young men had recommended, 'My father made your yoke heavy, but I shall add to it. My father controlled you with the whip, but I shall apply a spiked lash.' [15]Thus the king refused to listen to the people, and this was brought about by God, so that Yahweh might fulfil the promise which he had made through Ahijah of Shiloh to Jeroboam son of Nebat. [16]When all Israel saw that the king refused to listen to them, the people answered the king thus:

What share have we in David?
  —no heritage in the son of Jesse!
Each of you, to your tents, Israel!
  Now look to your own house, David!

So Israel went home again. [17]Rehoboam, however, reigned over those Israelites who lived in the towns of Judah. [18]When King Rehoboam sent Adoram who was in charge of forced labour, the Israelites stoned him to death, while King Rehoboam managed to mount his chariot and escape to Jerusalem. [19]And Israel has remained in rebellion against the House of David from that day to this.

11 When Rehoboam reached Jerusalem, he mustered a hundred and eighty thousand picked warriors of the House of Judah and Benjamin to fight Israel and win back the kingdom for Rehoboam. [2]But the word of Yahweh came to Shemaiah, man of God, [3]'Say this to Rehoboam son of Solomon, king of Judah, and to all Israel in Judah and Benjamin, [4]"Yahweh says this: Do not go and make war on your brothers; let everyone go home, for this is my doing." ' They obeyed Yahweh's command and went back instead of marching against Jeroboam.

[5]Rehoboam, residing in Jerusalem, fortified a number of towns for the defence of Judah. [6]He built Bethlehem, Etam, Tekoa, [7]Beth-Zur, Soco, Adullam, [8]Gath, Mareshah, Ziph, [9]Adoraim, Lachish, Azekah, [10]Zorah, Aijalon, Hebron, these being the fortified towns in Judah and Benjamin. [11]He equipped these fortresses, stationing commanders in them, with supplies of food, oil and wine, [12]and shields and spears in each of these towns, making them extremely strong and thus retaining control of Judah and Benjamin.

The priests and Levites migrate to Judah

[13]The priests and the Levites from all over Israel left their districts to put themselves at his disposal. [14]The Levites, indeed, abandoned their pasture lands and their holdings and came to Judah and Jerusalem because Jeroboam and his sons had excluded them from the priesthood of Yahweh. [15]Jeroboam had appointed his own priests for the high places dedicated to the satyrs and calves which he had made. [16]And those members of all the tribes of Israel who were determined to seek Yahweh, God of Israel, followed those priests and Levites to Jerusalem to sacrifice to Yahweh, God of their ancestors. [17]These added strength to the kingdom of Judah and gave their support to Rehoboam son of Solomon for three years. For three years they remained loyal to David and Solomon.

Rehoboam's family

[18]Rehoboam married Mahalath daughter of Jerimoth, son of David, and of Abihail daughter of Eliab son of Jesse, [19]and she bore him sons: Jeush, Shemariah and Zaham. [20]After her, he married Maacah daughter of Absalom, who bore him Abijah, Attai, Ziza and Shelomith. [21]Rehoboam loved Maacah daughter of Absalom, more than all his other wives and concubines. He had in fact a total of eighteen wives and sixty concubines and fathered twenty-eight sons and sixty daughters. [22]Rehoboam named Abijah son of Maacah as head, hence leader, of his brothers, with a view to making him king, [23]and acted wisely by distributing his sons throughout the territories of Judah and Benjamin, some in each fortified town, where he provided plenty of food for them and found them wives.

Rehoboam's unfaithfulness

12 When Rehoboam had consolidated the kingdom and become strong, he, and all Israel with him, abandoned the Law of Yahweh; [2]and thus it happened that in the fifth year of King Rehoboam, Shishak king of Egypt marched on Jerusalem, because they had been unfaithful to Yahweh, [3]with twelve hundred chariots and sixty thousand cavalry and countless hordes of Libyans, Sukkiim and Cushites who came from Egypt with him. [4]They captured the fortified towns

of Judah and reached Jerusalem. 5The
prophet Shemaiah then came to Rehoboam
and the generals of Judah, who had fallen
back on Jerusalem before Shishak's advance,
and said to them, 'Yahweh says this, "You
have abandoned me and so I have abandoned
you into Shishak's clutches."' 6At this, the
Israelite generals and the king humbled
themselves and said, 'Yahweh is just!' 7When
Yahweh saw that they had humbled them-
selves, the word of Yahweh came to Shemaiah
as follows, 'They have humbled themselves.
I shall not destroy them but shall grant them
some degree of deliverance. My retribution
will not be poured out on Jerusalem by means
of Shishak; 8they are nonetheless to become
his slaves, so that they may learn the differ-
ence between serving me and serving kings
of other countries.'
9So Shishak king of Egypt advanced on
Jerusalem and carried off the treasures of the
Temple and the treasures of the royal palace.
He took everything away, including the
golden shields which Solomon had made.
10To replace these, King Rehoboam made
bronze shields, entrusting them to the
commanders of the guard who guarded the
king's palace gate. 11Whenever the king went
to the Temple of Yahweh, the guards would
come out carrying them, returning them to
the guardroom afterwards.

Summary of the reign

12Because King Rehoboam had humbled
himself, the retribution of Yahweh turned
away from him so as not to destroy him
completely; and there were also some good
features in Judah. 13Thus he was able to
strengthen his position in Jerusalem and
continue as king; for Rehoboam was forty-
one years old when he came to the throne
and remained king for seventeen years in
Jerusalem, the city chosen by Yahweh from
all the tribes of Israel to put his name there.
His mother's name was Naamah the
Ammonite. 14But he did wrong in not setting
his heart on seeking Yahweh.
15The history of Rehoboam, from first to
last, is this not all written down in the records
of Shemaiah the prophet and of Iddo the
seer? Warfare between Rehoboam and Jero-
boam went on throughout the period.
16When Rehoboam fell asleep with his ances-
tors, he was buried in the City of David; his
son Abijah succeeded him.

B: ABIJAH AND LOYALTY TO THE LEGITIMATE PRIESTHOOD

War breaks out

13 In the eighteenth year of King Jero-
boam, Abijah became king of Judah
2and reigned for three years in Jerusalem.
His mother's name was Micaiah daughter
of Uriel of Gibeah. When war broke out
between Abijah and Jeroboam, 3Abijah took
the field with an army of four hundred thou-
sand picked warriors, while Jeroboam took
the field against him with eight hundred
thousand picked warriors.

Abijah addresses the Israelites

4Abijah took position on Mount Zemaraim,
in the highlands of Ephraim. 'Jeroboam and
all Israel,' he cried, 'listen to me! 5Do you
not know that Yahweh, God of Israel, has
given eternal sovereignty of Israel to David
and his sons by an inviolable covenant? 6Yet
Jeroboam son of Nebat, the slave of Solomon
son of David, rose in revolt against his master.
7Worthless men, scoundrels, rallied to him,
proving too strong for Rehoboam son of
Solomon, as Rehoboam was then inexperi-
enced and timid and unable to resist them.
8And now you propose to resist Yahweh's
sovereignty as exercised by the sons of David
because there is a great number of you and
you have the golden calves that Jeroboam
made you for gods! 9Have you not driven out
the priests of Yahweh, the sons of Aaron
and the Levites, to make priests of your own
like the peoples of foreign countries? Anyone
who comes with a bull and seven rams to get
himself consecrated can become priest of
these gods that are no gods. 10But for our
part, our God is Yahweh, and we have not
abandoned him; our priests are sons of Aaron
who minister to Yahweh, and those who
serve are Levites; 11morning after morning,
evening after evening, they present burnt
offerings and perfumed incense to Yahweh,
they put the bread of permanent offering on
the clean table and nightly light the lamps on
the golden lamp-stand; for we keep the decree
of Yahweh our God, although you have aban-
doned him. 12See how God is with us, at our
head, and his priests with trumpets to sound
the alarm against you! Israelites, do not make
war on Yahweh, God of your ancestors, for
you will not succeed.'

The battle

13 Now Jeroboam had sent a party round to ambush them from the rear; thus the main force confronted Judah and the ambush lay to their rear. 14 And when Judah looked round, they found themselves being attacked from front and rear. They called on Yahweh, the priests sounded the trumpets, 15 and the men of Judah raised the war cry and, as they raised the cry, God routed Jeroboam and all Israel before Abijah and Judah. 16 So the Israelites fled before Judah, because God had given Judah the upper hand, 17 and Abijah and his army inflicted a great slaughter on them: five hundred thousand of Israel's picked men fell, killed. 18 So the Israelites were humbled on that occasion, while the Judaeans won, since they had relied on Yahweh, God of their ancestors.

The end of the reign of Abijah

19 Abijah pursued Jeroboam, taking from him the towns of Bethel with its dependencies, Jeshanah with its dependencies and Ephron with its dependencies, 20 nor did Jeroboam regain strength during Abijah's lifetime. Eventually Yahweh struck him and he died, 21 but Abijah grew stronger than ever; he married fourteen wives and fathered twenty-two sons and sixteen daughters. 22 The rest of the history of Abijah, his conduct and his sayings, are recorded in the *midrash* of the prophet Iddo. 23 When Abijah fell asleep with his ancestors, he was buried in the City of David; his son Asa succeeded him.

C: ASA AND HIS REFORM OF PUBLIC WORSHIP

Peace under Asa

In his time the country was at peace for ten years.

14 Asa did what Yahweh his God regards as good and right. 2 He abolished the foreign altars and the high places, broke the pillars, cut down the sacred poles, 3 and urged Judah to seek Yahweh, God of their ancestors, and to observe the law and commandment. 4 Because he abolished the high places and incense altars through the towns of Judah, the kingdom under him was undisturbed. 5 He rebuilt the fortified towns of Judah, since the country was at peace and free of war during those years, because Yahweh had granted him peace.

6 'Let us rebuild these towns,' he told Judah, 'let us surround them with wall and tower, with gate and bar while the country is still ours, for we have sought Yahweh our God and he has sought us and given us peace all around.' They built and prospered.

7 Asa had an army of three hundred thousand men of Judah armed with shields and spears and two hundred and eighty thousand men of Benjamin armed with shields and bows, all of them outstanding soldiers.

Invasion by Zerah

8 Zerah the Cushite took the field against them with an army a million strong and three hundred chariots, and penetrated to Mareshah. 9 Asa took the field against him and the battle-lines were drawn up in the Valley of Zephathah, at Mareshah. 10 Asa then called on Yahweh his God and said, 'Yahweh, numbers and strength make no difference to you when you give your help. Help us, Yahweh our God, for, relying on you, we are confronting this horde in your name. Yahweh, you are our God. Human strength cannot prevail against you!'

11 Yahweh routed the Cushites before Asa and Judah. The Cushites fled, 12 and Asa pursued them with his army as far as Gerar. So many of the Cushites fell that they were unable to survive. They were cut to pieces by Yahweh and his army.

They carried off a great deal of booty, 13 they destroyed all the towns round Gerar—for a panic from Yahweh had seized the towns—and plundered all the towns since they were full of loot. 14 They also routed the cattle-owners and carried off great numbers of sheep and camels; then they returned to Jerusalem.

Azariah's sermon and the reform

15 The spirit of God then came on Azariah son of Oded; 2 he went out to meet Asa and said, 'Listen to me, Asa, and all you in Judah and in Benjamin: Yahweh will be with you so long as you are with him. If you seek him, he will let you find him; but if you desert him, he will desert you. 3 For a long time Israel did not have the true God or a teacher-priest or a law, 4but when in their distress they turned to Yahweh, God of Israel, and sought him, he let them find him. 5In those times there was no security for people as they went about their business, but great unrest affecting the inhabitants of all countries, 6nation being crushed by nation and city by city, since God caused confusion among them by every kind of distress. 7So be strong, do not be discouraged, for your deeds will be rewarded.'

Asa's religious reforms

8When Asa heard these words and the prophecy, he took courage and removed the abominable idols throughout the land of Judah and Benjamin as well as from the towns which he had captured in the highlands of Ephraim, and repaired the altar of Yahweh which stood in front of the portico of Yahweh. 9He summoned all Judah and Benjamin as well as those Ephraimites, Manassehites and Simeonites who had settled with them—for a great many people from Israel had gone over to Asa when they saw that Yahweh his God was with him. 10They assembled in Jerusalem in the third month of the fifteenth year of Asa's reign, 11that day sacrificing to Yahweh seven hundred oxen and seven thousand sheep from the booty which they had brought back. 12They then made a covenant to seek Yahweh, God of their ancestors, with all their heart and soul; 13anyone who would not seek Yahweh, God of Israel, was to be put to death, whether high or low, man or woman. 14They pledged their oath to Yahweh in ringing tones, with shouts of joy, to the sound of trumpet and horn; 15all Judah rejoiced over the oath, for they had sworn it wholeheartedly, and sought him so earnestly that he allowed them to find him; Yahweh gave them peace all round.

16King Asa even deprived his mother Maacah of the dignity of Great Lady for having made an obscenity for Asherah; Asa cut down her obscenity, smashed it and burnt it in the ravine of the Kidron. 17Though the high places were not abolished in Israel, Asa's heart was loyal throughout his life. 18He deposited his father's and his own dedicated gifts of silver, gold and sacred vessels, in the Temple of Yahweh.

19Up to the thirty-fifth year of Asa's reign there was no war.

War with Israel

16 In the thirty-sixth year of Asa's reign, Baasha king of Israel marched on Judah and fortified Ramah to block the communications of Asa king of Judah. 2Asa then took silver and gold from the treasuries of the Temple of Yahweh and the royal palace and sent this with the following message to Ben-Hadad king of Aram, who lived in Damascus, 3'Let us make an alliance between me and you, between my father and your father! Look, I have sent you silver and gold. Come, break off your alliance with Baasha king of Israel, which will make him withdraw from me.' 4Ben-Hadad listened favourably to King Asa and sent the generals of his armies to attack the towns of Israel; he ravaged Ijon, Dan, Abel-Maim and all the storage towns of Naphtali. 5When Baasha heard this he gave up fortifying Ramah, abandoning this work. 6King Asa then had all Judah carry away the stones and timber with which Baasha had been fortifying Ramah, and used them to fortify Geba and Mizpah.

7Then it was that Hanani the seer came to Asa king of Judah and said, 'Because you relied on the king of Aram and not on Yahweh your God, the king of Aram's army will slip through your fingers. 8Did not the Cushites and Libyans form a vast army with great numbers of chariots and cavalry? Even so, because you relied on Yahweh, he gave you the upper hand; 9for Yahweh's eyes rove to and fro across the whole world to support those whose hearts are loyal to him. You have acted like a fool in this respect; hence, from now on you will have wars.' 10Enraged with the seer, Asa had him put in the stocks in prison, being angry with him over this; at the same time Asa ill-treated some of the people too.

The end of the reign of Asa

11The history of Asa, from first to last, is recorded in the Book of the Kings of Judah and Israel. 12In the thirty-ninth year of his reign, Asa contracted a disease in his feet, which became very severe; in his illness, however, he consulted not Yahweh but the doctors. 13Asa then fell asleep with his ancestors, dying in the forty-first year of his reign. 14He was buried in the tomb which he had ordered to be cut for him in the City of David.

He was laid in the burial chamber which was
filled with perfume blended from all sorts of
oils, and a very great funeral fire was made
for him.

D: JEHOSHAPHAT AND HIS GOVERNMENT

Jehoshaphat's military policy

17 When his son Jehoshaphat succeeded
him, he made himself stronger against
Israel 2 by stationing troops in all the fortified
towns in Judah and by garrisoning Judah and
the towns of Ephraim which his father Asa
had captured.

His devotion to religion

3 Yahweh was with Jehoshaphat because he
followed the example of his father's earlier
days and did not have recourse to Baal,
4 but sought Yahweh, the God of his father,
following his commandments and not
behaving as Israel did. 5 Because of this,
Yahweh put him in secure control of the
kingdom, while all Judah gave Jehoshaphat
presents until ample riches and honour were
his. 6 He was so enthusiastic about obeying
Yahweh that once again he abolished the high
places and sacred poles in Judah.
7 In the third year of his reign he sent his
leading men—Ben-Hail, Obadiah, Zech-
ariah, Nethanel and Micaiah, to give instruc-
tion in the towns of Judah. 8 With them went
the Levites: Shemaiah, Nethaniah,
Zebadiah, Asahel, Shemiramoth, Jeho-
nathan, Adonijah and Tobijah, the Levites;
Elishama and Jehoram the priests went with
them. 9 They gave instruction in Judah,
having with them the book of the Law of
Yahweh, and went round all the towns of
Judah instructing the people.
10 A panic from Yahweh seized all the kings
of the countries surrounding Judah, as a
result of which they did not make war on
Jehoshaphat. 11 Some of the Philistines
brought Jehoshaphat presents and a load
of silver and the Arabs brought him seven
thousand seven hundred rams and seven
thousand seven hundred he-goats.
12 Jehoshaphat became more and more
powerful. He built fortresses and storage
towns in Judah.

The army

13 He accumulated ample supplies in the
towns of Judah.
He also had warriors, outstanding men, in
Jerusalem. 14 According to family, this is how
they were classified:
Over the commanders of the thousands of
Judah was General Adnah, who had three
hundred thousand outstanding men;
15 Under him was General Jehohanan, who
had two hundred and eighty thousand;
16 Under him was Amasiah son of Zichri,
who had volunteered for Yahweh and who
had two hundred thousand outstanding men;
17 That outstanding soldier, Eliada, repre-
sented Benjamin, and he had two hundred
thousand men armed with bow and shield;
18 And under him Jehozabad, who had one
hundred and eighty thousand equipped for
war.
19 These were in attendance on the king,
apart from those whom the king had stationed
in the fortified towns all over Judah.

His alliance with Ahab and the intervention of the prophets

18 Although Jehoshaphat enjoyed great
wealth and honour, he allied himself
by marriage to Ahab. 2 After some years
he paid a visit to Ahab in Samaria. Ahab
slaughtered an immense number of sheep
and oxen for him and his retinue, to induce
him to attack Ramoth-Gilead. 3 Ahab king of
Israel then said to Jehoshaphat king of Judah,
'Will you come with me to Ramoth-Gilead?'
He replied, 'I will share in battle with you,
my men with yours.'

The spurious prophets predict success

4 Jehoshaphat, however, said to the king of
Israel, 'First, please consult the word of
Yahweh.' 5 So the king of Israel called the
prophets together, four hundred of them.
'Should we go and attack Ramoth-Gilead,'
he asked, 'or should I hold back?' 'March,'
they replied, 'for God will deliver it into the
king's power.' 6 Jehoshaphat, however, said,
'Is there no other prophet of Yahweh here, for
us to consult?' 7 The king of Israel answered
Jehoshaphat, 'There is one more man
through whom we can consult Yahweh, but
I hate him because he never has a favourable
prophecy for me, always unfavourable ones;

he is Micaiah son of Imlah.' 'The king should
not say such things,' said Jehoshaphat. 8The
king of Israel then summoned a court official
and said, 'Bring Micaiah son of Imlah
immediately.'
9The king of Israel and Jehoshaphat king
of Judah were sitting each on his throne,
wearing their robes; in an open space just
outside the gate of Samaria, with all the
prophets prophesying before them, 10Zedek-
iah son of Chenaanah, who had made himself
some iron horns, said, 'Yahweh says, "With
horns like these, you will gore the Aramaeans
till you make an end of them." ' 11And all the
prophets prophesied in the same vein, saying,
'March on Ramoth-Gilead! Success is sure,
for Yahweh has already given it to the king!'

The prophet Micaiah predicts defeat

12The messenger who had gone to summon
Micaiah said to him, 'Look! What the
prophets are saying is uniformly favourable
to the king. So I hope you will say the same
as they do and speak favourably.' 13Micaiah
said, 'As Yahweh lives, I shall speak exactly
as Yahweh tells me!' 14When he came to the
king, the king said, 'Micaiah, should we
march to attack Ramoth-Gilead, or should I
hold back?' He replied, 'Go and conquer,
Yahweh will deliver them into your power!'
15The king went on, 'How often must I put
you on oath to tell me nothing but the truth
in the name of Yahweh?' 16Then he spoke
out.

I saw all Israel scattered on the mountains
like sheep without a shepherd.
And Yahweh said, 'These have no master,
let them all go peacefully home!'

17At this the king of Israel said to Jeho-
shaphat, 'Did I not tell you that he never
gives me favourable prophecies, but only
unfavourable ones?' 18Micaiah went on,
'Now listen to the word of Yahweh. I saw
Yahweh seated on his throne with the whole
array of heaven standing on his right and on
his left. 19Yahweh said, "Who will entice
Ahab king of Israel into marching to his
death at Ramoth-Gilead?" At which some
answered one way, and some another. 20A
spirit then came forward and stood before
Yahweh and said, "I will entice him."
"How?" Yahweh asked. 21He replied, "I
shall go and be a deceptive spirit in the
mouths of all his prophets." Yahweh said,
"You will succeed in enticing him. Go and
do it." 22And now, you see, Yahweh has put
a deceptive spirit into the mouths of your
prophets here, for in fact Yahweh has
pronounced disaster on you.'
23Zedekiah son of Chenaanah then came
up, struck Micaiah on the cheek and said,
'Which way did Yahweh's spirit leave me, to
speak to you?' 24'That is what you will find
out,' Micaiah retorted, 'the day you go from
room to room, trying to hide.' 25The king of
Israel said, 'Seize Micaiah and hand him over
to Amon governor of the city, and Joash the
king's son, 26and say, "These are the king's
orders: Put this man in prison and feed him
on nothing but bread and water until I am
safely home." ' 27Micaiah said, 'If you ever
do get home safely, Yahweh has not spoken
through me.'

The battle

28The king of Israel and Jehoshaphat king of
Judah marched on Ramoth-Gilead. 29The
king of Israel said to Jehoshaphat, 'I shall
disguise myself to go into battle, but you put
on your robes.' So the king of Israel disguised
himself, and they went into battle. 30Now,
the king of Aram had given his chariot
commanders the following order, 'Do not
attack anyone of whatever rank, except the
king of Israel.' 31So, when the chariot
commanders saw Jehoshaphat, they thought,
'That is the king of Israel,' and surrounded
him to attack. But when Jehoshaphat shouted
his war cry, Yahweh came to his help, God
drew them away from him, 32for the chariot
commanders, realising that he was not the
king of Israel, broke off their pursuit.
33Someone, however, drawing his bow
without any special aim, shot the king of
Israel between the joints of his armour. 'Turn
about!' he said to his charioteer. 'Get me out
of the fighting; I am collapsing.' 34But the
battle grew fiercer as the day went on, and
the king of Israel had to be held upright in
his chariot facing the Aramaeans until the
evening, and at sunset he died.

Jehoshaphat is rebuked by a prophet

19 Jehoshaphat king of Judah returned
home safely, however, to Jerusalem.
2Jehu son of Hanani the seer went to meet
him and said to King Jehoshaphat, 'Should
a man give help to the wicked? Should you

love those who hate Yahweh and so bring his retribution on yourself? 3All the same, there are good things to your credit, since you have removed the sacred poles from the country and have set your heart on seeking God.'

His judicial reforms

4Jehoshaphat resided in Jerusalem but regularly went on progress among the people, from Beersheba to the highlands of Ephraim, to convert them to Yahweh, God of their ancestors. 5He also appointed judges in the country in every one of the fortified towns of Judah, 6saying to the judges, 'Be careful what you do, since you are judging not by any human power but in the name of Yahweh, who will be with you when you pronounce sentence. 7This being so, let fear of Yahweh govern you; be careful what you do, for Yahweh our God will not tolerate malpractice, partiality or the taking of bribes.'

8Jehoshaphat also appointed some of the Levites, priests and heads of Israelite families in Jerusalem to settle disputes. They lived in Jerusalem 9and Jehoshaphat gave them the following charge: 'In fear of Yahweh and with conscientious integrity, this is how you are to act: 10whatever case your brothers living in other towns refer to you, whether involving blood feuds or law and commandment, statutes and judgements, you are to instruct them in such manner that they do not incur guilt before Yahweh and that you and your brothers do not incur his anger. If you act thus, you will not incur guilt. 11Amariah the chief priest himself will be your president in all religious cases, and Zebadiah son of Ishmael, leader of the House of Judah, in all civil ones, while the Levites will act as officers of the court. Be firm, put this into practice and may Yahweh protect the right!'

A holy war

20 Some time later, the Moabites and Ammonites, and with them the Meunites, advanced to war against Jehoshaphat. 2Jehoshaphat received the following intelligence, 'A vast horde is advancing on you from the other side of the Sea, from Edom; they are already at Hazazon-Tamar, that is, En-Gedi.'

3Jehoshaphat was alarmed and resolved to have recourse to Yahweh; he proclaimed a fast throughout all Judah. 4So Judah assembled to seek help from Yahweh; to seek Yahweh they came from every town in Judah.

5Then, standing in the Temple of Yahweh in front of the new court among the assembled people of Judah and Jerusalem, Jehoshaphat 6said, 'Yahweh, God of our ancestors, are you not God in heaven, and do you not rule all the kingdoms of the nations? Your power and might are such that no one can resist you. 7Did not you, our God, dispossess the inhabitants of this country for your people Israel and give it to the descendants of Abraham, your friend, for ever? 8They have lived in it and built you a sanctuary there for your name, 9saying, "If disaster, war, flood, pestilence or famine befall us, and we stand in front of this Temple, before you—for your name is in this Temple—and cry to you in our distress, then you will listen and rescue us."

10'Now see, the Ammonites and Moabites and the people of Mount Seir, whom you would not allow Israel to invade when they came out of Egypt—on the contrary, Israel avoided them, and did not destroy them—11see how they reward us, by coming to drive us out of your possession which you allotted to us! 12Our God, will you not pass sentence on them, since we are helpless against this vast horde about to attack us? Because we do not know what to do, we look to you.'

13All Judah, including their families, wives and children, were standing before Yahweh, 14when, in the middle of the assembly, the spirit of Yahweh came on Jahaziel son of Zechariah, son of Benaiah, son of Jeiel, son of Mattaniah the Levite, a member of the clan of Asaph, 15who then cried, 'Listen, all Judah and you citizens of Jerusalem, and you, King Jehoshaphat! Yahweh says this to you, "Do not be afraid, do not be daunted by this vast horde, for the war is not your affair but God's. 16Go down against them tomorrow; they are coming up by the Slope of Ziz and you will encounter them at the end of the ravine near the desert of Jeruel. 17You will not need to fight in this battle. Take up your position, stand firm, and see what salvation Yahweh has in store for you. Judah and Jerusalem, be fearless, be dauntless; march out against them tomorrow and Yahweh will be with you."'

18Jehoshaphat bowed his head, his face to

the ground, and all Judah and the citizens of Jerusalem fell down before Yahweh to worship Yahweh. [19]Then the Levites—both the Kohathites and Korahites—stood up to praise Yahweh, God of Israel, at the top of their voices.

[20]Early next morning they prepared to set out for the desert of Tekoa. As they were setting out, Jehoshaphat stood up and said, 'Listen to me, Judah and you citizens of Jerusalem! Believe in Yahweh your God and you will be secure; believe in his prophets and you will be successful.' [21]Then, having conferred with the people, he appointed singers who were to praise Yahweh and go out ahead of the army in sacred vestments, singing

Praise Yahweh,
for his faithful love endures for ever!

[22]The moment they began their shouts of praise, Yahweh sprang an ambush on the Ammonites, Moabites and the people of Mount Seir who were invading Judah, and that was the end of them, [23]for the Ammonites and Moabites turned on the people of Mount Seir, and put them under the curse of destruction and then, having finished off the people of Seir, set to work slaughtering one another.

[24]When Judah reached the point overlooking the desert and looked towards the horde, there were nothing but corpses lying on the ground; no one escaped. [25]When Jehoshaphat arrived to take the booty, they found quantities of cattle and innumerable possessions, clothes and valuables, which they seized for themselves; it was impossible to carry it, and it took them three days to collect it. [26]On the fourth day they assembled in the Valley of Beracah, where they blessed Yahweh—hence the place was given the name Valley of Beracah, which it still has today. [27]Then all the men of Judah and Jerusalem returned joyfully to Jerusalem with Jehoshaphat at their head as Yahweh had given them cause to rejoice over their enemies. [28]To the sound of lyre, harp and trumpet they came to Jerusalem, to the Temple of Yahweh, [29]and a panic from Yahweh seized all the neighbouring kings when they heard how Yahweh had fought against the enemies of Israel. [30]And henceforth Jehoshaphat's reign was undisturbed, for his God gave him peace all round.

The end of the reign of Jehoshaphat

[31]So Jehoshaphat reigned over Judah. He was thirty-five years old when he came to the throne and he reigned for twenty-five years in Jerusalem. His mother's name was Azubah daughter of Shilhi. [32]He followed the example of his father Asa undeviatingly, doing what Yahweh regards as right. [33]The high places, however, were not abolished; the people had still not set their hearts on the God of their ancestors. [34]The rest of the history of Jehoshaphat, from first to last, is written down in the records of Jehu son of Hanani, which are quoted in the Book of the Kings of Israel.

[35]Afterwards, Jehoshaphat formed a partnership with Ahaziah king of Israel, which was very wrong of him. [36]He joined him in building some ships to go to Tarshish; they built them at Ezion-Geber. [37]Eliezer son of Dodavahu of Mareshah then prophesied against Jehoshaphat as follows, 'Because you have become Ahaziah's partner, Yahweh has wrecked your efforts.' The ships were wrecked and were never fit to sail for Tarshish.

21 Then Jehoshaphat fell asleep with his ancestors and was buried with them in the city of David; his son Jehoram succeeded him.

E: IMPIETY AND DISASTERS UNDER JEHORAM, AHAZIAH, ATHALIAH AND JOASH

Accession of Jehoram; he massacres his brothers

[2]Jehoram's brothers, sons of Jehoshaphat, were Azariah, Jehiel, Zechariah, Azariahu, Michael and Shephatiah—all of them sons of Jehoshaphat king of Israel. [3]Their father had lavishly given them presents of silver, gold and other valuables as well as fortified towns in Judah; but the throne he bequeathed to Jehoram since he was the first-born. [4]Jehoram, having taken control of his father's kingdom and secured his own position, put all his brothers to the sword and some officials of Israel too.

[5]Jehoram was thirty-two years old when he came to the throne, and he reigned for eight years in Jerusalem. [6]He followed the

example of the kings of Israel as the House of Ahab were doing, he having married one of Ahab's daughters; and he did what is displeasing to Yahweh. 7But Yahweh would not destroy the House of David, because of the covenant which he had made with David, promising to provide him and his sons with a lamp for ever.

The disasters of his reign

8In his time Edom threw off the domination of Judah and set up a king for itself. 9Jehoram crossed the frontier, and with him his commanders and all his chariots. Under cover of dark, he and his chariot commanders broke through the Edomites surrounding him. 10Thus Edom threw off the domination of Judah and has remained free to the present day. Libnah revolted against him at the same time, because he had abandoned Yahweh, God of his ancestors. 11What is more, he set up high places in the highlands of Judah, leading the citizens of Jerusalem and the people of Judah into apostasy.

12Something written by the prophet Elijah then came into his hands. It said, 'Yahweh, God of your ancestor David, says this, "Since you have not followed the example of your father Jehoshaphat or of Asa king of Judah, 13but have followed the example of the kings of Israel and have led Judah and the citizens of Jerusalem into apostasy, just as the House of Ahab has led Israel into apostasy, and have even murdered your brothers, your own family, who were better men than you, 14Yahweh is going to afflict your people, your sons, your wives and all your property with a great calamity, 15and you yourself with a severe disease affecting your bowels, as a result of which disease, continuing day after day, you will suffer protrusion of your bowels." '

16Yahweh then roused the hostility of the Philistines and of the Arabs living near the Cushites against Jehoram. 17They invaded Judah, forcing their way into it and carrying off all the property to be found in the king's palace, as well as his sons and his wives, so that he was left no sons at all except his youngest son Jehoahaz. 18And after all this, Yahweh afflicted him with an incurable disease of the bowels; 19in due time, after about two years, his bowels protruded as a result of his disease and he died in acute pain. His people did not make a funeral pyre for him, as they had for his ancestors.

20He was thirty-two years old when he came to the throne and he reigned for eight years in Jerusalem. He passed away unlamented and was buried in the City of David, though not in the tombs of the kings.

Reign of Ahaziah

22 The inhabitants of Jerusalem then made his youngest son Ahaziah king in succession to him, since the marauders who had attacked the camp with the Arabs had killed all the older ones. That was why Ahaziah son of Jehoram, king of Judah became king. 2Ahaziah was forty-two years old when he came to the throne and he reigned for one year in Jerusalem. His mother's name was Athaliah, descendant of Omri. 3He too followed the example of the House of Ahab, for his mother being his adviser brought about his condemnation. 4He did what is displeasing to Yahweh as the House of Ahab did, for they were his advisers after his father's death, to his undoing. 5He followed their advice and went with Jehoram son of Ahab, king of Israel, to make war on Hazael king of Aram at Ramoth-Gilead. But the Aramaeans wounded Jehoram, 6who returned to Jezreel to recover from the wounds which he had received at Ramoth, fighting against Hazael king of Aram. Ahaziah son of Jehoram, king of Judah, went down to Jezreel to visit Jehoram son of Ahab because he was ailing. 7Through this visit to Jehoram God brought ruin on Ahaziah. On his arrival he went out with Jehoram to meet Jehu son of Nimshi whom Yahweh had anointed to make an end of the House of Ahab. 8While Jehu was executing sentence on the House of Ahab and came across the officers of Judah and Ahaziah's nephews who were in attendance on Ahaziah, he killed them, 9and then went in search of Ahaziah. The latter was captured while hiding in Samaria, and taken to Jehu who put him to death. But they gave him burial because, they said, 'He was the grandson of Jehoshaphat who sought Yahweh with all his heart.'

As a result, there was no member of Ahaziah's family left who was strong enough to rule the kingdom.

Athaliah massacres the royal family of Judah

10 When Athaliah mother of Ahaziah learned that her son was dead, she promptly did away with all the royal stock of the House of Judah. 11 But Jehosheba the king's daughter, surreptitiously rescued Joash son of Ahaziah from among the chiefs who were to be murdered, and put him with his nurse in the sleeping quarters; in this way Jehosheba daughter of King Joram and wife of Jehoiada the priest—she was the sister of Ahaziah—hid him from Athaliah, and he was not put to death. 12 He stayed hidden with them in the Temple of God for six years while Athaliah governed the country.

Accession of Joash and death of Athaliah

23 In the seventh year Jehoiada decided to take action and made a pact with the regimental commanders, Azariah son of Jeroham, Ishmael son of Jehohanan, Azariah son of Obed, Maaseiah son of Adaiah and Elishaphat son of Zichri. 2 These went all over Judah, gathering the Levites from all the towns of Judah, and the heads of the Israelite families, who then came to Jerusalem, 3 and the whole assembly made a pact with the king in the Temple of God. Jehoiada said to them, 'Look, the king's son is now to be king, as Yahweh has promised of the sons of David! 4 This is what you must do: a third of you priests and Levites who come on duty on the Sabbath must guard the gates, 5 a third the royal palace, a third the Foundation Gate, while the people must all stay in the courts of the Temple of Yahweh. 6 No one must enter the Temple of Yahweh except the priests and the ministering Levites; they may come in because they are consecrated. But the people must all observe Yahweh's regulations. 7 The Levites must surround the king, each man with his weapons in his hands; anyone who enters the Temple must be killed. And you will escort the king when he comes in and when he leaves.'

8 The Levites and all Judah did everything as Jehoiada the priest had ordered, and each one brought his men, those coming on duty on the Sabbath and those going off duty on the Sabbath, for Jehoiada the priest had not released any of the divisions from duty. 9 Jehoiada the priest then issued the regimental commanders with King David's spears and large and small shields, which were kept in the Temple of God. 10 He then positioned all the people, each man with his weapon in his hand, from the south side of the Temple to the north side of the Temple, close to the altar and the Temple, to form a circle round the king. 11 Then they brought the king's son out, crowned him, gave him a copy of the covenant and made him king. When Jehoiada and his sons had anointed him, they shouted, 'Long live the king!'

12 On hearing the people shouting as they ran to acclaim the king, Athaliah joined the people in the Temple of Yahweh. 13 When she looked, there stood the king on his dais by the entrance, with the officers and trumpeters at the king's side, and all the people of the country rejoicing and blowing the trumpets, and the singers with their musical instruments leading the hymns of praise. Then Athaliah tore her clothes and shouted, 'Treason, treason!' 14 Jehoiada the priest then gave the order to the regimental commanders in charge of the troops, 'Take her out between the ranks and put to the sword anyone who follows her.' For the priest had already said, 'Do not kill her inside the Temple of Yahweh.' 15 So they made way for her, and when she reached the entrance to the Horses' Gate of the palace, they killed her there.

Jehoiada's reform

16 Jehoiada made a covenant between himself, all the people and the king to remain Yahweh's people. 17 All the people then went to the temple of Baal and demolished it; they smashed its altars and its images and killed Mattan the priest of Baal in front of the altars.

18 Jehoiada entrusted the security of the Temple of Yahweh to the priests and Levites, whom David had put in charge of the Temple of Yahweh to present the burnt offerings of Yahweh as laid down in the Law of Moses, with joy and song as ordained by David. 19 He also appointed gatekeepers for the gates of the Temple of Yahweh, so that no one who was unclean might enter for any purpose at all.

20 He then took the regimental commanders, the nobles, the government officials and all the people of the land and he escorted the king down from the Temple of Yahweh. Entering the palace through the Upper Gate, they placed the king on the royal throne. 21 All the people of the land were

delighted, and the city made no move after
Athaliah had been put to death.
24 Joash was seven years old when he
came to the throne and he reigned for
forty years in Jerusalem. His mother's name
was Zibiah of Beersheba. [2]Joash did what
Yahweh regards as right throughout the life-
time of Jehoiada the priest. [3]Jehoiada found
him two wives and he fathered several sons
and daughters.

Joash repairs the Temple

[4]Later, Joash made up his mind to repair the
Temple of Yahweh. [5]Calling the priests and
the Levites together, he said, 'Go out to the
towns of Judah and collect money from all
Israel for annual repairs to the Temple of
Yahweh. Do this quickly.' But the Levites
were in no hurry, [6]so the king summoned
Jehoiada the chief priest and said, 'Why have
you not insisted on the Levites' bringing in
the tax from Judah and Jerusalem for the
Tent of Witness, as imposed by Moses
servant of Yahweh and the community of
Israel?'—[7]Athaliah and her sons, whom she
corrupted, despoiled the Temple of God and
even assigned all the sacred revenues of the
Temple of Yahweh to Baal. [8]So, at the king's
order, a chest was made and put outside
the gate of the Temple of Yahweh, [9]and a
proclamation was issued throughout Judah
and Jerusalem that the tax, which Moses
servant of God had imposed on Israel in the
desert, was to be brought to Yahweh. [10]Then
all the officials and all the people gladly
brought in their contributions, depositing
them in the chest until the payment was
complete.
[11]Whenever the chest was brought by the
Levites for royal inspection and found to
contain a large sum of money, the king's
secretary and the chief priest's representative
would come and empty the chest and then
have it returned to its place. This was done
day after day and a great deal of money was
collected. [12]The king and Jehoiada handed it
over to the foreman attached to the Temple
of Yahweh, and the hired masons and carpen-
ters set about repairing the Temple of
Yahweh; and iron-workers and bronze-
workers laboured to repair the Temple of
Yahweh. [13]The workmen got on with the
task—the repair work made good progress
at their hands—until they had restored the
Temple of God to its former state and recon-
ditioned it. [14]When they had finished, they
brought the balance of the money to the king
and Jehoiada, and with this vessels were
made for the Temple of Yahweh, vessels for
the liturgy and for the burnt offerings, bowls
and other gold and silver vessels. And the
perpetual burnt offering was offered in the
Temple of Yahweh throughout Jehoiada's
lifetime.
[15]But Jehoiada, growing old, had his fill of
days and died. He died at the age of a hundred
and thirty years, [16]and was buried with the
kings in the City of David because he had
served Israel and God and his Temple well.

Joash's decline and death

[17]After Jehoiada's death the officials of Judah
came to pay court to the king, and the king
listened to their advice, [18]and they abandoned
the Temple of Yahweh, God of their ances-
tors, for the worship of sacred poles and
idols. Judah and Jerusalem incurred wrath
because of this guilt of theirs. [19]He sent their
prophets to lead them back to Yahweh; these
put the case against them, but they would
not listen. [20]The spirit of God then invested
Zechariah son of Jehoiada the priest. He
stood up before the people and said, 'God
says this, "Why transgress Yahweh's
commands to your certain ruin? For if you
abandon Yahweh, he will abandon you." '
[21]They then plotted against him and, at the
king's order, stoned him in the court of
the Temple of Yahweh. [22]Thus King Joash,
forgetful of the devotion which Jehoiada
father of Zechariah had displayed on his
behalf, murdered his son, who cried out as
he died, 'Yahweh will see this and avenge it!'
[23]At the turn of the year, the Aramaean
army made war on Joash. When they reached
Judah and Jerusalem, they massacred all the
nation's government officials and sent all
their booty to the king of Damascus.
[24]Although the invading Aramaean army was
only a small body of men, Yahweh allowed
them to defeat a very large army because
they had abandoned Yahweh, God of their
ancestors; thus they executed judgement on
Joash.
After they had retired—for they left him
seriously wounded—[25]his own retainers
plotted against him to avenge the blood of
the son of Jehoiada the priest and murdered
him in his bed. When he died he was buried
in the City of David, but not in the tombs of

the kings. 26These were the conspirators:
Zabad son of Shimeath the Ammonite and
Jehozabad son of Shimrith the Moabite. 27As
regards his sons, the heavy tribute imposed
on him, and the restoration of the Temple of
God, this is recorded in the Commentary on
the Book of the Kings. His son Amaziah
succeeded him.

F: THE HALF-HEARTED PIETY AND PARTIAL SUCCESS OF AMAZIAH, UZZIAH AND JOTHAM

Accession of Amaziah

25 Amaziah was twenty-five years old
when he came to the throne and he
reigned for twenty-nine years in Jerusalem.
His mother's name was Jehoaddan of Jeru-
salem. 2He did what Yahweh regards as
right, though not wholeheartedly. 3Once the
kingdom was firmly under his control, he
killed those of his retainers who had
murdered the king his father. 4But he did not
put their sons to death; this was in accordance
with what is written in the Law, in the book
of Moses, where Yahweh had commanded,
'*Parents may not be put to death for children,*
nor children for parents, but each must be put to
death for his own crime.'[a]

His victorious campaign against Edom

5Amaziah summoned Judah and organised
all Judah and Benjamin by families under
commanders of thousands and commanders
of hundreds. He also made a register of those
who were twenty years old and upwards, and
found there were three hundred thousand
picked men, ready for service and capable of
wielding spear and shield. 6Furthermore, he
hired a hundred thousand tough fighting men
from Israel for a hundred talents of silver. 7A
man of God then came to him and said, 'My
lord king, do not let the Israelite troops march
with you, for Yahweh is not with Israel or
with any of the Ephraimites. 8For however
valiantly you act in war, God will bring you
down before the enemy, for God has the
power to uphold or to throw down.'
9Amaziah said to the man of God, 'But what
about the hundred talents which I have paid
for the Israelite troops?' 'Yahweh can give
you far more than that,' said the man of God.
10At this, Amaziah dismissed the troops who
had come to him from Ephraim and sent
them home again. They were furious with
Judah and went home in a great rage.
11Amaziah then, coming to a decision, led
out his own troops and, having reached the
Valley of Salt, struck down ten thousand
Seirites. 12The men of Judah captured ten
thousand more alive and, taking them to
the summit of the Rock, threw them off the
summit of the Rock so that they were all
dashed to pieces. 13Meanwhile, the troops
whom Amaziah had dismissed and not
allowed to go into battle with him rased
the towns of Judah, from Samaria to Beth-
Horon, killing three thousand of their inhabi-
tants and capturing great quantities of
plunder.
14On returning from his slaughter of the
Edomites, Amaziah brought the gods of the
Seirites with him; he set these up as his
gods, bowing down before them and burning
incense to them. 15Yahweh's anger was
aroused by Amaziah and he sent him a
prophet, who said to him, 'Why do you
consult those people's gods when they could
not save their own people from your clut-
ches?' 16He was still speaking when Amaziah
interrupted him. 'Have we appointed you a
royal counsellor? Stop, as you value your
life!' So the prophet stopped, and then said,
'I know that God has decided to destroy you
for having done this and for not listening to
my advice.'

His disastrous campaign against Israel

17After consultation, Amaziah king of Judah
then sent a message to Joash son of Jehoahaz
son of Jehu, king of Israel, saying, 'Come
and make a trial of strength!' 18Joash king
of Israel sent back word to Amaziah king
of Judah, 'The thistle of Lebanon sent a
message to the cedar of Lebanon, saying,
"Give my son your daughter in marriage";
but a wild animal of the Lebanon ran over
the thistle and squashed it. 19"Look at me,
the conqueror of Edom," you say, and now
aspire to even greater glory. But stay where
you belong! Why challenge disaster, to your
own and Judah's ruin?'
20But Amaziah would not listen, for this
was an act of God to deliver them up for
having consulted the gods of Edom. 21So
Joash king of Israel marched to the attack.

25a || Dt 24:16.

And at Beth-Shemesh, which belongs to
Judah, he and Amaziah king of Judah made
their trial of strength. 22Judah was defeated
by Israel, and everyone fled to his tent. 23The
king of Judah, Amaziah son of Joash, son of
Ahaziah, was taken prisoner at Beth-
Shemesh by Joash king of Israel who led him
off to Jerusalem, where he demolished four
hundred cubits of the city wall between the
Ephraim Gate and the Corner Gate; 24he then
took back with him to Samaria all the gold
and silver, and all the vessels to be found in
the Temple of God in the care of Obed-Edom,
the treasures in the palace, and hostages
besides.

His death

25Amaziah son of Joash, king of Judah, lived
for fifteen years after the death of Joash son
of Jehoahaz, king of Israel.
26The rest of the history of Amaziah, from
first to last, is this not recorded in the Book
of the Kings of Judah and Israel? 27Some time
after Amaziah had defected from Yahweh, a
plot having been hatched against him in
Jerusalem, he fled to Lachish where he was
murdered. 28He was then transported by
horse and buried with his ancestors in the
city of David.

Accession of Uzziah

26 All the people then chose Uzziah, who
was sixteen years old, and made him
king in succession to his father Amaziah. 2It
was he who rebuilt Elath, recovering it for
Judah, after the king had fallen asleep with
his ancestors. 3Uzziah was sixteen years old
when he came to the throne and he reigned
for fifty-two years in Jerusalem. His mother's
name was Jecoliah of Jerusalem. 4He did
what is pleasing to Yahweh, just as his father
Amaziah had done; 5he consulted God
throughout the lifetime of Zechariah, who
instructed him in the fear of God. And as
long as he consulted Yahweh, God gave him
success.

His military strength

6He went on campaign against the Phili-
stines, demolished the walls of Gath, the
walls of Jabneh and the walls of Ashdod,
and built towns in the area of Ashdod and
elsewhere in Philistine territory. 7God helped
him against the Philistines, the Arabs living at
Gur-Baal and the Meunites. 8The Meunites
paid tribute to Uzziah and his fame spread as
far as the frontier of Egypt, since he kept
growing stronger and stronger.
9Uzziah built towers in Jerusalem, at the
Corner Gate, at the Valley Gate and at the
Angle, and fortified them. 10He built towers
in the desert too, and dug many storage-
wells, for he had large herds in the lowlands
and on the tableland, and farmers and vine
dressers in the hills and fertile lands: for he
loved the land.
11Uzziah had a trained army ready to go on
campaign, organised in companies manned
as detailed by the scribe Jeiel and the staff-
officer Maaseiah, and commanded by
Hananiah one of the king's generals. 12The
heads of families of the military champions
numbered in all two thousand six hundred.
13Under them was an army of three hundred
and seven thousand five hundred men ready
for war, a powerful force to support the
king against the enemy. 14Uzziah provided
shields, spears, helmets, armour, bows and
sling-stones for the entire army. 15He also
erected expertly contrived devices for the
towers and angles of Jerusalem from which
to shoot arrows and drop large stones. His
fame spread far and wide, for he was miracu-
lously helped to become strong.

He is struck with a virulent skin-disease for his pride

16But once he was strong, his arrogance was
such that it led to his downfall; he was
unfaithful to Yahweh his God by entering
the Temple of Yahweh to burn incense on
the altar of incense. 17Azariah the priest with
eight brave priests of Yahweh followed him
in; 18confronting King Uzziah, they said to
him, 'Uzziah, you are not allowed to burn
incense to Yahweh; only the Aaronite priests
consecrated for the purpose may burn
incense. Leave the sanctuary, for you have
been unfaithful and will have no honour from
Yahweh God.' 19Uzziah, censer in hand to
burn incense, flew into a rage. But while he
was raging at the priests, a virulent skin-
disease broke out on his forehead in the
presence of the priests, in the Temple of
Yahweh, there by the altar of incense.
20When Azariah the chief priest and all the
other priests turned towards him, there was
skin-disease on his forehead and they hurried
him outside, and he himself was equally

anxious to get out, because Yahweh had struck him.

21 King Uzziah was afflicted with skin-disease till his dying day. Because of this, he lived confined to his room and was excluded from the Temple of Yahweh, while Jotham his son, who was master of the palace, governed the people of the country.

22 The rest of the history of Uzziah, from first to last, has been written by the prophet Isaiah son of Amoz. 23 Then Uzziah fell asleep with his ancestors and was buried with them in the field beside the burial ground of the kings since, it was reasoned, he was afflicted with virulent skin-disease. His son Jotham then succeeded him.

The reign of Jotham

27 Jotham was twenty-five years old when he came to the throne and he reigned for sixteen years in Jerusalem. His mother's name was Jerushah daughter of Zadok. 2 He did what Yahweh regards as right, just as his father Uzziah had done. Only he did not enter Yahweh's sanctuary. But the people continued to do wrong.

3 It was he who built the Upper Gate of the Temple of Yahweh and carried out considerable work on the wall of the Ophel. 4 He also built towns in the highlands of Judah and built forts and towers in the wooded areas.

5 He also went to war against the king of the Ammonites and defeated them; and the Ammonites had to give him a hundred talents of silver, ten thousand *kor* of wheat and ten thousand of barley that year. And the Ammonites paid him the same amount, the second and third years afterwards. 6 Jotham became powerful because he kept an unswerving course before Yahweh his God.

7 The rest of the history of Jotham, all his wars and his policy, are recorded in the Book of the Kings of Israel and Judah. 8 He was twenty-five years old when he came to the throne and he reigned for sixteen years in Jerusalem. 9 Then Jotham fell asleep with his ancestors, and was buried in the City of David; his son Ahaz succeeded him.

V: THE GREAT REFORMS UNDER HEZEKIAH AND JOSIAH

A: THE SINS OF AHAZ, FATHER OF HEZEKIAH

Accession of Ahaz: his idolatry

28 Ahaz was twenty years old when he came to the throne and he reigned for sixteen years in Jerusalem. He did not do what Yahweh regards as right, as his ancestor David had done. 2 He followed the example of the kings of Israel, even having images cast for the Baals; 3 he burned incense in the Valley of Ben-Hinnom, caused his sons to pass through the fire of sacrifice, copying the disgusting practices of the nations whom Yahweh had dispossessed for the Israelites. 4 He offered sacrifices and incense on the high places, on the hills and under every green tree.

The Syro-Ephraimite War

5 So Yahweh his God put him at the mercy of the king of Aram, who defeated him and took large numbers of captives, carrying them off to Damascus. He also put him at the mercy of the king of Israel, who inflicted heavy casualties on him. 6 In a single day, Pekah son of Remaliah killed a hundred and twenty thousand in Judah, all of them prominent men, because they had abandoned Yahweh, God of their ancestors. 7 Zichri, an Ephraimite champion, killed Maaseiah the king's son, Azrikam the controller of the household and Elkanah the king's second-in-command. 8 Of their brothers, the Israelites took two hundred thousand captive including wives, sons, daughters; they also took quantities of booty, carrying everything off to Samaria.

The Israelites obey the prophet Oded

9 Now there was a prophet of Yahweh there by the name of Oded, who went out to meet the troops returning to Samaria and said, 'Look, because Yahweh, God of your ancestors, was angry with Judah, he put them at your mercy, but you have slaughtered them with such fury as reached to heaven, 10 and

now you propose to reduce the children of
Judah and Jerusalem to being your male
and female slaves! Have you not yourselves
committed sins against Yahweh your God?
11 Now listen to me: release the captives you
have taken from your brothers, for the fierce
anger of Yahweh hangs over you.'
12 Some of the Ephraimite chieftains—
Azariah son of Jehohanan, Berechaiah son of
Meshillemoth, Jehizkiah son of Shallum and
Amasa son of Hadlai—then protested to
those returning from the war 13 and said to
them, 'You must not bring the captives here,
for we have already sinned against Yahweh
and you propose to add to our sin and guilt,
although our guilt is already great, and fierce
anger is hanging over Israel.' 14 So in the
presence of the officials and whole assembly,
the soldiers gave up the captives and the
booty. 15 Men nominated for the purpose then
took charge of the captives. From the booty
they clothed all those of them who were
naked; they gave them clothing and sandals,
provided them with food and drink, mounted
on donkeys all those who were infirm and
took them back to Jericho, the city of palm
trees, to their brothers. Then they returned
to Samaria.

Ahaz appeals to Assyria; his apostasy

16 This was when King Ahaz sent asking the
king of Assyria to come to his assistance.
17 The Edomites again invaded, defeated
Judah, and carried off captives, 18 while the
Philistines raided the towns in the lowlands
and in the Negeb of Judah, capturing Beth-
Shemesh, Aijalon, Gederoth, Soco and its
dependencies, Timnah and its dependencies
and Gimzo and its dependencies, and settled
there. 19 For Yahweh brought Judah low
because of Ahaz king of Israel, since he
behaved without restraint in Judah and had
been unfaithful to Yahweh. 20 Tiglath-Pileser
king of Assyria attacked and besieged him;
but he could not overpower him. 21 Although
Ahaz robbed the Temple of Yahweh and the
palaces of the king and princes and gave the
proceeds to the king of Assyria, he received
no help from him.
22 During the time when he was under siege
he disobeyed Yahweh even more grossly, this
King Ahaz. 23 For he offered sacrifices to the
gods of Damascus who had defeated him.
'Since the gods of the kings of Aram', he
thought, 'have supported them, I shall sacri-
fice to them, and perhaps they will help me.'
But they proved to be his and all Israel's
downfall.
24 Ahaz then collected the equipment of the
Temple of God, broke up the equipment of
the Temple of God, sealed the doors of the
Temple of Yahweh and put his own altars in
every corner of Jerusalem; 25 he set up high
places in every town of Judah to burn incense
to other gods, thus provoking the anger of
Yahweh, God of his ancestors.
26 The rest of his history, his whole policy,
from first to last, is recorded in the Book of
the Kings of Judah and Israel. 27 Then Ahaz
fell asleep with his ancestors and was buried
in the City, in Jerusalem, though he was not
taken to the tombs of the kings of Israel. His
son Hezekiah succeeded him.

B: REFORM UNDER HEZEKIAH

Accession of Hezekiah

29 Hezekiah was twenty-five years old
when he came to the throne and he
reigned for twenty-nine years in Jerusalem.
His mother's name was Abijah daughter of
Zechariah. 2 He did what Yahweh regards as
right, just as his ancestor David had done.

The purification of the Temple

3 In the first month of the first year of his
reign, he opened the doors of the Temple of
Yahweh, having repaired them. 4 He then
brought in the priests and the Levites,
assembled them in the eastern square, 5 and
said to them,
'Listen to me, Levites! First sanctify your-
selves, then sanctify the Temple of Yahweh,
God of your ancestors, and remove the filth
from the sanctuary. 6 Our ancestors were
unfaithful, and did what is displeasing to
Yahweh our God. They abandoned him,
turned their faces away from Yahweh's home
and turned their backs on him. 7 They even
closed the doors of the portico, put out
the lamps and stopped burning incense and
making burnt offerings in the sanctuary of
the God of Israel. 8 This was why Yahweh's
anger fell on Judah and Jerusalem and he
made them an object of terror, astonishment
and derision, as you can see for yourselves.
9 Yes, our ancestors were put to the sword,
and our sons, our daughters and our wives

were taken captive because of this. 10 I am now determined to make a covenant with Yahweh, God of Israel, so that his fierce anger may turn away from us. 11 Now, my sons, do not be remiss, for Yahweh has chosen you to stand in his presence and serve him by conducting his worship and offering him incense.'

12 The Levites set about it—Mahath son of Amasai and Joel son of Azariah, from the Kohathites; Kish son of Abdi and Azariah son of Jehallel, from the Merarites; Joah son of Zimmah and Eden son of Joah, from the Gershonites; 13 Shimri and Jeuel, of the sons of Elizaphan; Zechariah and Mattaniah of the sons of Asaph; 14 Jehiel and Shimei of the sons of Heman; Shemaiah and Uzziel of the sons of Jeduthun—15 and gathered their brothers together; they sanctified themselves, and in obedience to the king's order, in accordance with the words of Yahweh, they came to purify the Temple of Yahweh.

16 The priests went into the inner part of the Temple of Yahweh to purify it. They brought all the unclean things which they found in Yahweh's sanctuary, out into the court of the Temple of Yahweh, where the Levites collected them and took them out to the Kidron Valley. 17 They began sanctifying on the first day of the first month, and by the eighth day of the month had reached Yahweh's portico; thus they took eight days to sanctify the Temple of Yahweh, and by the sixteenth day of the first month everything was finished.

The sacrifice of expiation

18 They then waited on King Hezekiah and said, 'We have purified the whole Temple of Yahweh, the altar of burnt offering with all its equipment and the table for the loaves of permanent offering with all their equipment. 19 We have also got ready and sanctified all the equipment which King Ahaz in his infidelity had removed during his reign. It is all ready in front of Yahweh's altar.'

20 King Hezekiah lost no time but called the officials of the city together and went up to the Temple of Yahweh. 21 They brought seven bulls, seven rams, seven lambs and seven goats as a sin sacrifice for the royal house, for the sanctuary and for Judah, and he ordered the Aaronite priests to offer them on Yahweh's altar. 22 So they slaughtered the bulls and the priests took the blood and sprinkled it over the altar. They then slaughtered the rams and sprinkled the blood over the altar; and they slaughtered the lambs and sprinkled the blood over the altar. 23 Then they brought the goats, the sacrifice for sin, before the king and the assembly who laid their hands on them. 24 The priests slaughtered them and made a sacrifice for sin with their blood at the altar to expiate for all Israel, since the king had ordered the burnt offering and the sacrifice for sin on behalf of all Israel.

25 He positioned the Levites in the Temple of Yahweh with cymbals, lyres and harps, in accordance with the ordinance of David, of Gad the king's seer and of Nathan the prophet, for such was Yahweh's order conveyed through his prophets. 26 When the Levites stood with David's musical instruments, and the priests with the trumpets, 27 Hezekiah ordered the burnt offering to be presented on the altar. And as the burnt offering began, the hymns of Yahweh began too, and the trumpets sounded, to the accompaniment of the instruments of David king of Israel, 28 while the whole congregation worshipped, the singers singing and the trumpeters sounding the trumpets, continuously until the burnt offering was over.

The cult begins again

29 When the burnt offering was finished, the king and all those present with him fell to their knees and worshipped. 30 Then King Hezekiah and the officials told the Levites to sing praise to Yahweh in the words of David and Asaph the seer; and joyfully they sang their praises, then knelt in worship.

31 Hezekiah spoke again, 'Now that you have consecrated yourselves to Yahweh, come forward and bring thanksgiving sacrifices to the Temple of Yahweh.' Then the congregation brought thanksgiving sacrifices and those who were generous brought burnt offerings. 32 The number of burnt offerings brought by the congregation was seventy bulls, a hundred rams and two hundred lambs, all as burnt offerings for Yahweh. 33 The consecrated gifts amounted to six hundred bulls and three thousand sheep. 34 The priests were too few, however, and were unable to dismember all the burnt offerings, so their brothers, the Levites, helped them until the work was finished and the priests had sanctified themselves; for the Levites had been more conscientious about

sanctifying themselves than the priests had.
35In addition to the abundance of burnt offer-
ings, there were also the fatty pieces for
communion sacrifices and the libations for
the burnt offerings.

And so the liturgy of Yahweh's Temple
was restored, 36and Hezekiah and all the
people rejoiced over what God had provided
for the people, since everything had
happened so suddenly.

Preparations for the Passover

30 Hezekiah sent messengers to all Israel
and Judah, and also wrote letters to
Ephraim and Manasseh, bidding them come
to the Temple of Yahweh in Jerusalem to
celebrate the Passover in honour of Yahweh,
God of Israel. 2For the king and his officials
and the whole congregation in Jerusalem had
agreed to celebrate the Passover in the second
month, 3having been unable to celebrate it at
the proper time, since the priests had not
purified themselves in sufficient number, and
the people were not assembled in Jerusalem.
4And since this arrangement seemed fitting
to the king and the whole congregation, 5they
resolved to send a proclamation throughout
Israel, from Dan to Beersheba, calling on the
people to come to Jerusalem and celebrate a
Passover in honour of Yahweh, God of Israel,
since they had not celebrated it in a body
as prescribed. 6So, by order of the king,
courtiers set out with letters from the king
and his officials for every part of Israel and
Judah, saying, 'Israelites, return to Yahweh,
God of Abraham, Isaac and Israel, and he
will return to those of you who are left and
have escaped the grasp of the kings of Assyria.
7Do not be like your fathers and brothers
who were unfaithful to Yahweh, God of their
ancestors; he brought them to ruin, as you can
see. 8Do not be stubborn like your ancestors.
Submit to Yahweh, come to his sanctuary
which he has consecrated for ever, and serve
Yahweh your God, so that his fierce anger
may turn away from you. 9For if you return
to Yahweh, your brothers and your sons will
be treated mercifully by their captors and be
allowed to return to this country; for Yahweh
your God is gracious and merciful and will
not turn his face away from you, if you return
to him.'

10The courtiers went from town to town
through the territory of Ephraim and
Manasseh and as far as Zebulon but the
people laughed and scoffed at them; 11even
so, some people from Asher and Manasseh
and Zebulon were humble enough to come
to Jerusalem, 12while in Judah the hand of
God was also at work inspiring a unanimous
desire to obey the order of the king and
the officials in accordance with the word of
Yahweh.

The Passover and feast of Unleavened Bread

13A huge crowd assembled in Jerusalem to
celebrate the feast of Unleavened Bread in
the second month. An immense crowd 14set to
work removing the altars then in Jerusalem;
they also removed all the incense altars and
threw them into the Kidron Valley. 15They
then slaughtered the Passover victims on
the fourteenth day of the second month.
Ashamed of themselves, the priests and
Levites had in the meanwhile sanctified
themselves and brought burnt offerings to
the Temple of Yahweh, 16so they now stood
in their positions prescribed in the Law of
Moses man of God, the priests sprinkling the
blood handed to them by the Levites. 17Since
many people in the congregation had not
sanctified themselves, the Levites took care
of the slaughter of the Passover victims to
consecrate them to Yahweh for all who were
not clean. 18For a great many people,
especially from Ephraim, Manasseh, Issa-
char and Zebulon, had not purified them-
selves, since they did not eat the Passover as
prescribed. But Hezekiah prayed for them
as follows, 'May Yahweh in his goodness
pardon 19everyone whose heart is set on
seeking God, Yahweh, God of his ancestors,
even if he has not been purified as holy things
demand.' 20Yahweh listened to Hezekiah and
left the people unharmed.

21Amid great rejoicing, the Israelites
present in Jerusalem celebrated the feast of
Unleavened Bread for seven days, while day
after day the Levites and the priests praised
Yahweh with all their might. 22Hezekiah then
encouraged all the Levites who had such
understanding of Yahweh.

Having finished the seven-day festival,
during which they sacrificed communion
sacrifices and praised Yahweh, God of their
ancestors, 23the whole congregation decided
to celebrate for a further seven days. So they
joyfully celebrated for another seven days,
24Hezekiah king of Judah contributing a

thousand bulls and seven thousand sheep for the congregation, and the officials another thousand bulls and ten thousand sheep. And a large number of priests sanctified themselves. 25The whole congregation of Judah, the priests, the Levites, the whole congregation coming from Israel and the foreigners coming from the territory of Israel as well as those resident in Judah, rejoiced. 26There was great rejoicing in Jerusalem, for since the days of Solomon son of David, king of Israel, nothing comparable had ever occurred in Jerusalem. 27The levitical priests then stood up and blessed the people and their voice was heard, and their prayer reached his holy dwelling in heaven.

The purification of the country

31 When all this was complete, all Israel present went out to the towns of Judah, broke the pillars, cut down the sacred poles, wrecked the high places and the altars, and did away with them entirely throughout Judah, Benjamin, Ephraim, and Manasseh. Then all the Israelites returned to their towns, everyone to his property.

The reorganisation of the priests and Levites

2Hezekiah re-established the priestly and levitical orders, each man in his proper order according to his duties, whether priest or Levite, to bring burnt offerings and communion sacrifices, to serve and to give thanks and praise within the gates of Yahweh's camp. 3He also established a king's portion from his possessions for the morning and evening burnt offerings, and the burnt offerings for the Sabbaths, New Moons and festivals, as laid down in the Law of Yahweh. 4He furthermore requested the people living in Jerusalem to present the portion for the priests and Levites so that they might devote themselves to the Law of Yahweh. 5As soon as the order had been promulgated, the Israelites provided the first fruits of grain, new wine, olive oil, honey and every other kind of agricultural produce in abundance; they brought in an abundant tithe of everything. 6The Israelites and Judaeans living in the towns of Judah also brought in the tithe of cattle and sheep, and the tithe of sacred gifts consecrated to Yahweh their God, laying them in heaps. 7They began accumulating the heaps in the third month and had finished them by the seventh. 8When Hezekiah and the officials came to inspect the heaps they praised Yahweh and his people Israel.

9While Hezekiah was questioning the priests and Levites about the heaps, 10Azariah, the chief priest, of the family of Zadok, replied as follows, 'Since they began bringing the contributions to the Temple of Yahweh,' he said, 'we have had enough to eat and quantities left over, for Yahweh has blessed his people; this mass of stuff is left.' 11Hezekiah then ordered them to have storerooms prepared in the Temple of Yahweh and, when they had got them ready, 12they conscientiously brought in the contributions, tithes and consecrated gifts, Conaniah the Levite was put in charge of them, with Shimei his brother as his assistant, 13and with Jehiel, Azaziah, Nahath, Asahel, Jeremith, Jozabad, Eliel, Ismachiah, Mahath, and Benaiah as overseers under Conaniah and his brother Shimei, by order of King Hezekiah and of Azariah, the chief of the Temple of God. 14Kore son of Jimnah the Levite, keeper of the eastern gate, was made responsible for the voluntary offerings to God and for providing the portion set aside for Yahweh and the most holy gifts. 15Supporting him loyally in the priestly towns were Eden, Miniamin, Jeshua, Shemaiah, Amariah and Shechaniah, who made the distributions to their brothers in their various orders, whether high or low, 16irrespective of their official genealogy, to the males of thirty years and upwards—to each one who attended the Temple of Yahweh to fulfil his daily obligations—for the performance of their duties appropriate to their orders: 17the priests being registered according to family and the Levites of twenty years and upwards according to their duties within their orders. 18And the official genealogy included all their household, their wives, their sons and their daughters, throughout the community, since these men were obliged to keep sanctifying themselves anew. 19The Aaronite priests who lived on the pasture lands belonging to their towns, had men named in every town to distribute portions to every male among the priests and to everyone included in the official genealogy of the Levites.

20Hezekiah did this throughout all Judah. He did what Yahweh his God regards as good and right and loyal. 21Everything that he undertook, whether in the service of the

Temple of God or in connection with the law
or the commandments, he did in absolute
devotion to his God, and so succeeded.

Sennacherib's invasion

32 After these loyal actions, Sennacherib
king of Assyria advanced and invaded
Judah, and laid siege to the fortified towns,
intending to demolish them. [2]Hezekiah,
realising that Sennacherib's advance was the
preliminary to an attack on Jerusalem,
[3]consulted his officers and warriors about
sealing off the waters of the springs outside
the city, and they supported him. [4]So a large
number of people were called out to block
all the springs and cut off the watercourse
flowing through the country. 'Why', they
said, 'should the kings of Assyria find plenty
of water when they arrive?'
[5]Acting with determination, he also
repaired all the damaged parts of the wall,
built towers on it, constructed a second wall
on the outer side, strengthened the Millo of
the City of David and made quantities of
missiles and shields. [6]He then appointed
generals to command the people, summoned
them to him in the square by the city gate
and spoke as follows to encourage them, [7]'Be
strong and brave; do not be afraid or tremble
when you face the king of Assyria and the
whole horde he brings with him, for there
are more on our side than on his. [8]He has
only human strength, but we have Yahweh
our God to help us and fight our battles.' The
people took heart at the words of Hezekiah
king of Judah.

Sennacherib's blasphemous ultimatum and downfall

[9]Next, Sennacherib king of Assyria, who was
then besieging Lachish with all his forces,
sent his representatives to Jerusalem, to
Hezekiah king of Judah, and all Judah at
Jerusalem, with the following message,
[10]'Sennacherib king of Assyria says this,
"What gives you the confidence to remain in
the fortress of Jerusalem? [11]Isn't Hezekiah
deluding you, only to condemn you to die of
famine and thirst, when he says: Yahweh our
God will save us from the King of Assyria's
clutches? [12]Isn't Hezekiah the very man who
has suppressed his high places and altars, and
given the order to Judah and to Jerusalem:
You must worship before one altar and on
that alone offer incense? [13]Don't you know
what I and my ancestors have done to all the
peoples of the other countries? Have the
national gods of those countries had the
slightest success in saving their countries
from my clutches? [14]Of all the gods of those
nations whom my ancestors devoted to
destruction, which one has been able to save
his people from my clutches, for your god to
be able to save you from my clutches? [15]Do
not let Hezekiah mislead you. Do not let him
delude you like this. Do not believe him, for
no god of any nation or kingdom has been
able to save his people from me or from my
ancestors' clutches. No more will your god
be able to save you from my clutches." '
[16]And his representatives said a great deal
more, maligning Yahweh God, and his
servant Hezekiah.
[17]He also wrote a letter to insult Yahweh,
God of Israel, maligning him as follows, 'Just
as the national gods of the other countries
could not save their peoples from my clut-
ches, so Hezekiah's god cannot save his
people from my clutches.' [18]They then
shouted loudly in the Judaean language to
the people of Jerusalem on the ramparts to
frighten and confuse them, in the hope of
capturing the city, [19]maligning the God of
Jerusalem as though he were one of the man-
made gods of other peoples in the world.
[20]Then King Hezekiah and the prophet
Isaiah son of Amoz prayed and cried out to
Heaven about this, [21]and Yahweh sent an
angel who destroyed every warrior,
commander and officer in the king of Assyr-
ia's camp. So he had to retire shamefacedly
to his own country and when he went into
the temple of his god, some of his own sons
there struck him down with the sword. [22]So
Yahweh saved Hezekiah and the inhabitants
of Jerusalem from the clutches of Sennach-
erib king of Assyria and of everyone else, and
gave them peace on every side. [23]Many people
then brought gifts to Yahweh in Jerusalem
and valuable presents to Hezekiah king of
Judah; from then on, all the other nations
held him in high esteem.

The closing years of Hezekiah's reign

[24]About then Hezekiah fell ill and was at the
point of death. He prayed to Yahweh, who
heard him and granted him a sign. [25]But
Hezekiah made no return for the benefit
which he had received; he became proud and

brought retribution on himself and on Judah and Jerusalem. [26]Then, however, Hezekiah did humble himself in his pride, and so did the inhabitants of Jerusalem; as a result of which, Yahweh's retribution did not overtake them during Hezekiah's lifetime.

[27]Hezekiah enjoyed immense riches and honour. He built himself treasuries for gold, silver, precious stones, spices, jewels and every kind of desirable object, [28]as well as storehouses for his returns of grain, new wine and olive oil, and stalls for all kinds of cattle and pens for the flocks. [29]He also provided himself with donkeys in addition to his immense wealth of flocks and herds, since God had made him immensely wealthy.

[30]It was Hezekiah who stopped the upper outlet of the waters of Gihon and directed them straight down on the west side of the City of David. Hezekiah succeeded in all that he undertook, [31]although when the envoys were sent to him by the rulers of Babylon to enquire about the extraordinary thing which had taken place in the country, God left him alone to test him and discover what lay in his heart.

[32]The rest of the history of Hezekiah, and his deeds of faithful love, are recorded in the Vision of the prophet Isaiah son of Amoz, in the Book of the Kings of Judah and Israel. [33]Then Hezekiah fell asleep with his ancestors and was buried in the upper section of the tombs of the sons of David. All Judah and the inhabitants of Jerusalem paid him honours at his death. His son Manasseh succeeded him.

C: THE SINS OF MANASSEH AND OF AMON

Manasseh undoes the work of Hezekiah

33 Manasseh was twelve years old when he came to the throne, and he reigned for fifty-five years in Jerusalem. [2]He did what is displeasing to Yahweh, copying the disgusting practices of the nations whom Yahweh had dispossessed for the Israelites.

[3]He rebuilt the high places which his father Hezekiah had demolished, he set up altars to Baal and made sacred poles, he worshipped the whole array of heaven and served it. [4]He built altars in the Temple of Yahweh, of which Yahweh had said, 'My name will be in Jerusalem for ever.' [5]He built altars to the whole array of heaven in the two courts of the Temple of Yahweh. [6]He caused his sons to pass through the fire of sacrifice in the Valley of Ben-Hinnom. He practised soothsaying, divination and sorcery, and had dealings with mediums and spirit-guides. He did very many more things displeasing to Yahweh, thus provoking his anger. [7]He put a sculpted image, an idol which he had had made, inside the Temple of which God had said to David and his son Solomon, 'In this Temple and in Jerusalem, the city which I have chosen out of all the tribes of Israel, I shall put my name for ever. [8]Nor shall I ever again remove Israel's foot from the soil on which I established your ancestors on condition that they were careful to observe all I commanded them as laid down in the whole Law, the statutes and the ordinances, given through Moses.' [9]But Manasseh misled Judah and the inhabitants of Jerusalem into doing worse things than the nations which Yahweh had destroyed for the Israelites. [10]When Yahweh spoke to Manasseh and his people, they would not listen.

Manasseh's captivity and conversion

[11]Yahweh then brought down on them the generals of the king of Assyria's army who captured Manasseh with hooks, put him in chains and took him to Babylon. [12]While in his distress, he placated Yahweh his God by genuinely humbling himself before the God of his ancestors. [13]When he prayed to him, he was moved by his entreaty, heard his supplication and brought him back to Jerusalem to his kingdom. Manasseh realised then that Yahweh is God.

[14]Afterwards, he rebuilt the outer wall of the City of David, to the west of Gihon, in the valley, up to the Fish Gate and round the Ophel, and made it very much higher. And he stationed military governors in all the fortified towns of Judah.

[15]He also removed the foreign gods and the idol from the Temple of Yahweh, as well as all the altars which he had built on the mountain of the Temple of Yahweh and in Jerusalem, and threw them out of the city. [16]He repaired the altar of Yahweh and offered communion sacrifices and thanksgiving offerings on it, and commanded Judah to serve Yahweh, God of Israel. [17]The people, however, went on sacrificing at the high places, although only to Yahweh their God.

18 The rest of the history of Manasseh, his
prayer to his God, and the prophecies of the
seers who spoke to him in the name of
Yahweh, God of Israel, can be found in the
Annals of the Kings of Israel. 19 His prayer
and how God was moved by his entreaty, all
his sins, his infidelity, the sites where he built
high places and set up sacred poles and idols
before humbling himself, are set down in the
records of Hozai. 20 Then Manasseh fell asleep
with his ancestors and was buried in the
garden of his palace. His son Amon
succeeded him.

The obduracy of Amon

21 Amon was twenty-two years old when he
came to the throne, and he reigned for two
years in Jerusalem. 22 He did what is
displeasing to Yahweh, as his father
Manasseh had done, for Amon sacrificed to
all the images which his father Manasseh had
made, and served them. 23 He did not humble
himself before Yahweh as his father
Manasseh had done; on the contrary, Amon
wilfully added to his guilt. 24 His retinue
plotted against him and killed him in his own
palace. 25 The people of the country, however,
slaughtered all those who had plotted against
King Amon and proclaimed his son Josiah as
his successor.

D: REFORM UNDER JOSIAH

Accession of Josiah

34 Josiah was eight years old when he
came to the throne, and he reigned for
thirty-one years in Jerusalem. 2 He did what
is pleasing to Yahweh, and followed the
example of his ancestor David, not deviating
from it to right or to left.

The first reforms

3 In the eighth year of his reign, when he was
still a youth, he began to seek the God of his
ancestor David. In the twelfth year he began
to purge Judah and Jerusalem of the high
places, the sacred poles and the sculpted and
cast images. 4 He superintended the smashing
of the altars of Baal, he broke up the incense
altars standing above them, he shattered the
sacred poles and the sculpted and cast images
and reduced them to powder, scattering the
powder on the graves of those who had
sacrificed to them. 5 He burned the bones of
their priests on their altars and so purified
Judah and Jerusalem. 6 In the towns of
Manasseh, Ephraim and Simeon, as far as
Naphtali, and round their open spaces, 7 he
smashed the altars and sacred poles, reduced
the sculpted images to powder and broke up
all the incense altars throughout the territory
of Israel. Then he returned to Jerusalem.

Work on the Temple

8 In the eighteenth year of his reign, after
purging the country and the Temple, he
commissioned Shaphan son of Azaliah,
Maaseiah governor of the city and the herald
Joah son of Joahaz, to repair the Temple of
Yahweh his God. 9 When they came to the
high priest Hilkiah, they handed over the
money contributed to the Temple of God and
collected by the levitical guardians of the
threshold from Manasseh and Ephraim, from
all the rest of Israel, from all Judah and
Benjamin, and from the inhabitants of Jeru-
salem. 10 They handed it over to the masters
of works attached to the Temple of Yahweh,
and these gave it to the men working on the
Temple of Yahweh to repair and restore the
Temple; 11 they gave it to the craftsmen and
builders for buying dressed stone and timber
for beams, to underpin the buildings which
the kings of Judah had allowed to fall into
decay.

12 The men were conscientious in doing
their work; their foremen were Jahath and
Obadiah, Levites descended from Merari,
and Zechariah and Meshullam, descended
from Kohath, who supervised. The
Levites—all of whom were skilled instru-
mentalists— 13 were in charge of the carriers
and supervised all the workmen at their
various jobs, while some of the Levites acted
as secretaries, book-keepers and gate-
keepers.

The Book of the Law discovered

14 While bringing out the money contributed
to the Temple of Yahweh, the priest Hilkiah
found the book of the Law of Yahweh given
through Moses. 15 Hilkiah then said to
Shaphan the secretary, 'I have found the
Book of the Law in the Temple of Yahweh.'
And Hilkiah gave the book to Shaphan.

[16]Shaphan took the book to the king, reporting furthermore to him as follows, 'Your servants have done everything entrusted to them. [17]They have melted down the silver which was in the Temple of Yahweh and have handed it over to the supervisors and the masters of works.' [18]Shaphan the secretary also informed the king, 'The priest Hilkiah has given me a book'; and Shaphan read extracts from it in the king's presence.

[19]On hearing the words of the Law, the king tore his clothes. [20]Then the king gave the following order to Hilkiah, Ahikam son of Shaphan, Abdon son of Micah, Shaphan the secretary and Asaiah the king's minister, [21]'Go and consult Yahweh on behalf of me and of those left in Israel and Judah about the words of the book that has been discovered: for Yahweh's furious wrath has been pouring down on us because our ancestors did not obey the word of Yahweh by doing what this book says they ought to have done.'

Huldah the prophetess is consulted

[22]Hilkiah and those whom the king had designated went to the prophetess Huldah wife of Shallum, son of Tokhath, son of Hasrah, the keeper of the wardrobe; she lived in Jerusalem in the new town. They spoke to her about this, [23]and she replied, 'Yahweh, God of Israel, says this, "To the man who sent you to me reply: [24]Yahweh says this: I am going to bring disaster on this place and the people who live in it—all the curses set down in the book read in the king of Judah's presence. [25]Because they have abandoned me and burnt incense to other gods, so as to provoke my anger by their every action, my wrath is about to be poured down on this place, and nothing can stop it. [26]As for the king of Judah who sent you to consult Yahweh, say this to him: Yahweh, God of Israel, says this: The words you have heard . . . [27]But since your heart has been touched and you have humbled yourself before God on hearing what he has decreed against this place and the people who live in it, have torn your clothes and wept before me, I too have heard"—Yahweh says this. [28]"Look, when I gather you to your ancestors, you will be gathered into your grave in peace; you will not live to see the great disaster that I am going to bring on this place and on the people who live in it." ' They took this answer to the king.

The renewal of the covenant

[29]The king then had all the elders of Judah and of Jerusalem summoned, [30]and the king went up to the temple of Yahweh, with all the men of Judah and all the inhabitants of Jerusalem, priests, Levites and all the people, high and low. In their hearing he read out the entire contents of the Book of the Covenant discovered in the Temple of Yahweh. [31]The king then, standing on the dais, bound himself by the covenant before Yahweh, to follow Yahweh, to keep his commandments, decrees and laws with all his heart and soul and to carry out the terms of the covenant as written in this book. [32]He made all those present in Jerusalem and Benjamin pledge their allegiance to it.

The citizens of Jerusalem took action in keeping with the covenant of God, the God of their ancestors, [33]while Josiah removed all the abominations throughout the territories belonging to the Israelites and required all inhabitants of Israel to serve Yahweh their God; throughout his lifetime they did not deviate from following Yahweh, God of their ancestors.

Preparations for the Passover

35 Josiah then celebrated a Passover to Yahweh in Jerusalem. The Passover victims were slaughtered on the fourteenth day of the first month.

[2]He assigned the priests to their posts, encouraging them to do their duty in the Temple of Yahweh. [3]Then he said to the Levites, who had understanding for all Israel and were consecrated to Yahweh, 'Put the sacred ark in the Temple built by Solomon son of David, king of Israel. You need not carry it about on your shoulders any more. Now serve Yahweh your God and Israel his people! [4]Prepare yourselves by families according to your orders, as laid down in the decree of David king of Israel and that of Solomon his son, [5]and take up positions in the sanctuary corresponding to the family divisions of your brothers the laity, so that there are Levites for each family division. [6]Slaughter the Passover, sanctify yourselves and prepare it so that your brothers can

observe it in the way the word of Yahweh through Moses requires.'

[7]For the laity Josiah provided small livestock, that is, lambs and young goats—everything for the Passover offerings for all who attended—to the number of thirty thousand, as well as three thousand bullocks; these were from the king's own possessions. [8]His officials also made voluntary contributions for the people, the priests and the Levites; and Hilkiah, Zechariah and Jehiel, the chiefs of the Temple of God, gave two thousand six hundred lambs and three hundred bullocks to the priests for the Passover offerings; [9]while Conaniah, Shemaiah, Nethanel his brother, Hashabiah, Jeiel and Jozabad, the head Levites, provided five thousand lambs and five hundred bullocks as Passover offerings for the Levites.

The celebration of the Passover

[10]So the service was arranged, the priests stood in their places and the Levites in their orders as the king had commanded. [11]Then they slaughtered the Passover victims and while the priests sprinkled the blood as they received it from the Levites, the latter did the skinning. [12]Next they put the burnt offering aside for presentation to the family divisions of the laity, so that they could offer it to Yahweh in the way prescribed in the Book of Moses; they did the same with the bullocks. [13]They roasted the Passover victim over an open fire in accordance with the regulation and boiled the consecrated offerings in pots, kettles and pans, which they then distributed to all the laity as quickly as they could.

[14]Afterwards they provided for themselves and the priests, since the Aaronite priests were kept busy till nightfall making the burnt offerings and offering the fat; that was why the Levites prepared the Passover for themselves and for the Aaronite priests. [15]The Asaphite singers were at their places, in accordance with the command of David and Asaph, Heman and Jeduthun the king's seer; so were the gatekeepers at each gate. Because they could not leave their duties, their brothers the Levites prepared the Passover for them.

[16]So the whole service of Yahweh was arranged that day to celebrate the Passover and to bring burnt offerings on the altar of Yahweh, in accordance with King Josiah's command. [17]On that occasion the Israelites who were present celebrated the Passover and the feast of Unleavened Bread for seven days. [18]No Passover like this one had ever been celebrated in Israel since the days of the prophet Samuel, nor had any of the kings of Israel ever celebrated a Passover like the one celebrated by Josiah, the priests, the Levites, all Judah and Israel who were present, and the inhabitants of Jerusalem.

Death of Josiah

[19]This Passover was celebrated in the eighteenth year of Josiah's reign.

[20]After all this, when Josiah had provided for the Temple, Necho king of Egypt advanced to give battle at Carchemish on the Euphrates and Josiah went to intercept him. [21]Necho however sent him messengers to say, 'Why be concerned about me, king of Judah? I have not come today to attack you; my quarrel is with another dynasty. God has commanded me to move quickly, so keep well clear of the god who is with me!' [22]But Josiah was not to be deflected from his determination to fight him, and would not listen to Necho's words, which came from the mouth of God. He gave battle in the plain of Megiddo. [23]The archers shot King Josiah. The king then said to his retainers, 'Take me away; I am badly wounded.' [24]So his retainers lifted him out of his own chariot, transferred him to one which he had in reserve and brought him to Jerusalem, where he died and was buried in the tombs of his ancestors. All Judah and Jerusalem held mourning for Josiah. [25]Jeremiah composed a lament for Josiah and all the male and female singers to this day lament Josiah in their dirges; they have made it a rule in Israel; they are recorded in the Lamentations.

[26]The rest of the history of Josiah, his deeds of faithful love conforming to what is prescribed in the Law of Yahweh, [27]his history from first to last, are recorded in the Book of the Kings of Israel and Judah.

E: ISRAEL IN THE CLOSING YEARS OF THE MONARCHY

Jehoahaz

36 The people of the land then took Jehoahaz son of Josiah and proclaimed him king of Jerusalem in succession to his

father. 2 Jehoahaz was twenty-three years old
when he came to the throne, and he reigned
for three months in Jerusalem. 3 The king of
Egypt deposed him in Jerusalem and
imposed a levy of a hundred talents of silver
and one talent of gold on the country. 4 The
king of Egypt then made his brother Eliakim
king of Judah and Jerusalem, and changed his
name to Jehoiakim. Carrying off his brother
Jehoahaz, Necho took him to Egypt.

Jehoiakim

5 Jehoiakim was twenty-five years old when
he came to the throne, and he reigned for
eleven years in Jerusalem. He did what is
displeasing to Yahweh his God. 6 Nebuchad-
nezzar king of Babylon attacked him, loaded
him with chains and took him to Babylon.
7 To Babylon Nebuchadnezzar also took some
of the objects belonging to the Temple of
Yahweh and put them in his palace in
Babylon. 8 The rest of the history of Jeho-
iakim, the shameful things that he did and
what happened to him in consequence, these
are recorded in the Book of the Kings of
Israel and Judah. His son Jehoiachin
succeeded him.

Jehoiachin

9 Jehoiachin was eighteen years old when he
came to the throne, and he reigned for three
months and ten days in Jerusalem. He did
what is displeasing to Yahweh. 10 At the turn
of the year, King Nebuchadnezzar sent for
him and had him taken to Babylon, with
the valuables belonging to the Temple of
Yahweh, and made his brother Zedekiah
king of Judah and Jerusalem.

Zedekiah

11 Zedekiah was twenty-one years old when
he came to the throne, and he reigned for
eleven years in Jerusalem. 12 He did what is
displeasing to Yahweh his God. He did not
listen humbly to the prophet Jeremiah who
spoke for Yahweh. 13 Furthermore, he
rebelled against King Nebuchadnezzar who
had made him swear allegiance to him by
God. He became stubborn, and obstinately
refused to return to Yahweh, God of
Israel.

The nation

14 Furthermore, all the leaders of Judah, the
priests and the people too, added infidelity
to infidelity, copying all the shameful prac-
tices of the nations and defiling the Temple
of Yahweh which he himself had consecrated
in Jerusalem. 15 Yahweh, God of their ances-
tors, continuously sent them word through
his messengers because he felt sorry for his
people and his dwelling, 16 but they ridiculed
the messengers of God, they despised his
words, they laughed at his prophets, until
Yahweh's wrath with his people became so
fierce that there was no further remedy.

Ruin

17 So against them he summoned the king of
the Chaldaeans and he put their young men
to the sword within the very building of their
Temple, not sparing young man or girl, or
the old and infirm; he put them all at his
mercy. 18 All the things belonging to the
Temple of God, whether large or small,
the treasures of the Temple of Yahweh,
the treasures of the king and his officials,
everything he took to Babylon. 19 He burned
down the temple of God, demolished the
walls of Jerusalem, burned all its palaces to
the ground and destroyed everything of value
in it. 20 And those who had escaped the sword
he deported to Babylon, where they were
enslaved by him and his descendants until
the rise of the kingdom of Persia, 21 to fulfil
Yahweh's prophecy through Jeremiah: *Until
the country has paid off its Sabbaths, it will lie
fallow for all the days of its desolation—until
the seventy years are complete.*[a]

A new hope

22 In the first year of Cyrus king of Persia—to
fulfil the word of Yahweh through
Jeremiah—Yahweh roused the spirit of
Cyrus king of Persia to issue a proclamation
and to have it publicly displayed throughout
his kingdom: 23 'Cyrus king of Persia says
this, "Yahweh, the God of Heaven, has given
me all the kingdoms of the earth and has
appointed me to build him a Temple in
Jerusalem, which is in Judah. Whoever there
is among you of all his people, may his God
be with him! Let him go up." '

36a A combination of Lv 26:34–35 and Jr 25:11; 29:10.

THE BOOK OF EZRA

The Book of Ezra deals with the crucial period of the re-establishment of the Jewish community in Jerusalem after the release from exile (539 BC), a moment which is of the utmost importance for the future of Judaism. The return has been authorised, and sundry privileges have been decreed, by the central government of the Persian Empire in which Palestine now lies. But the book gives a fascinating picture of the efforts of the neighbouring communities to frustrate the attempts of the Jewish settlers to return to normality, even including appeals to the central government.

The story is difficult to follow. Decrees and counter-petitions are quoted at length in a surprisingly modern way, but events are related according to subject-matter rather than chronology, and the chronological order is further mixed up within sections. The relevant documents have been combined by the Chronicler with Ezra's report of his mission to give a picture of the restored community, devotedly centred on Temple and Law.

PLAN OF THE BOOKS

THE BOOK OF EZRA

I: THE RETURN FROM EXILE AND THE REBUILDING OF THE TEMPLE

The return of the exiles

1 In the first year of Cyrus king of Persia—to
fulfil the word of Yahweh spoken through
Jeremiah[a]—Yahweh roused the spirit of
Cyrus king of Persia to issue a proclamation
and to have it publicly displayed throughout
his kingdom:
2 'Cyrus king of Persia says this, "Yahweh,
the God of heaven, has given me all the
kingdoms of the earth and has appointed
me to build him a Temple in Jerusalem, in
Judah. 3 Whoever among you belongs to
the full tally of his people, may his God be
with him! Let him go up to Jerusalem, in
Judah, and build the Temple of Yahweh,
God of Israel, who is the God in Jerusalem.
4 And let each survivor, wherever he lives,
be helped by the people of his locality with
silver, gold, equipment and riding beasts,

1a Jr 25:11–12; 29:10.

as well as voluntary offerings for the
Temple of God which is in Jerusalem." '

5Then the heads of families of Judah and
of Benjamin, the priests and the Levites, in
fact all whose spirit had been roused by God,
prepared to go and rebuild the Temple of
Yahweh in Jerusalem; 6and all their neigh-
bours gave them every kind of help: silver,
gold, equipment, riding beasts and valuable
presents, in addition to their voluntary
offerings.
7Furthermore, King Cyrus handed over
the articles belonging to the Temple of
Yahweh which Nebuchadnezzar had carried
away from Jerusalem and put in the temple
of his god. 8Cyrus king of Persia handed
them over to Mithredath the treasurer who
checked them out to Sheshbazzar the prince
of Judah. 9The inventory was as follows:
thirty gold dishes; one thousand silver dishes,
twenty-nine repaired; 10thirty gold bowls; a
thousand silver bowls, four hundred and ten
damaged; one thousand other articles. 11In
all, five thousand four hundred articles of
gold and silver. Sheshbazzar took all these
with him when he led the exiles back from
Babylon to Jerusalem.

List of the first exiles to return

2 These were the people of the province who
returned[a] from the captivity of the Exile,
those whom Nebuchadnezzar king of
Babylon had deported to Babylon, and who
returned to Jerusalem and Judah, each to his
own town. 2They were the ones who arrived
with Zerubbabel, Jeshua, Nehemiah,
Seraiah, Reelaiah, Nahamani, Mordecai,
Bilshan, Mispar, Bigvai, Rehum and
Baanah.
The number of the men of the people of
the country of Israel: 3sons of Parosh, two
thousand one hundred and seventy-two;
4sons of Shephatiah, three hundred and
seventy-two; 5sons of Arah, seven hundred
and seventy-five; 6sons of Pahath-Moab, that
is to say the sons of Jeshua and Joab, two
thousand eight hundred and twelve; 7sons of
Elam, one thousand two hundred and fifty-
four; 8sons of Zattu, nine hundred and forty-
five; 9sons of Zaccai, seven hundred and
sixty; 10sons of Bani, six hundred and forty-
two; 11sons of Bebai, six hundred and twenty-
three; 12sons of Azgad, one thousand two
hundred and twenty-two; 13sons of
Adonikam, six hundred and sixty-six; 14sons
of Bigvai, two thousand and fifty-six;
15sons of Adin, four hundred and fifty-four;
16sons of Ater, that is to say of Hezekiah,
ninety-eight; 17sons of Bezai, three hundred
and twenty-three; 18sons of Jorah, one
hundred and twelve; 19sons of Hashum, two
hundred and twenty-three; 20sons of Gibbar,
ninety-five; 21sons of Bethlehem, one
hundred and twenty-three; 22men of Neto-
phah, fifty-six; 23men of Anathoth, one
hundred and twenty-eight; 24sons of Azma-
veth, forty-two; 25sons of Kiriath-Jearim,
Chephirah and Beeroth, seven hundred and
forty-three; 26sons of Ramah and Geba, six
hundred and twenty-one; 27men of Michmas,
one hundred and twenty-two; 28men of
Bethel and Ai, two hundred and twenty-
three; 29sons of Nebo, fifty-two; 30of
Magbish, one hundred and fifty-six; 31sons
of the other Elam, one thousand two hundred
and fifty-four; 32sons of Harim, three
hundred and twenty; 33sons of Lod, Hadid
and Ono, seven hundred and twenty-five;
34sons of Jericho, three hundred and forty-
five; 35sons of Senaah, three thousand six
hundred and thirty.
36The priests: sons of Jedaiah, of the House
of Jeshua, nine hundred and seventy-three;
37sons of Immer, one thousand and fifty-two;
38sons of Pashhur, one thousand two hundred
and forty-seven; 39sons of Harim, one thou-
sand and seventeen.
40The Levites: sons of Jeshua and
Kadmiel, of the line of Hodaviah, seventy-
four.
41The singers: sons of Asaph, one hundred
and twenty-eight.
42The sons of the gatekeepers: sons of
Shallum, sons of Ater, sons of Talmon, sons
of Akkub, sons of Hatita, sons of Shobai: in
all, one hundred and thirty-nine.
43The temple slaves: sons of Ziha, sons of
Hasupha, sons of Tabbaoth, 44sons of Keros,
sons of Siaha, sons of Padon, 45sons of
Lebanah, sons of Hagabah, sons of Akkub,
46sons of Hagab, sons of Shamlai, sons of
Hanan, 47sons of Giddel, sons of Gahar, sons
of Reaiah, 48sons of Rezin, sons of Nekoda,
sons of Gazzam, 49sons of Uzza, sons of
Paseah, sons of Besai, 50sons of Asnah, sons
of the Meunites, sons of the Nephisites,

2a || Ne 7:6–72.

51 sons of Bakbuk, sons of Hakupha, sons of
Harhur, 52 sons of Bazluth, sons of Mehida,
sons of Harsha, 53 sons of Barkos, sons of
Sisera, sons of Temah, 54 sons of Neziah, sons
of Hatipha.

55 The sons of Solomon's slaves: sons of
Sotai, sons of Hassophereth, sons of Peruda,
56 sons of Jaalah, sons of Darkon, sons of
Giddel, 57 sons of Shephatiah, sons of Hattil,
sons of Pochereth-ha-Zebaim, sons of Ami.
58 The total of the temple slaves and the
sons of Solomon's slaves: three hundred and
ninety-two.

59 The following, who came from Tel-
Melah, Tel-Harsha, Cherub, Addan and
Immer, could not prove that their families
and ancestry were of Israelite origin: 60 the
sons of Delaiah, the sons of Tobiah, the
sons of Nekoda: six hundred and fifty-two.
61 And among the sons of the priests: the sons
of Habaiah, the sons of Hakkoz, the sons
of Barzillai—who had married one of the
daughters of Barzillai the Gileadite, whose
name he adopted. 62 These had looked for
their entries in the official genealogies but
were not to be found there, and were hence
disqualified from the priesthood.
63 Consequently, His Excellency forbade
them to eat any of the consecrated food until
a priest appeared who could consult *urim* and
thummim.

64 The whole assembly numbered forty-two
thousand, three hundred and sixty people,
65 not counting their male and female slaves to
the number of seven thousand three hundred
and thirty-seven. They also had two hundred
male and female singers. 66 Their horses
numbered seven hundred and thirty-six,
their mules two hundred and forty-five,
67 their camels four hundred and thirty-five
and their donkeys six thousand seven
hundred and twenty.

68 When they arrived at the Temple of
Yahweh in Jerusalem, a certain number of
heads of families made voluntary offerings
for the Temple of God, for its rebuilding on
its site. 69 In accordance with their means they
gave sixty-one thousand gold drachmas, five
thousand silver minas and one hundred
priestly robes to the sacred treasury.

70 The priests, the Levites and some of the
people settled in Jerusalem; the singers, the
gatekeepers and the temple slaves in their
appropriate towns; and all the other Israelites
in their own towns.

Resumption of the sacrificial liturgy

3 When the seventh month came after the
Israelites had been resettled in their
towns, the people gathered as one person in
Jerusalem. 2 Then Jeshua son of Jozadak,
with his brother priests, and Zerubbabel son
of Shealtiel, with his brothers, set about
rebuilding the altar of the God of Israel, to
offer burnt offerings on it as prescribed in
the Law of Moses man of God. 3 They erected
the altar on its old site, despite their fear
of the people of the country, and on it they
presented burnt offerings to Yahweh, burnt
offerings morning and evening; 4 they
celebrated the feast of Shelters as pre-
scribed,[a] offering daily the number of burnt
offerings required from day to day, 5 and
in addition presented the continual burnt
offerings prescribed for the Sabbaths, for the
New Moons and for all the festivals sacred to
Yahweh, as well as those voluntary offerings
made by individuals to Yahweh. 6 From the
first day of the seventh month they began
presenting burnt offerings to Yahweh,
though the foundations of the Temple of
Yahweh had not yet been laid.

7 They also contributed money for the
masons and carpenters, and food, drink and
oil for the Sidonians and Tyrians for bringing
cedar wood from Lebanon by sea to Jaffa,
for which Cyrus king of Persia had given
permission. 8 It was in the second month of
the second year after their arrival at the
Temple of God in Jerusalem that Zerubbabel
son of Shealtiel and Jeshua son of Jozadak,
with the rest of their brothers, the priests,
the Levites and all the people who had
returned to Jerusalem from captivity, began
the work by appointing some of the Levites
who were twenty years old or more to superin-
tend the work on the Temple of Yahweh.
9 The Levites, Jeshua, his sons and his
brothers, with Kadmiel, Binnui and his sons,
the sons of Hodaviah, agreed to superintend
the men working on the Temple of God.
10 When the builders had laid the foundations
of the Temple of Yahweh, the priests in their
robes stood forward with trumpets, and the
Levites, the sons of Asaph, with cymbals, to
praise Yahweh according to the ordinances

3a Ex 23:14.

of David king of Israel. [11]They chanted praise and thanksgiving to Yahweh because for Israel, they said, 'he is good, and everlasting in his faithful love.' Then all the people raised a mighty shout of praise to Yahweh, since the foundations of the Temple of Yahweh had now been laid. [12]Many of the older priests, Levites and heads of families, who had seen the first temple, wept very loudly when the foundations of this one were laid before their eyes, but many others shouted aloud for joy, [13]so that nobody could distinguish the noise of the joyful shout from the noise of the people's weeping; for the people shouted so loudly that the noise could be heard far away.

Opposition from the Samaritans: their tactics under Cyrus

4 When the enemies of Judah and Benjamin heard that the exiles were building the Temple of Yahweh, God of Israel, [2]they came to Zerubbabel and Jeshua and the heads of families and said, 'Let us help you build, for we resort to your God as you do and we have been sacrificing to him since the time of Esarhaddon king of Assyria, who brought us here.' [3]Zerubbabel, Jeshua, and the other heads of Israelite families replied, 'It is out of the question that you should join us in building a Temple for our God. We shall build for Yahweh, God of Israel, on our own, as King Cyrus king of Persia has commanded us.' [4]The people of the country then set about demoralising the people of Judah and deterring them from building; [5]they also bribed counsellors against them to frustrate their purpose throughout the lifetime of Cyrus king of Persia right on into the reign of Darius king of Persia.

Samaritan tactics under Xerxes and Artaxerxes[a]

[6]In the reign of Xerxes, at the beginning of his reign, they drew up an accusation against the inhabitants of Judah and Jerusalem.

[7]In the days of Artaxerxes, Mithredath, Tabeel and their other associates wrote to Artaxerxes king of Persia against Jerusalem; the text of the letter was written in Aramaic writing and dialect.

[8]Then Rehum the governor and Shimshai the secretary wrote a letter to King Artaxerxes, denouncing Jerusalem as follows:

[9]'From Rehum the governor and Shimshai the secretary and their other associates, the judges, the legates, the Persian officials, the people of Uruk, Babylon and Susa—that is, the Elamites—[10]and the other peoples whom the great and illustrious Ashurbanipal deported and settled in the towns of Samaria and in the rest of Transeuphrates.'

[11]This is the text of the letter which they sent him:

'To King Artaxerxes, from your servants the people of Transeuphrates:

[12]'May the king now please be informed that the Jews, who have come up from you to us, have arrived in Jerusalem and are rebuilding the rebellious and evil city; they have begun rebuilding the walls and are laying the foundations; [13]and now the king should be informed that once this city is rebuilt and the walls are restored, they will refuse to pay tribute, tax or toll, thus the king will incur a loss; [14]and now, because we eat the palace salt, it is not proper for us to see this affront offered to the king; we therefore send this information to the king [15]so that a search may be made in the archives of your ancestors: in which archives you will find and learn that this city is a rebellious city, the bane of kings and provinces, and that sedition has been stirred up there from ancient times; that is why this city was destroyed. [16]We inform the king that if this city is rebuilt and its walls are restored, you will soon have no territories left in Transeuphrates.'

[17]The king sent this reply:

'To Rehum the governor, to Shimshai the secretary, and to their other associates resident in Samaria and elsewhere in Transeuphrates: Greetings!

[18]'And now, the document which you sent us has been accurately translated for me, [19]and by my orders search has been made, and it has been found that this city has rebelled against the kings in the past and that revolt and sedition have been contrived in it; [20]and that powerful kings

4a The passage 4:6—6:18 is written in Aramaic.

have reigned in Jerusalem, governing the
whole of Transeuphrates and exacting
tribute, tax and toll; 21 now give orders for
these men to cease work; this city is not to
be rebuilt until I give the order. 22 Beware
of acting negligently in this matter. Why
should the harm grow, to endanger the
king?'

23 As soon as the text of King Artaxerxes'
document had been read to Rehum the
governor, Shimshai the secretary and their
associates, they hurried to the Jews in Jerusalem
and stopped their work by force of
arms.

The rebuilding of the Temple (520–515 BC)

24 Work on the Temple of God in Jerusalem
then ceased, and was discontinued until the
second year of the reign of Darius King of
Persia.

5 When the prophets Haggai and Zechariah
son of Iddo prophesied to the Jews who
were in Judah and Jerusalem in the name
of the God of Israel who was over them,
2 Zerubbabel son of Shealtiel and Jeshua son
of Jozadak began rebuilding the Temple
of God in Jerusalem; with them were the
prophets of God, supporting them.
3 It was then that Tattenai governor of
Transeuphrates, Shethar-Bozenai and their
associates came to them and asked, 'Who
gave you the order to rebuild this Temple
and complete this structure? 4 What are the
names of the men putting up this building?'
5 But the eyes of their God were watching
over the elders of the Jews, so they were not
forced to stop until a report could reach
Darius and an official reply about the matter
could be received from him.

The governor's letter to King Darius

6 A copy of the letter which Tattenai,
governor of Transeuphrates, Shethar-Bozenai
and his associates, the officials in
Transeuphrates, sent to King Darius. 7 They
sent him a report which ran as follows:

'To King Darius, hearty greetings!
8 'The king should be informed that we
went to the province of Judah, to the
Temple of the great God, which is being
rebuilt with large stones; beams are
being embedded in the walls; the work
is being carried out energetically and is
making good progress. 9 Questioning these
elders, we asked them, "Who gave you
permission to rebuild this Temple and
complete this structure?" 10 We also asked
them their names, to inform you, so that
we could record the names of the men who
were their leaders.
11 'They gave us the following answer,
"We are the servants of the God of heaven
and earth; we are rebuilding the Temple
built many years ago, which a great king
of Israel had built and completed. 12 But
because our ancestors angered the God of
heaven, he handed them over to Nebuchadnezzar
the Chaldaean king of Babylon
who destroyed this Temple and deported
the people to Babylon. 13 In the first year
of Cyrus king of Babylon, however, King
Cyrus issued an official order that this
Temple of God should be rebuilt;
14 furthermore, those gold and silver articles
belonging to the Temple of God, which
Nebuchadnezzar had removed from the
temple in Jerusalem and brought to the
temple of Babylon, King Cyrus in turn
removed from the temple of Babylon and
handed back to a certain Sheshbazzar
whom he had appointed governor. 15 He
said to him, 'Take these articles; go and
return them to the Temple which is in
Jerusalem and let the Temple of God be
rebuilt on its original site;' 16 this Sheshbazzar
then came and laid the foundations
of the Temple of God in Jerusalem, and it
has been under construction ever since,
and is not yet finished."
17 'Hence, if it please the king, let search
be made in the royal treasuries in Babylon,
to find out if it is true that an official order
was issued by King Cyrus for this temple
of God in Jerusalem to be rebuilt; and let
the king's decision on this matter be sent
to us.'

King Darius replies

6 Then, on the order of King Darius, search
was made in the archives deposited in the
treasuries in Babylon 2 and a scroll was found
in the fortress of Ecbatana, which ran as
follows:

'Memorandum.

3 'In the first year of King Cyrus, King Cyrus issued this order:

"Temple of God in Jerusalem.

"The Temple is to be rebuilt as a place of offering sacrifice and its foundations retained. Its height is to be sixty cubits, its width sixty cubits, 4 with three layers of large stones and one layer of timber. The cost is to be met by the royal treasury. 5 Furthermore, the gold and silver articles belonging to the Temple of God which Nebuchadnezzar took from the Temple in Jerusalem and brought to Babylon are to be given back and returned to the temple in Jerusalem, each to its proper place, and deposited in the Temple of God."

6 'Hence, Tattenai governor of Transeuphrates, Shethar-Bozenai and your associates, the officials of Transeuphrates, keep away from there! 7 Leave the governor of the Jews and the elders of the Jews alone, to get on with their work on that Temple of God; they are permitted to rebuild that Temple of God on that site. 8 And herewith are my instructions as to how you will assist these elders of the Jews in the rebuilding of that Temple of God: the cost is to be paid in full to these men from the royal revenue, that is, from the taxes of Transeuphrates, and without interruption. 9 And whatever is required—young bulls, rams, lambs for burnt offerings to the God of heaven, wheat, salt, wine, oil, as the priests in Jerusalem request—is to be given them day by day without fail, 10 so that they may offer sacrifices acceptable to the God of heaven and pray for the life of the king and his sons. 11 Furthermore I have issued an instruction that if anyone disobeys this order, a beam is to be torn from his house, he is to be impaled on it and his house is to be reduced to a rubbish-heap for his offence; 12 and may the God who has caused his name to live there overthrow the king of any people who dares to defy this and destroy that Temple of God in Jerusalem! I, Darius, have issued this order. Let it be punctiliously obeyed!'

The Temple is completed

13 Tattenai governor of Transeuphrates, Shethar-Bozenai and their associates punctiliously obeyed the instructions sent by King Darius; 14 and the elders of the Jews made good progress over their building, thanks to the prophetic activity of the prophet Haggai and Zechariah son of Iddo, completing the reconstruction in accordance with the command of the God of Israel and the order of Cyrus and of Darius. 15 This Temple was completed on the twenty-third day of the month of Adar, in the sixth year of the reign of King Darius. 16 The Israelites—the priests, the Levites and the remainder of the exiles—joyfully celebrated the dedication of this Temple of God; 17 for the dedication of this Temple of God they offered one hundred bulls, two hundred rams, four hundred lambs and, as a sin offering for all Israel, twelve he-goats, corresponding to the number of the tribes of Israel. 18 Then they installed the priests in their orders and the Levites in their positions for the ministry of the Temple of God in Jerusalem, as prescribed in the Book of Moses.

The Passover of 515 BC

19 The exiles celebrated the Passover on the fourteenth day of the first month. 20 The Levites, as one man, had purified themselves; all were pure, so they sacrificed the Passover for all the exiles, for their brothers the priests and for themselves. 21 So the Israelites who had returned from exile and all those who had renounced the filthy practices of the people of the country to join them in resorting to Yahweh, God of Israel, ate the Passover. 22 For seven days they joyfully celebrated the feast of Unleavened Bread, for Yahweh had given them cause to rejoice, having moved the heart of the king of Assyria in their favour to support them in their work on the Temple of God, the God of Israel.

II: THE ORGANISATION OF THE COMMUNITY BY EZRA AND NEHEMIAH

The mission and personality of Ezra

7 After these events, in the reign of Artaxerxes king of Persia, Ezra son of Seraiah, son of Azariah, son of Hilkiah, [2]son of Shallum, son of Zadok, son of Ahitub, [3]son of Amariah, son of Azariah, son of Meraioth, [4]son of Zerahiah, son of Uzzi, son of Bukki, [5]son of Abishua, son of Phinehas, son of Eleazar, son of the chief priest Aaron—[6]this Ezra came up from Babylon. He was a scribe versed in the Law of Moses, which Yahweh, God of Israel, had given. The king gave him everything that he asked for, since the hand of Yahweh his God was over him. [7]A number of Israelites, priests, Levites, singers, gatekeepers and temple slaves went up to Jerusalem in the seventh year of the reign of King Artaxerxes. [8]Ezra arrived in Jerusalem in the fifth month, in the seventh year of the king's reign; [9]for he had ordered the departure from Babylon on the first day of the first month, and he arrived in Jerusalem on the first day of the fifth month, since the kindly hand of his God was over him. [10]For Ezra had devoted himself to studying the Law of Yahweh so as to put into practice and teach its statutes and rulings.

The order of Artaxerxes

[11]This is the text of the document which King Artaxerxes gave to Ezra, the priest-scribe, a student of matters pertaining to Yahweh's commandments and statutes relating to Israel:

[12]'Artaxerxes, king of kings, to the priest Ezra, Secretary of the Law of the God of heaven: greetings!

[13]'Now here are my orders. All members of the people of Israel in my kingdom, including their priests and Levites, who freely choose to go to Jerusalem, may go with you, [14]for you are being sent by the king and his seven counsellors to investigate how the Law of your God, in which you are expert, is being applied in Judah and Jerusalem, [15]and to transport the silver and gold which the king and his counsellors have voluntarily offered to the God of Israel who resides in Jerusalem, [16]as well as all the silver and gold which you receive throughout the province of Babylon and the voluntary offerings freely contributed by the people and the priests for the Temple of their God in Jerusalem.

[17]'This money you will punctiliously use for the purchase of bulls, rams, lambs and the materials for the oblations and libations which go with them, offering these on the altar of the Temple of your God in Jerusalem, [18]and using the remainder of the silver and gold in accordance with the will of your God as you and your brothers may think fit.

[19]'You will deliver the articles which have been given you for the ministry of the Temple of your God, to the God of Jerusalem, [20]and whatever else is needed and you are obliged to supply for the Temple of your God, you will supply from the royal treasury.

[21]'I, King Artaxerxes, have issued the following instruction to all the treasurers of Transeuphrates: Whatever the priest Ezra, Secretary of the Law of the God of heaven, may request of you is to be punctiliously complied with: [22]up to one hundred talents of silver, one hundred *kor* of wheat, one hundred *bat* of wine, one hundred *bat* of oil, and unlimited salt. [23]Whatever the God of heaven demands for the Temple of the God of heaven must be diligently provided; why should retribution come on the realm of the king and of his sons? [24]You are further informed that it is against the law to impose tribute, tax or toll on any of the priests, Levites, singers, gatekeepers, temple slaves or other servants of this temple of God.

[25]'And you, Ezra, by virtue of the wisdom of your God, which you possess, are to appoint magistrates and scribes to administer justice for the whole people of Transeuphrates, that is, for all who know the Law of your God; and you are to teach it to those who do not know it. [26]And on anyone who will not comply with the Law of your God and the Law of the king let sentence be swiftly executed, whether it be death, banishment, fine or imprisonment.'

Ezra's journey from Babylonia to Palestine

27 Blessed be Yahweh, God of our ancestors,
who moved the king's heart in this way to
restore the beauty of the Temple of Yahweh
in Jerusalem, 28 won for me the faithful love
of the king, his counsellors and all the most
powerful of the king's officials! Taking heart
since the hand of Yahweh my God was over
me, I assembled those Israelite heads of
families who were to go with me.

8 These, with their genealogies, were the
heads of families who set out from Babylon
with me in the reign of King Artaxerxes:
2 Of the sons of Phinehas: Gershom; of the
sons of Ithamar: Daniel; of the sons of David:
Hattush 3 son of Shechaniah; of the sons of
Parosh: Zechariah, and with him a hundred
and fifty males officially registered; 4 of the
sons of Pahath-Moab: Elioenai son of
Zerahiah, and with him two hundred males;
5 of the sons of Zattu: Shechaniah son of
Jahaziel, and with him three hundred males;
6 of the sons of Adin: Ebed son of Jonathan,
and with him fifty males; 7 of the sons of
Elam: Jeshaiah son of Athaliah, and with him
seventy males; 8 of the sons of Shephatiah:
Zebadiah son of Michael, and with him eighty
males; 9 of the sons of Joab: Obadiah son
of Jehiel, and with him two hundred and
eighteen males; 10 of the sons of Bani: Shelo-
mith son of Josiphiah, and with him a
hundred and sixty males; 11 of the sons of
Bebai: Zechariah son of Bebai, and with him
twenty-eight males; 12 of the sons of Azgad:
Johanan son of Hakkatan, and with him a
hundred and ten males; 13 of the sons of
Adonikam: the younger sons, whose names
are: Eliphelet, Jeiel and Shemaiah, and with
them sixty males; 14 and of the sons of Bigvai:
Uthai son of Zabud, and with him seventy
males.

15 I assembled them near the canal which
runs to Ahava, where we camped for three
days. I noticed laymen and priests, but I
could not discover any Levites there. 16 I then
sent for Eliezer, Ariel, Shemaiah, Elnathan,
Jarib, Elnathan, Nathan, Zechariah and
Meshullam, judicious men, 17 and sent them
to Iddo, the leading man of a place called
Casiphia; I told them what they were to say
to Iddo and his kinsmen, living at the place
called Casiphia, that is, to provide us with
people to serve the Temple of our God. 18 And
because the hand of God was good to us, they
sent us a wise man of the sons of Mahli son
of Levi, son of Israel, a certain Sherebiah
with his sons and kinsmen: eighteen men;
19 also Hashabiah and with him his brother
Jeshaiah of the sons of Merari with his
kinsmen and sons: twenty men; 20 and two
hundred and twenty temple slaves—
descendants of the temple slaves whom
David and the princes had assigned to serve
the Levites—all of them designated by name.

21 There, beside the Ahava Canal, I then
proclaimed a fast, to humble ourselves before
our God and to pray to him for a successful
journey for us, our dependants and all our
belongings. 22 For I should have been
ashamed to ask the king for a company of
cavalry to protect us from hostile people on
our road, as we had already said to the king,
'The hand of our God is over all who seek
him for their protection, but his mighty
retribution befalls all those who forsake him.'
23 So we fasted and pleaded with our God
about this, and he heard us.

24 I next chose twelve of the leading priests,
and also Sherebiah and Hashabiah with ten
of their kinsmen. 25 To them I weighed out
the silver, the gold and the utensils, the
contributions which the king, his counsel-
lors, his notables and all the Israelites there
present had made for the Temple of our God.
26 To them I weighed out and handed over
six hundred and fifty talents of silver, one
hundred utensils of silver valued at two
talents, one hundred talents of gold, 27 twenty
golden bowls valued at a thousand darics and
two utensils of fine burnished copper as
precious as gold. 28 I said to them, 'You are
consecrated to Yahweh; these utensils are
consecrated too; the silver and gold are a
voluntary offering to Yahweh, God of your
ancestors. 29 Guard them carefully until you
weigh them out to the leading priests, the
Levites, and the heads of families of Israel in
Jerusalem in the rooms of the Temple of
Yahweh.' 30 The priests and Levites then took
charge of the silver, the gold and the utensils
thus weighed, to bring them to Jerusalem to
the Temple of our God.

31 On the twelfth day of the first month we
left the Ahava Canal to make our way to
Jerusalem; the hand of our God was over us
and protected us from enemies and surprise
attacks on our way. 32 When we arrived in
Jerusalem, we rested for three days. 33 On the
fourth day the silver, the gold and the utensils
were weighed in the Temple of our God and
handed over to the priest Meremoth son of

Uriah and, with him, Eleazar son of Phinehas; with them were the Levites Jozabad son of Jeshua and Noadiah son of Binnui. [34]By number and weight all was there. The total weight was recorded at the same time.

[35]When the exiles arrived from their captivity, they offered burnt offerings to the God of Israel—twelve bulls on behalf of all Israel, ninety-six rams, seventy-two lambs, and as a sin offering twelve he-goats: the whole of this as a burnt offering to Yahweh.

[36]They also delivered the king's instructions to the king's satraps and the governors of Transeuphrates, who then supported the people and the Temple of God.

The marriages with foreigners dissolved

9 Once this was done, the officials approached me to say, 'The people of Israel, the priests and the Levites, have not renounced the disgusting practices of the people of the country—the Canaanites, the Hittites, the Perizzites, the Jebusites, the Moabites, the Egyptians and the Amorites—[2]since they and their sons have married some of their women, as a result of which the holy race has been contaminated by the people of the country. The officials and leaders have been the worst offenders in this act of infidelity.' [3]On hearing this, I tore my clothes and my cloak; I pulled hair from my head and beard and sat down in horror. [4]All who trembled at the words of the God of Israel gathered round me, when faced with the infidelity of the exiles, while I went on sitting there in horror until the evening sacrifice. [5]At the evening sacrifice I came out of my stupor and, falling on my knees in my torn clothes and cloak, stretched out my hands to Yahweh my God, [6]and said:

'My God, I am ashamed, I blush to lift my face to you, my God. For our iniquities have increased, until they are higher than our heads, and our guilt has risen as high as heaven. [7]From the days of our ancestors until now we have been deeply guilty and, because of our iniquities, we, our kings and our priests, have been handed over to the kings of other countries, to the sword, to captivity, to pillage, to shame, as is the case today. [8]And now, for a brief moment, the favour of Yahweh our God has allowed a remnant of us to escape and given us a stable home in his holy place, so that our God can raise our spirits and revive us a little in our slavery. [9]For we are slaves; but God has not forgotten us in our slavery; he has extended his faithful love to us even under the kings of Persia and revived us to rebuild the Temple of our God, restore its ruins and provide us with a refuge in Judah and in Jerusalem. [10]But now, our God, what can we say after this? For we have abandoned your commandments, [11]which you gave through your servants the prophets in these terms, "The country which you are about to possess is a polluted country, polluted by the people of the country and their disgusting practices, which have filled it with their filth from end to end. [12]Hence you are not to give your daughters in marriage to their sons, or let their daughters marry your sons, or ever concern yourselves about peace or good relations with them, if you want to grow stronger, to live off the fat of the land and bequeath it to your sons for ever."

[13]'After all that has befallen us because of our evil deeds and our deep guilt—though you, our God, have punished us less than our iniquities deserved and have allowed us to escape like this—[14]are we to break your commandments again and intermarry with people with these disgusting practices? Would you not be enraged with us to the point of destroying us, leaving neither remnant nor survivor? [15]Yahweh, God of Israel, you are upright. We survive only as the remnant we are today. We come before you in our guilt; because of it we cannot stand in your presence.'

10 While Ezra, weeping and prostrating himself in front of the Temple of God, was praying and making confession, a very large crowd of men, women and children of Israel gathered round him, the people weeping bitterly. [2]Then Shechaniah son of Jehiel, one of the sons of Elam, spoke up and said to Ezra, 'We have been unfaithful to our God by marrying foreign women from the people of the country. But, in spite of this, there is still some hope for Israel. [3]We will make a covenant with our God to send away all the foreign wives and their children in obedience to the advice of my lord and of those who tremble at the commandment of our God. Let us act in accordance with the Law. [4]Go ahead, do your duty; we support you. Be brave, take action!' [5]Then Ezra stood up and put the leading priests and Levites and all Israel on oath to do what had been

said. They took the oath. 6Ezra then left his
place in front of the Temple of God and went
to the room of Jehohanan son of Eliashib,
where he spent the night without eating
food or drinking water, because he was still
mourning over the exiles' infidelity.
7A proclamation was issued throughout
Judah and Jerusalem that all the exiles were
to assemble in Jerusalem, 8and that anyone
who failed within three days to answer the
summons of the officials and elders was to
forfeit all his possessions and himself be
excluded from the community of the exiles.
9As a result, all the men of Judah and
Benjamin assembled in Jerusalem within the
three days; it was the twentieth day of the
ninth month. All the people sat down in
the square in front of the Temple of God,
trembling because of the matter in hand and
because of the heavy rain. 10The priest Ezra
then stood up and said to them, 'You have
been unfaithful and have married foreign
wives, thus adding to Israel's guilt. 11So
now give thanks to Yahweh, God of your
ancestors, and do his will by holding aloof
from the people of the country and from
foreign wives.' 12In ringing tones, the whole
assembly answered, 'Yes, our duty is to do
as you say. 13But there are many people here
and it is the rainy season; we cannot stay out
in the open; besides, this is not something
that can be dealt with in one or two days,
since many of us have been unfaithful over
this. 14Let our officials deputise for the whole
community, and all the people in our towns
who have married foreign wives can come at
stated times, accompanied by elders and
judges from each town, until our God's fierce
anger over this is turned away from us.'
15Only Jonathan son of Asahel and Jahzeiah
son of Tikvah, supported by Meshullam and
Shabbethai the Levite, were opposed to this.
16The exiles did as had been proposed. And
the priest Ezra selected the family heads of
the various families, all of them by name,
who began their sittings on the first day of
the tenth month to look into the matter.
17And by the first day of the first month they
had dealt with all the men who had married
foreign women.

The list of the guilty

18Among the priests who were found to have
married foreign wives were:
of the sons of Jeshua son of Jozadak and
his brothers: Maaseiah, Eliezer, Jarib and
Gedaliah, 19who agreed to send their wives
away; their guilt offering was a ram from the
flock for their guilt;
20of the sons of Immer: Hanani and
Zebadiah;
21of the sons of Harim: Maaseiah, Elijah,
Shemaiah, Jehiel and Uzziah;
22of the sons of Pashhur: Elioenai,
Maaseiah, Ishmael, Nethanel, Jozabad and
Elasah;
23of the Levites: Jozabad, Shimei,
Kelaiah—that is, Kelita—Pethahiah, Judah,
and Eliezer;
24of the singers: Eliashib and Zaccur;
of the gatekeepers: Shallum, Telem and
Uri;
25and of the Israelites:
of the sons of Parosh: Ramiah, Izziah,
Malchijah, Mijamin, Eleazar, Malchijah and
Benaiah;
26of the sons of Elam: Mattaniah, Zech-
ariah, Jehiel, Abdi, Jeremoth and Elijah;
27of the sons of Zattu: Elioenai, Eliashib,
Mattaniah, Jeremoth, Zabad and Aziza;
28of the sons of Bebai: Jehohanan,
Hananiah, Zabbai, Atlai;
29of the sons of Bigvai: Meshullam,
Malluch, Jedaiah, Jashub, Sheal, Jere-
moth;
30of the sons of Pahath-Moab: Adna,
Chelal, Benaiah, Maaseiah, Mattaniah,
Bezalel, Binnui and Manasseh;
31of the sons of Harim: Eliezer, Isshijah,
Malchijah, Shemaiah, Shimeon, 32Benjamin,
Malluch, Shemariah;
33of the sons of Hashum: Mattenai,
Mattattah, Zabad, Eliphelet, Jeremai,
Manasseh, Shimei;
34of the sons of Bani: Maadai, Amram,
Uel, 35Benaiah, Bediah, Jeluhi, 36Vaniah,
Meremoth, Eliashib, 37Mattaniah, Mattenai
and Jaasau;
38of the sons of Binnui: Shimei,
39Shelemiah, Nathan and Adaiah;
40of the sons of Zaccai: Shashai, Sharai,
41Azarel, Shelemiah, Shemariah, 42Shallum,
Amariah, Joseph;
43of the sons of Nebo: Jeiel, Mattithiah,
Zabad, Zebina, Jaddai, Joel, Benaiah.
44All these had married foreign wives but
sent them away with their children.

THE BOOK OF NEHEMIAH

Nehemiah presided from 445 until 433 BC over the restoration of the community and the rebuilding of the walls of Jerusalem. As Ezra was responsible for the religious regeneration and reform of the community after the Exile, so Nehemiah was for organising its security and establishing a sound administration, despite continuing opposition from the inhabitants of the surrounding towns. The book is composed by the Chronicler largely from a *memoir* of Nehemiah, but also with the help of various lists.

THE BOOK OF NEHEMIAH

Nehemiah's call: his mission to Judah

1 The words of Nehemiah son of Hacaliah.
It happened in the month of Chislev, in
the twentieth year, while I was in the citadel
of Susa, 2 that Hanani, one of my brothers,
arrived with some men from Judah. I asked
them about the Jews—those who had escaped
and those who survived from the captivity—
and about Jerusalem. 3 They replied, 'The
survivors remaining there in the province
since the captivity are in a very bad and
demoralised condition: the walls of Jeru-
salem are in ruins and its gates have been
burnt down.' 4 On hearing this I sat down and
wept; for some days I mourned, fasting and
praying before the God of heaven.
5 I said, 'Yahweh, God of heaven—the
great and awe-inspiring God who keeps a
covenant of faithful love with those who love
him and obey his commandments—6 let your
ear be attentive and your eyes open, to listen
to your servant's prayer, which I now offer
to you day and night on behalf of your
servants the Israelites. I admit the sins of the
Israelites, which we have committed against
you. Both I and my father's House have
sinned; 7 we have acted very wickedly towards
you by not keeping the commandments, laws
and rulings which you enjoined on your
servant Moses.[a] 8 Remember, I beg you, the
promise which you solemnly made to your
servant Moses, "If you are unfaithful, I shall
scatter you among the peoples; 9 but if you
come back to me and keep my command-
ments and practise them, even though those
who have been banished are at the very sky's
end, I shall gather them from there and bring
them back to the place which I have chosen
as a dwelling-place for my name." 10 Since
they are your servants, your people, whom
you have redeemed with your mighty power
and strong hand, 11 O Lord, let your ear now
be attentive to your servant's prayer and to
the prayer of your servants who want to
revere your name. I beg you let your servant
be successful today and win this man's
compassion.'
At the time I was cupbearer to the king.

2 In the month of Nisan, in the twentieth
year of King Artaxerxes, since I was in
charge of the wine, I took the wine and
offered it to the king. Now, he had never
seen me looking depressed before. 2 So the
king said to me, 'Why are you looking
depressed? You are not sick! This must be a
sadness of the heart.' Thoroughly alarmed
by this, 3 I said to the king, 'May the king live
for ever! How can I not look depressed when
the city where the tombs of my ancestors are

1a Dt 30:1–4.

lies in ruins and its gates have been burnt down?' 4The king then said to me, 'What would you like me to do?' Praying to the God of heaven, 5I said to the king, 'If the king approves and your servant enjoys your favour, send me to Judah, to the city of the tombs of my ancestors, so that I can rebuild it.' 6The king—with the queen sitting beside him—said, 'How long will your journey take, and when will you come back?' Once I had given him a definite time, the king approved my mission.

7I then said to the king, 'If the king approves, may I be given orders for the governors of Transeuphrates to let me pass through on my way to Judah? 8Also an order for Asaph, keeper of the king's forest, to supply me with timber for the beams of the gates of the citadel of the Temple, for the city walls and for the house which I am to occupy?' These the king granted me because the kindly hand of my God was over me.

9When I reached the governors of Transeuphrates, I gave them the king's orders. The king had sent an escort of army officers and cavalry along with me.

10When Sanballat the Horonite and Tobiah the official of Ammon heard about this, they were exceedingly displeased that someone had come to promote the welfare of the Israelites.

The decision to rebuild the walls of Jerusalem

11And so I reached Jerusalem. After I had been there three days, 12I got up during the night with a few other men—I had not told anyone what my God had inspired me to do for Jerusalem—taking no animal with me other than my own mount. 13Under cover of dark I went out through the Valley Gate towards the Dragon's Fountain as far as the Dung Gate, and examined the wall of Jerusalem where it was broken down and its gates burnt out. 14I then crossed to the Fountain Gate and the King's Pool, but it was impassable to my mount. 15So I went up the Valley in the dark, examining the wall; I then went in again through the Valley Gate, coming back 16without the officials knowing where I had gone or what I had been doing. So far I had said nothing to the Jews: neither to the priests, the nobles, the officials nor any other persons involved in the undertaking.

17I then said to them, 'You see what a sorry state we are in: Jerusalem is in ruins and its gates have been burnt down. Come on, we must rebuild the walls of Jerusalem and put an end to our humiliating position!' 18And I told them how the kindly hand of my God had been over me, and the words which the king had said to me. At this they said, 'Let us start building at once!' and they set their hands to the good work.

19When Sanballat the Horonite, Tobiah the official of Ammon, and Geshem the Arab heard about this, they laughed at us and jeered. They said, 'What is this you are doing? Are you going to revolt against the king?' 20But I gave them this answer, 'The God of heaven will grant us success and we, his servants, mean to start building; as for you, you have neither share nor right nor memorial in Jerusalem.'

How the walls were rebuilt

3 Eliashib the high priest with his brother priests then set to work and rebuilt the Sheep Gate; they made the framework, hung its doors, fixed its bolts and bars and proceeded as far as the Tower of the Hundred and the Tower of Hananel. 2The men of Jericho built next to him; Zaccur son of Imri built next to them. 3The sons of Ha-Senaah rebuilt the Fish Gate; they made the framework, hung its doors and fixed its bolts and bars. 4Meremoth son of Uriah, son of Hakkoz, carried out repairs next to them; Meshullam son of Berechiah, son of Meshezabel, carried out repairs next to him; and Zadok son of Baana carried out repairs next to him. 5The men of Tekoa carried out repairs next to him, though their nobles would not demean themselves to help their masters. 6Joiada son of Paseah and Meshullam son of Besodeiah repaired the gate of the New Quarter; they made the framework, hung its doors and fixed its bolts and bars. 7Next to them repairs were carried out by Melatiah of Gibeon, Jadon of Meronoth, and the men of Gibeon and Mizpah, for the sake of the governor of Transeuphrates. 8Next to them repairs were carried out by Uzziel son of Harhaiah, a member of the metal-workers' guild, and next to him repairs were carried out by Hananiah of the perfumers' guild. These renovated the wall of Jerusalem as far as the Broad Wall.

9Next to them repairs were carried out by Rephaiah son of Hur, who was head of one

half of the district of Jerusalem. 10 Next to
them Jedaiah son of Harumaph carried out
repairs opposite his own house; next to him
repairs were carried out by Hattush son of
Hashabneiah. 11 Malchijah son of Harim and
Hasshub son of Pahath-Moab repaired
another section as far as the Furnace Tower.
12 Next to them repairs were carried out by
Shallum son of Hallohesh, head of the other
half of the district of Jerusalem, by him and
his sons. 13 Hanun and the inhabitants of
Zanoah repaired the Valley Gate: they rebuilt
it, hung its doors and fixed its bolts and bars;
they also repaired a thousand cubits of wall
up to the Dung Gate. 14 Malchijah son of
Rechab, head of the district of Beth-ha-
Cherem, repaired the Dung Gate; he rebuilt
it, hung its doors and fixed its bolts
and bars.

15 Shallum son of Col-Hozeh, head of the
district of Mizpah, repaired the Fountain
Gate; he rebuilt it, roofed it, hung its doors
and fixed its bolts and bars. He also rebuilt
the wall of the Pool of Siloah, adjoining the
king's garden, as far as the steps going down
from the City of David. 16 After him,
Nehemiah son of Azbuk, head of half the
district of Beth-Zur, carried out repairs from
a point opposite the Davidic Tombs to the
artificial pool and the House of the Cham-
pions. 17 After him, repairs were carried out
by the Levites: Rehum son of Bani; and next
to him Hashabiah, head of one half of the
district of Keilah, carried out repairs for
his own district. 18 After him, repairs were
carried out by their brothers: Binnui son of
Henadad, head of the other half of the district
of Keilah. 19 Next to him, Ezer son of Jeshua,
headman of Mizpah, repaired another section
in front of the ascent to the armoury at the
Angle.

20 After him, Baruch son of Zabbai repaired
another section from the Angle to the door
of the house of Eliashib the high priest.
21 After him, Meremoth son of Uriah, son of
Hakkoz, repaired another section from the
door of Eliashib's house as far as the end of
Eliashib's house. 22 And after him repairs
were carried out by the priests who lived in
the district. 23 After them repairs were carried
out by Benjamin and Hasshub, opposite their
own house. After them repairs were carried
out by Azariah son of Maaseiah, son of
Ananiah, beside his own house. 24 After him,
Binnui son of Henadad repaired another
section from Azariah's house as far as the
Angle at the corner. 25 After him, Palal son of
Uzai carried out repairs in front of the Angle
and the tower projecting from the king's
Upper Palace by the Court of the Guard; and
after him, Pedaiah son of Parosh carried out
the repairs 26 to a point by the Water Gate to
the east and the projecting tower. 27 After
him, the men of Tekoa repaired another
section from in front of the great projecting
tower as far as the wall of Ophel.

28 From the Horse Gate onwards repairs
were carried out by the priests, each in front
of his own house. 29 After them repairs were
carried out by Zadok son of Immer in front
of his house, and after him repairs were
carried out by Shemaiah son of Shechaniah,
keeper of the East Gate. 30 After him
Hananiah son of Shelemiah and Hanun sixth
son of Zalaph repaired another section, after
whom repairs were carried out by Meshullam
son of Berechiah in front of his room. 31 After
him Malchijah, of the metal-workers' guild,
repaired as far as the Hall of the temple slaves
and merchants, in front of the Muster Gate,
as far as the upper room at the corner. 32 And
between the upper room at the corner and
the Sheep Gate repairs were carried out by
the goldsmiths and the merchants.

The effect on the Jews' opponents

33 When Sanballat heard that we were
rebuilding the wall, he became furiously
angry. 34 He ridiculed the Jews and in front
of his kinsmen and the aristocracy of Samaria
he exclaimed, 'What are these pathetic Jews
doing . . . ? Are they going to give up? Or
offer sacrifices? Or complete the work in a
day? Can they put new life into stones taken
from rubbish heaps and even charred?' 35 And
beside him Tobiah of Ammon remarked, 'If
a jackal were to jump on what they are
building, it would knock their stone wall
down!' 36 Listen, our God, for we are
despised! Make their sneers fall back on their
own heads! Send them as booty to a land of
captivity! 37 Do not pardon their wicked-
ness, may their sin never be erased before
you, for they have insulted the builders to
their face!

38 Meanwhile we were rebuilding the wall,
which was soon joined up all the way round
to mid-height; the people put their hearts
into the work.

4 When Sanballat, Tobiah, the Arabs, the
Ammonites and the Ashdodites heard that

repairs to the walls of Jerusalem were going
forward—that the gaps were beginning to fill
up—they became very angry, 2and they all
plotted to come and attack Jerusalem and
upset my plans.
3We, however, prayed to our God and
organised a guard day and night to protect
the city from them. 4But in Judah the saying
went, 'The strength of the carrier falters, the
rubbish heap is so vast that by ourselves we
cannot rebuild the wall!' 5And our opponents
said, 'They will never know or see a thing,
until we are in there among them, and then
we shall massacre them and put a stop to the
work.'
6Now when the Jews who lived near them
had warned us ten times over, 'They are
coming up against us from every place they
live in,' 7men took up position in the space
behind the wall at those points where it was
lowest, and I organised the people by families
with their swords, spears and bows. 8Aware
of their anxiety, I then addressed the nobles,
the officials and the rest of the people, 'Do
not be afraid of them. Remember the great
and awe-inspiring Lord and fight for your
kinsmen, your sons, your daughters, your
wives and your homes.' 9Once our enemies
heard that we were forewarned and that God
had thwarted their plan, they withdrew and
we all went back to the wall, each one to his
work.
10From then on, half my own retainers
went on working, while the other half stood
by, armed with spears, shields, bows and
armour to protect the whole House of Judah
as they rebuilt the wall. 11The carriers were
armed, working with one hand and holding
a spear in the other. 12Each builder had his
sword strapped to his side as he built. Beside
me stood a trumpeter. 13I then said to the
nobles, the officials and the rest of the people,
'The work is great and widely spread out,
and we are deployed along the wall some way
from one another. 14Rally to us wherever you
hear the trumpet sounding; our God will
fight for us.' 15And so we went on with the
work from break of day until the stars came
out. 16At the same time I also told the people,
'Let every man, with his attendant, spend
the night inside Jerusalem; we shall spend
the night on guard and the day at work.'
17Neither I, nor my brothers, nor my attend-
ants, nor my bodyguards, ever took off our
clothes; each one kept his spear in his right
hand.

The social problems of Nehemiah
He vindicates his administration

5 There was a great outcry from the people,
and from their wives, against their brother
Jews. 2Some said, 'We are having to pledge
our sons and daughters to get enough grain
to eat and keep us alive.' 3Others said, 'We are
having to mortgage our fields, our vineyards
and our houses to get grain because of the
shortage.' 4Still others said, 'We have had to
borrow money on our fields and our vineyards
to pay the royal tax; 5and though we belong
to the same race as our brothers, and our
children are as good as theirs, we shall have to
sell our sons and our daughters into slavery;
some of our daughters have been sold into
slavery already. We can do nothing about it,
since our fields and our vineyards now belong
to others.'
6When I heard their complaints and these
words I was very angry. 7Having turned the
matter over in my mind, I reprimanded the
nobles and the officials as follows, 'Each of
you is imposing a burden on his brother.'
Summoning a great assembly to deal with
them, 8I said to them, 'To the best of our
power, we have redeemed our brother Jews
who were forced to sell themselves to foreign-
ers, and now you in turn are selling your
brothers, for them to be bought back by us!'
They were silent and could find nothing to
say. 9'What you are doing', I went on, 'is
wrong. Do you not want to walk in the fear
of our God and escape the sneers of the
nations, our enemies? 10I too, with my
brothers and retainers, have lent them money
and grain. Let us cancel these pledges. 11This
very day return them their fields, their vine-
yards, their olive groves and their houses,
and cancel the claim on the money, grain,
new wine and olive oil, which you have lent
them.' 12'We shall make restitution,' they
replied, 'we shall claim nothing more from
them; we shall do as you say.' Summoning
the priests, I then made them swear to do as
they had promised. 13Then, shaking out the
fold of my garment, I said, 'May God thus
shake out of house and possessions anyone
who does not make good this promise; may
he be shaken out thus and left empty!' And
the whole assembly answered, 'Amen' and
praised Yahweh. And the people kept this
promise.
14What is more, from the time when the
king appointed me to be their governor in

Judah, from the twentieth to the thirty-
second year of King Artaxerxes, for twelve
years, neither I nor my brothers ever levied
the governor's subsistence allowance,
[15]whereas the former governors, my prede-
cessors, had been a burden on the people,
from whom they took forty silver shekels a
day for food and wine, while their attendants
oppressed the people too. But I, fearing God,
never did this. [16]Also, not acquiring any land,
I concentrated on the work of this wall and
all my attendants joined in the work together,
too.
[17]Furthermore, magistrates and officials to
the number of a hundred and fifty ate at my
table, not to mention those who came to us
from the surrounding nations. [18]Every day,
one ox, six fine sheep, as well as poultry, were
prepared for me; every ten days, skins of
wine were brought in bulk. But even so,
I never claimed the governor's subsistence
allowance, since the people already had
burden enough to bear.
[19]To my credit, my God, remember all I
have done for this people.

The intrigues of Nehemiah's enemies
The wall is finished

6 When Sanballat, Tobiah, Geshem the
Arab and our other enemies heard that I
had rebuilt the wall and that not a single gap
was left—though at that time I had not
fixed the doors to the gates—[2]Sanballat and
Geshem sent me this message, 'Come and
meet us at Ha-Chephirim in the Vale of Ono.'
But they had evil designs on me. [3]So I sent
messengers to them to say, 'I am engaged in
a great undertaking, so I cannot come down.
Why should the work stop while I leave it
and come down to you?' [4]Four times they
sent me the same invitation and I made them
the same reply. [5]The fifth time, with the
same purpose in mind, Sanballat sent me his
servant bearing an open letter. [6]It ran, 'There
is a rumour among the nations—and Gashmu
confirms it—that you and the Jews are
thinking of rebelling, which is why you are
rebuilding the wall, and you intend to become
their king; [7]and that you have even briefed
prophets to acclaim you in Jerusalem with
the cry, "There is a king in Judah!" Now,
these rumours are going to reach the king; so
you had better come and discuss them with
us.' [8]To this I sent him the following reply,
'As regards what you say, nothing of the sort
has occurred; it is a figment of your own
imagination.' [9]For they were all trying to
terrorise us, thinking, 'They will become
demoralised over the work and it will not get
finished.' But my morale rose even higher.
[10]Then, when I went to visit Shemaiah son
of Delaiah, son of Mehetabel, since he was
prevented from coming to me, he said:

We must gather at the Temple of God,
inside the sanctuary itself;
we must shut the sanctuary doors,
for they are coming to kill you,
they are coming to kill you tonight!

[11]But I retorted, 'Should a man like me
run away? Would a man like me go into the
Temple to save his life? I shall not go in!' [12]I
realised that God had not sent him to say this,
but that he had produced this prophecy for
me because Tobiah was paying him [13]to
terrorise me into doing as he said and commit-
ting a sin, so that they would have grounds
for blackening my reputation and blaming
me.
[14]Remember Tobiah, my God, for what he
did; and Noadiah the prophetess, and the
other prophets who tried to terrorise me.
[15]The wall was finished within fifty-two
days, on the twenty-fifth of Elul. [16]When
all our enemies heard about it and all the
surrounding nations saw it, they thought it a
wonderful thing, because they realised that
this work had been accomplished by the
power of our God.
[17]During this same period, the nobles of
Judah kept sending letter after letter to
Tobiah, and letters from Tobiah kept
arriving for them; [18]for he had many sworn
to his interest in Judah, since he was son-in-
law to Shecaniah son of Arah, and his son
Jehohanan had married the daughter of
Meshullam son of Berechiah. [19]They even
cried up his good deeds in my presence, and
they reported what I said back to him. And
Tobiah kept sending letters to terrorise me.
7 Now, when the wall had been rebuilt and
I had hung the doors, the gatekeepers (the
singers and the Levites) were then appointed.
[2]I entrusted the administration of Jerusalem
to my brother Hanani, and to Hananiah the
commander of the citadel, for he was a more
trustworthy, God-fearing man than many
others. [3]I said to them, 'The gates of Jeru-
salem must not be opened until the sun gets
hot; and the doors must be shut and barred
before it begins to go down. Detail guards

from the residents of Jerusalem, each to his
post, in front of his own house.'

The repopulation of Jerusalem

4 The city was large and spacious but the
population was small, and the houses had not
been rebuilt. 5 My God then inspired me to
assemble the nobles, the officials and the
people for the purpose of taking a census
by families. I discovered the genealogical
register of those who had returned in the first
group, and there I found entered:

List of the first exiles to return[a]

6 These are the people of the province who
returned from the captivity of the Exile, those
whom Nebuchadnezzar king of Babylon had
deported, and who returned to Jerusalem
and Judah, each to his own town. 7 They
were the ones who arrived with Zerubbabel,
Jeshua, Nehemiah, Azariah, Raamiah,
Nahamani, Mordecai, Bilshan, Mispereth,
Bigvai, Nehum, Baanah.

The number of the men of the people of
Israel: 8 sons of Parosh, two thousand one
hundred and seventy-two; 9 sons of
Shephatiah, three hundred and seventy-two;
10 sons of Arah, six hundred and fifty-two;
11 sons of Pahath-Moab, that is to say sons of
Jeshua and Joab, two thousand eight
hundred and eighteen; 12 sons of Elam, one
thousand two hundred and fifty-four; 13 sons
of Zattu, eight hundred and forty-five; 14 sons
of Zaccai, seven hundred and sixty; 15 sons of
Binnui, six hundred and forty-eight; 16 sons
of Bebai, six hundred and twenty-eight;
17 sons of Azgad, two thousand three hundred
and twenty-two; 18 sons of Adonikam, six
hundred and sixty-seven; 19 sons of Bigvai,
two thousand and sixty-seven; 20 sons of Adin,
six hundred and fifty-five; 21 sons of Ater, that
is to say of Hezekiah, ninety-eight; 22 sons of
Hashum, three hundred and twenty-eight;
23 sons of Bezai, three hundred and twenty-
four; 24 sons of Hariph, one hundred and
twelve; 25 sons of Gibeon, ninety-five; 26 men
of Bethlehem and Netophah, one hundred
and eighty-eight; 27 men of Anathoth, one
hundred and twenty-eight; 28 men of Beth-
Azmaveth, forty-two; 29 men of Kiriath-
Jearim, Chephirah and Beeroth, seven
hundred and forty-three; 30 men of Ramah
and Geba, six hundred and twenty-one;
31 men of Michmas, one hundred and twenty-
two; 32 men of Bethel and Ai, one hundred
and twenty-three; 33 men of the other Nebo,
fifty-two; 34 sons of the other Elam, one thou-
sand two hundred and fifty-four; 35 sons of
Harim, three hundred and twenty; 36 sons of
Jericho, three hundred and forty-five; 37 sons
of Lod, Hadid and Ono, seven hundred and
twenty-one; 38 sons of Senaah, three thousand
nine hundred and thirty.

39 The priests: sons of Jedaiah, of the House
of Jeshua, nine hundred and seventy-three;
40 sons of Immer, one thousand and fifty-two;
41 sons of Pashhur, one thousand two hundred
and forty-seven; 42 sons of Harim, one thou-
sand and seventeen.

43 The Levites: sons of Jeshua, of Kadmiel,
of the sons of Hodiah, seventy-four.

44 The singers: sons of Asaph, one hundred
and forty-eight.

45 The gatekeepers: sons of Shallum, sons
of Ater, sons of Talmon, sons of Akkub, sons
of Hatita, sons of Shobai, one hundred and
thirty-eight.

46 The temple slaves: sons of Ziha, sons of
Hasupha, sons of Tabbaoth, 47 sons of Keros,
sons of Sia, sons of Padon, 48 sons of Lebana,
sons of Hagaba, sons of Shalmai, 49 sons of
Hanan, sons of Giddel, sons of Gahar, 50 sons
of Reaiah, sons of Rezin, sons of Nekoda,
51 sons of Gazzam, sons of Uzza, sons of
Paseah, 52 sons of Besai, sons of the Meunites,
sons of the Nephusites, 53 sons of Bakbuk,
sons of Hakupha, sons of Harhur, 54 sons of
Bazlith, sons of Mehida, sons of Harsha,
55 sons of Barkos, sons of Sisera, sons of
Temah, 56 sons of Nezaiah, sons of Hatipha.

57 The sons of Solomon's slaves: sons of
Sotai, sons of Sophereth, sons of Perida,
58 sons of Jaala, sons of Darkon, sons of
Giddel, 59 sons of Shephatiah, sons of Hattil,
sons of Pochereth-ha-Zebaim, sons of Amon.
60 The total of the temple slaves and the
sons of Solomon's slaves: three hundred and
ninety-two.

61 The following, who came from Tel-
Melah, Tel-Harsha, Cherub, Addon and
Immer, could not prove that their families
and ancestry were of Israelite origin: 62 the
sons of Delaiah, the sons of Tobiah, the sons
of Nekoda: six hundred and forty-two. 63 And
among the priests: the sons of Hobaiah, the
sons of Hakkoz, the sons of Barzillai—who

7a ‖ Ezr 2:1–70.

had married one of the daughters of Barzillai the Gileadite, whose name he adopted. 64 These had looked for their entries in the official genealogies but were not to be found there, and were hence disqualified from the priesthood. 65 Consequently, His Excellency forbade them to eat any of the consecrated food until a priest appeared who could consult *urim* and *thummim*.

66 The whole assembly numbered forty-two thousand three hundred and sixty people, 67 not counting their slaves and maidservants to the number of seven thousand three hundred and thirty-seven. They also had two hundred and forty-five male and female singers. 68 They had four hundred and thirty-five camels and six thousand seven hundred and twenty donkeys.

69 A certain number of heads of families contributed to the work. His Excellency contributed one thousand gold drachmas, fifty bowls, and thirty priestly robes to the fund. 70 And heads of families gave twenty thousand gold drachmas and two thousand two hundred silver minas to the work fund. 71 The gifts made by the rest of the people amounted to twenty thousand gold drachmas, two thousand silver minas, and sixty-seven priestly robes.

72 The priests, the Levites and some of the people lived in Jerusalem and thereabouts; the singers, the gatekeepers, and the temple slaves in their appropriate towns; and all the other Israelites, in their own towns.

Judaism is born. Ezra reads the Law
The feast of Shelters

Now when the seventh month came round—the Israelites being in their towns—

8 all the people gathered as one man in the square in front of the Water Gate, and asked the scribe Ezra to bring the Book of the Law of Moses which Yahweh had prescribed for Israel. 2 Accordingly, on the first day of the seventh month, the priest Ezra brought the Law before the assembly, consisting of men, women and all those old enough to understand. 3 In the square in front of the Water Gate, in the presence of the men and women, and of those old enough to understand, he read from the book from dawn till noon; all the people listened attentively to the Book of the Law.

4 The scribe Ezra stood on a wooden dais erected for the purpose; beside him stood, on his right, Mattithiah, Shema, Anaiah, Uriah, Hilkiah and Maaseiah; on his left, Pedaiah, Mishael, Malchijah, Hashum, Hashbaddanah, Zechariah, and Meshullam. 5 In full view of all the people—since he stood higher than them all—Ezra opened the book; and when he opened it, all the people stood up. 6 Then Ezra blessed Yahweh, the great God, and all the people raised their hands and answered, 'Amen! Amen!'; then they bowed down and, face to the ground, prostrated themselves before Yahweh. 7 And Jeshua, Bani, Sherebiah, Jamin, Akkub, Shabbethai, Hodiah, Maaseiah, Kelita, Azariah, Jozabab, Hanan, Pelaiah, who were Levites, explained the Law to the people, while the people all kept their places. 8 Ezra read from the book of the Law of God, translating and giving the sense; so the reading was understood.

9 Then His Excellency Nehemiah and the priest-scribe Ezra and the Levites who were instructing the people said to all the people, 'Today is sacred to Yahweh your God. Do not be mournful, do not weep.' For the people were all in tears as they listened to the words of the Law.

10 He then said, 'You may go; eat what is rich, drink what is sweet and send a helping to the man who has nothing prepared. For today is sacred to our Lord. Do not be sad: the joy of Yahweh is your stronghold.' 11 And the Levites calmed all the people down, saying, 'Keep quiet; this is a sacred day. Do not be sad.' 12 Then all the people went off to eat and drink and give helpings away and enjoy themselves to the full, since they had understood the meaning of what had been proclaimed to them.

13 On the second day, the heads of families of the whole people, and the priests and Levites, gathered round the scribe Ezra to study the words of the Law. 14 And written in the Law that Yahweh had prescribed through Moses[a] they found that the Israelites were to live in shelters during the feast of the seventh month. 15 So they issued a proclamation and had it circulated in all their towns and in Jerusalem: 'Go into the hills and bring branches of olive, pine, myrtle, palm and other leafy trees to make shelters, as it says in the book.' 16 The people went out; they

8a Lv 23:33–43.

brought branches and made shelters for
themselves, each man on his roof, in their
courtyards, in the precincts of the Temple of
God, in the square of the Water Gate and in
the square of the Ephraim Gate. 17The whole
assembly, all who had returned from the
captivity, put up shelters and lived in them;
this the Israelites had not done from the days
of Joshua son of Nun till that day, and there
was very great merrymaking.
18Each day, from the first day to the last
one, Ezra read from the Book of the Law of
God. They celebrated the feast for seven
days; on the eighth day, as prescribed, they
held a solemn assembly.

The ceremony of expiation

9 On the twenty-fourth day of this month
the Israelites, in sackcloth and with dust
on their heads, assembled for a fast. 2Then
those of Israelite stock who had severed
relations with all foreigners stood up and
confessed their sins and the iniquities of their
ancestors. 3Standing, each man in his place,
they read from the Book of the Law of
Yahweh their God for one quarter of the day;
for another quarter they confessed their sins
and worshipped Yahweh their God. 4On
the Levites' platform stood Jeshua, Binnui,
Kadmiel, Shebaniah, Bunni, Sherebiah,
Bani and Chenani, calling to Yahweh their
God in ringing tones. 5The Levites, Jeshua,
Kadmiel, Bani, Hashabneiah, Sherebiah,
Hodiah, Shebaniah and Pethahiah said,
'Stand up and bless Yahweh your God!

'Blessed are you, Yahweh our God
from everlasting to everlasting,
and blessed be your glorious name,
surpassing all blessing and praise!

6'You, Yahweh, are the one, only Yahweh,
you have created the heavens,
the heaven of heavens and all their array,
the earth and all it bears,
the seas and all they hold.
To all of them you give life,
and the array of heaven worships you.

7'You are Yahweh God,
who chose Abram,
brought him out of Ur in Chaldaea
and changed his name to Abraham.
8Finding his heart was faithful to you,
you made a covenant with him,
to give the country of the Canaanites,
the Hittites, the Amorites,
the Perizzites, the Jebusites
and the Girgashites
to him and his descendants.
And you have made good your promises,
for you are upright.

9'You saw the distress
of our ancestors in Egypt,
you heard their cry by the Sea of Reeds.
10You displayed signs and wonders
against Pharaoh,
against all his servants
and all the people of his land;
for you knew how arrogantly
they treated them.
You won a reputation
which you keep to this day.
11You opened up the sea in front of them:
they walked on dry ground
right through the sea.
Into the depths you hurled their pursuers
like a stone into the raging waters.
12With a pillar of cloud
you led them by day,
with a pillar of fire by night:
to light the way ahead of them
by which they were to go.
13You came down on Mount Sinai
and spoke with them from heaven;
you gave them right rules, reliable laws,
good statutes and commandments;
14you revealed your holy Sabbath to them;
you laid down commandments,
statutes and law for them
through your servant Moses.
15For their hunger
you gave them bread from heaven,
for their thirst
you brought them water out of a rock,
and you told them to go in
and take possession of the country
which you had sworn to give them.

16'But they and our ancestors
acted arrogantly,
grew obstinate
and flouted your commands.
17They refused to obey,
forgetful of the wonders
which you had worked for them;
they grew obstinate
and made up their minds to return
to their slavery in Egypt.
But because you are a forgiving God,
gracious and compassionate,
patient and rich in faithful love,
you did not abandon them!

18 'Even when they cast themselves a calf
out of molten metal
and said, "This is your God
who brought you up from Egypt!"
and committed monstrous impieties,
19 you, in your great compassion,
did not abandon them in the desert:
the pillar of cloud did not leave them,
leading them on their path by day,
nor the pillar of fire by night,
lighting the way ahead of them
by which they were to go.
20 You gave them your good spirit
to instruct them,
you did not withhold your manna
from their mouths,
you gave them water for their thirst.
21 For forty years you cared for them
in the desert,
so that they went short of nothing,
their clothes did not wear out,
nor were their feet swollen.

22 'You gave them kingdoms and peoples,
allotting them these as frontier lands;
they occupied the country
of Sihon king of Heshbon,
and the country of Og king of Bashan.
23 You gave them as many children
as there are stars in the sky,
and brought them into the country
which you had promised their ancestors
that they would enter and possess.
24 The children entered
and took possession of the country
and before them you subdued
the country's inhabitants, the Canaanites,
whom you put at their mercy,
with their kings
and the peoples of the country,
for them to treat as they pleased;
25 they captured fortified towns
and a fertile countryside,
they took possession of houses
stocked with all kinds of goods,
of storage-wells ready-hewn,
of vineyards, olive groves
and fruit trees in profusion;
so they ate, were full, grew fat
and revelled in your great goodness.

26 'But they grew disobedient,
rebelled against you
and thrust your law behind their backs;
they slaughtered your prophets
who had reproved them
to bring them back to you,
and committed monstrous impieties.
27 So you put them at the mercy
of their enemies
who oppressed them.
But when they were being oppressed
and called to you,
you heard them from heaven
and because of your great compassion
you gave them deliverers
who rescued them
from their oppressors' clutches.
28 But once at peace again,
again they did what was wrong
before you;
so you put them at the mercy
of their enemies
who then became their rulers.
When they called to you again,
you heard them from heaven
and, because of your compassion,
rescued them many times.
29 You warned them,
to bring them back to your law,
but they became arrogant,
did not obey your commandments
and sinned against your rules,
in whose observance is life;
they turned a stubborn shoulder,
were obstinate, and disobeyed.
30 You were patient with them
for many years
and warned them by your spirit
through your prophets,
but they would not listen;
so you put them at the mercy
of the people of the country.
31 But, because of your great compassion,
you did not destroy them completely
nor abandon them,
for you are a gracious,
compassionate God.
32 Now, our God—the great God,
the Mighty and Awe-inspiring One,
maintaining the covenant
and your faithful love—
count as no small thing this misery
which has befallen us,
our kings, our princes,
our priests, our prophets,
and all your people
from the times of the Assyrian kings
to the present day.
33 You have been upright
in all that has happened to us,
for you acted faithfully,
while we did wrong.

34 Our kings, our princes, our priests
and our ancestors did not keep your law
or pay attention to your commandments
 and obligations
which you imposed upon them.
35 Even in their own kingdom,
despite your great goodness
which you bestowed on them,
despite the wide and fertile country
which you had lavished on them,
they did not serve you
or renounce their evil deeds.
36 See, we are slaves today,
slaves in the country
 which you gave to our ancestors
for them to eat
 the good things it produces.
37 Its abundant produce goes to the kings
whom, for our sins, you have set over us,
who rule over our persons
and over our cattle as they please.
We are in great distress.'

A record of the promises made by the community

10 In view of all this we make a firm
agreement, in writing. Our princes,
our Levites, our priests and the rest of the
people have put their names to the document
under seal.

2 On the sealed document were the names
of: Nehemiah, son of Hacaliah, and Zede-
kiah; 3 Seraiah, Azariah, Jeremiah, 4 Pashhur,
Amariah, Malchijah, 5 Hattush, Shebaniah,
Malluch, 6 Harim, Meremoth, Obadiah,
7 Daniel, Ginnethon, Baruch, 8 Meshullam,
Abijah, Mijamin, 9 Maaziah, Bilgai,
Shemaiah: these were the priests.

10 The Levites were: Jeshua son of Azaniah,
Binnui of the sons of Henadad, Kadmiel,
11 and their kinsmen Shebaniah, Hodaviah,
Kelita, Pelaiah, Hanan, 12 Mica, Rehob,
Hashabiah, 13 Zaccur, Sherebiah, Shebaniah,
14 Hodiah, Bani, Chenani.

15 The leaders of the people were: Parosh,
Pahath-Moab, Elam, Zattu, Bani, 16 Bunni,
Azgad, Bebai, 17 Adonijah, Bigvai, Adin,
18 Ater, Hezekiah, Azzur, 19 Hodiah,
Hashum, Bezai, 20 Hariph, Anathoth,
Nebai, 21 Magpiash, Meshullam, Hezir,
22 Meshezabel, Zadok, Jaddua, 23 Pelatiah,
Hanan, Anaiah, 24 Hoshea, Hananiah,
Hasshub, 25 Hallohesh, Pilha, Shobek,
26 Rehum, Hashabnah, Maaseiah, 27 Ahijah,
Hanan, Anan, 28 Malluch, Harim, Baanah.

29 And the rest of the people, the priests,
the Levites, the gatekeepers, the singers, the
temple slaves and all those who had severed
relations with the people of the country to
adhere to the law of God, as also their wives,
their sons, their daughters, that is, all those
who had reached the age of discretion, 30 have
joined their esteemed brothers in a solemn
oath to follow the law of God given through
Moses, servant of God, and to observe and
practise all the commandments of Yahweh
our Lord, with his rules and his statutes.

31 We will not give our daughters in
marriage to the peoples of the country, nor
allow their daughters to marry our sons.

32 If the people of the country bring goods
or foodstuff of any kind to sell on the Sabbath
day, we will buy nothing from them on
Sabbath or holy day.

In the seventh year, we will forgo the
produce of the soil and the exaction of all
debts.

33 We recognise the following obligations:
to give one-third of a shekel yearly for the
service of the Temple of our God: 34 for
the loaves of permanent offering, for the
perpetual oblation, for the perpetual burnt
offering, for the sacrifices on Sabbaths, on
New Moons and on festivals, for the conse-
crated gifts, the sin offerings to expiate for
Israel, in short, for the whole work of the
Temple of our God;[a]

36 and further, to bring yearly to the Temple
of our God the first-fruits of our soil and the
first-fruits of all our orchards, 37 also the first-
born of our sons and of our cattle, as the law
prescribes, the first-born of our herds and
flocks should be taken to the Temple of our
God for the priests officiating in the Temple
of our God. 38 Furthermore, we shall bring
the best of our dough, of every kind of fruit,
of the new wine and of the oil to the priests,
to the storerooms of the Temple of our God,
and the tithe on our soil to the Levites—the
Levites will themselves collect the tithes from
all the towns of our religion. 39 An Aaronite
priest will accompany the Levites when they
collect the tithes, and the Levites will bring
a tenth part 40a,b of the tithes to the Temple of
our God, into the treasury storerooms; for
these rooms are where the Israelites and the
Levites are to bring the contributions of corn,

10a v. 35 is found after v. 40b.

wine and oil, and where the vessels of the
sanctuary are, and the officiating priests, the
gatekeepers and the singers.
35 Furthermore, as regards deliveries of
wood for burning on the altar of our God as
the law prescribes, we have arranged, by
drawing lots, how these deliveries are to be
made at the Temple of our God by the priests,
the Levites and the people by families, at
stated times every year.
40c We will no longer neglect the Temple of
our God.

Nehemiah's method of repopulating Jerusalem

11 Now the leaders of the people took up
residence in Jerusalem; so the rest of
the people drew lots: one man in ten was to
come and live in Jerusalem, the holy city,
while the other nine were to stay in the towns
outside. 2 The people praised all those who
volunteered to live in Jerusalem.
3 In the towns of Judah each man lived on
his own property, but these are the provincial
leaders, the Israelites, the priests, the
Levites, the temple slaves and the descend-
ants of Solomon's slaves, who made their
homes in Jerusalem:

The Jewish population at Jerusalem

4 Of the sons of Judah and the sons of
Benjamin who made their homes in Jeru-
salem there were:
Of the sons of Judah: Athaiah son of
Uzziah, son of Zechariah, son of Amariah,
son of Shephatiah, son of Mehalalel, of the
descendants of Perez; 5 and Maaseiah son of
Baruch, son of Col-Hozeh, son of Hazaiah,
son of Adaiah, son of Joiarib, son of Zech-
ariah, descendant of Shelah. 6 The total
number of the descendants of Perez living in
Jerusalem was four hundred and sixty-eight
outstanding people.
7 These are the sons of Benjamin: Sallu son
of Meshullam, son of Joed, son of Pedaiah,
son of Kolaiah, son of Maaseiah, son of Ithiel,
son of Jeshaiah, 8 and his brothers Gabbai and
Sallai; nine hundred and twenty-eight.
9 Joel son of Zichri was their chief, and
Judah son of Hassenuah was second in
command of the city.
10 Of the priests there were Jedaiah son of
Joiakim, son of 11 Seraiah, son of Hilkiah,
son of Meshullam, son of Zadok, son of
Meraioth, son of Ahitub, the chief of the
Temple of God, 12 and their kinsmen who
performed the Temple liturgy: eight
hundred and twenty-two; Adaiah son of
Jeroham, son of Pelaliah, son of Amzi, son of
Zechariah, son of Pashhur, son of Malchijah,
13 and his kinsfolk, heads of families: two
hundred and forty-two; and Amashai son of
Azarel, son of Ahzai, son of Meshillemoth,
son of Immer, 14 and his kinsfolk, outstand-
ing people: one hundred and twenty-eight.
Their chief was Zabdiel son of Haggadol.
15 Of the Levites there were Shemaiah son
of Hasshub, son of Azrikam, son of Hash-
abiah, son of Bunni; 16 Shabbethai and
Jozabad, the levitical leaders responsible for
work outside the Temple of God; 17 Mattaniah
son of Mica, son of Zabdi, son of Asaph, who
led the praises and intoned the thanksgiving
associated with the prayer, Bakbukiah being
his junior colleague; and Obadiah son of
Shammua, son of Galal, son of Jeduthun.
18 The total number of Levites in the holy city
was two hundred and eighty-four.

Supplementary notes

19 The gatekeepers: Akkub, Talmon and their
kinsmen, who kept watch at the gates: one
hundred and seventy-two.[a]
21 The temple slaves lived on Ophel; Ziha
and Gishpa were in charge of the temple
slaves. 22 The official in charge of the Levites
in Jerusalem was Uzzi son of Bani, son of
Hashabiah, son of Mattaniah, son of Mica,
of the sons of Asaph, who led the singing in
the liturgy of the Temple of God; 23 for the
singers were under royal orders, with regu-
lations laying down what was required of
them day by day. 24 Petahiah son of Meshez-
abel, of the sons of Zerah son of Judah, was
the king's minister for all matters connected
with the people.

The Jewish population outside Jerusalem

20 The rest of Israel, including the priests and
Levites, made their homes throughout the
towns of Judah, each man on his own inherit-
ance, 25 and in the villages near their lands.
Some of the sons of Judah made their homes
in Kiriath-Arba and its dependencies, Dibon

11a v. 20 is transposed to follow v. 24.

and its dependencies, Jekabzeel and its dependencies, [26]Jeshua, Moladah, Beth-Pelet, [27]Hazar-Shual, Beersheba and its dependencies, [28]Ziklag, Meconah and its dependencies, [29]En-Rimmon, Zorah, Jarmuth, [30]Zanoah, Adullam and their villages, Lachish and its lands, and Azekah and its dependencies; thus, they settled from Beersheba as far as the Valley of Hinnom.

[31]And some Benjaminites made their homes in Geba, Michmash, Aija, Bethel and its dependencies, [32]Anathoth, Nob, Ananiah, [33]Hazor, Ramah, Gittaim, [34]Hadid, Zeboim, Neballat, [35]Lod, Ono and the Valley of Craftsmen.

[36]Some levitical groups lived in Judah, some in Benjamin.

Priests and Levites who returned under Zerubbabel and Jeshua

12 These are the priests and the Levites who came back with Zerubbabel son of Shealtiel, and Jeshua:

[2]Seraiah, Jeremiah, Ezra, [3]Amariah, Malluch, Hattush, Shecaniah, Rehum, Meremoth, [4]Iddo, Ginnethoi, Abijah, [5]Mijamin, Maadiah, Bilgah, [6]Shemaiah, and Joiarib, Jedaiah, [7]Sallu, Amok, Hilkiah, Jedaiah—these were the heads of the priests and their kinsmen in the days of Jeshua.

[8]The Levites were Jeshua, Binnui, Kadmiel, Sherebiah, Judah, Mattaniah—this last, with his brothers, was in charge of the songs of praise, [9]while Bakbukiah and Unno, their colleagues, formed the alternate choir to theirs.

Genealogical list of high priests

[10]Jeshua fathered Joiakim, Joiakim fathered Eliashib, Eliashib fathered Joiada, [11]Joiada fathered Johanan, and Johanan fathered Jaddua.

Priests and Levites in the time of the High Priest Joiakim

[12]In the days of Joiakim the heads of the priestly families were: family of Seraiah, Meraiah; of Jeremiah, Hananiah; [13]of Ezra, Meshullam; of Amariah, Jehohanan; [14]of Malluch, Jonathan; of Shebaniah, Joseph; [15]of Harim, Adna; of Meremoth, Helkai; [16]of Iddo, Zechariah; of Ginnethon, Meshullam; [17]of Abijah, Zichri; of Minjamin, . . .; of Moadiah, Piltai; [18]of Bilgah, Shammua; of Shemaiah, Jehonathan; [19]and of Joiarib, Mattenai; of Jedaiah, *Uzzi*; [20]of Sallai, Kallai; of Amok, Eber; [21]of Hilkiah, Hashabiah; of Jedaiah, Nethanel.

[22]In the time of Eliashib, Joiada, Johanan and Jaddua, the heads of the families of priests were registered in the Book of Chronicles, up to the reign of Darius the Persian.

[23]The Levites who were heads of families were registered in the Book of Chronicles up to the time of Johanan, grandson of Eliashib.

[24]The heads of the Levites were Hashabiah, Sherebiah, Jeshua, Binnui, Kadmiel, while their brothers who formed an alternate choir for the hymns of praise and thanksgiving, as David, man of God, had prescribed, section corresponding to section, [25]were Mattaniah, Bakbukiah and Obadiah. Meshullam, Talmon and Akkub were the gatekeepers guarding the stores at the gates.

[26]These lived in the days of Joiakim son of Jeshua, son of Jozadak, and in the days of Nehemiah the governor and of Ezra the priest-scribe.

The dedication of the wall of Jerusalem

[27]At the dedication of the wall of Jerusalem the Levites were sent for, wherever they lived, to come to Jerusalem and joyfully perform the dedication with hymns of thanksgiving and songs to the accompaniment of cymbals, lyres and harps. [28]Accordingly, the levitical singers assembled from the district round Jerusalem, from the villages of the Netophathites, [29]from Beth-Gilgal and from their farms at Geba and Azmaveth—for the singers had built themselves villages all round Jerusalem. [30]When the priests and Levites had purified themselves, they then purified the people, the gates and the wall.

[31]I then made the leaders of Judah come on to the top of the wall and appointed two large choirs. One made its way along the top of the wall, to the right, towards the Dung Gate; [32]bringing up the rear were Hoshaiah and half the leaders of Judah, [33]and also Azariah, Ezra, Meshullam, [34]Judah, Benjamin, Shemaiah and Jeremiah, [35]of the priests, with trumpets; then Zechariah son of Jonathan, son of Shemaiah, son of Mattaniah, son of Micaiah, son of Zaccur, son of Asaph, [36]with his kinsmen, Shemaiah, Azarel, Milalai, Gilalai, Maai, Nethanel,

Juda, Hanani, with the musical instruments of David, man of God. The scribe Ezra walked at their head. 37 At the Fountain Gate they went straight on up the steps of the City of David, along the top of the rampart by the stairway of the wall, above the Palace of David as far as the Water Gate, on the east.

38 The other choir made its way to the left; I and half the leaders of the people followed them along the top of the wall from the Tower of the Furnaces to the Broad Wall, 39 from the Ephraim Gate, the Fish Gate, the Tower of Hananel and the Tower of the Hundred as far as the Sheep Gate, and they came to a halt at the Prison Gate.

40 The two choirs then took their places in the Temple of God. But I had half the magistrates with me 41 as well as the priests, Eliakim, Maaseiah, Miniamin, Micaiah, Elioenai, Zechariah, Hananiah with the trumpets, 42 and Maaseiah, Shemaiah, Eleazar, Uzzi, Jehohanan, Malchijah, Elam and Ezer. The singers sang loudly under the direction of Jezrahiah. 43 There were great sacrifices offered that day and the people rejoiced, God having given them good cause for rejoicing; the women and children rejoiced too, and the joy of Jerusalem could be heard from far away.

A golden age

44 For the rooms intended for the treasures, contributions, first-fruits and tithes, supervisors were then appointed whose business it was to collect in them those portions from the town lands awarded by the Law to the priests and Levites. For Judah rejoiced in the officiating priests and Levites, 45 since they—with the singers and gatekeepers—performed the liturgy of their God and the rites of purification as ordained by David and his son Solomon. 46 For from ancient times, from the days of David and Asaph, they had been the leaders in rendering hymns of praise and thanksgiving to God. 47 In the days of Zerubbabel and Nehemiah, all Israel supplied regular daily portions for the singers and gatekeepers, and gave the dedicated contributions to the Levites; and the Levites gave the dedicated contributions to the Aaronites.

13 At that time they were reading to the people from the Book of Moses, when they found this written in it, *'No Ammonite or Moabite is to be admitted* to the assembly of God, *and this is for all time,* 2 *since they did not come to meet* the Israelites *with bread and water, and even hired Balaam to oppose* them *by cursing* them; *but* our *God turned the curse into a blessing.'*[a] 3 Having heard the Law, they excluded all foreigners from Israel.

The second mission of Nehemiah

4 Earlier, Eliashib the priest, who was in charge of the rooms of the Temple of our God, and who was close to Tobiah, 5 had provided him with a large room where they previously used to store the meal offerings, incense, utensils, tithes of corn, wine and oil, that is, the part of the Levites, singers and gatekeepers, and the contributions for the priests. 6 While all this was going on I was away from Jerusalem, for in the thirty-second year of Artaxerxes king of Babylon I had gone to see the king. But after some time I asked the king for permission to leave, 7 and returned to Jerusalem, where I learned about the crime which Eliashib had committed for Tobiah's benefit, by providing him with a room in the courts of the Temple of God. 8 I was extremely displeased and threw all Tobiah's household goods out of the room and into the street. 9 I then gave orders for the room to be purified, and had the utensils of the Temple of God, the meal offerings and the incense, all replaced.

10 I also learned that the Levites had not been receiving their allocations, as a result of which the Levites and singers who performed the liturgy had all withdrawn to their farms. 11 I then reprimanded the officials. 'Why is the Temple of God deserted?' I asked. And I collected them together again and brought them back to their posts; 12 and all Judah then delivered the tithe of corn, wine and oil to the storehouses. 13 As supervisors of the storehouses I appointed Shelemiah the priest, Zadok the scribe, Pedaiah one of the Levites and, as their assistant, Hanan son of Zaccur, son of Mattaniah, since they were considered reliable people; their duty was to make the distributions to their kinsmen.

14 Remember me for this, my God, and do not blot out the good deeds which I have done for the Temple of my God and its observances!

13a Dt 23:4–6.

[15]At the same time I saw people in Judah treading the winepress, bringing in sacks of grain and loading donkeys on the Sabbath; they were also bringing wine, grapes, figs and every kind of merchandise into Jerusalem on the Sabbath day. So I forbade them to sell the food. [16]Tyrians living there were bringing in fish and every kind of merchandise which they were selling to the Judaeans on the Sabbath in Jerusalem itself. [17]So I also reprimanded the leading men of Judah, saying to them, 'What a wicked way to behave, profaning the Sabbath day! [18]Was this not exactly what your ancestors did, with the result that our God brought all this misery down on us and on this city? And now you are adding to the wrath hanging over Israel by profaning the Sabbath yourselves!' [19]So when the gates of Jerusalem were getting dark at the approach of the Sabbath, I gave orders for the doors to be shut and directed that they were not to be opened again until the Sabbath was over. I stationed some of my attendants at the gates to make sure that no merchandise was brought in on the Sabbath day. [20]So the traders and dealers in goods of all kinds spent the night outside Jerusalem once or twice, [21]until I reprimanded them. I said to them, 'Why are you spending the night in front of the wall? Do it again, and I shall use force on you.' After this, they did not come on the Sabbath. [22]I then ordered the Levites to purify themselves and act as guards at the gates, so that the Sabbath day might be kept holy.

Remember this also to my credit, have pity on me in the greatness of your faithful love.

[23]At that time too, I saw Jews who had married wives from Ashdod, Ammon and Moab; [24]as regards their children, half of them spoke the language of Ashdod or the language of one of the other peoples, but could no longer speak the language of Judah. [25]I reprimanded them, I cursed them, I struck several of them and tore out their hair and adjured them by God, 'You are not to give your daughters in marriage to their sons or let their daughters marry your sons, or marry them yourselves! [26]Was it not because of women like these that Solomon king of Israel sinned? Although among many nations there was no king like him and he was loved by his God, and God made him king of all Israel, even then foreign women led him into sinning! [27]Were you obedient when you committed this very grave crime: breaking faith with our God by marrying foreign wives?'

[28]One of the sons of Jehoiada, son of Eliashib the high priest, was a son-in-law of Sanballat the Horonite; I drove him from my presence.

[29]Remember them, my God, for having defiled the priesthood and the covenant of the priests and Levites!

[30]And so I purged them of everything foreign; I drew up regulations for the priests and Levites, defining each man's duty, [31]as well as for the deliveries of wood at the proper times, and for the first-fruits.

Remember this, my God, to my credit!

THE BOOK OF TOBIT

Tobit tells of the reward of perseverance in good works. Tobit's devotion to the Law and to the Jewish way of life is answered by God's watchful benevolence, as shown in the mission of the guiding angel who rights the family fortunes.

The story is set in Nineveh sometime during the Exile, but details of history and geography are telescoped and are not important to the appreciation of the story. The book was written *c.* 200 BC and existed only in Greek and Syriac translations until Hebr. fragments were recently found at Qumran.

TOBIT

1 The tale of Tobit son of Tobiel, son of
Ananiel, son of Aduel, son of Gabael, of
the lineage of Asiel and tribe of Naphtali. 2In
the days of Shalmaneser king of Assyria, he
was exiled from Thisbe, which is south of Kedesh-Naphtali in Upper Galilee, above Hazor, some distance to the west, north of Shephat.

I: TOBIT THE EXILE

3I, Tobit, have walked in paths of truth and
in good works all the days of my life. I have
given much in alms to my brothers and fellow
country-folk, exiled like me to Nineveh in
the country of Assyria. 4In my young days,
when I was still at home in the land of Israel, the whole tribe of Naphtali my ancestor broke away from the House of David and from Jerusalem, though this was the city chosen out of all the tribes of Israel for their sacrifices; here, the Temple—God's dwelling-place—had been built and hallowed
for all generations to come. 5All my brothers
and the House of Naphtali sacrificed on every hill-top in Galilee to the calf that Jeroboam king of Israel had made at Dan.

6Often I was quite alone in making the
pilgrimage to Jerusalem, fulfilling the Law that binds all Israel perpetually. I would hurry to Jerusalem with the first yield of fruits and beasts, the tithe of cattle and the
sheep's first shearings. 7I would give these to
the priests, the sons of Aaron, for the altar. To the Levites ministering at Jerusalem I would give my tithe of wine and corn, olives, pomegranates and other fruits. Six years in succession I took the second tithe in money
and went and paid it annually at Jerusalem.
8I gave the third to orphans and widows and
to the strangers who live among the Israelites; I brought it them as a gift every three years. When we ate, we obeyed both the ordinances of the law of Moses and the exhortations of Deborah the mother of our ancestor Ananiel;
for my father had died and left me an orphan.
9When I came to man's estate, I married a
woman from our kinsfolk whose name was Anna; she bore me a son whom I called Tobias.

10When the banishment into Assyria came,
I was taken away and went to Nineveh. All
my brothers and the people of my race ate
the food of the heathen, 11but for my part I
was careful not to eat the food of the heathen.
12And because I had kept faith with my
God with my whole heart, 13the Most High
granted me the favour of Shalmaneser, and I
became the king's purveyor. 14Until his
death I used to travel to Media, where I transacted business on his behalf, and I deposited sacks of silver worth ten talents with Gabael the brother of Gabrias at Rhages in Media.

15On the death of Shalmaneser his son
Sennacherib succeeded; the roads into Media
were barred, and I could no longer go there.
16In the days of Shalmaneser I had often given
alms to the people of my race; 17I gave my
bread to the hungry and clothes to those who lacked them; and I buried, when I saw them, the bodies of my country-folk thrown over the walls of Nineveh.

18I also buried those who were killed by
Sennacherib. When Sennacherib was beating a disorderly retreat from Judaea after the King of heaven had punished his blasphemies, he killed a great number of Israelites in his rage. So I stole their bodies to bury them; Sennacherib looked for them and
could not find them. 19A Ninevite went and
told the king it was I who had buried them secretly. When I knew that the king had been told about me and saw myself being hunted by men who would put me to death, I was
afraid and fled. 20All my goods were seized;
they were all confiscated by the treasury; nothing was left me but my wife Anna and my son Tobias.

21Less than forty days after this, the king
was murdered by his two sons, who then fled to the mountains of Ararat. His son Esarhaddon succeeded. Ahikar the son of my

brother Anael, was appointed chancellor of the exchequer for the kingdom and given the main ordering of affairs. [22]Ahikar then interceded for me and I was allowed to return to Nineveh, since Ahikar had been chief cupbearer, keeper of the signet, administrator and treasurer under Sennacherib king of Assyria, and Esarhaddon had kept him in office. He was a relation of mine; he was my nephew.

II: TOBIT BLINDED

2 In the reign of Esarhaddon, therefore, I returned home, and my wife Anna was restored to me with my son Tobias. At our feast of Pentecost (the feast of Weeks) there was a good dinner. I took my place for the meal; [2]the table was brought to me and various dishes were brought. I then said to my son Tobias, 'Go, my child, and seek out some poor, loyal-hearted man among our brothers exiled in Nineveh, and bring him to share my meal. I will wait until you come back, my child.' [3]So Tobias went out to look for some poor man among our brothers, but he came back again and said, 'Father!' I replied, 'What is it, my child?' He went on, 'Father, one of our nation has just been murdered; he has been strangled and then thrown down in the market place; he is there still.' [4]I sprang up at once, left my meal untouched, took the man from the market place and laid him in one of my rooms, waiting until sunset to bury him. [5]I came in again and washed myself and ate my bread in sorrow, [6]remembering the words of the prophet Amos concerning Bethel:

I shall turn your festivals into mourning
and all your singing into lamentation.[a]

[7]And I wept. When the sun was down, I went and dug a grave and buried him. [8]My neighbours laughed and said, 'See! He is not afraid any more.' (You must remember that a price had been set on my head earlier for this very thing.) 'Once before he had to flee, yet here he is, beginning to bury the dead again.'

[9]That night I took a bath; then I went into the courtyard and lay down by the courtyard wall. Since it was hot I left my face uncovered. [10]I did not know that there were sparrows in the wall above my head; their hot droppings fell into my eyes. This caused white spots to form, which I went to have treated by the doctors. But the more ointments they tried me with, the more the spots blinded me, and in the end, I became completely blind. I remained without sight four years; all my brothers were distressed on my behalf; and Ahikar provided for my upkeep for two years, until he left for Elymais.

[11]My wife Anna then undertook woman's work; she would spin wool and take cloth to weave; [12]she used to deliver whatever had been ordered from her and then receive payment. Now on the seventh day of the month of Dystros, she finished a piece of work and delivered it to her customers. They paid her all that was due, and into the bargain presented her with a kid for a meal. [13]When the kid came into my house, it began to bleat. I called to my wife and said, 'Where does this creature come from? Suppose it has been stolen! Let the owners have it back; we have no right to eat stolen goods'. [14]She said, 'No, it was a present given me over and above my wages.' I did not believe her, and told her to give it back to the owners (I felt deeply ashamed of her). To which, she replied, 'What about your own alms? What about your own good works? Everyone knows what return you have had for them.'

3 Then, sad at heart, I sighed and wept, and began this prayer of lamentation:

[2]You are just, O Lord,
and just are all your works.
All your ways are grace and truth,
and you are the Judge of the world.

[3]Therefore, Lord,
remember me, look on me.
Do not punish me for my sins
or for my needless faults
or those of my ancestors.

[4]For we have sinned against you

2a Am 8:10.

and broken your commandments;
and you have given us over
to be plundered,
to captivity and death,
to be the talk, the laughing-stock and scorn
of all the nations among whom
you have dispersed us.

5 And now all your decrees are true
when you deal with me
as my faults deserve,
and those of my ancestors.
For we have neither
kept your commandments
nor walked in truth before you.

6 So now, do with me as you will;
be pleased to take my life from me;
so that I may be delivered from earth
and become earth again.
Better death than life for me,
for I have endured groundless insult
and am in deepest sorrow.

Lord, be pleased
to deliver me from this affliction.
Let me go away to my everlasting home;
do not turn your face from me, O Lord.
Better death for me than life prolonged
in the face of unrelenting misery:
I can no longer bear to listen to insults.

III: SARAH

7 It chanced on the same day that Sarah the
daughter of Raguel, who lived in Media at
Ecbatana, also heard insults from one of her
father's maids. 8 For she had been given in
marriage seven times, and Asmodeus, the
worst of demons, had killed her bridegrooms
one after another before ever they had slept
with her as man with wife. The servant-
girl said, 'Yes, you kill your bridegrooms
yourself. That makes seven already to whom
you have been given, and you have not once
been in luck yet. 9 Just because your bride-
grooms have died, that is no reason for
punishing us. Go and join them, and may we
be spared the sight of any child of yours!'
10 That day, she grieved, she sobbed, and she
went up to her father's room intending to
hang herself. But then she thought, 'Suppose
they were to blame my father! They would
say, "You had an only daughter whom you
loved, and now she has hanged herself for
grief." I cannot cause my father a sorrow
which would bring down his old age to the
dwelling of the dead. I should do better not
to hang myself, but to beg the Lord to let me
die and not live to hear any more insults.'
11 And at this, by the window, with out-
stretched arms she said this prayer:

You are blessed, O God of mercy!
May your name be blessed for ever,
and may all things you have made
bless you everlastingly.

12 And now I turn my face
and I raise my eyes to you.

13 Let your word deliver me from earth;
I can hear myself insulted no longer.

14 O Lord, you know
that I have remained pure;
no man has touched me;
15 I have not dishonoured your name
or my father's name
in this land of exile.

I am my father's only daughter,
he has no other child as heir;
he has no brother at his side,
nor has he any kinsman left
for whom I ought to keep myself.

I have lost seven husbands already;
why should I live any longer?
If it does not please you to take my life,
then look on me with pity;
I can no longer bear
to hear myself defamed.

16 This time the prayer of each of them
found favour before the glory of God, 17 and
Raphael was sent to bring remedy to them
both. He was to take the white spots from
the eyes of Tobit, so that he might see God's
light with his own eyes; and he was to give
Sarah the daughter of Raguel as bride to
Tobias son of Tobit, and to rid her of Asmo-
deus, that worst of demons. For it was to
Tobias before all other suitors that she
belonged by right. Tobit was coming back
from the courtyard into the house at the same
moment as Sarah the daughter of Raguel was
coming down from the upper room.

IV: TOBIAS

4 The same day Tobit remembered the silver that he had left with Gabael at Rhages in Media [2]and thought, 'I have come to the point of praying for death; I should do well to call my son Tobias and tell him about the money before I die.' [3]He summoned his son Tobias and told him, 'When I die, give me an honourable burial. Honour your mother, and never abandon her all the days of your life. Do all that she wants, and give her no reason for sorrow. [4]Remember, my child, all the risks she ran for your sake when you were in her womb. And when she dies, bury her at my side in the same grave.

[5]'My child, be faithful to the Lord all your days. Never entertain the will to sin or to transgress his laws. Do good works all the days of your life, never follow ways that are not upright; [6]for if you act in truthfulness, you will be successful in all your actions, as everyone is who practises what is upright.

[7]'Set aside part of your goods for almsgiving. Never turn your face from the poor and God will never turn his from you. [8]Measure your alms by what you have; if you have much, give more; if you have little, do not be afraid to give less in alms. [9]So doing, you will lay up for yourself a great treasure for the day of necessity. [10]For almsgiving delivers from death and saves people from passing down to darkness. [11]Almsgiving is a most effective offering for all those who do it in the presence of the Most High.

[12]'My child, avoid all loose conduct. Choose a wife of your father's stock. Do not take a foreign wife outside your father's tribe, because we are the children of the prophets. Remember Noah, Abraham, Isaac and Jacob, our ancestors from the beginning. All of them took wives from their own kindred, and they were blessed in their children, and their race will inherit the earth. [13]You, too, my child, must love your own brothers; never presume to despise your brothers, the sons and daughters of your people; choose your wife from among them. For pride brings ruin and much worry; idleness causes need and poverty, for the mother of famine is idleness.

[14]'Do not keep back until next day the wages of those who work for you; pay them at once. If you serve God you will be rewarded. Be careful, my child, in all you do, well-disciplined in all your behaviour. [15]Do to no one what you would not want done to you. Do not drink wine to the point of drunkenness; do not let excess be your travelling companion.

[16]'Give your bread to those who are hungry, and your clothes to those who lack clothing. Of whatever you own in plenty, devote a proportion to almsgiving; and when you give alms, do it ungrudgingly. [17]Be generous with bread and wine on the graves of upright people, but not for the sinner.

[18]'Ask advice of every wise person; never scorn any profitable advice. [19]Bless the Lord God in everything; beg him to guide your ways and bring your paths and purposes to their end. For wisdom is not the property of every nation; their desire for what is good is conferred by the Lord. At his will he lifts up or he casts down to the depths of the dwelling of the dead. So now, my child, remember these precepts and never let them fade from your heart.

[20]'Now, my child, I must tell you I have left ten talents of silver with Gabael son of Gabrias, at Rhages in Media. [21]Do not be afraid, my child, if we have grown poor. You have great wealth if you fear God, if you shun every kind of sin and if you do what is pleasing to the Lord your God.'

V: RAPHAEL

5 Tobias then replied to his father Tobit, 'Father, I shall do everything you have told me. [2]But how am I to recover the silver from him? He does not know me, nor I him. What token am I to give him for him to believe me and hand the silver over to me? And besides, I do not know what roads to take for this journey into Media.' [3]Then Tobit answered his son Tobias, 'Each of us set his signature to a note which I cut in two,

so that each could keep half of it. I took one
piece, and put the other with the silver. To
think it was twenty years ago I left this silver
in his keeping! And now, my child, find a
trustworthy travelling companion—we shall
pay him for his time until you arrive back—
and then go and collect the silver from
Gabael.'
4Tobias went out to look for a man who
knew the way to go with him to Media.
Outside he found Raphael the angel standing
facing him, though he did not guess he was
an angel of God. 5He said, 'Where do you
come from, friend?' The angel replied, 'I am
one of your brother Israelites; I have come to
these parts to look for work.' Tobias asked,
'Do you know the road to Media?' 6The other
replied, 'Certainly I do, I have been there
many times; I have knowledge and experi-
ence of all the ways. I have often been to
Media and stayed with Gabael one of our
kinsmen who lives at Rhages in Media. It
usually takes two full days to get from Ecba-
tana to Rhages; Rhages lies in the mountains,
and Ecbatana is in the middle of the plain.'
7Tobias said, 'Wait for me, friend, while I go
and tell my father; I need you to come with
me; I shall pay you for your time.' 8The other
replied, 'Good, I shall wait; but do not be
long.'
9Tobias went in and told his father that he
had found one of their brother Israelites. And
the father said, 'Fetch him in; I want to find
out about his family and tribe. I must see if
he is going to be a reliable companion for
you, my child.' So Tobias went out and called
him, 'Friend,' he said, 'my father wants you.'
10The angel came into the house; Tobit
greeted him, and the other answered, wishing
him happiness in plenty. Tobit replied, 'Can
I ever be happy again? I am a blind man; I
no longer see the light of heaven; I am sunk
in darkness like the dead who see the light
no more. I am a man buried alive; I hear
people speak but cannot see them.' The angel
said, 'Take comfort; before long God will
heal you. Take comfort.' Tobit said, 'My son
Tobias wishes to go to Media. Will you join
him as his guide? Brother, I will pay you.'
He replied, 'I am willing to go with him; I
know all the ways; I have often been to
Media, I have crossed all its plains and
mountains, and I know all its roads.' 11Tobit
said, 'Brother, what family and what tribe do
you belong to? Will you tell me, brother?'
12'What does my tribe matter to you?' the
angel said. Tobit said, 'I want to be quite
sure whose son you are and what your name
is.' 13The angel said, 'I am Azarias, son of
the great Ananias, one of your kinsmen.'
14'Welcome and greetings, brother! Do not
be offended at my wanting to know the name
of your family; I find you are my kinsman of
a good and honourable line. I know Ananias
and Nathan, the two sons of the great
Shemaiah. They used to go to Jerusalem with
me; we have worshipped together there and
they have never strayed from the right path.
Your brothers are worthy men; you come of
good stock; welcome.'
15He went on, 'I engage you at a drachma
a day, with the same expenses as my own
son's. Complete the journey with my son
16and I shall go beyond the agreed wage.' The
angel replied, 'I shall complete the journey
with him. Do not be afraid. On the journey
outward all will be well; on the journey back
all will be well; the road is safe.' 17Tobit said,
'Blessings on you, brother!' Then he turned
to his son. 'My child', he said, 'prepare what
you need for the journey, and set off with
your brother. May God in heaven protect you
abroad and bring you both back to me safe
and sound! May his angel go with you and
protect you, my child!'
Tobias left the house to set out and kissed
his father and mother. Tobit said, 'A happy
journey!' 18His mother burst into tears and
said to Tobit, 'Why must you send my child
away? Is he not the staff of our hands, as
he goes about before us? 19Surely money is
not the only thing that matters? Surely it is
not as precious as our child? 20The way of life
God had already given us was good enough.'
21He said, 'Do not think such thoughts.
Going away and coming back, all will be well
with our child. You will see for yourself when
he comes back safe and sound! Do not think
such thoughts; do not worry on their account,
my sister. 22A good angel will go with him;
he will have a good journey and come back
to us well and happy.'
6 And she dried her tears.

VI: THE FISH

2 The boy left with the angel, and the dog followed behind. The two walked on, and when the first evening came they camped beside the Tigris. 3 The boy had gone down to the river to wash his feet, when a great fish leapt out of the water and tried to swallow his foot. The boy gave a shout 4 and the angel said, 'Catch the fish; do not let it go.' The boy mastered the fish and pulled it onto the bank. 5 The angel said, 'Cut it open; take out gall, heart and liver; set these aside and throw the entrails away, for gall and heart and liver have curative properties.' 6 The boy cut the fish open and took out gall and heart and liver. He fried part of the fish for his meal and kept some for salting. Then they walked on again together until they were nearly in Media.

7 Then the boy asked the angel this question, 'Brother Azarias, what can the fish's heart, liver and gall cure?' 8 He replied, 'You burn the fish's heart and liver, and their smoke is used in the case of a man or woman plagued by a demon or evil spirit; any such affliction disappears for good, leaving no trace. 9 As regards the gall, this is used as an eye ointment for anyone having white spots on his eyes; after using it, you have only to blow on the spots to cure them.'

10 They entered Media and had nearly reached Ecbatana 11 when Raphael said to the boy, 'Brother Tobias.' 'Yes?' he replied. The angel went on, 'Tonight we are to stay with Raguel, who is a kinsman of yours. He has a daughter called Sarah, 12 but apart from Sarah he has no other son or daughter. Now you are her next of kin; she belongs to you before anyone else and you may claim her father's inheritance. She is a thoughtful, courageous and very lovely girl, and her father loves her dearly. 13 You have the right to marry her. Listen, brother; this very evening I shall speak about the girl to her father and arrange for her to be betrothed to you, and when we come back from Rhages we can celebrate the marriage. I assure you, Raguel has no right whatever to refuse you or to betroth her to anyone else. That would be asking for death, as prescribed in the Book of Moses, once he is aware that kinship gives you the pre-eminent right to marry his daughter. So listen, brother. This very evening we shall speak about the girl and ask for her hand in marriage. When we come back from Rhages we shall fetch her and take her home with us.'

14 Tobias replied to Raphael, 'Brother Azarias, I have been told that she has already been given in marriage seven times and that each time her bridegroom has died in the bridal room. He died the same night as he entered her room; and I have heard people say it was a demon that killed them, 15 and this makes me afraid. To her the demon does no harm because he loves her, but as soon as a man tries to approach her, he kills him. I am my father's only son, and I have no wish to die. I do not want my father and mother to grieve over me for the rest of their lives; they have no other son to bury them.' 16 The angel said, 'Have you forgotten your father's advice? After all, he urged you to choose a wife from your father's family. Listen then, brother. Do not worry about the demon; take her. This very evening, I promise, she will be given you as your wife. 17 Then once you are in the bridal room, take the heart and liver of the fish and lay a little of it on the burning incense. The reek will rise, 18 the demon will smell it and flee, and there is no danger that he will ever be found near the girl again. Then, before you sleep together, first stand up, both of you, and pray. Ask the Lord of heaven to grant you his grace and protection. Do not be afraid; she was destined for you from the beginning, and you are the one to save her. She will follow you, and I pledge my word she will give you children who will be like brothers to you. Do not worry.' And when Tobias heard Raphael say this, when he understood that Sarah was his sister, a kinswoman of his father's family, he fell so deeply in love with her that he could no longer call his heart his own.

VII: RAGUEL

7 As they entered Ecbatana, Tobias said, 'Brother Azarias, take me at once to our brother Raguel's.' And he showed him the way to the house of Raguel, whom they found sitting beside his courtyard door. They greeted him first, and he replied, 'Welcome and greetings, brothers.' And he took them into his house. [2]He said to his wife Edna, 'How like my brother Tobit this young man is!' [3]Edna asked them where they came from; they said, 'We are sons of Naphtali exiled in Nineveh.' [4]'Do you know our brother Tobit?' 'Yes.' 'How is he?' [5]'He is alive and well.' And Tobias added, 'He is my father.' [6]Raguel leapt to his feet and kissed him and wept. [7]Then, finding words, he said, 'Blessings on you, child! You are the son of a noble father. How sad it is that someone so bright and full of good deeds should have gone blind!' He fell on the neck of his kinsman Tobias and wept. [8]And his wife Edna wept for him, and so did his daughter Sarah. [9]Raguel killed a ram from the flock, and they gave them a warm welcome.

They washed and bathed and sat down to table. Then Tobias said to Raphael, 'Brother Azarias, will you ask Raguel to give me my sister Sarah?' [10]Raguel overheard the words, and said to the young man, 'Eat and drink, and make the most of your evening; no one else has the right to take my daughter Sarah—no one but you, my brother. In any case even I am not at liberty to give her to anyone else, since you are her next of kin. However, my boy, I must be frank with you: [11]I have tried to find a husband for her seven times among our kinsmen, and all of them have died the first evening, on going to her room. But for the present, my boy, eat and drink; the Lord will grant you his grace and peace.' Tobias spoke out, 'I will not hear of eating and drinking till you have come to a decision about me.' Raguel answered, 'Very well. Since, by the prescription of the Book of Moses she is given to you, Heaven itself decrees she shall be yours. I therefore entrust your sister to you. From now on you are her brother and she is your sister. She is given to you from today for ever. The Lord of heaven favour you tonight, my child, and grant you his grace and peace.' [12]Raguel called for his daughter Sarah, took her by the hand and gave her to Tobias with these words, 'I entrust her to you; the law and the ruling recorded in the Book of Moses assign her to you as your wife. Take her; bring her home safe and sound to your father's house. The God of heaven grant you a good journey in peace.' [13]Then he turned to her mother and asked her to fetch him writing paper. He drew up the marriage contract, and so he gave his daughter as bride to Tobias according to the ordinance of the Law of Moses.

[14]After this they began to eat and drink. [15]Raguel called his wife Edna and said, 'My sister, prepare the second room and take her there.' [16]She went and made the bed in this room as he had ordered, and took her daughter to it. She wept over her, then wiped away her tears and said, 'Courage, daughter! May the Lord of heaven turn your grief to joy! Courage, daughter!' And she went out.

VIII: THE GRAVE

8 When they had finished eating and drinking and it seemed time to go to bed, the young man was taken from the dining room to the bedroom. [2]Tobias remembered Raphael's advice; he went to his bag, took the fish's heart and liver out of it and put some on the burning incense. [3]The reek of the fish distressed the demon, who fled through the air to Egypt. Raphael pursued him there, shackled him and strangled him forthwith.

[4]The parents meanwhile had gone out and shut the door behind them. Tobias rose from the bed, and said to Sarah, 'Get up, my sister! You and I must pray and petition our Lord to win his grace and his protection.' [5]She stood up, and they began praying for protection, and this was how he began:

You are blessed, O God of our fathers;
blessed too is your name
for ever and ever.

Let the heavens bless you
and all things you have made
for evermore.

6 You it was who created Adam,
you who created Eve his wife
to be his help and support;
and from these two
the human race was born.
You it was who said,
'It is not right that the man should be alone;
let us make him a helper like him.'[a]
7 And so I take my sister
not for any lustful motive,
but I do it in singleness of heart.
Be kind enough to have pity on her
and on me
and bring us to old age together.

8 And together they said, 'Amen, Amen,'
9 and lay down for the night.
But Raguel rose and called his servants,
who came and helped him dig a grave. 10 He
had thought, 'Heaven grant he does not die!
We should be overwhelmed with ridicule and
shame.' 11 When the grave was ready, Raguel
went back to the house, called his wife 12 and
said, 'Will you send a maid to the room to
see if Tobias is still alive? For if he is dead,
we may be able to bury him without anyone
else knowing.' 13 They sent the maid, lit the
lamp, opened the door and the maid went in.
She found the two fast asleep together; 14 she
came out again and whispered, 'He is not
dead; all is well.' 15 Then Raguel blessed the
God of heaven with these words:

You are blessed, my God,
with every blessing that is pure;
may you be blessed for evermore!
16 You are blessed for having made me glad.
What I feared has not happened,
instead you have shown us
your boundless mercy.
17 You are blessed for taking pity
on this only son, this only daughter.
Grant them, Master,
your mercy and your protection;
let them live out their lives
in happiness and in mercy.

18 And he made his servants fill the grave in
before dawn broke.
19 He told his wife to make an ovenful of
bread; he went to his flock, brought back two
oxen and four sheep and gave orders for them
to be cooked; and preparations began. 20 He
called Tobias and said, 'I will not hear of your
leaving here for a fortnight. You are to stay
where you are, eating and drinking, with me.
You will make my daughter happy again after
all her troubles. 21 After that, take away a half
of all I have, and take her safe and sound
back to your father. When my wife and I are
dead you shall have the other half. Courage,
my boy! I am your father, and Edna is your
mother. We are your parents in future, as we
are your sister's. Courage, my son!'

IX: THE WEDDING FEAST

9 Then Tobias turned to Raphael. 2 'Brother
Azarias,' he said, 'take four servants and
two camels and leave for Rhages. 3 Go to
Gabael's house, give him the receipt and see
about the money; then invite him to come
with you to my wedding feast. 4 You know
that my father must be counting the days
and that I cannot lose a single one without
worrying him. 5 You see what Raguel has
pledged himself to do; I am bound by his
oath.' So Raphael left for Rhages in Media
with the four servants and two camels. They
stayed with Gabael, and Raphael showed him
the receipt. He told him about the marriage
of Tobias son of Tobit and gave him his
invitation to the wedding feast. Gabael
started counting out the sacks to him—the
seals were intact—and they loaded them on
to the camels. 6 Early in the morning they
set off together for the feast, and reached
Raguel's house where they found Tobias
dining. He rose to greet Gabael, who burst
into tears and blessed him with the words,
'Excellent son of a father beyond reproach,
just and generous in his dealings! The Lord
give heaven's blessing to you, to your wife,

8a Gn 2:18.

to your wife's father and mother! Blessed be
God for granting me the sight of this living
image of my cousin Tobit!'

10 Every day, meanwhile, Tobit kept
reckoning the days required for the
journey there and the journey back. The full
number went by, and still his son had not
come. 2Then he thought, 'I hope he has
not been delayed there! I hope Gabael is not
dead, so that no one will give him the silver.'
3And he began to worry. 4His wife Anna kept
saying, 'My son is dead! He is no longer
among the living!' And she began to weep
and mourn over her son. She kept saying,
5'Alas! I should never have let you leave me,
my child, you, the light of my eyes.' 6And
Tobit would reply, 'Hush, my sister! Do not
worry. All is well with him. Something has
happened there to delay them. His
companion is someone we can trust, one of
our kinsmen at that. Do not lose heart, my
sister. 7He will soon be here.' But all she
would say was, 'Leave me alone; do not try
to deceive me. My child is dead.' And every
day she would go abruptly out to watch the
road by which her son had left. She trusted
no eyes but her own. Once the sun had set
she would come home again, only to weep
and moan all night, unable to sleep.

After the fourteen days of feasting that
Raguel had sworn to keep for his daughter's
marriage, Tobias came to him and said, 'Let
me go now; my father and mother must have
lost all hope of seeing me again. So I beg you,
father, to let me return to my father's house;
I have told you the plight he was in when I
left him.' 8Raguel said to Tobias, 'Stay, my
son, stay with me. I shall send messengers to
your father Tobit to give him news of you.'
9But Tobias pressed him, 'No, I beg you
to let me go back to my father's house.'
10Without more ado, Raguel committed
Sarah his bride into his keeping. He gave
Tobias half his wealth, slaves, men and
women, oxen and sheep, donkeys and
camels, clothes and money and household
things. 11And so he let them leave happily.
To Tobias he said these parting words, 'Good
health, my son, and a happy journey! May
the Lord of heaven be gracious to you and to
your wife Sarah! I hope to see your children
before I die.' 12To his daughter Sarah he said,
'Go now to your father-in-law's house, since
henceforward they are as much your parents
as those who gave you life. Go in peace, my
daughter, I hope to hear nothing but good of
you, as long as I live.' He said goodbye to
them and let them go.

Edna in her turn said to Tobias, 'Dear son
and brother, may it please the Lord to bring
you back again! I hope to live long enough to
see the children of you and my daughter
Sarah before I die. In the sight of the Lord I
give my daughter into your keeping. Never
make her unhappy as long as you live. Go in
peace, my son. Henceforward I am your
mother and Sarah is your sister. May we all
live happily for the rest of our lives!' And
she kissed them both and saw them set out
happily.

13Tobias left Raguel's house with his mind
at ease. In his gladness he blessed the Lord
of heaven and earth, the King of all that is,
for the happy issue of his travels. He gave
this blessing to Raguel and his wife Edna,
'May it be my happiness to honour you for
the rest of my life!'

X: TOBIT'S SIGHT RESTORED

11 They were nearly at Kaserin, opposite
Nineveh, 2when Raphael said, 'You
know the plight in which we left your father;
3let us go on ahead of your wife and prepare
the house ourselves while she travels behind
with the others.' 4They went on together
(Raphael warned Tobias to take the gall with
him) and the dog followed them.

5Anna was sitting, watching the road by
which her son would come. 6She was sure at
once it must be he and said to the father,
'Here comes your son, with his companion.'

7Raphael said to Tobias before he reached
his father, 'I give you my word that your
father's eyes will open. 8You must put the
fish's gall to his eyes; the medicine will smart
and will draw a filmy white skin off his eyes.
And your father will no more be blind but
will be able to see the light.'

9The mother ran forward and threw her

arms round her son's neck. 'Now I can die,'
she said, 'I have seen you again.' And she
wept. 10Tobit rose to his feet and stumbled
across the courtyard through the door.
Tobias came on towards him 11(he had the
fish's gall in his hand). He blew into his
eyes and said, steadying him, 'Take courage,
father!' With this he applied the medicine,
left it there a while, 12then with both hands
peeled away a filmy skin from the corners of
his eyes. 13Then his father fell on his neck
14and wept. He exclaimed, 'I can see you, my
son, the light of my eyes!' And he said:

Blessed be God!
Blessed be his great name!
Blessed be all his holy angels!
Blessed be his great name
for evermore!

15For, having afflicted me,
he has had pity on me
and now I see my son Tobias!

Tobias went indoors, joyfully blessing God
at the top of his voice. Then he told his
father everything; how his journey had been
successful and he had brought the silver
back; how he had married Sarah the daughter
of Raguel; how she was following him now,
close behind, and could not be far from the
gates of Nineveh.

16Tobit set off to the gates of Nineveh to
meet his daughter-in-law, giving joyful praise
to God as he went. When the people of
Nineveh saw him walking without a guide
and stepping forward as briskly as of old,
they were astonished. 17Tobit described to
them how God had taken pity on him and
had opened his eyes. Then Tobit met Sarah
the bride of his son Tobias, and blessed her
in these words. 'Welcome, daughter! Blessed
be your God for sending you to us, my
daughter. Blessings on your father, blessings
on my son Tobias, blessings on yourself, my
daughter. Welcome now to your own house
in joyfulness and in blessedness. Come in,
my daughter.' That day brought joy to the
Jews of Nineveh, 18and his cousins Ahikar
and Nadab came to share in Tobit's
happiness.

XI: THE REVELATION

12 When the wedding feast was over,
Tobit called his son Tobias and said,
'My son, you ought to think about paying
the amount due to your fellow traveller;
give him more than the figure agreed on.'
2'Father,' he replied, 'how much am I to give
him for his help? Even if I give him half the
goods he brought back with me, I shall not
be the loser. 3He has brought me back safe
and sound, he has cured my wife, he has
brought the money back too, and now he has
cured you as well. How much am I to give
him for all this?' 4Tobit said, 'He has richly
earned half what he brought back'. 5So
Tobias called his companion and said, 'Take
half of what you brought back, in payment
for all you have done, and go in peace.'

6Then Raphael took them both aside and
said, 'Bless God, utter his praise before all
the living for the favour he has shown you.
Bless and extol his name. Proclaim before all
people the deeds of God as they deserve,
and never tire of giving him thanks. 7It is
right to keep the secret of a king, yet right
to reveal and publish the works of God as
they deserve. Do what is good, and no evil
can befall you.

8'Prayer with fasting and alms with
uprightness are better than riches with
iniquity. Better to practise almsgiving than
to hoard up gold. 9Almsgiving saves from
death and purges every kind of sin. Those
who give alms have their fill of days; 10those
who commit sin and do evil bring harm on
themselves.

11'I am going to tell you the whole truth,
hiding nothing from you. I have already told
you that it is right to keep the secret of a king,
yet right too to reveal in a worthy way the
words of God. 12So you must know that when
you and Sarah were at prayer, it was I who
offered your supplications before the glory
of the Lord and who read them; so too when
you were burying the dead. 13When you did
not hesitate to get up and leave the table to
go and bury a dead man, I was sent to test
your faith, 14and at the same time God sent
me to heal you and your daughter-in-law
Sarah. 15I am Raphael, one of the seven angels

who stand ever ready to enter the presence of the glory of the Lord.'
[16]They were both overwhelmed with awe; they fell on their faces in terror. [17]But the angel said, 'Do not be afraid; peace be with you. Bless God for ever. [18]As far as I was concerned, when I was with you, my presence was not by any decision of mine, but by the will of God; he is the one whom you must bless as long as you live, he the one that you must praise. [19]You thought you saw me eating, but that was appearance and no more. [20]Now bless the Lord on earth and give thanks to God. I am about to return to him who sent me from above. Write down all that has happened.' And he rose in the air. [21]When they stood up again, he was no longer visible. They praised God with hymns; they thanked him for having performed such wonders; had not an angel of God appeared to them?

XII: ZION

13 And he said:

Blessed be God who lives for ever,
for his reign endures throughout all ages!
2 For he both punishes and pardons;
he sends people down to the depths
of the underworld
and draws them up
from utter Destruction;
no one can escape his hand.
3 Declare his praise before the nations,
you who are the children of Israel!
For if he has scattered you among them,
4 there too he has shown you his greatness.
Extol him before all the living;
he is our Lord
and he is our God;
he is our Father,
and he is God for ever and ever.

5 Though he punishes you
for your iniquities,
he will take pity on you all;
he will gather you from every nation
wherever you have been scattered.
6 If you return to him
with all your heart and all your soul,
behaving honestly towards him,
then he will return to you
and hide his face from you no longer.
Consider how well he has treated you;
loudly give him thanks.
Bless the Lord of justice
and extol the King of the ages.

I for my part sing his praise
in the country of my exile;
I make his power and greatness known
to a nation that has sinned.
Sinners, return to him;
let your conduct be upright before him;
perhaps he will be gracious to you
and take pity on you.
7 I for my part extol God
and my soul rejoices
in the King of heaven.
Let his greatness 8 be on every tongue,
his praises be sung in Jerusalem.

9 Jerusalem, Holy City,
God has scourged you
for what you have done
but will still take pity
on the children of the upright.
10 Thank the Lord as he deserves
and bless the King of the ages,
that your Temple may be rebuilt
with joy within you;
within you he may comfort every exile,
and within you he may love
all those who are distressed,
for all generations to come.

11 A bright light will shine
over all the regions of the earth;
many nations will come from far away,
from all the ends of the earth,
to dwell close to the holy name
of the Lord God,
with gifts in their hands
for the King of heaven.
Within you, generation after generation
will proclaim their joy,
and the name of her who is Elect
will endure
through the generations to come.

12 Cursed be any who affront you,
cursed be any who destroy you,
who throw down your walls,
who rase your towers,
who burn your houses!
Eternally blessed be he who rebuilds you!

13 Then you will exult, and rejoice
over the children of the upright,
for they will all have been gathered in
and will bless the Lord of the ages.

14 Blessed are those who love you,
blessed those who rejoice over your peace,
blessed those who have mourned
over all your punishment!
For they will soon rejoice within you,
witness all your blessedness
in days to come.
15 My soul blesses the Lord, the great King
16 because Jerusalem will be built anew
and his house for ever and ever.

What bliss, if one of my family be left
to see your glory
and praise the King of heaven!
The gates of Jerusalem will be built
of sapphire and of emerald,
and all your walls of precious stone,
the towers of Jerusalem
will be built of gold
and their battlements of pure gold.
17 The streets of Jerusalem will be paved
with ruby and with stones from Ophir;
the gates of Jerusalem will resound
with songs of exultation;
and all her houses will say,
'Alleluia! Blessed be the God of Israel.'
Within you they will bless the holy name
for ever and ever.

14 The end of the hymns of Tobit.

XIII: NINEVEH

Tobit died when he was a hundred and twelve
years old and received an honourable burial
in Nineveh. 2 He had been sixty-two when he
went blind; and after his cure, he lived in
comfort, practising almsgiving and continu-
ally praising God and extolling his greatness.
3 When he was at the point of death he
summoned his son Tobias and gave him these
instructions, 4 'My son, take your children
and hurry away to Media, since I believe the
word of God pronounced over Nineveh by
Nahum. Everything will come true, every-
thing happen that the emissaries of God, the
prophets of Israel, have predicted against
Assyria and Nineveh; not one of their words
will prove empty. It will all take place in due
time. You will be safer in Media than in
Assyria or in Babylonia. Since I for my part
know and believe that everything God has
said will come true; so it will be, and not a
word of the prophecies will fail.

'A census will be taken of our brothers
living in the land of Israel and they will be
exiled far from their own fair country. The
entire territory of Israel will become a desert,
and Samaria and Jerusalem will become a
desert, and the house of God, for a time, will
be laid waste and burnt. 5 Then once again
God will take pity on them and bring them
back to the land of Israel. They will rebuild
his house, although it will be less beautiful
than the first, until the time is fulfilled. But
after this, all will return from captivity and
rebuild Jerusalem in all her glory, and the
house of God will be rebuilt within her as
the prophets of Israel have foretold. 6 And
all the people of the whole earth will be
converted and will reverence God with all
sincerity. All will renounce their false gods
who have led them astray into error, 7 and
will bless the God of ages in uprightness.
All the Israelites spared in those days will
remember God in sincerity of heart. They will
come and gather in Jerusalem and thereafter
dwell securely in the land of Abraham, which
will be theirs. And those who sincerely love
God will rejoice. And those who commit sin
and wickedness will vanish from the earth.

8 'And now, my children, I lay this duty on
you; serve God sincerely, and do what is
pleasing to him. And lay on your children
the obligation to behave uprightly, to give
alms, to keep God in mind and to bless his
name always, sincerely and with all their
might.

9 'So then, my son, leave Nineveh, do not
stay here. 10 As soon as you have buried
your mother next to me, go the same day,
whenever it may be, and do not linger in this
country where I see wickedness and perfidy
unashamedly triumphant. Consider, my
child, all the things done by Nadab to his
foster-father Ahikar. Was not Ahikar forced
to go underground, though still a living man?
But God made the criminal pay for his outrage
before his victim's eyes, since Ahikar came

back to the light of day, while Nadab went
down to everlasting darkness in punishment
for plotting against Ahikar's life. Because of
his good works Ahikar escaped the deadly
snare Nadab had laid for him, and Nadab fell
into it to his own ruin. 11So, my children,
you see what comes of almsgiving, and what
wickedness leads to, I mean to death. But
now breath fails me.'

They laid him back on his bed; he died
and was buried with honour.

12When his mother died, Tobias buried
her beside his father. Then he left for Media
with his wife and children. He lived in Ecba-
tana with Raguel, his father-in-law. 13He
treated the ageing parents of his wife with
every care and respect, and later buried them
in Ecbatana in Media. Tobias inherited the
patrimony of Raguel besides that of his father
Tobit. 14Much honoured, he lived to the age
of a hundred and seventeen years. 15Before
he died he witnessed the ruin of Nineveh.
He saw the Ninevites taken prisoner and
deported to Media by Cyaxares king of
Media. He blessed God for everything he
inflicted on the Ninevites and Assyrians.
Before his death he had the opportunity of
rejoicing over the fate of Nineveh, and he
blessed the Lord God for ever and ever.
Amen.

THE BOOK OF JUDITH

A story of the triumph of faithful Jewry over the embattled forces of evil. 'Judith' means merely 'the Jewess', and she personifies the true daughter of Israel; it is remarkable that both here and in Esther the Jewish nation is saved by a woman. The fervent nationalism of the book is tempered by openness: the pagan Achior recognises the power of God, protector of the Jews.

The book may well have been written about 150 BC, but the setting of the story is indeterminate, for the main characters are unknown in any records, and the author's use of both geography and history is inexact and imaginative.

JUDITH

I: THE CAMPAIGN OF HOLOFERNES

Nebuchadnezzar and Arphaxad

1 It was the twelfth year of Nebuchadnezzar
who reigned over the Assyrians in the
great city of Nineveh. Arphaxad was then
reigning over the Medes in Ecbatana. 2He
surrounded this city with walls of dressed
stones three cubits thick and six cubits long,
making the rampart seventy cubits high and
fifty cubits wide. 3At the gates he placed
towers one hundred cubits high and, at the
foundations, sixty cubits wide, 4the gates
themselves being seventy cubits high and
forty wide to allow his forces to march out in
a body and his infantry to parade freely.
5About this time King Nebuchadnezzar

gave battle to King Arphaxad in the great
plain lying in the territory of Ragae.
6 Supporting him were all the peoples from
the highlands, all from the Euphrates and
Tigris and Hydaspes, and those from the
plains who were subject to Arioch, king
of the Elymaeans. Thus many nations had
mustered to take part in the battle of the
Cheleoudites.
7 Nebuchadnezzar king of the Assyrians
sent a message to all the inhabitants of Persia,
to all the inhabitants of the western countries,
Cilicia, Damascus, Lebanon, Anti-Lebanon,
to all those along the coast, 8 to the peoples of
Carmel, Gilead, Upper Galilee, the great
plain of Esdraelon, 9 to the people of Samaria
and its outlying towns, to those beyond
Jordan, as far away as Jerusalem, Bethany,
Chelous, Kadesh, the river of Egypt,
Tahpanhes, Rameses and the whole territory
of Goshen, 10 beyond Tanis too and Memphis,
and to all the inhabitants of Egypt as far as the
frontiers of Ethiopia. 11 But the inhabitants
of these countries ignored the summons of
Nebuchadnezzar king of the Assyrians and
did not rally to him to make war. They were
not afraid of him, since in their view he
appeared isolated. Hence they sent his
ambassadors back with nothing achieved and
in disgrace. 12 Nebuchadnezzar was furious
with all these countries. He swore by his
throne and kingdom to take revenge on all
the territories of Cilicia, Damascus and Syria,
of the Moabites and of the Ammonites, of
Judaea and Egypt as far as the limits of the
two seas, and to ravage them with the
sword.

The campaign against Arphaxad

13 In the seventeenth year, he gave battle with
his whole army to King Arphaxad and in this
battle defeated him. He routed Arphaxad's
entire army and all his cavalry and chariots;
14 he occupied his towns and advanced on
Ecbatana; he seized its towers and plundered
its market places, reducing its former
magnificence to a mockery. 15 He later
captured Arphaxad in the mountains of
Ragae and, thrusting him through with his
spears, destroyed him once and for all.
16 He then retired with his troops and all
who had joined forces with him: a vast horde
of armed men. Then he and his army gave
themselves up to carefree feasting for a
hundred and twenty days.

The campaign in the west

2 In the eighteenth year, on the twenty-
second day of the first month, a rumour
ran through the palace that Nebuchadnezzar
king of the Assyrians was to have his revenge
on all the countries, as he had threatened.
2 Summoning his general staff and senior
officers, he held a secret conference with
them, and with his own lips pronounced
utter destruction on the entire area. 3 It was
then decreed that everyone should be put
to death who had not answered the king's
appeal.
4 When the council was over, Nebuchad-
nezzar king of the Assyrians sent for Holo-
fernes, general-in-chief of his armies and
subordinate only to himself. He said to him,
5 'Thus speaks the Great King, lord of the
whole world, "Go; take men of proven
valour, about a hundred and twenty thousand
foot soldiers and a strong company of horse
with twelve thousand cavalrymen; 6 then
advance against all the western lands, since
these people have disregarded my call. 7 Bid
them have earth and water ready, because in
my rage I am about to march on them; the
feet of my soldiers will cover the whole face
of the earth, and I shall plunder it. 8 Their
wounded will fill the valleys and the torrents,
and rivers, blocked with their dead, will
overflow. 9 I shall lead them captive to the
ends of the earth. 10 Now go! Begin by
conquering this whole region for me. If they
surrender to you, hold them for me until the
time comes to punish them. 11 But if they
resist, look on no one with clemency, hand
them over to slaughter and plunder
throughout the territory entrusted to you.
12 For by my life and by the living power of
my kingdom I have spoken. All this I shall
do by my power. 13 And you, neglect none of
your master's commands, act strictly
according to my orders without further
delay." '
14 Leaving the presence of his sovereign,
Holofernes immediately summoned all the
marshals, generals and officers of the Assyr-
ian army 15 and detailed the picked troops as
his master had ordered, about a hundred and
twenty thousand men and a further twelve
thousand mounted archers. 16 He organised
these in the normal battle formation. 17 He
then secured vast numbers of camels,
donkeys and mules to carry the baggage, and
innumerable sheep, oxen and goats for food

supplies. [18]Every man received full rations and a generous sum of gold and silver from the king's purse.

[19]He then set out for the campaign with his whole army, in advance of King Nebuchadnezzar, to overwhelm the whole western region with his chariots, his horsemen and his picked body of foot. [20]A motley gathering followed in his rear, as numerous as locusts or the grains of sand on the ground; there was no counting their multitude.

The stages of Holofernes' advance

[21]Thus they set out from Nineveh and marched for three days towards the Plain of Bectileth. From Bectileth they went on to pitch camp near the mountains that lie to the north of Upper Cilicia. [22]From there Holofernes advanced into the highlands with his whole army, infantry, horsemen, chariots. [23]He cut his way through Put and Lud, carried away captive all the sons of Rassis and sons of Ishmael living on the verge of the desert south of Cheleon, [24]marched along the Euphrates, crossed Mesopotamia, rased all the fortified towns controlling the Wadi Abron and reached the sea. [25]Next he attacked the territories of Cilicia, butchering all who offered him resistance, advanced on the southern frontiers of Japheth, facing Arabia, [26]completely encircled the Midianites, burned their tents and plundered their sheep-folds, [27]made his way down to the Damascus plain at the time of the wheat harvest, set fire to the fields, destroyed the flocks and herds, sacked the towns, laid the countryside waste and put all the young men to the sword. [28]Fear and trembling seized all the coastal peoples; those of Sidon and Tyre, those of Sur, Ocina and Jamnia. The populations of Azotos and Ascalon were panic-stricken.

3 They therefore sent envoys to him to sue for peace, to say, [2]'We are servants of the great King Nebuchadnezzar; we lie prostrate before you. Treat us as you think fit. [3]Our cattle-farms, all our land, all our wheat fields, our flocks and herds, all the sheep-folds in our encampments are at your disposal. Do with them as you please. [4]Our towns and their inhabitants too are at your service; go and treat them as you think fit.' [5]These men came to Holofernes and delivered the message as above.

[6]He then made his way down to the coast with his army and stationed garrisons in all the fortified towns, levying outstanding men there as auxiliaries. [7]The people of these cities and of all the other towns in the neighbourhood welcomed him, wearing garlands and dancing to the sound of tambourines. [8]But he demolished their shrines and cut down their sacred trees, carrying out his commission to destroy all local gods so that the nations should worship Nebuchadnezzar alone and people of every language and nationality should hail him as a god.

[9]Thus he reached the edge of Esdraelon, in the neighbourhood of Dothan, a village facing the great ridge of Judaea. [10]He pitched camp between Geba and Scythopolis and stayed there a full month to re-provision his forces.

Judaea on the alert

4 When the Israelites living in Judaea heard how Holofernes, general-in-chief of Nebuchadnezzar king of the Assyrians, had treated the various nations, plundering their temples and destroying them, [2]they were thoroughly alarmed at his approach and trembled for Jerusalem and the Temple of the Lord their God. [3]They had returned from captivity only a short time before, and the resettlement of the people in Judaea and the reconsecration of the sacred furnishings, of the altar, and of the Temple, which had been profaned, were of recent date.

[4]They therefore alerted the whole of Samaria, Kona, Beth-Horon, Belmain, Jericho, Choba, Aesora and the Salem valley. [5]They occupied the summits of the highest mountains and fortified the villages on them; they laid in supplies for the coming war, as the fields had just been harvested. [6]Joakim the high priest, resident in Jerusalem at the time, wrote to the inhabitants of Bethulia and of Betomesthaim, two towns facing Esdraelon, towards the plain of Dothan. [7]He ordered them to occupy the mountain passes, the only means of access to Judaea, for there it would be easy for them to halt an attacking force, the narrowness of the approach not allowing men to advance more than two abreast. [8]The Israelites carried out the orders of Joakim the high priest and of the people's Council of Elders in session at Jerusalem.

A nation at prayer
9 All the men of Israel cried most fervently to
God and humbled themselves before him.
10 They, their wives, their children, their
cattle, all their resident aliens, hired or slave,
wrapped sackcloth round their loins. 11 All
the Israelites in Jerusalem, including women
and children, lay prostrate in front of the
Temple, and with ashes on their heads stret-
ched out their hands before the Lord. 12 They
draped the altar itself in sackcloth and
fervently joined together in begging the God
of Israel not to let their children be carried
off, their wives distributed as booty, the
towns of their heritage destroyed, the Temple
profaned and desecrated for the heathen to
gloat over. 13 The Lord heard them and
looked kindly on their distress.
The people fasted for many days
throughout Judaea as well as in Jerusalem
before the sanctuary of the Lord Almighty.
14 Joakim the high priest and all who stood
before the Lord, the Lord's priests and minis-
ters, wore sackcloth round their loins as they
offered the perpetual burnt offering and the
votive and voluntary offerings of the people.
15 With ashes on their turbans they earnestly
called on the Lord to look kindly on the
House of Israel.

A council of war in Holofernes' camp
5 Holofernes, general-in-chief of the Assyr-
ian army, received the intelligence that
the Israelites were preparing for war, that
they had closed the mountain passes, fortified
all the high peaks and laid obstructions in the
plains. 2 Holofernes was furious. He
summoned all the princes of Moab, all the
generals of Ammon and all the satraps of the
coastal regions. 3 'Men of Canaan,' he said,
'tell me: what people is this that occupies the
hill-country? What towns does it inhabit?
How large is its army? What are the sources
of its power and strength? Who is the king
who rules it and commands its army? 4 Why
have they disdained to wait on me, as all the
western peoples have?'
5 Achior, leader of all the Ammonites,
replied, 'May my lord be pleased to listen to
what your servant is going to say. I shall
give you the facts about these mountain folk
whose home lies close to you. You will hear
no lie from the mouth of your servant. 6 These
people are descended from the Chaldaeans.
7 They once came to live in Mesopotamia,
because they did not want to follow the gods
of their ancestors who lived in Chaldaea.
8 They abandoned the way of their ancestors
to worship the God of heaven, the God they
learnt to acknowledge. Banished from the
presence of their own gods, they fled to
Mesopotamia where they lived for a long
time. 9 When God told them to leave their
home and set out for Canaan, they settled
there and accumulated gold and silver and
great herds of cattle. 10 Next, famine having
overwhelmed the land of Canaan, they went
down to Egypt where they stayed till they
were well nourished. There they became a
great multitude, a race beyond counting.
11 But the king of Egypt turned against them
and exploited them by forcing them to make
bricks; he degraded them, reducing them to
slavery. 12 They cried to their God, who struck
the entire land of Egypt with incurable
plagues, and the Egyptians expelled them.
13 God dried up the Red Sea before them 14 and
led them forward by way of Sinai and Kadesh-
Barnea. Having driven off all the inhabitants
of the desert, 15 they settled in the land of the
Amorites and in their strength exterminated
the entire population of Heshbon. Then,
having crossed the Jordan, they took
possession of all the hill-country, 16 driving
out the Canaanites before them and the Periz-
zites, Jebusites, Shechemites and all the
Girgashites, and lived there for many years.
17 All the while they did not sin before their
God, prosperity was theirs, for they have a
God who hates wickedness. 18 But when they
turned from the path he had marked out for
them some were exterminated in a series of
battles, others were taken captive to a foreign
land. The Temple of their God was rased to
the ground and their towns were seized by
their enemies. 19 Then having turned once
again to their God, they came back from the
places to which they had been dispersed and
scattered, regained possession of Jerusalem,
where they have their Temple, and reoccu-
pied the hill-country which had been left
deserted. 20 So, now, master and lord, if this
people has committed any fault, if they have
sinned against their God, let us first be sure
that they really have this reason to fail, then
advance and attack them. 21 But if their nation
is guiltless, my lord would do better to
abstain, for fear that their Lord and God
should protect them. We should then become
the laughing-stock of the whole world.'

[22]When Achior had ended this speech, all the people crowding round the tent began protesting. Holofernes' own senior officers, as well as all the coastal peoples and the Moabites, threatened to tear him limb from limb. [23]'Why should we be afraid of the Israelites? They are a weak and powerless people, quite unable to stand a stiff attack. [24]Forward! Advance! Your army, Holofernes our master, will swallow them in one mouthful!'

Achior handed over to the Israelites

6 When the uproar of those crowding round the council had subsided, Holofernes, general-in-chief of the Assyrian army, reprimanded Achior in front of the whole crowd of foreigners and Ammonites. [2]'Achior, who do you think you are, you and the Ephraimite mercenaries, playing the prophet like this with us today, and trying to dissuade us from making war on the people of Israel? You claim their God will protect them. And who is God if not Nebuchadnezzar? He himself will display his power and wipe them off the face of the earth, and their God will certainly not save them. [3]But we, his servants, shall destroy them as easily as a single individual. They can never resist the strength of our cavalry. [4]We shall burn them all. Their mountains will be drunk with their blood and their plains filled with their corpses. Far from being able to resist us, every one of them will die; thus says King Nebuchadnezzar, lord of the whole world. For he has spoken, and his words will not prove empty. [5]As for you, Achior, you Ammonite mercenary, who in a rash moment said these words, you will not see my face again until the day when I have taken my revenge on this brood from Egypt. [6]And then the swords of my soldiers and the spears of my officers will pierce your sides. You will fall among their wounded, the moment I turn on Israel. [7]My servants will now take you into the hill-country and leave you near one of the towns in the passes; [8]you will not die, until you share their ruin. [9]No need to look so sad if you cherish the secret hope that they will not be captured! I have spoken; none of my words will prove idle.'

[10]Holofernes having commanded his tent-orderlies to seize Achior, to take him to Bethulia and to hand him over to the Israelites, [11]the orderlies took him, escorted him out of the camp and across the plain, and then, making for the hill-country, reached the springs below Bethulia. [12]As soon as the men of the town sighted them, they snatched up their weapons, left the town and made for the mountain tops, while all the slingers pelted them with stones to prevent them from coming up. [13]However, they managed to take cover at the foot of the slope, where they bound Achior and left him lying at the bottom of the mountain and returned to their master.

[14]The Israelites then came down from their town, stopped by him, unbound him and took him to Bethulia, where they brought him before the chief men of the town, [15]who at that time were Uzziah son of Micah of the tribe of Simeon, Chabris son of Gothoniel and Charmis son of Melchiel. [16]These summoned all the elders of the town. The young men and the women also hurried to the assembly. Achior was made to stand with all the people surrounding him, and Uzziah questioned him about what had happened. [17]He answered by telling them what had been said at Holofernes' council, and what he himself had said in the presence of the Assyrian leaders, and how Holofernes had bragged of what he would do to the House of Israel. [18]At this the people fell to the ground and worshipped God. [19]'Lord God of heaven,' they cried, 'take notice of their arrogance and have pity on the humiliation of our race. Look kindly today on those who are consecrated to you.' [20]They then spoke reassuringly to Achior and praised him warmly. [21]After the assembly Uzziah took him home and gave a banquet for the elders; all that night they called on the God of Israel for help.

II: THE SIEGE OF BETHULIA

The campaign against Israel

7 The following day Holofernes issued orders to his whole army and to the whole host of auxiliaries who had joined him, to break camp and march on Bethulia, to occupy the mountain passes and so open the campaign against the Israelites. [2]The troops

broke camp that same day. The actual
fighting force numbered one hundred and
twenty thousand infantry and twelve thou-
sand cavalry, not to mention the baggage
train with the vast number of men on foot
concerned with that. 3They penetrated the
valley in the neighbourhood of Bethulia, near
the spring, and deployed on a wide front
from Dothan to Balbaim and, in depth, from
Bethulia to Cyamon, which faces Esdraelon.
4When the Israelites saw this horde, they
were all appalled and said to each other, 'Now
they will lick the whole country clean. Not
even the loftiest peaks, the gorges or the hills
will be able to stand the weight of them.'
5Each man snatched up his arms; they lit
beacons on their towers and spent the whole
night on watch.

6On the second day Holofernes deployed
his entire cavalry in sight of the Israelites in
Bethulia. 7He reconnoitred the slopes leading
up to the town, located the water-points,
seized them and posted pickets over them and
returned to the main body. 8The chieftains
of the sons of Esau, all the leaders of the
Moabites and the generals of the coastal
district then came to him and said, 9'If our
master will be pleased to listen to us, his forces
will not sustain a single wound. 10These
Israelites do not rely so much on their spears
as on the height of the mountains where they
live. And admittedly it is not at all easy to
scale these heights of theirs.

11'This being the case, master, avoid
engaging them in a pitched battle and then
you will not lose a single man. 12Stay in camp,
keep all your troops there too, while your
servants seize the spring which rises at the
foot of the mountain, 13since that is what
provides the population of Bethulia with
their water supply. Thirst will then force
them to surrender their town. Meanwhile, we
and our men will climb the nearest mountain
tops and form advance posts there to prevent
anyone from leaving the town. 14Hunger will
waste them, with their wives and children,
and before the sword can reach them they
will already be lying in the streets outside
their houses. 15And you will make them pay
dearly for their defiance and their refusal to
meet you peaceably.'

16Their words pleased Holofernes as well
as all his officers, and he decided to do as
they suggested. 17Accordingly, a troop of
Moabites moved forward with a further five
thousand Assyrians. They penetrated the
valley and seized the Israelites' waterpoints
and springs. 18Meanwhile the Edomites and
Ammonites went and took up positions in the
highlands opposite Dothan, sending some of
their men to the south-east opposite Egrebel
near Chous on the Wadi Mochmur. The rest
of the Assyrian army took up positions in the
plain, covering every inch of the ground;
their tents and equipment made an immense
encampment, so vast were their numbers.

19The Israelites called on the Lord their
God, dispirited because the enemy had
surrounded them and cut all line of retreat.
20For thirty-four days the Assyrian army,
infantry, chariots, cavalrymen, had them
surrounded. Every water-jar the inhabitants
of Bethulia had was empty, 21their storage-
wells were drying up; on no day could a man
drink his fill, since their water was rationed.
22Their little children pined away, the women
and young men grew weak with thirst; they
collapsed in the streets and gateways of the
town; they had no strength left.

23Young men, women, children, the whole
people thronged clamouring round Uzziah
and the chief men of the town, shouting in
the presence of the assembled elders, 24'May
God be judge between you and us! For you
have done us great harm, by not suing for
peace with the Assyrians. 25And now there is
no one to help us. God has delivered us into
their hands to be prostrated before them in
thirst and utter helplessness. 26Call them in
at once; hand the whole town over to be
sacked by Holofernes' men and all his army.
27After all, we should be much better off as
their booty than we are now; no doubt we
shall be enslaved, but at least we shall be alive
and not see our little ones dying before our
eyes or our wives and children perishing.
28By heaven and earth and by our God, the
Lord of our fathers, who is punishing us for
our sins and the sins of our ancestors, we
implore you to take this course now, today.'
29Bitter lamentations rose from the whole
assembly, and they all cried loudly to the
Lord God.

30Then Uzziah spoke to them, 'Take heart,
brothers! Let us hold out five days more. By
then the Lord our God will take pity on us,
for he will not desert us altogether. 31At the
end of this time, if no help is forthcoming, I
shall do as you have said.' 32With that he
dismissed the people to their various quar-
ters. The men went to man the walls and
towers of the town, sending the women and
children home. The town was full of
despondency.

III: JUDITH

Description of Judith

8 Judith was informed at the time of what had happened. She was the daughter of Merari son of Ox, son of Joseph, son of Oziel, son of Elkiah, son of Ananias, son of Gideon, son of Raphaim, son of Ahitub, son of Elijah, son of Hilkiah, son of Eliab, son of Nathanael, son of Salamiel, son of Sarasadai, son of Israel. 2 Her husband Manasseh, of her own tribe and family, had died at the time of the barley harvest. 3 He was supervising the men as they bound up the sheaves in the field when he caught sunstroke and had to take to his bed. He died in Bethulia, his home town, and was buried with his ancestors in the field that lies between Dothan and Balamon. 4 As a widow, Judith stayed inside her home for three years and four months. 5 She had had an upper room built for herself on the roof. She wore sackcloth next to the skin and dressed in widow's weeds. 6 She fasted every day of her widowhood except for the Sabbath eve, the Sabbath itself, the eve of New Moon, the feast of New Moon and the joyful festivals of the House of Israel. 7 Now she was very beautiful, charming to see. Her husband Manasseh had left her gold and silver, menservants and maidservants, herds and land; and she lived among all her possessions 8 without anyone finding a word to say against her, so devoutly did she fear God.

Judith and the elders

9 Hearing how the water shortage had demoralised the people and how they had complained bitterly to the headman of the town, and being also told what Uzziah had said to them and how he had given them his oath to surrender the town to the Assyrians in five days' time, 10 Judith immediately sent the serving-woman who ran her household to summon Chabris and Charmis, two elders of the town. 11 When these came in she said:

'Listen to me, leaders of the people of Bethulia. You were wrong to speak to the people as you did today and to bind yourself by oath, in defiance of God, to surrender the town to our enemies if the Lord did not come to your help within a set number of days. 12 Who are you, to put God to the test today, you, of all people, to set yourselves above him? 13 You put the Lord Almighty to the test! You do not understand anything, and never will. 14 If you cannot sound the depths of the human heart or unravel the arguments of the human mind, how can you fathom the God who made all things, or sound his mind or unravel his purposes? No, brothers, do not provoke the anger of the Lord our God. 15 Although it may not be his will to help us within the next five days, he has the power to protect us for as many days as he pleases, just as he has the power to destroy us before our enemies. 16 But you have no right to demand guarantees where the designs of the Lord our God are concerned. For God is not to be threatened as a human being is, nor is he, like a mere human, to be cajoled. 17 Rather, as we wait patiently for him to save, let us plead with him to help us. He will hear our voice if such is his good pleasure.

18 'And indeed of recent times and still today there is not one tribe of ours, or family, or village, or town that has worshipped gods made by human hand, as once was done, 19 which was the reason why our ancestors were delivered over to sword and sack, and perished in misery at the hands of our enemies. 20 We for our part acknowledge no other God but him; and so we may hope he will not look on us disdainfully or desert our nation.

21 'If indeed they capture us, as you expect, then all Judaea will be captured too, and our holy places plundered, and we shall answer with our blood for their profanation. 22 The slaughter of our brothers, the captivity of our country, the unpeopling of our heritage, will recoil on our own heads among the nations whose slaves we shall become, and our new masters will look down on us as an outrage and a disgrace; 23 for our surrender will not reinstate us in their favour; no, the Lord our God will make it a thing to be ashamed of. 24 So now, brothers, let us set an example to our brothers, since their lives depend on us, and the sanctuary—Temple and altar—rests on us.

25 'All this being so, let us rather give thanks to the Lord our God who, as he tested our ancestors, is now testing us. 26 Remember

how he treated Abraham, all the ordeals of
Isaac, all that happened to Jacob in Syrian
Mesopotamia while he kept the sheep of
Laban, his mother's brother. 27 For as these
ordeals were intended by him to search their
hearts, so now this is not vengeance that God
is exacting on us, but a warning inflicted by
the Lord on those who are near his heart.'

28 Uzziah replied, 'Everything you have
just said comes from an honest heart and no
one will contradict a word of it. 29 Not that
today is the first time your wisdom has been
displayed; from your earliest years all the
people have known how shrewd you are and
of how sound a heart. 30 But, parched with
thirst, the people forced us to act as we had
promised them and to bind ourselves by an
inviolable oath. 31 You are a devout woman;
pray to the Lord, then, to send us a downpour
to fill our storage-wells, so that our faintness
may pass.'

32 Judith replied, 'Listen to me, I intend to
do something, the memory of which will be
handed down to the children of our race from
age to age. 33 Tonight you must be at the gate
of the town. I shall make my way out with
my attendant. Before the time fixed by you
for surrendering the town to our enemies,
the Lord will make use of me to rescue Israel.
34 You must not ask what I intend to do; I
shall not tell you until I have done it.' 35 Uzziah
and the chief men said, 'Go in peace. May
the Lord show you a way to take revenge on
our enemies.' 36 And leaving the upper room
they went back to their posts.

Judith's prayer

9 Judith threw herself face to the ground,
scattered ashes on her head, undressed as
far as the sackcloth she was wearing and cried
loudly to the Lord. At the same time in
Jerusalem the evening incense was being
offered in the Temple of God. Judith said:

2 Lord, God of my ancestor Simeon,
you armed him with a sword
to take vengeance on the foreigners
who had undone a virgin's belt
to her shame,
laid bare her thigh to her confusion,
violated her womb to her dishonour,
since, though you said,
'This must not be,' they did it.
3 For this you handed their leaders
over to slaughter,
and their bed, defiled by their treachery,
was itself betrayed in blood.
You struck the slaves with the chieftains
and the chieftains with their retainers.
4 You left their wives to be carried off,
their daughters to be taken captive,
and their spoils to be shared out
among the sons you loved,
who had been so zealous for you,
had loathed the stain put on their blood
and called on you for help.

O God, my God,
now hear this widow too;
5 for you have made the past,
and what is happening now,
and what will follow.
What is, what will be, you have planned;
what has been, you designed.
6 Your purposes stood forward;
'See, here we are!' they said.
For all your ways are prepared
and your judgements
delivered with foreknowledge.
7 See the Assyrians,
with their army abounding
glorying in their horses and their riders,
exulting in the strength of their infantry.
Trust as they may in shield and spear,
in bow and sling,
in you they have not recognised the Lord,
the breaker of battle-lines;
8 yours alone is the title of Lord.

Break their violence with your might,
in your anger bring down their strength.
For they plan to profane your holy places,
to defile the tabernacle,
the resting place of your glorious name,
and to hack down the horn of your altar.
9 Observe their arrogance,
send your fury on their heads,
give the strength I have in mind
to this widow's hand.
10 By guile of my lips
strike down slave with master,
and master with retainer.
Break their pride
by a woman's hand.

11 Your strength does not lie in numbers,
nor your might in strong men;
since you are the God of the humble,
the help of the oppressed,
the support of the weak,
the refuge of the forsaken,
the Saviour of the despairing.

[12]Please, please, God of my father,
God of the heritage of Israel,
Master of heaven and earth,
Creator of the waters,
King of your whole creation,
hear my prayer.
[13]Give me a beguiling tongue
to wound and kill
those who have formed such cruel designs
against your covenant,
against your holy dwelling-place,
against Mount Zion,
against the house belonging to your sons.
[14]And demonstrate to every nation,
every tribe,
that you are the Lord,
God of all power, all might,
and that the race of Israel
has no protector but you.

IV: JUDITH AND HOLOFERNES

Judith goes to the camp of Holofernes

10 Thus Judith called on the God of Israel.
When she had finished praying, [2]she
got up from the floor, summoned her maid
and went down into the rooms which she
used on Sabbath days and festivals. [3]There
she removed the sackcloth she was wearing
and taking off her widow's dress, she washed
all over, anointed herself plentifully with
perfumes, dressed her hair, wrapped a turban
round it and put on the robe of joy she used
to wear when her husband Manasseh was
alive. [4]She put sandals on her feet, put on her
necklaces, bracelets, rings, earrings and all
her jewellery, and made herself beautiful
enough to beguile the eye of any man who
saw her. [5]Then she handed her maid a skin
of wine and a flask of oil, filled a bag with
barley girdle-cakes, cakes of dried fruit and
pure loaves, and wrapping all these
provisions up gave them to her as well. [6]They
then went out, making for the town gate of
Bethulia. There they found Uzziah waiting
with the two elders of the town, Chabris and
Charmis. [7]When they saw Judith, her face so
changed and her clothes so different, they
were lost in admiration of her beauty. They
said to her:

[8]May the God of our ancestors
keep you in his favour!
May he crown your designs with success
to the glory of the children of Israel,
to the greater glory of Jerusalem!

[9]Judith worshipped God, and then she
said, 'Have the town gate opened for me so
that I can go out and fulfil all the wishes you
expressed to me.' They did as she asked and
gave orders to the young men to open the
gate for her. [10]This done, Judith went out
accompanied by her maid, while the men of
the town watched her all the way down the
mountain and across the valley, until they
lost sight of her.

[11]As the women were making straight
through the valley, an advance unit of Assyr-
ians intercepted them, [12]and, seizing Judith,
began to question her. 'Which side are you
on? Where do you come from? Where are
you going?' 'I am a daughter of the Hebrews,'
she replied, 'and I am fleeing from them since
they will soon be your prey. [13]I am on my
way to see Holofernes, the general of your
army, to give him trustworthy information.
I shall show him the road to take if he wants
to capture all the hill-country without losing
one man or one life.' [14]As the men listened to
what she was saying, they stared in astonish-
ment at the sight of such a beautiful woman.
[15]'It will prove the saving of you,' they said
to her, 'coming down to see our master of
your own accord. You had better go to his
tent; some of our men will escort you and
hand you over to him. [16]Once you are in his
presence do not be afraid. Tell him what you
have just told us and you will be well
treated.' [17]They then detailed a hundred of
their men as escort for herself and her
attendant, and these led them to the tent
of Holofernes.

[18]News of her coming had already spread
through the tents, and there was a general
stir in the camp. She was still outside the tent
of Holofernes waiting to be announced, when
a crowd began forming round her. [19]They
were immediately impressed by her beauty
and impressed with the Israelites because of
her. 'Who could despise a people who have
women like this?' they kept saying. 'Better
not leave one of them alive; let any go and

they could twist the whole world round their
fingers!'
[20]The bodyguard and adjutants of Holo-
fernes then came out and led Judith into the
tent. [21]Holofernes was resting on his bed
under a canopy of purple and gold studded
with emeralds and precious stones. [22]The
men announced her and he came out to
the entrance to the tent, with silver torches
carried before him.
[23]When Judith confronted the general and
his adjutant, the beauty of her face astonished
them all. She fell on her face and did homage
to him, but his servants raised her from the
ground.

The first meeting of Judith with Holofernes

11 'Courage, woman,' Holofernes said,
'do not be afraid. I have never hurt
anyone who chose to serve Nebuchadnezzar,
king of the whole world. [2]Even now, if your
nation of mountain dwellers had not insulted
me, I would not have raised a spear against
them. This was their fault, not mine. [3]But
tell me, why have you fled from them and
come to us? . . . Anyhow, this will prove the
saving of you. Courage! You will live through
this night, and many after. [4]No one will hurt
you. On the contrary, you will be treated
as well as any who serve my lord King
Nebuchadnezzar.'
[5]Judith said, 'Please listen favourably to
what your slave has to say. Permit your
servant to speak in your presence, I shall
speak no word of a lie to my lord tonight. [6]You
have only to follow your servant's advice and
God will bring your work to a successful
conclusion; in what my lord undertakes he
will not fail. [7]Long life to Nebuchadnezzar,
king of the whole world, who has sent you to
set every living soul to rights; may his power
endure! Since, thanks to you, he is served
not only by human beings, but because of
your might the wild animals themselves, the
cattle, and the birds of the air are to live in
the service of Nebuchadnezzar and his whole
House.
[8]'We have indeed heard of your genius and
adroitness of mind. It is known everywhere
in the world that throughout the empire you
have no rival for ability, wealth of experience
and brilliance in waging war. [9]We have also
heard what Achior said in his speech to your
council. The men of Bethulia having spared
him, he has told them everything that he said
to you. [10]Now, master and lord, do not
disregard what he said; keep it in your mind,
since it is true; our nation will not be
punished, the sword will indeed have no
power over them, unless they sin against their
God. [11]But as it is, my lord need expect no
repulse or setback, since death is about to fall
on their heads, for sin has gained a hold over
them, provoking the anger of their God each
time that they commit it. [12]As they are short
of food and their water is giving out, they
have resolved to fall back on their cattle and
decided to make use of all the things that God
has, by his laws, forbidden them to eat. [13]Not
only have they made up their minds to eat
the first-fruits of corn and the tithes of wine
and oil, though these have been consecrated
by them and set apart for the priests who
serve in Jerusalem in the presence of our
God, and may not lawfully even be handled
by ordinary people, [14]but they have sent
men to Jerusalem—where the inhabitants are
doing much the same—to bring them back
authorisation from the Council of Elders.
[15]Now this will be the outcome: when the
permission arrives and they act on it, that
very day they will be delivered over to you
for destruction.
[16]'When I, your servant, came to know all
this, I fled from them. God has sent me to do
things with you at which the world will be
astonished when it hears. [17]Your servant is
a devout woman; she honours the God of
heaven day and night. I therefore propose,
my lord, to stay with you. I, your servant,
shall go out every night into the valley and
pray to God to let me know when they have
committed their sin. [18]I shall then come and
tell you, so that you can march out with your
whole army; and none of them will be able to
resist you. [19]I shall be your guide right across
Judaea until you reach Jerusalem; there I
shall enthrone you in the very middle of the
city. And then you can round them up like
shepherd-less sheep, with never a dog daring
to bark at you. Foreknowledge tells me this;
this has been foretold to me and I have been
sent to reveal it to you.'
[20]Her words pleased Holofernes, and all his
adjutants. Full of admiration at her wisdom
they exclaimed, [21]'There is no woman like
her from one end of the earth to the other,
so lovely of face and so wise of speech!'
[22]Holofernes said, 'God has done well to send
you ahead of the others. Strength will be

ours, and ruin theirs who have insulted my lord. 23As for you, you are as beautiful as you are eloquent; if you do as you have promised, your God shall be my God, and you yourself shall make your home in the palace of King Nebuchadnezzar and be famous throughout the world.'

12 With that he had her brought in to where his silver dinner service was already laid, and had his own food served to her and his own wine poured out for her. 2But Judith said, 'I would rather not eat this, in case I incur some fault. What I have brought will be enough for me.' 3'Suppose your provisions run out,' Holofernes asked, 'how could we get more of the same sort? We have no one belonging to your race here.' 4'May your soul live, my lord,' Judith answered, 'the Lord will have used me to accomplish his plan, before your servant has finished these provisions.' 5Holofernes' adjutants then took her to a tent where she slept until midnight. A little before the morning watch, she got up. 6She had already sent this request to Holofernes, 'Let my lord kindly give orders for your servant to be allowed to go out and pray,' 7and Holofernes had ordered his guards not to prevent her. She stayed in the camp for three days; she went out each night to the valley of Bethulia and washed at the spring where the picket had been posted. 8As she went she prayed to the Lord God of Israel to guide her in her plan to relieve the children of her people. 9Having purified herself, she would return and stay in her tent until her meal was brought her in the evening.

Judith at the banquet of Holofernes

10On the fourth day Holofernes gave a banquet, inviting only his own staff and none of the other officers. 11He said to Bagoas, the officer in charge of his personal affairs, 'Go and persuade that Hebrew woman you are looking after to come and join us and eat and drink in our company. 12We shall be disgraced if we let a woman like this go without seducing her. If we do not seduce her, everyone will laugh at us!' 13Bagoas then left Holofernes and went to see Judith. 'Would this young and lovely woman condescend to come to my lord?' he asked. 'She will occupy the seat of honour opposite him, drink the joyful wine with us and be treated today like one of the Assyrian ladies who stand in the palace of Nebuchadnezzar.' 14'Who am I', Judith replied, 'to resist my lord? I shall not hesitate to do whatever he wishes, and doing this will be my joy to my dying day.'

15So she got up and put on her dress and all her feminine adornments. Her maid preceded her, and on the floor in front of Holofernes spread the fleece which Bagoas had given Judith for her daily use to lie on as she ate.

16Judith came in and took her place. The heart of Holofernes was ravished at the sight; his very soul was stirred. He was seized with a violent desire to sleep with her; and indeed since the first day he saw her, he had been waiting for an opportunity to seduce her. 17'Drink then!' Holofernes said. 'Enjoy yourself with us!' 18'I am delighted to do so, my lord, for since my birth I have never felt my life more worthwhile than today.' 19She took what her maid had prepared, and ate and drank facing him. 20Holofernes was so enchanted with her that he drank far more wine than he had drunk on any other day in his life.

13 It grew late and his staff hurried away. Bagoas closed the tent from the outside, having shown out those who still lingered in his lord's presence. They went to their beds wearied with too much drinking, 2and Judith was left alone in the tent with Holofernes who had collapsed wine-sodden on his bed. 3Judith then told her maid to stay just outside the bedroom and wait for her to come out, as she did every morning. She had let it be understood she would be going out to her prayers and had also spoken of her intention to Bagoas.

4By now everyone had left Holofernes, and no one, either important or unimportant, was left in the bedroom. Standing beside the bed, Judith murmured to herself:

Lord God, to whom all strength belongs,
prosper what my hands are now to do
for the greater glory of Jerusalem;
5now is the time to recover your heritage
and to further my plans
to crush the enemies arrayed against us.

6With that she went up to the bedpost by Holofernes' head and took down his scimitar; 7coming closer to the bed she caught him by the hair and said, 'Make me strong today, Lord God of Israel!' 8Twice she struck at his neck with all her might, and cut off his head.

9She then rolled his body off the bed and
pulled down the canopy from the bedposts.
After which, she went out and gave the head
of Holofernes to her maid 10who put it in
her food bag. The two then left the camp
together, as they always did when they went
to pray. Once they were out of the camp,
they skirted the ravine, climbed the slope to
Bethulia and made for the gates.

Judith brings the head of Holofernes to Bethulia

11From a distance, Judith shouted to the
guards on the gates, 'Open the gate! Open!
For the Lord our God is with us still,
displaying his strength in Israel and his might
against our enemies, as he has done today!'
12Hearing her voice, the townsmen hurried
down to the town gate and summoned the
elders. 13Everyone, great and small, came
running down, since her arrival was unex-
pected. They threw the gate open, welcomed
the women, lit a fire to see by and crowded
round them. 14Then Judith raised her voice
and said, 'Praise God! Praise him! Praise the
God who has not withdrawn his mercy from
the House of Israel, but has shattered our
enemies by my hand tonight!' 15She pulled
the head out of the bag and held it for
them to see. 'This is the head of Holofernes,
general-in-chief of the Assyrian army; here
is the canopy under which he lay drunk! The
Lord has struck him down by the hand of a
woman! 16Glory to the Lord who has
protected me in the course I took! My face
seduced him, only to his own undoing; he
committed no sin with me to shame me or
disgrace me.'

17Overcome with emotion, the people all
prostrated themselves and worshipped
God, exclaiming with one voice, 'Blessings
on you, our God, for confounding your
people's enemies today!' 18Uzziah then said
to Judith:

May you be blessed, my daughter,
  by God Most High,
beyond all women on earth;
and blessed be the Lord God,
Creator of heaven and earth,
who guided you to cut off the head
of the leader of our enemies!
19The trust which you have shown
will not pass from human hearts,
as they commemorate
the power of God for evermore.
20God grant you may be
  always held in honour
and rewarded with blessings,
since you did not consider your own life
when our nation was brought
  to its knees,
but warded off our ruin,
walking in the right path before our God.

And the people all said, 'Amen! Amen!'

V: VICTORY

The Jews attack the Assyrian camp

14 Judith said, 'Listen to me, brothers.
Take this head and hang it on your
battlements. 2When morning comes and the
sun is up, let every man take his arms and
every able-bodied man leave the town.
Appoint a leader for them, as if you meant to
march down to the plain against the Assyrian
advanced post. But you must not do this.
3The Assyrians will gather up their equip-
ment, make for their camp and wake up their
commanders; they in turn will rush to the
tent of Holofernes and not be able to find
him. They will then be seized with panic and
flee at your advance. 4All you and the others
who live in the territory of Israel will have to
do is to give chase and slaughter them as they
retreat.

5'But before you do this, call me Achior
the Ammonite, for him to see and identify
the man who held the House of Israel in
contempt, the man who sent him to us as
someone already doomed to die.' 6So they
had Achior brought from Uzziah's house. No
sooner had he arrived and seen the head of
Holofernes held by a member of the people's
assembly than he fell on his face in a faint.
7They lifted him up. He then threw himself
at Judith's feet and, prostrate before her,
exclaimed:

May you be blessed
  in all the tents of Judah

and in every nation;
those who hear your name
will be seized with dread!

8 'Now tell me everything that you have
done in these past few days.' And surrounded
by the people, Judith told him everything
she had done from the day she left Bethulia
to the moment when she was speaking.
9 When she came to the end, the people
cheered at the top of their voices until the
town echoed. 10 Achior, recognising all that
the God of Israel had done, believed ardently
in him and, accepting circumcision, was
permanently incorporated into the House of
Israel.
11 At daybreak they hung the head of Holo-
fernes on the ramparts. Every man took his
arms and they all went out in groups to the
slopes of the mountain. 12 Seeing this, the
Assyrians sent word to their leaders, who in
turn reported to the generals, the captains of
thousands and all the other officers; 13 and
these in their turn reported to the tent of
Holofernes. 'Rouse our master,' they said to
his major-domo, 'these slaves have dared to
march down on us to attack—and to be wiped
out to a man!' 14 Bagoas went inside and struck
the curtain dividing the tent, thinking that
Holofernes was sleeping with Judith. 15 But
as no one seemed to hear, he drew the curtain
and went into the bedroom, to find him
thrown down dead on the threshold, with his
head cut off. 16 He gave a great shout, wept,
sobbed, shrieked and rent his clothes. 17 He
then went into the tent which Judith had
occupied and could not find her either. Then,
rushing out to the men, he shouted, 18 'The
slaves have rebelled! A single Hebrew woman
has brought shame on the House of Nebuch-
adnezzar. Holofernes is lying dead on the
ground, without his head!'
19 When they heard this, the leaders of the
Assyrian army tore their tunics in conster-
nation, and the camp rang with their wild
cries and their shouting.

15 When the men who were still in their
tents heard the news they were
appalled. 2 Panic-stricken and trembling, no
two of them could keep together, the rout
was complete, with one accord they fled along
every track across the plain or through the
mountains. 3 The men who had been bivou-
acking in the mountains round Bethulia were
fleeing too. Then all the Israelite warriors
charged down on them. 4 Uzziah sent messen-
gers to Betomasthaim, Bebai, Choba, Kola,
throughout the whole territory of Israel, to
inform them of what had happened and to
urge them all to hurl themselves on the enemy
and annihilate them. 5 As soon as the Israelites
heard the news, they fell on them as one man
and massacred them all the way to Choba.
The men of Jerusalem and the entire moun-
tain country also rallied to them, once they
had been informed of the events in the enemy
camp. Then the men of Gilead and Galilee
attacked them on the flank and struck at them
fiercely till they neared Damascus and its
territory. 6 All the other inhabitants of
Bethulia fell on the Assyrian camp and looted
it to their great profit. 7 The Israelites
returning from the slaughter seized what was
left. The hamlets and villages of the mountain
country and the plain also captured a great
deal of booty, since there were vast stores
of it.

Thanksgiving

8 Joakim the high priest and the entire Council
of Elders of Israel, who were in Jerusalem,
came to gaze on the benefits that the Lord
had lavished on Israel and to see Judith and
congratulate her. 9 On coming to her house,
they blessed her with one accord, saying:

You are the glory of Jerusalem!
You are the great pride of Israel!
You are the highest honour of our race!

10 By doing all this with your own hand
you have deserved well of Israel,
and God has approved
what you have done.
May you be blessed by the Lord Almighty
in all the days to come!

And the people all said, 'Amen!'
11 The people looted the camp for thirty
days. They gave Judith the tent of Holo-
fernes, all his silver plate, his divans, his
drinking bowls and all his furniture. She took
this, loaded her mule, harnessed her carts
and heaped the things into them. 12 All the
women of Israel, hurrying to see her, formed
choirs of dancers in her honour. Judith took
wands of vine-leaves in her hand and distrib-
uted them to the women who accompanied
her; 13 she and her companions put on wreaths
of olive. Then she took her place at the head
of the procession and led the women as they
danced. All the men of Israel, armed and
garlanded, followed them, singing hymns.

14 With all Israel round her, Judith broke into this song of thanksgiving and the whole people sang this hymn:

16 Break into song for my God,
to the tambourine,
sing in honour of the Lord,
to the cymbal,
let psalm and canticle mingle for him,
extol his name, invoke it!
2 For the Lord is a God
who breaks battle-lines;
he has pitched his camp
in the middle of his people
to deliver me from the hands
of my oppressors.
3 Assyria came down
from the mountains of the north,
came with tens of thousands of his army.
Their multitude blocked the ravines,
their horses covered the hills.
4 He threatened to burn up my country,
destroy my young men with the sword,
dash my sucklings to the ground,
make prey of my little ones,
carry off my maidens;
5 but the Lord Almighty has thwarted them
by a woman's hand.
6 For their hero did not fall
at the young men's hands,
it was not the sons of Titans
struck him down,
no proud giants made that attack,
but Judith, the daughter of Merari,
who disarmed him
with the beauty of her face.
7 She laid aside her widow's dress
to raise up those
who were oppressed in Israel;
she anointed her face with perfume,
8 bound her hair under a turban,
put on a linen gown to seduce him.
9 Her sandal ravished his eye,
her beauty took his soul prisoner
and the scimitar cut through his neck!
10 The Persians trembled at her boldness,
the Medes were daunted by her daring.
11 These were struck with fear
when my lowly ones raised the war cry,
these were seized with terror
when my weak ones shouted,
and when they raised their voices
these gave ground.
12 The children of mere girls
ran them through,
pierced them
like the offspring of deserters.
They perished in the battle of my Lord!

13 I shall sing a new song to my God.
Lord, you are great, you are glorious,
wonderfully strong, unconquerable.
14 May your whole creation serve you!
For you spoke and things came into being,
you sent your breath
and they were put together,
and no one can resist your voice.
15 Should mountains be tossed
from their foundations
to mingle with the waves,
should rocks melt
like wax before your face,
to those who fear you,
you would still be merciful.
16 A little thing indeed
is a sweetly smelling sacrifice,
still less the fat
burned for you in burnt offering;
but whoever fears the Lord
is great for ever.
17 Woe to the nations
who rise against my race!
The Lord Almighty
will punish them on judgement day.
He will send fire and worms in their flesh
and they will weep with pain
for evermore.

18 When they reached Jerusalem they fell on
their faces before God and, once the people
had been purified, they presented their burnt
offerings, voluntary offerings and gifts. 19 All
Holofernes' property given her by the people,
and the canopy she herself had stripped from
his bed, Judith vowed to God as a dedicated
offering. 20 For three months the people gave
themselves up to rejoicings in front of the
Temple in Jerusalem, where Judith stayed
with them.

Judith lives to old age. Her death

21 When this was over, everyone returned
home. Judith went back to Bethulia and lived
on her property; as long as she lived, she
enjoyed a great reputation throughout the
country. 22 She had many suitors, but all her
days, from the time her husband Manasseh
died and was gathered to his people, she
never gave herself to another man. 23 Her
fame spread more and more, the older she

grew in her husband's house; she lived to the
age of one hundred and five. She emancipated
her maid, then died in Bethulia and was
buried in the cave where Manasseh her
husband lay. 24 The House of Israel mourned
her for seven days. Before her death she had
distributed her property among her own
relations and those of her husband
Manasseh.
25 Never again during the lifetime of Judith,
nor indeed for a long time after her death,
did anyone trouble the Israelites.

THE BOOK OF ESTHER

A delightfully vivid tale of intrigue and harem politics to illustrate the theme of God's protection of his people and the punishment of their opponents. It shows both Jewish nationalism and the unpopularity of the Jews as an alien body among the nations. The massacres are obviously fictitious, to illustrate the biblical theme of reversal of fortunes. The only character known to history is Ahasuerus, the more familiar form of whose name is Xerxes.

The book is read at the Feast of Purim, but the connection with that feast is perhaps secondary. It was written not long before 160 BC. The passages printed in italics are contained in the Gk text but are not in the Hebr.

ESTHER

PRELIMINARIES

Mordecai's dream

1 1a *In the second year of the reign of the Great*
King, Ahasuerus, on the first day of Nisan, a
dream came to Mordecai son of Jair, son of
Shimei, son of Kish, of the tribe of Benjamin,
1b *a Jew living at Susa and holding high office*
at the royal court. 1c *He was one of the captives*
whom Nebuchadnezzar king of Babylon had
deported from Jerusalem with Jeconiah king of
Judah.
1d *This was his dream. There were cries and*
noise, thunder and earthquakes, and disorder
over the whole earth. 1e *Then two great dragons*
came forward, each ready for the fray, and set
up a great roar. 1f *At the sound of them every*
nation made ready to wage war against the
nation of the just. 1g *A day of darkness and*
gloom, of affliction and distress, oppression and
great disturbance on earth! 1h *The entire upright*
nation was thrown into consternation at the fear
of the evils awaiting it and prepared for death,
crying out to God. 1i *Then from its cry, as from*
a little spring, there grew a great river, a flood
of water. 1k *Light came as the sun rose, and the*
humble were raised up and devoured the
mighty.
1l *On awakening from this dream and vision*
of God's designs, Mordecai thought deeply about
the matter, trying his best all day to discover
what its meaning might be.

A plot against the king

1m *Mordecai was lodging at court with Bigthan*
and Teresh, two of the king's eunuchs who

guarded the palace. [1n] *Having got wind of their plotting and gained knowledge of their designs, he discovered that they were preparing to assassinate King Ahasuerus, and he warned the king against them.* [1o] *The king gave orders for the two officers to be tortured; they confessed and were executed.* [1p] *He then had these events entered in his Record Book, while Mordecai himself also wrote an account of them.* [1q] *The king then appointed Mordecai to an office at court and rewarded him with presents.* [1r] *But Haman son of Hammedatha, the Agagite, who enjoyed high favour with the king, determined to injure Mordecai in revenge for the affair of the king's two officers.*

I: AHASUERUS AND VASHTI

Ahasuerus' banquet

1 It was in the days of Ahasuerus, the Ahasuerus whose empire stretched from India to Ethiopia and comprised one hundred and twenty-seven provinces. [2] In those days, when King Ahasuerus was sitting on his royal throne in the citadel of Susa, [3] in the third year of his reign, he gave a banquet at his court for all his officers-of-state and ministers, Persian and Median army-commanders, nobles and provincial governors. [4] Thus he displayed the riches and splendour of his empire and the pomp and glory of his majesty; the festivities went on for a long time, a hundred and eighty days.

[5] When this period was over, for seven days the king gave a banquet for all the people living in the citadel of Susa, to high and low alike, on the esplanade in the gardens of the royal palace. [6] There were white and violet hangings fastened with cords of fine linen and purple thread to silver rings on marble columns, couches of gold and silver on a pavement of porphyry, marble, mother-of-pearl and precious stones. [7] For drinking there were golden cups of various design and plenty of wine provided by the king with royal liberality. [8] The royal edict did not, however, make drinking obligatory, the king having instructed the officials of his household to treat each guest according to the guest's own wishes.

Disgrace of Queen Vashti

[9] Queen Vashti, for her part, gave a banquet for the women in the royal palace of King Ahasuerus. [10] On the seventh day, when the king was merry with wine, he commanded Mehuman, Biztha, Harbona, Bigtha, Abagtha, Zethar and Carkas, the seven officers in attendance on the person of King Ahasuerus, [11] to bring Queen Vashti before the king, crowned with her royal diadem, in order to display her beauty to the people and the officers-of-state, since she was very beautiful. [12] But Queen Vashti refused to come at the king's command delivered by the officers. The king was very angry at this and his rage grew hot. [13] Addressing himself to the wise men who were versed in the law—it being the practice to refer matters affecting the king to expert lawyers and jurists—[14] he summoned Carshena, Shethar, Admatha, Tarshish, Meres, Marsena and Memucan, seven Persian and Median officers-of-state who had privileged access to the royal presence and occupied the leading positions in the kingdom. [15] 'According to law,' he said, 'what is to be done to Queen Vashti for not obeying the command of King Ahasuerus delivered by the officers?' [16] In the presence of the king and the officers-of-state, Memucan replied, 'Queen Vashti has wronged not only the king but also all the officers-of-state and all the peoples inhabiting the provinces of King Ahasuerus. [17] The queen's conduct will soon become known to all the women, who will adopt a contemptuous attitude towards their own husbands. They will say, "King Ahasuerus himself commanded Queen Vashti to appear before him and she did not come." [18] Before the day is out, the wives of the Persian and Median officers-of-state will be telling every one of the king's officers-of-state what they have heard about the queen's behaviour; and that will mean contempt and anger all round. [19] If it is the king's pleasure, let him issue a royal edict, to be irrevocably incorporated into the laws of the Persians and Medes, to the effect that Vashti is never to appear again before King Ahasuerus, and let the king confer her royal dignity on a worthier woman. [20] Let this edict issued by the king be

proclaimed throughout his empire—which is great—and all the women will henceforth bow to the authority of their husbands, both high and low alike.'

21 This speech pleased the king and the officers-of-state, and the king did as Memucan advised. 22 He sent letters to all the provinces of the kingdom, to each province in its own script and to each nation in its own language, ensuring that every husband should be master in his own house.

II: MORDECAI AND ESTHER

Esther becomes queen

2 Some time after this, when the king's wrath had subsided, Ahasuerus remembered Vashti, how she had behaved, and the measures taken against her. 2 The king's gentlemen-in-waiting said, 'A search should be made on the king's behalf for beautiful young virgins, 3 and the king appoint commissioners throughout the provinces of his realm to bring all these beautiful young virgins to the citadel of Susa, to the harem under the authority of Hegai the king's eunuch, custodian of the women. Here he will give them whatever they need for enhancing their beauty, 4 and the girl who pleases the king can take Vashti's place as queen.' This advice pleased the king and he acted on it.

5 Now in the citadel of Susa there lived a Jew called Mordecai son of Jair, son of Shimei, son of Kish, of the tribe of Benjamin, 6 who had been deported from Jerusalem among the captives taken away with Jeconiah king of Judah by Nebuchadnezzar king of Babylon, 7 and was now bringing up a certain Hadassah, otherwise called Esther, his uncle's daughter, who had lost both father and mother; the girl had a good figure and a beautiful face, and on the death of her parents Mordecai had adopted her as his daughter.

8 On the promulgation of the royal command and edict a great number of girls were brought to the citadel of Susa where they were entrusted to Hegai. Esther, too, was taken to the king's palace and entrusted to Hegai, the custodian of the women. 9 The girl pleased him and won his favour. Not only did he quickly provide her with all she needed for her dressing room and her meals, but he gave her seven special maids from the king's household and transferred her and her maids to the best part of the harem. 10 Esther had not divulged her race or parentage, since Mordecai had forbidden her to do so. 11 Mordecai walked up and down in front of the courtyard of the harem all day and every day, to learn how Esther was and how she was being treated.

12 Each girl had to appear in turn before King Ahasuerus after a delay of twelve months fixed by the regulations for the women; this preparatory period was occupied as follows: six months with oil of myrrh, and six months with spices and lotions commonly used for feminine beauty treatment. 13 When each girl went to the king, she was given whatever she wanted to take with her, since she then moved from the harem into the royal household. 14 She went there in the evening, and the following morning returned to another harem entrusted to the care of Shaashgaz, the king's officer, custodian of the concubines. She did not go to the king any more, unless he was particularly pleased with her and had her summoned by name.

15 But when it was the turn of Esther the daughter of Abihail, whose nephew Mordecai had adopted her as his own daughter, to go into the king's presence, she did not ask for anything beyond what had been assigned her by Hegai, the king's officer, custodian of the women. Esther won the approval of all who saw her. 16 She was brought to King Ahasuerus in his royal apartments in the tenth month, which is called Tebeth, in the seventh year of his reign; 17 and the king liked Esther better than any of the other women; none of the other girls found so much favour and approval with him. So he set the royal diadem on her head and proclaimed her queen instead of Vashti.

18 The king then gave a great banquet, Esther's banquet, for all his officers-of-state and ministers, decreed a holiday for all the provinces and distributed largesse with royal prodigality.

Mordecai and Haman

19 When Esther, like the other girls, had been
transferred to the second harem, 20 she did not
divulge her parentage or race, in obedience to
the orders of Mordecai, whose instructions
she continued to follow as when she had been
under his care. 21 At this time Mordecai was
attached to the Chancellery and two malcon-
tents, Bigthan and Teresh, officers in the
king's service as Guards of the Threshold,
plotted to assassinate King Ahasuerus.
22 Mordecai came to hear of this and informed
Queen Esther, who in turn, on Mordecai's
authority, told the king. 23 The matter was
investigated and proved to be true. The two
conspirators were sent to the gallows, and
the incident was recorded in the Annals, in
the royal presence.

3 Shortly afterwards, King Ahasuerus
singled out Haman son of Hammedatha,
a native of Agāg, for promotion. He raised
him in rank, granting him precedence over
all his colleagues, the other officers-of-state,
2 and all the royal officials employed at the
Chancellery used to bow low and prostrate
themselves whenever Haman appeared—
such was the king's command. Mordecai
refused either to bow or to prostrate himself.
3 'Why do you flout the royal command?' the
officials of the Chancellery asked Mordecai.
4 Day after day they asked him this, but he
took no notice of them. In the end they
reported the matter to Haman, to see whether
Mordecai would persist in his attitude, since
he had told them that he was a Jew. 5 Haman
could see for himself that Mordecai did not
bow or prostrate himself in his presence; he
became furiously angry. 6 And, on being told
what race Mordecai belonged to, he thought
it beneath him merely to get rid of Mordecai,
but made up his mind to wipe out all the
members of Mordecai's race, the Jews, living
in Ahasuerus' entire empire.

III: THE JEWS IN PERIL

The decree of extermination against the Jews

7 In the first month, that is the month of
Nisan, of the twelfth year of King Ahasuerus,
the *pur*[a] (that is, the lot) was cast in Haman's
presence, to determine the day and the
month. The lot falling on the twelfth month,
which is Adar, 8 Haman said to King Ahasu-
erus, 'There is a certain unassimilated nation
scattered among the other nations through-
out the provinces of your realm; their laws
are different from those of all the other
nations, and the royal laws they ignore; hence
it is not in the king's interests to tolerate
them. 9 If their destruction be signed, so
please the king, I am ready to pay ten thou-
sand talents of silver to the king's receivers,
to be credited to the royal treasury.'
10 The king then took his signet ring off his
hand and gave it to Haman son of Hamme-
datha, the persecutor of the Jews. 11 'Keep
the money,' he said, 'and you can have the
people too; do what you like with them.'
12 The royal scribes were therefore
summoned for the thirteenth day of the first
month, when they wrote out the orders
addressed by Haman to the king's satraps, to
the governors ruling each province and to the
principal officials of each people, to each
province in its own script and to each people
in its own language. The edict was signed in
the name of King Ahasuerus and sealed with
his ring, 13 and letters were sent by runners
to every province of the realm, ordering the
destruction, slaughter and annihilation of all
Jews, young and old, including women and
children, on the same day—the thirteenth
day of the twelfth month, which is Adar—
and the seizing of their possessions.
13a *The text of the letter was as follows:*

'The Great King, Ahasuerus, to the governors of the hundred and twenty-seven provinces stretching from India to Ethiopia, and to their subordinate district commissioners:

13b *'Being placed in authority over many*
nations and ruling the whole world, I have
resolved never to be carried away by the
insolence of power, but always to rule with
moderation and clemency, so as to assure for
my subjects a life ever free from storms and,

3a From this the name of the feast on which the book is read, Purim, is derived. It is a joyful feast, characterised by banquets.

offering my kingdom the benefits of civilisation and free transit from end to end, to restore that peace which all men desire. 13c*In consultation with our advisers as to how this aim is to be effected, we have been informed by one of them, eminent among us for prudence and well proved for his unfailing devotion and unshakeable trustworthiness, and in rank second only to our majesty, Haman by name,* 13d*that there is, mingled among all the tribes of the earth, a certain ill-disposed people, opposed by its laws to every other nation and continually defying the royal ordinances, in such a way as to obstruct that form of government assured by us to the general good.*

13e*'Considering therefore that this people, unique of its kind, is in complete opposition to all humanity from which it differs by its outlandish laws, that it is hostile to our interests and that it commits the most heinous crimes, to the point of endangering the stability of the realm:*

13f*'We command that those persons designated to you in the letters written by Haman, who was appointed to watch over our interests and is a second father to us, be all destroyed, root and branch, including women and children, by the swords of their enemies, without any pity or mercy, on the fourteenth day of the twelfth month, Adar, of the present year,* 13g*so that, these past and present malcontents being in one day forcibly thrown down to Hades, our government may henceforward enjoy perpetual stability and peace.'*

14Copies of this decree, to be promulgated as law in each province, were published to the various peoples, so that each might be ready for the day aforementioned. 15At the king's command, the runners set out with all speed; the decree was first promulgated in the citadel of Susa.

While the king and Haman gave themselves up to feasting and drinking, consternation reigned in the city of Susa.

Mordecai and Esther try to avert the danger

4 When Mordecai learned what had happened, he tore his garments and put on sackcloth and ashes. Then he walked into the centre of the city, wailing loudly and bitterly, 2until he arrived in front of the Chancellery, which no one clothed in sackcloth was allowed to enter. 3And in every province, no sooner had the royal command and edict arrived, than among the Jews there was great mourning, fasting, weeping and wailing, and many lay on sackcloth and ashes.

4When Queen Esther's maids and officers came and told her, she was overcome with grief. She sent clothes for Mordecai to put on instead of his sackcloth, but he refused them. 5Esther then summoned Hathach, an officer whom the king had appointed to wait on her, and ordered him to go to Mordecai and enquire what the matter was and why he was acting in this way.

6Hathach went out to Mordecai in the city square in front of the Chancellery, 7and Mordecai told him what had happened to him personally, and also about the sum of money which Haman had offered to pay into the royal treasury to procure the destruction of the Jews. 8He also gave him a copy of the edict of extermination published in Susa for him to show Esther for her information, with the message that she was to go to the king and implore his favour and plead with him for the race to which she belonged. 8a *'Remember your humbler circumstances,' he said, 'when you were fed by my hand. Since Haman, the second person in the realm, has petitioned the king for our deaths,* 8b*invoke the Lord, speak to the king for us and save us from death!'*

9Hathach came back and told Esther what Mordecai had said; 10and she replied with the following message for Mordecai, 11'Royal officials and people living in the provinces alike all know that for anyone, man or woman, who approaches the king in the private apartments without having been summoned there, there is only one law: he must die, unless the king, by pointing his golden sceptre towards him, grants him his life. And I have not been summoned to the king for the last thirty days.'

12These words of Esther were reported to Mordecai, 13who sent back the following reply, 'Do not suppose that, because you are in the king's palace, you are going to be the one Jew to escape. 14No; if you persist in remaining silent at such a time, relief and deliverance will come to the Jews from another quarter, but both you and your father's whole family will perish. Who knows? Perhaps you have come to the throne for just such a time as this.'

15Whereupon Esther sent this reply to Mordecai, 16'Go and assemble all the Jews now in Susa and fast for me. Do not eat or

drink day or night for three days. For my part, I and my waiting-women shall keep the same fast, after which I shall go to the king in spite of the law; and if I perish, I perish.'
17Mordecai went away and carried out Esther's instructions.

Mordecai's prayer

17a *Then calling to mind all the wonderful works of the Lord, he offered this prayer:*

17b *Lord, Lord, Almighty King,*
everything is subject to your power,
and there is no one who can withstand you
in your determination to save Israel.

17c *You have made heaven and earth,*
and all the marvels that are under heaven.
You are the Master of the universe
and no one can resist you, Lord.

17d *You know all things,*
you, Lord, know
that neither pride, self-esteem nor vainglory
prompted me to do what I have done:
to refuse to prostrate myself
before proud Haman.
Gladly would I have kissed
the soles of his feet,
had this assured the safety of Israel.

17e *But what I have done, I have done,*
rather than place the glory of a man
above the glory of God;
and I shall not prostrate myself to anyone
except, Lord, to you,
and, in so doing,
I shall not be acting in pride.

17f *And now, Lord God,*
King, God of Abraham
spare your people!
For our ruin is being plotted,
there are plans to destroy
your ancient heritage.
17g *Do not overlook your inheritance,*
which you redeemed from Egypt to be yours.
17h *Hear my supplication,*
have mercy on your heritage,
and turn our grief into rejoicing,
so that we may live, Lord,
to hymn your name.
Do not suffer the mouths
of those who praise you to perish.

17i *And all Israel cried out with all their might, since death was staring them in the face.*

Esther's prayer

17k *Queen Esther also took refuge with the Lord in the mortal peril which had overtaken her. She took off her sumptuous robes and put on sorrowful mourning. Instead of expensive perfumes, she covered her head with ashes and dung. She mortified her body severely, and the former scenes of her happiness and elegance were now littered with tresses torn from her hair. She besought the Lord God of Israel in these words:*

17l *My Lord, our King, the Only One,*
come to my help, for I am alone
and have no helper but you
and am about to take my life in my hands.

17m *I have been taught from infancy*
in the bosom of my family
that you, Lord, have chosen
Israel out of all the nations
and our ancestors out of all before them,
to be your heritage for ever;
and that you have treated them
as you promised.

17n *But we have sinned against you*
and you have handed us over to our enemies
for paying honour to their gods.
Lord, you are upright.

17o *But they are not satisfied*
with the bitterness of our slavery:
they have pledged themselves to their idols
to abolish the decree
that your own lips have uttered,
to blot out your heritage,
to stop the mouths of those who praise you,
to quench your altar
and the glory of your House,
17p *and instead to open the mouths*
of the heathen,
to sing the praise of worthless idols
and for ever to idolise a king of flesh.

17q *Do not yield your sceptre, Lord,*
to what does not exist.
Never let our ruin be matter for laughter.
Turn these plots against their authors,
and make an example
of the man who leads the attack on us.
17r *Remember, Lord; reveal yourself*
in the time of our distress.

As for me, give me courage,
King of gods and Master of all powers!
17s *Put persuasive words into my mouth*
when I face the lion;
change his feeling into hatred for our enemy,

so that he may meet his end,
and all those like him!

17t *As for ourselves, save us by your hand,*
and come to my help, for I am alone
and have no one but you, Lord.
17u *You have knowledge of all things,*
and you know that I hate honours
from the godless,
that I loathe the bed of the uncircumcised,
of any foreigner whatever.
17w *You know I am under constraint,*
that I loathe the symbol of my high position
bound round my brow
when I appear at court;
I loathe it as if it were a filthy rag
and do not wear it on my days of leisure.
17x *Your servant has not eaten*
at Haman's table,
nor taken pleasure in the royal banquets,
nor drunk the wine of libations.
17y *Nor has your servant found pleasure*
from the day of her promotion until now
except in you, Lord, God of Abraham.
17z *O God, whose strength prevails over all,*
listen to the voice of the desperate,
save us from the hand of the wicked,
and free me from my fear!

Esther intrudes on the royal presence

5 1a *On the third day, when she had finished*
praying, she took off her suppliant's mourning
attire and dressed herself in her full splendour.
Radiant as she then appeared, she invoked God
who watches over all people and saves them.
With her, she took two ladies-in-waiting. With
a delicate air she leaned on one, while the other
accompanied her carrying her train. 1b *Rosy with*
the full flush of her beauty, her face radiated
joy and love: but her heart shrank with fear.
1c *Having passed through door after door, she*
found herself in the presence of the king. He was
sitting on his royal throne, dressed in all his
robes of state, glittering with gold and precious
stones—a formidable sight. 1d *He looked up,*
afire with majesty and, blazing with anger, saw
her. The queen sank to the floor. As she fainted,
the colour drained from her face and her head
fell against the lady-in-waiting beside her. 1e *But*
God changed the king's heart, inducing a milder
spirit. He sprang from his throne in alarm
and took her in his arms until she recovered,
comforting her with soothing words. 1f *'What is*
the matter, Esther?' he said. 'I am your brother.
Take heart, you are not going to die; our order
applies only to ordinary people. Come to me.'
2 *And raising his golden sceptre he laid it on*
Esther's neck, embraced her and said, 'Speak
to me.' 2a *'Sire,' she said, 'to me you looked like*
one of God's angels, and my heart was moved
with fear of your majesty. For you are a figure
of wonder, my lord, and your face is full of
graciousness.' 2b *But as she spoke she fell down*
in a faint. The king grew more agitated, and his
courtiers all set about reviving her. 3 'What is
the matter, Queen Esther?' the king said.
'Tell me what you want; even if it is half my
kingdom, I grant it you.' 4 'Would it please the
king,' Esther replied, 'to come with Haman
today to the banquet I have prepared for
him?' 5 The king said, 'Tell Haman to come
at once, so that Esther may have her wish.'

6 So the king and Haman came to the
banquet that Esther had prepared and,
during the banquet, the king again said to
Esther, 'Tell me your request; I grant it to
you. Tell me what you want; even if it is half
my kingdom, it is yours for the asking.'
7 'What do I want, what is my request?' Esther
replied. 8 'If I have found favour in the king's
eyes, and if it is his pleasure to grant what I
ask and to agree to my request, let the king
and Haman come to the banquet I intend to
give them tomorrow, and then I shall do as
the king says.'

9 Haman left full of joy and high spirits
that day; but when he saw Mordecai at the
Chancellery, neither standing up nor stirring
at his approach, he felt a gust of anger.
10 He restrained himself, however. Returning
home, he sent for his friends and Zeresh
his wife 11 and held forth to them about his
dazzling wealth, his many children, how the
king had raised him to a position of honour
and promoted him over the heads of the
king's officers-of-state and ministers.
12 'What is more,' he added, 'Queen Esther
has just invited me and the king—no one else
except me—to a banquet she was giving, and
better still she has invited me and the king
again tomorrow. 13 But what do I care about
all this when all the while I see Mordecai the
Jew sitting there at the Chancellery?' 14 'Have
a fifty-cubit gallows run up,' said Zeresh his
wife and all his friends, 'and in the morning
ask the king to have Mordecai hanged on it.
Then you can go with the king to the banquet,
without a care in the world!' Delighted with
this advice, Haman had the gallows erected.

IV: THE JEWS' REVENGE

The discomfiture of Haman

6 That night the king could not sleep; he called for the Record Book, or Annals, to be brought and read to him. 2 They contained an account of how Mordecai had denounced Bigthan and Teresh, two of the king's eunuchs serving as Guards of the Threshold, who had plotted to assassinate King Ahasuerus. 3 'And what honour and dignity', the king asked, 'was conferred on Mordecai for this?' 'Nothing has been done for him,' the gentlemen-in-waiting replied. 4 The king then said, 'Who is outside in the antechamber?' Haman had, that very moment, entered the outer antechamber of the private apartments, to ask the king to have Mordecai hanged on the gallows which he had just put up for the purpose. 5 So the king's gentlemen-in-waiting replied, 'It is Haman out in the antechamber.' 'Bring him in,' the king said, 6 and, as soon as Haman came in, went on to ask, 'What is the right way to treat a man whom the king wishes to honour?' 'Whom', thought Haman, 'would the king wish to honour, if not me?' 7 So he replied, 'If the king wishes to honour someone, 8 royal robes should be brought from the king's wardrobe, and a horse from the king's stable, sporting a royal diadem on its head. 9 The robes and horse should be entrusted to one of the noblest of the king's officers-of-state, who should then array the man whom the king wishes to honour and lead him on horseback through the city square, proclaiming before him: "This is the way a man shall be treated whom the king wishes to honour." ' 10 'Hurry,' the king said to Haman, 'take the robes and the horse, and do everything you have just said to Mordecai the Jew, who works at the Chancellery. On no account leave out anything that you have mentioned.'

11 So taking the robes and the horse, Haman arrayed Mordecai and led him on horseback through the city square, proclaiming before him: 'This is the way a man shall be treated whom the king wishes to honour.' 12 After this Mordecai returned to the Chancellery, while Haman went hurrying home in dejection and covering his face. 13 He told his wife Zeresh and all his friends what had just happened. His wife Zeresh and his friends said, 'You are beginning to fall, and Mordecai to rise; if he is Jewish, you will never get the better of him. With him against you, your fall is certain.'

Haman at Esther's banquet

14 While they were still talking, the king's officers arrived in a hurry to escort Haman to the banquet that Esther was giving.

7 The king and Haman went to Queen Esther's banquet, 2 and this second day, during the banquet, the king again said to Esther, 'Tell me your request, Queen Esther. I grant it to you. Whatever you want; even if it is half my kingdom, it is yours for the asking.' 3 'If I have found favour in your eyes, O king,' Queen Esther replied, 'and if it please your majesty, grant me my life—that is my request; and the lives of my people—that is what I want. 4 For we have been handed over, my people and I, to destruction, slaughter and annihilation; had we merely been sold as slaves and servant-girls, I should not have said anything; but in the present case, it will be beyond the persecutor's means to make good the loss that the king is about to sustain.' 5 King Ahasuerus interrupted Queen Esther, 'Who is this man?' he exclaimed. 'Where is the man who has thought of doing such a thing?' 6 Esther replied, 'The persecutor, the enemy? Why, this wretch Haman!' Haman quaked with terror in the presence of the king and queen. 7 In a rage the king got up from the banquet and went into the palace garden; while Haman, realising that the king was determined on his ruin, stayed behind to beg Queen Esther for his life.

8 When the king came back from the palace garden into the banqueting hall, he found Haman sprawled across the couch where Esther was reclining. 'What!' the king exclaimed. 'Is he going to rape the queen in my own palace?' The words were scarcely out of his mouth than a veil was thrown over Haman's face. 9 In the royal presence, Harbona, one of the officers, said, 'There is that fifty-cubit gallows, too, which Haman ran up for Mordecai, who spoke up to the king's great advantage. It is all ready at his house.' 'Hang him on it,' said the king. 10 So Haman was hanged on the gallows which he

had erected for Mordecai, and the king's wrath subsided.

The royal favour passes to the Jews

8 That same day King Ahasuerus gave Queen Esther the house of Haman, the persecutor of the Jews. Mordecai was presented to the king, Esther having revealed their mutual relationship. [2]The king, who had recovered his signet ring from Haman, took it off and gave it to Mordecai, while Esther gave Mordecai charge of Haman's house.

[3]Esther again went to speak to the king. She fell at his feet, weeping and imploring his favour, to frustrate the malice that Haman the Agagite had been plotting against the Jews. [4]The king held out the golden sceptre to her, whereupon Esther stood up and faced him. [5]'If such is the king's good pleasure,' she said, 'and if I have found favour before him, if my petition seems proper to him and if I myself am pleasing to his eyes, may he be pleased to issue a written revocation of the letters which Haman son of Hammedatha, the Agagite, has had written, ordering the destruction of the Jews throughout the royal provinces. [6]For how can I look on, while my people suffer what is proposed for them? How can I bear to witness the extermination of my relatives?'

[7]King Ahasuerus said to Queen Esther and to Mordecai the Jew, 'I for my part have given Esther Haman's house, and have had him hanged on the gallows for planning to destroy the Jews. [8]You, for your part, write what you please as regards the Jews, in the king's name, and seal it with the king's signet; for any edict written in the king's name and sealed with his signet is irrevocable.' [9]The royal scribes were summoned at once—it was the third month, the month of Sivan, on the twenty-third day—and at Mordecai's dictation an order was written to the Jews, the satraps, governors and principal officials of the provinces stretching from India to Ethiopia, a hundred and twenty-seven provinces, to each province in its own script, and to each people in its own language, and to the Jews in their own script and language. [10]These letters, written in the name of King Ahasuerus and sealed with the king's signet, were carried by couriers mounted on horses from the king's own stud-farms. [11]In them the king granted the Jews, in whatever city they lived, the right to assemble in self-defence, with permission to destroy, slaughter and annihilate any armed force of any people or province that might attack them, together with their women and children, and to plunder their possessions, [12]with effect from the same day throughout the provinces of King Ahasuerus—the thirteenth day of the twelfth month, which is Adar.

The decree of rehabilitation

[12a]*The text of the letter was as follows:*

[12b]*'The Great King, Ahasuerus, to the satraps of the hundred and twenty-seven provinces which stretch from India to Ethiopia, to the provincial governors and to all our loyal subjects, greeting:*

[12c]*'Many people, repeatedly honoured by the extreme bounty of their benefactors, only grow the more arrogant. It is not enough for them to seek our subjects' injury, but unable as they are to support the weight of their own surfeit they turn to scheming against their benefactors themselves.* [12d]*Not content with banishing gratitude from the human heart, but elated by the plaudits of people unacquainted with goodness, notwithstanding that all is for ever under the eye of God, they expect to escape his justice, so hostile to the wicked.* [12e]*Thus it has often happened to those placed in authority that, having entrusted friends with the conduct of affairs and allowed themselves to be influenced by them, they find themselves sharing with these the guilt of innocent blood and involved in irremediable misfortunes,* [12f]*the upright intentions of rulers having been misled by false arguments of the evilly disposed.* [12g]*This may be seen without recourse to the history of earlier times to which we have referred; you have only to look at what is before you, at the crimes perpetrated by a plague of unworthy officials.* [12h]*For the future, we shall exert our efforts to assure the tranquillity and peace of the realm for all,* [12i]*by adopting new policies and by always judging matters that are brought to our notice in the most equitable spirit.*

[12k]*'Thus Haman son of Hammedatha, a Macedonian, without a drop of Persian blood and far removed from our goodness, enjoyed our hospitality* [12l]*and was treated by us with the benevolence which we show to every nation, even to the extent of being proclaimed our 'father' and being accorded universally*

the prostration of respect as second in dignity
to the royal throne. 12m*But he, unable to keep*
within his own high rank, schemed to deprive
us of our realm and of our life. 12n*Furthermore,*
by tortuous wiles and arguments, he would
have had us destroy Mordecai, our saviour
and constant benefactor, with Esther the
blameless partner of our majesty, and their
whole nation besides. 12o*He thought by these*
means to leave us without support and so to
transfer the Persian empire to the
Macedonians.
12p*'But we find that the Jews, marked out*
for annihilation by this arch-scoundrel, are
not criminals: they are in fact governed by the
most just of laws. 12q*They are children of the*
Most High, the great and living God to whom
we and our ancestors owe the continuing
prosperity of our realm. 12r*You will therefore*
do well not to act on the letters sent by Haman
son of Hammedatha, since their author has
been hanged at the gates of Susa with his
whole household: a fitting punishment, which
God, Master of the Universe, has speedily
inflicted on him. 12s*Put up copies of this letter*
everywhere, allow the Jews to observe their
own customs without fear, and come to their
help against anyone who attacks them on the
day originally chosen for their maltreatment,
that is, the thirteenth day of the twelfth month,
which is Adar. 12t*For the all-powerful God*
has made this day a day of joy and not of ruin
for the chosen people. 12u*You, for your part,*
among your solemn festivals celebrate this as
a special day with every kind of feasting, so
that now and in the future, for you and for
Persians of good will, it may commemorate
your rescue, and for your enemies may stand
as a reminder of their ruin.
12v*'Every city and, more generally, every*
country, which does not follow these instruc-
tions, will be mercilessly devastated with fire
and sword, and made not only inaccessible to
human beings but hateful to wild animals and
even birds for ever.'

13Copies of this edict, to be promulgated
as law in each province, were published to
the various peoples, so that the Jews could
be ready on the day stated to avenge them-
selves on their enemies. 14The couriers,
mounted on the king's horses, set out in great
haste and urgency at the king's command.
The edict was also published in the citadel of
Susa. 15Mordecai left the royal presence in a
princely gown of violet and white, with a
great golden crown and a cloak of fine linen
and purple. The city of Susa shouted for joy.
16For the Jews there was light and gladness,
joy and honour. 17In every province and in
every city, wherever the king's command and
decree arrived, there was joy and gladness
among the Jews, with feasting and holiday-
making. Of the country's population many
became Jews, since now the Jews were feared.

The great Day of Purim

9 The king's command and decree came
into force on the thirteenth day of the
twelfth month, Adar, and the day on which
the enemies of the Jews had hoped to crush
them produced the very opposite effect: the
Jews it was who crushed their enemies. 2In
their towns throughout the provinces of King
Ahasuerus, the Jews assembled to strike at
those who had planned to injure them. No
one resisted them, since the various peoples
were now all afraid of them. 3Provincial
officers-of-state, satraps, governors and royal
officials, all supported the Jews for fear of
Mordecai. 4And indeed Mordecai was a
power in the palace and his fame was
spreading through all the provinces;
Mordecai was steadily growing more
powerful.
5So the Jews struck down all their enemies
with the sword, with resulting slaughter and
destruction, and worked their will on their
opponents. 6In the citadel of Susa alone,
the Jews put to death and slaughtered five
hundred men, 7notably Parshandatha,
Dalphon, Aspatha, 8Poratha, Adalia, Arid-
atha, 9Parmashtha, Arisai, Aridai and
Jezatha, 10the ten sons of Haman son of
Hammedatha, the persecutor of the Jews.
But they took no plunder.
11The number of those killed in the citadel
of Susa was reported to the king that same
day. 12The king said to Queen Esther, 'In the
citadel of Susa the Jews have killed five
hundred men and also the ten sons of Haman.
What must they have done in the other
provinces of the realm? Tell me your request;
I grant it to you. Tell me what else you would
like; it is yours for the asking.' 13'If such is
the king's pleasure,' Esther replied, 'let the
Jews of Susa be allowed to enforce today's
decree tomorrow as well. And as for the ten
sons of Haman, let their bodies be hanged on
the gallows.' 14Whereupon, the king having
given the order, the edict was promulgated

in Susa and the ten sons of Haman were
hanged. 15Thus the Jews of Susa reassembled
on the fourteenth day of the month of Adar
and killed three hundred men in the city. But
they took no plunder.
16The other Jews who lived in the king's
provinces also assembled to defend their lives
and rid themselves of their enemies. They
slaughtered seventy-five thousand of their
opponents. But they took no plunder. 17This
was on the thirteenth day of the month of
Adar. On the fourteenth day they rested and
made it a day of feasting and gladness. 18But
for the Jews of Susa, who had assembled
on the thirteenth and fourteenth days, the
fifteenth was the day they rested, making
that a day of feasting and gladness. 19This is
why Jewish country people, those who live
in undefended villages, keep the fourteenth
day of the month of Adar as a day of gladness,
feasting and holiday-making, and the
exchanging of presents with one another,
19a*whereas for those who live in cities the day of
rejoicing and exchanging presents with their
neighbours is the fifteenth day of Adar.*

V: THE FEAST OF PURIM

The official institution of the feast of Purim

20Mordecai committed these events to
writing. Then he sent letters to all the Jews
living in the provinces of King Ahasuerus,
both near and far, 21enjoining them to
celebrate the fourteenth and fifteenth days of
the month of Adar every year, 22as the days
on which the Jews had rid themselves of their
enemies, and the month in which their sorrow
had been turned into gladness, and mourning
into a holiday. He therefore told them to keep
these as days of festivity and gladness when
they were to exchange presents and make
gifts to the poor.
23Once having begun, the Jews continued
observing these practices, Mordecai having
written them an account 24of how Haman son
of Hammedatha, the Agagite, the persecutor
of all the Jews, had plotted their destruction
and had cast the *pur*, that is, the lot, for their
overthrow and ruin; 25but how, when he went
back to the king to ask him to order the
hanging of Mordecai, the wicked scheme
which he had devised against the Jews
recoiled on his own head, and both he and
his sons were hanged on the gallows; 26and
that, hence, these days were called Purim,
from the word *pur*. And so, because of what
was written in this letter, and because of
what they had seen for themselves and of what
had happened to them, 27the Jews willingly
bound themselves, their descendants and all
who should join them, to celebrate these two
days without fail, in the manner prescribed
and at the time appointed, year after year.
28Thus commemorated and celebrated from
generation to generation, in every family, in
every province, in every city, these days of
Purim will never be abrogated among the
Jews, nor will their memory perish from their
race.
29Queen Esther, the daughter of Abihail,
wrote with full authority to ratify this second
letter, 30and sent letters to all the Jews of the
hundred and twenty-seven provinces of the
realm of Ahasuerus, in terms of peace and
loyalty 31enjoining them to observe these days
of Purim at the appointed time, as Mordecai
the Jew had recommended, and in the
manner prescribed for themselves and their
descendants, with additional ordinances for
fasts and lamentations. 32The ordinance of
Esther fixed the law of Purim, which was
then recorded in a book.

Praise of Mordecai

10 King Ahasuerus put not only the main-
land under tribute but the Mediter-
ranean islands as well. 2All his feats of power
and valour, and the account of the high
honour to which he raised Mordecai: all this
is recorded in the Book of the Annals of the
Kings of Media and Persia.
3And Mordecai the Jew was next in rank
to King Ahasuerus. He was a man held
in respect among the Jews, esteemed by
thousands of his brothers, a man who sought
the good of his people and cared for the
welfare of his entire race.
3a*And Mordecai said, 'All this is God's doing.*
3b*I remember the dream I had about these
matters, nothing of which has failed to come
true:* 3c*the little spring that became a river, the*

light that shone, the sun, the flood of water. Esther is the river—she whom the king married and made queen. [3d]*The two dragons are Haman and myself.* [3e]*The nations are those that banded together to blot out the name of Jew.* [3f]*The single nation, mine, is Israel, those who cried out to God and were saved. Yes, the Lord has saved his people, the Lord has delivered us from all these evils, God has worked such signs and great wonders as have never occurred among the nations.*

[3g]*'Two destinies he appointed, one for his own people, one for the nations at large.* [3h]*And these two destinies were worked out at the hour and time and day laid down by God, involving all the nations.* [3i]*In this way God has remembered his people and vindicated his heritage;* [3k]*and for them these days, the fourteenth and fifteenth of the month of Adar, are to be days of assembly, of joy and of gladness before God, through all generations and for ever among his people Israel.'*

Note to the Greek translation of the book

[3l]*In the fourth year of the reign of Ptolemy and Cleopatra, Dositheus, who affirmed that he was a priest and Levite, and Ptolemy his son brought the foregoing letter concerning Purim. They vouched for its authenticity, the translation having been made by Lysimachus son of Ptolemy, a member of the Jerusalem community.*

THE FIRST BOOK OF MACCABEES

The two books of Maccabees record the fierce struggle of Judaism to resist absorption into the Hellenistic world from 167 to 151 BC. The kings of Syria, attempting to unify their empire, profited from factions within Judaism to try to stamp out the Jewish way of life. Elsewhere this attempt to impose a Greek-style religion and culture was universally successful, and Judaism might well have perished with other local religions and cultures. But the attempt produced a furious opposition from all those faithful to the Jewish Law. The opposition was led by Mattathias and his sons, a priestly family from a small village on the coastal plain, who soon became known as the Maccabees or 'hammers'. They set about their task with a reckless courage and faith in the unfailing help of their God. It soon became clear to the champions of the Law that political independence was a necessary condition of religious freedom.

The story of the forty-year struggle to establish this independence is the theme of 1 M. The author writes with a winning admiration for his heroes and an uncompromising commitment to his Jewish values. The account was written in Hebr., probably about 100 BC, but exists now only in a Gk version. There is a good deal of overlap with 2 M, which covers part of the same period from a different angle. Dates in 1 and 2 Maccabees are reckoned from 312 BC, the year of the foundation of Antioch.

PLAN OF THE BOOK

THE FIRST BOOK OF MACCABEES

I: INTRODUCTION

Alexander and his successors

1 Alexander of Macedon son of Philip had
come from the land of Kittim[a] and
defeated Darius king of the Persians and
Medes, whom he succeeded as ruler, at first
of Hellas. 2 He undertook many campaigns,
gained possession of many fortresses, and
put the local kings to death. 3 So he advanced
to the ends of the earth, plundering nation
after nation; the earth grew silent before him,
and his ambitious heart swelled with pride.
4 He assembled very powerful forces and
subdued provinces, nations and princes, and
they became his tributaries. 5 But the time
came when Alexander took to his bed, in the
knowledge that he was dying. 6 He
summoned his officers, noblemen who had
been brought up with him from his youth,
and divided his kingdom among them while
he was still alive. 7 Alexander had reigned
twelve years when he died. 8 Each of his
officers established himself in his own region.
9 All assumed crowns after his death, they
and their heirs after them for many years,
bringing increasing evils on the world.

Antiochus Epiphanes: Israel infected with Hellenism

10 From these there grew a wicked offshoot,
Antiochus Epiphanes son of King Antiochus;
once a hostage in Rome, he became king in
the 107th year[b] of the kingdom of the Greeks.
11 It was then that there emerged from Israel
a set of renegades who led many people
astray. 'Come,' they said, 'let us ally ourselves
with the gentiles surrounding us, for since
we separated ourselves from them many
misfortunes have overtaken us.' 12 This
proposal proved acceptable, 13 and a number
of the people eagerly approached the king,
who authorised them to practise the gentiles'
observances. 14 So they built a gymnasium in
Jerusalem, such as the gentiles have,
15 disguised their circumcision, and aban-
doned the holy covenant, submitting to
gentile rule as willing slaves of impiety.

First Egyptian campaign and pillage of the Temple

16 Once Antiochus had seen his authority
established, he determined to make himself
king of Egypt and the ruler of both kingdoms.
17 He invaded Egypt in massive strength, with
chariots and elephants (and cavalry) and a
large fleet. 18 He engaged Ptolemy king of
Egypt in battle, and Ptolemy turned back
and fled before his advance, leaving many
casualties. 19 The fortified cities of Egypt were
captured, and Antiochus plundered the
country. 20 After his conquest of Egypt, in
the year 143, Antiochus turned about and

1a Term extended from inhabitants of Kition to all Cypriots and then to all Greeks.
1b Dates in the text of 1—2 M are of the era starting with the foundation of Antioch in 312 BC.

advanced on Israel and Jerusalem in massive
strength.[c] 21 Insolently breaking into the
sanctuary, he removed the golden altar and
the lamp-stand for the light with all its
fittings, 22 together with the table for the
loaves of permanent offering, the libation
vessels, the cups, the golden censers, the veil,
the crowns, and the golden decoration on the
front of the Temple, which he stripped of
everything. 23 He made off with the silver and
gold and precious vessels; he discovered the
secret treasures and seized them 24 and,
removing all these, he went back to his own
country, having shed much blood and uttered
words of extreme arrogance.
25 There was deep mourning for Israel
throughout the country:

26 Rulers and elders groaned;
girls and young men wasted away;
the women's beauty suffered a change;
27 every bridegroom took up a dirge,
the bride sat grief-stricken
on her marriage-bed.
28 The earth quaked
because of its inhabitants
and the whole House of Jacob
was clothed with shame.

Intervention of the Mysarch and construction of the Acra

29 Two years later the king sent the Mysarch
through the cities of Judah. He came to
Jerusalem with an impressive force, 30 and
addressing them with what appeared to be
peaceful words, he gained their confidence;
then suddenly he fell on the city, dealing it a
terrible blow, and destroying many of the
people of Israel. 31 He pillaged the city and set
it on fire, tore down its houses and encircling
wall, 32 took the women and children captive
and commandeered the cattle. 33 They then
rebuilt the City of David with a great strong
wall and strong towers and made this their
Citadel. 34 There they installed a brood of
sinners, of renegades, who fortified them-
selves inside it, 35 storing arms and pro-
visions, and depositing there the loot they
had collected from Jerusalem; they were to
prove a great trouble.

36 It became an ambush for the sanctuary,
an evil adversary for Israel at all times.
37 They shed innocent blood
all round the sanctuary
and defiled the sanctuary itself.
38 The citizens of Jerusalem fled
because of them,
she became a dwelling-place of strangers;
estranged from her own offspring,
her children forsook her.
39 Her sanctuary became
as forsaken as a desert,
her feasts were turned into mourning,
her Sabbaths into a mockery,
her honour into reproach.
40 Her dishonour now fully matched
her former glory,
her greatness was turned into grief.

Installation of gentile cults

41 The king then issued a proclamation to his
whole kingdom that all were to become a
single people, each nation renouncing its
particular customs. 42 All the gentiles
conformed to the king's decree, 43 and many
Israelites chose to accept his religion, sacri-
ficing to idols and profaning the Sabbath.
44 The king also sent edicts by messenger to
Jerusalem and the towns of Judah, directing
them to adopt customs foreign to the country,
45 banning burnt offerings, sacrifices and
libations from the sanctuary, profaning
Sabbaths and feasts, 46 defiling the sanctuary
and everything holy, 47 building altars,
shrines and temples for idols, sacrificing pigs
and unclean beasts, 48 leaving their sons uncir-
cumcised, and prostituting themselves to all
kinds of impurity and abomination, 49 so that
they should forget the Law and revoke all
observance of it. 50 Anyone not obeying the
king's command was to be put to death.
51 Writing in such terms to every part of his
kingdom, the king appointed inspectors for
the whole people and directed all the towns
of Judah to offer sacrifice city by city. 52 Many
of the people—that is, every apostate from
the Law—rallied to them and so committed
evil in the country, 53 forcing Israel into hiding
in any possible place of refuge.
54 On the fifteenth day of Chislev in the year
145 the king built the appalling abomination[d]
on top of the altar of burnt offering; and
altars were built in the surrounding towns of
Judah 55 and incense offered at the doors of

1c || 2 M 5:11-16.
1d An idolatrous altar erected on the Jewish altar of burnt-offering.

houses and in the streets. 56Any books of the
Law that came to light were torn up and
burned. 57Whenever anyone was discovered
possessing a copy of the covenant or prac-
tising the Law, the king's decree sentenced
him to death. 58Month after month they
took harsh action against any offenders they
discovered in the towns of Israel. 59On the
twenty-fifth day of each month, sacrifice was
offered on the altar erected on top of the altar
of burnt offering. 60Women who had had
their children circumcised were put to death
according to the edict 61with their babies
hung round their necks, and the members of
their household and those who had
performed the circumcision were executed
with them.

62Yet there were many in Israel who stood
firm and found the courage to refuse unclean
food. 63They chose death rather than
contamination by such fare or profanation of
the holy covenant, and they were executed.
64It was a truly dreadful retribution that
visited Israel.

II: MATTATHIAS UNLEASHES THE HOLY WAR

Mattathias and his sons

2 About then, Mattathias son of John, son
of Simeon, a priest of the line of Joarib,
left Jerusalem and settled in Modein. 2He
had five sons, John known as Gaddi, 3Simon
called Thassi, 4Judas called Maccabaeus,
5Eleazar, called Avaran, and Jonathan called
Apphus. 6When he saw the blasphemies
being committed in Judah and Jerusalem,
7he said, 'Alas that I should have been born
to witness the ruin of my people and the ruin
of the Holy City, and to sit by while she
is delivered over to her enemies, and the
sanctuary into the hand of foreigners.

8'Her Temple has become
like someone of no repute,
9the vessels that were her glory
have been carried off as booty,
her babies have been slaughtered
in her streets,
her young men by the enemy's sword.
10Is there a nation that has not claimed
a share of her royal prerogatives,
that has not taken some of her spoils?
11All her ornaments
have been snatched from her,
her former freedom has become slavery.
12See how the Holy Place,
our beauty, our glory,
is now laid waste,
see how the gentiles have profaned it!
13What have we left to live for?'

14Mattathias and his sons tore their
garments, put on sackcloth, and observed
deep mourning.

The ordeal of the sacrifice at Modein

15The king's commissioners who were
enforcing the apostasy came to the town of
Modein for the sacrifices. 16Many Israelites
gathered round them, but Mattathias and his
sons drew apart. 17The king's commissioners
then addressed Mattathias as follows, 'You
are a respected leader, a great man in this
town; you have sons and brothers to support
you. 18Be the first to step forward and
conform to the king's decree, as all the nations
have done, and the leaders of Judah and the
survivors in Jerusalem; you and your sons
shall be reckoned among the Friends of the
King, you and your sons will be honoured
with gold and silver and many presents.'
19Raising his voice, Mattathias retorted,
'Even if every nation living in the king's
dominions obeys him, each forsaking its
ancestral religion to conform to his decrees,
20I, my sons and my brothers will still follow
the covenant of our ancestors. 21May Heaven
preserve us from forsaking the Law and its
observances. 22As for the king's orders, we
will not follow them: we shall not swerve
from our own religion either to right or to
left.' 23As he finished speaking, a Jew came
forward in the sight of all to offer sacrifice
on the altar in Modein as the royal edict
required. 24When Mattathias saw this, he was
fired with zeal; stirred to the depth of his
being, he gave vent to his legitimate anger,
threw himself on the man and slaughtered
him on the altar. 25At the same time he killed
the king's commissioner who was there to
enforce the sacrifice, and tore down the altar.
26In his zeal for the Law he acted as Phinehas

had against Zimri son of Salu.[a] 27 Then Matta-
thias went through the town, shouting at the
top of his voice, 'Let everyone who has any
zeal for the Law and takes his stand on the
covenant come out and follow me.' 28 Then
he fled with his sons into the hills, leaving all
their possessions behind in the town.

The ordeal of the Sabbath in the desert

29 Many people who were concerned for virtue
and justice went down to the desert and
stayed there, 30 taking with them their sons,
their wives and their cattle, so oppressive had
their sufferings become. 31 Word was brought
to the royal officials and forces stationed in
Jerusalem, in the City of David, that those
who had repudiated the king's edict had gone
down to the hiding places in the desert.
32 A strong detachment went after them, and
when it came up with them ranged itself
against them in battle formation, preparing
to attack them on the Sabbath day, 33 and
said, 'Enough of this! Come out and do as
the king orders and you will be spared.' 34 The
others, however, replied, 'We refuse to come
out, and we will not obey the king's orders
and profane the Sabbath day.' 35 The royal
forces at once went into action, 36 but the
others offered no opposition; not a stone was
thrown, there was no barricading of the
hiding places. 37 They only said, 'Let us all
die innocent; let heaven and earth bear
witness that you are massacring us with no
pretence of justice.' 38 The attack was pressed
home on the Sabbath itself, and they were
slaughtered, with their wives and children
and cattle, to the number of one thousand
persons.

The activity of Mattathias and his associates

39 When the news reached Mattathias and his
friends, they mourned them bitterly 40 and
said to one another, 'If we all do as our
brothers have done, and refuse to fight the
gentiles for our lives and institutions, they
will only destroy us the sooner from the
earth.' 41 So then and there they came to this
decision, 'If anyone attacks us on the Sabbath
day, whoever he may be, we shall resist him;
we must not all be killed, as our brothers
were in the hiding places.'

42 Soon they were joined by the Hasidaean
party,[b] stout fighting men of Israel, each one
a volunteer on the side of the Law. 43 All the
refugees from the persecution rallied to them,
giving them added support. 44 They organised
themselves into an armed force, striking
down the sinners in their anger, and the
renegades in their fury, and those who
escaped them fled to the gentiles for safety.
45 Mattathias and his friends made a tour,
overthrowing the altars 46 and forcibly
circumcising all the boys they found uncir-
cumcised in the territories of Israel. 47 They
hunted down the upstarts and managed their
campaign to good effect. 48 They wrested the
Law out of the control of the gentiles and the
kings and reduced the sinners to impotence.

The testament and death of Mattathias

49 As the days of Mattathias were drawing to
a close, he said to his sons, 'Arrogance and
outrage are now in the ascendant; it is a
period of turmoil and bitter hatred. 50 This is
the time, my children, for you to have a
burning zeal for the Law and to give your
lives for the covenant of our ancestors.

51 Remember the deeds
performed by our ancestors,
each in his generation,
and you will win great honour
and everlasting renown.
52 Was not Abraham tested
and found faithful,
was that not considered as justifying him?
53 Joseph in the time of his distress
maintained the Law,
and so became lord of Egypt.
54 Phinehas, our father,
in return for his burning zeal,
received the covenant
of everlasting priesthood.
55 Joshua, for carrying out his task,
became judge of Israel.
56 Caleb, for his testimony
before the assembled people,
received an inheritance in the land.
57 David for his generous heart
inherited the throne
of an everlasting kingdom.
58 Elijah for his consuming fervour
for the Law
was caught up to heaven itself.

2a Nb 25:6–15.
2b lit. 'the devout'. They soon split into two groups, the Pharisees and the Essenes.

59 Hananiah, Azariah and Mishael,
for their fidelity,
were saved from the flame.
60 Daniel for his singleness of heart
was rescued from the lion's jaws.
61 Know then that,
generation after generation,
no one who hopes in him
will be overcome.
62 Do not fear the threats of the sinner,
all his brave show
must come to the dunghill
and the worms.
63 Exalted today,
tomorrow he is nowhere to be found,
for he has returned to the dust
he came from
and his scheming is brought to nothing.
64 My children, be resolute and courageous
for the Law,
for it will bring you glory.

65 'Here is your brother Simeon, I know he
is a man of sound judgement. Listen to him
all your lives; let him take your father's place.
66 Judas Maccabaeus, strong and brave from
his youth, let him be your general and
conduct the war against the gentiles. 67 The
rest of you are to enrol in your ranks all
those who keep the Law, and to assure the
vengeance of your people. 68 Pay back the
gentiles to the full, and hold fast to the
ordinance of the Law.' 69 Then he blessed
them and was joined to his ancestors. 70 He
died in the year 146 and was buried in his
ancestral tomb at Modein, and all Israel
mourned him deeply.

III: JUDAS MACCABAEUS, LEADER OF THE JEWS (166–160 BC)

The eulogy of Judas Maccabaeus

3 His son, Judas, known as Maccabaeus,
then took his place. 2 All his brothers, and
all who had attached themselves to his father,
supported him, and they fought for Israel
with a will.

3 He extended the fame of his people.
Like a giant, he put on the breastplate
and buckled on his war harness;
he engaged in battle after battle,
protecting the ranks with his sword.
4 He was like a lion in his exploits,
like a young lion roaring over its prey.
5 He pursued and tracked down
the renegades,
he consigned those
who troubled his people to the flames.
6 The renegades quailed
with the terror he inspired,
all evil-doers were utterly confounded,
and deliverance went forward
under his leadership.
7 He brought bitterness to many a king
and rejoicing to Jacob by his deeds,
his memory is blessed for ever and ever.
8 He went through the towns of Judah
eliminating the irreligious from them,
and diverted the Retribution from Israel.
9 His name resounded
to the ends of the earth,
he rallied those
who were on the point of perishing.

Initial successes of Judas[a]

10 Next, Apollonius mustered the gentiles and
a large force from Samaria to make war on
Israel. 11 When Judas learned of it, he went
out to meet him and routed and killed him.
Many fell wounded, and the survivors took
to flight. 12 Their spoils were seized and the
sword of Apollonius was taken by Judas, who
used it to fight with throughout his life. 13 On
hearing that Judas had raised a mixed force
of believers and seasoned fighters, 14 Seron,
commander of the Syrian troops, said, 'I shall
make a name for myself and gain honour
in the kingdom if I fight Judas and those
supporters of his who are so contemptuous
of the king's orders.' 15 He therefore launched
another expedition, with a strong army of
unbelievers to support him in taking revenge
on the Israelites. 16 He had nearly reached the
descent of Beth-Horon when Judas went out
to confront him with a handful of men. 17 But
as soon as these saw the force advancing to
meet them, they said to Judas, 'How can we,

3a || 2 M 8.

few as we are, engage such overwhelming
numbers? We are exhausted as it is, not
having had anything to eat today.' 18'It is
easy', Judas answered, 'for a great number
to be defeated by a few; indeed, in the sight
of Heaven, deliverance, whether by many or
by few, is all one; 19for victory in war does
not depend on the size of the fighting force:
Heaven accords the strength. 20They are
coming against us in full-blown insolence and
lawlessness to destroy us, our wives and our
children, and to plunder us; 21but we are
fighting for our lives and our laws, 22and he
will crush them before our eyes; do not be
afraid of them.' 23When he had finished
speaking, he made a sudden sally against
Seron and his force and overwhelmed them.
24Judas pursued them down from Beth-
Horon as far as the plain. About eight
hundred of their men fell, and the rest took
refuge in the country of the Philistines.
25Judas and his brothers began to be feared,
and alarm seized the surrounding peoples.
26His name even reached the king's ears, and
among the nations there was talk of Judas
and his battles.

Antiochus prepares to invade Persia and Judaea

Regency of Lysias

27The news of these events infuriated Anti-
ochus, and he ordered mobilisation of all the
forces in his kingdom, a very powerful army.
28Opening his treasury, he distributed a
year's pay to his troops, telling them to
be prepared for any eventuality. 29He then
found that the money in his coffers had run
short and that the tribute of the province had
decreased, as a result of the dissension and
disaster brought on the country by his own
abrogation of laws that had been in force
from antiquity. 30He began to fear that, as
had happened more than once, he would not
have enough to cover the expenses and the
lavish bounties he had previously been accus-
tomed to make on a larger scale than his
predecessors on the throne. 31In this grave
quandary he resolved to invade Persia, there
to levy tribute on the provinces and so
accumulate substantial funds. 32He therefore
left Lysias, a nobleman and member of the
royal family, to manage the royal affairs
between the River Euphrates and the Egyp-
tian frontier, 33making him responsible for
the education of his son Antiochus, until he
should come back. 34To him Antiochus made
over half his forces, with the elephants, giving
him instructions about what he wanted done,
particularly with regard to the inhabitants of
Judaea and Jerusalem, 35against whom he
was to send a force, to crush and destroy the
power of Israel and the remnant of Jerusalem,
to wipe out their very memory from the place,
36to settle foreigners in all parts of their
territory and to distribute their land into lots.
37The king took the remaining half of his
troops with him and set out from Antioch,
the capital of his kingdom, in the year 147;
he crossed the River Euphrates and made his
way through the Upper Provinces.

Gorgias and Nicanor lead the Syrian army into Judaea

38Lysias chose Ptolemy son of Dorymenes,
with Nicanor and Gorgias, influential men
from among the Friends of the King, 39and,
under their command, despatched forty
thousand foot and seven thousand horse to
invade the land of Judah and devastate it, as
the king had ordered. 40The entire force
set out and reached the neighbourhood of
Emmaus in the lowlands, where they pitched
camp. 41The local merchants, hearing the
news of this, arrived at the camp, bringing
with them a large amount of gold and silver,
and fetters as well, proposing to buy the
Israelites as slaves; they were accompanied by
a company from Idumaea and the Philistine
country. 42Judas and his brothers saw that
the situation was going from bad to worse and
that armies were camping in their territory;
they were also well aware that the king had
ordered the people's total destruction. 43So
they said to each other, 'Let us restore the
ruins of our people and fight for our people
and our sanctuary.' 44The Assembly was
summoned, to prepare for war, to offer
prayer and to implore compassion and
mercy.

45Jerusalem was as empty as a desert,
none of her children to go in and out.
The sanctuary was trodden underfoot,
men of an alien race held the Citadel,
which had become a lodging for gentiles.
There was no more rejoicing for Jacob,
the flute and lyre were mute.

The Jews muster at Mizpah

46 After mustering, they made their way to Mizpah, opposite Jerusalem, since Mizpah was traditionally a place of prayer for Israel. 47 That day they fasted and put on sackcloth, covering their heads with ashes and tearing their garments. 48 For the guidance that the gentiles would have sought from the images of their false gods, they opened the Book of the Law. 49 They also brought out the priestly vestments, with first-fruits and tithes, and marshalled the Nazirites who had completed the period of their vow. 50 Then, raising their voices to Heaven, they cried, 'What shall we do with these people, and where are we to take them? 51 Your holy place has been trampled underfoot and defiled, your priests mourn in their humiliation, 52 and now the gentiles are in alliance to destroy us: you know what they have in mind for us. 53 How can we stand up and face them if you do not come to our aid?' 54 Then they sounded the trumpets and raised a great shout.

55 Next, Judas appointed leaders for the people, to command a thousand, a hundred, fifty or ten men. 56 Those who were in the middle of building a house, or were about to be married, or were planting a vineyard, or were afraid, he told to go home again, as the Law allowed. 57 The column then marched off and took up a position south of Emmaus. 58 'Stand to your arms,' Judas told them, 'acquit yourselves bravely, in the morning be ready to fight these gentiles massed against us to destroy us and our sanctuary. 59 Better for us to die in battle than to watch the ruin of our nation and our Holy Place. 60 Whatever be the will of Heaven, he will perform it.'

The battle of Emmaus

4 Gorgias took with him five thousand foot and a thousand picked cavalry, and the force moved off by night 2 with the object of attacking the Jewish position and dealing them an unexpected blow; the men from the Citadel were there to guide him. 3 Judas got wind of it and himself moved off with his fighters to strike at the royal army at Emmaus, 4 while its fighting troops were still dispersed outside the camp. 5 Hence, when Gorgias reached Judas' camp, he found no one and began looking for the Jews in the mountains. 'For', he said, 'we have got them on the run.' 6 First light found Judas in the plain with three thousand men, although these lacked the armour and swords they would have wished. 7 They could now see the gentile encampment with its strong fortifications and cavalry surrounding it, clearly people who understood warfare.

8 Judas said to his men, 'Do not be afraid of their numbers, and do not flinch at their attack. 9 Remember how our ancestors were delivered at the Red Sea when Pharaoh was pursuing them in force. 10 And now let us call on Heaven: if he cares for us, he will remember his covenant with our ancestors and will destroy this army confronting us today; 11 then all the nations will know for certain that there is One who ransoms and saves Israel.'

12 The foreigners looked up and, seeing the Jews advancing against them, 13 came out of the camp to join battle. Judas' men sounded the trumpet 14 and engaged them. The gentiles were defeated and fled towards the plain 15 and all the stragglers fell by the sword. The pursuit continued as far as Gezer and the plains of Idumaea, Azotus and Jamnia, and the enemy lost about three thousand men.

16 Breaking off the pursuit, Judas returned with his men 17 and said to the people, 'Never mind the booty, for we have another battle ahead of us. 18 Gorgias and his troops are still near us in the mountains. First stand up to our enemies and fight them, and then you can safely collect the booty.' 19 The words were hardly out of Judas' mouth, when a detachment came into view, peering down from the mountain. 20 Observing that their own troops had been routed and that the camp had been fired—since the smoke, which they could see, attested the fact—21 they were panic-stricken at the sight; and when, furthermore, they saw Judas' troops drawn up for battle on the plain, 22 they all fled into Philistine territory. 23 Judas then turned back to plunder the camp, and a large sum in gold and silver, with violet and sea-purple stuffs, and many other valuables were carried off. 24 On their return, the Jews chanted praises to Heaven, singing, 'He is kind and his love is everlasting!' 25 That day had seen a remarkable deliverance in Israel. 26 Those of the foreigners who had escaped came and gave Lysias an account of all that had happened. 27 The news shocked and dismayed him, for affairs in Israel had not gone as he intended, and the result was

quite the opposite to what the king had
ordered.

First campaign of Lysias[a]

28 The next year he mobilised sixty thousand
picked troops and five thousand cavalry with
the intention of finishing off the Jews. 29 They
advanced into Idumaea and made their base
at Beth-Zur, where Judas met them with ten
thousand men. 30 When he saw their military
strength he offered this prayer, 'Blessed are
you, Saviour of Israel, who shattered the
mighty warrior's attack at the hand of your
servant David, and delivered the Philistine
camp into the hands of Jonathan son of
Saul, and his armour-bearer. 31 Crush this
expedition in the same way at the hands of
your people Israel; let their troops and cavalry
bring them nothing but shame. 32 Sow panic
in their ranks, confound the confidence they
put in their numbers and send them reeling
in defeat. 33 Overthrow them by the sword of
those who love you, and all who acknowledge
your name will sing your praises.' 34 The two
forces engaged, and five thousand men of
Lysias' troops fell in hand-to-hand fighting.
35 Seeing the rout of his army and the courage
of Judas' troops and their readiness to live
or die nobly, Lysias withdrew to Antioch,
where he recruited mercenaries for a further
invasion of Judaea in even greater strength.

Purification and dedication of the Temple[b]

36 Judas and his brothers then said, 'Now that
our enemies have been defeated, let us go up
to purify the sanctuary and dedicate it.' 37 So
they marshalled the whole army, and went
up to Mount Zion. 38 There they found the
sanctuary deserted, the altar desecrated, the
gates burnt down, and vegetation growing in
the courts as it might in a wood or on some
mountain, while the storerooms were in
ruins. 39 They tore their garments and
mourned bitterly, putting dust on their
heads. 40 They prostrated themselves on the
ground, and when the trumpets gave the
signal they cried aloud to Heaven.

41 Judas then ordered his men to keep
the Citadel garrison engaged until he had
purified the sanctuary. 42 Next, he selected
priests who were blameless and zealous for
the Law 43 to purify the sanctuary and remove
the stones of the 'Pollution' to some unclean
place.

44 They discussed what should be done
about the altar of burnt offering which had
been profaned, 45 and very properly decided
to pull it down, rather than later be embar-
rassed about it since it had been defiled by
the gentiles. They therefore demolished it
46 and deposited the stones in a suitable place
on the hill of the Dwelling to await the
appearance of a prophet who should give
a ruling about them. 47 They took unhewn
stones, as the Law prescribed, and built a
new altar on the lines of the old one. 48 They
restored the Holy Place and the interior of
the Dwelling, and purified the courts. 49 They
made new sacred vessels, and brought the
lamp-stand, the altar of incense, and the table
into the Temple. 50 They burned incense on
the altar and lit the lamps on the lamp-stand,
and these shone inside the Temple. 51 They
placed the loaves on the table and hung the
curtains and completed all the tasks they had
undertaken.

52 On the twenty-fifth of the ninth month,
Chislev, in the year 148 they rose at dawn
53 and offered a lawful sacrifice on the new
altar of burnt offering which they had made.
54 The altar was dedicated, to the sound of
hymns, zithers, lyres and cymbals, at the
same time of year and on the same day on
which the gentiles had originally profaned it.
55 The whole people fell prostrate in adoration
and then praised Heaven who had granted
them success. 56 For eight days they
celebrated the dedication of the altar, joyfully
offering burnt offerings, communion and
thanksgiving sacrifices. 57 They ornamented
the front of the Temple with crowns and
bosses of gold, renovated the gates and store-
rooms, providing the latter with doors.
58 There was no end to the rejoicing among
the people, since the disgrace inflicted by the
gentiles had been effaced. 59 Judas, with his
brothers and the whole assembly of Israel,
made it a law that the days of the dedication
of the altar should be celebrated yearly at the
proper season, for eight days beginning on
the twenty-fifth of the month of Chislev, with
rejoicing and gladness.[c]

60 They then proceeded to build high walls

4a || 2 M 11:1–12.
4b || 2 M 10:1–8.
4c The Feast of Hanukkah, a feast of lights.

with strong towers round Mount Zion, to prevent the gentiles from coming and riding roughshod over it as in the past. 61 Judas stationed a garrison there to guard it; he also fortified Beth-Zur, so that the people would have a fortress confronting Idumaea.

The expedition against the Idumaeans and Ammonites

5 When the surrounding nations heard that the altar had been rebuilt and the sanctuary restored to what it had been before, they became very angry 2 and decided to destroy the descendants of Jacob living among them; they began to murder and evict our people.

3 Judas made war on the sons of Esau in Idumaea,[a] in the region of Acrabattene where they were besieging the Israelites. He dealt them a serious blow, drove them off and despoiled them. 4 He also remembered the wickedness of the sons of Baean, who were a menace and a trap for the people with their ambushes on the roads. 5 Having blockaded them in their town and besieged them, he put them under the curse of destruction; he then set fire to their towers and burned them down with everyone inside. 6 Next, he crossed over to the Ammonites where he found a strong fighting force and a numerous people, commanded by Timotheus. 7 He fought many battles with them, defeated them and cut them to pieces. 8 Having captured Jazer and its dependent villages, he retired to Judaea.

Preliminaries to campaigns in Galilee and Gilead

9 Next, the gentiles of Gilead banded together to destroy the Israelites living in their territory. The latter, however, took refuge in the fortress of Dathema, 10 and sent the following letter to Judas and his brothers:

'The gentiles round us have banded themselves together against us to destroy us, 11 and they are preparing to storm the fortress in which we have taken refuge; Timotheus is in command of their forces. 12 Come at once and rescue us from their clutches, for we have already suffered great losses. 13 All our countrymen living in Tobias' country have been killed, their women and children have been taken into captivity, their property has been seized, and about a thousand men have been destroyed there.'

14 While the letter was being read, other messengers arrived from Galilee with their garments torn, bearing similar news, 15 'The people of Ptolemais, Tyre and Sidon have joined forces with the whole of gentile Galilee to destroy us!'

16 When Judas and the people heard this, they held a great assembly to decide what should be done for their oppressed countrymen who were under attack from their enemies. 17 Judas said to his brother Simon, 'Pick your men and go and relieve your countrymen in Galilee, while my brother Jonathan and I make our way into Gilead.' 18 He left Joseph son of Zechariah and the people's leader Azariah with the remainder of the army in Judaea to keep guard, and gave them these orders, 19 'You are to be responsible for our people. Do not engage the gentiles until we return.' 20 Simon was allotted three thousand men for the expedition into Galilee, Judas eight thousand for Gilead.

The expeditions in Galilee and Gilead

21 Simon advanced into Galilee, engaged the gentiles in several battles and swept all before him; 22 he pursued them to the gate of Ptolemais, and they lost about three thousand men, whose spoils he collected. 23 With him, he took away the Jews of Galilee and Arbatta, with their wives and children and all their possessions, and brought them into Judaea with great rejoicing.

24 Meanwhile Judas Maccabaeus and his brother Jonathan crossed the Jordan[b] and made a three-days' march through the desert, 25 where they encountered the Nabataeans,[c] who gave them a friendly reception and told them everything that had been happening to their brothers in Gilead, 26 many of whom, they said, were shut up in Bozrah and Bosor, Alema, Chaspho, Maked and Carnaim, all large fortified towns. 27 Others were blockaded in the other towns of Gilead, and the

5a ‖ 2 M 10:15–23.
5b ‖ 2 M 12:10–31.
5c An Arab people, centred on Petra and controlling the trade routes for 200 years.

enemy planned to attack and capture these strongholds the very next day, and destroy all the people inside them on one day.

28 Judas and his army at once turned off by the desert road to Bozrah. He took the town and, having put all the males to the sword and collected the booty, burned it down. 29 When night came, he left the place, and they continued their march until they reached the fortress. 30 In the light of dawn they looked, and there was an innumerable horde, setting up ladders and engines to capture the fortress; the assault was just beginning. 31 When Judas saw that the attack had begun and that the war cry was rising to heaven from the city, mingled with trumpet calls and a great clamour, 32 he said to the men of his army, 'Into battle today for your brothers!' 33 Dividing them into three commands, he advanced on the enemy's rear, with trumpets sounding and prayers shouted aloud. 34 The troops of Timotheus, recognising that this was Maccabaeus, fled before his advance; Maccabaeus dealt them a crushing defeat; about eight thousand of their men fell that day. 35 Then, wheeling on Alema, he attacked and captured it and, having killed all the males and collected the booty, burned the place down. 36 From there he moved on and took Chaspho, Maked, Bosor and the remaining towns of Gilead. 37 After these events, Timotheus mustered another force and pitched camp opposite Raphon, on the far side of the stream-bed. 38 Judas sent men to reconnoitre the camp, and these reported back as follows, 'With him are massed all the gentiles surrounding us, making a very numerous army, 39 with Arab mercenaries as auxiliaries; they are encamped on the far side of the stream-bed, and ready to launch an attack on you.' Judas then advanced to engage them, 40 and was approaching the watercourse with his troops when Timotheus told the commanders of his army, 'If he crosses first we shall not be able to resist him, because he will have a great advantage over us; 41 but if he is afraid and camps on the other side of the stream, we shall cross over to him and the advantage will then be ours.'

42 As soon as Judas reached the watercourse, he posted people's scribes along it, giving them this order: 'Do not let anyone pitch his tent; all are to go into battle!' 43 He was himself the first across to the enemy side, with all the people following. He defeated all the opposing gentiles, who threw down their arms and ran for refuge in the sanctuary of Carnaim. 44 The Jews first captured the town and then burned down the temple with everyone inside. And so Carnaim was overthrown, and the enemy could offer no further resistance to Judas.

45 Next, Judas assembled all the Israelites living in Gilead, from the least to the greatest, with their wives, children and belongings, an enormous muster, to take them to Judaea. 46 They reached Ephron, a large town straddling the road and strongly fortified. As it was impossible to by-pass it either to right or to left, there was nothing for it but to march straight through. 47 But the people of the town denied them passage and barricaded the gates with stones. 48 Judas sent them a conciliatory message in these terms, 'We want to pass through your territory to reach our own; no one will do you any harm, we only want to go through on foot.' But they would not open up for him. 49 So Judas sent an order down the column for everyone to halt where he stood. 50 The fighting men took up their positions; Judas attacked the town all day and night, and the town fell to him. 51 He put all the males to the sword, rased the town to the ground, plundered it and marched through the town square over the bodies of the dead. 52 They then crossed the Jordan into the Great Plain, opposite Beth-Shean, 53 Judas all the time rallying the stragglers and encouraging the people the whole way until they reached Judaea. 54 They climbed Mount Zion in joy and gladness and presented burnt offerings because they had returned safe and sound without having lost a single man.

Reversal at Jamnia

55 While Judas and Jonathan were in Gilead and Simon his brother in Galilee outside Ptolemais, 56 Joseph son of Zechariah, and Azariah, who were in command of the army, heard of their valiant deeds and of the battles they had been fighting, 57 and said, 'Let us make a name for ourselves too and go and fight the nations around us.' 58 So they issued orders to the men under their command and marched on Jamnia. 59 Gorgias and his men came out of the town and gave battle. 60 Joseph and Azariah were routed and pursued as far as the frontiers of Judaea. That day about two thousand Israelites lost their lives. 61 Our people thus met with a great reverse, because they had not listened to Judas and his

brothers, thinking that they would do something equally valiant. [62]They were not, however, of the same breed of men as those to whom the deliverance of Israel was entrusted.

Successes in Idumaea and Philistia

[63]The noble Judas and his brothers, however, were held in high honour throughout Israel and among all the nations wherever their name was heard, [64]and people thronged round to acclaim them. [65]Judas marched out with his brothers to fight the Edomites in the country towards the south; he stormed Hebron and its dependent villages, threw down its fortifications and burned down its encircling towers. [66]Leaving there, he made for the country of the Philistines and passed through Marisa. [67]Among the fallen in that day's fighting were some priests who sought to prove their courage there by joining in the battle, a foolhardy venture. [68]Judas next turned on Azotus, which belonged to the Philistines; he overthrew their altars, burned the statues of their gods and, having pillaged their towns, withdrew to Judaea.

The last days of Antiochus Epiphanes[a]

6 King Antiochus, meanwhile, was making his way through the Upper Provinces; he had heard that in Persia there was a city called Elymais, renowned for its riches, its silver and gold, [2]and its very wealthy temple containing golden armour, breastplates and weapons, left there by Alexander son of Philip, the king of Macedon, the first to reign over the Greeks. [3]He therefore went and attempted to take the city and pillage it, but without success, the citizens having been forewarned. [4]They resisted him by force of arms. He was routed, and began retreating, very gloomily, towards Babylon. [5]But, while he was still in Persia, news reached him that the armies which had invaded Judaea had been routed, [6]and that Lysias in particular had advanced in massive strength, only to be forced to turn and flee before the Jews; that the latter were now stronger than ever, thanks to the arms, supplies and abundant spoils acquired from the armies they had cut to pieces, [7]and that they had pulled down the abomination which he had erected on the altar in Jerusalem, had encircled the sanctuary with high walls as in the past, and had fortified Beth-Zur, one of his cities. [8]When the king heard this news he was amazed and profoundly shaken; he threw himself on his bed and fell sick with grief, since things had not turned out for him as he had planned. [9]And there he remained for many days, subject to deep and recurrent fits of melancholy, until he realised that he was dying. [10]Then, summoning all his Friends, he said to them, 'Sleep evades my eyes, and my heart is cowed by anxiety. [11]I have been wondering how I could have come to such a pitch of distress, so great a flood as that which now engulfs me—I who was so generous and well-loved in my heyday. [12]But now I recall how wrongly I acted in Jerusalem when I seized all the vessels of silver and gold there and ordered the extermination of the inhabitants of Judah for no reason at all. [13]This, I am convinced, is why these misfortunes have overtaken me, and why I am dying of melancholy in a foreign land.'

The accession of Antiochus V

[14]He summoned Philip, one of his Friends, and made him regent of the whole kingdom. [15]He entrusted him with his diadem, his robe and his signet, on the understanding that he was to educate his son Antiochus and train him for the throne. [16]King Antiochus then died, in the year 149. [17]Lysias, learning that the king was dead, established on the throne in succession to him his son Antiochus, whom he had brought up from childhood—and styled him Eupator.

The siege of the Citadel of Jerusalem by Judas Maccabaeus

[18]The people in the Citadel at the time were blockading Israel round the sanctuary and were taking every opportunity to harm them and to support the gentiles. [19]Judas decided that they must be destroyed, and he mobilised the whole people to besiege them. [20]They assembled and laid siege to the Citadel in the year 150, building batteries and siege-engines. [21]But some of the besieged broke through the blockade, and to these a number of renegades from Israel attached themselves. [22]They made their way to the king and said, 'How much longer are you going to wait

6a || 2 M 1:11–17; 9.

before you see justice done and avenge our
fellows? 23 We were content to serve your
father, to comply with his orders, and to obey
his edicts. 24 As a result our own people will
have nothing to do with us; what is more,
they have killed all those of us they could
catch, and looted our family property. 25 Nor
is it on us alone that their blows have fallen,
but on all your territories. 26 At this moment,
they are laying siege to the Citadel of Jeru-
salem, to capture it, and they have fortified
the sanctuary and Beth-Zur. 27 Unless you
forestall them at once, they will go on to even
bigger things, and then you will never be able
to control them.'

Campaign of Antiochus V and Lysias
The battle of Beth-Zechariah

28 The king was furious when he heard this
and summoned all his Friends, the generals
of his forces and the marshals of horse. 29 He
recruited mercenaries from other kingdoms
and the Mediterranean islands. 30 His forces
numbered a hundred thousand foot soldiers,
twenty thousand cavalry and thirty-two
elephants with experience of battle
conditions. 31 They advanced through
Idumaea and besieged Beth-Zur, pressing
the attack for days on end; they also
constructed siege-engines, but the defenders
made a sortie and set these on fire, putting
up a brave resistance.
32 At this, Judas left the Citadel and pitched
camp at Beth-Zechariah opposite the royal
encampment. 33 The king rose at daybreak
and marched his army at top speed down the
road to Beth-Zechariah, where his forces
took up their battle formations and sounded
the trumpets. 34 The elephants were given a
syrup of grapes and mulberries to prepare
them for the battle. 35 These animals were
distributed among the phalanxes, to each
elephant being allocated a thousand men
dressed in coats of mail with bronze helmets
on their heads; five hundred picked
horsemen were also assigned to each beast.
36 The horsemen anticipated every move their
elephant made; wherever it went they went
with it, never quitting it. 37 On each elephant,
to protect it, was a stout wooden tower, kept
in position by girths, each with its three
combatants, as well as its mahout. 38 The
remainder of the cavalry was stationed on
one or other of the two flanks of the army,
to harass the enemy and cover the
phalanxes.
39 When the sun glinted on the bronze and
golden shields, the mountains caught the
glint and gleamed like fiery torches. 40 One
part of the royal army was deployed on the
upper slopes of the mountain and the other
in the valley below; they advanced in solid,
well-disciplined formation. 41 Everyone
trembled at the noise made by this vast
multitude, the thunder of the troops on the
march and the clanking of their armour, for
it was an immense and mighty army. 42 Judas
and his army advanced to give battle, and six
hundred of the king's army were killed.
43 Eleazar, called Avaran, noticing that one of
the elephants was royally caparisoned and
was also taller than all the others, and
supposing that the king was mounted on it,
44 sacrificed himself to save his people and
win an imperishable name. 45 Boldly charging
towards the creature through the thick of the
phalanx, dealing death to right and left, so
that the enemy scattered on either side at his
onslaught, 46 he darted in under the elephant,
thrust at it from underneath, and killed it.
The beast collapsed on top of him, and
he died on the spot. 47 The Jews however
realising how strong the king was and how
ferocious his army, retreated ahead of them.

The capture of Beth-Zur and siege of Mount Zion by the Syrians

48 The royal army moved up to encounter
them outside Jerusalem, and the king began
to blockade Judaea and Mount Zion. 49 He
granted peace terms to the people of Beth-
Zur, who evacuated the town; it lacked store
of provisions to withstand a siege, since the
land was enjoying a sabbatical year. 50 Having
occupied Beth-Zur, the king stationed a
garrison there to hold it. 51 He besieged the
sanctuary for a long time, erecting batteries
and siege-engines, flame-throwers and
ballistas, scorpions to discharge arrows, and
catapults. 52 The defenders countered these
by constructing their own engines and were
thus able to prolong their resistance. 53 But
they had no food in their stores since it was
the seventh year, and because those who had
taken refuge in Judaea from the gentiles had
eaten up the last of their reserves. 54 Only a
few men were left in the Holy Place, owing
to the severity of the famine; the rest had
dispersed and gone home.

The king grants the Jews religious freedom

55 Meanwhile Philip, whom King Antiochus before his death had appointed to train his son Antiochus for the throne, 56 had returned from Persia and Media with the forces that had accompanied the king, and was planning to seize control of affairs. 57 On hearing this, Lysias at once decided to leave,[b] and said to the king, the generals of the army and the men, 'We are growing weaker every day, we are short of food, and the place we are besieging is well fortified; moreover the affairs of the kingdom demand our attention. 58 Let us offer the hand of friendship to these men and make peace with them and with their whole nation. 59 Let us grant them permission to follow their own customs as before, since it is our abolition of these customs that has provoked them into acting like this.' 60 The king and his commanders approved this argument, and he offered the Jews peace terms, which they accepted. 61 The king and the generals ratified the treaty by oath, and the besieged accordingly left the fortress. 62 The king then entered Mount Zion, but on seeing how impregnable the place was, he broke the oath he had sworn and gave orders for the encircling wall to be demolished. 63 He then hurriedly withdrew, making off for Antioch, where he found Philip already master of the city. Antiochus gave battle and captured the city by force of arms.

Demetrius I becomes king, and sends Bacchides and Alcimus to Judaea[a]

7 In the year 151, Demetrius son of Seleucus left Rome and arrived with a few men at a town on the coast, where he inaugurated his reign. 2 It so happened that, as he was entering the royal residence of his ancestors, the army captured Antiochus and Lysias, and intended to bring them to him. 3 On hearing this, he said, 'Keep them out of my sight.' 4 The army put them to death, and Demetrius ascended his throne. 5 Next, all those Israelites without law or piety, led by Alcimus, whose ambition was to become high priest, 6 approached the king and denounced our people to him. 'Judas and his brothers', they said, 'have killed all your friends, and he has driven us out of our country. 7 Send someone now whom you can trust; let him go and see the wholesale ruin Judas has brought on us and on the king's dominions, and let him punish the wretches and all who assist them.'

8 The king chose Bacchides, one of the Friends of the King, governor of Transeuphrates, an important personage in the kingdom and loyal to the king. 9 He sent him with the godless Alcimus, whom he confirmed in the high priesthood, with orders to exact retribution from the Israelites. 10 So they set out with a large force and, on reaching Judaea, sent emissaries to Judas and his brothers with proposals peaceable yet treacherous. 11 The latter, however, did not put any faith in their words, aware that they had come with a large force. 12 Nevertheless, a commission of scribes presented themselves before Alcimus and Bacchides, to sue for just terms. 13 The first among the Israelites to ask them for peace terms were the Hasidaeans, 14 who reasoned thus, 'This is a priest of Aaron's line who has come with the armed forces; he will not wrong us.' 15 He did in fact discuss peace terms with them and gave them his oath, 'We shall not attempt to injure you or your friends.' 16 They believed him, but he arrested sixty of them and put them to death on one day, fulfilling the words of scripture: 17 *They have scattered the bodies of your faithful, and shed their blood all round Jerusalem, leaving no one to bury them!*[b] 18 At this, fear and dread gripped the whole people. 'There is no truth or virtue in them,' they said, 'they have broken their agreement and their sworn oath.'

19 Bacchides then left Jerusalem and encamped at Beth-Zeth, and from there sent and arrested many of the men who had deserted him and a few of our people too; he had them killed and thrown down the great well. 20 He then put Alcimus in charge of the province, leaving an army with him to support him; Bacchides himself returned to the king. 21 Alcimus continued his struggle to become high priest, 22 and all who were disturbing the peace of their own people rallied to him, and, having won control of Judaea, did much harm in Israel. 23 Seeing that all the wrongs done to the Israelites by Alcimus and his supporters exceeded what

6b || 2 M 11:13–33.
7a || 2 M 14:1–10.
7b || Ps 79:2–3.

the gentiles had done, 24 Judas went right round the whole territory of Judaea to take vengeance on those who had deserted him and to prevent their free movement about the country.

Nicanor in Judaea and battle of Caphar-Salama

25 When Alcimus saw how strong Judas and his supporters had grown and realised that he was powerless to resist them, he went back to the king, to whom he made malicious accusations against them. 26 The king sent Nicanor, one of his generals ranking as Illustrious and a bitter enemy of Israel, with orders to exterminate the people. 27 Reaching Jerusalem with a large force, Nicanor sent a friendly, yet treacherous, message to Judas and his brothers, as follows: 28 'Let us have no fighting between you and me; I shall come with a small escort for a peaceful meeting with you.' 29 He met Judas and they exchanged friendly greetings; the enemy, however, had made preparations to abduct Judas. 30 When Judas became aware of Nicanor's treacherous purpose in coming to see him, he took fright and refused any further meeting. 31 Nicanor then realised that his plan had been discovered, and took the field against Judas, to give battle near Caphar-Salama. 32 About five hundred of Nicanor's men fell; the rest took refuge in the City of David.

Threats against the Temple

33 After these events Nicanor went up to Mount Zion. Some of the priests came out of the Holy Place with some elders, to give him a friendly welcome and show him the burnt offering being presented for the king. 34 But he ridiculed them, laughed at them, defiled them and used insolent language, swearing in his rage, 35 'Unless Judas is handed over to me this time with his army, as soon as I am safely back, I promise you, I shall burn this building down!' 36 Then he went off in a fury. At this, the priests went in again, and stood weeping in front of the altar and the Temple, saying, 37 'You have chosen this house to be called by your name, to be a house of prayer and petition for your people. 38 Take vengeance on this man and on his army, and let them fall by the sword; remember their blasphemies and give them no respite.'

The 'Day of Nicanor' at Adasa

39 Nicanor left Jerusalem and encamped at Beth-Horon, where he was joined by an army from Syria. 40 Judas, meanwhile, camped at Adasa with three thousand men, and offered this prayer, 41 'When the king's envoys blasphemed, your angel went out and struck down one hundred and eighty-five thousand of his men. 42 In the same way let us see you crush this army today, so that everyone else may know that this man has spoken blasphemously against your sanctuary: pass judgement on him as his wickedness deserves!'

43 The armies met in battle on the thirteenth of the month Adar,[c] and Nicanor's army was crushed, he himself being the first to fall in the battle. 44 When Nicanor's soldiers saw him fall, they threw down their arms and fled. 45 The Jews pursued them a day's journey, from Adasa to the approaches of Gezer; they sounded their trumpets in warning as they followed them, 46 and people came out of all the surrounding Judaean villages to encircle the fugitives, who then turned back on their own men. All fell by the sword, not one being left alive. 47 Having collected the spoils and booty, they cut off Nicanor's head and the right hand he had stretched out in a display of insolence; these were taken and displayed within sight of Jerusalem. 48 The people were overjoyed and kept that day as a great holiday: 49 indeed they decided to celebrate it annually on the thirteenth of Adar. 50 For a short while Judaea enjoyed peace.

A eulogy of the Romans

8 Now Judas had heard of the reputation of the Romans: how strong they were, and how well disposed towards any who made common cause with them, making a treaty of friendship with anyone who approached them. 2 (And, indeed, they were extremely powerful.) He had been told of their wars and of their prowess among the Gauls, whom they had conquered and put under tribute; 3 and of all they had done in the province of

7c || 2 M 15:25–36.

Spain to gain possession of the silver and gold
mines there, 4making themselves masters of
the whole country by their determination and
perseverance, despite its great distance from
their own; of the kings who came from the
ends of the earth to attack them, only to
be crushed by them and overwhelmed with
disaster, and of others who paid them annual
tribute; 5Philip, Perseus king of the Kittim,
and others who had dared to make war on
them, had been defeated and reduced to
subjection, 6while Antiochus the Great, king
of Asia, who had advanced to attack them
with a hundred and twenty elephants,
cavalry, chariots and a very large army, had
also suffered defeat at their hands; 7they had
taken him alive and imposed on him and his
successors, on agreed terms, the payment
of an enormous tribute, the surrender of
hostages, and the cession 8of the Indian terri-
tory, with Media, Lydia, and some of their
best provinces, which they took from him
and gave to King Eumenes. 9Judas had also
heard how, when the Greeks planned an
expedition to destroy the Romans, 10the latter
had got wind of it and, sending a single
general against them, had fought a campaign
in which they inflicted heavy casualties,
carried their women and children away into
captivity, pillaged their goods, subdued their
country, tore down their fortresses and
reduced them to a slavery lasting to the
present day; 11and how they had destroyed
and subjugated all the other kingdoms and
islands that resisted them.
12But where their friends and those who
relied on them were concerned, they had
always stood by their friendship. They had
subdued kings far and near, and all who
heard their name went in terror of them.
13One man, if they determined to help him
and advance him to a throne, would certainly
occupy it, while another, if they so deter-
mined, would find himself deposed; their
influence was paramount. 14In spite of all
this, no single one of them had assumed a
crown or put on the purple for his own
aggrandisement. 15They had set up a senate,
where three hundred and twenty councillors
deliberated daily, constantly debating how
best to regulate public affairs. 16They en-
trusted their government to one man for a
year at a time, with absolute power over their
whole empire, and this man was obeyed by
all without envy or jealousy.

The alliance between the Jews and Romans

17Having chosen Eupolemus son of John, of
the family of Accos, and Jason son of Eleazar,
Judas sent them to Rome to make a treaty of
friendship and alliance with these people,
18in the hope of being rid of the yoke, for they
could see that Greek rule was reducing Israel
to slavery. 19The envoys made the lengthy
journey to Rome and presented themselves
before the Senate with their formal proposal:
20'Judas Maccabaeus and his brothers, with
the Jewish people, have sent us to you to
conclude a treaty of alliance and peace with
you, and to enrol ourselves as your allies and
friends.'
21The proposal met with the approval of
the senators. 22Here is a copy of the rescript
which they engraved on bronze tablets and
sent to Jerusalem to be kept there by the Jews
as a record of peace and alliance:

23'Good fortune attend the Romans and
the Jewish nation by sea and land for
ever; may sword or enemy be far from
them!
24'If war comes first to Rome or any of
her allies throughout her dominions, 25the
Jewish nation will take action as her ally,
as occasion may require, and do it
wholeheartedly. 26They will not give or
supply to the enemy any grain, arms,
money or ships: thus has Rome decided,
and they are to honour their obligations
without guarantees. 27In the same way, if
war comes first to the Jewish nation, the
Romans will support them energetically as
occasion may offer, 28and the aggressor
will not be furnished with grain, arms,
money or ships: such is the Roman
decision, and they will honour these obli-
gations without treachery. 29Such are the
articles under which the Romans have
concluded their treaty with the Jewish
people. 30If, later, either party should
decide to make any addition or deletion,
they will be free to do so, and any such
addition or deletion will be binding.
31'As regards the wrongs done to them
by King Demetrius, we have written to
him in these terms: Why have you made
your yoke lie heavy on our friends and
allies the Jews? 32If they appeal against you
again, we shall uphold their rights and
make war on you by sea and land.'

Battle of Beer-Zaith and death of Judas Maccabaeus

9 Demetrius, hearing that Nicanor and his army had fallen in battle, sent Bacchides and Alcimus a second time into Judaea, and with them the right wing of his army. 2 They took the road to Galilee and besieged Mesaloth in Arbela, and captured it, putting many people to death. 3 In the first month of the year 152, they encamped outside Jerusalem; 4 they then moved on, making their way to Beer-Zaith with twenty thousand foot and two thousand horse. 5 Judas lay in camp at Elasa, with three thousand picked men. 6 When they saw the huge size of the enemy forces they were terrified, and many slipped out of the camp, until no more than eight hundred of the force were left. 7 With battle now inevitable, Judas realised that his army had melted away; he was aghast, for he had no time to rally them. 8 Yet, dismayed as he was, he said to those who were left, 'Up! Let us face the enemy; we may yet have the strength to fight them.' 9 His men tried to dissuade him, declaring, 'We have no strength for anything but to escape with our lives this time; then we can come back with our brothers to fight them; by ourselves we are too few.' 10 Judas retorted, 'That I should do such a thing as run away from them! If our time has come, at least let us die like men for our countrymen, and leave nothing to tarnish our reputation.'

11 The army marched out of camp and drew up, facing the enemy. The cavalry was drawn up in two squadrons; the slingers and archers marched in the van of the army, and all the best fighters were put in the front rank; 12 Bacchides was on the right wing. The phalanx advanced from between the two squadrons, sounding the trumpets; the men on Judas' side also blew their trumpets, 13 and the earth shook with the noise of the armies. The engagement lasted from morning until evening.

14 Judas saw that Bacchides and the main strength of his army lay on the right; all the stout-hearted rallied to him, 15 and they crushed the right wing, pursuing them as far as the Azara Hills. 16 But when the Syrians on the left wing saw that the right had been broken, they turned and followed hot on the heels of Judas and his men to take them in the rear. 17 The fight became desperate, and there were many casualties on both sides. 18 Judas himself fell, and the remnant fled.

The funeral of Judas Maccabaeus

19 Jonathan and Simon took up their brother Judas and buried him in his ancestral tomb at Modein. 20 All Israel wept and mourned him deeply and for many days they repeated this dirge, 21 'What a downfall for the strong man, the man who kept Israel safe!' 22 The other deeds of Judas, the battles he fought, the exploits he performed, and all his titles to greatness have not been recorded; but they were very many.

IV: JONATHAN, LEADER OF THE JEWS AND HIGH PRIEST (160–143 BC)

The triumph of the Greek party Jonathan leads the resistance

23 After the death of Judas, the renegades came out of hiding throughout Israel and all the evil-doers reappeared. 24 At that time there was a severe famine, and the country went over to their side. 25 Bacchides deliberately chose the enemies of religion to administer the country. 26 These traced and searched out the friends of Judas and brought them before Bacchides, who ill-treated and mocked them. 27 A terrible oppression began in Israel; there had been nothing like it since the disappearance of prophecy among them.

28 The friends of Judas then all united in saying to Jonathan, 29 'Since your brother Judas died, there has been no one like him to head the resistance against our enemies, people like Bacchides and others who hate our nation. 30 Accordingly, we have today chosen you to take his place as our ruler and leader and to fight our campaigns.' 31 Whereupon, Jonathan took command, in succession to his brother Judas.

Jonathan in the desert of Tekoa
Bloody encounters round Medeba

32Bacchides, when he heard the news, made
plans to kill Jonathan. 33But this became
known to Jonathan, his brother Simon and
all his supporters, and they took refuge in
the desert of Tekoa, camping by the water-
supply at Asphar storage-well. 34(Bacchides
came to know of this on the Sabbath day, and
he too crossed the Jordan with his entire
army.)
35Jonathan sent his brother, who was one
of his commanders, to ask his friends the
Nabataeans to store their considerable
baggage for them. 36The sons of Amrai,
however, those of Medeba, intercepted
them, captured John and everything he had
and made off with their prize. 37Later,
Jonathan and his brother Simon were told
that the sons of Amrai were celebrating an
important wedding, and were escorting the
bride, a daughter of one of the great notables
of Canaan, from Nabata with a large retinue.
38Remembering the bloody end of their
brother John, they went up and hid under
cover of the mountain. 39As they were
keeping watch, a noisy procession came into
sight with a great deal of baggage, and the
bridegroom, with his groomsmen and his
family, came out to meet it with tambourines
and a band, and rich, warlike display. 40The
Jews rushed down on them from their
ambush and killed them, inflicting heavy
casualties; the survivors escaped to the moun-
tain, leaving their entire baggage train to be
captured. 41Thus, *the wedding was turned into
mourning and the music of their band into
lamentation.*[a] 42Having in this way avenged
in full the blood of their brother, they
returned to the marshes of the Jordan.

Crossing the Jordan

43As soon as Bacchides heard this, he came
on the Sabbath day with a considerable force
to the steep banks of the Jordan. 44Jonathan
said to his men, 'Up! Let us fight for our
lives, for today it is not as in the old days.
45You can see, we shall have to fight on our
front and to our rear; we have the waters of
the Jordan on one side, the marsh and scrub
on the other, and we have no line of with-
drawal. 46This is the moment to call on
Heaven, to deliver you from the clutches of
your enemies.' 47The engagement was begun
by Jonathan, who aimed a blow at Bacchides,
but the Syrian disengaged himself and with-
drew, 48whereupon Jonathan and his men
leapt into the Jordan and swam to the other
bank; the enemy did not, however, cross the
Jordan in pursuit. 49That day, Bacchides lost
about a thousand men.

Bacchides builds fortifications
The death of Alcimus

50Bacchides went back to Jerusalem and
began fortifying some of the Judaean towns:
the fortresses of Jericho, Emmaus, Beth-
Horon, Bethel, Timnath, Pharathon and
Tephon, with high walls and barred gates,
51and stationed a garrison in each of them to
harass Israel. 52He also fortified the town of
Beth-Zur, Gezer and the Citadel, and placed
troops in them with supplies of provisions.
53He took the sons of the leading men of the
country as hostages, and had them placed
under guard in the Citadel of Jerusalem.
54In the year 153, in the second month,
Alcimus ordered the demolition of the wall
of the inner court of the sanctuary, destroying
the work of the prophets. Alcimus had just
begun the demolition 55when he suffered a
stroke, and his work was interrupted. His
mouth became obstructed, and his paralysis
made him incapable of speaking at all or
giving directions to his household; 56it was
not long before he died in great agony. 57On
the death of Alcimus, Bacchides went back
to the king, and Judaea was left in peace for
two years.

The siege of Beth-Bassi

58The renegades then all agreed on a plan.
'Now is the time,' they said, 'while Jonathan
and his supporters are living in peace and
are full of confidence, for us to bring back
Bacchides, and he will arrest the lot of them
in one night.' 59So they went to him and
reached an understanding. 60Bacchides at
once set out with a large force, and sent secret
instructions to all his allies in Judaea to seize
Jonathan and his supporters. But they were
unable to do this because their plan became
known, 61and Jonathan and his men arrested

9a Am 8:10.

some fifty of the men of the country who were ringleaders in the plot, and put them to death.

62 Jonathan and Simon then retired with their partisans to Beth-Bassi in the desert; they rebuilt the ruinous parts of the place and fortified it. 63 When Bacchides heard this, he mustered his whole force and notified his adherents in Judaea. 64 He then proceeded to lay siege to Beth-Bassi, the fighting was protracted, and he constructed siege-engines. 65 Jonathan, however, leaving his brother Simon in the town, broke out into the countryside with a handful of men. 66 He launched a blow at Odomera and his brothers, and at the sons of Phasiron in their encampment; whereupon, these too came into the struggle, joining forces with him. 67 Simon and his people, meanwhile, made a sortie from the town and set fire to the siege-engines. 68 Taking the offensive against Bacchides, they defeated him. He was greatly disconcerted to find that his plan and his assault had come to nothing, 69 and vented his anger on those renegades who had induced him to enter the country, putting many of them to death; he then decided to take his own troops home. 70 Discovering this, Jonathan sent envoys to negotiate peace terms and the release of prisoners with him. 71 Bacchides agreed to this, accepting his proposals and swearing never to seek occasion to harm him for the rest of his life. 72 Having surrendered to Jonathan those prisoners he had earlier taken in Judaea, he turned about and withdrew to his own country, and never again came near their frontiers. 73 The sword no longer hung over Israel, and Jonathan settled in Michmash, where he began to judge the people and to rid Israel of the godless.

Alexander Balas competes for Jonathan's support and appoints him high priest

10 In the year 160, Alexander, son of Antiochus Epiphanes, raised an army and occupied Ptolemais. He was well received, and there inaugurated his reign. 2 On hearing this, King Demetrius assembled a very large army and marched off to do battle with him. 3 Demetrius furthermore sent Jonathan a most conciliatory letter, promising to promote him in rank, 4 for, as he said, 'We had better move first to come to terms with these people before he makes common cause with Alexander against us; 5 he will not have forgotten all the wrongs we inflicted on him and his brothers, and on his nation.' 6 He even authorised him to raise an army, to manufacture arms, and to describe himself as his ally, and ordered the hostages in the Citadel to be surrendered to him.

7 Jonathan went straight to Jerusalem and read the letter in the hearing of the whole people and of the men in the Citadel. 8 They were terrified when they heard that the king had given him authority to raise an army. 9 The men in the Citadel surrendered the hostages to Jonathan, who handed them back to their parents. 10 Jonathan then took up residence in Jerusalem and began the rebuilding and restoration of the city. 11 He ordered those responsible for the work to build the walls and the defences round Mount Zion of squared stone blocks to make them stronger, and this was done. 12 The foreigners in the fortresses built by Bacchides abandoned them, 13 one after another leaving his post to go back to his own country. 14 Only at Beth-Zur were a few left of those who had forsaken the Law and the precepts, since this was their refuge.

15 King Alexander heard of all the promises Demetrius had sent to Jonathan, and he was also given an account of the battles and exploits of this man and his brothers and of the hardships they had endured. 16 'Shall we ever find another man like him?' he exclaimed. 'We must make him our friend and ally!' 17 He therefore wrote him a letter, addressing him in these terms:

18 'King Alexander to his brother Jonathan, greetings.

> 19 'You have been brought to our notice as a strong man of action and as someone who deserves to be our friend. 20 Accordingly, we have today appointed you high priest of your nation, with the title of "Friend of the King" '—he also sent him a purple robe and a golden crown—'and you are to study our interests and maintain friendly relations with us.'

21 Jonathan put on the sacred vestments in the seventh month of the year 160, on the feast of Shelters; he then set about raising troops and manufacturing arms in quantity.

A letter from Demetrius I to Jonathan

22 Demetrius was displeased when he heard what had happened. 23 'What have we been

doing,' he said, 'for Alexander to forestall us in winning the friendship of the Jews and so improving his own position? 24 I too shall address an appeal to them, offering them advancement and riches as an inducement to support me.' 25 And he wrote to them as follows:

'King Demetrius to the Jewish nation, greetings.

26 'We have heard how you have kept your agreement with us and have maintained friendly relations with us and have not gone over to our enemies, and it has given us great satisfaction. 27 If you now continue to keep faith with us, we shall make you a handsome return for what you do on our behalf. 28 We shall accord you many exemptions and grant you privileges.

29 'Henceforth I release you and exempt all the Jews from the tribute, the salt dues and the crown levies, 30 and whereas I am entitled to one-third of the grain and one-half of the fruit of the trees, I release from this levy, from today and for the future, Judaea and the three districts annexed to it from Samaria-Galilee, from this day henceforth in perpetuity. 31 Jerusalem will be sacred and exempt, with its territory, from tithes and dues. 32 I relinquish control of the Citadel in Jerusalem and make it over to the high priest, so that he may man it with a garrison of his own choosing. 33 Every Jewish person taken from Judaea into captivity in any part of my kingdom I set free without ransom, and decree that all will be exempt from taxes, even on their livestock. 34 All festivals, Sabbaths, New Moons and days of special observance, and the three days before and three days after a festival, will be days of exemption and quittance for all the Jews in my kingdom, 35 and no one will have the right to exact payment from, or to molest, any of them for any matter whatsoever.

36 'Jews will be enrolled in the king's forces to the number of thirty thousand men and receive maintenance on the same scale as the rest of the king's forces. 37 Some of them will be stationed in the king's major fortresses, and from among others appointments will be made to positions of trust in the kingdom. Their officers and commanders will be appointed from their own number and will live under their own laws, as the king has prescribed for Judaea.

38 'As regards the three districts annexed to Judaea from the province of Samaria, these will be integrated into Judaea and considered as coming under one governor, obeying the high priest's authority and no other. 39 Ptolemais and the land thereto pertaining I present to the sanctuary in Jerusalem, to meet the necessary expenses of public worship. 40 And I make a personal grant of fifteen thousand silver shekels annually chargeable to the royal revenue from appropriate places. 41 And the entire surplus, which has not been paid in by the officials as in previous years, will henceforth be paid over by them for work on the Temple. 42 In addition, the sum of five thousand silver shekels, levied annually on the profits of the sanctuary, as shown in the annual accounts, is also relinquished as the perquisite of the priests who perform the liturgy. 43 Anyone who takes refuge in the Temple in Jerusalem or any of its precincts, when in debt to the royal exchequer or otherwise, will be discharged in full possession of all the goods he owns in my kingdom. 44 As regards the building and restoration of the sanctuary, the expense of the work will be met from the royal exchequer. 45 The reconstruction of the walls of Jerusalem and the fortification of the perimeter will also be a charge on the royal exchequer, as also the reconstruction of other city walls in Judaea.'

Jonathan rejects Demetrius' offers; death of Demetrius

46 When Jonathan and the people heard these proposals, they put no faith in them and refused to accept them, remembering what great wrongs Demetrius had done to Israel and how cruelly he had oppressed them. 47 They decided in favour of Alexander, since he seemed to offer the better inducements of the two, and they became his constant allies. 48 King Alexander now mustered large forces and advanced against Demetrius. 49 The two kings met in battle. Demetrius' army was defeated, and Alexander pursued him energetically. 50 He continued the battle with vigour until sunset. And that day Demetrius was killed.

Alexander's marriage with Cleopatra
Jonathan as commander-in-chief and governor-general

51 Alexander sent ambassadors to Ptolemy
king of Egypt, with this message:

52 'Since I have returned to my kingdom,
have ascended the throne of my ancestors,
have gained control by crushing Deme-
trius, and so recovered our country — 53 for
I fought him and we crushed both him and
his army, and I now occupy his royal
throne — 54 let us now make a treaty of
friendship. Give me your daughter in
marriage: as your son-in-law, I shall give
you, and her, presents which are worthy
of you.'

55 King Ptolemy replied as follows:

'Happy the day when you returned to the
land of your ancestors and ascended their
royal throne! 56 I shall at once do for you
what your letter proposes; but meet me at
Ptolemais, so that we can see one another,
and I shall become your father-in-law, as
you have asked.'

57 Ptolemy left Egypt with his daughter
Cleopatra and reached Ptolemais in the year
162. 58 King Alexander went to meet him, and
Ptolemy gave him the hand of his daughter
Cleopatra and celebrated her wedding in
Ptolemais with great magnificence, as kings
do. 59 King Alexander then wrote to Jonathan
to come and meet him. 60 Jonathan made his
way in state to Ptolemais and met the two
kings; he gave them and their friends silver
and gold, and many gifts, and made a favour-
able impression on them. 61 A number of
scoundrels, the pest of Israel, combined to
denounce him, but the king paid no attention
to them. 62 In fact, the king commanded
that Jonathan should be divested of his own
garments and clothed in the purple, which
was done. 63 The king then seated him by his
side and said to his officers, 'Escort him into
the centre of the city and proclaim that no
one is to bring charges against him on any
count; no one is to molest him for any reason.'
64 And so, when his accusers saw the honour
done him by this proclamation, and Jonathan
himself invested in the purple, they all fled.
65 The king did him the honour of enrolling
him among the First Friends, and appointed
him commander-in-chief and governor-
general. 66 Jonathan then returned to Jeru-
salem in peace and gladness.

Demetrius II
Apollonius, governor of Coele-Syria, defeated by Jonathan

67 In the year 165, Demetrius son of Deme-
trius came from Crete to the land of his
ancestors. 68 When King Alexander heard of
it he was plunged into gloom, and retired to
Antioch. 69 Demetrius confirmed Apollonius
as governor of Coele-Syria; the latter
assembled a large force, encamped at Jamnia
and sent the following message to Jonathan
the high priest:

70 'You are entirely alone in rising against
us, and now I find myself ridiculed and
reproached on your account. Why do you
use your authority to our disadvantage in
the mountains? 71 If you are so confident in
your forces, come down now to meet us
on the plain and let us take each other's
measure there; on my side I have the
strength of the towns. 72 Ask and learn who
I am and who the others supporting us are.
You will hear that you cannot stand up to
us, since your ancestors were twice routed
on their own ground, 73 nor will you now
be able to withstand the cavalry or so great
an army on the plain, where there is neither
rock, nor stone, nor refuge of any kind.'

74 On hearing Apollonius' words,
Jonathan's spirit was roused; he picked ten
thousand men and left Jerusalem, and his
brother Simon joined him with reinforce-
ments. 75 He drew up his forces outside Joppa,
the citizens having shut him out, since Apol-
lonius had a garrison in Joppa. When they
began the attack, 76 the citizens took fright
and opened the gates, and Jonathan occu-
pied Joppa. 77 Hearing this, Apollonius
marshalled three thousand cavalry and a large
army and made his way to Azotus as though
intending to march through, while in fact
pressing on into the plain, since he had a
great number of cavalry on which he was
relying. 78 Jonathan pursued him as far as
Azotus, where the armies joined battle.
79 Now, Apollonius had left a thousand
horsemen in concealment behind them.
80 Jonathan knew of this enemy position
behind him; the horsemen surrounded his
army, firing their arrows into his men from

morning till evening. [81]But the troops stood
firm, as Jonathan had ordered. Once the
cavalry was exhausted, [82]Simon sent his own
troops into attack against the phalanx, which
he cut to pieces and routed. [83]The cavalry
scattered over the plain and fled to Azotus,
where they took sanctuary in Beth-Dagon,
the temple of their idol. [84]Jonathan, however,
set fire to Azotus and the surrounding towns,
plundered them, and burned down the
temple of Dagon, with all the fugitives who
had crowded into it. [85]The enemy losses,
counting those who fell by the sword and
those burnt to death, totalled about eight
thousand men. [86]Jonathan then left and
pitched camp outside Ascalon, where the
citizens came out to meet him with great
ceremony. [87]Jonathan then returned to Jeru-
salem with his followers, laden with booty.
[88]In the event, when King Alexander heard
what had happened, he awarded Jonathan
further honours: [89]he sent him the golden
brooch, of the kind customarily presented to
the King's Cousins, and gave him proprietary
rights over Ekron and the land adjoining it.

Ptolemy VI supports Demetrius II but dies, as does Alexander Balas

11 The king of Egypt then assembled an
army as numerous as the sands of the
seashore, with many ships, and set out to
take possession of Alexander's kingdom by a
ruse and add it to his own kingdom. [2]He set
off for Syria with protestations of peace, and
the people of the towns opened their gates to
him and came out to meet him, since King
Alexander's orders were to welcome him,
Ptolemy being his father-in-law. [3]On
entering the towns, however, Ptolemy quar-
tered troops as a garrison in each one. [4]When
he reached Azotus he was shown the burnt-
out temple of Dagon, with Azotus and its
suburbs in ruins, corpses scattered here and
there, and the charred remains of those whom
Jonathan had burnt to death in the battle,
piled into heaps along his route. [5]They
explained to the king what Jonathan had
done, hoping for his disapproval; but the
king said nothing. [6]Jonathan went in state to
meet the king at Joppa, where they greeted
each other and spent the night. [7]Jonathan
accompanied the king as far as the river called
Eleutherus, and then returned to Jerusalem.
[8]King Ptolemy for his part occupied the
coastal towns as far as Seleucia on the coast,
all the while maturing his wicked designs
against Alexander. [9]He sent envoys to King
Demetrius to say, 'Come and let us make a
treaty; I shall give you my daughter, whom
Alexander now has, and you shall rule your
father's kingdom. [10]I regret having given my
daughter to that man, since he has tried to
kill me.' [11]He made this accusation because
he coveted his kingdom. [12]Having carried off
his daughter and bestowed her on Demetrius,
he broke with Alexander, and their enmity
became open. [13]Ptolemy next entered
Antioch and assumed the crown of Asia; he
now wore on his head the two crowns of
Egypt and Asia. [14]King Alexander was in
Cilicia at the time, since the people of those
parts had risen in revolt, [15]but when he heard
the news, he advanced on his rival to give
battle, while Ptolemy for his part also took
the field, met him with a strong force and
routed him. [16]Alexander fled to Arabia for
refuge, and King Ptolemy reigned supreme.
[17]Zabdiel the Arab cut off Alexander's head
and sent it to Ptolemy. [18]Three days later
King Ptolemy died, and the Egyptian garri-
sons in the strongholds were killed by the
local inhabitants. [19]So Demetrius became
king in the year 167.

Early relations between Demetrius and Jonathan

[20]At the same time, Jonathan mustered the
men of Judaea for an assault on the Citadel
of Jerusalem, and they set up numerous siege-
engines against it. [21]But some renegades who
hated their nation made their way to the king
and told him that Jonathan was besieging the
Citadel. [22]The king was angered by the news.
No sooner had he been informed than he set
out and came to Ptolemais. He wrote to
Jonathan, telling him to raise the siege and
to meet him for a conference in Ptolemais as
soon as possible. [23]When Jonathan heard
this, he gave orders for the siege to continue;
he then selected a deputation from the elders
of Israel and the priests, and took the delib-
erate risk [24]of himself taking silver and gold,
clothing and numerous other presents, and
going to Ptolemais to face the king, whose
favour he succeeded in winning; [25]and
although one or two renegades of his nation
brought charges against him, [26]the king
treated him as his predecessors had treated
him, and promoted him in the presence of all
his friends. [27]He confirmed him in the high-

priesthood and whatever other distinctions
he already held, and had him ranked among
the First Friends. 28 Jonathan asked the king
to exempt Judaea and the three Samaritan
districts from taxation, promising him three
hundred talents in return. 29 The king
consented, and wrote Jonathan a rescript
covering the whole matter, in these terms:

A new charter favouring the Jews

30 'King Demetrius to Jonathan his
brother, and to the Jewish nation,
greetings.
31 'We have written to Lasthenes our
cousin concerning you, and now send you
this copy of our rescript for your own
information:
32 "King Demetrius to his father Lasth-
enes, greetings.
33 "The nation of the Jews is our ally;
they fulfil their obligations to us, and in
view of their goodwill towards us we have
decided to show them our bounty. 34 We
confirm them in their possession of the
territory of Judaea and the three districts
of Aphairema, Lydda and Ramathaim;
these were annexed to Judaea from Sama-
ritan territory, with all their dependencies,
in favour of all who offer sacrifice in Jeru-
salem, instead of the royal dues which the
king formerly received from them every
year, from the yield of the soil and the fruit
crops. 35 As regards our other rights over
the tithes and taxes due to us, over the salt
marshes, and the crown taxes due to us, as
from today we release them from them all.
36 None of these grants will be revoked
henceforth or anywhere. 37 You will make
yourself responsible for having a copy of
this made, to be given to Jonathan and
displayed on the holy mountain in a
conspicuous place." '

**Demetrius II rescued by
Jonathan's troops at Antioch**

38 When King Demetrius saw that the country
was at peace under his rule and that no
resistance was offered him, he dismissed his
forces, and sent all the men home, except for
the foreign troops that he had recruited in
the foreign island, thus incurring the enmity
of the veterans who had served his ancestors.
39 Now Trypho, one of Alexander's former
supporters, noting that all the troops were
muttering against Demetrius, went to see
Iamleku, the Arab who was bringing up
Antiochus, Alexander's young son, 40 and
repeatedly urged him to let him have the boy,
so that he might succeed his father as king;
he told him of Demetrius' decision and of the
resentment it had aroused among his troops.
He spent a long time there. 41 Jonathan, mean-
while, sent to ask King Demetrius to with-
draw the garrisons from the Citadel in Jeru-
salem and from the other fortresses, since
they were constantly fighting Israel.
42 Demetrius sent word back to Jonathan,
'Not only will I do this for you and for your
nation, but I shall heap honours on you and
your nation if I find a favourable opportunity.
43 For the present, you would do well to send
me reinforcements, since all my troops have
deserted.' 44 Jonathan sent three thousand
experienced soldiers to him in Antioch; when
they reached the king, he was delighted at
their arrival. 45 The citizens crowded together
in the centre of the city, to the number of some
hundred and twenty thousand, intending to
kill the king. 46 The king took refuge in
the palace, while the citizens occupied the
thoroughfares of the city and began to attack.
47 The king then called on the Jews for help;
and these all rallied round him, then fanned
out through the city, and that day killed
about a hundred thousand of its inhabitants.
48 They fired the city, seizing a great deal of
plunder at the same time, and secured the
king's safety. 49 When the citizens saw that
the Jews had the city at their mercy, their
courage failed them, and they made an abject
appeal to the king, 50 'Give us the right hand
of peace, and let the Jews stop their fight
against us and the city.' 51 They threw down
their arms and made peace. The Jews were
covered in glory, in the eyes of the king and
of everyone else in his kingdom. Having won
renown in his kingdom, they returned to
Jerusalem laden with booty. 52 Thus, King
Demetrius sat all the more securely on his
royal throne, and the country was quiet under
his government. 53 But he gave the lie to all
the promises he had made, and changed his
attitude to Jonathan, giving nothing in return
for the services Jonathan had rendered him,
but thwarting him at every turn.

**Jonathan opposes Demetrius II
Simon retakes Beth-Zur
The Hazor incident**

54 After this, Trypho came back with the little
boy Antiochus, who became king and was

crowned. 55 All the troops that Demetrius had summarily dismissed rallied to Antiochus, and made war on Demetrius, who turned tail and fled. 56 Trypho captured the elephants and seized Antioch.

57 Young Antiochus then wrote as follows to Jonathan: 'I confirm you in the high-priesthood and set you over the four districts and appoint you one of the Friends of the King.' 58 He sent him a service of gold plate, and granted him the right to drink from gold vessels, and to wear the purple and the golden brooch. 59 He appointed his brother Simon commander-in-chief of the region from the Ladder of Tyre to the frontiers of Egypt. 60 Jonathan then set out and made a progress through Transeuphrates and its towns, and the entire Syrian army rallied to his support. He came to Ascalon and was received in state by the inhabitants. 61 From there he proceeded to Gaza, but the people of Gaza shut him out, so he laid siege to it, burning down its suburbs and plundering them. 62 The people of Gaza then pleaded with Jonathan, and he made peace with them; but he took the sons of their chief men as hostages and sent them away to Jerusalem. He then travelled through the country as far as Damascus.

63 Jonathan now learned that Demetrius' generals had arrived at Kadesh in Galilee with a large army, intending to remove him from office, 64 and went to engage them, leaving his brother Simon inside the country. 65 Simon laid siege to Beth-Zur, attacking it day after day, and blockading the inhabitants 66 till they sued for peace, which he granted them, though he expelled them from the town and occupied it, stationing a garrison there. 67 Jonathan and his army, meanwhile, having pitched camp by the Lake of Gennesar, rose early, and by morning were already in the plain of Hazor. 68 The foreigners' army advanced to fight them on the plain, having first positioned an ambush for him in the mountains. While the main body was advancing directly towards the Jews, 69 the troops in ambush broke cover and attacked first. 70 All the men with Jonathan fled; no one was left, except Mattathias son of Absalom and Judas son of Chalphi, the generals of his army. 71 At this, Jonathan tore his garments, put dust on his head, and prayed. 72 Then he returned to the fight and routed the enemy, who fled. 73 When the fugitives from his own forces saw this, they came back to him and joined in the pursuit as far as Kadesh where the enemy encampment was, and there they themselves pitched camp. 74 About three thousand of the foreign troops fell that day. Jonathan then returned to Jerusalem.

Jonathan's relations with Rome and Sparta

12 When Jonathan saw that circumstances were working in his favour, he sent a select mission to Rome to confirm and renew his treaty of friendship with the Romans. 2 He also sent letters to the same effect to the Spartans and to other places. 3 The envoys made their way to Rome, entered the Senate and said, 'Jonathan the high priest and the Jewish nation have sent us to renew your treaty of friendship and alliance with them as before.' 4 The Senate gave them letters to the authorities of each place, to procure their safe conduct to Judaea.

5 The following is the copy of the letter Jonathan wrote to the Spartans:

6 'Jonathan the high priest, the senate of the nation, the priests and the rest of the Jewish people to the Spartans their brothers, greetings.

7 'In the past, a letter was sent to Onias, the high priest, from Areios, one of your kings, stating that you are indeed our brothers, as the copy subjoined attests. 8 Onias received the envoy with honour, and accepted the letter, in which a clear declaration was made of friendship and alliance. 9 For our part, though we have no need of these, having the consolation of the holy books in our possession, 10 we venture to send to renew our fraternal friendship with you, so that we may not become strangers to you, a long time having elapsed since you last wrote to us. 11 We, for our part, on every occasion, at our festivals and on other appointed days, unfailingly remember you in the sacrifices we offer and in our prayers, as it is right and fitting to remember brothers. 12 We rejoice in your renown.

13 'We ourselves, however, have had many trials and many wars, the neighbouring kings making war on us. 14 We were unwilling to trouble you or our other allies and friends during these wars, 15 since we have the support of Heaven to help us,

thanks to which we have been delivered
from our enemies, and they are the ones
who have been brought low. 16 We have
therefore chosen Numenius son of Anti-
ochus, and Antipater son of Jason, and
sent them to the Romans to renew our
former treaty of friendship and alliance,
17 and we have ordered them also to visit
you, to greet you and deliver you this letter
of ours concerning the renewal of our
brotherhood; 18 we shall be grateful for an
answer to it.'

19 The following is the copy of the letter sent
to Onias:

20 'Areios king of the Spartans, to Onias the
high priest, greetings.
21 'It has been discovered in records
regarding the Spartans and Jews that they
are brothers, and of the race of Abraham.
22 Now that this has come to our knowl-
edge, we shall be obliged if you will send
us news of your welfare. 23 Our own
message to you is this: your flocks and your
possessions are ours, and ours are yours,
and we are instructing our envoys to give
you a message to this effect.'

Jonathan in Coele-Syria
Simon in Philistia

24 Jonathan learned that Demetrius' generals
had returned with a larger army than before
to make war on him. 25 He therefore left
Jerusalem and went to engage them in the
area of Hamath, not giving them the time to
invade his own territory. 26 He sent spies into
their camp, who told him on their return that
the enemy were taking up positions for a night
attack on the Jews. 27 At sunset, Jonathan
ordered his men to keep watch with their
weapons at hand, in readiness to fight at any
time during the night, and posted advance
guards all round the camp. 28 On learning that
Jonathan and his men were ready to fight,
the enemy took fright and, with quaking
hearts, lit fires in their bivouac and
decamped. 29 Jonathan and his men, watching
the glow of the fires, were unaware of their
withdrawal until morning, 30 and although
Jonathan pursued them, he failed to overtake
them, for they had already crossed the river
Eleutherus. 31 So Jonathan wheeled round on
the Arabs called Zabadaeans, beat them and
plundered them; 32 then, breaking camp, he
went to Damascus, thus crossing the whole
province. 33 Simon, meanwhile, had also set
out and had penetrated as far as Ascalon and
the neighbouring towns. He then turned on
Joppa and moved quickly to occupy it, 34 for
he had heard of their intention to hand over
this strong point to the supporters of Deme-
trius; he stationed a garrison there to hold it.

Building work in Jerusalem

35 Jonathan, on his return, called a meeting
of the elders of the people and decided with
them to build fortresses in Judaea 36 and to
heighten the walls of Jerusalem and erect a
high barrier between the Citadel and the city,
to cut the former off from the city and isolate
it, to prevent the occupants from buying
or selling. 37 Rebuilding the city was a co-
operative effort: part of the wall over the
eastern ravine had fallen down; he restored
the quarter called Chaphenatha. 38 Simon,
meanwhile, rebuilt Adida in the lowlands,
fortifying it, and erecting gates with bolts.

Jonathan falls into the hands of his enemies

39 Trypho's ambition was to become king of
Asia, assume the crown, and overpower King
Antiochus. 40 He was apprehensive that
Jonathan might not allow him to do this, and
might even make war on him, so he set out
and came to Beth-Shean, in the hopes of
finding some pretext for having him arrested
and put to death.
41 Jonathan went out to intercept him, with
forty thousand picked men in battle order,
and arrived at Beth-Shean. 42 When Trypho
saw him there with a large force, he hesitated
to make any move against him. 43 He even
received him with honour, commended him
to all his friends, gave him presents and
ordered his friends and his troops to obey
him as they would himself. 44 He said to
Jonathan, 'Why have you given all these
people so much trouble, when there is no
threat of war between us? 45 Send them back
home; pick yourself a few men as your body-
guard, and come with me to Ptolemais, which
I am going to hand over to you, with the other
fortresses and the remaining troops and all
the officials; after which, I shall take the road
for home. This was my purpose in coming
here.' 46 Jonathan trusted him and did as he
said; he dismissed his forces, who went back

to Judaea. 47With him he retained three
thousand men, of whom he left two thousand
in Galilee, while a thousand accompanied
him. 48But as soon as Jonathan had entered
Ptolemais, the people of Ptolemais closed the
gates, seized him, and put all those who had
entered with him to the sword. 49Trypho sent
troops and cavalry into Galilee and the Great
Plain to destroy all Jonathan's supporters.
50These, concluding that he had been taken
and had perished with his companions,
encouraged one another, marching with
closed ranks and ready to give battle, 51and
when their pursuers saw that they would
fight for their lives, they turned back. 52All
reached Judaea safe and sound, and there
they lamented Jonathan and his companions,
being very frightened indeed; all Israel was
plunged into mourning. 53The surrounding
nations were all now looking for ways of
destroying them: 'They have no leader,' they
said, 'no ally; we have only to attack them
now, and we shall blot out their very memory
from all peoples.'

V: SIMON, HIGH PRIEST AND ETHNARCH OF THE JEWS (143–134 BC)

Simon takes command

13 Simon heard that Trypho had collected
a large army to invade and devastate
Judaea, 2and when he saw how the people
were quaking with fear, he went up to Jeru-
salem, called the people together, 3and
exhorted them thus, 'You know yourselves
how much I and my brothers and my father's
family have done for the laws and the sanc-
tuary; you know what wars and hardships we
have experienced. 4That is why my brothers
are all dead, for Israel's sake, and I am the
only one left. 5Far be it from me, then, to
be sparing of my own life in any time of
oppression, for I am not worth more than my
brothers. 6Rather will I avenge my nation
and the sanctuary and your wives and chil-
dren, now that the foreigners are all united
in malice to destroy us.' 7The people's spirit
rekindled as they listened to his words, 8and
they shouted back at him, 'You are our leader
in place of Judas and your brother Jonathan.
9Fight our battles for us, and we will do
whatever you tell us.' 10So he assembled
all the fighting men and hurried on with
completing the walls of Jerusalem, fortifying
the whole perimeter. 11He sent a considerable
force to Joppa under Jonathan son of
Absalom who drove out the inhabitants and
remained there in occupation.

Simon repels Trypho from Judaea

12Trypho now left Ptolemais with a large
army to invade Judaea, taking Jonathan with
him under guard. 13Simon pitched camp
in Adida, facing the plain. 14When Trypho
learned that Simon had taken the place of his
brother Jonathan and that he intended to join
battle with him, he sent envoys to him with
this message, 15'Your brother Jonathan was
in debt to the royal exchequer for the offices
he held; that is why we are detaining him.
16If you send a hundred talents of silver and
two of his sons as hostages, to make sure that
on his release he does not revolt against us,
we shall release him.' 17Although Simon was
aware that the message was a ruse, he sent for
the money and the boys for fear of incurring
great hostility from the people, 18who would
have said that Jonathan had died because
Simon would not send Trypho the money
and the children. 19He therefore sent both
the boys and the hundred talents, but Trypho
broke his word and did not release Jonathan.
20Next, Trypho set about the invasion and
devastation of the country; he made a detour
along the Adora road, but Simon and his
army confronted him wherever he attempted
to go. 21The men in the Citadel kept sending
messengers to Trypho, urging him to get
through to them by way of the desert and
send them supplies. 22Trypho organised his
entire cavalry to go, but that night it snowed
so heavily that he could not get through for
the snow, so he left there and moved off
into Gilead. 23As he approached Baskama
he killed Jonathan, who was buried there.
24Trypho turned back and regained his own
country.

**Jonathan is buried in the mausoleum
built by Simon at Modein**

25 Simon sent and recovered the bones of his
brother Jonathan, and buried him in Modein,
the town of his ancestors. 26 All Israel kept
solemn mourning for him and long bewailed
him. 27 Over the tomb of his father and
brothers, Simon raised a monument high
enough to catch the eye, using dressed stone
back and front. 28 He erected seven pyramids
facing each other, for his father and mother
and his four brothers, 29 surrounding them
with a structure consisting of tall columns
surmounted by trophies of arms to their
everlasting memory and, beside the trophies
of arms, ships sculpted on a scale to be
seen by all who sail the sea. 30 Such was the
monument he constructed at Modein, and it
is still there today.

The favours of Demetrius II to Simon

31 Now Trypho, betraying the trust of young
King Antiochus, put him to death. 32 He
usurped his throne, assuming the crown of
Asia, and brought great havoc on the country.
33 Simon built up the fortresses of Judaea,
surrounding them with high towers, great
walls and gates with bolts, and stocked these
fortresses with food. 34 He also sent a
delegation to King Demetrius, to get him to
grant the province a remission, since all
Trypho did was to despoil. 35 King Demetrius
replied to his request in a letter framed as
follows:

36 'King Demetrius to Simon, high priest
and Friend of Kings, and to the elders and
nation of the Jews, greetings.

37 'It has pleased us to accept the golden
crown and the palm you have sent us, and
we are disposed to make a general peace
with you, and to write to the officials to
grant you remissions. 38 Everything that we
have decreed concerning you remains in
force, and the fortresses you have built
may remain in your hands. 39 We pardon
all offences, unwitting or intentional, hith-
erto committed, and remit the crown tax
you now owe us; and whatever other taxes
were levied in Jerusalem are no longer to
be levied. 40 If any of you are suitable for
enrolment in our bodyguard, let them be
enrolled, and let there be peace between
us.'

41 The gentile yoke was thus lifted from
Israel in the year 170, 42 when our people
began engrossing their documents and
contracts: 'In the first year of Simon, eminent
high priest, commander-in-chief and ethn-
arch of the Jews'.

The capture of Gezer by Simon

43 About that time Simon laid siege to Gezer,
surrounding it with his troops. He
constructed a mobile tower, brought it up to
the city, opened a breach in one of the
bastions and took it. 44 The men in the mobile
tower sprang out into the city, where great
confusion ensued. 45 The citizens,
accompanied by their wives and children,
mounted the ramparts with their garments
torn and loudly implored Simon to make
peace with them: 46 'Treat us', they said, 'not
as our wickedness deserves, but as your
mercy prompts you.' 47 Simon came to terms
with them and stopped the fighting; but he
expelled them from the city, purified the
houses which contained idols, and then made
his entry with songs of praise. 48 He banished
all impurity from it, settled in it people who
observed the Law, and having fortified it,
built a residence there for himself.

Simon occupies the Citadel in Jerusalem

49 The occupants of the Citadel in Jerusalem,
prevented as they were from coming out and
going into the countryside to buy and sell,
were in desperate need of food, and numbers
of them were being carried off by starvation.
50 They begged Simon to make peace with
them, and he granted this, though he expelled
them and purified the Citadel from its
pollutions. 51 The Jews made their entry on
the twenty-third day of the second month in
the year 171, with acclamations and carrying
palms, to the sound of lyres, cymbals and
harps, chanting hymns and canticles, since a
great enemy had been crushed and thrown
out of Israel. Simon made it a day of annual
rejoicing. 52 He fortified the Temple hill on
the Citadel side, and took up residence there
with his men. 53 Since his son John had come
to manhood, Simon appointed him general-
in-chief, with his residence in Gezer.

Eulogy of Simon

14 In the year 172, King Demetrius
assembled his forces and marched into
Media to raise help for the fight against
Trypho. 2 When Arsaces king of Persia and

Media heard that Demetrius had entered his territory, he sent one of his generals to capture him alive. [3]The general defeated the army of Demetrius, seized him and brought him to Arsaces, who imprisoned him. [4]The country was at peace throughout the days of Simon.

He sought the good of his nation
and they were well pleased
with his authority,
as with his magnificence,
throughout his life.
[5]To crown his titles to glory,
he took Joppa and made it a harbour,
gaining access to the Mediterranean Isles.
[6]He enlarged the frontiers of his nation,
keeping his mastery over the homeland,
[7]resettling a host of captives.
He conquered Gezer, Beth-Zur
and the Citadel,
ridding them of every impurity,
and no one could resist him.
[8]The people farmed their land in peace;
the land gave its produce,
the trees of the plain their fruit.
[9]The elders sat at ease in the squares,
all their talk was of their prosperity;
the young men wore splendid armour.
[10]He kept the towns supplied
with provisions
and furnished with fortifications,
until his fame resounded
to the ends of the earth.
[11]He established peace in the land,
and Israel knew great joy.
[12]Each man sat under his own vine
and his own fig tree,
and there was no one to make them afraid.
[13]No enemy was left in the land
to fight them,
the very kings of those times
had been crushed.
[14]He encouraged the afflicted members
of his people,
suppressing every wicked man
and renegade.
He strove to observe the Law,
[15]and gave new splendour to the Temple,
enriching it with many sacred vessels.

Renewal of the alliances with Sparta and with Rome

[16]When it became known in Rome and as far as Sparta that Jonathan was dead, people were deeply grieved. [17]But as soon as they heard that his brother Simon had succeeded him as high priest and was master of the country and the cities in it, [18]they wrote to him on bronze tablets to renew the treaty of friendship and alliance which they had made with his brothers, Judas and Jonathan, [19]and the document was read out before the assembly in Jerusalem.

[20]This is the copy of the letter sent by the Spartans:

'The rulers and the city of Sparta, to Simon the high priest and to the elders and priests and the rest of the people of the Jews, greetings.

[21]'The ambassadors whom you sent to our people have informed us of your glory and prosperity, and we are delighted with their visit. [22]We have recorded their declarations in the minutes of our public assemblies, as follows, "Numenius son of Antiochus, and Antipater son of Jason, ambassadors of the Jews, came to us to renew their friendship with us. [23]And it was the people's pleasure to receive these personages with honour and to deposit a copy of their statements in the public archives, so that the people of Sparta might preserve a record of them. A copy was also made for Simon the high priest." '

[24]After this, Simon sent Numenius to Rome as the bearer of a large golden shield weighing a thousand *mina*, to confirm the alliance with them.

Official honours decreed for Simon

[25]When these events were reported to our people, they said, 'What mark of appreciation shall we give to Simon and his sons? [26]He stood firm, he and his brothers and his father's house: he fought off the enemies of Israel and secured its freedom.' So they recorded an inscription on bronze tablets and set it up on pillars on Mount Zion. [27]This is a copy of the text:

'The eighteenth of Elul, in the year 172, being the third year of Simon, eminent high priest:

[28]'In Asaramel, in the Grand Assembly of priests and people, of princes of the nation and of elders of the country:

'We are acquainted with the matters following:

[29]'When there was almost incessant

fighting in the country Simon, son of
Mattathias, a priest of the line of Joarib,
and his brothers courted danger and with-
stood their nation's enemies to safeguard
the integrity of their sanctuary and of the
Law, and so brought their nation great
glory;
30 'For when, Jonathan having rallied his
nation and become its high priest and
having then been gathered to his ancestors,
31 the enemy planned to invade the country,
intending to devastate their territory and
to lay hands on their sanctuary, 32 Simon
next came forward to fight for his nation:
spending much of his personal wealth on
arming his nation's fighting men and on
providing their pay; 33 fortifying the towns
of Judaea, as well as Beth-Zur on the
Judaean frontier where the enemy arsenal
had formerly been, and stationing in it a
garrison of Jewish soldiers; 34 fortifying
Joppa on the coast, and Gezer on the
borders of Azotus, a place formerly
inhabited by the enemy, founding a Jewish
colony there, and providing the settlers
with everything they needed to set them
on their feet;
35 'In consequence of which, the people,
aware of Simon's loyalty and of the glory
which he was determined to win for his
nation, have made him their ethnarch and
high priest, for all his services and for the
integrity and loyalty which he has shown
towards his nation, and for having by
every means sought to enhance his people's
power;
36 'It has fallen to him in his time to expel
the foreigners from his country, including
those in the City of David in Jerusalem,
who had converted it into a citadel for their
own use, from which they would sally out
to defile the surroundings of the sanctuary
and to violate its sacred character; 37 to
station Jewish soldiers there instead for the
security of the country and the city; and to
heighten the walls of Jerusalem;
38 'And since King Demetrius has heard
that the Romans call the Jews their friends,
allies and brothers, 39 and that they have
given an honourable reception to Simon's
ambassadors, and, furthermore, 40 that the
Jews and priests are happy that Simon
should, pending the advent of a genuine
prophet, be their ethnarch and high priest
for life 41 therefore he has confirmed him
in the high-priestly office, has raised him
to the rank of Friend and has showered
great honours on him, also confirming him
as their commander-in-chief, 42 with the
right to appoint officials to oversee the
fabric of the sanctuary and to administer
the country, munitions and fortresses; 43 he
is to have personal charge of the sanctuary,
and to be obeyed by all; all official docu-
ments in the country must be drawn up in
his name; and he may assume the purple
and may wear golden ornaments;
44 'Furthermore, it is against the law
for any member of the public or of the
priesthood to contravene any of these
enactments or to contest his decisions, or
to convene a meeting anywhere in the
country without his permission, or to
assume the purple or wear the golden
brooch; 45 and anyone acting contrary to,
or rejecting any article of, these enactments
is liable to punishment;
46 'And since the people have unani-
mously agreed to grant Simon the right to
act as aforesaid, and 47 since Simon, for
his part, has given his assent, and has
consented to assume the high-priestly
office and to be commander-in-chief and
ethnarch of the Jews and their priests, and
to preside over all:
48 'So, be it now enacted: that this record
be inscribed on bronze tablets and be
erected at some conspicuous place within
the precincts of the Temple, 49 and that
copies be deposited in the Treasury for
Simon and his descendants.'

Letter of Antiochus VII and siege of Dora

15 Antiochus son of King Demetrius
addressed a letter from the Mediter-
ranean Isles to Simon, priest and ethnarch of
the Jews, and to the whole nation; 2 this was
how it read:

'King Antiochus to Simon, high priest
and ethnarch, and to the Jewish nation,
greetings.
3 'Whereas certain scoundrels have
seized control of the kingdom of our
fathers, and I propose to claim back the
kingdom so that I may re-establish it as it
was before, and whereas I have accordingly
recruited very large forces and fitted out
warships, 4 intending to make a landing in
the country and to hunt down the men who

have ruined it and laid waste many towns
in my kingdom;
5'I now, therefore, confirm in your
favour all remissions of taxes granted to
you by the kings my predecessors, as well
as the waiving of whatever presents they
may have conceded. 6I hereby authorise
you to mint your own coinage as legal
tender for your own country. 7I declare
Jerusalem and the sanctuary to be free; all
the arms you have manufactured and the
fortresses you have built and now occupy
may remain yours. 8All debts to the royal
treasury, present or future, are cancelled
henceforth in perpetuity. 9Furthermore,
when we have won back our kingdom, we
shall bestow such great honour on yourself,
your nation and the sanctuary as will make
your glory known throughout the world.'

10Antiochus invaded the land of his ances-
tors in the year 174 and, since the troops all
rallied to him, Trypho was left with few
supporters. 11Antiochus pursued the
usurper, who took refuge in Dora on the
coast, 12knowing that misfortunes were piling
up on him and that his troops had deserted
him. 13Antiochus pitched camp outside Dora
with a hundred and twenty thousand fighting
men and eight thousand cavalry. 14He laid
siege to the city while the ships closed in from
the sea, so that he had the city under attack
from land and sea, and allowed no one to go
in or come out.

The ambassadors return from Rome to Judaea The alliance with Rome proclaimed

15Numenius and his companions, mean-
while, arrived from Rome, bringing letters
addressed to various kings and states, in the
following terms:

16'Lucius, consul of the Romans, to King
Ptolemy, greetings.
17'The Jewish ambassadors have come
to us as our friends and allies to renew our
original friendship and alliance in the name
of the high priest Simon and the Jewish
people. 18They have brought a golden
shield worth a thousand *mina*.
19Accordingly, we have seen fit to write to
various kings and states, warning them
neither to molest the Jewish people nor to
attack either them or their towns or their
country, nor to ally themselves with any
such aggressors. 20We have seen fit to
accept the shield from them. 21If, there-
fore, any scoundrels have fled their country
to take refuge with you, hand them over
to Simon the high priest, to be punished
by him according to their law.'

22The consul sent the same letter to King
Demetrius, to Attalus, Ariarathes and
Arsaces, 23and to all states, including
Sampsames, the Spartans, Delos, Myndos,
Sicyon, Caria, Samos, Pamphylia, Lycia,
Halicarnassus, Rhodes, Phaselis, Cos, Side,
Arados, Gortyn, Cyprus and Cyrene. 24They
also drew up a copy for Simon the high priest.

Antiochus VII, besieging Dora, becomes hostile to Simon and sends him a reprimand

25Antiochus, meanwhile, from his positions
on the outskirts of Dora, was continually
throwing detachments against the town. He
constructed siege-engines, and blockaded
Trypho, preventing movement in or out.
26Simon sent him two thousand picked men
to support him in the fight, with silver and
gold and plenty of equipment. 27But Anti-
ochus would not accept them; instead, he
repudiated all his previous agreements with
Simon and completely changed his attitude
to him. 28He sent him Athenobius, one of his
Friends, to confer with him and say, 'You
are now occupying Joppa and Gezer and the
Citadel in Jerusalem, which are towns in
my kingdom. 29You have laid waste their
territory and done immense harm to the
country; and you have seized control of many
places properly in my kingdom. 30Either now
surrender the towns you have taken and the
taxes from the places you have seized outside
the frontiers of Judaea, 31or else pay me five
hundred talents of silver in compensation for
them and for the destruction you have done,
and another five hundred talents for the taxes
from the towns; otherwise we shall come and
make war on you.' 32When the King's Friend,
Athenobius, reached Jerusalem and saw
Simon's magnificence, his cabinet of gold
and silver plate and the state he kept, he
was dumbfounded. He delivered the king's
message, 33but Simon gave him this answer,
'We have not taken foreign territory or any
alien property but have occupied our ances-
tral heritage, for some time unjustly wrested
from us by our enemies; 34now that we have

a favourable opportunity, we are merely
recovering our ancestral heritage. 35 As
regards Joppa and Gezer, which you claim,
these were towns that did great harm to our
people and laid waste our country; we are
prepared to give a hundred talents for them.'
Without so much as a word in answer, 36 the
envoy went back to the king in a rage and
reported on Simon's answer and his magnifi-
cence, and on everything he had seen, at
which the king fell into a fury.

Cendebaeus, governor of the coastal region, harasses Judaea

37 Trypho now boarded a ship and escaped to
Orthosia. 38 The king appointed Cendebaeus
military governor of the coastal region and
allotted him a force of infantry and cavalry.
39 He ordered him to deploy his men facing
Judaea, and instructed him to rebuild
Kedron and fortify its gates, and to make war
on our people, while the king himself went
in pursuit of Trypho. 40 Cendebaeus arrived
at Jamnia and began to provoke our people
forthwith, invading Judaea, taking pris-
oners, and massacring. 41 Having rebuilt
Kedron, he stationed cavalry and troops
there to make sorties and patrol the roads of
Judaea, as the king had ordered.

The victory of Simon's sons over Cendebaeus

16 John then went up from Gezer and
reported to his father Simon what
Cendebaeus was busy doing. 2 At this, Simon
summoned his two elder sons, Judas and
John, and said to them, 'My brothers and I,
and my father's House, have fought the
enemies of Israel from our youth until today,
and many a time we have been successful in
rescuing Israel. 3 But now I am an old man,
while you, by the mercy of Heaven, are the
right age; take the place of my brother and
myself, go out and fight for our nation, and
may Heaven's aid be with you.' 4 He then
selected twenty thousand of the country's
fighting men and cavalry, and these marched
against Cendebaeus, spending the night at
Modein. 5 Making an early start, they
marched into the plain, to find a large army
opposing them, both infantry and cavalry;
there was, however, a stream-bed in between.
6 John drew up facing them, he and his army
and, seeing that the men were afraid to cross
the stream-bed, crossed over first himself.
When his men saw this, they too crossed after
him. 7 He divided his army into two, with the
cavalry in the centre and the infantry on
either flank, as the opposing cavalry was
very numerous. 8 The trumpets rang out;
Cendebaeus and his army were put to flight,
many of them falling mortally wounded and
the rest of them fleeing to the fortress. 9 Then
it was that Judas, John's brother, was
wounded, but John pursued them until
Cendebaeus reached Kedron, which he had
rebuilt. 10 Their flight took them as far as the
towers in the countryside of Azotus, and
John burnt these down. The enemy losses
amounted to ten thousand men; John
returned safely to Judaea.

Simon's tragic death at Dok His son John succeeds him

11 Ptolemy son of Abubos had been appointed
general in command of the Plain of Jericho;
he owned a great deal of silver and gold,
12 and was the high priest's son-in-law. 13 His
ambition was fired; he hoped to make himself
master of the whole country and therefore
treacherously began to plot the destruction
of Simon and his sons. 14 Simon, who was
inspecting the towns up and down the
country and attending to their adminis-
tration, had come down to Jericho with his
sons Mattathias and Judas, in the year 172,
in the eleventh month, the month of Shebat.
15 The son of Abubos lured them into a small
fortress called Dok, which he had built,
where he offered them a great banquet,
having previously hidden men in the place.
16 When Simon and his sons were drunk,
Ptolemy and his men reached for their
weapons, rushed on Simon in the banqueting
hall and killed him with his two sons and
some of his servants. 17 He thus committed a
great act of treachery and rendered evil for
good.

18 Ptolemy wrote a report of the affair and
sent it to the king, in the expectation of being
sent reinforcements and of having the cities
and the province made over to him. 19 He also
sent people to Gezer to murder John, and sent
written orders to the military commanders to
come to him so that he could give them silver,
gold and presents; 20 and he also sent others
to seize control of Jerusalem and the Temple
mount. 21 But someone had been too quick

for him and had already informed John in
Gezer that his father and brothers had
perished, adding, 'He is sending someone to
kill you too!' 22 Overcome as John was by the
news, he arrested the men who had come
to kill him and put them to death, being
forewarned of their murderous design. 23 The
rest of John's acts, the battles he fought and
the exploits he performed, the city walls he
built, and all his other achievements, 24 from
the day he succeeded his father as high priest,
are recorded in the annals of his pontificate.

THE SECOND BOOK OF MACCABEES

The second Book of Maccabees covers the same fifteen years as 1 M 1–7 (167–151 BC). But it is a far more literary and artistic work; rather than giving a continuous history, the author selects suitable incidents and dwells on them to show the heroism of the Jews and their special divine protection. It aims to edify and is often more a sermon than a history, complete with apparitions, divine interventions and noble stories of perseverance.

Each of the two parts of the book (dividing at 10:8) justifies a feast, the Dedication of the Temple and the Day of Nicanor. But apart from its memorable stories the chief importance of the book lies in its theological advance: it gives the first clear teaching on bodily resurrection (7:9), creation out of nothing (7:28), prayer for the dead (12:38) and the intercession of the saints (15:14). It was originally written in Gk and is based on a Hellenistic work by Jason of Cyrene; the compiler added the two initial letters to the Jews of Alexandria, and his own preface and final epilogue, writing probably in 124 BC. Dates in 1 and 2 Maccabees are reckoned from 312 BC.

PLAN OF THE BOOK

THE SECOND BOOK OF MACCABEES

I: LETTERS TO THE JEWS OF EGYPT

FIRST LETTER

1 'To their brothers, the Jews living in
Egypt, from their brothers, the Jews in
Jerusalem and Judaea, greetings and
untroubled peace.
2'May God prosper you, remembering his
covenant with Abraham, Isaac and Jacob, his
faithful servants. 3May he give you all a heart
to worship him and to do his will with a
generous mind and a willing spirit. 4May he
open your hearts to his Law and his precepts,
and give you peace. 5May he hear your
prayers and be reconciled with you, and not
abandon you in time of evil. 6Such is our
prayer for you.
7'During the reign of Demetrius, in the
year 169, we Jews wrote to you as follows,
"In the extremity of trouble that befell us in
the years after Jason and his associates had
betrayed the Holy Land and the kingdom,
8burning down the Temple gateway and
shedding innocent blood, we prayed to the
Lord and were then heard. And we then
offered a sacrifice, with wheat-flour, we lit
the lamps and we set out the loaves."
9'And we now recommend you too to keep
the feast of Shelters in the month of Chislev,
in the year one hundred and eighty-eight.'

SECOND LETTER

Address

10'The people of Jerusalem and of Judaea,
the senate and Judas, to Aristobulus, tutor
to King Ptolemy and one of the family of the
anointed priests, and to the Jews in Egypt,
greetings and good health.

Thanksgiving for the punishment of Antiochus

11'Since we have been rescued by God from
great danger, we give him great thanks for
championing our cause against the king, 12for
he it was who carried off those who had taken
up arms against the Holy City. 13For when
their leader reached Persia with his seemingly
irresistible army, he was cut to pieces in the
temple of Nanaea, as the result of a ruse
employed by the priests who served that
goddess. 14On the pretext of marrying
Nanaea, Antiochus came to the place with
his friends, intending to take its many treas-
ures as a dowry. 15The priests of Nanaea had
put these on display, and he for his part had
entered the temple precincts with only a small
retinue. As soon as Antiochus had gone inside
the temple, the priests shut him in, 16opened
a trap-door hidden in the ceiling and struck
the leader down by hurling stones like
thunderbolts. They then cut him into pieces
and threw his head to those who were waiting
outside. 17Blessed in all things be our God,
who has delivered the sacrilegious over to
death!

The miraculous preservation of the sacred fire

18'As we shall be celebrating the purification
of the Temple on the twenty-fifth of Chislev,
we consider it proper to notify you, so that
you too may celebrate it, as you do the feast
of Shelters and the fire that appeared when
Nehemiah, the builder of the Temple and
the altar, offered sacrifice. 19For when our
ancestors were being deported to Persia, the
devout priests of the time took some of the
fire from the altar and hid it secretly in a hole
like a dry well, where they concealed it in
such a way that the place was unknown to
anyone. 20When some years had elapsed, in
God's good time, Nehemiah, commissioned
by the king of Persia, sent the descendants
of the priests who had hidden the fire to look
for it. When they reported that in fact they
had found not fire but a thick liquid,
Nehemiah ordered them to draw some out
and bring it back. 21When they had done

this, Nehemiah ordered the priests to pour this liquid over the sacrificial materials, that is, the wood and what lay on it. [22]When this had been done, and when in due course the sun, which had previously been clouded over, shone out, a great fire flared up, to the astonishment of all. [23]While the sacrifice was being burned, the priests offered prayer, Jonathan intoning with all the priests, and the rest responding with Nehemiah. [24]The prayer took this form, "Lord, Lord God, Creator of all things, awesome, strong, just, merciful, the only king and benefactor, [25]the only provider, who alone are just, almighty and everlasting, the deliverer of Israel from every evil, who made our fathers your chosen ones and sanctified them, [26]accept this sacrifice on behalf of all your people Israel, and protect your heritage and consecrate it. [27]Bring together those of us who are dispersed, set free those in slavery among the heathen, look favourably on those held in contempt or abhorrence, and let the heathen know that you are our God. [28]Punish those who oppress us and affront us by their insolence, [29]and plant your people firmly in your Holy Place, as Moses promised."

[30]'The priests then chanted hymns accompanied by the harp. [31]When the sacrifice had been burnt, Nehemiah ordered the remaining liquid to be poured over large stones, [32]and when this was done a flame flared up, to be absorbed in a corresponding blaze of light from the altar. [33]When the matter became known and the king of the Persians heard that, in the place where the exiled priests had hidden the fire, a liquid had appeared, with which Nehemiah and his people had purified the sacrificial offerings, [34]the king, after verifying the facts, had the place enclosed and pronounced sacred. [35]To the people on whom the king bestowed it, he granted a part of the considerable revenue he derived from it. [36]Nehemiah and his people termed this stuff "nephtar", which means "purification", but it is commonly called "naphta".

Jeremiah conceals the tent, ark and altar

2 'It is on record that the prophet Jeremiah ordered the deportees to take the fire, as we have described, [2]and how, having given them the Law, the prophet warned the deportees never to forget the Lord's precepts, nor to let their thoughts be tempted by the sight of gold and silver statues or the finery adorning them. [3]Among other similar admonitions, he urged them not to let the Law depart from their hearts.

[4]'The same document also describes how the prophet, warned by an oracle, gave orders for the tent and the ark to go with him, when he set out for the mountain which Moses had climbed to survey God's heritage. [5]On his arrival, Jeremiah found a cave-dwelling, into which he put the tent, the ark and the altar of incense, afterwards blocking up the entrance. [6]Some of his companions went back later to mark out the path but were unable to find it. [7]When Jeremiah learned this, he reproached them, "The place is to remain unknown", he said, "until God gathers his people together again and shows them his mercy. [8]Then the Lord will bring these things once more to light, and the glory of the Lord will be seen, and so will the cloud, as it was revealed in the time of Moses[a] and when Solomon[b] prayed that the holy place might be gloriously hallowed."

[9]'It was also recorded how Solomon in his wisdom offered the sacrifice of the dedication and completion of the sanctuary. [10]As Moses had prayed to the Lord and fire had come down from heaven and burned up the sacrifice, so Solomon also prayed, and the fire from above consumed the burnt offerings. [11]Moses[c] had said, "Because the sacrifice for sin had not been eaten, it was burnt instead." [12]Solomon[d] similarly observed the eight-day festival.

Nehemiah's library

[13]'In addition to the above, it was also recorded, both in these writings and in the *Memoirs of Nehemiah*, how Nehemiah founded a library and made a collection of the books dealing with the kings and the prophets, the writings of David and the letters of the kings on the subject of offerings. [14]Similarly, Judas made a complete collection of the books dispersed in the late war, and

2a Ex 24:16.
2b 1 K 8:10–11.
2c Lv 10:16–17.
2d 1 K 8:65–66.

these we still have. 15 If you need any of them,
send someone to fetch them.

An invitation to the dedication

16 'Since we are about to celebrate the purifi-
cation, we now write, requesting you to
observe the same days. 17 God, who has saved
his whole people, conferring heritage,
kingdom, priesthood and sanctification on
all of us, 18 as he has promised in the Law,
will surely, as our hope is in him, be swift to
show us mercy and gather us together from
everywhere under heaven to the holy place,
since he has rescued us from great evils and
has purified it.'

II: COMPILER'S PREFACE

19 The story of Judas Maccabaeus and his
brothers, the purification of the great
Temple, the dedication of the altar,
20 together with the wars against Antiochus
Epiphanes and his son Eupator, 21 and the
celestial manifestations that came to hearten
the brave champions of Judaism, so that, few
though they were, they pillaged the whole
country, routed the barbarian hordes,
22 recovered the sanctuary renowned the
whole world over, liberated the city and re-
established the laws by then all but abolished,
the Lord showing his favour by all his
gracious help to them— 23 all this, already
related in five books by Jason of Cyrene, we
shall attempt to condense into a single work.
24 Considering the spate of figures and the
difficulty encountered, because of the mass
of material, by those who wish to immerse
themselves in historical records, 25 we have
aimed at providing diversion for those who
merely want something to read, a saving of
labour for those who enjoy committing
things to memory, and profit for each and
all. 26 For us who have undertaken the
drudgery of this abridgement, it has been no
easy task but a matter of sweat and midnight
oil, 27 comparable to the exacting task of
someone organising a banquet, whose aim is
to satisfy a variety of tastes. Nevertheless, for
the sake of rendering a general service, we
remain glad to endure this drudgery,
28 leaving accuracy of detail to the historian,
and concentrating our effort on tracing the
outlines in this condensed version. 29 Just as
the architect of a new house is responsible for
the construction as a whole, while the man
undertaking the ceramic painting has to take
into consideration only the decorative
requirements, so, I think, it is with us. 30 To
make the subject his own, to explore its by-
ways, to be meticulous about details, is the
business of the original historian, 31 but the
person making the adaptation must be
allowed to aim at conciseness of expression
and to forgo any exhaustive treatment of his
subject.

32 So now let us begin our narrative, without
adding any more to what has been said above;
there would be no sense in expanding the
preface to the history and curtailing the
history itself.

III: THE STORY OF HELIODORUS

The arrival of Heliodorus in Jerusalem

3 While the holy city was inhabited in all
peace and the laws were observed as
perfectly as possible, owing to the piety of
Onias the high priest and his hatred of
wickedness, 2 it came about that the kings
themselves honoured the holy place and
enhanced the glory of the Temple with the
most splendid offerings, 3 even to the extent
that Seleucus king of Asia defrayed from his
own revenues all the expenses arising out of
the sacrificial liturgy. 4 But a certain Simon,
of the tribe of Bilgah, on being appointed
administrator of the Temple, came into
conflict with the high priest over the regu-
lation of the city markets. 5 Unable to get the
better of Onias, he went off to Apollonius,
son of Thraseos, who was at that time
commander-in-chief of Coele-Syria and

Phoenicia, [6]and made out to him that the Treasury in Jerusalem was groaning with untold wealth, that the amount contributed was incalculable and out of all proportion to expenditure on the sacrifice, but that it could all be brought under the control of the king. [7]Apollonius met the king and told him about the wealth that had been disclosed to him; whereupon the king selected Heliodorus, his chancellor, and sent him with instructions to effect the removal of the reported wealth. [8]Heliodorus lost no time in setting out, ostensibly to inspect the towns of Coele-Syria and Phoenicia, but in fact to accomplish the king's purpose. [9]On his arrival in Jerusalem, and after a hospitable reception from the high priest and the city, he announced what had been disclosed, thus revealing the reason for his presence, and asked if this was indeed the true situation. [10]The high priest explained that there were funds set aside for widows and orphans, [11]with some belonging to Hyrcanus son of Tobias, a man occupying a very exalted position, and that the whole sum, in contrast to what the evil Simon had alleged, amounted to four hundred talents of silver and two hundred of gold. [12]He also added that it was entirely out of the question that an injustice should be done to those who had put their trust in the sanctity of the place and in the inviolable majesty of a Temple venerated throughout the entire world.

Consternation in Jerusalem

[13]But Heliodorus, because of his instructions from the king, peremptorily insisted that the funds must be confiscated for the royal exchequer. [14]Fixing a day for the purpose, he went in to draw up an inventory of the funds. There was no little consternation throughout the city; [15]the priests in their sacred vestments prostrated themselves before the altar and prayed to Heaven, to the Author of the law governing deposits, to preserve these funds intact for the depositors. [16]The appearance of the high priest was enough to pierce the heart of the beholder, his expression and his altered colour betraying the anguish of his soul; [17]the man was so overwhelmed by fear and bodily trembling that those who saw him could not possibly mistake the distress he was suffering. [18]People rushed headlong from the houses, intent on making public supplication because of the indignity threatening the holy place. [19]Women thronged the streets swathed in sackcloth below their breasts; girls secluded indoors came running, some to the doorways, some to the city walls, while others leaned out of the windows, [20]all stretching out their hands to Heaven in entreaty. [21]It was pitiful to see the people crowding together to prostrate themselves, and the foreboding of the high priest in his deep anguish. [22]While they were calling on the all-powerful Lord to preserve the deposits intact for the depositors, in full security, [23]Heliodorus set about his appointed task.

The punishment of Heliodorus

[24]He had already arrived with his bodyguard near the Treasury, when the Sovereign of spirits and of every power caused so great an apparition that all who had dared to accompany Heliodorus were dumbfounded at the power of God and reduced to abject terror. [25]Before their eyes appeared a horse richly caparisoned and carrying a fearsome rider. Rearing violently, it struck at Heliodorus with its forefeet. The rider was seen to be accoutred entirely in gold. [26]Two other young men of outstanding strength and radiant beauty, magnificently apparelled, appeared to him at the same time and, taking their stand on each side of him, flogged him unremittingly, inflicting stroke after stroke. [27]Suddenly Heliodorus fell to the ground, enveloped in thick darkness. His men came to his rescue and placed him in a litter, [28]this man who but a moment before had made his way into the Treasury, as we said above, with a great retinue and his whole bodyguard; and as they carried him away, powerless to help himself, they openly acknowledged the sovereign power of God.

[29]While Heliodorus lay prostrate under the divine visitation, speechless and bereft of all hope of deliverance, [30]the Jews blessed the Lord who had miraculously glorified his own holy place. And the Temple, which a little while before had been filled with terror and commotion, now overflowed with joy and gladness at the manifestation of the almighty Lord. [31]Some of Heliodorus' companions quickly begged Onias to entreat the Most High to grant the man his life, lying as he did at the very point of death.

[32]The high priest, afraid that the king might suspect the Jews of some foul play concerning Heliodorus, did indeed offer a

sacrifice for the man's recovery. 33And while the high priest was performing the rite of expiation, the same young men again appeared to Heliodorus, wearing the same apparel and, standing beside him, said, 'Be very grateful to Onias the high priest, since it is for his sake that the Lord has granted you your life. 34As for you, who have been scourged by Heaven, you must proclaim to everyone the grandeur of God's power.' So saying, they vanished.

The conversion of Heliodorus

35Heliodorus offered sacrifice to the Lord and made most solemn vows to the preserver of his life, and then took courteous leave of Onias and marched his forces back to the king. 36He openly testified to everyone about the works of the supreme God which he had seen with his own eyes. 37When the king asked Heliodorus what sort of man would be the right person to send to Jerusalem on a second occasion, he replied, 38'If you have some enemy or anyone disloyal to the state, send him there, and you will get him back well flogged, if he survives at all, since some peculiarly divine power attaches to the holy place. 39He who has his dwelling in heaven watches over the place and defends it, and he strikes down and destroys those who come to harm it.' 40This was the outcome of the affair of Heliodorus and the preservation of the Treasury.

IV: HELLENISTIC PROPAGANDA AND PERSECUTION UNDER ANTIOCHUS EPIPHANES

The misdeeds of Simon, administrator of the Temple

4 The Simon mentioned above as the informer against the funds and against his country began slandering Onias, insinuating that the latter had been responsible for the assault on Heliodorus and himself had contrived this misfortune. 2Simon now had the effrontery to name this benefactor of the city, this protector of his compatriots, this zealot for the laws, as an enemy of the public good. 3This hostility reached such proportions that murders were actually committed by some of Simon's agents, 4and at this point Onias, recognising how mischievous this rivalry was, and aware that Apollonius son of Menestheus, the general commanding Coele-Syria and Phoenicia, was encouraging Simon in his malice, 5went to see the king, not to play the accuser of his fellow-citizens, but having the public and private welfare of the entire people at heart. 6He saw that, without some intervention by the king, an orderly administration would no longer be possible, nor would Simon put a stop to his folly.

Jason, the high priest, introduces Hellenism

7When Seleucus had departed this life and Antiochus styled Epiphanes had succeeded to the kingdom, Jason, brother of Onias, usurped the high priesthood: 8he approached the king with a promise of three hundred and sixty talents of silver, with eighty talents to come from some other source of revenue. 9He further committed himself to paying another hundred and fifty, if the king would empower him to set up a gymnasium and youth centre, and to register the Antiochists of Jerusalem. 10When the king gave his assent, Jason, as soon as he had seized power, imposed the Greek way of life on his fellow-countrymen. 11He suppressed the liberties which the kings had graciously granted to the Jews at the instance of John, father of that Eupolemus who was later to be sent on an embassy to negotiate a treaty of friendship and alliance with the Romans and, overthrowing the lawful institutions, introduced new usages contrary to the Law. 12He went so far as to found a gymnasium at the very foot of the Citadel, and to fit out the noblest of his young men in the petasos. 13Godless wretch that he was and no true high priest, Jason set no bounds to his impiety; indeed the hellenising process reached such a pitch 14that the priests ceased to show any interest in serving the altar; but, scorning the Temple and neglecting the sacrifices, they would hurry, on the stroke of the gong, to take part in the distribution, forbidden by the Law, of the oil on the exercise ground; 15setting no

store by the honours of their fatherland, they
esteemed hellenic glories best of all. 16But all
this brought its own retribution; the very
people whose way of life they envied, whom
they sought to resemble in everything,
proved to be their enemies and executioners.
17It is no small thing to violate the divine
laws, as the period that followed will
demonstrate.

18On the occasion of the quadrennial games
at Tyre in the presence of the king, 19the vile
Jason sent an embassy of Antiochists from
Jerusalem, taking with them three hundred
silver drachmas for the sacrifice to Hercules.
But even those who brought the money did
not think it would be right to spend it on the
sacrifice and decided to reserve it for some
other item of expenditure; 20and so what
the sender had intended for the sacrifice to
Hercules was in fact applied, at the sugges-
tion of those who brought it, to the construc-
tion of triremes.

Antiochus Epiphanes is acclaimed in Jerusalem

21Apollonius son of Menestheus had been
sent to Egypt to attend the wedding of King
Philometor. Antiochus, having learnt that
the latter had become hostile to his affairs,
began thinking about his own safety: that
was why he had come to Joppa. He then
moved to Jerusalem, 22where he was given a
magnificent welcome by Jason and the city,
and escorted in by torchlight with accla-
mation. After which, he marched his army
into Phoenicia.

Menelaus becomes high priest

23When three years had passed, Jason sent
Menelaus, brother of the Simon mentioned
above, to convey the money to the king and
to complete negotiations on various essential
matters. 24But Menelaus, on being presented
to the king, flattered him by his own appear-
ance of authority, and so secured the high
priesthood for himself, outbidding Jason by
three hundred talents of silver. 25He returned
with the royal mandate, bringing nothing
worthy of the high priesthood and supported
only by the fury of a cruel tyrant and the rage
of a savage beast. 26Thus Jason, who had
supplanted his own brother, was in turn
supplanted by a third, and obliged to take
refuge in Ammanitis. 27As for Menelaus, he
secured the office, but defaulted altogether
on the sums promised to the king, 28although
Sostratus, the commandant of the Citadel,
whose business it was to collect the revenue,
kept demanding payment. The pair of them
in consequence were summoned before the
king, 29Menelaus leaving his brother Lysi-
machus as deputy high priest, while Sostratus
left Crates, the commander of the Cypriots,
to act for him.

The murder of Onias

30While all this was going on, it happened that
the people of Tarsus and Mallus revolted,
because their towns had been given as a
present to Antiochis, the king's concubine.
31The king therefore hurried off to settle
the affair, leaving Andronicus, one of his
dignitaries, to act as his deputy. 32Thinking
he had found a favourable opportunity,
Menelaus abstracted a number of golden
vessels from the Temple and presented them
to Andronicus, and managed to sell others
to Tyre and the surrounding cities. 33On
receiving clear evidence to this effect, Onias
retired to a place of sanctuary at Daphne
near Antioch and then taxed him with it.
34Menelaus then had a quiet word with An-
dronicus, urging him to get rid of Onias.
Andronicus sought out Onias and, resorting
to the trick of offering him his right hand on
oath, succeeded in persuading him, despite
the latter's lingering suspicions, to leave
sanctuary; whereupon, in defiance of all
justice, he immediately put him to death.
35The result was that not only Jews but
many people of other nationalities were
appalled and outraged by the unjust murder
of this man.

36On the king's return from the region of
Cilicia, the Jews of the capital, and those
Greeks who shared their hatred of the crime,
appealed to him about the unjustified murder
of Onias. 37Antiochus was profoundly
grieved and filled with pity, and he wept for
the prudence and moderation of the dead
man. 38Burning with indignation, he
immediately stripped Andronicus of the
purple, tore his garments off him and,
parading him through the length of the city,
rid the world of the assassin on the very spot
where he had laid impious hands on Onias,
the Lord dealing out to him the punishment
he deserved.

Lysimachus killed in an insurrection

[39]Now Lysimachus with the connivance of Menelaus had committed many sacrilegious thefts in the city, and when the facts became widely known, the populace rose against Lysimachus, who had already disposed of many pieces of gold plate. [40]The infuriated mob was becoming menacing, and Lysimachus armed nearly three thousand men and took aggressive action; the troops were led by a certain Auranus, a man advanced in years and no less in folly. [41]Recognising this act of aggression as the work of Lysimachus, some snatched up stones, others cudgels, while others scooped up handfuls of ashes lying at hand, and all hurled everything indiscriminately at Lysimachus' men, [42]to such effect that they wounded many of them, even killing a few, and routed them all; the sacrilegious thief himself they killed near the Treasury.

Menelaus buys his acquittal

[43]As a result of this, legal proceedings were taken against Menelaus. [44]When the king came down to Tyre, three men deputed by the Senate pleaded their case before him. [45]Menelaus, seeing the case had gone against him, promised a substantial sum to Ptolemy son of Dorymenes if he would influence the king in his favour. [46]Ptolemy then took the king aside into a colonnade, as though for a breath of fresh air, and persuaded him to change his mind; [47]the king then dismissed the charges against Menelaus, the cause of all this evil, while he condemned to death the other poor wretches who, had they pleaded even before Scythians, would have been let off scot-free. [48]No time was lost in carrying out this unjust punishment on those who had championed the cause of the city, the townships and the sacred vessels. [49]Some Tyrians even were so outraged by the crime that they provided sumptuously for their funeral, [50]while, as a result of the greed of the powerful, Menelaus remained in power, growing more wicked than ever and establishing himself as the chief enemy of his fellow-citizens.

Second Egyptian campaign

5 At about this time, Antiochus was preparing for his second attack on Egypt. [2]It then happened that all over the city for nearly forty days there were apparitions of horsemen galloping through the air in cloth of gold, troops of lancers fully armed, [3]squadrons of cavalry in order of battle, attacks and charges this way and that, a flourish of shields, a forest of pikes, a brandishing of swords, a hurling of missiles, a glittering of golden accoutrements and armour of all kinds. [4]So everyone prayed that this manifestation might prove a good omen.

Jason's insurrection; counteraction by Antiochus Epiphanes

[5]Then, on the strength of a false report that Antiochus was dead, Jason took at least a thousand men and launched an unexpected attack on the city. When the walls had been breached and the city was finally on the point of being taken, Menelaus took refuge in the Citadel. [6]Jason, however, made a pitiless slaughter of his fellow-citizens, oblivious of the fact that success against his own countrymen was the greatest of disasters, but rather picturing himself as winning trophies from some enemy, and not from his fellow-countrymen. [7]Even so, he did not manage to seize power; and, in the end, his machinations brought him nothing but shame, and he took refuge once more in Ammanitis. [8]His career of wickedness was thus brought to a halt: imprisoned by Aretas, the Arab despot, escaping from his town, hunted by everyone, detested for having overthrown the laws, abhorred as the butcher of his country and his countrymen, he drifted to Egypt. [9]He who had exiled so many from their fatherland, himself perished on foreign soil, having travelled to Sparta, hoping that, for kinship's sake, he might find harbour there. [10]So many carcases he had thrust out to lie unburied; now he himself had none to mourn him, no funeral rites, no place in the tomb of his ancestors.

[11]When the king came to hear of what had happened, he concluded that Judaea was in revolt. He therefore marched from Egypt, raging like a wild beast, and began by storming the city. [12]He then ordered his soldiers to cut down without mercy everyone they encountered, and to butcher all who took refuge in their houses. [13]It was a massacre of young and old, a slaughter of women and children, a butchery of young girls and infants. [14]There were eighty thousand

victims in the course of those three days, forty thousand dying by violence and as many again being sold into slavery.

Pillage of the Temple[a]

15 Not content with this, he had the audacity to enter the holiest Temple in the entire world, with Menelaus, that traitor to the laws and to his country, as his guide; 16 with impure hands he seized the sacred vessels; with impious hands he seized the offerings presented by other kings for the aggrandisement, glory and dignity of the holy place.

17 Holding so high an opinion of himself, Antiochus did not realise that the Lord was temporarily angry at the sins of the inhabitants of the city, hence his unconcern for the holy place. 18 Had they not been entangled in many sins, Antiochus too, like Heliodorus when King Seleucus sent him to inspect the Treasury, would have been flogged the moment he arrived and checked in his presumption. 19 The Lord, however, had not chosen the people for the sake of the holy place, but the holy place for the sake of the people; 20 and so the holy place itself, having shared the disasters that befell the people, in due course also shared their good fortune; having been abandoned by the Almighty in his anger, once the great Sovereign was placated it was reinstated in all its glory.

21 Antiochus, having extracted eighteen hundred talents from the Temple, hurried back to Antioch; in his pride he would have undertaken to make the dry land navigable and the sea passable on foot, so high his arrogance soared. 22 But he left officials behind to plague the nation: in Jerusalem, Philip, a Phrygian by race, and by nature more barbarous than the man who appointed him; 23 on Mount Gerizim, Andronicus; and, besides these, Menelaus, who lorded it over his countrymen worse than all the others.

Activities of Apollonius the Mysarch

In his rooted hostility to the Jews, 24 the king also sent the Mysarch Apollonius at the head of an army twenty-two thousand strong, with orders to put to death all men in their prime and to sell the women and children. 25 Arriving in Jerusalem and posing as a man of peace, this man waited until the holy day of the Sabbath and then, taking advantage of the Jews as they rested from work, ordered his men to parade fully armed; 26 all those who came out to watch he put to the sword; then, rushing into the city with his armed troops, he cut down an immense number of people.

27 Judas, also known as Maccabaeus, however, with about nine others, withdrew into the desert. He lived like the wild animals in the hills with his companions, eating nothing but wild plants to avoid contracting defilement.

Gentile cults imposed[a]

6 Shortly afterwards, the king sent Gerontes the Athenian to force the Jews to violate their ancestral customs and live no longer by the laws of God; 2 and to profane the Temple in Jerusalem and dedicate it to Olympian Zeus, and the one on Mount Gerizim to Zeus, Patron of Strangers, as the inhabitants of the latter place had requested. 3 The advent of these evils was painfully hard for all the people to bear. 4 The Temple was filled with revelling and debauchery by the gentiles, who took their pleasure with prostitutes and had intercourse with women in the sacred precincts, introducing other indecencies besides. 5 The altar of sacrifice was loaded with victims proscribed by the law as profane. 6 No one might either keep the Sabbath or observe the traditional feasts, or so much as admit to being a Jew. 7 People were driven by harsh compulsion to take part in the monthly ritual meal commemorating the king's birthday; and when a feast of Dionysus occurred, they were forced to wear ivy wreaths and walk in the Dionysiac procession. 8 A decree was issued at the instance of the people of Ptolemais for the neighbouring Greek cities, enforcing the same conduct on the Jews there, obliging them to share in the sacrificial meals, 9 and ordering the execution of those who would not voluntarily conform to Greek customs. So it became clear that disaster was imminent.

10 For example, two women were charged with having circumcised their children. They were paraded publicly round the town, with their babies hung at their breasts, and then

5a ‖ 1 M 1:20–24.
6a ‖ 1 M 1:45–51, 60–61; 2:32–38.

hurled over the city wall. 11Other people,
who had assembled in some near-by caves
to keep the seventh day without attracting
attention, were denounced to Philip, and
were then all burnt to death together, since
their consciences would not allow them to
defend themselves, out of respect for the
holiness of the day.

Providential significance of the persecution

12Now, I urge anyone who may read this
book not to be dismayed at these calamities,
but to reflect that such visitations are
intended not to destroy our race but to disci-
pline it. 13Indeed, when evil-doers are not
left for long to their own devices but incur
swift retribution, it is a sign of great benevol-
ence. 14In the case of other nations, the
Master waits patiently for them to attain the
full measure of their sins before he punishes
them, but with us he has decided to deal
differently, 15rather than have to punish us
later, when our sins come to full measure.
16And so he never entirely withdraws his
mercy from us; he may discipline us by some
disaster, but he does not desert his own
people. 17Let this be said simply by way
of reminder; we must return to our story
without more ado.

The martyrdom of Eleazar

18Eleazar, one of the foremost teachers of the
Law, a man already advanced in years and of
most noble appearance, had his mouth forced
open, to make him eat a piece of pork. 19But
he, resolving to die with honour rather than
to live disgraced, walked of his own accord
to the torture of the wheel, 20having spat the
stuff out, as befits those with the courage to
reject what is not lawful to taste, rather than
live. 21The people supervising the ritual meal,
forbidden by the Law, because of the length
of time for which they had known him, took
him aside and privately urged him to have
meat brought of a kind he could properly
use, prepared by himself, and only pretend
to eat the portions of sacrificial meat as
prescribed by the king; 22this action would
enable him to escape death, by availing
himself of an act of kindness prompted by
their long friendship. 23But having taken a
noble decision worthy of his years and the
dignity of his great age and the well-earned
distinction of his grey hairs, worthy too of
his impeccable conduct from boyhood, and
above all of the holy legislation established
by God himself, he answered accordingly,
telling them to send him at once to Hades.
24'Pretence', he said, 'does not befit our time
of life; many young people would suppose
that Eleazar at the age of ninety had
conformed to the foreigners' way of life 25and,
because I had played this part for the sake of
a paltry brief spell of life, might themselves
be led astray on my account; I should only
bring defilement and disgrace on my old
age. 26Even though for the moment I avoid
execution by man, I can never, living or dead,
elude the grasp of the Almighty. 27Therefore
if I am man enough to quit this life here and
now, I shall prove myself worthy of my old
age, 28and I shall have left the young a noble
example of how to make a good death, eagerly
and generously, for the venerable and holy
laws.'

So saying, he walked straight to the wheel,
29while those who were escorting him,
recently so well disposed towards him,
turned against him after this declaration,
which they regarded as sheer madness. 30He
for his part, just before he died under the
blows, gave a sigh and said, 'The Lord whose
knowledge is holy sees clearly that, though I
might have escaped death, from awe of him
I gladly endure these agonies of body under
the lash, and that in my soul I am glad to
suffer.'

31This was how he died, leaving his death
as an example of nobility and a record of
virtue not only for the young but for the
greater part of the nation.

The martyrdom of the seven brothers

7 It also happened that seven brothers were
arrested with their mother. The king tried
to force them to taste some pork, which the
Law forbids, by torturing them with whips
and scourges. 2One of them, acting as
spokesman for the others, said, 'What are
you trying to find out from us? We are
prepared to die rather than break the laws of
our ancestors.' 3The king, in a fury, ordered
pans and cauldrons to be heated over a fire.
4As soon as these were red-hot, he
commanded that their spokesman should
have his tongue cut out, his head scalped
and his extremities cut off, while the other
brothers and his mother looked on. 5When

he had been rendered completely helpless,
the king gave orders for him to be brought,
still breathing, to the fire and fried alive in a
pan. As the smoke from the pan drifted
about, his mother and the rest encouraged
one another to die nobly, with such words
as these, 6'The Lord God is watching and
certainly feels sorry for us, as Moses declared
in his song, which clearly states that "he will
take pity on his servants." '

7When the first had left the world in this
way, they brought the second forward to be
tortured. After stripping the skin from his
head, hair and all, they asked him, 'Will you
eat some pork, before your body is tortured
limb by limb?' 8Replying in his ancestral
tongue, he said, 'No!' So he too was put to
the torture in his turn. 9With his last breath
he exclaimed, 'Cruel brute, you may
discharge us from this present life, but the
King of the world will raise us up, since we
die for his laws, to live again for ever.'

10After him, they tortured the third, who
on being asked for his tongue promptly thrust
it out and boldly held out his hands,
11courageously saying, 'Heaven gave me
these limbs; for the sake of his laws I have no
concern for them; from him I hope to receive
them again.' 12The king and his attendants
were astounded at the young man's courage
and his utter indifference to suffering.

13When this one was dead they subjected
the fourth to the same torments and tortures.
14When he neared his end he cried, 'Ours is
the better choice, to meet death at men's
hands, yet relying on God's promise that
we shall be raised up by him; whereas for
you there can be no resurrection to new
life.'

15Next they brought forward the fifth and
began torturing him. 16But he looked at the
king and said, 'You have power over human
beings, mortal as you are, and can act as you
please. But do not think that our race has
been deserted by God. 17Only wait, and you
will see in your turn how his mighty power
will torment you and your descendants.'

18After him, they led out the sixth, and his
dying words were these, 'Do not delude
yourself: we are suffering like this through
our own fault, having sinned against our own
God; hence, appalling things have befallen
us—19but do not think you yourself will go
unpunished for attempting to make war on
God.'

20But the mother was especially admirable
and worthy of honourable remembrance, for
she watched the death of seven sons in the
course of a single day, and bravely endured
it because of her hopes in the Lord. 21Indeed
she encouraged each of them in their an-
cestral tongue; filled with noble conviction,
she reinforced her womanly argument with
manly courage, saying to them, 22'I do not
know how you appeared in my womb; it was
not I who endowed you with breath and life,
I had not the shaping of your every part.
23And hence, the Creator of the world, who
made everyone and ordained the origin of all
things, will in his mercy give you back breath
and life, since for the sake of his laws you
have no concern for yourselves.'

24Antiochus thought he was being ridi-
culed, suspecting insult in the tone of her
voice; and as the youngest was still alive he
appealed to him not with mere words but
with promises on oath to make him both rich
and happy if he would abandon the traditions
of his ancestors; he would make him his
Friend and entrust him with public office.
25The young man took no notice at all, and
so the king then appealed to the mother,
urging her to advise the youth to save his life.
26After a great deal of urging on his part
she agreed to try persuasion on her son.
27Bending over him, she fooled the cruel
tyrant with these words, uttered in their
ancestral tongue, 'My son, have pity on me;
I carried you nine months in my womb and
suckled you three years, fed you and reared
you to the age you are now, and provided for
you. 28I implore you, my child, look at the
earth and sky and everything in them, and
consider how God made them out of what
did not exist, and that human beings come
into being in the same way. 29Do not fear this
executioner, but prove yourself worthy of
your brothers and accept death, so that I may
receive you back with them in the day of
mercy.'

30She had hardly finished, when the young
man said, 'What are you all waiting for? I
will not comply with the king's ordinance; I
obey the ordinance of the Law given to our
ancestors through Moses. 31As for you, who
have contrived every kind of evil against the
Hebrews, you will certainly not escape the
hands of God. 32We are suffering for our own
sins; 33and if, to punish and discipline us, our
living Lord is briefly angry with us, he will
be reconciled with us in due course. 34But
you, unholy wretch and wickedest of villains,

what cause have you for pride, nourishing vain hopes and raising your hand against his servants?—[35]for you have not yet escaped the judgement of God the almighty, the all-seeing. [36]Our brothers, having endured brief pain, for the sake of ever-flowing life have died for the covenant of God, while you, by God's judgement, will have to pay the just penalty for your arrogance. [37]I too, like my brothers, surrender my body and life for the laws of my ancestors, begging God quickly to take pity on our nation, and by trials and afflictions to bring you to confess that he alone is God, [38]so that with my brothers and myself there may be an end to the wrath of the Almighty, rightly let loose on our whole nation.'

[39]The king fell into a rage and treated this one more cruelly than the others, for he was himself smarting from the young man's scorn. [40]And so the last brother met his end undefiled and with perfect trust in the Lord. [41]The mother was the last to die, after her sons.

[42]But let this be sufficient account of the ritual meals and monstrous tortures.

V: THE VICTORY OF JUDAISM

THE DEATH OF THE PERSECUTOR AND PURIFICATION OF THE TEMPLE

Judas Maccabaeus and the resistance

8 Judas, otherwise known as Maccabaeus, and his companions made their way secretly among the villages, rallying their fellow-countrymen; they recruited those who remained loyal to Judaism and assembled about six thousand. [2]They called on the Lord to have regard for the people oppressed on all sides, to take pity on the Temple profaned by the godless, [3]to have mercy on the city now being destroyed and levelled to the ground, to hear the blood of the victims that cried aloud to him, [4]to remember too the criminal slaughter of innocent babies and to avenge the blasphemies perpetrated against his name. [5]As soon as Maccabaeus had an organised force, he at once proved invincible to the foreigners, the Lord's anger having turned into compassion. [6]Making surprise attacks on towns and villages, he fired them; he captured favourable positions and inflicted very heavy losses on the enemy, [7]generally availing himself of the cover of night for such enterprises. The fame of his valour spread far and wide.

Campaign of Nicanor and Gorgias[a]

[8]When Philip saw Judas was making steady progress and winning more and more frequent successes, he wrote to Ptolemy, the general officer commanding Coele-Syria and Phoenicia, asking for reinforcements in the royal interest. [9]Ptolemy chose Nicanor son of Patroclus, one of the king's First Friends, and sent him without delay at the head of an international force of at least twenty thousand men to exterminate the entire Jewish race. As his associate he appointed Gorgias, a professional general of wide military experience. [10]Nicanor for his part proposed, by the sale of Jewish prisoners of war, to raise the two thousand talents of tribute money owed by the king to the Romans. [11]He lost no time in sending the seaboard towns an invitation to come and buy Jewish manpower, promising delivery of ninety head for one talent; but he did not reckon on the judgement from the Almighty that was soon to overtake him.

[12]When news reached Judas of Nicanor's advance, he warned his men of the enemy's approach, [13]whereupon the cowardly ones and those who lacked confidence in the justice of God took to their heels and ran away. [14]The rest sold all their remaining possessions, at the same time praying the Lord to deliver them from the godless Nicanor, who had sold them even in advance of any encounter—[15]if not for their own sakes, then at least out of consideration for the covenants made with their ancestors, and because they themselves bore his sacred and majestic name.

[16]Maccabaeus marshalled his men, who numbered about six thousand, and exhorted them not to be dismayed at the enemy or discouraged at the vast horde of gentiles

8a || 1 M 3:38—4:25.

wickedly advancing against them, but to fight bravely, 17keeping before their eyes the outrage committed by them against the holy place and the infamous and scornful treatment inflicted on the city, not to mention the destruction of their traditional way of life. 18'They may put their trust in their weapons and their exploits,' he said, 'but our confidence is in almighty God, who is able with a single nod to overthrow both those marching on us and the whole world with them.' 19He reminded them of the occasions on which their ancestors had received help: that time when, under Sennacherib, a hundred and eighty-five thousand men had perished;[b] 20that time in Babylonia when in the battle with the Galatians the Jewish combatants numbered only eight thousand, with four thousand Macedonians, yet when the Macedonians were hard pressed, the eight thousand had destroyed a hundred and twenty thousand, thanks to the help they had received from Heaven, and had taken great booty as a result.

21Having so roused their courage by these words that they were ready to die for the laws and their country, he then divided his army into four, 22putting his brothers, Simon, Joseph and Jonathan in command of one division each, and assigning them fifteen hundred men apiece. 23Next, he ordered Esdrias to read the Holy Book aloud and gave them their watchword 'Help from God'. Then, putting himself at the head of the first division, he attacked Nicanor. 24With the Almighty for their ally they slaughtered over nine thousand of the enemy, wounded and crippled the greater part of Nicanor's army and put them all to flight. 25The money of their prospective purchasers fell into their hands. After pursuing them for a good while, they turned back, since time was pressing: 26it was the eve of the Sabbath, and for that reason they did not prolong their pursuit. 27They collected the enemy's weapons and stripped them of their spoils, and because of the Sabbath even more heartily blessed and praised the Lord, who had saved them and who had chosen that day for the first manifestation of his compassion. 28When the Sabbath was over, they distributed some of the booty among the victims of the persecution and the widows and orphans; the rest they divided among themselves and their children. 29They then joined in public supplication, imploring the merciful Lord to be fully reconciled with his servants.

The defeat of Timotheus and Bacchides

30They also challenged the forces of Timotheus and Bacchides and destroyed over twenty thousand of them, gaining possession of several high fortresses. They divided their enormous booty into two equal shares, one for themselves, the other for the victims of the persecution and the orphans and widows, not forgetting the aged. 31They carefully collected the enemy's weapons and stored them in suitable places. The rest of the spoils they took to Jerusalem. 32They killed the tribal chieftain on Timotheus' staff, an extremely wicked man who had done great harm to the Jews. 33In the course of their victory celebrations in Jerusalem, they burned the men who had fired the Holy Gates; with Callisthenes they had taken refuge in one small house; so these received a fitting reward for their sacrilege.

The flight and testimony of Nicanor

34The triple-dyed scoundrel Nicanor, who had brought the thousand merchants to buy the Jews, 35finding himself with the Lord's help humbled by men he had himself reckoned as of very little account, stripped off his robes of state, and made his way across country unaccompanied, like a runaway slave, reaching Antioch by a singular stroke of fortune, since his army had been destroyed. 36Thus the man who had promised the Romans to make good their tribute money by selling the prisoners from Jerusalem, bore witness that the Jews had a defender and that they were in consequence invulnerable, since they followed the laws which that defender had ordained.

The last days of Antiochus Epiphanes[a]

9 At about the same time, Antiochus was beating a disorderly retreat from Persia. 2He had entered the city called Persepolis, planning to rob the temple and occupy the city; but the population at once sprang to

8b 2 K 19:35. The next incident is non-biblical.
9a || 1 M 6:1–16.

arms to defend themselves, with the result
that Antiochus was routed by the inhabitants
and forced to beat a humiliating retreat. 3On
his arrival in Ecbatana he learned what had
happened to Nicanor and to Timotheus'
forces. 4Flying into a passion, he resolved to
make the Jews pay for the disgrace inflicted
by those who had routed him, and with this
in mind he ordered his charioteer to drive
without stopping and get the journey over.
But the sentence of Heaven was already
hanging over him. In his pride, he had said,
'When I reach Jerusalem, I shall turn it into
a mass grave for the Jews.' 5But the all-seeing
Lord, the God of Israel, struck him with an
incurable and unseen complaint. The words
were hardly out of his mouth when he was
seized with an incurable pain in his bowels
and with excruciating internal torture; 6and
this was only right, since he had inflicted
many barbaric tortures on the bowels of
others. 7Even so, he in no way diminished
his arrogance; still bursting with pride,
breathing fire in his wrath against the Jews,
he was in the act of ordering an even keener
pace when the chariot gave a sudden lurch
and out he fell and, in this serious fall,
was dragged along, every joint of his body
wrenched out of place. 8He who only a little
while before had thought in his superhuman
boastfulness he could command the waves of
the sea, he who had imagined he could weigh
mountain peaks in a balance, found himself
flat on the ground and then being carried in
a litter, a visible demonstration to all of the
power of God, 9in that the very eyes of this
godless man teemed with worms and his flesh
rotted away while he lingered on in agonising
pain, and the stench of his decay sickened
the whole army. 10A short while before, he
had thought to grasp the stars of heaven; now
no one could bring himself to act as his
bearer, for the stench was intolerable.

11Then and there, as a consequence, in his
shattered state, he began to shed his excessive
pride and come to his senses under the divine
lash, spasms of pain overtaking him. 12His
stench being unbearable even to himself, he
exclaimed, 'It is right to submit to God; no
mortal should aspire to equality with the
Godhead.' 13The wretch began to pray to the
Master, who would never take pity on him
now, declaring 14that the holy city, towards
which he had been speeding to rase it to the
ground and turn it into a mass grave, should
be declared free; 15as for the Jews, whom he
had considered as not even worth burying,
so much carrion to be thrown out with their
children for birds and beasts to prey on, he
would give them all equal rights with the
Athenians; 16the holy Temple which he had
once plundered he would now adorn with the
finest offerings; he would restore all the
sacred vessels many times over; he would
defray from his personal revenue the
expenses incurred for the sacrifices; 17and, to
crown all, he would himself turn Jew and
visit every inhabited place, proclaiming the
power of God.

Antiochus writes to the Jews

18Finding no respite at all from his suffering,
God's just sentence having overtaken him,
he abandoned all hope for himself and wrote
the Jews the letter transcribed below, which
takes the form of an appeal in these terms:

19'To the excellent Jews, to the citizens,
Antiochus, king and commander-in-chief,
sends hearty greetings, wishing them all
health and prosperity.

20'If you and your children are well and
your affairs as you would wish, we are
profoundly thankful. 21For my part, I
cherish affectionate memories of you.

'On my return from the country of Persia
I fell seriously ill, and thought it necessary
to make provision for the common security
of all. 22Not that I despair of my condition,
for I have great hope of shaking off the
malady, 23but considering how my father,
whenever he was making an expedition
into the uplands, would designate his
successor 24so that, in case of any unfore-
seen event or disquieting rumour, the
people of the provinces might know to
whom he had left the conduct of affairs,
and thus remain undisturbed;
25furthermore, being well aware that the
sovereigns on our frontiers and the neigh-
bours of our realm are watching for oppor-
tunities and waiting to see what will
happen, I have designated as king my son
Antiochus, whom I have more than once
entrusted and commended to most of you
when I was setting out for the upland
satrapies; a transcript of my letter to him
is appended hereto. 26I therefore urge and
require you, being mindful of the benefits
both public and personal received from
me, that you each persist in those senti-

ments of goodwill that you harbour towards me. 27I am confident that he will pursue my own policy with benevolence and humanity, and will prove accommodating to your interests.'

28And so this murderer and blasphemer, having endured sufferings as terrible as those which he had made others endure, met his pitiable fate, and ended his life in the mountains far from his home. 29His comrade Philip brought back his body, and then, fearing Antiochus' son, withdrew to Egypt, to the court of Ptolemy Philometor.

The purification of the Temple[a]

10 Maccabaeus and his companions, under the Lord's guidance, restored the Temple and the city, 2and pulled down the altars erected by the foreigners in the market place, as well as the shrines. 3They purified the sanctuary and built another altar; then, striking fire from flints and using this fire, they offered the first sacrifice for two years, burning incense, lighting the lamps and setting out the loaves. 4When they had done this, prostrating themselves on the ground, they implored the Lord never again to let them fall into such adversity, but if they should ever sin, to correct them with moderation and not to deliver them over to blasphemous and barbarous nations. 5This day of the purification of the Temple fell on the very day on which the Temple had been profaned by the foreigners, the twenty-fifth of the same month, Chislev. 6They kept eight festal days with rejoicing, in the manner of the feast of Shelters, remembering how, not long before at the time of the feast of Shelters, they had been living in the mountains and caverns like wild beasts. 7Then, carrying thyrsuses, leafy boughs and palms, they offered hymns to him who had brought the cleansing of his own holy place to a happy outcome. 8They also decreed by public edict, ratified by vote, that the whole Jewish nation should celebrate those same days every year.

VI: THE STRUGGLE OF JUDAS AGAINST THE NEIGHBOURING PEOPLES AND AGAINST LYSIAS, MINISTER OF ANTIOCHUS V

Reign of Antiochus V: early years

9Such were the circumstances attending the death of Antiochus styled Epiphanes. 10Our task now is to unfold the history of Antiochus Eupator, son of that godless man, and briefly to relate the evil effects of the wars. 11On coming to the throne, this prince put at the head of affairs a certain Lysias, the general officer commanding Coele-Syria and Phoenicia, 12whereas Ptolemy, known as Macron, and the first person to govern the Jews justly, had done his best to govern them peacefully to make up for the wrongs inflicted on them in the past. 13Denounced, in consequence, to Eupator by the Friends of the King, he heard himself called traitor at every turn: for having abandoned Cyprus, which had been entrusted to him by Philometer, for having gone over to Antiochus Epiphanes, and for having shed no lustre on his illustrious office: he committed suicide by poisoning himself.

Gorgias and the Idumaean fortresses

14Gorgias now became general of the area; he maintained a force of mercenaries and a continual state of war with the Jews.[b] 15At the same time, the Idumaeans, who controlled important fortresses, were harassing the Jews, welcoming outlaws from Jerusalem and endeavouring to maintain a state of war. 16Maccabaeus and his men, after making public supplication to God, entreating him to support them, began operations against the Idumaean fortresses. 17Vigorously pressing home their attack, they seized possession of these vantage points, beating off all who fought on the ramparts; they slaughtered all who fell into their hands, accounting for no fewer than twenty thousand. 18Nine thou-

10a ‖ 1 M 4:36–61.
10b ‖ 1 M 5:1–8.

sand at least took refuge in two exceptionally
strong towers with everything they needed to
withstand a siege, 19whereupon, Maccabaeus
left Simon and Joseph, with Zacchaeus and
his forces, in sufficient numbers to besiege
them, and himself went off to other places
requiring his attention. 20But Simon's men
were greedy for money and allowed them-
selves to be bribed by some of the men in the
towers; accepting seventy thousand
drachmas, they let a number of them escape.
21When Maccabaeus was told what had
happened, he summoned the people's
commanders and accused the offenders of
having sold their brothers for money by
releasing their enemies to fight them.
22Having executed them as traitors, he at
once proceeded to capture both towers.
23Successful in all that he undertook by force
of arms, in these two fortresses he slaughtered
more than twenty thousand men.

Judas defeats Timotheus and captures Gezer

24Timotheus, who had been beaten by the
Jews once before, now assembled an enor-
mous force of mercenaries, mustering cavalry
from Asia in considerable numbers, and soon
appeared in Judaea, expecting to conquer it
by force of arms. 25At his approach, Macca-
baeus and his men made their supplications
to God, sprinkling earth on their heads and
putting sackcloth round their waists.
26Prostrating themselves on the terrace
before the altar, they begged him to support
them and to show himself the enemy of their
enemies, the adversary of their adversaries,
as the Law clearly states.
27After these prayers, they armed them-
selves and advanced a fair distance from the
city, halting when they were close to the
enemy. 28As the first light of dawn began to
spread, the two sides joined battle, the one
having as their pledge of success and victory
not only their own valour but their recourse
to the Lord, the other making their own
ardour their mainstay in the fight. 29When
the battle was at its height, the enemy saw
five magnificent men appear from heaven on
horses with golden bridles and put them-
selves at the head of the Jews; 30surrounding
Maccabaeus and screening him with their
own armour, they kept him unscathed, while
they rained arrows and thunderbolts on the
enemy until, blinded and confused, they
scattered in complete disorder. 31Twenty
thousand five hundred infantry and six
hundred cavalry were slaughtered.
32Timotheus himself fled to a strongly
guarded citadel called Gezer, where Chaereas
was in command. 33For four days Macca-
baeus and his men eagerly besieged the
fortress, 34while the defenders, confident in
the security of the place, hurled fearful blas-
phemies and godless insults at them. 35At
daybreak on the fifth day, twenty young men
of Maccabaeus' forces, fired with indignation
at the blasphemies, manfully assaulted the
wall, with wild courage cutting down
everyone they encountered. 36Others, in a
similar scaling operation, took the defenders
in the rear, and set fire to the towers, lighting
pyres on which they burned the blasphemers
alive. The first, meanwhile, breaking open
the gates, let the rest of the army in and, at
their head, captured the town. 37Timotheus
had hidden in a storage-well, but they killed
him, with his brother Chaereas, and Apollo-
phanes. 38When all this was over, with hymns
and thanksgiving they blessed the Lord, who
had shown such great kindness to Israel and
given them the victory.

The first campaign of Lysias[a]

11 Almost immediately afterwards,
Lysias, the king's tutor and cousin,
chief minister of the realm, much disturbed
at the turn of events, 2mustered about eighty
thousand foot soldiers and his entire cavalry
and advanced against the Jews, intending to
make the city a place for Greeks to live in,
3to levy a tax on the Temple as on other
national shrines, and to put the office of high
priest up for sale every year; 4he took no
account at all of the power of God, being
sublimely confident in his tens of thousands
of infantrymen, his thousands of cavalry, and
his eighty elephants.
5Invading Judaea, he approached Beth-
Zur, a fortified position about twenty miles
from Jerusalem, and began to subject it to
strong pressure. 6When Maccabaeus and his
men learned that Lysias was besieging the
fortresses, they and the populace with them
begged the Lord with lamentation and tears
to send a good angel to save Israel.

11a || 1 M 4:26–35.

7 Maccabaeus himself was the first to take up
his weapons, and he urged the rest to risk
their lives with him in support of their
brothers; so they sallied out resolutely, as
one man. 8 They were still near Jerusalem
when a rider attired in white appeared at their
head, brandishing golden weapons. 9 With
one accord they all blessed the God of mercy,
and found themselves filled with such
courage that they were ready to lay low not
men only but the fiercest beasts and walls of
iron. 10 They advanced in battle order with
the aid of their celestial ally, the Lord having
had mercy on them. 11 Charging like lions on
the enemy, they laid low eleven thousand of
the infantry and sixteen hundred horsemen,
and routed all the rest. 12 Of those, the
majority got away, wounded and weaponless.
Lysias himself escaped only by ignominious
flight.

Lysias makes peace with the Jews
Four letters concerning the treaty[b]

13 Now Lysias was not lacking in intelligence
and, as he reflected on the reverse he had just
suffered, he realised that the Hebrews were
invincible because the mighty God fought for
them. He therefore sent them a delegation
14 to persuade them to accept reasonable terms
all round, and promised to compel the king to
become their friend. 15 Maccabaeus, thinking
only of the common good, agreed to all that
Lysias proposed, and whatever Maccabaeus
submitted to Lysias in writing concerning
the Jews was granted by the king.
16 Here is the text of the letter Lysias wrote
to the Jews:

'Lysias to the Jewish people, greetings.
17 'John and Absalom, your envoys, have
delivered to me the communication tran-
scribed below, requesting me to approve
its provisions. 18 Anything requiring the
king's attention I have put before him;
whatever was possible, I have granted.
19 Provided you maintain your goodwill
towards the interests of the State, I shall
do my best in the future to promote your
well-being. 20 As regards the details, I have
given orders for your envoys and my own
officials to discuss these with you. 21 May
you prosper.

'The twenty-fourth day of Dioscorus, in
the year one hundred and forty-eight.'

22 The king's letter ran as follows:

'King Antiochus to his brother Lysias,
greetings.
23 'Now that our father has taken his
place among the gods, our will is that the
subjects of the realm be left undisturbed
to attend to their own affairs. 24 We under-
stand that the Jews do not approve our
father's policy, the adoption of Greek
customs, but prefer their own way of life
and ask to be allowed to observe their own
laws. 25 Accordingly, since we intend this
people to be free from vexation like any
other, our ruling is that the Temple be
restored to them and that they conduct
their affairs according to the customs of
their ancestors.
26 'It will therefore be your concern to
send them a mission of friendship, so
that on learning our policy they may have
confidence and happily go about their
business.'

27 The king's letter to the Jewish nation was
in these terms:

'King Antiochus to the Jewish Senate and
the rest of the Jews, greetings.
28 'If you are well, that is as we would
wish; we ourselves are in good health.
29 'Menelaus informs us that you wish
to return home and attend to your own
affairs. 30 Accordingly, all those who return
before the thirtieth day of Xanthicus may
rest assured that they have nothing to fear.
31 The Jews may make use of their own kind
of food and their own laws as formerly, and
none of them is to be molested in any way
for any unwitting offences. 32 I am in fact
sending Menelaus to set your minds at
rest. 33 Farewell.

'The fifteenth day of Xanthicus in the
year one hundred and forty-eight.'

34 The Romans also sent the Jews a letter,
which read as follows:

'Quintus Memmius, Titus Manilius,
Manius Sergius, legates of the Romans, to
the people of the Jews, greetings.
35 'Whatever Lysias, the king's Cousin,
has granted you we also approve. 36 As for
the matters he decided to refer to the king,
consider them carefully and send someone
without delay, if we are to interpret them

11b || 1 M 6:57.

to your advantage, because we are leaving for Antioch. 37 Lose no time, therefore, in sending us those who can tell us what your intentions are. 38 Farewell.

'The fifteenth day of Dioscorus in the year one hundred and forty-eight.'

Incidents at Joppa and Jamnia

12 These agreements once concluded, Lysias returned to the king and the Jews went back to their farming. 2 Among the local generals, Timotheus and Apollonius son of Gennaeus, as also Hieronymus and Demophon, and Nicanor the Cypriarch as well, would not allow the Jews to live in peace and quiet.

3 The people of Joppa committed a particularly wicked crime: they invited the Jews living among them to go aboard some boats they had lying ready, taking their wives and children. There was no hint of any intention to harm them; 4 there had been a public vote by the citizens, and the Jews accepted, as well they might, being peaceable people with no reason to suspect anything. But once out in the open sea they were all sent to the bottom, a company of at least two hundred.

5 When Judas heard of the cruel fate of his countrymen, he issued his orders to his men 6 and after invoking God, the just judge, he attacked his brothers' murderers. Under cover of dark he set fire to the port, burned the boats and put to the sword everyone who had taken refuge there. 7 As the town gates were closed, he withdrew, intending to come back and wipe out the whole community of Joppa. 8 But hearing that the people of Jamnia were planning to treat their resident Jews in the same way, 9 he made a night attack on the Jamnites and fired the port with its fleet; the glow of the flames was seen as far off as Jerusalem, thirty miles away.

The expedition in Gilead[a]

10 When they had left the town barely a mile behind them in their advance on Timotheus, Judas was attacked by an Arab force of at least five thousand foot soldiers, with five hundred cavalry. 11 A fierce engagement followed, and with God's help Judas' men won the day; the defeated nomads begged Judas to offer them the right hand of friendship, and promised to surrender their herds and make themselves generally useful to him. 12 Realising that they might indeed prove valuable in many ways, Judas consented to make peace with them and after an exchange of pledges the Arabs withdrew to their tents.

13 Judas also attacked a certain fortified town, closed by ramparts and inhabited by a medley of races; its name was Caspin. 14 Confident in the strength of their walls and their stock of provisions, the besieged adopted an insolent attitude to Judas and his men, reinforcing their insults with blasphemies and profanity. 15 But Judas and his men invoked the great Sovereign of the world who without battering-ram or siege-engine had overthrown Jericho in the days of Joshua; they then made a fierce assault on the wall. 16 By God's will, having captured the town, they made such indescribable slaughter that the nearby lake, a quarter of a mile across, seemed filled to overflowing with blood.

The battle of the Carnaim[b]

17 Ninety-five miles further on from there, they reached the Charax, in the country of Jews known as Tubians. 18 They did not find Timotheus himself in that neighbourhood; he had already left the district, having achieved nothing apart from leaving a very strong garrison at one point. 19 Dositheus and Sosipater, two of the Maccabaean generals, marched out and destroyed the force Timotheus had left behind in the fortress, amounting to more than ten thousand men. 20 Maccabaeus himself divided his army into cohorts to which he assigned commanders, and then hurried in pursuit of Timotheus, whose troops numbered one hundred and twenty thousand infantry and two thousand five hundred cavalry. 21 Timotheus' first move on learning of Judas' advance was to send away the women and children and the rest of the baggage train to the place called the Carnaim, since it was an impregnable position, difficult of access owing to the narrowness of all the approaches. 22 Judas' cohort came into sight first. The enemy, seized with fright and panic-stricken by the

12a ‖ 1 M 5:24–54.
12b ‖ 1 M 5:37–44.

manifestation of the All-seeing, began to flee,
one running this way, one running that, often
wounding one another in consequence and
running on the points of one another's
swords. 23 Judas pursued them with a will,
cutting the sinners to pieces and killing some-
thing like thirty thousand men. 24 Timotheus
himself, having fallen into the hands of Dosi-
theus and Sosipater and their men, very
craftily pleaded with them to let him go with
his life, on the grounds that he had the
relatives and even the brothers of many of
them in his power, and that these could
otherwise expect short shrift. 25 When at long
last he convinced them that he would honour
his promise and return these people safe and
sound, they let him go for the sake of saving
their brothers.

26 Reaching the Carnaim and the Atarga-
teion, Judas slaughtered twenty-five thou-
sand men.

The return by way of Ephron and Scythopolis

27 Having defeated and destroyed them, he
led his army against Ephron, a fortified town,
where Lysanias was living. Stalwart young
men drawn up outside the walls offered
vigorous resistance, while inside there were
quantities of war-engines and missiles in
reserve. 28 But the Jews, having invoked the
Sovereign who by his power shatters enemies'
defences, gained control of the town and cut
down nearly twenty-five thousand of the
people inside. 29 Moving off from there, they
pressed on to Scythopolis, 30 seventy-five
miles from Jerusalem. But as the Jews who
had settled there assured Judas that the
people of Scythopolis had always treated
them well and had been particularly kind to
them when times were at their worst, 31 he
and his men thanked them and urged them
to extend the same friendship to his race in
the future.

They reached Jerusalem shortly before the
feast of Weeks.

The campaign against Gorgias

32 After Pentecost, as it is called, they marched
against Gorgias, the general commanding
Idumaea. 33 He came out at the head of three
thousand infantry and four hundred cavalry;
34 in the course of the ensuing battle a few
Jews lost their lives.

35 A man called Dositheus, a horseman
of the Tubian contingent, a valiant man,
overpowered Gorgias and, gripping him by
the cloak, was forcibly dragging him along,
intending to take the accursed man alive, but
one of the Thracian cavalry, hurling himself
on Dositheus, slashed his shoulder, and
Gorgias escaped to Marisa. 36 Meanwhile,
since Esdrias and his men had been fighting
for a long time and were exhausted, Judas
called on the Lord to show himself their ally
and leader in battle.

37 Then, chanting the battle cry and hymns
at the top of his voice in his ancestral tongue,
by a surprise attack he routed Gorgias'
troops.

The sacrifice for the fallen

38 Judas then rallied his army and moved on
to the town of Adullam where, as it was
the seventh day of the week, they purified
themselves according to custom and kept the
Sabbath. 39 Next day, they came to find Judas
(since the necessity was by now urgent) to
have the bodies of the fallen taken up and
laid to rest among their relatives in their
ancestral tombs. 40 But when they found on
each of the dead men, under their tunics,
objects dedicated to the idols of Jamnia,
which the Law prohibits to Jews, it became
clear to everyone that this was why these men
had lost their lives. 41 All then blessed the
ways of the Lord, the upright judge who
brings hidden things to light, 42 and gave
themselves to prayer, begging that the sin
committed might be completely forgiven.
Next, the valiant Judas urged the soldiers to
keep themselves free from all sin, having
seen with their own eyes the effects of the
sin of those who had fallen; 43 after this he
took a collection from them individually,
amounting to nearly two thousand drachmas,
and sent it to Jerusalem to have a sacrifice for
sin offered, an action altogether fine and
noble, prompted by his belief in the resurrec-
tion. 44 For had he not expected the fallen to
rise again, it would have been superfluous
and foolish to pray for the dead, 45 whereas if
he had in view the splendid recompense
reserved for those who make a pious end,
the thought was holy and devout. Hence,
he had this expiatory sacrifice offered for
the dead, so that they might be released
from their sin.

The campaign of Antiochus V and Lysias
Horrible death of Menelaus

13 In the year one hundred and forty-
nine, Judas and his men discovered
that Antiochus Eupator was advancing in
force against Judaea, [2]and with him Lysias
his tutor and chief minister; he had moreover
a Greek force of one hundred and ten thou-
sand infantry, five thousand three hundred
cavalry, twenty-two elephants, and three
hundred chariots fitted with scythes.
[3]Menelaus, too, joined them and very
craftily kept urging Antiochus on, not for the
welfare of his own country but in the hope of
being restored to office. [4]But the King of
kings stirred up the anger of Antiochus
against the guilty wretch, and when Lysias
made it clear to the king that Menelaus was
the cause of all the troubles, Antiochus gave
orders for him to be taken to Beroea and there
put to death by the local method of execution.
[5]In that place there is a tower fifty cubits
high, full of ash, with an internal lip all
round overhanging the ashes. [6]If anyone is
convicted of sacrilegious theft or of some
other heinous crime, he is taken up to the top
and pushed over to perish. [7]In such a manner
was the renegade fated to die; Menelaus had
not even the privilege of burial. [8]Deserved
justice, this; since he had committed many
sins against the altar, the fire and ashes of
which were holy, it was in ashes that he met
his death.

The prayers and success of the Jews near Modein

[9]The king, then, was advancing, his mind
filled with barbarous designs, to give the Jews
a demonstration of far worse things than
anything that had happened under his father.
[10]When Judas heard of this, he ordered the
people day and night to call on the Lord as
never before, to come to the help of those
who were in peril of being deprived of the
Law, their fatherland and the holy Temple,
[11]and not to allow the people, just when they
were beginning to breathe again, to fall into
the power of ill-famed foreigners. [12]When
they had all, with one voice, obeyed his
instructions and had made their petitions to
the merciful Lord, weeping, fasting and
prostrating themselves for three days
continuously, Judas spoke words of encour-
agement and told them to keep close to him.
[13]After separate consultation with the elders,
he resolved not to wait for the king's army to
invade Judaea and take possession of the city,
but to march out and settle the whole matter
with the Lord's help.
[14]Having thus committed the outcome to
the Creator of the world, and having exhorted
his soldiers to fight bravely to the death for
the laws, the Temple, the city, their country
and their way of life, he encamped his army
near Modein. [15]Giving his men the password
'Victory from God', he made a night attack
on the king's pavilion with a picked band of
the bravest young men. Inside the camp he
destroyed about two thousand, and his men
cut down the largest of the elephants with its
mahout; [16]having eventually filled the camp
with terror and confusion, they successfully
withdrew, [17]just as dawn was breaking. This
was achieved, thanks to the protection which
the Lord granted Judas.

Antiochus V negotiates with the Jews[a]

[18]The king, having had a taste of Jewish
daring, now tried to capture their positions
by trickery. [19]He advanced on Beth-Zur, a
strong fortress of the Jews, but was checked,
overcome and so repulsed.
[20]Judas supplied the garrison with what
they needed, [21]but Rhodocus, of the Jewish
army, supplied the enemy with secret infor-
mation; the man was identified, arrested, and
dealt with. [22]A second time, the king parleyed
with the garrison of Beth-Zur; he offered and
accepted pledges of friendship, retired, then
attacked Judas and his men, but lost the
battle. [23]He was then told that Philip, left in
charge of affairs, had rebelled in Antioch. He
was stunned by this, opened negotiations
with the Jews, came to an agreement, and
swore to abide by all reasonable conditions.
Agreement reached, he offered a sacrifice,
honoured the Temple, and made generous
gifts to the holy place.
[24]He received Maccabaeus kindly and,
leaving Hegemonides to exercise command
from Ptolemais to the territory of the Gerren-
ians, [25]went to Ptolemais. The inhabitants of
the place disapproved of the treaty; they

13a || 1 M 6:48–63.

complained furiously and wanted to annul its
provisions. 26 Lysias mounted the rostrum
and made a convincing defence of the
provisions which convinced and calmed them
and won their goodwill. He then withdrew
to Antioch.

So much for the episode of the king's
offensive and retreat.

VII: THE CONFLICT WITH NICANOR, GENERAL OF DEMETRIUS I. THE DAY OF NICANOR[a]

Alcimus the high priest intervenes

14 Three years after this, Judas and his
men learned that Demetrius son of
Seleucus had landed at the port of Tripolis
with a strong army and a fleet, 2 and that he
had occupied the country and had killed
Antiochus and his tutor Lysias. 3 A certain
Alcimus, a former high priest, had wilfully
incurred defilement at the time of the insur-
rection; realising that whichever way he
turned there was no security for him, nor any
further access to the holy altar, 4 he went
to King Demetrius in about the year one
hundred and fifty-one and presented him
with a golden crown and a palm, together
with the traditional olive branches from the
Temple; there, for that day, he let the matter
rest.

5 Presently he found an opportunity to
further his mad plan. When Demetrius called
him into his council and questioned him
about the dispositions and intentions of the
Jews, he replied, 6 'Those Jews called
Hasidaeans, who are led by Judas Macca-
baeus, are war-mongers and rebels who are
preventing the kingdom from finding stab-
ility. 7 That is why, after being deprived
of my hereditary dignity—I mean the high
priesthood—I have come here now, 8 first out
of genuine concern for the king's interests,
and secondly, out of a regard for our own
fellow-citizens, because the irresponsible
behaviour of those I have mentioned has
brought no slight misery on our entire race.
9 When your majesty has taken note of all
these points, may it please you to make
provision for the welfare of our country and
our oppressed nation, as befits the gracious
benevolence you extend to all; 10 for, as long
as Judas remains alive, the State will never
enjoy peace.'

11 No sooner had he spoken thus than the
rest of the King's Friends, who were hostile
to Judas' activities, stoked Demetrius' anger.
12 The latter at once selected Nicanor, then
commander of the elephants, promoted him
to the command of Judaea and despatched
him 13 with instructions to dispose of Judas,
disperse his followers and instal Alcimus as
high priest of the greatest of temples. 14 The
foreigners in Judaea, who had fled before
Judas, flocked to join Nicanor, thinking that
the misfortunes and troubles of the Jews
would be to their own advantage.

Nicanor makes friends with Judas

15 When the Jews heard that Nicanor was
coming and that the foreigners were about to
attack, they sprinkled dust over themselves
and made supplication to him who had estab-
lished his people for ever and who never
failed to support his own heritage by direct
manifestations. 16 On their leader's orders,
they at once left the place where they were
and confronted the enemy at the village of
Dessau. 17 Simon, brother of Judas, engaged
Nicanor but, owing to the sudden arrival of
the enemy, suffered a slight reverse.
18 Nicanor, however, had heard how brave
Judas and his men were and how resolutely
they always fought for their country, and he
did not dare allow bloodshed to decide the
issue. 19 And so he sent Posidonius, Theo-
dotus and Mattathias to offer the Jews
pledges of friendship and to accept theirs.

20 After careful consideration of his terms,
the leader communicated them to his troops,
and since they were all clearly of one mind
they agreed to the treaty. 21 A day was fixed
on which the respective leaders were to meet
as individuals. A litter came out from either
side and seats were set up. 22 Judas had posted

14a || 1 M 7.

armed men in strategic positions, in case of a sudden treacherous move by the enemy. The leaders held their conference and reached agreement. 23Nicanor took up residence in Jerusalem and did nothing out of place there; indeed, he sent away the crowds that had flocked to join him. 24He kept Judas constantly with him, becoming deeply attached to him 25and encouraged him to marry and have children. Judas married, settled down and led a normal life.

Alcimus rekindles hostilities, and Nicanor threatens the Temple

26When Alcimus saw how friendly the two men had become, he went to Demetrius with a copy of the treaty they had signed and told him that Nicanor was harbouring thoughts against the interests of the State, and was planning that Judas, an enemy of the realm, should fill the next vacancy among the Friends of the King.

27The king flew into a rage; roused by the slanders of this villain, he wrote to Nicanor, telling him of his strong displeasure at these agreements and ordering him immediately to send Maccabaeus to Antioch in chains.

28When the letter reached Nicanor, he was very much upset, for he disliked the prospect of breaking an agreement with a man who had done nothing wrong. 29Since, however, there was no way of opposing the king, he waited for an opportunity to carry out the order by a stratagem. 30Maccabaeus began to notice that Nicanor was treating him more sharply and that his manner of speaking to him was more abrupt than it had been, and he concluded that such sharpness could have no very good motive. He therefore collected a considerable number of his followers and got away from Nicanor. 31The latter, realising that the man had well and truly outmanoeuvred him, went to the greatest and holiest of Temples when the priests were offering the customary sacrifices, and ordered them to surrender Judas. 32When they protested on oath that they did not know where the wanted man could be, 33he stretched out his right hand towards the Temple and swore this oath, 'If you do not hand Judas over to me as prisoner, I shall rase this dwelling of God to the ground, I shall demolish the altar, and on this very spot I shall erect a splendid temple to Dionysus.' 34With these words he left them. The priests stretched out their hands to heaven, calling on him who has at all times done battle for our nation; this was their prayer: 35'O Lord in need of nothing, it has pleased you that the Temple where you dwell should be here with us. 36Now, therefore, holy Lord of all holiness, preserve for ever from all profanation this House, so newly purified.'

The death of Razis

37Now, a man called Razis, one of the elders of Jerusalem, was denounced to Nicanor. He was a man who loved his countrymen and stood high in their esteem, and he was known as the father of the Jews because of his kindness. 38In the earlier days of the insurrection he had been convicted of Judaism, and he had risked both life and limb for Judaism with the utmost zeal. 39Nicanor, by way of demonstrating the enmity he had for the Jews, sent over five hundred soldiers to arrest him, 40reckoning that if he eliminated this man he would be dealing them a severe blow. 41When the troops were on the point of capturing the tower and were forcing the outer door and calling for fire to set the doors alight, Razis, finding himself completely surrounded, fell on his own sword, 42nobly resolving to die rather than fall into the clutches of these villains and suffer outrages unworthy of his noble birth. 43But in the heat of conflict he missed his thrust, and while the troops swarmed in through the doorways, he ran nimbly upstairs to the parapet and manfully threw himself down among the troops. 44But, as they immediately drew back, he fell into the middle of the empty space. 45Still breathing, and blazing with anger, he struggled to his feet, blood spurting in all directions, and despite his terrible wounds ran right through the crowd; then, taking his stand on a steep rock, 46although he had now lost every drop of blood, he tore out his entrails and taking them in both hands flung them down on the crowd, calling on the Master of his life and spirit to give them back to him one day. Thus he died.

Nicanor's blasphemies

15 Nicanor heard that Judas and his men were in the neighbourhood of Samaria, so he decided to attack them, at no risk to himself, on the day of rest. 2Those Jews who had been compelled to follow him, said,

'Do not massacre them in such a savage,
barbarous way. Respect the day on which the
All-seeing has conferred a special holiness.'
[3]At this the triple-dyed scoundrel asked if
there were in heaven a sovereign who had
ordered the keeping of the Sabbath day.
[4]When they answered, 'The living Lord
himself, the Heavenly Sovereign, has
ordered the observance of the seventh day,'
[5]he retorted, 'And I, as sovereign on earth,
order you to take up arms and do the king's
business.' For all that, he did not manage to
carry out his wicked plan.

Judas harangues his men. His dream

[6]While Nicanor, in his unlimited boastful-
ness and pride, was planning to erect a general
trophy with the spoils taken from Judas and
his men, [7]Maccabaeus remained firm in his
confident conviction that the Lord would
stand by him. [8]He urged his men not to
be dismayed by the foreigners' attacks but,
keeping in mind the help that had come to
them from Heaven in the past, to be confident
that this time too victory would be theirs with
the help of the Almighty. [9]He put fresh heart
into them by citing the Law and the Prophets
and, by stirring up memories of the battles
they had already won, he filled them with
new enthusiasm. [10]Having thus aroused their
courage, he ended his exhortation by demon-
strating the treachery of the foreigners and
how they had violated their oaths.

[11]Having armed each one of them not so
much with the safety given by shield and
lance as with that confidence which springs
from noble language, he encouraged them all
by describing to them a convincing dream—
a vision, as it were. [12]What he had seen was
this: Onias, the former high priest, that
paragon of men, modest of bearing and gentle
of manners, suitably eloquent and trained
from boyhood in the practice of every
virtue—Onias was stretching out his hands
and praying for the whole Jewish
community. [13]Next, there appeared a man
equally remarkable for his great age and
dignity and invested with a marvellous and
impressive air of majesty. [14]Onias began to
speak: 'This is a man', he said, 'who loves
his brothers and prays much for the people
and the holy city—Jeremiah, the prophet of
God.' [15]Jeremiah then stretched out his right
hand and presented Judas with a golden
sword, saying as he gave it, [16]'Take this holy
sword as a gift from God; with it you will
shatter the enemy.'

The disposition of the combatants

[17]Encouraged by the noble words of Judas,
which had the power to inspire valour and
give the young the spirit of mature men,
they decided not to entrench themselves in a
camp, but bravely to take the offensive and,
in hand-to-hand fighting, to commit the
result to the fortune of war, since the city,
their holy religion and the Temple were in
danger. [18]Their concern for their wives and
children, their brothers and relatives, had
shrunk to minute importance; their chief and
greatest fear was for the consecrated Temple.
[19]Those left behind in the city felt a similar
anxiety, alarmed as they were about the
forthcoming encounter in the open country.
[20]Everyone now awaited the coming issue.
The enemy had already concentrated their
forces and stood formed up in order of battle,
with the elephants drawn up in a strategic
position and the cavalry disposed on the
wings. [21]Maccabaeus took note of these
masses confronting him, the glittering array
of armour and the fierce aspect of the eleph-
ants; then, raising his hands to heaven, he
called on the Lord who works miracles, in
the knowledge that it is not by force of arms
but as he sees fit to decide, that victory is
granted by him to such as deserve it. [22]His
prayer was worded thus: 'You, Master, sent
your angel in the days of Hezekiah king of
Judaea, and he destroyed no less than one
hundred and eighty-five thousand of Sen-
nacherib's army; [23]now, once again, Sover-
eign of heaven, send a good angel before us
to spread terror and dismay. [24]May these men
be struck down by the might of your arm,
since they have come with blasphemy on
their lips to attack your holy people.' And on
these words he finished.

The defeat and death of Nicanor[a]

[25]Nicanor and his men advanced to the sound
of trumpets and war songs, [26]but the men
of Judas closed with the enemy uttering
invocations and prayers. [27]Fighting with
their hands and praying to God in their

15a || 1 M 7:43–50.

hearts, they cut down at least thirty-five
thousand men and were greatly cheered by
this manifestation of God. 28 When the
engagement was over and they were with-
drawing in triumph, they recognised
Nicanor, lying dead in full armour.
29 With shouting and confusion all around,
they blessed the sovereign Master in their
ancestral tongue. 30 He who, as protagonist,
had devoted himself, body and soul, to his
fellow-citizens, and had preserved the love
he felt even in youth for those of his own
race, gave orders for Nicanor's head to be cut
off, with his arm up to the shoulder, and
taken to Jerusalem. 31 When he arrived there
himself, he called his countrymen together,
stationed the priests in front of the altar and
then sent for the people from the Citadel.
32 He showed them the head of the abominable
Nicanor, and the hand which this infamous
man had stretched out so insolently against
the holy House of the Almighty. 33 Then,
cutting out godless Nicanor's tongue, he gave
orders for it to be fed piecemeal to the birds,
and for the salary of his folly to be hung up
in front of the Temple. 34 At this, everyone
sent blessings heavenwards to the glorious
Lord, saying, 'Blessed be he who has
preserved his holy place from pollution!'
35 He hung Nicanor's head from the
Citadel, a clear and evident sign to all of the
help of the Lord. 36 They all decreed by public
vote never to let that day go by unobserved,
but to celebrate the thirteenth day of the
twelfth month, called Adar in Aramaic, the
eve of what is called the Day of Mordecai.

Compiler's epilogue

37 So ends the episode of Nicanor, and as,
since then, the city has remained in the
possession of the Hebrews, I shall bring my
own work to an end here too. 38 If it is well
composed and to the point, that is just what
I wanted. If it is worthless and mediocre, that
is all I could manage. 39 Just as it is injurious
to drink wine by itself, or again water alone,
whereas wine mixed with water is pleasant
and produces a delightful sense of well-being,
so skill in presenting the incidents is what
delights the understanding of those who read
the book. And here I close.

INTRODUCTION TO THE WISDOM BOOKS

The five Wisdom books of the Bible are Job, Proverbs, Ecclesiastes (= Qoheleth), Ecclesiasticus (=Ben Sira) and Wisdom. With these are joined Psalms, which contain much Wisdom teaching, and the Song of Songs, because it was reputedly written by Solomon, the master of both Wisdom and song in Israel. These books span nearly 1,000 years: the earliest collection in Proverbs may well go back to Solomon himself (and some of the psalms to David), while the Book of Wisdom is the latest book of the OT.

Wisdom literature existed throughout the ancient East, crossing national boundaries, and the sages of Israel drew freely on Egyptian and Mesopotamian sources. It concerned principally the practical science of living, sane counsels of common sense, and acute observations of character which would enable a young man to avoid pitfalls and make his way in life. There was no particular religious basis, though in Israel there is always in the background the knowledge that true wisdom and true success come from Yahweh. This leads to two special concerns of Israel's Wisdom literature: a concern with human destiny, which, after the agonisings of Job and Qoheleth, and the tranquil confidence of Ben Sira, leads to the Book of Wisdom's assertion of the immortality of the soul. The other concern touches the origin of Wisdom with Yahweh: more and more clearly, through Job and Ben Sira until the latest section of Proverbs and the Book of Wisdom, personified Wisdom is seen as the agent of divine activity in the world, and eventually as participating in the divine nature itself. This prepares for the Christian understanding of the doctrine of the Trinity.

THE BOOK OF JOB

In this masterpiece of poetry the traditional Israelite solution to the problem of suffering as God's punishment for sin is radically reviewed. Job's innocent suffering calls into question the whole system of rewards and punishments in this life, despite the vain efforts of his friends to shore it up by urging him to admit his guilt, or at least his pride, or even that he must have sinned unwittingly. In protesting his innocence (which the reader knows from the Prologue) and rejecting the shallow solutions of these sages, Job clings blindly to God. Even when shrinking from God's torments, Job is confident of God's unfailing care. Paradoxically, though he sees no possibility of a future life, he is somehow sure that after his death he will know God's vindication. In the end his trust is justified by an overwhelming experience of the majesty, the power and the wisdom of God.

The discourses are best situated soon after the Exile, as a reflection on the sufferings then being undergone, though it is dramatically placed in an earlier nomadic period before the revelation of Yahweh. The clear structure of the dialogue is interrupted by two elements: by the hymn in praise of Wisdom, which differs in its view of Wisdom from that held by either Job or his friends, and by the speeches of Elihu, which merely repeat the problem already stated and pre-empt the solution still to come. Both these elements may well stem from the same author, but are not clearly integrated into the dialogue.

PLAN OF THE BOOK

- I Prologue 1—2
- II The Dialogue 3—31
  - **A** First Cycle of Discourses 3—14
  - **B** Second Cycle of Discourses 15—21
  - **C** Third Cycle of Discourses 22—27
  - **D** A Hymn in Praise of Wisdom 28
  - **E** Conclusion of the Dialogue 29—31
- III The Discourses of Elihu 32—37
- IV The Discourses of Yahweh 38:1—42:6
- V Epilogue 42:7–17

THE BOOK OF JOB

I: PROLOGUE

Satan tests Job

1 There was once a man in the land of Uz called Job: a sound and honest man who feared God and shunned evil. [2]Seven sons and three daughters were born to him. [3]And he owned seven thousand sheep, three thousand camels, five hundred yoke of oxen and five hundred she-donkeys, and many servants besides. This man was the most prosperous of all the Sons of the East. [4]It was the custom of his sons to hold banquets in one another's houses in turn, and to invite their three sisters to eat and drink with them. [5]Once each series of banquets was over, Job would send for them to come and be purified, and at dawn on the following day he would make a burnt offering for each of them. 'Perhaps', Job would say, 'my sons have sinned and in their heart blasphemed.' So that was what Job used to do each time.

[6]One day when the sons of God[a] came to attend on Yahweh, among them came Satan. [7]So Yahweh said to Satan, 'Where have you been?' 'Prowling about on earth,' he answered, 'roaming around there.' [8]So Yahweh asked him, 'Did you pay any attention to my servant Job? There is no one like him on the earth: a sound and honest man who fears God and shuns evil.' [9]'Yes,' Satan said, 'but Job is not God-fearing for nothing, is he? [10]Have you not put a wall round him and his house and all his domain? You have blessed all he undertakes, and his flocks throng the countryside. [11]But stretch out your hand and lay a finger on his possessions: then, I warrant you, he will curse you to your face.' [12]'Very well,' Yahweh said to Satan, 'all he has is in your power. But keep your hands off his person.' So Satan left the presence of Yahweh.

[13]On the day when Job's sons and daughters were eating and drinking in their eldest brother's house, [14]a messenger came to Job. 'Your oxen', he said, 'were at the plough, with the donkeys grazing at their side, [15]when the Sabaeans swept down on them and carried them off, and put the servants to the sword: I alone have escaped to tell you.' [16]He had not finished speaking when another messenger arrived. 'The fire of God', he said, 'has fallen from heaven and burnt the sheep and shepherds to ashes: I alone have escaped to tell you.' [17]He had not finished speaking when another messenger arrived. 'The Chaldaeans,' he said, 'three bands of them, have raided the camels and made off with them, and put the servants to the sword: I alone have escaped to tell you.' [18]He had not finished speaking when another messenger arrived. 'Your sons and daughters', he said, 'were eating and drinking at their eldest brother's house, [19]when suddenly from the desert a gale sprang up, and it battered all four corners of the house which fell in on the young people. They are dead: I alone have escaped to tell you.'

[20]Then Job stood up, tore his robe and shaved his head. Then, falling to the ground, he prostrated himself [21]and said:

Naked I came from my mother's womb,
naked I shall return again.
Yahweh gave, Yahweh has taken back.
Blessed be the name of Yahweh!

[22]In all this misfortune Job committed no sin, and he did not reproach God.

2 Another day, the sons of God came to attend on Yahweh and Satan came with them too. [2]So Yahweh said to Satan, 'Where have you been?' 'Prowling about on earth,' he answered, 'roaming around there.' [3]So Yahweh asked him, 'Did you pay any attention to my servant Job? There is no one like him on the earth: a sound and honest man who fears God and shuns evil. He persists in his integrity still; you achieved nothing by provoking me to ruin him.' [4]'Skin after

---

1a God's court and council, the angels. These include Satan, 'the accuser', who is responsible for testing human beings in their faithfulness to God. He is later identified with the spirit of evil.

skin!'[a] Satan replied. 'Someone will give
away all he has to save his life. 5But stretch
out your hand and lay a finger on his bone
and flesh; I warrant you, he will curse you to
your face.' 6'Very well,' Yahweh said to
Satan, 'he is in your power. But spare his
life.' 7So Satan left the presence of
Yahweh.

He struck Job down with malignant ulcers
from the sole of his foot to the top of his head.
8Job took a piece of pot to scrape himself,
and went and sat among the ashes. 9Then his
wife said to him, 'Why persist in this integrity
of yours? Curse God and die.' 10'That is how
a fool of a woman talks,' Job replied. 'If we
take happiness from God's hand, must we
not take sorrow too?' And in all this misfor-
tune Job uttered no sinful word.

11The news of all the disasters that had
fallen on Job came to the ears of three of his
friends. Each of them set out from home—
Eliphaz of Teman, Bildad of Shuah and
Zophar of Naamath—and by common
consent they decided to go and offer him
sympathy and consolation. 12Looking at him
from a distance, they could not recognise
him; they wept aloud and tore their robes
and threw dust over their heads. 13They sat
there on the ground beside him for seven
days and seven nights. To Job they spoke
never a word, for they saw how much he was
suffering.

II: THE DIALOGUE

A: FIRST CYCLE OF DISCOURSES

Job curses the day of his birth

3 In the end it was Job who broke the silence and cursed the day of his birth. 2This is what
he said:

3Perish the day on which I was born
and the night that told of a boy conceived.
4May that day be darkness,
may God on high have no thought for it,
may no light shine on it.
5May murk and shadow dark as death claim it for their own,
clouds hang over it,
eclipse swoop down on it.
6See! Let obscurity seize on it,
from the days of the year let it be excluded,
into the reckoning of the months not find its way.
7And may that night be sterile,
devoid of any cries of joy!
8Let it be cursed by those who curse certain days[a]
and are ready to rouse Leviathan.
9Dark be the stars of its morning,
let it wait in vain for light
and never see the opening eyes of dawn.
10Since it would not shut the doors of the womb on me
to hide sorrow from my eyes.

11Why was I not still-born,
or why did I not perish as I left the womb?
12Why were there knees to receive me,
breasts for me to suck?

2a Proverb, meaning perhaps that physical hurt is worse than progressive loss of goods.
3a Sorcerers. Leviathan is the monster of primeval chaos, always lurking to engulf order.

13 Now I should be lying in peace,
wrapped in a restful slumber,
14 with the kings and high viziers of earth
who have built their dwellings in desolate places,
15 or with princes who have quantities of gold
and silver cramming their tombs;
16 or, put away like an abortive child, I should not have existed,
like little ones that never see the light.
17 Down there, the wicked bustle no more,
there the weary rest.
18 Prisoners, all left in peace,
hear no more the shouts of the oppressor.
19 High and low are there together,
and the slave is free of his master.
20 Why give light to a man of grief?
Why give life to those bitter of heart,
21 who long for a death that never comes,
and hunt for it more than for buried treasure?
22 They would be glad to see the grave-mound
and shout with joy if they reached the tomb.
23 Why give light to one who does not see his way,
whom God shuts in all alone?

24 My only food is sighs,
and my groans pour out like water.
25 Whatever I fear comes true,
whatever I dread befalls me.
26 For me, there is no calm, no peace;
my torments banish rest.

Confidence in God

4 Eliphaz of Teman spoke next. He said:

2 If we say something to you, will you bear with us?
Who in any case could refrain from speaking now?
3 You have schooled many others,
giving strength to feeble hands;
4 your words supported any who wavered
and strengthened every failing knee.
5 And now your turn has come, and you lose patience,
at the first touch on yourself you are overwhelmed!
6 Does not your piety give you confidence,
and your integrity of life give you hope?
7 Can you recall anyone guiltless that perished?
Where then have the honest been wiped out?
8 I speak from experience: those who plough iniquity
and sow disaster, reap just that.
9 Under the breath of God, they perish:
a blast of his anger, and they are destroyed;
10 the lion's roars, his savage growls,
like the fangs of a lion cub, are broken off.
11 The lion dies for lack of prey
and the lioness's whelps are dispersed.
12 I have received a secret revelation,
a whisper has come to my ears;

13 by night when dreams confuse the mind
and slumber lies heavy on everyone,
14 a shiver of horror ran through me
and filled all my bones with fright.
15 A breath slid over my face,
the hairs of my body bristled.
16 Someone stood there—I did not know his face,
but the form stayed there before my eyes.
Silence—then I heard a voice,
17 'Can a mortal seem upright to God,
would anybody seem pure in the presence of his Maker?
18 God cannot rely even on his own servants,
even with his angels he finds fault.
19 What then of those who live in houses of clay,
who are founded on dust?
20 They are crushed as easily as a moth,
between morning and evening they are ground to powder.
They vanish for ever, with no one to bring them back.
21 Their tent-peg is snatched from them,
and they die devoid of wisdom.'

5 Make your appeal then. Will you find an answer?
To which of the holy ones will you turn?
2 Resentment kills the senseless,
and anger brings death to the fool.
3 I have seen the senseless taking root,
when a curse fell suddenly on his house.
4 His children are deprived of prop and stay,
ruined at the gate, and no one to defend them;
5 their harvest goes to feed the hungry,
God snatches it from their mouths,
and covetous people thirst for their possessions.
6 No, misery does not grow out of the soil,
nor sorrow spring from the ground.
7 It is people who breed trouble for themselves
as surely as eagles fly to the height.
8 If I were you, I should appeal to God
and lay my case before him.
9 His works are great, past all reckoning,
marvels beyond all counting.
10 He sends down rain to the earth,
pours down water on the fields.
11 If his will is to raise up the downcast,
or exalt the afflicted to the heights of prosperity,
12 he frustrates the plans of the artful
so that they cannot succeed in their intrigues.
13 He traps the crafty in the snare of their own trickery,
throws the plans of the cunning into disarray.
14 In daylight they come up against darkness,
and grope their way as if noon were night.
15 He rescues the bankrupt from their jaws,
and the needy from the grasp of the mighty.
16 Hope springs afresh for the weak,
and wickedness must shut its mouth.

17 Blessed are those whom God corrects!

Do not then scorn the lesson of Shaddai![a]
18 For he who wounds is he who soothes the sore,
and the hand that hurts is the hand that heals.
19 Six times he will deliver you from sorrow,
and the seventh time, evil will not touch you.
20 In time of famine, he will save you from death,
and in wartime from the stroke of the sword.
21 You will be safe from the lash of the tongue,
unafraid at the approach of the despoiler.
22 You will laugh at drought and frost,
and have no fear of the beasts of the earth.
23 You will have a pact with the stones of the field,
and live in amity with wild beasts.
24 You will know that your tent is secure,
and your sheepfold unharmed when you inspect it.
25 You will see your descendants multiply,
your offspring grow like the grass in the fields.
26 At a ripe age you will go to the grave,
like a wheatsheaf stacked in due season.
27 All this we have observed and it is so!
Heed it, you will be the wiser for it!

Only the sufferer knows his own grief

6 Job spoke next. He said:

2 If only my misery could be weighed,
and all my ills be put together on the scales!
3 But they outweigh the sands of the seas:
what wonder then if my words are wild?
4 The arrows of Shaddai stick fast in me,
my spirit absorbs their poison,
God's terrors stand paraded against me.
5 Does a wild donkey bray when it has grass,
or an ox low when its fodder is within reach?
6 Is not food insipid, eaten without salt,
is there any taste in egg-white?
7 But the very things my appetite revolts at
are now my diet in sickness.
8 Will no one hear my prayer,
will not God himself grant my hope?
9 May it please God to crush me,
to give his hand free play and do away with me!
10 This thought, at least, would give me comfort
(a thrill of joy in unrelenting pain),
that I never rebelled against the Holy One's decrees.
11 But have I the strength to go on waiting?
And why be patient, when doomed to such an end?
12 Is mine the strength of stone,
is my flesh made of bronze?
13 Can I support myself on nothing?
Has not all help deserted me?
14 Refuse faithful love to your neighbour
and you forsake the fear of Shaddai.

5a A name of God in patriarchal times, the dramatic setting of the dialogues.

15 Like the torrent, my brothers have proved deceptive,
as fleeting torrents they flow:
16 the ice makes their waters turgid
when, above them, the snow melts,
17 but, come the burning summer, they run dry,
they vanish in the heat of the sun.
18 Caravans leave the trail to find them,
go deep into wastelands, and are lost.
19 The caravans of Tema look to them,
and on them Sheba's convoys build their hopes.
20 Their trust brings only embarrassment,
they reach them only to be thwarted.

21 And this is how you now treat me,
terrified at the sight of me, you take fright.
22 Have I said to you, 'Give me something,
make some present for me at your own cost,
23 snatch me from the grasp of an oppressor,
ransom me from the grip of a violent man'?
24 Put me right, and I shall say no more;
show me where I have been at fault.
25 Fair comment can be borne without resentment,
but what are your strictures aimed at?
26 Do you think mere words deserve censure,
desperate speech that the wind blows away?
27 Soon you will be haggling over the price of an orphan,
and selling your friend at bargain price!
28 Come, I beg you, look at me:
man to man, I shall not lie.
29 Relent then, no harm is done;
relent then, since I am upright.
30 Is evil to be found on my lips?
Can I not recognise misfortune when I taste it?

7 Is not human life on earth just conscript service?
Do we not live a hireling's life?
2 Like a slave, sighing for the shade,
or a hireling with no thought but for his wages,
3 I have months of futility assigned to me,
nights of suffering to be my lot.
4 Lying in bed I wonder, 'When will it be day?'
No sooner up than, 'When will evening come?'
And crazy thoughts obsess me till twilight falls.
5 Vermin and loathsome scabs cover my body;
my skin is cracked and oozes pus.
6 Swifter than a weaver's shuttle my days have passed,
and vanished, leaving no hope behind.
7 Remember that my life is but a breath,
and that my eyes will never again see joy.
8 The eye that once saw me will look on me no more,
your eyes will turn my way, and I shall not be there.
9 A cloud dissolves and is gone,
so no one who goes down to Sheol ever comes up again,
10 ever comes home again,
and his house knows that person no more.
11 That is why I cannot keep quiet:
in my anguish of spirit I shall speak,

in my bitterness of soul I shall complain.
12 Am I the Sea,[a] or some sea monster,
that you should keep me under guard?
13 If I say, 'My bed will comfort me,
my couch will lighten my complaints,'
14 you then frighten me with dreams
and terrify me with visions,
15 so that strangling would seem welcome in comparison,
yes, death preferable to what I suffer.
16 I am wasting away, my life is not unending;
leave me then, for my days are but a breath.
17 What are human beings that you should take them so seriously,
subjecting them to your scrutiny,
18 that morning after morning you should examine them
and at every instant test them?
19 Will you never take your eyes off me
long enough for me to swallow my spittle?
20 Suppose I have sinned, what have I done to you,
you tireless watcher of humanity?
Why do you choose me as your target?
Why should I be a burden to you?
21 Can you not tolerate my sin,
not overlook my fault?
For soon I shall be lying in the dust,
you will look for me and I shall be no more.

The unswerving course of God's justice

8 Bildad of Shuah spoke next. He said:
2 How much longer are you going to talk like this
and go blustering on in this way?
3 Can God deflect the course of right
or Shaddai falsify justice?
4 If your sons sinned against him,
he has punished them for their wrong-doing.
6a You for your part, if you are pure and honest,
5 must now seek God, plead with Shaddai.
6b Forthwith his light will shine on you and he will restore
an upright man's house to prosperity.
7 Your former state will seem as nothing to you,
so great will your future be.

8 Question the generation that has passed,
meditate on the experience of its ancestors—
9 for we children of yesterday, we know nothing,
our life on earth passes like a shadow—
10 but they will teach you, they will tell you,
and their thought is expressed in these sayings,
11 'Can papyrus flourish except in marshes?
Without water can the rushes grow?
12 Even when green and before being cut,
fastest of all plants they wither.
13 Such is the fate of all who forget God;
so perishes the hope of the godless.

7a In Babylonian myths the Sea was a goddess, held back from sweeping civilisation away.

14 His hope is nothing but gossamer,
his confidence a spider's web.
15 Let him lean on his house, it will not stand firm;
cling to it, it will not hold.
16 Like some lush plant in the sunlight,
he sent his young shoots sprouting over the garden;
17 but his roots were twined in a heap of stones,
he drew his life among the rocks.
18 Snatch him from his bed,
and it denies it ever saw him.
19 Now he rots on the roadside,
and others are springing up in the soil.
20 Believe me, God neither spurns anyone of integrity,
nor lends his aid to the evil.
21 Once again laughter may fill your mouth
and cries of joy break from your lips.
22 Your enemies will be covered with shame
and the tent of the wicked will vanish!'

God's justice is above all law

9 Job spoke next. He said:

2 Indeed, I know it is as you say:
how could anyone claim to be upright before God?
3 Anyone trying to argue matters with him,
could not give him one answer in a thousand.
4 Among the wisest and the hardiest,
who then can successfully defy him?
5 He moves the mountains, though they do not know it;
he throws them down when he is angry.
6 He shakes the earth, and moves it from its place,
making all its pillars tremble.
7 The sun, at his command, forbears to rise,
and on the stars he sets a seal.
8 He and no other has stretched out the heavens
and trampled on the back of the Sea.
9 He has made the Bear and Orion,
the Pleiades and the Mansions of the South.
10 The works he does are great and unfathomable,
and his marvels cannot be counted.
11 If he passes me, I do not see him;
he slips by, imperceptible to me.
12 If he snatches his prey, who is going to stop him
or dare to ask, 'What are you doing?'
13 God does not renounce his anger:
beneath him, Rahab's[a] minions still lie prostrate.

14 And here am I, proposing to defend myself
and select my arguments against him!
15 Even if I am upright, what point is there in answering him?
I can only plead for mercy with my judge!
16 And if he deigned to answer my citation,
I cannot believe he would listen to what I said,

9a Another name for the Sea as monster of chaos, also used of the Red Sea.

17 he who crushes me for one hair,
who, for no reason, wounds and wounds again,
18 not even letting me regain my breath,
with so much bitterness he fills me!
19 Shall I try force? Look how strong he is!
Or go to court? But who will summon him?
20 If I prove myself upright, his mouth may condemn me,
even if I am innocent, he may pronounce me perverse.
21 But am I innocent? I am no longer sure,
and life itself I despise!
22 It is all one, and hence I boldly say:
he destroys innocent and guilty alike.
23 When a sudden deadly scourge descends,
he laughs at the plight of the innocent.
24 When a country falls into the power of the wicked,
he veils the faces of its judges.
Or if not he, who else?
25 My days pass: more swiftly than a runner
they flee away with never a glimpse of happiness,
26 they skim past like a reed canoe,
like an eagle swooping on its prey.
27 If I decide to stifle my complaining,
change countenance, and wear a smiling face,
28 fear seizes me at the thought of all my woes,
for I know you do not regard me as innocent.
29 And if I have done wrong,
why should I put myself to useless trouble?
30 If I wash myself in melted snow,
clean my hands with soda,
31 you will only plunge me into the dung,
till my clothes themselves recoil from me!
32 For he is not human like me: impossible for me to answer him
or appear alongside him in court.
33 There is no arbiter between us,
to lay his hand on both,
34 to stay his rod from me,
or keep away his daunting terrors.
35 Nonetheless, unafraid of him, I shall speak:
since I do not see myself like that at all!

10 Since I have lost all taste for life,
I shall give free rein to my complaining;
I shall let my embittered soul speak out.
2 I shall say to God, 'Do not condemn me,
tell me what your case is against me.
3 Is it right for you to attack me,
in contempt for what you yourself have made,
thus abetting the schemes of the wicked?
4 Are your eyes mere human eyes,
do you see as human beings see?
5 Are you mortal like human beings?
do your years pass as human days pass?
6 You, who enquire into my faults
and investigate my sins,
7 you know very well that I am innocent,
and that no one can rescue me from your grasp.

8 Your hands having shaped and created me,
now you change your mind and mean to destroy me!
9 Having made me, remember, as though of clay,
now you mean to turn me back into dust!
10 Did you not pour me out like milk,
and then let me thicken like curds,
11 clothe me with skin and flesh,
and weave me of bone and sinew?
12 In your love you gave me life,
and in your care watched over my every breath.
13 Yet, all the while, you had a secret plan:
I know that you were biding your time
14 to see if I should sin
and then not acquit me of my faults.
15 Woe to me, if I am guilty;
even if I am upright, I dare not lift my head,
so overwhelmed with shame and drunk with pain am I!
16 Proud as a lion, you hunt me down,
multiplying your exploits at my expense,
17 attacking me again and again,
your fury against me ever increasing,
your troops assailing me, wave after wave.

18 Why did you bring me out of the womb?
I should have perished then, unseen by any eye,
19 a being that had never been,
to be carried from womb to grave.
20 The days of my life are few enough:
turn your eyes away, leave me a little joy,
21 before I go to the place of no return,
to the land of darkness and shadow dark as death,
22 where dimness and disorder hold sway,
and light itself is like dead of night.

Job must acknowledge God's wisdom

11 Zophar of Naamath spoke next. He said:
2 Is babbling to go without an answer?
Is wordiness a proof of uprightness?
3 Do you think your talking strikes people dumb,
will you jeer with no one to refute you?
4 These were your words, 'My conduct is pure,
in your eyes I am free of blame!'
5 Will no one let God speak,
open his lips and give you answer,
6 show you the secrets of wisdom
which put all cleverness to shame?
Then you would realise that God is calling you to account for your sin.
7 Can you claim to fathom the depth of God,
can you reach the limit of Shaddai?
8 It is higher than the heavens: what can you do?
It is deeper than Sheol: what can you know?
9 It would be longer to measure than the earth
and broader than the sea.
10 If he intervenes to close or convoke the assembly,
who is to prevent him?

[11]He knows how deceptive human beings are,
and he sees their misdeeds too, and marks them well.
[12]Hence empty-headed people would do well to study sense
and people who behave like wild donkeys to let themselves be tamed.

[13]Come, reconsider your attitude,
stretch out your hands towards him!
[14]If you repudiate the sin which you have doubtless committed
and do not allow wickedness to live on in your tents,
[15]you will be able to raise an unsullied face,
unwavering and free from fear,
[16]for you will forget about your misery,
thinking of it only as a flood that passed long ago.
[17]Then begins an existence more radiant than noon,
and the very darkness will be bright as morning.
[18]Confident because there is hope;
after your troubles, you will sleep secure.
[19]When you lie down to rest, no one will trouble you,
and many will seek your favour.
[20]But as for the wicked, their eyes are weary,
there is no refuge for them;
their only hope is to breathe their last.

God's wisdom is best seen in the awesome works of his omnipotence

12 Job spoke next. He said:
[2]Doubtless, you are the voice of the people,
and when you die, wisdom will die with you!
[3]But I have a brain, as well as you,
I am in no way inferior to you,
and who, in any case, does not know all that?
[4]Anyone becomes a laughing-stock to his friends
if he cries to God and expects an answer.
People laugh at anyone who has integrity and is upright.
[5]'Add insult to injury,' think the prosperous,
'strike the fellow now that he is staggering!'
[6]And yet the tents of brigands are left in peace:
those who provoke God dwell secure
and so does anyone who makes a god of his fist!
[7]You have only to ask the cattle, for them to instruct you,
and the birds of the sky, for them to inform you.
[8]The creeping things of earth will give you lessons,
and the fish of the sea provide you an explanation:
[9]there is not one such creature but will know
that the hand of God has arranged things like this!
[10]In his hand is the soul of every living thing
and the breath of every human being!
[11]Can the ear not distinguish the value of what is said,
just as the palate can tell one food from another?
[12]Wisdom is found in the old,
and discretion comes with great age.
[13]But in him there is wisdom, and power too,
and good counsel no less than discretion.
[14]What he destroys, no one can rebuild;
whom he imprisons, no one can release.

15 Is there a drought? He has withheld the waters.
Do they play havoc on earth? He has let them loose.
16 In him is strength, in him resourcefulness,
beguiler and beguiled alike are his.
17 He robs a country's counsellors of their wits,
turns judges into fools.
18 He undoes the belts of kings
and knots a rope round their waists.
19 He makes priests walk barefoot,
and overthrows the powers that are established.
20 He strikes the most assured of speakers dumb
and robs old people of their discretion.
21 He pours contempt on the nobly born,
and unbuckles the belt of the strong.
22 He unveils the depths of darkness,
brings shadow dark as death to the light.
23 He builds nations up, then ruins them,
he makes peoples expand, then suppresses them.
24 He strips a country's leaders of their judgement,
and leaves them to wander in a trackless waste,
25 to grope about in unlit darkness,
lurching to and fro as though drunk.

13 I have seen all this with my own eyes,
heard with my own ears and understood.
2 Whatever you know, I know too;
I am in no way inferior to you.
3 But my words are intended for Shaddai;
I mean to remonstrate with God.
4 As for you, you are only charlatans,
all worthless as doctors!
5 Will no one teach you to be quiet
—the only wisdom that becomes you!
6 Kindly listen to my accusation
and give your attention to the way I shall plead.
7 Do you mean to defend God by prevarication
and by dishonest argument,
8 and, taking his side like this,
appoint yourselves as his advocates?
9 How would you fare, if he were to scrutinise you?
Can he be duped as mortals are duped?
10 He would inflict a harsh rebuke on you
for your covert partiality.
11 Does his majesty not affright you?
Does his terror not overcome you?
12 Your received ideas are maxims of ash,
your retorts, retorts of clay.
13 Be quiet! Kindly let me do the talking,
happen to me what may.
14 I am putting my flesh between my teeth,
I am taking my life in my hands;
15 let him kill me if he will; I have no other hope
than to justify my conduct in his eyes.
16 And this is what will save me,
for the wicked would not dare to appear before him.

17 Listen carefully to my words,
and pay attention to what I am going to say.
18 You see, I shall proceed by form of law,
knowing that I am upright.
19 Who wants to contest my case?
In advance, I agree to be silenced and to die!
20 Only grant me two concessions,
and then I shall not hide away from your face:
21 remove your hand, which lies so heavy on me,
no longer make me cower from your terror.
22 Then call me forward and I shall answer,
or rather, I shall speak and you will answer.
23 How many faults and crimes have I committed?
Tell me what my misdeed has been, what my sin?
24 Why do you hide your face
and look on me as your enemy?
25 Do you want to intimidate a wind-blown leaf,
do you want to pursue a dry straw?
26 You who lay bitter allegations against me
and tax me with the faults of my youth
27 and have put my feet in the stocks;
you examine my every step
and measure my footprints one by one!

28 For his part, he crumbles away like rotten wood,
or like a moth-eaten garment,
14 a human being, born of woman,
whose life is short but full of trouble.
2 Like a flower, such a one blossoms and withers,
fleeting as a shadow, transient.
3 And this is the creature on whom you fix your gaze,
and bring to judgement before you!
4 But will anyone produce the pure from what is impure?
No one can!
5 Since his days are measured out,
since his tale of months depends on you,
since you assign him bounds he cannot pass,
6 turn your eyes from him, leave him alone,
like a hired labourer, to finish his day in peace.
7 There is always hope for a tree:
when felled, it can start its life again;
its shoots continue to sprout.
8 Its roots may have grown old in the earth,
its stump rotting in the ground,
9 but let it scent the water, and it buds,
and puts out branches like a plant newly set.
10 But a human being? He dies, and dead he remains,
breathes his last, and then where is he?
11 The waters of the sea will vanish,
the rivers stop flowing and run dry:
12 a human being, once laid to rest, will never rise again,
the heavens will wear out before he wakes up,
or before he is roused from his sleep.

13 Will no one hide me in Sheol,
and shelter me there till your anger is past,
fixing a certain day for calling me to mind—

14 can the dead come back to life?—
day after day of my service, I should be waiting
for my relief to come.
15 Then you would call, and I should answer,
you would want to see once more what you have made.
16 Whereas now you count every step I take,
you would then stop spying on my sin;
17 you would seal up my crime in a bag,
and put a cover over my fault.

18 Alas! Just as, eventually, the mountain falls down,
the rock moves from its place,
19 water wears away the stones,
the cloudburst erodes the soil;
so you destroy whatever hope a person has.
20 You crush him once for all, and he is gone;
first you disfigure him, then you dismiss him.
21 His children may rise to honours—he does not know it;
they may come down in the world—he does not care.
22 He feels no pangs, except for his own body,
makes no lament, except for his own self.

B: SECOND CYCLE OF DISCOURSES

Job's own words condemn him

15 Eliphaz of Teman spoke next. He said:

2 Does anyone wise respond with windy arguments,
or feed on an east wind?
3 Or make a defence with ineffectual words
and speeches good for nothing?
4 You do worse: you suppress reverence,
you discredit discussion before God.
5 Your very fault incites you to speak like this,
hence you adopt this language of cunning.
6 Your own mouth condemns you, and not I;
your own lips bear witness against you.

7 Are you the first-born of the human race,
brought into the world before the hills?
8 Have you been a listener at God's council,
or established a monopoly of wisdom?
9 What knowledge do you have that we have not,
what understanding that is not ours too?
10 One of us is an old, grey-headed man
loaded with more years than your father!
11 Can you ignore these divine consolations
and the moderate tone of our words?
12 How passion carries you away!
And how you roll your eyes,
13 when you vent your anger on God
and speeches come tripping off your tongue!
14 How can anyone be pure,
anyone born of woman be upright?
15 God cannot rely even on his holy ones,
to him, even the heavens seem impure.

16How much more, this hateful, corrupt thing,
humanity, which soaks up wickedness like water!
17Listen to me, I have a lesson for you:
I am going to impart my own experience
18and the tradition of the sages
who have remained faithful to their ancestors,
19to whom alone the land was given—
no foreigner included among them.
20The life of the wicked is unceasing torment,
the years allotted to the tyrant are numbered.
21A cry of panic echoes in his ear;
when all is peace, his destroyer swoops down on him.
22No more can he count on escaping from the dark,
but knows that he is destined for the sword,
23marked down as meat for the vulture.
He knows that his ruin is at hand.
24The hour of darkness terrifies him,
distress and anguish assail him
as when a king is poised for the assault.
25He raised his hand against God,
boldly he defied Shaddai!
26Head lowered, he charged him,
with his massively bossed shield.
27His face had grown full and fat,
and his thighs too heavy with flesh.
28He had occupied the towns he had destroyed,
with their uninhabited houses
about to fall into ruins;
29but no great profit to him, his luck will not hold,
he will cast his shadow over the country no longer,
30(he will not escape the dark).
A flame will scorch his young shoots,
the wind will carry off his blossom.
31Let him not trust in his great height
or delusion will be his.
32His palm trees will wither before their time
and his branches never again be green.
33Like the vine, he will shake off his unripe fruit,
like the olive tree, shed his blossom.
34Yes, sterile is the spawn of the sinner,
and fire consumes the tents of the venal.
35Whoever conceives malice, breeds disaster,
bears as offspring only a false hope.

Human injustice and divine justice

16 Job spoke next. He said:
2How often have I heard all this before!
What sorry comforters you are!
3'When will these windy arguments be over?'
or again, 'What sickness drives you to defend yourself?'
4Oh yes! I too could talk as you do,
if you were in my place;
I could overwhelm you with speeches,
shaking my head over you,

5and speak words of encouragement,
and then have no more to say.
6When I speak, my suffering does not stop;
if I say nothing, is it in any way reduced?
7And now it is driving me to distraction;
you have struck my whole acquaintanceship with horror,
8now it rounds on me, my slanderer has now turned witness,
he appears against me, accusing me face to face;
9his anger tears and hounds me
with gnashing teeth.
My enemies look daggers at me,
10and open gaping jaws.
Their sneers strike like slaps in the face;
and they all set on me at once.
11Yes, God has handed me over to the godless,
and cast me into the hands of the wicked.

12I was living at peace, until he made me totter,
taking me by the neck to shatter me.
He has set me up as his target:
13he shoots his arrows at me from all sides,
pitilessly pierces my loins,
and pours my gall out on the ground.
14Breach after breach he drives through me,
charging on me like a warrior.
15I have sewn sackcloth over my skin,
thrown my forehead in the dust.
16My face is red with tears,
and shadow dark as death covers my eyelids.
17Nonetheless, my hands are free of violence,
and my prayer is pure.
18Cover not my blood, O earth,
and let my cry mount without cease!
19Henceforth I have a witness in heaven,
my defender is there on high.
20Interpreter of my thoughts there with God,
before whom flow my tears,
21let my anguish plead the cause of a man at grips with God,
just as a man might defend his fellow.
22For the years of my life are numbered,
and I am leaving by the road of no return.

17 My breathing is growing weaker
and the gravediggers are gathering for me.
2Scoffers are my only companions,
their harshness haunts my nights.
3So you must go bail for me to yourself,
for which of them cares to clap his hand on mine?
4For you have shut their hearts to reason,
hence not a hand is lifted.
5Just so is a man who invites his friends to share his property
while the eyes of his own children languish.

6I have become a byword among foreigners,
and a creature on whose face to spit,
7since I am nearly blind with grief
and my limbs are reduced to a shadow.

8 Any honest person is appalled at the sight,
the innocent is indignant at the sinner.
9 Anyone upright grows stronger step by step:
and anyone whose hands are clean grows ever in vigour!

10 Come on then, all of you, back to the attack!
I shall not find one wise man among you!
11 My days are over, so are my plans,
my heart-strings are broken;
12 yet they would have me believe that night is day,
that light to dispel the darkness is at hand,
13 when all I want, in fact, is to dwell in Sheol
and in that darkness there to make my bed!
14 To the tomb, I cry, 'You are my father!'—
to the worm, 'You are my mother—you, my sister!'
15 Where then is my hope?
Who can see any happiness for me?
16 unless they come down to Sheol with me,
all of us sinking into the dust together?

The inevitable fate of the wicked

18 Bildad of Shuah spoke next. He said:
2 What prevents you others from saying something?
Think—for it is our turn to speak!
3 Why do you regard us as animals,
considering us no more than brutes?
4 Tear yourself to pieces if you will,
but the world, for all your rage, will not turn to desert,
the rocks will not shift from their places.
5 The light of the wicked must certainly be put out,
the lamp that gives him light cease to shine.
6 In his tent the light is dimmed,
the lamp that shone on him is snuffed.
7 His vigorous stride loses its power,
his own designs falter.
8 For into the net his own feet carry him,
he walks into the snares.
9 A spring grips him by the heel,
a trap snaps shut, and he is caught.
10 Hidden in the ground is a snare to catch him,
pitfalls lie across his path.
11 Terrors threaten him from all sides
following him step by step.
12 Hunger becomes his companion,
by his side Disaster stands.
13 Disease devours his skin,
Death's First-Born gnaws his limbs.
14 He will be torn from the shelter of his tent,
and you will drag him to the King of Terrors.[a]
15 You can live in the tent, since it is no longer his,
and brimstone will be scattered on his sheepfold.
16 Below, his roots dry out
and his branches are blasted above.

18a Figures of oriental mythology.

[17]His memory fades from the land,
his name is forgotten in the countryside.
[18]Driven from the light into the darkness,
he is banished from the world,
[19]without issue or posterity among his own people
or a single survivor where he used to live.
[20]His end appals the west
and fills the east with terror.
[21]Such indeed is the fate of the places where wickedness dwells—
the home of everyone who knows not God.

Faith at its height in total desertion

19 Job spoke next. He said:

[2]How much longer are you going to torment me
and crush me by your speeches?
[3]You have insulted me ten times already:
have you no shame at maltreating me?
[4]Even if I had gone astray,
my error would still be my own affair.
[5]But, whereas you take this superior attitude
and claim that my disgrace is my own fault,
[6]I tell you that God has wronged me
and enveloped me in his net.
[7]If I protest against such violence, I am not heard,
if I appeal against it, judgement is never given.
[8]He has built an impassable wall across my path
and covered my way with darkness.
[9]He has deprived me of my glory
and taken the crown from my head.
[10]He assails me from all directions to make me vanish;
he uproots my hope as he might a tree.
[11]Inflamed with anger against me,
he regards me as his foe.
[12]His troops have come in force,
directing their line of advance towards me,
they are now encamped round my tent.

[13]He has alienated my brothers from me,
my relatives take care to avoid me,
[14]my intimate friends have gone away
and the guests in my house have forgotten me.
[15]My slave-girls regard me as an intruder,
a stranger as far as they are concerned.
[16]My servant does not answer when I call him,
I am obliged to beg favours from him!
[17]My breath is unbearable to my wife,
my stench to my own brothers.
[18]Even the children look down on me,
whenever I stand up, they start jeering at me.
[19]All my dearest friends recoil from me in horror:
those I loved best have turned against me.
[20]My flesh is rotting under my skin,
my bones are sticking out like teeth.
[21]Pity me, pity me, my friends,
since I have been struck by the hand of God.

22 Must you persecute me just as God does,
and give my body no peace?

23 Will no one let my words be recorded,
inscribed on some monument
24 with iron chisel and engraving tool,
cut into the rock for ever?
25 I know that I have a living Defender[a]
and that he will rise up last, on the dust of the earth.
26 After my awakening, he will set me close to him,
and from my flesh I shall look on God.
27 He whom I shall see will take my part:
my eyes will be gazing on no stranger.
My heart sinks within me.
28 When you say, 'How can we confound him?
What pretext can we discover against him?'
29 You yourselves had best beware the sword,
since the wrath bursts into flame at wicked deeds
and then you will learn that there is indeed a judgement!

The course of justice admits of no exception

20 Zophar of Naamath spoke next. He said:

2 My thoughts urge me to reply to this,
and hence the impatience that grips me.
3 I have put up with prating that outrages me
and now my mind inspires me with an answer.
4 Do you not know, that since time began
and human beings were set on the earth,
5 the triumph of the wicked has always been brief,
and the sinner's gladness has never lasted long?
6 Towering to the sky he may have been,
his head touching the clouds;
7 but he vanishes, like a phantom, once for all,
while those who used to see him, ask, 'Where is he?'
8 Like a dream that leaves no trace he takes his flight,
like a vision in the night he flies away.
9 The eye accustomed to see him sees him no more,
his home will never set eyes on him again.
10 His sons will have to reimburse the poor
and his children pay back his riches.
11 His bones used to be full of youthful vigour:
and there it lies, in the dust with him, now!
12 Evil was sweet to his mouth,
he would shelter it under his tongue;
13 cultivating it carefully,
he would let it linger on his palate.
14 Such food goes bad in his belly,
working inside him like the poison of a viper.
15 Now he has to vomit up the wealth that he has swallowed,
God makes him disgorge it.

19a Technical term for the closest relative, the avenger of blood. Having no belief in life after death, Job yet bursts the bounds of his belief and asserts that he will somehow see his vindication by God himself. 'Rise up' is a technical term for the action of defendant or judge.

16He used to suck vipers' venom,
and the tongue of the adder kills him.
17No more will he know the streams of oil
or the torrents of honey and cream.
18When he gives back his winnings, his cheerfulness will fade,
and the satisfied air he had when business was thriving.
19Since he once destroyed the huts of the poor,
plundering houses instead of building them up,
20since his avarice could never be satisfied,
now all his hoarding will not save him;
21since nothing could escape his greed,
his prosperity will not last.
22When he has everything he needs, want will seize him,
and misery will light on him with all its force.
23On him God looses all his burning wrath,
hurling against his flesh a hail of arrows.
24If he escapes the weapons of iron,
the bow of bronze will transfix him.
25Out of his back sticks an arrow,
from his gall a shining point.
The terrors advance on him,
26all the hidden darknesses are waiting to carry him off.
A fire unlit by human hand devours him,
and consumes what is left in his tent.
27The heavens lay bare his iniquity,
and the earth rises up against him.
28The income of his house pours away,
like the torrents, on the day of retribution.
29Such is the fate God reserves for the wicked,
the inheritance he assigns to the accursed!

Facts give the lie

21 Job spoke next. He said:
2Listen carefully to my words;
let this be the consolation you allow me.
3Permit me to speak in my turn;
you may jeer when I have spoken.
4Is my complaint just about a fellow-mortal?
I have good grounds to be perturbed!
5Give your attention to me; you will be dumbfounded
and will place your hand over your mouth.
6I myself am appalled at the very thought,
and my flesh creeps.
7Why do the wicked still live on,
their power increasing with their age?
8They see their posterity assured,
and their offspring secure before their eyes.
9The peace of their houses has nothing to fear,
the rod that God wields is not for them.
10No mishap with their bull at breeding-time,
nor miscarriage with their cow at calving.
11They let their infants frisk like lambs,
their children dance like deer.

12 They sing to the tambourine and harp,
and rejoice to the sound of the pipe.
13 They end their lives in happiness
and go down in peace to Sheol.

14 Yet these are the ones who say to God, 'Go away!
We do not want to learn your ways.
15 What is the point of our serving Shaddai?
What should we gain from praying to him?'
16 Surely they have won their own prosperity,
since God is kept so far from their plans?

17 Do we often see the light of the wicked put out,
or disaster overtake him,
or the retribution of God destroy his possessions,
18 or the wind blow him away like a straw,
or a whirlwind carry him off like chaff?
19 So God is storing up punishment for his children?
But the wicked himself should be punished, and should know it!
20 He himself should witness his own ruin,
and himself drink the anger of Shaddai.
21 Once he is gone, what joy can he gain from his family,
once the number of his months has been cut off?
22 But who can teach wisdom to God,
to him who is judge of those on high?
23 And again: one person dies in the fullness of strength,
in all possible happiness and ease,
24 thighs padded with fat
and the marrow in the bones good and moist.
25 Another dies in bitterness of heart,
never having tasted happiness.
26 They lie together down in the dust
and the worms soon cover them both.

27 Oh, I know what is in your minds,
what you so spitefully think about me!
28 'What has become of the great lord's house,' you say,
'where is the tent where the wicked used to live?'
29 Have you never questioned people who travel,
do you not understand the testimony they give:
30 on the day of disaster, the wicked is spared,
on the day of retribution, he is kept safe?
31 And who is there then to reproach him for his deeds
and to pay him back for the things he has done?
32 He is carried away to the cemetery,
and a watch is kept at his tomb.
33 The clods of the ravine lie easy on him,
and the whole population walk behind.
34 So what sense is there in your empty consolation?
your answers are the left-overs of infidelity!

C: THIRD CYCLE OF DISCOURSES

Admission of guilt leads to reconciliation with God

22 Eliphaz of Teman spoke next. He said:

2Can a human being contribute anything to God,
when even someone intelligent can benefit only himself?
3Does Shaddai derive any benefit from your uprightness,
or profit from your blameless conduct?
4Do you think he is punishing you for your piety
and bringing you to justice for that?
5No, for your great wickedness, more likely,
for your unlimited sins!
6You have exacted unearned pledges from your brothers,
stripped people naked of their clothes,
7failed to give water to the thirsty
and refused bread to the hungry;
8handed the land over to a strong man,
for some favoured person to move in,
9sent widows away empty-handed
and crushed the arms of orphans.
10No wonder, then, if snares are all around you,
and sudden terrors make you afraid;
11if light has turned to darkness, so that you cannot see,
and you have been submerged in the flood.

12Does not God live high in the heavens,
does he not see the zenith of the stars?
13And because he is up there, you have said, 'What does God know?
Can he judge through the dark cloud?
14The clouds, to him, are an impenetrable veil,
as he goes his way on the rim of the heavens.'
15And will you still follow the ancient trail
trodden by the wicked,
16those who were borne off before their time,
whose foundations were swamped by a flood,
17for having said to God, 'Go away!
What can Shaddai do to us?'
18Yet he himself had filled their houses with good things,
although excluded from the plans of the wicked!
19At such a spectacle, the upright rejoice,
and the innocent deride them:
20'See how our enemies have been destroyed!
See how their wealth has perished in the flames!'

21Well then! Make peace with him, be reconciled,
and all your happiness will be restored to you.
22Welcome the teaching from his lips,
and keep his words close to your heart.
23If you return, humbled, to Shaddai
and drive wickedness far from your tent,
24if you lay your gold down on the dust,
Ophir down among the pebbles of the torrent,
25Shaddai will be bars of gold to you
and silver piled in heaps.
26Then Shaddai will be all your delight,
and you will lift your face to God.
27You will pray, and he will hear;
and you will be able to fulfil your vows.
28Whatever you undertake will go well,
and light will shine on your path;

29 for he casts down the pride of the arrogant,
but he saves those of downcast eyes.
30 He rescues anyone who is innocent;
have your hands clean, and you will be saved.

God is far off, and evil triumphant

23 Job spoke next. He said:

2 My lament is still rebellious;
despite my groans, his hand is just as heavy.
3 Will no one help me to know
how to travel to his dwelling?
4 I should set out my case to him,
advancing any number of grievances.
5 Then I could learn his defence, every word of it,
taking note of everything he said to me.
6 Would he put all his strength into this debate with me?
No, he would only have to give his attention to me,
7 to recognise his opponent as upright
and so I should win my case for ever.

8 If I go to the east, he is not there;
or to the west, I still cannot see him.
9 If I seek him in the north, he is not to be found,
invisible as ever, if I turn to the south.
10 And yet he knows every step I take!
Let him test me in the crucible: I shall come out pure gold.
11 My footsteps have followed close in his,
I have walked in his way without swerving;
12 I have not neglected the commandment of his lips,
in my heart I have cherished the words of his mouth.
13 But once he has made up his mind, who can change it?
Whatever he plans, that he carries out.
14 No doubt, then, but he will carry out my sentence,
like so many other decrees that he has made.
15 That is why I am full of fear before him,
and the more I think, the greater grows my dread of him.
16 God has undermined my courage,
Shaddai has filled me with fear.
17 The darkness having failed to destroy me,
I am plunged back into obscurity by him!

24 Why does Shaddai not make known the times he has fixed;
why do his faithful never see his Days?[a]
2 The wicked move boundary-marks away,
they carry off flock and shepherd.
3 They drive away the orphan's donkey,
as security, they seize the widow's ox.
4 The needy have to keep out of the way,
poor country people have to keep out of sight.
5 Like wild desert donkeys, they go out to work,
searching from dawn for food,
and at evening for something on which to feed their children.
6 They go harvesting in the field of some scoundrel,
they go pilfering in the vineyards of the wicked.

24a i.e., his Days of Retribution, as the Day of Yahweh in prophetic writings.

[10]They go about naked, lacking clothes,
and starving while they carry the sheaves.
[11]Two little walls, their shelter at high noon;
parched with thirst, they have to tread the winepress.
[7]They spend the night naked, lacking clothes,
with no covering against the cold.
[8]Mountain rainstorms cut them through,
unsheltered, they hug the rocks.
[9]The orphan child is torn from the breast,
the child of the poor is exacted as security.
[12]From the towns come the groans of the dying
and the gasp of the wounded crying for help.
Yet God remains deaf to prayer!

[13]In contrast, there are those who reject the light:
who know nothing of its ways
and who do not frequent its paths.
[14]When all is dark the murderer leaves his bed
to kill the poor and needy.
During the night the thief goes on the prowl,
[16a]breaking into houses while the darkness lasts.
[15]The eye of the adulterer watches for twilight,
'No one will see me,' he mutters
as he masks his face.
[16b]In the daytime they keep out of sight,
these people who do not want to know the light.
[17]For all of them, morning is a time of shadow dark as death,
since that is when they know what fear is.[b]

[25]Is this not so? Who can prove me a liar
or show that my words have no substance?

A hymn to God's omnipotence

25 Bildad of Shuah spoke next. He said:
[2]What sovereignty, what awe, is his
who creates peace on his heights!
[3]Who can count his armies?
Against whom does his lightning not surge forth?
[4]Could anyone think God regards him as virtuous,
the child of woman as pure!
[5]Why, the very moon lacks lustre,
the very stars seem impure to him!
[6]How much less a human, this maggot,
the child of man, this worm![a]

26 [5]The Shadows[a] tremble underneath the earth,
the waters and their denizens are afraid.
[6]Before his eyes, Sheol is bare,
Perdition itself is uncovered.
[7]He it was who spread the North above the void
and poised the earth on nothingness.
[8]He fastens up the waters in his clouds,
without the clouds giving way under their weight.

24b vv. 18–24 are conjecturally placed after 27:23. The text is corrupt.
25a 26:1–4 are conjecturally placed after 26:14. They belong to Job's speech.
26a i.e., the powerless dead.

[9]He covers the face of the full moon,
spreading his cloud across it.
[10]He has traced a ring on the surface of the waters,
at the boundary between light and dark.
[11]The pillars of the heavens tremble,
awe-struck at his threats.
[12]By his power, he has whipped up the Sea,
by his skill, he has crushed Rahab.
[13]His breath has made the heavens luminous,
his hand transfixed the Fleeing Serpent.
[14]This is only a fraction of what he has done
and all we catch of it is the feeblest echo.
But who can conceive the thunder of his power?

Bildad's rhetoric is beside the point

26 [1]Job spoke next. He said:
[2]To one so weak, what a help you are,
for the arm that is powerless, what a rescuer!
[3]What excellent advice you give the unlearned,
you are never at a loss for a helpful suggestion!
[4]For whom are these words of yours intended
and whence comes that wit you are now displaying?

Job reaffirms his innocence while acknowledging God's power

27 And Job continued his solemn discourse. He said:
[2]I swear by the living God who denies me justice,
by Shaddai who has filled me with bitterness,
[3]that as long as a shred of life is left in me,
and the breath of God breathes in my nostrils,
[4]my lips will never speak evil
nor my tongue utter any lie.
[5]Far from admitting you to be in the right,
I shall maintain my integrity to my dying day.
[6]I take my stand on my uprightness, I shall not stir:
in my heart I need not be ashamed of my days.
[7]Let my enemy meet the fate of the wicked,
my adversary, the lot of the evil-doer!
[8]For what hope does the godless have when he prays
and raises his soul to God?
[9]Is God likely to hear his cries
when disaster descends on him?
[10]Did he make Shaddai all his delight,
calling on him at every turn?
[11]But I am showing you the way that God works,
making no secret of Shaddai's designs.
[12]And if you had all understood them for yourselves,
you would not have wasted your breath in empty words.

Discourse of Zophar
The fate of the wicked

[13]This is the fate that God assigns to the wicked,
the inheritance that the violent receive from Shaddai.

14 Though he have many children, it is but for the sword;
his descendants will never have enough to eat.
15 Plague will bury those he leaves behind him,
and their widows will have no chance to mourn them.
16 Though he amass silver like dust
and gather fine clothes like clay,
17 let him gather!—some good man will wear them,
while his silver is shared among the upright.
18 All he has built himself is a spider's web,
made himself a watchman's shack.
19 He goes to bed rich, but never again:
he wakes to find it has all gone.
20 Terror assails him in broad daylight,
and at night a whirlwind sweeps him off.
21 An east wind picks him up and drags him away,
snatching him up from his homestead.
22 Pitilessly he is turned into a target,
and forced to flee from the hands that menace him.
23 His downfall is greeted with applause,
he is hissed wherever he goes.
24 18acb He is no more than a straw floating on the water,
his estate is accursed throughout the land,
nobody goes near his vineyard.
19 As drought and heat make snow disappear,
so does Sheol anyone who has sinned.
20 The womb that shaped him forgets him
and his name is recalled no longer.
Thus wickedness is blasted as a tree is struck.
21 He used to ill-treat the childless woman
and show no kindness to the widow.
22 But he who lays mighty hold on tyrants
rises up to take away a life that seemed secure.
23 He let him build his hopes on false security,
but kept his eyes on every step he took.
24 He had his time of glory, now he vanishes,
wilting like the saltwort once it is picked,
and withering like an ear of corn.

D: A HYMN IN PRAISE OF WISDOM

Wisdom is beyond human reach

28 Silver has its mines,
and gold a place for refining.
2 Iron is extracted from the earth,
the smelted rocks yield copper.
3 Man makes an end of darkness,
to the utmost limit he digs
the black rock in shadow dark as death.
4 Foreigners bore into ravines
in unfrequented places,
swinging suspended far from human beings.
5 That earth from which bread comes
is ravaged underground by fire.
6 There, the rocks have veins of sapphire
and their dust contains gold.

[7]That is a path unknown to birds of prey,
unseen by the eye of any vulture;
[8]a path not trodden by the lordly beasts,
where no lion ever walked.
[9]Man attacks the flint,
upturning mountains by their roots.
[10]He cuts canals through the rock,
on the watch for anything precious.
[11]He explores the sources of rivers,
bringing hidden things to light.
[12]But where does Wisdom come from?
Where is Intelligence to be found?

[13]No human being knows the way to her,
she is not to be found on earth where they live.
[14]'She is not in me,' says the Abyss;
'Nor here,' replies the Sea.
[15]She cannot be bought with solid gold,
nor paid for with any weight of silver,
[16]nor valued against gold of Ophir,
precious agate or sapphire.
[17]Neither gold nor glass compares with her,
for her, a vase of fine gold would be no exchange,
[18]let alone coral or crystal:
better go fishing for Wisdom than for pearls!
[19]Topaz from Cush is worthless in comparison,
and gold, even refined, is valueless.
[20]But where does Wisdom come from?
Where is Intelligence to be found?

[21]She cannot be seen by any living creature,
she is hidden from the birds of the sky.
[22]Perdition and Death both say,
'We have heard only rumours of her.'
[23]God alone understands her path
and knows where she is to be found.
[24](For he sees to the remotest parts of the earth,
and observes all that lies under heaven.)
[25]When he willed to give weight to the wind
and measured out the waters with a gauge,
[26]when he imposed a law on the rain
and mapped a route for thunderclaps to follow,
[27]then he saw and evaluated her,
looked her through and through, assessing her.
[28]Then he said to human beings,
'Wisdom?—that is fear of the Lord;
Intelligence?—avoidance of evil.'

E: CONCLUSION OF THE DIALOGUE

Job's complaints and apologia
a. His former happiness

29 And Job continued his solemn discourse. He said:
[2]Will no one bring back to me the months that have gone,
and the days when God was my guardian,

3 when his lamp shone over my head,
and his light was my guide in the darkness?
4 Shall I ever see my days of harvest again
when God protected my tent;
5 when Shaddai still dwelt with me,
and my children were around me;
6 when my feet were bathed in milk,
and streams of oil poured from the rocks?
7 When I went out to the gate of the city,
when I took my seat in the square,
8 as soon as I appeared, the young men stepped aside,
and the old men rose to their feet.
9 Men of note broke off their speeches,
and put their hands over their mouths;
10 the voices of rulers were silenced,
and their tongues stayed still in their mouths.
21 They[a] waited anxiously to hear me,
and listened in silence to what I had to say.
22 When I had finished, no one contradicted,
my words dropping on them, one by one.
23 They waited for me as though for rain,
open-mouthed as though for a late shower.
24 If I smiled at them, it was too good to be true,
they watched my face for the least sign of favour.
25 As their chief, I told them which course to take,
like a king living among his troops,
and I led them wherever I chose.

11 On hearing me, people congratulated me,
on seeing me, people deferred to me,
12 because I freed the poor in distress
and the orphan who had no helper.
13 The dying man's blessing rested on me
and I gave the widow's heart cause to rejoice.
14 Uprightness I wore as a garment,
fair judgement was my cloak and my turban.
15 I was eyes for the blind,
and feet for the lame.
16 Who but me was father of the poor?
The stranger's case had a hearing from me.
17 I used to break the fangs of the wicked,
and snatch their prey from their jaws.

18 And I used to say, 'I shall die in honour,
after days as numerous as the sand.
19 My roots can reach the water,
the dews of night settle on my leaves.
20 My glory will be for ever new
and the bow in my hand for ever strong.'

b. His present misery

30 And now I am the laughing-stock
of people who are younger than I am
and whose parents I would have disdained
to put with the dogs guarding my flock.

29a vv. 21–25 are inserted here because they follow on better from v. 10 and lead up to v. 11.

2 And what use to me was the strength of their hands?—
enfeebled as they were,
3 worn out by want and hunger,
for they used to gnaw the roots of the thirsty ground—
that place of gloom, ruin and desolation—
4 they used to pick saltwort among the scrub,
making their meals off roots of broom.
5 Outlawed from human company,
which raised hue and cry against them, as against thieves,
6 they made their homes in the sides of ravines,
in holes in the earth or in clefts of rock.
7 You could hear them braying from the bushes
as they huddled together in the thistles.
8 Children of scoundrels, worse, nameless people,
the very outcasts of society!
9 And these are the ones who now make up songs about me
and use me as a byword!
10 Filled with disgust, they keep their distance,
on seeing me, they spit without restraint.
11 And since God has loosened my bow-string and afflicted me,
they too throw off the bridle in my presence.
12 Their brats surge forward on my right,
to see when I am having a little peace,
and advance on me with threatening strides.
13 They cut off all means of escape
seizing the chance to destroy me, and no one stops them.
14 They move in, as if through a wide breach,
and I go tumbling beneath the rubble.
15 Terror rounds on me,
my confidence is dispersed as though by the wind,
my hope of safety vanishes like a cloud.

16 And now the life in me trickles away,
days of grief have gripped me.
17 At night-time sickness saps my bones
I am gnawed by wounds that never sleep.
18 Violently, he has caught me by my clothes,
has gripped me by the collar of my coat.
19 He has thrown me into the mud;
I am no more than dust and ashes.

20 I cry to you, and you give me no answer;
I stand before you, but you take no notice.
21 You have grown cruel to me,
and your strong hand torments me unmercifully.
22 You carry me away astride the wind
and blow me to pieces in a tempest.
23 Yes, I know that you are taking me towards death,
to the common meeting-place of all the living.

24 Yet have I ever laid a hand on the poor
when they cried out for justice in calamity?
25 Have I not wept for those whose life is hard,
felt pity for the penniless?
26 I hoped for happiness, but sorrow came;
I looked for light, but there was darkness.

27 My stomach seethes, is never still,
days of suffering have struck me.
28 Sombre I go, yet no one comforts me,
and if I rise in the council, I rise to weep.
29 I have become brother to the jackal
and companion to the ostrich.
30 My skin has turned black on me,
my bones are burnt with fever.
31 My harp is tuned to dirges,
my pipe to the voice of mourners.

Job's apologia

31 I had made an agreement with my eyes
not to linger on any virgin.
2 Now what portion does God allot from above,
what fate does Shaddai apportion from his heaven—
3 if not the disasters appropriate to the wicked
and the calamities fit for evil-doers?
4 But surely he sees how I behave,
does he not count all my steps?
5 Have I been a fellow-traveller with falsehood,
or hastened my steps towards deceit?
6 Let him weigh me on accurate scales:
then he, God, will recognise my integrity!
7 If my feet have wandered from the rightful path,
or if my eyes have led my heart astray,
or if my hands are smirched with any stain,
8 let someone else eat what I have sown
and let my young shoots all be rooted out.
9 If my heart has been seduced by a woman,
or if I have lurked at my neighbour's door,
10 let my wife go and grind for someone else,
let others have intercourse with her!
11 For I would have committed a sin of lust,
a crime punishable by the law,
12 a fire, indeed, burning all to Perdition,
which would have devoured my whole revenue.
13 If I have ever infringed the rights of slave
or slave-girl in legal actions against me—
14 what shall I do, when God stands up?
What shall I say, when he holds his assize?
15 Did he not create them in the womb like me,
the same God forming us in the womb?
38 If my land cries for vengeance against me
and its furrows weep in concert,
39 if I have eaten its produce without paying,
and caused the death of its owners,
40a let brambles grow instead of wheat,
rank weeds instead of barley!

16 Have I been insensible to the needs of the poor,
or let a widow's eyes grow dim?
17 Have I eaten my bit of bread on my own
without sharing it with the orphan?

[18]I, whom God has fostered father-like from childhood,
and guided since I left my mother's womb,
[19]have I ever seen a wretch in need of clothing,
or the poor with nothing to wear,
[20]without his having cause to bless me from his heart,
as he felt the warmth of the fleece from my lambs?
[21]Have I raised my hand against an orphan,
presuming on my credit at the gate?
[22]If so, let my shoulder fall from its socket,
let my arm break off at the elbow!
[23]For the terror of God would fall on me
and I could not then stand my ground before his majesty.

[24]Have I put my faith in gold,
saying to fine gold, 'Ah, my security'?
[25]Have I ever gloated over my great wealth,
or the riches that my hands have won?
[26]Or has the sight of the sun in its glory,
or the glow of the moon as it walked the sky,
[27]secretly stolen my heart,
so that I blew them a kiss?
[28]That too would be a criminal offence,
to have denied the supreme God.
[29]Have I rejoiced at my enemy's misfortune,
or exulted when disaster overtook him?—
[30]I, who would not allow my tongue to sin
or to lay his life under a curse.
[31]The people of my tent, did they not say,
'Will anyone name a person whom he has not filled with meat?'
[32]No stranger ever had to sleep outside,
my door was always open to the traveller.
[33]Have I ever concealed my transgression from others
or kept my fault a secret in my breast?
[34]Have I ever stood in fear of common gossip,
or dreaded any family's contempt,
and so kept quiet, not venturing out of doors?
[35]Will no one give me a hearing?
I have said my last word; now let Shaddai reply!
When my adversary has drafted his writ against me
[36]I shall wear it on my shoulder,
and bind it round my head like a royal turban.
[37]I shall give him an account of my every step
and go as boldly as a prince to meet him.

[40b]End of the words of Job.

III: THE DISCOURSES OF ELIHU

Elihu joins the discussion

32 These three men stopped arguing with Job, because he was convinced of his
uprightness. [2]But Elihu son of Barachel the Buzite, of the clan of Ram, became very
angry. He fumed with rage against Job for thinking that he was right and God was wrong;
[3]and he was equally angry with the three friends for giving up the argument and thus putting
God in the wrong. [4]While they and Job were talking, Elihu had waited, because they were
older than he was; [5]but when he saw that the three men had not another word to say in
answer, his anger burst out. [6]And Elihu son of Barachel the Buzite began to speak. He said:

Prologue

I am still young,
and you are old,
so I was shy and hesitant
to tell you what I know.
7 I thought, 'Age ought to speak,
advancing years will convey wisdom.'
8 There is, you see, a spirit residing in humanity,
the breath of God conferring intelligence.
9 Great age does not give wisdom,
nor seniority fair judgement.
10 And so I ask you for a hearing;
now it is my turn to tell what I know.
11 Up to now, I was hanging on your words,
I paid attention to your arguments
as each of you chose his words.
12 I paid very close attention;
and I see that none of you has confounded Job,
not one of you has refuted what he says.
13 So do not say, 'We have found wisdom;
our teaching is divine and not human.'
14 I am not going to follow the same line of argument;
my reply to Job will be couched in different terms.

15 They are nonplussed for an answer,
words have failed them.
16 I have been waiting. Since they do not speak,
since they have given up the argument,
17 now I shall have my say,
my turn has come to say what I know.
18 For I am full of words
and forced to speak by a spirit within me;
19 within me, it feels like new wine seeking a vent,
bursting out of new wine-skins.
20 To gain relief, I must speak,
I must open my lips and reply.
21 I shall not take anyone's side,
I shall not flatter anyone.
22 I do not know how to flatter—
or my Creator would make short work of me.

Job's presumption

33 So, Job, please listen to my words
and attend to all I have to say.
2 Now as I open my mouth,
and my tongue shapes words against my palate,
3 I shall utter words of wisdom from the heart,
my lips will speak in all sincerity.
5 Refute me, if you can.
Prepare yourself, take up your position!
6 Look, I am your equal, not some god,
like you I was moulded out of clay.
4 God's was the spirit that made me,
Shaddai's the breath that gave me life.

7 No fear of me, therefore, need affright you,
my hand will not lie heavy over you.
8 How could you say in my hearing—
for the sound of your words did not escape me—
9 'I am clean, and sinless,
I am pure, without fault.
10 But he keeps inventing excuses against me
and regards me as his enemy.
11 He puts me in the stocks,
he watches my every path'?
12 In saying so, I tell you, you are wrong:
for God is greater than any human being.
13 Why then quarrel with him
for not replying to you, word for word?
14 God speaks first in one way,
and then in another, although we do not realise it.
15 In dreams and in night-visions,
when slumber has settled on humanity
and people are asleep in bed,
16 he speaks in someone's ear,
frightens him with apparitions
17 to turn him from what he is doing
and to put an end to his pride.
18 And thus he preserves his soul from the abyss,
his life from passing down the Canal.
19 Or again, he corrects by the sufferings of the sick-bed,
when someone's bones tremble continuously
20 and the thought of food revolts him,
however tasty it is,
21 and his flesh rots away while you watch it
and the bones beneath begin to show,
22 and his soul is drawing nearer to the abyss
and his life to the dwelling of the dead.
23 Then, if there is an Angel near him,
a Mediator, one in a thousand,
to remind him where his duty lies,
24 to take pity on him and to say,
'Spare him from going down to the abyss:
I have found the ransom for his life,'
25 his flesh will recover its childhood freshness,
he will return to the days of his youth.
26 He will pray to God who has restored him to favour,
and will come into his presence with joy.
He will tell others how he has received saving justice
27 and sing this hymn before his companions,
'I sinned and left the path of right,
but God has not punished me as my sin deserved.
28 He has spared my soul from going down to the abyss
and is making my life see the light.'
29 All this is what God keeps doing
again and yet again for human beings,
30 to snatch souls back from the abyss
and to make the light of the living still shine.

31 Pay attention, Job, listen to me:
keep quiet, I have more to say.

32 If you have anything to say, refute me,
speak out, for I would gladly accept that you are upright.
33 If not, then listen to me:
keep quiet, and I will teach you wisdom.

The three sages have failed to justify God

34 Elihu continued his speech. He said:

2 And now, you sages, listen to what I say,
lend me your ears, you learned men.
3 The ear distinguishes the value of what is said,
just as the palate can tell one food from another.
4 Let us consider together God's ruling
and decide what we all mean by good.
5 Job has been saying, 'I am upright
and God denies me fair judgement.
6 My judge is treating me cruelly,
my wound is incurable, for no fault of mine.'
7 Can anyone else exist like Job,
who laps up mockery like water,
8 who consorts with evil-doers
and marches in step with the wicked?
9 Did he not say, 'No one derives any benefit
from enjoying the society of God'?

10 Listen to me then, like intelligent people.
Far be evil from God
or injustice from Shaddai!
11 For he pays people back for what they do,
treating each as his own conduct deserves.
12 Be sure of it: God never does wrong,
Shaddai does not pervert what is just.
13 Did someone else entrust the world to his care
was he given charge of the universe by someone else?
14 If he were to recall his spirit,
to concentrate his breath back in himself,
15 all flesh would instantly perish
and all people would return to dust.
16 If you have any intelligence, listen to this,
lend your ear to the sound of my words.
17 Could an enemy of fair judgement ever govern?
Would you dare condemn the Upright One, the Almighty,
18 who says to a king, 'You are a scoundrel!'
and to nobles, 'You are wicked!',
19 who is unimpressed by princes
and makes no distinction between rich and poor,
since all alike have been made by him?
20 They die suddenly, at dead of night,
they perish—these great ones—and disappear:
it costs him no effort to remove a tyrant.
21 For his eyes keep watch on human ways,
and he observes every step.
22 No darkness, no shadow dark as death
where wrong-doers can hide!
23 He serves no writ on anyone,
no summons to appear before God's court:

[24]he breaks the powerful without enquiry
and sets up others in their places.
[25]He knows the sort of things they do!
He overthrows them at night, to be trampled on.
[26]He beats them like criminals
chained up for all to see,
[27]since they have turned their backs on him,
having understood so little of his ways
[28]as to make the cries of the weak rise to him
and let him hear the appeal of the afflicted.

[29]But if he is still silent and no one can move him,
if he veils his face, so that no one can see him,
he is taking pity on nations and individuals,
[30]is setting some wrong-doer free from the meshes of affliction.
[31]When such a one says to God,
'I was misled, I shall not do wrong any more;
[32]although I have sinned, instruct me;
although I did wrong, I will not do it again,'
[33]in your opinion, should he punish such a one—
you who have rejected his decisions?
This is for you to decide—not for me!—
so kindly enlighten us!
[34]Ordinary sensible people, however, will say to me,
and so will any sage who has been listening to me,
[35]'Job's words are spoken without any knowledge,
what he says shows no intelligence.
[36]Kindly examine him thoroughly,
since his answers imply that he is a criminal.
[37]For to his sin he now adds rebellion,
bringing law to an end among us
and heaping abuse on God.'

God's transcendence

35 Elihu continued his speech. He said:
[2]Do you think you can prove yourself upright
and establish your uprightness before God
[3]by daring to say to him, 'What does it matter to you,
or how does it benefit me, whether I have sinned or not?'
[4]Very well, I shall tell you
and your friends as well.
[5]Take a look at the skies and see,
observe how high the clouds are above you.
[6]If you sin, how can you affect him?
If you heap up crimes, what effect has it on him?
[7]If you are upright, what do you give him,
what benefit does he receive at your hands?
[8]Your wickedness affects only your fellows,
your uprightness, other human beings.
[9]They too groan under the weight of oppression,
they cry for help under the tyranny of the mighty,
[10]but none of them thinks of saying, 'Where is God, my Maker,
who makes glad songs ring out at night,
[11]who has made us more intelligent than wild animals
wiser than birds in the sky?'

[12]Cry they may, but get no answer,
to be spared from the arrogance of the wicked.
[13]Of course God does not listen to trivialities,
Shaddai pays no attention to them.
[14]And how much less when you say, 'I cannot see him,
my case is open and I am waiting for him.'
[15]Or, 'His anger never punishes,
he does not seem aware of human rebellion.'
[16]Hence, when Job speaks, he talks nonsense,
ignorantly babbling on and on.

The real meaning of Job's sufferings

36 Elihu went on speaking. He said:
[2]Be patient a little longer while I explain,
for I have more to say on God's behalf.
[3]I shall range far afield for my arguments
to prove my Maker just.
[4]I guarantee, nothing I shall say will be untrue:
you have a man of sound learning here.
[5]God does not reject anyone whose heart is pure
[6]or let the sinner live on in all his power.
He does accord fair judgement to the afflicted;
[7]he does uphold what the upright deserve.
When he raises kings to thrones,
if they grow proud of their unending rule,
[8]then he fetters them with chains,
they are caught in the bonds of affliction.
[9]He shows them the import of their deeds,
of the sins of pride they have committed.
[10]In their ears he sounds a warning,
ordering them to turn back from doing wrong.
[11]If they take notice and obey him,
the rest of their days are prosperous
and the years pass pleasantly.
[12]If not, they go down the Canal
and perish in their stupidity.
[13]The stubborn, who cherish their anger
and do not cry for help when he chains them,
[14]die in the bloom of youth
or live among the male prostitutes of the temple.
[15]But God saves the afflicted by his affliction,
warning him in his misery.
[16]You, too, he would like to snatch from torment.
While you were enjoying boundless abundance,
with rich food piled high on your table,
[17]you did not bring the wicked to trial
and did not give fair judgement to the orphan.
[18]Beware of being led astray by abundance,
of being corrupted by expensive presents.
[19]Take the powerful to law, not merely the penniless,
those whose arm is strong, not merely the weak.
[20]Do not crush people you do not know
to install your relations in their place.
[21]Avoid any tendency to wrong-doing,
for this is why affliction is testing you now.

Hymn to God's omnipotence

22 See, God is sublime in his strength
and who can teach lessons as he does?
23 Who has ever told him which course to take,
or dared to say to him, 'You have done wrong'?
24 Consider, rather, how you may praise his work,
a theme that many have sung.
25 This is something that everyone can see,
gazing, as we do, from afar.
26 Yes, the greatness of God exceeds our knowledge,
the number of his years is past counting.
27 It is he who makes the raindrops small
and pulverises the rain into mist.
28 And the clouds then pour this out,
sending it streaming down on the human race.
31 By these means, he sustains the peoples,
giving them plenty to eat.
29 And who can fathom how he spreads the clouds,
or why such crashes thunder from his tent?
30 He spreads a mist before him
and covers the tops of the mountains.
32 He gathers up the lightning in his hands,
assigning it the mark where to strike.
33 His crashing gives warning of its coming,
anger flashes out against iniquity.

37 At this, my very heart quakes
and leaps out of its place.
2 Listen, oh listen, to the blast of his voice
and the sound that issues from his mouth.
3 His lightning is hurled across the heaven,
it strikes to the extremities of earth.
4 After it comes a roaring sound,
God thunders with majestic voice.
He does not check his thunderbolts
until his voice resounds no more.
5 Yes, certainly God shows us marvels
and does great deeds that we cannot understand.
6 When he says to the snow, 'Fall on the earth!'
to the showers, 'Now rain hard!'
7 he brings all human activity to a standstill,
for everyone to acknowledge his work.
8 The animals go back to their dens
and take shelter in their lairs.
9 The storm wind comes from the Mansion of the South,
and the north winds usher in the cold.
10 At the breath of God, ice comes next,
the surface of the waters hardens over.
11 He weighs the clouds down with moisture,
and the storm clouds radiate his lightning.
12 He himself guides their wheeling motion
presiding over their seasonal changes.
They carry out his orders to the letter
all over this earthly world.
13 Whether to punish earth's peoples
or as a work of faithful love, he despatches them.

[14]Listen to this, Job, without flinching
and reflect on the marvellous works of God.
[15]Do you know how God controls them
or how his clouds make the lightning flash?
[16]Do you know how he balances the clouds—
a miracle of consummate skill?
[17]When your clothes are hot to your body
and the earth lies still under the south wind,
[18]can you, like him, stretch out the sky,
tempered like a mirror of cast metal?
[19]Teach me what we should say to him:
but better discuss no further, since we are in the dark.
[20]Does he take note when I speak?
When human beings give orders, does he take it in?
[21]There are times when the light vanishes,
behind darkening clouds;
then comes the wind, sweeping them away.
[22]and brightness spreads from the north.
God is clothed in fearful splendour:
[23]he, Shaddai, is far beyond our reach.
Supreme in power, in equity,
excelling in saving justice, yet no oppressor—
[24]no wonder then that people fear him:
everyone thoughtful holds him in awe!

IV: THE DISCOURSES OF YAHWEH

FIRST DISCOURSE

Job must bow to the Creator's wisdom

38 Then from the heart of the tempest Yahweh gave Job his answer. He said:
[2]Who is this, obscuring my intentions
with his ignorant words?
[3]Brace yourself like a fighter;
I am going to ask the questions, and you are to inform me!
[4]Where were you when I laid the earth's foundations?
Tell me, since you are so well-informed!
[5]Who decided its dimensions, do you know?
Or who stretched the measuring line across it?
[6]What supports its pillars at their bases?
Who laid its cornerstone
[7]to the joyful concert of the morning stars
and unanimous acclaim of the sons of God?
[8]Who pent up the sea behind closed doors
when it leapt tumultuous from the womb,
[9]when I wrapped it in a robe of mist
and made black clouds its swaddling bands;
[10]when I cut out the place I had decreed for it
and imposed gates and a bolt?
[11]'Come so far,' I said, 'and no further;
here your proud waves must break!'

12Have you ever in your life given orders to the morning
or sent the dawn to its post,
13to grasp the earth by its edges
and shake the wicked out of it?
14She turns it as red as a clay seal,
she tints it as though it were a dress,
15stealing the light from evil-doers
and breaking the arm raised to strike.
16Have you been right down to the sources of the sea
and walked about at the bottom of the Abyss?
17Have you been shown the gates of Death,
have you seen the janitors of the Shadow dark as death?
18Have you an inkling of the extent of the earth?
Tell me all about it if you have!
19Which is the way to the home of the Light,
and where does darkness live?—
20You could then show them the way to their proper places,
you could put them on the path home again!
21If you do know, you must have been born when they were,
you must be very old by now!

22Have you visited the place where the snow is stored?
Have you seen the stores of hail,
23which I keep for times of distress,
for days of battle and war?
24From which direction does the lightning fork,
where in the world does the east wind blow itself out?
25Who bores a channel for the downpour
or clears the way for the rolling thunder
26so that rain may fall on lands where no one lives,
and the deserts void of human dwelling,
27to meet the needs of the lonely wastes
and make grass sprout on the thirsty ground?
28Has the rain a father?
Who begets the dewdrops?
29What womb brings forth the ice,
who gives birth to the frost of heaven,
30when the waters grow hard as stone
and the surface of the deep congeals?

31Can you fasten the harness of the Pleiades,
or untie Orion's bands?
32Can you guide the Crown season by season
and show the Bear and its cubs which way to go?
33Have you grasped the celestial laws?
Could you make their writ run on the earth?
34Can your voice carry as far as the clouds
and make the pent-up waters do your bidding?
35Will lightning flashes come at your command
and answer, 'Here we are'?
36Who endowed the ibis with wisdom
and gave the cock his intelligence?
37Whose skill details every cloud
and tilts the water-skins of heaven
38until the dust solidifies
and the cracks in the ground close up?

39 Do you go hunting prey for the lioness;
do you satisfy the hunger of young lions
40 where they crouch in their den,
waiting eagerly in the bushes?
41 Who makes provision for the raven
when his little ones cry out to God
craning their necks in search of food?

39

Do you know when mountain goats give birth?
Have you ever watched deer in labour?
2 Have you ever counted the months that they carry their young?
Do you know when they give birth?
3 They crouch to drop their young,
they get rid of their burdens
4 and the calves, having grown big and strong,
go off into the desert and never come back to them.
5 Who has given the wild donkey his freedom,
who has undone the harness of the brayer?
6 I have given him the wastelands as his home,
the salt plain as his habitat.
7 He scorns the turmoil of the town,
obeys no donkey-man's shouts.
8 The mountains are the pastures that he ranges
in quest of anything green.
9 Is the wild ox willing to serve you
or spend a night beside your manger?
10 If you tie a rope round his neck
will he harrow the furrows for you?
11 Can you rely on his massive strength
and leave him to do your heavy work?
12 Can you depend on him to come home
and pile your grain on your threshing-floor?

13 Can the wing of the ostrich be compared
with the plumage of stork or falcon?
14 She leaves her eggs on the ground
with only earth to warm them;
15 forgetting that a foot may tread on them
or a wild animal crush them.
16 Cruel to her chicks as if they were not hers,
little she cares if her labour goes for nothing.
17 God, you see, has deprived her of wisdom
and given her no share of intelligence.
18 Yet, if she bestirs herself to use her height,
she can make fools of horse and rider too.

19 Are you the one who makes the horse so brave
and covers his neck with flowing mane?
20 Do you make him leap like a grasshopper?
His haughty neighing inspires terror.
21 Exultantly he paws the soil of the valley,
and charges the battle-line in all his strength.
22 He laughs at fear; he is afraid of nothing,
he recoils before no sword.
23 On his back the quiver rattles,
the flashing spear and javelin.
24 Trembling with impatience, he eats up the miles;
when the trumpet sounds, there is no holding him.

25 At each trumpet blast he neighs exultantly.
He scents the battle from afar,
the thundering of the commanders and the war cry.

26 Is it your wisdom that sets the hawk flying
when he spreads his wings to travel south?
27 Does the eagle soar at your command
to make her eyrie in the heights?
28 She spends her nights among the crags
with a needle of rock as her fortress,
29 from which she watches for prey,
fixing it with her far-ranging eye.
30 Even her young drink blood;
where anyone has been killed, she is there.

40 Still speaking to Job, Yahweh said:

2 Is Yahweh's opponent going to give way?
Has God's critic thought up an answer?

3 Job replied to Yahweh:

4 My words have been frivolous: what can I reply?
I had better lay my hand over my mouth.
5 I have spoken once, I shall not speak again;
I have spoken twice, I have nothing more to say.

SECOND DISCOURSE

God is master of the forces of evil

6 Yahweh gave Job his answer from the heart of the tempest. He said:

7 Brace yourself like a fighter,
I am going to ask the questions, and you are to inform me!
8 Do you really want to reverse my judgement,
put me in the wrong and yourself in the right?
9 Has your arm the strength of God's,
can your voice thunder as loud?
10 Come on, display your majesty and grandeur,
robe yourself in splendour and glory.
11 Let the fury of your anger burst forth,
humble the haughty at a glance!
12 At a glance, bring down all the proud,
strike down the wicked where they stand.
13 Bury the lot of them in the ground,
shut them, every one, in the Dungeon.
14 And I shall be the first to pay you homage,
since your own right hand is strong enough to save you.

Behemoth[a]

15 But look at Behemoth, my creature, just as you are!
He feeds on greenstuff like the ox,
16 but what strength he has in his loins,
what power in his stomach muscles!

40a Lit. 'the Beast', sometimes a mythical buffalo, but here the hippopotamus.

[17]His tail is as stiff as a cedar,
the sinews of his thighs are tightly knit.
[18]His bones are bronze tubes,
his frame like forged iron.
[19]He is the first of the works of God.
His Maker threatened him with the sword,
[20]forbidding him the mountain regions
and all the wild animals that play there.
[21]Under the lotus he lies,
he hides among the reeds in the swamps.
[22]The leaves of the lotus give him shade,
the willows by the stream shelter him.
[23]If the river overflows, he does not worry:
Jordan might come up to his mouth, but he would not care.
[24]Who is going to catch him by the eyes
or put poles through his nose?

Leviathan[b]

[25]Leviathan, too! Can you catch him with a fish-hook
or hold his tongue down with a rope?
[26]Can you put a cane through his nostrils
or pierce his jaw with a hook?
[27]Will he plead lengthily with you,
addressing you in diffident tones?
[28]Will he strike a bargain with you
to become your slave for life?
[29]Will you make a pet of him, like a bird,
keep him on a lead to amuse your little girls?
[30]Is he to be sold by the fishing guild
and then retailed by merchants?
[31]Riddle his hide with darts?
Or his head with fishing spears?
[32]You have only to lay a finger on him
never to forget the struggle or risk it again!
41 Any hope you might have would be futile,
the mere sight of him would overwhelm you.
[2]When roused, he grows ferocious,
who could ever stand up to him?
[3]Who has ever attacked him with impunity?
No one beneath all heaven!
[4]Next I will talk of his limbs
and describe his matchless strength—
[5]who can undo the front of his tunic
or pierce the double armour of his breastplate?
[6]Who dare open the gates of his mouth?
Terror reigns round his teeth!
[7]His back is like rows of shields,
sealed with a stone seal,
[8]touching each other so close
that no breath could pass between,
[9]sticking to one another
making an impervious whole.

40b Properly the monster of chaos, see 26:13, but here described as a crocodile.

10His sneezes radiate light,
his eyes are like the eyelashes of the dawn.
11From his mouth come fiery torches,
sparks of fire fly out of it.
12His nostrils belch smoke
like a cauldron boiling on the fire.
13His breath could kindle coals,
flame issues from his mouth.
14His strength resides in his neck,
violence leaps before him as he goes.
17When he stands up, the waves take fright
and the billows of the sea retreat.
15The strips of his flesh are jointed together,
firmly set in and immovable.
16His heart is as hard as rock
unyielding as the lower millstone.
18Sword may strike but will not stick in him,
no more will spear, javelin or lance.
19Iron means no more to him than straw,
nor bronze than rotten wood.
20No arrow can make him flee,
a sling-stone tickles him like hay.
21Club seems to him like straw,
he laughs at the whirring javelin.
22He has sharp potsherds underneath,
and moves across the slime like a harrow.
23He makes the depths seethe like a cauldron,
he makes the sea fume like a scent burner.
24Behind him he leaves a glittering wake—
a white fleece seems to float on the deeps.
25He has no equal on earth,
being created without fear.
26He looks the haughtiest in the eye;
of all the lordly beasts he is king.

Job's final answer

42 This was the answer Job gave to Yahweh:
2I know that you are all-powerful:
what you conceive, you can perform.
3I was the man who misrepresented your intentions
with my ignorant words.
You have told me about great works that I cannot understand,
about marvels which are beyond me, of which I know nothing.
4(Listen, please, and let me speak:
I am going to ask the questions, and you are to inform me.)
5Before, I knew you only by hearsay
but now, having seen you with my own eyes,
6I retract what I have said,
and repent in dust and ashes.

V: EPILOGUE

Yahweh rebukes the three sages

7 When Yahweh had finished saying this to
Job, he said to Eliphaz of Teman, 'I burn
with anger against you and your two friends,
for not having spoken correctly about me as
my servant Job has done. 8 So now find seven
bullocks and seven rams, and take them back
with you to my servant Job and make a
burnt offering for yourselves, while Job, my
servant, offers prayers for you. I shall show
him favour and shall not inflict my
displeasure on you for not having spoken
about me correctly, as my servant Job has
done.' 9 Eliphaz of Teman, Bildad of Shuah
and Zophar of Naamath went away to do as
Yahweh had ordered, and Yahweh listened
to Job with favour.

Yahweh restores Job's fortunes

10 And Yahweh restored Job's condition,
while Job was interceding for his friends.
More than that, Yahweh gave him double
what he had before. 11 And all his brothers
and all his sisters and all his friends of former
times came to see him. Over dinner in his
house, they showed their sympathy and
comforted him for all the evils Yahweh had
inflicted on him. Each of them gave him a
silver coin, and each a gold ring. 12 Yahweh
blessed Job's latter condition even more than
his former one. He came to own fourteen
thousand sheep, six thousand camels, a thou-
sand yoke of oxen and a thousand she-
donkeys. 13 He had seven sons and three
daughters; 14 his first daughter he called
'Turtledove', the second 'Cassia' and the
third 'Mascara'. 15 Throughout the land there
were no women as beautiful as the daughters
of Job. And their father gave them inherit-
ance rights like their brothers.
16 After this, Job lived for another one
hundred and forty years, and saw his children
and his children's children to the fourth
generation. 17 Then, old and full of days, Job
died.

THE PSALMS

The Psalter is Israel's hymnbook. It includes prayers for every occasion in the nation's life: for the solemn Temple liturgy as well as private, meditative prayer; prayers after victory and defeat, in joy and in sorrow; prayers of thankful praise and prayers of sad entreaty. Many are royal prayers, at an enthronement or royal wedding, and show the messianic hopes centred on David's line; others celebrate the kingship of Yahweh.

Although the historical data given in the italicised titles are later and unreliable, historical allusions in the psalms themselves and the language show a vast range of dates, spreading from David's time right down to the Maccabaean era. The tradition of David's own association with the liturgy and the psalms is so strong that some may even stem from him. Some were composed for different schools of Temple singers, and other earlier, partial collections existed, which explains some duplication and overlap.

This is the poetry of a vivid and passionate people. It uses colourful, even wild, imagery of despair, of God's intervention, of hopes for future prosperity, and prays for violent revenge on opponents, protesting innocence and guilt with similar whole-hearted sincerity.

In this edition the Hebr. numbering of the Pss is used. From Ps 10 to Ps 147 this is ahead of the Gk and Vulgate numbering, which is given in the margin.

THE PSALMS

PSALM 1

The two paths

1 How blessed is anyone who rejects the advice of the wicked
and does not take a stand in the path that sinners tread,
nor a seat in company with cynics,
2 but who delights in the law of Yahweh
and murmurs his law day and night.

3 Such a one is like a tree planted near streams;
it bears fruit in season
and its leaves never wither,
and every project succeeds.
4 How different the wicked, how different!

Just like chaff blown around by the wind
5 the wicked will not stand firm at the Judgement
nor sinners in the gathering of the upright.
6 For Yahweh watches over the path of the upright,
but the path of the wicked is doomed.

PSALM 2

The messianic drama

1 Why this uproar among the nations,
this impotent muttering of the peoples?
2 Kings of the earth take up position,
princes plot together
against Yahweh and his anointed,
3 'Now let us break their fetters!
Now let us throw off their bonds!'

4 He who is enthroned in the heavens laughs,
Yahweh makes a mockery of them,
5 then in his anger rebukes them,
in his rage he strikes them with terror.
6 'I myself have anointed my king
on Zion my holy mountain.'

7 I will proclaim the decree of Yahweh:

He said to me, 'You are my son,
today have I fathered you.
8 Ask of me, and I shall give you the nations as your birthright,
the whole wide world as your possession.
9 With an iron sceptre you will break them,
shatter them like so many pots.'

10 So now, you kings, come to your senses,
you earthly rulers, learn your lesson!
11 In fear be submissive to Yahweh;
12 with trembling kiss his feet,
lest he be angry and your way come to nothing,
for his fury flares up in a moment.

How blessed are all who take refuge in him!

PSALM 3

Morning prayer of the upright in persecution

Psalm *Of David* *When he was fleeing from his son Absalom*

1 Yahweh, how countless are my enemies,
how countless those who rise up against me,
2 how countless those who say of me,
'No salvation for him from his God!' *Pause*

3 But you, Yahweh, the shield at my side,
my glory, you hold my head high.
4 I cry out to Yahweh;
he answers from his holy mountain. *Pause*

5 As for me, if I lie down and sleep,
I shall awake, for Yahweh sustains me.
6 I have no fear of people in their thousands upon thousands,
who range themselves against me wherever I turn.

7 Arise, Yahweh, rescue me, my God!
You strike all my foes across the face,
you break the teeth of the wicked.
8 In Yahweh is salvation,
on your people, your blessing! *Pause*

PSALM 4

Evening prayer

For the choirmaster *For strings* *Psalm* *Of David*

1 When I call, answer me, God, upholder of my right.
In my distress you have set me at large;
take pity on me and hear my prayer!

2 Children of men, how long will you be heavy of heart,
why love what is vain and chase after illusions? *Pause*

3 Realise that Yahweh performs wonders for his faithful,
Yahweh listens when I call to him.

4 Be careful not to sin,
speak in your hearts, and on your beds keep silence. *Pause*

5 Loyally offer sacrifices, and trust in Yahweh.

6 Many keep saying, 'Who will put happiness before our eyes?'
Let the light of your face shine on us.

Yahweh, 7 to my heart you are a richer joy
than all their corn and new wine.

8 In peace I lie down and at once fall asleep,
for it is you and none other, Yahweh, who make me rest secure.

PSALM 5

Morning prayer

For the choirmaster For flutes Psalm Of David

1 Give ear to my words, Yahweh,
spare a thought for my sighing.
2 Listen to my cry for help,
my King and my God!

To you I pray, 3 Yahweh.
At daybreak you hear my voice;
at daybreak I lay my case before you
and fix my eyes on you.

4 You are not a God who takes pleasure in evil,
no sinner can be your guest.
5 Boasters cannot stand their ground
under your gaze.

You hate evil-doers,
6 liars you destroy;
the violent and deceitful
Yahweh detests.

7 But, so great is your faithful love,
I may come into your house,
and before your holy temple
bow down in reverence of you.

8 In your saving justice, Yahweh, lead me,
because of those who lie in wait for me;
make your way plain before me.

9 Not a word from their lips can be trusted,
through and through they are destruction,
their throats are wide-open graves,
their tongues seductive.

10 Lay the guilt on them, God,
make their intrigues their own downfall;

for their countless offences, thrust them from you,
since they have rebelled against you.

11 But joy for all who take refuge in you,
endless songs of gladness!
You shelter them, they rejoice in you,
those who love your name.

12 It is you who bless the upright, Yahweh,
you surround them with favour as with a shield.

PSALM 6[a]

Supplication in time of trial

For the choirmaster For strings For the octachord Psalm Of David

1 Yahweh, let your rebuke to me not be in anger,
your punishment not in the heat of wrath.
2 Have pity on me, Yahweh, for I am fading away.
Heal me, Yahweh, my bones are shaken,
3 my spirit is shaken to its very depths.
But you, Yahweh . . . how long?

4 Yahweh, relent and save my life
rescue me because of your faithful love,
5 for in death there is no remembrance of you;
who could sing your praises in Sheol?

6 I am worn out with groaning,
every night I drench my pillow
and soak my bed with tears.
7 My eyes waste away with vexation.
Arrogance from all my foes!
8 Away from me, all evil-doers!

For Yahweh has heard the sound of my weeping,
9 Yahweh has heard my pleading.
Yahweh will accept my prayer.
10 Let all my enemies be put to confusion, shaken to their depths,
let them retreat in sudden confusion.

PSALM 7

Prayer of the upright in persecution

Lament Of David Which he sang to Yahweh about Cush the Benjaminite

1 Yahweh my God, I take refuge in you,
save me from all my pursuers and rescue me,
2 or he will savage me like a lion,
carry me off with no one to rescue me.

6a The first of the seven Penitential Psalms (6; 32; 38; 51; 102; 130; 142).

3 Yahweh my God, if I have done this:
if injustice has stained my hands,
4 if I have repaid my ally with treachery
or spared one who attacked me unprovoked,
5 may an enemy hunt me down and catch me,
may he trample my life into the ground
and crush my vital parts into the dust. *Pause*

6 Arise, Yahweh, in your anger,
rise up against the arrogance of my foes.
Awake, my God,
you demand judgement.
7 Let the assembly of nations gather round you;
return above it on high!
8 (Yahweh judges the nations.)

Judge me, Yahweh, as my uprightness
and my integrity deserve.
9 Put an end to the malice of the wicked,
make the upright stand firm,
you who discern hearts and minds,
God the upright.

10 God is a shield that protects me,
saving the honest of heart.
11 God is an upright judge,
slow to anger,
but a God at all times threatening
12 for those who will not repent.

Let the enemy whet his sword,
draw his bow and make ready;
13 but he is making ready instruments of death for himself
and tipping his arrows with fire;
14 look at him: pregnant with malice,
conceiving spite, he gives birth to treachery.

15 He digs a trap, scoops it out,
but he falls into the snare he made himself.
16 His spite recoils on his own head,
his brutality falls back on his own skull.

17 I thank Yahweh for his saving justice.
I sing to the name of the Most High.

PSALM 8

The power of God's name

For the choirmaster On the . . . of Gath[a] Psalm Of David

1 Yahweh our Lord,
how majestic is your name throughout the world!

Whoever keeps singing of your majesty higher than the heavens,
2 even through the mouths of children, or of babes in arms,

8a Perhaps on the harp or on a melody of Gath, i.e. Philistine.

you make him a fortress, firm against your foes,
to subdue the enemy and the rebel.

3 I look up at your heavens, shaped by your fingers,
at the moon and the stars you set firm—
4 what are human beings that you spare a thought for them,
or the child of Adam that you care for him?

5 Yet you have made him little less than a god,
you have crowned him with glory and beauty,
6 made him lord of the works of your hands,
put all things under his feet,

7 sheep and cattle, all of them,
and even the wild beasts,
8 birds in the sky, fish in the sea,
when he makes his way across the ocean.

9 Yahweh our Lord,
how majestic your name throughout the world!

PSALMS 9–10[a]

God strikes the wicked and saves the humble

For the choirmaster On oboe and harp Psalm Of David

Aleph 1 I thank you, Yahweh, with my whole heart,
I recount all your wonders,

2 I rejoice and delight in you,
I sing to your name, Most High.

Bet 3 My enemies are in retreat,
they stumble and perish at your presence,
4 for you have given fair judgement in my favour,
seated on your throne as upright judge.

Gimel 5 You have rebuked the nations, destroyed the wicked,
blotted out their name for ever and ever;
6 the enemy is wiped out—mere ruins for ever—
you have annihilated their cities, their memory has perished.

He See, 7 Yahweh is enthroned for ever,
keeping his throne firm for judgement;
8 he will himself judge the world in uprightness,
will give a true verdict on the nations.

Waw 9 May Yahweh be a stronghold for the oppressed,
a stronghold in times of trouble!
10 Those who revere your name can rely on you,
you never desert those who seek you, Yahweh.

Zain 11 Sing to Yahweh who dwells in Zion,
tell the nations his mighty deeds,
12 for the avenger of blood does not forget them,
he does not ignore the cry of the afflicted.

9–10a One poem with initial letters in alphabetical order, though in our corrupt text some are missing.

Het [13]Have pity on me, Yahweh, see my affliction,
pull me back from the gates of death,
[14]that I may recount all your praises at the gates of the daughter of Zion
and rejoice in your salvation.

Tet [15]The nations have fallen into the trap they made,
their feet caught in the snare they laid.
[16]Yahweh has made himself known, given judgement,
he has ensnared the wicked in the work of their own hands. *Muted music Pause*

Yod [17]May the wicked turn away to Sheol,
all the nations forgetful of God.
Kaph [18]For the needy is not forgotten for ever,
not for ever does the hope of the poor come to nothing.

[19]Arise, Yahweh; human strength shall not prevail.
The nations shall stand trial before you.
[20]Strike them with terror, Yahweh;
the nations shall know that they are no more than human! *Pause*

10

Lamed [1]Why, Yahweh, do you keep so distant,
stay hidden in times of trouble?
[2]In his pride the wicked hunts down the weak,
who is caught in the schemes he devises.
(Mem) [3]The wicked is proud of his inmost desires,
by his blasphemies the grasping spurns Yahweh,
(Nun) [4]the wicked in his arrogance does not look very far;
'There is no God,' is his only thought.

[5]In all circumstances his step is assured;
your judgements are above his head.
His rivals? He scoffs at them all.

[6]He says in his heart, 'I shall never be shaken,'
free of trouble himself, [7]he wishes it on others.

(Samek)
Pe His speech is full of lies and browbeating,
under his tongue lurk spite and wickedness.
[8]In the undergrowth he lies in ambush,
in his hiding-place he murders the innocent.

Ain He watches intently for the downtrodden,
[9]lurking unseen like a lion in his lair,
lurking to pounce on the poor;
he pounces on him and drags him off in his net.

(Zade)
[10]He keeps watch, crouching down low,
the poor wretch falls into his clutches;
[11]he says in his heart, 'God forgets,
he has turned away his face to avoid seeing the end.'

Qoph [12]Rise, Yahweh! God, raise your hand,
do not forget the afflicted!
[13]Why should the wicked spurn God,
assuring himself you will never follow it up?

Resh [14]You have seen for yourself the trouble and vexation,
you watch so as to take it in hand.

The oppressed relies on you;
you are the only recourse of the orphan.

Shin 15 Break the arm of the wicked and evil,
seek out wickedness till there is none left to be found.
16 Yahweh is king for ever and ever,
the heathen has vanished from his country.

Taw 17 Yahweh, you listen to the laments of the poor,
you give them courage, you grant them a hearing,
18 to give judgement for the orphaned and exploited,
so that earthborn humans may strike terror no more.

PSALM 11

V 10

The confidence of the upright

For the choirmaster Of David

1 In Yahweh I have found refuge.
How can you say to me,
'Bird, flee to your mountain?

2 'For look, the wicked are drawing their bows,
fitting their arrows to the string
to shoot honest men from the shadows.
3 If the foundations fall to ruin, what can the upright do?'

4 Yahweh in his holy temple!
Yahweh, his throne is in heaven;
his eyes watch over the world,
his gaze scrutinises the children of Adam.

5 Yahweh examines the upright and the wicked,
the lover of violence he detests.
6 He will rain down red-hot coals,
fire and sulphur on the wicked,
a scorching wind will be their lot.

7 For Yahweh is upright and loves uprightness,
the honest will ever see his face.

PSALM 12

V 11

Against a treacherous world

For the choirmaster On the octachord Psalm Of David

1 Help, Yahweh! No one loyal is left,
the faithful have vanished from among the children of Adam.
2 Friend tells lies to friend,
and, smooth-tongued, speaks from an insincere heart.

3 May Yahweh cut away every smooth lip,
every boastful tongue,

4 those who say, 'In our tongue lies our strength,
our lips are our allies; who can master us?'
5 'For the poor who are plundered, the needy who groan,
now will I act,' says Yahweh,
'I will grant salvation to those who sigh for it.'

6 Yahweh's promises are promises unalloyed,
natural silver which comes from the earth seven times refined.

7 You, Yahweh, will watch over them,
you will protect them from that brood for ever.
8 The wicked will scatter in every direction,
as the height of depravity among the children of Adam.

PSALM 13

V 12

A confident appeal

For the choirmaster Psalm Of David

1 How long, Yahweh, will you forget me? For ever?
How long will you turn away your face from me?
2 How long must I nurse rebellion in my soul,
sorrow in my heart day and night?
How long is the enemy to domineer over me?
3 Look down, answer me, Yahweh my God!
Give light to my eyes or I shall fall into the sleep of death.

4 Or my foe will boast, 'I have overpowered him,'
and my enemy have the joy of seeing me stumble.
5 As for me, I trust in your faithful love, Yahweh.
Let my heart delight in your saving help,
let me sing to Yahweh for his generosity to me,
let me sing to the name of Yahweh the Most High!

PSALM 14[a]

V 13

The fate of the godless

For the choirmaster Of David

1 The fool has said in his heart,
'There is no God.'
Their deeds are corrupt and vile,
not one of them does right.

2 Yahweh looks down from heaven
at the children of Adam.
To see if a single one is wise,
a single one seeks God.

3 All have turned away,
all alike turned sour,

14a Almost identical with Ps 53 except that the proper name 'Yahweh' here occurs for 'God'.

not one of them does right,
not a single one.

4 Are they not aware, all these evil-doers?
They are devouring my people,
this is the bread they eat,
and they never call to Yahweh.

5 They will be gripped with fear,
where there is no need for fear,
for God takes the side of the upright;
6 you may mock the plans of the poor,
but Yahweh is their refuge.

7 Who will bring from Zion salvation for Israel?
When Yahweh brings his people home,
what joy for Jacob, what happiness for Israel!

PSALM 15

V 14

The guest of Yahweh

Psalm *Of David*

1 Yahweh, who can find a home in your tent,
who can dwell on your holy mountain?

2 Whoever lives blamelessly,
who acts uprightly,
who speaks the truth from the heart,
3 who keeps the tongue under control,

who does not wrong a comrade,
who casts no discredit on a neighbour,
4 who looks with scorn on the vile,
but honours those who fear Yahweh,

who stands by an oath at any cost,
5 who asks no interest on loans,
who takes no bribe to harm the innocent.
No one who so acts can ever be shaken.

PSALM 16

V 15

Yahweh my heritage

In a quiet voice *Of David*

1 Protect me, O God, in you is my refuge.

2 To Yahweh I say, 'You are my Lord,
my happiness is in none 3 of the sacred spirits of the earth.'

They only take advantage of all who love them.
4 People flock to their teeming idols.
Never shall I pour libations to them!
Never take their names on my lips.

5 My birthright, my cup is Yahweh;
you, you alone, hold my lot secure.
6 The measuring-line marks out for me a delightful place,
my birthright is all I could wish.

7 I bless Yahweh who is my counsellor,
even at night my heart instructs me.
8 I keep Yahweh before me always,
for with him at my right hand, nothing can shake me.

9 So my heart rejoices, my soul delights,
my body too will rest secure,
10 for you will not abandon me to Sheol,
you cannot allow your faithful servant to see the abyss.
11 You will teach me the path of life,
unbounded joy in your presence,
at your right hand delight for ever.

PSALM 17

V 16

The plea of the innocent

Prayer *Of David*

1 Listen, Yahweh, to an upright cause,
pay attention to my cry,
lend an ear to my prayer,
my lips free from deceit.
2 From your presence will issue my vindication,
your eyes fixed on what is right.

3 You probe my heart, examine me at night,
you test me by fire and find no evil.
I have not sinned with my mouth 4 as most people do.

I have treasured the word from your lips,
5 my steps never stray from the paths you lay down,
from your tracks; so my feet never stumble.
6 I call upon you, God, for you answer me;
turn your ear to me, hear what I say.
7 Show the evidence of your faithful love,
saviour of those who hope in your strength against attack.

8 Guard me as the pupil of an eye,
shelter me in the shadow of your wings
9 from the presence of the wicked who would maltreat me;
deadly enemies are closing in on me.
10 Engrossed in themselves
they are mouthing arrogant words.
11 They are advancing against me, now they are closing in,
watching for the chance to hurl me to the ground,
12 like a lion preparing to pounce,
like a young lion crouching in ambush.

13 Arise, Yahweh, confront him and bring him down,
with your sword save my life from the wicked,

14 Yahweh, from mortals, by your hand,
from mortals whose part in life is in this world.

You fill their bellies from your store,
their children will have all they desire,
and leave their surplus to their children.
15 But I in my uprightness will see your face,
and when I awake I shall be filled with the vision of you.

PSALM 18[a] V 17

A king's thanksgiving

For the choirmaster Of David, the servant of Yahweh, who addressed the words of this song to Yahweh when Yahweh had delivered him from all his enemies and from the clutches of Saul. He said:

1 I love you, Yahweh, my strength
(my Saviour, you have saved me from violence).

2 Yahweh is my rock and my fortress,
my deliverer is my God.
I take refuge in him, my rock,
my shield, my saving strength,
my stronghold, my place of refuge.

3 I call to Yahweh who is worthy of praise,
and I am saved from my foes.

4 With Death's breakers closing in on me,
Belial's torrents ready to swallow me,
5 Sheol's snares every side of me,
Death's traps lying ahead of me,

6 I called to Yahweh in my anguish,
I cried for help to my God;
from his Temple he heard my voice,
my cry came to his ears.

7 Then the earth quaked and rocked,
the mountains' foundations shuddered,
they quaked at his blazing anger.
8 Smoke rose from his nostrils,
from his mouth devouring fire
(coals were kindled at it).

9 He parted the heavens and came down,
a storm-cloud underneath his feet;
10 riding one of the winged creatures, he flew,
soaring on the wings of the wind.

11 His covering he made the darkness,
his pavilion dark waters and dense cloud.
12 A brightness lit up before him,
hail and blazing fire.

18a || 2 S 22.

13 Yahweh thundered from the heavens,
the Most High made his voice heard.
14 He shot his arrows and scattered them,
he hurled his lightning and routed them.

15 The very springs of ocean were exposed,
the world's foundations were laid bare,
at your roaring, Yahweh,
at the blast of breath from your nostrils!

16 He reached down from on high, snatched me up,
pulled me from the watery depths,
17 rescued me from my mighty foe,
from my enemies who were stronger than I.

18 They assailed me on my day of disaster
but Yahweh was there to support me;
19 he freed me, set me at large,
he rescued me because he loves me.

20 Yahweh rewards me for my uprightness,
as my hands are pure, so he repays me,
21 since I have kept the ways of Yahweh,
and not fallen away from my God.

22 His judgements are all before me,
his statutes I have not put away from me.
23 I am blameless before him,
I keep myself clear of evil.

24 So Yahweh repaid me for acting uprightly
because he could see I was pure.
25 You are faithful to the faithful,
blameless with the blameless,

26 sincere to the sincere,
but cunning to the crafty,
27 you save a people that is humble
and humiliate those with haughty looks.

28 Yahweh, you yourself are my lamp,
my God lights up my darkness;
29 with you I storm the rampart,
with my God I can scale any wall.

30 This God, his way is blameless;
the word of Yahweh is refined in the furnace,
for he alone is the shield
of all who take refuge in him.

31 For who is God but Yahweh,
who is a rock but our God?
32 This God who girds me with strength,
who makes my way free from blame,

33 who makes me as swift as a deer
and sets me firmly on the heights,
34 who trains my hands for battle,
my arms to bend a bow of bronze.

35 You give me your invincible shield

(your right hand upholds me)
you never cease to listen to me,
36 you give me the strides of a giant,
give me ankles that never weaken.

37 I pursue my enemies and overtake them,
not turning back till they are annihilated;
38 I strike them down and they cannot rise,
they fall, they are under my feet.

39 You have girded me with strength for the fight,
bent down my assailants beneath me,
40 made my enemies retreat before me;
and those who hate me I destroy.

41 They cry out, there is no one to save;
to Yahweh, but no answer comes.
42 I crumble them like dust before the wind,
trample them like the mud of the streets.

43 You free me from the quarrels of my people,
you place me at the head of the nations,
a people I did not know are now my servants;

44 foreigners come wooing my favour,
no sooner do they hear than they obey me;
45 foreigners grow faint of heart,
they come trembling out of their fastnesses.

46 Life to Yahweh! Blessed be my rock!
Exalted be the God of my salvation,
47 the God who gives me vengeance,
and subjects whole peoples to me,

48 who rescues me from my raging enemies.
You lift me high above those who attack me,
you deliver me from the man of violence.

49 For this I will praise you, Yahweh, among the nations,
and sing praise to your name.

50 He saves his king time after time,
displays his faithful love for his anointed,
for David and his heirs for ever.

PSALM 19

V 18

Yahweh, sun of saving justice

For the choirmaster Psalm Of David

1 The heavens declare the glory of God,
the vault of heaven proclaims his handiwork,
2 day discourses of it to day,
night to night hands on the knowledge.

3 No utterance at all, no speech,
not a sound to be heard,
4 but from the entire earth the design stands out,
this message reaches the whole world.

High above, he pitched a tent for the sun,
5 who comes forth from his pavilion like a bridegroom,
delights like a champion in the course to be run.

6 Rising on the one horizon
he runs his circuit to the other,
and nothing can escape his heat.

7 The Law of Yahweh is perfect,
refreshment to the soul;
the decree of Yahweh is trustworthy,
wisdom for the simple.

8 The precepts of Yahweh are honest,
joy for the heart;
the commandment of Yahweh is pure,
light for the eyes.

9 The fear of Yahweh is pure,
lasting for ever;
the judgements of Yahweh are true,
upright, every one,

10 more desirable than gold,
even than the finest gold;
his words are sweeter than honey,
that drips from the comb.

11 Thus your servant is formed by them;
observing them brings great reward.
12 But who can detect his own failings?
Wash away my hidden faults.

13 And from pride preserve your servant,
never let it be my master.
So shall I be above reproach,
free from grave sin.

14 May the words of my mouth always find favour,
and the whispering of my heart,
in your presence, Yahweh,
my rock, my redeemer.

PSALM 20

V 19

Prayer for the king

For the choirmaster Psalm Of David

1 May Yahweh answer you in time of trouble,
may the name of the God of Jacob protect you!
2 May he send you help from the sanctuary,
give you support from Zion!

3 May he remember all your sacrifices
and delight in your burnt offerings! *Pause*
4 May he grant you your heart's desire
and crown all your plans with success!

5 So that with joy we can hail your victory
and draw up our ranks in the name of our God.

May Yahweh grant all your petitions.

6 Now I know that Yahweh
gives victory to his anointed.
He will respond from his holy heavens
with great deeds of victory from his right hand.

7 Some call on chariots, some on horses,
but we on the name of Yahweh our God.
8 They will crumple and fall,
while we stand upright and firm.

9 Yahweh, save the king,
answer us when we call.

PSALM 21

V 20

For a coronation ceremony

For the choirmaster Psalm Of David

1 Yahweh, the king rejoices in your power;
How your saving help fills him with joy!
2 You have granted him his heart's desire,
not denied him the prayer of his lips. *Pause*

3 For you come to meet him with blessings of prosperity,
put a crown of pure gold on his head.
4 He has asked for life, you have given it him,
length of days for ever and ever.

5 Great his glory through your saving help;
you invest him with splendour and majesty.
6 You confer on him everlasting blessings,
you gladden him with the joy of your presence.
7 For the king puts his trust in Yahweh;
the faithful love of the Most High will keep him from falling.

8 Your hand will reach all your enemies,
your right hand all who hate you.
9 You will hurl them into a blazing furnace
on the day when you appear;
Yahweh will engulf them in his anger,
and fire will devour them.
10 You will purge the earth of their descendants,
the human race of their posterity.

11 They have devised evil against you
but, plot as they may, they will not succeed,
12 since you will make them turn tail,
by shooting your arrows in their faces.

13 Rise, Yahweh, in your power!
We will sing and make music in honour of your strength.

PSALM 22

V 21

The sufferings and hopes of the upright

For the choirmaster To 'the Doe of the Dawn' Psalm Of David

1 My God, my God, why have you forsaken me?
The words of my groaning do nothing to save me.
2 My God, I call by day but you do not answer,
at night, but I find no respite.

3 Yet you, the Holy One,
who make your home in the praises of Israel,
4 in you our ancestors put their trust,
they trusted and you set them free.
5 To you they called for help and were delivered;
in you they trusted and were not put to shame.

6 But I am a worm, less than human,
scorn of mankind, contempt of the people;
7 all who see me jeer at me,
they sneer and wag their heads,
8 'He trusted himself to Yahweh, let Yahweh set him free!
Let him deliver him, as he took such delight in him.'

9 It was you who drew me from the womb
and soothed me on my mother's breast.
10 On you was I cast from my birth,
from the womb I have belonged to you.
11 Do not hold aloof, for trouble is upon me,
and no one to help me!

12 Many bulls are encircling me,
wild bulls of Bashan closing in on me.
13 Lions ravening and roaring
open their jaws at me.

14 My strength is trickling away,
my bones are all disjointed,
my heart has turned to wax,
melting inside me.
15 My mouth is dry as earthenware,
my tongue sticks to my jaw.
You lay me down in the dust of death.

16 A pack of dogs surrounds me,
a gang of villains closing in on me
as if to hack off my hands and my feet.
17 I can count every one of my bones,
while they look on and gloat;
18 they divide my garments among them
and cast lots for my clothing.

19 Yahweh, do not hold aloof!
My strength, come quickly to my help,
20 rescue my soul from the sword,
the one life I have from the grasp of the dog!
21 Save me from the lion's mouth,
my poor life from the wild bulls' horns!

22I shall proclaim your name to my brothers,
praise you in full assembly:
23'You who fear Yahweh, praise him!
All the race of Jacob, honour him!
Revere him, all the race of Israel!'

24For he has not despised
nor disregarded the poverty of the poor,
has not turned away his face,
but has listened to the cry for help.

25Of you is my praise in the thronged assembly,
I will perform my vows before all who fear him.
26The poor will eat and be filled,
those who seek Yahweh will praise him,
'May your heart live for ever.'

27The whole wide world will remember and return to Yahweh,
all the families of nations bow down before him.
28For to Yahweh, ruler of the nations, belongs kingly power!
29All who prosper on earth will bow before him,
all who go down to the dust will do reverence before him.
And those who are dead, 30their descendants will serve him,
will proclaim his name to generations 31still to come;
and these will tell of his saving justice to a people yet unborn:
he has fulfilled it.

PSALM 23

V 22

The good Shepherd

Psalm Of David

1Yahweh is my shepherd, I lack nothing.
2In grassy meadows he lets me lie.

By tranquil streams he leads me
3to restore my spirit.
He guides me in paths of saving justice
as befits his name.

4Even were I to walk in a ravine as dark as death
I should fear no danger, for you are at my side.
Your staff and your crook are there to soothe me.

5You prepare a table for me
under the eyes of my enemies;
you anoint my head with oil;
my cup brims over.

6Kindness and faithful love pursue me
every day of my life.
I make my home in the house of Yahweh
for all time to come.

PSALM 24

V 23

For a solemn entry into the sanctuary

Psalm *Of David*

[1]To Yahweh belong the earth and all it contains,
the world and all who live there;
[2]it is he who laid its foundations on the seas,
on the flowing waters fixed it firm.

[3]Who shall go up to the mountain of Yahweh?
Who shall take a stand in his holy place?

[4]The clean of hands and pure of heart,
whose heart is not set on vanities,
who does not swear an oath in order to deceive.

[5]Such a one will receive blessing from Yahweh,
saving justice from the God of his salvation.
[6]Such is the people that seeks him,
that seeks your presence, God of Jacob. *Pause*

[7]Gates, lift high your heads,
raise high the ancient gateways,
and the king of glory shall enter!

[8]Who is he, this king of glory?
It is Yahweh, strong and valiant,
Yahweh valiant in battle.

[9]Gates, lift high your heads,
raise high the ancient gateways,
and the king of glory shall enter!

[10]Who is he, this king of glory?
Yahweh Sabaoth,
he is the king of glory. *Pause*

PSALM 25

V 24

Prayer in danger

Of David

Aleph [1]ADORATION I offer, Yahweh,
[2]to you, my God.

Bet BUT in my trust in you do not put me to shame,
let not my enemies gloat over me.

Gimel [3]CALLING to you, none shall ever be put to shame,
but shame is theirs who groundlessly break faith.

Dalet [4]DIRECT me in your ways, Yahweh,
and teach me your paths.

He [5]ENCOURAGE me to walk in your truth and teach me
since you are the God who saves me.

(Waw) FOR my hope is in you all day long—
7c such is your generosity, Yahweh.
Zain 6 GOODNESS and faithful love have been yours for ever,
Yahweh, do not forget them.

Het 7 HOLD not my youthful sins against me,
but remember me as your faithful love dictates.

Tet 8 INTEGRITY and generosity are marks of Yahweh
for he brings sinners back to the path.

Yod 9 JUDICIOUSLY he guides the humble,
instructing the poor in his way.

Kaph 10 KINDNESS unfailing and constancy mark all Yahweh's paths,
for those who keep his covenant and his decrees.

Lamed 11 LET my sin, great though it is, be forgiven,
Yahweh, for the sake of your name.

Mem 12 MEN who respect Yahweh, what of them?
He teaches them the way they must choose.
Nun 13 NEIGHBOURS to happiness will they live,
and their children inherit the land.
Samek 14 ONLY those who fear Yahweh have his secret
and his covenant, for their understanding.

Ain 15 PERMANENTLY my eyes are on Yahweh,
for he will free my feet from the snare.
Pe 16 QUICK, turn to me, pity me,
alone and wretched as I am!

Zade 17 RELIEVE the distress of my heart,
bring me out of my constraint.
(Qoph) 18 SPARE a glance for my misery and pain,
take all my sins away.

Resh 19 TAKE note how countless are my enemies,
how violent their hatred for me.
Shin 20 UNLESS you guard me and rescue me
I shall be put to shame, for you are my refuge.
Taw 21 VIRTUE and integrity be my protection,
for my hope, Yahweh, is in you.

22 Ransom Israel, O God,
from all its troubles.

PSALM 26

V 25

Prayer of the blameless

Of David

1 Yahweh, be my judge!
I go on my way in innocence,
my trust in Yahweh never wavers.

2 Probe me, Yahweh, examine me,
Test my heart and my mind in the fire.

3 For your faithful love is before my eyes,
and I live my life by your truth.

4 No sitting with wastrels for me,
no travelling with hypocrites;
5 I hate the company of sinners,
I refuse to sit down with the wicked.

6 I will wash my hands in innocence
and join the procession round your altar, Yahweh,
7 to make heard the sound of thanksgiving,
to proclaim all your wonders.
8 Yahweh, I love the beauty of your house
and the place where your glory dwells.

9 Do not couple me with sinners,
nor my life with men of violence,
10 whose hands are stained with guilt,
their right hands heavy with bribes.

11 In innocence I will go on my way;
ransom me, take pity on me.
12 I take my stand on the right path;
I will bless you, Yahweh, in the assemblies.

PSALM 27 V 26

In God's company there is no fear

Of David

1 Yahweh is my light and my salvation,
whom should I fear?
Yahweh is the fortress of my life,
whom should I dread?

2 When the wicked advance against me
to eat me up,
they, my opponents, my enemies,
are the ones who stumble and fall.

3 Though an army pitch camp against me,
my heart will not fear,
though war break out against me,
my trust will never be shaken.

4 One thing I ask of Yahweh,
one thing I seek:
to dwell in Yahweh's house
all the days of my life,
to enjoy the sweetness of Yahweh,
to seek out his temple.

5 For he hides me away under his roof
on the day of evil,
he folds me in the recesses of his tent,
sets me high on a rock.

6 Now my head is held high
above the enemies who surround me;
in his tent I will offer
sacrifices of acclaim.

I will sing, I will make music for Yahweh.

7 Yahweh, hear my voice as I cry,
pity me, answer me!
8 Of you my heart has said,
'Seek his face!'
Your face, Yahweh, I seek;
9 do not turn away from me.

Do not thrust aside your servant in anger,
without you I am helpless.
Never leave me, never forsake me,
God, my Saviour.
10 Though my father and mother forsake me,
Yahweh will gather me up.

11 Yahweh, teach me your way,
lead me on the path of integrity
because of my enemies;
12 do not abandon me to the will of my foes—
false witnesses have risen against me,
and are breathing out violence.

13 This I believe: I shall see the goodness of Yahweh,
in the land of the living.
14 Put your hope in Yahweh, be strong, let your heart be bold,
put your hope in Yahweh.

PSALM 28

V 27

Petition and thanksgiving

Of David

1 To you, Yahweh, I cry,
my rock, do not be deaf to me!
If you stay silent
I shall be like those who sink into oblivion.

2 Hear the sound of my prayer
when I call upon you,
when I raise my hands, Yahweh,
towards your Holy of Holies.

3 Do not drag me away with the wicked,
with evil-doers,
who talk to their partners of peace
with treachery in their hearts.

4 Repay them as their deeds deserve,
as befits their treacherous actions;
as befits their handiwork repay them,
let their deserts fall back on themselves.

5 They do not comprehend the deeds of Yahweh,
the work of his hands.
May he pull them down and not rebuild them!

6 Blessed be Yahweh
for he hears the sound of my prayer.

7 Yahweh is my strength and my shield,
in him my heart trusts.
I have been helped; my body has recovered its vigour,
with all my heart I thank him.

8 Yahweh is the strength of his people,
a safe refuge for his anointed.
9 Save your people, bless your heritage,
shepherd them and carry them for ever!

PSALM 29

V 28

Hymn to the Lord of the storm

Psalm *Of David*

1 Give Yahweh his due, sons of God,
give Yahweh his due of glory and strength,
2 give Yahweh the glory due to his name,
adore Yahweh in the splendour of holiness.

3 Yahweh's voice over the waters, the God of glory thunders;
Yahweh over countless waters,
4 Yahweh's voice in power, Yahweh's voice in splendour;

5 Yahweh's voice shatters cedars,
Yahweh shatters cedars of Lebanon,
6 he makes Lebanon skip like a calf,
Sirion like a young wild ox.

7 Yahweh's voice carves out lightning-shafts,
8 Yahweh's voice convulses the desert,
Yahweh convulses the desert of Kadesh,
9 Yahweh's voice convulses terebinths,
strips forests bare.

In his palace all cry, 'Glory!'
10 Yahweh was enthroned for the flood,
Yahweh is enthroned as king for ever.
11 Yahweh will give strength to his people,
Yahweh blesses his people with peace.

PSALM 30 V 29

Thanksgiving after mortal danger

Psalm Canticle for the Dedication of the House Of David

1 I praise you to the heights, Yahweh, for you have raised me up,
you have not let my foes make merry over me.
2 Yahweh, my God, I cried to you for help and you healed me.
3 Yahweh, you have lifted me out of Sheol,
from among those who sink into oblivion you have given me life.

4 Make music for Yahweh, all you who are faithful to him,
praise his unforgettable holiness.
5 His anger lasts but a moment, his favour through life;
In the evening come tears, but with dawn cries of joy.

6 Carefree, I used to think,
'Nothing can ever shake me!'
7 Your favour, Yahweh, set me on impregnable heights,
but you turned away your face and I was terrified.

8 To you, Yahweh, I call,
to my God I cry for mercy.
9 What point is there in my death, my going down to the abyss?
Can the dust praise you or proclaim your faithfulness?

10 Listen, Yahweh, take pity on me,
Yahweh, be my help!
11 You have turned my mourning into dancing,
you have stripped off my sackcloth and clothed me with joy.
12 So my heart will sing to you unceasingly,
Yahweh, my God, I shall praise you for ever.

PSALM 31 V 30

Prayer in time of ordeal

For the choirmaster Psalm Of David

1 In you, Yahweh, I have taken refuge,
let me never be put to shame,
in your saving justice deliver me, rescue me,
2 turn your ear to me, make haste.

Be for me a rock-fastness,
a fortified citadel to save me.
3 You are my rock, my rampart;
true to your name, lead me and guide me!

4 Draw me out of the net they have spread for me,
for you are my refuge;
5 to your hands I commit my spirit,
by you have I been redeemed.

God of truth, 6 you hate
those who serve useless idols;

but my trust is in Yahweh:
7 I will delight and rejoice in your faithful love!

You, who have seen my misery,
and witnessed the miseries of my soul,
8 have not handed me over to the enemy,
but have given me freedom to roam at large.

9 Take pity on me, Yahweh,
for I am in trouble.
Vexation is gnawing away my eyes,
my soul deep within me.

10 For my life is worn out with sorrow,
and my years with sighs.
My strength gives way under my misery,
and my bones are all wasted away.

11 The sheer number of my enemies
makes me contemptible,
loathsome to my neighbours,
and my friends shrink from me in horror.

When people see me in the street
they take to their heels.
12 I have no more place in their hearts than a corpse,
or something lost.

13 All I hear is slander
—terror wherever I turn—
as they plot together against me,
scheming to take my life.

14 But my trust is in you, Yahweh;
I say, 'You are my God,'
15 every moment of my life is in your hands, rescue me
from the clutches of my foes who pursue me;
16 let your face shine on your servant,
save me in your faithful love.

17 I call on you, Yahweh, so let disgrace fall not on me,
but on the wicked.
Let them go down to Sheol in silence,
18 muzzles on their lying mouths,
which speak arrogantly against the upright
in pride and contempt.

19 Yahweh, what quantities of good things
you have in store for those who fear you,
and bestow on those who make you their refuge,
for all humanity to see.

20 Safe in your presence you hide them,
far from human plotting,
shielding them in your tent,
far from contentious tongues.

21 Blessed be Yahweh who works for me
miracles of his faithful love
(in a fortified city)!
22 In a state of terror I cried,
'I have been cut off from your sight!'

Yet you heard my plea for help
when I cried out to you.

23 Love Yahweh, all his faithful:
Yahweh protects his loyal servants,
but he repays the arrogant
with interest.
24 Be brave, take heart,
all who put your hope in Yahweh.

PSALM 32

V 31

Candid admission of sin

Of David Poem

1 How blessed are those whose offence is forgiven,
whose sin blotted out.
2 How blessed are those to whom Yahweh imputes no guilt,
whose spirit harbours no deceit.

3 I said not a word, but my bones wasted away
from groaning all the day;
4 day and night
your hand lay heavy upon me;
my heart grew parched as stubble
in summer drought. *Pause*

5 I made my sin known to you,
did not conceal my guilt.
I said, 'I shall confess
my offence to Yahweh.'
And you, for your part, took away my guilt,
forgave my sin. *Pause*

6 That is why each of your faithful ones prays to you
in time of distress.
Even if great floods overflow,
they will never reach your faithful.
7 You are a refuge for me,
you guard me in trouble,
with songs of deliverance you surround me. *Pause*

8 I shall instruct you and teach you the way to go;
I shall not take my eyes off you.

9 Be not like a horse or a mule;
that does not understand bridle or bit;
if you advance to master them,
there is no means of bringing them near.

10 Countless troubles are in store for the wicked,
but one who trusts in Yahweh is enfolded in his faithful love.

11 Rejoice in Yahweh,
exult all you upright,
shout for joy, you honest of heart.

PSALM 33

V 32

Hymn to Providence

1 Shout for joy, you upright;
praise comes well from the honest.
2 Give thanks to Yahweh on the lyre,
play for him on the ten-stringed lyre.
3 Sing to him a new song,
make sweet music for your cry of victory.

4 The word of Yahweh is straightforward,
all he does springs from his constancy.
5 He loves uprightness and justice;
the faithful love of Yahweh fills the earth.

6 By the word of Yahweh the heavens were made,
by the breath of his mouth all their array.
7 He collects the waters of the sea like a dam,
he stores away the abyss in his treasure-house.

8 Let the whole earth fear Yahweh,
let all who dwell in the world revere him;
9 for, the moment he spoke, it was so,
no sooner had he commanded, than there it stood!

10 Yahweh thwarts the plans of nations,
frustrates the counsels of peoples;
11 but Yahweh's own plan stands firm for ever,
his heart's counsel from age to age.
12 How blessed the nation whose God is Yahweh,
the people he has chosen as his heritage.

13 From heaven Yahweh looks down,
he sees all the children of Adam,
14 from the place where he sits he watches
all who dwell on the earth;
15 he alone moulds their hearts,
he understands all they do.

16 A large army will not keep a king safe,
nor his strength save a warrior's life;
17 it is delusion to rely on a horse for safety,
for all its power it cannot save.

18 But see how Yahweh watches over those who fear him,
those who rely on his faithful love,
19 to rescue them from death
and keep them alive in famine.

20 We are waiting for Yahweh;
he is our help and our shield,
21 for in him our heart rejoices,
in his holy name we trust.
22 Yahweh, let your faithful love rest on us,
as our hope has rested in you.

PSALM 34

V 33

In praise of God's justice

Of David, when he had feigned insanity before Abimelech, and Abimelech sent him away

Aleph 1 I will bless Yahweh at all times,
his praise continually on my lips.
Bet 2 I will praise Yahweh from my heart;
let the humble hear and rejoice.

Gimel 3 Proclaim with me the greatness of Yahweh,
let us acclaim his name together.
Dalet 4 I seek Yahweh and he answers me,
frees me from all my fears.

He 5 Fix your gaze on Yahweh and your face will grow bright,
you will never hang your head in shame.
Zain 6 A pauper calls out and Yahweh hears,
saves him from all his troubles.

Het 7 The angel of Yahweh encamps
around those who fear him, and rescues them.
Tet 8 Taste and see that Yahweh is good.
How blessed are those who take refuge in him.

Yod 9 Fear Yahweh, you his holy ones;
those who fear him lack for nothing.
Kaph 10 Young lions may go needy and hungry,
but those who seek Yahweh lack nothing good.

Lamed 11 Come, my children, listen to me,
I will teach you the fear of Yahweh.
Mem 12 Who among you delights in life,
longs for time to enjoy prosperity?

Nun 13 Guard your tongue from evil,
your lips from any breath of deceit.
Samek 14 Turn away from evil and do good,
seek peace and pursue it.

Ain 15 The eyes of Yahweh are on the upright,
his ear turned to their cry.
Pe 16 But Yahweh's face is set against those who do evil,
to cut off the memory of them from the earth.

Zade 17 They cry in anguish and Yahweh hears,
and rescues them from all their troubles.
Qoph 18 Yahweh is near to the broken-hearted,
he helps those whose spirit is crushed.

Resh 19 Though hardships without number beset the upright,
Yahweh brings rescue from them all.
Shin 20 Yahweh takes care of all their bones,
not one of them will be broken.

Taw 21 But to the wicked evil brings death,
those who hate the upright will pay the penalty.
22 Yahweh ransoms the lives of those who serve him,
and there will be no penalty for those who take refuge in him.

PSALM 35

V 34

Prayer of the virtuous in persecution

Of David

1 Accuse my accusers, Yahweh,
attack my attackers.
2 Grasp your buckler and shield,
up, and help me.
3 Brandish spear and pike
to confront my pursuers,
give me the assurance, 'I am your Saviour.'

4 Shame and humiliation on those
who are out to kill me!
Defeat and repulse in dismay
on those who plot my downfall.

5 May they be like chaff before the wind,
with the angel of Yahweh to chase them.
6 May their way be dark and slippery,
with the angel of Yahweh to hound them.

7 Unprovoked they laid their snare for me,
unprovoked dug a trap to kill me.
8 Ruin comes upon them unawares;
the snare they have laid will catch them,
and into their own trap they will fall.

9 Then I shall delight in Yahweh,
rejoice that he has saved me.
10 My very bones will all exclaim,
Yahweh, who can compare with you
in rescuing the poor from the oppressor;
the needy from the exploiter?

11 False witnesses come forward against me
asking me questions I cannot answer,
they cross-examine me, 12 repay my kindness with cruelty,
make my life barren.

13 But I, when they were ill, had worn sackcloth,
and mortified myself with fasting,
praying ever anew in my heart,
14 as if for a friend or brother; I had wandered restless,
as if mourning a mother,
so bowed had I been in sorrow.

15 When I stumble they gather in glee,
gather around me;
strangers I never even knew
tear me apart incessantly.
16 If I fall they surround me,
grinding their teeth at me.

17 How much longer, Lord, will you look on?
Rescue me from their onslaughts,
from young lions rescue the one life that I have.

18 I will give you thanks in the great assembly
praise you where the people gather.

19 Let not my lying enemies
gloat over me;
those who hate me unprovoked
look askance at me.

20 They have no greeting of peace
to the peace-loving people of the land;
they think up deceptive speeches.
21 Their mouths wide open to accuse me,
they say, 'Come on now, we saw you.'

22 You saw it, Yahweh, do not stay silent;
Lord, do not stand aloof from me.
23 Up, awake, to my defence,
my God and my Lord, to my cause.
24 In your saving justice give judgement for me, Yahweh my God,
and do not let them gloat over me.

25 Do not let them think, 'Just as we hoped,'
nor, 'Now we have swallowed him up.'
26 Shame and dismay on them all
who gloat over my misfortunes.
Let all who profit at my expense
be covered with shame and disgrace.

27 But let all who delight in my uprightness
shout for joy and gladness;
let them constantly say,
'Great is Yahweh,
who delights to see his servant in peace.'

28 And my tongue shall recount your saving justice,
all day long sing your praise.

PSALM 36[a]

V 35

The perversity of sinners and the benevolence of God

For the choirmaster Of the servant of Yahweh Of David

1 Sin is the oracle of the wicked
in the depths of his heart;
there is no fear of God
before his eyes.

2 He sees himself with too flattering an eye
to detect and detest his guilt;
3 all he says is malicious and deceitful,
he has turned his back on wisdom.

To get his way 4 he hatches malicious plots
even in his bed;
once set on his evil course
no wickedness is too much for him.

36a The two parts of the Ps in different rhythms may have existed separately.

5 Yahweh, your faithful love is in the heavens,
your constancy reaches to the clouds,
6 your saving justice is like towering mountains,
your judgements like the mighty deep.

Yahweh, you support both man and beast;
7 how precious, God, is your faithful love.
So the children of Adam
take refuge in the shadow of your wings.

8 They feast on the bounty of your house,
you let them drink from your delicious streams;
9 in you is the source of life,
by your light we see the light.

10 Maintain your faithful love to those who acknowledge you,
and your saving justice to the honest of heart.
11 Do not let the foot of the arrogant overtake me
or wicked hands drive me away.

12 There they have fallen, the evil-doers,
flung down, never to rise again.

PSALM 37 V 36

The fate of the upright and the wicked

Of David

Aleph 1 Do not get heated about the wicked
or envy those who do wrong.
2 Quick as the grass they wither,
fading like the green of the fields.

Bet 3 Put your trust in Yahweh and do right,
make your home in the land and live secure.
4 Make Yahweh your joy
and he will give you your heart's desires.

Gimel 5 Commit your destiny to Yahweh,
be confident in him, and he will act,
6 making your uprightness clear as daylight,
and the justice of your cause as the noon.

Dalet 7 Stay quiet before Yahweh, wait longingly for him,
do not get heated over someone who is making a fortune,
succeeding by devious means.

He 8 Refrain from anger, leave rage aside,
do not get heated—it can do no good;
9 for evil-doers will be annihilated,
while those who hope in Yahweh shall have the land for their own.

Waw 10 A little while and the wicked will be no more,
however well you search for the place, the wicked will not be there;
11 but the poor will have the land for their own,
to enjoy untroubled peace.

Zain 12 The wicked plots against the upright
and gnashes his teeth at him,

13 but Yahweh only laughs at his efforts,
knowing that his end is in sight.

Het 14 Though the wicked draw his sword
and bend his bow to slaughter the honest
and bring down the poor and the needy,
15 his sword will pierce his own heart,
and his bow will be shattered.

Tet 16 What little the upright possesses
outweighs all the wealth of the wicked;
17 for the weapons of the wicked shall be shattered,
while Yahweh supports the upright.

Yod 18 The lives of the just are in Yahweh's care,
their birthright will endure for ever;
19 they will not be put to shame when bad times come,
in time of famine they will have plenty.

Kaph 20 The wicked, enemies of Yahweh, will be destroyed,
they will vanish like the green of the pasture,
they will vanish in smoke.

Lamed 21 The wicked borrows and will not repay,
but the upright is generous in giving;
22 those he blesses will have the land for their own,
and those he curses be annihilated.

Mem 23 Yahweh guides a strong man's steps and keeps them firm;
and takes pleasure in him.
24 When he trips he is not thrown sprawling,
since Yahweh supports him by the hand.

Nun 25 Now I am old, but ever since my youth
I never saw an upright person abandoned,
or the descendants of the upright forced to beg their bread.
26 The upright is always compassionate, always lending,
so his descendants reap a blessing.

Samek 27 Turn your back on evil and do good,
you will have a home for ever,
28 for Yahweh loves justice
and will not forsake his faithful.

Ain Evil-doers will perish eternally,
the descendants of the wicked be annihilated,
29 but the upright shall have the land for their own,
there they shall live for ever.

Pe 30 Wisdom comes from the lips of the upright,
and his tongue speaks what is right;
31 the law of his God is in his heart,
his foot will never slip.

Zade 32 The wicked keeps a close eye on the upright,
looking out for a chance to kill him;
33 Yahweh will never abandon him to the clutches of the wicked,
nor let him be condemned if he is tried.

Qoph 34 Put your hope in Yahweh, keep to his path,
he will raise you up to make the land your own;
you will look on while the wicked are annihilated.

Resh 35 I have seen the wicked exultant,
towering like a cedar of Lebanon.
36 When next I passed he was gone,
I searched for him and he was nowhere to be found.

Shin 37 Observe the innocent, consider the honest,
for the lover of peace will not lack children.
38 But the wicked will all be destroyed together,
and their children annihilated.

Taw 39 The upright have Yahweh for their Saviour,
their refuge in times of trouble;
40 Yahweh helps them and rescues them,
he will rescue them from the wicked,
and save them because they take refuge in him.

PSALM 38

V 37

Prayer in distress

Psalm *Of David* *In commemoration*

1 Yahweh, do not correct me in anger,
do not discipline me in wrath.
2 For your arrows have pierced deep into me,
your hand has pressed down upon me.
3 Your indignation has left no part of me unscathed,
my sin has left no health in my bones.

4 My sins stand higher than my head,
they weigh on me as an unbearable weight.
5 I have stinking, festering wounds,
thanks to my folly.
6 I am twisted and bent double,
I spend my days in gloom.

7 My loins burn with fever,
no part of me is unscathed.
8 Numbed and utterly crushed
I groan in distress of heart.

9 Lord, all my longing is known to you,
my sighing no secret from you,
10 my heart is throbbing, my strength has failed,
the light has gone out of my eyes.

11 Friends and companions shun my disease,
even the dearest of them keep their distance.
12 Those with designs on my life lay snares,
those who wish me ill speak of violence
and hatch treachery all day long.

13 But I hear nothing, as though I were deaf,
as though dumb, saying not a word.
14 I am like the one who, hearing nothing,
has no sharp answer to make.

15 For in you, Yahweh, I put my hope,
you, Lord my God, will give answer.
16 I said, 'Never let them gloat over me,
do not let them take advantage of me if my foot slips.'

17 There is no escape for me from falling,
no relief from my misery.
18 But I make no secret of my guilt,
I am anxious at the thought of my sin.

19 There is no numbering those who oppose me without cause,
no counting those who hate me unprovoked,
20 repaying me evil for good,
slandering me for trying to do them good.

21 Yahweh, do not desert me,
my God, do not stand aloof from me.
22 Come quickly to my help,
Lord, my Saviour!

PSALM 39

V 38

Insignificance of human beings before God

For the choirmaster For Jeduthun Psalm Of David

1 I said, 'I will watch how I behave
so that I do not sin by my tongue.
I will keep a muzzle on my mouth
as long as any sinner is near.'
2 I stayed dumb, silent, speechless,
but the sinner's prosperity redoubled my torment.

3 My heart had been smouldering within me,
but at the thought of this it flared up
and the words came bursting out,
4 'Yahweh, let me know my fate,
how much longer I have to live.
Show me just how frail I am.

5 'Look, you have given me but a hand's breadth or two of life,
the length of my life is as nothing to you.
Every human being that stands on earth is a mere puff of wind,
6 every human being that walks only a shadow;
a mere puff of wind is the wealth stored away—
no knowing who will profit from it.'

7 So now, Lord, what am I to hope for?
My hope is in you.
8 Save me from all my sins,
do not make me the butt of fools.
9 I keep silence, I speak no more
since you yourself have been at work.

10 Take your scourge away from me.
I am worn out by the blows you deal me.

11 You correct human beings by punishing sin,
like a moth you eat away all their desires—
a human being is a mere puff of wind.

12 Yahweh, hear my prayer,
listen to my cry for help,
do not remain deaf to my weeping.
For I am a stranger in your house,
a nomad like all my ancestors.
13 Turn away your gaze that I may breathe freely
before I depart and am no more!

PSALM 40

V 39

Song of praise and prayer for help

For the choirmaster Of David Psalm

1 I waited, I waited for Yahweh,
then he stooped to me
and heard my cry for help.

2 He pulled me up from the seething chasm,
from the mud of the mire.
He set my feet on rock,
and made my footsteps firm.

3 He put a fresh song in my mouth,
praise of our God.
Many will be awestruck at the sight,
and will put their trust in Yahweh.

4 How blessed are those
who put their trust in Yahweh,
who have not sided with rebels
and those who have gone astray in falsehood.

5 How much you have done,
Yahweh, my God—
your wonders, your plans for us—
you have no equal.
I will proclaim and speak of them;
they are beyond number.

6 You wanted no sacrifice or cereal offering,
but you gave me an open ear,
you did not ask for burnt offering or sacrifice for sin;
7 then I said, 'Here I am, I am coming.'

In the scroll of the book it is written of me,
8 my delight is to do your will;
your law, my God,
is deep in my heart.

9 I proclaimed the saving justice of Yahweh
in the great assembly.
See, I will not hold my tongue,
as you well know.

[10]I have not kept your saving justice locked in the depths of my heart,
but have spoken of your constancy and saving help.
I have made no secret of your faithful and steadfast love,
in the great assembly.

[11]You, Yahweh, have not withheld
your tenderness from me;
your faithful and steadfast love
will always guard me.

[12]For troubles surround me,
until they are beyond number;
my sins have overtaken me;
I cannot see my way.
They outnumber the hairs of my head,
and my heart fails me.

[13]Be pleased, Yahweh, to rescue me,[a]
Yahweh, come quickly and help me!
[14]Shame and dismay to all
who seek to take my life.

Back with them, let them be humiliated
who delight in my misfortunes.
[15]Let them be aghast with shame,
those who say to me, 'Aha, aha!'

[16]But joy and happiness in you
to all who seek you!
Let them ceaselessly cry, 'Great is Yahweh'
who love your saving power.

[17]Poor and needy as I am,
the Lord has me in mind.
You, my helper, my Saviour,
my God, do not delay.

PSALM 41

V 40

Prayer of a sufferer deserted

For the choirmaster Psalm Of David

[1]Blessed is anyone who cares for the poor and the weak;
in time of trouble Yahweh rescues him.
[2]Yahweh protects him, gives him life and happiness on earth.
Do not abandon him to his enemies' pleasure!
[3]Yahweh sustains him on his bed of sickness;
you transform altogether the bed where he lies sick.

[4]For my part I said, 'Yahweh, take pity on me!
Cure me for I have sinned against you.'
[5]My enemies speak to me only of disaster,
'When will he die and his name disappear?'
[6]When people come to see me their talk is hollow,
when they get out they spread the news with spite in their hearts.

40a vv. 13–17 recur in Ps 70.

7All who hate me whisper together about me
and reckon I deserve the misery I suffer.
8'A fatal sickness has a grip on him;
now that he is down, he will never get up again.'
9Even my trusted friend on whom I relied,
who shared my table, takes advantage of me.

10But you, Yahweh, take pity on me!
Put me on my feet and I will give them their due.
11This will convince me that you delight in me,
if my enemy no longer exults over me.
12Then you will keep me unscathed,
and set me in your presence for ever.

13Blessed be Yahweh, the God of Israel,
from eternity to eternity.
Amen, Amen.[a]

PSALMS 42–43

V 41–42

Lament of a Levite in exile

For the choirmaster Poem Of the sons of Korah

1As a deer yearns
for running streams,
so I yearn
for you, my God.

2I thirst for God,
the living God;
when shall I go to see
the face of God?

3I have no food but tears
day and night,
as all day long I am taunted,
'Where is your God?'

4This I remember
as I pour out my heart,
how I used to pass under the roof of the Most High
used to go to the house of God,
among cries of joy and praise,
the sound of the feast.

5Why be so downcast,
why all these sighs?
Hope in God! I will praise him still,
my Saviour, 6my God.

When I am downcast
I think of you:
from the land of Jordan and Hermon,
I think of you, humble mountain.

41a A doxology closes each book of the Psalter: Pss 72, 89, 106, 150.

7 Deep is calling to deep
by the roar of your cataracts,
all your waves and breakers
have rolled over me.

8 In the daytime God sends his faithful love,
and even at night;
the song it inspires in me
is a prayer to my living God.

9 I shall say to God, my rock,
'Why have you forgotten me?
Why must I go around in mourning,
harrassed by the enemy?'

10 With death in my bones,
my enemies taunt me,
all day long they ask me,
'Where is your God?'

11 Why so downcast,
why all these sighs?
Hope in God! I will praise him still,
my Saviour, my God.

43

1 Judge me, God, defend my cause
against a people who have no faithful love;
from those who are treacherous and unjust,
rescue me.

2 For you are the God of my strength;
why abandon me?
Why must I go around in mourning,
harrassed by the enemy?

3 Send out your light and your truth;
they shall be my guide,
to lead me to your holy mountain
to the place where you dwell.

4 Then I shall go to the altar of God,
to the God of my joy.
I will rejoice and praise you on the harp,
O God, my God.

5 Why so downcast,
why all these sighs?
Hope in God! I will praise him still,
my Saviour, my God.

PSALM 44

V 43

National lament

For the choirmaster Of the sons of Korah Poem

1 God, we have heard for ourselves,
our ancestors have told us,
of the deeds you did in their days,
in days of old, 2 by your hand.

To establish them in the land you drove out nations,
to make room for them you harried peoples.
3 It was not their own sword that won the land,
nor their own arms which made them victorious,
but your hand it was and your arm,
and the light of your presence, for you loved them.

4 You are my king, my God,
who decreed Jacob's victories;
5 through you we conquered our opponents,
in your name we trampled down those who rose up against us.

6 For my trust was not in my bow,
my victory was not won by my sword;
7 it was you who saved us from our opponents,
you who put to shame those who hate us.
8 Our boast was always of God,
we praised your name without ceasing. *Pause*

9 Yet now you have abandoned and humiliated us,
you no longer take the field with our armies,
10 you leave us to fall back before the enemy,
those who hate us plunder us at will.

11 You hand us over like sheep for slaughter,
you scatter us among the nations,
12 you sell your people for a trifle
and make no profit on the sale.

13 You make us the butt of our neighbours,
the mockery and scorn of those around us,
14 you make us a by-word among nations,
other peoples shake their heads over us.

15 All day long I brood on my disgrace,
the shame written clear on my face,
16 from the sound of insult and abuse,
from the sight of hatred and vengefulness.

17 All this has befallen us though we had not forgotten you,
nor been disloyal to your covenant,
18 our hearts never turning away,
our feet never straying from your path.
19 Yet you have crushed us in the place where jackals live,
and immersed us in shadow dark as death.

20 Had we forgotten the name of our God
and stretched out our hands to a foreign god,

21 would not God have found this out,
for he knows the secrets of the heart?
22 For your sake we are being massacred all day long,
treated as sheep to be slaughtered.

23 Wake, Lord! Why are you asleep?
Awake! Do not abandon us for good.
24 Why do you turn your face away,
forgetting that we are poor and harrassed?

25 For we are bowed down to the dust,
and lie prone on the ground.
26 Arise! Come to our help!
Ransom us, as your faithful love demands.

PSALM 45

V 44

Royal wedding song

For the choirmaster Tune: 'Lilies . . .' Of the sons of Korah Poem Love song

1 My heart is stirred by a noble theme,
I address my poem to the king,
my tongue the pen of an expert scribe.

2 Of all men you are the most handsome,
gracefulness is a dew upon your lips,
for God has blessed you for ever.

3 Warrior, strap your sword at your side,
in your majesty and splendour advance, 4 ride on
in the cause of truth, gentleness and uprightness.

Stretch the bowstring tight, lending terror to your right hand.
5 Your arrows are sharp, nations lie at your mercy,
the king's enemies lose heart.

6 Your throne is from God, for ever and ever,
the sceptre of your kingship a sceptre of justice,
7 you love uprightness and detest evil.

This is why God, your God, has anointed you
with oil of gladness, as none of your rivals,
8 your robes all myrrh and aloes.

From palaces of ivory, harps bring you joy,
9 in your retinue are daughters of kings,
the consort at your right hand in gold of Ophir.

10 Listen, my daughter, attend to my words and hear;
forget your own nation and your ancestral home,
11 then the king will fall in love with your beauty;
he is your lord, bow down before him.
12 The daughter of Tyre will court your favour with gifts,
and the richest of peoples 13 with jewels set in gold.

Clothed 14 in brocade, the king's daughter is led within
to the king with the maidens of her retinue;
her companions are brought to her,

[15]they enter the king's palace with joy and rejoicing.
[16]Instead of your ancestors you will have sons;
you will make them rulers over the whole world.

[17]I will make your name endure from generation to generation,
so nations will sing your praise for ever and ever.

PSALM 46

V 45

God is with us

For the choirmaster Of the sons of Korah For oboe Song

[1]God is both refuge and strength for us,
a help always ready in trouble;
[2]so we shall not be afraid though the earth be in turmoil,
though mountains tumble into the depths of the sea,
[3]and its waters roar and seethe,
and the mountains totter as it heaves.

(Yahweh Sabaoth is with us,
our citadel, the God of Jacob.) *Pause*

[4]There is a river whose streams bring joy to God's city,
it sanctifies the dwelling of the Most High.
[5]God is in the city, it cannot fall;
at break of day God comes to its rescue.
[6]Nations are in uproar, kingdoms are tumbling,
when he raises his voice the earth crumbles away.

[7]Yahweh Sabaoth is with us,
our citadel, the God of Jacob. *Pause*

[8]Come, consider the wonders of Yahweh,
the astounding deeds he has done on the earth;
[9]he puts an end to wars over the whole wide world,
he breaks the bow, he snaps the spear,
shields he burns in the fire.
[10]'Be still and acknowledge that I am God,
supreme over nations, supreme over the world.'

[11]Yahweh Sabaoth is with us,
our citadel, the God of Jacob. *Pause*

PSALM 47

V 46

Yahweh king of Israel, king of the world

For the choirmaster Of the sons of Korah Psalm

[1]Clap your hands, all peoples,
acclaim God with shouts of joy.

[2]For Yahweh, the Most High, is glorious,
the great king over all the earth.
[3]He brings peoples under our yoke
and nations under our feet.

4He chooses for us our birthright,
the pride of Jacob whom he loves. *Pause*

5God goes up to shouts of acclaim,
Yahweh to a fanfare on the ram's horn.

6Let the music sound for our God, let it sound,
let the music sound for our king, let it sound.

7For he is king of the whole world;
learn the music, let it sound for God!
8God reigns over the nations,
seated on his holy throne.

9The leaders of the nations rally
to the people of the God of Abraham.
The shields of the earth belong to God,
who is exalted on high.

PSALM 48 **V 47**

Zion, the mountain of God

Song Psalm Of the sons of Korah

1Great is Yahweh and most worthy of praise
in the city of our God,
the holy mountain, 2towering in beauty,
the joy of the whole world:

Mount Zion in the heart of the north,
the settlement of the great king;
3God himself among its palaces
has proved himself its bulwark.

4For look, kings made alliance,
together they advanced;
5without a second glance, when they saw,
they panicked and fled away.

6Trembling seized them on the spot,
pains like those of a woman in labour;
7it was the east wind,
that wrecker of ships from Tarshish.

8What we had heard we saw for ourselves
in the city of our God,
in the city of Yahweh Sabaoth,
which God has established for ever. *Pause*

9We reflect on your faithful love, God,
in your temple!
10Both your name and your praise, God,
are over the whole wide world.

Your right hand is full of saving justice,
11Mount Zion rejoices,
the daughters of Judah delight
because of your saving justice.

12 Go round Zion, walk right through her,
count her bastions,
13 admire her walls,
examine her palaces,

to tell future generations
14 that such is God;
our God for ever and ever,
he is our guide!

PSALM 49

V 48

The futility of wealth

For the choirmaster Of the sons of Korah Psalm

1 Hear this, all nations,
listen, all who dwell on earth,
2 people high and low,
rich and poor alike!

3 My lips have wisdom to utter,
my heart good sense to whisper.
4 I listen carefully to a proverb,
I set my riddle to the music of the harp.

5 Why should I be afraid in times of trouble?
Malice dogs me and hems me in.
6 They trust in their wealth,
and boast of the profusion of their riches.

7 But no one can ever redeem himself
or pay his own ransom to God,
8 the price for himself is too high;
it can never be 9 that he will live on for ever
and avoid the sight of the abyss.

10 For he will see the wise also die
no less than the fool and the brute,
and leave their wealth behind for others.

11 For ever no home but their tombs,
their dwelling-place age after age,
though they gave their name to whole territories.

12 In prosperity people lose their good sense,
they become no better than dumb animals.
13 So they go on in their self-assurance,
right up to the end they are content with their lot. *Pause*

14 They are penned in Sheol like sheep,
Death will lead them to pasture,
and those who are honest will rule over them.

In the morning all trace of them will be gone,
Sheol will be their home.
15 But my soul God will ransom
from the clutches of Sheol, and will snatch me up. *Pause*

[16]Do not be overawed when someone gets rich,
and lives in ever greater splendour;
[17]when he dies he will take nothing with him,
his wealth will not go down with him.

[18]Though he pampered himself while he lived
—and people praise you for looking after yourself—
[19]he will go to join the ranks of his ancestors,
who will never again see the light.

[20]In prosperity people lose their good sense,
they become no better than dumb animals.

PSALM 50

V 49

Worship in spirit and truth

Psalm *Of Asaph*

[1]The God of gods, Yahweh, is speaking,
from east to west he summons the earth.
[2]From Zion, perfection of beauty, he shines forth;
[3]he is coming, our God, and will not be silent.

Devouring fire ahead of him,
raging tempest around him,
[4]he summons the heavens from on high,
and the earth to judge his people.

[5]'Gather to me my faithful,
who sealed my covenant by sacrifice.'
[6]The heavens proclaim his saving justice,
'God himself is judge.' *Pause*

[7]'Listen, my people, I am speaking,
Israel, I am giving evidence against you,
I, God, your God.

[8]'It is not with your sacrifices that I find fault,
those burnt offerings constantly before me;
[9]I will not accept any bull from your homes,
nor a single goat from your folds.

[10]'For all forest creatures are mine already,
the animals on the mountains in their thousands.
[11]I know every bird in the air,
whatever moves in the fields is mine.

[12]'If I am hungry I shall not tell you,
since the world and all it holds is mine.
[13]Am I to eat the flesh of bulls
or drink the blood of goats?

[14]'Let thanksgiving be your sacrifice to God,
fulfil the vows you make to the Most High;
[15]then if you call to me in time of trouble
I will rescue you and you will honour me.'

16But to the wicked, God says:

'What right have you to recite my statutes,
to take my covenant on your lips,
17when you detest my teaching,
and thrust my words behind you?

18'You make friends with a thief as soon as you see one,
you feel at home with adulterers,
19your conversation is devoted to wickedness,
and your tongue to inventing lies.

20'You sit there, slandering your own brother,
you malign your own mother's son.
21You do this, and am I to say nothing?
Do you think that I am really like you?
I charge you, indict you to your face.

22'Think it out, you who forget God,
or I will tear you apart without hope of a rescuer.
23Honour to me is a sacrifice of thanksgiving;
to the upright I will show God's salvation.'

PSALM 51

V 50

A prayer of contrition

For the choirmaster Of David When the prophet Nathan had come to him because he had gone to Bathsheba

1Have mercy on me, O God, in your faithful love,
in your great tenderness wipe away my offences;
2wash me clean from my guilt,
purify me from my sin.

3For I am well aware of my offences,
my sin is constantly in mind.
4Against you, you alone, I have sinned,
I have done what you see to be wrong,

that you may show your saving justice when you pass sentence,
and your victory may appear when you give judgement,
5remember, I was born guilty,
a sinner from the moment of conception.

6But you delight in sincerity of heart,
and in secret you teach me wisdom.
7Purify me with hyssop till I am clean,
wash me till I am whiter than snow.

8Let me hear the sound of joy and gladness,
and the bones you have crushed will dance.
9Turn away your face from my sins,
and wipe away all my guilt.

10God, create in me a clean heart,
renew within me a resolute spirit,
11do not thrust me away from your presence,
do not take away from me your spirit of holiness.

12 Give me back the joy of your salvation,
sustain in me a generous spirit.
13 I shall teach the wicked your paths,
and sinners will return to you.

14 Deliver me from bloodshed, God, God of my salvation,
and my tongue will acclaim your saving justice.
15 Lord, open my lips,
and my mouth will speak out your praise.

16 Sacrifice gives you no pleasure,
burnt offering you do not desire.
17 Sacrifice to God is a broken spirit,
a broken, contrite heart you never scorn.

18 In your graciousness do good to Zion,
rebuild the walls of Jerusalem.
19 Then you will delight in upright sacrifices,
—burnt offerings and whole oblations—
and young bulls will be offered on your altar.

PSALM 52

V 51

The fate of cynics

For the choirmaster Poem Of David When Doeg the Edomite went and warned Saul, 'David has gone to Abimelech's house'

1 Why take pride in being wicked,
you champion in villainy,
all day long 2 plotting crime?
Your tongue is razor-sharp,
you artist in perfidy.

3 You prefer evil to good,
lying to uprightness. *Pause*
4 You revel in destructive talk,
treacherous tongue!

5 That is why God will crush you,
destroy you once and for all,
snatch you from your tent,
uproot you from the land of the living. *Pause*

6 The upright will be awestruck as they see it,
they will mock him,
7 'So much for someone who would not place
his reliance in God,
but relied on his own great wealth,
and made himself strong by crime.'

8 But I, like a flourishing olive tree
in the house of God,
put my trust in God's faithful love,
for ever and ever.

9 I shall praise you for ever
for what you have done,

and shall trust in your name, so full of goodness,
in the presence of your faithful.

PSALM 53[a] V 52

The fate of the godless

For the choirmaster In sickness Poem Of David

1The fool has said in his heart,
'There is no God!'
They are corrupt, vile and unjust,
not one of them does right.

2God looks down from heaven
at the children of Adam,
to see if a single one is wise,
a single one seeks God.

3All have proved faithless,
all alike turned sour,
not one of them does right,
not a single one.

4Are they not aware, these evil-doers?
They are devouring my people;
this is the bread they eat,
and they never call upon God.

5They will be gripped with fear,
just where there is no need for fear,
for God scatters the bones of him who besieges you;
they are mocked because God rejects them.

6Who will bring from Zion salvation for Israel?
When God brings his people home,
what joy for Jacob, what happiness for Israel!

PSALM 54 V 53

Appeal to God, the just judge

For the choirmaster On stringed instruments Poem Of David When the Ziphites went to Saul and said, 'Is not David hiding with us?'

1God, save me by your name,
in your power vindicate me.
2God, hear my prayer,
listen to the words I speak.

3Arrogant men are attacking me,
bullies hounding me to death,
no room in their thoughts for God. *Pause*

53a Almost identical with Ps 14 except that the name 'Yahweh' is not used.

4 But now God is coming to my help,
the Lord, among those who sustain me.
5 May their wickedness recoil on those who lie in wait for me.
Yahweh, in your constancy destroy them.

6 How gladly will I offer you sacrifice,
and praise your name, for it is good,
7 for it has rescued me from all my troubles,
and my eye has feasted on my enemies.

PSALM 55

V 54

Prayer when slandered

For the choirmaster For strings Poem Of David

1 God, hear my prayer,
do not hide away from my plea,
2 give me a hearing, answer me,
my troubles give me no peace.

I shudder 3 at the enemy's shouts,
at the outcry of the wicked;
they heap up charges against me,
in their anger bring hostile accusations against me.

4 My heart writhes within me,
the terrors of death come upon me,
5 fear and trembling overwhelm me,
and shuddering grips me.

6 And I say,
'Who will give me wings like a dove,
to fly away and find rest?'
7 How far I would escape,
and make a nest in the desert! *Pause*

8 I would soon find a refuge
from the storm of abuse,
from the 9 destructive tempest, Lord,
from the flood of their tongues.

For I see violence
and strife in the city,
10 day and night they make their rounds
along the city walls,

Inside live malice and mischief,
11 inside lives destruction,
tyranny and treachery never absent
from its central square.

12 Were it an enemy who insulted me,
that I could bear;
if an opponent pitted himself against me,
I could turn away from him.

13 But you, a person of my own rank,
a comrade and dear friend,

14 to whom I was bound by intimate friendship
in the house of God!

May they recoil in disorder,
15 may death descend on them,
may they go down alive to Sheol,
since evil shares their home with them.

16 For my part, I appeal to God,
and Yahweh saves me;
17 evening, morning, noon,
I complain and I groan.

He hears my cry,
18 he ransoms me and gives me peace
from the feud against me,
for they are taking me to law.

19 But God will listen and will humble them,
he who has been enthroned from the beginning;
no change of heart for them,
for they do not fear God.

20 They attack those at peace with them,
going back on their oaths;
21 though their mouth is smoother than butter,
enmity is in their hearts;
their words more soothing than oil,
yet sharpened like swords.

22 Unload your burden onto Yahweh
and he will sustain you;
never will he allow
the upright to stumble.

23 You, God, will thrust them down
to the abyss of destruction,
men bloodthirsty and deceptive,
before half their days are spent.

For my part, I put my trust in you.

PSALM 56

V 55

Trust in God

For the choirmaster Tune: 'The oppression of distant princes' Of David In a quiet voice
When the Philistines seized him in Gath

1 Take pity on me, God, as they harry me,
pressing their attacks home all day.
2 Those who harry me lie in wait for me all day,
countless are those who attack me from the heights.

3 When I am afraid, I put my trust in you,
4 in God, whose word I praise,
in God I put my trust and have no fear,
what power has human strength over me?

5 All day long they carp at my words,
their only thought is to harm me,
6 they gather together, lie in wait and spy on my movements,
as though determined to take my life.

7 Because of this crime reject them,
in your anger, God, strike down the nations.
8 You yourself have counted up my sorrows,
collect my tears in your wineskin.
9 Then my enemies will turn back
on the day when I call.

This I know, that God is on my side.
10 In God whose word I praise,
in Yahweh whose word I praise,
11 in God I put my trust and have no fear;
what can mortal man do to me?

12 I am bound by the vows I have made, God,
I will pay you the debt of thanks,
13 for you have saved my life from death
to walk in the presence of God,
in the light of the living.

PSALM 57

V 56

Among ferocious enemies

For the choirmaster Tune: 'Do not destroy' Of David In a quiet voice When he escaped from Saul in the cave

1 Take pity on me, God, take pity on me,
for in you I take refuge,
in the shadow of your wings I take refuge,
until the destruction is past.

2 I call to God the Most High,
to God who has done everything for me;
3 may he send from heaven and save me,
and check those who harry me; *Pause*
may God send his faithful love and his constancy.

4 I lie surrounded by lions,
greedy for human prey,
their teeth are spears and arrows,
their tongue a sharp sword.

5 Be exalted above the heavens, God!
Your glory over all the earth!
6 They laid a snare in my path
—I was bowed with care—
they dug a pit ahead of me,
but fell in it themselves. *Pause*

7 My heart is ready, God,
my heart is ready;
I will sing, and make music for you.

[8]Awake, my glory,
awake, lyre and harp,
that I may awake the Dawn.

[9]I will praise you among the peoples, Lord,
I will make music for you among nations,
[10]for your faithful love towers to heaven,
your constancy to the clouds.
[11]Be exalted above the heavens, God!
Your glory over all the earth!

PSALM 58

V 57

The judge of earthly judges

For the choirmaster Tune: 'Do not destroy' Of David In a quiet voice

[1]Divine as you are, do you truly give upright verdicts?
do you judge fairly the children of Adam?
[2]No! You devise injustice in your hearts,
and with your hands you administer tyranny on the earth.

[3]Since the womb they have gone astray, the wicked,
on the wrong path since their birth, with their unjust verdicts.
[4]They are poisonous as any snake,
deaf as an adder that blocks its ears
[5]so as not to hear the magician's music,
however skilful his spells.

[6]God, break the teeth in their mouths,
snap off the fangs of these young lions, Yahweh.
[7]May they drain away like water running to waste,
may they wither like trampled grass,
[8]like the slug that melts as it moves
or a still-born child that never sees the sun.

[9]Before they sprout thorns like the bramble,
green or burnt up, may retribution whirl them away.
[10]The upright will rejoice to see vengeance done,
and will bathe his feet in the blood of the wicked.
[11]'So', people will say, 'the upright does have a reward;
there is a God to dispense justice on earth.'

PSALM 59

V 58

Against the wicked

For the choirmaster Tune: 'Do not destroy' Of David In a quiet voice When Saul sent men to watch David's house in order to have him killed

[1]Rescue me from my enemies, my God,
be my stronghold from my assailants,
[2]rescue me from evil-doers,
from men of violence save me.

3 Look at them, lurking to ambush me,
violent men are attacking me,
for no fault, no sin of mine, Yahweh, 4 for no guilt,
they come running to take up position.

Wake up, stand by me and keep watch,
5 Yahweh, God of Sabaoth, God of Israel,
rise up, to punish all the nations,
show no mercy to all these malicious traitors. *Pause*

6 Back they come at nightfall,
snarling like curs,
prowling through the town.

7 Look how they rant in speech
with swords on their lips,
'Who is there to hear us?'

8 For your part, Yahweh, you laugh at them,
you make mockery of all nations.
9 My strength, I keep my eyes fixed on you.

For my stronghold is God,
10 the God who loves me faithfully is coming to meet me,
God will let me feast my eyes on those who lie in wait for me.

11 Do not annihilate them, or my people may forget;
shake them in your power, bring them low,
Lord, our shield.

12 Sin is in their mouths, sin on their lips,
so let them be trapped in their pride
for the curses and lies that they utter.

13 Destroy them in your anger, destroy them till they are no more,
and let it be known that God is Master
in Jacob and the whole wide world. *Pause*

14 Back they come at nightfall,
snarling like curs,
prowling through the town,
15 scavenging for something to eat,
growling unless they have their fill.

16 And so I will sing of your strength,
in the morning acclaim your faithful love;
you have been a stronghold for me,
a refuge when I was in trouble.

17 My strength, I will make music for you,
for my stronghold is God,
the God who loves me faithfully.

PSALM 60

V 59

National prayer after defeat

For the choirmaster To the tune 'The decree is a lily' In a quiet voice Of David To be learnt When he was at war with Aram-Naharaim and Aram-Zobah, and Joab marched back to destroy twelve thousand Edomites in the Valley of Salt

1 God, you have rejected us, broken us,
you were angry, come back to us!
2 You made the earth tremble, split it open;
now mend the rifts, it is tottering still.

3 You have forced your people to drink a bitter draught,
forced us to drink a wine that made us reel.
4 You gave a signal to those who fear you
to let them escape out of range of the bow. *Pause*

5 To rescue those you love,
save with your right hand and answer us.

6 God has spoken from his sanctuary,
'In triumph I will divide up Shechem,
and share out the Valley of Succoth.

7 'Mine is Gilead, mine Manasseh,
Ephraim the helmet on my head,
Judah my commander's baton,

8 'Moab a bowl for me to wash in,
on Edom I plant my sandal.
Now try shouting "Victory!" over me, Philistia!'

9 Who will lead me against a fortified city,
who will guide me into Edom,
10 if not you, the God who has rejected us?
God, you no longer march with our armies.

11 Bring us help in our time of crisis,
any human help is worthless.
12 With God we shall do deeds of valour,
he will trample down our enemies.

PSALM 61

V 60

Prayer of an exile

For the choirmaster For strings Of David

1 God, hear my cry,
listen to my prayer.
2 From the end of the earth I call to you
with fainting heart.
Lead me to the high rock that stands far out of my reach.

3 For you are my refuge,
a strong tower against the enemy.

4 Let me stay in your tent for ever,
taking refuge in the shelter of your wings!
5 For you, God, accept my vows,
you grant me the heritage of those who fear your name.

6 Let the king live on and on,
let his years continue age after age.
7 May his throne be always in God's presence,
your faithful love and constancy watch over him.

8 Then I shall always sing to your name,
day after day fulfilling my vows.

PSALM 62

V 61

Hope in God alone

For the choirmaster . . . Jeduthun Psalm Of David

1 In God alone there is rest for my soul,
from him comes my safety;
2 he alone is my rock, my safety,
my stronghold so that I stand unshaken.

3 How much longer will you set on a victim,
all together, intent on murder,
like a rampart already leaning over,
a wall already damaged?
4 Trickery is their only plan,
deception their only pleasure,
with lies on their lips they pronounce a blessing,
with a curse in their hearts. *Pause*

5 Rest in God alone, my soul!
He is the source of my hope.
6 He alone is my rock, my safety,
my stronghold, so that I stand unwavering.
7 In God is my safety and my glory,
the rock of my strength.

In God is my refuge; 8 trust in him,
you people, at all times.
Pour out your hearts to him,
God is a refuge for us. *Pause*

9 Ordinary people are a mere puff of wind,
important people a delusion;
set both on the scales together,
and they are lighter than a puff of wind.

10 Put no trust in extortion,
no empty hopes in robbery;
however much wealth may multiply,
do not set your heart on it.

11 Once God has spoken,
twice have I heard this:
Strength belongs to God,
12 to you, Lord, faithful love;
and you repay everyone as their deeds deserve.

PSALM 63

V 62

Yearning for God

Psalm *Of David* *When he was in the desert of Judah*

1 God, you are my God, I pine for you;
my heart thirsts for you,
my body longs for you,
as a land parched, dreary and waterless.
2 Thus I have gazed on you in the sanctuary,
seeing your power and your glory.

3 Better your faithful love than life itself;
my lips will praise you.
4 Thus I will bless you all my life,
in your name lift up my hands.
5 All my longings fulfilled as with fat and rich foods,
a song of joy on my lips and praise in my mouth.

6 On my bed when I think of you,
I muse on you in the watches of the night,
7 for you have always been my help;
in the shadow of your wings I rejoice;
8 my heart clings to you,
your right hand supports me.

9 May those who are hounding me to death
go down to the depths of the earth,
10 given over to the blade of the sword,
and left as food for jackals.
11 Then the king shall rejoice in God,
all who swear by him shall gain recognition,
for the mouths of liars shall be silenced.

PSALM 64

V 63

Punishment for slanderers

For the choirmaster *Psalm* *Of David*

1 Listen, God, to my voice as I plead,
protect my life from fear of the enemy;
2 hide me from the league of the wicked,
from the gang of evil-doers.

3 They sharpen their tongues like a sword,
aim their arrows of poisonous abuse,
4 shoot at the innocent from cover,
shoot suddenly, with nothing to fear.

5 They support each other in their evil designs,
they discuss how to lay their snares.
'Who will see us?' they say,
6 'or will penetrate our secrets?'
He will do that, he who penetrates human nature to its depths,
the depths of the heart.

7 God has shot them with his arrow,
sudden were their wounds.
8 He brings them down because of their tongue,
and all who see them shake their heads.

9 Everyone will be awestruck,
proclaim what God has done,
and understand why he has done it.

10 The upright will rejoice in Yahweh,
will take refuge in him,
and all the honest will praise him.

PSALM 65

V 64

Thanksgiving hymn

For the choirmaster Psalm Of David Song

1 Praise is rightfully yours,
God, in Zion.
Vows to you shall be fulfilled,
2 for you answer prayer.

All humanity must come to you
3 with its sinful deeds.
Our faults overwhelm us,
but you blot them out.

4 How blessed those whom you choose
and invite to dwell in your courts.
We shall be filled with the good things of your house,
of your holy temple.

5 You respond to us with the marvels of your saving justice,
God our Saviour,
hope of the whole wide world,
even the distant islands.

6 By your strength you hold the mountains steady,
being clothed in power,
7 you calm the turmoil of the seas,
the turmoil of their waves.

The nations are in uproar,
in panic those who live at the ends of the earth;
8 your miracles bring shouts of joy
to the gateways of morning and evening.

9 You visit the earth and make it fruitful,
you fill it with riches;
the river of God brims over with water,
you provide the grain.

To that end
10 you water its furrows abundantly, level its ridges,
soften it with showers and bless its shoots.

11 You crown the year with your generosity,
richness seeps from your tracks,
12 the pastures of the desert grow moist,
the hillsides are wrapped in joy,
13 the meadows are covered with flocks,
the valleys clothed with wheat;
they shout and sing for joy.

PSALM 66 V 65

Corporate prayer of thanksgiving

For the choirmaster Song Psalm

1 Acclaim God, all the earth,
2 sing psalms to the glory of his name,
glorify him with your praises,
3 say to God, 'How awesome you are!

'Your achievements are the measure of your power,
your enemies woo your favour,
4 all the earth bows down before you,
sings psalms to you, sings psalms to your name.' *Pause*

5 Come and see the marvels of God,
his awesome deeds for the children of Adam:
6 he changed the sea into dry land,
they crossed the river on foot.

So let us rejoice in him,
7 who rules for ever by his power;
his eyes keep watch on the nations
to forestall rebellion against him. *Pause*

8 Nations, bless our God,
let the sound of his praise be heard;
9 he brings us to life
and keeps our feet from stumbling.

10 God, you have put us to the test,
refined us like silver,
11 let us fall into the net;
you have put a heavy strain on our backs,
12 let men ride over our heads;
but now the ordeal by fire and water is over,
you have led us out to breathe again.

13 I bring burnt offerings to your house,
I fulfil to you my vows,
14 the vows that rose to my lips,
that I pronounced when I was in trouble.

15 I will offer you rich burnt offerings,
with the smoke of burning rams.
I will sacrifice to you bullocks and goats. *Pause*

16 Come and listen, all who fear God,
while I tell what he has done for me.

17 To him I cried aloud,
high praise was on my tongue.
18 Had I been aware of guilt in my heart,
the Lord would not have listened,
19 but in fact God did listen,
attentive to the sound of my prayer.

20 Blessed be God
who has not turned away my prayer,
nor his own faithful love from me.

PSALM 67

V 66

Harvest song

For the choirmaster For strings Psalm Song

1 May God show kindness and bless us,
and make his face shine on us. *Pause*
2 Then the earth will acknowledge your ways,
and all nations your power to save.

3 Let the nations praise you, God,
let all the nations praise you.

4 Let the nations rejoice and sing for joy,
for you judge the world with justice,
you judge the peoples with fairness,
you guide the nations on earth. *Pause*

5 Let the nations praise you, God,
let all the nations praise you.

6 The earth has yielded its produce;
God, our God has blessed us.
7 May God continue to bless us,
and be revered by the whole wide world.

PSALM 68

V 67

An epic of Israel's glory

For the choirmaster Of David Psalm Song

1 Let God arise, let his enemies scatter,
let his opponents flee before him.
2 You disperse them like smoke;
as wax melts in the presence of a fire,
so the wicked melt at the presence of God.

3 The upright rejoice in the presence of God,
delighted and crying out for joy.
4 Sing to God, play music to his name,
build a road for the Rider of the Clouds,
rejoice in Yahweh, dance before him.

5 Father of orphans, defender of widows,
such is God in his holy dwelling.
6 God gives the lonely a home to live in,
leads prisoners out into prosperity,
but rebels must live in the bare wastelands.

7 God, when you set out at the head of your people,
when you strode over the desert, 8 the earth rocked, *Pause*
the heavens pelted down rain at the presence of God,
at the presence of God, the God of Israel.

9 God, you rained down a shower of blessings,
when your heritage was weary you gave it strength.
10 Your family found a home, which you
in your generosity provided for the humble.

11 The Lord gave a command,
the good news of a countless army.
12 The chieftains of the army are in flight, in flight,
and the fair one at home is sharing out the spoils.

13 While you are at ease in the sheepfolds,
the wings of the Dove[a] are being covered with silver,
and her feathers with a sheen of green gold;
14 when Shaddai scatters the chieftains,
through her it snows[b] on the Dark Mountain.

15 A mountain of God, the mountain of Bashan!
a haughty mountain, the mountain of Bashan!
16 Why be envious, haughty mountains,
of the mountain God has chosen for his dwelling?
There God will dwell for ever.

17 The chariots of God are thousand upon thousand;
God has come from Sinai to the sanctuary.
18 You have climbed the heights, taken captives,
you have taken men as tribute, even rebels
that Yahweh God might have a dwelling-place.

19 Blessed be the Lord day after day,
he carries us along, God our Saviour. *Pause*

20 This God of ours is a God who saves;
from Lord Yahweh comes escape from death;
21 but God smashes the head of his enemies,
the long-haired skull of the prowling criminal.

22 The Lord has said, 'I will bring them back from Bashan,
I will bring them back from the depths of the sea,
23 so that you may bathe your feet in blood,
and the tongues of your dogs feast on your enemies.'

24 Your processions, God, are for all to see,
the processions of my God, of my king, to the sanctuary;
25 singers ahead, musicians behind,
in the middle come girls, beating their drums.

26 In choirs they bless God,
Yahweh, since the foundation of Israel.

68a Two obscure vv., referring perhaps to Jg 5; some tribes missed Israel's glorious victory.
68b Perhaps the salt sown on devastated Shechem after the victory.

27 Benjamin was there, the youngest in front,
the princes of Judah in bright-coloured robes,
the princes of Zebulun, the princes of Naphtali.

28 Take command, my God, as befits your power,
the power, God, which you have wielded for us,
29 from your temple high above Jerusalem.
Kings will come to you bearing tribute.

30 Rebuke the Beast of the Reeds,
that herd of bulls, that people of calves,
who bow down with ingots of silver.
Scatter the people who delight in war.
31 From Egypt nobles will come,
Ethiopia will stretch out its hands to God.

32 Kingdoms of the earth, sing to God,
play for 33 the Rider of the Heavens, the primeval heavens. *Pause*
There he speaks, with a voice of power!
34 Acknowledge the power of God.

Over Israel his splendour, in the clouds his power.
35 Awesome is God in his sanctuary.
He, the God of Israel,
gives strength and power to his people.

Blessed be God.

PSALM 69

V 68

Lament

For the choirmaster Tune: 'Lilies . . .' Of David

1 Save me, God, for the waters
have closed in on my very being.

2 I am sinking in the deepest swamp
and there is no firm ground.
I have stepped into deep water
and the waves are washing over me.

3 I am exhausted with calling out, my throat is hoarse,
my eyes are worn out with searching for my God.

4 More numerous than the hairs of my head
are those who hate me without reason.
Those who seek to get rid of me are powerful,
my treacherous enemies.
(Must I give back what I have never stolen?)

5 God, you know how foolish I am,
my offences are not hidden from you.

6 Those who hope in you must not be made fools of,
Yahweh Sabaoth, because of me!

Those who seek you must not be disgraced,
God of Israel, because of me!

7 It is for you I bear insults,
my face is covered with shame,
8 I am estranged from my brothers,
alienated from my own mother's sons;
9 for I am eaten up with zeal for your house,
and insults directed against you fall on me.

10 I mortify myself with fasting,
and find myself insulted for it,
11 I dress myself in sackcloth
and become their laughing-stock,
12 the gossip of people sitting at the gate,
and the theme of drunkards' songs.

13 And so, I pray to you, Yahweh,
at the time of your favour;
in your faithful love answer me,
in the constancy of your saving power.
14 Rescue me from the mire before I sink in;
so I shall be saved from those who hate me,
from the watery depths.
15 Let not the waves wash over me,
nor the deep swallow me up,
nor the pit close its mouth on me.

16 Answer me, Yahweh, for your faithful love is generous;
in your tenderness turn towards me;
17 do not turn away from your servant,
be quick to answer me, for I am in trouble.
18 Come to my side, redeem me,
ransom me because of my enemies.

19 You know well the insults,
the shame and disgrace I endure.
Every one of my oppressors is known to you.
20 Insult has broken my heart past cure.
I hoped for sympathy, but in vain,
for consolers—not one to be found.

21 To eat they gave me poison,
to drink, vinegar when I was thirsty.
22 May their own table prove a trap for them,
and their abundance a snare;
23 may their eyes grow so dim that they cannot see,
all their muscles lose their strength.

24 Vent your fury on them,
let your burning anger overtake them.
25 Reduce their encampment to ruin,
and leave their tents untenanted,
26 for hounding someone you had already stricken,
for redoubling the pain of one you had wounded.

27 Charge them with crime after crime,
exclude them from your saving justice,
28 erase them from the book of life,
do not enrol them among the upright.

29 For myself, wounded wretch that I am,
by your saving power raise me up!

30 I will praise God's name in song,
I will extol him by thanksgiving,
31 for this will please Yahweh more than an ox,
than a bullock horned and hoofed.

32 The humble have seen and are glad.
Let your courage revive, you who seek God.
33 For God listens to the poor,
he has never scorned his captive people.
34 Let heaven and earth and seas,
and all that stirs in them, acclaim him!

35 For God will save Zion,
and rebuild the cities of Judah,
and people will live there on their own land;
36 the descendants of his servants will inherit it,
and those who love his name will dwell there.

PSALM 70[a] V 69

A cry of distress

For the choirmaster Of David In commemoration

1 Be pleased, God, to rescue me,
Yahweh, come quickly and help me!
2 Shame and dismay to those
who seek my life!

Back with them! Let them be humiliated
who delight in my misfortunes.
3 Let them shrink away covered with shame,
those who say to me, 'Aha, aha!'

4 But joy and happiness in you
to all who seek you.
Let them ceaselessly cry, 'God is great',
who love your saving power.

5 Poor and needy as I am,
God, come quickly to me!
Yahweh, my helper, my Saviour,
do not delay!

PSALM 71 V 70

A prayer in old age

1 In you, Yahweh, I take refuge,
I shall never be put to shame.
2 In your saving justice rescue me, deliver me,
listen to me and save me.

70a = 40:13–17.

3 Be a sheltering rock for me,
always accessible;
you have determined to save me,
for you are my rock, my fortress.
4 My God, rescue me from the clutches of the wicked,
from the grasp of the rogue and the ruthless.

5 For you are my hope, Lord,
my trust, Yahweh, since boyhood.
6 On you I have relied since my birth,
since my mother's womb you have been my portion,
the constant theme of my praise.

7 Many were bewildered at me,
but you are my sure refuge.
8 My mouth is full of your praises,
filled with your splendour all day long.

9 Do not reject me in my old age,
nor desert me when my strength is failing,
10 for my enemies are discussing me,
those with designs on my life are plotting together.

11 'Hound him down, for God has deserted him!
Seize him, there is no one to rescue him.'
12 God, do not stand aloof,
my God, come quickly to help me.

13 Shame and ruin
on those who slander me,
may those intent on harming me
be covered with insult and infamy.

14 As for me, my hope will never fade,
I will praise you more and more.
15 My lips shall proclaim your saving justice,
your saving power all day long.

16 I will come in the power of Yahweh
to tell of your justice, yours alone.
17 God, you have taught me from boyhood,
and I am still proclaiming your marvels.

18 Now that I am old and grey-haired,
God, do not desert me,
till I have proclaimed your strength
to generations still to come,
your power 19 and justice to the skies.

You have done great things,
God, who is like you?
20 You have shown me much misery and hardship,
but you will give me life again,
You will raise me up again from the depths of the earth,
21 prolong my old age, and comfort me again.

22 For my part, I will thank you on the lyre
for your constancy, my God.
I will play the harp in your honour,
Holy One of Israel.

[23]My lips sing for joy as I play to you,
because you have redeemed me,
[24]and all day long my tongue
muses on your saving justice.
Shame and disgrace
on those intent to harm me!

PSALM 72

V 71

The promised king

Of Solomon

[1]God, endow the king with your own fair judgement,
the son of the king with your own saving justice,
[2]that he may rule your people with justice,
and your poor with fair judgement.

[3]Mountains and hills,
bring peace to the people!
With justice [4]he will judge the poor of the people,
he will save the children of the needy
and crush their oppressors.

[5]In the sight of the sun and the moon he will endure,
age after age.
[6]He will come down like rain on mown grass,
like showers moistening the land.

[7]In his days uprightness shall flourish,
and peace in plenty till the moon is no more.
[8]His empire shall stretch from sea to sea,
from the river to the limits of the earth.

[9]The Beast will cower before him,
his enemies lick the dust;
[10]the kings of Tarshish and the islands
will pay him tribute.

The kings of Sheba and Saba
will offer gifts;
[11]all kings will do him homage,
all nations become his servants.

[12]For he rescues the needy who calls to him,
and the poor who has no one to help.
[13]He has pity on the weak and the needy,
and saves the needy from death.

[14]From oppression and violence he redeems their lives,
their blood is precious in his sight.
[15](Long may he live; may the gold of Sheba be given him!)
Prayer will be offered for him constantly,
and blessings invoked on him all day.

[16]May wheat abound in the land,
waving on the heights of the hills,

like Lebanon with its fruits and flowers at their best,
like the grasses of the earth.

17 May his name be blessed for ever,
and endure in the sight of the sun.
In him shall be blessed every race in the world,
and all nations call him blessed.

18 Blessed be Yahweh, the God of Israel,
who alone works wonders;
19 blessed for ever his glorious name.
May the whole world be filled with his glory!
Amen! Amen!

20 End of the prayers of David, son of Jesse.

PSALM 73

V 72

The triumph of justice

Psalm *Of Asaph*

1 Indeed God is good to Israel,
the Lord to those who are pure of heart.

2 My feet were on the point of stumbling,
a little more and I had slipped,
3 envying the arrogant as I did,
and seeing the prosperity of the wicked.

4 For them no such thing as pain,
untroubled, their comfortable portliness;
5 exempt from the cares which are the human lot,
they have no part in Adam's afflictions.

6 So pride is a necklace to them,
violence the garment they wear.
7 From their fat oozes out malice,
their hearts drip with cunning.

8 Cynically they advocate evil,
loftily they advocate force.
9 Their mouth claims heaven for themselves,
and their tongue is never still on earth.

10 That is why my people turn to them,
and enjoy the waters of plenty,
11 saying, 'How can God know?
What knowledge can the Most High have?'
12 That is what the wicked are like,
piling up wealth without any worries.

13 Was it useless, then, to have kept my own heart clean,
to have washed my hands in innocence?

14 When I was under a hail of blows all day long,
and punished every morning,
15 had I said, 'I shall talk like them,'
I should have betrayed your children's race.

16 So I set myself to understand this:
how difficult I found it!
17 Until I went into the sanctuaries of the gods
and understood what was destined to become of them.
18 You place them on a slippery slope
and drive them down into chaos.

19 How sudden their hideous destruction!
They are swept away, annihilated by terror!
20 Like a dream upon waking, Lord,
when you awake, you dismiss their image.

21 My heart grew embittered,
my affections dried up,
22 I was stupid and uncomprehending,
a clumsy animal in your presence.

23 Even so, I stayed in your presence,
you grasped me by the right hand;
24 you will guide me with advice,
and will draw me in the wake of your glory.

25 Who else is there for me in heaven?
And, with you, I lack nothing on earth.
26 My heart and my flesh are pining away:
my heart's rock, my portion, God for ever!

27 Truly, those who abandon you will perish;
you destroy those who adulterously desert you,
28 whereas my happiness is to be near God.
I have made the Lord Yahweh my refuge,
to tell of all your works.

PSALM 74 V 73

Lament on the sack of the Temple

Poem Of Asaph

1 God, why have you finally rejected us,
your anger blazing against the flock you used to pasture?
2 Remember the people you took to yourself long ago,
your own tribe which you redeemed,
and this Mount Zion where you came to live.

3 Come up to these endless ruins!
The enemy have sacked everything in the sanctuary;
4 your opponents made uproar in the place of assemblies,
they fixed their emblems over the entrance,
emblems 5 never known before.

Their axes deep in the wood, 6 hacking at the panels,
they battered them down with axe and pick;
7 they set fire to your sanctuary,
profanely rased to the ground the dwelling-place of your name.

8 They said to themselves, 'Let us crush them at one stroke!'
They burned down every sacred shrine in the land.

9 We see no signs, no prophet any more,
and none of us knows how long it will last.

10 How much longer, God, will the enemy blaspheme?
Is the enemy to insult your name for ever?
11 Why hold back your hand,
keep your right hand hidden in the folds of your robe?

12 Yet, God, my king from the first,
author of saving acts throughout the earth,
13 by your power you split the sea in two,
and smashed the heads of the monsters on the waters.

14 You crushed Leviathan's[a] heads,
gave him as food to the wild animals.
15 You released the springs and brooks,
and turned primordial rivers into dry land.

16 Yours is the day and yours the night,
you caused sun and light to exist,
17 you fixed all the boundaries of the earth,
you created summer and winter.

18 Remember, Yahweh, the enemy's blasphemy,
a foolish people insults your name.
19 Do not surrender your turtledove to the beast;
do not forget for ever the life of your oppressed people.

20 Look to the covenant!
All the hiding-places of the land are full,
haunts of violence.
21 Do not let the downtrodden retreat in confusion,
give the poor and needy cause to praise your name.

22 Arise, God, champion your own cause,
remember how fools blaspheme you all day long!
23 Do not forget the shouting of your enemies,
the ever-mounting uproar of your adversaries.

PSALM 75 V 74

The universal judge

For the choirmaster Tune: 'Do not destroy' Psalm Of Asaph Song

1 We give thanks to you, God, we give thanks to you,
as we call upon your name, as we recount your wonders.

2 'At the appointed time
I myself shall dispense justice.
3 The earth quakes and all its inhabitants;
it is I who hold its pillars firm. *Pause*

4 "I said to the boastful, "Do not boast!"
to the wicked, "Do not flaunt your strength!
5 Do not flaunt your strength so proudly,
do not talk with that arrogant stance.""

74a Properly a mythical monster of chaos, it stands here for the evil power of Egypt.

6 No longer from east to west,
no longer in the mountainous desert,
7 is God judging in uprightness,
bringing some down, raising others.
8 Yahweh is holding a cup
filled with a heady blend of wine;
he will pour it, they will drink it to the dregs,
all the wicked on earth will drink it.

9 But I shall speak out for ever,
shall make music for the God of Jacob.
10 I shall break down all the strength of the wicked,
and the strength of the upright will rise high.

PSALM 76 V 75

Hymn to God the awe-inspiring

For the choirmaster For strings Psalm Of Asaph Song

1 God is acknowledged in Judah,
his name is great in Israel,
2 his tent is pitched in Salem,
his dwelling is in Zion;
3 there he has broken the lightning-flashes of the bow,
shield and sword and war. *Pause*

4 Radiant you are, and renowned
for the mountains of booty 5 taken from them.
Heroes are now sleeping their last sleep,
the warriors' arms have failed them;
6 at your reproof, God of Jacob,
chariot and horse stand stunned.

7 You, you alone, strike terror! Who can hold his ground
in your presence when your anger strikes?
8 From heaven your verdicts thunder,
the earth is silent with dread
9 when God takes his stand to give judgement,
to save all the humble of the earth. *Pause*

10 Human anger serves only to praise you,
the survivors of your anger will huddle round you.
11 Make and fulfil your vows to Yahweh your God,
let those who surround him make offerings to the Awesome One.
12 He cuts short the breath of princes,
strikes terror in earthly kings.

PSALM 77

V 76

Meditation on Israel's past

For the choirmaster . . . Jeduthun Of Asaph Psalm

1 I cry to God in distress,
I cry to God and he hears me.

2 In the day of my distress I sought the Lord;
all night I tirelessly stretched out my hands,
my heart refused to be consoled.
3 I sigh as I think of God,
my spirit faints away as I ponder on him. *Pause*

4 You kept me from closing my eyes,
I was too distraught to speak;
5 I thought of former times,
years long past
6 I recalled;
through the night I ponder in my heart,
as I reflect, my spirit asks this question:

7 Is the Lord's rejection final?
Will he never show favour again?
8 Is his faithful love gone for ever?
Has his Word come to an end for all time?
9 Does God forget to show mercy?
In anger does he shut off his tenderness? *Pause*

10 And I said, 'This is what wounds me,
the right hand of the Most High has lost its strength.'
11 Remembering Yahweh's great deeds,
remembering your wonders in the past,
12 I reflect on all that you did,
I ponder all your great deeds.

13 God, your ways are holy!
What god is as great as our God?
14 You are the God who does marvellous deeds,
brought nations to acknowledge your power,
15 with your own arm redeeming your people,
the children of Jacob and Joseph. *Pause*

16 When the waters saw you, God,
when the waters saw you they writhed in anguish,
the very depths shook with fear.
17 The clouds pelted down water,
the sky thundered,
your arrows shot back and forth.

18 The rolling of your thunder was heard,
your lightning-flashes lit up the world,
the earth shuddered and shook.
19 Your way led over the sea,
your path over the countless waters,
and none could trace your footsteps.

20 You guided your people like a flock
by the hand of Moses and Aaron.

PSALM 78

V 77

The lessons of Israelite history

Psalm Of Asaph

1 My people, listen to my teaching,
pay attention to what I say.
2 I will speak to you in poetry,
unfold the mysteries of the past.

3 What we have heard and know,
what our ancestors have told us
4 we shall not conceal from their descendants,
but will tell to a generation still to come:

the praises of Yahweh, his power,
the wonderful deeds he has done.
5 He instituted a witness in Jacob,
he established a law in Israel,

he commanded our ancestors
to hand it down to their descendants,
6 that a generation still to come might know it,
children yet to be born.

They should be sure to tell their own children,
7 and should put their trust in God,
never forgetting God's great deeds,
always keeping his commands,

8 and not, like their ancestors,
be a stubborn and rebellious generation,
a generation weak of purpose,
their spirit fickle towards God.

9 The archer sons of Ephraim
turned tail when the time came for fighting;
10 they failed to keep God's covenant,
they refused to follow his Law;

11 they had forgotten his great deeds,
the marvels he had shown them;
12 he did marvels in the sight of their ancestors
in Egypt, in the plains of Tanis.

13 He split the sea and brought them through,
made the waters stand up like a dam;
14 he led them with a cloud by day,
and all the night with the light of a fire;

15 he split rocks in the desert,
let them drink as though from the limitless depths;
16 he brought forth streams from a rock,
made waters flow down in torrents.

17 But they only sinned against him more than ever,
defying the Most High in barren country;
18 they deliberately challenged God
by demanding food to their hearts' content.

19 They insulted God by saying,
'Can God make a banquet in the desert?
20 True, when he struck the rock,
waters gushed out and flowed in torrents;
but what of bread? Can he give that,
can he provide meat for his people?'

21 When he heard them Yahweh vented his anger,
fire blazed against Jacob,
his anger mounted against Israel,
22 because they had no faith in God,
no trust in his power to save.

23 Even so he gave orders to the skies above,
he opened the sluice-gates of heaven;
24 he rained down manna to feed them,
he gave them the wheat of heaven;
25 mere mortals ate the bread of the Mighty,
he sent them as much food as they could want.

26 He roused an east wind in the heavens,
despatched a south wind by his strength;
27 he rained down meat on them like dust,
birds thick as sand on the seashore,
28 tumbling into the middle of his camp,
all around his dwelling-place.

29 They ate as much food as they wanted,
he satisfied all their cravings;
30 but their cravings were still upon them,
the food was still in their mouths,
31 when the wrath of God attacked them,
slaughtering their strongest men,
laying low the flower of Israel.

32 Despite all this, they went on sinning,
they put no faith in his marvels.
33 He made their days vanish in mist,
their years in sudden ruin.

34 Whenever he slaughtered them, they began to seek him,
they turned back and looked eagerly for him,
35 recalling that God was their rock,
God the Most High, their redeemer.

36 They tried to hoodwink him with their mouths,
their tongues were deceitful towards him;
37 their hearts were not loyal to him,
they were not faithful to his covenant.

38 But in his compassion he forgave their guilt
instead of killing them,
time and again repressing his anger
instead of rousing his full wrath,
39 remembering they were creatures of flesh,
a breath of wind that passes, never to return.

40 How often they defied him in the desert!
How often they grieved him in the wastelands!
41 Repeatedly they challenged God,
provoking the Holy One of Israel,

42 not remembering his hand,
the time when he saved them from the oppressor,

43 he who did his signs in Egypt,
his miracles in the plains of Tanis,
44 turning their rivers to blood,
their streams so that they had nothing to drink.

45 He sent horseflies to eat them up,
and frogs to devastate them,
46 consigning their crops to the caterpillar,
the fruit of their hard work to the locust;

47 he killed their vines with hail,
their sycamore trees with frost,
48 delivering up their cattle to hail,
and their flocks to thunderbolts.

49 He loosed against them the full heat of his anger,
fury, rage and destruction,
a detachment of destroying angels;
50 he gave free course to his anger.

He did not exempt their own selves from death,
delivering up their lives to the plague.
51 He struck all the first-born in Egypt,
the flower of the youth in the tents of Ham.

52 He brought out his people like sheep,
guiding them like a flock in the desert,
53 leading them safe and unafraid,
while the sea engulfed their enemies.

54 He brought them to his holy land,
the hill-country won by his right hand;
55 he dispossessed nations before them,
measured out a heritage for each of them,
and settled the tribes of Israel in their tents.

56 But still they challenged the Most High God and defied him,
refusing to keep his decrees;
57 as perverse and treacherous as their ancestors,
they gave way like a faulty bow,
58 provoking him with their high places,
rousing his jealousy with their idols.

59 God listened and vented his wrath,
he totally rejected Israel;
60 he forsook his dwelling in Shiloh,
the tent where he used to dwell on the earth.

61 He abandoned his power to captivity,
his splendour to the enemy's clutches;
62 he gave up his people to the sword,
he vented his wrath on his own heritage.

63 Fire devoured their young men,
their young girls had no wedding-song;
64 their priests fell by the sword
and their widows sang no dirge.

65 The Lord arose as though he had been asleep,
like a strong man fighting-mad with wine,
66 he struck his enemies on the rump,
and put them to everlasting shame.

67 Rejecting the tents of Joseph,
passing over the tribe of Ephraim,
68 he chose the tribe of Judah,
his well-loved mountain of Zion;
69 he built his sanctuary like high hills,
like the earth set it firm for ever.

70 He chose David to be his servant,
took him from the sheepfold,
71 took him from tending ewes
to pasture his servant Jacob,
and Israel his heritage.
72 He pastured them with unblemished heart,
with a sensitive hand he led them.

PSALM 79

V 78

National lament

Psalm *Of Asaph*

1 God, the pagans have invaded your heritage,
they have defiled your holy temple,
they have laid Jerusalem in ruins,
2 they have left the corpses of your servants
as food for the birds of the air,
the bodies of your faithful for the wild beasts.

3 Around Jerusalem they have shed blood like water,
leaving no one to bury them.
4 We are the scorn of our neighbours,
the butt and laughing-stock of those around us.
5 How long will you be angry, Yahweh? For ever?
Is your jealousy to go on smouldering like a fire?

6 Pour out your anger on the nations
who do not acknowledge you,
and on the kingdoms
that do not call on your name;
7 for they have devoured Jacob
and devastated his home.

8 Do not count against us the guilt of former generations,
in your tenderness come quickly to meet us,
for we are utterly weakened;
9 help us, God our Saviour,
for the glory of your name;
Yahweh, wipe away our sins,
rescue us for the sake of your name.

10 Why should the nations ask,
'Where is their God?'

Let us see the nations suffer vengeance
for shedding your servants' blood.
11 May the groans of the captive reach you,
by your great strength save those who are condemned to death!

12 Repay our neighbours sevenfold
for the insults they have levelled at you, Lord.
13 And we, your people, the flock that you pasture,
will thank you for ever,
will recite your praises from age to age.

PSALM 80

V 79

Prayer for the restoration of Israel

For the choirmaster Tune: 'The decrees are lilies' Of Asaph Psalm

1 Shepherd of Israel, listen,
you who lead Joseph like a flock,
enthroned on the winged creatures, shine forth
2 over Ephraim, Benjamin and Manasseh;
rouse your valour
and come to our help.

3 God, bring us back,
let your face shine on us and we shall be safe.

4 Yahweh, God Sabaoth, how long
will you flare up at your people's prayer?
5 You have made tears their food,
redoubled tears their drink.
6 You let our neighbours quarrel over us,
our enemies mock us.

7 God Sabaoth, bring us back,
let your face shine on us and we shall be safe.

8 You brought a vine out of Egypt,
to plant it you drove out nations;
9 you cleared a space for it,
it took root and filled the whole country.

10 The mountains were covered with its shade,
and the cedars of God with its branches,
11 its boughs stretched as far as the sea,
its shoots as far as the River.

12 Why have you broken down its fences?
Every passer-by plucks its grapes,
13 boars from the forest tear at it,
wild beasts feed on it.

14 God Sabaoth, come back, we pray,
look down from heaven and see,
visit this vine;
15 protect what your own hand has planted.
16 They have thrown it on the fire like dung,
the frown of your rebuke will destroy them.

17 May your hand protect those at your side,
the child of Adam you have strengthened for yourself!
18 Never again will we turn away from you,
give us life and we will call upon your name.

19 God Sabaoth, bring us back,
let your face shine on us and we shall be safe.

PSALM 81

V 80

For the feast of Shelters

For the choirmaster On the . . . of Gath Of Asaph

1 Sing for joy to God our strength,
shout in triumph to the God of Jacob.

2 Strike up the music, beat the tambourine,
play the melodious harp and the lyre;
3 blow the trumpet for the new month,
for the full moon, for our feast day!

4 For Israel has this statute,
a decision of the God of Jacob,
5 a decree he imposed on Joseph,
when he went to war against Egypt.

I heard a voice unknown to me,
6 'I freed his shoulder from the burden,
his hands were able to lay aside the labourer's basket.
7 You cried out in your distress, so I rescued you.

'Hidden in the storm, I answered you,
I tested you at the waters of Meribah. *Pause*
8 Listen, my people, while I give you warning;
Israel, if only you would listen to me!

9 'You shall have no strange gods,
shall worship no alien god.
10 I, Yahweh, am your God,
who brought you here from Egypt,
you have only to open your mouth for me to fill it.

11 'My people would not listen to me,
Israel would have none of me.
12 So I left them to their stubborn selves,
to follow their own devices.

13 'If only my people would listen to me,
if only Israel would walk in my ways,
14 at one stroke I would subdue their enemies,
turn my hand against their opponents.

15 'Those who hate Yahweh would woo his favour,
though their doom was sealed for ever,
16 while I would feed him on pure wheat,
would give you your fill of honey from the rock.'

PSALM 82

V 81

Against the judges of the nations

Psalm Of Asaph

1 God takes his stand in the divine assembly,
surrounded by the gods he gives judgement.

2 'How much longer will you give unjust judgements
and uphold the prestige of the wicked?
3 Let the weak and the orphan have justice,
be fair to the wretched and the destitute. *Pause*

4 'Rescue the weak and the needy,
save them from the clutches of the wicked.

5 'Ignorant and uncomprehending, they wander in darkness,
while the foundations of the world are tottering.
6 I had thought, "Are you gods,
are all of you sons of the Most High?"
7 No! you will die as human beings do,
as one man, princes, you will fall.'

8 Arise, God, judge the world,
for all nations belong to you.

PSALM 83

V 82

Against the enemies of Israel

Song Psalm Of Asaph

1 God, do not remain silent,
do not stay quiet or unmoved, God!
2 See how your enemies are in uproar,
how those who hate you are rearing their heads.

3 They are laying plans against your people,
conspiring against those you cherish;
4 they say, 'Come, let us annihilate them as a nation,
the name of Israel shall be remembered no more!'

5 They conspire with a single mind,
they conclude an alliance against you,
6 the tents of Edom and the Ishmaelites,
Moab and the Hagrites,
7 Gebal, Ammon, Amalek,
Philistia and the Tyrians;
8 even Assyria has joined them
to reinforce the children of Lot. *Pause*

9 Treat them like Midian and Sisera,
like Jabin at the river Kishon;
10 wiped out at En-Dor,
they served to manure the ground.
11 Treat their leaders like Oreb and Zeeb,
all their commanders like Zebah and Zalmunna,

12 for they said, 'Let us take for ourselves
God's settlements.'

13 My God, treat them like thistledown,
like chaff at the mercy of the wind.
14 As fire devours a forest,
as a flame sets mountains ablaze,
15 so drive them away with your tempest,
by your whirlwind fill them with terror.
16 Shame written all over their faces,
let them seek your name, Yahweh!
17 Dishonour and terror be always theirs,
death also and destruction.
18 Let them know that you alone bear the name of Yahweh,
Most High over all the earth.

PSALM 84 V 83

Pilgrimage song

For the choirmaster On the . . . of Gath Of the sons of Korah Psalm

1 How lovely are your dwelling-places,
Yahweh Sabaoth.
2 My whole being yearns and pines
for Yahweh's courts,
My heart and my body cry out for joy
to the living God.

3 Even the sparrow has found a home,
the swallow a nest to place its young:
your altars, Yahweh Sabaoth,
my King and my God.

4 How blessed are those who live in your house;
they shall praise you continually. *Pause*
5 Blessed those who find their strength in you,
whose hearts are set on pilgrimage.

6 As they pass through the Valley of the Balsam,
they make there a water-hole,
and—a further blessing—early rain fills it.
7 They make their way from height to height,
God shows himself to them in Zion.

8 Yahweh, God Sabaoth, hear my prayer,
listen, God of Jacob.
9 God, our shield, look,
and see the face of your anointed.

10 Better one day in your courts
than a thousand at my own devices,
to stand on the threshold of God's house
than to live in the tents of the wicked.

11 For Yahweh God is a rampart and shield,
he gives grace and glory;

Yahweh refuses nothing good
to those whose life is blameless.

12 Yahweh Sabaoth,
blessed is he who trusts in you.

PSALM 85

V 84

Prayer for peace and justice

For the choirmaster Of the sons of Korah Psalm

1 Yahweh, you are gracious to your land,
you bring back the captives of Jacob,
2 you take away the guilt of your people,
you blot out all their sin. *Pause*

3 You retract all your anger,
you renounce the heat of your fury.

4 Bring us back, God our Saviour,
appease your indignation against us!
5 Will you be angry with us for ever?
Will you prolong your wrath age after age?

6 Will you not give us life again,
for your people to rejoice in you?
7 Show us, Lord, your faithful love,
grant us your saving help.

8 I am listening. What is God's message?
Yahweh's message is peace
for his people, for his faithful,
if only they renounce their folly.
9 His saving help is near for those who fear him,
his glory will dwell in our land.

10 Faithful Love and Loyalty join together,
Saving Justice and Peace embrace.
11 Loyalty will spring up from the earth,
and Justice will lean down from heaven.

12 Yahweh will himself give prosperity,
and our soil will yield its harvest.
13 Justice will walk before him,
treading out a path.

PSALM 86

V 85

Prayer in time of trial

Prayer Of David

1 Listen to me, Yahweh, answer me,
for I am poor and needy.
2 Guard me, for I am faithful,
save your servant who relies on you.

You are my God, 3take pity on me, Lord,
for to you I cry all the day.
4Fill your servant's heart with joy, Lord,
for to you I raise up my heart.

5Lord, you are kind and forgiving,
rich in faithful love for all who call upon you.
6Yahweh, hear my prayer,
listen to the sound of my pleading.

7In my day of distress I call upon you,
because you answer me, Lord;
8among the gods there is none to compare with you,
no great deeds to compare with yours.

9All nations will come and adore you, Lord,
and give glory to your name.
10For you are great and do marvellous deeds,
you, God, and none other.

11Teach me, Yahweh, your ways,
that I may not stray from your loyalty;
let my heart's one aim be to fear your name.

12I thank you with all my heart, Lord my God,
I will glorify your name for ever,
13for your faithful love for me is so great
that you have rescued me from the depths of Sheol.

14Arrogant men, God, are rising up against me,
a brutal gang is after my life,
in their scheme of things you have no place.

15But you, Lord, God of tenderness and mercy,
slow to anger, rich in faithful love and loyalty,
16turn to me and pity me.

Give to your servant your strength,
to the child of your servant your saving help,
17give me a sign of your kindness.

18My enemies will see to their shame
that you, Yahweh, help and console me.

PSALM 87

V 86

Zion, mother of nations

Of the sons of Korah Psalm Song

1With its foundations on the holy mountains,
2Yahweh loves his city,
he prefers the gates of Zion
to any dwelling-place in Jacob.

3He speaks of glory for you,
city of God, *Pause*

4'I number Rahab and Babylon
among those that acknowledge me;
look at Tyre, Philistia, Ethiopia,
so and so was born there.'

5But of Zion it will be said,
'Every one was born there,'
her guarantee is the Most High.

6Yahweh in his register of peoples
will note against each, 'Born there', *Pause*
7princes no less than native-born;
all make their home in you.

PSALM 88

V 87

Prayer in great distress

Song Psalm Of the sons of Korah In sickness In suffering Poem For Heman the native-born

1Yahweh, God of my salvation,
when I cry out to you in the night,
2may my prayer reach your presence,
hear my cry for help.

3For I am filled with misery,
my life is on the brink of Sheol;
4already numbered among those who sink into oblivion,
I am as one bereft of strength,
5left alone among the dead,
like the slaughtered lying in the grave,
whom you remember no more,
cut off as they are from your protection.

6You have plunged me to the bottom of the grave,
in the darkness, in the depths;
7weighted down by your anger,
kept low by your waves. *Pause*

8You have deprived me of my friends,
made me repulsive to them,
imprisoned, with no escape;
9my eyes are worn out with suffering.
I call to you, Yahweh, all day,
I stretch out my hands to you.

10Do you work wonders for the dead,
can shadows rise up to praise you? *Pause*
11Do they speak in the grave of your faithful love,
of your constancy in the place of perdition?
12Are your wonders known in the darkness,
your saving justice in the land of oblivion?

13But, for my part, I cry to you, Yahweh,
every morning my prayer comes before you;
14why, Yahweh, do you rebuff me,
turn your face away from me?

[15]Wretched and close to death since childhood,
I have borne your terrors—I am finished!
[16]Your anger has overwhelmed me,
your terrors annihilated me.

[17]They flood around me all day long,
close in on me all at once.
[18]You have deprived me of friends and companions,
and all that I know is the dark.

PSALM 89

V 88

Hymn and prayer to God the faithful

Poem For Ethan the native-born

[1]I shall sing the faithful love of Yahweh for ever,
from age to age my lips shall declare your constancy,
[2]for you have said: love is built to last for ever,
you have fixed your constancy firm in the heavens.

[3]'I have made a covenant with my Chosen One,
sworn an oath to my servant David:
[4]I have made your dynasty firm for ever,
built your throne stable age after age.' *Pause*

[5]The heavens praise your wonders, Yahweh,
your constancy in the gathering of your faithful.
[6]Who in the skies can compare with Yahweh?
Who among the sons of god can rival him?

[7]God, awesome in the assembly of holy ones,
great and dreaded among all who surround him,
[8]Yahweh, God Sabaoth, who is like you?
Mighty Yahweh, your constancy is all round you!

[9]You control the pride of the ocean,
when its waves ride high you calm them.
[10]You split Rahab[a] in two like a corpse,
scattered your enemies with your mighty arm.

[11]Yours are the heavens and yours the earth,
the world and all it holds, you founded them;
[12]you created the north and the south,
Tabor and Hermon hail your name with joy.

[13]Yours is a strong arm,
mighty your hand, your right hand raised high;
[14]Saving Justice and Fair Judgement the foundations of your throne,
Faithful Love and Constancy march before you.

[15]How blessed the nation that learns to acclaim you!
They will live, Yahweh, in the light of your presence.
[16]In your name they rejoice all day long,
by your saving justice they are raised up.

89a Usually the sea as a monster of chaos, subdued at creation; or Egypt subdued at the exodus.

17 You are the flower of their strength,
by your favour our strength is triumphant;
18 for to Yahweh belongs our shield,
to the Holy One of Israel our king.

19 Once you spoke in a vision,
to your faithful you said:
'I have given strength to a warrior,
I have raised up a man chosen from my people.

20 'I have found David my servant,
and anointed him with my holy oil.
21 My hand will always be with him,
my arm will make him strong.

22 'No enemy will be able to outwit him,
no wicked man overcome him;
23 I shall crush his enemies before him,
strike his opponents dead.

24 'My constancy and faithful love will be with him,
in my name his strength will be triumphant.
25 I shall establish his power over the sea,
his dominion over the rivers.

26 'He will cry to me, "You are my father,
my God, the rock of my salvation!"
27 So I shall make him my first-born,
the highest of earthly kings.

28 'I shall maintain my faithful love for him always,
my covenant with him will stay firm.
29 I have established his dynasty for ever,
his throne to be as lasting as the heavens.

30 'Should his descendants desert my law,
and not keep to my rulings,
31 should they violate my statutes,
and not observe my commandments,

32 'then I shall punish their offences with the rod,
their guilt with the whip,
33 but I shall never withdraw from him my faithful love,
I shall not belie my constancy.

34 'I shall not violate my covenant,
I shall not withdraw the word once spoken.
35 I have sworn by my holiness, once and for all,
never will I break faith with David.

36 'His dynasty shall endure for ever,
his throne like the sun before me,
37 as the moon is established for ever,
a faithful witness in the skies.' *Pause*

38 Yet you yourself—you have spurned and rejected,
and have vented your wrath on your anointed,
39 you have repudiated the covenant with your servant,
dishonoured his crown in the dust.

40 You have pierced all his defences,
and laid his strongholds in ruins,

41 everyone passing by plunders him,
he has become the butt of his neighbours.

42 You have raised high the right hand of his opponents,
have made all his enemies happy;
43 you have snapped off his sword on a rock,
and failed to support him in battle.

44 You have stripped him of his splendid sceptre,
and toppled his throne to the ground.
45 You have aged him before his time,
enveloped him in shame. *Pause*

46 How long, Yahweh, will you remain hidden? For ever?
Is your anger to go on smouldering like a fire?
47 Remember me; how long have I left?
For what pointless end did you create all the children of Adam?
48 Who can live and never see death?
Who can save himself from the clutches of Sheol? *Pause*

49 Lord, what of those pledges of your faithful love?
You made an oath to David by your constancy.
50 Do not forget the insults to your servant;
I take to heart the taunts of the nations,
51 which your enemies have levelled, Yahweh,
have levelled at the footsteps of your anointed!

52 Blessed be Yahweh for ever.
Amen, Amen.

PSALM 90

V 89

On human frailty

Prayer *Of Moses, man of God*

1 Lord, you have been our refuge
from age to age.

2 Before the mountains were born,
before the earth and the world came to birth,
from eternity to eternity you are God.

3 You bring human beings to the dust,
by saying, 'Return, children of Adam.'
4 A thousand years are to you
like a yesterday which has passed,
like a watch of the night.

5 You flood them with sleep
—in the morning they will be like growing grass:
6 in the morning it is blossoming and growing,
by evening it is withered and dry.

7 For we have been destroyed by your wrath,
dismayed by your anger.
8 You have taken note of our guilty deeds,
our secrets in the full light of your presence.

9 All our days pass under your wrath,
our lives are over like a sigh.
10 The span of our life is seventy years—
eighty for those who are strong—
but their whole extent is anxiety and trouble,
they are over in a moment and we are gone.

11 Who feels the power of your anger,
or who that fears you, your wrath?

12 Teach us to count up the days that are ours,
and we shall come to the heart of wisdom.
13 Come back, Yahweh! How long must we wait?
Take pity on your servants.

14 Each morning fill us with your faithful love,
we shall sing and be happy all our days;
15 let our joy be as long as the time that you afflicted us,
the years when we experienced disaster.

16 Show your servants the deeds you do,
let their children enjoy your splendour!
17 May the sweetness of the Lord be upon us,
to confirm the work we have done!

PSALM 91

V 90

Under God's protection

1 You who live in the secret place of Elyon,
spend your nights in the shelter of Shaddai,
2 saying to Yahweh, 'My refuge, my fortress,
my God in whom I trust!'

3 He rescues you from the snare
of the fowler set on destruction;
4 he covers you with his pinions,
you find shelter under his wings.
His constancy is shield and protection.

5 You need not fear the terrors of night,
the arrow that flies in the daytime,
6 the plague that stalks in the darkness,
the scourge that wreaks havoc at high noon.

7 Though a thousand fall at your side,
ten thousand at your right hand,
you yourself will remain unscathed.
8 You have only to keep your eyes open
to see how the wicked are repaid,
9 you who say, 'Yahweh my refuge!'
and make Elyon your fortress.

10 No disaster can overtake you,
no plague come near your tent;
11 he has given his angels orders about you
to guard you wherever you go.

12 They will carry you in their arms
in case you trip over a stone.
13 You will walk upon wild beast and adder,
you will trample young lions and snakes.

14 'Since he clings to me I rescue him,
I raise him high, since he acknowledges my name.
15 He calls to me and I answer him:
in distress I am at his side,
I rescue him and bring him honour.
16 I shall satisfy him with long life,
and grant him to see my salvation.'

PSALM 92 V 91

The song of the upright

Psalm Song *For the Sabbath*

1 It is good to give thanks to Yahweh,
to make music for your name, Most High,
2 to proclaim your faithful love at daybreak,
and your constancy all through the night,
3 on the lyre, the ten-stringed lyre,
to the murmur of the harp.

4 You have brought me joy, Yahweh, by your deeds,
at the work of your hands I cry out,
5 'How great are your works, Yahweh,
immensely deep your thoughts!'
6 Stupid people cannot realise this,
fools do not grasp it.

7 The wicked may sprout like weeds,
and every evil-doer flourish,
but only to be eternally destroyed;
8 whereas you are supreme for ever, Yahweh.

9 Look how your enemies perish,
how all evil-doers are scattered!
10 You give me the strength of the wild ox,
you anoint me with fresh oil;
11 I caught sight of the ambush against me,
overheard the plans of the wicked.

12 The upright will flourish like the palm tree,
will grow like a cedar of Lebanon.
13 Planted in the house of Yahweh,
they will flourish in the courts of our God.

14 In old age they will still bear fruit,
will remain fresh and green,
15 to proclaim Yahweh's integrity;
my rock, in whom no fault can be found.

PSALM 93

V 92

The majesty of God

1 Yahweh is king, robed in majesty,
robed is Yahweh and girded with power.

2 The world is indeed set firm, it can never be shaken;
your throne is set firm from of old,
from all eternity you exist.

3 The rivers lift up, Yahweh,
the rivers lift up their voices,
the rivers lift up their thunder.

4 Greater than the voice of many waters,
more majestic than the breakers of the sea,
Yahweh is majestic in the heights.

5 Your decrees stand firm, unshakeable,
holiness is the beauty of your house,
Yahweh, for all time to come.

PSALM 94

V 93

The God of justice

1 God of vengeance, Yahweh,
God of vengeance, shine forth!
2 Arise, judge of the world,
give back the proud what they deserve!

3 How long are the wicked, Yahweh,
how long are the wicked to triumph?
4 They bluster and boast,
they flaunt themselves, all the evil-doers.

5 They crush your people, Yahweh,
they oppress your heritage,
6 they murder the widow and the stranger,
bring the orphan to a violent death.

7 They say, 'Yahweh is not looking,
the God of Jacob is taking no notice.'
8 Take notice yourselves, you coarsest of people!
Fools, when will you learn some sense?

9 Shall he who implanted the ear not hear,
he who fashioned the eye not see?
10 Shall he who instructs nations not punish?
Yahweh, the teacher of all people,
11 knows human plans and how insipid they are.

12 How blessed are those you instruct, Yahweh,
whom you teach by means of your law,
13 to give them respite in evil times,
till a pit is dug for the wicked.

[14]Yahweh will not abandon his people,
he will not desert his heritage;
[15]for judgement will again become saving justice,
and in its wake all upright hearts will follow.

[16]Who rises up on my side against the wicked?
Who stands firm on my side against all evil-doers?
[17]If Yahweh did not come to my help,
I should soon find myself dwelling in the silence.

[18]I need only say, 'I am slipping,'
for your faithful love, Yahweh, to support me;
[19]however great the anxiety of my heart,
your consolations soothe me.

[20]Are you partner to a destructive court,
that gives disorder the status of law?
[21]They make an attack on the life of the upright,
and condemn innocent blood.

[22]No! Yahweh is a stronghold to me,
my God is my rock of refuge.
[23]He turns back their guilt on themselves,
annihilates them for their wickedness,
he annihilates them, Yahweh our God.

PSALM 95

V 94

Invitation to praise

[1]Come, let us cry out with joy to Yahweh,
acclaim the rock of our salvation.
[2]Let us come into his presence with thanksgiving,
acclaim him with music.

[3]For Yahweh is a great God,
a king greater than all the gods.
[4]In his power are the depths of the earth,
the peaks of the mountains are his;
[5]the sea belongs to him, for he made it,
and the dry land, moulded by his hands.

[6]Come, let us bow low and do reverence;
kneel before Yahweh who made us!
[7]For he is our God,
and we the people of his sheepfold,
the flock of his hand.

If only you would listen to him today!
[8]Do not harden your hearts as at Meribah,
as at the time of Massah in the desert,[a]
[9]when your ancestors challenged me,
put me to the test, and saw what I could do!

95a Incidents during the desert journey: *Meribah* =dispute, *Massah* =temptation.

10 For forty years that generation sickened me,
and I said, 'Always fickle hearts;
they cannot grasp my ways.'
11 Then in my anger I swore
they would never enter my place of rest.

PSALM 96

V 95

Yahweh, king and judge

1 Sing a new song to Yahweh!
Sing to Yahweh, all the earth!
2 Sing to Yahweh, bless his name!

Proclaim his salvation day after day,
3 declare his glory among the nations,
his marvels to every people!

4 Great is Yahweh, worthy of all praise,
more awesome than any of the gods.
5 All the gods of the nations are idols!

It was Yahweh who made the heavens;
6 in his presence are splendour and majesty,
in his sanctuary power and beauty.

7 Give to Yahweh, families of nations,
give to Yahweh glory and power,
8 give to Yahweh the glory due to his name!

Bring an offering and enter his courts,
9 adore Yahweh in the splendour of his holiness.
Tremble before him, all the earth.

10 Say among the nations, 'Yahweh is king.'
The world is set firm, it cannot be moved.
He will judge the nations with justice.

11 Let the heavens rejoice and earth be glad!
Let the sea thunder, and all it holds!
12 Let the countryside exult, and all that is in it,
and all the trees of the forest cry out for joy,

13 at Yahweh's approach, for he is coming,
coming to judge the earth;
he will judge the world with saving justice,
and the nations with constancy.

PSALM 97

V 96

The triumph of Yahweh

1 Yahweh is king! Let earth rejoice,
the many isles be glad!
2 Cloud, black cloud enfolds him,
saving justice and judgement the foundations of his throne.

3 Fire goes before him,
sets ablaze his enemies all around;
4 his lightning-flashes light up the world,
the earth sees it and quakes.

5 The mountains melt like wax,
before the Lord of all the earth.
6 The heavens proclaim his saving justice,
all nations see his glory.

7 Shame on all who serve images,
who pride themselves on their idols;
bow down to him, all you gods!

8 Zion hears and is glad,
the daughters of Judah exult,
because of your judgements, Yahweh.

9 For you are Yahweh,
Most High over all the earth,
far transcending all gods.

10 Yahweh loves those who hate evil,
he keeps safe his faithful,
rescues them from the clutches of the wicked.

11 Light dawns for the upright,
and joy for honest hearts.
12 Rejoice in Yahweh, you who are upright,
praise his unforgettable holiness.

PSALM 98

V 97

The judge of the world

Psalm

1 Sing a new song to Yahweh,
for he has performed wonders,
his saving power is in his right hand
and his holy arm.

2 Yahweh has made known his saving power,
revealed his saving justice for the nations to see,
3 mindful of his faithful love and his constancy
to the House of Israel.

The whole wide world has seen
the saving power of our God.
4 Acclaim Yahweh, all the earth,
burst into shouts of joy!

5 Play to Yahweh on the harp,
to the sound of instruments;
6 to the sound of trumpet and horn,
acclaim the presence of the King.

7 Let the sea thunder, and all that it holds,
the world and all who live in it.

8 Let the rivers clap their hands,
and the mountains shout for joy together,

9 at Yahweh's approach, for he is coming
to judge the earth;
he will judge the world with saving justice
and the nations with fairness.

PSALM 99

V 98

God, the upright and holy king

1 Yahweh is king, the peoples tremble;
he is enthroned on the winged creatures, the earth shivers;
2 Yahweh is great in Zion.

He is supreme over all nations;
3 let them praise your name, great and awesome;
holy is he 4 and mighty!

You are a king who loves justice,
you established honesty, justice and uprightness;
in Jacob it is you who are active.

5 Exalt Yahweh our God,
bow down at his footstool;
holy is he!

6 Moses and Aaron are among his priests, and Samuel,
calling on his name; they called on Yahweh
and he answered them.

7 He spoke with them in the pillar of fire,
they obeyed his decrees, the Law he gave them.

8 Yahweh our God, you answered them,
you were a God of forgiveness to them,
but punished them for their sins.

9 Exalt Yahweh our God,
bow down at his holy mountain;
holy is Yahweh our God!

PSALM 100

V 99

Invitation to praise

Psalm For thanksgiving

1 Acclaim Yahweh, all the earth,
2 serve Yahweh with gladness,
come into his presence with songs of joy!

3 Be sure that Yahweh is God,
he made us, we belong to him,
his people, the flock of his sheepfold.

4Come within his gates giving thanks,
to his courts singing praise,
give thanks to him and bless his name!

5For Yahweh is good,
his faithful love is everlasting,
his constancy from age to age.

PSALM 101

V 100

The ideal ruler

Of David Psalm

1I will sing of faithful love and judgement;
to you, Yahweh, will I make music.
2I will go forward in the path of the blameless;
when will you come to me?

I will live in purity of heart,
in my house,
3I will not set before my eyes
anything sordid.

I hate those who act crookedly;
this has no attraction for me.
4Let the perverse of heart keep away from me;
the wicked I disregard.

5One who secretly slanders a comrade,
I reduce to silence;
haughty looks, proud heart,
these I cannot abide.

6I look to the faithful of the land
to be my companions,
only he who walks in the path of the blameless
shall be my servant.

7There is no room in my house
for anyone who practises deceit;
no liar will stand his ground
where I can see him.

8Morning after morning I reduce to silence
all the wicked in the land,
banishing from the city of Yahweh
all evil-doers.

PSALM 102[a]

V 101

Prayer in misfortune

Prayer of someone afflicted, who in misfortune pours out sorrows before Yahweh

1 Yahweh, hear my prayer,
let my cry for help reach you.
2 Do not turn away your face from me
when I am in trouble;
bend down and listen to me,
when I call, be quick to answer me!

3 For my days are vanishing like smoke,
my bones burning like an oven;
4 like grass struck by blight, my heart is withering,
I forget to eat my meals.
5 From the effort of voicing my groans
my bones stick out through my skin.

6 I am like a desert-owl in the wastes,
a screech-owl among ruins,
7 I keep vigil and moan
like a lone bird on a roof.
8 All day long my enemies taunt me,
those who once praised me now use me as a curse.

9 Ashes are the food that I eat,
my drink is mingled with tears,
10 because of your fury and anger,
since you have raised me up only to cast me away;
11 my days are like a fading shadow,
I am withering up like grass.

12 But you, Yahweh, are enthroned for ever,
each generation in turn remembers you.
13 Rise up, take pity on Zion!
the time has come to have mercy on her,
the moment has come;
14 for your servants love her very stones,
are moved to pity by her dust.

15 Then will the nations revere the name of Yahweh,
and all the kings of the earth your glory;
16 when Yahweh builds Zion anew,
he will be seen in his glory;
17 he will turn to hear the prayer of the destitute,
and will not treat their prayer with scorn.

18 This shall be put on record for a future generation,
and a people yet to be born shall praise God:
19 Yahweh has leaned down from the heights of his sanctuary,
has looked down from heaven to earth,
20 to listen to the sighing of the captive,
and set free those condemned to death,
21 to proclaim the name of Yahweh in Zion,
his praise in Jerusalem;

102a Two poems: vv. 1–11 + 23–27 form a personal lament, vv. 12–22 a prayer for pity.

22 nations will gather together,
and kingdoms to worship Yahweh.

23 In my journeying my strength has failed on the way;
24 let me know the short time I have left.
Do not take me away before half my days are done,
for your years run on from age to age.

25 Long ago you laid earth's foundations,
the heavens are the work of your hands.
26 They pass away but you remain;
they all wear out like a garment,
like outworn clothes you change them;
27 but you never alter, and your years never end.

28 The children of those who serve you will dwell secure,
and their descendants live on in your presence.

PSALM 103

V 102

God is love

Of David

1 Bless Yahweh, my soul,
from the depths of my being, his holy name;
2 bless Yahweh, my soul,
never forget all his acts of kindness.

3 He forgives all your offences,
cures all your diseases,
4 he redeems your life from the abyss,
crowns you with faithful love and tenderness;
5 he contents you with good things all your life,
renews your youth like an eagle's.

6 Yahweh acts with uprightness,
with justice to all who are oppressed;
7 he revealed to Moses his ways,
his great deeds to the children of Israel.

8 Yahweh is tenderness and pity,
slow to anger and rich in faithful love;
9 his indignation does not last for ever,
nor his resentment remain for all time;
10 he does not treat us as our sins deserve,
nor repay us as befits our offences.

11 As the height of heaven above earth,
so strong is his faithful love for those who fear him.
12 As the distance of east from west,
so far from us does he put our faults.

13 As tenderly as a father treats his children,
so Yahweh treats those who fear him;
14 he knows of what we are made,
he remembers that we are dust.

15 As for a human person—his days are like grass,
he blooms like the wild flowers;
16 as soon as the wind blows he is gone,
never to be seen there again.

17 But Yahweh's faithful love for those who fear him
is from eternity and for ever;
and his saving justice to their children's children;
18 as long as they keep his covenant,
and carefully obey his precepts.

19 Yahweh has fixed his throne in heaven,
his sovereign power rules over all.
20 Bless Yahweh, all his angels,
mighty warriors who fulfil his commands,
attentive to the sound of his words.

21 Bless Yahweh, all his armies,
servants who fulfil his wishes.
22 Bless Yahweh, all his works,
in every place where he rules.

Bless Yahweh, my soul.

PSALM 104

V 103

The glories of creation

1 Bless Yahweh, my soul,
Yahweh, my God, how great you are!
Clothed in majesty and splendour,
2 wearing the light as a robe!

You stretch out the heavens like a tent,
3 build your palace on the waters above,
making the clouds your chariot,
gliding on the wings of the wind,
4 appointing the winds your messengers,
flames of fire your servants.

5 You fixed the earth on its foundations,
for ever and ever it shall not be shaken;
6 you covered it with the deep like a garment,
the waters overtopping the mountains.

7 At your reproof the waters fled,
at the voice of your thunder they sped away,
8 flowing over mountains, down valleys,
to the place you had fixed for them;
9 you made a limit they were not to cross,
they were not to return and cover the earth.

10 In the ravines you opened up springs,
running down between the mountains,
11 supplying water for all the wild beasts;
the wild asses quench their thirst,
12 on their banks the birds of the air make their nests,
they sing among the leaves.

13 From your high halls you water the mountains,
satisfying the earth with the fruit of your works:
14 for cattle you make the grass grow,
and for people the plants they need,
to bring forth food from the earth,
15 and wine to cheer people's hearts,
oil to make their faces glow,
food to make them sturdy of heart.

16 The trees of Yahweh drink their fill,
the cedars of Lebanon which he sowed;
17 there the birds build their nests,
on the highest branches the stork makes its home;
18 for the wild goats there are the mountains,
in the crags the coneys find refuge.

19 He made the moon to mark the seasons,
the sun knows when to set.
20 You bring on darkness, and night falls,
when all the forest beasts roam around;
21 young lions roar for their prey,
asking God for their food.

22 The sun rises and away they steal,
back to their lairs to lie down,
23 and man goes out to work,
to labour till evening falls.

24 How countless are your works, Yahweh,
all of them made so wisely!
The earth is full of your creatures.

25 Then there is the sea, with its vast expanses
teeming with countless creatures,
creatures both great and small;
26 there ships pass to and fro,
and Leviathan whom you made to sport with.

27 They all depend upon you,
to feed them when they need it.
28 You provide the food they gather,
your open hand gives them their fill.

29 Turn away your face and they panic;
take back their breath and they die
and revert to dust.
30 Send out your breath and life begins;
you renew the face of the earth.

31 Glory to Yahweh for ever!
May Yahweh find joy in his creatures!
32 At his glance the earth trembles,
at his touch the mountains pour forth smoke.

33 I shall sing to Yahweh all my life,
make music for my God as long as I live.
34 May my musings be pleasing to him,
for Yahweh gives me joy.
35 May sinners vanish from the earth,
and the wicked exist no more!

Bless Yahweh, my soul.

PSALM 105

The wonderful history of Israel

Alleluia!

1Give thanks to Yahweh, call on his name,
proclaim his deeds to the peoples!
2Sing to him, make music for him,
recount all his wonders!
3Glory in his holy name,
let the hearts that seek Yahweh rejoice!

4Seek Yahweh and his strength,
tirelessly seek his presence!
5Remember the marvels he has done,
his wonders, the judgements he has spoken.

6Stock of Abraham, his servant,
children of Jacob whom he chose!
7He is Yahweh our God,
his judgements touch the whole world.

8He remembers his covenant for ever,
the promise he laid down for a thousand generations,
9which he concluded with Abraham,
the oath he swore to Isaac.

10He established it as a statute for Jacob,
an everlasting covenant with Israel,
11saying, 'To you I give a land,
Canaan, your allotted birthright.'

12When they were insignificant in numbers,
a handful of strangers in the land,
13wandering from country to country,
from one kingdom and nation to another,

14he allowed no one to oppress them;
for their sake he instructed kings,
15'Do not touch my anointed ones,
to my prophets you may do no harm.'

16He called down famine on the land,
he took away their food supply;
17he sent a man ahead of them,
Joseph, sold as a slave.

18So his feet were weighed down with shackles,
his neck was put in irons.
19In due time his prophecy was fulfilled,
the word of Yahweh proved him true.

20The king sent orders to release him,
the ruler of nations set him free;
21he put him in charge of his household,
the ruler of all he possessed,

22to instruct his princes as he saw fit,
to teach his counsellors wisdom.

23 Then Israel migrated to Egypt,
Jacob settled in the country of Ham.

24 He made his people increase in numbers,
he gave them more strength than their enemies,
25 whose heart he turned to hate his own people,
to double-cross his servants.

26 He sent his servant Moses,
and Aaron, the man of his choice.
27 They worked there the wonders he commanded,
marvels in the country of Ham.

28 Darkness he sent, and darkness fell,
but that nation defied his orders.
29 He turned their rivers to blood,
and killed all the fish in them.

30 Their country was overrun with frogs,
even in the royal apartments;
31 at his word came flies,
and mosquitoes throughout the country.

32 He gave them hail as their rain,
flames of fire in their land;
33 he blasted their vine and their fig tree,
and shattered the trees of the country.

34 At his word came locusts,
hoppers beyond all counting;
35 they devoured every green thing in the land,
devoured all the produce of the soil.

36 He struck all the first-born in their land,
the flower of all their manhood;
37 he led Israel out with silver and gold;
in their tribes there was none who stumbled.

38 Egypt was glad at their leaving,
for terror of Israel had seized them.
39 He spread out a cloud to cover them,
and fire to light up the night.

40 They asked and he brought them quails,
food from heaven to their hearts' content;
41 he opened a rock, the waters gushed out,
and flowed in dry ground as a river.

42 Faithful to his sacred promise,
given to his servant Abraham,
43 he led out his people with rejoicing,
his chosen ones with shouts of joy.

44 He gave them the territories of nations,
they reaped the fruit of other people's labours,
45 on condition that they kept his statutes,
and remained obedient to his laws.

PSALM 106

National confession of guilt

1 Alleluia!

Give thanks to Yahweh, for he is good,
his faithful love is everlasting!
2 Who can recount all Yahweh's triumphs,
who can fully voice his praise?

3 How blessed are those who keep to what is just,
whose conduct is always upright!
4 Remember me, Yahweh,
in your love for your people.

Come near to me with your saving power,
5 let me share the happiness of your chosen ones,
let me share the joy of your people,
the pride of your heritage.

6 Like our ancestors, we have sinned,
we have acted wickedly, guiltily;
7 our ancestors in Egypt never grasped
the meaning of your wonders.

They did not bear in mind your countless acts of love,
at the Sea of Reeds they defied the Most High;
8 but for the sake of his name he saved them,
to make known his mighty power.

9 At his rebuke the Sea of Reeds dried up,
he let them pass through the deep as though it were desert,
10 so he saved them from their opponents' clutches,
rescued them from the clutches of their enemies.

11 The waters enveloped their enemies,
not one of whom was left.
12 Then they believed what he had said,
and sang his praises.

13 But they soon forgot his achievements,
they did not even wait for his plans;
14 they were overwhelmed with greed in the wastelands,
in the solitary wastes they challenged God.

15 He gave them all they asked for,
but struck them with a deep wasting sickness;
16 in the camp they grew jealous of Moses,
and of Aaron, Yahweh's holy one.

17 The earth opened and swallowed up Dathan,
closed in on Abiram's faction;
18 fire flamed out against their faction,
the renegades were engulfed in flames.

19 At Horeb they made a calf,
bowed low before cast metal;
20 they exchanged their glory
for the image of a grass-eating bull.

21 They forgot the God who was saving them,
who had done great deeds in Egypt,
22 such wonders in the land of Ham,
such awesome deeds at the Sea of Reeds.

23 He thought of putting an end to them,
had not Moses, his chosen one,
taken a stand in the breach and confronted him,
to turn his anger away from destroying them.

24 They counted a desirable land for nothing,
they put no trust in his promise;
25 they stayed in their tents and grumbled,
they would not listen to Yahweh's voice.

26 So he lifted his hand against them,
to strike them down in the desert,
27 to strike down their descendants among the nations,
to scatter them all over the world.

28 They committed themselves to serve Baal-Peor,
and ate sacrifices made to lifeless gods.
29 They so provoked him by their actions
that a plague broke out among them.

30 Then up stood Phinehas to intervene,
and the plague was checked;
31 for this he is the example of uprightness,
from age to age for ever.

32 At the waters of Meribah they so angered Yahweh,
that Moses suffered on their account,
33 for they had embittered his spirit,
and he spoke without due thought.

34 They did not destroy the nations,
as Yahweh had told them to do,
35 but intermarried with them,
and adopted their ways.

36 They worshipped those nations' false gods,
till they found themselves entrapped,
37 and sacrificed their own sons
and their daughters to demons.

38 Innocent blood they shed,
the blood of their sons and daughters;
offering them to the idols of Canaan,
they polluted the country with blood.

39 They defiled themselves by such actions,
their behaviour was that of a harlot.
40 Yahweh's anger blazed out at his people,
his own heritage filled him with disgust.

41 He handed them over to the nations,
and their opponents became their masters;
42 their enemies lorded it over them,
crushing them under their rule.

43 Time and again he rescued them,

but they still defied him deliberately,
and sank ever deeper in their guilt;
44 even so he took pity on their distress,
as soon as he heard them cry out.

45 Bearing his covenant with them in mind,
he relented in his boundless and faithful love;
46 he ensured that they received compassion,
in their treatment by all their captors.

47 Save us, Yahweh our God,
gather us from among the nations,
that we may give thanks to your holy name,
and may glory in praising you.

48 Blessed be Yahweh, the God of Israel,
from all eternity and for ever!
Let all the people say, 'Amen'.

PSALM 107

V 106

God, a refuge in every danger

Alleluia!

1 Give thanks to Yahweh for he is good,
his faithful love lasts for ever.

2 So let them say whom Yahweh redeemed,
whom he redeemed from the power of their enemies,
3 bringing them back from foreign lands,
from east and west, north and south.

4 They were wandering in the desert, in the wastelands,
could find no way to an inhabited city;
5 they were hungry and thirsty,
their life was ebbing away.

6 They cried out to Yahweh in their distress,
he rescued them from their plight,
7 he set them on the road,
straight to an inhabited city.

8 Let them thank Yahweh for his faithful love,
for his wonders for the children of Adam!
9 He has fed the hungry to their hearts' content,
filled the starving with good things.

10 Sojourners in gloom and shadow dark as death,
fettered in misery and chains,
11 for defying the orders of Yahweh,
for scorning the plan of the Most High—
12 he subdued their spirit by hard labour;
if they fell there was no one to help.

13 They cried out to Yahweh in their distress,
he rescued them from their plight,
14 he brought them out from gloom and shadow dark as death,
and shattered their chains.

15 Let them thank Yahweh for his faithful love,
for his wonders for the children of Adam!
16 He broke open gates of bronze
and smashed iron bars.

17 Fools for their rebellious ways,
wretched because of their sins,
18 finding all food repugnant,
brought close to the gates of death—

19 they cried out to Yahweh in their distress;
he rescued them from their plight,
20 he sent out his word and cured them,
and rescued their life from the abyss.

21 Let them thank Yahweh for his faithful love,
for his wonders for the children of Adam!
22 Let them offer thanksgiving sacrifices,
and recount with shouts of joy what he has done!

23 Voyagers on the sea in ships,
plying their trade on the great ocean,
24 have seen the works of Yahweh,
his wonders in the deep.

25 By his word he raised a storm-wind,
lashing up towering waves.
26 Up to the sky then down to the depths!
Their stomachs were turned to water;
27 they staggered and reeled like drunkards,
and all their skill went under.

28 They cried out to Yahweh in their distress,
he rescued them from their plight,
29 he reduced the storm to a calm,
and all the waters subsided,
30 and he brought them, overjoyed at the stillness,
to the port where they were bound.

31 Let them thank Yahweh for his faithful love,
for his wonders for the children of Adam!
32 Let them extol him in the assembly of the people,
and praise him in the council of elders.

33 He has turned rivers into desert,
bubbling springs into arid ground,
34 fertile country into salt-flats,
because the people living there were evil.

35 But he has turned desert into stretches of water,
arid ground into bubbling springs,
36 and has given the hungry a home,
where they have built themselves a city.

37 There they sow fields and plant vines,
and reap a harvest of their produce.
38 He blesses them and their numbers increase,
he keeps their cattle at full strength.

39 Their numbers had fallen, they had grown weak,
under pressure of disaster and hardship;

40he covered princes in contempt,
left them to wander in trackless wastes.

41But the needy he raises from their misery,
makes their families as numerous as sheep.
42At the sight the honest rejoice,
and the wicked have nothing to say.

43Who is wise? Such a one should take this to heart,
and come to understand Yahweh's faithful love.

PSALM 108[a]

V 107

Morning hymn and national prayer

Song Psalm Of David

1My heart is ready, God,
I will sing and make music;
come, my glory!
2Awake, lyre and harp,
I will awake the Dawn!

3I will praise you among the peoples, Yahweh,
I will play to you among nations,
4for your faithful love towers to heaven,
and your constancy to the clouds.

5Be exalted above the heavens, God.
Your glory over the whole earth!

6To rescue those you love,
save with your right hand and answer us.

7God has spoken from his sanctuary,
'In triumph I will divide up Shechem,
and share out the Valley of Succoth.

8'Mine is Gilead, mine Manasseh,
Ephraim the helmet on my head,
Judah my commander's baton,

9'Moab a bowl for me to wash in,
on Edom I plant my sandal,
over Philistia I cry victory.'

10Who will lead me against a fortified city,
who will guide me into Edom,
11if not you, the God who has rejected us?
God, you no longer march with our armies.

12Bring us help in our time of crisis,
any human assistance is worthless.
13With God we shall do deeds of valour,
he will trample down our enemies.

108a = 57:7–11 + 60:5–12.

PSALM 109

V 108

An imprecation

For the choirmaster Of David Psalm

1 God whom I praise, do not be silent!
2 Wicked and deceiving words
are being said about me,
false accusations are cast in my teeth.
3 Words of hate fly all around me,
though I give no cause for hostility.

4 In return for my friendship they denounce me,
and all I can do is pray!
5 They repay my kindness with evil,
and friendship with hatred.

6 'Set up a wicked man against him
as accuser to stand on his right.
7 At his trial may he emerge as guilty,
even his prayer construed as a crime!

8 'May his life be cut short,
someone else take over his office,
9 his children be orphaned,
his wife be widowed.

10 'May his children wander perpetually,
beggars, driven from the ruins of their house,
11 a creditor seize all his goods,
and strangers make off with his earnings.

12 'May there be none left faithful enough to show him love,
no one take pity on his orphans,
13 the line of his descendants cut off,
his name wiped out in one generation.

14 'May Yahweh never forget the crimes of his ancestors,
and his mother's sins not be wiped out;
15 may Yahweh keep these constantly in mind,
to cut off the remembrance of them from the earth.'

16 He had no thought of being loyal,
but hounded the poor and the needy
and the broken-hearted to their death.
17 He had a taste for cursing; let it recoil on him!
No taste for blessing; let it never come his way!

18 Cursing has been the uniform he wore;
let it soak into him like water,
like oil right into his bones.
19 Let it be as a robe which envelops him completely,
a sash which he always wears.

20 Let this be the salary Yahweh pays
the accusers who blacken my name.
21 Yahweh, treat them as your name demands;
as your faithful love is generous, deliver me.

22 Poor and needy as I am,
my wounds go right to the heart;
23 I am passing away like a fading shadow,
they have shaken me off like a locust.

24 My knees are weak from lack of food,
my body lean for lack of fat.
25 I have become the butt of their taunts,
they shake their heads at the sight of me.

26 Help me, Yahweh my God,
save me as your faithful love demands.
27 Let them know that yours is the saving hand,
that this, Yahweh, is your work.

28 Let them curse, provided that you bless;
let their attacks bring shame to them and joy to your servant!
29 Let my accusers be clothed in disgrace,
enveloped in a cloak of shame.

30 With generous thanks to Yahweh on my lips,
I shall praise him before all the people,
31 for he stands at the side of the poor,
to save their lives from those who sit in judgement on them.

PSALM 110

V 109

The Priest Messiah

Of David Psalm

1 Yahweh declared to my Lord, 'Take your seat at my right hand,
till I have made your enemies your footstool.'

2 Yahweh will stretch out the sceptre of your power;
from Zion you will rule your foes all around you.

3 Royal[a] dignity has been yours from the day of your birth,
sacred honour from the womb, from the dawn of your youth.

4 Yahweh has sworn an oath he will never retract,
you are a priest for ever of the order of Melchizedek.

5 At your right hand, Lord,
he shatters kings when his anger breaks out.
6 He judges nations, heaping up corpses,
he breaks heads over the whole wide world.
7 He drinks from a stream as he goes,
and therefore he holds his head high.

110a Conjectural translation of a textually corrupt and obscure v.

PSALM 111 V 110

In praise of Yahweh's deeds

1 Alleluia!
Aleph I give thanks to Yahweh with all my heart,
Bet in the meeting-place of honest people, in the assembly.
Gimel 2 Great are the deeds of Yahweh,
Dalet to be pondered by all who delight in them.

He 3 Full of splendour and majesty his work,
Waw his saving justice stands firm for ever.
Zain 4 He gives us a memorial of his great deeds;
Het Yahweh is mercy and tenderness.

Tet 5 He gives food to those who fear him,
Yod he keeps his covenant ever in mind.
Kaph 6 His works show his people his power
Lamed in giving them the birthright of the nations.

Mem 7 The works of his hands are fidelity and justice,
Nun all his precepts are trustworthy,
Samek 8 established for ever and ever,
Ain accomplished in fidelity and honesty.

Pe 9 Deliverance he sends to his people,
Zade his covenant he imposes for ever;
Qoph holy and awesome his name.
Resh 10 The root of wisdom is fear of Yahweh;
Shin those who attain it are wise.
Taw His praise will continue for ever.

PSALM 112 V 111

Praise of the upright

1 Alleluia!
Aleph How blessed is anyone who fears Yahweh,
Bet who delights in his commandments!
Gimel 2 His descendants shall be powerful on earth,
Dalet the race of the honest shall receive blessings:

He 3 Riches and wealth for his family;
Waw his uprightness stands firm for ever.
Zain 4 For the honest he shines as a lamp in the dark,
Het generous, tender-hearted, and upright.

Tet 5 All goes well for one who lends generously,
Yod who is honest in all his dealing;
Kaph 6 for all time to come he will not stumble,
Lamed for all time to come the upright will be remembered.

Mem 7 Bad news holds no fears for him,
Nun firm is his heart, trusting in Yahweh.
Samek 8 His heart held steady, he has no fears,
Ain till he can gloat over his enemies.

Pe [9]To the needy he gives without stint,
Zade his uprightness stands firm for ever;
Qoph his reputation is founded on strength.

Resh [10]The wicked are vexed at the sight,
Shin they grind their teeth and waste away.
Taw The desires of the wicked will be frustrated.

PSALM 113

V 112

To the God of glory and mercy

[1]Alleluia!

Praise, servants of Yahweh,
praise the name of Yahweh.
[2]Blessed be the name of Yahweh,
henceforth and for ever.
[3]From the rising of the sun to its setting,
praised be the name of Yahweh!

[4]Supreme over all nations is Yahweh,
supreme over the heavens his glory.
[5]Who is like Yahweh our God?
His throne is set on high,
[6]but he stoops to look down on heaven and earth.

[7]He raises the poor from the dust,
he lifts the needy from the dunghill,
[8]to give them a place among princes,
among princes of his people.
[9]He lets the barren woman be seated at home,
the happy mother of sons.

PSALM 114

V 113A

Passover hymn

Alleluia!

[1]When Israel came out of Egypt,
the House of Jacob from a people of foreign speech,
[2]Judah became his sanctuary,
and Israel his domain.

[3]The sea fled at the sight,
the Jordan turned back,
[4]the mountains skipped like rams,
the hills like sheep.

[5]Sea, what makes you flee?
Jordan, why turn back?
[6]Why skip like rams, you mountains?
Why like sheep, you hills?

7 Tremble, earth, at the coming of the Lord,
at the coming of the God of Jacob,
8 who turns rock into pool,
flint into fountain.

PSALM 115

V 113B

The one true God

1 Not to us, Yahweh, not to us,
but to your name give the glory,
for your faithful love and your constancy!
2 Why should the nations ask, 'Where is their God?'

3 Our God is in heaven,
he creates whatever he chooses.
4 They have idols of silver and gold,
made by human hands.

5 These have mouths but say nothing,
have eyes but see nothing,
6 have ears but hear nothing,
have noses but smell nothing.

7 They have hands but cannot feel,
have feet but cannot walk,
no sound comes from their throats.
8 Their makers will end up like them,
and all who rely on them.

9 House of Israel, rely on Yahweh;
he is their help and their shield.
10 House of Aaron, rely on Yahweh;
he is their help and their shield.
11 You who fear Yahweh, rely on Yahweh;
he is their help and their shield.

12 Yahweh will keep us in mind, he will bless,
he will bless the House of Israel,
he will bless the House of Aaron,
13 he will bless those who fear Yahweh,
small and great alike.

14 May Yahweh add to your numbers,
yours and your children's too!
15 May you be blessed by Yahweh,
who made heaven and earth.

16 Heaven belongs to Yahweh,
but earth he has given to the children of Adam.

17 The dead cannot praise Yahweh,
those who sink into silence,
18 but we, the living, shall bless Yahweh,
henceforth and for ever.

PSALM 116

V 114–115

Thanksgiving

Alleluia!

1 I am filled with love when Yahweh listens
to the sound of my prayer,
2 when he bends down to hear me,
as I call.

3 The bonds of death were all round me,
the snares of Sheol held me fast;
distress and anguish held me in their grip,
4 I called on the name of Yahweh.

Deliver me, Yahweh, I beg you.

5 Yahweh is merciful and upright,
our God is tenderness.
6 Yahweh looks after the simple,
when I was brought low he gave me strength.

7 My heart, be at peace once again,
for Yahweh has treated you generously.
8 He has rescued me from death, my eyes from tears,
and my feet from stumbling.
9 I shall pass my life in the presence of Yahweh,
in the land of the living.

10 My trust does not fail even when I say,
'I am completely wretched.'
11 In my terror I said,
'No human being can be relied on.'
12 What return can I make to Yahweh
for his generosity to me?
13 I shall take up the cup of salvation
and call on the name of Yahweh.

14 I shall fulfil my vows to Yahweh,
witnessed by all his people.

15 Costly in Yahweh's sight
is the death of his faithful.

16 I beg you, Yahweh! I am your servant,
I am your servant and my mother was your servant;
you have undone my fetters.
17 I shall offer you a sacrifice of thanksgiving
and call on the name of Yahweh.

18 I shall fulfil my vows to Yahweh,
witnessed by all his people,
19 in the courts of the house of Yahweh,
in your very heart, Jerusalem.

PSALM 117

V 116

Summons to praise

Alleluia!

1 Praise Yahweh, all nations,
extol him, all peoples,
2 for his faithful love is strong
and his constancy never-ending.

PSALM 118

V 117

Processional hymn for the feast of Shelters

Alleluia!

1 Give thanks to Yahweh for he is good,
for his faithful love endures for ever.

2 Let the House of Israel say,
'His faithful love endures for ever.'
3 Let the House of Aaron say,
'His faithful love endures for ever.'
4 Let those who fear Yahweh say,
'His faithful love endures for ever.'

5 In my distress I called to Yahweh,
he heard me and brought me relief.
6 With Yahweh on my side I fear nothing;
what can human beings do to me?
7 With Yahweh on my side as my help,
I gloat over my enemies.

8 It is better to take refuge in Yahweh
than to rely on human beings;
9 better to take refuge in Yahweh
than to rely on princes.

10 Nations were swarming around me,
in the name of Yahweh I cut them down;
11 they swarmed around me, pressing upon me,
in the name of Yahweh I cut them down.
12 They swarmed around me like bees,
they flared up like a brushwood fire,
in the name of Yahweh I cut them down.

13 I was pushed hard, to make me fall,
but Yahweh came to my help.
14 Yahweh is my strength and my song,
he has been my Saviour.

15 Shouts of joy and salvation,
in the tents of the upright,
'Yahweh's right hand is triumphant,
16 Yahweh's right hand is victorious,
Yahweh's right hand is triumphant!'

[17]I shall not die, I shall live
to recount the great deeds of Yahweh.
[18]Though Yahweh punished me sternly,
he has not abandoned me to death.

[19]Open for me the gates of saving justice,
I shall go in and thank Yahweh.
[20]This is the gate of Yahweh,
where the upright go in.
[21]I thank you for hearing me,
and making yourself my Saviour.

[22]The stone which the builders rejected
has become the cornerstone;
[23]This is Yahweh's doing,
and we marvel at it.
[24]This is the day which Yahweh has made,
a day for us to rejoice and be glad.

[25]We beg you, Yahweh, save us,
we beg you, Yahweh, give us victory!
[26]Blessed in the name of Yahweh is he who is coming!
We bless you from the house of Yahweh.
[27]Yahweh is God,
he gives us light.

Link your processions, branches in hand,
up to the horns of the altar.
[28]You are my God, I thank you,
all praise to you, my God.
I thank you for hearing me,
and making yourself my Saviour.

[29]Give thanks to Yahweh for he is good,
for his faithful love endures for ever.

PSALM 119 — V 118

In praise of the divine Law

Aleph [1]How blessed are those whose way is blameless,
who walk in the Law of Yahweh!
[2]Blessed are those who observe his instructions,
who seek him with all their hearts,
[3]and, doing no evil,
who walk in his ways.
[4]You lay down your precepts
to be carefully kept.
[5]May my ways be steady
in doing your will.
[6]Then I shall not be shamed,
if my gaze is fixed on your commandments.
[7]I thank you with a sincere heart
for teaching me your upright judgements.
[8]I shall do your will;
do not ever abandon me wholly.

Bet

9 How can a young man keep his way spotless?
By keeping your words.
10 With all my heart I seek you,
do not let me stray from your commandments.
11 In my heart I treasure your promises,
to avoid sinning against you.
12 Blessed are you, Yahweh,
teach me your will!
13 With my lips I have repeated
all the judgements you have given.
14 In the way of your instructions lies my joy,
a joy beyond all wealth.
15 I will ponder your precepts
and fix my gaze on your paths.
16 I find my delight in your will,
I do not forget your words.

Gimel

17 Be generous to your servant and I shall live,
and shall keep your words.
18 Open my eyes and I shall fix my gaze
on the wonders of your Law.
19 Wayfarer though I am on the earth,
do not hide your commandments from me.
20 My heart is pining away with longing
at all times for your judgements.
21 You have rebuked the arrogant, the accursed,
who stray from your commandments.
22 Set me free from taunts and contempt
since I observe your instructions.
23 Though princes sit plotting against me,
your servant keeps pondering your will.
24 Your instructions are my delight,
your wishes my counsellors.

Dalet

25 Down in the dust I lie prostrate;
true to your word, revive me.
26 I tell you my ways and you answer me;
teach me your wishes.
27 Show me the way of your precepts,
that I may reflect on your wonders.
28 I am melting away for grief;
true to your word, raise me up.
29 Keep me far from the way of deceit,
grant me the grace of your Law.
30 I have chosen the way of constancy,
I have moulded myself to your judgements.
31 I cling to your instructions,
Yahweh, do not disappoint me.
32 I run the way of your commandments,
for you have given me freedom of heart.

He

33 Teach me, Yahweh, the way of your will,
and I will observe it.
34 Give me understanding and I will observe your Law,
and keep it wholeheartedly.
35 Guide me in the way of your commandments,
for my delight is there.

36 Bend my heart to your instructions,
not to selfish gain.
37 Avert my eyes from pointless images,
by your word give me life.
38 Keep your promise to your servant
so that all may hold you in awe.
39 Avert the taunts that I dread,
for your judgements are generous.
40 See how I yearn for your precepts;
in your saving justice give me life.

Waw 41 Let your faithful love come to me, Yahweh,
true to your promise, save me!
42 Give me an answer to the taunts against me,
since I rely on your word.
43 Do not deprive me of that faithful word,
since my hope lies in your judgements.
44 I shall keep your Law without fail
for ever and ever.
45 I shall live in all freedom
because I have sought your precepts.
46 I shall speak of your instructions before kings
and will not be shamed.
47 Your commandments fill me with delight,
I love them dearly.
48 I stretch out my hands to your commandments that I love,
and I ponder your judgements.

Zain 49 Keep in mind your promise to your servant
on which I have built my hope.
50 It is my comfort in distress,
that your promise gives me life.
51 Endlessly the arrogant have jeered at me,
but I have not swerved from your Law.
52 I have kept your age-old judgements in mind,
Yahweh, and I am comforted.
53 Fury grips me when I see the wicked
who abandon your Law.
54 Your judgements are my song
where I live in exile.
55 All night, Yahweh, I hold your name in mind,
I keep your Law.
56 This is what it means to me,
observing your precepts.

Het 57 My task, I have said, Yahweh,
is to keep your word.
58 Wholeheartedly I entreat your favour;
true to your promise, take pity on me!
59 I have reflected on my ways,
and I turn my steps to your instructions.
60 I hurry without delay
to keep your commandments.
61 Though caught in the snares of the wicked,
I do not forget your Law.
62 At midnight I rise to praise you
for your upright judgements.

63 I am a friend to all who fear you
and keep your precepts.
64 Your faithful love fills the earth,
Yahweh, teach me your judgements.

Tet

65 You have been generous to your servant, Yahweh,
true to your promise.
66 Teach me judgement and knowledge,
for I rely on your commandments.
67 Before I was punished I used to go astray,
but now I keep to your promise.
68 You are generous and act generously,
teach me your will.
69 The arrogant blacken me with lies
though I wholeheartedly observe your precepts.
70 Their hearts are gross like rich fat,
but my delight is in your Law.
71 It was good for me that I had to suffer,
the better to learn your judgements.
72 The Law you have uttered is more precious to me
than all the wealth in the world.

Yod

73 Your hands have made me and held me firm,
give me understanding and I shall learn your commandments.
74 Those who fear you rejoice at the sight of me
since I put my hope in your word.
75 I know, Yahweh, that your judgements are upright,
and in punishing me you show your constancy.
76 Your faithful love must be my consolation,
as you have promised your servant.
77 Treat me with tenderness and I shall live,
for your Law is my delight.
78 Let the arrogant who tell lies against me be shamed,
while I ponder your precepts.
79 Let those who fear you rally to me,
those who understand your instructions.
80 My heart shall be faultless towards your will;
then I shall not be ashamed.

Kaph

81 I shall wear myself out for your salvation,
for your word is my hope.
82 My eyes, too, are worn out waiting for your promise,
when will you have pity on me?
83 For I am like a smoked wineskin,
but I do not forget your will.
84 How long has your servant to live?
When will you bring my persecutors to judgement?
85 The arrogant have dug pitfalls for me
in defiance of your Law.
86 All your commandments show constancy.
Help me when they pursue me dishonestly.
87 They have almost annihilated me on earth,
but I have not deserted your precepts.
88 True to your faithful love, give me life,
and I shall keep the instructions you have laid down.

Lamed

89 For ever, Yahweh, your word
is planted firm in heaven.

90 Your constancy endures from age to age;
you established the earth and it stands firm.
91 Through your judgements all stands firm to this day,
for all creation is your servant.
92 Had your Law not been my delight,
I would have perished in my misery.
93 I shall never forget your precepts,
for by them you have given me life.
94 I am yours, save me,
for I seek your precepts.
95 The wicked may hope to destroy me,
but all my thought is of your instructions.
96 I have seen that all perfection is finite,
but your commandment has no limit.

Mem

97 How I love your Law!
I ponder it all day long.
98 You make me wiser than my enemies
by your commandment which is mine for ever.
99 I am wiser than all my teachers
because I ponder your instructions.
100 I have more understanding than the aged
because I keep your precepts.
101 I restrain my foot from evil paths
to keep your word.
102 I do not turn aside from your judgements,
because you yourself have instructed me.
103 How pleasant your promise to my palate,
sweeter than honey in my mouth!
104 From your precepts I learn wisdom,
so I hate all deceptive ways.

Nun

105 Your word is a lamp for my feet,
a light on my path.
106 I have sworn—and shall maintain it—
to keep your upright judgements.
107 I am utterly wretched, Yahweh;
true to your promise, give me life.
108 Accept, Yahweh, the tribute from my mouth,
and teach me your judgements.
109 My life is in your hands perpetually,
I do not forget your Law.
110 The wicked have laid out a snare for me,
but I have not strayed from your precepts.
111 Your instructions are my eternal heritage,
they are the joy of my heart.
112 I devote myself to obeying your statutes,
their recompense is eternal.

Samek

113 I hate a divided heart,
I love your Law.
114 You are my refuge and shield,
I put my hope in your word.
115 Leave me alone, you wicked,
I shall observe the commandments of my God.
116 True to your word, support me and I shall live;
do not disappoint me of my hope.

117 Uphold me and I shall be saved,
my gaze fixed on your will.
118 You shake off all who stray from your will;
deceit fills their horizon.
119 In your sight all the wicked of the earth are like rust,
so I love your instructions.
120 My whole body trembles before you,
your judgements fill me with fear.

Ain

121 All my conduct has been just and upright,
do not hand me over to my oppressors.
122 Guarantee the well-being of your servant,
do not let the proud oppress me.
123 My eyes are languishing for your salvation
and for the saving justice you have promised.
124 Show your faithful love to your servant,
teach me your judgements.
125 Your servant am I; give me understanding
and I shall know your instructions.
126 It is time to take action, Yahweh,
your Law is being broken.
127 So I love your commandments
more than gold, purest gold.
128 So I rule my life by your precepts,
I hate all deceptive paths.

Pe

129 Wonderful are your instructions,
so I observe them.
130 As your word unfolds it gives light,
and even the simple understand.
131 I open wide my mouth,
panting eagerly for your commandments.
132 Turn to me, pity me;
those who love your name deserve it.
133 Keep my steps firm in your promise;
that no evil may triumph over me.
134 Rescue me from human oppression,
and I will observe your precepts.
135 Let your face shine on your servant,
teach me your will.
136 My eyes stream with tears
because your Law is disregarded.

Zade

137 You are upright, Yahweh,
and your judgements are honest.
138 You impose uprightness as a witness to yourself,
it is constancy itself.
139 My zeal is burning me up
because my oppressors forget your word.
140 Your promise is well tested,
your servant holds it dear.
141 Puny and despised as I am,
I do not forget your precepts.
142 Your saving justice is for ever just,
and your Law is trustworthy.
143 Though anguish and distress grip me
your commandments are my delight.

144 Your instructions are upright for ever,
give me understanding and I shall live.

Qoph 145 I call with all my heart; answer me, Yahweh,
and I will observe your judgements.
146 I call to you; save me,
and I will keep your instructions.
147 I am awake before dawn to cry for help,
I put my hope in your word.
148 My eyes are awake before each watch of the night,
to ponder your promise.
149 In your faithful love, Yahweh, listen to my voice,
let your judgements give me life.
150 My pursuers are coming closer to their wicked designs,
and further from your Law.
151 You are close to me, Yahweh,
and all your commandments are true.
152 Long have I known that your instructions
were laid down to last for ever.

Resh 153 Look at my suffering and rescue me,
for I do not forget your Law.
154 Plead my cause and defend me;
as you promised, give me life.
155 Salvation is far from the wicked,
for they do not seek your will.
156 Your kindnesses to me are countless, Yahweh;
true to your judgements, give me life.
157 Though my enemies and oppressors are countless,
I do not turn aside from your instructions.
158 The sight of these renegades appals me;
they do not observe your promise.
159 See how I love your precepts;
true to your faithful love, give me life.
160 Faithfulness is the essence of your word,
your upright judgements hold good for ever.

Shin 161 Though princes hound me unprovoked,
what fills me with awe is your word.
162 I rejoice in your promise
like one who finds a vast treasure.
163 Falsehood I hate and detest,
my love is for your Law.
164 Seven times a day I praise you
for your upright judgements.
165 Great peace for those who love your Law;
no stumbling-blocks for them!
166 I am waiting for your salvation, Yahweh,
I fulfil your commandments.
167 I observe your instructions,
I love them dearly.
168 I observe your precepts, your judgements,
for all my ways are before you.

Taw 169 May my cry approach your presence, Yahweh;
by your word give me understanding.
170 May my prayer come into your presence,
rescue me as you have promised.

171 May my lips proclaim your praise,
for you teach me your will.
172 May my tongue recite your promise,
for all your commandments are upright.
173 May your hand be there to help me,
since I have chosen your precepts.
174 I long for your salvation, Yahweh,
your Law is my delight.
175 May I live only to praise you,
may your judgements be my help.
176 I am wandering like a lost sheep,
come and look for your servant,

for I have not forgotten your commandments.

PSALM 120

V 119

The enemies of peace

Song of Ascents[a]

1 To Yahweh when I am in trouble
I call and he answers me.
2 Yahweh, save me from lying lips
and a treacherous tongue!

3 What will he repay you, what more,
treacherous tongue?
4 War-arrows made sharp
over red-hot charcoal.

5 How wretched I am, living in Meshech,
dwelling in the tents of Kedar!

6 Too long have I lived
among people who hate peace.
7 When I speak of peace
they are all for war!

PSALM 121

V 120

The guardian of Israel

Song of Ascents

1 I lift up my eyes to the mountains;
where is my help to come from?
2 My help comes from Yahweh
who made heaven and earth.

3 May he save your foot from stumbling;
may he, your guardian, not fall asleep!
4 You see—he neither sleeps nor slumbers,
the guardian of Israel.

120a The Songs of Ascents (Pss 120—134) were sung by pilgrims on their way up to Jerusalem.

[5]Yahweh is your guardian, your shade,
Yahweh, at your right hand.
[6]By day the sun will not strike you,
nor the moon by night.

[7]Yahweh guards you from all harm
Yahweh guards your life,
[8]Yahweh guards your comings and goings,
henceforth and for ever.

PSALM 122 V 121

Hail, Jerusalem

Song of Ascents Of David

[1]I rejoiced that they said to me,
'Let us go to the house of Yahweh.'
[2]At last our feet are standing
at your gates, Jerusalem!

[3]Jerusalem, built as a city,
in one united whole,
[4]there the tribes go up,
the tribes of Yahweh,
a sign for Israel to give thanks
to the name of Yahweh.
[5]For there are set the thrones of judgement,
the thrones of the house of David.

[6]Pray for the peace of Jerusalem,
prosperity for your homes!
[7]Peace within your walls,
prosperity in your palaces!

[8]For love of my brothers and my friends
I will say, 'Peace upon you!'
[9]For love of the house of Yahweh our God
I will pray for your well-being.

PSALM 123 V 122

Prayer in distress

Song of Ascents

[1]I lift up my eyes to you
who are enthroned in heaven.
[2]Just as the eyes of slaves
are on their masters' hand,

or the eyes of a slave-girl
on the hand of her mistress,
so our eyes are on Yahweh our God,
for him to take pity on us.

[3]Have pity on us, Yahweh, have pity,
for we have had our full share of scorn,
[4]more than our share
of jeers from the complacent.

(Scorn is for the proud.)

PSALM 124

V 123

The Saviour of Israel

Song of Ascents Of David

[1]If Yahweh had not been on our side
—let Israel repeat it—
[2]if Yahweh had not been on our side
when people attacked us,
[3]they would have swallowed us alive
in the heat of their anger.

[4]Then water was washing us away,
a torrent running right over us;
[5]running right over us then
were turbulent waters.

[6]Blessed be Yahweh for not letting us fall
a prey to their teeth!
[7]We escaped like a bird
from the fowlers' net.

The net was broken
and we escaped;
[8]our help is in the name of Yahweh,
who made heaven and earth.

PSALM 125

V 124

God protects his faithful

Song of Ascents

[1]Whoever trusts in Yahweh is like Mount Zion:
unshakeable, it stands for ever.
[2]Jerusalem! The mountains encircle her:
so Yahweh encircles his people,
henceforth and for ever.

[3]The sceptre of the wicked will not come to rest
over the heritage of the upright;
or the upright might set
their own hands to evil.

[4]Do good, Yahweh, to those who are good,
to the sincere at heart.

5 But the crooked, the twisted, turn them away,
Yahweh, with evil-doers.

Peace to Israel!

PSALM 126 V 125

Song of the returning exiles

Song of Ascents

1 When Yahweh brought back Zion's captives
we lived in a dream;
2 then our mouths filled with laughter,
and our lips with song.

Then the nations kept saying, 'What great deeds
Yahweh has done for them!'
3 Yes, Yahweh did great deeds for us,
and we were overjoyed.

4 Bring back, Yahweh, our people from captivity
like torrents in the Negeb!
5 Those who sow in tears
sing as they reap.

6 He went off, went off weeping,
carrying the seed.
He comes back, comes back singing,
bringing in his sheaves.

PSALM 127 V 126

Trust in Providence

Song of Ascents Of Solomon

1 If Yahweh does not build a house
in vain do its builders toil.
If Yahweh does not guard a city
in vain does its guard keep watch.

2 In vain you get up earlier,
and put off going to bed,
sweating to make a living,
since it is he who provides for his beloved as they sleep.

3 Sons are a birthright from Yahweh,
children are a reward from him.
4 Like arrows in a warrior's hand
are the sons you father when young.

5 How blessed is the man
who has filled his quiver with them;
in dispute with his enemies at the city gate
he will not be worsted.

PSALM 128 V 127

Blessing on the faithful

Song of Ascents

1 How blessed are all who fear Yahweh,
who walk in his ways!

2 Your own labours will yield you a living,
happy and prosperous will you be.
3 Your wife a fruitful vine
in the inner places of your house.
Your children round your table
like shoots of an olive tree.

4 Such are the blessings that fall
on those who fear Yahweh.
5 May Yahweh bless you from Zion!
May you see Jerusalem prosper
all the days of your life,
6 and live to see your children's children!

Peace to Israel!

PSALM 129 V 128

Against Zion's enemies

Song of Ascents

1 Often as men have attacked me since I was young
—let Israel repeat it—
2 often as men have attacked me since I was young,
they have never overcome me.

3 On my back ploughmen have set to work,
making long furrows,
4 but Yahweh the upright has shattered
the yoke of the wicked.

5 Let all who hate Zion
be thrown back in confusion,
6 let them be like grass on a roof,
dried up before it is cut,
7 never to fill the reaper's arm
nor the binder's lap.
8 And no passer-by will say,
'The blessing of Yahweh be on you!

'We bless you in the name of Yahweh.'

PSALM 130 V 129

Out of the depths

Song of Ascents

1 From the depths I call to you, Yahweh:
2 Lord, hear my cry.
Listen attentively
to the sound of my pleading!

3 If you kept a record of our sins,
Lord, who could stand their ground?
4 But with you is forgiveness,
that you may be revered.

5 I rely, my whole being relies,
Yahweh, on your promise.
6 My whole being hopes in the Lord,
more than watchmen for daybreak;
more than watchmen for daybreak
7 let Israel hope in Yahweh.

For with Yahweh is faithful love,
with him generous ransom;
8 and he will ransom Israel
from all its sins.

PSALM 131 V 130

Childlike trust

Song of Ascents

1 Yahweh, my heart is not haughty,
I do not set my sights too high.
I have taken no part in great affairs,
in wonders beyond my scope.
2 No, I hold myself in quiet and silence,
like a little child in its mother's arms,
like a little child, so I keep myself.
3 Let Israel hope in Yahweh
henceforth and for ever.

PSALM 132 V 131

For the anniversary of the transfer of the ark

Song of Ascents

1 Yahweh, remember David
and all the hardships he endured,
2 the oath he swore to Yahweh,
his vow to the Mighty One of Jacob:

3 'I will not enter tent or house,
will not climb into bed,
4 will not allow myself to sleep,
not even to close my eyes,
5 till I have found a place for Yahweh,
a dwelling for the Mighty One of Jacob!'

6 Listen, we heard of it in Ephrathah,
we found it at Forest-Fields.
7 Let us go into his dwelling-place,
and worship at his footstool.

8 Go up, Yahweh, to your resting-place,
you and the ark of your strength.
9 Your priests are robed in saving justice,
your faithful are shouting for joy.
10 For the sake of your servant David,
do not reject your anointed.

11 Yahweh has sworn to David,
and will always remain true to his word,
'I promise that I will set
a son of yours upon your throne.
12 If your sons observe my covenant
and the instructions I have taught them,
their sons too for evermore
will occupy your throne.'

13 For Yahweh has chosen Zion,
he has desired it as a home.
14 'Here shall I rest for evermore,
here shall I make my home as I have wished.

15 'I shall generously bless her produce,
give her needy their fill of food,
16 I shall clothe her priests with salvation,
and her faithful will sing aloud for joy.

17 'There I shall raise up a line of descendants for David,
light a lamp for my anointed;
18 I shall clothe his enemies with shame,
while his own crown shall flourish.'

PSALM 133 V 132

Brotherly love

Song of Ascents

1 How good, how delightful it is
to live as brothers all together!

2 It is like a fine oil on the head,
running down the beard,
running down Aaron's beard,
onto the collar of his robes.

3 It is like the dew of Hermon
falling on the heights of Zion;
for there Yahweh bestows his blessing,
everlasting life.

PSALM 134

V 133

For the evening liturgy

Song of Ascents

1 Come, bless Yahweh,
all you who serve Yahweh,
serving in the house of Yahweh,
in the courts of the house of our God.
Through the night watches
2 stretch out your hands towards the sanctuary
and bless Yahweh.

3 May Yahweh bless you from Zion,
he who made heaven and earth!

PSALM 135[a]

V 134

Hymn of praise

1 Alleluia!

Praise the name of Yahweh,
you who serve Yahweh, praise him,
2 serving in the house of Yahweh,
in the courts of the house of our God.

3 Praise Yahweh, for Yahweh is good,
make music for his name—it brings joy—
4 for Yahweh has chosen Jacob for himself,
Israel as his own possession.

5 For I know that Yahweh is great,
our Lord is above all gods.
6 Yahweh does whatever he pleases
in heaven, on earth,
in the waters and all the depths.

7 He summons up clouds from the borders of earth,
sends rain with lightning-flashes,
and brings the wind out of his storehouse.

8 He struck the first-born in Egypt,
man and beast alike,
9 he sent signs and wonders into the heart of Egypt,
against Pharaoh and all his officials.

135a Composed entirely of fragments or reminiscences of other Pss.

10 He struck down many nations,
he slaughtered mighty kings,
11 Sihon king of the Amorites,
and Og king of Bashan,
and all the kingdoms of Canaan.
12 He gave their land as a birthright,
a birthright to his people Israel.

13 Yahweh, your name endures for ever,
Yahweh, your memory is fresh from age to age.
14 For Yahweh vindicates his people,
feels compassion for his servants.

15 The idols of the nations are silver and gold,
made by human hands.
16 These have mouths but say nothing,
have eyes but see nothing,

17 have ears but hear nothing,
and they have no breath in their mouths.
18 Their makers will end up like them,
everyone who relies on them.

19 House of Israel, bless Yahweh,
House of Aaron, bless Yahweh,
20 House of Levi, bless Yahweh,
you who fear Yahweh, bless Yahweh.

21 Blessed be Yahweh from Zion,
he who dwells in Jerusalem!

PSALM 136

V 135

Litany of thanksgiving

Alleluia!

1 Give thanks to Yahweh for he is good,
for his faithful love endures for ever.
2 Give thanks to the God of gods,
for his faithful love endures for ever.
3 Give thanks to the Lord of lords,
for his faithful love endures for ever.

4 He alone works wonders,
for his faithful love endures for ever.
5 In wisdom he made the heavens,
for his faithful love endures for ever.
6 He set the earth firm on the waters,
for his faithful love endures for ever.

7 He made the great lights,
for his faithful love endures for ever.
8 The sun to rule the day,
for his faithful love endures for ever.
9 Moon and stars to rule the night,
for his faithful love endures for ever.

10 He struck down the first-born of Egypt,
for his faithful love endures for ever.
11 He brought Israel out from among them,
for his faithful love endures for ever.
12 With mighty hand and outstretched arm,
for his faithful love endures for ever.

13 He split the Sea of Reeds in two,
for his faithful love endures for ever.
14 Let Israel pass through the middle,
for his faithful love endures for ever.
15 And drowned Pharaoh and all his army,
for his faithful love endures for ever.

16 He led his people through the desert,
for his faithful love endures for ever.
17 He struck down mighty kings,
for his faithful love endures for ever.
18 Slaughtered famous kings,
for his faithful love endures for ever.
19 Sihon king of the Amorites,
for his faithful love endures for ever.
20 And Og king of Bashan,
for his faithful love endures for ever.

21 He gave their land as a birthright,
for his faithful love endures for ever.
22 A birthright to his servant Israel,
for his faithful love endures for ever.
23 He kept us in mind when we were humbled,
for his faithful love endures for ever.
24 And rescued us from our enemies,
for his faithful love endures for ever.

25 He provides food for all living creatures,
for his faithful love endures for ever.
26 Give thanks to the God of heaven,
for his faithful love endures for ever.

PSALM 137

V 136

Song of the exiles

1 By the rivers of Babylon
we sat and wept
at the memory of Zion.
2 On the poplars there
we had hung up our harps.

3 For there our gaolers had asked us
to sing them a song,
our captors to make merry,
'Sing us one of the songs of Zion.'

4 How could we sing a song of Yahweh
on alien soil?

5 If I forget you, Jerusalem,
may my right hand wither!

6 May my tongue remain stuck to my palate
if I do not keep you in mind,
if I do not count Jerusalem
the greatest of my joys.

7 Remember, Yahweh, to the Edomites' cost,
the day of Jerusalem,
how they said, 'Down with it! Rase it to the ground!'

8 Daughter of Babel, doomed to destruction,
a blessing on anyone
who treats you as you treated us,
9 a blessing on anyone who seizes your babies
and shatters them against a rock!

PSALM 138

V 137

Hymn of thanksgiving

Of David

1 I thank you, Yahweh, with all my heart,
for you have listened to the cry I uttered.
In the presence of angels I sing to you,
2 I bow down before your holy Temple.

I praise your name for your faithful love and your constancy;
your promises surpass even your fame.
3 You heard me on the day when I called,
and you gave new strength to my heart.

4 All the kings of the earth give thanks to you, Yahweh,
when they hear the promises you make;
5 they sing of Yahweh's ways,
'Great is the glory of Yahweh!'
6 Sublime as he is, Yahweh looks on the humble,
the proud he picks out from afar.

7 Though I live surrounded by trouble
you give me life—to my enemies' fury!
You stretch out your right hand and save me,
8 Yahweh will do all things for me.
Yahweh, your faithful love endures for ever,
do not abandon what you have made.

PSALM 139 V 138

In praise of God's omniscience

For the choirmaster Of David Psalm

1 Yahweh, you examine me and know me,
2 you know when I sit, when I rise,
you understand my thoughts from afar.
3 You watch when I walk or lie down,
you know every detail of my conduct.

4 A word is not yet on my tongue
before you, Yahweh, know all about it.
5 You fence me in, behind and in front,
you have laid your hand upon me.
6 Such amazing knowledge is beyond me,
a height to which I cannot attain.

7 Where shall I go to escape your spirit?
Where shall I flee from your presence?
8 If I scale the heavens you are there,
if I lie flat in Sheol, there you are.

9 If I speed away on the wings of the dawn,
if I dwell beyond the ocean,
10 even there your hand will be guiding me,
your right hand holding me fast.

11 I will say, 'Let the darkness cover me,
and the night wrap itself around me,'
12 even darkness to you is not dark,
and night is as clear as the day.

13 You created my inmost self,
knit me together in my mother's womb.
14 For so many marvels I thank you;
a wonder am I, and all your works are wonders.

You knew me through and through,
15 my being held no secrets from you,
when I was being formed in secret,
textured in the depths of the earth.

16 Your eyes could see my embryo.
In your book all my days were inscribed,
every one that was fixed is there.

17 How hard for me to grasp your thoughts,
how many, God, there are!
18 If I count them, they are more than the grains of sand;
if I come to an end, I am still with you.

19 If only, God, you would kill the wicked!—
Men of violence, keep away from me!—
20 those who speak blasphemously about you,
and take no account of your thoughts.

21 Yahweh, do I not hate those who hate you,
and loathe those who defy you?
22 My hate for them has no limits,
I regard them as my own enemies.

23 God, examine me and know my heart,
test me and know my concerns.
24 Make sure that I am not on my way to ruin,
and guide me on the road of eternity.

PSALM 140 V 139

Against the wicked

For the choirmaster Psalm Of David

1 Rescue me, Yahweh, from evil men,
protect me from violent men,
2 whose heart is bent on malice,
day after day they harbour strife;
3 their tongues as barbed as a serpent's,
viper's venom behind their lips. *Pause*

4 Keep me, Yahweh, from the clutches of the wicked,
protect me from violent men,
who are bent on making me stumble,
5b laying out snares where I walk,
5a in their arrogance hiding pitfall and noose
5c to trap me as I pass. *Pause*

6 I said to Yahweh, 'You are my God.'
Listen, Yahweh, to the sound of my prayer.
7 Yahweh my Lord, my saving strength,
you shield my head when battle comes.
8 Yahweh, do not grant the wicked their wishes,
do not let their plots succeed. *Pause*

Do not let my attackers 9 prevail,
but let them be overwhelmed by their own malice.
10 May red-hot embers rain down on them,
may they be flung into the mire once and for all.
11 May the slanderer find no rest anywhere,
may evil hunt down violent men implacably.

12 I know that Yahweh will give judgement for the wretched,
justice for the needy.
13 The upright shall praise your name,
the honest dwell in your presence.

PSALM 141 V 140

Against the attractions of evil

Psalm Of David

1 Yahweh, I am calling, hurry to me,
listen to my voice when I call to you.
2 May my prayer be like incense in your presence,
my uplifted hands like the evening sacrifice.

3 Yahweh, mount a guard over my mouth,
a guard at the door of my lips.
4 Check any impulse to speak evil,
to share the foul deeds of evil-doers.

I shall not sample their delights!
5 May the upright correct me with a friend's rebuke;
but the wicked shall never anoint my head with oil,
for that would make me party to their crimes.

6 They are delivered into the power of the rock, their judge,
those who took pleasure in hearing me say,
7 'Like a shattered millstone on the ground
our bones are scattered at the mouth of Sheol.'

8 To you, Yahweh, I turn my eyes,
in you I take refuge, do not leave me unprotected.
9 Save me from the traps that are set for me,
the snares of evil-doers.

10 Let the wicked fall each into his own net,
while I pass on my way.

PSALM 142

V 141

Prayer in persecution

Psalm Of David When he was in the cave Prayer

1 To Yahweh I cry out with my plea.
To Yahweh I cry out with entreaty.
2 I pour out my worry in his presence,
in his presence I unfold my troubles.
3 However faint my spirit;
you are watching over my path.

On the road I have to travel
they have hidden a trap for me.
4 Look on my right and see—
there is no one who recognises me.
All refuge is denied me,
no one cares whether I live or die.

5 I cry out to you, Yahweh,
I affirm, 'You are my refuge,
my share in the land of the living!'
6 Listen to my calling,
for I am miserably weak.

Rescue me from my persecutors,
for they are too strong for me.
7 Lead me out of prison
that I may praise your name.
The upright gather round me
because of your generosity to me.

PSALM 143 V 142

A humble entreaty

Psalm Of David

1 Yahweh, hear my prayer,
listen to my pleading;
in your constancy answer me,
in your saving justice;
2 do not put your servant on trial,
for no one living can be found guiltless at your tribunal.

3 An enemy is in deadly pursuit,
crushing me into the ground,
forcing me to live in darkness,
like those long dead.
4 My spirit is faint,
and within me my heart is numb with fear.

5 I recall the days of old,
reflecting on all your deeds,
I ponder the works of your hands.
6 I stretch out my hands to you,
my heart like a land thirsty for you. *Pause*

7 Answer me quickly, Yahweh,
my spirit is worn out;
do not turn away your face from me,
or I shall be like those who sink into oblivion.

8 Let dawn bring news of your faithful love,
for I place my trust in you;
show me the road I must travel
for you to relieve my heart.

9 Rescue me from my enemies, Yahweh,
since in you I find protection.
10 Teach me to do your will,
for you are my God.
May your generous spirit lead me
on even ground.

11 Yahweh, for the sake of your name,
in your saving justice give me life,
rescue me from distress.
12 In your faithful love annihilate my enemies,
destroy all those who oppress me,
for I am your servant.

PSALM 144[a] V 143

Hymn for war and victory

Of David

1Blessed be Yahweh, my rock,
who trains my hands for war
and my fingers for battle,
2my faithful love, my bastion,
my citadel, my Saviour;
I shelter behind him, my shield,
he makes the peoples submit to me.

3Yahweh, what is a human being for you to notice,
a child of Adam for you to think about?
4Human life, a mere puff of wind,
days as fleeting as a shadow.

5Yahweh, part the heavens and come down,
touch the mountains, make them smoke.
6Scatter them with continuous lightning-flashes,
rout them with a volley of your arrows.

7Stretch down your hand from above,
save me, rescue me from deep waters,
from the clutches of foreigners,
8whose every word is worthless,
whose right hand is raised in perjury.

9God, I sing to you a new song,
I play to you on the ten-stringed lyre,
10for you give kings their victories,
you rescue your servant David.

From the sword of evil 11save me,
rescue me from the clutches of foreigners
whose every word is worthless,
whose right hand testifies to falsehood.

12May our sons be like plants
growing tall from their earliest days,
our daughters like pillars
carved fit for a palace,

13our barns filled to overflowing
with every kind of crop,
the sheep in our pastures be numbered
in thousands and tens of thousands,

14our cattle well fed,
free of raids and pillage,
free of outcry in our streets.

15How blessed the nation of whom this is true,
blessed the nation whose God is Yahweh!

144a After prayers for help (vv. 1–11) drawn from other Pss, vv. 12–15 envisage messianic blessings.

PSALM 145

V 144

Praise to Yahweh the King

Hymn of Praise Of David

Aleph 1 I shall praise you to the heights, God my King,
I shall bless your name for ever and ever.
Bet 2 Day after day I shall bless you,
I shall praise your name for ever and ever.
Gimel 3 Great is Yahweh and worthy of all praise,
his greatness beyond all reckoning.

Dalet 4 Each age will praise your deeds to the next,
proclaiming your mighty works.
He 5 Your renown is the splendour of your glory,
I will ponder the story of your wonders.

Waw 6 They will speak of your awesome power,
and I shall recount your greatness.
Zain 7 They will bring out the memory of your great generosity,
and joyfully acclaim your saving justice.

Het 8 Yahweh is tenderness and pity,
slow to anger, full of faithful love.
Tet 9 Yahweh is generous to all,
his tenderness embraces all his creatures.

Yod 10 All your creatures shall thank you, Yahweh,
and your faithful shall bless you.
Kaph 11 They shall speak of the glory of your kingship
and tell of your might,
Lamed 12 making known your mighty deeds to the children of Adam,
the glory and majesty of your kingship.
Mem 13 Your kingship is a kingship for ever,
your reign lasts from age to age.

(Nun) Yahweh is trustworthy in all his words,
and upright in all his deeds.
Samek 14 Yahweh supports all who stumble,
lifts up those who are bowed down.

Ain 15 All look to you in hope
and you feed them with the food of the season.
Pe 16 And, with generous hand,
you satisfy the desires of every living creature.

Zade 17 Upright in all that he does,
Yahweh acts only in faithful love.
Qoph 18 He is close to all who call upon him,
all who call on him from the heart.

Resh 19 He fulfils the desires of all who fear him,
he hears their cry and he saves them.
Shin 20 Yahweh guards all who love him,
but all the wicked he destroys.

Taw 21 My mouth shall always praise Yahweh,
let every creature bless his holy name
for ever and ever.

PSALM 146 V 145

Hymn to the God of help

1 Alleluia!
Praise Yahweh, my soul!
2 I will praise Yahweh all my life,
I will make music to my God as long as I live.

3 Do not put your trust in princes,
in any child of Adam, who has no power to save.
4 When his spirit goes forth he returns to the earth,
on that very day all his plans come to nothing.

5 How blessed is he who has Jacob's God to help him,
his hope is in Yahweh his God,
6 who made heaven and earth,
the sea and all that is in them.

He keeps faith for ever,
7 gives justice to the oppressed,
gives food to the hungry;
Yahweh sets prisoners free.

8 Yahweh gives sight to the blind,
lifts up those who are bowed down.
9 Yahweh protects the stranger,
he sustains the orphan and the widow.

8c Yahweh loves the upright,
9c but he frustrates the wicked.
10 Yahweh reigns for ever,
your God, Zion, from age to age.

PSALM 147 V 146–147

Hymn to the All-Powerful

Alleluia!

1 Praise Yahweh—it is good to sing psalms
to our God—how pleasant to praise him.
2 Yahweh, Builder of Jerusalem!
He gathers together the exiles of Israel,
3 healing the broken-hearted
and binding up their wounds;
4 he counts out the number of the stars,
and gives each one of them a name.

5 Our Lord is great, all-powerful,
his wisdom beyond all telling.
6 Yahweh sustains the poor,
and humbles the wicked to the ground.

7 Sing to Yahweh in thanksgiving,
play the harp for our God.

8 He veils the sky with clouds,
and provides the earth with rain,
makes grass grow on the hills
and plants for people to use,
9 gives fodder to cattle
and to young ravens when they cry.

10 He takes no delight in the power of horses,
no pleasure in human sturdiness;
11 his pleasure is in those who fear him,
in those who hope in his faithful love.

12 Praise Yahweh, Jerusalem,
Zion, praise your God.

13 For he gives strength to the bars of your gates,
he blesses your children within you,
14 he maintains the peace of your frontiers,
gives you your fill of finest wheat.

15 He sends his word to the earth,
his command runs quickly,
16 he spreads the snow like flax,
strews hoarfrost like ashes,

17 he sends ice-crystals like breadcrumbs,
and who can withstand that cold?
18 When he sends his word it thaws them,
when he makes his wind blow, the waters are unstopped.

19 He reveals his word to Jacob,
his statutes and judgements to Israel.
20 For no other nation has he done this,
no other has known his judgements.

PSALM 148

Cosmic hymn of praise

1 Alleluia!

Praise Yahweh from the heavens,
praise him in the heights.
2 Praise him, all his angels,
praise him, all his host!

3 Praise him, sun and moon,
praise him, all shining stars,
4 praise him, highest heavens,
praise him, waters above the heavens.

5 Let them praise the name of Yahweh
at whose command they were made;
6 he established them for ever and ever
by an unchanging decree.

7 Praise Yahweh from the earth,
sea-monsters and all the depths,

8 fire and hail, snow and mist,
storm-winds that obey his word,

9 mountains and every hill,
orchards and every cedar,
10 wild animals and all cattle,
reptiles and winged birds,

11 kings of the earth and all nations,
princes and all judges on earth,
12 young men and girls,
old people and children together.

13 Let them praise the name of Yahweh,
for his name alone is sublime,
his splendour transcends earth and heaven.
14 For he heightens the strength of his people,
to the praise of all his faithful,
the children of Israel, the people close to him.

PSALM 149

Song of triumph

1 Alleluia!

Sing a new song to Yahweh:
his praise in the assembly of the faithful!
2 Israel shall rejoice in its Maker,
the children of Zion delight in their king;
3 they shall dance in praise of his name,
play to him on tambourines and harp!

4 For Yahweh loves his people,
he will crown the humble with salvation.
5 The faithful exult in glory,
shout for joy as they worship him,
6 praising God to the heights with their voices,
a two-edged sword in their hands,

7 to wreak vengeance on the nations,
punishment on the peoples,
8 to load their kings with chains
and their nobles with iron fetters,
9 to execute on them the judgement passed—
to the honour of all his faithful.

PSALM 150

Final chorus of praise

1 Alleluia!

Praise God in his holy place,
praise him in the heavenly vault of his power,

2praise him for his mighty deeds,
praise him for all his greatness.

3Praise him with fanfare of trumpet,
praise him with harp and lyre,
4praise him with tambourines and dancing,
praise him with strings and pipes,
5praise him with the clamour of cymbals,
praise him with triumphant cymbals,
6Let everything that breathes praise Yahweh.

Alleluia!

THE BOOK OF PROVERBS

The core of this collection of wise sayings is the two collections of proverbs attributed to Solomon. They are succinct, witty and pungent reflections on life; they fit well with the origins of such collections of wise sayings, advice given to those who wanted to get on at court. In Israel Solomon was responsible for the development of the court, and himself had the reputation of unrivalled wisdom. The vast majority of the sayings show no particular connection with religion or faith, being purely a matter of deep good sense, but every now and then they reveal a belief that all wisdom comes from Yahweh. They reflect a sharp, competitive, cynical, secular society, where compassion too has its place.

To this central core are added various supplements. There are four little collections at the end, appendices which speak for themselves; but the two most important are sections III and I. Section III is founded on the very ancient Egyptian *Wisdom of Amenemophis* (written down *c.* 1000 BC but already then ancient), which shows how Israel learnt from the neighbouring cultures. Section I is the latest part of the book, probably post-exilic; it is an invitation to acquire wisdom, acquired by faith in Yahweh, which reaches its climax in Wisdom's own self-description at 8:22.

PLAN OF THE BOOK

THE PROVERBS

Title and purpose of the book

1 The proverbs of Solomon son of David, king of Israel:
[2]for learning what wisdom and discipline are,
for understanding words of deep meaning,
[3]for acquiring a disciplined insight,
uprightness, justice and fair dealing;
[4]for teaching sound judgement to the simple,
and knowledge and reflection to the young;
[6]for perceiving the meaning of proverbs and obscure sayings,
the sayings of the sages and their riddles.
[5]Let the wise listen and learn yet more,
and a person of discernment will acquire the art of guidance.

[7]The fear of Yahweh is the beginning of knowledge;
fools spurn wisdom and discipline.

I: PROLOGUE

COMMENDATION OF WISDOM

The sage speaks: avoid bad company

[8]Listen, my child, to your father's instruction,
do not reject your mother's teaching:
[9]they will be a crown of grace for your head,
a circlet for your neck.
[10]My child, if sinners try to seduce you,
do not go with them.
[11]If they say, 'Come with us:
let us lie in ambush to shed blood;
if we plan an ambush for the innocent without provocation,
[12]we can swallow them alive, like Sheol,
and whole, like those who sink into oblivion.
[13]We shall find treasures of every sort,
we shall fill our houses with plunder;
[14]throw in your lot with us:
one purse between us all.'
[15]My child, do not follow them in their way,
keep your steps out of their path

16 *for their feet hasten to evil,*
they are quick to shed blood;[a]
17 for the net is spread in vain
if any winged creature can see it.
18 It is for their own blood such people lie in wait,
their ambush is against their own selves!
19 Such are the paths of all who seek dishonest gain:
which robs of their lives all who take it for their own.

Wisdom speaks: a warning to the heedless

20 Wisdom calls aloud in the streets,
she raises her voice in the public squares;
21 she calls out at the street corners,
she delivers her message at the city gates.
22 'You simple people, how much longer will you cling
to your simple ways?
How much longer will mockers revel in their mocking
and fools go on hating knowledge?
23 Pay attention to my warning.
To you I will pour out my heart
and tell you what I have to say.
24 Since I have called and you have refused me,
since I have beckoned and no one has taken notice,
25 since you have ignored all my advice
and rejected all my warnings,
26 I, for my part, shall laugh at your distress,
I shall jeer when terror befalls you,
27 when terror befalls you, like a storm,
when your distress arrives, like a whirlwind,
when ordeal and anguish bear down on you.
28 Then they will call me, but I shall not answer,
they will look eagerly for me and will not find me.
29 They have hated knowledge,
they have not chosen the fear of Yahweh,
30 they have taken no notice of my advice,
they have spurned all my warnings:
31 so they will have to eat the fruits of their own ways of life,
and choke themselves with their own scheming.
32 For the errors of the simple lead to their death,
the complacency of fools works their own ruin;
33 but whoever listens to me may live secure,
will have quiet, fearing no mischance.'

Wisdom, a safeguard against bad company

2 My child, if you take my words to heart,
if you set store by my commandments,
2 tuning your ear to wisdom,
tuning your heart to understanding,
3 yes, if your plea is for clear perception,
if you cry out for understanding,
4 if you look for it as though for silver,
search for it as though for buried treasure,

1a A quotation of Is 59:7, absent from the best Gk MSS.

[5]then you will understand what the fear of Yahweh is,
and discover the knowledge of God.
[6]For Yahweh himself is giver of wisdom,
from his mouth issue knowledge and understanding.
[7]He reserves his advice for the honest,
a shield to those whose ways are sound;
[8]he stands guard over the paths of equity,
he keeps watch over the way of those faithful to him.
[9]Then you will understand uprightness, equity and fair dealing,
the paths that lead to happiness.
[10]When wisdom comes into your heart
and knowledge fills your soul with delight,
[11]then prudence will be there to watch over you,
and understanding will be your guardian
[12]to keep you from the way that is evil,
from those whose speech is deceitful,
[13]from those who leave the paths of honesty
to walk the roads of darkness:
[14]those who find their joy in doing wrong,
and their delight in deceitfulness,
[15]whose tracks are twisted,
and the paths that they tread crooked.
[16]To keep you, too, from the woman who belongs to another,[a]
from the stranger, with her wheedling words;
[17]she has left the partner of her younger days,
she has forgotten the covenant of her God;
[18]her house is tilting towards Death,
down to the Shades go her paths.
[19]Of those who go to her not one returns,
they never regain the paths of life.

[20]Thus you will tread the way of good people,
persisting in the paths of the upright.
[21]For the land will be for the honest to live in,
the innocent will have it for their home;
[22]while the wicked will be cut off from the land,
and the faithless rooted out of it.

How to acquire wisdom

3 My child, do not forget my teaching,
let your heart keep my principles,
[2]since they will increase your length of days,
your years of life and your well-being.

[3]Let faithful love and constancy never leave you:
tie them round your neck,
write them on the tablet of your heart.
[4]Thus you will find favour and success
in the sight of God and of people.
[5]Trust wholeheartedly in Yahweh,
put no faith in your own perception;
[6]acknowledge him in every course you take,
and he will see that your paths are smooth.

2a Adultery, besides its literal meaning, also symbolises desertion of Yahweh, Israel's spouse.

7 Do not congratulate yourself on your own wisdom,
fear Yahweh and turn your back on evil:
8 health-giving, this, to your body,
relief to your bones.

9 Honour Yahweh with what goods you have
and with the first-fruits of all your produce;
10 then your barns will be filled with corn,
your vats overflowing with new wine.

11 My child, do not scorn correction from Yahweh,
do not resent his reproof;
12 for Yahweh reproves those he loves,
as a father the child whom he loves.

The joys of wisdom

13 Blessed are those who have discovered wisdom,
those who have acquired understanding!
14 Gaining her is more rewarding than silver,
her yield is more valuable than gold.
15 She is beyond the price of pearls;
nothing you could covet is her equal.
16 In her right hand is length of days;
in her left hand, riches and honour.
17 Her ways are filled with delight,
her paths all lead to contentment.
18 She is a tree of life for those who hold her fast,
those who cling to her live happy lives.

19 In wisdom, Yahweh laid the earth's foundations,
in understanding he spread out the heavens.
20 Through his knowledge the depths were cleft open,
and the clouds distil the dew.

21 My child, hold to sound advice and prudence,
never let them out of sight;
22 they will give life to your soul
and beauty to your neck.
23 You will go on your way in safety,
your feet will not stumble.
24 When you go to bed, you will not be afraid;
once in bed, your sleep will be sweet.
25 Have no fear either of sudden terror
or of attack mounted by wicked men,
26 since Yahweh will be your guarantor,
he will keep your steps from the snare.

27 Refuse no kindness to those who have a right to it,
if it is in your power to perform it.
28 Do not say to your neighbour, 'Go away! Come another time!
I will give it you tomorrow,' if you can do it now.
29 Do not plot harm against your neighbour
who is living unsuspecting beside you.
30 Do not pick a groundless quarrel with anyone
who has done you no harm.
31 Do not envy the man of violence,
never model your conduct on his;

32 for the wilful wrong-doer is abhorrent to Yahweh,
who confides only in the honest.
33 Yahweh's curse lies on the house of the wicked,
but he blesses the home of the upright.
34 He mocks those who mock,
but accords his favour to the humble.
35 Glory is the portion of the wise,
all that fools inherit is contempt.

On choosing wisdom

4 Listen, my children, to a father's instruction;
pay attention, and learn what understanding is.
2 What I am offering you is sound doctrine:
do not forsake my teaching.
3 I too was once a child with a father,
in my mother's eyes a tender child, unique.
4 This was what he used to teach me,
'Let your heart treasure what I have to say,
keep my principles and you will live;
5 acquire wisdom, acquire understanding,
never forget her, never deviate from my words.
6 Do not desert her, she will keep you safe;
love her, she will watch over you.
7 The first principle of wisdom is: acquire wisdom;
at the cost of all you have, acquire understanding!
8 Hold her close, and she will make you great;
embrace her, and she will be your pride;
9 she will provide a graceful garland for your head,
bestow a crown of honour on you.'

10 Listen, my child, take my words to heart,
and the years of your life will be multiplied.
11 I have educated you in the ways of wisdom,
I have guided you along the path of honesty.
12 When you walk, your going will be unhindered,
if you run, you will not stumble.
13 Hold fast to discipline, never let her go,
keep your eyes on her, she is your life.
14 Do not follow the path of the wicked,
do not walk the way that the evil go.
15 Avoid it, do not take it,
turn your back on it, pass it by.
16 For they cannot sleep unless they have first done wrong,
they miss their sleep if they have not made someone stumble;
17 for the bread of wickedness is what they eat,
and the wine of violence is what they drink.

18 The path of the upright is like the light of dawn,
its brightness growing to the fullness of day;
19 the way of the wicked is as dark as night,
they cannot tell the obstacles they stumble over.

20 My child, pay attention to what I am telling you,
listen carefully to my words;
21 do not let them out of your sight,
keep them deep in your heart.

22For they are life to those who find them
and health to all humanity.
23More than all else, keep watch over your heart,
since here are the wellsprings of life.
24Turn your back on the mouth that misleads,
keep your distance from lips that deceive.
25Let your eyes be fixed ahead,
your gaze be straight before you.
26Let the path you tread be level
and all your ways be firm.
27Turn neither to right nor to left,
keep your foot clear of evil.

Against adultery. Where the wise man's love should be

5 My son, pay attention to my wisdom,
listen carefully to what I know;
2so that you may preserve discretion
and your lips may guard knowledge.
Take no notice of a loose-living woman,
3for the lips of the adulteress drip with honey,
her palate is more unctuous than oil,
4but in the end she is bitter as wormwood,
sharp as a two-edged sword.
5Her feet go down to death,
Sheol the goal of her steps;
6far from following the path of life,
her course is uncertain and she does not know it.

7And now, son, listen to me,
never deviate from what I say:
8set your course as far from her as possible,
go nowhere near the door of her house,
9or she will hand over your honour to others,
the years of your life to a man without pity,
10and strangers will batten on your property,
and your produce go to the house of a stranger,
11and, at your ending,
your body and flesh having been consumed,
you will groan 12and exclaim,
'Alas, I hated discipline,
my heart spurned all correction;
13I would not attend to the voice of my masters,
I would not listen to those who tried to teach me.
14Now I have come to nearly every kind of misery,
in the assembly and in the community.'

15Drink the water from your own storage-well,
fresh water from your own spring.
16Even if your fountains overflow outside,
your streams of water in the public squares:
17let them be for you alone,
and not for strangers with you.
18May your fountain-head be blessed!

Find joy with the wife you married in your youth,

[19]fair as a hind, graceful as a fawn:
hers the breasts that ever fill you with delight,
hers the love that ever holds you captive.
[20]Why be seduced, my son, by someone else's wife,
and fondle the breast of a woman who belongs to another?
[21]For the eyes of Yahweh observe human ways,
and survey all human paths.
[22]The wicked is snared in his own misdeeds,
is caught in the meshes of his own sin.
[23]For want of discipline, he dies,
led astray by his own excessive folly.

On surety rashly offered

6 My child, if you have gone surety for your neighbour,
if you have guaranteed the bond of a stranger,
[2]if you have committed yourself with your lips,
if through words of yours you have been entrapped,
[3]do this, my child, to extricate yourself—
since you have put yourself in the power of your neighbour:
go, humble yourself, plead with your neighbour,
[4]give your eyes no sleep,
your eyelids no rest,
[5]break free like a gazelle from the trap,
like a bird from the fowler's clutches.

The idler and the ant

[6]Idler, go to the ant;
ponder her ways and grow wise:
[7]no one gives her orders,
no overseer, no master,
[8]yet all through the summer she gets her food ready,
and gathers her supplies at harvest time.
[9]How long do you intend to lie there, idler?
When are you going to rise from your sleep?
[10]A little sleep, a little drowsiness,
a little folding of the arms to lie back,
[11]and poverty comes like a vagrant
and, like a beggar, dearth.[a]

Portrait of a scoundrel

[12]A scoundrel, a vicious man,
he goes with a leer on his lips,
[13]winking his eye, shuffling his foot,
beckoning with his finger.
[14]Trickery in his heart, always scheming evil,
he sows dissension.
[15]Disaster will overtake him sharply for this,
suddenly, irretrievably, he will be broken.

6a =24:33–34.

Seven things abhorrent to God

16 There are six things that Yahweh hates,
seven that he abhors:
17 a haughty look, a lying tongue,
hands that shed innocent blood,
18 a heart that weaves wicked plots,
feet that hurry to do evil,
19 a false witness who lies with every breath,
and one who sows dissension among brothers.

More fatherly advice

20 Keep your father's precept, my child,
do not spurn your mother's teaching.
21 Bind them ever to your heart,
tie them round your neck.
22 While you are active, they will guide you,
when you fall asleep, they will watch over you,
when you wake up, they will converse with you.

23 For the precept is a lamp,
the teaching is a light;
correction and discipline are the way to life,
24 preserving you from the woman of bad character,
from the wheedling talk of a woman who belongs to another.
25 Do not covet her beauty in your heart
or let her captivate you with the play of her eyes;
26 a prostitute can be bought for a hunk of bread,
but a married woman aims to snare a precious life.
27 Can a man carry fire inside his shirt
without setting his clothes alight?
28 Can you walk on red-hot coals
without burning your feet?
29 Just so, the man who makes love to his neighbour's wife:
no one who touches her will get off unpunished.
30 People attach but little blame to a thief
who steals only to satisfy his hunger;
31 yet even he, if caught, will have to repay sevenfold
and hand over all his family resources.
32 But the adulterer has no sense;
he works his own destruction.
33 All he will get is blows and contempt,
and dishonour never to be blotted out.
34 For jealousy inflames the husband
who will show no mercy when the day comes for revenge;
35 he will not consider any compensation;
lavish what gifts you may, he will not be placated.

7 My child, keep my words,
and treasure my precepts,
2 keep my precepts and you will live,
keep my teaching as the apple of your eye.
3 Bind these to your fingers,
write them on the tablet of your heart.
4 Say to Wisdom, 'You are my sister!'
Call Understanding your relation,

5 to save yourself from the woman that belongs to another,
from the stranger, with her seductive words.

6 While I was at the window of my house,
I was looking out through the lattice
7 and I saw, among the callow youths,
I noticed among the lads,
one boy who had no sense.
8 Going along the lane, near the corner where she lives,
he reaches the path to her house,
9 at twilight when day is declining,
at dead of night and in the dark.
10 And look, a woman is coming to meet him,
dressed like a prostitute, false of heart.
11 She is loud and brazen;
her feet cannot rest at home.
12 Once in the street, once in the square,
she lurks at every corner.
13 She catches hold of him, she kisses him,
the bold-faced creature says to him,
14 'I had to offer a communion sacrifice,
I have discharged my vows today;
15 that is why I came out to meet you,
to look for you, and now I have found you.
16 I have spread coverlets over my divan,
embroidered stuff, Egyptian material,
17 I have sprinkled my bed with myrrh,
with aloes and cinnamon.
18 Come on, we'll make love as much as we like, till morning.
Let us enjoy the delights of love!
19 For my husband is not at home,
he has gone on a very long journey,
20 taking his moneybags with him;
he will not be back till the moon is full.'
21 With her persistent coaxing she overcomes him,
lures him on with her wheedling patter.
22 Forthwith he follows her,
like an ox on its way to the slaughterhouse,
like a madman on his way to the stocks,
23 until an arrow pierces him to the liver,
like the bird that dashes into the net
without realising that its life is at stake.
24 And now, son, listen to me,
pay attention to the words I have to say:
25 do not let your heart stray into her ways,
or wander into her paths;
26 she has done so many to death,
and the strongest have all been her victims.
27 Her house is the way to Sheol,
the descent to the courts of death.

Wisdom speaks again

8 Is not Wisdom calling?
Is not Understanding raising her voice?
2 On the heights overlooking the road,
at the crossways, she takes her stand;

3by the gates, at the entrance to the city,
on the access-roads, she cries out,
4'I am calling to you, all people,
my words are addressed to all humanity.
5Simpletons, learn how to behave,
fools, come to your senses.
6Listen, I have something important to tell you,
when I speak, my words are right.
7My mouth proclaims the truth,
for evil is abhorrent to my lips
8All the words from my mouth are upright,
nothing false there, nothing crooked,
9everything plain, if you can understand,
straight, if you have acquired knowledge.
10Accept my discipline rather than silver,
and knowledge of me in preference to finest gold.
11For Wisdom is more precious than jewels,
and nothing else is so worthy of desire.

Wisdom sings her own praises. Wisdom, the guide of kings

12'I, Wisdom, share house with Discretion,
I am mistress of the art of thought.
13(Fear of Yahweh means hatred of evil.)
I hate pride and arrogance,
wicked behaviour and a lying mouth.
14To me belong good advice and prudence,
I am perception: power is mine!
15By me monarchs rule
and princes decree what is right;
16by me rulers govern,
so do nobles, the lawful authorities.
17I love those who love me;
whoever searches eagerly for me finds me.
18With me are riches and honour,
lasting wealth and saving justice.
19The fruit I give is better than gold, even the finest,
the return I make is better than pure silver.
20I walk in the way of uprightness
in the path of justice,
21to endow my friends with my wealth
and to fill their treasuries.

Wisdom as Creator[a]

22'Yahweh created me, first-fruits of his fashioning,
before the oldest of his works.
23From everlasting, I was firmly set,
from the beginning, before the earth came into being.
24The deep was not, when I was born,
nor were the springs with their abounding waters.
25Before the mountains were settled,
before the hills, I came to birth;

8a Wisdom's creation by God was on a different plane to all his other works. Wisdom almost seems to be a distinct personality, sharing in God's activity, and his agent in the world. The concept given here will be used in the NT to express Christ's relationship to his Father.

26 before he had made the earth, the countryside,
and the first elements of the world.
27 When he fixed the heavens firm, I was there,
when he drew a circle on the surface of the deep,
28 when he thickened the clouds above,
when the sources of the deep began to swell,
29 when he assigned the sea its boundaries
—and the waters will not encroach on the shore—
when he traced the foundations of the earth,
30 I was beside the master craftsman,
delighting him day after day,
ever at play in his presence,
31 at play everywhere on his earth,
delighting to be with the children of men.

The supreme invitation

32 'And now, my children, listen to me.
Happy are those who keep my ways.
33 Listen to instruction and become wise,
do not reject it.
34 Blessed, whoever listens to me,
who day after day keeps watch at my gates
to guard my portals.
35 For whoever finds me finds life,
and obtains the favour of Yahweh;
36 but whoever misses me harms himself,
all who hate me are in love with death.'

Wisdom as hostess

9 Wisdom has built herself a house,
she has hewn her seven pillars,
2 she has slaughtered her beasts, drawn her wine,
she has laid her table.
3 She has despatched her maidservants
and proclaimed from the heights above the city,
4 'Who is simple? Let him come this way.'
To the fool she says,
5 'Come and eat my bread,
drink the wine which I have drawn!
6 Leave foolishness behind and you will live,
go forwards in the ways of perception.'

Against cynics

7 Reprove a mocker and you attract contempt,
rebuke the wicked and you attract dishonour.
8 Do not rebuke the mocker, he will hate you.
Rebuke the wise and he will love you for it.
9 Be open with the wise, he grows wiser still,
teach the upright, he will gain yet more.
10 The first principle of wisdom is the fear of Yahweh,
What God's holy ones know—this is understanding.
11 For by me your days will be multiplied,
and your years of life increased.

12 Are you wise? You are wise to your own good.
A mocker? The burden is yours alone.

A silly woman apes Wisdom

13 A silly woman acts on impulse,
is foolish and knows nothing.
14 She sits at the door of her house,
on a throne high up in the city,
15 calling to the passers-by,
who are walking straight past on their way,
16 'Who is simple? Turn aside, come over here.'
To the fool she says,
17 'Stolen waters are sweet,
and bread tastes better when eaten in secret.'
18 But the fool does not know that this is where the Shades are
and that her guests are already in the vales of Sheol.

II: THE MAJOR COLLECTION ATTRIBUTED TO SOLOMON

10 The proverbs of Solomon.

A wise child is a father's joy,[a]
a foolish child a mother's grief.

2 Treasures wickedly come by give no benefit,
but uprightness brings delivery from death.[b]

3 Yahweh does not let the upright go hungry,
but he thwarts the greed of the wicked.

4 A slack hand brings poverty,
but the hand of the diligent brings wealth.

5 Reaping at harvest-time is the mark of the prudent,
sleeping at harvest-time is the sign of the worthless.

6 Blessings are on the head of the upright,
but the mouth of the godless is a cover for violence.

7 The upright is remembered with blessings,
the name of the wicked rots away.

8 The wise of heart takes orders,
but a gabbling fool heads for ruin.

9 Anyone whose ways are honourable walks secure,
but whoever follows crooked ways is soon unmasked.

10 A wink of the eye brings trouble,
a bold rebuke brings peace.

11 The mouth of the upright is a life-giving fountain,
but the mouth of the godless is a cover for violence.

12 Hatred provokes disputes,
but love excuses all offences.

10a =15:20.
10b =11:4.

[13]On the lips of the discerning is found wisdom,
on the back of a fool, the stick.

[14]Wise people store up knowledge,
but the mouth of a fool makes ruin imminent.

[15]The wealth of the rich is their stronghold,[c]
poverty is the undoing of the weak.

[16]The wage of the upright affords life,
but sin is all the wicked earns.

[17]Whoever abides by discipline, walks towards life,
whoever ignores correction goes astray.

[18]Liars' lips are a cover for hatred,
whoever utters slander is a fool.

[19]A flood of words is never without fault;
whoever controls the lips is wise.

[20]The tongue of the upright is purest silver,
the heart of the wicked is of trumpery value.

[21]The lips of the upright nourish many peoples,
but fools die for want of sense.

[22]The blessing of Yahweh is what brings riches,
to this, hard toil has nothing to add.

[23]A fool takes pleasure in doing wrong,
the intelligent in cultivating wisdom.

[24]What the wicked fears overtakes him,
what the upright desires comes to him as a present.

[25]When the storm is over, the wicked is no more,
but the upright stands firm for ever.

[26]As vinegar to the teeth, smoke to the eyes,
so the sluggard to the one who sends him.

[27]The fear of Yahweh adds length to life,
the years of the wicked will be cut short.

[28]The hope of the upright is joy,
the expectations of the wicked come to nothing.

[29]The way of Yahweh is a rampart for the honest,
for evil-doers nothing but ruin.

[30]The upright will never have to give way,
but the land will offer no home for the wicked.

[31]The mouth of the upright utters wisdom,
the tongue that deceives will be cut off.

[32]The lips of the upright know about kindness,
the mouth of the wicked about deceit.

11 A false balance is abhorrent to Yahweh,
a just weight is pleasing to him.

[2]Pride comes first; disgrace soon follows;
with the humble is wisdom found.

10c =18:11.

3 The honest have their own honesty for guidance,
the treacherous are ruined by their own perfidy.

4 In the day of retribution riches will be useless,
but uprightness delivers from death.[a]

5 The uprightness of the good makes their way straight,
the wicked fall by their own wickedness.

6 Their uprightness sets the honest free,
the treacherous are imprisoned by their own desires.

7 The hope of the wicked perishes with death,
hope placed in riches comes to nothing.

8 The upright escapes affliction,
the wicked incurs it instead.

9 Through his mouth the godless is the ruin of his neighbour,
but by knowledge the upright are safeguarded.

10 When the upright prosper the city rejoices,
when the wicked are ruined there is a shout of joy.

11 A city is raised on the blessing of the honest,
and demolished by the mouth of the wicked.

12 Whoever looks down on a neighbour lacks good sense;
the intelligent keeps a check on the tongue.

13 A tittle-tattler lets secrets out,
the trustworthy keeps things hidden.

14 For want of leadership a people perishes,
safety lies in many advisers.

15 Whoever goes bail for a stranger does himself harm,
but one who shuns going surety is safe.

16 A gracious woman acquires honour,
violent people acquire wealth.

17 Faithful love brings its own reward,
the inflexible injure their own selves.

18 Disappointment crowns the labours of the wicked,
whoever sows uprightness reaps a solid reward.

19 Whoever establishes uprightness is on the way to life,
whoever pursues evil, on the way to death.

20 Tortuous hearts are abhorrent to Yahweh,
dear to him, those whose ways are blameless.

21 Be sure of it, the wicked will not go unpunished,
but the race of the upright will come to no harm.

22 A golden ring in the snout of a pig
is a lovely woman who lacks discretion.

23 The hope of the upright is nothing but good,
the expectation of the wicked is retribution.

24 One scatters money around, yet only adds to his wealth,
another is excessively mean, but only grows the poorer.

11a =10:2.

25 The soul who blesses will prosper,
whoever satisfies others will also be satisfied.

26 The people's curse is on those who hoard the wheat,
their blessing on the head of those who sell it.

27 Whoever strives for good obtains favour,
whoever looks for evil will get an evil return.

28 Whoever trusts in riches will have a fall,
the upright will flourish like the leaves.

29 Whoever misgoverns a house inherits the wind,
and the fool becomes slave to the wise.

30 The fruit of the upright is a tree of life:
the sage captivates souls.

31 If here on earth the upright gets due reward,
how much more the wicked and the sinner!

12 Whoever loves discipline, loves knowledge,
stupid are those who hate correction.

2 The honest obtains Yahweh's favour,
the schemer incurs his condemnation.

3 No one is made secure by wickedness,
but nothing shakes the roots of the upright.

4 A capable wife, her husband's crown,
a shameless wife, a cancer in his bones.

5 The plans of the upright are honest,
the intrigues of the wicked are full of deceit.

6 The words of the wicked are snares to shed blood,
what the honest say keeps them safe.

7 Once thrown down, the wicked are no more,
but the house of the upright stands firm.

8 Prudence wins praise,
but a tortuous heart incurs only contempt.

9 Better a common fellow who has a slave
than someone who gives himself airs and has nothing to eat.

10 The upright has compassion on his animals,
but the heart of the wicked is ruthless.

11 Whoever works his land shall have bread and to spare,
but no one who chases fantasies has any sense.[a]

12 The godless delights in the snare of the wicked,
but the root of the upright bears fruit.

13 In the sin of the lips lies a disastrous trap,
but the upright finds a way out of misfortune.

14 Abundance of good things is the fruit of the lips;
labour brings its own return.

15 Fools think the way they go is straight,
the wise listens to advice.

12a =28:19.

16 The fool shows anger straightaway,
the discreet conceals dislike.

17 To tell the truth is to further justice,
a false witness is nothing but deceit.

18 Thoughtless words can wound like a sword,
but the tongue of the wise brings healing.

19 Sincere lips endure for ever,
the lying tongue lasts only a moment.

20 Deceit is in the heart of the schemer,
joy with those who give counsels of peace.

21 No harm can come to the upright,
but the wicked are swamped by misfortunes.

22 Lying lips are abhorrent to Yahweh;
dear to him those who make truth their way of life.

23 The discreet keeps knowledge hidden,
the heart of fools proclaims their folly.

24 For the diligent hand, authority;
for the slack hand, forced labour.

25 Worry makes a heart heavy,
a kindly word makes it glad.

26 The upright shows the way to a friend;
the way of the wicked leads them astray.

27 The idle has no game to roast;
diligence is anyone's most precious possession.

28 In the way of uprightness is life,
the ways of the vengeful lead to death.

13 A wise child listens to a father's discipline,
a cynic will not listen to reproof.

2 The fruit of the mouth provides a good meal,
but the soul of the treacherous feeds on violence.

3 A guard on the mouth makes life secure,
whoever talks too much is lost.

4 The idler hungers but has no food;
hard workers get their fill.

5 The upright hates a lying word,
but the wicked slanders and defames.

6 Uprightness stands guard over one whose way is honest,
sin causes the ruin of the wicked.

7 There are some who, on nothing, pretend to be rich,
some, with great wealth, pretend to be poor.

8 The ransom for life is a person's wealth;
but the poor will not hear the reproof.

9 The light of the upright is joyful,
the lamp of the wicked goes out.

10 Insolence breeds only disputes,
wisdom lies with those who take advice.

11 A sudden fortune will dwindle away,
accumulation little by little is the way to riches.

12 Hope deferred makes the heart sick,
desire fulfilled is a tree of life.

13 Contempt for the word is self-destructive,
respect for the commandment wins salvation.

14 The teaching of the wise is a life-giving fountain
for eluding the snares of death.[a]

15 Good sense wins favour,
but the way of the treacherous is hard.

16 Anyone of discretion acts by the light of knowledge,
the fool parades his folly.

17 A bad messenger falls into misfortune,
a trusty messenger brings healing.

18 Whoever rejects discipline wins poverty and scorn;
for anyone who accepts correction: honour.

19 Desire fulfilled is sweet to the soul;
fools are loth to turn—from evil.

20 Whoever walks with the wise becomes wise,
whoever mixes with fools will be ruined.

21 Evil will pursue the sinner,
but good will reward the upright.

22 The good bequeaths a heritage to children's children,
the wealth of the sinner is stored away for the upright.

23 Though the farms of the poor yield much food,
some perish for lack of justice.

24 Whoever fails to use the stick hates his child;
whoever is free with correction loves him.

25 The upright eats to the full,
the belly of the wicked goes empty.

14 Wisdom builds herself a house;
with her own hands Folly pulls it down.

2 Whoever keeps to an honest course fears Yahweh,
whoever deserts his paths shows contempt for him.

3 Pride sprouts in the mouth of the fool,
the lips of the wise keep them safe.

4 No oxen, empty manger;
strong bull, much cash.

5 The truthful witness tells no lies,
the false witness lies with every breath.

6 In vain the mocker looks for wisdom,
knowledge comes easy to the intelligent.

7 Keep well clear of the fool,
you will not find wise lips there.

13a =14:27.

8 With people of discretion, wisdom keeps a watch over their conduct,
but the folly of fools leads them astray.

9 Fools mock at the sacrifice for sin,
but favour resides among the honest.

10 The heart knows its own grief best,
nor can a stranger share its joy.

11 The house of the wicked will be destroyed,
the tent of the honest will prosper.

12 There are ways that some think straight,
but they lead in the end to death.[a]

13 Even in laughter the heart finds sadness,
and joy makes way for sorrow.

14 The miscreant will reap the reward of his conduct,
and the good the reward of his deeds.

15 The simpleton believes any message,
a person of discretion treads a careful path.

16 The wise fears evil and avoids it,
the fool is insolent and conceited.

17 A quick-tempered person commits rash acts,
but a schemer is detestable.

18 Simpletons have folly for their portion,
people of discretion knowledge for their crown.

19 The evil bow down before the good,
the wicked, at the gates of the upright.

20 The poor is detestable even to a friend,
but many are they who love someone rich.

21 One who despises the needy is at fault,
one who takes pity on the poor is blessed.

22 Plan evil—isn't this to go astray?
Those who plan for good can earn faithful love and constancy.

23 Hard work always yields its profit,
idle talk brings only want.

24 The crown of the wise is their riches;
the folly of fools is folly.

25 A truthful witness saves lives,
whoever utters lies is a deceiver.

26 In the fear of Yahweh is powerful security;
for his children he is a refuge.

27 The fear of Yahweh is a life-giving spring
for eluding the snares of death.[b]

28 Large population, monarch's glory;
dwindling population, ruler's ruin.

29 Mastery of temper is high proof of intelligence,
a quick temper makes folly worse than ever.

14a =16:25.
14b =13:14.

30 The life of the body is a tranquil heart,
but envy is a cancer in the bones.

31 To oppress the weak insults the Creator,
kindness to the needy honours the Creator.

32 For evil-doing, the wicked will be flung headlong,
but in integrity the upright will find refuge.

33 Wisdom resides in an understanding heart;
she is not to be found in the hearts of fools.

34 Uprightness makes a nation great,
by sin whole races are disgraced.

35 A king shows favour to a wise minister,
but anger to one who shames him.

15 A mild answer turns away wrath,
sharp words stir up anger.

2 The tongue of the wise makes knowledge welcome,
the mouth of a fool spews folly.

3 The eyes of Yahweh are everywhere:
observing the wicked and the good.

4 The tongue that soothes is a tree of life;
the perverse tongue, a breaker of hearts.

5 Only a fool spurns a father's discipline,
whoever accepts correction is discreet.

6 In the house of the upright there is no lack of treasure,
the earnings of the wicked are fraught with anxiety.

7 The lips of the wise spread knowledge,
not so the hearts of fools.

8 The sacrifice of the wicked is abhorrent to Yahweh,
dear to him is the prayer of the honest.

9 The conduct of the wicked is abhorrent to Yahweh,
but he loves the person whose goal is uprightness.

10 Correction is severe for one who leaves the way;
whoever hates being reprimanded will die.

11 Sheol and Perdition lie open to Yahweh;
how much more the human heart!

12 The mocker does not care to be reprimanded,
and will not choose the wise as companions.

13 Glad heart means happy face,
where the heart is sad the spirit is broken.

14 The heart of the wise seeks knowledge,
a fool's mouth feeds on folly.

15 For the poor every day is evil,
for the joyous heart it is always festival time.

16 Better to have little and with it fear of Yahweh
than immense wealth and with it anxiety.

17 Better a dish of herbs when love is there
than a fattened ox and hatred to go with it.

18 The hot-headed provokes disputes,
the equable allays dissension.

19 The way of the lazy is like a thorny hedge,
the path of the honest is a broad highway.

20 A wise child is a father's joy;[a]
only a brute despises his mother.

21 Folly appeals to someone without sense,
a person of understanding goes straight forward.

22 Without deliberation plans come to nothing.
Plans succeed where counsellors are many.

23 Anyone who has a ready answer has joy too:
how satisfying is the apt reply!

24 For the prudent, the path of life leads upwards
thus avoiding Sheol below.

25 Yahweh pulls down the house of the proud,
but he keeps the widow's boundaries intact.

26 Wicked scheming is abhorrent to Yahweh,
but words that are kind are pure.

27 Craving for dishonest gain brings trouble on a house,
hatred of bribery earns life.

28 The heart of the upright reflects before answering,
the mouth of the wicked spews out wickedness.

29 Yahweh keeps his distance from the wicked,
but he listens to the prayers of the upright.

30 A kindly glance gives joy to the heart,
good news lends strength to the bones.

31 The ear attentive to wholesome correction
finds itself at home in the company of the wise.

32 Whoever rejects correction lacks self-respect,
whoever accepts reproof grows in understanding.

33 The fear of Yahweh is a school of wisdom,
before there can be glory, there must be humility.[b]

16 A human heart makes the plans,
Yahweh gives the answer.

2 A person's own acts seem right to the doer,
but Yahweh is the weigher of souls.

3 Commend what you do to Yahweh,
and what you plan will be achieved.

4 Yahweh made everything for its own purpose,
yes, even the wicked for the day of disaster.

5 Every arrogant heart is abhorrent to Yahweh:
be sure this will not go unpunished.

15a =10:1.
15b =18:12.

6 By faithful love and constancy sin is expiated;
by fear of Yahweh evil is avoided.

7 Let Yahweh be pleased with someone's way of life
and he makes that person's very enemies into friends.

8 Better have little and with it uprightness
than great revenues with injustice.

9 The human heart may plan a course,
but it is Yahweh who makes the steps secure.

10 The lips of the king utter prophecies,
he keeps faith when he speaks in judgement.

11 The balances and scales belong to Yahweh,
all the weights in the bag are of his making.

12 Evil-doing is abhorrent to kings,
since uprightness is a throne's foundation.

13 Upright lips are welcome to a king,
he loves someone of honest words.

14 The king's wrath is the herald of death,
but the wise will appease it.

15 When the king's face brightens it spells life,
his favour is like the rain in spring.

16 Better gain wisdom than gold,
choose understanding in preference to silver.

17 To turn from evil is the way of the honest;
whoever watches the path keeps life safe.

18 Pride goes before destruction,
a haughty spirit before a fall.

19 Better be humble with the poor
than share the booty with the proud.

20 Whoever listens closely to the word finds happiness;
whoever trusts Yahweh is blessed.

21 The wise of heart is acclaimed as intelligent,
sweetness of speech increases knowledge.

22 Shrewdness is a fountain of life for its possessor,
the folly of fools is their own punishment.

23 The heart of the wise lends shrewdness to speech
and makes words more persuasive.

24 Kindly words are a honeycomb,
sweet to the taste, wholesome to the body.

25 There is a way that some think straight,
but it leads in the end to death.[a]

26 A worker's appetite works on his behalf,
for his hunger urges him on.

27 A worthless person concocts evil,
such a one's talk is like a scorching fire.

16a =14:12.

28 A troublemaker sows strife,
a slanderer divides friend from friend.

29 The violent lures his neighbour astray
and leads him by a way that is not good.

30 Whoever narrows the eyes to think up tricks
and purses the lips has already done wrong.

31 White hairs are a crown of honour,
they are found in the ways of uprightness.

32 Better an equable person than a hero,
someone with self-mastery than one who takes a city.

33 In the fold of the garment the lot is thrown,
but from Yahweh comes the decision.

17 Better a mouthful of dry bread with peace
than a house filled with quarrelsome sacrifices.

2 A shrewd servant comes off better than an unworthy child,
he will share the inheritance with the brothers.

3 A furnace for silver, a foundry for gold,[a]
but Yahweh for the testing of hearts!

4 An evil-doer pays heed to malicious talk,
a liar listens to a slanderous tongue.

5 To mock the poor is to insult the Creator,
no one who laughs at distress will go unpunished.

6 The crown of the aged is their children's children;
the children's glory is their father.

7 Fine words do not become the foolish,
false words become a prince still less.

8 A gift works like a talisman for one who holds it:
it brings prosperity at every turn.

9 Whoever covers an offence promotes love,
whoever again raises the matter divides friends.

10 A reproof makes more impression on a person of understanding
than a hundred strokes on a fool.

11 The wicked person thinks of nothing but rebellion,
but a cruel messenger will be sent to such a one.

12 Rather come on a bear robbed of her cubs
than on a fool in his folly.

13 Disaster will never be far from the house
of one who returns evil for good.

14 As well unleash a flood as start a dispute;
desist before the quarrel breaks out.

15 To absolve the guilty and condemn the upright,
both alike are abhorrent to Yahweh.

16 What good is money in the hand of a fool?
To buy wisdom with it? The desire is not there.

17a =27:21.

17 A friend is a friend at all times,
it is for adversity that a brother is born.

18 Whoever offers guarantees lacks sense
and goes surety for a neighbour.

19 The double-dealer loves sin,
the proud courts ruin.

20 The tortuous of heart finds no happiness,
the perverse of speech falls into misery.

21 He who fathers a stupid child does so to his sorrow,
the father of a fool knows no joy.

22 A glad heart is excellent medicine,
a depressed spirit wastes the bones away.

23 Under cover of his cloak a bad man takes a gift
to pervert the course of justice.

24 The intelligent has wisdom there before him,
but the eyes of a fool range to the ends of the earth.

25 A foolish child is a father's sorrow,
and the grief of her who gave the child birth.

26 To fine the upright is indeed a crime,
to strike the noble is an injustice.

27 Whoever can control the tongue knows what knowledge is,
someone of understanding keeps a cool temper.

28 If the fool holds his tongue, he may pass for wise;
if he seals his lips, he may pass for intelligent.

18 Whoever lives alone follows private whims,
and is angered by advice of any kind.

2 A fool takes no pleasure in understanding
but only in airing an opinion.

3 When wickedness comes, indignity comes too,
and, with contempt, dishonour.

4 Deep waters, such are human words:
a gushing stream, the utterance of wisdom.

5 It is not good to show partiality for the wicked
and so to deprive the upright when giving judgement.

6 The lips of a fool go to the law-courts
with a mouth that pleads for a beating.

7 The mouth of the fool works its owner's ruin,
the lips of a fool are a snare for their owner's life.

8 The words of a slanderer are tasty morsels
that go right down into the belly.[a]

9 Whoever is idle at work
is blood-brother to the destroyer.

10 The name of Yahweh is a strong tower;
the upright runs to it and is secure.

18a =26:22.

11 The wealth of the rich forms a stronghold,[b]
a high wall, as the rich supposes.

12 The human heart is haughty until destruction comes,
before there can be glory there must be humility.[c]

13 To retort without first listening
is both foolish and embarrassing.

14 Sickness the human spirit can endure,
but when the spirit is broken, who can bear this?

15 The heart of the intelligent acquires learning,
the ears of the wise search for knowledge.

16 A present will open all doors
and win access to the great.

17 The first to plead is adjudged to be upright,
until the next comes and cross-examines him.

18 The lot puts an end to disputes
and decides between men of power.

19 A brother offended is worse than a fortified city,
and quarrels are like the locks of a keep.

20 From the fruit of the mouth is a stomach filled,
it is the yield of the lips that gives contentment.

21 Death and life are in the gift of the tongue,
those who indulge it must eat the fruit it yields.

22 He who finds a wife finds happiness,
receiving a mark of favour from Yahweh.

23 The language of the poor is entreaty,
the answer of the rich harshness.

24 There are friends who point the way to ruin,
others are closer than a brother.

19 Better the poor living an honest life
than the adept at double-talk who is a fool.

2 Where knowledge is wanting, zeal is not good;
whoever goes too quickly stumbles.

3 Folly leads conduct astray,
yet it is against Yahweh that the heart rages.

4 Wealth multiplies friends,
but the one friend the poor has is taken away.

5 The false witness will not go unpunished,[a]
no one who utters lies will go free.

6 The nobleman has many to court his favour,
to a giver of gifts, everyone is friend.

7 The poor man's brothers hate him, every one;
his friends—how much the more do these desert him!

He goes in search of words, but there are none to be had.[b]

18b =10:15.
18c =15:33.
19a =19:9.
19b A fragment, probably lacking the first line.

[8]Whoever acquires sense wins profit from it,
whoever treasures understanding finds happiness.

[9]The false witness will not go unpunished,[c]
whoever utters lies will be destroyed.

[10]It is not fitting for a fool to live in luxury,
still less for a slave to govern princes.

[11]Good sense makes for self-control,
and for pride in overlooking an offence.

[12]Like the roaring of a lion, the anger of a king,
but like dew on the grass his favour.

[13]A foolish child is a disaster for the father,
the bickerings of a wife are like an ever-dripping gutter.

[14]From fathers comes inheritance of house and wealth,
from Yahweh a wife who is discreet.

[15]Idleness lulls to sleep,
the feckless soul will go hungry.

[16]Keeping the commandment is self-preservation,
but whoever despises these ways will die.

[17]Whoever is kind to the poor is lending to Yahweh
who will repay him the kindness done.

[18]While there is hope for him, chastise your child,
but do not get so angry as to kill him.

[19]The violent lays himself open to a penalty;
spare him, and you aggravate his crime.

[20]Listen to advice, accept correction,
to be the wiser in the time to come.

[21]Many are the plans in the human heart,
but the purpose of Yahweh—that stands firm.

[22]Faithful love is what people look for in a person;
they prefer the poor to a liar.

[23]The fear of Yahweh leads to life,
it brings food and shelter, without fear of evil.

[24]Into the dish the idler dips his hand,
but bring it back to his mouth he cannot.[d]

[25]Strike a cynic, and simpletons will be more wary;
reprove the intelligent and he will understand your meaning.

[26]He who ill-treats his father and drives out his mother
is a child both worthless and depraved.

[27]Give up listening to instruction, my child,
if you mean to stray from words of knowledge.

[28]A perjured witness holds the law in scorn;
the mouth of the wicked feasts on evil-doing.

19c =19:5.
19d =26:15.

29 Punishments were made for mockers,
and beating for the backs of fools.

20 Wine is reckless, liquor rowdy;
unwise is anyone whom it seduces.

2 Like the roaring of a lion is the fury of a king;
whoever provokes him sins against himself.

3 It is praiseworthy to stop short of a law-suit;
only a fool flies into a rage.

4 In autumn the idler does not plough,
at harvest time he looks—nothing there!

5 The resources of the human heart are like deep waters:
an understanding person has only to draw on them.

6 Many describe themselves as people of faithful love,
but who can find someone really to be trusted?

7 The upright whose ways are blameless—
blessed the children who come after!

8 A king enthroned on the judgement seat
with one look scatters all that is evil.

9 Who can say, 'I have cleansed my heart,
I am purified of my sin'?

10 One weight here, another there; here one measure, there another:
both alike are abhorrent to Yahweh.

11 A young man's character appears in what he does,
if his behaviour is pure and straight.

12 Ear that hears, eye that sees,
Yahweh has made both of these.

13 Do not love sleep or you will know poverty;
keep your eyes open and have your fill of food.

14 'No good, no good!' says the buyer,
but he goes off congratulating himself.

15 There are gold and jewels of every type,
but a priceless ornament is speech informed by knowledge.

16 Take the man's clothes! He has gone surety for a stranger.
Take a pledge from him to the profit of persons unknown![a]

17 Bread is sweet when it is got by fraud,
but later the mouth is full of grit.

18 Plans are matured by consultation;
take wise advice when waging war.

19 The bearer of gossip lets out secrets;
do not mingle with chatterers.

20 Whoever curses father or mother
will have his lamp put out in the deepest darkness.

21 Property quickly come by at first
will not be blessed in the end.

22 Do not say, 'I shall repay evil';
put your hope in Yahweh and he will keep you safe.

20a =27:13.

23 One weight here, another there: this is abhorrent to Yahweh,
false scales are not good.

24 Yahweh guides the steps of the powerful:
but who can comprehend human ways?

25 Anyone is trapped who cries 'Dedicated!'
and begins to reflect only after the vow.

26 A wise king winnows the wicked
and makes the wheel pass over them.

27 The human spirit is the lamp of Yahweh—
searching the deepest self.

28 Faithful love and loyalty mount guard over the king,
his throne is founded on saving justice.

29 The pride of the young is their strength,
the ornament of the old, grey hairs.

30 Wounding strokes are good medicine for evil,
blows have an effect on the inmost self.

21 Like flowing water is a king's heart in Yahweh's hand;
he directs it wherever he pleases.

2 All actions are straight in the doer's own eyes,
but it is Yahweh who weighs hearts.

3 To do what is upright and just
is more pleasing to Yahweh than sacrifice.

4 Haughty eye, proud heart,
lamp of the wicked, nothing but sin.

5 The hardworking is thoughtful, and all is gain;
too much haste, and all that comes of it is want.

6 To make a fortune with the help of a lying tongue:
such is the idle fantasy of those who look for death.

7 The violence of the wicked proves their ruin,
for they refuse to do what is right.

8 The way of the felon is devious,
the conduct of the innocent straight.

9 Better the corner of a roof to live on
than a house shared with a quarrelsome woman.[a]

10 The soul of the wicked is intent on evil,
to such a person no neighbour can ever do right.

11 When a cynic is punished, simpletons grow wiser,
but someone of understanding acquires knowledge by instruction.

12 The Upright One watches the house of the wicked;
he hurls the wicked to destruction.

13 Whoever refuses to listen to the cry of the weak,
will in turn plead and not be heard.

14 Anger is mollified by a covert gift,
raging fury by a present under cover of the cloak.

21a =25:24.

15 Doing what is right fills the upright with joy,
but evil-doers with terror.

16 Whoever strays far from the way of prudence
will rest in the assembly of shadows.

17 Pleasure-lovers stay poor,
no one will grow rich who loves wine and good living.

18 The wicked is a ransom for the upright;
and the law-breaker for the honest.

19 Better to live in a desert land
than with a quarrelsome and irritable woman.

20 The wise has valuables and oil at home,
but a fool soon runs through both.

21 Whoever pursues uprightness and faithful love
will find life, uprightness and honour.

22 A sage can scale a garrisoned city
and shatter the rampart on which it relied.

23 Watch kept over mouth and tongue
keeps the watcher safe from disaster.

24 Insolent, haughty—the name is 'Cynic';
overweening pride marks such behaviour.

25 The idler's desires are the death of him,
since his hands will do no work.

26 All day long the godless is racked by desire,
the upright gives without ever refusing.

27 The sacrifice of the wicked is abhorrent,
above all if it is offered for bad motives.

28 The false witness will perish,
but no one who knows how to listen will ever be silenced.

29 The wicked man's strength shows on his face,
but the honest it is whose steps are firm.

30 No wisdom, no understanding,
no advice is worth anything before Yahweh.

31 Fit out the cavalry for the day of battle,
but the victory is Yahweh's.

22 Fame is preferable to great wealth,
favour, to silver and gold.

2 Rich and poor rub shoulders,
Yahweh has made them both.

3 The discreet sees danger and takes shelter,
simpletons go ahead and pay the penalty.[a]

4 The reward of humility is the fear of Yahweh,
and riches, honour and life.

5 Thorns and snares line the path of the wilful,
whoever values life will stay at a distance.

22a =27:12.

[6]Give a lad a training suitable to his character
and, even when old, he will not go back on it.

[7]The rich lords it over the poor,
the borrower is the lender's slave.

[8]Whoever sows injustice reaps disaster,
and the rod of such anger will disappear.

[9]A kindly eye will earn a blessing,
such a person shares out food with the poor.

[10]Expel the mocker and strife goes too,
law-suits and dislike die down.

[11]Whoever loves the pure of heart
and is gracious of speech has the king for a friend.

[12]Yahweh's eyes protect knowledge,
but he confounds deceitful speeches.

[13]'There is a lion outside,' says the idler,
'I shall be killed in the street!'

[14]The mouth of an adulterous woman is a deep pit,
into it falls the man whom Yahweh rebukes.

[15]Folly is anchored in the heart of a youth,
the whip of instruction will rid him of it.

[16]Harsh treatment enriches the poor,
but a gift impoverishes the rich.

III: A SELECTION FROM THE SAGES

[17]Give ear, listen to the sayings of the sages,
and apply your heart to what I know,
[18]for it will be a delight to keep them deep within you
to have them all ready on your lips.
[19]So that your trust may be in Yahweh,
it is you whom I wish to instruct today.

[20]Have I not written for you thirty chapters
of advice and knowledge,
[21]to make you know the certainty of true sayings,
so that you can return with sound answers to those who sent you?

[22]Do not despoil the weak, for he is weak,
and do not oppress the poor at the gate,
[23]for Yahweh takes up their cause,
and extorts the life of their extortioners.

[24]Do not make friends with one who gives way to anger,
make no one quick-tempered a companion of yours,
[25]for fear you learn such behaviour
and in it find a snare for yourself.

[26]Do not be one of those who go guarantor,
who go surety for debts:
[27]if you have no means of paying
your bed will be taken from under you.

28 Do not displace the ancient boundary-stone[b]
set by your ancestors.

29 You see someone alert at his business?
His aim will be to serve kings;
not for him the service of the obscure.

23 If you take your seat at a great man's table,
take careful note of what you have before you;
2 if you have a big appetite
put a knife to your throat.
3 Do not hanker for his delicacies,
for they are deceptive food.

4 Do not wear yourself out in quest of wealth,
stop applying your mind to this.
5 Fix your gaze on it, and it is there no longer,
for it is able to sprout wings
like an eagle that flies off to the sky.

6 Do not eat the food of anyone whose eye is jealous,
do not hanker for his delicacies.
7 For what he is really thinking about is himself:
'Eat and drink,' he tells you, but his heart is not with you.
8 You will spit out whatever you have eaten
and find your compliments wasted.

9 Do not waste words on a fool,
who will not appreciate the shrewdness of your remarks.

10 Do not displace the ancient boundary-stone,[a]
or encroach on orphans' lands,
11 for they have a powerful avenger,
and he will take up their cause against you.

12 Apply your heart to discipline,
and your ears to instructive sayings.

13 Do not be chary of correcting a child,
a stroke of the cane is not likely to be fatal.
14 Give him a stroke of the cane,
you will save his soul from Sheol.

15 My child, if your heart is wise,
then my own heart is glad,
16 and my inmost self rejoices
when from your lips come honest words.

17 Do not let your heart be envious of sinners
but remain steady every day in the fear of Yahweh;
18 for there is a future,
and your hope will not come to nothing.

19 Listen, my child, and be wise,
and guide your heart in the way.

20 Do not be one of those forever tippling wine
nor one of those who gorge themselves with meat;
21 for the drunkard and glutton impoverish themselves,
and sleepiness is clothed in rags.

22b =23:10.
23a =22:28.

22 Listen to your father from whom you are sprung,
do not despise your mother in her old age.
23 Purchase truth—never sell it—
wisdom, discipline, and discernment.
24 The father of the upright will rejoice indeed,
he who fathers a wise child will have joy of it.
25 Your father and mother will be happy,
and she who bore you joyful.

26 My child, pay attention to me,
let your eyes take pleasure in my way:
27 a prostitute is a deep pit,
a narrow well, the woman who belongs to another.
28 Yes, like a brigand, she lies in wait,
increasing the number of law-breakers.

29 For whom is pity, for whom contempt,
for whom is strife, for whom complaint,
for whom blows struck at random,
for whom the clouded eye?
30 For those who linger over wine too long,
ever on the look-out for the blended liquors.
31 Do not gaze at wine, how red it is,
how it sparkles in the cup!
How smoothly it slips down the throat!
32 In the end its bite is like a serpent's,
its sting as sharp as an adder's.
33 Your eyes will see peculiar things,
you will talk nonsense from your heart.
34 You will be like someone sleeping in mid-ocean,
like one asleep at the mast-head.
35 'Struck me, have they? But I'm not hurt.
Beaten me? I don't feel anything.
When shall I wake up? . .
I'll ask for more of it!'

24 Do not be envious of the wicked
or wish for their company,
2 for their hearts are scheming violence,
their lips talking mischief.

3 By wisdom a house is built,
by understanding it is made strong;
4 by knowledge its storerooms are filled
with riches of every kind, rare and desirable.

5 The wise is mighty in power,
strength is reinforced by science;
6 for it is by strategy that you wage war,
and victory depends on having many counsellors.

7 For a fool wisdom is an inaccessible fortress:
at the city gate he does not open his mouth.

8 Anyone intent on evil-doing
is known as a master in cunning.

9 Folly dreams of nothing but sin,
the mocker is abhorrent.

10 If you lose heart when things go wrong,
your strength is not worth much.

11 Save those being dragged towards death,
but can you rescue those on their way to execution?
12 If you say, 'But look, we did not know,'
will the Weigher of the heart pay no attention?
Will not the Guardian of your soul be aware
and repay you as your deeds deserve?

13 Eat honey, my child, since it is good;
honey that drips from the comb is sweet to the taste:
14 and so, for sure, will wisdom be to your soul:
find it and you will have a future
and your hope will not be cut short.

15 Do not lurk, wicked man, round the upright man's dwelling,
do not despoil his house.
16 For though the upright falls seven times, he gets up again;
the wicked are the ones who stumble in adversity.

17 Should your enemy fall, do not rejoice,
when he stumbles do not let your heart exult:
18 for fear that Yahweh will be displeased at the sight
and turn his anger away from him.

19 Do not be indignant about the wicked,
do not be envious of the evil,
20 for there is no future for the evil,
the lamp of the wicked will go out.

21 Fear Yahweh, my child, and fear the king;
do not ally yourself with innovators;
22 for suddenly disaster will loom for them,
and who knows what ruin will seize them and their friends?

IV: A FURTHER SELECTION FROM THE SAGES

23 The following are also taken from the sages:

To show partiality in judgement is not good.
24 Whoever tells the wicked, 'You are upright,'
peoples curse him, nations revile him;
25 but those who correct him, come out of it well,
on them will come a happy blessing.

26 Whoever returns an honest answer,
plants a kiss on the lips.

27 Plan what you want on the open ground,
make your preparation in the field;
then go and build your house.

28 Do not bear witness lightly against your neighbour,
nor deceive with your lips.

29 Do not say, 'I will treat my neighbour as my neighbour treated me;
I will repay everyone what each has earned.'

30 By the idler's field I was passing,
by the vineyard of a man who had no sense,
31 there it all lay, deep in thorns,
entirely overgrown with weeds,
and its stone wall broken down.
32 And as I gazed I pondered,
I drew this lesson from the sight,
33 'A little sleep, a little drowsiness,
a little folding of the arms to lie back
34 and poverty comes like a vagrant,
and, like a beggar, dearth.'[a]

V: THE SECOND COLLECTION ATTRIBUTED TO SOLOMON

25 Here are some more of Solomon's proverbs, transcribed at the court of Hezekiah king of Judah:

2 To conceal a matter, this is the glory of God,
to sift it thoroughly, the glory of kings.
3 The heavens for height and the earth for depth,
unfathomable, as are the hearts of kings.

4 From silver remove the dross
and it emerges wholly purified;
5 from the king's presence remove the wicked
and on uprightness his throne is founded.

6 In the presence of the king do not give yourself airs,
do not take a place among the great;
7 better to be invited, 'Come up here',
than be humiliated in the presence of the prince.

8 What your eyes have witnessed
do not produce too quickly at the trial,
for what are you to do at the end
should your neighbour confute you?

9 Have the quarrel out with your neighbour,
but do not disclose another's secret,
10 for fear your listener put you to shame,
and the loss of repute be irremediable.

11 Like apples of gold inlaid with silver
is a word that is aptly spoken.
12 A golden ring, an ornament of finest gold,
is a wise rebuke to an attentive ear.

13 The coolness of snow in harvest time,
such is a trustworthy messenger to those who send him:
he revives the soul of his master.

14 Clouds and wind, but no rain:
such is anyone whose promises are princely but never kept.

15 With patience a judge may be cajoled:
a soft tongue breaks bones.

24a =6:10–11.

16 Eat to your satisfaction what honey you may find,
but not to excess or you will bring it up again.

17 Do not set foot too often in your neighbour's house,
for fear the neighbour tire of you and come to hate you.

18 A mace, a sword, a piercing arrow,
such is anyone who bears false witness against a companion.

19 Decaying tooth, lame foot,
such is the fickle when trusted in time of trouble:
20 as well take off your coat in bitter weather.

You are pouring vinegar on a wound
when you sing songs to a sorrowing heart.

21 If your enemy is hungry, give him something to eat;
if thirsty, something to drink.
22 By this you will be heaping red-hot coals on his head,
and Yahweh will reward you.
23 The north wind begets the rain,
and a backbiting tongue, black looks.

24 Better the corner of a roof to live on
than a house shared with a quarrelsome woman.[a]

25 Cold water to a thirsty throat;
such is good news from a distant land.

26 A churned-up spring, a fountain fouled;
such is the upright person trembling before the wicked.

27 It is not good to eat too much honey,
nor to seek for glory on top of glory.

28 An open town, and without defences:
such is anyone who lacks self-control.

26 Snow no more befits the summer, nor rain the harvest-time,
than honours befit a fool.

2 As the sparrow escapes, and the swallow flies away,
so the undeserved curse will never hit its mark.

3 A whip for the horse, a bridle for the donkey,
and for the backs of fools, a stick.

4 Do not answer a fool in the terms of his folly
for fear you grow like him yourself.

5 Answer a fool in the terms of his folly
for fear he imagine himself wise.

6 He wounds himself, he takes violence for his drink,
who sends a message by a fool.

7 Unreliable as the legs of the lame,
so is a proverb in the mouth of fools.

8 As well tie the stone to the sling
as pay honour to a fool.

9 A thorn branch in a drunkard's hand,
such is a proverb in the mouth of fools.

25a =21:9.

10 An archer wounding everyone,
such is he who hires the passing fool and drunkard.

11 As a dog returns to its vomit,
so a fool reverts to his folly.

12 You see someone who thinks himself wise?
More to be hoped for from a fool than from him!

13 'A wild beast on the road!' says the idler,
'a lion in the streets!'

14 The door turns on its hinges,
the idler on his bed.

15 Into the dish the idler dips his hand,
but is too tired to bring it back to his mouth.[a]

16 The idler thinks himself wiser
than seven people who answer with discretion.

17 He takes a stray dog by the ears,
who meddles in someone else's quarrel.

18 Like a madman hurling firebrands,
arrows and death,
19 so is anyone who lies to a companion
and then says, 'Aren't I amusing?'

20 No wood, and the fire goes out;
no slanderer, and quarrelling dies down.

21 Charcoal for live embers, wood for fire,
and the quarrelsome for kindling strife.

22 The words of a slanderer are tasty morsels
that go right down into the belly.[b]

23 Base silver-plate on top of clay:
such are fervent lips and a wicked heart.

24 Whoever hates may hide it in speech,
but deep within lies treachery;
25 do not trust such a person's pretty speeches,
since in the heart lurk seven abominations.
26 Hatred may disguise itself with guile,
to reveal its wickedness later in the assembly.

27 Whoever digs a pit falls into it,
the stone comes back on him that rolls it.

28 The lying tongue hates its victims,
the wheedling mouth causes ruin.

27 Do not congratulate yourself about tomorrow,
since you do not know what today will bring forth.

2 Let someone else sing your praises, but not your own mouth,
a stranger, but not your own lips.

3 Heavy is the stone, weighty is the sand;
heavier than both—a grudge borne by a fool.

26a =19:24.
26b =18:8.

4 Cruel is wrath, overwhelming is anger;
but jealousy, who can withstand that?

5 Better open reproof
than feigned love.

6 Trustworthy are blows from a friend,
deceitful are kisses from a foe.

7 The gorged throat revolts at honey,
the hungry throat finds all bitterness sweet.

8 Like a bird that strays from its nest,
so is anyone who strays away from home.

9 Oil and perfume gladden the heart,
and the sweetness of friendship rather than self-reliance.

10 Do not give up your friend or your father's friend;
when trouble comes, do not go off to your brother's house,
better a near neighbour than a distant brother.

11 Learn to be wise, my child, and gladden my heart,
that I may have an answer for anyone who insults me.

12 The discreet sees danger and takes shelter,
simpletons go ahead and pay the penalty.[a]

13 Take the man's clothes! He has gone surety for a stranger.
Take a pledge from him, for persons unknown.[b]

14 Whoever at dawn loudly blesses his neighbour—
it will be reckoned to him as a curse.

15 The dripping of a gutter on a rainy day
and a quarrelsome woman are alike;
16 whoever can restrain her, can restrain the wind,
and take a firm hold on grease.

17 Iron is sharpened by iron,
one person is sharpened by contact with another.

18 Whoever tends the fig tree eats its figs,
whoever looks after his master will be honoured.

19 As water reflects face back to face,
so one human heart reflects another.

20 Sheol and Perdition are never satisfied,
insatiable, too, are human eyes.

21 A furnace for silver, a foundry for gold:
a person is worth what his reputation is worth.

22 Pound a fool in a mortar,
among grain with a pestle,
his folly will not leave him.

23 Know your flocks' condition well,
take good care of your herds;
24 for riches do not last for ever,
crowns do not hand themselves on from age to age.
25 The grass once gone, the aftergrowth appearing,
the hay gathered in from the mountains,

27a =22:3.
27b =20:16.

26 you should have lambs to clothe you,
goats to buy you a field,
27 goat's milk sufficient to feed you,
to feed your household and provide for your serving girls.

28 The wicked flees when no one is pursuing,
the upright is bold as a lion.

2 A country in revolt throws up many leaders:
with one person wise and experienced, you have stability.

3 The wicked oppresses the weak:
here is a devastating rain—and farewell, bread!

4 Those who forsake the law sing the praises of the wicked,
those who observe the law are angered by them.

5 The wicked do not know what justice means,
those who seek Yahweh understand everything.

6 Better someone poor living an honest life
than someone of devious ways however rich.

7 An intelligent child is one who keeps the Law;
an associate of profligates brings shame on his father.

8 Whoever increases wealth by usury and interest
amasses it for someone else who will bestow it on the poor.

9 Whoever refuses to listen to the Law,
such a one's very prayer is an abomination.

10 Whoever seduces the honest to evil ways
will fall into his own pit.
The blameless are the heirs to happiness.

11 The rich may think himself wise,
but the intelligent poor will unmask him.

12 When the upright triumph, there is great exultation:
when the wicked are in the ascendant, people take cover.[a]

13 No one who conceals his sins will prosper,
whoever confesses and renounces them will find mercy.

14 Blessed the person who is never without fear,
whoever hardens his heart will fall into distress.

15 Like a roaring lion or a springing bear
is a wicked ruler of a powerless people.

16 An unenlightened ruler is rich in rapacity,
one who hates greed will lengthen his days.

17 A man guilty of murder will flee till he reaches his tomb:
let no one halt him!

18 Whoever lives an honest life will be safe,
whoever wavers between two ways falls down in one of them.

19 Whoever works his land shall have bread and to spare,
but no one who chases fantasies has any sense.[b]

28a =28:28.
28b =12:11.

20 A trustworthy person will be overwhelmed with blessings,
but no one who tries to get rich quickly will go unpunished.

21 It is not good to show partiality,
but people will do wrong for a mouthful of bread.

22 The person of greedy eye chases after wealth,
not knowing that want will be the result.

23 Anyone who reproves another
will enjoy more favour in the end than the flatterer.

24 Whoever robs father and mother saying, 'Nothing wrong in that!'
is comrade for a brigand.

25 The covetous provokes disputes,
whoever trusts in Yahweh will prosper.

26 Whoever trusts his own wit is a fool,
anyone whose ways are wise will be safe.

27 No one who gives to the poor will ever go short,
but whoever closes his eyes will have curses in plenty.

28 When the wicked are in the ascendant, people take cover,[c]
but when they perish, the upright multiply.

29 Whoever is stiff-necked under reproof
will be suddenly and irremediably broken.

2 When the upright are on the increase, the people rejoice;
when the wicked are in power, the people groan.

3 The lover of Wisdom makes his father glad,
but the patron of prostitutes fritters his wealth away.

4 A king gives a country stability by justice,
an extortioner brings it to ruin.

5 Whoever flatters his companion
spreads a net for his feet.

6 In the sin of the wicked lies a snare,
but the upright exults and rejoices.

7 The upright understands the cause of the weak,
the wicked has not the wit to understand it.

8 Scoffers set a city in ferment,
but the wise moderate anger.

9 Let someone wise argue with a fool,
anger and good humour alike will be wasted.

10 The bloodthirsty hate the honest,
but the upright seek them out.

11 The fool blurts out every angry feeling,
but the wise subdues and restrains them.

12 When a ruler listens to false reports,
all his ministers will be scoundrels.

13 Poor and oppressor are found together,
Yahweh gives light to the eyes of both.

28c =28:12.

14 The king who judges the weak with equity
sees his throne set firm for ever.

15 The stick and the reprimand bestow wisdom,
a young man left to himself brings shame on his mother.

16 When the wicked are on the increase, sin multiplies,
but the upright will witness their downfall.

17 Correct your child, and he will give you peace of mind;
he will delight your soul.

18 Where there is no vision the people get out of hand;
happy are they who keep the law.

19 Not by words is a slave corrected:
even if he understands, he will take no notice.

20 You see someone too ready of speech?
There is more to be hoped for from a fool!

21 If a slave is pampered from childhood,
he will prove ungrateful in the end.

22 The hot-head provokes disputes,
someone in a rage commits all sorts of sins.

23 Pride brings humiliation,
whoever humbles himself will win honour.

24 To hear the curse and disclose nothing
is to share with the thief and to hate oneself.

25 To be afraid of human beings is a snare,
whoever trusts in Yahweh is secure.

26 Many people seek a ruler's favour,
but the rights of each come from Yahweh.

27 Abhorrent to the upright is the sinful,
abhorrent to the wicked is one whose way is straight.

VI: THE SAYINGS OF AGUR

30 The sayings of Agur son of Jakeh, of Massa.[a] Prophecy of this man for Ithiel, for Ithiel and for Ucal.

2 I am myself the stupidest of people,
bereft of human intelligence,
3 I have not learnt wisdom,
and I lack the knowledge of the holy ones.
4 Who has mounted to the heavens, then come down again?
Who has gathered the wind in the clasp of his hand?
Who has wrapped the waters in his cloak?
Who has set all the ends of the earth firm?
What is his name?
What is his child's name?
Do you know?

30a In northern Arabia, home also of Lemuel (31:1). The wisdom of eastern sages was proverbial.

5 Every word of God is unalloyed,
a shield to those who take refuge in him.
6 To his words make no addition,
lest he reprove you
and account you a liar.

7 Two things I beg of you,
do not grudge me them before I die:
8 keep falsehood and lies far from me,
give me neither poverty nor riches,
grant me only my share of food,
9 for fear that, surrounded by plenty, I should fall away
and say, 'Yahweh—who is Yahweh?'
or else, in destitution, take to stealing
and profane the name of my God.

10 Do not blacken a slave's name to his master,
lest he curse you, and you suffer for it.

11 There is a breed of person that curses his father
and does not bless his mother;
12 a breed that, laying claim to purity,
has not yet been cleansed of its filth;
13 a breed haughty of eye,
with disdain in every glance;
14 a breed with swords for teeth,
with knives for jaws,
devouring the oppressed from the earth
and the needy from the land.

VII: NUMERICAL PROVERBS

15 The leech has two daughters: 'Give! Give!'
There are three insatiable things,
four, indeed, that never say, 'Enough!'
16 Sheol, the barren womb,
earth which can never have its fill of water,
fire which never says, 'Enough!'

17 The eye which looks jeeringly on a father,
and scorns the obedience due to a mother,
will be pecked out by the ravens of the valley,
and eaten by the vultures.

18 There are three things beyond my comprehension,
four, indeed, that I do not understand:
19 the way of an eagle through the skies,
the way of a snake over the rock,
the way of a ship in mid-ocean,
the way of a man with a girl.

20 This is how an adulteress behaves:
she eats, then wipes her mouth and says,
'I have done nothing wrong!'

21 There are three things at which the earth trembles,
four, indeed, which it cannot endure:

22a slave become king,
 a brute gorged with food,
23a hateful woman wed at last,
 a servant girl inheriting from her mistress.

24There are four creatures little on the earth,
 though they are wisest of the wise:
25ants, a race with no strength,
 yet in the summer they make sure of their food;
26the coneys, a race without defences,
 yet they make their home in the rocks;
27locusts, which have no king,
 yet they all march in good order;
28lizards, which you can catch in your hand,
 yet they frequent the palaces of kings.

29There are three things of stately tread,
 four, indeed, of stately walk:
30the lion, bravest of beasts,
 he will draw back from nothing;
31a vigorous cock, a he-goat,
 and the king when he harangues his people.

32If you have been foolish enough to fly into a passion
 and now have second thoughts, lay your hand on your lips.
33For by churning the milk you produce butter,
 by wringing the nose you produce blood,
 and by whipping up anger you produce strife.

VIII: THE SAYINGS OF LEMUEL

31 The sayings of Lemuel king of Massa, taught him by his mother:

2What, my son! What, son of my womb!
 What, son of my vows!
3Do not expend your energy on women
 nor your wealth on those who ruin kings.

4Not for kings, O Lemuel,
 not for kings the drinking of wine,
 not for princes the love of liquor,
5for fear that in liquor they forget what they have decreed
 and pervert the course of justice against all the poor.

6Procure strong drink for someone about to die,
 wine for him whose heart is heavy:
7let him drink and forget his misfortune,
 and remember his misery no more.

8Make your views heard, on behalf of the dumb,
 on behalf of all the unwanted;
9make your views heard, pronounce an upright verdict,
 defend the cause of the poor and the wretched.

IX: THE PERFECT HOUSEWIFE

Aleph 10 The truly capable woman—who can find her?
She is far beyond the price of pearls.

Bet 11 Her husband's heart has confidence in her,
from her he will derive no little profit.

Gimel 12 Advantage and not hurt she brings him
all the days of her life.

Dalet 13 She selects wool and flax,
she does her work with eager hands.

He 14 She is like those merchant vessels,
bringing her food from far away.

Waw 15 She gets up while it is still dark
giving her household their food,
giving orders to her serving girls.

Zain 16 She sets her mind on a field, then she buys it;
with what her hands have earned she plants a vineyard.

Het 17 She puts her back into her work
and shows how strong her arms can be.

Tet 18 She knows that her affairs are going well;
her lamp does not go out at night.

Yod 19 She sets her hands to the distaff,
her fingers grasp the spindle.

Kaph 20 She holds out her hands to the poor,
she opens her arms to the needy.

Lamed 21 Snow may come, she has no fears for her household,
with all her servants warmly clothed.

Mem 22 She makes her own quilts,
she is dressed in fine linen and purple.

Nun 23 Her husband is respected at the city gates,
taking his seat among the elders of the land.

Samek 24 She weaves materials and sells them,
she supplies the merchant with sashes.

Ain 25 She is clothed in strength and dignity,
she can laugh at the day to come.

Pe 26 When she opens her mouth, she does so wisely;
on her tongue is kindly instruction.

Zade 27 She keeps good watch on the conduct of her household,
no bread of idleness for her.

Qoph 28 Her children stand up and proclaim her blessed,
her husband, too, sings her praises:

Resh 29 'Many women have done admirable things,
but you surpass them all!'

Shin 30Charm is deceitful, and beauty empty;
the woman who fears Yahweh is the one to praise.

Taw 31Give her a share in what her hands have worked for,
and let her works tell her praises at the city gates.

THE BOOK OF ECCLESIASTES

The author of this book is puzzled. In his meandering and disorderly quest he repeatedly rejects all solutions based on traditional morality, not without a trace of bitterness. He veers from one extreme to another: at one moment he seems to reject the after-life (3:18), at another to accept it (12:7). Struck by the futility of life, love, work and wealth, he remains dissatisfied, though he still accepts God as creator, ruler and goal of human destiny.

This mentality reflects the disillusionment following the Exile, when the old certainties had perished, and the upsurge of faith and devotion in the Maccabean period had not yet occurred. The identity of the author is unknown. He presents himself as Solomon, the father of Wisdom in Israel, but this is a recognised literary fiction. 'Qoheleth' means only 'man of the Assembly', perhaps its speaker or president. At all events, the book is valuable for its uncomfortable and questioning faith, and its inclusion in the Bible is a reassurance for all who share this attitude.

ECCLESIASTES

1 Composition of Qoheleth son of David,
king in Jerusalem.

PART ONE

Prologue

2Sheer futility, Qoheleth says. Sheer futility:
everything is futile! 3What profit can we show
for all our toil, toiling under the sun? 4A
generation goes, a generation comes, yet the
earth stands firm for ever. 5The sun rises, the
sun sets; then to its place it speeds and there
it rises. 6Southward goes the wind, then turns
to the north; it turns and turns again; then
back to its circling goes the wind. 7Into the
sea go all the rivers, and yet the sea is never
filled, and still to their goal the rivers go. 8All
things are wearisome. No one can say that
eyes have not had enough of seeing, ears their
fill of hearing.

9What was, will be again,
what has been done, will be done again,
and there is nothing new under the sun!

10Take anything which people acclaim as
being new: it existed in the centuries
preceding us. 11No memory remains of the
past, and so it will be for the centuries to
come—they will not be remembered by their
successors.

Life of Solomon

12I, Qoheleth, have reigned over Israel in
Jerusalem. 13Wisely I have applied myself to
investigation and exploration of everything
that happens under heaven. What a weari-
some task God has given humanity to keep
us busy! 14I have seen everything that is done
under the sun: how futile it all is, mere
chasing after the wind!

15What is twisted cannot be straightened,
what is not there cannot be counted.

16I thought to myself: I have acquired a
greater stock of wisdom than anyone before
me in Jerusalem. I myself have mastered
every kind of wisdom and science. 17I have
applied myself to understanding philosophy
and science, stupidity and folly, and I now
realise that all this too is chasing after the
wind.

18Much wisdom, much grief;
the more knowledge, the more sorrow.

2I thought to myself, 'Very well, I will try
pleasure and see what enjoyment has to
offer.' And this was futile too. 2This laughter,
I reflected, is a madness, this pleasure no use
at all. 3I decided to hand my body over to
drinking wine, my mind still guiding me
in wisdom; I resolved to embrace folly, to
discover the best way for people to spend
their days under the sun. 4I worked on a
grand scale: built myself palaces, planted
vineyards; 5made myself gardens and
orchards, planting every kind of fruit tree in
them; 6had pools made for watering the
young trees of my plantations. 7I bought
slaves, male and female, had home-born
slaves as well; herds and flocks I had too,
more than anyone in Jerusalem before me. 8I
amassed silver and gold, the treasures of
kings and provinces; acquired singers, men
and women, and every human luxury, chest
upon chest of it. 9So I grew great, greater
than anyone in Jerusalem before me; nor did
my wisdom leave me. 10I denied my eyes
nothing that they desired, refused my heart
no pleasure, for I found all my hard work a
pleasure, such was the return for all my
efforts. 11I then reflected on all that my hands
had achieved and all the effort I had put into
its achieving. What futility it all was, what
chasing after the wind! There is nothing to
be gained under the sun.

12My reflections then turned to wisdom,
stupidity and folly. For instance, what can
the successor of a king do? What has been
done already. 13More is to be gained from
wisdom than from folly, just as one gains
more from light than from darkness; this, of
course, I see:

14The wise have their eyes open,
the fool walks in the dark.

No doubt! But I know, too, that one fate
awaits them both. 15'Since the fool's fate', I
thought to myself, 'will be my fate too, what
is the point of my having been wise?' I realised
that this too is futile. 16For there is no lasting
memory for the wise or the fool, and in the
days to come both will be forgotten; the wise,
no less than the fool, must die. 17Life I have
come to hate, for what is done under the sun
disgusts me, since all is futility and chasing
after the wind. 18All I have toiled for under
the sun and now bequeath to my successor I
have come to hate; 19who knows whether he
will be wise or a fool? Yet he will be master
of all the work into which I have put my
efforts and wisdom under the sun. That is
futile too. 20I have come to despair of all the
efforts I have expended under the sun. 21For
here is one who has laboured wisely, skilfully
and successfully and must leave what is his
own to someone who has not toiled for it at
all. This is futile too, and grossly unjust; 22for
what does he gain for all the toil and strain
that he has undergone under the sun—23since
his days are full of sorrow, his work is full of
stress and even at night he has no peace of
mind? This is futile too.

24There is no happiness except in eating
and drinking, and in enjoying one's achieve-
ments; and I see that this too comes from
God's hand; 25for who would get anything to
eat or drink, unless all this came from him?
26Wisdom, knowledge and joy, God gives to
those who please him, but on the sinner he
lays the task of gathering and storing up
for someone else who is pleasing to him.
This too is futility and chasing after the
wind.

Death

3 There is a season for everything, a time
for every occupation under heaven:

2 A time for giving birth,
a time for dying;
a time for planting,
a time for uprooting what has been planted.
3 A time for killing,
a time for healing;
a time for knocking down,
a time for building.
4 A time for tears,
a time for laughter;
a time for mourning,
a time for dancing.
5 A time for throwing stones away,
a time for gathering them;
a time for embracing,
a time to refrain from embracing.
6 A time for searching,
a time for losing;
a time for keeping,
a time for discarding.
7 A time for tearing,
a time for sewing;
a time for keeping silent,
a time for speaking.
8 A time for loving,
a time for hating;
a time for war,
a time for peace.

9 What do people gain from the efforts they
make? 10 I contemplate the task that God gives
humanity to labour at. 11 All that he does is
apt for its time; but although he has given us
an awareness of the passage of time, we can
grasp neither the beginning nor the end of
what God does.
12 I know there is no happiness for a human
being except in pleasure and enjoyment
through life. 13 And when we eat and drink
and find happiness in all our achievements,
this is a gift from God.
14 I know that whatever God does will be
for ever.

To this there is nothing to add,
from this there is nothing to subtract,
and the way God acts inspires dread.

15 What is, has been already,
what will be, is already;
God seeks out anyone who is persecuted.

16 Again I observe under the sun:
crime is where justice should be,
the criminal is where the upright
should be.

17 And I think to myself: the upright and
the criminal will both be judged by God,
since there is a time for every thing and every
action here.
18 I think to myself: where human beings
are concerned, this is so that God can test
them and show them that they are animals.
19 For the fate of human and the fate of animal
is the same: as the one dies, so the other dies;
both have the selfsame breath. Human is in
no way better off than animal—since all is
futile.

20 Everything goes to the same place,
everything comes from the dust,
everything returns to the dust.

21 Who knows if the human spirit mounts
upward or if the animal spirit goes downward
to the earth?
22 I see there is no contentment for a human
being except happiness in achievement; such
is the lot of a human beings. No one can tell
us what will happen after we are gone.

Society

4 Then again, I contemplate all the
oppression that is committed under
the sun. Take for instance the tears of the
oppressed. No one to comfort them! The
power their oppressors wield. No one to
comfort them! 2 So, rather than the living
who still have lives to live, I congratulate the
dead who have already met death; 3 happier
than both of these are those who are yet
unborn and have not seen the evil things that
are done under the sun. 4 I see that all effort
and all achievement spring from mutual jeal-
ousy. This too is futility and chasing after the
wind.

5 The fool folds his arms
and eats his own flesh away.

6 Better one hand full of repose
than two hands full of achievements
to chase after the wind.

7 And something else futile I observe under
the sun: 8 a person is quite alone—no child,
no brother; and yet there is no end to his
efforts, his eyes can never have their fill of
riches. For whom, then, do I work so hard
and grudge myself pleasure? This too is
futile, a sorry business.

9 Better two than one alone, since thus their
work is really rewarding. 10 If one should fall,
the other helps him up; but what of the
person with no one to help him up when he
falls? 11 Again: if two sleep together they keep
warm, but how can anyone keep warm alone?
12 Where one alone would be overcome, two
will put up resistance; and a threefold cord
is not quickly broken.

13 Better a youngster poor and wise
than a monarch old and silly
who will no longer take advice—
14 even though stepping from prison
to the throne,
even though born a beggar
in that kingdom.

15 I observe that all who live and move
under the sun support the young newcomer
who takes over. 16 He takes his place at the
head of innumerable subjects; but his
successors will not think the more kindly of
him for that. This too is futile and chasing
after the wind.
17 Watch your step when you go to the
House of God: drawing near to listen is better
than the offering of a sacrifice by fools,
though they do not know that they are doing
wrong.

5 Be in no hurry to speak; do not hastily
declare yourself before God; for God is in
heaven, you on earth. Be sparing, then, of
speech:

2 From too much worrying comes illusion,
from too much talking, the accents of folly.

3 If you make a vow to God, discharge it
without delay, for God has no love for fools.
Discharge your vow. 4 Better a vow unmade
than made and not discharged. 5 Do not allow
your mouth to make a sinner of you, and do
not say to the messenger that it was a mistake.
Why give God occasion to be angry with you
and ruin all the work that you have done?

6 From too many illusions
come futility and too much talk.

Therefore, fear God.
7 If in a province you see the poor
oppressed, fair judgement and justice viol-
ated, do not be surprised, for over every
official there watches a higher official, and
over these, higher officials still. 8 But what
the land yields is for the benefit of all, a king
is served by the fields.

Money

9 No one who loves money ever has enough,
no one who loves luxury has any income;

this, too, is futile.

10 Where goods abound, parasites abound:

where is the owner's profit, apart from
feasting his eyes?
11 The labourer's sleep is sweet, whether he
has eaten little or much, but the surfeit of the
rich will not let him sleep at all.
12 Something grossly unjust I observe
under the sun: riches stored and turning to
loss for their owner. 13 An unlucky venture,
and those riches are lost; a son is born to him,
and he has nothing to leave him. 14 Naked
from his mother's womb he came; as naked
as he came will he depart; not one of his
achievements can he take with him. 15 And
something else grossly unjust: that as he
came, so must he go; what profit can he show
after toiling to earn the wind, 16 as he spends
the rest of his days in darkness, mourning,
many sorrows, sickness and exasperation.
17 So my conclusion is this: true happiness
lies in eating and drinking and enjoying
whatever has been achieved under the sun,
throughout the life given by God: for this is
the lot of humanity. 18 And whenever God
gives someone riches and property, with the
ability to enjoy them and to find contentment
in work, this is a gift from God. 19 For such a
person will hardly notice the passing of time,
so long as God keeps his heart occupied with
joy.

6 I see another evil under the sun, which
goes hard with people: 2 suppose someone
has received from God riches, property,
honours—nothing at all left to wish for; but
God does not give the chance to enjoy them,
and some stranger enjoys them. This is futile,
and grievous suffering too. 3 Or take someone
who has had a hundred children and lived for
many years, and, having reached old age, has
never enjoyed the good things of life and has
not even got a tomb; it seems to me, a still-
born child is happier.

4 In futility it came, into darkness it departs,
and in darkness will its name be buried.

5 It has never so much as seen or known the
sun; all the same, it will rest more easily than
that person, 6 who would never have known
the good things of life, even by living a

thousand years twice over. Do we not all go to the same place in the end?

[7]All toil is for the mouth,
yet the appetite is never satisfied.

[8]What advantage has the wise over the fool?
And what of the pauper
who knows how to behave in society?

[9]Better the object seen
than the sting of desire:
for the latter too is futile
and chasing after the wind.

[10]What has been is already defined—
we know what people are:
They cannot bring to justice
one who is stronger than themselves.

[11]The more we say, the more futile it is:
what good can we derive from it? [12]And who
knows what is best for someone during life,
during the days of futile life which are spent
like a shadow? Who can tell anyone what will
happen after him under the sun?

PART TWO

Prologue

7 Better a good name than costly oil,
the day of death than the day of birth.
[2]Better go to the house of mourning
than to the house of feasting;
for to this end everyone comes,
let the living take this to heart.
[3]Better sadness than laughter:
a joyful heart may be concealed
behind sad looks.
[4]The heart of the wise
is in the house of mourning,
the heart of fools in the house of gaiety.
[5]Better attend to the reprimand of the wise
than listen to a song sung by a fool.
[6]For like the crackling of thorns
under the cauldron
is the laughter of fools:
and that too is futile.
[7]But being oppressed drives a sage mad,
and a present corrupts the heart.

Warnings

[8]Better the end of a matter
than its beginning,
better patience than ambition.

[9]Do not be too easily exasperated, for
exasperation dwells in the heart of fools. [10]Do
not ask why the past was better than the
present, for this is not a question prompted
by wisdom.

[11]Wisdom is as good as a legacy,
profitable to those
who enjoy the light of the sun.
[12]For as money protects, so does wisdom,
and the advantage of knowledge is this:
that wisdom bestows life
on those who possess her.
[13]Consider God's creation:
who, for instance, can straighten
what God has bent?
[14]When things are going well,
enjoy yourself,
and when they are going badly,
consider this:
God has designed the one
no less than the other
so that we should take nothing for granted.
[15]In my futile life, I have seen everything:
the upright person
perishing in uprightness
and the wicked person
surviving in wickedness.
[16]Do not be upright to excess
and do not make yourself unduly wise:
why should you destroy yourself?
[17]Do not be wicked to excess,
and do not be a fool:
why die before your time?
[18]It is wise to hold on to one
and not let go of the other,
since the godfearing will find both.

[19]Wisdom makes the wise stronger than a
dozen governors in a city.

[20]No one on earth is sufficiently upright to
do good without ever sinning.

[21]Again, do not listen to all that people say,
then you will not hear your servant abusing
you.

[22]For often, as you very well know, you
have abused others.

[23]Thanks to wisdom, I have found all this
to be true; I resolved to be wise, but this was
beyond my reach!

24 The past is out of reach,
buried deep—who can discover it?

25 But I have reached the point where,
having learnt, explored and investigated
wisdom and reflection, I recognise evil as
being a form of madness, and folly as some-
thing stupid.

26 And I find woman more bitter than Death,
she is a snare,
her heart is a net, and her arms are chains.
The man who is pleasing to God
eludes her,
but the sinner is captured by her.
27 This is what I think, says Qoheleth,
having examined one thing after another
to draw some conclusion,
28 which I am still looking for,
although unsuccessfully:
one man in a thousand, I may find,
but a woman better than other women—
never.
29 This alone is my conclusion:
God has created man straightforward,
and human artifices are human inventions.

8 Who compares with the sage?
Who else knows how to explain things?
Wisdom lights up the face,
enlivening a grim expression.
2 Obey the king's command and,
because of the divine promise,
3 be in no hurry to depart from it;
do not be obstinate in a bad cause,
since the king will do as he likes
in any case.
4 Since the word of a king is sovereign,
what is the point of saying, 'Why do that?'
5 One who obeys the command
will come to no harm;
the heart of the sage
knows the right moment and verdict,
6 for there is a right moment
and verdict for everything;
but misfortune lies heavy upon anyone
7 who does not know
what the outcome will be,
no one is going to say
how things will turn out.
8 No one can control the wind
and stop it from blowing,
no one can control the day of death.
From war there is no escape,
no more can wickedness save the person
who commits it.

9 I have seen all this to be so, having care-
fully studied everything taking place under
the sun, while one person tyrannises over
another to the former's detriment.
10 And again, I have observed the wicked
carried to their graves, and people leaving
the holy place and, once out in the city,
forgetting how the wicked used to behave;
how futile this is too!
11 Because the sentence on the evil-doer is
not carried out on the instant, people's hearts
are full of desire to do wrong. 12 The sinner
who does wrong a hundred times lives on.
But this too I know, that there is good in
store for people who fear God, because they
fear him, 13 but there is no good in store for
the wicked because he does not fear God, and
so, like a shadow, he will not prolong his
days. 14 Another futile thing that happens on
earth: upright people being treated as though
they were wicked and wicked people being
treated as though they were upright. To me
this is one more example of futility.
15 And therefore I praise joy, since human
happiness lies only in eating and drinking
and in taking pleasure; this comes from what
someone achieves during the days of life that
God gives under the sun.
16 Having applied myself to acquiring
wisdom and to observing the activity taking
place in the world—for day and night our
eyes enjoy no rest— 17 I have scrutinised God's
whole creation: you cannot get to the bottom
of everything taking place under the sun; you
may wear yourself out in the search, but you
will never find it. Not even a sage can get to
the bottom of it, even if he says that he has
done so.

Destiny

9 Yes, I have applied myself to all this and
experienced all this to be so: that is to say,
that the upright and the wise, with their
activities, are in the hands of God.

We do not understand either love or hate,
where we are concerned,
both of them are [2]futile.
And for all of us is reserved
a common fate,
for the upright and for the wicked,
for the good and for the bad;
whether we are ritually pure or not,
whether we offer sacrifice or not:
it is the same for the good
and for the sinner,

for someone who takes a vow,
as for someone who fears to do so.

3This is another evil among those occurring under the sun: that there should be the same fate for everyone. The human heart, however, is full of wickedness; folly lurks in our hearts throughout our lives, until we end among the dead.

4But there is hope for someone
still linked to the rest of the living:
better be a live dog than a dead lion.

5The living are at least aware that they are going to die, but the dead know nothing whatever. No more wages for them, since their memory is forgotten. 6Their love, their hate, their jealousy, have perished long since, and they will never have any further part in what goes on under the sun.

7So, eat your bread in joy,
drink your wine with a glad heart,
since God has already approved
your actions.
8At all times, dress in white
and keep your head well scented.
9Spend your life with the woman you love,
all the days of futile life
God gives you under the sun,
throughout your futile days,
since this is your lot in life
and in the effort you expend
under the sun.
10Whatever work you find to do,
do it with all your might,
for there is neither achievement,
nor planning, nor science,
nor wisdom in Sheol where you are going.
11Another thing I have observed
under the sun:
that the race is not won by the speediest,
nor the battle by the champions;
it is not the wise who get food,
nor the intelligent wealth,
nor the learned favour:
chance and mischance befall them all.
12We do not know when our time will come:
like fish caught in the treacherous net,
like birds caught in the snare,
just so are we all trapped by misfortune
when it suddenly overtakes us.

Wisdom and folly

13Here is another example of the wisdom I have acquired under the sun and it strikes me as important:

14There was once a small town, with only a few inhabitants; a mighty king made war on it, laying siege to it and building great siege-works round it. 15But there was in that town a poverty-stricken sage who by his wisdom saved the town. No one remembered this poor man afterwards. 16So I say:

Wisdom is more effective
than brute force,
but the wisdom of a poor man
is not valued:
no one listens to what he has to say.

17The calm words of the wise make themselves heard above the shouts of someone commanding an army of fools.

18Wisdom is worth more
than weapons of war,
but a single sin undoes a deal of good.

10 One dead fly
can spoil the scent-maker's oil:
a grain of stupidity
outweighs wisdom and glory.

2The sage's heart leads him aright,
the fool's leads him astray.

3A fool walks down the road,
he has no wit—
and everyone remarks,
'How silly he is!'

4If the anger of the ruler rises against you, do not leave your post; composure mitigates grave offences.

5One evil I observe under the sun: the sort of misjudgement to which rulers are prone—
6folly promoted to the top and the rich taking the lowest place. 7I see slaves riding on horses and princes on foot like slaves.

8He who digs a pit falls into it,
he who undermines a wall
gets bitten by a snake,
9he who quarries stones gets hurt by them,
he who chops wood takes a risk from it.

10If, for want of sharpening, the blade is blunt, you have to work twice as hard; but it is the outcome that makes wisdom rewarding.

11If, for want of charming, the snake bites,
the snake-charmer gets nothing out of it.

12The sayings of a sage give pleasure,
what a fool says procures his own ruin:
13his words have their origin in stupidity
and their ending in treacherous folly.

14A fool talks a great deal,
but none of us in fact can tell the future;
what will happen after us, who can tell?

15A fool finds hard work very tiring,
he cannot even find his own way into town.

16Woe to you, country with a lad for king,
and where princes start feasting
in the morning!
17Happy the land whose king is nobly born,
where princes eat at a respectable hour
to keep themselves strong
and not merely to revel!

18Thanks to idleness,
the roof-tree gives way,
thanks to carelessness,
the house lets in the rain.

19We give parties to enjoy ourselves,
wine makes us cheerful
and money has an answer for everything.

20Do not abuse the king, even in thought,
do not abuse a rich man,
even in your bedroom,
for a bird of the air might carry the news,
a winged messenger might repeat
what you have said.

11 Cast your bread on the water,
eventually you will recover it.
2Offer a share to seven or to eight people,
you can never tell what disaster may occur.
3When clouds are full of rain,
they will shed it on the earth.
If a tree falls, whether south or north,
where it falls, there it will lie.
4Keep watching the wind
and you will never sow,
keep staring at the clouds
and you will never reap.
5You do not understand
how the wind blows,
or how the embryo grows
in a woman's womb:
no more can you understand
the work of God, the Creator of all.
6In the morning, sow your seed,
until evening, do not cease from labour,
for of any two things
you do not know which will succeed,
or which of the two is the better.

Old age

7How sweet light is,
how delightful it is to see the sun!
8However many years you live,
enjoy them all,
but remember, the days of darkness
will be many:
futility awaits you at the end.

9Young man, enjoy yourself
while you are young,
make the most of the days of your youth,
follow the prompting and desire
of heart and eye,
but remember, God will call you
to account for everything.
10Rid your heart of indignation,
keep your body clear of suffering,
though youth and the age of black hair
are both futile.

12 Remember your Creator
while you are still young,
before the bad days come,
before the years come which,
you will say, give you no pleasure;
2before the sun and the light grow dim
and the moon and stars,
before the clouds return after the rain;
3the time when your watchmen
become shaky,
when strong men are bent double,
when the women, one by one,
quit grinding,
and, as they look out of the window,
find their sight growing dim.
4When the street-door is kept shut,
when the sound of grinding fades away,
when the first cry of a bird wakes you up,
when all the singing has stopped;
5when going uphill is an ordeal
and you are frightened
at every step you take—
yet the almond tree is in flower
and the grasshopper is weighed down
and the caper-bush loses its tang;
while you are on the way
to your everlasting home
and the mourners are assembling
in the street;
6before the silver thread snaps,
or the golden bowl is cracked,
or the pitcher shattered at the fountain,
or the pulley broken at the well-head:
7the dust returns to the earth
from which it came,
and the spirit returns to God who gave it.

8Sheer futility, Qoheleth says, everything is futile.

Epilogue[a]

[9]Besides being a sage, Qoheleth taught the
people what he himself knew, having
weighed, studied and emended many prov-
erbs. [10]Qoheleth took pains to write in an
attractive style and by it to convey truths.
[11]The sayings of a sage are like goads,
like pegs positioned by shepherds: the same
shepherd finds a use for both.
[12]Furthermore, my child, you must realise
that writing books involves endless hard
work, and that much study wearies the
body.
[13]To sum up the whole matter: fear God
and keep his commandments, for that is the
duty of everyone. [14]For God will call all our
deeds to judgement, all that is hidden, be it
good or bad.

THE SONG OF SONGS

The Song of Songs, that is, the greatest of all songs, is a collection of love lyrics. Traditionally it has long been understood as an allegory of the love of God for his people. But in origin it is surely a collection of purely secular love-songs, celebrating the God-given love of the Lover for his Beloved and of the Beloved for her Lover. Its passionate imagery is sometimes startling, but each image expresses a quality of love.

The origin of the Song may be sought in wedding-festivities, though it is attributed to Solomon as master of song in Israel. It is post-exilic, probably 5th or 4th century, in the tradition of Egyptian and Syrian love-poetry.

THE SONG OF SONGS

TITLE AND PROLOGUE

1 Solomon's Song of Songs.

BELOVED: [2]Let him kiss me with the kisses of his mouth,
for your love-making is sweeter than wine;
[3]delicate is the fragrance of your perfume,
your name is an oil poured out,
and that is why girls love you.

12a Not by the same hand as the rest. Perhaps by a disciple with a similar cast of mind.

FIRST POEM

4 Draw me in your footsteps, let us run.
The king has brought me into his rooms;
you will be our joy and our gladness.
We shall praise your love more than wine;
how right it is to love you.

DIALOGUE OF THE LOVERS

BELOVED: 5 I am black but lovely, daughters of Jerusalem,
like the tents of Kedar,
like the pavilions of Salmah.
6 Take no notice of my dark colouring,
it is the sun that has burnt me.
My mother's sons turned their anger on me,
they made me look after the vineyards.
My own vineyard I had not looked after!

7 Tell me then, sweetheart,
where will you lead your flock to graze,
where will you rest it at noon?
That I may no more wander like a vagabond
beside the flocks of your companions.

CHORUS: 8 If you do not know this, O loveliest of women,
follow the tracks of the flock,
and take your kids to graze
close by the shepherds' tents.

LOVER: 9 I compare you, my love,
to my mare harnessed to Pharaoh's chariot.
10 Your cheeks show fair between their pendants
and your neck within its necklaces.
11 We shall make you golden earrings
and beads of silver.

DUO: 12 —While the king rests in his own room
my nard yields its perfume.
13 My love is a sachet of myrrh
lying between my breasts.
14 My love is a cluster of henna flowers
among the vines of En-Gedi.[a]

15 —How beautiful you are, my beloved,
how beautiful you are!
Your eyes are doves.

16 —How beautiful you are, my love,
and how you delight me!
Our bed is the greensward.

17 —The beams of our house are cedar trees,
its panelling the cypress.

1a A fertile oasis of vines and palms on the desolate west shore of the Dead Sea.

2

[1] —I am the rose of Sharon,
the lily of the valleys.

[2] —As a lily among the thistles,
so is my beloved among girls.

[3] —As an apple tree among the trees of the wood,
so is my love among young men.
In his delightful shade I sit,
and his fruit is sweet to my taste.
[4] He has taken me to his cellar,
and his banner over me is love.
[5] Feed me with raisin cakes,
restore me with apples,
for I am sick with love.

[6] His left arm is under my head,
his right embraces me.

[7] —I charge you,
daughters of Jerusalem,
by all gazelles and wild does,
do not rouse, do not wake my beloved
before she pleases.

SECOND POEM

BELOVED: [8] I hear my love.
See how he comes
leaping on the mountains,
bounding over the hills.
[9] My love is like a gazelle,
like a young stag.

See where he stands
behind our wall.
He looks in at the window,
he peers through the opening.

[10] My love lifts up his voice,
he says to me,
'Come then, my beloved,
my lovely one, come.
[11] For see, winter is past,
the rains are over and gone.

[12] 'Flowers are appearing on the earth.
The season of glad songs has come,
the cooing of the turtledove is heard in our land.
[13] The fig tree is forming its first figs
and the blossoming vines give out their fragrance.
Come then, my beloved,
my lovely one, come.

[14] 'My dove, hiding in the clefts of the rock,
in the coverts of the cliff,
show me your face,

let me hear your voice;
for your voice is sweet
and your face is lovely.'
15 Catch the foxes for us,
the little foxes
that make havoc of the vineyards,
for our vineyards are in fruit.

16 My love is mine and I am his.
He pastures his flock among the lilies.

17 Before the day-breeze rises,
before the shadows flee, return!
Be, my love, like a gazelle, like a young stag,
on the mountains of Bether.

3

1 On my bed at night I sought
the man who is my sweetheart:
I sought but could not find him!
2 So I shall get up and go through the city;
in the streets and in the squares,
I shall seek my sweetheart.
I sought but could not find him!

3 I came upon the watchmen—
those who go on their rounds in the city:
'Have you seen my sweetheart?'

4 Barely had I passed them
when I found my sweetheart.
I caught him, would not let him go,
not till I had brought him
to my mother's house,
to the room where she conceived me!

LOVER: 5 I charge you,
daughters of Jerusalem,
by gazelles and wild does,
do not rouse, do not wake my beloved
before she pleases.

THIRD POEM

POET: 6 What is this coming up from the desert
like a column of smoke,
breathing of myrrh and frankincense
and every exotic perfume?

7 Here comes Solomon's litter.
Around it are sixty champions,
the flower of the warriors of Israel;
8 all of them skilled swordsmen,
expert in war.
Each man has his sword at his side,
against alarms by night.

9 King Solomon

has had a palanquin made
of wood from Lebanon.
10 He has had the posts made of silver,
the canopy of gold,
the seat of purple;
the centre is inlaid with ebony.

11 Daughters of Zion,
come and see King Solomon,
wearing the diadem with which his mother crowned him
on his wedding day,
on the day of his heart's joy.

4 LOVER: 1 How beautiful you are, my beloved,
how beautiful you are!
Your eyes are doves,
behind your veil;
your hair is like a flock of goats
surging down Mount Gilead.
2 Your teeth, a flock of sheep to be shorn
when they come up from the washing.
Each one has its twin,
not one unpaired with another.
3 Your lips are a scarlet thread
and your words enchanting.
Your cheeks, behind your veil,
are halves of pomegranate.
4 Your neck is the Tower of David
built on layers,
hung round with a thousand bucklers,
and each the shield of a hero.
5 Your two breasts are two fawns,
twins of a gazelle,
that feed among the lilies.

6 Before the day-breeze rises,
before the shadows flee,
I shall go to the mountain of myrrh,
to the hill of frankincense.

7 You are wholly beautiful, my beloved,
and without a blemish.

8 Come from Lebanon, my promised bride,
come from Lebanon, come on your way.
Look down from the heights of Amanus,
from the crests of Senir and Hermon,
the haunt of lions,
the mountains of leopards.

9 You ravish my heart,
my sister, my promised bride,
you ravish my heart
with a single one of your glances,
with a single link of your necklace.
10 What spells lie in your love,
my sister, my promised bride!
How delicious is your love, more delicious than wine!

How fragrant your perfumes,
more fragrant than all spices!
11 Your lips, my promised bride,
distil wild honey.
Honey and milk
are under your tongue;
and the scent of your garments
is like the scent of Lebanon.

12 She is a garden enclosed,
my sister, my promised bride;
a garden enclosed,
a sealed fountain.
13 Your shoots form an orchard of pomegranate trees,
bearing most exquisite fruit:
14 nard and saffron,
calamus and cinnamon,
with all the incense-bearing trees;
myrrh and aloes,
with the subtlest odours.
15 Fountain of the garden,
well of living water,
streams flowing down from Lebanon!

BELOVED: 16 Awake, north wind,
come, wind of the south!
Breathe over my garden,
to spread its sweet smell around.
Let my love come into his garden,
let him taste its most exquisite fruits.

5 LOVER: 1 I come into my garden,
my sister, my promised bride,
I pick my myrrh and balsam,
I eat my honey and my honeycomb,
I drink my wine and my milk.

POET: Eat, friends, and drink,
drink deep, my dearest friends.

FOURTH POEM

BELOVED: 2 I sleep, but my heart is awake.
I hear my love knocking.
'Open to me, my sister, my beloved,
my dove, my perfect one,
for my head is wet with dew,
my hair with the drops of night.'

3 —'I have taken off my tunic,
am I to put it on again?
I have washed my feet,
am I to dirty them again?'
4 My love thrust his hand
through the hole in the door;
I trembled to the core of my being.

5 Then I got up
to open to my love,
myrrh ran off my hands,
pure myrrh off my fingers,
on to the handle of the bolt.

6 I opened to my love,
but he had turned and gone.
My soul failed at his flight,
I sought but could not find him,
I called, but he did not answer.

7 The watchmen met me,
those who go on their rounds in the city.
They beat me, they wounded me,
they took my cloak away from me:
those guardians of the ramparts!

8 I charge you,
daughters of Jerusalem,
if you should find my love,
what are you to tell him?
—That I am sick with love!

CHORUS: 9 What makes your lover better than other lovers,
O loveliest of women?
What makes your lover better than other lovers,
to put us under such an oath?

BELOVED: 10 My love is fresh and ruddy,
to be known among ten thousand.
11 His head is golden, purest gold,
his locks are palm fronds
and black as the raven.
12 His eyes are like doves
beside the water-courses,
bathing themselves in milk,
perching on a fountain-rim.
13 His cheeks are beds of spices,
banks sweetly scented.
His lips are lilies,
distilling pure myrrh.
14 His hands are golden, rounded,
set with jewels of Tarshish.
His belly a block of ivory
covered with sapphires.
15 His legs are alabaster columns
set in sockets of pure gold.
His appearance is that of Lebanon,
unrivalled as the cedars.
16 His conversation is sweetness itself,
he is altogether lovable.
Such is my love, such is my friend,
O daughters of Jerusalem.

6

CHORUS: 1 Where did your lover go,
O loveliest of women?
Which way did your lover turn
so that we can help you seek him?

BELOVED: 2 My love went down to his garden,
to the beds of spices,
to pasture his flock on the grass
and gather lilies.

3 I belong to my love, and my love to me.
He pastures his flock among the lilies.

FIFTH POEM

LOVER: 4 You are fair as Tirzah,[a] my beloved,
enchanting as Jerusalem,
formidable as an army!
5 Turn your eyes away from me,
they take me by assault!
Your hair is like a flock of goats
surging down the slopes of Gilead.
6 Your teeth are like a flock of ewes
as they come up from being washed.
Each one has its twin,
not one unpaired with another.
7 Your cheeks, behind your veil,
are halves of pomegranate.

8 There are sixty queens
and eighty concubines
(and countless girls).
9 My dove is my only one,
perfect and mine.
She is the darling of her mother,
the favourite of the one who bore her.
Girls have seen her and proclaimed her blessed,
queens and concubines have sung her praises,
10 'Who is this arising like the dawn,
fair as the moon,
resplendent as the sun,
formidable as an army?'

11 I went down to the nut orchard
to see the fresh shoots in the valley,
to see if the vines were budding
and the pomegranate trees in flower.
12 Before I knew . . . my desire had hurled me
onto the chariots of Amminadib![b]

7 CHORUS: 1 Come back, come back, girl from Shulam,[a]
come back, come back, where we can look at you!
Why are you looking at the girl from Shulam,
dancing between two lines of dancers?

LOVER: 2 How beautiful are your feet in their sandals,
O prince's daughter!

6a Early capital of the northern kingdom. The name means 'agreeable, pleasant'.
6b Perhaps a mythical figure who rides around on a chariot interfering in love-affairs.
7a Obscure; it may also be a name derived from Solomon, 'she who belongs to Solomon'.

The curve of your thighs is like the curve of a necklace,
work of a master hand.
3 Your navel is a bowl well rounded
with no lack of wine,
your belly a heap of wheat
surrounded with lilies.
4 Your two breasts are two fawns,
twins of a gazelle.
5 Your neck is an ivory tower.
Your eyes, the pools of Heshbon,
by the gate of Bath-Rabbim.
Your nose, the Tower of Lebanon,
sentinel facing Damascus.
6 Your head is held high like Carmel,
and its hair is as dark as purple;
a king is held captive in your tresses.

7 How beautiful you are, how charming,
my love, my delight!
8 In stature like the palm tree,
its fruit-clusters your breasts.
9 I have decided, 'I shall climb the palm tree,
I shall seize its clusters of dates!'
May your breasts be clusters of grapes,
your breath sweet-scented as apples,
10 and your palate like sweet wine.

BELOVED: Flowing down the throat of my love,
as it runs on the lips of those who sleep.
11 I belong to my love,
and his desire is for me.

12 Come, my love,
let us go to the fields.
We will spend the night in the villages,
13 and in the early morning we will go to the vineyards.
We will see if the vines are budding,
if their blossoms are opening,
if the pomegranate trees are in flower.
Then I shall give you
the gift of my love.
14 The mandrakes yield their fragrance,
the most exquisite fruits are at our doors;
the new as well as the old,
I have stored them for you, my love.

8 1 Ah, why are you not my brother,
nursed at my mother's breast!
Then if I met you out of doors, I could kiss you
without people thinking ill of me.
2 I should lead you, I should take you into my mother's house,
and you would teach me!
I should give you spiced wine to drink,
juice of my pomegranates.

3 His left arm is under my head
and his right embraces me.

LOVER: 4I charge you,
daughters of Jerusalem,
do not rouse, do not wake my beloved,
before she pleases!

EPILOGUE

5Who is this coming up from the desert
leaning on her lover?

I awakened you under the apple tree,
where your mother conceived you,
where she who bore you conceived you.

BELOVED: 6Set me like a seal on your heart,
like a seal on your arm.
For love is strong as Death,
passion as relentless as Sheol.
The flash of it is a flash of fire,
a flame of Yahweh himself.
7Love no flood can quench,
no torrents drown.
Were a man to offer all his family wealth
to buy love,
contempt is all that he would gain.

APPENDICES

Two epigrams

8Our sister is little: her breasts are not yet
formed. What shall we do for our sister on
the day she is spoken for? 9If she is a rampart,
on the crest we shall build a battlement of
silver; if she is a door, we shall board her up
with planks of cedar.
10I am a wall, and my breasts represent its
towers. And under their eyes I have found
true peace.
11Solomon had a vineyard at Baal-Hamon.
He entrusted it to overseers, and each one
was to pay him the value of its produce, a
thousand shekels of silver. 12But I tend my
own vineyard myself. You, Solomon, may
have your thousand shekels, and those who
oversee its produce their two hundred.

Final additions

13You who dwell in the gardens, my
companions listen for your voice; let me hear
it.
14Haste away, my love,
be like a gazelle,
a young stag,
on the spice-laden mountains.

THE BOOK OF WISDOM

The Book of Wisdom is unique in the Bible as being the product of a Greek frame of mind, for the author is a hellenised Jew, thoroughly familiar with Greek culture, writing probably at Alexandria in about 50 BC.

Against the background of Egyptian worship of animals and mockery of Jewish trust in God, the author devotes much of the first part of the book to the ineffectiveness of such mockery when God has promised immortality to those who remain faithful. Using Greek modes of thought, he is the first to express the hope of after-life in terms of immortality of the individual soul (3:4). In the second section Solomon, the master of Wisdom (to whom authorship of the book is conventionally attributed), speaks in praise of Wisdom. This reaches its high point in the description of Wisdom as God's own power at work in the world. The third section of the book is devoted to a rather flowery history, concentrating chiefly on the ineffective opposition of the Egyptians to God's people at the time of the exodus. Using Jewish legends and other amplification of the biblical account, the author points a contrast between the wonders God worked for Israel and the adverse effect of the same wonders on the Egyptians, stressing constantly the folly of Egyptian worship of animals and idols.

Perhaps the single most important contribution of the book consists in its reflections on Wisdom, and especially the personification of Wisdom as God's agent in the world, yet sharing intimately in his nature (7:22). The ground is prepared for the understanding of Jesus as the incarnate Wisdom of God. It is also valuable to see Judaism beyond the frontiers of Palestine, at grips with the varied worship of the Graeco-Roman world, and to see it developing such ideas as that of the individual as a child of God.

PLAN OF THE BOOK

THE BOOK OF WISDOM

I: WISDOM AND HUMAN DESTINY

On seeking God and rejecting evil

1 Love uprightness you who are rulers on earth,
be properly disposed towards the Lord
and seek him in simplicity of heart;
2 for he will be found by those who do not put him to the test,
revealing himself to those who do not mistrust him.
3 Perverse thoughts, however, separate people from God,
and power, when put to the test, confounds the stupid.
4 Wisdom will never enter the soul of a wrong-doer,
nor dwell in a body enslaved to sin;
5 for the holy spirit of instruction flees deceitfulness,
recoils from unintelligent thoughts,
is thwarted by the onset of vice.

6 Wisdom is a spirit friendly to humanity,
though she will not let a blasphemer's words go unpunished;
since God observes the very soul
and accurately surveys the heart,
listening to every word.
7 For the spirit of the Lord fills the world,
and that which holds everything together knows every word said.
8 No one who speaks what is wrong will go undetected,
nor will avenging Justice pass by such a one.
9 For the schemes of the godless will be examined,
and a report of his words will reach the Lord
to convict him of his crimes.
10 There is a jealous ear that overhears everything,
not even a murmur of complaint escapes it.
11 So beware of uttering frivolous complaints,
restrain your tongue from finding fault;
even what is said in secret has repercussions,
and a lying mouth deals death to the soul.

12 Do not court death by the errors of your ways,
nor invite destruction through the work of your hands.
13 For God did not make Death,
he takes no pleasure in destroying the living.
14 To exist—for this he created all things;
the creatures of the world have health in them,
in them is no fatal poison,
and Hades has no power over the world:
15 for uprightness is immortal.

Life as the godless see it

16 But the godless call for Death with deed and word,
counting him friend, they wear themselves out for him;

with him they make a pact,
worthy as they are to belong to him.

2 And this is the false argument they use,
'Our life is short and dreary,
there is no remedy when our end comes,
no one is known to have come back from Hades.
2 We came into being by chance
and afterwards shall be as though we had never been.
The breath in our nostrils is a puff of smoke,
reason a spark from the beating of our hearts;
3 extinguish this and the body turns to ashes,
and the spirit melts away like the yielding air.
4 In time, our name will be forgotten,
nobody will remember what we have done;
our life will pass away like wisps of cloud,
dissolving like the mist
that the sun's rays drive away
and that its heat dispels.
5 For our days are the passing of a shadow,
our end is without return,
the seal is affixed and nobody comes back.

6 'Come then, let us enjoy the good things of today,
let us use created things with the zest of youth:
7 take our fill of the dearest wines and perfumes,
on no account forgo the flowers of spring
8 but crown ourselves with rosebuds before they wither,
9 no meadow excluded from our orgy;
let us leave the signs of our revelry everywhere,
since this is our portion, this our lot!

10 'As for the upright man who is poor, let us oppress him;
let us not spare the widow,
nor respect old age, white-haired with many years.
11 Let our might be the yardstick of right,
since weakness argues its own futility.
12 Let us lay traps for the upright man, since he annoys us
and opposes our way of life,
reproaches us for our sins against the Law,
and accuses us of sins against our upbringing.
13 He claims to have knowledge of God,
and calls himself a child of the Lord.
14 We see him as a reproof to our way of thinking,
the very sight of him weighs our spirits down;
15 for his kind of life is not like other people's,
and his ways are quite different.
16 In his opinion we are counterfeit;
he avoids our ways as he would filth;
he proclaims the final end of the upright as blessed
and boasts of having God for his father.
17 Let us see if what he says is true,
and test him to see what sort of end he will have.
18 For if the upright man is God's son, God will help him
and rescue him from the clutches of his enemies.
19 Let us test him with cruelty and with torture,
and thus explore this gentleness of his

and put his patience to the test.
20 Let us condemn him to a shameful death
since God will rescue him—or so he claims.'

Error of the godless

21 This is the way they reason, but they are misled,
since their malice makes them blind.
22 They do not know the hidden things of God,
they do not hope for the reward of holiness,
they do not believe in a reward for blameless souls.
23 For God created human beings to be immortal,
he made them as an image of his own nature;
24 Death came into the world only through the Devil's envy,
as those who belong to him find to their cost.

Destinies of the good and bad compared

3 But the souls of the upright are in the hands of God,
and no torment can touch them.
2 To the unenlightened, they appeared to die,
their departure was regarded as disaster,
3 their leaving us like annihilation;
but they are at peace.
4 If, as it seemed to us, they suffered punishment,
their hope was rich with immortality;
5 slight was their correction, great will their blessings be.
God was putting them to the test
and has proved them worthy to be with him;
6 he has tested them like gold in a furnace,
and accepted them as a perfect burnt offering.
7 At their time of visitation, they will shine out;
as sparks run through the stubble, so will they.
8 They will judge nations, rule over peoples,
and the Lord will be their king for ever.
9 Those who trust in him will understand the truth,
those who are faithful will live with him in love;
for grace and mercy await his holy ones,
and he intervenes on behalf of his chosen.

10 But the godless will be duly punished for their reasoning,
for having neglected the upright and deserted the Lord.
11 Yes, wretched are they who scorn wisdom and discipline:
their hope is void,
their toil unavailing,
their achievements unprofitable;
12 their wives are reckless,
their children depraved,
their descendants accursed.

Better be sterile than have godless children

13 Blessed the sterile woman if she be blameless,
and has not known an unlawful bed,
for she will have fruit at the visitation of souls.
14 Blessed, too, the eunuch whose hand commits no crime,

and who harbours no resentment against the Lord:
a special favour will be granted to him for his loyalty,
a most desirable portion in the temple of the Lord.
15 For the fruit of honest labours is glorious,
and the root of understanding does not decay.
16 But the children of adulterers will not reach maturity,
the offspring of an unlawful bed will disappear.
17 Even if they live long, they will count for nothing,
their old age will go unhonoured at the last;
18 while if they die early, they have neither hope
nor comfort on the day of judgement,
19 for the end of a race of evil-doers is harsh.

4 Better to have no children yet to have virtue,
since immortality perpetuates its memory;
for God and human beings both recognise it.
2 Present, we imitate it,
absent, we long for it;
crowned, it holds triumph through eternity,
having striven for untainted prizes and emerged the victor.

3 But the offspring of the godless come to nothing, however prolific,
sprung from a bastard stock, they will never strike deep roots,
never put down firm foundations.
4 They may branch out for a time,
but, on unsteady foundations, they will be rocked by the wind
and uprooted by the force of the storm;
5 their branches, yet unformed, will be snapped off,
their fruit be useless,
too unripe to eat,
fit for nothing.
6 For children begotten of unlawful bed
witness, when put on trial, to their parents' wickedness.

The premature death of the upright

7 The upright, though he die before his time, will find rest.
8 Length of days is not what makes age honourable,
nor number of years the true measure of life;
9 understanding, this is grey hairs,
untarnished life, this is ripe old age.
10 Having won God's favour, he has been loved
and, as he was living among sinners, has been taken away.
11 He has been carried off so that evil may not warp his understanding
or deceitfulness seduce his soul;
12 for the fascination of evil throws good things into the shade,
and the whirlwind of desire corrupts a simple heart.
13 Having come to perfection so soon, he has lived long;
14 his soul being pleasing to the Lord,
he has hurried away from the wickedness around him.

Yet people look on, uncomprehending;
and it does not enter their heads
15 that grace and mercy await his chosen ones
and that he intervenes on behalf of his holy ones.
16 The upright who dies condemns the godless who survive,
and youth quickly perfected condemns the lengthy old age of the wicked.
17 These people see the end of the wise

without understanding what the Lord has in store
or why he has taken such a one to safety;
18 they look on and sneer,
but the Lord will laugh at them.
19 Soon they will be corpses without honour,
objects of horror among the dead for ever.
For he will shatter them and fling them headlong and dumbfounded.
He will shake them from their foundations;
they will be utterly laid waste,
a prey to grief,
and their memory will perish.

The godless called to judgement

20 When the count of their sins has been drawn up, in terror they will come,
and their crimes, confronting them, will accuse them.
5 Then the upright will stand up boldly
to face those who had oppressed him
and had thought so little of his sufferings.
2 And, seeing him, they will be seized with terrible fear,
amazed that he should have been so unexpectedly saved.
3 Stricken with remorse, they will say to one another
with groans and labouring breath,
4 'This is the one whom we used to mock,
making him the butt of our insults, fools that we were!
His life we regarded as madness,
his ending as without honour.
5 How has he come to be counted as one of the children of God
and to have his lot among the holy ones?
6 Clearly we have strayed from the way of truth;
the light of justice has not shone for us,
the sun has not risen for us.
7 We have left no path of lawlessness or ruin unexplored,
we have crossed deserts where there was no track,
but the way of the Lord is one we have never known.
8 What good has arrogance been to us?
What has been the purpose of our riches and boastfulness?
9 All those things have passed like a shadow,
passed like a fleeting rumour.
10 Like a ship that cuts through heaving waves—
leaving no trace to show where it has passed,
no wake from its keel in the waves.
11 Or like a bird flying through the air—
leaving no proof of its passing;
it whips the light air with the stroke of its pinions,
tears it apart in its whirring rush,
drives its way onward with sweeping wing,
and afterwards no sign is seen of its passage.
12 Or like an arrow shot at a mark,
the pierced air closing so quickly on itself,
there is no knowing which way the arrow has passed.
13 So with us: scarcely born, we disappear;
of virtue not a trace have we to show,
we have spent ourselves in our own wickedness!'

14 For the hope of the godless is like chaff carried on the wind,

like fine spray driven by the storm;
it disperses like smoke before the wind,
goes away like the memory of a one-day guest.

Glorious destiny of the upright and punishment of the godless

15 But the upright live for ever,
their recompense is with the Lord,
and the Most High takes care of them.
16 So they will receive the glorious crown
and the diadem of beauty from the Lord's hand;
for he will shelter them with his right hand
and with his arm he will shield them.

17 For armour he will take his jealous love,
he will arm creation to punish his enemies;
18 he will put on justice as a breastplate,
and for helmet wear his forthright judgement;
19 he will take up invincible holiness for shield,
20 of his pitiless wrath he will forge a sword,
and the universe will march with him to fight the reckless.
21 Bolts truly aimed, the shafts of lightning will leap,
and from the clouds, as from a full-drawn bow, fly to their mark;
22 and the catapult will hurl hailstones charged with fury.
The waters of the sea will rage against them,
the rivers engulf them without pity,
23 a mighty gale will rise against them
and winnow them like a hurricane.
Thus wickedness will lay the whole earth waste
and evil-doing bring down the thrones of the mighty.

II: SOLOMON AND THE QUEST FOR WISDOM

Kings should seek Wisdom

6 Listen then, kings, and understand;
rulers of remotest lands, take warning;
2 hear this, you who govern great populations,
taking pride in your hosts of subject nations!
3 For sovereignty is given to you by the Lord
and power by the Most High,
who will himself probe your acts and scrutinise your intentions.

4 If therefore, as servants of his kingdom, you have not ruled justly
nor observed the law,
nor followed the will of God,
5 he will fall on you swiftly and terribly.
On the highly placed a ruthless judgement falls;
6 the lowly are pardoned, out of pity,
but the mighty will be mightily tormented.
7 For the Lord of all does not cower before anyone,
he does not stand in awe of greatness,
since he himself has made small and great
and provides for all alike;
8 but a searching trial awaits those who wield power.

9So, monarchs, my words are meant for you,
so that you may learn wisdom and not fall into error;
10for those who in holiness observe holy things will be adjudged holy,
and, accepting instruction from them, will find their defence in them.
11Set your heart, therefore, on what I have to say,
listen with a will, and you will be instructed.

Wisdom sought is Wisdom found

12Wisdom is brilliant, she never fades.
By those who love her, she is readily seen,
by those who seek her, she is readily found.
13She anticipates those who desire her by making herself known first.
14Whoever gets up early to seek her will have no trouble
but will find her sitting at the door.
15Meditating on her is understanding in its perfect form,
and anyone keeping awake for her will soon be free from care.
16For she herself searches everywhere for those who are worthy of her,
benevolently appearing to them on their ways,
anticipating their every thought.
17For Wisdom begins with the sincere desire for instruction,
care for instruction means loving her,
18loving her means keeping her laws,
attention to her laws guarantees incorruptibility,
19and incorruptibility brings us near to God;
20the desire for Wisdom thus leads to sovereignty.
21If then thrones and sceptres delight you, monarchs of the nations,
honour Wisdom, so that you may reign for ever.

Solomon proposes to describe Wisdom

22What Wisdom is and how she was born, I shall now explain;
I shall hide no mysteries from you,
but shall follow her steps from the outset of her origin,
setting out what we know of her in full light,
without departing from the truth.
23Blighting envy is no companion for me,
for envy has nothing in common with Wisdom.
24In the greatest number of the wise lies the world's salvation,
in a sagacious king the stability of a people.
25Learn, therefore, from my words; the gain will be yours.

Solomon a man like other men

7 I too am mortal like everyone else,
a descendant of the first man formed from the earth.
I was modelled in flesh inside a mother's womb,
2where, for ten months, in blood I acquired substance—
the result of virile seed and pleasure, sleep's companion.
3I too, when I was born, drew in the common air,
I fell on the same ground that bears us all,
and crying was the first sound I made, like everyone else.
4I was nurtured in swaddling clothes, with every care.
5No king has known any other beginning of existence;
6for there is only one way into life, and one way out of it.

Solomon's respect for Wisdom

7 And so I prayed,[a] and understanding was given me;
I entreated, and the spirit of Wisdom came to me.
8 I esteemed her more than sceptres and thrones;
compared with her, I held riches as nothing.
9 I reckoned no precious stone to be her equal,
for compared with her, all gold is a pinch of sand,
and beside her, silver ranks as mud.
10 I loved her more than health or beauty,
preferred her to the light,
since her radiance never sleeps.
11 In her company all good things came to me,
and at her hands incalculable wealth.
12 All these delighted me, since Wisdom brings them,
though I did not then realise that she was their mother.
13 What I learned diligently, I shall pass on liberally,
I shall not conceal how rich she is.
14 For she is to human beings an inexhaustible treasure,
and those who acquire this win God's friendship,
commended to him by the gifts of instruction.

His appeal for divine inspiration

15 May God grant me to speak as he would wish
and conceive thoughts worthy of the gifts I have received,
since he is both guide to Wisdom and director of sages;
16 for we are in his hand, yes, ourselves and our sayings,
and all intellectual and all practical knowledge.
17 He it was who gave me sure knowledge of what exists,
to understand the structure of the world and the action of the elements,
18 the beginning, end and middle of the times,
the alternation of the solstices and the succession of the seasons,
19 the cycles of the year and the position of the stars,
20 the natures of animals and the instincts of wild beasts,
the powers of spirits and human mental processes,
the varieties of plants and the medical properties of roots.
21 And now I understand everything, hidden or visible,
for Wisdom, the designer of all things, has instructed me.

Eulogy of Wisdom

22 For within her is a spirit[b] intelligent, holy,
unique, manifold, subtle,
mobile, incisive, unsullied,
lucid, invulnerable, benevolent, shrewd,
23 irresistible, beneficent, friendly to human beings,
steadfast, dependable, unperturbed,
almighty, all-surveying,
penetrating all intelligent, pure and most subtle spirits.
24 For Wisdom is quicker to move than any motion;
she is so pure, she pervades and permeates all things.
25 She is a breath of the power of God,

7a cf. 1 K 3:4–14.
7b The peak of OT writing on Wisdom (cf. Jb 28; Pr 8:22). The twenty-one qualities show Wisdom originating and participating in God, inseparable from him but working in the world.

pure emanation of the glory of the Almighty;
so nothing impure can find its way into her.
26 For she is a reflection of the eternal light,
untarnished mirror of God's active power,
and image of his goodness.

27 Although she is alone, she can do everything;
herself unchanging, she renews the world,
and, generation after generation, passing into holy souls,
she makes them into God's friends and prophets;
28 for God loves only those who dwell with Wisdom.
29 She is indeed more splendid than the sun,
she outshines all the constellations;
compared with light, she takes first place,
30 for light must yield to night,
but against Wisdom evil cannot prevail.
8 Strongly she reaches from one end of the world to the other
and she governs the whole world for its good.

Solomon's love for Wisdom

2 Wisdom I loved and searched for from my youth;
I resolved to have her as my bride,
I fell in love with her beauty.
3 She enhances her noble birth by sharing God's life,
for the Master of All has always loved her.
4 Indeed, she shares the secrets of God's knowledge,
and she chooses what he will do.
5 If in this life wealth is a desirable possession,
what is more wealthy than Wisdom whose work is everywhere?
6 Or if it be the intellect that is at work,
who, more than she, designs whatever exists?
7 Or if it be uprightness you love,
why, virtues are the fruit of her labours,
since it is she who teaches temperance and prudence,
justice and fortitude;
nothing in life is more useful for human beings.
8 Or if you are eager for wide experience,
she knows the past, she forecasts the future;
she knows how to turn maxims, and solve riddles;
she has foreknowledge of signs and wonders,
and of the unfolding of the ages and the times.

Wisdom indispensable to rulers

9 I therefore determined to take her to share my life,
knowing that she would be my counsellor in prosperity
and comfort me in cares and sorrow.
10 'Thanks to her, I shall be admired by the masses
and honoured, though young, by the elders.
11 I shall be reckoned shrewd as a judge,
and the great will be amazed at me.
12 They will wait on my silences,
and pay attention when I speak;
if I speak at some length, they will lay their hand on their lips.
13 By means of her, immortality will be mine,

I shall leave an everlasting memory to my successors.
14 I shall govern peoples, and nations will be subject to me;
15 at the sound of my name fearsome despots will be afraid;
I shall show myself kind to the people and valiant in battle.

16 'When I go home I shall take my ease with her,
for nothing is bitter in her company,
when life is shared with her there is no pain,
nothing but pleasure and joy.'

Solomon prepares to ask for Wisdom

17 Having meditated on all this,
and having come to the conclusion
that immortality resides in kinship with Wisdom,
18 noble contentment in her friendship,
inexhaustible riches in her activities,
understanding in cultivating her society,
and renown in conversing with her,
I went all ways, seeking how to get her.
19 I was a boy of happy disposition,
I had received a good soul as my lot,
20 or rather, being good, I had entered an undefiled body;
21 but, realising that I could never possess Wisdom unless God gave her to me,
—a sign of intelligence in itself, to know in whose gift she lay—
I prayed to the Lord and entreated him,
and with all my heart I said:

Solomon's prayer [a] for Wisdom

9 'God of our ancestors, Lord of mercy,
who by your word have made the universe,
2 and in your wisdom have fitted human beings
to rule the creatures that you have made,
3 to govern the world in holiness and saving justice
and in honesty of soul to dispense fair judgement,
4 grant me Wisdom, consort of your throne,
and do not reject me from the number of your children.
5 For I am your servant, son of your serving maid,
a feeble man, with little time to live,
with small understanding of justice and the laws.
6 Indeed, were anyone perfect among the sons of men,
if he lacked the Wisdom that comes from you, he would still count for nothing.

7 'You have chosen me to be king over your people,
to be judge of your sons and daughters.
8 You have bidden me build a temple on your holy mountain,
and an altar in the city where you have pitched your tent,
a copy of the holy Tent which you prepared at the beginning.
9 With you is Wisdom, she who knows your works,
she who was present when you made the world;
she understands what is pleasing in your eyes
and what agrees with your commandments.
10 Despatch her from the holy heavens,
send her forth from your throne of glory

9a cf. 1 K 3:6–9.

to help me and to toil with me
and teach me what is pleasing to you;
11 since she knows and understands everything
she will guide me prudently in my actions
and will protect me with her glory.
12 Then all I do will be acceptable,
I shall govern your people justly
and be worthy of my father's throne.

13 'What human being indeed can know the intentions of God?
And who can comprehend the will of the Lord?
14 For the reasoning of mortals is inadequate,
our attitudes of mind unstable;
15 for a perishable body presses down the soul,
and this tent of clay weighs down the mind with its many cares.
16 It is hard enough for us to work out what is on earth,
laborious to know what lies within our reach;
who, then, can discover what is in the heavens?
17 And who could ever have known your will, had you not given Wisdom
and sent your holy Spirit from above?
18 Thus have the paths of those on earth been straightened
and people have been taught what pleases you,
and have been saved, by Wisdom.'

III: WISDOM AT WORK IN HISTORY

From Adam to Moses[a]

10 It was Wisdom who protected the first man to be fashioned,
the father of the world, who had been created all alone,
she it was who rescued him from his fall
2 and gave him the strength to subjugate all things.
3 But when in his wrath a wicked man deserted her,
he perished in his fratricidal fury.

4 When because of him the earth was drowned, it was Wisdom again who saved it,
piloting the upright man on valueless timber.
5 Again, when, concurring in wickedness, the nations had been thrown into confusion,
she singled out the upright man, preserved him blameless before God
and fortified him against pity for his child.
6 She it was who, while the godless perished, saved the upright man
as he fled from the fire raining down on the Five Cities,
7 in witness against whose evil ways
a desolate land still smokes,
where plants bear fruit that never ripens
and where, monument to an unbelieving soul, there stands a pillar of salt.
8 For, by ignoring the path of Wisdom,
not only did they suffer the loss of not knowing the good,
but they left the world a memorial to their folly,
so that their offences could not pass unnoticed.

9 But Wisdom delivered her servants from their ordeals.
10 The upright man, fleeing from the anger of his brother,

10a v. 1 Adam, v. 3 Cain, v. 4 Noah, v. 5 Abraham, v. 6 Lot, v. 10 Jacob, v. 13 Joseph.

was led by her along straight paths.
She showed him the kingdom of God
and taught him the knowledge of holy things.
She brought him success in his labours
and gave him full return for all his efforts;
11 she stood by him against grasping and oppressive men
and she made him rich.
12 She preserved him from his enemies
and saved him from the traps they set for him.
In an arduous struggle she awarded him the prize,
to teach him that piety is stronger than all.

13 She did not forsake the upright man when he was sold,
but snatched him away from sin;
14 she accompanied him down into the pit,
nor did she abandon him in his chains
until she had brought him the sceptre of a kingdom
and authority over his despotic masters,
thus exposing as liars those who had traduced him,
and giving him honour everlasting.

The Exodus

15 It was Wisdom who delivered a holy people,
a blameless race, from a nation of oppressors.
16 She entered the soul of a servant of the Lord,
and withstood fearsome kings with wonders and signs.
17 To the holy people she gave the wages of their labours;
she guided them by a marvellous road,
herself their shelter by day—
and their starlight through the night.
18 She brought them across the Red Sea,
leading them through an immensity of water,
19 whereas she drowned their enemies,
then spat them out from the depths of the abyss.
20 So the upright despoiled the godless;
Lord, they extolled your holy name,
and with one accord praised your protecting hand;
21 for Wisdom opened the mouths of the dumb
and made eloquent the tongues of babes.
11 She made their actions successful, by means of a holy prophet.
2 They journeyed through an unpeopled desert
and pitched their tents in inaccessible places.
3 They stood firm against their enemies, fought off their foes.

First antithesis: miracle of the water

4 On you they called when they were thirsty,
and from the rocky cliff water was given them,
from hard stone a remedy for their thirst.
5 Thus, what had served to punish their enemies
became a benefit for them in their difficulties.
6 Whereas their enemies had only the ever-flowing source
of a river fouled with mingled blood and mud,
7 to punish them for their decree of infanticide,
you gave your people, against all hope, water in abundance,

8once you had shown by the thirst that they were experiencing
how severely you were punishing their enemies.
9From their own ordeals, which were only loving correction,
they realised how an angry sentence was tormenting the godless;
10for you had tested your own as a father admonishes,
but the others you had punished as a pitiless king condemns,
11and, whether far or near, they were equally afflicted.
12For a double sorrow seized on them,
and a groaning at the memory of the past;
13when they learned that the punishments they were receiving
were beneficial to the others, they realised it was the Lord,
14while for the man whom long before they had exposed and later mockingly rebuffed,
they felt only admiration when all was done,
having suffered a thirst so different from that of the upright.

God's forbearance with Egypt

15For their foolish and wicked notions which led them astray
into worshipping mindless reptiles and contemptible beetles,
you sent a horde of mindless animals to punish them
16and to teach them that the agent of sin is the agent of punishment.
17And indeed your all-powerful hand which created
the world from formless matter, did not lack means
to unleash a horde of bears or savage lions on them
18or unknown beasts, newly created, full of rage,
breathing out fire,
or puffing out stinking smoke,
or flashing fearful sparks from their eyes,
19beasts able not only to destroy them, being so savage,
but even to strike them dead by their terrifying appearance.
20However, without these, one breath could have blown them over,
pursued by Justice,
whirled away by the breath of your power.
You, however, ordered all things by measure, number and weight.

This forbearance explained

21For your great power is always at your service,
and who can withstand the might of your arm?
22The whole world, for you, can no more than tip a balance,
like a drop of morning dew falling on the ground.
23Yet you are merciful to all, because you are almighty,
you overlook people's sins, so that they can repent.
24Yes, you love everything that exists,
and nothing that you have made disgusts you,
since, if you had hated something, you would not have made it.
25And how could a thing subsist, had you not willed it?
Or how be preserved, if not called forth by you?
26No, you spare all, since all is yours, Lord, lover of life!
12 For your imperishable spirit is in everything!
2And thus, gradually, you correct those who offend;
you admonish and remind them of how they have sinned,
so that they may abstain from evil and trust in you, Lord.

God's forbearance with Canaan

3 The ancient inhabitants of your holy land
4 you hated for their loathsome practices,
their acts of sorcery, and unholy rites.
5 Those ruthless murderers of children,
those eaters of entrails at feasts of human flesh and of blood,
those initiates of secret brotherhoods,
6 those murderous parents of defenceless beings,
you determined to destroy at our ancestors' hands,
7 so that this land, dearer to you than any other,
might receive a worthy colony of God's children.

8 Even so, since these were human, you treated them leniently,
sending hornets as forerunners of your army,
to exterminate them little by little.
9 Not that you were unable to hand the godless over to the upright in pitched battle
or destroy them at once by savage beasts or one harsh word;
10 but, by carrying out your sentences gradually, you gave them a chance to repent,
although you knew that they were inherently evil,
innately wicked,
11 and fixed in their cast of mind;
for they were a race accursed from the beginning.

This forbearance explained

Nor was it from awe of anyone that you let their sins go unpunished.
12 For who is there to ask, 'What have you done?'
Or who is there to disagree with your sentence?
Who to arraign you for destroying nations which you have created?
Who to confront you by championing the wicked?
13 For there is no god, other than you, who cares for every one,
to whom you have to prove that your sentences have been just.
14 No more could any king or despot challenge you over those whom you have punished.
15 For, being upright yourself, you rule the universe uprightly,
and hold it as incompatible with your power
to condemn anyone who has not deserved to be punished.
16 For your strength is the basis of your saving justice,
and your sovereignty over all makes you lenient to all.
17 You show your strength when people will not believe in your absolute power,
and you confound any insolence in those who do know it.
18 But you, controlling your strength, are mild in judgement, and govern us with great lenience,
for you have only to will, and your power is there.

God's lessons for Israel

19 By acting thus, you have taught your people
that the upright must be kindly to his fellows,
and you have given your children the good hope
that after sins you will grant repentance.
20 For, if with such care and indulgence you have punished
your children's enemies, though doomed to death,
and have given them time and place to be rid of their wickedness,
21 with what exact attention have you not judged your children,
to whose ancestors, by oaths and covenants, you made such generous promises?
22 Thus, you instruct us, when you punish our enemies in moderation,

that we should reflect on your kindness when we judge,
and, when we are judged, we should look for mercy.

Progressive punishment of the Egyptians

23 And this is why people leading foolish and wicked lives
were tortured by you with their own abominations;
24 for they had strayed too far on the paths of error
by taking the vilest and most despicable of animals for gods,
being deluded like silly little children.
25 So, as to children with no sense,
you gave them a sentence making fools of them.
26 Those, however, who would not take warning from a mocking reproof
were soon to endure a sentence worthy of God.
27 The creatures that made them suffer and against which they protested,
those very creatures that they had taken for gods
and by which they were punished they saw in their true light;
and he whom hitherto they had refused to know, they realised was true God.
And this is why the final condemnation fell on them.

Indictment of idolatry: the deification of nature

13 Yes, naturally stupid are all who are unaware of God,
and who, from good things seen, have not been able to discover Him-who-is,
or, by studying the works, have not recognised the Artificer.
2 Fire, however, or wind, or the swift air,
the sphere of the stars, impetuous water, heaven's lamps,
are what they have held to be the gods who govern the world.

3 If, charmed by their beauty, they have taken these for gods,
let them know how much the Master of these excels them,
since he was the very source of beauty that created them.
4 And if they have been impressed by their power and energy,
let them deduce from these how much mightier is he that has formed them,
5 since through the grandeur and beauty of the creatures
we may, by analogy, contemplate their Author.

6 Small blame, however, attaches to them,
for perhaps they go astray
only in their search for God and their eagerness to find him;
7 familiar with his works, they investigate them
and fall victim to appearances, seeing so much beauty.
8 But even so, they have no excuse:
9 if they are capable of acquiring enough knowledge
to be able to investigate the world,
how have they been so slow to find its Master?

The cult of idols

10 But wretched are they, with their hopes set on dead things,
who have given the title of gods to human artefacts,
gold or silver, skilfully worked,
figures of animals,
or useless stone, carved by some hand long ago.

11 Take a woodcutter. He fells a suitable tree,
neatly strips off the bark all over
and then with admirable skill

works the wood into an object useful in daily life.
12 The bits left over from his work
he uses for cooking his food, then eats his fill.
13 There is still a good-for-nothing bit left over,
a gnarled and knotted billet:
he takes it and whittles it with the concentration of his leisure hours,
he shapes it with the skill of experience,
he gives it a human shape
14 or perhaps he makes it into some vile animal,
smears it with ochre, paints its surface red,
coats over all its blemishes.
15 He next makes a worthy home for it,
lets it into the wall, fixes it with an iron clamp.
16 Thus he makes sure that it will not fall down—
being well aware that it cannot help itself,
since it is only an image, and needs to be helped.
17 And yet, if he wishes to pray for his goods, for his marriage, for his children,
he does not blush to harangue this lifeless thing—
for health, he invokes what is weak,
18 for life, he pleads with what is dead,
for help, he goes begging to total inexperience,
for a journey, what cannot even use its feet,
19 for profit, an undertaking, and success in pursuing his craft,
he asks skill from something whose hands have no skill whatever.
14 Or someone else, taking ship to cross the wild waves,
loudly invokes a piece of wood[a] frailer than the vessel that bears him.
2 Agreed, the ship is the product of a craving for gain,
its building embodies the wisdom of the shipwright;
3 but your providence, Father, is what steers it,
you having opened a pathway even through the sea,
and a safe way over the waves,
4 showing that you can save, whatever happens,
so that, even without experience, someone may put to sea.
5 It is not your will that the works of your Wisdom should be sterile,
so people entrust their lives to the smallest piece of wood,
cross the waves on a raft, yet are kept safe and sound.
6 Why, in the beginning, when the proud giants were perishing,
the hope of the world took refuge on a raft
and, steered by your hand, preserved the seed of a new generation
for the ages to come.

7 For blessed is the wood which serves the cause of uprightness
8 but accursed the man-made idol, yes, it and its maker,
he for having made it, and it because, though perishable, it has been called god.
9 For God holds the godless and his godlessness in equal hatred;
10 both work and workman will alike be punished.
11 Hence even the idols of the nations will have a visitation
since, in God's creation, they have become an abomination,
a scandal for human souls,
a snare for the feet of the foolish.

Origin of the cult of idols

12 The idea of making idols was the origin of fornication,
their discovery corrupted life.

14a A ship's figurehead.

13They did not exist at the beginning, they will not exist for ever;
14human vanity brought them into the world,
and a quick end is therefore reserved for them.
15A father afflicted by untimely mourning
has an image made of his child so soon carried off,[b]
and now pays divine honours to what yesterday was only a corpse,
handing on mysteries and ceremonies to his people;
16time passes, the custom hardens and is observed as law.
17Rulers were the ones who ordered that statues should be worshipped:
people who could not honour them in person, because they lived too far away,
would have a portrait made of their distant countenance,
to have an image that they could see of the king whom they honoured;
meaning, by such zeal, to flatter the absent as if he were present.
18Even people who did not know him
were stimulated into spreading his cult by the artist's enthusiasm;
19for the latter, doubtless wishing to please his ruler,
exerted all his skill to surpass the reality,
20and the crowd, attracted by the beauty of the work,
mistook for a god someone whom recently they had honoured as a man.
21And this became a snare for life:
that people, whether enslaved by misfortune or by tyranny,
should have conferred the ineffable Name on sticks and stones.

The consequences of idolatry

22It is not enough, however, for them to have such misconceptions about God;
for, living in the fierce warfare of ignorance,
they call these terrible evils peace.
23With their child-murdering rites, their occult mysteries,
or their frenzied orgies with outlandish customs,
24they no longer retain any purity in their lives or their marriages,
one treacherously murdering another or wronging him by adultery.
25Everywhere a welter of blood and murder, theft and fraud,
corruption, treachery, riot, perjury,
26disturbance of decent people, forgetfulness of favours,
pollution of souls, sins against nature,
disorder in marriage, adultery and debauchery.
27For the worship of idols with no name
is the beginning, cause, and end of every evil.
28For these people either carry their merrymaking to the point of frenzy,
or they prophesy what is not true, or they live wicked lives,
or they perjure themselves without hesitation;
29since they put their trust in lifeless idols
they do not reckon their false oaths can harm them.
30But they will be justly punished for this double crime:
for degrading the concept of God by adhering to idols;
and for wickedly perjuring themselves in contempt for what is holy.
31For it is not the power of the things by which they swear
but the punishment reserved for sinners
that always follows the offences of wicked people.

14b The Gk custom of giving the dead divine rank.

Israel not idolatrous

15 But you, our God, are kind and true,
slow to anger, governing the universe with mercy.
2 Even if we sin, we are yours, since we acknowledge your power,
but we will not sin, knowing we count as yours.
3 To know you is indeed the perfect virtue,
and to know your power is the root of immortality.
4 We have not been duped by inventions of misapplied human skill,
or by the sterile work of painters,
by figures daubed with assorted colours,
5 the sight of which sets fools yearning
and hankering for the lifeless form of an unbreathing image.
6 Lovers of evil and worthy of such hopes
are those who make them, those who want them and those who worship them.

The makers of idols are fools

7 Take a potter, now, laboriously working the soft earth,
shaping each object for us to use.
Out of the self-same clay,
he models vessels intended for a noble use
and those for a contrary purpose, all alike:
but which of these two uses each will have
is for the potter himself to decide.
8 Then—ill-spent effort!—from the same clay he models a futile god,
although so recently made out of earth himself
and shortly to return to what he was taken from,
when asked to give back the soul that has been lent to him.

9 Even so, he does not worry about having to die
or about the shortness of his life,
but strives to outdo the goldsmiths and silversmiths,
imitates the bronzeworkers,
and prides himself on modelling counterfeits.
10 Ashes, his heart;
more vile than earth, his hope;
more wretched than clay, his life!
11 For he has misconceived the One who has modelled him,
who breathed an active soul into him
and inspired a living spirit.
12 What is more, he looks on this life of ours as a kind of game,
and our time here like a fair, full of bargains.
'However foul the means,' he says, 'a man must make a living.'
13 He, more than any other, knows he is sinning,
he who from one earthy stuff makes both brittle pots and idols.

The folly of the Egyptians: their indiscriminate idolatry

14 But most foolish, more pitiable even than the soul of a little child,
are the enemies who once played the tyrant with your people,
15 and have taken all the idols of the heathen for gods;
these can use neither their eyes for seeing
nor their nostrils for breathing the air
nor their ears for hearing
nor the fingers on their hands for handling
nor their feet for walking.

[16]They have been made, you see, by a human being,
modelled by a being whose own breath is borrowed.
No man can model a god to resemble himself;
[17]subject to death, his impious hands can produce
only something dead.
He himself is worthier than the things he worships;
he will at least have lived, but never they.
[18]And they worship even the most loathsome of animals,
worse than the rest in their degree of stupidity,
[19]without a trace of beauty—if that is what is attractive in animals—
and excluded from God's praises and blessing.

Second antithesis: frogs and quails

16 Thus they were appropriately punished by similar creatures
and tormented by swarms of vermin.
[2]In contrast to this punishment, you did your people a kindness
and, to satisfy their sharp appetite,
provided quails—a luscious rarity—for them to eat.
[3]Thus the Egyptians,
at the repulsive sight of the creatures sent against them,
were to find that, though they longed for food,
they had lost their natural appetite;
whereas your own people, after a short privation,
were to have a rare relish for their portion.
[4]Inevitable that relentless want should seize on the former oppressors;
enough for your people to be shown
how their enemies were being tortured.

Third antithesis: locusts and bronze serpent

[5]Even when the fearful rage of wild animals overtook them
and they were perishing from the bites of writhing snakes,
your retribution did not continue to the end.
[6]Affliction struck them briefly, by way of warning,
and they had a saving token[a] to remind them of the commandment of your Law,
[7]for whoever turned to it was saved, not by what he looked at,
but by you, the Saviour of all.
[8]And by such means you proved to our enemies
that you are the one who delivers from every evil;
[9]for them, the bites of locusts and flies proved fatal
and no remedy could be found to save their lives,
since they deserved to be punished by such creatures.

[10]But your children,
not even the fangs of poisonous snakes could bring them down;
for your mercy came to their help and cured them.
[11]One sting—how quickly healed!—
to remind them of your pronouncements
rather than that, by sinking into deep forgetfulness,
they should be cut off from your kindness.
[12]No herb, no poultice cured them,
but your all-healing word, Lord.

[13]Yes, you are the one with power over life and death,

16a The bronze snake, Nb 21:4–9.

bringing to the gates of Hades and back again.
14 A human being out of malice may put to death,
but cannot bring the departed spirit back
or free the soul that Hades has once received.

Fourth antithesis: hail and manna

15 It is not possible to escape your hand.
16 The godless who refused to acknowledge you
were scourged by the strength of your arm,
pursued by no ordinary rains, hail and unrelenting downpours,
and consumed by fire.
17 Even more wonderful, in the water—which quenches all—
the fire[b] raged fiercer than ever;
for the elements fight for the upright.
18 At one moment, the fire would die down,
to avoid consuming the animals sent against the godless
and to make clear to them by that sight, that the sentence of God was pursuing them;
19 at another, in the very heart of the water, it would burn more fiercely than fire
to ruin the produce of a wicked land.
20 How differently with your people! You gave them the food of angels,
from heaven untiringly providing them bread already prepared,
containing every delight, to satisfy every taste.
21 And the substance you gave
showed your sweetness towards your children,
for, conforming to the taste of whoever ate it,
it transformed itself into what each eater wished.
22 Snow and ice endured the fire, without melting;
this was to show them that, to destroy the harvests of their enemies,
fire would burn even in hail and flare in falling rain,
23 whereas, on the other hand, it would even forget its own strength
in the service of feeding the upright.

24 For the creation, being at the service of you, its Creator,
tautens to punish the wicked
and slackens for the benefit of those who trust in you.
25 And this is why, by changing into all things,
it obediently served your all-nourishing bounty,
conforming to the wishes of those who were in need;
26 so that your beloved children, Lord, might learn
that the various crops are not what provide nourishment,
but your word which preserves all who believe in you.
27 For that which fire could not destroy
melted in the heat of a single fleeting sunbeam,
28 to show that, to give you thanks, we must rise before the sun
and meet you at the dawning of the day;
29 whereas the hope of the ungrateful melts like winter frost
and flows away like water running to waste.

Fifth antithesis: darkness and pillar of fire[a]

17 Yes, your judgements are great and impenetrable,
which is why uninstructed souls have gone astray.
2 While the wicked supposed they had a holy nation in their power,

---

16b cf. the lightning of Ex 9:24.
17a cf. Ex 10:21–23. It is here supposed that darkness came on some while light continued for others.

they themselves lay prisoners of the dark, in the fetters of long night,
confined under their own roofs, banished from eternal providence.
3 While they thought to remain unnoticed with their secret sins,
curtained by dark forgetfulness,
they were scattered in fearful dismay,
terrified by apparitions.
4 The hiding place sheltering them could not ward off their fear;
terrifying noises echoed round them;
and gloomy, grim-faced spectres haunted them.
5 No fire had power enough to give them light,
nor could the brightly blazing stars
illuminate that dreadful night.
6 The only light for them was a great, spontaneous blaze—
a fearful sight to see!
And in their terror, once that sight had vanished,
they thought what they had seen more terrible than ever.
7 Their magical illusions were powerless now,
and their claims to intelligence were ignominiously confounded;
8 for those who promised to drive out fears and disorders from sick souls
were now themselves sick with ludicrous fright.
9 Even when there was nothing frightful to scare them,
the vermin creeping past and the hissing of reptiles filled them with panic;
10 they died convulsed with fright,
refusing even to look at empty air, which cannot be eluded anyhow!
11 Wickedness is confessedly very cowardly, and it condemns itself;
under pressure from conscience it always assumes the worst.
12 Fear, indeed, is nothing other
than the failure of the help offered by reason;
13 the less you rely within yourself on this,
the more alarming it is not to know the cause of your suffering.
14 And they, all locked in the same sleep,
while that darkness lasted—which was in fact quite powerless
and had issued from the depths of equally powerless Hades—
15 were now chased by monstrous spectres,
now paralysed by the fainting of their souls;
for a sudden, unexpected terror had attacked them.

16 And thus, whoever it might be that fell there
stayed clamped to the spot in this prison without bars.
17 Whether he was ploughman or shepherd,
or somebody at work in the desert,
he was still overtaken and suffered the inevitable fate,
for all had been bound by the one same chain of darkness.
18 The soughing of the wind,
the tuneful noise of birds in the spreading branches,
the measured beat of water in its powerful course,
the headlong din of rocks cascading down,
19 the unseen course of bounding animals,
the roaring of the most savage of wild beasts,
the echo rebounding from the clefts in the mountains,
all held them paralysed with fear.
20 For the whole world shone with the light of day
and, unhindered, went about its work;
21 over them alone there spread a heavy darkness,
image of the dark that would receive them.
But heavier than the darkness was the burden they were to themselves.

18 For your holy ones, however, there was a very great light.
The Egyptians, who could hear them but not see them,
called them fortunate because they had not suffered too;
2 they thanked them for doing no injury in return for previous wrongs
and asked forgiveness for their past ill-will.
3 In contrast to the darkness, you gave your people a pillar of blazing fire
to guide them on their unknown journey,
a mild sun for their ambitious migration.
4 But well those others deserved to be deprived of light
and imprisoned in darkness,
for they had kept in captivity your children,
by whom the incorruptible light of the Law was to be given to the world.

Sixth antithesis: night of bereavement and night of deliverance

5 As they had resolved to kill the infants of the holy ones,
and as of those exposed only one child had been saved,
you punished them by carrying off their horde of children
and by destroying them all in the wild water.
6 That night had been known in advance to our ancestors,
so that, well knowing him in whom they had put their trust,
they would be sure of his promises.
7 Your people thus were waiting
both for the rescue of the upright and for the ruin of the enemy;
8 for by the very vengeance that you exacted on our adversaries,
you glorified us by calling us to you.
9 So the holy children of the good offered sacrifice in secret
and with one accord enacted this holy law:
that the holy ones should share good things and dangers alike;
and forthwith they chanted the hymns of the ancestors.

10 In echo came the discordant cries of their enemies,
and the pitiful wails of people mourning for their children
could be heard from far away.
11 One and the same punishment had struck slave and master alike,
and now commoner and king had the same sufferings to endure.
12 Struck by the same death, all had innumerable dead.
There were not enough living left to bury them,
for, at one stroke, the flower of their offspring had perished.
13 Those whose spells had made them completely incredulous,
when faced with the destruction of their first-born,
acknowledged this people to be child of God.

14 When peaceful silence lay over all,
and night had run the half of her swift course,
15 down from the heavens, from the royal throne,
leapt your all-powerful Word
like a pitiless warrior into the heart of a land doomed to destruction.
Carrying your unambiguous command like a sharp sword,
16 it stood, and filled the universe with death;
though standing on the earth, it touched the sky.
17 Immediately, dreams and gruesome visions
overwhelmed them with terror,
unexpected fears assailed them.
18 Hurled down, some here, some there, half dead,
they were able to say why they were dying;

[19]for the dreams that had troubled them
had warned them why beforehand,
so that they should not perish without knowing why they were being afflicted.

Threat of annihilation in the desert

[20]Experience of death, however, touched the upright too,
and a great many were struck down in the desert.
But the Retribution did not last long,
[21]for a blameless man hurried to their defence.
Wielding the weapons of his sacred office,
prayer and expiating incense,
he confronted Retribution and put an end to the plague,
thus showing that he was your servant.
[22]He overcame Hostility, not by physical strength,
nor by force of arms;
but by word he prevailed over the Punisher,
by recalling the oaths made to the Fathers, and the covenants.
[23]Already the corpses lay piled in heaps,
when he interposed and beat Retribution back
and cut off its approach to the living.
[24]For the whole world was on his flowing robe,
the glorious names of the Fathers engraved on the four rows of stones,
and your Majesty on the diadem on his head.
[25]From these the Destroyer recoiled, he was afraid of these.
This one experience of Retribution was enough.

Seventh antithesis: the Red Sea

19 But the godless were assailed by merciless anger to the very end,
for he knew beforehand what they would do,
[2]how, after letting his people leave and hastening their departure,
they would change their minds and give chase.
[3]They were actually still conducting their mourning rites
and lamenting at the tombs of their dead,
when another mad scheme came into their heads
and they set out to pursue, as though runaways,
the people whom they had expelled and begged to go.
[4]A well-deserved fate urged them to this extreme
and made them forget what had already happened,
so that they would add to their torments
the one punishment outstanding
[5]and, while your people were experiencing a journey
contrary to all expectations,
would themselves meet an extraordinary death.

[6]For the whole creation, submissive to your commands,
had its very nature re-created,
so that your children should be preserved from harm.
[7]Overshadowing the camp there was the cloud;
where there had been water, dry land was seen to rise;
the Red Sea became an unimpeded way,
the tempestuous waves, a green plain;
[8]sheltered by your hand, the whole nation passed across,
gazing at these amazing prodigies.

9 They were like horses at pasture,
they skipped like lambs,
singing your praises, Lord, their deliverer.
10 For they still remembered the events of their exile,
how the land had bred mosquitoes instead of animals
and the River had disgorged millions of frogs instead of fish.
11 Later they were to see a new way for birds to come into being,
when, goaded by greed, they demanded something tasty,
12 and quails came up out of the sea to satisfy them.

Egypt guiltier than Sodom

13 On the sinners, however, punishments rained down
not without violent thunder as early warning;
and they suffered what their own crimes had justly deserved
since they had shown such bitter hatred to foreigners.
14 Others, indeed, had failed to welcome strangers who came to them,
but the Egyptians had enslaved their own guests and benefactors.
15 The sinners, moreover, will certainly be punished for it,
since they gave the foreigners a hostile welcome;
16 but the latter, having given a festive reception
to people who already shared the same rights as themselves,
later overwhelmed them with terrible labours.
17 Hence they were struck with blindness,
like the sinners at the gate of the upright,
when, yawning darkness all around them,
each had to grope his way through his own door.

A new harmony in nature

18 A new attuning of the elements occurred,
as on a harp the notes may change their rhythm,
though all the while preserving the same tone;
and this is just what happened:
19 land animals became aquatic,
swimming ones took to the land,
20 fire reinforced its strength in water,
and water forgot the power of extinguishing it;
21 flames, on the other hand, did not char the flesh
of delicate animals that ventured into them;
nor did they melt the heavenly food
resembling ice and as easily melted.

Conclusion

22 Yes, Lord, in every way you have made your people great and glorious;
you have never failed to help them at any time or place.

ECCLESIASTICUS

Ben Sira (called 'Ecclesiasticus' in the Gk translation), the wise and perceptive scribe of Jerusalem, writes movingly of the chief loves of his life, the Law and the Temple liturgy; he also shows a touching devotion to the great figures of Israel's past. He gives us a pithy collection of reflections, mostly on worldly wisdom, good behaviour, tact and good sense. But he insists that Wisdom comes from God, mediated through the Law. He always has death, the moment of reckoning, before his eyes, though he gives no clear teaching about the after-life or what the reward for good deeds will be.

The 'Wisdom of Ben Sira' was originally written in Hebr., but, as the foreword says, it was translated into Gk by the author's grandson in 132 BC. It is this translation which is accepted as 'Ecclesiasticus', though sizeable fragments of the original Hebr. text have recently been discovered. Ben Sira wrote about 190/180 BC.

PLAN OF THE BOOK

Translator's Foreword
I A Collection of Maxims 1:1—42:14
II The Glory of God 42:15—50
A In Nature 42:15—43
B In History 44—50
Appendices

NOTE: The numbering of the verses is based on a Latin text which included several additions to the original. In some cases whole verses are missed out in this edition.

ECCLESIASTICUS

TRANSLATOR'S FOREWORD

1The Law, the Prophets, 2and the other writers succeeding them have passed on to us great lessons, 3in consequence of which Israel must be commended for learning and wisdom. 4Furthermore, it is a duty, not only to acquire learning by reading, 5but also, once having acquired it, to make oneself of use to people outside 6by what one can say or write. 7My grandfather Jesus, having long devoted himself to the reading 8of the Law, 9the Prophets 10and other books of the Fathers 11and having become very learned in them, 12himself decided to write something on the subjects of learning and wisdom, 13so that people who wanted to learn might, by themselves accepting these disciplines, 14learn how better to live according to the Law.

15You are therefore asked 16to read this book 17with good will and attention 18and to show indulgence 19in those places where, notwithstanding our efforts at interpretation, we may seem 20to have failed to give an adequate rendering of this or that expression; 21the fact is that there is no equivalent 22for things originally written in Hebrew when it is a question of translating them into another language; 23what is more, 24the Law itself, the Prophets [25]and the other books [26]differ considerably in translation from what appears in the original text.

[27]It was in the thirty-eighth year of the late King Euergetes[a] [28]that, coming to Egypt and spending some time here, [29]and finding life here consistent with a high degree of wisdom, [30]I became convinced of an immediate duty to apply myself in my turn with pains and diligence to the translation of the book that follows; [31]and I spent much time and learning on it [32]in the course of this period, [33]to complete the work and to publish the book [34]for the benefit of those too who, domiciled abroad, wish to study, [35]to reform their behaviour, and to live as the Law requires.

I: A COLLECTION OF MAXIMS

The origin of wisdom

1 All wisdom comes from the Lord,
she is with him for ever.
2 The sands of the sea, the drops of rain,
the days of eternity—who can count them?
3 The height of the sky, the breadth of the earth,
the depth of the abyss—who can explore them?
4 Wisdom was created before everything,
prudent understanding subsists from remotest ages.
6 For whom has the root of wisdom ever been uncovered?
Her resourceful ways, who knows them?
8 One only is wise, terrible indeed,
9 seated on his throne, the Lord.
It was he who created, inspected and weighed her up,
and then poured her out on all his works—
10 as much to each living creature as he chose—
bestowing her on those who love him.

The fear of God

11 The fear of the Lord is glory and pride,
happiness and a crown of joyfulness.
12 The fear of the Lord gladdens the heart,
giving happiness, joy and long life.
13 For those who fear the Lord, all will end well:
on their dying day they will be blessed.
14 The basis of wisdom is to fear the Lord;
she was created with the faithful in their mothers' womb;
15 she has made a home in the human race, an age-old foundation,
and to their descendants will she faithfully cling.
16 The fullness of wisdom is to fear the Lord;
she intoxicates them with her fruits;
17 she fills their entire house with treasures
and their storerooms with her produce.
18 The crown of wisdom is to fear the Lord:
she makes peace and health flourish.
19 The Lord has seen and assessed her,
he has showered down knowledge and intelligence,
he has exalted the renown of those who possess her.

Foreword *a* Ptolemy VII Euergetes Physcon (170–117 BC). So the date is 132 BC.

20 The root of wisdom is to fear the Lord,
and her branches are long life.

Patience and self-control

22 The rage of the wicked cannot put him in the right,
for the weight of his rage is his downfall.
23 A patient person puts up with things until the right time comes:
but his joy will break out in the end.
24 Till the time comes he keeps his thoughts to himself,
and many a lip will affirm how wise he is.

Wisdom and uprightness

25 Wisdom's treasuries contain the maxims of knowledge,
the sinner, however, holds piety in abhorrence.
26 If you desire wisdom, keep the commandments,
and the Lord will bestow it on you.
27 For the fear of the Lord is wisdom and instruction,
and what pleases him is faithfulness and gentleness.
28 Do not stand out against fear of the Lord,
do not practise it with a double heart.
29 Do not act a part in public,
keep watch over your lips.
30 Do not grow too high and mighty, for fear you fall
and cover yourself in disgrace;
for the Lord would then reveal your secrets
and overthrow you before the whole community
for not having practised fear of the Lord
and for having a heart full of deceit.

The fear of God in time of ordeal

2 My child, if you aspire to serve the Lord,
prepare yourself for an ordeal.
2 Be sincere of heart, be steadfast,
and do not be alarmed when disaster comes.
3 Cling to him and do not leave him,
so that you may be honoured at the end of your days.
4 Whatever happens to you, accept it,
and in the uncertainties of your humble state, be patient,
5 since gold is tested in the fire,
and the chosen in the furnace of humiliation.
6 Trust him and he will uphold you,
follow a straight path and hope in him.
7 You who fear the Lord, wait for his mercy;
do not turn aside, for fear you fall.
8 You who fear the Lord, trust him,
and you will not be robbed of your reward.
9 You who fear the Lord, hope for those good gifts of his,
everlasting joy and mercy.
10 Look at the generations of old and see:
who ever trusted in the Lord and was put to shame?
Or who ever, steadfastly fearing him, was forsaken?
Or who ever called to him and was ignored?
11 For the Lord is compassionate and merciful,
he forgives sins and saves in the time of distress.

12 Woe to faint hearts and listless hands,
and to the sinner who treads two paths.
13 Woe to the listless heart that has no faith,
for such will have no protection.
14 Woe to you who have lost the strength to endure;
what will you do at the Lord's visitation?
15 Those who fear the Lord do not disdain his words,
and those who love him keep his ways.
16 Those who fear the Lord do their best to please him,
and those who love him will find satisfaction in the Law.
17 Those who fear the Lord keep their hearts prepared
and humble themselves in his presence.
18 Let us fall into the hands of the Lord, not into any human clutches;
for as his majesty is, so too is his mercy.

Duties towards parents

3 Children, listen to me for I am your father:
do what I tell you, and so be safe;
2 for the Lord honours the father above his children
and upholds the rights of a mother over her sons.
3 Whoever respects a father expiates sins,
4 whoever honours a mother is like someone amassing a fortune.
5 Whoever respects a father will in turn be happy with children,
the day he prays for help, he will be heard.
6 Long life comes to anyone who honours a father,
whoever obeys the Lord makes a mother happy.
7 Such a one serves parents as well as the Lord.
8 Respect your father in deed as well as word,
so that blessing may come on you from him;
9 since a father's blessing makes his children's house firm,
while a mother's curse tears up its foundations.
10 Do not make a boast of disgrace overtaking your father,
your father's disgrace reflects no honour on you;
11 for a person's own honour derives from the respect shown to his father,
and a mother held in dishonour is a reproach to her children.
12 My child, support your father in his old age,
do not grieve him during his life.
13 Even if his mind should fail, show him sympathy,
do not despise him in your health and strength;
14 for kindness to a father will not be forgotten
but will serve as reparation for your sins.
15 On your own day of ordeal God will remember you:
like frost in sunshine, your sins will melt away.
16 Whoever deserts a father is no better than a blasphemer,
and whoever distresses a mother is accursed of the Lord.

Humility

17 My child, be gentle in carrying out your business,
and you will be better loved than a lavish giver.
18 The greater you are, the more humbly you should behave,
and then you will find favour with the Lord;
20 for great though the power of the Lord is,
he accepts the homage of the humble.

21Do not try to understand things that are too difficult for you,
or try to discover what is beyond your powers.
22Concentrate on what has been assigned you,
you have no need to worry over mysteries.
23Do not meddle with matters that are beyond you;
what you have been taught already exceeds the scope of the human mind.
24For many have been misled by their own notions,
wicked presumption having warped their judgement.

Pride

26A stubborn heart will come to a bad end,
and whoever dallies with danger will perish in it.
27A stubborn heart is weighed down with troubles,
the sinner heaps sin on sin.
28For the disease of the proud there is no cure,
since an evil growth has taken root there.
29The heart of the sensible will reflect on parables,
an attentive ear is the sage's dream.

Charity to the poor

30Water puts out a blazing fire,
almsgiving expiates sins.
31Whoever gives favours in return is mindful of the future;
at the moment of falling, such a person will find support.

4 1My child, do not refuse the poor a livelihood,
do not tantalise the needy.
2Do not add to the sufferings of the hungry,
do not bait anyone in distress.
3Do not aggravate a heart already angry,
nor keep the destitute waiting for your alms.
4Do not repulse a hard-pressed beggar,
nor turn your face from the poor.
5Do not avert your eyes from the needy,
give no one occasion to curse you;
6for if someone curses you in distress,
his Maker will give ear to the imprecation.
7Gain the love of the community,
in the presence of the great bow your head.
8To the poor lend an ear,
and courteously return the greeting.
9Save the oppressed from the hand of the oppressor,
and do not be mean-spirited in your judgements.
10Be like a father to the fatherless
and as good as a husband to their mothers.
And you will be like a child to the Most High,
who will love you more than your own mother does.

Wisdom as educator

11Wisdom brings up her own children
and cares for those who seek her.
12Whoever loves her loves life,
those who seek her early will be filled with joy.

13 Whoever possesses her will inherit honour,
and wherever he walks the Lord will bless him.
14 Those who serve her minister to the Holy One,
and the Lord loves those who love her.
15 Whoever obeys her rules the nations,
whoever pays attention to her dwells secure.
16 If he trusts himself to her he will inherit her,
and his descendants will remain in possession of her;
17 for though she takes him at first through winding ways,
bringing fear and faintness on him,
trying him out with her discipline till she can trust him,
and testing him with her ordeals,
18 she then comes back to him on the straight road, makes him happy
and reveals her secrets to him.
19 If he goes astray, however, she abandons him
and leaves him to his own destruction.

Modesty and deference to others

20 Take circumstances into account and beware of evil,
and have no cause to be ashamed of yourself;
21 for there is a shame that leads to sin
and a shame that is honourable and gracious.
22 Do not be too severe on yourself,
do not let shame lead you to ruin.
23 Do not refrain from speaking when it will do good,
and do not hide your wisdom;
24 for your wisdom is made known by what you say,
your erudition by the words you utter.
25 Do not contradict the truth,
rather blush for your own ignorance.
26 Do not be ashamed to confess your sins,
do not struggle against the current of the river.
27 Do not grovel to the foolish,
do not show partiality to the influential.
28 Fight to the death for truth,
and the Lord God will war on your side.
29 Do not be bold of tongue,
yet idle and slack in deed;
30 do not be like a lion at home,
or cowardly towards your servants.
31 Do not let your hands be outstretched to receive,
yet tight-fisted when the time comes to give back.

Wealth and presumption

5 Do not put your confidence in your money
or say, 'With this I am self-sufficient.'
2 Do not be led by your appetites and energy
to follow the passions of your heart.
3 And do not say, 'Who has authority over me?'
for the Lord will certainly give you your deserts.
4 Do not say, 'I have sinned, but what harm has befallen me?'
for the Lord's forbearance is long.
5 Do not be so sure of forgiveness
that you add sin to sin.

6 And do not say, 'His compassion is great,
he will forgive me my many sins';
for with him are both mercy and retribution,
and his anger does not pass from sinners.
7 Do not delay your return to the Lord,
do not put it off day after day;
for suddenly the Lord's wrath will blaze out,
and on the day of punishment you will be utterly destroyed.
8 Do not set your heart on ill-gotten gains,
they will be of no use to you on the day of disaster.

Straightforwardness and self-possession

9 Do not winnow in every wind,
or walk along every by-way
(as the double-talking sinner does).
10 Be steady in your convictions,
and be a person of your word.
11 Be quick to listen,
and deliberate in giving an answer.
12 If you understand the matter, give your neighbour an answer,
if not, keep your hand over your mouth.
13 Both honour and disgrace come from talking,
the tongue is its owner's downfall.
14 Do not get a name for scandal-mongering,
do not set traps with your tongue;
for as shame lies in store for the thief,
so harsh condemnation awaits the deceitful.
15 Avoid offences in great as in small matters,
and do not exchange friendship for enmity,
6 1 for a bad name will earn you shame and reproach,
as happens to the double-talking sinner.
2 Do not get carried aloft on the wings of passion,
for fear your strength tear itself apart like a bull,
3 and you devour your own foliage and destroy your own fruit
and end by making yourself like a piece of dried-up wood.
4 An evil temper destroys the person who has it
and makes him the laughing-stock of his enemies.

Friendship

5 A kindly turn of speech attracts new friends,
a courteous tongue invites many a friendly response.
6 Let your acquaintances be many,
but for advisers choose one out of a thousand.
7 If you want to make a friend, take him on trial,
and do not be in a hurry to trust him;
8 for one kind of friend is so only when it suits him
but will not stand by you in your day of trouble.
9 Another kind of friend will fall out with you
and to your dismay make your quarrel public,
10 and a third kind of friend will share your table,
but not stand by you in your day of trouble:
11 when you are doing well he will be your second self,
ordering your servants about;

12 but, if disaster befalls you, he will recoil from you
and keep out of your way.
13 Keep well clear of your enemies,
and be wary of your friends.
14 A loyal friend is a powerful defence:
whoever finds one has indeed found a treasure.
15 A loyal friend is something beyond price,
there is no measuring his worth.
16 A loyal friend is the elixir of life,
and those who fear the Lord will find one.
17 Whoever fears the Lord makes true friends,
for as a person is, so is his friend too.

Apprenticeship to wisdom

18 My child, from your earliest youth choose instruction,
and till your hair is white you will keep finding wisdom.
19 Like ploughman and sower, cultivate her
and wait for her fine harvest,
for in tilling her you will toil a little while,
but very soon you will be eating her crops.
20 How very harsh she is to the undisciplined!
The senseless does not stay with her for long:
21 she will weigh as heavily on the senseless as a touchstone
and such a person will lose no time in throwing her off;
22 for Wisdom is true to her name,
she is not accessible to many.
23 Listen, my child, and take my advice,
do not reject my counsel:
24 put your feet into her fetters,
and your neck into her collar;
25 offer your shoulder to her burden,
do not be impatient of her bonds;
26 court her with all your soul,
and with all your might keep in her ways;
27 search for her, track her down: she will reveal herself;
once you hold her, do not let her go.
28 For in the end you will find rest in her
and she will take the form of joy for you:
29 her fetters you will find a mighty defence,
her collars, a precious necklace.
30 Her yoke will be a golden ornament,
and her bonds be purple ribbons;
31 you will wear her like a robe of honour,
you will put her on like a crown of joy.
32 If you wish it, my child, you can be taught;
apply yourself, and you will become intelligent.
33 If you love listening, you will learn,
if you pay attention, you will become wise.
34 Attend the gathering of elders;
if there is a wise man there, attach yourself to him.
35 Listen willingly to any discourse coming from God,
do not let wise proverbs escape you.
36 If you see a man of understanding, visit him early,
let your feet wear out his doorstep.

37 Reflect on the injunctions of the Lord,
busy yourself at all times with his commandments.
He will strengthen your mind,
and the wisdom you desire will be granted you.

Miscellaneous advice

7 Do no evil, and evil will not befall you;
2 shun wrong, and it will avoid you.
3 My child, do not sow in the furrows of wickedness,
for fear you have to reap them seven times over.

4 Do not ask the Lord for the highest place,
or the king for a seat of honour.
5 Do not parade your uprightness before the Lord,
or your wisdom before the king.
6 Do not scheme to be appointed judge,
for fear you should not be strong enough to stamp out injustice,
for fear of being swayed by someone influential
and so of risking the loss of your integrity.
7 Do not wrong the general body of citizens
and so lower yourself in popular esteem.
8 Do not be drawn to sin twice over,
for you will not go unpunished even once.
9 Do not say, 'God will be impressed by my numerous offerings;
when I sacrifice to God Most High, he is bound to accept.'

10 Do not be hesitant in prayer;
do not neglect to give alms.

11 Do not laugh at someone who is sad of heart,
for he who brings low can lift up high.

12 Do not make up lies against your brother,
nor against a friend either.
13 Mind you tell no lies,
for no good can come of it.

14 Do not talk too much at the gathering of elders,
and do not repeat yourself at your prayers.

15 Do not shirk tiring jobs
or farm work, ordained by the Most High.

16 Do not swell the ranks of sinners,
remember that the retribution will not delay.
17 Be very humble,
since the recompense for the godless is fire and worms.

18 Do not barter a friend away for the sake of profit,
nor a true brother for the gold of Ophir.
19 Do not turn against a wise and good wife;
her gracious presence is worth more than gold.
20 Do not ill-treat a slave who is an honest worker,
or a wage-earner who is devoted to you.
21 Love an intelligent slave with all your heart,
and do not deny such a slave his freedom.

Children

22 Have you cattle? Look after them;
if they are making you a profit, keep them.
23 Have you children? Educate them,
from childhood make them bow the neck.
24 Have you daughters? Take care of their bodies,
but do not be over-indulgent.
25 Marry a daughter off, and you have finished a great work;
but give her to a man of sense.
26 Have you a wife to your liking? Do not turn her out;
but if you do not love her, never trust her.

Parents

27 With all your heart honour your father,
never forget the birthpangs of your mother.
28 Remember that you owe your birth to them;
how can you repay them for what they have done for you?

Priests

29 With all your soul, fear the Lord
and revere his priests.
30 With all your might love him who made you,
and do not abandon his ministers.
31 Fear the Lord and honour the priest
and give him the portion enjoined on you:
first-fruits, sacrifice of reparation, shoulder-gift,
sanctification sacrifice, first-fruits of the holy things.

The poor and afflicted

32 And also give generously to the poor,
so that your blessing may lack nothing.
33 Let your generosity extend to all the living,
do not withhold it even from the dead.
34 Do not turn your back on those who weep,
but share the grief of the grief-stricken.
35 Do not shrink from visiting the sick;
in this way you will make yourself loved.
36 In everything you do, remember your end,
and you will never sin.

Prudence and commonsense

8 Do not try conclusions with anyone influential,
in case you later fall into his clutches.
2 Do not quarrel with anyone rich,
in case he puts his weight against you;
for gold has destroyed many,
and has swayed the hearts of kings.
3 Do not argue with anyone argumentative,
do not pile wood on that fire.

4 Do not joke with anyone uncouth,
for fear of hearing your ancestors insulted.

5 Do not revile a repentant sinner;
remember that we all are guilty.
6 Do not despise anyone in old age;
after all, some of us too are growing old.
7 Do not gloat over anyone's death;
remember that we all have to die.

Tradition

8 Do not scorn the discourse of the wise,
but make yourself familiar with their maxims,
since from these you will learn the theory
and the art of serving the great.
9 Do not dismiss what the old people have to say,
for they too were taught by their parents;
from them you will learn how to think,
and the art of the timely answer.

Prudence

10 Do not kindle the coals of the sinner,
in case you scorch yourself in his blaze.
11 Refuse to be provoked by the insolent,
for fear that such a one try to trap you in your words.

12 Do not lend to anyone who is stronger than you are—
if you do lend, resign yourself to loss.

13 Do not stand surety beyond your means;
if you do stand surety, be prepared to pay up.

14 Do not go to law with a judge,
since judgement will be given in his favour.

15 Do not go travelling with a rash man,
for fear he becomes burdensome to you;
he will act as the whim takes him,
and you will both be ruined by his folly.
16 Do not argue with a quick-tempered man,
do not go with him where there are no other people,
since blood counts for nothing in his eyes,
and where no help is to be had, he will strike you down.

17 Do not ask a fool for advice,
since a fool will not be able to keep a confidence.
18 In a stranger's presence do nothing that should be kept secret,
since you cannot tell what use the stranger will make of it.
19 Do not open your heart to all comers,
nor lay claim to their good offices.

Women

9 Do not be jealous of the wife you love,
do not teach her lessons in how to harm you.
2 Do not put yourself in a woman's hands
or she may come to dominate you completely.

3 Do not keep company with a prostitute,
in case you get entangled in her snares.
4 Do not dally with a singing girl,
in case you get caught by her wiles.
5 Do not stare at a pretty girl,
in case you and she incur the same punishment.
6 Do not give your heart to whores,
or you will ruin your inheritance.
7 Keep your eyes to yourself in the streets of a town,
do not prowl about its unfrequented quarters.
8 Turn your eyes away from a handsome woman,
do not stare at a beauty belonging to someone else.
Because of a woman's beauty, many have been undone;
this makes passion flare up like a fire.
9 Never sit down with a married woman,
or sit at table with her drinking wine,
in case you let your heart succumb to her
and you lose all self-control and slide to disaster.

Relations with people

10 Do not desert an old friend;
the new one will not be his match.
New friend, new wine;
when it grows old, you drink it with pleasure.

11 Do not envy the sinner his success;
you do not know how that will end.
12 Do not take pleasure in what pleases the godless;
remember they will not go unpunished here below.

13 Keep your distance from the man who has the power to put to death,
and you will not be haunted by the fear of dying.
If you do approach him, make no false move,
or he may take your life.
Realise that you are treading among trip-lines,
that you are strolling on the battlements.

14 Cultivate your neighbours to the best of your ability,
and consult with the wise.
15 For conversation seek the intelligent,
let all your discussions bear on the law of the Most High.
16 Have the upright for your table companions,
and let your pride be in fearing the Lord.

17 Work from skilled hands will earn its praise,
but a leader of the people must be skilful in words.
18 A chatterbox is a terror to his town,
a loose talker is detested.

Government

10 A sagacious ruler educates his people,
and he makes his subjects understand order.
2 As the magistrate is, so will his officials be,
as the governor is, so will be the inhabitants of his city.
3 An undisciplined king will be the ruin of his people,
a city owes its prosperity to the intelligence of its leading men.

4 The government of the earth is in the hands of the Lord,
he sets the right leader over it at the right time.
5 Human success is in the hands of the Lord.
He invests the scribe with honour.

Against pride

6 Do not resent your neighbour's every offence,
and never act in a fit of passion.
7 Pride is hateful to God and humanity,
and injustice is abhorrent to both.
8 Sovereignty passes from nation to nation
because of injustice, arrogance and money.
9 What has dust and ashes to pride itself on?
Even in life its entrails are repellent.
10 A long illness makes a fool of the doctor;
a king today is a corpse tomorrow.
11 For in death the portion of all alike will be
insects, wild animals and worms.
12 The first stage of pride is to desert the Lord
and to turn one's heart away from one's Maker.
13 Since the first stage of pride is sin,
whoever clings to it will pour forth filth.
This is why the Lord inflicts unexpected punishments
on such people, utterly destroying them.
14 The Lord has turned mighty princes off their thrones
and seated the humble there instead.
15 The Lord has plucked up the proud by the roots,
and planted the lowly in their place.
16 The Lord has overthrown the lands of the nations
and destroyed them to the very foundations of the earth.
17 Sometimes he has taken them away and destroyed them,
and blotted out their memory from the earth.
18 Pride was not created for human beings,
nor furious rage for those born of woman.

Persons deserving honour

19 What race deserves honour? The human race.
What race deserves honour? Those who fear the Lord.
What race deserves contempt? The human race.
What race deserves contempt? Those who break the Law.
20 A leader is honoured by his brothers,
and those who fear the Lord are honoured by him.
22 The rich, the noble, the poor,
let them pride themselves on fearing the Lord.
23 It is not right to despise one who is poor but intelligent,
and it is not good to honour one who is a sinner.
24 Magnate, magistrate, potentate, all are to be honoured,
but none is greater than the one who fears the Lord.
25 A wise slave will have free men waiting on him,
and the enlightened will not complain.

Frankness and humility

26 Do not try to be smart when you do your work,
do not put on airs when you are in difficulties.
27 Better the hardworking who has plenty of everything,
than the pretentious at a loss for a meal.
28 My child, be modest in your self-esteem,
and value yourself at your proper worth.
29 Who can justify one who inflicts injuries on himself,
or respect one who is full of self-contempt?
30 The poor is honoured for wit,
and the rich for wealth.
31 Honoured in poverty, how much the more in wealth!
Dishonoured in wealth, how much the more in poverty!

The deceptiveness of appearances

11 Wisdom enables the poor to stand erect,
and gives to the poor a place with the great.

2 Do not praise anyone for good looks,
nor dislike anyone for mere appearance.

3 Small among winged creatures is the bee
but her produce is the sweetest of the sweet.

4 Do not grow proud when people honour you;
for the works of the Lord are wonderful
but hidden from human beings.

5 Many monarchs have been made to sit on the ground,
and the person nobody thought of has worn the crown.
6 Many influential people have been utterly disgraced,
and prominent people have fallen into the power of others.

Deliberation and reflection

7 Do not find fault before making thorough enquiry;
first reflect, then give a reprimand.
8 Listen before you answer,
and do not interrupt a speech before it is finished.

9 Do not wrangle about something that does not concern you,
do not interfere in the quarrels of sinners.

10 My child, do not take on a great amount of business;
if you multiply your interests, you are bound to suffer for it;
hurry as fast as you can, yet you will never arrive,
nor will you escape by running away.
11 Some people work very hard at top speed,
only to find themselves falling further behind.

Trust in God alone

12 Or there is the slow kind of person, needing help,
poor in possessions and rich in poverty;
and the Lord turns a favourable eye on him,
lifts him out of his wretched condition,

13 and enables him to hold his head high,
thus causing general astonishment.
14 Good and bad, life and death,
poverty and wealth, all come from the Lord.
17 To the devout the Lord's gift remains constant,
and his favour will be there to lead them for ever.
18 Others grow rich by pinching and scraping,
and here is the reward they receive for it:
19 although they say, 'Now I can sit back
and enjoy the benefit of what I have got,'
they do not know how long this will last;
they will have to leave their goods to others and die.
20 Stick to your job, work hard at it
and grow old at your work.
21 Do not admire the achievements of sinners,
trust the Lord and mind your own business;
since it is a trifle in the eyes of the Lord,
in a moment, suddenly to make the poor rich.
22 The blessing of the Lord is the reward of the devout,
in a moment God brings his blessing to flower.
23 Do not say, 'What are my needs,
how much shall I have in the future?'
24 And do not say, 'I am self-sufficient,
what disaster can affect me now?'
25 In prosperous times, disasters are forgotten
and in times of disaster, no one remembers prosperity.
26 Yet it is a trifle for the Lord on the day someone dies
to repay him as his conduct deserves.
27 A moment's adversity, and pleasures are forgotten;
in a person's last hour his deeds will stand revealed.
28 Call no one fortunate before his death;
it is by his end that someone will be known.

Distrust the wicked

29 Do not bring everyone home with you,
for many are the traps of the crafty.
30 Like a captive partridge in a cage, so is the heart of the proud:
like a spy he watches for your downfall,
31 ever on the look-out, turning good into bad
and finding fault with what is praiseworthy.
32 A hearthful of glowing coals starts from a single spark,
and the sinner lurks for the chance to spill blood.
33 Beware of a scoundrel and his evil contrivances,
in case he puts a smear on you for ever.
34 Give a home to a stranger and he will start trouble
and estrange you from your own family.

Rules for doing good

12 If you mean to do a kindness, choose the right person,
then your good deeds will not be wasted.
2 Do good to someone devout, and you will be rewarded,
if not by that person, then certainly by the Most High.
3 No good will come to one who persists in evil,
or who refuses to give alms.

4Give to the devout,
do not go to the help of a sinner.
5Do good to the humble,
give nothing to the godless.
Refuse him bread, do not give him any,
it might make him stronger than you are;
then you would be repaid evil twice over
for all the good you had done him.
6For the Most High himself detests sinners,
and will repay the wicked with what they deserve.
7Give to the good,
and do not go to the help of a sinner.

True and false friends

8In prosperity you cannot always tell a true friend,
but in adversity you cannot mistake an enemy.
9When someone is doing well that person's enemies are sad,
when someone is doing badly, even a friend will keep at a distance.
10Do not ever trust an enemy;
as bronze tarnishes, so does an enemy's malice.
11Even if he behaves humbly and comes bowing and scraping,
maintain your reserve and be on your guard against him.
Behave towards him as if you were polishing a mirror,
you will find that his tarnish cannot last.
12Do not stand him beside you
in case he thrusts you out and takes your place.
Do not seat him on your right,
or he will be after your position,
and then you will remember what I have said
and sadly admit that I was right.
13Who feels sorry for a snake-charmer bitten by a snake,
or for those who take risks with savage animals?—
14just so for one who consorts with a sinner,
and becomes an accomplice in his sins.
15He will stay with you for a while,
but if you once give way he will press his advantage.
16An enemy may have sweetness on his lips,
and in his heart a scheme to throw you into the ditch.
An enemy may have tears in his eyes,
but if he gets a chance there can never be too much blood for him.
17If you meet with misfortune, you will find him there before you,
and, pretending to help you, he will trip you up.
18He will wag his head and clap his hands,
he will whisper a lot and his expression will change.

Mix with your equals

13 Whoever touches pitch will be defiled,
and anyone who associates with the proud will come
to be like them.
2Do not try to carry a burden too heavy for you,
do not associate with someone more powerful and wealthy than yourself.
Why put the clay pot next to the iron cauldron?
It will only break when they bang against each other.

3 The rich does wrong and takes a high line;
the poor is wronged and has to beg for pardon.
4 If you are useful the rich will exploit you,
if you go bankrupt he will desert you.
5 Are you well off?—he will live with you,
he will clean you out without a single qualm.
6 Does he need you?—he will hoodwink you,
smile at you and raise your hopes;
he will speak politely to you
and say, 'Is there anything you need?'
7 He will make you feel small at his dinner parties
and, having cleaned you out two or three times over,
will end by laughing at you.
Afterwards, when he sees you, he will avoid you
and shake his head about you.

8 Take care you are not hoodwinked
and thus humiliated through your own stupidity.
9 When an influential person invites you, show reluctance,
and he will press his invitation all the more.
10 Do not thrust yourself forward, in case you are pushed aside,
but do not stand aloof, or you will be overlooked.
11 Do not affect to treat him as an equal,
do not trust his flow of words;
since all this talking is expressly meant to test you,
under cover of geniality he will be weighing you up.

12 Pitiless is anyone who retails gossip;
he will not spare you either blows or chains.
13 Be wary, take very great care,
because you are walking with your own downfall.

15 Every living thing loves its own sort,
and every man his fellow.
16 Every creature mixes with its kind,
and human beings stick to their own sort.
17 How can wolf and lamb agree?—
Just so with sinner and devout.
18 What peace can there be between hyena and dog?
And what peace between rich and poor?
19 Wild desert donkeys are the prey of lions;
so too, the poor is the quarry of the rich.
20 The proud thinks humility abhorrent;
so too, the rich abominates the poor.
21 When the rich stumbles he is supported by friends;
when the poor falls, his friends push him away.
22 When the rich slips, there are many hands to catch him,
if he talks nonsense he is congratulated.
The poor slips, and is blamed for it,
he may talk good sense, but no room is made for him.
23 The rich speaks and everyone stops talking,
and then they praise his discourse to the skies.
The poor speaks and people say, 'Who is this?'
and if he stumbles, they trip him up yet more.

24 Wealth is good where there is no sin,
poverty is evil, the godless say.

25 The heart moulds a person's expression
whether for better or worse.
26 Happy heart, cheerful expression;
but wearisome work, inventing proverbs.

True happiness

14 Blessed is anyone who has not sinned in speech
and who needs feel no remorse for sins.
2 Blessed is anyone whose conscience brings no reproach
and who has never given up hope.

Envy and greed

3 Wealth is not the right thing for the niggardly,
and what use are possessions to the covetous?
4 Whoever hoards by stinting himself is hoarding for others,
and others will live sumptuously on his riches.

5 If someone is mean to himself, whom does he benefit?
he does not even enjoy what is his own.
6 No one is meaner than the person who is mean to himself,
this is how his wickedness repays him.
7 If he does any good, he does it unintentionally,
and in the end he himself reveals his wickedness.
8 Wicked the person who has an envious eye,
averting his face, and careless of others' lives.

9 The eye of the grasping is not content with what he has,
greed shrivels up the soul.

10 The miser is grudging of bread,
there is famine at his table.

11 My child, treat yourself as well as you can afford,
and bring worthy offerings to the Lord.
12 Remember that death will not delay,
and that you have never seen Sheol's contract.
13 Be kind to your friend before you die,
treat him as generously as you can afford.
14 Do not refuse yourself the good things of today,
do not let your share of what is lawfully desired pass you by.
15 Will you not have to leave your fortune to another,
and the fruit of your labour to be divided by lot?
16 Give and receive, enjoy yourself—
there are no pleasures to be found in Sheol.
17 Like clothes, every body will wear out,
the age-old law is, 'Everyone must die.'
18 Like foliage growing on a bushy tree,
some leaves falling, others growing,
so are the generations of flesh and blood:
one dies, another is born.
19 Every achievement rots away and perishes,
and with it goes its author.

The happiness of the sage

20 Blessed is anyone who meditates on wisdom,
and reasons with intelligence,
21 who studies her ways in his heart,
and ponders her secrets.
22 He pursues her like a hunter,
and lies in wait by her path;
23 he peeps in at her windows,
and listens at her doors;
24 he lodges close to her house,
and fixes his peg in her walls;
25 he pitches his tent at her side,
and lodges in an excellent lodging;
26 he sets his children in her shade,
and camps beneath her branches;
27 he is sheltered by her from the heat,
and in her glory he makes his home.

15 1 Whoever fears the Lord will act like this,
and whoever grasps the Law will obtain wisdom.
2 She will come to meet him like a mother,
and receive him like a virgin bride.
3 She will give him the bread of understanding to eat,
and the water of wisdom to drink.
4 He will lean on her and will not fall,
he will rely on her and not be put to shame.
5 She will raise him high above his neighbours,
and in full assembly she will open his mouth.
6 He will find happiness and a crown of joy,
he will inherit an everlasting name.
7 Fools will not gain possession of her,
nor will sinners set eyes on her.
8 She stands remote from pride,
and liars cannot call her to mind.
9 Praise is unseemly in a sinner's mouth,
since it has not been put there by the Lord.
10 For praise should be uttered only in wisdom,
and the Lord himself then prompts it.

Freedom of choice

11 Do not say, 'The Lord was responsible for my sinning,'
for he does not do what he hates.
12 Do not say, 'It was he who led me astray,'
for he has no use for a sinner.
13 The Lord hates all that is foul,
and no one who fears him will love it either.
14 He himself made human beings in the beginning,
and then left them free to make their own decisions.
15 If you choose, you will keep the commandments
and so be faithful to his will.
16 He has set fire and water before you;
put out your hand to whichever you prefer.
17 A human being has life and death before him;
whichever he prefers will be given him.

18 For vast is the wisdom of the Lord;
he is almighty and all-seeing.
19 His eyes are on those who fear him,
he notes every human action.
20 He never commanded anyone to be godless,
he has given no one permission to sin.

The fate of the obstinate

16 Do not long for a brood of worthless children,
and do not take pleasure in godless sons.
2 However many you have, take no pleasure in them,
unless the fear of the Lord lives among them.
3 Do not count on their having long life,
do not put too much faith in their number;
for better have one than a thousand,
better die childless than have children who are godless.
4 One person of sense can populate a city,
but a race of lawless people will be destroyed.
5 My eyes have seen many such things,
my ears have heard things even more impressive.
6 Fire is kindled in a sinful society,
Retribution blazes in a rebellious nation.
7 God did not pardon the giants of old
who, confident in their strength, had rebelled.
8 He did not spare the people with whom Lot lived;
he abhorred them, rather, for their pride.
9 He was pitiless to the nation of perdition—
those people who gloried in their sins—
10 as also to the six hundred thousand men on the march,
who had banded together in their obstinacy.
11 And had there been only one man stubborn,
it would have been amazing had he escaped unpunished,
since mercy and wrath alike belong to the Lord
who is mighty to forgive and to pour out wrath.
12 As great as his mercy, so is his severity;
he judges each person as his deeds deserve:
13 the sinner will not escape with his ill-gotten gains
nor the patience of the devout go for nothing.
14 He takes note of every charitable action,
and everyone is treated as he deserves.

Certainty of retribution

17 Do not say, 'I shall hide from the Lord;
who is going to remember me up there?
I shall not be noticed among so many people;
what am I in the immensity of creation?'
18 For see, the sky and the heavens above the sky,
the abyss and the earth shake at his visitation.
19 The mountains and earth's foundations alike
quail and tremble when he looks at them.
20 But to all this no one gives thought.
Who keeps his movements in mind?
21 The storm wind itself is invisible,
and most of what he does goes undetected.

22 'Who will report whether justice has been done?
Who will be watching? The covenant is remote!'
23 Such are the thoughts of the person of little sense,
stupid, misguided, cherishing his folly.

Human beings in the creation

24 Listen to me, my child, and learn knowledge,
and give your whole mind to my words.
25 I shall expound discipline methodically
and proclaim knowledge with precision.

26 When God created his works in the beginning,
he assigned them their places as soon as they were made.
27 He determined his works for all time,
from their origins to their distant generations.
They know neither hunger nor weariness,
and they never desert their duties.
28 Not one has ever got in the way of another,
and they will never disobey his word.
29 And afterwards the Lord looked at the earth,
and filled it with his good things.
30 He covered its surface with every kind of animal,
and to it they will return.

17 1 The Lord fashioned human beings from the earth,
to consign them back to it.
2 He gave them so many days and so much time,
he gave them authority over everything on earth.
3 He clothed them in strength, like himself,
and made them in his own image.
4 He filled all living things with dread of human beings,
making them masters over beasts and birds.
6 He made them a tongue, eyes and ears,
and gave them a heart to think with.
7 He filled them with knowledge and intelligence,
and showed them what was good and what evil.
8 He put his own light in their hearts
to show them the magnificence of his works,
10 so that they would praise his holy name
as they told of his magnificent works.
11 He set knowledge before them,
he endowed them with the law of life.
12 He established an eternal covenant with them,
and revealed his judgements to them.
13 Their eyes saw the majesty of his glory,
and their ears heard the glory of his voice.
14 He said to them, 'Beware of all wrong-doing';
he gave each a commandment concerning his neighbour.

The divine judge

15 Their ways are always under his eye,
they cannot be hidden from his sight.
17 Over each nation he has set a governor,
but Israel is the Lord's own portion.

19 Their actions are all as plain as the sun to him,
and his eyes rest constantly on their conduct.
20 Their iniquities are not hidden from him,
all their sins are before the Lord.
22 Almsgiving is like a signet ring to him,
he cherishes generosity like the pupil of an eye.
23 One day he will rise and reward them,
he will repay their deserts on their own heads.
24 But to those who repent he permits return,
and he encourages those who have lost hope.

Exhortation to repentance

25 Return to the Lord and renounce your sins,
plead before his face, stop offending him.
26 Come back to the Most High, turn away from iniquity
and hold all that is foul in abhorrence.
27 Who is going to praise the Most High in Sheol
if we do not glorify him while we are alive?
28 The dead can praise no more than those who do not exist,
only those with life and health can praise the Lord.
29 How great is the mercy of the Lord,
his pardon for those who turn to him!
30 For we cannot have everything,
human beings are not immortal.
31 What is brighter than the sun? And yet it fades.
Flesh and blood think of nothing but evil.
32 He surveys the armies of the lofty sky,
and all of us are only dust and ashes.

The greatness of God

18 He who lives for ever has created the sum of things.
2 The Lord alone will be found just.
4 He has given no one the power to proclaim his works to the end,
and who can fathom his magnificent deeds?
5 Who can assess his magnificent strength,
and who can go further and tell all of his mercies?
6 Nothing can be added to them, nothing subtracted,
it is impossible to fathom the marvels of the Lord.
7 When someone finishes he is only beginning,
and when he stops he is as puzzled as ever.

The nothingness of human beings

8 What is a human being, what purpose does he serve?
What is good and what is bad for him?
9 The length of his life: a hundred years at most.
10 Like a drop of water from the sea, or a grain of sand,
such are these few years compared with eternity.
11 This is why the Lord is patient with them
and pours out his mercy on them.
12 He sees and recognises how wretched their end is,
and so he makes his forgiveness the greater.
13 Human compassion extends to neighbours,
but the Lord's compassion extends to everyone;

rebuking, correcting and teaching,
bringing them back as a shepherd brings his flock.
14 He has compassion on those who accept correction,
and who fervently search for his judgements.

The art of giving

15 My child, do not temper your favours with blame
nor any of your gifts with words that hurt.
16 Does not dew relieve the heat?
In the same way a word is worth more than a gift.
17 Why surely, a word is better than a good present,
but a generous person is ready with both.
18 A fool will offer nothing but insult,
and a grudging gift makes the eyes smart.

Reflection and foresight

19 Learn before you speak,
take care of yourself before you fall ill.
20 Examine yourself before judgement comes,
and on the day of visitation you will be acquitted.
21 Humble yourself before you fall ill,
repent as soon as the sin is committed.
22 Let nothing prevent your discharging a vow in good time,
and do not wait till death to set matters right.
23 Prepare yourself before making a vow,
and do not be like someone who tempts the Lord.
24 Bear in mind the retribution of the last days,
the time of vengeance when God averts his face.
25 In a time of plenty remember times of famine,
think of poverty and want when you are rich.
26 The time slips by between dawn and dusk,
everything passes quickly for the Lord.
27 The wise will be cautious in everything,
in sinful times will take care not to offend.
28 Every person of sense recognises wisdom,
and will respect anyone who has found her.
29 Those who understand sayings have toiled for their wisdom
and have poured out accurate maxims.

Self-control

30 Do not be governed by your passions,
restrain your desires.
31 If you allow yourself to satisfy your desires,
this will make you the laughing-stock of your enemies.
32 Do not indulge in luxurious living,
do not get involved in such society.
33 Do not beggar yourself by banqueting on credit
when there is nothing in your pocket.

19 1 A drunken workman will never grow rich,
and one who makes light of small matters will gradually sink.
2 Wine and women corrupt intelligent men,
the customer of whores loses all sense of shame.
3 Grubs and worms will have him as their legacy,
and the man who knows no shame will lose his life.

Against loose talk

4 Being too ready to trust shows shallowness of mind,
and sinning harms the sinner.
5 Taking pleasure in evil earns condemnation;
6 by hating gossip one avoids evil.
7 Never repeat what you are told
and you will come to no harm;
8 whether to friend or foe, do not talk about it,
unless it would be sinful not to, do not reveal it;
9 you would be heard out, then mistrusted,
and in due course you would be hated.
10 Have you heard something? Let it die with you.
Courage! It will not burst you!
11 A fool will suffer birthpangs over a piece of news,
like a woman labouring with child.
12 Like an arrow stuck in the flesh of the thigh,
so is a piece of news inside a fool.

Do not trust everything you hear

13 Question your friend, he may have done nothing at all;
and if he has done anything, he will not do it again.
14 Question your neighbour, he may have said nothing at all;
and if he has said anything, he will not say it again.
15 Question your friend, for slander is very common,
do not believe all you hear.
16 People sometimes make a slip, without meaning what they say;
and which of us has never sinned by speech?
17 Question your neighbour before you threaten him,
and defer to the Law of the Most High.

True and false wisdom

20 Wisdom consists entirely in fearing the Lord,
and wisdom is entirely constituted by the fulfilling of the Law.
22 Being learned in evil, however, is not wisdom,
there is no prudence in the advice of sinners.
23 There is a cleverness that is detestable;
whoever has no wisdom is a fool.
24 Better be short of sense and full of fear,
than abound in shrewdness and violate the Law.
25 There is a wickedness which is scrupulous but nonetheless dishonest,
and there are those who misuse kindness to win their case.
26 There is the person who will walk bowed down with grief,
when inwardly this is nothing but deceit:
27 he hides his face and pretends to be deaf,
if he is not unmasked, he will take advantage of you.
28 There is the person who is prevented from sinning by lack of strength,
yet he will do wrong when he gets the chance.
29 You can tell a person by his appearance,
you can tell a thinker by the look on his face.
30 The way a person dresses, the way he laughs,
the way he walks, tell you what he is.

Silence and speech

20 There is the rebuke that is untimely,
and there is the person who keeps quiet, and he is the shrewd one.
2 But how much better to rebuke than to fume!
3 The person who acknowledges a fault wards off punishment.

4 Like a eunuch trying to take a girl's virginity
is someone who tries to impose justice by force.

5 There is the person who keeps quiet and is considered wise,
another incurs hatred for talking too much.

6 There is the person who keeps quiet, not knowing how to answer,
another keeps quiet, knowing when to speak.

7 The wise will keep quiet till the right moment,
but a garrulous fool will always misjudge it.

8 Someone who talks too much will earn dislike,
and someone who usurps authority will earn hatred.

Paradoxes

9 There is the person who finds misfortune a boon,
and the piece of luck that turns to loss.

10 There is the gift that affords you no profit,
and the gift that repays you double.

11 There is the honour that leads to humiliation,
and there are people in a low state who raise their heads.

12 There is the person who buys much for little,
yet pays for it seven times over.

13 The wise wins love with words,
while fools may shower favours in vain.
14 The gift of the stupid will bring you no advantage,
his eyes look for seven times as much in return.
15 He gives little and reviles much,
he opens his mouth like the town crier,
he lends today and demands payment tomorrow;
he is a detestable fellow.
16 The fool will say, 'I have no friends,
I get no gratitude for my good deeds;
17 those who eat my bread have malicious tongues.'
How often he will be laughed at, and by how many!

Inappropriate talk

18 Better a slip on the pavement than a slip of the tongue;
this is how ruin takes the wicked by surprise.

19 A coarse-grained person is like an indiscreet story
endlessly retold by the ignorant.

20 A maxim is rejected when coming from a fool,
since the fool does not utter it on the apt occasion.

21 There is a person who is prevented from sinning by poverty;
no qualms of conscience disturb that person's rest.

22 There is a person who courts destruction out of false shame,
courts destruction for the sake of a fool's opinion.

23 There is a person who out of false shame makes promises to a friend,
and so makes an enemy for nothing.

Lying

24 Lying is an ugly blot on anyone,
and ever on the lips of the undisciplined.

25 A thief is preferable to an inveterate liar,
but both are heading for ruin.

26 Lying is an abominable habit,
the liar's disgrace lasts for ever.

Wisdom

27 The wise gains advancement by words,
the shrewd wins favour from the great.

28 Whoever tills the soil will have a full harvest,
whoever wins favour from the great will secure pardon for offences.

29 Presents and gifts blind the eyes of the wise
and stifle rebukes like a muzzle on the mouth.

30 Wisdom concealed, and treasure undiscovered,
what use is either of these?
31 Better one who conceals his folly
than one who conceals his wisdom.[a]

Various sins

21 My child, have you sinned? Do so no more,
and ask forgiveness for your previous faults.
2 Flee from sin as from a snake,
if you approach it, it will bite you;
its teeth are lion's teeth,
they take human life away.
3 All law-breaking is like a two-edged sword,
the wounds it inflicts are beyond cure.

4 Terror and violence make havoc of riches,
similarly, desolation overtakes the houses of the proud.
5 A plea from the mouth of the poor goes straight to the ear of God,
whose judgement comes without delay.

6 Whoever resents reproof walks in the sinner's footsteps;
whoever fears the Lord is repentant of heart.

7 The glib speaker is known far and wide,
but the wary detects every slip.

8 To build your house with other people's money
is like collecting stones for your own tomb.

9 A meeting of the lawless is like a heap of tow:
they will end in a blazing fire.

20a =41:14–15.

[10]The sinner's road is smoothly paved,
but it ends at the pit of Sheol.

The wise and the foolish

[11]Whoever keeps the Law will master his instincts;
the fear of the Lord is made perfect in wisdom.

[12]No one who lacks aptitude can be taught,
but certain aptitudes give rise to bitterness.

[13]The sage's knowledge is as rich as the abyss
and his advice is like a living spring.
[14]The heart of a fool is like a broken jar,
it will not hold any knowledge.
[15]If the educated hears a wise saying,
he praises it and caps it with another;
if a debauchee hears it, he does not like it
and tosses it behind his back.

[16]The talk of a fool is like a load on a journey,
but it is a pleasure to listen to the intelligent.
[17]The utterance of the shrewd will be eagerly awaited in the assembly,
what he says will be given serious consideration.

[18]The wisdom of a fool is like the wreckage of a house,
the knowledge of a dolt is incoherent talk.

[19]To the senseless fellow instruction is like fetters on the feet,
like manacles on the right hand.

[20]A fool laughs at the top of his voice,
but the intelligent quietly smiles.

[21]To the shrewd instruction is like a golden ornament,
like a bracelet on the right arm.

[22]The step of a fool goes straight into a house,
but a person of much experience makes a respectful approach;
[23]the stupid peeps inside through the door,
a well-bred person waits outside.
[24]Listening at doors is a sign of bad upbringing,
the perceptive would be ashamed to do so.

[25]The lips of gossips repeat the words of others,
the words of the wise are carefully weighed.

[26]The heart of fools is in their mouth,
but the mouth of the wise is in their heart.

[27]When the godless curses Satan,
he is cursing himself.
[28]The scandal-monger sullies himself
and earns the hatred of the neighbourhood.

The idler

22 An idler is like a stone covered in filth,
everyone whistles at his disgrace.
[2]An idler is like a lump of dung,
anyone picking it up shakes it off his hand.

Degenerate children

3 It is a disgrace to have fathered a badly brought-up son,
but the birth of any daughter is a loss;
4 a sensible daughter will find a husband,
but a shameless one is a grief to her father.
5 A brazen daughter puts father and mother to shame,
and will be disowned by both.

6 An untimely remonstrance is like music at a funeral,
but a thrashing and correction are wisdom at all times.

Wisdom and folly

9 Teaching a fool is like gluing bits of pottery together—
you are rousing someone who is besotted with sleep.
10 You might as well talk to someone sound asleep;
when you have finished the fool will say, 'What's up?'

11 Shed tears for the dead, who has left the light behind;
shed tears for the fool, who has left his wits behind.
Shed quieter tears for the dead who is at rest,
for the fool life is worse than death.
12 Mourning for the dead lasts seven days,
for the foolish and ungodly all the days of their lives.

13 Do not waste many words on the stupid,
do not go near a dolt.

Beware of him, or you will have trouble
and be soiled by contact with him;
keep away from him, and you will have peace of mind
and not be exasperated by his folly.

14 What is heavier than lead,
and what is its name if not 'fool'?
15 Sand and salt and a lump of iron
are a lighter burden than a dolt.

16 A tie-beam bonded into a building
will not be dislodged by an earthquake;
so too, a heart resolved after due reflection
will not flinch at the critical moment.

17 A heart founded on intelligent reflection
is like a stucco decoration on a smooth wall.

18 Pebbles placed on top of a wall
will not stand up to the wind;
no more can the heart of a fool frightened at his own thoughts
stand up to fear.

Friendship

19 Prick an eye and you will draw a tear,
prick a heart and you reveal its feelings.

20 Throw stones at birds and you scare them away,
reproach a friend and you destroy a friendship.

21 If you have drawn your sword on a friend,
do not despair; there is a way back.

22 If you have opened your mouth against your friend,
do not worry; there is hope for reconciliation;
but insult, arrogance, betrayal of secrets, and the stab in the back—
in these cases any friend is lost.

23 Win your neighbour's confidence when he is poor,
so that you may enjoy his later good fortune with him;
stand by him in times of trouble,
in order to have your share when he comes into a legacy.

24 Fire is heralded by the reek of the furnace and smoke,
so too, bloodshed by insults.

25 I shall not be ashamed to shelter a friend
nor shall I hide away from him,
26 and if evil comes to me through him,
everyone who hears about it will beware of him.

Vigilance

27 Who will set a guard on my mouth,
and an efficient seal on my lips,
to keep me from falling,
and my tongue from causing my ruin?

23 1 Lord, father and master of my life,
do not abandon me to their whims,
do not let me fall because of them.
2 Who will lay whips to my thoughts,
and the discipline of wisdom to my heart,
to be merciless to my errors
and not let my sins go unchecked,
3 for fear my errors should multiply
and my sins then abound
and I fall before my adversaries,
and my enemy gloat over me?
4 Lord, father and God of my life,
do not let my eyes be proud,
5 turn envy away from me,
6 do not let lechery and lust grip me,
do not leave me a prey to shameless desire.

Swearing

7 Children, listen to what I teach,
no one who keeps it will be caught out.
8 The sinner is ensnared by his own lips,
both the abusive and the proud are tripped by them.
9 Do not get into the habit of swearing,
do not make a habit of naming the Holy One;
10 for just as a slave who is constantly overseen
will never be without bruises,
so someone who is always swearing and uttering the Name
will not be exempt from sin.
11 A man for ever swearing is full of iniquity,
and the scourge will not depart from his house.
If he offends, his sin will be on him,
if he did it unheedingly, he has doubly sinned;

if he swears a false oath, he will not be treated as innocent,
for his house will be filled with calamities.

Foul language

12 One way of talking is like death,
let it not be found in the heritage of Jacob
since devout people have nothing to do with that:
they will not wallow in sin.
13 Do not get into the habit of using coarse and foul language
since this involves sinful words.
14 Remember your father and mother
when you are sitting with the great,
for fear you forget yourself in their presence
and behave like a fool,
and then wish you had not been born
and curse the day of your birth.
15 No one in the habit of using shameful language
will break himself of it as long as he lives.

Lechery

16 There are two types of people who commit sin after sin
and a third who attracts retribution—
17 desire, blazing like a furnace,
will not die down until it has been sated—
the man who lusts after members of his own family
is not going to stop until he is quite burnt out;
every food is sweet to the promiscuous,
and he will not desist until he dies;
18 and the man who sins against the marriage bed
and says to himself, 'Who can see me?
There is darkness all round me, the walls hide me,
no one can see me, why should I worry?
The Most High will not remember my sins.'
19 What he fears are human eyes,
he does not realise that the eyes of the Lord
are ten thousand times brighter than the sun,
observing every aspect of human behaviour,
seeing into the most secret corners.
20 All things were known to him before they were created,
and are still, now that they are finished.
21 This man will be punished in view of the whole town,
and will be seized when he least expects it.

The adulteress

22 Similarly the woman unfaithful to her husband,
who provides him with an heir by another man:
23 first, she has disobeyed the Law of the Most High;
secondly, she has been false to her husband;
and thirdly, she has gone whoring in adultery
24 and conceived children by another man.
She will be led before the assembly,
an enquiry will be held about her children.

25 Her children will strike no root,
her branches will bear no fruit.
26 She will leave an accursed memory behind her,
her shame will never be wiped out.
27 And those who survive her will recognise
that nothing is better than fearing the Lord,
and nothing sweeter than adherence to the Lord's commandments.

Discourse of Wisdom

24 Wisdom[a] speaks her own praises,
in the midst of her people she glories in herself.
2 She opens her mouth in the assembly of the Most High,
she glories in herself in the presence of the Mighty One:
3 'I came forth from the mouth of the Most High,
and I covered the earth like mist.
4 I had my tent in the heights,
and my throne was a pillar of cloud.
5 Alone, I have made the circuit of the heavens
and walked through the depths of the abyss.
6 Over the waves of the sea and over the whole earth,
and over every people and nation I have held sway.
7 Among all these I searched for rest,
and looked to see in whose territory I might pitch camp.
8 Then the Creator of all things instructed me
and he who created me fixed a place for my tent.
He said, "Pitch your tent in Jacob,
make Israel your inheritance."
9 From eternity, in the beginning, he created me,
and for eternity I shall remain.
10 In the holy tent I ministered before him
and thus became established in Zion.
11 In the beloved city he has given me rest,
and in Jerusalem I wield my authority.
12 I have taken root in a privileged people,
in the Lord's property, in his inheritance.
13 I have grown tall as a cedar on Lebanon,
as a cypress on Mount Hermon;
14 I have grown tall as a palm in En-Gedi,
as the rose bushes of Jericho;
as a fine olive in the plain,
as a plane tree, I have grown tall.
15 Like cinnamon and acanthus, I have yielded a perfume,
like choice myrrh, have breathed out a scent,
like galbanum, onycha, labdanum,
like the smoke of incense in the tent.
16 I have spread my branches like a terebinth,
and my branches are glorious and graceful.
17 I am like a vine putting out graceful shoots,
my blossoms bear the fruit of glory and wealth.
19 Approach me, you who desire me,
and take your fill of my fruits,

24a A high point: personified Wisdom shares God's throne (the cloud) but also chooses Israel for an inheritance and more specifically serves in the Temple. Sira then identifies Wisdom with the Law.

20 for memories of me are sweeter than honey,
inheriting me is sweeter than the honeycomb.
21 They who eat me will hunger for more,
they who drink me will thirst for more.
22 No one who obeys me will ever have to blush,
no one who acts as I dictate will ever sin.'

Wisdom and the Law

23 All this is no other than the Book of the Covenant of the Most High God,
the Law that Moses enjoined on us,
an inheritance for the communities of Jacob.
25 This is what makes wisdom brim over like the Pishon,
like the Tigris in the season of fruit,
26 what makes intelligence overflow like the Euphrates,
like the Jordan at harvest time;
27 and makes discipline flow like the Nile,
like the Gihon when the grapes are harvested.
28 The first man did not finish discovering about her,
nor has the most recent tracked her down;
29 for her thoughts are wider than the sea,
and her designs more profound than the abyss.
30 And I, like a conduit from a river,
like a watercourse running into a garden,
31 I said, 'I am going to water my orchard,
I intend to irrigate my flower beds.'
And see, my conduit has grown into a river,
and my river has grown into a sea.
32 Making discipline shine forth from daybreak,
I shall send its light far and wide.
33 I shall pour out teaching like prophecy,
as a legacy to all future generations.
34 And note, I have been working not merely for myself,
but for all who are seeking wisdom.

Proverbs

25 There are three things my soul delights in,
and which are delightful to God and to all people:
concord between brothers, friendship between neighbours,
and a wife and husband who live happily together.

2 There are three sorts of people my soul hates,
and whose existence I consider an outrage:
the poor swollen with pride, the rich who is a liar
and an adulterous old man who has no sense.

The aged

3 If you have gathered nothing in your youth,
how can you discover anything in your old age?
4 How fine a thing: sound judgement with grey hairs,
and for greybeards to know how to advise!
5 How fine a thing: wisdom in the aged,
and considered advice coming from people of distinction!
6 The crown of the aged is ripe experience,
their glory, the fear of the Lord.

Numerical proverbs

7 There are nine things I can think of which strike me as happy,
and a tenth which is now on my tongue:
the man who can be proud of his children,
he who lives to see the downfall of his enemies;
8 happy is he who keeps house with a sensible wife;
he who does not toil with ox and donkey;[a]
he who has never sinned with his tongue;
he who does not serve a man less worthy than himself;
9 happy is he who has acquired good sense
and can find attentive ears for what he has to say;
10 how great is he who has acquired wisdom;
but unsurpassed is one who fears the Lord.
11 The fear of the Lord surpasses everything;
what can compare with someone who has mastered that?

Women

13 Any wound rather than a wound of the heart!
Any spite rather than the spite of woman!
14 Any evil rather than an evil caused by an enemy!
Any vengeance rather than the vengeance of a foe!
15 There is no poison worse than the poison of a snake,
there is no fury worse than the fury of an enemy.
16 I would sooner keep house with a lion or a dragon
than keep house with a spiteful wife.

17 A woman's spite changes her appearance
and makes her face as grim as a bear's.
18 When her husband goes out to dinner with his neighbours,
he cannot help heaving bitter sighs.

19 No spite can approach the spite of a woman,
may a sinner's lot be hers!

20 Like the climbing of a sandhill for elderly feet,
such is a garrulous wife for a quiet husband.
21 Do not be taken in by a woman's beauty,
never lose your head over a woman.

22 Bad temper, insolence and shame hold sway
where the wife supports the husband.
23 Low spirits, gloomy face, stricken heart:
such is a spiteful wife.
Slack hands and sagging knees:
such is the wife who does not make her husband happy.

24 Sin began with a woman,
and thanks to her we must all die.

25 Do not let water find a leak,
nor a spiteful woman give free rein to her tongue.
26 If she will not do as you tell her,
get rid of her.

26

1 How blessed is the husband of a really good wife;
the number of his days will be doubled.

25a Such an uneven team is prohibited by Dt 22:10.

[2]A perfect wife is the joy of her husband,
he will live out the years of his life in peace.
[3]A good wife is the best of portions,
reserved for those who fear the Lord;
[4]rich or poor, their hearts will be glad,
their faces cheerful, whatever the season.

[5]There are three things that I dread,
and a fourth which terrifies me:
slander by a whole town, the gathering of a mob,
and a false accusation—these are all worse than death;
[6]but a woman jealous of a woman means heartbreak and sorrow,
and all this is the scourge of the tongue.

[7]A bad wife is a badly fitting ox-yoke,
trying to master her is like grasping a scorpion.
[8]A drunken wife will goad anyone to fury,
she cannot conceal her own degradation.

[9]A woman's wantonness shows in her wide-eyed look,
her eyelashes leave no doubt.
[10]Keep a headstrong daughter under firm control,
or, feeling free, she will take advantage of it.
[11]Keep a strict watch on her shameless eye,
do not be surprised if she disgraces you.
[12]Like a thirsty traveller she will open her mouth
and drink any water she comes across;
she will sit down in front of every tent-peg
and open her quiver to any arrow.

[13]The grace of a wife will charm her husband,
her understanding will make him the stronger.
[14]A silent wife is a gift from the Lord,
no price can be put on a well-trained character.
[15]A modest wife is a boon twice over,
a chaste character cannot be over-valued.
[16]Like the sun rising over the mountains of the Lord,
such is the beauty of a good wife in a well-run house.
[17]Like a lamp shining on the sacred lamp-stand,
such is a beautiful face on a well-proportioned body.
[18]Like golden pillars on a silver base,
such are shapely legs on firm-set heels.

Depressing things

[28]There are two things which grieve my heart
and a third arouses my anger:
a warrior wasting away through poverty,
the intelligent treated with contempt,
someone turning back from virtue to sin—
the Lord marks out such a person for a violent death.

Commerce

[29]It is difficult for a merchant to avoid doing wrong
and for a trader not to incur sin.
27 [1]Many have sinned for the sake of profit,
one who hopes to be rich must turn a blind eye.

[2]A peg will stick in the joint between two stones,
and sin will wedge itself between selling and buying.
[3]Whoever does not firmly hold to the fear of the Lord,
his house will soon be overthrown.

Speech

[4]In a shaken sieve the rubbish is left behind,
so too the defects of a person appear in speech.
[5]The kiln tests the work of the potter,
the test of a person is in conversation.
[6]The orchard where the tree grows is judged by its fruit,
similarly words betray what a person feels.
[7]Do not praise anyone who has not yet spoken,
since this is where people are tested.

Virtue

[8]If you pursue virtue, you will attain it
and put it on like a festal gown.
[9]Birds consort with their kind,
truth comes home to those who practise it.
[10]The lion lies in wait for its prey,
so does sin for those who do wrong.
[11]The conversation of the devout is wisdom at all times,
but the fool is as changeable as the moon.
[12]When visiting stupid people, choose the right moment,
but among the thoughtful take your time.
[13]The conversation of fools is disgusting,
raucous their laughter in their sinful pleasures.
[14]The talk of hard-swearing people makes your hair stand on end,
their brawling makes you stop your ears.
[15]A quarrel between the proud leads to bloodshed,
and their insults are embarrassing to hear.

Secrets

[16]A betrayer of secrets forfeits all trust
and will never find the kind of friend he wants.
[17]Be fond of a friend and keep faith with him,
but if you have betrayed his secrets, do not go after him any more;
[18]for, as one destroys a person by killing him,
so you have killed your neighbour's friendship,
[19]and as you let a bird slip through your fingers,
so you have let your friend go, and will not catch him.
[20]Do not go after him—he is far away,
he has fled like a gazelle from the snare.
[21]For a wound can be bandaged and abuse forgiven,
but for the betrayer of a secret there is no hope.

Hypocrisy

[22]Someone with a sly wink is plotting mischief,
no one can dissuade him from it.

23 Honey-tongued to your face,
he is lost in admiration at your words;
but behind your back he has other things to say,
and turns your words into a stumbling-block.
24 I have found many things to hate, but nothing as much as him,
and the Lord hates him too.

25 Whoever throws a stone in the air, throws it on to his own head;
a treacherous blow cuts both ways.
26 The man who digs a pit falls into it,
whoever sets a snare will be caught by it.
27 On anyone who does evil, evil will recoil,
without his knowing where it comes from.

28 Sarcasm and abuse are the mark of the arrogant,
but vengeance lies in wait like a lion for such a one.
29 The trap will close on all who rejoice in the downfall of the devout,
and pain will eat them up before they die.

Resentment

30 Resentment and anger, these are foul things too,
and a sinner is a master at them both.

28

1 Whoever exacts vengeance will experience the vengeance of the Lord,
who keeps strict account of sin.
2 Pardon your neighbour any wrongs done to you,
and when you pray, your sins will be forgiven.
3 If anyone nurses anger against another,
can one then demand compassion from the Lord?
4 Showing no pity for someone like oneself,
can one then plead for one's own sins?
5 Mere creature of flesh, yet cherishing resentment!—
who will forgive one for sinning?
6 Remember the last things, and stop hating,
corruption and death, and be faithful to the commandments.
7 Remember the commandments, and do not bear your fellow ill-will,
remember the covenant of the Most High, and ignore the offence.

Quarrels

8 Avoid quarrelling and you will sin less;
for the hot-tempered provokes quarrels,
9 a sinner sows trouble between friends,
introducing discord among the peaceful.
10 The way a fire burns depends on its fuel,
a quarrel spreads in proportion to its violence;
a man's rage depends on his strength,
his fury grows fiercer in proportion to his wealth.
11 A sudden quarrel kindles fire,
a hasty dispute leads to bloodshed.
12 Blow on a spark and up it flares,
spit on it and out it goes;
both are the effects of your mouth.

The tongue

13 A curse on the scandal-monger and double-talker,
such a person has ruined many who lived in concord.

[14]That third tongue has shattered the peace of many
and driven them from nation to nation;
it has pulled down fortified cities,
and overthrown the houses of the great.
[15]The third tongue has had upright wives divorced,
depriving them of reward for their hard work.
[16]No one who listens to it will ever know peace of mind,
will ever live in peace again.
[17]A stroke of the whip raises a weal,
but a stroke of the tongue breaks bones.
[18]Many have fallen by the edge of the sword,
but many more have fallen by the tongue.
[19]Blessed is anyone who has been sheltered from it,
and has not experienced its fury,
who has not dragged its yoke about,
or been bound in its chains;
[20]for its yoke is an iron yoke,
its chains are bronze chains;
[21]the death it inflicts is a miserable death,
Sheol is preferable to it.
[22]It cannot gain a hold over the devout,
they are not burnt by its flames.
[23]Those who desert the Lord will fall into it,
it will flare up inextinguishably among them,
it will be let loose against them like a lion,
it will tear them like a leopard.
[24]Be sure you put a thorn-hedge round your property,
lock away your silver and gold;
[25]then make scales and weights for your words,
and put a door with bolts across your mouth.
[26]Take care you take no false step through it,
in case you fall a prey to him who lies in wait.

Loans

29 Making your neighbour a loan is an act of mercy,
to lend him a helping hand is to keep the commandments.
[2]Lend to your neighbour in his time of need,
and in your turn repay your neighbour on time.
[3]Be as good as your word and keep faith with him,
and you will find your needs met every time.
[4]Many treat a loan as a windfall,
and embarrass those who have come to their rescue.
[5]Until he gets something, a man will kiss his neighbour's hand,
and refer diffidently to his wealth;
but when the loan falls due, he puts this off,
he repays with offhand words,
and pleads the inconvenience of the time
[6]Even if he can be made to pay, his creditor will recover barely half,
and consider even that a windfall.
But otherwise he will be cheated of his money,
and undeservedly gain himself an enemy;
the man will pay him back in curses and abuse,
and with insults instead of honour.
[7]Many, not out of malice, refuse to lend;
they are merely anxious not to be cheated for nothing.

Almsgiving

[8]Nevertheless, be patient with those who are badly off,
do not keep them waiting on your generosity.
[9]In obedience to the commandment, help the poor;
do not turn the poor away empty-handed in their need.
[10]Spend your money on your brother or your friend,
do not leave it under a stone to rust away.
[11]Use your wealth as the Most High has decreed;
you will find that more profitable than gold.
[12]Stock your store-rooms with almsgiving;
this will save you from all misfortune.
[13]Better than sturdy shield or weighty spear,
this will fight for you against the enemy.

Guarantees

[14]A good man will go surety for his neighbour;
only a shameless wretch would desert him.
[15]Do not forget the favour your guarantor has done you;
he has given his life for you.
[16]A sinner is careless of his guarantor's prosperity,
the ungrateful forgets his deliverer.
[17]Going surety has ruined many who were prosperous,
tossing them about in a heavy sea.
[18]It has driven the powerful from home
to wander among foreign nations.
[19]A wicked man in a hurry to stand guarantor
in the hope of profit, is hurrying to be sentenced.
[20]Come to your neighbour's help as far as you can,
but take care not to fall into the same plight.

Staying in other people's houses

[21]The first thing in life is water, and bread, and clothing,
and a house for the sake of privacy.
[22]Better the life of the poor under a roof of planks,
than lavish fare in somebody else's house.
[23]Whether you have little or much, be content with it,
and you will not hear your household complaining.
[24]It is a miserable life, going from house to house;
wherever you stay, you dare not open your mouth,
[25]you do not belong, you receive no thanks for the drink you pour out
and hear embittering words into the bargain:
[26]'Come along, stranger, lay the table,
what have you got ready? give me something to eat!'
[27]'Go away, stranger, make room for someone important;
my brother is coming to stay, I need the house.'
[28]It is hard for the reasonable
to be begrudged hospitality
to be shamed like a debtor.

Bringing up children

30 Whoever loves his son will beat him frequently
so that in after years the son may be his comfort.

2 Whoever is strict with his son will reap the benefit,
and be able to boast of him to his acquaintances.

3 Whoever educates his son will be the envy of his enemy,
and will be proud of him among his friends.

4 Even when the father dies, he might well not be dead,
since he leaves his likeness behind him.
5 In life he has had the joy of his company,
dying, he has no anxieties.
6 He leaves an avenger against his enemies
and a rewarder of favours for his friends.

7 Whoever coddles his son will bandage his wounds,
his heart will turn over at every cry.
8 A badly broken-in horse turns out stubborn,
a son left to himself turns out headstrong.
9 Pamper your child and he will terrorise you,
play along with him and he will bring you sorrow.

10 Do not laugh with him, or one day you will weep with him
and end up gnashing your teeth.
11 While he is young, do not allow him his freedom
and do not wink at his mistakes.
12 Bend his neck in youth,
bruise his ribs while he is a child,
or else he will grow stubborn and disobedient,
and hurt you very deeply.
13 Be strict with your son, and persevere with him,
or you will rue his insolence.

Health

14 Better be poor if healthy and fit
than rich if tormented in body.
15 Health and strength are better than any gold,
a robust body than untold wealth.
16 No riches can outweigh bodily health,
no enjoyment surpass a cheerful heart.
17 Better death than a wretched life,
and everlasting rest than chronic illness.
18 Good things lavished on a closed mouth
are like food offerings put on a grave.
19 What use is an offering to an idol
which can neither eat nor smell?
How describe someone pursued by the Lord's displeasure?
20 He looks and sighs
like a eunuch embracing a pretty girl—how he sighs!

Happiness

21 Do not abandon yourself to sorrow,
do not torment yourself with brooding.
22 Gladness of heart is life to anyone,
joy is what gives length of days.
23 Give your cares the slip, console your heart,
chase sorrow far away;

for sorrow has been the ruin of many,
and is no use to anybody.
24 Jealousy and anger shorten your days,
and worry brings premature old age.
25 A genial heart makes a good trencherman,
someone who enjoys a good meal.

Riches

31 The sleeplessness brought by wealth makes a person lose weight,
the worry it causes drives away sleep.
2 The worries of the daytime prevent you from sleeping,
like a serious illness, they keep sleep at bay.
3 The rich for ever toils, piling up money,
and then, leaving off, he is gorged with luxuries;
4 the poor for ever toils, barely making a living,
and then, leaving off, is poorer than ever.

5 No one who loves money can easily avoid sinning,
whoever pursues profit will be corrupted by it.
6 Gold has been the ruin of many;
their coming destruction was self-evident,
7 since it is a snare for those who sacrifice to it
and stupid people all get caught in it.
8 Happy the rich who is found to be blameless
and does not go chasing after gold.
9 Who is he, so that we can congratulate him,
for he has achieved marvels among his fellows?
10 Who has been through this test and emerged perfect?
He may well be proud of that!
Who has had the chance to sin and has not sinned,
had the chance to do wrong and has not done it?
11 His fortune will be firmly based
and the assembly will acclaim his generosity.

Dinner parties

12 If you are sitting down to a lavish table,
do not display your greed,
do not say, 'What a lot to eat!'
13 Remember, it is bad to have a greedy eye.
Is any creature more wicked than the eye?
—That is why it is always weeping!
14 Do not reach out for anything your host has his eye on,
do not jostle him at the dish.
15 Judge your fellow-guest's needs by your own,
be thoughtful in every way.
16 Eat what is offered you like a well brought-up person,
do not wolf your food or you will earn dislike.
17 For politeness' sake be the first to stop;
do not act the glutton, or you will give offence,
18 and if you are sitting with a large party,
do not help yourself before the others do.
19 A little is quite enough for a well-bred person;
his breathing is easy when he lies in bed.
20 A moderate diet ensures sound sleep,
one gets up early, in the best of spirits.

Sleeplessness, biliousness and gripe
are what the glutton has to endure.
21 If you are forced to eat too much,
get up, go and vomit, and you will feel better.
22 Listen to me, my child, do not disregard me,
eventually you will see the force of my words.
Be moderate in all your activities
and illness will never overtake you.

23 People praise the person who keeps a splendid table,
and their opinion of his munificence is sound.
24 But a niggardly host provokes universal resentment
and people will retail instances of his meanness.

Wine

25 Do not play the valiant at your wine,
for wine has been the undoing of many.
26 The furnace proves the temper of steel,
and wine proves hearts in the drinking bouts of braggarts.
27 Wine gives life
if drunk in moderation.
What is life worth without wine?
It came into being to make people happy.
28 Drunk at the right time and in the right amount,
wine makes for a glad heart and a cheerful mind.
29 Bitterness of soul comes of wine drunk to excess
out of temper or bravado.
30 Drunkenness excites the stupid to a fury to his own harm,
it reduces his strength while leading to blows.
31 Do not provoke your fellow-guest at a wine feast,
do not make fun of him when he is enjoying himself,
do not take him to task
or annoy him by reclaiming money owed.

Banquets

32 Have they made you the presider? Do not let it go to your head,
behave like everyone else in the party,
see that they are happy and then sit down yourself.
2 Having discharged your duties, take your place
so that your joy may be through theirs,
and you may receive the crown for your competence.

3 Speak, old man—it is proper that you should—
but with discretion: do not spoil the music.
4 If someone is singing, do not ramble on
and do not play the sage at the wrong moment.
5 An amber seal on a precious stone,
such is a concert of music at a wine feast.
6 An emerald seal in a golden setting,
such are strains of music with a vintage wine.

7 Speak, young man, when you must,
but twice at most, and then only if questioned.
8 Keep to the point, say much in few words;
give the impression of knowing but not wanting to speak.

9Among eminent people do not behave as though you were their equal;
do not make frivolous remarks when someone else is speaking.
10Lightning comes before the thunder,
favour goes ahead of a modest person.
11Leave in good time, do not bring up the rear,
and hurry home without loitering.
12There amuse yourself, and do what you have a mind to,
but do not sin by arrogant talk.
13And for all this bless your Creator,
who intoxicates you with his favours.

The fear of God

14Whoever fears the Lord will accept his correction;
those who look for him will win his favour.
15Whoever seeks the Law will be nourished by it,
the hypocrite will find it a stumbling-block.
16Those who fear the Lord win his approval,
their good deeds shining like a light.

17The sinner waves reproof aside,
he finds an excuse for headstrong behaviour.
18A sensible person never scorns a warning;
foreigners and the proud do not know about fear.

19Never act without reflection,
and you will not regret your actions.
20Do not venture on a rough road,
for fear of stumbling over the stones.
21Do not be over-confident on an even road
22and beware of your own children.
23Watch yourself in everything you do;
this is also the way to keep the commandments.

24Anyone who trusts in the Law obeys its precepts,
no one who has confidence in the Lord will come to harm.

33 1No evil will befall one who fears the Lord,
such a one will be rescued even in the ordeal.
2No one who hates the Law is wise,
one who is hypocritical about it is like a storm-tossed ship.
3An intelligent person will put faith in the Law,
for such a one the Law is as dependable as a prophecy.

4Prepare what you have to say and you will get a hearing,
marshal your information before you answer.
5The feelings of a fool are like a cart-wheel,
a fool's thought revolves like a turning axle.
6A rutting stallion is like a sarcastic friend;
he neighs, whoever rides him.

Inequality

7Why is one day better than another,
though the sun gives the same daylight throughout the year?
8They have been differentiated in the mind of the Lord,
who has diversified the seasons and feasts;
9some he has made more important and has hallowed,
others he has made ordinary days.

10 Human beings come from the ground,
Adam himself was formed out of earth;
11 in the fullness of his wisdom
the Lord has made distinctions between them,
and diversified their conditions.
12 Some of them he has blessed,
hallowing and setting them near him;
others he has cursed and humiliated
by degrading them from their positions.
13 Like clay in the hands of the potter
to mould as it pleases him,
so are human beings in the hands of their Maker
to reward as he judges right.
14 Opposite evil stands good,
opposite death, life;
so too opposite the devout stands the sinner.
15 Contemplate all the works of the Most High,
you will find they go in pairs, by opposites.

16 Although the last to come, I have kept my eyes open
like a man picking up what the grape-pickers have left.
17 By the blessing of the Lord I have come in first,
and like a true grape-picker have filled my winepress.
18 And note, I have not been working merely for myself,
but for all who seek instruction.

19 Listen to me, important public figures,
presidents of the assembly, give ear!

Independence

20 Neither to son nor wife, brother nor friend,
give power over yourself during your own lifetime.
And do not give your property to anyone else,
in case you regret it and have to ask for it back.
21 As long as you live and there is breath in your body,
do not yield power over yourself to anyone;
22 better for your children to come begging to you,
than for you to have to go begging to them.
23 In all you do be the master,
and leave a reputation unstained.
24 The day your life draws to a close,
at the hour of death, then distribute your heritage.

Slaves

25 Fodder, the stick and burdens for a donkey,
bread, discipline and work for a slave.
26 Work your slave hard, and you will have peace of mind,
leave his hands idle, and he will be asking for his freedom.
27 Yoke and harness will bow the neck,
for a bad servant, torments and the rack.
28 Set him to work, so that he will not be idle;
idleness teaches every kind of mischief.
29 Keep him at his duties, where he should be,
if he is disobedient, clap him in irons.

[30]But do not be over-exacting with anyone,
and do nothing contrary to justice.

[31]You have only one slave? Treat him like yourself,
since you have acquired him with blood.
[32]You have only one slave? Treat him as a brother,
since you need him as you need yourself.
[33]If you ill-treat him and he runs away,
which way will you go to look for him?

Dreams

34 Vain and deceptive hopes are for the foolish,
and dreams lend wings to fools.
[2]As well clutch at shadows and chase the wind
as put any faith in dreams.
[3]Dreams are no different from mirrors;
confronting a face, the reflection of that face.
[4]What can be cleansed by uncleanness,
what can be verified by falsehood?
[5]Divinations, auguries and dreams are nonsense,
like the fantasies of a pregnant woman.
[6]Unless sent as emissaries from the Most High,
do not give them a thought;
[7]for dreams have led many astray,
and those who relied on them have come to grief.
[8]Fulfilling the Law requires no such falsehood,
and wisdom is perfected in veracity.

Travelling

[9]A much travelled man knows many things,
and a man of great experience will talk sound sense.
[10]Someone who has never had his trials knows little;
but the travelled man is master of every situation.
[11]I have seen many things on my travels,
I have understood more than I can put into words.
[12]I have often been in danger of death,
but I have been spared, and this is why:
[13]the spirit of those who fear the Lord can survive,
for their hope is in someone with power to save them.
[14]No one who fears the Lord need ever hesitate,
or ever be daunted, since the Lord is his hope.
[15]Happy the soul of one who fears the Lord.
On whom does he rely? Who supports him?
[16]The eyes of the Lord watch over those who love him,
he is their powerful protection and their strong support,
their screen from the desert wind, their shelter from the midday sun,
a guard against stumbling, an assurance against a fall.
[17]He revives the spirit and brightens the eyes,
he gives health, life and blessing.

Sacrifices

[18]The sacrifice of an offering unjustly acquired is a mockery;
the gifts of the impious are unacceptable.

19 The Most High takes no pleasure in offerings from the godless,
multiplying sacrifices will not gain pardon for sin.
20 Offering sacrifice from the property of the poor
is as bad as slaughtering a son before his father's eyes.
21 A meagre diet is the very life of the poor,
to deprive them of it is to commit murder.
22 To take away a fellow-man's livelihood is to kill him,
to deprive an employee of his wages is to shed blood.
23 If one person builds while another pulls down,
what will they get out of it but trouble?
24 If one person prays and another calls down a curse,
to which one's voice is the Master going to listen?
25 If someone washes after touching a corpse, and then touches it again,
what is the good of his washing?
26 Just so with someone who fasts for sin,
and then goes and commits it again.
Who is going to hear that person's prayer?
What is the good of the self-abasement?

The Law and sacrifices

35 One who keeps the Law multiplies offerings;
one who follows the commandments offers communion sacrifices.
2 Proof of gratitude is an offering of fine flour,
almsgiving a sacrifice of praise.
3 To abandon wickedness is what pleases the Lord,
to give up wrong-doing is an expiatory sacrifice.
4 Do not appear empty-handed in the Lord's presence;
for all these things are due under the commandment.
5 The offering of the upright graces the altar,
and its savour rises before the Most High.
6 The sacrifice of the upright is acceptable,
its memorial will not be forgotten.
7 Honour the Lord with generosity,
do not stint the first-fruits you bring.
8 Add a smiling face to all your gifts,
and be cheerful as you dedicate your tithes.
9 Give to the Most High as he has given to you,
as generously as your means can afford;
10 for the Lord is a good rewarder,
he will reward you seven times over.

Divine justice

11 Do not try to bribe him with presents, he will not accept them,
do not put your faith in wrongly motivated sacrifices;
12 for the Lord is a judge
who is utterly impartial.
13 He never shows partiality to the detriment of the poor,
he listens to the plea of the injured party.
14 He does not ignore the orphan's supplication,
nor the widow's as she pours out her complaint.
15 Do the widow's tears not run down her cheeks,
as she accuses the man who is the cause of them?
16 Whoever wholeheartedly serves God will be accepted,
his petitions will carry to the clouds.

[17]The prayer of the humble pierces the clouds:
and until it does, he is not to be consoled,
[18]nor will he desist until the Most High takes notice of him,
acquits the upright and delivers judgement.
[19]And the Lord will not be slow,
nor will he be dilatory on their behalf,
[20]until he has crushed the loins of the merciless
and exacted vengeance on the nations,
[21]until he has eliminated the hordes of the arrogant
and broken the sceptres of the wicked,
[22]until he has repaid all people as their deeds deserve
and human actions as their intentions merit,
[23]until he has judged the case of his people
and made them rejoice in his mercy.
[24]Mercy is welcome in time of trouble,
like rain clouds in time of drought.

Prayer for the deliverance and restoration of Israel

36 Take pity on us, Master, Lord of the universe, look at us,
spread fear of yourself throughout all other nations.
[2]Raise your hand against the foreign nations
and let them see your might.
[3]As, in their sight, you have proved yourself holy to us,
so now, in our sight, prove yourself great to them.
[4]Let them acknowledge you, just as we have acknowledged
that there is no God but you, Lord.
[5]Send new portents, do fresh wonders,
win glory for your hand and your right arm.
[6]Rouse your fury, pour out your rage,
destroy the opponent, annihilate the enemy.
[7]Hasten the day, remember the oath,
and let people tell of your mighty deeds.
[8]Let fiery wrath swallow up the survivor,
and destruction overtake those who oppress your people.
[9]Crush the heads of hostile rulers
who say, 'There is no one else but us!'
[10]Gather together all the tribes of Jacob,
restore them their heritage as at the beginning.
[11]Take pity, Lord, on the people called by your name,
on Israel whom you have made your first-born.
[12]Have compassion on your holy city,
on Jerusalem, the place where you rest.
[13]Fill Zion with your praises
and your sanctuary with your glory.
[14]Vindicate those whom you created first,
fulfil what has been prophesied in your name.
[15]Give those who wait for you their reward,
let your prophets be proved true.
[16]Grant, Lord, the prayer of your servants,
in the terms of Aaron's blessing on your people,
[17]so that all the earth's inhabitants may acknowledge
that you are the Lord, the everlasting God.

Discrimination

18 The stomach takes in all kinds of food,
but some foods are better than others.
19 As the palate discerns the flavour of game,
so a shrewd listener detects lying words.
20 A perverse character causes depression in others;
it needs experience to know how to repay such a one.

Choosing a wife

21 A woman will accept any husband,
but some daughters are better than others.
22 A woman's beauty delights the beholder,
a man likes nothing better.
23 If her tongue is kind and gentle,
her husband is the happiest of men.
24 The man who takes a wife has the makings of a fortune,
a helper to match himself, a pillar of support.
25 When property has no fence, it is open to plunder,
when a man has no wife, he is aimless and querulous.
26 Will anyone trust an armed thief
who flits from town to town?
27 So it is with the man who has no nest,
and lodges wherever night overtakes him.

False friends

37 Any friend will say, 'I am your friend too,'
but some friends are friends only in name.
2 Is it not a deadly sorrow
when a comrade or a friend turns enemy?
3 O evil inclination, why were you created,
to cover the earth with deceit?
4 One kind of comrade congratulates a friend in prosperity
but in time of trouble appears on the other side.
5 One kind of comrade genuinely feels for a friend
and when it comes to a fight, springs to arms.
6 Do not forget the genuine friend,
do not push him out of mind once you are rich.

Advisers

7 Any adviser will offer advice,
but some are governed by self-interest.
8 Beware of someone who offers advice;
first find out what he wants himself—
since his advice coincides with his own interest—
in case he has designs on you
9 and tells you, 'You are on the right road,'
but stands well clear to see what will happen to you.
10 Do not consult anyone who looks at you askance,
conceal your plans from people jealous of you.
11 Do not consult a woman about her rival,
or a coward about war,

a merchant about prices,
or a buyer about selling,
anyone mean about gratitude,
or anyone selfish about kindness,
a lazy fellow about any sort of work,
or a casual worker about finishing a job,
an idle servant about a major undertaking—
do not rely on these for any advice.
12But have constant recourse to some devout person,
whom you know to be a keeper of the commandments,
whose soul matches your own,
and who, if you go wrong, will be sympathetic.
13Finally, stick to the advice your own heart gives you,
no one can be truer to you than that;
14since a person's soul often gives a clearer warning
than seven watchmen perched on a watchtower.
15And besides all this beg the Most High
to guide your steps into the truth.

True and false wisdom

16Reason should be the basis for every activity,
reflection must come before any undertaking.
17Thoughts are rooted in the heart,
and this sends out four branches:
18good and evil, life and death,
and mistress of them always is the tongue.
19One kind of person is clever at teaching others,
yet is no good whatever to himself;
20another, very eloquent, is detested
and ends by starving to death,
21not having won the favour of the Lord,
and being destitute of all wisdom.
22Another considers himself wise
and proclaims his intellectual conclusions as certainties.
23But the truly wise instructs his people
and his intellectual conclusions are certainties.
24The wise is showered with blessings,
and all who see him will call him happy.
25Human life lasts a number of days,
but the days of Israel are beyond counting.
26The wise will earn confidence among the people,
his name will live for ever.

Moderation

27During your life, my child, see what suits your constitution,
do not give it what you find disagrees with it;
28for not everything is good for everybody,
nor does everybody like everything.
29Do not be insatiable for any delicacy,
do not be greedy for food,
30for over-eating leads to illness
and excess leads to liver-attacks.
31Many people have died from over-eating;
control yourself, and so prolong your life.

Medicine and illness

38 Treat the doctor with the honour that is his due,
in consideration of his services;
for he too has been created by the Lord.
2 Healing itself comes from the Most High,
like a gift received from a king.
3 The doctor's learning keeps his head high,
and the great regard him with awe.
4 The Lord has brought forth medicinal herbs from the ground,
and no one sensible will despise them.
5 Did not a piece of wood once sweeten the water,
thus giving proof of its power?[a]
6 He has also given some people knowledge,
so that they may draw credit from his mighty works.
7 He uses these for healing and relieving pain;
the druggist makes up a mixture from them.
8 Thus, there is no end to his activities;
thanks to him, well-being exists throughout the world.

9 My child, when you are ill, do not rebel,
but pray to the Lord and he will heal you.
10 Renounce your faults, keep your hands unsoiled,
and cleanse your heart from all sin.
11 Offer incense and a memorial of fine flour,
make as rich an offering as you can afford.
12 Then let the doctor take over—the Lord created him too—
do not let him leave you, for you need him.
13 There are times when good health depends on doctors.
14 For they, in their turn, will pray the Lord
to grant them the grace to relieve
and to heal, and so prolong your life.
15 Whoever sins in the eyes of his Maker,
let such a one come under the care of the doctor!

Mourning

16 My child, shed tears over the dead,
lament for the dead to show your sorrow,
then bury the body with due ceremony
and do not fail to honour the grave.
17 Weep bitterly, beat your breast,
observe the mourning the dead deserves
for a day or two, to avoid censorious comment,
and then be comforted in your sorrow;
18 for grief can lead to death,
a grief-stricken heart loses all energy.
19 In affliction sorrow persists,
a life of grief is hard to bear.
20 Do not abandon your heart to grief,
drive it away, bear your own end in mind.
21 Do not forget, there is no coming back;
you cannot help the dead, and you will harm yourself.
22 'Remember my doom, since it will be yours too;
I yesterday, you today!'

38a Ex 15:23–25.

23 Once the dead are laid to rest, let their memory rest,
do not fret for them, once their spirit departs.

Trades and crafts

24 Leisure gives the scribe the chance to acquire wisdom;
a man with few commitments can grow wise.
25 How can the ploughman become wise,
whose sole ambition is to wield the goad,
driving his oxen, engrossed in their work,
his conversation limited to bullocks,
26 his thoughts absorbed in the furrows he traces
and his long evenings spent in fattening heifers?
27 Similarly with all workmen and craftsmen,
toiling day and night;
those who engrave seals,
for ever trying to think of a new design,
concentrating on catching a good likeness
and staying up late to get the work done.
28 Similarly with the blacksmith sitting by his anvil;
he considers what to do with the pig-iron,
the breath of the fire scorches his skin,
as he contends with the heat of the furnace;
the noise of the hammer deafens him,
his eyes are fixed on the pattern;
he concentrates on getting the job done well
and stays up late to apply the finishing touches.
29 Similarly with the potter, sitting at his work,
turning the wheel with his feet;
constantly on the alert over his work,
each flick of the finger premeditated;
30 he pummels the clay with his arm,
and with his feet he kneads it;
he concentrates on applying the glaze right
and stays up late to clean the kiln.
31 All these people rely on their hands
and each is skilled at his own craft.
32 A town could not be inhabited without them,
there would be no settling, no travelling.
33 But you will not find them in the parliament,
they do not hold high rank in the assembly.
They do not sit on the judicial bench,
and they do not meditate on the Law.
34 They are not remarkable for their culture or judgement,
nor are they found frequenting the philosophers.
They sustain the structure of the world,
and their prayer is concerned with their trade.

The scribe

39 Not so with one who concentrates his mind
and his meditation on the Law of the Most High.
He researches into the wisdom of all the Ancients,
he occupies his time with the prophecies.
2 He preserves the discourses of famous men,
he is at home with the niceties of parables.

3 He researches into the hidden sense of proverbs,
he ponders the obscurities of parables.
4 He enters the service of princes,
he is seen in the presence of rulers.
He travels in foreign countries,
he has experienced human good and human evil.
5 At dawn and with all his heart
he turns to the Lord his Creator;
he pleads in the presence of the Most High,
he opens his mouth in prayer
and makes entreaty for his sins.
6 If such be the will of the great Lord,
he will be filled with the spirit of intelligence,
he will shower forth words of wisdom,
and in prayer give thanks to the Lord.
7 He will grow upright in purpose and learning,
he will ponder the Lord's hidden mysteries.
8 He will display the instruction he has received,
taking his pride in the Law of the Lord's covenant.
9 Many will praise his intelligence
and it will never be forgotten.
His memory will not disappear,
generation after generation his name will live.
10 Nations will proclaim his wisdom,
the assembly will celebrate his praises.[a]
11 If he lives long, his name will be more glorious than a thousand others,
and if he dies, that will satisfy him just as well.

Invitation to praise God

12 And here are some more of my reflections:
yes, I am as full as the moon at the full!
13 Listen to me, devout children, and blossom
like the rose that grows on the bank of a watercourse.
14 Give off a sweet smell like incense,
flower like the lily, spread your fragrance abroad,
sing a song of praise
blessing the Lord for all his works.
15 Declare the greatness of his name,
proclaim his praise
with song and with lyre,
and this is how you must sing his praises:
16 'How wonderful, the actions of the Lord!
Whatever he orders is done at the proper time!'
You must not say, 'What is this? Why is that?'
There is a proper time for every question.
17 At his word, the water stops and piles up high,
at his voice, the watery reservoirs take shape,
18 at his command, whatever he wants is done,
no one can stop him, if he intends to save.
19 He can see whatever human beings are doing,
nothing can be hidden from his eye;
20 his gaze stretches from eternity to eternity,
and nothing can astonish him.

39a =44:15.

21 You must not say, 'What is this? Why is that?'
for everything has been made for a purpose.

22 As his blessing covers the dry land like a river
and soaks it like a flood,
23 so retribution is his legacy to the nations,
just as he has turned fresh waters to salt.
24 His ways are as smooth for the devout,
as they are full of obstacles for the wicked.
25 Good things were created from the beginning for good people,
as bad ones were for sinners.
26 The prime needs of human beings for living
are water and fire, iron and salt,
wheat-flour, milk and honey,
the juice of the grape, oil and clothing.
27 All these are good for those who are good,
but turn out bad for sinners.

28 Some winds have been created for punishing,
in his fury, he uses them as scourges;
on the day of doom, they unleash their violence
and appease the wrath of their Creator.
29 Fire and hail, famine and death,
have all been created for punishing.
30 Wild animals' fangs, scorpions, vipers,
the avenging sword for the ruin of the godless:
31 all of them exult in discharging his orders,
ready on earth whenever the need arises
and, when their time comes, not falling short of his word.

32 That is why I was determined from the outset,
why I have pondered and why I have written,
33 'The works of the Lord are all good,
when the time is right, he gives whatever is needed.
34 You must not say, "This is worse than that,"
for, sooner or later, everything proves its worth.
35 So now, sing with all your heart and voice,
and bless the name of the Lord!'

Human wretchedness

40 A hard lot has been created for human beings,
a heavy yoke lies on the children of Adam
from the day they come out of their mother's womb,
till the day they return to the mother of them all.
2 What fills them with foreboding and their hearts with fear
is dread of the day of death.
3 From the one who sits on a glorious throne
to the wretch in dust and ashes,
4 from the one who wears purple and a crown
to the one dressed in sacking,
all is fury and jealousy, turmoil and unrest,
fear of death, rivalry, strife.
5 And even at night while he rests on his bed
his sleep only gives a new twist to his worries:
6 scarcely has he lain down to rest,
when in his sleep, as if in broad daylight,

he is troubled with nightmares,
like one who has escaped from a battle,
7 and at the moment of rescue he wakes up,
amazed that there was nothing to be afraid of!
8 For all creatures, human and animal—
and seven times more for sinners—
9 there is death and blood and strife and the sword,
disasters, famine, affliction, plague.
10 These things were all created for the wicked,
and the Flood came because of them.
11 All that comes from the earth returns to the earth,[a]
and what comes from the water returns to the sea.

Various maxims

12 All bribery and injustice will be blotted out,
but good faith will stand for ever.
13 Ill-gotten wealth will vanish like a torrent,
like the single thunder-clap that heralds rain.
14 When he opens his hand, he rejoices,
by the same token, sinners come to ruin.
15 The sprigs of the godless will not make many branches,
tainted roots find only hard rock.
16 The reed that grows by every lake and river's edge
is the first plant to be uprooted.
17 Charity is a very paradise of blessing
and almsgiving endures for ever.
18 For a person of private means and one who works hard, life is pleasant,
better off than either, one who finds a treasure.
19 Children and the founding of a city perpetuate a name:
more esteemed than either, a perfect wife.
20 Wine and music cheer the heart;
better than either, the love of wisdom.
21 Flute and harp add sweetness to a song;
better than either, a melodious voice.
22 The eye longs for grace and beauty;
better than either, the green of spring corn.
23 Friend or comrade—it is always well met;
better than either, a wife and husband.
24 Brothers and allies are good in times of trouble;
better than either, almsgiving to the rescue.
25 Gold and silver will steady your feet;
more esteemed than either, good advice.
26 Money and strength make a confident heart;
better than either, the fear of the Lord.
With fear of the Lord, nothing is lacking:
no need to seek for other help.
27 Fear of the Lord is a paradise of blessing,
a better protection than the highest reputation.

Sponging

28 My child, do not live by sponging off others,
better be dead than be a sponger.

40a =41:10.

29 A life spent in eyeing someone else's table
cannot be accounted a life at all.
Other people's food defiles the gullet;
a wise, well-brought-up person will beware of doing this.
30 What a sponger says may sound very sweet
but in his belly there burns a fire.

Death

41 O death, how bitter it is to remember you
for someone peacefully living with his possessions,
for someone with no worries and everything going well
and who can still enjoy his food!

2 O death, your sentence is welcome
to one in want, whose strength is failing,
to one worn out with age and a thousand worries,
resentful and impatient!

3 Do not dread death's sentence;
remember those who came before you and those who will come after.
4 This is the sentence passed on all living creatures by the Lord,
so why object to what seems good to the Most High?
Whether your life lasts ten or a hundred or a thousand years,
its length will not be held against you in Sheol.

The fate of the wicked

5 Hateful brats, such are the children of sinners,
who foregather in the haunts of the godless.
6 The inheritance of sinners' children is doomed to perish,
their posterity will endure lasting reproach.
7 A godless father will be blamed by his children
for the reproach he has brought on them.
8 A bad outlook for you, godless people,
who have forsaken the Law of God Most High.
9 When you were born, you were born to be accursed,
and when you die, that curse will be your portion.
10 All that comes from the earth returns to the earth,[a]
so too the wicked proceed from curse to destruction.
11 Mourning concerns only the bodies of the dead,
but the worthless name of sinners will be blotted out.

12 Be careful of your reputation, for it will last you longer
than a thousand great hoards of gold.
13 A good life lasts a certain number of days,
but a good reputation lasts for ever.

Sense of shame

14 Keep my instructions and be at peace, my children.

Wisdom[b] hidden away and treasure undisplayed,
what use is either of these?
15 Better someone who hides his folly
than one who hides his wisdom.

41a =40:11.
41b =20:30–31.

16 Preserve a sense of shame in the following matters,
for not every kind of shame is right to harbour,
nor is every situation correctly appraised by all.
17 Be ashamed, before father and mother, of depraved behaviour,
and before prince or potentate of telling lies;
18 of wrong-doing before judge or magistrate,
and of impiety before the assembly of the people;
19 of sharp practice before your companion and your friend,
and of theft before the neighbourhood you live in.
20 Before the truth and covenant of God,
be ashamed of leaning elbows on the table,
21 of being ungracious when giving or receiving,
of ignoring those who greet you,
22 of gazing at a loose woman,
of repulsing your fellow-countryman,
23 of misappropriating another's portion or gift,
of paying court to another man's wife,
24 of making advances to his servant-girl
—do not go near her bed—
25 of saying disagreeable things to friends
—do not follow up a gift with a taunt—
26 of repeating everything you hear
and of betraying confidences.
27 Then you will know what true shame is,
and you will find yourself in everyone's graces.

42 1 The following things you should not be ashamed of,
and do not sin from fear of what others think:
2 of the Law of the Most High or of the covenant,
of a verdict that acquits the godless,
3 of keeping accounts with a travelling companion,
of settling property on your friends,
4 of being accurate over scales and weights,
of making small and large profits,
5 of gaining from commercial transactions,
of disciplining your children strictly,
of lashing a wicked slave till you draw blood.
6 With an interfering wife, it is as well to use your seal,
and where there are many hands, lock things up.
7 Whatever stores you issue, do it by number and weight,
spendings and takings, put everything in writing.
8 Do not be ashamed to correct a stupid person or a fool,
or an old dotard who bickers with young people.
Then you will show yourself really educated
and win the approval of everyone.

Worries of a father with a daughter

9 Unknown to her, a daughter keeps her father awake,
the worry she gives him drives away his sleep:
in her youth, in case she never marries,
married, in case she should be disliked,
10 as a virgin, in case she should be defiled
and found with child in her father's house,
having a husband, in case she goes astray,
married, in case she should be sterile!

[11]Your daughter is headstrong? Keep a sharp look-out
that she does not make you the laughing-stock of your enemies,
the talk of the town, the object of common gossip,
and put you to public shame.

Women

[12]Do not stare at any man for his good looks,
do not sit down with women;
[13]for moth comes out of clothes,
and woman's spite out of woman.
[14]Better a man's spite than a woman's kindness:
women give rise to shame and reproach.

II: THE GLORY OF GOD

A: IN NATURE

[15]Next, I shall remind you of the works of the Lord,
and tell of what I have seen.
By the words of the Lord his works come into being
and all creation obeys his will.
[16]The shining sun looks down on all things,
and the work of the Lord is full of his glory.
[17]The Lord has not granted the Holy Ones the power
to tell of all his marvels
which the Almighty Lord has solidly constructed
for the universe to stand firm in his glory.
[18]He has fathomed both the abyss and the human heart
and seen into their devious ways;
for the Most High knows all there is to know
and sees the signs of the times.
[19]He declares what is past and what will be,
and reveals the trend of hidden things.
[20]Not a thought escapes him,
not a single word is hidden from him.
[21]He has embellished the magnificent works of his wisdom,
he is from everlasting to everlasting,
nothing can be added to him, nothing taken away,
he needs no one's advice.
[22]How lovely, all his works,
how dazzling to the eye!
[23]They all live and last for ever,
and, whatever the circumstances, all obey.
[24]All things go in pairs, by opposites,
he has not made anything imperfect:
[25]one thing complements the excellence of another.
Who could ever grow tired of gazing at his glory?

The sun

43 Pride of the heights, a clear vault of the sky—
such is the beauty of the heavens, a glorious sight.

2The sun, as he emerges, proclaims at his rising,
'How wonderful a thing, the work of the Most High!'
3At his zenith, he parches the ground,
who can withstand his blaze?
4We have to blow the furnace to produce any heat,
the sun burns the mountains three times as much;
breathing out blasts of fire,
flashing his rays, he dazzles the eyes.
5Great is the Lord who created him
and whose word speeds him on his course.

The moon

6And then the moon, ever punctual
to mark the times, an everlasting sign:
7It is the moon that signals the feasts,
a luminary that wanes after being full.
8The month derives its name from hers,
she waxes wonderfully in her phases,
banner of the hosts on high,
shining in the vault of heaven.

The stars

9The glory of the stars makes the beauty of the sky,
a brilliant adornment of the Lord on High.
10At the words of the Holy One they stand as he decrees,
and never grow slack at their watch.

The rainbow

11See the rainbow and praise its Maker,
so superbly beautiful in its splendour.
12Across the sky it forms a glorious arc
drawn by the hands of the Most High.

The wonders of nature

13By his command he sends the snow,
he speeds the lightning by his command.
14In the same way, his treasuries open
and the clouds fly out like birds.
15His great power solidifies the clouds,
then pulverises them into hail.
17aAt the roar of his thunder, the earth writhes in labour,
16 at the sight of him, the mountains quake.
At his will the south wind blows,
17bor the storm from the north and the whirlwind.
18He sprinkles snow like birds alighting,
it comes down like locusts settling.
The eye marvels at the beauty of its whiteness,
and the mind is amazed at its falling.
19Over the earth, like salt, he also pours hoarfrost,
which, when it freezes, bristles like thorns.
20The cold wind blows from the north,
and ice forms on the water;

it forms on every piece of standing water,
covering it like a breastplate.
21 The wind swallows up the mountains and scorches the desert,
like a fire it consumes the vegetation.
22 But cloud brings swift healing,
and dew brings joy after the heat.

23 By his own resourcefulness he has tamed the abyss,
and planted it with islands.
24 Those who sail the sea tell of its dangers,
their accounts fill our ears with amazement:
25 for there too exist strange and wonderful works,
animals of every kind and huge sea creatures.
26 Thanks to God, his messenger reaches port,
everything works out according to his word.

27 We could say much more and still fall short;
to put it concisely, 'He is all.'
28 Where shall we find sufficient power to glorify him,
since he is the Great One, above all his works,
29 the awe-inspiring Lord, stupendously great,
and wonderful in his power?
30 Exalt the Lord in your praises
as high as you may—still he surpasses you.
Exert all your strength when you exalt him,
do not grow tired—you will never come to the end.
31 Who has ever seen him to describe him?
Who can glorify him as he deserves?
32 Many mysteries remain even greater than these,
for we have seen only a few of his works,
33 the Lord himself having created all things
and given wisdom to those who are devout.

B: IN HISTORY

Eulogy of the ancestors

44 Next let us praise illustrious men,
our ancestors in their successive generations.
2 The Lord has created an abundance of glory,
and displayed his greatness from earliest times.
3 Some wielded authority as kings
and were renowned for their strength;
others were intelligent advisers
and uttered prophetic sayings.
4 Others directed the people by their advice,
by their understanding of the popular mind,
and by the wise words of their teaching;
5 others composed musical melodies
and set down ballads;
6 others were rich and powerful,
living peacefully in their homes.
7 All these were honoured by their contemporaries
and were the glory of their day.
8 Some of them left a name behind them,
so that their praises are still sung.

[9]While others have left no memory,
and disappeared as though they had not existed.
They are now as though they had never been,
and so too, their children after them.

[10]But here is a list of illustrious men
whose good works have not been forgotten.
[11]In their descendants they find
a rich inheritance, their posterity.
[12]Their descendants stand by the commandments
and, thanks to them, so do their children's children.
[13]Their offspring will last for ever,
their glory will not fade.
[14]Their bodies have been buried in peace,
and their name lives on for all generations.
[15]The peoples will proclaim their wisdom,
the assembly will celebrate their praises.[a]

Enoch

[16]Enoch pleased the Lord and was transferred to heaven,
an example for the conversion of all generations.

Noah

[17]Noah was found perfectly upright,
in the time of retribution he became the heir:
because of him a remnant was preserved for the earth
at the coming of the Flood.
[18]Everlasting covenants were made with him
that never again should every living creature perish by flood.

Abraham

[19]Abraham, the great ancestor of a host of nations,
no one was ever his equal in glory.
[20]He observed the Law of the Most High,
and entered into a covenant with him.
He confirmed the covenant in his own flesh,
and proved himself faithful under ordeal.
[21]The Lord therefore promised him on oath
to bless the nations through his descendants,
to multiply him like the dust on the ground,
to exalt his descendants like the stars,
and to give them the land as their heritage,
from one sea to the other,
from the River to the ends of the earth.

Isaac and Jacob

[22]To Isaac too, for the sake of Abraham his father,
he assured [23]the blessing of all humanity;
he caused the covenant to rest on the head of Jacob.

44a =39:10.

He confirmed him in his blessings
and gave him the land as his inheritance;
he divided it into portions,
and shared it out among the twelve tribes.

Moses

45 From Jacob's stock he produced a generous man
who found favour in the eyes of all humanity,
beloved by God and people,
Moses, of blessed memory.
2 He made him the equal of the holy ones in glory
and made him strong, to the terror of his enemies.
3 By the word of Moses, he made prodigies cease
and raised him high in the respect of kings;
he gave him commandments for his people,
and showed him something of his glory.
4 For his loyalty and gentleness he sanctified him,
choosing him alone out of all human beings;
5 he allowed him to hear his voice,
and led him into the darkness;
6 he gave him the commandments face to face,
the law of life and knowledge,
to teach Jacob his ordinances
and Israel his decrees.

Aaron

He raised up Aaron, a holy man like Moses,
his brother, of the tribe of Levi.
7 He made an everlasting covenant with him,
and gave him the priesthood of the people.
He adorned him with impressive vestments,
he dressed him in a robe of glory.
8 He clothed him in glorious perfection
and invested him with rich ornaments,
the breeches, the long robe, the *ephod*.
9 To surround the robe he gave him pomegranates,
and many gold bells all round
to chime at every step,
for their sound to be heard in the Temple
as a reminder to the children of his people;
10 and a sacred vestment of gold and aquamarine
and scarlet, the work of an embroiderer;
the pectoral of judgement, the *urim* and *thummim*,
of plaited crimson, the work of a craftsman;
11 precious stones cut like seals
mounted in gold, the work of a jeweller,
as a reminder with their engraved inscriptions
of the number of the tribes of Israel;
12 and a golden diadem on his turban,
engraved with the seal of consecration;
superb ornamentation, magnificent work,
adornment to delight the eye.
13 There had never been such lovely things before him,
and no one else has ever put them on,

but only his own sons,
and his descendants for all time.
14 His sacrifices were to be burnt entirely,
twice each day and for ever.
15 Moses consecrated him
and anointed him with holy oil;
and this was an everlasting covenant for him,
and for his descendants as long as the heavens endure,
that he should preside over worship, act as priest,
and bless the people in the name of the Lord.
16 He chose him out of all the living
to offer sacrifices to the Lord,
incense and perfume as a memorial
to make expiation for the people.
17 He entrusted him with his commandments,
committed to him the statutes of the Law
for him to teach Jacob his decrees
and enlighten Israel on his Law.
18 Others plotted against him,
they were jealous of him in the desert,
Dathan and Abiram and their men,
Korah and his crew in fury and rage.
19 The Lord saw it and was displeased,
his raging fury made an end of them;
he worked miracles on them,
consuming them by his flaming fire.
20 And he added to Aaron's glory,
he gave him an inheritance;
he allotted him the offerings of the first-fruits,
before all else, as much bread as he could want.
21 Thus they eat the sacrifices of the Lord
which he gave to him and his posterity.
22 But of the people's territory he inherits nothing,
he alone of all the people has no share,
'For I myself am your share and heritage.'

Phinehas

23 Phinehas son of Eleazar is third in glory
because of his zeal in the fear of the Lord,
because he stood firm when the people revolted,
with a staunch and courageous heart;
and in this way made expiation for Israel.
24 Hence a covenant of peace was sealed with him,
making him governor of both sanctuary and people,
and securing to him and his descendants
the high priestly dignity for ever.
25 There was also a covenant with David
son of Jesse, of the tribe of Judah,
a royal succession by exclusively linear descent,
but the succession of Aaron passes to all his descendants.
26 May God endow your hearts with wisdom
to judge his people uprightly,
so that the virtues of your ancestors may never fade,
and their glory may pass to all their descendants!

Joshua

46 Mighty in war was Joshua son of Nun,
successor to Moses in the prophetic office,
who well deserved his name,[a]
and was a great saviour of the chosen people,
wreaking vengeance on the enemies who opposed him,
and so bringing Israel into its inheritance.
2 How splendid he was when, arms uplifted,
he brandished his sword against cities!
3 Who had ever shown such determination as his?
He himself led the battles of the Lord.
4 Was not the sun held back by his hand,
and one day drawn out into two?
5 He called on the Most High, the Mighty One,
while pressing the enemies from all directions,
and the great Lord answered him
with hard and violent hailstones.
6 He fell on that enemy nation,
and at the Descent destroyed all resistance
to make the nations acknowledge his warlike prowess
and that he was waging war on behalf of the Lord.

Caleb

7 For he was a follower of the Mighty One,
in the time of Moses showing his devotion,
he and Caleb son of Jephunneh,
by opposing the whole community,
by preventing the people from sinning,
and by silencing the mutters of rebellion.
8 Hence these two alone were preserved
out of six hundred thousand men on the march,
and brought into their inheritance,
into a land where milk and honey flow.
9 And the Lord conferred strength on Caleb too,
which stayed by him into old age,
so that he could invest the highlands of the country
which his descendants kept as their inheritance,
10 so that every Israelite might see
that it is good to follow the Lord.

The Judges

11 The Judges too, each when he was called,
all men whose hearts were never disloyal,
who never turned their backs on the Lord—
may their memory be blessed!
12 May their bones flourish again from the tomb,
and may the names of those illustrious men
be worthily borne by their sons!

46a *Yehoshua'* (=Joshua) means 'Yahweh saves'.

Samuel

13 Samuel was the beloved of his Lord;
prophet of the Lord, he instituted the kingdom,
and anointed rulers over his people.
14 By the Law of the Lord he judged the assembly,
and the Lord watched over Jacob.
15 By his loyalty he was recognised as a prophet,
by his words he was known to be a trustworthy seer.
16 He called on the Lord, the Mighty One,
when his enemies pressed in from all directions,
by offering a sucking lamb.
17 And the Lord thundered from heaven,
and made his voice heard in a rolling peal;
18 he massacred the leaders of the enemy,
and all the rulers of the Philistines.
19 Before the time of his everlasting rest
he bore witness to the Lord and his anointed,
'Of no property, not even a pair of sandals,
have I ever deprived a soul.'
Nor did anyone accuse him.
20 And, having fallen asleep, he prophesied again,
warning the king of his end;
he spoke from the depths of the earth in prophecy,
to blot out the wickedness of the people.

Nathan

47 After him arose Nathan,
to prophesy in the time of David.

David

2 As the fat is set apart from the communion sacrifice,
so was David chosen out of the Israelites.
3 He played with lions as though with kids,
and with bears as though with lambs.
4 While still a boy, did he not slay the giant
and take away the people's shame,
by hurling a stone from his sling
and cutting short the boasting of Goliath?
5 For he called on the Lord Most High,
who gave strength to his right arm
to put a mighty warrior to death
and assert the strength of his own people.
6 Hence they gave him credit for ten thousand,
and praised him while they blessed the Lord,
by offering him a crown of glory.
7 For he destroyed the enemies on every front,
he annihilated his foes, the Philistines,
and crushed their strength for ever.
8 In all his activities he gave thanks
to the Holy One Most High in words of glory;
he put all his heart into his songs
out of love for his Creator.

9 He placed singers before the altar,
melodiously to sing;
10 he gave the feasts their splendour,
the festivals their solemn pomp,
causing the Lord's holy name to be praised
and the sanctuary to resound from dawn.
11 The Lord took away his sins,
making his strength ever greater;
he gave him a royal covenant,
and a glorious throne in Israel.

Solomon

12 A wise son succeeded him,
who lived content, thanks to him.
13 Solomon reigned in a time of peace,
and God gave him peace all round
so that he could raise a house to his name
and prepare an everlasting sanctuary.
14 How wise you were despite your youth,
like a river, brimming over with intelligence!
15 Your mind ranged the earth,
you filled it with mysterious sayings.
16 Your name reached the distant islands,
and you were loved for your peace.[a]
17 Your songs, your proverbs, your sayings
and your answers were the wonder of the world.
18 In the name of the Lord God,
of him who is called the God of Israel,
you amassed gold like so much tin,
and made silver as common as lead.
19 You abandoned your body to women,
you became the slave of your appetites.
20 You stained your honour,
you profaned your stock,
so bringing retribution on your children
and affliction for your folly:
21 the empire split in two,
from Ephraim arose a rebel kingdom.
22 But the Lord never goes back on his mercy,
never cancels any of his words,
will neither deny offspring to his elect
nor stamp out the line of the man who loved him.
And hence, he has granted a remnant to Jacob
and to David a root sprung from him.

Rehoboam

23 Solomon rested with his ancestors,
leaving one of his stock as his successor,
the stupidest member of the nation,
brainless Rehoboam, who drove the people to rebel.

47a Solomon means 'man of peace'.

Jeroboam

[24]Next, Jeroboam son of Nebat, who made Israel sin,
and set Ephraim on the way of evil;
from then on their sins multiplied so excessively
as to drive them out of their country;
[25]for they tried out every kind of wickedness,
until vengeance overtook them.

Elijah

48 Then the prophet Elijah arose like a fire,
his word flaring like a torch.
[2]It was he who brought famine on them
and decimated them in his zeal.
[3]By the word of the Lord he shut up the heavens,
three times also he brought down fire.
[4]How glorious you were in your miracles, Elijah!
Has anyone reason to boast as you have?—
[5]rousing a corpse from death,
from Sheol, by the word of the Most High;
[6]dragging kings down to destruction,
and high dignitaries from their beds;
[7]hearing a rebuke on Sinai
and decrees of punishment on Horeb;
[8]anointing kings as avengers,
and prophets to succeed you;
[9]taken up in the whirlwind of fire,
in a chariot with fiery horses;
[10]designated in the prophecies of doom
to allay God's wrath before the fury breaks,
to turn the hearts of fathers towards their children,[a]
and to restore the tribes of Jacob.
[11]Blessed, those who will see you,
and those who have fallen asleep in love;
for we too shall certainly have life.

Elisha

[12]Such was Elijah, who was enveloped in a whirlwind;
and Elisha was filled with his spirit;
throughout his life no ruler could shake him,
and no one could subdue him.
[13]No task was too hard for him,
and even in death his body prophesied.
[14]In his lifetime he performed wonders,
and in death his works were marvellous.

Infidelity and punishment

[15]Despite all this the people did not repent,
nor did they give up their sins,
until they were herded out of their country
and scattered all over the earth;

48a Ml 3:24.

16 only a few of the people were left,
with a ruler of the House of David.
Some of them did what pleased the Lord,
others piled sin on sin.

Hezekiah

17 Hezekiah fortified his city,
and laid on a water-supply inside it;
with iron he tunnelled through the rock
and constructed storage-tanks.
18 In his days Sennacherib invaded
and sent Rabshakeh;
he lifted his hand against Zion,
and boasted loudly in his arrogance.
19 Then their hearts and hands trembled,
they felt the pangs of a woman in labour,
20 but they called on the merciful Lord,
stretching out their hands towards him.
Swiftly the Holy One heard them from heaven
and delivered them by the agency of Isaiah;
21 he struck the camp of the Assyrians
and his Angel annihilated them.

Isaiah

22 For Hezekiah did what is pleasing to the Lord,
and was steadfast[b] in the ways of David his father,
enjoined on him by the prophet Isaiah,
a great man trustworthy in his vision.
23 In his days the sun moved back;
he prolonged the life of the king.
24 In the power of the spirit he saw the last things,
he comforted the mourners of Zion,
25 he revealed the future to the end of time,
and hidden things long before they happened.

Josiah

49 The memory of Josiah is like blended incense
prepared by the perfumer's art;
it is as sweet as honey to all mouths,
and like music at a wine feast.
2 He took the right course, of converting the people,
he rooted out the iniquitous abominations,
3 he set his heart on the Lord,
in godless times he upheld the cause of religion.

The last kings and prophets

4 Apart from David, Hezekiah and Josiah,
they all heaped wrong on wrong,
they abandoned the Law of the Most High:
the kings of Judah disappeared;

48b Word-play on 'Hezekiah' (=Yahweh makes strong).

5 for they handed their power over to others
and their honour to a foreign nation.
6 The holy, chosen city was burnt down,
her streets were left deserted,
7 as Jeremiah had predicted; for they had ill-treated him,
though consecrated a prophet in his mother's womb,
to tear up and afflict *and destroy*,
but also *to build up and to plant*.[a]
8 Ezekiel saw a vision of glory
which God showed to him
above the chariot of the great winged creatures,
9 for he mentioned the enemies in the downpour
to the advantage of those who follow the right way.
10 As for the twelve prophets,
may their bones flower again from the tomb,
since they have comforted Jacob
and redeemed him in faith and hope.

Zerubbabel and Joshua

11 How shall we extol Zerubbabel?
He was like a signet ring on the right hand,
12 so too was Joshua son of Jozadak;
they who in their days built the Temple
and raised a sanctuary sacred to the Lord,
destined to everlasting glory.

Nehemiah

13 Great too is the memory of Nehemiah,
who rebuilt our walls which lay in ruins,
erected the bolted gates
and rebuilt our houses.

Retrospect

14 No one else has ever been created on earth to equal Enoch,
for he was taken up from earth.
15 And no one else ever born has been like Joseph,
the leader of his brothers, the prop of his people;
his bones received a visitation.
16 Shem and Seth were the most honoured of men,
but above every living creature is Adam.

Simon[a] the high priest

50 It was the High Priest Simon son of Onias
who repaired the Temple during his lifetime
and in his day fortified the sanctuary.
2 He laid the foundations of double depth,
the high buttresses of the Temple precincts.
3 In his day the pool was excavated,
a reservoir as huge as the sea.

49a Jr 1:10.
50a Simon II, son of Onias III, high priest *c.* 220–195 BC.

4Anxious to save the people from ruin,
he fortified the city against siege.
5How splendid he was with the people thronging round him,
when he emerged from the curtained shrine,
6like the morning star among the clouds,
like the moon at the full,
7like the sun shining on the Temple of the Most High,
like the rainbow gleaming against brilliant clouds,
8like a rose in springtime,
like a lily by a spring,
like a branch of the incense tree in summer,
9like fire and incense in the censer,
like a massive golden vessel
encrusted with every kind of precious stone,
10like an olive tree loaded with fruit,
like a cypress soaring to the clouds;
11when he took his ceremonial robe
and put on his magnificent ornaments,
when he went up to the holy altar
and filled the sanctuary precincts with his grandeur;
12when he received the portions from the hands of the priests,
himself standing by the altar hearth,
crowned with the circle of his brothers,
as a cedar of Lebanon is by its foliage,
as though surrounded by the trunks of palm trees.
13When all the sons of Aaron in their glory,
with the offerings of the Lord in their hands,
stood before the whole assembly of Israel,
14while he completed the rites at the altars,
nobly presenting the offerings to the Almighty, Most High!
15He would reach out his hand to the cup
and pour a libation of wine,
pouring it at the foot of the altar,
a fragrance pleasing to the Most High, King of All;
16then the sons of Aaron would shout
and blow their metal trumpets,
making a mighty sound ring out
as a reminder before the Most High;
17and immediately the people all together
would fall on their faces to the ground,
in adoration of their Lord,
the Almighty, God Most High,
18and with the cantors chanting their hymns of praise.
Sweet was the melody of all these voices,
19as the people pleaded with the Lord Most High
and prayed in the presence of the Merciful,
until the service of the Lord was completed
and the ceremony at an end.
20Then he would come down and raise his hands
over the whole assembly of the Israelites,
to give them the Lord's blessing from his lips,
being privileged to pronounce his name;
21and once again the people would bow low
to receive the blessing of the Most High.

Exhortation

22 And now bless the God of all things,
the doer of great deeds everywhere,
who has exalted our days from the womb
and has acted mercifully towards us.
23 May he grant us cheerful hearts
and bring peace in our time,
in Israel for ages on ages.
24 May his mercy be faithfully with us,
may he redeem us in our own times!

Numerical proverb

25 There are two nations that my soul detests,
the third is not a nation at all:
26 the inhabitants of Mount Seir, the Philistines,
and the stupid people living at Shechem.

Conclusion

27 Instruction in wisdom and knowledge
is what has been written in this book
by Jesus son of Sira Eleazar of Jerusalem,
who has poured a rain of wisdom from his heart.
28 Blessed is he who devotes his time to these
and grows wise by taking them to heart!
29 If he practises them he will be strong enough for anything,
since the light of the Lord is his path.

APPENDICES

Hymn of thanksgiving

51 I shall give thanks to you, Lord and King,
and praise you, God my Saviour,
I give thanks to your name;
2 for you have been my guard and support
and redeemed my body from destruction,
from the snare of the lying tongue,
from lips that fabricate falsehood;
in the presence of my assailants, you were on my side;
you have been my support, you have redeemed me,
3 true to your abounding kindness
—and the greatness of your name—you liberated me
from the fangs of those seeking to devour me,
from the clutches of those seeking my life,
from the many ordeals which I have endured,
4 from the stifling heat which hemmed me in,
from the heart of a fire which I had not kindled,
5 from deep in the belly of Sheol,
6 treacherous denunciations to the king.
My soul has been close to death,
my life had gone down to the brink of Sheol.

7 I was completely surrounded, there was no one to help me;
I looked for someone to help me, there was no one.
8 Then I remembered your mercy, Lord,
and your deeds from earliest times,
how you deliver those who wait for you patiently,
and save them from the clutches of their enemies.
9 And I sent up my plea from the earth,
I begged to be delivered from death.
10 I called on the Lord, the father of my Lord,
'Do not desert me in the days of ordeal,
in the days of the proud, when we are helpless.
I shall praise your name unceasingly
and gratefully sing its praises.'
11 And my plea was heard,
for you saved me from destruction,
you delivered me from that time of evil.
12 And therefore I shall thank you and praise you,
and bless the name of the Lord.

Poem on the quest for wisdom

13 When I was still a youth, before I went travelling,
in my prayers I asked outright for wisdom.
14 Outside the sanctuary I would pray for her,
and to the last I shall continue to seek her.
15 From her blossoming to the ripening of her grape
my heart has taken its delight in her.
My foot has pursued a straight path,
I have sought her ever since my youth.
16 By bowing my ear a little, I have received her,
and have found much instruction.
17 Thanks to her I have advanced;
glory be to him who has given me wisdom!
18 For I was determined to put her into practice,
have earnestly pursued the good, and shall not be put to shame.
19 My soul has fought to possess her,
I have been scrupulous in keeping the Law;
I have stretched out my hands to heaven
and bewailed how little I knew of her;
20 I have directed my soul towards her,
and in purity I have found her;
having my heart fixed on her from the outset,
I shall never be deserted;
21 my very core having yearned to discover her,
I have now acquired a good possession.
22 In reward the Lord has given me a tongue
with which I shall sing his praises.
23 Come close to me, you ignorant,
take your place in my school.
24 Why complain about lacking these things
when your souls are so thirsty for them?
25 I have opened my mouth, I have said:
'Buy her without money,
26 put your necks under her yoke,
let your souls receive instruction,
she is near, within your reach.'

27 See for yourselves: how slight my efforts have been
to win so much peace.
28 Buy instruction with a large sum of silver,
thanks to her you will gain much gold.
29 May your souls rejoice in the mercy of the Lord,
may you never be ashamed of praising him.
30 Do your work before the appointed time
and at the appointed time he will give you your reward.

(*Subscript:*) Wisdom of Jesus, son of Sira.

INTRODUCTION TO THE PROPHETS

Inspired speakers who claim to give a divine message are not confined to Israel. Balaam of Moab and the prophets of Baal appear in the Bible. In the early monarchy we glimpse two groups of prophets: brotherhoods of prophets such as those with whom the young Saul and Elisha were associated, and court prophets who claimed to interpret God's will to their royal masters. More often than not – Nathan is one exception – these were more concerned with pleasing the king than with giving him God's message.

In the time of crisis which preceded the end of the monarchy, first in the northern kingdom (overrun by Assyria in 721 BC) then in the south (conquered by Babylon in 586) great prophets emerged whose message is recorded and whose sayings were written down in book form. At first their function was to warn the people against their prevailing faults and bring them back to fidelity and trust in Yahweh – so Amos and Hosea in the north and the great prophets Isaiah and Jeremiah in the south. Contemporary with Isaiah, Micah tried to draw the people and rulers from their corruption, and Jeremiah's part in the great reform of 622 was anticipated by Zephaniah's ministry. Both before and after the fall of Jerusalem Ezekiel brought to the exiles those promises of a new heart and a new covenant which Jeremiah had made in Jerusalem, and Second Isaiah soon afterwards encouraged them with a promise of return. After the return Haggai and Zechariah encouraged the beleaguered community to rebuild the Temple and soon afterwards Malachi criticised their faults of observance. In the last stage of prophecy Joel, the second part of Zechariah and finally Daniel look forward to a deliverance at a final Day of the Lord. Thus for six centuries the prophets were the guides and mediators of God's message to Israel. But their message of the transcendence and love of God for his people, and of his demand for reciprocal fidelity and holiness, go far beyond their immediate audience.

The divine message came to the prophets in various ways, sometimes by visions or through ordinary sights such as two baskets of figs (Jr 24), sometimes through personal experiences such as Hosea's passionate love for his unfaithful wife. They expressed the message just as diversely by symbolic actions; by parables, satires and funeral laments – addressed to kings, leaders or the people at large. Only in very few cases was the message written down by, or at the order of, the prophet. In most cases the sayings and narratives were collected later by disciples and combined, seldom in chronological order, more often in some kind of logical order or by verbal links. In most cases additions and adjustments to make the prophecies applicable to later circumstances have made the original message even harder to recover.

THE BOOK OF ISAIAH

The message of the prophet Isaiah is shaped by his opening vision (ch. 6) of the glory and sanctity of God confronting human sin. Always in awe of God's majesty, Isaiah speaks out against moral corruption and the fatal zeal of the kings of Judah to seek alliance with other nations rather than rely solely on Yahweh. Called in 740 BC, Isaiah delivers most of his prophecies at the time of three military threats to the kingdom, in 735 (the Syro-Ephraimite alliance of three local kings), 711 and 701 (Sargon and Sennacherib, kings of Assyria). Besides threats of disaster if Israel persists in putting its trust elsewhere than in Yahweh, he promises also the survival of a faithful remnant of Israel and the fulfilment of the promises to David of a kingdom of messianic peace. With some later insertions these prophecies form the content of chapters 1—35.

Some 150 years later an anonymous prophet, named Second Isaiah, took up this same message (chh. 40—55), foretelling the consolation of Israel by the end of the Babylonian exile. These chapters are marked by a vision of the Holy One of Israel as the Redeemer who will renew the miracles of the exodus, and by polemic against the idols of Babylon, where he was prophesying to the remnant of Israel. Notable among these chapters are four Songs of a Servant of Yahweh (42:1–9; 49:1–6; 50:4–11; 52:13—53:12) who will fulfil his task by bringing salvation to the nations through his own suffering. This mysterious figure has been variously thought to be the prophet himself, a personification of Israel, or the Messiah, and it was certainly one of the ways in which the early Church understood Jesus.

The third part of the book (56—66), written later still, mostly after the return from exile, takes up the same themes, with a wider openness to the salvation of all nations. These will flow to a restored Jerusalem to draw salvation from the City of Yahweh.

Spread over some 300 years, the prophecies of the Book of Isaiah are united not only by recurrent phrases and modes of thought but by a fundamental vision of the destiny of Israel inthe hand of the awesome, holy God who will cleanse the remnant of his erring people and bring them to a kingdom of peace.

PLAN OF THE BOOK

ISAIAH

I: THE FIRST PART OF THE BOOK OF ISAIAH

A: PROPHECIES BEFORE THE SYRO-EPHRAIMITE WAR

Title

1 The vision of Isaiah son of Amoz concerning Judah and Jerusalem, which he received in the reigns of Uzziah, Jotham, Ahaz and Hezekiah kings of Judah.

Against an ungrateful people

2 Listen, you heavens; earth, attend,
for Yahweh is speaking,
'I have reared children
and brought them up,
but they have rebelled against me.
3 The ox knows its owner
and the donkey its master's crib;
Israel does not know,
my people do not understand.'
4 Disaster, sinful nation,
people weighed down with guilt,
race of wrong-doers, perverted children!
They have abandoned Yahweh,
despised the Holy One of Israel,
they have turned away from him.
5 Where shall I strike you next,
if you persist in treason?
The whole head is sick,
the whole heart is diseased,
6 from the sole of the foot to the head
there is nothing healthy:
only wounds, bruises and open sores
not dressed, not bandaged,
not soothed with ointment,
7 your country a desolation,
your towns burnt down,
your soil, foreigners lay it waste
before your eyes,
a desolation like devastation by foreigners.
8 The daughter of Zion is left
like a shanty in a vineyard,
like a shed in a cucumber field,
like a city besieged.
9 Had Yahweh Sabaoth not left us
a few survivors,
we should be like Sodom,
we should be the same as Gomorrah.

Against hypocrisy

10 Hear what Yahweh says,
you rulers of Sodom;

listen to what our God teaches,
you people of Gomorrah.
11 'What are your endless sacrifices to me?'
says Yahweh.
'I am sick of burnt offerings of rams
and the fat of calves.
I take no pleasure in the blood
of bulls and lambs and goats.
12 When you come
and present yourselves before me,
who has asked you
to trample through my courts?
13 Bring no more futile cereal offerings,
the smoke from them fills me with disgust.
New Moons, Sabbaths, assemblies—
I cannot endure solemnity
combined with guilt.
14 Your New Moons and your meetings
I utterly detest;
to me they are a burden
I am tired of bearing.
15 When you stretch out your hands
I turn my eyes away.
You may multiply your prayers,
I shall not be listening.
Your hands are covered in blood,
16 wash, make yourselves clean.
Take your wrong-doing out of my sight.
Cease doing evil. 17 Learn to do good,
search for justice, discipline the violent,
be just to the orphan, plead for the widow.
18 'Come, let us talk this over,' says Yahweh.
'Though your sins are like scarlet,
they shall be white as snow;
though they are red as crimson,
they shall be like wool.
19 If you are willing to obey,
you shall eat the good things of the earth.
20 But if you refuse and rebel,
the sword shall eat you instead—
for Yahweh's mouth has spoken.'

Lament for Jerusalem

21 The faithful city,
what a harlot[a] she has become!
Zion, once full of fair judgement,
where saving justice used to dwell,
but now assassins!

22 Your silver has turned into dross,
your wine is watered.
23 Your princes are rebels,
accomplices of brigands.
All of them greedy for presents
and eager for bribes,
they show no justice to the orphan,
and the widow's cause
never reaches them.

24 Hence, the Lord Yahweh Sabaoth,
the Mighty One of Israel, says this,
'Disaster, I shall get the better
of my enemies,
I shall avenge myself on my foes.

25 'I shall turn my hand against you,
I shall purge your dross
as though with potash,
I shall remove all your alloy.

26 'And I shall restore your judges as at first,
your counsellors as in bygone days,
after which you will be called
City of Saving Justice,
Faithful City.'

27 Zion will be redeemed by fair judgement,
and those who return, by saving justice.
28 Rebels and sinners alike will be destroyed,
and those who abandon Yahweh
will perish.

Against sacred trees

29 How ashamed you will be
of the terebinths
which gave you such delight;
and how you will blush
for the gardens which you chose!
30 For you will be like a terebinth
with faded leaves,
like a garden without water;
31 the strong will become like tinder,
his work like the spark;
both will go up in flames together,
with no one to put them out.

Everlasting peace

2 The vision of Isaiah son of Amoz, concerning Judah and Jerusalem.

2 It will happen in the final days
that the mountain of Yahweh's house
will rise higher than the mountains
and tower above the heights.
Then all the nations will stream to it,
3 many peoples will come to it and say,

1a Prostitution is a frequent figure for unfaithfulness to Yahweh.

'Come, let us go up
to the mountain of Yahweh,
to the house of the God of Jacob
that he may teach us his ways
so that we may walk in his paths.'
For the Law will issue from Zion
and the word of Yahweh from Jerusalem.

4 Then he will judge between the nations
and arbitrate between many peoples
They will hammer their swords
into ploughshares
and their spears into sickles.
Nation will not lift sword against nation,
no longer will they learn how to make war.[a]

5 House of Jacob, come,
let us walk in Yahweh's light.

The brilliance of Yahweh's majesty

6 You have rejected your people,
the House of Jacob,
for it has long been full of sorcerers
like the Philistines,
and is overrun with foreigners.
7 The country is full of silver and gold
and treasures unlimited,
the country is full of horses,
its chariots are unlimited;
8 the country is full of idols.
They bow down
before the work of their hands,
before what their own fingers
have made.

9 Human nature has been humbled,
humankind brought low:
do not raise them again!
10 Go into the rock, hide in the dust,
in terror of Yahweh,
at the brilliance of his majesty,
when he arises to make the earth quake.

11 Human pride will lower its eyes,
human arrogance will be humbled,
and Yahweh alone will be exalted,
on that day.
12 That will be a day for Yahweh Sabaoth,
for all who are majestic and haughty,
for all who are proud, to be brought low,
13 for all the cedars of Lebanon,
high and proud,
and for all the oaks of Bashan;
14 for all the high mountains
and for all the proud hills;
15 for every lofty tower
and for every towering wall;
16 for all the ships of Tarshish
and for everything held precious.

17 Human pride will be humbled,
human arrogance brought low,
and Yahweh alone will be exalted,
on that day.

18 When the idols all disappear,
19 they will go into the caverns of the rocks
and into the fissures of the earth
in terror of Yahweh,
at the brilliance of his majesty,
when he arises to make the earth quake.

20 That day, people will fling to moles and
bats the silver idols and golden idols which
have been made for them to worship,

21 and go into the crevices of the rocks
and the clefts in the cliffs,
in terror of Yahweh,
at the brilliance of his majesty,
when he arises to make the earth quake.

22 Have no more to do with humankind,
which has only the breath in its nostrils.
How much is this worth?

Anarchy in Jerusalem

3 Now the Lord Yahweh Sabaoth
is about to deprive Jerusalem and Judah
of resources and provisions—
all reserves of food, all reserves of water—
2 of hero, warrior, judge, prophet,
diviner, elder, 3 captain, dignitary,
counsellor, architect, soothsayer.
4 'I shall give them boys for princes,
raw lads to rule over them.'
5 People will be ill-treated by one another,
each by his neighbour;
the young will insult the aged,
and the low, the respected.
6 Yes, a man will catch hold of his brother
in their father's house, to say,
'You have a cloak, so you be leader,
and rule this heap of ruins.'
7 And, that day, the other will protest,
'I am no healer;
in my house there is neither food
nor clothing;
do not make me leader of the people.'
8 For Jerusalem has collapsed
and Judah has fallen,

2a || Mi 4:1–3.

because their words and deeds
affront Yahweh
and insult his glorious gaze.
9 Their complacency bears witness
against them,
they parade their sin like Sodom;
they do not conceal it,
all the worse for them,
for they have hatched their own downfall.
10 Say, 'Blessed the upright,
for he will feed on the fruit of his deeds;
11 woe to the wicked, it will go ill with him,
for he will be treated
as his actions deserve.'
12 O my people,
their oppressors pillage them
and extortioners rule over them!
O my people, your rulers mislead you
and efface the paths you ought to follow!
13 Yahweh has risen to accuse,
is standing to pass judgement
on the people.
14 Yahweh is about to try
the elders and the princes of his people,
'You are the ones
who have ravaged the vineyard,
the spoils of the poor are in your houses.
15 By what right do you crush my people
and grind the faces of the poor?'
says the Lord Yahweh Sabaoth.

The women of Jerusalem

16 Yahweh says:

Because Zion's daughters are proud
and walk with heads held high
and enticing eyes—
with mincing steps they go,
jingling the bangles on their feet—
17 the Lord will give Zion's daughters
scabby heads,
Yahweh will lay their foreheads bare.

18 That day the Lord will take away the
ornamental chains, medallions, crescents,
19 pendants, bracelets, trinkets, 20 diadems,
ankle-chains, necklaces, scent bottles,
amulets, 21 finger-rings, nose-rings, 22 party
dresses, cloaks, scarves, purses, 23 mirrors,
linen clothes, turbans and mantillas.

24 Then, instead of perfume, a stink;
instead of belt, a rope,
instead of hair elaborately dressed,
a shaven scalp,
instead of gorgeous clothes,
sacking round the waist,
and brand marks instead of beauty.

Misery in Jerusalem

25 Your men will fall by the sword,
your warriors in battle,
26 and her gates will moan and mourn;
she will sit on the ground, deserted.

4 That day, seven women will catch hold of
one man and say, 'We will eat our own
food, and wear our own clothing, but just let
us bear your name. Take our disgrace away.'

Yahweh's seedling

2 That day, Yahweh's seedling
will turn to beauty and glory,
what the earth brings forth
will turn to the pride and ornament
of Israel's survivors.
3 Those who are left in Zion
and remain in Jerusalem
will be called holy,
all those in Jerusalem
noted down to live.
4 When the Lord has washed away
the filth of Zion's daughters
and with the wind of judgement
and the wind of burning cleansed
Jerusalem of the blood shed in her,
5 Yahweh will create,
over every house on Mount Zion
and over those who assemble there,
a cloud by day,
and by night smoke
with the brightness of a flaring fire.
For over all will be the Glory
as canopy 6 and tent
to give shade by day from the heat,
refuge and shelter from the storm
and the rain.

The song of the vineyard

5 Let me sing my beloved
the song of my friend for his vineyard.

My beloved had a vineyard
on a fertile hillside.
2 He dug it, cleared it of stones,
and planted it with red grapes.
In the middle he built a tower,
he hewed a press there too.
He expected it to yield fine grapes:
wild grapes were all it yielded.

[3]And now, citizens of Jerusalem
and people of Judah,
I ask you to judge between me
and my vineyard.
[4]What more could I have done
for my vineyard
that I have not done?
Why, when I expected it
to yield fine grapes,
has it yielded wild ones?

[5]Very well, I shall tell you
what I am going to do to my vineyard:
I shall take away its hedge,
for it to be grazed on,
and knock down its wall,
for it to be trampled on.
[6]I shall let it go to waste, unpruned, undug,
overgrown by brambles
and thorn-bushes,
and I shall command the clouds
to rain no rain on it.
[7]Now, the vineyard of Yahweh Sabaoth
is the House of Israel,
and the people of Judah
the plant he cherished.
He expected fair judgement,
but found injustice,
uprightness, but found cries of distress.

Curses

[8]Woe to those who add house to house
and join field to field
until there is nowhere left
and they are the sole inhabitants
of the country.
[9]Yahweh Sabaoth has sworn this
in my hearing,
'Many houses will be brought to ruin,
great and fine ones left untenanted;
[10]for ten acres of vineyard
will yield only one barrel,
and ten bushel of seed
will yield only one bushel.'

[11]Woe to those who get up early
to go after strong drink,
and stay up late at night
inflamed with wine.
[12]Nothing but harp and lyre,
tambourine and pipe,
and wine for their drinking bouts.

Never a thought for the works of Yahweh,
never a glance
for what his hands have done.
[13]That is why my people is in exile,
for want of perception;
her dignitaries starving,
her populace parched with thirst.
[14]That is why Sheol opens wide its throat
and gapes with measureless jaw
and down go her noblemen and populace
and her loud revellers merry to the last!

[15]Human nature has been humbled,
humankind brought low,[a]
and the eyes of the proud
have been humbled.
[16]Yahweh Sabaoth is the more respected
for his judgement,
God the Holy One
has displayed his holiness by his justice!
[17]Now the lambs will graze
in their old pastures,
and the fields laid waste by fat cattle
will feed the kids.

[18]Woe to those who drag guilt along
by the reins of duplicity,
drag along sin as though with a cart rope;
[19]to those who say,
'Why doesn't he do his work quickly
so that we can see it;
why doesn't the Holy One
of Israel's design
hurry up and come true
so that we can experience it?'

[20]Woe to those who call what is bad, good,
and what is good, bad,
who substitute darkness for light
and light for darkness,
who substitute bitter for sweet
and sweet for bitter.

[21]Woe to those who think themselves wise
and believe themselves enlightened.

[22]Woe to those whose might lies
in wine bibbing,
their heroism in mixing strong drinks,
[23]who acquit the guilty for a bribe
and deny justice to the upright.
[24]Yes, as the flame devours the stubble,
as the straw flares up and disappears,
their root will be like decay
and their shoot be carried off like dust,
for having rejected the law
of Yahweh Sabaoth,

5a The refrain of the poem in 2:6–22; perhaps vv. 14–16 belong there.

for having despised the word
of the Holy One of Israel.

Yahweh's anger

25 This is why Yahweh's anger
has blazed out against his people;
and he has raised his hand against them
to strike them;
why the mountains have shuddered
and why corpses are lying like dung
in the streets.
After all this, his anger is not spent.
No, his hand is still raised!

Yahweh summons the invaders

26 He hoists a signal for a distant nation,
he whistles them up
from the ends of the earth;
and see how swift, how fleet they come!

27 None of them tired,
none of them stumbling,
none of them asleep or drowsy,
none of them with belt unfastened,
none of them with broken sandal-strap.

28 Their arrows are sharpened,
their bows all strung,
their horses' hoofs
you would think were flint
and their wheels, a whirlwind!

29 Their roar is like that of a lioness,
like fierce young lions they roar,
growling they seize their prey
and carry it off,
with no one to prevent it,

30 growling at it, that day,
like the growling of the sea.
Only look at the country:
darkness and distress,
and the light turned to darkness
by the clouds.

B: THE BOOK OF IMMANUEL

The call of Isaiah

6 In the year of King Uzziah's death I saw
the Lord seated on a high and lofty throne;
his train filled the sanctuary.
2 Above him
stood seraphs, each one with six wings: two
to cover its face, two to cover its feet and two
for flying;
3 and they were shouting these
words to each other:

Holy, holy, holy is Yahweh Sabaoth.
His glory fills the whole earth.

4 The door-posts shook at the sound of their
shouting, and the Temple was full of smoke.
5 Then I said:

'Woe is me! I am lost,
for I am a man of unclean lips
and I live among a people of unclean lips,
and my eyes have seen the King,
Yahweh Sabaoth.'

6 Then one of the seraphs flew to me,
holding in its hand a live coal which it had
taken from the altar with a pair of tongs.
7 With this it touched my mouth and said:

'Look, this has touched your lips,
your guilt has been removed
and your sin forgiven.'

8 I then heard the voice of the Lord saying:

'Whom shall I send? Who will go for us?'

And I said, 'Here am I, send me.'
9 He said:

'Go, and say to this people,
"Listen and listen, but never understand!
Look and look, but never perceive!"
10 Make this people's heart coarse,
make their ears dull, shut their eyes tight,
or they will use their eyes to see,
use their ears to hear,
use their heart to understand,
and change their ways and be healed.'

11 I then said, 'Until when, Lord?' He
replied, 'Until towns are in ruins and
deserted, houses untenanted and a great
desolation reigns in the land,
12 and Yahweh
has driven the people away and the country
is totally abandoned.
13 And suppose one-
tenth of them are left in it, that will be
stripped again, like the terebinth, like the
oak, cut back to the stock; their stock is a
holy seed.'

Isaiah intervenes

7 In the reign of Ahaz son of Jotham, son of
Uzziah king of Judah, Razon king of Aram
advanced on Jerusalem with Pekah son of
Remaliah king of Israel, to attack it; but he
was unable to attack it.
2 The House of David
was informed: 'Aram has halted in
Ephraimite territory.' At this, his heart and
his people's hearts shook like forest trees
shaking in the wind.

[3]Yahweh then said to Isaiah, 'Go out with your son Shear-Jashub,[a] and meet Ahaz at the end of the conduit of the upper pool, on the road to the Fuller's Field, [4]and say to him, "Pay attention and keep calm. Do not be frightened or demoralised by these two smouldering sticks of firewood, by the fierce anger of Razon, Aram and the son of Remaliah, [5]or because Aram, Ephraim and the son of Remaliah have been plotting against you and saying: [6]Let us mount an attack on Judah, destroy it, force it onto our side and install the son of Tabeel there as king.

[7]"Lord Yahweh says this:

This will not happen, it will never occur,
[8]for the head of Aram is Damascus,
and the head of Damascus is Razon;
another sixty-five years,
and Ephraim will cease to be a people.
[9]The head of Ephraim is Samaria,
and the head of Samaria
is the son of Remaliah.
If you will not take your stand on me
you will not stand firm." '

Isaiah intervenes again

[10]Yahweh spoke to Ahaz again and said:

[11]Ask Yahweh your God for a sign,
either in the depths of Sheol
or in the heights above.

[12]But Ahaz said, 'I will not ask. I will not put Yahweh to the test.'

[13]He then said:

Listen now, House of David:
are you not satisfied
with trying human patience
that you should try
my God's patience too?
[14]The Lord will give you a sign in any case:
It is this: the young woman[b] is with child
and will give birth to a son
whom she will call Immanuel.
[15]On curds and honey will he feed
until he knows how to refuse the bad
and choose the good.
[16]Before the child knows
how to refuse the bad
and choose the good,
the lands whose two kings
are frightening you
will be deserted.
[17]Yahweh will bring times for you,
your people and your ancestral House,
such as have not been seen
since Ephraim broke away from Judah
(the king of Assyria).

Prediction of an invasion

[18]When that day comes,
Yahweh will whistle up mosquitoes
from the distant streams of Egypt
and bees from the land of Assyria,
[19]and they will all come and settle
on the streams in the gullies,
in the holes in the rocks,
on all the thorn-bushes
and on all the water-points.
[20]That day the Lord will shave,
with a razor hired
from the other side of the River
(with the king of Assyria),
the head and the hair of the leg,
and take off the beard, too.
[21]When that day comes, each man will raise
one heifer and two sheep,
[22]and because of the abundant milk
they give
(on curds will he feed)
all who are left in the country
will feed on curds and honey.
[23]When that day comes,
wherever there used to be
a thousand vines
worth a thousand pieces of silver,
all will be brambles and thorn-bushes;
[24]to be ventured into
only with arrows and bow,
for the country will be nothing
but brambles and thorn-bushes.
[25]No more will you venture
on any hillside formerly under the hoe
for fear of the brambles and thorn-bushes;
it will be fit only for pasturing the cattle,
a tramping-ground for sheep.

The birth of a son to Isaiah

8 Yahweh said to me, 'Take a large tablet and on it with an ordinary stylus write, "Maher-Shalal-Hash-Baz". [2]And take reliable witnesses, the priest Uriah and Zechariah son of Jeberechiah.'

[3]I then had intercourse with the prophetess, who then conceived and gave birth to

7a The name means 'a remnant will return'.
7b Perhaps Ahaz's wife, about to give birth to Hezekiah, but Isaiah sees it as symbolic of the fulfilment of royal messianic prophecies. For 'young woman' Gk reads 'virgin', interpreted by Mt of Mary.

a son.[a] Yahweh said to me, 'Call him Maher-
Shalal-Hash-Baz, 4for before the child knows
how to say "mother" or "father", the wealth
of Damascus and the booty of Samaria will
be carried away while the king of Assyria
looks on.'

Shiloah and the Euphrates

5Yahweh spoke to me again and said, 6'Since
this people has rejected the waters of Shiloah
which flow smoothly, and has trembled
before Razon and the son of Remaliah, 7now,
against it, the Lord will bring the mighty,
swelling waters of the River (the king of
Assyria and all his glory); the River will flood
up all its channels and overflow all its banks;
8it will flow into Judah, flooding everything
and passing on; it will reach right up to the
neck, and the spreading of its wings will cover
the whole extent of your country, Immanuel!

9Realise this, peoples, and be afraid,
listen, all members of far-off nations!
Arm yourselves yet be afraid!
Arm yourselves yet be afraid!
10Devise plans as you may:
they will come to nothing!
Make what pronouncements you like;
it will not come about!
For God is with us!'

Isaiah's mission

11For this was how Yahweh spoke to me
when his hand seized hold of me
and he taught me not to follow
the path of this people, saying,
12'Do not call conspiracy
all that this people calls conspiracy;
do not dread what they dread,
have no fear of that.
13Yahweh Sabaoth is the one
you will proclaim holy,
him you will dread, him you will fear.
14He will be a sanctuary,
a stumbling-stone,
a rock to trip up
the two Houses of Israel;
a snare and a trap
for the inhabitants of Jerusalem,
15over which many of them will stumble,
fall and be broken,
be ensnared and made captive.
16Bind up the testimony,
seal the instruction
in the heart of my disciples.'
17My trust is in Yahweh who hides his face
from the House of Jacob;
I put my hope in him.
18Look, I and the children
whom Yahweh has given me
shall become signs and portents in Israel
on behalf of Yahweh Sabaoth
who dwells on Mount Zion.
19And should people say to you,
'Go and consult ghosts and wizards
that whisper and mutter'—
a people should certainly
consult its gods
and the dead on behalf of the living!
20As regards instruction and testimony,
without doubt this is how they will talk,
and hence there will be
no dawn for them.

Wandering in darkness

21Oppressed and starving
he will wander the country;
and, once starving,
he will become frenzied
and curse his king and his God;
turning his gaze upward,
22then down to earth,
there will be only anguish,
gloom, the confusion of night,
swirling darkness.
23For is not everything dark as night
for a country in distress?

Deliverance

As the past humbled the land of Zebulun and the land of Naphtali, so the future will glorify the Way of the Sea, beyond the Jordan, the territory of the nations.

9 The people that walked in darkness
have seen a great light;
on the inhabitants of a country
in shadow dark as death
light has blazed forth.
2You have enlarged the nation,
you have increased its joy;
they rejoice before you
as people rejoice at harvest time,

8a His name means 'Speedy-spoil-quick-booty', a prediction of the destruction of Damascus and Samaria in 722 BC.

as they exult
when they are dividing the spoils.

3For the yoke that weighed on it,
the bar across its shoulders,
the rod of its oppressor,
these you have broken
as on the day of Midian.

4For all the footgear
clanking over the ground
and all the clothing rolled in blood,
will be burnt, will be food for the flames.

5For a son has been born for us,
a son has been given to us,
and dominion has been laid
on his shoulders;
and this is the name he has been given,
'Wonder-Counsellor, Mighty-God,
Eternal-Father, Prince-of-Peace'
6to extend his dominion
in boundless peace,
over the throne of David
and over his kingdom
to make it secure and sustain it
in fair judgement and integrity.
From this time onwards and for ever,
the jealous love of Yahweh Sabaoth
will do this.

The ordeals of the Northern Kingdom

7The Lord has launched a word at Jacob
and it has fallen on Israel;
8and the people will all soon know it,
Ephraim and the inhabitants of Samaria,
who say in the pride
of their arrogant hearts,
9'The bricks have fallen down
but we shall rebuild with dressed stone;
the sycamores have been felled
but we shall replace them with cedars.'
10But, against them,
Yahweh has raised their foe Razon,
he has whipped up their enemies,
11Aram to the east, Philistines to the west,
to devour Israel with gaping jaws.
After all this, his anger is not spent.
No, his hand is still raised!

12But the people would not come back
to him who struck them,
they would not seek out Yahweh Sabaoth;
13hence Yahweh has topped
and tailed Israel,
cutting off palm and reed in a single day.
14(The 'top' is the elder and the man of rank;
the 'tail' is the prophet teaching lies.)
15This people's leaders have led them astray,
and those who are led by them
are swallowed up.
16Hence the Lord
will no longer take delight
in their young people,
or pity on their orphans and widows,
since all of them are godless and evil,
and everything they say is madness.
After all this, his anger is not spent.
No, his hand is still raised!

17Yes, wickedness has been burning
like a fire,
devouring bramble and thorn-bush,
setting the forest thickets ablaze—
up they go in billowing smoke!
18The country has been set on fire
by the fury of Yahweh Sabaoth,
and the people are like food for the flames.
No one spares a thought for his brother.
19They have sliced to the right
and are still hungry,
they have eaten to the left
and are not satisfied;
each devours the flesh of his own arm.
20Manasseh devours Ephraim,
Ephraim Manasseh,
together they turn against Judah.
After all this, his anger is not spent.
No, his hand is still raised!

10 Woe to those
who enact unjust decrees,
who compose oppressive legislation
2to deny justice to the weak
and to cheat the humblest of my people
of fair judgement,
to make widows their prey
and to rob the orphan.
3What will you do
on the day of punishment,
when disaster comes from far away?
To whom will you run for help
and where will you leave your riches,
4to avoid squatting among the captives
or falling among the slain?
After all this, his anger is not spent.
No, his hand is still raised!

Against the king of Assyria

5Woe to Assyria, rod of my anger,
the club in their hands is my fury!

6 I was sending him
against a godless nation,
commissioning him
against the people who enraged me,
to pillage and plunder at will
and trample on them
like the mud in the streets.
7 But this was not his intention
nor did his heart plan it so,
for he dreamed
of putting an end to them,
of liquidating nations without number!
8 For he thought,
'Are not my officers all kings?
9 Is not Calno like Carchemish,
Hamath like Arpad,
Samaria like Damascus?
10 As my hand has found
the kingdoms of the false gods,
where there were more images
than in Jerusalem and Samaria,
11 as I have treated Samaria
and her false gods
shall I not treat Jerusalem
and her statues too?'

12 When the Lord has completed all his
work on Mount Zion and in Jerusalem, he
will punish the fruit of the king of Assyria's
boastful heart and the insolence of his
haughty looks.
13 For he thinks:

'By the strength of my own arm
I have done this
and by my own wisdom:
how intelligent I have been!
I have abolished the frontiers
between peoples,
I have plundered their treasures,
like a hero, I have subjugated
their inhabitants.
14 My hand has found,
as though a bird's nest,
the riches of the peoples.
Like someone collecting deserted eggs,
I have collected the whole world
while no one has fluttered a wing
or opened a beak to squawk.'

15 Does the axe claim more credit
than the man who wields it,
or the saw more strength
than the man who handles it?
As though a staff controlled
those who raise it,
or the club could raise
what is not made of wood!
16 That is why Yahweh Sabaoth
is going to inflict
leanness on his stout men,
and beneath his glory
kindle a fever burning like a fire.
17 The light of Israel will become a fire
and its Holy One a flame
burning and devouring
his thorn-bushes and brambles in a day.
18 He will consume his luxuriant forest
and productive ground,
he will ravage body and soul:
it will be like a consumptive wasting away;
19 and what remain of the trees of his forest
will be so few
that a child could write their number.

The little remnant

20 When that day comes,
the remnant of Israel
and the survivors of the House of Jacob
will stop relying on the man
who strikes them
and will truly rely on Yahweh,
the Holy One of Israel.
21 A remnant will return,
the remnant of Jacob,
to the mighty God.
22 Israel, though your people
are like the sand of the sea,
only a remnant of them will return:
a destruction has been decreed
which will make justice overflow,
23 for, throughout the country,
the Lord Yahweh Sabaoth
will enforce the destruction
now decreed.

Trust in God

24 That is why the Lord Yahweh Sabaoth says
this:

My people who live in Zion,
do not be afraid of Assyria!
He may strike you with the rod,
he may raise the club against you
(on the way from Egypt),
25 but in a very short time
the retribution will come to an end,
and my anger will destroy them.
26 Yahweh Sabaoth will brandish
a whip at him

as he struck Midian at Oreb's Rock,
will brandish his rod at the Sea
as he raised it on the way from Egypt.
27 When that day comes,
his burden will fall from your shoulder,
and his yoke from your neck,
and the yoke will be destroyed . . .

The invasion

28 He has reached Aiath,
he has moved on to Migron,
he has left his baggage train
at Michmash.
29 They have passed through the defile,
they have bivouacked at Geba.
Ramah quaked, Gibeah of Saul has fled.
30 Cry your loudest, Bath-Gallim!
Pay attention, Laish!
Answer her, Anathoth!
31 Madmenah has run away,
the inhabitants of Gebim
have taken cover.
32 This very day, as he halts at Nob,
he will shake his fist at the mountain
of the daughter of Zion,
the hill of Jerusalem.
33 See how the Lord Yahweh Sabaoth
violently lops off the foliage!
The ones standing highest are cut down,
the proudest are laid low!
34 The forest thickets fall beneath the axe,
and the Lebanon falls
to the blows of a Mighty One.

The descendant of David

11 A shoot will spring
from the stock of Jesse,
a new shoot will grow from his roots.
2 On him will rest the spirit of Yahweh,
the spirit of wisdom and insight,
the spirit of counsel and power,
the spirit of knowledge
and fear of Yahweh:
3 his inspiration will lie in fearing Yahweh.
His judgement will not be
by appearances,
his verdict not given on hearsay.
4 He will judge the weak with integrity
and give fair sentence
for the humblest in the land.
He will strike the country
with the rod of his mouth
and with the breath of his lips
bring death to the wicked.
5 Uprightness will be
the belt around his waist,
and constancy the belt about his hips.

6 The wolf will live with the lamb,
the panther lie down with the kid,
calf, lion and fat-stock beast together,
with a little boy to lead them.
7 The cow and the bear will graze,
their young will lie down together.
The lion will eat hay like the ox.
8 The infant will play
over the den of the adder;
the baby will put his hand
into the viper's lair.
9 No hurt, no harm will be done
on all my holy mountain,
for the country will be full
of knowledge of Yahweh
as the waters cover the sea.

Return from the dispersion

10 That day, the root of Jesse,
standing as a signal for the peoples,
will be sought out by the nations
and its home will be glorious.
11 When that day comes,
the Lord will raise his hand
a second time
to ransom the remnant of his people,
those still left, from Assyria,
from Egypt,
from Pathros, Cush and Elam,
from Shinar, Hamath
and the islands of the Sea.
12 He will hoist a signal for the nations
and assemble the outcasts of Israel;
he will gather the scattered people
of Judah
from the four corners of the earth.
13 Then Ephraim's jealousy will cease
and Judah's enemies be suppressed;
Ephraim will no longer
be jealous of Judah
nor Judah any longer hostile to Ephraim,
14 but together they will swoop
on the Philistines' back, to the west,
and together pillage
the people of the east.
Edom and Moab
will be subject to their sway
and the Ammonites will obey them.

15 Then Yahweh will dry up
the gulf of the Sea of Egypt,
he will raise his hand against the River
with the heat of his breath.
He will divide it into seven streams
for them to cross dry-shod.
16 And there will be a highway
for the remnant of his people
for those still left, from Assyria,
as there was for Israel
when he came out of Egypt.

Psalm

12 And, that day, you will say:

'I praise you, Yahweh,
you have been angry with me
but your anger is now appeased
and you have comforted me.
2 Look, he is the God of my salvation:
I shall have faith and not be afraid,
for Yahweh is my strength and my song,
he has been my salvation.'[a]

3 Joyfully you will draw water
from the springs of salvation
4 and, that day, you will say,
'Praise Yahweh, invoke his name.[b]
Proclaim his deeds to the people,
declare his name sublime.
5 Sing of Yahweh,
for his works are majestic,
make them known throughout the world.
6 Cry and shout for joy,
you who live in Zion,
For the Holy One of Israel
is among you in his greatness.'

C: PROCLAMATIONS ABOUT FOREIGN NATIONS

Against Babylon

13 Proclamation about Babylon, seen by Isaiah son of Amoz.

2 On a bare hill hoist a signal,
shout for them,
beckon them to come
to the Nobles' Gate.
3 I have issued orders
to my sacred warriors,
I have summoned my heroes
to serve my anger,
my proud champions.
4 The noise of a great crowd
in the mountains,
like an immense people,
the tumultuous sound of kingdoms,
of nations mustering:
it is Yahweh Sabaoth
marshalling the troops for battle.
5 They come from a distant country,
from the far horizons,
Yahweh and the instruments of his fury
to lay the whole country waste.
6 Howl! For the Day of Yahweh is near,
coming like devastation from Shaddai.
7 This is why all hands fall limp,
why all the men are losing heart;
8 they are panic-stricken,
seized with pains and convulsions;
they writhe like a woman in labour,
they look at one another appalled,
with feverish faces.
9 Look, the Day of Yahweh is coming,
merciless, with wrath and burning anger,
to reduce the country to a desert
and root out the sinners from it.
10 For in the sky the stars and Orion
will shed their light no longer,
the sun will be dark when it rises,
and the moon will no longer give its light.
11 I am going to punish the world
for its wickedness
and the wicked for their guilt,
and put an end to the pride of the arrogant
and humble the haughtiness of despots.
12 I shall make people scarcer than pure gold,
human life scarcer than the gold of Ophir.
13 This is why I am going to shake
the heavens,
why the earth will reel on its foundations,
under the wrath of Yahweh Sabaoth,
the day when his anger ignites.
14 Then like a hunted gazelle,
like sheep that nobody gathers in,
everyone will head back to his people,
everyone will flee to his native land.
15 All those who are found will be stabbed,
all those captured will fall by the sword,
16 their babies dashed to pieces
before their eyes,
their houses plundered, their wives raped.

12a ‖ Ex 15:2.
12b ‖ Ps 105:1.

17 Look, against them
I am stirring up the Medes
who care nothing for silver,
who set no value by gold.
18 Bows will annihilate the young men,
they will have no pity
for the fruit of the womb,
or mercy in their eyes for children.
19 And Babylon, that pearl of kingdoms,
that splendid jewel of the Chaldaeans,
will, like Sodom and Gomorrah,
be overthrown by God.
20 Never again will anyone live there
or reside there
for all generations to come.
Never again will the Arab
pitch his tent there,
or the shepherds
bring their flocks to rest.
21 But beasts of the desert
will make their haunt there
and owls fill their houses,
there ostriches will settle their home,
there goats will dance.
22 Hyenas will howl in its towers,
jackals in its delightful palaces,
for its doom is about to come
and its days will not last long.

The end of the Exile

14 Yahweh will have pity on Jacob, he will
choose Israel once more and resettle
them on their native soil. Foreigners will join
them, attaching themselves to the House of
Jacob. 2 Peoples will take them and escort
them home, and the House of Israel will take
them as slaves, men and women on Yahweh's
soil. They will enslave those who enslaved
them and will master their oppressors.

The death of the king of Babylon

3 When that day comes, and Yahweh gives
you rest from your suffering and torment and
the grim servitude to which you have been
subjected, 4 you will recite this satire on the
king of Babylon and say:

'How did the tyrant end?
How did his arrogance end?
5 Yahweh has broken the staff
of the wicked,
the sceptre of rulers,
6 furiously lashing peoples
with continual blows,
angrily hammering nations,
pursuing without respite.
7 The whole world is at rest and calm,
shouts of joy resounding,
8 the cypresses, the cedars of Lebanon,
rejoice aloud at your fate,
"Now that you have been laid low,
no one comes up to fell us."

9 'On your account, Sheol below
is astir to greet your arrival.
He has roused the ghosts to greet you,
all the rulers of the world.
He has made all the kings of the nations
get up from their thrones.
10 They will all greet you with the words,
"So, you too are now as weak as we are!
You, too, have become like us.
11 Your pride has been flung down to Sheol
with the music of your lyres;
under you a mattress of maggots,
over you a blanket of worms.
12 How did you come to fall
from the heavens,
Daystar, son of Dawn?
How did you come
to be thrown to the ground,
conqueror of nations?
13 You who used to think to yourself:
I shall scale the heavens;
higher than the stars of God
I shall set my throne.
I shall sit on the Mount of Assembly
far away to the north.
14 I shall climb high above the clouds,
I shall rival the Most High."
15 Now you have been flung down to Sheol,
into the depths of the abyss!

16 'When they see you,
they will scrutinise you
and consider what you have become,
"Is this the man
who made the world tremble,
who overthrew kingdoms?
17 He made the world a desert,
he levelled cities
and never freed his prisoners to go home."
18 All other kings of nations, all of them,
lie honourably, each in his own tomb;
19 but you have been thrown away,
unburied,
like a loathsome branch,
covered with heaps of the slain
pierced by the sword
who fall on the rocks of the abyss
like trampled carrion.

20 'You will not rejoin them in the grave,
for you have brought your country to ruin
and destroyed your people.
The offspring of the wicked
leave no name behind them.
21 Make ready to slaughter his sons
for the guilt of their father!
Never again must they rise
to conquer the world
and cover the face of the earth
with their cities.

22 'I will rise against them, declares Yahweh
Sabaoth, and deprive Babylon of name,
remnant, offspring and posterity, declares
Yahweh. 23 I shall turn it into the haunt of
hedgehogs, a swamp. I shall sweep it with
the broom of destruction, declares Yahweh
Sabaoth.'

Against Assyria

24 Yahweh Sabaoth has sworn it,
'Yes, what I have planned will take place,
what I have decided will be so:

25 'I shall break Assyria in my country,
I shall trample on him on my mountains.
Then his yoke will slip off them,
his burden will slip from their shoulders.'

26 This is the decision taken
in defiance of the whole world;
this, the hand outstretched
in defiance of all nations.

27 Once Yahweh Sabaoth has decided,
who will stop him?
Once he stretches out his hand,
who can withdraw it?

Against the Philistines

28 In the year Ahaz died came this proclamation:

29 All Philistia, do not rejoice
because the rod which used to beat you
is now broken,
for the serpent stock will produce a viper,
its offspring will be a flying dragon.

30 While the first-born of the poor are grazing
and the destitute are resting in safety,
I shall make your stock die of hunger
and then slaughter what remains of you.

31 Howl, gate! Shriek, city!
Totter, all Philistia!
For a smoke is coming from the north,
and there are no deserters
in those battalions.

32 What reply will be given then
to the messengers of that nation?—
That Yahweh founded Zion
and there the poor of his people
will find refuge.

On Moab[a]

15 Proclamation about Moab:

Laid waste in a night,
Ar-Moab lies silent;
Laid waste in a night,
Kir-Moab lies silent.

2 The daughter of Dibon has climbed
to the high places to weep;
on Nebo and in Medeba
Moab laments.

Every head shaven,
every beard cut off,
3 they wear sackcloth in their streets;
on their roofs and in their squares,
everyone is lamenting
and collapsing in tears.

4 Heshbon and Elealeh are crying out
in distress,
their voices can be heard as far as Jahaz.
That is why the warriors of Moab
are shivering,
his soul trembles at the sound.
5 His heart cries out in distress for Moab,
whose fugitives are already at Zoar,
nearly at Eglath-Shelishiyah.

They climb the slope of Luhith,[b]
weeping as they go;
on the road to Horonaim
they utter heart-rending cries.

6 The Waters of Nimrim
have become a waste land,
the grass dried up,
the plants withered away,
nothing green any more.

7 That is why they are carrying
what they could save of their stores
across the Ravine of the Willows.

15a cf. Jr 48.
15b || Jr 48:5.

[8]For the cry for help re-echoes
round the territory of Moab;
their wailing, right to Eglaim,
to Beer-Elim, their wailing;

[9]Dimon's waters are swollen with blood,
and I have worse in store for Dimon:
a lion for those of Moab who survive,
for those left on its soil.

The Moabites' petition

16 Send the lamb
to the ruler of the land,
from Sela by the desert,
to the mountain of the daughter of Zion,
[2]for soon, like a fluttered bird,
like nestlings cast out,
will be the women of Moab
at the fords of the Arnon.

[3]Hold a council, make a decision.
At noon spread your shadow
as if it were night.
Hide those who have been driven out,
do not betray the fugitive,
[4]let those who have been driven out of Moab
come and live with you;
be their refuge in the face of the devastator.
Once the oppression is past,
and the devastation has stopped
and those now trampling on the country
have gone away,
[5]the throne will be made secure
in faithful love,
and on it will sit in constancy
within the tent of David
a judge seeking fair judgement
and pursuing uprightness.

[6]We have heard about Moab's pride,
about how very proud it is,
about its arrogance, its pride, its rage,
its bravado, which will come to nothing!

Moab's lament

[7]And so Moab is wailing for Moab,
wailing, every one of them.
For the raisin cakes of Kir-Hareseth[a]
you mourn, stricken with grief.
[8]For Heshbon's vineyards are withering,
the vine of Sibmah
whose red grapes used to overcome
the overlords of the nations.
It used to reach to Jazer,
had wound its way into the desert,
its shoots grew so numerous
they spread across the sea.
[9]And so I weep, as Jazer weeps,
for the vine of Sibmah.
I water you with my tears,
Heshbon and Elealeh.
For over your harvest and vintage
the cheering has died away;
[10]joy and gladness
have vanished from the orchards.
No more revelry in the vineyards,
no more happy shouting;
no more the treader treads wine
in the presses,
the cheering has ceased.
[11]That is why my whole being
quivers like harp strings for Moab,
my very heart, for Kir-Heres.
[12]Moab will be seen,
wearing itself out on the high places
and going to its temple to pray,
but it will accomplish nothing.

[13]Such was the word which Yahweh spoke
about Moab in the past. [14]And now Yahweh
has spoken in these terms, 'Within three
years, as a hired worker reckons them, the
glory of Moab will be humbled, despite its
teeming population. It will be reduced to
nothing, an insignificant remnant.'

Against Damascus and Israel

17 Proclamation about Damascus:

Damascus will soon cease to be a city,
it will become a heap of ruins.
[2]Its towns, abandoned for ever,
will be pastures for flocks;
there they will rest
with no one to disturb them.
[3]Ephraim will be stripped of its defences
and Damascus of its sovereignty;
and the remnant of Aram will be treated
like the glory of the Israelites—
declares Yahweh Sabaoth.

[4]When that day comes,
Jacob's glory will diminish,
from being fat he will grow lean;
[5]as when a reaper gathers in
the standing corn,
harvesting the ears of corn with his arm,

16a || Jr 48:29–30.

or when they glean the ears
in the Valley of Rephaim,
6 nothing will remain but pickings,
as when an olive tree is beaten;
two or three berries left
on the topmost bough,
four or five berries
on the branches of the tree—
declares Yahweh, God of Israel.

7 That day, a man will look to his Creator
and his eyes will turn to the Holy One of
Israel. 8 He will no longer look to altars, his
own handiwork, or to what his own fingers
have made: the sacred poles and incense-
altars.

9 That day, its cities of refuge
will be abandoned
as were the woods and heaths
at the Israelites' advance:
there will be desolation.
10 Since you have forgotten
the God of your salvation,
and failed to keep the Rock,
your refuge, in mind,
you plant pleasure-gardens,
you sow exotic seeds;
11 the day you plant them,
you get them to sprout,
and, next morning,
your seedlings are in flower;
but the harvest will vanish
on the day of disease
and incurable pain.

12 Disaster! The thunder of vast hordes,
a thunder like the thunder of the seas,
the roar of nations
roaring like the roar of mighty floods,
13 of nations roaring like the roar of ocean!
He rebukes them and far away they flee,
driven like chaff on the mountains
before the wind,
like an eddy of dust before the storm.
14 At evening all is terror,
by morning all have disappeared.
Such will be the lot
of those who plunder us,
such, the fate of our despoilers.

Against Cush

18 Disaster! Land of the whirring locust
beyond the rivers of Cush,
2 who send ambassadors by sea,
in little reed-boats across the waters!
Go, swift messengers
to a nation tall and bronzed,
to a people feared far and near,
a mighty and masterful nation
whose country is criss-crossed with rivers.
3 All you who inhabit the world,
you who people the earth,
when the signal is hoisted
on the mountains,
you will see,
when the ram's-horn is sounded,
you will hear.
4 For this is what Yahweh has told me,
'I shall sit here quietly looking down,
like the burning heat in the daytime,
like a dewy mist in the heat of harvest.'
5 For, before the harvest,
once the flowering is over
and blossom turns into ripening grape,
the branches will be cut off
with pruning knives,
and the shoots taken off, cut away.
6 All has been abandoned
to the mountain birds of prey
and the wild animals:
the birds of prey will summer on them,
and all the wild animals winter on them.

7 Then, an offering will be brought to
Yahweh Sabaoth on behalf of a people tall
and bronzed, on behalf of a people feared far
and near, on behalf of a mighty and masterful
nation whose country is criss-crossed with
rivers: to the place where the name of Yahweh
Sabaoth resides, Mount Zion.

Against Egypt

19 Proclamation about Egypt:

Look! Yahweh, riding a swift cloud,
is coming to Egypt.
The false gods of Egypt totter before him
and Egypt's heart quails within her.
2 I shall stir up Egypt against Egypt,
they will fight one another,
brother against brother,
friend against friend,
city against city,
kingdom against kingdom.
3 Egypt's spirit will fail within her
and I shall confound her deliberations.
They will consult false gods and wizards,
ghosts and sorcerers.
4 And I shall hand Egypt over
to the clutches of a cruel master,
a ruthless king will rule them—
declares Yahweh Sabaoth.

5 The waters will ebb from the sea,
the river will dry up and run low,
6 the streams will become foul,
the rivers of Egypt sink and dry up.
Rush and reed will turn black,
7 the Nile-plants on the banks of the Nile;
all the vegetation of the Nile,
will wither, blow away and be no more.
8 The fishermen will groan,
it will be mourning
for all who cast hook in the Nile;
those who spread nets on the waters
will lose heart.
9 The workers of carded flax
and the weavers of white cloth
will be confounded,
10 the weavers dismayed,
all the workmen dejected.
11 Yes, the princes of Zoan are fools,
Pharaoh's wisest councillors
make up a stupid council.
How dare you say to Pharaoh,
'I am descended from sages,
I am descended from bygone kings'?
12 Where are these sages of yours?
Let them tell you, so that all may know,
the plans Yahweh Sabaoth has made
against Egypt!
13 The princes of Zoan are fools,
the princes of Noph, self-deceivers,
the top men of her provinces
have led Egypt astray.
14 Yahweh has infused them
with a giddy spirit;
they have led Egypt astray
in all she undertakes
like a drunkard straying about
as he vomits.
15 Nowadays no one does for Egypt
what top and tail,
palm and reed used to do.

The conversion of Egypt

16 That day Egypt will be like women, trem-
bling and terrified at the threatening hand of
Yahweh Sabaoth, when he raises it against
her. 17 The land of Judah will become Egypt's
shame; whenever she is reminded of it, she
will be terrified, because of the plan which
Yahweh Sabaoth has laid against her. 18 That
day in Egypt there will be five towns speaking
the language of Canaan and pledging them-
selves to Yahweh Sabaoth; one of them will
be called City of the Sun. 19 That day there
will be an altar dedicated to Yahweh in the
centre of Egypt and, close to the frontier, a
pillar dedicated to Yahweh, 20 and this will be
a sign and a witness to Yahweh Sabaoth in
Egypt. When they cry to Yahweh for help
because of oppressors, he will send them a
Saviour and leader to deliver them. 21 Yahweh
will reveal himself to Egypt, and the Egyp-
tians will acknowledge Yahweh that day and
will offer sacrifices and cereal offerings, and
will make vows to Yahweh and perform
them. 22 And if Yahweh strikes Egypt, having
struck he will heal, and they will turn to
Yahweh who will hear their prayers and heal
them. 23 That day there will be a highway
from Egypt to Assyria. Assyria will have
access to Egypt and Egypt have access to
Assyria. Egypt will serve with Assyria.

24 That day Israel will make a third with
Egypt and Assyria, a blessing at the centre of
the world, 25 and Yahweh Sabaoth will bless
them in the words, 'Blessed be my people
Egypt, Assyria my creation, and Israel my
heritage.'

Relating to the capture of Ashdod

20 The year the general-in-chief, sent by
Sargon king of Assyria, came to
Ashdod and stormed and captured it 2 at that
time Yahweh spoke through Isaiah son of
Amoz and said, 'Go, undo the sackcloth
round your waist and take the sandals off
your feet.' And he did so, and walked about,
naked and barefoot. 3 Yahweh then said, 'As
my servant Isaiah has been walking about
naked and barefoot for the last three years as
a sign and portent for Egypt and Cush, 4 so
the king of Assyria will lead the captives of
Egypt and the exiles of Cush, young and old,
naked and barefoot, their buttocks bared, to
the shame of Egypt. 5 Then they will be afraid
and ashamed of Cush their hope and Egypt
their pride, 6 and the inhabitants of this coast
will say on that day, "Look what has
happened to our hope, to those to whom we
fled for help, to escape from the king of
Assyria. How are we going to escape?" '

The fall of Babylon

21 Proclamation about the coastal desert:

As whirlwinds sweeping over the Negeb,
he comes from the desert,
from a fearsome country.
2 A harsh vision has been shown me,

'The traitor betrays
and the despoiler despoils.
Advance, Elam, lay siege, Media!'
I have cut short all groaning.
3This is why my loins are racked with pain,
why I am seized with pangs
like the pangs of a woman in labour;
I am too distressed to hear,
too afraid to look.
4My heart is bewildered,
dread overwhelms me,
the twilight I longed for
has become my horror.
5They lay the table, spread the cloth,
they eat, they drink.
Up, princes, grease the shield!

6For this is what the Lord has told me,
'Go, post a look-out,
let him report what he sees.
7He will see cavalry, horsemen two by two,
men mounted on donkeys,
men mounted on camels;
let him watch alertly,
be very alert indeed!'
8Then the look-out shouted,
'On the watchtower, Lord,
I stay all day
and at my post
I stand all night.
9Now the cavalry is coming,
horsemen two by two.'
He shouted again and said,
'Babylon has fallen, has fallen,
and all the images of her gods
he has shattered to the ground!'
10You whom I have threshed,
grain of my threshing-floor,
what I have heard
from Yahweh Sabaoth, God of Israel,
I am telling you now.

On Edom

11Proclamation about Dumah:

From Seir, someone shouts to me,
'Watchman, what time of night?
Watchman, what time of night?'

12The watchman answers,
'Morning is coming, then night again.
If you want to ask, ask!
Come back! Come here!'

Against the Arabs

13Proclamation about the wastelands:

In the thickets, on the wastelands,
you spend the night,
you caravans of Dedanites.
14Bring water for the thirsty!
The inhabitants of Tema went
with bread to greet the fugitive.
15For these have fled before the sword,
the naked sword and the bent bow,
the press of battle.

16For this is what the Lord has told me,
'In one year's time as a hired worker
reckons it, all the glory of Kedar will be
finished 17and, of the valiant archers, the
Kedarites, hardly any will be left, for
Yahweh, God of Israel, has spoken.'

Against rejoicing in Jerusalem

22 Prophecy on the Valley of Vision:

Now what is the matter with you
for you all to be up on the housetops,
2full of excitement, boisterous town,
joyful city?
Your slain have not fallen to the sword
nor died in battle.
3Your leaders have all fled together,
captured without a bow between them,
all who could be found
have been captured at a blow,
far though they had fled.
4That is why I said,
'Turn your eyes away from me,
let me weep bitterly;
do not try to comfort me
over the ruin of the daughter
of my people.'

5For this is a day of rout,
panic and confusion,
the work of the Lord Yahweh Sabaoth
in the Valley of Vision.
The wall is sapped,
cries for help ring out to the mountains.
6Elam has picked up his quiver,
with manned chariots and horsemen,
and Kir has bared his shield.
7Your fairest valleys are full of chariots
and the horsemen take up positions
at the gates;
8thus falls the defence of Judah.

That day you turned your gaze
to the weapons in the House of the Forest.
9 You saw how many breaches there were
in the City of David.
You collected the waters of the lower pool.
10 You surveyed the houses in Jerusalem
and pulled houses down
to strengthen the wall.
11 Between the two walls
you made a reservoir
for the waters of the old pool.
But you did not look
to the Creator of these things,
you did not look to the One
who fashioned them long ago.

12 That day the Lord Yahweh Sabaoth
called on you
to weep and mourn,
to shave your heads, to put on sackcloth.
13 But instead there is joy and merriment,
killing of oxen, slaughtering of sheep,
eating of meat, drinking of wine,
'Let us eat and drink,
for tomorrow we shall be dead.'
14 Then Yahweh Sabaoth revealed this
to my ears,
'This guilt will never be forgiven you,
until you are dead,'
says the Lord Yahweh Sabaoth.

Against Shebna

15 The Lord Yahweh Sabaoth says this:

Go and find that steward,
Shebna, the master of the palace:
16 'What do you own here,
who gave you the right
for you to hew yourself a tomb here?'
He is hewing himself a tomb,
is digging a resting-place for himself
in the rock.
17 But Yahweh will throw you away,
strong as you are,
will grasp you in his grip,
18 will screw you up into a ball,
a ball thrown into a vast space.
There you will die,
with your splendid chariots,
disgrace to your master's palace!
19 I shall hound you from your office,
I shall snatch you from your post
20 and, when that day comes,
I shall summon my servant
Eliakim son of Hilkiah.
21 I shall dress him in your tunic,
I shall put your sash round his waist,
I shall invest him with your authority;
and he will be a father
to the inhabitants of Jerusalem
and to the House of Judah.
22 I shall place the key of David's palace
on his shoulder;
when he opens, no one will close,
when he closes, no one will open.
23 I shall drive him like a nail
into a firm place;
and he will become a throne of glory
for his family.

24 'On him will depend all the glory of his
family, the descendants and offspring, all the
vessels of small capacity too, from cups to
pitchers. 25 That day, declares Yahweh
Sabaoth, the nail driven into a firm place will
give way, will be torn out and fall. And the
whole load hanging on it will be lost. For
Yahweh has spoken.'

Against Tyre

23 Proclamation about Tyre:

Howl, ships of Tarshish,
for all has been destroyed—
no more houses, no way of getting in:
the news has reached them from Kittim.
2 Be struck dumb, inhabitants of the coast,
you merchants of Sidon,
whose messengers cross the sea
3 to the wide ocean.
The grain of the Canal,
the harvest of the Nile,
formed her revenue.
She was the market for the nations.
4 Blush, Sidon (citadel of the seas),
for this is what the sea has said,
'I have felt no birth-pangs,
never given birth,
never reared boys nor brought up girls.'

5 When the news reaches Egypt,
they will tremble to hear Tyre's fate.
6 Cross to Tarshish, howl,
inhabitants of the coast.

7 Is this your proud city
founded far back in the past,
whose steps led her far afield
to found her colonies?
8 Who took this decision
against Tyre,
who used to hand out crowns,

whose traders were princes,
whose merchants,
men honoured in the city?
9 Yahweh Sabaoth took this decision
to wither the pride of all beauty
and humiliate those honoured in the city.
10 Cultivate your country like the Delta,
daughter of Tarshish,
for your marine docks are no more.
11 He has raised his hand against the sea,
he has shaken kingdoms,
Yahweh has ordained the destruction
of the fortresses of Canaan.

12 He has said, 'Exult no more,
ill-treated virgin daughter of Sidon!
Get up, cross to Kittim,
no respite for you there, either.'
13 Look at the land of the Chaldaeans,
a people who used not to exist!
Assyria assigned it
to the creatures of the wilds;
they raised their siege-towers against it,
demolished its bastions,
reduced it to ruin.
14 Howl, ships of Tarshish,
for your fortress has been destroyed.

15 When that day comes, Tyre will be forgotten for seventy years, the length of one king's life. But when the seventy years are over, Tyre will become like the whore in the song:

16 'Take your harp, walk the town,
whore whom men have forgotten!
Play sweetly, song after song,
to make them remember you.'

17 At the end of the seventy years Yahweh will visit Tyre. She will receive her pay again and play the whore with all the kingdoms of the world on the surface of the earth. 18 But her profits and wages will be dedicated to Yahweh. They will not be stored or hoarded, but her profits will go to those who live in Yahweh's presence, for them to have as much food as they want and splendid clothes.

D: APOCALYPSE

Yahweh's judgement

24 See how Yahweh lays the earth waste,
makes it a desert, buckles its surface,
scatters its inhabitants,
2 priest and people alike, master and slave,
mistress and maid, seller and buyer,
lender and borrower, creditor and debtor.
3 Ravaged, ravaged the earth will be,
despoiled, despoiled,
for Yahweh has uttered this word.
4 The earth is mourning, pining away,
the pick of earth's people
are withering away.
5 The earth is defiled
by the feet of its inhabitants,
for they have transgressed the laws,
violated the decree,
broken the everlasting covenant.
6 That is why the curse
has consumed the earth
and its inhabitants pay the penalty,
that is why the inhabitants of the earth
have been burnt up
and few people are left.

Song about the ruined city

7 The new wine is mourning,
the vine is withering away,
the once merry-hearted are sighing.
8 The cheerful sound of tambourines
is silent,
the sound of revelling is over,
the cheerful sound of the harp is silent.
9 No more will they sing over their wine,
liquor will taste bitter to the drinker.
10 The city of nothingness is in ruins,
every house is shut, no one can enter.
11 People shout in the streets
to try to get wine;
all joy has vanished,
happiness has been banished
from the country.
12 Nothing but rubble in the city,
the gate has collapsed in ruins.
13 For at the heart of earth's life,
among the peoples,
it is as at the beating of the olive trees,
as at the gleaning of the grapes
when the grape harvest is over.
14 They raise their voices,
shouting for joy,
in Yahweh's honour
they shout from the west.
15 'Yes, in the east, give glory to Yahweh,
in the islands of the sea,
to the name of Yahweh, God of Israel!'
16 We have heard psalms
from the remotest parts of earth,
'Glory to the Upright One!'

The last battle

But I thought, 'What an ordeal,
what an ordeal! What misery for me!'
The traitors have betrayed,
the traitors have acted
most treacherously.
17 Fear, the pit and the snare for you,
inhabitants of the city!
18 And whoever flees from the cry of fear
will fall into the pit,
and whoever climbs out of the pit
will be caught in the snare.[a]
Yes, the sluice-gates above are open,
the foundations of the earth are quaking.
19 A cracking, the earth cracks open,
a jolting, the earth gives a jolt,
a lurching, the earth lurches
backwards and forwards.
20 The earth will reel to and fro
like a drunkard,
it will be shaken like a shanty;
so heavy will be its sin on it,
it will fall, never to rise again.
21 When that day comes,
Yahweh will punish
the armies of the sky above
and on earth the kings of the earth;
22 they will be herded together,
herded together like prisoners
in a dungeon
and shut up in gaol,
and, after long years, punished.
23 The moon will be confused
and the sun ashamed,
for Yahweh Sabaoth is king
on Mount Zion and in Jerusalem,
and the Glory will radiate on their elders.

A hymn of thanksgiving

25 Yahweh, you are my God,
I shall praise you to the heights,
I shall praise your name;
for you have accomplished marvels,
plans long-conceived, faithfully, firmly.
2 For you have made the town
a heap of stones,
the fortified city a ruin.
The foreigners' citadel is a city no longer,
it will never be rebuilt.
3 Hence mighty peoples will honour you,
the city of pitiless nations hold you in awe;
4 For you have been a refuge for the weak,
a refuge for the needy in distress,
a shelter from the storm,
shade from the heat;
for the breath of the pitiless
is like a winter storm.
5 Like heat in a dry land
you calm the foreigners' tumult;
as heat under the shadow of a cloud,
so the song of the pitiless dies away.

The divine banquet

6 On this mountain, for all peoples,
Yahweh Sabaoth is preparing
a banquet of rich food,
a banquet of fine wines,
of succulent food, of well-strained wines.
7 On this mountain, he has destroyed
the veil which used to veil all peoples,
the pall enveloping all nations;
8 he has destroyed death for ever.
Lord Yahweh has wiped away the tears
from every cheek;
he has taken his people's shame away
everywhere on earth,
for Yahweh has spoken.
9 And on that day, it will be said,
'Look, this is our God,
in him we put our hope
that he should save us,
this is Yahweh, we put our hope in him.
Let us exult and rejoice
since he has saved us.'
10 For Yahweh's hand will rest
on this mountain,
and Moab will be trodden under his feet
as straw is trodden into the dung-heap.
11 He may stretch his hands wide
on the mountain
like a swimmer stretching out his hands
to swim.
But he will humble his pride
despite what his hands may attempt.
12 And the impregnable fortress
of your walls,
he has overthrown, laid low,
flung to the ground, in the dust.

A hymn of thanksgiving

26 That day, this song will be sung in Judah:

24a || Jr 48:43–44.

'We have a fortress city,
the walls and ramparts provide safety.
2 Open the gates!
Let the upright nation come in,
the nation that keeps faith!
3 This is the plan decreed:
you will guarantee peace,
the peace entrusted to you.
4 Trust in Yahweh for ever,
for Yahweh is a rock for ever.
5 He has brought low
the dwellers on the heights,
the lofty citadel;
he lays it low, brings it to the ground,
flings it down in the dust.
6 It will be trodden under foot,
by the feet of the needy,
the steps of the weak.'

A psalm

7 The path of the Upright One is honesty;
you smooth the honest way of the upright.
8 Following the path of your judgements,
Yahweh, we set our hopes in you,
your name, your memory
are all our soul desires.
9 At night my soul longs for you
and my spirit within me seeks you out;
for when your judgements appear on earth
the inhabitants of the world
learn what saving justice is.
10 If pity is shown to the wicked
without his learning what saving justice is,
he will act wrongly
in the land of right conduct
and not see the majesty of Yahweh.
11 Yahweh, your hand is raised
but they do not see!
The antagonists of your people
will look and grow pale;
with your fiery wrath
you will devour your enemies.

12 Yahweh, you will grant us peace,
having completed all our undertakings
for us.
13 Yahweh our God, other lords than you
have ruled us
but, loyal to you alone,
we invoke your name.
14 The dead will not come back to life,
the shadows will not rise again,
for you have punished them,
annihilated them,
wiping out their very memory.
15 You have made the nation larger, Yahweh,
made the nation larger
and won yourself glory,
you have rolled back
the frontiers of the country.

16 Yahweh, in distress they had recourse
to you,
they expended themselves in prayer,
since your punishment was on them.
17 As a pregnant woman
near her time of delivery
writhes and cries out in her pangs,
so have we been, Yahweh, in your eyes:
18 we have been pregnant, we have writhed,
but we have given birth only to wind:
we have not given salvation to the earth,
no inhabitants for the world
have been brought to birth.
19 Your dead will come back to life,
your corpses will rise again.
Wake up and sing,
you dwellers in the dust,
for your dew will be a radiant dew,
but the earth will give birth to the shades.

The Lord's judgement

20 Go, my people, go to your private room,
shut yourselves in.
Hide yourselves a little while
until the retribution has passed.

21 For see, Yahweh emerges
from his dwelling
to punish the inhabitants of earth
for their guilt;
and the earth will reveal the blood
shed on it
and no longer hide its slain.

27 That day Yahweh will punish,
with his unyielding sword,
massive and strong,
Leviathan[a] the fleeing serpent,
Leviathan the coiling serpent;
he will kill that dragon that lives in the sea.

Yahweh's vineyard

2 That day,
sing of the splendid vineyard!
3 I, Yahweh, am its guardian,
from time to time I water it;

27a A mythical monster of primeval chaos.

so that no harm befall it,
I guard it night and day.

4—I do not have a wall.
Who can reduce me to brambles
and thorn-bushes?
—I shall make war and trample on it
and at the same time burn it.

5Or should they beg for my protection,
let them make their peace with me,
peace let them make with me.

Pardon and punishment

6In days to come, Jacob will take root,
Israel will bud and blossom
and the surface of the world
be one vast harvest.
7Has he struck him as he was struck
by those who struck him?
Has he murdered him
as he was murdered
by those who murdered him?
8By expelling, by excluding him,
you have executed a sentence,
he has blown him away with a breath
as rough as the east wind.
9For that is how Jacob's guilt
will be forgiven,
such will be the result
of renouncing his sin,
when all the altar-stones
have been smashed to pieces
like lumps of chalk,
when the sacred poles and incense-altars
stand no longer.
10For the fortified city is abandoned now,
deserted, forsaken as a desert
where calves browse,
where they lie down,
destroying its branches.
11When boughs go dry, they get burnt,
women come and use them for firewood.
Now, this is a people
that does not understand,
and so its Maker will not take pity on it,
he who formed it
will not show it any mercy.

The Israelites return

12When that day comes,
Yahweh will start his threshing
from the course of the River
to the Torrent of Egypt,
and you will be gathered one by one,
Israelites!
13When that day comes,
the great ram's-horn will be sounded,
and those lost in Assyria will come,
and those banished to Egypt,
and they will worship Yahweh
on the holy mountain, in Jerusalem.

E: POEMS ON ISRAEL AND JUDAH

Against Samaria

28 Woe to the haughty crown
of Ephraim's drunkards,
to the fading flower
of its proud splendour
sited at the head of the lush valley,
to those prostrated by wine!
2See, a strong and mighty man
in the Lord's service,
like a storm of hail, a destroying tempest,
like immense flood-waters overflowing,
with his hand he throws them
to the ground.
3They will be trampled underfoot,
the haughty crown
of Ephraim's drunkards,
4and the faded flower of its proud splendour
sited at the head of the lush valley.
Like a fig ripe before summer comes:
whoever spots it
forthwith picks and swallows it.

5That day Yahweh Sabaoth
will be a crown of splendour
and a proud diadem
for the remnant of his people,
6a spirit of fair judgement
for him who sits in judgement,
and the strength of those
who repel the assault on the gate.

Against false prophets

7These too have been confused by wine,
have gone astray owing to liquor.
Priest and prophet have become
confused by liquor,
are sodden with wine,
have strayed owing to liquor,
have become confused in their visions,
have strayed in their decisions.
8Yes, every table is covered
in filthy vomit,
not one is clean!

9 'Whom does he think he is lecturing?
Whom does he think his message is for?
Babies just weaned?
Babies just taken from the breast?
10 With his
"Sav lasav, sav lasav,
kav lakav, kav lakav,
zeer sham, zeer sham!" '

11 Now, with stammering lips
and in a foreign language,
he will talk to this nation.
12 He used to say to them,
'Here you can rest!
Here you can let the weary rest!
Here all is quiet.'
But they refused to listen.
13 Now Yahweh is going to say this to them,
'Sav lasav, sav lasav,
kav lakav, kav lakav,
zeer sham, zeer sham.'
So that when they walk
they will fall over backwards
and so be broken, trapped
and taken captive.

Against evil counsellors

14 Hence listen to Yahweh's word,
you insolent men,
rulers of this people in Jerusalem.
15 Because you have said,
'We have made a treaty with Death
and have struck a pact with Sheol.
When the scourging flood comes over,
it will not touch us,
for we have made lies our refuge
and hidden under falsehood.'
16 So the Lord Yahweh says this,
'Now I shall lay a stone in Zion,
a granite stone, a precious corner-stone,
a firm foundation-stone:
no one who relies on this will stumble.
17 And I will make fair judgement
the measure,
and uprightness the plumb-line.'

But hail will sweep away the refuge of lies
and floods wash away the hiding-place;
18 your treaty with Death will be broken
and your pact with Sheol will not hold.
When the scourging flood comes over,
you will be trodden down by it;
19 every time it comes over,
it will seize on you,
for it will come over,
morning after morning,
day by day and night by night.
Nothing but fear
will make you understand
what you hear.
20 For the bed is too short to stretch in,
the blanket too narrow for covering.
21 Yes, as on Mount Perazim,
Yahweh will rise,
as in the Valley of Gibeon, he will storm
to do his work, his mysterious work,
to do his deed, his extraordinary deed.
22 Stop scoffing, then,
or your bonds will be tightened further,
for I have heard it:
it has been irrevocably decided
as regards the whole country
by the Lord Yahweh Sabaoth.

A parable

23 Listen closely to my words,
be attentive,
understand what I am saying.
24 Does the ploughman
plough all day to sow,
breaking up and harrowing his ground?
25 Once he has levelled its surface,
does he not scatter fennel, sow cummin?
Then he puts in wheat, millet, barley
and, round the edges, spelt,
26 for his God has taught him this rule
and instructed him.
27 Fennel must not be crushed
with a sledge,
nor cart-wheels driven over cummin;
fennel must be beaten with a stick,
and cummin with a flail.
28 When you are threshing wheat,
you do not waste time crushing it;
you get the horse
and cart-wheel moving,
but you do not grind it fine.
29 All this is a gift from Yahweh Sabaoth,
marvellous advice
leading to great achievements.

On Jerusalem

29 Woe, Ariel,[a] Ariel,
city where David encamped.
Let year after year pass,
let the feasts make their full round,

29a Symbolic name for Jerusalem (=? lion of God).

[2]then I shall inflict trouble on Ariel,
and there will be sighing and sobbing,
and I shall make it truly Ariel.
[3]I shall encamp all round you,
I shall lay siege to you
and mount siege-works against you.
[4]You will be laid low,
will speak from the underworld,
your words will rise like a murmur
from the dust.
Your voice from the earth
will be like a ghost's,
it will whisper
as though coming from the dust.

[5]The horde of your enemies
will be like fine dust,
the horde of the warriors like flying chaff.
And suddenly, in an instant,
[6]you will be visited by Yahweh Sabaoth
with thunder, earthquake, mighty din,
hurricane, tempest,
flame of devouring fire.
[7]It will be like a dream,
like a vision at night:
the horde of all the nations
at war with Ariel,
all those fighting,
besieging and troubling it.
[8]It will be like the dream of a hungry man:
he eats, then wakes up with an empty belly;
or like the dream of a thirsty man:
he drinks, then wakes up exhausted
with a parched throat.
So will it be with the horde of all the nations
making war on Mount Zion.

[9]Be stupefied and stunned,
go blind, unseeing,
drunk but not on wine,
staggering but not through liquor.
[10]For Yahweh has infused you
with a spirit of lethargy,
he has closed your eyes (the prophets),
he has veiled your heads (the seers).

[11]For to you every vision has become like
the words of a sealed book. You give it to
someone able to read and say, 'Read that.'
He replies, 'I cannot, because it is sealed.'
[12]You then give the book to someone who
cannot read, and say, 'Read that.' He replies,
'I cannot read.'

Prophecy

[13]The Lord then said:
Because this people approaches me
only in words,
honours me only with lip-service
while their hearts are far from me,
and reverence for me,
as far as they are concerned,
is nothing but human commandment,
a lesson memorised,
[14]very well, I shall have to go on
astounding this people
with prodigies and wonders:
for the wisdom of its wise men is doomed,
the understanding of any who understand
will vanish.

The triumph of right

[15]Woe to those who burrow down
to conceal their plans from Yahweh,
who scheme in the dark
and say, 'Who can see us?
Who knows who we are?'
[16]How perverse you are!
Is the potter no better than the clay?
Something that was made,
can it say of its maker,
'He did not make me'?
Or a pot say of the potter,
'He does not know his job'?
[17]Is it not true that in a very short time
the Lebanon
will become productive ground,
so productive you might take it
for a forest?
[18]That day the deaf
will hear the words of the book
and, delivered from shadow and darkness,
the eyes of the blind will see.
[19]The lowly will find ever more joy
in Yahweh
and the poorest of people
will delight in the Holy One of Israel;
[20]for the tyrant will be no more,
the scoffer has vanished
and all those on the look-out for evil
have been destroyed:
[21]those who incriminate others
by their words,
those who lay traps for the arbitrator
at the gate
and groundlessly deprive the upright
of fair judgement.
[22]That is why Yahweh,
God of the House of Jacob,
Abraham's redeemer, says this,

'No longer shall Jacob be disappointed,
no more shall his face grow pale,
23 for when he sees his children,
my creatures, home again with him,
he will acknowledge my name as holy,
he will acknowledge
the Holy One of Jacob to be holy
and will hold the God of Israel in awe.
24 Erring spirits will learn to understand
and murmurers accept instruction.'

Against the embassy to Egypt

30 Woe to the rebellious children—
declares Yahweh—
who make plans
which do not come from me
and make alliances not inspired by me,
and so add sin to sin!
2 They are leaving for Egypt,
without consulting me,
to take refuge in Pharaoh's protection,
to shelter in Egypt's shadow.
3 Pharaoh's protection will be your shame,
the shelter of Egypt's shadow
your confounding.
4 For his princes have gone to Zoan
and his messengers have reached Hanes.
5 Everyone has been disappointed
by a people who cannot help,
who bring neither aid nor profit,
only disappointment and confusion.

Another prophecy against an embassy

6 Proclamation about the beasts of the Negeb:

Into the land of distress and of anguish,
of lioness and roaring lion,
of viper and flying dragon,
they bear their riches on donkeys' backs,
their treasures on camels' humps,
to a nation that cannot help:
7 Egypt, whose help is vain and futile;
and so I call her 'Rahab[a]-the-collapsed'.

Testament

8 Now go, inscribe this on a tablet,
write it on a scroll,
so that it may serve for time to come
for ever and for ever.
9 This is a rebellious people,
they are lying children,
children who will not listen
to Yahweh's Law.
10 To the seers they say, 'See nothing!'
To the prophets, 'Do not prophesy
the truth to us;
tell us flattering things;
have illusory visions;
11 turn aside from the way, leave the path,
rid us of the Holy One of Israel.'

12 So the Holy One of Israel says this,
'Since you have rejected this word
and put your trust in fraud
and disloyalty
and rely on these,
13 for you this guilt will prove to be
a breach opening up,
a bulge at the top of a wall
which suddenly and all at once
comes crashing down.
14 He will shatter it like an earthenware pot,
ruthlessly knocking it to pieces,
so that of the fragments not one shard
can be found
with which to take up fire from the hearth
or scoop water from the storage-well.'

15 For Lord Yahweh, the Holy One of Israel,
says this,
'Your salvation lay in conversion
and tranquillity,
your strength in serenity and trust
and you would have none of it.
16 "No," you said, "we shall flee on horses."
And so flee you will!
And again, "We shall ride on swift ones."
And so your pursuers will be swift!
17 A thousand will quake at the threat of one
and when five threaten you will flee,
until what is left of you will be
like a flagstaff on a mountain top,
like a signal on a hill.'

God will forgive

18 But Yahweh is waiting
to be gracious to you,
the Exalted One, to take pity on you,
for Yahweh is a God of fair judgement;
blessed are all who hope in him.

19 Yes, people of Zion living in Jerusalem,
you will weep no more.
He will be gracious to you
when your cry for help rings out;

30a =Egypt.

as soon as he hears it,
he will answer you.
20 When the Lord has given you
the bread of suffering
and the water of distress,
he who is your teacher will hide no longer,
and you will see your teacher
with your own eyes.
21 Your ears will hear these words
behind you,
'This is the way, keep to it,'
whether you turn to right or left.
22 You will hold unclean
the silverplating of your idols
and the goldplating of your images.
You will throw them away
like the polluted things they are,
shouting after them, 'Good riddance!'
23 He will send rain
for the seed you sow in the ground,
and the bread that the ground provides
will be rich and nourishing.
That day, your cattle will graze
in wide pastures.
24 Oxen and donkeys that work the land
will eat for fodder wild sorrel,
spread by the shovel-load and fork-load.
25 On every lofty mountain,
on every high hill
there will be streams and water-courses,
on the day of the great slaughter
when the strongholds fall.
26 Then moonlight will be
bright as sunlight
and sunlight itself be
seven times brighter
—like the light of seven days in one—
on the day Yahweh dresses
his people's wound
and heals the scars of the blows
they have received.

Against Assyria

27 See, the name of Yahweh
comes from afar,
blazing his anger, heavy his threat.
His lips are brimming over with fury,
his tongue is like a devouring fire.
28 His breath is like a river in spate
coming up to the neck,
to sift the nations
with the sieve of destruction,
to harness the peoples in a bridle,
that will lead them astray.
29 Your song will be like that
on a festal night,
and there will be joy in your hearts
as when to the sound of the flute
people make a pilgrimage
to the mountain of Yahweh,
the Rock of Israel.
30 Yahweh will make his majestic voice
ring out,
he will show the weight of his arm
in the heat of his anger,
with a devouring fire,
with thunderbolt,
downpour and hailstones.
31 Yes, at Yahweh's voice
Assyria will be terrified,
he will strike him with his rod;
32 each time he goes by,
will fall the punishing rod
that Yahweh will lay on him,
to the sound of tambourines and harps,
in the battles which he will wage
against him with uplifted hand.
33 Yes, Topheth[b] has been ready
for a long time now,
that too is ready for the king,
deep and wide his pyre,
fire and wood in plenty.
Yahweh's breath,
like a stream of brimstone,
will set fire to it.

Against the Egyptian alliance

31 Woe to those going down to Egypt
for help,
who put their trust in horses,
who rely on the quantity of chariots,
and on great strength of cavalrymen,
but do not look to the Holy One of Israel
or consult Yahweh.
2 Yet he too is wise and can bring disaster
and he will not go back on his word;
he will rise against the breed of evil-doers
and against those
who protect wrong-doers.
3 The Egyptian is human, not divine,
his horses are flesh, not spirit;
Yahweh will stretch out his hand:
the protector will stumble,
the protected will fall
and all will perish together.

30b The rubbish-dump of Jerusalem.

Against Assyria

4 Yes, this is what Yahweh has said to me:
As a lion or lion cub
growls over its prey,
when scores of shepherds
are summoned to drive it off,
without being frightened
by their shouting
or cowed by the noise they make,
just so will Yahweh Sabaoth descend
to fight for Mount Zion and for its hill.
5 Like hovering birds,
so will Yahweh Sabaoth
protect Jerusalem;
by protecting it, he will save it,
by supporting it, he will deliver it.
6 Come back to the one whom the Israelites
have so deeply betrayed!
7 For, that day, each of you will throw away
the false gods of silver
and the false gods of gold
which your own sinful hands have made.
8 Assyria will fall by the sword,
not that of a man,
will be devoured by the sword,
of no human being,
he will flee before the sword
and his young warriors will be enslaved.
9 In his terror he will abandon his rock,
and his panic-stricken officers
desert the standard—
declares Yahweh, whose fire is in Zion,
whose furnace, in Jerusalem.

A good king

32 There will be a king
who reigns uprightly
and princes who rule with fair judgement;
2 each will be like a shelter from the wind,
a refuge from the storm,
like streams on arid ground,
like the shade of a solid rock
in a desolate land.
3 The eyes of seers will no longer be closed,
the ears of hearers will be alert,
4 the heart of the hasty
will learn to think things over,
and the tongue of stammerers
will speak promptly and clearly.
5 The fool will no longer be called generous,
nor the rascal be styled bountiful.

Niggard and noble

6 For the fool speaks folly
and his heart is set on villainy;
he is godless in his actions
and his words ascribe error to Yahweh;
he starves the hungry of their food
and refuses drink to the thirsty.
7 Everything to do with the rascal is evil,
he devises infamous plans
to ruin the poor with lying words
even when the needy
has right on his side;
8 but the noble person
plans only noble things,
noble his every move.

Against the women of Jerusalem

9 Stand up, you haughty women,
listen to my words;
you over-confident daughters,
pay attention to what I say.

10 Within one year and a few days
you will tremble,
you over-confident women;
grape-harvesting will be finished,
gathering will never happen again.

11 Shudder, you haughty women,
tremble, you over-confident women;
strip, undress, put sackcloth
round your waists.

12 Beat your breasts for the pleasant fields,
for the fruitful vine,
13 for my people's soil
where the bramble-bush will be growing
and for all the happy houses,
for the rejoicing city.

14 For the citadel will be abandoned
and the thronged city deserted,
Ophel[a] and the Keep
will be denuded for ever,
the playground of wild donkeys
and the pasture of flocks,

Outpouring of the spirit

15 until the spirit is poured out on us
from above,
and the desert becomes an orchard,
and an orchard that seems like a forest.

32a The hill of the earliest city of Jerusalem; the keep is presumably a great tower.

16 Fair judgement will fix its home
in the desert,
and uprightness live in this orchard,
17 and the product of uprightness
will be peace,
the effect of uprightness
being quiet and security for ever.

18 My people will live in a peaceful home,
in peaceful houses, tranquil dwellings.
19 And should the forest
be totally destroyed
and the city gravely humiliated,
20 You will be happy to sow
wherever there is water
and to let the ox and donkey roam free.

The expected deliverance

33 Woe to you, destroying
though not yourself destroyed,
betraying though not yourself betrayed;
when you have finished destroying,
you will be destroyed,
when you have stopped betraying,
you will be betrayed.
2 Yahweh, show us your mercy,
we hope in you.
Be our arm every morning
and our salvation in time of distress.
3 At the sound of tumult the peoples flee,
when you stand up the nations scatter.
4 Your spoil is gathered in
as a grasshopper gathers in,
like a swarm of locusts
people descend on it.
5 Yahweh is exalted,
for he is enthroned above,
he has filled Zion with fair judgement
and saving justice.

6 You can count on this all your days:
wisdom and knowledge
are the riches that save,
the fear of Yahweh is his treasure.

7 Look, Ariel is lamenting in the streets,
the ambassadors of peace
are weeping bitterly.
8 The highways are deserted,
no travellers any more on the roads.
Agreements are broken,
witnesses held in contempt,
there is respect for no one.
9 The land pines away in mourning,
the Lebanon is withering with shame,
Sharon has become like the wasteland,
Bashan and Carmel are shuddering.
10 'Now I shall stand up,' says Yahweh,
'now I shall rise, now draw myself up.
11 You conceive chaff, you give birth to straw:
like fire, my breath will devour you.
12 The peoples will be burnt up
as though by quicklime,
like cut thorns they will be burnt
on the fire.
13 You who are far away,
listen to what I have done,
and you who are near, realise my strength.'
14 The sinners in Zion are panic-stricken
and fear seizes on the godless,
'Which of us can survive
the devouring fire,
which of us survive everlasting burning?'
15 The one who acts uprightly
and speaks honestly,
who scorns to get rich by extortion,
who rejects bribes out of hand,
who refuses to listen to plans
involving bloodshed
and shuts his eyes
rather than countenance crime:
16 such a man will live on the heights,
the craggy rocks will be his refuge,
he will be fed, he will not want for water.

The return to Jerusalem

17 Your eyes will gaze on the king
in his beauty,
they will look on a country
stretching far and wide.
18 Your heart will meditate on past terrors,
'Where is the man who did the counting?
Where is the man who did the weighing?
Where is the man
who counted off the towers?'
19 No more will you see that insolent people,
that people of unintelligible speech,
of barbarous and meaningless tongue.
20 Gaze at Zion, city of our feasts;
your eyes will see Jerusalem
as a home that is secure,
a tent not to be moved,
none of its tent-pegs ever to be pulled out,
none of its guy-ropes ever to be broken.

21 There it is that Yahweh
shows us his power,
like a place of rivers and very wide canals
on which will row no galley,
over which will pass no majestic ship.

22 (For Yahweh is our judge,
Yahweh our lawgiver,
Yahweh is our king and our Saviour.)
23 Your tackle has given way,
it cannot support the mast,
it cannot hoist the pennon.
And so there is much booty
to be shared out;
the lame fall to plundering,
24 and no one living there will say,
'I am sickly';
the people living there
will find their guilt forgiven.

The sentence on Edom

34 Come near and listen, you nations,
pay attention, you peoples.
Let the earth and its contents listen,
the world and its entire population.
2 For Yahweh is angry with all the nations,
enraged with all their hordes.
He has vowed them to destruction,
handed them over to slaughter.
3 Their dead will be thrown away,
the stench will rise from their corpses,
the mountains will run with their blood,
4 the entire array of heaven will fall apart.
The heavens will be rolled up like a scroll
and all their array will fade away,
as fade the leaves falling from the vine,
as fade those falling from the fig tree.

5 For my sword has drunk deep
in the heavens:
see how it now falls on Edom,
on the people vowed to destruction,
to punish them.
6 Yahweh's sword is gorged with blood,
it is greasy with fat,
with the blood of lambs and goats,
with the fat of the kidneys of rams.
For Yahweh has a sacrifice in Bozrah,
a great slaughter in the land of Edom.
7 The wild oxen will fall with them,
the bullocks with the bulls;
their land will be drenched with blood
and their dust will be greasy with fat.
8 For this will be Yahweh's day
of vengeance,
the year of retribution in Zion's lawsuit.

9 Its streams will turn into pitch,
its dust into brimstone,
its country will turn into blazing pitch.
10 Never quenched night or day,
its smoke rising for ever,
it will lie waste age after age,
no one will travel through it
for ever and ever.
11 It will be the haunt of pelican
and hedgehog,
the owl and the raven will live there;
over it Yahweh will stretch
the measuring line of chaos
and the plumb-line of emptiness.

12 There will be no more nobles
to proclaim the royal authority;
there will be an end of all its princes.
13 Brambles will grow in its bastions,
nettles and thorn-bushes in its fortresses,
it will be the lair of jackals,
an enclosure for ostriches.
14 Wild cats will meet hyenas there,
satyr will call to satyr,
there Lilith too will lurk
and find somewhere to rest.
15 The snake will nest and lay eggs there,
will hatch and gather its young
into the shade;
and there the vultures will assemble,
each one with its mate.
16 Search in Yahweh's book, and read,
not one of these will be missing,
not one of them lacking a mate;
for thus his mouth has ordained it,
and his spirit has brought them together.
17 He has thrown the lot for each,
his hand has measured out their share;
they will possess it for ever,
and live there age after age.

The triumph of Jerusalem

35 Let the desert and the dry lands
be glad,
let the wasteland rejoice and bloom;
like the asphodel, 2 let it burst into flower,
let it rejoice and sing for joy.
The glory of Lebanon is bestowed on it,
the splendour of Carmel and Sharon;
then they will see the glory of Yahweh,
the splendour of our God.
3 Strengthen all weary hands,
steady all trembling knees
4 and say to the faint-hearted,
'Be strong! Do not be afraid.
Here is your God,
vengeance is coming,
divine retribution;
he is coming to save you.'

[5]Then the eyes of the blind will be opened,
the ears of the deaf unsealed,
[6]then the lame will leap like a deer
and the tongue of the dumb sing for joy;
for water will gush in the desert
and streams in the wastelands,
[7]the parched ground will become a marsh
and the thirsty land springs of water;
the lairs where the jackals used to live
will become plots of reed and papyrus.

[8]And through it will run a road for them
and a highway
which will be called the Sacred Way;
the unclean will not be allowed to use it;
He will be the one to use this road,
the fool will not stray along it.
[9]No lion will be there,
no ferocious beast set foot on it,
nothing of the sort be found;
it will be used by the redeemed.
[10]For those whom Yahweh has ransomed
will return,
they will come to Zion shouting for joy,
their heads crowned with joy unending;
rejoicing and gladness will escort them
and sorrow and sighing will take flight.

APPENDICES[a]

Sennacherib's invasion

36 In the fourteenth year of King
Hezekiah, Sennacherib king of Assyria
advanced on all the fortified towns of Judah
and captured them. [2]From Lachish the king
of Assyria sent the cupbearer-in-chief with a
large force to King Hezekiah in Jerusalem.
The cupbearer-in-chief took up position
near the conduit of the upper pool on the
road to the Fuller's Field. [3]The master of the
palace, Eliakim son of Hilkiah, Shebna the
secretary and the herald Joah son of Asaph
went out to him. [4]The cupbearer-in-chief
said to them, 'Say to Hezekiah, "The great
king, the king of Assyria, says this: What
makes you so confident? [5]Do you think
empty words are as good as strategy and
military strength? Who are you relying on,
to dare to rebel against me? [6]There you are,
relying on that broken reed, Egypt, which
pricks and pierces the hand of the person
who leans on it. That is what Pharaoh king
of Egypt is like to all who rely on him. [7]You
may say to me: We rely on Yahweh our God.
But haven't his high places and altars been
suppressed by Hezekiah, who told Judah and
Jerusalem: This is the altar before which you
must worship? [8]Very well, then, make a
wager with my lord the king of Assyria: I will
give you two thousand horses if you can find
horsemen to ride them. [9]How could you
repulse a single one of the least of my master's
soldiers? And yet you have relied on Egypt
for chariots and horsemen. [10]And lastly, have
I marched on this country to lay it waste
without warrant from Yahweh? Yahweh
himself said to me: March on this country
and lay it waste." '

[11]Eliakim, Shebna and Joah said to the
cupbearer-in-chief, 'Please speak to your
servants in Aramaic, for we understand it;
do not speak to us in the Judaean language
within earshot of the people on the ramparts.'
[12]But the cupbearer-in-chief said, 'Do you
think my lord sent me here to say these things
to your master or to you? On the contrary, it
was to the people sitting on the ramparts
who, like you, are doomed to eat their own
dung and drink their own urine.'

[13]The cupbearer-in-chief then drew
himself up and shouted loudly in the Judaean
language, 'Listen to the words of the great
king, the king of Assyria. [14]The king says
this, "Do not let Hezekiah delude you! He
will be powerless to save you. [15]Do not let
Hezekiah persuade you to rely on Yahweh
by saying: Yahweh is sure to save us; this city
will not fall into the king of Assyria's clutches.
[16]Do not listen to Hezekiah, for the king
of Assyria says this: Make peace with me,
[17]surrender to me, and every one of you will
be free to eat the fruit of his own vine and of
his own fig tree and to drink the water of his
own storage-well until I come and take you
away to a country like your own, a land of
corn and good wine, a land of bread and
vineyards. [18]Do not let Hezekiah delude you
by saying: Yahweh will save us. Has any
god of any nation been able to save his
country from the king of Assyria's clutches?
[19]Where are the gods of Hamath and Arpad?
Where are the gods of Sepharvaim? Where
are the national gods of Samaria? Did they
save Samaria from my clutches? [20]Of all the
national gods, which ones have saved their

36a chh. 36—39 form a historical appendix, reproducing the story of Isaiah given in 2 K 18:13, 17—20:19.

countries from my clutches, that Yahweh
should be able to save Jerusalem from my
clutches?" '
21They, however, kept quiet and said
nothing in reply, since the king had given the
order, 'You are not to answer him.' 22The
master of the palace, Eliakim son of Hilkiah,
Shebna the secretary and the herald Joah son
of Asaph, with their clothes torn, went to
Hezekiah and reported what the cupbearer-
in-chief had said.

The prophet Isaiah is consulted

37 On hearing this, King Hezekiah tore
his clothes, put on sackcloth and went
to the Temple of Yahweh. 2He sent Eliakim
master of the palace, Shebna the secretary
and the elders of the priests, wearing sack-
cloth, to the prophet Isaiah son of Amoz.
3They said to him, 'This is what Hezekiah
says, "Today is a day of suffering, of punish-
ment, of disgrace. Children come to birth
and there is no strength to bring them forth.
4May Yahweh your God hear the words of
the cupbearer-in-chief whom his master, the
king of Assyria, has sent to insult the living
God, and may Yahweh your God punish the
words he has heard! Offer your prayer for
the remnant still left." '
5When King Hezekiah's ministers came to
Isaiah, 6he said to them, 'Say to your master,
"Yahweh says this: Do not be afraid of the
words which you have heard or the blas-
phemies which the king of Assyria's minions
have uttered against me. 7Look, I am going
to put a spirit in him and, on the strength of
a rumour, he will go back to his own country,
and in that country I shall make him fall by
the sword." '

The cupbearer returns to his master

8The cupbearer turned about and rejoined
the king of Assyria, who was then attacking
Libnah, the cupbearer having learnt that the
king had already left Lachish 9on hearing
that Tirhakah king of Cush was on his way
to attack him.

Second account of Sennacherib's activities

Sennacherib again sent messengers to
Hezekiah, saying, 10'Tell Hezekiah king of
Judah this, "Do not let your God on whom
you are relying deceive you with the promise:
Jerusalem will not fall into the king of As-
syria's clutches. 11You have learnt by now
what the kings of Assyria have done to all the
other countries, putting them under the curse
of destruction. Are you likely to be saved?
12Did the gods of the nations whom my
ancestors devastated save them—Gozan,
Haran, Rezeph and the Edenites who were
in Tel Basar? 13Where is the king of Hamath,
the king of Arpad, the king of Lair, of
Sepharvaim, of Hena, of Ivvah?" '
14Hezekiah took the letter from the mess-
engers' hands and read it; he then went up to
the Temple of Yahweh and spread it out
before Yahweh. 15Hezekiah said this prayer
in the presence of Yahweh, 16'Yahweh
Sabaoth, God of Israel, enthroned on the
winged creatures, you alone are God of all
the kingdoms of the world, you made heaven
and earth. 17Give ear, Yahweh, and listen;
open your eyes, Yahweh, and see! Hear the
words of Sennacherib, who has sent to insult
the living God. 18It is true, Yahweh, that the
kings of Assyria have destroyed all the nations
(and their countries); 19they have thrown
their gods on the fire, for these were not gods
but human artefacts—wood and stone—and
hence they have destroyed them. 20But now,
Yahweh our God, save us from his clutches,
I beg you, and let all the kingdoms of the
world know that you alone are God, Yahweh.'

Isaiah intervenes

21Isaiah son of Amoz then sent the following
message to Hezekiah, 'Yahweh, God of
Israel, says this, "In answer to the prayer
which you have addressed to me about
Sennacherib king of Assyria. 22Here is the
pronouncement which Yahweh has made
about him:

She despises you, she scorns you,
the virgin daughter of Zion;
she tosses her head at you,
the daughter of Jerusalem!
23Whom have you insulted,
whom did you blaspheme?
Against whom raised your voice
and lifted your haughty eyes?
Against the Holy One of Israel.
24Through your minions
you have insulted the Lord,
thinking: With my many chariots
I have climbed the mountain-tops,

the utmost peaks of Lebanon.
I have felled its mighty cedars,
its finest cypresses,
have reached its furthest peak,
its forest garden.
25 Yes, I have dug and drunk
of foreign waters;
under the soles of my feet
I have dried up all Egypt's rivers.

26 Do you hear? Long ago
I prepared this,
from days of old I actually planned it,
now I carry it out.
You were to lay walled cities
in heaps of ruins;
27 that was why their inhabitants,
feeble of hand,
were dismayed and discomfited,
were weak as grass,
were frail as plants,
were like grass of housetop and meadow
under the east wind.
28 But whether you stand up or sit down,
whether you go out or come in, I know it
(and how you rave against me).
29 Because you have raved against me
and your arrogance has reached my ears,
I shall put a hook through your nostrils
and a muzzle on your lips,
and make you return by the road
by which you came.

A sign for Hezekiah

30 And this will be the sign for you:
This year will be eaten the self-sown grain,
next year what sprouts in the fallow;
but in the third year sow and reap,
plant vineyards and eat their fruit.
31 The surviving remnant
of the House of Judah will bring forth
new roots below and fruits above;
32 for a remnant will issue from Jerusalem,
and survivors from Mount Zion.
Yahweh Sabaoth's jealous love
will accomplish this." '

A prophecy on Assyria

33 'This, then, is what Yahweh says about the king of Assyria:

He will not enter this city,
will shoot no arrow at it,
confront it with no shield,
throw up no earthwork against it.
34 By the road by which he came,
by that he will return;
he will not enter this city,
declares Yahweh.
35 I shall protect this city and save it
for my sake and my servant David's sake.'

Sennacherib is punished

36 That same night the angel of Yahweh went
out and struck down a hundred and eighty-
five thousand men in the Assyrian camp. In
the early morning when it was time to get up,
there they lay, so many corpses.
37 Sennacherib struck camp and left; he
returned home and stayed in Nineveh. 38 One
day when he was worshipping in the temple
of his god Nisroch, his sons Adrammelech
and Sharezer struck him down with the sword
and escaped into the territory of Ararat. His
son Esarhaddon succeeded him.

The illness and cure of Hezekiah

38 About then, Hezekiah fell ill and was
at the point of death. The prophet
Isaiah son of Amoz came and said to him,
'Yahweh says this, "Put your affairs in order,
for you are going to die, you will not live." '
2 Hezekiah turned his face to the wall and
addressed this prayer to Yahweh, 3 'Ah,
Yahweh, remember, I beg you, that I have
behaved faithfully and with sincerity of heart
in your presence and done what you regard
as right.' And Hezekiah shed many tears.
4 Then the word of Yahweh came to Isaiah,
5 'Go and say to Hezekiah, "Yahweh, the God
of your ancestor David, says this: I have
heard your prayer and seen your tears. I shall
cure you: in three days' time you will go up
to the Temple of Yahweh. I shall add fifteen
years to your life. 6 I shall save you and this
city from the king of Assyria's clutches and
defend this city for my sake and my servant
David's sake." '
21 'Bring a fig poultice,' Isaiah said, 'apply
it to the ulcer and he will recover.' 22 Hezekiah
said, 'What is the sign to tell me that I shall
be going up to the Temple of Yahweh?'[a]
7 'Here', Isaiah replied, 'is the sign from
Yahweh that he will do what he has said.
8 Look, I shall make the shadow cast by the

38a vv. 21–22 were misplaced when the canticle of Hezekiah was inserted. They are here restored.

declining sun on the steps—the steps to Ahaz's roof-room—go back ten steps.' And the sun went back the ten steps by which it had declined.

The canticle of Hezekiah

9 Canticle of Hezekiah king of Judah after his illness and recovery.

10 I thought: In the noon of my life
I am to depart.
At the gates of Sheol I shall be held
for the rest of my days.
11 I thought: I shall never see Yahweh again
in the land of the living,
I shall never see again a single one
of those who live on earth.
12 My home has been pulled up,
and thrown away
like a shepherd's tent;
like a weaver, I have rolled up my life,
he has cut me from the loom.
From dawn to dark,
you have been making an end of me;
13 till daybreak, I cried for help;
like a lion, he has crushed all my bones,
from dawn to dark,
you have been making an end of me.
14 I twitter like a swallow,
I moan like a dove,
my eyes have grown dim from looking up.
Lord, I am overwhelmed,
come to my help.
15 How can I speak
and what can I say to him?
He is the one to act.
I must eke out the rest of my years
in bitterness of soul.

16 The Lord is over them; they live,
and everything in them lives by his spirit.
You will cure me. Restore me to life.
17 At once, my bitterness turns to well-being.
For you have preserved my soul
from the pit of nothingness,
you have thrust all my sins behind you.
18 For Sheol cannot praise you,
nor Death celebrate you;
those who go down to the pit
can hope no longer in your constancy.
19 The living, the living are the ones
who praise you,
as I do today.
Fathers tell their sons
about your constancy.
20 Yahweh, come to my help
and we will make our harps resound
all the days of our life
in the Temple of Yahweh.

The Babylonian embassy

39 At that time, the king of Babylon,
Merodach-Baladan son of Baladan,
sent letters and a gift to Hezekiah, for he
had heard of his illness and his recovery.
2 Hezekiah was delighted at this and showed
the ambassadors his entire treasury, the
silver, gold, spices, precious oil, his armoury
too, and everything to be seen in his store-
houses. There was nothing in his palace or in
his whole domain that Hezekiah did not show
them.
3 The prophet Isaiah then came to King
Hezekiah and asked him, 'What have these
men said, and where have they come to you
from?' Hezekiah answered, 'They have come
from a distant country, from Babylon.'
4 Isaiah said, 'What have they seen in your
palace?' 'They have seen everything in my
palace,' Hezekiah answered. 'There is
nothing in my storehouses that I have not
shown them.'
5 Then Isaiah said to Hezekiah, 'Listen to
the word of Yahweh Sabaoth, 6 "The days
are coming when everything in your palace,
everything that your ancestors have amassed
until now, will be carried off to Babylon. Not
a thing will be left," Yahweh says. 7 "Sons
sprung from you, sons begotten by you, will
be abducted to be eunuchs in the palace of
the king of Babylon." ' 8 Hezekiah said to
Isaiah, 'This word of Yahweh that you
announce is reassuring,' for he was thinking,
'There is going to be peace and security
during my lifetime.'

II: THE BOOK OF THE CONSOLATION OF ISRAEL

Prediction of deliverance

40 'Console[a] my people, console them,'
says your God.
2'Speak to the heart of Jerusalem
and cry to her
that her period of service is ended,
that her guilt has been atoned for,
that, from the hand of Yahweh,
she has received
double punishment for all her sins.'

3A voice cries, 'Prepare in the desert
a way for Yahweh.
Make a straight highway for our God
across the wastelands.
4Let every valley be filled in,
every mountain and hill be levelled,
every cliff become a plateau,
every escarpment a plain;
5then the glory of Yahweh will be revealed
and all humanity will see it together,
for the mouth of Yahweh has spoken.'

6A voice said, 'Cry aloud!' and I said,
'What shall I cry?'
—'All humanity is grass
and all its beauty like the wild flower's.
7The grass withers, the flower fades
when the breath of Yahweh blows on them.
(The grass is surely the people.)
8The grass withers, the flower fades,
but the word of our God remains for ever.'

9Go up on a high mountain,
messenger of Zion.
Shout as loud as you can,
messenger of Jerusalem!
Shout fearlessly,
say to the towns of Judah,
'Here is your God.'

10Here is Lord Yahweh coming with power,
his arm maintains his authority,
his reward is with him
and his prize precedes him.[b]
11He is like a shepherd feeding his flock,
gathering lambs in his arms,
holding them against his breast
and leading to their rest the mother ewes.

The majesty of God

12Who was it measured the water of the sea
in the hollow of his hand
and calculated the heavens
to the nearest inch,
gauged the dust of the earth
to the nearest bushel,
weighed the mountains in scales,
the hills in a balance?

13Who directed the spirit of Yahweh,
what counsellor could have
instructed him?
14Whom has he consulted to
enlighten him,
to instruct him in the path of judgement,
to teach him knowledge
and show him how to understand?
15See, the nations are like a drop
in a bucket,
they count as a grain of dust
on the scales.
See, coasts and islands
weigh no more than fine powder.
16The Lebanon is not enough
for the burning fires
nor its animals enough
for the burnt offering.
17All the nations are as nothing
before him,
for him they count as nothingness
and emptiness.
18To whom can you compare God?
What image can you contrive of him?

19The craftsman casts an idol,
a goldsmith overlays it with gold
and casts silver chains for it.
20Someone too poor to afford a sacrifice
chooses a piece of wood
that will not rot;
he then seeks out a skilled craftsman
to set up an idol that will not totter.
21Did you not know,
had you not heard?
Was it not told you from the beginning?
Have you not understood
how the earth was set on its foundations?
22He who sits enthroned
above the circle of the earth,

40a Hence the title of this second part of Isaiah.
40b =62:11.

the inhabitants of which
are like grasshoppers,
stretches out the heavens like a cloth,
spreads them out like a tent to live in.
23 He reduces princes to nothing,
the rulers of the world
to mere emptiness.
24 Scarcely are they planted,
scarcely sown,
scarcely has their stem
taken root in the soil,
than he blows on them and they wither
and the storm carries them away
like chaff.

25 'To whom can you compare me,
or who is my equal?' says the Holy One.
26 Lift your eyes and look:
he who created these things
leads out their army in order,
summoning each of them by name.
So mighty is his power,
so great his strength,
that not one fails to answer.
27 How can you say, Jacob,
how can you repeat, Israel,
'My way is hidden from Yahweh,
my rights are ignored by my God'?
28 Did you not know? Had you not heard?
Yahweh is the everlasting God,
he created the remotest parts
of the earth.
He does not grow tired or weary,
his understanding is beyond fathoming.
29 He gives strength to the weary,
he strengthens the powerless.
30 Youths grow tired and weary,
the young stumble and fall,
31 but those who hope in Yahweh
will regain their strength,
they will sprout wings like eagles,
though they run
they will not grow weary,
though they walk they will never tire.

Cyrus, the instrument of Yahweh

41 Coasts and islands,
fall silent before me,
and let the peoples renew their strength,
let them come forward and speak;
let us assemble for judgement.
2 'Who has raised from the east
him whom saving justice
summons in its train,
him to whom Yahweh
delivers up the nations
and subjects kings,
him who reduces them to dust
with his sword,
and to driven stubble with his bow,
3 him who pursues them
and advances unhindered,
his feet scarcely touching the road?
4 Who has acted thus, who has done this?
He who calls each generation
from the beginning:
I, Yahweh, who am the first
and till the last I shall still be there.'
5 The coasts and islands have seen
and taken fright,
the remotest parts of earth are trembling:
they are approaching, they are here!
6 People help one another,
they say to each other, 'Take heart!'
7 The woodworker encourages the smelter,
the polisher encourages the hammerer,
saying of the soldering, 'It is sound';
and he fastens it with nails
to keep it steady.

Israel, chosen and protected by Yahweh

8 But you, Israel, my servant,
Jacob whom I have chosen,
descendant of Abraham my friend,
9 whom I have taken to myself,
from the remotest parts of the earth
and summoned from countries far away,
to whom I have said, 'You are my servant,
I have chosen you, I have not rejected you,'
10 do not be afraid, for I am with you;
do not be alarmed, for I am your God.
I give you strength, truly I help you,
truly I hold you firm
with my saving right hand.
11 Look, all those who rage against you
will be put to shame and humiliated;
those who picked quarrels with you
will be reduced to nothing and will perish.
12 You will look for them
but will not find them,
those who used to fight you;
they will be destroyed
and brought to nothing,
those who made war on you.
13 For I, Yahweh, your God,
I grasp you by your right hand;
I tell you, 'Do not be afraid,
I shall help you.'
14 Do not be afraid, Jacob, you worm!

You little handful of Israel!
I shall help you, declares Yahweh;
your redeemer[a] is the Holy One of Israel.
15 Look, I am making you
into a threshing-sledge,
new, with double teeth;
you will thresh
and beat the mountains to dust
and reduce the hills to straw.
16 You will winnow them
and the wind will carry them off,
the gale will scatter them;
whereas you will rejoice in Yahweh,
will glory in the Holy One of Israel.
17 The oppressed and needy
search for water,
and there is none,
their tongue is parched with thirst.
I, Yahweh, shall answer them,
I, the God of Israel,
shall not abandon them.
18 I shall open up rivers on barren heights
and water-holes down in the ravines;
I shall turn the desert into a lake
and dry ground into springs of water.
19 I shall plant the desert with cedar trees,
acacias, myrtles and olives;
in the wastelands I shall put cypress trees,
plane trees and box trees side by side;
20 so that people may see and know,
so that they may all observe
and understand
that the hand of Yahweh has done this,
that the Holy One of Israel has created it.

The fatuity of idols

21 'Present your case,' says Yahweh,
'Produce your arguments,'
says Jacob's king.
22 'Let them produce and reveal to us
what is going to happen.
What happened in the past?
Reveal it so that we can consider it
and know what the outcome will be.
Or tell us about the future,
23 reveal what is to happen next,
and then we shall know
that you are gods.
At least, do something,
be it good or bad,
so that we may feel alarm and fear.
24 Look, you are less than nothingness,
and what you do is less than nothing;
to choose you is an outrage.'
25 I have raised him from the north
and he has come,
from the east he has been summoned
by name.
He tramples on rulers like mud,
like a potter treading clay.
26 Who revealed this from the beginning
for us to know,
and in the past for us to say,
'That is right'?
No one in fact revealed it,
no one proclaimed it,
no one has heard you speak.
27 First-fruits of Zion, look,
here they come!
I send a messenger to Jerusalem,
28 and I look—no one,
not a single counsellor among them
who, if I asked, could give an answer.
29 Taken altogether they are nothingness,
what they do is nothing,
their statues, wind and emptiness.

First song of the servant

42 Here is my servant[a] whom I uphold,
my chosen one
in whom my soul delights.
I have sent my spirit upon him,
he will bring fair judgement to the nations.
2 He does not cry out or raise his voice,
his voice is not heard in the street;
3 he does not break the crushed reed
or snuff the faltering wick.
Faithfully he presents fair judgement;
4 he will not grow faint,
he will not be crushed
until he has established
fair judgement on earth,
and the coasts and islands
are waiting for his instruction.
5 Thus says God, Yahweh,
who created the heavens
and spread them out,
who hammered into shape the earth
and what comes from it,
who gave breath to the people on it,
and spirit to those who walk on it:
6 I, Yahweh, have called you
in saving justice,

41a The *go'el*, the closest relative, defender and avenger of blood, often used of Yahweh in the Pss.
42a The first of the four Songs of the Servant (*see* Introd. p. 879).

I have grasped you by the hand
and shaped you;
I have made you a covenant of the people
and light to the nations,
7 to open the eyes of the blind,
to free captives from prison,
and those who live in darkness
from the dungeon.
8 I am Yahweh, that is my name!
I shall not yield my glory to another,
nor my honour to idols.
9 See how the former predictions
have come true.
Fresh things I now reveal;
before they appear I tell you of them.

Song of victory

10 Sing a new song to Yahweh!
Let his praise be sung
from remotest parts of the earth
by those who sail the sea
and by everything in it,
by the coasts and islands
and those who inhabit them.
11 Let the desert and its cities
raise their voices,
the encampments where Kedar lives.
Let the inhabitants of the Rock
cry aloud for joy
and shout from the mountain tops.
12 Let them give glory to Yahweh
and, in the coasts and islands,
let them voice his praise.
13 Yahweh advances like a hero,
like a warrior he rouses his fire.
He shouts, he raises the war cry,
he shows his might against his foes.
14 'From long ago I have been silent,
I have kept quiet, held myself in check,
groaning like a woman in labour,
panting and gasping for air.
15 I shall ravage mountain and hill,
shall wither all their vegetation;
I shall turn the torrents into firm ground
and dry up the marshes.
16 I shall lead the blind by a road
they do not know,
by paths they do not know
I shall conduct them.
I shall turn the darkness into light
before them
and the quagmires into solid ground.
This I shall do—without fail.'
17 Those who trust in idols will recoil,
they will blush for shame,
who say to metal images,
'You are our gods.'

Israel's blindness

18 Listen, you deaf!
Look and see, you blind!
19 Who so blind as my servant,
so deaf as the messenger I send?
(Who so blind as the friend
I have taken to myself,
so deaf as Yahweh's servant?)
20 You have seen many things
but not observed them;
your ears are open but you do not hear.
21 Yahweh wished,
because of his saving justice,
to make the Law great and glorious.
22 Yet here is a people pillaged
and plundered,
all of them shut up in caves,
imprisoned in dungeons.
They have been pillaged,
with no one to rescue them,
plundered, with no one to say,
'Give it back!'
23 Which of you will listen to this,
who pay attention and listen in future?
24 Who surrendered Jacob
to the plunderer
and Israel to the pillagers?
Was it not Yahweh, against whom
we had sinned,
in whose ways they would not walk
and whose Law they would not obey?
25 On him he poured out his blazing anger
and the fury of war;
it enveloped him in flames
and yet he did not understand;
it burned him up,
but he did not learn a lesson.

God, Israel's protector and liberator

43 And now, thus says Yahweh,
he who created you, Jacob,
who formed you, Israel:
Do not be afraid, for I have redeemed you;
I have called you by your name,
you are mine.
2 Should you pass through the waters,
I shall be with you;
or through rivers,
they will not swallow you up.

Should you walk through fire,
you will not suffer,
and the flame will not burn you.
3 For I am Yahweh, your God,
the Holy One of Israel, your Saviour.
I have given Egypt for your ransom,
Cush and Seba in exchange for you.
4 Since I regard you as precious,
since you are honoured and I love you,
I therefore give people
in exchange for you,
and nations in return for your life.
5 Do not be afraid, for I am with you.
I shall bring your offspring from the east,
and gather you from the west.
6 To the north I shall say, 'Give them up!'
and to the south, 'Do not hold them back!'
Bring back my sons from far away,
and my daughters from the remotest part
of the earth,
7 everyone who bears my name,
whom I have created for my glory,
whom I have formed, whom I have made.

Yahweh alone is God

8 Bring forward the people that is blind,
yet has eyes,
that is deaf and yet has ears.
9 Let all the nations assemble,
let the peoples gather here!
Which of them has proclaimed this
and revealed things to us in the past?
Let them bring their witnesses
to justify themselves,
let others hear and say, 'It is true.'
10 You yourselves are my witnesses,
declares Yahweh,
and the servant whom I have chosen,
so that you may know and believe me
and understand that it is I.
No god was formed before me,
nor will be after me.
11 I, I am Yahweh,
and there is no other Saviour but me.
12 I have revealed, have saved,
and have proclaimed,
not some foreigner among you.
You are my witnesses,
declares Yahweh,

I am God, 13 yes, from eternity I am.
No one can deliver from my hand;
when I act, who can thwart me?

Against Babylon

14 Thus says Yahweh,
your redeemer, the Holy One of Israel:
For your sake I have sent to Babylon,
I shall knock down all the prison bars,
and the Chaldaeans' shouts of joy
will change to lamentations.
15 I am Yahweh, your Holy One,
the Creator of Israel, your king.

Miracles of the new Exodus

16 Thus says Yahweh,
who made a way through the sea,
a path in the raging waters,
17 who led out chariot and horse
together with an army of picked troops:
they lay down never to rise again,
they were snuffed out, put out like a wick.
18 No need to remember past events,
no need to think about
what was done before.
19 Look, I am doing something new,
now it emerges; can you not see it?
Yes, I am making a road in the desert
and rivers in wastelands.
20 The wild animals will honour me,
the jackals and the ostriches,
for bestowing water in the desert
and rivers on the wastelands
for my people, my chosen one, to drink.
21 The people I have shaped for myself
will broadcast my praises.

Israel's ingratitude

22 But, Jacob, you have not invoked me;
no, Israel, you have grown weary of me.
23 You have not brought me lambs
as your burnt offerings
and have not honoured me
with your sacrifices.
I have not subjected you
to cereal offering,
I have not wearied you
by demanding incense.
24 You have not bought expensive reed
for me
or sated me with the fat
of your sacrifices.
Instead by your sins
you have treated me like a slave,
you have wearied me with your crimes,

25 I, I it is who blot out your acts of revolt
for my own sake
and shall not call your sins to mind.
26 Remind me,
and we will judge this together;
state your own case and justify yourself.
27 Your first ancestor sinned,
your interpreters revolted against me.
28 That is why I deposed the chief men
of my sanctuary,
why I put Jacob
under the curse of destruction
and subjected Israel to insult.

The blessing in store for Israel

44 And now listen, Jacob my servant,
Israel whom I have chosen.
2 Thus says Yahweh who made you,
who formed you in the womb;
he will help you.
Do not be afraid, Jacob my servant,
Jeshurun[a] whom I have chosen.
3 For I shall pour out water
on the thirsty soil
and streams on the dry ground.
I shall pour out my spirit
on your descendants,
my blessing on your offspring,
4 and they will spring up among the grass,
like willows on the banks of a stream.
5 One person will say, 'I belong to Yahweh,'
another will call himself by Jacob's name.
On his hand another will write 'Yahweh's'
and be surnamed 'Israel'.

There is only one God

6 Thus says Yahweh, Israel's king,
Yahweh Sabaoth, his redeemer:
I am the first and I am the last;
there is no God except me.
7 Who is like me? Let him call out,
let him affirm it and convince me it is so;
let him say what has been happening
since I instituted an eternal people,
and predict to them what will happen next!
8 Have no fear, do not be afraid:
have I not told you
and revealed it long ago?
You are my witnesses.
Is there any God except me?
There is no Rock; I know of none.

The fatuity of idols

9 The makers of idols are all nothingness; the
works they delight in serve no purpose. And
these are the witness against them: they see
nothing, they know nothing; and so they will
be put to shame. 10 Who ever fashioned a
god or cast an image without hope of gain?
11 Watch how all its devotees will be put to
shame, and the men who made it too, who
are only human. Let them all assemble, let
them stand forward and feel both fear and
shame!

12 The blacksmith makes an axe over the
charcoal, beats it into shape with a hammer,
works on it with his strong arm. Then he
feels hungry and his strength deserts him;
having drunk no water, he is exhausted.

13 The wood carver[b] takes his measure-
ments, outlines the image with chalk,
executes it with the chisel, following the
outline with a compass. He makes it look like
a human being, with human standards of
beauty, so that it can reside in a house. 14 He
has cut down cedars, has selected an oak and
a terebinth which he has grown for himself
among the trees in the forest and has planted
a pine tree which the rain has nourished.
15 Once it is suitable to burn, he takes some
of it to warm himself; having kindled it, he
bakes bread. But he also makes a god and
worships it; he makes an idol from it and
bows down before it. 16 Half of it he burns on
the fire, over this half he roasts meat, eats it
and is replete; at the same time he warms
himself and says, 'Ah, how warm I am,
watching the flames!' 17 With the remainder
he makes a god, his idol, bows down before
it, worships it and prays to it. 'Save me,' he
says, 'for you are my god.'

18 They know nothing, they understand
nothing, since their eyes are incapable of
seeing and their hearts of reflecting. 19 Not
one of them looks into his heart, not one of
them has the knowledge and wit to think, 'I
burned half of it on the fire and cooked
food over the embers. Am I right to make
something disgusting out of what is left?
Am I right to bow down before a block
of wood?'

20 He hankers after ashes, his deluded heart
has led him astray; he will not save himself,
he will not think, 'What I have in my hand
is nothing but a lie!'

44a Rare poetic name of Israel, perhaps meaning 'the upright one'.
44b ‖ Ws 13:11–16.

Loyalty to Yahweh

21 Remember these things, Jacob,
and Israel, since you are my servant.
I formed you, you are my servant;
Israel, I shall not forget you.
22 I have dispelled your acts of revolt
like a cloud
and your sins like a mist.
Come back to me,
for I have redeemed you.
23 Heavens, shout for joy, for
Yahweh has acted!
Underworld, shout aloud!
Shout for joy, you mountains,
forests and all your trees!
For Yahweh has redeemed Jacob
and displayed his glory in Israel.

God, Creator of the world and lord of history

24 Thus says Yahweh, your redeemer,
he who formed you in the womb:
I, Yahweh, have made all things,
I alone spread out the heavens.
When I hammered the earth into shape,
who was with me?
25 I, who foil the omens of soothsayers
and make fools of diviners,
who confound sages
turning their knowledge into folly,
26 who confirm the word of my servant
and make the plans of my
envoys succeed;
who say to Jerusalem,
'You will be inhabited,'
and to the towns of Judah,
'You will be rebuilt
and I shall restore the ruins
of Jerusalem';
27 who say to the ocean, 'Dry up!
I shall make your rivers run dry';
28 who say to Cyrus, 'My shepherd.'
He will perform my entire will
by saying to Jerusalem,
'You will be rebuilt,'
and to the Temple,
'You will be refounded.'

Cyrus, the instrument of God

45 Thus says Yahweh
to his anointed one,
to Cyrus whom, he says,
I have grasped by his right hand,
to make the nations bow before him
and to disarm kings,
to open gateways before him
so that their gates be closed no more:
2 I myself shall go before you,
I shall level the heights,
I shall shatter the bronze gateways,
I shall smash the iron bars.
3 I shall give you secret treasures
and hidden hoards of wealth,
so that you will know that I am Yahweh,
who call you by your name,
the God of Israel.
4 It is for the sake of my servant Jacob
and of Israel my chosen one,
that I have called you by your name,
have given you a title
though you do not know me.
5 I am Yahweh, and there is no other,
there is no other God except me.
Though you do not know me,
I have armed you
6 so that it may be known from east to west
that there is no one except me.
I am Yahweh, and there is no other,
7 I form the light and I create the darkness,
I make well-being, and I create disaster,
I, Yahweh, do all these things.

Prayer

8 Rain down, you heavens, from above,
and let the clouds pour down
saving justice,
let the earth open up
and blossom with salvation,
and let justice sprout with it;
I, Yahweh, have created it!

The supreme power of Yahweh

9 Woe to anyone who argues with his Maker,
one earthenware pot among many!
Does the clay say to its potter,
'What are you doing?
Your work has no hands!'
10 Woe to anyone who asks a father,
'Why are you begetting?'
and a woman, 'Why are you giving birth?'
11 Thus says Yahweh,
the Holy One of Israel and his Maker:
I am asked for signs regarding my sons,
I am given orders about the work I do.
12 It was I who made the earth
and I created human beings on it,

mine were the hands
that spread out the heavens
and I have given the orders
to all their array.
13 I myself have raised him in saving justice
and I shall make all paths level for him.
He will rebuild my city
and bring my exiles home
without ransom or indemnity,
says Yahweh Sabaoth.

The conversion of the nations

14 Thus says Yahweh:
The produce of Egypt,
the commerce of Cush
and the men of Seba, tall of stature,
will come over to you and belong to you.
They will follow you, walking in chains,
they will bow before you,
they will pray to you,
'With you alone is God,
and there is no other!
The gods do not exist.'
15 Truly, you are a God
who conceals himself,
God of Israel, Saviour!
16 They are shamed and humbled,
every one of them,
humiliated they go, the makers of idols.
17 Israel will be saved by Yahweh,
saved everlastingly.
You will never be ashamed or humiliated
for ever and ever.
18 For thus says Yahweh,
the Creator of the heavens—
he is God, who shaped the earth
and made it,
who set it firm;
he did not create it to be chaos,
he formed it to be lived in:
I am Yahweh, and there is no other.
19 I have not spoken in secret,
in some dark corner of the underworld.
I did not say, 'Offspring of Jacob,
search for me in chaos!'
I am Yahweh: I proclaim saving justice,
I say what is true.

God, lord of the whole universe

20 Assemble, come,
all of you gather round,
survivors of the nations.
They have no knowledge,
those who parade their wooden idols
and pray to a god
that cannot save.
21 Speak up, present your case,
let them put their heads together!
Who foretold this in the past,
who revealed it long ago?
Was it not I, Yahweh?
There is no other god except me,
no saving God, no Saviour except me!
22 Turn to me and you will be saved,
all you ends of the earth,
for I am God, and there is no other.
23 By my own self I swear it;
what comes from my mouth
is saving justice,
it is an irrevocable word:
All shall bend the knee to me,
by me every tongue shall swear,
24 saying, 'In Yahweh alone
are saving justice and strength,'
until all those who used to rage at him
come to him in shame.
25 In Yahweh the whole race of Israel
finds justice and glory.

The fall of Babylon

46 Bel[a] is crouching, Nebo cowering,
their idols are being put on animals,
on beasts of burden,
the loads you have been carrying
are a burden to a weary beast.
2 They are cowering
and crouching together,
no one can save this burden,
they themselves have gone into captivity.
3 Listen to me, House of Jacob,
all who remain of the House of Israel,
whom I have carried since the womb,
whom I have supported
since you were conceived.
4 Until your old age I shall be the same,
until your hair is grey I shall carry you.
As I have done, so I shall support you,
I myself shall carry and shall save you.
5 With whom can you compare me,
equate me,
to whom can you liken me,
making equals of us?
6 They lavish gold from their purses
and weigh out silver on the scales.

46a Bel and Nebo are Babylonian chief gods, of the sky and wisdom respectively.

They engage a goldsmith to make a god,
then bow low and actually adore!
7 They lift it on their shoulders and carry it,
and put it down where it is meant to stand,
so that it never moves from the spot.
You may cry out to it in distress,
it never replies,
it never saves anyone in trouble.
8 Remember this and stand firm;
rebels, look into your hearts.
9 Remember the things
that happened long ago,
for I am God, and there is no other;
I am God, and there is none like me.
10 From the beginning I revealed the future,
in advance, what has not yet occurred.
I say: My purpose will come about,
I shall do whatever I please;
11 I call a bird of prey from the east,
my man predestined, from a distant land.
What I have said, I shall do,
what I have planned, I shall perform.
12 Listen to me, you hard-hearted people
far removed from saving justice:
13 I am bringing my justice nearer,
it is not far away,
my salvation will not delay.
I shall place my salvation in Zion
and my glory in Israel.

Lament for Babylon

47 Step down! Sit in the dust,
virgin daughter of Babylon.
Sit on the ground, no throne,
daughter of the Chaldaeans,
for never again will you be called
tender and delicate.
2 Take the grinding mill, crush up the meal.
Remove your veil,
tie up your skirt, bare your legs,
cross the rivers.
3 Let your nakedness be displayed
and your shame exposed.
I am going to take vengeance
and no one will stand in my way.
4 Our redeemer,
Yahweh Sabaoth is his name,
the Holy One of Israel, says:
5 Sit in silence, bury yourself in darkness,
daughter of the Chaldaeans,
for never again will you be called
the mistress of kingdoms.
6 Being angry with my people,
I rejected my heritage,
surrendering them into your clutches.
You showed them no mercy,
you made your yoke very heavy
on the aged.
7 You thought, 'I shall be a queen for ever.'
You did not reflect on these matters
or think about the future.

8 Now listen to this, voluptuous woman,
lolling at ease
and thinking to yourself,
'I am the only one who matters.
I shall never be widowed,
never know bereavement.'
9 Yet both these things will befall you,
suddenly, in one day.
Bereavement and widowhood
will suddenly befall you
in spite of all your witchcraft
and the potency of your spells.
10 Confident in your wickedness,
you thought, 'No one can see me.'
Your wishes and your knowledge
were what deluded you,
as you thought to yourself,
'I am the only one who matters.'
11 Hence, disaster will befall you
which you will not know
how to charm away,
calamity overtake you
which you will not be able to avert,
ruination will suddenly befall you,
such as you have never known.
12 Keep to your spells then,
and all your sorceries,
at which you have worked so hard
since you were young.
Perhaps you will succeed,
perhaps you will strike terror!
13 You have had many tiring consultations:
let the astrologers come forward now
and save you,
the star-gazers
who announce month by month
what will happen to you next.
14 Look, they are like wisps of straw,
the fire will burn them up.
They will not save their lives
from the power of the flame.
No embers these, for keeping warm,
no fire to sit beside!
15 Such will your wizards prove to be for you,
for whom you have worked so hard
since you were young;
each wandering his own way,
none of them can save you.

Yahweh has foretold everything

48 Listen to this, House of Jacob,
you who are called by the name of Israel
and issued from the waters of Judah,
who swear by the name of Yahweh
and invoke the God of Israel,
though not in good faith or uprightness;
2 for they call themselves after the holy city
and rely on the God of Israel,
Yahweh Sabaoth is his name.
3 Things now past I revealed long ago,
they issued from my mouth,
I proclaimed them;
suddenly I acted and they happened.
4 For I knew you to be obstinate,
your neck an iron sinew
and your forehead bronze.
5 As I told you about it long before,
before it happened I revealed it to you,
so that you could not say,
'My statue did it,
my idol, my metal image, ordained this.'
6 You have heard and seen all this,
why won't you admit it?
Now I am going to reveal
new things to you,
secrets that you do not know;
7 they have just been created, not long ago,
and until today you have heard
nothing about them,
so that you cannot say,
'Yes, I knew about this.'
8 No, you have not heard,
you have not known,
for a long time your ear
has not been attentive,
for I knew how treacherous you were;
you have been called a rebel
since the womb.
9 For the sake of my name
I shall defer my anger,
for the sake of my honour
I shall be patient with you,
rather than destroy you.
10 Look, I have purchased you,
but not for silver,
I have chosen you
out of the cauldron of affliction.
11 For my sake and my sake only shall I act,
for why should my name be profaned?
I will not yield my glory to another.

Yahweh has chosen Cyrus

12 Listen to me, Jacob,
Israel whom I have called:
I, and none else, am the first,
I am also the last.
13 My hand laid the foundations of earth
and my right hand spread out the heavens.
I summon them
and they all present themselves together.
14 Assemble, all of you, and listen;
which of them has revealed this?
Yahweh loves him; he will do his pleasure
on Babylon and the race of the Chaldaeans;
15 I, I have spoken,
yes, I have summoned him,
I have brought him, and he will succeed.

Israel's destiny

16 Come near and listen to this:
from the first, I never spoke obscurely;
when it happened, I was there,
and now Lord Yahweh has sent me
with his spirit.
17 Thus says Yahweh, your redeemer,
the Holy One of Israel:
I am Yahweh your God
and teach you for your own good,
I lead you in the way you ought to go.
18 If only you had listened
to my commandments!
Your prosperity would have been
like a river
and your saving justice
like the waves of the sea.
19 Your descendants would have been
numbered like the sand,
your offspring as many as its grains.
Their name would never be cancelled
or blotted out from my presence.

The end of the Exile

20 Come out from Babylon!
Flee from the Chaldaeans!
Declare this with cries of joy,
proclaim it,
carry it to the remotest parts of earth,
say, 'Yahweh has redeemed
his servant Jacob.'
21 Those he led through the arid country
never went thirsty;
he made water flow for them
from the rock,
he split the rock
and out streamed the water.
22 There is no peace, says Yahweh,
for the wicked.

Second song of the servant

49 Coasts and islands, listen to me,
pay attention, distant peoples.
Yahweh called me when I was in the womb,
before my birth
he had pronounced my name.
2 He made my mouth like a sharp sword,
he hid me in the shadow of his hand.
He made me into a sharpened arrow
and concealed me in his quiver.
3 He said to me, 'Israel, you are my servant,
through whom I shall manifest my glory.'
4 But I said, 'My toil has been futile,
I have exhausted myself for nothing,
to no purpose.'
Yet all the while
my cause was with Yahweh
and my reward with my God.
5 And now Yahweh has spoken,
who formed me in the womb
to be his servant,
to bring Jacob back to him
and to re-unite Israel to him;
—I shall be honoured in Yahweh's eyes,
and my God has been my strength.—
6 He said, 'It is not enough for you
to be my servant,
to restore the tribes of Jacob
and bring back the survivors of Israel;
I shall make you a light to the nations
so that my salvation may reach
the remotest parts of earth.'
7 Thus says Yahweh,
the redeemer, the Holy One of Israel,
to the one who is despised,
detested by the nation,
to the slave of despots:
Kings will stand up when they see,
princes will see and bow low,
because of Yahweh who is faithful,
the Holy One of Israel
who has chosen you.

The joyful homecoming

8 Thus says Yahweh:
At the time of my favour
I have answered you,
on the day of salvation I have helped you.
I have formed you and have appointed you
to be the covenant for a people,
to restore the land,
to return ravaged properties,
9 to say to prisoners, 'Come out,'
to those who are in darkness,
'Show yourselves.'
Along the roadway they will graze,
and any bare height will be their pasture.
10 They will never hunger or thirst,
scorching wind and sun
will never plague them;
for he who pities them will lead them,
will guide them to springs of water.
11 I shall turn all my mountains into a road
and my highways will be raised aloft.
12 Look! Here they come from far away,
look, these from the north and the west,
those from the land of Sinim.[a]

13 Shout for joy, you heavens; earth, exult!
Mountains, break into joyful cries!
For Yahweh has consoled his people,
is taking pity on his afflicted ones.
14 Zion was saying,
'Yahweh has abandoned me,
the Lord has forgotten me.'
15 Can a woman forget her baby at the breast,
feel no pity for the child she has borne?
Even if these were to forget,
I shall not forget you.
16 Look, I have engraved you
on the palms of my hands,
your ramparts are ever before me.
17 Your rebuilders are hurrying,
your destroyers and despoilers
will soon go away.

18 Raise your eyes and look around you:
all are assembling, coming to you.[b]
By my life, declares Yahweh,
you will put them all on like jewels,
like a bride, you will fasten them on.
19 For your desolate places and your ruins
and your devastated country
from now on will be too cramped
for your inhabitants,
and your devourers will be far away.
20 Once more they will say in your hearing,
the children of whom you were bereft,
'The place is too cramped for me,
make room for me to live.'
21 Then you will think to yourself,
'Who has borne me these?
I was bereft and barren,
exiled, turned out of my home;

49a Syene in Egypt, modern Aswan, where there was a large Jewish colony.
49b =60:4.

who has reared these?
I was left all alone,
so where have these come from?'

22 Thus says Lord Yahweh:
Look, I am beckoning to the nations
and hoisting a signal to the peoples:
they will bring your sons in their arms
and your daughters will be carried
on their shoulders.
23 Kings will be your foster-fathers
and their princesses, your foster-mothers.
They will fall prostrate before you,
faces to the ground,
and lick the dust at your feet.
And you will know that I am Yahweh;
those who hope in me
will not be disappointed.
24 Can the body be snatched from the warrior,
can the tyrant's captive be set free?
25 But thus says Yahweh:
The warrior's captive
will indeed be snatched away
and the tyrant's booty
will indeed be set free;
I myself shall fight those who fight you
and I myself shall save your children.
26 I shall make your oppressors
eat their own flesh,
they will be as drunk on their own blood
as on new wine.
And all humanity will know
that I am Yahweh, your Saviour,
your redeemer, the Mighty One of Jacob.

Israel's punishment

50 Thus says Yahweh:
Where is your mother's writ of divorce
by which I repudiated her?
Or to which of my creditors
have I sold you?
Look, you have been sold
for your own misdeeds,
your mother was repudiated
for your acts of rebellion.
2 Why was there no one there when I came?
Why did no one answer when I called?
Is my hand too short to redeem?
Have I not strength to save?
Look, with a threat I can dry the sea,
and turn rivers to desert;
the fish in them go rotten for want of water
and die of thirst.
3 I dress the heavens in black,
I cover them in sackcloth.

Third song of the servant

4 Lord Yahweh has given me
a disciple's tongue,
for me to know how to give
a word of comfort to the weary.
Morning by morning
he makes my ear alert
to listen like a disciple.
5 Lord Yahweh has opened my ear
and I have not resisted,
I have not turned away.
6 I have offered my back
to those who struck me,
my cheeks to those
who plucked my beard;
I have not turned my face away
from insult and spitting.
7 Lord Yahweh comes to my help,
this is why insult has not touched me,
this is why I have set my face like flint
and know that I shall not
be put to shame.
8 He who grants me saving justice is near!
Who will bring a case against me?
Let us appear in court together!
Who has a case against me?
Let him approach me!
9 Look, Lord Yahweh is coming
to my help!
Who dares condemn me?
Look at them, all falling apart
like moth-eaten clothes!
10 Which of you fears Yahweh
and listens to his servant's voice?
Which of you walks in darkness
and sees no light?
Let him trust in the name of Yahweh
and lean on his God!
11 Look, all you who light a fire
and arm yourselves with firebrands,
walk by the light of your fire
and the firebrands you have kindled!
This is what you will get from me:
you will lie down in torment!

The blessings in store for the chosen people

51 Listen to me,
you who pursue saving justice,
you who seek Yahweh.
Consider the rock
from which you were hewn,
the quarry from which you were dug.
2 Consider Abraham your father

and Sarah who gave you birth.
When I called him he was the only one
but I blessed him and made him numerous.
3 Yes, Yahweh has pity on Zion,
has pity on all her ruins;
he will turn her desert into an Eden
and her wastelands
into the garden of Yahweh.
Joy and gladness will be found in her,
thanksgiving and the sound of music.

God's reign of saving justice

4 Pay attention to me, my people,
listen to me, my nation,
for a law will come from me,
and I shall make my saving justice
the light of peoples.
5 My justice is suddenly approaching,
my salvation appears,
my arm is about to judge the peoples.
The coasts and islands
will put their hope in me
and put their trust in my arm.
6 Raise your eyes to the heavens,
look down at the earth;
for the heavens will vanish like smoke,
the earth wear out like clothing
and its inhabitants die like vermin,
but my salvation will last for ever
and my saving justice remain inviolable.

7 Listen to me, you who know
what saving justice means,
a people who take my laws to heart:
do not fear people's taunts,
do not be alarmed by their insults,
8 for the moth will eat them like clothing,
the grub will devour them like wool,
but my saving justice will last for ever
and my salvation for all generations.

The awakening of Yahweh

9 Awake, awake!
Clothe yourself in strength,
arm of Yahweh.
Awake, as in the olden days,
generations long ago!
Was it not you who split Rahab[a] in half,
who pierced the Dragon through?
10 Was it not you who dried up the sea,
the waters of the great Abyss;
who made the sea-bed into a road
for the redeemed to go across?
11 This is why
those whom Yahweh has ransomed
will return,
they will enter Zion shouting for joy,
their heads crowned with a joy unending;
joy and gladness will escort them
and sorrow and sighing will take flight.

Yahweh, the consoler

12 I, I am your consoler.
Why then should you be afraid
of mortal human beings,
of a child of man,
whose fate is that of the grass?
13 You forget about Yahweh your Creator
who spread out the heavens
and laid the earth's foundations;
you have never stopped trembling
all day long
before the fury of the oppressor
when he was bent on destruction.
Where is the oppressor's fury now?
14 The despairing captive
is soon to be set free;
he will not die in the dungeon,
nor will his food run out.
15 I am Yahweh your God
who stirs up the sea,
making its waves roar—
Yahweh Sabaoth is my name.
16 I put my words into your mouth,
I hid you in the shadow of my hand,
to spread out the heavens
and lay the earth's foundations
and say to Zion, 'You are my people.'

The awakening of Jerusalem

17 Awake, awake!
To your feet, Jerusalem!
You who from Yahweh's hand
have drunk the cup of his wrath.
The chalice, the stupefying cup,
you have drained to the dregs.
18 There is no one to guide her
of all the children she has borne,
no one to grasp her hand
of all the children she has reared.
19 Double disaster has befallen you—
who is there to sympathise?
Pillage and ruin, famine and sword—
who is there to console you?
20 Your children are lying helpless

51a Creation is represented as a triumph over the monsters of chaos, especially the sea.

at the end of every street
like an antelope trapped in a net;
they are filled to the brim
with Yahweh's wrath,
with the rebuke of your God.
21 So listen to this, afflicted one,
drunk, though not with wine.
22 Thus says your Lord Yahweh,
your God, defender of your people:
Look, I am taking
the stupefying cup from your hand,
the chalice, the cup of my wrath,
you will not have to drink again.
23 I shall hand it to your tormentors
who used to say to you,
'On the ground!
So that we can walk over you!'
And you would flatten your back
like the ground,
like a street for them to walk on.

The liberation of Jerusalem

52 Awake, awake!
Clothe yourself in strength, Zion.
Put on your finest clothes,
Jerusalem, Holy City;
for the uncircumcised and the unclean
will enter you no more.
2 Shake off your dust; get up,
captive Jerusalem!
The chains have fallen from your neck,
captive daughter of Jerusalem!

3 For Yahweh says this,
'You were sold for nothing;
you will be redeemed without money.'
4 For the Lord Yahweh says this,
'Long ago my people went to Egypt
and settled there as aliens;
finally Assyria oppressed them
for no reason.
5 So now what is to be done,'
declares Yahweh,
'since my people have been carried off
for nothing,
their masters howl in triumph,'
declares Yahweh,
'and my name is held in contempt
all day, every day?
6 Because of this
my people will know my name,
because of this
they will know when the day comes,
that it is I saying, Here I am!'

A prediction of salvation

7 How beautiful on the mountains,
are the feet of the messenger
announcing peace,
of the messenger of good news,
who proclaims salvation
and says to Zion,
'Your God is king!'
8 The voices of your watchmen!
Now they raise their voices,
shouting for joy together,
for with their own eyes they have seen
Yahweh returning to Zion.
9 Break into shouts together,
shouts of joy, you ruins of Jerusalem;
for Yahweh has consoled his people,
he has redeemed Jerusalem.
10 Yahweh has bared his holy arm
for all the nations to see,
and all the ends of the earth
have seen the salvation of our God.
11 Go away, go away, leave that place,
do not touch anything unclean.
Get out of her, purify yourselves,
you who carry Yahweh's vessels!
12 For you are not to hurry away,
you are not to leave like fugitives.
No, Yahweh marches at your head
and the God of Israel is your rearguard.

Fourth song of the servant

13 Look, my servant will prosper,
will grow great, will rise to great heights.

14 As many people were aghast at him
—he was so inhumanly disfigured
that he no longer looked like a man—
15 so many nations will be astonished
and kings will stay tight-lipped
before him,
seeing what had never been told them,
learning what they had not heard before.
53 Who has given credence
to what we have heard?
And who has seen in it
a revelation of Yahweh's arm?
2 Like a sapling he grew up before him,
like a root in arid ground.
He had no form or charm to attract us,
no beauty to win our hearts;
3 he was despised, the lowest of men,
a man of sorrows, familiar with suffering,
one from whom, as it were,
we averted our gaze,
despised, for whom we had no regard.

4Yet ours were the sufferings
he was bearing,
ours the sorrows he was carrying,
while we thought of him
as someone being punished
and struck with affliction by God;
5whereas he was being wounded
for our rebellions,
crushed because of our guilt;
the punishment reconciling us fell on him,
and we have been healed by his bruises.
6We had all gone astray like sheep,
each taking his own way,
and Yahweh brought the acts of rebellion
of all of us to bear on him.
7Ill-treated and afflicted,
he never opened his mouth,
like a lamb led to the slaughter-house,
like a sheep dumb before its shearers
he never opened his mouth.

8Forcibly, after sentence, he was taken.
Which of his contemporaries
was concerned
at his having been cut off
from the land of the living,
at his having been struck dead
for his people's rebellion?
9He was given a grave with the wicked,
and his tomb is with the rich,
although he had done no violence,
had spoken no deceit.

10It was Yahweh's good pleasure
to crush him with pain;
if he gives his life as a sin offering,
he will see his offspring
and prolong his life,
and through him
Yahweh's good pleasure will be done.

11After the ordeal he has endured,
he will see the light and be content.
By his knowledge, the upright one,
my servant will justify many
by taking their guilt on himself.

12Hence I shall give him a portion
with the many,
and he will share the booty
with the mighty,
for having exposed himself to death
and for being counted
as one of the rebellious,
whereas he was bearing the sin of many
and interceding for the rebellious.

Jerusalem restored to Yahweh's favour

54 Shout for joy, barren one
who has borne no children!
Break into cries and shouts of joy,
you who were never in labour!
For the children of the forsaken one
are more in number
than the children of the wedded wife,
says Yahweh.
2Widen the space of your tent,
extend the curtains of your home,
do not hold back!
Lengthen your ropes,
make your tent-pegs firm,
3for you will burst out to right and to left,
your race will dispossess the nations
and repopulate deserted towns.
4Do not fear,
you will not be put to shame again,
do not worry,
you will not be disgraced again;
for you will forget the shame of your youth
and no longer remember
the dishonour of your widowhood.
5For your Creator is your husband,
Yahweh Sabaoth is his name,
the Holy One of Israel is your redeemer,
he is called God of the whole world.
6Yes, Yahweh has called you back
like a forsaken, grief-stricken wife,
like the repudiated wife of his youth,
says your God.
7I did forsake you for a brief moment,
but in great compassion
I shall take you back.
8In a flood of anger, for a moment
I hid my face from you.
But in everlasting love
I have taken pity on you,
says Yahweh, your redeemer.
9For me it will be as in the days of Noah
when I swore that Noah's waters
should never flood the world again.
So now I swear never to be angry with you
and never to rebuke you again.
10For the mountains may go away
and the hills may totter,
but my faithful love will never leave you,
my covenant of peace will never totter,
says Yahweh who takes pity on you.

The new Jerusalem

11Unhappy creature, storm-tossed,
unpitied,

look, I shall lay your stones on agates
and your foundations on sapphires.
12 I shall make your battlements rubies,
your gateways firestone
and your entire wall precious stones.
13 All your children
will be taught by Yahweh
and great will be
your children's prosperity.
14 In saving justice you will be made firm,
free from oppression:
you will have nothing to fear;
free from terror:
it will not approach you.
15 Should anyone attack you,
that will not be my doing,
and whoever does attack you,
for your sake will fall.
16 I created the smith
who blows on the charcoal-fire
to produce a weapon for his use;
I also created the destroyer
to ruin it.
17 No weapon forged against you
will succeed.
Any voice raised against you in court
you will refute.
Such is the lot
of the servants of Yahweh,
the saving justice I assure them,
declares Yahweh.

Final invitation

55 Oh, come to the water
all you who are thirsty;
though you have no money, come!
Buy and eat; come, buy wine and milk
without money, free!
2 Why spend money on what cannot nourish
and your wages on what fails to satisfy?
Listen carefully to me,
and you will have good things to eat
and rich food to enjoy.
3 Pay attention, come to me;
listen, and you will live.

I shall make an everlasting covenant
with you
in fulfilment of the favours
promised to David.
4 Look, I have made him a witness
to peoples,
a leader and lawgiver to peoples.
5 Look, you will summon a nation
unknown to you,
a nation unknown to you will hurry to you
for the sake of Yahweh your God,
because the Holy One of Israel
has glorified you.

6 Seek out Yahweh
while he is still to be found,
call to him while he is still near.
7 Let the wicked abandon his way
and the evil one his thoughts.
Let him turn back to Yahweh
who will take pity on him,
to our God, for he is rich in forgiveness;
8 for my thoughts are not your thoughts
and your ways are not my ways,
declares Yahweh.
9 For the heavens are as high above earth
as my ways are above your ways,
my thoughts above your thoughts.
10 For, as the rain and the snow
come down from the sky
and do not return
before having watered the earth,
fertilising it and making it germinate
to provide seed for the sower
and food to eat,
11 so it is with the word
that goes from my mouth:
it will not return to me unfulfilled
or before having carried out
my good pleasure
and having achieved
what it was sent to do.

Conclusion

12 Yes, you will go out with joy
and be led away in safety.
Mountains and hills
will break into joyful cries before you
and all the trees of the countryside
clap their hands.
13 Cypress will grow instead of thorns,
myrtle instead of nettles.
And this will be fame for Yahweh,
an eternal monument
never to be effaced.

III: THE THIRD PART OF THE BOOK OF ISAIAH

Promises to foreigners

56 Thus says Yahweh:
Make fair judgement your concern,
act with justice,
for soon my salvation will come
and my saving justice be manifest.
2 Blessed is anyone who does this,
anyone who clings to it,
observing the Sabbath, not profaning it,
and abstaining from every evil deed.
3 No foreigner adhering to Yahweh
should say,
'Yahweh will utterly exclude me
from his people.'
No eunuch should say,
'Look, I am a dried-up tree.'
4 For Yahweh says this:
To the eunuchs
who observe my Sabbaths
and choose to do my good pleasure
and cling to my covenant,
5 I shall give them in my house
and within my walls
a monument and a name
better than sons and daughters;
I shall give them an everlasting name
that will never be effaced.
6 As for foreigners
who adhere to Yahweh to serve him,
to love Yahweh's name
and become his servants,
all who observe the Sabbath,
not profaning it,
and cling to my covenant:
7 these I shall lead to my holy mountain
and make them joyful
in my house of prayer.
Their burnt offerings and sacrifices
will be accepted on my altar,
for my house will be called
a house of prayer for all peoples.
8 Lord Yahweh
who gathers the exiles of Israel declares:
There are others I shall gather
besides those already gathered.
9 Come and gorge, all you wild beasts,
all you beasts of the forest!

The unworthiness of the nation's leaders

10 Its watchmen are all blind,
they know nothing.
Dumb watchdogs all, unable to bark,
they dream, lie down, and love to sleep.
11 Greedy dogs, never satisfied,
such are the shepherds,
who understand nothing;
they all go their own way,
each to the last man after his own interest.
12 'Come, let me fetch wine;
we will get drunk on strong drink,
tomorrow will be just as wonderful
as today
and even more so!'
57 The upright person perishes
and no one cares.
The faithful is taken off
and no one takes it to heart.
Yes, because of the evil times
the upright is taken off;
2 he will enter peace,
and those who follow the right way
will find rest on their beds.

Against idolatry

3 But you, you children of a witch,
come here,
adulterous race prostituting yourselves!
4 At whom are you jeering,
at whom are you making faces
and sticking out your tongue?
Are you not the spawn of rebellion,
a lying race?
5 Lusting among the terebinths,
and under every spreading tree,
sacrificing children in the ravines,
below the clefts in the rocks.
6 The smooth stones of the ravines
will be your portion,
yes, these will be your lot.
To these you have poured libations,
have brought your cereal offering.
Can all this appease me?
7 On a mountain high and lofty
you have put your bed.
Thither, too, you have climbed
to offer sacrifice.
8 Behind door and doorpost
you have set your reminder.
Yes, far from me, you exposed yourself,
climbed on to your bed,
and made the most of it.
You struck a profitable bargain
with those whose bed you love,

whoring with them often,
with your eyes on the sacred symbol.
9 You went to Molech[a] with oil,
you were prodigal with your perfumes;
you sent your envoys far afield,
down to Sheol itself.
10 Though tired by so much travelling,
you never said, 'It is no use.'
Finding your strength revive,
you never gave up.
11 Who was it you dreaded, and feared,
that you should betray me,
no longer remember me
and not spare a thought for me?
Was I not silent for a long time?
So you cannot have been afraid of me.
12 Now I shall expose
this uprightness of yours,
and little good it did you.
13 When you cry for help,
let those thronging round you save you!
The wind will carry them all away,
one puff will take them off.
But whoever trusts in me
will inherit the country,
he will own my holy mountain.

Salvation for the weak

14 Then it will be said:
Level up, level up, clear the way,
remove the obstacle
from my people's way,
15 for thus says the High and Exalted One
who lives eternally
and whose name is holy,
'I live in the holy heights
but I am with the contrite and humble,
to revive the spirit of the humble,
to revive the heart of the contrite.

16 'For I do not want to be forever accusing
nor always to be angry,
or the spirit would fail
under my onslaught,
the souls that I myself have made.

17 'Angered by his wicked cupidity,
I hid and struck him in anger,
but he rebelliously went the way
of his choice.

18 'I saw how he behaved,
but I shall heal him,
I shall lead him,
fill him with consolation,
him and those who mourn for him,
19 bringing praise to their lips.
Peace, peace to far and near,
Yahweh says,
and I shall heal him.'
20 The wicked, however,
are like the restless sea
that cannot be still,
whose waters throw up mud and dirt.
21 'No peace', says Yahweh,
'for the wicked.'

Fasting pleasing to God

58 Shout for all you are worth,
do not hold back,
raise your voice like a trumpet.
To my people
proclaim their rebellious acts,
to the House of Jacob, their sins.
2 They seek for me day after day,
they long to know my ways,
like a nation that has acted uprightly
and not forsaken the law of its God.
They ask me for laws that are upright,
they long to be near God:
3 'Why have we fasted, if you do not see,
why mortify ourselves if you never notice?'
Look, you seek your own pleasure
on your fastdays
and you exploit all your workmen;
4 look, the only purpose of your fasting
is to quarrel and squabble
and strike viciously with your fist.
Fasting like yours today
will never make your voice heard on high.
5 Is that the sort of fast that pleases me,
a day when a person
inflicts pain on himself?
Hanging your head like a reed,
spreading out sackcloth and ashes?
Is that what you call fasting,
a day acceptable to Yahweh?
6 Is not this the sort of fast that pleases me:
to break unjust fetters,
to undo the thongs of the yoke.
to let the oppressed go free,
and to break all yokes?
7 Is it not sharing your food with the hungry,
and sheltering the homeless poor;
if you see someone lacking clothes,
to clothe him,
and not to turn away from your own kin?

57a 'The King', a Semitic deity to whom children were sacrificed.

8Then your light will blaze out
like the dawn
and your wound be quickly healed over.
Saving justice will go ahead of you
and Yahweh's glory come behind you.
9Then you will cry for help
and Yahweh will answer;
you will call and he will say, 'I am here.'
If you do away with the yoke,
the clenched fist and malicious words,
10if you deprive yourself for the hungry
and satisfy the needs of the afflicted,
your light will rise in the darkness,
and your darkest hour will be like noon.
11Yahweh will always guide you,
will satisfy your needs
in the scorched land;
he will give strength to your bones
and you will be like a watered garden,
like a flowing spring
whose waters never run dry.
12Your ancient ruins will be rebuilt;
you will build on age-old foundations.
You will be called 'Breach-mender',
'Restorer of streets to be lived in'.

The Sabbath

13If you refrain
from breaking the Sabbath,
from taking your own pleasure
on my holy day,
if you call the Sabbath 'Delightful',
and the day sacred to Yahweh
'Honourable',
if you honour it
by abstaining from travel,
from seeking your own pleasure
and from too much talk,
14then you will find true happiness
in Yahweh,
and I shall lead you in triumph
over the heights of the land.
I shall feed you on the heritage
of your father Jacob,
for the mouth of Yahweh has spoken.

Penitential psalm

59 No, the arm of Yahweh
is not too short to save,
nor his ear too dull to hear,
2but your guilty deeds have made a gulf
between you and your God.
Your sins have made him
hide his face from you
so as not to hear you,
3since your hands are stained with blood
and your fingers with guilt;
your lips utter lies,
your tongues murmur wickedness.
4No one makes upright accusations
or pleads sincerely.
All rely on empty words, utter falsehood,
conceive trouble and give birth to evil.

5They are hatching adders' eggs
and weaving a spider's web;
eat one of their eggs and you die,
crush one and a viper emerges.
6Their webs are useless for clothing,
their deeds are useless for wearing;
their deeds are deeds of guilt,
violence fills their hands.
7Their feet run to do evil;
they are quick to shed innocent blood.
Their thoughts are thoughts of guilt,
wherever they go there is havoc and ruin.
8They do not know the way of peace,
there is no fair judgement in their course,
they have made their own crooked paths,
and no one treading them knows any peace.

9Thus fair judgement is remote from us
nor can uprightness overtake us.
We looked for light and all is darkness,
for brightness and we walk in gloom.
10Like the blind we feel our way along walls,
we grope our way like people without eyes.
We stumble as though noon were twilight,
among the robust we are like the dead.
11We growl, all of us, like bears,
like doves we make no sound but moaning,
waiting for the fair judgement
that never comes,
for salvation, but that is far away.

12How often we have rebelled against you
and our sins bear witness against us.
Our rebellious acts are indeed with us,
we are well aware of our guilt:
13rebellion and denial of Yahweh,
turning our back on our God,
talking violence and revolt,
murmuring lies in our heart.
14Fair judgement is driven away
and saving justice stands aloof,
for good faith has stumbled in the street
and sincerity cannot enter.
15Good faith has vanished;
anyone abstaining from evil is victimised.

Yahweh saw this and was displeased
that there was no fair judgement.
16He saw there was no one

and wondered there was no one
to intervene.
So he made his own arm his mainstay,
his own saving justice his support.
17 He put on saving justice like a breastplate,
on his head the helmet of salvation.
He put on the clothes of vengeance
like a tunic
and wrapped himself in jealousy
like a cloak.
18 To each he repays his due,
retribution to his enemies,
reprisals on his foes,
to the coasts and islands
he will repay their due.
19 From the west,
Yahweh's name will be feared,
and from the east, his glory,
for he will come like a pent-up stream
impelled by the breath of Yahweh.
20 Then for Zion will come a redeemer,
for those who stop rebelling in Jacob,
declares Yahweh.

Prophecy

21 'For my part, this is my covenant with
them, says Yahweh. My spirit with which I
endowed you, and my words that I have put
in your mouth, will not leave your mouth, or
the mouths of your children, or the mouths
of your children's children, says Yahweh,
henceforth and for ever.'

The splendour of Jerusalem

60 Arise, shine out,
for your light has come,
and the glory of Yahweh has risen on you.
2 Look! though night still covers the earth
and darkness the peoples,
on you Yahweh is rising
and over you his glory can be seen.
3 The nations will come to your light
and kings to your dawning brightness.
4 Lift up your eyes and look around:
all are assembling
and coming towards you,[a]
your sons coming from far away
and your daughters
being carried on the hip.
5 At this sight you will grow radiant,
your heart will throb and dilate,
since the riches of the sea will flow to you,
the wealth of the nations come to you;
6 camels in throngs will fill your streets,
the young camels of Midian and Ephah;
everyone in Saba will come,
bringing gold and incense
and proclaiming Yahweh's praises.
7 All the flocks of Kedar
will gather inside you,
the rams of Nebaioth will be at your service
as acceptable victims on my altar,
and I shall glorify my glorious house.

8 Who are these flying like a cloud,
like doves to their dovecote?
9 Why, the coasts and islands
put their hope in me
and the vessels of Tarshish take the lead
in bringing your children from far away,
and their silver and gold with them,
for the sake of the name of Yahweh
your God,
of the Holy One of Israel
who has made you glorious.
10 Foreigners will rebuild your walls
and their kings will serve you.
For though I struck you in anger,
in mercy I have pitied you.
11 Your gates will always be open,
never closed, either day or night,
for the riches of the nations
to be brought you
and their kings to be let in.

12 For the nation and kingdom
that will not serve you will perish,
and the nations will be utterly destroyed.

13 The glory of the Lebanon
will come to you,
cypress, plane-tree, box-tree, one and all,
to adorn the site of my sanctuary,
for me to honour the place where I stand.
14 Your oppressors' children
will humbly approach you,
at your feet all who despised you will fall
addressing you as 'City of Yahweh',
'Zion of the Holy One of Israel'.
15 Instead of your being forsaken and hated,
avoided by everyone,
I will make you an object of eternal pride,
a source of joy from age to age.
16 You will suck the milk of nations,
you will suck the wealth of kings,
and you will know that I,
Yahweh, am your Saviour,

60a =49:18.

that your redeemer
is the Mighty One of Jacob.
17 For bronze I shall bring gold
and for iron I shall bring silver,
and for wood, bronze,
and for stone, iron;
I shall make Peace your administration
and Saving Justice your government.
18 Violence will no longer be heard of
in your country,
nor devastation and ruin
within your frontiers.
You will call your walls 'Salvation'
and your gates 'Praise'.

19 No more will the sun give you daylight,
nor moonlight shine on you,
but Yahweh will be your everlasting light,
your God will be your splendour.
20 Your sun will set no more
nor will your moon wane,
for Yahweh will be your everlasting light
and your days of mourning will be over.
21 Your people, all of them upright,
will possess the country for ever,
the shoot I myself have planted,
my handiwork, for my own glory.
22 The smallest will grow into a thousand,
the weakest one into a mighty nation.
When the time is ripe, I, Yahweh,
shall quickly bring it about.

A prophet's mission

61 The spirit of Lord Yahweh
is on me
for Yahweh has anointed me.
He has sent me to bring the news
to the afflicted,
to soothe the broken-hearted,
2 to proclaim liberty to captives,
release to those in prison,
to proclaim a year of favour from Yahweh
and a day of vengeance for our God,
to comfort all who mourn
3 (to give to Zion's mourners),
to give them for ashes a garland,
for mourning-dress, the oil of gladness,
for despondency, festal attire;
and they will be called
'terebinths of saving justice',
planted by Yahweh to glorify him.
4 They will rebuild the ancient ruins,
they will raise what has long lain waste,
they will restore the ruined cities,
all that has lain waste for ages past.
5 Strangers will come forward
to feed your flocks,
foreigners be your ploughmen
and vinedressers;
6 but you will be called 'priests of Yahweh'
and be addressed as 'ministers of our God'.
You will feed on the wealth of nations,
you will supplant them in their glory.
7 To make up for your shame,
you will receive double;
instead of disgrace,
shouts of joy will be their lot;
yes, they will have a double portion
in their country
and everlasting joy will be theirs.
8 For I am Yahweh: I love fair judgement,
I hate robbery and wrong-doing,
and I shall reward them faithfully
and make an everlasting covenant
with them.
9 Their race will be famous
throughout the nations
and their offspring
throughout the peoples.
All who see them will admit
that they are a race
whom Yahweh has blessed.

Thanksgiving

10 I exult for joy in Yahweh,
my soul rejoices in my God,
for he has clothed me
in garments of salvation,
he has wrapped me in a cloak
of saving justice,
like a bridegroom wearing his garland,
like a bride adorned in her jewels.
11 For as the earth sends up its shoots
and a garden makes seeds sprout,
so Lord Yahweh makes saving justice
and praise
spring up in the sight of all nations.

The splendour of Jerusalem

62 About Zion I will not be silent,
about Jerusalem I shall not rest
until saving justice dawns for her
like a bright light
and her salvation like a blazing torch.
2 The nations will then see
your saving justice,
and all kings your glory,
and you will be called a new name
which Yahweh's mouth will reveal.

3You will be a crown of splendour
in Yahweh's hand,
a princely diadem in the hand of your God.
4No more will you be known as 'Forsaken'
or your country be known as 'Desolation';
instead, you will be called
'My Delight is in her'
and your country 'The Wedded';
for Yahweh will take delight in you
and your country will have its wedding.
5Like a young man marrying a virgin,
your rebuilder will wed you,
and as the bridegroom rejoices in his bride,
so will your God rejoice in you.

6On your walls, Jerusalem,
I have posted watchmen;
they will never fall silent, day or night.
No peace for you,
as you keep Yahweh's attention!
7And give him no peace either
until he restores Jerusalem
and makes her the pride of the world!
8Yahweh has sworn by his right hand
and by his mighty arm:
Never again shall I give your grain
to feed your enemies.
Never again will foreigners drink the wine
for which you have toiled.
9No, the reapers will eat it
and praise Yahweh,
the harvesters will drink it
in my sacred courts!

Conclusion

10Pass through, pass through the gates.
Clear a way for my people!
Level up, level up the highway,
remove the stones!
Hoist a signal to the peoples!
11This is what Yahweh has proclaimed
to the remotest part of earth:
Say to the daughter of Zion,
'Look, your salvation is coming;
with him comes his reward,
his achievement precedes him!'[a]

12They will be called 'The Holy People',
'Yahweh's Redeemed',
while you will be called 'Sought-after',
'City-not-forsaken'.

Judgement of the nations

63 Who is this coming from Edom,
from Bozrah in crimson garments,
so magnificently dressed,
marching so full of strength?
—It is I, whose word is saving justice,
whose power is to save.
2—Why are your garments red,
your clothes like someone
treading the winepress?
3—I have trodden the winepress alone;
of my people, not one was with me.
So I trod them down in my anger,
I trampled on them in my wrath.
Their blood squirted over my garments
and all my clothes are stained.
4For I have decided on a day of vengeance,
my year of retribution has come.
5I looked: there was no one to help me;
I was appalled but could find no supporter!
Then my own arm came to my rescue
and my own fury supported me.
6I crushed the peoples in my anger,
I shattered them in my fury
and sent their blood streaming
to the ground.

Meditation on the history of Israel

7I shall recount Yahweh's acts
of faithful love,
Yahweh's praises,
in return for all
that Yahweh has done for us,
for his great kindness
to the House of Israel,
for all that he has done in his mercy,
for the abundance of his acts
of faithful love.

8For he said, 'Truly they are my people,
children who will not betray me,'
and he became their Saviour.
9In all their troubles,
it was no messenger or angel
but his presence that saved them.
In his love and pity
he himself redeemed them,
lifted them up and carried them
throughout the days of old.
10But they rebelled
and vexed his holy Spirit.
Then he became their enemy
and himself waged war on them.

62a =40:10.

[11]But he called the past to mind,
Moses his servant.
Where is he who saved them
from the sea,
the Shepherd of his flock?
Where was he who put
his holy Spirit among them,
[12]whose glorious arm led the way
by Moses' right hand?
Who divided the waters before them
to win himself everlasting renown,
[13]who led them through the depths
as easily as a horse through the desert?
They stumbled as little
[14]as cattle going down to the plain.
Yahweh's Spirit led them to rest.
This was how you guided your people
to win yourself glorious renown.

[15]Look down from heaven and see
from your holy and glorious dwelling.
Where is your zeal and your might?
Are your deepest feelings,
your mercy to me, to be restrained?
[16]After all, you are our Father.
If Abraham will not own us,
if Israel will not acknowledge us,
you, Yahweh, are our Father,
'Our Redeemer' is your name from of old.
[17]Why, Yahweh, do you let us wander
from your ways
and let our hearts grow too hard
to fear you?
Return, for the sake of your servants,
the tribes of your heritage.
[18]Your holy people have owned it
for so short a time,
our enemies have trampled
on your sanctuary.
[19]We have long been like those
you do not rule,
people who do not bear your name.

Oh, that you would tear the heavens open
and come down
—in your presence
the mountains would quake,
64 as fire sets brushwood alight,
as fire makes water boil—
to make your name known to your foes;
the nations would tremble
at your presence,
[2]at the unexpected miracles you would do.
(Oh, that you would come down,
in your presence
the mountains would quake!)
[3]Never has anyone heard,
no ear has heard, no eye has seen
any god but you act like this
for the sake of those who trust him.
[4]You come to meet those
who are happy to act uprightly;
keeping your ways reminds them of you.
Yes, you have been angry
and we have been sinners;
now we persist in your ways
and we shall be saved.
[5]We have all been like unclean things
and our upright deeds like filthy rags.
We wither, all of us, like leaves,
and all our misdeeds
carry us off like the wind.
[6]There is no one to invoke your name,
to rouse himself to hold fast to you,
for you have hidden your face from us
and given us up
to the power of our misdeeds.
[7]And yet, Yahweh, you are our Father;
we the clay and you our potter,
all of us are the work of your hands.
[8]Yahweh, do not let your anger go too far
and do not remember guilt for ever.
Look, please, we are all your people;
[9]your holy cities have become a desert,
Zion has become a desert,
Jerusalem a wasteland.
[10]Our holy and glorious Temple,
in which our ancestors used to praise you,
has been burnt to the ground;
all our delight lies in ruins.
[11]Yahweh, can you restrain yourself
at all this?
Will you stay silent
and afflict us beyond endurance?

The coming judgement

65 I have let myself be approached
by those who did not consult me,
I have let myself be found
by those who did not seek me.
I said, 'Here I am, here I am!'
to a nation that did not invoke my name.
[2]Each day I stretched out my hands
to a rebellious people
who follow a way which is not good,
as the fancy takes them;
[3]a people constantly provoking me
to my face
by sacrificing in gardens,
burning incense on bricks,
[4]living in tombs,

spending the night in dark corners,
eating the meat of pigs,
putting unclean foods on their plates.
5 'Keep your distance,' they say,
'do not touch me,
lest my sanctity come near you!'
Such words are like stifling smoke to me,
an ever-burning fire.
6 Look, it is inscribed before me:
I shall not be silent
until I have repaid them,
repaid them in full,
7 punished your guilt
and your ancestors' guilt together,
Yahweh declares.
For having burnt incense on the mountains
and insulted me on the hills,
I shall pay them back in full
for what they have done.

8 Yahweh says this:
As when a bunch of grapes is found
still to have juice in it,
people say, 'Do not destroy it,
for it contains a blessing,'
so I shall act for my servants' sake,
I shall not destroy them all.
9 I shall produce descendants from Jacob
and heirs to my mountains from Judah,
my chosen ones will own them
and my servants will live there.
10 Sharon will be a pasture for flocks,
the Valley of Achor
a feeding ground for cattle,
for those of my people
who have sought me.
11 But as for those of you
who abandon Yahweh,
who forget my holy mountain,
who lay the table for Gad,[a]
who fill cups of mixed wine for Meni,
12 you I shall destine to the sword
and all of you will stoop to be slaughtered,
because I called and you would not answer,
I spoke and you would not listen;
you have done what I consider evil,
you chose to do what displeases me.
13 Therefore Lord Yahweh says this:
You will see my servants eating
while you go hungry;
you will see my servants drinking
while you go thirsty;
you will see my servants rejoicing
while you are put to shame;
14 you will hear my servants
shouting for joy of heart,
while you shriek for sorrow of heart
and howl with a broken spirit.
15 And you will leave your name behind
as a curse for my chosen ones,
'May Lord Yahweh strike you dead!'
But to his servants
he will give another name.
16 Whoever blesses himself on earth
will bless himself by the God of truth,
and whoever swears an oath on earth
will swear by the God of truth,
for past troubles will be forgotten
and hidden from my eyes.
17 For look, I am going to create
new heavens and a new earth,
and the past will not be remembered
and will come no more to mind.
18 Rather be joyful, be glad for ever
at what I am creating,
for look, I am creating Jerusalem
to be 'Joy'
and my people to be 'Gladness'.
19 I shall be joyful in Jerusalem
and I shall rejoice in my people.
No more will the sound of weeping
be heard there,
nor the sound of a shriek;
20 never again will there be an infant there
who lives only a few days,
nor an old man who does not run
his full course;
for the youngest will die at a hundred,
and at a hundred
the sinner will be accursed.
21 They will build houses and live in them,
they will plant vineyards and eat their fruit.
22 They will not build for others to live in,
or plant for others to eat;
for the days of my people
will be like the days of a tree,
and my chosen ones will themselves use
what they have made.
23 They will not toil in vain,
nor bear children destined to disaster,
for they are the race
of Yahweh's blessed ones
and so are their offspring.
24 Thus, before they call I shall answer,
before they stop speaking
I shall have heard.
25 The wolf and the young lamb
will feed together,

65a Gad is the Aramaean god of luck, Meni an unknown god, possibly of fate.

the lion will eat hay like the ox,
and dust be the serpent's food.
No hurt, no harm will be done
on all my holy mountain,[b]
Yahweh says.

Prophecy on the Temple

66 Thus says Yahweh:
With heaven my throne
and earth my footstool,
what house could you build me,
what place for me to rest,
2 when all these things were made by me
and all belong to me?—declares Yahweh.
But my eyes are drawn to the person
of humbled and contrite spirit,
who trembles at my word.

3 Some slaughter a bull,
some kill a human being,
some sacrifice a lamb, some strangle a dog,
some present an offering of pig's blood,
some burn memorial incense,
a revolting blessing;
all these people have chosen
their own ways
and take delight
in their disgusting practices.
4 I too take delight in making fools of them,
I shall bring what they most fear
down on them
because I have called
and no one would answer,
I spoke and no one listened.
They have done what I regard as evil,
have chosen what displeases me.

Judgement on Jerusalem

5 Listen to the word of Yahweh,
you who tremble at his word.
Your brothers, who hate and reject you
because of my name, have said,
'Let Yahweh show his glory,
let us witness your joy!'
But they will be put to shame.

6 Listen! An uproar from the city!
A voice from the Temple!
The voice of Yahweh
bringing retribution on his enemies.

7 Before being in labour
she has given birth.
Before the birth pangs came,
she has been delivered of a child.

8 Who ever heard of such a thing,
who ever saw anything like this?
Can a country be born in one day?
Can a nation be brought forth
all at once?
For Zion, scarcely in labour,
has brought forth her children!

9 Shall I open the womb
and not bring to birth?
says Yahweh.
Shall I, who bring to birth,
close the womb?
says your God.

10 Rejoice with Jerusalem,
be glad for her, all you who love her!
Rejoice, rejoice with her,
all you who mourned her!

11 So that you may be suckled and satisfied
from her consoling breast,
so that you may drink deep with delight
from her generous nipple.

12 For Yahweh says this:
Look, I am going to send peace
flowing over her like a river,
and like a stream in spate
the glory of the nations.

You will be suckled, carried on her hip
and fondled in her lap.
13 As a mother comforts a child,
so I shall comfort you;
you will be comforted in Jerusalem.

14 At the sight your heart will rejoice,
and your limbs regain vigour
like the grass.
To his servants
Yahweh will reveal his hand,
but to his enemies his fury.

15 For see how Yahweh comes in fire,
his chariots like the whirlwind,
to assuage his anger with burning,
his rebukes with flaming fire.

16 For by fire will Yahweh execute
fair judgement,
and by his sword, on all people;
and Yahweh's victims will be many.
17 As for those who sanctify themselves
and purify themselves
to enter the gardens,
following the one in the centre,
who eat the flesh of pigs,
revolting things and rats:

65b =11:7, 9.

their deeds and their thoughts
will perish together,
declares Yahweh.

An eschatological discourse

18 I am coming to gather every nation and
every language. They will come to witness
my glory. 19 I shall give them a sign and send
some of their survivors to the nations: to
Tarshish, Put, Lud, Meshech, Tubal and
Javan,[a] to the distant coasts and islands that
have never heard of me or seen my glory.
They will proclaim my glory to the nations,
20 and from all the nations they will bring all
your brothers as an offering to Yahweh, on
horses, in chariots, in litters, on mules and
on camels, to my holy mountain, Jerusalem,
Yahweh says, like Israelites bringing offer-
ings in clean vessels to Yahweh's house.
21 And some of them I shall make into priests
and Levites, Yahweh says.
22 For as the new heavens and the new earth
I am making will endure before me, declares
Yahweh, so will your race and your name
endure.

23 From New Moon to New Moon,
from Sabbath to Sabbath,
all humanity will come and bow
in my presence, Yahweh says.
24 And on their way out they will see
the corpses of those
who rebelled against me;
for their worm will never die
nor their fire be put out,
and they will be held in horror
by all humanity.

THE BOOK OF JEREMIAH

Jeremiah is personally a most attractive character. He is of a retiring nature and never wanted to be a prophet; he protests frequently, in his wonderfully frank and intimate conversations with Yahweh, his dislike of proclaiming the strident message of destruction. He was caught up in the turmoil of the last years of Jerusalem's monarchy and found himself compelled to prophesy doom and defeat in the face of hostility from his own townsfolk, disdain from the king and eventually imprisonment as the only means of silencing this influence so subversive of the war effort.

Jeremiah possibly took part in the national revival inspired by the deuteronomic reform of 622 BC. But after King Josiah's death he had the unpopular task of proclaiming the coming disaster as Nebuchadnezzar advanced into Palestine (605), besieged rebellious Jerusalem (597) and deported many of the inhabitants. At a second revolt Nebuchadnezzar burnt the Temple (587 or 586) and deported all but a rabble. Even so, the governor was assassinated, and Jeremiah was hustled off to Egypt by a group of fugitives. But in spite of his constant sayings and actions symbolising disaster, Jeremiah also has a message of hope. He promises a new covenant of the heart and a new intimacy of personal relationship to Yahweh. It is perhaps this which made him one of the best loved and most important figures in the Jewish tradition.

The book is by no means in chrono-

66a Possible identifications: Spain, Lybia, Lydia, Phrygia, Cilicia, or Greece.

logical order. The scroll of Jeremiah's early prophecies was callously burnt by the king in 605 – only to be rewritten by the prophet's secretary, Baruch, who probably supplied also the biographical anecdotes. But there is a good deal of repetition of sayings, and they are often grouped by subject-matter (e.g. prophecies about a number of kings, grouped in 21:11–23:8) or linked together by the chance occurrence of a key word or name.

PLAN OF THE BOOK

JEREMIAH

Title

1 The words of Jeremiah son of Hilkiah,
one of the priests living at Anathoth in the
territory of Benjamin. 2The word of Yahweh
came to him in the days of Josiah son of
Amon, king of Judah, in the thirteenth year
of his reign; 3then in the days of Jehoiakim
son of Josiah, king of Judah, until the end of
the eleventh year of Zedekiah son of Josiah,
king of Judah, until the deportation of Jerusalem, in the fifth month.

I: PROPHECIES AGAINST JUDAH AND JERUSALEM

A: IN THE REIGN OF JOSIAH

The call of Jeremiah

4The word of Yahweh came to me, saying:

5'Before I formed you in the womb
I knew you;
before you came to birth
I consecrated you;
I appointed you as prophet to the nations.'

6I then said, 'Ah, ah, ah, Lord Yahweh;
you see, I do not know how to speak: I am
only a child!'

7But Yahweh replied,

'Do not say, "I am only a child,"
for you must go to all to whom I send you
and say whatever I command you.
8 Do not be afraid of confronting them,
for I am with you to rescue you,
Yahweh declares.'

9 Then Yahweh stretched out his hand and
touched my mouth, and Yahweh said to me:

'There! I have put my words
into your mouth.
10 Look, today I have set you
over the nations and kingdoms,
to uproot and to knock down,
to destroy and to overthrow,
to build and to plant.'

11 The word of Yahweh came to me, asking,
'Jeremiah, what do you see?' I answered, 'I
see a branch of the Watchful Tree.' 12 Then
Yahweh said, 'Well seen, for I am watching
over my word to perform it.'
13 A second time the word of Yahweh came
to me, asking, 'What do you see?' I answered,
'I see a cooking pot on the boil, with its mouth
tilting from the north.' 14 Then Yahweh said:

'From the north disaster will come
boiling over
on all who live in the country,
15 for I am now summoning
all the families of the kingdoms
of the north,
Yahweh declares.
They will come,
and each will set his throne
in front of the gates of Jerusalem,
all round, against its walls
and against all the towns of Judah.
16 I shall pronounce my judgements on them
because of all their wickedness,
since they have abandoned me,
offering incense to other gods
and worshipping what their own hands
have made.

17 'As for you, prepare yourself for action.
Stand up and tell them
all I command you.
Have no fear of them
and in their presence
I will make you fearless.
18 For look, today I have made you
into a fortified city,
a pillar of iron,
a wall of bronze
to stand against the whole country:
the kings of Judah, its princes,
its priests and the people of the country.
19 They will fight against you
but will not overcome you,
for I am with you,
Yahweh declares,
to rescue you.'

The earliest preaching of Jeremiah: the infidelity of Israel

2 The word of Yahweh came to me, saying,
2 'Go and shout this in Jerusalem's ears:

'Yahweh says this:
"I remember your faithful love,
the affection of your bridal days,
when you followed me through the desert,
through a land unsown.
3 Israel was sacred to Yahweh;
the first-fruits of his harvest;
all who ate this incurred guilt,
disaster befell them,
Yahweh declares." '
4 Listen to Yahweh's word, House of Jacob
and all the families of the House of Israel.
5 Yahweh says this,
'What did your ancestors
find wrong in me
for them to have deserted me so far
as to follow Futility
and become futile themselves?
6 They never said, "Where is Yahweh,
who brought us out of Egypt
and led us through the desert,
through a land of plains and ravines,
through a land of drought,
of shadow dark as death,
a land through which no one passes
and where no human being lives?"
7 I brought you to a country of plenty,
to enjoy its produce and good things;
but when you entered
you defiled my country
and made my heritage loathsome.
8 The priests never asked,
"Where is Yahweh?"
Those skilled in the Law
did not know me,
the shepherds too rebelled against me
and the prophets prophesied by Baal
and followed the Useless Ones.
9 So I must state my case
against you once more,
Yahweh declares,
and state my case
against your children's children:

10 Cross to the isles of the Kittim[a] and look,
send to Kedar and carefully observe,
see if anything like this
has happened before!
11 Does a nation change its gods?
—and these are not gods at all!
Yet my people have exchanged their Glory
for the Useless One!
12 You heavens, stand aghast at this,
horrified, utterly appalled,
Yahweh declares.
13 For my people have committed
two crimes:
they have abandoned me,
the fountain of living water,
and dug water-tanks for themselves,
cracked water-tanks
that hold no water.

14 'Is Israel a slave?
Was he born into serfdom,
for him to be preyed on like this?
15 Lions have roared at him,
they have made their voices heard.
They have left this country a desert,
his towns lie burnt and uninhabited.
16 The people of Noph and Tahpanhes[b]
have shaved your skull!
17 Have you not brought this on yourself,
by abandoning Yahweh your God,
when he was guiding you on your way?
18 What is the good of going to Egypt now
to drink the water of the Nile?
What is the good of going to Assyria
to drink the water of the River?
19 Your wickedness will bring
its own punishment,
your infidelities will bring you to book,
so give thought and see
how evil and bitter it is
to abandon Yahweh your God
and not to stand in awe of me,
the Lord Yahweh Sabaoth declares.

20 'It is long ago now
since you broke your yoke,
burst your bonds
and said, "I will not serve!"
Yet on every high hill
and under every green tree
you have sprawled and played the whore.
21 Yet I had planted you, a red vine
of completely sound stock.
How is it you have turned into seedlings
of a vine that is alien to me?
22 Even though you scrub yourself with soda
and put in quantities of soap,
the stain of your guilt
would still be visible to me,
the Lord Yahweh declares.
23 How dare you say, "I am not defiled,
I have not run after the Baals?"
Look at your behaviour in the Valley,
realise what you have done.
24 A wild she-donkey, at home in the desert,
snuffing the breeze in desire;
who can control her when she is on heat?
Males need not trouble to look for her,
they will find her in her month.
25 Beware! Your own foot will go unshod,
your own throat grow dry!
But you said, "It is no use! No!
For I love the Strangers
and they are the ones I shall follow."

26 'Like a thief ashamed at being caught,
so will the House of Israel be:
they, their kings, their chief men,
their priests and their prophets,
27 who say to a piece of wood,
"You are my father,"
and to a stone, "You gave birth to me."
For they turn to me their backs,
never their faces;
yet when trouble comes they shout,
"Get up! Save us!"
28 Where are your gods
you made for yourself?
Let them get up if they can save you
when trouble comes!
For you have as many gods
as you have towns, Judah![c]
29 Why make out a case against me?
You have all rebelled against me,
Yahweh declares.
30 In vain I have struck your children,
they have not accepted correction;
your own sword has devoured
your prophets
like a marauding lion.
31 Now you of this generation,
listen to what Yahweh says:
Have I been a desert for Israel,
or a land of gloom?
Why do my people say,

2a i.e. the Greeks. Kedar is a nomadic Arab tribe, so 'Go east or west'.
2b Noph and Tahpanhes are towns in the Egyptian Delta.
2c =11:13.

"We are our own masters,
we will come to you no more"?
32 Does a girl forget her ornaments,
a bride her sash?
And yet my people have forgotten me,
days beyond number.

33 'How well you set your course
in pursuit of love!
And so you have schooled your ways
to wicked deeds.
34 The very skirts of your robe are stained
with the blood of the poor,
of innocent men you never caught
breaking and entering!
And in spite of all this,
35 you say, "I am innocent,
let his anger turn from me!"
Now I pass sentence on you
for saying, "I have not sinned."

36 'How frivolously you undertake
a change of course!
But you will be disappointed by Egypt
just as you were by Assyria.
37 You will have to leave there too
with your hands on your head,
for Yahweh has rejected
those that you rely on,
you will come to no good with them.'

Conversion

3 'If a man divorces his wife
and she leaves him
and becomes someone else's,
has he the right to go back to her?
Has not that piece of land
been totally polluted?
And you, having played the whore
with many lovers,
you claim the right to come back to me!
Yahweh demands.

2 'Lift your eyes to the bare heights
and look!
Where have you not offered your sex!
You waited by the roadside for them
like an Arab in the desert.
You have polluted the country
with your prostitution and your vices:
3 this is why the showers
have been withheld,
the late rains have not come.

'But you maintained
a prostitute's bold front,
with no trace of a blush.
4 From now on, do not cry out at me,
"My father!
My beloved ever since I was young!
5 Will he keep up his anger for ever,
maintain his wrath to the end?"
You say this but still go on sinning,
being so obstinate.'

The Northern Kingdom urged to repent

6 In the days of King Josiah, Yahweh said to
me, 'Have you seen what disloyal Israel has
done? How she has made her way up every
high hill and to every green tree, and played
the whore there? 7 I thought, "After doing all
this she will come back to me." But she did
not come back. Her faithless sister Judah saw
this. 8 She also saw that I had repudiated
disloyal Israel for all her adulteries and given
her her divorce papers. Her faithless sister
Judah, however, was not afraid: she too
went and played the whore. 9 And with her
shameless whoring, she polluted the country;
she committed adultery with stones and
pieces of wood. 10 Worse than all this: Judah,
her faithless sister, has come back to me not
in sincerity, but only in pretence, Yahweh
declares.'

11 And Yahweh said to me, 'Disloyal Israel
is upright, compared with faithless Judah.
12 So go and shout words towards the north,
and say:

"Come back, disloyal Israel,
Yahweh declares,
I shall frown on you no more,
since I am merciful,
Yahweh declares.
I shall not keep my anger for ever.
13 Only acknowledge your guilt:
how you have rebelled
against Yahweh your God,
how you have prostituted yourself
with the Strangers
under every green tree
and have not listened to my voice,
Yahweh declares.

Zion in the messianic age

14 "Come back, disloyal children, Yahweh
declares, for I alone am your Master, and I
will take you, one from a town, two from a
family, and bring you to Zion. 15 I shall give
you shepherds after my own heart, who will
pasture you wisely and discreetly. 16 Then,
when you have increased and grown

numerous in the country, Yahweh declares, no one will ever again say: The ark of the covenant of Yahweh! It will not enter their minds, they will not remember it or miss it, nor will another one be made. 17When that time comes, Jerusalem will be called: The Throne of Yahweh, and all the nations will converge on her, on Yahweh's name, on Jerusalem, and will no longer follow their own stubborn and wicked inclinations.

18"When those days come, the House of Judah will join the House of Israel; together they will come from the land of the north to the country I gave your ancestors as their heritage."

Continuation of the poem on conversion

19'And I was thinking:
How am I to rank you as my children?
I shall give you a country of delights,
the fairest heritage of all the nations!
I thought: You will call me Father
and will never cease to follow me.
20But like a woman betraying her lover,
House of Israel, you have betrayed me,'
Yahweh declares.

21A noise is heard on the bare heights:
the weeping and entreaty of the Israelites,
for they have gone wildly astray,
have forgotten Yahweh their God.
22'Come back, disloyal sons,
I want to cure your disloyalty.'
'We are here, we are coming to you,
for you are Yahweh our God.
23The hills are a delusion after all,
so is the tumult of the mountains.
Yahweh our God is, after all,
the saving of Israel.
24Shame has devoured
what our ancestors worked for
ever since we were young,
their flocks and herds,
their sons and their daughters.
25Let us lie down in our shame,
let our confusion cover us,
for we have sinned
against Yahweh our God,
we and our ancestors,
from our youth until today,
and have not listened
to the voice of Yahweh our God.'

4 'If you come back, Israel,
Yahweh declares,
if you come back to me,
if you take your Horrors out of my sight,
if you go roving no more,
2if you swear, "As Yahweh lives!"
truthfully, justly, uprightly,
then the nations will bless themselves
by him
and glory in him.

3'For Yahweh says this
to the men of Judah and Jerusalem,
"Clear the ground that lies neglected,
do not sow among thorns.
4Circumcise yourselves for Yahweh,
apply circumcision to your hearts,
men of Judah
and inhabitants of Jerusalem,
or my wrath will leap out like a fire
and burn with no one to quench it,
in return for the wickedness
of your deeds." '[a]

Invasion from the north

5Announce it in Judah,
proclaim it in Jerusalem, say,
'Sound the trumpet in the countryside,
shout the message aloud:
Mobilise!
Take to the fortified towns![b]
6Signpost the way to Zion!
Run! Do not delay!
For I am bringing disaster from the north,
an immense calamity.
7The lion is up from his thicket,
the destroyer of nations is on his way,
he has come from his home
to reduce your land to a desert;
your towns will be in ruins, uninhabited.
8So wrap yourselves in sackcloth,
lament and wail,
since Yahweh's burning anger
has not turned away from us.

9"That day,' Yahweh declares,
'the king's heart will fail him,
the princes' hearts will fail them too,
the priests will stand aghast,
the prophets stupefied.'
10Then I said, 'Ah, Lord Yahweh,
how sadly you deceived this people
and Jerusalem

4a =21:12.
4b =8:14.

when you used to say,
"You will have peace,"
whereas the sword is now at our throats!
11 When that time comes, this will be said
to this people and to Jerusalem:
The scorching wind
from the desert heights
comes towards the daughter of my people
—and not to winnow or to cleanse!
12 A gale of wind comes to me
from over there.
Now I myself shall pass sentence on them!'

13 Look, he is advancing like the clouds,
his chariots like a hurricane,
his horses swifter than eagles.
Disaster for us! We are lost!
14 Wash your heart clean of wickedness,
Jerusalem,
and so be saved.
How long will you go on harbouring
your pernicious thoughts?
15 For a voice from Dan shouts the news,
proclaims disaster
from the highlands of Ephraim.
16 Report it to the nations,
proclaim it to Jerusalem,
'Enemies are coming
from a distant country,
shouting their war cry
against the towns of Judah;
17 they surround her
like watchmen round a field
because she has rebelled against me',
Yahweh declares.
18 'Your own behaviour and actions
have brought this on yourself.
Your wickedness, how bitter,
has stabbed you to the heart!'

19 In the pit of my stomach
how great my agony!
Walls of my heart!
My heart is throbbing!
I cannot keep quiet,
for I have heard the trumpet call,
the battle cry.
20 Ruin on ruin is the news:
the whole land is laid waste,
my tents are suddenly destroyed,
in one moment all that sheltered me.
21 How long must I see the standard
and hear the trumpet call?

22 'This is because my people are stupid,
they do not know me,
they are slow-witted children,
they have no understanding,
they are clever enough at doing wrong,
but do not know how to do right.'

23 I looked to the earth—
it was a formless waste;
to the heavens, and their light had gone.
24 I looked to the mountains—
they were quaking
and all the hills rocking to and fro.
25 I looked—there was no one at all,
the very birds of heaven had all fled.
26 I looked—the fruitful land was a desert,
all its towns in ruins
before Yahweh,
before his burning anger.
27 Yes, Yahweh has said this,
'The whole country will be laid waste,
though I shall not annihilate it completely.
28 For this, the earth will go into mourning
and the heavens above grow dark.
For I have spoken, I have decided,
I shall not change my mind
or go back on it.'

29 At the din of horseman and archer
the entire city takes to flight:
some plunge into the thickets,
others scale the rocks;
every town is abandoned,
not a single person is left there.
30 And, once despoiled,
what are you going to do?
You may dress yourself in scarlet,
put on ornaments of gold,
enlarge your eyes with paint
but you make yourself pretty in vain.
Your former lovers disdain you,
your life is what they are seeking.
31 Yes, I hear screams
like those of a woman in labour,
anguish like that of a woman
giving birth to her first child;
they are the screams
of the daughter of Zion, gasping,
hands outstretched,
'Unhappy me! I am dying,
the murderers have killed me!'

Reasons for the invasion

5 Rove the streets of Jerusalem,
now look and enquire,
see in her squares
if you can find an individual,
one individual who does right
and seeks the truth,

and I will pardon her,
Yahweh says.
2 Although they say, 'As Yahweh lives,'
they are, in fact, swearing a false oath.
3 Yahweh, do your eyes not look for truth?
You have struck them;
they have not felt it.
You have annihilated them,
for they ignored the lesson.
They have set their faces harder than rock,
they have refused to repent.
4 I thought, 'These are only the poor!
They behave stupidly
since they do not know Yahweh's way
or the ruling of their God.
5 I shall approach the great men
and speak to them,
for these will know Yahweh's way
and the ruling of their God.'
But these, too, have broken the yoke,
have burst the bonds.
6 And so, a lion from the forest
will slaughter them,
a wolf from the plains will despoil them,
a leopard will be lurking
round their towns:
anyone who goes out
will be torn to pieces—
because of their many crimes,
their countless infidelities.

7 'Why should I pardon you?
Your sons have abandoned me,
to swear by gods that are not gods at all.
I fed them full,
and they became adulterers,
they hurried to the brothel.
8 They are well-fed, roving stallions,
each neighing for his neighbour's wife.
9 Shall I fail to punish this,
Yahweh demands,
or on such a nation
to exact vengeance?[a]
10 Scale her terraces! Destroy!
But do not annihilate her completely!
Strip off her branches,
for Yahweh does not own them!
11 How treacherously they have treated me,
the House of Israel
and the House of Judah!
Yahweh declares.

12 'They have denied Yahweh,
they have said, "He is nothing;
no evil will overtake us,
we shall not see sword or famine.
13 And the prophets? Nothing but wind;
the word is not in them;
let those very things happen to them!" '
14 Because of this,
Yahweh, God Sabaoth, says this,
'Since you have said such things,
now I shall make my words
a fire in your mouth,
and make this people wood,
for the fire to devour.
15 Now I shall bring on you
a nation from afar, House of Israel,
Yahweh declares,
an enduring nation,
an ancient nation,
a nation whose language you do not know,
nor can you grasp what they say.
16 Their quiver a gaping tomb,
they are all of them fighters.
17 They will devour your harvest
and your food,
devour your sons and daughters,
devour your flocks and herds,
devour your vines and fig trees,
and demolish your fortified towns
in which you trust—with the sword!'

Lesson to be drawn from the punishment

18 'Yet even in those days, Yahweh declares,
I shall not annihilate you completely.
19 'And when you ask, "Why has Yahweh
our God done all this to us?" you will give
them this answer, "As you abandon me to
serve alien gods in your own country, so you
must serve aliens in a country not your own."

In a time of famine (?)

20 'Announce this in the House of Jacob,
proclaim it in Judah, and say,
21 "Now listen to this,
stupid, brainless people
who have eyes and do not see,
who have ears and do not hear!
22 Have you no fear of me?
Yahweh demands.
Will you not tremble before me
who set the sand as limit to the sea,
as an everlasting barrier it cannot pass?
Its waves may toss but not prevail,
they may roar but cannot pass beyond.

5a =5:29; 9:8.

23 But this people
has a rebellious, unruly heart;
they have rebelled and gone!
24 Nor do they say to themselves:
Now we ought to fear Yahweh our God
who gives the rain, of autumn
and of spring, at the right season,
and reserves us
the weeks appointed for harvest.
25 Your misdeeds have upset all this,
your sins have deprived you
of these blessings." '

Resumption of the theme of the invasion

26 Yes, there are wicked men
among my people
who watch like fowlers on the alert;
they set traps
and they catch human beings.
27 Like a cage full of birds
so are their houses full of loot;
they have grown rich and powerful
because of it,
28 they are fat, they are sleek,
in wickedness they go to any lengths:
they have no respect for rights,
for orphans' rights, and yet they succeed!
They have not upheld
the cause of the needy.
29 Shall I fail to punish this,
Yahweh demands,
or on such a nation
to exact vengeance?[b]
30 Horrible, disgusting things
are happening in the land:
31 the prophets prophesy falsely
and the priests exploit the people.
And my people love it!
But when the end comes,
what will you do?

More about the invasion

6 Flee in a body, Benjaminites,
right away from Jerusalem!
Sound the trumpet in Tekoa![a]
Light the beacon on Beth-ha-Cherem!
For disaster lowers from the north,
an immense calamity.
2 Beautiful, delicate as she is,
I shall destroy the daughter of Zion!
3 Shepherds are advancing on her
with their flocks.
They have pitched their tents
all round her,
each grazes his part.
4 Prepare for holy war against her!
To arms! We shall attack at noon!
Disaster for us! The light is fading,
the evening shadows lengthen.
5 To arms! We shall attack at night
and destroy her palaces.
6 For Yahweh Sabaoth says this,
'Cut down trees,
throw up an earthwork outside Jerusalem:
this is the city to be punished,
with nothing but oppression in her.
7 As a well keeps its water fresh
so she keeps her wickedness fresh.
Violence and ruin
are what you hear in her,
wounds and blows
always forced on my attention.
8 Reform, Jerusalem,
or I shall turn my attention away from you
and reduce you to a desert,
a land without people.'
9 Yahweh Sabaoth says this,
'They will glean, glean what is left of Israel
like a vine.
Like a grape-picker,
pass your hand again
over the branches!'
10 To whom should I speak, whom warn,
for them to hear?
Look, their ears are uncircumcised,
they cannot listen.
Look, for them Yahweh's word
is something to sneer at,
they have no taste for it.
11 So I am full of Yahweh's wrath,
I am weary of holding it in.
Then pour it on the children in the streets,
and on the bands of youths as well,
for husband and wife will both be taken,
the greybeard
and the man weighed down with years.
12 Their houses will pass to other men,
so will their fields and wives.
Yes, I shall stretch my hand
over those living in this country,
Yahweh declares.
13 For, from the least to greatest,
they are all greedy for gain;
prophet no less than priest,
all of them practise fraud.

5b =5:9; 9:8.
6a Both towns are south, but in sight, of Jerusalem.

14 Without concern
they dress my people's wound,
saying, 'Peace! Peace!'
whereas there is no peace.
15 They should be ashamed
of their loathsome deeds.
Not they! They feel no shame,
they do not even know how to blush.
And so as others fall, they too will fall,
will be thrown down
when I come and punish them,
Yahweh says.[b]

16 Yahweh says this,
'Stand at the crossroads and look,
ask for the ancient paths:
which was the good way? Take it
and you will find rest for yourselves.
But they have said, "We will not take it."
17 I posted look-outs on your behalf:
Listen to the sound of the trumpet!
But they said, "We will not listen."
18 Then hear, you nations,
and know, assembly,
what is going to happen to them!
19 Listen, earth!
Watch, I shall bring disaster
on this people:
it is the fruit of the way they think,
since they have not listened to my words
nor to my law, but have rejected it.
20 What do I care about incense
imported from Sheba,
or fragrant cane
from a distant country?
Your burnt offerings are not acceptable,
your sacrifices do not please me.'
21 And so, Yahweh says this,
'In front of this people
I shall now lay obstacles
for them to stumble over;
father and son alike,
neighbour and friend will perish.'

22 Yahweh says this,
'Look, a people is coming
from the land of the north,
from the far ends of the earth
a great nation is rising;
23 they are armed with bow and spear,
they are cruel and pitiless;
their noise is like the roaring of the sea;
they are riding horses,
they are ready to fight against you
as one man,
against you, daughter of Zion.[c]
24 We have heard the news,
our hands fall limp,
anguish has gripped us,
pain like that of a woman in labour.
25 Do not go out into the countryside,
do not venture onto the roads,
for the enemy's sword is there,
terror on every side.
26 Put on sackcloth, daughter of my people,
roll in ashes;
mourn as for an only son,
a very bitter dirge.
For on us suddenly
the destroyer is coming.

27 'I have appointed you
as tester of my people,
to learn and to test how they behave.
28 All of them are total rebels
peddlers of slander,
hard as bronze and iron,
all agents of corruption.
29 The bellows blast away
to make the fire burn away the lead.
In vain the smelter does his work,
for the dross is not purged out.
30 "Silver-reject", men call them,
and indeed Yahweh has rejected them!'

B: PROPHECIES MAINLY IN THE REIGN OF JEHOIAKIM

True worship
a: Against the Temple

7 The word that came to Jeremiah from
Yahweh, saying, 2 'Stand at the gate of the
Temple of Yahweh and there proclaim this
message. Say, "Listen to the word of
Yahweh, all you of Judah who come in by
these gates to worship Yahweh. 3 Yahweh
Sabaoth, the God of Israel, says this: Amend
your behaviour and your actions and I will
let you stay in this place. 4 Do not put your
faith in delusive words, such as: This is
Yahweh's sanctuary, Yahweh's sanctuary,
Yahweh's sanctuary! 5 But if you really amend
your behaviour and your actions, if you really
treat one another fairly, 6 if you do not exploit

6b =8:10–12.
6c =50:41–43.

the stranger, the orphan and the widow, if
you do not shed innocent blood in this place
and if you do not follow other gods, to your
own ruin, [7]then I shall let you stay in this
place, in the country I gave for ever to your
ancestors of old. [8]Look, you are putting your
faith in delusive, worthless words! [9]Steal,
would you, murder, commit adultery,
perjure yourselves, burn incense to Baal,
follow other gods of whom you know
nothing?— [10]and then come and stand before
me in this Temple that bears my name,
saying: Now we are safe to go on doing all
these loathsome things! [11]Do you look on this
Temple that bears my name as a den of
bandits? I, at any rate, can see straight,
Yahweh declares.

[12]"Now go to the place which used to be
mine at Shiloh, where I once gave my name
a home; see what I have done to it because of
the wickedness of my people Israel! [13]And
now, since you have done all these things,
Yahweh declares, and refused to listen when
I spoke so urgently, so persistently, or to
answer when I called you, [14]I shall treat this
Temple that bears my name, and in which
you put your heart, the place that I gave you
and your ancestors, just as I treated Shiloh,
[15]and I shall drive you out of my sight, as
I did all your kinsfolk, the whole race of
Ephraim."

b: Alien gods

[16]'You, for your part, must not intercede for
this people, nor raise either plea or prayer on
their behalf; do not plead with me, for I will
not listen to you. [17]Can you not see what they
are doing in the towns of Judah and in the
streets of Jerusalem? [18]The children collect
the wood, the fathers light the fire, the women
knead the dough, to make cakes for the
Queen of Heaven;[a] and, to spite me, they
pour libations to alien gods. [19]Is it really me
they spite, Yahweh demands, is it not in fact
themselves, to their own confusion? [20]So,
Lord Yahweh says this, "My anger, my
wrath will be poured down on this place, on
man and beast, on the trees of the countryside
and the fruits of the soil; it will burn, and not
be quenched."

c: Worship without sincerity

[21]'Yahweh Sabaoth, the God of Israel, says
this, "Add your burnt offerings to your sacri-
fices and eat all the meat. [22]For when I
brought your ancestors out of Egypt, I said
nothing to them, gave them no orders, about
burnt offerings or sacrifices. [23]My one
command to them was this: Listen to my
voice, then I will be your God and you shall
be my people. In everything, follow the way
that I mark out for you, and you shall prosper.
[24]But they did not listen, they did not pay
attention; they followed their own devices,
their own stubborn and wicked inclinations,
and got worse rather than better. [25]From the
day your ancestors left Egypt until today, I
have sent you all my servants the prophets,
persistently sending them day after day.
[26]But they have not listened to me, have
not paid attention; they have deliberately
resisted, behaving worse than their ances-
tors. [27]So you will tell them all this, but they
will not listen to you; you will call them, but
they will not answer you." [28]Then you are to
say to them, "This is the nation that will
neither listen to the voice of Yahweh its God
nor take correction. Sincerity is no more, it
has vanished from their mouths.

d: More about idolatrous worship: a threat of exile

[29]"Cut off your tresses, throw them away!
On the bare heights raise a dirge,
for Yahweh has rejected, has abandoned,
a brood that enrages him!"

[30]'Yes, the people of Judah have done what
displeases me, Yahweh declares. They have
set up their Horrors in the Temple that bears
my name, to defile it, [31]and have built the
high places of Topheth[b] in the Valley of Ben-
Hinnom, to burn their sons and daughters: a
thing I never ordered, that had never entered
my thoughts.[c] [32]So now the days are coming,
Yahweh declares, when people will no longer
say Topheth or Valley of Ben-Hinnom, but
Valley of Slaughter. Topheth will become a
burial ground, for lack of other space; [33]the
corpses of this people will be food for the
birds of the sky and the animals of earth, and
there will be no one to drive them off. [34]I

7a Mesopotamian goddess of fertility.
7b The rubbish-dump of Jerusalem, where children were also sacrificed.
7c =32:34–35.

shall silence the shouts of rejoicing and mirth and the voices of bridegroom and bride, in the towns of Judah and the streets of Jerusalem, for the country will be reduced to desert.'

8 'When that time comes, Yahweh declares, the bones of the kings of Judah, the bones of its chief men, the bones of the priests, the bones of the prophets and the bones of the inhabitants of Jerusalem, will be taken from
their tombs. 2 They will be spread out before
the sun, the moon, the whole array of heaven, whom they have loved and served, followed, consulted and worshipped. They will not be gathered or reburied but will be left lying on
the surface like dung.[a] 3 And death will seem
preferable to life to all the survivors of this wicked race, wherever I have driven them, Yahweh Sabaoth declares.

Threats, laments, advice
Israel's perversity

4 "You are to tell them, "Yahweh says this:
If someone falls,
can he not stand up again?
If people stray, can they not turn back?
5 Why does this people
persist in acts of infidelity,
why does Jerusalem
persist in continuous infidelity?
They cling to illusion,
they refuse to turn back.
6 I have listened attentively:
they have never said anything like that.
Not one repents of wickedness
saying: What have I done?
Each one keeps returning to the course
like a horse charging into battle.
7 Even the stork in the sky
knows the appropriate season;
turtledove, swallow and crane
observe their time of migration.
But my people do not know
Yahweh's laws!" '

The Law as administered by the priests

8 How can you say, 'We are wise,
since we have Yahweh's Law?'
Look how it has been falsified
by the lying pen of the scribes!
9 The wise are put to shame,
alarmed, caught out
because they have rejected
Yahweh's word.
What price their wisdom now?

Repetition of an earlier threat[b]

10 So I shall give their wives to other men,
their fields to new masters,
for, from the least to greatest,
they are all greedy for gain;
prophet no less than priest,
all of them practise fraud.
11 Without concern they dress
the wound of the daughter of my people,
saying, 'Peace! Peace!'
whereas there is no peace.
12 They should be ashamed
of their loathsome deeds.
Not they! They feel no shame,
they do not even know how to blush.
And so as others fall, they too will fall,
will be thrown down
when the time for punishing them
comes,
Yahweh says.

Threats against Judah the Vine

13 I shall put an end to them,
Yahweh declares,
no more grapes on the vine,
no more figs on the fig tree
only withered leaves:
I have found them people
to trample on them!
14 Why are we sitting still?
Mobilise!
Take to the fortified towns[c]
and there fall silent,
since Yahweh our God means to silence us
by giving us poisoned water to drink
because we have sinned against him.
15 We are hoping for peace—
no good came of it!
For the time of healing—
nothing but terror![d]
16 From Dan you can hear
the snorting of his horses;
at the neighing of his stallions
the whole country quakes;

8a =25:33.
8b A duplicate of 6:12–15, absent in the Gk text.
8c =4:5.
8d =14:19.

they are coming to devour the country
and its contents,
the town and those that live in it.
17 Yes, now I am sending you
poisonous snakes
against which no charm exists;
and they will bite you,
Yahweh declares.

A lament of the prophet during a famine

18 Incurable sorrow overtakes me,
my heart fails me.
19 Hark, from the daughter of my people
the cry for help,
ringing far and wide throughout the land!
'Is Yahweh no longer in Zion,
her King no longer there?'
(Why have they provoked me
with their idols,
with their futile foreign gods?)
20 'Harvest is over, summer at an end,
and we have not been saved!'
21 The wound of the daughter of my people
wounds me too,
all looks dark to me, terror grips me.
22 Is there no balm in Gilead any more?
Is no doctor there?
Then why is there no progress
in the cure of the daughter of my people?
23 Who will turn my head into a fountain,
and my eyes into a spring of tears,
that I can weep day and night
over the slain of the daughter of my people?

The moral corruption of Judah

9 Who will find me a wayfarer's shelter
in the desert,
for me to quit my people,
and leave them far behind?
For all of them are adulterers,
a conspiracy of traitors.
2 They bend their tongues like a bow;
not truth but falsehood
holds sway in the land;
yes, they go from crime to crime,
but me they do not know,
Yahweh declares.
3 Let each be on his guard against his friend;
do not trust a brother,
for every brother aims but to supplant,
and every friend is a peddler of slander.
4 Each one cheats his friend,
never telling the truth;
they have trained their tongues to lie
and devote all their energies
to doing wrong.
5 You live in a world of bad faith!
Out of bad faith, they refuse to know me,
Yahweh declares.
6 And, so, Yahweh Sabaoth declares,
now I shall purge them and test them,
no other way to treat
the daughter of my people!
7 Their tongue is a deadly arrow,
their words are in bad faith;
with his mouth
each wishes his neighbour peace,
while in his heart plotting a trap for him.
8 Shall I fail to punish them for this,
Yahweh demands,
or on such a nation
fail to exact vengeance?[a]

Sorrow in Zion

9 I raise the wail and lament
for the mountains,
the dirge for the desert pastures,
for they have been burnt:
no one passes there,
the sound of flocks is heard no more.
Birds of the sky and animals,
all have fled, all are gone.
10 I shall make Jerusalem a heap of ruins,
a lair for jackals,
and the towns of Judah
an uninhabited wasteland.

11 Who is wise enough to understand this?
To whom has Yahweh's mouth spoken to
explain it?

Why is the country annihilated,
burnt like the desert where no one passes?

12 Yahweh says, 'This is because they have
forsaken my Law which I gave them and have
not listened to my voice or followed it,
13 but
have followed their own stubborn hearts,
have followed the Baals as their ancestors
taught them.'
14 So Yahweh Sabaoth, the God
of Israel, says this, 'Now I shall give this
people wormwood to eat and poisoned water
to drink.[b]
15 I shall scatter them among
nations unknown to their ancestors or to

9a =5:9, 29.
9b =23:15.

them; and I shall pursue them with the sword
until I have annihilated them.'

16 Yahweh Sabaoth says this,
'Prepare to call for the mourning women!
Send for those who are best at it!
17 Let them lose no time
in raising the lament over us!
Let our eyes rain tears,
our eyelids run with weeping!
18 A lament makes itself heard in Zion,
"What ruin is ours,
what utter shame!
For we must leave the country,
our homes have been knocked down!" '
19 Now listen, you women,
to Yahweh's word,
let your ears take in the word
his own mouth speaks.
Teach your daughters how to wail
and teach one another this dirge,
20 'Death has climbed in at our windows,
and made its way into our palaces;
it has cut down the children in the street,
the young people in the squares—
21 Speak! Yahweh declares this—
human corpses are strewn
like dung in the open field,
like sheaves left by the reaper,
with no one to gather them.'

True wisdom

22 Yahweh says this,
'Let the sage not boast of wisdom,
nor the valiant of valour,
nor the wealthy of riches!
23 But let anyone who wants to boast,
boast of this:
of understanding and knowing me.
For I am Yahweh,
who acts with faithful love,
justice, and uprightness on earth;
yes, these are what please me,'
Yahweh declares.

Circumcision, a false guarantee

24 'Look, the days are coming, Yahweh
declares, when I shall punish all who are
circumcised only in the flesh: 25 Egypt, Judah,
Edom, the Ammonites, Moab, and all the
men with shaven temples who live in the
desert. For all those nations, and the whole
House of Israel too, are uncircumcised at
heart.'

Idols and the true God

10 Listen, House of Israel, to the word
that Yahweh addresses to you. Yahweh
says this:

2 'Do not learn the ways of the nations
or take alarm at the heavenly signs,
alarmed though the nations may be
at them.
3 Yes, the customs of the peoples
are quite futile:
wood, nothing more, cut out of a forest,
worked with a blade by a carver's hand,
4 then embellished with silver and gold,
then fastened with hammer and nails
to keep it from moving.
5 Like scarecrows in a melon patch,
they cannot talk,
they have to be carried,
since they cannot walk.
Have no fear of them: they can do no harm
—nor any good either!'

6 Yahweh, there is no one like you,
so great you are,
so great your mighty name.
7 Who would not revere you,
King of nations?
Yes, this is your due.
Since of all the wise among the nations,
and in all their kingdoms,
there is not a single one like you.

8 All of them are brutish and stupid:
the Futile Ones' teaching is but wood,
9 silver leaf imported from Tarshish
and gold from Ophir,
the work of carver or goldsmith;
then dressed up in violet and purple,
all the work of skilled men.
10 But Yahweh is the true God.
He is the living God,
the everlasting King.
The earth quakes when he is wrathful,
the nations cannot endure his fury.

11 'Tell them this, "The gods who did not
make the heavens and the earth will vanish
from the earth and from under these
heavens." '

12 By his power he made the earth,
by his wisdom set the world firm,
but his discernment
spread out the heavens.
13 When he thunders
there is a roaring of waters in heaven;

he raises clouds
from the remotest parts of the earth,
makes the lightning flash
for the downpour,
and brings the wind from his storehouse.
14 At this all people stand stupefied,
uncomprehending,
every goldsmith blushes for his idols;
his castings are but delusion,
with no breath in them.
15 They are futile, a laughable production;
when the time comes
for them to be punished,
they will vanish.
16 The Heritage of Jacob is not like these,
for he is the maker of everything,
and Israel is the tribe that is his heritage.
His name is Yahweh Sabaoth.[a]

Panic in the country

17 Pick up your pack from the ground,
you the besieged!
18 For Yahweh says this,
'Now I shall throw out
the inhabitants of the country,
this time,
and bring distress on them,
so that they may find me!'
19 Disaster is on me! What a wound!
My injury is incurable!
And I used to think,
'If this is the worst, I can bear it!'
20 But now my tent is destroyed,
all my ropes are snapped,
my sons have left me and are no more;
no one is left to put my tent up again
or to hang the side-cloths.
21 The shepherds are the ones
who have been stupid:
they have not searched for Yahweh.
This is why they have not prospered
and why their whole flock
has been dispersed.
22 Listen! A terrible noise!
A mighty uproar from the land of the north
to reduce the towns of Judah
to desert, to a lair for jackals!

23 I know, Yahweh,
no one's course is in his control,
nor is it in anyone's power,
as he goes his way,
to guide his own steps.
24 Correct me, Yahweh,
but with moderation,
not in your anger,
or you will reduce me to nothing.

25 Pour out your anger on the nations
who do not acknowledge you,
and on the families
that do not call on your name,
for they have devoured Jacob,
have devoured and made an end of him
and reduced his home to desolation.

Jeremiah and observance of the covenant

11 The word that came to Jeremiah from
Yahweh, 2 'Hear the terms of this
covenant; tell them to the people of Judah
and to the inhabitants of Jerusalem. 3 Tell
them, "Yahweh, God of Israel, says this:
Cursed be anyone who will not listen to the
terms of this covenant 4 which I ordained for
your ancestors when I brought them out of
Egypt, out of that iron-foundry. Listen to
my voice, I told them, carry out all my orders,
then you will be my people and I shall be
your God, 5 so that I may fulfil the oath I
swore to your ancestors, that I may give them
a country flowing with milk and honey, as
is the case today." ' I replied, 'So be it,
Yahweh!' 6 Then Yahweh said to me,
'Proclaim all these terms in the towns of
Judah and in the streets of Jerusalem, saying,
"Listen to the terms of this covenant and
obey them. 7 For when I brought your ances-
tors out of Egypt, I solemnly warned them,
and have persistently warned them until
today, saying: Listen to my voice. 8 But they
did not listen, did not pay attention; instead,
each followed his own stubborn and wicked
inclinations. And against them, in conse-
quence, I put into action the words of this
covenant which I had ordered them to obey
and which they had not obeyed." '
9 Yahweh said to me, 'Plainly there is
conspiracy among the people of Judah and
the citizens of Jerusalem. 10 They have
reverted to the sins of their ancestors who
refused to listen to my words: they too are
following other gods and serving them. The
House of Israel and the House of Judah have
broken my covenant which I made with their
ancestors. 11 And so, Yahweh says this, "I
shall now bring a disaster on them which they
cannot escape; they will call to me for help,

10a =51:15–19.

but I shall not listen to them. 12 The towns of
Judah and the citizens of Jerusalem will then
go and call for help to the gods to whom they
burn incense, but these will be no help at all
to them in their time of distress!

13 "For you have as many gods
as you have towns, Judah![a]
You have built as many altars to Shame,
as many incense altars to Baal,
as Jerusalem has streets!

14 "You, for your part, must not intercede for this people, nor raise either plea or prayer on their behalf, for I will not listen when their distress forces them to call to me for help."

Rebuke to the frequenters of the Temple

15 'What is my beloved doing in my house?
She has achieved her wicked plans.
Can vows and consecrated meat
turn disaster from you
for you to be so happy?
16 "Green olive-tree covered in fine fruit",
was Yahweh's name for you.
With a shattering noise
he has set fire to it,
its branches are broken.'

17 And Yahweh Sabaoth, who planted you, has decreed disaster for you because of the evil the House of Israel and the House of Judah have done, provoking me by burning incense to Baal.

Jeremiah persecuted at Anathoth

18 Yahweh informed me and I knew it; you
then revealed their scheming to me. 19 I for
my part was like a trustful lamb being led
to the slaughterhouse, not knowing the
schemes they were plotting against me, 'Let
us destroy the tree in its strength, let us cut
him off from the land of the living, so that
his name may no longer be remembered!'

20 Yahweh Sabaoth,
whose judgement is upright,
tester of motives and thoughts,
I shall see your vengeance on them,
for I have revealed my cause to you.[b]

21 Against the people of Anathoth who are
determined to kill me and say to me, 'Do not
prophesy in the name of Yahweh or you will
die at our hands!' 22 Yahweh says this, 'I am
about to punish them. Their young people
will die by the sword, their sons and daughters by famine. 23 Not one will be left when I
bring disaster on the people of Anathoth,
when the year for punishing them comes.'

The prosperity of the wicked

12 Your uprightness is too great,
Yahweh,
for me to dispute with you.
But I should like to discuss
some points of justice with you:
Why is it
that the way of the wicked prospers?
Why do all treacherous people thrive?
2 You plant them, they take root,
they flourish, yes, and bear fruit.
You are on their lips,
yet far from their heart.
3 You know me, Yahweh, you see me,
you probe my heart,
which is close to yours.
Drag them off like sheep
for the slaughterhouse,
reserve them for the day of butchery.

4 (How long will the land be in mourning, and the grass wither all over the countryside? The animals and birds are dying as a result of the wickedness of the inhabitants.)

For they say,
'God does not see our fate.'

5 "If you find it exhausting
to race against me on foot,
how will you compete against horses?
In a country at peace you feel secure,
but how will you fare
in the thickets of the Jordan?

6 "For even your brothers and your own family will betray you. They will pursue you in full cry. Put no faith in them when they speak you fair!'

Yahweh laments his ravaged inheritance

7 I have abandoned my house,
left my heritage,
I have delivered what I dearly loved
into the clutches of its enemies.
8 To me, my heritage has behaved

11a =2:28.
11b =20:12.

like a lion in the forest,
it roared at me ferociously:
so I now hate it.
[9]I see my heritage
as a brightly-coloured bird of prey
attacked by birds of prey on every side!
Go, assemble all the wild animals,
make them come and dine!
[10]Many shepherds
have laid my vineyard waste,
have trampled over my plot of land,
the plot of land which was my joy,
reducing my favourite estate
to a deserted wilderness.
[11]They have made it a waste;
wasted, it mourns before me.
The whole country has been devastated
and no one takes it to heart.
[12]The devastators have arrived
on all the bare heights of the desert
(for Yahweh wields a devouring sword);
from one end of the country to the other,
there is no peace for any living thing.
[13]Wheat they have sown, thorns they reap:
they have worn themselves out,
to no profit.
They are disappointed in their harvests,
because of Yahweh's burning anger.

The neighbouring peoples: their judgement and salvation

[14]Yahweh says this, 'As regards all my evil
neighbours who have laid hands on the
heritage I granted my people Israel, look, I
shall uproot them from their soil, (though I
shall uproot the House of Judah from among
them). [15]But having uprooted them, I shall
take pity on them again and bring them back
each to its own heritage, each to its own
country, [16]and if they carefully learn my
people's ways and swear by my name, "As
Yahweh lives", as they have taught my people
to swear by Baal, then they will be re-
established among my people. [17]But if any
nation refuses to listen, I shall uproot it for
ever and destroy it, Yahweh declares.'

The useless waistcloth[a]

13 Yahweh said this to me, 'Go and buy a
linen waistcloth and put it round your
waist. But do not dip it in water.' [2]And so,
as Yahweh had ordered, I bought a waistcloth
and put it round my waist. [3]A second time
the word of Yahweh came to me, [4]'Take the
waistcloth that you have bought and are
wearing round your waist. Up, go to the
Euphrates and hide it there in a hole in the
rock.' [5]So I went and hid it by the Euphrates
as Yahweh had ordered me. [6]A long time
later, Yahweh said to me, 'Up, go to the
Euphrates and fetch the waistcloth I ordered
you to hide there.' [7]So I went to the
Euphrates, and I searched, and I took the
waistcloth from the place where I had hidden
it. And there was the waistcloth ruined, no
use for anything. [8]Then the word of Yahweh
was addressed to me as follows, [9]'Yahweh
says this, "In the same way I shall ruin
the pride of Judah, the immense pride of
Jerusalem. [10]This evil people, these people
who refuse to listen to my words, who follow
their own stubborn inclinations and run after
other gods, serving and worshipping them—
this people will become like this waistcloth,
no good for anything. [11]For just as a
waistcloth clings to a man's waist, so I made
the whole House of Israel and the whole
House of Judah cling to me, Yahweh
declares, to be my people, my glory, my
honour and my pride. But they have not
listened."

The wine jugs smashed together

[12]'You will also say this to them, "Yahweh,
God of Israel, says this: Any jug can be filled
with wine." And if they answer you, "Do
you think we do not know that any jug
can be filled with wine?" [13]you are to say,
"Yahweh says this: Look, I shall fill all the
inhabitants of this country, the kings who
occupy the throne of David, the priests, the
prophets and all the citizens of Jerusalem,
with drunkenness. [14]Then I shall smash them
one against the other, parents and children
all together, Yahweh declares. Mercilessly,
relentlessly, pitilessly, I shall destroy
them." '

A vision of exile

[15]Listen and pay attention,
do not be proud:
Yahweh is speaking!
[16]Give glory to Yahweh your God
before the darkness comes,

13a The Euphrates is probably symbolised by the river Parah near Jr's home.

before your feet stumble
on the darkened mountains.
You hope for light,
but he will turn it to shadow dark as death,
will change it to blackness.
17 If you do not listen to this warning,
I shall weep in secret for your pride;
my eyes will weep bitterly
and stream with tears,
for Yahweh's flock
is being led into captivity.

Jehoiachin threatened

18 Tell the king and the queen mother,
'Sit in a lower place,
since your glorious crown
has fallen from your head.
19 The towns of the Negeb are shut off
with no one to give access to them.
All Judah has been deported,
deported wholesale.'

An admonition to impenitent Jerusalem

20 Raise your eyes and look at these
now coming from the north.
Where is the flock once entrusted to you,
the flock which was your pride?
21 What will you say
when they come and punish you,
you yourself having taught them?
Against you, in the lead,
will come your friends.
Then will not anguish grip you
as it grips a woman in labour?
22 And should you ask yourself,
'Why is all this happening to me?'
it is because of your great guilt
that your skirts have been pulled up
and you have been manhandled.
23 Can the Ethiopian change his skin,
or the leopard his spots?
And you, can you do right,
being so accustomed to wrong?
24 'I shall scatter you like chaff
on the desert wind.
25 This is your share, the part allotted you,
from me, Yahweh declares,
because you have forgotten me
and put your trust in Delusion.
26 I am the one who pulls your skirts up
over your face
to let your shame be seen.
27 Oh! Your adulteries,
your shrieks of pleasure,
your vile prostitution!
On the hills, in the fields,
I have seen your Horrors.
Jerusalem, disaster is coming for you!
How much longer till you are made clean?'

The great drought

14 The word of Yahweh that came to
Jeremiah on the occasion of the
drought.

2 'Judah is in mourning,
her towns are pining,
sinking to the ground;
a cry goes up from Jerusalem.
3 The nobles send their servants for water,
they come to the water-tanks,
find no water,
and return with their pitchers empty.
Dismayed and bewildered,
they cover their heads.
4 Because the soil is all cracked
since the country has had no rain;
the farmers are dismayed,
they cover their heads.
5 Even the doe in the countryside
giving birth abandons her young,
for there is no grass;
6 the wild donkeys standing
on the bare heights
gasp for air like jackals:
their eyes grow dim
for lack of pasture.'
7 Although our sins witness against us,
Yahweh, for your name's sake, intervene!
Yes, our acts of infidelity have been many,
we have sinned against you!
8 Yahweh, hope of Israel,
its Saviour in time of distress,
why are you like a stranger in this country,
like a traveller staying only for one night?
9 Why are you like someone bemused,
like a warrior who has no power to rescue?
And yet, Yahweh, you are among us,
we are called by your name.
Do not desert us!

10 Yahweh says this about this people,
'They take such pleasure in darting hither
and thither, they cannot restrain their feet!
But Yahweh takes pleasure in them no
longer; now he will keep their guilt in mind
and punish their sins.'

11 Yahweh then said to me, 'Do not inter-
cede for this people or their welfare. 12 If they
fast, I will not listen to their plea; if they offer

burnt offerings and cereal offerings I will not
accept them. Rather, I shall make an end of
them by sword, famine and plague.'
13 'Ah, Lord Yahweh,' I answered, 'here
are the prophets telling them, "You will not
see the sword, famine will not touch you; I
promise you true peace in this place." '
14 Then Yahweh said to me, 'The prophets
are prophesying lies in my name; I have not
sent them, I gave them no orders, I never
spoke to them. Delusive visions, hollow
predictions, daydreams of their own, that is
what they prophesy to you. 15 Therefore,
Yahweh says this: The prophets who
prophesy in my name when I have not sent
them, and tell you there will be no sword or
famine in this country, these same prophets
will meet their end by sword and famine.
16 And as for the people to whom they
prophesy, they will be tossed into the streets
of Jerusalem, victims of famine and the
sword, with not a soul to bury them: neither
them nor their wives, nor their sons, nor their
daughters. I shall pour their own wickedness
down on them.

17 'So say this word to them:
May my eyes shed tears
night and day, unceasingly,
since the daughter of my people
has sustained a fearsome wound,
a crippling injury.
18 If I go into the countryside,
there lie those killed by the sword;
if I go into the city,
I see people tortured with hunger;
even prophets and priests
roam the country at their wits' end.'

19 Have you rejected Judah altogether?
Does your very soul revolt at Zion?
Why have you struck us down
without hope of cure?
We were hoping for peace—
no good came of it!
For the moment of cure—
nothing but terror![a]
20 Yahweh, we acknowledge our wickedness
and our ancestors' guilt:
we have indeed sinned against you.
21 For your name's sake do not reject us,
do not dishonour the throne of your glory.
Remember us;
do not break your covenant with us.
22 Can any of the nations' Futile Ones
make it rain?
Can the heavens of their own accord
give showers?
Are you not the one, Yahweh our God?
In you is our hope,
since you make all these things.

15 Yahweh said to me, 'Even if Moses and
Samuel pleaded before me, I could not
sympathise with this people! Drive them out
of my sight; away with them! 2 And if they
ask you, "Where shall we go?" tell them this,
"Yahweh says this:

Those for the plague, to the plague;
those for the sword, to the sword;
those for famine, to famine;
those for captivity, to captivity![a]

3 "I shall consign them to four kinds of
thing, Yahweh declares: the sword to kill,
the dogs to drag away, the birds of heaven
and wild animals of earth to devour and to
destroy. 4 I shall make them an object of
horror to all the kingdoms of the earth,
because of Manasseh son of Hezekiah, king
of Judah, and what he did in Jerusalem." '

The horrors of war

5 Who is there to pity you, Jerusalem,
who to grieve for you,
who to go out of his way
and ask how you are?
6 'You yourself have rejected me,
Yahweh declares,
you have turned your back on me;
so I have stretched my hand over you
and destroyed you.
Tired of relenting,
7 I have winnowed them with a winnow
at the country's gates.
They have been bereft,
I have destroyed my people,
but they refuse to leave their ways.
8 I have made their widows outnumber
the sand of the sea.
On the mother of young warriors
I bring the destroyer in broad daylight.
Suddenly I bring
anguish and terror down on her.
9 The mother of seven sons grows faint
and gasps for breath.
It is still day, but already her sun has set,

14a =8:15.
15a =43:11.

she is dismayed and distracted;
and the rest of them
I shall consign to the sword,
to their enemies, Yahweh declares.'

The call[b] of Jeremiah renewed

10 A disaster for me, mother,
that you bore me
to be a man of strife
and dissension for the whole country.
I neither lend nor borrow,
yet all of them curse me.
11 Have I not genuinely done my best
to serve you, Yahweh?
Have I not interceded with you
in time of disaster and distress!
12 'Can iron break the iron of the north
and the bronze?
13 Your wealth and your treasures
I shall hand over to plunder,
without repayment,
because of all your sins,
throughout your territory.
14 I shall enslave you to your enemies
in a country which you do not know,
for my anger has kindled a fire
that will burn you up.'[c]

15 Yahweh, you know!
Remember me, take care of me,
and avenge me on my persecutors.
However long your anger endures,
do not snatch me away.
Realise that I suffer insult for your sake.
16 When your words came, I devoured them:
your word was my delight
and the joy of my heart;
for I was called by your Name,
Yahweh, God Sabaoth.
17 I never sat in the company of scoffers
amusing myself;
with your hands on me I held myself aloof,
since you had filled me with indignation.
18 Why is my suffering continual,
my wound incurable,
refusing to be healed?
Truly, for me you are a deceptive stream
with uncertain waters!

19 To which Yahweh replied,
'If you repent, I shall restore you
to plead before me.
If you distinguish between the precious
and the base,
you shall be as my own mouth.
They will come back to you,
but you must not go back to them.
20 As far as these people are concerned,
I shall make you
a fortified wall of bronze.
They will fight against you
but will not overcome you,
because I am with you
to save you and rescue you,
Yahweh declares.
21 I shall rescue you
from the clutches of the wicked
and redeem you
from the grasp of the violent.'

The prophet's life is itself symbolic

16 The word of Yahweh was addressed to
me as follows:
2 'You are not to marry or have sons and
daughters in this place. 3 For Yahweh says
this regarding the sons and daughters to be
born in this place, about the mothers who
give birth to them, and about the fathers who
beget them in this land, 4 "They will die of
deadly diseases, unlamented and unburied;
they will be like dung spread on the ground;
they will meet their end by sword and famine,
and their corpses will be food for the birds of
the sky and the beasts of earth."
5 'Yes, Yahweh says this, "Go into no house
where there is mourning, do not go and
lament or grieve with them; for I have with-
drawn my peace from this people, Yahweh
declares, and faithful love and pity too. 6 High
or low, they will die in this country, without
burial or lament; there will be no gashing, no
shaving of the head for them. 7 No bread will
be broken for the mourner to comfort him
for the dead; no cup of consolation will be
offered him for his father or his mother.
8 "And do not enter a house where there is
feasting, to sit with them and eat and drink.
9 For Yahweh Sabaoth, the God of Israel, says
this: In this place, before your eyes, in your
own days, I will silence the shouts of rejoicing
and mirth and the voices of bridegroom and
bride.
10 "When you tell these people this and

15b The 'confessions of Jr' (11:18—12:5; 15:10–21; 17:14–18; 18:18–23; 20:7–18) show Jr in a dialogue of astounding intimacy with Yahweh.
15c =17:3–4.

they ask you: Why has Yahweh decreed such
complete and total disaster for us? What have
we done wrong? What sin have we committed
against Yahweh our God? [11]then you are to
answer: It is because your ancestors aban-
doned me, Yahweh declares, and followed
other gods, and served and worshipped them.
They abandoned me and did not keep my
Law. [12]And you for your part have behaved
even worse than your ancestors. Look, each
of you follows his own stubborn and wicked
inclinations, without listening to me. [13]And
so, I shall eject you from this country into a
country unknown to you or to your ancestors,
and there you can serve other gods, day and
night, for I shall show you no more favour."

The return of the scattered Israelites

[14]'Look, the days are coming, Yahweh
declares, when people will no longer say, "As
Yahweh lives who brought the Israelites out
of Egypt!" [15]but, "As Yahweh lives who
brought the Israelites back from the land of
the north and all the countries to which he
had driven them." I shall bring them back to
the very soil I gave their ancestors.'[a]

The invasion foretold

[16]'Watch, I shall send for many fishermen,
Yahweh declares, and these will fish them
up; next, I shall send for many huntsmen, and
these will hunt them out of every mountain,
every hill, and out of the holes in the rocks.
[17]For my eyes watch all their ways, these are
not hidden from me, and their guilt does not
escape my gaze. [18]I shall requite their guilt
and their sin twice over, since they have
polluted my country with the carcases of their
Horrors, and filled my heritage with their
Abominations.'[b]

The conversion of the nations

[19]Yahweh, my strength, my stronghold,
my refuge in time of distress!
To you the nations will come
from the remotest parts of the earth
and say,
'Our fathers inherited nothing
but Delusion,
Futility of no use whatever.
[20]Can human beings make their own gods?
These are not gods at all!'
[21]'Now listen,
I will make them acknowledge,
this time I will make them acknowledge
my hand and my might;
and then they will know
that Yahweh is my name.'

Judah's contaminated worship

17 'The sin of Judah is written
with an iron pen,
engraved with a diamond point
on the tablet of the heart
and on the horns of their altars,
[2]while their children remember
their altars and their sacred pole
beside the green trees, on the lofty hills.
[3]My mountain on the plain,
your wealth and all your treasures
I shall hand over to be plundered,
because of the sin of your high places
throughout your territory.
[4]You will have to relinquish your heritage
which I gave you;
I will enslave you to your enemies
in a country which you do not know,
for my fiery anger kindled by you
will burn for ever.'[a]

A group of wisdom sayings

[5]Yahweh says this,
'Accursed be anyone
who trusts in human beings,
who relies on human strength
and whose heart turns from Yahweh.
[6]Such a person is like scrub
in the wastelands:
when good comes, it does not affect him
since he lives in the parched places
of the desert,
uninhabited, salt land.

[7]'Blessed is anyone who trusts in Yahweh,
with Yahweh to rely on.
[8]Such a person is like a tree by the waterside
that thrusts its roots to the stream:
when the heat comes it has nothing to fear,
its foliage stays green;
untroubled in a year of drought,
it never stops bearing fruit.

16a =23:7–8.
16b The Horrors and Abominations are idols.
17a =15:13–14.

[9]'The heart is more devious
than any other thing,
and is depraved;
who can pierce its secrets?
[10]I, Yahweh, search the heart,
test the motives,
to give each person what his conduct
and his actions deserve.

[11]'The partridge will hatch eggs
it has not laid.
No different is the person
who gets riches unjustly:
his days half done, they will desert him
and he prove a fool after all.'

Confidence in the Temple and in Yahweh

[12]A glorious throne,
sublime from the beginning,
such is our Holy Place.
[13]Yahweh, hope of Israel,
all who abandon you will be put to shame,
those who turn from you
will be registered in the underworld,
since they have abandoned Yahweh,
the fountain of living water.

A prayer for vengeance

[14]Heal me, Yahweh, and I shall be healed,
save me, and I shall be saved,
for you are my praise.
[15]Look, they keep saying to me,
'Where is Yahweh's word?
Let it come true then!'
[16]Yet I have never urged you to send disaster,
I never desired the fatal day,
this you know;
what came from my lips
was not concealed from you.
[17]Do not be a terror to me,
you, my refuge in time of disaster.
[18]Let my persecutors be confounded,
not me,
let them, not me, be terrified.
On them bring the day of disaster,
destroy them, destroy them twice over!

Observance of the Sabbath

[19]Yahweh said this to me, 'Go and stand at
the Gate of the Sons of the People by which
the kings of Judah go in and out—and at
all the gates of Jerusalem. [20]Say to them,
"Listen to the word of Yahweh, you kings of
Judah, all you people of Judah too, and
all you inhabitants of Jerusalem who pass
through the gates. [21]Yahweh says this: As
you value your lives, on no account carry a
burden on the Sabbath day or bring it in
through the gates of Jerusalem. [22]Bring no
burden out of your houses on the Sabbath
day, and do no work. Keep the Sabbath day
holy, as I ordered your ancestors. [23]They
would not hear, would not pay attention;
they deliberately refused to listen or accept
instruction. [24]But if you listen carefully to
me, Yahweh declares, and bring no burden
in through the gates of this city on the Sabbath
day, if you keep the Sabbath holy and do no
work on that day, [25]then, through the gates
of this city, kings and princes occupying the
throne of David will continue to make their
entry, riding in chariots or on horseback,
they, their chief men, the people of Judah
and the inhabitants of Jerusalem. And this
city will be inhabited for ever. [26]They will
come from the towns of Judah, from the
districts round Jerusalem, from the territory
of Benjamin, from the lowlands, from the
highlands, from the Negeb, to offer burnt
offering and sacrifice, and cereal offering and
incense, to offer thanksgiving sacrifices in
the Temple of Yahweh. [27]But if you do not
listen to me to keep the Sabbath day holy,
and to refrain from entering the gates of
Jerusalem with burdens on the Sabbath day,
then I shall set fire to its gates; fire will
devour the palaces of Jerusalem and not be
quenched." '

Jeremiah visits the potter

18 The word that came to Jeremiah from
Yahweh as follows, [2]'Get up and make
your way down to the potter's house, and
there I shall tell you what I have to say.' [3]So
I went down to the potter's house; and there
he was, working at the wheel. [4]But the vessel
he was making came out wrong, as may
happen with clay when a potter is at work.
So he began again and shaped it into another
vessel, as he thought fit. [5]Then the word of
Yahweh came to me as follows, [6]'House of
Israel, can I not do to you what this potter
does? Yahweh demands. Yes, like clay in the
potter's hand, so you are in mine, House of
Israel. [7]Sometimes I announce that I shall
uproot, break down and destroy a certain
nation or kingdom, [8]but should the nation I
have threatened abandon its wickedness, I

then change my mind about the disaster
which I had intended to inflict on it.
9 Sometimes I announce that I shall build up
and plant a certain nation or kingdom, 10 but
should that nation do what displeases me and
refuse to listen to my voice, I then change my
mind about the good which I was intending
to confer on it. 11 So now, say this to the people
of Judah and the inhabitants of Jerusalem,
"Yahweh says this: Listen, I am preparing a
disaster for you, I am working out a plan
against you. So now, each one of you, turn
back from your evil ways, amend your
conduct and actions." 12 They, however, will
say, "It is no use! We shall follow our own
plans; each of us will act on his own wicked
inclinations." '

About Israel's repudiation of Yahweh

13 Therefore, Yahweh says this,
'Ask, please, among the nations
if anyone has heard anything like this.
The Virgin of Israel
has done a very horrible thing.
14 Does the snow of Lebanon
ever leave the rocks of its slopes?
Do the rivers of foreign lands,
their cold flowing waters, ever run dry?
15 And yet my people have forgotten me!
They burn incense to a Nothing!
They have been made to stumble
in their ways,
the ancient paths,
to walk in paths,
on an unmade road,
16 to make their country an object of horror,
everlastingly derided:
every passer-by will be appalled at it
and shake his head.
17 Like the east wind, I shall scatter them
before the enemy.
I shall show them my back, not my face,
the day they are ruined.'

A plot against Jeremiah

18 'Come on,' they said, 'let us concoct a plot
against Jeremiah, for the Law will not perish
for lack of priests, nor advice for lack of wise
men, nor the word for lack of prophets. Come
on, let us slander him and pay no attention
to anything he says.'

19 Pay attention to me, Yahweh,
hear what my adversaries are saying.
20 Should evil be returned for good?
Now they are digging a pit for me.
Remember how I pleaded before you
and spoke good of them,
to turn your retribution away from them.
21 So, hand their sons over to famine,
abandon them to the edge of the sword.
Let their wives become
childless and widowed.
Let their husbands die of plague,
their young men be cut down
by the sword in battle.
22 Let cries re-echo from their houses
as you bring raiders suddenly on them.
For they have dug a pit to catch me,
they have laid snares to trap my feet.
23 But you, Yahweh, know
all about their murderous plot against me.
Do not forgive their guilt,
do not efface their sin from your sight.
Let them be hurled down before you,
deal with them while you are angry!

The broken jug and the altercation with Pashhur

19 Then Yahweh said to Jeremiah, 'Go
and buy a potter's earthenware jug.
Take some of the people's elders and some
of the senior priests with you. 2 Go out
towards the Valley of Ben-Hinnom, just
outside the Gate of the Potsherds. There
proclaim the words I shall say to you. 3 You
must say, "Kings of Judah, inhabitants of
Jerusalem! Listen to the word of Yahweh!
Yahweh Sabaoth, the God of Israel, says this:
I am about to bring such a disaster on this
place that the ears of every one who hears of
it will ring. 4 For they have abandoned me
and have made this place unrecognisable,
and offered incense here to other gods which
neither they nor their ancestors nor the kings
of Judah ever knew before. They have filled
this place with the blood of the innocent; 5 for
they have built high places for Baal to burn
their sons as burnt offerings to Baal, a thing
I never ordered, never mentioned, that had
never entered my thoughts. 6 So now the days
are coming, Yahweh declares, when people
will no longer call this place Topheth, or
Valley of Ben-Hinnom, but Valley of
Slaughter. 7 Because of this place, I shall
empty Judah and Jerusalem of sound advice;
I shall make them fall by the sword before
their enemies, by the hand of those deter-
mined to kill them; I shall give their corpses

as food to the birds of the sky and the animals of earth. 8 And I shall make this city an object of horror and derision; every passer-by will be appalled at it and whistle at the sight of all the wounds it has sustained. 9 I shall make them eat the flesh of their own sons and daughters: they will eat one another during the siege, in the shortage to which their enemies, and those determined to kill them, will reduce them."

10 'You must break this jug in front of the men who are with you, 11 and say to them, "Yahweh Sabaoth says this: I am going to break this people and this city just as one breaks a potter's pot, so that it can never be mended again.

"Topheth will become a burial ground, for lack of other burial space. 12 That is how I shall treat this place, Yahweh declares, and its inhabitants, by making this city like Topheth. 13 The houses of Jerusalem and those of the kings of Judah, all the houses on the roofs of which they offered incense to the whole array of heaven and poured libations to other gods, will be unclean, like this place Topheth." '

14 Jeremiah then came back from Topheth where Yahweh had sent him to prophesy, and stood in the court of the Temple of Yahweh and said to all the people, 15 'Yahweh Sabaoth, the God of Israel, says this, "Yes, on this city, and on all the towns belonging to it, I shall bring all the disaster which I had decreed for it, since they have stubbornly refused to listen to my words." '

20 Now the priest Pashhur son of Immer, who was the chief of police in the Temple of Yahweh, heard Jeremiah making this prophecy. 2 Pashhur struck the prophet Jeremiah and then put him in the stocks, in the Upper Benjamin Gate leading into the Temple of Yahweh. 3 Next day, Pashhur had Jeremiah taken out of the stocks; Jeremiah then said to him, 'Not Pashhur but Terror-on-every-Side is Yahweh's name for you. 4 For Yahweh says this, "I am going to hand you over to terror, you and all your friends; they will fall by the sword of their enemies, your own eyes will see it. The whole of Judah, too, I shall hand over to the king of Babylon; he will carry them off captive to Babylon and put them to the sword. 5 And all the wealth of this city, all its stores, all its valuables, all the treasures of the kings of Judah, I shall hand over to their enemies who will plunder them, round them up and carry them off to Babylon. 6 As for you, Pashhur, and your whole household, you will go into captivity; you will go to Babylon; there you will die, and there be buried, you and all your friends to whom you have prophesied lies." '

Selections from the 'Confessions' of Jeremiah

7 You have seduced me, Yahweh,
and I have let myself be seduced;
you have overpowered me:
you were the stronger.
I am a laughing-stock all day long,
they all make fun of me.
8 For whenever I speak, I have to howl
and proclaim, 'Violence and ruin!'
For me, Yahweh's word has been the cause
of insult and derision all day long.
9 I would say to myself,
'I will not think about him,
I will not speak in his name any more,'
but then there seemed to be a fire
burning in my heart,
imprisoned in my bones.
The effort to restrain it wearied me,
I could not do it.
10 I heard so many disparaging me,
'Terror on every side!
Denounce him! Let us denounce him!'
All those who were on good terms with me
watched for my downfall,
'Perhaps he will be seduced into error.
Then we shall get the better of him
and take our revenge!'
11 But Yahweh is at my side
like a mighty hero;
my opponents will stumble, vanquished,
confounded by their failure;
everlasting, unforgettable disgrace
will be theirs.
12 Yahweh Sabaoth,
you[a] who test the upright,
observer of motives and thoughts,
I shall see your vengeance on them,
for I have revealed my cause to you.
13 Sing to Yahweh,
praise Yahweh,
for he has delivered the soul of one in need
from the clutches of evil doers.

14 A curse on the day when I was born!

20a =11:20.

May the day my mother bore me
be unblessed!
15 A curse on the man
who brought my father the news,
'A son, a boy has been born to you!'
making him overjoyed.
16 May this man be like the towns
that Yahweh overthrew without mercy;
may he hear the warning-cry at dawn
and the shout of battle at high noon,
17 for not killing me in the womb;
my mother would have been my grave
and her womb pregnant for ever.
18 Why ever did I come out of the womb
to see toil and sorrow
and end my days in shame?

C: PROPHECIES MAINLY LATER THAN THE REIGN OF JEHOIAKIM

Jeremiah answers the envoys of Zedekiah

21 The word that came to Jeremiah from
Yahweh when King Zedekiah sent
Pashhur[a] son of Malchiah to him, with the
priest Zephaniah son of Maaseiah, to say
this, 2 'Please consult Yahweh for us, since
Nebuchadnezzar king of Babylon is making
war on us: perhaps Yahweh will work one of
his many miracles for us and force him to
withdraw.' 3 Jeremiah said to them, 'Take
this answer to Zedekiah, 4 "Yahweh, God
of Israel, says this: I shall bring back the
weapons of war which you are now carrying,
and with which you are fighting the king of
Babylon and the Chaldaeans now besieging
you; from outside the walls, I shall stack
them in the centre of this city. 5 And I shall
fight against you myself with outstretched
hand and mighty arm, in anger, fury and
great wrath. 6 I shall strike down the inhabi-
tants of this city, human and animal; they
will die of a great plague. 7 Then, Yahweh
declares, I shall deliver Zedekiah king of
Judah, his officials, the people and those of
this city who have escaped the plague, the
sword, or the famine, into the clutches of
Nebuchadnezzar king of Babylon, into the
clutches of their enemies and into the clutches
of those determined to kill them; mercilessly,
relentlessly, pitilessly, he will put them to
the sword."
8 'And you must say to this people,
"Yahweh says this: Look, I offer you a choice
between the way of life and the way of death.
9 Anyone who stays in this city will die by
sword, by famine, or by plague; but anyone
who leaves it and surrenders to the Chal-
daeans now besieging you will live; he will
escape with his life.[b] 10 For I am determined
on disaster, and not prosperity, for this city,
Yahweh declares. It will be handed over to
the king of Babylon, and he will burn it
down." '

Address to the royal family of Judah

11 To the royal House of Judah. Listen to the
word of Yahweh, 12 House of David! Yahweh
says this:

Each morning give fair judgement,
rescue anyone who has been wronged
from the hands of his oppressor,
or else my wrath will leap out like a fire,
it will burn and no one
will be able to quench it,
because of the wickedness
of your actions.[c]
13 My quarrel is with you,
resident of the valley,
Rock-in-the-Plain,
Yahweh declares,
with you that say,
'Who would dare attack us
and enter our lairs?'
14 I shall punish you as your actions deserve,
Yahweh declares,
I shall set fire to its forest
and it will devour all around it.

22 Yahweh said this, 'Go down to the
palace of the king of Judah and there say
this word, 2 "Listen to the word of Yahweh,
king of Judah now occupying the throne of
David, you, your officials and your people
who go through these gates. 3 Yahweh says
this: Act uprightly and justly; rescue from
the hands of the oppressor anyone who has
been wronged, do not exploit or ill-treat the
stranger, the orphan, the widow; shed no
innocent blood in this place. 4 For if you are
scrupulous in obeying this command, then
kings occupying the throne of David will

21a Not to be confused with the Pashhur of ch. 20, a different person.
21b =38:2.
21c =4:4.

continue to make their entry through the gates of this palace riding in chariots or on horseback, they, their officials and their
people. [5]But if you do not listen to these words, then I swear by myself, Yahweh declares, this palace shall become a ruin!
[6]"Yes, this is what Yahweh says about the palace of the king of Judah:

You are like Gilead to me,
like a peak of Lebanon.
All the same, I will reduce you to a desert,
to uninhabited towns.
[7]I dedicate men to destroy you,
each man with his weapons;
they will cut down your finest cedars
and throw them on the fire.

[8]"And when many nations pass this city, they will say to one another: Why has Yahweh treated this great city like this? [9]And the
answer will be: Because they abandoned the covenant of Yahweh their God to worship other gods and serve them." '

Prophecies against various kings: against Jehoahaz

[10]Do not weep for the man who is dead,
do not raise the dirge for him.
Weep rather for the one
who has gone away,
since he will never come back,
never see his native land again.

[11]For this is what Yahweh has said about Shallum son of Josiah, king of Judah, who succeeded Josiah his father and was forced to leave this place, 'He will never come back to it
[12]but will die in the place to which he has been taken captive; and he will never see this country again.

Against Jehoiakim

[13]'Disaster for the man
who builds his house
without uprightness,
his upstairs rooms without fair judgement,
who makes his fellow-man
work for nothing,
without paying him his wages,
[14]who says,
"I shall build myself a spacious palace
with airy upstairs rooms,"
who makes windows in it,
panels it with cedar,
and paints it vermilion.
[15]Are you more of a king
because of your passion for cedar?
Did your father go hungry or thirsty?
But he did what is just and upright,
so all went well for him.
[16]He used to examine the cases
of poor and needy,
then all went well.
Is not that what it means to know me?
Yahweh demands.
[17]You on the other hand have eyes and heart
for nothing but your own interests,
for shedding innocent blood
and perpetrating violence and oppression.'

[18]That is why Yahweh says this about Jehoiakim son of Josiah, king of Judah:

'No lamenting for him,
"My poor brother! My poor sister!"
No lamenting for him,
"His poor lordship! His poor majesty!"
[19]He will have a donkey's funeral
—dragged away and thrown
out of the gates of Jerusalem.'

Against Jehoiachin

[20]'Climb the Lebanon range and shriek,
raise your voice in Bashan,
shriek from the Abarim,
for all your lovers have been ruined!
[21]I spoke to you in your prosperity,
but you said, "I will not listen!"
From your youth
this has been how you behaved,
refusing to listen to my voice.
[22]The wind will shepherd
all your shepherds away
and your lovers will go into captivity.
Then you will blush deep with shame
at the thought of all your wickedness.
[23]You who have made
the Lebanon your home
and made your nest among the cedars,
how you will groan
when anguish overtakes you,
pangs like those of a woman in labour!

[24]'As I live, Yahweh declares, even if Coniah[a] son of Jehoiakim, king of Judah, were the signet ring on my right hand, I would still wrench you off!
[25]I shall hand you

22a Alternative name for Jeconiah.

over to those determined to kill you, to
those you dread, to Nebuchadnezzar king of
Babylon, to the Chaldaeans. 26I shall hurl you
and the mother who bore you into another
country; you were not born there but you
will both die there. 27They will not return to
the country to which they desperately long
to return.'

28Is he a shoddy broken pot,
this man Coniah,
a crock that no one wants?
Why are he and his offspring ejected,
hurled into a country
they know nothing of?
29O land, land, land,
listen to the word of Yahweh!
30Yahweh says this,
'List this man as: Childless;
a man who made a failure of his life,
since none of his offspring will succeed
in occupying the throne of David,
or ruling in Judah again.'

Messianic prophecies. The future king

23 'Disaster for the shepherds who lose
and scatter the sheep of my pasture,
Yahweh declares. 2This, therefore, is what
Yahweh, God of Israel, says about the
shepherds who shepherd my people, "You
have scattered my flock, you have driven
them away and have not taken care of them.
Right, I shall take care of you for your
misdeeds, Yahweh declares! 3But the
remnant of my flock I myself shall gather
from all the countries where I have driven
them, and bring them back to their folds;
they will be fruitful and increase in numbers.
4For them I shall raise up shepherds to
shepherd them and pasture them. No fear,
no terror for them any more; not one shall be
lost, Yahweh declares!

5Look, the days are coming,
Yahweh declares,
when I shall raise an upright Branch
for David;
he will reign as king and be wise,
doing what is just and upright
in the country.
6In his days Judah will triumph
and Israel live in safety.
And this is the name[a] he will be called,
'Yahweh-is-our-Saving-Justice.' "

7'So, look, the days are coming, Yahweh
declares, when people will no longer say, "As
Yahweh lives who brought the Israelites out
of Egypt," 8but, "As Yahweh lives who led
back and brought home the offspring of the
House of Israel from the land of the north
and all the countries to which he had driven
them, to live on their own soil." '[b]

A tract against the false prophets

9On the prophets.

My heart is broken within me,
I tremble in all my bones;
I am like a drunken man,
like a man overcome with wine,
because of Yahweh and his holy words:

10'For the country is full of adulterers;
yes, because of a curse,
the country is in mourning
and the pasturage in the desert
has dried up;
they are prompt to do wrong,
make no effort to do right.
11Yes, even prophet and priest are godless,
I have detected their wickedness
in my own House,
Yahweh declares.
12Because of this, their way will prove
treacherous going for them;
in the darkness where they are driven,
there they will fall.
For I shall bring disaster on them,
when the year for punishing them comes,
Yahweh declares.

13'In the prophets of Samaria
I have seen insanity:
they prophesied in the name of Baal
and led my people Israel astray.
14But in the prophets of Jerusalem
I have seen something horrible:
adultery, persistent lying,
such abetting of the wicked
that no one renounces his wickedness.
To me they are all like Sodom
and its inhabitants are like Gomorrah.
15So this is what Yahweh Sabaoth
says about the prophets,
"Now I shall give them wormwood to eat

23a This messianic title contrasts with Zedekiah (=Yahweh is my Saving Justice), cf. 33:15–16.
23b =16:14–15.

and make them drink poisoned water,[c]
since from the prophets of Jerusalem
godlessness has spread
throughout the land."

16'Yahweh Sabaoth says this,
"Do not listen to what those prophets
prophesy to you;
they are deluding you,
they retail visions of their own,
and not what comes
from Yahweh's mouth.
17To those who despise me,
they keep saying:
Yahweh has spoken: you will have peace!
and to all who follow
their own stubborn inclinations:
No disaster will touch you."

18But who has been present in Yahweh's
council and seen, and heard his word? Who
has paid attention to his word and listened
to it?

19Look, Yahweh's hurricane,
his wrath, bursts out,
a fearsome hurricane,
to burst on the heads of the wicked;
20Yahweh's anger will not withdraw
until he has performed, has carried out,
what he has in mind.
In the final days,
you will understand this clearly,[d]
21'I did not send these prophets,
yet they ran!
I did not speak to them,
yet they prophesied!
22Had they been present in my council,
they could have proclaimed my words
to my people
and turned them from their evil way
and from the wickedness of their deeds!

23'Am I a God when near, Yahweh demands,
and not a God when far away?
24Can anyone hide somewhere secret
without my seeing him? Yahweh demands.
Do I not fill heaven and earth?
Yahweh demands.

25'I have heard what the prophets say who
make their lying prophecies in my name. "I
have had a dream," they say, "I have had a
dream!" 26How long are there to be those
among the prophets who prophesy lies and
are in fact prophets of their own delusions?
27They are doing their best, by means of the
dreams that they keep telling each other, to
make my people forget my name, just as
their ancestors forgot my name in favour
of Baal. 28Let the prophet who has had a
dream tell it for a dream! And let him who
receives a word from me, deliver my word
accurately!

'What have straw and wheat in common?
Yahweh demands.
29Is my word not like fire,
Yahweh demands,
is it not like a hammer shattering a rock?

30'So, then, I have a quarrel with the
prophets, Yahweh declares, that steal my
words from one another. 31I have a quarrel
with the prophets, Yahweh declares, who
wag their tongues to utter prophecies. 32I
have a quarrel with the prophets who make
prophecies out of lying dreams, Yahweh
declares, who recount them, and lead my
people astray by their lies and their bragging.
I certainly never sent them or commissioned
them, and they serve no good purpose for
this people, Yahweh declares.

33'And when this people, or a prophet,
or a priest, asks you, "What is Yahweh's
burden?" you must answer, "You are the
burden, and I shall get rid of you, Yahweh
declares!"

34'As for the prophet, the priest, or anyone
else, who says, "Yahweh's burden", I shall
punish that man, and his household too.
35This is what you must say to one another,
among yourselves, "What answer has
Yahweh given?" or "What has Yahweh
said?" 36But stop using the expression
"Yahweh's burden", for what each man says
will be his own responsibility. And you twist
the words of the living God, of Yahweh
Sabaoth, our God. 37This is the way to speak
to a prophet, "What answer has Yahweh
given?" or "What has Yahweh said?" 38But
if you say, "Yahweh's burden", then Yahweh
says this, "Since you use the expression
'Yahweh's burden', when I have warned you
to stop saying, 'Yahweh's burden', 39believe
me, I shall pick you up and fling you from
my presence, you and the city I gave to you
and to your ancestors. 40I shall bring down
everlasting shame on you, everlasting and
unforgettable disgrace." '

23c =9:14.
23d =30:23–24.

The two baskets of figs[a]

24 Yahweh gave me a vision: set out in front of the Temple of Yahweh were two baskets of figs. This was after Nebuchadnezzar king of Babylon had led Jeconiah son of Jehoiakim, king of Judah, away into exile from Jerusalem, with the chief men of Judah, the blacksmiths and metalworkers, and had taken them to Babylon. 2One basket contained excellent figs, like those that ripen first; the other contained very bad figs, so bad they were uneatable. 3Yahweh said to me, 'What do you see, Jeremiah?' 'Figs,' I answered, 'the good ones excellent, the bad ones very bad, so bad as to be uneatable.' 4Then the word of Yahweh was addressed to me, 5'Yahweh, the God of Israel, says this, "As these figs are good, so I mean to concern myself with the welfare of the exiles of Judah whom I have sent from this place to the country of the Chaldaeans. 6My eyes will watch over them for their good, to bring them back to this country, to build them up and not to break them down, to plant them and not to uproot them. 7I shall give them a heart to acknowledge that I am Yahweh. They will be my people and I shall be their God, for they will return to me with all their heart. 8As for the bad figs, the figs so bad as to be uneatable—yes, Yahweh says this—that is how I shall treat Zedekiah king of Judah, his chief men and what is left of Jerusalem, those who remain in this country and those living in Egypt. 9I shall make them an object of horror, a disaster, to all the kingdoms of the earth, a thing of shame, a byword, a laughing-stock, a curse, wherever I shall drive them. 10Sword, famine and plague I shall send against them until they have vanished from the soil I gave to them and to their ancestors." '

D: BABYLON
THE SCOURGE OF YAHWEH

25 The word that was addressed to Jeremiah about all the people of Judah in the fourth year of Jehoiakim son of Josiah, king of Judah (that is to say the first year of Nebuchadnezzar king of Babylon). 2The prophet Jeremiah proclaimed it before all the people of Judah and all the inhabitants of Jerusalem:

3'For twenty-three years, from the thirteenth year of Josiah son of Amon, king of Judah, until today, the word of Yahweh has been addressed to me and I have never tired of speaking to you (but you have not listened. 4Furthermore, Yahweh has untiringly sent you all his servants the prophets, but you have not listened or paid attention). 5The message was this, "Turn back, each one of you, from your evil behaviour and your evil actions, and you will go on living on the soil Yahweh long ago gave to you and your ancestors for ever. 6(And do not follow other gods to serve and worship them, do not provoke me with things you yourselves have made, and then I shall not harm you.) 7But you have not listened to me (Yahweh declares, so that you have now provoked me with things you yourselves have made, and thus harmed yourselves)."

8'So—this is what Yahweh Sabaoth says, "Since you have not listened to my words, 9I shall now send for all the families of the north (Yahweh declares, that is, for Nebuchadnezzar king of Babylon, my servant) and bring them down on this country and its inhabitants (and on all these surrounding nations); I shall curse them with utter destruction and make them an object of horror, of scorn, and ruin them for ever. 10From them I shall banish the shouts of rejoicing and mirth, the voices of bridegroom and bride, the sound of the handmill and the light of the lamp; 11and this whole country will be reduced to ruin and desolation, and these nations will be enslaved to the king of Babylon for seventy years. 12(But when the seventy years are over, I shall punish the king of Babylon and that nation, Yahweh declares, for the wrong they have done, that is, the country of the Chaldaeans, and make it desolate for ever), 13and against that country I shall perform all the words with which I have threatened it, that is, everything written in this book." '

24a || Ezk 11:14–21.

II: INTRODUCTION TO THE PROPHECIES AGAINST THE NATIONS

The vision of the cup

What Jeremiah prophesied against all the nations.
14('For these in their turn are to be enslaved
to powerful nations and great kings, and
I shall pay them back as their deeds and
handiwork deserve.')
15For Yahweh, the God of Israel, said this
to me, 'Take this cup of the wine of wrath
and make all the nations to whom I send you
drink it; 16they will drink and reel and lose
their wits, because of the sword I am sending
among them.' 17I took the cup from Yahweh's
hand and made all the nations to whom
Yahweh sent me drink it 18(Jerusalem and
the towns of Judah, its kings and its chief
men, to make them a ruin, an object of horror
and derision and a curse, as is the case today):
19Pharaoh king of Egypt, his officials, his
chief men and all his people, 20with the whole
conglomeration of peoples there (all the kings
of the country of Uz); all the kings of the
country of the Philistines, Ashkelon, Gaza,
Ekron and what is still left of Ashdod;
21Edom, Moab and the Ammonites; 22(all)
the kings of Tyre, (all) the kings of Sidon, the
kings of the island across the sea; 23Dedan,
Tema, Buz, all the people with shaven
temples; 24all the kings of Arabia (and all the
kings of the conglomeration of peoples) who
live in the desert 25(all the kings of Zimri), all
the kings of Elam, and all the kings of Media;
26all the kings of the north, near and far, one
after another: in short, all the kingdoms on
the face of the earth. (As for the king of
Sheshak, he will drink last of all.)
27'You will say to them, "Yahweh Sabaoth,
the God of Israel, says this: Drink! Get
drunk! Vomit! Fall, never to rise again,
before the sword that I am sending among
you!" 28If they refuse to take the cup from
your hand and drink, you will say to them,
"Yahweh Sabaoth says this: You must drink!
29Look, for a start, I am bringing disaster on
the city that bears my name, so are you likely
to go unpunished? You certainly will not go
unpunished, for next I shall summon a sword
against all the inhabitants of the land,
Yahweh declares."
30'For your part, you are to prophesy all
these words to them. Say to them:

"Yahweh roars from on high,
he thunders from his holy dwelling-place,
loudly he roars at his own fold,
shouts aloud
like those who tread the grape
at all the inhabitants of the land.
31The noise resounds
to the remotest parts of the earth.
For Yahweh is indicting the nations,
arraigning all humanity for judgement;
the wicked he assigns to the sword,
Yahweh declares.
32Yahweh Sabaoth says this:
Look, disaster is spreading
from nation to nation,
a mighty tempest is rising
from the far ends of the earth.

33"Those slaughtered by Yahweh that day
will be scattered across the world from end
to end. No dirge will be raised for them; no
one will gather them or bury them; they will
stay lying on the surface like dung.[a]

34"Howl, shepherds, shriek,
roll on the ground, you lords of the flock,
for your days have come to be slaughtered
and to be scattered,
and like a choice vase you will fall.
35No refuge then for the shepherds,
no escape for the lords of the flock!
36Listen! A shriek from the shepherds,
a howl from the lords of the flock!
For Yahweh has laid their pasture waste,
37the peaceful sheepfolds
are reduced to silence
owing to Yahweh's furious anger.
38The lion has left his lair
and their country is a wasteland now,
owing to the devastating fury,
owing to his furious anger." '

25a =8:2.

III: PROPHECIES OF HAPPINESS

A: INTRODUCTION: JEREMIAH THE TRUE PROPHET

Arrest and trial of Jeremiah

26 At the beginning of the reign of Jehoi-
akim son of Josiah, king of Judah,
this word came to Jeremiah from Yahweh,
2'Yahweh says this, "Stand in the court of
the Temple of Yahweh. To all the people
from the towns of Judah who come to worship
in the Temple of Yahweh you will say every-
thing I have ordered you to say, not omitting
one syllable. 3Perhaps they will listen and
each turn from his evil way: if so, I shall
relent and not bring the disaster on them
which I intend because of their misdeeds."
4Say to them, "Yahweh says this: If you will
not listen to me and follow my Law which I
have given you, 5and pay attention to the
words of my servants the prophets whom I
have never tired of sending to you, although
you never have paid attention, 6I shall treat
this Temple as I treated Shiloh, and make
this city a curse for all the nations of the
world." '

7The priests and prophets and all the
people heard Jeremiah say these words in
the Temple of Yahweh. 8When Jeremiah had
finished saying everything that Yahweh had
ordered him to say to all the people, the
priests and prophets and all the people seized
hold of him and said, 'You will die for
this! 9Why have you made this prophecy in
Yahweh's name, "This Temple will become
like Shiloh, and this city become an unin-
habited ruin"?' And the people all crowded
in on Jeremiah in the Temple of Yahweh.
10Hearing of this, the chief men of Judah
came up from the royal palace to the Temple
of Yahweh and took their seats at the entry
of the New Gate of the Temple of Yahweh.

11The priests and prophets then said to the
chief men and all the people, 'This man
deserves to die, since he has prophesied
against this city, as you have heard with your
own ears.' 12Jeremiah, however, replied to
all the chief men and all the people as follows,
'Yahweh himself sent me to prophesy against
this Temple and this city all the things you
have heard. 13So now amend your behaviour
and actions, listen to the voice of Yahweh
your God, and Yahweh will relent about the
disaster that he has decreed for you. 14For
myself, I am, as you see, in your hands. Do
whatever you please or think right with me.
15But be sure of this, that if you put me to
death, you will be bringing innocent blood on
yourselves, on this city and on its inhabitants,
since Yahweh has truly sent me to you to say
all this for you to hear.'

16The chief men and all the people then
said to the priests and prophets, 'This man
does not deserve to die: he has spoken to us
in the name of Yahweh our God.' 17And some
of the country's elders rose to address all the
assembled people. 18'Micah of Moresheth,'
they said, 'who prophesied in the days of
Hezekiah king of Judah, had this to say to all
the people of Judah, "Yahweh Sabaoth says
this:

Zion will become ploughland,
Jerusalem a heap of rubble
and the Temple Mount a wooded height."[a]

19'Did Hezekiah king of Judah and all
Judah put him to death for this? Did they
not rather, fearing Yahweh, plead with him,
to such effect that Yahweh relented about
the disaster which he had decreed for them?
Are we now to burden our souls with such a
crime?'

20There was another man, too, who used
to prophesy in Yahweh's name, Uriah son of
Shemaiah, from Kiriath-Jearim. He proph-
esied exactly the same things against this city
and this country as Jeremiah. 21When King
Jehoiakim with all his officers and all the
chief men heard what he said, the king was
determined to put him to death. On hearing
this, Uriah took fright and, fleeing, escaped
to Egypt. 22King Jehoiakim, however, sent
Elnathan son of Achbor to Egypt with others,
23who brought Uriah back from Egypt and
took him to King Jehoiakim, who had him
put to the sword and his body thrown into
the common burial ground. 24But Jeremiah
had a protector in Ahikam son of Shaphan,
so he was not handed over to the people to
be put to death.

26a =Mi 3:12.

B: THE PAMPHLET FOR THE EXILES

The symbolic yoke and the message to the neighbouring kings

27 (At the beginning of the reign of Zedek-
iah son of Josiah, king of Judah, this
word came to Jeremiah from Yahweh:)
2Yahweh said this to me, 'Make yourself
thongs and yokes and put them on your neck.
3Then send them to the king of Edom, the
king of Moab, the king of the Ammonites,
the king of Tyre, and the king of Sidon,
through their envoys accredited to Zedekiah
king of Judah in Jerusalem. 4Give them the
following message for their masters,
"Yahweh Sabaoth, God of Israel, says this:
You must tell your masters this: 5I by my
great power and outstretched arm made the
earth, the human beings and the animals that
are on earth, and I give them to whom I
please. 6For the present, I have handed all
these countries over to Nebuchadnezzar king
of Babylon, my servant; I have even put the
wild animals at his service. 7(All the nations
will serve him, his son and his grandson,
until the time for his own country comes in
its turn, when mighty nations and great kings
will enslave him.) 8Any nation or kingdom
that will not serve Nebuchadnezzar king of
Babylon and will not bow its neck to the yoke
of the king of Babylon, I shall punish that
nation with sword, famine and plague,
Yahweh declares, until I have destroyed it by
his hand. 9For your own part, do not listen
to your prophets, your diviners, dreamers,
magicians and sorcerers, who tell you: You
will not be enslaved by the king of Babylon.
10They prophesy lies to you, the result of
which will be that you will be banished from
your soil, that I shall drive you out, and you
will perish. 11The nation, however, that is
prepared to bend its neck to the yoke of the
king of Babylon and serve him, I shall leave
in peace on its own soil, Yahweh declares, to
farm it and stay on it." '
12To Zedekiah king of Judah I spoke in
exactly the same terms. 'Bend your necks', I
told him, 'to the yoke of the king of Babylon;
serve him and his people and you will survive.
13(Why so anxious to die, you and your
people, by sword, famine and plague, with
which Yahweh has threatened the nation
refusing to serve the king of Babylon?) 14Do
not listen to the words the prophets say to
you, "You will not be enslaved by the king
of Babylon." They prophesy lies to you.
15Since I have not sent them, Yahweh
declares, they prophesy untruths to you in
my name. The result will be that I shall drive
you out, you will perish, and so will the
prophets who prophesy to you.'
16I also spoke to the priests and to all this
people as follows, 'Yahweh says this, "Do
not listen to the words of your prophets who
prophesy to you as follows: Look, the vessels
of the Temple of Yahweh will very shortly be
brought back from Babylon. They prophesy
lies to you. 17(Do not listen to them; serve
the king of Babylon and you will survive.
Why should this city become a ruin?) 18If
they are real prophets, if Yahweh's word is
really with them, they ought now to be
pleading with Yahweh Sabaoth that the
remaining vessels in the Temple of Yahweh,
in the palace of the king of Judah and else-
where in Jerusalem, do not go to Babylon
too! 19For this is what Yahweh Sabaoth says
about (the pillars, the Sea, the stands and)
the other vessels still remaining in this city,
20those not carried off by Nebuchadnezzar
king of Babylon when he took Jeconiah son
of Jehoiakim, king of Judah, into exile from
Jerusalem to Babylon (with all the leading
men of Judah and Jerusalem). 21Yes, this is
what Yahweh Sabaoth, God of Israel, says
about the vessels still remaining in the
Temple of Yahweh, in the palace of the king
of Judah and elsewhere in Jerusalem: 22They
will be carried off to Babylon (and stay there
until the day I punish them), Yahweh
declares. (Then I shall bring them back and
restore them to this place.)" '

The dispute with Hananiah

28 That same year, at the beginning of the
reign of Zedekiah king of Judah, in the
fifth month of the fourth year, the prophet
Hananiah son of Azzur, a Gibeonite, spoke
as follows to Jeremiah in the Temple of
Yahweh in the presence of the priests and of
all the people, 2'Yahweh Sabaoth, the God of
Israel, says this, "I have broken the yoke of
the king of Babylon. 3In exactly two years'
time I shall bring back all the vessels of the
Temple of Yahweh which Nebuchadnezzar
king of Babylon took away from here and
carried off to Babylon. 4And I shall also bring
back Jeconiah son of Jehoiakim, king of
Judah and all the exiles of Judah who have

gone to Babylon, Yahweh declares, for I shall
break the yoke of the king of Babylon." '
5The prophet Jeremiah then replied to the
prophet Hananiah in front of the priests
and all the people present in the Temple of
Yahweh. 6'So be it!' the prophet Jeremiah
said, 'May Yahweh do so! May he fulfil the
words that you have prophesied and bring all
the vessels of the Temple of Yahweh and all
the exiles back to this place from Babylon.
7Listen carefully, however, to this word that
I am now going to say for you and all the
people to hear: 8From remote times, the
prophets who preceded you and me proph-
esied war, disaster and plague for many coun-
tries and for great kingdoms; 9the prophet
who prophesies peace can be recognised as
one truly sent by Yahweh only when his word
comes true.'
10The prophet Hananiah then snatched the
yoke off the neck of the prophet Jeremiah
and broke it. 11In front of all the people
Hananiah then said, 'Yahweh says this,
"This is how, in exactly two years' time, I
shall break the yoke of Nebuchadnezzar king
of Babylon and take it off the necks of all the
nations." ' At this, the prophet Jeremiah
went away.
12After the prophet Hananiah had broken
the yoke he had snatched off the prophet
Jeremiah's neck, the word of Yahweh came
to Jeremiah, 13'Go to Hananiah and tell him
this, "Yahweh says this: You have broken
the wooden yokes only to make iron yokes to
replace them! 14For Yahweh Sabaoth, the
God of Israel, says this: An iron yoke is what
I now lay on the necks of all these nations to
enslave them to Nebuchadnezzar king of
Babylon. (They will be enslaved to him; I
have even given him the wild animals.)" '
15The prophet Jeremiah said to the prophet
Hananiah, 'Listen carefully, Hananiah:
Yahweh has not sent you; and thanks to you
this people is now relying on what is false.
16And so, Yahweh says this, "I am going to
send you off the face of the earth: you will die
this year (since you have preached rebellion
against Yahweh)." '
17The prophet Hananiah died the same
year, in the seventh month.

The letter to the exiles

29 This is the text of the letter that the
prophet Jeremiah sent from Jerusalem
to those who were left of the elders in exile,
to the priests, the prophets and all the people
whom Nebuchadnezzar had deported from
Jerusalem to Babylon. 2This was after King
Jeconiah had left Jerusalem with the queen
mother, the eunuchs, the chief men of Judah
and Jerusalem, and the blacksmiths and
metalworkers. 3The letter was entrusted to
Elasah son of Shaphan and to Gemariah son
of Hilkiah, whom Zedekiah king of Judah
had sent to Babylon, to Nebuchadnezzar
king of Babylon. The letter said:

4"Yahweh Sabaoth, the God of Israel, says
this to all the exiles deported from Jeru-
salem to Babylon: 5Build houses, settle
down; plant gardens and eat what they
produce; 6marry and have sons and daugh-
ters; choose wives for your sons, find
husbands for your daughters so that these
can bear sons and daughters in their turn;
you must increase there and not decrease.
7Work for the good of the city to which I
have exiled you; pray to Yahweh on its
behalf, since on its welfare yours depends.
8For Yahweh Sabaoth, the God of Israel,
says this: Do not be deceived by the
prophets who are with you or by your
diviners; do not listen to the dreams you
have, 9since they prophesy lies to you in
my name. I have not sent them, Yahweh
declares. 10For Yahweh says this: When
the seventy years granted to Babylon are
over, I shall intervene on your behalf and
fulfil my favourable promise to you by
bringing you back to this place. 11Yes, I
know what plans I have in mind for you,
Yahweh declares, plans for peace, not for
disaster, to give you a future and a hope.
12When you call to me and come and pray
to me, I shall listen to you. 13When you
search for me, you will find me; when you
search wholeheartedly for me, 14I shall let
you find me (Yahweh declares. I shall
restore your fortunes and gather you in
from all the nations and wherever I have
driven you, Yahweh declares. I shall bring
you back to the place from which I exiled
you).

15'Since you say: Yahweh has raised up
prophets for us in Babylon—16this is what
Yahweh says about the king now occu-
pying the throne of David and all the
people living in this city, your brothers
who did not go with you into exile:
17Yahweh Sabaoth says this: I am now
going to send them sword, famine and

plague; I shall make them like rotten figs,
so bad as to be uneatable. 18 I shall pursue
them with sword, famine and plague. I
shall make them an object of terror to all
the kingdoms of the earth, a curse, a thing
of horror, scorn and derision to all the
nations where I have driven them,
19 because they have refused to listen to my
words, Yahweh declares, although I have
persistently sent them all my servants the
prophets; but they would not listen,
Yahweh declares. 20 But all you exiles,
whom I have sent from Jerusalem to
Babylon, listen to Yahweh's word!

21 'This is what Yahweh Sabaoth, God of
Israel, says about Ahab son of Kolaiah, and
Zedekiah son of Maaseiah, who prophesy
lies to you in my name: I shall hand them
over now to Nebuchadnezzar king of
Babylon who will put them to death before
your very eyes. 22 This curse, based on their
fate, will be used by all the exiles of Judah
in Babylon: May Yahweh treat you like
Zedekiah and Ahab, roasted alive by the
king of Babylon, 23 because they have done
a scandalous thing in Israel, committing
adultery with their neighbour's wives and
speaking lying words in my name without
orders from me. I know all the same and
am witness to it, Yahweh declares.'

Prophecy against Shemaiah

24 'And to Shemaiah of Nehelam you will
speak as follows: 25 Yahweh Sabaoth, God
of Israel, says this: Since you, on your own
initiative, have sent a letter to all the people
in Jerusalem, to the priest Zephaniah son
of Maaseiah (and to all the priests), saying:
26 Yahweh has appointed you priest in place
of the priest Jehoiada to keep order in the
Temple of Yahweh, to put any crazy fellow
posing as a prophet in the stocks and
collar, 27 why then have you not disciplined
Jeremiah of Anathoth, now posing as a
prophet to you? 28 Why, he has even sent
us a message in Babylon, saying: It will be
a long time. Build houses, settle down;
plant gardens and eat what they
produce.'. . .

29 (Now, after the priest Zephaniah had
read this letter to the prophet Jeremiah),
30 the word of Yahweh came then to Jeremiah
as follows, 31 'Send this message to all the
exiles, "This is what Yahweh says about
Shemaiah of Nehelam: Since Shemaiah has
prophesied to you without my sending him,
and since he has caused you to rely on what
is false 32 for that reason, Yahweh declares, I
shall punish Shemaiah of Nehelam and his
descendants; no male member of his family
will survive among this people to see the
happiness that I will bestow on my people
(Yahweh declares, since he has preached
rebellion against Yahweh)." '

C: THE BOOK OF CONSOLATION

Promise of recovery for Israel

30 The word which came to Jeremiah
from Yahweh, as follows, 2 'Yahweh,
God of Israel, says this, "Write for yourself
in a book all the words I have spoken to you.
3 For look, the days are coming, Yahweh
declares, when I shall bring back the captives
of my people Israel (and Judah), Yahweh
says. I shall make them come back and take
possession of the country I gave to their
ancestors." '

4 These are the words Yahweh spoke about
Israel (and Judah):

5 Yahweh says this:
We have heard a cry of panic,
of terror, not of peace.
6 Now ask and see:
can a man bear children?
Then why do I see each man
with his hands on his loins
like a woman in labour?
Why has every face grown pale?
7 Disaster! This is the great day,
no other like it:
a time of distress for Jacob,
though he will be saved from it.

8 (That day, Yahweh Sabaoth declares, I
shall break the yoke now on your neck and
snap your chains; and foreigners will enslave
you no more, 9 but Israel and Judah will serve
Yahweh their God, and David their king
whom I shall raise up for them.)

10 So do not be afraid, my servant Jacob,
Yahweh declares,
Israel, do not be alarmed:
for look, I shall rescue you
from distant countries
and your descendants from the country
where they are captive.

Jacob will return and be at peace,
secure, with no one to trouble him.
11 For I am with you to save you,
Yahweh declares,
I shall make an end of all the nations
where I have driven you,
but I shall not make an end of you,
only discipline you in moderation,
not to let you go quite unpunished.[a]

12 Yes, Yahweh says this:
Your wound is incurable,
your injury past healing.
13 There is no one to plead your cause;
for an ulcer there are remedies,
but for you no cure at all.
14 All your lovers have forgotten you,
they look for you no more.
Yes, I have struck you as an enemy strikes,
with cruel punishment
(because of your great guilt
and countless sins).
15 Why cry out because of your wound?
Your pain is incurable!
Because of your great guilt
and countless sins,
I have treated you like this.
16 But all those who devoured you
will be devoured,
all your enemies, all, go into captivity,
those who despoiled you will be despoiled,
and all who pillaged you be pillaged.
17 For I shall restore you to health
and heal your wounds, Yahweh declares,
you who used to be called 'Outcast',
'Zion for whom no one cares'.

18 Yahweh says this:
Look, I shall restore the tents of Jacob
and take pity on his dwellings:
the town will be rebuilt on its mound,
the stronghold where it ought to stand.
19 From them will come thanksgiving
and shouts of joy.
I shall make them increase,
they will not decrease;
I shall make them honoured,
no more to be humbled.
20 Their sons will be as once they were,
their community fixed firmly before me,
and I shall punish all their oppressors.
21 Their prince will be one of their own,
their ruler come from their own people,
and I shall permit him
to approach me freely;
for who, otherwise, would be so bold
as to approach me, Yahweh demands?
22 You will be my people
and I shall be your God.
23 Look, Yahweh's hurricane,
his wrath, bursts out,
a roaring hurricane,
to burst on the heads of the wicked;
24 Yahweh's burning anger will not turn aside
until he has performed, has carried out,
what he has in mind.
In the final days, you will understand this.[b]

31 When that time comes, Yahweh
declares, I shall be the God of all the
families of Israel, and they will be my people.

2 Yahweh says this:
They have found pardon in the desert,
those who have survived the sword.
Israel is marching to his rest.
3 Yahweh has appeared to me from afar;
I have loved you with an everlasting love
and so I still maintain
my faithful love for you.
4 I shall build you once more,
yes, you will be rebuilt,
Virgin of Israel!
Once more in your best attire,
and with your tambourines,
you will go out dancing gaily.
5 Once more you will plant vineyards
on the mountains of Samaria
(those who plant will themselves
enjoy the fruit).
6 Yes, a day will come
when the watchmen shout
on the mountains of Ephraim,
'Up! Let us go up to Zion,
to Yahweh our God!'

7 For Yahweh says this:
Shout with joy for Jacob!
Hail the chief of nations!
Proclaim! Praise! Shout,
'Yahweh has saved his people,
the remnant of Israel!'

8 Watch, I shall bring them back
from the land of the north
and gather them in
from the far ends of the earth.
With them, the blind and the lame,

30a =46:27–28.
30b =23:19–20.

women with child, women in labour,
all together: a mighty throng
will return here!
9 In tears they will return,
in prayer I shall lead them.
I shall guide them to streams of water,
by a smooth path
where they will not stumble.
For I am a father to Israel,
and Ephraim is my first-born son.

10 Listen, nations, to the word of Yahweh.
On the farthest coasts and islands
proclaim it, say,
'He who scattered Israel is gathering him,
will guard him as a shepherd
guarding his flock.'
11 For Yahweh has ransomed Jacob,
rescued him from a hand
stronger than his own.
12 They will come, shouting for joy
on the heights of Zion,
thronging towards Yahweh's lavish gifts,
for wheat, new wine and oil,
sheep and cattle;
they will be like a well-watered garden,
they will sorrow no more.
13 The young girl will then take pleasure
in the dance,
and young men and old alike;
I shall change their mourning
into gladness,
comfort them, give them joy
after their troubles;
14 I shall refresh my priests with rich food,
and my people will gorge themselves
on my lavish gifts,
Yahweh declares.

15 Yahweh says this:
A voice is heard in Ramah,
lamenting and weeping bitterly:
it is Rachel[a] weeping for her children,
refusing to be comforted for her children,
because they are no more.
16 Yahweh says this:
Stop your lamenting
dry your eyes,
for your labour will have a reward,
Yahweh declares,
and they will return
from the enemy's country.
17 There is hope for your future after all,
Yahweh declares,
your children will return
to their homeland.
18 I have indeed heard Ephraim's grieving,
'You flogged me, I took a flogging,
like a young, untrained bull.
Bring me back, let me come back,
for you are Yahweh my God!
19 For, since I turned away, I have repented;
having understood, I beat my breast.
I was deeply ashamed, I blushed,
aware of the disgrace
incurred when I was young.'
20 Is Ephraim, then, so dear a son to me,
a child so favoured,
that whenever I mention him
I remember him lovingly still?
That is why I yearn for him,
why I must take pity on him,
Yahweh declares.

21 Set up your signposts,
raise yourself landmarks,
fix your mind on the road,
the way by which you went.
Come home, Virgin of Israel,
come home to these towns of yours.
22 How long will you hesitate,
rebellious daughter?
For Yahweh is creating
something new on earth:
the Woman sets out
to find her Husband again.

Promise of restoration to Judah

23 Yahweh Sabaoth, the God of Israel, says
this, 'In the country of Judah and in its towns,
they will use these words once more, when I
bring their captives home:

"Yahweh bless you,
home of saving justice,
holy mountain!"

24 'And in this country, Judah and all its
towns, the ploughmen and those who wander
with their flocks, will live together, 25 for I
shall give the weary all they need and satisfy
all those whose strength has gone.'

26 At this, I awoke and saw
that my sleep had been sweet to me.

Israel and Judah

27 'Look, the days are coming, Yahweh
declares, when I shall sow the House of Israel

31a Ancestor of the deported tribe of Benjamin.

and the House of Judah with the seed both
of people and of cattle. 28And as I once
watched over them to uproot, to knock down,
to overthrow, destroy and bring disaster, so
now I shall watch over them to build and to
plant, Yahweh declares.

Individual retribution

29'In those days people will no longer say:

"The fathers have eaten unripe grapes;
the children's teeth are set on edge."[b]

30But each will die for his own guilt. Everyone
who eats unripe grapes will have his own
teeth set on edge.

The new covenant

31'Look, the days are coming, Yahweh
declares, when I shall make a new covenant
with the House of Israel (and the House of
Judah), 32but not like the covenant I made
with their ancestors the day I took them by
the hand to bring them out of Egypt, a
covenant which they broke, even though I
was their Master, Yahweh declares. 33No,
this is the covenant I shall make with the
House of Israel when those days have come,
Yahweh declares. Within them I shall plant
my Law, writing it on their hearts. Then I
shall be their God and they will be my people.
34There will be no further need for everyone
to teach neighbour or brother, saying,
"Learn to know Yahweh!" No, they will all
know me, from the least to the greatest,
Yahweh declares, since I shall forgive their
guilt and never more call their sin to mind.'

Israel will endure

35Yahweh who provides the sun
to shine by day,
who regulates moon and stars
to shine by night,
who stirs the sea, making its waves roar,
he whose name is Yahweh Sabaoth,
says this,
36'Were this established order
ever to pass away
before me, Yahweh declares,
then the race of Israel would also cease
being a nation for ever before me!'
37Yahweh says this,
'Were the heavens above
ever to be measured,
the foundations of the earth below
ever to be fathomed,
then I too would reject
the whole race of Israel
for all that they have done,
Yahweh declares.'

Jerusalem magnificently rebuilt

38'Look, the days are coming, Yahweh
declares, when the City will be rebuilt for
Yahweh, from the Tower of Hananel to the
Corner Gate. 39Then once again the meas-
uring line will stretch straight to the Hill of
Gareb, turning then to Goah. 40And the whole
valley, with its corpses and ashes, and all the
ground beside the ravine of the Kidron as far
as the corner of the Horse Gate, eastwards,
will be consecrated to Yahweh. It will never
be destroyed or demolished again.

D: ADDITIONS TO THE BOOK OF CONSOLATION

Jeremiah buys a field in token of future prosperity

32 The word that came to Jeremiah from
Yahweh in the tenth year of Zedekiah
king of Judah, which was the eighteenth year
of Nebuchadnezzar. 2The army of the king
of Babylon was then besieging Jerusalem,
and the prophet Jeremiah was confined in
the Court of the Guard in the king of Judah's
palace, 3where Zedekiah king of Judah had
confined him, saying, 'Why do you keep
prophesying like this, "Yahweh says this: I
am going to hand this city over to the king of
Babylon and he will capture it; 4and Zedekiah
king of Judah will not escape the clutches of
the Chaldaeans, but will certainly be handed
over to the king of Babylon, speak to him
personally and see him face to face. 5He will
take Zedekiah away to Babylon and there he
will stay (until I attend to him, Yahweh
declares. If you fight the Chaldaeans you will
not succeed!)" '

6Jeremiah said, 'The word of Yahweh has
been addressed to me as follows, 7"Look,
Hanamel the son of your uncle Shallum
will come to you and say: Buy my field at

31b || Ezk 18:2.

Anathoth, for you have the right of redemption to purchase it." 8And, as Yahweh had said, my cousin Hanamel came to me, in the Court of the Guard and said, "Buy my field at Anathoth in the territory of Benjamin, for you have the right of inheritance and right of redemption; buy it." I knew then that this was Yahweh's order. 9Accordingly, I bought the field from my cousin Hanamel of Anathoth and weighed him out the money: seventeen silver shekels. 10I drew up the deeds and sealed it, called in witnesses and weighed out the money on the scales. 11I then took both the sealed deed of purchase (with its stipulations and clauses) and its open copy 12and handed over the deed of purchase to Baruch son of Neriah, son of Mahseiah, in the presence of my cousin Hanamel, of the witnesses who had signed the deed of purchase, and of all the Judaeans who then happened to be in the Court of the Guard. 13In their presence I gave Baruch this order, 14"Yahweh Sabaoth, God of Israel, says this: Take these deeds, the sealed deed of purchase and its open copy, and put them in an earthenware pot, so that they may be preserved for a long time. 15For Yahweh Sabaoth, God of Israel, says this: Houses, fields and vineyards will again be bought in this country."

16'After I had entrusted the deed of purchase to Baruch son of Neriah, I prayed to Yahweh as follows, 17"Ah, Lord Yahweh, you made the heavens and the earth by your great power and outstretched arm. To you nothing is impossible. 18You show faithful love to thousands but repay the fathers' guilt in full to their children after them. Great and mighty God, whose name is Yahweh Sabaoth, 19great in purpose, mighty in deed, whose eyes are open on all human ways, rewarding every individual as that person's ways and actions deserve! 20You performed signs and wonders in Egypt, as you still do in Israel and among humanity today. You have won the name for yourself which is yours today. 21You brought your people Israel out of Egypt with signs and wonders, with mighty hand and outstretched arm and fearsome terror. 22Then you gave them this country which you had promised on oath to their ancestors, a country flowing with milk and honey. 23They then entered it, taking possession of it, but they would not listen to your voice nor follow your Law: they would do nothing you ordered them to do; and so you made this total disaster befall them. 24Look! The earthworks are already in place to take the city and, by means of sword, famine and plague, the city is now within the clutches of the Chaldaeans attacking it. What you said has now come true, as you see. 25Yet you yourself, Lord Yahweh, told me: Buy the field, pay for it, have it witnessed although the city is already in the Chaldaeans' clutches." '

26The word of Yahweh was addressed to me as follows, 27'Look, I am Yahweh, God of all humanity. Is anything impossible to me?

28'So, Yahweh says this, "I shall hand this city over to the Chaldaeans and to Nebuchadnezzar king of Babylon, and he will capture it; 29the Chaldaeans attacking this city will enter it, fire it and burn it to the ground, with the houses on whose roofs incense has been offered to Baal and libations poured to other gods, to provoke my anger. 30For the people of Israel and Judah alike have done nothing but what displeases me since they were young. (The people of Israel in fact have done nothing but provoke my anger by their actions, Yahweh declares.) 31Yes, from the day when this city was built until today, it has been such cause of anger and wrath to me that I mean to remove it from my sight, 32on account of all the wickedness the people of Israel and the people of Judah have done to provoke my anger; they, their kings, their chief men, their priests, their prophets, the people of Judah and the inhabitants of Jerusalem. 33They turned to me their backs, never their faces; and though I taught them so urgently, so untiringly, they would not listen and accept correction. 34Instead, they set up their Horrors in the Temple that bears my name to defile it, 35and built the high places of Baal in the Valley of Ben-Hinnom, to burn their sons and daughters alive in honour of Molech:[a] a thing I have never ordered, that had never entered my thoughts—that they would cause Judah to sin by anything so loathsome!

36"So now, this is what Yahweh, God of Israel, says about this city of which you now say: By means of sword, famine and plague, it is already within the king of Babylon's clutches: 37Look, I shall gather them in from all the countries where I have driven them in

---

32a =7:30–31.

my anger, my fury and great wrath. I shall bring them back to this place and make them live in safety. 38Then they will be my people, and I shall be their God. 39I shall give them singleness of heart and singleness of conduct so that they will always fear me, for their own good and that of their children after them. 40I shall make an everlasting covenant with them, never to cease in my efforts for their welfare, and I shall put respect for me in their hearts, so that they will never turn away from me again. 41My joy will lie in them and in doing them good, and I shall plant them firmly in this country, with all my heart and soul. 42For Yahweh says this: Just as I have brought this complete and total disaster on this people, so I shall bring them all the good things I have promised them. 43Fields will again be bought in this country of which you now say: It is a wasteland without human or animal, already in the clutches of the Chaldaeans. 44People will buy fields, pay money, draw up deeds, seal them and have them witnessed in the territory of Benjamin, in the districts round Jerusalem, in the towns of Judah, of the highlands, of the lowlands and of the Negeb. For I shall bring back their captives, Yahweh declares." '

Another promise of recovery

33 Jeremiah was still confined to the Court of the Guard when the word of Yahweh came to him a second time, as follows, 2'Yahweh who made the earth, who formed it and set it firm—Yahweh is his name—says this, 3"Call to me and I will answer you; I will tell you great secrets of which you know nothing. 4For this is what Yahweh, God of Israel, says about the houses of this city and the palaces of the kings of Judah which are about to be destroyed by means of the earthworks and the sword; 5about those now fighting the Chaldaeans, only to fill the city with corpses, those whom I have slaughtered in my furious anger, those whose wickedness has made me hide my face from this city: 6Look, I shall bring them remedy and cure; I shall cure them and reveal a new order of peace and loyalty to them. 7I shall bring back the captives of Judah and the captives of Israel and shall rebuild them as before. 8I shall cleanse them of all their guilt, by which they have offended me, I shall forgive all their guilty actions, by which they have offended me and rebelled against me. 9And, for me, Jerusalem will become a name of joy and praise and pride for all the nations on earth to see; when they hear of all the prosperity that I shall give, they will be seized with fear and trembling at all the prosperity and the peace that I provide for it."

10'Yahweh says this, "In this place of which you now say: It is a ruin, without human or animal, in the towns of Judah and desolate streets of Jerusalem where there is neither human nor animal, once more will be heard 11shouts of rejoicing and mirth, the voices of bridegroom and bride, and the singing of those who bring thanksgiving sacrifices to the Temple of Yahweh: Give thanks to Yahweh Sabaoth, for Yahweh is good, for his faithful love is everlasting. For I shall bring back the country's captives, as before, Yahweh says."

12'Yahweh Sabaoth says this, "In this ruinous place, without human or animal, in all its towns, once again there will be pastures for the shepherds to rest their flocks. 13In the towns of the highlands, of the lowlands and the Negeb, in the territory of Benjamin, in the districts round Jerusalem and in the towns of Judah, once again the flocks shall pass under the hand of someone who counts them, Yahweh says.

The institutions of the future

14"Look, the days are coming, Yahweh declares, when I shall fulfil the promise of happiness I made to the House of Israel and the House of Judah:

15In those days and at that time,
I shall make an upright Branch
grow for David,
who will do what is just and upright
in the country.
16In those days Judah will triumph
and Israel live in safety.
And this is the name the city will be called:
Yahweh-is-our-Saving-Justice."[a]

17'For Yahweh says this, "David will never lack a male descendant to occupy the throne of the House of Israel, 18nor will the levitical priests ever lack male descendants to stand before me and offer the burnt offering, to burn the cereal offering and offer sacrifice every day." '

33a =23:5–6.

19The word of Yahweh came to Jeremiah
as follows, 20'Yahweh says this, "If you could
break my covenant with the day and my
covenant with the night so that day and night
do not come at their due time, 21then my
covenant with David my servant might also
be broken and he would have no son to reign
on his throne, and so also might my covenant
with the levitical priests, who are my minis-
ters. 22As surely as the array of heaven cannot
be counted, nor the sand of the sea be meas-
ured, so surely shall I increase the heirs
of David my servant and the Levites who
minister to me." '

23The word of Yahweh came to Jeremiah
as follows, 24'Have you not noticed what
these people say, "The two families which
Yahweh chose he has now rejected"? So they
despise my people, whom they no longer
think of as a nation. 25Yahweh says this, "If
I have not created day and night and fixed
the laws governing heaven and earth, 26why,
then I shall reject the descendants of Jacob
and of David my servant and cease to choose
rulers from his descendants for the heirs of
Abraham, Isaac and Jacob! For I shall bring
back their captives and take pity on them." '

E: MISCELLANEOUS PROPHECIES

The fate of Zedekiah

34 The word came to Jeremiah from
Yahweh when Nebuchadnezzar king
of Babylon and his whole army, with all the
kingdoms of the earth under his dominion
and all the peoples, were waging war on
Jerusalem and all its towns, 2'Yahweh, God of
Israel, says this, "Go and speak to Zedekiah
king of Judah and tell him, Yahweh says this:
I am going to hand this city over to the power
of the king of Babylon, and he will burn it
down. 3And you yourself will not escape his
clutches but will certainly be captured and
handed over to him. You will see the king
of Babylon face to face and speak to him
personally. Then you will go to Babylon.
4Even so, listen to the word of Yahweh,
Zedekiah king of Judah! This is what Yahweh
says about you: You will not die by the sword;
5you will die in peace. And as spices were
burnt for your ancestors, the kings who in
times past preceded you, so spices will be
burnt for you and a dirge sung for you: Alas
for his highness! I have spoken, Yahweh
declares." '

6The prophet Jeremiah repeated all these
words to Zedekiah king of Judah in Jeru-
salem, 7while the army of the king of Babylon
was attacking Jerusalem and all such towns
of Judah as still held out, namely Lachish
and Azekah, these being the only fortified
towns of Judah remaining.

The episode of the liberated slaves

8The word came to Jeremiah from Yahweh
after King Zedekiah had made a covenant
with all the people in Jerusalem to issue a
proclamation freeing their slaves: 9each man
was to free his Hebrew slaves, men and
women, no one was any longer to keep a
brother Judaean in slavery. 10All the chief
men and all the people who had entered into
the covenant had agreed that everyone should
free his slaves, men or women, and no longer
keep them as slaves: they had agreed on this
and set them free. 11Afterwards, however,
they changed their minds, recovered the
slaves, men and women, whom they had set
free, and reduced them to slavery again.
12The word of Yahweh came then to Jeremiah
as follows, 13'Yahweh, God of Israel, says
this, "I made a covenant with your ancestors
when I brought them out of Egypt, out of the
house of slavery; it said: 14At the end of seven
years each one of you is to free his brother
Hebrew who has sold himself to you: he may
be your slave for six years, then you must
send him away free. But your ancestors did
not listen to me and would not pay attention.
15Now, today you repented and did what
pleases me by proclaiming freedom for your
neighbour; you made a covenant before me
in the Temple that bears my name. 16And
then you changed your minds and, profaning
my name, each of you has recovered his
slaves, men and women, whom you had sent
away free to live their own lives, and has
forced them to become your slaves again."

17'So Yahweh says this: "You have
disobeyed me, by failing to grant freedom to
brother and neighbour. Very well, I in my
turn, Yahweh declares, shall leave sword,
famine and plague free to deal with you and
I shall make you an object of horror to all the
kingdoms of the earth. 18As for the people
who have broken my covenant, who have not
observed the terms of the covenant which
they made before me, I shall treat them like
the calf that people cut in two to pass between
its pieces. 19The chief men of Judah and
Jerusalem, the eunuchs, the priests, and all

the country people who have passed between
the pieces of the calf, 20 I shall hand over to
their enemies and those determined to kill
them, and their corpses will be food for the
birds of the sky and the animals of earth. 21 As
for Zedekiah king of Judah and his chief
men, I shall hand them to their enemies, to
those determined to kill them, and to the
army of the king of Babylon which has just
withdrawn. 22 Listen, I shall give the order,
Yahweh declares, and bring them back to
this city to attack it and capture it and burn
it down. And I shall make an uninhabited
waste of the towns of Judah." '

The example of the Rechabites

35 The word which came to Jeremiah
from Yahweh in the days of Jehoiakim
son of Josiah, king of Judah, 2 'Go to the clan
of the Rechabites and speak to them; bring
them into one of the rooms of the Temple of
Yahweh and offer them wine to drink.' 3 So
I took Jaazaniah son of Jeremiah, son of
Habazziniah, with his brothers and all his
sons, the whole Rechabite clan, 4 and brought
them to the Temple of Yahweh into the room
of Ben-Johanan son of Igdaliah, a man of
God, which was next to that of the chief men,
above the room of Maaseiah son of Shallum,
guardian of the threshold. 5 I then set pitchers
full of wine, and some cups, before the
members of the Rechabite clan and said,
'Drink some wine.'

6 But they replied, 'We do not drink wine,
because our ancestor Jonadab son of Rechab
gave us this order, "You must not drink
wine, neither you nor your sons for ever;
7 nor must you build houses, sow seed, plant
vineyards or own them, but must live in tents
all your lives, so that you may live long on
the soil to which you are alien." 8 We have
punctiliously obeyed the orders of our
ancestor, Jonadab son of Rechab, never
drinking wine ourselves, nor our wives, our
sons or our daughters, 9 not building houses
to live in, owning neither vineyard nor field
nor seed, 10 living in tents. We have obeyed
the orders of our ancestor Jonadab,
respecting them in every particular. 11 How-
ever, when Nebuchadnezzar king of Babylon
invaded this country, we decided, "We must
get away! We will go to Jerusalem to escape
the armies of the Chaldaeans and
Aramaeans." So that is why we are living in
Jerusalem.'

12 Then the word of Yahweh came to
Jeremiah as follows, 13 'Yahweh Sabaoth, the
God of Israel, says this, "Go and say to
the people of Judah and the inhabitants of
Jerusalem: Will you never learn the lesson
and listen to my words, Yahweh demands?
14 The words of Jonadab son of Rechab,
ordering his sons to drink no wine, have
been observed; obedient to their ancestor's
command, they drink none even today. But
to me, who spoke to you so urgently, so
untiringly, you have not listened. 15 I have
urgently and untiringly sent you all my
servants the prophets to say: Turn back, each
one of you, from your evil behaviour and
amend your actions, do not follow other gods
to serve them, and you will go on living on
the soil I gave to you and your ancestors. But
you have not paid attention or listened to me.
16 Thus the sons of Jonadab son of Rechab
have kept the command their ancestor gave
them, but this people has not listened to me.
17 And so, Yahweh, God Sabaoth, God of
Israel, says this: Look, on Judah and the
citizens of Jerusalem I am going to bring
all the disaster which I have decreed for
them, because I spoke to them and they
would not listen, called to them and they
would not answer." '

18 Then Jeremiah said to the Rechabite
clan, 'Yahweh Sabaoth, the God of Israel,
says this, "Because you have obeyed the
orders of your ancestor Jonadab and observed
all his rules and done everything he ordered
you to do, 19 therefore, Yahweh Sabaoth, the
God of Israel, says this: Jonadab son of
Rechab will never lack a male descendant to
stand before me for ever." '

IV: THE SUFFERINGS OF JEREMIAH

The scroll written in 605–604 BC

36 In the fourth year of Jehoiakim son of
Josiah, king of Judah, this word came
to Jeremiah from Yahweh, 2 'Take a scroll
and on it write all the words I have spoken to
you about Israel, Judah and all the nations,
from the day I first spoke to you, in the time

of Josiah, until today. 3Perhaps when the
House of Judah hears about all the disaster I
intend to inflict on them, they will turn, each
one of them, from their evil behaviour, so that
I can forgive their sinful guilt.' 4Jeremiah
then summoned Baruch son of Neriah, who
at his dictation wrote down on the scroll all
the words Yahweh had spoken to him.

5Jeremiah then gave Baruch this order, 'As
I am prevented from entering the Temple of
Yahweh, 6you yourself must go and, from
the scroll you wrote at my dictation, read all
Yahweh's words to the people in his Temple
on the day of the fast, and in this way you
can read them in the hearing also of all the
Judaeans who come in from their towns.
7Perhaps their prayers will move Yahweh
and they will turn one and all from their evil
behaviour, for great is the furious anger with
which Yahweh has threatened this people.'
8Baruch son of Neriah duly carried out the
order that the prophet Jeremiah had given
him, to read all Yahweh's words from the
book in his Temple.

9Now, in the fifth year of Jehoiakim son of
Josiah, king of Judah, in the ninth month,
all the people of Jerusalem and all the people
who could get to Jerusalem from the towns
of Judah were summoned to a fast before
Yahweh. 10Baruch then read Jeremiah's
words from the book; this happened in the
room of Gemariah son of the scribe Shaphan,
in the upper court at the entry of the New
Gate of the Temple of Yahweh, where all the
people could hear.

11Micaiah son of Gemariah, son of
Shaphan, having heard all Yahweh's words
read from the book, 12went down to the royal
palace, to the scribe's room. All the chief
men were in session: the scribe Elishama,
Delaiah son of Shemaiah, Elnathan son of
Achbor, Gemariah son of Shaphan, Zedekiah
son of Hananiah and all the other chief men;
13and to them Micaiah reported all the words
he heard as Baruch was reading the book
aloud to the people. 14The chief men then by
common consent sent Jehudi son of Netaniah
to Baruch, with Shelemiah son of Cushi, to
say, 'Come, and bring the scroll with you
which you have been reading to the people.'
15Bringing the scroll with him, Baruch son
of Neriah appeared before them. 'Sit down,'
they said, 'and read it out.' So Baruch read
it to them. 16Having heard all the words they
turned to one another in alarm and said to
Baruch, 'We must certainly inform the king
of this.' 17They then questioned Baruch,
'Tell us', they said, 'how you came to write
all these words.' 18'Jeremiah dictated them
all to me,' Baruch replied, 'and I wrote them
down in ink in this book.' 19The chief men
said to Baruch, 'You and Jeremiah had better
go into hiding; and do not tell anyone where
you are.' 20Whereupon they went off to the
king in the palace court, depositing the scroll
in the room of the scribe Elishama. They
then informed the king of the whole affair.

21The king sent Jehudi for the scroll, and
he brought it from the room of the scribe
Elishama and read it to the king and all the
chief men standing round the king. 22The
king was sitting in his winter apartments—it
was the ninth month—with a fire burning in
a brazier in front of him. 23Each time Jehudi
had read three or four columns, the king cut
them off with a scribe's knife and threw them
into the fire in the brazier until the whole of
the scroll had been burnt in the brazier fire.
24But in spite of hearing all these words,
neither the king nor any of his courtiers took
alarm or tore their clothes; 25and although
Elnathan and Delaiah and Gemariah had
urged the king not to burn the scroll he would
not listen to them, 26but ordered the king's
son Jerahmeel and Seraiah son of Azriel and
Shelemiah son of Abdeel to arrest the scribe
Baruch and the prophet Jeremiah. But
Yahweh had hidden them.

27Then the word of Yahweh came to
Jeremiah, after the king had burnt the
scroll containing the words Baruch had
written at Jeremiah's dictation, 28'Take
another scroll and write down all the words
that were written on the first scroll burnt by
Jehoiakim king of Judah. 29And as regards
Jehoiakim king of Judah, you are to say,
"Yahweh says this: You have burnt that
scroll, saying: Why have you written down:
The king of Babylon will certainly come and
lay this country waste and leave it without
human or animal? 30So, this is what Yahweh
says about Jehoiakim king of Judah: He will
have no one to occupy the throne of David,
and his corpse will be tossed out to the heat
of the day and the frost of the night. 31I shall
punish him, his offspring and his courtiers
for their guilt; on them, on the citizens of
Jerusalem and on the people of Judah I shall
bring the total disaster which I had decreed
for them but to which they have paid no
attention." '

32Jeremiah then took another scroll and

gave it to the scribe Baruch son of Neriah,
who in it at Jeremiah's dictation wrote all the
words of the book that Jehoiakim king of
Judah had burnt, with many similar words
in addition.

A verdict on Zedekiah

37 Zedekiah son of Josiah became king,
succeeding Coniah son of Jehoiakim.
Nebuchadnezzar king of Babylon had made
him king of Judah. 2 But neither he nor his
courtiers nor the people of the country paid
any attention to the words Yahweh spoke
through the prophet Jeremiah.

Zedekiah consults Jeremiah during the respite of 588 BC

3 King Zedekiah sent Jehucal son of Shele-
miah and the priest Zephaniah son of
Maaseiah to the prophet Jeremiah with this
message, 'Intercede for us with Yahweh our
God.' 4 Now Jeremiah was still moving freely
among the people: he had not yet been put
in prison. 5 Meanwhile Pharaoh's army was
on the move from Egypt and the Chaldaeans
besieging Jerusalem had raised the siege
when they heard the news.

6 Then the word of Yahweh came to the
prophet Jeremiah as follows, 7 'Yahweh, God
of Israel, says this, "To the king of Judah
who sent you to consult me make this reply:
Is Pharaoh's army marching to your aid? It
will withdraw to its own country, Egypt.
8 The Chaldaeans will return to attack this
city; they will capture it and burn it down.
9 Yahweh says this: Do not cheer yourselves
up by thinking: The Chaldaeans are leaving
us for good. They are not leaving. 10 Even if
you cut to pieces the whole Chaldaean army
now fighting against you until there were
only the wounded left, they would stand up
again, each man in his tent, to burn this city
down." '

The arrest of Jeremiah Improvement in his treatment

11 At the time when the Chaldaean army,
threatened by Pharaoh's army, had raised the
siege of Jerusalem, 12 Jeremiah set out from
Jerusalem for the territory of Benjamin to see
about a piece of his property among the
people there. 13 He was at the Benjamin Gate
when the guard commander there, a certain
Irijah son of Shelemiah, son of Hananiah,
arrested the prophet Jeremiah, shouting,
'You are deserting to the Chaldaeans!'
14 Jeremiah answered, 'It is a lie! I am not
deserting to the Chaldaeans.' But Irijah
would not listen to Jeremiah and took him
under arrest to the chief men. 15 And the chief
men, furious with Jeremiah, had him beaten
and shut up in the house of the scribe
Jonathan, which had been turned into a
prison. 16 Thus Jeremiah found himself in an
underground vault. And there for a long time
he stayed.

17 Later, King Zedekiah had him sent for,
and the king questioned him privately in his
palace. 'Is there any word from Yahweh?' he
asked. 'There is,' Jeremiah answered, and
added, 'you will be handed over to the king
of Babylon.' 18 Jeremiah then said to King
Zedekiah, 'What wrong have I done you, or
your courtiers or this people, for you to have
put me in prison? 19 Where are your prophets
now who prophesied, "The king of Babylon
will not attack you or this country"? 20 So now
I beg you to hear me, my lord king! I beg you
to approve my request! Do not have me taken
back to the house of the scribe Jonathan, or
I shall die there.' 21 King Zedekiah then gave
an order, and Jeremiah was confined in the
Court of the Guard and given a loaf of bread
a day from the Street of the Bakers as long as
there was bread left in the city. So Jeremiah
stayed in the Court of the Guard.

Jeremiah is thrown into the storage-well. Ebed-Melech intervenes

38 But Shephatiah son of Mattan, Geda-
liah son of Pashhur, Jucal son of Shele-
miah and Pashhur son of Malchiah heard the
words which Jeremiah was saying to all the
people, 2 'Yahweh says this, "Anyone who
stays in this city will die by sword, famine
or plague; but anyone who leaves it and
surrenders to the Chaldaeans will live; he will
escape with his life.[a] 3 Yahweh says this: This
city will certainly be handed over to the army
of the king of Babylon, and he will capture
it." '

4 The chief men then said to the king, 'You
must have this man put to death: he is
unquestionably disheartening the remaining

38a =21:9.

soldiers in the city, and all the people too, by talking like this. This man is seeking not the welfare of the people but their ruin.' 5King Zedekiah answered, 'He is in your hands as you know, for the king is powerless to oppose you.' 6So they took Jeremiah and put him into the storage-well of the king's son Malchiah in the Court of the Guard, letting him down with ropes. There was no water in the storage-well, only mud, and into the mud Jeremiah sank.

7But Ebed-Melech the Cushite, a eunuch attached to the palace, heard that Jeremiah had been put into the storage-well. As the king was sitting in the Benjamin Gate, 8Ebed-Melech came out from the palace and spoke to the king. 9'My lord king,' he said, 'these men have done a wicked thing by treating the prophet Jeremiah like this: they have thrown him into the storage-well. He will starve to death there, since there is no more food in the city.' 10At this the king gave Ebed-Melech the Cushite the following order: 'Take thirty men with you from here and pull the prophet Jeremiah out of the storage-well before he dies.' 11Ebed-Melech took the men with him and went into the palace to the Treasury wardrobe; out of it he took some torn, worn-out rags which he lowered on ropes to Jeremiah in the storage-well. 12Ebed-Melech the Cushite then said to Jeremiah, 'These torn, worn-out rags are for you to put under your armpits to pad the ropes.' Jeremiah did this. 13Then they hauled Jeremiah up with the ropes and pulled him out of the storage-well. And Jeremiah stayed in the Court of the Guard.

The last conversation between Jeremiah and Zedekiah

14King Zedekiah had the prophet Jeremiah summoned to him at the third entrance to the Temple of Yahweh. 'I want to ask you for a word,' the king said to Jeremiah, 'keep nothing back from me.' 15Jeremiah answered Zedekiah, 'If I do proclaim it to you, are you not sure to have me put to death? And if I give you advice, you will not listen to me.' 16King Zedekiah then secretly swore this oath to Jeremiah, 'As Yahweh lives, giver of this life of ours, I will have you neither put to death nor handed over to these men who are determined to kill you.' 17Jeremiah then said to Zedekiah, 'Yahweh, God Sabaoth, God of Israel, says this, "If you go out and surrender to the king of Babylon's generals, your life will be safe and this city will not be burnt down; you and your family will survive. 18But if you do not go out and surrender to the king of Babylon's generals, this city will be handed over to the Chaldaeans and they will burn it down; nor will you yourself escape their clutches." ' 19King Zedekiah then said to Jeremiah, 'I am afraid of the Judaeans who have already gone over to the Chaldaeans: I might be handed over to them and they would ill-treat me.' 20'You will not be handed over to them,' Jeremiah replied. 'Please listen to Yahweh's voice as I have relayed it to you, and then all will go well with you and your life will be safe. 21But if you refuse to surrender, this is what Yahweh has shown me: 22the sight of all the women left in the king of Judah's palace being led off to the king of Babylon's generals and saying:

"They have misled you,
  they have triumphed over you,
those friends of yours!
Your feet have sunk in the mud!
They are up and away!"

23'Yes, all your wives and children will be led off to the Chaldaeans, and you yourself will not escape their clutches but will be a prisoner in the clutches of the king of Babylon. And as for this city, it will be burnt down.'

24Zedekiah then said to Jeremiah, 'Do not let anyone else hear these words or you will die. 25If the chief men hear that I have been talking to you, and come and say, "Tell us what you said to the king and what the king said to you; keep nothing back from us, or we shall put you to death," 26you must reply, "I presented this request to the king: that he would not have me sent back to Jonathan's house to die." '

27And in fact all the chief men came to Jeremiah and questioned him. He told them exactly what the king had ordered him to say. They then left him in peace, since the conversation had not been overheard. 28And Jeremiah stayed in the Court of the Guard until the day Jerusalem was captured. And he was there when Jerusalem actually was captured.

The fall of Jerusalem and what happened to Jeremiah

39 In the ninth year of Zedekiah king of Judah, in the tenth month, Nebuchad-

nezzar king of Babylon advanced on Jeru-
salem with his entire army, and they laid
siege to it. [2]In the eleventh year of Zedekiah,
in the fourth month, a breach was made in
the city wall.
[3]The king of Babylon's officials, all having
made their entry, took their seats in the
Middle Gate: Nergal-Sharezer, Samgar-
Nebo, Sar-Sechim a high dignitary of state,
Nergal-Sharezer the chief astrologer, and all
the king of Babylon's other officials . . .
[4]On seeing them, Zedekiah king of Judah
and all the fighting men fled, leaving the city
under cover of dark, by way of the king's
garden through the gate between the two
walls, and made their way towards the
Arabah. [5]But the Chaldaean troops pursued
them and caught up with Zedekiah in the
plains of Jericho. They captured him and
took him to Nebuchadnezzar king of Babylon
at Riblah in the territory of Hamath, where
he passed sentence on him. [6]The king of
Babylon had Zedekiah's sons slaughtered
before his eyes at Riblah; the king of Babylon
also had all the leading men of Judah put to
death. [7]He then put out Zedekiah's eyes and,
loading him with chains, carried him off to
Babylon. [8]The Chaldaeans burnt down the
royal palace and the private houses, and
demolished the walls of Jerusalem.
[9]Nebuzaradan commander of the guard
deported the remainder of the population left
behind in the city, the deserters who had
gone over to him, and the rest of the artisans
to Babylon. [10]But Nebuzaradan commander
of the guard left some of the poor people
behind in the country of Judah, those who
had nothing, at the same time giving them
vineyards and fields.
[11]With regard to Jeremiah, Nebuchad-
nezzar king of Babylon had given the
following orders to Nebuzaradan, com-
mander of the guard, [12]'Take him, look after
him; do him no harm, but treat him as he
may ask you.'
[13]He entrusted this mission to (Nebuzar-
adan commander of the guard,) Nebushaz-
ban the high dignitary of state, Nergal-
Sharezer the chief astrologer and all the king
of Babylon's other officials.
[14]These despatched men to take Jeremiah
from the Court of the Guard and turned him
over to Gedaliah son of Ahikam, son of
Shaphan for safe conduct home. So he
remained among the people.

A prophecy assuring the safety of Ebed-Melech

[15]While Jeremiah was confined in the Court
of the Guard, the word of Yahweh came to
him as follows, [16]'Go and say to Ebed-Melech
the Cushite, "Yahweh, God of Israel says
this: Look, I am about to perform my words
about this city for its ruin and not for its
prosperity. That day they will come true
before your eyes. [17]But I shall rescue you that
day, Yahweh declares, and you will not be
handed over to the hands of the men you fear.
[18]Yes, I shall certainly rescue you: you will
not fall to the sword; you will escape with
your life, because you have put your trust in
me, Yahweh declares." '

Further details about the treatment of Jeremiah

40 The word which came to Jeremiah
from Yahweh after Nebuzaradan
commander of the guard had released him
from Ramah, where he had found him in
chains with all the other captives from Jeru-
salem and Judah who were being deported
to Babylon:
[2]The commander of the guard took
Jeremiah and said to him, 'Yahweh your God
foretold calamity for this country, [3]and now
he has brought it. He has done what he
threatened to do, because you had sinned
against Yahweh and would not listen to his
voice; so all this has happened to you. [4]Look,
today I am having your hands unchained. If
you like to come with me to Babylon, come:
I shall look after you. If you do not want to
come with me to Babylon, do not. Look,
you have the whole country before you: go
wherever you think it best and most suitable
to go.' [5]And before Jeremiah retired, he
added, 'You can go back to Gedaliah son of
Ahikam, son of Shaphan, whom the king of
Babylon has appointed governor of the towns
of Judah, and stay with him among the
people, or go anywhere else you think suit-
able.' With that, the commander of the guard
gave him provisions and a present, and
dismissed him. [6]Jeremiah went to Mizpah,
to Gedaliah son of Ahikam and stayed with
him, among those people still left in the
country.

Gedaliah the governor; his assassination

7When the military leaders who with their
men were still in the field, all heard that the
king of Babylon had appointed Gedaliah
son of Ahikam as governor of the country,
making him responsible for the men, women
and children, and those of the poor country
people who had not been deported to
Babylon, 8they came to Gedaliah at Mizpah:
Ishmael son of Nethaniah, Johanan and
Jonathan sons of Kareah, Seraiah son of
Tanhumeth, the sons of Ephai the Netoph-
athite, Jezaniah son of the Maacathite, they
and their men. 9To them and to their men
Gedaliah son of Ahikam, son of Shaphan,
swore an oath. 'Do not be afraid', he said, 'of
serving the Chaldaeans, stay in the country,
serve the king of Babylon, and all will go
well with you. 10I for my part, as the man
answerable to the Chaldaeans when they
come to us, shall stay here at Mizpah, whereas
you can harvest the wine, summer fruit and
oil, fill your storage jars and settle in the
towns which you have seized.'

11Similarly, when all the Judaeans living
in Moab, with the Ammonites, in Edom and
elsewhere, heard that the king of Babylon had
left a remnant in Judah and had appointed
Gedaliah son of Ahikam, son of Shaphan as
their governor, 12the Judaeans all came back
from wherever they had been driven. On
their return to the land of Judah, to Gedaliah
at Mizpah, they harvested an immense quan-
tity of wine and summer fruit.

13Now Johanan son of Kareah and all the
military leaders still in the field, came to
Gedaliah at Mizpah 14and said to him, 'Are
you aware that Baalis king of the Ammonites
has sent Ishmael son of Nethaniah to
assassinate you?' But Gedaliah son of Ahikam
would not believe them. 15Johanan son of
Kareah then spoke in secret to Gedaliah at
Mizpah, as follows: 'Please let me go and kill
Ishmael son of Nethaniah, and no one will
be any the wiser. Why should he assassinate
you and cause the dispersal of all the Judaeans
who have rallied round you. Why should the
remnant of Judah perish?' 16But Gedaliah
son of Ahikam replied to Johanan son of
Kareah, 'You will do no such thing, for what
you say about Ishmael is false.'

41 In the seventh month, however,
Ishmael son of Nethaniah son of
Elishama, who was of royal descent, came
with officers of the king and ten men to
Gedaliah son of Ahikam at Mizpah. And as
they were taking their meal together, there
at Mizpah, 2Ishmael son of Nethaniah stood
up with his ten men, and attacking Gedaliah
son of Ahikam, son of Shaphan, with their
swords, they killed the man whom the king of
Babylon had made governor of the country.
3And all the Judaeans who were with him,
that is with Gedaliah at Mizpah, and the
Chaldaean soldiers who happened to be
there, Ishmael killed too.

4On the day after the murder of Gedaliah,
before the news had become known, 5eighty
men arrived from Shechem, Shiloh and
Samaria, with their beards shaved off, their
clothing torn, and covered in self-inflicted
gashes; they were bringing cereal offerings
and incense with them to present to the
Temple of Yahweh. 6Ishmael son of
Nethaniah went out of Mizpah to meet them,
weeping as he went. When he met them he
said, 'Come to Gedaliah son of Ahikam.' 7But
once they were well inside the town, Ishmael
son of Nethaniah slaughtered them, with the
help of his men, and had them thrown into
the storage-well. 8There were ten of them,
however, who said to Ishmael, 'Do not kill
us: we have stocks of wheat and barley, oil
and honey, hidden away in the fields.' So he
spared them and did not kill them with
their brothers. 9The storage-well into which
Ishmael threw the corpses of all the men he
had killed was a large one, the one which
King Asa had built as a precaution against
Baasha king of Israel. Ishmael son of
Nethaniah filled it with the slaughtered men.
10Ishmael then took all the rest of the people
prisoner who were at Mizpah, the king's
daughters and all the remaining people in
Mizpah, whom Nebuzaradan, commander
of the guard, had entrusted to Gedaliah son
of Ahikam. Ishmael son of Nethaniah took
them prisoner and set out, intending to cross
over to the Ammonites.

11When Johanan son of Kareah and all the
military leaders who were with him heard
about all the crimes committed by Ishmael
son of Nethaniah, 12they mustered all their
men and set out to attack Ishmael son of
Nethaniah. They caught up with him at
the great Pool of Gibeon. 13At the sight of
Johanan son of Kareah and all the military
leaders with him, all the people with Ishmael
were delighted. 14All the people whom
Ishmael had taken as prisoners from Mizpah
turned about, went back and joined Johanan

son of Kareah. [15]Ishmael son of Nethaniah,
however, escaped from Johanan with eight
of his men and fled to the Ammonites.
[16]Johanan son of Kareah and all the military
leaders with him then rallied all the remaining
people whom Ishmael son of Nethaniah had
taken as prisoners from Mizpah after killing
Gedaliah son of Ahikam: men—fighting
men—women, children and eunuchs, whom
they brought back from Gibeon. [17]Setting
off, they made a halt at Khan Kimham near
Bethlehem, intending to go on to Egypt, [18]to
get away from the Chaldaeans. They were
now terrified of them, since Ishmael son of
Nethaniah had killed Gedaliah son of Ahikam
whom the king of Babylon had made
governor of the country.

The flight to Egypt

42 Then all the military leaders, in
particular Johanan son of Kareah and
Azariah son of Hoshaiah, and all the people
from least to greatest, approached [2]the
prophet Jeremiah and said, 'Please hear our
petition and intercede with Yahweh your
God for us and for all this remnant—and how
few of us are left out of many, your own eyes
can see—[3]so that Yahweh your God may
show us the way we are to go and what we
must do.' [4]The prophet Jeremiah replied, 'I
hear you; I will indeed pray to Yahweh your
God as you ask; and whatever answer Yahweh
your God gives you, I will tell you, keeping
nothing back from you.' [5]They in their turn
said to Jeremiah, 'May Yahweh be a true and
faithful witness against us, if we do not follow
the instructions that Yahweh your God sends
us through you. [6]Whether we like it or not,
we shall obey the voice of Yahweh our God
to whom we are sending you, so that we may
prosper by obeying the voice of Yahweh our
God.'
[7]Ten days later the word of Yahweh came
to Jeremiah. [8]He then summoned Johanan
son of Kareah and all the military leaders
who were with him, and all the people from
least to greatest, [9]and said, 'Yahweh, God of
Israel, to whom you deputed me to present
your petition says this, [10]"If you will only
stay in this country, I shall build you and not
overthrow you; I shall plant you and not
uproot you, for I am sorry about the disaster
I have inflicted on you. [11]Do not be afraid of
the king of Babylon, whom you fear now; do
not fear him, Yahweh declares, for I am with
you to save you and rescue you from his
clutches. [12]I shall take pity on you, so that he
pities you and lets you return to your native
soil. [13]But if you say: We will not stay in this
country; if you disobey the voice of Yahweh
your God, [14]and say: No, Egypt is where we
shall go, where we shall not see war or hear
the trumpet-call or go short of food; that is
where we want to live; [15]in that case, remnant
of Judah, listen to Yahweh's word: Yahweh
Sabaoth, God of Israel, says this: If you are
determined to go to Egypt, and if you do go
and settle there, [16]the sword you fear will
overtake you there in Egypt, and there you
will die. [17]Yes, all those who are determined
to go to Egypt and settle there, will die by
sword, famine and plague: not a single one
of them will survive or escape the disaster I
shall inflict on them. [18]Yes, Yahweh Sabaoth,
the God of Israel, says this: Just as my furious
anger was poured out on the inhabitants of
Jerusalem, so will my fury be poured out on
you if you go to Egypt: you will become an
object of execration and horror, a curse, a
laughing-stock; and you will never see this
place again." [19]Remnant of Judah, Yahweh
has told you, "Do not go into Egypt." Under-
stand clearly that today I have given you a
solemn warning. [20]You were not being
sincere when you sent me to Yahweh your
God and said, "Intercede for us with Yahweh
our God; tell us exactly what Yahweh our
God says and we will do it." [21]Today I have
told you, but you have not obeyed the voice
of Yahweh your God or any part of the
message he sent me to give you. [22]So under-
stand this clearly: you will die by sword,
famine and plague in the place where you
want to go and settle.'

43 When Jeremiah had finished telling all
the people all the words of Yahweh
their God, which Yahweh their God had
sent him to tell them—all the words quoted
above—[2]Azariah son of Hoshaiah, and
Johanan son of Kareah, and all those arrogant
men, said to Jeremiah, 'You are lying.
Yahweh our God did not send you to say,
"Do not go to Egypt and settle there." [3]It
was Baruch son of Neriah, who keeps inciting
you against us, to hand us over to the Chal-
daeans so that they can put us to death or
deport us to Babylon.'
[4]So neither Johanan nor any of the military
leaders nor any of the people obeyed the voice
of Yahweh by staying in the country of Judah.
[5]Instead, Johanan son of Kareah and all the

military leaders led off the entire remnant of Judah, those who had come back from all the nations where they had been driven to live in the country of Judah: 6men, women, children, the royal princesses too, and every single person that Nebuzaradan commander of the guard had left with Gedaliah son of Ahikam, son of Shaphan, including the prophet Jeremiah and Baruch son of Neriah. 7And so, in disobedience to the voice of Yahweh, they reached Egypt and arrived at Tahpanhes.

Jeremiah foretells the invasion of Egypt by Nebuchadnezzar

8At Tahpanhes the word of Yahweh was addressed to Jeremiah as follows, 9'Take some large stones and bury them in the cement on the terrace outside the entrance of Pharaoh's palace in Tahpanhes, where the Judaeans can see you. 10Then say to them, "Yahweh, God of Israel, says this: Look, I shall send for my servant Nebuchadnezzar, king of Babylon, and he will place his throne on these stones I have buried, and spread his canopy above them. 11When he comes, he will defeat Egypt:

Those for the plague, to the plague;
those for captivity, to captivity;
those for the sword, to the sword![a]

12"He will set fire to the temples of the gods of Egypt; he will burn these gods or take them prisoner; like a shepherd wrapping his cloak round him, so he will wrap Egypt round him, and then leave without anyone laying hands on him. 13He will break the obelisks of the temple of the Sun in Egypt, and burn down the temples of the gods of Egypt." '

The last episode of Jeremiah's ministry: the Judaeans in Egypt and the Queen of Heaven

44 The word that came to Jeremiah for all the Judaeans living in Egypt, those, that is, living in Migdol, Tahpanhes, Noph and the territory of Pathros.

2'Yahweh Sabaoth, God of Israel, says this, "You have seen all the disaster I have brought on Jerusalem and all the towns of Judah; today they lie in ruins and uninhabited. 3This was because of the wicked deeds they committed to provoke my anger, by going and offering incense and serving other gods whom neither they, nor you, nor your ancestors knew anything about, 4although I urgently and untiringly sent you all my servants the prophets to say: You must not do this loathsome thing, which I hate. 5But they would not listen or pay attention, and turn from their wickedness and stop offering incense to other gods. 6And so my furious anger overflowed, burning down the towns of Judah and the streets of Jerusalem, which were reduced to ruins and wasteland, as they still are today. 7And now, Yahweh, God Sabaoth, God of Israel, says this: Why bring complete disaster on yourselves by cutting yourselves off from Judah—your men, women, children and babes in arms—so as to leave yourselves no remnant, 8by provoking my wrath by your actions, offering incense to other gods in Egypt where you have come to settle, as though bent on your own destruction and on becoming a curse and a laughing-stock for all the nations of the earth? 9Have you forgotten the wicked deeds of your ancestors, of the kings of Judah and of your princes, your own wicked deeds and those of your wives, committed in the country of Judah and in the streets of Jerusalem? 10To this day they have felt neither contrition nor fear; they have not observed my Law or my statutes, which I prescribed for you, as for your ancestors. 11So, Yahweh Sabaoth, God of Israel, says this: Look, I have determined on disaster and shall destroy Judah completely. 12I shall take the remnant of Judah who were determined to come to Egypt and settle there, and in Egypt they will perish; they will fall to the sword or perish of famine, from least to greatest; by sword and famine they will die and be an object of execration and horror, a curse, a laughing-stock. 13I shall punish those who live in Egypt just as I punished Jerusalem: by sword, famine and plague. 14Of the remnant of Judah which has come to settle in Egypt, not a single one will escape or survive to return to the country of Judah where they long to return and live. For none of them will return, except a few refugees." '

15At this, all the men who knew that their wives offered incense to other gods, and all the women who were standing there, a great crowd (and all the people living in Egypt,

43a =15:2.

in Pathros), answered Jeremiah as follows,
16'We have no intention of listening to the
word you have just spoken to us in Yahweh's
name, 17but intend to go on doing all we have
vowed to do: offering incense to the Queen
of Heaven and pouring libations in her
honour, as we used to do, we and our ances-
tors, our kings and our chief men, in the
towns of Judah and the streets of Jerusalem:
we had food in plenty then, we lived well, we
suffered no disasters. 18But since we gave up
offering incense to the Queen of Heaven and
pouring libations in her honour, we have
been destitute and have perished either by
sword or by famine. 19Besides, when we offer
incense to the Queen of Heaven and pour
libations in her honour, do you think we
make cakes for her with her features on
them, and pour libations to her, without our
husbands' knowledge?'

20To all the people, men and women, all
those who had made this answer, Jeremiah
retorted, 21'The incense you offered in the
towns of Judah and the streets of Jerusalem,
you, your ancestors, your kings, your chief
men and the people at large—was this not
what Yahweh kept remembering, and found
so repellent 22that Yahweh could not endure
your misdeeds and your loathsome practices
any longer, with the result that your country
has become the uninhabited ruin, the object
of horror and cursing it is today? 23Because
you offered incense, because you sinned
against Yahweh, refusing to listen to the
voice of Yahweh, or to observe his Law, his
statutes and his decrees—that is why the
present disaster has overtaken you.'

24Further, Jeremiah said to all the people,
and particularly to all the women, 'Listen to
the word of Yahweh, all you Judaeans in
Egypt, 25Yahweh Sabaoth, God of Israel,
says this, "You and your wives, what your
mouths promised, your hands have indeed
performed! You said: We shall punctiliously
fulfil the vows we have made and offer incense
to the Queen of Heaven and pour libations
in her honour. Very well, keep your vows,
perform them punctiliously! 26But listen to
the word of Yahweh, all you Judaeans living
in Egypt: I swear by my great name, Yahweh
says, that my name will no longer be uttered
by any man of Judah throughout Egypt; no
one will say: As Lord Yahweh lives. 27No, I
am going to keep my eye on them for disaster,
not for prosperity, and all the Judaeans in
Egypt will perish either by the sword or
by famine until they are wiped out. 28Yet,
though few in number, those who escape the
sword will return to the country of Judah
from Egypt. Then the entire remnant of
Judah which has come and settled in Egypt
will know whose word comes true, mine or
theirs.

29"And here is the sign for you, Yahweh
declares, that I shall punish you in this place:
so that you will know that the words with
which I threaten you will come true:
30Yahweh says this: Look, I shall hand
Pharaoh Hophra, king of Egypt, over to his
enemies and to those determined to kill him,
just as I handed Zedekiah king of Judah
over to his enemy Nebuchadnezzar king of
Babylon, who was determined to kill him." '

A prophecy of comfort for Baruch

45 The word that the prophet Jeremiah
addressed to Baruch son of Neriah
when the latter wrote these words down in a
book at Jeremiah's dictation in the fourth
year of Jehoiakim son of Josiah, king of
Judah, 2'This is what Yahweh God of Israel
says about you, Baruch! 3"You have been
thinking: what disaster for me, and Yahweh
has added further grief to my troubles! I am
worn out with groaning, and find no relief!"
4Say to him as follows, "Yahweh says this:
Now I am knocking down what I have built,
am uprooting what I have planted, over the
whole country! 5And you ask for special
treatment! Do not ask, for I am now going
to bring disaster on all humanity, Yahweh
declares, but you I shall allow to escape with
your life, wherever you may go." '

V: PROPHECIES AGAINST THE NATIONS[a]

46 The words of Yahweh that were addressed to the prophet Jeremiah against the nations.

Prophecies against Egypt
The defeat at Carchemish

2On Egypt.
Against the army of Pharaoh Necho king of Egypt, which was at Carchemish on the River Euphrates when Nebuchadnezzar king of Babylon defeated it in the fourth year of Jehoiakim son of Josiah, king of Judah.

3Buckler and shield at the ready!
Onward to battle!
4Harness the horses:
into the saddle, horsemen!
To your ranks! On with your helmets!
Sharpen your spears,
put on your breastplates!
5Why do I see them
retreating, panic-stricken?
Their heroes, beaten back,
are fleeing headlong,
with not a look behind.
Terror on every side,
Yahweh declares!
6No flight for the swift,
no escape for the strong!
Up in the north on the River Euphrates,
they have collapsed, have fallen.

7Who was it rose like the Nile,
his waters foaming like a torrent?
8Why, Egypt rose like the Nile,
his waters foaming like a torrent.
'I shall rise', he said, 'and drown the earth;
sweep away town and its inhabitants!
9Charge, horses!
Forward, chariots!
Let the warriors advance,
men from Cush and Put
with shield in hand,
men from Lud[b] who bend the bow!'
10For this is the Day of Lord
Yahweh Sabaoth,
a day of vengeance
when he takes revenge on his foes:
the sword will devour until gorged,
until drunk with their blood,
for Lord Yahweh Sabaoth
is holding a sacrificial feast
in the land of the north,
on the River Euphrates.
11Go up to Gilead and fetch balm,
virgin daughter of Egypt!
You multiply remedies in vain,
nothing can cure you!
12The nations have heard of your shame,
your wailing fills the world,
for warrior has stumbled against warrior,
and both have fallen together.

The invasion of Egypt

13The word that came from Yahweh to the prophet Jeremiah when Nebuchadnezzar king of Babylon advanced to attack Egypt.

14Publish it in Egypt,
proclaim it in Migdol,
proclaim it in Noph and Tahpanhes!
Say, 'Stand your ground, be prepared,
for the sword is devouring all round you!'
15Why has Apis fled?
Why has your Mighty One not stood firm?
Why, Yahweh has overturned him,
16he has caused many to fall!
Falling over one another,
they say, 'Up, and back to our own people,
to the country where we were born,
away from the devastating sword!'
17They have given Pharaoh king of Egypt
the nickname,
'Much-noise-but-he-lets-the-chance-slip-by'!
18As I live, the King declares,
whose name is Yahweh Sabaoth,
he is coming,
a very Tabor among mountains,
a Carmel high above the sea!
19Get your bundle ready for exile,
fair inhabitant of Egypt!
Noph will be reduced to a desert,
desolate, uninhabited.
20Egypt was a splendid heifer,
but a gadfly from the north
has settled on her.
21The mercenaries she had with her,
these too

46a In Hebr. the prophecies are transferred here; in Gk they occur after ch. 25.
46b Cush, Put and Lud are perhaps Ethiopia, Lybia and Lydia respectively.

were like fattened calves:
but they too have taken to their heels,
have all run away, not held their ground,
for their day of disaster
has overtaken them,
their time for being punished.

22 Hear her hissing like a snake
as they advance in force
to fall on her with their axes,
like woodcutters,
23 they will fell her forest, Yahweh declares,
however impenetrable it was
for they are more numerous than locusts,
there is no counting them.
24 The daughter of Egypt is put to shame,
handed over to a people from the north.

25 Yahweh Sabaoth, God of Israel, has said,
'Look, I shall punish Amon of No, Pharaoh,
Egypt, its gods, its kings, Pharaoh and those
who put their trust in him. 26 I shall hand him
over to those who are determined to kill him,
to Nebuchadnezzar king of Babylon, to his
generals. But afterwards, Egypt will be
inhabited again as in the past, Yahweh
declares.

27 But do not be afraid, my servant Jacob,
Israel, do not be alarmed:
for look, I shall rescue you from afar
and your descendants
from the country where they are captive.
Jacob will return and be at peace,
secure, with no one to trouble him.
28 Do not be afraid, my servant Jacob,
Yahweh declares, for I am with you:
I shall make an end of all the nations
where I have driven you,
but I shall not make an end of you,
I shall discipline you only as you deserve,
not leaving you quite unpunished.[c]

Prophecy against the Philistines

47 The word of Yahweh that came to
Jeremiah about the Philistines before
Pharaoh attacked Gaza. 2 'Yahweh says this:

Look, the waters are rising from the north
to become an overwhelming flood,
overwhelming the country and all in it,
the town and its inhabitants!
People cry for help, and there is wailing
from all the country's inhabitants
3 at the thunder of his chargers' hoofs,
the crash of his chariots,
the grinding of his wheels.
Fathers forget about their children,
their hands fall limp
4 because the day has come
for all the Philistines to be destroyed,
for Tyre and Sidon to be stripped
to the last of their allies.
Yes, Yahweh is destroying the Philistines,
the remnant from the Isle of Caphtor.
5 Baldness has befallen Gaza,
Ashkelon has been reduced to silence.
You who remain in the valley,
how long will you gash yourselves?
6 Oh, sword of Yahweh,
how long before you rest?
Back into your scabbard,
stop, keep still!
7 Yet how can it rest
when Yahweh has given it an order,
Ashkelon and the sea coast,
the targets assigned to it?

Prophecies against Moab

48 On Moab. Yahweh, God of Israel, says
this:

Wretched Nebo, for it has been ravaged,
Kiriathaim has been shamed and taken,
shame and distraction on the citadel,
2 the pride of Moab is no more!
At Heshbon they plotted her downfall,
'Come, let us put an end to her
as a nation!'
And you too, inhabitants of Madmen,
will be silenced,
the sword will be after you.

3 A cry of agony goes up from Horonaim,
'Devastation! Dire calamity.
4 Moab has been shattered,'
the agonised cries of her little ones
ring out.
5 Up the slope of Luhith,
weeping they go.
On the road down to Horonaim
is heard the shriek of disaster,[a]
6 'Away! Flee for your lives
like the wild donkey into the desert!'
7 Yes, since you relied on your deeds
and your wealth,
you will be captured too.

46c =30:10–11.
48a ‖ Is 15:5.

Chemosh will go into exile,
with all his priests and princes.
8The despoiler will descend on every town,
not one will escape;
the Valley will be ravaged,
the Plain be plundered
as Yahweh has said.
9Give Moab wings
so that she can fly away,
for her towns will be laid in ruins
where no one will ever live again.

10(Accursed be he who does Yahweh's
work negligently! Accursed be he who
deprives his sword of blood!)

11From his youth Moab lived at ease,
he settled on his lees,
never having been decanted,
never having gone into exile:
and so he kept his own flavour,
his aroma was unchanged.

12And so the days are coming, Yahweh
declares, when I shall send him decanters to
decant him; they will empty his pitchers and
break his wine jars to bits. 13Moab will be
shamed by Chemosh then, as the House of
Israel was shamed by Bethel in which they
put their trust.

14How can you say, 'We are heroes,
sturdy fighting men'?
15Moab has been ravaged, his cities scaled,
the flower of his youth
goes down to the slaughter,
declares the King,
whose name is Yahweh Sabaoth.
16Moab's ruin is coming soon,
his downfall comes at top speed.
17Grieve for him, all you living near him,
all you who knew his name.
Say, 'How shattered it is, that mighty rod,
that splendid sceptre!'

18Come down from your glory,
sit on the parched ground,
daughter of Dibon,
for the despoiler of Moab
has advanced on you,
he has destroyed your strongholds.
19Stand by the roadside, keep watch,
daughter of Aroer.
Question fugitive and runaway,
ask, 'What has happened?'
20'Moab has been shattered and shamed.
Wail and shriek!
Shout along the Arnon,
Moab has been laid waste!'

21Judgement has also come on the Plain, on
Holon, Jahzah, Mephaath, 22Dibon, Nebo,
Beth-Diblathaim, 23Kiriathaim, Beth-
Gamul, Beth-Meon, 24Kerioth, Bozrah, and
all the towns of Moab, far and near.

25Moab's horn has been cut off,
his arm is broken, Yahweh declares.

26Make him drunk! He has set himself up
against Yahweh; let Moab wallow in his
vomit and become a laughing-stock in his
turn. 27Was Israel not a laughing-stock to
you? Was he caught red-handed with the
thieves, for you to shake your head whenever
you mention him?

28Leave the towns,
make the rocks your home,
inhabitants of Moab.
Learn from the dove that makes its nest
in the walls of the gaping gorge.

29We have heard about Moab's pride,
so very proud!
What arrogance! What pride!
What conceit!
What a haughty heart!
30—I know all about his presumption,
Yahweh declares,
his empty boasting,
those empty deeds of his!
31—and so I lament for Moab,
for all Moab I raise my cry
and mourn for the people of Kir-Heres.[b]
32More than for Jazer I weep for you,
vineyard of Sibmah:
your shoots stretched beyond the sea,
they reached all the way to Jazer.
On your harvest and vintage
the despoiler has descended.
33Gladness and joy have vanished
from the orchards of Moab.
I have dried up the wine in the presses,
the treader of grapes treads no more,
the joyful shouting has ceased.

34The cries of Heshbon and Elealeh can be
heard as far as Jahaz. The shrieks resound
from Zoar to Horonaim and Eglath-
Shelishiyah, for even the Waters of Nimrim
have become a wasteland.
35And in Moab I shall make an end,
Yahweh declares, of anyone offering sacrifice

48b || Is 16:6–7.

on the high places and anyone offering
incense to his gods.
36 That is why my heart sobs like a flute for
Moab, sobs like a flute for the people of Kir-
Heres, since the wealth he had acquired is
lost. 37 Yes, every head is shaved, every beard
cut off, gashes are on every hand, sackcloth
round every waist. 38 On all the housetops of
Moab and in all its squares there is nothing
but lamenting, for I have broken Moab like
an unwanted pot, Yahweh declares. 39 How
shattered he is! Wail! Moab so shamefully in
retreat! Moab has become a laughing-stock,
a thing of horror to all his neighbours.

40 For Yahweh says this:
(Look, like an eagle, he will hover,
spreading his wings over Moab.)
41 The towns have been captured,
the strongholds seized.
(And the heart of Moab's warriors,
that day,
will be like that of a woman
in labour pains.)
42 Moab will be destroyed,
no longer a people,
for setting itself up against Yahweh.
43 Terror, the pit and the snare for you,
inhabitant of Moab,
Yahweh declares.

44 And anyone who escapes from terror
will fall into the pit,
and anyone who climbs out of the pit
will be caught in the snare.[c]
Yes, I shall bring all this on Moab
when the year comes for punishing them,
Yahweh declares.

45 In the shelter of Heshbon the fugitives
have paused, exhausted.
But fire will burst from Heshbon,
a flame from the palace of Sihon,
consuming the brows of Moab,
the head of a turbulent brood.
46 Disaster for you, Moab!
The people of Chemosh are lost!
For your sons have been taken into exile
and your daughters into captivity.

47 But I shall bring back Moab's captives
in the final days, Yahweh declares.

Thus far the judgement on Moab.

Prophecy against Ammon

49 To the Ammonites.

Yahweh says this:
Has Israel no sons?
Has he no heir?
Why should Milcom have inherited Gad
and his people have settled in its towns?
2 And so the days are coming,
Yahweh declares,
when I shall make the war cry ring out
for Rabbah-of-the-Ammonites.
She will become a desolate mound
and her daughter towns
will be burnt down.
Then Israel will inherit from his heirs,
Yahweh says.
3 Wail, Heshbon,
for Ar has been laid waste!
Shriek, daughters of Rabbah!
Wrap yourself in sackcloth,
raise the dirge,
run to and fro among the sheep-pens!
For Milcom is going into exile,
with all his priests and princes.
4 How you used to glory in your Valley,
rebellious daughter,
confident in your resources,
'Who will dare to attack me?'
5 Look, I shall bring terror on you,
Lord Yahweh Sabaoth declares,
from all directions;
you shall be driven away,
everyone for himself,
with no one to rally the fugitives.

6 (But later I shall bring back the captive
Ammonites, Yahweh declares.)

Prophecy against Edom[a]

7 To Edom.

Yahweh says this:
Is there no wisdom left in Teman?
Have the shrewd
run out of commonsense,
has their wisdom vanished?
8 Away! Take to your heels! Go into hiding,
inhabitants of Dedan,
for I shall bring ruin on Esau
when the time comes for me
to punish him.
9 If grape-pickers were to come to you,

48c || Is 24:17–18.
49a || Ob 1–6.

would they not leave a few gleanings?
If robbers came during the night,
would they not steal
only as much as they wanted?
10 But I for my part have stripped Esau,
have laid his hiding places bare:
he can hide no longer.
His race is destroyed,
so are his brothers and neighbours;
he is no more!
11 Leave your orphans, I shall support them,
and let your widows rely on me!

12 For Yahweh says this, 'Look, those who
would not have had to drink the cup will have
to drink it all the same; so why should you
go unpunished? You will not go unpunished,
but will certainly have to drink. 13 For by my
own self I have sworn, Yahweh declares, that
Bozrah will become an object of horror, a
laughing-stock, a desert, a curse, and all its
towns ruins for ever.'

14 I have received a message from Yahweh,
a herald has been sent
throughout the nations,
'Muster! March against this people!
Prepare for battle!'
15 For look, I shall reduce you
to the smallest of nations,
to the most despised of people.
16 Your reputation for ferocity,
your proud heart has misled you.
You whose home
is in the crannies of the Rock,
who cling to the top of the peak!
Though you make your nest
as high as the eagle's,
I shall bring you down from there,
Yahweh declares.

17 Edom will become an object of horror;
everyone going near will be appalled, and
whistle at the sight of all her wounds. 18 As at
the overthrow of Sodom and Gomorrah and
their neighbouring towns, no one will live
there any more, Yahweh says, no human
being settle there again.[b]

19 Look, like a lion he climbs
from the thickets of the Jordan
to the perennial pasture!
In a flash, I shall make them run away,
and there appoint someone I shall choose.
For who is there like me?
Who can hale me into court?
Name me the shepherd
who can stand up to me.
20 So now hear the plan
that Yahweh has laid against Edom,
the schemes he has in mind
against the inhabitants of Teman:
they will certainly be dragged away
like the smallest of the flock!
Their pastures will certainly be sacked
before their eyes!
21 The earth quakes
at the sound of their downfall,[c]
the sound of it echoes to the Sea of Reeds.
22 Look, like an eagle, he will soar and hover,
spreading his wings over Bozrah.
And the heart of Edom's warriors,
that day,
will be like that of a woman in labour pains.

Prophecy against the towns of Syria

23 To Damascus.

Hamath and Arpad are shamed,
for they have heard bad news.
They are convulsed with anxiety
like the sea that cannot be calmed.
24 Damascus is aghast,
she prepares for flight,
she is seized with trembling
(anguish and sorrow have laid hold on her
as on a woman in labour).
25 What now! That famous town deserted,
that city of gaiety?

26 And so in her squares her young men will
fall, and all her fighting men will perish, that
day, Yahweh Sabaoth declares.[d]

27 I shall light a fire
inside the walls of Damascus,
to devour the palaces of Ben-Hadad.

Prophecy against the Arab tribes

28 To Kedar and the kingdoms of Hazor,
which were conquered by Nebuchadnezzar
king of Babylon. Yahweh says this:

Up! March on Kedar,
destroy the sons of the east!

49b =50:40.
49c =50:44–46.
49d =50:30.

29 Let their tents and their flocks
be captured,
their tent-cloths and all their gear;
let their camels be seized
and the shout go up,
'Terror on every side!'
30 Away! Get into hiding as fast as you can,
inhabitants of Hazor, Yahweh declares,
for Nebuchadnezzar king of Babylon
has made a plan against you,
he has a scheme in mind against you,
31 Up! March on a nation at its ease,
living secure, Yahweh declares,
that has no gates, no bars,
that lives in a remote place!
32 Their camels will be the plunder,
their countless sheep the spoil.
I shall scatter them to the winds,
those Crop-Heads,
and bring ruin on them from every side,
Yahweh declares.
33 Hazor will become the lair of jackals,
desolate for ever.
No one will live there any more,
no human being settle there again.

Prophecy against Elam

34 The word of Yahweh that came to the
prophet Jeremiah about Elam, at the begin-
ning of the reign of Zedekiah king of Judah.
35 'Yahweh Sabaoth says this:

Look, I shall break Elam's bow,
the source of his might.
36 I shall bring four winds on Elam
from the four corners of the sky,
and I shall scatter them to all these winds:
there will not be a single nation
to which people expelled from Elam
do not go.

37 I shall make the Elamites tremble
before their enemies,
before those determined to kill them.
I shall bring disaster on them,
my burning anger, Yahweh declares.
I shall pursue them with the sword
until I have destroyed them all.
38 I shall set up my throne in Elam,
uprooting its king and princes,
Yahweh declares.

39 In the final days, I shall bring Elam's
captives back, Yahweh declares.'

Prophecy against Babylon

50 The word that Yahweh spoke against
Babylon, against the country of the
Chaldaeans, through the prophet Jeremiah.

**The fall of Babylon
and the liberation of Israel**

2 Announce it to the nations, proclaim it,
hoist a signal and proclaim it,
making no secret of it, say,
'Babylon is captured, Bel disgraced,
Marduk[a] shattered.
(Her idols are disgraced,
her Obscenities shattered.)'
3 For a nation is marching on her
from the north,
to turn her country into a desert:
no one will live there any more;
human and animal have fled and gone.

4 In those days and at that time
the people of Israel will return
(they and the people of Judah);
they will come weeping
in search of Yahweh their God.
5 They will ask the way to Zion
and turn their faces towards her,
'Come, let us bind ourselves to Yahweh
by an everlasting covenant
never to be forgotten!'

6 Lost sheep, such were my people;
their shepherds led them astray,
the mountains misled them;
from mountain to hill they went,
forgetful of their fold.
7 Whoever came across them
devoured them,
their enemies said, 'We are not to blame,
since they have sinned against Yahweh,
the Home of Justice,
against Yahweh,
the Hope of their ancestors.'
8 Escape from Babylon,
leave the country of the Chaldaeans.
Be like he-goats, leading the sheep!
9 For look, I shall raise a league
of mighty nations to attack Babylon,
from the land of the north.
They will take up position against her;
by them she will be taken.

50a Bel and Marduk are the chief gods of Babylon.

Their arrows,
like an experienced soldier's,
never return in vain.
10 Chaldaea will be plundered,
all her plunderers will be satisfied,
Yahweh declares.

11 Rejoice! Have your triumph,
you plunderers of my heritage!
Be playful like a heifer let out to grass!
Neigh like stallions!
12 But your mother is covered with shame,
disgraced is the woman who bore you;
she is the least of nations now;
a desert, a parched land, a wasteland.
13 Because of Yahweh's anger,
no one will live there any more,
she will become a total solitude.
All who pass by Babylon will be appalled
and whistle at the sight of all her wounds.

14 Take position against Babylon,
surround her,
all you who bend the bow.
Shoot at her! Do not spare your arrows,
for she has sinned against Yahweh!
15 Raise the war cry against her from all sides.
She surrenders! Her bastions fall!
Her walls collapse!
This is Yahweh's vengeance!
Take revenge on her.
Treat her as she has treated others.
16 Deprive Babylon of the man who sows,
of the man who wields the sickle at harvest.
Away from the devastating sword,
let everyone return to his own people,
let everyone flee to his own country!

17 Israel was a straying sheep
pursued by lions.

First, the king of Assyria devoured him,
and latterly Nebuchadnezzar king of Babylon
crunched his bones.
18 So Yahweh Sabaoth,
God of Israel, says this: Look, I shall punish
the king of Babylon and his country as I
punished the king of Assyria.

19 I will bring Israel back to his pastures
to browse on Carmel and in Bashan,
on the highlands of Ephraim
and in Gilead,
and he will be satisfied.
20 In those days and at that time,
Yahweh declares,
you may look for Israel's guilt,
it will not be there,
for Judah's sins, you will not find them,
for I shall pardon the remnant that I leave.

The fall of Babylon proclaimed to Jerusalem

21 March on the country of Merathaim,
march on it
and on the inhabitants of Pekod;
slaughter and curse with destruction
every last one of them,
Yahweh declares,
carry out my orders to the letter!
22 The din of battle fills the country,
immense destruction.

23 How utterly shattered
that hammer of the whole world!
What a thing of horror Babylon has become
throughout the nations!
24 I set a snare for you, Babylon;
you were caught
before you knew it.
You have been found and overpowered
for having defied Yahweh.

25 Yahweh has opened his armoury
and taken out the weapons of his fury.
For Lord Yahweh Sabaoth has work to do
in the country of the Chaldaeans.
26 Fall on her from every side,
open her granaries,
pile her in heaps,
curse her with destruction,
until nothing is left of her.

27 Slaughter all her bulls,
down to the slaughterhouse with them!
Disaster on them, their day has come,
their time for being punished.

28 Listen! Fugitives and runaways
from the country of Babylon
arrive in Zion and proclaim
the revenge of Yahweh our God,
revenge for his Temple!

The sin of arrogance

29 Call up the archers against Babylon!
All you who bend the bow,
invest her on all sides,
leave her no way of escape.
Repay her as her deeds deserve;
treat her as she has treated others,
for she was arrogant to Yahweh,
to the Holy One of Israel.

30 And so in her squares her young men will

fall, and all her fighting men will perish, that day, Yahweh declares.[b]

31 My quarrel is with you, 'Arrogance!'
Lord Yahweh Sabaoth declares,
your day has come,
the time for me to punish you.
32 'Arrogance' will stumble, she will fall,
no one will lift her up:
I shall set fire to her towns
and it will devour all around it.

Yahweh the redeemer of Israel

33 Yahweh Sabaoth says this:
The people of Israel are oppressed
(and the people of Judah too),
all their captors hold them fast,
they will not let them go.
34 But their redeemer is strong:
Yahweh Sabaoth is his name.
He will take up their cause,
to give our country rest
but make the inhabitants of Babylon
tremble.

35 A sword against the Chaldaeans,
Yahweh declares,
against the inhabitants of Babylon,
against her princes and her sages!
36 A sword against her diviners:
may they lose their wits!
A sword against her warriors:
may they panic!
37 A sword against her horses, her chariots
and the conglomeration of people
inside her:
may they be like women!
A sword against her treasures:
may they be plundered!
38 Drought on her waters: may they dry up!
For it is a country of idols,
and they are mad about those bogeys
of theirs!

39 Hence wild cats and jackals will live there,
and ostriches make their home there.
She will never again be inhabited, for ever,
but remain uninhabited age after age.
40 As when God overthrew
Sodom and Gomorrah,
and their neighbouring towns,
Yahweh declares,
no one will live there any more,
no human being settle there again.[c]

The enemy from the north and the lion of Jordan

41 Look, a people is coming from the north,
a mighty nation;
from the far ends of the earth
many kings are stirring.
42 They are armed with bow and spear,
they are cruel and pitiless;
their noise is like the roaring of the sea;
they ride horses,
ready as one man to fight you,
daughter of Babylon!
43 The king of Babylon[d] has heard the news,
his hands fall limp,
anguish has seized him,
pain like that of a woman in labour.

44 Look, like a lion
he climbs the thickets of the Jordan
to the perennial pasture!
In a flash I shall make them run away
and there appoint someone I shall choose.
For who is there like me?
Who can hale me into court?
Name me the shepherd
who can stand up to me.
45 So now hear the plan
that Yahweh has laid against Babylon,
the schemes he has in mind
against the country of the Chaldaeans:
they will certainly be dragged away
like the smallest in the flock!
Their pastures will certainly be sacked
before their eyes!
46 The earth quakes
at the sound of Babylon's capture,[e]
and the shouting echoes
through the nations.

Yahweh makes war on Babylon

51 Yahweh says this:
Against Babylon
and the inhabitants of Leb-Kamai
I shall rouse a destructive wind.
2 I shall send winnowers to Babylon
to winnow her
and leave her country bare,

50b =49:26.
50c =49:18.
50d =6:22–23.
50e =49:19–21.

for she will be beleaguered on all sides,
on the day of disaster.
3 Let no archer bend his bow!
Let no man swagger in his breastplate!
—No quarter for her young men!
Curse her whole army with destruction!
4 In the country of the Chaldaeans
the slaughtered will fall,
in the streets of Babylon,
those run through by the sword.
5 For Israel and Judah have not been bereft
of their God, Yahweh Sabaoth,
although their country was full of sin
against the Holy One of Israel.

6 Escape from Babylon
(save your lives, each one of you);
do not perish for her guilt,
for now is the time
for Yahweh's vengeance:
he will pay her her reward!
7 Babylon was a golden cup
in Yahweh's hand,
she made the whole world drunk,
the nations drank her wine
and then went mad.
8 Babylon has suddenly fallen, is broken:
wail for her!
Fetch balm for her wounds,
perhaps she can be cured!
9 —'We tried to cure Babylon;
she has got no better.
Leave her alone
and let us each go to his own country.'
—Yes, her sentence reaches to the sky,
rises to the very clouds.
10 Yahweh has shown
the uprightness of our cause.
Come, let us tell in Zion
what Yahweh our God has done.

11 Sharpen the arrows,
fill the quivers!

Yahweh has roused the spirit of the kings of the Medes, because he has a plan against Babylon to destroy it; this is Yahweh's revenge, revenge for his Temple.

12 Against the walls of Babylon
raise the standard!
Strengthen the guard!
Post the sentries!
Take up concealed positions!

For Yahweh has both planned and done what he promised he would to the inhabitants of Babylon.

13 Enthroned beside abundant waters,
rich in treasures,
you now meet your end,
the finish of your pillaging.
14 By his own self
Yahweh Sabaoth has sworn:
I shall fill you with men
as though with grasshoppers,
and over you
they will raise the triumph-shout.

15 By his power he made the earth,
by his wisdom set the world firm,
by his discernment spread out the heavens.
16 When he thunders
there is a roaring of waters in heaven;
he raises clouds
from the furthest limits of the earth,
makes the lightning flash
for the downpour,
and brings the wind from his storehouse.
17 At this everyone stands stupefied,
uncomprehending,
every goldsmith blushes for his idols;
his castings are but delusion,
with no breath in them.
18 They are futile, a laughable production,
when the time comes
for them to be punished,
they will vanish.
19 The Heritage of Jacob is not like these,
for he is the maker of everything,
and Israel is the tribe that is his heritage;
His name is Yahweh Sabaoth.[a]

Yahweh's hammer and the giant mountain

20 You were my mace,
a weapon of war.
With you I crushed nations,
struck kingdoms down,
21 with you crushed horse and rider,
with you crushed chariot and charioteer,
22 with you crushed man and woman,
with you crushed old man and young,
with you crushed young man and girl,
23 with you crushed shepherd and flock,
with you crushed ploughman and team,
with you crushed governors
and magistrates,

24 and I shall repay Babylon and the inhabi-

51a =10:12–16.

tants of Chaldaea, before your eyes, for all the wrongs they have done to Zion, Yahweh declares.

25 I am setting myself against you,
mountain of destruction,
Yahweh declares,
destroyer of the whole world!
I shall reach out my hand for you
and send you tumbling from the crags
and make you a burnt-out mountain.
26 No corner-stone will be taken
from you again
and no foundation-stone,
for you will be a desert for ever,
Yahweh declares.

The end of Babylon is imminent

27 Raise the standard throughout the world,
sound the trumpet among the nations!
Consecrate nations to make war on her;
summon kingdoms against her:
Ararat, Minni, Ashkenaz;
appoint a recruiting-officer
for her enemies,
bring up the cavalry, bristling like locusts.

28 Consecrate nations to make war on her: the kings of Media, her governors, all her magistrates and the whole territory under their rule.

29 Then the earth trembled and writhed,
for Yahweh's plan against Babylon
was being executed:
to change the country of Babylon
into an unpopulated desert.

30 The warriors of Babylon
have done with fighting,
they have stayed inside their fortresses;
their courage exhausted,
they are now like women.
Her houses are on fire,
her gates are shattered.
31 Courier follows close on courier,
messenger on messenger,
to tell the king of Babylon
that his city has been taken from all sides,
32 the fords occupied,
the bastions burnt down
and the fighting men seized with panic.
33 For Yahweh Sabaoth,
the God of Israel, says this:
the daughter of Babylon
is like a threshing-floor
when it is being trodden:
a little while, and then the time
for harvesting her will come.

Yahweh's vengeance

34 He devoured me, consumed me,
Nebuchadnezzar king of Babylon,
left me like an empty dish,
like the Dragon
he has swallowed me whole,
filled his belly with my titbits
and threw me out.
35 'On Babylon be the wounds I suffered!'
the daughter of Zion will say.
'On the inhabitants of Chaldaea
be my blood!'
Jerusalem will say.

36 So, Yahweh says this:
Look, I am taking up your cause
to make sure you are avenged.
I shall dry her river up,
make her springs run dry.
37 Babylon will become a heap of stones,
the lair of jackals,
a thing of horror and of scorn,
with no one living in it.
38 Like lions they roar together,
they growl like lions' whelps.
39 Are they feverish?
I will prepare them a drink
and make them drink until they are tipsy
and fall into an everlasting sleep,
never to wake again,
Yahweh declares.
40 I will drag them away
to the slaughterhouse like lambs,
like rams and goats.

A dirge for Babylon

41 What! Has Sheshak been taken,
been conquered,
the pride of the whole world?
What a thing of horror
Babylon has become
throughout the nations!
42 The sea has risen over Babylon,
she sinks beneath its boisterous waves.
43 Her towns have been turned
into wasteland,
a parched land, a desert,
a country where no one lives
and where nobody goes.

Yahweh punishes the idols

44I shall punish Bel in Babylon
and make him disgorge
what he has swallowed.
In future the nations
will stream to him no more.
The very walls of Babylon
will fall.
45Get out of her, my people;
save your lives, each one of you,
from Yahweh's furious anger.

46But do not be faint-hearted! Do not take
fright at rumours hawked round the country:
one rumour spreads one year, next year
another follows; violence rules on earth and
one tyrant succeeds another.

47So look, the days are coming
when I shall punish the idols of Babylon.
Her entire country will be humbled,
with all her slaughtered
lying on home-soil.
48The heaven and earth and all within them
will shout for joy over Babylon,
for the destroyers from the north
are coming to her, Yahweh declares.
49Babylon in her turn must fall,
you slaughtered ones of Israel,
just as through Babylon there fell
men slaughtered all over the world.
50You who have escaped her sword,
leave her, do not wait!
Remember Yahweh from afar,
let Jerusalem come into your mind.
51—'We were ashamed
when we heard of the outrage,
we were covered in confusion
because foreigners had entered
the Temple of Yahweh's holy places.'
52—So look, the days are coming,
Yahweh declares,
when I shall punish her idols,
and the wounded will groan
throughout her country.

53Were Babylon to scale the heavens
or reinforce her towering citadel,
destroyers would still come to her
on my orders,
Yahweh declares.
54The din of shouting from Babylon,
of immense destruction,
from the country of the Chaldaeans!
55Yes, Yahweh is laying Babylon waste
and silencing her monstrous din,
whose waves used to roar like the ocean
and their tumultuous voices rang out.
56For the destroyer has fallen on Babylon,
her warriors are captured,
their bows are broken.
Yes, Yahweh is a God of retribution,
he never fails to repay.
57I shall make her princes
and her sages drink,
her governors,
her magistrates, her warriors;
they will fall into an everlasting sleep,
never to wake again,
declares the King,
whose name is Yahweh Sabaoth.

Babylon rased to the ground

58Yahweh Sabaoth says this:
The walls of Babylon the Great
will be rased to the ground,
and her lofty gates
will be burnt down.
Thus peoples toil for nothing
and nations wear themselves out,
for the flames.

The written prophecy thrown into the Euphrates

59This is the order that the prophet Jeremiah
gave to Seraiah son of Neriah, son of
Mahseiah when Seraiah left for Babylon with
Zedekiah king of Judah, in the fourth year
of his reign. Seraiah was lord chamberlain.
60Now, on one sheet, Jeremiah had written
down the entire disaster that was to befall
Babylon, that is, all these words recorded
here against Babylon. 61Jeremiah then said
to Seraiah, 'When you reach Babylon, see to
it that you read all these words aloud. 62Then
say, "You, Yahweh, have promised to
destroy this place, so that no one will live
here ever again, neither human nor animal,
and it will be desolate for ever." 63Then,
when you have finished reading this sheet,
tie a stone to it and throw it into the middle
of the Euphrates, 64with the words, "So shall
Babylon sink, never to rise again from the
disaster which I am going to bring on her." '
Thus far the words of Jeremiah.

VI: APPENDIX[a]

The destruction of Jerusalem and the pardon of Jehoiachin

52 Zedekiah was twenty-one years old
when he came to the throne, and he
reigned for eleven years in Jerusalem. His
mother's name was Hamital daughter of
Jeremiah, of Libnah. 2He did what is
displeasing to Yahweh, just as Jehoiakim had
done. 3That this should happen to Jerusalem
and Judah was due to Yahweh's anger,
resulting in his casting them away from his
presence.
Zedekiah rebelled against the king of
Babylon. 4In the ninth year of his reign, in
the tenth month, on the tenth day of the
month, Nebuchadnezzar king of Babylon
advanced on Jerusalem with his entire army;
he pitched camp in front of the city and threw
up earthworks round it. 5The city lay under
siege till the eleventh year of King Zedekiah.
6In the fourth month, on the ninth day of the
month, when famine was raging in the city
and there was no food for the populace, 7a
breach was made in the city wall. The king
and all the fighting men then fled, leaving the
city under cover of dark, by way of the gate
between the two walls, which is near the
king's garden—the Chaldaeans had
surrounded the city—and made his way
towards the Arabah. 8The Chaldaean troops
pursued the king and caught up with Zedek-
iah in the plains of Jericho, where all his
troops deserted. 9But the Chaldaeans
captured the king and took him to the king of
Babylon at Riblah in the territory of Hamath,
where he passed sentence on him. 10He had
Zedekiah's sons slaughtered before his eyes;
he also had all the chief men of Judah put to
death at Riblah. 11He then put out Zedekiah's
eyes and, loading him with chains, the king
of Babylon carried him off to Babylon where
he kept him prisoner until his dying day.
12In the fifth month, on the tenth day of
the month—it was in the nineteenth year of
Nebuchadnezzar king of Babylon—Nebu-
zaradan commander of the guard, a member
of the king of Babylon's staff, entered Jeru-
salem. 13He burnt down the Temple of
Yahweh, the royal palace and all the houses
in Jerusalem. 14The Chaldaean troops who
accompanied the commander of the guard
demolished all the walls surrounding
Jerusalem.
15Nebuzaradan commander of the guard
deported (some of the poor people and) the
remainder of the population left in the city,
the deserters who had gone over to the king
of Babylon, and the rest of the artisans. 16But
Nebuzaradan commander of the guard left
some of the poor country-people behind as
vineyard workers and ploughmen.
17The Chaldaeans broke up the bronze
pillars from the Temple of Yahweh, the
wheeled stands and the bronze Sea, which
were in the Temple of Yahweh, and took all
the bronze away to Babylon. 18They also
took the ash containers, the scoops, the
knives, the sprinkling bowls, the incense
bowls, and all the bronze furnishings used in
worship. 19The commander of the guard also
took the bowls, the censers, the sprinkling
bowls, the ash containers, the lamp-stands,
the goblets and the saucers: everything that
was made of gold and everything made of
silver. 20As regards the two pillars, the one
Sea, the twelve bronze oxen supporting the
Sea, and the wheeled stands, which King
Solomon had made for the Temple of
Yahweh, there was no reckoning the weight
of bronze in all these objects. 21As regards the
pillars, the height of one pillar was eighteen
cubits, its circumference was twelve cubits,
it was four fingers thick, and hollow inside;
22on it stood a capital of bronze, the height of
the capital being five cubits; round the capital
were filigree and pomegranates, all in bronze.
So also for the second pillar. 23There were
ninety-six pomegranates round the sides,
making a hundred pomegranates round the
filigree in all.
24The commander of the guard took pris-
oner Seraiah the chief priest, Zephaniah the
priest next in rank, and the three guardians
of the threshold. 25In the city he took prisoner
an official who was in command of the
fighting men, seven of the king's personal
friends who were discovered in the city, the
secretary to the army commander responsible
for military conscription, and sixty men of
distinction discovered in the city.
26Nebuzaradan commander of the guard took

52a || 2 K 24:18—25:30.

these men and brought them to the king of
Babylon at Riblah, 27and at Riblah, in the
territory of Hamath, the king of Babylon had
them put to death. Thus Judah was deported
from its country.
28The number of people deported by
Nebuchadnezzar was as follows. In the
seventh year: three thousand and twenty-
three Judaeans; 29in the eighteenth year of
Nebuchadnezzar, eight hundred and thirty-
two persons were deported from Jerusalem;
30in the twenty-third year of Nebuchad-
nezzar, Nebuzaradan commander of the
guard deported seven hundred and forty-five
Judaeans. In all: four thousand six hundred
persons.

31But in the thirty-seventh year of the exile
of Jehoiachin king of Judah, in the twelfth
month, on the twenty-fifth day of the month,
Evil-Merodach king of Babylon, in the year
he came to the throne, pardoned Jehoiachin
king of Judah and released him from prison.
32He treated him kindly and allotted him a
seat above those of the other kings who were
with him in Babylon. 33So Jehoiachin laid
aside his prisoner's garb and for the rest of
his life always ate at the king's table. 34And
his upkeep was permanently ensured by the
king, day after day, for the rest of his life
until the day he died.

LAMENTATIONS

These five laments were written soon after the fall of Jerusalem in 587 BC. Shining through their sorrow is a ray of unconquerable trust in Yahweh and whole-hearted repentance. The first four are alphabetical poems, their verses beginning with all the letters of the Hebr. alphabet in series. Their attribution to Jeremiah merely shows the influence of that great prophet in later Judaism.

LAMENTATIONS

FIRST LAMENTATION

1 *Aleph* How deserted she sits,
the city once thronged with people!
Once the greatest of nations,
she is now like a widow.
Once the princess of states,
she is now put to forced labour.

Bet 2All night long she is weeping,
tears running down her cheeks.
Not one of all her lovers
remains to comfort her.
Her friends have all betrayed her
and become her enemies.

Gimel 3 Judah has gone into exile
after much pain and toil.
Living among the nations
she finds no respite;
her persecutors all overtake her
where there is no way out.

Dalet 4 The roads to Zion are in mourning;
no one comes to her festivals now.
Her gateways are all deserted;
her priests groan;
her young girls are grief-stricken;
she suffers bitterly.

He 5 Her foes now have the upper hand,
her enemies prosper,
for Yahweh has made her suffer
for her many, many crimes;
her children have gone away into captivity
driven in front of the oppressor.

Waw 6 And from the daughter of Zion
all her splendour has departed.
Her princes were like stags
which could find no pasture,
exhausted, as they flee
before the hunter.

Zain 7 Jerusalem remembers
her days of misery and distress;
when her people fell into the enemy's clutches
there was no one to help her.
Her enemies looked on
and laughed at her downfall.

Het 8 Jerusalem has sinned so gravely
that she has become a thing unclean.
All who used to honour her despise her,
having seen her nakedness;
she herself groans aloud
and turns her face away.

Tet 9 Her filth befouls her skirts—
she never thought to end like this,
and hence her astonishing fall
with no one to comfort her.
Yahweh, look at my misery,
for the enemy is triumphant!

Yod 10 The enemy stretched out his hand
for everything she treasured;
she saw the heathen
enter her sanctuary,
whom you had forbidden
to enter your Assembly.

Kaph 11 All her people are groaning,
looking for something to eat;
they have bartered their treasures for food,
to keep themselves alive.

Look, Yahweh, and consider
how despised I am!

Lamed 12 All you who pass this way,
look and see:
is any sorrow like the sorrow
inflicted on me,
with which Yahweh struck me
on the day of his burning anger?

Mem 13 He sent fire from on high
deep into my bones;
he stretched a net for my feet,
he pulled me back;
he left me shattered,
sick all day long.

Nun 14 He has watched out for my offences,
with his hand he enmeshes me,
his yoke is on my neck,
he has deprived me of strength.
The Lord has put me into clutches
which I am helpless to resist.

Samek 15 The Lord has rejected
all my warriors within my walls,
he has summoned a host against me
to crush my young men;
in the winepress the Lord trampled
the young daughter of Judah.

Ain 16 And that is why I weep;
my eyes stream with water,
since a comforter who could revive me
is far away.
My children are shattered,
for the enemy has proved too strong.

Pe 17 Zion stretches out her hands,
with no one to comfort her.
Yahweh has commanded Jacob's enemies
to surround him;
they treat Jerusalem
as though she were unclean.

Zade 18 Yahweh is in the right,
for I rebelled against his command.
Listen, all you peoples,
and see my sorrow.
My young girls and my young men
have gone into captivity.

Qoph 19 I called to my lovers;
they failed me.
My priests and my elders
expired in the city,
as they searched for food
to keep themselves alive.

Resh 20 Look, Yahweh. I am in distress!
My inmost being is in ferment;

my heart turns over inside me—
how rebellious I have been!
Outside, the sword bereaves;
inside it is like death.

Shin 21 Listen, for I am groaning,
with no one to comfort me.
All my enemies have heard of my disaster,
they are glad about what you have done.
Bring the Day you once foretold,
so that they may be like me!

Taw 22 Let all their wickedness come before you,
and treat them
as you have treated me
for all my crimes;
numberless are my groans,
and I am sick at heart.

SECOND LAMENTATION

2 *Aleph* In his anger, with what darkness
has the Lord enveloped the daughter of Zion!
He has flung the beauty of Israel
from heaven to the ground,
without regard for his footstool
on the day of his anger.

Bet 2 The Lord pitilessly engulfed
all the homes of Jacob;
in his fury he tore down
the fortresses of the daughter of Judah;
he threw to the ground, he desecrated
the kingdom and its princes.

Gimel 3 In his burning anger
he broke all the might of Israel,
withdrew his protecting right hand
at the coming of the enemy,
and blazed against Jacob like a fire
that burns up everything near it.

Dalet 4 Like an enemy he bent his bow,
and his right hand held firm;
like a foe he slaughtered
all those who were a delight to see;
on the tent of the daughter of Zion
he poured out his fury like fire.

He 5 The Lord behaved like an enemy;
he engulfed Israel,
he engulfed all its citadels,
he destroyed its fortresses
and for the daughter of Judah
multiplied weeping on wailing.

Waw [6]He wrecked his domain like a garden,
destroyed his assembly-points,
Yahweh erased the memory
of festivals and Sabbaths in Zion;
in the heat of his anger he treated
king and priest with contempt.

Zain [7]The Lord has rejected his altar,
he has come to loathe his sanctuary
and has given her palace walls
into the clutches of the enemy;
from the uproar they made in Yahweh's temple
it might have been a festival day!

Het [8]Yahweh has resolved to destroy
the walls of the daughter of Zion,
stretching out the line, not staying his hand
until he has engulfed everything,
thus bringing mourning on wall and rampart;
alike they crumbled.

Tet [9]Her gates have sunk into the ground;
he has broken and shattered their bars.
Her king and her princes are among the gentiles,
there is no instruction,
furthermore her prophets cannot find
any vision from Yahweh.

Yod [10]Mute, they sit on the ground,
the elders of the daughter of Zion;
they have put dust on their heads
and wrapped themselves in sackcloth.
The young girls of Jerusalem bow their heads
to the ground.

Kaph [11]My eyes are worn out with weeping,
my inmost being is in ferment,
my heart plummets
at the destruction of my young people,
as the children and babies grow faint
in the streets of the city.

Lamed [12]They keep saying to their mothers,
'Where is some food?'
as they faint like wounded men
in the streets of the city,
as they breathe their last
on their mothers' breasts.

Mem [13]To what can I compare or liken you,
daughter of Jerusalem?
Who can rescue and comfort you,
young daughter of Zion?
For huge as the sea is your ruin:
who can heal you?

Nun [14]The visions your prophets had for you
were deceptive whitewash;
they did not lay bare your guilt
so as to change your fortunes:

the visions they told you
were deceptive.

Samek 15 All who pass your way
clap their hands at the sight;
they whistle and shake their heads
over the daughter of Jerusalem,
'Is this the city they call Perfection of Beauty,
the joy of the whole world?'

Pe 16 Your enemies open their mouths
in chorus against you;
they whistle and grind their teeth;
they say, 'We have swallowed her up.
This is the day we were waiting for;
at last we have seen it!'

Ain 17 Yahweh has done what he planned,
has carried out his threat,
as he ordained long ago:
he has destroyed without pity,
increasing the might of your foes—
and letting your foes get the credit.

Zade 18 Cry then to the Lord,
rampart of the daughter of Zion;
let your tears flow like a torrent,
day and night;
allow yourself no respite,
give your eyes no rest!

Qoph 19 Up, cry out in the night-time
as each watch begins!
Pour your heart out like water
in Yahweh's presence!
Raise your hands to him
for the lives of your children
(who faint with hunger
at the end of every street)!

Resh 20 Look, Yahweh, and consider:
whom have you ever treated like this?
Should women eat their little ones,
the children they have nursed?
Should priest and prophet be slaughtered
in the Lord's sanctuary?

Shin 21 Children and old people are lying
on the ground in the streets;
my young men and young girls
have fallen by the sword;
you have killed them, on the day of your anger,
you have slaughtered them pitilessly.

Taw 22 As though to a festival you called together
terrors from all sides,
so that, on the day of Yahweh's anger,
none escaped and none survived.
Those whom I had nursed and reared,
my enemy has annihilated them all.

THIRD LAMENTATION

3 *Aleph* I am the man familiar with misery
under the rod of his fury.
2 He has led and guided me
into darkness, not light.
3 Against none but me does he turn his hand,
again and again, all day.

Bet 4 He has wasted my flesh and skin away,
has broken my bones.
5 He has besieged me and made hardship
a circlet round my head.
6 He has forced me to dwell where all is dark,
like those long-dead in their everlasting home.

Gimel 7 He has walled me in so that I cannot escape;
he has weighed me down with chains;
8 even when I shout for help,
he shuts out my prayer.
9 He has closed my way with blocks of stone,
he has obstructed my paths.

Dalet 10 For me he is a lurking bear,
a lion in hiding.
11 Heading me off, he has torn me apart,
leaving me shattered.
12 He has bent his bow and used me
as a target for his arrows.

He 13 He has shot deep into me
with shafts from his quiver.
14 I have become a joke to all my own people,
their refrain all day long.
15 He has given me my fill of bitterness,
he has made me drunk with wormwood.

Waw 16 He has broken my teeth with gravel,
he has fed me on ashes.
17 I have been deprived of peace,
I have forgotten what happiness is
18 and thought, 'My lasting hope
in Yahweh is lost.'

Zain 19 Bring to mind my misery and anguish;
it is wormwood and gall!
20 My heart dwells on this continually
and sinks within me.
21 This is what I shall keep in mind
and so regain some hope:

Het 22 Surely Yahweh's mercies are not over,
his deeds of faithful love not exhausted;
23 every morning they are renewed;
great is his faithfulness!
24 'Yahweh is all I have,' I say to myself,
'and so I shall put my hope in him.'

Tet
25 Yahweh is good to those who trust him,
to all who search for him.
26 It is good to wait in silence
for Yahweh to save.
27 It is good for someone to bear the yoke
from a young age,

Yod
28 to sit in solitude and silence
when it weighs heavy,
29 to lay one's head in the dust—
maybe there is hope—
30 to offer one's cheek to the striker,
to have one's fill of disgrace!

Kaph
31 For the Lord will not reject
anyone for ever.
32 If he brings grief, he will have pity
out of the fullness of his faithful love,
33 for it is not for his own pleasure
that he torments and grieves the human race.

Lamed
34 When all the prisoners in a country
are crushed underfoot,
35 when human rights are overridden
in defiance of the Most High,
36 when someone is cheated of justice,
does not the Lord see it?

Mem
37 Who has only to speak and it is so done?
Who commands, if not the Lord?
38 From where, if not from the mouth of the Most High,
do evil and good come?
39 Why then should anyone complain?
Better to be bold against one's sins.

Nun
40 Let us examine our path, let us ponder it
and return to Yahweh.
41 Let us raise our hearts and hands
to God in heaven.
42 We are the ones who have sinned, who have rebelled,
and you have not forgiven.

Samek
43 You have enveloped us in anger,
pursuing us, slaughtering without pity.
44 You have wrapped yourself in a cloud
too thick for prayer to pierce.
45 You have reduced us to rubbish
and refuse among the nations.

Pe
46 Our enemies open their mouths
in chorus against us.
47 Terror and pitfall have been our lot,
ravage and ruin.
48 My eyes dissolve in torrents of tears
at the ruin of my beloved people.

Ain
49 My eyes will weep ceaselessly,
without relief,
50 until Yahweh looks down
and sees from heaven.

51 My eyes have grown sore
over all the daughters of my city.

Zade 52 Unprovoked, my enemies
hunted me down like a bird.
53 They shut me finally in a pit,
they closed me in with a stone.
54 The waters rose over my head;
I thought, 'I am lost!'

Qoph 55 Yahweh, I called on your name
from the deep pit.
56 You heard my voice, do not close your ear
to my prayer, to my cry.
57 You are near when I call to you.
You said, 'Do not be afraid!'

Resh 58 Lord, you defended my cause,
you have redeemed my life.
59 Yahweh, you have seen the wrong done to me,
grant me redress.
60 You have seen their vindictiveness,
all their plots against me.

Shin 61 You have heard their insults, Yahweh,
all their plots against me,
62 the whispering and murmuring of my enemies
against me all day long.
63 Look, whether they sit or stand,
I am their refrain.

Taw 64 Yahweh, repay them
as their deeds deserve.
65 Lay hardness of heart
as your curse on them.
66 Angrily pursue them, root them out
from under your heavens!

FOURTH LAMENTATION

4 *Aleph* How the gold has tarnished,
how the fine gold has changed!
The sacred stones lie scattered
at the corner of every street.

Bet 2 The children of Zion,
as precious as finest gold—
to think that they should now be reckoned
like crockery made by a potter!

Gimel 3 The very jackals give the breast,
and suckle their young:
but the daughter of my people is as cruel
as the ostriches of the desert.

Dalet 4 The tongue of the baby at the breast
sticks to its palate for thirst;

little children ask for bread,
no one gives them any.

He 5Those who used to eat only the best,
now lie dying in the streets;
those who were reared in the purple
claw at the rubbish heaps,

Waw 6for the wickedness of the daughter of my people
exceeded the sins of Sodom,
which was overthrown in a moment
without a hand being laid on it.

Zain 7Once her young people were brighter than snow,
whiter than milk;
rosier than coral their bodies,
their hue like sapphire.

Het 8Now their faces are blacker than soot,
they are not recognised in the streets,
the skin has shrunk over their bones,
as dry as a stick.

Tet 9Happier those killed by the sword
than those killed by famine:
they waste away, sunken
for lack of the fruits of the earth.

Yod 10With their own hands, kindly women
cooked their children;
this was their food
when the daughter of my people was ruined.

Kaph 11Yahweh indulged his fury,
he vented his fierce anger,
he lit a fire in Zion
which devoured her foundations.

Lamed 12The kings of the earth never believed,
nor did any of the inhabitants of the world,
that foe or enemy would ever penetrate
the gates of Jerusalem.

Mem 13Owing to the sins of her prophets
and the crimes of her priests,
who had shed the blood of the upright,
in the heart of the city,

Nun 14they wandered blindly through the streets,
polluted with blood,
so that no one dared
to touch their clothes.

Samek 15'Keep away! Unclean!' people shouted,
'Keep away! Keep away! Don't touch!'
If they left and fled to the nations,
they were not allowed to stay there either.

Pe 16The face of Yahweh destroyed them,
he will look on them no more.
There was no respect for the priests,
no deference for the elders.

Ain 17 Continually we were wearing out our eyes,
watching for help—in vain.
From our towers we watched for a nation
which could not save us anyway.

Zade 18 Men dogged our steps,
to keep us out of our streets.
Our end was near, our days were done,
our end had come.

Qoph 19 Our pursuers were swifter
than eagles in the sky;
they hounded our steps through the mountains,
they lay in ambush for us in the wilds.

Resh 20 The breath of our nostrils, Yahweh's anointed,
was caught in their traps,
he of whom we said, 'In his shadow
we shall live among the nations.'

Shin 21 Rejoice, exult, daughter of Edom,
you who reside in Uz![a]
To you in turn the cup will pass;
you will get drunk and strip yourself naked!

Taw 22 Your wickedness is atoned for, daughter of Zion,
he will never banish you again.
But your wickedness, daughter of Edom, will he punish,
your sins he will lay bare!

FIFTH LAMENTATION

5 Yahweh, remember what has happened to us;
consider, and see our degradation.

2 Our heritage has passed to strangers,
our homes to foreigners.

3 We are orphans, we are fatherless;
our mothers are like widows.

4 We have to buy our own water to drink,
our own wood we can get only at a price.

5 The yoke is on our necks; we are persecuted;
exhausted we are, allowed no rest.

6 We made a pact with Egypt,
with Assyria, to have plenty of food.

7 Our ancestors sinned; they are no more,
and we bear the weight of their guilt.

8 Slaves rule us;
there is no one to rescue us from their clutches.

9 At peril of our lives we earn our bread,
by risking the sword of the desert.

4a South of Edom. The neighbouring peoples joined in the destruction of Jerusalem.

[10]Our skin is as hot as an oven,
from the scorch of famine.

[11]The women in Zion have been raped,
the young girls in the towns of Judah.

[12]Princes have been hanged by their hands;
the face of the old has won no respect.

[13]Youths have been put to the mill,
boys stagger under loads of wood.

[14]The elders have deserted the gateway;
the young have given up their music.

[15]Joy has vanished from our hearts;
our dancing has turned to mourning.

[16]The crown has fallen from our heads.
Alas that ever we sinned!

[17]This is why our hearts are sick;
this is why our eyes are dim:

[18]because Mount Zion is desolate;
jackals roam to and fro on it.

[19]Yet you, Yahweh, rule from eternity;
your throne endures from age to age.

[20]Why do you never remember us?
Why do you abandon us so long?

[21]Make us come back to you, Yahweh, and we will come back.
Restore us as we were before!

[22]Unless you have utterly rejected us,
in an anger which knows no limit.

THE BOOK OF BARUCH

This book assembles four quite separate pieces, two in prose and two in poetry. It is a valuable expression of the spirituality of the Jews dispersed in exile, their devotion to the Jewish Law, their spirit of penance and their messianic hopes. Although it is conventionally attributed to Baruch, Jeremiah's secretary, it was probably written in the first century BC (chapter 6 at least a century earlier).

PLAN OF THE BOOK

THE BOOK OF BARUCH

INTRODUCTION

Baruch and the Jews in Babylon

1 This is the text of the book written in Babylon by Baruch son of Neraiah, son of Mahseiah, son of Zedekiah, son of Hasadiah, son of Hilkiah, [2]in the fifth year, on the seventh day of the month, at the time when the Chaldaeans had captured Jerusalem and burned it down.

[3]Baruch read the text of this book aloud to Jeconiah son of Jehoiakim, king of Judah, and to all the people who had come to hear the reading, [4]to the nobles and the sons of the king, and to the elders; to the whole people, that is, to the least no less than to the greatest, to all who lived in Babylon beside the river Sud. [5]On hearing it they wept, fasted and prayed before the Lord; [6]and they collected as much money as each could afford [7]and sent it to Jerusalem to the priest Jehoiakim son of Hilkiah, son of Shallum, and the other priests, and all the people who were with him in Jerusalem. [8]Also on the tenth day of Sivan he was given the utensils of the house of the Lord, which had been removed from the Temple, to take them back to the land of Judah; these were silver utensils which Zedekiah son of Josiah, king of Judah, had had made [9]after Nebuchadnezzar king of Babylon had deported Jeconiah from Jerusalem to Babylon, together with the princes, the metalworkers, the nobles and the common people.

[10]Now, they wrote, we are sending you money to pay for burnt offerings, offerings for sin, and incense. Prepare oblations and offer them on the altar of the Lord our God; [11]and pray for the long life of Nebuchadnezzar king of Babylon, and of his son Belshazzar, that they may endure on earth as long as the heavens endure; [12]and that the Lord may give us strength and enlighten our eyes, so that we may lead our lives under the protection of Nebuchadnezzar king of Babylon and of his son Belshazzar, and that we may serve them for a long time and win their favour. [13]Also pray to the Lord our God for us, because we have sinned against him, and the anger, the fury of the Lord, has still not turned away from us. [14]Lastly, you must read the booklet which we are sending you, publicly in the house of the Lord on the feastday and appropriate days. [15]You must say:

I: THE PRAYER OF THE EXILES

Confession of sins

Saving justice is the Lord's, we have only the look of shame we bear, as is the case today for the people of Judah and the inhabitants of Jerusalem, [16]for our kings and princes, our priests, our prophets, and for our ancestors, [17]because we have sinned before the Lord, [18]have disobeyed him, and have not listened to the voice of the Lord our God telling us to follow the commandments which the Lord had ordained for us. [19]From the day when the Lord brought our ancestors out of Egypt until today we have been disobedient to the Lord our God, we have been disloyal, refusing to listen to his voice. [20]And we are not free even today of the disasters and the curse which the Lord pronounced through

his servant Moses the day he brought our
ancestors out of Egypt to give us a land
flowing with milk and honey. 21 We have not
listened to the voice of the Lord our God in
all the words of those prophets he sent us;
22 but, each following the dictates of our evil
heart, we have taken to serving alien gods,
and doing what is displeasing to the Lord
our God.

2 And so the Lord has carried out the
sentence which he passed on us, on our
judges who governed Israel, on our kings and
leaders and on the people of Israel and of
Judah; 2 what he did to Jerusalem has never
been paralleled under the wide heavens—in
conformity with what was written in the Law
of Moses; 3 we were each reduced to eating
the flesh of our own sons and daughters.
4 Furthermore, he has handed them over into
the power of all the kingdoms that surround
us, to be the contempt and execration of all
the neighbouring peoples among whom the
Lord scattered them. 5 Instead of being
masters, they found themselves enslaved,
because we had sinned against the Lord our
God by not listening to his voice.

6 Saving justice is the Lord's; we and our
ancestors have only the look of shame we
bear today. 7 All those disasters which the
Lord pronounced against us have now
befallen us. 8 And yet we have not tried to
win the favour of the Lord by each of us
renouncing the dictates of our own wicked
heart; 9 so the Lord has been alert to our
misdeeds and has brought disaster down on
us, since the Lord is upright in everything
he had commanded us to do, 10 and we have
not listened to his voice so as to follow the
commandments which the Lord had
ordained for us.

The prayer

11 And now, Lord, God of Israel, who brought
your people out of Egypt with a mighty hand,
with signs and wonders, with great power
and with outstretched arm, to win yourself a
name such as you have today, 12 we have
sinned, we have committed sacrilege; Lord
our God, we have broken all your precepts.
13 Let your anger turn from us since we are
no more than a little remnant among the
nations where you have dispersed us.
14 Listen, Lord, to our prayers and our
entreaties; deliver us for your own sake and
let us win the favour of the people who have
deported us, 15 so that the whole world may
know that you are the Lord our God, since
Israel and his descendants bear your name.
16 Look down, Lord, from your holy
dwelling-place and think of us, bow your ear
and listen, 17 open your eyes, Lord, and look;
the dead down in Sheol, whose breath has
been taken from their bodies, are not the
ones to give glory and due recognition to the
Lord; 18 whoever is overcome with affliction,
who goes along bowed down and frail, with
failing eyes and hungering soul, that is the
one to give you glory and due recognition,
Lord.

19 We do not rely on the merits of our
ancestors and of our kings to offer you our
humble plea, Lord our God. 20 No, you have
sent down your anger and your fury on us,
as you threatened through your servants the
prophets when they said, 21 'The Lord says
this: *Bend your necks and serve the king of
Babylon,*[a] and you will remain in the country
which I gave to your ancestors. 22 But if you
do not listen to the voice of the Lord and
serve the king of Babylon 23 then *I shall silence
the shouts of rejoicing and mirth and the voices
of bridegroom and bride in the towns of Judah
and the streets of Jerusalem, and the whole
country will be reduced to desert,*[b] with no
inhabitants.' 24 But we would not listen to
your voice and serve the king of Babylon, and
so you carried out what you had threatened
through your servants the prophets: that the
bones of our kings and of our ancestors would
be dragged from their resting places. 25 They
were indeed *tossed out to the heat of the day
and the frost of the night.*[c] And people died in
dreadful agony, from famine, sword and
plague. 26 And so, because of the wickedness
of the House of Israel and the House of
Judah, you have made this House, that bears
your name, what it is today.

27 And yet, Lord our God, you have treated
us in a way worthy of all your goodness
and boundless tenderness, 28 just as you had
promised through your servant Moses, the
day you told him to write your Law in the
presence of the Israelites, and said, 29 'If you

2a Jr 27:12.
2b Jr 7:34.
2c Jr 36:30.

do not listen to my voice, this great and
innumerable multitude will certainly be
reduced to a tiny few among the nations
where I shall scatter them—30 for I knew that,
being an obstinate people, they would not
listen to me. But in the country of their
exile, they will come to themselves 31 and
acknowledge that I am the Lord their God. I
shall give them a heart and an attentive ear,
32 and they will sing my praises in the country
of their exile, they will remember my name;
33 they will stop being obstinate and, remem-
bering what became of their ancestors who
sinned before the Lord, will turn from their
evil deeds. 34 Then I shall bring them back to
the country which I promised on oath to their
ancestors Abraham, Isaac and Jacob, and
make them masters in it. I shall make their
numbers grow; they will not dwindle again.
35 And I shall make an everlasting covenant
with them; so that I am their God and they
are my people. And never again shall I drive
my people Israel out of the country which I
have given them.'

3 Almighty Lord, God of Israel, a soul in
anguish, a troubled heart now cries to
you: 2 Listen and have pity, Lord, for we
have sinned before you. 3 You sit enthroned
for ever, while we are perishing for ever.
4 Almighty Lord, God of Israel, hear the
prayer of the dead of Israel, of the children
of those who have sinned against you and
have not listened to the voice of the Lord
their God; hence the disasters which dog us.
5 Do not call to mind the misdeeds of our
ancestors, but remember instead your power
and your name. 6 You are indeed the Lord
our God and we will praise you, Lord, 7 since
you have put respect for you in our hearts to
encourage us to call on your name. We long
to praise you in our exile, for we have rid our
hearts of the wickedness of our ancestors
who sinned against you. 8 Look, today we
are still in exile where you have scattered us
as something contemptible, accursed, con-
demned, for all the misdeeds of our ancestors
who had abandoned the Lord our God.

II: WISDOM, THE PREROGATIVE OF ISRAEL

9 Listen, Israel, to commands
that bring life;
hear, and learn what knowledge means.
10 Why, Israel, why are you in the country
of your enemies,
growing older and older in an alien land,
11 defiling yourselves with the dead,
reckoned with those who go to Sheol?
12 It is because you have forsaken
the fountain of wisdom!
13 Had you walked in the way of God,
you would be living in peace for ever.
14 Learn where knowledge is,
where strength,
where understanding, and so learn
where length of days is, where life,
where the light of the eyes
and where peace.

15 But who has found out where she lives,
who has entered her treasure house?
16 Where now are the leaders of the nations
and those who ruled
even the beasts of earth,
17 those who sported with the birds of heaven,
those who accumulated silver and gold
on which all people rely,
and whose possessions had no end,
18 those who worked so carefully in silver
—but of whose works
no trace is to be found?
19 They have vanished, gone down to Sheol.
Others have risen to their places,
20 more recent generations have seen the day
and peopled the earth in their turn,
but the way of knowledge
they have not found;
21 they have not recognised
the paths she treads.
Nor have their children
had any grasp of her,
remaining far from her way.
22 Nothing has been heard of her in Canaan,
nothing has been seen of her in Teman;
23 the children of Hagar
in search of worldly wisdom,
the merchants of Midian and Teman,
the tale-spinners and the philosophers
have none of them
found the way to wisdom
or remembered the paths she treads.

24 How great, Israel, is the house of God,
how wide his domain,
25 immeasurably wide,
infinitely lofty!
26 In it were born the giants,
famous from the beginning,
immensely tall, expert in war;
27 God's choice did not fall on these,
he did not show them
the way of knowledge;
28 they perished for lack of wisdom,
perished by their own folly.
29 Who has ever climbed the sky
and seized her
to bring her down from the clouds?
30 Who has ever crossed the ocean
and found her
to bring her back
in exchange for the finest gold?
31 No one can learn the way to her,
no one can understand the path she treads.

32 But the One who knows all discovers her,
he has grasped her with his own intellect,
he has set the earth firm for evermore
and filled it with four-footed beasts,
33 he sends the light—and it goes,
he recalls it—and trembling it obeys;
34 the stars shine joyfully at their posts;
35 when he calls them, they answer,
'Here we are';
they shine to delight their Creator.
36 It is he who is our God,
no other can compare with him.
37 He has uncovered the whole way
of knowledge
and shown it to his servant Jacob,
to Israel his well-beloved;
38 only then did she appear on earth
and live among human beings.
4 She is the book of God's commandments,
the Law that stands for ever;
those who keep her shall live,
those who desert her shall die.
2 Turn back, Jacob, seize her,
in her radiance make your way to light:
3 do not yield your glory to another,
your privilege to a people not your own.
4 Israel, blessed are we:
what pleases God has been revealed to us!

III: THE COMPLAINTS AND HOPES OF JERUSALEM

5 Take courage, my people,
memorial of Israel!
6 You were sold to the nations,
but not for extermination.
You provoked God;
and so were delivered to your enemies,
7 since you had angered your Creator
by offering sacrifices to demons,
and not to God.
8 You had forgotten the eternal God
who reared you.
You had also grieved Jerusalem
who nursed you,
9 for when she saw God's anger
falling on you, she said:

Listen, you neighbours of Zion:
God has sent me great sorrow.
10 I have seen my sons and daughters
taken into captivity,
which the Eternal brought down on them.
11 I had reared them joyfully;
in tears, in sorrow,
I watched them go away.
12 Do not, any of you, exult over me,
a widow, deserted by so many;
I am bereaved
because of the sins of my children,
who turned away from the Law of God,
13 who did not want to know his precepts
and would not follow
the ways of his commandments
or tread the paths of discipline
as his justice directed.
14 Come here, neighbours of Zion!
Remember my sons'
and daughters' captivity,
which the Eternal brought down on them.
15 How he brought a distant nation
down on them,
a ruthless nation
speaking a foreign language,
they showed neither respect for the aged,
nor pity for the child;
16 they carried off
the widow's cherished sons,
they left her quite alone,
bereft of her daughters.
17 For my part, how could I help you?

18 He who brought those disasters
down on you,
is the one to deliver you
from your enemies' clutches.
19 Go, my children, go your way!
I must stay bereft and lonely;
20 I have taken off the clothes of peace
and put on the sackcloth of entreaty;
all my life I shall cry to the Eternal.

21 Take courage, my children, call on God:
he will deliver you from tyranny,
from the clutches of your enemies;
22 for I look to the Eternal for your rescue,
and joy has come to me from the Holy One
at the mercy soon to reach you
from your Saviour, the Eternal.
23 In sorrow and tears I watched you go away,
but God will give you back to me
in joy and gladness for ever.
24 As the neighbours of Zion
have now witnessed your captivity,
so will they soon see your rescue by God,
which will come upon you with great glory
and splendour of the Eternal.
25 My children, patiently bear the anger
brought on you by God.
Your enemy has persecuted you,
but soon you will witness his destruction
and set your foot on his neck.
26 My favourite children
have travelled by rough roads,
carried off like a flock
by a marauding enemy.
27 Take courage, my children, call on God:
he who brought this on you
will remember you.
28 As by your will you first strayed from God,
so now turn back
and search for him ten times harder;
29 for as he has been bringing down
those disasters on you,
so will he rescue you
and give you eternal joy.
30 Take courage, Jerusalem:
he who gave you your name
will console you.
31 Disaster will come to all
who have ill-treated you
and gloated over your fall.
32 Disaster will come to the cities
where your children were slaves;
disaster to whichever one
received your children,
33 for just as she rejoiced at your fall
and was happy to see you ruined,
so will she grieve over her own desolation.
34 I shall deprive her of the joy
of a populous city,
and her insolence will turn to mourning;
35 fire from the Eternal
will befall her for many a day,
and demons will dwell in her for ages.
36 Jerusalem, turn your eyes to the east,
see the joy that is coming to you from God.
37 Look, the children you watched go away
are on their way home;
reassembled from east and west,
they are on their way home
at the Holy One's command,
rejoicing in God's glory.

5 Jerusalem, take off your dress of sorrow
and distress,
put on the beauty of God's glory
for evermore,
2 wrap the cloak of God's saving justice
around you,
put the diadem of the Eternal One's glory
on your head,
3 for God means to show your splendour
to every nation under heaven,
4 and the name God gives you
for evermore will be,
'Peace-through-Justice,
and Glory-through-Devotion'.
5 Arise, Jerusalem, stand on the heights
and turn your eyes to the east:
see your children reassembled
from west and east
at the Holy One's command,
rejoicing because God has remembered.
6 Though they left you on foot
driven by enemies,
now God brings them back to you,
carried gloriously, like a royal throne.
7 For God has decreed the flattening
of each high mountain,
of the everlasting hills,
the filling of the valleys
to make the ground level
so that Israel can walk safely
in God's glory.
8 And the forests and every fragrant tree
will provide shade
for Israel, at God's command;
9 for God will guide Israel in joy
by the light of his glory,
with the mercy and saving justice
which come from him.

IV: THE LETTER OF JEREMIAH

*A copy of the letter which Jeremiah sent to those
about to be led captive to Babylon by the king
of the Babylonians, to tell them what he had
been commanded by God:*

6 'Because of the sins which you have
committed before God you are to be
deported to Babylon by Nebuchadnezzar
king of the Babylonians. [2]Once you have
reached Babylon you will stay there for many
years, as long as seven generations; after
which I shall bring you home in peace. [3]Now
in Babylon you will see gods made of silver,
of gold, of wood, being carried shoulder-
high, and filling the gentiles with fear. [4]Be
on your guard! Do not imitate the foreigners,
do not have any fear of their gods [5]as you
see their worshippers prostrating themselves
before and behind them. Instead, say in
your hearts, "Master, it is you that we must
worship." [6]For my angel is with you; your
lives will be in his care.

[7]'Overlaid with gold and silver, their
tongues polished smooth by a craftsman,
they are counterfeit and have no power to
speak. [8]As though for a girl fond of finery,
these people take gold and make crowns for
the heads of their gods. [9]And sometimes, the
priests filch gold and silver from their gods
to spend on themselves, even giving some of
it to the prostitutes on the terrace. [10]They
dress up these gods of silver, gold and wood,
in clothes, like human beings; on their own
they cannot protect themselves from either
tarnish or woodworm; [11]when they have been
dressed in purple cloaks, their faces have to
be dusted, because of the temple dust which
settles thick on them. [12]One holds a sceptre
like the governor of a province, yet is power-
less to put to death anyone who offends him;
[13]another holds sword and mace in his right
hand, yet is powerless to defend himself
against war or thieves. [14]From this it is
evident that they are not gods; do not be
afraid of them.

[15]'Just as a pot in common use becomes
useless once it is broken, so are these gods
enshrined inside their temples. [16]Their eyes
are full of dust raised by the feet of those who
enter. [17]Just as the doors are locked on all
sides on someone who has offended a king
and is under sentence of death, so the priests
secure the temples of these gods with gates
and bolts and bars for fear of burglary. [18]They
light more lamps for them than they do for
themselves, and the gods see none of them.
[19]They are like one of the temple beams,
which are said to be gnawed away from
within; the termites creep out of the ground
and eat them and their clothes too, and they
feel nothing. [20]Their faces are blackened by
the smoke that rises from the temple. [21]Bats,
swallows, birds of every kind perch on their
bodies and heads, and so do cats. [22]From
this, you can see for yourselves that they are
not gods; do not be afraid of them.

[23]'The gold with which they are parading
their futility before the world is supposed to
make them look beautiful, but if someone
does not rub off the tarnish, these gods will
not be shining much on their own, and even
while they were being cast, they felt nothing.
[24]However much was paid for them, there is
still no breath of life in them. [25]Being unable
to walk, they have to be carried on men's
shoulders, which shows how futile they are.
It is humiliating for their worshippers, too,
who have to stand them up again if they fall
over. [26]Once they have been stood up, they
cannot move on their own; if they tilt askew,
they cannot right themselves; offerings made
to them might as well be made to the dead.
[27]Whatever is sacrificed to them, the priests
re-sell and pocket the profit; while their wives
salt down part of it, but give nothing to the
poor or to the helpless. As to the sacrifices
themselves, why, women during their
periods and women in childbed are not afraid
to touch them! [28]From all this you can tell
that they are not gods; do not be afraid of
them.

[29]'Indeed, how can they even be called
gods, when women do the offering to these
gods of silver, gold and wood? [30]In their
temples, the priests stay sitting down, their
garments torn, heads and beard shaved and
heads uncovered; [31]they roar and shriek
before their gods as people do at funeral
feasts. [32]The priests take robes from the
gods to clothe their own wives and children.
[33]Whether these gods are treated badly or
well, they are incapable of paying back either
treatment; as incapable too of making or

unmaking kings, 34 equally incapable of distributing wealth or money. If anyone fails to honour a vow he has made to them, they cannot call him to account. 35 They can neither save anyone from death nor rescue the weak from the strong, 36 nor restore sight to the blind, nor save anyone in trouble, 37 nor take pity on a widow, nor be generous to an orphan. 38 These wooden gods overlaid with gold and silver are about as much use as rocks cut out of the mountain side. Their worshippers will be confounded! 39 So how can anyone think or say that they are gods?

40 'The Chaldaeans themselves do them no honour; if they find someone who is dumb and cannot speak, they present him to Bel, entreating him for the gift of speech, as though he could perceive it! 41 And they are incapable of drawing the conclusion and abandoning those gods—such is their lack of perception. 42 Women with strings round their waists sit in the streets, burning bran like incense; 43 when one of these has been picked up by a passer-by and been to bed with him, she then gloats over her neighbour for not having been thought as worthy as herself and for not having had her string broken. 44 Whatever is done for them is spurious. So how can anyone think or say that they are gods?

45 'Made by woodworkers and goldsmiths, they are only what those workmen decide to make them. 46 Their makers have not long to live themselves, so how can the things they make be gods? 47 Their legacy to their descendants is nothing but delusion and dishonour. 48 If war or disasters befall them, the priests discuss where best to hide themselves and these gods; 49 how can anyone fail to realise that they are not gods, if they cannot save themselves from war or from disasters? 50 And since they are only made of wood overlaid with gold or silver, it will later become apparent that they are spurious; it will be obvious to everyone, to nations as to kings, that they are not gods but the work of human hands, and that there is no divine activity in them. 51 Does anyone still need convincing that they are not gods?

52 'They can neither appoint a king over a country, nor give rain to humankind, 53 nor regulate their own affairs, nor rescue anyone who suffers a wrong; they are as helpless as crows between sky and ground. 54 If fire falls on the temple of these wooden gods overlaid with gold or silver, their priests fly to safety while they for their part stay there like beams, to be burnt. 55 They cannot put up any resistance to a king or to enemies. 56 So how can anyone think or say that they are gods?

57 'These wooden gods overlaid with gold or silver cannot evade thieves or marauders; strong men may rob them of their gold and silver and make off with the robes they are dressed in; yet they are powerless to help even themselves. 58 Better to be a king displaying his prowess, a household pot of use to its owner, than to be these counterfeit gods; or merely the door of a house, protecting what is inside, than these counterfeit gods; or a wooden pillar in a palace than these counterfeit gods. 59 The sun, the moon and the stars, which shine and have been given work to do, are obedient; 60 similarly, the lightning, as it flashes, is a fine sight; in the same way, the wind blows across every country, 61 the clouds execute the order God gives them to pass over the whole earth, and the fire, sent from above to consume mountain and forest, carries out its orders. 62 Now these gods are not their equals, either in beauty or in power. 63 So, no one can think or say that they are gods, powerless as they are to administer justice or to do anyone any good. 64 Therefore, knowing that they are not gods, do not be afraid of them.

65 'For they can neither curse nor bless kings, 66 nor produce signs in heaven for the nations, nor shine like the sun, nor shed light like the moon. 67 The animals are better off than they are, being able to look after themselves by making for cover. 68 There is not the slightest shred of evidence that they are gods; so do not be afraid of them!

69 'Their wooden gods overlaid with gold and silver are like a scarecrow in a field of cucumbers—protecting nothing. 70 Or again, their wooden gods overlaid with gold and silver are like a thorn-bush in a garden—any kind of bird may perch on it—or like a corpse thrown out into the dark. 71 From the purple and linen rotting on their backs you can tell that they are not gods; and in the end, eaten away, they will be the dishonour of the country. 72 Better, then, someone upright who has no idols; dishonour will never come near him.'

THE BOOK OF EZEKIEL

Ezekiel describes his visions, especially the opening vision of God which inspires and pervades the book, with an imaginative power which has stimulated religious artists down the centuries. He gives his message also by means of weird mimes and fantastic poetic allegories. But the burden of his message is clear: after the capture of Jerusalem the hope of Israel lies in the exiles in Babylon, not in the contaminated rabble remaining in Jerusalem. Ezekiel calls the exiles to conversion: they can forget the failings of their ancestors, for all are now responsible only for their own sins. Yahweh has promised them a new spirit and a new covenant; he himself will be their shepherd who will look to his own name and reputation as the champion of Israel. The prophet of hope, Ezekiel concludes his visions with a blueprint for the new Temple and the new Jerusalem, modelled on the old but superior to it, the centre of a new Holy Land, sanctified by the holiness and presence of God.

Ezekiel prophesied in Babylon between 593 and 571 BC. He must have been deported after the first siege of Jerusalem in 598; he foretells the final destruction of the city in 586. But, as usual with the prophets, his prophecies were arranged by his disciples often by sequence of thought rather than in chronological order.

PLAN OF THE BOOK

EZEKIEL

INTRODUCTION

1 In the thirtieth year, on the fifth day of
the fourth month, as I was among the
exiles by the River Chebar, heaven opened
and I saw visions from God. [2]On the fifth of
the month—it was the fifth year of exile for
King Jehoiachin—[3]the word of Yahweh was
addressed to the priest Ezekiel son of Buzi,
in Chaldaea by the River Chebar. There the
hand of Yahweh came on him.

The vision of the Chariot of Yahweh

[4]I looked; a stormy wind blew from the north,
a great cloud with flashing fire and brilliant
light round it, and in the middle, in the heart
of the fire, a brilliance like that of amber,
[5]and in the middle what seemed to be four
living creatures. They looked like this: They
were of human form. [6]Each had four faces,

each had four wings. 7Their legs were
straight; they had hooves like calves, glit-
tering like polished brass. 8Below their
wings, they had human hands on all four
sides corresponding to their four faces and
four wings. 9They touched one another with
their wings; they did not turn as they moved;
each one moved straight forward. 10As to the
appearance of their faces, all four had a
human face, and a lion's face to the right,
and all four had a bull's face to the left, and
all four had an eagle's face. 11Their wings
were spread upwards, each had one pair
touching its neighbour's, and the other pair
covering its body. 12And each one moved
straight forward; they went where the
spirit urged them, they did not turn as
they moved.

13Between these living creatures were what
looked like blazing coals, like torches,
darting backwards and forwards between the
living creatures; the fire gave a brilliant light,
and lightning flashed from the fire, 14and
the living creatures kept disappearing and
reappearing like flashes of lightning.

15Now, as I looked at the living creatures,
I saw a wheel touching the ground beside
each of the four-faced living creatures. 16The
appearance and structure of the wheels were
like glittering chrysolite. All four looked
alike, and their appearance and structure
were such that each wheel seemed to have
another wheel inside it. 17In whichever of the
four directions they moved, they did not need
to turn as they moved. 18Their circumference
was of awe-inspiring size, and the rims of all
four sparkled all the way round. 19When the
living creatures moved, the wheels moved
beside them; and when the living creatures
left the ground, the wheels too left the
ground. 20They moved in whichever direc-
tion the spirit chose to go, and the wheels
rose with them, since the wheels shared
the spirit of the animals. 21When the living
creatures moved on, they moved on; when
the former halted, the latter halted; when the
former left the ground, the wheels too left
the ground, since the wheels shared the spirit
of the animals. 22Over the heads of the living
creatures was what looked like a solid surface
glittering like crystal, spread out over their
heads, above them, 23and under the solid
surface, their wings were spread out straight,
touching one another, and each had a pair
covering its body. 24I also heard the noise of
their wings; when they moved, it was like
the noise of flood-waters, like the voice of
Shaddai, like the noise of a storm, like the
noise of an armed camp; and when they
halted, they lowered their wings; 25there was
a noise too.

26Beyond the solid surface above their
heads, there was what seemed like a sapphire,
in the form of a throne. High above on
the form of a throne was a form with the
appearance of a human being.

27I saw a brilliance like amber, like fire,
radiating from what appeared to be the waist
upwards; and from what appeared to be the
waist downwards, I saw what looked like
fire, giving a brilliant light all round. 28The
radiance of the encircling light was like the
radiance of the bow in the clouds on rainy
days. The sight was like the glory of Yahweh.
I looked and fell to the ground, and I heard
the voice of someone speaking to me.

The vision of the scroll

2 He said, 'Son of man, get to your feet; I
will speak to you.' 2As he said these words
the spirit came into me and put me on my
feet, and I heard him speaking to me. 3He
said, 'Son of man, I am sending you to the
Israelites, to the rebels who have rebelled
against me. They and their ancestors have
been in revolt against me up to the present
day. 4Because they are stubborn and obsti-
nate children, I am sending you to them, to
say, "Lord Yahweh says this." 5Whether
they listen or not, this tribe of rebels will
know there is a prophet among them. 6And
you, son of man, do not be afraid of them or
of what they say, though you find yourself
surrounded with brambles and sitting on
scorpions. Do not be afraid of their words or
alarmed by their looks, for they are a tribe of
rebels. 7You are to deliver my words to them
whether they listen or not, for they are a tribe
of rebels. 8But you, son of man, are to listen
to what I say to you; do not be a rebel like
that rebellious tribe. Open your mouth and
eat what I am about to give you.'

9When I looked, there was a hand stretch-
ing out to me, holding a scroll. 10He un-
rolled it in front of me; it was written on, front
and back; on it was written 'Lamentations,
dirges and cries of grief'.

3 He then said, 'Son of man, eat what you
see; eat this scroll, then go and speak to
the House of Israel.' 2I opened my mouth;
he gave me the scroll to eat 3and then said,

'Son of man, feed on this scroll which I am giving you and eat your fill.' So I ate it, and it tasted sweet as honey.

[4]He then said, 'Son of man, go to the House of Israel and tell them what I have said. [5]You are not being sent to a nation that speaks a difficult foreign language; you are being sent to the House of Israel. [6]Not to big nations that speak difficult foreign languages, and whose words you would not understand—if I sent you to them, they would listen to you; [7]but the House of Israel will not listen to you because it will not listen to me. The whole House of Israel is defiant and obstinate. [8]But now, I am making you as defiant as they are, and as obstinate as they are; [9]I am making your resolution as hard as a diamond, harder than flint. So do not be afraid of them, do not be overawed by them, for they are a tribe of rebels.'

[10]Then he said, 'Son of man, take to heart everything I say to you, listen carefully, [11]then go to your exiled countrymen and talk to them. Say to them, "Lord Yahweh says this," whether they listen or not.'

[12]The spirit lifted me up, and behind me I heard a great vibrating sound, 'Blessed be the glory of Yahweh in his dwelling-place!' [13]This was the sound of the living creatures' wings beating against each other, and the sound of the wheels beside them: a great vibrating sound. [14]The spirit lifted me up and took me, and I went, bitter and angry, and the hand of Yahweh lay heavy on me. [15]I came to Tel Abib, to the exiles beside the River Chebar where they were living, and there I stayed with them in a stupor for seven days.

The prophet as watchman[a]

[16]After seven days the word of Yahweh was addressed to me as follows, [17]'Son of man, I have appointed you as watchman for the House of Israel. When you hear a word from my mouth, warn them from me. [18]If I say to someone wicked, "You will die," and you do not warn this person; if you do not speak to warn someone wicked to renounce evil and so save his life, it is the wicked person who will die for the guilt, but I shall hold you responsible for that death. [19]If, however, you do warn someone wicked who then fails to renounce wickedness and evil ways, the wicked person will die for the guilt, but you yourself will have saved your life. [20]When someone upright renounces uprightness to do evil and I set a trap for him, it is he who will die; since you failed to warn him, he will die for his guilt, and the uprightness he practised will no longer be remembered; but I shall hold you responsible for his death. [21]If, however, you warn someone upright not to sin and this person does not sin, such a one will live, thanks to your warning, and you too will have saved your life.'

I: BEFORE THE SIEGE OF JERUSALEM

Ezekiel is struck dumb

[22]While I was there the hand of Yahweh came on me; he said, 'Get up, go out into the valley, and there I shall speak to you.' [23]I got up and went out into the valley; the glory of Yahweh was resting there, like the glory I had seen by the River Chebar, and I fell to the ground. [24]The spirit of Yahweh then entered me and put me on my feet and spoke to me.

He said, 'Go and shut yourself in your house. [25]Son of man, you are about to be tied and bound, and unable to mix with other people. [26]I am going to make your tongue stick to the roof of your mouth; you will be dumb, and no longer able to reprove them, for they are a tribe of rebels. [27]When I speak to you, however, I shall open your mouth and then you will say to them, "Lord Yahweh says this: Let anyone prepared to listen, listen; let anyone who refuses, refuse!"—for they are a tribe of rebels.'

The siege of Jerusalem foretold

4 'For your part, son of man, take a brick and lay it in front of you; on it scratch a city, Jerusalem. [2]You are then to besiege it, trench round it, build earthworks, pitch camps and bring up battering-rams all round.

3a A summary of the fuller version in 33:1–9.

3Then take an iron pan and place it as though
it were an iron wall between you and the city.
Then fix your gaze on it; it is being besieged
and you are besieging it. This is a sign for the
House of Israel.

4'Lie down on your left side and take the
guilt of the House of Israel on yourself. You
will bear their guilt for as many days as you
lie on that side. 5Allowing one day for every
year of their guilt, I ordain that you bear it
for three hundred and ninety days; this is
how you will bear the House of Israel's guilt.
6And when you have finished doing this, you
are to lie down again, on your right side, and
bear the guilt of the House of Judah for forty
days. I have set the length for you as one day
for one year. 7Then fix your gaze on the
siege of Jerusalem, raise your bared arm and
prophesy against her. 8Look, I am going to
tie you up and you will not be able to turn
over from one side to the other until the
period of your seclusion is over.

9'Now take wheat, barley, beans, lentils,
millet and spelt; put them all in the same pot
and make them into bread for yourself. You
are to eat it for as many days as you are
lying on your side—three hundred and ninety
days. 10Of this food, you are to weigh out a
daily portion of twenty shekels and eat it a
little piece at a time. 11And you are to ration
the water you drink—a sixth of a *hin*—
drinking that a little at a time. 12You are to
eat this in the form of a barley cake baked
where they can see you, on human dung.'
13And Yahweh said, 'This is how the Israel-
ites will have to eat their defiled food, wher-
ever I disperse them among the nations.' 14I
then said, 'Lord Yahweh, my soul is not
defiled. From my childhood until now, I
have never eaten an animal that has died a
natural death or been savaged; no tainted
meat has ever entered my mouth.' 15'Very
well,' he said, 'I grant you cow-dung instead
of human dung; you are to bake your bread
on that.' 16He then said, 'Son of man, I am
going to cut off Jerusalem's food supply; in
their extremity, the food they eat will be
weighed out; to their horror, the water they
drink will be rationed, 17until there is no food
or water left, and they fall into a stupor and
waste away because of their guilt.'

5 'Son of man, take a sharp sword, use it
like a barber's razor and run it over your
head and beard. Then take scales and divide
the hair you have cut off. 2Burn one-third
inside the city, while the days of the siege are
working themselves out. Then take another
third and chop it up with the sword all round
the city. The last third you are to scatter to
the wind, while I unsheathe the sword behind
them. 3Also take a few hairs and tie them up
in the folds of your cloak; 4and of these again
take a few, and throw them on the fire and
burn them. From them fire will come on the
whole House of Israel.

5'The Lord Yahweh says this, "This is
Jerusalem, which I have placed in the middle
of the nations, surrounded with foreign coun-
tries. 6She has rebelled more perversely
against my observances than the nations
have, and against my laws than the
surrounding countries have; for they have
rejected my observances and not kept my
laws."

7'Therefore, the Lord Yahweh says this,
"Because your disorders are worse than those
of the nations round you, since you do not
keep my laws or respect my observances, and
since you do not respect even the observances
of the surrounding nations, 8very well, the
Lord Yahweh says this: I, too, am against
you and shall execute my judgements on you
for the nations to see. 9Because of all your
loathsome practices I shall do such things as
I have never done before, nor shall ever do
again. 10Those of you who are parents will
eat their children, and children will eat their
parents. I shall execute judgement on you
and disperse what remains of you to the
winds. 11For, as I live—declares Lord
Yahweh—as sure as you have defiled my
sanctuary with all your horrors and all your
loathsome practices, so I too shall reject you
without a glance of pity, I shall not spare you.
12A third of your citizens will die of plague
or starve to death inside you; a third will fall
by the sword round you; and a third I shall
scatter to the winds, unsheathing the sword
behind them. 13I shall sate my anger and
bring my fury to rest on them until I am
avenged; and when I have sated my fury on
them, then they will know that I, Yahweh,
spoke out of jealousy for you. 14Yes, I shall
reduce you to a ruin, an object of derision to
the surrounding nations, in the eyes of all
who pass by. 15You will be an object of
derision and insults, an example, an object
of amazement to the surrounding nations,
when I execute judgement on you in furious
anger and furious punishments. I, Yahweh,
have spoken. 16On them I shall send the
deadly arrows of famine, which will destroy

you—for I shall send them to destroy you; then I shall make the famine worse and cut off your food supply. 17I shall send famine and wild animals on you to rob you of your children; plague and bloodshed will sweep through you, and I shall bring the sword down on you. I, Yahweh, have spoken." '

Against the mountains of Israel

6 The word of Yahweh was addressed to me as follows, 2'Son of man, turn towards the mountains of Israel and prophesy against them. 3Say, "Mountains of Israel, hear the word of the Lord Yahweh. The Lord Yahweh says this to mountains and hills and ravines and valleys: Look, I am going to summon the sword against you and destroy your high places. 4Your altars will be wrecked, and your incense burners smashed; I shall fling your butchered inhabitants down in front of your foul idols; 5I shall lay the corpses of the Israelites in front of their foul idols and scatter their bones all round your altars. 6Wherever you live, the towns will be destroyed and the high places wrecked, to the ruin and wrecking of your altars, the shattering and abolition of your foul idols, the smashing of your incense burners and the utter destruction of all your works. 7As the butchered fall about you, you will know that I am Yahweh.

8"But I shall spare some of you to escape the sword among the nations, when you have been dispersed in their lands; 9and your survivors will remember me among the nations where they are held captive, since I shall have broken their adulterous hearts for having deserted me, and destroyed their eyes for having turned adulterously towards their foul idols. They will loathe themselves for all the wrong they have caused by their loathsome practices. 10Then they will know that I am Yahweh and that I was not talking lightly when I said that I would inflict these disasters on them."

The sins of Israel

11'The Lord Yahweh says this, "Clap your hands, stamp your feet, and say: Alas for all the loathsome sins of the House of Israel, which is about to fall by sword, famine and plague! 12Far off, they will die by plague; near at hand they will fall by the sword; and any who survive or are spared will die of famine. This is how I shall sate my fury on them. 13Then you will know that I am Yahweh, when their butchered corpses lie among their foul idols, all round their altars, on every high hill, on every mountain top, under every green tree, under every leafy oak, wherever they offer a smell pleasing to all their idols. 14I shall point my finger at them and reduce the country to an empty wasteland from the desert to Riblah, everywhere they live, and they will know that I am Yahweh." '

The end is near

7 The word of Yahweh was addressed to me as follows, 2'Son of man, say, "Lord Yahweh says this to the land of Israel: Finished! The end is coming for the four corners of the country. 3This is the end for you; I shall unleash my anger on you, and judge you as your conduct deserves and call you to account for all your loathsome practices. 4I shall show you no pity, I shall not spare you; I shall repay you for your conduct and for the loathsome practices in which you persist. Then you will know that I am Yahweh.

5"The Lord Yahweh says this: Disaster, a unique disaster, is coming. 6The end is coming, the end is coming, it is on the move towards you, it is coming now. 7Now it is your turn, you who dwell in this country. Doom is coming, the day is near; no joy now, only tumult, on the mountains. 8Now I shall soon vent my fury on you and sate my anger on you: I shall judge you as your conduct deserves and repay you for all your loathsome practices. 9I shall show neither pity nor mercy, but shall repay you for your conduct and the loathsome practices in which you persist. Then you will know that I am Yahweh and that I strike.

10"Now is the day, your turn has come, it has come, it appears, the sceptre has blossomed, pride is at its peak. 11Violence has risen to become the scourge of wickedness . . . 12Doom is coming, the day is near. Neither should buyer rejoice, nor seller regret, for the fury rests on everyone alike. 13The seller will not be able to go back on his bargain; each persists in his sins; they take no defensive measures. 14The trumpet sounds, all is ready, but no one goes into battle, since my fury rests on all alike.

The sins of Israel

15"Outside, the sword; inside, plague and
famine. Whoever is living in the countryside
will die by the sword; whoever is living in the
city will be devoured by famine and plague.
16And those who escape will escape to the
mountains and there, like doves of the
valleys, I shall slaughter them all, each one
for his sin. 17Every hand will grow limp,
every knee turn to water. 18They will put on
sackcloth, each one trembling. Every face
will be ashamed and every head be shaved.
19They will throw their silver away in the
streets and their gold they will regard as a
pollution; neither their silver nor their gold
will be able to save them on the day of
Yahweh's fury. Never again will they have
enough to eat, never again will they fill their
bellies, since that was the occasion for their
guilt. 20They used to pride themselves on the
beauty of their jewellery, out of which they
made their loathsome images, their horrors;
so now I have made it pollute them. 21I shall
hand it over as plunder to foreigners, as loot
to the most evil people on earth. They will
profane it. 22I shall turn my face away from
them, while my treasure-house is profaned
and robbers will force their way in and
profane it.

23"Forge yourself a chain; for the country
is full of bloody executions and the city full
of deeds of violence, 24so I shall bring the
cruellest of the nations to seize their houses.
I shall put an end to the pride of their élite,
and their sanctuary will be profaned. 25Terror
is on the way: they will look for peace and
there will be none. 26Disaster will follow on
disaster, rumour on rumour; they will pester
the prophet for a vision; the priest will be at
a loss over the law and the elders on how to
advise. 27The king will go into mourning, the
prince be plunged in grief, the hands of the
country people tremble. I shall treat them as
their conduct deserves, and judge them as
their own verdicts merit. Then they will
know that I am Yahweh!"'

A vision of the sins of Jerusalem[a]

8 In the sixth year, on the fifth day of the
sixth month, I was sitting at home and the
elders of Judah were sitting with me, when
suddenly the hand of the Lord Yahweh fell
on me there.

2I looked, and there was a form with the
appearance of a human being. Downwards
from what seemed to be the waist there was
fire; and upwards from the waist there was a
brilliance like the glitter of amber.
3Something like a hand was stretched out and
it took me by a lock of my hair; and the spirit
lifted me between heaven and earth and, in
visions from God, took me to Jerusalem, to
the entrance of the inner north gate, where
stands the idol that provokes jealousy. 4There
was the glory of the God of Israel; it looked
like what I had seen in the valley. 5He said,
'Son of man, raise your eyes to the north.' I
raised my eyes to the north, and there, to the
north of the altar gate, stood this statue of
jealousy at the entrance. 6He said, 'Son of
man, do you see what they are doing, the
monstrous, loathsome things that the House
of Israel is practising here, to drive me out of
my sanctuary? And you will see practices
more loathsome still.'

7He next took me to the entrance to the
court. I looked; there was a hole in the wall.
8He said, 'Son of man, bore through the
wall.' I bored through the wall, until I had
made an opening. 9He said, 'Go in and look
at the loathsome things they are doing inside.'
10I went in and looked and there was every
kind of reptile and repulsive animal, and all
the foul idols of the House of Israel, carved
all round the walls. 11Seventy elders of the
House of Israel were worshipping the idols—
among them Jaazaniah son of Shaphan—
each one with his censer in his hand, from
which rose a fragrant cloud of incense. 12He
said, 'Son of man, have you seen what the
elders of the House of Israel do in the dark,
each in his personal image-shrine? They say,
"Yahweh cannot see us; Yahweh has aban-
doned the country." ' 13He said, 'You will
see them at practices more loathsome still.'

14He next took me to the entrance of the
north gate of the Temple of Yahweh where
women were sitting, weeping for Tammuz.[b]
15He said, 'Son of man, do you see that? You
will see even more loathsome things than
that.'

16He then led me to the inner court of
the Temple of Yahweh. And there, at the
entrance to Yahweh's sanctuary, between

8a chh. 8—11 are a vision four years before the final siege.
8b A vegetation god whose annual death and rebirth were mourned and greeted.

the portico and the altar, there were about
twenty-five men, with their backs to
Yahweh's sanctuary and their faces turned
towards the east. They were prostrating
themselves to the east, before the rising sun.
17He said to me, 'Son of man, do you see
that? Is it not bad enough for the House of
Judah to be doing the loathsome things they
are doing here? But they fill the country with
violence and provoke my anger further; look
at them now putting that branch to their
nostrils. 18And so I shall react in fury; I shall
show neither pity nor mercy. They may cry
as loudly as they like to me; I will not listen.'

The punishment

9 Then he shouted loudly for me to hear,
'The scourges of the city are approaching,
each carrying his weapon of destruction!'
2Immediately six men advanced from the
upper north gate, each holding a deadly
weapon. Among them was a man dressed in
linen, with a scribe's ink-horn in his belt.
They came in and halted in front of the
bronze altar. 3The glory of the God of Israel
rose from above the winged creature where
it had been, towards the threshold of the
Temple. He called to the man dressed in
linen with a scribe's ink-horn in his belt 4and
Yahweh said to him, 'Go all through the city,
all through Jerusalem, and mark a cross on
the foreheads of all who grieve and lament
over all the loathsome practices in it.' 5I heard
him say to the others, 'Follow him through
the city and strike. Not one glance of pity;
show no mercy; 6old men, young men, girls,
children, women, kill and exterminate them
all. But do not touch anyone with a cross on
his forehead. Begin at my sanctuary.' So they
began with the old men who were in the
Temple. 7He said to them, 'Defile the
Temple; fill the courts with corpses; then go
out!' They went out and hacked their way
through the city.

8While they were hacking them down, I
was left alone; I fell on my face, crying
out, 'Ah, Lord Yahweh, are you going to
annihilate all that is left of Israel by venting
your fury on Jerusalem?' 9He said, 'The guilt
of the House of Israel and Judah is immense;
the country is full of bloodshed, the city full
of perversity, for they say, "Yahweh has
abandoned the country, Yahweh cannot
see." 10Then, I too shall neither give one
glance of pity nor show any mercy. I shall
repay them for what they have done.' 11The
man dressed in linen with the scribe's ink-
horn in his belt then came back and made his
report, 'I have carried out your orders.'

10 Then, in vision I saw that above the
solid surface over the heads of the
winged creatures there was above them some-
thing like sapphire, which seemed to be like
a throne. 2He then said to the man dressed
in linen, 'Go in between the wheels below the
winged creatures; take a handful of burning
coal from between the winged creatures and
scatter it over the city.' He went in as I
watched.

3The winged creatures were on the right
of the Temple as the man went in, and the
cloud filled the inner court. 4The glory of
Yahweh rose from above the winged crea-
tures, towards the threshold of the Temple;
the Temple was filled by the cloud and the
court was full of the brightness of the glory of
Yahweh. 5The noise of the winged creatures'
wings could be heard even in the outer court,
like the voice of God Almighty when he
speaks.

6When he had given the order to the man
dressed in linen, 'Take the fire from between
the wheels, between the winged creatures,'
the man went in and stood by one of the
wheels. 7One of the winged creatures then
reached his hand out towards the fire between
the winged creatures, took some of it and put
it into the hands of the man dressed in linen,
who took it and came out again.

8There appeared to be what looked like a
human hand under the winged creatures'
wings. 9And I looked, and there were four
wheels beside the winged creatures, one
wheel beside each winged creature, and the
appearance of the wheels was like the sparkle
of chrysolite. 10In appearance, all four looked
alike, as though each wheel had another
wheel inside it.

11In whichever of the four directions
they moved, they did not need to turn as they
moved, but whichever way the head was
facing there they followed; they did not turn
as they moved, 12and their entire bodies, their
backs, their hands, their wings, as well as
the wheels, had eyes all the way round (the
wheels of all four). 13In my hearing, these
wheels were called 'galgal'. 14Each had four
faces; the first was a winged creature's face,
the second a human face, the third a lion's
face and the fourth an eagle's face. 15The
winged creatures rose; this was the being I

had seen by the River Chebar. 16When the winged creatures moved, the wheels moved beside them; and when the winged creatures raised their wings to leave the ground, the wheels did not turn beside them. 17When the former halted the latter halted; when the former rose, the latter rose with them, since they shared the same living spirit.

The glory of Yahweh leaves the Temple

18The glory of Yahweh then came out over the Temple threshold and paused over the winged creatures. 19These raised their wings and rose from the ground as I watched, and the wheels were beside them. They paused at the entrance to the east gate of the Temple of Yahweh, with the glory of the God of Israel over them, above. 20This was the winged creature I had seen beneath the God of Israel by the River Chebar; I knew that they were winged creatures. 21Each had four faces and four wings and what seemed to be human hands under their wings. 22Their faces were like those I had seen by the River Chebar. Each one moved straight forward.

The sins of Jerusalem (continued)

11 The spirit lifted me up and brought me to the east gate of the Temple of Yahweh, the gate that looks eastwards. There at the entrance to the gate stood twenty-five men, among whom I saw Jaazaniah son of Azzur and Pelatiah son of Benaiah, leaders of the people.

2He said to me, 'Son of man, these are the wicked schemers who are spreading their bad advice through this city. 3They say, "There will be no house-building yet awhile. The city is the cooking pot and we are the meat." 4So prophesy against them, prophesy, son of man!' 5The spirit of Yahweh fell on me, and he said to me, 'Say, "Yahweh says this: I know what you are saying, House of Israel, I know how insolent you are. 6You have filled this city with more and more of your victims; you have strewn its streets with victims. 7And so the Lord Yahweh says this: Your victims, whom you have put in it, are the meat, and the city is the cooking pot; but I shall take you out of it. 8You are afraid of the sword and I shall bring the sword down on you—declares the Lord Yahweh—9and I shall take you out of it and hand you over to foreigners and bring you to justice; 10you will fall by the sword on the soil of Israel; I shall execute justice on you, and you will know that I am Yahweh. 11This city will be no cooking pot for you, nor will you be the meat inside; I shall execute justice on you on the soil of Israel; 12and you will know that I am Yahweh, whose laws you have not obeyed and whose judgements you have not kept; instead, you have adopted the customs of the nations round you." '

13Now as I was prophesying, Pelatiah son of Benaiah dropped dead. I fell to the ground and cried out, 'Ah, Lord Yahweh, are you going to annihilate the remnant of Israel?'

The new covenant promised to the exiles

14The word of Yahweh was then addressed to me as follows, 15'Son of man, to your brothers one and all, to your kinsfolk and to the whole House of Israel, the inhabitants of Jerusalem have said, "Keep well away from Yahweh. This country has now been made over to us!" 16So say, "The Lord Yahweh says this: Yes, I have sent them far away among the nations and I have dispersed them to foreign countries; and for a while I have been a sanctuary for them in the country to which they have gone." 17So say, "The Lord Yahweh says this: I shall gather you back from the peoples, I shall collect you in from the countries where you have been scattered and give you the land of Israel. 18When they come back, they will purge it of all its horrors and loathsome practices. 19I shall give them a single heart and I shall put a new spirit in them; I shall remove the heart of stone from their bodies and give them a heart of flesh, 20so that they can keep my laws and respect my judgements and put them into practice. Then they will be my people and I shall be their God. 21But those whose hearts are set on their horrors and loathsome practices I shall repay for their conduct—declares the Lord Yahweh." '

The glory of Yahweh leaves Jerusalem

22The winged creatures then raised their wings and the wheels moved with them, with the glory of the God of Israel over them, above. 23And the glory of Yahweh rose from the centre of the city and halted on the mountain to the east of the city.

24Then the spirit lifted me up and took me, in vision, in the spirit of God, to the exiles in

Chaldaea, and the vision which I had seen
faded. 25I then told the exiles everything that
Yahweh had shown me.

The mime of the exile

12 The word of Yahweh was addressed to
me as follows, 2'Son of man, you are
living among a tribe of rebels who have eyes
and never see, they have ears and never hear,
because they are a tribe of rebels. 3So, son of
man, pack an exile's bundle and set off for
exile by daylight while they watch. You will
leave your home and go somewhere else while
they watch. Then perhaps they will see that
they are a tribe of rebels. 4You will pack your
baggage like an exile's bundle, by daylight,
while they watch, and leave like an exile in
the evening, while they watch. 5While they
watch, make a hole in the wall, and go
out through it. 6While they watch, you will
shoulder your pack and go out into the dark;
you will cover your face so that you cannot
see the ground, since I have made you an
omen for the House of Israel.'

7I did as I had been told. I packed my
baggage like an exile's bundle, by daylight;
and in the evening I made a hole through the
wall with my hands; then I went out into the
dark and shouldered my pack while they
watched.

8Next morning the word of Yahweh was
addressed to me as follows, 9'Son of man, did
not the House of Israel, did not that tribe of
rebels, ask you, "What are you doing?"
10Say, "The Lord Yahweh says this: This
prophecy concerns Jerusalem and the whole
House of Israel who live there." 11Say, "I am
an omen for you; as I have done, so will be
done to them; they will be deported into
exile. 12Their prince will shoulder his pack
in the dark and go out through the wall; a
hole will be made to let him out; he will cover
his face, so that he cannot see the country.
13I shall throw my net over him and catch
him in my mesh; I shall take him to Babylon,[a]
to the land of the Chaldaeans, though he will
not see it; and there he will die. 14And all
those in attendance on him, his army and all
his troops, I shall scatter to all the winds and
unsheathe the sword behind them. 15Then
they will know that I am Yahweh, when
I scatter them throughout the nations and
disperse them in foreign countries. 16But I
shall let a few of them escape the sword,
famine and plague, to describe all their loath-
some practices to the peoples among whom
they will go, so that these too may know that
I am Yahweh." '

17The word of Yahweh was addressed to
me as follows, 18'Son of man, you are to
tremble as you eat your food and shudder
apprehensively as you drink your water,
19and you are to say to the people of the
country, "The Lord Yahweh says this to the
inhabitants of Jerusalem. They will shudder
apprehensively as they eat their food, and
drink their water in fear, so that the country
and its population may be freed from the
violence of its inhabitants. 20When the popu-
lous cities have been destroyed and the
country has been reduced to desert, then you
will know that I am Yahweh." '

Popular proverbs

21The word of Yahweh was addressed to
me as follows, 22'Son of man, what do you
understand by the saying pronounced over
the land of Israel, "Days go by and visions
fade"?

23'Very well, tell them, "The Lord Yahweh
says this: I shall put an end to this saying; it
will never be used in Israel again." Instead,
tell them:

"The days are coming when every vision
will come true, 24for there will be no more
futile visions or deceptive prophecy in the
House of Israel, 25since I, Yahweh, shall
speak. And what I shall say will come true
without delay; for what I shall say, I shall
perform in your own lifetime, you tribe of
rebels—declares the Lord Yahweh." '

26The word of Yahweh was addressed to
me as follows, 27'Son of man, the House of
Israel is now saying, "The vision that this
man sees concerns the distant future; he is
prophesying for times far ahead." 28Very
well, tell them, "The Lord Yahweh says this:
There will be no further delay in the fulfilling
of any of my words. What I have said shall
be done now—declares the Lord Yahweh." '

Against the false prophets

13 The word of Yahweh was addressed to
me as follows, 2'Son of man, prophesy
against the prophets of Israel; prophesy, and

12a =17:20.

say to those who make up prophecies out of
their own heads, "Hear what Yahweh says:
3The Lord Yahweh says this: Disaster is in
store for the foolish prophets who follow
their own spirit and have seen nothing! 4Your
prophets, Israel, are like ruin-haunting
jackals!
5"You have not ventured into the breach;
you have not built up the wall round the
House of Israel, to hold fast in battle on the
Day of Yahweh. 6Theirs are futile visions
and false predictions, who say: A prophecy
from Yahweh, when Yahweh has not sent
them; yet they expect their words to come
true. 7Have not the visions you see been
futile, have not the predictions you make
been false, although you say: A prophecy of
Yahweh, when I have not spoken?
8"Very well, the Lord Yahweh says this:
Because of your futile words and false predic-
tions, I am now against you—declares Lord
Yahweh. 9My hand will be against the
prophets who have futile visions and give
false predictions; they will not be admitted
to the council of my people, their names will
not be entered in the roll of the House of
Israel, they will not set foot on the soil of
Israel; and they will know that I am the Lord
Yahweh. 10This is because they have misled
my people by saying Peace! when there is no
peace. When my people were repairing a
wall, these men came and plastered it over!
11Tell these plasterers: It will rain hard, it
will hail, it will blow a gale, 12and down will
come the wall! Will not people ask you: What
has become of the plaster you slapped on it?
13Well then, the Lord Yahweh says this: I am
going to unleash a stormy wind in my fury,
torrential rain in my anger, hailstones in my
destructive fury, 14and I shall shatter the wall
you plastered and knock it down and lay its
foundations bare. It will fall and you will
perish under it; then you will know that I am
Yahweh."
15'When I have sated my anger on the wall
and those who plastered it, I shall say to you,
"The wall is gone, and so are those who
plastered over it, 16the prophets of Israel who
prophesy about Jerusalem and have visions
of peace for her when there is no peace—
declares the Lord Yahweh."

Against the false prophetesses

17'Also, son of man, turn to the women of
your people who make up prophecies out of
their own heads; prophesy against them.
18Say, "The Lord Yahweh says this: Disaster
is in store for women who sew ribbons round
each wrist and make head-cloths for people
of all sizes, in their hunt for souls! Are you
to hunt the souls of my people and keep your
own souls safe? 19You dishonour me in front
of my people for a few handfuls of barley, a
few bits of bread, killing those who ought not
to die and sparing those who ought not to
live, lying to my people who love listening to
lies.
20"Very well, the Lord Yahweh says this:
Look, I am now against your ribbons, with
which you hunt souls like birds, and I shall
tear them off your arms and free those souls
whom you hunt like birds. 21I shall tear your
head-cloths to pieces and rescue my people
from your clutches; no longer will they be
fair game for you to ensnare. Then you will
know that I am Yahweh.
22"For having intimidated with lies the
heart of the upright whom I had done nothing
to alarm, and for having encouraged the
wicked not to give up wicked ways and so be
saved, 23very well, you will have no more
futile visions and make no more predictions,
for I shall rescue my people from your
clutches, and you will know that I am
Yahweh." '

Against idolatry

14 Next, some elders of Israel visited me
and while they were sitting with me,
2the word of Yahweh was addressed to me
as follows, 3'Son of man, these men have
enshrined their foul idols in their hearts and
placed the cause of their sinning right before
their eyes. Why should I let myself be
consulted by them? 4So speak to them; tell
them this, "Lord Yahweh says this: Every
member of the House of Israel who enshrines
his foul idols in his heart and places the cause
of his sinning right before his eyes, and who
then approaches the prophet, will get this
answer from me, Yahweh, as the multiplicity
of his idols deserves, 5and in this way I hope
to win back the hearts of the House of Israel
who have all been estranged from me by their
foul idols."
6'So say to the House of Israel, "The Lord
Yahweh says this: Come back, turn away
from your foul idols, turn your backs on all
your loathsome practices; 7for if any member
of the House of Israel—or any foreigner

living in Israel—deserts me to enshrine his
foul idols in his heart and places the cause of
his sinning right before his eyes and then
approaches a prophet to consult me through
him, he will get his answer from me, Yahweh.
8 I shall set my face against that person; I shall
make him an example and a byword; I shall
rid my people of him, and you will know that
I am Yahweh. 9 And if the prophet is seduced
into saying something, I, Yahweh, shall have
seduced that prophet; I shall point my finger
at him and rid my people Israel of him. 10 Both
will be punished for their guilt; the prophet's
punishment will be the same as that of the
person who consults him, 11 so that the House
of Israel will never stray from me again or
defile themselves again with these crimes,
but be my people and I their God—declares
the Lord Yahweh." '

Individual responsibility[a]

12 The word of Yahweh was addressed to me:
13 'Son of man, when a country sins against
me by being unfaithful and I point my finger
at it and destroy its supply of food, inflicting
famine on it and denuding it of human and
animal, 14 even if the three men, Noah, Danel
and Job,[b] were living in it, they would save
no one but themselves by their uprightness—
declares the Lord Yahweh. 15 Were I to
unleash wild beasts on that country to rob it
of its children and reduce it to a desert which
no one would dare to cross because of the
animals, 16 even if these three men were living
there, as I live—declares the Lord Yahweh—
they would not be able to save either son or
daughter; they alone would be saved, and the
country would become a desert. 17 Were I to
bring the sword down on that country and
say, "Sword, cross the country!" so as to
denude it of human and animal, 18 even if
these three men were living there, as I live—
declares the Lord Yahweh—they would not
be able to save either son or daughter; they
alone would be saved. 19 If I were to send the
plague on that country and vent my fury on
it by bloodshed, so as to denude it of human
and animal, 20 even if Noah and Danel and
Job were living there, as I live—declares the
Lord Yahweh—they would be able to save
neither son nor daughter, only themselves by
their uprightness.

21 'The Lord Yahweh says this, "Even if I
send my four dreadful scourges on Jerusalem—sword, famine, wild beasts and
plague—to denude it of human and animal,
22 even so, there will be a remnant left, a few
men and women who come through; when
they come to you and you see their conduct
and actions, you will take comfort in spite
of the disaster which I have brought on
Jerusalem, in spite of all I have brought on
her. 23 They will comfort you, when you see
their conduct and actions, and so you will
know that I have not done in vain all
I have done to her—declares the Lord
Yahweh." '

A parable of the vine

15 The word of Yahweh was addressed to
me as follows:

2 Son of man, how is the wood
of the vine better
than wood from the branch of a forest tree?
3 Is its wood used for making anything?
Are pegs on which to hang things
made from it?
4 There it is, thrown on the fire for fuel.
The fire burns off both ends;
the middle is charred;
can it be kept for anything now?
5 While it was intact,
you could make nothing with it;
burned and charred,
is it any more useful now?

6 So, the Lord Yahweh says this:

As the wood of the vine
among the forest trees,
which I have thrown on the fire for fuel,
so shall I treat
the inhabitants of Jerusalem.
7 I shall set my face against them.
They have escaped one fire,
but fire will devour them yet.
And you will know that I am Yahweh,
when I set my face against them.
8 I shall reduce the country to a desert,
because of their infidelity—
declares the Lord Yahweh.

14a cf. 18; 33:10–20, and Dt 24; Jr 31 on individual responsibility.
14b Three celebrated heroes of uprightness. Danel is known from other Near Eastern ancient poetry.

An allegorical history of Jerusalem[a]

16 The word of Yahweh was addressed to me as follows, 2"Son of man, confront Jerusalem with her loathsome practices! 3Say, "The Lord Yahweh says this: By origin and birth you belong to the land of Canaan. Your father was an Amorite and your mother a Hittite. 4At birth, the very day you were born, there was no one to cut your navel-string, or wash you in water to clean you, or rub you with salt, or wrap you in swaddling clothes. 5No one looked at you with pity enough to do any of these things out of sympathy for you. You were exposed in the open fields in your own dirt on the day you were born.

6"I saw you kicking on the ground in your blood as I was passing, and I said to you as you lay in your blood: Live! 7and I made you grow like the grass of the fields. You developed, you grew, you reached marriageable age. Your breasts became firm and your hair grew richly, but you were stark naked. 8Then I saw you as I was passing. Your time had come, the time for love. I spread my cloak over you and covered your nakedness; I gave you my oath, I made a covenant with you—declares the Lord Yahweh—and you became mine. 9I bathed you in water, I washed the blood off you, I anointed you with oil. 10I gave you embroidered dresses, fine leather shoes, a linen headband and a cloak of silk. 11I loaded you with jewels, gave you bracelets for your wrists and a necklace for your throat. 12I gave you nose-ring and earrings; I put a beautiful diadem on your head. 13You were loaded with gold and silver and dressed in linen and silk and brocade. Your food was the finest flour, honey and oil. You grew more and more beautiful; and you rose to be queen. 14The fame of your beauty spread through the nations, since it was perfect, because I had clothed you with my own splendour—declares the Lord Yahweh.

15"But you became infatuated with your own beauty and used your fame to play the whore, lavishing your debauchery on all comers. 16You took some of your clothes to make for yourself high places bright with colours and there you played the whore. 17You also took your jewellery, made with my gold and silver which I had given you, and made yourself male images to serve your whorings. 18You took your embroidered clothes and used these to dress them up, and you offered them my oil and my incense. 19And the bread I gave you, the finest flour, the oil and honey with which I fed you, you offered them as a pleasing smell.

"What is more—declares the Lord Yahweh—20you took the sons and daughters you had borne me and sacrificed them as food to the images. Was not your whoring enough in itself, 21for you to slaughter my children and hand them over to be burnt in their honour?22And in all your loathsome practices and your whorings you never called your early days to mind, when you were stark naked, kicking on the ground in your own blood.

23"To crown your wickedness—disaster upon you, disaster! declares the Lord Yahweh—24you built yourself a mound and made yourself a high place in every open space. 25At the entry to every alley you made yourself a high place, defiling your beauty and opening your legs to all comers in countless acts of fornication. 26You have also fornicated with your big-membered neighbours, the Egyptians, provoking my anger with further acts of fornication. 27So now I have raised my hand against you, I have cut down on your food, I have put you at the mercy of your enemies, the Philistine women, who blush at your lewd behaviour. 28Still unsatisfied, you prostituted yourself to the Assyrians; you played the whore with them, but were not satisfied even then. 29You committed further acts of fornication in the country of merchants, with the Chaldaeans, and these did not satisfy you either.

30"How simple-minded you are!—declares the Lord Yahweh—for although you do all the things that a professional prostitute would, 31in building a mound and making yourself a high place in every street, you do not act like a proper prostitute because you disdain to take a fee. 32An adulteress welcomes strangers instead of her husband. 33All prostitutes accept presents, but you give presents to all your lovers, you bribe them to come from all over the place to fornicate with you! 34In fornicating, you are the opposite of other women, since no one runs after you to fornicate with you; since you give the fee and do not get one, you are the very opposite!

35"Very well, whore, hear the word of

16a =23.

Yahweh! 36The Lord Yahweh says this: For having squandered your money and let yourself be seen naked while whoring with your lovers and all the foul idols of your loathsome practices and for giving them your children's blood—37for all this, I shall assemble all the lovers to whom you have given pleasure, all the ones you liked and also all the ones you disliked; yes, I shall assemble them round you and strip you naked in front of them, and let them see you naked from head to foot. 38I shall pass on you the sentence that adulteresses and murderesses receive; I shall hand you over to their jealous fury; 39I shall hand you over to them; they will destroy your mound and pull down your high place; they will tear off your clothes, take away your jewels and leave you stark naked. 40Then they will call an assembly of citizens to deal with you, who will stone you to death and hack you to pieces with their swords, 41and burn down your premises and execute justice on you, while many other women look on; and I shall put an end to your whoring: no more paid lovers for you! 42Once my fury is exhausted with you, then my jealousy will leave you; I shall be calm and not angry any more. 43Since you never called to mind your early days and have done nothing but provoke me, now I in my turn shall bring your conduct down on your own head—declares the Lord Yahweh!

"Have you not added this lewd behaviour to your other loathsome practices? 44So now all dealers in proverbs will apply this one to you: Like mother, like daughter. 45Yes; you are a true daughter of your mother, who hated her husband and her children; you are a true sister of your sisters, who hated their husbands and their children. Your mother was a Hittite and your father an Amorite. 46Your elder sister is Samaria, who lives to the north of you with her daughters. Your younger sister is Sodom, who lives to the south of you with her daughters. 47You never failed to imitate their behaviour and copy their loathsome practices, and soon your behaviour was more corrupt than theirs was. 48As I live—declares the Lord Yahweh—your sister Sodom and her daughters never did what you and your daughters have done. 49The crime of your sister Sodom was pride, gluttony, calm complacency; such were hers and her daughters' crimes. They never helped the poor and needy; 50they were proud, and engaged in loathsome practices before me, and so I swept them away as you have seen. 51And yet Samaria never committed half the crimes that you have.

"You have done more loathsome things than they have. By all your loathsome practices you have made your sisters seem innocent, 52and now you bear the shame of which you have freed your sisters; since the sins which you have committed are more revolting than theirs, they are more upright than you are. So now, bear the disgrace and shame of having put your sisters in the right.

53"I shall restore their fortunes, I shall restore Sodom and her daughters, I shall restore Samaria and her daughters, and then I shall restore your fortune with theirs, 54so that you can bear your shame and disgrace for all you have done, and so console them. 55When your sisters, Sodom and her daughters, are restored to what they were, and Samaria and her daughters are restored to what they were, then you too and your daughters will be restored to what you were. 56Did you not gloat over your sister Sodom when you were so proud, 57before you were stripped naked? Like her, you are now the laughing-stock of the women of Edom, of all the women round, of the women of Philistia, who pour out their contempt on you. 58You have brought this on yourself, with your lewdness and your loathsome practices—declares the Lord Yahweh.

59"For the Lord Yahweh says this: I shall treat you as you have deserved for making light of an oath and breaking a covenant, 60but I shall remember my covenant with you when you were a girl and shall conclude a covenant with you that will last for ever. 61And you for your part will remember your behaviour and feel ashamed of it when you receive your elder and younger sisters and I make them your daughters, although this is not included in my covenant with you. 62I shall renew my covenant with you; and you will know that I am Yahweh, 63and so remember and feel ashamed and in your confusion be reduced to silence, when I forgive you for everything you have done—declares the Lord Yahweh." '

The allegory of the eagle

17 The word of Yahweh was addressed to me as follows, 2'Son of man, put a riddle, propound a parable to the House of Israel. 3Say, "The Lord Yahweh says this:

A great eagle with great wings,
long-pinioned,
rich with many-coloured plumage,
came to the Lebanon.
4He took the top of the cedar tree,
he plucked off the top branch,
he carried it off
to the country of merchants
and set it down in a city of shopkeepers.
5Next, he took one of the country's seeds
and put it in a fertile field;
by the side of a generous stream,
like a willow tree, he placed it.
6It grew and became a fruitful vine
of modest size,
grew up towards the eagle,
its roots grew downwards.
So it became a vine,
branching out and sprouting new shoots.

7But there was another great eagle
with great wings and thick plumage.
And now the vine twisted its roots
towards him
and stretched its branches towards him,
for him to water it
away from the bed where it was planted.
8It was in a fertile field,
by the side of a wide stream
that the vine had been planted,
to branch out and bear fruit
and become a noble vine."

9Say, "The Lord Yahweh says this:
Will it succeed?
Will the eagle not tear out its roots
and strip off its fruit,
so that all the new leaves it puts out
will wither,
and no great strength is needed
nor many people
to pull it up by the roots?
10Planted it may be—will it succeed?
Will it not shrivel up
when the east wind blows?
It will wither in the bed
where it was growing!" '

11The word of Yahweh was addressed to
me as follows:
12'Say to that tribe of rebels, "Do you not
know what this means?" Say this, 'Look,
the king of Babylon came to Jerusalem; he
carried away the king and the princes, and
took them to his home in Babylon. 13He took
a member of the royal family and made a
treaty with him, forcing him to swear loyalty,
having already deported the leading men of
the country, 14so that the kingdom would
remain modest and without ambitions, and
would keep and honour his treaty. 15But the
prince rebelled against him and sent envoys
to Egypt to procure himself horses and a large
number of troops. Will he succeed? Will a
man who has done this go unpunished? Can
he break a treaty and go unpunished? 16As I
live, I swear it—declares the Lord Yahweh—
in Babylon, in the country of the king who
put him on the throne, whose oath he has
disregarded and whose treaty he has broken,
there he will die. 17Despite the pharaoh's
great army and hordes of men, he will not be
able to save him by fighting, however many
earthworks are raised, however many tren-
ches dug to the loss of many lives. 18He has
disregarded the oath by breaking the treaty
to which he had pledged himself and, having
done all this, will not go unpunished.
19"So, the Lord Yahweh says this: As
I live, I swear it: my oath which he has
disregarded, my treaty which he has broken,
I shall make them both recoil on his own
head. 20I shall throw my net over him, he will
be caught in my mesh; I shall take him to
Babylon[a] and punish him there for being
unfaithful to me. 21All the pick of all his
troops will fall by the sword, and the
survivors be scattered to all the winds. And
you will know that I, Yahweh, have spoken.
22"The Lord Yahweh says this:

From the top of the tall cedar tree,
from the highest branch
I shall take a shoot
and plant it myself
on a high and lofty mountain.
23I shall plant it
on the highest mountain in Israel.
It will put out branches and bear fruit
and grow into a noble cedar tree.
Every kind of bird will live beneath it,
every kind of winged creature
will rest in the shade of its branches.
24And all the trees of the countryside
will know that I, Yahweh, am the one
who lays the tall tree low
and raises the low tree high,
who makes the green tree wither
and makes the withered bear fruit.

17a =12:13.

I, Yahweh, have spoken,
and I will do it." '

Individual responsibility

18 The word of Yahweh was addressed to
me as follows, 2'Why do you keep
repeating this proverb in the land of Israel:

The parents have eaten unripe grapes;
and the children's teeth are set on edge?[a]

3'As I live—declares the Lord Yahweh—
you will have no further cause to repeat this
proverb in Israel. 4Look, all life belongs to
me; the father's life and the son's life, both
alike belong to me. The one who has sinned
is the one to die.
5'But if a man is upright, his actions law-
abiding and upright, 6and he does not eat on
the mountains or raise his eyes to the foul
idols of the House of Israel, does not defile
his neighbour's wife or touch a woman during
her periods, 7oppresses no one, returns the
pledge on a debt, does not rob, gives his own
food to the hungry, his clothes to those who
lack clothing, 8does not lend for profit, does
not charge interest, abstains from evil, gives
honest judgement between one person and
another, 9keeps my laws and sincerely
respects my judgements—someone like this
is truly upright and will live—declares the
Lord Yahweh.
10'But if he has a son prone to violence
and bloodshed, who commits one of these
misdeeds—11even though the father never
has—a son who dares to eat on the mountains,
who defiles his neighbour's wife, 12who
oppresses the poor and needy, robs, fails to
return pledges, raises his eyes to foul idols,
engages in loathsome practices, 13lends for
profit, or charges interest, such a person will
by no means live; having committed all these
appalling crimes he will die, and his blood be
on his own head.
14'But if he in turn has a son who, in spite
of seeing all the sins that his father has
committed, does not imitate him, 15does not
eat on the mountains or raise his eyes to the
foul idols of the House of Israel, does not
defile his neighbour's wife, 16oppresses no
one, takes no pledges, does not rob, gives his
own food to the hungry, his clothes to those
who lack clothing, 17abstains from evil, does
not lend for profit or charge interest, respects
my judgements and keeps my laws, he will
not die for his father's sins: he will most
certainly live. 18But his father, because he
was violent, robbed others and never did
good among his people, will most certainly
die in his guilt.
19'Now, you say, "Why doesn't the son
bear his father's guilt?" If the son has been
law-abiding and upright, has kept all my laws
and followed them, most certainly he will
live. 20The one who has sinned is the one who
must die; a son is not to bear his father's
guilt, nor a father his son's guilt. The upright
will be credited with his uprightness, and the
wicked with his wickedness.
21'If the wicked, however, renounces all
the sins he has committed, respects my laws
and is law-abiding and upright, he will most
certainly live; he will not die. 22None of the
crimes he committed will be remembered
against him from then on; he will most
certainly live[b] because of his upright actions.
23Would I take pleasure in the death of the
wicked—declares the Lord Yahweh—and
not prefer to see him renounce his wickedness
and live?
24'But if the upright abandons uprightness
and does wrong by copying all the loathsome
practices of the wicked, is he to live? All his
upright actions will be forgotten from then
on; for the infidelity of which he is guilty and
the sin which he has committed, he will most
certainly die.
25'Now, you say, "What the Lord does is
unjust." Now listen, House of Israel: is what
I do unjust? Is it not what you do that is
unjust? 26When the upright abandons
uprightness and does wrong and dies, he dies
because of the wrong which he himself has
done. 27Similarly, when the wicked abandons
wickedness to become law-abiding and
upright, he saves his own life. 28Having
chosen to renounce all his previous crimes,
he will most certainly live: he will not die.
29And yet the House of Israel says, "What
the Lord does is unjust." Is what I do unjust,
House of Israel? Is it not what you do that is
unjust? 30So in future, House of Israel, I shall
judge each of you by what that person does—
declares the Lord Yahweh.[c] Repent,
renounce all your crimes, avoid all occasions

18a || Jr 31:29, cf. Ezk 14:12.
18b =33:16.
18c =33:20

for guilt. 31 Shake off all the crimes you have
committed, and make yourselves a new heart
and a new spirit! Why die, House of Israel?
32 I take no pleasure in the death of anyone—
declares the Lord Yahweh—so repent and
live!'

A lament for the queen-mother and princes of Israel

19 1 'Now, raise a lament for the princes of
Israel. 2 Say:

What was your mother?
A lioness among lions;
lying among the cubs
she nursed her whelps.
3 She reared one of her whelps:
he grew into a young lion;
he learnt to tear his prey;
he became a man-eater.
4 The nations came to hear of him;
he was caught in their pit;
they dragged him away with hooks
to Egypt.[a]
5 Her expectation thwarted,
and seeing her hope dashed,
she took another of her whelps
and made a young lion of him.
6 He prowled among the lions,
he grew into a young lion,
he learnt to tear his prey;
he became a man-eater.
7 He tore down their palaces,
he destroyed their cities;
the land and all its inhabitants
were appalled
by the sound of his roars.
8 The nations marched out against him
from the surrounding provinces;
they spread their net over him;
he was caught in their pit.
9 They shackled him with hooks,
they took him to the king of Babylon
and threw him into a fortress,
so that his voice could never again
be heard
on the mountains of Israel.

10 Your mother was like a vine
planted beside the water,
fruitful and leafy,
because the water flowed so full.
11 She had stout stems
which became kingly sceptres;
she grew higher and higher,
up into the clouds;
she was admired for her height
and the number of her branches.
12 But she was furiously uprooted
and thrown on the ground;
the east wind dried up her fruit,
she was broken to pieces;
her stout stem dried up,
the fire devoured it.
13 Now she has been transplanted
to the desert,
to a dry and thirsty land.
14 Fire burst out of her stem
devouring her branches and fruit.
No more stout stem for her,
no more kingly sceptre.'

This is a lament; it was used as such.

An account of Israel's infidelities

20 1 In the seventh year, on the tenth day
of the fifth month, some of the elders
of Israel came to consult Yahweh and were
sitting with me, 2 when the word of Yahweh
was addressed to me as follows, 3 'Son of man,
speak to the elders of Israel. Say, "The Lord
Yahweh says this: Have you come to consult
me? As I live, I will not be consulted by you—
declares the Lord Yahweh."
4 'Are you ready to judge them? Are you
ready to judge them, son of man? Confront
them with the loathsome practices of their
ancestors. 5 Say, "The Lord Yahweh says
this: On the day when I chose Israel, when
I pledged my word to the House of Jacob, I
made myself known to them in Egypt;
I pledged my word to them and said: I am
Yahweh your God. 6 That day I pledged them
my word that I would bring them out of
Egypt to a country which I had reconnoitred
for them, a country flowing with milk and
honey, and the loveliest of them all. 7 And I
said to them: Each of you must reject the
horrors which attract you; do not pollute
yourselves with the foul idols of Egypt; I am
Yahweh your God. 8 But they rebelled against
me and would not listen to me. Not one of
them rejected the horrors which attracted
them; they did not give up the foul idols of
Egypt. I then resolved to vent my fury on
them, to sate my anger on them in Egypt.
9 But respect for my own name kept me from

19a King Jehoahaz, the whelp of Israel, was deposed and taken to Egypt.

letting it be profaned in the eyes of the nations
among whom they were living, and before
whom I had made myself known to them and
promised to bring them out of Egypt. 10So I
brought them out of Egypt and led them into
the desert. 11I gave them my laws and taught
them my judgements, in whose observance
people find life. 12And I also gave them my
Sabbaths as a sign between me and them, so
that they might know that I, Yahweh, am the
one who sanctifies them. 13The House of
Israel, however, rebelled against me in the
desert; they refused to keep my laws, they
scorned my judgements, in whose observ-
ance people find life, and they grossly
profaned my Sabbaths. I then resolved to
vent my fury on them in the desert and
destroy them. 14But respect for my own name
kept me from letting it be profaned in the
eyes of the nations, before whom I had
brought them out. 15Even so, I pledged them
my word in the desert that I would not lead
them to the country which I had given them,
a country flowing with milk and honey, and
the loveliest of them all, 16since they had
scorned my judgements, had refused to keep
my laws and had profaned my Sabbaths,
their hearts being attached to foul idols. 17In
spite of this, I took pity on them; I refrained
from destroying them and did not make an
end of them in the desert.
18"'I said to their children in the desert: Do
not follow the laws of your ancestors, do
not practise their judgements, do not defile
yourselves with their foul idols. 19I am
Yahweh your God. Keep my laws, respect
my judgements and practise them. 20Keep
my Sabbaths holy; let them be a sign between
me and you, so that people may know that
I am Yahweh your God. 21Their children,
however, rebelled against me; they refused
to keep my laws, they did not respect or
practise my judgements, which must be prac-
tised by all who want to live; they profaned
my Sabbaths. I then resolved to vent my fury
on them, to sate my anger on them in the
desert. 22But I restrained my hand; respect
for my own name kept me from letting it be
profaned in the eyes of the nations, before
whom I had brought them out. 23Once again,
however, I pledged them my word that I
would scatter them throughout the nations
and disperse them in foreign countries,
24because they had not followed my judge-
ments but had rejected my laws and profaned
my Sabbaths, their eyes being fastened on
the foul idols of their ancestors. 25And for
this reason I gave them laws that were not
good and judgements by which they could
never live; 26and I polluted them with their
own offerings, making them sacrifice every
first-born son in order to fill them with revul-
sion, so that they would know that I am
Yahweh."
27'For this reason, son of man, speak to the
House of Israel. Say to them, "The Lord
Yahweh says this: Here is another way by
which your ancestors outraged me by their
infidelity. 28Once I had brought them into
the country which I had pledged my word to
give them, they then saw all sorts of high
hills, all kinds of leafy trees, and there they
performed their sacrifices and made offerings
that provoked my anger; there they set out
their pleasing smell and poured their
libations. 29I then said to them: What is this
high place where you go? And they gave, and
still give it, the name of Bamah."
30'So, say to the House of Israel, "The
Lord Yahweh says this: If you are polluting
yourselves as your ancestors did by forni-
cating with their horrors—31for by offering
your gifts and by burning your children as
sacrifices, you have been polluting yourselves
with all your foul idols to this very day—shall
I let myself be consulted by you, House of
Israel? As I live—declares Lord Yahweh—I
shall not let myself be consulted by you.
32And what you sometimes imagine will never
be so, when you say: We shall be like the
peoples, the tribes of foreign lands, worship-
ping wood and stone. 33As I live I swear it—
declares the Lord Yahweh—I am the one
who will reign over you, with a strong hand
and outstretched arm, once my fury is sated.
34With a strong hand and outstretched arm,
once my fury is sated, I shall bring you back
from the peoples and gather you again from
the countries throughout which you have
been scattered. 35I shall lead you into the
desert of the nations and there I shall judge
you face to face. 36As I judged your ancestors
in the desert of Egypt, so will I judge you—
declares the Lord Yahweh. 37I shall make
you pass under the crook, bring you to respect
the covenant 38and rid you of the rebels who
have revolted against me; I shall bring them
out of the country where they are staying,
but they will not enter the country of Israel,
and you will know that I am Yahweh. 39House
of Israel, Lord Yahweh says this: Go on, all
of you, worship your foul idols, but later we

shall see if you don't listen to me! Then you
will stop profaning my holy name with your
offerings and your foul idols. 40For on my
holy mountain, on the high mountain of
Israel—declares the Lord Yahweh—is where
the whole House of Israel, everyone in the
country, will worship me. There I shall
accept and there expect your presents, your
choicest offering and all your consecrated
gifts. 41I shall welcome you like a pleasing
smell when I bring you back from the peoples
and gather you from the countries through-
out which you have been scattered, and
through you I shall display my holiness for
all the nations to see; 42and you will know
that I am Yahweh, when I bring you back to
the soil of Israel, to the country which I
pledged my word to give to your ancestors.
43There you will remember your past behav-
iour and all the actions by which you have
defiled yourselves, and you will loathe your-
selves for all the wrongs which you have
committed. 44And you will know that I am
Yahweh, when I treat you as respect for my
own name requires, and not as your wicked
behaviour and corrupt actions deserve,
House of Israel—declares the Lord
Yahweh." '

The sword[a] of Yahweh

21 The word of Yahweh was addressed to
me as follows, 2'Son of man, turn to
the right; utter your word towards the south,
prophesy against the forest land of the Negeb.
3Say to the forest of Negeb, "Hear the word
of Yahweh! The Lord Yahweh says this:
Listen; I am about to kindle a fire in you
which will burn up every green tree in you as
well as every dry one; it will be an unquench-
able blaze and every face will be scorched by
it from the Negeb to the north. 4All humanity
will see that it was I, Yahweh, who kindled
it, and it will not be extinguished." ' 5I said,
'Lord Yahweh, they say of me, "He does
nothing but speak in riddles!" '
6Then the word of Yahweh was addressed
to me as follows, 7'Son of man, turn towards
Jerusalem, utter your word towards the sanc-
tuary and prophesy against the land of Israel.
8Say to the land of Israel, "Yahweh says
this: Now I am against you; I am about to
unsheathe my sword and rid you of the
upright and the wicked alike. 9Since I am
going to rid you of upright and wicked alike,
I shall unsheathe my sword against everyone
alive, from the Negeb to the north, 10so that
everyone alive will know that I, Yahweh, am
the one who has unsheathed my sword; it
will not go back again."
11'Son of man, groan as though your heart
were breaking. Utter your bitter groans
where they can see you. 12And if they say,
"Why these groans?" reply, "Because of the
news which is about to come, all hearts will
sink, all hands grow weak, all spirits grow
faint and all knees turn to water. It is coming
now, it is here!—declares Lord Yahweh." '
13The word of Yahweh was addressed to
me as follows, 14'Son of man, prophesy. Say,
"The Lord says this. Say:

The sword, the sword
has been sharpened and polished,
15sharpened for slaughter,
polished to flash like lightning . . .
16He has had it polished to be wielded,
this sword sharpened and polished
to put in the slaughterer's hand!
17Shout and wail, son of man,
for it will come on my people,
on all the chief men of Israel
doomed like my people to the sword!
So beat your breast,
18for this will be an ordeal . . .
declares the Lord Yahweh.
19So prophesy, son of man,
and clap your hands!
Let the sword pass three times,
that sword for victims,
that sword for a great victim,
threatening them from every side!
20To make hearts sink
and make sure many fall,
I have posted the slaughtering sword
at every gate
to flash like lightning,
polished for slaughter.
21Be sharp, on the right,
be ready on the left,
whichever way your blade is needed!
22I too shall clap my hands
and sate my fury!
I, Yahweh, have spoken." '

The king of Babylon at the crossroads

23The word of Yahweh was addressed to me
as follows, 24'Son of man, mark out two roads

21a Four separate sayings (1–12; 13–22; 23–32; 33–37) linked only by this word.

for the sword of the king of Babylon to come along, making both of them begin from the same country. Then put up a signpost, put it where the road leaves for the city, [25]trace the route which the sword should take for Rabbah-of-the-Ammonites, and for Judah, to the fortress of Jerusalem. [26]For the king of Babylon has halted at the fork where these two roads diverge, to take the omens. He has shaken the arrows, questioned the household gods, inspected the liver. [27]The lot marked 'Jerusalem' is in his right hand: there to set up battering-rams, give the word for slaughter, raise the war cry, level battering-rams against the gates, cast up earthworks, build entrenchments. [28]The inhabitants will believe that these omens are idle, for they have received sworn guarantees, but he will bring their guilt to mind and capture them. [29]And so the Lord Yahweh says this, "Since you have brought your guilt to mind by parading your misdeeds and flaunting your sins in everything you do: because you have drawn attention to yourselves, you will be captured. [30]As for you, impious and wicked prince of Israel, whose doom is approaching to put an end to your crimes, [31]the Lord Yahweh says this: They will take away your diadem and remove your crown. Everything will be changed; the low will be raised and the high brought low! [32]Ruin, ruin, I shall bring such ruin as never was before, until the rightful ruler comes, on whom I shall bestow it."

The punishment of Ammon

[33]'Son of man, prophesy and say, "The Lord Yahweh says this: In reply to the Ammonites and their jeers, say: The sword, the sword is drawn for slaughter, polished to devour, to flash like lightning—[34]while you have empty visions and consult lying omens—to cut the throats of the wicked, whose doom is approaching to put an end to their crimes. [35]Put it back in the scabbard. The place where you were created, the land of your origin, will be where I judge you. [36]I shall vent my fury on you, breathe the fire of my rage against you and hand you over to barbarous men whose trade is destruction. [37]You will be fuel for the fire, your blood will flow through the country, you will leave no memory behind you; for I, Yahweh, have spoken!" '

The crimes of Jerusalem

22 The word of Yahweh was addressed to me as follows, [2]'Son of man, are you ready to judge? Are you ready to judge the blood-stained city? Confront her with all her loathsome practices! [3]Say, "The Lord Yahweh says this: City shedding blood inside yourself to hasten your doom, making foul idols on your soil to defile yourself, [4]you have incurred guilt by the blood you have shed, you have defiled yourself with the foul idols you have made, you have shortened your days, you have come to the end of your years. This is why I have made you an object of scorn to the nations and a laughing-stock to every country. [5]From far and near they will taunt you with your infamous disorders.

[6]"Look! In you the princes of Israel, one and all, have furthered their own interests at the cost of bloodshed; [7]in you people have despised their fathers and mothers; in you they have ill-treated the settler; in you they have oppressed the widow and orphan. [8]You have treated my sanctuary with contempt, you have profaned my Sabbaths. [9]In you informers incite to bloodshed; in you people eat on the mountains and act licentiously; [10]in you they have sexual intercourse with their fathers; in you they force themselves on women in their periods; [11]in you one man engages in loathsome practices with his neighbour's wife, another lewdly defiles his daughter-in-law, another violates his sister, his own father's daughter. [12]In you people take bribes for shedding blood; you lend for profit and charge interest, you profit from your fellow by extortion and have forgotten about me—declares the Lord Yahweh.

[13]"Now I shall clap my hands at your acts of banditry and the blood that flows in you. [14]Will your heart be able to resist, will your hands be steady, the day when I call you to account? I, Yahweh, have spoken and shall act. [15]I shall scatter you among the nations and disperse you in foreign countries, and so put an end to the filthiness now inside you; [16]through your own fault, you will be profaned in the eyes of the nations, and you will know that I am Yahweh!" '

[17]The word of Yahweh was addressed to me as follows, [18]'Son of man, for me, the House of Israel has become dross: copper, tin, iron, lead, all mixed up together in the melting-pot; they are dross. [19]And so, Lord Yahweh says this, "Since you have all become

dross, right! I shall collect you inside Jeru-
salem. [20]As silver, copper, iron, lead and tin
are collected in the melting-pot, and the fire
is blown underneath to melt them down, so
I shall collect you in my furious anger and
have you melted down; [21]I shall collect you
and blow up the fire of my rage for you and
have you melted down inside the city. [22]As
silver is melted in the melting-pot, so you
will be melted down inside the city, and you
will know that I, Yahweh, have vented my
fury on you." '
[23]The word of Yahweh was addressed to
me as follows, [24]'Son of man, say to her,
"You are a land that has not received rain or
shower on the day of anger. [25]In you, the
princes are like a roaring lion tearing its prey.
They have eaten the people, seized wealth
and jewels and widowed many inside her.
[26]Her priests have violated my law and
desecrated my sanctuary; they have made no
distinction between sacred and profane, they
have not taught people the difference
between clean and unclean; they have turned
their eyes away from my Sabbaths and I have
been dishonoured by them. [27]In her the
leaders are wolves tearing their prey, shed-
ding blood and killing people to steal their
possessions. [28]Her prophets have plastered
these things over with their empty visions
and lying prophecies, saying: Yahweh says
this, although Yahweh has not spoken. [29]The
people of the country have taken to extortion
and banditry; they have oppressed the poor
and needy and ill-treated the settler in a way
that is unjustifiable. [30]I have been looking for
someone among them to build a barricade
and oppose me in the breach, to defend the
country and prevent me from destroying it;
but I have found no one. [31]Hence I have
vented my fury on them; I have put an end
to them in the fire of my rage. I have made
their conduct recoil on their own heads—
declares the Lord Yahweh." '

An allegorical history of Jerusalem and Samaria[a]

23 The word of Yahweh was addressed to
me as follows, [2]'Son of man, there were
once two women, daughters of the same
mother. [3]They played the whore in Egypt;
they played the whore when they were still
girls. There their nipples were handled, there
their virgin breasts were first fondled. [4]Their
names were: Oholah the elder, Oholibah her
sister. They belonged to me and bore sons and
daughters. As regards their names, Samaria is
Oholah, Jerusalem Oholibah. [5]Now Oholah
played the whore, although she belonged to
me; she lusted after her lovers, her neigh-
bours the Assyrians, [6]dressed in purple,
governors and magistrates, all of them young
and desirable, and skilful horsemen. [7]She
played the whore with all of them, the pick
of Assyria, and defiled herself with all the
foul idols of all those with whom she was in
love, [8]nor did she give up the whoring begun
in Egypt, where men had slept with her from
her girlhood, fondling her virgin breasts,
debauching her over and over again.
[9]'That is why I have handed her over to
her lovers, to the Assyrians with whom she
was in love. [10]They stripped her naked, seized
her sons and daughters and put her to the
sword. She became notorious among women
for the justice done on her.
[11]'Her sister Oholibah saw all this, but she
was even more depraved, and her whorings
were worse than her sister's. [12]She fell in love
with her neighbours the Assyrians, governors
and magistrates, dressed in sumptuous
clothes, skilful horsemen, all young and
desirable. [13]Then I saw that she had defiled
herself, that both sisters were equally bad.
[14]She began whoring worse than ever; no
sooner had she seen wall-carvings of men,
pictures of Chaldaeans coloured vermilion,
[15]men with sashes round their waists and
elaborate turbans on their heads, all so lordly
of bearing, depicting the Babylonians,
natives of Chaldaea, [16]than she fell in love
with them at first sight and sent messengers
to them in Chaldaea. [17]The Babylonians came
to her, shared her love-bed and defiled her
with their whoring. Once defiled by them,
she withdrew her affection from them.
[18]Thus she flaunted her whoring, exposing
her body, until I withdrew my affection from
her as I had withdrawn it from her sister.
[19]But she began whoring worse than ever,
remembering her girlhood, when she had
played the whore in Egypt, [20]when she had
been in love with their profligates, big-
membered as donkeys, ejaculating as vio-
lently as stallions.
[21]'You were hankering for the debauchery
of your girlhood, when they used to handle

23a =16.

your nipples in Egypt and fondle your young
breasts. 22And so, Oholibah, Lord Yahweh
says this, "I shall set all your lovers against
you, from whom you have withdrawn your
affection, and bring them to assault you from
all directions: 23the Babylonians and all the
Chaldaeans, the men of Pekod and Shoa and
Koa, and all the Assyrians with them, young
and desirable, all governors and magistrates,
all famous lords and skilful horsemen.
24From the north, they will advance on you
with chariots and wagons and an inter-
national army and beset you with shield,
buckler and helmet on all sides. I shall charge
them to pass sentence on you and they will
pass sentence on you as they think fit. 25I
shall direct my jealousy against you; they will
treat you with fury; they will cut off your
nose and ears, and what is left of your family
will fall by the sword; they will seize your
sons and daughters, and what is left will be
burnt. 26They will strip off your garments
and rob you of your jewels. 27I shall put an
end to your debauchery and to the whorings
you began in Egypt; you will not look to the
Egyptians any more, you will never think of
them again. 28For the Lord Yahweh says this:
Now, I shall hand you over to those you
hate, to those for whom you no longer feel
affection. 29They will treat you with hatred,
they will rob you of the entire fruit of your
labours and leave you stark naked. And thus
your shameful whorings will be exposed,
your debauchery and your whorings. 30This
will happen to you because you have played
the whore with the nations and have defiled
yourself with their foul idols. 31Since you
have copied your sister's behaviour, I shall
put her cup in your hand." 32The Lord
Yahweh says this:

You will drink your sister's cup,
a cup both deep and wide,
leading to laughter and mockery,
so ample the draught it holds.
33You will be filled
with drunkenness and sorrow.
Cup of affliction and devastation,
the cup of your sister Samaria,
34you will drink it, you will drain it;
then you will break it in pieces
and lacerate your own breasts.

For I have spoken—declared the Lord
Yahweh.
35"And so, the Lord Yahweh says this:
Since you have forgotten me and have turned
your back on me, you too will have to bear the
weight of your debauchery and whorings." '
36And Yahweh said to me, 'Son of man, are
you ready to judge Oholah and Oholibah and
charge them with their loathsome practices?
37They have been adulteresses, their hands
are dripping with blood, they have com-
mitted adultery with their foul idols. As for
the children they had borne me, they have
offered them as burnt sacrifices to feed them.
38And here is something else they have done
to me: they have defiled my sanctuary today
and have profaned my Sabbaths. 39The same
day as sacrificing their children to their idols,
they have been to my sanctuary and profaned
it. Yes, this is what they have done in my
own house.

40'Worse still, they summoned men from
far away, invited by messenger, and they
came. For them you bathed, you painted
your eyes, put on your jewels 41and sat on a
sumptuous bed, by which a table was laid
out. On this you had put my incense and my
oil. 42The noise of the carefree company
resounded, made by the crowd of men
brought in from the desert; they put bracelets
on the women's arms and magnificent crowns
on their heads. 43I thought, "That woman,
worn out with adultery! Are they going to
fornicate with her too?" 44Yet they visit her
like any common prostitute, just as they
visited those profligate women Oholah and
Oholibah. 45All the same, there are upright
men who will judge them as adulteresses
and murderesses are judged, since they are
adulteresses and their hands are dripping
with blood."

46'The Lord Yahweh says this, "Summon
an assembly to deal with them, and hand
them over to terror and pillage; 47let the
assembly stone them and dispatch them with
their swords; let their sons and daughters be
slaughtered and their houses set on fire.
48This is how I shall purge the country of
debauchery, so that all women will be taught
the lesson never to ape your debauchery
again. 49Your debauchery will recoil on your-
selves, and you will bear the weight of the
sins committed with your foul idols and you
will know that I am the Lord Yahweh." '

Announcement of the siege of Jerusalem

24 In the ninth year, on the tenth day of
the tenth month, the word of Yahweh
was addressed to me as follows, 2'Son of man,

write down today's date, yes, today's, for this
very day the king of Babylon began his attack
on Jerusalem. 3So pronounce a parable for
this tribe of rebels. Say, "The Lord Yahweh
says this:

Put the pot on the fire;
put it on; pour the water in!
4Now put the cuts of meat all in together,
all the best cuts, leg and shoulder.
Fill it with the best bones.
5Take the best of the flock,
then heap wood underneath;
boil it thoroughly
until even the bones are cooked.

6"For the Lord Yahweh says this:

Disaster is in store for the bloody city,
for that rusty cooking pot
whose rust will not come off!
Empty it, bit by bit,
not bothering to draw lots;
7for she is still full of bloodshed,
she has put blood on the naked rock;
she did not pour it on the ground
so as to cover it with dust.
8To make anger rise, to exact vengeance,
I have put her blood on the naked rock,
so that it should not be covered:

9"So, the Lord Yahweh says this:

Disaster is in store for the bloody city!
I too plan to build a great fire.
10Heap on the wood, light it,
cook the meat, prepare the seasoning
let the bones burn!
11Put the empty pot on the coals
to make it hot,
until the bronze glows,
the filth inside melts
and the rust is burnt away!

12"But all that rust would not come off in
the fire. 13Your filth is infamous. Since I have
tried to purge you and you would not let
yourself be purged of your filth, so now you
will never be purged of your filth until I have
sated my anger on you. 14I, Yahweh, have
spoken; this will happen; I shall act and not
relent; I shall show no pity, no compassion.
You will be judged as your conduct and
actions deserve—declares the Lord
Yahweh." '

Ordeals for the prophet

15The word of Yahweh was addressed to me
as follows, 16'Son of man, at a blow I am
about to deprive you of the delight of your
eyes. But you are not to lament, not to weep,
not to let your tears run down. 17Groan in
silence, do not go into mourning for the dead,
knot your turban round your head, put your
sandals on your feet, do not cover your beard,
do not eat the usual food.' 18I told this to the
people in the morning, and my wife died in
the evening, and the next morning I did as I
had been ordered. 19The people then said to
me, 'Will you not explain what meaning these
actions have for us?' 20I replied, 'The word
of Yahweh has been addressed to me as
follows, 21"Say to the House of Israel, the
Lord Yahweh says this: I am about to profane
my sanctuary, the pride of your strength, the
delight of your eyes, the joy of your hearts.
Your sons and daughters whom you have left
behind will fall by the sword. 22Then you will
do as I have done: you will not cover your
beards or eat the usual food; 23you will keep
your turbans on your heads and your sandals
on your feet; you will not lament or weep but
will waste away for your crimes, groaning
among yourselves. 24Thus Ezekiel is a sign
for you. You will do exactly what he has
done. And when this happens, you will know
that I am Lord Yahweh! "
25'And, son of man, the day that I deprive
them of their strength, their crowning joy,
the delight of their eyes, the joy of their
hearts, their sons and daughters, 26that day a
survivor will bring you the news. 27That day
your mouth will be opened to speak to the
survivor; you will speak and no longer be
dumb; you will be a sign for them, and they
will know that I am Yahweh.'

II: PROPHECIES AGAINST THE NATIONS

Against the Ammonites

25 The word of Yahweh was addressed
to me as follows, 2'Son of man, turn
towards the Ammonites and prophesy
against them. 3Say to the Ammonites, "Hear
the word of the Lord Yahweh. The Lord
Yahweh says this:

"Since you gloated over my sanctuary
when it was profaned, and over the land of
Israel when it was ravaged, and over the
House of Judah when it went into exile, 4I
shall let the sons of the East take possession
of you; they will pitch their camps inside
you, they will make their home in you. They
will be the ones to eat your produce and drink
your milk. 5I shall turn Rabbah into a camel
yard and the towns of Ammon into sheep-
folds. And so you will know that I am
Yahweh.
6"The Lord Yahweh says this: Since you
have clapped your hands and danced for joy,
full of malicious delight at Israel's fate, 7my
hand will be against you for this; I shall
hand you over to be looted by the peoples,
obliterate you as a nation and wipe you out
as a country. I shall reduce you to nothing,
and you will know that I am Yahweh.

Against Moab

8"The Lord Yahweh says this:
"Since Moab and Seir have said: Look at
the House of Judah; it is no different from
any other nation; 9very well, I shall expose
Moab's heights; its cities will no longer be
cities throughout the land—the jewels of the
country, Beth-Jeshimoth, Baal-Meon and
Kiriathaim. 10I shall let the sons of the East
and the Ammonites take possession of them,
so that they will no longer be remembered
by the nations. 11I shall bring Moab to justice,
and they will know that I am Yahweh.

Against Edom

12"The Lord Yahweh says this:
"Since Edom has taken revenge on the
House of Judah and committed great crimes
in doing so, 13very well, the Lord Yahweh
says this: My hand will be against Edom and
denude it of human and animal. I shall lay it
waste, from Teman as far as Dedan they will
be put to the sword. 14I shall take vengeance
on Edom by means of my people Israel. They
will treat Edom as my anger and fury dictate,
and they will know this is my vengeance—
declares the Lord Yahweh.

Against the Philistines

15"The Lord Yahweh says this,
"Since the Philistines have acted in
revenge and, motivated by malice, have taken
revenge, doing their best to destroy because
of their long-standing hatred, 16very well, the
Lord Yahweh says this: My hand will be
against the Philistines; I shall exterminate
the Cherethites and destroy the rest of the
coastal peoples. 17I shall perform frightful
acts of vengeance and inflict furious punish-
ments on them; and they will know that I am
Yahweh, when I exact my vengeance on
them." '

Against Tyre

26 In the eleventh year, on the first of
the month, the word of Yahweh was
addressed to me as follows,
2'Son of man, since Tyre has said of
Jerusalem:

"Aha! She is shattered,
the Gateway to the Nations;
she now gives way to me.
Her riches are ruined!"
3Very well, the Lord Yahweh says this,
"Now, Tyre, I am against you,
4I shall raise many nations against you
as the sea raises its waves.
They will destroy the walls of Tyre,
they will demolish her towers;
I shall sweep the dust of her away
and reduce her to a naked rock.
5She will be a drying-ground out to sea
for fishing-nets.
For I have spoken—
declares Lord Yahweh.
She will be the prey of the nations.
6As for her daughters on the mainland,
these will be put to the sword,
and they will know that I am Yahweh."

7'For the Lord Yahweh says this, "From
the north, I shall bring Nebuchadnezzar,
king of Babylon, king of kings, down on
Tyre with horses, chariots, cavalry and an
enormous army.

8He will put your daughters
on the mainland to the sword.
He will build siege-works against you,
cast up a siege-ramp against you,
raise a screen against you;
9he will pound your walls with his
battering-rams,
and demolish your towers
with his siege-engines.
10His horses are so many
that their dust will hide you.

The noise of his horsemen
and his chariot-wheels
will make your walls tremble
as he enters your gates
as though storming into a city
through the breach.
11 With his horses' hoofs
he will trample through all your streets;
he will put your people to the sword,
and throw your massive pillars
to the ground.
12 Your wealth will be seized,
your merchandise looted,
your walls rased,
your luxurious houses shattered,
your stones, your timbers,
your very dust, thrown into the sea.
13 I shall put an end
to the sound of your songs;
the sound of your harps
will not be heard again.
14 I shall reduce you to a naked rock,
and make you into a drying-ground
for fishing-nets,
never to be rebuilt;
for I, Yahweh, have spoken
—declares the Lord Yahweh."

Lament over Tyre

15 'The Lord Yahweh says this to Tyre, "Will
not the islands quake at the sound of your fall,
while the wounded groan and the slaughter
takes place inside you? 16 All the princes of
the sea will leave their thrones, lay aside their
cloaks, take off their embroidered robes.
Dressed in terror they will sit on the ground
trembling incessantly, stunned at your fate.
17 "They will raise the lament for you as
follows:

You are destroyed then,
vanished from the seas,
famous city, former sea-power,
who with her citizens,
used to spread terror
all over the mainland!
18 Now the islands are trembling
on the day of your fall;
the islands of the sea
are terrified by your end.

19 "For the Lord Yahweh says this:
"When I make you a ruined city like other
deserted cities, when I raise the deep against
you and the ocean covers you, 20 when I fling
you down with those who go down into the
abyss, with the people of long ago, and put
you deep in the underworld, in the ruins of
long ago with those who sink into oblivion,
so that you can never come back or be restored
to the land of the living, 21 I will make you an
object of terror; you will not exist. People
will look for you but never find you again—
declares the Lord Yahweh!" '

Second lament over the fall of Tyre

27 The word of Yahweh was addressed to
me as follows, 2 'Son of man, raise the
lament for Tyre. 3 Say to Tyre, "City
enthroned at the gateway of the sea, agent
between the peoples and the many islands,
Lord Yahweh says this:

Tyre, you used to say: I am a ship
perfect in beauty.
4 Your frontiers were far out to sea;
those who built you
made you perfect in beauty.
5 Cypress from Senir they used
for all your planking.
They took a cedar from Lebanon
to make a mast above you.
6 From oaks of Bashan
they made your oars.
They built you a deck of cedar
inlaid with ivory
from the Kittim isles.
7 Embroidered linen from Egypt
was used for your sail
and for your flag.
Purple and scarlet
from the Elishah islands
formed your deck-tent.
8 The people of Sidon and Arvad
were your oarsmen.
The sages of Tyre were aboard,
serving as sailors.
9 The elders and craftsmen of Gebal
were there
to caulk your seams.

"Every sea-going ship and crew fre-
quented you to guarantee your trade. 10 Men
from Persia, Lud and Put served as warriors
in your army; hanging up shield and helmet
in you, they displayed your splendour. 11 The
sons of Arvad with their army manned your
walls all round, while the Gammadians
manned your towers; hanging their shields
all round your walls, they completed your
beauty. 12 Tarshish traded with you because
of your abundant resources and exchanged

your merchandise for silver, iron, tin and
lead. 13Javan, Tubal and Meshech traded
with you. For your merchandise they traded
slaves and bronze artefacts. 14The people of
Beth-Togarmah traded your horses, char-
gers, mules. 15The people of Dedan traded
with you; many islands were your customers
and paid you in ivory tusks and ebony.
16Edom traded with you for the sake of
your many manufactured goods, exchanging
garnets, purple, embroideries, fine linen,
coral and rubies for your goods. 17Judah
and the land of Israel also traded with you,
bringing corn from Minnith, *pannag*, honey,
oil and balm. 18Damascus traded with you,
for quantities of your manufactured goods
and other goods of all kinds, furnishing you
with wine from Helbon and wool from Zahar.
19Dan and Javan, from Uzal onwards,
supplied you with wrought iron, cassia and
reeds in exchange for your goods. 20Dedan
traded with you in saddle-cloths. 21Arabia
and all the sheikhs of Kedar were your
customers; they paid in lambs, rams and he-
goats. 22The merchants of Sheba and Raamah
traded with you; they supplied you with the
finest spices, precious stones and gold for
your merchandise. 23Haran, Canneh and
Eden, the merchants of Sheba, Asshur and
Chilmad traded with you. 24They traded
rich clothes, embroidered and purple cloaks,
multi-coloured materials and strong plaited
cords for your markets.

25Ships of Tarshish sailed on your business;
you were full and heavily loaded
far out to sea.
26Out to the open sea
your oarsmen rowed you.
The east wind has wrecked you
far out to sea.
27Your riches, your goods, your cargo,
your seamen, your sailors,
your caulkers, your commercial agents,
all the warriors you carry,
and all the passengers who are aboard
will founder far out to sea
on the day of your shipwreck.

28When they hear the cries of your sailors
the coasts will tremble.
29Then the oarsmen will all desert
their ships.
The sailors and seafaring people
will stay ashore.
30They will raise their voices for you
and weep bitterly.
They will throw dust on their heads
and roll in ashes;
31they will shave their heads for you
and put sackcloth round their waists.
With heartfelt bitterness
they will weep for you,
bitterly wail.
32Wailing, they will raise the lament
for you,
they will lament over you:

Who is like Tyre,
far out to sea?
33When you unloaded your goods
to satisfy so many peoples,
you enriched the kings of the earth
with your excess of wealth and goods.
34Now you have been wrecked
by the waves,
by the depths of the sea.
Your cargo and all your passengers
have foundered with you.
35All those who live in the islands
will be stunned at your fate.
Their kings will quake with horror,
with downcast expressions.
36The merchants of the nations
will whistle at your fate.
You will be an object of terror,
gone for ever." '

Against the king of Tyre

28 The word of Yahweh was addressed to
me as follows, 2'Son of man, say to the
ruler of Tyre, "The Lord Yahweh says this:

Because your heart has grown proud,
you thought: I am a god;
I am divinely enthroned
far out to sea.
Though you are human, not divine,
you have allowed yourself
to think like God.[a]
3So, you are wiser than Danel;
no sage as wise as you!
4By your wisdom and your intelligence
you have made yourself a fortune,
you have put gold and silver
into your treasuries.
5Such is your skill in trading,
your fortune has continued to increase,

28a Some features of the story of Adam's fall in Eden recur here.

and your fortune has made your heart
grow prouder.

6"And so, the Lord Yahweh says this:

Since you have allowed yourself
to think like God,
7very well, I am going to bring foreigners
against you,
the most barbarous of the nations.
They will draw sword against
your fine wisdom,
they will desecrate your splendour,
8they will throw you down into the grave
and you will die a violent death
far out to sea.
9Will you still think: I am a god,
when your slaughterers confront you?
But you will be human, not divine,
in the clutches of the ones
who strike you down!
10You will die like the uncircumcised
at the hand of foreigners.

"For I have spoken—declares the Lord Yahweh." '

The fall of the king of Tyre

11The word of Yahweh was addressed to me
as follows, 12'Son of man, raise a lament for
the king of Tyre. Say to him, "The Lord
Yahweh says this:

You used to be a model of perfection,
full of wisdom,
perfect in beauty;
13you were in Eden, in the garden of God.
All kinds of gem formed your mantle:
sard, topaz, diamond, chrysolite, onyx,
jasper, sapphire, garnet, emerald,
and your ear-pendants and spangles
were made of gold;
all was ready on the day you were created.
14I made you a living creature
with outstretched wings, as guardian,
you were on the holy mountain of God;
you walked amid red-hot coals.
15Your behaviour was exemplary
from the day you were created
until guilt first appeared in you,
16because your busy trading
has filled you with violence and sin.
I have thrown you down
from the mountain of God
and destroyed you,
guardian winged creature,
amid the coals.
17Your heart has grown proud
because of your beauty,
your wisdom has been corrupted
by your splendour.
I have thrown you to the ground;
I have made you a spectacle for kings.
18By the immense number of your crimes,
by the dishonesty of your trading,
you have defiled your sanctuary.
So I have brought fire out of you
to devour you;
I have reduced you to ashes on the ground
before the eyes of all who saw you.
19Of the nations, all who know you
are stunned at your fate.
You are an object of terror;
gone for ever." '

Against Sidon

20The word of Yahweh was addressed to me
as follows, 21'Son of man, turn towards Sidon
and prophesy against her. 22Say, "The Lord
Yahweh says this:

I am against you, Sidon,
I will show my glory in you!
They will know I am Yahweh,
once I execute sentence on her
and display my holiness in her.
23For I shall send her the plague,
and there will be blood in her streets,
and in her the dead will fall
under the sword raised against her
from all sides,
and they will know that I am Yahweh.

Israel delivered from the nations

24"No more, for the House of Israel, shall
any of the hostile nations surrounding
them be a thorn that wounds or a briar that
tears; and they will know that I am
Yahweh.
25"The Lord Yahweh says this: When I
gather the House of Israel back from the
peoples where they are dispersed, I shall
display my glory in them for the nations to
see. They will live on the soil which I gave to
my servant Jacob. 26They will live there in
confidence, build houses, plant vineyards.
They will live in safety, once I inflict punish-
ments on all the hostile nations surrounding
them, and they will know that I am Yahweh
their God." '

Against Egypt

29 In the tenth year, on the twelfth day of
the tenth month, the word of Yahweh
was addressed to me as follows, 2‘Son of man,
turn towards Pharaoh king of Egypt and
prophesy against him and against the whole of
Egypt. 3Speak and say, “The Lord Yahweh
says this:

Look, I am against you,
  Pharaoh king of Egypt—
the great crocodile wallowing in his Niles
who thought: My Nile is mine, I made it.
4I shall put hooks through your jaws,
make your Nile fish stick to your scales,
and pull you out of your Niles
with all your Nile fish
  sticking to your scales.
5I shall drop you in the desert,
  with all your Nile fish.
You will fall in the wilds
and not be taken up or buried.
I shall give you as food
to the wild animals
  and the birds of heaven,
6and all the inhabitants of Egypt
  will know that I am Yahweh,
for they have given no more support
  than a reed to the House of Israel.
7Wherever they grasped you,
  you broke in their hands
and cut their hands all over.
Whenever they leaned on you, you broke,
making all their limbs give way.

8“So, the Lord Yahweh says this: I shall
send the sword against you to denude you of
human and animal. 9Egypt will become a
desolate waste, and they will know that I am
Yahweh. Because he thought: The Nile is
mine, I made it, 10very well, I am against you
and your Niles. I shall make Egypt a waste
and a desolation, from Migdol to Syene and
beyond to the frontiers of Ethiopia. 11No
human foot will pass through it, no animal
foot will pass through it. For forty years it
will remain uninhabited. 12I shall make Egypt
the most desolate of countries; for forty years
its cities will be the most desolate of wasted
cities. And I shall scatter the Egyptians
among the nations and disperse them among
the countries. 13The Lord Yahweh, however,
says this: After forty years have passed, I
shall gather the Egyptians back from the
nations where they were dispersed. 14I shall
bring the Egyptian captives back and re-
install them in the land of Pathros, in the
country of their origin. There they will
constitute a modest kingdom. 15Egypt will
be the most modest of kingdoms and no
longer dominate other nations; for I shall
reduce it, so that it will not rule other nations
ever again. 16It will no longer be anything for
the House of Israel to trust in, but will be a
reminder of the guilt which lay in turning to
it for help. And they will know that I am
Lord Yahweh.” ’

17In the twenty-seventh year, on the first
day of the first month, the word of Yahweh
was addressed to me as follows:

18‘Son of man, Nebuchadnezzar king of
Babylon has taken his army in a great
expedition against Tyre. Their heads have all
gone bald, their shoulders are all chafed, but
even so he has derived no profit, either for
himself or for his army, from the expedition
mounted against Tyre. 19Since this is so, the
Lord Yahweh says this, “Look, I shall hand
Egypt over to Nebuchadnezzar king of
Babylon. He will carry off its riches, loot it,
put it to the sack; that will be the wages for
his army. 20As wages for the trouble he has
taken, I am giving him Egypt instead (for
they have been working for me)—declares
the Lord Yahweh.

21“That day, I shall raise up a new stock
for the House of Israel and allow you to open
your mouth among them. And they will know
that I am Yahweh.” ’

Against Egypt: the day of Yahweh

30 The word of Yahweh was addressed to
me as follows, 2‘Son of man, prophesy
and say, “The Lord Yahweh says this: Howl:
Disaster day! 3For the day is near, the day of
Yahweh is near; it will be a day dark with
cloud, a time of doom for the nations.

4“The sword will come on Egypt, and
anguish on the country of Cush when the
slaughtered fall in Egypt, when her riches
are carried away and her foundations are
destroyed. 5Cush, Put and Lud, all Arabia,
Cub and the children of the country of the
covenant will fall by the sword with them.

6“Yahweh says this:

“The supports of Egypt will fall; the pride
of her strength will crumble; they will fall by
the sword from Migdol to Syene—declares
the Lord Yahweh.

7“They will be the most desolate of des-
olate countries, and its cities the most ruined

of cities. 8And they will know that I am
Yahweh when I set fire to Egypt and all its
supports are shattered.
9"That day, I shall send messengers by
ship to terrify the carefree Cushites, and
anguish will overtake them on the day of
Egypt—it is coming now! 10The Lord
Yahweh says this: I shall destroy the huge
population of Egypt at the hand of Nebuch-
adnezzar king of Babylon. 11He and his
people, the most barbarous of nations, will
be brought to ravage the country. They will
draw the sword against Egypt and fill the
country with corpses. 12I shall dry up the
courses of the Nile and sell the country to
the wicked. I shall lay the whole country
waste and everything in it, at the hand of
foreigners. I, Yahweh, have spoken.
13"The Lord Yahweh says this: I shall
destroy the foul idols and take the false gods
away from Noph. Egypt will be left without
a ruler. I shall spread fear through Egypt. 14I
shall lay Pathros waste, set Zoan on fire,
inflict my punishments on No. 15I shall vent
my fury on Sin, the bastion of Egypt; I shall
wipe out the throngs of No. 16I shall set fire
to Egypt; Sin will be seized with convulsions;
a breach will be opened at No and the waters
flood out. 17The young men of On and Pi-
Beseth will fall by the sword and the cities
themselves go into captivity. 18At Tahpanhes
day will turn to darkness when I shatter the
sceptres of Egypt there, when the pride of
her strength ceases. A cloud will cover Egypt
itself, and its daughters will go into captivity.
19Such will be the punishments I inflict on
Egypt. And they will know that I am
Yahweh." '
20In the eleventh year, on the seventh day
of the first month, the word of Yahweh was
addressed to me as follows, 21'Son of man, I
have broken the arm of Pharaoh king of
Egypt; you can see that no one has dressed
his wound by applying remedies to it, by
bandaging it and by dressing it, to make it
strong enough to wield the sword. 22This
being so, the Lord Yahweh says this, "Look,
I am against Pharaoh king of Egypt; I shall
break his arms, the sound one and the broken
one, and make the sword drop from his hand.
23I shall scatter Egypt among the nations and
disperse it among the countries. 24I shall
strengthen the arms of the king of Babylon
and put my sword in his hand. I shall break
Pharaoh's arms and, confronted with his
enemy, he will groan like a dying man. 25I
shall strengthen the arms of the king of
Babylon, and the arms of Pharaoh will fall.
And they will know that I am Yahweh, when
I put my sword into the hands of the king of
Babylon and he wields it against Egypt. 26I
shall scatter Egypt among the nations and
disperse it among the countries; and they will
know that I am Yahweh." '

The cedar tree

31 In the eleventh year, on the first day of
the third month, the word of Yahweh
was addressed to me as follows, 2'Son of man,
say to Pharaoh king of Egypt and his throng
of subjects:

"What can compare with you
for greatness?
3I know: a cedar tree in the Lebanon
with noble branches, dense foliage,
lofty height.
Its top pierces the clouds.
4The waters have made it grow,
the deep has made it tall,
pouring its rivers round the place
where it is planted,
sending rivulets to all the wild trees.
5This is why its height was greater
than that of other wild trees,
its branches increased in number,
its boughs stretched wide,
because of the plentiful waters
making it grow.
6All the birds of heaven
nested in its branches;
under its boughs all wild animals
dropped their young;
in its shade sat many, many people.
7It was beautiful in its size,
in the span of its boughs;
for its roots were in plentiful waters.
8There was no cedar like it
in the garden of God,
no cypress had branches such as these,
no plane tree could match its boughs,
no tree in the garden of God
could rival its beauty.
9I had made it so lovely
with its many branches
that it was the envy of every tree in Eden,
in the garden of God.

10"Very well, the Lord Yahweh says this:
"Since it has raised itself to its full height,
has lifted its top into the clouds, and has
grown arrogant about its height, 11I have

handed it over to the prince of the nations, for him to treat as its wickedness deserves; I have rejected it. 12 Foreigners, the most barbarous of nations, have cut it down and deserted it. On the mountains, in all the valleys, lie its branches; its broken boughs are in every ravine throughout the country; everybody in the country has fled its shade and deserted it. 13 On its wreckage perch all the birds of heaven; all the wild animals have advanced on its branches.

14 "So in future let no tree rear its height beside the waters, none push its top into the clouds, no watered tree stretch its height towards them. For all of them are doomed to death, to the depths of the underworld, with the common run of humanity, with those who sink into oblivion.

15 "The Lord Yahweh says this: The day it went down to Sheol, I imposed mourning, I closed the deep over it. I stopped its rivers and the plentiful waters dried up; I made Lebanon dark because of it, and all the wild trees wilted because of it. 16 With the noise when it fell I made the nations quake, as I hurled it down to Sheol, with those who sink into oblivion. In the depths of the underworld all the trees of Eden took comfort, the pick of the loveliest trees of the Lebanon, all irrigated by the waters. 17 And its offspring among the nations, once living in its shade, went down to Sheol with it, to those who have been slaughtered by the sword.

18 "Which of the trees of Eden compares with you for glory and greatness? Yet you have been hurled down with the trees of Eden, to the depths of the underworld, among the uncircumcised, and there you lie with those who have been slaughtered by the sword. So much for Pharaoh and all his throng—declares the Lord Yahweh." '

The crocodile

32 In the twelfth year, on the first day of the twelfth month, the word of Yahweh was addressed to me as follows, 2 'Son of man, raise a lament for Pharaoh king of Egypt. Say to him:

"Young lion of nations,
you are destroyed!
Once you were like a crocodile
in the lagoons;
emerging from your rivers,
you churned up the water
with your trampling
and fouled their streams.

3 "The Lord Yahweh says this:

I shall throw my net over you
in a great concourse of nations;
and they will trawl you up in my net.
Then I shall leave you high and dry,
4 I shall throw you out into the wilds
and make all the birds of heaven
settle on you,
and glut all the beasts of the earth
with you.
5 I shall strew your flesh on your mountains
and fill the valleys with your corruption;
6 I shall water the country
with what flows from you,
with your blood, on the mountainsides,
and you will fill the ravines.
7 When I extinguish you
I shall cover the skies
and darken the stars.
I shall cover the sun with clouds
and the moon will not give its light.
8 I shall dim every luminary in heaven
because of you
and cover your country in darkness
—declares the Lord Yahweh.

9 "I shall grieve the heart of many peoples when I bring about your destruction among the nations, in countries unknown to you. 10 I shall stun many peoples with shock at your fate; their kings will tremble with horror at your fate, when I brandish my sword before their eyes. The day you fall, each will tremble in terror for his life. 11 For the Lord Yahweh says this: The sword of the king of Babylon will overtake you. 12 I shall make your throngs of subjects fall at the swords of my warriors. They are the most barbarous of nations. They will annihilate the pride of Egypt, and all its throngs will be destroyed. 13 I shall also destroy all its cattle beside the plentiful waters. No human foot will churn them, no animal foot will churn them up again; 14 then I shall let their waters settle and make their rivers glide like oil—declares the Lord Yahweh.

15 "When I reduce Egypt to a ruin and the country is stripped of its contents, when I strike all those who live there, they will know that I am Yahweh.

16 "Such is the lament which the daughters of the nations will raise. They will raise it

over Egypt and all its throng. This is the lament they will raise—declares the Lord Yahweh." '

Pharaoh goes down to Sheol

17In the twelfth year, on the fifteenth day of the first month, the word of Yahweh was addressed to me as follows, 18'Son of man, lament over the throng of Egypt, for down she must go with the daughters of majestic nations to the depths of the underworld with those who sink into oblivion.

19'Whom do you surpass in beauty? Down with you, make your bed with the uncircumcised, 20with those who have been slaughtered by the sword. (The sword has been given, it has been drawn.) She and all her throngs have fallen. 21From the depths of Sheol, the mightiest heroes, her allies, will say to her, "They have come down, they have lain down, uncircumcised, slaughtered by the sword."

22'Assyria is there and all her hordes, with their graves all round her; all of them slaughtered, fallen by the sword; 23their graves have been made in the deepest part of the abyss, and her hordes, with their graves all round her; all of them slaughtered, killed by the sword, who once spread terror through the world of the living.

24'Elam is there and all her throng round her grave, all of them slaughtered, fallen by the sword; they have gone down uncircumcised to the depths of the underworld, who once spread terror throughout the world of the living. They have borne their shame with those who sink into oblivion. 25Among the slaughtered, they have put a bed for her, among her throng with their tombs round her, all of them uncircumcised, slaughtered by the sword for having spread terror throughout the world of the living. They have borne their shame with those who sink into oblivion. They have been put among the slaughtered.

26'Meshech, Tubal are there and all her throng, with their graves round her, all of them uncircumcised, slaughtered by the sword for having spread terror through the world of the living. 27They do not lie with the heroes who fell long ago, those who went down to Sheol fully armed, who had their swords laid under their heads and their shields put under their bones, since the heroes inspired the world of the living with terror. 28But you will be broken with the uncircumcised and lie with those slaughtered by the sword.

29'Edom is there, her kings and all her princes who, despite their valour, have been laid with those slaughtered by the sword. They lie with the uncircumcised, with those who sink into oblivion.

30'All the princes of the north and all the Sidonians are there, who have gone down with the slaughtered, because of the terror which their power inspired. Ashamed, uncircumcised, they lie among those slaughtered by the sword and bear their shame with those who sink into oblivion.

31'Pharaoh will see them and take comfort at the sight of all this throng slaughtered by the sword—Pharaoh and all his throng—declares the Lord Yahweh. 32For having spread terror through the world of the living, he will be laid with the uncircumcised, with those slaughtered by the sword, Pharaoh and all his throng—declares the Lord Yahweh.'

III: DURING AND AFTER THE SIEGE OF JERUSALEM

The prophet as watchman

33 The word of Yahweh was addressed to me as follows, 2'Son of man, speak to the people of your country. Say to them, "When I send the sword against the people of that country, take one of their number and post him as a watchman; 3if he sees the sword coming against the country, he must sound his horn to warn the people. 4If someone hears the sound of the horn but pays no attention and the sword overtakes him and destroys him, he will have been responsible for his own death. 5He has heard the sound of the horn and paid no attention; his death will be his own responsibility. But the life of someone who pays attention will be secure.

6"If, however, the watchman has seen the sword coming but has not blown his horn, and so the people are not alerted and the

sword overtakes them and destroys a single
one of them, that person will indeed die for
his guilt, but I shall hold the watchman
responsible for his death."
7'Son of man I have appointed you as
watchman for the House of Israel. When you
hear a word from my mouth, warn them from
me. 8If I say to someone wicked, "Evil-
doer, you are to die," and you do not speak
to warn the wicked person to renounce such
ways, the wicked person will die for this
guilt, but I shall hold you responsible for the
death. 9If, however, you do warn someone
wicked to renounce such ways and repent,
and that person does not repent, then the
culprit will die for this guilt, but you yourself
will have saved your life.

Conversion and perversity

10'Son of man, say to the House of Israel,
"You are continually saying: Our crimes and
sins weigh heavily on us; we are wasting away
because of them. How are we to go on living?"
11Say to them, "As I live—declares the Lord
Yahweh—I do not take pleasure in the death
of the wicked but in the conversion of the
wicked who changes his ways and saves his
life. Repent, turn back from your evil ways.
Why die, House of Israel?"
12'Son of man, say to the members of
your nation, "The uprightness of an upright
person will not save him once he takes to
wrong-doing; the wickedness of a wicked
person will not ruin him once he renounces
his wickedness. No one upright will be able
to live on the strength of uprightness, having
once taken to sinning. 13If I say to someone
upright: You are to live, and then, trusting
in this uprightness, he does wrong, none of
the uprightness will be remembered; because
of the wrong-doing, he will die. 14If, however,
I say to someone wicked: You are to die, and
he turns back from sin and does what is lawful
and upright, 15if he returns pledges, restores
what he has stolen, keeps the laws that give
life and no longer does wrong, he will live
and will not die. 16None of his previous sins
will be remembered against him; having done
what is lawful and upright, he will live.[a]
17"But the members of your nation say:
What the Lord does is unjust. But it is what
you do that is unjust. 18When an upright
person gives up being upright and does
wrong, he dies for it. 19And when a wicked
person gives up being wicked and does what
is lawful and upright, because of this he lives.
20But you say: What the Lord does is unjust!
I shall judge each of you by what you do,
House of Israel." '[b]

The taking of the city

21In the twelfth year of our captivity, on the
fifth day of the tenth month, a fugitive arrived
from Jerusalem and said to me, 'The city has
been taken.' 22Now the hand of the Lord had
been on me the evening before the fugitive
arrived; he had opened my mouth before the
fugitive came to me the next morning; my
mouth had been opened and I was dumb no
longer.

The ravaging of the country

23The word of Yahweh was then addressed
to me as follows, 24'Son of man, the people
living in those ruins on the soil of Israel say
this, "Abraham was alone when he was given
possession of this country. But we are many;
the country has been given us as our
heritage."
25'Very well, tell them, "The Lord Yahweh
says this: You eat blood, you raise your eyes
to your foul idols, you shed blood; are you to
own the country? 26You rely on your swords,
you engage in loathsome practices, each of
you defiles his neighbour's wife; are you to
own the country?" 27Tell them this, "The
Lord Yahweh says this: As I live, I swear it,
those in the ruins will fall to the sword, those
in the countryside I shall give to the wild
animals for them to eat, and those among the
crags and in caves will die of plague. 28I shall
make the country a desolate waste, and the
pride of its strength will be at an end. The
mountains of Israel will be deserted and no
one will pass that way again. 29Then they will
know that I am Yahweh, when I make the
country a desolate waste because of all the
filthy things they have done."

The results of the preaching

30'Son of man, the members of your nation
are talking about you on the ramparts and in
doorways. They keep saying to one another,
"Come and hear the word that has come from
Yahweh." 31They throng towards you; my

33a =18:22.
33b =18:29–30.

people sit down in front of you and listen to your words, but they do not act on them. What they act on is the lie in their mouths, and their hearts are set on dishonest gain. 32 As far as they are concerned, you are like a love song pleasantly sung to a good musical accompaniment. They listen to your words, but no one acts on them. 33 When the thing takes place—and it is beginning now—they will know that there has been a prophet among them.'

The shepherds of Israel

34 The word of Yahweh was addressed to me as follows, 2 'Son of man, prophesy against the shepherds of Israel; prophesy and say to them, "Shepherds, the Lord Yahweh says this: Disaster is in store for the shepherds of Israel who feed themselves! Are not shepherds meant to feed a flock? 3 Yet you have fed on milk, you have dressed yourselves in wool, you have sacrificed the fattest sheep, but failed to feed the flock. 4 You have failed to make weak sheep strong, or to care for the sick ones, or bandage the injured ones. You have failed to bring back strays or look for the lost. On the contrary, you have ruled them cruelly and harshly. 5 For lack of a shepherd they have been scattered, to become the prey of all the wild animals; they have been scattered. 6 My flock is astray on every mountain and on every high hill; my flock has been scattered all over the world; no one bothers about them and no one looks for them.

7 "Very well, shepherds, hear the word of Yahweh: 8 As I live, I swear it—declares the Lord Yahweh—since my flock has been pillaged and for lack of a shepherd is now the prey of every wild animal, since my shepherds have ceased to bother about my flock, since my shepherds feed themselves rather than my flock, 9 very well, shepherds, hear the word of Yahweh: 10 The Lord Yahweh says this: Look, I am against the shepherds. I shall take my flock out of their charge and henceforth not allow them to feed my flock. And the shepherds will stop feeding themselves, because I shall rescue my sheep from their mouths to stop them from being food for them.

11 "For the Lord Yahweh says this: Look, I myself shall take care of my flock and look after it. 12 As a shepherd looks after his flock when he is with his scattered sheep, so shall I look after my sheep. I shall rescue them from wherever they have been scattered on the day of clouds and darkness. 13 I shall bring them back from the peoples where they are; I shall gather them back from the countries and bring them back to their own land. I shall pasture them on the mountains of Israel, in the ravines and in all the inhabited parts of the country. 14 I shall feed them in good pasturage, the highest mountains of Israel will be their grazing ground. There they will rest in good grazing grounds; they will browse in rich pastures on the mountains of Israel. 15 I myself shall pasture my sheep, I myself shall give them rest—declares the Lord Yahweh. 16 I shall look for the lost one, bring back the stray, bandage the injured and make the sick strong. I shall watch over the fat and healthy. I shall be a true shepherd to them.

17 "As for you, my sheep, the Lord Yahweh says this: I shall judge between sheep and sheep, between rams and he-goats. 18 Not content to drink the clearest of the water, you foul the rest with your feet. 19 And my sheep must graze on what your feet have trampled and drink what your feet have fouled. 20 Very well, the Lord Yahweh says this: I myself shall judge between the fat sheep and the thin sheep. 21 Since you have jostled with flank and shoulder and butted all the ailing sheep with your horns, until you have scattered them outside, 22 I shall come and save my sheep and stop them from being victimised. I shall judge between sheep and sheep.

23 "I shall raise up one shepherd, my servant David, and put him in charge of them to pasture them; he will pasture them and be their shepherd. 24 I, Yahweh, shall be their God, and my servant David will be ruler among them. I, Yahweh, have spoken. 25 I shall make a covenant of peace with them; I shall rid the country of wild animals. They will be able to live secure in the desert and go to sleep in the woods. 26 I shall settle them round my hill; I shall send rain at the proper time; it will be a rain of blessings. 27 The trees of the countryside will yield their fruit and the soil will yield its produce; they will be secure on their soil. And they will know that I am Yahweh when I break the bars of their yoke and rescue them from the clutches of their slave-masters. 28 No more will they be a prey to the nations, no more will the wild animals of the country devour them. They will live secure, with no one to frighten them.

29 I shall make splendid vegetation grow for
them; no more will they suffer from famine
in the country; no more will they have to bear
the insults of other nations. 30 So they will
know that I, their God, am with them and that
they, the House of Israel, are my people—
declares the Lord Yahweh. 31 And you, my
sheep, are the flock of my human pasture,
and I am your God—declares the Lord
Yahweh." '

Against the mountains of Edom

35 The word of Yahweh was addressed
to me as follows, 2 'Son of man, turn
towards Mount Seir and prophesy against it.
3 Say to it, "The Lord Yahweh says this:
Look, I am against you, Mount Seir; I shall
stretch out my hand against you; I shall make
you a desolate waste; 4 I shall lay your towns
in ruins. You will become a waste and you will
know that I am Yahweh. 5 Since, following
a long-standing hatred, you betrayed the
Israelites to the sword on the day of their
distress, on the day when an end came for
their guilt, 6 very well, as I live—declares the
Lord Yahweh—I destine you to bloodshed,
and bloodshed will pursue you. I swear it;
you have incurred guilt by shedding blood,
and bloodshed will pursue you. 7 I shall make
Mount Seir a desolate waste and denude it of
anyone travelling to and fro. 8 I shall fill its
mountains with its slaughtered; on your hills,
in your valleys and in all your ravines, those
slaughtered by the sword will fall. 9 I shall
make you a perpetual waste, your towns will
never be inhabited again, and you will know
that I am Yahweh.

10 "Since you said: The two nations and the
two countries will be mine; we are going to
take possession of it, although Yahweh was
there, 11 very well, as I live—declares the
Lord Yahweh—I shall act with the same
anger and jealousy as you acted in your hatred
for them. I shall make myself known for their
sake, when I punish you, 12 and you will
know that I, Yahweh, have heard all the
blasphemies which you have uttered against
the mountains of Israel, such as: They have
been laid waste, they have been given to us
for us to devour. 13 Great was your insolence
towards me, many your speeches against me;
I have heard! 14 Lord Yahweh says this: To
the joy of the whole world, I shall make you
a waste. 15 Since you rejoiced because the
heritage of the House of Israel had been laid
waste, I shall do the same to you, Mount
Seir; and you will become a waste, and so
will the whole of Edom; and they will know
that I am Yahweh.' "

Prophecy about the mountains of Israel

36 'Son of man, prophesy to the moun-
tains of Israel. Say, "Mountains of
Israel, hear the word of Yahweh. 2 The Lord
Yahweh says this: Since the enemy has
gloated over you by saying: Aha! These
eternal heights are owned by us now, 3 very
well, prophesy! Say: The Lord Yahweh says
this: Since you have been ravaged and seized
on from all sides, and have become the prop-
erty of the rest of the nations, and become
the subject of people's talk and gossip, 4 very
well, mountains of Israel, hear the word of
the Lord Yahweh! The Lord Yahweh says
this to the mountains and hills, to the ravines
and valleys, to the devastated ruins and aban-
doned cities which have been put to the sack
and have become a laughing-stock to the rest
of the nations all round; 5 very well, the Lord
Yahweh says this: I swear it in the heat of
my jealousy; I am speaking to the rest of
the nations and to the whole of Edom who
so exultantly and contemptuously took
possession of my country to despoil its
pastureland."

6 'Because of this, prophesy about the land
of Israel. Say to the mountains and hills, to
the ravines and valleys, "The Lord Yahweh
says this: I am speaking in my jealousy and
rage; because you are enduring the insults of
the nations, 7 very well, the Lord Yahweh
says this: I raise my hand and I swear that
the nations all around you shall have their
own insults to bear.

8 "Mountains of Israel, you will grow bran-
ches and bear fruit for my people Israel, who
will soon return. 9 Yes, I am coming to you,
I shall turn to you; you will be tilled and
sown. 10 I shall increase your population, the
whole House of Israel, yes, all. The cities will
be inhabited and the ruins rebuilt. 11 I shall
increase your population, both human and
animal; they will be fertile and reproduce. I
shall repopulate you as you were before; I
shall make you more prosperous than you
were before, and you will know that I am
Yahweh. 12 Thanks to me, men will tread
your soil again, my people Israel; they will
own you and you will be their heritage,

and never again will you rob them of their children.

13"The Lord Yahweh says this: Since people have said of you: You are a man-eater, you have robbed your nation of its children, 14very well, you will eat no more men, never rob your nation of its children again—declares the Lord Yahweh. 15I shall never again let you hear the insults of the nations, you will never again have to bear the taunts of the peoples, you will never again rob the nation of its children—declares the Lord Yahweh." '

16The word of Yahweh was addressed to me as follows, 17'Son of man, the members of the House of Israel used to live in their own territory, but they defiled it by their conduct and actions; to me their conduct was as unclean as a woman's menstruation. 18I then vented my fury on them because of the blood they shed in the country and the foul idols with which they defiled it. 19I scattered them among the nations and they were dispersed throughout the countries. I sentenced them as their conduct and actions deserved. 20They have profaned my holy name among the nations where they have gone, so that people say of them, "These are the people of Yahweh; they have been exiled from his land." 21But I have been concerned about my holy name, which the House of Israel has profaned among the nations where they have gone. 22And so, say to the House of Israel, "The Lord Yahweh says this: I am acting not for your sake, House of Israel, but for the sake of my holy name, which you have profaned among the nations where you have gone. 23I am going to display the holiness of my great name, which has been profaned among the nations, which you have profaned among them. And the nations will know that I am Yahweh—declares the Lord Yahweh—when in you I display my holiness before their eyes. 24For I shall take you from among the nations and gather you back from all the countries, and bring you home to your own country. 25I shall pour clean water over you and you will be cleansed; I shall cleanse you of all your filth and of all your foul idols. 26I shall give you a new heart, and put a new spirit in you; I shall remove the heart of stone from your bodies and give you a heart of flesh instead. 27I shall put my spirit in you, and make you keep my laws, and respect and practise my judgements. 28You will live in the country which I gave your ancestors. You will be my people and I shall be your God. 29I shall save you from everything that defiles you, I shall summon the wheat and make it plentiful and impose no more famines on you. 30I shall increase the yield of tree and field, so that you will never again bear the ignominy of famine among the nations. 31Then you will remember your evil conduct and actions. You will loathe yourselves for your guilt and your loathsome practices. 32I assure you that I am not doing this for your sake—declares the Lord Yahweh. Be ashamed and blush for your conduct, House of Israel.

33"The Lord Yahweh says this: On the day I cleanse you from all your guilt, I shall repopulate the cities and cause the ruins to be rebuilt. 34Waste land, once desolate for every passer-by to see, will now be farmed again. 35And people will say: This land, so recently a waste, is now like a garden of Eden, and the ruined cities once abandoned and levelled to the ground are now strongholds with people living in them. 36And the nations left round you will know that I, Yahweh, have rebuilt what was levelled and replanted what was ruined. I, Yahweh, have spoken and shall do it.

37"The Lord Yahweh says this: As a further mark of favour, I shall let myself be consulted by the House of Israel; I shall increase their numbers like a human flock, 38like a flock of sacrificial animals, like the flock in Jerusalem on her solemn feasts. So your ruined cities will be filled with human flocks, and they will know that I am Yahweh." '

The dry bones

37 The hand of Yahweh was on me; he carried me away by the spirit of Yahweh and set me down in the middle of the valley, a valley full of bones. 2He made me walk up and down and all around among them. There were vast quantities of these bones on the floor of the valley; and they were completely dry. 3He said to me, 'Son of man, can these bones live?' I said, 'You know, Lord Yahweh.' 4He said, 'Prophesy over these bones. Say, "Dry bones, hear the word of Yahweh. 5The Lord Yahweh says this to these bones: I am now going to make breath enter you, and you will live. 6I shall put sinews on you, I shall make flesh grow on you, I shall cover you with skin and give you

breath, and you will live; and you will know that I am Yahweh." ' 7I prophesied as I had been ordered. While I was prophesying, there was a noise, a clattering sound; it was the bones coming together. 8And as I looked, they were covered with sinews; flesh was growing on them and skin was covering them, yet there was no breath in them. 9He said to me, 'Prophesy to the breath; prophesy, son of man. Say to the breath, "The Lord Yahweh says this: Come from the four winds, breath; breathe on these dead, so that they come to life!" ' 10I prophesied as he had ordered me, and the breath entered them; they came to life and stood up on their feet, a great, an immense army.

11Then he said, 'Son of man, these bones are the whole House of Israel. They keep saying, "Our bones are dry, our hope has gone; we are done for." 12So, prophesy. Say to them, "The Lord Yahweh says this: I am now going to open your graves; I shall raise you from your graves, my people, and lead you back to the soil of Israel. 13And you will know that I am Yahweh, when I open your graves and raise you from your graves, my people, 14and put my spirit in you, and you revive, and I resettle you on your own soil. Then you will know that I, Yahweh, have spoken and done this—declares the Lord Yahweh." '

Judah and Israel in one kingdom

15The word of Yahweh was addressed to me as follows, 16'Son of man, take a stick and write on it, "Judah and those Israelites loyal to him." Take another stick and write on it, "Joseph (Ephraim's wood) and all the House of Israel loyal to him."

17'Join one to the other to make a single piece of wood, a single stick in your hand. 18And when the members of your nation say, "Will you not tell us what you mean?" 19say, "The Lord Yahweh says this: I am taking the stick of Joseph (now in Ephraim's hand) and those tribes of Israel loyal to him and shall join them to the stick of Judah. I shall make one stick out of the two, a single stick in my hand."

20'When the pieces of wood you have written on are in your hand in full sight of them, 21say, "The Lord Yahweh says this: I shall take the Israelites from the nations where they have gone. I shall gather them together from everywhere and bring them home to their own soil. 22I shall make them into one nation in the country, on the mountains of Israel, and one king is to be king of them all; they will no longer form two nations, nor be two separate kingdoms. 23They will no longer defile themselves with their foul idols, their horrors and any of their crimes. I shall save them from the acts of infidelity which they have committed and shall cleanse them; they will be my people and I shall be their God. 24My servant David will reign over them, one shepherd for all; they will follow my judgements, respect my laws and practise them. 25They will live in the country which I gave to my servant Jacob, the country in which your ancestors lived. They will live in it, they, their children, their children's children, for ever. David my servant is to be their prince for ever. 26I shall make a covenant of peace with them, an eternal covenant with them. I shall resettle them and make them grow; I shall set my sanctuary among them for ever. 27I shall make my home above them; I shall be their God, and they will be my people. 28And the nations will know that I am Yahweh the sanctifier of Israel, when my sanctuary is with them for ever." '

Against Gog, king of Magog

38 The word of Yahweh was addressed to me as follows, 2'Son of man, turn towards Gog, to the country of Magog, towards the paramount prince of Meshech and Tubal, and prophesy against him. 3Say, "The Lord Yahweh says this: I am against you, Gog, paramount prince of Meshech and Tubal. 4I shall turn you about, I shall fix hooks in your jaws and bring you out with your entire army, horses and horsemen, all perfectly equipped, a huge array armed with shields and bucklers, and all wielding swords. 5Persia and Cush and Put are with them, all with buckler and helmet; 6Gomer and all its troops, Beth-Togarmah in the far north and all its troops, and many nations with you. 7Be ready, be well prepared, you and all your troops and the others rallying to you, and hold yourself at my service.

8"Many days will pass before you are given orders; in the final years you will march on this country, whose inhabitants will have been living in confidence, remote from other peoples, since they escaped the sword and were gathered in from various nations, here

in the long-deserted mountains of Israel.
9 Like a storm you will approach, you will
advance and cover the country like a cloud,
you, all your troops and many nations with
you.
10 "The Lord Yahweh says this: That day,
a thought will enter your mind and you will
form a sinister plan. 11 You will think: I shall
attack this undefended country and march
on this peaceful nation living secure, all living
in towns without walls or bars or gates. 12 You
will come to plunder and loot and turn your
might against the ruins they live in, against
this people gathered back from the nations,
these stock-breeders and traders who live at
the Navel of the World. 13 Sheba and Dedan,
the merchants and all the magnates of
Tarshish will ask you: Have you come for
plunder? Are you massing your troops with
a view to looting? To make off with gold and
silver, seize cattle and goods, and come away
with unlimited spoil?"
14 "So, son of man, prophesy. Say to Gog,
"The Lord Yahweh says this: Is it not true
that you will set out at a time when my people
Israel is living secure? 15 You will leave your
home in the far north, you and many nations
with you, a great army of countless troops
all mounted. 16 You will invade Israel, my
people. You will be like a cloud covering the
country. In the final days, I myself shall bring
you to attack my country, so that the nations
will know who I am, when I display my
holiness to them, by means of you, Gog.
17 "The Lord Yahweh says this: It was of
you that I spoke in the past through my
servants the prophets of Israel, who proph-
esied in those days, foretelling your invasion.
18 The day Gog attacks the land of Israel—
declares the Lord Yahweh—my furious
wrath will boil up. In my anger, 19 in my
jealousy, in the heat of my fury I say it: That
day, I swear, there will be such a huge
earthquake in the land of Israel, 20 that the
fish in the sea and the birds of heaven, the
wild beasts, all the reptiles creeping along
the ground, and all people on the surface of
the earth will quake before me. Mountains
will fall, cliffs crumble, all walls collapse, and
21 I shall summon every kind of sword against
him—declares the Lord Yahweh—and each
will turn his sword against his comrade. 22 I
shall punish him with plague and bloodshed,
and rain down torrential rain, hailstones, fire
and brimstone on him, on his troops and on
the many nations with him. 23 I shall display
my greatness and holiness and bring the
many nations to acknowledge me; and they
will know that I am Yahweh." '

39 'So, son of man, prophesy against Gog.
Say, "The Lord Yahweh says this:
Look, I am against you, Gog, paramount
prince of Meshech and Tubal. 2 I shall turn
you about, lead you on, and bring you from
the farthest north against the mountains of
Israel. 3 I shall break the bow in your left
hand and dash the arrows out of your right.
4 You will fall on the mountains of Israel, you,
all your troops and the nations with you. I
shall make you food for every kind of bird of
prey and wild animals. 5 You will fall in the
wilds, for I have spoken—declares the Lord
Yahweh. 6 I shall send down fire on Magog
and on those living undisturbed in the
islands, and they will know that I am
Yahweh. 7 I shall see that my holy name is
acknowledged by my people Israel, and no
longer allow my holy name to be profaned;
and the nations will know that I am Yahweh,
holy in Israel.
8 "All this is to happen, all this is to take
place—declares the Lord Yahweh. This is
the day I predicted.
9 "The inhabitants of the towns of Israel
will go out and set fire to and burn the
weapons, the shields and bucklers, bows and
arrows, javelins and spears. They will burn
these for seven years 10 and not fetch wood
from the countryside or cut it in the forests,
since they will be burning the weapons. They
will plunder those who plundered them, and
despoil those who despoiled them—declares
the Lord Yahweh.
11 "That day, I shall give Gog a famous spot
in Israel for his grave, the valley of the
Obarim, east of the Sea—the valley that halts
the traveller—and there Gog and his whole
throng will be buried, and it will be called
the Valley of Hamon-Gog. 12 The House of
Israel will take seven months to bury them
and cleanse the country. 13 All the people
of the country will dig their graves, thus
winning themselves renown, the day when I
display my glory—declares the Lord
Yahweh. 14 And men will be detailed to the
permanent duty of going through the country
and burying those left above ground and
cleansing it. They will begin their search
once the seven months are over, 15 and as they
go through the country, if one of them sees
any human bones, he will set up a marker
beside them until the gravediggers have

buried them in the valley of Hamon-Gog [16](and Hamonah is also the name of a town) and have cleansed the country."

[17]'Son of man, the Lord Yahweh says this, "Say to the birds of every kind and to all the wild animals: Muster, come, gather from everywhere around for the sacrifice I am making for you, a great sacrifice on the mountains of Israel, so that you can eat flesh and drink blood. [18]You will eat the flesh of heroes, you will drink the blood of the princes of the world. They are all rams and lambs, goats and fat bulls of Bashan. [19]You will glut yourselves on fat and drink yourselves drunk on blood at this sacrifice I am making for you. [20]You will glut yourselves at my table on horses and chargers, on heroes and every kind of warrior—declares the Lord Yahweh."

Conclusion

[21]'I shall display my glory to the nations, and all nations will see my sentence when I inflict it and my hand when I strike them. [22]The House of Israel will know that I am Yahweh their God, from that day forward for ever. [23]The nations too will know that the House of Israel were exiled for their guilt; because they were unfaithful to me, I hid my face from them and put them into the clutches of their enemies, so that they all fell by the sword. [24]I treated them as their loathsome acts of infidelity deserved and hid my face from them.

[25]'So, the Lord Yahweh says this, "Now I shall bring Jacob's captives back and take pity on the whole House of Israel and show myself jealous for my holy name. [26]They will forget their disgrace and all the acts of infidelity which they committed against me when they were living safely in their own country, with no one to disturb them. [27]When I bring them home from the peoples, when I gather them back from the countries of their enemies, when I display my holiness in them for many nations to see, [28]they will know that I am Yahweh their God who, having sent them into exile among the nations, have reunited them in their own country, not leaving a single one behind. [29]I shall never hide my face from them again, since I shall pour out my spirit on the House of Israel—declares the Lord Yahweh." '

IV: THE TORAH OF EZEKIEL[a]

The future Temple

40 In the twenty-fifth year of our captivity, at the beginning of the year, on the tenth day of the month, fourteen years to the day from the capture of the city, the hand of Yahweh was on me. He carried me away: [2]in divine visions, he carried me away to the land of Israel and put me down on a very high mountain, on the south of which there seemed to be built a city. [3]He took me to it, and there I saw a man, whose appearance was like brass. He had a flax cord and a measuring rod in his hand and was standing in the gateway. [4]The man said to me, 'Son of man, look carefully, listen closely and pay attention to everything I show you, since you have been brought here only for me to show it to you. Tell the House of Israel everything that you see.'

The outer wall

[5]Now, the Temple was surrounded on all sides by an outer wall. The man was holding a measuring rod six cubits long, each cubit a forearm and a handsbreadth. He measured the thickness of this construction—one rod; and its height—one rod.

The east gate

[6]He went to the east gate, climbed the steps and measured its threshold: one rod deep. [7]Each guardroom one rod by one rod; and the piers between the guardrooms five cubits thick, and the threshold of the gate inwards from the porch of the gate: one rod.[b] [9]He measured the porch of the gate: eight cubits; its piers: two cubits; the porch of the gate was at the inner end. [10]There were three

40a This last section is a blueprint for the restored community, alive to the presence of God in his spirit and inspired by the ideal of holiness.
40b v. 8 is omitted: it doubles v. 7.

guardrooms on each side of the east gate, all three of the same size; the piers between them all of the same thickness each side. 11 He measured the width of the entrance: ten cubits; and the width all down the gateway: thirteen cubits. 12 There was a rail in front of the guardrooms; each rail on either side was one cubit. And the guardrooms on either side were six cubits square. 13 He measured the width of the gate from the back wall of one guardroom to the back wall of the other; it was twenty-five cubits across, the openings being opposite each other. 14 He measured the porch: twenty cubits; the court surrounded the gate on all sides. 15 From the front of the entrance gate, to the far end of the porch of the inner gate: fifty cubits. 16 All round inside the gate there were trellised windows in the guardrooms and in their piers; similarly, in the porch there were windows all round and palm trees on the piers.

The outer court

17 He then took me to the outer court, which had rooms and a paved terrace going all the way round; there were thirty rooms on this terrace. 18 This terrace, which came up to the sides of the gates and matched their depth, was the Lower Terrace. He measured the width of the court, 19 from the front of the lower gate to the façade of the inner court, outside: a hundred cubits (on the east and on the north).

The north gate

20 He measured the length and breadth of the north gate of the outer court. 21 It had three guardrooms on each side; its piers and porch were of the same size as those of the first gate: fifty cubits long and twenty-five cubits wide. 22 Its windows, its porch and its palm trees were of the same size as those of the east gate. There were seven steps up to it, and its porch was at the inner end. 23 In the inner court there was, opposite the north gate, a gate like the one opposite the east gate. He measured the distance from one gate to the other: a hundred cubits.

The south gate

24 He took me to the south side where there was a south gate; he measured its guardrooms, piers and porch; they were of the same size as the others. 25 The gateway, as well as its porch, had windows all round, like the windows of the others; it was fifty cubits long and twenty-five cubits wide, 26 and it had seven steps up to it; its porch was at the inner end and had palm trees on its piers, one on either side. 27 The inner court had a south gate; he measured the distance southwards from one gate to the other: a hundred cubits.

The inner court. The south gate

28 He then took me into the inner court by the south gate; he measured the south gate which was of the same size as the others. 29 Its guardrooms, piers and porch were of the same size as the others. 30 The gateway, as well as its porch, had windows all round; it was fifty cubits long and twenty-five cubits wide. 31 The porch gave on to the outer court. It had palm trees on its piers and eight steps leading up to it.

The east gate

32 He took me to the eastern part of the inner court and measured the gate. It was of the same size as the others. 33 Its guardrooms, piers and porch were of the same size as the others. The gateway, as well as its porch, had windows all round; it was fifty cubits long and twenty-five cubits wide. 34 Its porch gave on to the outer court. There were palm trees on its piers on either side and eight steps leading up to it.

The north gate

35 He then took me to the north gate and measured it. 36 Its guardrooms, piers and porch were of the same size as the others. The gateway had windows all round; it was fifty cubits long and twenty-five cubits wide. 37 Its porch gave on to the outer court. There were palm trees on its piers on either side and eight steps leading up to it.

Subsidiary buildings at the gate

38 There was a room, the entrance to which was in the porch of the gateway, where they washed the burnt offerings. 39 And inside the porch of the gateway were slabs, two on either side, for slaughtering the burnt offerings, the sacrifice for sin and the sacrifice of reparation.

40 Outside, at the approach to the entrance of the north gate, were two slabs, and on the other side, at the porch end of the gate were two slabs. 41 There were four slabs on one side and four slabs on the other side of the gateway, eight slabs in all, on which the slaughtering was done. 42 There were also four slabs of dressed stone for the burnt offerings, a cubit and a half long, a cubit and a half wide and a cubit high, on which the instruments for slaughtering the burnt offerings and sacrifice were placed; 43 runnels a handsbreadth wide went all round the top, and on these slabs was put the sacrificial flesh.

44 Then he took me into the inner court; there were two rooms in the inner court, one on the side of the north gate, facing south, the other on the side of the south gate, facing north. 45 He told me, 'The room looking south is for the priests responsible for the service of the Temple, 46 and the room looking north is for the priests responsible for the service of the altar. These are the sons of Zadok, those of the sons of Levi who approach Yahweh to serve him.'

The inner court

47 He measured the court; it was a hundred cubits long and a hundred cubits wide, a square with the altar standing in front of the Temple.

The Temple. The Ulam

48 He took me to the Ulam of the Temple and measured the piers of the Ulam: five cubits either side; and the width of the entrance was three cubits either side. 49 The length of the Ulam was twenty cubits and its width twelve cubits. There were ten steps leading up to it, and there were columns by the piers, one on either side.

The Hekal

41 He took me to the Hekal and measured its piers: six cubits wide on the one side, six cubits wide on the other. 2 The width of the entrance was ten cubits, and the returns of the entrance were five cubits on the one side and five cubits on the other. He measured its length: forty cubits; and its width: twenty cubits.

The Debir

3 He then went inside and measured the pier at the entrance: two cubits; then the entrance; six cubits; and the returns of the entrance: seven cubits. 4 He measured its length; twenty cubits; and its width against the Hekal: twenty cubits. He then said to me, 'This is the Holy of Holies.'

The side cells

5 He then measured the wall of the Temple: six cubits. The width of the lateral structure was four cubits, all round the Temple. 6 The cells were one above the other in three tiers of thirty cells each. The cells were recessed into the wall, the wall of the structure comprising the cells, all round, forming offsets; but there were no offsets in the wall of the Temple itself. 7 The width of the cells increased, storey by storey, corresponding to the amount taken in from the wall from one storey to the next, all round the Temple.

8 Then I saw that there was a paved terrace all round the Temple. The height of this, which formed the base of the side cells, was one complete rod of six cubits. 9 The outer wall of the side cells was five cubits thick. There was a passage between the cells of the Temple 10 and the rooms, twenty cubits wide, all round the Temple. 11 As a way in to the lateral cells on the passage there was one entrance on the north side and one entrance on the south side. The width of the passage was five cubits right round.

The building on the west side

12 The building on the west side of the court was seventy cubits wide, the wall of the building was five cubits thick all round and its length was ninety cubits. 13 He measured the length of the Temple: a hundred cubits. 14 The length of the court plus the building and its walls: a hundred cubits. 15 He measured the length of the building, along the court, at the back, and its galleries on either side: a hundred cubits.

Particulars of the Temple itself

The inside of the Hekal and the porches of the court, 16 the thresholds, the windows, the galleries on three sides, facing the threshold, were panelled with wood all round from floor to windows, and the windows were screened with latticework. 17 From the door to the inner part of the Temple, as well as outside, and on the wall all round, both inside and out, 18 were carved great winged creatures and palm trees, one palm tree between two winged creatures; each winged creature had two faces: 19 a human face turned towards the palm tree on one side and the face of a lion towards the palm tree on the other side, throughout the Temple, all round. 20 Winged creatures and palm trees were carved on the wall from the floor to above the entrance. 21 The doorposts of the Temple were square.

The wooden altar

In front of the sanctuary there was something like 22 a wooden altar, three cubits high and two cubits square. Its corners, base and sides were of wood. He said to me, 'This is the table in the presence of Yahweh.'

The doors

23 The Hekal had double doors and the sanctuary 24 double doors. These doors had two hinged leaves, two leaves for the one door, two leaves for the other. 25 On them (on the doors of the Hekal), were carved great winged creatures and palm trees like those carved on the walls. There was a wooden porch roof on the front of the Ulam on the outside, 26 and windows with flanking palm trees on the sides of the Ulam, the cells to the side of the Temple and the porch-roofs.

Subsidiary buildings of the Temple

42 He then took me out into the outer court on the north side and led me to the room facing the court, that is to say, to the front of the building on the north side. 2 Along the front, it was a hundred cubits long on the north side and fifty cubits wide. 3 Facing the gateways of the inner court and facing the paving of the outer court was a gallery in front of the triple gallery, 4 and in front of the rooms was a walk, ten cubits measured inwards and a hundred cubits long; their doors looked north. 5 The top-floor rooms were narrow because the galleries took up part of the width, being narrower than those on the ground floor or those on the middle floor of the building; 6 these were divided into three storeys and had no columns such as the court had. Hence they were narrower than the ground floor ones or the middle-floor ones (below them). 7 The outer wall parallel to the rooms, facing them and giving onto the outer court, was fifty cubits long, 8 the length of the rooms facing the outer court being fifty cubits, while for those facing the hall of the Temple it was a hundred cubits. 9 Beneath the rooms there was an entrance from the east, leading in from the outer court.

10 In the thickness of the wall of the court, on the south side fronting the court and the building, were rooms. 11 A walk ran in front of them, as with the rooms built on the north side; they were of the same length and breadth, and were of similar design with similar doors in and out. 12 Before the rooms on the south side there was an entrance at the end of each walk, opposite the corresponding wall on the east side, at their entries. 13 He said to me, 'The northern and southern rooms giving onto the court are the rooms of the sanctuary, in which the priests who approach Yahweh will eat the most holy things. In them will be placed the most holy things: the oblation, the sacrifice for sin and the sacrifice of reparation, since this is a holy place. 14 Once the priests have entered, they will not go out of the holy place into the outer court without leaving their liturgical vestments there, since these vestments are holy; they will put on other clothes before going near places assigned to the people.'

Measurements of the court

15 When he had finished measuring the inside of the Temple, he took me out to the east gate and measured it right round the sides. 16 He measured the east side with his measuring rod: a total of five hundred cubits by the measuring rod. 17 He then measured the north side: a total of five hundred cubits by the measuring rod. 18 He then measured the south side: five hundred cubits by the measuring rod 19 was the total. On the west side he measured five hundred cubits by the measuring rod. 20 He measured the entire enclosing wall on all four sides: length five hundred, breadth five hundred, separating the sacred from the profane.

The return of Yahweh

43 He took me to the gate, the one facing east. [2]I saw the glory of the God of Israel approaching from the east. A sound came with him like the sound of the ocean, and the earth shone with his glory. [3]This vision was like the one I had seen when I had come for the destruction of the city, and like the one I had seen by the River Chebar. Then I fell to the ground.

[4]The glory of Yahweh arrived at the Temple by the east gate. [5]The Spirit lifted me up and brought me into the inner court; I saw the glory of Yahweh fill the Temple. [6]And I heard someone speaking to me from the Temple while the man stood beside me. [7]He said, 'Son of man, this is the dais of my throne, the step on which I rest my feet. I shall live here among the Israelites for ever; and the House of Israel, they and their kings, will never again defile my holy name with their whorings and the corpses of their kings, [8]by putting their threshold beside my threshold and their doorposts beside my doorposts, with a party wall shared by them and me. They used to defile my holy name by their loathsome practices, and this is why I put an end to them in my anger. [9]From now on they will banish their whorings and the corpses of their kings from my presence and I shall live among them for ever.

[10]'Son of man, describe this Temple to the House of Israel, to shame them out of their loathsome practices. (Let them draw up the plan of it.) [11]And, if they are ashamed of their behaviour, show them the design and plan of the Temple, its exits and entrances, its shape, how all of it is arranged, the entire design and all its principles. Give them all this in writing so that they can see and take note of its design and the way it is all arranged and carry it out. [12]This is the charter of the Temple: all the surrounding space on the mountain top is an especially holy area. (Such is the charter of the Temple.)'

The altar

[13]These were the dimensions of the altar, in cubits each of a cubit plus a handsbreadth. The base: one cubit high and one cubit wide; the space by the runnel, all round the edge of the altar, one handsbreadth. [14]From the ground level of the base up to the lower plinth, two cubits high and one cubit wide; from the lesser plinth to the greater plinth, four cubits high and one cubit wide. [15]The altar hearth: four cubits high, with four horns projecting from the hearth, [16]the hearth was four-square: twelve cubits by twelve cubits; [17]and the square plinth: fourteen cubits by fourteen cubits; and the ledge all round: half a cubit; and the base: one cubit all round. The steps were on the east side.

The consecration of the altar

[18]He said to me, 'Son of man, the Lord Yahweh says this, "As regards the altar, this is how things must be done when it has been built for the sacrifice of the burnt offering and for the pouring of blood. [19]To the levitical priests—those of the race of Zadok—who approach me to serve me—declares the Lord Yahweh—you must give a young bull as a sacrifice for sin. [20]You must take some of its blood and put it on the four horns, on the four corners of the plinth and on the surrounding ledge. In this way you will purify it and make expiation on it. [21]Then take the bull of the sacrifice for sin and burn it in that part of the Temple which is cut off from the sanctuary. [22]On the second day, you must offer an unblemished he-goat as the sacrifice for sin, and the altar must be purified again as was done with the bull. [23]When you have finished the purification, you must offer a young, unblemished bull and an unblemished ram from the flock. [24]You must present them before Yahweh, and the priests will sprinkle salt on them and offer them as burnt offerings to Yahweh. [25]As a sacrifice for sin, every day for seven days you must offer a he-goat, a bull and an unblemished ram from the flock. [26]In this way the altar will be expiated and will be purified and inaugurated. [27]At the end of that time, on the eighth day and afterwards, the priest will offer your burnt offerings and your communion sacrifices on the altar, and I shall look favourably on you—declares the Lord Yahweh." '

The use of the east gate

44 He brought me back to the outer east gate of the sanctuary. It was shut. [2]Yahweh said to me, 'This gate will be kept shut. No one may open it or go through it, since Yahweh, God of Israel, has been through it. And so it must be kept shut. [3]The prince himself, however, may sit there to

take his meal in the presence of Yahweh. He
must enter and leave through the porch of
the gate.'

Rules of admission to the Temple

4He led me through the north gate to the
front of the Temple. And then I looked; I
saw the glory of Yahweh filling the Temple
of Yahweh; and I fell to the ground. 5Yahweh
said to me, 'Son of man, pay attention, look
carefully and listen closely to everything I
explain; these are all the arrangements of the
Temple of Yahweh and all its laws. Be careful
about who is admitted to the Temple and
who is excluded from the sanctuary. 6And
say to the rebels of the House of Israel,
"The Lord Yahweh says this: You have gone
beyond all bounds with all your loathsome
practices, House of Israel, 7by admitting
aliens, uncircumcised in heart and body,
to frequent my sanctuary and profane my
Temple, while offering my food, the fat and
the blood, and breaking my covenant with
all your loathsome practices. 8Instead of
maintaining the service of my holy things,
you have deputed someone else to maintain
my service in my sanctuary. 9The Lord
Yahweh says this: No alien, uncircumcised
in heart and body, may enter my sanctuary,
none of the aliens living among the Israelites.

The Levites

10"As regards the Levites who abandoned me
when Israel strayed far from me by following
its idols, they must bear the weight of their
own sin. 11They must be servants in my
sanctuary, responsible for guarding the
Temple gates and serving the Temple. They
will kill the burnt offerings and the sacrifice
for the people, and hold themselves at the
service of the people. 12Since they used to be
at their service in front of their idols and were
an occasion of guilt for the House of Israel,
very well, I stretch out my hand against
them—declares the Lord Yahweh—they will
bear the weight of their guilt. 13They may
never approach me again to perform the
priestly office in my presence, nor touch my
holy things and my most holy things; they
must bear the disgrace of their loathsome
practices. 14I shall give them the responsi-
bility of serving the Temple; I shall make
them responsible for serving it and for every-
thing to be done in it.

The priests

15"As regards the levitical priests, the sons of
Zadok, who maintained the service of my
sanctuary when the Israelites strayed far from
me, they will approach me to serve me; they
will stand in my presence to offer me the
fat and blood—declares the Lord Yahweh.
16They will enter my sanctuary and approach
my table to serve me; they will maintain my
service. 17Once they enter the gates of the
inner court, they must wear linen vestments;
they must wear no wool when they serve
inside the gates of the inner court and in the
Temple. 18They must wear linen caps on
their heads and linen breeches on their loins;
they may not wear anything round their
waists that makes them sweat. 19When they
go out to the people in the outer court,
they must remove the vestments in which
they have performed the liturgy and leave
them in the rooms of the Holy Place, and put
on other clothes, so as not to hallow the
people with their vestments. 20They may
neither shave their heads nor let their hair
grow long, but must cut their hair carefully.
21No priest may drink wine on the day he
enters the inner court. 22They may not marry
widows or divorced women, but only virgins
of the race of Israel; they may, however,
marry a widow, if she is the widow of a priest.
23They must teach my people the difference
between what is sacred and what is profane
and make them understand the difference
between what is clean and what is unclean.
24They must be judges in law-suits; they must
judge in the spirit of my judgements; they
must follow my laws and ordinances at all my
feasts and keep my Sabbaths holy. 25They
may not go near a dead person, in case they
become unclean, except in these permissible
cases, that is, for father, mother, daughter,
son, brother or unmarried sister. 26After one
of them has been purified, seven days must
elapse; 27then, the day he enters the Holy
Place in the inner court to minister in the
Holy Place, he must offer his sacrifice for
sin—declares the Lord Yahweh. 28They may
have no heritage; I myself shall be their
heritage. You may give them no patrimony
in Israel; I myself shall be their patrimony.
29Their food must be the oblation, the sacri-
fice for sin and the sacrifice of reparation.
Everything dedicated by vow in Israel shall
be for them. 30The best of all your first-fruits
and of all the dues and of everything you

offer, must go to the priests; and the best of
your dough you must also give to the priests,
so that a blessing may rest on your house.
31Priests must not eat the flesh of anything
that has died a natural death or been savaged,
be it bird or animal." '

The division of the country
The portion for Yahweh

45 ' "When you draw lots to divide the
country by heritage, you must set a
sacred portion of the country aside for
Yahweh: twenty-five thousand cubits long
and twenty thousand wide. The whole of this
land must be sacred, 2and of this an area five
hundred by five hundred cubits must be for
the sanctuary, with a boundary fifty cubits
wide right round. 3Out of this area you must
also measure a section twenty-five thousand
by ten thousand cubits, in which will be the
sanctuary, the Holy of Holies. 4This will be
the sacred portion of the country, belonging
to the priests who officiate in the sanctuary
and approach Yahweh to serve him. It will
contain room for their houses and room
for the sanctuary. 5A portion twenty-five
thousand by ten thousand cubits will be
owned by the Levites serving the Temple,
with towns for them to live in. 6You must give
the city possession of an area five thousand by
twenty-five thousand cubits, near the land
belonging to the sanctuary; this must be for
the whole House of Israel.

The portion for the prince

7"The prince must have a territory either
side of the sacred portion and of the property
of the city, adjacent to the sacred portion and
the property of the city, stretching westwards
from the west and eastwards from the east,
its size equal to one of the portions between
the west and the east frontiers 8of the country.
This will be his property in Israel. Then my
princes will no longer oppress my people;
they must leave the rest of the country for
the House of Israel, for its tribes.

9"The Lord Yahweh says this: Enough,
princes of Israel! Give up your violence and
plundering, do what is upright and just, stop
crushing my people with taxation—declares
the Lord Yahweh. 10Have fair scales, a fair
ephah, a fair *bat*. 11Let the *ephah* and *bat* be
equal, let the *bat* hold one-tenth of a *homer*
and the *ephah* one-tenth of a *homer*. Let the
measures be based on the *homer*. 12The shekel
must be twenty *gerah*. Twenty shekels,
twenty-five shekels and fifteen shekels must
make one *mina*.

Offerings for worship

13"This is the offering that you must levy:
the sixth of an *ephah* for every *homer* of wheat,
and the sixth of an *ephah* for every *homer* of
barley. 14The dues on oil: one *bat* of oil out
of every ten *bat* or out of every *kor* (which is
equal to ten *bat* or one *homer*, since ten *bat*
equal one *homer*). 15You must levy one sheep
on every flock of two hundred from the
pastures of Israel for the oblation, the burnt
offerings and the communion sacrifice. This
must form your expiation—declares the Lord
Yahweh. 16Let all the people of the country
be subject to this due for the prince of Israel.
17The prince must make himself responsible
for providing the burnt offerings, the
oblation and the libations for feasts, New
Moons, Sabbaths and all the solemn festivals
of the House of Israel. He must provide
the sacrifice for sin, the oblation, the burnt
offerings and the communion sacrifices to
make expiation for the House of Israel.

The feast of the Passover

18"The Lord Yahweh says this: On the first
day of the first month, you must take a young
bull without blemish, to purify the sanctuary.
19The priest must take blood from the sacri-
fice for sin and put it on the doorposts of the
Temple, on the four corners of the altar
plinth and on the doorposts of the gates of
the inner court. 20You must do the same on
the seventh of the month, on behalf of anyone
who has sinned through inadvertence or
ignorance. This is how you must make expia-
tion for the Temple. 21On the fourteenth day
of the first month, you must celebrate the
feast of the Passover. For seven days everyone
must eat unleavened loaves. 22On that day,
the prince must offer a bull as a sacrifice for
sin, for himself and all the people of the
country. 23For the seven days of the feast, he
must offer Yahweh burnt offerings of seven
bulls and seven rams without blemish, daily
for a week, and one he-goat daily as a sacrifice
for sin, 24and as an oblation, one *ephah* for
each bull and one *ephah* for each ram, and a
hin of oil for every *ephah*.

The feast of Shelters

25“For the feast that falls on the fifteenth day of the seventh month, he must do the same for seven days, offering the sacrifice for sin, the burnt offerings, the oblation and the oil.” ’

Miscellaneous regulations

46 ‘ “The Lord Yahweh says this: The east gate of the inner court must be kept shut for the six working days. On the Sabbath day, however, it must be opened, as also on the day of the New Moon; 2and the prince must go in through the porch of the outer gate and take his position by the doorposts of the gate. The priests must then offer his burnt offerings and his communion sacrifice. He must prostrate himself on the threshold of the gate and go out, and the gate must not be shut again until the evening. 3The people of the country must prostrate themselves in the presence of Yahweh at the entrance to the gate on Sabbaths and days of the New Moon. 4The burnt offering offered to Yahweh by the prince on the Sabbath day must consist of six unblemished lambs and one unblemished ram, 5with an oblation of one *ephah* for the ram, and such oblation as he pleases for the lambs, and a *hin* of oil for every *ephah*. 6On the day of the New Moon it must consist of an unblemished young bull, six unblemished lambs and one unblemished ram, 7when he must make an oblation of one *ephah* for the bull and one *ephah* for the ram, and what he pleases for the lambs, and a *hin* of oil for every *ephah*.

8“When the prince goes in, he must enter by the porch of the gate, and he must leave by the same way. 9When the people of the country come into the presence of Yahweh at the solemn festivals, those who have come in by the north gate to prostrate themselves must go out by the south gate, and those who have come in by the south gate must go out by the north gate; no one must turn back to leave through the gate by which he entered but must go out on the opposite side. 10The prince will be with them, coming in like them and going out like them.

11“On feast days and solemn festivals the oblation must be one *ephah* for every bull, one *ephah* for every ram, what he pleases for the lambs, and a *hin* of oil for every *ephah*. 12When the prince offers Yahweh voluntary burnt offerings or a voluntary communion sacrifice, the east gate must be opened for him, and he must offer his burnt offerings and his communion sacrifice as he does on the Sabbath day; when he has gone out, the gate must be shut after him. 13Every day he must offer an unblemished lamb one year old as a burnt offering to Yahweh; he must offer this every morning. 14Every morning in addition he must offer an oblation of one-sixth of an *ephah* and one-third of a *hin* of oil, for mixing with the flour. This is the oblation to Yahweh, a perpetual decree, fixed for ever. 15The lamb, the oblation and the oil must be offered morning after morning for ever.

16“Lord Yahweh says this: If the prince presents part of his hereditary portion to one of his sons, the gift must pass into the ownership of his sons and become their hereditary property. 17If, however, he presents part of his hereditary portion to one of his slaves, it will belong to the man only until the year of liberation and then must revert to the prince. Only his sons may retain his hereditary portion. 18The prince may not take any part of the people’s hereditary portion, thus robbing them of what is theirs; he must provide the patrimony of his sons out of his own property, so that no member of my people is robbed of what is his!” ’

19He took me through the entrance at the side of the north gate that leads to the rooms of the Holy Place set apart for the priests. And there before us, to the west, was a space at the end. 20He said to me, ‘This is where the priests must boil the slaughtered animals for the sacrifice for sin and the sacrifice of reparation, and where they must bake the oblation, without having to carry them into the outer court and so run the risk of hallowing the people.’ 21He then took me into the outer court and led me to each of its four corners; in each corner of the outer court was a compound; 22in other words, the four corners of the court contained four small compounds, forty cubits by thirty, all four being the same size. 23All four were enclosed by a wall, with hearths all round the bottom of the wall. 24He said, ‘These are the kitchens where the Temple servants must boil the sacrifices offered by the people.’

The spring in the Temple

47 He brought me back to the entrance of the Temple, where a stream flowed

eastwards from under the Temple threshold,
for the Temple faced east. The water flowed
from under the right side of the Temple,
south of the altar. 2He took me out by the
north gate and led me right round outside as
far as the outer east gate where the water
flowed out on the right-hand side. 3The man
went off to the east holding his measuring
line and measured off a thousand cubits; he
then made me wade across the stream; the
water reached my ankles. 4He measured off
another thousand and made me wade across
the stream again; the water reached my
knees. He measured off another thousand
and made me wade across the stream again;
the water reached my waist. 5He measured
off another thousand; it was now a river
which I could not cross; the stream had
swollen and was now deep water, a river
impossible to cross. 6He then said, 'Do you
see, son of man?' He then took me and
brought me back to the bank on the river.
7Now, when I reached it, I saw an enormous
number of trees on each bank of the river.
8He said, 'This water flows east down to
the Arabah and to the sea; and flowing into
the sea it makes its waters wholesome.
9Wherever the river flows, all living creatures
teeming in it will live. Fish will be very
plentiful, for wherever the water goes it
brings health, and life teems wherever the
river flows. 10There will be fishermen on its
banks. Fishing nets will be spread from En-
Gedi to En-Eglaim. The species of fish will
be the same as the fish of the Great Sea.
11The marshes and lagoons, however, will
not become wholesome, but will remain salt.
12Along the river, on either bank, will grow
every kind of fruit tree with leaves that never
wither and fruit that never fails; they will
bear new fruit every month, because this
water comes from the sanctuary. And their
fruit will be good to eat and the leaves
medicinal.'

The frontiers of the Holy Land

13'The Lord Yahweh says this, "This will
be the territory which you must distribute
among the twelve tribes of Israel, with two
portions for Joseph. 14You will each have a
fair share of it, since I swore to your fathers
that I would give it to them, and this country
now falls to you as your heritage. 15These will
be the frontiers of the country. On the north,
from the Great Sea, the road from Hethlon
to the Pass of Hamath, Zedad, 16Berothah,
Sibraim lying between the territories of
Damascus and Hamath, to Hazer-ha-Tikon
on the borders of Hauran; 17the frontier will
extend from the sea to Hazer-Enon, with the
territory of Damascus and the territory of
Hamath to the north; that will be the northern
frontier. 18On the east, the Jordan will serve
as frontier between Hauran and Damascus,
between Gilead and Israel, down to the
Eastern Sea as far as Tamar; that will be the
eastern frontier. 19On the south, from Tamar
southward to the Waters of Meribah in
Kadesh, to the Wadi and the Great Sea; that
will be the southern frontier. 20And to the
west, the Great Sea will serve as frontier up
to the point opposite the Pass of Hamath;
that will be the western frontier. 21You must
distribute this country among yourselves,
among the tribes of Israel. 22You must
distribute it as a heritage for yourselves and
the aliens settled among you who have fath-
ered children among you, since you must
treat them as citizens of Israel. They must
draw lots for their heritage with you, among
the tribes of Israel. 23You will give the alien
his heritage in the tribe where he has settled—
declares the Lord Yahweh." '

Distribution of the Holy Land

48 1' "This is the list of the tribes. One
portion in the far north by way of
Hethlon to the Pass of Hamath, to Hazer-
Enon, with the territory of Damascus to the
north, and marching with Hamath, from the
eastern limit to the western limit: Dan. 2One
portion bordering Dan, from the eastern
limit to the western limit: Asher. 3One
portion bordering Asher, from the eastern
limit to the western limit: Naphtali. 4One
portion bordering Naphtali, from the eastern
limit to the western limit: Manasseh. 5One
portion bordering Manasseh, from the
eastern limit to the western limit: Ephraim.
6One portion bordering Ephraim, from the
eastern limit to the western limit: Reuben.
7One portion bordering Reuben, from the
eastern limit to the western limit: Judah.
8One portion bordering Judah, from the
eastern limit to the western limit, is the
portion which you must set aside, twenty-
five thousand cubits wide, and as long as each
of the other portions from the eastern limit
to the western limit. The sanctuary will be in
the centre of it.

9"The portion which you must set aside for Yahweh must be twenty-five thousand cubits long and ten thousand cubits wide.
10This sacred portion must belong to the priests, being, on the north side, twenty-five thousand cubits; on the west side ten thousand cubits wide, on the east side ten thousand cubits wide and on the south side twenty-five thousand cubits long; the sanctuary of Yahweh will be in the centre of it.
11This will be for the consecrated priests, those of the sons of Zadok who maintained my liturgy and did not go astray with the straying Israelites, as the Levites went astray.
12And so their portion must be taken out of the especially holy portion of the land, near the territory of the Levites. 13The territory of the Levites, like the territory of the priests, must be twenty-five thousand cubits long and ten thousand wide—the whole length being twenty-five thousand and the width ten thousand. 14It will be illegal for them to sell or exchange any part of it, and the domain can never be alienated, since it is consecrated to Yahweh. 15As regards the remainder, an area of five thousand cubits by twenty-five thousand, this must be for the common use of the city, for houses and pastures. In the middle will be the city. 16These will be its dimensions: on the north side, four thousand five hundred cubits; on the south side, four thousand five hundred cubits; on the east side, four thousand five hundred cubits; on the west side, four thousand five hundred cubits.
17The pasture land of the city must extend two hundred and fifty cubits to the north, two hundred and fifty to the south, two hundred and fifty to the east, two hundred and fifty to the west. 18One strip, contiguous to the sacred portion, must be left over, consisting of ten thousand cubits to eastward and ten thousand to westward, marching with the sacred portion; this will bring in a revenue for feeding the municipal workmen.
19And the municipal workmen, drawn from all the tribes of Israel, will farm it. 20The portion must have a total area of twenty-five thousand cubits by twenty-five thousand. You must allocate a square area from the sacred portion to constitute the city. 21What is left over will be for the prince, on either side of the sacred portion and of the property of the city, marching with the twenty-five thousand cubits to eastward to the eastern frontier, and marching with the twenty-five thousand cubits to westward to the western frontier—running parallel with the other portions and belonging to the prince. In the centre will be the sacred portion and the sanctuary of the Temple. 22Thus, apart from the property of the Levites and the property of the city which lie in the middle of the prince's portion, everything between the borders of Judah and the borders of Benjamin must belong to the prince.

23"As regards the rest of the tribes: One portion from the eastern limit to the western limit: Benjamin. 24One portion bordering Benjamin, from the eastern limit to the western limit: Simeon. 25One portion bordering Simeon, from the eastern limit to the western limit: Issachar. 26One portion bordering Issachar, from the eastern limit to the western limit: Zebulun. 27One portion bordering Zebulun, from the eastern limit to the western limit: Gad. 28On the southern border of Gad, on the south side, the border will run from Tamar to the Waters of Meribah in Kadesh, to the Wadi and the Great Sea.
29This is how you must distribute the country to the tribes of Israel as their heritage, and these must be their portions—declares the Lord Yahweh.

The gates of Jerusalem

30"Here are the exits from the city. On the north side, four thousand five hundred cubits are to be measured off. 31The gates of the city are to be named after the tribes of Israel. Three gates to the north: one the gate of Reuben; one the gate of Judah; one the gate of Levi. 32On the east side, there will be four thousand five hundred cubits and three gates: one the gate of Joseph; one the gate of Benjamin; one the gate of Dan. 33On the south side, four thousand five hundred cubits are to be measured off, and there are to be three gates: one the gate of Simeon; one the gate of Issachar; one the gate of Zebulun.
34On the west side, there will be four thousand five hundred cubits and three gates: one the gate of Gad; one the gate of Asher; one the gate of Naphtali. 35Total perimeter: eighteen thousand cubits.

"The name of the city in future must be: Yahweh-is-there." '[a]

48a Hebr. *yahweh-sham* suggests 'Jerusalem'.

THE BOOK OF DANIEL

The book was written during the persecution of the Jews by the Syrian king Antiochus Epiphanes (167–164 BC); his attempts to seduce the Jews from the observance of the Law (*see* 1—2 M) form the background of its message. The first six chapters describe the life of Daniel, a Jewish sage, at the brilliant court of Babylon under Nebuchadnezzar (605–562 BC) and his successors; they stress the reward for fidelity to the Law and God's unfailing protection against impious persecution. The next six chapters contain allegorical visions given to Daniel which guarantee the collapse of the persecution and a glorious future for the people of God. The vivid imagery of these chapters uses coded symbolic terms to convey a secret, the message of comfort for the future. The message of a future kingdom, founded by God and ruled by the son of man, stretches far beyond its immediate purpose of strengthening the Jews under persecution.

The inaccuracy and vagueness of historical detail in the stories about Daniel, as well as the date of writing, some 400 years later, confirm that they are edifying fiction of the type known from Tb, Est and Jdt. Daniel is otherwise unknown to history, though a sage 'Danel' was revered in the ancient Near East. Similarly, the predictions of the future in the second part of the book contain remarkable detail for the period between the supposed and the actual date of writing, but after that they become more general and allusive.

Chh. 13 and 14 are later additions, extant only in the Gk version. The book was mostly written in Hebr., though 2:4—7:28 existed only in Aramaic. Additions to chapter 3 which exist only in the Gk text are printed in italics.

DANIEL

INTRODUCTION: THE YOUNG HEBREWS AT THE COURT OF NEBUCHADNEZZAR

1 In the third year of the reign of Jehoiakim
king of Judah, Nebuchadnezzar king of
Babylon marched on Jerusalem and besieged
it. 2 The Lord let Jehoiakim king of Judah
fall into his power, as well as some of the
vessels belonging to the Temple of God.
These he took away to Shinar, putting the
vessels into the treasury of his own gods.
3 From the Israelites, the king ordered
Ashpenaz, his chief eunuch, to bring a certain
number of boys of royal or noble descent;
4 they had to be without any physical defect,
of good appearance, versed in every branch of
wisdom, well-informed, discerning, suitable
for service at the royal court. Ashpenaz was
to teach them to speak and write the language
of the Chaldaeans. 5 The king assigned them
a daily allowance of food and wine from the
royal table. They were to receive an education
lasting for three years, after which they would

enter the royal service. 6Among them were
the Judaeans Daniel, Hananiah, Mishael and
Azariah. 7The chief eunuch gave them other
names, calling Daniel Belteshazzar,
Hananiah Shadrach, Mishael Meshach, and
Azariah Abed-Nego.
8Daniel, who was determined not to incur
pollution by food and wine from the royal
table, begged the chief eunuch to spare him
this defilement. 9God allowed Daniel to
receive faithful love and sympathy from the
chief eunuch. 10But the eunuch warned
Daniel, 'I am afraid of my lord the king: he
has assigned you food and drink, and if he
sees you looking thinner in the face than the
other boys of your age, my head will be in
danger with the king because of you.' 11To
the guard assigned to Daniel, Hananiah,
Mishael and Azariah by the chief eunuch,
Daniel then said, 12'Please allow your
servants a ten days' trial, during which we
are given only vegetables to eat and water to
drink. 13You can then compare our looks
with those of the boys who eat the king's
food; go by what you see, and treat your
servants accordingly.' 14The man agreed to
do what they asked and put them on ten days'
trial. 15When the ten days were over, they
looked better and fatter than any of the boys
who had eaten their allowance from the royal
table; 16so the guard withdrew their allow-
ance of food and the wine they were to drink,
and gave them vegetables. 17To these four
boys God gave knowledge and skill in every
aspect of literature and learning; Daniel also
had the gift of interpreting every kind of
vision and dream.
18When the time stipulated by the king for
the boys to be presented to him came round,
the chief eunuch presented them to Nebuch-
adnezzar. 19The king conversed with them,
and among all the boys found none to equal
Daniel, Hananiah, Mishael and Azariah. So
they became members of the king's court,
20and on whatever point of wisdom or under-
standing he might question them, he found
them ten times better than all the magicians
and soothsayers in his entire kingdom.
21Daniel remained there until the first year of
King Cyrus.

NEBUCHADNEZZAR'S DREAM: THE COMPOSITE STATUE

The king questions his soothsayers

2 In the second year of his reign, Nebuchad-
nezzar had a series of dreams; he was
perturbed by this and sleep deserted him.
2The king then had magicians and sooth-
sayers, sorcerers and Chaldaeans summoned
to tell him what his dreams meant. They
arrived and stood in the king's presence.
3The king said to them, 'I have had a dream,
and my mind is troubled by a wish to under-
stand it.' 4The Chaldaeans answered the
king:
'May your majesty live for ever! Tell your
servants the dream, and we shall reveal its
meaning for you.' 5The king answered the
Chaldaeans, 'This is my firm resolve: if you
cannot tell me what I dreamt and what it
means, I shall have you torn limb from limb
and your houses turned into dunghills. 6If,
on the other hand, you can tell me what I
dreamt and what it means, I shall give you
presents, rewards and high honour. So tell
me what I dreamt and what it means.' 7A
second time they said, 'Let the king tell his
dream to his servants, and we shall reveal its
meaning.' 8But the king retorted, 'It is plain
to me that you are trying to gain time,
knowing my proclaimed resolve. 9If you do
not interpret my dream for me, there will be
but one sentence passed on you all; you
have agreed among yourselves to make me
misleading and tortuous speeches while the
time goes by. So tell me what my dream
was, and then I shall know whether you can
interpret it.' 10The Chaldaeans answered the
king, 'Nobody in the world could explain the
king's problem; what is more, no other king,
governor or chief would think of putting such
a question to any magician, soothsayer or
Chaldaean. 11The question the king asks is
difficult, and no one can find the king an
answer to it, except the gods, whose dwelling
is not with mortals.' 12At this the king flew
into a rage and ordered all the Babylonian
sages to be put to death. 13On publication of
the decree to have the sages killed, search
was made for Daniel and his companions to
have them put to death.

Daniel intervenes

14 Then, with shrewd and cautious words,
Daniel approached Arioch, the king's chief
executioner, when he was on his way to kill
the Babylonian sages. 15 To this royal official
Arioch he said, 'Why has the king issued such
a harsh decree?' Arioch explained matters to
Daniel, 16 and Daniel went off to ask the
king for a stay of execution to give him the
opportunity of revealing his interpretation to
the king. 17 Daniel then went home and told
his friends Hananiah, Mishael and Azariah
what had happened, 18 urging them to beg the
God of heaven to show his mercy and explain
the mysterious secret, so that Daniel and his
friends might be spared the fate of the other
Babylonian sages. 19 The mystery was then
revealed to Daniel in a night-vision, and
Daniel blessed the God of heaven. 20 This is
what Daniel said:

May the name of God
be blessed for ever and ever,
since wisdom and power are his alone.
21 It is he who controls
the procession of times and seasons,
who makes and unmakes kings,
who confers wisdom on the wise,
and knowledge
on those with discernment,
22 who uncovers depths and mysteries,
who knows what lies in darkness;
and light dwells with him.
23 To you, God of my fathers,
I give thanks and praise
for having given me wisdom and strength:
to me you have explained
what we asked you,
to us you have explained
the king's problem.

24 So Daniel went to see Arioch, whom the
king had made responsible for putting the
Babylonian sages to death. Going in, he said,
'Do not put the Babylonian sages to death.
Take me into the king's presence and I will
reveal the meaning to the king.' 25 Arioch lost
no time in bringing Daniel to the king.
'Among the exiles from Judah,' he said, 'I
have discovered a man who can reveal the
meaning to the king.' 26 The king said to
Daniel (who had been given the name
Belteshazzar), 'Can you tell me what I dreamt
and what it means?' 27 Facing the king, Daniel
replied, 'None of the sages, soothsayers,
magicians or exorcists has been able to tell
the king the truth of the mystery which the
king has propounded; 28 but there is a God in
heaven who reveals mysteries and who has
shown King Nebuchadnezzar what is to take
place in the final days. These, then, are the
dream and the visions that passed through
your head as you lay in bed:[a]

29 'Your Majesty, on your bed your
thoughts turned to what would happen in
the future, and the Revealer of Mysteries
disclosed to you what is to take place. 30 This
mystery has been revealed to me, not that I
am wiser than anyone else, but for this sole
purpose: that the king should learn what it
means, and that you should understand your
inmost thoughts.

31 'You have had a vision, Your Majesty;
this is what you saw: a statue, a great statue
of extreme brightness, stood before you,
terrible to see. 32 The head of this statue was
of fine gold, its chest and arms were of silver,
its belly and thighs of bronze, 33 its legs of
iron, its feet part iron, part clay. 34 While you
were gazing, a stone broke away, untouched
by any hand, and struck the statue, struck
its feet of iron and clay and shattered them.
35 Then, iron and clay, bronze, silver and
gold, all broke into pieces as fine as chaff on
the threshing-floor in summer. The wind
blew them away, leaving not a trace behind.
And the stone that had struck the statue grew
into a great mountain, filling the whole world.
36 This was the dream; we shall now explain
to the king what it means.

37 'You, Your Majesty, king of kings, to
whom the God of heaven has given sov-
ereignty, power, strength and honour—
38 human beings, wild animals, birds of the
air, wherever they live, he has entrusted to
your rule, making you king of them all—you
are the golden head. 39 And, after you, another
kingdom will rise, not as great as yours, and
then a third, of bronze, which will rule
the whole world. 40 There will be a fourth
kingdom, hard as iron, as iron that pulverises
and crushes all. Like iron that breaks every-
thing to pieces, it will crush and break all the
earlier kingdoms. 41 The feet you saw, part
earthenware, part iron, are a kingdom which
will be split in two, but which will retain
something of the strength of iron, just as you
saw the iron and the clay of the earthenware
mixed together. 42 The feet were part iron,

2a Under the image of metals these allegories describe successive empires, Babylonian, Median, Persian, Greek, which finally give way to the messianic kingdom.

part potter's clay: the kingdom will be partly
strong and partly brittle. 43 And just as you
saw the iron and the clay of the earthenware
mixed together, so the two will be mixed
together in human seed;[b] but they will not
hold together any more than iron will blend
with clay. 44 In the days of those kings, the
God of heaven will set up a kingdom which
will never be destroyed, and this kingdom
will not pass into the hands of another race:
it will shatter and absorb all the previous
kingdoms and itself last for ever— 45 just as
you saw a stone, untouched by hand, break
away from the mountain and reduce iron,
bronze, earthenware, silver and gold to
powder. The Great God has shown the king
what is to take place. The dream is true, the
interpretation exact.'

The king's profession of faith

46 At this, King Nebuchadnezzar fell pros-
trate before Daniel; he gave orders for Daniel
to be offered an oblation and a fragrant
sacrifice. 47 The king said to Daniel, 'Your
god is indeed the God of gods, the Master of
kings, and the Revealer of Mysteries, since
you have been able to reveal this mystery.'
48 The king then conferred high rank on
Daniel and gave him many handsome
presents. He also made him governor of the
whole province of Babylon and head of all
the sages of Babylon. 49 At Daniel's request,
the king entrusted the affairs of the province
of Babylon to Shadrach, Meshach and
Abed-Nego; Daniel himself remained in
attendance on the king.

THE ADORATION OF THE GOLDEN STATUE

Nebuchadnezzar sets up a golden statue

3 King Nebuchadnezzar had a golden statue
made, sixty cubits high and six cubits
wide, which he set up on the plain of Dura,
in the province of Babylon. 2 King Nebuchad-
nezzar then summoned the satraps, magis-
trates, governors, counsellors, treasurers,
judges, lawyers, and all the provincial auth-
orities to assemble and attend the dedication
of the statue set up by King Nebuchadnezzar.
3 Satraps, magistrates, governors, counsel-
lors, treasurers, judges, lawyers and all the
provincial authorities then assembled for the
dedication of the statue set up by King Nebu-
chadnezzar and stood in front of the statue
which King Nebuchadnezzar had set up.
4 A herald then loudly proclaimed: 'Peoples,
nations, languages! Thus are you com-
manded: 5 the moment you hear the sound of
horn, pipe, lyre, zither, harp, bagpipe and
every other kind of instrument, you will
prostrate yourselves and worship the golden
statue set up by King Nebuchadnezzar.
6 Anyone who does not prostrate himself and
worship will immediately be thrown into the
burning fiery furnace.' 7 And so, the instant
all the peoples heard the sound of horn,
pipe, lyre, zither, harp, bagpipe and all the
other instruments, all the peoples, nations
and languages prostrated themselves and
worshipped the statue set up by King
Nebuchadnezzar.

The denunciation and condemnation of the Jews

8 Some Chaldaeans then came forward and
maliciously accused the Jews. 9 They said to
King Nebuchadnezzar, 'May Your Majesty
live for ever! 10 You have issued a decree,
Your Majesty, to the effect that everyone on
hearing the sound of horn, pipe, lyre, zither,
harp, bagpipe and every other kind of instru-
ment is to prostrate himself and worship the
golden statue; 11 and that anyone who does
not prostrate himself and worship is to be
thrown into the burning fiery furnace.
12 Now, there are certain Jews to whom you
have entrusted the affairs of the province
of Babylon: Shadrach, Meshach and Abed-
Nego; these men have ignored your
command, Your Majesty; they do not serve
your gods, and refuse to worship the golden
statue you have set up.' 13 Shaking with fury,
Nebuchadnezzar sent for Shadrach, Mesh-
ach and Abed-Nego. The men were immedi-
ately brought before the king.
14 Nebuchadnezzar addressed them, 'Shad-
rach, Meshach and Abed-Nego, is it true that
you do not serve my gods, and that you refuse
to worship the golden statue I have set up?

2b The short-lived marriage alliance between the Seleucids of Syria and the Ptolemies of Egypt.

15 When you hear the sound of horn, pipe,
lyre, zither, harp, bagpipe and every other
kind of instrument, are you prepared to
prostrate yourselves and worship the statue
I have made? If you refuse to worship it, you
will be thrown forthwith into the burning
fiery furnace; then which of the gods could
save you from my power?' 16 Shadrach,
Meshach and Abed-Nego replied to King
Nebuchadnezzar, 'Your question needs no
answer from us: 17 if our God, the one we
serve, is able to save us from the burning
fiery furnace and from your power, Your
Majesty, he will save us; 18 and even if he does
not, then you must know, Your Majesty,
that we will not serve your god or worship
the statue you have set up.' 19 This infuriated
King Nebuchadnezzar; his expression was
changed now as he looked at Shadrach,
Meshach and Abed-Nego. He gave orders
for the furnace to be made seven times hotter
than usual 20 and commanded certain stal-
warts from his army to bind Shadrach,
Meshach and Abed-Nego and throw them
into the burning fiery furnace. 21 They were
then bound in their cloaks, trousers, head-
gear and other garments, and thrown into the
burning fiery furnace. 22 The king's command
was so urgent and the heat of the furnace was
so fierce, that the men carrying Shadrach,
Meshach and Abed-Nego were burnt to death
by the flames from the fire; 23 the three men,
Shadrach, Meshach and Abed-Nego fell,
bound, into the burning fiery furnace.

The song of Azariah in the furnace[a]

24 *And they walked in the heart of the flames,*
praising God and blessing the Lord. 25 *Azariah*
stood in the heart of the fire, praying aloud thus:

26 *May you be blessed and revered,*
Lord, God of our ancestors,
may your name be held glorious for ever.
27 *For you are upright*
in all that you have done for us,
all your deeds are true,
all your ways right,
all your judgements true.
28 *True is the sentence you have given*
in all that you have brought down on us
and on Jerusalem,
the holy city of our ancestors,
for you have treated us rightly and truly,
as our sins deserve.
29 *Yes, we have sinned*
and committed a crime by deserting you,
yes, we have greatly sinned;
we have not listened to your commandments,
30 *we have not observed them,*
we have not done
what you commanded us to do
for our own good.
31 *Yes, all that you have brought down on us,*
all that you have done to us,
you have been fully justified in doing.
32 *You have handed us over to our enemies,*
to a lawless people, the worst of the godless,
to an unjust king,
the worst in the whole world;
33 *today we have no right to open our mouths,*
shame and dishonour are the lot
of those who serve and worship you.

34 *Do not abandon us for ever,*
for the sake of your name;
do not repudiate your covenant,
35 *do not withdraw your favour from us,*
for the sake of Abraham, your friend,
of Isaac, your servant,
and of Israel, your holy one,
36 *to whom you promised*
to make their descendants
as many as the stars of heaven
and as the grains of sand on the seashore.
37 *Lord, we have become the least of all nations,*
we are put to shame today
throughout the world,
because of our sins.

38 *We now have no leader, no prophet, no prince,*
no burnt offering, no sacrifice, no oblation,
no incense,
no place where we can make offerings to you
39 *and win your favour.*
But may the contrite soul, the humbled spirit,
be as acceptable to you
40 *as burnt offerings of rams and bullocks,*
as thousands of fat lambs:
such let our sacrifice be to you today,
and may it please you
that we follow you whole-heartedly,
since those who trust in you will not be shamed.
41 *And now we put our whole heart*
into following you,
into fearing you
and seeking your face once more.
42 *Do not abandon us to shame*
but treat us in accordance with your gentleness,
in accordance with the greatness of your mercy.

3a The italicised passages are preserved only in Gk.

[43]*Rescue us in accordance*
with your wonderful deeds
and win fresh glory for your name, O Lord.
[44]*Confusion seize all who ill-treat your servants:*
may they be covered with shame,
deprived of all their power,
and may their strength be broken.
[45]*Let them learn that you alone are God*
and Lord,
glorious over the whole world.

[46]*All this time, the king's servants, who had*
thrown them into the furnace, had been stoking
it with crude oil, pitch, tow and brushwood
[47]*until the flames rose forty-nine cubits above the*
furnace [48]*and, leaping out, burnt those Chal-*
daeans to death who were standing round it.
[49]*But the angel of the Lord came down into the*
furnace beside Azariah and his companions; he
drove the flames of the fire outwards from the
furnace [50]*and, in the heart of the furnace, wafted*
a coolness to them as of the breeze and dew, so
that the fire did not touch them at all and caused
them no pain or distress.

The song of the three young men

[51]*Then all three in unison began to sing, glori-*
fying and blessing God in the furnace, with the
words:

[52]*May you be blessed,*
Lord, God of our ancestors,
be praised and extolled for ever.
Blessed be your glorious and holy name,
praised and extolled for ever.
[53]*May you be blessed in the Temple*
of your sacred glory,
exalted and glorified above all for ever:
[54]*blessed on the throne of your kingdom,*
exalted above all, glorified for ever:
[55]*blessed are you who fathom the abyss,*
enthroned on the winged creatures,
praised and exalted above all for ever:
[56]*blessed in the expanse of the heavens,*
exalted and glorified for ever.

[57]*Bless the Lord, all the Lord's creation:*
praise and glorify him for ever!
[58]*Bless the Lord, angels of the Lord,*
praise and glorify him for ever!
[59]*Bless the Lord, heavens,*
praise and glorify him for ever!
[60]*Bless the Lord, all the waters*
above the heavens,
praise and glorify him for ever!
[61]*Bless the Lord, powers of the Lord,*
praise and glorify him for ever!
[62]*Bless the Lord, sun and moon,*
praise and glorify him for ever!
[63]*Bless the Lord, stars of heaven,*
praise and glorify him for ever!

[64]*Bless the Lord, all rain and dew,*
praise and glorify him for ever!
[65]*Bless the Lord, every wind,*
praise and glorify him for ever!
[66]*Bless the Lord, fire and heat,*
praise and glorify him for ever!
[67]*Bless the Lord, cold and warmth,*
praise and glorify him for ever!
[68]*Bless the Lord, dew and snow-storm,*
praise and glorify him for ever!
[69]*Bless the Lord, frost and cold,*
praise and glorify him for ever!
[70]*Bless the Lord, ice and snow,*
praise and glorify him for ever!
[71]*Bless the Lord, nights and days,*
praise and glorify him for ever!
[72]*Bless the Lord, light and darkness,*
praise and glorify him for ever!
[73]*Bless the Lord, lightning and cloud,*
praise and glorify him for ever!

[74]*Let the earth bless the Lord:*
praise and glorify him for ever!
[75]*Bless the Lord, mountains and hills,*
praise and glorify him for ever!
[76]*Bless the Lord, every plant that grows,*
praise and glorify him for ever!
[77]*Bless the Lord, springs of water,*
praise and glorify him for ever!
[78]*Bless the Lord, seas and rivers,*
praise and glorify him for ever!
[79]*Bless the Lord, whales,*
and everything that moves in the waters,
praise and glorify him for ever!
[80]*Bless the Lord, every kind of bird,*
praise and glorify him for ever!
[81]*Bless the Lord, all animals wild and tame,*
praise and glorify him for ever!

[82]*Bless the Lord, all the human race:*
praise and glorify him for ever!
[83]*Bless the Lord, O Israel,*
praise and glorify him for ever!
[84]*Bless the Lord, priests,*
praise and glorify him for ever!
[85]*Bless the Lord, his servants,*
praise and glorify him for ever!
[86]*Bless the Lord, spirits and souls*
of the upright,
praise and glorify him for ever!

87 *Bless the Lord, faithful,*
humble-hearted people,
praise and glorify him for ever!

88 *Hananiah, Azariah and Mishael,*
bless the Lord,
praise and glorify him for ever! —
For he has rescued us from the Underworld,
he has saved us from the hand of Death,
he has snatched us
from the burning fiery furnace,
he has drawn us from the heart of the flame!
89 *Give thanks to the Lord, for he is good,*
for his love is everlasting.
90 *Bless the Lord, the God of gods,*
all who fear him,
give praise and thanks to him,
for his love is everlasting!

The king acknowledges the miracle[b]

24/91 King Nebuchadnezzar sprang to his feet
in amazement. He said to his advisers, 'Did
we not have these three men thrown bound
into the fire?' They answered the king,
'Certainly, Your Majesty'. 25/92 'But', he went
on, 'I can see four men walking free in the
heart of the fire and quite unharmed! And
the fourth looks like a child of the gods!'
26/93 Nebuchadnezzar approached the mouth
of the burning fiery furnace and said, 'Shad-
rach, Meshach and Abed-Nego, servants of
God Most High, come out, come here!' And
from the heart of the fire out came Shadrach,
Meshach and Abed-Nego. 27/94 The satraps,
magistrates, governors, and advisers of the
king crowded round the three men to
examine them: the fire had had no effect on
their bodies: not a hair of their heads had
been singed, their cloaks were not scorched,
no smell of burning hung about them. Nebu-
chadnezzar said, 28/95 'Blessed be the God of
Shadrach, Meshach and Abed-Nego: he has
sent his angel to rescue his servants who,
putting their trust in him, defied the order of
the king, and preferred to forfeit their bodies
rather than serve or worship any god but
their God. 29/96 I therefore decree as follows,
"Peoples, nations, and languages! Let any
of you speak disrespectfully of the God of
Shadrach, Meshach and Abed-Nego, and I
shall have him torn limb from limb and his
house turned into a dunghill; for there is no
other god who can save like this." '

30/97 The king then showered favours on
Shadrach, Meshach and Abed-Nego in the
province of Babylon.

THE WARNING DREAM AND THE MADNESS OF NEBUCHADNEZZAR

Nebuchadnezzar's proclamation

31/98 'King Nebuchadnezzar, to all peoples,
nations and languages dwelling throughout
the world: may you prosper more and more!
32/99 'It is my pleasure to make known the
signs and wonders with which the Most High
God has favoured me.

33/100 How great his signs,
how mighty his wonders!
His kingdom is an everlasting kingdom,
his empire endures age after age!'

Nebuchadnezzar describes his dream

4 'I, Nebuchadnezzar, was living comfort-
ably in my house, prosperously in my
palace. 2 I had a dream; it appalled me. Dread
assailed me as I lay in bed; the visions that
passed through my head tormented me. 3 So
I decreed that all the sages of Babylon be
summoned to explain to me what the dream
meant. 4 Magicians, soothsayers, Chaldaeans
and exorcists came, and I told them what I
had dreamt, but they could not interpret it
for me. 5 Daniel, renamed Belteshazzar after
my own god, and in whom the spirit of
the holy gods resides, then came into my
presence. I told him my dream:

6 ' "Belteshazzar, chief of magicians," I
said, "I know that the spirit of the holy gods
resides in you and that no mystery puts you
at a loss. This is the dream I have had; tell
me what it means.

7 ' "The visions that passed through my
head as I lay in bed were these:

3b At this point the Hebr. resumes. The verse numbering is therefore given according to both Hebr. and Gk.

I saw a tree
in the middle of the world;
it was very tall.
8 The tree grew taller and stronger,
until its top reached the sky
and it could be seen
from the very ends of the earth.
9 Its foliage was beautiful,
its fruit abundant,
in it was food for all.
For the wild animals it provided shade,
the birds of heaven nested in its branches,
all living creatures found their food on it.

10 ' "I watched the visions passing through my head as I lay in bed:

Next, a Watchful One,[a] a holy one,
came down from heaven.
11 At the top of his voice he shouted:
Cut the tree down, lop off its branches,
strip off its leaves, throw away its fruit;
let the animals flee from its shelter
and the birds from its branches.
12 But leave the stump with its roots
in the ground,
bound with hoops of iron and bronze,
in the grass of the countryside.
Let it be drenched by the dew of heaven
and have its lot
with the animals, eating grass!
13 Let it cease to have a human heart,
and be given the heart of a beast,
and seven times shall pass over him!

14 Such is the sentence
proclaimed by the Watchers,
the verdict announced by the holy ones—
so that every living thing may learn
that the Most High
rules over human sovereignty;
he confers it on whom he pleases,
and raises the lowest of humankind.

15 ' "This was the dream I had—I, Nebuchadnezzar the king. Now it is for you, Belteshazzar, to pronounce on its meaning, since not one of the sages in my kingdom has been able to interpret it for me; you, however, can do so, since the spirit of the holy gods resides in you." '

Daniel interprets the dream

16 Daniel, known as Belteshazzar, was confused for a time and upset.
The king said, 'Belteshazzar, do not be
upset at the dream and its meaning.' Beltesh-
azzar answered, 'My lord, may the dream
apply to those who hate you, and its meaning
to your foes!
17 The tree you saw, so large and
strong and tall that it reached the sky and
could be seen throughout the world,
18 the
tree with beautiful foliage and abundant
fruit, with food for all in it, providing shade
for the wild animals, with the birds of heaven
nesting in its branches:
19 that tree is yourself,
Your Majesty, for you have grown great and
strong; your stature is now so great that it
reaches the sky, and your empire extends to
the ends of the earth.

20 'And the Watchful One seen by the king,
the holy one coming down from heaven and
saying, "Cut the tree down and destroy it,
but leave stump and roots in the ground,
bound with hoops of iron and bronze in the
grass of the countryside; let it be drenched
by the dew and have its lot with the wild
animals until seven times have passed over
it":
21 the meaning of this, Your Majesty, the
verdict of the Most High passed on my lord
the king, is this:

22 You will be driven from human society
and will make your home
with the wild animals,
you will feed on grass, as oxen do,
you will be drenched
by the dew of heaven;
seven times will pass over you
until you have learnt
that the Most High rules
over human sovereignty
and confers it on whom he pleases.

23 'And the order, "Leave the stump and
roots of the tree", means that your kingdom
will be kept for you until you come to under-
stand that Heaven rules all.
24 May it please
the king to accept my advice: by upright
actions break with your sins, break with your
crimes by showing mercy to the poor, and so
live long and peacefully.'

The dream comes true

25 This all happened to King Nebuchad-
nezzar.
26 At the end of twelve months, while
strolling on the roof of the royal palace in
Babylon,
27 the king was saying, 'Great

4a An angel, one of God's attendants, a term common in extra-biblical contemporary works.

Babylon! Was it not built by me as a royal
residence, by the force of my might and for
the majesty of my glory?' 28 The words were
not out of his mouth when a voice came down
from heaven:

'Of you, King Nebuchadnezzar,
it is decreed:
the empire has been taken from you,
29 you will be driven from human society
and will make your home
with the wild animals;
you will feed on grass, as oxen do,
and seven times will pass over you
until you have learnt
that the Most High
rules over human sovereignty
and gives it to whom he pleases.'

30 The words were immediately fulfilled:
Nebuchadnezzar was driven from human
society and ate grass as oxen do; he was
drenched by the dew of heaven; his hair grew
like an eagle's feathers, and his nails became
like a bird's talons.
31 'When the time was over, I, Nebuchad-
nezzar, raised my eyes to heaven: my reason
returned. And I blessed the Most High,

praising and glorifying him
who lives for ever,
for his empire is an everlasting empire,
his kingship endures, age after age.
32 All who dwell on earth count for nothing;
as he thinks fit,
he disposes the army of heaven
and those who dwell on earth.
No one can arrest his hand
or ask him, "What have you done?"

33 'At that moment my reason returned
and, for the honour of my royal state, my
glory and splendour returned too. My coun-
sellors and noblemen acclaimed me; I was
restored to my throne, and to my past great-
ness even more was added. 34 And now I,
Nebuchadnezzar,

praise, extol and glorify
the King of heaven,
all of whose deeds are true,
all of whose ways are right,
and who can humble those
who walk in pride.'

BELSHAZZAR'S FEAST

5 King Belshazzar gave a great banquet for
his noblemen, a thousand of them, and,
in the presence of this thousand, he drank
his wine. 2 Having tasted the wine, Belshazzar
gave orders for the gold and silver vessels to
be brought which his father Nebuchadnezzar
had taken from the sanctuary in Jerusalem,
so that the king, his noblemen, his wives and
the women who sang for him could drink out
of them. 3 The gold and silver vessels taken
from the sanctuary of the Temple of God in
Jerusalem were brought in, and the king, his
noblemen, his wives and the women who
sang for him drank out of them. 4 They drank
their wine and praised their idols of gold and
silver, of bronze and iron, of wood and stone.
5 Suddenly, the fingers of a human hand
appeared and began to write on the plaster of
the palace wall, directly behind the lamp-
stand; and the king could see the hand as it
wrote. 6 The king turned pale with alarm: his
hip-joints went slack and his knees began
to knock. 7 He shouted for his soothsayers,
Chaldaeans, and exorcists. And the king said
to the Babylonian sages, 'Anyone who can
read this writing and tell me what it means
shall be dressed in purple, and have a chain
of gold put round his neck, and be one of the
three men who govern the kingdom.' 8 The
king's sages all crowded forward, but they
could neither read the writing nor explain to
the king what it meant. 9 Greatly alarmed,
King Belshazzar turned even paler, and his
noblemen were equally disturbed. 10 Then
the queen, attracted by the noise made by
the king and his noblemen, came into the
banqueting hall. 'May Your Majesty live for
ever!' said the queen. 'Do not be alarmed,
do not look so pale. 11 In your kingdom there
is a man in whom lives the spirit of the holy
gods. In your father's days he was known
for a perception, intelligence and wisdom
comparable to that of the gods. King Nebu-
chadnezzar, your father, made him head of
the magicians, soothsayers, Chaldaeans and
exorcists. 12 Since this man Daniel, whom the

king had renamed Belteshazzar, is filled with
such a marvellous spirit and such knowledge
and intelligence in interpreting dreams,
solving enigmas and unravelling difficult
problems, send for him; he will be able to tell
you what this means.'
13 Daniel was brought into the king's pres-
ence; the king said to Daniel, 'Are you the
Daniel who was one of the Judaean exiles
brought by my father the king from Judah?
14 I am told that the spirit of the gods lives
in you, and that you are known for your
perception, intelligence and marvellous
wisdom. 15 The sages and soothsayers have
already been brought to me to read this
writing and tell me what it means, but they
have been unable to reveal its meaning. 16 I
am told that you are able to give interpreta-
tions and to unravel difficult problems, so if
you can read the writing and tell me what it
means, you shall be dressed in purple, and
have a chain of gold put round your neck,
and be one of the three men who govern the
kingdom.'
17 Then Daniel spoke up in the presence of
the king. 'Keep your gifts for yourself,' he
said, 'and give your rewards to others! I can
certainly read the writing to the king and tell
him what it means. 18 Your Majesty, the Most
High God gave Nebuchadnezzar your father
sovereignty, greatness, majesty and glory.
19 He made him so great that all peoples,
nations and languages shook with dread
before him: he killed whom he pleased,
spared whom he pleased, promoted whom
he pleased, degraded whom he pleased. 20 But
because his heart grew swollen with pride,
and his spirit stiff with arrogance, he was
deposed from his sovereign throne and
stripped of his glory. 21 He was driven from
human society, his heart was more like an
animal's than a man's; he lived with the wild
donkeys; he fed on grass like oxen; his body
was drenched by the dew of heaven, until he
had learnt that the Most High rules over
human sovereignty and appoints whom he
pleases to rule it. 22 But you, Belshazzar, who
are his son, you have not humbled your heart,
in spite of knowing all this. 23 You have defied
the Lord of heaven, you have had the vessels
from his Temple brought to you, and you,
your noblemen, your wives and the women
singing for you have drunk your wine out of
them. You have praised gods of gold and
silver, of bronze and iron, of wood and stone,
which can neither see, hear nor understand;
but you have given no glory to the God in
whose hands are your breath itself and all
your fortunes. 24 That is why he has sent the
hand which has written these words. 25 The
writing reads: *mene, mene, teqel* and *parsin*.
26 The meaning of the words is this:[a] *mene*:
God has *measured* your sovereignty and put
an end to it; 27 *teqel*: you have been *weighed* in
the balance and found wanting; 28 *parsin*: your
kingdom has been *divided* and given to the
Medes and the *Persians*.'
29 At Belshazzar's order Daniel was dressed
in purple, a chain of gold was put round his
neck and he was proclaimed as one of the
three men who governed the kingdom.
30 That same night, the Chaldaean king
Belshazzar was murdered,
6 and Darius the Mede received the
kingdom, at the age of sixty-two.

DANIEL IN THE LION PIT

The satraps resent Daniel's promotion

2 It pleased Darius to appoint a hundred and
twenty satraps over his kingdom for the
various parts, 3 and over them three presi-
dents—of whom Daniel was one—to whom
the satraps were to be responsible. This
was to safeguard the king's interests. 4 This
Daniel, by virtue of the marvellous spirit
residing in him, was so evidently superior to
the other presidents and satraps that the king
considered appointing him to rule the whole
kingdom. 5 The presidents and satraps, in
consequence, started hunting for some affair
of state by which they could discredit Daniel;
but they could find nothing to his discredit,
and no case of negligence; he was so punc-
tilious that they could not find a single
instance of maladministration or neglect.
6 These men then thought, 'We shall never
find a way of discrediting Daniel unless we
try something to do with the law of his God.'

5a The untranslatable play on Aramaic words is shown in the text by italics.

7The presidents and satraps then went in a body to the king. 'King Darius,' they said, 'live for ever! 8We are all agreed, presidents of the realm, magistrates, satraps, councillors and governors, that the king should issue an edict enforcing the following regulation: Whoever within the next thirty days prays to anyone, divine or human, other than to yourself, Your Majesty, is to be thrown into the lions' den. 9Your Majesty, ratify the edict at once by signing this document, making it unalterable, as befits the law of the Medes and the Persians, which cannot be revoked.' 10King Darius accordingly signed the document embodying the edict.

Daniel continues to pray

11When Daniel heard that the document had been signed, he retired to his house. The windows of his upstairs room faced towards Jerusalem. Three times each day, he went down on his knees, praying and giving praise to God as he had always done. 12These men came along in a body and found Daniel praying and pleading with God. 13They then went to the king and reminded him of the royal edict, 'Have you not signed an edict forbidding anyone for the next thirty days to pray to anyone, divine or human, other than to yourself, Your Majesty, on pain of being thrown into the lions' den?' 'The decision stands', the king replied, 'as befits the law of the Medes and the Persians, which cannot be revoked.' 14They then said to the king, 'Your Majesty, this man Daniel, one of the exiles from Judah, disregards both you and the edict which you have signed: he is at his prayers three times each day.' 15When the king heard these words he was deeply distressed and determined to save Daniel; he racked his brains until sunset to find some way to save him. 16But the men kept pressing the king, 'Your Majesty, remember that in conformity with the law of the Medes and the Persians, no edict or decree can be altered when once issued by the king.'

Daniel is thrown to the lions

17The king then ordered Daniel to be brought and thrown into the lion pit. The king said to Daniel, 'Your God, whom you have served so faithfully, will have to save you.' 18A stone was then brought and laid over the mouth of the pit; and the king sealed it with his own signet and with that of his noblemen, so that there could be no going back on the original decision about Daniel. 19The king returned to his palace, spent the night in fasting and refused to receive any of his concubines. Sleep eluded him, 20and at the first sign of dawn he got up and hurried to the lion pit. 21As he approached the pit he called in anguished tones to Daniel, 'Daniel, servant of the living God! Has your God, whom you serve so faithfully, been able to save you from the lions?' 22Daniel answered the king, 'May Your Majesty live for ever! 23My God sent his angel who sealed the lions' jaws; they did me no harm, since in his sight I am blameless; neither have I ever done you any wrong, Your Majesty.' 24The king was overjoyed and ordered Daniel to be released from the pit. Daniel was released from the pit and found to be quite unhurt, because he had trusted in his God. 25The king then sent for the men who had accused Daniel and had them thrown into the lion pit, and their wives and children too; and before they reached the floor of the pit the lions had seized them and crushed their bones to pieces.

The king's profession of faith

26King Darius then wrote to all nations, peoples and languages dwelling throughout the world:

'May you prosper more and more! 27This is my decree: Throughout every dominion of my realm, let all tremble with fear before the God of Daniel:

He is the living God, he endures for ever,
his kingdom will never be destroyed
and his empire never come to an end.
28He saves, sets free,
and works signs and wonders
in the heavens and on earth;
he has saved Daniel
from the power of the lions.'

29This Daniel flourished in the reign of Darius and the reign of Cyrus the Persian.

DANIEL'S DREAM: THE FOUR BEASTS

The vision of the beasts, the One most venerable and the son of man

7 In the first year of Belshazzar king of
Babylon, Daniel had a dream and visions
that passed through his head as he lay in bed.
He wrote the dream down, and this is how
the narrative began: 2 Daniel said, 'I have
been seeing visions in the night. I saw that
the four winds of heaven were stirring up the
Great Sea; 3 four great beasts emerged from
the sea, each different from the others. 4 The
first was like a lion with eagle's wings and, as
I looked, its wings were torn off, and it was
lifted off the ground and set standing on its
feet like a human; and it was given a human
heart. 5 And there before me was a second
beast, like a bear, rearing up on one side,
with three ribs in its mouth, between its
teeth. "Up!" came the command. "Eat quan-
tities of flesh!" 6 After this I looked; and there
before me was another beast, like a leopard,
and with four bird's wings on its flanks; it
had four heads and was granted authority.
7 Next, in the visions of the night, I saw
another vision: there before me was a fourth
beast, fearful, terrifying, very strong; it had
great iron teeth, and it ate its victims, crushed
them, and trampled their remains underfoot.
It was different from the previous beasts and
had ten horns.[a]

8 'While I was looking at these horns, I saw
another horn sprouting among them, a little
one; three of the original horns were pulled
out by the roots to make way for it; and in
this horn I saw eyes like human eyes, and a
mouth full of boasting.

9 While I was watching,
thrones were set in place
and one most venerable took his seat.
His robe was white as snow,
the hair of his head as pure as wool.
His throne was a blaze of flames,
its wheels were a burning fire.
10 A stream of fire poured out,
issuing from his presence.
A thousand thousand waited on him,
ten thousand times ten thousand
stood before him.
The court was in session
and the books lay open.

11 'I went on watching: then, because of the
noise made by the boastings of the horn, as I
watched, the beast was put to death, and its
body destroyed and committed to the flames.
12 The other beasts were deprived of their
empire, but received a lease of life for a season
and a time.

13 I was gazing into the visions of the night,
when I saw,
coming on the clouds of heaven,
as it were a son of man.[b]
He came to the One most venerable
and was led into his presence.
14 On him was conferred rule,
honour and kingship,
and all peoples, nations and languages
became his servants.
His rule is an everlasting rule
which will never pass away,
and his kingship will never come to an end.

The interpretation of the vision

15 'I, Daniel, was deeply disturbed and the
visions that passed through my head alarmed
me. 16 So I approached one of those who were
standing by and asked him about all this.
And in reply he revealed to me what these
things meant. 17 "These four great beasts are
four kings who will rise up from the earth.
18 Those who receive royal power are the holy
ones of the Most High, and kingship will be
theirs for ever, for ever and ever." 19 Then I
asked about the fourth beast, different from
all the rest, very terrifying, with iron teeth
and bronze claws; it ate its victims, crushed
them, and trampled their remains underfoot;
20 and about the ten horns on its head—and
why the other horn sprouted and the three
original horns fell, and why this horn had
eyes and a mouth full of boasting, and why
it looked more impressive than its fellows.
21 This was the horn I had watched making
war on the holy ones and proving the
stronger, 22 until the coming of the One most
venerable who gave judgement in favour of

7a The ten Seleucid kings. The little horn (v. 8) will be Antiochus Epiphanes the persecutor.
7b This human figure represents the people of God, but may well bear an individual sense too, as their leader and representative.

the holy ones of the Most High, when the time came for the holy ones to assume kingship.
[23]This is what he said:

"The fourth beast
is to be a fourth kingdom on earth,
different from all other kingdoms.
It will devour the whole world,
trample it underfoot and crush it.
[24]As for the ten horns: from this kingdom
will rise ten kings, and another after them;
this one will be different
from the previous ones
and will bring down three kings;
[25]he will insult the Most High,
and torment
the holy ones of the Most High.
He will plan to alter the seasons
and the Law,
and the Saints will be handed over to him
for a time, two times, and half a time.
[26]But the court will sit,
and he will be stripped
of his royal authority
which will be finally destroyed
and reduced to nothing.
[27]And kingship and rule
and the splendours of all the kingdoms
under heaven
will be given to the people
of the holy ones of the Most High,
whose royal power is an eternal power,
whom every empire will serve and obey."

[28]'Here the narrative ends.
'I, Daniel, was greatly disturbed in mind, and I grew pale; but I kept these things to myself.'

DANIEL'S VISION: THE RAM AND THE HE-GOAT

The vision

8 In the third year of King Belshazzar a
vision appeared to me, Daniel, after the
one that had originally appeared to me. [2]I
gazed at the vision, and as I gazed I found
myself in Susa, the citadel in the province of
Elam; gazing at the vision, I found myself at
the Ulai Gate. [3]I raised my eyes to look, and
I saw a ram standing in front of the gate. It
had two horns; both were tall, but one taller
than the other, and the one that rose the
higher was the second. [4]I saw the ram butting
westwards, northwards and southwards. No
animal could stand up to it, nothing could
escape its power. It did as it pleased and
became strong.
[5]This is what I observed: a he-goat from
the west, encroaching over the entire surface
of the world though never touching the
ground, and between its eyes the goat had
one majestic horn. [6]It advanced on the two-
horned ram, which I had seen standing in
front of the gate, and charged at it in the full
force of its fury. [7]I saw it reach the ram; it
was enraged with the ram and struck it,
breaking both its horns, so that the ram was
not strong enough to hold its ground; it threw
it to the ground and trampled it underfoot;
no one was there to rescue the ram. [8]The he-
goat then grew more powerful than ever; but
at the height of its strength the great horn
snapped, and in its place sprouted four
majestic horns, pointing to the four winds of
heaven.
[9]From one of these, the small one, sprang
a horn which grew to great size towards south
and east and towards the Land of Splendour.
[10]It grew right up to the armies of heaven and
flung armies and stars to the ground, and
trampled them underfoot. [11]It even chal-
lenged the power of the Prince of the army;
it abolished the perpetual sacrifice and over-
threw the foundation of his sanctuary, [12]and
the army too; over the sacrifice it installed
iniquity and flung truth to the ground; the
horn was active and successful.
[13]I heard a holy one speaking, and another
holy one say to the speaker, 'How long is
this vision to be—of perpetual sacrifice, of
horrifying iniquity, of sanctuary and army
trampled underfoot?' [14]The first replied,
'Until two thousand three hundred evenings
and mornings have gone by: then the sanc-
tuary will have its rights restored.'

The angel Gabriel interprets the vision

[15]As I, Daniel, gazed at the vision and tried
to understand it, I saw someone standing in
front of me who looked like a man. [16]I heard
a human voice cry over the Ulai, 'Gabriel,
tell him the meaning of the vision!' [17]He
approached the place where I was standing;

as he approached, I was seized with terror and fell prostrate on the ground. 'Son of man,' he said to me, 'understand this: the vision shows the time of the End.'
18He was still speaking, when I fainted, face downwards on the ground. He touched me, however, and raised me to my feet.
19'Come,' he said, 'I shall tell you what is going to happen when the Retribution is over, about the final times.
20As for the ram which you saw, its two horns are the kings of Media and of Persia.
21The hairy he-goat is the king of Greece, the large horn between its eyes is the first king.
22The horn which snapped and the four horns which sprouted in its place are four kingdoms rising from his nation but not having his strength.

23'And at the end of their reign,
when the measure of their sins is full,
a king will arise, a proud-faced,
ingenious-minded man.
24His power will grow greater and greater,
though not through any power of his own;
he will plot incredible schemes,
he will succeed in whatever he undertakes,
he will destroy powerful men
and the holy ones, God's people.
25Such will be his resourcefulness of mind
that all his treacherous activities
will succeed.
He will grow arrogant of heart
and destroy many people
by taking them unawares.
He will challenge the power
of the Prince of princes
but, without any human intervention,
he will be broken.
26The vision of the evenings
and the mornings
which has been revealed is true,
but you must keep the vision secret,
for there are still many days to go.'

27At this I, Daniel, lost consciousness; I was ill for several days. Then I got up to discharge my duties in the king's service, keeping the vision a secret and still not understanding what it meant.

THE PROPHECY OF THE SEVENTY WEEKS

Daniel's prayer

9 It was the first year of Darius son of Artaxerxes, a Mede by race who assumed the throne of Chaldaea.
2In the first year of his reign I, Daniel, was studying the scriptures, counting over the number of years—as revealed by Yahweh to the prophet Jeremiah—that were to pass before the desolation of Jerusalem would come to an end, namely seventy years.
3I turned my face to the Lord God begging for time to pray and to plead, with fasting, sackcloth and ashes.
4I pleaded with Yahweh my God and made this confession:

'O my Lord, God great and to be feared, you keep the covenant and show faithful love towards those who love you and who observe your commandments:
5we have sinned, we have done wrong, we have acted wickedly, we have betrayed your commandments and rulings and turned away from them.
6We have not listened to your servants the prophets, who spoke in your name to our kings, our chief men, our ancestors and all people of the country.
7Saving justice, Lord, is yours; we have only the look of shame we wear today, we, the people of Judah, the inhabitants of Jerusalem, the whole of Israel, near and far away, in every country to which you have dispersed us because of the treachery we have committed against you.
8To us, our kings, our chief men and our ancestors, belongs the look of shame, O Yahweh, since we have sinned against you.
9And it is for the Lord our God to have mercy and to pardon, since we have betrayed him,
10and have not listened to the voice of Yahweh our God nor followed the laws he has given us through his servants the prophets.
11The whole of Israel has flouted your Law and turned away, unwilling to listen to your voice; and the curse and imprecation written in the Law of Moses, the servant of God, have come pouring down on us, because we have sinned against him.
12He has carried out the threats which he made against us and the chief men who governed us—that he would bring so great a disaster down on us that the fate of Jerusalem would find no parallel under all heaven.
13And now, as written in the Law of Moses, this whole calamity has befallen us;

even so, we have not appeased Yahweh our
God by renouncing our crimes and learning
your truth.
14 Yahweh has watched for the
right moment to bring disaster on us, since
Yahweh our God is just in all his dealings
with us, and we have not listened to his voice.
15 And now, Lord our God, who by your
mighty hand brought us out of Egypt—the
renown you won then endures to this day—
we have sinned, we have done wrong.
16 Lord,
by all your acts of saving justice, turn away
your anger and your fury from Jerusalem,
your city, your holy mountain, for as a result
of our sins and the crimes of our ancestors,
Jerusalem and your people are objects of
scorn to all who surround us.
17 And now, our
God, listen to the prayer and pleading of your
servant. For your own sake, Lord, let your
face smile again on your desolate sanctuary.
18 Listen, my God, listen to us; open your
eyes and look at our plight and at the city that
bears your name. Relying not on our upright
deeds but on your great mercy, we pour out
our plea to you.
19 Listen, Lord! Forgive,
Lord! Hear, Lord, and act! For your own
sake, my God, do not delay—since your city
and your people alike bear your name.'

The angel Gabriel explains the prophecy

20 I was still speaking, still at prayer, con-
fessing my own sins and the sins of my people
Israel, and placing my plea before Yahweh
my God for the holy mountain of my God,
21 still speaking, still at prayer, when Gabriel,
the being I had originally seen in vision,
swooped on me in full flight at the hour of
the evening sacrifice.
22 He came, he spoke,
he said to me, 'Now, Daniel; I have come
down to teach you how to understand.
23 When your pleading began, a word was
uttered, and I have come to tell you. You are
a man specially chosen. Grasp the meaning
of the word, understand the vision:

24 'Seventy weeks are decreed
for your people and your holy city,
for putting an end to transgression,
for placing the seal on sin,
for expiating crime,
for introducing everlasting uprightness
for setting the seal
on vision and on prophecy,
for anointing the holy of holies.
25 Know this, then, and understand:
From the time there went out this message:
"Return and rebuild Jerusalem"
to the coming of an Anointed Prince,
seven weeks and sixty-two weeks,
with squares and ramparts restored
and rebuilt,
but in a time of trouble.
26 And after the sixty-two weeks
an Anointed One
put to death without his . . .
city and sanctuary ruined
by a prince who is to come.
The end of that prince will be catastrophe
and, until the end, there will be war
and all the devastation decreed.
27 He will strike a firm alliance
with many people
for the space of a week;
and for the space of one half-week
he will put a stop to sacrifice and oblation,
and on the wing of the Temple
will be the appalling abomination[a]
until the end, until the doom
assigned to the devastator.'

THE GREAT VISION

THE TIME OF RETRIBUTION

The vision of the man dressed in linen

10 In the third year of Cyrus king of
Persia, a revelation was made to Daniel
known as Belteshazzar, a true revelation of a
great conflict. He grasped the meaning of the
revelation; what it meant was disclosed to
him in a vision.
2 At that time, I, Daniel, was doing a three-
week penance;
3 I ate no agreeable food,
touched no meat or wine, and did not anoint
myself, until these three weeks were over.
4 On the twenty-fourth day of the first month,
as I stood on the bank of that great river, the

9a The Hebr. evokes idols of Baal. Antiochus set up a statue of Zeus in the Temple.

Tigris, [5]I raised my eyes to look about me,
and this is what I saw:

A man dressed in linen,
with a belt of pure gold round his waist:
[6]his body was like beryl,
his face looked like lightning,
his eyes were like fiery torches,
his arms and his face
had the gleam of burnished bronze,
the sound of his voice
was like the roar of a multitude.

[7]I, Daniel, alone saw the apparition; the
men who were with me did not see the vision,
but so great a trembling overtook them that
they fled to hide. [8]I was left alone, gazing
on this great vision; I was powerless, my
appearance was changed and contorted; my
strength deserted me.

The apparition of the angel

[9]I heard a voice speaking, and at the sound
of the voice I fell fainting, face downwards
on the ground. [10]I felt a hand touching me,
setting my knees and my hands trembling.
[11]He said, 'Daniel, you are a man specially
chosen; understand the words that I am about
to say; stand up; I have been sent to you
now.' He said this, and I stood up trembling.
[12]He then said, 'Daniel, do not be afraid: from
that first day when, the better to understand,
you resolved to mortify yourself before God,
your words have been heard; and your words
are the reason why I have come. [13]The Prince
of the kingdom of Persia has been resisting
me for twenty-one days, but Michael, one of
the Chief Princes, came to my assistance. I
have left him confronting the kings of Persia
[14]and have come to tell you what will happen
to your people in the final days. For here is a
new vision about those days.'

[15]When he had said these things to me, I
prostrated myself on the ground, without
saying a word; [16]then someone looking like a
man touched my lips. I opened my mouth to
speak, and I said to the person standing in
front of me, 'My lord, anguish overcomes me
at this vision, and my strength deserts me.
[17]How can your servant speak to my lord now
that I have no strength left and my breath
fails me?' [18]Once again, the person like a man
touched me; he gave me strength. [19]'Do not
be afraid,' he said, 'you are a man specially
chosen; peace be with you; play the man, be
strong!' And as he spoke to me I felt strong
again and said, 'Let my lord speak, you have
given me strength.'

The prelude to the prophecy

[20a]He then said, 'Do you know why I have
come to you? [21a]It is to tell you what is written
in the Book of Truth. [20b]I must go back
to fight the Prince of Persia; when I have
overcome him, the Prince of Javan will come
next. [21b]In all this, there is no one to lend me
support except Michael your Prince,

11 on whom I rely to give me support and
to reinforce me. [2]And now I shall tell
you the truth about these things.

Early struggles between Seleucids and Ptolemies

'Three more kings are going to rise in Persia;
a fourth will come and be richer than all the
others, and when, thanks to his wealth, he
has grown powerful, he will make war on all
the kingdoms of Greece. [3]A mighty king will
rise and govern a vast empire and do whatever
he pleases. [4]But once he has come to power,
his empire will be broken up and parcelled
out to the four winds of heaven, though not
to his descendants: it will not be ruled as he
ruled it, for his sovereignty will be uprooted
and will pass to others than his own
descendants.

[5]'The king of the south will grow powerful,
but one of his princes will grow more
powerful still, with an empire greater than his
own. [6]Some years later, these will conclude
a treaty and, to ratify the agreement, the
daughter of the king of the south will go to
the king of the north. Her arm will not,
however, retain its strength, nor his posterity
endure: she will be handed over, she, her
escorts and her child, and he who has had
authority over her. In due time [7]a sprig from
her roots will rise in his place, will march on
the defences, force the stronghold of the king
of the north, and succeed in overcoming
them. [8]He will even carry off all their gods,
their statues, their precious gold and silver
vessels as booty to Egypt. For some years he
will leave the king of the north in peace, [9]but
the latter will invade the kingdom of the king
of the south, then retire to his own country.
[10]His sons will next be on the march,
mustering a host of powerful forces; and he
will advance, deploy, break through and
march on the southern stronghold once

again. 11 The king of the south will fly into a
rage and set out to give battle to the king of
the north, who will have an immense army
on his side, but this army will be defeated by
him. 12 The army will be annihilated; he will
be triumphant; he will overthrow tens of
thousands; yet he will have no enduring
strength. 13 The king of the north will come
back, having recruited an even larger army
than before, and finally, after some years, he
will advance a second time with a great army
and plentiful supplies. 14 At that time, many
will take up arms against the king of the
south, and the more violent of your own
people will rebel in the hope of realising the
vision; but they will fail. 15 The king of the
north will then come and throw up siege-
works to capture a strongly fortified city.
The forces of the south will not stand their
ground; the pick of the people will not be
strong enough to resist. 16 The invader will
do as he pleases, no one will be able to resist
him: he will take his stand in the Land of
Splendour, destruction in his hands. 17 He
will set about conquering his entire kingdom,
but will then make a treaty with him and, to
overthrow the kingdom, give him a woman's
hand; but this will not last or be to his
advantage. 18 He will next turn to the coasts
and islands and conquer many of them, but
a magistrate will put a stop to his outrages in
such a way that he will be unable to repay
outrage for outrage.

19 'He will then turn on the strongholds of
his own country, but will stumble, fall, and
never be seen again. 20 In his place there will
rise a man who will send an extortioner to
despoil the royal splendour; in a few days he
will be shattered, though neither publicly
nor in battle.

Antiochus Epiphanes

21 'In his place will rise a wretch: royal honours
will not be given to him, but rather he will
insinuate himself into them at his pleasure
and will gain possession of the kingdom by
intrigue. 22 Armies will be utterly routed and
crushed by him, the Prince of the covenant
too. 23 Through his alliances he will act treach-
erously and, despite the smallness of his
following, grow ever stronger. 24 At his
pleasure, he will invade rich provinces, acting
as his fathers or his fathers' fathers never
acted, distributing among them plunder,
spoil and wealth, plotting his stratagems
against the fortresses—for a time.

25 'He will summon up his might and
courage against the king of the south with a
great army. The king of the south will march
to war with a huge and powerful army but
will not succeed, since he will be outwitted
by trickery. 26 Those who shared his food will
ruin him; his army will be swept away, many
will fall in the slaughter.

27 'The two kings, seated at one table, hearts
bent on evil, will tell their lies; but they will
not have their way, for the appointed time is
still to come. 28 Then the wretch will return
greatly enriched to his own country, his heart
set against the holy covenant; he will take
action and then return to his own country.
29 In due time, he will make his way south-
wards again, but this time the outcome will
not be as before. 30 The ships of the
Kittim will oppose him, and he will be
worsted. He will retire and take furious action
against the holy covenant and, as before, will
favour those who forsake that holy covenant.

31 'Forces of his will come and profane
the Citadel-Sanctuary; they will abolish the
perpetual sacrifice and install the appalling
abomination there. 32 Those who break the
covenant he will seduce by his blandish-
ments, but the people who know their God
will stand firm and take action. 33 Those of
the people who are wise leaders will instruct
many; for some days, however, they will
stumble from sword and flame, captivity and
pillage. 34 And thus stumbling, little help will
they receive, though many will be scheming
in their support. 35 Of the wise leaders some
will stumble, and so a number of them will
be purged, purified and made clean—until
the time of the End, for the appointed time
is still to come.

36 'The king will do as he pleases, growing
more and more arrogant, considering himself
greater than all the gods; he will utter incred-
ible blasphemies against the God of gods,
and he will thrive until the wrath reaches
bursting point; for what has been decreed
will certainly be fulfilled. 37 Heedless of his
fathers' gods, heedless of the god whom
women love, heedless of any god whatever,
he will consider himself greatest of all.
38 Instead of them, he will honour the god of
fortresses, will honour a god unknown to
his ancestors with gold and silver, precious
stones and valuable presents. 39 He will use
the people of an alien god to defend the

fortresses; he will confer great honours on
those whom he acknowledges, by giving
them wide authority and by parcelling the
country out for rent.

THE TIME OF THE END

The end of the persecutor

40 'When the time comes for the End, the king
of the south will try conclusions with him;
but the king of the north will come storming
down on him with chariots, cavalry, and a
large fleet. He will invade countries, overrun
them and drive on. 41 He will invade the Land
of Splendour, and many will fall; but Edom,
Moab, and what remains of the sons of
Ammon will escape him.
42 'He will reach out to attack countries:
Egypt will not escape him. 43 The gold and
silver treasures and all the valuables of Egypt
will lie in his power. Libyans and Cushites
will be at his feet: 44 but reports coming from
the East and the north will worry him, and
in great fury he will set out to bring ruin and
complete destruction to many. 45 He will pitch
the tents of his royal headquarters between
the sea and the mountains of the Holy Splen-
dour. Yet he will come to his end—there will
be no help for him.'
12 'At that time Michael will arise—the
great Prince, defender of your people.
That will be a time of great distress, unpar-
alleled since nations first came into existence.
When that time comes, your own people will
be spared—all those whose names are found
written in the Book.

Resurrection and retribution

2 'Of those who are sleeping in the Land of
Dust, many will awaken, some to everlasting
life, some to shame and everlasting disgrace.
3 Those who are wise will shine as brightly as
the expanse of the heavens, and those who
have instructed many in uprightness, as
bright as stars for all eternity.
4 'But you, Daniel, must keep these words
secret and keep the book sealed until the time
of the End. Many will roam about, this way
and that, and wickedness will continue to
increase.'

The sealed prophecy

5 I, Daniel, then looked and saw two other
people standing, one on the near bank of the
river, the other on the far. 6 One of them said
to the man dressed in linen who was standing
further up the stream, 'How long until these
wonders take place?' 7 I heard the man speak
who was dressed in linen, standing further
up the stream: he raised his right hand and
his left to heaven and swore by him who lives
for ever, 'A time and two times, and half a
time; and all these things will come true,
once the crushing of the holy people's power
is over.' 8 I listened but did not understand.
I then said, 'My lord, what is to be the
outcome?' 9 'Go, Daniel,' he said. 'These
words are to remain secret and sealed until
the time of the End. 10 Many will be cleansed,
made white and purged; the wicked will
persist in doing wrong; the wicked will never
understand; those who are wise will under-
stand. 11 From the moment that the perpetual
sacrifice is abolished and the appalling abom-
ination set up: a thousand two hundred and
ninety days. 12 Blessed is he who perseveres
and attains a thousand three hundred and
thirty-five days. 13 But you, go away and rest;
and you will rise for your reward at the end
of time.'

SUSANNA[a] AND THE JUDGEMENT OF DANIEL

13 In Babylon there lived a man named
Joakim. 2 He was married to a woman
called Susanna daughter of Hilkiah, a woman
of great beauty; and she was God-fearing, for
3 her parents were worthy people and had
instructed their daughter in the Law of
Moses. 4 Joakim was a very rich man and had
a garden by his house; he used to be visited
by a considerable number of the Jews, since
he was held in greater respect than any other
man. 5 Two elderly men had been selected
from the people, that year, to act as judges.

13a chh. 13—14 occur in Gk but not in the Hebr. text.

Of such the Lord had said, 'Wickedness has
come to Babylon through the elders and
judges posing as guides to the people.' 6These
men were often at Joakim's house, and all
who were engaged in litigation used to come
to them. 7At midday, when the people had
gone away, Susanna would take a walk in her
husband's garden. 8The two elders, who used
to watch her every day as she came in to take
her walk, gradually began to desire her.
9They threw reason aside, making no effort
to turn their eyes to Heaven, and forgetting
the demands of virtue. 10Both were inflamed
by passion for her, but they hid their desire
from each other, 11for they were ashamed to
admit the longing to sleep with her, 12but
they made sure of watching her every day.
13One day, having parted with the words,
'Let us go home, then, it is time for the
midday meal,' they went off in different
directions, 14only to retrace their steps and
find themselves face to face again. Obliged
then to explain, they admitted their desire
and agreed to look for an opportunity of
surprising her alone. 15So they waited for a
favourable moment; and one day Susanna
came as usual, accompanied only by two
young maidservants. The day was hot and
she wanted to bathe in the garden. 16There
was no one about except the two elders,
spying on her from their hiding place. 17She
said to the servants, 'Bring me some oil and
balsam and shut the garden door while I
bathe.' 18They did as they were told, shutting
the garden door and going back to the house
by a side entrance to fetch what she had asked
for; they knew nothing about the elders, for
they had concealed themselves.

19Hardly were the maids gone than the
two elders sprang up and rushed upon her.
20'Look,' they said, 'the garden door is shut,
no one can see us. We want to have you, so
give in and let us! 21Refuse, and we shall both
give evidence that a young man was with you
and that this was why you sent your maids
away.' 22Susanna sighed. 'I am trapped,' she
said, 'whatever I do. If I agree, it means death
for me; if I resist, I cannot get away from
you. 23But I prefer to fall innocent into your
power than to sin in the eyes of the Lord.'
24She then cried out as loud as she could. The
two elders began shouting too, putting the
blame on her, 25and one of them ran to open
the garden door. 26The household, hearing
the shouting in the garden, rushed out by the
side entrance to see what had happened to
her. 27Once the elders had told their story,
the servants were thoroughly taken aback,
since nothing of this sort had ever been said
of Susanna.

28Next day a meeting was held at the
house of her husband Joakim. The two elders
arrived, full of their wicked plea against
Susanna, to have her put to death. 29They
addressed the company, 'Summon Susanna
daughter of Hilkiah and wife of Joakim.' She
was sent for, 30and came accompanied by her
parents, her children and all her relations.
31Susanna was very graceful and beautiful to
look at; 32she was veiled, so the wretches
made her unveil in order to feast their eyes
on her beauty. 33All her own people were
weeping, and so were all the others who saw
her. 34The two elders stood up, with all the
people round them, and laid their hands on
her head. 35Tearfully she turned her eyes to
Heaven, her heart confident in God. 36The
elders then spoke, 'While we were walking by
ourselves in the garden, this woman arrived
with two maids. She shut the garden door
and then dismissed the servants. 37A young
man, who had been hiding, went over to her
and they lay together. 38From the end of the
garden where we were, we saw this crime
taking place and hurried towards them.
39Though we saw them together, we were
unable to catch the man: he was too strong
for us; he opened the door and took to his
heels. 40We did, however, catch this woman
and ask her who the young man was.
41She refused to tell us. That is our
evidence.'

Since they were elders of the people and
judges, the assembly accepted their word:
Susanna was condemned to death. 42She cried
out as loud as she could, 'Eternal God, you
know all secrets and everything before it
happens; 43you know that they have given
false evidence against me. And now I must
die, innocent as I am of everything their
malice has invented against me!'

44The Lord heard her cry 45and, as she was
being led away to die, he roused the holy
spirit residing in a young boy called Daniel
46who began to shout, 'I am innocent of
this woman's death!' 47At this all the people
turned to him and asked, 'What do you mean
by that?' 48Standing in the middle of the
crowd, he replied, 'Are you so stupid, chil-
dren of Israel, as to condemn a daughter of
Israel unheard, and without troubling to find
out the truth? 49Go back to the scene of the

trial: these men have given false evidence
against her.'
50All the people hurried back, and the
elders said to Daniel, 'Come and sit with us
and tell us what you mean, since God has
given you the gifts that elders have.' 51Daniel
said, 'Keep the men well apart from each
other, for I want to question them.' 52When
the men had been separated, Daniel had one
of them brought to him. 'You have grown
old in wickedness,' he said, 'and now the sins
of your earlier days have overtaken you,
53you with your unjust judgements, your
condemnation of the innocent, your acquittal
of the guilty, although the Lord has said,
"You must not put the innocent and upright
to death." 54Now then, since you saw her so
clearly, tell me what sort of tree you saw them
lying under.' He replied, 'Under an acacia
tree.' 55Daniel said, 'Indeed! Your lie recoils
on your own head:[b] the angel of God has
already received from him your sentence and
will cut you in half.' 56He dismissed the man,
ordered the other to be brought and said to
him, 'Son of Canaan, not of Judah, beauty
has seduced you, lust has led your heart
astray! 57This is how you have been behaving
with the daughters of Israel, and they have
been too frightened to resist; but here is a
daughter of Judah who could not stomach
your wickedness! 58Now then, tell me what
sort of tree you surprised them under.' He
replied, 'Under an aspen tree.' 59Daniel said,
'Indeed! Your lie recoils on your own head:
the angel of God is waiting with a sword to
rend you in half, and destroy the pair of you.'
60Then the whole assembly shouted,
blessing God, the Saviour of those who trust
in him. 61And they turned on the two elders
whom Daniel had convicted of false evidence
out of their own mouths. 62As the Law of
Moses prescribes, they were given the same
punishment as they had schemed to inflict
on their neighbour. They were put to death.
And thus, that day, an innocent life was
saved. 63Hilkiah and his wife gave thanks to
God for their daughter Susanna, and so did
her husband Joakim and all his relations,
because she had been acquitted of anything
dishonourable.
64From that day onwards, Daniel's repu-
tation stood high with the people.

BEL AND THE DRAGON

Daniel and the priests of Bel[a]

14 When King Astyages joined his ances-
tors, Cyrus of Persia succeeded him.
2Daniel was very close to the king, who
respected him more than any of his other
friends. 3Now, in Babylon there was an idol
called Bel, to which twelve bushels of the
finest flour, forty sheep and six measures
of wine were offered every day. 4The king
venerated this idol and used to go and worship
it every day. Daniel, however, worshipped
his own God. 5'Why do you not worship Bel?'
the king asked Daniel. 'I do not worship idols
made by human hand,' Daniel replied, 'I
worship the living God who made heaven and
earth and who is lord over all living creatures.'
6'Do you not believe, then,' said the king,
'that Bel is a living god? Can you not see how
much he eats and drinks each day?' 7Daniel
laughed. 'Your Majesty,' he said, 'do not be
taken in; he is clay inside, and bronze outside,
and has never eaten or drunk anything.'
8This made the king angry; he summoned
his priests, 'Tell me who eats all this food,'
he said, 'or die. Prove to me that Bel really
eats it, and I will have Daniel put to death
for blaspheming him.' 9Daniel said to the
king, 'Let it be as you say.'
10There were seventy of these priests, to
say nothing of their wives and children. The
king went to the temple of Bel, taking Daniel
with him. 11The priests of Bel said to him,
'We shall now go out, and you, Your Majesty,
will lay out the meal and mix the wine and
set it out. Then, lock the door and seal it with
your personal seal. If, when you return in the
morning, you do not find that everything has
been eaten by Bel, let us be put to death;
otherwise let Daniel, that slanderer!' 12They
were thinking—hence their confidence—of
a secret entrance which they had made under
the table, and by which they came in regularly
and took the offerings away. 13When the

13b In Gk, the punishment and the tree in both cases have similar sounds: *shinos/schisei*, *prinos/katapriseí*.
14a Another name for Marduk, chief god of Babylon.

priests had gone and the king had set out the
food for Bel, [14]Daniel made his servants bring
ashes and spread them all over the temple
floor, with no other witness than the king.
They then left the building, shut the door
and, sealing it with the king's seal, went
away. [15]That night, as usual, the priests came
with their wives and children; they ate and
drank everything.

[16]The king was up very early next morning,
and Daniel with him. [17]'Daniel,' said the
king, 'are the seals intact?' 'They are intact,
Your Majesty,' he replied. [18]The king then
opened the door and, taking one look at the
table, exclaimed, 'You are great, O Bel!
There is no deception in you!' [19]But Daniel
laughed; and, restraining the king from going
in any further, he said, 'Look at the floor and
take note whose footmarks these are!' [20]'I can
see the footmarks of men, of women and of
children,' said the king, [21]and angrily ordered
the priests to be arrested, with their wives
and children. They then showed him the
secret door through which they used to come
and take what was on the table. [22]The king
had them put to death and handed Bel over
to Daniel who destroyed both the idol and its
temple.

Daniel kills the dragon

[23]There was a great dragon which the Baby-
lonians worshipped too. [24]The king said to
Daniel, 'Are you going to tell me that this is
made of bronze? Look, it is alive; it eats and
drinks; you cannot deny that this is a living
god; worship it, then.' [25]Daniel replied, 'I
will worship the Lord my God; he is the
living God. With your permission, Your
Majesty, without using either sword or club,
I shall kill this dragon.' [26]'You have my
permission,' said the king. [27]Whereupon,
Daniel took some pitch, some fat and some
hair and boiled them up together, rolled the
mixture into balls and fed them to the dragon;
the dragon swallowed them and burst. Daniel
said, 'Now look at the sort of thing you
worship!' [28]The Babylonians were furious
when they heard about this and rose against
the king. 'The king has turned Jew,' they
said, 'he has allowed Bel to be overthrown,
and the dragon to be killed, and he has put
the priests to death.' [29]So they went to the
king and said, 'Hand Daniel over to us or
else we shall kill you and your family.' [30]They
pressed him so hard that the king found
himself forced to hand Daniel over to them.

Daniel in the lion pit

[31]They threw Daniel into the lion pit, and
there he stayed for six days. [32]In the pit were
seven lions, which were given two human
bodies and two sheep every day; but for this
period they were not given anything, to make
sure they would eat Daniel.

[33]Now, the prophet Habakkuk was in
Judaea: he had been making a stew and
breaking up bread into a basket. He was
on his way to the fields, taking this to the
harvesters, [34]when the angel of the Lord
spoke to him, 'Take the meal you are carrying
to Babylon, and give it to Daniel in the lion
pit.' [35]'Lord,' replied Habakkuk, 'I have not
even seen Babylon and know nothing about
this pit.' [36]The angel of the Lord took hold
of his head and carried him off by the hair to
Babylon where, with a great blast of his
breath, he set Habakkuk down on the edge
of the pit. [37]'Daniel, Daniel,' Habakkuk
shouted, 'take the meal that God has sent
you.' [38]And Daniel said, 'You have kept me
in mind, O God; you have not deserted those
who love you.' [39]Rising to his feet, he ate
the meal, while the angel of God carried
Habakkuk back in a moment to his own
country.

[40]On the seventh day, the king came to
lament over Daniel; on reaching the pit he
looked inside, and there sat Daniel. [41]'You
are great, O Lord, God of Daniel,' he
exclaimed, 'there is no god but you!' [42]He
then had Daniel released from the pit and the
plotters of Daniel's ruin thrown in instead,
where they were instantly eaten before his
eyes.

THE BOOK OF HOSEA

Hosea was preaching during the last years of the northern kingdom of Israel, as it vainly attempted to stave off the advance of Assyria. Denouncing contaminated worship and injustice, he proclaimed that fidelity to Yahweh, not foreign alliance, was the only solution. By contrast to the deep gloom of his contemporary Amos, Hosea's thinking is dominated by his passionate love for his faithless wife, which he saw as an image of Yahweh's unfaltering love for Israel.

PLAN OF THE BOOK

HOSEA

Title

1 The word of Yahweh which came to Hosea
son of Beeri during the reigns of Uzziah,
Jotham, Ahaz and Hezekiah kings of Judah,
and of Jeroboam son of Joash, king of Israel.

I: THE MARRIAGE OF HOSEA AND ITS SYMBOLISM

Hosea's marriage: his three children

2 The beginning of what Yahweh said through
Hosea:
Yahweh said to Hosea, 'Go, marry a whore,
and get children with a whore; for the country
itself has become nothing but a whore by
abandoning Yahweh.'
3 So he went and married Gomer daughter
of Diblaim, who conceived and bore him a
son. 4 Yahweh then said to him, 'Call him
Jezreel, for in a little while I shall punish the
House of Jehu for the bloodshed at Jezreel[a]
and put an end to the sovereignty of the
House of Israel. 5 When that day comes, I
shall break the bow of Israel in the Valley of
Jezreel.'
6 She conceived a second time and gave
birth to a daughter. Yahweh then said to
him, 'Call her Lo-Ruhamah, for I shall show
no more pity for the House of Israel, I shall
never forgive them again. 7 (Instead, I
shall take pity on the House of Judah and
shall save them, not by bow or sword or force
of arms, not by horses or horsemen, but by
Yahweh their God.)'
8 After weaning Lo-Ruhamah, she con-
ceived and gave birth to a son. 9 Yahweh said,
'Call him Lo-Ammi, for you are not my
people and I do not exist for you.'

1a 2 K 9:15—10:14.

Hope for the future

2 But the Israelites will become as numerous
as the sands of the sea, which cannot be
measured or counted. In the very place where
they were told, 'You are not my people,'

they will be told
they are 'Children of the living God'.
2 The Judaeans and Israelites
will be reunited
and will choose themselves a single head,
and will spread far beyond their country,
for great will be the Day of Jezreel!
3 Then call your brothers, 'My people',
and your sisters, 'You have been pitied'.

Yahweh and his unfaithful wife

4 To court, take your mother to court!
For she is no longer my wife
nor am I her husband.
She must either remove her whoring ways
from her face
and her adulteries
from between her breasts,
5 or I shall strip her and expose her
naked as the day she was born;
I shall make her as bare as the desert,
I shall make her as dry as arid country,
and let her die of thirst.
6 And I shall feel no pity for her children
since they are the children of her whorings.
7 Yes, their mother has played the whore,
she who conceived them
has disgraced herself
by saying, 'I shall chase after my lovers;
they will assure me my keep,
my wool, my flax, my oil and my drinks.'

8 This is why I shall block her way
with thorns,
and wall her in to stop her in her tracks;
9 then if she chases her lovers
she will not catch them,
if she looks for them she will not find them,
and then she will say,
'I shall go back to my first husband,
I was better off then than I am now;'
10 she had never realised before
that I was the one who was giving her
the grain, new wine and oil,
giving her more and more silver and gold
which they have spent on Baal!

11 This is why I shall take back my grain
when it is due
and my new wine,
when the season for it comes.
I shall withdraw my wool and my flax
which were to cover her naked body,
12 and then display her infamy
before her lovers' eyes—
no one will take her from me then!
13 I shall put an end to all her merrymaking,
her festivals, her New Moons
and her Sabbaths
and all her solemn feasts.
14 I shall make her vines and fig trees derelict
of which she used to say,
'These are the pay my lovers gave me.'
I shall turn them into a jungle:
wild animals will feed on them.
15 I mean to make her pay for the feast-days
on which she burnt incense to the Baals,
when she tricked herself out
in her earrings and necklaces
to chase after her lovers,
and forget me!
—declares Yahweh.

Reconciliation

16 But look, I am going to seduce her
and lead her into the desert
and speak to her heart.
17 There I shall give her back her vineyards,
and make the Vale of Achor[a]
a gateway of hope.
There she will respond
as when she was young,
as on the day when she came up
from Egypt.

18 When that day comes—
declares Yahweh—
you will call me, 'My husband',
no more will you call me, 'My Baal'.
19 I shall banish the names of the Baals
from her lips
and their name will be mentioned no more.
20 When that day comes
I shall make a treaty for them
with the wild animals,
with the birds of heaven
and the creeping things of the earth;
I shall break the bow and the sword
and warfare, and banish them
from the country,

2a The scene of Achan's sin, Jos 7:24.

and I will let them sleep secure.
[21]I shall betroth you to myself for ever,
I shall betroth you
in uprightness and justice,
and faithful love and tenderness.
[22]Yes, I shall betroth you to myself in loyalty
and in the knowledge of Yahweh.
[23]When that day comes, I shall respond
—declares Yahweh—
I shall respond to the heavens
and they will respond to the earth
[24]and the earth will respond to the grain,
the new wine and oil,
and they will respond to Jezreel.
[25]I shall sow her in the country to be mine,
I shall take pity on Lo-Ruhamah,
I shall tell Lo-Ammi, 'You are my people,'
and he will say, 'You are my God.'

Second account of Hosea's marriage

3 Yahweh said to me, 'Go again, love a
woman who loves another man, an
adulteress, and love her as Yahweh
loves the Israelites although they turn to
other gods and love raisin cakes.' [2]So I
bought her for fifteen shekels of silver, a
homer of barley and a skin of wine, [3]and I
said to her, 'You will have to spend a long
time waiting for me without playing the
whore and without giving yourself to any
man, and I will behave in the same way
towards you.'

The explanation

[4]For the Israelites will have to spend a
long time without king or leader, without
sacrifice or sacred pillar, without *ephod* or
domestic images; [5]but after that, the Israel-
ites will return and again seek Yahweh
their God and David their king, and turn
trembling to Yahweh for his bounty in the
final days.

II: THE CRIMES AND PUNISHMENT OF ISRAEL

General corruption

4 Israelites, hear what Yahweh says,
for Yahweh indicts
the citizens of the country:
there is no loyalty, no faithful love,
no knowledge of God in the country,
[2]only perjury and lying, murder, theft,
adultery and violence,
bloodshed after bloodshed.
[3]This is why the country is in mourning
and all its citizens pining away,
the wild animals also and birds of the sky,
even the fish in the sea will disappear.

Against the priests

[4]But let no one denounce, no one rebuke;
it is you, priest, that I denounce.
[5]Priest, you will stumble in broad daylight,
and the prophet will stumble with you
in the dark,
and I will make your mother perish.
[6]My people perish for want of knowledge.
Since you yourself
have rejected knowledge,
so I shall reject you from my priesthood;
since you have forgotten
the teaching of your God,
I in my turn shall forget your children.

[7]The more of them there have been,
the more they have sinned against me;
they have bartered their Glory for Shame.[a]
[8]They feed on the sin of my people,
they are greedy for their iniquity.
[9]But as with the people, so with the priest,
I shall punish them for their conduct,
I shall pay them back for their deeds.
[10]They will eat but never be satisfied,
they will play the whore
but not grow more prolific,
since they have deserted Yahweh
to give themselves up [11]to whoring.

Worship in Israel is idolatrous and debauched

Old wine and new wine
addle my people's wits,
[12]they consult their block of wood,

4a A contemptuous name for Baal.

and their stick explains
what they should do.
For an urge to go whoring
has led them astray
and whoring they go
and desert their God;
13 they offer sacrifice on the mountain tops,
they burn incense on the hills,
under oak and poplar and terebinth,
for pleasant is their shade.
So, although your daughters
play the whore
and your daughters-in-law
commit adultery,
14 I shall not punish your daughters
for playing the whore
nor your daughters-in-law
for committing adultery,
when the men themselves
are wandering off with whores
and offering sacrifice
with sacred prostitutes,
for a people with no understanding
is doomed.

A warning to Judah and Israel

15 Though you, Israel, play the whore,
there is no need for Judah to sin too.
Do not go to Gilgal,
do not go up to Beth-Aven,[b]
do not swear oaths 'by Yahweh's life',
16 for Israel is as stubborn
as a stubborn heifer;
so is Yahweh likely to pasture him
like a lamb in a broad meadow?
17 Ephraim has made a pact with idols—
let him alone!
18 Their drunken orgy over,
they do nothing but play the whore,
preferring Shame to their Pride;
19 the wind with its wings
will carry them off
and their sacrifices will bring them
nothing but disgrace.

Against the priests and royal family

5 Hear this, you priests,
listen, House of Israel,
pay attention, royal House,
for it is you who have justice in your care,
but you have been a snare at Mizpah
and a net outspread on Tabor.
2 They have dug the ditch deep at Shittim
and so I am going to punish them all.

The effects of obduracy

3 Ephraim have I known,
Israel is not hidden from me;
and yet, Ephraim,
you have played the whore,
Israel is befouled.
4 Their deeds do not allow them
to return to their God,
since an urge to play the whore
possesses them
and they no longer know Yahweh.
5 Israel's arrogance is his accuser,
the guilt of Israel and Ephraim
is their undoing,
Judah too will be undone with them.
6 Though they go in search of Yahweh
with their sheep and cattle,
they will not find him;
he has withdrawn from them.
7 They have betrayed Yahweh
because they have fathered bastards;
now the new moon will devour
them and their fields.

Brother wars against brother

8 Sound the horn in Gibeah,
the trumpet in Ramah,
raise the war cry in Beth-Aven,
'We are behind you, Benjamin!'
9 When the day of punishment comes,
Ephraim will be a wasteland;
on the tribes of Israel
I have pronounced certain doom.
10 The rulers of Judah act like men
who move the boundary stone;
I shall pour my wrath out on them
like a flood.
11 Ephraim is oppressed,
crushed by the sentence,
for having deliberately followed a Lie.
12 Because of this, I shall be like ringworm
for Ephraim
and like gangrene for the House of Judah.

The folly of foreign alliances

13 Once Ephraim realised that he was sick
and Judah that he had an ulcer,
Ephraim then went to Assyria,

4b A nickname (=House of Evil) for the northern national sanctuary at Bethel (=House of God).

he sent messengers to the Great King;
but he has no power to cure you
or to heal you of your sore;
14 for I shall be like a lion to Ephraim,
like a young lion to the House of Judah;
I myself shall rend them,
then go my way,
shall carry them off,
beyond hope of rescue.

15 I shall go back to my place
until they confess their guilt and seek me,
seek me eagerly in their distress.

The Israelites reply

6 Come, let us return to Yahweh.
He has rent us and he will heal us;
he has struck us
and he will bind up our wounds;
2 after two days he will revive us,
on the third day he will raise us up
and we shall live in his presence.
3 Let us know,
let us strive to know Yahweh;
that he will come is as certain as the dawn.
He will come to us like a shower,
like the rain of springtime to the earth.

4 What am I to do with you, Ephraim?
What am I to do with you, Judah?
For your love is like morning mist,
like the dew that quickly disappears.
5 This is why I have hacked them to pieces
by means of the prophets,
why I have killed them
with words from my mouth,
why my sentence will blaze forth
like the dawn—
6 for faithful love is what pleases me,
not sacrifice;
knowledge of God, not burnt offerings.

Disorders in Israel

7 But they have broken
the covenant at Adam,
there they have betrayed me.
8 Gilead is a city of evil-doers,
full of bloody footprints.
9 Like so many robbers in ambush,
a gang of priests commits murder
on the road to Shechem—
what infamous behaviour!
10 At Bethel I have seen a horrible thing;
there Ephraim plays the whore,
Israel is befouled.

11 For you too, Judah, a harvest is in store,
when I restore my people's fortunes.

7 Whenever I would heal Israel,
I am confronted by the guilt of Ephraim
and the evil-doings of Samaria;
for deceit is their principle of behaviour;
the thief breaks into the house,
marauders raid in the open;
2 and they never pause to consider
that I remember all their wicked deeds;
and now their own deeds hem them in
and stare me in the face.

Conspiracy the order of the day in Israel

3 They amuse the king
with their wickedness
and the chief men with their lies.
4 They are all adulterers, hot as an oven
which the baker need not stoke
from the time he has kneaded the dough
until it rises.
5 At the holiday for our king,
the ministers become inflamed
with wine,
while he accepts the homage of people
6 who laugh at him.
Their hearts are like an oven as they plot,
all night their passion slumbers,
then in the morning it bursts into flame;
7 yes, all of them as hot as ovens,
they consume their rulers.
All their kings have fallen thus,
not one of them has ever called on me.

Israel ruined by relying on foreign powers

8 Ephraim mixes with the nations.
Ephraim is a half-baked cake.
9 Foreigners have eaten his strength away
but he is unconscious of it;
even his hair is turning grey
but he is unconscious of it.
10 (Israel's arrogance is his own accuser;
but they do not come back to Yahweh
their God
or seek him, despite all this.)
11 Ephraim is like a silly, witless pigeon
calling on Egypt, turning to Assyria.
12 Wherever they turn,
I shall spread my net over them,
I shall bring them down
like the birds of the sky,
I shall punish them for their perversity.

The ingratitude and punishment of Israel

13 Woe to them for having fled from me!
Ruin seize them for having wronged me!
I have rescued them again and again
and they have only told lies about me.
14 Theirs is no heartfelt cry to me
when they lament on their beds;
when they gash themselves over the grain
and new wine,
they are still rebelling against me.
15 Though I supported
and gave strength to their arms,
they plan how to hurt me.
16 They turn to what does not exist,
they are like a faulty bow.
Their leaders will fall by the sword
because of their arrogant talk;
how they will be laughed at in Egypt!

An omen

8 Put the trumpet to your lips!
Like an eagle, disaster is swooping
on Yahweh's home!
Because they have violated my covenant
and been unfaithful to my Law,
2 in vain will they cry, 'My God!'
In vain, 'We, Israel, know you!'
3 Israel has rejected the good,
the enemy will pursue them.
4 They have set up kings,
but without my consent,
and appointed princes,
but without my knowledge.
With their silver and gold,
they have made themselves idols,
but only to be destroyed.
5 I spurn your calf,[a] Samaria!
My anger blazes against them!
How long will it be
before they recover their innocence?
6 For it is the product of Israel—
a craftsman made the thing,
it is no god at all!
The calf of Samaria
will be broken to pieces!
7 Since they sow the wind,
they will reap the whirlwind;
stalk without ear,
it will never yield flour—
or if it does, foreigners will swallow it.

Israel ruined by relying on foreign powers

8 Israel has himself been swallowed;
now they are lost among the nations
like something no one wants,
9 for having made approaches to Assyria—
like a wild donkey, all alone.
Ephraim has rented lovers
10 and because he has rented them
from the nations
I am now going to round them up;
soon they will feel the weight
of the king of princes!

Against the outward show of worship

11 Ephraim keeps building altars
for his sins,
these very altars are themselves a sin.
12 However much of my Law
I write for him,
Ephraim regards it as alien to him.
13 They offer sacrifices to me
and eat the meat,
they do not win Yahweh's favour.
On the contrary,
he will remember their guilt
and punish their sins;
they will have to go back to Egypt.
14 Israel has forgotten his Maker
and has built palaces,
while Judah keeps on building
fortified towns;
but I shall send fire down on his cities
to devour their citadels.

The sorrows of exile

9 No merrymaking, Israel, for you,
no rejoicing like other peoples,
for you have deserted your God
to play the whore,
you have loved the fee of prostitution
on every threshing-floor.
2 The threshing-floor and wine-press
will not feed them;
they will be disappointed of new wine.
3 No more will they live
in Yahweh's country;
Ephraim will have to go back to Egypt,
and eat polluted food in Assyria
4 No more will they pour libations of wine
to Yahweh,
and their sacrifices will not win his favour

8a The golden bull on which the sanctuary at Bethel was centred.

but will be like funeral fare for them:
whoever eats them will be polluted;
for their food will be for themselves alone,
not being offered in Yahweh's home.
5 What will you do
on the solemn feast-day,
on the day of Yahweh's festival?
6 What a scene of devastastion
they have left!
Egypt will round them up,
Memphis will bury them,
nettles will inherit their fields
and thorn-bushes
invade their homesteads.

Persecution, the prophet's reward for foretelling punishment

7 The days of punishment have come,
the days of retribution are here;
Israel knows it!
'The prophet is mad
and the inspired man a fool!'
Great has been your guilt—
all the greater then the hostility!
8 The watchman of Ephraim
is with my God:
it is the prophet—
and a fowler's trap is placed
on all his paths;
and in the shrine of his God
there is enmity towards him.
9 They have become deeply corrupt
as in the days of Gibeah;
he will remember their guilt,
he will punish their sins.

Punishment for the crime at Baal-Peor

10 It was like finding grapes in the desert
when I found Israel,
like seeing early fruit on a fig tree
when I saw your ancestors;
but when they reached Baal-Peor
they devoted themselves to Shame[a]
and became as loathsome
as the thing they loved.
11 The glory of Ephraim
will fly away like a bird:
no giving birth, no pregnancy,
no conceiving.
12 If they rear their children,
I shall take them away
before they grow up!
Woe to them indeed when I leave them!
13 Ephraim looked to me like Tyre,
planted in a meadow,
so Ephraim will present his children
to the slaughterer.
14 Give them, Yahweh—
what are you to give?—
give them wombs that miscarry
and dried-up breasts.

Gilgal

15 Their wickedness appeared in full
at Gilgal,
there I came to hate them.
Because of the wickedness of their deeds
I shall drive them from my home,
I shall love them no longer;
all their princes are rebels.
16 Ephraim is blasted,
their root has dried out,
they will bear no more fruit.
And even if they do bear children
I shall slaughter
the darlings of their womb.
17 Because they have not listened to him,
my God will cast them off
and they will become wanderers
among the nations.

The destruction of Israel's cultic objects

10 Israel was a luxuriant vine
yielding plenty of fruit.
The more his fruit increased,
the more altars he built;
the richer his land became,
the richer he made the sacred pillars.
2 Theirs is a divided heart;
now they will have to pay for it.
He himself will hack down their altars
and wreck their sacred pillars.
3 Then they will say,
'We have no king
because we have not feared Yahweh,
but what could the king do for us?'
4 Speeches are made,
oaths sworn to no purpose,
agreements concluded,
and so-called justice spreads
like a poisonous weed
along the furrows of the fields!
5 Samaria's citizens will tremble

9a A nickname for Baal, worshipped at Baal-Peor, Nb 25.

for the calf of Beth-Aven;
the people there will mourn for it,
so will its idol-priests,
as they exult in its glory
once it has been carried away!
6 It will be carried off to Assyria
as tribute to the Great King.
Ephraim will reap the shame,
and Israel blush for his intentions.
7 Samaria has had her day.
Her king is like a straw
drifting on the water.
8 The high places of Aven, the sin of Israel,
will be destroyed;
thorns and thistles
will grow over their altars.
Then they will say to the mountains,
'Cover us!'
and to the hills, 'Fall on us!'

9 Since the days of Gibeah, Israel,
you have sinned.
There they have taken their stand,
and will not war overtake the guilty
at Gibeah?
10 I am coming to punish them;
nations will muster against them
to punish them for their two crimes.

Israel has disappointed Yahweh's hope

11 Ephraim is a well-trained heifer
that loves to tread the grain.
But I have laid a yoke on her fine neck,
I shall put Ephraim into harness,
Judah will have to plough,
Jacob must draw the harrow.

12 Sow saving justice for yourselves,
reap a harvest of faithful love;
break up your fallow ground:
it is time to seek out Yahweh
until he comes to rain saving justice
down on you.

13 You have ploughed wickedness,
you have reaped iniquity,
you have eaten the fruit of falsehood.
Because you have trusted in your chariots,
in your great numbers of warriors,
14 turmoil is going to break out
among your people,
and all your fortresses will be laid waste.
As Shalman laid Beth-Arbel waste
on the day of battle,
dashing mothers to pieces
on their children,
15 so it shall be done to you, Bethel,
because of your great wickedness;
at dawn, the king of Israel will be no more.

God's love despised: his vengeance

11 When Israel was a child I loved him,
and I called my son out of Egypt.
2 But the more I called,
the further they went away from me;
they offered sacrifice to Baal
and burnt incense to idols.
3 I myself taught Ephraim to walk,
I myself took them by the arm,
but they did not know
that I was the one caring for them,
4 that I was leading them with human ties,
with leading-strings of love,
that, with them, I was like someone
lifting an infant to his cheek,
and that I bent down to feed him.

5 He will not have to go back to Egypt,
Assyria will be his king instead!
Since he has refused to come back to me,
6 the sword will rage through his cities,
destroying the bars of his gates,
devouring them because of their plots.

God's love stronger than his vengeance

7 My people are bent on disregarding me;
if they are summoned to come up,
not one of them makes a move.

8 Ephraim, how could I part with you?
Israel, how could I give you up?
How could I make you like Admah
or treat you like Zeboiim?
My heart within me is overwhelmed,
fever grips my inmost being.
9 I will not give rein to my fierce anger,
I will not destroy Ephraim again,
for I am God, not man,
the Holy One in your midst,
and I shall not come to you in anger.

The return from exile

10 They will follow Yahweh;
he will roar like a lion,
and when he roars,
his children will come fluttering
from the west,
11 fluttering like sparrows from Egypt,
like pigeons from Assyria,
and I shall settle them in their homes
—declares Yahweh.

Political and religious perversity of Israel

12 Ephraim besieges me with lying,
the House of Israel with duplicity.
(But Judah still is on God's side,
he is faithful to the Holy One.)
2 Ephraim feeds himself on wind,
all day he chases the wind from the East,
he heaps up cheating and violence;
they make a treaty with Assyria,
at the same time sending oil to Egypt.

Against Jacob and Ephraim

3 Yahweh has a case against Judah,
he will punish Jacob as his conduct merits,
he will repay him as his deeds deserve.
4 In the very womb
he overreached his brother,
in maturity he wrestled against God.
5 He wrestled with the angel and beat him,
he wept and pleaded with him.
He met him at Bethel
and there God spoke to us—
6 yes, Yahweh, God Sabaoth,
Yahweh is his title!
7 So turn back with God's help,
maintain faithful love and loyalty
and always put your trust in your God.
8 Merchants use fraudulent scales.
To defraud is his delight.
9 'How rich I have become!' says Ephraim,
'I have made a fortune.'
But of all his gains he will keep nothing
because of the sin of which he is guilty.

Reconciliation

10 But I have been Yahweh your God
since your days in Egypt
and will make you live in tents again
as in the days of Meeting.
11 I will speak through prophets,
I will give vision after vision
and through the ministry of prophets
will speak in parables.

New threats

12 Is Gilead a sink of iniquity?
Yes, they are a worthless lot!
At Gilgal they sacrifice to bulls,
that is why their altars
are like heaps of stones
in a ploughed field.
13 Jacob fled to the countryside of Aram,
Israel slaved to win a wife,
to win a wife he looked after sheep.
14 By a prophet Yahweh brought Israel
out of Egypt
and by a prophet Israel was preserved.
15 Ephraim gave bitter provocation—
Yahweh will bring his bloodshed
down on him,
his Lord will repay him for his insult.

Idolatry punished

13 When Ephraim used to speak,
all trembled;
he was a power in Israel;
but once he had incurred guilt with Baal,
he died.
2 And now they compound their sins
by casting images for themselves
out of their silver,
idols of their own invention,
the work of craftsmen, all of it!
'Sacrifice to them,' they say!
Men bestow kisses to calves!
3 That is why they will be
like morning mist,
like the dew that quickly disappears,
like the chaff whirled
from the threshing-floor,
like smoke escaping through the window.

The punishment for ingratitude

4 But I have been Yahweh your God
since your days in Egypt
when you knew no god but me,
since you had no one else to save you.
5 I cared for you in the desert,
in the land of dreadful drought.
6 I pastured them, and they were satisfied;
once satisfied, their hearts grew proud,
and therefore they forgot me.
7 So now I shall be like a lion to them,
like a leopard I shall lurk beside the road,
8 like a bear robbed of her cubs
I shall meet them
and rend the membrane of their heart,
and there like a lioness I shall eat them,
like a wild beast tear them to shreds.

The end of the monarchy

9 Israel, you have destroyed yourself
though in me lies your help.
10 Your king, where is he now, to save you,

or the governors in all your cities?–
whom you once pleaded for, saying,
'Give me a king and princes!'
11 In my anger I gave you a king
and in my wrath I have taken him away.

The inevitability of ruin

12 Ephraim's guilt is packed away,
his sin is locked up.
13 Pangs as of childbirth overtake him,
and a stupid child he is;
his time is due,
but he does not leave the womb.
14 Shall I save them from the
clutches of Sheol?
Shall I buy them back from Death?
Where are your plagues, Death?
Where are your scourges, Sheol?
Compassion will be banished
from my sight!
15 Though Ephraim bears more fruit
than his brothers,
the wind from the East will come,
Yahweh's breath blowing up
from the desert
to dry his spring, to dry up his fountain,
to strip his treasury
of everything worth having.
14 Samaria will pay the penalty
for having rebelled against her God.
They will fall by the sword,
their little children
will be dashed to pieces
and their pregnant women
disembowelled.

III: THE REPENTANCE AND RECONCILIATION OF ISRAEL

The sincere conversion of Israel to Yahweh

2 Israel, come back to Yahweh your God
your guilt was the cause of your downfall.
3 Provide yourself with words
and come back to Yahweh.
Say to him, 'Take all guilt away
and give us what is good,
instead of bulls we will dedicate to you
our lips.
4 Assyria cannot save us,
we will not ride horses any more,
or say, "Our God!"
to our own handiwork,
for you are the one
in whom orphans find compassion.'

5 I shall cure them of their disloyalty,
I shall love them with all my heart,
for my anger has turned away from them.
6 I shall fall like dew on Israel,
he will bloom like the lily
and thrust out roots
like the cedar of Lebanon;
7 he will put out new shoots,
he will have the beauty of the olive tree
and the fragrance of Lebanon.
8 They will come back to live in my shade;
they will grow wheat again,
they will make the vine flourish,
their wine will be as famous as Lebanon's.
9 What has Ephraim to do with idols
any more
when I hear him and watch over him?
I am like an evergreen cypress,
you owe your fruitfulness to me.

Concluding admonition

10 Let the wise understand these words,
let the intelligent grasp their meaning,
for Yahweh's ways are straight
and the upright will walk in them,
but sinners will stumble.

THE BOOK OF JOEL

The first two chapters form an almost liturgical call to repentance, the last two a promise of Yahweh's renewal and salvation for all nations, both being centred on the final Day of Yahweh. This literary prophecy was probably composed after the return from exile, c. 400 BC.

PLAN OF THE BOOK

JOEL

Title

1 The word of Yahweh that was addressed
to Joel son of Pethuel.

I: THE PLAGUE OF LOCUSTS

A: LITURGY OF MOURNING AND ENTREATY

Lament over the ruin of the country

2 Listen to this, you elders;
everybody in the country, attend!
Has anything like this
ever happened in your day,
or in your ancestors' days?
3 Tell your children about it
and let your children tell their children,
and their children the next generation!

4 What the nibbler has left,
the grown locust has eaten,
what the grown locust has left,
the hopper has eaten,
and what the hopper has left,
the shearer has eaten.
5 Wake up, you drunkards, and weep!
All you wine-bibbers, lament
for the new wine:
it has been snatched from your lips.
6 For a nation has invaded my country,
mighty and innumerable,
with teeth like a lion's teeth,
with the fangs of a lioness.
7 It has reduced my vines to a desolation
and my fig trees to splinters,
stripped them and broken them down,
leaving their branches white.

8 Mourn, as a virgin-bride in sackcloth
for the bridegroom of her youth!

9Cereal offering and libation
are lost to Yahweh's Temple.
The priests, the ministers of Yahweh,
are in mourning.
10The fields are ruined,
the land is in mourning,
for the grain has been ruined,
the new wine has failed,
of olive oil only a trickle.

11Stand dismayed, you farmers,
wail, you vinedressers,
for the wheat, for the barley!
The harvest of the fields has been lost!
12The vine has withered,
the fig tree wilts away;
pomegranate, palm tree, apple tree,
every tree in the countryside is dry,
and for human beings
joy has run dry too.

A call to repentance and prayer

13Priests, put on sackcloth and lament!
You ministers of the altar, wail!
Come here, lie in sackcloth all night long,
you ministers of my God!
For the Temple of your God
has been deprived
of cereal offering and libation.
14Order a fast,
proclaim a solemn assembly;
you elders,
summon everybody in the country
to the Temple of Yahweh your God.
Cry out to Yahweh:
15'Alas for the day!
For the Day of Yahweh is near,
coming as destruction from Shaddai.'

16Has not the food disappeared
before our very eyes?
Have not joy and gladness vanished
from the Temple of our God?
17The seeds shrivel
under their clods;
the granaries are deserted,
the barns are in ruins,
because the harvest has dried out.
18Loudly the cattle groan!
The herds of oxen are bewildered
because they have no pasture.
The flocks of sheep
bear the punishment too.

19Yahweh, to you I cry:
for fire has devoured the desert pastures,
flame has burnt up
all the trees in the countryside.
20Even the wild animals
pant loudly for you,
for the watercourses have run dry,
and fire has devoured the desert pastures.

A warning about the Day of Yahweh

2 Blow the ram's-horn in Zion,
sound the alarm on my holy mountain!
Let everybody in the country tremble,
for the Day of Yahweh is coming,
yes, it is near.

2Day of darkness and gloom,[a]
Day of cloud and blackness.
Like the dawn, across the mountains
spreads a vast and mighty people,
such as has never been before,
such as will never be again
to the remotest ages.

The invasion of locusts

3In their van a fire devours,
in their rear a flame consumes.
The country is like a garden of Eden
ahead of them
and a desert waste behind them.
Nothing escapes them.
4They look like horses,
like chargers they gallop on,
5with a racket like that of chariots
they spring over the mountain tops,
with a crackling like a blazing fire
devouring the stubble,
a mighty army in battle array.

6At the sight of them, people are appalled
and every face grows pale.
7Like fighting men they press forward,
like warriors they scale the walls,
each marching straight ahead,
not turning from his path;
8they never jostle each other,
each marches straight ahead:
arrows fly, they still press forward,
never breaking ranks.
9They hurl themselves at the city,
they leap onto the walls,
swarm up the houses,
getting in through the windows
like thieves.

2a || Zp 1:15.

A vision of the Day of Yahweh

10 As they come on, the earth quakes,
the skies tremble,
sun and moon grow dark,
the stars lose their brilliance.[b]
11 Yahweh's voice rings out
at the head of his troops!
For mighty indeed is his army,
strong, the enforcer of his orders,
for great is the Day of Yahweh,
and very terrible—who can face it?

A call to repentance

12 'But now—declares Yahweh—
come back to me with all your heart,
fasting, weeping, mourning.'
13 Tear your hearts and not your clothes,
and come back to Yahweh your God,
for he is gracious and compassionate,
slow to anger, rich in faithful love,
and he relents about inflicting disaster.
14 Who knows if he will not come back,
relent
and leave a blessing behind him,
a cereal offering and a libation
to be presented to Yahweh your God?

15 Blow the ram's-horn in Zion!
Order a fast,
proclaim a solemn assembly,
16 call the people together,
summon the community,
assemble the elders,
gather the children,
even infants at the breast!
Call the bridegroom from his bedroom
and the bride from her bower!
17 Let the priests, the ministers of Yahweh,
stand weeping between portico and altar,
saying, 'Spare your people, Yahweh!
Do not expose your heritage
to the contempt,
to the sarcasm of the nations!
Why give the peoples cause to say,
"Where is their God?" '

B: YAHWEH'S ANSWER

18 Then, becoming jealous over his country,
Yahweh took pity on his people.

The plague stops

19 Yahweh said in answer to his people,
'Now I shall send you
wheat, wine and olive oil
until you have enough.
Never again will I expose you
to the contempt of the nations.
20 I shall take the northerner
far away from you
and drive him into an arid, desolate land,
his vanguard to the eastern sea,
his rearguard to the western sea.
He will give off a stench,
he will give off a foul stink
(for what he made bold to do).'

A vision of plenty

21 Land, do not be afraid;
be glad, rejoice,
for Yahweh has done great things.
22 Wild animals, do not be afraid;
the desert pastures are green again,
the trees bear fruit,
vine and fig tree yield their richness.

23 Sons of Zion, be glad,
rejoice in Yahweh your God;
for he has given you
autumn rain as justice demands,
and he will send the rains down for you,
the autumn and spring rain as of old.
24 The threshing-floors will be full of grain,
the vats overflow with wine and oil.

25 'I will make up to you for the years
devoured by grown locust and hopper,
by shearer and young locust,
my great army
which I sent to invade you.

26 'You will eat to your heart's content,
and praise the name of Yahweh your God
who has treated you so wonderfully.
(My people will never
be humiliated again!)

27 'And you will know that I am among you
in Israel,
I, Yahweh your God, and no one else.
My people will never
be humiliated again!'

2b =4:15.

II: THE NEW AGE AND THE DAY OF YAHWEH

A: THE OUTPOURING OF THE SPIRIT

3 [1]'After this
I shall pour out my spirit on all humanity.
Your sons and daughters shall prophesy,
your old people shall dream dreams,
and your young people see visions.
[2]Even on the slaves, men and women,
shall I pour out my spirit in those days.
[3]I shall show portents in the sky
and on earth,
blood and fire and columns of smoke.'

[4]The sun will be turned into darkness,
and the moon into blood,
before the Day comes,
that great and terrible Day.
[5]All who call on the name of Yahweh
will be saved,
for *on Mount Zion will be those
who have escaped*,[a]
as Yahweh has said,
and in Jerusalem a remnant
whom Yahweh is calling.

B: THE JUDGEMENT OF THE NATIONS

The judgement announced

4 [1]'For in those days and at that time,
when I restore the fortunes
of Judah and Jerusalem,
[2]I shall gather all the nations together
and take them down
to the Valley of Jehoshaphat;[a]
there I shall put them on trial
because of Israel,
my people and my heritage,
for having scattered them
among the nations
and having divided my land
among themselves.
[3]They drew lots for my people,
bartering a boy for a whore
and selling a girl for wine to drink.

Charges against the Phoenicians and Philistines

[4]'And what are you to me, Tyre and Sidon
and all you regions of Philistia?
Can you take revenge on me?
If you take revenge on me,
I shall quickly, instantly,
make your revenge
recoil on your own heads
[5]for having taken my silver and gold away
and carried off my valuable treasures
to your temples,
[6]and for having sold
the children of Judah and Jerusalem
to the Ionians,
to be taken far away
from their own frontiers.
[7]Look, I shall rouse them from the places
to which you have sold them;
I shall make your actions
recoil on your own heads
[8]by selling your sons and daughters
to the sons of Judah,
who in turn will sell them to the Sabaeans,
to a nation far away—
Yahweh has spoken!'

A summons to the nations

[9]Proclaim this among the nations.
Prepare for war!
Rouse the champions!
All you troops, advance,
march!
[10]Hammer your ploughshares into swords,
your bill-hooks into spears;
let the weakling say, 'I am tough!'
[11]Hurry and come,
all the nations around,
and assemble there!
(Yahweh, send down your champions!)
[12]'Let the nations rouse themselves
and march
to the Valley of Jehoshaphat,
for there I shall sit in judgement
on all the nations around.
[13]Ply the sickle,
for the harvest is ripe;
come and tread,

3a Ob 17.
4a A symbolic name (= Yahweh judges).

for the winepress is full;
the vats are overflowing,
so great is their wickedness!'

14 Multitude on multitude
in the Valley of Decision!
For the Day of Yahweh is near
in the Valley of the Verdict!

The Day of Yahweh

15 Sun and moon grow dark,
the stars lose their brilliance.[b]
16 Yahweh roars from Zion,
he thunders from Jerusalem;[c]
heaven and earth tremble.

But Yahweh will be a shelter
for his people,
a stronghold for the Israelites.

17 'Then you will know
that I am Yahweh your God
residing on Zion, my holy mountain.
Jerusalem will then be a sanctuary,
no foreigners will overrun it ever again.'

C: THE GLORIOUS FUTURE OF ISRAEL

18 When that Day comes,
the mountains will run with new wine
and the hills will flow with milk,
and all the stream-beds of Judah
will run with water.
A fountain will spring
from Yahweh's Temple
and water the Gorge of the Acacias.
19 Egypt will become a desolation,
and Edom a desert waste
on account of the violence
done to the children of Judah
whose innocent blood
they shed in their country.
20 But Judah will be inhabited for ever,
and Jerusalem
from generation to generation!
21 'I shall avenge their blood
and let none go unpunished,'
and Yahweh will dwell in Zion.

THE BOOK OF AMOS

A shepherd from the south, Amos preached briefly, with fine, rural imagery, in the rich northern kingdom, against the corruptions of wealth, luxury, perversion of justice and external religion. The punishment of the Day of the Lord was already looming, in the form of the threat of invasion by Assyria, soon (in 721) to overrun Israel. Amos is the first to teach that a faithful remnant will survive – unless this one ray of hope was added later.

PLAN OF THE BOOK

I Judgement on the neighbouring Nations and on Israel itself 1–2
II Israel warned and threatened 3–6
III The Visions 7:1–9:10
IV Prospects of Restoration and of Idyllic Prosperity 9:11–15

4b =2:10.
4c ‖ Am 1:2.

AMOS

Title

1 Words of Amos one of the shepherds of Tekoa. The visions he had about Israel, in the time of Uzziah king of Judah and Jeroboam son of Joash, king of Israel, two years before the earthquake.

Introduction

2 He said:

Yahweh roars from Zion,
and makes himself heard from
Jerusalem;[a]
the shepherds' pastures mourn,
and the crown of Carmel dries up.

I: JUDGEMENT ON THE NEIGHBOURING NATIONS AND ON ISRAEL ITSELF

Damascus

3 Yahweh says this:

For the three crimes, the four crimes
of Damascus,
I have made my decree and will not relent:
because they have threshed Gilead
with iron threshing-sledges,
4 I shall send fire down
on the House of Hazael
to devour the palaces of Ben-Hadad;
5 I shall break the gate-bar of Damascus,
I shall destroy
the inhabitant of Bikath-Aven,
the holder of the sceptre in Beth-Eden,
and the people of Aram
will be deported to Kir,
Yahweh says.

Gaza and Philistia

6 Yahweh says this:

For the three crimes, the four crimes
of Gaza,
I have made my decree and will not relent:
because they have deported
entire nations as slaves to Edom,
7 I shall send fire down on the walls of Gaza
to devour its palaces;
8 I shall destroy the inhabitant of Ashdod,
the holder of the sceptre in Ashkelon;
I shall turn my hand against Ekron
and the remnant of the Philistines
will perish,
says the Lord Yahweh.

Tyre and Phoenicia

9 Yahweh says this:

For the three crimes, the four crimes
of Tyre,
I have made my decree and will not relent:
because they have handed
hosts of captives over to Edom,
heedless of a covenant of brotherhood,
10 I shall send fire down on the walls of Tyre
to devour its palaces.

Edom

11 Yahweh says this:

For the three crimes, the four crimes
of Edom,
I have made my decree and will not relent:
because he has pursued his brother
with the sword,
because he has stifled any sense of pity,
and perpetually nursed his anger
and constantly cherished his rage,
12 I shall send fire down on Teman
to devour the palaces of Bozrah.

1a || Jr 4:16.

Ammon

13Yahweh says this:

For the three crimes, the four crimes
of the Ammonites,
I have made my decree and will not relent:
because they have disembowelled
the pregnant women of Gilead
in order to extend their own frontiers,
14I shall light a fire
against the walls of Rabbah
to devour its palaces
amid war cries on the day of battle,
in a whirlwind on the day of storm,
15and their king shall go into captivity,
he and his chief men with him,
says Yahweh.

Moab

2 Yahweh says this:

For the three crimes, the four crimes
of Moab,
I have made my decree and will not relent:
because they have burnt the bones
of the king of Edom to ash,
2I shall send fire down into Moab
to devour the palaces of Kerioth,
and Moab will die in the tumult,
amid war cries and the blare of trumpets;
3I shall destroy the ruler there
and slaughter all the chief men there
with him,
says Yahweh.

Judah

4Yahweh says this:

For the three crimes, the four crimes
of Judah,
I have made my decree and will not relent:
because they have despised Yahweh's law
and not kept his commandments,
since their Falsehoods,
which their ancestors followed,
have led them astray,
5I shall send fire down on Judah
to devour the palaces of Jerusalem.

Israel

6Yahweh says this:

For the three crimes, the four crimes
of Israel,
I have made my decree and will not relent:
because they have sold the upright
for silver
and the poor for a pair of sandals,[a]
7because they have crushed the heads
of the weak into the dust
and thrust the rights of the oppressed
to one side,
father and son sleeping with the same girl
and thus profaning my holy name,
8lying down beside every altar
on clothes acquired as pledges,
and drinking the wine of the people
they have fined
in the house of their god.

9Yet it was I who destroyed the Amorite
before them,
he who was as tall as the cedars,
as strong as the oaks;
I who destroyed his fruit above ground
and his roots below.
10It was I who brought you up from Egypt
and for forty years led you
through the desert
to take possession
of the Amorite's country;
11I who raised up prophets from your sons
and Nazirites from your young men.
Israelites, is this not true?
—declares Yahweh!

12But you have made the Nazirite
drink wine
and given orders to the prophets,
'Do not prophesy.'
13Very well! Like a cart
overloaded with sheaves
I shall crush you where you stand;
14flight will be cut off for the swift,
the strong will have no chance
to exert his strength
nor the warrior be able to save his life;
15the archer will not stand his ground,
the swift of foot will not escape,
nor will the horseman save his life;
16even the bravest of warriors
will jettison his arms and run away,
that day!
—declares Yahweh!

2a =8:6.

II: ISRAEL WARNED AND THREATENED

Election and punishment

3 Listen, Israelites, to this prophecy which Yahweh pronounces against you, against the whole family which I brought up from Egypt:

2 You alone have I intimately known
of all the families of earth,
that is why I shall punish you
for all your wrong-doings.

The prophetic call cannot be resisted

3 Do two people travel together
unless they have agreed to do so?
4 Does the lion roar in the forest
if it has no prey?
Does the young lion growl in his lair
if it has caught nothing?
5 Does a bird fall on the ground in a net
unless a trap has been set for it?
Will the net spring up from the ground
without catching something?
6 Does the trumpet sound in the city
without the people being alarmed?
Does misfortune come to a city
if Yahweh has not caused it?

7 No indeed, Lord Yahweh does nothing
without revealing his secret
to his servants the prophets.
8 The lion roars: who is not afraid?
Lord Yahweh has spoken:
who will not prophesy?

Samaria will perish for her corruption

9 From the palace roofs of Assyria
and from the palace roofs of Egypt,
proclaim aloud,
'Assemble on the hills of Samaria
and observe the grave disorders inside her
and the acts of oppression there!'
10 Little they know of right conduct
—declares Yahweh—
who cram their palaces with violence
and extortion.
11 This is why—Lord Yahweh says this—
an enemy will soon besiege the land,
he will bring down your strength
and your palaces will be looted.

12 Yahweh says this:

As the shepherd rescues two legs
or the tip of an ear
from the lion's mouth,
so will the children of Israel be salvaged
who now loll in Samaria
in the corners of their beds,
on their divans of Damascus.

Against Bethel and domestic luxury

13 Listen and testify against
the House of Jacob
—declares the Lord Yahweh,
God Sabaoth—
14 the day when I punish Israel for his crimes
I shall also punish the altars of Bethel;
the horns of the altar will be hacked off
and will fall to the ground.
15 I shall blast winter house
with summer house,
ivory houses will be destroyed
and many mansions cease to be
—declares Yahweh.

Against the women of Samaria

4 Listen to this saying,
you cows of Bashan
living on the hill of Samaria,
exploiting the weak
and ill-treating the poor,
saying to your husbands,
'Bring us something to drink!'
2 The Lord God has sworn by his holiness:
Look, the days will soon be on you
when he will use hooks to drag you away
and fish-hooks for the very last of you;
3 through the breaches in the wall
you will leave,
each one straight ahead,
and be herded away towards Hermon
—declares Yahweh.

The self-deception, obstinacy and punishment of Israel

4 Go to Bethel, and sin,
to Gilgal, and sin even harder!
Bring your sacrifices each morning,
your tithes every third day,
5 burn your thank-offering of leaven
and widely publicise
your free-will offerings,

for this, children of Israel,
is what makes you happy
—declares the Lord Yahweh.

6 I even gave you clean teeth
in all your towns
and a shortage of food in all your villages
and still you would not come back to me
—declares Yahweh.

7 I even withheld the rain from you
full three months before harvest-time;
I caused rain to fall in one town
and caused no rain to fall in another;
one field was rained on
and the next for want of rain dried up;
8 two towns, three towns went tottering
to one town for water to drink
but went unsatisfied,
and still you would not come back to me
—declares Yahweh.

9 I struck you with blight and mildew,
I dried up your gardens and vineyards;
the locust devoured your fig trees
and olive trees
and still you would not come back to me
—declares Yahweh.

10 I sent plague on you like Egypt's plague,
I slaughtered your young men
with the sword
and at the same time your horses
were captured;
I filled your nostrils
with the stench of your camps
and still you would not come back to me
—declares Yahweh.

11 I overturned you
as God overturned Sodom
and Gomorrah;
you were like a brand
snatched from the blaze
and still you would not come back to me
—declares Yahweh.

12 So this, Israel, is what I plan to do to you.
Because I am going to do this to you,
Israel, prepare to meet your God!

Doxology[a]

13 For look, he it is
who forges the mountains,
creates the wind,
who reveals his mind to humankind,
changes the dawn into darkness
and strides on the heights of the world:
Yahweh, God Sabaoth, is his name.

Lament for Israel

5 Listen to this word
which I utter against you,
it is a dirge, House of Israel:
2 She has fallen down, never to rise again,
the virgin Israel.
There she lies on her own soil,
with no one to lift her up.

3 For Lord Yahweh says this:
The town
which used to put a thousand
in the field
will be left with a hundred,
and the one which used to put a hundred
will be left with ten,
to fight for the House of Israel.

No salvation without repentance

4 For Yahweh says this
to the House of Israel:
Seek me out and you will survive,
5 but do not seek out Bethel,
do not go to Gilgal,
do not journey to Beersheba,
for Gilgal is going into captivity
and Bethel will be brought to nothing.
6 Seek out Yahweh and you will survive
or else he will sweep like fire
upon the House of Joseph
and burn it down, with no one at Bethel
able to quench the flames.
7 They turn justice into wormwood
and throw uprightness to the ground.

Doxology

8 He it is who makes the Pleiades and Orion,
who turns shadow dark as death
into morning
and day to darkest night,
who summons the waters of the sea
and pours them over the surface
of the land.
Yahweh is his name.[a]
9 He brings destruction on the strong
and ruin comes on the fortress.

4a A hymnic fragment, probably added later, as 5:8–9 and 9:5–6.
5a =9:6.

Threats

10 They hate the man who teaches justice
at the city gate
and detest anyone who declares the truth.
11 For trampling on the poor man
and for extorting levies on his wheat:
although you have built houses
of dressed stone,
you will not live in them;
although you have planted
pleasant vineyards,
you will not drink wine from them:
12 for I know how many your crimes are
and how outrageous your sins,
you oppressors of the upright,
who hold people to ransom
and thrust the poor aside at the gates.
13 That is why anyone prudent
keeps silent now,
since the time is evil.

Exhortation

14 Seek good and not evil
so that you may survive,
and Yahweh, God Sabaoth, be with you
as you claim he is.
15 Hate evil, love good,
let justice reign at the city gate:
it may be that Yahweh, God Sabaoth,
will take pity on the remnant of Joseph.

Impending punishment

16 Therefore Yahweh Sabaoth,
the Lord, says this:
In every public square
there will be lamentation,
in every street they will cry out,
'Alas! Alas!'
The farmer will be called on to mourn,
the professional mourners to lament,
17 and there will be wailing
in every vineyard,
for I mean to pass through among you,
Yahweh says.

The Day[b] of Yahweh

18 Disaster for you
who long for the Day of Yahweh!
What will the Day of Yahweh
mean for you?
It will mean darkness, not light,
19 as when someone runs away from a lion,
only to meet a bear;
he goes into his house
and puts his hand on the wall,
only for a snake to bite him.
20 Will not the Day of Yahweh
be darkness, not light,
totally dark, without a ray of light?

Against formalism in religion

21 I hate, I scorn your festivals,
I take no pleasure
in your solemn assemblies.
22 When you bring me burnt offerings . . .[c]
your oblations, I do not accept them
and I do not look
at your communion sacrifices
of fat cattle.
23 Spare me the din of your chanting,
let me hear none of your strumming
on lyres,
24 but let justice flow like water,
and uprightness
like a never-failing stream!
25 Did you bring me sacrifices and oblations
those forty years in the desert,
House of Israel?
26 Now you must shoulder
Sakkuth your king
and the star of your God, Kaiwan,
those idols you made for yourselves;
27 for I am about to drive you into captivity
beyond Damascus,
Yahweh says—God Sabaoth is his name.

Against the self-indulgent and their false sense of security

6 Disaster for those
so comfortable in Zion
and for those so confident
on the hill of Samaria,
the notables of this first of nations,
those to whom the House of Israel
has recourse!
2 Travel to Calneh and look,
go on from there to Hamath the great,

5b A day of retribution, punishment of the wicked and vindication of God's faithful people. It figures prominently in all the prophets.
5c A line seems to be missing here.

then go down to Gath[a] in Philistia.
Are they more powerful
than these kingdoms?
Is their territory larger than yours?
3 Thinking to defer the evil day,
you are hastening the reign of violence.

4 Lying on ivory beds
and sprawling on their divans,
they dine on lambs from the flock,
and stall-fattened veal;
5 they bawl to the sound of the lyre
and, like David,
they invent musical instruments;
6 they drink wine by the bowlful,
and lard themselves with the finest oils,
but for the ruin of Joseph
they care nothing.
7 That is why they will now go
into captivity,
heading the column of captives.
The sprawlers' revelry is over.

The punishment:
plague, earthquake, invasion

8 Lord Yahweh has sworn by his own self
—declares Yahweh, God Sabaoth:
I detest the pride of Jacob,
I hate his palaces,
I shall hand over the city and all in it.
9 If ten people are left in a single house,
they will die
10 and a few will be left to carry
the bones from the house,
and they will say to anyone
deep inside the house,
'Any more there?'
and he will answer, 'No.'
Then he will say, 'Hush!—
Yahweh's name must not be mentioned.'
11 For look, Yahweh gives the command:
as he strikes,
the great house falls to pieces
and the small house is in fragments.

12 Can horses gallop over rocks?
Can the sea be ploughed with oxen?
Yet you have changed justice into poison,
and the fruit of uprightness
into wormwood,
13 while rejoicing over Lo-Debar
and saying,
'Wasn't it by our own strength
that we captured Karnaim?'
14 But look, House of Israel, against you
—declares Yahweh, God Sabaoth—
I am raising a nation to oppress you
from the Pass of Hamath
to the Gorge of the Arabah.

III: THE VISIONS

First vision: the locusts

7 This is what Lord Yahweh showed me:
there was a swarm of locusts
when the second crop was sprouting,
full-grown locusts, after the king's hay
had been cut.
2 When they had eaten all the grass
in the land,
I said, 'Lord Yahweh, forgive, I beg you.
How can Jacob survive, being so small?'
3 Then Yahweh relented;
'It will not happen,' said Yahweh.

Second vision: the drought

4 This is what Lord Yahweh showed me:
Lord Yahweh summoning fire
in punishment;
it had devoured the great Abyss
and was encroaching on the land,
5 when I said, 'Lord Yahweh, stop,
I beg you.
How can Jacob survive, being so small?'
6 Then Yahweh relented;
'This will not happen either,'
said the Lord Yahweh.

Third vision: the plumb-line

7 This is what he showed me:
the Lord standing by a wall,
with a plumb-line in his hand.
8 'What do you see, Amos?'
Yahweh asked me.
'A plumb-line,' I said.
Then the Lord said,
'Look, I am going to put a plumb-line

6a Calneh, Hamath and Gath were taken by Assyria in 738, 720, 711 BC respectively.

in among my people Israel;
never again will I overlook their offences.
9The high places of Isaac will be ruined
and the sanctuaries of Israel laid waste,
and, sword in hand, I will attack
the House of Jeroboam.'

Amaziah challenges Amos' right to prophesy

10Amaziah the priest of Bethel then sent word
to Jeroboam king of Israel as follows, 'Amos
is plotting against you in the heart of the
House of Israel; the country cannot tolerate
his speeches. 11For this is what Amos says,
"Jeroboam is going to die by the sword, and
Israel will go into captivity far from its native
land." ' 12To Amos himself Amaziah said,
'Go away, seer, take yourself off to Judah,
earn your living there, and there you can
prophesy! 13But never again will you
prophesy at Bethel, for this is a royal sanc-
tuary, a national temple.' 14'I am not a pro-
phet,' Amos replied to Amaziah, 'nor do I
belong to a prophetic brotherhood. I am
merely a herdsman and dresser of sycamore-
figs. 15But Yahweh took me as I followed the
flock, and Yahweh said to me, "Go and
prophesy to my people Israel." 16So now
listen to what Yahweh says:

"You say: Do not prophesy against Israel,
do not foretell doom
on the House of Isaac!"
17Very well, this is what Yahweh says,
"Your wife will become a prostitute
in the streets,
your sons and daughters will fall
by the sword,
your land will be parcelled out
by measuring line,
and you yourself will die on polluted soil
and Israel will go into captivity
far from its own land!" '

Fourth vision: the basket of ripe fruit

8 This is what Lord Yahweh showed me:
A basket of ripe fruit.
2'What do you see, Amos?' he asked.
'A basket of ripe fruit,' I said.
Then Yahweh said,
'The time is ripe for my people Israel;
I will not continue
to overlook their offences.
3That day, the palace songs
will turn to howls,
—declares the Lord Yahweh—
the corpses will be many
that are thrown down everywhere.
Keep silent!'

Against swindlers and exploiters

4Listen to this, you who crush the needy
and reduce the oppressed to nothing,
5you who say,
'When will New Moon be over
so that we can sell our corn,
and Sabbath, so that we can market
our wheat?
Then, we can make
the bushel-measure smaller
and the shekel-weight bigger,
by fraudulently tampering
with the scales.
6We can buy up the weak for silver
and the poor for a pair of sandals,[a]
and even get a price
for the sweepings of the wheat.'
7Yahweh has sworn by the pride of Jacob,
'Never will I forget
anything they have done.'

8Will not the earth tremble for this
and all who live on it lament,
as it all rises together
like the Nile in Egypt,
it swells and then subsides
like the Egyptian Nile?[b]

Prediction of punishment: darkness and mourning

9'On that Day—
declares the Lord Yahweh—
I shall make the sun go down at noon
and darken the earth in broad daylight.
10I shall turn your festivals into mourning
and all your singing into lamentation;
I shall make you all wear sacking
round your waists
and have all your heads shaved.
I shall make it like the mourning
for an only child,
and it will end like the bitterest of days.

8a =2:6.
8b =9:5.

Famine and drought of the word of God

11 'The days are coming—
declares the Lord Yahweh—
when I shall send a famine on the country,
not hunger for food, not thirst for water,
but famine for hearing Yahweh's word.
12 People will stagger from sea to sea,
will wander from the north to the east,
searching for Yahweh's word,
but will not find it.

Fresh prediction of punishment

13 'That Day, fine girls and stalwart youths
will faint from thirst.
14 The people who swear
by the Sin[c] of Samaria,
who say, "Long live your god, Dan!"
and "Hurrah for the pilgrimage
to Beersheba!"
will all fall, never to rise again.'

Fifth vision: the fall of the sanctuary

9 I saw the Lord standing by the altar,
and he said,
'Strike the top of the pillar
so that the thresholds shake!
Smash their heads in, one and all!
And I shall put any survivors to the sword;
whoever runs away will not run far,
whoever escapes
will not make good his escape.
2 Should they burrow into Sheol,
my hand will haul them out;
should they climb to heaven,
I shall bring them down.
3 Should they hide on the top of Carmel,
I shall track them down and catch them;
should they hide from me on the sea bed,
I shall order the Serpent there
to bite them;
4 if their enemies herd them into captivity,
I shall order the sword to kill them there,
and I shall fix my eyes on them
for evil and not for good.'

Doxology

5 Lord Yahweh Sabaoth—
he touches the earth and it melts,
and all living things on it lament,
as all rises together like the Nile in Egypt
and then subsides
like the Egyptian Nile.[a]
6 He who builds his mansions
in the heavens,
supporting his vault on the earth;
who summons the waters of the sea
and pours them
over the surface of the land:
Yahweh is his name.[b]

Sinners will all perish

7 Are not you and the Cushites
all the same to me,
children of Israel?—declares Yahweh.
Did I not bring Israel up from Egypt
and the Philistines from Caphtor,
and the Aramaeans from Kir?
8 Look, Lord Yahweh's eyes
are on the sinful kingdom,
I shall wipe it off the face of the earth,
although I shall not destroy
the House of Jacob completely
—declares Yahweh.
9 For look, I shall give the command
and shall shake out the House of Israel
among all nations
as a sieve is shaken out
without one grain falling on the ground.
10 All the sinners of my people
will perish by the sword, who say,
'Disaster will never approach
or overtake us.'

8c The Hebr. word is *'ashemah*, a pun on the name of the goddess Ashimah.
9a =8:8.
9b =5:8.

IV: PROSPECTS OF RESTORATION AND OF IDYLLIC PROSPERITY[c]

11 On that Day, I shall rebuild
the tottering hut of David,
make good the gaps in it, restore its ruins
and rebuild it as it was in the days of old,
12 for them to be master
of what is left of Edom
and of all the nations once called mine
—Yahweh declares,
and he will perform it.

13 The days are coming—
declares Yahweh—
when the ploughman will tread
on the heels of the reaper,
and the treader of grapes
on the heels of the sower of seed,
and the mountains will run with new wine
and the hills all flow with it.
14 I shall restore the fortunes
of my people Israel;
they will rebuild the ruined cities
and live in them,
they will plant vineyards
and drink their wine,
they will lay out gardens
and eat their produce.
15 And I shall plant them in their own soil
and they will never be uprooted again
from the country
which I have given them,
declares Yahweh, your God.

THE BOOK OF OBADIAH

This short prophecy, half of which (vv. 1–9) is closely paralleled in Jeremiah 49, proclaims revenge on the Edomites who helped destroy Jerusalem after the siege of 587 BC. It must date from soon after this.

OBADIAH

Title

Vision of Obadiah: about Edom.

Prologue

1c I have received a message from Yahweh,
a herald has been sent
throughout the nations:
'Up! Let us march against this people.
Into battle!'

Sentence pronounced on Edom

1b The Lord Yahweh says this:
2 Look, I have reduced you
to the smallest of nations,
you are now beneath contempt.

3 Your proud heart has misled you,
you whose home is in the crannies
of the Rock,
who make the heights your dwelling,

9c The only hopeful passage in Amos, perhaps added later.

who think to yourself,
'Who can bring me down to earth?'
4 Though you soar like an eagle,
though you set your nest among the stars,
I shall bring you down from there!—
declares Yahweh.[a]

The annihilation of Edom

5 If thieves were to come to you
(or robbers during the night)
surely they would steal only as much
as they wanted?
If grape-pickers were to come to you,
surely they would leave a few gleanings?

But how you have been pillaged!
6 How Esau has been looted,
his hidden treasures routed out![b]
7 Your allies all pursued you
right to the frontier,
your confederates kept you in suspense,
then got the better of you,
your own guests laid a trap for you,
'He has quite lost his wits.'

8 When that day comes—
declares Yahweh—
shall I not eliminate sages from Edom
and intelligence from Mount Esau?

9 Your warriors, Teman,
will be so demoralised
that the people of Mount Esau
will be massacred
to the last one.

The guilt of Edom

For the slaughter,
10 for the violence
done to your brother Jacob,
shame will cover you
and you will be annihilated for ever.

11 On the day, when you stood aloof
while strangers carried off his riches,
while foreigners passed through his gate
and cast lots for Jerusalem,
you were as bad as the rest of them.

12 Do not feast your eyes on your brother
on the day of his misfortune.
Do not gloat over the children of Judah
on the day of their ruin.
Do not play the braggart
on the day of distress.

13 Do not enter my people's gate
on their day of calamity.
Do not, you especially,
feast your eyes on their suffering
on their day of calamity.
Do not touch their possessions
on their day of calamity.

14 Do not wait at the crossroads
to annihilate their fugitives.
Do not hand over their survivors
on the day of distress.
15 For the Day of Yahweh is near
for all the nations.
As you have done,
so will it be done to you:
your deeds will recoil on your own head.

The Day of Yahweh
Israel revenged on Edom

16 Just as you have drunk
on my holy mountain,
so will all the nations drink continually,
they will drink, will drink greedily,
but they will be
as though they had never been!

17 But on Mount Zion
will be those who have escaped
—it will be a sanctuary—
and the House of Jacob will recover
what is rightfully theirs.

18 Then the House of Jacob will be a fire,
the House of Joseph a flame,
and the House of Esau like stubble.
They will set it alight and burn it up,
and no one of the House of Esau
will survive.
Yahweh has spoken.

The new Israel

19 People from the Negeb will occupy
the Mount of Esau,
people from the lowlands
the country of the Philistines;
they will occupy Ephraim and Samaria,
and Benjamin will occupy Gilead.
20 The exiles of this army, the sons of Israel,
will have the Canaanites' land
as far as Zarephthah,

a || Jr 49:14–16.
b || Jr 49:9–10.

while the exiles from Jerusalem
now in Sepharad
will have the cities of the Negeb.

21 Victorious, they will climb Mount Zion
to rule over Mount Esau,
and sovereignty will be Yahweh's!

THE BOOK OF JONAH

A light satire, with no pretensions to being historical. It teaches the universality of God's love, probably to correct the exclusiveness of the post-exilic community. The willing obedience of the Ninevites contrasts pointedly with Jonah's obstinacy and bad temper. This fictional form is unique in the prophetic tradition.

JONAH

Jonah rebels against his mission

1 The word of Yahweh was addressed to
Jonah son of Amittai: 2 'Up!' he said, 'Go
to Nineveh, the great city, and proclaim to
them that their wickedness has forced itself
upon me.' 3 Jonah set about running away
from Yahweh, and going to Tarshish. He
went down to Jaffa and found a ship bound
for Tarshish; he paid his fare and boarded it,
to go with them to Tarshish, to get away from
Yahweh. 4 But Yahweh threw a hurricane at
the sea, and there was such a great storm at
sea that the ship threatened to break up. 5 The
sailors took fright, and each of them called
on his own god, and to lighten the ship they
threw the cargo overboard. Jonah, however,
had gone below, had lain down in the hold
and was fast asleep, 6 when the boatswain
went up to him and said, 'What do you
mean by sleeping? Get up! Call on your god!
Perhaps he will spare us a thought and not
leave us to die.' 7 Then they said to each other,
'Come on, let us draw lots to find out who is
to blame for bringing us this bad luck.' So
they cast lots, and the lot pointed to Jonah.
8 Then they said to him, 'Tell us, what is your
business? Where do you come from? What
is your country? What is your nationality?'
9 He replied, 'I am a Hebrew, and I worship
Yahweh, God of Heaven, who made both sea
and dry land.' 10 The sailors were seized with
terror at this and said, 'Why ever did you do
this?' since they knew that he was trying to
escape from Yahweh, because he had told
them so. 11 They then said, 'What are we to
do with you, to make the sea calm down for
us?' For the sea was growing rougher and
rougher. 12 He replied, 'Take me and throw
me into the sea, and then it will calm down
for you. I know it is my fault that this great
storm has struck you.' 13 The sailors rowed
hard in an effort to reach the shore, but in
vain, since the sea was growing rougher and
rougher. 14 So at last they called on Yahweh
and said, 'O, Yahweh, do not let us perish
for the sake of this man's life, and do not
hold us responsible for causing an innocent
man's death; for you, Yahweh, have acted as
you saw fit.' 15 And taking hold of Jonah they
threw him into the sea; and the sea stopped
raging. 16 At this, the men were seized with
dread of Yahweh; they offered a sacrifice to
Yahweh and made vows to him.

Jonah is saved

2 Now Yahweh ordained that a great fish
should swallow Jonah; and Jonah
remained in the belly of the fish for three

days and three nights. 2 From the belly of the
fish, Jonah prayed[a] to Yahweh, his God; he
said:

3 Out of my distress I cried to Yahweh
and he answered me,
from the belly of Sheol I cried out;
you heard my voice!

4 For you threw me into the deep,
into the heart of the seas,
and the floods closed round me.
All your waves and billows
passed over me;
5 then I thought, 'I am banished
from your sight;
how shall I ever see your holy Temple
again?'

6 The waters round me rose to my neck,
the deep was closing round me,
seaweed twining round my head.
7 To the roots of the mountains,
I sank into the underworld,
and its bars closed round me for ever.

But you raised my life from the Pit,
Yahweh my God!
8 When my soul was growing ever weaker,
Yahweh, I remembered you,
and my prayer reached you
in your holy Temple.

9 Some abandon their faithful love
by worshipping false gods,
10 but I shall sacrifice to you
with songs of praise.
The vow I have made I shall fulfil!
Salvation comes from Yahweh!

11 Yahweh spoke to the fish, which then
vomited Jonah onto the dry land.

The conversion of Nineveh and God's pardon

3 The word of Yahweh was addressed to
Jonah a second time. 2 'Up!' he said, 'Go
to Nineveh, the great city, and preach to it
as I shall tell you.' 3 Jonah set out and went
to Nineveh in obedience to the word of
Yahweh. Now Nineveh was a city great
beyond compare; to cross it took three days.
4 Jonah began by going a day's journey into
the city and then proclaimed, 'Only forty
days more and Nineveh will be overthrown.'
5 And the people of Nineveh believed in God;
they proclaimed a fast and put on sackcloth,
from the greatest to the least. 6 When the
news reached the king of Nineveh, he rose
from his throne, took off his robe, put on
sackcloth and sat down in ashes. 7 He then
had it proclaimed throughout Nineveh, by
decree of the king and his nobles, as follows:
'No person or animal, herd or flock, may eat
anything; they may not graze, they may not
drink any water. 8 All must put on sackcloth
and call on God with all their might; and let
everyone renounce his evil ways and violent
behaviour. 9 Who knows? Perhaps God will
change his mind and relent and renounce his
burning wrath, so that we shall not perish.'
10 God saw their efforts to renounce their evil
ways. And God relented about the disaster
which he had threatened to bring on them,
and did not bring it.

The grievance of the prophet and God's answer

4 This made Jonah very indignant; he fell
into a rage. 2 He prayed to Yahweh and
said, 'Please, Yahweh, isn't this what I said
would happen when I was still in my own
country? That was why I first tried to flee to
Tarshish, since I knew you were a tender,
compassionate God, slow to anger, rich in
faithful love, who relents about inflicting
disaster. 3 So now, Yahweh, please take my
life, for I might as well be dead as go on
living.' 4 Yahweh replied, 'Are you right to
be angry?'
5 Jonah then left the city and sat down to
the east of the city. There he made himself a
shelter and sat under it in the shade, to see
what would happen to the city. 6 Yahweh God
then ordained that a castor-oil plant should
grow up over Jonah to give shade for his
head and soothe his ill-humour; Jonah was
delighted with the castor-oil plant. 7 But at
dawn the next day, God ordained that a worm
should attack the castor-oil plant—and it
withered. 8 Next, when the sun rose, God
ordained that there should be a scorching
east wind; the sun beat down so hard on
Jonah's head that he was overcome and
begged for death, saying, 'I might as well be
dead as go on living.' 9 God said to Jonah,
'Are you right to be angry about the castor-
oil plant?' He replied, 'I have every right to
be angry, mortally angry!' 10 Yahweh replied,

2a The prayer is a later mosaic of psalms.

'You are concerned for the castor-oil plant which has not cost you any effort and which you did not grow, which came up in a night and has perished in a night. 11 So why should I not be concerned for Nineveh, the great city, in which there are more than a hundred and twenty thousand people who cannot tell their right hand from their left, to say nothing of all the animals?'

THE BOOK OF MICAH

Micah was a contemporary of Isaiah, and shares Isaiah's messianic hope in the line of David. He also attempts to convert swindlers, tyrants and corrupt judges. Some of the prophecies of hope may be of later date, to mitigate the terrible threats, as also the symmetrical arrangement into four sections.

PLAN OF THE BOOK

MICAH

1 The word of Yahweh which came to Micah of Moresheth during the reigns of Jotham, Ahaz and Hezekiah kings of Judah. His visions about Samaria and Jerusalem.

I: ISRAEL ON TRIAL

THREAT AND CONDEMNATION

The judgement of Samaria

2 Listen, all you peoples,
attend, earth and everyone on it!
Yahweh intends to give evidence
against you,
the Lord, from his holy temple.
3 For look, Yahweh is leaving his home,
down he comes,
he treads the heights of earth.
4 Beneath him, the mountains melt,
and valleys are torn open,
like wax near a fire,
like water pouring down a slope.
5 All this is because of the crime of Jacob,
the sin of the House of Israel.
What is the crime of Jacob?
Is it not Samaria?
What is the sin of the House of Judah?
Is it not Jerusalem?
6 So I shall make Samaria a ruin
in the open country,

a place for planting vines.
I shall send her stones
rolling into the valley,
until I have laid her foundations bare.
7 All her images will be shattered,
all her earnings consumed by fire.
I shall leave all her idols derelict—
they were amassed
out of prostitutes' earnings
and prostitutes' earnings
once more they will be.

Lament for Jerusalem and the lowland towns

8 This is why I shall howl and wail,
why I shall go barefoot and naked,
why I shall howl like the jackals,
why I shall shriek like the owls;
9 for there is no cure for the wounds
that Yahweh inflicts:
the blow falls on Judah,
it falls on the gateway of my people,
on Jerusalem itself.
10 *Do not announce it in Gath*,[a]
in . . .[b] shed no tears!
In Beth-Leaphrah
roll in the dust!
11 Sound the horn,
inhabitant of Shaphir!
She has not left her city,
she who lives in Zaanan.
Beth-Ezel is torn from its foundations,
from its strong supports.
12 What hope has she of happiness,
she who lives in Maroth?
Instead Yahweh sent down disaster
on the gateway of Jerusalem itself!
13 Harness the horse to the chariot,
you inhabitant of Lachish!
That is where the sin of the daughter
of Zion began;
the crimes of Israel can be traced to you!
14 And so you must provide a dowry
for Moresheth-Gath.
Beth-Achzib will prove a disappointment
for the kings of Israel.
15 The plunderer will come to you again,
you citizen of Mareshah!
And into Adullam will vanish
the glory of Israel.

16 Off with your hair, shave your head,
for the children that were your joy.
Make yourselves bald like the vulture,
for they have left you for exile.

Against land-grabbers

2 Disaster for those who plot evil,
who lie in bed planning mischief!
No sooner is it dawn than they do it,
since they have the power to do so.
2 Seizing the fields that they covet,
they take over houses as well,
owner and house they seize alike,
the man himself as well as his inheritance.
3 So Yahweh says this:
Look, I am now plotting
a disaster for this breed
from which you will not extricate
your necks;
you will not hold your heads up then,
for the times will be disastrous indeed.
4 That day they will make a satire on you,
they will strike up a dirge and say,
'We have been stripped of everything;
my people's land has been divided up,
no one else can restore it to them,
our fields have been awarded
to our despoiler.'

5 Because of this, you will have no one
to measure out a share
in Yahweh's community.

The prophet of misfortune

6 'Do not drivel,' they drivel,
'do not drivel like this!
Disgrace will not overtake us!
7 'Can the House of Jacob be accursed?
Has Yahweh grown short-tempered?
Is that his way of going to work?
His prophecies can only be favourable
for his people Israel!'
8 But you are the ones who play the enemy
to my people.
From the inoffensive man
you snatch his cloak,
on those who feel safe
you inflict the damage of war.
9 My people's women you evict
from the homes they love,
and deprive the children
of my glory for ever,
10 saying, 'Up and off with you!
You can't stay here!'

1a 2 S 1:20. The predictions pun on the names of the towns, e.g. Shaphir and *shophar* =horn.
1b Only one letter is left of this place-name.

For a worthless thing you exact
an extortionate pledge.
11 If a man of the spirit came
and invented this lie,
'I prophesy wine and liquor for you,'
he would be the prophet
for a people like this.

Promises of restoration

12 I shall assemble the whole of Jacob,
I shall gather the remnant of Israel,
I shall gather them together
like sheep in an enclosure.
And like a flock within their fold,
they will bleat far away from anyone,
13 their leader will break out first,
then all break out through the gate
and escape,
with their king leading the way
and with Yahweh at their head.

Against the rulers who oppress the people

3 Then I said,
'Kindly listen, you leaders
of the House of Jacob,
you princes of the House of Israel.
Surely you are the ones
who ought to know what is right,
2 and yet you hate what is good
and love what is evil,
skinning people alive,
pulling the flesh off their bones,
3 eating my people's flesh,
stripping off their skin,
breaking up their bones,
chopping them up small
like flesh for the pot,
like meat in the stew-pan?'
4 Then they will call to Yahweh,
but he will not answer them.
When the time comes
he will hide his face from them
because of the crimes
they have committed.

Against venal prophets

5 Yahweh says this against the prophets
who lead my people astray:
So long as they have something to eat
they cry 'Peace'.
But on anyone who puts nothing
into their mouths
they declare war.
6 And so, for you,
night will be without vision
and for you the darkness
without divination.
The sun will set for the prophets,
the daylight will go black above them.
7 Then the seers will be covered
with shame,
the diviners with confusion;
they will all put their hands
over their mouths
because there is no answer from God.
8 Not so with me, I am full of strength
(full of Yahweh's spirit),
of the sense of right, of energy
to accuse Jacob of his crime
and Israel of his sin.

To the rulers: prophecy of the ruin of Zion

9 Kindly listen to this,
you leaders of the House of Jacob,
you princes of the House of Israel,
who detest justice,
wresting it from its honest course,
10 who build Zion with blood,
and Jerusalem with iniquity!
11 Her leaders give verdicts for presents,
her priests take a fee for their rulings,
her prophets divine for money
and yet they rely on Yahweh!
'Isn't Yahweh among us?' they say,
'No disaster is going to overtake us.'
12 That is why, thanks to you,
Zion will become ploughland,
Jerusalem a heap of rubble
and the Temple Mount a wooded height.

II: PROMISES TO ZION

The future reign of Yahweh in Zion[a]

4 But in days to come
Yahweh's Temple Mountain
will tower above the mountains,
rise higher than the hills.
2 Then the peoples will stream to it,
then many nations will come and say,
'Come, we will go up
to Yahweh's mountain,
to the Temple of the God of Jacob,
so that he may teach us his ways
and we may walk in his paths;
for the Law issues from Zion
and Yahweh's word from Jerusalem.'
3 He will judge between many peoples
and arbitrate between mighty nations.
They will hammer their swords
into ploughshares
and their spears into bill-hooks.
Nation will not lift sword against nation
or ever again be trained to make war.
4 But each man will sit under his vine
and fig tree
with no one to trouble him.
The mouth of Yahweh Sabaoth
has spoken.

5 For all peoples go forward,
each in the name of its god,
while we go forward in the name
of Yahweh our God
for ever and ever.

The scattered flock is gathered to Zion

6 That day—declares Yahweh—
I shall gather in the lame
and bring together the strays
and those whom I have treated harshly.
7 From the footsore I shall make a remnant,
and from the far-flung a mighty nation.
And Yahweh will reign over them
on Mount Zion
thenceforth and for ever.

8 And to you, Tower of the Flock,
Ophel of the daughter of Zion,
to you your former sovereignty
will return,
the royal power
of the daughter of Jerusalem.

The siege, exile and liberation of Zion

9 Why are you crying out now?
Have you no king?
Has your counsellor perished,
for pangs to grip you
like those of a woman in labour?
10 Writhe in pain and cry aloud,
daughter of Zion, like a woman in labour,
for now you must leave the city
and camp in the open country;
to Babylon you must go,
and there you will be rescued;
there Yahweh will ransom you
from the clutches of your enemies.

Her enemies to be crushed on the threshing-floor

11 Now many nations
have mustered against you.
They say, 'Let us desecrate her,
let us gloat over Zion!'
12 But they do not know
Yahweh's thoughts,
they do not understand his design:
he has collected them
like sheaves on the threshing-floor.
13 Start your threshing, daughter of Zion,
for I shall make your horn like iron,
I shall make your hooves like bronze,
so that you can crush many peoples.
And you will devote
what they have stolen to Yahweh,
their wealth to the Lord
of the whole earth.

The distress and glory of the Davidic dynasty

14 Now look to your fortifications, Fortress!
They have laid siege to us;
the ruler of Israel will be struck
on the cheek with a rod.

5 But you (Bethlehem) Ephrathah,
the least of the clans of Judah,
from you will come for me
a future ruler of Israel
whose origins go back to the distant past,
to the days of old.
2 Hence Yahweh will abandon them

4a vv. 1–3 = Is 2:2–4. The universalist theme fits better in Isaiah.

only until she who is in labour gives birth,
and then those who survive of his race
will be reunited to the Israelites.
3He will take his stand
and he will shepherd them
with the power of Yahweh,
with the majesty of the name of his God,
and they will be secure,
for his greatness will extend
henceforth to the most distant parts
of the country.

The future conqueror of Assyria

4He himself will be peace!
Should the Assyrian invade our country,
should he set foot in our land,
we shall raise seven shepherds
against him,
eight leaders of men;
5they will shepherd Assyria with the sword,
the country of Nimrod with naked blade.
He will save us from the Assyrian,
should he invade our country,
should he set foot inside our frontiers.

The future role of the remnant

6Then what is left of Jacob,
surrounded by many peoples,
will be like a dew from Yahweh,
like showers on the grass,
which do not depend on human agency
and are beyond human control.

7Then what is left of Jacob,
surrounded by many peoples,
will be like a lion among the forest beasts,
like a fierce lion among flocks of sheep
trampling as he goes,
mangling his prey
which no one takes from him.

Yahweh will destroy all temptations

8You will be victorious over your foes
and all your enemies will be torn to pieces.
9When that day comes—
declares Yahweh—
I shall tear your horses away from you,
I shall destroy your chariots;
10I shall tear the cities from your country,
I shall overthrow all your fortresses;
11I shall tear the spells out of your hands
and you will have no more soothsayers;
12I shall tear away your images
and your sacred pillars from among you,
and no longer will you worship
things which your own hands have made!
13I shall uproot your sacred poles
and shall destroy your cities!

14In furious anger I shall wreak vengeance
on the nations who have disobeyed me!

III: ISRAEL AGAIN ON TRIAL

REPROACHES AND THREATS

Yahweh's case against Israel

6 Now listen to what Yahweh says:
'Stand up, state your case
to the mountains
and let the hills hear
what you have to say!'
2Listen, mountains,
to the case as Yahweh puts it,
give ear, you foundations of the earth,
for Yahweh has a case against his people
and he will argue it with Israel.
3'My people, what have I done to you,
how have I made you tired of me?
Answer me!
4For I brought you up from Egypt,
I ransomed you
from the place of slave-labour
and sent Moses, Aaron and Miriam
to lead you.
5My people, please remember:
what was Balak king of Moab's plan
and how did Balaam son of Beor
answer him?
. . .[a] from Shittim to Gilgal,
for you to know Yahweh's saving justice.

6'With what shall I enter
Yahweh's presence
and bow down before God All-high?
Shall I enter with burnt offerings,
with calves one year old?

6a Some words are missing in the Hebrew text.

7 Will he be pleased with rams
by the thousand,
with ten thousand streams of oil?
Shall I offer my eldest son
for my wrong-doing,
the child of my own body for my sin?
8 'You have already been told what is right
and what Yahweh wants of you.
Only this, to do what is right,
to love loyalty
and to walk humbly with your God.'

Against tricksters in the city

9 Yahweh's voice! He thunders to the city,
'Listen, tribe of assembled citizens!
10 Can I overlook the false measure,
that abomination, the short bushel?
11 Can I connive at rigged scales
and at the bag of fraudulent weights?
12 For the rich there are steeped in violence,
and the citizens there are habitual liars.
13 'I myself have therefore
begun to strike you down,
to bring you to ruin for your sins.
14 You will eat but not be satisfied;
you will store up but never keep safe;
what you do keep safe
I shall hand over to the sword;
15 you will sow but will not reap,
press the olive
but will not rub yourself with oil,
tread the grape
but will not drink the wine.

The example of Samaria

16 'For you keep the laws of Omri;
what the House of Ahab did,
you have done;
by modelling yourselves
on their standards,
you force me to make
an appalling example of you
and reduce your citizens
to a laughing-stock;
hence you will endure the scorn
of other peoples.'

Universal injustice

7 How wretched I am,
a harvester in summer time,
like a gleaner at the vintage:
not a single cluster to eat,
none of those early figs I love!
2 The faithful have vanished from the land:
there is no one honest left.
All of them are on the alert for blood,
every man hunting his brother with a net.
3 Their hands are adept at wrong-doing:
the official makes his demands,
the judge gives judgement for a bribe,
the man in power
pronounces as he pleases.
4 The best of them is like a briar,
the most honest of them
like a thorn-hedge.
Now from the north
their punishment approaches!
That will be when they are confounded!
5 Trust no neighbour,
put no confidence in a friend;
do not open your mouth
to the wife who shares your bed.
6 For son insults father,
daughter rebels against mother,
daughter-in-law against mother-in-law;
a person's enemies come
from within the household itself.

7 But I shall look to Yahweh,
my hope is in the God who will save me;
my God will hear me.[a]

IV: HOPE FOR THE FUTURE

Zion insulted by enemies

8 Do not gloat over me, my enemy:
though I have fallen, I shall rise;
though I live in darkness,
Yahweh is my light.

9 I must endure Yahweh's anger
for I have sinned against him,
until he takes up my cause
and rights my wrongs;
he will bring me out into the light,

7a Originally the end of the book. vv. 8–11 are exilic, vv. 14–17 even later, and vv. 18–20 a final psalm.

and then I shall contemplate
his saving justice.
10 When my enemy sees this,
she will be covered with shame,
having sneered,
'Where is Yahweh your God?'
This time, I shall be watching
as she is trampled underfoot
like mud in the streets.

A prophecy of restoration

11 That will be the day
for rebuilding your walls!
The day for expanding your frontiers!
12 The day when others come to you
all the way from Assyria, from Egypt,
from Tyre and all the way
from the Euphrates,
from sea to sea, from the mountains
to the mountains!
13 The earth will become a desert
by reason of its inhabitants,
in return for what they have done.

A prayer for the confusion of Zion's enemies

14 With shepherd's crook
lead your people to pasture,
the flock that is your heritage,
living confined in a forest
with meadow land all round.
Let them graze in Bashan and Gilead
as in the days of old!
15 As in the days
when you came out of Egypt,
grant us to see wonders!
16 The nations will see and be confounded
in spite of all their power;
they will put their hands
over their mouths,
their ears will be deafened.
17 They will lick the dust like snakes,
like reptiles that crawl on the earth.
They will creep trembling
out of their lairs,
in terror before you.

A plea for God's forgiveness

18 What god can compare with you
for pardoning guilt
and for overlooking crime?
He does not harbour anger for ever,
since he delights in showing faithful love.
19 Once more have pity on us,
tread down our faults;
throw all our sins
to the bottom of the sea.
20 Grant Jacob your faithfulness,
and Abraham your faithful love,
as you swore to our ancestors
from the days of long ago.

THE BOOK OF NAHUM

A fine, short alphabetical poem on the wrath of Yahweh leads into a prophecy of the fall of Nineveh. Nineveh fell in 612 BC and the prophecy must be close to this date.

NAHUM

1 Prophecy about Nineveh. Book of the vision of Nahum of Elkosh.

PRELUDE

Psalm. The wrath of Yahweh

Aleph 2 Yahweh is a jealous
and vengeful God,
Yahweh takes vengeance,
he is rich in wrath;
Yahweh takes vengeance on his foes,
he stores up fury for his enemies.
3 Yahweh is slow to anger
but great in power,
Yahweh never lets evil
go unpunished.
Bet In storm and whirlwind
he takes his way,
the clouds are the dust
stirred up by his feet.
Gimel 4 He rebukes the sea, dries it up,
and makes all the rivers run dry.
Dalet . . . Bashan and Carmel wither,
the greenery of the Lebanon
withers too.
He 5 The mountains tremble before him,
the hills reel;
Waw the earth collapses before him,
the world and all who live in it.
Zain 6 His fury—who can withstand it?
Who can endure his burning wrath?
Het His anger pours out like fire
and the rocks break apart
before him.
Tet 7 Yahweh is better than a fortress
in time of distress;
Yod he recognises those who trust in him
8 even when the flood rushes on;
Kaph he will make an end once and for all
of those who defy him,
and pursue his foes into darkness.

Prophetic judgement on Judah and Assyria

9 What are your thoughts about Yahweh?
He it is who makes a final end:
his adversaries
will not rise up a second time;
10 like a thicket of tangled brambles,
like dry straw,
they will be burnt up completely.

To Assyria
11 From you has emerged
someone plotting evil against Yahweh,
one of Belial's counsellors.[a]

To Judah
12 Yahweh says this:
Unopposed and many though they be,
they will be cut down and pass away.
Though I have made you suffer,
I shall make you suffer no more,
13 for now I shall break his yoke
which presses hard on you
and snap your chains.

1a Belial (=useless) stands for the power of evil.

To the king of Nineveh
14As for you, this is Yahweh's decree:
You will have no heirs to your name,
from the temple of your gods I shall remove
carved image and cast image,
and I shall devastate your tomb,
for you are accursed!

2 *To Judah*
See on the mountains the feet of the herald!
'Peace!' he proclaims.
Judah, celebrate your feasts,
carry out your vows,
for Belial
will never pass through you again;
he has been utterly destroyed.

THE FALL OF NINEVEH

The assault

2The destroyer has advanced on you,
guarding the siege-works,
watching the road,
bracing himself, mustering great strength!
3(For Yahweh has restored
the vine of Jacob,
yes, the vine of Israel,
although the plunderers
had plundered them,
although they had snapped off
their vine-shoots!)
4The shields of his fighting men show red,
his warriors are dressed in scarlet;
the metal of the chariots sparkles
as he prepares for battle;
the horsemen are impatient for action;
5the chariots storm through the streets,
jostling one another in the squares;
they look like blazing flames,
like lightning they dash to and fro.
6His captains are called out;
stumbling as they go,
they speed towards the wall,
and the mantelet is put in position.
7The sluices of the River are opened,
and the palace melts in terror.
8Beauty[a] is taken captive, carried away,
her slave-girls moaning like doves
9and beating their breasts.
Nineveh is like a lake,
whose waters are draining away.
'Stop! Stop!'
But no one turns back.
10'Plunder the silver! Plunder the gold!'
There is no end to the treasure,
a mass of everything you could desire!
11Ravaged, wrecked, ruined!
Heart fails and knees give way,
anguish is in the loins of all,
and every face grows pale!

Sentence passed on the lion of Assyria

12Where is the lions' den now,
the cave of the lion's whelps,
where the lion and lioness
walked with their cubs
and no one molested them,
13where the lion would tear up food
for his whelps
and strangle the kill for his mates,
where he filled his caverns with prey
and his lairs with spoil?
14Look, I am against you!—
declares Yahweh Sabaoth—
I shall send your chariots up in smoke,
and the sword will devour your whelps;
I shall cut short
your depredations on earth,
and the voices of your envoys
will be heard no more.

Sentence passed on Nineveh the harlot

3 Disaster to the city of blood,
packed throughout with lies,
stuffed with booty,
where plundering has no end!
2The crack of the whip!
The rumble of wheels!
Galloping horse,
jolting chariot,
3charging cavalry,
flashing swords,
gleaming spears,
a mass of wounded,
hosts of dead,
countless corpses;
they stumble over corpses—
4because of the countless whorings
of the harlot,
the graceful beauty, the cunning witch,

2a The statue of the goddess Ishtar, a fertility deity.

who enslaved nations by her harlotries
and tribes by her spells.

5 Look, I am against you!—
declares Yahweh Sabaoth—
I shall lift your skirts as high as your face
and show your nakedness to the nations,
your shame to the kingdoms.
6 I shall pelt you with filth,
I shall shame you
and put you in the pillory.
7 Then all who look at you
will shrink from you and say,
'Nineveh has been ruined!'
Who will mourn for her?
Where would I find
people to comfort you?

The lesson of Thebes

8 Are you better off than No-Amon[a]
situated among rivers,
her defences the seas,
her rampart the waters?
9 In Ethiopia and Egypt
lay her strength, and it was boundless;
Put and the Libyans served in her army.
10 But she too went into exile,
into captivity;
her little ones too were dashed to pieces
at every crossroad;
lots were drawn for her nobles,
all her great men were put in chains.

11 You too will become drunk,
you will go into hiding;
you too will have to search
for a refuge from the enemy.

Nineveh's preparations useless

12 Your fortifications are all fig trees,
with early ripening figs:
as soon as they are shaken,
they fall into the mouth of the eater.
13 Look at your people:
you are a nation of women!
The gates of your country
gape open to your enemies;
fire has devoured their bars!
14 Draw yourselves water for the siege,
strengthen your fortifications!
Into the mud with you, puddle the clay,
repair the brick-kiln!
15 There the fire will burn you up,
the sword will cut you down.

The locusts fly away

Make yourselves as numerous as locusts,
make yourselves as numerous
as the hoppers,
16a let your commercial agents
outnumber the stars of heaven,
17a your garrisons, like locusts,
and your marshals,
like swarms of hoppers!
They settle on the walls
when the day is cold.
The sun appears,
16b the locusts spread their wings,
they fly away,
17b away they fly, no one knows where.

A funeral lament

Alas, 18 your shepherds are asleep,
king of Assyria,
your bravest men slumber;
your people are scattered
on the mountains
with no one to gather them.
19 There is no remedy for your wound,
your injury is past healing.
All who hear the news of you
clap their hands at your downfall.
For who has not felt
your unrelenting cruelty?

3a Thebes in Upper Egypt, taken by Assyria in 633 BC.

THE BOOK OF HABAKKUK

In this carefully composed book, Part I considers the problem of the triumph of the wicked; Part II curses the oppressor, the threatening Babylonians (so that the book should be dated 605–597). The final liturgical psalm celebrates God's victory.

PLAN OF THE BOOK

HABAKKUK

Title

1 The charge that Habakkuk the prophet received in a vision.

I: DIALOGUE BETWEEN THE PROPHET AND HIS GOD

First complaint of the prophet: lawlessness prevails

2 How long, Yahweh, am I to cry for help
while you will not listen;
to cry, 'Violence!' in your ear
while you will not save?

3 Why do you make me see wrong-doing,
why do you countenance oppression?
Plundering and violence confront me,
contention and discord flourish.

4 And so the law loses its grip
and justice never emerges,
since the wicked outwits the upright
and so justice comes out perverted.

First answer: the Chaldaeans as instrument of God's justice

5 Cast your eyes over the nations, look,
and be amazed, astounded.
For I am doing something
in your own days
which you will not believe
if you are told of it.
6 For look, I am stirring up the Chaldaeans,
that fierce and fiery nation
who march miles across country
to seize the homes of others.
7 They are dreadful and awesome,
a law and authority to themselves.

8 Their horses are swifter than leopards,
fiercer than wolves at night;
their horsemen gallop on,
their horsemen advance from afar,
swooping like an eagle anxious to feed.

9 They are all bent on violence,
their faces scorching like an east wind;
they scoop up prisoners like sand.

10 They scoff at kings,
they despise princes.
They make light of all fortresses:
they heap up earth and take them.
11 Then the wind changes and is gone . . .
Guilty is he
who makes his strength his god.

Second complaint of the prophet: the tyranny of the conqueror

12 Surely you, Yahweh,
are from ancient times,
my holy God, who never dies!
Yahweh, you have appointed him
to execute judgement;
O Rock, you have set him firm to punish.

13 Your eyes are too pure to rest on evil,
you cannot look on at oppression.
Why do you look on at those
who play the traitor,
why say nothing
while the wicked swallows someone
more upright than himself?
14 Why treat people like fish of the sea,
like gliding creatures who have no leader?
15 They haul them all up on their hook,
they catch them in their net,
they sweep them up in their dragnet
and then make merry and rejoice.

16 And so they offer a sacrifice to their net,
and burn incense to their dragnet,
for by these they get a rich living
and live off the fat of the land.
17 Are they to go on
emptying their net unceasingly,
slaughtering the nations without pity?

Second answer: the upright will live through faithfulness

2 I shall stand at my post,
I shall station myself on my watch-tower,
watching to see what he will say to me,
what answer he will make
to my complaints.

2 Then Yahweh answered me and said,
'Write the vision down,
inscribe it on tablets
to be easily read.
3 For the vision is for its appointed time,
it hastens towards its end
and it will not lie;
although it may take some time,
wait for it,
for come it certainly will before too long.

4 'You see, anyone
whose heart is not upright
will succumb,
but the upright will live
through faithfulness.'[a]

II: CURSES ON THE OPPRESSOR

Prelude

5 Now, surely, wealth is treacherous!
He is arrogant, for ever on the move,
with appetite as large as Sheol
and as insatiable as Death,
gathering in all the nations,
and making a harvest of all peoples.
6 Are not the peoples all bound to satirise
and make up cryptic riddles about him?
As for instance:

Five imprecations

I

Disaster to anyone
who amasses goods not his
(for how long?)
and to anyone who weighs himself down
with goods taken in pledge!
7 Will not your creditors
suddenly stand up,
will not those who make you shiver
wake up,
and you will fall a prey to them?
8 Since you have plundered many nations,
all the nations that remain
will plunder you,
because of the bloodshed and violence
done to the country,
to the city and to all who live in it.

II

9 Disaster to anyone
who amasses ill-gotten gains
for his house,
so as to fix his nest on high
and so evade the reach of misfortune!

2a Paul uses the Gk version 'faith' for the doctrine of justification by faith in Rm 1:17.

10 You have conspired
to bring shame on your house:
by overthrowing many peoples
you have worked your own ruin.

11 For the very stone
will protest from the wall,
and the beam will respond
from the framework.

III

12 Disaster to anyone
who builds a town with bloodshed
and founds a city on wrong-doing!

13 Is it not thanks to Yahweh Sabaoth
that the peoples' toil is fuel for the fire,
and the nations' labour came to nothing?

14 *But the earth will be full*
of the knowledge of the glory of Yahweh
as the waters cover the depths of the sea. [b]

IV

15 Disaster to anyone
who makes his neighbours drink,
pouring out his poison
until they are drunk,
so that he can see them naked!
16 You are full of shame, not glory!
Your turn now to drink
and show your foreskin.
The cup in Yahweh's right hand
comes round to you,
and disgrace will overshadow your glory.

17 For the violence done to the Lebanon
will overwhelm you
and the massacre of animals
will terrify you,
because of the bloodshed and violence
done to the country,
to the city and to all who live in it.

V

19 [c] Disaster to anyone who says to the log,
'Wake up!',
to the dumb stone, 'On your feet!'
(This is the prophecy!)
Look, he is encased in gold and silver,
—but not a breath of life inside it!

18 What use is a sculpted image
that a sculptor should make it?
—a metal image, a lying instructor!
And why does the image-maker
put his trust in it,
that he should make dumb idols?

20 But Yahweh is in his holy Temple:
let the whole earth be silent before him.

III: PLEA TO YAHWEH FOR DELIVERANCE

Title

3 A prayer of the prophet Habakkuk; tone as for dirges.

Prayer

2 Yahweh, I have heard of your renown;
your work, Yahweh,
inspires me with dread.
Make it live again in our time,
make it known in our time;
in wrath remember mercy.

Theophany: Yahweh's approach

3 Eloah[a] comes from Teman,
and the Holy One
from Mount Paran. *Pause*
His majesty covers the heavens,
and his glory fills the earth.

4 His brightness is like the day,
rays flash from his hands,
that is where his power lies hidden.

5 Pestilence goes before him
and Plague follows close behind.

6 When he stands up,
he makes the earth tremble,
with his glance
he makes the nations quake.
And the eternal mountains are dislodged,
the everlasting hills sink down,
his pathway from of old.

7 I saw the tents of Cushan in trouble,
the tent-curtains of Midian shuddering.

2b Is 11:9.
2c vv. 18 and 19 have been transposed.
3a An ancient name for God. Teman is a district, Paran a mountain in Edom.

Yahweh's battle

8 Yahweh, are you enraged with the rivers,
are you angry with the sea,
that you should mount your chargers,
your rescuing chariots?

9 You uncover your bow,
and give the string its fill of arrows.
Pause

You drench the soil with torrents;
10 the mountains see you and tremble,
great floods sweep by,
the abyss roars aloud,
lifting high its waves.

11 Sun and moon stay inside their dwellings,
they flee at the light of your arrows,
at the flash of your lightning-spear.

12 In rage you stride across the land,
in anger you trample the nations.

13 You marched to save your people,
to save your anointed one;
you wounded
the head of the house of the wicked,
laid bare the foundation to the rock.
Pause

14 With your shafts
you pierced the leader of his warriors
who stormed out with shouts of joy
to scatter us,
as if they meant to devour
some poor wretch in their lair.

15 With your horses
you trampled through the sea,
through the surging abyss!

Conclusion: human fear and faith in God

16 When I heard, I trembled to the core,
my lips quivered at the sound;
my bones became disjointed
and my legs gave way beneath me.

Calmly I await the day of anguish
which is dawning
on the people now attacking us.

17 (For the fig tree is not to blossom,
nor will the vines bear fruit,
the olive crop will disappoint
and the fields will yield no food;
the sheep will vanish from the fold;
no cattle in the stalls.)

18 But I shall rejoice in Yahweh,
I shall exult in God my Saviour.

19 Yahweh my Lord is my strength,
he will make my feet as light as a doe's,
and set my steps on the heights.

For the choirmaster; on stringed instruments.

THE BOOK OF ZEPHANIAH

Zephaniah preached reform shortly before the deuteronomic reform occurred, early in the reign of King Josiah (640–609 BC). His principal theme is the Day of the Lord, which will purify Judah and the nations. Those who are left will form a humble remnant devoted to Yahweh.

PLAN OF THE BOOK

ZEPHANIAH

1 The word of Yahweh which was addressed to Zephaniah son of Cushi, son of Gedaliah, son of Amariah, son of Hezekiah, in the days of Josiah son of Amon king of Judah.

I: THE DAY OF YAHWEH FOR JUDAH

Prelude: judgement on all creation

2 I shall sweep away everything
off the face of the earth,
declares Yahweh.
3 I shall sweep away humans and animals,
the birds of the air and the fish of the sea,
I shall topple the wicked
and wipe all people
off the face of the earth
—declares Yahweh.

Against the worshippers of alien gods

4 I shall raise my hand against Judah
and against all who live in Jerusalem,
and from this place
I will wipe out Baal's remnant,
the very name of his priests,
5 and those who prostrate themselves
on the roofs
before the array of heaven,
and those who prostrate themselves
before Yahweh
but swear by Milcom,[a]
6 and those who have turned their back
on Yahweh,
who do not seek Yahweh
and do not consult him.

7 Silence before Lord Yahweh,
for the Day of Yahweh is near!
Yahweh has prepared a sacrifice,
he has consecrated his guests.

Against the courtiers

8 On the Day of Yahweh's sacrifice,
I shall punish the courtiers,
the royal princes
and all who dress
in outlandish clothes.
9 On that day I shall punish
all who go up the Step
and fill the Temple of their lords,
with violence and deceit.

Against the merchants of Jerusalem

10 On that Day—declares Yahweh—
uproar will be heard from the Fish Gate,
wailing from the New Quarter
and a great crash from the hills.
11 Wail, you who live in the Hollow,
for it is all over with the merchants,
all the money-bags have been wiped out!

Against unbelievers

12 When that time comes
I shall search Jerusalem by lamplight
and punish the men
stagnating over the remains of their wine,
who say in their hearts,
'Yahweh can do nothing,
either good or bad.'
13 For this, their wealth will be looted
and their houses laid in ruins;
they will build houses
but not live in them,
they will plant vineyards
but not drink their wine.

The Day of Yahweh

14 The great Day of Yahweh is near,
near, and coming with great speed.
How bitter the sound
of the Day of Yahweh,
the Day when the warrior
shouts his cry of war.
15 That Day is a day of retribution,
a day of distress and tribulation,

1a A god of Ammon.

a day of ruin and of devastation,
a day of darkness and gloom,
a day of cloud and thick fog,
16 a day of trumpet blast and battle cry
against fortified town
and high corner-tower.
17 I shall bring such distress on humanity
that they will grope their way
like the blind
for having sinned against Yahweh.
Their blood will be poured out like mud,
yes, their corpses like dung;
18 nor will their silver or gold
be able to save them.
On the Day of Yahweh's anger,
by the fire of his jealousy,
the whole earth will be consumed.
For he will destroy, yes, annihilate
everyone living on earth.

Conclusion: a call to conversion

2 Gather together, gather together,
nations without shame,
2 before you are dispersed like chaff
which disappears in a day;
before Yahweh's burning anger
overtakes you
(before the Day of Yahweh's anger
overtakes you).
3 Seek Yahweh,
all you humble of the earth,
who obey his commands.
Seek uprightness,
seek humility:
you may perhaps find shelter
on the Day of Yahweh's anger.

II: AGAINST THE NATIONS

The enemy to the west: the Philistines

4 For Gaza will be abandoned
and Ashkelon reduced to ruins;
Ashdod will be driven out
in broad daylight
and Ekron[a] uprooted.
5 Disaster to the members
of the coastal league,
to the nation of the Cherethites!
This is the word of Yahweh against you:
I shall subdue you, land of the Philistines,
I shall destroy you
till there are no inhabitants left;
6 and the coastal league
will be reduced to pasture land,
to grazing grounds for shepherds
and folds for sheep;
7 and the league will belong
to the remnant of the House of Judah;
they will pasture their flocks there,
at night they will rest
in the houses of Ashkelon;
for, when Yahweh their God
has punished them,
he will restore their fortunes.

The enemies to the east: Moab and Ammon

8 I have heard the taunt of Moab
and the insults of the Ammonites,
as they taunted my people
and boasted of their own domains.
9 For this, as I live—
declares Yahweh Sabaoth,
God of Israel—
Moab will become like Sodom
and the Ammonites like Gomorrah:
a realm of nettles, a heap of salt,
a desolation for ever.
What is left of my people
will plunder them,
the survivors of my nation
will take their heritage.
10 This will be the price of their pride
for having taunted and boasted
over the people of Yahweh Sabaoth.
11 Yahweh will be fearsome to them,
for he will scatter all the gods of the earth,
and they will bow down to him,
each from his own place—
all the islands of the nations.

2a Four of the five Philistine coastal cities. Gath was already in ruins.

The enemy to the south: Ethiopia

12 You Ethiopians too
will be run through by my sword.

The enemy to the north: Assyria

13 He will raise his hand against the north
and bring Assyria down in ruins;
he will make Nineveh a waste,
as dry as a desert.
14 Flocks will rest inside there,
so will wild animals;
pelican and porcupine
will nest round her cornices at night;
the owl will hoot at the window
and the raven croak on the doorstep—
for the cedar has been torn down.
15 This is what the city will be like,
once living happy and carefree
and thinking to itself,
'I have no rival—not I!'
And what will it be now? A ruin,
a lair for wild beasts to rest in,
and everyone who passes by
will whistle and throw up his hands.

III: AGAINST JERUSALEM

Against the rulers of Judah

3 Disaster to the rebellious,
the befouled,
the tyrannical city!
2 She has not listened to the call,
she has not bowed to correction,
she has not trusted in Yahweh,
she has not drawn near to her God.
3 The rulers she has
are roaring lions,
her judges are wolves of the wastelands
which leave nothing over
for the morning,
4 her prophets are braggarts,
impostors,
her priests have profaned what is holy
and violated the Law.

5 Yahweh the Upright is in her,
he does no wrong;
morning by morning he gives judgement,
each dawn unfailingly
(but the wrong-doer knows no shame).

The example of the nations

6 I have exterminated the nations,
their corner-towers lie in ruins;
I have emptied their streets,
no one walks through them;
their cities have been destroyed
and are now deserted and unpeopled.
7 I thought, 'At least you will fear me,
at least you will bow to correction,'
and none of the punishments
I brought on them
will disappear from their view.
But no, it only made them more anxious
to do whatever was corrupt.

8 So wait for me—declares Yahweh—
for the day when I rise as accuser,
for I am determined to gather the nations,
to assemble the kingdoms,
and on you to vent my fury,
the whole heat of my anger
(for the whole earth will be devoured
by the fire of my jealousy).

IV: PROMISES

Conversion of the nations

9 Yes, then I shall purge
the lips of the peoples,
so that all may invoke
the name of Yahweh
and serve him shoulder to shoulder.
10 From beyond the rivers of Ethiopia,
my suppliants will bring me tribute.

The humble remnant of Israel

11 When that Day comes
you will never again be ashamed
of all the deeds
with which you once rebelled against me,
for I shall rid you
of those who exult in your pride;
never again will you strut
on my holy mountain.

12 But in you I shall leave surviving
a humble[a] and lowly people,
13 and those who are left in Israel
will take refuge in the name of Yahweh.
They will do no wrong,
will tell no lies;
nor will a deceitful tongue
be found in their mouths.
But they will be able to graze and rest
with no one to alarm them.

Psalms of joy in Zion[b]

14 Shout for joy, daughter of Zion,
Israel, shout aloud!
Rejoice, exult with all your heart,
daughter of Jerusalem!
15 Yahweh has repealed your sentence;
he has turned your enemy away.
Yahweh is king among you, Israel,
you have nothing more to fear.

16 When that Day comes,
the message for Jerusalem will be:
Zion, have no fear,
do not let your hands fall limp.
17 Yahweh your God is there with you,
the warrior-Saviour.
He will rejoice over you with happy song,
he will renew you by his love,
he will dance with shouts of joy for you,
18 as on a day of festival.

Return of the exiles

I have taken away your misfortune,
no longer need you bear
the disgrace of it.
19 I am taking action here and now
against your oppressors.
When that time comes
I will rescue the lame,
and gather the strays,
and I will win them praise and renown
when I restore their fortunes.

20 At that time I shall be your guide,
at the time when I gather you in,
I shall give you praise and renown
among all the peoples of the earth
when I restore your fortunes
under your own eyes,
declares Yahweh.

THE BOOK OF HAGGAI

Haggai is the first prophet of the restored community after the Exile, prophesying in Jerusalem from August to December 520 BC. His message, amid the depression after the return from exile, is encouragement to rebuild the Temple and offer pure worship there.

3a In the prophets the humble and oppressed, specially dependent on Yahweh, are the object of his special care. here and in the Pss poverty is a spiritual quality, openness to God's love.
3b These two final psalms were probably added later.

HAGGAI

The summons to rebuild the Temple

1 In the second year of King Darius, on the first day of the sixth month, the word of Yahweh was addressed through the prophet Haggai to Zerubbabel son of Shealtiel governor of Judah and to Joshua son of Jehozadak the high priest as follows, 2'Yahweh Sabaoth says this, "This people says: The time has not yet come to rebuild the Temple of Yahweh." ' 3(And the word of Yahweh was addressed through the prophet Haggai, as follows,) 4"Is this a time for you to live in your panelled houses, when this House lies in ruins? 5So now, Yahweh Sabaoth says this, "Think carefully about your behaviour. 6You have sown much and harvested little; you eat but never have enough, drink but never have your fill, put on clothes but feel no warmth. The wage-earner gets his wages only to put them in a bag with a hole in it." 7Yahweh Sabaoth says this, "Think carefully about your behaviour. 8Go up into the hills, fetch timber and rebuild the House; and I shall take pleasure in it and manifest my glory there—Yahweh says. 9The abundance you expected proved to be little. When you brought the harvest in, I blasted it. And why?—Yahweh Sabaoth declares. Because while my House lies in ruins, each of you is busy with his own house. 10That is why the sky has withheld the rain and the earth withheld its yield. 11I have called down drought on land and hills, on grain, on new wine, on olive oil and on all the produce of the ground, on humans and animals and all your labours." '

12Zerubbabel son of Shealtiel, Joshua son of Jehozadak the high priest and the entire remnant of the people, paid attention to the voice of Yahweh their God and to the words of the prophet Haggai, which Yahweh their God had sent him to deliver. And the people were filled with fear before Yahweh. 13Haggai, the messenger of Yahweh, then passed on Yahweh's message to the people, 'I am with you—declares Yahweh.' 14And Yahweh roused the spirit of Zerubbabel son of Shealtiel governor of Judah, the spirit of Joshua son of Jehozadak the high priest and the spirit of the entire remnant of the people; they came and set to work in the Temple of Yahweh Sabaoth, their God. 15This was on the twenty-fourth day of the sixth month.

The future glory of the Temple

In the second year of King Darius,

2 on the twenty-first day of the seventh month, the word of Yahweh was addressed through the prophet Haggai, as follows, 2'You are to speak to Zerubbabel son of Shealtiel governor of Judah, to Joshua son of Jehozadak the high priest and to the remnant of the people. Say this, 3"Is there anyone left among you who saw this Temple in its former glory? And how does it look to you now? Does it not seem as though there is nothing there? 4But take courage now, Zerubbabel!—Yahweh declares. Courage, Joshua son of Jehozadak high priest! Courage, all you people of the country!—Yahweh declares. To work! I am with you—Yahweh Sabaoth declares—5and my spirit is present among you. Do not be afraid! 6For Yahweh Sabaoth says this: A little while now, and I shall shake the heavens and the earth, the sea and the dry land. 7I shall shake all the nations, and the treasures of all the nations will flow in, and I shall fill this Temple with glory, says Yahweh Sabaoth. 8Mine is the silver, mine the gold!—Yahweh Sabaoth declares. 9The glory of this new Temple will surpass that of the old, says Yahweh Sabaoth, and in this place I shall give peace—Yahweh Sabaoth declares." '

Haggai consults the priests

10On the twenty-fourth day of the ninth month, in the second year of Darius, the word of Yahweh was addressed to the prophet Haggai as follows, 11'Yahweh Sabaoth says this, "Ask the priests to give a ruling on this: 12If someone is carrying consecrated meat in the fold of his gown and allows the fold to touch bread, broth, wine, oil or food of any kind, will that become holy?" ' The priests replied, 'No.' 13Haggai then said, 'If anyone rendered unclean by contact with a corpse touches any of these things, will that become unclean?' The priests replied, 'It will become unclean.' [14]Haggai then spoke out. 'It is the same with this people,' he said, 'the same with this nation, in my view—Yahweh declares—the same with everything they turn their hands to; and whatever they offer here is unclean.

A promise of agricultural prosperity

[15]'So now think carefully, today and henceforth: before one stone had been laid on another in the sanctuary of Yahweh, [16]what state were you in? You would come to a twenty-measure heap and find only ten; you would come to a vat to draw fifty measures and find only twenty. [17]Everything you turned your hands to, I struck with wind-blast, mildew and hail, and still you would not return to me—Yahweh declares. [18]So think carefully, today and henceforth (from the twenty-fourth day of the ninth month, from the day the foundation of the sanctuary of Yahweh was laid, think carefully) [19]if seed-corn is still short in the barn, and if vine and fig tree, pomegranate and olive tree still bear no fruit.

'From today onwards I intend to bless you.'

The promise to Zerubbabel

[20]On the twenty-fourth day of the month the word of Yahweh was addressed a second time to Haggai, as follows, [21]'Speak to Zerubbabel governor of Judah. Say this, "I am going to shake the heavens and the earth. [22]I shall overturn the thrones of kingdoms and destroy the power of the kings of the nations. I shall overthrow the chariots and their crews; horses and their riders will fall, every one to the sword of his comrade. [23]When that day comes—Yahweh Sabaoth declares—I shall take you, Zerubbabel son of Shealtiel my servant—Yahweh declares—and make you like a signet ring. For I have chosen you—Yahweh Sabaoth declares." '

THE BOOK OF ZECHARIAH

The book falls into two parts. The first (chh. 1–8), chiefly in prose, is marked by eight symbolic visions and their interpretation; it is the work of the prophet Zechariah and is dated 520–517 BC. Occurring soon after the return from exile, it concentrates on the questions which concerned also Haggai, the restoration of the Temple and purity of observance. It is shot through with the hope of a royal Messiah.

The second part (chh. 9–14) probably dates from 200 years later: chapters 9–11 provide a poetic account of the messianic hope, and chapters 12–14 a prose prediction of the triumph of Yahweh at Jerusalem in the last days.

ZECHARIAH

FIRST PART

A summons to conversion

1 In the second year of Darius, in the eighth
month, the word of Yahweh was
addressed to the prophet Zechariah (son of
Berechiah), son of Iddo, as follows, [2]'Yahweh
was deeply angry with your ancestors. [3]So
say this to them, "Yahweh Sabaoth[a] says this:
Return to me—Yahweh Sabaoth declares—
and I will return to you, says Yahweh
Sabaoth. [4]Do not be like your ancestors
when the prophets in the past cried to them:
Yahweh Sabaoth says this: Turn back from
your evil ways and evil deeds—they would
not listen or pay attention to me—Yahweh
declares. [5]Where are your ancestors now?
And the prophets, do they live for ever? [6]But
did not my words and statutes, with which
I had charged my servants the prophets,
overtake your ancestors just the same?" '

So they repented and said, 'Yahweh
Sabaoth has treated us as he resolved to do,
and as our ways and deeds deserved.'

First vision: the horsemen

[7]On the twenty-fourth day of the eleventh
month (the month of Shebat), in the second
year of Darius, the word of Yahweh was
addressed to the prophet Zechariah (son of
Berechiah), son of Iddo, as follows, [8]'I had a
vision during the night. There was a man
riding a red horse standing among the deep-
rooted myrtles; behind him were other
horses—red, chestnut and white. [9]I said,
"What are these, my lord?" And the angel
who was talking to me said, "I will show you
what they are." [10]The man standing among
the myrtles then replied, "Those are they
whom Yahweh has sent to patrol the world."
[11]They reported to the angel of Yahweh as he
stood among the myrtles, "We have been
patrolling the world, and indeed the whole
world is still and at peace." [12]The angel
of Yahweh then spoke and said, "Yahweh
Sabaoth, how long will you wait before taking
pity on Jerusalem and the cities of Judah, on
which you have inflicted your anger for the
past seventy years?" [13]Yahweh then replied
with kind and comforting words to the angel
who was talking to me. [14]The angel who was
talking to me then said to me, "Make this
proclamation: Yahweh Sabaoth says this: I
am burning with jealousy for Jerusalem and
Zion [15]but am deeply angry with the nations
now at ease; before, I was only mildly angry,
but they contributed to the disaster. [16]So now
Yahweh says this: In compassion I have
returned to Jerusalem; my Temple will be
rebuilt there—Yahweh Sabaoth declares—
and the measuring line will be stretched over
Jerusalem. [17]Make this proclamation too:
Yahweh Sabaoth says this: My cities are once
more to be very prosperous. Yahweh will
comfort Zion once again, and again make
Jerusalem his choice." '

Second vision: the horns and the smiths

2 Then, raising my eyes, I had a vision. It
was this: There were four horns. [2]I said
to the angel who was talking to me, 'What
are these?' He said to me, 'These are the
horns which scattered Judah (Israel) and
Jerusalem.' [3]Yahweh then showed me four
smiths. [4]And I said, 'What are these coming
to do?' He said to me, '(Those horns scattered
Judah so completely that no one dared to
raise his head; but) these have come to terrify
them, to throw down the horns of the nations
who raised their horns over the land of Judah
to scatter it.'

Third vision: the measurer

[5]Then, raising my eyes, I had a vision. There
was a man with a measuring line in his hand.
[6]I asked him, 'Where are you going?' He
said, 'To measure Jerusalem, to calculate her
width and length.' [7]And then, while the angel
who was talking to me walked away, another
angel came out to meet him. [8]He said to
him, 'Run, and tell that young man this,

1a || Ml 3:7.

"Jerusalem is to remain unwalled, because
of the great number of men and cattle inside.
9For I—Yahweh declares—shall be a wall of
fire all round her and I shall be the Glory
within her." '

Two exhortations to the exiles

10Look out! Look out!
  Flee from the land of the north
—Yahweh declares—
for I have scattered you
  to the four winds of heaven
—Yahweh declares.
11Look out! Make your escape, Zion,
now living with the daughter of Babylon!
12For Yahweh Sabaoth says this,
since the Glory commissioned me,
about the nations who plundered you,
'Whoever touches you
  touches the apple of my eye.
13Now look, I shall wave my hand over them
and they will be plundered
  by those whom they have enslaved.'
Then you will know
  that Yahweh Sabaoth has sent me!

14Sing, rejoice, daughter of Zion,
for now I am coming
to live among you
—Yahweh declares!

15And on that day many nations
will be converted to Yahweh.
Yes, they will become his people,
and they will live among you.
Then you will know
  that Yahweh Sabaoth
    has sent me to you!
16Yahweh will take possession of Judah,
his portion in the Holy Land,
and again make Jerusalem his choice.
17Let all people be silent before Yahweh,
now that he is stirring
  from his holy Dwelling!

Fourth vision: the investiture of Joshua

3 He then showed me the high priest Joshua,
standing before the angel of Yahweh, with
Satan standing on his right to accuse him.
2The angel of Yahweh said to Satan, 'May
Yahweh rebuke you, Satan! May Yahweh
rebuke you, since he has made Jerusalem his
choice. Is not this man a brand snatched from
the fire?' 3Now Joshua was dressed in dirty
clothes as he stood before the angel. 4aThe
latter then spoke as follows to those who were
standing before him, 'Take off his dirty
clothes 4cand dress him in splendid robes
5and put a clean turban on his head.' So they
put a clean turban on his head and dressed
him in clean clothes, while the angel of
Yahweh stood by 4band said, 'You see, I have
taken your guilt away.' 6The angel of Yahweh
then made this declaration to Joshua,
7'Yahweh Sabaoth says this, "If you walk in
my ways and keep my ordinances, you shall
govern my house, you shall watch over my
courts, and I will give you free access among
those in attendance here. 9aFor this is the
stone which I have put before Joshua, a stone
on which are seven eyes; and I myself shall
cut the inscription on it—Yahweh Sabaoth
declares."

The coming of the 'Branch'

8'So listen, High Priest Joshua, you and the
colleagues over whom you preside—for they
are an omen of things to come—for now I
shall bring in my servant the Branch,[a] 9band
I shall remove this country's guilt in a single
day. 10On that day—Yahweh Sabaoth
declares—invite each other to come under
your vine and your fig tree." '

Fifth vision: the lamp-stand and the olive trees

4 The angel who was talking to me came
back and roused me as though rousing
someone who was asleep. 2And he asked me,
'What do you see?' I replied, 'As I look, there
is a lamp-stand entirely of gold with a bowl
at the top of it; it holds seven lamps, with
seven openings for the lamps on it. 3By it are
two olive trees, one to the right and the other
to the left.' 4I then said to the angel who was
talking to me, 'What are those things, my
lord?' 5The angel who was talking to me
replied, 'Do you not know what they are?' I
said, 'No, my lord.' 6aHe then gave me
this answer, 10b'These seven are the eyes of
Yahweh, which range over the whole world.'
11Then I went on to ask him, 'What is the
meaning of these two olive trees, to right and
left of the lamp-stand?' 12(And I went on to
ask him further, 'What is the meaning of the

3a A messianic title (*see* Jr 23:5) later applied to Zerubbabel (6:12).

two olive branches discharging oil through
the two golden openings?') 13He replied, 'Do
you not know what they are?' I said, 'No, my
lord.' 14He said, 'These are the two anointed
ones in attendance on the Lord of the whole
world.

Three sayings about Zerubbabel

6bThis is the word of Yahweh with regard to
Zerubbabel, 'Not by might and not by power,
but by my spirit'—says Yahweh Sabaoth.

7'What are you, great mountain? Beside
Zerubbabel you shall become a plain! He will
bring out the keystone while it is cheered
with Hurrah! Hurrah!'

8The word of Yahweh was addressed to
me as follows, 9'The hands of Zerubbabel
have laid the foundation of this Temple; his
hands will finish it. (Then you will know that
Yahweh Sabaoth has sent me to you.) 10aA
day of little things, no doubt, but who would
dare despise it? How they will rejoice when
they see the chosen stone in the hands of
Zerubbabel!'

Sixth vision: the flying scroll

5 Again raising my eyes, I had a vision.
There was a flying scroll. 2The angel who
was talking to me said, 'What do you see?' I
replied, 'I see a flying scroll; it is twenty
cubits long and ten cubits wide.' 3He then
said to me, 'This is God's curse sweeping
across the face of the whole country; for,
according to what it says on one side, every
thief will be banished and, according to what
it says on the other, everyone who commits
perjury in my name will be banished from it.
4I am going to release it—Yahweh Sabaoth
declares—for it to enter the house of the thief
and of anyone who commits perjury in my
name, for it to settle deep within his house
and consume it, timber, stone and all.'

Seventh vision: the woman in the bushel measure

5The angel who was talking to me appeared
and said to me, 'Raise your eyes, and see
what this is, going along.' 6I said, 'What is
it?' He said, 'It is a bushel measure going
along.' He went on, 'This is their guilt
throughout the country.' 7At this, a disc of
lead was raised, and I saw a woman sitting
inside the barrel. 8He said, 'This is Wicked-
ness.' And he rammed her back into the
barrel and jammed its mouth shut with the
mass of lead. 9I raised my eyes, and there
were two women appearing. The wind caught
their wings—they had wings like a stork's;
they raised the barrel midway between earth
and heaven. 10I then said to the angel who
was talking to me, 'Where are they taking
the barrel?' 11He replied, 'To build a temple
for it in the land of Shinar[a] and make a
pedestal on which to put it.'

Eighth vision: the chariots

6 Again I raised my eyes, and this is what I
saw: four chariots coming out between
two mountains, and the mountains were
mountains of bronze. 2The first chariot had
red horses, the second chariot had black
horses, 3the third chariot had white horses
and the fourth chariot had vigorous, piebald
horses. 4I asked the angel who was talking to
me, 'What are these, my lord?' 5The angel
replied, 'They are the four winds of heaven
now leaving, after attending the Lord of the
whole world. 6The black horses are leaving
for the land of the north; the white are
following them, and the piebald are leaving
for the land of the south.' 7They came out
vigorously, eager to patrol the world. He said
to them, 'Go and patrol the world.' And they
patrolled the world. 8He called to me and
said, 'Look, the ones going to the land of the
north brought my spirit to rest on the land of
the north.'

The votive crown

9Then the word of Yahweh was addressed to
me as follows, 10'Collect silver and gold from
the exiles, from Heldai, Tobijah and Jedaiah,
then (you yourself go the same day) go to the
house of Josiah son of Zephaniah, who has
arrived from Babylon. 11Then, taking the
silver and gold, make a crown and place it on
the head of the high priest Joshua[a] son of
Jehozadak. 12And say this to him, "Yahweh
Sabaoth says this: Here is a man whose
name is Branch; where he is, there will be a

5a Babylon, where Wickedness has its temple, leaving the Holy Land pure.
6a The original reading must have been 'Zerubbabel'; 'Joshua' was later substituted, when the high priest became the unique head of the community after the disappearance of the royal house.

branching out (and he will rebuild Yahweh's sanctuary). 13 Yes, he is the one who will rebuild Yahweh's sanctuary; he will wear the royal insignia and sit on his throne and govern, with a priest on his right. Perfect peace will reign between these two. 14 And the crown will serve Heldai, Tobijah, Jedaiah and the son of Zephaniah as a memorial of favour in Yahweh's sanctuary. 15 And those now far away will come and work on the building of Yahweh's sanctuary."

'Then you will know that Yahweh Sabaoth has sent me to you. It will happen if you diligently obey the voice of Yahweh your God.'

A question about fasting

7 In the fourth year of King Darius, the word of Yahweh was addressed to Zechariah on the fourth day of the ninth month, the month of Chislev. 2 Bethel sent Sharezer with a deputation to entreat Yahweh's favour 3 and to ask the priests in the Temple of Yahweh Sabaoth and the prophets, 'Ought I to go on mourning and fasting in the fifth month as I have been doing for so many years past?'

A survey of the nation's past

4 Then the word of Yahweh Sabaoth was addressed to me as follows, 5 'Say to all the people of the country and to the priests, "While you have been fasting and mourning in the fifth and seventh months for the past seventy years, have you really been fasting for my sake? 6 And when you were eating and drinking, were you not eating and drinking for your own sake? 7 Do you not know the words which Yahweh proclaimed through the prophets in the past, when Jerusalem was inhabited and secure, as were her surrounding towns, and when the Negeb and the lowlands were inhabited?" ' (8 The word of Yahweh was addressed to Zechariah as follows, 9 'Yahweh Sabaoth says this.) He said, "Apply the law fairly, and show faithful love and compassion towards one another. 10 Do not oppress the widow and the orphan, the foreigner and the poor, and do not secretly plan evil against one another." 11 But they would not listen; they turned a rebellious shoulder; they stopped their ears rather than hear; 12 they made their hearts adamant rather than listen to the teaching and the words that Yahweh Sabaoth had sent—by his spirit—through the prophets in the past; and consequently the fury of Yahweh Sabaoth overtook them. 13 And so, since when he called they would not listen, "I would not listen when they called", says Yahweh Sabaoth, 14 "but scattered them among all the nations unknown to them. Hence, after they had gone, the country was deserted, and no one came or went. They had turned a land of delights into a desert." '

A prospect of salvation

8 The word of Yahweh Sabaoth came as follows:

2 Yahweh Sabaoth says this:
I have been burning
with jealousy for Zion,
with furious jealousy for her sake.

3 Yahweh says this:
I am coming back to Zion
and shall live in the heart of Jerusalem.
Jerusalem will be called Faithful City
and the mountain of Yahweh Sabaoth,
the Holy Mountain.

4 Yahweh Sabaoth says this:
Aged men and women once again will sit
in the squares of Jerusalem,
each with a stick to lean on
because of their great age.
5 And the squares of the city will be full
of boys and girls
playing there.

6 Yahweh Sabaoth says this:
If this seems a miracle
to the remnant of this people
(in those days),
will it seem one to me?
declares Yahweh.

7 Yahweh Sabaoth says this:
Look, I shall rescue my people
from the countries of the east
and from the countries of the west.
8 I shall bring them back
to live in the heart of Jerusalem,
and they will be my people
and I shall be their God,
faithful and just.

9 'Yahweh Sabaoth says this, "Take heart, you who today hear these promises uttered by the prophets since the day when the

foundations of the Temple of Yahweh
Sabaoth were laid, that the sanctuary would
indeed be rebuilt. 10For up to now, men were
not paid their wages and nothing was paid
for the animals either; and it has not been
safe for anyone to come and go, because of
the enemy, since I had set each one against
everyone else. 11But from now on, I shall not
treat the remnant of this people as I have
treated them in time past—declares Yahweh
Sabaoth. 12Now they will sow in peace; the
vine will give its fruit, the soil will give its
produce and heaven will give its dew. I shall
bestow all these on the remnant of this people.
13Just as once you were a curse among the
nations, House of Judah and House of
Israel, so now I shall save you, and you
will be a blessing. Do not be afraid. Take
heart!"
14'For Yahweh Sabaoth says this, "Just as
I resolved to ill-treat you when your ancestors
provoked me to anger and did not relent—
says Yahweh Sabaoth—15so now I have
changed my mind and intend to treat Jeru-
salem and the House of Judah well. Do not
be afraid!
16"These are the things that you must do.
Speak the truth to one another; at your gates,
administer fair judgement conducive to
peace; 17do not secretly plot evil against one
another; do not love perjury; since I hate all
this—Yahweh declares." '

The answer to the question on fasting

18The word of Yahweh Sabaoth was
addressed to me as follows:
19'Yahweh Sabaoth says this, "The fast of
the fourth month, the fast of the fifth, the
fast of the seventh and the fast of the tenth
are to become glad, joyful, happy festivals
for the House of Judah. So love truth and
peace!" '

A prospect of salvation

20'Yahweh Sabaoth says this, "In the future,
peoples and citizens of many cities will come;
21and citizens of one city will go to the next
and say: We must certainly go to entreat
Yahweh's favour and seek out Yahweh
Sabaoth; I am going myself. 22Yes, many
peoples and great nations will seek out
Yahweh Sabaoth in Jerusalem and entreat
Yahweh's favour."
23'Yahweh Sabaoth says this, "In those
days, ten men from nations of every language
will take a Jew by the sleeve and say: We
want to go with you, since we have learnt
that God is with you." '

SECOND PART

9 A proclamation.

The new promised land

The word of Yahweh is against Hadrach,
it has come to rest on Damascus,
for the source of Aram belongs to Yahweh
no less than all the tribes of Israel;
2on Hamath too, which borders on it,
and on (Tyre and) Sidon,
  despite her acumen.
3Tyre has built herself a fortress,
has heaped up silver like dust
and gold like the dirt of the streets.
4And now the Lord
  is going to dispossess her;
at sea he will break her power,
and she herself will go up in flames.
5Seeing this, Ashkelon will be terrified,
Gaza too, and writhe with grief,
Ekron too, at the ruin of her prospects;
the king will vanish from Gaza
and Ashkelon be unpeopled,
6while a half-breed will live in Ashdod!
Yes, I shall destroy
  the pride of the Philistine;
7I shall snatch his blood from his mouth,
his abominations from between his teeth.
But his remnant too
  will belong to our God,
becoming like a clan in Judah,
and Ekron will become like a Jebusite.
8I shall stand guard before my home
to defend it against all comers,
and no oppressor will overrun them
  ever again,
for now I am on the alert.

The Royal Saviour

[9]Rejoice heart and soul, daughter of Zion!
Shout for joy, daughter of Jerusalem!
Look, your king is approaching,
he is vindicated and victorious,
humble and riding on a donkey,
on a colt, the foal of a donkey.
[10]He will banish chariots from Ephraim
and horses from Jerusalem;
the bow of war will be banished.
He will proclaim peace to the nations,
his empire will stretch from sea to sea,
from the River to the limits of the earth.

The restoration of Israel

[11]As for you,
because of the blood of your covenant
I have released your prisoners
from the pit
in which there is no water.
[12]Come back to the fortress,
you prisoners waiting in hope.
This very day, I vow,
I shall make it up to you twice over.
[13]For I have strung Judah
as a bow for myself,
laid Ephraim on the string as an arrow,
have roused your sons, Zion,
against your sons, Javan,[a]
and have made you like a warrior's sword.
[14]Then Yahweh will appear above them
and his arrow will flash out like lightning.
(The Lord) Yahweh
will sound the trumpet
and advance in the storm-winds
of the south.
[15]Yahweh Sabaoth will protect them!
They will devour,
will trample on the sling-stones,
they will drink blood like wine,
awash like bowls,
like the corners of the altar.
[16]Yahweh their God will give them victory
when that day comes,
like the sheep who are his people;
yes, the stones of a diadem
will sparkle over his country.
[17]How fine, how splendid that will be,
with wheat
to make the young men flourish,
and new wine the maidens!

Faithfulness to Yahweh

10 [1]Ask Yahweh for rain in autumn
and at the time of the spring rains.
Yahweh is the one
to make the storm-clouds.
He will give them showers of rain;
to each, grass in his field.
[2]Since the domestic idols
have talked nonsense,
and the diviners have seen false signs,
and dreams have purveyed delusions,
affording empty comfort,
that is why they have strayed like sheep,
in distress for want of a shepherd.

Israel's deliverance and return

[3]My anger has been roused
by the shepherds,
and I shall vent it on the he-goats.
When Yahweh Sabaoth comes
to visit his flock,
the House of Judah,
he will make it his royal war-horse.
[4]From it will emerge Cornerstone
and Tent-peg,
from it, Bow-ready-for-Battle,
from it, every type of leader.
Together [5]they will be like warriors
trampling the dirt of the streets in battle;
when they fight,
because Yahweh is with them,
they will put mounted men to rout.

[6]Then I shall make
the House of Judah mighty
and the House of Joseph victorious.
I shall restore them,
because I have taken pity on them,
and they will be as though
I had never cast them off,
for I am Yahweh their God
and shall answer their prayer.
[7]Ephraim will be like a warrior.
Their hearts will be cheered
as though by wine.
Their children will see this and rejoice,
their hearts will exult in Yahweh.

[8]I shall whistle to them
and gather them in,
for I have redeemed them;
they will be as numerous
as they used to be.

9a Greece, now conquering the East under Alexander the Great.

9 I shall scatter them among the peoples
but in distant countries
they will remember me,
they will instruct their children
and then return.
10 I shall bring them home from Egypt
and gather them back from Assyria;
I shall lead them into Gilead
and the Lebanon,
and even that
will not be large enough for them.

11 They will cross the sea of Egypt
(and the waves of the sea will be struck);
all the depths of the River
will be dried up.
The arrogance of Assyria
will be cast down
and the sceptre of Egypt taken away.
12 I shall make them mighty in Yahweh,
and they will march in my name
—Yahweh declares.

A taunt against enemies

11 Open your gateways, Lebanon,
and the fire shall burn down
your cedar trees!
2 Wail, juniper,
for the cedar tree has fallen,
the majestic ones have been ravaged!
Wail, oaks of Bashan,
for the impenetrable forest
has been felled!
3 The sound of the wailing of shepherds!
Their majesty has been ravaged.
The sound of the roaring of young lions!
The pride of the Jordan has been ravaged.

The two shepherds

4 Yahweh my God says this, 'Pasture the
sheep for slaughter, 5 whose buyers kill them
and go unpunished, whose sellers say of
them, "Blessed be Yahweh; now I am rich!"
and whose own shepherds show them no
pity. 6 For I shall show no further pity for the
inhabitants of the country—Yahweh
declares! Instead, I shall put everyone into
the clutches of a neighbour, into the clutches
of the king. They will crush the country and
I shall not rescue anyone from their clutches.'

7 Then I pastured for slaughter the sheep
belonging to the sheep-dealers. I took two
staves: the one I called 'Goodwill', the other
'Couplers'; and I pastured the sheep myself,
8 getting rid of three shepherds in one month.
But I lost patience with them, and they
equally detested me. 9 I then said, 'I am not
going to pasture you any more; the one
doomed to die can die; the one doomed to
perish can perish; and the rest can devour one
another.' 10 I then took my staff, 'Goodwill',
and broke it in half, to break my covenant,
which I had made with all the peoples.
11 When it was broken, that day the sheep-
dealers, who were watching me, realised that
this had been a word of Yahweh. 12 I then said
to them, 'If you see fit, give me my wages; if
not, never mind.' So they weighed out my
wages: thirty shekels of silver. 13 Yahweh said
to me, 'Throw it to the smelter, this princely
sum at which they have valued me!' Taking
the thirty shekels of silver, I threw them into
the Temple of Yahweh, for the smelter. 14 I
then broke my second staff, 'Couplers,' in
half, to rupture the brotherly relationship
between Judah and Israel.

15 Next, Yahweh said to me, 'This time,
take the gear of a good-for-nothing shepherd.
16 For I am now going to raise a shepherd in
this country, who will not bother about the
lost, who will not go in search of the stray,
who will not heal the injured, who will not
support the swollen, but who will eat the
meat of the fat ones, tearing off their very
hoofs.

17 Disaster to the shepherd
who deserts his flock!
May the sword attack his arm
and his right eye!
May his arm shrivel completely
and his right eye be totally blinded!'

The deliverance and restoration of Jerusalem

12 A proclamation.
The word of Yahweh about Israel
(2b and also about Judah). Yahweh, who
spread out the heaven and founded the earth
and formed the human spirit within,
declares:

2a 'Look, I shall make Jerusalem a cup to
set all the surrounding peoples reeling. (That
will be at the time of the siege of Jerusalem.)

3 'When that day comes, I shall make Jeru-
salem a stone too heavy for all the peoples to
lift; all those who try to lift it will hurt
themselves severely, although all the nations
of the world will be massed against her.

4When that day comes—declares Yahweh—
I shall strike all the horses with panic and
their riders with madness. And I shall strike
all the peoples with blindness. (But I shall
keep watch over Judah.) 5Then the rulers of
Judah will say to themselves, "The strength
of the inhabitants of Jerusalem lies in Yahweh
Sabaoth their God." 6When that day comes,
I shall make the rulers of Judah like a brazier
burning in a pile of wood, like a torch flaming
in a sheaf; and they will devour all the peoples
round them to right and left. And Jerusalem
will be full of people as before, where she
stands (in Jerusalem). 7Yahweh will first save
the tents of Judah, so that the glory of the
House of David and the glory of the inhabi-
tants of Jerusalem do not increase at Judah's
expense. 8When that day comes, Yahweh
will protect the inhabitants of Jerusalem; and
the frailest of them will be like David when
that day comes, and the House of David will
be like God, like the angel of Yahweh, at
their head.
9'When that day comes, I shall set about
destroying all the nations who advance
against Jerusalem. 10But over the House of
David and the inhabitants of Jerusalem I
shall pour out a spirit of grace and prayer,
and they will look to me. They will mourn
for the one whom they have pierced as though
for an only child, and weep for him as people
weep for a first-born child. 11When that day
comes, the mourning in Jerusalem will be as
great as the mourning for Hadad Rimmon in
the Plain of Megiddo. 12And the country will
mourn clan by clan:

The clan of the House of David by itself,
and their women by themselves;
the clan of the House of Nathan by itself,
and their women by themselves;
13the clan of the House of Levi by itself,
and their women by themselves;
the clan of the House of Shimei by itself,
and their women by themselves;
14all the rest of the clans,
every clan by itself,
and their women by themselves.'

13 'When that day comes, a fountain will
be opened for the House of David and
the inhabitants of Jerusalem, to wash sin and
impurity away.
2'When that day comes—Yahweh
declares—I shall cut off the names of the
idols from the country, and they will never
be remembered again; I shall also rid the
country of the prophets, and of the spirit
of impurity. 3Then, if anyone still goes on
prophesying, his parents, his own father and
mother will say to him, "You shall not live,
since you utter lies in Yahweh's name." And
even while he is prophesying, his parents,
his own father and mother will pierce him
through. 4When that day comes, the
prophets will all be ashamed to relate their
visions when they prophesy and no longer
put on their hair cloaks with intent to deceive.
5Instead, they will say, "I am no prophet. I
am a man who tills the soil, for the land has
been my living since I was a boy." 6And if
anyone asks him, "What are those gashes on
your chest?[a]" he will reply, "I got them when
I was with my friends." '

Invocation to the sword; the new people

7Awake, sword, against my shepherd,
against the man who is close to me—
declares Yahweh Sabaoth!
Strike the shepherd, scatter the sheep!
And I shall turn my hand
against the young!
8So it will be, throughout the country—
declares Yahweh Sabaoth—
two-thirds in it will be cut off (be killed)
and the other third will be left.
9I shall pass this third through the fire,
refine them as silver is refined,
test them as gold is tested.
He will call on my name
and I shall answer him;
I shall say, 'He is my people,'
and he will say, 'Yahweh is my God!'

The eschatological battle; the splendour of Jerusalem

14 Look, the Day of Yahweh is coming,
when the spoils taken from you will be
shared out among you. 2For I shall gather all
the nations to Jerusalem for battle. The city
will be taken, the houses plundered, the
women ravished. Half the city will go into
exile, but the rest of the people will not be
ejected from the city. 3Then Yahweh will
sally out and fight those nations as once he
fought on the day of battle. 4When that day
comes, his feet will rest on the Mount of

13a Such scars were once the hallmark of a prophet (1 K 18:28).

Olives, which faces Jerusalem on the east, and the Mount of Olives will be split in half from east to west, forming a huge valley; half the Mount will recede northwards, the other half southwards.
5The valley between the hills will be filled in, yes, it will be blocked as far as Jasol, it will be filled in as it was by the earthquake in the days of Uzziah king of Judah. And Yahweh my God will come, and all the holy ones with him.

6That Day, there will be no light, but only cold and frost.
7And it will be one continuous day—Yahweh knows—there will be no more day and night, and it will remain light right into the time of evening.
8When that Day comes, living waters will issue from Jerusalem, half towards the eastern sea, half towards the western sea; they will flow summer and winter.
9Then Yahweh will become king of the whole world. When that Day comes, Yahweh will be the one and only and his name the one name.
10The entire country will be transformed into plain, from Geba to Rimmon in the Negeb, but Jerusalem will stand high in her place and be full of people from the Benjamin Gate to the site of the earlier gate, to the Corner Gate, and from the Tower of Hananel to the king's winepresses.
11People will make their homes there. The curse of destruction will be lifted; Jerusalem will be safe to live in.

12And this is the plague with which Yahweh will strike all the nations who have fought against Jerusalem; their flesh will rot while they are still standing on their feet; their eyes will rot in their sockets; their tongues will rot in their mouths.
15And the plague afflicting the horses, mules, camels, donkeys and all the other animals in those armies will be the same.
13When that Day comes, a great terror will fall on them from Yahweh; each man will grab his neighbour's hand and they will fall to fighting among themselves.
14Even Judah will fight against Jerusalem. The wealth of all the surrounding nations will be heaped together: gold, silver, clothing, in vast quantity.

16After this, all the survivors of all the nations which have attacked Jerusalem will come up year after year to worship the King, Yahweh Sabaoth, and to keep the feast of Shelters.
17Should one of the races of the world fail to come up to Jerusalem to worship the King, Yahweh Sabaoth, there will be no rain for that one.
18Should the race of Egypt fail to come up and pay its visit, on it will fall the plague which Yahweh will inflict on each of those nations which fail to come up to keep the feast of Shelters.
19Such will be the punishment for Egypt and the punishment for all the nations which fail to come up to keep the feast of Shelters.

20When that Day comes, the very bells on the horses will be inscribed with the words, 'Sacred to Yahweh', and the cooking pots of the house of Yahweh will be as holy as the sprinkling bowls before the altar.
21Yes, every cooking pot in Jerusalem and in Judah shall be sacred to Yahweh Sabaoth, and all who come to offer sacrifice will help themselves and do their cooking in them, and there will be no more traders in the Temple of Yahweh Sabaoth, when that Day comes.

THE BOOK OF MALACHI

The book consists of six short passages, alternately on the Day of Yahweh and on purity of observance. It is anonymous, for 'Malachi' means merely 'my messenger'. It stems from the mid fifth century, some years after the return from the Babylonian exile.

MALACHI

1 A message.
The word of Yahweh to Israel through
Malachi.

The love of Yahweh for Israel

[2]'I have loved you, says Yahweh. But you
ask, "How have you shown your love?" Was
not Esau[a] Jacob's brother? declares Yahweh;
even so, I loved Jacob [3]but I hated Esau. I
turned his mountains into a desert and his
heritage into dwellings in the wastelands. [4]If
Edom says, "We have been struck down but
we shall rebuild our ruins," Yahweh Sabaoth
says this, "Let them build, but I shall pull
down! They will be known as Land of
Wickedness and Nation-with-which-
Yahweh-is-angry-for-ever. [5]You will see this
yourselves and you will say: Yahweh is
mighty beyond the borders of Israel."

An indictment of the priests

[6]"The son honours his father, the slave stands
in awe of his master. But if I am indeed
father, where is the honour due to me? And
if I am indeed master, where is the awe due
to me? says Yahweh Sabaoth to you priests
who despise my name. You ask, "How have
we despised your name?" [7]By putting
polluted food on my altar. You ask, "How
have we polluted you?" By saying, "The
table of Yahweh deserves no respect."
[8]When you bring blind animals for sacrifice,
is this not wrong? When you bring the lame
and the diseased, is this not wrong? If you
offer them to your governor, see if he is
pleased with them or receives you graciously,
says Yahweh Sabaoth. [9]In that case, try
pleading with God to take pity on us (that is
what you have done), and will he take any
notice? says Yahweh Sabaoth. [10]Why does
one of you not close the doors and so stop the
pointless lighting of fires on my altar? I am
not pleased with you, says Yahweh Sabaoth;
from your hands I find no offerings acceptable.
[11]But from farthest east to farthest west
my name is great among the nations, and
everywhere incense and a pure gift are offered
to my name, since my name is great among
the nations, says Yahweh Sabaoth.
[12]'But you have profaned it by saying,
"The table of the Lord is polluted, hence the
food offered on it deserves no respect." [13]You
say, "How tiresome it all is!" and sniff
disdainfully at me, says Yahweh Sabaoth.
You bring a stolen, lame or diseased animal,
you bring that as an offering! Am I to accept
this from you? says Yahweh Sabaoth.
[14]Cursed be the rogue who has a male in
his flock but pays his vow by sacrificing a
blemished animal to me! For I am a great
king, says Yahweh Sabaoth, and among the
nations my name inspires awe.'

2 'And now, priests, this commandment is
for you. [2]If you will not listen, if you will
not sincerely resolve to glorify my name, says
Yahweh Sabaoth, I shall certainly lay a curse
on you and I shall curse your blessing. Indeed
I will lay a curse, for none of you makes this
resolve. [3]Now, I am going to break your arm

1a Considered the ancestor of Edom, which is often also called Esau.

and throw offal in your faces—the offal of
your solemn feasts—and sweep you away
with it. 4Then you will know that I sent this
commandment to you, to affirm my intention
to maintain my covenant with Levi, says
Yahweh Sabaoth. 5My covenant was with
him—a covenant of life and peace, and these
were what I gave him—a covenant of respect,
and he respected me and held my name in
awe. 6The law of truth was in his mouth and
guilt was not found on his lips; he walked in
peace and justice with me and he converted
many from sinning. 7The priest's lips ought
to safeguard knowledge; his mouth is where
the law should be sought, since he is Yahweh
Sabaoth's messenger. 8But you yourselves
have turned aside from the way; you have
caused many to lapse by your teaching. Since
you have destroyed the covenant of Levi,
says Yahweh Sabaoth, 9so I in my turn have
made you contemptible and vile to the whole
people, for not having kept my ways and for
being partial in applying the law.

Mixed marriage and divorce

10'Is there not one Father of us all? Did not
one God create us? Why, then, do we break
faith with one another, profaning the
covenant of our ancestors? 11Judah has
broken faith; a detestable thing has been
done in Israel and in Jerusalem. For Judah
has profaned Yahweh's beloved sanctuary;
he has married the daughter of an alien god.
12May Yahweh deprive such an offender of
witness and advocate in the tents of Jacob
among those who present offerings to
Yahweh Sabaoth!

13'And here is something else you do: you
cover the altar of Yahweh with tears, with
weeping and wailing, because he now refuses
to consider the offering or to accept it
from you. 14And you ask, "Why?" Because
Yahweh stands as witness between you and
the wife of your youth, with whom you
have broken faith, even though she was your
partner and your wife by covenant. 15Did he
not create a single being, having flesh and the
breath of life? And what does this single being
seek? God-given offspring! Have respect for
your own life then, and do not break faith
with the wife of your youth. 16For I hate
divorce, says Yahweh, God of Israel, and
people concealing their cruelty under
a cloak, says Yahweh Sabaoth. Have
respect for your own life then, and do not
break faith.

The Day of Yahweh

17'You have wearied Yahweh with your talk.
You ask, "How have we wearied him?"
When you say, "Any evil-doer is good as
far as Yahweh is concerned; indeed he is
delighted with them"; or when you say,
"Where is the God of fair judgement
now?"

3 'Look, I shall send my messenger to clear
a way before me. And suddenly the Lord
whom you seek will come to his Temple; yes,
the angel of the covenant, for whom you long,
is on his way, says Yahweh Sabaoth. 2Who
will be able to resist the day of his coming?
Who will remain standing when he appears?
For he will be like a refiner's fire, like fullers'
alkali. 3He will take his seat as refiner and
purifier; he will purify the sons of Levi and
refine them like gold and silver, so that
they can make the offering to Yahweh with
uprightness. 4The offering of Judah and
Jerusalem will then be acceptable to Yahweh
as in former days, as in the years of old. 5I
am coming to put you on trial and I shall be
a ready witness against sorcerers, adulterers,
perjurers, and against those who oppress the
wage-earner, the widow and the orphan, and
who rob the foreigner of his rights and do not
respect me, says Yahweh Sabaoth.

Temple tithes

6'No; I, Yahweh, do not change; and you
have not ceased to be children of Jacob! 7Ever
since the days of your ancestors, you have
evaded my statutes and not observed them.
Return to me and I will return to you, says
Yahweh Sabaoth.[a] You ask, "How are we to
return? 8Can a human being cheat God?" Yet
you try to cheat me! You ask, "How do we try
to cheat you?" Over tithes and contributions.
9A curse lies on you because you, this whole
nation, try to cheat me. 10Bring the tithes in
full to the treasury, so that there is food in
my house; put me to the test now like this,
says Yahweh Sabaoth, and see if I do not
open the floodgates of heaven for you and
pour out an abundant blessing for you. 11For
your sakes, I shall forbid the locust to destroy

3a || Zc 1:3.

the produce of your soil or prevent the vine from bearing fruit in your field, says Yahweh Sabaoth, 12and all the nations will call you blessed, for you will be a land of delights, says Yahweh Sabaoth.

The triumph of the upright on the Day of Yahweh

13'You have said harsh things about me, says Yahweh. And yet you say, "What have we said against you?" 14You have said, "It is useless to serve God; what is the good of keeping his commands or of walking mournfully before Yahweh Sabaoth? 15In fact, we now call the proud the happy ones; the evildoers are the ones who prosper; they put God to the test, yet come to no harm!" '

16Then those who feared Yahweh talked to one another about this, and Yahweh took note and listened; and a book of remembrance was written in his presence recording those who feared him and kept his name in mind. 17'On the day when I act, says Yahweh Sabaoth, they will be my most prized possession, and I shall spare them in the way a man spares the son who serves him. 18Then once again you will see the difference between the upright person and the wicked one, between the one who serves God and the one who does not serve him.

19'For look, the Day is coming, glowing like a furnace. All the proud and all the evildoers will be the stubble, and the Day, when it comes, will set them ablaze, says Yahweh Sabaoth, leaving them neither root nor branch. 20But for you who fear my name, the Sun of justice will rise with healing in his rays, and you will come out leaping like calves from the stall, 21and trample on the wicked, who will be like ashes under the soles of your feet on the day when I act, says Yahweh Sabaoth.

Appendices

22'Remember the Law of my servant Moses to whom at Horeb I prescribed decrees and rulings for all Israel.

23'Look, I shall send you the prophet Elijah before the great and awesome Day of Yahweh comes. 24He will reconcile parents to their children and children to their parents, to forestall my putting the country under the curse of destruction.'

THE
NEW TESTAMENT

INTRODUCTION TO THE SYNOPTIC GOSPELS

The gospels are not 'lives' or biographies of Jesus, but are four versions of the record of the Good News brought by Jesus. Jesus himself preached the coming of God's rule, the establishment of his sovereignty, breaking through the bonds of evil, sin and death to which all people had been subject. The gospels are full also of wonder at the mystery of Jesus himself, and why a shameful death was the means by which God must triumph in him.

At the heart of the gospel tradition is the first preaching of the Good News of Jesus by the apostles. The tradition was handed down in the community in the form of stories, parables and short sayings remembered for their teaching or the light they threw on the person or message of Jesus. To some extent these stories would be moulded to bring out their lesson, e.g. the fulfilment of Scripture in the life, death and resurrection of Jesus, or their application to Christian behaviour in the world. The tradition was expressed also in hymns and short summaries to be learnt by heart.

Which of the gospels was the first to be written is still in dispute, although it is clear that the three 'synoptic' (i.e. 'with the same eye') gospels are interrelated. The most common view is that Mk was the first, and that this was expanded independently by Mt and Lk, each using a now lost collection of the Sayings of Jesus. The traditional view is that Mt came first and was used by Lk, with Mk finally making a digest of them both. In either view the gospels are the end product of a long process of development in the Christian community under the guidance of the Spirit.

Nor is it possible to establish firmly the date or authorship of these gospels. Tradition from the 2nd century holds that Matthew the apostle stands authority for Mt, that Mk represents the tradition of Peter, and that the author of Lk was a companion of Paul. But the identity of the authors is less important than the guarantee of their material by the tradition of the early community, of which each must have been an authorised interpreter. Of the date, we can only be sure that they all stem from the last forty years of the 1st century.

THE GOSPEL OF MATTHEW

Mt is the gospel of the Kingdom of Heaven. This points to three principal emphases: (i) While Mk concentrates on the gradual unfolding of the disciples' understanding of Jesus, Mt stresses from the first that Jesus is a king; he is a noble and dignified figure who deserves and receives homage from all around him; already in his earthly life he is seen as the exalted

Christ. (ii) The Kingdom of Heaven, still to be completed, but already strongly associated with the community which Jesus founded, is the fulfilment of God's plan for Israel. So the Church is the true Israel, the recipient of God's promises, which goes out to all nations in the power of Christ. (iii) Mt is the most Semitic of the gospels, constantly touching on Jewish and rabbinic customs and ways of thought and argument, stressing that Jesus fulfils the hopes of the OT both in general and in minute detail. There is a strong and typically Jewish interest in the final retribution, about which Mt is full of warnings.

The main part of the gospel, apart from the infancy stories and the passion narrative, is divided into five sections (each with a narrative and a teaching section) by analogy with the five books of the Jewish Law. Mt is more interested than Mk in Jesus' teaching, which he assembles in five great discourses, each with its own subject: the Sermon on the Mount (5—7), the Missionary Discourse (10—11), Parables (13), the Community (18) and the Last Discourse (24—25). So this Jewish-Christian scribe shows that Jesus is not only the Davidic Messiah but also the Lawgiver or second Moses.

PLAN OF THE BOOK

THE GOSPEL ACCORDING TO MATTHEW

I: THE BIRTH AND INFANCY OF JESUS

The ancestry of Jesus

1 Roll of the genealogy of Jesus Christ, son of David, son of Abraham:

2 Abraham fathered Isaac,
Isaac fathered Jacob,
Jacob fathered Judah and his brothers,
3 Judah fathered Perez and Zerah,
whose mother was Tamar,
Perez fathered Hezron,
Hezron fathered Ram,
4 Ram fathered Amminadab,
Amminadab fathered Nahshon,
Nahshon fathered Salmon,
5 Salmon fathered Boaz,
whose mother was Rahab,
Boaz fathered Obed,
whose mother was Ruth,
Obed fathered Jesse;
6 and Jesse fathered King David.

David fathered Solomon,
whose mother had been Uriah's wife,

7 Solomon fathered Rehoboam,
Rehoboam fathered Abijah,
Abijah fathered Asa,
8 Asa fathered Jehoshaphat,
Jehoshaphat fathered Joram,
Joram fathered Uzziah,
9 Uzziah fathered Jotham,
Jotham fathered Ahaz,
Ahaz fathered Hezekiah,
10 Hezekiah fathered Manasseh,
Manasseh fathered Amon,
Amon fathered Josiah;
11 and Josiah fathered Jechoniah
and his brothers.
Then the deportation to Babylon
took place.

12 After the deportation to Babylon:
Jechoniah fathered Shealtiel,
Shealtiel fathered Zerubbabel,
13 Zerubbabel fathered Abiud,
Abiud fathered Eliakim,
Eliakim fathered Azor,
14 Azor fathered Zadok,
Zadok fathered Achim,
Achim fathered Eliud,
15 Eliud fathered Eleazar,
Eleazar fathered Matthan,
Matthan fathered Jacob;
16 and Jacob fathered Joseph
the husband of Mary;
of her was born Jesus
who is called Christ.

17 The sum of generations is therefore: fourteen from Abraham to David; fourteen from David to the Babylonian deportation; and fourteen from the Babylonian deportation to Christ.

Joseph adopts Jesus as his son

18 This is how Jesus Christ came to be born.
His mother Mary was betrothed to Joseph;
but before they came to live together she was
found to be with child through the Holy
Spirit. 19 Her husband Joseph, being an
upright man and wanting to spare her
disgrace, decided to divorce her informally.
20 He had made up his mind to do this when
suddenly the angel of the Lord appeared to
him in a dream and said, 'Joseph son of
David, do not be afraid to take Mary home
as your wife, because she has conceived what
is in her by the Holy Spirit. 21 She will give
birth to a son and you must name him Jesus,
because he is the one who is to save his people
from their sins.' 22 Now all this took place to
fulfil what the Lord had spoken through the
prophet:

23 *Look! the virgin is with child*
and will give birth to a son
whom they will call Immanuel,[a]

a name which means 'God-is-with-us'.
24 When Joseph woke up he did what the
angel of the Lord had told him to do: he
took his wife to his home; 25 he had not had
intercourse with her when she gave birth to
a son; and he named him Jesus.

The visit of the Magi

2 After Jesus had been born at Bethlehem
in Judaea during the reign of King Herod,
suddenly some wise men came to Jerusalem
from the east 2 asking, 'Where is the infant
king of the Jews? We saw his star as it rose
and have come to do him homage.' 3 When
King Herod heard this he was perturbed,
and so was the whole of Jerusalem. 4 He called
together all the chief priests and the scribes
of the people, and enquired of them where
the Christ was to be born. 5 They told him,
'At Bethlehem in Judaea, for this is what the
prophet wrote:

6 *And you, Bethlehem*,
in the land of Judah,
you are by no means the *least*
among the leaders of Judah,
for *from you will come a leader*
who will *shepherd* my people Israel.'[a]

7 Then Herod summoned the wise men to see
him privately. He asked them the exact date
on which the star had appeared 8 and sent
them on to Bethlehem with the words, 'Go
and find out all about the child, and when
you have found him, let me know, so that I
too may go and do him homage.' 9 Having
listened to what the king had to say, they set
out. And suddenly the star they had seen
rising went forward and halted over the place
where the child was. 10 The sight of the star
filled them with delight, 11 and going into the
house they saw the child with his mother
Mary, and falling to their knees they did him

1a Is 7:14.
2a Mi 5:1.

homage. Then, opening their treasures, they
offered him gifts of gold and frankincense
and myrrh. 12But they were given a warning
in a dream not to go back to Herod, and
returned to their own country by a different
way.

The flight into Egypt
The massacre of the Innocents

13After they had left, suddenly the angel of
the Lord appeared to Joseph in a dream and
said, 'Get up, take the child and his mother
with you, and escape into Egypt, and stay
there until I tell you, because Herod intends
to search for the child and do away with him.'
14So Joseph got up and, taking the child and
his mother with him, left that night for
Egypt, 15where he stayed until Herod was
dead. This was to fulfil what the Lord had
spoken through the prophet:

I called my son out of Egypt.[b]

16Herod was furious on realising that he
had been fooled by the wise men, and in
Bethlehem and its surrounding district he
had all the male children killed who were two
years old or less, reckoning by the date he
had been careful to ask the wise men. 17Then
were fulfilled the words spoken through the
prophet Jeremiah:

18*A voice is heard in Ramah,*
lamenting and weeping bitterly:
it is Rachel weeping for her children,
refusing to be comforted
because they are no more.[c]

From Egypt to Nazareth

19After Herod's death, suddenly the angel of
the Lord appeared in a dream to Joseph in
Egypt 20and said,[d] 'Get up, take the child and
his mother with you and go back to the land
of Israel, for those who wanted to kill the
child are dead.' 21So Joseph got up and,
taking the child and his mother with him,
went back to the land of Israel. 22But when
he learnt that Archelaus had succeeded his
father Herod as ruler of Judaea he was afraid
to go there, and being warned in a dream he
withdrew to the region of Galilee. 23There he
settled in a town called Nazareth. In this way
the words spoken through the prophets were
to be fulfilled:

He will be called a Nazarene.

II: THE KINGDOM OF HEAVEN IS ANNOUNCED

A: NARRATIVE SECTION

The proclamation of John the Baptist

3 In due course John the Baptist appeared;
he proclaimed this message in the desert
of Judaea, 2'Repent, for the kingdom of
Heaven is close at hand.' 3This was the man
spoken of by the prophet Isaiah when he said:

A voice of one that cries in the desert,
'Prepare a way for the Lord,
make his paths straight.'[a]

4This man John wore a garment made of
camel-hair with a leather loin-cloth round his
waist,[b] and his food was locusts and wild
honey. 5Then Jerusalem and all Judaea and
the whole Jordan district made their way to
him, 6and as they were baptised by him in
the river Jordan they confessed their sins.
7But when he saw a number of Pharisees and
Sadducees coming for baptism he said to
them, 'Brood of vipers, who warned you to
flee from the coming retribution? 8Produce
fruit in keeping with repentance, 9and do
not presume to tell yourselves, "We have
Abraham as our father," because, I tell you,
God can raise children for Abraham from
these stones. 10Even now the axe is being laid
to the root of the trees, so that any tree failing
to produce good fruit will be cut down and
thrown on the fire. 11I baptise you in water
for repentance, but the one who comes after
me is more powerful than I, and I am not fit

2b Nb 23:22.
2c In Jr 31:15 she weeps for the northern tribes. But traditionally she was buried near Bethlehem.
2d cf. Ex. 4:19–20. There are several parallels with the stories of Moses' infancy.
3a Is 40:3.
3b As Elijah, 2 K 1:8.

to carry his sandals; he will baptise you with
the Holy Spirit and fire. 12His winnowing-
fan is in his hand; he will clear his threshing-
floor and gather his wheat into his barn; but
the chaff he will burn in a fire that will never
go out.'

Jesus is baptised

13Then Jesus appeared: he came from Galilee
to the Jordan to be baptised by John. 14John
tried to dissuade him, with the words, 'It is I
who need baptism from you, and yet you
come to me!' 15But Jesus replied, 'Leave it
like this for the time being; it is fitting that
we should, in this way, do all that uprightness
demands.' Then John gave in to him.

16And when Jesus had been baptised he at
once came up from the water, and suddenly
the heavens opened and he saw the Spirit of
God descending like a dove and coming down
on him. 17And suddenly there was a voice
from heaven, 'This is my Son, the Beloved;
my favour rests on him.'[c]

Testing in the desert

4 Then Jesus was led by the Spirit out into
the desert to be put to the test by the devil.
2He fasted for forty days and forty nights,
after which he was hungry, 3and the tester
came and said to him, 'If you are Son of God,
tell these stones to turn into loaves.' 4But he
replied, 'Scripture says:

Human beings live not on bread alone
but on every word
that comes from the mouth of God.'[a]

5The devil then took him to the holy city and
set him on the parapet of the Temple. 6'If
you are Son of God,' he said, 'throw yourself
down; for scripture says:

He has given his angels orders about you,
and *they will carry you in their arms*
in case you trip over a stone.'[b]

7Jesus said to him, 'Scripture also says:

Do not put the Lord your God to the test.'[c]

8Next, taking him to a very high mountain,
the devil showed him all the kingdoms of the
world and their splendour. 9And he said to
him, 'I will give you all these, if you fall at
my feet and do me homage.' 10Then Jesus
replied, 'Away with you, Satan! For scripture
says:

The Lord your God is the one
to whom you must do homage,
him alone you must serve.'[d]

11Then the devil left him, and suddenly
angels appeared and looked after him.

Return to Galilee

12Hearing that John had been arrested he
withdrew to Galilee, 13and leaving Nazara he
went and settled in Capernaum, beside the
lake, on the borders of Zebulun and
Naphtali. 14This was to fulfil what was spoken
by the prophet Isaiah:

15*Land of Zebulun! Land of Naphtali!*
Way of the sea beyond Jordan.
Galilee of the nations!
16*The people that lived in darkness*
have seen a great light;
on those who lived
in a country of shadow dark as death
a light has dawned.[e]

17From then onwards Jesus began his procla-
mation with the message, 'Repent, for the
kingdom of Heaven is close at hand.'

The first four disciples are called

18As he was walking by the Lake of Galilee
he saw two brothers, Simon, who was called
Peter, and his brother Andrew; they were
making a cast into the lake with their net, for
they were fishermen. 19And he said to them,
'Come after me and I will make you fishers
of people.' 20And at once they left their nets
and followed him.

21Going on from there he saw another pair
of brothers, James son of Zebedee and his
brother John; they were in their boat with
their father Zebedee, mending their nets,
and he called them. 22And at once, leaving
the boat and their father, they followed him.

3c cf. Is 42:1.
4a Dt 8:3.
4b Ps 91:10–12.
4c Dt 6:16.
4d Dt 6:13.
4e Is 8:23–9:1.

Jesus proclaims the message and heals the sick

[23]He went round the whole of Galilee teaching in their synagogues, proclaiming the good news of the kingdom and curing all kinds of disease and illness among the people. [24]His fame spread throughout Syria, and those who were suffering from diseases and painful complaints of one kind or another, the possessed, epileptics, the paralysed, were all brought to him, and he cured them. [25]Large crowds followed him, coming from Galilee, the Decapolis, Jerusalem, Judaea and Transjordan.

B: THE SERMON ON THE MOUNT

The Beatitudes[a]

5 Seeing the crowds, he went onto the mountain. And when he was seated his disciples came to him. [2]Then he began to speak. This is what he taught them:

[3]How blessed are the poor in spirit:
the kingdom of Heaven is theirs.
[4]Blessed are *the gentle*:[b]
they shall have the earth as inheritance.[c]
[5]Blessed are those who mourn:
they shall be comforted.
[6]Blessed are those
who hunger and thirst for uprightness:
they shall have their fill.
[7]Blessed are the merciful:
they shall have mercy shown them.
[8]Blessed are the pure in heart:
they shall see God.
[9]Blessed are the peacemakers:
they shall be recognised
as children of God.
[10]Blessed are those who are persecuted
in the cause of uprightness:
the kingdom of Heaven is theirs.

[11]'Blessed are you when people abuse you and persecute you and speak all kinds of calumny against you falsely on my account. [12]Rejoice and be glad, for your reward will be great in heaven; this is how they persecuted the prophets before you.

Salt for the earth and light for the world

[13]'You are salt for the earth. But if salt loses its taste, what can make it salty again? It is good for nothing, and can only be thrown out to be trampled under people's feet.

[14]'You are light for the world. A city built on a hill-top cannot be hidden. [15]No one lights a lamp to put it under a tub; they put it on the lamp-stand where it shines for everyone in the house. [16]In the same way your light must shine in people's sight, so that, seeing your good works, they may give praise to your Father in heaven.

The fulfilment of the Law

[17]'Do not imagine that I have come to abolish the Law or the Prophets. I have come not to abolish but to complete them. [18]In truth I tell you, till heaven and earth disappear, not one dot, not one little stroke, is to disappear from the Law until all its purpose is achieved. [19]Therefore, anyone who infringes even one of the least of these commandments and teaches others to do the same will be considered the least in the kingdom of Heaven; but the person who keeps them and teaches them will be considered great in the kingdom of Heaven.

The new standard higher than the old

[20]'For I tell you, if your uprightness does not surpass that of the scribes and Pharisees, you will never get into the kingdom of Heaven.

[21]'You have heard how it was said to our ancestors, *You shall not kill*;[d] and if anyone does kill he must answer for it before the court. [22]But I say this to you, anyone who is angry with a brother will answer for it before the court; anyone who calls a brother "Fool" will answer for it before the Sanhedrin; and anyone who calls him "Traitor" will answer for it in hell fire. [23]So then, if you are bringing your offering to the altar and there remember that your brother has something against you, [24]leave your offering there before the altar, go and be reconciled with your brother first, and then come back and present your offering. [25]Come to terms with your opponent in good time while you are still on

5a Lk 6:20–23.
5b Ps 37:11.
5c Gn 13:15.
5d Ex 20:13.

the way to the court with him, or he may
hand you over to the judge and the judge to
the officer, and you will be thrown into
prison. [26]In truth I tell you, you will not get
out till you have paid the last penny.
[27]'You have heard how it was said, *You
shall not commit adultery.*[e] [28]But I say this to
you, if a man looks at a woman lustfully, he
has already committed adultery with her in
his heart. [29]If your right eye should be your
downfall, tear it out and throw it away; for it
will do you less harm to lose one part of
yourself than to have your whole body thrown
into hell. [30]And if your right hand should be
your downfall, cut it off and throw it away;
for it will do you less harm to lose one part of
yourself than to have your whole body go to
hell.
[31]'It has also been said, *Anyone who divorces
his wife must give her a writ of dismissal.*[f] [32]But
I say this to you, everyone who divorces his
wife, except for the case of an illicit marriage,[g]
makes her an adulteress; and anyone who
marries a divorced woman commits adultery.
[33]'Again, you have heard how it was said
to our ancestors, *You must not break your oath,
but must fulfil your oaths to the Lord.*[h] [34]But I
say this to you, do not swear at all, either by
heaven, since that is *God's throne*; [35]or by
earth, since that is *his footstool*; or by Jeru-
salem, since that is *the city of the great King.*[i]
[36]Do not swear by your own head either,
since you cannot turn a single hair white or
black. [37]All you need say is "Yes" if you
mean yes, "No" if you mean no; anything
more than this comes from the Evil One.
[38]'You have heard how it was said: *Eye for
eye and tooth for tooth.*[j] [39]But I say this to you:
offer no resistance to the wicked. On the
contrary, if anyone hits you on the right
cheek, offer him the other as well; [40]if some-
one wishes to go to law with you to get your
tunic, let him have your cloak as well. [41]And
if anyone requires you to go one mile, go two
miles with him. [42]Give to anyone who asks
you, and if anyone wants to borrow, do not
turn away.
[43]'You have heard how it was said, *You will
love your neighbour*[k] and hate your enemy.
[44]But I say this to you, love your enemies and
pray for those who persecute you; [45]so that
you may be children of your Father in heaven,
for he causes his sun to rise on the bad as well
as the good, and sends down rain to fall on
the upright and the wicked alike. [46]For if you
love those who love you, what reward will
you get? Do not even the tax collectors do as
much? [47]And if you save your greetings for
your brothers, are you doing anything excep-
tional? [48]Do not even the gentiles do as much?
You must therefore be perfect, just as your
heavenly Father is perfect.'

Almsgiving in secret

6 'Be careful not to parade your uprightness
in public to attract attention; otherwise
you will lose all reward from your Father in
heaven. [2]So when you give alms, do not have
it trumpeted before you; this is what the
hypocrites do in the synagogues and in the
streets to win human admiration. In truth I
tell you, they have had their reward. [3]But
when you give alms, your left hand must
not know what your right is doing; [4]your
almsgiving must be secret, and your Father
who sees all that is done in secret will
reward you.

Prayer in secret

[5]'And when you pray, do not imitate the
hypocrites: they love to say their prayers
standing up in the synagogues and at the
street corners for people to see them. In truth
I tell you, they have had their reward. [6]But
when you pray, *go to your private* room, shut
yourself in, and so pray[a] to your Father who
is in that secret place, and your Father who
sees all that is done in secret will reward you.

How to pray. The Lord's Prayer

[7]'In your prayers do not babble as the gentiles
do, for they think that by using many words
they will make themselves heard. [8]Do not be

5e Ex 20:14.
5f Dt 24:1.
5g Marriage within the Jewish forbidden degrees, allowed by the Romans but not in Christianity.
5h Ex 20:7.
5i Ps 48:2.
5j Ex 21:24.
5k Lv 19:18. The rest of the sentence is not from the OT.
6a Is 26:20.

like them; your Father knows what you need
before you ask him. 9So you should pray like
this:

Our Father in heaven,
may your name be held holy,
10your kingdom come,
your will be done,
on earth as in heaven.
11Give us today our daily bread.
12And forgive us our debts,
as we have forgiven those
who are in debt to us.
13And do not put us to the test,
but save us from the Evil One.[b]

14'Yes, if you forgive others their failings,
your heavenly Father will forgive you yours;
15but if you do not forgive others, your Father
will not forgive your failings either.

Fasting in secret

16'When you are fasting, do not put on a
gloomy look as the hypocrites do: they go
about looking unsightly to let people know
they are fasting. In truth I tell you, they have
had their reward. 17But when you fast, put
scent on your head and wash your face, 18so
that no one will know you are fasting except
your Father who sees all that is done in secret;
and your Father who sees all that is done in
secret will reward you.

True treasures

19'Do not store up treasures for yourselves
on earth, where moth and woodworm destroy
them and thieves can break in and steal. 20But
store up treasures for yourselves in heaven,
where neither moth nor woodworm destroys
them and thieves cannot break in and steal.
21For wherever your treasure is, there will
your heart be too.

The eye, the lamp of the body

22'The lamp of the body is the eye. It follows
that if your eye is clear, your whole body will
be filled with light. 23But if your eye is
diseased, your whole body will be darkness.
If then, the light inside you is darkened, what
darkness that will be!

God and money

24'No one can be the slave of two masters: he
will either hate the first and love the second,
or be attached to the first and despise the
second. You cannot be the slave both of God
and of money.

Trust in Providence

25'That is why I am telling you not to worry
about your life and what you are to eat, nor
about your body and what you are to wear.
Surely life is more than food, and the body
more than clothing! 26Look at the birds in
the sky. They do not sow or reap or gather
into barns; yet your heavenly Father feeds
them. Are you not worth much more than
they are? 27Can any of you, however much
you worry, add one single cubit to your span
of life? 28And why worry about clothing?
Think of the flowers growing in the fields;
they never have to work or spin; 29yet I assure
you that not even Solomon in all his royal
robes was clothed like one of these. 30Now if
that is how God clothes the wild flowers
growing in the field which are there today
and thrown into the furnace tomorrow, will
he not much more look after you, you who
have so little faith? 31So do not worry; do not
say, "What are we to eat? What are we to
drink? What are we to wear?" 32It is the
gentiles who set their hearts on all these
things. Your heavenly Father knows you
need them all. 33Set your hearts on his
kingdom first, and on God's saving justice,
and all these other things will be given you
as well. 34So do not worry about tomorrow:
tomorrow will take care of itself. Each day
has enough trouble of its own.'

Do not judge

7 'Do not judge, and you will not be judged;
2because the judgements you give are the
judgements you will get, and the standard
you use will be the standard used for you.
3Why do you observe the splinter in your
brother's eye and never notice the great log
in your own? 4And how dare you say to your
brother, "Let me take that splinter out of
your eye," when, look, there is a great log
in your own? 5Hypocrite! Take the log out
of your own eye first, and then you will see

6b Lk 11:2-4.

clearly enough to take the splinter out of your brother's eye.

Do not profane sacred things

6 'Do not give dogs what is holy; and do not throw your pearls in front of pigs, or they may trample them and then turn on you and tear you to pieces.

Effective prayer

7 'Ask, and it will be given to you; search, and you will find; knock, and the door will be opened to you. 8 Everyone who asks receives; everyone who searches finds; everyone who knocks will have the door opened. 9 Is there anyone among you who would hand his son a stone when he asked for bread? 10 Or would hand him a snake when he asked for a fish? 11 If you, then, evil as you are, know how to give your children what is good, how much more will your Father in heaven give good things to those who ask him!

The golden rule

12 'So always treat others as you would like them to treat you; that is the Law and the Prophets.

The two ways

13 'Enter by the narrow gate, since the road that leads to destruction is wide and spacious, and many take it; 14 but it is a narrow gate and a hard road that leads to life, and only a few find it.

False prophets

15 'Beware of false prophets who come to you disguised as sheep but underneath are ravenous wolves. 16 You will be able to tell them by their fruits. Can people pick grapes from thorns, or figs from thistles? 17 In the same way, a sound tree produces good fruit but a rotten tree bad fruit. 18 A sound tree cannot bear bad fruit, nor a rotten tree bear good fruit. 19 Any tree that does not produce good fruit is cut down and thrown on the fire. 20 I repeat, you will be able to tell them by their fruits.

The true disciple

21 'It is not anyone who says to me, "Lord, Lord," who will enter the kingdom of Heaven, but the person who does the will of my Father in heaven. 22 When the day comes many will say to me, "Lord, Lord, did we not prophesy in your name, drive out demons in your name, work many miracles in your name?" 23 Then I shall tell them to their faces: I have never known you; *away from me, all evil doers!*[a]

24 'Therefore, everyone who listens to these words of mine and acts on them will be like a sensible man who built his house on rock. 25 Rain came down, floods rose, gales blew and hurled themselves against that house, and it did not fall: it was founded on rock. 26 But everyone who listens to these words of mine and does not act on them will be like a stupid man who built his house on sand. 27 Rain came down, floods rose, gales blew and struck that house, and it fell; and what a fall it had!'

The amazement of the crowds

28 Jesus had now finished what he wanted to say, and his teaching made a deep impression on the people 29 because he taught them with authority, unlike their own scribes.

III: THE KINGDOM OF HEAVEN IS PREACHED

A: NARRATIVE SECTION: TEN MIRACLES

Cure of a man with skin-disease

8 After he had come down from the mountain large crowds followed him. 2 Suddenly a man with a virulent skin-disease came up and bowed low in front of him, saying, 'Lord, if you are willing, you can cleanse me.' 3 Jesus stretched out his hand and touched him saying, 'I am willing. Be cleansed.' And his skin-disease was cleansed at once. 4 Then Jesus said to him, 'Mind you tell no one, but

7a Ps 6:8.

go and show yourself to the priest and make the offering prescribed by Moses,[a] as evidence to them.'

Cure of the centurion's servant

5 When he went into Capernaum a centurion came up and pleaded with him. 6 'Sir,' he said, 'my servant is lying at home paralysed and in great pain.' 7 Jesus said to him, 'I will come myself and cure him.' 8 The centurion replied, 'Sir, I am not worthy to have you under my roof; just give the word and my servant will be cured. 9 For I am under authority myself and have soldiers under me; and I say to one man, "Go," and he goes; to another, "Come here," and he comes; to my servant, "Do this," and he does it.' 10 When Jesus heard this he was astonished and said to those following him, 'In truth I tell you, in no one in Israel have I found faith as great as this. 11 And I tell you that many will come from east and west and sit down with Abraham and Isaac and Jacob at the feast in the kingdom of Heaven; 12 but the children of the kingdom will be thrown out into the darkness outside, where there will be weeping and grinding of teeth.' 13 And to the centurion Jesus said, 'Go back, then; let this be done for you, as your faith demands.' And the servant was cured at that moment.

Cure of Peter's mother-in-law

14 And going into Peter's house Jesus found Peter's mother-in-law in bed and feverish. 15 He touched her hand and the fever left her, and she got up and began to serve him.

A number of cures

16 That evening they brought him many who were possessed by devils. He drove out the spirits with a command and cured all who were sick. 17 This was to fulfil what was spoken by the prophet Isaiah:

He himself bore our sicknesses away
and carried our diseases.[b]

Unconditional commitment

18 When Jesus saw the crowd all about him he gave orders to leave for the other side. 19 One of the scribes then came up and said to him, 'Master, I will follow you wherever you go.' 20 Jesus said, 'Foxes have holes and the birds of the air have nests, but the Son of man has nowhere to lay his head.'

21 Another man, one of the disciples, said to him, 'Lord, let me go and bury my father first.' 22 But Jesus said, 'Follow me, and leave the dead to bury their dead.'

The calming of the storm

23 Then he got into the boat followed by his disciples. 24 Suddenly a storm broke over the lake, so violent that the boat was being swamped by the waves. But he was asleep. 25 So they went to him and woke him saying, 'Save us, Lord, we are lost!' 26 And he said to them, 'Why are you so frightened, you who have so little faith?' And then he stood up and rebuked the winds and the sea; and there was a great calm. 27 They were astounded and said, 'Whatever kind of man is this, that even the winds and the sea obey him?'

The demoniacs of Gadara

28 When he reached the territory of the Gadarenes on the other side, two demoniacs came towards him out of the tombs—they were so dangerously violent that nobody could use that path. 29 Suddenly they shouted, 'What do you want with us, Son of God? Have you come here to torture us before the time?' 30 Now some distance away there was a large herd of pigs feeding, 31 and the devils pleaded with Jesus, 'If you drive us out, send us into the herd of pigs.' 32 And he said to them, 'Go then,' and they came out and made for the pigs; and at that the whole herd charged down the cliff into the lake and perished in the water. 33 The herdsmen ran off and made for the city, where they told the whole story, including what had happened to the demoniacs. 34 Suddenly the whole city set out to meet Jesus; and as soon as they saw him they implored him to leave their neighbourhood.

Cure of a paralytic

9 He got back in the boat, crossed the water and came to his home town. 2 And suddenly some people brought him a para-

8a Lv 14:1–32.
8b Is 53:4.

lytic stretched out on a bed. Seeing their faith, Jesus said to the paralytic, 'Take comfort, my child, your sins are forgiven.' 3And now some scribes said to themselves, 'This man is being blasphemous.' 4Knowing what was in their minds Jesus said, 'Why do you have such wicked thoughts in your hearts? 5Now, which of these is easier: to say, "Your sins are forgiven," or to say, "Get up and walk"? 6But to prove to you that the Son of man has authority on earth to forgive sins,'—then he said to the paralytic—'get up, pick up your bed and go off home.' 7And the man got up and went home. 8A feeling of awe came over the crowd when they saw this, and they praised God for having given such authority to human beings.

The call of Matthew

9As Jesus was walking on from there he saw a man named Matthew sitting at the tax office, and he said to him, 'Follow me.' And he got up and followed him.

Eating with sinners

10Now while he was at table in the house it happened that a number of tax collectors and sinners came to sit at the table with Jesus and his disciples. 11When the Pharisees saw this, they said to his disciples, 'Why does your master eat with tax collectors and sinners?' 12When he heard this he replied, 'It is not the healthy who need the doctor, but the sick. 13Go and learn the meaning of the words: *Mercy is what pleases me, not sacrifice.*[a] And indeed I came to call not the upright, but sinners.'

A discussion on fasting

14Then John's disciples came to him and said, 'Why is it that we and the Pharisees fast, but your disciples do not?' 15Jesus replied, 'Surely the bridegroom's attendants cannot mourn as long as the bridegroom is still with them? But the time will come when the bridegroom is taken away from them, and then they will fast. 16No one puts a piece of unshrunken cloth onto an old cloak, because the patch pulls away from the cloak and the tear gets worse. 17Nor do people put new wine into old wineskins; otherwise, the skins burst, the wine runs out, and the skins are lost. No; they put new wine in fresh skins and both are preserved.'

Cure of the woman with a haemorrhage
The official's daughter raised to life

18While he was speaking to them, suddenly one of the officials came up, who bowed low in front of him and said, 'My daughter has just died, but come and lay your hand on her and her life will be saved.' 19Jesus rose and, with his disciples, followed him.

20Then suddenly from behind him came a woman, who had been suffering from a haemorrhage for twelve years, and she touched the fringe of his cloak, 21for she was thinking, 'If only I can touch his cloak I shall be saved.' 22Jesus turned round and saw her; and he said to her, 'Courage, my daughter, your faith has saved you.' And from that moment the woman was saved.

23When Jesus reached the official's house and saw the flute-players, with the crowd making a commotion, he said, 24'Get out of here; the little girl is not dead; she is asleep.' And they ridiculed him. 25But when the people had been turned out he went inside and took her by the hand; and she stood up. 26And the news of this spread all round the countryside.

Cure of two blind men

27As Jesus went on his way two blind men followed him shouting, 'Take pity on us, son of David.' 28And when Jesus reached the house the blind men came up to him and he said to them, 'Do you believe I can do this?' They said, 'Lord, we do.' 29Then he touched their eyes saying, 'According to your faith, let it be done to you.' 30And their sight returned. Then Jesus sternly warned them, 'Take care that no one learns about this.' 31But when they had gone away, they talked about him all over the countryside.

Cure of a dumb demoniac

32They had only just left when suddenly a man was brought to him, a dumb demoniac. 33And when the devil was driven out, the dumb man spoke and the people were amazed and said, 'Nothing like this has ever been

9a Ho 6:6.

seen in Israel.' 34But the Pharisees said, 'It is
through the prince of devils that he drives
out devils.'

The distress of the crowds

35Jesus made a tour through all the towns
and villages, teaching in their synagogues,
proclaiming the good news of the kingdom
and curing all kinds of disease and all kinds
of illness.
36And when he saw the crowds he felt sorry
for them because they were harassed and
dejected, like sheep without a shepherd.
37Then he said to his disciples, 'The harvest
is rich but the labourers are few, so ask the
Lord of the harvest to send out labourers to
his harvest.'

B: INSTRUCTION FOR APOSTLES

The mission of the Twelve[a]

10 He summoned his twelve disciples and
gave them authority over unclean
spirits with power to drive them out and to
cure all kinds of disease and all kinds of
illness.
2These are the names of the twelve
apostles: first, Simon who is known as Peter,
and his brother Andrew; James the son of
Zebedee, and his brother John; 3Philip and
Bartholomew; Thomas, and Matthew the tax
collector; James the son of Alphaeus, and
Thaddaeus; 4Simon the Zealot and Judas
Iscariot, who was also his betrayer. 5These
twelve Jesus sent out, instructing them as
follows:
'Do not make your way to gentile territory,
and do not enter any Samaritan town; 6go
instead to the lost sheep of the House of
Israel. 7And as you go, proclaim that the
kingdom of Heaven is close at hand. 8Cure the
sick, raise the dead, cleanse those suffering
from virulent skin-diseases, drive out devils.
You received without charge, give without
charge. 9Provide yourselves with no gold or
silver, not even with coppers for your purses,
10with no haversack for the journey or spare
tunic or footwear or a staff, for the labourer
deserves his keep.
11'Whatever town or village you go into,
seek out someone worthy and stay with him
until you leave. 12As you enter his house,
salute it, 13and if the house deserves it, may
your peace come upon it; if it does not,
may your peace come back to you. 14And if
anyone does not welcome you or listen to
what you have to say, as you walk out of the
house or town shake the dust from your feet.
15In truth I tell you, on the Day of Judgement
it will be more bearable for Sodom and
Gomorrah than for that town. 16Look, I am
sending you out like sheep among wolves; so
be cunning as snakes and yet innocent as
doves.

Missionaries will be persecuted

17'Be prepared for people to hand you over
to sanhedrins and scourge you in their syna-
gogues. 18You will be brought before gover-
nors and kings for my sake, as evidence to
them and to the gentiles. 19But when you are
handed over, do not worry about how to
speak or what to say; what you are to say
will be given to you when the time comes,
20because it is not you who will be speaking;
the Spirit of your Father will be speaking in
you.
21'Brother will betray brother to death,
and a father his child; children will come
forward against their parents and have them
put to death. 22You will be universally hated
on account of my name; but anyone who
stands firm to the end will be saved. 23If they
persecute you in one town, take refuge in the
next; and if they persecute you in that, take
refuge in another. In truth I tell you, you will
not have gone the round of the towns of Israel
before the Son of man comes.
24'Disciple is not superior to teacher, nor
slave to master. 25It is enough for disciple to
grow to be like teacher, and slave like master.
If they have called the master of the house
"Beelzebul", how much more the members
of his household?

Open and fearless speech

26'So do not be afraid of them. Everything
now covered up will be uncovered, and every-
thing now hidden will be made clear. 27What
I say to you in the dark, tell in the daylight;
what you hear in whispers, proclaim from
the housetops.
28'Do not be afraid of those who kill the

10a Mk 3:14–19; Lk 6:13–16; the order and even some of the names vary in the different lists.

body but cannot kill the soul; fear him rather who can destroy both body and soul in hell. 29Can you not buy two sparrows for a penny? And yet not one falls to the ground without your Father knowing. 30Why, every hair on your head has been counted. 31So there is no need to be afraid; you are worth more than many sparrows.

32'So if anyone declares himself for me in the presence of human beings, I will declare myself for him in the presence of my Father in heaven. 33But the one who disowns me in the presence of human beings, I will disown in the presence of my Father in heaven.

Jesus, the cause of dissension

34'Do not suppose that I have come to bring peace to the earth: it is not peace I have come to bring, but a sword. 35For I have come to set son against *father, daughter against mother, daughter-in-law against mother-in-law;* 36*a person's enemies will be the members of his own household.*[b]

Renouncing self to follow Jesus

37'No one who prefers father or mother to me is worthy of me. No one who prefers son or daughter to me is worthy of me. 38Anyone who does not take his cross and follow in my footsteps is not worthy of me. 39Anyone who finds his life will lose it; anyone who loses his life for my sake will find it.

Conclusion of the Instruction

40'Anyone who welcomes you welcomes me; and anyone who welcomes me welcomes the one who sent me.

41'Anyone who welcomes a prophet because he is a prophet will have a prophet's reward; and anyone who welcomes an upright person because he is upright will have the reward of an upright person.

42'If anyone gives so much as a cup of cold water to one of these little ones because he is a disciple, then in truth I tell you, he will most certainly not go without his reward.'

IV: THE MYSTERY OF THE KINGDOM OF HEAVEN

A: NARRATIVE SECTION

11 When Jesus had finished instructing his twelve disciples he moved on from there to teach and preach in their towns.

The Baptist's question
Jesus commends him

2Now John had heard in prison what Christ was doing and he sent his disciples to ask him, 3'Are you the one who is to come, or are we to expect someone else?' 4Jesus answered, 'Go back and tell John what you hear and see; 5the blind see again, and the lame walk, those suffering from virulent skin-diseases are cleansed, and the deaf hear, the dead are raised to life and the good news is proclaimed to the poor;[a] 6and blessed is anyone who does not find me a cause of falling.'

7As the men were leaving, Jesus began to talk to the people about John, 'What did you go out into the desert to see? A reed swaying in the breeze? No? 8Then what did you go out to see? A man wearing fine clothes? Look, those who wear fine clothes are to be found in palaces. 9Then what did you go out for? To see a prophet? Yes, I tell you, and much more than a prophet: 10he is the one of whom scripture says:

Look, I am going to send my messenger
in front of you
to prepare your way before you.[b]

11'In truth I tell you, of all the children born to women, there has never been anyone greater than John the Baptist; yet the least in the kingdom of Heaven is greater than he. 12Since John the Baptist came, up to this present time, the kingdom of Heaven has been subjected to violence and the violent are taking it by storm. 13Because it was towards John that all the prophecies of the prophets and of the Law were leading; 14and he, if you will believe me, is the Elijah who was to return. 15Anyone who has ears should listen!

10b Mi 7:6.
11a cf. Is 35:5; 61:1.
11b Ml 3:1.

Jesus condemns his contemporaries

16 'What comparison can I find for this genera-
tion? It is like children shouting to each other
as they sit in the market place:

17 We played the pipes for you,
and you wouldn't dance;
we sang dirges,
and you wouldn't be mourners.

18 'For John came, neither eating nor
drinking, and they say, "He is possessed."
19 The Son of man came, eating and drinking,
and they say, "Look, a glutton and a
drunkard, a friend of tax collectors and
sinners." Yet wisdom is justified by her
deeds.'

Lament over the lake-towns

20 Then he began to reproach the towns in
which most of his miracles had been worked,
because they refused to repent.
21 'Alas for you, Chorazin! Alas for you,
Bethsaida! For if the miracles done in you
had been done in Tyre and Sidon, they would
have repented long ago in sackcloth and
ashes. 22 Still, I tell you that it will be more
bearable for Tyre and Sidon on Judgement
Day than for you. 23 And as for you, Caper-
naum, did you want to be *raised as high as*
heaven? You shall be flung down to hell.[c] For
if the miracles done in you had been done in
Sodom, it would have been standing yet.
24 Still, I tell you that it will be more bearable
for Sodom on Judgement Day than for you.'

The good news revealed to the simple
The Father and the Son

25 At that time Jesus exclaimed, 'I bless you,
Father, Lord of heaven and of earth, for
hiding these things from the learned and the
clever and revealing them to little children.
26 Yes, Father, for that is what it pleased you
to do. 27 Everything has been entrusted to me
by my Father; and no one knows the Son
except the Father, just as no one knows the
Father except the Son and those to whom the
Son chooses to reveal him.

The gentle mastery of Christ

28 'Come to me, all you who labour and are
overburdened, and I will give you rest.
29 Shoulder my yoke and learn from me, for I
am gentle and humble in heart, *and you will*
find rest for your souls.[d] 30 Yes, my yoke is easy
and my burden light.'

Picking corn on the Sabbath

12 At that time Jesus went through the
cornfields one Sabbath day. His
disciples were hungry and began to pick ears
of corn and eat them. 2 The Pharisees noticed
it and said to him, 'Look, your disciples are
doing something that is forbidden on the
Sabbath.' 3 But he said to them, 'Have you
not read what David did when he and his
followers were hungry—4 how he went into
the house of God and they ate the loaves
of the offering although neither he nor his
followers were permitted to eat them, but
only the priests? 5 Or again, have you not read
in the Law that on the Sabbath day the
Temple priests break the Sabbath without
committing any fault? 6 Now here, I tell you,
is something greater than the Temple. 7 And
if you had understood the meaning of the
words: *Mercy is what pleases me, not sacrifice*,[a]
you would not have condemned the blame-
less. 8 For the Son of man is master of the
Sabbath.'

Cure of the man with a withered hand

9 He moved on from there and went to their
synagogue; 10 now a man was there with a
withered hand. They asked him, 'Is it
permitted to cure somebody on the Sabbath
day?' hoping for something to charge him
with. 11 But he said to them, 'If any one of
you here had only one sheep and it fell down
a hole on the Sabbath day, would he not get
hold of it and lift it out? 12 Now a man is far
more important than a sheep, so it follows
that it is permitted on the Sabbath day to do
good.' 13 Then he said to the man, 'Stretch
out your hand.' He stretched it out and his
hand was restored, as sound as the other one.
14 At this the Pharisees went out and began
to plot against him, discussing how to
destroy him.

11c Is 14:13, 15.
11d Jr 6:16.
12a Ho 6:6.

Jesus the 'servant of Yahweh'

[15]Jesus knew this and withdrew from the
district. Many followed him and he cured
them all [16]but warned them not to make him
known. [17]This was to fulfil what was spoken
by the prophet Isaiah:[b]

[18]*Look! My servant whom I have chosen,*
my beloved, in whom my soul delights,
I will send my Spirit upon him,
and he will *present* judgement
to the nations;
[19]*he will not brawl or cry out,*
his voice is not heard in the streets,
[20]*he will not break the crushed reed,*
or snuff the faltering wick,
[21]*until he has made judgement victorious;*
in him the nations will put their hope.[b]

Jesus and Beelzebul

[22]Then they brought to him a blind and dumb
demoniac; and he cured him, so that the
dumb man could speak and see. [23]All the
people were astounded and said, 'Can this be
the son of David?' [24]But when the Pharisees
heard this they said, 'The man drives out
devils only through Beelzebul, the chief of
the devils.'
[25]Knowing what was in their minds he said
to them, 'Every kingdom divided against
itself is heading for ruin; and no town, no
household divided against itself can last.
[26]Now if Satan drives out Satan, he is divided
against himself; so how can his kingdom last?
[27]And if it is through Beelzebul that I drive
devils out, through whom do your own
experts drive them out? They shall be your
judges, then. [28]But if it is through the Spirit
of God that I drive out devils, then be sure
that the kingdom of God has caught you
unawares.
[29]'Or again, how can anyone make his way
into a strong man's house and plunder his
property unless he has first tied up the strong
man? Only then can he plunder his house.
[30]'Anyone who is not with me is against
me, and anyone who does not gather in with
me throws away. [31]And so I tell you, every
human sin and blasphemy will be forgiven,
but blasphemy against the Spirit will not be
forgiven. [32]And anyone who says a word
against the Son of man will be forgiven; but
no one who speaks against the Holy Spirit
will be forgiven either in this world or in the
next.

Words betray the heart

[33]'Make a tree sound and its fruit will be
sound; make a tree rotten and its fruit will
be rotten. For the tree can be told by its fruit.
[34]You brood of vipers, how can your speech
be good when you are evil? For words flow
out of what fills the heart. [35]Good people draw
good things from their store of goodness; bad
people draw bad things from their store of
badness. [36]So I tell you this, that for every
unfounded word people utter they will
answer on Judgement Day, [37]since it is by
your words you will be justified, and by your
words condemned.'

The sign of Jonah

[38]Then some of the scribes and Pharisees
spoke up. 'Master,' they said, 'we should like
to see a sign from you.' [39]He replied, 'It is an
evil and unfaithful generation that asks for a
sign! The only sign it will be given is the sign
of the prophet Jonah. [40]For as Jonah *re-*
mained in the belly of the sea-monster for three
days and three nights,[c] so will the Son of man
be in the heart of the earth for three days and
three nights. [41]On Judgement Day the men of
Nineveh will appear against this generation
and they will be its condemnation, because
when Jonah preached they repented; and
look, there is something greater than Jonah
here. [42]On Judgement Day the Queen of the
South will appear against this generation and
be its condemnation, because she came from
the ends of the earth to hear the wisdom
of Solomon; and look, there is something
greater than Solomon here.

The return of the unclean spirit

[43]'When an unclean spirit goes out of
someone it wanders through waterless
country looking for a place to rest, and cannot
find one. [44]Then it says, "I will return to the
home I came from." But on arrival, finding
it unoccupied, swept and tidied, [45]it then
goes off and collects seven other spirits more
wicked than itself, and they go in and set up

12b Is 42:1–4.
12c Jon 2:1.

house there, and so that person ends up worse
off than before. That is what will happen to
this wicked generation.'

The true kinsfolk of Jesus

[46]He was still speaking to the crowds when
suddenly his mother and his brothers[d] were
standing outside and were anxious to have a
word with him.[47][e] [48]But to the man who
told him this Jesus replied, 'Who is my
mother? Who are my brothers?' [49]And
stretching out his hand towards his disciples
he said, 'Here are my mother and my
brothers. [50]Anyone who does the will of my
Father in heaven is my brother and sister and
mother.'

B: DISCOURSE OF PARABLES

Introduction

13 That same day, Jesus left the house and
sat by the lakeside, [2]but such large
crowds gathered round him that he got into
a boat and sat there. The people all stood on
the shore, [3]and he told them many things in
parables.

Parable of the sower

He said, 'Listen, a sower went out to sow.
[4]As he sowed, some seeds fell on the edge of
the path, and the birds came and ate them
up. [5]Others fell on patches of rock where
they found little soil and sprang up at once,
because there was no depth of earth; [6]but as
soon as the sun came up they were scorched
and, not having any roots, they withered
away. [7]Others fell among thorns, and the
thorns grew up and choked them. [8]Others
fell on rich soil and produced their crop,
some a hundredfold, some sixty, some thirty.
[9]Anyone who has ears should listen!'

Why Jesus speaks in parables

[10]Then the disciples went up to him and
asked, 'Why do you talk to them in parables?'
[11]In answer, he said, 'Because to you is
granted to understand the mysteries of the
kingdom of Heaven, but to them it is not
granted. [12]Anyone who has will be given
more and will have more than enough; but
anyone who has not will be deprived even of
what he has. [13]The reason I talk to them in
parables is that they look without seeing and
listen without hearing or understanding. [14]So
in their case what was spoken by the prophet
Isaiah is being fulfilled:

Listen and listen, but never understand!
Look and look, but never perceive!
[15]*This people's heart has grown coarse,*
their ears dulled,
they have shut their eyes tight
to avoid using their eyes to see,
their ears to hear,
their heart to understand,
changing their ways
and being healed by me.[a]

[16]'But blessed are your eyes because they
see, your ears because they hear! [17]In truth I
tell you, many prophets and upright people
longed to see what you see, and never saw it;
to hear what you hear, and never heard it.

The parable of the sower explained

[18]'So pay attention to the parable of the
sower. [19]When anyone hears the word of the
kingdom without understanding, the Evil
One comes and carries off what was sown in
his heart: this is the seed sown on the edge of
the path. [20]The seed sown on patches of rock
is someone who hears the word and welcomes
it at once with joy. [21]But such a person has
no root deep down and does not last; should
some trial come, or some persecution on
account of the word, at once he falls away.
[22]The seed sown in thorns is someone who
hears the word, but the worry of the world
and the lure of riches choke the word and so
it produces nothing. [23]And the seed sown in
rich soil is someone who hears the word and
understands it; this is the one who yields a
harvest and produces now a hundredfold,
now sixty, now thirty.'

Parable of the darnel

[24]He put another parable before them, 'The
kingdom of Heaven may be compared to a

12d Not necessarily Mary's children. The Hebr. and Aram. word includes cousins and close relations.
12e v. 47 ('Someone said to him: Your mother and brothers are standing outside and want to speak to you') is omitted by some important textual witnesses. It is probably a restatement of v. 46 modelled on Mk and Lk.
13a Is 6:9–10.

man who sowed good seed in his field. 25While
everybody was asleep his enemy came, sowed
darnel all among the wheat, and made off.
26When the new wheat sprouted and ripened,
then the darnel appeared as well. 27The
owner's labourers went to him and said, "Sir,
was it not good seed that you sowed in your
field? If so, where does the darnel come
from?" 28He said to them, "Some enemy has
done this." And the labourers said, "Do you
want us to go and weed it out?" 29But he said,
"No, because when you weed out the darnel
you might pull up the wheat with it. 30Let
them both grow till the harvest; and at harvest
time I shall say to the reapers: First collect
the darnel and tie it in bundles to be burnt,
then gather the wheat into my barn." '

Parable of the mustard seed

31He put another parable before them, 'The
kingdom of Heaven is like a mustard seed
which a man took and sowed in his field. 32It
is the smallest of all the seeds, but when it
has grown it is the biggest of shrubs and
becomes a tree, so that the birds of the air
can come and shelter in its branches.'

Parable of the yeast

33He told them another parable, 'The
kingdom of Heaven is like the yeast a woman
took and mixed in with three measures of
flour till it was leavened all through.'

The people are taught only in parables

34In all this Jesus spoke to the crowds in
parables; indeed, he would never speak to
them except in parables. 35This was to fulfil
what was spoken by the prophet:

I will speak to you in parables,
unfold what has been hidden
since the foundation of the world.[b]

The parable of the darnel explained

36Then, leaving the crowds, he went to the
house; and his disciples came to him and
said, 'Explain to us the parable about the
darnel in the field.' 37He said in reply, 'The
sower of the good seed is the Son of man.
38The field is the world; the good seed is
the subjects of the kingdom; the darnel, the
subjects of the Evil One; 39the enemy who
sowed it, the devil; the harvest is the end of
the world; the reapers are the angels. 40Well
then, just as the darnel is gathered up and
burnt in the fire, so it will be at the end of
time. 41The Son of man will send his angels
and they will gather out of his kingdom all
causes of falling and all who do evil, 42and
throw them into the blazing furnace, where
there will be weeping and grinding of teeth.
43Then the upright will shine like the sun in
the kingdom of their Father. Anyone who
has ears should listen!

Parables of the treasure and of the pearl

44'The kingdom of Heaven is like treasure
hidden in a field which someone has found;
he hides it again, goes off in his joy, sells
everything he owns and buys the field.

45'Again, the kingdom of Heaven is like a
merchant looking for fine pearls; 46when he
finds one of great value he goes and sells
everything he owns and buys it.

Parable of the dragnet

47'Again, the kingdom of Heaven is like a
dragnet that is cast in the sea and brings in a
haul of all kinds of fish. 48When it is full, the
fishermen bring it ashore; then, sitting down,
they collect the good ones in baskets and
throw away those that are no use. 49This is
how it will be at the end of time: the angels
will appear and separate the wicked from the
upright, 50to throw them into the blazing
furnace, where there will be weeping and
grinding of teeth.

Conclusion

51'Have you understood all these?' They said,
'Yes.' 52And he said to them, 'Well then,
every scribe who becomes a disciple of the
kingdom of Heaven is like a householder who
brings out from his storeroom new things as
well as old.'

13b Ps 78:2.

V: THE CHURCH
FIRST-FRUITS OF THE KINGDOM OF HEAVEN

A: NARRATIVE SECTION

A visit to Nazareth

53When Jesus had finished these parables he
left the district; 54and, coming to his home
town, he taught the people in their synagogue
in such a way that they were astonished and
said, 'Where did the man get this wisdom
and these miraculous powers? 55This is the
carpenter's son, surely? Is not his mother the
woman called Mary, and his brothers James
and Joseph and Simon and Jude? 56His
sisters, too, are they not all here with us? So
where did the man get it all?' 57And they
would not accept him. But Jesus said to them,
'A prophet is despised only in his own country
and in his own house,' 58and he did not work
many miracles there because of their lack of
faith.

Herod and Jesus

14 At that time Herod the tetrarch heard
about the reputation of Jesus 2and said
to his court, 'This is John the Baptist himself;
he has risen from the dead, and that is why
miraculous powers are at work in him.'

John the Baptist beheaded

3Now it was Herod who had arrested John,
chained him up and put him in prison because
of Herodias, his brother Philip's wife. 4For
John had told him, 'It is against the Law for
you to have her.' 5He had wanted to kill him
but was afraid of the people, who regarded
John as a prophet. 6Then, during the cele-
brations for Herod's birthday, the daughter
of Herodias danced before the company and
so delighted Herod 7that he promised on oath
to give her anything she asked. 8Prompted
by her mother she said, 'Give me John the
Baptist's head, here, on a dish.' 9The king
was distressed but, thinking of the oaths he
had sworn and of his guests, he ordered it
to be given her, 10and sent and had John
beheaded in the prison. 11The head was
brought in on a dish and given to the girl,
who took it to her mother. 12John's disciples
came and took the body and buried it; then
they went off to tell Jesus.

First miracle of the loaves[a]

13When Jesus received this news he withdrew
by boat to a lonely place where they could be
by themselves. But the crowds heard of this
and, leaving the towns, went after him on
foot. 14So as he stepped ashore he saw a large
crowd; and he took pity on them and healed
their sick.

15When evening came, the disciples went
to him and said, 'This is a lonely place, and
time has slipped by; so send the people
away, and they can go to the villages to
buy themselves some food.' 16Jesus replied,
'There is no need for them to go: give them
something to eat yourselves.' 17But they
answered, 'All we have with us is five loaves
and two fish.' 18So he said, 'Bring them here
to me.' 19He gave orders that the people were
to sit down on the grass; then he took the five
loaves and the two fish, raised his eyes to
heaven and said the blessing. And breaking
the loaves he handed them to his disciples,
who gave them to the crowds. 20They all ate
as much as they wanted, and they collected
the scraps left over, twelve baskets full.
21Now about five thousand men had eaten,
to say nothing of women and children.

Jesus walks on the water and, with him, Peter

22And at once he made the disciples get into
the boat and go on ahead to the other side
while he sent the crowds away. 23After
sending the crowds away he went up into the
hills by himself to pray. When evening came,
he was there alone, 24while the boat, by now
some furlongs from land, was hard pressed
by rough waves, for there was a head-wind.
25In the fourth watch of the night he came
towards them, walking on the sea, 26and
when the disciples saw him walking on the
sea they were terrified. 'It is a ghost,' they
said, and cried out in fear. 27But at once Jesus

14a This and 15:32–39 are probably varying accounts of the same incident. This one echoes 2 K 4:42.

called out to them, saying, 'Courage! It's me! Don't be afraid.' [28]It was Peter who answered. 'Lord,' he said, 'if it is you, tell me to come to you across the water.' [29]Jesus said, 'Come.' Then Peter got out of the boat and started walking towards Jesus across the water, [30]but then noticing the wind, he took fright and began to sink. 'Lord,' he cried, 'save me!' [31]Jesus put out his hand at once and held him. 'You have so little faith,' he said, 'why did you doubt?' [32]And as they got into the boat the wind dropped. [33]The men in the boat bowed down before him and said, 'Truly, you are the Son of God.'

Cures at Gennesaret

[34]Having made the crossing, they came to land at Gennesaret. [35]When the local people recognised him they spread the news through the whole neighbourhood and took all that were sick to him, [36]begging him just to let them touch the fringe of his cloak. And all those who touched it were saved.

The traditions of the Pharisees

15 Then Pharisees and scribes from Jerusalem came to Jesus and said, [2]'Why do your disciples break away from the tradition of the elders? They eat without washing their hands.' [3]He answered, 'And why do you break away from the commandment of God for the sake of your tradition? [4]For God said, *"Honour your father and your mother"* and *"Anyone who curses his father or mother will be put to death."*[a] [5]But you say, "If anyone says to his father or mother: Anything I might have used to help you is dedicated to God, [6]he is rid of his duty to father or mother." In this way you have made God's word ineffective by means of your tradition. [7]Hypocrites! How rightly Isaiah prophesied about you when he said:

[8]*This people honours me*
only with lip-service,
while their hearts are far from me.
[9]*Their reverence of me is worthless;*
the lessons they teach are nothing
but human commandments.'[b]

On clean and unclean

[10]He called the people to him and said, 'Listen, and understand. [11]What goes into the mouth does not make anyone unclean; it is what comes out of the mouth that makes someone unclean.'

[12]Then the disciples came to him and said, 'Do you know that the Pharisees were shocked when they heard what you said?' [13]He replied, 'Any plant my heavenly Father has not planted will be pulled up by the roots. [14]Leave them alone. They are blind leaders of the blind; and if one blind person leads another, both will fall into a pit.'

[15]At this, Peter said to him, 'Explain the parable for us.' [16]Jesus replied, 'Even you—don't you yet understand? [17]Can't you see that whatever goes into the mouth passes through the stomach and is discharged into the sewer? [18]But whatever comes out of the mouth comes from the heart, and it is this that makes someone unclean. [19]For from the heart come evil intentions: murder, adultery, fornication, theft, perjury, slander. [20]These are the things that make a person unclean. But eating with unwashed hands does not make anyone unclean.'

The daughter of the Canaanite woman healed

[21]Jesus left that place and withdrew to the region of Tyre and Sidon. [22]And suddenly out came a Canaanite woman from that district and started shouting, 'Lord, Son of David, take pity on me. My daughter is tormented by a devil.' [23]But he said not a word in answer to her. And his disciples went and pleaded with him, saying, 'Give her what she wants, because she keeps shouting after us.' [24]He said in reply, 'I was sent only to the lost sheep of the House of Israel.' [25]But the woman had come up and was bowing low before him. 'Lord,' she said, 'help me.' [26]He replied, 'It is not fair to take the children's food and throw it to little dogs.' [27]She retorted, 'Ah yes, Lord; but even little dogs eat the scraps that fall from their masters' table.' [28]Then Jesus answered her, 'Woman, you have great faith. Let your desire be granted.' And from that moment her daughter was well again.

15a Ex 20:12 and 21:17.
15b Is 29:13.

Cures near the lake

29 Jesus went on from there and reached the
shores of the Lake of Galilee, and he went up
onto the mountain. He took his seat, 30 and
large crowds came to him bringing the lame,
the crippled, the blind, the dumb and many
others; these they put down at his feet, and
he cured them. 31 The crowds were astonished
to see the dumb speaking, the cripples whole
again, the lame walking and the blind with
their sight, and they praised the God
of Israel.

Second miracle of the loaves

32 But Jesus called his disciples to him and
said, 'I feel sorry for all these people; they
have been with me for three days now and
have nothing to eat. I do not want to send
them off hungry, or they might collapse on
the way.' 33 The disciples said to him, 'Where
in a deserted place could we get sufficient
bread for such a large crowd to have enough
to eat?' 34 Jesus said to them, 'How many
loaves have you?' They said, 'Seven, and a
few small fish.' 35 Then he instructed the
crowd to sit down on the ground, 36 and he
took the seven loaves and the fish, and after
giving thanks he broke them and began
handing them to the disciples, who gave them
to the crowds. 37 They all ate as much as they
wanted, and they collected what was left of
the scraps, seven baskets full. 38 Now four
thousand men had eaten, to say nothing of
women and children. 39 And when he had
sent the crowds away he got into the boat and
went to the territory of Magadan.

The Pharisees ask for a sign from heaven

16 The Pharisees and Sadducees came,
and to put him to the test they asked if
he would show them a sign from heaven. 2 He
replied, 'In the evening you say, "It will be
fine; there's a red sky," 3 and in the morning,
"Stormy weather today; the sky is red and
overcast." You know how to read the face of
the sky, but you cannot read the signs of the
times. 4 It is an evil and unfaithful generation
asking for a sign, and the only sign it will be
given is the sign of Jonah.' And he left them
and went off.

The yeast of the Pharisees and Sadducees

5 The disciples, having crossed to the other
side, had forgotten to take any food. 6 Jesus
said to them, 'Keep your eyes open, and
be on your guard against the yeast of the
Pharisees and Sadducees.' 7 And they said
among themselves, 'It is because we have not
brought any bread.' 8 Jesus knew it, and he
said, 'You have so little faith, why are you
talking among yourselves about having no
bread? 9 Do you still not understand? Do you
not remember the five loaves for the five
thousand and the number of baskets you
collected? 10 Or the seven loaves for the four
thousand and the number of baskets you
collected? 11 How could you fail to understand
that I was not talking about bread? What I
said was: Beware of the yeast of the Pharisees
and Sadducees.' 12 Then they understood that
he was telling them to be on their guard,
not against yeast for making bread, but
against the teaching of the Pharisees and
Sadducees.

Peter's profession of faith; his pre-eminence

13 When Jesus came to the region of Caesarea
Philippi he put this question to his disciples,
'Who do people say the Son of man is?' 14 And
they said, 'Some say John the Baptist, some
Elijah, and others Jeremiah or one of the
prophets.' 15 'But you,' he said, 'who do you
say I am?' 16 Then Simon Peter spoke up and
said, 'You are the Christ, the Son of the living
God.' 17 Jesus replied, 'Simon son of Jonah,
you are a blessed man! Because it was no
human agency that revealed this to you but
my Father in heaven. 18 So I now say to you:
You are Peter[a] and on this rock I will build my
community. And the gates of the underworld
can never overpower it. 19 I will give you the
keys of the kingdom of Heaven: whatever
you bind on earth will be bound in heaven;
whatever you loose on earth will be loosed in
heaven.' 20 Then he gave the disciples strict
orders not to say to anyone that he was the
Christ.

First prophecy of the Passion

21 From then onwards Jesus began to make it
clear to his disciples that he was destined to

16a The name means 'rock'.

go to Jerusalem and suffer grievously at the hands of the elders and chief priests and scribes and to be put to death and to be raised up on the third day. [22]Then, taking him aside, Peter started to rebuke him. 'Heaven preserve you, Lord,' he said, 'this must not happen to you.' [23]But he turned and said to Peter, 'Get behind me, Satan! You are an obstacle in my path, because you are thinking not as God thinks but as human beings do.'

The condition of following Christ

[24]Then Jesus said to his disciples, 'If anyone wants to be a follower of mine, let him renounce himself and take up his cross and follow me. [25]Anyone who wants to save his life will lose it; but anyone who loses his life for my sake will find it. [26]What, then, will anyone gain by winning the whole world and forfeiting his life? Or what can anyone offer in exchange for his life?

[27]'For the Son of man is going to come in the glory of his Father with his angels, and then he will reward each one according to his behaviour. [28]In truth I tell you, there are some standing here who will not taste death before they see the Son of man coming with his kingdom.'

The transfiguration

17 Six days later, Jesus took with him Peter and James and his brother John and led them up a high mountain by themselves. [2]There in their presence he was transfigured: his face shone like the sun and his clothes became as dazzling as light. [3]And suddenly Moses and Elijah appeared to them; they were talking with him. [4]Then Peter spoke to Jesus. 'Lord,' he said, 'it is wonderful for us to be here; if you want me to, I will make three shelters here, one for you, one for Moses and one for Elijah.' [5]He was still speaking when suddenly a bright cloud[a] covered them with shadow, and suddenly from the cloud there came a voice which said, 'This is my Son, the Beloved; he enjoys my favour. Listen to him.'[b] [6]When they heard this, the disciples fell on their faces, overcome with fear. [7]But Jesus came up and touched them, saying, 'Stand up, do not be afraid.' [8]And when they raised their eyes they saw no one but Jesus.

The question about Elijah

[9]As they came down from the mountain Jesus gave them this order, 'Tell no one about this vision until the Son of man has risen from the dead.' [10]And the disciples put this question to him, 'Why then do the scribes say that Elijah must come first?' [11]He replied, 'Elijah is indeed coming, and he will set everything right again; [12]however, I tell you that Elijah has come already and they did not recognise him but treated him as they pleased; and the Son of man will suffer similarly at their hands.' [13]Then the disciples understood that he was speaking of John the Baptist.

The epileptic demoniac

[14]As they were rejoining the crowd a man came up to him and went down on his knees before him. [15]'Lord,' he said, 'take pity on my son: he is demented and in a wretched state; he is always falling into fire and into water. [16]I took him to your disciples and they were unable to cure him.' [17]In reply, Jesus said, 'Faithless and perverse generation! How much longer must I be with you? How much longer must I put up with you? Bring him here to me.' [18]And when Jesus rebuked it the devil came out of the boy, who was cured from that moment.

[19]Then the disciples came privately to Jesus. 'Why were we unable to drive it out?' they asked. [20]He answered, 'Because you have so little faith. In truth I tell you, if your faith is the size of a mustard seed you will say to this mountain, "Move from here to there," and it will move; nothing will be impossible for you.'[21][c]

Second prophecy of the Passion

[22]When they were together in Galilee, Jesus said to them, 'The Son of man is going to be delivered into the power of men; [23]they will put him to death, and on the third day he will be raised up again.' And a great sadness came over them.

17a cf. Ex 13:22.
17b Dt 18:15, 19; Is 42:1.
17c Some authorities add v. 21, 'As for this kind, it is cast out only by prayer and fasting.' Cf. Mk 9:29.

The Temple tax paid by Jesus and Peter

[24]When they reached Capernaum, the collectors of the half-shekel[d] came to Peter and said, 'Does your master not pay the half-
shekel?' [25]'Yes,' he replied, and went into the house. But before he could speak, Jesus said, 'Simon, what is your opinion? From whom do earthly kings take toll or tribute? From their sons or from foreigners?' [26]And when
he replied, 'From foreigners,' Jesus said, 'Well then, the sons are exempt. [27]However,
so that we shall not be the downfall of others, go to the lake and cast a hook; take the first fish that rises, open its mouth and there you will find a shekel; take it and give it to them for me and for yourself.'

B: THE DISCOURSE ON THE CHURCH

Who is the greatest?

18 At this time the disciples came to Jesus and said, 'Who is the greatest in the kingdom of Heaven?' [2]So he called a little
child to him whom he set among them. [3]Then
he said, 'In truth I tell you, unless you change and become like little children you will never enter the kingdom of Heaven. [4]And so, the
one who makes himself as little as this little child is the greatest in the kingdom of Heaven.

On leading others astray

[5]'Anyone who welcomes one little child like this in my name welcomes me. [6]But anyone
who is the downfall of one of these little ones who have faith in me would be better drowned in the depths of the sea with a great millstone round his neck. [7]Alas for the world
that there should be such causes of falling! Causes of falling indeed there must be, but alas for anyone who provides them!

[8]'If your hand or your foot should be your downfall, cut it off and throw it away: it is better for you to enter into life crippled or lame, than to have two hands or two feet and be thrown into eternal fire. [9]And if your eye
should be your downfall, tear it out and throw it away: it is better for you to enter into life with one eye, than to have two eyes and be thrown into the hell of fire.

[10]'See that you never despise any of these little ones, for I tell you that their angels in heaven are continually in the presence of my Father in heaven.[11][a]

The lost sheep

[12]'Tell me. Suppose a man has a hundred sheep and one of them strays; will he not leave the ninety-nine on the hillside and go
in search of the stray? [13]In truth I tell you, if
he finds it, it gives him more joy than do the ninety-nine that did not stray at all.
[14]Similarly, it is never the will of your Father in heaven that one of these little ones should be lost.

Brotherly correction

[15]'If your brother does something wrong, go and have it out with him alone, between your two selves. If he listens to you, you have won
back your brother. [16]If he does not listen, take one or two others along with you: *whatever the misdemeanour, the evidence of two or three witnesses is required to sustain the charge.*[b] [17]But
if he refuses to listen to these, report it to the community; and if he refuses to listen to the community, treat him like a gentile or a tax collector.

[18]'In truth I tell you, whatever you bind on earth will be bound in heaven; whatever you loose on earth will be loosed in heaven.

Prayer in common

[19]'In truth I tell you once again, if two of you on earth agree to ask anything at all, it will be granted to you by my Father in heaven.
[20]For where two or three meet in my name, I am there among them.'

Forgiveness of injuries

[21]Then Peter went up to him and said, 'Lord, how often must I forgive my brother if he wrongs me? As often as seven times?' [22]Jesus
answered, 'Not seven, I tell you, but seventy-seven times.

17d A yearly tax on all Jews for the upkeep of the Temple.
18a Some authorities add v. 11, 'For the Son of man has come to save what was lost.' cf. Lk 19:10.
18b Dt 19:15.

Parable of the unforgiving debtor

23‘And so the kingdom of Heaven may be
compared to a king who decided to settle
his accounts with his servants. 24When the
reckoning began, they brought him a man
who owed ten thousand talents; 25he had no
means of paying, so his master gave orders
that he should be sold, together with his wife
and children and all his possessions, to meet
the debt. 26At this, the servant threw himself
down at his master's feet, with the words,
"Be patient with me and I will pay the whole
sum." 27And the servant's master felt so sorry
for him that he let him go and cancelled the
debt. 28Now as this servant went out, he
happened to meet a fellow-servant who owed
him one hundred denarii;[c] and he seized him
by the throat and began to throttle him,
saying, "Pay what you owe me." 29His fellow-
servant fell at his feet and appealed to him,
saying, "Be patient with me and I will pay
you." 30But the other would not agree; on
the contrary, he had him thrown into prison
till he should pay the debt. 31His fellow-
servants were deeply distressed when they
saw what had happened, and they went to
their master and reported the whole affair to
him. 32Then the master sent for the man and
said to him, "You wicked servant, I cancelled
all that debt of yours when you appealed to
me. 33Were you not bound, then, to have pity
on your fellow-servant just as I had pity on
you?" 34And in his anger the master handed
him over to the torturers till he should pay
all his debt. 35And that is how my heavenly
Father will deal with you unless you each
forgive your brother from your heart.’

VI: THE APPROACHING ADVENT OF THE KINGDOM OF HEAVEN

A: NARRATIVE SECTION

The question about divorce

19 Jesus had now finished what he wanted
to say, and he left Galilee and came into
the territory of Judaea on the far side of the
Jordan. 2Large crowds followed him and he
healed them there.

3Some Pharisees approached him, and to
put him to the test they said, ‘Is it against the
Law for a man to divorce his wife on any
pretext whatever?’ 4He answered, ‘Have you
not read that the Creator from the beginning
made them male and female 5and that he said:
*This is why a man leaves his father and mother
and becomes attached to his wife, and the two
become one flesh?*[a] 6They are no longer two,
therefore, but one flesh. So then, what God
has united, human beings must not divide.’

7They said to him, ‘Then why did Moses
command that a writ of dismissal should be
given in cases of divorce?’[b] 8He said to them,
‘It was because you were so hard-hearted,
that Moses allowed you to divorce your wives,
but it was not like this from the beginning.
9Now I say this to you: anyone who divorces
his wife—I am not speaking of an illicit
marriage—and marries another, is guilty of
adultery.’

Continence

10The disciples said to him, ‘If that is how
things are between husband and wife, it is
advisable not to marry.’ 11But he replied, ‘It
is not everyone who can accept what I have
said, but only those to whom it is granted.
12There are eunuchs born so from their
mother's womb, there are eunuchs made so
by human agency and there are eunuchs who
have made themselves so for the sake of the
kingdom of Heaven. Let anyone accept this
who can.’

Jesus and the children

13Then people brought little children to him,
for him to lay his hands on them and pray.
The disciples scolded them, 14but Jesus said,
‘Let the little children alone, and do not stop
them from coming to me; for it is to such as

18c About $200, contrasted with the other debt of over $60 million.
19a Gn 1:17; 2:24.
19b Dt 24:1. On Mt's exception in v. 9, *see* 5:32.

these that the kingdom of Heaven belongs.'
15 Then he laid his hands on them and went
on his way.

The rich young man

16 And now a man came to him and asked,
'Master, what good deed must I do to possess
eternal life?' 17 Jesus said to him, 'Why do
you ask me about what is good? There is one
alone who is good. But if you wish to enter
into life, keep the commandments.' 18 He
said, 'Which ones?' Jesus replied, 'These:
*You shall not kill. You shall not commit
adultery. You shall not steal. You shall not give
false witness.* 19 *Honour your father and your
mother. You shall love your neighbour as
yourself.*'[c] 20 The young man said to him, 'I
have kept all these. What more do I need to
do?' 21 Jesus said, 'If you wish to be perfect,
go and sell your possessions and give the
money to the poor, and you will have treasure
in heaven; then come, follow me.' 22 But when
the young man heard these words he went
away sad, for he was a man of great wealth.

The danger of riches

23 Then Jesus said to his disciples, 'In truth I
tell you, it is hard for someone rich to enter
the kingdom of Heaven. 24 Yes, I tell you
again, it is easier for a camel to pass through
the eye of a needle than for someone rich to
enter the kingdom of Heaven.' 25 When the
disciples heard this they were astonished.
'Who can be saved, then?' they said. 26 Jesus
gazed at them. 'By human resources', he told
them, 'this is impossible; for God everything
is possible.'

The reward of renunciation

27 Then Peter answered and said, 'Look, we
have left everything and followed you. What
are we to have, then?' 28 Jesus said to them,
'In truth I tell you, when everything is made
new again and the Son of man is seated on
his throne of glory, you yourselves will sit on
twelve thrones to judge the twelve tribes of
Israel. 29 And everyone who has left houses,
brothers, sisters, father, mother, children or
land for the sake of my name will receive a
hundred times as much, and also inherit
eternal life.
30 'Many who are first will be last, and the
last, first.'

Parable of the labourers in the vineyard

20 1 'Now the kingdom of Heaven is like a
landowner going out at daybreak to
hire workers for his vineyard. 2 He made an
agreement with the workers for one denarius
a day and sent them to his vineyard. 3 Going
out at about the third hour he saw others
standing idle in the market place 4 and said to
them, "You go to my vineyard too and I will
give you a fair wage." 5 So they went. At
about the sixth hour and again at about the
ninth hour, he went out and did the same.
6 Then at about the eleventh hour he went
out and found more men standing around,
and he said to them, "Why have you been
standing here idle all day?" 7 "Because no one
has hired us," they answered. He said to
them, "You go into my vineyard too." 8 In
the evening, the owner of the vineyard said
to his bailiff, "Call the workers and pay them
their wages, starting with the last arrivals and
ending with the first." 9 So those who were
hired at about the eleventh hour came for-
ward and received one denarius each. 10 When
the first came, they expected to get more, but
they too received one denarius each. 11 They
took it, but grumbled at the landowner
saying, 12 "The men who came last have done
only one hour, and you have treated them
the same as us, though we have done a heavy
day's work in all the heat." 13 He answered
one of them and said, "My friend, I am not
being unjust to you; did we not agree on one
denarius? 14 Take your earnings and go. I
choose to pay the lastcomer as much as I pay
you. 15 Have I no right to do what I like with
my own? Why should you be envious because
I am generous?" 16 Thus the last will be first,
and the first, last.'

Third prophecy of the Passion

17 Jesus was going up to Jerusalem, and on the
road he took the Twelve aside by themselves
and said to them, 18 'Look, we are going up
to Jerusalem, and the Son of man is about
to be handed over to the chief priests and
scribes. They will condemn him to death
19 and will hand him over to the gentiles to be

19c Ex 20:12–16.

mocked and scourged and crucified; and on the third day he will be raised up again.'

The mother of Zebedee's sons makes her request

20 Then the mother of Zebedee's sons came with her sons to make a request of him, and bowed low; 21 and he said to her, 'What is it you want?' She said to him, 'Promise that these two sons of mine may sit one at your right hand and the other at your left in your kingdom.' 22 Jesus answered, 'You do not know what you are asking. Can you drink the cup that I am going to drink?' They replied, 'We can.' 23 He said to them, 'Very well; you shall drink my cup, but as for seats at my right hand and my left, these are not mine to grant; they belong to those to whom they have been allotted by my Father.'

Leadership with service

24 When the other ten heard this they were indignant with the two brothers. 25 But Jesus called them to him and said, 'You know that among the gentiles the rulers lord it over them, and great men make their authority felt. 26 Among you this is not to happen. No; anyone who wants to become great among you must be your servant, 27 and anyone who wants to be first among you must be your slave, 28 just as the Son of man came not to be served but to serve, and to give his life as a ransom for many.'

The two blind men of Jericho

29 As they left Jericho a large crowd followed him. 30 And now there were two blind men sitting at the side of the road. When they heard that it was Jesus who was passing by, they shouted, 'Lord! Have pity on us, son of David.' 31 And the crowd scolded them and told them to keep quiet, but they only shouted the louder, 'Lord! Have pity on us, son of David.' 32 Jesus stopped, called them over and said, 'What do you want me to do for you?' 33 They said to him, 'Lord, let us have our sight back.' 34 Jesus felt pity for them and touched their eyes, and at once their sight returned and they followed him.

The Messiah enters Jerusalem

21 When they were near Jerusalem and had come to Bethphage on the Mount of Olives, then Jesus sent two disciples, 2 saying to them, 'Go to the village facing you, and you will at once find a tethered donkey and a colt with her. Untie them and bring them to me. 3 If anyone says anything to you, you are to say, "The Master needs them and will send them back at once." ' 4 This was to fulfil what was spoken by the prophet:

5 *Say to the daughter of Zion:*
Look, your king is approaching,
humble and riding on a donkey
and on a colt,
the foal of a beast of burden.[a]

6 So the disciples went and did as Jesus had told them. 7 They brought the donkey and the colt, then they laid their cloaks on their backs and he took his seat on them. 8 Great crowds of people spread their cloaks on the road, while others were cutting branches from the trees and spreading them in his path. 9 The crowds who went in front of him and those who followed were all shouting:

Hosanna to the son of David!
Blessed is he
who is coming in the name of the Lord![b]
Hosanna in the highest heavens!

10 And when he entered Jerusalem, the whole city was in turmoil as people asked, 'Who is this?' 11 and the crowds answered, 'This is the prophet Jesus from Nazareth in Galilee.'

The expulsion of the dealers from the Temple

12 Jesus then went into the Temple and drove out all those who were selling and buying there; he upset the tables of the money-changers and the seats of the dove-sellers. 13 He said to them, 'According to scripture, *my house will be called a house of prayer*; but you are turning it into a *bandits' den*.'[c] 14 There were also blind and lame people who came to him in the Temple, and he cured them. 15 At the sight of the wonderful things he did and of the children shouting, 'Hosanna to the son of David' in the Temple, the chief priests and

21a Zc 9:9.
21b Ps 118:26.
21c Is 56:7; Jr 7:11.

the scribes were indignant and said to him,
16'Do you hear what they are saying?' Jesus
answered, 'Yes. Have you never read this:

By the mouths of children, babes in arms,
you have made sure of praise?'[d]

17With that he left them and went out of the
city to Bethany, where he spent the night.

The barren fig tree withers
Faith and prayer

18As he was returning to the city in the early
morning, he felt hungry. 19Seeing a fig tree
by the road, he went up to it and found
nothing on it but leaves. And he said to
it, 'May you never bear fruit again,' and
instantly the fig tree withered. 20The disciples
were amazed when they saw it and said, 'How
is it that the fig tree withered instantly?'
21Jesus answered, 'In truth I tell you, if you
have faith and do not doubt at all, not only
will you do what I have done to the fig tree,
but even if you say to this mountain, "Be
pulled up and thrown into the sea," it will be
done. 22And if you have faith, everything you
ask for in prayer, you will receive.'

The authority of Jesus is questioned

23He had gone into the Temple and was
teaching, when the chief priests and the
elders of the people came to him and said,
'What authority have you for acting like this?
And who gave you this authority?' 24In reply
Jesus said to them, 'And I will ask you a
question, just one; if you tell me the answer
to it, then I will tell you my authority for
acting like this. 25John's baptism: what was
its origin, heavenly or human?' And they
argued this way among themselves, 'If we
say heavenly, he will retort to us, "Then why
did you refuse to believe him?"; 26but if we
say human, we have the people to fear, for
they all hold that John was a prophet.' 27So
their reply to Jesus was, 'We do not know.'
And he retorted to them, 'Nor will I tell you
my authority for acting like this.'

Parable of the two sons

28'What is your opinion? A man had two
sons. He went and said to the first, "My boy,
go and work in the vineyard today." 29He
answered, "I will not go," but afterwards
thought better of it and went. 30The man
then went and said the same thing to the
second who answered, "Certainly, sir," but
did not go. 31Which of the two did the father's
will?' They said, 'The first.' Jesus said to
them, 'In truth I tell you, tax collectors and
prostitutes are making their way into the
kingdom of God before you. 32For John came
to you, showing the way of uprightness, but
you did not believe him, and yet the tax
collectors and prostitutes did. Even after
seeing that, you refused to think better of it
and believe in him.

Parable of the wicked tenants

33'Listen to another parable. There was a
man, a landowner, who planted a vineyard;
he fenced it round, dug a winepress in it and
built a tower; then he leased it to tenants and
went abroad. 34When vintage time drew near
he sent his servants to the tenants to collect
his produce. 35But the tenants seized his
servants, thrashed one, killed another and
stoned a third. 36Next he sent some more
servants, this time a larger number, and they
dealt with them in the same way. 37Finally
he sent his son to them thinking, "They will
respect my son." 38But when the tenants saw
the son, they said to each other, "This is the
heir. Come on, let us kill him and take over
his inheritance." 39So they seized him and
threw him out of the vineyard and killed
him. 40Now when the owner of the vineyard
comes, what will he do to those tenants?'
41They answered, 'He will bring those wret-
ches to a wretched end and lease the vineyard
to other tenants who will deliver the produce
to him at the proper time.' 42Jesus said to
them, 'Have you never read in the scriptures:

The stone which the builders rejected
has become the cornerstone;
this is the Lord's doing
and we marvel at it?[e]

43'I tell you, then, that the kingdom of God
will be taken from you and given to a people
who will produce its fruit.'[44][f]

45When they heard his parables, the chief
priests and the scribes realised he was
speaking about them, 46but though they

21d Ps 8:2.
21e Ps 118:22–23.
21f Some authorities add v. 44, taken from Lk 20:18.

would have liked to arrest him they were
afraid of the crowds, who looked on him as a
prophet.

Parable of the wedding feast

22 Jesus began to speak to them in
parables once again, 2 'The kingdom of
Heaven may be compared to a king who gave
a feast for his son's wedding. 3 He sent his
servants to call those who had been invited,
but they would not come. 4 Next he sent some
more servants with the words, "Tell those
who have been invited: Look, my banquet is
all prepared, my oxen and fattened cattle
have been slaughtered, everything is ready.
Come to the wedding." 5 But they were not
interested: one went off to his farm, another
to his business, 6 and the rest seized his
servants, maltreated them and killed them.
7 The king was furious. He despatched his
troops, destroyed those murderers and burnt
their town. 8 Then he said to his servants,
"The wedding is ready; but as those who
were invited proved to be unworthy, 9 go to
the main crossroads and invite everyone you
can find to come to the wedding." 10 So these
servants went out onto the roads and collected
together everyone they could find, bad and
good alike; and the wedding hall was filled
with guests. 11 When the king came in to look
at the guests he noticed one man who was not
wearing a wedding garment, 12 and said to
him, "How did you get in here, my friend,
without a wedding garment?" And the man
was silent. 13 Then the king said to the attend-
ants, "Bind him hand and foot and throw
him into the darkness outside, where there
will be weeping and grinding of teeth." 14 For
many are invited but not all are chosen.'

On tribute to Caesar

15 Then the Pharisees went away to work out
between them how to trap him in what he
said. 16 And they sent their disciples to him,
together with some Herodians, to say,
'Master, we know that you are an honest man
and teach the way of God in all honesty, and
that you are not afraid of anyone, because
human rank means nothing to you. 17 Give us
your opinion, then. Is it permissible to pay
taxes to Caesar or not?' 18 But Jesus was aware
of their malice and replied, 'You hypocrites!
Why are you putting me to the test? 19 Show
me the money you pay the tax with.' They
handed him a denarius, 20 and he said, 'Whose
portrait is this? Whose title?' 21 They replied,
'Caesar's.' Then he said to them, 'Very well,
pay Caesar what belongs to Caesar—and God
what belongs to God.' 22 When they heard
this they were amazed; they left him alone
and went away.

The resurrection of the dead

23 That day some Sadducees—who deny that
there is a resurrection—approached him and
they put this question to him, 24 'Master,
Moses said[a] that if a man dies childless, his
brother is to marry the widow, his sister-in-
law, to raise children for his brother. 25 Now
we had a case involving seven brothers; the
first married and then died without children,
leaving his wife to his brother; 26 the same
thing happened with the second and third
and so on to the seventh, 27 and then last of
all the woman herself died. 28 Now at the
resurrection, whose wife among the seven
will she be, since she had been married to
them all?' 29 Jesus answered them, 'You are
wrong, because you understand neither the
scriptures nor the power of God. 30 For at the
resurrection men and women do not marry;
no, they are like the angels in heaven. 31 And
as for the resurrection of the dead, have you
never read what God himself said to you: 32 *I
am the God of Abraham, the God of Isaac and
the God of Jacob?*[b] He is God, not of the dead,
but of the living.' 33 And his teaching made a
deep impression on the people who heard it.

The greatest commandment of all

34 But when the Pharisees heard that he had
silenced the Sadducees they got together
35 and, to put him to the test, one of them put
a further question, 36 'Master, which is the
greatest commandment of the Law?' 37 Jesus
said to him, '*You must love the Lord your God
with all your heart, with all your soul*, and with
all your mind. 38 This is the greatest and the
first commandment. 39 The second resembles
it: *You must love your neighbour as yourself.*[c]
40 On these two commandments hang the
whole Law, and the Prophets too.'

22a Dt 25:5–6.
22b Ex 3:6.
22c Dt 6:5 combined with Lv 19:18.

Christ not only son but also Lord of David

41While the Pharisees were gathered round,
Jesus put to them this question, 42'What is
your opinion about the Christ? Whose son is
he?' They told him, 'David's.' 43He said to
them, 'Then how is it that David, moved by
the Spirit, calls him Lord, where he says:

44*The Lord declared to my Lord,*
take your seat at my right hand,
till I have made your enemies
your footstool?[d]

45'If David calls him Lord, how then can he
be his son?' 46No one could think of anything
to say in reply, and from that day no one
dared to ask him any further questions.

The scribes and Pharisees: their hypocrisy and vanity

23 Then addressing the crowds and his
disciples Jesus said, 2'The scribes and
the Pharisees occupy the chair of Moses.
3You must therefore do and observe what
they tell you; but do not be guided by what
they do, since they do not practise what they
preach. 4They tie up heavy burdens and lay
them on people's shoulders, but will they lift
a finger to move them? Not they! 5Everything
they do is done to attract attention, like
wearing broader headbands and longer
tassels, 6like wanting to take the place of
honour at banquets and the front seats in the
synagogues, 7being greeted respectfully in
the market squares and having people call
them Rabbi.

8'You, however, must not allow yourselves
to be called Rabbi, since you have only one
Master, and you are all brothers. 9You must
call no one on earth your father, since you
have only one Father, and he is in heaven.
10Nor must you allow yourselves to be called
teachers, for you have only one Teacher, the
Christ. 11The greatest among you must be
your servant. 12Anyone who raises himself up
will be humbled, and anyone who humbles
himself will be raised up.

The sevenfold indictment of the scribes and Pharisees

13'Alas for you, scribes and Pharisees, you
hypocrites! You shut up the kingdom of
Heaven in people's faces, neither going in
yourselves nor allowing others to go in who
want to.[14][a]

15'Alas for you, scribes and Pharisees, you
hypocrites! You travel over sea and land to
make a single proselyte, and anyone who
becomes one you make twice as fit for hell as
you are.

16'Alas for you, blind guides! You say, "If
anyone swears by the Temple, it has no force;
but anyone who swears by the gold of the
Temple is bound." 17Fools and blind! For
which is of greater value, the gold or the
Temple that makes the gold sacred? 18Again,
"If anyone swears by the altar it has no force;
but anyone who swears by the offering on the
altar, is bound." 19You blind men! For which
is of greater worth, the offering or the altar
that makes the offering sacred? 20Therefore,
someone who swears by the altar is swearing
by that and by everything on it. 21And
someone who swears by the Temple is swear-
ing by that and by the One who dwells in it.
22And someone who swears by heaven is
swearing by the throne of God and by the
One who is seated there.

23'Alas for you, scribes and Pharisees, you
hypocrites! You pay your tithe of mint and
dill and cummin and have neglected the
weightier matters of the Law—justice,
mercy, good faith! These you should have
practised, those not neglected. 24You blind
guides, straining out gnats and swallowing
camels!

25'Alas for you, scribes and Pharisees, you
hypocrites! You clean the outside of cup and
dish and leave the inside full of extortion and
intemperance. 26Blind Pharisee! Clean the
inside of cup and dish first so that it and the
outside are both clean.

27'Alas for you, scribes and Pharisees, you
hypocrites! You are like whitewashed tombs
that look handsome on the outside, but inside
are full of the bones of the dead and every
kind of corruption. 28In just the same way,
from the outside you look upright, but inside
you are full of hypocrisy and lawlessness.

29'Alas for you, scribes and Pharisees, you
hypocrites! You build the sepulchres of the
prophets and decorate the tombs of the
upright, 30saying, "We would never have
joined in shedding the blood of the prophets,
had we lived in our ancestors' day." 31So!

22d Ps 110:1.
23a Some authorities add v. 14, taken from Mk 12:40.

Your own evidence tells against you! You are
the children of those who murdered the
prophets! [32]Very well then, finish off the
work that your ancestors began.

Their crimes and approaching punishment

[33]'You serpents, brood of vipers, how can
you escape being condemned to hell? [34]This
is why—look—I am sending you prophets
and wise men and scribes; some you will
slaughter and crucify, some you will scourge
in your synagogues and hunt from town
to town; [35]and so you will draw down on
yourselves the blood of every upright person
that has been shed on earth, from the blood
of Abel the holy to the blood of Zechariah
son of Barachiah whom you murdered
between the sanctuary and the altar. [36]In
truth I tell you, it will all recoil on this
generation.

Jerusalem admonished

[37]'Jerusalem, Jerusalem, you that kill the
prophets and stone those who are sent to you!
How often have I longed to gather your
children together, as a hen gathers her chicks
under her wings, and you refused! [38]Look!
Your house will be deserted, [39]for, I promise,
you shall not see me any more until you are
saying:

Blessed is he
who is coming in the name of the Lord!'[b]

B: THE END AND THE SECOND COMING[a]

Introduction

24 Jesus left the Temple, and as he was
going away his disciples came up to
draw his attention to the Temple buildings.
[2]He said to them in reply, 'You see all these?
In truth I tell you, not a single stone here will
be left on another: everything will be pulled
down.' [3]And while he was sitting on the
Mount of Olives the disciples came and asked
him when they were by themselves, 'Tell us,
when is this going to happen, and what sign
will there be of your coming and of the end
of the world?'

The beginning of sorrows

[4]And Jesus answered them, 'Take care that
no one deceives you, [5]because many will
come using my name and saying, "I am the
Christ," and they will deceive many. [6]You
will hear of wars and rumours of wars; see
that you are not alarmed, for this is something
that must happen, but the end will not be
yet. [7]For nation will fight against nation, and
kingdom against kingdom. There will be
famines and earthquakes in various places.
[8]All this is only the beginning of the
birthpangs.

[9]'Then you will be handed over to be
tortured and put to death; and you will be
hated by all nations on account of my name.
[10]And then many will fall away; people will
betray one another and hate one another.
[11]Many false prophets will arise; they will
deceive many, [12]and with the increase of
lawlessness, love in most people will grow
cold; [13]but anyone who stands firm to the end
will be saved.

[14]'This good news of the kingdom will be
proclaimed to the whole world as evidence to
the nations. And then the end will come.

The great tribulation of Jerusalem

[15]'So when you see *the appalling abomination*,[b]
of which the prophet Daniel spoke, set up in
the holy place (let the reader understand),
[16]then those in Judaea must escape to the
mountains; [17]if anyone is on the housetop, he
must not come down to collect his belongings
from the house; [18]if anyone is in the fields,
he must not turn back to fetch his cloak.
[19]Alas for those with child, or with babies at
the breast, when those days come! [20]Pray
that you will not have to make your escape in
winter or on a Sabbath. [21]For then there will
be *great distress, unparalleled since*[c] the world
began, and such as will never be again. [22]And
if that time had not been shortened, no
human being would have survived; but shor-

23b Ps 118:26.
24a In this discourse on the future of Christ's community, Mt links the destruction of Jerusalem in AD 70 to the final coming of Christ.
24b Dn 9:27; 11:31; 12:11.
24c Dn 12:1.

tened that time shall be, for the sake of those
who are chosen.
23'If anyone says to you then, "Look, here
is the Christ," or "Over here," do not believe
it; 24for false Christs and false prophets will
arise and provide great signs and portents,
enough to deceive even the elect, if that were
possible. 25Look! I have given you warning.

The coming of the Son of man

26'If, then, they say to you, "Look, he is in
the desert," do not go there; "Look, he is
in some hiding place," do not believe it;
27because the coming of the Son of man will
be like lightning striking in the east and
flashing far into the west. 28Wherever the
corpse is, that is where the vultures will
gather.

The universal significance of this coming

29'Immediately after the distress of those days
the sun will be darkened,[d] the moon will not
give its light, the stars will fall from the sky
and the powers of the heavens will be shaken.
30And then the sign of the Son of man will
appear in heaven; then, too, all the peoples
of the earth will beat their breasts; and they
will see the *Son of man coming on the clouds of*
heaven with power and great glory.[e] 31And he
will send his angels with a loud trumpet to
gather his elect from the four winds, from
one end of heaven to the other.

The time of this coming

32'Take the fig tree as a parable: as soon as its
twigs grow supple and its leaves come out,
you know that summer is near. 33So with you
when you see all these things: know that he
is near, right at the gates. 34In truth I tell
you, before this generation has passed away,
all these things will have taken place. 35Sky
and earth will pass away, but my words will
never pass away. 36But as for that day and
hour, nobody knows it, neither the angels of
heaven, nor the Son, no one but the Father
alone.

Be on the alert

37'As it was in Noah's day, so will it be when
the Son of man comes. 38For in those days
before the Flood people were eating,
drinking, taking wives, taking husbands,
right up to the day Noah went into the ark,[f]
39and they suspected nothing till the Flood
came and swept them all away. This is what
it will be like when the Son of man comes.
40Then of two men in the fields, one is taken,
one left; 41of two women grinding at the mill,
one is taken, one left.
42'So stay awake, because you do not know
the day when your master is coming. 43You
may be quite sure of this, that if the house-
holder had known at what time of the night
the burglar would come, he would have
stayed awake and would not have allowed
anyone to break through the wall of his
house. 44Therefore, you too must stand ready
because the Son of man is coming at an hour
you do not expect.

Parable of the conscientious steward

45'Who, then, is the wise and trustworthy
servant whom the master placed over his
household to give them their food at the
proper time? 46Blessed that servant if his
master's arrival finds him doing exactly that.
47In truth I tell you, he will put him in charge
of everything he owns. 48But if the servant is
dishonest and says to himself, "My master is
taking his time," 49and sets about beating his
fellow-servants and eating and drinking with
drunkards, 50his master will come on a day
he does not expect and at an hour he does not
know. 51The master will cut him off and send
him to the same fate as the hypocrites, where
there will be weeping and grinding of teeth.'

Parable of the ten wedding attendants

25 'Then the kingdom of Heaven will be
like this: Ten wedding attendants took
their lamps and went to meet the bridegroom.
2Five of them were foolish and five were
sensible: 3the foolish ones, though they took
their lamps, took no oil with them, 4whereas
the sensible ones took flasks of oil as well as
their lamps. 5The bridegroom was late, and
they all grew drowsy and fell asleep. 6But
at midnight there was a cry, "Look! The
bridegroom! Go out and meet him." 7Then
all those wedding attendants woke up and
trimmed their lamps, 8and the foolish ones

24d Am 8:9.
24e Dn 7:13–14.
24f Gn 7:11–23.

said to the sensible ones, "Give us some of
your oil: our lamps are going out." 9 But they
replied, "There may not be enough for us
and for you; you had better go to those who
sell it and buy some for yourselves." 10 They
had gone off to buy it when the bridegroom
arrived. Those who were ready went in with
him to the wedding hall and the door was
closed. 11 The other attendants arrived later.
"Lord, Lord," they said, "open the door for
us." 12 But he replied, "In truth I tell you, I
do not know you." 13 So stay awake, because
you do not know either the day or the hour.

Parable of the talents

14 "It is like a man about to go abroad who
summoned his servants and entrusted his
property to them. 15 To one he gave five
talents, to another two, to a third one, each
in proportion to his ability. Then he set out
on his journey. 16 The man who had received
the five talents promptly went and traded
with them and made five more. 17 The man
who had received two made two more in the
same way. 18 But the man who had received
one went off and dug a hole in the ground
and hid his master's money. 19 Now a long
time afterwards, the master of those servants
came back and went through his accounts
with them. 20 The man who had received the
five talents came forward bringing five more.
"Sir," he said, "you entrusted me with five
talents; here are five more that I have made."
21 His master said to him, "Well done, good
and trustworthy servant; you have shown
you are trustworthy in small things; I will
trust you with greater; come and join in your
master's happiness." 22 Next the man with
the two talents came forward. "Sir," he said,
"you entrusted me with two talents; here are
two more that I have made." 23 His master said
to him, "Well done, good and trustworthy
servant; you have shown you are trustworthy
in small things; I will trust you with greater;
come and join in your master's happiness."
24 Last came forward the man who had the
single talent. "Sir," said he, "I had heard
you were a hard man, reaping where you had
not sown and gathering where you had not
scattered; 25 so I was afraid, and I went off
and hid your talent in the ground. Here it is;
it was yours, you have it back." 26 But his
master answered him, "You wicked and lazy
servant! So you knew that I reap where I
have not sown and gather where I have
not scattered? 27 Well then, you should have
deposited my money with the bankers, and
on my return I would have got my money
back with interest. 28 So now, take the talent
from him and give it to the man who has the
ten talents. 29 For to everyone who has will be
given more, and he will have more than
enough; but anyone who has not, will be
deprived even of what he has. 30 As for this
good-for-nothing servant, throw him into
the darkness outside, where there will be
weeping and grinding of teeth."

The Last Judgement

31 "When the Son of man comes in his glory,
escorted by all the angels, then he will take
his seat on his throne of glory. 32 All nations
will be assembled before him and he will
separate people one from another as the
shepherd separates sheep from goats. 33 He
will place the sheep on his right hand and the
goats on his left. 34 Then the King will say to
those on his right hand, "Come, you whom
my Father has blessed, take as your heritage
the kingdom prepared for you since the foun-
dation of the world. 35 For I was hungry and
you gave me food, I was thirsty and you gave
me drink, I was a stranger and you made me
welcome, 36 lacking clothes and you clothed
me, sick and you visited me, in prison and
you came to see me." 37 Then the upright will
say to him in reply, "Lord, when did we see
you hungry and feed you, or thirsty and give
you drink? 38 When did we see you a stranger
and make you welcome, lacking clothes and
clothe you? 39 When did we find you sick or
in prison and go to see you?" 40 And the King
will answer, "In truth I tell you, in so far as
you did this to one of the least of these
brothers of mine, you did it to me." 41 Then
he will say to those on his left hand, "Go
away from me, with your curse upon you, to
the eternal fire prepared for the devil and his
angels. 42 For I was hungry and you never
gave me food, I was thirsty and you never
gave me anything to drink, 43 I was a stranger
and you never made me welcome, lacking
clothes and you never clothed me, sick and
in prison and you never visited me." 44 Then
it will be their turn to ask, "Lord, when did
we see you hungry or thirsty, a stranger or
lacking clothes, sick or in prison, and did not
come to your help?" 45 Then he will answer,
"In truth I tell you, in so far as you neglected

to do this to one of the least of these, you neglected to do it to me." [46]And they will go away to eternal punishment, and the upright to eternal life.'

VII: PASSION AND RESURRECTION

The conspiracy against Jesus

26 Jesus had now finished all he wanted to say, and he told his disciples, [2]'It will be Passover, as you know, in two days' time, and the Son of man will be handed over to be crucified.'

[3]Then the chief priests and the elders of the people assembled in the palace of the high priest, whose name was Caiaphas, [4]and made plans to arrest Jesus by some trick and have him put to death. [5]They said, however, 'It must not be during the festivities; there must be no disturbance among the people.'

The anointing at Bethany

[6]Jesus was at Bethany in the house of Simon, a man who had suffered from a virulent skin-disease, when [7]a woman came to him with an alabaster jar of very expensive ointment, and poured it on his head as he was at table. [8]When they saw this, the disciples said indignantly, 'Why this waste? [9]This could have been sold for a high price and the money given the poor.' [10]But Jesus noticed this and said, 'Why are you upsetting the woman? What she has done for me is indeed a good work! [11]You have the poor with you always, but you will not always have me. [12]When she poured this ointment on my body, she did it to prepare me for burial. [13]In truth I tell you, wherever in all the world this gospel is proclaimed, what she has done will be told as well, in remembrance of her.'

Judas betrays Jesus

[14]Then one of the Twelve, the man called Judas Iscariot, went to the chief priests [15]and said, 'What are you prepared to give me if I hand him over to you?' They paid him thirty silver pieces, [16]and from then onwards he began to look for an opportunity to betray him.

Preparations for the Passover supper

[17]Now on the first day of Unleavened Bread the disciples came to Jesus to say, 'Where do you want us to make the preparations for you to eat the Passover?' [18]He said, 'Go to a certain man in the city and say to him, "The Master says: My time is near. It is at your house that I am keeping Passover with my disciples." ' [19]The disciples did what Jesus told them and prepared the Passover.

The treachery of Judas foretold

[20]When evening came he was at table with the Twelve. [21]And while they were eating he said, 'In truth I tell you, one of you is about to betray me.' [22]They were greatly distressed and started asking him in turn, 'Not me, Lord, surely?' [23]He answered, 'Someone who has dipped his hand into the dish with me will betray me. [24]The Son of man is going to his fate, as the scriptures say he will, but alas for that man by whom the Son of man is betrayed! Better for that man if he had never been born!' [25]Judas, who was to betray him, asked in his turn, 'Not me, Rabbi, surely?' Jesus answered, 'It is you who say it.'

The institution of the Eucharist

[26]Now as they were eating, Jesus took bread, and when he had said the blessing he broke it and gave it to the disciples. 'Take it and eat,' he said, 'this is my body.' [27]Then he took a cup, and when he had given thanks he handed it to them saying, 'Drink from this, all of you, [28]for this is my blood, the blood of the covenant, poured out for many for the forgiveness of sins. [29]From now on, I tell you, I shall never again drink wine until the day I drink the new wine with you in the kingdom of my Father.'

Peter's denial foretold

[30]After the psalms had been sung they left for the Mount of Olives. [31]Then Jesus said to them, 'You will all fall away from me tonight, for the scripture says: *I shall strike the shepherd*

and the sheep of the flock will be scattered,[a] [32]but after my resurrection I shall go ahead of you to Galilee.' [33]At this, Peter said to him, 'Even if all fall away from you, I will never fall away.' [34]Jesus answered him, 'In truth I tell you, this very night, before the cock crows, you will have disowned me three times.' [35]Peter said to him, 'Even if I have to die with you, I will never disown you.' And all the disciples said the same.

Gethsemane

[36]Then Jesus came with them to a plot of land called Gethsemane; and he said to his disciples, 'Stay here while I go over there to pray.' [37]He took Peter and the two sons of Zebedee with him. And he began to feel sadness and anguish.

[38]Then he said to them, 'My soul is sorrowful to the point of death. Wait here and stay awake with me.' [39]And going on a little further he fell on his face and prayed. 'My Father,' he said, 'if it is possible, let this cup pass me by. Nevertheless, let it be as you, not I, would have it.' [40]He came back to the disciples and found them sleeping, and he said to Peter, 'So you had not the strength to stay awake with me for one hour? [41]Stay awake, and pray not to be put to the test. The spirit is willing enough, but human nature is weak.' [42]Again, a second time, he went away and prayed: 'My Father,' he said, 'if this cup cannot pass by, but I must drink it, your will be done!'[b] [43]And he came back again and found them sleeping, their eyes were so heavy. [44]Leaving them there, he went away again and prayed for the third time, repeating the same words. [45]Then he came back to the disciples and said to them, 'You can sleep on now and have your rest. Look, the hour has come when the Son of man is to be betrayed into the hands of sinners. [46]Get up! Let us go! Look, my betrayer is not far away.'

The arrest

[47]And suddenly while he was still speaking, Judas, one of the Twelve, appeared, and with him a large number of men armed with swords and clubs, sent by the chief priests and elders of the people. [48]Now the traitor had arranged a sign with them saying, 'The one I kiss, he is the man. Arrest him.' [49]So he went up to Jesus at once and said, 'Greetings, Rabbi,' and kissed him. [50]Jesus said to him, 'My friend, do what you are here for.' Then they came forward, seized Jesus and arrested him. [51]And suddenly, one of the followers of Jesus grasped his sword and drew it; he struck the high priest's servant and cut off his ear. [52]Jesus then said, 'Put your sword back, for all who draw the sword will die by the sword. [53]Or do you think that I cannot appeal to my Father, who would promptly send more than twelve legions of angels to my defence? [54]But then, how would the scriptures be fulfilled that say this is the way it must be?' [55]It was at this time that Jesus said to the crowds, 'Am I a bandit, that you had to set out to capture me with swords and clubs? I sat teaching in the Temple day after day and you never laid a hand on me.' [56]Now all this happened to fulfil the prophecies in scripture. Then all the disciples deserted him and ran away.

Jesus before the Sanhedrin[c]

[57]The men who had arrested Jesus led him off to the house of Caiaphas the high priest, where the scribes and the elders were assembled. [58]Peter followed him at a distance right to the high priest's palace, and he went in and sat down with the attendants to see what the end would be.

[59]The chief priests and the whole Sanhedrin were looking for evidence against Jesus, however false, on which they might have him executed. [60]But they could not find any, though several lying witnesses came forward. Eventually two came forward [61]and made a statement, 'This man said, "I have power to destroy the Temple of God and in three days build it up." ' [62]The high priest then rose and said to him, 'Have you no answer to that? What is this evidence these men are bringing against you?' [63]But Jesus was silent. And the high priest said to him, 'I put you on oath by the living God to tell us if you are the Christ, the Son of God.' [64]Jesus answered him, 'It is you who say it. But, I tell you that from this time onward you will see the *Son of man seated at the right hand of*

26a Zc 13:7.
26b =6:10.
26c The gospels differ: Lk and Jn mention an interrogation at night and a Sanhedrin session in the morning. Mt and Mk place this morning session in the night.

the Power and *coming on the clouds of heaven*.'[d]
65 Then the high priest tore his clothes and
said, 'He has blasphemed. What need of
witnesses have we now? There! You have
just heard the blasphemy. 66 What is your
opinion?' They answered, 'He deserves to
die.'
67 Then they spat in his face and hit him
with their fists; others said as they struck
him, 68 'Prophesy to us, Christ! Who hit you
then?'

Peter's denials

69 Meanwhile Peter was sitting outside in the
courtyard, and a servant-girl came up to
him saying, 'You, too, were with Jesus the
Galilean.' 70 But he denied it in front of them
all. 'I do not know what you are talking
about,' he said. 71 When he went out to the
gateway another servant-girl saw him and
said to the people there, 'This man was with
Jesus the Nazarene.' 72 And again, with an
oath, he denied it, 'I do not know the man.'
73 A little later the bystanders came up and
said to Peter, 'You are certainly one of them
too! Why, your accent[e] gives you away.'
74 Then he started cursing and swearing, 'I
do not know the man.' And at once the cock
crowed, 75 and Peter remembered what Jesus
had said, 'Before the cock crows you will
have disowned me three times.' And he went
outside and wept bitterly.

Jesus is taken before Pilate

27 When morning came, all the chief
priests and the elders of the people met
in council to bring about the death of Jesus.
2 They had him bound and led him away to
hand him over to Pilate, the governor.

The death of Judas

3 When he found that Jesus had been
condemned, then Judas, his betrayer, was
filled with remorse and took the thirty silver
pieces back to the chief priests and elders
4 saying, 'I have sinned. I have betrayed inno-
cent blood.' They replied, 'What is that to
us? That is your concern.' 5 And flinging
down the silver pieces in the sanctuary he
made off, and went and hanged himself. 6 The
chief priests picked up the silver pieces and
said, 'It is against the Law to put this into
the treasury; it is blood-money.' 7 So they
discussed the matter and with it bought the
potter's field as a graveyard for foreigners,
8 and this is why the field is still called the
Field of Blood. 9 The word spoken through
the prophet Jeremiah was then fulfilled: *And
they took the thirty silver pieces, the sum at which
the precious One was priced by the children of
Israel,* 10 *and they gave them for the potter's field,
just as the Lord directed me.*[a]

Jesus before Pilate

11 Jesus, then, was brought before the
governor, and the governor put to him this
question, 'Are you the king of the Jews?'
Jesus replied, 'It is you who say it.' 12 But
when he was accused by the chief priests and
the elders he refused to answer at all. 13 Pilate
then said to him, 'Do you not hear how many
charges they have made against you?' 14 But
to the governor's amazement, he offered not
a word in answer to any of the charges.
15 At festival time it was the governor's
practice to release a prisoner for the people,
anyone they chose. 16 Now there was then a
notorious prisoner whose name was
Barabbas. 17 So when the crowd gathered,
Pilate said to them, 'Which do you want me
to release for you: Barabbas, or Jesus who is
called Christ?' 18 For Pilate knew it was out
of jealousy that they had handed him over.
19 Now as he was seated in the chair of
judgement, his wife sent him a message,
'Have nothing to do with that upright man;
I have been extremely upset today by a dream
that I had about him.'
20 The chief priests and the elders,
however, had persuaded the crowd to
demand the release of Barabbas and the
execution of Jesus. 21 So when the governor
spoke and asked them, 'Which of the two do
you want me to release for you?' they said,
'Barabbas.' 22 Pilate said to them, 'But in that
case, what am I to do with Jesus who is called
Christ?' They all said, 'Let him be crucified!'
23 He asked, 'But what harm has he done?'
But they shouted all the louder, 'Let him be
crucified!' 24 Then Pilate saw that he was

26d Ps 110:1 and Dn 7:13.
26e Presumably Galileans had a local accent.
27a Zc 11:12–13.

making no impression, that in fact a riot was imminent. So he took some water, washed his hands in front of the crowd and said, 'I am innocent of this man's blood. It is your concern.' [25]And the people, every one of them, shouted back, 'Let his blood be on us and on our children!' [26]Then he released Barabbas for them. After having Jesus scourged he handed him over to be crucified.

Jesus is crowned with thorns

[27]Then the governor's soldiers took Jesus with them into the Praetorium and collected the whole cohort round him. [28]And they stripped him and put a scarlet cloak round him, [29]and having twisted some thorns into a crown they put this on his head and placed a reed in his right hand. To make fun of him they knelt to him saying, 'Hail, king of the Jews!' [30]And they spat on him and took the reed and struck him on the head with it. [31]And when they had finished making fun of him, they took off the cloak and dressed him in his own clothes and led him away to crucifixion.

The crucifixion

[32]On their way out, they came across a man from Cyrene, called Simon, and enlisted him to carry his cross. [33]When they had reached a place called Golgotha, that is, the place of the skull, [34]they gave him wine to drink mixed with gall,[b] which he tasted but refused to drink. [35]When they had finished crucifying him they shared out his clothing by casting lots, [36]and then sat down and stayed there keeping guard over him.

[37]Above his head was placed the charge against him; it read: 'This is Jesus, the King of the Jews.' [38]Then two bandits were crucified with him, one on the right and one on the left.

The crucified Jesus is mocked

[39]The passers-by jeered at him; they shook their heads [40]and said, 'So you would destroy the Temple and in three days rebuild it! Then save yourself if you are God's son and come down from the cross!' [41]The chief priests with the scribes and elders mocked him in the same way, [42]with the words, 'He saved others; he cannot save himself. He is the king of Israel; let him come down from the cross now, and we will believe in him. [43]He has put his trust in God; now let God rescue him if he wants him. For he did say, "I am God's son."'[c] [44]Even the bandits who were crucified with him taunted him in the same way.

The death of Jesus

[45]From the sixth hour there was darkness over all the land until the ninth hour. [46]And about the ninth hour, Jesus cried out in a loud voice, *'Eli, eli, lama sabachthani?'* that is, *'My God, my God, why have you forsaken me?'*[d] [47]When some of those who stood there heard this, they said, 'The man is calling on Elijah,' [48]and one of them quickly ran to get a sponge which he filled with vinegar and, putting it on a reed, gave it him to drink. [49]But the rest of them said, 'Wait! And see if Elijah will come to save him.' [50]But Jesus, again crying out in a loud voice, yielded up his spirit.

[51]And suddenly, the veil of the Sanctuary was torn in two from top to bottom, the earth quaked, the rocks were split, [52]the tombs opened and the bodies of many holy people rose from the dead, [53]and these, after his resurrection, came out of the tombs, entered the holy city and appeared to a number of people. [54]The centurion, together with the others guarding Jesus, had seen the earthquake and all that was taking place, and they were terrified and said, 'In truth this man was son of God.'

[55]And many women were there, watching from a distance, the same women who had followed Jesus from Galilee and looked after him. [56]Among them were Mary of Magdala, Mary the mother of James and Joseph, and the mother of Zebedee's sons.

The burial

[57]When it was evening, there came a rich man of Arimathaea, called Joseph, who had himself become a disciple of Jesus. [58]This man went to Pilate and asked for the body of Jesus. Then Pilate ordered it to be handed over. [59]So Joseph took the body, wrapped it

---

27b cf. Ps 69:21.
27c cf. Ws 2:18–20.
27d Ps 22:1.

in a clean shroud 60and put it in his own new
tomb which he had hewn out of the rock. He
then rolled a large stone across the entrance
of the tomb and went away. 61Now Mary of
Magdala and the other Mary were there,
sitting opposite the sepulchre.

The guard at the tomb

62Next day, that is, when Preparation Day
was over, the chief priests and the Pharisees
went in a body to Pilate 63and said to him,
'Your Excellency, we recall that this impostor
said, while he was still alive, "After three
days I shall rise again." 64Therefore give the
order to have the sepulchre kept secure until
the third day, for fear his disciples come and
steal him away and tell the people, "He has
risen from the dead." This last piece of fraud
would be worse than what went before.'
65Pilate said to them, 'You may have your
guard; go and make all as secure as you know
how.' 66So they went and made the sepulchre
secure, putting seals on the stone and
mounting a guard.

The empty tomb. The angel's message

28 After the Sabbath, and towards dawn
on the first day of the week, Mary of
Magdala and the other Mary went to visit the
sepulchre. 2And suddenly there was a violent
earthquake, for an angel of the Lord,
descending from heaven, came and rolled
away the stone and sat on it. 3His face was
like lightning, his robe white as snow. 4The
guards were so shaken by fear of him that
they were like dead men. 5But the angel
spoke; and he said to the women, 'There is
no need for you to be afraid. I know you are
looking for Jesus, who was crucified. 6He is
not here, for he has risen, as he said he would.
Come and see the place where he lay, 7then
go quickly and tell his disciples, "He has
risen from the dead and now he is going ahead
of you to Galilee; that is where you will see
him." Look! I have told you.' 8Filled with
awe and great joy the women came quickly
away from the tomb and ran to tell his
disciples.

Appearance to the women

9And suddenly, coming to meet them, was
Jesus. 'Greetings,' he said. And the women
came up to him and, clasping his feet, they
did him homage. 10Then Jesus said to them,
'Do not be afraid; go and tell my brothers
that they must leave for Galilee; there they
will see me.'

**Precautions taken
by the leaders of the people**

11Now while they were on their way, some of
the guards went off into the city to tell the
chief priests all that had happened. 12These
held a meeting with the elders and, after
some discussion, handed a considerable sum
of money to the soldiers 13with these instruc-
tions, 'This is what you must say, "His
disciples came during the night and stole him
away while we were asleep." 14And should
the governor come to hear of this, we under-
take to put things right with him ourselves
and to see that you do not get into trouble.'
15So they took the money and carried out
their instructions, and to this day that is the
story among the Jews.

**Appearance in Galilee
The mission to the world**

16Meanwhile the eleven disciples set out for
Galilee, to the mountain where Jesus had
arranged to meet them. 17When they saw him
they fell down before him, though some
hesitated. 18Jesus came up and spoke to them.
He said, 'All authority in heaven and on earth
has been given to me.[a] 19Go, therefore, make
disciples of all nations; baptise them in the
name of the Father and of the Son and of the
Holy Spirit, 20and teach them to observe
all the commands I gave you. And look, I
am with you always; yes, to the end of
time.'

28a cf. Dn 7:14.

THE GOSPEL OF MARK

Mark is often considered the earliest gospel to have been written. If so, Mark is responsible for evolving a new type of literature, neither history nor biography but the imparting of the Good News (the Old English word is 'Gospel') of the reign of God in Jesus. It is the most compact gospel, concentrating not on Jesus' teaching but on the mystery of his person, the gradual way in which the disciples reach an understanding of him which still remains hidden from the crowds. The paradox is that Jesus is acknowledged as Son of God by the Father and by evil spirits, and yet he is rejected by the leaders of the Jews and is even misunderstood by his own disciples. The gospel has been called a passion narrative with extended introduction; or it may be seen in two halves, the first being the revelation that Jesus is Messiah, the second — after the decisive turning-point at Caesarea Philippi (8:29) — being the revelation of his role of suffering. Mark shows that the rejection was an essential part of God's plan, foretold in the Scriptures, and crowned by Jesus' awesome resurrection.

PLAN OF THE BOOK

I Prelude to the Public Ministry of Jesus 1:1–13
II The Galilean Ministry 1:14—7:23
III Journeys outside Galilee 7:24—10
IV The Jerusalem Ministry 11—13
V Passion and Resurrection 14—16

THE GOSPEL ACCORDING TO MARK

I: PRELUDE TO THE PUBLIC MINISTRY OF JESUS

The proclamation of John the Baptist

1 The beginning of the gospel about Jesus
Christ, the Son of God. 2 It is written in
the prophet Isaiah:

Look, I am going to send my messenger
in front of you
to prepare your way before you. [a]

3 *A voice of one that cries in the desert:*
Prepare a way for the Lord,
make his paths straight.

4 John the Baptist was in the desert,
proclaiming a baptism of repentance for the
forgiveness of sins. 5 All Judaea and all the
people of Jerusalem made their way to him,
and as they were baptised by him in the river

1a Ml 3:1 followed by Is 40:3.

Jordan they confessed their sins. 6 John wore
a garment of camel-skin, and he lived on
locusts and wild honey. 7 In the course of
his preaching he said, 'After me is coming
someone who is more powerful than me, and
I am not fit to kneel down and undo the strap
of his sandals. 8 I have baptised you with
water, but he will baptise you with the Holy
Spirit.'

Jesus is baptised

9 It was at this time that Jesus came from
Nazareth in Galilee and was baptised in the
Jordan by John. 10 And at once, as he was
coming up out of the water, he saw the
heavens torn apart and the Spirit, like a dove,
descending on him. 11 And a voice came from
heaven, 'You are my Son, the Beloved; my
favour rests on you.'

Testing in the desert

12 And at once the Spirit drove him into the
desert 13 and he remained there for forty days,
and was put to the test by Satan. He was
with the wild animals, and the angels looked
after him.

II: THE GALILEAN MINISTRY

Jesus begins to proclaim the message

14 After John had been arrested, Jesus went
into Galilee. There he proclaimed the gospel
from God saying, 15 'The time is fulfilled, and
the kingdom of God is close at hand. Repent,
and believe the gospel.'

The first four disciples are called

16 As he was walking along by the Lake of
Galilee he saw Simon and Simon's brother
Andrew casting a net in the lake—for they
were fishermen. 17 And Jesus said to them,
'Come after me and I will make you into
fishers of people.' 18 And at once they left
their nets and followed him.
19 Going on a little further, he saw James
son of Zebedee and his brother John; they
too were in their boat, mending the nets. 20 At
once he called them and, leaving their father
Zebedee in the boat with the men he
employed, they went after him.

Jesus teaches in Capernaum and cures a demoniac

21 They went as far as Capernaum, and at once
on the Sabbath he went into the synagogue
and began to teach. 22 And his teaching
made a deep impression on them because,
unlike the scribes, he taught them with
authority.
23 And at once in their synagogue there was
a man with an unclean spirit, and he shouted,
24 'What do you want with us, Jesus of Naza-
reth? Have you come to destroy us? I know
who you are: the Holy One of God.' 25 But
Jesus rebuked it saying, 'Be quiet! Come out
of him!' 26 And the unclean spirit threw the
man into convulsions and with a loud cry
went out of him. 27 The people were so aston-
ished that they started asking one another
what it all meant, saying, 'Here is a teaching
that is new, and with authority behind it: he
gives orders even to unclean spirits and they
obey him.' 28 And his reputation at once
spread everywhere, through all the
surrounding Galilean countryside.

Cure of Simon's mother-in-law

29 And at once on leaving the synagogue, he
went with James and John straight to the
house of Simon and Andrew. 30 Now Simon's
mother-in-law was in bed and feverish, and
at once they told him about her. 31 He went
in to her, took her by the hand and helped
her up. And the fever left her and she began
to serve them.

A number of cures

32 That evening, after sunset, they brought to
him all who were sick and those who were
possessed by devils. 33 The whole town came
crowding round the door, 34 and he cured
many who were sick with diseases of one kind
or another; he also drove out many devils,
but he would not allow them to speak,
because they knew who he was.

Jesus quietly leaves Capernaum and travels through Galilee

35 In the morning, long before dawn, he got up and left the house and went off to a lonely place and prayed there. 36 Simon and his companions set out in search of him, 37 and when they found him they said, 'Everybody is looking for you.' 38 He answered, 'Let us go elsewhere, to the neighbouring country towns, so that I can proclaim the message there too, because that is why I came.' 39 And he went all through Galilee, preaching in their synagogues and driving out devils.

Cure of a man suffering from a virulent skin-disease

40 A man suffering from a virulent skin-disease came to him and pleaded on his knees saying, 'If you are willing, you can cleanse me.' 41 Feeling sorry for him, Jesus stretched out his hand, touched him and said to him, 'I am willing. Be cleansed.' 42 And at once the skin-disease left him and he was cleansed. 43 And at once Jesus sternly sent him away and said to him, 44 'Mind you tell no one anything, but go and show yourself to the priest, and make the offering for your cleansing prescribed by Moses as evidence to them.' 45 The man went away, but then started freely proclaiming and telling the story everywhere, so that Jesus could no longer go openly into any town, but stayed outside in deserted places. Even so, people from all around kept coming to him.

Cure of a paralytic

2 When he returned to Capernaum, some time later word went round that he was in the house; 2 and so many people collected that there was no room left, even in front of the door. He was preaching the word to them 3 when some people came bringing him a paralytic carried by four men, 4 but as they could not get the man to him through the crowd, they stripped the roof over the place where Jesus was; and when they had made an opening, they lowered the stretcher on which the paralytic lay. 5 Seeing their faith, Jesus said to the paralytic, 'My child, your sins are forgiven.' 6 Now some scribes were sitting there, and they thought to themselves, 7 'How can this man talk like that? He is being blasphemous. Who but God can forgive sins?' 8 And at once, Jesus, inwardly aware that this is what they were thinking, said to them, 'Why do you have these thoughts in your hearts? 9 Which of these is easier: to say to the paralytic, "Your sins are forgiven" or to say, "Get up, pick up your stretcher and walk"? 10 But to prove to you that the Son of man has authority to forgive sins on earth'— 11 he said to the paralytic—'I order you: get up, pick up your stretcher, and go off home.' 12 And the man got up, and at once picked up his stretcher and walked out in front of everyone, so that they were all astonished and praised God saying, 'We have never seen anything like this.'

The call of Levi

13 He went out again to the shore of the lake; and all the people came to him, and he taught them. 14 As he was walking along he saw Levi the son of Alphaeus sitting at the tax office, and he said to him, 'Follow me.' And he got up and followed him.

Eating with sinners

15 When Jesus was at dinner in his house, a number of tax collectors and sinners were also sitting at table with Jesus and his disciples; for there were many of them among his followers. 16 When the scribes of the Pharisee party saw him eating with sinners and tax collectors, they said to his disciples, 'Why does he eat with tax collectors and sinners?' 17 When Jesus heard this he said to them, 'It is not the healthy who need the doctor, but the sick. I came to call not the upright, but sinners.'

A discussion on fasting

18 John's disciples and the Pharisees were keeping a fast, when some people came to him and said to him, 'Why is it that John's disciples and the disciples of the Pharisees fast, but your disciples do not?' 19 Jesus replied, 'Surely the bridegroom's attendants cannot fast while the bridegroom is still with them? As long as they have the bridegroom with them, they cannot fast. 20 But the time will come when the bridegroom is taken away from them, and then, on that day, they will fast. 21 No one sews a piece of unshrunken cloth on an old cloak; otherwise, the patch pulls away from it, the new from the old, and

the tear gets worse. 22And nobody puts new
wine into old wineskins; otherwise, the wine
will burst the skins, and the wine is lost and
the skins too. No! New wine into fresh skins!'

Picking corn on the Sabbath

23It happened that one Sabbath day he was
taking a walk through the cornfields, and his
disciples began to make a path by plucking
ears of corn. 24And the Pharisees said to him,
'Look, why are they doing something on the
Sabbath day that is forbidden?' 25And he
replied, 'Have you never read what David
did in his time of need when he and his
followers were hungry—26how he went into
the house of God when Abiathar[a] was high
priest, and ate the loaves of the offering which
only the priests are allowed to eat, and how
he also gave some to the men with him?'
27And he said to them, 'The Sabbath was
made for man, not man for the Sabbath; 28so
the Son of man is master even of the Sabbath.'

Cure of the man with a withered hand

3 Another time he went into the synagogue,
and there was a man present whose hand
was withered. 2And they were watching him
to see if he would cure him on the Sabbath
day, hoping for something to charge him
with. 3He said to the man with the withered
hand, 'Get up and stand in the middle!'
4Then he said to them, 'Is it permitted on the
Sabbath day to do good, or to do evil; to save
life, or to kill?' But they said nothing. 5Then
he looked angrily round at them, grieved to
find them so obstinate, and said to the man,
'Stretch out your hand.' He stretched it out
and his hand was restored. 6The Pharisees
went out and began at once to plot with the
Herodians[a] against him, discussing how to
destroy him.

The crowds follow Jesus

7Jesus withdrew with his disciples to the
lakeside, and great crowds from Galilee
followed him. From Judaea, 8and from Jeru-
salem, and from Idumaea and Transjordan
and the region of Tyre and Sidon, great
numbers who had heard of all he was doing
came to him. 9And he asked his disciples to
have a boat ready for him because of the
crowd, to keep him from being crushed.
10For he had cured so many that all who were
afflicted in any way were crowding forward
to touch him. 11And the unclean spirits,
whenever they saw him, would fall down
before him and shout, 'You are the Son of
God!' 12But he warned them strongly not to
make him known.

The appointment of the Twelve

13He now went up onto the mountain and
summoned those he wanted. So they came to
him 14and he appointed twelve; they were
to be his companions and to be sent out to
proclaim the message, 15with power to drive
out devils. 16And so he appointed the Twelve,
Simon to whom he gave the name Peter,
17James the son of Zebedee and John the
brother of James, to whom he gave the name
Boanerges or 'Sons of Thunder'; 18Andrew,
Philip, Bartholomew, Matthew, Thomas,
James the son of Alphaeus, Thaddaeus,
Simon the Zealot 19and Judas Iscariot, the
man who was to betray him.

His family are concerned about Jesus

20He went home again, and once more such
a crowd collected that they could not even
have a meal. 21When his relations heard of
this, they set out to take charge of him; they
said, 'He is out of his mind.'

Allegations of the scribes

22The scribes who had come down from
Jerusalem were saying, 'Beelzebul is in him,'
and, 'It is through the prince of devils that
he drives devils out.' 23So he called them to
him and spoke to them in parables, 24'How
can Satan drive out Satan? If a kingdom is
divided against itself, that kingdom cannot
last. 25And if a household is divided against
itself, that household can never last. 26Now
if Satan has rebelled against himself and is
divided, he cannot last either—it is the end
of him. 27But no one can make his way into a
strong man's house and plunder his property
unless he has first tied up the strong man.
Only then can he plunder his house.
28'In truth I tell you, all human sins will

2a In fact his father, Ahimelech, was high priest, 1 S 21:1–7.
3a Supporters of the Herodian dynasty, campaigning for the return of all Palestine to their rule.

be forgiven, and all the blasphemies ever
uttered; [29]but anyone who blasphemes
against the Holy Spirit will never be forgiven,
but is guilty of an eternal sin.' [30]This was
because they were saying, 'There is an
unclean spirit in him.'

The true kinsmen of Jesus

[31]Now his mother and his brothers arrived
and, standing outside, sent in a message
asking for him. [32]A crowd was sitting round
him at the time the message was passed to
him, 'Look, your mother and brothers and
sisters are outside asking for you.' [33]He
replied, 'Who are my mother and my
brothers?' [34]And looking at those sitting in a
circle round him, he said, 'Here are my
mother and my brothers. [35]Anyone who does
the will of God, that person is my brother
and sister and mother.'

Parable of the sower

4 Again he began to teach them by the
lakeside, but such a huge crowd gathered
round him that he got into a boat on the water
and sat there. The whole crowd were at the
lakeside on land. [2]He taught them many
things in parables, and in the course of his
teaching he said to them, [3]'Listen! Imagine
a sower going out to sow. [4]Now it happened
that, as he sowed, some of the seed fell on the
edge of the path, and the birds came and ate
it up. [5]Some seed fell on rocky ground where
it found little soil and at once sprang up,
because there was no depth of earth; [6]and
when the sun came up it was scorched and,
not having any roots, it withered away. [7]Some
seed fell into thorns, and the thorns grew up
and choked it, and it produced no crop. [8]And
some seeds fell into rich soil, grew tall and
strong, and produced a good crop; the yield
was thirty, sixty, even a hundredfold.' [9]And
he said, 'Anyone who has ears for listening
should listen!'

Why Jesus spoke in parables

[10]When he was alone, the Twelve, together
with the others who formed his company,
asked what the parables meant. [11]He told
them, 'To you is granted the secret of the
kingdom of God, but to those who are outside
everything comes in parables,

[12]so that *they may look and look,*
but never perceive;
listen and listen, but never understand;
to avoid changing their ways
and being healed.'[a]

The parable of the sower explained

[13]He said to them, 'Do you not understand
this parable? Then how will you understand
any of the parables? [14]What the sower is
sowing is the word. [15]Those on the edge of
the path where the word is sown are people
who have no sooner heard it than Satan at
once comes and carries away the word that
was sown in them. [16]Similarly, those who are
sown on patches of rock are people who,
when first they hear the word, welcome it at
once with joy. [17]But they have no root deep
down and do not last; should some trial come,
or some persecution on account of the word,
at once they fall away. [18]Then there are others
who are sown in thorns. These have heard
the word, [19]but the worries of the world, the
lure of riches and all the other passions come
in to choke the word, and so it produces
nothing. [20]And there are those who have been
sown in rich soil; they hear the word and
accept it and yield a harvest, thirty and sixty
and a hundredfold.'

Receiving and handing on the teaching of Jesus

[21]He also said to them, 'Is a lamp brought in
to be put under a tub or under the bed?
Surely to be put on the lamp-stand? [22]For
there is nothing hidden, but it must be dis-
closed, nothing kept secret except to be
brought to light. [23]Anyone who has ears for
listening should listen!'

Parable of the measure

[24]He also said to them, 'Take notice of what
you are hearing. The standard you use will
be used for you—and you will receive more
besides; [25]anyone who has, will be given
more; anyone who has not, will be deprived
even of what he has.'

4a Is 6:9–10.

Parable of the seed growing by itself

26 He also said, 'This is what the kingdom of
God is like. A man scatters seed on the land.
27 Night and day, while he sleeps, when he is
awake, the seed is sprouting and growing;
how, he does not know. 28 Of its own accord
the land produces first the shoot, then the
ear, then the full grain in the ear. 29 And when
the crop is ready, at once he starts to reap
because the harvest has come.'

Parable of the mustard seed

30 He also said, 'What can we say that the
kingdom is like? What parable can we find
for it? 31 It is like a mustard seed which, at the
time of its sowing, is the smallest of all the
seeds on earth. 32 Yet once it is sown it grows
into the biggest shrub of them all and puts
out big branches so that the birds of the air
can shelter in its shade.'

The use of parables

33 Using many parables like these, he spoke
the word to them, so far as they were capable
of understanding it. 34 He would not speak to
them except in parables, but he explained
everything to his disciples when they were
by themselves.

The calming of the storm

35 With the coming of evening that same day,
he said to them, 'Let us cross over to the
other side.' 36 And leaving the crowd behind
they took him, just as he was, in the boat;
and there were other boats with him. 37 Then
it began to blow a great gale and the waves
were breaking into the boat so that it was
almost swamped. 38 But he was in the stern,
his head on the cushion, asleep. 39 They woke
him and said to him, 'Master, do you not
care? We are lost!' And he woke up and
rebuked the wind and said to the sea, 'Quiet
now! Be calm!' And the wind dropped, and
there followed a great calm. 40 Then he said
to them, 'Why are you so frightened? Have
you still no faith?' 41 They were overcome
with awe and said to one another, 'Who
can this be? Even the wind and the sea
obey him.'

The Gerasene demoniac

5 They reached the territory of the Ger-
asenes on the other side of the lake, 2 and
when he disembarked, a man with an unclean
spirit at once came out from the tombs
towards him. 3 The man lived in the tombs
and no one could secure him any more, even
with a chain, 4 because he had often been
secured with fetters and chains but had
snapped the chains and broken the fetters,
and no one had the strength to control him.
5 All night and all day, among the tombs and
in the mountains, he would howl and gash
himself with stones. 6 Catching sight of Jesus
from a distance, he ran up and fell at his feet
7 and shouted at the top of his voice, 'What
do you want with me, Jesus, son of the Most
High God? In God's name do not torture
me!' 8 For Jesus had been saying to him,
'Come out of the man, unclean spirit.' 9 Then
he asked, 'What is your name?' He answered,
'My name is Legion, for there are many of
us.' 10 And he begged him earnestly not to
send them out of the district. 11 Now on the
mountainside there was a great herd of pigs
feeding, 12 and the unclean spirits begged
him, 'Send us to the pigs, let us go into them.'
13 So he gave them leave. With that, the
unclean spirits came out and went into the
pigs, and the herd of about two thousand
pigs charged down the cliff into the lake, and
there they were drowned. 14 The men looking
after them ran off and told their story in the
city and in the country round about; and the
people came to see what had really happened.
15 They came to Jesus and saw the demoniac
sitting there—the man who had had the
legion in him—properly dressed and in his
full senses, and they were afraid. 16 And those
who had witnessed it reported what had
happened to the demoniac and what had
become of the pigs. 17 Then they began to
implore Jesus to leave their neighbourhood.
18 As he was getting into the boat, the man
who had been possessed begged to be allowed
to stay with him. 19 Jesus would not let him
but said to him, 'Go home to your people and
tell them all that the Lord in his mercy has
done for you.' 20 So the man went off and
proceeded to proclaim in the Decapolis all
that Jesus had done for him. And everyone
was amazed.

Cure of the woman with a haemorrhage
The daughter of Jairus raised to life

[21]When Jesus had crossed again in the boat
to the other side, a large crowd gathered
round him and he stayed by the lake. [22]Then
the president of the synagogue came up,
named Jairus, and seeing him, fell at his feet
[23]and begged him earnestly, saying, 'My little
daughter is desperately sick. Do come and
lay your hands on her that she may be saved
and may live.' [24]Jesus went with him and a
large crowd followed him; they were pressing
all round him.
[25]Now there was a woman who had
suffered from a haemorrhage for twelve
years; [26]after long and painful treatment
under various doctors, she had spent all she
had without being any the better for it; in
fact, she was getting worse. [27]She had heard
about Jesus, and she came up through the
crowd and touched his cloak from behind,
thinking, [28]'If I can just touch his clothes, I
shall be saved.' [29]And at once the source of
the bleeding dried up, and she felt in herself
that she was cured of her complaint. [30]And
at once aware of the power that had gone out
from him, Jesus turned round in the crowd
and said, 'Who touched my clothes?' [31]His
disciples said to him, 'You see how the crowd
is pressing round you; how can you ask,
"Who touched me?" ' [32]But he continued to
look all round to see who had done it. [33]Then
the woman came forward, frightened and
trembling because she knew what had
happened to her, and she fell at his feet and
told him the whole truth. [34]'My daughter,'
he said, 'your faith has restored you to health;
go in peace and be free of your complaint.'
[35]While he was still speaking some people
arrived from the house of the president of the
synagogue to say, 'Your daughter is dead;
why put the Master to any further trouble?'
[36]But Jesus overheard what they said and he
said to the president of the synagogue, 'Do
not be afraid; only have faith.' [37]And he
allowed no one to go with him except Peter
and James and John the brother of James.
[38]So they came to the house of the president
of the synagogue, and Jesus noticed all the
commotion, with people weeping and wailing
unrestrainedly. [39]He went in and said to
them, 'Why all this commotion and crying?
The child is not dead, but asleep.' [40]But they
ridiculed him. So he turned them all out and,
taking with him the child's father and mother
and his own companions, he went into the
place where the child lay. [41]And taking the
child by the hand he said to her, '*Talitha
kum!*' which means, 'Little girl, I tell you to
get up.' [42]The little girl got up at once and
began to walk about, for she was twelve
years old. At once they were overcome with
astonishment, [43]and he gave them strict
orders not to let anyone know about it, and
told them to give her something to eat.

A visit to Nazareth

6 Leaving that district, he went to his home
town, and his disciples accompanied him.
[2]With the coming of the Sabbath he began
teaching in the synagogue, and most of them
were astonished when they heard him. They
said, 'Where did the man get all this? What
is this wisdom that has been granted him,
and these miracles that are worked through
him? [3]This is the carpenter, surely, the son
of Mary, the brother of James and Joset and
Jude and Simon? His sisters, too, are they
not here with us?' And they would not accept
him. [4]And Jesus said to them, 'A prophet is
despised only in his own country, among his
own relations and in his own house'; [5]and he
could work no miracle there, except that he
cured a few sick people by laying his hands
on them. [6]He was amazed at their lack of
faith.

The mission of the Twelve

He made a tour round the villages, teaching.
[7]Then he summoned the Twelve and began to
send them out in pairs, giving them authority
over unclean spirits. [8]And he instructed them
to take nothing for the journey except a
staff—no bread, no haversack, no coppers
for their purses. [9]They were to wear sandals
but, he added, 'Don't take a spare tunic.'
[10]And he said to them, 'If you enter a house
anywhere, stay there until you leave the
district. [11]And if any place does not welcome
you and people refuse to listen to you, as you
walk away shake off the dust under your feet
as evidence to them.' [12]So they set off to
proclaim repentance; [13]and they cast out
many devils, and anointed many sick people
with oil and cured them.

Herod and Jesus

[14]King Herod had heard about him, since by
now his name was well known. Some were

saying, 'John the Baptist has risen from the
dead, and that is why miraculous powers are
at work in him.' 15 Others said, 'He is Elijah,'
others again, 'He is a prophet, like the
prophets we used to have.' 16 But when Herod
heard this he said, 'It is John whose head I
cut off; he has risen from the dead.'

John the Baptist beheaded

17 Now it was this same Herod who had sent
to have John arrested, and had had him
chained up in prison because of Herodias, his
brother Philip's wife whom he had married.
18 For John had told Herod, 'It is against the
law for you to have your brother's wife.' 19 As
for Herodias, she was furious with him and
wanted to kill him, but she was not able to
do so, 20 because Herod was in awe of John,
knowing him to be a good and upright man,
and gave him his protection. When he had
heard him speak he was greatly perplexed,
and yet he liked to listen to him.
21 An opportunity came on Herod's
birthday when he gave a banquet for the
nobles of his court, for his army officers and
for the leading figures in Galilee. 22 When the
daughter of this same Herodias came in and
danced, she delighted Herod and his guests;
so the king said to the girl, 'Ask me anything
you like and I will give it you.' 23 And he
swore her an oath, 'I will give you anything
you ask, even half my kingdom.' 24 She went
out and said to her mother, 'What shall I ask
for?' She replied, 'The head of John the
Baptist.' 25 The girl at once rushed back to
the king and made her request, 'I want
you to give me John the Baptist's head,
immediately, on a dish.' 26 The king was
deeply distressed but, thinking of the oaths
he had sworn and of his guests, he was
reluctant to break his word to her. 27 At once
the king sent one of the bodyguard with
orders to bring John's head. 28 The man went
off and beheaded him in the prison; then he
brought the head on a dish and gave it to the
girl, and the girl gave it to her mother.
29 When John's disciples heard about this,
they came and took his body and laid it in a
tomb.

First miracle of the loaves

30 The apostles rejoined Jesus and told him
all they had done and taught. 31 And he said
to them, 'Come away to some lonely place all
by yourselves and rest for a while'; for there
were so many coming and going that there
was no time for them even to eat. 32 So they
went off in the boat to a lonely place where
they could be by themselves. 33 But people
saw them going, and many recognised them;
and from every town they all hurried to the
place on foot and reached it before them. 34 So
as he stepped ashore he saw a large crowd;
and he took pity on them because they were
like sheep without a shepherd, and he set
himself to teach them at some length. 35 By
now it was getting very late, and his disciples
came up to him and said, 'This is a lonely
place and it is getting very late, 36 so send
them away, and they can go to the farms and
villages round about, to buy them-
selves something to eat.' 37 He replied, 'Give
them something to eat yourselves.' They
answered, 'Are we to go and spend two
hundred denarii on bread for them to eat?'
38 He asked, 'How many loaves have you? Go
and see.' And when they had found out they
said, 'Five, and two fish.' 39 Then he ordered
them to get all the people to sit down in
groups on the green grass, 40 and they sat
down on the ground in squares of hundreds
and fifties. 41 Then he took the five loaves and
the two fish, raised his eyes to heaven and
said the blessing; then he broke the loaves
and began handing them to his disciples to
distribute among the people. He also shared
out the two fish among them all. 42 They all
ate as much as they wanted. 43 They collected
twelve basketfuls of scraps of bread and
pieces of fish. 44 Those who had eaten the
loaves numbered five thousand men.

Jesus walks on the water

45 And at once he made his disciples get into
the boat and go on ahead to the other side
near Bethsaida, while he himself sent the
crowd away. 46 After saying goodbye to them
he went off into the hills to pray. 47 When
evening came, the boat was far out on the
sea, and he was alone on the land. 48 He could
see that they were hard pressed in their
rowing, for the wind was against them; and
about the fourth watch of the night he came
towards them, walking on the sea. He was
going to pass them by, 49 but when they saw
him walking on the sea they thought it was a
ghost and cried out; 50 for they had all seen
him and were terrified. But at once he spoke
to them and said, 'Courage! It's me! Don't

be afraid.' [51]Then he got into the boat with them and the wind dropped. They were utterly and completely dumbfounded, [52]because they had not seen what the miracle of the loaves meant; their minds were closed.

Cures at Gennesaret

[53]Having made the crossing, they came to land at Gennesaret and moored there. [54]When they disembarked people at once recognised him, [55]and started hurrying all through the countryside and brought the sick on stretchers to wherever they heard he was. [56]And wherever he went, to village or town or farm, they laid down the sick in the open spaces, begging him to let them touch even the fringe of his cloak. And all those who touched him were saved.

The traditions of the Pharisees

7 The Pharisees and some of the scribes who had come from Jerusalem gathered round him, [2]and they noticed that some of his disciples were eating with unclean hands, that is, without washing them. [3]For the Pharisees, and all the Jews, keep the tradition of the elders and never eat without washing their arms as far as the elbow; [4]and on returning from the market place they never eat without first sprinkling themselves. There are also many other observances which have been handed down to them to keep, concerning the washing of cups and pots and bronze dishes. [5]So the Pharisees and scribes asked him, 'Why do your disciples not respect the tradition of the elders but eat their food with unclean hands?' [6]He answered, 'How rightly Isaiah prophesied about you hypocrites in the passage of scripture:

This people honours me
only with lip-service,
while their hearts are far from me.
[7]*Their reverence of me is worthless;*
the lessons they teach
are nothing but human commandments.[a]

[8]You put aside the commandment of God to observe human traditions.' [9]And he said to them, 'How ingeniously you get round the commandment of God in order to preserve your own tradition! [10]For Moses said: *Honour your father and your mother*, and, *Anyone who curses father or mother must be put to death.*[b] [11]But you say, "If a man says to his father or mother: Anything I have that I might have used to help you is Korban[c] (that is, dedicated to God)," [12]then he is forbidden from that moment to do anything for his father or mother. [13]In this way you make God's word ineffective for the sake of your tradition which you have handed down. And you do many other things like this.'

On clean and unclean

[14]He called the people to him again and said, 'Listen to me, all of you, and understand. [15]Nothing that goes into someone from outside can make that person unclean; it is the things that come out of someone that make that person unclean. [16]Anyone who has ears for listening should listen!'

[17]When he had gone into the house, away from the crowd, his disciples questioned him about the parable. [18]He said to them, 'Even you—don't you understand? Can't you see that nothing that goes into someone from outside can make that person unclean, [19]because it goes not into the heart but into the stomach and passes into the sewer?' (Thus he pronounced all foods clean.) [20]And he went on, 'It is what comes out of someone that makes that person unclean. [21]For it is from within, from the heart, that evil intentions emerge: fornication, theft, murder, [22]adultery, avarice, malice, deceit, indecency, envy, slander, pride, folly. [23]All these evil things come from within and make a person unclean.'

7a Is 29:13.
7b Ex 20:12; 21:17.
7c Nothing Korban could be used for anyone else – a convenient legal fiction.

III: JOURNEYS OUTSIDE GALILEE

The daughter of the Syro-Phoenician woman healed

24He left that place and set out for the territory of Tyre. There he went into a house and did not want anyone to know he was there; but he could not pass unrecognised. 25At once a woman whose little daughter had an unclean spirit heard about him and came and fell at his feet. 26Now this woman was a gentile, by birth a Syro-Phoenician, and she begged him to drive the devil out of her daughter. 27And he said to her, 'The children should be fed first, because it is not fair to take the children's food and throw it to little dogs.' 28But she spoke up, 'Ah yes, sir,' she replied, 'but little dogs under the table eat the scraps from the children.' 29And he said to her, 'For saying this you may go home happy; the devil has gone out of your daughter.' 30So she went off home and found the child lying on the bed and the devil gone.

Healing of the deaf man

31Returning from the territory of Tyre, he went by way of Sidon towards the Lake of Galilee, right through the Decapolis territory. 32And they brought him a deaf man who had an impediment in his speech; and they asked him to lay his hand on him. 33He took him aside to be by themselves, away from the crowd, put his fingers into the man's ears and touched his tongue with spittle. 34Then looking up to heaven he sighed; and he said to him, '*Ephphatha*,' that is, 'Be opened.' 35And his ears were opened, and at once the impediment of his tongue was loosened and he spoke clearly. 36And Jesus ordered them to tell no one about it, but the more he insisted, the more widely they proclaimed it. 37Their admiration was unbounded, and they said, 'Everything he does is good, he makes the deaf hear and the dumb speak.'

Second miracle of the loaves

8 And now once again a great crowd had gathered, and they had nothing to eat. So he called his disciples to him and said to them, 2'I feel sorry for all these people; they have been with me for three days now and have nothing to eat. 3If I send them off home hungry they will collapse on the way; some have come a great distance.' 4His disciples replied, 'Where could anyone get these people enough bread to eat in a deserted place?' 5He asked them, 'How many loaves have you?' And they said to him, 'Seven.' 6Then he instructed the crowd to sit down on the ground, and he took the seven loaves, and after giving thanks he broke them and began handing them to his disciples to distribute; and they distributed them among the crowd. 7They had a few small fishes as well, and over these he said a blessing and ordered them to be distributed too. 8They ate as much as they wanted, and they collected seven basketfuls of the scraps left over. 9Now there had been about four thousand people. He sent them away 10and at once, getting into the boat with his disciples, went to the region of Dalmanutha.

The Pharisees ask for a sign from heaven

11The Pharisees came up and started a discussion with him; they demanded of him a sign from heaven, to put him to the test. 12And with a profound sigh he said, 'Why does this generation demand a sign? In truth I tell you, no sign shall be given to this generation.' 13And, leaving them again, he re-embarked and went away to the other side.

The yeast of the Pharisees and of Herod

14The disciples had forgotten to take any bread and they had only one loaf with them in the boat. 15Then he gave them this warning, 'Keep your eyes open; look out for the yeast of the Pharisees and the yeast of Herod.' 16And they said to one another, 'It is because we have no bread.' 17And Jesus knew it, and he said to them, 'Why are you talking about having no bread? Do you still not understand, still not realise? Are your minds closed? 18Have you *eyes and do not see, ears and do not hear?*[a] Or do you not remember? 19When I broke the five loaves for the five thousand, how many baskets full of scraps did you collect?' They answered, 'Twelve.' 20'And

8a Jr 5:21; Ezk 12:2.

when I broke the seven loaves for the four thousand, how many baskets full of scraps did you collect?' And they answered, 'Seven.' 21 Then he said to them, 'Do you still not realise?'

Cure of a blind man at Bethsaida

22 They came to Bethsaida, and some people brought to him a blind man whom they begged him to touch. 23 He took the blind man by the hand and led him outside the village. Then, putting spittle on his eyes and laying his hands on him, he asked, 'Can you see anything?' 24 The man, who was beginning to see, replied, 'I can see people; they look like trees as they walk around.' 25 Then he laid his hands on the man's eyes again and he saw clearly; he was cured, and he could see everything plainly and distinctly. 26 And Jesus sent him home, saying, 'Do not even go into the village.'

Peter's profession of faith

27 Jesus and his disciples left for the villages round Caesarea Philippi. On the way he put this question to his disciples, 'Who do people say I am?' 28 And they told him, 'John the Baptist, others Elijah, others again, one of the prophets.' 29 'But you,' he asked them, 'who do you say I am?' Peter spoke up and said to him, 'You are the Christ.' 30 And he gave them strict orders not to tell anyone about him.

First prophecy of the Passion

31 Then he began to teach them that the Son of man was destined to suffer grievously, and to be rejected by the elders and the chief priests and the scribes, and to be put to death, and after three days to rise again; 32 and he said all this quite openly. Then, taking him aside, Peter tried to rebuke him. 33 But, turning and seeing his disciples, he rebuked Peter and said to him, 'Get behind me, Satan! You are thinking not as God thinks, but as human beings do.'

The condition of following Christ

34 He called the people and his disciples to him and said, 'If anyone wants to be a follower of mine, let him renounce himself and take up his cross and follow me. 35 Anyone who wants to save his life will lose it; but anyone who loses his life for my sake, and for the sake of the gospel, will save it. 36 What gain, then, is it for anyone to win the whole world and forfeit his life? 37 And indeed what can anyone offer in exchange for his life? 38 For if anyone in this sinful and adulterous generation is ashamed of me and of my words, the Son of man will also be ashamed of him when he comes in the glory of his Father with the holy angels.'

9 And he said to them, 'In truth I tell you, there are some standing here who will not taste death before they see the kingdom of God come with power.'

The Transfiguration

2 Six days later, Jesus took with him Peter and James and John and led them up a high mountain on their own by themselves. There in their presence he was transfigured: 3 his clothes became brilliantly white, whiter than any earthly bleacher could make them. 4 Elijah appeared to them with Moses; and they were talking to Jesus. 5 Then Peter spoke to Jesus, 'Rabbi,' he said, 'it is wonderful for us to be here; so let us make three shelters, one for you, one for Moses and one for Elijah.' 6 He did not know what to say; they were so frightened. 7 And a cloud came, covering them in shadow; and from the cloud there came a voice, 'This is my Son, the Beloved. Listen to him.' 8 Then suddenly, when they looked round, they saw no one with them any more but only Jesus.

The question about Elijah

9 As they were coming down from the mountain he warned them to tell no one what they had seen, until after the Son of man had risen from the dead. 10 They observed the warning faithfully, though among themselves they discussed what 'rising from the dead' could mean. 11 And they put this question to him, 'Why do the scribes say that Elijah must come first?' 12 He said to them, 'Elijah is indeed first coming to set everything right again; yet how is it that the scriptures say about the Son of man that he must suffer grievously and be treated with contempt? 13 But I tell you that Elijah has come and they have treated him as they pleased, just as the scriptures say about him.'

The epileptic demoniac

14As they were rejoining the disciples they
saw a large crowd round them and some
scribes arguing with them. 15At once, when
they saw him, the whole crowd were struck
with amazement and ran to greet him. 16And
he asked them, 'What are you arguing about
with them?' 17A man answered him from the
crowd, 'Master, I have brought my son to
you; there is a spirit of dumbness in him,
18and when it takes hold of him it throws him
to the ground, and he foams at the mouth
and grinds his teeth and goes rigid. And I
asked your disciples to drive it out and they
were unable to.' 19In reply he said to them,
'Faithless generation, how much longer must
I be among you? How much longer must I
put up with you? Bring him to me.' 20They
brought the boy to him, and at once the spirit
of dumbness threw the boy into convulsions,
and he fell to the ground and lay writhing
there, foaming at the mouth. 21Jesus asked
the father, 'How long has this been
happening to him?' 'From childhood,' he
said, 22'and it has often thrown him into fire
and into water, in order to destroy him. 23But
if you can do anything, have pity on us
and help us.' 24'If you can?' retorted Jesus.
'Everything is possible for one who has faith.'
At once the father of the boy cried out, 'I
have faith. Help my lack of faith!' 25And
when Jesus saw that a crowd was gathering,
he rebuked the unclean spirit. 'Deaf and
dumb spirit,' he said, 'I command you: come
out of him and never enter him again.' 26Then
it threw the boy into violent convulsions and
came out shouting, and the boy lay there so
like a corpse that most of them said, 'He is
dead.' 27But Jesus took him by the hand and
helped him up, and he was able to stand.
28When he had gone indoors, his disciples
asked him when they were by themselves,
'Why were we unable to drive it out?' 29He
answered, 'This is the kind that can be driven
out only by prayer.'

Second prophecy of the Passion

30After leaving that place they made their
way through Galilee; and he did not want
anyone to know, 31because he was instructing
his disciples; he was telling them, 'The Son
of man will be delivered into the power of
men; they will put him to death; and three
days after he has been put to death he will
rise again.' 32But they did not understand
what he said and were afraid to ask him.

Who is the greatest?

33They came to Capernaum, and when he got
into the house he asked them, 'What were
you arguing about on the road?' 34They said
nothing, because on the road they had been
arguing which of them was the greatest. 35So
he sat down, called the Twelve to him and
said, 'If anyone wants to be first, he must
make himself last of all and servant of all.'
36He then took a little child whom he set
among them and embraced, and he said to
them, 37'Anyone who welcomes a little child
such as this in my name, welcomes me; and
anyone who welcomes me, welcomes not me
but the one who sent me.'

On using the name of Jesus

38John said to him, 'Master, we saw someone
who is not one of us driving out devils in your
name, and because he was not one of us we
tried to stop him.' 39But Jesus said, 'You
must not stop him; no one who works a
miracle in my name could soon afterwards
speak evil of me. 40Anyone who is not against
us is for us.

Generosity shown to Christ's disciples

41'If anyone gives you a cup of water to drink
because you belong to Christ, then in truth I
tell you, he will most certainly not lose his
reward.

On leading others astray

42'But anyone who is the downfall of one of
these little ones who have faith, would be
better thrown into the sea with a great mill-
stone hung round his neck. 43And if your
hand should be your downfall, cut it off; it is
better for you to enter into life crippled, than
to have two hands and go to hell, into the fire
that can never be put out. [44][a] 45And if your
foot should be your downfall, cut it off; it is
better for you to enter into life lame, than
to have two feet and be thrown into hell.

9a Omitting, with the best MSS, vv. 44 and 46 (Vulg.), as repetitions of v. 48.

[46][b] [47]And if your eye should be your downfall, tear it out; it is better for you to enter into the kingdom of God with one eye, than to have two eyes and be thrown into hell [48]where *their worm will never die nor their fire be put out.*[c] [49]For everyone will be salted with fire. [50]Salt is a good thing, but if salt has become insipid, how can you make it salty again? Have salt in yourselves and be at peace with one another.'

The question about divorce

10 After leaving there, he came into the territory of Judaea and Transjordan. And again crowds gathered round him, and again he taught them, as his custom was. [2]Some Pharisees approached him and asked, 'Is it lawful for a man to divorce his wife?' They were putting him to the test. [3]He answered them, 'What did Moses command you?' [4]They replied, 'Moses allowed us to draw up a writ of dismissal in cases of divorce.'[a] [5]Then Jesus said to them, 'It was because you were so hard hearted that he wrote this commandment for you. [6]But from the beginning of creation *he made them male and female.* [7]*This is why a man leaves his father and mother,* [8]*and the two become one flesh.*[b] They are no longer two, therefore, but one flesh. [9]So then, what God has united, human beings must not divide.' [10]Back in the house the disciples questioned him again about this, [11]and he said to them, 'Whoever divorces his wife and marries another is guilty of adultery against her. [12]And if a woman divorces her husband and marries another she is guilty of adultery too.'

Jesus and the children

[13]People were bringing little children to him, for him to touch them. The disciples scolded them, [14]but when Jesus saw this he was indignant and said to them, 'Let the little children come to me; do not stop them; for it is to such as these that the kingdom of God belongs. [15]In truth I tell you, anyone who does not welcome the kingdom of God like a little child will never enter it.' [16]Then he embraced them, laid his hands on them and gave them his blessing.

The rich young man

[17]He was setting out on a journey when a man ran up, knelt before him and put this question to him, 'Good master, what must I do to inherit eternal life?' [18]Jesus said to him, 'Why do you call me good? No one is good but God alone. [19]You know the commandments: *You shall not kill; You shall not commit adultery; You shall not steal; You shall not give false witness;* You shall not defraud; *Honour your father and mother.*'[c] [20]And he said to him, 'Master, I have kept all these since my earliest days.' [21]Jesus looked steadily at him and he was filled with love for him, and he said, 'You need to do one thing more. Go and sell what you own and give the money to the poor, and you will have treasure in heaven; then come, follow me.' [22]But his face fell at these words and he went away sad, for he was a man of great wealth.

The danger of riches

[23]Jesus looked round and said to his disciples, 'How hard it is for those who have riches to enter the kingdom of God!' [24]The disciples were astounded by these words, but Jesus insisted, 'My children,' he said to them, 'how hard it is to enter the kingdom of God! [25]It is easier for a camel to pass through the eye of a needle than for someone rich to enter the kingdom of God.' [26]They were more astonished than ever, saying to one another, 'In that case, who can be saved?' [27]Jesus gazed at them and said, 'By human resources it is impossible, but not for God: because for God everything is possible.'

The reward of renunciation

[28]Peter took this up. 'Look,' he said to him, 'we have left everything and followed you.' [29]Jesus said, 'In truth I tell you, there is no one who has left house, brothers, sisters, mother, father, children or land for my sake and for the sake of the gospel [30]who will not

9b See 9a above.
9c Is 66:24. The word for hell is 'Gehenna', the rubbish-dump of Jerusalem, with its perpetual fires.
10a Dt 24:1.
10b Gn 1:27; 2:24.
10c Ex 20:12–16.

receive a hundred times as much, houses,
brothers, sisters, mothers, children and
land—and persecutions too—now in this
present time and, in the world to come,
eternal life. 31 Many who are first will be last,
and the last, first.'

Third prophecy of the Passion

32 They were on the road, going up to Jeru-
salem; Jesus was walking on ahead of them;
they were in a daze, and those who followed
were apprehensive. Once more taking the
Twelve aside he began to tell them what was
going to happen to him, 33 'Now we are going
up to Jerusalem, and the Son of man is about
to be handed over to the chief priests and the
scribes. They will condemn him to death and
will hand him over to the gentiles, 34 who will
mock him and spit at him and scourge him
and put him to death; and after three days he
will rise again.'

The sons of Zebedee make their request

35 James and John, the sons of Zebedee,
approached him. 'Master,' they said to him,
'We want you to do us a favour.' 36 He said to
them, 'What is it you want me to do for you?'
37 They said to him, 'Allow us to sit one at
your right hand and the other at your left in
your glory.' 38 But Jesus said to them, 'You
do not know what you are asking. Can you
drink the cup that I shall drink, or be baptised
with the baptism with which I shall be
baptised?' 39 They replied, 'We can.' Jesus
said to them, 'The cup that I shall drink you
shall drink, and with the baptism with which
I shall be baptised you shall be baptised,
40 but as for seats at my right hand or my left,
these are not mine to grant; they belong to
those to whom they have been allotted.'

Leadership with service

41 When the other ten heard this they began
to feel indignant with James and John, 42 so
Jesus called them to him and said to them,
'You know that among the gentiles those they
call their rulers lord it over them, and their
great men make their authority felt. 43 Among
you this is not to happen. No; anyone who
wants to become great among you must be
your servant, 44 and anyone who wants to be
first among you must be slave to all. 45 For
the Son of man himself came not to be served
but to serve, and to give his life as a ransom
for many.'

The blind man of Jericho

46 They reached Jericho; and as he left Jericho
with his disciples and a great crowd,
Bartimaeus—that is, the son of Timaeus—a
blind beggar, was sitting at the side of the
road. 47 When he heard that it was Jesus of
Nazareth, he began to shout and cry out,
'Son of David, Jesus, have pity on me.' 48 And
many of them scolded him and told him to
keep quiet, but he only shouted all the louder,
'Son of David, have pity on me.' 49 Jesus
stopped and said, 'Call him here.' So they
called the blind man over. 'Courage,' they
said, 'get up; he is calling you.' 50 So throwing
off his cloak, he jumped up and went to
Jesus. 51 Then Jesus spoke, 'What do you
want me to do for you?' The blind man said
to him, 'Rabbuni, let me see again.' 52 Jesus
said to him, 'Go; your faith has saved you.'
And at once his sight returned and he
followed him along the road.

IV: THE JERUSALEM MINISTRY

The Messiah enters Jerusalem

11 When they were approaching Jeru-
salem, at Bethphage and Bethany, close
by the Mount of Olives, he sent two of his
disciples 2 and said to them, 'Go to the village
facing you, and as you enter it you will at
once find a tethered colt that no one has yet
ridden. Untie it and bring it here. 3 If anyone
says to you, "What are you doing?" say,
"The Master needs it and will send it back
here at once." ' 4 They went off and found a
colt tethered near a door in the open street.
As they untied it, 5 some men standing there
said, 'What are you doing, untying that colt?'
6 They gave the answer Jesus had told them,
and the men let them go. 7 Then they took
the colt to Jesus and threw their cloaks on its
back, and he mounted it. 8 Many people
spread their cloaks on the road, and others

greenery which they had cut in the fields.
9 And those who went in front and those who
followed were all shouting, '*Hosanna! Blessed
is he who is coming in the name of the Lord!*[a]
10 Blessed is the coming kingdom of David
our father![b] *Hosanna* in the highest heavens!'
11 He entered Jerusalem and went into the
Temple; and when he had surveyed it all, as
it was late by now, he went out to Bethany
with the Twelve.

The barren fig tree

12 Next day as they were leaving Bethany, he
felt hungry. 13 Seeing a fig tree in leaf some
distance away, he went to see if he could find
any fruit on it, but when he came up to it he
found nothing but leaves; for it was not the
season for figs. 14 And he addressed the fig
tree, 'May no one ever eat fruit from you
again.' And his disciples heard him say this.

The expulsion of the dealers from the Temple

15 So they reached Jerusalem and he went into
the Temple and began driving out the men
selling and buying there; he upset the tables
of the money changers and the seats of the
dove sellers. 16 Nor would he allow anyone to
carry anything through the Temple. 17 And
he taught them and said, 'Does not scripture
say: *My house will be called a house of prayer
for all peoples*? But you have turned it into *a
bandits' den*.'[c] 18 This came to the ears of the
chief priests and the scribes, and they tried
to find some way of doing away with him;
they were afraid of him because the people
were carried away by his teaching. 19 And
when evening came he went out of the city.

The fig tree withered. Faith and prayer

20 Next morning, as they passed by, they saw
the fig tree withered to the roots. 21 Peter
remembered. 'Look, Rabbi,' he said to Jesus,
'the fig tree that you cursed has withered
away.' 22 Jesus answered, 'Have faith in God.
23 In truth I tell you, if anyone says to this
mountain, "Be pulled up and thrown into
the sea," with no doubt in his heart, but
believing that what he says will happen, it
will be done for him. 24 I tell you, therefore,
everything you ask and pray for, believe that
you have it already, and it will be yours.
25 And when you stand in prayer, forgive
whatever you have against anybody, so that
your Father in heaven may forgive your
failings too.'[26][d]

The authority of Jesus is questioned

27 They came to Jerusalem again, and as Jesus
was walking in the Temple, the chief priests
and the scribes and the elders came to him,
28 and they said to him, 'What authority have
you for acting like this? Or who gave you
authority to act like this?' 29 Jesus said to
them, 'And I will ask you a question, just one;
answer me and I will tell you my authority for
acting like this. 30 John's baptism, what was
its origin, heavenly or human? Answer me
that.' 31 And they argued this way among
themselves, 'If we say heavenly, he will say,
"Then why did you refuse to believe him?"
32 But dare we say human?'—they had the
people to fear, for everyone held that John
had been a real prophet. 33 So their reply to
Jesus was, 'We do not know.' And Jesus said
to them, 'Nor will I tell you my authority for
acting like this.'

Parable of the wicked tenants

12 He went on to speak to them in
parables, 'A man planted a vineyard;
he fenced it round, dug out a trough for the
winepress and built a tower; then he leased
it to tenants and went abroad. 2 When the
time came, he sent a servant to the tenants to
collect from them his share of the produce of
the vineyard. 3 But they seized the man,
thrashed him and sent him away empty
handed. 4 Next he sent another servant to
them; him they beat about the head and
treated shamefully. 5 And he sent another and
him they killed; then a number of others, and
they thrashed some and killed the rest. 6 He
had still someone left: his beloved son. He
sent him to them last of all, thinking, "They
will respect my son." 7 But those tenants said
to each other, "This is the heir. Come on, let
us kill him, and the inheritance will be ours."
8 So they seized him and killed him and threw

11a Ps 118:25–26.
11b 2 S 7:16.
11c Is 56:7 followed by Jr 7:11.
11d Some authorities add a v. borrowed from Mt 6:15.

him out of the vineyard. 9Now what will the owner of the vineyard do? He will come and make an end of the tenants and give the vineyard to others. 10Have you not read this text of scripture:

The stone which the builders rejected
has become the cornerstone;
11*this is the Lord's doing,*
and we marvel at it?'[a]

12And they would have liked to arrest him, because they realised that the parable was aimed at them, but they were afraid of the crowds. So they left him alone and went away.

On tribute to Caesar

13Next they sent to him some Pharisees and some Herodians to catch him out in what he said. 14These came and said to him, 'Master, we know that you are an honest man, that you are not afraid of anyone, because human rank means nothing to you, and that you teach the way of God in all honesty. Is it permissible to pay taxes to Caesar or not? Should we pay or not?' 15Recognising their hypocrisy he said to them, 'Why are you putting me to the test? Hand me a denarius and let me see it.' 16They handed him one and he said to them, 'Whose portrait is this? Whose title?' They said to him, 'Caesar's.' 17Jesus said to them, 'Pay Caesar what belongs to Caesar—and God what belongs to God.' And they were amazed at him.

The resurrection of the dead

18Then some Sadducees—who deny that there is a resurrection—came to him and they put this question to him, 19'Master, Moses prescribed for us that if a man's brother dies leaving a wife but no child, the man must marry the widow to raise up children for his brother. 20Now there were seven brothers; the first married a wife and then died leaving no children. 21The second married the widow, and he too died leaving no children; with the third it was the same, 22and none of the seven left any children. Last of all the woman herself died. 23Now at the resurrection, when they rise again, whose wife will she be, since she had been married to all seven?'

24Jesus said to them, 'Surely the reason why you are wrong is that you understand neither the scriptures nor the power of God. 25For when they rise from the dead, men and women do not marry; no, they are like the angels in heaven. 26Now about the dead rising again, have you never read in the Book of Moses, in the passage about the bush, how God spoke to him and said: *I am the God of Abraham, the God of Isaac and the God of Jacob?*[b] 27He is God, not of the dead, but of the living. You are very much mistaken.'

The greatest commandment of all

28One of the scribes who had listened to them debating appreciated that Jesus had given a good answer and put a further question to him, 'Which is the first of all the commandments?' 29Jesus replied, 'This is the first:[c] *Listen, Israel, the Lord our God is the one, only Lord,* 30*and you must love the Lord your God with all your heart, with all your soul,* with all your mind *and with all your strength.* 31The second is this:[d] *You must love your neighbour as yourself.* There is no commandment greater than these.' 32The scribe said to him, 'Well spoken, Master; what you have said is true, that *he is one and there is no other.* 33To *love him with all your heart, with all your understanding and strength,* and to *love your neighbour as yourself,* this is far more important than any burnt offering or sacrifice.' 34Jesus, seeing how wisely he had spoken, said, 'You are not far from the kingdom of God.' And after that no one dared to question him any more.

Jesus not only son but also Lord of David

35While teaching in the Temple, Jesus said, 'How can the scribes maintain that the Christ is the son of David? 36David himself, moved by the Holy Spirit, said:

The Lord declared to my Lord,
take your seat at my right hand

12a Ps 118:22–23.
12b Ex 3:6.
12c Dt 6:4–5.
12d Lv 19:18.

till I have made your enemies
your footstool.[e]

37David himself calls him Lord; in what way
then can he be his son?' And the great crowd
listened to him with delight.

The scribes condemned by Jesus

38In his teaching he said, 'Beware of the
scribes who like to walk about in long robes,
to be greeted respectfully in the market
squares, 39to take the front seats in the syna-
gogues and the places of honour at banquets;
40these are the men who devour the property
of widows and for show offer long prayers.
The more severe will be the sentence they
receive.'

The widow's mite

41He sat down opposite the treasury and
watched the people putting money into the
treasury, and many of the rich put in a great
deal. 42A poor widow came and put in two
small coins, the equivalent of a penny. 43Then
he called his disciples and said to them, 'In
truth I tell you, this poor widow has put
more in than all who have contributed to the
treasury; 44for they have all put in money
they could spare, but she in her poverty has
put in everything she possessed, all she had
to live on.'

The eschatological discourse: Introduction[a]

13 As he was leaving the Temple one of
his disciples said to him, 'Master, look
at the size of those stones! Look at the size of
those buildings!' 2And Jesus said to him,
'You see these great buildings? Not a single
stone will be left on another; everything will
be pulled down.'

3And while he was sitting on the Mount of
Olives, facing the Temple, Peter, James,
John and Andrew questioned him when they
were by themselves, 4'Tell us, when is this
going to happen, and what sign will there be
that it is all about to take place?'

The beginning of sorrows

5Then Jesus began to tell them, 'Take care
that no one deceives you. 6Many will come
using my name and saying, "I am he," and
they will deceive many. 7When you hear of
wars and rumours of wars, do not be alarmed;
this is something that must happen, but the
end will not be yet. 8For nation will fight
against nation, and kingdom against
kingdom. There will be earthquakes in
various places; there will be famines. This is
the beginning of the birth-pangs.

9'Be on your guard: you will be handed
over to sanhedrins; you will be beaten in
synagogues; and you will be brought before
governors and kings for my sake, as evidence
to them, 10since the gospel must first be
proclaimed to all nations.

11'And when you are taken to be handed
over, do not worry beforehand about what to
say; no, say whatever is given to you when
the time comes, because it is not you who
will be speaking; it is the Holy Spirit.
12Brother will betray brother to death, and a
father his child; children will come forward
against their parents and have them put to
death. 13You will be universally hated on
account of my name; but anyone who stands
firm to the end will be saved.

The great tribulation of Jerusalem

14'When you see *the appalling abomination*[b]
set up where it ought not to be (let the reader
understand), then those in Judaea must
escape to the mountains; 15if a man is on the
housetop, he must not come down or go
inside to collect anything from his house; 16if
a man is in the fields, he must not turn back
to fetch his cloak. 17Alas for those with child,
or with babies at the breast, when those days
come! 18Pray that this may not be in winter.
19For in those days there will be *great distress,*
unparalleled since[c] God created the world, and
such as will never be again. 20And if the Lord
had not shortened that time, no human being
would have survived; but he did shorten the
time, for the sake of the elect whom he chose.

21'And if anyone says to you then, "Look,
here is the Christ" or, "Look, he is there,"

12e Ps 110:1.
13a By contrast with Mt 24—25, Mk's discourse concerns only the destruction of Jerusalem as an act of God delivering his people.
13b Dn 9:27; 11:31; 12:11.
13c Dn 12:1.

do not believe it; [22]for false Christs and false
prophets will arise and produce signs and
portents to deceive the elect, if that were
possible. [23]You, therefore, must be on your
guard. I have given you full warning.

The coming of the Son of man

[24]'But in those days, after that time of
distress, the sun will be darkened, the moon
will not give its light, [25]the stars will come
falling out of the sky and the powers in the
heavens will be shaken. [26]And then they will
see the *Son of man coming in the clouds* with
great power and glory.[d] [27]And then he will
send the angels to gather his elect from the
four winds, from the ends of the world to the
ends of the sky.[e]

The time of this coming

[28]'Take the fig tree as a parable: as soon as its
twigs grow supple and its leaves come out,
you know that summer is near. [29]So with you
when you see these things happening: know
that he is near, right at the gates. [30]In truth I
tell you, before this generation has passed
away all these things will have taken place.
[31]Sky and earth will pass away, but my words
will not pass away.

[32]'But as for that day or hour, nobody
knows it, neither the angels in heaven, nor
the Son; no one but the Father.

Be on the alert

[33]'Be on your guard, stay awake, because you
never know when the time will come. [34]It is
like a man travelling abroad: he has gone
from his home, and left his servants in charge,
each with his own work to do; and he has
told the doorkeeper to stay awake. [35]So stay
awake, because you do not know when the
master of the house is coming, evening,
midnight, cockcrow or dawn; [36]if he comes
unexpectedly, he must not find you asleep.
[37]And what I am saying to you I say to all:
Stay awake!'

V: PASSION AND RESURRECTION

The conspiracy against Jesus

14 It was two days before the Passover and
the feast of Unleavened Bread, and the
chief priests and the scribes were looking for
a way to arrest Jesus by some trick and have
him put to death. [2]For they said, 'It must not
be during the festivities, or there will be a
disturbance among the people.'

The anointing at Bethany

[3]He was at Bethany in the house of Simon, a
man who had suffered from a virulent skin-
disease; he was at table when a woman came in
with an alabaster jar of very costly ointment,
pure nard. She broke the jar and poured the
ointment on his head. [4]Some who were there
said to one another indignantly, 'Why this
waste of ointment? [5]Ointment like this could
have been sold for over three hundred denarii
and the money given to the poor'; and they
were angry with her. [6]But Jesus said, 'Leave
her alone. Why are you upsetting her? What
she has done for me is a good work. [7]You
have the poor with you always, and you can
be kind to them whenever you wish, but you
will not always have me. [8]She has done
what she could: she has anointed my body
beforehand for its burial. [9]In truth I tell you,
wherever throughout all the world the gospel
is proclaimed, what she has done will be told
as well, in remembrance of her.'

Judas betrays Jesus

[10]Judas Iscariot, one of the Twelve,
approached the chief priests with an offer
to hand Jesus over to them. [11]They were
delighted to hear it, and promised to give
him money; and he began to look for a
way of betraying him when the opportunity
should occur.

Preparations for the Passover supper

[12]On the first day of Unleavened Bread, when
the Passover lamb was sacrificed, his disciples

13d Dn 7:13–14.
13e Dt 30:4.

said to him, 'Where do you want us to go and make the preparations for you to eat the Passover?' [13]So he sent two of his disciples, saying to them, 'Go into the city and you will meet a man carrying a pitcher of water. Follow him, [14]and say to the owner of the house which he enters, "The Master says: Where is the room for me to eat the Passover with my disciples?" [15]He will show you a large upper room furnished with couches, all prepared. Make the preparations for us there.' [16]The disciples set out and went to the city and found everything as he had told them, and prepared the Passover.

The treachery of Judas foretold

[17]When evening came he arrived with the Twelve. [18]And while they were at table eating, Jesus said, 'In truth I tell you, one of you is about to betray me, one of you *eating with me*.'[a] [19]They were distressed and said to him, one after another, 'Not me, surely?' [20]He said to them, 'It is one of the Twelve, one who is dipping into the same dish with me. [21]Yes, the Son of man is going to his fate, as the scriptures say he will, but alas for that man by whom the Son of man is betrayed! Better for that man if he had never been born.'

The institution of the Eucharist

[22]And as they were eating he took bread, and when he had said the blessing he broke it and gave it to them. 'Take it,' he said, 'this is my body.' [23]Then he took a cup, and when he had given thanks he handed it to them, and all drank from it, [24]and he said to them, 'This is my blood, the blood of the covenant, poured out for many. [25]In truth I tell you, I shall never drink wine any more until the day I drink the new wine in the kingdom of God.'

Peter's denial foretold

[26]After the psalms had been sung they left for the Mount of Olives. [27]And Jesus said to them, 'You will all fall away, for the scripture says: *I shall strike the shepherd and the sheep will be scattered*;[b] [28]however, after my resurrection I shall go before you into Galilee.' [29]Peter said, 'Even if all fall away, I will not.' [30]And Jesus said to him, 'In truth I tell you, this day, this very night, before the cock crows twice, you will have disowned me three times.' [31]But he repeated still more earnestly, 'If I have to die with you, I will never disown you.' And they all said the same.

Gethsemane

[32]They came to a plot of land called Gethsemane, and he said to his disciples, 'Stay here while I pray.' [33]Then he took Peter and James and John with him. [34]And he began to feel terror and anguish. And he said to them, 'My soul is sorrowful to the point of death. Wait here, and stay awake.' [35]And going on a little further he threw himself on the ground and prayed that, if it were possible, this hour might pass him by. [36]'*Abba*,[c] Father!' he said, 'For you everything is possible. Take this cup away from me. But let it be as you, not I, would have it.' [37]He came back and found them sleeping, and he said to Peter, 'Simon, are you asleep? Had you not the strength to stay awake one hour? [38]Stay awake and pray not to be put to the test. The spirit is willing enough, but human nature is weak.' [39]Again he went away and prayed, saying the same words. [40]And once more he came back and found them sleeping, their eyes were so heavy; and they could find no answer for him. [41]He came back a third time and said to them, 'You can sleep on now and have your rest. It is all over. The hour has come. Now the Son of man is to be betrayed into the hands of sinners. [42]Get up! Let us go! My betrayer is not far away.'

The arrest

[43]And at once, while he was still speaking, Judas, one of the Twelve, came up and with him a number of men armed with swords and clubs, sent by the chief priests and the scribes and the elders. [44]Now the traitor had arranged a signal with them saying, 'The one I kiss, he is the man. Arrest him, and see he is well guarded when you lead him away.' [45]So when the traitor came, he went up to

14a Ps 41:9.
14b Zc 13:7.
14c An affectionate Aramaic word, address of child to father.

Jesus at once and said, 'Rabbi!' and kissed him. 46The others seized him and arrested him. 47Then one of the bystanders drew his sword and struck out at the high priest's servant and cut off his ear.

48Then Jesus spoke. 'Am I a bandit,' he said, 'that you had to set out to capture me with swords and clubs? 49I was among you teaching in the Temple day after day and you never laid a hand on me. But this is to fulfil the scriptures.' 50And they all deserted him and ran away. 51A young man followed with nothing on but a linen cloth. They caught hold of him, 52but he left the cloth in their hands and ran away naked.

Jesus before the Sanhedrin

53They led Jesus off to the high priest; and all the chief priests and the elders and the scribes assembled there. 54Peter had followed him at a distance, right into the high priest's palace, and was sitting with the attendants warming himself at the fire.

55The chief priests and the whole Sanhedrin were looking for evidence against Jesus in order to have him executed. But they could not find any. 56Several, indeed, brought false witness against him, but their evidence was conflicting. 57Some stood up and submitted this false evidence against him, 58'We heard him say, "I am going to destroy this Temple made by human hands, and in three days build another, not made by human hands." ' 59But even on this point their evidence was conflicting. 60The high priest then rose before the whole assembly and put this question to Jesus, 'Have you no answer to that? What is this evidence these men are bringing against you?' 61But he was silent and made no answer at all. The high priest put a second question to him saying, 'Are you the Christ, the Son of the Blessed One?' 62'I am,' said Jesus, 'and you will see the *Son of man seated at the right hand of the Power and coming with the clouds of heaven*.'[d] 63The high priest tore his robes and said, 'What need of witnesses have we now? 64You heard the blasphemy. What is your finding?' Their verdict was unanimous: he deserved to die.

65Some of them started spitting at his face, hitting him and saying, 'Play the prophet!' And the attendants struck him too.

Peter's denials

66While Peter was down below in the courtyard, one of the high priest's servant-girls came up. 67She saw Peter warming himself there, looked closely at him and said, 'You too were with Jesus, the man from Nazareth.' 68But he denied it. 'I do not know, I do not understand what you are talking about,' he said. And he went out into the forecourt, and a cock crowed. 69The servant-girl saw him and again started telling the bystanders, 'This man is one of them.' 70But again he denied it. A little later the bystanders themselves said to Peter, 'You are certainly one of them! Why, you are a Galilean.' 71But he started cursing and swearing, 'I do not know the man you speak of.' 72And at once the cock crowed for the second time, and Peter recalled what Jesus had said to him, 'Before the cock crows twice, you will have disowned me three times.' And he burst into tears.

Jesus before Pilate

15 First thing in the morning, the chief priests, together with the elders and scribes and the rest of the Sanhedrin, had their plan ready. They had Jesus bound and took him away and handed him over to Pilate.

2Pilate put to him this question, 'Are you the king of the Jews?' He replied, 'It is you who say it.' 3And the chief priests brought many accusations against him. 4Pilate questioned him again, 'Have you no reply at all? See how many accusations they are bringing against you!' 5But, to Pilate's surprise, Jesus made no further reply.

6At festival time Pilate used to release a prisoner for them, any one they asked for. 7Now a man called Barabbas was then in prison with the rebels who had committed murder during the uprising. 8When the crowd went up and began to ask Pilate the customary favour, 9Pilate answered them, 'Do you want me to release for you the king of the Jews?' 10For he realised it was out of jealousy that the chief priests had handed Jesus over. 11The chief priests, however, had incited the crowd to demand that he should release Barabbas for them instead. 12Then Pilate spoke again, 'But in that case, what am I to do with the man you call king of the Jews?' 13They shouted back, 'Crucify him!'

14d Dn 7:13; Ps 110:1.

14 Pilate asked them, 'What harm has he
done?' But they shouted all the louder,
'Crucify him!' 15 So Pilate, anxious to placate
the crowd, released Barabbas for them and,
after having Jesus scourged, he handed him
over to be crucified.

Jesus crowned with thorns

16 The soldiers led him away to the inner part
of the palace, that is, the Praetorium, and
called the whole cohort together. 17 They
dressed him up in purple, twisted some
thorns into a crown and put it on him. 18 And
they began saluting him, 'Hail, king of the
Jews!' 19 They struck his head with a reed and
spat on him; and they went down on their
knees to do him homage. 20 And when they
had finished making fun of him, they took
off the purple and dressed him in his own
clothes.

The way of the cross

They led him out to crucify him. 21 They
enlisted a passer-by, Simon of Cyrene, father
of Alexander and Rufus,[a] who was coming
in from the country, to carry his cross. 22 They
brought Jesus to the place called Golgotha,
which means the place of the skull.

The crucifixion

23 They offered him wine mixed with myrrh,
but he refused it. 24 Then they crucified him,
and shared out his clothing, casting lots to
decide what each should get. 25 It was the
third hour when they crucified him. 26 The
inscription giving the charge against him
read, 'The King of the Jews'. 27 And they
crucified two bandits with him, one on his
right and one on his left.[28][b]

The crucified Jesus is mocked

29 The passers-by jeered at him; they shook
their heads and said, 'Aha! So you would
destroy the Temple and rebuild it in three
days! 30 Then save yourself; come down from
the cross!' 31 The chief priests and the scribes
mocked him among themselves in the same
way with the words, 'He saved others, he
cannot save himself. 32 Let the Christ, the
king of Israel, come down from the cross
now, for us to see it and believe.' Even those
who were crucified with him taunted him.

The death of Jesus

33 When the sixth hour came there was dark-
ness over the whole land until the ninth hour.
34 And at the ninth hour Jesus cried out in a
loud voice, '*Eloi, eloi,*[c] *lama sabachthani?*'
which means, '*My God, my God, why have
you forsaken me?*' 35 When some of those who
stood by heard this, they said, 'Listen, he is
calling on Elijah.' 36 Someone ran and soaked
a sponge in vinegar and, putting it on a reed,
gave it to him to drink saying, 'Wait! And
see if Elijah will come to take him down.'
37 But Jesus gave a loud cry and breathed his
last. 38 And the veil of the Sanctuary was torn
in two from top to bottom. 39 The centurion,
who was standing in front of him, had seen
how he had died, and he said, 'In truth this
man was Son of God.'

The women on Calvary

40 There were some women watching from a
distance. Among them were Mary of
Magdala, Mary who was the mother of James
the younger and Joset, and Salome. 41 These
used to follow him and look after him when
he was in Galilee. And many other women
were there who had come up to Jerusalem
with him.

The burial

42 It was now evening, and since it was Prep-
aration Day—that is, the day before the
Sabbath—43 there came Joseph of Arim-
athaea, a prominent member of the Council,
who himself lived in the hope of seeing the
kingdom of God, and he boldly went to Pilate
and asked for the body of Jesus. 44 Pilate,
astonished that he should have died so soon,
summoned the centurion and enquired if he
had been dead for some time. 45 Having been
assured of this by the centurion, he granted

15a cf. Rm 16:13.
15b Some authorities add a verse similar to Lk 22:37.
15c This Aramaic form cf. Ps 22:1, explains the soldiers' pun about Elijah better than Mt's Hebr form *eli*.

the corpse to Joseph 46who bought a shroud,
took Jesus down from the cross, wrapped
him in the shroud and laid him in a tomb
which had been hewn out of the rock. He
then rolled a stone against the entrance to
the tomb. 47Mary of Magdala and Mary the
mother of Joset took note of where he was
laid.

The empty tomb. The angel's message

16 When the Sabbath was over, Mary of
Magdala, Mary the mother of James,
and Salome, bought spices with which to
go and anoint him. 2And very early in the
morning on the first day of the week they
went to the tomb when the sun had risen.
3They had been saying to one another,
'Who will roll away the stone for us from the
entrance to the tomb?' 4But when they looked
they saw that the stone—which was very
big—had already been rolled back. 5On
entering the tomb they saw a young man in
a white robe seated on the right-hand side,
and they were struck with amazement. 6But
he said to them, 'There is no need to be
so amazed. You are looking for Jesus of
Nazareth, who was crucified: he has risen,
he is not here. See, here is the place where
they laid him. 7But you must go and tell his
disciples and Peter, "He is going ahead of
you to Galilee; that is where you will see him,
just as he told you." ' 8And the women came
out and ran away from the tomb because they
were frightened out of their wits; and they
said nothing to anyone, for they were afraid.[a]

Appearances of the risen Christ

9Having risen in the morning on the first day
of the week, he appeared first to Mary of
Magdala from whom he had cast out seven
devils. 10She then went to those who had been
his companions, and who were mourning and
in tears, and told them. 11But they did not
believe her when they heard her say that he
was alive and that she had seen him.
12After this, he showed himself under
another form to two of them as they were on
their way into the country. 13These went back
and told the others, who did not believe them
either.
14Lastly, he showed himself to the Eleven
themselves while they were at table. He
reproached them for their incredulity and
obstinacy, because they had refused to
believe those who had seen him after he had
risen. 15And he said to them, 'Go out to
the whole world; proclaim the gospel to all
creation. 16Whoever believes and is baptised
will be saved; whoever does not believe will
be condemned. 17These are the signs that will
be associated with believers: in my name they
will cast out devils; they will have the gift of
tongues; 18they will pick up snakes in their
hands and be unharmed should they drink
deadly poison; they will lay their hands on
the sick, who will recover.'
19And so the Lord Jesus, after he had
spoken to them, was taken up into heaven;
there at the right hand of God he took his
place, 20while they, going out, preached
everywhere, the Lord working with them
and confirming the word by the signs that
accompanied it.

16a Originally Mk probably ended abruptly on this note of awe and wonder. The next 12 vv., missing in some MSS, are a summary of material gathered from other NT writings.

THE GOSPEL OF LUKE

Luke's gospel is very warm and human, concentrating on Jesus' mercy and forgiveness, his call especially to the poor and underprivileged, inviting both Jew and gentile to salvation. Luke writes a more sophisticated Greek than the other evangelists, giving the impression that he is providing a history for the civilised Greek reader. Perhaps for this reason much of his special material consists of teaching on points of individual morality, especially the danger of material possessions and misuse of wealth. Luke also brings out the importance of individual spiritual qualities, especially prayer, joy and praise of God, and the essential part played by the Holy Spirit in the Christian life. But in spite of his attention to Greek readers, Luke is very much aware that Jesus is the completion of the OT: the stories of Jesus' infancy, especially, are shot through with reminiscences of the OT.

Many of these emphases occur also in Acts, which once formed the second part of a single two-volume work. The turning-point is Jerusalem, for Luke begins and ends the gospel in Jerusalem, much of Jesus' instruction being brought together in the great final journey up to Jerusalem (section IV); the resurrection appearances are in and around Jerusalem, and it is from Jerusalem that the faith spreads in Acts.

PLAN OF THE BOOK

THE GOSPEL ACCORDING TO LUKE

Prologue

1 Seeing that many others have undertaken
to draw up accounts of the events that
have reached their fulfilment among us, 2 as
these were handed down to us by those who
from the outset were eyewitnesses and
ministers of the word, 3 I in my turn, after
carefully going over the whole story from the
beginning, have decided to write an ordered
account for you, Theophilus,[a] 4 so that your
Excellency may learn how well founded the
teaching is that you have received.

1a Theophilus (='God-lover') may be real or imaginary.

I: THE BIRTH AND HIDDEN LIFE OF JOHN THE BAPTIST AND OF JESUS

The birth of John the Baptist foretold

5In the days of King Herod of Judaea there lived a priest called Zechariah who belonged to the Abijah section of the priesthood, and he had a wife, Elizabeth by name, who was a descendant of Aaron. 6Both were upright in the sight of God and impeccably carried out all the commandments and observances of the Lord. 7But they were childless: Elizabeth was barren and they were both advanced in years.

8Now it happened that it was the turn of his section to serve, and he was exercising his priestly office before God 9when it fell to him by lot, as the priestly custom was, to enter the Lord's sanctuary and burn incense there. 10And at the hour of incense all the people were outside, praying.

11Then there appeared to him the angel of the Lord, standing on the right of the altar of incense. 12The sight disturbed Zechariah and he was overcome with fear. 13But the angel said to him, 'Zechariah, do not be afraid, for your prayer has been heard. Your wife Elizabeth is to bear you a son and you shall name him John. 14He will be your joy and delight and many will rejoice at his birth, 15for he will be great in the sight of the Lord; he must drink no wine, no strong drink;[b] even from his mother's womb he will be filled with the Holy Spirit, 16and he will bring back many of the Israelites to the Lord their God. 17With the spirit and power of Elijah, he will go before him *to reconcile fathers to their children*[c] and the disobedient to the good sense of the upright, preparing for the Lord a people fit for him.' 18Zechariah said to the angel, '*How can I know this?*[d] I am an old man and my wife is getting on in years.' 19The angel replied, 'I am Gabriel, who stand in God's presence, and I have been sent to speak to you and bring you this good news. 20Look! Since you did not believe my words, which will come true at their appointed time, you will be silenced and have no power of speech until this has happened.' 21Meanwhile the people were waiting for Zechariah and were surprised that he stayed in the sanctuary so long. 22When he came out he could not speak to them, and they realised that he had seen a vision in the sanctuary. But he could only make signs to them and remained dumb.

23When his time of service came to an end he returned home. 24Some time later his wife Elizabeth conceived and for five months she kept to herself, saying, 25'The Lord has done this for me, now that it has pleased him to take away the humiliation I suffered in public.'

The annunciation

26In the sixth month the angel Gabriel was sent by God to a town in Galilee called Nazareth, 27to a virgin betrothed to a man named Joseph, of the House of David; and the virgin's name was Mary. 28He went in and said to her, 'Rejoice, you who enjoy God's favour! The Lord is with you.' 29She was deeply disturbed by these words and asked herself what this greeting could mean, 30but the angel said to her, 'Mary, do not be afraid; you have won God's favour. 31Look! You are to conceive in your womb and bear a son, and you must name him Jesus. 32He will be great and will be called Son of the Most High. The Lord God will give him the throne of his ancestor David; 33he will rule over the House of Jacob for ever and his reign will have no end.'[e] 34Mary said to the angel, 'But how can this come about, since I have no knowledge of man?' 35The angel answered, 'The Holy Spirit will come upon you, and the power of the Most High will cover you with its shadow. And so the child will be holy and will be called Son of God. 36And I tell you this too: your cousin Elizabeth also, in her old age, has conceived a son, and she whom people called barren is now in her sixth month, 37*for nothing is impossible to God.*'[f] 38Mary said, 'You see before you the Lord's

---

1b cf. Nb 6:2–3.
1c Ml 3:23–24.
1d Gn 15:8.
1e cf. 2 S 7:12–16.
1f Gn 18:14.

servant, let it happen to me as you have said.'
And the angel left her.

The visitation

39 Mary set out at that time and went as
quickly as she could into the hill country to
a town in Judah. 40 She went into Zechariah's
house and greeted Elizabeth. 41 Now it
happened that as soon as Elizabeth heard
Mary's greeting, the child leapt in her womb
and Elizabeth was filled with the Holy Spirit.
42 She gave a loud cry and said, 'Of all women
you are the most blessed, and blessed is
the fruit of your womb. 43 Why should I be
honoured with a visit from the mother of my
Lord? 44 Look, the moment your greeting
reached my ears, the child in my womb leapt
for joy. 45 Yes, blessed is she who believed
that the promise made her by the Lord would
be fulfilled.'

The Magnificat[g]

46 And Mary said:

My soul proclaims
the greatness of the Lord
47 and my spirit *rejoices*
in God my Saviour;
48 because *he has looked upon*
the humiliation of his servant.
Yes, from now onwards
all generations will call me blessed,
49 for the Almighty
has done great things for me.
Holy is his name,
50 and *his faithful love extends age after age*
to those who fear him.
51 He has used the power of his arm,
he has routed the arrogant of heart.
52 *He has pulled down princes*
from their thrones
and raised high the lowly.
53 *He has filled the starving with good things*,
sent the rich away empty.
54 *He has come to the help*
of Israel his servant,
mindful of his faithful love
55 —according to the promise
he made to our ancestors—
of his mercy to Abraham
and to his descendants for ever.

56 Mary stayed with her some three months
and then went home.

The birth of John the Baptist and visit of the neighbours

57 The time came for Elizabeth to have her
child, and she gave birth to a son; 58 and when
her neighbours and relations heard that the
Lord had lavished on her his faithful love,
they shared her joy.

The circumcision of John the Baptist

59 Now it happened that on the eighth day
they came to circumcise the child; they were
going to call him Zechariah after his father,
60 but his mother spoke up. 'No,' she said,
'he is to be called John.' 61 They said to her,
'But no one in your family has that name,'
62 and made signs to his father to find out what
he wanted him called. 63 The father asked for
a writing-tablet and wrote, 'His name is
John.' And they were all astonished. 64 At
that instant his power of speech returned
and he spoke and praised God. 65 All their
neighbours were filled with awe and the
whole affair was talked about throughout the
hill country of Judaea. 66 All those who heard
of it treasured it in their hearts. 'What will
this child turn out to be?' they wondered.
And indeed the hand of the Lord was with
him.

The Benedictus[h]

67 His father Zechariah was filled with the
Holy Spirit and spoke this prophecy:

68 *Blessed be the Lord, the God of Israel*,
for he has visited his people,
he has *set them free*,
69 and he has established for us
a saving power
in the House of his servant David,
70 just as he proclaimed,
by the mouth of his holy prophets
from ancient times,
71 that he would save us from our *enemies*
and *from the hands of all those*
who hate us,
72 and show *faithful love to our ancestors*,
and so *keep in mind his* holy *covenant*.

1g Mary's canticle echoes Hannah's 1 S 2:1–10, and also 1 S 1:11; Ps 103:17; 111:9; Jb 5:11; 12:19; Ps 98:2; 107:9; Is 41:8–9.
1h The canticle uses Ps 41:13; 111:9; Lv 26:42; Is 9:1.

73 This was the oath he swore
to our father Abraham,
74 that he would grant us, free from fear,
to be delivered
from the hands of our enemies,
75 to serve him in holiness and uprightness
in his presence, all our days.
76 And you, little child,
you shall be called
Prophet of the Most High,
for you will go before *the Lord*
to prepare a way for him,
77 to give his people knowledge of salvation
through the forgiveness of their sins,
78 because of the faithful love of our God
in which the rising Sun
has come from on high to visit us,
79 to give light to *those who live*
in darkness and the shadow dark as death,
and to guide our feet
into *the way of peace*.

The hidden life of John the Baptist

80 Meanwhile the child grew up and his spirit
grew strong. And he lived in the desert until
the day he appeared openly to Israel.

The birth of Jesus and visit of the shepherds

2 Now it happened that at this time Caesar
Augustus issued a decree that a census
should be made of the whole inhabited world.
2 This census—the first—took place while
Quirinius was governor of Syria, 3 and
everyone went to be registered, each to his
own town. 4 So Joseph set out from the town
of Nazareth in Galilee for Judaea, to David's
town called Bethlehem, since he was of
David's House and line, 5 in order to be
registered together with Mary, his betrothed,
who was with child. 6 Now it happened that,
while they were there, the time came for her
to have her child, 7 and she gave birth to a
son, her first-born. She wrapped him in
swaddling clothes and laid him in a manger
because there was no room for them in the
living-space. 8 In the countryside close by
there were shepherds out in the fields keeping
guard over their sheep during the watches of
the night. 9 An angel of the Lord stood over
them and the glory of the Lord shone round
them. They were terrified, 10 but the angel
said, 'Do not be afraid. Look, I bring you
news of great joy, a joy to be shared by the
whole people. 11 Today in the town of David
a Saviour has been born to you; he is Christ
the Lord. 12 And here is a sign for you: you
will find a baby wrapped in swaddling clothes
and lying in a manger.' 13 And all at once with
the angel there was a great throng of the hosts
of heaven, praising God with the words:

14 Glory to God in the highest heaven,
and on earth peace for those he favours.

15 Now it happened that when the angels
had gone from them into heaven, the
shepherds said to one another, 'Let us go to
Bethlehem and see this event which the Lord
has made known to us.' 16 So they hurried
away and found Mary and Joseph, and the
baby lying in the manger. 17 When they saw
the child they repeated what they had been
told about him, 18 and everyone who heard it
was astonished at what the shepherds said to
them. 19 As for Mary, she treasured all these
things and pondered them in her heart. 20 And
the shepherds went back glorifying and
praising God for all they had heard and seen,
just as they had been told.

The circumcision of Jesus

21 When the eighth day came and the child
was to be circumcised, they gave him the
name Jesus, the name the angel had given
him before his conception.

Jesus is presented in the Temple

22 And when the day came for them to be
purified in keeping with the Law of Moses,
they took him up to Jerusalem to present him
to the Lord—23 observing what is written in
the Law of the Lord: *Every first-born male*
must be consecrated to the Lord—[a] 24 and also
to offer in sacrifice, in accordance with what
is prescribed in the Law of the Lord, *a pair*
of turtledoves or two young pigeons.[b] 25 Now in
Jerusalem there was a man named Simeon.
He was an upright and devout man; he looked
forward to the restoration of Israel and the
Holy Spirit rested on him. 26 It had been
revealed to him by the Holy Spirit that he
would not see death until he had set eyes on

2a Ex 13:2.
2b Lv 5:7.

the Christ of the Lord. 27 Prompted by the Spirit he came to the Temple; and when the parents brought in the child Jesus to do for him what the Law required, 28 he took him into his arms and blessed God; and he said:

The Nunc Dimittis

29 Now, Master, you are letting
your servant go in peace
as you promised;
30 for my eyes have seen the salvation
31 which you have made ready
in the sight of the nations;
32 a light of revelation for the gentiles
and glory for your people Israel.

The prophecy of Simeon

33 As the child's father and mother were wondering at the things that were being said about him, 34 Simeon blessed them and said to Mary his mother, 'Look, he is destined for the fall and for the rise of many in Israel, destined to be a sign that is opposed— 35 and a sword will pierce your soul too—so that the secret thoughts of many may be laid bare.'

The prophecy of Anna

36 There was a prophetess, too, Anna the daughter of Phanuel, of the tribe of Asher. She was well on in years. Her days of girlhood over, she had been married for seven years 37 before becoming a widow. She was now eighty-four years old and never left the Temple, serving God night and day with fasting and prayer. 38 She came up just at that moment and began to praise God; and she spoke of the child to all who looked forward to the deliverance of Jerusalem.

The hidden life of Jesus at Nazareth

39 When they had done everything the Law of the Lord required, they went back to Galilee, to their own town of Nazareth. 40 And as the child grew to maturity, he was filled with wisdom; and God's favour was with him.

Jesus among the doctors of the Law

41 Every year his parents used to go to Jerusalem for the feast of the Passover. 42 When he was twelve years old, they went up for the feast as usual. 43 When the days of the feast were over and they set off home, the boy Jesus stayed behind in Jerusalem without his parents knowing it. 44 They assumed he was somewhere in the party, and it was only after a day's journey that they went to look for him among their relations and acquaintances. 45 When they failed to find him they went back to Jerusalem looking for him everywhere.

46 It happened that, three days later, they found him in the Temple, sitting among the teachers, listening to them, and asking them questions; 47 and all those who heard him were astounded at his intelligence and his replies. 48 They were overcome when they saw him, and his mother said to him, 'My child, why have you done this to us? See how worried your father and I have been, looking for you.' 49 He replied, 'Why were you looking for me? Did you not know that I must be in my Father's house?' 50 But they did not understand what he meant.

The hidden life at Nazareth resumed

51 He went down with them then and came to Nazareth and lived under their authority. His mother stored up all these things in her heart. 52 And Jesus increased in wisdom, in stature, and in favour with God and with people.

II: PRELUDE TO THE PUBLIC MINISTRY OF JESUS

The proclamation of John the Baptist

3 In the fifteenth year of Tiberius Caesar's reign, when Pontius Pilate was governor of Judaea, Herod tetrarch of Galilee, his brother Philip tetrarch of the territories of Ituraea and Trachonitis, Lysanias tetrarch of Abilene, 2 and while the high-priesthood was held by Annas and Caiaphas, the word of God came to John the son of Zechariah, in the desert. 3 He went through the whole Jordan area proclaiming a baptism of repent-

ance for the forgiveness of sins, 4as it is
written in the book of the sayings of Isaiah
the prophet:

A voice of one that cries in the desert:
Prepare a way for the Lord,
make his paths straight!
5*Let every valley be filled in,*
every mountain and hill be levelled,
winding ways be straightened
and rough roads made smooth,
6*and all humanity*
will see the salvation of God.[a]

7He said, therefore, to the crowds who
came to be baptised by him, 'Brood of vipers,
who warned you to flee from the coming
retribution? 8Produce fruit in keeping with
repentance, and do not start telling your-
selves, "We have Abraham as our father,"
because, I tell you, God can raise children for
Abraham from these stones. 9Yes, even
now the axe is being laid to the root of the
trees, so that any tree failing to produce
good fruit will be cut down and thrown on
the fire.'
10When all the people asked him, 'What
must we do, then?' 11he answered, 'Anyone
who has two tunics must share with the one
who has none, and anyone with something
to eat must do the same.' 12There were tax
collectors, too, who came for baptism, and
these said to him, 'Master, what must we
do?' 13He said to them, 'Exact no more than
the appointed rate.' 14Some soldiers asked
him in their turn, 'What about us? What
must we do?' He said to them, 'No intimi-
dation! No extortion! Be content with your
pay!'
15A feeling of expectancy had grown among
the people, who were beginning to wonder
whether John might be the Christ, 16so John
declared before them all, 'I baptise you with
water, but someone is coming, who is more
powerful than me, and I am not fit to undo
the strap of his sandals; he will baptise you
with the Holy Spirit and fire. 17His winnow-
ing-fan is in his hand, to clear his threshing-
floor and to gather the wheat into his barn;
but the chaff he will burn in a fire that will
never go out.' 18And he proclaimed the good
news to the people with many other exhor-
tations too.

John the Baptist imprisoned

19But Herod the tetrarch, censured by John
for his relations with his brother's wife
Herodias and for all the other crimes he had
committed, 20added a further crime to all the
rest by shutting John up in prison.

Jesus is baptised

21Now it happened that when all the people
had been baptised and while Jesus after his
own baptism was at prayer, heaven opened
22and the Holy Spirit descended on him in a
physical form, like a dove. And a voice came
from heaven, '*You are my Son; today have I*
fathered you.'[b]

The ancestry of Jesus

23When he began, Jesus was about thirty
years old, being the son, as it was thought,
of Joseph son of Heli, 24son of Matthat, son
of Levi, son of Melchi, son of Jannai, son of
Joseph, 25son of Mattathias, son of Amos,
son of Nahum, son of Esli, son of Naggai,
26son of Maath, son of Mattathias, son of
Semein, son of Josech, son of Joda, 27son of
Joanan, son of Rhesa, son of Zerubbabel,
son of Shealtiel, son of Neri, 28son of Melchi,
son of Addi, son of Cosam, son of Elmadam,
son of Er, 29son of Jesus, son of Eliezer, son
of Jorim, son of Matthat, son of Levi, 30son
of Symeon, son of Judah, son of Joseph,
son of Jonam, son of Eliakim, 31son of Melea,
son of Menna, son of Mattatha, son of
Nathan, son of David, 32son of Jesse, son
of Obed, son of Boaz, son of Sala, son of
Nahshon, 33son of Amminadab, son
of Admin, son of Arni, son of Hezron, son of
Perez, son of Judah, 34son of Jacob, son
of Isaac, son of Abraham, son of Terah, son
of Nahor, 35son of Serug, son of Reu, son of
Peleg, son of Eber, son of Shelah, 36son of
Cainan, son of Arphaxad, son of Shem, son
of Noah, son of Lamech, 37son of Methu-
selah, son of Enoch, son of Jared, son of
Mahalaleel, son of Cainan, 38son of Enos, son
of Seth, son of Adam, son of God.

3a Is 40:3–5.
3b Ps 2:7.

Testing in the desert

4 Filled with the Holy Spirit, Jesus left the
Jordan and was led by the Spirit into the
desert, 2for forty days being put to the test
by the devil. During that time he ate nothing
and at the end he was hungry. 3Then the
devil said to him, 'If you are Son of God, tell
this stone to turn into a loaf.' 4But Jesus
replied, 'Scripture says:

Human beings live not on bread alone.'[a]

5Then leading him to a height, the devil
showed him in a moment of time all the
kingdoms of the world 6and said to him,
'I will give you all this power and their
splendour, for it has been handed over to me,
for me to give it to anyone I choose. 7Do
homage, then, to me, and it shall all be yours.'
8But Jesus answered him, 'Scripture says:

You must do homage to the Lord your God,
him alone you must serve.'[b]

9Then he led him to Jerusalem and set him
on the parapet of the Temple. 'If you are Son
of God,' he said to him, 'throw yourself down
from here, 10for scripture says:

He has given his angels orders about you,
to guard you,

and again:

11*They will carry you in their arms*
in case you trip over a stone.'[c]

12But Jesus answered him, 'Scripture says:

Do not put the Lord your God to the test.'[d]

13Having exhausted every way of putting him
to the test, the devil left him, until the
opportune moment.

III: THE GALILEAN MINISTRY

Jesus begins to preach

14Jesus, with the power of the Spirit in him,
returned to Galilee; and his reputation spread
throughout the countryside. 15He taught in
their synagogues and everyone glorified him.

Jesus at Nazareth

16He came to Nazara, where he had been
brought up, and went into the synagogue on
the Sabbath day as he usually did. He stood
up to read, 17and they handed him the scroll
of the prophet Isaiah. Unrolling the scroll he
found the place where it is written:

18*The spirit of the Lord is on me,*
for he has anointed me
to bring the good news to the afflicted.
He has sent me
to proclaim liberty to captives,
sight to the blind,
to let the oppressed go free,
19*to proclaim a year of favour*
from the Lord.[e]

20He then rolled up the scroll, gave it back to
the assistant and sat down. And all eyes in
the synagogue were fixed on him. 21Then he
began to speak to them, 'This text is being
fulfilled today even while you are listening.'
22And he won the approval of all, and they
were astonished by the gracious words that
came from his lips.

They said, 'This is Joseph's son, surely?'
23But he replied, 'No doubt you will quote
me the saying, "Physician, heal yourself,"
and tell me, "We have heard all that
happened in Capernaum, do the same here
in your own country." ' 24And he went on, 'In
truth I tell you, no prophet is ever accepted in
his own country.

25'There were many widows in Israel, I can
assure you, in Elijah's day, when heaven
remained shut for three years and six months
and a great famine raged throughout the
land, 26but Elijah was not sent to any one of
these: he was sent *to a widow at Zarephath, a*
town in Sidonia.[f] 27And in the prophet
Elisha's time there were many suffering from

4a Dt 8:3.
4b Dt 6:13.
4c Ps 91:11–12.
4d Dt 6:16.
4e Is 61:1–2.
4f 1 K 17:9.

virulent skin-diseases in Israel, but none of
these was cured—only Naaman the Syrian.'[g]
28 When they heard this everyone in the
synagogue was enraged. 29 They sprang to
their feet and hustled him out of the town;
and they took him up to the brow of the hill
their town was built on, intending to throw
him off the cliff, 30 but he passed straight
through the crowd and walked away.

Jesus teaches in Capernaum and cures a demoniac

31 He went down to Capernaum, a town in
Galilee, and taught them on the Sabbath.
32 And his teaching made a deep impression
on them because his word carried authority.
33 In the synagogue there was a man
possessed by the spirit of an unclean devil,
and he shouted at the top of his voice, 34 'Ha!
What do you want with us, Jesus of Nazareth?
Have you come to destroy us? I know who
you are: the Holy One of God.' 35 But Jesus
rebuked it, saying, 'Be quiet! Come out of
him!' And the devil, throwing the man into
the middle, went out of him without hurting
him at all. 36 Astonishment seized them and
they were all saying to one another, 'What is
it in his words? He gives orders to unclean
spirits with authority and power and they
come out.' 37 And the news of him travelled
all through the surrounding countryside.

Cure of Simon's mother-in-law

38 Leaving the synagogue he went to Simon's
house. Now Simon's mother-in-law was in
the grip of a high fever and they asked him
to do something for her. 39 Standing over her
he rebuked the fever and it left her. And she
immediately got up and began to serve them.

A number of cures

40 At sunset all those who had friends suffering
from diseases of one kind or another brought
them to him, and laying his hands on each he
cured them. 41 Devils too came out of many
people, shouting, 'You are the Son of God.'
But he warned them and would not allow
them to speak because they knew that he was
the Christ.

Dawn departure from Capernaum and travels through Judaea

42 When daylight came he left the house and
made his way to a lonely place. The crowds
went to look for him, and when they had
caught up with him they wanted to prevent
him leaving them, 43 but he answered, 'I must
proclaim the good news of the kingdom of
God to the other towns too, because that is
what I was sent to do.' 44 And he continued
his proclamation in the synagogues of Judaea.

The first four disciples are called

5 Now it happened that he was standing one
day by the Lake of Gennesaret, with the
crowd pressing round him listening to the
word of God, 2 when he caught sight of two
boats at the water's edge. The fishermen had
got out of them and were washing their
nets. 3 He got into one of the boats—it was
Simon's—and asked him to put out a little
from the shore. Then he sat down and taught
the crowds from the boat.
4 When he had finished speaking he said to
Simon, 'Put out into deep water and pay
out your nets for a catch.' 5 Simon replied,
'Master, we worked hard all night long and
caught nothing, but if you say so, I will pay
out the nets.' 6 And when they had done this
they netted such a huge number of fish that
their nets began to tear, 7 so they signalled to
their companions in the other boat to come
and help them; when these came, they filled
both boats to sinking point.
8 When Simon Peter saw this he fell at the
knees of Jesus saying, 'Leave me, Lord; I am
a sinful man.' 9 For he and all his companions
were completely awestruck at the catch they
had made; 10 so also were James and John,
sons of Zebedee, who were Simon's partners.
But Jesus said to Simon, 'Do not be afraid;
from now on it is people you will be catching.'
11 Then, bringing their boats back to land
they left everything and followed him.

Cure of a man suffering from a virulent skin-disease

12 Now it happened that Jesus was in one of
the towns when suddenly a man appeared,
covered with a skin-disease. Seeing Jesus he
fell on his face and implored him saying, 'Sir,

4g 2 K 5:14.

if you are willing you can cleanse me.' 13He stretched out his hand, and touched him saying, 'I am willing. Be cleansed.' At once the skin-disease left him. 14He ordered him to tell no one, 'But go and show yourself to the priest and make the offering for your cleansing just as Moses prescribed, as evidence to them.'

15But the news of him kept spreading, and large crowds would gather to hear him and to have their illnesses cured, 16but he would go off to some deserted place and pray.

Cure of a paralytic

17Now it happened that he was teaching one day, and Pharisees and teachers of the Law, who had come from every village in Galilee, from Judaea and from Jerusalem, were sitting there. And the power of the Lord was there so that he should heal. 18And now some men appeared, bringing on a bed a paralysed man whom they were trying to bring in and lay down in front of him. 19But as they could find no way of getting the man through the crowd, they went up onto the top of the house and lowered him and his stretcher down through the tiles into the middle of the gathering, in front of Jesus. 20Seeing their faith he said, 'My friend, your sins are forgiven you.' 21The scribes and the Pharisees began to think this over. 'Who is this man, talking blasphemy? Who but God alone can forgive sins?' 22But Jesus, aware of their thoughts, made them this reply, 'What are these thoughts you have in your hearts? 23Which of these is easier: to say, "Your sins are forgiven you," or to say, "Get up and walk"? 24But to prove to you that the Son of man has authority on earth to forgive sins,'—he said to the paralysed man—'I order you: get up, and pick up your stretcher and go home.' 25And immediately before their very eyes he got up, picked up what he had been lying on and went home praising God.

26They were all astounded and praised God and were filled with awe, saying, 'We have seen strange things today.'

The call of Levi

27When he went out after this, he noticed a tax collector, Levi by name, sitting at the tax office, and said to him, 'Follow me.' 28And leaving everything Levi got up and followed him.

Eating with sinners in Levi's house

29In his honour Levi held a great reception in his house, and with them at table was a large gathering of tax collectors and others. 30The Pharisees and their scribes complained to his disciples and said, 'Why do you eat and drink with tax collectors and sinners?' 31Jesus said to them in reply, 'It is not those that are well who need the doctor, but the sick. 32I have come to call not the upright but sinners to repentance.'

Discussion on fasting

33They then said to him, 'John's disciples are always fasting and saying prayers, and the disciples of the Pharisees, too, but yours go on eating and drinking.' 34Jesus replied, 'Surely you cannot make the bridegroom's attendants fast while the bridegroom is still with them? 35But the time will come when the bridegroom is taken away from them; then, in those days, they will fast.'

36He also told them a parable, 'No one tears a piece from a new cloak to put it on an old cloak; otherwise, not only will the new one be torn, but the piece taken from the new will not match the old.

37'And nobody puts new wine in old wineskins; otherwise, the new wine will burst the skins and run to waste, and the skins will be ruined. 38No; new wine must be put in fresh skins. 39And nobody who has been drinking old wine wants new. "The old is good," he says.'

Picking corn on the Sabbath

6 It happened that one Sabbath he was walking through the cornfields, and his disciples were picking ears of corn, rubbing them in their hands and eating them. 2Some of the Pharisees said, 'Why are you doing something that is forbidden on the Sabbath day?' 3Jesus answered them, 'So you have not read what David did[a] when he and his followers were hungry—4how he went into the house of God and took the loaves of the offering and ate them and gave them to his

6a 1 S 21:2–7.

followers, loaves which the priests alone are allowed to eat?' 5And he said to them, 'The Son of man is master of the Sabbath.'

Cure of the man with a withered hand

6Now on another Sabbath he went into the synagogue and began to teach, and a man was present, and his right hand was withered. 7The scribes and the Pharisees were watching him to see if he would cure somebody on the Sabbath, hoping to find something to charge him with. 8But he knew their thoughts; and he said to the man with the withered hand, 'Get up and stand out in the middle!' And he came forward and stood there. 9Then Jesus said to them, 'I put it to you: is it permitted on the Sabbath to do good, or to do evil; to save life, or to destroy it?' 10Then he looked round at them all and said to the man, 'Stretch out your hand.' He did so, and his hand was restored. 11But they were furious and began to discuss the best way of dealing with Jesus.

The choice of the Twelve

12Now it happened in those days that he went onto the mountain to pray; and he spent the whole night in prayer to God. 13When day came he summoned his disciples and picked out twelve of them; he called them 'apostles': 14Simon whom he called Peter, and his brother Andrew, James, John, Philip, Bartholomew, 15Matthew, Thomas, James son of Alphaeus, Simon called the Zealot, 16Judas son of James, and Judas Iscariot who became a traitor.

The crowds follow Jesus

17He then came down with them and stopped at a piece of level ground where there was a large gathering of his disciples, with a great crowd of people from all parts of Judaea and Jerusalem and the coastal region of Tyre and Sidon 18who had come to hear him and to be cured of their diseases. People tormented by unclean spirits were also cured, 19and everyone in the crowd was trying to touch him because power came out of him that cured them all.

The first sermon. The Beatitudes[b]

20Then fixing his eyes on his disciples he said:

How blessed are you who are poor:
the kingdom of God is yours.
21Blessed are you who are hungry now:
you shall have your fill.
Blessed are you who are weeping now:
you shall laugh.

22'Blessed are you when people hate you, drive you out, abuse you, denounce your name as criminal, on account of the Son of man. 23Rejoice when that day comes and dance for joy, look!—your reward will be great in heaven. This was the way their ancestors treated the prophets.

The curses

24But alas for you who are rich:
you are having your consolation now.
25Alas for you who have plenty to eat now:
you shall go hungry.
Alas for you who are laughing now:
you shall mourn and weep.

26'Alas for you when everyone speaks well of you! This was the way their ancestors treated the false prophets.

Love of enemies

27'But I say this to you who are listening: Love your enemies, do good to those who hate you, 28bless those who curse you, pray for those who treat you badly. 29To anyone who slaps you on one cheek, present the other cheek as well; to anyone who takes your cloak from you, do not refuse your tunic. 30Give to everyone who asks you, and do not ask for your property back from someone who takes it. 31Treat others as you would like people to treat you. 32If you love those who love you, what credit can you expect? Even sinners love those who love them. 33And if you do good to those who do good to you, what credit can you expect? For even sinners do that much. 34And if you lend to those from whom you hope to get money back, what credit can you expect? Even sinners lend to sinners to get back the same amount. 35Instead, love your enemies and do good to them, and lend without any hope of return. You will have a great reward, and you will be children of the

6b Mt 5:1.

Most High, for he himself is kind to the
ungrateful and the wicked.

Compassion and generosity

36 'Be compassionate just as your Father is
compassionate. 37 Do not judge, and you will
not be judged; do not condemn, and you
will not be condemned; forgive, and you will
be forgiven. 38 Give, and there will be gifts
for you: a full measure, pressed down, shaken
together, and overflowing, will be poured
into your lap; because the standard you use
will be the standard used for you.'

Integrity

39 He also told them a parable, 'Can one blind
person guide another? Surely both will fall
into a pit? 40 Disciple is not superior to
teacher; but fully trained disciple will be like
teacher. 41 Why do you observe the splinter
in your brother's eye and never notice the
great log in your own? 42 How can you say to
your brother, "Brother, let me take out that
splinter in your eye," when you cannot see
the great log in your own? Hypocrite! Take
the log out of your own eye first, and then
you will see clearly enough to take out the
splinter in your brother's eye.

43 'There is no sound tree that produces
rotten fruit, nor again a rotten tree that
produces sound fruit. 44 Every tree can be
told by its own fruit: people do not pick
figs from thorns, nor gather grapes from
brambles. 45 Good people draw what is good
from the store of goodness in their hearts;
bad people draw what is bad from the store
of badness. For the words of the mouth flow
out of what fills the heart.

The true disciple

46 'Why do you call me, "Lord, Lord" and
not do what I say?

47 'Everyone who comes to me and listens
to my words and acts on them—I will show
you what such a person is like. 48 Such a
person is like the man who, when he built a
house, dug, and dug deep, and laid the
foundations on rock; when the river was in
flood it bore down on that house but could
not shake it, it was so well built. 49 But
someone who listens and does nothing is like
the man who built a house on soil, with no
foundations; as soon as the river bore down
on it, it collapsed; and what a ruin that house
became!'

Cure of the centurion's servant

7 When he had come to the end of all he
wanted the people to hear, he went into
Capernaum. 2 A centurion there had a
servant, a favourite of his, who was sick and
near death. 3 Having heard about Jesus he
sent some Jewish elders to him to ask him to
come and heal his servant. 4 When they came
to Jesus they pleaded earnestly with him
saying, 'He deserves this of you, 5 because he
is well disposed towards our people; he built
us our synagogue himself.' 6 So Jesus went
with them, and was not very far from the
house when the centurion sent word to him
by some friends to say to him, 'Sir, do not
put yourself to any trouble because I am not
worthy to have you under my roof; 7 and that
is why I did not presume to come to you
myself; let my boy be cured by your giving
the word. 8 For I am under authority myself,
and have soldiers under me; and I say to one
man, "Go," and he goes; to another, "Come
here," and he comes; to my servant, "Do
this," and he does it.' 9 When Jesus heard
these words he was astonished at him and,
turning round, said to the crowd following
him, 'I tell you, not even in Israel have I
found faith as great as this.' 10 And when the
messengers got back to the house they found
the servant in perfect health.

The son of the widow of Nain restored to life

11 It happened that soon afterwards he went
to a town called Nain, accompanied by his
disciples and a great number of people.
12 Now when he was near the gate of the town
there was a dead man being carried out, the
only son of his mother, and she was a widow.
And a considerable number of the towns-
people was with her. 13 When the Lord saw
her he felt sorry for her and said to her, 'Don't
cry.' 14 Then he went up and touched the bier
and the bearers stood still, and he said,
'Young man, I tell you: get up.' 15 And the
dead man sat up and began to talk, and Jesus
gave him to his mother.[a] 16 Everyone was filled

7a 1 K 17:23.

with awe and glorified God saying, 'A great
prophet has risen up among us; God has
visited his people.' 17And this view of him
spread throughout Judaea and all over the
countryside.

The Baptist's question
Jesus commends him

18The disciples of John gave him all this news,
and John, summoning two of his disciples,
19sent them to the Lord to ask, 'Are you the
one who is to come, or are we to expect
someone else?' 20When the men reached
Jesus they said, 'John the Baptist has sent us
to you to ask, "Are you the one who is to
come or are we to expect someone else?" '
21At that very time he cured many people of
diseases and afflictions and of evil spirits,
and gave the gift of sight to many who were
blind. 22Then he gave the messengers their
answer, 'Go back and tell John what you
have seen and heard: the blind see again, the
lame walk, those suffering from virulent
skin-diseases are cleansed, and the deaf
hear, the dead are raised to life, the good
news is proclaimed to the poor; 23and
blessed is anyone who does not find me a
cause of falling.'

24When John's messengers had gone he
began to talk to the people about John,
25'What did you go out into the desert to see?
A reed swaying in the breeze? No! Then what
did you go out to see? A man dressed in fine
clothes? Look, those who go in magnificent
clothes and live luxuriously are to be found
at royal courts! 26Then what did you go out
to see? A prophet? Yes, I tell you, and much
more than a prophet: 27he is the one of whom
scripture says:

Look, I am going to send my messenger
in front of you
to prepare your *way before you.*[b]

28'I tell you, of all the children born to
women, there is no one greater than John;
yet the least in the kingdom of God is greater
than he.' 29All the people who heard him,
and the tax collectors too, acknowledged
God's saving justice by accepting baptism
from John; 30but by refusing baptism from
him the Pharisees and the lawyers thwarted
God's plan for them.

Jesus condemns his contemporaries

31'What comparison, then, can I find for the
people of this generation? What are they like?
32They are like children shouting to one
another while they sit in the market place:

We played the pipes for you,
and you wouldn't dance;
we sang dirges,
and you wouldn't cry.

33'For John the Baptist has come, not
eating bread, not drinking wine, and you say,
"He is possessed." 34The Son of man has
come, eating and drinking, and you say,
"Look, a glutton and a drunkard, a friend of
tax collectors and sinners." 35Yet wisdom is
justified by all her children.'

The woman who was a sinner

36One of the Pharisees invited him to a meal.
When he arrived at the Pharisee's house and
took his place at table, 37suddenly a woman
came in, who had a bad name in the town.
She had heard he was dining with the Pharisee
and had brought with her an alabaster jar of
ointment. 38She waited behind him at his
feet, weeping, and her tears fell on his feet,
and she wiped them away with her hair; then
she covered his feet with kisses and anointed
them with the ointment.

39When the Pharisee who had invited him
saw this, he said to himself, 'If this man were
a prophet, he would know who this woman
is and what sort of person it is who is touching
him and what a bad name she has.' 40Then
Jesus took him up and said, 'Simon, I have
something to say to you.' He replied, 'Say
on, Master.' 41'There was once a creditor who
had two men in his debt; one owed him five
hundred denarii, the other fifty. 42They were
unable to pay, so he let them both off.
Which of them will love him more?' 43Simon
answered, 'The one who was let off more, I
suppose.' Jesus said, 'You are right.'

44Then he turned to the woman and said
to Simon, 'You see this woman? I came into
your house, and you poured no water over
my feet, but she has poured out her tears over
my feet and wiped them away with her hair.
45You gave me no kiss, but she has been
covering my feet with kisses ever since I came
in. 46You did not anoint my head with oil,

7b Ml 3:1.

but she has anointed my feet with ointment.
[47]For this reason I tell you that her sins, many
as they are, have been forgiven her, because
she has shown such great love.[c] It is someone
who is forgiven little who shows little love.'
[48]Then he said to her, 'Your sins are
forgiven.' [49]Those who were with him at table
began to say to themselves, 'Who is this man,
that even forgives sins?' [50]But he said to the
woman, 'Your faith has saved you; go in
peace.'

The women accompanying Jesus

8 Now it happened that after this he made
his way through towns and villages
preaching and proclaiming the good news of
the kingdom of God. With him went the
Twelve, [2]as well as certain women who had
been cured of evil spirits and ailments: Mary
surnamed the Magdalene, from whom seven
demons had gone out, [3]Joanna the wife of
Herod's steward Chuza, Susanna, and many
others who provided for them out of their
own resources.

Parable of the sower

[4]With a large crowd gathering and people
from every town finding their way to him, he
told this parable:

[5]'A sower went out to sow his seed. Now
as he sowed, some fell on the edge of the path
and was trampled on; and the birds of the air
ate it up. [6]Some seed fell on rock, and when
it came up it withered away, having no
moisture. [7]Some seed fell in the middle of
thorns and the thorns grew with it and choked
it. [8]And some seed fell into good soil and
grew and produced its crop a hundredfold.'
Saying this he cried, 'Anyone who has ears
for listening should listen!'

Why Jesus speaks in parables

[9]His disciples asked him what this parable
might mean, [10]and he said, 'To you is granted
to understand the secrets of the kingdom of
God; for the rest it remains in parables, so
that

they may look but not perceive,
listen but not understand.[a]

The parable of the sower explained

[11]'This, then, is what the parable means: the
seed is the word of God. [12]Those on the edge
of the path are people who have heard it, and
then the devil comes and carries away the
word from their hearts in case they should
believe and be saved. [13]Those on the rock are
people who, when they first hear it, welcome
the word with joy. But these have no root;
they believe for a while, and in time of
trial they give up. [14]As for the part that fell
into thorns, this is people who have heard,
but as they go on their way they are choked
by the worries and riches and pleasures of
life and never produce any crops. [15]As for the
part in the rich soil, this is people with a
noble and generous heart who have heard the
word and take it to themselves and yield a
harvest through their perseverance.

Parable of the lamp

[16]'No one lights a lamp to cover it with a bowl
or to put it under a bed. No, it is put on a
lamp-stand so that people may see the light
when they come in. [17]For nothing is hidden
but it will be made clear, nothing secret but
it will be made known and brought to light.
[18]So take care how you listen; anyone who
has, will be given more; anyone who has not,
will be deprived even of what he thinks
he has.'

The true family of Jesus

[19]His mother and his brothers came looking
for him, but they could not get to him because
of the crowd. [20]He was told, 'Your mother
and brothers are standing outside and want
to see you.' [21]But he said in answer, 'My
mother and my brothers are those who hear
the word of God and put it into practice.'

The calming of the storm

[22]It happened that one day he got into a boat
with his disciples and said to them, 'Let us
cross over to the other side of the lake.' So
they set out, [23]and as they sailed he fell asleep.
When a squall of wind came down on the
lake the boat started shipping water and they
found themselves in danger. [24]So they went

7c In most of the story love wins forgiveness, but in vv. 40–43 and 47a, forgiveness nourishes love.
8a Is 6:9.

to rouse him saying, 'Master! Master! We are
lost!' Then he woke up and rebuked the wind
and the rough water; and they subsided and
it was calm again. 25 He said to them, 'Where
is your faith?' They were awestruck and
astounded and said to one another, 'Who can
this be, that gives orders even to winds and
waves and they obey him?'

The Gerasene demoniac

26 They came to land in the territory of the
Gerasenes, which is opposite Galilee. 27 He
was stepping ashore when a man from the
city who was possessed by devils came
towards him; for a long time the man had
been living with no clothes on, not in a
house, but in the tombs.

28 Catching sight of Jesus he gave a shout,
fell at his feet and cried out at the top of his
voice, 'What do you want with me, Jesus,
son of the Most High God? I implore you, do
not torture me.' 29 For Jesus had been telling
the unclean spirit to come out of the man. It
had seized on him a great many times, and
then they used to secure him with chains and
fetters to restrain him, but he would always
break the fastenings, and the devil would
drive him out into the wilds. 30 Jesus asked
him, 'What is your name?' He said,
'Legion'—because many devils had gone into
him. 31 And these begged him not to order
them to depart into the Abyss.

32 Now there was a large herd of pigs feeding
there on the mountain, and the devils begged
him to let them go into these. So he gave
them leave. 33 The devils came out of the
man and went into the pigs, and the herd
charged down the cliff into the lake and
was drowned.

34 When the swineherds saw what had
happened they ran off and told their story in
the city and in the country round about;
35 and the people went out to see what had
happened. When they came to Jesus they
found the man from whom the devils had
gone out sitting at the feet of Jesus, wearing
clothes and in his right mind; and they were
afraid. 36 Those who had witnessed it told
them how the man who had been possessed
came to be saved. 37 The entire population of
the Gerasene territory was in great fear and
asked Jesus to leave them. So he got into the
boat and went back.

38 The man from whom the devils had gone
out asked to be allowed to stay with him, but
he sent him away saying, 39 'Go back home
and report all that God has done for you.' So
the man went off and proclaimed throughout
the city all that Jesus had done for him.

Cure of the woman with a haemorrhage
Jairus' daughter raised to life

40 On his return Jesus was welcomed by the
crowd, for they were all there waiting for him.
41 And suddenly there came a man named
Jairus, who was president of the synagogue.
He fell at Jesus' feet and pleaded with him to
come to his house, 42 because he had an only
daughter about twelve years old, who was
dying. And the crowds were almost stifling
Jesus as he went.

43 Now there was a woman suffering from
a haemorrhage for the past twelve years,
whom no one had been able to cure. 44 She
came up behind him and touched the fringe
of his cloak; and the haemorrhage stopped at
that very moment. 45 Jesus said, 'Who was it
that touched me?' When they all denied it,
Peter said, 'Master, it is the crowds round
you, pushing.' 46 But Jesus said, 'Somebody
touched me. I felt that power had gone out
from me.' 47 Seeing herself discovered, the
woman came forward trembling, and falling
at his feet explained in front of all the people
why she had touched him and how she had
been cured at that very moment. 48 'My
daughter,' he said, 'your faith has saved you;
go in peace.'

49 While he was still speaking, someone
arrived from the house of the president of the
synagogue to say, 'Your daughter has died.
Do not trouble the Master any further.' 50 But
Jesus heard this, and he spoke to the man,
'Do not be afraid, only have faith and she
will be saved.' 51 When he came to the house
he allowed no one to go in with him except
Peter and John and James, and the child's
father and mother. 52 They were all crying
and mourning for her, but Jesus said, 'Stop
crying; she is not dead, but asleep.' 53 But
they ridiculed him, knowing she was dead.
54 But taking her by the hand himself he spoke
to her, 'Child, get up.' 55 And her spirit
returned and she got up at that very moment.
Then he told them to give her something to
eat. 56 Her parents were astonished, but he
ordered them not to tell anyone what had
happened.

The mission of the Twelve

9 He called the Twelve together and gave them power and authority over all devils and to cure diseases, [2]and he sent them out to proclaim the kingdom of God and to heal. [3]He said to them, 'Take nothing for the journey: neither staff, nor haversack, nor bread, nor money; and do not have a spare tunic. [4]Whatever house you enter, stay there; and when you leave let your departure be from there. [5]As for those who do not welcome you, when you leave their town shake the dust from your feet as evidence against them.' [6]So they set out and went from village to village proclaiming the good news and healing everywhere.

Herod and Jesus

[7]Meanwhile Herod the tetrarch had heard about all that was going on; and he was puzzled, because some people were saying that John had risen from the dead, [8]others that Elijah had reappeared, still others that one of the ancient prophets had come back to life. [9]But Herod said, 'John? I beheaded him. So who is this I hear such reports about?' And he was anxious to see him.

The return of the apostles
Miracle of the loaves

[10]On their return the apostles gave him an account of all they had done. Then he took them with him and withdrew towards a town called Bethsaida where they could be by themselves. [11]But the crowds got to know and they went after him. He made them welcome and talked to them about the kingdom of God; and he cured those who were in need of healing.

[12]It was late afternoon when the Twelve came up to him and said, 'Send the people away, and they can go to the villages and farms round about to find lodging and food; for we are in a lonely place here.' [13]He replied, 'Give them something to eat yourselves.' But they said, 'We have no more than five loaves and two fish, unless we are to go ourselves and buy food for all these people.' [14]For there were about five thousand men. But he said to his disciples, 'Get them to sit down in parties of about fifty.' [15]They did so and made them all sit down. [16]Then he took the five loaves and the two fish, raised his eyes to heaven, and said the blessing over them; then he broke them and handed them to his disciples to distribute among the crowd. [17]They all ate as much as they wanted, and when the scraps left over were collected they filled twelve baskets.

Peter's profession of faith

[18]Now it happened that he was praying alone, and his disciples came to him and he put this question to them, 'Who do the crowds say I am?' [19]And they answered, 'Some say John the Baptist; others Elijah; others again one of the ancient prophets come back to life.' [20]'But you,' he said to them, 'who do you say I am?' It was Peter who spoke up. 'The Christ of God,' he said. [21]But he gave them strict orders and charged them not to say this to anyone.

First prophecy of the Passion

[22]He said, 'The Son of man is destined to suffer grievously, to be rejected by the elders and chief priests and scribes and to be put to death, and to be raised up on the third day.'

The condition of following Christ

[23]Then, speaking to all, he said, 'If anyone wants to be a follower of mine, let him renounce himself and take up his cross every day and follow me. [24]Anyone who wants to save his life will lose it; but anyone who loses his life for my sake, will save it. [25]What benefit is it to anyone to win the whole world and forfeit or lose his very self? [26]For if anyone is ashamed of me and of my words, of him the Son of man will be ashamed when he comes in his own glory and in the glory of the Father and the holy angels.

The kingdom will come soon

[27]'I tell you truly, there are some standing here who will not taste death before they see the kingdom of God.'

The transfiguration

[28]Now about eight days after this had been said, he took with him Peter, John and James and went up the mountain to pray. [29]And it happened that, as he was praying, the aspect

of his face was changed and his clothing
became sparkling white. 30 And suddenly
there were two men talking to him; they were
Moses and Elijah 31 appearing in glory, and
they were speaking of his passing which he
was to accomplish in Jerusalem. 32 Peter and
his companions were heavy with sleep, but
they woke up and saw his glory and the two
men standing with him. 33 As these were
leaving him, Peter said to Jesus, 'Master, it
is wonderful for us to be here; so let us make
three shelters, one for you, one for Moses
and one for Elijah.' He did not know what
he was saying. 34 As he was saying this, a
cloud came and covered them with shadow;
and when they went into the cloud the
disciples were afraid. 35 And a voice came
from the cloud saying, 'This is my Son, the
Chosen One. Listen to him.'[a] 36 And after the
voice had spoken, Jesus was found alone.
The disciples kept silence and, at that time,
told no one what they had seen.

The epileptic demoniac

37 Now it happened that on the following
day when they were coming down from the
mountain a large crowd came to meet him.
38 And suddenly a man in the crowd cried out.
'Master,' he said, 'I implore you to look at
my son: he is my only child. 39 A spirit will
suddenly take hold of him, and all at once it
gives a sudden cry and throws the boy into
convulsions with foaming at the mouth; it is
slow to leave him, but when it does, it leaves
the boy worn out. 40 I begged your disciples
to drive it out, and they could not.' 41 In reply
Jesus said, 'Faithless and perverse gener-
ation! How much longer must I be among
you and put up with you? Bring your son
here.' 42 Even while the boy was coming, the
devil threw him to the ground in convulsions.
But Jesus rebuked the unclean spirit and
cured the boy and gave him back to his
father, 43 and everyone was awestruck by the
greatness of God.

Second prophecy of the Passion

But while everyone was full of admiration for
all he did, he said to his disciples, 44 'For your
part, you must have these words constantly
in mind: The Son of man is going to be
delivered into the power of men.' 45 But they
did not understand what he said; it was
hidden from them so that they should not see
the meaning of it, and they were afraid to ask
him about it.

Who is the greatest?

46 An argument started between them about
which of them was the greatest. 47 Jesus knew
what thoughts were going through their
minds, and he took a little child whom he set
by his side 48 and then he said to them,
'Anyone who welcomes this little child in
my name welcomes me; and anyone who
welcomes me, welcomes the one who sent
me. The least among you all is the one who
is the greatest.'

On using the name of Jesus

49 John spoke up. 'Master,' he said, 'we saw
someone driving out devils in your name,
and because he is not with us we tried to stop
him.' 50 But Jesus said to him, 'You must not
stop him: anyone who is not against you is
for you.'

IV: THE JOURNEY TO JERUSALEM

A Samaritan village is inhospitable

51 Now it happened that as the time drew near
for him to be taken up, he resolutely turned
his face towards Jerusalem 52 and sent messen-
gers ahead of him. These set out, and they
went into a Samaritan village to make prep-
arations for him, 53 but the people would
not receive him because he was making for
Jerusalem. 54 Seeing this, the disciples James
and John said, 'Lord, do you want us to call
down fire from heaven to burn them up?'
55 But he turned and rebuked them, 56 and
they went on to another village.

Hardships of the apostolic calling

57 As they travelled along they met a man on
the road who said to him, 'I will follow you
wherever you go.' 58 Jesus answered, 'Foxes

9a Dt 18:15, 19; Is 42:1.

have holes and the birds of the air have nests, but the Son of man has nowhere to lay his head.'

[59]Another to whom he said, 'Follow me,' replied, 'Let me go and bury my father first.' [60]But he answered, 'Leave the dead to bury their dead; your duty is to go and spread the news of the kingdom of God.'

[61]Another said, 'I will follow you, sir, but first let me go and say good-bye to my people at home.' [62]Jesus said to him, 'Once the hand is laid on the plough, no one who looks back is fit for the kingdom of God.'

The mission of the seventy-two disciples

10 After this the Lord appointed seventy-two others and sent them out ahead of him in pairs, to all the towns and places he himself would be visiting. [2]And he said to them, 'The harvest is rich but the labourers are few, so ask the Lord of the harvest to send labourers to do his harvesting. [3]Start off now, but look, I am sending you out like lambs among wolves. [4]Take no purse with you, no haversack, no sandals. Salute no one on the road. [5]Whatever house you enter, let your first words be, "Peace to this house!" [6]And if a man of peace lives there, your peace will go and rest on him; if not, it will come back to you. [7]Stay in the same house, taking what food and drink they have to offer, for the labourer deserves his wages; do not move from house to house. [8]Whenever you go into a town where they make you welcome, eat what is put before you. [9]Cure those in it who are sick, and say, "The kingdom of God is very near to you." [10]But whenever you enter a town and they do not make you welcome, go out into its streets and say, [11]"We wipe off the very dust of your town that clings to our feet, and leave it with you. Yet be sure of this: the kingdom of God is very near." [12]I tell you, on the great Day it will be more bearable for Sodom than for that town.

[13]'Alas for you, Chorazin! Alas for you, Bethsaida! For if the miracles done in you had been done in Tyre and Sidon, they would have repented long ago, sitting in sackcloth and ashes. [14]And still, it will be more bearable for Tyre and Sidon at the Judgement than for you. [15]And as for you, Capernaum, did you want to be *raised high as heaven? You shall be flung down to hell.*[a]

[16]'Anyone who listens to you listens to me; anyone who rejects you rejects me, and those who reject me reject the one who sent me.'

True cause for the apostles to rejoice

[17]The seventy-two came back rejoicing. 'Lord,' they said, 'even the devils submit to us when we use your name.' [18]He said to them, 'I watched Satan fall like lightning from heaven. [19]Look, I have given you power to tread down serpents and scorpions and the whole strength of the enemy; nothing shall ever hurt you. [20]Yet do not rejoice that the spirits submit to you; rejoice instead that your names are written in heaven.'

The good news revealed to the simple
The Father and the Son

[21]Just at this time, filled with joy by the Holy Spirit, he said, 'I bless you, Father, Lord of heaven and of earth, for hiding these things from the learned and the clever and revealing them to little children. Yes, Father, for that is what it has pleased you to do. [22]Everything has been entrusted to me by my Father; and no one knows who the Son is except the Father, and who the Father is except the Son and those to whom the Son chooses to reveal him.'

The privilege of the disciples

[23]Then turning to his disciples he spoke to them by themselves, 'Blessed are the eyes that see what you see, [24]for I tell you that many prophets and kings wanted to see what you see, and never saw it; to hear what you hear, and never heard it.'

The great commandment

[25]And now a lawyer stood up and, to test him, asked, 'Master, what must I do to inherit eternal life?' [26]He said to him, 'What is written in the Law? What is your reading of it?' [27]He replied, '*You must love the Lord your God with all your heart, with all your soul, with all your strength*, and with all your mind, *and your neighbour as yourself.*'[b] [28]Jesus said to

10a Is 14:13–15.
10b Dt 6:5 and Lv 19:18.

him, 'You have answered right, do this and
life is yours.'

Parable of the good Samaritan

29But the man was anxious to justify himself
and said to Jesus, 'And who is my neighbour?'
30In answer Jesus said, 'A man was once on
his way down from Jerusalem to Jericho and
fell into the hands of bandits; they stripped
him, beat him and then made off, leaving
him half dead. 31Now a priest happened to
be travelling down the same road, but when
he saw the man, he passed by on the other
side. 32In the same way a Levite who came to
the place saw him, and passed by on the other
side. 33But a Samaritan traveller who came
on him was moved with compassion when he
saw him. 34He went up to him and bandaged
his wounds, pouring oil and wine on them.
He then lifted him onto his own mount and
took him to an inn and looked after him.
35Next day, he took out two denarii and
handed them to the innkeeper and said,
"Look after him, and on my way back I will
make good any extra expense you have."
36Which of these three, do you think, proved
himself a neighbour to the man who fell into
the bandits' hands?' 37He replied, 'The one
who showed pity towards him.' Jesus said to
him, 'Go, and do the same yourself.'

Martha and Mary

38In the course of their journey he came to a
village, and a woman named Martha
welcomed him into her house. 39She had a
sister called Mary, who sat down at the Lord's
feet and listened to him speaking. 40Now
Martha, who was distracted with all the
serving, came to him and said, 'Lord, do you
not care that my sister is leaving me to do the
serving all by myself? Please tell her to help
me.' 41But the Lord answered, 'Martha,
Martha,' he said, 'you worry and fret about
so many things, 42and yet few are needed,
indeed only one. It is Mary who has chosen
the better part, and it is not to be taken from
her.'

The Lord's prayer

11 Now it happened that he was in a
certain place praying, and when he had
finished, one of his disciples said, 'Lord,
teach us to pray, as John taught his disciples.'
2He said to them, 'When you pray, this is
what to say:

Father, may your name be held holy,
your kingdom come;
3give us each day our daily bread,
and forgive us our sins,
4for we ourselves forgive each one
who is in debt to us.
And do not put us to the test.'[a]

The importunate friend

5He also said to them, 'Suppose one of you
has a friend and goes to him in the middle of
the night to say, "My friend, lend me three
loaves, 6because a friend of mine on his
travels has just arrived at my house and I
have nothing to offer him;" 7and the man
answers from inside the house, "Do not
bother me. The door is bolted now, and my
children are with me in bed; I cannot get up
to give it to you." 8I tell you, if the man does
not get up and give it to him for friendship's
sake, persistence will make him get up and
give his friend all he wants.

Effective prayer

9'So I say to you: Ask, and it will be given to
you; search, and you will find; knock, and
the door will be opened to you. 10For
everyone who asks receives; everyone who
searches finds; everyone who knocks will
have the door opened. 11What father among
you, if his son asked for a fish, would hand
him a snake? 12Or if he asked for an egg, hand
him a scorpion? 13If you then, evil as you are,
know how to give your children what is good,
how much more will the heavenly Father
give the Holy Spirit to those who ask him!'

Jesus and Beelzebul

14He was driving out a devil and it was dumb;
and it happened that when the devil had gone
out the dumb man spoke, and the people
were amazed. 15But some of them said, 'It is
through Beelzebul, the prince of devils, that
he drives devils out.' 16Others asked him, as
a test, for a sign from heaven; 17but, knowing
what they were thinking, he said to them,

11a Mt 6:9–13.

cubit to your span of life? [26]If a very small thing is beyond your powers, why worry about the rest? [27]Think how the flowers grow; they never have to spin or weave; yet, I assure you, not even Solomon in all his royal robes was clothed like one of them. [28]Now if that is how God clothes a flower which is growing wild today and is thrown into the furnace tomorrow, how much more will he look after you, who have so little faith! [29]But you must not set your hearts on things to eat and things to drink; nor must you worry. [30]It is the gentiles of this world who set their hearts on all these things. Your Father well knows you need them. [31]No; set your hearts on his kingdom, and these other things will be given you as well.

[32]'There is no need to be afraid, little flock, for it has pleased your Father to give you the kingdom.

On almsgiving

[33]'Sell your possessions and give to those in need. Get yourselves purses that do not wear out, treasure that will not fail you, in heaven where no thief can reach it and no moth destroy it. [34]For wherever your treasure is, that is where your heart will be too.

On being ready for the Master's return

[35]'See that you have your belts done up and your lamps lit. [36]Be like people waiting for their master to return from the wedding feast, ready to open the door as soon as he comes and knocks. [37]Blessed those servants whom the master finds awake when he comes. In truth I tell you, he will do up his belt, sit them down at table and wait on them. [38]It may be in the second watch that he comes, or in the third, but blessed are those servants if he finds them ready. [39]You may be quite sure of this, that if the householder had known at what time the burglar would come, he would not have let anyone break through the wall of his house. [40]You too must stand ready, because the Son of man is coming at an hour you do not expect.'

[41]Peter said, 'Lord, do you mean this parable for us, or for everyone?' [42]The Lord replied, 'Who, then, is the wise and trustworthy steward whom the master will place over his household to give them at the proper time their allowance of food? [43]Blessed that servant if his master's arrival finds him doing exactly that. [44]I tell you truly, he will put him in charge of everything that he owns. [45]But if the servant says to himself, "My master is taking his time coming," and sets about beating the menservants and the servant-girls, and eating and drinking and getting drunk, [46]his master will come on a day he does not expect and at an hour he does not know. The master will cut him off and send him to the same fate as the unfaithful.

[47]'The servant who knows what his master wants, but has got nothing ready and done nothing in accord with those wishes, will be given a great many strokes of the lash. [48]The one who did not know, but has acted in such a way that he deserves a beating, will be given fewer strokes. When someone is given a great deal, a great deal will be demanded of that person; when someone is entrusted with a great deal, of that person even more will be expected.

Jesus and his Passion

[49]'I have come to bring fire to the earth, and how I wish it were blazing already! [50]There is a baptism I must still receive, and what constraint I am under until it is completed!

Jesus the cause of dissension

[51]'Do you suppose that I am here to bring peace on earth? No, I tell you, but rather division. [52]For from now on, a household of five will be divided: three against two and two against three; [53]*father opposed to son*, son to father, mother to daughter, *daughter to mother*, mother-in-law to daughter-in-law, *daughter-in-law to mother-in-law*.'[a]

On reading the signs of the times

[54]He said again to the crowds, 'When you see a cloud looming up in the west you say at once that rain is coming, and so it does. [55]And when the wind is from the south you say it's going to be hot, and it is. [56]Hypocrites! You know how to interpret the face of the earth and the sky. How is it you do not know how to interpret these times?

[57]'Why not judge for yourselves what is upright? [58]For example: when you are going

12a Mi 7:6.

to court with your opponent, make an effort
to settle with him on the way, or he may drag
you before the judge and the judge hand you
over to the officer and the officer have you
thrown into prison. 59I tell you, you will not
get out till you have paid the very last penny.'

Examples inviting repentance

13 It was just about this time that some
people arrived and told him about the
Galileans whose blood Pilate had mingled
with that of their sacrifices. At this he said to
them, 2'Do you suppose that these Galileans
were worse sinners than any others, that this
should have happened to them? 3They were
not, I tell you. No; but unless you repent you
will all perish as they did. 4Or those eighteen
on whom the tower at Siloam fell, killing
them all? Do you suppose that they were
more guilty than all the other people living
in Jerusalem? 5They were not, I tell you. No;
but unless you repent you will all perish as
they did.'

Parable of the barren fig tree

6He told this parable, 'A man had a fig tree
planted in his vineyard, and he came looking
for fruit on it but found none. 7He said to his
vinedresser, "For three years now I have
been coming to look for fruit on this fig tree
and finding none. Cut it down: why should
it be taking up the ground?" 8"Sir," the man
replied, "leave it one more year and give me
time to dig round it and manure it: 9it may
bear fruit next year; if not, then you can cut
it down." '

Healing of a crippled woman on the Sabbath

10One Sabbath day he was teaching in one of
the synagogues, 11and there before him was
a woman who for eighteen years had been
possessed by a spirit that crippled her; she
was bent double and quite unable to stand
upright. 12When Jesus saw her he called her
over and said, 'Woman, you are freed from
your disability,' 13and he laid his hands on
her. And at once she straightened up, and
she glorified God.

14But the president of the synagogue was
indignant because Jesus had healed on the
Sabbath, and he addressed all those present
saying, 'There are six days when work is to
be done. Come and be healed on one of those
days and not on the Sabbath.' 15But the Lord
answered him and said, 'Hypocrites! Is there
one of you who does not untie his ox or his
donkey from the manger on the Sabbath and
take it out for watering? 16And this woman,
a daughter of Abraham whom Satan has held
bound these eighteen years—was it not right
to untie this bond on the Sabbath day?'
17When he said this, all his adversaries were
covered with confusion, and all the people
were overjoyed at all the wonders he worked.

Parable of the mustard seed

18He went on to say, 'What is the kingdom
of God like? What shall I compare it with?
19It is like a mustard seed which a man took
and threw into his garden: it grew and became
a tree, and the birds of the air sheltered in its
branches.'

Parable of the yeast

20Again he said, 'What shall I compare the
kingdom of God with? 21It is like the yeast a
woman took and mixed in with three meas-
ures of flour till it was leavened all through.'

The narrow door; rejection of the Jews, call of the gentiles

22Through towns and villages he went
teaching, making his way to Jerusalem.
23Someone said to him, 'Sir, will there be
only a few saved?' He said to them, 24'Try
your hardest to enter by the narrow door,
because, I tell you, many will try to enter and
will not succeed.

25'Once the master of the house has got up
and locked the door, you may find yourself
standing outside knocking on the door,
saying, "Lord, open to us," but he will
answer, "I do not know where you come
from." 26Then you will start saying, "We
once ate and drank in your company; you
taught in our streets," 27but he will reply, "I
do not know where you come from; *away
from me, all evil doers!*"[a]

28'Then there will be weeping and grinding
of teeth, when you see Abraham and Isaac
and Jacob and all the prophets in the kingdom

13a Ps 6:8.

of God, and yourselves thrown out. 29 And
people from east and west, from north and
south, will come and sit down at the feast in
the kingdom of God.
30 'Look, there are those now last who
will be first, and those now first who will
be last.'

Herod the fox

31 Just at this time some Pharisees came up.
'Go away,' they said. 'Leave this place,
because Herod[b] means to kill you.' 32 He
replied, 'You may go and give that fox this
message: Look! Today and tomorrow I drive
out devils and heal, and on the third day I
attain my end. 33 But for today and tomorrow
and the next day I must go on, since it would
not be right for a prophet to die outside
Jerusalem.

Jerusalem admonished

34 'Jerusalem, Jerusalem, you that kill the
prophets and stone those who are sent to you!
How often have I longed to gather your
children together, as a hen gathers her brood
under her wings, and you refused! 35 Look!
Your house will be left to you. Yes, I promise
you, you shall not see me till the time comes
when you are saying:

Blessed is he
who is coming in the name of the Lord!'[c]

Healing of a dropsical man on the Sabbath

14 Now it happened that on a Sabbath day
he had gone to share a meal in the house
of one of the leading Pharisees; and they
watched him closely. 2 Now there in front of
him was a man with dropsy, 3 and Jesus
addressed the lawyers and Pharisees with the
words, 'Is it against the law to cure someone
on the Sabbath, or not?' 4 But they remained
silent, so he took the man and cured him
and sent him away. 5 Then he said to them,
'Which of you here, if his son falls into a well,
or his ox, will not pull him out on a Sabbath
day without any hesitation?' 6 And to this
they could find no answer.

On choosing places at table

7 He then told the guests a parable, because
he had noticed how they picked the places
of honour. He said this, 8 'When someone
invites you to a wedding feast, do not take
your seat in the place of honour. A more
distinguished person than you may have been
invited, 9 and the person who invited you
both may come and say, "Give up your place
to this man." And then, to your embarrass-
ment, you will have to go and take the lowest
place. 10 No; when you are a guest, make your
way to the lowest place and sit there, so that,
when your host comes, he may say, "My
friend, move up higher." Then, everyone
with you at the table will see you honoured.
11 For everyone who raises himself up will be
humbled, and the one who humbles himself
will be raised up.'

On choosing guests to be invited

12 Then he said to his host, 'When you give a
lunch or a dinner, do not invite your friends
or your brothers or your relations or rich
neighbours, in case they invite you back and
so repay you. 13 No; when you have a party,
invite the poor, the crippled, the lame, the
blind; 14 then you will be blessed, for they
have no means to repay you and so you will
be repaid when the upright rise again.'

The invited guests who made excuses

15 On hearing this, one of those gathered
round the table said to him, 'Blessed is anyone
who will share the meal in the kingdom of
God!' 16 But he said to him, 'There was a man
who gave a great banquet, and he invited a
large number of people. 17 When the time for
the banquet came, he sent his servant to say
to those who had been invited, "Come along:
everything is ready now." 18 But all alike
started to make excuses. The first said, "I
have bought a piece of land and must go and
see it. Please accept my apologies." 19 Another
said, "I have bought five yoke of oxen and
am on my way to try them out. Please accept
my apologies." 20 Yet another said, "I have
just got married and so am unable to come."
21 'The servant returned and reported this
to his master. Then the householder, in a
rage, said to his servant, "Go out quickly into

13b Herod Antipas, son of Herod the Great.
13c Ps 118:26.

the streets and alleys of the town and bring in here the poor, the crippled, the blind and the lame." 22 "Sir," said the servant, "your orders have been carried out and there is still room." 23 Then the master said to his servant, "Go to the open roads and the hedgerows and press people to come in, to make sure my house is full; 24 because, I tell you, not one of those who were invited shall have a taste of my banquet." '

Renouncing all that one holds dear

25 Great crowds accompanied him on his way and he turned and spoke to them. 26 'Anyone who comes to me without hating father, mother, wife, children, brothers, sisters, yes and his own life too, cannot be my disciple. 27 No one who does not carry his cross and come after me can be my disciple.

Renouncing possessions

28 'And indeed, which of you here, intending to build a tower, would not first sit down and work out the cost to see if he had enough to complete it? 29 Otherwise, if he laid the foundation and then found himself unable to finish the work, anyone who saw it would start making fun of him and saying, 30 "Here is someone who started to build and was unable to finish." 31 Or again, what king marching to war against another king would not first sit down and consider whether with ten thousand men he could stand up to the other who was advancing against him with twenty thousand? 32 If not, then while the other king was still a long way off, he would send envoys to sue for peace. 33 So in the same way, none of you can be my disciple without giving up all that he owns.

On loss of enthusiasm in a disciple

34 'Salt is a good thing. But if salt itself loses its taste, what can make it salty again? 35 It is good for neither soil nor manure heap. People throw it away. Anyone who has ears for listening should listen!'

The three parables of God's mercy

15 The tax collectors and sinners, however, were all crowding round to listen to him, 2 and the Pharisees and scribes complained saying, 'This man welcomes sinners and eats with them.' 3 So he told them this parable:

The lost sheep

4 'Which one of you with a hundred sheep, if he lost one, would fail to leave the ninety-nine in the desert and go after the missing one till he found it? 5 And when he found it, would he not joyfully take it on his shoulders 6 and then, when he got home, call together his friends and neighbours, saying to them, "Rejoice with me, I have found my sheep that was lost." 7 In the same way, I tell you, there will be more rejoicing in heaven over one sinner repenting than over ninety-nine upright people who have no need of repentance.

The lost drachma

8 'Or again, what woman with ten drachmas would not, if she lost one, light a lamp and sweep out the house and search thoroughly till she found it? 9 And then, when she had found it, call together her friends and neighbours, saying to them, "Rejoice with me, I have found the drachma I lost." 10 In the same way, I tell you, there is rejoicing among the angels of God over one repentant sinner.'

The lost son (the 'prodigal') and the dutiful son

11 Then he said, 'There was a man who had two sons. 12 The younger one said to his father, "Father, let me have the share of the estate that will come to me." So the father divided the property between them. 13 A few days later, the younger son got together everything he had and left for a distant country where he squandered his money on a life of debauchery.

14 "When he had spent it all, that country experienced a severe famine, and now he began to feel the pinch; 15 so he hired himself out to one of the local inhabitants who put him on his farm to feed the pigs. 16 And he would willingly have filled himself with the husks the pigs were eating but no one would let him have them. 17 Then he came to his senses and said, "How many of my father's hired men have all the food they want and more, and here am I dying of hunger! 18 I will leave this place and go to my father and say: Father, I have sinned against heaven and

against you; [19]I no longer deserve to be called
your son; treat me as one of your hired men."
[20]So he left the place and went back to his
father.

'While he was still a long way off, his father
saw him and was moved with pity. He ran to
the boy, clasped him in his arms and kissed
him. [21]Then his son said, "Father, I have
sinned against heaven and against you. I no
longer deserve to be called your son." [22]But
the father said to his servants, "Quick! Bring
out the best robe and put it on him; put a
ring on his finger and sandals on his feet.
[23]Bring the calf we have been fattening, and
kill it; we will celebrate by having a feast,
[24]because this son of mine was dead and has
come back to life; he was lost and is found."
And they began to celebrate.

[25]'Now the elder son was out in the fields,
and on his way back, as he drew near the
house, he could hear music and dancing.
[26]Calling one of the servants he asked what it
was all about. [27]The servant told him, "Your
brother has come, and your father has killed
the calf we had been fattening because he has
got him back safe and sound." [28]He was
angry then and refused to go in, and his father
came out and began to urge him to come in;
[29]but he retorted to his father, "All these
years I have slaved for you and never once
disobeyed any orders of yours, yet you never
offered me so much as a kid for me to
celebrate with my friends. [30]But, for this
son of yours, when he comes back after
swallowing up your property—he and his
loose women—you kill the calf we had been
fattening."

[31]'The father said, "My son, you are with
me always and all I have is yours. [32]But it was
only right we should celebrate and rejoice,
because your brother here was dead and has
come to life; he was lost and is found." '

The crafty steward

16 He also said to his disciples, 'There was
a rich man and he had a steward who
was denounced to him for being wasteful
with his property. [2]He called for the man and
said, "What is this I hear about you? Draw
me up an account of your stewardship
because you are not to be my steward any
longer." [3]Then the steward said to himself,
"Now that my master is taking the steward-
ship from me, what am I to do? Dig? I am
not strong enough. Go begging? I should be
too ashamed. [4]Ah, I know what I will do to
make sure that when I am dismissed from
office there will be some to welcome me into
their homes."

[5]"Then he called his master's debtors one
by one. To the first he said, "How much
do you owe my master?" [6]"One hundred
measures of oil," he said. The steward said,
"Here, take your bond; sit down and quickly
write fifty." [7]To another he said, "And you,
sir, how much do you owe?" "One hundred
measures of wheat," he said. The steward
said, "Here, take your bond and write
eighty."

[8]'The master praised the dishonest steward
for his astuteness. For the children of this
world are more astute in dealing with their
own kind than are the children of light.'

The right use of money

[9]'And so I tell you this: use money, tainted
as it is, to win you friends, and thus make
sure that when it fails you, they will welcome
you into eternal dwellings. [10]Anyone who is
trustworthy in little things is trustworthy in
great; anyone who is dishonest in little things
is dishonest in great. [11]If then you are not
trustworthy with money, that tainted thing,
who will trust you with genuine riches? [12]And
if you are not trustworthy with what is not
yours, who will give you what is your very
own?

[13]'No servant can be the slave of two
masters: he will either hate the first and love
the second, or be attached to the first and
despise the second. You cannot be the slave
both of God and of money.'

Against the Pharisees and their love of money

[14]The Pharisees, who loved money, heard all
this and jeered at him. [15]He said to them,
'You are the very ones who pass yourselves
off as upright in people's sight, but God
knows your hearts. For what is highly
esteemed in human eyes is loathsome in the
sight of God.

The kingdom stormed

[16]'Up to the time of John it was the Law
and the Prophets; from then onwards, the
kingdom of God has been preached, and
everyone is forcing their way into it.

The Law remains

17'It is easier for heaven and earth to
disappear than for one little stroke to drop
out of the Law.

Marriage indissoluble

18'Everyone who divorces his wife and
marries another is guilty of adultery, and the
man who marries a woman divorced by her
husband commits adultery.

The parable of the rich man and Lazarus

19'There was a rich man who used to dress in
purple and fine linen and feast magnificently
every day. 20And at his gate there used to lie
a poor man called Lazarus, covered with
sores, 21who longed to fill himself with what
fell from the rich man's table. Even dogs
came and licked his sores. 22Now it happened
that the poor man died and was carried away
by the angels into Abraham's embrace. The
rich man also died and was buried.
23'In his torment in Hades he looked up
and saw Abraham a long way off with Lazarus
in his embrace. 24So he cried out, "Father
Abraham, pity me and send Lazarus to dip
the tip of his finger in water and cool my
tongue, for I am in agony in these flames."
25Abraham said, "My son, remember that
during your life you had your fill of good
things, just as Lazarus his fill of bad. Now
he is being comforted here while you are in
agony. 26But that is not all: between us and
you a great gulf has been fixed, to prevent
those who want to cross from our side to
yours or from your side to ours."
27'So he said, "Father, I beg you then to
send Lazarus to my father's house, 28since I
have five brothers, to give them warning so
that they do not come to this place of torment
too." 29Abraham said, "They have Moses
and the prophets, let them listen to them."
30The rich man replied, "Ah no, father
Abraham, but if someone comes to them
from the dead, they will repent." 31Then
Abraham said to him, "If they will not listen
either to Moses or to the prophets, they will
not be convinced even if someone should rise
from the dead." '

On leading others astray

17 He said to his disciples, 'Causes of
falling are sure to come, but alas for the
one through whom they occur! 2It would be
better for such a person to be thrown into the
sea with a millstone round the neck than to
be the downfall of a single one of these little
ones. 3Keep watch on yourselves!

Brotherly correction

'If your brother does something wrong,
rebuke him and, if he is sorry, forgive him.
4And if he wrongs you seven times a day and
seven times comes back to you and says, "I
am sorry," you must forgive him.'

The power of faith

5The apostles said to the Lord, 'Increase our
faith.' 6The Lord replied, 'If you had faith
like a mustard seed you could say to this
mulberry tree, "Be uprooted and planted in
the sea," and it would obey you.

Humble service

7'Which of you, with a servant ploughing or
minding sheep, would say to him when he
returned from the fields, "Come and have
your meal at once"? 8Would he not be more
likely to say, "Get my supper ready; fasten
your belt and wait on me while I eat and drink.
You yourself can eat and drink afterwards"?
9Must he be grateful to the servant for doing
what he was told? 10So with you: when you
have done all you have been told to do, say,
"We are useless servants: we have done no
more than our duty." '

The ten victims of skin-disease

11Now it happened that on the way to Jeru-
salem he was travelling in the borderlands of
Samaria and Galilee. 12As he entered one of
the villages, ten men suffering from a virulent
skin-disease came to meet him. They stood
some way off 13and called to him, 'Jesus!
Master! Take pity on us.' 14When he saw
them he said, 'Go and show yourselves to the
priests.' Now as they were going away they
were cleansed. 15Finding himself cured, one
of them turned back praising God at the top
of his voice 16and threw himself prostrate at
the feet of Jesus and thanked him. The man
was a Samaritan. 17This led Jesus to say,
'Were not all ten made clean? The other nine,
where are they? 18It seems that no one has
come back to give praise to God, except this

foreigner.' [19]And he said to the man, 'Stand
up and go on your way. Your faith has
saved you.'

The coming of the kingdom of God

[20]Asked by the Pharisees when the kingdom
of God was to come, he gave them this
answer, 'The coming of the kingdom of God
does not admit of observation [21]and there will
be no one to say, "Look, it is here! Look, it
is there!" For look, the kingdom of God is
among you.'

The Day of the Son of man

[22]He said to the disciples, 'A time will come
when you will long to see one of the days of
the Son of man and will not see it. [23]They
will say to you, "Look, it is there!" or,
"Look, it is here!" Make no move; do not set
off in pursuit; [24]for as the lightning flashing
from one part of heaven lights up the other,
so will be the Son of man when his Day
comes. [25]But first he is destined to suffer
grievously and be rejected by this
generation.

[26]'As it was in Noah's day, so will it also
be in the days of the Son of man. [27]People
were eating and drinking, marrying wives
and husbands, right up to the day Noah
went into the ark, and the Flood came and
destroyed them all. [28]It will be the same as it
was in Lot's day: people were eating and
drinking, buying and selling, planting and
building, [29]but the day Lot left Sodom, it
rained fire and brimstone from heaven and it
destroyed them all. [30]It will be the same when
the day comes for the Son of man to be
revealed.

[31]'When that Day comes, no one on the
housetop, with his possessions in the house,
must come down to collect them, nor must
anyone in the fields turn back. [32]Remember
Lot's wife. [33]Anyone who tries to preserve
his life will lose it; and anyone who loses it
will keep it safe. [34]I tell you, on that night,
when two are in one bed, one will be taken,
the other left; [35]when two women are
grinding corn together, one will be taken,
the other left.' [36][a] [37]The disciples spoke up
and asked, 'Where, Lord?' He said, 'Where
the body is, there too will the vultures gather.'

The unscrupulous judge and the importunate widow

18 Then he told them a parable about the
need to pray continually and never lose
heart. [2]'There was a judge in a certain town,'
he said, 'who had neither fear of God nor
respect for anyone. [3]In the same town there
was also a widow who kept on coming to him
and saying, "I want justice from you against
my enemy!" [4]For a long time he refused, but
at last he said to himself, "Even though I
have neither fear of God nor respect for any
human person, [5]I must give this widow her
just rights since she keeps pestering me, or
she will come and slap me in the face." '

[6]And the Lord said, 'You notice what the
unjust judge has to say? [7]Now, will not God
see justice done to his elect if they keep calling
to him day and night even though he still
delays to help them? [8]I promise you, he will
see justice done to them, and done speedily.
But when the Son of man comes, will he find
any faith on earth?'

The Pharisee and the tax collector

[9]He spoke the following parable to some
people who prided themselves on being
upright and despised everyone else, [10]'Two
men went up to the Temple to pray, one
a Pharisee, the other a tax collector. [11]The
Pharisee stood there and said this prayer to
himself, "I thank you, God, that I am not
grasping, unjust, adulterous like everyone
else, and particularly that I am not like this
tax collector here. [12]I fast twice a week; I pay
tithes on all I get." [13]The tax collector stood
some distance away, not daring even to raise
his eyes to heaven; but he beat his breast and
said, "God, be merciful to me, a sinner."
[14]This man, I tell you, went home again
justified; the other did not. For everyone who
raises himself up will be humbled, but anyone
who humbles himself will be raised up.'

Jesus and the children

[15]People even brought babies to him, for him
to touch them; but when the disciples saw
this they scolded them. [16]But Jesus called
the children to him and said, 'Let the little
children come to me, and do not stop them;
for it is to such as these that the kingdom of

17a Add. v. 36, 'There will be two men in the fields; one will be taken, the other left,' cf. Mt 24:40.

God belongs. 17In truth I tell you, anyone
who does not welcome the kingdom of God
like a little child will never enter it.'

The rich aristocrat

18One of the rulers put this question to him,
'Good Master, what shall I do to inherit
eternal life?' 19Jesus said to him, 'Why do
you call me good? No one is good but God
alone. 20You know the commandments: *You
shall not commit adultery; You shall not kill;
You shall not steal; You shall not give false
witness; Honour your father and your mother*.'[a]
21He replied, 'I have kept all these since my
earliest days.' 22And when Jesus heard this
he said, 'There is still one thing you lack. Sell
everything you own and distribute the money
to the poor, and you will have treasure in
heaven; then come, follow me.' 23But when
he heard this he was overcome with sadness,
for he was very rich.

The danger of riches

24Jesus looked at him and said, 'How hard it
is for those who have riches to make their
way into the kingdom of God! 25Yes, it is
easier for a camel to pass through the eye of
a needle than for someone rich to enter the
kingdom of God.' 26Those who were listening
said, 'In that case, who can be saved?' 27He
replied, 'Things that are impossible by
human resources, are possible for God.'

The reward of renunciation

28But Peter said, 'Look, we left all we had to
follow you.' 29He said to them, 'In truth I tell
you, there is no one who has left house, wife,
brothers, parents or children for the sake of
the kingdom of God 30who will not receive
many times as much in this present age and,
in the world to come, eternal life.'

Third prophecy of the Passion

31Then taking the Twelve aside he said to
them, 'Look, we are going up to Jerusalem,
and everything that is written by the prophets
about the Son of man is to come true. 32For
he will be handed over to the gentiles and
will be mocked, maltreated and spat on, 33and
when they have scourged him they will put
him to death; and on the third day he will
rise again.' 34But they could make nothing of
this; what he said was quite obscure to them,
they did not understand what he was telling
them.

Entering Jericho: the blind man

35Now it happened that as he drew near to
Jericho there was a blind man sitting at the
side of the road begging. 36When he heard
the crowd going past he asked what it was all
about, 37and they told him that Jesus the
Nazarene was passing by. 38So he called out,
'Jesus, Son of David, have pity on me.' 39The
people in front scolded him and told him to
keep quiet, but he only shouted all the louder,
'Son of David, have pity on me.' 40Jesus
stopped and ordered them to bring the man
to him, and when he came up, asked him,
41'What do you want me to do for you?' 'Sir,'
he replied, 'let me see again.' 42Jesus said to
him, 'Receive your sight. Your faith has
saved you.' 43And instantly his sight returned
and he followed him praising God, and all
the people who saw it gave praise to God.

Zacchaeus

19 He entered Jericho and was going
through the town 2and suddenly a man
whose name was Zacchaeus made his appear-
ance; he was one of the senior tax collectors
and a wealthy man. 3He kept trying to see
which Jesus was, but he was too short and
could not see him for the crowd; 4so he ran
ahead and climbed a sycamore tree to catch
a glimpse of Jesus who was to pass that way.
5When Jesus reached the spot he looked up
and spoke to him, 'Zacchaeus, come down.
Hurry, because I am to stay at your house
today.' 6And he hurried down and welcomed
him joyfully. 7They all complained when
they saw what was happening. 'He has gone
to stay at a sinner's house,' they said. 8But
Zacchaeus stood his ground and said to the
Lord, 'Look, sir, I am going to give half my
property to the poor, and if I have cheated
anybody I will pay him back four times the
amount.' 9And Jesus said to him, 'Today
salvation has come to this house, because this
man too is a son of Abraham; 10for the Son
of man has come to seek out and save what
was lost.'

Parable of the pounds

11While the people were listening to this he
went on to tell a parable, because he was near

18a Ex 20:12–16.

Jerusalem and they thought that the kingdom
of God was going to show itself then and
there. [12]Accordingly he said, 'A man of noble
birth went to a distant country to be
appointed king and then return. [13]He
summoned ten of his servants and gave them
ten pounds, telling them, "Trade with these,
until I get back." [14]But his compatriots
detested him and sent a delegation to follow
him with this message, "We do not want this
man to be our king."

[15]'Now it happened that on his return,
having received his appointment as king, he
sent for those servants to whom he had given
the money, to find out what profit each had
made by trading. [16]The first came in, "Sir,"
he said, "your one pound has brought in
ten." [17]He replied, "Well done, my good
servant! Since you have proved yourself
trustworthy in a very small thing, you shall
have the government of ten cities." [18]Then
came the second, "Sir," he said, "your one
pound has made five." [19]To this one also he
said, "And you shall be in charge of five
cities." [20]Next came the other, "Sir," he said,
"here is your pound. I put it away safely
wrapped up in a cloth [21]because I was afraid
of you; for you are an exacting man: you
gather in what you have not laid out and reap
what you have not sown." [22]He said to him,
"You wicked servant! Out of your own
mouth I condemn you. So you knew that I
was an exacting man, gathering in what I
have not laid out and reaping what I have not
sown? [23]Then why did you not put my money
in the bank? On my return I could have
drawn it out with interest." [24]And he said to
those standing by, "Take the pound from
him and give it to the man who has ten
pounds." [25]And they said to him, "But, sir,
he has ten pounds . . ." [26]"I tell you, to
everyone who has will be given more; but
anyone who has not will be deprived even of
what he has.

[27]"As for my enemies who did not want me
for their king, bring them here and execute
them in my presence." '

V: TEACHING IN JERUSALEM

The Messiah enters Jerusalem

[28]When he had said this he went on ahead,
going up to Jerusalem. [29]Now it happened
that when he was near Bethphage and
Bethany, close by the Mount of Olives as it
is called, he sent two of the disciples, saying,
[30]'Go to the village opposite, and as you enter
it you will find a tethered colt that no one has
ever yet ridden. Untie it and bring it here.
[31]If anyone asks you, "Why are you untying
it?" you are to say this, "The Master needs
it." ' [32]The messengers went off and found
everything just as he had told them. [33]As they
were untying the colt, its owners said, 'Why
are you untying it?' [34]and they answered,
'The Master needs it.'

[35]So they took the colt to Jesus and,
throwing their cloaks on its back, they lifted
Jesus on to it. [36]As he moved off, they spread
their cloaks in the road, [37]and now, as he
was approaching the downward slope of the
Mount of Olives, the whole group of disciples
joyfully began to praise God at the top of
their voices for all the miracles they had seen.
[38]They cried out:

Blessed is he who is coming
as King *in the name of the Lord!*[a]
Peace in heaven
and glory in the highest heavens!

Jesus defends his disciples for acclaiming him

[39]Some Pharisees in the crowd said to him,
'Master, reprove your disciples,' [40]but he
answered, 'I tell you, if these keep silence,
the stones will cry out.'

Lament for Jerusalem

[41]As he drew near and came in sight of the
city he shed tears over it [42]and said, 'If you
too had only recognised on this day the way
to peace! But in fact it is hidden from your
eyes! [43]Yes, a time is coming when your
enemies will raise fortifications all round you,
when they will encircle you and hem you in

19a Ps 118:26.

on every side; [44]they will dash you and the children inside your walls to the ground; they will leave not one stone standing on another within you, because you did not recognise the moment of your visitation.'

The expulsion of the dealers from the Temple

[45]Then he went into the Temple and began driving out those who were busy trading, saying to them, [46]'According to scripture, *my house shall be a house of prayer* but you have turned it into *a bandits' den*.'[b]

Jesus teaches in the Temple

[47]He taught in the Temple every day. The chief priests and the scribes, in company with the leading citizens, tried to do away with him, [48]but they could not find a way to carry this out because the whole people hung on his words.

The Jews question the authority of Jesus

20 Now it happened that one day while he was teaching the people in the Temple and proclaiming the good news, the chief priests and the scribes came up, together with the elders, [2]and spoke to him. 'Tell us,' they said, 'what authority have you for acting like this? Or who gives you this authority?' [3]In reply he said to them, 'And I will ask you a question, just one. Tell me: [4]John's baptism: what was its origin, heavenly or human?' [5]And they debated this way among themselves, 'If we say heavenly, he will retort, "Why did you refuse to believe him?"; [6]and if we say human, the whole people will stone us, for they are convinced that John was a prophet.' [7]So their reply was that they did not know where it came from. [8]And Jesus said to them, 'Nor will I tell you my authority for acting like this.'

Parable of the wicked tenants

[9]And he went on to tell the people this parable, 'A man planted a vineyard and leased it to tenants, and went abroad for a long while. [10]When the right time came, he sent a servant to the tenants to get his share of the produce of the vineyard. But the tenants thrashed him, and sent him away empty-handed. [11]But he went on to send a second servant; they thrashed him too and treated him shamefully and sent him away empty-handed. [12]He still went on to send a third; they wounded this one too, and threw him out. [13]Then the owner of the vineyard thought, "What am I to do? I will send them my own beloved son. Perhaps they will respect him." [14]But when the tenants saw him they put their heads together saying, "This is the heir, let us kill him so that the inheritance will be ours." [15]So they threw him out of the vineyard and killed him.

'Now what will the owner of the vineyard do to them? [16]He will come and make an end of these tenants and give the vineyard to others.' Hearing this they said, 'God forbid!' [17]But he looked hard at them and said, 'Then what does this text in the scriptures mean:

The stone which the builders rejected
has become the cornerstone?[a]

[18]Anyone who falls on that stone will be dashed to pieces; anyone it falls on will be crushed.'

[19]And the scribes and the chief priests would have liked to lay hands on him that very moment, because they realised that this parable was aimed at them, but they were afraid of the people.

On tribute to Caesar

[20]So they awaited their opportunity and sent agents to pose as upright men, and to catch him out in something he might say and so enable them to hand him over to the jurisdiction and authority of the governor. [21]They put to him this question, 'Master, we know that you say and teach what is right; you favour no one, but teach the way of God in all honesty. [22]Is it permissible for us to pay taxes to Caesar or not?' [23]But he was aware of their cunning and said, [24]'Show me a denarius. Whose portrait and title are on it?' They said, 'Caesar's.' [25]He said to them, 'Well then, pay Caesar what belongs to Caesar—and God what belongs to God.'

[26]They were unable to catch him out in anything he had to say in public; they were amazed at his answer and were silenced.

19b Is 56:7 and Jr 7:11.
20a Ps 118:22.

The resurrection of the dead

27 Some Sadducees—those who argue that
there is no resurrection—approached him
and they put this question to him, 28 'Master,
Moses prescribed for us, if a man's married
brother dies childless, the man must marry
the widow to raise up children for his brother.
29 Well then, there were seven brothers; the
first, having married a wife, died childless.
30 The second 31 and then the third married
the widow. And the same with all seven, they
died leaving no children. 32 Finally the woman
herself died. 33 Now, at the resurrection,
whose wife will she be, since she had been
married to all seven?'
34 Jesus replied, 'The children of this world
take wives and husbands, 35 but those who
are judged worthy of a place in the other
world and in the resurrection from the dead
do not marry 36 because they can no longer
die, for they are the same as the angels, and
being children of the resurrection they are
children of God. 37 And Moses himself implies
that the dead rise again, in the passage about
the bush where he calls the Lord *the God of
Abraham, the God of Isaac and the God of
Jacob*.[b] 38 Now he is God, not of the dead, but
of the living; for to him everyone is alive.'
39 Some scribes then spoke up. They said,
'Well put, Master.' 40 They did not dare to
ask him any more questions.

Christ not only son but also Lord of David

41 He then said to them, 'How can people
maintain that the Christ is son of David?
42 Why, David himself says in the Book of
Psalms:

The Lord declared to my Lord,
take your seat at my right hand,
43 *till I have made your enemies*
your footstool.[c]

44 David here calls him Lord; how then can
he be his son?'

The scribes condemned by Jesus

45 While all the people were listening he said
to the disciples, 46 'Beware of the scribes who
like to walk about in long robes and love to
be greeted respectfully in the market squares,
to take the front seats in the synagogues and
the places of honour at banquets, 47 who
devour the property of widows, and for show
offer long prayers. The more severe will be
the sentence they receive.'

The widow's mite

21 Looking up, he saw rich people putting
their offerings into the treasury; 2 and
he noticed a poverty-stricken widow putting
in two small coins, 3 and he said, 'I tell you
truly, this poor widow has put in more than
any of them; 4 for these have all put in money
they could spare, but she in her poverty has
put in all she had to live on.'

Discourse on the destruction of Jerusalem: Introduction

5 When some were talking about the Temple,
remarking how it was adorned with fine
stonework and votive offerings, he said, 6 'All
these things you are staring at now—the time
will come when not a single stone will be left
on another; everything will be destroyed.'
7 And they put to him this question, 'Master,'
they said, 'when will this happen, then, and
what sign will there be that it is about to take
place?'

The warning signs

8 But he said, 'Take care not to be deceived,
because many will come using my name and
saying, "I am the one" and "The time is near
at hand." Refuse to join them. 9 And when
you hear of wars and revolutions, do not be
terrified, for this is something that must
happen first, but the end will not come at
once.' 10 Then he said to them, 'Nation will
fight against nation, and kingdom against
kingdom. 11 There will be great earthquakes
and plagues and famines in various places;
there will be terrifying events and great signs
from heaven.
12 'But before all this happens, you will be
seized and persecuted; you will be handed
over to the synagogues and to imprisonment,
and brought before kings and governors for
the sake of my name 13—and that will be your
opportunity to bear witness. 14 Make up your

20b Ex 3:6.
20c Ps 110:1.

minds not to prepare your defence, [15]because
I myself shall give you an eloquence and a
wisdom that none of your opponents will be
able to resist or contradict. [16]You will be
betrayed even by parents and brothers,
relations and friends; and some of you will
be put to death. [17]You will be hated univer-
sally on account of my name, [18]but not a hair
of your head will be lost. [19]Your perseverance
will win you your lives.

The siege

[20]'When you see Jerusalem surrounded by
armies, then you must realise that it will soon
be laid desolate. [21]Then those in Judaea must
escape to the mountains, those inside the city
must leave it, and those in country districts
must not take refuge in it. [22]For this is the
time of retribution when all that scripture
says must be fulfilled. [23]Alas for those with
child, or with babies at the breast, when those
days come!

The disaster and the age of the gentiles

[24]'For great misery will descend on the land
and retribution on this people. They will fall
by the edge of the sword and be led captive
to every gentile country; and Jerusalem will
be trampled down by the gentiles until their
time is complete.

Cosmic disasters and the glorious appearing of the Son of man

[25]'There will be signs in the sun and moon
and stars; on earth nations in agony, bewil-
dered by the turmoil of the ocean and its
waves; [26]men fainting away with terror and
fear at what menaces the world, for the
powers of heaven will be shaken. [27]And then
they will see the *Son of man coming in a cloud*
with power and great glory.[a] [28]When these
things begin to take place, stand erect, hold
your heads high, because your liberation is
near at hand.'

The time of this coming

[29]And he told them a parable, 'Look at the
fig tree and indeed every tree. [30]As soon as
you see them bud, you can see for yourselves
that summer is now near. [31]So with you when
you see these things happening: know that
the kingdom of God is near. [32]In truth I tell
you, before this generation has passed away
all will have taken place. [33]Sky and earth will
pass away, but my words will never pass
away.

Be on the alert

[34]'Watch yourselves, or your hearts will be
coarsened by debauchery and drunkenness
and the cares of life, and that day will come
upon you unexpectedly, [35]like a trap. For it
will come down on all those living on the face
of the earth. [36]Stay awake, praying at all times
for the strength to survive all that is going to
happen, and to hold your ground before the
Son of man.'

The last days of Jesus

[37]All day long he would be in the Temple
teaching, but would spend the night in the
open on the hill called the Mount of Olives.
[38]And from early morning the people
thronged to him in the Temple to listen
to him.

VI: THE PASSION[a]

The conspiracy against Jesus: Judas betrays him

22 The feast of Unleavened Bread, called
the Passover, was now drawing near,
[2]and the chief priests and the scribes were
looking for some way of doing away with
him, because they were afraid of the people.
[3]Then Satan entered into Judas, surnamed
Iscariot, who was one of the Twelve. [4]He
approached the chief priests and the officers
of the guard to discuss some way of handing

21a Dn 7:13–14.
22a For this section Lk has a good deal of information which he does not share with Mt and Mk. It is often close to Jn.

Jesus over to them. [5]They were delighted and agreed to give him money. [6]He accepted and began to look for an opportunity to betray him to them without people knowing about it.

Preparation for the Passover supper

[7]The day of Unleavened Bread came round, on which the Passover had to be sacrificed, [8]and he sent Peter and John, saying, 'Go and make the preparations for us to eat the Passover.' [9]They asked him, 'Where do you want us to prepare it?' [10]He said to them, 'Look, as you go into the city you will meet a man carrying a pitcher of water. Follow him into the house he enters [11]and tell the owner of the house, "The Master says this to you: Where is the room for me to eat the Passover with my disciples?" [12]The man will show you a large upper room furnished with couches. Make the preparations there.' [13]They set off and found everything as he had told them and prepared the Passover.

The supper

[14]When the time came he took his place at table, and the apostles with him. [15]And he said to them, 'I have ardently longed to eat this Passover with you before I suffer; [16]because, I tell you, I shall not eat it until it is fulfilled in the kingdom of God.'

[17]Then, taking a cup, he gave thanks and said, 'Take this and share it among you, [18]because from now on, I tell you, I shall never again drink wine until the kingdom of God comes.'

The institution of the Eucharist

[19]Then he took bread, and when he had given thanks, he broke it and gave it to them, saying, 'This is my body given for you; do this in remembrance of me.' [20]He did the same with the cup after supper, and said, 'This cup is the new covenant in my blood poured out for you.

The treachery of Judas foretold

[21]'But look, here with me on the table is the hand of the man who is betraying me. [22]The Son of man is indeed on the path which was decreed, but alas for that man by whom he is betrayed!' [23]And they began to ask one another which of them it could be who was to do this.

Who is the greatest?

[24]An argument also began between them about who should be reckoned the greatest; [25]but he said to them, 'Among the gentiles it is the kings who lord it over them, and those who have authority over them are given the title Benefactor. [26]With you this must not happen. No; the greatest among you must behave as if he were the youngest, the leader as if he were the one who serves. [27]For who is the greater: the one at table or the one who serves? The one at table, surely? Yet here am I among you as one who serves!

The reward promised to the apostles

[28]'You are the men who have stood by me faithfully in my trials; [29]and now I confer a kingdom on you, just as my Father conferred one on me: [30]you will eat and drink at my table in my kingdom, and you will sit on thrones to judge the twelve tribes of Israel.

Peter's denial and repentance foretold

[31]'Simon, Simon! Look, Satan has got his wish to sift you all like wheat; [32]but I have prayed for you, Simon, that your faith may not fail, and once you have recovered, you in your turn must strengthen your brothers.' [33]'Lord,' he answered, 'I would be ready to go to prison with you, and to death.' [34]Jesus replied, 'I tell you, Peter, by the time the cock crows today you will have denied three times that you know me.'

A time of crisis

[35]He said to them, 'When I sent you out without purse or haversack or sandals, were you short of anything?' [36]'No, nothing,' they said. He said to them, 'But now if you have a purse, take it, and the same with a haversack; if you have no sword, sell your cloak and buy one, [37]because I tell you these words of scripture are destined to be fulfilled in me: *He was counted as one of the rebellious.*[b] Yes, what it says about me is even now

22b Is 53:12.

reaching its fulfilment.' 38They said, 'Lord,
here are two swords.' He said to them, 'That
is enough!'

The Mount of Olives

39He then left to make his way as usual to the
Mount of Olives, with the disciples
following. 40When he reached the place he
said to them, 'Pray not to be put to the test.'
41Then he withdrew from them, about a
stone's throw away, and knelt down and
prayed. 42'Father,' he said, 'if you are willing,
take this cup away from me. Nevertheless,
let your will be done, not mine.' 43Then an
angel appeared to him, coming from heaven
to give him strength. 44In his anguish he
prayed even more earnestly, and his sweat
fell to the ground like great drops of blood.
45When he rose from prayer he went to the
disciples and found them sleeping for sheer
grief. 46And he said to them, 'Why are you
asleep? Get up and pray not to be put to the
test.'

The arrest

47Suddenly, while he was still speaking, a
number of men appeared, and at the head
of them the man called Judas, one of the
Twelve, who went up to Jesus to kiss him.
48Jesus said, 'Judas, are you betraying the
Son of man with a kiss?' 49His followers,
seeing what was about to happen, said, 'Lord,
shall we use our swords?' 50And one of them
struck the high priest's servant and cut off
his right ear. 51But at this Jesus said, 'That is
enough.' And touching the man's ear he
healed him.
52Then Jesus said to the chief priests and
captains of the Temple guard and elders who
had come for him, 'Am I a bandit, that you
had to set out with swords and clubs? 53When
I was among you in the Temple day after day
you never made a move to lay hands on me.
But this is your hour; this is the reign of
darkness.'

Peter's denials

54They seized him then and led him away,
and they took him to the high priest's house.
Peter followed at a distance. 55They had lit a
fire in the middle of the courtyard and Peter
sat down among them, 56and as he was sitting
there by the blaze a servant-girl saw him,
peered at him, and said, 'This man was with
him too.' 57But he denied it. 'Woman, I do
not know him,' he said. 58Shortly afterwards
someone else saw him and said, 'You are one
of them too.' But Peter replied, 'I am not,
my friend.' 59About an hour later another
man insisted, saying, 'This fellow was
certainly with him. Why, he is a Galilean.'
60Peter said, 'My friend, I do not know what
you are talking about.' At that instant, while
he was still speaking, the cock crowed, 61and
the Lord turned and looked straight at Peter,
and Peter remembered the Lord's words
when he had said to him, 'Before the cock
crows today, you will have disowned me
three times.' 62And he went outside and wept
bitterly.

Jesus mocked by the guards

63Meanwhile the men who guarded Jesus
were mocking and beating him. 64They blind-
folded him and questioned him, saying,
'Prophesy! Who hit you then?' 65And they
heaped many other insults on him.

Jesus before the Sanhedrin

66When day broke there was a meeting of the
elders of the people, the chief priests and
scribes. He was brought before their council,
67and they said to him, 'If you are the Christ,
tell us.' He replied, 'If I tell you, you will
not believe, 68and if I question you, you will
not answer. 69But from now on, the *Son of*
man will be *seated at the* right hand of the
Power *of God*.'[c] 70They all said, 'So you are
the Son of God then?' He answered, 'It is you
who say I am.' 71Then they said, 'Why do we
need any evidence? We have heard it for
ourselves from his own lips.'

23 The whole assembly then rose, and
they brought him before Pilate.

Jesus before Pilate

2They began their accusation by saying, 'We
found this man inciting our people to revolt,
opposing payment of the tribute to Caesar,
and claiming to be Christ, a king.' 3Pilate put
to him this question, 'Are you the king of the
Jews?' He replied, 'It is you who say it.'

22c Ps 110:1.

[4]Pilate then said to the chief priests and the
crowd, 'I find no case against this man.' [5]But
they persisted, 'He is inflaming the people
with his teaching all over Judaea and all the
way from Galilee, where he started, down to
here.' [6]When Pilate heard this, he asked if
the man were a Galilean; [7]and finding that he
came under Herod's jurisdiction, he passed
him over to Herod, who was also in Jerusalem
at that time.

Jesus before Herod

[8]Herod was delighted to see Jesus; he had
heard about him and had been wanting for a
long time to set eyes on him; moreover, he
was hoping to see some miracle worked by
him. [9]So he questioned him at some length,
but without getting any reply. [10]Meanwhile
the chief priests and the scribes were there,
vigorously pressing their accusations. [11]Then
Herod, together with his guards, treated him
with contempt and made fun of him; he put
a rich cloak on him and sent him back to
Pilate. [12]And though Herod and Pilate had
been enemies before, they were reconciled
that same day.

Jesus before Pilate again

[13]Pilate then summoned the chief priests and
the leading men and the people. [14]He said to
them, 'You brought this man before me as a
popular agitator. Now I have gone into the
matter myself in your presence and found no
grounds in the man for any of the charges
you bring against him. [15]Nor has Herod
either, since he has sent him back to us. As
you can see, the man has done nothing that
deserves death, [16]so I shall have him flogged
and then let him go.'[17][a] [18]But as one man
they howled, 'Away with him! Give us
Barabbas!' [19](This man had been thrown into
prison because of a riot in the city and
murder.)

[20]In his desire to set Jesus free, Pilate
addressed them again, [21]but they shouted
back, 'Crucify him! Crucify him!' [22]And for
the third time he spoke to them, 'But what
harm has this man done? I have found no
case against him that deserves death, so I
shall have him flogged and then let him go.'
[23]But they kept on shouting at the top of
their voices, demanding that he should be
crucified. And their shouts kept growing
louder.

[24]Pilate then gave his verdict: their demand
was to be granted. [25]He released the man they
asked for, who had been imprisoned because
of rioting and murder, and handed Jesus over
to them to deal with as they pleased.

The way to Calvary

[26]As they were leading him away they seized
on a man, Simon from Cyrene, who was
coming in from the country, and made him
shoulder the cross and carry it behind Jesus.
[27]Large numbers of people followed him, and
women too, who mourned and lamented for
him. [28]But Jesus turned to them and said,
'Daughters of Jerusalem, do not weep for
me; weep rather for yourselves and for your
children. [29]For look, the days are surely
coming when people will say, "Blessed are
those who are barren, the wombs that have
never borne children, the breasts that have
never suckled!" [30]Then they will begin to *say
to the mountains, "Fall on us!"; to the hills,
"Cover us!"*[b] [31]For if this is what is done to
green wood, what will be done when the
wood is dry?' [32]Now they were also leading
out two others, criminals, to be executed
with him.

The crucifixion

[33]When they reached the place called The
Skull, there they crucified him and the two
criminals, one on his right, the other on his
left. [34]Jesus said, 'Father, forgive them; they
do not know what they are doing.' Then they
cast lots to share out his clothing.

The crucified Christ is mocked

[35]The people stayed there watching. As for
the leaders, they jeered at him with the
words, 'He saved others, let him save himself
if he is the Christ of God, the Chosen One.'
[36]The soldiers mocked him too, coming up
to him, offering him vinegar, [37]and saying,
'If you are the king of the Jews, save yourself.'
[38]Above him there was an inscription: 'This
is the King of the Jews'.

23a Some authorities add v. 17, borrowed from Mt 27:15.
23b Ho 10:8.

The good thief

39One of the criminals hanging there abused him: 'Are you not the Christ? Save yourself and us as well.' 40But the other spoke up and rebuked him. 'Have you no fear of God at all?' he said. 'You got the same sentence as he did, 41but in our case we deserved it: we are paying for what we did. But this man has done nothing wrong.' 42Then he said, 'Jesus, remember me when you come into your kingdom.' 43He answered him, 'In truth I tell you, today you will be with me in paradise.'

The death of Jesus

44It was now about the sixth hour and the sun's light failed, so that darkness came over the whole land until the ninth hour. 45The veil of the Sanctuary was torn right down the middle. 46Jesus cried out in a loud voice saying, 'Father, *into your hands I commit my spirit.*'[c] With these words he breathed his last.

After the death

47When the centurion saw what had taken place, he gave praise to God and said, 'Truly, this was an upright man.' 48And when all the crowds who had gathered for the spectacle saw what had happened, they went home beating their breasts.

49All his friends stood at a distance; so also did the women who had accompanied him from Galilee and saw all this happen.

The burial

50And now a member of the Council arrived, a good and upright man named Joseph. 51He had not consented to what the others had planned and carried out. He came from Arimathaea, a Jewish town, and he lived in the hope of seeing the kingdom of God. 52This man went to Pilate and asked for the body of Jesus. 53He then took it down, wrapped it in a shroud and put it in a tomb which was hewn in stone and which had never held a body. 54It was Preparation day and the Sabbath was beginning to grow light.

55Meanwhile the women who had come from Galilee with Jesus were following behind. They took note of the tomb and how the body had been laid.

56Then they returned and prepared spices and ointments. And on the Sabbath day they rested, as the Law required.

VII: AFTER THE RESURRECTION

The empty tomb. The angel's message

24 On the first day of the week, at the first sign of dawn, they went to the tomb with the spices they had prepared. 2They found that the stone had been rolled away from the tomb, 3but on entering they could not find the body of the Lord Jesus. 4As they stood there puzzled about this, two men in brilliant clothes suddenly appeared at their side. 5Terrified, the women bowed their heads to the ground. But the two said to them, 'Why look among the dead for someone who is alive? 6He is not here; he has risen. Remember what he told you when he was still in Galilee: 7that the Son of man was destined to be handed over into the power of sinful men and be crucified, and rise again on the third day.' 8And they remembered his words.

The apostles refuse to believe the women

9And they returned from the tomb and told all this to the Eleven and to all the others. 10The women were Mary of Magdala, Joanna, and Mary the mother of James. And the other women with them also told the apostles, 11but this story of theirs seemed pure nonsense, and they did not believe them.

Peter at the tomb

12Peter, however, went off to the tomb, running. He bent down and looked in and saw the linen cloths but nothing else; he then went back home, amazed at what had happened.

23c Ps 31:5.

The road to Emmaus

13 Now that very same day, two of them were
on their way to a village called Emmaus,
seven miles from Jerusalem, 14 and they were
talking together about all that had happened.
15 And it happened that as they were talking
together and discussing it, Jesus himself
came up and walked by their side; 16 but their
eyes were prevented from recognising him.
17 He said to them, 'What are all these things
that you are discussing as you walk along?'
They stopped, their faces downcast.
18 Then one of them, called Cleopas,
answered him, 'You must be the only person
staying in Jerusalem who does not know the
things that have been happening there these
last few days.' 19 He asked, 'What things?'
They answered, 'All about Jesus of Nazareth,
who showed himself a prophet powerful in
action and speech before God and the whole
people; 20 and how our chief priests and our
leaders handed him over to be sentenced to
death, and had him crucified. 21 Our own
hope had been that he would be the one to
set Israel free. And this is not all: two whole
days have now gone by since it all happened;
22 and some women from our group have
astounded us: they went to the tomb in the
early morning, 23 and when they could not
find the body, they came back to tell us they
had seen a vision of angels who declared he
was alive. 24 Some of our friends went to the
tomb and found everything exactly as the
women had reported, but of him they saw
nothing.'
25 Then he said to them, 'You foolish men!
So slow to believe all that the prophets have
said! 26 Was it not necessary that the Christ
should suffer before entering into his glory?'
27 Then, starting with Moses and going
through all the prophets, he explained to
them the passages throughout the scriptures
that were about himself.
28 When they drew near to the village to
which they were going, he made as if to go
on; 29 but they pressed him to stay with them
saying, 'It is nearly evening, and the day is
almost over.' So he went in to stay with them.
30 Now while he was with them at table, he
took the bread and said the blessing; then he
broke it and handed it to them. 31 And their
eyes were opened and they recognised him;
but he had vanished from their sight. 32 Then
they said to each other, 'Did not our hearts
burn within us as he talked to us on the road
and explained the scriptures to us?'
33 They set out that instant and returned
to Jerusalem. There they found the Eleven
assembled together with their companions,
34 who said to them, 'The Lord has indeed
risen and has appeared to Simon.' 35 Then
they told their story of what had happened
on the road and how they had recognised him
at the breaking of bread.

Jesus appears to the apostles

36 They were still talking about all this when
he himself stood among them and said to
them, 'Peace be with you!' 37 In a state of
alarm and fright, they thought they were
seeing a ghost. 38 But he said, 'Why are you
so agitated, and why are these doubts stirring
in your hearts? 39 See by my hands and my
feet that it is I myself. Touch me and see for
yourselves; a ghost has no flesh and bones as
you can see I have.' 40 And as he said this he
showed them his hands and his feet. 41 Their
joy was so great that they still could not
believe it, as they were dumbfounded; so he
said to them, 'Have you anything here to
eat?' 42 And they offered him a piece of grilled
fish, 43 which he took and ate before their
eyes.

Last instructions to the apostles

44 Then he told them, 'This is what I meant
when I said, while I was still with you, that
everything written about me in the Law of
Moses, in the Prophets and in the Psalms,
was destined to be fulfilled.' 45 He then
opened their minds to understand the scrip-
tures, 46 and he said to them, 'So it is written
that the Christ would suffer and on the third
day rise from the dead, 47 and that, in his
name, repentance for the forgiveness of sins
would be preached to all nations, beginning
from Jerusalem. 48 You are witnesses to this.
49 'And now I am sending upon you what
the Father has promised. Stay in the city,
then, until you are clothed with the power
from on high.'

The ascension

50 Then he took them out as far as the outskirts
of Bethany, and raising his hands he blessed
them. 51 Now as he blessed them, he withdrew
from them and was carried up to heaven.
52 They worshipped him and then went back
to Jerusalem full of joy; 53 and they were
continually in the Temple praising God.

THE GOSPEL OF JOHN

The fourth gospel stands apart from the others in several ways. Instead of the patchwork quilt of little incidents of the Synoptics, this gospel is conceived on broader lines. Episodes are followed by a developed discourse or dialogue which explains the meaning of the signs: Jesus is the revelation of the Father. He replaces in his own person the Temple and the religious institutions of the Jews. All those who encounter Jesus judge themselves by their response to him and to his message. Finally, the Hour of Jesus, his passion and resurrection, is not a disgrace but is the triumph of the King Messiah.

The plan and pattern of the gospel are also different. Instead of a Galilean ministry followed by a final week in Jerusalem, there is a passing backwards and forwards between Galilee and Jerusalem, and the highly significant cleansing of the Temple dramatises Jesus' message not at the end but at the beginning of the ministry. Many of the themes of the gospel are gathered up in the great discourse at the Last Supper (chh. 14–17) when Jesus assures his followers of his continuing presence in his Spirit, who will guide them into all truth. The stress on the Spirit of truth now present brings a new emphasis: many of the blessings of the final coming are seen as already present whereas the first three gospels look for them in the future. The final conflict with the powers of evil is already taking place, and eternal life is already granted to believers.

Ancient tradition associates the gospel with John the Apostle, but modern studies show that a complex process of development occurred, either from a primitive core or from several separate sources. Such a development, through a group of John's disciples in the latter half of the first century, would account for numerous repetitions and overlaps, the result of a determination to lose nothing of the tradition of the teaching of the Beloved Disciple.

PLAN OF THE BOOK

THE GOSPEL ACCORDING TO JOHN

A: PROLOGUE

1 In the beginning was the Word:[a]
the Word was with God
and the Word was God.
2 He was with God in the beginning.
3 Through him all things came into being,
not one thing came into being
except through him.
4 What has come into being in him was life,
life that was the light of men;
5 and light shines in darkness,
and darkness could not overpower it.

6 A man came, sent by God.
His name was John.
7 He came as a witness,
to bear witness to the light,
so that everyone might believe
through him.
8 He was not the light,
he was to bear witness to the light.

9 The Word was the real light
that gives light to everyone;
he was coming into the world.
10 He was in the world
that had come into being through him,
and the world did not recognise him.
11 He came to his own
and his own people did not accept him.
12 But to those who did accept him
he gave power to become children of God,
to those who believed in his name
13 who were[b] born not from human stock
or human desire
or human will
but from God himself.
14 The Word became flesh,
he lived among us,
and we saw his glory,
the glory that he has from the Father
as only Son of the Father,
full of grace and truth.

15 John witnesses to him. He proclaims:
'This is the one of whom I said:
He who comes after me
has passed ahead of me
because he existed before me.'

16 Indeed, from his fullness
we have, all of us, received—
one gift replacing another,
17 for the Law was given through Moses,
grace and truth have come
through Jesus Christ.
18 No one has ever seen God;
it is the only Son,
who is close to the Father's heart,
who has made him known.

1a In the OT the Word or Wisdom of God is present with God before the world existed and reveals God to the world. Jn sees this Word-Wisdom in the person of Jesus.
1b Some MSS have the singular 'was', which would refer to Jesus' divine origin.

B: JESUS' MINISTRY

I: PROCLAMATION OF THE NEW ORDER: THE MINISTRY OF JESUS

A: THE OPENING WEEK

The witness of John

[19]This was the witness of John, when the
Jews sent to him priests and Levites from
Jerusalem to ask him, 'Who are you?' [20]He
declared, he did not deny but declared, 'I am
not the Christ.' [21]So they asked, 'Then are
you Elijah?' He replied, 'I am not.' 'Are you
the Prophet?' He answered, 'No.' [22]So they
said to him, 'Who are you? We must take
back an answer to those who sent us. What
have you to say about yourself?' [23]So he said,
'I am, as Isaiah prophesied:

A voice of one that cries in the desert:
Prepare a way for the Lord.
Make his paths straight!'[c]

[24]Now those who had been sent were Phar-
isees, [25]and they put this question to him,
'Why are you baptising if you are not the
Christ, and not Elijah, and not the Prophet?'
[26]John answered them, 'I baptise with water;
but standing among you—unknown to you—
[27]is the one who is coming after me; and I am
not fit to undo the strap of his sandal.' [28]This
happened at Bethany, on the far side of the
Jordan, where John was baptising.
[29]The next day, he saw Jesus coming
towards him and said, 'Look, there is the
lamb of God that takes away the sin of the
world. [30]It was of him that I said, "Behind
me comes one who has passed ahead of me
because he existed before me." [31]I did not
know him myself, and yet my purpose in
coming to baptise with water was so that he
might be revealed to Israel.' [32]And John
declared, 'I saw the Spirit come down on him
like a dove from heaven and rest on him. [33]I
did not know him myself, but he who sent
me to baptise with water had said to me,
"The man on whom you see the Spirit come
down and rest is the one who is to baptise
with the Holy Spirit." [34]I have seen and I
testify that he is the Chosen One of God.'

The first disciples

[35]The next day as John stood there again with
two of his disciples, Jesus went past, [36]and
John looked towards him and said, 'Look,
there is the lamb of God.' [37]And the two
disciples heard what he said and followed
Jesus. [38]Jesus turned round, saw them
following and said, 'What do you want?'
They answered, 'Rabbi'—which means
Teacher—'where do you live?' [39]He replied,
'Come and see'; so they went and saw where
he lived, and stayed with him that day. It was
about the tenth hour.
[40]One of these two who became followers
of Jesus after hearing what John had said was
Andrew, the brother of Simon Peter. [41]The
first thing Andrew did was to find his brother
and say to him, 'We have found the
Messiah'—which means the Christ—[42]and
he took Simon to Jesus. Jesus looked at him
and said, 'You are Simon son of John; you
are to be called Cephas'—which means Rock.
[43]The next day, after Jesus had decided to
leave for Galilee, he met Philip and said,
'Follow me.' [44]Philip came from the same
town, Bethsaida, as Andrew and Peter.
[45]Philip found Nathanael and said to him,
'We have found him of whom Moses in the
Law and the prophets wrote, Jesus son of
Joseph, from Nazareth.' [46]Nathanael said to
him, 'From Nazareth? Can anything good
come from that place?' Philip replied, 'Come
and see.' [47]When Jesus saw Nathanael
coming he said of him, 'There, truly, is an
Israelite in whom there is no deception.'
[48]Nathanael asked, 'How do you know me?'
Jesus replied, 'Before Philip came to call you,
I saw you under the fig tree.' [49]Nathanael
answered, 'Rabbi, you are the Son of God,
you are the king of Israel.' [50]Jesus replied,
'You believe that just because I said: I

1c Is 40:3.

saw you under the fig tree. You are going to see greater things than that.' [51]And then he added, 'In all truth I tell you, you will see heaven open and the angels of God ascending and descending over the Son of man.'

The wedding at Cana

2 On the third day there was a wedding at Cana in Galilee. The mother of Jesus was there, [2]and Jesus and his disciples had also been invited. [3]And they ran out of wine, since the wine provided for the feast had all been used, and the mother of Jesus said to him, 'They have no wine.' [4]Jesus said, 'Woman, what do you want from me? My hour has not come yet.' [5]His mother said to the servants, '*Do whatever he tells you.*'[a] [6]There were six stone water jars standing there, meant for the ablutions that are customary among the Jews: each could hold twenty or thirty gallons. [7]Jesus said to the servants, 'Fill the jars with water,' and they filled them to the brim. [8]Then he said to them, 'Draw some out now and take it to the president of the feast.' [9]They did this; the president tasted the water, and it had turned into wine. Having no idea where it came from—though the servants who had drawn the water knew—the president of the feast called the bridegroom [10]and said, 'Everyone serves good wine first and the worse wine when the guests are well wined; but you have kept the best wine till now.'

[11]This was the first of Jesus' signs: it was at Cana in Galilee. He revealed his glory, and his disciples believed in him. [12]After this he went down to Capernaum with his mother and his brothers and his disciples, but they stayed there only a few days.

B: THE PASSOVER

The cleansing of the Temple

[13]When the time of the Jewish Passover was near Jesus went up to Jerusalem, [14]and in the Temple he found people selling cattle and sheep and doves, and the money changers sitting there. [15]Making a whip out of cord, he drove them all out of the Temple, sheep and cattle as well, scattered the money changers' coins, knocked their tables over [16]and said to the dove sellers, 'Take all this out of here and stop using my Father's house as a market.' [17]Then his disciples remembered the words of scripture: ***I am eaten up with zeal for your house.***[b] [18]The Jews intervened and said, 'What sign can you show us that you should act like this?' [19]Jesus answered, 'Destroy this Temple, and in three days I will raise it up.' [20]The Jews replied, 'It has taken forty-six years to build this Temple:[c] are you going to raise it up again in three days?' [21]But he was speaking of the Temple that was his body, [22]and when Jesus rose from the dead, his disciples remembered that he had said this, and they believed the scripture and what he had said.

Jesus in Jerusalem

[23]During his stay in Jerusalem for the feast of the Passover many believed in his name when they saw the signs that he did, [24]but Jesus knew all people and did not trust himself to them; [25]he never needed evidence about anyone; he could tell what someone had within.

The conversation with Nicodemus

3 There was one of the Pharisees called Nicodemus, a leader of the Jews, [2]who came to Jesus by night and said, 'Rabbi, we know that you have come from God as a teacher; for no one could perform the signs that you do unless God were with him.' [3]Jesus answered:

In all truth I tell you,
no one can see the kingdom of God
without being born from above.

[4]Nicodemus said, 'How can anyone who is already old be born? Is it possible to go back into the womb again and be born?' [5]Jesus replied:

In all truth I tell you,
no one can enter the kingdom of God
without being born
  through water and the Spirit;
[6]what is born of human nature is human;
what is born of the Spirit is spirit.

2a Gn 41:55.
2b Ps 69:9.
2c Reconstruction work began in 19 BC, so this is Passover AD 28.

[7]Do not be surprised when I say:
You must be born from above.
[8]The wind blows where it pleases;
you can hear its sound,
but you cannot tell where it comes from
or where it is going.
So it is with everyone
who is born of the Spirit.

[9]'How is that possible?' asked Nicodemus.
[10]Jesus replied, 'You are the Teacher of
Israel, and you do not know these things!

[11]'In all truth I tell you,
we speak only about what we know
and witness only to what we have seen
and yet you people reject our evidence.
[12]If you do not believe me
when I speak to you about earthly things,
how will you believe me
when I speak to you about heavenly things?
[13]No one has gone up to heaven
except the one
who came down from heaven,
the Son of man;
[14]as Moses lifted up the snake in the desert,
so must the Son of man be lifted up
[15]so that everyone who believes
may have eternal life in him.
[16]For this is how God loved the world:
he gave his only Son,
so that everyone who believes in him
may not perish
but may have eternal life.
[17]For God sent his Son into the world
not to judge the world,
but so that through him
the world might be saved.
[18]No one who believes in him
will be judged;
but whoever does not believe
is judged already,
because that person does not believe
in the Name of God's only Son.
[19]And the judgement is this:
though the light has come into the world
people have preferred
darkness to the light
because their deeds were evil.
[20]And indeed, everybody who does wrong
hates the light and avoids it,
to prevent his actions
from being shown up;
[21]but whoever does the truth
comes out into the light,
so that what he is doing
may plainly appear as done in God.'

Jesus' ministry in Judaea
John bears witness for the last time

[22]After this, Jesus went with his disciples
into the Judaean countryside and stayed with
them there and baptised. [23]John also was
baptising at Aenon near Salim, where there
was plenty of water, and people were going
there and were being baptised. [24]For John
had not yet been put in prison.

[25]Now a discussion arose between some of
John's disciples and a Jew about purification,
[26]so they went to John and said, 'Rabbi, the
man who was with you on the far side of the
Jordan, the man to whom you bore witness,
is baptising now, and everyone is going to
him.' [27]John replied:

'No one can have anything
except what is given him from heaven.

[28]'You yourselves can bear me out. I said, "I
am not the Christ; I am the one who has been
sent to go in front of him."

[29]'It is the bridegroom who has the bride;
and yet the bridegroom's friend,
who stands there and listens to him,
is filled with joy at the bridegroom's voice.
This is the joy I feel, and it is complete.
[30]He must grow greater,
I must grow less.
[31]He who comes from above
is above all others;
he who is of the earth
is earthly himself
and speaks in an earthly way.
He who comes from heaven
[32]bears witness to the things
he has seen and heard,
but his testimony
is not accepted by anybody;
[33]though anyone
who does accept his testimony
is attesting that God is true,
[34]since he whom God has sent
speaks God's own words,
for God gives him the Spirit
without reserve.
[35]The Father loves the Son
and has entrusted everything to his hands.
[36]Anyone who believes in the Son
has eternal life,
but anyone who refuses
to believe in the Son
will never see life:
God's retribution hangs over him.'

Jesus among the Samaritans

4 When Jesus heard that the Pharisees had
found out that he was making and
baptising more disciples than John — 2 though
in fact it was his disciples who baptised, not
Jesus himself — 3 he left Judaea and went back
to Galilee. 4 He had to pass through Samaria.
5 On the way he came to the Samaritan town
called Sychar near the land that Jacob gave
to his son Joseph. 6 Jacob's well was there and
Jesus, tired by the journey, sat down by the
well. It was about the sixth hour. 7 When a
Samaritan woman came to draw water, Jesus
said to her, 'Give me something to drink.'
8 His disciples had gone into the town to buy
food. 9 The Samaritan woman said to him,
'You are a Jew. How is it that you ask me, a
Samaritan, for something to drink?' — Jews,
of course, do not associate with Samaritans.
10 Jesus replied to her:

If you only knew what God is offering
and who it is that is saying to you,
'Give me something to drink,'
you would have been the one to ask,
and he would have given you living water.

11 'You have no bucket, sir,' she answered,
'and the well is deep: how do you get this
living water? 12 Are you a greater man than
our father Jacob, who gave us this well and
drank from it himself with his sons and his
cattle?' 13 Jesus replied:

Whoever drinks this water
will be thirsty again;
14 but no one who drinks the water
  that I shall give
will ever be thirsty again:
the water that I shall give
will become a spring of water within,
  welling up for eternal life.

15 'Sir,' said the woman, 'give me some of
that water, so that I may never be thirsty or
come here again to draw water.' 16 'Go and
call your husband,' said Jesus to her, 'and
come back here.' 17 The woman answered, 'I
have no husband.' Jesus said to her, 'You are
right to say, "I have no husband"; 18 for
although you have had five, the one you now
have is not your husband. You spoke the
truth there.' 19 'I see you are a prophet, sir,'
said the woman. 20 'Our fathers worshipped
on this mountain,[a] though you say that Jeru-
salem is the place where one ought to
worship.' 21 Jesus said:

Believe me, woman, the hour is coming
when you will worship the Father
neither on this mountain
  nor in Jerusalem.
22 You worship what you do not know;
we worship what we do know;
for salvation comes from the Jews.
23 But the hour is coming —
  indeed is already here —
when true worshippers
  will worship the Father
    in spirit and truth:
that is the kind of worshipper
the Father seeks.
24 God is spirit,
and those who worship
must worship in spirit and truth.

25 The woman said to him, 'I know that
Messiah — that is, Christ — is coming; and
when he comes he will explain everything.'
26 Jesus said, 'That is who I am, I who speak
to you.'
27 At this point his disciples returned and
were surprised to find him speaking to a
woman, though none of them asked, 'What
do you want from her?' or, 'What are you
talking to her about?' 28 The woman put down
her water jar and hurried back to the town to
tell the people, 29 'Come and see a man who
has told me everything I have done; could
this be the Christ?' 30 This brought people
out of the town and they made their way
towards him.
31 Meanwhile, the disciples were urging
him, 'Rabbi, do have something to eat'; 32 but
he said, 'I have food to eat that you do not
know about.' 33 So the disciples said to one
another, 'Has someone brought him food?'
34 But Jesus said:

My food
is to do the will of the one who sent me,
and to complete his work.
35 Do you not have a saying:
Four months and then the harvest?
Well, I tell you,
look around you, look at the fields;
already they are white,
  ready for harvest!
36 Already the reaper
  is being paid his wages,

4a Gerizim, where there had been a Temple rivalling Jerusalem's. To Jesus both are provisional.

already he is bringing in the grain
for eternal life,
so that sower and reaper
can rejoice together.
37 For here the proverb holds true:
one sows, another reaps;
38 I sent you to reap
a harvest you have not laboured for.
Others have laboured for it;
and you have come
into the rewards of their labour.

39 Many Samaritans of that town believed
in him on the strength of the woman's words
of testimony, 'He told me everything I have
done.' 40 So, when the Samaritans came up to
him, they begged him to stay with them. He
stayed for two days, and 41 many more came
to believe on the strength of the words he
spoke to them; 42 and they said to the woman,
'Now we believe no longer because of what
you told us; we have heard him ourselves
and we know that he is indeed the Saviour of
the world.'

Jesus in Galilee

43 When the two days were over Jesus left for
Galilee. 44 He himself had declared that a
prophet is not honoured in his own home
town. 45 On his arrival the Galileans received
him well, having seen all that he had done at
Jerusalem during the festival which they too
had attended.

Second sign at Cana
The cure of a royal official's son

46 He went again to Cana in Galilee, where he
had changed the water into wine. And there
was a royal official whose son was ill at
Capernaum; 47 hearing that Jesus had arrived
in Galilee from Judaea, he went and asked
him to come and cure his son, as he was at
the point of death. 48 Jesus said to him, 'Unless
you see signs and portents you will not
believe!' 49 'Sir,' answered the official, 'come
down before my child dies.' 50 'Go home,'
said Jesus, 'your son will live.' The man
believed what Jesus had said and went on his
way home; 51 and while he was still on the
way his servants met him with the news that
his boy was alive. 52 He asked them when the
boy had begun to recover. They replied, 'The
fever left him yesterday at the seventh hour.'
53 The father realised that this was exactly the
time when Jesus had said, 'Your son will
live'; and he and all his household believed.
54 This new sign, the second, Jesus
performed on his return from Judaea to
Galilee.

II: THE SECOND FEAST AT JERUSALEM: FIRST OPPOSITION TO REVELATION

The cure of a sick man at the Pool of Bethesda

5 After this there was a Jewish festival, and
Jesus went up to Jerusalem. 2 Now in
Jerusalem next to the Sheep Pool there is a
pool called Bethesda in Hebrew, which has
five porticos; 3 and under these were crowds
of sick people, blind, lame, paralysed.[a] 5 One
man there had an illness which had lasted
thirty-eight years, 6 and when Jesus saw him
lying there and knew he had been in that
condition for a long time, he said, 'Do you
want to be well again?' 7 'Sir,' replied the sick
man, 'I have no one to put me into the pool
when the water is disturbed; and while I am
still on the way, someone else gets down there
before me.' 8 Jesus said, 'Get up, pick up your
sleeping-mat and walk around.' 9 The man
was cured at once, and he picked up his mat
and started to walk around.

Now that day happened to be the Sabbath,
10 so the Jews said to the man who had been
cured, 'It is the Sabbath; you are not allowed
to carry your sleeping-mat.' 11 He replied,
'But the man who cured me told me, "Pick
up your sleeping-mat and walk around." '
12 They asked, 'Who is the man who said to
you, "Pick up your sleeping-mat and walk
around"? ' 13 The man had no idea who it

5a Some ancient MSS add: 'waiting for the water to move;[4] for at intervals the angel of the Lord came down into the pool, and the water was disturbed, and the first person to enter the water after this disturbance was cured of any ailment from which he was suffering'.

was, since Jesus had disappeared, as the place
was crowded. 14 After a while Jesus met him
in the Temple and said, 'Now you are well
again, do not sin any more, or something
worse may happen to you.' 15 The man went
back and told the Jews that it was Jesus who
had cured him. 16 It was because he did things
like this on the Sabbath that the Jews began
to harass Jesus. 17 His answer to them was,
'My Father still goes on working, and I am
at work, too.' 18 But that only made the Jews
even more intent on killing him, because not
only was he breaking the Sabbath, but he
spoke of God as his own Father and so made
himself God's equal.

19 To this Jesus replied:

In all truth I tell you,
by himself the Son can do nothing;
he can do only
what he sees the Father doing:
and whatever the Father does
the Son does too.
20 For the Father loves the Son
and shows him everything
he himself does,
and he will show him
even greater things than these,
works that will astonish you.
21 Thus, as the Father raises the dead
and gives them life,
so the Son gives life to anyone he chooses;
22 for the Father judges no one;
he has entrusted all judgement to the Son,
23 so that all may honour the Son
as they honour the Father.
Whoever refuses honour to the Son
refuses honour to the Father
who sent him.
24 In all truth I tell you,
whoever listens to my words,
and believes in the one who sent me,
has eternal life;
without being brought to judgement
such a person
has passed from death to life.
25 In all truth I tell you,
the hour is coming—
indeed it is already here—
when the dead
will hear the voice of the Son of God,
and all who hear it will live.
26 For as the Father has life in himself,
so he has granted the Son also
to have life in himself;
27 and, because he is the Son of man,
has granted him power
to give judgement.
28 Do not be surprised at this,
for the hour is coming
when the dead will leave their graves
at the sound of his voice:
29 those who did good
will come forth to life;
and those who did evil
will come forth to judgement.
30 By myself I can do nothing;
I can judge only as I am told to judge,
and my judging is just,
because I seek to do not my own will
but the will of him who sent me.
31 Were I to testify on my own behalf,
my testimony would not be true;
32 but there is another witness
who speaks on my behalf,
and I know that his testimony is true.
33 You sent messengers to John,
and he gave his testimony to the truth—
34 not that I depend on human testimony;
no, it is for your salvation
that I mention it.
35 John was a lamp lit and shining
and for a time you were content
to enjoy the light that he gave.
36 But my testimony is greater than John's:
the deeds my Father has given me
to perform,
these same deeds of mine
testify that the Father has sent me.
37 Besides, the Father who sent me
bears witness to me himself.
You have never heard his voice,
you have never seen his shape,
38 and his word finds no home in you
because you do not believe
in the one whom he has sent.

39 You pore over the scriptures,
believing that in them
you can find eternal life;
it is these scriptures that testify to me,
40 and yet you refuse to come to me
to receive life!
41 Human glory means nothing to me.
42 Besides, I know you too well:
you have no love of God in you.
43 I have come in the name of my Father
and you refuse to accept me;
if someone else should come
in his own name
you would accept him.

44How can you believe,
since you look to each other for glory
and are not concerned
with the glory that comes
from the one God?
45Do not imagine
that I am going to accuse you
before the Father:
you have placed your hopes on Moses,
and Moses will be the one
who accuses you.
46If you really believed him
you would believe me too,
since it was about me that he was writing;
47but if you will not believe what he wrote,
how can you believe what I say?

III: THE PASSOVER OF THE BREAD OF LIFE: FURTHER OPPOSITION TO REVELATION

The miracle of the loaves

6After this, Jesus crossed the Sea of
Galilee—or of Tiberias— 2and a large
crowd followed him, impressed by the signs
he had done in curing the sick. 3Jesus climbed
the hillside and sat down there with his
disciples. 4The time of the Jewish Passover
was near.
5Looking up, Jesus saw the crowds
approaching and said to Philip, 'Where can
we buy some bread for these people to eat?'
6He said this only to put Philip to the test; he
himself knew exactly what he was going to
do. 7Philip answered, 'Two hundred denarii
would not buy enough to give them a little
piece each.' 8One of his disciples, Andrew,
Simon Peter's brother, said, 9'Here is a small
boy with five barley loaves and two fish; but
what is that among so many?' 10Jesus said to
them, 'Make the people sit down.' There was
plenty of grass there, and as many as five
thousand men sat down. 11Then Jesus took
the loaves, gave thanks, and distributed them
to those who were sitting there; he then did
the same with the fish, distributing as much
as they wanted. 12When they had eaten
enough he said to the disciples, 'Pick up the
pieces left over, so that nothing is wasted.'
13So they picked them up and filled twelve
large baskets with scraps left over from the
meal of five barley loaves. 14Seeing the sign
that he had done, the people said, 'This is
indeed the prophet who is to come into the
world.' 15Jesus, as he realised they were about
to come and take him by force and make him
king, fled back to the hills alone.

Jesus comes to his disciples walking on the waters

16That evening the disciples went down to
the shore of the sea 17and got into a boat to
make for Capernaum on the other side of the
sea. It was getting dark by now and Jesus
had still not rejoined them. 18The wind was
strong, and the sea was getting rough. 19They
had rowed three or four miles when they saw
Jesus walking on the sea and coming towards
the boat. They were afraid, 20but he said,
'It's me. Don't be afraid.' 21They were ready
to take him into the boat, and immediately it
reached the shore at the place they were
making for.

The discourse in the synagogue at Capernaum

22Next day, the crowd that had stayed on the
other side saw that only one boat had been
there, and that Jesus had not got into the
boat with his disciples, but that the disciples
had set off by themselves. 23Other boats,
however, had put in from Tiberias, near
the place where the bread had been eaten.
24When the people saw that neither Jesus nor
his disciples were there, they got into those
boats and crossed to Capernaum to look for
Jesus. 25When they found him on the other
side, they said to him, 'Rabbi, when did you
come here?' 26Jesus answered:

In all truth I tell you,
you are looking for me
not because you have seen the signs
but because you had all the bread
you wanted to eat.
27Do not work for food that goes bad,
but work for food
that endures for eternal life,
which the Son of man will give you,
for on him the Father, God himself,
has set his seal.

28Then they said to him, 'What must we
do if we are to carry out God's work?' 29Jesus

gave them this answer, 'This is carrying out
God's work: you must believe in the one he
has sent.' 30So they said, 'What sign will you
yourself do, the sight of which will make us
believe in you? What work will you do? 31Our
fathers ate manna in the desert; as scripture
says: *He gave them bread from heaven to eat.*'[a]
32Jesus answered them:

In all truth I tell you,
it was not Moses
who gave you the bread from heaven,
it is my Father
who gives you the bread from heaven,
the true bread;
33for the bread of God
is the bread
which comes down from heaven
and gives life to the world.

34'Sir,' they said, 'give us that bread always.'
35Jesus answered them:

I am the bread of life.
No one who comes to me will ever hunger;
no one who believes in me will ever thirst.
36But, as I have told you,
you can see me and still you do not believe.
37Everyone whom the Father gives me
will come to me;
I will certainly not reject
anyone who comes to me,
38because I have come from heaven,
not to do my own will,
but to do the will of him who sent me.
39Now the will of him who sent me
is that I should lose nothing
of all that he has given to me,
but that I should raise it up
on the last day.
40It is my Father's will
that whoever sees the Son
and believes in him
should have eternal life,
and that I should raise that person up
on the last day.

41Meanwhile the Jews were complaining
to each other about him, because he had said,
'I am the bread that has come down from
heaven.' 42They were saying, 'Surely this is
Jesus son of Joseph, whose father and mother
we know. How can he now say, "I have come
down from heaven?" ' 43Jesus said in reply
to them, 'Stop complaining to each other.

44'No one can come to me
unless drawn by the Father who sent me,
and I will raise that person up
on the last day.
45It is written in the prophets:
They will all be taught by God;[b]
everyone who has listened to the Father,
and learnt from him,
comes to me.
46Not that anybody has seen the Father,
except him who has his being from God:
he has seen the Father.
47In all truth I tell you,
everyone who believes has eternal life.
48I am the bread of life.
49Your fathers ate manna in the desert
and they are dead;
50but this is the bread
which comes down from heaven,
so that a person may eat it and not die.
51I am the living bread
which has come down from heaven.
Anyone who eats this bread
will live for ever;
and the bread that I shall give
is my flesh, for the life of the world.'

52Then the Jews started arguing among
themselves, 'How can this man give us his
flesh to eat?' 53Jesus replied to them:

In all truth I tell you,
if you do not eat
the flesh of the Son of man
and drink his blood,
you have no life in you.
54Anyone who does eat my flesh
and drink my blood
has eternal life,
and I shall raise that person up
on the last day.
55For my flesh is real food
and my blood is real drink.
56Whoever eats my flesh
and drinks my blood
lives in me
and I live in that person.
57As the living Father sent me
and I draw life from the Father,
so whoever eats me
will also draw life from me.
58This is the bread
which has come down from heaven;
it is not like the bread our ancestors ate:

6a Ps 78:24. 'Bread from heaven' is commented vv. 32–48 and 'to eat' vv. 49–58.
6b Is 54:13.

they are dead,
but anyone who eats this bread
will live for ever.

59 This is what he taught at Capernaum in
the synagogue. 60 After hearing it, many of his
followers said, 'This is intolerable language.
How could anyone accept it?' 61 Jesus was
aware that his followers were complaining
about it and said, 'Does this disturb you?
62 What if you should see the Son of man
ascend to where he was before?

63 'It is the spirit that gives life,
the flesh has nothing to offer.
The words I have spoken to you are spirit
and they are life.

64 'But there are some of you who do not
believe.' For Jesus knew from the outset who
did not believe and who was to betray him.
65 He went on, 'This is why I told you that no
one could come to me except by the gift of
the Father.' 66 After this, many of his disciples
went away and accompanied him no more.

Peter's profession of faith

67 Then Jesus said to the Twelve, 'What about
you, do you want to go away too?' 68 Simon
Peter answered, 'Lord, to whom shall we go?
You have the message of eternal life, 69 and
we believe; we have come to know that you
are the Holy One of God.' 70 Jesus replied to
them, 'Did I not choose the Twelve of you?
Yet one of you is a devil.' 71 He meant Judas
son of Simon Iscariot, since this was the man,
one of the Twelve, who was to betray him.

IV: THE FEAST OF SHELTERS: THE GREAT REJECTION

Jesus goes up to Jerusalem for the feast and teaches there

7 After this Jesus travelled round Galilee;
he could not travel round Judaea, because
the Jews were seeking to kill him.
2 As the Jewish feast of Shelters drew near,
3 his brothers said to him, 'Leave this place
and go to Judaea, so that your disciples, too,
can see the works you are doing; 4 no one who
wants to be publicly known acts in secret; if
this is what you are doing, you should reveal
yourself to the world.' 5 Not even his brothers
had faith in him. 6 Jesus answered, 'For me
the right time has not come yet, but for you
any time is the right time. 7 The world cannot
hate you, but it does hate me, because I give
evidence that its ways are evil. 8 Go up to the
festival yourselves: I am not going to this
festival, because for me the time is not ripe
yet.' 9 Having said that, he stayed behind in
Galilee.
10 However, after his brothers had left for
the festival, he went up as well, not publicly
but secretly. 11 At the festival the Jews were
on the look-out for him: 'Where is he?' they
said. 12 There was a great deal of talk about
him in the crowds. Some said, 'He is a good
man'; others, 'No, he is leading the people
astray.' 13 Yet no one spoke about him openly,
for fear of the Jews.
14 When the festival was half over, Jesus
went to the Temple and began to teach. 15 The
Jews were astonished and said, 'How did he
learn to read? He has not been educated.'
16 Jesus answered them:

'My teaching is not from myself:
it comes from the one who sent me;
17 anyone who is prepared to do his will,
will know whether my teaching
is from God
or whether I speak on my own account.
18 When someone speaks
on his own account,
he is seeking honour for himself;
but when he is seeking
the honour of the person who sent him,
then he is true
and altogether without dishonesty.
19 Did not Moses give you the Law?
And yet not one of you keeps the Law!

'Why do you want to kill me?' 20 The crowd
replied, 'You are mad! Who wants to kill
you?' 21 Jesus answered, 'One work I did, and
you are all amazed at it. 22 Moses ordered you
to practise circumcision—not that it began
with him, it goes back to the patriarchs—and
you circumcise on the Sabbath. 23 Now if
someone can be circumcised on the Sabbath
so that the Law of Moses is not broken, why
are you angry with me for making someone

completely healthy on a Sabbath? [24]Do not
keep judging according to appearances; let
your judgement be according to what is
right.'

"You will look for me
and will not find me;
where I am,
you cannot come?" '

The people discuss the origin of the Messiah

[25]Meanwhile some of the people of Jerusalem
were saying, 'Isn't this the man they want to
kill? [26]And here he is, speaking openly, and
they have nothing to say to him! Can it be
true the authorities have recognised that he
is the Christ? [27]Yet we all know where he
comes from, but when the Christ appears no
one will know where he comes from.'
[28]Then, as Jesus was teaching in the
Temple, he cried out:

You know me
and you know where I came from.
Yet I have not come of my own accord:
but he who sent me is true;
You do not know him,
[29]but I know him
because I have my being from him
and it was he who sent me.

[30]They wanted to arrest him then, but
because his hour had not yet come no one
laid a hand on him.

Jesus foretells his approaching departure

[31]There were many people in the crowds,
however, who believed in him; they were
saying, 'When the Christ comes, will he give
more signs than this man has?' [32]Hearing
that talk like this about him was spreading
among the people, the Pharisees sent the
Temple guards to arrest him.
[33]Then Jesus said:

For a short time I am with you still;
then I shall go back to the one
who sent me.
[34]You will look for me
and will not find me;
where I am
you cannot come.

[35]So the Jews said to one another, 'Where
is he intending to go that we shall not be able
to find him? Is he intending to go abroad to
the people who are dispersed among the
Greeks and to teach the Greeks? [36]What does
he mean when he says:

The promise of living water

[37]On the last day, the great day of the festival,
Jesus stood and cried out:

'Let anyone who is thirsty come to me!
[38]Let anyone who believes in me
come and drink!

As scripture says, "From his heart shall flow
streams of living water." '
[39]He was speaking of the Spirit which those
who believed in him were to receive; for there
was no Spirit as yet because Jesus had not yet
been glorified.

Fresh discussions on the origin of the Messiah

[40]Some of the crowd who had been listening
said, 'He is indeed the prophet,' [41]and some
said, 'He is the Christ,' but others said,
'Would the Christ come from Galilee? [42]Does
not scripture say that the Christ must be
descended from David and come from
Bethlehem, the village where David was?'
[43]So the people could not agree about him.
[44]Some wanted to arrest him, but no one
actually laid a hand on him.
[45]The guards went back to the chief priests
and Pharisees who said to them, 'Why
haven't you brought him?' [46]The guards
replied, 'No one has ever spoken like this
man.' [47]'So,' the Pharisees answered, 'you,
too, have been led astray? [48]Have any of the
authorities come to believe in him? Any of
the Pharisees? [49]This rabble knows nothing
about the Law—they are damned.' [50]One of
them, Nicodemus—the same man who had
come to Jesus earlier—said to them, [51]'But
surely our Law does not allow us to pass
judgement on anyone without first giving
him a hearing and discovering what he is
doing?' [52]To this they answered, 'Are you a
Galilean too? Go into the matter, and see
for yourself: prophets do not arise in
Galilee.'

The adulterous woman[a]

53They all went home,
8 and Jesus went to the Mount of Olives.
2At daybreak he appeared in the Temple
again; and as all the people came to him, he
sat down and began to teach them.
3The scribes and Pharisees brought a
woman along who had been caught commit-
ting adultery; and making her stand there in
the middle 4they said to Jesus, 'Master, this
woman was caught in the very act of commit-
ting adultery, 5and in the Law Moses has
ordered us to stone women of this kind. What
have you got to say?' 6They asked him this
as a test, looking for an accusation to use
against him. But Jesus bent down and started
writing on the ground with his finger. 7As
they persisted with their question, he
straightened up and said, 'Let the one among
you who is guiltless be the first to throw
a stone at her.' 8Then he bent down and
continued writing on the ground. 9When
they heard this they went away one by one,
beginning with the eldest, until the last one
had gone and Jesus was left alone with the
woman, who remained in the middle. 10Jesus
again straightened up and said, 'Woman,
where are they? Has no one condemned you?'
11'No one, sir,' she replied. 'Neither do I
condemn you,' said Jesus. 'Go away, and
from this moment sin no more.'

Jesus, the light of the world

12When Jesus spoke to the people again, he
said:

I am the light of the world;
anyone who follows me
will not be walking in the dark,
but will have the light of life.

A discussion on the testimony of Jesus to himself

13At this the Pharisees said to him, 'You are
testifying on your own behalf; your testimony
is not true.' 14Jesus replied:

Even though I am testifying
on my own behalf,
my testimony is still true,
because I know
where I have come from
and where I am going;
but you do not know
where I come from or where I am going.
15You judge by human standards;
I judge no one,
16but if I judge,
my judgement will be true,
because I am not alone:
the one who sent me is with me;
17and in your Law it is written
that the testimony of two witnesses is
true.
18I testify on my own behalf,
but the Father who sent me
testifies on my behalf, too.

19They asked him, 'Where is your Father
then?' Jesus answered:

You do not know me,
nor do you know my Father;
if you did know me,
you would know my Father as well.

20He spoke these words in the Treasury,
while teaching in the Temple. No one
arrested him, because his hour had not yet
come.
21Again he said to them:

I am going away; you will look for me
and you will die in your sin.
Where I am going, you cannot come.

22So the Jews said to one another, 'Is he
going to kill himself, that he says, "Where
I am going, you cannot come?"' 23Jesus
went on:

You are from below;
I am from above.
You are of this world;
I am not of this world.
24I have told you already:
You will die in your sins.
Yes, if you do not believe that I am He,[a]
you will die in your sins.

25So they said to him, 'Who are you?' Jesus
answered:

What I have told you from the outset.
26About you I have much to say
and much to judge;
but the one who sent me is true,
and what I declare to the world
I have learnt from him.

7a Many ancient MSS omit 7:53—8:11.
8a Here and in vv. 28, 58 Jesus appropriates the divine name revealed to Moses in Ex 3:14.

27 They did not recognise that he was talking to them about the Father. 28 So Jesus said:

When you have lifted up the Son of man,
then you will know that I am He
and that I do nothing of my own accord.
What I say
is what the Father has taught me;
29 he who sent me is with me,
and has not left me to myself,
for I always do what pleases him.

30 As he was saying this, many came to believe in him.

Jesus and Abraham

31 To the Jews who believed in him Jesus said:

If you make my word your home
you will indeed be my disciples;
32 you will come to know the truth,
and the truth will set you free.

33 They answered, 'We are descended from
Abraham and we have never been the slaves
of anyone; what do you mean, "You will be
set free?" ' 34 Jesus replied:

In all truth I tell you,
everyone who commits sin is a slave.
35 Now a slave has no permanent standing
in the household,
but a son belongs to it for ever.
36 So if the Son sets you free,
you will indeed be free.
37 I know that you are descended
from Abraham;
but you want to kill me
because my word finds no place in you.
38 What I speak of
is what I have seen at my Father's side,
and you too put into action
the lessons you have learnt
from your father.

39 They repeated, 'Our father is Abraham.' Jesus said to them:

If you are Abraham's children,
do as Abraham did.
40 As it is, you want to kill me,
a man who has told you the truth
as I have learnt it from God;
that is not what Abraham did.
41 You are doing your father's work.

They replied, 'We were not born illegit-
imate, the only father we have is God.'
42 Jesus answered:

If God were your father,
you would love me,
since I have my origin in God
and have come from him;
I did not come of my own accord,
but he sent me.
43 Why do you not understand what I say?
Because you cannot bear to listen
to my words.
44 You are from your father, the devil,
and you prefer to do
what your father wants.
He was a murderer from the start;
he was never grounded in the truth;
there is no truth in him at all.
When he lies
he is speaking true to his nature,
because he is a liar, and the father of lies.
45 But it is because I speak the truth
that you do not believe me.
46 Can any of you convict me of sin?
If I speak the truth,
why do you not believe me?
47 Whoever comes from God
listens to the words of God;
the reason why you do not listen
is that you are not from God.

48 The Jews replied, 'Are we not right in saying that you are a Samaritan and possessed by a devil?' Jesus answered:

49 I am not possessed;
but I honour my Father,
and you deny me honour.
50 I do not seek my own glory;
there is someone who does seek it
and is the judge of it.
51 In all truth I tell you,
whoever keeps my word
will never see death.

52 The Jews said, 'Now we know that you
are possessed. Abraham is dead, and the
prophets are dead, and yet you say,
"Whoever keeps my word will never know
the taste of death." 53 Are you greater than
our father Abraham, who is dead? The
prophets are dead too. Who are you claiming
to be?' 54 Jesus answered:

If I were to seek my own glory
my glory would be worth nothing;
in fact, my glory
is conferred by the Father,
by the one of whom you say,
'He is our God,'
55 although you do not know him.

But I know him,
and if I were to say, 'I do not know him,'
I should be a liar, as you yourselves are.
But I do know him, and I keep his word.
56Your father Abraham rejoiced
to think that he would see my Day;
he saw it and was glad.

57The Jews then said, 'You are not fifty
yet, and you have seen Abraham!' 58Jesus
replied:

In all truth I tell you,
before Abraham ever was,
I am.

59At this they picked up stones to throw
at him; but Jesus hid himself and left the
Temple.

The cure of the man born blind

9 As he went along, he saw a man who
had been blind from birth. 2His disciples
asked him, 'Rabbi, who sinned, this man or
his parents, that he should have been born
blind?' 3'Neither he nor his parents sinned,'
Jesus answered, 'he was born blind so that
the works of God might be revealed in him.

4'As long as day lasts
we must carry out the work of the one
who sent me;
the night will soon be here
when no one can work.
5As long as I am in the world
I am the light of the world.'

6Having said this, he spat on the ground,
made a paste with the spittle, put this over
the eyes of the blind man, 7and said to him,
'Go and wash in the Pool of Siloam' (the name
means 'one who has been sent'). So he went
off and washed and came back able to see.
8His neighbours and the people who used
to see him before (for he was a beggar) said,
'Isn't this the man who used to sit and beg?'
9Some said, 'Yes, it is the same one.' Others
said, 'No, but he looks just like him.' The
man himself said, 'Yes, I am the one.' 10So
they said to him, 'Then how is it that your
eyes were opened?' 11He answered, 'The man
called Jesus made a paste, daubed my eyes
with it and said to me, "Go off and wash at
Siloam"; so I went, and when I washed I
gained my sight.' 12They asked, 'Where is
he?' He answered, 'I don't know.'
13They brought to the Pharisees the man
who had been blind. 14It had been a Sabbath
day when Jesus made the paste and opened
the man's eyes, 15so when the Pharisees asked
him how he had gained his sight, he said, 'He
put a paste on my eyes, and I washed, and I
can see.' 16Then some of the Pharisees said,
'That man cannot be from God: he does not
keep the Sabbath.' Others said, 'How can a
sinner produce signs like this?' And there
was division among them. 17So they spoke to
the blind man again, 'What have you to say
about him yourself, now that he has opened
your eyes?' The man answered, 'He is a
prophet.'
18However, the Jews would not believe
that the man had been blind without first
sending for the parents of the man who had
gained his sight and 19asking them, 'Is this
man really the son of yours who you say was
born blind? If so, how is it that he is now able
to see?' 20His parents answered, 'We know
he is our son and we know he was born blind,
21but how he can see, we don't know, nor
who opened his eyes. Ask him. He is old
enough: let him speak for himself.' 22His
parents spoke like this out of fear of the Jews,
who had already agreed to ban from the
synagogue anyone who should acknowledge
Jesus as the Christ. 23This was why his
parents said, 'He is old enough; ask him.'
24So the Jews sent for the man again and
said to him, 'Give glory to God! We are
satisfied that this man is a sinner.' 25The man
answered, 'Whether he is a sinner I don't
know; all I know is that I was blind and now
I can see.' 26They said to him, 'What did he
do to you? How did he open your eyes?'
27He replied, 'I have told you once and you
wouldn't listen. Why do you want to hear it
all again? Do you want to become his disciples
yourselves?' 28At this they hurled abuse at
him, 'It is you who are his disciple, we are
disciples of Moses: 29we know that God spoke
to Moses, but as for this man, we don't know
where he comes from.' 30The man replied,
'That is just what is so amazing! You don't
know where he comes from and he has opened
my eyes! 31We know that God doesn't listen
to sinners, but God does listen to people who
are devout and do his will. 32Ever since the
world began it is unheard of for anyone to
open the eyes of someone born blind; 33if this
man were not from God, he wouldn't have
been able to do anything.' 34They retorted,
'Are you trying to teach us, and you a sinner

through and through ever since you were
born!' And they ejected him.
35 Jesus heard they had ejected him, and
when he found him he said to him, 'Do you
believe in the Son of man?' 36 'Sir,' the man
replied, 'tell me who he is so that I may
believe in him.' 37 Jesus said, 'You have seen
him; he is speaking to you.' 38 The man said,
'Lord, I believe,' and worshipped him.
39 Jesus said:

It is for judgement
that I have come into this world,
so that those without sight may see
and those with sight may become blind.

40 Hearing this, some Pharisees who were
present said to him, 'So we are blind, are
we?' 41 Jesus replied:

If you were blind,
you would not be guilty,
but since you say, 'We can see,'
your guilt remains.

The good shepherd[a]

10 'In all truth I tell you, anyone who does
not enter the sheepfold through the
gate, but climbs in some other way, is a thief
and a bandit. 2 He who enters through the
gate is the shepherd of the flock; 3 the gate-
keeper lets him in, the sheep hear his voice,
one by one he calls his own sheep and leads
them out. 4 When he has brought out all those
that are his, he goes ahead of them, and the
sheep follow because they know his voice.
5 They will never follow a stranger, but will
run away from him because they do not
recognise the voice of strangers.'
6 Jesus told them this parable but they
failed to understand what he was saying to
them.
7 So Jesus spoke to them again:

In all truth I tell you,
I am the gate of the sheepfold.
8 All who have come before me
are thieves and bandits,
but the sheep took no notice of them.
9 I am the gate.
Anyone who enters through me
will be safe:
such a one will go in and out
and will find pasture.
10 The thief comes
only to steal and kill and destroy.
I have come
so that they may have life
and have it to the full.
11 I am the good shepherd:
the good shepherd lays down his life
for his sheep.
12 The hired man,
since he is not the shepherd
and the sheep do not belong to him,
abandons the sheep
as soon as he sees a wolf coming,
and runs away,
and then the wolf attacks
and scatters the sheep;
13 he runs away
because he is only a hired man
and has no concern for the sheep.
14 I am the good shepherd;
I know my own
and my own know me,
15 just as the Father knows me
and I know the Father;
and I lay down my life for my sheep.
16 And there are other sheep I have
that are not of this fold,
and I must lead these too.
They too will listen to my voice,
and there will be only one flock,
one shepherd.
17 The Father loves me,
because I lay down my life
in order to take it up again.
18 No one takes it from me;
I lay it down of my own free will,
and as I have power to lay it down,
so I have power to take it up again;
and this is the command
I have received from my Father.

19 These words caused a fresh division
among the Jews. 20 Many said, 'He is
possessed, he is raving; why do you listen to
him?' 21 Others said, 'These are not the words
of a man possessed by a devil: could a devil
open the eyes of the blind?'

10a cf. Jr 23; Ezk 34.

V: THE FEAST OF DEDICATION: THE DECISION TO KILL JESUS

Jesus claims to be the Son of God

22 It was the time of the feast of Dedication in
Jerusalem. It was winter, 23 and Jesus was in
the Temple walking up and down in the
Portico of Solomon. 24 The Jews gathered
round him and said, 'How much longer are
you going to keep us in suspense? If you are
the Christ, tell us openly.' 25 Jesus replied:

I have told you, but you do not believe.
The works I do in my Father's name
are my witness;
26 but you do not believe,
because you are no sheep of mine.
27 The sheep that belong to me
listen to my voice;
I know them and they follow me.
28 I give them eternal life;
they will never be lost
and no one will ever steal them
from my hand.
29 The Father, for what he has given me,
is greater than anyone,
and no one can steal anything
from the Father's hand.
30 The Father and I are one.

31 The Jews fetched stones to stone him,
32 so Jesus said to them, 'I have shown you
many good works from my Father; for which
of these are you stoning me?' 33 The Jews
answered him, 'We are stoning you, not for
doing a good work, but for blasphemy;
though you are only a man, you claim to be
God.' 34 Jesus answered:

Is it not written in your Law:
I said, you are gods?[b]
35 So it uses the word 'gods'
of those people to whom
the word of God was addressed
—and scripture cannot be set aside.
36 Yet to someone
whom the Father has consecrated
and sent into the world you say,
'You are blaspheming'
because I said, 'I am Son of God.'
37 If I am not doing my Father's work,
there is no need to believe me;
38 but if I am doing it,
then even if you refuse to believe in me,
at least believe in the work I do;
then you will know for certain
that the Father is in me
and I am in the Father.

39 They again wanted to arrest him then,
but he eluded their clutches.

Jesus withdraws to the other side of the Jordan

40 He went back again to the far side of the
Jordan to the district where John had been
baptising at first and he stayed there. 41 Many
people who came to him said, 'John gave no
signs, but all he said about this man was
true'; 42 and many of them believed in him.

VI: JESUS MOVES TOWARDS HIS DEATH

The resurrection of Lazarus

11 There was a man named Lazarus of
Bethany, the village of Mary and her
sister, Martha, and he was ill. 2 It was the same
Mary, the sister of the sick man Lazarus, who
anointed the Lord with ointment and wiped
his feet with her hair. 3 The sisters sent this
message to Jesus, 'Lord, the man you love is
ill.' 4 On receiving the message, Jesus said,
'This sickness will not end in death, but it is
for God's glory so that through it the Son of
God may be glorified.'

5 Jesus loved Martha and her sister and
Lazarus, 6 yet when he heard that he was ill
he stayed where he was for two more days
7 before saying to the disciples, 'Let us go
back to Judaea.' 8 The disciples said, 'Rabbi,

10b Ps 82:6.

it is not long since the Jews were trying to
stone you; are you going back there again?'
9 Jesus replied:

Are there not twelve hours in the day?
No one who walks in the daytime
stumbles,
having the light of this world to see by;
10 anyone who walks around at night
stumbles,
having no light as a guide.

11 He said that and then added, 'Our friend
Lazarus is at rest; I am going to wake him.'
12 The disciples said to him, 'Lord, if he is at
rest he will be saved.' 13 Jesus was speaking
of the death of Lazarus, but they thought
that by 'rest' he meant 'sleep'; 14 so Jesus put
it plainly, 'Lazarus is dead; 15 and for your
sake I am glad I was not there because now
you will believe. But let us go to him.' 16 Then
Thomas—known as the Twin—said to the
other disciples, 'Let us also go to die with
him.'

17 On arriving, Jesus found that Lazarus
had been in the tomb for four days already.
18 Bethany is only about two miles from Jeru-
salem, 19 and many Jews had come to Martha
and Mary to comfort them about their
brother. 20 When Martha heard that Jesus was
coming she went to meet him. Mary remained
sitting in the house. 21 Martha said to Jesus,
'Lord, if you had been here, my brother
would not have died, 22 but even now I know
that God will grant whatever you ask of him.'
23 Jesus said to her, 'Your brother will
rise again.' 24 Martha said, 'I know he will rise
again at the resurrection on the last day.'
25 Jesus said:

I am the resurrection.
Anyone who believes in me,
even though that person dies, will live,
26 and whoever lives and believes in me
will never die.
Do you believe this?

27 'Yes, Lord,' she said, 'I believe that you
are the Christ, the Son of God, the one who
was to come into this world.'

28 When she had said this, she went and
called her sister Mary, saying in a low voice,
'The Master is here and wants to see you.'
29 Hearing this, Mary got up quickly and went
to him. 30 Jesus had not yet come into the
village; he was still at the place where Martha
had met him. 31 When the Jews who were in
the house comforting Mary saw her get up
so quickly and go out, they followed her,
thinking that she was going to the tomb to
weep there.

32 Mary went to Jesus, and as soon as she
saw him she threw herself at his feet, saying,
'Lord, if you had been here, my brother
would not have died.' 33 At the sight of her
tears, and those of the Jews who had come
with her, Jesus was greatly distressed, and
with a profound sigh he said, 34 'Where have
you put him?' They said, 'Lord, come and
see.' 35 Jesus wept; 36 and the Jews said, 'See
how much he loved him!' 37 But there were
some who remarked, 'He opened the eyes of
the blind man. Could he not have prevented
this man's death?' 38 Sighing again, Jesus
reached the tomb: it was a cave with a stone
to close the opening. 39 Jesus said, 'Take the
stone away.' Martha, the dead man's sister,
said to him, 'Lord, by now he will smell; this
is the fourth day since he died.' 40 Jesus
replied, 'Have I not told you that if you
believe you will see the glory of God?' 41 So
they took the stone away. Then Jesus lifted
up his eyes and said:

Father, I thank you
for hearing my prayer.
42 I myself knew that you hear me always,
but I speak
for the sake of all these
who are standing around me,
so that they may believe
it was you who sent me.

43 When he had said this, he cried in a loud
voice, 'Lazarus, come out!' 44 The dead man
came out, his feet and hands bound with
strips of material, and a cloth over his face.
Jesus said to them, 'Unbind him, let him go
free.'

The Jewish leaders decide on the death of Jesus

45 Many of the Jews who had come to visit
Mary, and had seen what he did, believed in
him, 46 but some of them went to the Pharisees
to tell them what Jesus had done. 47 Then the
chief priests and Pharisees called a meeting.
'Here is this man working all these signs,'
they said, 'and what action are we taking?
48 If we let him go on in this way everybody
will believe in him, and the Romans will
come and suppress the Holy Place and our
nation.' 49 One of them, Caiaphas, the high
priest that year, said, 'You do not seem to

have grasped the situation at all; [50]you fail to
see that it is to your advantage that one man
should die for the people, rather than that
the whole nation should perish.'[51] He did not
speak in his own person, but as high priest
of that year he was prophesying that Jesus
was to die for the nation—[52]and not for the
nation only, but also to gather together into
one the scattered children of God. [53]From
that day onwards they were determined to
kill him. [54]So Jesus no longer went about
openly among the Jews, but left the district
for a town called Ephraim, in the country
bordering on the desert, and stayed there
with his disciples.

The Passover draws near

[55]The Jewish Passover was drawing near, and
many of the country people who had gone up
to Jerusalem before the Passover to purify
themselves [56]were looking out for Jesus,
saying to one another as they stood about in
the Temple, 'What do you think? Will he
come to the festival or not?' [57]The chief
priests and Pharisees had by now given their
orders: anyone who knew where he was must
inform them so that they could arrest him.

The anointing at Bethany

12 Six days before the Passover, Jesus
went to Bethany, where Lazarus was,
whom he had raised from the dead. [2]They
gave a dinner for him there; Martha waited
on them and Lazarus was among those at
table. [3]Mary brought in a pound of very costly
ointment, pure nard, and with it anointed the
feet of Jesus, wiping them with her hair;
the house was filled with the scent of the
ointment. [4]Then Judas Iscariot—one of his
disciples, the man who was to betray him—
said, [5]'Why was this ointment not sold for
three hundred denarii and the money given
to the poor?' [6]He said this, not because he
cared about the poor, but because he was a
thief; he was in charge of the common fund
and used to help himself to the contents. [7]So
Jesus said, 'Leave her alone; let her keep it
for the day of my burial. [8]You have the poor
with you always, you will not always have
me.'

[9]Meanwhile a large number of Jews heard
that he was there and came not only on
account of Jesus but also to see Lazarus
whom he had raised from the dead. [10]Then
the chief priests decided to kill Lazarus as
well, [11]since it was on his account that many
of the Jews were leaving them and believing
in Jesus.

The Messiah enters Jerusalem

[12]The next day the great crowd of people who
had come up for the festival heard that Jesus
was on his way to Jerusalem. [13]They took
branches of palm and went out to receive
him, shouting:

'Hosanna!
Blessed is he
who is coming in the name of the Lord,[a]
the king of Israel.'

[14]Jesus found a young donkey and mounted
it—as scripture says:

[15]*Do not be afraid, daughter of Zion;*
look, your king is approaching,
riding on the foal of a donkey.[b]

[16]At first his disciples did not understand
this, but later, after Jesus had been glorified,
they remembered that this had been written
about him and that this was what had
happened to him. [17]The crowd who had been
with him when he called Lazarus out of the
tomb and raised him from the dead kept
bearing witness to it; [18]this was another
reason why the crowd came out to receive
him: they had heard that he had given this
sign. [19]Then the Pharisees said to one
another, 'You see, you are making no
progress; look, the whole world has gone
after him!'

Jesus foretells his death and subsequent glorification

[20]Among those who went up to worship
at the festival were some Greeks. [21]These
approached Philip, who came from Bethsaida
in Galilee, and put this request to him, 'Sir,
we should like to see Jesus.' [22]Philip went to
tell Andrew, and Andrew and Philip together
went to tell Jesus.

[23]Jesus replied to them:

Now the hour has come
for the Son of man to be glorified.
[24]In all truth I tell you,
unless a wheat grain falls into the earth
and dies,

12a Ps 118:25–26.
12b Zc 9:9–10.

it remains only a single grain;
but if it dies
it yields a rich harvest.
25 Anyone who loves his life loses it;
anyone who hates his life in this world
will keep it for eternal life.
26 Whoever serves me, must follow me,
and my servant will be with me
wherever I am.
If anyone serves me,
my Father will honour him.
27 Now my soul is troubled.
What shall I say:
Father, save me from this hour?[c]
But it is for this very reason
that I have come to this hour.
28 Father, glorify your name!

A voice came from heaven, 'I have glorified it, and I will again glorify it.'
29 The crowd standing by, who heard this, said it was a clap of thunder; others said, 'It was an angel speaking to him.' 30 Jesus answered, 'It was not for my sake that this voice came, but for yours.

31 'Now sentence is being passed
on this world;
now the prince of this world
is to be driven out.
32 And when I am lifted up from the earth,
I shall draw all people to myself.'

33 By these words he indicated the kind of death he would die. 34 The crowd answered, 'The Law has taught us that the Christ will remain for ever. So how can you say, "The Son of man must be lifted up"? Who is this Son of man?' 35 Jesus then said:

The light will be with you
only a little longer now.
Go on your way while you have the light,
or darkness will overtake you,
and nobody who walks in the dark
knows where he is going.
36 While you still have the light,
believe in the light
so that you may become children of light.

Having said this, Jesus left them and was hidden from their sight.

Conclusion: the unbelief of the Jews

37 Though they had been present when he gave so many signs, they did not believe in him; 38 this was to fulfil the words of the prophet Isaiah:

Lord, who has given credence
to what they have heard from us,
and who has seen in it
a revelation of the Lord's arm?[d]

39 Indeed, they were unable to believe because, as Isaiah says again:

40 *He has blinded their eyes,*
he has hardened their heart,
to prevent them from using their eyes to see,
using their heart to understand,
changing their ways and being healed by me.[e]

41 Isaiah said this because he saw his glory, and his words referred to Jesus.
42 And yet there were many who did believe in him, even among the leading men, but they did not admit it, because of the Pharisees and for fear of being banned from the synagogue: 43 they put human glory before God's glory.
44 Jesus declared publicly:

Whoever believes in me
believes not in me
but in the one who sent me,
45 and whoever sees me,
sees the one who sent me.
46 I have come into the world as light,
to prevent anyone who believes in me
from staying in the dark any more.
47 If anyone hears my words
and does not keep them faithfully,
it is not I who shall judge such a person,
since I have come not to judge the world,
but to save the world:
48 anyone who rejects me
and refuses my words
has his judge already:
the word itself that I have spoken
will be his judge on the last day.
49 For I have not spoken of my own accord;
but the Father who sent me
commanded me what to say
and what to speak,
50 and I know that his commands
mean eternal life.
And therefore what the Father
has told me
is what I speak.

12c cf. Lk 22:40–46par.
12d Is 53:1.
12e Is 6:10.

C: JESUS' HOUR COMES: THE PASSION AND THE RESURRECTION

I: JESUS' LAST MEAL WITH HIS DISCIPLES

The washing of feet

13 Before the festival of the Passover, Jesus, knowing that his hour had come to pass from this world to the Father, having loved those who were his in the world, loved them to the end.

[2]They were at supper, and the devil had already put it into the mind of Judas Iscariot son of Simon, to betray him. [3]Jesus knew that the Father had put everything into his hands, and that he had come from God and was returning to God, [4]and he got up from table, removed his outer garments and, taking a towel, wrapped it round his waist; [5]he then poured water into a basin and began to wash the disciples' feet and to wipe them with the towel he was wearing.

[6]He came to Simon Peter, who said to him, 'Lord, are you going to wash my feet?' [7]Jesus answered, 'At the moment you do not know what I am doing, but later you will understand.' [8]'Never!' said Peter. 'You shall never wash my feet.' Jesus replied, 'If I do not wash you, you can have no share with me.' Simon Peter said, [9]'Well then, Lord, not only my feet, but my hands and my head as well!' [10]Jesus said, 'No one who has had a bath needs washing, such a person is clean all over. You too are clean, though not all of you are.' [11]He knew who was going to betray him, and that was why he said, 'though not all of you are'.

[12]When he had washed their feet and put on his outer garments again he went back to the table. 'Do you understand', he said, 'what I have done to you? [13]You call me Master and Lord, and rightly; so I am. [14]If I, then, the Lord and Master, have washed your feet, you must wash each other's feet. [15]I have given you an example so that you may copy what I have done to you.

[16]'In all truth I tell you,
no servant is greater than his master,
no messenger is greater
than the one who sent him.

[17]'Now that you know this, blessed are you if you behave accordingly. [18]I am not speaking about all of you: I know the ones I have chosen; but what scripture says must be fulfilled:

'He who shares my table
takes advantage of me.[a]

[19]I tell you this now, before it happens,
so that when it does happen
you may believe that I am He.
[20]In all truth I tell you,
whoever welcomes the one I send,
welcomes me,
and whoever welcomes me,
welcomes the one who sent me.'

The treachery of Judas foretold

[21]Having said this, Jesus was deeply disturbed and declared, 'In all truth I tell you, one of you is going to betray me.' [22]The disciples looked at each other, wondering whom he meant. [23]The disciple Jesus loved was reclining next to Jesus; [24]Simon Peter signed to him and said, 'Ask who it is he means,' [25]so leaning back close to Jesus' chest he said, 'Who is it, Lord?' [26]Jesus answered, 'It is the one to whom I give the piece of bread that I dip in the dish.' And when he had dipped the piece of bread he gave it to Judas son of Simon Iscariot. [27]At that instant, after Judas had taken the bread, Satan entered him. Jesus then said, 'What you are going to do, do quickly.' [28]None of the others at table understood why he said this. [29]Since Judas had charge of the common fund, some of them thought Jesus was telling him, 'Buy what we need for the festival,' or telling him to give something to the poor. [30]As soon as Judas had taken the piece of bread he went out. It was night.

13a Ps 41:9.

Farewell discourses[b]

[31]When he had gone, Jesus said:

Now has the Son of man been glorified,
and in him God has been glorified.
[32]If God has been glorified in him,
God will in turn glorify him in himself,
and will glorify him very soon.
[33]Little children,
I shall be with you only a little longer.
You will look for me,
and, as I told the Jews,
where I am going,
you cannot come.
[34]I give you a new commandment:
love one another;
you must love one another
just as I have loved you.
[35]It is by your love for one another,
that everyone will recognise you
as my disciples.

[36]Simon Peter said, 'Lord, where are you
going?' Jesus replied, 'Now you cannot
follow me where I am going, but later you
shall follow me.' [37]Peter said to him, 'Why
can I not follow you now? I will lay down my
life for you.' [38]'Lay down your life for me?'
answered Jesus. 'In all truth I tell you, before
the cock crows you will have disowned me
three times.'

14 Do not let your hearts be troubled.
You trust in God, trust also in me.
[2]In my Father's house
there are many places to live in;
otherwise I would have told you.
I am going now to prepare a place for you,
[3]and after I have gone
and prepared you a place,
I shall return to take you to myself,
so that you may be with me
where I am.
[4]You know the way
to the place where I am going.

[5]Thomas said, 'Lord, we do not know
where you are going, so how can we know
the way?' [6]Jesus said:

I am the Way; I am Truth and Life.
No one can come to the Father
except through me.
[7]If you know me,
you will know my Father too.
From this moment you know him
and have seen him.

[8]Philip said, 'Lord, show us the Father
and then we shall be satisfied.' Jesus said to
him, [9]'Have I been with you all this time,
Philip, and you still do not know me?

'Anyone who has seen me
has seen the Father,
so how can you say,
"Show us the Father"?
[10]Do you not believe
that I am in the Father
and the Father is in me?
What I say to you
I do not speak of my own accord:
it is the Father, living in me,
who is doing his works.
[11]You must believe me when I say
that I am in the Father
and the Father is in me;
or at least believe it
on the evidence of these works.
[12]In all truth I tell you,
whoever believes in me
will perform the same works
as I do myself,
and will perform even greater works,
because I am going to the Father.
[13]Whatever you ask in my name
I will do,
so that the Father may be glorified
in the Son.
[14]If you ask me anything in my name,
I will do it.
[15]If you love me
you will keep my commandments.
[16]I shall ask the Father,
and he will give you another Paraclete[a]
to be with you for ever,
[17]the Spirit of truth
whom the world can never accept
since it neither sees nor knows him;
but you know him,
because he is with you, he is in you.
[18]I shall not leave you orphans;
I shall come to you.
[19]In a short time
the world will no longer see me;

13b These contain teaching given also on other occasions, and perhaps in different versions. Ch. 16 may be another version of ch. 14, and ch. 17 yet another.
14a The Gk word means 'advocate', 'counsellor', 'protector'.

but you will see that I live
and you also will live.
20 On that day
you will know that I am in my Father
and you in me and I in you.
21 Whoever holds to my commandments
and keeps them
is the one who loves me;
and whoever loves me
will be loved by my Father,
and I shall love him
and reveal myself to him.'

22 Judas—not Judas Iscariot—said to him,
'Lord, what has happened, that you intend
to show yourself to us and not to the world?'
23 Jesus replied:

Anyone who loves me will keep my word,
and my Father will love him,
and we shall come to him
and make a home in him.
24 Anyone who does not love me
does not keep my words.
And the word that you hear
is not my own:
it is the word of the Father who sent me.
25 I have said these things to you
while still with you;
26 but the Paraclete, the Holy Spirit,
whom the Father will send in my name,
will teach you everything
and remind you of all I have said to you.
27 Peace I bequeath to you,
my own peace I give you,
a peace which the world cannot give,
this is my gift to you.
Do not let your hearts be troubled
or afraid.
28 You heard me say:
I am going away and shall return.
If you loved me you would be glad
that I am going to the Father,
for the Father is greater than I.
29 I have told you this now,
before it happens,
so that when it does happen
you may believe.
30 I shall not talk to you much longer,
because the prince of this world
is on his way.
He has no power over me,
31 but the world must recognise
that I love the Father
and that I act
just as the Father commanded.
Come now, let us go.

The true vine[a]

15 I am the true vine,
and my Father is the vinedresser.
2 Every branch in me that bears no fruit
he cuts away,
and every branch that does bear fruit
he prunes
to make it bear even more.
3 You are clean already,
by means of the word
that I have spoken to you.
4 Remain in me, as I in you.
As a branch cannot bear fruit all by itself,
unless it remains part of the vine,
neither can you unless you remain in me.
5 I am the vine,
you are the branches.
Whoever remains in me, with me in him,
bears fruit in plenty;
for cut off from me you can do nothing.
6 Anyone who does not remain in me
is thrown away like a branch
—and withers;
these branches are collected
and thrown on the fire
and are burnt.
7 If you remain in me
and my words remain in you,
you may ask for whatever you please
and you will get it.
8 It is to the glory of my Father
that you should bear much fruit
and be my disciples.
9 I have loved you
just as the Father has loved me.
Remain in my love.
10 If you keep my commandments
you will remain in my love,
just as I have kept
my Father's commandments
and remain in his love.
11 I have told you this
so that my own joy may be in you
and your joy be complete.
12 This is my commandment:
love one another,
as I have loved you.
13 No one can have greater love
than to lay down his life for his friends.

15a cf. Is 5:1–7; Mk 12:1–12.

14You are my friends,
if you do what I command you.
15I shall no longer call you servants,
because a servant does not know
the master's business;
I call you friends,
because I have made known to you
everything I have learnt from my Father.
16You did not choose me,
no, I chose you;
and I commissioned you
to go out and to bear fruit,
fruit that will last;
so that the Father will give you
anything you ask him in my name.
17My command to you
is to love one another.

The disciples and the world

18If the world hates you,
you must realise that it hated me
before it hated you.
19If you belonged to the world,
the world would love you as its own;
but because you do not belong to the world,
because my choice of you
has drawn you out of the world,
that is why the world hates you.
20Remember the words I said to you:
A servant is not greater than his master.
If they persecuted me,
they will persecute you too;
if they kept my word,
they will keep yours as well.
21But it will be on my account
that they will do all this to you,
because they do not know
the one who sent me.
22If I had not come,
if I had not spoken to them,
they would have been blameless;
but as it is they have no excuse
for their sin.
23Anyone who hates me hates my Father.
24If I had not performed
such works among them
as no one else has ever done,
they would be blameless;
but as it is, in spite of what they have seen,
they hate both me and my Father.
25But all this was only to fulfil
the words written in their Law:
They hated me without reason.[b]
26When the Paraclete comes,
whom I shall send to you from the Father,
the Spirit of truth
who issues from the Father,
he will be my witness.
27And you too will be witnesses,
because you have been with me
from the beginning.

16 I have told you all this
so that you may not fall away.
2They will expel you
from the synagogues,
and indeed the time is coming
when anyone who kills you
will think he is doing
a holy service to God.
3They will do these things
because they have never known
either the Father or me.
4But I have told you all this,
so that when the time for it comes
you may remember that I told you.

The coming of the Paraclete

I did not tell you this from the beginning,
because I was with you;
5but now I am going to the one
who sent me.
Not one of you asks,
'Where are you going?'
6Yet you are sad at heart
because I have told you this.
7Still, I am telling you the truth:
it is for your own good that I am going,
because unless I go,
the Paraclete will not come to you;
but if I go,
I will send him to you.
8And when he comes,
he will show the world how wrong it was,
about sin,
and about who was in the right,
and about judgement:
9about sin:
in that they refuse to believe in me;
10about who was in the right:
in that I am going to the Father
and you will see me no more;
11about judgement:
in that the prince of this world
is already condemned.
12I still have many things to say to you

15b Ps 69:4.

but they would be too much for you
to bear now.
13 However, when the Spirit of truth comes
he will lead you to the complete truth,
since he will not be speaking
of his own accord,
but will say only what he has been told;
and he will reveal to you
the things to come.
14 He will glorify me,
since all he reveals to you
will be taken from what is mine.
15 Everything the Father has is mine;
that is why I said:
all he reveals to you
will be taken from what is mine.

Jesus to return very soon

16 In a short time you will no longer see me,
and then a short time later
you will see me again.

17 Then some of his disciples said to one
another, 'What does he mean, "In a short
time you will no longer see me, and then a
short time later you will see me again," and,
"I am going to the Father"? 18 What is this
"short time"? We don't know what he
means.' 19 Jesus knew that they wanted to
question him, so he said, 'You are asking one
another what I meant by saying, "In a short
time you will no longer see me, and then a
short time later you will see me again."

20 'In all truth I tell you,
you will be weeping and wailing
while the world will rejoice;
you will be sorrowful,
but your sorrow will turn to joy.
21 A woman in childbirth suffers,
because her time has come;
but when she has given birth to the child
she forgets the suffering
in her joy that a human being
has been born into the world.
22 So it is with you: you are sad now,
but I shall see you again,
and your hearts will be full of joy,
and that joy no one shall take from you.
23 When that day comes,
you will not ask me any questions.
In all truth I tell you,
anything you ask from the Father
he will grant in my name.
24 Until now you have not asked
anything in my name.
Ask and you will receive,
and so your joy will be complete.
25 I have been telling you these things
in veiled language.
The hour is coming
when I shall no longer speak to you
in veiled language
but tell you about the Father
in plain words.
26 When that day comes
you will ask in my name;
and I do not say
that I shall pray to the Father for you,
27 because the Father himself loves you
for loving me,
and believing that I came from God.
28 I came from the Father
and have come into the world
and now I am leaving the world
to go to the Father.'

29 His disciples said, 'Now you are speaking
plainly and not using veiled language. 30 Now
we see that you know everything and need
not wait for questions to be put into words;
because of this we believe that you came from
God.' 31 Jesus answered them:

Do you believe at last?
32 Listen; the time will come—
indeed it has come already—
when you are going to be scattered,
each going his own way
and leaving me alone.
And yet I am not alone,
because the Father is with me.
33 I have told you all this
so that you may find peace in me.
In the world you will have hardship,
but be courageous:
I have conquered the world.

The prayer of Jesus

17 After saying this, Jesus raised his eyes
to heaven and said:

Father, the hour has come:
glorify your Son
so that your Son may glorify you;
2 so that, just as you have given him
power over all humanity,
he may give eternal life
to all those you have entrusted to him.
3 And eternal life is this:
to know you,
the only true God,
and Jesus Christ whom you have sent.

4 I have glorified you on earth
by finishing the work
that you gave me to do.
5 Now, Father, glorify me
with that glory I had with you
before ever the world existed.
6 I have revealed your name
to those whom you took from the world
to give me.
They were yours
and you gave them to me,
and they have kept your word.
7 Now at last they have recognised
that all you have given me
comes from you
8 for I have given them
the teaching you gave to me,
and they have indeed accepted it
and know for certain
that I came from you,
and have believed
that it was you who sent me.
9 It is for them that I pray.
I am not praying for the world
but for those you have given me,
because they belong to you.
10 All I have is yours
and all you have is mine,
and in them I am glorified.
11 I am no longer in the world,
but they are in the world,
and I am coming to you.
Holy Father,
keep those you have given me
true to your name,
so that they may be one like us.
12 While I was with them,
I kept those you had given me
true to your name.
I have watched over them
and not one is lost
except one who was destined to be lost,
and this was to fulfil the scriptures.
13 But now I am coming to you
and I say these things in the world
to share my joy with them to the full.
14 I passed your word on to them,
and the world hated them,
because they belong to the world
no more than I belong to the world.
15 I am not asking you
to remove them from the world,
but to protect them from the Evil One.
16 They do not belong to the world
any more than I belong to the world.
17 Consecrate them in the truth;
your word is truth.
18 As you sent me into the world,
I have sent them into the world,
19 and for their sake I consecrate myself
so that they too
may be consecrated in truth.
20 I pray not only for these
but also for those
who through their teaching
will come to believe in me.
21 May they all be one,
just as, Father, you are in me
and I am in you,
so that they also may be in us,
so that the world may believe
it was you who sent me.
22 I have given them the glory
you gave to me,
that they may be one as we are one.
23 With me in them and you in me,
may they be so perfected in unity
that the world will recognise
that it was you who sent me
and that you have loved them
as you have loved me.
24 Father,
I want those you have given me
to be with me where I am,
so that they may always see my glory
which you have given me
because you loved me
before the foundation of the world.
25 Father, Upright One,
the world has not known you,
but I have known you,
and these have known
that you have sent me.
26 I have made your name known to them
and will continue to make it known,
so that the love with which you loved me
may be in them,
and so that I may be in them.

II: THE PASSION

The arrest of Jesus

18 After he had said all this, Jesus left with
his disciples and crossed the Kidron
valley where there was a garden into which
he went with his disciples. 2Judas the traitor
knew the place also, since Jesus had often
met his disciples there, 3so Judas brought the
cohort to this place together with guards sent
by the chief priests and the Pharisees, all with
lanterns and torches and weapons. 4Knowing
everything that was to happen to him, Jesus
came forward and said, 'Who are you looking
for?' 5They answered, 'Jesus the Nazarene.'
He said, 'I am he.' Now Judas the traitor was
standing among them. 6When Jesus said to
them, 'I am he,' they moved back and fell on
the ground. 7He asked them a second time,
'Who are you looking for?' They said, 'Jesus
the Nazarene.' 8Jesus replied, 'I have told
you that I am he. If I am the one you are
looking for, let these others go.' 9This was to
fulfil the words he had spoken, 'Not one of
those you gave me have I lost.'
10Simon Peter, who had a sword, drew it
and struck the high priest's servant, cutting
off his right ear. The servant's name was
Malchus. 11Jesus said to Peter, 'Put your
sword back in its scabbard; am I not to drink
the cup that the Father has given me?'

Jesus before Annas and Caiaphas
Peter disowns him

12The cohort and its tribune and the Jewish
guards seized Jesus and bound him. 13They
took him first to Annas, because Annas was
the father-in-law of Caiaphas, who was high
priest that year. 14It was Caiaphas who had
counselled the Jews, 'It is better for one man
to die for the people.'
15Simon Peter, with another disciple,
followed Jesus. This disciple, who was
known to the high priest, went with Jesus
into the high priest's palace, 16but Peter
stayed outside the door. So the other disciple,
the one known to the high priest, went out,
spoke to the door-keeper and brought Peter
in. 17The girl on duty at the door said to
Peter, 'Aren't you another of that man's
disciples?' He answered, 'I am not.' 18Now
it was cold, and the servants and guards had
lit a charcoal fire and were standing there
warming themselves; so Peter stood there
too, warming himself with the others.
19The high priest questioned Jesus about
his disciples and his teaching. 20Jesus
answered, 'I have spoken openly for all the
world to hear; I have always taught in the
synagogue and in the Temple where all the
Jews meet together; I have said nothing in
secret. 21Why ask me? Ask my hearers what
I taught; they know what I said.' 22At these
words, one of the guards standing by gave
Jesus a slap in the face, saying, 'Is that the
way you answer the high priest?' 23Jesus
replied, 'If there is some offence in what I
said, point it out; but if not, why do you
strike me?' 24Then Annas sent him, bound,
to Caiaphas the high priest.[a]
25As Simon Peter stood there warming
himself, someone said to him, 'Aren't you
another of his disciples?' He denied it saying,
'I am not.' 26One of the high priest's servants,
a relation of the man whose ear Peter had cut
off, said, 'Didn't I see you in the garden with
him?' 27Again Peter denied it; and at once a
cock crowed.

Jesus before Pilate

28They then led Jesus from the house of
Caiaphas to the Praetorium. It was now
morning. They did not go into the Praeto-
rium themselves to avoid becoming defiled
and unable to eat the Passover. 29So Pilate
came outside to them and said, 'What charge
do you bring against this man?' They replied,
30'If he were not a criminal, we should not
have handed him over to you.' 31Pilate said,
'Take him yourselves, and try him by your
own Law.' The Jews answered, 'We are not
allowed to put anyone to death.' 32This was
to fulfil the words Jesus had spoken indi-
cating the way he was going to die.
33So Pilate went back into the Praetorium
and called Jesus to him and asked him, 'Are
you the king of the Jews?' 34Jesus replied,
'Do you ask this of your own accord, or have
others said it to you about me?' 35Pilate
answered, 'Am I a Jew? It is your own people
and the chief priests who have handed you
over to me: what have you done?' 36Jesus
replied, 'Mine is not a kingdom of this world;

18a Jn has no Sanhedrin session as the other gospels have, only a private interrogation at night.

if my kingdom were of this world, my men would have fought to prevent my being surrendered to the Jews. As it is, my kingdom does not belong here.' [37]Pilate said, 'So, then you are a king?' Jesus answered, 'It is you who say that I am a king. I was born for this, I came into the world for this, to bear witness to the truth; and all who are on the side of truth listen to my voice.' [38]'Truth?' said Pilate. 'What is that?' And so saying he went out again to the Jews and said, 'I find no case against him. [39]But according to a custom of yours I should release one prisoner at the Passover; would you like me, then, to release for you the king of the Jews?' [40]At this they shouted, 'Not this man,' they said, 'but Barabbas.' Barabbas was a bandit.

19 Pilate then had Jesus taken away and scourged; [2]and after this, the soldiers twisted some thorns into a crown and put it on his head and dressed him in a purple robe. [3]They kept coming up to him and saying, 'Hail, king of the Jews!' and slapping him in the face.

[4]Pilate came outside again and said to them, 'Look, I am going to bring him out to you to let you see that I find no case against him.' [5]Jesus then came out wearing the crown of thorns and the purple robe. Pilate said, 'Here is the man.' [6]When they saw him, the chief priests and the guards shouted, 'Crucify him! Crucify him!' Pilate said, 'Take him yourselves and crucify him: I find no case against him.' [7]The Jews replied, 'We have a Law, and according to that Law he ought to be put to death, because he has claimed to be Son of God.'

[8]When Pilate heard them say this his fears increased. [9]Re-entering the Praetorium, he said to Jesus, 'Where do you come from?' But Jesus made no answer. [10]Pilate then said to him, 'Are you refusing to speak to me? Surely you know I have power to release you and I have power to crucify you?' [11]Jesus replied, 'You would have no power over me at all if it had not been given you from above; that is why the man who handed me over to you has the greater guilt.'

Jesus is condemned to death

[12]From that moment Pilate was anxious to set him free, but the Jews shouted, 'If you set him free you are no friend of Caesar's; anyone who makes himself king is defying Caesar.' [13]Hearing these words, Pilate had Jesus brought out, and seated him on the chair of judgement at a place called the Pavement, in Hebrew Gabbatha. [14]It was the Day of Preparation, about the sixth hour. 'Here is your king,' said Pilate to the Jews. [15]But they shouted, 'Away with him, away with him, crucify him.' Pilate said, 'Shall I crucify your king?' The chief priests answered, 'We have no king except Caesar.' [16]So at that Pilate handed him over to them to be crucified.

The crucifixion

They then took charge of Jesus, [17]and carrying his own cross he went out to the Place of the Skull or, as it is called in Hebrew, Golgotha, [18]where they crucified him with two others, one on either side, Jesus being in the middle. [19]Pilate wrote out a notice and had it fixed to the cross; it ran: 'Jesus the Nazarene, King of the Jews'. [20]This notice was read by many of the Jews, because the place where Jesus was crucified was near the city, and the writing was in Hebrew, Latin and Greek. [21]So the Jewish chief priests said to Pilate, 'You should not write "King of the Jews", but that the man said, "I am King of the Jews". ' [22]Pilate answered, 'What I have written, I have written.'

Jesus' garments divided

[23]When the soldiers had finished crucifying Jesus they took his clothing and divided it into four shares, one for each soldier. His undergarment was seamless, woven in one piece from neck to hem; [24]so they said to one another, 'Instead of tearing it, let's throw dice to decide who is to have it.' In this way the words of scripture were fulfilled:

They divide my garments among them
and cast lots for my clothes.[a]

That is what the soldiers did.

Jesus and his mother

[25]Near the cross of Jesus stood his mother and his mother's sister, Mary the wife of Clopas, and Mary of Magdala. [26]Seeing his mother and the disciple whom he loved

---

19a Ps 22:18.

standing near her, Jesus said to his mother,
'Woman, this is your son.' 27Then to the
disciple he said, 'This is your mother.' And
from that hour the disciple took her into his
home.

The death of Jesus

28After this, Jesus knew that everything had
now been completed and, so that the scrip-
ture should be completely fulfilled, he said:

I am thirsty.[b]

29A jar full of sour wine stood there; so,
putting a sponge soaked in the wine on a
hyssop stick, they held it up to his mouth.
30After Jesus had taken the wine he said, 'It
is fulfilled'; and bowing his head he gave up
his spirit.

The pierced Christ

31It was the Day of Preparation, and to avoid
the bodies' remaining on the cross during the
Sabbath—since that Sabbath was a day of
special solemnity—the Jews asked Pilate to
have the legs broken and the bodies taken
away. 32Consequently the soldiers came and
broke the legs of the first man who had been
crucified with him and then of the other.
33When they came to Jesus, they saw he was
already dead, and so instead of breaking his
legs 34one of the soldiers pierced his side with
a lance; and immediately there came out
blood and water. 35This is the evidence of
one who saw it—true evidence, and he knows
that what he says is true—and he gives it so
that you may believe as well. 36Because all
this happened to fulfil the words of scripture:

Not one bone of his will be broken;[c]

37and again, in another place scripture says:

They will look to the one
whom they have pierced.[d]

The burial

38After this, Joseph of Arimathaea, who was
a disciple of Jesus—though a secret one
because he was afraid of the Jews—asked
Pilate to let him remove the body of Jesus.
Pilate gave permission, so they came and
took it away. 39Nicodemus came as well—
the same one who had first come to Jesus at
night-time—and he brought a mixture of
myrrh and aloes, weighing about a hundred
pounds. 40They took the body of Jesus and
bound it in linen cloths with the spices,
following the Jewish burial custom. 41At the
place where he had been crucified there was
a garden, and in this garden a new tomb in
which no one had yet been buried. 42Since it
was the Jewish Day of Preparation and the
tomb was nearby, they laid Jesus there.

III: THE DAY OF CHRIST'S RESURRECTION

The empty tomb

20 It was very early on the first day of the
week and still dark, when Mary of
Magdala came to the tomb. She saw that the
stone had been moved away from the tomb
2and came running to Simon Peter and the
other disciple, the one whom Jesus loved.
'They have taken the Lord out of the tomb,'
she said, 'and we don't know where they have
put him.'

3So Peter set out with the other disciple to
go to the tomb. 4They ran together, but the
other disciple, running faster than Peter,
reached the tomb first; 5he bent down and
saw the linen cloths lying on the ground, but
did not go in. 6Simon Peter, following him,
also came up, went into the tomb, saw the
linen cloths lying on the ground 7and also the
cloth that had been over his head; this was
not with the linen cloths but rolled up in a
place by itself. 8Then the other disciple who
had reached the tomb first also went in; he
saw and he believed. 9Till this moment they
had still not understood the scripture, that
he must rise from the dead. 10The disciples
then went back home.

19b Ps 69:21.
19c Ex 12:46 and Ps 34:20.
19d Zc 12:10.

The appearance to Mary of Magdala

[11]But Mary was standing outside near the tomb, weeping. Then, as she wept, she stooped to look inside, [12]and saw two angels in white sitting where the body of Jesus had been, one at the head, the other at the feet. [13]They said, 'Woman, why are you weeping?' 'They have taken my Lord away,' she replied, 'and I don't know where they have put him.' [14]As she said this she turned round and saw Jesus standing there, though she did not realise that it was Jesus. [15]Jesus said to her, 'Woman, why are you weeping? Who are you looking for?' Supposing him to be the gardener, she said, 'Sir, if you have taken him away, tell me where you have put him, and I will go and remove him.' [16]Jesus said, 'Mary!' She turned round then and said to him in Hebrew, 'Rabbuni!'—which means Master. [17]Jesus said to her, 'Do not cling to me, because I have not yet ascended to the Father. But go to the brothers, and tell them: I am ascending to my Father and your Father, to my God and your God.' [18]So Mary of Magdala told the disciples, 'I have seen the Lord,' and that he had said these things to her.

Appearances to the disciples

[19]In the evening of that same day, the first day of the week, the doors were closed in the room where the disciples were, for fear of the Jews. Jesus came and stood among them. He said to them, 'Peace be with you,' [20]and, after saying this, he showed them his hands and his side. The disciples were filled with joy at seeing the Lord, [21]and he said to them again, 'Peace be with you.

'As the Father sent me,
so am I sending you.'

[22]After saying this he breathed on them and said:

Receive the Holy Spirit.
[23]If you forgive anyone's sins,
they are forgiven;
if you retain anyone's sins,
they are retained.

[24]Thomas, called the Twin, who was one of the Twelve, was not with them when Jesus came. [25]So the other disciples said to him, 'We have seen the Lord,' but he answered, 'Unless I can see the holes that the nails made in his hands and can put my finger into the holes they made, and unless I can put my hand into his side, I refuse to believe.' [26]Eight days later the disciples were in the house again and Thomas was with them. The doors were closed, but Jesus came in and stood among them. 'Peace be with you,' he said. [27]Then he spoke to Thomas, 'Put your finger here; look, here are my hands. Give me your hand; put it into my side. Do not be unbelieving any more but believe.' [28]Thomas replied, 'My Lord and my God!' [29]Jesus said to him:

You believe because you can see me.
Blessed are those who have not seen
and yet believe.

IV: FIRST CONCLUSION

[30]There were many other signs that Jesus worked in the sight of the disciples, but they are not recorded in this book. [31]These are recorded so that you may believe that Jesus is the Christ, the Son of God, and that believing this you may have life through his name.

D: EPILOGUE[a]

I: THE APPEARANCE ON THE SHORE OF TIBERIAS

21 Later on, Jesus revealed himself again
to the disciples. It was by the Sea of
Tiberias, and it happened like this: 2 Simon
Peter, Thomas called the Twin, Nathanael
from Cana in Galilee, the sons of Zebedee
and two more of his disciples were together.
3 Simon Peter said, 'I'm going fishing.' They
replied, 'We'll come with you.' They went
out and got into the boat but caught nothing
that night.

4 When it was already light, there stood
Jesus on the shore, though the disciples did
not realise that it was Jesus. 5 Jesus called out,
'Haven't you caught anything, friends?' And
when they answered, 'No,' 6 he said, 'Throw
the net out to starboard and you'll find some-
thing.' So they threw the net out and could
not haul it in because of the quantity of fish.
7 The disciple whom Jesus loved said to Peter,
'It is the Lord.' At these words, 'It is the
Lord,' Simon Peter tied his outer garment
round him (for he had nothing on) and
jumped into the water. 8 The other disciples
came on in the boat, towing the net with the
fish; they were only about a hundred yards
from land.

9 As soon as they came ashore they saw that
there was some bread there and a charcoal
fire with fish cooking on it. 10 Jesus said,
'Bring some of the fish you have just caught.'
11 Simon Peter went aboard and dragged the
net ashore, full of big fish, one hundred and
fifty-three of them; and in spite of there being
so many the net was not broken. 12 Jesus said
to them, 'Come and have breakfast.' None
of the disciples was bold enough to ask, 'Who
are you?'. They knew quite well it was the
Lord. 13 Jesus then stepped forward, took the
bread and gave it to them, and the same with
the fish. 14 This was the third time that Jesus
revealed himself to the disciples after rising
from the dead.

15 When they had eaten, Jesus said to Simon
Peter, 'Simon son of John, do you love me
more than these others do?' He answered,
'Yes, Lord, you know I love you.' Jesus said
to him, 'Feed my lambs.' 16 A second time he
said to him, 'Simon son of John, do you love
me?' He replied, 'Yes, Lord, you know I love
you.' Jesus said to him, 'Look after my
sheep.' 17 Then he said to him a third time,
'Simon son of John, do you love me?' Peter
was hurt that he asked him a third time, 'Do
you love me?' and said, 'Lord, you know
everything; you know I love you.' Jesus said
to him, 'Feed my sheep.

18 In all truth I tell you,
when you were young
you put on your own belt
and walked where you liked;
but when you grow old
you will stretch out your hands,
and somebody else
  will put a belt round you
and take you
  where you would rather not go.'

19 In these words he indicated the kind of
death by which Peter would give glory to
God. After this he said, 'Follow me.'

20 Peter turned and saw the disciple whom
Jesus loved[b] following them—the one who
had leant back close to his chest at the supper
and had said to him, 'Lord, who is it that will
betray you?' 21 Seeing him, Peter said to Jesus,
'What about him, Lord?' 22 Jesus answered,
'If I want him to stay behind till I come, what
does it matter to you? You are to follow
me.' 23 The rumour then went out among the
brothers that this disciple would not die. Yet
Jesus had not said to Peter, 'He will not
die,' but, 'If I want him to stay behind till
I come.'

21a Added by the evangelist or one of his disciples.
21b The source of Jn's tradition; but his identity is uncertain.

II: SECOND CONCLUSION

24 This disciple is the one who vouches for
these things and has written them down, and
we know that his testimony is true.
25 There was much else that Jesus did; if it
were written down in detail, I do not suppose
the world itself would hold all the books that
would be written.

ACTS OF THE APOSTLES

This is the story of the spread of the Christian faith across the Mediterranean world, first in Judaea, then further in Palestine and finally in the capital of the empire, Rome. The main figures are Peter, leader of the apostles, and Paul, apostle of the gentiles, closely related in their work by similarities in preaching and in miracles.

The whole Christian community is filled with the Spirit of Jesus, whose guidance inspires every new initiative, and who ensures the harmony of the early community in its prayer, joy and praise. Even persecution brings only joy and thanksgiving, for the early Jerusalem community is presented as a model of perseverance, generosity and devotion. But although it is stressed that Christianity is the logical outcome of Judaism and is in full continuity with it, the Jews reject it again and again, even stirring up trouble with the Roman authorities and forcing the missionaries to turn to the gentiles.

The author, like any historian, moulds his material to bring out its message. Paul the Roman citizen, and the other Christians are unfailingly loyal to the authorities, and Christianity is a benign influence. By comparison with Paul's letters and other NT epistles the picture of the early Church seems idealised: there were differences of opinion and even bitter dissensions in the Church, particularly over relationships between gentile and Jewish Christians. Modern historians and archaeologists, however, have confirmed the accuracy of the legal and constitutional information given.

Certain passages in the travel-story are related in the first person, showing that the author of these actually travelled with Paul. Nevertheless considerable divergences from Paul's own account of some events and particularly of his theological views (e.g. on observance of the Jewish Law) raise doubts about how well the author actually knew Paul—unless he adjusted the picture to fit his theme of church harmony. He certainly followed contemporary convention in composing speeches for Peter and Paul: each sermon follows a set pattern (story of Jesus' death and resurrection, his ministry, an appeal to Scripture, a call to commitment to Christ and repentance), and the argumentation from Scripture is highly elaborate, often relying on the Gk text of the Bible, though the speech must originally have been delivered in Hebrew or Aramaic.

Of all the books of the Bible Acts is the one most at home in the classical Roman world: the author is a civilised and urbane hellenistic Jew. Style, vocabulary and theological emphases all combine to show that Acts and Luke issue from the same pen. Acts is the latter part of a two-volume work, split when the four gospels were gathered together about AD 150. There is no clear evidence of the date of the book. No event later than the early 60s is mentioned, but Paul's arrival in Rome is a natural cut-off point for the story, and no conclusions about the date may be drawn from Acts' failure to narrate later history. It must have been written in the last quarter of the century.

PLAN OF THE BOOK

I The Church in Jerusalem 1:12—5
II The Earliest Missions 6—12
III The Mission of Barnabas and Paul. The Council of Jerusalem 13:1—15:35
IV Paul's Missions 15:36—19:20
V The End of Paul's Missionary Journeys. A Prisoner for Christ 19:21—28:31

ACTS OF THE APOSTLES

Prologue

1 In my earlier work, Theophilus, I dealt
with everything Jesus had done and taught
from the beginning 2 until the day he gave his
instructions to the apostles he had chosen
through the Holy Spirit, and was taken up to
heaven. 3 He had shown himself alive to them
after his Passion by many demonstrations:
for forty days he had continued to appear to
them and tell them about the kingdom of
God. 4 While at table with them, he had told
them not to leave Jerusalem, but to wait there
for what the Father had promised. 'It is', he
had said, 'what you have heard me speak
about: 5 John baptised with water but, not
many days from now, you are going to be
baptised with the Holy Spirit.'

The ascension

6 Now having met together, they asked him,
'Lord, has the time come for you to restore
the kingdom to Israel?' 7 He replied, 'It is not
for you to know times or dates that the Father
has decided by his own authority, 8 but you
will receive the power of the Holy Spirit
which will come on you, and then you will
be my witnesses not only in Jerusalem but
throughout Judaea and Samaria, and indeed
to earth's remotest end.'

9 As he said this he was lifted up while they
looked on, and a cloud took him from their
sight. 10 They were still staring into the sky
as he went, when suddenly two men in white
were standing beside them, 11 and they said,
'Why are you Galileans standing here looking
into the sky? This Jesus who has been taken
up from you into heaven will come back in
the same way as you have seen him go to
heaven.'

I: THE CHURCH IN JERUSALEM

The group of apostles

12 So from the Mount of Olives, as it is called, they went back to Jerusalem, a short distance away, no more than a Sabbath walk; 13 and when they reached the city they went to the upper room where they were staying; there were Peter and John, James and Andrew, Philip and Thomas, Bartholomew and Matthew, James son of Alphaeus and Simon the Zealot, and Jude son of James. 14 With one heart all these joined constantly in prayer, together with some women, including Mary the mother of Jesus, and with his brothers.

Judas is replaced

15 One day Peter stood up to speak to the brothers—there were about a hundred and twenty people in the congregation, 16 'Brothers,' he said, 'the passage of scripture had to be fulfilled in which the Holy Spirit, speaking through David, foretells the fate of Judas, who acted as guide to the men who arrested Jesus—17 after being one of our number and sharing our ministry. 18 As you know, he bought a plot of land with the money he was paid for his crime. He fell headlong and burst open, and all his entrails poured out.[a] 19 Everybody in Jerusalem heard about it and the plot came to be called "Bloody Acre", in their language Hakeldama. 20 Now in the Book of Psalms it says:

Reduce his encampment to ruin
and leave his tent unoccupied.

And again:

Let someone else take over his office.

21 'Out of the men who have been with us the whole time that the Lord Jesus was living with us, 22 from the time when John was baptising until the day when he was taken up from us, one must be appointed to serve with us as a witness to his resurrection.'

23 Having nominated two candidates, Joseph known as Barsabbas, whose surname was Justus, and Matthias, 24 they prayed, 'Lord, you can read everyone's heart; show us therefore which of these two you have chosen 25 to take over this ministry and apostolate, which Judas abandoned to go to his proper place.' 26 They then drew lots for them, and as the lot fell to Matthias, he was listed as one of the twelve apostles.

Pentecost

2 When Pentecost day came round, they had all met together, 2 when suddenly there came from heaven a sound as of a violent wind which filled the entire house in which they were sitting; 3 and there appeared to them tongues as of fire; these separated and came to rest on the head of each of them. 4 They were all filled with the Holy Spirit and began to speak different languages as the Spirit gave them power to express themselves.

5 Now there were devout men living in Jerusalem from every nation under heaven, 6 and at this sound they all assembled, and each one was bewildered to hear these men speaking his own language. 7 They were amazed and astonished. 'Surely,' they said, 'all these men speaking are Galileans? 8 How does it happen that each of us hears them in his own native language? 9 Parthians, Medes and Elamites; people from Mesopotamia, Judaea and Cappadocia, Pontus and Asia, 10 Phrygia and Pamphylia, Egypt and the parts of Libya round Cyrene; residents of Rome—11 Jews and proselytes alike—Cretans and Arabs, we hear them preaching in our own language about the marvels of God.' 12 Everyone was amazed and perplexed; they asked one another what it all meant. 13 Some, however, laughed it off. 'They have been drinking too much new wine,' they said.

Peter's address to the crowd

14 Then Peter stood up with the Eleven and addressed them in a loud voice:

'Men of Judaea, and all you who live in Jerusalem, make no mistake about this, but listen carefully to what I say. 15 These men are not drunk, as you imagine; why, it is only the third hour of the day. 16 On the contrary, this is what the prophet was saying:

1a cf. Ws 4:19. Ps 69:5; 109:8 are also used.

17 In the last days—the Lord declares—
I shall pour out my Spirit on all humanity.
Your sons and daughters shall prophesy,
your young people shall see visions,
your old people dream dreams.
18 *Even on the slaves, men and women,*
shall I pour out my Spirit.
19 *I will show portents in the sky* above
and signs on the earth below.
20 *The sun will be turned into darkness*
and the moon into blood
before the day of the Lord comes,
that great and terrible Day.
21 *And all who call on the name of the Lord*
will be saved.[a]

22 'Men of Israel, listen to what I am going
to say: Jesus the Nazarene was a man
commended to you by God by the miracles
and portents and signs that God worked
through him when he was among you, as you
know. 23 This man, who was put into your
power by the deliberate intention and fore-
knowledge of God, you took and had cruci-
fied and killed by men outside the Law. 24 But
God raised him to life, freeing him from the
pangs of Hades; for it was impossible for him
to be held in its power since, 25 as David says
of him:

I kept the Lord before my sight always,
for with him at my right hand
nothing can shake me.
26 *So my heart rejoiced*
my tongue delighted;
my body, too, will rest secure,
27 *for you will not abandon me to Hades*
or allow your holy one to see corruption.
28 *You have taught me the way of life,*
you will fill me with joy in your presence.[b]

29 'Brothers, no one can deny that the patri-
arch David himself is dead and buried: his
tomb is still with us. 30 But since he was a
prophet, and knew that God *had sworn him*
an oath *to make one of his descendants succeed*
him on the throne, 31 he spoke with foreknowl-
edge about the resurrection of the Christ: he
is the one who was *not abandoned to Hades*,
and whose body did not *see corruption*. 32 God
raised this man Jesus to life, and of that we
are all witnesses. 33 Now raised to the heights
by God's right hand, he has received from
the Father the Holy Spirit, who was prom-
ised, and what you see and hear is the
outpouring of that Spirit. 34 For David
himself never went up to heaven, but yet he
said:

The Lord declared to my Lord,
take your seat at my right hand,
35 *till I have made your enemies*
your footstool.[c]

36 'For this reason the whole House of Israel
can be certain that the Lord and Christ
whom God has made is this Jesus whom you
crucified.'

The first conversions

37 Hearing this, they were cut to the heart and
said to Peter and the other apostles, 'What
are we to do, brothers?' 38 'You must repent,'
Peter answered, 'and every one of you must
be baptised in the name of Jesus Christ for
the forgiveness of your sins, and you will
receive the gift of the Holy Spirit. 39 The
promise that was made is for you and your
children, and for all *those who are far away,*
for all those whom the Lord our God *is calling*
to himself.'[d] 40 He spoke to them for a long
time using many other arguments, and he
urged them, 'Save yourselves from this
perverse generation.' 41 They accepted what
he said and were baptised. That very day
about three thousand were added to their
number.

The early Christian community

42 These remained faithful to the teaching
of the apostles, to the brotherhood, to the
breaking of bread and to the prayers.
43 And everyone was filled with awe; the
apostles worked many signs and miracles.
44 And all who shared the faith owned
everything in common; 45 they sold their
goods and possessions and distributed the
proceeds among themselves according to
what each one needed.
46 Each day, with one heart, they regularly
went to the Temple but met in their houses
for the breaking of bread; they shared their
food gladly and generously; 47 they praised
God and were looked up to by everyone. Day
by day the Lord added to their community
those destined to be saved.

2a Jl 3:1–5.
2b Ps 16:8–11 LXX.
2c Ps 110:1.
2d Ps 57:19.

The cure of a lame man[a]

3 Once, when Peter and John were going up to the Temple for the prayers at the ninth hour, [2]it happened that there was a man being carried along. He was a cripple from birth; and they used to put him down every day near the Temple entrance called the Beautiful Gate so that he could beg from the people going in. [3]When this man saw Peter and John on their way into the Temple he begged from them. [4]Peter, and John too, looked straight at him and said, 'Look at us.' [5]He turned to them expectantly, hoping to get something from them, [6]but Peter said, 'I have neither silver nor gold, but I will give you what I have: in the name of Jesus Christ the Nazarene, walk!' [7]Then he took him by the right hand and helped him to stand up. Instantly his feet and ankles became firm, [8]he jumped up, stood, and began to walk, and he went with them into the Temple, walking and jumping and praising God. [9]Everyone could see him walking and praising God, [10]and they recognised him as the man who used to sit begging at the Beautiful Gate of the Temple. They were all astonished and perplexed at what had happened to him.

Peter's address to the people

[11]Everyone came running towards them in great excitement, to the Portico of Solomon, as it is called, where the man was still clinging to Peter and John. [12]When Peter saw the people he addressed them, 'Men of Israel, why are you so surprised at this? Why are you staring at us as though we had made this man walk by our own power or holiness? [13]It is *the God of Abraham, Isaac and Jacob, the God of our ancestors, who has glorified his servant*[b] Jesus whom you handed over and then disowned in the presence of Pilate after he had given his verdict to release him. [14]It was you who accused the Holy and Upright One, you who demanded that a murderer should be released to you [15]while you killed the prince of life. God, however, raised him from the dead, and to that fact we are witnesses; [16]and it is the name of Jesus which, through faith in him, has brought back the strength of this man whom you see here and who is well known to you. It is faith in him that has restored this man to health, as you can all see.

[17]'Now I know, brothers, that neither you nor your leaders had any idea what you were really doing; [18]but this was the way God carried out what he had foretold, when he said through all his prophets that his Christ would suffer. [19]Now you must repent and turn to God, so that your sins may be wiped out, [20]and so that the Lord may send the time of comfort. Then he will send you the Christ he has predestined, that is Jesus, [21]whom heaven must keep till the universal restoration comes which God proclaimed, speaking through his holy prophets. [22]Moses, for example, said, *"From among your brothers the Lord God will raise up for you a prophet like me; you will listen to whatever he tells you. [23]Anyone who refuses to listen to that prophet shall be cut off from the people."*[c] [24]In fact, all the prophets that have ever spoken, from Samuel onwards, have predicted these days.

[25]'You are the heirs of the prophets, the heirs of the covenant God made with your ancestors when he told Abraham, *"All the nations of the earth will be blessed in your descendants"*.[d] [26]It was for you in the first place that God raised up his servant and sent him to bless you as every one of you turns from his wicked ways.'

Peter and John before the Sanhedrin

4 While they were still talking to the people the priests came up to them, accompanied by the captain of the Temple and the Sadducees. [2]They were extremely annoyed at their teaching the people the resurrection from the dead by proclaiming the resurrection of Jesus. [3]They arrested them, and, as it was already late, they kept them in prison till the next day. [4]But many of those who had listened to their message became believers; the total number of men had now risen to something like five thousand.

[5]It happened that the next day the rulers, elders and scribes held a meeting in Jerusalem [6]with Annas the high priest, Caiaphas, Jonathan, Alexander and all the members of the high-priestly families. [7]They made the

3a cf. Ac 14:8–10; Lk 8:51.
3b Ex 3:6 with Is 52:13.
3c Dt 18:15, 19.
3d Gn 22:18.

prisoners stand in the middle and began to
interrogate them, 'By what power, and by
whose name have you men done this?' 8Then
Peter, filled with the Holy Spirit, addressed
them, 'Rulers of the people, and elders! 9If
you are questioning us today about an act of
kindness to a cripple and asking us how he
was healed, 10you must know, all of you, and
the whole people of Israel, that it is by the
name of Jesus Christ the Nazarene, whom
you crucified, and God raised from the dead,
by this name and by no other that this man
stands before you cured. 11This is *the stone*
which you, *the builders, rejected* but which *has*
become the cornerstone.[a] Only in him is there
salvation; 12for of all the names in the world
given to men, this is the only one by which
we can be saved.'

13They were astonished at the fearlessness
shown by Peter and John, considering that
they were uneducated laymen; and they
recognised them as associates of Jesus; 14but
when they saw the man who had been cured
standing by their side, they could find no
answer. 15So they ordered them to stand
outside while the Sanhedrin had a private
discussion. 16'What are we going to do with
these men?' they asked. 'It is obvious to
everybody in Jerusalem that a notable miracle
has been worked through them, and we
cannot deny it. 17But to stop the whole thing
spreading any further among the people, let
us threaten them against ever speaking to
anyone in this name again.'

18So they called them in and gave them a
warning on no account to make statements
or to teach in the name of Jesus. 19But Peter
and John retorted, 'You must judge whether
in God's eyes it is right to listen to you and
not to God. 20We cannot stop proclaiming
what we have seen and heard.' 21The court
repeated the threats and then released them;
they could not think of any way to punish
them, since all the people were giving glory
to God for what had happened. 22The man
who had been miraculously cured was over
forty years old.

The apostles' prayer under persecution

23As soon as they were released they went to
the community and told them everything the
chief priests and elders had said to them.
24When they heard it they lifted up their voice
to God with one heart. 'Master,' they prayed,
'it is you who made sky and earth and sea,
and everything in them; 25it is you who
said through the Holy Spirit and speaking
through our ancestor David, your servant:

Why this uproar among the nations,
this impotent muttering of the peoples?
26*Kings on earth take up position,*
princes plot together
against the Lord and his Anointed.[b]

27'This is what has come true: in this very
city Herod and Pontius Pilate *plotted together*
with the gentile *nations* and the *peoples* of
Israel, against your holy servant Jesus whom
you *anointed*, 28to bring about the very thing
that you in your strength and your wisdom
had predetermined should happen. 29And
now, Lord, take note of their threats and
help your servants to proclaim your message
with all fearlessness, 30by stretching out your
hand to heal and to work miracles and marvels
through the name of your holy servant Jesus.'
31As they prayed, the house where they were
assembled rocked. From this time they
were all filled with the Holy Spirit and began
to proclaim the word of God fearlessly.

The early Christian community

32The whole group of believers was united,
heart and soul; no one claimed private owner-
ship of any possessions, as everything they
owned was held in common.

33The apostles continued to testify to the
resurrection of the Lord Jesus with great
power, and they were all accorded great
respect.

34None of their members was ever in want,
as all those who owned land or houses would
sell them, and bring the money from the sale
of them, 35to present it to the apostles; it was
then distributed to any who might be in need.

The generosity of Barnabas

36There was a Levite of Cypriot origin called
Joseph whom the apostles surnamed
Barnabas (which means 'son of encourage-
ment'). 37He owned a piece of land and he
sold it and brought the money and presented
it to the apostles.

4a Ps 118:22.
4b Ps 2:1–2.

The fraud of Ananias and Sapphira

5 There was also a man called Ananias. He
and his wife, Sapphira, agreed to sell a
property; 2 but with his wife's connivance he
kept back part of the price and brought the
rest and presented it to the apostles. 3 Peter
said, 'Ananias, how can Satan have so
possessed you that you should lie to the Holy
Spirit and keep back part of the price of the
land? 4 While you still owned the land, wasn't
it yours to keep, and after you had sold it
wasn't the money yours to do with as you
liked? What put this scheme into your mind?
You have been lying not to men, but to God.'
5 When he heard this Ananias fell down dead.
And a great fear came upon everyone present.
6 The younger men got up, wrapped up the
body, carried it out and buried it.
7 About three hours later his wife came in,
not knowing what had taken place. 8 Peter
challenged her, 'Tell me, was this the price
you sold the land for?' 'Yes,' she said, 'that
was the price.' 9 Peter then said, 'Why did
you and your husband agree to put the Spirit
of the Lord to the test? Listen! At the door
are the footsteps of those who have buried
your husband; they will carry you out, too.'
10 Instantly she dropped dead at his feet.
When the young men came in they found she
was dead, and they carried her out and buried
her by the side of her husband. 11 And a great
fear came upon the whole church and on all
who heard it.

The general situation

12 The apostles worked many signs and
miracles among the people. One in heart,
they all used to meet in the Portico of
Solomon. 13 No one else dared to join them,
but the people were loud in their praise 14 and
the numbers of men and women who came
to believe in the Lord increased steadily.
Many signs and wonders were worked among
the people at the hands of the apostles 15 so
that the sick were even taken out into the
streets and laid on beds and sleeping-mats in
the hope that at least the shadow of Peter
might fall across some of them as he went
past. 16 People even came crowding in from
the towns round about Jerusalem, bringing
with them their sick and those tormented by
unclean spirits, and all of them were cured.

The apostles' arrest and miraculous deliverance[a]

17 Then the high priest intervened with all his
supporters from the party of the Sadducees.
Filled with jealousy, 18 they arrested the
apostles and had them put in the public gaol.
19 But at night the angel of the Lord opened
the prison gates and said as he led them out,
20 'Go and take up position in the Temple,
and tell the people all about this new Life.'
21 They did as they were told; they went
into the Temple at dawn and began to
preach.

A summons to appear before the Sanhedrin

When the high priest arrived, he and his
supporters convened the Sanhedrin—this
was the full Senate of Israel—and sent to the
gaol for them to be brought. 22 But when the
officials arrived at the prison they found
they were not inside, so they went back
and reported, 23 'We found the gaol securely
locked and the warders on duty at the gates,
but when we unlocked the door we found no
one inside.' 24 When the captain of the Temple
and the chief priests heard this news they
wondered what could be happening. 25 Then
a man arrived with fresh news. 'Look!' he
said, 'the men you imprisoned are in the
Temple. They are standing there preaching
to the people.' 26 The captain went with his
men and fetched them—though not by force,
for they were afraid that the people might
stone them.
27 When they had brought them in to face
the Sanhedrin, the high priest demanded
an explanation. 28 'We gave you a strong
warning', he said, 'not to preach in this name,
and what have you done? You have filled
Jerusalem with your teaching, and seem
determined to fix the guilt for this man's
death on us.' 29 In reply Peter and the apostles
said, 'Obedience to God comes before obedi-
ence to men; 30 it was the God of our ancestors
who raised up Jesus, whom you executed by
hanging on a tree. 31 By his own right hand
God has now raised him up to be leader and
Saviour, to give repentance and forgiveness
of sins through him to Israel. 32 We are
witnesses to this, we and the Holy Spirit
whom God has given to those who obey him.'

5a cf. 12:6–11; 16:26–27.

33This so infuriated them that they wanted
to put them to death.

Gamaliel's intervention

34One member of the Sanhedrin, however, a
Pharisee called Gamaliel, who was a teacher
of the Law respected by the whole people,
stood up and asked to have the men taken
outside for a time. 35Then he addressed the
Sanhedrin, 'Men of Israel, be careful how
you deal with these people. 36Some time
ago there arose Theudas. He claimed to be
someone important, and collected about four
hundred followers; but when he was killed,
all his followers scattered and that was the
end of them. 37And then there was Judas the
Galilean, at the time of the census, who
attracted crowds of supporters; but he was
killed too, and all his followers dispersed.
38What I suggest, therefore, is that you leave
these men alone and let them go. If this
enterprise, this movement of theirs, is of
human origin it will break up of its own
accord; 39but if it does in fact come from God
you will be unable to destroy them. Take
care not to find yourselves fighting against
God.'

His advice was accepted; 40and they had
the apostles called in, gave orders for them
to be flogged, warned them not to speak in
the name of Jesus and released them. 41And
so they left the presence of the Sanhedrin,
glad to have had the honour of suffering
humiliation for the sake of the name.

42Every day they went on ceaselessly
teaching and proclaiming the good news of
Christ Jesus, both in the temple and in private
houses.

II: THE EARLIEST MISSIONS

The institution of the Seven

6 About this time, when the number of
disciples was increasing, the Hellenists[a]
made a complaint against the Hebrews: in
the daily distribution their own widows were
being overlooked. 2So the Twelve called a
full meeting of the disciples and addressed
them, 'It would not be right for us to neglect
the word of God so as to give out food; 3you,
brothers, must select from among yourselves
seven men of good reputation, filled with the
Spirit and with wisdom, to whom we can
hand over this duty. 4We ourselves will
continue to devote ourselves to prayer and to
the service of the word.' 5The whole assembly
approved of this proposal and elected
Stephen, a man full of faith and of the Holy
Spirit, together with Philip, Prochorus,
Nicanor, Timon, Parmenas, and Nicolaus
of Antioch, a convert to Judaism. 6They
presented these to the apostles, and after
prayer they laid their hands on them.

7The word of the Lord continued to
spread: the number of disciples in Jerusalem
was greatly increased, and a large group of
priests made their submission to the faith.

Stephen's arrest

8Stephen was filled with grace and power and
began to work miracles and great signs among
the people. 9Then certain people came
forward to debate with Stephen, some from
Cyrene and Alexandria who were members
of the synagogue called the Synagogue of
Freedmen, and others from Cilicia and Asia.
10They found they could not stand up against
him because of his wisdom, and the Spirit
that prompted what he said. 11So they
procured some men to say, 'We heard him
using blasphemous language against Moses
and against God.' 12Having turned the people
against him as well as the elders and scribes,
they took Stephen by surprise, and arrested
him and brought him before the Sanhedrin.
13There they put up false witnesses to say,
'This man is always making speeches against
this Holy Place and the Law. 14We have heard
him say that Jesus, this Nazarene, is going to
destroy this Place and alter the traditions that
Moses handed down to us.' 15The members of
the Sanhedrin all looked intently at Stephen,
and his face appeared to them like the face of
an angel.

6a Jews from outside Palestine, or Gk-speakers.

Stephen's speech[a]

7 The high priest asked, 'Is this true?' [2]He replied, 'My brothers, my fathers, listen to what I have to say. The God of glory appeared to our ancestor Abraham, while he was in Mesopotamia before settling in Haran, [3]and *said to* him, *"Leave your country, your kindred and your father's house for this country which I shall show you."* [4]So he left Chaldaea and settled in Haran; and after his father died God made him leave that place and come to this land where you are living today. [5]God did not give him any property in this land or even a foothold, yet he promised to *give it to him and after him to his descendants, childless* though he was. [6]The actual words God used when he spoke to him are that *his descendants would be exiles in a land not their own, where they would be enslaved and oppressed for four hundred years.* [7]*"But I will bring judgement on the nation that enslaves them,"* God said, *"and after this they will leave, and worship me in this place."* [8]Then he made the *covenant of circumcision* with him: and so when his son Isaac was born Abraham *circumcised him on the eighth day*; similarly Isaac circumcised Jacob, and Jacob the twelve patriarchs.

[9]'The patriarchs were *jealous of Joseph and sold him into slavery in Egypt.* But *God was with him,* [10]and rescued him from all his miseries by making him so wise that he *won the favour* of Pharaoh king of Egypt, who *made him governor of Egypt* and *put him in charge of his household.* [11]*Then a famine set in* that caused much suffering *throughout Egypt and Canaan*, and our ancestors could find nothing to eat. [12]When Jacob *heard that there were supplies in Egypt*, he sent our ancestors there on a first visit; [13]and on the second *Joseph made himself known to his brothers*, and Pharaoh came to know his origin. [14]Joseph then sent for his father Jacob and his whole family, a total of *seventy-five people.* [15]Jacob went down into Egypt and after he and our ancestors had died there, [16]their bodies were brought back to Shechem and buried in the tomb that Abraham had bought for money from the sons of Hamor, the father of Shechem.

[17]'As the time drew near for God to fulfil the promise he had solemnly made to Abraham, our nation in Egypt *became very powerful and numerous,* [18]*there came to power in Egypt a new king who had never heard of Joseph.* [19]*He took precautions and wore down* our race, forcing our ancestors to expose their babies rather than *letting them live.* [20]It was at this time that Moses was born, *a fine child* before God. He was looked after for *three months* in his father's house, [21]and after he had been exposed, *Pharaoh's daughter adopted* him and brought him up *like a son.* [22]So Moses was taught all the wisdom of the Egyptians and became a man with power both in his speech and in his actions.

[23]'At the age of forty he decided to visit *his kinsmen, the Israelites.* [24]When he saw one of them being ill-treated he went to his defence and rescued the man by *killing the Egyptian.* [25]He thought his brothers would realise that through him God would liberate them, but they did not. [26]The next day, when he came across some of them fighting, he tried to reconcile them, and said, "Friends, you are brothers; why are you hurting each other?" [27]But *the man who was attacking his kinsman* pushed him aside, saying, *"And who appointed you to be prince over us and judge?* [28]*Do you intend to kill me as you killed the Egyptian yesterday?"* [29]Moses fled when he heard this and *he went to dwell in the land of Midian*, where he fathered two sons.

[30]'When forty years were fulfilled, *in the desert near Mount* Sinai, *an angel appeared to him in a flame blazing from a bush* that was on fire. [31]Moses was amazed by what he saw. *As he went nearer to look at it, the voice of the Lord was* heard, [32]"I am the God of your ancestors, the God of Abraham, Isaac and Jacob." Moses trembled and *was afraid to look.* [33]The Lord said to him, *"Take off your sandals,* for the place where you are standing is holy ground. [34]*I have seen the misery of my people in Egypt, I have heard them crying for help, and I have come down to rescue them. So come here; I am sending you into Egypt."*

[35]'It was the same Moses that they had disowned when they said, *"Who appointed you to be our leader and judge?"* whom God sent to be both leader and redeemer through the angel who had appeared to him in the bush. [36]It was this man who led them out, after performing *miracles and signs in Egypt* and at the Red Sea and *in the desert for forty years.* [37]It was this Moses who told the sons of Israel, *"From among your own brothers God will raise up a prophet like me."* [38]When they

7a A survey using chiefly Gn and Ex.

held the assembly in the desert it was he who was with our ancestors and the angel who had spoken to him on Mount Sinai; it was he who was entrusted with words of life to hand on to us. 39 This is the man that our ancestors refused to listen to; they pushed him aside, *went back to Egypt* in their thoughts, 40 *and said to Aaron, "Make us a god to go at our head; for that Moses, the man who brought us here from Egypt, we do not know what has become of him."* 41 It was then that *they made the statue of a calf and offered sacrifice* to the idol. They were perfectly happy with something they had made for themselves. 42 God turned away from them and abandoned them to the worship of the army of heaven, as scripture says in the book of the prophets:

Did you bring me sacrifices and oblations
those forty years in the desert,
House of Israel?
43 *No, you carried the tent of Moloch*
on your shoulders
and the star of the god Rephan,
the idols you made
for yourselves to adore,
and so now I am about to drive you
into captivity beyond Babylon.[b]

44 'While they were in the desert our ancestors possessed the Tent of Testimony that had been constructed according to the instructions God gave Moses, telling him to *work to the design* he had been shown. 45 It was handed down from one ancestor of ours to another until Joshua brought it into the country that had belonged to the nations which were driven out by God before us. Here it stayed until the time of David. 46 He won God's favour and asked permission *to find a dwelling for* the House of *Jacob*, 47 though it was *Solomon* who actually *built a house for God*. 48 Even so the Most High does not live in a house that human hands have built: for as the prophet says:

49 *With heaven my throne*
and earth my footstool,
what house could you build me,
says the Lord,
what place for me to rest,
50 *when all these things were made by me?*[c]

51 'You stubborn people, with uncircumcised hearts and ears. You are always resisting the Holy Spirit, just as your ancestors used to do. 52 Can you name a single prophet your ancestors never persecuted? They killed those who foretold the coming of the Upright One, and now you have become his betrayers, his murderers. 53 In spite of being given the Law through angels, you have not kept it.'

54 They were infuriated when they heard this, and ground their teeth at him.

The stoning of Stephen
Saul as persecutor

55 But Stephen, filled with the Holy Spirit, gazed into heaven and saw the glory of God, and Jesus standing at God's right hand. 56 'Look! I can see heaven thrown open,' he said, 'and the Son of man standing at the right hand of God.' 57 All the members of the council shouted out and stopped their ears with their hands; then they made a concerted rush at him, 58 thrust him out of the city and stoned him. The witnesses put down their clothes at the feet of a young man called Saul. 59 As they were stoning him, Stephen said in invocation, 'Lord Jesus, receive my spirit.' 60 Then he knelt down and said aloud, 'Lord, do not hold this sin against them.' And with these words he fell asleep.

8 Saul approved of the killing.
That day a bitter persecution started against the church in Jerusalem, and everyone except the apostles scattered to the country districts of Judaea and Samaria.

2 There were some devout people, however, who buried Stephen and made great mourning for him.

3 Saul then began doing great harm to the church; he went from house to house arresting both men and women and sending them to prison.

Philip in Samaria

4 Once they had scattered, they went from place to place preaching the good news. 5 And Philip went to a Samaritan town and proclaimed the Christ to them. 6 The people unanimously welcomed the message Philip preached, because they had heard of the miracles he worked and because they saw them for themselves. 7 For unclean spirits

7b Am 5:25–27.
7c Is 66:1–2.

came shrieking out of many who were
possessed, and several paralytics and cripples
were cured. [8]As a result there was great
rejoicing in that town.

Simon the magician

[9]Now a man called Simon had for some time
been practising magic arts in the town and
astounded the Samaritan people. He had
given it out that he was someone momentous,
[10]and everyone believed in him; eminent
citizens and ordinary people alike had
declared, 'He is the divine power that is called
Great.' [11]He had this following because for a
considerable period they had been astounded
by his wizardry. [12]But when they came to
accept Philip's preaching of the good news
about the kingdom of God and the name of
Jesus Christ, they were baptised, both men
and women, [13]and even Simon himself
became a believer. After his baptism Simon
went round constantly with Philip and was
astonished when he saw the wonders and
great miracles that took place.
[14]When the apostles in Jerusalem heard
that Samaria had accepted the word of God,
they sent Peter and John to them, [15]and they
went down there and prayed for them to
receive the Holy Spirit, [16]for as yet he had
not come down on any of them: they had only
been baptised in the name of the Lord Jesus.
[17]Then they laid hands on them, and they
received the Holy Spirit.
[18]When Simon saw that the Spirit was
given through the laying on of the apostles'
hands, he offered them money, [19]with the
words, 'Give me the same power so that
anyone I lay my hands on will receive the
Holy Spirit.' [20]Peter answered, 'May your
silver be lost for ever, and you with it, for
thinking that money could buy what God has
given for nothing! [21]You have no share, no
part, in this: God can see how your heart
is warped. [22]Repent of this wickedness of
yours, and pray to the Lord that this scheme
of yours may be forgiven; [23]it is plain to me
that you are held in the bitterness of gall and
the chains of sin.' [24]Simon replied, 'Pray to
the Lord for me yourselves so that none
of the things you have spoken about may
happen to me.'
[25]Having given their testimony and
proclaimed the word of the Lord, they went
back to Jerusalem, preaching the good news
to a number of Samaritan villages.

Philip baptises a eunuch

[26]The angel of the Lord spoke to Philip
saying, 'Set out at noon and go along the road
that leads from Jerusalem down to Gaza, the
desert road.' [27]So he set off on his journey.
Now an Ethiopian had been on pilgrimage to
Jerusalem; he was a eunuch and an officer
at the court of the kandake, or queen, of
Ethiopia; he was her chief treasurer. [28]He
was now on his way home; and as he sat in
his chariot he was reading the prophet Isaiah.
[29]The Spirit said to Philip, 'Go up and join
that chariot.' [30]When Philip ran up, he heard
him reading Isaiah the prophet and asked,
'Do you understand what you are reading?'
[31]He replied, 'How could I, unless I have
someone to guide me?' So he urged Philip to
get in and sit by his side. [32]Now the passage
of scripture he was reading was this:

Like a lamb led to the slaughter-house,
like a sheep dumb in front of its shearers,
he never opens his mouth.
[33]*In his humiliation*
fair judgement was denied him.
Who will ever talk about his descendants,
since his life on earth has been cut short?[a]

[34]The eunuch addressed Philip and said,
'Tell me, is the prophet referring to himself
or someone else?' [35]Starting, therefore, with
this text of scripture Philip proceeded to
explain the good news of Jesus to him.
[36]Further along the road they came to some
water, and the eunuch said, 'Look, here is
some water; is there anything to prevent
my being baptised?'[37][b] [38]He ordered the
chariot to stop, then Philip and the eunuch
both went down into the water and he
baptised him. [39]But after they had come up
out of the water again Philip was taken away
by the Spirit of the Lord, and the eunuch
never saw him again but went on his way
rejoicing. [40]Philip appeared in Azotus and
continued his journey, proclaiming the good
news in every town as far as Caesarea.

8a Is 53:7–8.
8b v. 37, omitted here, is a very ancient gloss: 'And Philip said, "If you believe with all your heart, you may." And he replied, "I believe that Jesus is the Son of God." '

The conversion of Saul[a]

9 Meanwhile Saul was still breathing threats to slaughter the Lord's disciples. He went to the high priest [2]and asked for letters addressed to the synagogues in Damascus, that would authorise him to arrest and take to Jerusalem any followers of the Way, men or women, that he might find.

[3]It happened that while he was travelling to Damascus and approaching the city, suddenly a light from heaven shone all round him. [4]He fell to the ground, and then he heard a voice saying, 'Saul, Saul, why are you persecuting me?' [5]'Who are you, Lord?' he asked, and the answer came, 'I am Jesus, whom you are persecuting. [6]Get up and go into the city, and you will be told what you are to do.' [7]The men travelling with Saul stood there speechless, for though they heard the voice they could see no one. [8]Saul got up from the ground, but when he opened his eyes he could see nothing at all, and they had to lead him into Damascus by the hand. [9]For three days he was without his sight and took neither food nor drink.

[10]There was a disciple in Damascus called Ananias, and he had a vision in which the Lord said to him, 'Ananias!' When he replied, 'Here I am, Lord,' [11]the Lord said, 'Get up and go to Straight Street and ask at the house of Judas for someone called Saul, who comes from Tarsus. At this moment he is praying, [12]and has seen a man called Ananias coming in and laying hands on him to give him back his sight.'

[13]But in response, Ananias said, 'Lord, I have heard from many people about this man and all the harm he has been doing to your holy people in Jerusalem. [14]He has come here with a warrant from the chief priests to arrest everybody who invokes your name.' [15]The Lord replied, 'Go, for this man is my chosen instrument to bring my name before gentiles and kings and before the people of Israel; [16]I myself will show him how much he must suffer for my name.' [17]Then Ananias went. He entered the house, and laid his hands on Saul and said, 'Brother Saul, I have been sent by the Lord Jesus, who appeared to you on your way here, so that you may recover your sight and be filled with the Holy Spirit.' [18]It was as though scales fell away from his eyes and immediately he was able to see again. So he got up and was baptised, [19]and after taking some food he regained his strength.

Saul's preaching at Damascus

After he had spent only a few days with the disciples in Damascus, [20]he began preaching in the synagogues, 'Jesus is the Son of God.' [21]All his hearers were amazed, and said, 'Surely, this is the man who did such damage in Jerusalem to the people who invoke this name, and who came here for the sole purpose of arresting them to have them tried by the chief priests?' [22]Saul's power increased steadily, and he was able to throw the Jewish colony at Damascus into complete confusion by the way he demonstrated that Jesus was the Christ.

[23]Some time passed, and the Jews worked out a plot to kill him, [24]but news of it reached Saul. They were keeping watch at the gates day and night in order to kill him, [25]but the disciples took him by night and let him down from the wall, lowering him in a basket.

Saul's visit to Jerusalem[b]

[26]When he got to Jerusalem he tried to join the disciples, but they were all afraid of him: they could not believe he was really a disciple. [27]Barnabas, however, took charge of him, introduced him to the apostles, and explained how the Lord had appeared to him and spoken to him on his journey, and how he had preached fearlessly at Damascus in the name of Jesus. [28]Saul now started to go round with them in Jerusalem, preaching fearlessly in the name of the Lord. [29]But after he had spoken to the Hellenists and argued with them, they became determined to kill him. [30]When the brothers got to know of this, they took him to Caesarea and sent him off from there to Tarsus.

A lull

[31]The churches throughout Judaea, Galilee and Samaria were now left in peace, building themselves up and living in the fear of the Lord; encouraged by the Holy Spirit, they continued to grow.

9a =22; 26; cf. 2 M 3.
9b ‖ Ga 1:18–19?

went in to meet all the people assembled there, 28and Peter said to them, 'You know it is forbidden for Jews to mix with people of another race and visit them; but God has made it clear to me that I must not call anyone profane or unclean. 29That is why I made no objection to coming when I was sent for; but I should like to know exactly why you sent for me.' 30Cornelius replied, 'At this time three days ago I was in my house saying the prayers for the ninth hour, when I suddenly saw a man in front of me in shining robes. 31He said, "Cornelius, your prayer has been heard and your charitable gifts have not been forgotten by God; 32so now you must send to Jaffa and fetch Simon known as Peter who is lodging in the house of Simon the tanner, by the sea." 33So I sent for you at once, and you have been kind enough to come. Here we all are, assembled in front of you to hear all the instructions God has given you.'

Peter's address in the house of Cornelius

34Then Peter addressed them, 'I now really understand', he said, 'that God has no favourites, 35but that anybody of any nationality who fears him and does what is right is acceptable to him.

36'God sent his word to the people of Israel, and it was to them that *the good news of peace was brought*[a] by Jesus Christ—he is the Lord of all. 37You know what happened all over Judaea, how Jesus of Nazareth began in Galilee, after John had been preaching baptism. 38*God had anointed him with the Holy Spirit* and with power, and because God was with him, Jesus went about doing good and curing all who had fallen into the power of the devil. 39Now we are witnesses to everything he did throughout the countryside of Judaea and in Jerusalem itself: and they killed him by hanging him on a tree, 40yet on the third day God raised him to life and allowed him to be seen, 41not by the whole people but only by certain witnesses that God had chosen beforehand. Now we are those witnesses—we have eaten and drunk with him after his resurrection from the dead—42and he has ordered us to proclaim this to his people and to bear witness that God has appointed him to judge everyone, alive or dead. 43It is to him that all the prophets bear this witness: that all who believe in Jesus will have their sins forgiven through his name.'

Baptism of the first gentiles

44While Peter was still speaking the Holy Spirit came down[b] on all the listeners. 45Jewish believers who had accompanied Peter were all astonished that the gift of the Holy Spirit should be poured out on gentiles too, 46since they could hear them speaking strange languages and proclaiming the greatness of God. Peter himself then said, 47'Could anyone refuse the water of baptism to these people, now they have received the Holy Spirit just as we have?' 48He then gave orders for them to be baptised in the name of Jesus Christ. Afterwards they begged him to stay on for some days.

Jerusalem: Peter justifies his conduct

11 The apostles and the brothers in Judaea heard that gentiles too had accepted the word of God, 2and when Peter came up to Jerusalem the circumcised believers protested to him 3and said, 'So you have been visiting the uncircumcised and eating with them!' 4Peter in reply gave them the details point by point, 5'One day, when I was in the town of Jaffa,' he began, 'I fell into a trance as I was praying and had a vision of something like a big sheet being let down from heaven by its four corners. This sheet came right down beside me. 6I looked carefully into it and saw four-footed animals of the earth, wild beasts, reptiles, and birds of heaven. 7Then I heard a voice that said to me, "Now, Peter, kill and eat!" 8But I answered, "Certainly not, Lord; nothing profane or unclean has ever crossed my lips." 9And a second time the voice spoke from heaven, "What God has made clean, you have no right to call profane." 10This was repeated three times, before the whole of it was drawn up to heaven again.

11'Just at that moment, three men stopped outside the house where we were staying; they had been sent from Caesarea to fetch me, 12and the Spirit told me to have no hesitation about going back with them. The six brothers here came with me as well, and we entered the man's house. 13He told us he had seen an angel standing in his house who

10a Is 52:7 and in v. 38 Is 61:1.
10b cf. 2:3–4.

Peter cures a paralytic at Lydda

32 It happened that Peter visited one place after another and eventually came to God's holy people living down in Lydda. 33 There he found a man called Aeneas, a paralytic who had been bedridden for eight years. 34 Peter said to him, 'Aeneas, Jesus Christ cures you: get up and make your bed.' Aeneas got up immediately; 35 everybody who lived in Lydda and Sharon saw him, and they were converted to the Lord.

Peter raises a woman to life at Jaffa

36 At Jaffa there was a disciple called Tabitha, or in Greek, Dorcas, who never tired of doing good or giving to those in need. 37 But it happened that at this time she became ill and died, and they washed her and laid her out in an upper room. 38 Lydda is not far from Jaffa, so when the disciples heard that Peter was there, they sent two men to urge him, 'Come to us without delay.'

39 Peter went back with them immediately, and on his arrival they took him to the upper room, where all the widows stood round him in tears, showing him tunics and other clothes Dorcas had made when she was with them. 40 Peter sent everyone out of the room and knelt down and prayed. Then he turned to the dead woman and said, 'Tabitha, stand up.' She opened her eyes, looked at Peter and sat up. 41 Peter helped her to her feet, then he called in the members of the congregation and widows and showed them she was alive. 42 The whole of Jaffa heard about it and many believed in the Lord.

43 Peter stayed on some time in Jaffa, lodging with a leather-tanner called Simon.

Peter visits a Roman centurion

10 One of the centurions of the Italica cohort stationed in Caesarea was called Cornelius. 2 He and the whole of his household were devout and God-fearing, and he gave generously to Jewish causes and prayed constantly to God.

3 One day at about the ninth hour he had a vision in which he distinctly saw the angel of God come into his house and call out to him, 'Cornelius!' 4 He stared at the vision in terror and exclaimed, 'What is it, Lord?' The angel answered, 'Your prayers and charitable gifts have been accepted by God. 5 Now you must send some men to Jaffa and fetch a man called Simon, known as Peter, 6 who is lodging with Simon the tanner whose house is by the sea.' 7 When the angel who said this had gone, Cornelius called two of the slaves and a devout soldier of his staff, 8 told them all that had happened, and sent them off to Jaffa.

9 Next day, while they were still on their journey and had only a short distance to go before reaching the town, Peter went to the housetop at about the sixth hour to say his prayers. 10 He felt hungry and was looking forward to his meal, but before it was ready he fell into a trance 11 and saw heaven thrown open and something like a big sheet being let down to earth by its four corners; 12 it contained every kind of animal, reptile and bird. 13 A voice then said to him, 'Now, Peter, kill and eat!' 14 But Peter answered, 'Certainly not, Lord; I have never yet eaten anything profane or unclean.' 15 Again, a second time, the voice spoke to him, 'What God has made clean, you have no right to call profane.' 16 This was repeated three times, and then suddenly the container was drawn up to heaven again.

17 Peter was still at a loss over the meaning of the vision he had seen, when the men sent by Cornelius arrived. They had asked where Simon's house was and they were now standing at the door, 18 calling out to know if the Simon known as Peter was lodging there. 19 While Peter's mind was still on the vision, the Spirit told him, 'Look! Some men have come to see you. 20 Hurry down, and do not hesitate to return with them; it was I who told them to come.' 21 Peter went down and said to them, 'I am the man you are looking for; why have you come?' 22 They said, 'The centurion Cornelius, who is an upright and God-fearing man, highly regarded by the entire Jewish people, was told by God through a holy angel to send for you and bring you to his house and to listen to what you have to say.' 23 So Peter asked them in and gave them lodging.

Next day, he was ready to go off with them, accompanied by some of the brothers from Jaffa. 24 They reached Caesarea the following day, and Cornelius was waiting for them. He had asked his relations and close friends to be there, 25 and as Peter reached the house Cornelius went out to meet him, fell at his feet and did him reverence. 26 But Peter helped him up. 'Stand up,' he said, 'after all, I am only a man!' 27 Talking together they left them to go back to Jerusalem. [14]The others carried on from Perga till they reached Antioch in Pisidia. Here they went to synagogue on the Sabbath and took their seats. [15]After the passages from the Law and the Prophets had been read, the presidents of the synagogue sent them a message, 'Brothers, if you would like to address some words of encouragement to the congregation, please do so.' [16]Paul stood up, raised his hand for silence and began to speak:

Paul's preaching before the Jews[a]

'Men of Israel, and fearers of God, listen! [17]The God of our nation Israel chose our ancestors and made our people great when they were living in Egypt, a land not their own; then by divine power he led them out [18]and for about forty years *took care of* them in the desert. [19]*When he had destroyed seven nations in Canaan, he put them in possession* of their land [20]for about four hundred and fifty years. After this he gave them judges, down to the prophet Samuel. [21]Then they demanded a king, and God gave them Saul son of Kish, a man of the tribe of Benjamin. After forty years, [22]he deposed him and raised up David to be king, whom he attested in these words, "*I have found David* son of Jesse, *a man after my own heart, who will perform my entire will.*" [23]To keep his promise, God has raised up for Israel one of David's descendants, Jesus, as Saviour, [24]whose coming was heralded by John when he proclaimed a baptism of repentance for the whole people of Israel. [25]Before John ended his course he said, "I am not the one you imagine me to be; there is someone coming after me whose sandal I am not fit to undo."

[26]'My brothers, sons of Abraham's race, and all you godfearers, this message of salvation is meant for you. [27]What the people of Jerusalem and their rulers did, though they did not realise it, was in fact to fulfil the prophecies read on every Sabbath. [28]Though they found nothing to justify his execution, they condemned him and asked Pilate to have him put to death. [29]When they had carried out everything that scripture foretells about him they took him down from the tree and buried him in a tomb. [30]But God raised him from the dead, [31]and for many days he appeared to those who had accompanied him from Galilee to Jerusalem: and it is these same companions of his who are now his witnesses before our people.

[32]'We have come here to tell you the good news that the promise made to our ancestors has come about. [33]God has fulfilled it to their children by raising Jesus from the dead. As scripture says in the psalms: *You are my son: today I have fathered you.* [34]The fact that God raised him from the dead, never to return to corruption, is no more than what he had declared: *To you I shall give the holy things promised to David which can be relied upon.* [35]This is also why it says in another text: *You will not allow your Holy One to see corruption.* [36]Now when David in his own time had served God's purposes he died; he was buried with his ancestors and has certainly *seen corruption*. [37]The one whom God has raised up, however, has not *seen corruption*.

[38]'My brothers, I want you to realise that it is through him that forgiveness of sins is being proclaimed to you. Through him justification from all sins from which the Law of Moses was unable to justify [39]is being offered to every believer.

[40]'So be careful—or what the prophets say will happen to you.

[41]*Cast your eyes around you, mockers;*
be amazed, and perish!
For I am doing something in your own days
that you would never believe
if you were told of it.'

[42]As they left they were urged to continue this preaching the following Sabbath. [43]When the meeting broke up many Jews and devout converts followed Paul and Barnabas, and in their talks with them Paul and Barnabas urged them to remain faithful to the grace God had given them.

Paul and Barnabas preach to the gentiles

[44]The next Sabbath almost the whole town assembled to hear the word of God. [45]When they saw the crowds, the Jews, filled with jealousy, used blasphemies to contradict everything Paul said. [46]Then Paul and Barnabas spoke out fearlessly. 'We had to proclaim the word of God to you first, but since you have rejected it, since you do not think yourselves worthy of eternal life, here and now we turn to the gentiles. [47]For this is

---

13a Paul uses Dt 1:31; 7:1; Ps 89:14; 2:7; Is 55:3; Ps 16:9; Hab 1:5.

what the Lord commanded us to do when he
said:

I have made you a light to the nations,
so that my salvation may reach
the remotest parts of the earth.'[b]

48 It made the gentiles very happy to hear
this and they gave thanks to the Lord for his
message; all who were destined for eternal
life became believers. 49 Thus the word of the
Lord spread through the whole countryside.
50 But the Jews worked on some of the
devout women of the upper classes and the
leading men of the city; they stirred up a
persecution against Paul and Barnabas and
expelled them from their territory. 51 So they
shook the dust from their feet in protest
against them and went off to Iconium; but
the converts were filled with joy and the Holy
Spirit.

Iconium evangelised

14 It happened that at Iconium they went
to the Jewish synagogue, in the same
way, and they spoke so effectively that a great
many Jews and Greeks became believers.
2 (However, the Jews who refused to
believe stirred up the gentiles against the
brothers and set them in opposition.)
3 Accordingly Paul and Barnabas stayed on
for some time, preaching fearlessly in the
Lord; and he attested all they said about his
gift of grace, allowing signs and wonders to
be performed by them.
4 The people in the city were divided; some
supported the Jews, others the apostles, 5 but
eventually with the connivance of the auth-
orities a move was made by gentiles as well
as Jews to make attacks on them and to stone
them. 6 When they came to hear of this, they
went off for safety to Lycaonia where, in
the towns of Lystra and Derbe and in the
surrounding country, 7 they preached the
good news.

Healing of a cripple

8 There was a man sitting there who had never
walked in his life, because his feet were
crippled from birth; 9 he was listening to Paul
preaching, and Paul looked at him intently
and saw that he had the faith to be cured.
10 Paul said in a loud voice, 'Get to your feet—
stand up,' and the cripple jumped up and
began to walk.
11 When the crowds saw what Paul had
done they shouted in the language of
Lycaonia, 'The gods have come down to us
in human form.' 12 They addressed Barnabas
as Zeus, and since Paul was the principal
speaker they called him Hermes. 13 The
priests of Zeus-outside-the-Gate, proposing
that all the people should offer sacrifice with
them, brought garlanded oxen to the gates.
14 When the apostles Barnabas and Paul heard
what was happening they tore their clothes,
and rushed into the crowd, shouting,
15 'Friends, what do you think you are doing?
We are only human beings, mortal like your-
selves. We have come with good news to
make you turn from these empty idols to the
living God who made sky and earth and the
sea and all that these hold. 16 In the past he
allowed all the nations to go their own way;
17 but even then he did not leave you without
evidence of himself in the good things he
does for you: he sends you rain from heaven
and seasons of fruitfulness; he fills you with
food and your hearts with merriment.' 18 With
this speech they just managed to prevent the
crowd from offering them sacrifice.

End of the mission

19 Then some Jews arrived from Antioch and
Iconium and turned the people against them.
They stoned Paul and dragged him outside
the town, thinking he was dead. 20 The
disciples came crowding round him but, as
they did so, he stood up and went back to the
town. The next day he and Barnabas left for
Derbe.
21 Having preached the good news in that
town and made a considerable number of
disciples, they went back through Lystra,
Iconium and Antioch. 22 They put fresh heart
into the disciples, encouraging them to
persevere in the faith, saying, 'We must all
experience many hardships before we enter
the kingdom of God.' 23 In each of these
churches they appointed elders, and with
prayer and fasting they commended them to
the Lord in whom they had come to believe.
24 They passed through Pisidia and reached
Pamphylia. 25 Then after proclaiming the
word at Perga they went down to Attalia
26 and from there sailed for Antioch, where

13b Is 49:6; cf. 18:6; 28:25.

they had originally been commended to the grace of God for the work they had now completed.

[27]On their arrival they assembled the church and gave an account of all that God had done with them, and how he had opened the door of faith to the gentiles. [28]They stayed there with the disciples for some time.

Controversy at Antioch

15 Then some men came down from Judaea and taught the brothers, 'Unless you have yourselves circumcised in the tradition of Moses you cannot be saved.' [2]This led to disagreement, and after Paul and Barnabas had had a long argument with these men it was decided that Paul and Barnabas and others of the church should go up to Jerusalem and discuss the question with the apostles and elders.

[3]The members of the church saw them off, and as they passed through Phoenicia and Samaria they told how the gentiles had been converted, and this news was received with the greatest satisfaction by all the brothers. [4]When they arrived in Jerusalem they were welcomed by the church and by the apostles and elders, and gave an account of all that God had done through them.

Controversy at Jerusalem

[5]But certain members of the Pharisees' party who had become believers objected, insisting that gentiles should be circumcised and instructed to keep the Law of Moses. [6]The apostles and elders met[a] to look into the matter, [7]and after a long discussion, Peter stood up and addressed them.

Peter's speech

'My brothers,' he said, 'you know perfectly well that in the early days God made his choice among you: the gentiles were to learn the good news from me and so become believers. [8]And God, who can read everyone's heart, showed his approval of them by giving the Holy Spirit to them just as he had to us. [9]God made no distinction between them and us, since he purified their hearts by faith. [10]Why do you put God to the test now by imposing on the disciples the very burden that neither our ancestors nor we ourselves were strong enough to support? [11]But we believe that we are saved in the same way as they are: through the grace of the Lord Jesus.'

[12]The entire assembly fell silent, and they listened to Barnabas and Paul describing all the signs and wonders God had worked through them among the gentiles.

James' speech

[13]When they had finished it was James who spoke. 'My brothers,' he said, 'listen to me. [14]Simeon has described how God first arranged to enlist a people for his name out of the gentiles. [15]This is entirely in harmony with the words of the prophets, since the scriptures say:

[16]*After that I shall return*
and rebuild the fallen hut of David;
I shall make good the gaps in it
and restore it.
[17]*Then the rest of humanity,*
and of all the nations once called mine,
will look for the Lord,
says the Lord who made this [18]known
so long ago.[b]

[19]'My verdict is, then, that instead of making things more difficult for gentiles who turn to God, [20]we should send them a letter telling them merely to abstain from anything polluted by idols, from illicit marriages, from the meat of strangled animals and from blood. [21]For Moses has always had his preachers in every town and is read aloud in the synagogues every Sabbath.'

The apostolic letter

[22]Then the apostles and elders, with the whole church, decided to choose delegates from among themselves to send to Antioch with Paul and Barnabas. They chose Judas, known as Barsabbas, and Silas, both leading men in the brotherhood, [23]and gave them this letter to take with them:

'The apostles and elders, your brothers,

15a Two disputes are combined: Peter's speech concerns obligations of gentiles to keep the Jewish Law, James' concerns social contact.
15b Am 9:11–12.

send greetings to the brothers of gentile
birth in Antioch, Syria and Cilicia. 24We
hear that some people coming from here,
but acting without any authority from
ourselves, have disturbed you with their
demands and have unsettled your minds;
25and so we have decided unanimously to
elect delegates and to send them to you
with our well-beloved Barnabas and
Paul, 26who have committed their lives
to the name of our Lord Jesus Christ.
27Accordingly we are sending you Judas
and Silas, who will confirm by word of
mouth what we have written. 28It has been
decided by the Holy Spirit and by ourselves
not to impose on you any burden beyond
these essentials: 29you are to abstain from
food sacrificed to idols, from blood, from
the meat of strangled animals and
from illicit marriages. Avoid these, and
you will do what is right. Farewell.'

The delegates at Antioch

30The party left and went down to Antioch,
where they summoned the whole community
and delivered the letter. 31The community
read it and were delighted with the encour-
agement it gave them. 32Judas and Silas,
being themselves prophets, spoke for a long
time, encouraging and strengthening the
brothers. 33These two spent some time there,
and then the brothers wished them peace
and they went back to those who had sent
them.[34][c] 35Paul and Barnabas, however,
stayed on in Antioch, and there with many
others they taught and proclaimed the good
news, the word of the Lord.

IV: PAUL'S MISSIONS

Paul separates from Barnabas and recruits Silas

36On a later occasion Paul said to Barnabas,
'Let us go back and visit the brothers in all
the towns where we preached the word of the
Lord, so that we can see how they are doing.'
37Barnabas suggested taking John Mark,
38but Paul was not in favour of taking along
the man who had deserted them in Pamphylia
and had refused to share in their work.
39There was sharp disagreement so that
they parted company, and Barnabas sailed
off with Mark to Cyprus. 40Before Paul left,
he chose Silas to accompany him and was
commended by the brothers to the grace
of God.

Lycaonia: Paul recruits Timothy

41He travelled through Syria and Cilicia,
consolidating the churches.
16 From there he went to Derbe, and then
on to Lystra, where there was a disciple
called Timothy, whose mother was Jewish
and had become a believer; but his father was
a Greek. 2The brothers at Lystra and Iconium
spoke well of him, 3and Paul, who wanted to
have him as a travelling companion, had him
circumcised. This was on account of the Jews
in the locality where everyone knew his father
was a Greek.
4As they visited one town after another,
they passed on the decisions reached by
the apostles and elders in Jerusalem, with
instructions to observe them.
5So the churches grew strong in the faith,
as well as growing daily in numbers.

The crossing into Asia Minor

6They travelled through Phrygia and the
Galatian country, because they had been told
by the Holy Spirit not to preach the word in
Asia. 7When they reached the frontier of
Mysia they tried to go into Bithynia, but as
the Spirit of Jesus would not allow them,
8they went through Mysia and came down to
Troas.
9One night Paul had a vision: a Mace-
donian appeared and kept urging him in
these words, 'Come across to Macedonia and
help us.' 10Once he had seen this vision
we lost no time in arranging a passage to
Macedonia, convinced that God had called
us to bring them the good news.

15c Some MSS add v. 34 'But Silas decided to stay there'.

Arrival at Philippi

11 Sailing from Troas we made a straight run
for Samothrace; the next day for Neapolis,
12 and from there for Philippi, a Roman
colony and the principal city of that district
of Macedonia. 13 After a few days in this city
we went outside the gates beside a river as it
was the Sabbath and this was a customary
place for prayer. We sat down and preached
to the women who had come to the meeting.
14 One of these women was called Lydia, a
woman from the town of Thyatira who was
in the purple-dye trade, and who revered
God. She listened to us, and the Lord opened
her heart to accept what Paul was saying.
15 After she and her household had been
baptised she kept urging us, 'If you judge me
a true believer in the Lord,' she said, 'come
and stay with us.' And she would take no
refusal.

Imprisonment of Paul and Silas

16 It happened one day that as we were going
to prayer, we were met by a slave-girl who
was a soothsayer and made a lot of money
for her masters by foretelling the future.
17 This girl started following Paul and the rest
of us and shouting, 'Here are the servants of
the Most High God; they have come to tell
you how to be saved!' 18 She did this day
after day until Paul was exasperated and
turned round and said to the spirit, 'I order
you in the name of Jesus Christ to leave that
woman.' The spirit went out of her then
and there.
19 When her masters saw that there was no
hope of making any more money out of
her, they seized Paul and Silas and dragged
them into the market place before the auth-
orities. 20 Taking them before the magistrates
they said, 'These people are causing a
disturbance in our city. They are Jews 21 and
are advocating practices which it is unlawful
for us as Romans to accept or follow.' 22 The
crowd joined in and showed its hostility to
them, so the magistrates had them stripped
and ordered them to be flogged. 23 They were
given many lashes and then thrown into
prison, and the gaoler was told to keep a
close watch on them. 24 So, following such
instructions, he threw them into the inner
prison and fastened their feet in the
stocks.

The miraculous deliverance of Paul and Silas

25 In the middle of the night Paul and Silas
were praying and singing God's praises, while
the other prisoners listened. 26 Suddenly there
was an earthquake that shook the prison to
its foundations. All the doors flew open and
the chains fell from all the prisoners. 27 When
the gaoler woke and saw the doors wide open
he drew his sword and was about to commit
suicide, presuming that the prisoners had
escaped. 28 But Paul shouted at the top of his
voice, 'Do yourself no harm; we are all here.'
29 He called for lights, then rushed in,
threw himself trembling at the feet of Paul
and Silas, 30 and escorted them out, saying,
'Sirs, what must I do to be saved?' 31 They
told him, 'Become a believer in the Lord
Jesus, and you will be saved, and your house-
hold too.' 32 Then they preached the word of
the Lord to him and to all his household.
33 Late as it was, he took them to wash their
wounds, and was baptised then and there
with all his household. 34 Afterwards he took
them into his house and gave them a meal,
and the whole household celebrated their
conversion to belief in God.
35 When it was daylight the magistrates sent
the lictors with the order: 'Release those
men.' 36 The gaoler reported the message to
Paul, 'The magistrates have sent an order for
your release; you can go now and be on your
way.' 37 'What!' Paul replied. 'Without trial
they gave us a public flogging, though we are
Roman citizens, and threw us into prison,
and now they want to send us away on the
quiet! Oh no! They must come and escort us
out themselves.'
38 The lictors reported this to the magis-
trates, who were terrified when they heard
they were Roman citizens. 39 They came and
urged them to leave the town. 40 From the
prison they went to Lydia's house where they
saw all the brothers and gave them some
encouragement; then they left.

Thessalonica: difficulties with the Jews

17 Passing through Amphipolis and
Apollonia, they eventually reached
Thessalonica, where there was a Jewish syna-
gogue. 2 Paul as usual went in and for three
consecutive Sabbaths developed the argu-
ments from scripture for them, 3 explaining
and proving how it was ordained that the

Christ should suffer and rise from the dead.
'And the Christ', he said, 'is this Jesus whom
I am proclaiming to you.' 4Some of them
were convinced and joined Paul and Silas,
and so did a great many godfearing people
and Greeks, as well as a number of the leading
women.
5The Jews, full of resentment, enlisted the
help of a gang from the market place, stirred
up a crowd, and soon had the whole city in
an uproar. They made for Jason's house,
hoping to bring them before the People's
Assembly; 6however, they found only Jason
and some of the brothers, and these they
dragged before the city council, shouting,
'The people who have been turning the whole
world upside down have come here now;
7they have been staying at Jason's. They have
broken Caesar's edicts by claiming that there
is another king, Jesus.' 8Hearing this, the
citizens and the city councillors were
alarmed, 9and they made Jason and the rest
give security before setting them free.

Fresh difficulties at Beroea

10When it was dark the brothers immediately
sent Paul and Silas away to Beroea, where
they went to the Jewish synagogue as soon as
they arrived. 11Here the Jews were more
noble-minded than those in Thessalonica,
and they welcomed the word very readily;
every day they studied the scriptures to check
whether it was true. 12Many of them became
believers, and so did many Greek women of
high standing and a number of the men.
13When the Jews of Thessalonica came to
learn that the word of God was being
preached by Paul in Beroea as well, they went
there to make trouble and stir up the people.
14So the brothers arranged for Paul to go
immediately as far as the coast, leaving Silas
and Timothy behind. 15Paul's escort took
him as far as Athens, and went back with
instructions for Silas and Timothy to rejoin
Paul as soon as they could.

Paul in Athens

16Paul waited for them in Athens and there
his whole soul was revolted at the sight of a
city given over to idolatry. 17In the synagogue
he debated with the Jews and the godfearing,
and in the market place he debated every day
with anyone whom he met. 18Even a few
Epicurean and Stoic philosophers argued
with him. Some said, 'What can this parrot
mean?' And, because he was preaching about
Jesus and Resurrection, others said, 'He
seems to be a propagandist for some
outlandish gods.'
19They got him to accompany them to the
Areopagus, where they said to him, 'Can we
know what this new doctrine is that you
are teaching? 20Some of the things you say
seemed startling to us and we would like to
find out what they mean.' 21The one amuse-
ment the Athenians and the foreigners living
there seem to have is to discuss and listen to
the latest ideas.
22So Paul stood before the whole council
of the Areopagus and made this speech:

Paul's speech before the council of the Areopagus

'Men of Athens, I have seen for myself how
extremely scrupulous you are in all religious
matters, 23because, as I strolled round
looking at your sacred monuments, I noticed
among other things an altar inscribed: To An
Unknown God. In fact, the unknown God
you revere is the one I proclaim to you.
24'Since the God who made the world and
everything in it is himself Lord of heaven and
earth, he does not make his home in shrines
made by human hands. 25Nor is he in need
of anything, that he should be served by
human hands; on the contrary, it is he
who gives everything—including life and
breath—to everyone. 26From one single prin-
ciple he not only created the whole human
race so that they could occupy the entire
earth, but he decreed the times and limits of
their habitation. 27And he did this so that
they might seek the deity and, by feeling
their way towards him, succeed in finding
him; and indeed he is not far from any of us,
28since it is in him that we live, and move,
and exist,[a] as indeed some of your own writers
have said:

We are all his children.[b]

29'Since we are the children of God, we
have no excuse for thinking that the deity
looks like anything in gold, silver or stone

17a From the Gk poet Epimenides.
17b The Gk philosopher Aratus.

that has been carved and designed by a man.

30 'But now, overlooking the times of ignorance, God is telling everyone everywhere that they must repent, 31 because he has fixed a day when the whole world will be judged in uprightness by a man he has appointed. And God has publicly proved this by raising him from the dead.'

32 At this mention of rising from the dead, some of them burst out laughing; others said, 'We would like to hear you talk about this another time.' 33 After that Paul left them, 34 but there were some who attached themselves to him and became believers, among them Dionysius the Aeropagite and a woman called Damaris, and others besides.

Foundation of the church of Corinth

18 After this Paul left Athens and went to Corinth, 2 where he met a Jew called Aquila whose family came from Pontus. He and his wife Priscilla had recently left Italy because an edict of Claudius had expelled all the Jews from Rome. Paul went to visit them, 3 and when he found they were tentmakers, of the same trade as himself, he lodged with them, and they worked together. 4 Every Sabbath he used to hold debates in the synagogues, trying to convert Jews as well as Greeks.

5 After Silas and Timothy had arrived from Macedonia, Paul devoted all his time to preaching, declaring to the Jews that Jesus was the Christ. 6 When they turned against him and started to insult him, he took his cloak and shook it out in front of them,[a] saying, 'Your blood be on your own heads; from now on I will go to the gentiles with a clear conscience.' 7 Then he left the synagogue and moved to the house next door that belonged to a worshipper of God called Justus. 8 Crispus, president of the synagogue, and his whole household, all became believers in the Lord. Many Corinthians when they heard this became believers and were baptised. 9 One night the Lord spoke to Paul in a vision, 'Be fearless; speak out and do not keep silence: 10 I am with you. I have so many people that belong to me in this city that no one will attempt to hurt you.' 11 So Paul stayed there preaching the word of God among them for eighteen months.

The Jews take Paul to court

12 But while Gallio was proconsul of Achaia, the Jews made a concerted attack on Paul and brought him before the tribunal, saying, 13 'We accuse this man of persuading people to worship God in a way that breaks the Law.' 14 Before Paul could open his mouth, Gallio said to the Jews, 'Listen, you Jews. If this were a misdemeanour or a crime, it would be in order for me to listen to your plea; 15 but if it is only quibbles about words and names, and about your own Law, then you must deal with it yourselves—I have no intention of making legal decisions about these things.' 16 Then he began to hustle them out of the court, 17 and at once they all turned on Sosthenes, the synagogue president, and beat him in front of the tribunal. Gallio refused to take any notice at all.

Return to Antioch and departure for the third journey

18 After staying on for some time, Paul took leave of the brothers and sailed for Syria, accompanied by Priscilla and Aquila. At Cenchreae he had his hair cut off, because of a vow he had made.

19 When they reached Ephesus, he left them, but first he went alone to the synagogue to debate with the Jews. 20 They asked him to stay longer, but he declined, 21 though when he took his leave he said, 'I will come back another time, God willing.' Then he sailed from Ephesus.

22 He landed at Caesarea and went up to greet the church. Then he came down to Antioch 23 where he spent a short time before continuing his journey through the Galatian country and then through Phrygia, encouraging all the followers.

Apollos

24 An Alexandrian Jew named Apollos[b] now arrived in Ephesus. He was an eloquent man, with a sound knowledge of the scriptures, and yet, 25 though he had been given instruction in the Way of the Lord and preached with great

18a cf. 13:47; 28:25.
18b cf. 1 Co 1:12; 3:4–11.

spiritual fervour and was accurate in all the
details he taught about Jesus, he had experi-
enced only the baptism of John. 26He began
to teach fearlessly in the synagogue and,
when Priscilla and Aquila heard him, they
attached themselves to him and gave him
more detailed instruction about the Way.
27When Apollos thought of crossing over
to Achaia, the brothers encouraged him and
wrote asking the disciples to welcome him.
When he arrived there he was able by God's
grace to help the believers considerably 28by
the energetic way he refuted the Jews in
public, demonstrating from the scriptures
that Jesus was the Christ.

The disciples of John at Ephesus

19 It happened that while Apollos was in
Corinth, Paul made his way overland
as far as Ephesus, where he found a number
of disciples. 2When he asked, 'Did you
receive the Holy Spirit when you became
believers?' they answered, 'No, we were
never even told there was such a thing as a
Holy Spirit.' 3He asked, 'Then how were
you baptised?' They replied, 'With John's
baptism.' 4Paul said, 'John's baptism was a
baptism of repentance; but he insisted that
the people should believe in the one who was
to come after him—namely Jesus.' 5When
they heard this, they were baptised in the
name of the Lord Jesus, 6and the moment
Paul had laid hands on them the Holy Spirit
came down on them, and they began to speak
with tongues and to prophesy. 7There were
about twelve of these men in all.

Foundation of the church of Ephesus

8He began by going to the synagogue, where
he spoke out fearlessly and argued persuas-
ively about the kingdom of God. He did this
for three months, 9till the attitude of some of
the congregation hardened into unbelief. As
soon as they began attacking the Way in
public, he broke with them and took his
disciples apart to hold daily discussions in
the lecture room of Tyrannus. 10This went
on for two years, with the result that all the
inhabitants of Asia, both Jews and Greeks,
were able to hear the word of the Lord.

The Jewish exorcists

11So remarkable were the miracles worked
by God at Paul's hands 12that handkerchiefs
or aprons which had touched him were taken
to the sick, and they were cured of their
illnesses, and the evil spirits came out of
them.
13But some itinerant Jewish exorcists too
tried pronouncing the name of the Lord
Jesus over people who were possessed by evil
spirits; they used to say, 'I adjure you by the
Jesus whose spokesman is Paul.' 14Among
those who did this were seven sons of Sceva,
a Jewish chief priest. 15The evil spirit replied,
'Jesus I recognise, and Paul I know, but who
are you?' 16and the man with the evil spirit
hurled himself at them and overpowered first
one and then another, and handled them
so violently that they fled from that house
stripped of clothing and badly mauled.
17Everybody in Ephesus, both Jews and
Greeks, heard about this episode; everyone
was filled with awe, and the name of the Lord
Jesus came to be held in great honour.
18Some believers, too, came forward to
admit in detail how they had used spells
19and a number of them who had practised
magic collected their books and made a bon-
fire of them in public. The value of these
was calculated to be fifty thousand silver
pieces.
20In this powerful way the word of the
Lord spread more and more widely and
successfully.

V: THE END OF PAUL'S MISSIONARY JOURNEYS
A PRISONER FOR CHRIST

Paul's plans

21When all this was over Paul made up his
mind to go back to Jerusalem through Mace-
donia and Achaia. 'After I have been there,'
he said, 'I must go on to see Rome as well.'
22So he sent two of his helpers, Timothy and
Erastus, ahead of him to Macedonia, while
he remained for a time in Asia.

Ephesus: the silversmiths' riot

23 It was during this time that a serious disturbance broke out in connection with the Way. 24 A silversmith called Demetrius, who provided work for a large number of craftsmen making silver shrines of Diana, 25 called a general meeting of them with others in the same trade. 'As you know,' he said, 'it is on this industry that we depend for our prosperity. 26 Now you must have seen and heard how, not just in Ephesus but nearly everywhere in Asia, this man Paul has persuaded and converted a great number of people with his argument that gods made by hand are not gods at all. 27 This threatens not only to discredit our trade, but also to reduce the sanctuary of the great goddess Diana to unimportance. It could end up by taking away the prestige of a goddess venerated all over Asia, and indeed all over the world.' 28 This speech roused them to fury, and they started to shout, 'Great is Diana of the Ephesians!' 29 The whole town was filled with the uproar and the mob made a concerted rush to the theatre, dragging along two of Paul's Macedonian travelling companions, Gaius and Aristarchus. 30 Paul wanted to make an appeal to the people, but the disciples refused to let him; 31 in fact, some of the Asiarchs, who were friends of his, sent messages urging him not to take the risk of going into the theatre.

32 By now everybody was shouting different things, till the assembly itself had no idea what was going on; most of them did not even know why they had gathered together. 33 Some of the crowd prevailed upon Alexander, whom the Jews pushed forward; he raised his hand for silence with the intention of explaining things to the people. 34 As soon as they realised he was a Jew, they all started shouting in unison, 'Great is Diana of the Ephesians!' and they kept this up for two hours. 35 When the town clerk eventually succeeded in calming the crowd, he said, 'Citizens of Ephesus! Is there anybody who does not know that the city of the Ephesians is the guardian of the temple of great Diana and of her statue that fell from heaven? 36 Nobody can contradict this and there is no need for you to get excited or do anything rash. 37 These men you have brought here are not guilty of any sacrilege or blasphemy against our goddess. 38 If Demetrius and the craftsmen he has with him want to complain about anyone, there are the assizes and the proconsuls; let them take the case to court. 39 And if you want to ask any more questions you must raise them in the regular assembly. 40 We could easily be charged with rioting for today's happenings: there is no ground for it all, and we can give no justification for this gathering.' When he had finished this speech he dismissed the assembly.

Paul leaves Ephesus

20 When the disturbance was over, Paul sent for the disciples and, after speaking words of encouragement to them, said good-bye and set out for Macedonia. 2 On his way through those areas he said many words of encouragement to them and then made his way into Greece, 3 where he spent three months. He was leaving by ship for Syria when a plot organised against him by the Jews made him decide to go back by way of Macedonia. 4 He was accompanied by Sopater, son of Pyrrhus, who came from Beroea; Aristarchus and Secundus who came from Thessalonica; Gaius from Derbe, and Timothy, as well as Tychicus and Trophimus who were from Asia. 5 They all went on to Troas where they waited for us. 6 We ourselves left Philippi by ship after the days of Unleavened Bread and joined them five days later at Troas, where we stayed for a week.

Troas: Paul raises a dead man to life

7 On the first day of the week we met for the breaking of bread. Paul was due to leave the next day, and he preached a sermon that went on till the middle of the night. 8 A number of lamps were lit in the upstairs room where we were assembled, 9 and as Paul went on and on, a young man called Eutychus who was sitting on the window-sill grew drowsy and was overcome by sleep and fell to the ground three floors below. He was picked up dead. 10 Paul went down and stooped to clasp the boy to him, saying, 'There is no need to worry, there is still life in him.' 11 Then he went back upstairs where he broke the bread and ate and carried on talking till he left at daybreak. 12 They took the boy away alive, and were greatly encouraged.

From Troas to Miletus

13We were now to go on ahead by sea, so we
set sail for Assos, where we were to take Paul
on board; this was what he had arranged, for
he wanted to go overland. 14When he rejoined
us at Assos we took him aboard and went on
to Mitylene. 15The next day we sailed from
there and arrived opposite Chios. The second
day we touched at Samos and, after stopping
at Trogyllium, made Miletus the next day.
16Paul had decided to pass wide of Ephesus
so as to avoid spending time in Asia, since he
was anxious to be in Jerusalem, if possible,
for the day of Pentecost.

Farewell to the elders of Ephesus

17From Miletus he sent for the elders of the
church of Ephesus. 18When they arrived he
addressed these words to them:

'You know what my way of life has been
ever since the first day I set foot among you
in Asia, 19how I have served the Lord in all
humility, with all the sorrows and trials that
came to me through the plots of the Jews. 20I
have not hesitated to do anything that would
be helpful to you; I have preached to you and
instructed you both in public and in your
homes, 21urging both Jews and Greeks to
turn to God and to believe in our Lord Jesus.

22'And now you see me on my way to
Jerusalem in captivity to the Spirit; I have no
idea what will happen to me there, 23except
that the Holy Spirit, in town after town, has
made it clear to me that imprisonment and
persecution await me. 24But I do not place
any value on my own life, provided that I
complete the mission the Lord Jesus gave
me—to bear witness to the good news of
God's grace.

25'I now feel sure that none of you among
whom I have gone about proclaiming the
kingdom will ever see my face again. 26And
so on this very day I swear that my conscience
is clear as far as all of you are concerned, 27for
I have without faltering put before you the
whole of God's purpose.

28'Be on your guard for yourselves and for
all the flock of which the Holy Spirit has
made you the guardians, to feed the Church
of God which he bought with the blood of his
own Son.

29'I know quite well that when I have gone
fierce wolves will invade you and will have
no mercy on the flock. 30Even from your own
ranks there will be men coming forward with
a travesty of the truth on their lips to induce
the disciples to follow them. 31So be on your
guard, remembering how night and day for
three years I never slackened in counselling
each one of you with tears. 32And now I
commend you to God and to the word of his
grace that has power to build you up and
to give you your inheritance among all the
sanctified.

33'I have never asked anyone for money or
clothes; 34you know for yourselves that these
hands of mine earned enough to meet my
needs and those of my companions. 35By
every means I have shown you that we must
exert ourselves in this way to support the
weak, remembering the words of the Lord
Jesus, who himself said, "There is more
happiness in giving than in receiving." '[a]

36When he had finished speaking he knelt
down with them all and prayed. 37By now
they were all in tears; they put their arms
round Paul's neck and kissed him; 38what
saddened them most was his saying they
would never see his face again. Then they
escorted him to the ship.

The journey to Jerusalem

21 When we had at last torn ourselves
away from them and put to sea, we set
a straight course and arrived at Cos; the next
day we reached Rhodes, and from there went
on to Patara. 2Here we found a ship bound
for Phoenicia, so we went on board and sailed
in her. 3After sighting Cyprus and leaving it
to port, we sailed to Syria and put in at Tyre,
since the ship was to unload her cargo there.
4We sought out the disciples and stayed there
a week. Speaking in the Spirit, they kept
telling Paul not to go on to Jerusalem, 5but
when our time was up we set off. Together
with the women and children they all escorted
us on our way till we were out of the town.
When we reached the beach, we knelt down
and prayed; 6then, after saying good-bye to
each other, we went aboard and they returned
home.

7The end of our voyage from Tyre came
when we landed at Ptolemais, where we
greeted the brothers and stayed one day with
them. 8The next day we left and came to

20a This saying does not occur in the gospels.

Caesarea. Here we called on Philip the evan-
gelist, one of the Seven, and stayed with him.
9He had four unmarried daughters who were
prophets. 10When we had been there several
days a prophet called Agabus arrived from
Judaea. 11He came up to us, took Paul's belt
and tied up his own feet and hands, and said,
'This is what the Holy Spirit says, "The man
to whom this girdle belongs will be tied up
like this by the Jews in Jerusalem and handed
over to the gentiles." ' 12When we heard
this, we and all the local people urged Paul
not to go on to Jerusalem. 13To this he replied,
'What are you doing, weeping and breaking
my heart? For my part, I am ready not only
to be bound but even to die in Jerusalem for
the name of the Lord Jesus.' 14And so, as he
would not be persuaded, we gave up the
attempt, saying, 'The Lord's will be done.'

Paul's arrival in Jerusalem

15After this we made our preparations and
went on up to Jerusalem. 16Some of the
disciples from Caesarea accompanied us and
took us to the house of a Cypriot with whom
we were to lodge; he was called Mnason and
had been one of the earliest disciples.
17On our arrival in Jerusalem the brothers
gave us a very warm welcome. 18The next
day Paul went with us to visit James, and all
the elders were present. 19After greeting them
he gave a detailed account of all that God
had done among the gentiles through his
ministry. 20They gave glory to God when
they heard this. Then they said, 'You see,
brother, how thousands of Jews have now
become believers, all of them staunch
upholders of the Law; 21and what they have
heard about you is that you instruct all Jews
living among the gentiles to break away from
Moses, authorising them not to circumcise
their children or to follow the customary
practices. 22What is to be done? A crowd is
sure to gather, for they will hear that you
have come. 23So this is what we suggest that
you should do; we have four men here who
are under a vow; 24take these men along and
be purified with them and pay all the expenses
connected with the shaving of their heads.
This will let everyone know there is no truth
in the reports they have heard about you, and
that you too observe the Law by your way of
life. 25About the gentiles who have become
believers, we have written giving them our
decision that they must abstain from things
sacrificed to idols, from blood, from the
meat of strangled animals and from illicit
marriages.'
26So the next day Paul took the men along
and was purified with them, and he visited
the Temple to give notice of the time when
the period of purification would be over
and the offering would have to be presented
on behalf of each of them.

Paul's arrest

27The seven days were nearly over when some
Jews from Asia caught sight of him in the
Temple and stirred up the crowd and seized
him, 28shouting, 'Men of Israel, help! This is
the man who preaches to everyone every-
where against our people, against the Law
and against this place. He has even profaned
this Holy Place by bringing Greeks into the
Temple.' 29They had, in fact, previously seen
Trophimus the Ephesian in the city with him
and thought that Paul had brought him into
the Temple.
30This roused the whole city; people came
running from all sides; they seized Paul and
dragged him out of the Temple, and the gates
were closed behind them. 31While they were
setting about killing him, word reached the
tribune of the cohort that there was tumult
all over Jerusalem. 32He immediately called
out soldiers and centurions and charged
down on the crowd, who stopped beating
Paul when they saw the tribune and the
soldiers. 33When the tribune came up he took
Paul into custody, had him bound with two
chains and enquired who he was and what he
had done. 34People in the crowd called out
different things, and since the noise made
it impossible for him to get any positive
information, the tribune ordered Paul to be
taken into the fortress. 35When Paul reached
the steps, the crowd became so violent that
he had to be carried by the soldiers; 36and
indeed the whole mob was after them,
shouting, 'Do away with him!'
37Just as Paul was being taken into the
fortress, he asked the tribune if he could have
a word with him. The tribune said, 'You
speak Greek, then? 38Aren't you the Egyptian
who started the recent revolt and led those
four thousand cut-throats out into the
desert?' 39'I?' said Paul, 'I am a Jew and a
citizen of the well-known city of Tarsus in
Cilicia. Please give me permission to speak
to the people.' 40The man gave his consent

and Paul, standing at the top of the steps, raised his hand to the people for silence. A profound silence followed, and he started speaking to them in Hebrew.

Paul's address to the Jews of Jerusalem

22 'My brothers, my fathers, listen to what I have to say to you in my defence.'
2When they realised he was speaking in Hebrew, the silence was even greater than before. 3'I am a Jew', Paul said, 'and was born at Tarsus in Cilicia. I was brought up here in this city. It was under Gamaliel that I studied and was taught the exact observance of the Law of our ancestors. In fact, I was as full of duty towards God as you all are today.
4I even persecuted this Way to the death and sent women as well as men to prison in chains
5as the high priest and the whole council of elders can testify. I even received letters from them to the brothers in Damascus, which I took with me when I set off to bring prisoners back from there to Jerusalem for punishment.
6'It happened[a] that I was on that journey and nearly at Damascus when in the middle of the day a bright light from heaven suddenly shone round me. 7I fell to the ground and heard a voice saying, "Saul, Saul, why are you persecuting me?" 8I answered, "Who are you, Lord?" and he said to me, "I am Jesus the Nazarene, whom you are persecuting." 9The people with me saw the light but did not hear the voice which spoke to me.
10I said, "What am I to do, Lord?" The Lord answered, "Get up and go into Damascus, and there you will be told what you have been appointed to do." 11Since the light had been so dazzling that I was blind, I got to Damascus only because my companions led me by the hand.
12'Someone called Ananias, a devout follower of the Law and highly thought of by all the Jews living there, 13came to see me; he stood beside me and said, "Brother Saul, receive your sight." Instantly my sight came back and I was able to see him. 14Then he said, "The God of our ancestors has chosen you to know his will, to see the Upright One and hear his own voice speaking, 15because you are to be his witness before all humanity, testifying to what you have seen and heard.
16And now why delay? Hurry and be baptised and wash away your sins, calling on his name."
17'It happened that, when I got back to Jerusalem, and was praying in the Temple, I fell into a trance 18and then I saw him. "Hurry," he said, "leave Jerusalem at once; they will not accept the testimony you are giving about me." 19"Lord," I answered, "they know that I used to go from synagogue to synagogue, imprisoning and flogging those who believed in you; 20and that when the blood of your witness Stephen was being shed, I, too, was standing by, in full agreement with his murderers, and in charge of their clothes." 21Then he said to me, "Go! I am sending you out to the gentiles far away." '

Paul the Roman citizen

22So far they had listened to him, but at these words they began to shout, 'Rid the earth of the man! He is not fit to live!' 23They were yelling, waving their cloaks and throwing dust into the air, 24and so the tribune had him brought into the fortress and ordered him to be examined under the lash, to find out the reason for the outcry against him.
25But when they had strapped him down Paul said to the centurion on duty, 'Is it legal for you to flog a man who is a Roman citizen and has not been brought to trial?' 26When he heard this the centurion went and told the tribune; 'Do you realise what you are doing?' he said. 'This man is a Roman citizen.' 27So the tribune came and asked him, 'Tell me, are you a Roman citizen?' Paul answered 'Yes'. 28To this the tribune replied, 'It cost me a large sum to acquire this citizenship.' 'But I was born to it,' said Paul. 29Then those who were about to examine him hurriedly withdrew, and the tribune himself was alarmed when he realised that he had put a Roman citizen in chains.

His appearance before the Sanhedrin

30The next day, since he wanted to know for sure what charge the Jews were bringing, he freed Paul and gave orders for a meeting of the chief priests and the entire Sanhedrin; then he brought Paul down and set him in front of them.

22a =9; 26.

23 Paul looked steadily at the Sanhedrin
and began to speak, 'My brothers, to
this day I have conducted myself before God
with a perfectly clear conscience.' 2 At this the
high priest Ananias ordered his attendants to
strike him on the mouth. 3 Then Paul said
to him, 'God will surely strike you, you
whitewashed wall! How can you sit there to
judge me according to the Law, and then
break the Law by ordering a man to strike
me?' 4 The attendants said, 'Are you insulting
the high priest of God?' 5 Paul answered,
'Brothers, I did not realise it was the high
priest; certainly scripture says, "*You will not
curse your people's leader.*" '[a]
6 Now Paul was well aware that one party
was made up of Sadducees and the other of
Pharisees, so he called out in the Sanhedrin,
'Brothers, I am a Pharisee and the son of
Pharisees. It is for our hope in the resurrec-
tion of the dead that I am on trial.' 7 As soon
as he said this, a dispute broke out between
the Pharisees and Sadducees, and the
assembly was split between the two parties.
8 For the Sadducees say there is neither resur-
rection, nor angel, nor spirit, while the Phar-
isees accept all three. 9 The shouting grew
louder, and some of the scribes from the
Pharisees' party stood up and protested
strongly, 'We find nothing wrong with this
man. Suppose a spirit has spoken to him, or
an angel?' 10 Feeling was running high, and
the tribune, afraid that they would tear Paul
to pieces, ordered his troops to go down and
haul him out and bring him into the fortress.
11 Next night, the Lord appeared to him
and said, 'Courage! You have borne witness
for me in Jerusalem, now you must do the
same in Rome.'

The conspiracy of the Jews against Paul

12 When it was day, the Jews held a secret
meeting at which they made a vow not to eat
or drink until they had killed Paul. 13 More
than forty of them entered this pact, 14 and
they went to the chief priests and elders and
told them, 'We have made a solemn vow to
let nothing pass our lips until we have killed
Paul. 15 Now it is up to you and the Sanhedrin
together to apply to the tribune to bring
him down to you, as though you meant to
examine his case more closely; we, on our
side, are prepared to dispose of him before
he reaches you.'
16 But the son of Paul's sister heard of the
ambush they were laying and made his way
into the fortress and told Paul, 17 who called
one of the centurions and said, 'Take this
young man to the tribune; he has something
to tell him.' 18 So the man took him to the
tribune, and reported, 'The prisoner Paul
summoned me and requested me to bring
this young man to you; he has something to
tell you.' 19 Then the tribune took him by the
hand and drew him aside and questioned him
in private, 'What is it you have to tell me?'
20 He replied, 'The Jews have made a plan to
ask you to take Paul down to the Sanhedrin
tomorrow, as though they meant to enquire
more closely into his case. 21 Do not believe
them. There are more than forty of them
lying in wait for him, and they have vowed
not to eat or drink until they have got rid of
him. They are ready now and only waiting
for your order to be given.' 22 The tribune let
the young man go with this order, 'Tell no
one that you have given me this information.'

Paul transferred to Caesarea

23 Then he summoned two of the centurions
and said, 'Get two hundred soldiers ready to
leave for Caesarea by the third hour of the
night with seventy cavalry and two hundred
auxiliaries; 24 provide horses for Paul, and
deliver him unharmed to Felix the governor.'
25 He also wrote a letter in these terms:

26 'Claudius Lysias to his Excellency the
governor Felix, greetings. 27 This man had
been seized by the Jews and would have
been murdered by them; but I came on the
scene with my troops and got him away,
having discovered that he was a Roman
citizen. 28 Wanting to find out what charge
they were making against him, I brought
him before their Sanhedrin. 29 I found that
the accusation concerned disputed points
of their Law, but that there was no charge
deserving death or imprisonment.
30 Acting on information that there was a
conspiracy against the man, I hasten to
send him to you, and have notified his
accusers that they must state their case
against him in your presence.'

31 The soldiers carried out their orders;

23a Ex 22:27. Ananias became high priest in AD 47.

they took Paul and escorted him by night to Antipatris. 32Next day they left the mounted escort to go on with him and returned to the fortress. 33On arriving at Caesarea the escort delivered the letter to the governor and handed Paul over to him. 34When he had read it, he asked Paul what province he came from. Learning that he was from Cilicia he said, 35'I will hear your case as soon as your accusers are here too.' Then he ordered him to be held in Herod's praetorium.

The case before Felix

24 Five days later the high priest Ananias came down with some of the elders and an advocate named Tertullus, and they laid information against Paul before the governor. 2Paul was called, and Tertullus opened for the prosecution, 'Your Excellency, Felix, the unbroken peace we enjoy and the reforms this nation owes to your foresight 3are matters we accept, always and everywhere, with all gratitude. 4I do not want to take up too much of your time, but I urge you in your graciousness to give us a brief hearing. 5We have found this man a perfect pest; he stirs up trouble among Jews the world over and is a ringleader of the Nazarene sect. 6He has even attempted to profane the Temple. We placed him under arrest.[a] [7] 8If you ask him you can find out for yourself the truth of all our accusations against this man.' 9The Jews supported him, asserting that these were the facts.

10When the governor motioned him to speak, Paul answered:

Paul's speech before the Roman governor

'I know that you have administered justice over this nation for many years, and I can therefore speak with confidence in my defence. 11As you can verify for yourself, it is no more than twelve days since I went up to Jerusalem on pilgrimage, 12and it is not true that they ever found me arguing with anyone or stirring up the mob, either in the Temple, in the synagogues, or about the town; 13neither can they give you any proof of the accusations they are making against me now.

14'What I do admit to you is this: it is according to the Way, which they describe as a sect, that I worship the God of my ancestors, retaining my belief in all points of the Law and in what is written in the prophets; 15and I hold the same hope in God as they do that there will be a resurrection of the upright and the wicked alike. 16In these things, I, as much as they, do my best to keep a clear conscience at all times before God and everyone.

17'After several years I came to bring relief-money to my nation[b] and to make offerings; 18it was in connection with these that they found me in the Temple; I had been purified, and there was no crowd involved, and no disturbance. 19But some Jews from Asia—these are the ones who should have appeared before you and accused me of whatever they had against me. 20At least let those who are present say what crime they held against me when I stood before the Sanhedrin, 21unless it were to do with this single claim, when I stood up among them and called out, "It is about the resurrection of the dead that I am on trial before you today." '

Paul's captivity at Caesarea

22At this, Felix, who was fairly well informed about the Way, adjourned the case, saying, 'When Lysias the tribune comes down I will give judgement about your case.' 23He then gave orders to the centurion that Paul should be kept under arrest but free from restriction, and that none of his own people should be prevented from seeing to his needs.

24Some days later Felix came with his wife Drusilla who was a Jewess. He sent for Paul and gave him a hearing on the subject of faith in Christ Jesus. 25But when Paul began to treat of uprightness, self-control and the coming Judgement, Felix took fright and said, 'You may go for the present; I will send for you when I find it convenient.' 26At the same time he had hopes of receiving money from Paul, and for this reason he sent for him frequently and had talks with him.

27When two years came to an end, Felix was succeeded by Porcius Festus and, being anxious to gain favour with the Jews, Felix left Paul in custody.

24a Several witnesses add 'intending to judge him according to our Law, [7] but the tribune Lysias intervened and took him out of our hands by force,[8] ordering the accusers to appear before you'.
24b cf. 1 Co 16:1.

Paul appeals to Caesar

25 Three days after his arrival in the province, Festus went up to Jerusalem from Caesarea. 2The chief priests and leaders of the Jews informed him of the case against Paul, 3urgently asking him to support them against him, and to have him transferred to Jerusalem. They were preparing an ambush to murder him on the way. 4But Festus replied that Paul was in custody in Caesarea, and that he would be going back there shortly himself. 5He said, 'Let your authorities come down with me, and if there is anything wrong about the man, they can bring a charge against him.'

6After staying with them for eight or ten days at the most, he went down to Caesarea and the next day he took his seat on the tribunal and had Paul brought in. 7As soon as Paul appeared, the Jews who had come down from Jerusalem surrounded him, making many serious accusations which they were unable to substantiate. 8Paul's defence was this, 'I have committed no offence whatever against either Jewish law, or the Temple, or Caesar.' 9Festus was anxious to gain favour with the Jews, so he said to Paul, 'Are you willing to go up to Jerusalem and be tried on these charges before me there?' 10But Paul replied, 'I am standing before the tribunal of Caesar and this is where I should be tried. I have done the Jews no wrong, as you very well know. 11If I am guilty of committing any capital crime, I do not ask to be spared the death penalty. But if there is no substance in the accusations these persons bring against me, no one has a right to surrender me to them. I appeal to Caesar.' 12Then Festus conferred with his advisers and replied, 'You have appealed to Caesar; to Caesar you shall go.'

Paul appears before King Agrippa

13Some days later King Agrippa and Bernice arrived in Caesarea and paid their respects to Festus. 14Their visit lasted several days, and Festus put Paul's case before the king, saying, 'There is a man here whom Felix left behind in custody, 15and while I was in Jerusalem the chief priests and elders of the Jews laid information against him, demanding his condemnation. 16But I told them that Romans are not in the habit of surrendering any man, until the accused confronts his accusers and is given an opportunity to defend himself against the charge. 17So they came here with me, and I wasted no time but took my seat on the tribunal the very next day and had the man brought in. 18When confronted with him, his accusers did not charge him with any of the crimes I had expected; 19but they had some argument or other with him about their own religion and about a dead man called Jesus whom Paul alleged to be alive. 20Not feeling qualified to deal with questions of this sort, I asked him if he would be willing to go to Jerusalem to be tried there on this issue. 21But Paul put in an appeal for his case to be reserved for the judgement of the emperor, so I ordered him to be remanded until I could send him to Caesar.' 22Agrippa said to Festus, 'I should like to hear the man myself.' He answered, 'Tomorrow you shall hear him.'

23So the next day Agrippa and Bernice arrived in great state and entered the audience chamber attended by the tribunes and the city notables; and Festus ordered Paul to be brought in. 24Then Festus said, 'King Agrippa, and all here present with us, you see before you the man about whom the whole Jewish community has petitioned me, both in Jerusalem and here, loudly protesting that he ought not to be allowed to remain alive. 25For my own part I am satisfied that he has committed no capital crime, but when he himself appealed to the emperor I decided to send him. 26But I have nothing definite that I can write to his Imperial Majesty about him; that is why I have produced him before you all, and before you in particular, King Agrippa, so that after the examination I may have something to write. 27It seems to me pointless to send a prisoner without indicating the charges against him.'

26 Then Agrippa said to Paul, 'You have leave to speak on your own behalf.' And Paul held up his hand and began his defence:

Paul's speech before King Agrippa

2'I consider myself fortunate, King Agrippa, in that it is before you I am to answer today all the charges made against me by the Jews, 3the more so because you are an expert in matters of custom and controversy among the Jews. So I beg you to listen to me patiently.

4'My manner of life from my youth, a life spent from the beginning among my own

people and in Jerusalem, is common knowl-
edge among the Jews. 5They have known me
for a long time and could testify, if they
would, that I followed the strictest party in
our religion and lived as a Pharisee. 6And
now it is for my hope in the promise made by
God to our ancestors that I am on trial, 7the
promise that our twelve tribes, constant in
worship night and day, hope to attain. For
that hope, Your Majesty, I am actually put
on trial by Jews! 8Why does it seem incredible
to you that God should raise the dead?

9'As for me, I once thought it was my duty
to use every means to oppose the name of
Jesus the Nazarene. 10This I did in Jerusalem;
I myself threw many of God's holy people
into prison, acting on authority from the
chief priests, and when they were being
sentenced to death I cast my vote against
them. 11I often went round the synagogues
inflicting penalties, trying in this way to
force them to renounce their faith; my fury
against them was so extreme that I even
pursued them into foreign cities.

12'On such an expedition I was going to
Damascus, armed with full powers and a
commission from the chief priests,[a] 13and
in the middle of the day as I was on my way,
Your Majesty, I saw a light from heaven
shining more brilliantly than the sun round
me and my fellow-travellers. 14We all fell to
the ground, and I heard a voice saying to
me in Hebrew, "Saul, Saul, why are you
persecuting me? It is hard for you, kicking
against the goad." 15Then I said, "Who are
you, Lord?" And the Lord answered, "I am
Jesus, whom you are persecuting. 16But get
up and stand on your feet, for I have appeared
to you for this reason: to appoint you as my
servant and as witness of this vision in which
you have seen me, and of others in which I
shall appear to you. 17*I shall rescue you* from
the people and from *the nations to whom I send*
you 18*to open their eyes*, so that they may turn
from darkness to light,[b] from the dominion of
Satan to God, and receive, through faith in
me, forgiveness of their sins and a share in
the inheritance of the sanctified."

19'After that, King Agrippa, I could not
disobey the heavenly vision. 20On the
contrary I started preaching, first to the
people of Damascus, then to those of Jeru-
salem and all Judaean territory, and also to
the gentiles, urging them to repent and turn
to God, proving their change of heart by their
deeds. 21This was why the Jews laid hands
on me in the Temple and tried to do away
with me. 22But I was blessed with God's help,
and so I have stood firm to this day, testifying
to great and small alike, saying nothing more
than what the prophets and Moses himself
said would happen: 23that the Christ was to
suffer and that, as the first to rise from the
dead, he was to proclaim a light for our people
and for the gentiles.'

His hearers' reactions

24He had reached this point in his defence
when Festus shouted out, 'Paul, you are out
of your mind; all that learning of yours is
driving you mad.' 25But Paul answered,
'Festus, your Excellency, I am not mad: I am
speaking words of sober truth and good
sense. 26The king understands these matters,
and to him I now speak fearlessly. I am
confident that nothing of all this comes as a
surprise to him; after all, these things were
not done in a corner. 27King Agrippa, do you
believe in the prophets? I know you do.' 28At
this Agrippa said to Paul, 'A little more, and
your arguments would make a Christian of
me.' 29Paul replied, 'Little or much, I wish
before God that not only you but all who are
listening to me today would come to be as I
am—except for these chains.'

30At this the king rose to his feet, with the
governor and Bernice and those who sat there
with them. 31When they had retired they
talked together and agreed, 'This man is
doing nothing that deserves death or impris-
onment.' 32And Agrippa remarked to Festus,
'The man could have been set free if he had
not appealed to Caesar.'

The departure for Rome

27 When it had been decided that we
should sail to Italy, Paul and some other
prisoners were handed over to a centurion
called Julius, of the Augustan cohort. 2We
boarded a vessel from Adramyttium bound
for ports on the Asiatic coast and put to sea;
we had Aristarchus with us, a Macedonian
of Thessalonica. 3Next day we put in at
Sidon, and Julius was considerate enough to

26a =9: 22
26b Jr 1:5–8 followed by Is 42:16.

allow Paul to go to his friends to be looked
after.
4 From there we put to sea again, but as the
winds were against us we sailed under the lee
of Cyprus, 5 then across the open sea off
Cilicia and Pamphylia, taking a fortnight to
reach Myra in Lycia. 6 There the centurion
found an Alexandrian ship leaving for Italy
and put us aboard.
7 For some days we made little headway,
and we had difficulty in making Cnidus. The
wind would not allow us to touch there, so
we sailed under the lee of Crete off Cape
Salmone 8 and struggled along the coast until
we came to a place called Fair Havens, near
the town of Lasea.

Storm and shipwreck

9 A great deal of time had been lost, and
navigation was already hazardous, since it
was now well after the time of the Fast, so
Paul gave them this warning, 10 'Friends, I
can see this voyage will be dangerous and
that we will run considerable risk of losing
not only the cargo and the ship but also our
lives as well.' 11 But the centurion took more
notice of the captain and the ship's owner
than of what Paul was saying; 12 and since the
harbour was unsuitable for wintering, the
majority were for putting out from there in
the hope of wintering at Phoenix—a harbour
in Crete, facing south-west and north-west.
13 A southerly breeze sprang up and,
thinking their objective as good as reached,
they weighed anchor and began to sail past
Crete, close inshore. 14 But it was not long
before a hurricane, the 'north-easter' as they
call it, burst on them from across the island.
15 The ship was caught and could not keep
head to wind, so we had to give way to the
wind and let ourselves be driven. 16 We ran
under the lee of a small island called Cauda
and managed with some difficulty to bring the
ship's boat under control. 17 Having hauled it
up they used it to undergird the ship; then,
afraid of running aground on the Syrtis
banks, they floated out the sea-anchor and so
let themselves drift. 18 As we were thoroughly
storm-bound, the next day they began to
jettison the cargo, 19 and the third day they
threw the ship's gear overboard with their
own hands. 20 For a number of days both the
sun and the stars were invisible and the storm
raged unabated until at last we gave up all
hope of surviving.
21 Then, when they had been without food
for a long time, Paul stood up among the
men. 'Friends,' he said, 'you should have
listened to me and not put out from Crete.
You would have spared yourselves all this
damage and loss. 22 But now I ask you not to
give way to despair. There will be no loss of
life at all, only of the ship. 23 Last night there
appeared beside me an angel of the God to
whom I belong and whom I serve, 24 and
he said, "Do not be afraid, Paul. You are
destined to appear before Caesar, and God
grants you the safety of all who are sailing
with you." 25 So take courage, friends; I trust
in God that things will turn out just as I was
told; 26 but we are to be stranded on some
island.'
27 On the fourteenth night we were being
driven one way and another in the Adriatic,
when about midnight the crew sensed that
land of some sort was near. 28 They took
soundings and found twenty fathoms; after
a short interval they sounded again and found
fifteen fathoms. 29 Then, afraid that we might
run aground somewhere on a reef, they
dropped four anchors from the stern and
prayed for daylight. 30 When the crew tried
to escape from the ship and lowered the ship's
boat into the sea as though they meant to lay
out anchors from the bows, Paul said to the
centurion and his men, 31 'Unless those men
stay on board you cannot hope to be saved.'
32 So the soldiers cut the boat's ropes and let
it drop away.
33 Just before daybreak Paul urged them all
to have something to eat. 'For fourteen days',
he said, 'you have been in suspense, going
hungry and eating nothing. 34 I urge you to
have something to eat; your safety depends
on it. Not a hair of any of your heads will be
lost.' 35 With these words he took some bread,
gave thanks to God in view of them all, broke
it and began to eat. 36 They all plucked up
courage and took something to eat them-
selves. 37 In all we were two hundred and
seventy-six souls on board that ship. 38 When
they had eaten what they wanted they light-
ened the ship by throwing the corn overboard
into the sea.
39 When day came they did not recognise
the land, but they could make out a bay with
a beach; they planned to run the ship aground
on this if they could. 40 They slipped the
anchors and let them fall into the sea, and
at the same time loosened the lashings of

the rudders; then, hoisting the foresail to the
wind, they headed for the beach. [41]But the
cross-currents carried them into a shoal and
the vessel ran aground. The bows were
wedged in and stuck fast, while the stern
began to break up with the pounding of the
waves.
[42]The soldiers planned to kill the prisoners
for fear that any should swim off and escape.
[43]But the centurion was determined to bring
Paul safely through and would not let them
carry out their plan. He gave orders that those
who could swim should jump overboard first
and so get ashore, [44]and the rest follow either
on planks or on pieces of wreckage. In this
way it happened that all came safe and sound
to land.

Waiting in Malta

28 Once we had come safely through, we
discovered that the island was called
Malta. [2]The inhabitants treated us with
unusual kindness. They made us all welcome
by lighting a huge fire because it had started
to rain and the weather was cold. [3]Paul had
collected a bundle of sticks and was putting
them on the fire when a viper brought out by
the heat attached itself to his hand. [4]When
the inhabitants saw the creature hanging
from his hand they said to one another,
'That man must be a murderer; he may have
escaped the sea, but divine justice would not
let him live.' [5]However, he shook the creature
off into the fire and came to no harm,
[6]although they were expecting him at any
moment to swell up or drop dead on the spot.
After they had waited a long time without
seeing anything out of the ordinary happen
to him, they changed their minds and began
to say he was a god.
[7]In that neighbourhood there were estates
belonging to the chief man of the island,
whose name was Publius. He received us and
entertained us hospitably for three days. [8]It
happened that Publius' father was in bed,
suffering from fever and dysentery. Paul
went in to see him, and after a prayer he laid
his hands on the man and healed him. [9]When
this happened, the other sick people on the
island also came and were cured; [10]they
honoured us with many marks of respect,
and when we sailed they put on board the
provisions we needed.

From Malta to Rome

[11]At the end of three months we set sail in a
ship that had wintered in the island; she came
from Alexandria and her figurehead was the
Twins. [12]We put in at Syracuse and spent
three days there; [13]from there we followed
the coast up to Rhegium. After one day there
a south wind sprang up and on the second
day we made Puteoli, [14]where we found some
brothers and had the great encouragement of
staying a week with them. And so we came
to Rome.
[15]When the brothers there heard about us
they came to meet us, as far as the Forum of
Appius and the Three Taverns. When Paul
saw them he thanked God and took courage.
[16]On our arrival in Rome Paul was allowed
to stay in lodgings of his own with the soldier
who guarded him.

Paul makes contact with the Roman Jews

[17]After three days he called together the
leading Jews. When they had assembled, he
said to them, 'Brothers, although I have done
nothing against our people or the customs of
our ancestors, I was arrested in Jerusalem
and handed over to the Romans. [18]They
examined me and would have set me free,
since they found me guilty of nothing
involving the death penalty; [19]but the Jews
lodged an objection, and I was forced to
appeal to Caesar, though not because I had
any accusation to make against my own
nation. [20]That is why I have urged you to see
me and have a discussion with me, for it is
on account of the hope of Israel that I wear
this chain.'
[21]They answered, 'We have received no
letters from Judaea about you, nor has any
of the brothers arrived here with any report
or story of anything to your discredit. [22]We
think it would be as well to hear your own
account of your position; all we know about
this sect is that it encounters opposition
everywhere.'

Paul's declaration to the Roman Jews

[23]So they arranged a day with him and a large
number of them visited him at his lodgings.
He put his case to them, testifying to the
kingdom of God and trying to persuade them
about Jesus, arguing from the Law of Moses

and the prophets from early morning until
evening; 24 and some were convinced by what
he said, while the rest were sceptical. 25 So
they disagreed among themselves and, as
they went away, Paul had one last thing to
say to them, 'How aptly the Holy Spirit spoke
when he told your ancestors through the
prophet Isaiah:

26 *Go and say to this people:*
Listen and listen but never understand!
Look and look but never perceive!
27 *This people's heart is torpid,*
their ears dulled,
they have shut their eyes tight,
to avoid using their eyes to see,
their ears to hear,
using their heart to understand,
changing their ways
and being healed by me. [a]

28 'You must realise, then, that this sal-
vation of God has been sent to the gentiles;
and they will listen to it.'[29] [b]

Epilogue

30 He spent the whole of the two years in his
own rented lodging. He welcomed all who
came to visit him, 31 proclaiming the kingdom
of God and teaching the truth about the Lord
Jesus Christ with complete fearlessness and
without any hindrance from anyone.

INTRODUCTION TO
THE LETTERS OF PAUL

The general lines of Paul's life as a Christian missionary are clear enough from Acts, though there are some inconsistencies between that picture and the information from Paul's own letters. In the last decade of his apostolate he wrote to the churches he had founded, in response to questions, worries and difficulties they were experiencing. With these as his starting-point he ranges widely over the vital issues of Christian theology and life, discussing often very local issues in the light of basic principles. The letters also provide a fascinating portrait of Paul, capable of affection and anger, working passionately and selflessly for Christ and the churches he loved. Bearing suffering and persecution in unison with his Master, Paul is inspired always by his knowledge of sharing Christ's life as servant of God.

The letters are traditionally printed in decreasing order of length, first letters to communities, then those to individuals. The most probable chronological order is:

1 EARLY EPISTLES	1–2 Thessalonians
2 THE GREAT EPISTLES	1–2 Corinthians, Galatians, Romans, possibly Philippians

28a Is 6:9–10; cf. 13:47; 18:6.
28b Some MSS add v. 29 'And when he had said this, the Jews left, arguing hotly among themselves.'

3 CAPTIVITY EPISTLES — Colossians, Ephesians (authorship disputed), Philemon

4 PASTORAL EPISTLES — (authorship doubtful) 1–2 Timothy, Titus

THE LETTER TO THE ROMANS

As well as being the longest of Paul's letters (and so printed first) Rm is a noble synthesis of his teaching on the Law and faith, a theme already treated in Ga. Writing to the mixed community of Jewish and gentile origin at Rome, Paul wants partly to introduce himself before a proposed visit and partly to give help on the problems which caused friction between the two sections in the community. It is a calmer treatment than Ga, and Paul is less negative towards the Law.

The main point of the letter is that the Law is powerless to save, and gives only knowledge of sin, not strength. Salvation is offered to all humanity through faith in Christ, who delivers from the retribution of God. This faith is expressed in baptism, by which Christians are buried with Christ and rise with Christ to new life as adopted sons and members of Christ, sharing his life and his experiences. Among the most striking of all Pauline passages are chh. 9—11: by reflection on Scripture, Paul explores the agonising problem of the mystery of the refusal of his brothers the Jews to recognise Christ.

PLAN OF THE LETTER

ROMANS
THE LETTER OF PAUL TO THE CHURCH IN ROME

Address

1 From Paul, a servant of Christ Jesus,
called to be an apostle, [2]set apart for the
service of the gospel that God promised long
ago through his prophets in the holy
scriptures.
[3]This is the gospel concerning his Son
who, in terms of human nature [4]was born a
descendant of David and who, in terms of
the Spirit and of holiness, was designated
Son of God in power by resurrection from
the dead: Jesus Christ, our Lord, [5]through
whom we have received grace and our apos-
tolic mission of winning the obedience of
faith among all the nations for the honour of
his name. [6]You are among these, and by his
call you belong to Jesus Christ. [7]To you all,
God's beloved in Rome, called to be his holy
people. Grace and peace from God our Father
and the Lord Jesus Christ.

Thanksgiving and prayer

[8]First I give thanks to my God through Jesus
Christ for all of you because your faith is
talked of all over the world. [9]God, whom I
serve with my spirit in preaching the gospel
of his Son, is my witness that I continually
mention you in my prayers, [10]asking always
that by some means I may at long last be
enabled to visit you, if it is God's will. [11]For
I am longing to see you so that I can convey
to you some spiritual gift that will be a
lasting strength, [12]or rather that we may be
strengthened together through our mutual
faith, yours and mine. [13]I want you to be
quite certain too, brothers, that I have often
planned to visit you—though up to the
present I have always been prevented—in the
hope that I might work as fruitfully among
you as I have among the gentiles elsewhere.
[14]I have an obligation to Greeks as well as
barbarians, to the educated as well as the
ignorant, [15]and hence the eagerness on my
part to preach the gospel to you in Rome too.

SALVATION BY FAITH

I: JUSTIFICATION

The theme stated

[16]For I see no reason to be ashamed of the
gospel; it is God's power for the salvation
of everyone who has faith—Jews first, but
Greeks as well—[17]for in it is revealed the
saving justice of God: a justice based on faith
and addressed to faith. As it says in scripture:
Anyone who is upright through faith will live.[a]

A: THE RETRIBUTION OF GOD AGAINST GENTILE AND JEW

God's retribution against the gentiles

[18]The retribution of God from heaven is being
revealed against the ungodliness and injustice
of human beings who in their injustice hold
back the truth. [19]For what can be known

1a Hab 2:4 LXX.

about God is perfectly plain to them, since God has made it plain to them: 20ever since the creation of the world, the invisible existence of God and his everlasting power have been clearly seen by the mind's understanding of created things. And so these people have no excuse: 21they knew God and yet they did not honour him as God or give thanks to him, but their arguments became futile and their uncomprehending minds were darkened. 22While they claimed to be wise, in fact they were growing so stupid 23that *they exchanged the glory* of the immortal God *for an imitation*,[b] for the image of a mortal human being, or of birds, or animals, or crawling things.

24That is why God abandoned them in their inmost cravings to filthy practices of dishonouring their own bodies—25because they *exchanged God's truth* for a lie and have worshipped and served the creature instead of the Creator, who is blessed for ever. Amen.

26That is why God abandoned them to degrading passions: 27why their women have exchanged natural intercourse for unnatural practices; and the men, in a similar fashion, too, giving up normal relations with women, are consumed with passion for each other, men doing shameful things with men and receiving in themselves due reward for their perversion.

28In other words, since they would not consent to acknowledge God, God abandoned them to their unacceptable thoughts and indecent behaviour. 29And so now they are steeped in all sorts of injustice, rottenness, greed and malice; full of envy, murder, wrangling, treachery and spite, 30libellers, slanderers, enemies of God, rude, arrogant and boastful, enterprising in evil, rebellious to parents, 31without brains, honour, love or pity. 32They are well aware of God's ordinance: that those who behave like this deserve to die—yet they not only do it, but even applaud others who do the same.

The Jews are not exempt from the retribution of God

2 So no matter who you are, if you pass judgement you have no excuse. It is yourself that you condemn when you judge others, since you behave in the same way as those you are condemning. 2We are well aware that people who behave like that are justly condemned by God. 3But you—when you judge those who behave like this while you are doing the same yourself—do you think you will escape God's condemnation? 4Or are you not disregarding his abundant goodness, tolerance and patience, failing to realise that this generosity of God is meant to bring you to repentance? 5Your stubborn refusal to repent is only storing up retribution for yourself on that Day of retribution when God's just verdicts will be made known. 6*He will repay everyone as their deeds deserve*.[a] 7For those who aimed for glory and honour and immortality by persevering in doing good, there will be eternal life; 8but for those who out of jealousy have taken for their guide not truth but injustice, there will be the fury of retribution. 9Trouble and distress will come to every human being who does evil—Jews first, but Greeks as well; 10glory and honour and peace will come to everyone who does good—Jews first, but Greeks as well. 11*There is no favouritism with God*.[b]

The Law will not save them

12All those who have sinned without the Law will perish without the Law; and those under the Law who have sinned will be judged by the Law. 13For the ones that God will justify are not those who have heard the Law but those who have kept the Law. 14So, when gentiles, not having the Law, still through their own innate sense behave as the Law commands, then, even though they have no Law, they are a law for themselves. 15They can demonstrate the effect of the Law engraved on their hearts, to which their own conscience bears witness; since they are aware of various considerations, some of which accuse them, while others provide them with a defence . . . on the day when, 16according to the gospel that I preach, God, through Jesus Christ, judges all human secrets.

17If you can call yourself a Jew, and you really trust in the Law, and are proud of your God, 18and know his will, and tell right from wrong because you have been taught by the

1b Jr 2:11.
2a Ps 62:12.
2b Dt 10:17.

Law; [19]if you are confident that you are a guide to the blind and a beacon to those in the dark, [20]that you can teach the ignorant and instruct the unlearned because the Law embodies all knowledge and all truth—[21]so then, in teaching others, do you teach yourself as well? You preach that there is to be no stealing, but do you steal? [22]You say that adultery is forbidden, but do you commit adultery? You detest the worship of objects, but do you desecrate holy things yourself? [23]If, while you are boasting of the Law, you disobey it, then you are bringing God into contempt. [24]As scripture says: *It is your fault that the name of God is held in contempt among the nations.*[c]

Circumcision will not save them

[25]Circumcision has its value if you keep the Law; but if you go on breaking the Law, you are no more circumcised than the uncircumcised. [26]And if an uncircumcised man keeps the commands of the Law, will not his uncircumcised state count as circumcision? [27]More, the man who, in his native uncircumcised state, keeps the Law, is a condemnation of you, who, by your concentration on the letter and on circumcision, actually break the Law. [28]Being a Jew is not only having the outward appearance of a Jew, and circumcision is not only a visible physical operation. [29]The real Jew is the one who is inwardly a Jew, and real circumcision is in the heart, a thing not of the letter but of the spirit. He may not be praised by any human being, but he will be praised by God.

God's promises will not save them

3 Is there any benefit, then, in being a Jew? Is there any advantage in being circumcised? [2]A great deal, in every way. First of all, it was to the Jews that the message of God was entrusted. [3]What if some of them were unfaithful? Do you think their lack of faith could cancel God's faithfulness? [4]Out of the question! God will always be true even if *no human being can be relied on.*[a] As scripture says: *That you may show your saving justice when you pass sentence and your victory may appear when you give judgement.* [5]But if our injustice serves to bring God's saving justice into view, can we say that God is unjust when—to use human terms—he brings his retribution down on us? [6]Out of the question! It would mean that God could not be the judge of the world. [7]You might as well say that if my untruthfulness makes God demonstrate his truthfulness, to his greater glory, then I should not be judged to be a sinner at all. [8]In this case, the slanderous report some people are spreading would be true, that we teach that one should do evil that good may come of it. In fact such people are justly condemned.

All are guilty

[9]Well: are we any better off? Not at all: we have already indicted Jews and Greeks as being all alike under the dominion of sin. [10]As scripture says:

Not one of them is upright, not a single one,
[11]*not a single one is wise,*
not a single one seeks God.
[12]*All have turned away, all alike turned sour,*
not one of them does right, not a single one.
[13]*Their throats are wide-open graves,*
their tongues seductive.
Viper's venom behind their lips;
[14]*their speech is full of cursing and bitterness.*
[15]*Their feet quick to shed innocent blood,*
[16]*wherever they go there is havoc and ruin.*
[17]*They do not know the way of peace,*
[18]*there is no fear of God before their eyes.*

[19]Now we are well aware that whatever the Law says is said for those who are subject to the Law, so that every mouth may be silenced, and the whole world brought under the judgement of God. [20]So then, *no human being can be found upright at the tribunal* of God by keeping the Law; all that the Law does is to tell us what is sinful.

B: FAITH AND THE JUDGEMENT OF GOD

The revelation of God's judgement

[21]God's saving justice was witnessed by the Law and the Prophets, but now it has been revealed altogether apart from law: [22]God's saving justice given through faith in Jesus

---

2c Ezk 36:20.
3a In vv. 4–20 Paul uses numerous quotations from the Pss and Is 59:7–8.

Christ to all who believe. [23]No distinction is made: all have sinned and lack God's glory, [24]and all are justified by the free gift of his grace through being set free in Christ Jesus. [25]God appointed him as a sacrifice for reconciliation, through faith, by the shedding of his blood, and so showed his justness; first for the past, when sins went unpunished because he held his hand; [26]and now again for the present age, to show how he is just and justifies everyone who has faith in Jesus.

What faith does

[27]So what becomes of our boasts? There is no room for them. On what principle—that only actions count? No; that faith is what counts, [28]since, as we see it, a person is justified by faith and not by doing what the Law tells him to do. [29]Do you think God is the God only of the Jews, and not of gentiles too? Most certainly of gentiles too, [30]since there is only one God; he will justify the circumcised by their faith, and he will justify the uncircumcised through their faith. [31]Are we saying that the Law has been made pointless by faith? Out of the question; we are placing the Law on its true footing.

C: THE EXAMPLE OF ABRAHAM

Abraham justified by faith

4 Then what do we say about Abraham, the ancestor from whom we are descended physically? [2]If Abraham had been justified because of what he had done, then he would have had something to boast about. But not before God: [3]does not scripture say: *Abraham put his faith in God and this was reckoned to him as uprightness?*[a] [4]Now, when someone works, the wages for this are not considered as a favour but as due; [5]however, when someone, without working, puts faith in the one who justifies the godless, it is this faith that is reckoned as uprightness. [6]David, too, says the same: he calls someone blessed if God attributes uprightness to that person, apart from any action undertaken:

[7]How blessed are those
whose offence is forgiven,
whose sin is blotted out.
[8]How blessed are those
to whom the Lord imputes no guilt.[b]

Justified before circumcision

[9]Is this blessing only for the circumcised, or is it said of the uncircumcised as well? Well, we said of Abraham that *his faith was reckoned to him as uprightness*. [10]Now how did this come about? When he was already circumcised, or before he had been circumcised? Not when he had been circumcised, but while he was still uncircumcised; [11]and *circumcision*[c] was given to him later, *as a sign* and a guarantee that the faith which he had while still uncircumcised was reckoned to him as uprightness. In this way, Abraham was to be the ancestor of all believers who are uncircumcised, so that they might be reckoned as upright; [12]as well as the ancestor of those of the circumcision who not only have their circumcision but who also follow our ancestor Abraham along the path of faith that he trod before he was circumcised.

Not justified by obedience to the Law

[13]For the promise to Abraham and his descendants that he should inherit the world was not through the Law, but through the uprightness of faith. [14]For if it is those who live by the Law who will gain the inheritance, faith is worthless and the promise is without force; [15]for the Law produces nothing but God's retribution, and it is only where there is no Law that it is possible to live without breaking the Law. [16]That is why the promise is to faith, so that it comes as a free gift and is secure for all the descendants, not only those who rely on the Law but all those others who rely on the faith of Abraham, the ancestor of us all [17](as scripture says: *I have made you the father of many nations*). Abraham is our father in the eyes of God, in whom he put his faith, and who brings the dead to life and calls into existence what does not yet exist.

Abraham's faith a model of Christian faith

[18]Though there seemed no hope, he hoped and believed that he was to become *father of*

4a Gn 15:6.
4b Ps 32:1–2.
4c Quotations about Abraham from Gn (17:10; 17:5; 15:5; 17:17).

many nations in fulfilment of the promise:
Just so will your descendants be. [19]Even the
thought that his body was as good as dead—
he was about a hundred years old—and that
Sarah's womb was dead too did not shake his
faith. [20]Counting on the promise of God,
he did not doubt or disbelieve, but drew
strength from faith and gave glory to God,
[21]fully convinced that whatever God prom-
ised he has the power to perform. [22]This is the
faith that was *reckoned to him as uprightness*.
[23]And the word 'reckoned' in scripture
applies not only to him; [24]it is there for our
sake too—our faith, too, will be 'reckoned'
[25]because we believe in him who raised from
the dead our Lord Jesus who was *handed over
to death for our sins*[d] and raised to life for our
justification.

II: SALVATION

Faith guarantees salvation

5 So then, now that we have been justified
by faith, we are at peace with God through
our Lord Jesus Christ; [2]it is through him, by
faith, that we have been admitted into God's
favour in which we are living, and look
forward exultantly to God's glory. [3]Not only
that; let us exult, too, in our hardships,
understanding that hardship develops
perseverance, [4]and perseverance develops a
tested character, something that gives us
hope, [5]and a hope which will not let us down,
because the love of God has been poured into
our hearts by the Holy Spirit which has been
given to us. [6]When we were still helpless,
at the appointed time, Christ died for the
godless. [7]You could hardly find anyone ready
to die even for someone upright; though it is
just possible that, for a really good person,
someone might undertake to die. [8]So it is
proof of God's own love for us, that Christ
died for us while we were still sinners. [9]How
much more can we be sure, therefore, that,
now that we have been justified by his death,
we shall be saved through him from the
retribution of God. [10]For if, while we were
enemies, we were reconciled to God through
the death of his Son, how much more can we
be sure that, being now reconciled, we shall
be saved by his life. [11]What is more, we are
filled with exultant trust in God, through our
Lord Jesus Christ, through whom we have
already gained our reconciliation.

A: DELIVERANCE FROM SIN, DEATH AND LAW

Adam and Jesus Christ

[12]Well then; it was through one man that sin
came into the world,[a] and through sin death,
and thus death has spread through the whole
human race because everyone has sinned.
[13]Sin already existed in the world before there
was any law, even though sin is not reckoned
when there is no law. [14]Nonetheless death
reigned over all from Adam to Moses, even
over those whose sin was not the breaking
of a commandment, as Adam's was. He
prefigured the One who was to come . . .
[15]There is no comparison between the free
gift and the offence. If death came to many
through the offence of one man, how much
greater an effect the grace of God has had,
coming to so many and so plentifully as a
free gift through the one man Jesus Christ!
[16]Again, there is no comparison between the
gift and the offence of one man. One single
offence brought condemnation, but now,
after many offences, have come the free gift
and so acquittal! [17]It was by one man's offence
that death came to reign over all, but how
much greater the reign in life of those who
receive the fullness of grace and the gift of
saving justice, through the one man, Jesus
Christ. [18]One man's offence brought
condemnation on all humanity; and one
man's good act has brought justification and
life to all humanity. [19]Just as by one man's
disobedience many were made sinners, so by
one man's obedience are many to be made
upright. [20]When law came on the scene, it
was to multiply the offences. But however

4d Is 53:6.
5a Ws 2:24.

much sin increased, grace was always greater;
21 so that as sin's reign brought death, so grace
was to rule through saving justice that leads
to eternal life through Jesus Christ our Lord.

Baptism

6 What should we say then? Should we
remain in sin so that grace may be given
the more fully? 2 Out of the question! We
have died to sin; how could we go on living
in it? 3 You cannot have forgotten that all of
us, when we were baptised into Christ Jesus,
were baptised into his death. 4 So by our
baptism into his death we were buried with
him, so that as Christ was raised from the
dead by the Father's glorious power, we too
should begin living a new life. 5 If we have
been joined to him by dying a death like
his, so we shall be by a resurrection like his;
6 realising that our former self was crucified
with him, so that the self which belonged to
sin should be destroyed and we should be
freed from the slavery of sin. 7 Someone who
has died, of course, no longer has to answer
for sin.

8 But we believe that, if we died with Christ,
then we shall live with him too. 9 We know
that Christ has been raised from the dead and
will never die again. Death has no power over
him any more. 10 For by dying, he is dead to
sin once and for all, and now the life that he
lives is life with God. 11 In the same way, you
must see yourselves as being dead to sin but
alive for God in Christ Jesus.

Holiness, not sin, to be the master

12 That is why you must not allow sin to reign
over your mortal bodies and make you obey
their desires; 13 or give any parts of your
bodies over to sin to be used as instruments
of evil. Instead, give yourselves to God, as
people brought to life from the dead, and
give every part of your bodies to God to be
instruments of uprightness; 14 and then sin
will no longer have any power over you—you
are living not under law, but under grace.

The Christian is freed from the slavery of sin

15 What is the implication? That we are free
to sin, now that we are not under law but
under grace? Out of the question! 16 You
know well that if you undertake to be some-
body's slave and obey him, you are the slave
of him you obey: you can be the slave either
of sin which leads to death, or of obedience
which leads to saving justice. 17 Once you
were slaves of sin, but thank God you have
given whole-hearted obedience to the pattern
of teaching to which you were introduced;
18 and so, being freed from serving sin, you
took uprightness as your master. 19 I am
putting it in human terms because you are still
weak human beings: as once you surrendered
yourselves as servants to immorality and to a
lawlessness which results in more lawless-
ness, now you have to surrender yourselves
to uprightness which is to result in sancti-
fication.

The reward of sin and the reward of uprightness

20 When you were the servants of sin, you felt
no obligation to uprightness, 21 and what did
you gain from living like that? Experiences
of which you are now ashamed, for that sort
of behaviour ends in death. 22 But, now you
are set free from sin and bound to the service
of God, your gain will be sanctification and
the end will be eternal life. 23 For the wage
paid by sin is death; the gift freely given by
God is eternal life in Christ Jesus our Lord.

The Christian is freed from slavery to the Law

7 As people who are familiar with the Law,
brothers, you cannot have forgotten that
the law can control a person only during that
person's lifetime. 2 A married woman, for
instance, is bound to her husband by law, as
long as he lives, but when her husband dies
all her legal obligation to him as husband is
ended. 3 So if she were to have relations with
another man while her husband was still
alive, she would be termed an adulteress; but
if her husband dies, her legal obligation
comes to an end and if she then has relations
with another man, that does not make her
an adulteress. 4 In the same way you, my
brothers, through the body of Christ have
become dead to the Law and so you are able
to belong to someone else, that is, to him who
was raised from the dead to make us live
fruitfully for God. 5 While we were still living
by our natural inclinations, the sinful
passions aroused by the Law were working
in all parts of our bodies to make us live lives

which were fruitful only for death. 6But now
we are released from the Law, having died to
what was binding us, and so we are in a new
service, that of the spirit, and not in the old
service of a written code.

The function of the Law

7What should we say, then? That the Law
itself is sin? Out of the question! All the same,
if it had not been for the Law, I should not
have known what sin was; for instance, I
should not have known what it meant to
covet if the Law had not said: *You are not to*
covet.[a] 8But, once it found the opportunity
through that commandment, sin produced
in me all kinds of covetousness; as long as
there is no Law, sin is dead.
9Once, when there was no Law, I used to
be alive; but when the commandment came,
sin came to life 10and I died. The command-
ment was meant to bring life but I found
it brought death, 11because sin, finding its
opportunity by means of the commandment,
beguiled[b] me and, by means of it, killed me.
12So then, the Law is holy, and what it
commands is holy and upright and good.
13Does that mean that something good
resulted in my dying? Out of the question!
But sin, in order to be identified as sin, caused
my death through that good thing, and so it
is by means of the commandment that sin
shows its unbounded sinful power.

The inward struggle

14We are well aware that the Law is spiritual:
but I am a creature of flesh and blood sold as
a slave to sin. 15I do not understand my own
behaviour; I do not act as I mean to, but I do
things that I hate. 16While I am acting as I
do not want to, I still acknowledge the Law
as good, 17so it is not myself acting, but the
sin which lives in me. 18And really, I know
of nothing good living in me—in my natural
self, that is—for though the will to do what
is good is in me, the power to do it is not:
19the good thing I want to do, I never do; the
evil thing which I do not want—that is what
I do. 20But every time I do what I do not want
to, then it is not myself acting, but the sin
that lives in me.
21So I find this rule: that for me, where I
want to do nothing but good, evil is close at
my side. 22In my inmost self I dearly love
God's law, 23 but I see that acting on my
body there is a different law which battles
against the law in my mind. So I am brought
to be a prisoner of that law of sin which lives
inside my body.
24What a wretched man I am! Who will
rescue me from this body doomed to death?
25God—thanks be to him—through Jesus
Christ our Lord.

So it is that I myself with my mind obey
the law of God, but in my disordered nature
I obey the law of sin.

B: THE CHRISTIAN'S SPIRITUAL LIFE

The life of the spirit

8 Thus, condemnation will never come to
those who are in Christ Jesus, 2because
the law of the Spirit which gives life in Christ
Jesus has set you free from the law of sin and
death. 3What the Law could not do because
of the weakness of human nature, God did,
sending his own Son in the same human
nature as any sinner to be a sacrifice for sin,
and condemning sin in that human nature.
4This was so that the Law's requirements
might be fully satisfied in us as we direct our
lives not by our natural inclinations but by
the Spirit. 5Those who are living by their
natural inclinations have their minds on the
things human nature desires; those who live
in the Spirit have their minds on spiritual
things. 6And human nature has nothing to
look forward to but death, while the Spirit
looks forward to life and peace, 7because
the outlook of disordered human nature is
opposed to God, since it does not submit to
God's Law, and indeed it cannot, 8and those
who live by their natural inclinations can
never be pleasing to God. 9You, however,
live not by your natural inclinations, but by
the Spirit, since the Spirit of God has made
a home in you. Indeed, anyone who does not
have the Spirit of Christ does not belong to
him. 10But when Christ is in you, the body is
dead because of sin but the spirit is alive
because you have been justified; 11and if the
Spirit of him who raised Jesus from the dead

7a Ex 20:17.
7b Gn 3:13.

has made his home in you, then he who raised Christ Jesus from the dead will give life to your own mortal bodies through his Spirit living in you.

12 So then, my brothers, we have no obligation to human nature to be dominated by it. 13 If you do live in that way, you are doomed to die; but if by the Spirit you put to death the habits originating in the body, you will have life.

Children of God

14 All who are guided by the Spirit of God are sons of God; 15 for what you received was not the spirit of slavery to bring you back into fear; you received the Spirit of adoption, enabling us to cry out, '*Abba*, Father!' 16 The Spirit himself joins with our spirit to bear witness that we are children of God. 17 And if we are children, then we are heirs, heirs of God and joint-heirs with Christ, provided that we share his suffering, so as to share his glory.

Glory as our destiny

18 In my estimation, all that we suffer in the present time is nothing in comparison with the glory which is destined to be disclosed for us, 19 for the whole creation is waiting with eagerness for the children of God to be revealed. 20 It was not for its own purposes that creation had frustration imposed on it, but for the purposes of him who imposed it— 21 with the intention that the whole creation itself might be freed from its slavery to corruption and brought into the same glorious freedom as the children of God. 22 We are well aware that the whole creation, until this time, has been groaning in labour pains. 23 And not only that: we too, who have the first-fruits of the Spirit, even we are groaning inside ourselves, waiting with eagerness for our bodies to be set free. 24 In hope, we already have salvation; in hope, not visibly present, or we should not be hoping— nobody goes on hoping for something which is already visible. 25 But having this hope for what we cannot yet see, we are able to wait for it with persevering confidence.

26 And as well as this, the Spirit too comes to help us in our weakness, for, when we do not know how to pray properly, then the Spirit personally makes our petitions for us in groans that cannot be put into words; 27 and he who can see into all hearts knows what the Spirit means because the prayers that the Spirit makes for God's holy people are always in accordance with the mind of God.

God has called us to share his glory

28 We are well aware that God works with those who love him, those who have been called in accordance with his purpose, and turns everything to their good. 29 He decided beforehand who were the ones destined to be moulded to the pattern of his Son, so that he should be the eldest of many brothers; 30 it was those so destined that he called; those that he called, he justified, and those that he has justified he has brought into glory.

A hymn to God's love

31 After saying this, what can we add? If God is for us, who can be against us? 32 Since he did not spare his own Son, but gave him up for the sake of all of us, then can we not expect that with him he will freely give us all his gifts? 33 Who can bring any accusation against those that God has chosen? *When God grants saving justice* 34 *who can condemn?*[a] Are we not sure that it is Christ Jesus, who died— yes and more, who was raised from the dead and is at God's right hand—and who is adding his plea for us? 35 Can anything cut us off from the love of Christ—can hardships or distress, or persecution, or lack of food and clothing, or threats or violence; 36 as scripture says:

For your sake we are being massacred
all day long,
treated as sheep to be slaughtered?[b]

37 No; we come through all these things triumphantly victorious, by the power of him who loved us. 38 For I am certain of this: neither death nor life, nor angels, nor principalities, nothing already in existence and nothing still to come, nor any power, 39 nor the heights nor the depths, nor any created thing whatever, will be able to come between us and the love of God, known to us in Christ Jesus our Lord.

8a Is 50:8.
8b Ps 44:22.

Humility and charity

3And through the grace that I have been given, I say this to every one of you: never pride yourself on being better than you really are, but think of yourself dispassionately, recognising that God has given to each one his measure of faith. 4Just as each of us has various parts in one body, and the parts do not all have the same function: 5in the same way, all of us, though there are so many of us, make up one body in Christ, and as different parts we are all joined to one another. 6Then since the gifts that we have differ according to the grace that was given to each of us: if it is a gift of prophecy, we should prophesy as much as our faith tells us; 7if it is a gift of practical service, let us devote ourselves to serving; if it is teaching, to teaching; 8if it is encouraging, to encouraging. When you give, you should give generously from the heart; if you are put in charge, you must be conscientious; if you do works of mercy, let it be because you enjoy doing them. 9Let love be without any pretence. Avoid what is evil; stick to what is good. 10In brotherly love let your feelings of deep affection for one another come to expression and regard others as more important than yourself. 11In the service of the Lord, work not halfheartedly but with conscientiousness and an eager spirit. 12Be joyful in hope, persevere in hardship; keep praying regularly; 13share with any of God's holy people who are in need; look for opportunities to be hospitable.

Charity to everyone, including enemies

14Bless your persecutors; never curse them, bless them. 15Rejoice with others when they rejoice, and be sad with those in sorrow. 16Give the same consideration to all others alike. Pay no regard to social standing, but meet humble people on their own terms. *Do not congratulate yourself on your own wisdom.*[a] 17Never pay back evil with evil, but *bear in mind the ideals that all regard with respect.* 18As much as possible, and to the utmost of your ability, be at peace with everyone. 19Never try to get revenge: leave that, my dear friends, to the Retribution. As scripture says: *Vengeance is mine—I will pay them back*, the Lord promises. 20And more: *If your enemy is hungry, give him something to eat; if thirsty, something to drink. By this, you will be heaping red-hot coals on his head.* 21Do not be mastered by evil, but master evil with good.

Submission to civil authority

13 Everyone is to obey the governing authorities, because there is no authority except from God and so whatever authorities exist have been appointed by God. 2So anyone who disobeys an authority is rebelling against God's ordinance; and rebels must expect to receive the condemnation they deserve. 3Magistrates bring fear not to those who do good, but to those who do evil. So if you want to live with no fear of authority, live honestly and you will have its approval; 4it is there to serve God for you and for your good. But if you do wrong, then you may well be afraid; because it is not for nothing that the symbol of authority is the sword: it is there to serve God, too, as his avenger, to bring retribution to wrongdoers. 5You must be obedient, therefore, not only because of this retribution, but also for conscience's sake. 6And this is why you should pay taxes, too, because the authorities are all serving God as his agents, even while they are busily occupied with that particular task. 7Pay to each one what is due to each: taxes to the one to whom tax is due, tolls to the one to whom tolls are due, respect to the one to whom respect is due, honour to the one to whom honour is due.

Love and Law

8The only thing you should owe to anyone is love for one another, for to love the other person is to fulfil the law. 9All these: *You shall not commit adultery, You shall not kill, You shall not steal, You shall not covet*, and all the other commandments that there are, are summed up in this single phrase: *You must love your neighbour*[a] *as yourself.* 10Love can cause no harm to your neighbour, and so love is the fulfilment of the Law.

Children of the light

11Besides, you know the time has come; the moment is here for you to stop sleeping and

---

12a Pr 3:7, followed by Lv 19:18; Pr 25:21–22.
13a Ex 20:13–17 summed up in Lv 19:18.

brought salvation for the gentiles, in order to stir them to envy. [12]And if their fall has proved a great gain to the world, and their loss has proved a great gain to the gentiles—how much greater a gain will come when all is restored to them!

[13]Let me say then to you gentiles that, as far as I am an apostle to the gentiles, I take pride in this work of service; [14]and I want it to be the means of rousing to envy the people who are my own blood-relations and so of saving some of them. [15]Since their rejection meant the reconciliation of the world, do you know what their re-acceptance will mean? Nothing less than life from the dead!

The Jews are still the chosen people

[16]When the first-fruits are made holy, so is the whole batch; and if the root is holy, so are the branches. [17]Now suppose that some branches were broken off, and you are wild olive, grafted among the rest to share with the others the rich sap of the olive tree; [18]then it is not for you to consider yourself superior to the other branches; and if you start feeling proud, think: it is not you that sustain the root, but the root that sustains you. [19]You will say, 'Branches were broken off on purpose for me to be grafted in.' True; [20]they through their unbelief were broken off, and you are established through your faith. So it is not pride that you should have, but fear: [21]if God did not spare the natural branches, he might not spare you either. [22]Remember God's severity as well as his goodness: his severity to those who fell, and his goodness to you as long as you persevere in it; if not, you too will be cut off. [23]And they, if they do not persevere in their unbelief, will be grafted in; for it is within the power of God to graft them back again. [24]After all, if you, cut off from what was by nature a wild olive, could then be grafted unnaturally on to a cultivated olive, how much easier will it be for them, the branches that naturally belong there, to be grafted on to the olive tree which is their own.

The conversion of the Jews

[25]I want you to be quite certain, brothers, of this mystery, to save you from *congratulating yourselves on your own good sense*: part of Israel had its mind hardened, but only until the gentiles have wholly come in; [26]and this is how all Israel will be saved. As scripture says:

From Zion will come the Redeemer,
he will remove godlessness from Jacob.
[27]*And this will be my covenant with them,*
when I take their sins away.

[28]As regards the gospel, they are enemies, but for your sake; but as regards those who are God's choice, they are still well loved for the sake of their ancestors. [29]There is no change of mind on God's part about the gifts he has made or of his choice.

[30]Just as you were in the past disobedient to God but now you have been shown mercy, through their disobedience; [31]so in the same way they are disobedient now, so that through the mercy shown to you they too will receive mercy. [32]God has imprisoned all human beings in their own disobedience only to show mercy to them all.

A hymn to God's mercy and wisdom

[33]How rich and deep are the wisdom and the knowledge of God! We cannot reach to the root of his decisions or his ways. [34]*Who has ever known the mind of the Lord? Who has ever been his adviser?* [35]*Who has given anything to him, so that his presents come only as a debt returned?* [36]Everything there is comes from him and is caused by him and exists for him. To him be glory for ever! Amen.

EXHORTATION

Spiritual worship

12 I urge you, then, brothers, remembering the mercies of God, to offer your bodies as a living sacrifice, dedicated and acceptable to God; that is the kind of worship for you, as sensible people. [2]Do not model your behaviour on the contemporary world, but let the renewing of your minds transform you, so that you may discern for yourselves what is the will of God—what is good and acceptable and mature.

wake up, because by now our salvation is nearer than when we first began to believe. 12The night is nearly over, daylight is on the way; so let us throw off everything that belongs to the darkness and equip ourselves for the light. 13Let us live decently, as in the light of day; with no orgies or drunkenness, no promiscuity or licentiousness, and no wrangling or jealousy. 14Let your armour be the Lord Jesus Christ, and stop worrying about how your disordered natural inclinations may be fulfilled.

Charity towards the scrupulous

14 Give a welcome to anyone whose faith is not strong, but do not get into arguments about doubtful points. 2One person may have faith enough to eat any kind of food; another, less strong, will eat only vegetables. 3Those who feel free to eat freely are not to condemn those who are unwilling to eat freely; nor must the person who does not eat freely pass judgement on the one who does—because God has welcomed him. 4And who are you, to sit in judgement over somebody else's servant? Whether he deserves to be upheld or to fall is for his own master to decide; and he shall be upheld, for the Lord has power to uphold him. 5One person thinks that some days are holier than others, and another thinks them all equal. Let each of them be fully convinced in his own mind. 6The one who makes special observance of a particular day observes it in honour of the Lord. So the one who eats freely, eats in honour of the Lord, making his thanksgiving to God; and the one who does not, abstains from eating in honour of the Lord and makes his thanksgiving to God. 7For none of us lives for himself and none of us dies for himself; 8while we are alive, we are living for the Lord, and when we die, we die for the Lord: and so, alive or dead, we belong to the Lord. 9It was for this purpose that Christ both died and came to life again: so that he might be Lord of both the dead and the living. 10Why, then, does one of you make himself judge over his brother, and why does another among you despise his brother? All of us will have to stand in front of the judgement-seat of God: 11as scripture says: *By my own life* says the Lord, *every knee shall bow before me, every tongue shall give glory to God.*[a] 12It is to God, then, that each of us will have to give an account of himself.

13Let us each stop passing judgement, therefore, on one another and decide instead that none of us will place obstacles in any brother's way, or anything that can bring him down. 14I am sure, and quite convinced in the Lord Jesus, that no food is unclean in itself; it is only if someone classifies any kind of food as unclean, then for him it is unclean. 15And indeed, if through any kind of food you are causing offence to a brother, then you are no longer being guided by love. You are not to let the food that you eat cause the ruin of anyone for whom Christ died. 16A privilege of yours must not be allowed to give rise to harmful talk; 17for it is not eating and drinking that make the kingdom of God, but the saving justice, the peace and the joy brought by the Holy Spirit. 18It is the person who serves Christ in these things that will be approved by God and respected by everyone. 19So then, let us be always seeking the ways which lead to peace and the ways in which we can support one another. 20Do not wreck God's work for the sake of food. Certainly all foods are clean; but all the same, any kind can be evil for someone to whom it is an offence to eat it. 21It is best to abstain from eating any meat, or drinking any wine, or from any other activity which might cause a brother to fall away, or to be scandalised, or to weaken.

22Within yourself, before God, hold on to what you already believe. Blessed is the person whose principles do not condemn his practice. 23But anyone who eats with qualms of conscience is condemned, because this eating does not spring from faith—and every action which does not spring from faith is sin.

15 It is for us who are strong to bear with the susceptibilities of the weaker ones, and not please ourselves. 2Each of us must consider his neighbour's good, so that we support one another. 3Christ did not indulge his own feelings, either; indeed, as scripture says: *The insults of those who insult you fall on me.*[a] 4And all these things which were written so long ago were written so that we, learning perseverance and the encouragement which the scriptures give, should have hope. 5Now

14a Is 45:23.
15a Ps 69:9.

the God of perseverance and encouragement give you all the same purpose, following the example of Christ Jesus, [6]so that you may together give glory to the God and Father of our Lord Jesus Christ with one heart.

[7]Accept one another, then, for the sake of God's glory, as Christ accepted you. [8]I tell you that Christ's work was to serve the circumcised, fulfilling the truthfulness of God by carrying out the promises made to the fathers, [9]and his work was also for the gentiles, so that they should give glory to God for his faithful love; as scripture says: *For this I shall praise you among the nations and sing praise to your name.*[b] [10]And in another place it says: *Nations, rejoice, with his people,* [11]and in another place again: *Praise the Lord, all nations, extol him, all peoples.* [12]And in Isaiah, it says: *The root of Jesse will appear, he who rises up to rule the nations, and in him the nations will put their hope.*

[13]May the God of hope fill you with all joy and peace in your faith, so that in the power of the Holy Spirit you may be rich in hope.

EPILOGUE

Paul's ministry

[14]My brothers, I am quite sure that you, in particular, are full of goodness, fully instructed and capable of correcting each other. [15]But I have special confidence in writing on some points to you, to refresh your memories, because of the grace that was given to me by God. [16]I was given grace to be a minister of Christ Jesus to the gentiles, dedicated to offer them the gospel of God, so that gentiles might become an acceptable offering, sanctified by the Holy Spirit.

[17]So I can be proud, in Christ Jesus, of what I have done for God. [18]Of course I can dare to speak only of the things which Christ has done through me to win the allegiance of the gentiles, using what I have said and done, [19]by the power of signs and wonders, by the power of the Spirit of God. In this way, from Jerusalem and all round, even as far as Illyricum, I have fully carried out the preaching of the gospel of Christ; [20]and what is more, it has been my rule to preach the gospel only where the name of Christ has not already been heard, for I do not build on another's foundations; [21]in accordance with scripture: *Those who have never been told about him will see him, and those who have never heard about him will understand.*[c]

Paul's plans[d]

[22]That is why I have been so often prevented from coming to see you; [23]now, however, as there is nothing more to keep me in these parts, I hope, after longing for many years past to visit you, to see you when I am on the way to Spain—[24]and after enjoying at least something of your company, to be sent on my way with your support. [25]But now I have undertaken to go to Jerusalem in the service of the holy people of God there, [26]since Macedonia and Achaia have chosen to make a generous contribution to the poor among God's holy people at Jerusalem.

[27]Yes, they chose to; not that they did not owe it to them. For if the gentiles have been given a share in their spiritual possessions, then in return to give them help with material possessions is repaying a debt to them. [28]So when I have done this, and given this harvest into their possession, I shall visit you on the way to Spain. [29]I am sure that, when I do come to you, I shall come with the fullest blessing of Christ.

[30]Meanwhile I urge you, brothers, by our Lord Jesus Christ and by the love of the Spirit, that in your prayers to God for me you exert yourselves to help me; [31]praying that I may escape the unbelievers in Judaea, and that the aid I am carrying to Jerusalem will be acceptable to God's holy people. [32]Then I shall come to you, if God wills, for a happy time of relaxation in your company. [33]The God of peace be with you all. Amen.

15b Ps 18:49, followed by Dt 32:43; Ps 117:1; Is 11:10.
15c Is 52:15.
15d We do not know whether Paul completed this journey.

Greetings and good wishes[a]

16 I commend to you our sister Phoebe, a
deaconess of the church at Cenchreae;
[2]give her, in the Lord, a welcome worthy
of God's holy people, and help her with
whatever she needs from you—she herself
has come to the help of many people,
including myself.
[3]My greetings to Prisca and Aquila, my
fellow-workers in Christ Jesus, [4]who risked
their own necks to save my life; to them,
thanks not only from me, but from all the
churches among the gentiles; [5]and my greet-
ings to the church at their house.
Greetings to my dear friend Epaenetus,
the first of Asia's offerings to Christ.
[6]Greetings to Mary, who worked so hard
for you. [7]Greetings to those outstanding
apostles, Andronicus and Junias, my
kinsmen and fellow-prisoners, who were in
Christ before me. [8]Greetings to Ampliatus,
my dear friend in the Lord. [9]Greetings to
Urban, my fellow-worker in Christ, and to
my dear friend Stachys. [10]Greetings
to Apelles, proved servant of Christ. Greet-
ings to all the household of Aristobulus.
[11]Greetings to my kinsman, Herodion, and
greetings to those who belong to the Lord in
the household of Narcissus. [12]Greetings to
Tryphaena and Tryphosa who work hard
in the Lord; greetings to my dear friend
Persis, also a very hard worker in the Lord.
[13]Greetings to Rufus, chosen servant of the
Lord, and to his mother—a mother to
me too. [14]Greetings to Asyncritus, Phlegon,
Hermes, Patrobas, Hermas, and the
brothers who are with them. [15]Greetings to
Philologus and Julia, Nereus and his sister,
and Olympas and all God's holy people who
are with them. [16]Greet each other with the
holy kiss. All the churches of Christ send
their greetings.

A warning and first postscript

[17]I urge you, brothers, be on your guard
against the people who are out to stir up
disagreements and bring up difficulties
against the teaching which you learnt. Avoid
them. [18]People of that sort are servants not
of our Lord Christ, but of their own greed;
and with talk that sounds smooth and reason-
able they deceive the minds of the unwary.
[19]Your obedience has become known to
everyone, and I am very pleased with you for
it; but I should want you to be learned only
in what is good, and unsophisticated about
all that is evil. [20]The God of peace will soon
crush Satan under your feet. The grace of
our Lord Jesus Christ be with you.

Last greetings and second postscript

[21]Timothy, who is working with me, sends
greetings to you, and so do my kinsmen
Lucius, Jason and Sosipater. [22]I, Tertius,
who am writing this letter, greet you in the
Lord. [23]Greetings to you from Gaius, my host
here, and host of the whole church. Erastus,
the city treasurer, sends greetings to you,
and our brother Quartus.[24] [b]

Doxology[c]

[25]And now to him
who can make you strong
in accordance with the gospel that I preach
and the proclamation of Jesus Christ,
in accordance with that mystery
which for endless ages was kept secret
[26]but now (as the prophets wrote)
is revealed,
as the eternal God commanded,
to be made known to all the nations,
so that they obey in faith:
[27]to him, the only wise God,
give glory through Jesus Christ
for ever and ever. Amen.

16a vv. 1–23 possibly formed no part of the original letter.
16b Some authorities add v. 24, 'The grace . . . with you' as in v. 20.
16c A solemn summary, placed by some authorities after 15:33.

FIRST CORINTHIANS

The busy port of Corinth had a lively and turbulent Christian community. Their first surviving letter from Paul treats difficulties in the community reported to Paul (at Ephesus, probably in AD 57) by their envoys, then answers various questions they brought to him. Finally Paul teaches about the resurrection. In dealing with these moral and practical issues Paul imparts invaluable teaching about Christ as the Wisdom of God, the Church as his Body, and the gifts of the Spirit in the Christian community. He stresses the primacy of conscience and the independent value of every Christian, for each has a particular part to play as a unique member of the Body of Christ. The gifts of the Spirit, no matter how spectacular, are to be assessed only by their contribution towards building up the Body of Christ.

PLAN OF THE LETTER

1 CORINTHIANS
THE FIRST LETTER OF PAUL TO THE CHURCH AT CORINTH

INTRODUCTION

Address and greetings. Thanksgiving

1 Paul, called by the will of God to be an
apostle of Christ Jesus, and Sosthenes,
our brother, 2 to the church of God in Corinth,
to those who have been consecrated in Christ
Jesus and called to be God's holy people,
with all those everywhere who call on the
name of our Lord Jesus Christ, their Lord as
well as ours. 3 Grace to you and peace from
God our Father and the Lord Jesus Christ.
4 I am continually thanking God about you,

for the grace of God which you have been
given in Christ Jesus; 5in him you have
been richly endowed in every kind of utter-
ance and knowledge; 6so firmly has witness
to Christ taken root in you. 7And so you are
not lacking in any gift as you wait for our
Lord Jesus Christ to be revealed; 8he will
continue to give you strength till the very
end, so that you will be irreproachable on the
Day of our Lord Jesus Christ. 9You can rely
on God, who has called you to be partners
with his Son Jesus Christ our Lord.

I: DIVISIONS AND SCANDALS

A: FACTIONS IN THE CORINTHIAN CHURCH

Dissensions among the faithful

10Brothers, I urge you, in the name of our
Lord Jesus Christ, not to have factions among
yourselves but all to be in agreement in what
you profess; so that you are perfectly united
in your beliefs and judgements. 11From what
Chloe's people have been telling me about
you, brothers, it is clear that there are serious
differences among you. 12What I mean is
this: every one of you is declaring, 'I belong
to Paul,' or 'I belong to Apollos,' or 'I
belong to Cephas,'[a] or 'I belong to Christ.'
13Has Christ been split up? Was it Paul that
was crucified for you, or was it in Paul's name
that you were baptised? 14I am thankful I did
not baptise any of you, except Crispus and
Gaius, 15so that no one can say that you were
baptised in my name. 16Yes, I did baptise the
family of Stephanas, too; but besides these I
do not think I baptised anyone.

The true wisdom and the false

17After all, Christ sent me not to baptise, but
to preach the gospel; and not by means of
wisdom of language, wise words which would
make the cross of Christ pointless. 18The
message of the cross is folly for those who are
on the way to ruin, but for those of us who
are on the road to salvation it is the power of
God. 19As scripture says: *I am going to destroy
the wisdom of the wise and bring to nothing the
understanding of any who understand.* 20*Where
are the philosophers? Where are the experts?*[b]
And where are the debaters of this age? Do
you not see how God has shown up human
wisdom as folly? 21Since in the wisdom of
God the world was unable to recognise God
through wisdom, it was God's own pleasure
to save believers through the folly of the
gospel. 22While the Jews demand miracles
and the Greeks look for wisdom, 23we are
preaching a crucified Christ: to the Jews an
obstacle they cannot get over, to the gentiles
foolishness, 24but to those who have been
called, whether they are Jews or Greeks, a
Christ who is both the power of God and the
wisdom of God. 25God's folly is wiser than
human wisdom, and God's weakness is
stronger than human strength. 26Consider,
brothers, how you were called; not many of
you are wise by human standards, not many
influential, not many from noble families.
27No, God chose those who by human stan-
dards are fools to shame the wise; he chose
those who by human standards are weak to
shame the strong, 28those who by human
standards are common and contemptible—
indeed those who count for nothing—to
reduce to nothing all those that do count for
something, 29so that no human being might
feel boastful before God. 30It is by him that
you exist in Christ Jesus, who for us was
made wisdom from God, and saving justice
and holiness and redemption. 31As scripture
says: *If anyone wants to boast, let him boast of
the Lord.*[c]

2 Now when I came to you, brothers, I did
not come with any brilliance of oratory
or wise argument to announce to you the
mystery of God. 2I was resolved that the only
knowledge I would have while I was with you
was knowledge of Jesus, and of him as the
crucified Christ. 3I came among you in weak-
ness, in fear and great trembling 4and what
I spoke and proclaimed was not meant to

1a *Cephas* is the Aramaic word for 'Peter'. For Apollos *see* Ac 18:24.
1b Is 29:14; 19:12.
1c cf. Jr 9:22–23.

convince by philosophical argument, but to demonstrate the convincing power of the Spirit, 5so that your faith should depend not on human wisdom but on the power of God.

6But still, to those who have reached maturity, we do talk of a wisdom, not, it is true, a philosophy of this age or of the rulers of this age, who will not last long now. 7It is of the mysterious wisdom of God that we talk, the wisdom that was hidden, which God predestined to be for our glory before the ages began. 8None of the rulers of the age recognised it; for if they had recognised it, they would not have crucified the Lord of glory; 9but it is as scripture says: *What no eye has seen and no ear has heard, what the mind of man cannot visualise; all that God has prepared for those who love him;*[a] 10to us, though, God has given revelation through the Spirit, for the Spirit explores the depths of everything, even the depths of God. 11After all, is there anyone who knows the qualities of anyone except his own spirit, within him; and in the same way, nobody knows the qualities of God except the Spirit of God. 12Now, the Spirit we have received is not the spirit of the world but God's own Spirit, so that we may understand the lavish gifts God has given us. 13And these are what we speak of, not in the terms learnt from human philosophy, but in terms learnt from the Spirit, fitting spiritual language to spiritual things. 14The natural person has no room for the gifts of God's Spirit; to him they are folly; he cannot recognise them, because their value can be assessed only in the Spirit. 15The spiritual person, on the other hand, can assess the value of everything, and that person's value cannot be assessed by anybody else. 16For: *who has ever known the mind of the Lord? Who has ever been his adviser?*[b] But we are those who have the mind of Christ.

3 And so, brothers, I was not able to talk to you as spiritual people; I had to talk to you as people still living by your natural inclinations, still infants in Christ; 2I fed you with milk and not solid food, for you were not yet able to take it—and even now, you are still not able to, 3for you are still living by your natural inclinations. As long as there are jealousy and rivalry among you, that surely means that you are still living by your natural inclinations and by merely human principles. 4While there is one that says, 'I belong to Paul' and another that says, 'I belong to Apollos' are you not being only too human?

The place of the Christian preacher

5For what is Apollos and what is Paul? The servants through whom you came to believe, and each has only what the Lord has given him. 6I did the planting, Apollos did the watering, but God gave growth. 7In this, neither the planter nor the waterer counts for anything; only God, who gives growth. 8It is all one who does the planting and who does the watering, and each will have the proper pay for the work that he has done. 9After all, we do share in God's work; you are God's farm, God's building.

10By the grace of God which was given to me, I laid the foundations like a trained master-builder, and someone else is building on them. Now each one must be careful how he does the building. 11For nobody can lay down any other foundation than the one which is there already, namely Jesus Christ. 12On this foundation, different people may build in gold, silver, jewels, wood, hay or straw 13but each person's handiwork will be shown for what it is. The Day which dawns in fire will make it clear and the fire itself will test the quality of each person's work. 14The one whose work stands up to it will be given his wages; 15the one whose work is burnt down will suffer the loss of it, though he himself will be saved; he will be saved as someone might expect to be saved from a fire.

16Do you not realise that you are a temple of God with the Spirit of God living in you? 17If anybody should destroy the temple of God, God will destroy that person, because God's temple is holy; and you are that temple.

Conclusions

18There is no room for self-delusion. Any one of you who thinks he is wise by worldly standards must learn to be a fool in order to be really wise. 19For the wisdom of the world is folly to God. As scripture says: *He traps the crafty in the snare of their own cunning* 20and again: *The Lord knows the plans of* the wise

2a A free combination of Is 64:3 and Jr 3:16.
2b Is 40:13.

and how insipid they are.[a] [21]So there is to be no boasting about human beings: everything belongs to you, [22]whether it is Paul, or Apollos, or Cephas, the world, life or death, the present or the future—all belong to you; [23]but you belong to Christ and Christ belongs to God.

4 People should think of us as Christ's servants, stewards entrusted with the mysteries of God. [2]In such a matter, what is expected of stewards is that each one should be found trustworthy. [3]It is of no importance to me how you or any other human court may judge me: I will not even be the judge of my own self. [4]It is true that my conscience does not reproach me, but that is not enough to justify me: it is the Lord who is my judge. [5]For that reason, do not judge anything before the due time, until the Lord comes; he will bring to light everything that is hidden in darkness and reveal the designs of all hearts. Then everyone will receive from God the appropriate commendation.

[6]I have applied all this to myself and Apollos for your sakes, so that you can learn how the saying, 'Nothing beyond what is written' is true of us: no individual among you must become filled with his own importance and make comparisons, to another's detriment. [7]Who made you so important? What have you got that was not given to you? And if it was given to you, why are you boasting as though it were your own? [8]You already have everything—you are rich already—you have come into your kingdom, without any help from us! Well, I wish you were kings and we could be kings with you! [9]For it seems to me that God has put us apostles on show right at the end, like men condemned to death: we have been exhibited as a spectacle to the whole universe, both angelic and human. [10]Here we are, fools for Christ's sake, while you are the clever ones in Christ; we are weak, while you are strong; you are honoured, while we are disgraced. [11]To this day, we go short of food and drink and clothes, we are beaten up and we have no homes; [12]we earn our living by labouring with our own hands; when we are cursed, we answer with a blessing; when we are hounded, we endure it passively; [13]when we are insulted, we give a courteous answer. We are treated even now as the dregs of the world, the very lowest scum.

An appeal

[14]I am writing all this not to make you ashamed but simply to remind you, as my dear children; [15]for even though you might have ten thousand slaves to look after you in Christ, you still have no more than one father, and it was I who fathered you in Christ Jesus, by the gospel. [16]That is why I urge you to take me as your pattern [17]and why I have sent you Timothy, a dear and faithful son to me in the Lord, who will remind you of my principles of conduct in Christ, as I teach them everywhere in every church.

[18]On the assumption that I was not coming to you, some of you have become filled with your own self-importance; [19]but I shall be coming to you soon, the Lord willing, and then I shall find out not what these self-important people say, but what power they have. [20]For the kingdom of God consists not in spoken words but in power. [21]What do you want then? Am I to come to you with a stick in my hand or in love, and with a spirit of gentleness?

B: INCEST IN CORINTH

5 It is widely reported that there is sexual immorality among you, immorality of a kind that is not found even among gentiles: that one of you is living with his stepmother.[a] [2]And you so filled with your own self-importance! It would have been better if you had been grieving bitterly, so that the man who has done this thing were turned out of the community. [3]For my part, however distant I am physically, I am present in spirit and have already condemned the man who behaved in this way, just as though I were present in person. [4]When you have gathered together in the name of our Lord Jesus, with the presence of my spirit, and in the power of our Lord Jesus, [5]hand such a man over to Satan, to be destroyed as far as natural life is concerned, so that on the Day of the Lord his spirit may be saved.

[6]Your self-satisfaction is ill founded. Do

3a Jb 5:13 followed by Ps 94:11.
5a Against OT and Roman law, but seemingly not Corinthian law, it was forbidden by the Jerusalem decision (Ac 15:20).

you not realise that only a little yeast leavens
the whole batch of dough? 7Throw out the
old yeast so that you can be the fresh dough,
unleavened as you are. For our Passover has
been sacrificed, that is, Christ; 8let us keep
the feast, then, with none of the old yeast and
no leavening of evil and wickedness, but only
the unleavened bread of sincerity and truth.
9In my letter, I wrote to you that you
should have nothing to do with people living
immoral lives. 10I was not including every-
body in this present world who is sexually
immoral, or everybody who is greedy, or
dishonest or worships false gods—that would
mean you would have to cut yourselves off
completely from the world. 11In fact what I
meant was that you were not to have anything
to do with anyone going by the name of
brother who is sexually immoral, or is greedy,
or worships false gods, or is a slanderer or a
drunkard or dishonest; never even have a
meal with anybody of that kind. 12It is no
concern of mine to judge outsiders. It is for
you to judge those who are inside, is it not?
13But outsiders are for God to judge.

You must banish this evil-doer from among you.[b]

C: RECOURSE TO THE GENTILE COURTS

6 Is one of you with a complaint against
another so brazen as to seek judgement
from sinners and not from God's holy people?
2Do you not realise that the holy people of
God are to be the judges of the world? And if
the world is to be judged by you, are you
not competent for petty cases? 3Do you not
realise that we shall be the judges of angels?—
then quite certainly over matters of this life.
4But when you have matters of this life to be
judged, you bring them before those who are
of no account in the Church! 5I say this to
make you ashamed of yourselves. Can it
really be that it is impossible to find in the
community one sensible person capable of
deciding questions between brothers, 6and
that this is why brother goes to law against
brother, and that before unbelievers? 7No; it
is a fault in you, by itself, that one of you
should go to law against another at all: why
do you not prefer to suffer injustice, why not
prefer to be defrauded? 8And here you are,
doing the injustice and the defrauding, and
to your own brothers.
9Do you not realise that people who do evil
will never inherit the kingdom of God? Make
no mistake—the sexually immoral, idolaters,
adulterers, the self-indulgent, sodomites,
10thieves, misers, drunkards, slanderers and
swindlers, none of these will inherit the
kingdom of God. 11Some of you used to be of
that kind: but you have been washed clean,
you have been sanctified, and you have been
justified in the name of the Lord Jesus Christ
and through the Spirit of our God.

D: SEXUAL IMMORALITY

12'For me everything is permissible';[a] maybe,
but not everything does good. True, for me
everything is permissible, but I am deter-
mined not to be dominated by anything.
13Foods are for the stomach, and the stomach
is for foods; and God will destroy them both.
But the body is not for sexual immorality;
14it is for the Lord, and the Lord is for the
body. God raised up the Lord and he will
raise us up too by his power. 15Do you
not realise that your bodies are members of
Christ's body; do you think one can take
parts of Christ's body and join them to the
body of a prostitute? Out of the question!
16Or do you not realise that anyone who
attaches himself to a prostitute is one body
with her, since *the two*, as it is said, *become
one flesh*.[b] 17But anyone who attaches himself
to the Lord is one spirit with him.
18Keep away from sexual immorality. All
other sins that people may commit are done
outside the body; but the sexually immoral
person sins against his own body. 19Do you
not realise that your body is the temple of the
Holy Spirit, who is in you and whom you
received from God? 20You are not your own
property, then; you have been bought at a
price. So use your body for the glory
of God.

5b Dt 13:6.
6a Perhaps a saying of Paul now (and 10:23) quoted against him.
6b Gn 2:24.

II: ANSWERS TO VARIOUS QUESTIONS

A: MARRIAGE AND VIRGINITY

7 Now for the questions about which you wrote. Yes, it is a good thing for a man not to touch a woman; [2] yet to avoid immorality every man should have his own wife and every woman her own husband. [3] The husband must give to his wife what she has a right to expect, and so too the wife to her husband. [4] The wife does not have authority over her own body, but the husband does; and in the same way, the husband does not have authority over his own body, but the wife does. [5] You must not deprive each other, except by mutual consent for a limited time, to leave yourselves free for prayer, and to come together again afterwards; otherwise Satan may take advantage of any lack of self-control to put you to the test. [6] I am telling you this as a concession, not an order. [7] I should still like everyone to be as I am myself; but everyone has his own gift from God, one this kind and the next something different.

[8] To the unmarried and to widows I say: it is good for them to stay as they are, like me. [9] But if they cannot exercise self-control, let them marry, since it is better to be married than to be burnt up.

[10] To the married I give this ruling, and this is not mine but the Lord's: a wife must not be separated from her husband—[11] or if she has already left him, she must remain unmarried or else be reconciled to her husband—and a husband must not divorce his wife.

[12] For other cases these instructions are my own, not the Lord's. If one of the brothers has a wife who is not a believer, and she is willing to stay with him, he should not divorce her; [13] and if a woman has a husband who is not a believer and he is willing to stay with her, she should not divorce her husband. [14] You see, the unbelieving husband is sanctified through his wife and the unbelieving wife is sanctified through the brother. If this were not so, your children would be unclean, whereas in fact they are holy. [15] But if the unbeliever chooses to leave, then let the separation take place: in these circumstances, the brother or sister is no longer tied. But God has called you to live in peace: [16] as a wife, how can you tell whether you are to be the salvation of your husband; as a husband, how can you tell whether you are to be the salvation of your wife?

[17] Anyway let everyone continue in the part which the Lord has allotted to him, as he was when God called him. This is the rule that I give to all the churches. [18] If a man who is called has already been circumcised, then he must stay circumcised; when an uncircumcised man is called, he may not be circumcised. [19] To be circumcised is of no importance, and to be uncircumcised is of no importance; what is important is the keeping of God's commandments. [20] Everyone should stay in whatever state he was in when he was called. [21] So, if when you were called, you were a slave, do not think it matters—even if you have a chance of freedom, you should prefer to make full use of your condition as a slave. [22] You see, anyone who was called in the Lord while a slave, is a freeman of the Lord; and in the same way, anyone who was free when called, is a slave of Christ. [23] You have been bought at a price; do not be slaves now to any human being. [24] Each one of you, brothers, is to stay before God in the state in which you were called.

[25] About people remaining virgin, I have no directions from the Lord, but I give my own opinion as a person who has been granted the Lord's mercy to be faithful. [26] Well then, because of the stress which is weighing upon us, the right thing seems to be this: it is good for people to stay as they are. [27] If you are joined to a wife, do not seek to be released; if you are freed of a wife, do not look for a wife. [28] However, if you do get married, that is not a sin, and it is not sinful for a virgin to enter upon marriage. But such people will have the hardships consequent on human nature, and I would like you to be without that.

[29] What I mean, brothers, is that the time has become limited, and from now on, those who have spouses should live as though they had none; [30] and those who mourn as though they were not mourning; those who enjoy life as though they did not enjoy it; those who have been buying property as though they had no possessions; [31] and those who are involved with the world as though they were people not engrossed in it. Because this world as we know it is passing away.

32I should like you to have your minds free
from all worry. The unmarried man gives his
mind to the Lord's affairs and to how he can
please the Lord; 33but the man who is married
gives his mind to the affairs of this world and
to how he can please his wife, and he is
divided in mind. 34So, too, the unmarried
woman, and the virgin, gives her mind to the
Lord's affairs and to being holy in body and
spirit; but the married woman gives her mind
to the affairs of this world and to how she can
please her husband. 35I am saying this only
to help you, not to put a bridle on you, but
so that everything is as it should be, and you
are able to give your undivided attention to
the Lord.

36If someone with strong passions thinks
that he is behaving badly towards his fiancée
and that things should take their due course,
he should follow his desires. There is no sin
in it; they should marry. 37But if he stands
firm in his resolution, without any compul-
sion but with full control of his own will, and
decides to let her remain as his fiancée, then
he is acting well. 38In other words, he who
marries his fiancée is doing well, and he who
does not, better still.

39A wife is tied as long as her husband is
alive. But if the husband dies, she is free to
marry anybody she likes, only it must be in
the Lord. 40She would be happier if she
stayed as she is, to my way of thinking—
and I believe that I too have the Spirit
of God.

B: FOOD OFFERED TO FALSE GODS

General principles

8 Now about food which has been dedicated
to false gods.[a] We are well aware that all
of us have knowledge; but while knowledge
puffs up, love is what builds up. 2Someone
may think that he has full knowledge of
something and yet not know it as well as
he should; 3but someone who loves God is
known by God. 4On the subject of eating
foods dedicated to false gods, we are well
aware that none of the false gods exists in
reality and that there is no God other than
the One. 5Though there are so-called gods,
in the heavens or on earth—and there are
plenty of gods and plenty of lords—6yet for
us there is only one God, the Father from
whom all things come and for whom we
exist, and one Lord, Jesus Christ, through
whom all things come and through whom
we exist.

The claims of knowledge

7However, not everybody has this knowl-
edge. There are some in whose consciences
false gods still play such a part that they take
the food as though it had been dedicated to a
god; then their conscience, being vulnerable,
is defiled. 8But of course food cannot make
us acceptable to God; we lose nothing by not
eating it, we gain nothing by eating it. 9Only
be careful that this freedom of yours does not
in any way turn into an obstacle to trip those
who are vulnerable. 10Suppose someone sees
you, who have the knowledge, sitting eating
in the temple of some false god, do you not
think that his conscience, vulnerable as it is,
may be encouraged to eat foods dedicated to
false gods? 11And then it would be through
your knowledge that this brother for whom
Christ died, vulnerable as he is, has been
lost. 12So, sinning against your brothers and
wounding their vulnerable consciences, you
would be sinning against Christ. 13That is
why, if food can be the cause of a brother's
downfall, I will never eat meat any more,
rather than cause my brother's downfall.

Paul invokes his own example

9 Am I not free? Am I not an apostle? Have
I not seen Jesus our Lord? Are you not
my work in the Lord? 2Even if to others I am
not an apostle, to you at any rate I am, for
you are the seal of my apostolate in the Lord.
3To those who want to interrogate me, this is
my answer. 4Have we not every right to eat
and drink? 5And every right to be
accompanied by a Christian wife, like the
other apostles, like the brothers of the Lord,
and like Cephas? 6Are Barnabas and I the
only ones who have no right to stop working?
7What soldier would ever serve in the army
at his own expense? And who is there who
would plant a vineyard and never eat the fruit
from it; or would keep a flock and not feed
on the milk from his flock? 8Do not think
that this is merely worldly wisdom. Does not
the Law say exactly the same? It is written in

8a Food, especially meat, left over from sacrifices, was offered for sale cheap in the markets.

the Law of Moses: 9*You must not muzzle an ox when it is treading out the corn.*[a] Is it about oxen that God is concerned here, 10or is it not said entirely for our sake? Clearly it was written for our sake, because it is right that whoever ploughs should plough with the expectation of having his share, and whoever threshes should thresh with the expectation of having his share. 11If we have sown the seed of spiritual things in you, is it too much to ask that we should receive from you a crop of material things? 12Others have been given such rights over you and do we not deserve more? In fact, we have never exercised this right; on the contrary, we have put up with anything rather than obstruct the gospel of Christ in any way. 13Do you not realise that the ministers in the Temple get their food from the Temple, and those who serve at the altar can claim their share from the altar? 14In the same way, the Lord gave the instruction that those who preach the gospel should get their living from the gospel.

15However, I have never availed myself of any rights of this kind; and I have not written this to secure such treatment for myself; I would rather die than that . . . No one shall take from me this ground of boasting. 16In fact, preaching the gospel gives me nothing to boast of, for I am under compulsion and I should be in trouble if I failed to do it. 17If I did it on my own initiative I would deserve a reward; but if I do it under compulsion I am simply accepting a task entrusted to me. 18What reward do I have, then? That in my preaching I offer the gospel free of charge to avoid using the rights which the gospel allows me.

19So though I was not a slave to any human being, I put myself in slavery to all people, to win as many as I could. 20To the Jews I made myself as a Jew, to win the Jews; to those under the Law as one under the Law (though I am not), in order to win those under the Law; 21to those outside the Law as one outside the Law, though I am not outside the Law but under Christ's law, to win those outside the Law. 22To the weak, I made myself weak, to win the weak. I accommodated myself to people in all kinds of different situations, so that by all possible means I might bring some to salvation. 23All this I do for the sake of the gospel, that I may share its benefits with others.

24Do you not realise that, though all the runners in the stadium take part in the race, only one of them gets the prize? Run like that—to win. 25Every athlete concentrates completely on training, and this is to win a wreath that will wither, whereas ours will never wither. 26So that is how I run, not without a clear goal; and how I box, not wasting blows on air. 27I punish my body and bring it under control, to avoid any risk that, having acted as herald for others, I myself may be disqualified.

A warning and the lessons of Israel's history

10 I want you to be quite certain, brothers, that our ancestors all had the cloud over them and all passed through the sea. 2In the cloud and in the sea they were all baptised into Moses; 3all ate the same spiritual food 4and all drank the same spiritual drink, since they drank from the spiritual rock which followed them,[a] and that rock was Christ. 5In spite of this, God was not pleased with most of them, and their corpses *were scattered over the desert.*[b] 6Now these happenings were examples, for our benefit, so that we should never set our hearts, as they did, on evil things; 7nor are you to worship false gods, as some of them did, as it says in scripture: *The people sat down to eat and drink, and afterwards got up to amuse themselves.*[c] 8Nor, again, are we to fall into sexual immorality; some of them did this, and twenty-three thousand met their downfall in one day. 9And we are not to put the Lord to the test; some of them put him to the test, and they were killed by snakes. 10Never complain; some of them complained, and they were killed by the Destroyer. 11Now all these things happened to them by way of example, and they were described in writing to be a lesson for us, to whom it has fallen to live in the last days of the ages. 12Everyone, no matter how firmly he thinks he is standing, must be careful he does not fall. 13None of the trials which have come upon you is more than a human being can stand. You can trust that God will not let you be put to the test beyond your strength,

9a Dt 25:4.
10a In rabbinic tradition the rock of Nb 20:8 followed them.
10b Nb 14:16.
10c Ex 32:6.

but with any trial will also provide a way out
by enabling you to put up with it.

Sacrificial feasts
No compromise with idolatry

[14]For that reason, my dear friends, have
nothing to do with the worship of false gods.
[15]I am talking to you as sensible people; weigh
up for yourselves what I have to say. [16]The
blessing-cup, which we bless, is it not a
sharing in the blood of Christ; and the loaf of
bread which we break, is it not a sharing in
the body of Christ? [17]And as there is one loaf,
so we, although there are many of us, are one
single body, for we all share in the one loaf.
[18]Now compare the natural people of Israel:
is it not true that those who eat the sacrifices
share the altar? [19]What does this mean? That
the dedication of food to false gods amounts
to anything? Or that false gods themselves
amount to anything? [20]No, it does not; simply
that when pagans sacrifice, *what is sacrificed
by them is sacrificed to demons who are not
God.*[d] I do not want you to share with demons.
[21]You cannot drink the cup of the Lord and
the cup of demons as well; you cannot have
a share at the Lord's table and the demons'
table as well. [22]Do we really want to arouse
the Lord's jealousy; are we stronger than he
is?

Food sacrificed to idols
Practical solutions

[23]'Everything is permissible'; maybe so, but
not everything does good. True, everything
is permissible, but not everything builds
people up. [24]Nobody should be looking for
selfish advantage, but everybody for someone
else's. [25]Eat anything that is sold in butchers'
shops; there is no need to ask questions for
conscience's sake, [26]since *To the Lord belong
the earth and all it contains.*[e] [27]If an unbeliever
invites you to a meal, go if you want to, and
eat whatever is put before you; you need not
ask questions of conscience first. [28]But if
someone says to you, 'This food has been
offered in sacrifice,' do not eat it, out of
consideration for the person that told you,
for conscience's sake—[29]not your own
conscience, I mean, but the other person's.
Why should my freedom be governed by
somebody else's conscience? [30]Provided that
I accept it with gratitude, why should I be
blamed for eating food for which I give
thanks? [31]Whatever you eat, then, or drink,
and whatever else you do, do it all for the
glory of God. [32]Never be a cause of offence,
either to Jews or to Greeks or to the Church
of God, [33]just as I try to accommodate every-
body in everything, not looking for my own
advantage, but for the advantage of every-
body else, so that they may be saved.

11 Take me as your pattern, just as I take
Christ for mine.

C: DECORUM IN PUBLIC WORSHIP

Women's behaviour at services

[2]I congratulate you for remembering me so
consistently and for maintaining the
traditions exactly as I passed them on to you.
[3]But I should like you to understand that the
head of every man is Christ, the head of
woman is man, and the head of Christ is God.
[4]For any man to pray or to prophesy with his
head covered shows disrespect for his head.
[5]And for a woman to pray or prophesy with
her head uncovered shows disrespect for her
head; it is exactly the same as if she had her
hair shaved off. [6]Indeed, if a woman does go
without a veil, she should have her hair cut
off too; but if it is a shameful thing for a
woman to have her hair cut off or shaved off,
then she should wear a veil.

[7]But for a man it is not right to have his
head covered, since he is the image of God
and reflects God's glory; but woman is the
reflection of man's glory. [8]For man did not
come from woman; no, woman came from
man; [9]nor was man created for the sake of
woman, but woman for the sake of man:
[10]and this is why it is right for a woman to
wear on her head a sign of the authority over
her, because of the angels. [11]However, in the
Lord, though woman is nothing without
man, man is nothing without woman; [12]and
though woman came from man, so does every
man come from a woman, and everything
comes from God.

[13]Decide for yourselves: does it seem fitting
that a woman should pray to God without a
veil? [14]Does not nature itself teach you that

10d Dt 32:17.
10e Ps 24:1.

if a man has long hair, it is a disgrace to him, [15]but when a woman has long hair, it is her glory? After all, her hair was given to her to be a covering.

[16]If anyone wants to be contentious, I say that we have no such custom, nor do any of the churches of God.

The Lord's Supper

[17]Now that I am on the subject of instructions, I cannot congratulate you on the meetings you hold; they do more harm than good. [18]In the first place, I hear that when you all come together in your assembly, there are separate factions among you, and to some extent I believe it. [19]It is no bad thing, either, that there should be differing groups among you so that those who are to be trusted among you can be clearly recognised. [20]So, when you meet together, it is not the Lord's Supper that you eat; [21]for when the eating begins, each one of you has his own supper first, and there is one going hungry while another is getting drunk. [22]Surely you have homes for doing your eating and drinking in? Or have you such disregard for God's assembly that you can put to shame those who have nothing? What am I to say to you? Congratulate you? On this I cannot congratulate you.

[23]For the tradition I received[a] from the Lord and also handed on to you is that on the night he was betrayed, the Lord Jesus took some bread, [24]and after he had given thanks, he broke it, and he said, 'This is my body, which is for you; do this in remembrance of me.' [25]And in the same way, with the cup after supper, saying, 'This cup is the new covenant in my blood. Whenever you drink it, do this as a memorial of me.' [26]Whenever you eat this bread, then, and drink this cup, you are proclaiming the Lord's death until he comes. [27]Therefore anyone who eats the bread or drinks the cup of the Lord unworthily is answerable for the body and blood of the Lord.

[28]Everyone is to examine himself and only then eat of the bread or drink from the cup; [29]because a person who eats and drinks without recognising the body is eating and drinking his own condemnation. [30]That is why many of you are weak and ill and a good number have died. [31]If we were critical of ourselves we would not be condemned, [32]but when we are judged by the Lord, we are corrected by the Lord to save us from being condemned along with the world.

[33]So then, my brothers, when you meet for the Meal, wait for each other; [34]anyone who is hungry should eat at home. Then your meeting will not bring your condemnation. The other matters I shall arrange when I come.

Spiritual gifts

12 About the gifts of the Spirit, brothers, I want you to be quite certain. [2]You remember that, when you were pagans, you were irresistibly drawn to inarticulate heathen gods. [3]Because of that, I want to make it quite clear to you that no one who says 'A curse on Jesus' can be speaking in the Spirit of God, and nobody is able to say, 'Jesus is Lord' except in the Holy Spirit.

The variety and the unity of gifts

[4]There are many different gifts, but it is always the same Spirit; [5]there are many different ways of serving, but it is always the same Lord. [6]There are many different forms of activity, but in everybody it is the same God who is at work in them all. [7]The particular manifestation of the Spirit granted to each one is to be used for the general good. [8]To one is given from the Spirit the gift of utterance expressing wisdom; to another the gift of utterance expressing knowledge, in accordance with the same Spirit; [9]to another, faith, from the same Spirit; and to another, the gifts of healing, through this one Spirit; [10]to another, the working of miracles; to another, prophecy; to another, the power of distinguishing spirits; to one, the gift of different tongues and to another, the interpretation of tongues. [11]But at work in all these is one and the same Spirit, distributing them at will to each individual.

The analogy of the body

[12]For as with the human body which is a unity although it has many parts—all the parts of the body, though many, still making up one single body—so it is with Christ. [13]We were baptised into one body in a single Spirit,

---

11a cf. 15:3.

Jews as well as Greeks, slaves as well as free
men, and we were all given the same Spirit
to drink. 14And indeed the body consists not
of one member but of many. 15If the foot
were to say, 'I am not a hand and so I do not
belong to the body,' it does not belong to the
body any the less for that. 16Or if the ear
were to say, 'I am not an eye, and so I do not
belong to the body,' that would not stop its
belonging to the body. 17If the whole body
were just an eye, how would there be any
hearing? If the whole body were hearing,
how would there be any smelling?

18As it is, God has put all the separate parts
into the body as he chose. 19If they were all
the same part, how could it be a body? 20As
it is, the parts are many but the body is one.
21The eye cannot say to the hand, 'I have no
need of you,' and nor can the head say to the
feet, 'I have no need of you.'

22What is more, it is precisely the parts of
the body that seem to be the weakest which
are the indispensable ones. 23It is the parts of
the body which we consider least dignified
that we surround with the greatest dignity;
and our less presentable parts are given
greater presentability 24which our present-
able parts do not need. God has composed
the body so that greater dignity is given to
the parts which were without it, 25and so that
there may not be disagreements inside the
body but each part may be equally concerned
for all the others. 26If one part is hurt, all
the parts share its pain. And if one part is
honoured, all the parts share its joy.

27Now Christ's body is yourselves, each of
you with a part to play in the whole. 28And
those whom God has appointed in the Church
are, first apostles, secondly prophets, thirdly
teachers; after them, miraculous powers,
then gifts of healing, helpful acts, guidance,
various kinds of tongues. 29Are all of them
apostles? Or all prophets? Or all teachers? Or
all miracle-workers? 30Do all have the gifts
of healing? Do all of them speak in tongues
and all interpret them?

The order of importance in spiritual gifts
Hymn to Love

31Set your mind on the higher gifts. And now
I am going to put before you the best way
of all.

13 Though I command languages both
human and angelic—if I speak without
love, I am no more than a gong booming or
a cymbal clashing. 2And though I have the
power of prophecy, to penetrate all mysteries
and knowledge, and though I have all the
faith necessary to move mountains—if I am
without love, I am nothing. 3Though I should
give away to the poor all that I possess, and
even give up my body to be burned—if I am
without love, it will do me no good whatever.

4Love is always patient and kind; love is
never jealous; love is not boastful or
conceited, 5it is never rude and never seeks
its own advantage, it does not take offence or
store up grievances. 6Love does not rejoice
at wrongdoing, but finds its joy in the truth.
7It is always ready to make allowances, to
trust, to hope and to endure whatever comes.

8Love never comes to an end. But if there
are prophecies, they will be done away with;
if tongues, they will fall silent; and if knowl-
edge, it will be done away with. 9For we
know only imperfectly, and we prophesy
imperfectly; 10but once perfection comes, all
imperfect things will be done away with.
11When I was a child, I used to talk like a
child, and see things as a child does, and
think like a child; but now that I have become
an adult, I have finished with all childish
ways. 12Now we see only reflections in a
mirror, mere riddles, but then we shall be
seeing face to face. Now I can know only
imperfectly; but then I shall know just as
fully as I am myself known.

13As it is, these remain: faith, hope and
love, the three of them; and the greatest of
them is love.

Spiritual gifts:
their respective importance
in the community

14 Make love your aim; but be eager, too,
for spiritual gifts, and especially for
prophesying. 2Those who speak in a tongue
speak to God, but not to other people,
because nobody understands them; they are
speaking in the Spirit and the meaning is
hidden. 3On the other hand, someone who
prophesies speaks to other people, building
them up and giving them encouragement and
reassurance. 4Those who speak in a tongue
may build themselves up, but those who
prophesy build up the community. 5While I
should like you all to speak in tongues, I
would much rather you could prophesy; since
those who prophesy are of greater importance
than those who speak in tongues, unless they

can interpret what they say so that the church is built up by it.

6 Now suppose, brothers, I come to you and speak in tongues, what good shall I do you if my speaking provides no revelation or knowledge or prophecy or instruction? 7 It is the same with an inanimate musical instrument. If it does not make any distinction between notes, how can one recognise what is being played on flute or lyre? 8 If the trumpet sounds a call which is unrecognisable, who is going to get ready for the attack? 9 It is the same with you: if you do not use your tongue to produce speech that can be readily understood, how can anyone know what you are saying? You will be talking to the air. 10 However many the languages used in the world, all of them use sound; 11 but if I do not understand the meaning of the sound, I am a barbarian[a] to the person who is speaking, and the speaker is a barbarian to me. 12 So with you, as you are eager to have spiritual powers, aim to be rich in those which build up the community.

13 That is why anybody who speaks in a tongue must pray that he may be given the interpretation. 14 For if I pray in a tongue, my spirit may be praying but my mind derives no fruit from it. 15 What then? I shall pray with the spirit, but I shall pray with the mind as well: I shall sing praises with the spirit and I shall sing praises with the mind as well. 16 Otherwise, if you say your blessing only with the spirit, how is the uninitiated person going to answer 'Amen' to your thanksgiving, without understanding what you are saying? 17 You may be making your thanksgiving well, but the other person is not built up at all. 18 I thank God that I speak with tongues more than any of you; 19 all the same, when I am in the assembly I would rather say five words with my mind, to instruct others as well, than ten thousand words in a tongue.

20 Brothers, do not remain children in your thinking; infants in wickedness—agreed, but in your thinking grown-ups. 21 It says in the written Law: *In strange tongues and in a foreign language I will talk to this nation, and* even so *they will refuse to listen*,[b] says the Lord. 22 So then, strange languages are significant not for believers, but for unbelievers; whereas on the other hand, prophesying is not for unbelievers, but for believers. 23 Suppose that, if the whole congregation were meeting and all of them speaking in tongues, and some uninitiated people or unbelievers were to come in, don't you think they would say that you were all raving? 24 But if you were all prophesying when an unbeliever or someone uninitiated came in, he would find himself put to the test by all and judged by all 25 and the secrets of his heart revealed; and so he would fall down on his face and worship God, declaring that *God is indeed among you.*[c]

Regulating spiritual gifts

26 Then what should it be like, brothers? When you come together each of you brings a psalm or some instruction or a revelation, or speaks in a tongue or gives an interpretation. Let all these things be done in a way that will build up the community. 27 If there are to be any people speaking in a tongue, then let there be only two, or at the most three, and those one at a time, and let one of these interpret. 28 If there is no interpreter, then let each of them be quiet in the assembly, and speak only to himself and God. 29 Let two prophets, or three, speak while the rest weigh their words; 30 and if a revelation comes to someone else who is sitting by, the speaker should stop speaking. 31 You can all prophesy, but one at a time, then all will learn something and all receive encouragement. 32 The prophetic spirit is to be under the prophets' control, 33 for God is a God not of disorder but of peace.

As in all the churches of God's holy people, 34 women are to remain quiet in the assemblies, since they have no permission to speak: theirs is a subordinate part, as the Law itself says. 35 If there is anything they want to know, they should ask their husbands at home: it is shameful for a woman to speak in the assembly.

36 Do you really think that you are the source of the word of God? Or that you are the only people to whom it has come? 37 Anyone who claims to be a prophet, or to have any spiritual powers must recognise that what I am writing to you is a commandment from the Lord. 38 If anyone does not recognise

14a i.e. someone who does not understand Gk.
14b Is 28:11–12.
14c Is 45:14.

this, it is because that person is not recognised himself.

[39]So, my brothers, be eager to prophesy, and do not suppress the gift of speaking in tongues. [40]But make sure that everything is done in a proper and orderly fashion.

III: THE RESURRECTION OF THE DEAD

The fact of the resurrection

15 I want to make quite clear to you, brothers, what the message of the gospel that I preached to you is; you accepted it and took your stand on it, [2]and you are saved by it, if you keep to the message I preached to you; otherwise your coming to believe was in vain. [3]The tradition I handed on to you in the first place, a tradition which I had myself received,[a] was that Christ died for our sins, in accordance with the scriptures, [4]and that he was buried; and that on the third day, he was raised to life, in accordance with the scriptures; [5]and that he appeared to Cephas; and later to the Twelve; [6]and next he appeared to more than five hundred of the brothers at the same time, most of whom are still with us, though some have fallen asleep; [7]then he appeared to James, and then to all the apostles. [8]Last of all he appeared to me too, as though I was a child born abnormally.

[9]For I am the least of the apostles and am not really fit to be called an apostle, because I had been persecuting the Church of God; [10]but what I am now, I am through the grace of God, and the grace which was given to me has not been wasted. Indeed, I have worked harder than all the others—not I, but the grace of God which is with me. [11]Anyway, whether it was they or I, this is what we preach and what you believed.

[12]Now if Christ is proclaimed as raised from the dead, how can some of you be saying that there is no resurrection of the dead? [13]If there is no resurrection of the dead, then Christ cannot have been raised either, [14]and if Christ has not been raised, then our preaching is without substance, and so is your faith. [15]What is more, we have proved to be false witnesses to God, for testifying against God that he raised Christ to life when he did not raise him—if it is true that the dead are not raised. [16]For, if the dead are not raised, neither is Christ; [17]and if Christ has not been raised, your faith is pointless and you have not, after all, been released from your sins. [18]In addition, those who have fallen asleep in Christ are utterly lost. [19]If our hope in Christ has been for this life only, we are of all people the most pitiable.

[20]In fact, however, Christ has been raised from the dead, as the first-fruits of all who have fallen asleep. [21]As it was by one man that death came, so through one man has come the resurrection of the dead. [22]Just as all die in Adam, so in Christ all will be brought to life; [23]but all of them in their proper order: Christ the first-fruits, and next, at his coming, those who belong to him. [24]After that will come the end, when he will hand over the kingdom to God the Father, having abolished every principality, every ruling force and power. [25]For he is to be king *until he has made* his enemies his footstool, [26]and the last of the enemies to be done away with is death, for *he has put all things under his feet*.[b] [27]But when it is said everything is subjected, this obviously cannot include the One who subjected everything to him. [28]When everything has been subjected to him, then the Son himself will be subjected to the One who has subjected everything to him, so that God may be all in all.

[29]Otherwise, what are people up to who have themselves baptised on behalf of the dead? If the dead are not raised at all, what is the point of being baptised on their behalf? [30]And what about us? Why should we endanger ourselves every hour of our lives? [31]I swear by the pride that I take in you, in Christ Jesus our Lord, that I face death every day. [32]If I fought wild animals at Ephesus in a purely human perspective, what had I to gain by it? [33]If the dead are not going to be raised, then *Let us eat and drink, for tomorrow we shall be dead*.[c] [34]So do not let anyone lead

15a cf. 11:23.
15b Ps 110:1.
15c Is 22:13.

you astray, 'Bad company corrupts good ways.'[d] Wake up from your stupor as you should and leave sin alone; some of you have no understanding of God; I tell you this to instil some shame in you.

The manner of the resurrection

35 Someone may ask: How are dead people raised, and what sort of body do they have when they come? 36 How foolish! What you sow must die before it is given new life; 37 and what you sow is not the body that is to be, but only a bare grain, of wheat I dare say, or some other kind; 38 it is God who gives it the sort of body that he has chosen for it, and for each kind of seed its own kind of body.

39 Not all flesh is the same flesh: there is human flesh; animals have another kind of flesh, birds another and fish yet another. 40 Then there are heavenly bodies and earthly bodies; the heavenly have a splendour of their own, and the earthly a different splendour. 41 The sun has its own splendour, the moon another splendour, and the stars yet another splendour; and the stars differ among themselves in splendour. 42 It is the same too with the resurrection of the dead: what is sown is perishable, but what is raised is imperishable; 43 what is sown is contemptible but what is raised is glorious; what is sown is weak, but what is raised is powerful; 44 what is sown is a natural body, and what is raised is a spiritual body.

If there is a natural body, there is a spiritual body too. 45 So the first *man*, Adam, as scripture says, *became a living soul*;[e] and the last Adam has become a life-giving spirit. 46 But first came the natural body, not the spiritual one; that came only afterwards. 47 The first man, being made of earth, is earthly by nature; the second man is from heaven. 48 The earthly man is the pattern for earthly people, the heavenly man for heavenly ones. 49 And as we have borne the likeness of the earthly man, so we shall bear the likeness of the heavenly one.

50 What I am saying, brothers, is that mere human nature cannot inherit the kingdom of God: what is perishable cannot inherit what is imperishable. 51 Now I am going to tell you a mystery: we are not all going to fall asleep, 52 but we are all going to be changed, instantly, in the twinkling of an eye, when the last trumpet sounds. The trumpet is going to sound, and then the dead will be raised imperishable, and we shall be changed, 53 because this perishable nature of ours must put on imperishability, this mortal nature must put on immortality.

A hymn of triumph. Conclusion

54 And after this perishable nature has put on imperishability and this mortal nature has put on immortality, then will the words of scripture come true: *Death is swallowed up in victory.* 55 *Death, where is your victory? Death, where is your sting?*[f] 56 The sting of death is sin, and the power of sin comes from the Law. 57 Thank God, then, for giving us the victory through Jesus Christ our Lord.

58 So, my dear brothers, keep firm and immovable, always abounding in energy for the Lord's work, being sure that in the Lord none of your labours is wasted.

CONCLUSION

Commendations. Greetings

16 Now about the collection for God's holy people;[a] you are to do the same as I prescribed for the churches in Galatia. 2 On the first day of the week, each of you should put aside and reserve as much as each can spare; do not delay the collection till I arrive. 3 When I come, I will send to Jerusalem with letters of introduction those people you approve to deliver your gift; 4 if it is worth my going too, they can travel with me.

5 In any case, I shall be coming to you after I have passed through Macedonia, as I have to go through Macedonia; 6 and I may be staying some time with you, perhaps

15d A proverb found also in Menander's *Thais*.
15e Gn 2:7.
15f A free version of Is 25:8 and Hos 13:14.
16a cf. Ac 24:17; 2 Co 8–9.

wintering, so that you can start me on my
next journey, wherever I may be going. 7I do
not want to make only a passing visit to you,
and I am hoping to spend quite a time with
you, the Lord permitting. 8But I shall remain
at Ephesus until Pentecost, 9for a very prom-
ising door is standing wide open to me and
there are many against us.
10If Timothy comes, make sure that he has
nothing to fear from you; he is doing the
Lord's work, just as I am, 11and nobody is to
underrate him. Start him off in peace on his
journey to come on to me: the brothers and I
are waiting for him. 12As for our brother
Apollos, I urged him earnestly to come to
you with the brothers, but he was quite firm
that he did not want to go yet, and he will
come when he finds an opportunity.
13Be vigilant, stay firm in the faith, be
brave and strong. 14Let everything you do be
done in love.
15There is something else I must urge you
to do, brothers. You know how Stephanas'
family have been the first-fruits of Achaia
and have devoted themselves to the service
of God's holy people; 16I ask you in turn to
put yourselves at the service of people like
this and all that work with them in this
arduous task. 17I am delighted that Stephanas
and Fortunatus and Achaicus have arrived;
they have made up for your not being here.
18They have set my mind at rest, just as they
did yours; you should appreciate people like
them.
19The churches of Asia send their greet-
ings. Aquila and Prisca send their best wishes
in the Lord, together with the church that
meets in their house. 20All the brothers send
their greetings. Greet one another with the
holy kiss.
21This greeting is in my own hand—PAUL.
22If there is anyone who does not love the
Lord, a curse on such a one. *Maran atha.*[b]
23The grace of the Lord Jesus Christ be
with you.
24My love is with you all in Christ Jesus.

SECOND CORINTHIANS

Between 1 Co and 2 Co frequent and stormy interchanges with Corinth intervene, *see* 1[a] note. Paul is still anxious to improve his relations with the community. This gives rise to his reflections on the apostolate, the spreading of the glorious light of Christ, by which we are transformed into the image we reflect. The collection for the Jerusalem community (section II) was close to Paul's heart; he mentions it several times in his letters as a means to unity, showing the devotion of the new communities to the mother church; here he urges especially the example of Christ's generosity. The final section is the fullest piece of Paul's autobiographical writing we possess, giving a fascinating picture of the opposition and difficulties which he met by means of his love of Christ.

It is possible that 2 Co is not a single letter but a collection of separate notes; each of the three sections below may be distinct, and there may be divisions even within these, *see* notes at 6*b* and 9*a*.

PLAN OF THE LETTER

16*b* Aram. 'The Lord is coming' (or perhaps 'Lord, come').

II Organisation of the Collection 8—9
III Paul's Apologia 10—13:10
Conclusion 13:11–13

2 CORINTHIANS

THE SECOND LETTER OF PAUL TO THE CHURCH AT CORINTH

INTRODUCTION

Address and greetings. Thanksgiving

1 Paul, by the will of God an apostle of
Christ Jesus, and Timothy, our brother,
to the church of God in Corinth and to all
God's holy people in the whole of Achaia.
[2]Grace to you and peace from God our Father
and the Lord Jesus Christ.
[3]Blessed be the God and Father of our
Lord Jesus Christ, the merciful Father and
the God who gives every possible encourage-
ment; [4]he supports us in every hardship, so
that we are able to come to the support of
others, in every hardship of theirs because of
the encouragement that we ourselves receive
from God. [5]For just as the sufferings of
Christ overflow into our lives; so too does the
encouragement we receive through Christ.
[6]So if we have hardships to undergo, this will
contribute to your encouragement and your
salvation; if we receive encouragement, this
is to gain for you the encouragement which
enables you to bear with perseverance the
same sufferings as we do. [7]So our hope for
you is secure in the knowledge that you share
the encouragement we receive, no less than
the sufferings we bear.
[8]So in the hardships we underwent in Asia,
we want you to be quite certain, brothers,
that we were under extraordinary pressure,
beyond our powers of endurance, so that we
gave up all hope even of surviving. [9]In fact
we were carrying the sentence of death within
our own selves, so that we should be forced
to trust not in ourselves but in God, who
raises the dead. [10]He did save us from such a
death and will save us—we are relying on
him to do so. [11]Your prayer for us will
contribute to this, so that, for God's favour
shown to us as the result of the prayers of so
many, thanks too may be given by many on
our behalf.

I: SOME RECENT EVENTS REVIEWED

Why Paul changed his plans

[12]There is one thing that we are proud of,
namely our conscientious conviction that we
have always behaved towards everyone, and
especially towards you, with that unalloyed
holiness that comes from God, relying not on
human reasoning but on the grace of God.
[13]In our writing, there is nothing that you
cannot read clearly and understand; [14]and it
is my hope that, just as you have already
understood us partially, so you will under-
stand fully that you can be as proud of us as
we shall be of you when the Day of our Lord
Jesus comes.
[15]It was with this assurance that I had been
meaning to come to you first, so that you
would benefit doubly; [16]both to visit you on
my way to Macedonia, and then to return to
you again from Macedonia, so that you could
set me on my way to Judaea. [17]Since that was
my purpose, do you think I lightly changed

my mind? Or that my plans are based on
ordinary human promptings and I have in
my mind Yes, yes[a] at the same time as No,
no? [18]As surely as God is trustworthy, what
we say to you is not both Yes and No.
[19]The Son of God, Jesus Christ, who was
proclaimed to you by us, that is, by me and
by Silvanus and Timothy, was never Yes-
and-No; his nature is all Yes. [20]For in him is
found the Yes to all God's promises and
therefore it is 'through him' that we answer
'Amen' to give praise to God. [21]It is God who
gives us, with you, a sure place in Christ
[22]and has both anointed us and marked us
with his seal, giving us as pledge the Spirit in
our hearts.

[23]By my life I call on God to be my witness
that it was only to spare you that I did not
come to Corinth again.[b] [24]We have no wish
to lord it over your faith, but to work with
you for your joy; for your stand in the faith
is firm.

2 I made up my mind, then, that my next
visit to you would not be a painful one,
[2]for if I cause you distress I am causing
distress to my only possible source of joy.
[3]Indeed, I wrote as I did precisely to spare
myself distress when I visited you, from the
very people who should have given me joy,
in the conviction that for all of you my joy
was yours too. [4]I wrote to you in agony of
mind, not meaning to cause you distress
but to show you how very much love I have
for you.

[5]If anyone did cause distress, he caused it
not to me, but—not to exaggerate—in some
degree to all of you. [6]The punishment already
imposed by the majority was quite enough
for such a person; [7]and now by contrast you
should forgive and encourage him all the
more, or he may be overwhelmed by the
extent of his distress. [8]That is why I urge
you to give your love towards him definite
expression. [9]This was in fact my reason for
writing, to test your quality and whether you
are completely obedient. [10]But if you forgive
anybody, then I too forgive that person; and
whatever I have forgiven, if there is anything
I have forgiven, I have done it for your
sake in Christ's presence, [11]to avoid being
outwitted by Satan, whose scheming we
know only too well.

From Troas to Macedonia
The apostolate: its importance

[12]When I came to Troas for the sake of the
gospel of Christ and a door was opened for
me there in the Lord, [13]I had no relief from
anxiety, not finding my brother Titus there,
and I said goodbye to them and went on to
Macedonia. [14]But, thanks be to God who
always gives us in Christ a part in his
triumphal procession, and through us is
spreading everywhere the fragrance of the
knowledge of himself. [15]To God we are the
fragrance of Christ, both among those who
are being saved and among those who are on
the way to destruction; [16]for these last, the
smell of death leading to death, but for the
first, the smell of life leading to life. Who is
equal to such a task? [17]At least we do not
adulterate the word of God, as so many do,
but it is in all purity, as envoys of God and in
God's presence, that we speak in Christ.

3 Are we beginning to commend ourselves
to you afresh—as though we needed, like
some others, to have letters of commendation
either to you or from you? [2]You yourselves
are our letter, written in our hearts, that
everyone can read and understand; [3]and it
is plain that you are a letter from Christ,
entrusted to our care, written not with ink
but with the Spirit of the living God; not on
stone tablets but on the tablets of human
hearts.

[4]Such is the confidence we have through
Christ in facing God; [5]it is not that we are so
competent that we can claim any credit for
ourselves; all our competence comes from
God. [6]He has given us the competence to be
ministers of a new covenant, a covenant
which is not of written letters, but of the
Spirit; for the written letters kill, but the
Spirit gives life. [7]Now if the administering of
death, engraved in letters on stone, occurred
in such glory that the Israelites could not look
Moses steadily in the face,[a] because of its
glory, transitory though this glory was, [8]how
much more will the ministry of the Spirit
occur in glory! [9]For if it is glorious to admin-
ister condemnation, to administer saving

1a The argument is based on the Hebr. word *Amen* = Yes. The root meaning is 'faithful', 'solid'.
1b After writing 1 Co Paul *1* paid a brief, stern visit to Corinth and promised to return, *2* sent a messenger who was insulted, *3* sent a severe reprimand which was effective, and *4* wrote this letter.
3a cf. Ex 34:29–35.

justice is far richer in glory. 10Indeed, what was once considered glorious has lost all claim to glory, by contrast with the glory which transcends it. 11For if what was transitory had any glory, how much greater is the glory of that which lasts for ever.

12With a hope like this, we can speak with complete fearlessness; 13not like Moses who put a veil over his face so that the Israelites should not watch the end of what was transitory. 14But their minds were closed; indeed, until this very day, the same veil remains over the reading of the Old Testament: it is not lifted, for only in Christ is it done away with. 15As it is, to this day, whenever Moses is read, their hearts are covered with a veil, 16and this veil will not be taken away till they turn to the Lord. 17Now this Lord is the Spirit and where the Spirit of the Lord is, there is freedom. 18And all of us, with our unveiled faces like mirrors reflecting the glory of the Lord, are being transformed into the image that we reflect in brighter and brighter glory; this is the working of the Lord who is the Spirit.

4 Such by God's mercy is our ministry, and therefore we do not waver 2but have renounced all shameful secrecy. It is not our way to be devious, or to falsify the word of God; instead, in God's sight we commend ourselves to every human being with a conscience by showing the truth openly. 3If our gospel seems to be veiled at all, it is so to those who are on the way to destruction, 4the unbelievers whose minds have been blinded by the god of this world, so that they cannot see shining the light of the gospel of the glory of Christ, who is the image of God. 5It is not ourselves that we are proclaiming, but Christ Jesus as the Lord, and ourselves as your servants for Jesus' sake. 6It is God who said, 'Let light shine out of darkness,' that has shone into our hearts to enlighten them with the knowledge of God's glory, the glory on the face of Christ.

The hardships and hopes of the apostolate

7But we hold this treasure in pots of earthenware, so that the immensity of the power is God's and not our own. 8We are subjected to every kind of hardship, but never distressed; we see no way out but we never despair; 9we are pursued but never cut off; knocked down, but still have some life in us; 10always we carry with us in our body the death of Jesus so that the life of Jesus, too, may be visible in our body. 11Indeed, while we are still alive, we are continually being handed over to death, for the sake of Jesus, so that the life of Jesus, too, may be visible in our mortal flesh. 12In us, then, death is at work; in you, life.

13But as we have the same spirit of faith as is described in scripture—*I believed and therefore I spoke*[a]—we, too, believe and therefore we, too, speak, 14realising that he who raised up the Lord Jesus will raise us up with Jesus in our turn, and bring us to himself—and you as well. 15You see, everything is for your benefit, so that as grace spreads, so, to the glory of God, thanksgiving may also overflow among more and more people.

16That is why we do not waver; indeed, though this outer human nature of ours may be falling into decay, at the same time our inner human nature is renewed day by day. 17The temporary, light burden of our hardships is earning us for ever an utterly incomparable, eternal weight of glory, 18since what we aim for is not visible but invisible. Visible things are transitory, but invisible things eternal.

5 For we are well aware that when the tent that houses us on earth is folded up, there is a house for us from God, not made by human hands but everlasting, in the heavens. 2And in this earthly state we do indeed groan, 3longing to put on our heavenly home over the present one; if indeed we are to be found clothed rather than stripped bare. 4Yes, indeed, in this present tent, we groan under the burden, not that we want to be stripped of our covering, but because we want to be covered with a second garment on top, so that what is mortal in us may be swallowed up by life. 5It is God who designed us for this very purpose, and he has given us the Spirit as a pledge.

6We are always full of confidence, then, realising that as long as we are at home in the body we are exiled from the Lord, 7guided by faith and not yet by sight; 8we are full of confidence, then, and long instead to be exiled from the body and to be at home with the Lord. 9And so whether at home or exiled, we make it our ambition to please him. 10For at the judgement seat of Christ we are all to

4a Ps 116:10.

be seen for what we are, so that each of us may receive what he has deserved in the body, matched to whatever he has done, good or bad.

The apostolate in action

11 And so it is with the fear of the Lord always in mind that we try to win people over. But God sees us for what we are, and I hope your consciences do too. 12 Again we are saying this not to commend ourselves to you, but simply to give you the opportunity to take pride in us, so that you may have an answer for those who take pride in appearances and not inner reality. 13 If we have been unreasonable, it was for God; if reasonable, for you. 14 For the love of Christ overwhelms us when we consider that if one man died for all, then all have died; 15 his purpose in dying for all humanity was that those who live should live not any more for themselves, but for him who died and was raised to life.

16 From now onwards, then, we will not consider anyone by human standards: even if we were once familiar with Christ according to human standards, we do not know him in that way any longer. 17 So for anyone who is in Christ, there is a new creation: the old order is gone and a new being is there to see. 18 It is all God's work; he reconciled us to himself through Christ and he gave us the ministry of reconciliation. 19 I mean, God was in Christ reconciling the world to himself, not holding anyone's faults against them, but entrusting to us the message of reconciliation.

20 So we are ambassadors for Christ; it is as though God were urging you through us, and in the name of Christ we appeal to you to be reconciled to God. 21 For our sake he made the sinless one a victim for sin, so that in him we might become the uprightness of God.

6 As his fellow-workers, we urge you not to let your acceptance of his grace come to nothing. 2 As he said, '*At the time of my favour I have answered you; on the day of salvation I have helped you*';[a] well, now is the real time of favour, now the day of salvation is here. 3 We avoid putting obstacles in anyone's way, so that no blame may attach to our work of service; 4 but in everything we prove ourselves authentic servants of God; by resolute perseverance in times of hardships, difficulties and distress; 5 when we are flogged or sent to prison or mobbed; labouring, sleepless, starving; 6 in purity, in knowledge, in patience, in kindness; in the Holy Spirit, in a love free of affectation; 7 in the word of truth and in the power of God; by using the weapons of uprightness for attack and for defence: 8 in times of honour or disgrace, blame or praise; taken for impostors and yet we are genuine; 9 unknown and yet we are acknowledged; dying, and yet here we are, alive; scourged but not executed; 10 in pain yet always full of joy; poor and yet making many people rich; having nothing, and yet owning everything.

A warning

11 People of Corinth, we have spoken frankly and opened our heart to you. 12 Any distress you feel is not on our side; the distress is in your own selves. 13 In fair exchange—I speak as though to children of mine—you must open your hearts too.

14 Do[b] not harness yourselves in an uneven team with unbelievers; how can uprightness and law-breaking be partners, or what can light and darkness have in common? 15 How can Christ come to an agreement with Beliar and what sharing can there be between a believer and an unbeliever? 16 The temple of God cannot compromise with false gods, and that is what we are—the temple of the living God. We have God's word for it: *I shall fix my home among them and live among them; I will be their God and they will be my people.* 17 *Get away from them, purify yourselves,* says the Lord. *Do not touch anything unclean, and then I shall welcome you.* 18 *I shall be father to you, and* you *will be sons* and daughters *to me*,[c] says the almighty Lord.

7 Since these promises have been made to us, my dear friends, we should wash ourselves clean of everything that pollutes either body or spirit, bringing our sanctification to completion in the fear of God.

2 Keep a place for us in your hearts. We have not injured anyone, or ruined anyone, or taken advantage of anyone. 3 I am not saying this to condemn anybody; as I have already told you, you are in our hearts—so

6a Is 49:8.
6b 6:14—7:1 may be a fragment on its own, a warning against infiltration of gentile ways.
6c Lv 26:11–12; Is 52:11; 2 S 7:14.

that together we live and together we die. 4I can speak with the greatest frankness to you; and I can speak with the greatest pride about you: in all our hardship, I am filled with encouragement and overflowing with joy.

Paul in Macedonia; he is joined by Titus

5Even after we had come to Macedonia, there was no rest for this body of ours. Far from it; we were beset by hardship on all sides, there were quarrels all around us and misgivings within us. 6But God, who encourages all those who are distressed, encouraged us through the arrival of Titus; 7and not simply by his arrival only, but also by means of the encouragement that you had given him, as he told us of your desire to see us, how sorry you were and how concerned for us; so that I was all the more joyful.

8So now, though I did distress you with my letter, I do not regret it. Even if I did regret it—and I realise that the letter distressed you, even though not for long—9I am glad now, not because you were made to feel distress, but because the distress that you were caused led to repentance; your distress was the kind that God approves and so you have come to no kind of harm through us. 10For to be distressed in a way that God approves leads to repentance and then to salvation with no regrets; it is the world's kind of distress that ends in death. 11Just look at this present case: at what the result has been of your being made to feel distress in the way that God approves—what concern, what defence, what indignation and what alarm; what yearning, and what enthusiasm, and what justice done. In every way you have cleared yourselves of blame in this matter. 12So although I wrote a letter to you, it was not for the sake of the offender, nor for the one offended, but only so that you yourselves should fully realise in the sight of God what concern you have for us. 13That is what I have found encouraging.

In addition to all this to encourage us, we were made all the more joyful by Titus' joy, now that his spirit has been refreshed by you all. 14And if I boasted about you to him in any way, then I have not been made to look foolish; indeed, our boast to Titus has been proved to be as true as anything we said to you. 15His personal affection for you is all the stronger when he remembers how obedient you have all been, and how you welcomed him with fear and trembling. 16I am glad that I have every confidence in you.

II: ORGANISATION OF THE COLLECTION

Why the Corinthians should be generous

8 Next, brothers, we will tell you of the grace of God which has been granted to the churches of Macedonia, 2and how, throughout continual ordeals of hardship, their unfailing joy and their intense poverty have overflowed in a wealth of generosity on their part. 3I can testify that it was of their own accord that they made their gift, which was not merely as far as their resources would allow, but well beyond their resources; 4and they had kept imploring us most insistently for the privilege of a share in the fellowship of service to God's holy people—5it was not something that we expected of them, but it began by their offering themselves to the Lord and to us at the prompting of the will of God. 6In the end we urged Titus, since he had already made a beginning, also to bring this work of generosity to completion among you. 7More, as you are rich in everything—faith, eloquence, understanding, concern for everything, and love for us too—then make sure that you excel in this work of generosity too. 8I am not saying this as an order, but testing the genuineness of your love against the concern of others. 9You are well aware of the generosity which our Lord Jesus Christ had, that, although he was rich, he became poor for your sake, so that you should become rich through his poverty. 10I will give you my considered opinion in the matter; this will be the right course for you as you were the first, a year ago, not only to take any action but also even to conceive the project. 11Now, then, complete the action as well, so that the fulfilment may—so far as your resources permit—be proportionate to your enthusiasm for the project. 12As long as the enthusiasm is there, the basis on which it is acceptable is what someone has, not what

someone does not have. 13 It is not that you ought to relieve other people's needs and leave yourselves in hardship; but there should be a fair balance— 14 your surplus at present may fill their deficit, and another time their surplus may fill your deficit. So there may be a fair balance; 15 as scripture says: *No one who had collected more had too much, no one who collected less had too little.*[a]

The delegates recommended to the Corinthians

16 Thank God for putting into Titus' heart the same sincere concern for you. 17 He certainly took our urging to heart; but greater still was his own enthusiasm, and he went off to you of his own accord. 18 We have sent with him the brother who is praised as an evangelist in all the churches 19 and who, what is more, was elected by the churches to be our travelling companion in this work of generosity, a work to be administered by us for the glory of the Lord and our complete satisfaction. 20 We arranged it this way so that no one should be able to make any accusation against us about this large sum we are administering. 21 And so *we have been careful to do right* not only *in the sight of the Lord* but also *in the sight of people.*[b] 22 Along with these, we have sent a brother of ours whose eagerness we have tested over and over again in many ways and who is now all the more eager because he has so much faith in you. 23 If Titus is in question—he is my own partner and fellow-worker in your interests; and if our brothers—they are the emissaries of the churches and the glory of Christ. 24 So then, in full view of all the churches, give proof that you love them, and that we were right to boast of you to them.

9 About the help to God's holy people, there is really no need for me to write to you;[a] 2 for I am well aware of your enthusiasm, and I have been boasting of it to the Macedonians that 'Achaia has been ready for a year'; your enthusiasm has been a spur to many others. 3 All the same, I have sent the brothers, to make sure that our boast about you may not prove hollow in this respect and that you may be ready, as I said you would be; 4 so that if by chance some of the Macedonians came with me and found you unprepared we—to say nothing of yourselves—would not be put to shame by our confidence in you. 5 So I have thought it necessary to encourage the brothers to go to you ahead of us and make sure in advance of the gift that you have already promised, so that it is all at hand as a real gift and not an imposition.

Blessings to be expected from the collection

6 But remember: anyone who sows sparsely will reap sparsely as well—and anyone who sows generously will reap generously as well. 7 Each one should give as much as he has decided on his own initiative, not reluctantly or under compulsion, for *God loves a cheerful giver.*[b] 8 God is perfectly able to enrich you with every grace, so that you always have enough for every conceivable need, and your resources overflow in all kinds of good work. 9 As scripture says: *To the needy he gave without stint, his uprightness stands firm for ever.*[c]

10 The one who so freely provides *seed for the sower and food to eat*[d] will provide you with ample store of seed for sowing and make *the harvest of your uprightness*[e] a bigger one: 11 you will be rich enough in every way for every kind of generosity that makes people thank God for what we have done. 12 For the help provided by this contribution not only satisfies the needs of God's holy people, but also overflows into widespread thanksgiving to God; 13 because when you have proved your quality by this help, they will give glory to God for the obedience which you show in professing the gospel of Christ, as well as for the generosity of your fellowship towards them and towards all. 14 At the same time, their prayer for you will express the affection they feel for you because of the unbounded grace God has given you. 15 Thanks be to God for his gift that is beyond all telling!

8a Ex 16:18.
8b Pr 3:4 LXX.
9a As he has just done so, this chapter may be a separate note.
9b Pr 22:8 LXX.
9c Ps 112:9.
9d Is 55:10.
9e Ho 12:12.

III: PAUL'S APOLOGIA

Paul's reply to accusations of weakness

10 I urge you by the gentleness and forbearance of Christ—this is Paul now speaking personally—I, the one who is so humble when he is facing you but full of boldness at a distance. [2]Yes, my appeal to you is that I should not have to be bold when I am actually with you, or show the same self-assurance as I reckon to use when I am challenging those who reckon that we are guided by human motives. [3]For although we are human, it is not by human methods that we do battle. [4]The weapons with which we do battle are not those of human nature, but they have the power, in God's cause, to demolish fortresses. It is ideas that we demolish, [5]every presumptuous notion that is set up against the knowledge of God, and we bring every thought into captivity and obedience to Christ; [6]once you have given your complete obedience, we are prepared to punish any disobedience. [7]Look at the evidence of your eyes. Anybody who is convinced that he belongs to Christ should go on to reflect that we belong to Christ no less than he does. [8]Maybe I have taken rather too much pride in our authority, but the Lord gave us that for building you up, not for knocking you down, and I am not going to be shamed [9]into letting you think that I can put fear into you only by letter. [10]Someone said, 'His letters are weighty enough, and full of strength, but when you see him in person, he makes no impression and his powers of speaking are negligible.' [11]I should like that sort of person to take note that our deeds when we are present will show the same qualities as our letters when we were at a distance.

His reply to the accusation of ambition

[12]We are not venturing to rank ourselves, or even to compare ourselves with certain people who provide their own commendations. By measuring themselves by themselves and comparing themselves to themselves, they only show their folly. [13]By contrast we do not intend to boast beyond measure, but will measure ourselves by the standard which God laid down for us, namely that of having come all the way to you. [14]We are not overreaching ourselves as we would be if we had not come all the way to you; in fact we were the first to come as far as you with the good news of Christ. [15]So we are not boasting beyond measure, about other men's work; in fact, we hope, as your faith increases, to grow greater and greater by this standard of ours, [16]by preaching the gospel to regions beyond you, rather than boasting about work already done in someone else's province. [17]*Let anyone who wants to boast, boast of the Lord.*[a] [18]For it is not through self-commendation that recognition is won, but through commendation.

Paul is driven to sound his own praises

11 I wish you would put up with a little foolishness from me—not that you don't do this already. [2]The jealousy that I feel for you is, you see, God's own jealousy: I gave you all in marriage to a single husband, a virgin pure for presentation to Christ. [3]But I am afraid that, just as the snake with his cunning seduced Eve, your minds may be led astray from single-minded devotion to Christ. [4]Because any chance comer has only to preach a Jesus other than the one we preached, or you have only to receive a spirit different from the one you received, or a gospel different from the one you accepted—and you put up with that only too willingly. [5]Now, I consider that I am not in the least inferior to the super-apostles. [6]Even if there is something lacking in my public speaking, this is not the case with my knowledge, as we have openly shown to you at all times and before everyone.

[7]Have I done wrong, then, humbling myself so that you might be raised up, by preaching the gospel of God to you for nothing? [8]I was robbing other churches, taking wages from them in order to work for you. [9]When I was with you and needed money, I was no burden to anybody, for the brothers from Macedonia brought me as much as I needed when they came; I have

10a Jr 9:22–23.

always been careful not to let myself be a burden to you in any way, and I shall continue to be so. [10]And as Christ's truth is in me, this boast of mine is not going to be silenced in the regions of Achaia. [11]Why should it be? Because I do not love you? God knows that I do. [12]I will go on acting as I do at present, to cut the ground from under the feet of those who are looking for a chance to be proved my equals in grounds for boasting. [13]These people are counterfeit apostles, dishonest workers disguising themselves as apostles of Christ. [14]There is nothing astonishing in this; even Satan disguises himself as an angel of light. [15]It is nothing extraordinary, then, when his servants disguise themselves as the servants of uprightness. They will come to the end appropriate to what they have done.

[16]To repeat: let no one take me for a fool, but if you do, then treat me as a fool, so that I, too, can do a little boasting. [17]I shall not be following the Lord's way in what I say now, but will be speaking out of foolishness in the conviction that I have something to boast about. [18]So many people boast on merely human grounds that I shall too. [19]I know how happy you are to put up with fools, being so wise yourselves; [20]and how you will still go on putting up with a man who enslaves you, eats up all you possess, keeps you under his orders and sets himself above you, or even slaps you in the face. [21]I say it to your shame; perhaps we have been too weak.

Whatever bold claims anyone makes—now I am talking as a fool—I can make them too. [22]Are they Hebrews? So am I. Are they Israelites? So am I. Are they descendants of Abraham? So am I. [23]Are they servants of Christ? I speak in utter folly—I am too, and more than they are: I have done more work, I have been in prison more, I have been flogged more severely, many times exposed to death. [24]Five times I have been given the thirty-nine lashes by the Jews; [25]three times I have been beaten with sticks; once I was stoned; three times I have been shipwrecked, and once I have been in the open sea for a night and a day; [26]continually travelling, I have been in danger from rivers, in danger from brigands, in danger from my own people and in danger from the gentiles, in danger in the towns and in danger in the open country, in danger at sea and in danger from people masquerading as brothers; [27]I have worked with unsparing energy, for many nights without sleep; I have been hungry and thirsty, and often altogether without food or drink; I have been cold and lacked clothing. [28]And, besides all the external things, there is, day in day out, the pressure on me of my anxiety for all the churches. [29]If anyone weakens, I am weakened as well; and when anyone is made to fall, I burn in agony myself.

[30]If I have to boast, I will boast of all the ways in which I am weak. [31]The God and Father of the Lord Jesus—who is for ever to be blessed—knows that I am not lying. [32]When I was in Damascus, the governor who was under King Aretas put guards round Damascus city to catch me, [33]and I was let down in a basket through a window in the wall, and that was how I escaped from his hands.

12 I am boasting because I have to. Not that it does any good, but I will move on to visions and revelations from the Lord. [2]I know a man in Christ who fourteen years ago—still in the body? I do not know; or out of the body? I do not know: God knows—was caught up right into the third heaven. [3]And I know that this man—still in the body? or outside the body? I do not know, God knows—[4]was caught up into Paradise and heard words said that cannot and may not be spoken by any human being. [5]On behalf of someone like that I am willing to boast, but I am not going to boast on my own behalf except of my weaknesses; [6]and then, if I do choose to boast I shall not be talking like a fool because I shall be speaking the truth. But I will not go on in case anybody should rate me higher than he sees and hears me to be, because of the exceptional greatness of the revelations.

[7]Wherefore, so that I should not get above myself, I was given a thorn in the flesh, a messenger from Satan to batter me and prevent me from getting above myself. [8]About this, I have three times pleaded with the Lord that it might leave me; [9]but he has answered me, 'My grace is enough for you: for power is at full stretch in weakness.' It is, then, about my weaknesses that I am happiest of all to boast, so that the power of Christ may rest upon me; [10]and that is why I am glad of weaknesses, insults, constraints, persecutions and distress for Christ's sake. For it is when I am weak that I am strong.

[11]I have turned into a fool, but you forced me to it. It is you that should have been commending me; those super-apostles had no advantage over me, even if I am nothing

at all. 12All the marks characteristic of a
true apostle have been at work among you:
complete perseverance, signs, marvels,
demonstrations of power. 13Is there any way
in which you have been given less than the
rest of the churches, except that I did not
make myself a burden to you? Forgive me
for this unfairness!

14Here I am, ready to come to you for the
third time and I am not going to be a burden
on you: it is not your possessions that I want,
but yourselves. Children are not expected to
save up for their parents, but parents for their
children, 15and I am more than glad to spend
what I have and to be spent for the sake of
your souls. Is it because I love you so much
more, that I am loved the less?

16All right, then; I did not make myself a
burden to you, but, trickster that I am,
I caught you by trickery. 17Have I taken
advantage of you through any of the people
I have sent to you? 18Titus came at my
urging, and I sent his companion with him.
Did Titus take advantage of you? Can you
deny that he and I were following the gui-
dance of the same Spirit and were on the
same tracks?

Paul's fears and anxieties

19All this time you have been thinking that
we have been pleading our own cause before
you; no, we have been speaking in Christ and
in the presence of God—and all, dear friends,
to build you up. 20I am afraid that in one way
or another, when I come, I may find you
different from what I should like you to be,
and you may find me what you would not
like me to be; so that in one way or the other
there will be rivalry, jealousy, bad temper,
quarrels, slander, gossip, arrogance and
disorders; 21and when I come again, my God
may humiliate me in front of you and I shall
be grieved by all those who sinned in the past
and have still not repented of the impurities
and sexual immorality and debauchery that
they have committed.

13 This will be the third time I have
confronted you. *Whatever the mis-
demeanour, the evidence of two or three witnesses
is required to sustain a charge.*[a] 2I gave you
notice once, and now, though I am not with
you, I give notice again, just as when I was
with you for a second time, to those who
sinned before, and to all others; and it is to
this effect, that when I do come next time, I
shall have no mercy. 3Since you are asking
for a proof that it is Christ who speaks in me;
he is not weak with you but his power is at
work among you; 4for, though it was out of
weakness that he was crucified, he is alive
now with the power of God. We, too, are
weak in him, but with regard to you we shall
live with him by the power of God.

5Put yourselves to the test to make sure
you are in the faith. Examine yourselves. Do
you not recognise yourselves as people in
whom Jesus Christ is present?—unless, that
is, you fail the test. 6But we, as I hope you
will come to recognise, do not fail the test.
7It is our prayer to God that you may do
nothing wrong—not so that we have the
credit of passing a test, but because you will
be doing what is right, even if we do not pass
the test. 8We have no power to resist the
truth; only to further the truth; 9and we are
delighted to be weak if only you are strong.
What we ask in our prayers is that you should
be made perfect. 10That is why I am writing
this while still far away, so that when I am
with you I shall not have to be harsh, with
the authority that the Lord has given me, an
authority that is for building up and not for
breaking down.

CONCLUSION

Recommendations, greetings, final good wishes

11To end then, brothers, we wish you joy; try
to grow perfect; encourage one another; have
a common mind and live in peace, and the
God of love and peace will be with you.

12Greet one another with the holy kiss. All
God's holy people send you their greetings.

13The grace of the Lord Jesus Christ, the
love of God and the fellowship of the Holy
Spirit be with you all.

13a Dt 19:15.

THE LETTER TO THE GALATIANS

A burning problem in the early Church was the attitude to Judaism, and the new Christians of Galatia had been persuaded of the need to keep to Jewish observance. Here is Paul's answer, written with all his characteristic vigour: he points out his own special call and special authority from God, and insists that the cross and faith set aside the Law, for the Law brings only a curse. Using rabbinic arguments especially appealing to the Jews, he shows that true sons of God are sons through faith and God's promise to Abraham, not through physical descent from Abraham.

PLAN OF THE LETTER

I Paul's Apologia 1:11—2:21
II Doctrinal Matters 3—4
III Exhortation 5—6

GALATIANS

THE LETTER OF PAUL TO THE CHURCH IN GALATIA

Address[a]

1 From Paul, an apostle appointed not by human beings nor through any human being but by Jesus Christ and God the Father who raised him from the dead, [2]and all the brothers who are with me, to the churches of Galatia. [3]Grace and peace from God the Father and our Lord Jesus Christ [4]who gave himself for our sins to liberate us from this present wicked world, in accordance with the will of our God and Father, [5]to whom be glory for ever and ever. Amen.

A warning

[6]I am astonished that you are so promptly turning away from the one who called you in the grace of Christ and are going over to a different gospel—[7]not that it is another gospel; except that there are trouble-makers among you who are seeking to pervert the gospel of Christ. [8]But even if we ourselves or an angel from heaven preaches to you a gospel other than the one we preached to you, let God's curse be on him. [9]I repeat again what we declared before: anyone who preaches to you a gospel other than the one you were first given is to be under God's curse. [10]Whom am I trying to convince now, human beings or God? Am I trying to please human beings? If I were still doing that I should not be a servant of Christ.

1a Unusually, this contains no thanks or praise.

1:3–14, a hymn in praise of God's plan; 1:15—2:10, concentrating on Christ's position; and 2:11–22 concentrating on the unity of all in the New Man.

There is some doubt whether Paul is the actual author of this letter. Besides the development in thought, has changed, and Ep is written in florid and almost liturgical languag is closely related to Col, sometimes reusing phrases from that letter.

PLAN OF THE LETTER

- I The Mystery of Salvation and of the Church 1:3—3
- II Exhortation 4—6

EPHESIANS

THE LETTER OF PAUL TO THE CHURCH AT EPHESUS

Address and greetings

1 Paul, by the will of God an apostle of Christ Jesus, to God's holy people,[a] faithful in Christ Jesus. 2 Grace and peace to you from God our Father and from the Lord Jesus Christ.

I: THE MYSTERY OF SALVATION AND OF THE CHURCH

God's plan of salvation

3 Blessed be God
the Father of our Lord Jesus Christ,
who has blessed us
with all the spiritual blessings of heaven
in Christ.
4 Thus he chose us in Christ
before the world was made
to be holy and faultless
before him in love,
5 marking us out for himself beforehand,
to be adopted sons,
through Jesus Christ.
Such was his purpose and good pleasure,
6 to the praise of the glory of his grace,
his free gift to us in the Beloved,
7 in whom, through his blood,
we gain our freedom,
the forgiveness of our sins.
Such is the richness of the grace
8 which he has showered on us
in all wisdom and insight.
9 He has let us know
the mystery of his purpose,
according to his good pleasure
which he determined beforehand
in Christ,
10 for him to act upon
when the times had run their course:
that he would bring everything together
under Christ, as head,
everything in the heavens
and everything on earth.
11 And it is in him
that we have received our heritage,
marked out beforehand as we were,
under the plan of the One
who guides all things
as he decides by his own will,

1a Some authorities add 'who are at Ephesus' or 'who are . . .', leaving a gap for a place-name to be filled in.

[12]chosen to be,
for the praise of his glory,
the people who
would put their hopes in Christ
before he came.
[13]Now you too, in him,
have heard the message of the truth
and the gospel of your salvation,
and having put your trust in it
you have been stamped with the seal
of the Holy Spirit of the Promise,
[14]who is the pledge of our inheritance,
for the freedom of the people
whom God has taken for his own,
for the praise of his glory.

The triumph and the supremacy of Christ

[15]That is why I, having once heard about
your faith in the Lord Jesus, and your love
for all God's holy people, [16]have never failed
to thank God for you and to remember you
in my prayers. [17]May the God of our Lord
Jesus Christ, the Father of glory, give you a
spirit of wisdom and perception of what is
revealed, to bring you to full knowledge of
him. [18]May he enlighten the eyes of your
mind so that you can see what hope his call
holds for you, how rich is the glory of the
heritage he offers among his holy people,
[19]and how extraordinarily great is the power
that he has exercised for us believers; this
accords with the strength of his power [20]at
work in Christ, the power which he exercised
in raising him from the dead and enthroning
him at his right hand, in heaven, [21]far above
every principality, ruling force, power or
sovereignty,[b] or any other name that can be
named, not only in this age but also in the
age to come. [22]*He has put all things under his
feet*,[c] and made him, as he is above all
things, the head of the Church; [23]which is
his Body, the fullness of him who is filled,
all in all.

Salvation in Christ a free gift

2 And you were dead, through the crimes
and the sins [2]which used to make up your
way of life when you were living by the
principles of this world, obeying the ruler
who dominates the air, the spirit who is at
work in those who rebel. [3]We too were all
among them once, living only by our natural
inclinations, obeying the demands of human
self-indulgence and our own whim; our
nature made us no less liable to God's retri-
bution than the rest of the world. [4]But God,
being rich in faithful love, through the great
love with which he loved us, [5]even when we
were dead in our sins, brought us to life with
Christ—it is through grace that you have
been saved—[6]and raised us up with him and
gave us a place with him in heaven, in Christ
Jesus.

[7]This was to show for all ages to come,
through his goodness towards us in Christ
Jesus, how extraordinarily rich he is in grace.
[8]Because it is by grace that you have been
saved, through faith; not by anything of your
own, but by a gift from God; [9]not by anything
that you have done, so that nobody can claim
the credit. [10]We are God's work of art, created
in Christ Jesus for the good works which God
has already designated to make up our way
of life.

Reconciliation of the Jews and the gentiles with each other and with God

[11]Do not forget, then, that there was a time
when you who were gentiles by physical
descent, termed the uncircumcised by those
who speak of themselves as the circumcised
by reason of a physical operation, [12]do not
forget, I say, that you were at that time
separate from Christ and excluded from
membership of Israel, aliens with no part in
the covenants of the Promise, limited to this
world, without hope and without God. [13]But
now in Christ Jesus, you that used to be so
far off have been brought close, by the blood
of Christ. [14]For he is the peace between us,
and has made the two into one entity and
broken down the barrier which used to keep
them apart, by destroying in his own person
the hostility, [15]that is, the Law of command-
ments with its decrees. His purpose in this
was, by restoring peace, to create a single
New Man out of the two of them, [16]and
through the cross, to reconcile them both to
God in one Body; in his own person he killed
the hostility. [17]He came to bring the good
news of *peace to you who were far off and peace*

1b Names for cosmic powers.
1c Ps 8:6.

to those who were near.[a] [18]Through him, then, we both in the one Spirit have free access to the Father.

[19]So you are no longer aliens or foreign visitors; you are fellow-citizens with the holy people of God and part of God's household. [20]You are built upon the foundations of the apostles and prophets, and Christ Jesus himself is the cornerstone. [21]Every structure knit together in him grows into a holy temple in the Lord; [22]and you too, in him, are being built up into a dwelling-place of God in the Spirit.

Paul, a servant of the mystery

3 It is because of this that I, Paul, a prisoner of the Lord Jesus on behalf of you gentiles. . . [2]You have surely heard the way in which God entrusted me with the grace he gave me for your sake; [3]he made known to me by a revelation the mystery I have just described briefly—[4]a reading of it will enable you to perceive my understanding of the mystery of Christ. [5]This mystery, as it is now revealed in the Spirit to his holy apostles and prophets, was unknown to humanity in previous generations: [6]that the gentiles now have the same inheritance and form the same Body and enjoy the same promise in Christ Jesus through the gospel. [7]I have been made the servant of that gospel by a gift of grace from God who gave it to me by the workings of his power. [8]I, who am less than the least of all God's holy people, have been entrusted with this special grace, of proclaiming to the gentiles the unfathomable treasure of Christ [9]and of throwing light on the inner workings of the mystery kept hidden through all the ages in God, the Creator of everything. [10]The purpose of this was, that now, through the Church, the principalities and ruling forces should learn how many-sided God's wisdom is, [11]according to the plan which he had formed from all eternity in Christ Jesus our Lord. [12]In him we are bold enough to approach God in complete confidence, through our faith in him; [13]so, I beg you, do not let the hardships I go through on your account make you waver; they are your glory.

Paul's prayer

[14]This, then, is what I pray, kneeling before the Father, [15]from whom every fatherhood, in heaven or on earth, takes its name. [16]In the abundance of his glory may he, through his Spirit, enable you to grow firm in power with regard to your inner self, [17]so that Christ may live in your hearts through faith, and then, planted in love and built on love, [18]with all God's holy people you will have the strength to grasp the breadth and the length, the height and the depth; [19]so that, knowing the love of Christ, which is beyond knowledge, you may be filled with the utter fullness of God.

[20]Glory be to him whose power, working in us, can do infinitely more than we can ask or imagine; [21]glory be to him from generation to generation in the Church and in Christ Jesus for ever and ever. Amen.

II: EXHORTATION

A call to unity

4 I, the prisoner in the Lord, urge you therefore to lead a life worthy of the vocation to which you were called. [2]With all humility and gentleness, and with patience, support each other in love. [3]Take every care to preserve the unity of the Spirit by the peace that binds you together. [4]There is one Body, one Spirit, just as one hope is the goal of your calling by God. [5]There is one Lord, one faith, one baptism, [6]and one God and Father of all, over all, through all and within all.

[7]On each one of us God's favour has been bestowed in whatever way Christ allotted it. [8]That is why it says:

He went up to the heights, took captives,
he gave gifts to humanity.[a]

[9]When it says, 'he went up', it must mean that he had gone down to the deepest levels of the earth. [10]The one who went down is none other than the one who went up above

2a Is 57:19.
4a Ps 68:18.

not be thoughtless but must recognise what
is the will of the Lord. 18*Do not get drunk with*
wine;[b] this is simply dissipation; be filled with
the Spirit. 19Sing psalms and hymns and
inspired songs among yourselves, singing
and chanting to the Lord in your hearts,
20always and everywhere giving thanks to
God who is our Father in the name of our
Lord Jesus Christ.

The morals of the home

21Be subject to one another out of reverence
for Christ. 22Wives should be subject to their
husbands as to the Lord, 23since, as Christ is
head of the Church and saves the whole
body, so is a husband the head of his wife;
24and as the Church is subject to Christ,
so should wives be to their husbands, in
everything. 25Husbands should love their
wives, just as Christ loved the Church and
sacrificed himself for her 26to make her holy
by washing her in cleansing water with a form
of words, 27so that when he took the Church
to himself she would be glorious, with no
speck or wrinkle or anything like that, but
holy and faultless. 28In the same way,
husbands must love their wives as they love
their own bodies; for a man to love his wife
is for him to love himself. 29A man never
hates his own body, but he feeds it and looks
after it; and that is the way Christ treats the
Church, 30because we are parts of his Body.
31*This is why a man leaves his father and mother*
and becomes attached to his wife, and the two
become one flesh.[c] 32This mystery has great
significance, but I am applying it to Christ
and the Church. 33To sum up: you also, each
one of you, must love his wife as he loves
himself; and let every wife respect her
husband.

6 Children, be obedient to your parents
in the Lord—that is what uprightness
demands. 2The first commandment that has
a promise attached to it is: *Honour your*
father and your mother, 3and the promise is:
so that you may have long life and prosper in
the land.[a] 4And parents, never drive your
children to resentment but bring them up
with correction and advice inspired by the
Lord.

5Slaves, be obedient to those who are,
according to human reckoning, your
masters, with deep respect and sincere
loyalty, as you are obedient to Christ: 6not
only when you are under their eye, as if you
had only to please human beings, but as
slaves of Christ who wholeheartedly do the
will of God. 7Work willingly for the sake of
the Lord and not for the sake of human
beings. 8Never forget that everyone, whether
a slave or a free man, will be rewarded by the
Lord for whatever work he has done well.
9And those of you who are employers, treat
your slaves in the same spirit; do without
threats, and never forget that they and you
have the same Master in heaven and there is
no favouritism with him.

The spiritual war

10Finally, grow strong in the Lord, with
the strength of his power. 11Put on the full
armour of God so as to be able to resist the
devil's tactics. 12For it is not against human
enemies that we have to struggle, but against
the principalities and the ruling forces who
are masters of the darkness in this world, the
spirits of evil in the heavens. 13That is why
you must take up all God's armour, or you
will not be able to put up any resistance on
the evil day, or stand your ground even
though you exert yourselves to the full.

14So stand your ground, with *truth a belt*
round your waist, and *uprightness a breastplate*,
15wearing for shoes on your feet *the eagerness*
to spread the gospel of peace[b] 16and always
carrying the shield of faith so that you can
use it to quench the burning arrows of the
Evil One. 17And then you must take *salvation*
as your helmet and the sword of the Spirit,
that is, the word of God.

18In all your prayer and entreaty keep
praying in the Spirit on every possible
occasion. Never get tired of staying awake to
pray for all God's holy people, 19and pray for
me to be given an opportunity to open my
mouth and fearlessly make known the
mystery of the gospel 20of which I am an
ambassador in chains; pray that in
proclaiming it I may speak as fearlessly as I
ought to.

5b Pr 23:31.
5c Gn 2:24.
6a Ex 20:12.
6b Is 59:17; 40:9.

all the heavens to fill all things. 11 And to
some, his 'gift' was that they should be
apostles; to some prophets; to some, evangel-
ists; to some, pastors and teachers; 12 to knit
God's holy people together for the work of
service to build up the Body of Christ, 13 until
we all reach unity in faith and knowledge of
the Son of God and form the perfect Man,
fully mature with the fullness of Christ
himself.
14 Then we shall no longer be children, or
tossed one way and another, and carried
hither and thither by every new gust of
teaching, at the mercy of all the tricks people
play and their unscrupulousness in deliberate
deception. 15 If we live by the truth and in
love, we shall grow completely into Christ,
who is the head 16 by whom the whole Body
is fitted and joined together, every joint
adding its own strength, for each individual
part to work according to its function. So the
body grows until it has built itself up in love.

The new life in Christ

17 So this I say to you and attest to you in the
Lord, do not go on living the empty-headed
life that the gentiles live. 18 Intellectually they
are in the dark, and they are estranged from
the life of God, because of the ignorance
which is the consequence of closed minds.
19 Their sense of right and wrong once dulled,
they have abandoned all self-control and
pursue to excess every kind of uncleanness.
20 Now that is hardly the way you have learnt
Christ, 21 unless you failed to hear him prop-
erly when you were taught what the truth is
in Jesus. 22 You were to put aside your old
self, which belongs to your old way of life
and is corrupted by following illusory desires.
23 Your mind was to be renewed in spirit 24 so
that you could put on the New Man that has
been created on God's principles, in the
uprightness and holiness of the truth.
25 So from now on, there must be no more
lies. *Speak the truth to one another,*[b] since we
are all parts of one another. 26 *Even if you are
angry, do not sin:*[c] never let the sun set on your
anger 27 or else you will give the devil a
foothold. 28 Anyone who was a thief must stop
stealing; instead he should exert himself at
some honest job with his own hands so that
he may have something to share with those
in need. 29 No foul word should ever cross
your lips; let your words be for the improve-
ment of others, as occasion offers, and do
good to your listeners; 30 do not grieve the
Holy Spirit of God who has marked you with
his seal, ready for the day when we shall be
set free. 31 Any bitterness or bad temper or
anger or shouting or abuse must be far
removed from you—as must every kind of
malice. 32 Be generous to one another,
sympathetic, forgiving each other as readily
as God forgave you in Christ.

5 As God's dear children, then, take him as
your pattern, 2 and follow Christ by loving
as he loved you, giving himself up for us *as
an offering and a sweet-smelling sacrifice to
God.*[a] 3 Among you there must be not even a
mention of sexual vice or impurity in any
of its forms, or greed: this would scarcely
become the holy people of God! 4 There must
be no foul or salacious talk or coarse jokes—
all this is wrong for you; there should rather
be thanksgiving. 5 For you can be quite
certain that nobody who indulges in sexual
immorality or impurity or greed—which is
worshipping a false god—can inherit the
kingdom of God. 6 Do not let anyone deceive
you with empty arguments: it is such behav-
iour that draws down God's retribution on
those who rebel against him. 7 Make sure that
you do not throw in your lot with them. 8 You
were darkness once, but now you are light in
the Lord; behave as children of light, 9 for the
effects of the light are seen in complete
goodness and uprightness and truth. 10 Try
to discover what the Lord wants of you,
11 take no part in the futile works of darkness
but, on the contrary, show them up for what
they are. 12 The things which are done in
secret are shameful even to speak of; 13 but
anything shown up by the light will be illumi-
nated 14 and anything illuminated is itself a
light. That is why it is said:

Wake up, sleeper,
rise from the dead,
and Christ will shine on you.

15 So be very careful about the sort of lives
you lead, like intelligent and not like senseless
people. 16 Make the best of the present time,
for it is a wicked age. 17 This is why you must

4b Zc 8:16.
4c Ps 4:4.
5a Ex 29:18.

15 Please give my greetings to the brothers
at Laodicea and to Nympha and the church
which meets in her house. 16 After this letter
has been read among you, send it on to be
read in the church of the Laodiceans; and get
the letter from Laodicea[b] for you to read
yourselves. 17 Give Archippus this message,
'Remember the service that the Lord
assigned to you, and try to carry it out.'
18 This greeting is in my own hand—PAUL.
Remember the chains I wear. Grace be
with you.

THE LETTERS TO THE THESSALONIANS

First Thessalonians is probably the earliest letter of Paul that we have, written in AD 50. It begins with affectionate praise for the community and their example of faith. Its main single topic is the imminence of the Second Coming of Christ. Paul describes this by means of rich biblical imagery, the conventional symbols of God's judgement. He stresses especially the suddenness with which God's judgement will come. So strong was his emphasis that he found that he needed to quieten their excitement with the explanation in Second Thessalonians that the time was not yet ripe.

1 THESSALONIANS

THE FIRST LETTER OF PAUL TO THE CHURCH IN THESSALONICA

Address

1 Paul, Silvanus and Timothy, to the
Church in Thessalonica which is in God
the Father and the Lord Jesus Christ. Grace
to you and peace.

Thanksgiving and congratulations

2 We always thank God for you all,
mentioning you in our prayers continually.
3 We remember before our God and Father
how active is the faith, how unsparing the
love, how persevering the hope which you
have from our Lord Jesus Christ.
4 We know, brothers loved by God, that
you have been chosen, 5 because our gospel
came to you not only in words, but also in
power and in the Holy Spirit and with great
effect. And you observed the sort of life we
lived when we were with you, which was for
your sake. 6 You took us and the Lord as your
model, welcoming the word with the joy of
the Holy Spirit in spite of great hardship.
7 And so you became an example to all
believers in Macedonia and Achaia 8 since it
was from you that the word of the Lord rang
out—and not only throughout Macedonia
and Achaia, for your faith in God has spread
everywhere. We do not need to tell other

4b Possibly this letter is Ep.

people about it: [9]other people tell us how we started the work among you, how you broke with the worship of false gods when you were converted to God and became servants of the living and true God; [10]and how you are now waiting for Jesus, his Son, whom he raised from the dead, to come from heaven. It is he who saves us from the Retribution which is coming.

Paul's example in Thessalonica

2 You know yourselves, my brothers, that our visit to you has not been pointless. [2]Although, as you know, we had received rough treatment and insults at Philippi, God gave us the courage to speak his gospel to you fearlessly, in spite of great opposition. [3]Our encouragement to you does not come from any delusion or impure motives or trickery. [4]No, God has approved us to be entrusted with the gospel, and this is how we preach, seeking to please not human beings but God who *tests* our *hearts*.[a] [5]Indeed, we have never acted with the thought of flattering anyone, as you know, nor as an excuse for greed, God is our witness; [6]nor have we ever looked for honour from human beings, either from you or anybody else, [7]when we could have imposed ourselves on you with full weight, as apostles of Christ.

Instead, we lived unassumingly among you. Like a mother feeding and looking after her children, [8]we felt so devoted to you, that we would have been happy to share with you not only the gospel of God, but also our own lives, so dear had you become. [9]You remember, brothers, with what unsparing energy we used to work, slaving night and day so as not to be a burden on any one of you while we were proclaiming the gospel of God to you. [10]You are witnesses, and so is God, that our treatment of you, since you believed, has been impeccably fair and upright. [11]As you know, we treated every one of you as a father treats his children, [12]urging you, encouraging you and appealing to you to live a life worthy of God, who calls you into his kingdom and his glory.

The faith and the patience of the Thessalonians

[13]Another reason why we continually thank God for you is that as soon as you heard the word that we brought you as God's message, you welcomed it for what it really is, not the word of any human being, but God's word, a power that is working among you believers. [14]For you, my brothers, have modelled yourselves on the churches of God in Christ Jesus which are in Judaea, in that you have suffered the same treatment from your own countrymen as they have had from the Jews, [15]who put the Lord Jesus to death, and the prophets too, and persecuted us also. Their conduct does not please God, and makes them the enemies of the whole human race, [16]because they are hindering us from preaching to gentiles to save them. Thus all the time they are *reaching the full extent of* their *iniquity*,[b] but retribution has finally overtaken them.

Paul's anxiety

[17]Although we had been deprived of you for only a short time in body but never in affection, brothers, we had an especially strong desire and longing to see you face to face again, [18]and we tried hard to come and visit you; I, Paul, tried more than once, but Satan prevented us. [19]What do you think is our hope and our joy, and what *our crown of honour*[c] in the presence of our Lord Jesus when he comes? [20]You are, for you are our pride and joy.

Timothy's mission to Thessalonica

3 When we could not bear it any longer, we decided it would be best to be left without a companion at Athens, [2]and sent our brother Timothy, who is God's helper in spreading the gospel of Christ, to keep you firm and encourage you about your faith [3]and prevent any of you from being unsettled by the present hardships. As you know, these are bound to come our way: [4]indeed, when we were with you, we warned you that we are certain to have hardships to bear, and that is what has happened now, as you have found out. [5]That is why, when I could not bear it any longer, I sent to assure myself of your

2a Jr 11:20.
2b Gn 15:16.
2c Pr 16:31.

faith: I was afraid the Tester might have put you to the test, and all our work might have been pointless.

Paul thanks God for good reports of the Thessalonians

6 However, Timothy has returned from you and has given us good news of your faith and your love, telling us that you always remember us with pleasure and want to see us quite as much as we want to see you. 7 And so, brothers, your faith has been a great encouragement to us in the middle of our own distress and hardship; 8 now we can breathe again, as you are holding firm in the Lord. 9 How can we thank God enough for you, for all the joy we feel before our God on your account? 10 We are earnestly praying night and day to be able to see you face to face again and make up any shortcomings in your faith.

11 May God our Father himself, and our Lord Jesus, ease our path to you. 12 May the Lord increase and enrich your love for each other and for all, so that it matches ours for you. 13 And may he so confirm your hearts in holiness that you may be blameless in the sight of our God and Father when our Lord Jesus comes *with all his holy ones.*[a]

Live in holiness and charity

4 Finally, brothers, we urge you and appeal to you in the Lord Jesus; we instructed you how to live in the way that pleases God, and you are so living; but make more progress still. 2 You are well aware of the instructions we gave you on the authority of the Lord Jesus.

3 God wills you all to be holy. He wants you to keep away from sexual immorality, 4 and each one of you to know how to control his body in a way that is holy and honourable, 5 not giving way to selfish lust like *the nations who do not acknowledge God.*[a] 6 He wants nobody at all ever to sin by taking advantage of a brother in these matters; the Lord always *pays back*[b] sins of that sort, as we told you before emphatically. 7 God called us to be holy, not to be immoral; 8 in other words, anyone who rejects this is rejecting not human authority, but God, *who gives you his Holy Spirit.*[c]

9 As for brotherly love, there is no need to write to you about that, since you have yourselves learnt from God to love one another, 10 and in fact this is how you treat all the brothers throughout the whole of Macedonia. However, we do urge you, brothers, to go on making even greater progress 11 and to make a point of living quietly, attending to your own business and earning your living, just as we told you to, 12 so that you may earn the respect of outsiders and not be dependent on anyone.

The dead and the living at the time of the Lord's coming

13 We want you to be quite certain, brothers, about those who have fallen asleep, to make sure that you do not grieve for them, as others do who have no hope. 14 We believe that Jesus died and rose again, and that in the same way God will bring with him those who have fallen asleep in Jesus. 15 We can tell you this from the Lord's own teaching, that we who are still alive for the Lord's coming will not have any advantage over those who have fallen asleep. 16 At the signal given by the voice of the Archangel and the trumpet of God, the Lord himself will come down from heaven; those who have died in Christ will be the first to rise, 17 and only after that shall we who remain alive be taken up in the clouds, together with them, to meet the Lord in the air. This is the way we shall be with the Lord for ever. 18 With such thoughts as these, then, you should encourage one another.

Watchfulness while awaiting the coming of the Lord

5 About times and dates, brothers, there is no need to write to you 2 for you are well aware in any case that the Day of the Lord is going to come like a thief in the night. 3 It is when people are saying, 'How quiet and peaceful it is' that sudden destruction falls on them, as suddenly as labour pains come on a pregnant woman; and there is no escape.

4 But you, brothers, do not live in the dark,

3a Zc 14:5.
4a Ps 79:6.
4b Dt 32:35.
4c Ezk 37:14.

that the Day should take you unawares like a thief. 5No, you are all children of light and children of the day: we do not belong to the night or to darkness, 6so we should not go on sleeping, as everyone else does, but stay wide awake and sober. 7Night is the time for sleepers to sleep and night the time for drunkards to be drunk, 8but we belong to the day and we should be sober; let us put on faith and love for a *breastplate*, and the hope of *salvation* for a *helmet*.[a] 9God destined us not for his retribution, but to win salvation through our Lord Jesus Christ, 10who died for us so that, awake or asleep, we should still live united to him. 11So give encouragement to each other, and keep strengthening one another, as you do already.

12We appeal to you, my brothers, to be considerate to those who work so hard among you as your leaders in the Lord and those who admonish you. 13Have the greatest respect and affection for them because of their work.

Be at peace among yourselves. 14We urge you, brothers, to admonish those who are undisciplined, encourage the apprehensive, support the weak and be patient with everyone. 15Make sure that people do not try to repay evil for evil; always aim at what is best for each other and for everyone. 16Always be joyful; 17pray constantly; 18and for all things give thanks; this is the will of God for you in Christ Jesus.

19Do not stifle the Spirit 20or despise the gift of prophecy with contempt; 21test everything and hold on to what is good 22and *shun every* form of *evil*.[b]

Closing prayer and farewell

23May the God of peace make you perfect and holy; and may your spirit, life and body be kept blameless for the coming of our Lord Jesus Christ. 24He who has called you is trustworthy and will carry it out.

25Pray for us, my brothers.

26Greet all the brothers with a holy kiss. 27My orders, in the Lord's name, are that this letter is to be read to all the brothers.

28The grace of our Lord Jesus Christ be with you.

2 THESSALONIANS

THE SECOND LETTER OF PAUL TO THE CHURCH IN THESSALONICA

Address

1 Paul, Silvanus and Timothy, to the Church in Thessalonica which is in God our Father and the Lord Jesus Christ 2Grace to you and peace from God the Father and the Lord Jesus Christ.

Thanksgiving and encouragement
The Last Judgement

3We must always thank God for you, brothers; quite rightly, because your faith is growing so wonderfully and the mutual love that each one of you has for all never stops increasing. 4Among the churches of God we take special pride in you for your perseverance and faith under all the persecutions and hardships you have to bear. 5It all shows that God's judgement is just, so that you may be found worthy of the kingdom of God; it is for the sake of this that you are suffering now.

6For God's justice will surely mean hardship being inflicted on those who are now inflicting hardship on you, 7and for you who are now suffering hardship, relief with us, when the Lord Jesus appears from heaven

5a Is 59:17.
5b Jb 1:8.

with the angels of his power. [8]He will come *amid flaming fire*; *he will impose a penalty*[a] on those who *do not acknowledge God* and *refuse to accept* the gospel of our Lord Jesus. [9]Their punishment is to be lost eternally, excluded *from the presence of the Lord and from the glory of his strength* [10]*on that day* when he comes *to be glorified among his holy ones* and *marvelled at* by all who believe in him; and you are among those who believed our witness.

[11]In view of this we also pray continually that our God will make you worthy of his call, and by his power fulfil all your desires for goodness, and complete all that you have been doing through faith; [12]so that the *name* of our Lord Jesus Christ *may be glorified* in you and you in him, by the grace of our God and the Lord Jesus Christ.

The coming of the Lord and the prelude to it

2 About the coming of our Lord Jesus Christ, brothers, and our being gathered to him: [2]please do not be too easily thrown into confusion or alarmed by any manifestation of the Spirit or any statement or any letter claiming to come from us, suggesting that the Day of the Lord has already arrived. [3]Never let anyone deceive you in any way.

It cannot happen until the Great Revolt[a] has taken place and there has appeared the wicked One, the lost One, [4]the Enemy, who *raises himself above every* so-called *God* or object of worship to *enthrone himself in God's* sanctuary and flaunts the claim that he is God. [5]Surely you remember my telling you about this when I was with you? [6]And you know, too, what is still holding him back from appearing before his appointed time. [7]The mystery of wickedness is already at work, but let him who is restraining it once be removed, [8]and the wicked One will appear openly. The Lord *will destroy him with the breath of his mouth* and will annihilate him with his glorious appearance at his coming.

[9]But the coming of the wicked One will be marked by Satan being at work in all kinds of counterfeit miracles and signs and wonders, [10]and every wicked deception aimed at those who are on the way to destruction because they would not accept the love of the truth and so be saved. [11]And therefore God sends on them a power that deludes people so that they believe what is false, [12]and so that those who do not believe the truth and take their pleasure in wickedness may all be condemned.

Encouragement to persevere

[13]But we must always thank God for you, brothers whom the Lord loves, because God chose you from the beginning to be saved by the Spirit who makes us holy and by faith in the truth. [14]Through our gospel he called you to this so that you should claim as your own the glory of our Lord Jesus Christ. [15]Stand firm, then, brothers, and keep the traditions that we taught you, whether by word of mouth or by letter. [16]May our Lord Jesus Christ himself, and God our Father who has given us his love and, through his grace, such ceaseless encouragement and such sure hope, [17]encourage you and strengthen you in every good word and deed.

3 Finally, brothers, pray for us that the Lord's message may spread quickly, and be received with honour as it was among you; [2]and pray that we may be preserved from bigoted and evil people, for not everyone has faith. [3]You can rely on the Lord, who will give you strength and guard you from the evil One, [4]and we, in the Lord, have every confidence in you, that you are doing and will go on doing all that we tell you. [5]May the Lord turn your hearts towards the love of God and the perseverance of Christ.

Against idleness and disunity

[6]In the name of the Lord Jesus Christ, we urge you, brothers, to keep away from any of the brothers who lives an undisciplined life, not in accordance with the tradition you received from us.

[7]You know how you should take us as your model: we were not undisciplined when we were with you, [8]nor did we ever accept food from anyone without paying for it; no, we worked with unsparing energy, night and day, so as not to be a burden on any of you. [9]This was not because we had no right to be, but in order to make ourselves a model for you to imitate.

[10]We urged you when we were with you not to let anyone eat who refused to work.

1a This threatening imagery of the Day of the Lord uses Is 66:15; Jr 10:25; Is 2:10–17; 49:3; 66:5.
2a Paul uses biblical symbolism: Is 11:4; 14:13; Ezk 28:2; Ps 33:6.

[11]Now we hear that there are some of you who are living lives without any discipline, doing no work themselves but interfering with other people's. [12]In the Lord Jesus Christ, we urge and call on people of this kind to go on quietly working and earning the food that they eat.

[13]My brothers, never slacken in doing what is right. [14]If anyone refuses to obey what I have written in this letter, take note of him and have nothing to do with him, so that he will be ashamed of himself, [15]though you are not to treat him as an enemy, but to correct him as a brother.

Prayer and farewell wishes

[16]May the Lord of peace himself give you peace at all times and in every way. The Lord be with you all.

[17]This greeting is in my own hand—PAUL. It is the mark of genuineness in every letter; this is my own writing. [18]May the grace of our Lord Jesus Christ be with you all.

THE PASTORAL EPISTLES

The letters to Timothy and Titus or 'Pastoral Epistles' form a group, giving advice to disciples of Paul on the pastoral care of his communities. They give a valuable insight into those communities as they move into the second generation of Christians, especially of the structures of the churches and of the qualities needed by Christian ministers. They also show the Church adapting to the hellenistic environment in the last years of the century. The hymns quoted may well be taken from the liturgy.

The absence of characteristic Pauline doctrines and a certain timidity of outlook combine with a change of literary style and vocabulary to suggest either that the apostle is old and tired, or that the letters spring from another pen. The historical data are not easy to join together, and certainly do not fit the period in Paul's life known from other sources. It may be, therefore, that these letters were not written by Paul but were simply attributed to him as a great authority—a practice not uncommon at the time.

1 TIMOTHY

THE FIRST LETTER FROM PAUL TO TIMOTHY

Address

1 Paul, apostle of Christ Jesus appointed by the command of God our Saviour and of Christ Jesus our hope, [2]to Timothy, true child of mine in the faith. Grace, mercy and peace from God the Father and from Christ Jesus our Lord.

Suppress the false teachers

[3]When I was setting out for Macedonia I urged you to stay on in Ephesus to instruct certain people not to spread wrong teaching [4]or to give attention to myths and unending genealogies; these things only foster doubts instead of furthering God's plan which is

founded on faith. 5The final goal at which this instruction aims is love, issuing from a pure heart, a clear conscience and a sincere faith. 6Some people have missed the way to these things and turned to empty speculation, 7trying to be teachers of the Law; but they understand neither the words they use nor the matters about which they make such strong assertions.

The purpose of the Law

8We are well aware that the Law is good, but only provided it is used legitimately, 9on the understanding that laws are not framed for people who are upright. On the contrary, they are for criminals and the insubordinate, for the irreligious and the wicked, for the sacrilegious and the godless; they are for people who kill their fathers or mothers and for murderers, 10for the promiscuous, homosexuals, kidnappers, for liars and for perjurers—and for everything else that is contrary to the sound teaching 11that accords with the gospel of the glory of the blessed God, the gospel that was entrusted to me.

Paul on his own calling

12I thank Christ Jesus our Lord, who has given me strength. By calling me into his service he has judged me trustworthy, 13even though I used to be a blasphemer and a persecutor and contemptuous. Mercy, however, was shown me, because while I lacked faith I acted in ignorance; 14but the grace of our Lord filled me with faith and with the love that is in Christ Jesus. 15Here is a saying that you can rely on and nobody should doubt: that Christ Jesus came into the world to save sinners. I myself am the greatest of them; 16and if mercy has been shown to me, it is because Jesus Christ meant to make me the leading example of his inexhaustible patience for all the other people who were later to trust in him for eternal life. 17To the eternal King, the undying, invisible and only God, be honour and glory for ever and ever. Amen.

Timothy's responsibility

18Timothy, my son, these are the instructions that I am giving you, in accordance with the words once spoken over you by the prophets, so that in their light you may fight like a good soldier 19with faith and a good conscience for your weapons. Some people have put conscience aside and wrecked their faith in consequence. 20I mean men like Hymenaeus and Alexander, whom I have handed over to Satan so that they may learn not to be blasphemous.

Liturgical prayer

2 I urge then, first of all that petitions, prayers, intercessions and thanksgiving should be offered for everyone, 2for kings and others in authority, so that we may be able to live peaceful and quiet lives with all devotion and propriety. 3To do this is right, and acceptable to God our Saviour: 4he wants everyone to be saved and reach full knowledge of the truth. 5For there is only one God, and there is only one mediator between God and humanity, himself a human being, Christ Jesus, 6who offered himself as a ransom for all. This was the witness given at the appointed time, 7of which I was appointed herald and apostle and—I am telling the truth and no lie—a teacher of the gentiles in faith and truth.

8In every place, then, I want the men to lift their hands up reverently in prayer, with no anger or argument.

Women in the assembly

9Similarly, women are to wear suitable clothes and to be dressed quietly and modestly, without braided hair or gold and jewellery or expensive clothes; 10their adornment is to do the good works that are proper for women who claim to be religious. 11During instruction, a woman should be quiet and respectful. 12I give no permission for a woman to teach or to have authority over a man. A woman ought to be quiet, 13because Adam was formed first and Eve afterwards, 14and it was not Adam who was led astray but the woman who was led astray and fell into sin. 15Nevertheless, she will be saved by child-bearing, provided she lives a sensible life and is constant in faith and love and holiness.

The elder-in-charge

3 Here is a saying that you can rely on: to want to be a presiding elder is to desire a

noble task. [2]That is why the presiding elder must have an impeccable character. Husband of one wife, he must be temperate, discreet and courteous, hospitable and a good teacher; [3]not a heavy drinker, nor hot-tempered, but gentle and peaceable, not avaricious, [4]a man who manages his own household well and brings his children up to obey him and be well-behaved: [5]how can any man who does not understand how to manage his own household take care of the Church of God? [6]He should not be a new convert, in case pride should turn his head and he incur the same condemnation as the devil. [7]It is also necessary that he be held in good repute by outsiders, so that he never falls into disrepute and into the devil's trap.

Deacons

[8]Similarly, deacons must be respectable, not double-tongued, moderate in the amount of wine they drink and with no squalid greed for money. [9]They must hold to the mystery of the faith with a clear conscience. [10]They are first to be examined, and admitted to serve as deacons only if there is nothing against them. [11]Similarly, women must be respectable, not gossips, but sober and wholly reliable. [12]Deacons must be husbands of one wife and must be people who manage their children and households well. [13]Those of them who carry out their duties well as deacons will earn a high standing for themselves and an authoritative voice in matters concerning faith in Christ Jesus.

The Church and the mystery of the spiritual life

[14]I write this to you in the hope that I may be able to come to you soon; [15]but in case I should be delayed, I want you to know how people ought to behave in God's household—that is, in the Church of the living God, pillar and support of the truth. [16]Without any doubt, the mystery of our religion is very deep indeed:

He was made visible in the flesh,
justified in the Spirit,
seen by angels,
proclaimed to the gentiles,
believed in throughout the world,
taken up in glory.

False teachers

4 The Spirit has explicitly said that during the last times some will desert the faith and pay attention to deceitful spirits and doctrines that come from devils, [2]seduced by the hypocrisy of liars whose consciences are branded as though with a red-hot iron: [3]they forbid marriage and prohibit foods which God created to be accepted with thanksgiving by all who believe and who know the truth. [4]Everything God has created is good, and no food is to be rejected, provided it is received with thanksgiving: [5]the word of God and prayer make it holy. [6]If you put all this to the brothers, you will be a good servant of Christ Jesus and show that you have really digested the teaching of the faith and the good doctrine which you have always followed. [7]Have nothing to do with godless myths and old wives' tales. Train yourself for religion. [8]Physical exercise is useful enough, but the usefulness of religion is unlimited, since it holds out promise both for life here and now and for the life to come; [9]that is a saying that you can rely on and nobody should doubt it. [10]I mean that the point of all our toiling and battling is that we have put our trust in the living God and he is the Saviour of the whole human race but particularly of all believers. [11]This is what you are to instruct and teach.

[12]Let no one disregard you because you are young, but be an example to all the believers in the way you speak and behave, and in your love, your faith and your purity. [13]Until I arrive, devote yourself to reading to the people, encouraging and teaching. [14]You have in you a spiritual gift which was given to you when the prophets spoke and the body of elders laid their hands on you; do not neglect it. [15]Let this be your care and your occupation, and everyone will be able to see your progress. [16]Be conscientious about what you do and what you teach; persevere in this, and in this way you will save both yourself and those who listen to you.

Pastoral practice

5 Never speak sharply to a man older than yourself, but appeal to him as you would to your own father; treat younger men as brothers, [2]older women as mothers and young women as sisters with all propriety.

Widows

3 Be considerate to widows—if they really are widowed. 4 If a widow has children or grandchildren, they are to learn first of all to do their duty to their own families and repay their debt to their parents, because this is what pleases God. 5 But a woman who is really widowed and left on her own has set her hope on God and perseveres night and day in petitions and prayer. 6 The one who thinks only of pleasure is already dead while she is still alive: 7 instruct them in this, too, so that their lives may be blameless. 8 Anyone who does not look after his own relations, especially if they are living with him, has rejected the faith and is worse than an unbeliever.

9 Enrolment as a widow is permissible only for a woman at least sixty years old who has had only one husband. 10 She must be a woman known for her good works—whether she has brought up her children, been hospitable to strangers and washed the feet of God's holy people, helped people in hardship or been active in all kinds of good work. 11 Do not accept young widows because if their natural desires distract them from Christ, they want to marry again, 12 and then people condemn them for being unfaithful to their original promise. 13 Besides, they learn how to be idle and go round from house to house; and then, not merely idle, they learn to be gossips and meddlers in other people's affairs and to say what should remain unsaid. 14 I think it is best for young widows to marry again and have children and a household to look after, and not give the enemy any chance to raise a scandal about them; 15 there are already some who have turned aside to follow Satan. 16 If a woman believer has widowed relatives, she should support them and not make the Church bear the expense but enable it to support those who are really widowed.

The elders

17 Elders who do their work well while they are in charge earn double reward, especially those who work hard at preaching and teaching. 18 As scripture says: *You must not muzzle an ox when it is treading out the corn;*[a] and again: *The worker deserves his wages.* 19 Never accept any accusation brought against an elder unless it is supported *by two or three witnesses.* 20 If anyone is at fault, reprimand him publicly, as a warning to the rest. 21 Before God, and before Jesus Christ and the angels he has chosen, I charge you to keep these rules impartially and never to be influenced by favouritism. 22 Do not be too quick to lay hands on anyone, and never make yourself an accomplice in anybody else's sin; keep yourself pure.

23 You should give up drinking only water and have a little wine for the sake of your digestion and the frequent bouts of illness that you have.

24 The faults of some people are obvious long before they come to the reckoning, while others have faults that are not discovered until later. 25 Similarly, the good that people do can be obvious; but even when it is not, it cannot remain hidden.

Slaves

6 All those under the yoke of slavery must have unqualified respect for their masters, so that the name of God and our teaching are not brought into disrepute. 2 Those whose masters are believers are not to respect them less because they are brothers; on the contrary, they should serve them all the better, since those who have the benefit of their services are believers and dear to God.

The true teacher and the false teacher

This is what you are to teach and urge. 3 Anyone who teaches anything different and does not keep to the sound teaching which is that of our Lord Jesus Christ, the doctrine which is in accordance with true religion, 4 is proud and has no understanding, but rather a weakness for questioning everything and arguing about words. All that can come of this is jealousy, contention, abuse and evil mistrust; 5 and unending disputes by people who are depraved in mind and deprived of truth, and imagine that religion is a way of making a profit. 6 Religion, of course, does bring large profits, but only to those who are content with what they have. 7 We brought nothing into the world, and we can take nothing out of it; 8 but as long as we have food and clothing, we shall be content with that.

5a Dt 25:4 followed by Lk 10:7; Dt 19:15.

9People who long to be rich are a prey to trial;
they get trapped into all sorts of foolish and
harmful ambitions which plunge people into
ruin and destruction. 10'The love of money
is the root of all evils' and there are some
who, pursuing it, have wandered away from
the faith and so given their souls any number
of fatal wounds.

Timothy's vocation recalled

11But, as someone dedicated to God, avoid
all that. You must aim to be upright and
religious, filled with faith and love, persever-
ance and gentleness. 12Fight the good fight
of faith and win the eternal life to which you
were called and for which you made your
noble profession of faith before many
witnesses. 13Now, before God, the source
of all life, and before Jesus Christ, who
witnessed to his noble profession of faith
before Pontius Pilate, I charge you 14to do all
that you have been told, with no faults or
failures, until the appearing of our Lord Jesus
Christ,

15who at the due time will be revealed
by God, the blessed and only Ruler of all,
the King of kings and the Lord of lords,
16who alone is immortal,
whose home is in inaccessible light,
whom no human being has seen
or is able to see:
to him be honour and everlasting power.
Amen.

Rich Christians

17Instruct those who are rich in this world's
goods that they should not be proud and
should set their hopes not on money, which
is untrustworthy, but on God who gives us
richly all that we need for our happiness.
18They are to do good and be rich in good
works, generous in giving and always ready
to share—19this is the way they can amass a
good capital sum for the future if they want
to possess the only life that is real.

Final warning and conclusion

20My dear Timothy, take great care of all that
has been entrusted to you. Turn away from
godless philosophical discussions and the
contradictions of the 'knowledge' which is
not knowledge at all; 21by adopting this, some
have missed the goal of faith. Grace be with
you.

2 TIMOTHY
THE SECOND LETTER FROM PAUL TO TIMOTHY

Greeting and thanksgiving

1 From Paul, apostle of Christ Jesus
through the will of God in accordance
with his promise of life in Christ Jesus, 2to
Timothy, dear son of mine. Grace, mercy
and peace from God the Father and from
Christ Jesus our Lord.
3Night and day I thank God whom I serve
with a pure conscience as my ancestors did.
I remember you in my prayers constantly
night and day; 4I remember your tears and
long to see you again to complete my joy. 5I
also remember your sincere faith, a faith
which first dwelt in your grandmother Lois,
and your mother Eunice, and I am sure dwells
also in you.

The gifts that Timothy has received

6That is why I am reminding you now to fan
into a flame the gift of God that you possess
through the laying on of my hands. 7God did
not give us a spirit of timidity, but the Spirit
of power and love and self-control. 8So you
are never to be ashamed of witnessing to
our Lord, or ashamed of me for being his
prisoner; but share in my hardships for the
sake of the gospel, relying on the power of
God 9who has saved us and called us to be
holy—not because of anything we ourselves
had done but for his own purpose and by
his own grace. This grace had already been
granted to us, in Christ Jesus, before the
beginning of time, 10but it has been revealed
only by the appearing of our Saviour Christ
Jesus. He has abolished death, and he has
brought to light immortality and life through
the gospel, 11in whose service I have been
made herald, apostle and teacher.

12That is why I am experiencing my present
sufferings; but I am not ashamed, because I
know in whom I have put my trust, and I
have no doubt at all that he is able to safeguard
until that Day what I have entrusted to him.

13Keep as your pattern the sound teaching
you have heard from me, in the faith and love
that are in Christ Jesus. 14With the help of
the Holy Spirit who dwells in us, look after
that precious thing given in trust.

15As you know, Phygelus and Hermogenes
and all the others in Asia have deserted me.
16I hope the Lord will be kind to all the family
of Onesiphorus, because he has often been a
comfort to me and has never been ashamed
of my chains. 17On the contrary, as soon as
he reached Rome, he searched hard for me
and found me. 18May the Lord grant him to
find the Lord's mercy on that Day. You know
better than anyone else how much he helped
me at Ephesus.

How Timothy should face hardships

2 As for you, my dear son, take strength
from the grace which is in Christ Jesus.
2Pass on to reliable people what you have
heard from me through many witnesses so
that they in turn will be able to teach others.

3Bear with your share of difficulties, like a
good soldier of Christ Jesus. 4No one on
active service involves himself in the affairs
of civilian life, because he must win the
approval of the man who enlisted him; 5or
again someone who enters an athletic contest
wins only by competing in the sports—a prize
can be won only by competing according
to the rules; 6and again, it is the farmer who
works hard that has the first claim on any
crop that is harvested. 7Think over what I
have said, and the Lord will give you full
understanding.

8Remember the gospel that I carry, 'Jesus
Christ risen from the dead, sprung from the
race of David'; 9it is on account of this that I
have to put up with suffering, even to being
chained like a criminal. But God's message
cannot be chained up. 10So I persevere for
the sake of those who are chosen, so that
they, too, may obtain the salvation that is in
Christ Jesus with eternal glory.

11Here is a saying that you can rely on:

If we have died with him,
then we shall live with him.
12If we persevere,
then we shall reign with him.
If we disown him, then he will disown us.
13If we are faithless, he is faithful still,
for he cannot disown his own self.

The struggle against the immediate danger from false teachers

14Remind them of this; and tell them in the
name of God that there must be no wrangling
about words: all that this ever achieves is
the destruction of those who are listening.
15Make every effort to present yourself before
God as a proven worker who has no need to
be ashamed, but who keeps the message of
truth on a straight path. 16Have nothing to
do with godless philosophical discussions—
they only lead further and further away from
true religion. 17Talk of this kind spreads
corruption like gangrene, as in the case of
Hymenaeus and Philetus, 18the men who
have gone astray from the truth, claiming
that the resurrection has already taken place.
They are upsetting some people's faith.

19However, God's solid foundation-stone
stands firm, and this is the seal on it: '*The
Lord knows those who are his own*' and 'All
who *call on the name of the Lord*[a] must avoid
evil.'

20Not all the dishes in a large house are

2a Nb 16:5; Is 26:13.

made of gold and silver; some are made of wood or earthenware: the former are held in honour, the latter held cheap. 21 If someone holds himself aloof from these faults I speak of, he will be a vessel held in honour, dedicated and fit for the Master, ready for any good work.

22 Turn away from the passions of youth, concentrate on uprightness, faith, love and peace, in union with all those who call on the Lord with a pure heart. 23 Avoid these foolish and undisciplined speculations, understanding that they only give rise to quarrels; 24 and a servant of the Lord must not engage in quarrels, but must be kind to everyone, a good teacher, and patient. 25 He must be gentle when he corrects people who oppose him, in the hope that God may give them a change of mind so that they recognise the truth 26 and come to their senses, escaping the trap of the devil who made them his captives and subjected them to his will.

The dangers of the last days

3 You may be quite sure that in the last days there will be some difficult times. 2 People will be self-centred and avaricious, boastful, arrogant and rude; disobedient to their parents, ungrateful, irreligious; 3 heartless and intractable; they will be slanderers, profligates, savages and enemies of everything that is good; 4 they will be treacherous and reckless and demented by pride, preferring their own pleasure to God. 5 They will keep up the outward appearance of religion but will have rejected the inner power of it. Keep away from people like that.

6 Of the same kind, too, are those men who insinuate themselves into families in order to get influence over silly women who are obsessed with their sins and follow one craze after another, 7 always seeking learning, but unable ever to come to knowledge of the truth. 8 Just as Jannes and Jambres defied Moses,[a] so these men defy the truth, their minds corrupt and their faith spurious. 9 But they will not be able to go on much longer: their folly, like that of the other two, must become obvious to everybody.

10 You, though, have followed my teaching, my way of life, my aims, my faith, my patience and my love, my perseverance 11 and the persecutions and sufferings that came to me in places like Antioch, Iconium and Lystra—all the persecutions I have endured; and the Lord has rescued me from every one of them. 12 But anybody who tries to live in devotion to Christ is certain to be persecuted; 13 while these wicked impostors will go from bad to worse, deceiving others, and themselves deceived.

14 You must keep to what you have been taught and know to be true; remember who your teachers were, 15 and how, ever since you were a child, you have known the holy scriptures[b]—from these you can learn the wisdom that leads to salvation through faith in Christ Jesus. 16 All scripture is inspired by God and useful for refuting error, for guiding people's lives and teaching them to be upright. 17 This is how someone who is dedicated to God becomes fully equipped and ready for any good work.

A solemn charge

4 Before God and before Christ Jesus who is to be judge of the living and the dead, I charge you, in the name of his appearing and of his kingdom: 2 proclaim the message and, welcome or unwelcome, insist on it. Refute falsehood, correct error, give encouragement—but do all with patience and with care to instruct. 3 The time is sure to come when people will not accept sound teaching, but their ears will be itching for anything new and they will collect themselves a whole series of teachers according to their own tastes; 4 and then they will shut their ears to the truth and will turn to myths. 5 But you must keep steady all the time; put up with suffering; do the work of preaching the gospel; fulfil the service asked of you.

Paul in the evening of his life

6 As for me, my life is already being poured away as a libation, and the time has come for me to depart. 7 I have fought the good fight to the end; I have run the race to the finish; I have kept the faith; 8 all there is to come for me now is the crown of uprightness which the Lord, the upright judge, will give to me on that Day; and not only to me but to all those who have longed for his appearing.

3a In Jewish tradition (but not the Bible) the leaders of the Egyptian magicians, cf. Ex 7:11.
3b Probably the OT. There is no sign that the NT writings were yet set on the same level.

Final advice

9 Make every effort to come and see me as soon as you can. 10 As it is, Demas has deserted me for love of this life and gone to Thessalonica, Crescens has gone to Galatia and Titus to Dalmatia; 11 only Luke is with me. Bring Mark with you; I find him a useful helper in my work. 12 I have sent Tychicus to Ephesus. 13 When you come, bring the cloak I left with Carpus in Troas, and the scrolls, especially the parchment ones. 14 Alexander the coppersmith has done me a lot of harm; *the Lord will repay him as his deeds deserve.*[a] 15 Be on your guard against him yourself, because he has been bitterly contesting everything that we say.

16 The first time I had to present my defence, no one came into court to support me. Every one of them deserted me—may they not be held accountable for it. 17 But the Lord stood by me and gave me power, so that through me the message might be fully proclaimed for all the gentiles to hear; and so I was *saved from the lion's mouth.*[b] 18 The Lord will rescue me from all evil attempts on me, and bring me safely to his heavenly kingdom. To him be glory for ever and ever. Amen.

Farewells and final good wishes

19 Greetings to Prisca and Aquila, and the family of Onesiphorus. 20 Erastus stayed behind at Corinth, and I left Trophimus ill at Miletus. 21 Make every effort to come before the winter.

Greetings to you from Eubulus, Pudens, Linus, Claudia and all the brothers.

22 The Lord be with your spirit. Grace be with you.

TITUS

THE LETTER FROM PAUL TO TITUS

Address

1 From Paul, servant of God, an apostle of Jesus Christ to bring those whom God has chosen to faith and to the knowledge of the truth that leads to true religion, 2 and to give them the hope of the eternal life that was promised so long ago by God. He does not lie 3 and so, in due time, he made known his message by a proclamation which was entrusted to me by the command of God our Saviour. 4 To Titus, true child of mine in the faith that we share. Grace and peace from God the Father and from Christ Jesus our Saviour.

The appointment of elders

5 The reason I left you behind in Crete was for you to organise everything that still had to be done and appoint elders in every town, in the way that I told you, 6 that is, each of them must be a man of irreproachable character, husband of one wife, and his children must be believers and not liable to be charged with disorderly conduct or insubordination. 7 The presiding elder has to be irreproachable since he is God's representative: never arrogant or hot-tempered, nor a heavy drinker or violent, nor avaricious; 8 but hospitable and a lover of goodness; sensible,

4a Ps 28:4.
4b Ps 22:21.

upright, devout and self-controlled; [9]and he
must have a firm grasp of the unchanging
message of the tradition, so that he can be
counted on both for giving encouragement
in sound doctrine and for refuting those who
argue against it.

Opposing the false teachers

[10]And in fact there are many people who are
insubordinate, who talk nonsense and try to
make others believe it, particularly among
those of the circumcision. [11]They must be
silenced: people of this kind upset whole
families, by teaching things that they ought
not to, and doing it for the sake of sordid
gain. [12]It was one of themselves, one of
their own prophets, who said,[a] 'Cretans were
never anything but liars, dangerous animals,
all greed and laziness'; [13]and that is a true
statement. So be severe in correcting them,
and make them sound in the faith [14]so that
they stop taking notice of Jewish myths and
the orders of people who turn away from the
truth.

[15]To those who are pure themselves, every-
thing is pure; but to those who have been
corrupted and lack faith, nothing can be
pure—the corruption is both in their minds
and in their consciences. [16]They claim to
know God but by their works they deny him;
they are outrageously rebellious and quite
untrustworthy for any good work.

Some specific moral instruction

2 It is for you, then, to preach the behaviour
which goes with healthy doctrine. [2]Older
men should be reserved, dignified, moderate,
sound in faith and love and perseverance.
[3]Similarly, older women should behave as
befits religious people, with no scandal-
mongering and no addiction to wine—they
must be the teachers of right behaviour [4]and
show younger women how they should love
their husbands and love their children, [5]how
they must be sensible and chaste, and how to
work in their homes, and be gentle, and obey
their husbands, so that the message of God
is not disgraced. [6]Similarly, urge younger
men to be moderate in everything that they
do, [7]and you yourself set an example of good
works, by sincerity and earnestness, when
you are teaching, and by a message sound
and irreproachable [8]so that any opponent
will be at a loss, with no accusation to make
against us. [9]Slaves must be obedient to their
masters in everything, and do what is wanted
without argument; [10]and there must be no
pilfering—they must show complete honesty
at all times, so that they are in every way a
credit to the teaching of God our Saviour.

The basis of the Christian moral life

[11]You see, God's grace has been revealed to
save the whole human race; [12]it has taught us
that we should give up everything contrary
to true religion and all our worldly passions;
we must be self-restrained and live upright
and religious lives in this present world,
[13]waiting in hope for the blessing which will
come with the appearing of the glory of our
great God and Saviour Christ Jesus. [14]He
offered himself for us in order to ransom us
from all our *faults* and *to purify a people to be*
his very own[a] and eager to do good.

[15]This is what you must say, encouraging
or arguing with full authority; no one should
despise you.

General instruction for believers

3 Remind them to be obedient to the officials
in authority; to be ready to do good at
every opportunity; [2]not to go slandering
other people but to be peaceable and gentle,
and always polite to people of all kinds.
[3]There was a time when we too were ignorant,
disobedient and misled and enslaved by
different passions and dissipations; we lived
then in wickedness and malice, hating each
other and hateful ourselves.

[4]But when the kindness and love of God
our Saviour for humanity were revealed, [5]it
was not because of any upright actions we
had done ourselves; it was for no reason
except his own faithful love that he saved us,
by means of the cleansing water of rebirth
and renewal in the Holy Spirit [6]which he has
so generously poured over us through Jesus
Christ our Saviour; [7]so that, justified by his
grace, we should become heirs in hope of
eternal life. [8]This is doctrine that you can
rely on.

1a Attributed to the Cretan poet Epimenides.
2a Ex 19:5.

Personal advice to Titus

I want you to be quite uncompromising in teaching all this, so that those who now believe in God may keep their minds constantly occupied in doing good works. All this is good, and useful for everybody. [9]But avoid foolish speculations, and those genealogies, and the quibbles and disputes about the Law—they are useless and futile. [10]If someone disputes what you teach, then after a first and a second warning, have no more to do with him: [11]you will know that anyone of that sort is warped and is self-condemned as a sinner.

Practical recommendations, farewells and good wishes

[12]As soon as I have sent Artemas or Tychicus to you, do your best to join me at Nicopolis, where I have decided to spend the winter. [13]Help eagerly on their way Zenas the lawyer and Apollos, and make sure they have everything they need. [14]All our people must also learn to occupy themselves in doing good works for their practical needs, and not to be unproductive.

[15]All those who are with me send their greetings. Greetings to those who love us in the faith. Grace be with you all.

THE LETTER TO PHILEMON

A note from Paul carried back to his master by a runaway slave who has become a Christian and one of Paul's helpers. It is an affectionate expression of Christian fellowship and humanity.

PHILEMON
THE LETTER FROM PAUL TO PHILEMON

Address

From Paul, a prisoner of Christ Jesus and from our brother Timothy; to our dear fellow worker Philemon, [2]our sister Apphia, our fellow soldier Archippus and the church that meets in your house. [3]Grace and the peace of God our Father and the Lord Jesus Christ.

Thanksgiving and prayer

[4]I always thank my God, mentioning you in my prayers, [5]because I hear of the love and the faith which you have for the Lord Jesus and for all God's holy people. [6]I pray that your fellowship in faith may come to expression in full knowledge of all the good we can do for Christ. [7]I have received much joy and encouragement by your love; you have set the hearts of God's holy people at rest.

The request about Onesimus

[8]Therefore, although in Christ I have no hesitations about telling you what your duty is, [9]I am rather appealing to your love, being what I am, Paul, an old man, and now also a prisoner of Christ Jesus. [10]I am appealing to

you for a child of mine, whose father I
became while wearing these chains: I mean
Onesimus.[a] 11 He was of no use to you before,
but now he is useful both to you and to me.
12 I am sending him back to you—that is to
say, sending you my own heart. 13 I should
have liked to keep him with me; he could
have been a substitute for you, to help me
while I am in the chains that the gospel has
brought me. 14 However, I did not want to do
anything without your consent; it would have
been forcing your act of kindness, which
should be spontaneous. 15 I suppose you have
been deprived of Onesimus for a time, merely
so that you could have him back for ever,
16 no longer as a slave, but something much
better than a slave, a dear brother; especially
dear to me, but how much more to you, both
on the natural plane and in the Lord. 17 So if
you grant me any fellowship with yourself,
welcome him as you would me; 18 if he has
wronged you in any way or owes you
anything, put it down to my account. 19 I am
writing this in my own hand: I, Paul, shall
pay it back—I make no mention of a further
debt, that you owe your very self to me!
20 Well then, brother, I am counting on you,
in the Lord; set my heart at rest, in Christ.
21 I am writing with complete confidence in
your compliance, sure that you will do even
more than I ask.

A personal request. Good wishes

22 There is another thing: will you get a place
ready for me to stay in? I am hoping through
your prayers to be restored to you.

23 Epaphras, a prisoner with me in Christ
Jesus, sends his greetings; 24 so do my fellow-
workers Mark, Aristarchus, Demas and
Luke.

25 May the grace of our Lord Jesus Christ
be with your spirit.

THE LETTER TO THE HEBREWS

This anonymous letter, joined on to the letters of Paul, was aptly entitled (in the 2nd century) 'To the Hebrews'. It uses scriptural passages throughout to show that the sacrifice and covenant of Christ fulfil God's promises, and bring the faithful to perfection, where the old dispensation failed. It contains a rich theology not only of Christ's effective priesthood but of his human and divine nature. The letter's emphasis on ceremonial suggests that it was addressed to Jewish priests who hankered after the splendour of the Temple worship and its ineffectual sacrifices. The author stresses that the pilgrimage of the Israelites through the desert was only an image of the Christian pilgrimage to the final place of rest, and that the faith of the great patriarchs was a model for Christian faith and perseverance.

It is unclear whether the letter was written before or after the destruction of the Temple in AD 70, and its authorship is similarly unknown. Italy is mentioned as the place of origin (13:24).

a A pun: Onesimus means 'useful'.

PLAN OF THE LETTER

THE LETTER TO THE HEBREWS

PROLOGUE

The greatness of the incarnate Son of God

1 At many moments in the past and by
many means, God spoke to our ancestors
through the prophets; but 2 in our time, the
final days, he has spoken to us in the person
of his Son, whom he appointed heir of all
things and through whom he made the ages.
3 He is the reflection of God's glory and bears
the impress of God's own being,[a] sustaining
all things by his powerful command; and now
that he has purged sins away, he has taken
his seat at the right hand of the divine Majesty
on high. 4 So he is now as far above the angels
as the title which he has inherited is higher
than their own name.

I: THE SON IS GREATER THAN THE ANGELS

Proof from the scriptures[b]

5 To which of the angels, then, has God ever
said:

You are my Son, today I have fathered you,

or:

I shall be a father to him and he a son to me?

6 Again, when he brings the First-born into
the world, he says:

Let all the angels of God pay him homage.

7 To the angels, he says:

appointing the winds his messengers
and flames of fire his servants,

8 but to the Son he says:

Your throne, God, is for ever and ever;

and:

the *sceptre of* his *kingdom*
is *a sceptre of justice*;

1a cf. Ws 7:25–26.
1b Texts used: Ps 2:7; 2 S 7:14; Ps 97:7; 104:4; 45:6–7; 102:25–27; 110:1.

9 you love uprightness and detest evil.
This is why God,
your God, has anointed you
with the oil of gladness,
as none of your rivals.

10 And again:

Long ago, Lord,
you laid earth's foundations,
the heavens are the work of your hands.
11 They pass away but you remain,
they all wear out like a garment.
12 Like a cloak you will roll them up,
like a garment,
and they will be changed.
But you never alter
and your years are unending.

13 To which of the angels has God ever said:

Take your seat at my right hand
till I have made your enemies your footstool?

14 Are they not all ministering spirits, sent to serve for the sake of those who are to inherit salvation?

An exhortation

2 We ought, then, to turn our minds more attentively than before to what we have
been taught, so that we do not drift away. 2 If
a message that was spoken through angels proved to be so reliable that every infringement and disobedience brought its own
proper punishment, 3 then we shall certainly
not go unpunished if we neglect such a great salvation. It was first announced by the Lord himself, and is guaranteed to us by those who
heard him; 4 God himself confirmed their witness with signs and marvels and miracles of all kinds, and by distributing the gifts of the Holy Spirit in the various ways he wills.

Redemption brought by Christ, not by angels

5 It was not under angels that he put the world to come, about which we are speaking.
6 Someone witnesses to this somewhere with the words:

What are human beings
that you spare a thought for them,
a child of Adam that you care for him?
7 For a short while you have made him
less than the angels;
you have crowned him
with glory and honour,
8 put all things under his feet.[a]

For in *putting all things under* him he made no exceptions. At present, it is true, we are not able to see that *all things are under him,*
9 but we do see Jesus, who was *for a short while made less than the angels*, now *crowned with glory and honour* because he submitted to death; so that by God's grace his experience of death should benefit all humanity.
10 It was fitting that God, for whom and through whom everything exists, should, in bringing many sons to glory, make perfect through suffering the leader of their
salvation. 11 For consecrator and consecrated are all of the same stock; that is why he is not
ashamed to call them *brothers* 12 in the text: *I shall proclaim your name to my brothers, praise*
you in full assembly; or in the text: 13 *I shall put my hope in him*; followed by *Look, I and the children whom God has given me.*[b]
14 Since all the *children* share the same human nature, he too shared equally in it, so that by his death he could set aside him who held the power of death, namely the devil,
15 and set free all those who had been held in slavery all their lives by the fear of death.
16 For it was not the angels that he took to himself; he took to himself *the line of*
Abraham. 17 It was essential that he should in this way be made completely like his brothers so that he could become a compassionate and trustworthy high priest for their relationship to God, able to expiate the sins of the people.
18 For the suffering he himself passed through while being put to the test enables him to help others when they are being put to the test.

2a Ps 8:4–6.
2b Ps 22:22; Is 8:17, 18.

II: JESUS THE FAITHFUL AND MERCIFUL HIGH PRIEST

Christ higher than Moses

3 That is why all you who are holy brothers
and share the same heavenly call should
turn your minds to Jesus, the apostle and the
high priest of our profession of faith. 2He
was *trustworthy* to the one who appointed him,
just like *Moses*, who remained trustworthy *in
all his household*;[a] 3but he deserves a greater
glory than Moses, just as the builder of a
house is more honoured than the house itself.
4Every house is built by someone, of course;
but God built everything that exists. 5It
is true that Moses was *trustworthy in the
household* of God, as a *servant* is, acting as
witness to the things which were yet to be
revealed, 6but Christ is trustworthy as a
son is, over his household. And we are his
household, as long as we fearlessly maintain
the hope in which we glory.

How to reach God's land of rest[b]

7That is why, as the Holy Spirit says:

If only you would listen to him today!
8*Do not harden your hearts,*
as at the rebellion,
as at the time of testing in the desert,
9*when your ancestors challenged me,*
and put me to the test,
and saw what I could do
10*for forty years.*
That was why
that generation sickened me
and I said, 'Always fickle hearts,
that cannot grasp my ways!'
11*And then in my anger I swore*
that they would never enter my place of rest.

12Take care, brothers, that none of you ever
has a wicked heart, so unbelieving as to turn
away from the living God. 13Every day, as
long as this *today* lasts, keep encouraging one
another so that none of you is *hardened* by the
lure of sin, 14because we have been granted a
share with Christ only if we keep the grasp
of our first confidence firm to the end. 15In
this saying: *If only you would listen to him
today; do not harden your hearts, as at the
Rebellion*, 16who was it who *listened* and then
rebelled? Surely all those whom Moses led out
of Egypt. 17And with whom was he *angry for
forty years*? Surely with those who sinned and
whose *dead bodies fell in the desert*. 18To whom
did he *swear they would never enter his place of
rest*? Surely those who would not believe. 19So
we see that it was their refusal to believe
which prevented them from entering.

4 Let us beware, then: since the promise
never lapses, none of you must think that
he has come too late for the promise of *entering
his place of rest*. 2We received the gospel
exactly as they did; but hearing the message
did them no good because they did not share
the faith of those who did listen. 3We,
however, who have faith, are *entering a place
of rest*, as in the text: *And then in my anger I
swore that they would never enter my place of
rest*. Now God's work was all finished at the
beginning of the world; 4as one text says,
referring to the seventh day: *And God rested
on the seventh day after all the work he had been
doing*. 5And, again, the passage above says:
They will never reach my place of rest. 6It
remains the case, then, that there would be
some people who would reach it, and since
those who first heard the good news were
prevented from entering by their refusal to
believe, 7God fixed another day, a *Today*,
when he said through David in the text
already quoted: *If only you would listen to him
today; do not harden your hearts*. 8If Joshua
had led them into this place of rest, God
would not later have spoken of another day.
9There must still be, therefore, a seventh-
day rest reserved for God's people, 10since to
enter the place of rest is to *rest after your work*,
as God did after his. 11Let us, then, press
forward to *enter this place of rest*, or some of
you might copy this example of refusal to
believe and be lost.

12The word of God is something alive and
active: it cuts more incisively than any two-
edged sword: it can seek out the place where
soul is divided from spirit, or joints from
marrow; it can pass judgement on secret
emotions and thoughts. 13No created thing is
hidden from him; everything is uncovered
and stretched fully open to the eyes of the one
to whom we must give account of ourselves.

3a Nb 12:7.
3b An elaboration on Ps 95:7–11.

Jesus the compassionate high priest

[14]Since in Jesus, the Son of God, we have the supreme high priest who has gone through to the highest heaven, we must hold firm to our profession of faith. [15]For the high priest we have is not incapable of feeling our weaknesses with us, but has been put to the test in exactly the same way as ourselves, apart from sin. [16]Let us, then, have no fear in approaching the throne of grace to receive mercy and to find grace when we are in need of help.

5 Every high priest is taken from among human beings and is appointed to act on their behalf in relationships with God, to offer gifts and sacrifices for sins; [2]he can sympathise with those who are ignorant or who have gone astray, because he too is subject to the limitations of weakness. [3]That is why he has to make sin offerings for himself as well as for the people. [4]No one takes this honour on himself; it needs a call from God, as in Aaron's case. [5]And so it was not Christ who gave himself the glory of becoming high priest, but the one who said to him: *You are my Son, today I have fathered you*,[a] [6]and in another text: *You are a priest for ever, of the order of Melchizedek.* [7]During his life on earth, he offered up prayer and entreaty, with loud cries and with tears, to the one who had the power to save him from death, and, winning a hearing by his reverence, [8]he learnt obedience, Son though he was, through his sufferings; [9]when he had been perfected, he became for all who obey him the source of eternal salvation [10]and was acclaimed by God with the title of high *priest of the order of Melchizedek.*

III: THE AUTHENTIC PRIESTHOOD OF JESUS CHRIST

Christian life and theology

[11]On this subject we have many things to say, and they are difficult to explain because you have grown so slow at understanding. [12]Indeed, when you should by this time have become masters, you need someone to teach you all over again the elements of the principles of God's sayings; you have gone back to needing milk, and not solid food. [13]Truly, no one who is still living on milk can digest the doctrine of saving justice, being still a baby. [14]Solid food is for adults with minds trained by practice to distinguish between good and bad.

The author explains his intention

6 Let us leave behind us then all the elementary teaching about Christ and go on to its completion, without going over the fundamental doctrines again: the turning away from dead actions, faith in God, [2]the teaching about baptisms and the laying-on of hands, about the resurrection of the dead and eternal judgement. [3]This, God willing, is what we propose to do.

[4]As for those people who were once brought into the light, and tasted the gift from heaven, and received a share of the Holy Spirit, [5]and tasted the goodness of God's message and the powers of the world to come [6]and yet in spite of this have fallen away—it is impossible for them to be brought to the freshness of repentance a second time, since they are crucifying the Son of God again for themselves, and making a public exhibition of him. [7]A field that drinks up the rain that has fallen frequently on it, and yields the crops that are wanted by the owners who grew them, receives God's blessing; [8]but one that grows brambles and thistles is worthless, and near to being cursed. It will end by being burnt.

Words of hope and encouragement

[9]But you, my dear friends—in spite of what we have just said, we are sure you are in a better state and on the way to salvation. [10]God would not be so unjust as to forget all you have done, the love that you have for his name or the services you have done, and are still doing, for the holy people of God. [11]Our desire is that every one of you should go on showing the same enthusiasm till the ultimate fulfilment of your hope, [12]never growing careless, but taking as your model those who

5a Ps 2:7 followed by Ps 110:4.

by their faith and perseverance are heirs of
the promises.
13 When God made the promise to
Abraham, he *swore by his own self*, since there
was no one greater he could swear by: 14 *I will
shower blessings on you and give you many
descendants.*[a] 15 Because of that, Abraham
persevered and received fulfilment of the
promise. 16 Human beings, of course, swear
an oath by something greater than them-
selves, and between them, confirmation by
an oath puts an end to all dispute. 17 In the
same way, when God wanted to show the
heirs of the promise even more clearly how
unalterable his plan was, he conveyed it by
an oath 18 so that through two unalterable
factors in which God could not be lying, we
who have fled to him might have a vigorous
encouragement to grasp the hope held out to
us. 19 This is the anchor our souls have, as
sure as it is firm, reaching right through
inside the curtain 20 where Jesus has entered as
a forerunner on our behalf, having become a
high *priest for ever, of the order of Melchizedek.*

A: CHRIST'S PRIESTHOOD HIGHER THAN LEVITICAL PRIESTHOOD

Melchizedek[a]

7 *Melchizedek, king of Salem, a priest of God
Most High, came to meet Abraham when he
returned from defeating the kings*, and *blessed
him*; 2 and Abraham gave him *a tenth of every-
thing.* By the interpretation of his name, he
is, first, 'king of saving justice' and also *king
of Salem*, that is, 'king of peace'; 3 he has no
father, mother or ancestry, and his life has
no beginning or ending; he is like the Son of
God. He remains a priest for ever.

Melchizedek accepted tithes from Abraham

4 Now think how great this man must have
been, if the patriarch *Abraham gave him a
tenth* of the finest plunder. 5 We know that
any of the descendants of Levi who are
admitted to the priesthood are obliged by the
Law to take tithes from the people, that is,
from their own brothers although they too
are descended from Abraham. 6 But this man,
who was not of the same descent, took his
tithe from Abraham, and he gave his blessing
to the holder of the promises. 7 Now it is
indisputable that a blessing is given by a
superior to an inferior. 8 Further, in the
normal case it is ordinary mortal men who
receive the tithes, whereas in that case it was
one who is attested as being alive. 9 It could
be said that Levi himself, who receives tithes,
actually paid tithes, in the person of
Abraham, 10 because he was still in the loins
of his ancestor when *Melchizedek came to
meet him.*

From levitical priesthood to the priesthood of Melchizedek

11 Now if perfection had been reached
through the levitical priesthood—and this
was the basis of the Law given to the people—
why was it necessary for a different kind of
priest to arise, spoken of as being *of the order
of Melchizedek* rather than of the order of
Aaron? 12 Any change in the priesthood must
mean a change in the Law as well.
13 So our Lord, of whom these things were
said, belonged to a different tribe, the
members of which have never done service
at the altar; 14 everyone knows he came from
Judah, a tribe which Moses did not mention
at all when dealing with priests.

The abrogation of the old law

15 This becomes even more clearly evident if
another priest, of the type of Melchizedek,
arises who is a priest 16 not in virtue of a law
of physical descent, but in virtue of the power
of an indestructible life. 17 For he is attested
by the prophecy: *You are a priest for ever of
the order of Melchizedek.* 18 The earlier
commandment is thus abolished, because of
its weakness and ineffectiveness 19 since the
Law could not make anything perfect; but
now this commandment is replaced by some-
thing better—the hope that brings us close
to God.

Christ's priesthood is unchanging

20 Now the former priests became priests
without any oath being sworn, 21 but this one
with the swearing of an oath by him who said

6a Gn 22:16.
7a A commentary on Gn 14:17–20.

to him, *The Lord has sworn an oath he will
never retract: you are a priest for ever*; 22 the
very fact that it occurred with the swearing
of an oath makes the covenant of which Jesus
is the guarantee all the greater. 23 Further, the
former priests were many in number, because
death put an end to each one of them; 24 but
this one, because he remains *for ever*, has a
perpetual priesthood. 25 It follows, then, that
his power to save those who come to God
through him is absolute, since he lives for
ever to intercede for them.

The perfection of the heavenly high priest

26 Such is the high priest that met our need,
holy, innocent and uncontaminated, set apart
from sinners, and raised up above the
heavens; 27 he has no need to offer sacrifices
every day, as the high priests do, first for
their own sins and only then for those of the
people; this he did once and for all by offering
himself. 28 The Law appoints high priests
who are men subject to weakness; but the
promise on oath, which came after the
Law, appointed the Son who is made perfect
for ever.

B: SUPERIORITY OF THE WORSHIP, SANCTUARY AND MEDIATION OF CHRIST

The new priesthood and the new sanctuary

8 The principal point of all that we have said
is that we have a high priest of exactly this
kind. He *has taken his seat at the right*[a] of the
throne of divine Majesty in the heavens, 2 and
he is the minister of the sanctuary and of the
true *Tent* which *the Lord*, and not any man,
set up.[b] 3 Every high priest is constituted to
offer gifts and sacrifices, and so this one too
must have something to offer. 4 In fact, if he
were on earth, he would not be a priest at all,
since there are others who make the offerings
laid down by the Law, 5 though these main-
tain the service only of a model or a reflection
of the heavenly realities; just as Moses, when
he had the Tent to build, was warned by God
who said: *See that you work to the design that
was shown you on the mountain*.[c]

Christ is the mediator of a greater covenant

6 As it is, he has been given a ministry as far
superior as is the covenant of which he is
the mediator, which is founded on better
promises. 7 If that first covenant had been
faultless, there would have been no room for
a second one to replace it. 8 And in fact God
does find fault with them; he says:

Look, the days are coming, the Lord
declares,
when I will make a new covenant
with the House of Israel
and the House of Judah,
9 *but not a covenant*
like the one I made with their ancestors,
the day I took them by the hand
to bring them out of Egypt,
which covenant of mine they broke,
and I too abandoned them,
the Lord declares.
10 *No, this is the covenant*
I will make with the House of Israel,
when those days have come,
the Lord declares:
In their minds I shall plant my laws
writing them on their hearts.
Then I shall be their God,
and they shall be my people.
11 *There will be no further need*
for each to teach his neighbour,
and each his brother,
saying 'Learn to know the Lord!'
No, they will all know me,
from the least to the greatest,
12 *since I shall forgive their guilt*
and never more call their sins to mind.[d]

13 By speaking of a *new* covenant, he implies
that the first one is old. And anything old and
ageing is ready to disappear.

Christ enters the heavenly sanctuary

9 The first covenant also had its laws
governing worship and its sanctuary, a
sanctuary on this earth. 2 There was a tent
which comprised two compartments: the
first, in which the lamp-stand, the table and
the loaves of permanent offering were kept,
was called the Holy Place; 3 then beyond the
second veil, a second compartment which

8a Ps 110:1.
8b Nb 24:6.
8c Ex 25:40.
8d Jr 31:31–34.

was called the Holy of Holies 4 to which belonged the gold altar of incense, and the ark of the covenant, plated all over with gold. In this were kept the gold jar containing the manna, Aaron's branch that grew the buds, and the tables of the covenant. 5 On top of it were the glorious winged creatures, overshadowing the throne of mercy. This is not the time to go into detail about this.

6 Under these provisions, priests go regularly into the outer tent to carry out their acts of worship, 7 but the second tent is entered only once a year, and then only by the high priest who takes in the blood to make an offering for his own and the people's faults of inadvertence. 8 By this, the Holy Spirit means us to see that as long as the old tent stands, the way into the holy place is not opened up; 9 it is a symbol for this present time. None of the gifts and sacrifices offered under these regulations can possibly bring any worshipper to perfection in his conscience; 10 they are rules about outward life, connected with food and drink and washing at various times, which are in force only until the time comes to set things right.

11 But now Christ has come, as the high priest of all the blessings which were to come. He has passed through the greater, the more perfect tent, not made by human hands, that is, not of this created order; 12 and he has entered the sanctuary once and for all, taking with him not the blood of goats and bull calves, but his own blood, having won an eternal redemption. 13 The blood of goats and bulls and the ashes of a heifer, sprinkled on those who have incurred defilement, may restore their bodily purity. 14 How much more will the blood of Christ, who offered himself, blameless as he was, to God through the eternal Spirit, purify our conscience from dead actions so that we can worship the living God.

Christ seals the new covenant with his blood

15 This makes him the mediator of a new covenant, so that, now that a death has occurred to redeem the sins committed under an earlier covenant, those who have been called to an eternal inheritance may receive the promise. 16 Now wherever a will is in question, the death of the testator must be established; 17 a testament comes into effect only after a death, since it has no force while the testator is still alive. 18 That is why even the earlier covenant was inaugurated with blood, 19 and why, after Moses had promulgated all the commandments of the Law to the people, he took the calves' blood, the goats' blood and some water, and with these he sprinkled the book itself and all the people, using scarlet wool and hyssop; 20 saying as he did so: *This is the blood of the covenant that God has made with you.*[a] 21 And he sprinkled both the tent and all the liturgical vessels with blood in the same way. 22 In fact, according to the Law, practically every purification takes place by means of blood; and if there is no shedding of blood, there is no remission. 23 Only the copies of heavenly things are purified in this way; the heavenly things themselves have to be purified by a higher sort of sacrifice than this. 24 It is not as though Christ had entered a man-made sanctuary which was merely a model of the real one; he entered heaven itself, so that he now appears in the presence of God on our behalf. 25 And he does not have to offer himself again and again, as the high priest goes into the sanctuary year after year with the blood that is not his own, 26 or else he would have had to suffer over and over again since the world began. As it is, he has made his appearance once and for all, at the end of the last age, to do away with sin by sacrificing himself. 27 Since human beings die only once, after which comes judgement, 28 so Christ too, having offered himself only once *to bear the sin of many*,[b] will manifest himself a second time, sin being no more, to those who are waiting for him, to bring them salvation.

SUMMARY: CHRIST'S SACRIFICE SUPERIOR TO THE SACRIFICES OF THE MOSAIC LAW

The old sacrifices ineffective

10 So, since the Law contains no more than a reflection of the good things which were still to come, and no true image of them, it is quite incapable of bringing the worshippers to perfection, by means of the

9a Ex 24:8.
9b Is 53:12.

same sacrifices repeatedly offered year after
year. 2 Otherwise, surely the offering of them
would have stopped, because the worship-
pers, when they had been purified once,
would have no awareness of sins. 3 But in fact
the sins are recalled year after year in the
sacrifices. 4 Bulls' blood and goats' blood are
incapable of taking away sins, 5 and that is
why he said, on coming into the world:

You wanted no sacrifice or cereal offering,
but you gave me a body.
6 *You took no pleasure in burnt offering*
or sacrifice for sin;
7 *then I said, 'Here I am, I am coming,'*
in the scroll of the book it is written of me,
to do your will, God.[a]

8 He says first *You did not want* what the Law
lays down as the things to be offered, that is:
*the sacrifices, the cereal offerings, the burnt
offerings and the sacrifices for sin*, and *you took
no pleasure* in them; 9 and then he says: *Here
I am! I am coming to do your will.* He is
abolishing the first sort to establish the
second. 10 And this *will* was for us to be made
holy by the *offering* of the *body* of Jesus Christ
made once and for all.

The efficacy of Christ's sacrifice

11 Every priest stands at his duties every day,
offering over and over again the same sacri-
fices which are quite incapable of taking away
sins. 12 He, on the other hand, has offered one
single sacrifice for sins, and then *taken his
seat for ever, at the right hand of God*, 13 where
he is now waiting *till his enemies are made
his footstool.*[b] 14 By virtue of that one single
offering, he has achieved the eternal perfec-
tion of all who are sanctified. 15 The Holy
Spirit attests this to us, for after saying:

16 *No, this is the covenant*
I will make with them,
when those days have come.

the Lord says:

In their minds I will plant my Laws
writing them on their hearts,
17 *and I shall never more*
call their sins to mind,[c]
or their offences.

18 When these have been forgiven, there can
be no more sin offerings.

IV: PERSEVERING FAITH

The Christian opportunity

19 We have then, brothers, complete confi-
dence through the blood of Jesus in entering
the sanctuary, 20 by a new way which he has
opened for us, a living opening through the
curtain, that is to say, his flesh. 21 And we
have the *high priest* over all *the sanctuary of
God.*[d] 22 So as we go in, let us be sincere
in heart and filled with faith, our hearts
sprinkled and free from any trace of bad
conscience, and our bodies washed with pure
water. 23 Let us keep firm in the hope we
profess, because the one who made the
promise is trustworthy. 24 Let us be
concerned for each other, to stir a response
in love and good works. 25 Do not absent
yourself from your own assemblies, as some
do, but encourage each other; the more so as
you see the Day drawing near.

The danger of apostasy

26 If, after we have been given knowledge of
the truth, we should deliberately commit any
sins, then there is no longer any sacrifice
for them. 27 There is left only the dreadful
prospect of judgement and of *the fiery wrath*
that is to *devour your enemies.*[e] 28 Anyone who
disregards the Law of Moses is ruthlessly *put
to death on the word of two witnesses or three;*[f]
29 and you may be sure that anyone who
tramples on the Son of God, and who treats
the blood of the covenant which sanctified him
as if it were not holy, and who insults the
Spirit of grace, will be condemned to a far

10a Ps 40:6–8.
10b Ps 110:1.
10c Jr 31:33–34.
10d Zc 6:11–12.
10e Is 26:11.
10f Dt 17:6.

severer punishment. 30We are all aware who it was that said: *Vengeance is mine; I will pay them back.*[g] And again: *The Lord will vindicate his people.* 31It is a dreadful thing to fall into the hands of the living God.

Motives for perseverance

32Remember the great challenge of the sufferings that you had to meet after you received the light, in earlier days; 33sometimes by being yourselves publicly exposed to humiliations and violence, and sometimes as associates of others who were treated in the same way. 34For you not only shared in the sufferings of those who were in prison, but you accepted with joy being stripped of your belongings, knowing that you owned something that was better and lasting. 35Do not lose your fearlessness now, then, since the reward is so great. 36You will need perseverance if you are to do God's will and gain what he has promised.

37Only *a little while now, a very little while,*
for come he certainly will before too long.[h]
38*My upright person will live through faith*
but if he draws back,
my soul will take no pleasure in him.[i]

39We are not the sort of people who *draw back*, and are lost by it; we are the sort who keep *faith* until our souls are saved.

The exemplary faith of our ancestors

11 Only faith can guarantee the blessings that we hope for, or prove the existence of realities that are unseen. 2It is for their faith that our ancestors are acknowledged.

3It is by faith that we understand that the ages were created by a word from God, so that from the invisible the visible world came to be.

4It was because of his faith that Abel offered God a better sacrifice than Cain, and for that he was acknowledged as upright when *God* himself made acknowledgement of *his offerings*. Though he is dead, he still speaks by faith.

5It was because of his faith that Enoch was taken up and did not experience death: *he was no more, because God took him*;[a] because before his assumption he was acknowledged to *have pleased God*. 6Now it is impossible to please God without faith, since anyone who comes to him must believe that he exists and rewards those who seek him.

7It was through his faith that Noah, when he had been warned by God of something that had never been seen before, took care to build an ark to save his family. His faith was a judgement on the world, and he was able to claim the uprightness which comes from faith.

8It was by faith that Abraham obeyed the call to *set out* for a country that was the inheritance given to him and his descendants, and that *he set out* without knowing where he was going. 9By faith he *sojourned* in the Promised Land as though it were not his, living in tents with Isaac and Jacob, who were heirs with him of the same promise. 10He looked forward to the well-founded city, designed and built by God.

11It was equally by faith that Sarah, in spite of being past the age, was made able to conceive, because she believed that he who had made the promise was faithful to it. 12Because of this, there came from one man, and one who already had the mark of death on him, descendants *as numerous as the stars of heaven and the grains of sand on the seashore which cannot be counted.*[b]

13All these died in faith, before receiving any of the things that had been promised, but they saw them in the far distance and welcomed them, recognising that they were only *strangers and nomads on earth.* 14People who use such terms about themselves make it quite plain that they are in search of a homeland. 15If they had meant the country they came from, they would have had the opportunity to return to it; 16but in fact they were longing for a better homeland, their heavenly homeland. That is why God is not ashamed to be called their God, since he has founded the city for them.

17It was by faith that Abraham, *when put to the test, offered up Isaac.*[c] He offered to sacrifice *his only son* even though he had yet

10g Dt 32:35–36.
10h Is 26:20.
10i Hab 2:3–4.
11a Gn 5:24.
11b Gn 22:17.
11c Gn 22:1–14.

to receive what had been promised, 18 and he had been told: *Isaac is the one through whom your name will be carried on.*[d] 19 He was confident that God had the power even to raise the dead; and so, figuratively speaking, he was given back Isaac from the dead.

20 It was by faith that this same Isaac gave his blessing to Jacob and Esau for the still distant future. 21 By faith Jacob, when he was dying, blessed each of Joseph's sons, *bowed in reverence, as he leant on his staff.*[e] 22 It was by faith that, when he was about to die, Joseph mentioned the Exodus of the Israelites and gave instructions about his own remains.

23 It was by faith that Moses, when he was born, *was kept hidden by his parents for three months;*[f] because they *saw* that he was a *fine* child; they were not afraid of the royal edict. 24 It was by faith that, *when he was grown up,* Moses refused to be known as the son of Pharaoh's daughter 25 and chose to be ill-treated in company with God's people rather than to enjoy the transitory pleasures of sin. 26 He considered that the humiliations offered to the Anointed were something more precious than all the treasures of Egypt, because he had his eyes fixed on the reward. 27 It was by faith that he left Egypt without fear of the king's anger; he held to his purpose like someone who could see the Invisible. 28 It was by faith that he kept *the Passover* and sprinkled *the blood* to prevent *the Destroyer* from touching any of their first-born sons. 29 It was by faith they crossed the Red Sea as easily as dry land, while the Egyptians, trying to do the same, were drowned.

30 It was through faith that the walls of Jericho fell down when the people had marched round them for seven days. 31 It was by faith that Rahab the prostitute welcomed the spies and so was not killed with the unbelievers.

32 What more shall I say? There is not time for me to give an account of Gideon, Barak, Samson, Jephthah, or of David, Samuel and the prophets. 33 These were men who through faith conquered kingdoms, did what was upright and earned the promises. They could keep a lion's mouth shut, 34 put out blazing fires and emerge unscathed from battle. They were weak people who were given strength to be brave in war and drive back foreign invaders. 35 Some returned to their wives from the dead by resurrection; and others submitted to torture, refusing release so that they would rise again to a better life. 36 Some had to bear being pilloried and flogged, or even chained up in prison. 37 They were stoned, or sawn in half,[g] or killed by the sword; they were homeless, and wore only the skins of sheep and goats; they were in want and hardship, and maltreated. 38 They were too good for the world and they wandered in deserts and mountains and in caves and ravines. 39 These all won acknowledgement through their faith, but they did not receive what was promised, 40 since God had made provision for us to have something better, and they were not to reach perfection except with us.

The example of Jesus Christ

12 With so many witnesses in a great cloud all around us, we too, then, should throw off everything that weighs us down and the sin that clings so closely, and with perseverance keep running in the race which lies ahead of us. 2 Let us keep our eyes fixed on Jesus, who leads us in our faith and brings it to perfection: for the sake of the joy which lay ahead of him, he endured the cross, disregarding the shame of it, and *has taken his seat at the right* of God's throne. 3 Think of the way he persevered against such opposition from sinners and then you will not lose heart and come to grief. 4 In the fight against sin, you have not yet had to keep fighting to the point of bloodshed.

God's fatherly instruction

5 Have you forgotten that encouraging text in which you are addressed as sons?

My son, do not scorn correction
from the Lord,
do not resent his training,
6 *for the Lord trains those he loves,*
and chastises every son he accepts.[a]

11d Gn 21:12.
11e Gn 47:31.
11f Ex 2:2, 11.
11g Some apocryphal texts say that Isaiah was executed in this way by King Manasseh.
12a Pr 3:11–12.

7 Perseverance is part of your *training*; God is treating you as his *sons*. Has there ever been any *son* whose father did not *train* him? 8 If you were not getting this training, as all of you are, then you would be not *sons* but bastards. 9 Besides, we have all had our human fathers who punished us, and we respected them for it; all the more readily ought we to submit to the Father of spirits, and so earn life. 10 Our human fathers were training us for a short life and according to their own lights; but he does it all for our own good, so that we may share his own holiness. 11 Of course, any discipline is at the time a matter for grief, not joy; but later, in those who have undergone it, it bears fruit in peace and uprightness. 12 So *steady all weary hands and trembling knees*[b] 13 and make your crooked paths straight; then the injured limb will not be maimed, it will get better instead.

Unfaithfulness is punished

14 *Seek peace*[c] with all people, and the holiness without which no one can ever see the Lord. 15 Be careful that no one is deprived of the grace of God and that no *root of bitterness should begin to grow and make trouble*;[d] this can poison a large number. 16 And be careful that there is no immoral person, or anyone worldly minded like Esau, *who sold his birthright*[e] for one single meal. 17 As you know, when he wanted to obtain the blessing afterwards, he was rejected and, though he pleaded for it with tears, he could find no way of reversing the decision.

The two covenants

18 What you have come to is nothing known to the senses: not a *blazing fire*,[f] or *gloom* or *total darkness*, or a *storm*; 19 or *trumpet-blast* or the *sound of a voice speaking* which made everyone that heard it beg that no more should be said to them. 20 They could not bear the order that was given: *If even a beast touches the mountain, it must be stoned.*[g] 21 The whole scene was so terrible that Moses said, 'I am afraid and trembling.' 22 But what you have come to is Mount Zion and the city of the living God, the heavenly Jerusalem where the millions of angels have gathered for the festival, 23 with the whole Church of first-born sons, enrolled as citizens of heaven. You have come to God himself, the supreme Judge, and to the spirits of the upright who have been made perfect; 24 and to Jesus, the mediator of a new covenant, and to purifying blood which pleads more insistently than Abel's. 25 Make sure that you never refuse to listen when he speaks. If the people who on earth refused to listen to a warning could not escape their punishment, how shall we possibly escape if we turn away from a voice that warns us from heaven? 26 That time his voice made the earth shake, but now he has given us this promise: *I am going to shake the earth once more and* not only the earth but *heaven as well.*[h] 27 The words *once more* indicate the removal of what is shaken, since these are created things, so that what is not shaken remains. 28 We have been given possession of an unshakeable kingdom. Let us therefore be grateful and use our gratitude to worship God in the way that pleases him, in reverence and fear. 29 For our *God* is a *consuming fire.*[i]

APPENDIX

Final recommendations

13 Continue to love each other like brothers, 2 and remember always to welcome strangers, for by doing this, some people have entertained angels without knowing it. 3 Keep in mind those who are in prison, as though you were in prison with

12b Is 35:3.
12c Ps 34:14.
12d Dt 29:17.
12e Gn 25:33.
12f Ex 19—20, followed by Dt 9:19; Hg 2:6; Dt 4:24.
12g Ex 19:12seq.
12h Hg 2:6.
12i Dt 4:24.

them; and those who are being badly treated, since you too are in the body. 4Marriage must be honoured by all, and marriages must be kept undefiled, because the sexually immoral and adulterers will come under God's judgement. 5Put avarice out of your lives and be content with whatever you have; God himself has said: *I shall not fail you or desert you*,[a] 6and so we can say with confidence: *With the Lord on my side, I fear nothing: what can human beings do to me?*[b]

Faithfulness

7Remember your leaders, who preached the word of God to you, and as you reflect on the outcome of their lives, take their faith as your model. 8Jesus Christ is the same today as he was yesterday and as he will be for ever. 9Do not be led astray by all sorts of strange doctrines: it is better to rely on grace for inner strength than on food, which has done no good to those who concentrate on it. 10We have our own altar from which those who serve the Tent have no right to eat. 11The bodies of the animals *whose blood is taken into the sanctuary* by the high priest *for the rite of expiation are burnt outside the camp*,[c] 12and so Jesus too suffered outside the gate to sanctify the people with his own blood. 13Let us go to him, then, *outside the camp*, and bear his humiliation. 14There is no permanent city for us here; we are looking for the one which is yet to be. 15Through him, *let us offer God* an unending *sacrifice* of praise, the fruit of the lips of those who acknowledge his name. 16Keep doing good works and sharing your resources, for these are the kinds of sacrifice that please God.

Obedience to religious leaders

17Obey your leaders and give way to them; they watch over your souls because they must give an account of them; make this a joy for them to do, and not a grief—you yourselves would be the losers. 18Pray for us; we are sure that our own conscience is clear and we are certainly determined to behave honourably in everything we do. 19I ask you very particularly to pray that I may come back to you all the sooner.

EPILOGUE

News, good wishes and greetings

20I pray that the God of peace, *who brought back* from the dead our Lord Jesus, the great *Shepherd of the sheep, by the blood that sealed an eternal covenant*,[d] 21may prepare you to do his will in every kind of good action; effecting in us all whatever is acceptable to himself through Jesus Christ, to whom be glory for ever and ever. Amen.

22I urge you, brothers, to take these words of encouragement kindly; that is why I have written to you briefly.

23I want you to know that our brother Timothy has been set free. If he arrives in time, he will be with me when I see you. 24Greetings to all your leaders and to all God's holy people. God's holy people in Italy send you greetings. 25Grace be with you all.

13a Dt 31:6.
13b Ps 118:6.
13c Lv 16:27.
13d A combination of Is 63:11 with Ezk 34:23; 37:26.

INTRODUCTION TO THE LETTERS TO ALL CHRISTIANS

Most of these seven letters are addressed to Christians in general rather than any particular community, and they are often called the 'Catholic' or 'Universal Epistles'. In some cases their authorship is disputed: they claim to stem from the apostles, and they have been accepted by Christians as truly representing the apostolic tradition. They reflect a world towards the end of the 1st century when the spreading Christian communities are at grips with their first difficulties both from within and from outside.

THE LETTER OF JAMES

More a sermon than a letter, Jm blends OT and gospel tradition with Gk elegance. The author insists that Christian faith must issue in good works: a faith not expressed in good works is no faith at all. In the Wisdom tradition of the OT he gives sharp and sensible advice on many practical points of conduct, especially stressing the danger and transitoriness of wealth.

Some scholars consider Jm the earliest writing of the NT; others place it at the end of the century and deny that it was written by James, brother of the Lord and leader of the Jewish–Christian party in the Jerusalem church.

THE LETTER OF JAMES

Address and greetings

1 From James, servant of God and of the
Lord Jesus Christ. Greetings to the twelve
tribes of the Dispersion.[a]

Trials a privilege

[2]My brothers, consider it a great joy when
trials of many kinds come upon you, [3]for you
well know that the testing of your faith
produces perseverance, and [4]perseverance
must complete its work so that you will
become fully developed, complete, not
deficient in any way.

Prayer with confidence

[5]Any of you who lacks wisdom must ask
God, who gives to all generously and without
scolding; it will be given. [6]But the prayer
must be made with faith, and no trace of

1a Properly, Jews scattered in the gentile world, successors of the twelve tribes.

doubt, because a person who has doubts is
like the waves thrown up in the sea by the
buffeting of the wind. 7That sort of person,
in two minds, 8inconsistent in every activity,
must not expect to receive anything from
the Lord.

The lot of the rich

9It is right that the brother in humble circum-
stances should glory in being lifted up, 10and
the rich in being brought low. For the rich
will last no longer than *the wild flower*; 11the
scorching sun comes up, and the *grass withers*,
its *flower falls*,[b] its beauty is lost. It is the
same with the rich: in the middle of a busy
life, the rich will wither.

Temptation

12*Blessed is anyone who perseveres*[c] when trials
come. Such a person is of proven worth and
will win the prize of life, the crown that the
Lord has promised to those who love him.
13Never, when you are being put to the
test, say, 'God is tempting me'; God cannot
be tempted by evil, and he does not put
anybody to the test. 14Everyone is put to the
test by being attracted and seduced by that
person's own wrong desire. 15Then the desire
conceives and gives birth to sin, and when
sin reaches full growth, it gives birth to death.

Receiving the Word and putting it into practice

16Make no mistake about this, my dear
brothers: 17all that is good, all that is perfect,
is given us from above; it comes down from
the Father of all light; with him there is no
such thing as alteration, no shadow caused
by change.
18By his own choice he gave birth to us by
the message of the truth so that we should be
a sort of first-fruits of all his creation.

True religion

19Remember this, my dear brothers:
everyone should be *quick to listen*[d] but *slow* to
speak and slow to human anger; 20God's
saving justice is never served by human
anger; 21 so do away with all impurities and
remnants of evil. Humbly welcome the Word
which has been planted in you and can save
your souls.
22But you must do what the Word tells
you and not just listen to it and deceive
yourselves. 23Anyone who listens to the Word
and takes no action is like someone who looks
at his own features in a mirror and, 24once he
has seen what he looks like, goes off and
immediately forgets it. 25But anyone who
looks steadily at the perfect law of freedom
and keeps to it—not listening and forgetting,
but putting it into practice—will be blessed
in every undertaking.
26Nobody who fails to keep a tight rein on
the tongue can claim to be religious; this is
mere self-deception; that person's religion is
worthless. 27Pure, unspoilt religion, in the
eyes of God our Father, is this: coming to
the help of orphans and widows in their
hardships, and keeping oneself uncontami-
nated by the world.

Respect for the poor

2 My brothers, do not let class distinction
enter into your faith in Jesus Christ, our
glorified Lord. 2Now suppose a man comes
into your synagogue, well-dressed and with
a gold ring on, and at the same time a poor
man comes in, in shabby clothes, 3and you
take notice of the well-dressed man, and say,
'Come this way to the best seats'; then you
tell the poor man, 'Stand over there' or 'You
can sit on the floor by my foot-rest.' 4In
making this distinction among yourselves
have you not used a corrupt standard?
5Listen, my dear brothers: it was those
who were poor according to the world that
God chose, to be rich in faith and to be the
heirs to the kingdom which he promised to
those who love him. 6You, on the other hand,
have dishonoured the poor. Is it not the rich
who lord it over you? 7Are not they the ones
who drag you into court, who insult the
honourable name which has been
pronounced over you? 8Well, the right thing
to do is to keep the supreme Law of scripture:
you will love your neighbour as yourself;[a] 9but
as soon as you make class distinctions, you

1b Is 40:6–7.
1c Dn 12:2.
1d Si 5:11.
2a Lv 19:18.

are committing sin and under condemnation for breaking the Law.

[10]You see, anyone who keeps the whole of the Law but trips up on a single point, is still guilty of breaking it all. [11]He who said, '*You must not commit adultery*' said also, '*You must not kill.*'[b] Now if you commit murder, you need not commit adultery as well to become a breaker of the Law. [12]Talk and behave like people who are going to be judged by the law of freedom. [13]Whoever acts without mercy will be judged without mercy but mercy can afford to laugh at judgement.

Faith and good deeds

[14]How does it help, my brothers, when someone who has never done a single good act claims to have faith? Will that faith bring salvation? [15]If one of the brothers or one of the sisters is in need of clothes and has not enough food to live on, [16]and one of you says to them, 'I wish you well; keep yourself warm and eat plenty,' without giving them these bare necessities of life, then what good is that? [17]In the same way faith, if good deeds do not go with it, is quite dead.

[18]But someone may say: So you have faith and I have good deeds? Show me this faith of yours without deeds, then! It is by my deeds that I will show you my faith. [19]You believe in the one God—that is creditable enough, but even the demons have the same belief, and they tremble with fear. [20]Fool! Would you not like to know that faith without deeds is useless? [21]Was not Abraham our father justified by his deed, because he *offered his son Isaac on the altar?*[c] [22]So you can see that his faith was working together with his deeds; his faith became perfect by what he did. [23]In this way the scripture was fulfilled: *Abraham put his faith in God, and this was considered as making him upright*;[d] and he received the name 'friend of God'.

[24]You see now that it is by deeds, and not only by believing, that someone is justified. [25]There is another example of the same kind: Rahab the prostitute,[e] was she not justified by her deeds because she welcomed the messengers and showed them a different way to leave? [26]As a body without a spirit is dead, so is faith without deeds.

Uncontrolled language

3 Only a few of you, my brothers, should be teachers, bearing in mind that we shall receive a stricter judgement. [2]For we all trip up in many ways.

Someone who does not trip up in speech has reached perfection and is able to keep the whole body on a tight rein. [3]Once we put a bit in the horse's mouth, to make it do what we want, we have the whole animal under our control. [4]Or think of ships: no matter how big they are, even if a gale is driving them, they are directed by a tiny rudder wherever the whim of the helmsman decides. [5]So the tongue is only a tiny part of the body, but its boasts are great. Think how small a flame can set fire to a huge forest; [6]The tongue is a flame too. Among all the parts of the body, the tongue is a whole wicked world: it infects the whole body; catching fire itself from hell, it sets fire to the whole wheel of creation. [7]Wild animals and birds, reptiles and fish of every kind can all be tamed, and have been tamed, by humans; [8]but nobody can tame the tongue—it is a pest that will not keep still, full of deadly poison. [9]We use it to bless the Lord and Father, but we also use it to curse people who are made in God's image: [10]the blessing and curse come out of the same mouth. My brothers, this must be wrong—[11]does any water supply give a flow of fresh water and salt water out of the same pipe? [12]Can a fig tree yield olives, my brothers, or a vine yield figs? No more can sea water yield fresh water.

Real wisdom and its opposite

[13]Anyone who is wise or understanding among you should from a good life give evidence of deeds done in the gentleness of wisdom. [14]But if at heart you have the bitterness of jealousy, or selfish ambition, do not be boastful or hide the truth with lies; [15]this is not the wisdom that comes from above, but earthly, human and devilish. [16]Wherever there are jealousy and ambition, there are also disharmony and wickedness of every kind; [17]whereas the wisdom that comes down from above is essentially something pure; it is also peaceable, kindly and

2b Ex 20:3, 14.
2c Gn 22:9.
2d Gn 15:6.
2e Jos 2:1seq.

considerate; it is full of mercy and shows itself by doing good; nor is there any trace of partiality or hypocrisy in it. [18]The peace sown by peacemakers brings a harvest of justice.

Disunity among Christians

4 Where do these wars and battles between yourselves first start? Is it not precisely in the desires fighting inside your own selves? [2]You want something and you lack it; so you kill. You have an ambition that you cannot satisfy; so you fight to get your way by force. It is because you do not pray that you do not receive; [3]when you do pray and do not receive, it is because you prayed wrongly, wanting to indulge your passions.

[4]Adulterers! Do you not realise that love for the world is hatred for God? Anyone who chooses the world for a friend is constituted an enemy of God. [5]Can you not see the point of the saying in scripture, 'The longing of the spirit he sent to dwell in us is a jealous longing.'? [6]But he has given us an even greater grace, as scripture says:[a] *God opposes the proud but he accords his favour to the humble.* [7]Give in to God, then; resist the devil, and he will run away from you. [8]The nearer you go to God, the nearer God will come to you. Clean your hands, you sinners, and clear your minds, you waverers. [9]Appreciate your wretchedness, and weep for it in misery. Your laughter must be turned to grief, your happiness to gloom. [10]Humble yourselves before the Lord and he will lift you up.

[11]Brothers, do not slander one another. Anyone who slanders a brother, or condemns one, is speaking against the Law and condemning the Law. But if you condemn the Law, you have ceased to be subject to it and become a judge over it.

[12]There is only one lawgiver and he is the only judge and has the power to save or to destroy. Who are you to give a verdict on your neighbour?

A warning for the rich and self-confident

[13]Well now, you who say, 'Today or tomorrow, we are off to this or that town; we are going to spend a year there, trading, and make some money.' [14]You never know what will happen tomorrow: you are no more than a mist that appears for a little while and then disappears. [15]Instead of this, you should say, 'If it is the Lord's will, we shall still be alive to do this or that.' [16]But as it is, how boastful and loud-mouthed you are! Boasting of this kind is always wrong. [17]Everyone who knows what is the right thing to do and does not do it commits a sin.

5 Well now, you rich! Lament, weep for the miseries that are coming to you. [2]Your wealth is rotting, your clothes are all moth-eaten. [3]All your gold and your silver are corroding away, and the same corrosion will be a witness against you and eat into your body. It is like a fire which you have stored up for the final days. [4]Can you hear crying out against you the wages which you kept back from the labourers mowing your fields? The cries of the reapers have reached the ears of the Lord Sabaoth. [5]On earth you have had a life of comfort and luxury; in the time of slaughter you went on eating to your heart's content. [6]It was you who condemned the upright and killed them; they offered you no resistance.

The coming of the Lord

[7]Now be patient, brothers, until the Lord's coming. Think of a farmer: how patiently he waits for the precious fruit of the ground until it has had the autumn rains and the spring rains! [8]You too must be patient; do not lose heart, because the Lord's coming will be soon. [9]Do not make complaints against one another, brothers, so as not to be brought to judgement yourselves; the Judge is already to be seen waiting at the gates. [10]For your example, brothers, in patiently putting up with persecution, take the prophets who spoke in the Lord's name; [11]remember it is those who had perseverance that we say are the blessed ones. You have heard of the perseverance of Job and understood the Lord's purpose, realising that *the Lord is kind and compassionate.*[a]

[12]Above all, my brothers, do not swear by heaven or by the earth or use any oaths at all. If you mean 'yes', you must say 'yes'; if you mean 'no', say 'no'. Otherwise you make yourselves liable to judgement.

[13]Any one of you who is in trouble should pray; anyone in good spirits should sing a

4a Pr 3:34. The saying in v. 5 is not in the OT.
5a Ps 103:8.

psalm. [14]Any one of you who is ill should
send for the elders of the church, and they
must anoint the sick person with oil in the
name of the Lord and pray over him. [15]The
prayer of faith will save the sick person and
the Lord will raise him up again; and if he
has committed any sins, he will be forgiven.
[16]So confess your sins to one another, and
pray for one another to be cured; the heartfelt
prayer of someone upright works very powerfully.
[17]Elijah was a human being as frail as
ourselves— he prayed earnestly for it not to
rain, and no rain fell for three and a half
years; [18]then he prayed again and the sky
gave rain and the earth gave crops.

[19]My brothers, if one of you strays away
from the truth, and another brings him back
to it, [20]he may be sure that anyone who can
bring back a sinner from his erring ways will
be saving his soul from death and *covering
over many a sin.*[b]

THE FIRST LETTER OF PETER

First Peter is written to Christians of Asia Minor to encourage them in time of trial or persecution. The Christian must prove true worth by sharing in Christ's sufferings. The letter is full of practical advice, and the constant return to the idea of the new life of baptism suggests that the letter was written for the newly baptised.

The letter has always been accepted by tradition as Peter's own. If the standard of Gk is too high for a Galilean fisherman, this may be due to the secretary Silvanus.

1 PETER

THE FIRST LETTER OF PETER

Address. Greetings

1 Peter, apostle of Jesus Christ, to all those
living as aliens in the Dispersion[a] of
Pontus, Galatia, Cappadocia, Asia and
Bithynia, who have been chosen, [2]in the
foresight of God the Father, to be made holy
by the Spirit, obedient to Jesus Christ and
sprinkled with his blood: Grace and peace be
yours in abundance.

Introduction
The inheritance of Christians

[3]Blessed be God the Father of our Lord Jesus
Christ, who in his great mercy has given us a
new birth into a living hope through the
resurrection of Jesus Christ from the dead
[4]and into a heritage that can never be spoilt
or soiled and never fade away. It is reserved
in heaven for you [5]who are being kept safe

5b Pr 10:12; Tb 12:9.
1a *See* Jm 1a note.

by God's power through faith until the
salvation which has been prepared is revealed
at the final point of time.

Faithfulness to Christ and love of Christ

6 This is a great joy to you, even though for a
short time yet you must bear all sorts of trials;
7 so that the worth of your faith, more valuable
than gold, which is perishable even if it has
been tested by fire, may be proved—to your
praise and honour when Jesus Christ is
revealed. 8 You have not seen him, yet you
love him; and still without seeing him you
believe in him and so are already filled with
a joy so glorious that it cannot be described;
9 and you are sure of the goal of your faith,
that is, the salvation of your souls.

The hope of the prophets

10 This salvation was the subject of the search
and investigation of the prophets who spoke
of the grace you were to receive, 11 searching
out the time and circumstances for which the
Spirit of Christ, bearing witness in them, was
revealing the sufferings of Christ and the
glories to follow them. 12 It was revealed to
them that it was for your sake and not their
own that they were acting as servants deliv-
ering the message which has now been
announced to you by those who preached to
you the gospel through the Holy Spirit sent
from heaven. Even the angels long to catch a
glimpse of these things.

The demands of the new life
Holiness of the newly baptised

13 Your minds, then, must be sober and ready
for action; put all your hope in the grace
brought to you by the revelation of Jesus
Christ. 14 Do not allow yourselves to be
shaped by the passions of your old ignorance,
15 but as obedient children, be yourselves holy
in all your activity, after the model of the
Holy One who calls us, 16 since scripture says,
'*Be holy, for I am holy*.'[b] 17 And if you address
as Father him who judges without favour-
itism according to each individual's deeds,
live out the time of your exile here in reverent
awe. 18 For you know that the price of your
ransom from the futile way of life handed
down from your ancestors was paid, not in
anything perishable like silver or gold,[c] 19 but
in precious blood as of a blameless and spot-
less lamb, Christ. 20 He was marked out before
the world was made, and was revealed at the
final point of time for your sake. 21 Through
him you now have faith in God, who raised
him from the dead and gave him glory for
this very purpose—that your faith and hope
should be in God.

Regeneration by the Word

22 Since by your obedience to the truth you
have purified yourselves so that you can
experience the genuine love of brothers, love
each other intensely from the heart; 23 for
your new birth was not from any perishable
seed but from imperishable seed, the living
and enduring Word of God. 24 For *all
humanity is grass, and all its beauty like the wild
flower's. As grass withers, the flower fades,* 25 *but
the Word of the Lord remains for ever.*[d] And
this Word is the Good News that has been
brought to you.

2 Rid yourselves, then, of all spite, deceit,
hypocrisy, envy and carping criticism.
2 Like new-born babies all your longing
should be for milk—the unadulterated spiri-
tual milk—which will help you to grow up to
salvation, 3 at any rate if *you have tasted that
the Lord is good*[a].

The new priesthood

4 He is the living stone, rejected by human
beings but chosen by God and precious to
him; set yourselves close to him 5 so that you,
too, may be living stones making a spiritual
house as a holy priesthood to offer the spiri-
tual sacrifices made acceptable to God
through Jesus Christ. 6 As scripture says:
*Now I am laying a stone in Zion, a chosen,
precious cornerstone* and *no one who relies on
this will be brought to disgrace.*[b] 7 To you
believers it brings honour. But for unbe-
lievers, it is rather a *stone which the builders*

1b Lv 19:2.
1c Is 52:3.
1d Is 40:6–8.
2a Ps 34:8.
2b Is 28:16.

rejected that became a cornerstone,[c] 8 *a stumbling stone, a rock to trip people up*.[d] They stumble over it because they do not believe in the Word; it was the fate in store for them.

9 But you are *a chosen race, a kingdom of priests, a holy nation, a people to be a personal possession*[e] to sing the praises of God who called you out of the darkness into his wonderful light. 10 Once you were *a non-people* and now you are the People of God; once you were *outside his pity*; now you *have received pity*.[f]

The obligations of Christians: towards unbelievers

11 I urge you, my dear friends, as *strangers and nomads*,[g] to keep yourselves free from the disordered natural inclinations that attack the soul. 12 Always behave honourably among gentiles so that they can see for themselves what moral lives you lead, and when the day of reckoning comes, give thanks to God for the things which now make them denounce you as criminals.

Towards civil authority

13 For the sake of the Lord, accept the authority of every human institution: the emperor, as the supreme authority, 14 and the governors as commissioned by him to punish criminals and praise those who do good. 15 It is God's will that by your good deeds you should silence the ignorant talk of fools. 16 You are slaves of no one except God, so behave like free people, and never use your freedom as a cover for wickedness. 17 Have respect for everyone and love for your fellow-believers; fear God and honour the emperor.

Towards masters

18 Slaves, you should obey your masters respectfully, not only those who are kind and reasonable but also those who are difficult to please. 19 You see, there is merit if, in awareness of God, you put up with the pains of undeserved punishment; 20 but what glory is there in putting up with a beating after you have done something wrong? The merit in the sight of God is in putting up with it patiently when you are punished for doing your duty.

21 This, in fact, is what you were called to do, because Christ suffered for you and left an example for you to follow in his steps. 22 He had done nothing wrong, and *had spoken no deceit*.[h] 23 He was insulted and did not retaliate with insults; when he was suffering he made no threats but put his trust in the upright judge. 24 He was *bearing our sins* in his own body on the cross, so that we might die to our sins and live for uprightness; *through his bruises you have been healed*. 25 You had *gone astray like sheep* but now you have returned to the shepherd and guardian of your souls.

In marriage

3 In the same way, you wives should be obedient to your husbands. Then if there are some husbands who do not believe the Word, they may find themselves won over, without a word spoken, by the way their wives behave, 2 when they see the reverence and purity of your way of life. 3 Your adornment should be not an exterior one, consisting of braided hair or gold jewellery or fine clothing, 4 but the interior disposition of the heart, consisting in the imperishable quality of a gentle and peaceful spirit, so precious in the sight of God. 5 That was how the holy women of the past dressed themselves attractively—they hoped in God and were submissive to their husbands; 6 like Sarah, who was obedient to Abraham, and called him her *lord*.[a] You are now her children, as long as you live good lives free from fear and worry.

7 In the same way, husbands must always treat their wives with consideration in their life together, respecting a woman as one who, though she may be the weaker partner, is equally an heir to the generous gift of life. This will prevent anything from coming in the way of your prayers.

2c Ps 118:22.
2d Is 8:14.
2e Is 43:20–21.
2f Ho 1:9 and allusions to Ho 2.
2g Ps 39:12.
2h Several quotations from Is 53:5–9.
3a Gn 18:12.

Love the brothers

[8]Finally: you should all agree among yourselves and be sympathetic; love the brothers, have compassion and be self-effacing. [9]Never repay one wrong with another, or one abusive word with another; instead, repay with a blessing. That is what you are called to do, so that you inherit a blessing. [10]For

Who among you delights in life,
longs for time to enjoy prosperity?
Guard your tongue from evil,
your lips from any breath of deceit.
[11]*Turn away from evil and do good,*
seek peace and pursue it.
[12]*For the eyes of the Lord are on the upright,*
his ear turned to their cry.
But the Lord's face is set
against those who do evil.[b]

In persecution

[13]No one can hurt you if you are determined to do only what is right; [14]and blessed are you if you have to suffer for being upright. *Have no dread of them; have no fear.*[c] [15]Simply *proclaim the Lord* Christ *holy* in your hearts, and always have your answer ready for people who ask you the reason for the hope that you have. [16]But give it with courtesy and respect and with a clear conscience, so that those who slander your good behaviour in Christ may be ashamed of their accusations. [17]And if it is the will of God that you should suffer, it is better to suffer for doing right than for doing wrong.

The resurrection and the descent into hell

[18]Christ himself died once and for all for sins, the upright for the sake of the guilty, to lead us to God. In the body he was put to death, in the spirit he was raised to life, [19]and, in the spirit, he went to preach to the spirits in prison. [20]They refused to believe long ago, while God patiently waited to receive them, in Noah's time when the ark was being built. In it only a few, that is eight souls, were saved through water. [21]It is the baptism corresponding to this water which saves you now—not the washing off of physical dirt but the pledge of a good conscience given to God through the resurrection of Jesus Christ, [22]who has entered heaven and is at God's right hand, with angels, ruling forces and powers subject to him.

The break with sin

4 As Christ has undergone bodily suffering, you too should arm yourselves with the same conviction, that anyone who has undergone bodily suffering has broken with sin, [2]because for the rest of life on earth that person is ruled not by human passions but only by the will of God. [3]You spent quite long enough in the past living the sort of life that gentiles choose to live, behaving in a debauched way, giving way to your passions, drinking to excess, having wild parties and drunken orgies and sacrilegiously worshipping false gods. [4]So people are taken aback that you no longer hurry off with them to join this flood which is rushing down to ruin, and then abuse you for it. [5]They will have to answer for it before the judge who is to judge the living and the dead. [6]And this was why the gospel was brought to the dead as well, so that, though in their bodies they had undergone the judgement that faces all humanity, in their spirit they might enjoy the life of God.

The revelation of Christ is close

[7]The end of all things is near, so keep your minds calm and sober for prayer. [8]Above all preserve an intense love for each other, since *love covers over many a sin.*[a] [9]Welcome each other into your houses without grumbling. [10]Each one of you has received a special grace, so, like good stewards responsible for all these varied graces of God, put it at the service of others. [11]If anyone is a speaker, let it be as the words of God, if anyone serves, let it be as in strength granted by God; so that in everything God may receive the glory, through Jesus Christ, since to him alone belong all glory and power for ever and ever. Amen.

Suffering for Christ

[12]My dear friends, do not be taken aback at the testing by fire which is taking place among you, as though something strange were happening to you; [13]but in so far as you share

---

3b Ps 34:12–16.
3c Is 8:12–13.
4a Pr 10:12; Tb 12:9.

in the sufferings of Christ, be glad, so that you may enjoy a much greater gladness when his glory is revealed. [14]If you are insulted for bearing Christ's name, blessed are you, for *on* you *rests the Spirit of God*,[b] the Spirit of glory. [15]None of you should ever deserve to suffer for being a murderer, a thief, a criminal or an informer; [16]but if any one of you should suffer for being a Christian, then there must be no shame but thanksgiving to God for bearing this name. [17]The time has come for the judgement to begin at the household of God; and if it begins with us, what will be the end for those who refuse to believe God's gospel? [18]*If it is hard for the upright to be saved, what will happen to the wicked and to sinners?*[c] [19]So even those whom God allows to suffer should commit themselves to a Creator who is trustworthy, and go on doing good.

Instructions: to the elders

5 I urge the elders among you, as a fellow-elder myself and a witness to the sufferings of Christ, and as one who is to have a share in the glory that is to be revealed: [2]give a shepherd's care to the flock of God that is entrusted to you: watch over it, not simply as a duty but gladly, as God wants; not for sordid money, but because you are eager to do it. [3]Do not lord it over the group which is in your charge, but be an example for the flock. [4]When the chief shepherd appears, you will be given the unfading crown of glory.

To the faithful

[5]In the same way, younger people, be subject to the elders. Humility towards one another must be the garment you all wear constantly, because *God opposes the proud but accords his favour to the humble.*[a] [6]Bow down, then, before the power of God now, so that he may raise you up in due time; [7]*unload all your burden on to him*,[b] since he is concerned about you. [8]Keep sober and alert, because your enemy the devil is on the prowl like a *roaring lion*,[c] looking for someone to devour. [9]Stand up to him, strong in faith and in the knowledge that it is the same kind of suffering that the community of your brothers throughout the world is undergoing. [10]You will have to suffer only for a little while: the God of all grace who called you to eternal glory in Christ will restore you, he will confirm, strengthen and support you. [11]His power lasts for ever and ever. Amen.

Last words. Greetings

[12]I write these few words to you through Silvanus, who is a trustworthy brother, to encourage you and attest that this is the true grace of God. Stand firm in it!

[13]Your sister in Babylon, who is with you among the chosen, sends you greetings; so does my son, Mark.

[14]Greet one another with a kiss of love.

Peace to you all who are in Christ.

THE SECOND LETTER OF PETER

Second Peter encourages its readers to wait for the Day of the Lord Jesus Christ with patience and alert perseverance. It warns against false teachers, and especially ones who value only knowledge at the expense of generosity and self-control. A large section, 2:1—3:3, coincides closely with the Letter of Jude and is probably dependent on it.

4b Is 11:2.
4c Pr 11:31 LXX.
5a Pr 3:34 LXX.
5b Ps 55:22.
5c Ps 22:13.

The letter may well be the latest writing of the NT, and is widely accepted as dating from the 2nd century, well after Peter's death. It is given the authority of Peter by a literary convention.

2 PETER
THE SECOND LETTER OF PETER

Greetings

1 Simon Peter, servant and apostle of Jesus
Christ, to those who have received a faith
as precious as our own, given through the
saving justice of our God and Saviour Jesus
Christ. 2Grace and peace be yours in abun-
dance through the knowledge of our Lord.

The generosity of God

3By his divine power, he has lavished on us
all the things we need for life and for true
devotion, through the knowledge of him who
has called us by his own glory and goodness.
4Through these, the greatest and priceless
promises have been lavished on us, that
through them you should share the divine
nature and escape the corruption rife in the
world through disordered passion. 5With this
in view, do your utmost to support your faith
with goodness, goodness with under-
standing, 6understanding with self-control,
self-control with perseverance, perseverance
with devotion, 7devotion with kindness to
the brothers, and kindness to the brothers
with love. 8The possession and growth of
these qualities will prevent your knowledge
of our Lord Jesus Christ from being ineffec-
tual or unproductive. 9But without them, a
person is blind or short-sighted, forgetting
how the sins of the past were washed away.
10Instead of this, brothers, never allow your
choice or calling to waver; then there will be
no danger of your stumbling, 11for in this
way you will be given the generous gift of
entry to the eternal kingdom of our Lord and
Saviour Jesus Christ.

The apostolic witness

12That is why I will always go on recalling the
same truths to you, even though you already
know them and are firmly fixed in these
truths. 13I am sure it is my duty, as long as I
am in this tent, to keep stirring you up with
reminders, 14since I know the time for me to
lay aside this tent is coming soon, as our Lord
Jesus Christ made clear to me. 15And I shall
take great care that after my own departure
you will still have a means to recall these
things to mind.
16When we told you about the power and
the coming of our Lord Jesus Christ, we
were not slavishly repeating cleverly invented
myths; no, we had seen his majesty with our
own eyes. 17He was honoured and glorified
by God the Father, when a voice came to him
from the transcendent Glory, *This is my Son,
the Beloved; he enjoys my favour.*[a] 18We
ourselves heard this voice from heaven, when
we were with him on the holy mountain.

The value of prophecy

19So we have confirmation of the words of
the prophets; and you will be right to pay
attention to it as to a lamp for lighting a way
through the dark, until the dawn comes and
the morning star rises in your minds. 20At
the same time, we must recognise that the
interpretation of scriptural prophecy is never
a matter for the individual. 21For no prophecy
ever came from human initiative. When
people spoke for God it was the Holy Spirit
that moved them.

1a Mt 17:5par.

False teachers

2 As there were false prophets in the past
history of our people, so you too will have
your false teachers, who will insinuate their
own disruptive views and, by disowning the
Lord who bought them freedom, will bring
upon themselves speedy destruction. [2]Many
will copy their debauched behaviour, and the
Way of Truth will be brought into disrepute
on their account. [3]In their greed they will try
to make a profit out of you with untrue tales.
But the judgement made upon them long ago
is not idle, and the destruction awaiting them
is for ever on the watch.

Lessons of the past

[4]When angels sinned, God did not spare
them: he sent them down into the underworld
and consigned them to the dark abyss to be
held there until the Judgement. [5]He did not
spare the world in ancient times: he saved
only Noah, the preacher of uprightness,
along with seven others, when he sent the
Flood over a world of sinners. [6]He
condemned the cities of Sodom and
Gomorrah by reducing them to ashes as a
warning to future sinners; [7]but rescued Lot,
an upright man who had been sickened by
the debauched way in which these vile people
behaved—[8]for that upright man, living
among them, was outraged in his upright
soul by the crimes that he saw and heard
every day. [9]All this shows that the Lord is
well able to rescue the good from their trials,
and hold the wicked for their punishment
until the Day of Judgement, [10]especially
those who follow the desires of their corrupt
human nature and have no respect for the
Lord's authority.

The punishment to come

Such self-willed people with no reverence are
not afraid of offending against the glorious
ones, [11]but the angels in their greater strength
and power make no complaint or accusation
against them in the Lord's presence. [12]But
these people speak evil of what they do not
understand; they are like brute beasts, born
only to be caught and killed, and like beasts
they will be destroyed, being injured in
return for the injuries they have inflicted.
[13]Debauchery even by day they make their
pleasure; they are unsightly blots, and amuse
themselves by their trickery even when they
are sharing your table; [14]with their eyes
always looking for adultery, people with an
insatiable capacity for sinning, they will
seduce any but the most stable soul. Where
greed is concerned they are at their peak of
fitness. They are under a curse. [15]They have
left the right path and wandered off to follow
the path of Balaam son of Bosor, who set his
heart on a dishonest reward, but soon had his
fault pointed out to him: [16]a dumb beast of
burden, speaking with a human voice, put a
stop to the madness of the prophet.

[17]People like this are dried-up springs,
fogs swirling in the wind, and the gloom of
darkness is stored up for them. [18]With their
high-sounding but empty talk they tempt
back people who have scarcely escaped from
those who live in error, by playing on the
disordered desires of their human nature
and by debaucheries. [19]They may promise
freedom but are themselves slaves to corrup-
tion; because if anyone lets himself be domi-
nated by anything, then he is a slave to it;
[20]and anyone who has escaped the pollution
of the world by coming to know our Lord
and Saviour Jesus Christ, and who then
allows himself to be entangled and mastered
by it a second time, ends up by being worse
than he was before. [21]It would have been
better for them never to have learnt the way
of uprightness, than to learn it and then desert
the holy commandment that was entrusted to
them. [22]What they have done is exactly as the
proverb rightly says: *The dog goes back to its
vomit*[a] and: As soon as the sow has been
washed, it wallows in the mud.

The Day of the Lord; the prophets and the apostles

3 My dear friends, this is the second letter
I have written to you, trying to awaken in
you by my reminders an unclouded under-
standing. [2]Remember what was said in the
past by the holy prophets and the command of
the Lord and Saviour given by your apostles.

False teachers

[3]First of all, do not forget that in the final
days there will come sarcastic scoffers whose

2a Pr 26:11.

life is ruled by their passions. [4]'What has
happened to the promise of his coming?' they
will say, 'Since our Fathers died everything
has gone on just as it has since the beginning
of creation!' [5]They deliberately ignore the
fact that long ago there were the heavens and
the earth, formed out of water and through
water by the Word of God, [6]and that it was
through these same factors that the world of
those days was destroyed by the floodwaters.
[7]It is the same Word which is reserving the
present heavens and earth for fire, keeping
them till the Day of Judgement and of the
destruction of sinners.

[8]But there is one thing, my dear friends,
that you must never forget: that with the
Lord, a day is like a thousand years, and *a
thousand years are like a day.*[a] [9]The Lord is
not being slow in carrying out his promises,
as some people think he is; rather is he being
patient with you, wanting nobody to be lost
and everybody to be brought to repentance.
[10]The Day of the Lord will come like
a thief, and then with a roar the sky will
vanish, the elements will catch fire and melt
away, the earth and all that it contains will
be burned up.

Fresh call to holiness. Doxology

[11]Since everything is coming to an end like
this, what holy and saintly lives you should
be living [12]while you wait for the Day of God
to come, and try to hasten its coming: on that
Day the sky will dissolve in flames and the
elements melt in the heat. [13]What we are
waiting for, relying on his promises, is the
new heavens and new earth, where upright-
ness will be at home. [14]So then, my dear
friends, while you are waiting, do your best
to live blameless and unsullied lives so that
he will find you at peace. [15]Think of our
Lord's patience as your opportunity to be
saved; our brother Paul, who is so dear to us,
told you this when he wrote to you with the
wisdom that he was given. [16]He makes this
point too in his letters as a whole wherever
he touches on these things. In all his letters
there are of course some passages which are
hard to understand, and these are the ones
that uneducated and unbalanced people
distort, in the same way as they distort the
rest of scripture[b]—to their own destruction.
[17]Since you have been forewarned about this,
my dear friends, be careful that you do not
come to the point of losing the firm ground
that you are standing on, carried away by
the errors of unprincipled people. [18]Instead,
continue to grow in the grace and in the
knowledge of our Lord and Saviour Jesus
Christ. To him be glory, in time and eternity.
Amen.

THE LETTERS OF JOHN

First John dwells on many of the themes of John's Gospel. It reflects on the position of Christ: he is the revelation of the Father, the source of light, love and truth. The Christian's life must be centred on the twin commandments of faith in Jesus Christ as Son of God, and of love of the brethren. So the Christian will share with Christ the life which he himself shares with the Father.

The letter is addressed to communities threatened by false teaching, and warns Christians to be on guard against an Antichrist who is to be part of the final crisis of the world. It seems to envisage a definite group, who once formed part of the community but who

3a Ps 90:4.
3b Paul's letters seemingly already exist as a collection, and are put on the same level as the OT.

have embraced false teaching on Christ.

The other two letters are mere notes, 2 Jn warning against those who deny the reality of the incarnation, and 3 Jn dealing with an unruly church leader who is causing dissension.

PLAN OF THE LETTER

1 JOHN
THE FIRST LETTER OF JOHN

INTRODUCTION

The Incarnate Word and sharing with the Father and the Son

1 Something which has existed
since the beginning,
which we have heard,
which we have seen with our own eyes,
which we have watched
and touched with our own hands,
the Word of life—
this is our theme.
2 That life was made visible;
we saw it and are giving our testimony,
declaring to you the eternal life,
which was present to the Father
and has been revealed to us.
3 We are declaring to you
what we have seen and heard,
so that you too may share our life.
Our life is shared with the Father
and with his Son Jesus Christ.
4 We are writing this to you
so that our joy may be complete.

I: TO WALK IN THE LIGHT

5 This is what we have heard from him
and are declaring to you:
God is light,
and there is no darkness in him at all.
6 If we say that we share in God's life
while we are living in darkness,
we are lying,
because we are not living the truth.
7 But if we live in light,
as he is in light,
we have a share in another's life,
and the blood of Jesus, his Son,
cleanses us from all sin.

First condition: to break with sin

8 If we say, 'We have no sin,'
we are deceiving ourselves,
and truth has no place in us;
9 if we acknowledge our sins,
he is trustworthy and upright,
so that he will forgive our sins
and will cleanse us from all evil.
10 If we say, 'We have never sinned,'
we make him a liar,
and his word has no place in us.

2 My children, I am writing this
to prevent you from sinning;
but if anyone does sin,
we have an advocate with the Father,
Jesus Christ, the upright.
2 He is the sacrifice to expiate our sins,
and not only ours,
but also those of the whole world.

Second condition: to keep the commandments, especially that of love

3 In this way we know
that we have come to know him,
if we keep his commandments.
4 Whoever says, 'I know him'
without keeping his commandments,
is a liar,
and truth has no place in him.
5 But anyone who does keep his word,
in such a one
God's love truly reaches its perfection.
This is the proof
that we are in God.
6 Whoever claims
to remain in him
must act as he acted.
7 My dear friends,
this is not a new commandment
I am writing for you,
but an old commandment
that you have had from the beginning;
the old commandment
is the message you have heard.
8 Yet in another way, I am writing
a new commandment for you
—and this is true for you,
just as much as for him—
for darkness is passing away
and the true light is already shining.
9 Whoever claims to be in light
but hates his brother
is still in darkness.
10 Anyone who loves his brother
remains in light
and there is in him
nothing to make him fall away.
11 But whoever hates his brother
is in darkness
and is walking about in darkness
not knowing where he is going,
because darkness has blinded him.

Third condition: detachment from the world

12 I am writing to you, children,
because your sins have been forgiven
through his name.
13 I am writing to you, fathers,
because you have come to know
the One who has existed
since the beginning.
I am writing to you, young people,
because you have overcome the Evil One.
14 I have written to you, children,
because you have come to know
the Father.
I have written to you, parents,
because you have come to know
the One who has existed
since the beginning.
I have written to you, young people,
because you are strong,
and God's word remains in you,
and you have overcome the Evil One.
15 Do not love the world
or what is in the world.
If anyone does love the world,
the love of the Father
finds no place in him,
16 because everything there is
in the world—
disordered bodily desires,
disordered desires of the eyes,
pride in possession—
is not from the Father
but is from the world.
17 And the world,
with all its disordered desires,
is passing away.
But whoever does the will of God
remains for ever.

Fourth condition: to be on guard against Antichrists

18 Children, this is the final hour;
you have heard
that the Antichrist[a] is coming,
and now many Antichrists
have already come;
from this we know
that it is the final hour.
19 They have gone from among us,
but they never really belonged to us;

2a cf. 2 Th 2:3–4.

if they had belonged to us,
they would have stayed with us.
But this was to prove
that not one of them belonged to us.
20 But you have been anointed
by the Holy One,
and have all received knowledge.
21 I have written to you
not because you are ignorant of the truth,
but because you are well aware of it,
and because no lie
can come from the truth.
22 Who is the liar,
if not one who claims
that Jesus is not the Christ?
This is the Antichrist,
who denies both the Father and the Son.
23 Whoever denies the Son
cannot have the Father either;
whoever acknowledges the Son
has the Father too.
24 Let what you heard in the beginning
remain in you;
as long as
what you heard in the beginning
remains in you,
you will remain in the Son
and in the Father.
25 And the promise he made you himself
is eternal life.
26 So much have I written to you
about those
who are trying to lead you astray.
27 But as for you,
the anointing you received from him
remains in you,
and you do not need anyone to teach you;
since the anointing he gave you
teaches you everything,
and since it is true, not false,
remain in him just as he has taught you.
28 Therefore remain in him now, children,
so that when he appears
we may be fearless,
and not shrink from him in shame
at his coming.

II: TO LIVE AS GOD'S CHILDREN

29 If you know that he is upright
you must recognise that everyone
whose life is upright
is a child of his.
3 You must see what great love
the Father has lavished on us
by letting us be called God's children—
which is what we are!
The reason why the world
does not acknowledge us
is that it did not acknowledge him.
2 My dear friends,
we are already God's children,
but what we shall be in the future
has not yet been revealed.
We are well aware that when he appears
we shall be like him,
because we shall see him as he really is.

First condition: to break with sin

3 Whoever treasures this hope of him
purifies himself, to be as pure as he is.
4 Whoever sins, acts wickedly,
because all sin is wickedness.
5 Now you are well aware
that he has appeared
in order to take sins away,
and that in him there is no sin.
6 No one who remains in him sins,
and whoever sins
has neither seen him nor recognised him.
7 Children, do not let anyone
lead you astray.
Whoever acts uprightly is upright,
just as he is upright.
8 Whoever lives sinfully
belongs to the devil,
since the devil has been a sinner
from the beginning.
This was the purpose
of the appearing of the Son of God,
to undo the work of the devil.
9 No one who is a child of God sins
because God's seed remains in him.
Nor can he sin,
because he is a child of God.
10 This is what distinguishes
the children of God
from the children of the devil:
whoever does not live uprightly

and does not love his brother
is not from God.

Second condition:
to keep the commandments,
especially that of love

11 This is the message
which you heard from the beginning,
that we must love one another,
12 not to be like Cain,
who was from the Evil One
and murdered his brother.
And why did he murder his brother?
Because his own actions were evil
and his brother's upright.
13 Do not be surprised, brothers,
if the world hates you.
14 We are well aware
that we have passed over
from death to life
because we love our brothers.
Whoever does not love, remains in death.
15 Anyone who hates his brother
is a murderer,
and you are well aware that no murderer
has eternal life remaining in him.
16 This is the proof of love,
that he laid down his life for us,
and we too ought to lay down our lives
for our brothers.
17 If anyone is well-off
in worldly possessions
and sees his brother in need
but closes his heart to him,
how can the love of God
be remaining in him?
18 Children,
our love must be not just words
or mere talk,
but something active and genuine.
19 This will be the proof
that we belong to the truth,
and it will convince us in his presence,
20 even if our own feelings condemn us,
that God is greater than our feelings
and knows all things.
21 My dear friends,
if our own feelings do not condemn us,
we can be fearless before God,
22 and whatever we ask
we shall receive from him,
because we keep his commandments
and do what is acceptable to him.
23 His commandment is this,
that we should believe
in the name of his Son Jesus Christ
and that we should love one another
as he commanded us.
24 Whoever keeps his commandments
remains in God, and God in him.
And this is the proof
that he remains in us:
the Spirit that he has given us.

Third condition:
to be on guard against Antichrists
and against the world

4 My dear friends,
not every spirit is to be trusted,
but test the spirits
to see whether they are from God,
for many false prophets
are at large in the world.
2 This is the proof of the spirit of God:
any spirit
which acknowledges Jesus Christ,
come in human nature,
is from God,
3 and no spirit
which fails to acknowledge Jesus
is from God;
it is the spirit of Antichrist,
whose coming you have heard of;
he is already at large in the world.
4 Children, you are from God
and have overcome them,
because he who is in you
is greater than he who is in the world.
5 They are from the world,
and therefore the world
inspires what they say,
and listens to them.
6 We are from God;
whoever recognises God listens to us;
anyone who is not from God
refuses to listen to us.
This is how we can distinguish
the spirit of truth
from the spirit of falsehood.

III: THE SOURCE OF LOVE AND FAITH

The source of love

[7]My dear friends,
let us love one another,
since love is from God
and everyone who loves
is a child of God and knows God.
[8]Whoever fails to love does not know God,
because God is love.
[9]This is the revelation
of God's love for us,
that God sent his only Son into the world
that we might have life through him.
[10]Love consists in this:
it is not we who loved God,
but God loved us and sent his Son
to expiate our sins.
[11]My dear friends,
if God loved us so much,
we too should love one another.
[12]No one has ever seen God,
but as long as we love one another
God remains in us
and his love comes to its perfection in us.
[13]This is the proof that we remain in him
and he in us,
that he has given us a share in his Spirit.
[14]We ourselves have seen and testify
that the Father sent his Son
as Saviour of the world.
[15]Anyone who acknowledges
that Jesus is the Son of God,
God remains in him and he in God.
[16]We have recognised for ourselves,
and put our faith in,
the love God has for us.
God is love,
and whoever remains in love
remains in God
and God in him.
[17]Love comes to its perfection in us
when we can face
the Day of Judgement fearlessly,
because even in this world
we have become as he is.
[18]In love there is no room for fear,
but perfect love drives out fear,
because fear implies punishment
and no one who is afraid
has come to perfection in love.
[19]Let us love, then,
because he first loved us.
[20]Anyone who says 'I love God'
and hates his brother,
is a liar,
since whoever does not love the brother
whom he can see
cannot love God whom he has not seen.
[21]Indeed this is the commandment
we have received from him,
that whoever loves God,
must also love his brother.

5 Whoever believes that Jesus is the Christ
is a child of God,
and whoever loves the father
loves the son.
[2]In this way we know
that we love God's children,
when we love God
and keep his commandments.
[3]This is what the love of God is:
keeping his commandments.
Nor are his commandments
burdensome,
[4]because every child of God
overcomes the world.
And this is the victory
that has overcome the world—
our faith.

The source of faith

[5]Who can overcome the world
but the one who believes
that Jesus is the Son of God?
[6]He it is who came by water and blood,[a]
Jesus Christ,
not with water alone
but with water and blood,
and it is the Spirit that bears witness,
for the Spirit is Truth.
[7]So there are three witnesses,
[8]the Spirit, water and blood;
and the three of them coincide.
[9]If we accept
the testimony of human witnesses,
God's testimony is greater,
for this is God's testimony
which he gave about his Son.
[10]Whoever believes in the Son of God
has this testimony within him,

5a cf. Jn 19:34.

and whoever does not believe
is making God a liar,
because he has not believed
the testimony
God has given about his Son.
11 This is the testimony:
God has given us eternal life,
and this life is in his Son.
12 Whoever has the Son has life,
and whoever has not the Son of God
has not life.
13 I have written this to you
who believe
in the name of the Son of God
so that you may know
that you have eternal life.

SUPPLEMENTS

Prayer for sinners

14 Our fearlessness towards him
consists in this,
that if we ask anything
in accordance with his will
he hears us.
15 And if we know
that he listens to whatever we ask him,
we know that we already possess
whatever we have asked of him.
16 If anyone sees his brother commit a sin
that is not a deadly sin,
he has only to pray,
and God will give life to this brother
—provided that it is not a deadly sin.
There is sin that leads to death
and I am not saying
you must pray about that.
17 Every kind of wickedness is sin,
but not all sin leads to death.

Summary of the letter

18 We are well aware
that no one who is a child of God sins,
because he who was born from God
protects him,
and the Evil One has no hold over him.
19 We are well aware that we are from God,
and the whole world
is in the power of the Evil One.
20 We are well aware also
that the Son of God has come,
and has given us understanding
so that we may know
the One who is true.
We are in the One who is true
as we are in his Son, Jesus Christ.
He is the true God
and this is eternal life.
Children, be on your guard
against false gods.

2 JOHN

THE SECOND LETTER OF JOHN

From the Elder:[a] my greetings to the Lady, the chosen one,[b] and to her children, whom I love in truth—and I am not the only one, for so do all who have come to know the Truth—2 because of the truth that remains in us and will be with us for ever. 3 In our life of truth and love, we shall have grace, faithful love and peace from God the Father and from Jesus Christ, the Son of the Father.

---

a The elders were the leaders in each community; '*the* Elder' must indicate a special leadership.
b i.e. one of the local churches.

The law of love

[4]It has given me great joy to find that children
of yours have been living the life of truth as
we were commanded by the Father. [5]And
now I am asking you—dear lady, not as
though I were writing you a new command-
ment, but only the one which we have had
from the beginning—that we should love one
another.
[6]To love is to live according to his
commandments: this is the commandment
which you have heard since the beginning,
to live a life of love.

The enemies of Christ

[7]There are many deceivers at large in the
world, refusing to acknowledge Jesus Christ
as coming in human nature. They are the
Deceiver; they are the Antichrist. [8]Watch
yourselves, or all our work will be lost and
you will forfeit your full reward. [9]If anybody
does not remain in the teaching of Christ but
goes beyond it, he does not have God with
him: only those who remain in what he taught
can have the Father and the Son with them.
[10]If anyone comes to you bringing a different
doctrine, you must not receive him into your
house or even give him a greeting. [11]Whoever
greets him has a share in his wicked activities.
[12]There are several things I have to tell
you, but I have thought it best not to trust
them to paper and ink. I hope instead to visit
you and talk to you in person, so that our joy
may be complete.
[13]Greetings to you from the children of
your sister,[c] the chosen one.

3 JOHN

THE THIRD LETTER OF JOHN

From the Elder: greetings to my dear friend
Gaius, whom I love in truth. [2]My dear
friend, I hope everything is going happily
with you and that you are as well physically
as you are spiritually. [3]It was a great joy to
me when some brothers came and told of
your faithfulness to the truth, and of your
life in the truth. [4]It is always my greatest joy
to hear that my children are living according
to the truth.
[5]My dear friend, you have done loyal work
in helping these brothers, even though they
were strangers to you. [6]They are a proof to
the whole Church of your love and it would
be a kindness if you could help them on
their journey as God would approve. [7]It was
entirely for the sake of the name that they set
out, without depending on the non-believers
for anything: [8]it is our duty to welcome
people of this sort and contribute our share
to their work for the truth.

Beware of the example of Diotrephes

[9]I have written a note for the members of the
church, but Diotrephes, who enjoys being in
charge of it, refuses to accept us. [10]So if I
come, I shall tell everyone how he has
behaved, and about the wicked accusations
he has been circulating against us. As if that
were not enough, he not only refuses to
welcome our brothers, but prevents from
doing so other people who would have liked
to, and expels them from the church. [11]My
dear friend, never follow a bad example, but
keep following the good one; whoever does
what is right is from God, but no one who
does what is wrong has ever seen God.

Commendation of Demetrius

[12]Demetrius has been approved by everyone,
and indeed by Truth itself. We too will vouch
for him and you know that our testimony is
true.

c A neighbouring church.

Epilogue

[13]There were several things I had to tell you but I would rather not trust them to pen and ink. [14]However, I hope to see you soon and talk to you in person. [15]Peace be with you; greetings from your friends; greet each of our friends by name.

THE LETTER OF JUDE

A short letter warning against certain false teachers and their evil way of life, it also encourages its readers to entrust themselves to Christ's mercy and protection. The author claims to be Jude, brother of the Lord; he stands firmly within the Jewish tradition, using both OT and other Jewish writings to express and illustrate his message, but it is equally a fully Christian work. The Second Letter of Peter draws freely upon the letter, which probably stems from the end of the 1st century.

THE LETTER OF JUDE

Address

From Jude, servant of Jesus Christ and brother of James; to those who are called, to those who are dear to God the Father and kept safe for Jesus Christ, [2]mercy, peace and love be yours in abundance.

The reason for this letter

[3]My dear friends, at a time when I was eagerly looking forward to writing to you about the salvation that we all share, I felt that I must write to you encouraging you to fight hard for the faith which has been once and for all entrusted to God's holy people. [4]Certain people have infiltrated among you, who were long ago marked down for condemnation on this account; without any reverence they pervert the grace of our God to debauchery and deny all religion, rejecting our only Master and Lord, Jesus Christ.

The false teachers: the certainty of punishment

[5]I should like to remind you—though you have already learnt it once and for all—that the Lord rescued the nation from Egypt, but afterwards he still destroyed the people who refused to believe him; [6]and the angels who did not keep to the authority they had, but left their appointed sphere,[a] he has kept in darkness in eternal bonds until the judgement of the great Day. [7]Sodom and Gomorrah, too, and the neighbouring towns, who with the same sexual immorality pursued unnatural lusts,[b] are put before us

a Gn 6:1–2, elaborated in *The Book of Enoch*.
b Gn 19:1–11, elaborated in *The Testament of the Twelve Patriarchs*.

as an example since they are paying the
penalty of eternal fire.

Their violent language

8 Nevertheless, these people are doing the
same: in their delusions they not only defile
their bodies and disregard Authority, but
abuse the Glories as well. 9 Not even the
archangel Michael, when he was engaged in
argument with the devil about the corpse
of Moses,[c] dared to denounce him in the
language of abuse; all he said was, '*May the
Lord rebuke you.*'[d] 10 But these people abuse
anything they do not understand; and the
only things they do understand—merely by
nature like unreasoning animals—will turn
out to be fatal to them.

Their vicious behaviour

11 Alas for them, because they have followed
Cain;[e] they have thrown themselves into the
same delusion as Balaam[f] for a reward; they
have been ruined by the same rebellion as
Korah[g]—and share the same fate. 12 They
are a dangerous hazard at your community
meals, coming for the food and quite shame-
lessly only looking after themselves. They
are like the clouds blown about by the winds
and bringing no rain, or like autumn trees,
barren and uprooted and so twice dead; 13 like
wild sea waves with their own shame for
foam; or like wandering stars for whom the
gloom of darkness is stored up for ever. 14 It
was with them in mind that Enoch, the
seventh patriarch from Adam, made his
prophecy when he said, 'I tell you, the Lord
will come with his holy ones in their tens of
thousands, 15 to pronounce judgement on all
humanity and to sentence the godless for
all the godless things they have done, and for
all the defiant things said against him by god-
less sinners.'[h] 16 They are mischief-makers,
grumblers governed only by their own
desires, with *mouths full of boastful talk*,[i]
ready to flatter others for gain.

A warning

17 But remember, my dear friends, what the
apostles of our Lord Jesus Christ foretold.
18 'At the final point of time', they told you,
'there will be mockers who follow nothing
but their own godless desires.' 19 It is they
who cause division, who live according to
nature and do not possess the Spirit.

The duties of love

20 But you, my dear friends, must build your-
selves up on the foundation of your most holy
faith, praying in the Holy Spirit; 21 keep
yourselves within the love of God and wait
for the mercy of our Lord Jesus Christ to give
you eternal life. 22 To some you must be
compassionate because they are wavering;
23 others you must save by snatching them
from the fire; to others again you must be
compassionate but wary, hating even the
tunic stained by their bodies.

Doxology

24 To him who can keep you from falling
and bring you safe to his glorious presence,
innocent and joyful, 25 to the only God, our
Saviour, through Jesus Christ our Lord, be
glory, majesty, authority and power, before
all ages, now and for ever. Amen.

---

c *See* the apocryphal *Assumption of Moses*.
d Zc 3:2.
e Gn 4:8.
f Nb 22:2.
g Nb 16.
h *Enoch* 1:9.
i Lv 19:15.

THE REVELATION TO JOHN

The Bible is summed up in the message of hope and the rich symbolism of this book. It is a vision of rescue from the trials which beset God's people, and a promise of a glorious future. The message is expressed by means of imagery which draws on the whole of the Bible, so that every feature, animals, colours, numbers, is evocative and full of overtones to a reader familiar with the OT. In this way it is a secret and allusive revelation of what is to come, though the natural symbolism of the great acts of worship and the final vision of the messianic splendour of the new Holy City are clear enough. There was a tradition of such writing in Judaism from Dn onwards, to strengthen God's people in persecution with assurance of eventual deliverance and triumph.

Written to encourage Christians in a time of persecution by the Roman empire, perhaps under Nero, *c.* AD 68, or more probably under Domitian, *c.* AD 55, it has wider reference than any particular persecution and provides a promise of eventual deliverance for Christians under any circumstances of trial and oppression.

Much of the imagery is strikingly similar to that of John's Gospel, though some of the theological ideas (e.g. on the Second Coming) are very different. The book probably issues from the Johannine tradition rather than from the same pen. Furthermore, the frequent repetitions suggest that two apocalypses by the same author may have been combined. The initial letters to the seven churches form a preface to the visions.

PLAN OF THE BOOK

THE REVELATION TO JOHN

Prologue

1 A revelation of Jesus Christ, which God gave him so that he could tell his servants *what is* now *to take place*[a] very soon; he sent his angel to make it known to his servant John, 2and John has borne witness to the Word of God and to the witness of Jesus Christ, everything that he saw. 3Blessed is anyone who reads the words of this prophecy, and blessed those who hear them, if they treasure the content, because the Time is near.

1a Dn 2:28.

I: THE LETTERS TO THE CHURCHES OF ASIA

Address and greeting[b]

[4]John, to the seven churches of Asia: grace and peace to you from him who is, who was, and who is to come, from the seven spirits who are before his throne, [5]and from Jesus Christ, *the faithful witness, the First-born* from the dead, *the highest of earthly kings*. He loves us and has washed away our sins with his blood, [6]and made us a *Kingdom of Priests* to serve his God and Father; to him, then, be glory and power for ever and ever. Amen. [7]Look, he *is coming on the clouds*; everyone will see him, even *those who pierced him*, and *all the races of the earth will mourn over him*. Indeed this shall be so. Amen. [8]'I am the Alpha and the Omega,' says the Lord God, who is, who was, and who is to come, the Almighty.

Preliminary vision

[9]I, John, your brother and partner in hardships, in the kingdom and in perseverance in Jesus, was on the island of Patmos on account of the Word of God and of witness to Jesus; [10]it was the Lord's Day and I was in ecstasy, and I heard a loud voice behind me, like the sound of a trumpet, saying, [11]'Write down in a book all that you see, and send it to the seven churches of Ephesus, Smyrna, Pergamum, Thyatira, Sardis, Philadelphia and Laodicea.' [12]I turned round to see who was speaking to me, and when I turned I saw seven golden lamp-stands [13]and, in the middle of them, one *like a Son of man*,[c] dressed in a long robe tied at the waist with a *belt of gold*. [14]*His head and his hair were white with the whiteness of wool, like snow, his eyes* like a *burning* flame, [15]*his feet like burnished bronze* when it has been refined in a furnace, and *his voice like the sound of the ocean*. [16]In his right hand he was holding seven stars, out of his mouth came a sharp sword, double-edged, and his face was like the sun shining with all its force.

[17]When I saw him, I fell at his feet as though dead, but he laid his right hand on me and said, 'Do not be afraid; it is I, *the First* and *the Last*; I am the Living One, [18]I was dead and look—I am alive for ever and ever, and I hold the keys of death and of Hades. [19]Now write down all that you see of present happenings and *what is still to come*.[d] [20]The secret of the seven stars you have seen in my right hand, and of the seven golden lamp-stands, is this: the seven stars are the angels of the seven churches, and the seven lamp-stands are the seven churches themselves.'

1 Ephesus

2 'Write to the angel of the church in Ephesus and say, "Here is the message of the one who holds the seven stars in his right hand and who lives among the seven golden lamp-stands: [2]I know your activities, your hard work and your perseverance. I know you cannot stand wicked people, and how you put to the test those who were self-styled apostles, and found them false. [3]I know too that you have perseverance, and have suffered for my name without growing tired. [4]Nevertheless, I have this complaint to make: you have less love now than formerly. [5]Think where you were before you fell; repent, and behave as you did at first, or else, if you will not repent, I shall come to you and take your lamp-stand from its place. [6]It is in your favour, nevertheless, that you loathe as I do the way the Nicolaitans are behaving. [7]Let anyone who can hear, listen to what the Spirit is saying to the churches: those who prove victorious I will feed *from the tree of life* set *in* God's *paradise*."'[a]

2 Smyrna

[8]'Write to the angel of the church in Smyrna and say, "Here is the message of *the First* and *the Last*, who was dead and has come to life again: [9]I know your hardships and your poverty, and—though you are rich—the slander of the people who falsely claim to be Jews but are really members of the synagogue

1b The quotations point to the glorious Messiah: Ps 89:37, 27; Is 55:4; Ex 19:6; Dn 7:13; Zc 12:10, 44.
1c Allusions to Dn 7 and 10 and Ezk 43:2.
1d Dn 2:28.
2a Gn 2:9.

of Satan. 10 Do not be afraid of the sufferings that are coming to you. Look, the devil will send some of you to prison *to put you to the test*, and you must face hardship for *ten days.*[b] Even if you have to die, keep faithful, and I will give you the crown of life for your prize. 11 Let anyone who can hear, listen to what the Spirit is saying to the churches: for those who prove victorious will come to no harm from the second death."

3 Pergamum

12 'Write to the angel of the church in Pergamum and say, "Here is the message of the one who has the sharp sword, double-edged: 13 I know where you live, in the place where Satan is enthroned, and that you still hold firmly to my name, and did not disown your faith in me even when my faithful witness, Antipas, was killed among you, where Satan lives.

14 "Nevertheless, I have one or two charges against you: some of you are followers of Balaam, who taught Balak to set a trap for the Israelites so that they committed adultery by eating food that had been sacrificed to idols; 15 and among you too there are some also who follow the teaching of the Nicolaitans. 16 So repent, or I shall soon come to you and attack these people with the sword out of my mouth. 17 Let anyone who can hear, listen to what the Spirit is saying to the churches: to those who prove victorious I will give some hidden manna and a white stone, with *a new name* written on it, known only to the person who receives it."

4 Thyatira

18 'Write to the angel of the church in Thyatira and say, "Here is the message of the Son of God who has eyes like a burning flame and feet like burnished bronze: 19 I know your activities, your love, your faith, your service and your perseverance, and I know how you are still making progress. 20 Nevertheless, I have a complaint to make: you tolerate the woman Jezebel[c] who claims to be a prophetess, and by her teaching she is luring my servants away to commit the adultery of eating food which has been sacrificed to idols. 21 I have given her time to repent but she is not willing to repent of her adulterous life. 22 Look, I am consigning her to a bed of pain, and all her partners in adultery to great hardship, unless they repent of their practices; 23 and I will see that her children die, so that all the churches realise that it is I who *test motives and thoughts and repay* you *as your deeds deserve.*[d] 24 But on the rest of you in Thyatira, all of you who have not accepted this teaching or learnt the deep secrets of Satan, as they are called, I am not laying any other burden; 25 but hold on firmly to what you already have until I come. 26 To anyone who proves victorious, and keeps working for me until the end, *I will give* the authority over *the nations* 27 which I myself have been given by my Father, *to rule them with an iron sceptre and shatter them like so many pots.*[e] 28 And I will give such a person the Morning Star. 29 Let anyone who can hear, listen to what the Spirit is saying to the churches."

5 Sardis

3 'Write to the angel of the church in Sardis and say, "Here is the message of the one who holds the seven spirits of God and the seven stars: I know about your behaviour: how you are reputed to be alive and yet are dead. 2 Wake up; put some resolve into what little vigour you have left: it is dying fast. So far I have failed to notice anything in your behaviour that my God could possibly call perfect; 3 remember how you first heard the message. Hold on to that. Repent! If you do not wake up, I shall come to you like a thief, and you will have no idea at what hour I shall come upon you. 4 There are a few in Sardis, it is true, who have kept their robes unstained, and they are fit to come with me, dressed in white. 5 Anyone who proves victorious will be dressed, like these, in white robes; I shall not blot that name out of the book of life, but acknowledge it in the presence of my Father and his angels. 6 Let anyone who can hear, listen to what the Spirit is saying to the churches."

6 Philadelphia

7 'Write to the angel of the church in Philadelphia and say, "Here is the message of the

2b Dn 1:12.
2c cf. 2 K 9:22.
2d Jr 11:20; 17:10.
2e Ps 2:8–9.

holy and true one who *has the key of David*, so that *when he opens, no one will close, and when he closes, no one will open:*[a] [8]I know about your activities. Look, I have opened in front of you a door that no one will be able to close—and I know that though you are not very strong, you have kept my commandments and not disowned my name. [9]Look, I am going to make the synagogue of Satan—those who falsely claim to be Jews, but are liars, because they are no such thing—I will make them *come and fall at your feet* and recognize that *I have loved you.*[b] [10]Because you have kept my commandment to persevere, I will keep you safe in the time of trial which is coming for the whole world, to put the people of the world to the test. [11]I am coming soon: hold firmly to what you already have, and let no one take your victor's crown away from you. [12]Anyone who proves victorious I will make into a pillar in the sanctuary of my God, and it will stay there for ever; I will inscribe on it the name of my God and the name of the city of my God, the new Jerusalem which is coming down from my God in heaven, and my own new name as well. [13]Let anyone who can hear, listen to what the Spirit is saying to the churches."

7 Laodicea

[14]'Write to the angel of the church in Laodicea and say, "Here is the message of the Amen,[c] the trustworthy, the true witness, the Principle of God's creation: [15]I know about your activities: how you are neither cold nor hot. I wish you were one or the other, [16]but since you are neither hot nor cold, but only lukewarm, I will spit you out of my mouth. [17]You say to yourself: I am rich, I have made a fortune and have everything I want, never realising that you are wretchedly and pitiably poor, and blind and naked too. [18]I warn you, buy from me the gold that has been tested in the fire to make you truly rich, and white robes to clothe you and hide your shameful nakedness, and ointment to put on your eyes to enable you to see. [19]I *reprove* and *train those whom I love:*[d] so repent in real earnest. [20]Look, I am standing at the door, knocking. If one of you hears me calling and opens the door, I will come in to share a meal at that person's side. [21]Anyone who proves victorious I will allow to share my throne, just as I have myself overcome and have taken my seat with my Father on his throne. [22]Let anyone who can hear, listen to what the Spirit is saying to the churches." '

II: THE PROPHETIC VISIONS

A: THE PRELUDE TO THE GREAT DAY OF GOD

God entrusts the future of the world to the Lamb[a]

4 Then, in my vision, I saw a door open in heaven and heard the same voice speaking to me, the voice like a trumpet, saying, 'Come up here: I will show you *what is to take place* in the future.' [2]With that, I fell into ecstasy and I saw a throne standing in heaven, and the *One* who was *sitting on the throne*, [3]and the One sitting there looked like a diamond and a ruby. There was a rainbow encircling the throne, and this looked like an emerald. [4]Round the throne in a circle were twenty-four thrones, and on them twenty-four elders sitting, dressed in white robes with golden crowns on their heads. [5]Flashes of lightning were coming from the throne, and the sound of peals of thunder, and in front of the throne there were seven flaming lamps burning, the seven Spirits of God. [6]In front of the throne was a sea as transparent as crystal. *In the middle* of the throne and around it, were *four living creatures all studded with eyes*, in front and behind. [7]*The first* living creature was like *a lion, the second* like *a bull, the third* living creature had a *human face*, and *the fourth* living creature was like a flying *eagle*. [8]*Each* of the four living creatures had *six wings* and

3a Is 22:22.
3b Is 43:3.
3c *Amen* is Hebr. for truth, firmness.
3d Pr 3:12.
4a The scene draws on Ezk 1; 10 and Is 6.

was studded with eyes all the way round as well
as inside; and day and night they never
stopped singing:

Holy, Holy, Holy
is the Lord God, the Almighty;
who was, and is and is to come.'

9 Every time the living creatures glorified and
honoured and gave thanks to the One sitting
on the throne, *who lives for ever and ever*, 10 the
twenty-four elders prostrated themselves
before him to worship the One *who lives for
ever and ever*, and threw down their crowns
in front of the throne, saying:

11 You are worthy, our Lord and God,
to receive glory and honour and power,
for you made the whole universe;
by your will, when it did not exist,
it was created.

5 I saw that in the right hand of the One
sitting on the throne there was *a scroll that
was written on back and front*[a] and was sealed
with seven seals. 2 Then I saw a powerful
angel who called with a loud voice, 'Who is
worthy to open the scroll and break its seals?'
3 But there was no one, in heaven or on the
earth or under the earth, who was able to
open the scroll and read it. 4 I wept bitterly
because nobody could be found to open the
scroll and read it, 5 but one of the elders said
to me, 'Do not weep. Look, *the Lion* of
the tribe *of Judah, the Root*[b] of David, has
triumphed, and so he will open the scroll and
its seven seals.'

6 Then I saw, in the middle of the throne
with its four living creatures and the circle of
the elders, a Lamb standing that seemed to
have been sacrificed; it had seven horns, and
it had seven eyes, which are the seven Spirits
that God has *sent out over the whole world.*[c]
7 The Lamb came forward to take the scroll
from the right hand of the One sitting on the
throne, 8 and when he took it, the four living
creatures prostrated themselves before him
and with them the twenty-four elders; each
one of them was holding a harp and had
a golden bowl full of incense which are the
prayers of the saints. 9 They sang a new
hymn:

You are worthy to take the scroll
and to break its seals,
because you were sacrificed,
and with your blood
you bought people for God
of every race, language, people and nation
10 and made them
a line of kings and priests[d] for God,
to rule the world.

11 In my vision, I heard the sound of an
immense number of angels gathered round
the throne and the living creatures and the
elders; there were *ten thousand times ten thou-
sand of them* and *thousands upon thousands*,[e]
12 loudly chanting:

Worthy is the Lamb that was sacrificed
to receive power, riches, wisdom,
strength, honour, glory and blessing.

13 Then I heard all the living things in
creation—everything that lives in heaven,
and on earth, and under the earth, and in the
sea, crying:

To the One seated on the throne
and to the Lamb,
be all praise, honour, glory and power,
for ever and ever.

14 And the four living creatures said, 'Amen';
and the elders prostrated themselves to
worship.

The Lamb breaks the seven seals

6 Then, in my vision, I saw the Lamb break
one of the seven seals, and I heard one of
the four living creatures shout in a voice like
thunder, 'Come!' 2 Immediately I saw a white
horse[a] appear, and its rider was holding a
bow; he was given a victor's crown and he
went away, to go from victory to victory.

3 When he broke the second seal, I heard
the second living creature shout, 'Come!'
4 And out came another horse, bright red,
and its rider was given this duty: to take away
peace from the earth and set people killing
each other. He was given a huge sword.

5 When he broke the third seal, I heard the
third living creature shout, 'Come!' Immedi-

5a Ezk 2:9.
5b Gn 49:9; Is 11:10.
5c Zc 4:10.
5d Is 61:6.
5e Dn 7:10.
6a The horsemen echo Zc 1:8–10; 6:1–3.

ately I saw a black horse appear, and its rider
was holding a pair of scales; 6and I seemed to
hear a voice shout from among the four living
creatures and say, 'A day's wages for a quart
of corn, and a day's wages for three quarts of
barley, but do not tamper with the oil or the
wine.'
7When he broke the fourth seal, I heard
the voice of the fourth living creature shout,
'Come!' 8Immediately I saw another horse
appear, deathly pale, and its rider was called
Death, and Hades followed at its heels.

They were given authority over a quarter
of the earth, *to kill by the sword, by famine, by
plague and through wild beasts.*[b]
9When he broke the fifth seal, I saw under-
neath the altar the souls of all the people who
had been killed on account of the Word of
God, for witnessing to it. 10They shouted in
a loud voice, 'Holy, true Master, how much
longer will you wait before you pass sentence
and take vengeance for our death on the
inhabitants of the earth?' 11Each of them was
given a white robe, and they were told to be
patient a little longer, until the roll was
completed of their fellow-servants and
brothers who were still to be killed as they
had been.
12In my vision, when he broke the sixth
seal, there was a violent earthquake and the
sun went as black as coarse sackcloth;
the moon turned red as blood all over, 13and
the stars of the sky fell[c] onto the earth *like figs*
dropping from a fig tree when a high wind
shakes it; 14the *sky disappeared like a scroll
rolling up* and all the mountains and islands
were shaken from their places. 15Then all the
kings of the earth, the governors and the
commanders, the rich people and the men of
influence, the whole population, slaves and
citizens, *hid in caverns and among the rocks of
the mountains.*[d] 16*They said to the mountains*[e]
and the rocks, '*Fall on us* and hide us away
from the One who sits on the throne and from
the retribution of the Lamb. 17For *the Great
Day of his retribution* has come, *and who can
face it?*'[f]

God's servants will be preserved[a]

7 Next I saw four angels, standing at *the four
corners of the earth,*[b] holding back the
four winds of the world to keep them from
blowing over the land or the sea or any tree.
2Then I saw another angel rising where the
sun rises, carrying the seal of the living God;
he called in a powerful voice to the four angels
whose duty was to devastate land and sea,
3'Wait before you do any damage on land or
at sea or to the trees, until we have put the
seal on the foreheads[c] of the servants of our
God.' 4And I heard how many had been
sealed: a hundred and forty-four thousand,[d]
out of all the tribes of Israel.

5From the tribe of Judah, twelve thousand
had been sealed;
from the tribe of Reuben, twelve thousand;
from the tribe of Gad, twelve thousand;
6from the tribe of Asher, twelve thousand;
from the tribe of Naphtali, twelve
thousand;
from the tribe of Manasseh, twelve
thousand;
7from the tribe of Simeon, twelve thousand;
from the tribe of Levi, twelve thousand;
from the tribe of Issachar, twelve
thousand;
8from the tribe of Zebulun, twelve
thousand;
from the tribe of Joseph, twelve thousand;
and from the tribe of Benjamin, twelve
thousand had been sealed.

The rewarding of the saints[e]

9After that I saw that there was a huge
number, impossible for anyone to count, of
people from every nation, race, tribe and
language; they were standing in front of the
throne and in front of the Lamb, dressed in
white robes and holding palms in their hands.
They shouted in a loud voice, 10'Salvation to
our God, who sits on the throne, and to
the Lamb!' 11And all the angels who were
standing in a circle round the throne,

6b Ezk 14:21.
6c Is 34:4.
6d Ho 10:8.
6e Is 2:10, 18, 19.
6f Jl 2:11; 3:4.
7a =14:1–5.
7b Ezk 7:2.
7c Ezk 9:4.
7d The sacred number 12 squared and multiplied by 1000 indicates the totality of the saved.
7e =15:2–5.

surrounding the elders and the four living
creatures, prostrated themselves before the
throne, and touched the ground with their
foreheads, worshipping God 12 with these
words:

> Amen. Praise and glory and wisdom,
> thanksgiving and honour
> and power and strength
> to our God for ever and ever. Amen.

13 One of the elders then spoke and asked
me, 'Who are these people, dressed in white
robes, and where have they come from?' 14 I
answered him, 'You can tell me, sir.' Then
he said, 'These are the people who have been
through the great trial; they have washed
their robes white again in the blood of the
Lamb. 15 That is why they are standing in
front of God's throne and serving him day
and night in his sanctuary; and the One who
sits on the throne will spread his tent over
them. 16 *They will never hunger or thirst* again;
sun and scorching wind will never plague them,
17 because the Lamb who is at the heart of the
throne *will be their shepherd and will guide
them to springs of living water*;[f] and God *will
wipe away all tears from their eyes*.'[g]

The seventh seal

8 The Lamb then broke the seventh seal,
and there was silence in heaven for about
half an hour.

The prayers of the saints bring the coming of the Great Day nearer

2 Next I saw seven trumpets being given to
the seven angels who stand in the presence
of God. 3 Another angel, who had a golden
censer, came and stood at the altar. A large
quantity of incense was given to him to offer
with the prayers of all the saints on the golden
altar that stood in front of the throne; 4 and
so from the angel's hand the smoke of the
incense went up in the presence of God and
with it the prayers of the saints. 5 Then the
angel took the censer and *filled it from the fire
of the altar*,[a] which he then hurled down onto
the earth; immediately there came peals of
thunder and flashes of lightning, and the
earth shook.

The first four trumpets[b]

6 The seven angels that had the seven trum-
pets now made ready to sound them. 7 The
first blew his trumpet and, with that, hail and
fire, mixed with blood, were hurled on the
earth: a third of the earth was burnt up, and
a third of all trees, and every blade of grass was
burnt. 8 The second angel blew his trumpet,
and it was as though a great mountain blazing
with fire was hurled into the sea: a third of
the sea turned into blood, 9 a third of all the
living things in the sea were killed, and a
third of all ships were destroyed. 10 The third
angel blew his trumpet, and a huge star fell
from the sky, burning like a ball of fire, and
it fell on a third of all rivers and on the
springs of water; 11 this was the star called
Wormwood, and a third of all water turned
to wormwood, so that many people died; the
water had become so bitter. 12 The fourth
angel blew his trumpet, and a third of the
sun and a third of the moon and a third of
the stars were blasted, so that the light went
out of a third of them and the day lost a third
of its illumination, and likewise the night.

13 In my vision, I heard an eagle, calling
aloud as it flew high overhead, 'Disaster,
disaster, disaster, on all the people on earth
at the sound of the other three trumpets
which the three angels have yet to blow!'

The fifth trumpet

9 Then the fifth angel blew his trumpet, and
I saw a star that had fallen from heaven
onto the earth, and the angel was given the
key to the shaft leading down to the Abyss.
2 When he unlocked the shaft of the
Abyss, *smoke rose* out of the Abyss *like the
smoke from a* huge *furnace*[a] so that the sun
and the sky were darkened by the smoke from
the Abyss, 3 and out of the smoke dropped
locusts onto the earth: they were given the
powers that scorpions have on the earth:
4 they were forbidden to harm any fields or
crops or trees and told to attack only those
people who were without God's seal on their

7f Is 49:10.
7g =21:4; Is 25:8.
8a Lv 16:12; Ezk 10:2.
8b =16:1–9.
9a Ex 19:18.

foreheads. 5They were not to kill them, but to give them anguish for five months, and the anguish was to be the anguish of a scorpion's sting. 6When this happens, *people will long for death and not find it anywhere*;[b] they will want to die and death will evade them.

7These locusts *looked like horses*[c] armoured *for battle*; they had what looked like gold crowns on their heads, and their faces looked human, 8and their hair was like women's hair, and *teeth like lion's teeth.* 9They had body-armour like iron breastplates, and the noise of their wings sounded like *the racket of chariots with many horses charging.* 10Their tails were like scorpions' tails, with stings, and with their tails they were able to torture people for five months. 11As their leader they had their emperor, the angel of the Abyss, whose name in Hebrew is Abaddon, and in Greek Apollyon.[d]

12That was the first of the disasters; there are still two more to come.

The sixth trumpet

13The sixth angel blew his trumpet, and I heard a single voice issuing from the four horns of the golden altar in God's presence. 14It spoke to the sixth angel with the trumpet, and said, 'Release the four angels that are chained up at the great river Euphrates.' 15These four angels had been ready for this hour of this day of this month of this year, and ready to destroy a third of the human race. 16I learnt how many there were in their army: twice ten thousand times ten thousand mounted men. 17In my vision I saw the horses, and the riders with their breastplates of flame colour, hyacinth-blue and sulphur-yellow; the horses had lions' heads, and fire, smoke and sulphur were coming from their mouths. 18It was by these three plagues, the fire, the smoke and the sulphur coming from their mouths, that the one third of the human race was killed. 19All the horses' power was in their mouths and their tails: their tails were like snakes, and had heads which inflicted wounds. 20But the rest of the human race, who escaped death by these plagues, refused either to abandon *their own handiwork*[e] or to stop worshipping devils, the *idols made of gold, silver, bronze, stone and wood*[f] that can neither see nor hear nor move. 21Nor did they give up their murdering, or witchcraft, or fornication or stealing.

The imminence of the last punishment

10 Then I saw another powerful angel coming down from heaven, wrapped in cloud, with a rainbow over his head; his face was like the sun, and his legs were pillars of fire. 2In his hand he had a small scroll, unrolled; he put his right foot in the sea and his left foot on the land 3and he shouted so loud, it was *like a lion roaring.*[a] At this, the seven claps of thunder made themselves heard 4and when the seven thunderclaps had sounded, I was preparing to write, when I heard a voice from heaven say to me, 'Keep the words of the seven thunderclaps secret and do not write them down.' 5Then the angel that I had seen, standing on the sea and the land, *raised his right hand to heaven,*[b] 6and *swore by him who lives for ever* and ever, *and made heaven and all that it contains,*[c] and *earth and all it contains*, and *the sea and all it contains*, 'The time of waiting is over; 7at the time when the seventh angel is heard sounding his trumpet, the mystery of God will be fulfilled, just as he announced in the gospel to *his servants the prophets*.'

The seer eats the small scroll

8Then I heard the voice I had heard from heaven speaking to me again. 'Go', it said, 'and take that open scroll from the hand of the angel standing on sea and land.' 9I went to the angel and asked him to give me the small scroll, and he said, 'Take it and eat it; it will turn your stomach sour, but it will taste as sweet as honey.' 10So I took it out of the angel's hand, and *I ate it and it tasted sweet as honey*,[d] but when I had eaten it my stomach turned sour. 11Then I was told, 'You are

9b Jb 3:21.
9c The details of vv. 7–9 echo Jl 1 and 2.
9d Both names mean 'Destroyer'.
9e Is 17:8.
9f Dn 5:4.
10a Am 1:2; 3:8.
10b Dt 32:40.
10c Ne 9:6.
10d Ezk 3:1–13.

to prophesy again, this time against many different nations and countries and languages and kings.'

The two witnesses

11 Then I was given a long cane like a measuring rod, and I was told, 'Get up and measure God's sanctuary, and the altar, and the people who worship there; [2]but exclude the outer court and do not measure it, because it has been handed over to gentiles—they will trample on the holy city for forty-two months.[a] [3]But I shall send my two witnesses to prophesy for twelve hundred and sixty days, wearing sackcloth. [4]These are the *two olive trees*[b] and the two lamps *in attendance on the Lord of the world*.[c] [5]Fire comes from their mouths and consumes their enemies if anyone tries to harm them; and anyone who tries to harm them will certainly be killed in this way. [6]They have the power to lock up the sky so that it does not rain as long as they are prophesying; they have the power to turn water into blood and strike the whole world with any plague as often as they like. [7]When they have completed their witnessing, the beast that comes out of the Abyss *is going to make war on them and overcome them*[d] and kill them. [8]Their corpses lie in the main street of the great city[e] known by the symbolic names Sodom and Egypt, in which their Lord was crucified. [9]People of every race, tribe, language and nation stare at their corpses, for three-and-a-half days, not letting them be buried, [10]and the people of the world are glad about it and celebrate the event by giving presents to each other, because these two prophets have been a plague to the people of the world.'

[11]After the three-and-a-half days, *God breathed life into them and they stood up on their feet*,[f] and everybody who saw it happen was terrified; [12]then I heard a loud voice from heaven say to them, 'Come up here,' and while their enemies were watching, they went up to heaven in a cloud. [13]Immediately, there was a violent earthquake, and a tenth of the city collapsed; seven thousand persons were killed in the earthquake, and the survivors, overcome with fear, could only praise the God of heaven.

[14]That was the second of the disasters; the third is to come quickly after it.

The seventh trumpet

[15]Then the seventh angel blew his trumpet, and voices could be heard shouting in heaven, calling, 'The kingdom of the world has become the kingdom of our Lord and his Christ, and he will reign for ever and ever.' [16]The twenty-four elders, enthroned in the presence of God, prostrated themselves and touched the ground with their foreheads worshipping God [17]with these words, 'We give thanks to you, Almighty Lord God, He who is, He who was, for assuming your great power and beginning your reign. [18]*The nations were in uproar*[g] and now the time has come for your retribution, and for the dead to be judged, and for *your servants the prophets*, for the saints and for *those who fear* your name, *small and great alike*, to be rewarded. The time has come to destroy those who are destroying the earth.'

[19]Then the sanctuary of God in heaven opened, and the ark of the covenant could be seen inside it. Then came flashes of lightning, peals of thunder and an earthquake and violent hail.

The vision of the woman and the dragon

12 Now a great sign appeared in heaven: a woman, robed with the sun, standing on the moon, and on her head a crown of twelve stars. [2]She was pregnant, and in labour, crying aloud in the pangs of childbirth. [3]Then a second sign appeared in the sky: there was a huge red dragon with seven heads and ten horns, and each of the seven heads crowned with a coronet. [4]Its tail swept a third of *the stars from the sky and hurled them to the ground*,[a] and the dragon

---

11a Cf. Dn 7:25. Half seven years, so the opposite of completion, a short and incomplete time of persecution.
11b Zc 4:3, 14.
11c 2 K 1:10.
11d Dn 7:21.
11e Also called Babylon. It is the centre of evil and persecution, possibly Rome.
11f Ezk 37:5, 10.
11g Ps 2:1, 5, followed by Am 3:7; Ps 115:13.
12a Dn 8:10.

stopped in front of the woman as she was at
the point of giving birth, so that it could eat
the child as soon as it was born. 5The woman
was delivered of a boy,[b] the son who was *to*
rule all the nations with an iron sceptre, and the
child was taken straight up to God and to his
throne, 6while the woman escaped into the
desert, where God had prepared a place for
her to be looked after for twelve hundred and
sixty days.
7And now war broke out in heaven, when
Michael[c] with his angels attacked the dragon.
The dragon fought back with his angels, 8but
they were defeated and driven out of heaven.
9The great dragon, the primeval serpent,
known as the devil or Satan, who had led all
the world astray, was hurled down to the
earth and his angels were hurled down with
him. 10Then I heard a voice shout from
heaven, 'Salvation and power and empire for
ever have been won by our God, and all
authority for his Christ, now that the accuser,
who accused our brothers day and night
before our God, has been brought down.
11They have triumphed over him by the blood
of the Lamb and by the word to which they
bore witness, because even in the face of
death they did not cling to life. 12So let the
heavens rejoice and all who live there; but
for you, earth and sea, disaster is coming—
because the devil has gone down to you
in a rage, knowing that he has little time
left.'
13As soon as the dragon found himself
hurled down to the earth, he sprang in pursuit
of the woman, the mother of the male child,
14but she was given a pair of the great eagle's
wings to fly away from the serpent into the
desert, to the place where she was to be
looked after for *a time, two times and half a*
time.[d] 15So the serpent vomited water from
his mouth, like a river, after the woman, to
sweep her away in the current, 16but the earth
came to her rescue; it opened its mouth and
swallowed the river spewed from the dragon's
mouth. 17Then the dragon was enraged with
the woman and went away to make war on
the rest of her children, who obey God's
commandments and have in themselves the
witness of Jesus.

The dragon delegates his power to the beast

18And I took my stand on the seashore.
13 Then I saw *a beast*[a] *emerge from the sea*:
it had seven heads and ten horns, with
a coronet on each of its ten horns, and its
heads were marked with blasphemous titles.
2I saw that the beast *was like a leopard*, with
paws like *a bear* and a mouth like *a lion*; the
dragon had handed over to it his own power
and his throne and his immense authority. 3I
saw that one of its heads seemed to have had
a fatal wound but that this deadly injury had
healed and the whole world had marvelled
and followed the beast. 4They prostrated
themselves in front of the dragon because
he had given the beast his authority; and
they prostrated themselves in front of the
beast, saying, 'Who can compare with the
beast? Who can fight against it?' 5The beast
was allowed *to mouth its boasts* and blas-
phemies and to be active for forty-two
months; 6and it mouthed its blasphemies
against God, against his name, his heavenly
Tent and all those who are sheltered there.
7It was allowed *to make war against the saints*
and conquer them, and given power over every
race, people, language and nation; 8and all
people of the world will worship it, that is,
everybody whose name has not been written
down since the foundation of the world in
the sacrificial Lamb's book of life. 9Let
anyone who can hear, listen: 10*Those for*
captivity to captivity; those for death by *the*
sword to death by *the sword*.[b] This is why the
saints must have perseverance and faith.

The false prophet as the slave of the beast

11Then I saw a second beast, emerging from
the ground; it had two horns like a lamb, but
made a noise like a dragon. 12This second
beast exercised all the power of the first beast,
on its behalf making the world and all its
people worship the first beast, whose deadly
injury had healed. 13And it worked great
miracles, even to calling down fire from
heaven onto the earth while people watched.
14Through the miracles which it was allowed
to do on behalf of the first beast, it was able

12b Is 66:7, followed by Ps 2:9. The woman is the people of God, and the boy is the Messiah.
12c God's champion in Dn 10:13; 12:1.
12d *See* 11*a* note.
13a The vision draws on Dn 7.
13b Jr 15:2.

to lead astray the people of the world and persuade them to put up a statue in honour of the beast that had been wounded by the sword and still lived. 15It was allowed to breathe life into this statue, so that the statue of the beast was able to speak, and to have *anyone who refused to worship the statue*[c] of the beast put to death. 16It compelled everyone—small and great alike, rich and poor, slave and citizen—to be branded on the right hand or on the forehead, 17and made it illegal for anyone to buy or sell anything unless he had been branded with the name of the beast or with the number of its name.

18There is need for shrewdness here: anyone clever may interpret the number of the beast: it is the number of a human being, the number 666.[d]

The companions of the Lamb[a]

14 Next in my vision I saw Mount Zion, and standing on it the Lamb who had with him a hundred and forty-four thousand people, all with his name and his Father's name written on their foreheads. 2I heard a sound coming out of heaven like the sound of the ocean or the roar of thunder; it was like the sound of harpists playing their harps. 3There before the throne they were singing a new hymn in the presence of the four living creatures and the elders, a hymn that could be learnt only by the hundred and forty-four thousand who had been redeemed from the world. 4These are the sons who have kept their virginity and not been defiled with women; they *follow* the Lamb wherever he goes; they, out of all people, have been redeemed to be *the first-fruits for God*[b] and for the Lamb. 5*No lie*[c] was found in their mouths and no fault can be found in them.

Angels announce the Day of Judgement

6Then I saw another angel, flying high overhead, sent to announce the gospel of eternity to all who live on the earth, every nation, race, language and tribe. 7He was calling, 'Fear God and glorify him, because the time has come for him to sit in judgement; worship *the maker of heaven and earth and sea*[d] and the springs of water.'

8A second angel followed him, calling, '*Babylon has fallen, Babylon the Great has fallen*, Babylon which gave the whole world *the wine of retribution* to drink.'[e]

9A third angel followed, shouting aloud, 'All those who worship the beast and his statue, or have had themselves branded on the hand or forehead, 10will be made to drink the wine of God's fury which is ready, undiluted, in his cup of retribution; in *fire and brimstone*[f] they will be tortured in the presence of the holy angels and the Lamb 11and *the smoke* of their torture will *rise for ever and ever.*[g] There will be no respite, *night or day*, for those who worship the beast or its statue or accept branding with its name.' 12This is why there must be perseverance in the saints who keep the commandments of God and faith in Jesus. 13Then I heard a voice from heaven say to me, 'Write down: Blessed are those who die in the Lord! Blessed indeed, the Spirit says; now they can rest for ever after their work, since their good deeds go with them.'

The harvest and vintage of the gentiles[h]

14Now in my vision I saw a white *cloud* and, *sitting on it, one like a son of man* with a gold crown on his head and a sharp sickle in his hand. 15Then another angel came out of the sanctuary and shouted at the top of his voice to the one sitting on the cloud, '*Ply* your *sickle* and reap: harvest time has come and *the harvest* of the earth *is ripe*.' 16Then the one sitting on the cloud set his sickle to work on the earth, and the harvest of earth was reaped.

17Another angel, who also carried a sharp sickle, came out of the temple in heaven, 18and the angel in charge of the fire left the altar and shouted at the top of his voice to the one with the sharp sickle, 'Put your sickle in,

---

13c Dn 3:5–7, 15.
13d 6=7–1, so 666=triple imperfection. It may also symbolise a name.
14a =7:1–8.
14b Jr 2:2–3.
14c Zp 3:13.
14d Ex 20:11.
14e =18:2–3; cf. Is 21:9; 51:17.
14f Gn 19:24.
14g Is 34:9–10.
14h Dn 7:13; Jl 4:12–13.

and harvest the bunches from the vine of the
earth; all its grapes are ripe.' 19 So the angel
set his sickle to work on the earth and
harvested the whole vintage of the earth
and put it into a huge winepress, the wine-
press of God's anger, 20 outside the city, where
it was trodden until the blood that came out
of the winepress was up to the horses' bridles
as far away as sixteen hundred furlongs.

The hymn of Moses and the Lamb[a]

15 And I saw in heaven another sign,
great and wonderful: seven angels were
bringing the seven plagues that are the last
of all, because they exhaust the anger of God.
2 I seemed to be looking at a sea of crystal
suffused with fire, and standing by the lake
of glass, those who had fought against the
beast and won, and against his statue and the
number which is his name. They all had
harps from God, 3 and they were singing the
hymn of Moses,[b] the servant of God, and the
hymn of the Lamb:

How great and wonderful
  are all your works,
Lord God Almighty;
upright and true are all your ways,
King of nations.
4 *Who does not revere*
  and *glorify your name, O Lord?*
For you alone are holy,
and all nations will come and adore you
for the many acts of saving justice
  you have shown.

The seven bowls of plagues

5 After this, in my vision, the sanctuary, the
tent of the Testimony, opened in heaven,
6 and out came the seven angels with the seven
plagues, wearing pure white linen, fastened
round their waists with belts of gold. 7 One
of the four living creatures gave the seven
angels seven golden bowls filled with the
anger of God who lives for ever and ever.
8 *The smoke from the glory* and the power *of*
God filled the temple[c] so that no one could go
into it until the seven plagues of the seven
angels were completed.

16 Then I heard a loud voice[a] from the
sanctuary calling to the seven angels,
'Go, and empty the seven bowls of God's
anger over the earth.'

2 The first angel went and emptied his bowl
over the earth; at once, on all the people who
had been branded with the mark of the beast
and had worshipped its statue, there came
disgusting and virulent sores.

3 The second angel emptied his bowl over
the sea, and it turned to blood, like the blood
of a corpse, and every living creature in the
sea died.

4 The third angel emptied his bowl into the
rivers and springs of water and they turned
into blood. 5 Then I heard the angel of water
say, 'You are the Upright One, He who is,
He who was, the Holy One, for giving this
verdict: 6 they spilt the blood of the saints and
the prophets, and blood is what you have
given them to drink; it is what they deserve.'
7 And I heard the altar itself say, 'Truly, Lord
God Almighty, the punishments you give are
true and just.'

8 The fourth angel emptied his bowl over
the sun and it was made to scorch people with
its flames; 9 but though people were scorched
by the fierce heat of it, they cursed the name
of God who had the power to cause such
plagues, and they would not repent and
glorify him.

10 The fifth angel emptied his bowl over the
throne of the beast and its whole empire was
plunged into darkness. People were biting
their tongues for pain, 11 but instead of
repenting for what they had done, they
cursed the God of heaven because of their
pains and sores.

12 The sixth angel emptied his bowl over
the great river Euphrates; all the water dried
up so that a way was made for the kings of
the East to come in. 13 Then from the jaws of
dragon and beast and false prophet I saw
three foul spirits come; they looked like frogs
14 and in fact were demon spirits, able to work
miracles, going out to all the kings of the
world to call them together for the war of the
Great Day of God the Almighty. — 15 Look, I
shall come like a thief. Blessed is anyone who
has kept watch, and has kept his clothes on,
so that he does not go out naked and expose

15a =7:1–8.
15b Ex 15; in fact the hymn uses Jr 10:7; Ps 86:9.
15c 1 K 8:10.
16a =8:6–12.

his shame. — [16]They called the kings together
at the place called, in Hebrew, Armageddon.[b]

[17]The seventh angel emptied his bowl into
the air, and a great voice boomed out from
the sanctuary, 'The end has come.' [18]Then
there were flashes of lightning and peals of
thunder and a violent earthquake, *unparalleled since* humanity *first came into existence*.[c]
[19]The Great City was split into three parts
and the cities of the world collapsed; Babylon
the Great was not forgotten: God made her
drink the full winecup of his retribution.
[20]Every island vanished and the mountains
disappeared; [21]and hail, with great hailstones
weighing a talent each, fell from the sky on
the people. They cursed God for sending a
plague of hail; it was the most terrible plague.

B: THE PUNISHMENT OF BABYLON

The great prostitute

17 One of the seven angels that had the
seven bowls came to speak to me, and
said, 'Come here and I will show you the
punishment of the great prostitute *who* is
enthroned beside abundant waters,[a] [2]with
whom all the kings of the earth have prostituted themselves, and who has made all the
population of the world drunk with the wine
of her adultery.' [3]He took me in spirit to a
desert, and there I saw a woman riding a
scarlet beast which had seven heads and ten
horns and had blasphemous titles written all
over it. [4]The woman was dressed in purple
and scarlet and glittered with gold and jewels
and pearls, and she was holding a gold
winecup filled with the disgusting filth of her
prostitution; [5]on her forehead was written a
name, a cryptic name: 'Babylon the Great,
the mother of all the prostitutes and all the
filthy practices on the earth.' [6]I saw that she
was drunk, drunk with the blood of the
saints, and the blood of the martyrs of Jesus;
and when I saw her, I was completely mystified. [7]The angel said to me, 'Do you not
understand? I will tell you the meaning of
this woman, and of the beast she is riding,
with the seven heads and the ten horns.

The symbolism of the beast and the prostitute

[8]'The beast you have seen was once alive and
is alive no longer; it is yet to come up from
the Abyss, but only to go to its destruction.
And the people of the world, whose names
have not been written since the beginning of
the world in the book of life, will be astonished when they see how the beast was once
alive and is alive no longer, and is still to
come.

[9]'This calls for shrewdness. The seven
heads are the seven hills, on which the woman
is sitting. [10]The seven heads are also seven
emperors. Five of them have already gone,
one is here now, and one is yet to come; once
here, he must stay for a short while. [11]The
beast, who was alive and is alive no longer,
is at the same time the eighth and one of the
seven, and he is going to his destruction.

[12]'*The ten horns* which you saw *are ten kings*[b]
who have not yet been given their royal power
but will have royal authority only for a single
hour and in association with the beast. [13]They
are all of one mind in putting their strength
and their powers at the beast's disposal, [14]and
they will go to war against the Lamb; but
because the Lamb is *Lord of lords* and *King
of kings*,[c] he will defeat them, he and his
followers, the called, the chosen, the
trustworthy.'

[15]The angel continued, 'The waters you
saw, beside which the prostitute was sitting,
are all the peoples, the populations, the
nations and the languages. [16]But the ten
horns and the beast will turn against the
prostitute, and *tear off* her *clothes* and leave
her stark naked;[d] then they will eat her flesh
and burn the remains in the fire. [17]In fact,
God has influenced their minds to do what
he intends, to agree together to put their
royal powers at the beast's disposal until the
time when God's words shall be fulfilled.
[18]The woman you saw is the great city which
has authority over all the rulers on earth.'

16b i.e. the mountains of Megiddo, symbol of disaster since King Josiah was killed there, 2 K 23:29.
16c Dn 12:1.
17a Jr 51:13. The seven heads are the seven hills of Rome.
17b Dn 7:24.
17c Dn 10:17.
17d Ezk 16:39.

An angel announces the fall of Babylon[a]

18 After this, I saw another angel come
down from heaven, with great author-
ity given to him; *the earth shone with his glory*.
2 At the top of his voice he shouted,[b] '*Babylon
has fallen, Babylon* the Great *has fallen*, and
has become *the haunt of devils* and a lodging
for every foul spirit and dirty, loathsome
bird. 3 All the nations have drunk deep of the
wine of her prostitution; every king on the
earth has prostituted himself with her, and
every merchant grown rich through her
debauchery.'

The people of God summoned to flee

4 Another voice spoke from heaven; I heard
it say, 'Come out, my people, away from her,
so that you do not share in her crimes and
have the same plagues to bear. 5 *Her sins have
reached up to the sky*, and God has her crimes
in mind: *treat her as she has treated others*. 6 She
must be paid double the amount she exacted.
She is to have a doubly strong cup of her own
mixture. 7 Every one of her pomps and orgies
is to be matched by a torture or an agony. *I
am enthroned as queen, she thinks; I am no
widow and will never know bereavement*. 8 For
that, *in one day*, the plagues will fall on her:
disease and mourning and famine. She will
be burned to the ground. The Lord God who
has condemned her is mighty.'

The people of the world mourn for Babylon.

9 'There will be mourning and weeping for
her by the kings of the earth who have
prostituted themselves with her and held
orgies with her. They see the smoke as she
burns, 10 while they keep at a safe distance
through fear of her anguish. They will say:

Mourn, mourn for this great city,
Babylon, so powerful a city,
in one short hour
your doom has come upon you.

11 'There will be weeping and distress over
her among all the traders of the earth when
no one is left to buy their cargoes of goods;
12 their stocks of gold and silver, jewels and
pearls, linen and purple and silks and scarlet;
all the sandalwood, every piece in ivory or
fine wood, in bronze or iron or marble;
13 the cinnamon and spices, the myrrh and
ointment and incense; wine, oil, flour and
corn; their stocks of cattle, sheep, horses
and chariots, their slaves and their human
cargo.

14 'All the fruits you had set your hearts
on have failed you; gone for ever, never to
return again, is your life of magnificence
and ease.

15 'The traders who had made a fortune out
of her will be standing at a safe distance
through fear of her anguish, mourning and
weeping. 16 They will be saying:

Mourn, mourn for this great city;
for all the linen and purple and scarlet
that you wore,
for all your finery of gold and jewels
and pearls;
17 your huge riches are all destroyed
within a single hour.'

All the captains and seafaring men, sailors
and all those who make a living from the sea
kept a safe distance, 18 watching the smoke as
she burned, and crying out, 'Has there ever
been a city as great as this!' 19 They threw
dust on their heads and said, with tears and
groans:

'Mourn, mourn for this great city
whose lavish living has made a fortune
for every owner of a sea-going ship,
ruined within a single hour.

20 'Now heaven, celebrate her downfall, and
all you saints, apostles and prophets: God
has given judgement for you against her.'

21 Then a powerful angel picked up a
boulder like a great millstone, and as he
hurled it into the sea, he said, 'That is how
the great city of Babylon is going to be hurled
down, never to be seen again.

22 Never again in you
will be heard
the song of harpists and minstrels,
the music of flute and trumpet;
never again will craftsmen of every skill
be found in you
or *the sound of the handmill*[c] be heard;

18a These songs of doom draw on OT threats to a proud city, especially Jr 50—51; Ezk 26—28; Is 47.
18b =14:8.
18c Jr 25:10, followed by Jr 7:34; Is 23:8.

23never again
will shine *the light of the lamp* in you,
never again will be heard in you
the voices of bridegroom and bride.
Your traders were the princes
of the earth,
all the nations were led astray
by your sorcery.

24In her was found the blood of prophets and
saints, and all the blood that was ever shed
on earth.'

Songs of victory in heaven

19 After this I heard what seemed to be
the great sound of a huge crowd in
heaven, singing, 'Alleluia! Salvation and
glory and power to our God! 2He judges
fairly, he punishes justly, and he has
condemned the great prostitute who
corrupted the earth with her prostitution; he
has avenged the blood of his servants which
she shed.' 3And again they sang, 'Alleluia!
The smoke of her *will rise for ever and ever.*'[a]
4Then the twenty-four elders and the four
living creatures threw themselves down and
worshipped God seated on his throne, and
they cried, 'Amen, Alleluia.'
5Then a voice came from the throne; it
said, 'Praise our God, you servants of his and
those who fear him, small and great alike.'[b]
6And I heard what seemed to be the voices of
a huge crowd, like the sound of the ocean
or the great roar of thunder, answering,
'Alleluia! The reign of the Lord our God
Almighty has begun; 7let us be glad and
joyful and give glory to God, because this is
the time for the marriage of the Lamb. 8His
bride is ready, and she has been able to dress
herself in dazzling white linen, because her
linen is made of the good deeds of the saints.'
9The angel said, 'Write this, "Blessed are
those who are invited to the wedding feast of
the Lamb," ' and he added, 'These words of
God are true.' 10Then I knelt at his feet to
worship him, but he said to me, 'Never do
that: I am your fellow-servant and the fellow-
servant of all your brothers who have in
themselves the witness of Jesus. God alone
you must worship.' The witness of Jesus is
the spirit of prophecy.

C: THE DESTRUCTION OF THE UNBELIEVERS

The first eschatological battle[c]

11And now I saw heaven open, and a white
horse appear; its rider was called Trust-
worthy and True; *in uprightness he judges* and
makes war. 12His eyes were flames of fire,
and he was crowned with many coronets; the
name written on him was known only to
himself, 13*his cloak was soaked in blood.* He is
known by the name, The Word of God.
14Behind him, dressed in linen of dazzling
white, rode the armies of heaven on white
horses. 15From his mouth came a sharp sword
with which to strike the unbelievers; he is
the one *who will rule them with an iron sceptre*,
and tread out the wine of Almighty God's
fierce retribution. 16On his cloak and on his
thigh a name was written: *King of kings* and
Lord of lords.
17I saw an angel standing in the sun, and
he shouted aloud to all the birds that were
flying high overhead in the sky, 'Come here.
Gather together at God's *great feast.* 18*You will
eat the flesh of kings*, and the flesh of great
generals and heroes, the flesh of horses and
their riders and of all kinds of people, citizens
and slaves, small and great alike.'
19Then I saw the beast, with all the kings
of the earth and their armies, gathered toge-
ther to fight the Rider and his army. 20But
the beast was taken prisoner, together with
the false prophet who had worked miracles on
the beast's behalf and by them had deceived
those who had accepted branding with the
mark of the beast and those who had wor-
shipped his statue. These two were hurled
alive into the fiery lake of burning sulphur.
21All the rest were killed by the sword of the
Rider, which came out of his mouth, and *all
the birds glutted themselves with their flesh.*

The reign of a thousand years

20 Then I saw an angel come down from
heaven with the key of the Abyss in his
hand and an enormous chain. 2He over-
powered the dragon, that primeval serpent
which is the devil and Satan, and chained

19a Is 34:10.
19b Ps 115:13.
19c =20:7–10. The OT allusions show this avenger to be the Messiah: Is 11:4; 63:1; Ps 2:9; Ezk 39:17, 20.

him up for a thousand years. 3He hurled him
into the Abyss and shut the entrance and
sealed it over him, to make sure he would
not lead the nations astray again until the
thousand years had passed. At the end of that
time he must be released, but only for a short
while.
4Then I saw thrones, where they took their
seats, and *on them was conferred the power to*
give judgement.[a] I saw the souls of all who had
been beheaded for having witnessed for Jesus
and for having preached God's word, and
those who refused to worship the beast or his
statue and would not accept the brand-mark
on their foreheads or hands; they came to
life, and reigned with Christ for a thousand
years.[b] 5The rest of the dead did not come to
life until the thousand years were over; this
is the first resurrection. 6Blessed and holy are
those who share in the first resurrection; the
second death has no power over them but
they will be priests of God and of Christ and
reign with him for a thousand years.
7When the thousand years are over,[c] Satan
will be released from his prison 8and will
come out to lead astray all the nations in the
four quarters of the earth, *Gog and Magog,*[d]
and mobilise them for war, his armies being
as many as the sands of the sea. 9They
came swarming over the entire country and
besieged the camp of the saints, which is the
beloved City. *But fire rained down on them*
from heaven[e] and consumed them. 10Then the
devil, who led them astray, was hurled into
the lake of fire and sulphur, where the beast
and the false prophet are, and their torture
will not come to an end, day or night, for
ever and ever.

The Last Judgement

11Then I saw a great white throne and the
One who was sitting on it. In his presence,
earth and sky vanished, leaving no trace. 12I
saw the dead, great and small alike, standing
in front of his throne while *the books lay open.*[f]
And another book was opened, which is the
book of life, and the dead were judged from
what was written in the books, as their deeds
deserved.
13The sea gave up all the dead who were in
it; 14Death and Hades were emptied of the
dead that were in them; and every one was
judged as his deeds deserved. Then Death
and Hades were hurled into the burning lake.
This burning lake is the second death; 15and
anybody whose name could not be found
written in the book of life was hurled into the
burning lake.

D: THE JERUSALEM OF THE FUTURE

The heavenly Jerusalem

21 Then I saw *a new heaven and a new*
earth;[a] the first heaven and the first
earth had disappeared now, and there was no
longer any sea. 2I saw the holy city, the new
Jerusalem, coming down out of heaven from
God, prepared as a bride dressed for her
husband. 3Then I heard a loud voice call from
the throne, 'Look, here God lives among
human beings. He will make *his home among*
them; they will be his people,[b] and he will be
their God, *God-with-them.* 4*He will wipe* away
all *tears from their eyes;*[c] there will be no more
death, and no more mourning or sadness or
pain. The world of the past has gone.'
5Then the One sitting on the throne spoke.
'Look, I am making the whole of creation
new. Write this, "What I am saying is trust-
worthy and will come true." ' 6Then he said
to me, 'It has already happened. I am the
Alpha and the Omega, the Beginning and the
End. I will give water from the well of life
free to anybody who is thirsty; 7anyone who
proves victorious will inherit these things;
and *I will be his* God and *he will be my son.*[d]
8But the legacy for cowards, for those who
break their word, or worship obscenities, for
murderers and the sexually immoral, and for
sorcerers, worshippers of false gods or any

20a Dn 7:22.
20b The time of the Church after the end of the persecution, not a reign of a returned Christ.
20c =19:11–21.
20d Ezk 38:2.
20e Ezk 38:22.
20f Dn 7:10. A register of human deeds and a list of the predestined.
21a Is 65:17.
21b Ezk 37:27.
21c Is 8:8; 25:8.
21d 2 S 7:14.

other sort of liars, is the second death in the
burning lake of sulphur.'

The messianic Jerusalem

9 One of the seven angels that had the seven
bowls full of the seven final plagues came to
speak to me and said, 'Come here and I
will show you the bride that the Lamb has
married.' 10 *In the spirit, he carried me to the
top of a very high mountain,*[e] and showed me
Jerusalem, the holy city, coming down out
of heaven from God. 11 It had *all the glory of
God*[f] and glittered like some precious jewel
of crystal-clear diamond. 12 Its wall was of a
great height and had twelve gates; at each of
the twelve gates there was an angel, and over
the gates were written the names *of the twelve
tribes of Israel;* 13 *on the east there were three
gates, on the north three gates, on the south three
gates, and on the west three gates.*[g] 14 The city
walls stood on twelve foundation stones, each
one of which bore the name of one of the
twelve apostles of the Lamb.

15 The angel that was speaking to me was
carrying a gold measuring rod to measure the
city and its gates and wall. 16 The plan of the
city is perfectly square, its length the same
as its breadth. He measured the city with his
rod and it was twelve thousand furlongs,
equal in length and in breadth, and equal in
height. 17 He measured its wall, and this was
a hundred and forty-four cubits high—by
human measurements. 18 The wall was built
of diamond, and the city of pure gold, like
clear glass. 19 The foundations of the city wall
were faced with all kinds of precious stone:
the first with diamond, the second lapis
lazuli, the third turquoise, the fourth crystal,
20 the fifth agate, the sixth ruby, the seventh
gold quartz, the eighth malachite, the ninth
topaz, the tenth emerald, the eleventh
sapphire and the twelfth amethyst. 21 The
twelve gates were twelve pearls, each gate
being made of a single pearl, and the main
street of the city was pure gold, transparent
as glass. 22 I could not see any temple in the
city since the Lord God Almighty and the
Lamb were themselves the temple, 23 and
the city did not need the sun or the moon for
light, since it was lit by the radiant glory of
God, and the Lamb was a lighted torch for
it. 24 *The nations will come to its light*[h] and the
kings of the earth will bring it their treasures.
25 Its *gates will never be closed by day*—and
there will be no night there—26 and *the nations
will come, bringing their treasure* and their
wealth. 27 Nothing unclean may come into it:
no one who does what is loathsome or false,
but only those who are listed in the Lamb's
book of life.

22 Then the angel showed me the river of
life, rising from the throne of God
and of the Lamb and flowing crystal-clear.
2 Down the middle of the city street, *on either
bank of the river were the trees of life, which
bear twelve crops of fruit in a year, one in each
month, and the leaves of which are the cure for
the nations.*[a]

3 *The curse of destruction will be abolished.*[b]
The throne of God and of the Lamb will be
in the city; his servants will worship him,
4 they will see him face to face, and his name
will be written on their foreheads. 5 And
night will be abolished; they will not need
lamplight or sunlight, because the Lord God
will be shining on them. They will reign for
ever and ever.

6 The angel said to me, 'All that you have
written is sure and will come true: the Lord
God who inspires the prophets has sent his
angel to reveal to his servants *what is soon to
take place.* 7 I am coming soon!' Blessed are
those who keep the prophetic message of this
book.

8 I, John, am the one who heard and saw
these things. When I had heard and seen
them all, I knelt at the feet of the angel who
had shown them to me, to worship him; 9 but
he said, 'Do no such thing: I am your fellow-
servant and the fellow-servant of your
brothers the prophets and those who keep
the message of this book. God alone you must
worship.'

10 This, too, he said to me, 'Do not keep
the prophecies in this book a secret, because
the Time is close. 11 Meanwhile let the sinner
continue sinning, and the unclean continue
to be unclean; let the upright continue in his
uprightness, and those who are holy continue

21e Ezk 40:2.
21f Is 60:1–2.
21g Ezk 48:31–35.
21h Is 60:3.
22a Ezk 47:12.
22b Zc 14:11.

SUPPLEMENTS

THEOLOGICAL GLOSSARY

*refers the reader for further information to another entry in this glossary.

abba An Aramaic word, an affectionate term of endearment used by children to their father. It was used by Jesus to his Father, and became for Christians a guarantee, almost a talisman, of their close relationship with the Father as children of God. Mk 14:36; Rm 8:15; Ga 4:6.

Adam See 'Second Adam'.

almsgiving With prayer and fasting one of the three principal good works in Judaism. Jesus warns against hypocrisy in their exercise, but Lk especially stresses the importance of generosity to the poor. Paul lays down guidelines for it. Mt 6:2–4; Mk 12:41–44; Lk 18:22; 1 Co 8:7–15.

amen From the Hebr root 'truth', it expresses acceptance or confirmation by the speaker of a statement, prayer or oath of another. Jesus is the 'Amen' of the Father as the fulfilment of his promises. Jesus himself uses the expression, in a unique way, to give emphasis to certain claims. Neh 8:6; Ps 41:13; Jn 3:3, 11; 2 Co 1:20; Rv 3:14.

angel of Yahweh God's agent in the world, or God acting in the world, hardly distinct from God, and sometimes standing for God in visible form. Gn 21:17; Ex 14:19; 23:20–21.

angels Members of the heavenly court, God's retinue, they are depicted as sent to protect God's friends and deliver messages ('angel' = 'messenger') or interpret events. Some are called cherubim* or seraphim* Some of the messengers are named, Gabriel etc. 1 K 22:19; Jb 1:6; Tob 5:4; Mt 28:2; Lk 1–2.

anger of God An aspect of God's awesome holiness and his absolute demand for loyalty, it manifests itself, often unpredictably, in fearful natural phenomena (storm, lightning, etc) and the punishment of offenders. It is to be fully expressed in the great judgement of the Day of the Lord. Nb 11:1; 1 K 14:15; Is 9:11–10:4; Na 1; Rv 16:1.

anointing In ancient Israel the king was made a sacred person by anointing with oil; God's chosen king in the renewal of all things was to be 'the anointed', *Messiah** or *Christ*. Later the high priest also was anointed, and after the Exile, all priests*. Ex 29:7; 1 S 10:1; 16:1; 2 S 19:22; Ps 132:10; Ac 2:36.

antichrist This figure, diametrically opposed to Christ, is the symbolic personification of all evil, also represented as Gog, the Enemy, the Beast. Ezk 38; 2 Th 2:3–12; 1 Jn 2:18, 22; Rv 11:7; 13:1.

apocalyptic A form of literature promising, normally in coded imagery, release from present misery and a glorious future for God's people. It is first seen in Ezk 38–39, is popular in Judaism from 200 BC onwards, and occurs in the NT in Mk 13par and Rv.

apostle Literally an 'envoy', it is used in the Christian sense to refer to those sent to preach the gospel. More narrowly it designates the Twelve chosen by Jesus to be his witnesses*. In the power of the Spirit*, they are the leaders of the young community and continue the ministry of Jesus. After the model of the 12 sons of Jacob, they are the foundation stones of the new Jerusalem. Mk 3:16–19; Mt 28:16; Ac 1:21; 6:2; Rv 21:14.

Ark of the Covenant A wooden box containing the stone tablets of the Law, carried by the Israelites on their journey through the desert, and symbol of God's presence among his people. The actual meeting-point was thought to be the 'mercy-seat', a gold plate on top of the ark where God was enthroned. The ark was the guarantee of God's help in battle. It was lost to the Philistines, then brought back by David, and finally disappeared presumably in the Sack of Jerusalem in 587 BC. Ex 25:10; Lv 16:13; Nm 10:33; 1 S 4:10; 2 S 6; 1 K 8:6.

atonement See 'expiation'.

authority Authority derives from God, who will scrutinise the holder on how it has been exercised. The risen Christ enjoys all authority in heaven and on earth, but authority to make binding decisions is granted also to Peter and to the community itself. Christian authority is linked to service rather than domination. Ws 6:3; Mt 16:19; 18:18; 28:18; Mk 10:42–43.

Baal Hebr for 'Lord', it is the individual and collective name of Canaanite gods, often representing the male fertility principle. Jg 2:11–13; 1 K 18:18; Ho 2:10–15.

baptism A rite of immersion used by John the Baptist to signify entry into a community of repentance awaiting the Messiah. Later, as the rite of entry into the Christian community, it purifies and makes the initiate a new person by incorporation into Christ, and especially into his death and resurrection, and by the gift of his Spirit. Mt 3:6, 15; Ac 2:38; Rm 6:4; Ep 5:26.

blessing God blesses by imparting life, success, fertility, happiness. God's representative also may pronounce this gift by an effective word; once it is spoken it cannot be withdrawn. When others bless God it is an acknowledgement of and thanks for these gifts and a prayer for their continuance. Gn 12:2; 27; Ps 66:20; 67:6–7; Ep 1:3.

blood Blood, which signifies life, belongs to God; it may not be eaten. Because of this mysterious significance it is used in solemn oaths, covenants and purification. Particularly the covenant* with Israel is solemnised in blood, and the New Covenant in the blood of Christ, which also cleanses from sin. Christ's blood was also the price by which humanity is redeemed. Gn 9:6; Lv 1:5; Ex 24:8; Mt 26:28; Ep 1:7; Heb 9:12–15.

body In Hebr thought not normally opposed to the soul, the body is conceived as the material aspect of a living person. In Paul the Christian is incorporated into the body of Christ, becoming a member of his body at baptism; the Christian members make up the body of Christ, or later, form the body which Christ is the head*. The eucharistic body of Christ is shared by his members who partake of it. Finally it is the body transformed in Christ which will rise again. Dn 12:3; Rm 7:24; 1 Co 12:12; 15:44; Ep 1:23; Col 2:10.

breath See 'spirit'.

bride Following Ho, Israel is conceived as the bride of Yahweh, temporarily unfaithful to him and flirting with other partners, but finally united with him. So Jesus likens his coming to the marriage feast and himself to the bridegroom. The image is used to teach Christ's self-sacrifice for his bride. Ho 1:2; Ezk 16; Mt 9:15; 22:1; Jn 3:29; Ep 5:22.

canon of scripture The books regarded by the Jews as holy were being distinguished in the 2nd century BC, the collection reaching its final form soon after the sack of Jerusalem in 70 AD. The books and parts of books originally written in Gk were not included. Christian books began to be considered as equally sacred in the 2nd century, and the present canon of the New Testament was virtually standard by the 4th century. One tradition within the Church excluded the Gk books, and this tradition was taken up by the 15th century Reformers, who relegated these books to the Apocrypha. 1 Mc 12:9.

cherubim Great winged creatures similar to the carved stone *karibu* guarding Babylonian temples and palaces. In Solomon's Temple they formed a frame for the Ark*, a throne for Yahweh. In the post-exilic Temple a smaller pair remained on the mercy-seat. Ex 25:18; 2 K 19:15; Ps 99:1.

Christos See 'Messiah'.

church The Gk word *ekklesia*, originally designating the Israelite religious assembly, was applied to local Jewish communities, then to their Christian equivalents (Ac, Paul), finally to the Christian community as a whole (Ep, Col). In the gospels it occurs only at Mt 16:18; 18:17. The Pauline churches were organised after the model of Jewish communities, with elders* and a president, but the Spirit inspired many other ministries* in them, contributing to the building up of Christ's body*. Other NT images of the Church are God's bride*, a flock, a building, a vine*, the New Jerusalem. Jn 10:1; 15:1; Ac 15:4; 20:17; Ga 1:2; Ep 2:19; Rv 21–22.

circumcision Originally a rite preparatory

to marriage, removal of the foreskin of the penis becomes a reminder of the covenant between God and his people. It gains its full importance as an identifying sign only after the Exile. In the face of hypocrisy the prophets teach circumcision of the heart. Gn 34:15; Ex 12:44; Jr 4:4; 1 M 1:60.

coming See 'Day of the Lord'.

commandments The Ten Commandments, existing in several different versions in the OT, are the basis of the Law*, and were treasured in Judaism as words of life. Jesus taught that the chief commandments were not only to love God but also to love one's neighbour. Especially in Jn love* is the basis of all obedience to God's commands. Ex 20; Dt 8:3; Mk 12:28–34; Jn 13:34; 1 Jn 2:8.

conscience The concept as such enters the Bible only through Gk philosophy; the word occurs in the OT only in Ws 17:11, but frequently in Paul. He speaks mostly of a good and clear conscience, founded on faith. But conscience can also show gentiles that they are at fault. Weak consciences must not be hurt by the more robust. Rm 2:8; 1 Co 4:4; 8:7–12; 1 Tm 1:5, 19.

conversion Literally 'turning back', entry upon a new way of life after a renunciation of sin, a necessary condition for entry into the Baptist's or Jesus' community. Christian conversion entails acknowledging Jesus as Lord and the gift of the holy Spirit*. Mt 3:2; Ac 3:19; 9:35; 1 P 2:25.

covenant A treaty or alliance on certain conditions, made between equal or unequal parties, sealed by oaths and usually by blood*. The terms to which God bound himself by the covenant with Abraham are the basis of all Israel's hopes, and made Israel God's special people. This covenant was likened to a marriage-bond. But Israel broke the terms of allegiance to God, and when the institutions of Israel are accordingly being destroyed, the prophets look forward to a new covenant of the heart*, expressing individual loyalty. Jesus seals this new covenant in his blood. Gn 15:1; Ex 19:5; Jr 31:31; Ezk 36:27; Mk 14:24; Heb 8:6.

creation In Gn creation is described by means of seemingly historical myths to stress God's sovereign power and the superiority of the human race in God's plan for the world. Elsewhere God's continuous care is stressed, without which everything would lapse into nothingness, and his absolute right, like a potter, to make what he will. In the later OT God is seen to create through his Wisdom* or his Word*. Christ is this Word, and is the exemplar of creation. Gn 1–2; Ps 104; Jr 18:6; Prov 8:22; Jn 1:3; Col 1:15–18.

cross The humiliating and agonizing death of Jesus by crucifixion completed once and for all what the demands of the Law* could not achieve. His obedience there undid the disobedience of Adam. By 'taking up the cross' Christians can share in this sacrifice. Mk 8:34; Rm 5:8–18; Ga 6:14; Heb 7:27.

cup A metaphor for the destiny of individuals or nations, more often unfavourable than favourable. The cup of God's anger* is to be handed to the nations who oppress Israel. In the NT it becomes an image of sharing in Jesus' suffering. Ps 11:6; 16:5; Jr 25:15; Mk 10:38.

curse of destruction *See herem.*

darkness See 'light'.

day of the Lord In the OT a day of retribution when Israel, hardened in sin, is to be punished. After the Fall of Jerusalem it becomes a day of hope when Israel's oppressors are to be punished. The imagery becomes more and more lurid, including cosmic signs, earthquake, eclipse. In the NT it becomes the Day of Christ, when Christ the Lord will come as judge*, often amid similar imagery, to renew the world, requite the wicked, reward the just and hand over the kingdom* to his Father. Jl 2; Am 5:18; 8:9; Mt 24:29–31; 25:31–46; 1 Co 15:24; 1 Th 4:15–17.

deacon Seven officials are appointed *deaconein* in Ac 6. Notionally in charge of distributions to the needy, they in fact seem to be a hierarchy subordinate to the Twelve, and in charge of the Hellenist* Christians, but preaching and baptising just like the Twelve. Later, deacons seem to be authoritative officers, mentioned after presbyters*. Ac 6; Rm 16:1; Ph 1:1; 1 T 3:8–13.

death In early Israel death means 'being gathered to the forefathers', but soon the dead are thought to lead a shadowy existence in Sheol*. But the conviction that God cannot abandon his faithful ones eventually flowers in the concept of a life after death, vindication for the faithful and disgrace for the wicked. Paul sees death as a moment of coming even closer to Christ. Gn 25:8; Ps 6:5; 16:11; Jb 19:25–26; Is 53; Dn 12:2; Mk 12:27; Ph 1:21–23.

descent into hell In 1 P 3:18 Christ 'went to preach to the spirits in prison'. This is a flimsy basis for the belief that Christ descended into Sheol*. It is even uncertain who these spirits were, the chained demons of Jewish legend or the righteous dead. Rm 10:6 and Ep 4:8 merely declare the reality of Jesus' death.

desert In the thought of Israel the desert is the abode of evil spirits, into which the scapegoat* is driven to its death. But it is also the place where Israel first became God's people and lived with him in a honeymoon period of faithful love. In the messianic renewal of the world the barrenness of the desert will turn to fertile blossom. Lv 17:7; Is 35:1; Ho 2:16; Am 5:25.

devil See 'spirits', 'Satan'.

divorce Permitted under the old Law, on condition that it be irrevocable, divorce is forbidden by Jesus with an appeal to the fusing of personalities envisaged by Gn. Mt adds a clause allowing divorce in the case of 'illicit marriage', generally understood to mean marriages illicit by Jewish law but permitted in other codes. Dt 24:1; Mt 19:3–6.

dreams Despite the widespread ancient belief in dreams as a means of divine communication, they appear as such in the Bible rarely outside specific clusters, e.g. Gn 37–41; Dn; Mt 1–2; Ac 16–27. There are also warnings that dreams may contain deceptive messages, reflecting only the viewer. Dt 13:2–6; Si 34:1–8.

elders After the model of the 70 elders appointed by Moses, local Jewish communities were governed by a committee of elders (*presbyteroi*). This structure was taken over by Christian communities. Elders were carefully selected and their office was seen to depend on the holy Spirit*. The president (*episcopos*) was probably chosen from among them. Ex 18:13; Ac 11:30; 14:23; 20:28; Ti 1:5–9.

ephod Three distinct objects are thus named: **1**. an instrument of divination, used for consulting Yahweh, 1 S 2:28. **2**. a linen loincloth worn by sacred ministers, 1 S 2:18. **3**. a kind of breastplate worn by the high priest in post-exilic times, Ex 28:6.

eschatology The doctrine of the last things, usually referring to teaching about the Day of the Lord*, e.g. the eschatological discourse of Mk 13 par. Jn however displays a 'realised eschatology', i.e. with the coming of the Spirit* the last age of the world has already begun.

eternal life Christ himself is life, and gives life to those who believe in him. This life is eternal, in that the believer has already entered into this ageless, unchanging quality of God. It has only to be completed by the resurrection. Jn 1:4; 3:15, 36; 6:40, 54; 1 Co 15:42; 2 Co 4:17.

eucharist The rite instituted by Jesus at his last supper with his disciples and repeated by them on his instructions. It is the new Passover of Christ, at which he seals the new covenant* in his blood*, shed for the remission of sins. Christ's body* which is his members is portrayed and fed by sharing in his eucharistic body, the true bread from heaven which gives eternal life*. Mt 26:26 par; Jn 6:31–58; 1 Co 11:17–34.

expiation Expiation or atonement is a process by which sin is removed (the Hebr word is related to 'cover') in order to achieve reconciliation and peace with God or a fellow human. In the old Law there was an annual Day of Expiation, on which the scapegoat* was sent out and the high priest offered sacrifice* for the sins of all the people. Jesus' sacrifice of expiation is seen as the perfect fulfilment of this repeated rite. Lv 16; 2 Co 5:18–19; Heb 9:11–14; 13:11–12; 1 Jn 2:2.

faith Trust in and commitment to God in response to his promises. Christian faith is the acceptance of Christ as Lord* and Saviour*; it unites with Christ and makes the believer a child of God, who imparts his Spirit* to the believer. Faith is normally expressed in baptism* and the works of the Spirit. In contrast to the Law, faith is a reliance not on self but on God, but it requires strength and tenacity. Rm 3:21–5:11; Ga 3:2–9; 2 Th 3:2–8.

fall, the One seemingly historical account of the origin of human sin. It draws heavily upon the myths of the surrounding cultures but purifies them to teach its own lesson. The sin is perhaps represented as sexual, but certainly as consisting in arrogant disobedience, with which Christ's humble obedience is contrasted. Traces of other accounts of the origin of evil survive, e.g. in Ezk 28:11–19. Gn 3; Ws 2:22–25; Rm 5:12–21; Phil 2:6–11.

fasting A natural expression of grief, in the Law* fasting is prescribed only for the Day of Expiation. Other fasts were added to implore God's mercy, and fasting became one of the three principal good works of Judaism. The prophets and Jesus warn against hypocrisy* in this matter, and there is no evidence that Jesus encouraged fasting. Lv 16:29; 2 S 12:16; Is 58:1; Mt 9:14.

father See 'abba'.

fear of Yahweh The absolute holiness of God can inspire absolute terror as well as obedience, but there is also an awe at the majesty of God which is compatible with delight in him and love. Nevertheless, a sense of human unworthiness lays even the prophets prostrate before God. Dt 6:2; Ps 112:1; Is 2:6–21; Ezk 1:28; Rv 1:17.

fire A symbol of the presence of God, whose holiness makes him, like fire, unapproachable. Also the most radical purifying and refining agent, whence hell or Gehenna (a valley full of burning rubbish-dumps) is represented as fiery. The Baptist expected the Messiah* to come with fire. Ex 13:22; Is 6:7; Mt 3:11–12; Mk 9:43.

flesh Basically meat, animal or human, flesh comes to mean humanity as a whole, often what is frail and perishable in humanity, the natural human desires, inclinations etc, which need to be brought under the divine influence. Hebr has no word for 'body' as opposed to 'soul', for the spirit animates the flesh and gives it life. Gn 2:23; 6:17; Is 40:6; Jn 3:6; 6:63; Rm 8.

forgiveness A willingness to forgive is one of the salient characteristics of Yahweh from the earliest times. Forgiveness is an element in the messianic future. When Jesus forgives sin, he is judged to be assuming a divine prerogative. But he also stresses that fellow-Christians must forgive each other. Gn 18:26–32; Ex 34:7; Mt 6:14; 9:2–6; 18:23–35; Lk 7:36–50.

freedom Christ came to bring freedom from slavery to sin. The Christian now willingly serves a new master, God or Christ. Paul seems to have been indifferent to political freedom and to have accepted the institution of slavery without a qualm. Rm 6:15–22; 1 Co 7:21–22; Ep 6:5–9.

fulfilment Jesus is the fulfilment of the Father's promises in the OT, completing his plan for Israel. He also brings the old Law* to completion by removing its imperfections. Mt particularly sets out to show Jesus deliberately fulfilling OT passages in exact detail. Mt 1:22; 5:17–48; Heb 11:40.

fullness This difficult term (*pleroma* in Gk) is used of Christ in Col and Ep. In him lives the fullness of divinity, and Christians too find their fulfilment in him. Further, all fullness is found in him, for all creation reaches its term and completion in him. Ep 1:23; 4:13; Col 1:19; 2:9.

gentile Anyone not a Jew. In later Jewish literature, even the gospels, they are sometimes judged harshly. Mt 5:47; 18:17; Rm 1:18–32; 1 Co 5:11. But after some controversy it was decided that gentiles too, not Jews only, could be Christians. Ac 10; 15:7; Ga 2:14.

glory Often an awesome visible manifestation of the unapproachable God in brightness and fire, conveying his majesty and splendour. To give glory to God is to recognise his divinity and omnipotence; so the earth is full of his glory. Jesus shares in and reveals this glory, and the Christian too is to share it. Ex 24:16; Lk 2:14; 19:38; Jn 1:14; 12:23; 17:22–24.

gospel The English 'god spell' = 'good news' mirrors the Gk *euangelion*. Originally used in the emperor-cult, where it denoted news of any great imperial event, victory, birth of an heir etc, the term was adopted already in Paul for the good news brought by Jesus and preached by Paul.

Mk so uses the term, but from Mt onwards it comes increasingly to mean the text or a part of it. Mt 26:13; Mk 1:15; 2 Co 2:12; Ga 1:7–8.

grace A fluid term related to favour (Gk *charis*, whence 'grace'). It may be a quality of graciousness, loveliness which arouses favour, or the unearned favour of a powerful ruler who need give no account of his actions. Basically it is the pleasingness of the favourite or the pleasure of the favourer, but it may also be the favours bestowed. Pr 11:16; Jn 1:14, 17; Phil 1:2; Rv 22:21.

head In medical thought of Jesus' time the head is considered the superior guiding principle, and also the source of life for the body. So when Christ is designated the head of his body the Church, he is nominated its guiding authority and source of life. Ep 1:22; 4:16; 5:23; Col 1:18; 2:19.

healing Sickness was regarded as the grasp of evil on a person, so that healing is a sign that evil is being overcome. Jesus' cures are part of the triumph over evil expected for the renewal of the world in the last times. It is not necessary that all the cures should be miraculous in the sense of being scientifically inexplicable. Mt 4:23; 8:16; 11:2–5; Jn 5:14.

heart The source of thoughts, feelings, decision, the centre of religious awareness, through which God is perceived, sought, heard, praised and loved. Dt 6:5; Ps 51:10; Jr 31:31; Ezk 36:26.

heaven In the primitive Hebr conception of a three-tier universe heaven is the dwelling-place of God, and 'Heaven' is used as a reverent circumlocution to avoid using the sacred name of God (so in Mt 'the Kingdom of Heaven' = 'the Kingdom of God' elsewhere). The homeland of the Christian is in heaven, by which is meant that the Christian's thoughts, interests, etc are there centred. Gn 1:6–8; Jb 22:12–13; Ps 11:4; Mt 3:2, 16; 6:20; Phil 3:20.

hell See 'fire'.

Hellenists Jews from outside Palestine, who used Gk as their language of worship. The Hellenist Christians of Jerusalem soon became a distinctive group, with their own hierarchy, the Seven 'deacons'*, and were the first to be persecuted. Ac 6:1; 8:1.

***herem*/curse of destruction** A regulation of the 'holy war' of ancient Israel, by which all captives and booty were destroyed in acknowledgement that all victory is won by Yahweh. This barbaric custom is last mentioned at Samuel's butchering of Agag. Its general use in stories of Joshua's conquests may be more a later theological warning against mixing with foreigners than a historical reality. Jos 6:16–21; Dt 7:2; 1 S 15.

high priest The high priesthood as such may not have existed until after the Exile; it includes politico-religious leadership from about 200 BC until 70 AD. Jesus is called 'priest' or 'high priest' only in Heb: his sacrifice is effective; he has access to the heavenly sanctuary; he is the perfect mediator*. 2 Mc 3:1; Jn 18:13; Heb 2:17; 7:26–28; 9:11–28.

holiness Awe, terror, fascination, reverence are human reactions to the otherness of God. He is so holy that no human being can see him and live; they can only be staggered and awestruck at experiencing him. Yet association with him demands some share in his holiness, moral purity and (in some circumstances) ritual purity, consisting in separation from the ordinary processes of life. God asserts his holiness by protecting his people from all enemies, and when their sins prevent this, it is a slur on his holiness. Ex 3:5; Lv 19:2; Is 5:16; 6:3; Ezk 36:23; Rv 4:8.

hope Closely allied to faith* as trust in Yahweh, hope is reliance on God's faithful love and confidence that his promises will be fulfilled. Abraham's hope is the model of Christian hope in that it relied on no human possibilities. Jr 17:5–8; Ho 2:17; Rm 4:18–5:11; Heb 11:1.

hour of Jesus In Jn the moment of Jesus' passion, death and resurrection, considered as the moment of exaltation and glorification. From Cana onwards Jesus and the reader are conscious of this goal to which the whole of Jesus' life is directed. Jn 2:4; 7:30; 12:23, 27; 16:22.

humility In the sense of 'lowliness' this quality calls for God's mercy and favour; the humble are specially dear to him, for those who accept their own helplessness must rely only on God. This was very central to Jewish spirituality during the oppressed period after the Fall of Jerusalem. In the modern sense of self-deprecation it has little place in the Bible; especially Paul seems to offend against it. 1 S 2:1; Ps 113:7–9; Lk 1:46–55; 6:20–23; 1 Co 11:1.

hypocrisy The prophets castigate hypocritical religious observance, ritual without due dispositions or social justice. The gospels similarly warn against the hypocrisy of the Pharisees. Is 1:10–16; Ho 8:11; Am 5:21; Mt 6:1–18; 23; Jn 7:53–8:11.

immortality See 'death'.

intercession In all parts of the OT various figures are asked to intercede for those in spiritual and temporal need: Abraham, Moses, Job, Jeremiah. It seems to have been thought especially appropriate to those men of prayer, the prophets. After the last supper Jesus intercedes for his followers. At the end of the OT, sacrifice* and intercession for the dead occur. Gn 18:24; Jb 42:8; Jr 42:2; 2 Mc 12:38; Jn 17.

individual responsibility Corporate responsibility is very strong in Israel, each liable to be punished for the sins of forbears, until Ezk and Jr both teach that henceforth this shall no longer hold. The change is linked to the change from promises rooted in the religion of institutions to promises rooted in a religion of the heart. Gn 18; Dt 24:16; Jr 31:29; Ezk 18:2.

Israel Three meanings: **1.** A personal name given to Jacob, Gn 32:29, whence the other meanings. **2.** A politico-geographical name, the northern territories, 1 S 11:8, or the united kingdom, 1 K 11:42. **3.** The holy people of God, a religious entity, for God chose Israel to be his very own people, a consecrated nation, set apart from other nations by the covenant*, but destined to bring salvation to all. Jesus makes a new holy people for himself, to which the same theology is applied. Dt 7; Ex 19:5; Is 45:14–17; Rm 9–11; Ga 6:16; Heb 8:8–10; 1 P 2:9.

Jesus See under separate titles: 'Lord', 'messiah', 'prophet', 'son of David', 'son of God', 'son of man', 'truth', 'word'.

judge The judges of the 'period of the judges' immediately after the settlement of Israel in Canaan are of two kinds: charismatic leaders or warlike liberators raised up in crisis, and authoritative figures to whom people of a certain district bring lawsuits for decision. Jg 3:9; 10:2, 3; 12:7. God is the supreme judge of all nations, and of the oppressed, often in the sense of vindicator; he will judge all nations at the end. Dt 10:18; Ps 9:7–8; Is 2:4; Jl 4:12. But he gives all judgement to the Son. Mt 25:32; Jn 5:22; Ac 10:42.

justice God's saving justice consists in punishing, but also in pardoning the repentant sinner, because he is then just by fidelity to his promises of salvation. To this corresponds human justice, or 'uprightness' which may be gained only by trust in these promises, ultimately by faith* in Jesus. Is 5:16; Ho 2:21; Rm 3:21; 4:1–25; Ga 3:8.

king/kingship Israel, God's people, has no king but Yahweh. But at a certain stage military necessity made an earthly king unavoidable. David, God's chosen king, became the ideal for the future king who would renew God's kingship in Israel, and thence over the whole world. Jesus preached that God's rule or kingship had been inaugurated, showing it by his triumph over evil in all its forms, sickness, demonic possession, moral evil, death itself. God's kingship was still to be completed. 1 S 8:1–9; Ps 93; 97; Is 11:1–9; Ezk 34:23; Mk 1:15; 4:26–32; 11:10; Mt 25:31.

korban =dedicated to God. The rabbis taught that nothing so dedicated could be given away for any other purpose, no matter how laudable. Thus the owner retained its use. Mk 7:11; Mt 15:15.

lamb A Johannine image for Christ, combining the idea of a sacrificial lamb with that of the Servant* of the Lord who takes all sin on himself. Ex 12:5; Lv 14:10; Jn 1:29; 19:36; 1 P 1:19. The Lamb of Rv, slain and yet living and enthroned, is expressed in Gk by a different word. Rv 5:6; 17:14; 21:27.

Law The first five books of the Bible, the 'Pentateuch' formed the written Law of Israel, revered as the terms of God's covenant* with Israel, so a source of life to Israel. Also a body of tradition had grown up which enjoyed equal status as the 'oral Law'. Jesus fulfills the Law by his life and teaching. Paul sees the Law at best as a temporary guide, or as showing the enormity of sin by making it formal and conscious; so Christ rescues from slavery to the Law those who believe in him. Dt 8:3; Ps 119; Mt 5:17; 15:1–9; Rm 7:7; Ga 3.

leprosy The word traditionally used far more widely than the modern medical term, to cover many forms of skin diseases, serious or trivial, or even signs of decay in clothing or on walls. See Lv 13–14.

levite A member of a group assisting the priests in the sanctuary, probably originally priests themselves, and claiming Levi as their ancestor. Gn 29:34; Nm 16–17; Dt 18:1–8; Ezr 2:40–42.

liberty See 'freedom'.

life Life is given by God and belongs to God, who remains master of life. The fullness of life is eternal life*, which Jesus, who is himself life, came to bring. The believer's life is hidden in Christ and implies holiness* and living to God in the spirit. Gn 2:7; 9:4; Ps 104:29; Jn 10:10; Rm 8:1; Phil 1:21; Co 3:3.

light A feature of divine manifestations and a messianic title. God is light and his Servant* is a light to the nations. God's Law* is a light to the steps. In the NT Jesus is the true light. By contrast, darkness symbolises the reign of evil. Ps 27:1; Is 9:1; 42:6; 60:1; Jn 1:4–5; 8:12.

Lord In the Gk OT the divine name Yahweh* is translated 'Lord'. But the expression can bear a far weaker sense, merely 'Sir!'. However in the early community to call Jesus 'Lord' was the test of faith, and Christians were 'those who invoke the name of the Lord', in the sense of the divine name. Mk 7:28; Lk 10:40; Ac 2:21; 9:14; 1 Co 12:3; Phil 2:11.

love The Hebr concept of love involves a generous, responsive, active self-giving, modelled on that of God. God's relationship to Israel is that of passionate married love; the Israelite must love God with his whole being, and similarly his neighbour. Jesus extends this obligation to love to all human beings, with Jesus' own selfless love as model. Dt 6:5; Ho 2:21; Ezk 16; Mk 12:28–34; Jn 13:34; 1 Co 13; 1 Jn 4:7–5:4.

marriage See 'bride', 'divorce'.

mediator Various figures in the OT act as mediators, see 'intercession'. In the NT Christ is the one mediator. In him is the fullness* of divinity, yet he is the Head* of the Body*. Through him come grace* and truth*. He is the mediator of the perfect covenant*. Jn 1:16–17; Col 2:9; 1 Tm 2:5; Heb 8:6.

mercy See 'forgiveness'.

messiah ='anointed' (Gk *christos*), normally a royal title, see 'anointing'. In the decades before the Jewish revolts in 66 AD and 132 AD it was popular as a title of revolutionary leaders. Jesus was so hailed by his followers, by the crowds and by his opponents (to construct a charge against him). He, however, was non-committal in regard to it, probably because of its political implications. The tradition after him is more positive, and in Paul 'Christos' becomes part of Jesus' name. 2 S 7:12–16; Ps 2; Is 6–9; Mk 8:29; 12:35; 14:61; 15:32; Ac 2:36.

ministry Jesus' concept of ministry is one of service. The earliest Christian communities were governed by elders* but there were many other ministries, such as that of the apostles* to witness to Jesus' resurrection, and the Seven, deacons*, leaders of the Gk community in Jerusalem. Paul mentions also prophets, teachers, healers, etc. Mt 20:26; 23:11; Ac 1:15–22; 6:1–6; 1 Co 12:28–30.

miracle Not exactly a biblical concept, centred as it is on contravention of the laws of nature. The Bible speaks rather of the 'wonders of God', signs of his power exercised for the sake of his people, especially in delivering them from Egypt. So Jesus' works of power or wonders are signs of the outbreak of the kingship/kingdom* of God and the presence of God's power in a new way. Jos 3:5; Ps 9:1; 107:24; Mt 12:38–39; Mk 6:2, 5, 14; Jn 2:11, 18, 23; Ac 4:22.

mystery A concept borrowed by Paul from Jewish apocalyptic*, of the mysterious plan long hidden in God and finally revealed. He applies it to the climax of history, the cross and resurrection, salvation preached to all nations and the restoration of all things in Christ. Rm 16:25; 1 Co 2:8; Ep 1:9–10; 3:3–12.

name Names in the Bible determine the nature of what is named. When Adam names the animals he determines their nature. Similarly, by a new naming a person is given a new significance and a new power (Israel, Emmanuel, Peter). Hence many Hebr names are etymologised to show a special significance. God's name carries with it his power; so to speak his name invokes his power, to make his name known is to display his power. Those who call on the name of Jesus (e.g. in baptism*) submit themselves to his power. Gn 1:19; 32:29; Ps 54:1; Mt 1:23; 16:18; Ac 2:38; 10:43; Phil 2:9.

nazirite ='one set apart' ritually by a vow whose terms are given in Nm 6; Jg 13:5–7; Am 2:11; Ac 18:18.

numbers In the Bible numbers often have a set significance, e.g. 4 for the quarters of the world, so the whole universe, Gn 2:10; 7 for completion, Lk 8:2, so 6 for radical incompletion, Rv 13:18 (similarly 3½, Dn 7:25); 12 for fullness (so 144,000 for utter totality, Rv 7:4); 40 a round, large approximate number, Ex 16:34. Since in Gk letters are used as digits, a number may also be a cryptogram for a name whose digits add up to that number, Rv 13:18.

obstinacy The obstinacy of Israel is a frequent theme especially in the prophets. God will correct his people with punishment but not desert them. This obstinacy is given as the reason why Jesus speaks in parables. But Jesus' own disciples also are in Mk (softened in the other gospels) rebuked for their hardness of heart and failure to believe. Dt 9:13; Is 48:4; Mt 13:13; Mk 4:40; 7:18; Ac 28:25; Rm 11:7.

parable Short stories told for comparison or to illustrate a point, a method of teaching much used in popular teaching, in the OT and especially by Jesus in the gospels. The underlying Hebr term *mashal* includes also other imaged sayings, similes and riddles. The gospel parables are often adjusted by the evangelists to apply to their own situations. Jg 9:7–15; 2 S 12:1–14; Mt 13; Mk 4; Lk 15–16.

paraclete A helper, counsellor, advocate, Jesus, himself a 'paraclete', will send another 'paraclete' to guide his disciples into all truth. This will be the holy Spirit*. The term is used in Judaism, but in the Bible only in Jn 14:16, 26; 15:26; 16:7; 1 Jn 12:1.

Passover Originally an annual nomadic feast for the flocks at the first full moon of spring, it came to commemorate the liberation from Egypt. Later it was combined with the feast for the beginning of harvest, Unleavened Bread, and so acquires the symbolism of a fresh start, free from corruption. Jesus probably used a Passover supper to seal his new Covenant*. The name itself (Hebr *pessah*, Aram *pascha*) is obscure. Ex 12; 2 Chr 35:18; Mt 26:26; 1 Co 5:8.

peace 'Shalom!' is the normal Jewish greeting, but its realisation is a messianic blessing, presupposing justice and fidelity to God. So Christ is our bond of peace, and the gospel is the word of peace. Ps 122:6–8; Is 48:18; Jn 14:27; Ep 2:14–16.

Pharisees A party within Judaism, the strictest observers of the Law, both written and oral, sometimes prone to casuistry and hypocrisy, but also known for great warmth of devotion. Jesus' independence with regard to the Law often brought him into opposition with them. Mt 12:2; 15:1–20; 23; Lk 7:36; Ac 23:6.

poverty In the OT the poor are specially protected by Yahweh, and specially favoured if they call to him. He will punish their oppressors and render them justice. The remnant* of God's people will be poor, and the messianic king* a humble king. In the wisdom literature, however, poverty is regarded as a curse of idleness and folly. In the NT the poor are included among the outcasts to whom the gospel message is especially addressed; their misery will be reversed. Ex 22:21; Jb 24:2–12; Ps 22:26; Pr 6:11; Am 4:1; Lk 6:20; 16:19–31.

prayer The Psalms form the largest collection of prayers in the OT, but other intimate and confident prayers to Yahweh abound. In the NT Jesus is seen to be constantly praying to his Father, as he teaches his followers to do. Praise and thanksgiving, inspired by the holy Spirit, especially mark the early communities. Jr 15:10–21; Mt 6:5–13; Lk 22:39–46; Jn 17; Ac 2:42; 4:24; Rm 8:26–27.

priest The English word is derived from *presbyteros*=elder*. In primitive Israel any head of a family would offer sacrifice, though there were priests of the various sanctuaries throughout the land. The Temple priesthood cannot predate Solomon's Temple, and its importance grows with the centralisation of cult there shortly before the exile. See also 'high priest'. In the NT only Christ is called priest or high priest*. Ex 12:6; 2 S 8:17; 1 K 8:6; Neh 10:3–9.

prophet The task of the prophet is not so much to foretell as to pronounce God's will, to mediate God's view of a situation, sometimes backing this up with predictions. Some professional court prophets are mentioned, but the prophetic movement was more often critical of the establishment. A final prophet was expected who would initiate God's renewal of all things, and Jesus is seen as this prophet. There were also prophets in the earliest Christian communities. Dt 18:15–18; 1 K 18:22; 19:16; 22:6; Lk 4:16–24; 7:15; Ac 11:27.

prostitution In the Bible an image of Israel's unfaithfulness to Yahweh, whose bride* she is. Ex 34:16; Ho 1:2; Ezk 16.

punishment See 'anger'.

purity The concept of clean and unclean was most important in OT ritual, many (but not all) of the prescriptions being based on primitive health precautions for hot countries and reverence for life-processes. Such ritual uncleanness was not necessarily morally culpable but rendered a person unfit for the cult. Jesus removed the basis of such prohibitions, and this was applied more widely by the early community. Lv 11–22; Mk 7:14–23; Ac 10:9–16; 15:19–29; Rm 14:14.

recapitulation in Christ See 'head'.

redeemer A technical term of family law, the closest male relative, the *go'el*, who is bound to extricate his relative from disasters such as childlessness or debt. God is the *go'el*, so redeemer or saviour of his people. Of Christ the term 'Saviour' is used almost exclusively in the Pastoral Letters and 2 P. Jb 19:25; Ps 19:14; Is 41:14; Phil 3:20; Ti 1:3–4; 2 P 1:1, 11.

redemption A general term used in the OT for the deliverance of Israel from Egypt by God's mighty power, without any price or ransom being paid, to be his own possession; then for the deliverance from exile in Babylon, especially as an image of final deliverance from sin. Christ delivers the new Israel from slavery to the Law* and to sin, making her his own people. The mention of Christ's blood as a ransom-price is rare. Dt 7:6–8; Jer 31:11; Ps 44:26; Mk 10:45; Rm 3:24; 1 Co 6:20; Col 1:13; 1 P 1:18.

remnant An important theme in the prophets is that, though Israel will be punished for infidelity, a faithful remnant will be preserved and will be the spearhead of the messianic renewal. Is 10:19–21; Ezk 6:8–10; Am 9:8–10; Zc 13:8–10.

resurrection By the mid 2nd century BC belief in a general resurrection after death* at the end of time, to glory or disgrace, is apparent. The resurrection of Jesus before the end of time is different, though Paul still sees it as the fulfilment of the hope of Israel. God raised him to new life as the glorious Lord with all authority in heaven and on earth, first-born from the dead and so the leader of a new humanity. Those who have entered into his death and resurrection by baptism* are raised and glorified with him, transformed into the sphere of the divine. Dn 2:12; Mt 28:18; Mk 16: Ac 23:6; Rm 1:4; 1 Co 15; Phil 2:9–11; Heb 2:10.

revenge See 'vengeance'.

rock An image for a reliable foundation which can be trusted, used of God, Ps 18:2; 95:1; of Christ, 1 Co 10:4; and of Peter, the rock on which Christ built his community, Mt 16:18.

Sabbath A weekly day of rest dedicated to Yahweh, but also to ensure human freedom to God. Of very ancient origin, it gained its full importance at the time of the Exile and became one of the touchstones of fidelity to Judaism. Gn 2:2; Ex 23:12; Neh 13:15; Mt 12:1.

sacrifice Laws and ritual for the various

sacrifices which played such an important part in the OT are set out in Lv 1–7. The prophets, echoed by Jesus, strongly criticised the sacrificial practice as insincere, external rites at variance with dispositions and blindness to injustice. Jesus sealed his new covenant by the sacrifice of his blood, fulfilling the purpose of OT sacrifices in a way which they could not. Ps 50; Is 1:10–17; Ho 6:4–5; Mt 26:26–29; Ep 5:2, 25; Heb 7–10.

Sadducees The traditionalist party of the Jews, mostly from the great priestly families, they sought and held political power. They kept to the written Law and rejected new developments such as angels* and the doctrine of resurrection*. Mt 22:23; Mk 12:18; Ac 23:6–8.

Samaritans Inhabitants of Samaria, the region midway between Galilee and Judaea, disliked and despised by the Jews for their mixed race and mixed religion. Of the Bible they accepted only the first five books. The dislike was mutual. But Jesus, especially in Lk, contrasts Samaritan openness with Jewish rigidity. Lk 10:30–37; 17:16; Jn 4; Ac 8:25.

Satan The Hebr word means 'adversary' and is used in a general sense, then in particular of one of the 'sons of God' who is responsible on God's behalf for testing and proving human beings. Only in 1 Ch 21:1 does it become a proper name. In the NT he is interchangeably called the 'devil' (Gk *diabolos*=accuser), and also actively promotes evil, claiming power over the world. In the Johannine writings the devil/Satan is a fundamentally evil entity. 1 K 5:18; Jb 1:6; 2:1; Zc 3:1–2; Mt 4:1; 13:19; 25:41; Jn 8:44; 1 Jn 3:8–10.

saviour See 'redeemer'.

scapegoat A goat sent out annually, ritually bearing the sins of the people, into the desert to perish in this abode of evil spirits. Lv 16:20–22.

scribes At the time of Jesus Jewish scholars learned in the Law and the scriptures, to whom people turned for authoritative guidance and interpretations. Many were Pharisees, and they opposed Jesus actively. But not all were hostile. Mt is often called a Christian scribe. Mt 12:38; 13:52; Mk 11:27; 12:28–34; Jn 8:3; Ac 4:5.

Second Adam Inverting Jewish legend that the Adam of Gn was preceded by a first, heavenly Adam, Paul teaches that the founder of the human race was the first Adam and Jesus the Second, heavenly, Adam. The first Adam fell by his sin of pride and disobedience, dragging down the human race. The Second Adam raises and renews the human race by his humility and obedience. Rm 5:12–21; 1 Co 15:21, 45; Phil 2:6–11.

seraphim Fiery dragons in Nm 21:7, sent by God to punish the guilty. In Is 6 fiery beings which form God's retinue.

servant In the Semitic world often a title of honour because of the confidential relationship between servant and master. The Servant of the Lord in Isaiah is a redemptive figure, perhaps Israel, perhaps an individual representing Israel, whose mission is, by suffering willingly borne, to free from sin and bring God's salvation to the nations. Subtle allusions suggest that Jesus, and certainly the evangelists, identified himself with this figure. Is 42:1–4; 49:1–6; 50:4–9; 52:13–53:12; Mt 3:17; 8:17; 26:28; Phil 2:6–11; 1 P 2:21–25.

Sheol In Hebr thought a place where the dead continue to exist in darkness, dust and helplessness, without wisdom and unable to know or praise God. Jb 17:13–16; Ps 88:3–12; Is 14:9–11; Rv 20:14.

shepherd A common image of kingship in the near East, used by Jr and Ezk to accuse the selfish rulers of Israel. Ezk also uses it to foretell a messianic shepherd who will pasture his people in Yahweh's name and renew the covenant*. Jesus uses it in his parable of the lost sheep and his own claim to be the good shepherd. Jr 23:1–6; Ezk 34; Zc 11:4–17; Mt 18:12–14; Mk 6:34; Jn 10.

sign The miracles of Jesus are signs of his messianic mission and of the Father's glory; Jn 1–12 is conventionally known as The Book of Signs. Jesus himself, however, prefers the expression 'the works of my Father' and at times refused to manifest the signs which the Jews demanded. Mt 12:38; Jn 2:11; 4:48–54; 10:32–38; 1 Co 1:22.

sin Consciousness of sin and failure is deep in Israel. But admission of guilt leads on always to confidence in God's forgiveness; the paradigm case is the sin of Eve and Adam, followed by the other stories of primitive sin till the Flood. Especially after Israel's infidelity is sealed by the Exile, this awareness is intensified. In Paul Sin (as a personification) has ruled over all people by solidarity with the sin of Adam*, and is overcome only by solidarity through faith* with the sacrifice of Christ. Gn 3; Ps 51; Bar 1:15–22; Rm 1:18–3:20; 5:8–21; 6:17–23.

son of David A messianic title stemming from the promise to David, and stressed thenceforth in the OT and at the time of Jesus. Mt especially shows Jesus being so hailed and emphasises its importance. Jesus himself was hesitant towards this title, perhaps because it suggested too human a notion of the Messiah*. 2 S 7:8–16; Ps 89; Is 11:1–5; Ezk 34:23–24; Mt 1; 9:23; Mk 12:35; Lk 1:32; Jn 7:42; Ac 2:30; Rm 1:4.

son of God A title expressing a special choice by God, a special mission from God and special protection by him. It is applied in the OT to the angels, to Israel, to its leaders and to other individuals. Jesus is so hailed by Satan and the possessed, by the voice from heaven at his baptism and transfiguration, and finally by the centurion. Jn and particularly Paul use the title more widely of Jesus. Jesus himself speaks only of 'the Son' with relation to his Father. Ex 4:22; Ps 2:7; Ws 18:13; Ho 11:1; Mt 3:17; 4:3, 6; 8:29; 11:27; 17:5; 26:63; 27:54; Jn 1:34; 11:4, 27; 17:1; Rm 1:3–4; Ga 2:20.

son of man An Aramaic expression by which a speaker self-effacingly points to himself. It was a favourite self-designation of Jesus. It is understood by the evangelists by reference to Dn as a title of glory*, but scholars dispute whether it could already have held this sense in Jesus' own lifetime. Dn 7:13; Mt 8:20; 13:13; 25:31; 26:64; Ac 7:56; Rv 1:13.

soul In the NT corresponds to the Hebr *nephesh*, meaning the life or the self, the centre of desire, emotions and loyalty. Mt 26:38; Lk 2:35; 12:19; Heb 10:39.

spirit In Hebr and Gk the same word means 'breath', 'wind', 'spirit', often the principle of life and activity in human beings, given by God and withdrawn by him. Prophets and charismatic leaders receive the spirit of God in a special way for a special task. In the last days the spirit is to be poured out on the whole people and on individuals, in a new covenant of the spirit. Gn 1:2; Nm 11:17; Jg 3:10; 6:34; Is 11:2; Ezk 37:1–14; Jl 3:1–2.

In the NT the Spirit comes upon Jesus at his baptism and upon the Apostles at Pentecost, after which every decisive move in the early community is seen to be guided by the Spirit. Similarly in Paul the Spirit, the Spirit of God or of Christ, makes Christians children of God and empowers them to all Christian activity, including prayer and love. Jn teaches especially that this Spirit, the Paraclete*, brings the continuing personal presence of Christ. That this Spirit of God or of Christ is a distinct person is implied also by the frequent triadic formulae in Paul. Mk 1:10; Jn 1–33; 14:16; Ac 1:8; 15:28; Rm 5:5; 1 Co 14:14–16; 2 Co 13:13; Ga 5:13–36.

spirits In Judaism spirits bulked large in the popular imagination. Various mental disorders were attributed to unclean spirits, and Jesus shows his conquest of evil by expelling them. There was also a range of cosmic spirits, intermediaries between God and the world, controlling events and nations ('principalities', 'powers', etc); the supremacy of the risen Christ is expressed by his command over them. Mk 1:23, 32; Ac 16:16; Ga 4:3; Ep 1:21.

suffering God tests his faithful by suffering. Job's endurance gives power to his prayer, and the Servant* of the Lord in Isaiah atones for the sins of others by his suffering. Christ teaches that persecution is part of the mission of apostles*, and Paul regards it as a sign of his apostolate. He attributes to the Christ who is in him the sufferings he bears. Jb 42:8; Is 53:4–7; Mk 13:9–13; 2 Co 11:23; Col 1:24.

temple The importance of the temple in Jerusalem was as the dwelling-place of God in the centre of his people. Already the prophets taught that in the new covenant* God would dwell in each individual heart, and Paul teaches that Christians are temples of the spirit*. In the final vision of Rv there is no temple because God fills his whole people. 1 K 8:10; Ezk 9–11; Jr 31:33; Jn 2:21; 1 Co 3:16; Rv 21:22.

ongues 'Speaking in tongues', a form of ecstatic speech inspired by the Spirit, is bursts of praise unintelligible to the ordinary listener and needing an interpreter. Paul recognises but does not fully encourage this phenomenon. At Pentecost Ac describes a similar happening, when the apostles preach intelligibly in tongues unknown to themselves. Ac 2:4; 1 Co 14:1–25.

truth In the NT truth is related to the divine. Jesus is the true vine, the true bread from heaven, the true shepherd, the true light, the fulfilment of these OT figures, promises of God. He is also the Truth itself, and his Spirit* will guide his followers into all truth, which will sanctify them and set them free. Jn 8; 14:6; 17:17–19; 2 Co 6:7; Ep 4:21.

vengeance In a society without police the law did not so much enjoin revenge as limit punishment to the equal of the damage caused. But in Israel the nearest relative was obliged to protect the living rather than to avenge the dead. Forgiveness within Israel was prescribed, and Jesus strongly demanded mutual forgiveness. Nb 35:33; Lv 19:17; Mt 5:38; 18:21.

vine An image for Israel, the vine or vineyard of the Lord, tended by him but unresponsive. Similarly the grape-harvest is an image of the final judgement. Jesus is the true vine fulfilling perfectly the vocation of Israel. Is 5:1–7; Jr 2:21; Jn 15:1.

virgin In the OT the virgin daughter of Zion is a symbol of Israel, emphasising her vulnerability and her dependence on Yahweh. It is the firm tradition of the gospels that Jesus was born of a virgin mother. Paul commends virginity in view of the pressing eschatological crisis. Lam 1:6; 2:1; Am 8:2; Mt 1:25; 1 Co 7:25.

war See '*herem*/curse of destruction'.

wisdom See Introduction to the Wisdom Books, p. 540.

witness A witness (Gk *martyr*) in the NT sense does not simply witness to an observed fact but bears personal testimony to a truth, putting personal weight behind it. So Jesus witnesses to the truth, and the Father, the scriptures and the Spirit witness to Jesus. The apostles witness to the resurrection in the sense of proclaiming it. The Gospel of Jn is laid out as a great trial scene, in which people reject or accept the witness to Jesus. Jn 1:7–8; 5:31–37; 18:37; Ac 1:8; 1 Tm 6:13.

word God created by his Word and reveals by it, so that the Word is an image of God at work in the world. The Word is distinct from God and yet divine, always united to him and dependent on him, sent by him in power to reveal his salvation. Si 42:15; Is 55:1; Jn 1:1; Rv 19:13.

Yahweh The personal name of God revealed to Moses, and treasured as a sign of intimacy and favour. The later Jews regarded it as too sacred to be pronounced; only the consonants YHWH were written. The meaning 'I am what I am' or 'He who is' is perhaps a refusal to give a meaning; or it may suggest that God is the cause of being. Ex 3:13; 34:6.

Zion The holy mountain of Jerusalem, the dwelling-place of God and the symbol of his presence. All nations will flow thither to receive salvation and to revere God. It will be a city of joy and source of the river of salvation, the city of the Lamb. Ps 122; Is 60:1; 66:18–20; Zc 14; Rv 21–22.

CHRONOLOGICAL TABLE

GENERAL HISTORY		BIBLICAL HISTORY
Egypt, old kingdom (great pyramids)	3000	*Abraham's ancestors nomads in Mesopotamia*
	2000	
		c.1850 Abraham in Canaan
	1800	
c.1750 *Hammurabi's Code of Law*		The Patriarchs in Egypt
Egypt: 1377–1358 Akhenaton	1300	
1290–1224 Rameses II		c.1250 The Exodus – Moses – Covenant on Sinai
		c.1220 Joshua invades Palestine
1184–1170 Rameses III	1200	1200–1025 The Judges
		c.1040 Samuel
		1030–1010 Saul
		1010–970 David
		970–931 Solomon

GENERAL HISTORY	BIBLICAL HISTORY		
Revival of Assyria	ISRAEL		JUDAH
	931–910 Jeroboam I		931–913 Rehoboam
883–859 Assurnasirpal	885–874 Omri		
858–824 Shalmaneser III			
			870–848 Jehoshaphat
	841–814 Jehu		841–835 Athaliah
	798–783 Joash	Elijah	
	783–743 Jeroboam II	Elisha	781–740 Uzziah
745–727 Tiglath-Pileser III		**Amos, Hosea** **Isaiah, Micah**	740–736 Jotham
721–705 Sargon II	721 *Capture of Samaria*		
704–681 Sennacherib			716–687 **Hezekiah**
669–630 Ashurbanipal		**Zephaniah, Jeremiah, Nahum,** **Deuteronomic History edited**	740–609 Josiah
Neo-Babylonians			
626–605 Nebupolassar		**Habakkuk, Jeremiah**	609–598 Jehoiakim
605–562 Nebuchadnezzar			
		597 *Siege of Jerusalem – deportations – Ezekiel* 586 *Sack of Jerusalem – more deportations*	
		Ezekiel, Second Isaiah	

GENERAL HISTORY	BIBLICAL HISTORY
Persian Period	
555–530 Cyrus king of Medes & Persians	
539 *Cyrus captures Babylon*	538 *Cyrus decrees return of Jews*
522–486 Darius I	520 *Temple rebuilt* – Zerubbabel commissioner
490 ⚔ *Marathon*	**Haggai, Zechariah, final edition of Pentateuch**
486–465 Xerxes I	**?Job, Proverbs, Song of Songs, Ruth**
480 ⚔ *Salamis*	
478–432 Athenian Empire, Pericles	445 Nehemiah's first Mission **Malachiah, Obadiah**
Socrates	398 Ezra's Mission **?Joel, Jonah, Tobit,**
Plato	**?Chronicles, Ezra-Nehemiah**
336–323 Alexander the Great Aristotle	**?Qoheleth**
Egypt ruled by Ptolemies, Syria by Seleucid kings	300–200 *Egypt dominates Palestine*
218–204 *Rome defeats Hannibal in 2nd Punic War*	200–167 *Syria dominates Palestine* **?Esther**
189 *Rome defeats Antiochus III of Syria*	**?Ben Sira**
175–164 Antiochus IV Epiphanes king of Syria	167 *Jews revolt against Syria, led by Maccabees*
	166–160 Judas
	Daniel
	160–143 Jonathan
	143–134 Simon
133 *Asia a Roman province*	134–63 Hasmonean kings in Judaea **Judith, 1–2 Maccabees**
66–62 *Pompey the Great's eastern campaigns*	63 *Pompey captures Jerusalem* **?Wisdom**

GENERAL HISTORY

44 *Julius Caesar assassinated*
31 *Octavian (Augustus) defeats Antony at ⚔ Actium*

31 BC–14 AD Augustus supreme

14–37 Tiberius emperor

37–41 Caligula

41–54 Claudius

54–68 Nero

69–71 Titus

81–96 Domitian

96–98 Nerva

98–117 Trajan

BIBLICAL HISTORY

40–4 BC Herod king of Judaea — ?6 BC–?30 AD *Jesus*

4 BC–6 AD Archelaus king of Judaea

4 BC–39 AD Herod Antipas tetrarch of Galilee

6–41 Judaea a Roman province — 6–15 Annas high priest

26–36 Pontius Pilate prefect — 18–36 Caiaphas high priest

Paul's letters

66–70 *Siege of Jerusalem* — **Synoptic Gospels**

John's Gospel

MEASURES AND MONEY

APPROXIMATE EQUIVALENTS

Length	*cubit*	=	50 cm (2 feet)
Capacity	*homer*	=	500 litres (100 gallons)
	kor	=	500 litres (100 gallons)
	bat	=	50 litres (10 gallons)
	hin	=	8 litres (1½ gallons)
	log	=	1½ litre (1 pint)
Weight	talent	=	30 kilograms (70 lbs)
	mina	=	50 grams (1 lb)
	sheqel	=	1 gram (½ oz)

Money 'silver piece' = 4 drachmas

drachma (Gk) = denarius (Roman) = day's wage of casual labourer

'penny' = cheapest coin available

INDEX OF PERSONS

Principal references are given, but the list is not exhaustive. Sometimes only the first verse of a passage is cited.